INTELLECTUAL PROPERTY LAW

INTELLECTUAL PROPERTY LAW

Third Edition

L. BENTLY AND B. SHERMAN

OXFORD

UNIVERSITY PRESS

OXFORD
UNIVERSITY PRESS

Great Clarendon Street, Oxford OX2 6DP

Oxford University Press is a department of the University of Oxford.
It furthers the University's objective of excellence in research, scholarship,
and education by publishing worldwide in

Oxford New York

Auckland Cape Town Dar es Salaam Hong Kong Karachi
Kuala Lumpur Madrid Melbourne Mexico City Nairobi
New Delhi Shanghai Taipei Toronto

With offices in

Argentina Austria Brazil Chile Czech Republic France Greece
Guatemala Hungary Italy Japan Poland Portugal Singapore
South Korea Switzerland Thailand Turkey Ukraine Vietnam

Oxford is a registered trade mark of Oxford University Press
in the UK and in certain other countries

Published in the United States
by Oxford University Press Inc., New York

British Library Cataloguing in Publication Data

Data available

Library of Congress Cataloging in Publication Data

Bently, Lionel, 1964–
Intellectual property law / L. Bently and B. Sherman.—3rd ed.
p. cm.
Includes index.
ISBN 978–0–19–929204–2
1. Intellectual property—Great Britain.   I. Sherman, Brad.   II. Title.
KD1269.B375 2008
346.4104'8—dc22   2008033838

Typeset by Newgen Imaging Systems (P) Ltd., Chennai, India
Printed in Great Britain
on acid-free paper by
Ashford Colour Press Ltd., Gosport, Hants

ISBN 978–0–19–929204–2

3 5 7 9 10 8 6 4

For Clair.
For Leanne, Liam, Joe and Lucy.

PREFACE

The task of writing the third edition of this book on intellectual property law brought with it a number of challenges. In writing this new edition, we have taken account of a number of important changes. These include the introduction in December 2007 of the European Patent Convention 2000 (EPC 2000), which replaced the 1973 European Patent Convention. Similar changes were also made to British patent law. While the EPC 2000 did not bring about many substantive changes in the law, it did renumber and alter many of the articles. The rules that accompany the EPC 2000 and the 1977 Patents Act were also overhauled. We have taken account, as well, of jurisprudential developments in the other areas where there has been less legislative change. These include the House of Lords' decisions in *Campbell v. MGN, Douglas v. Hello, Synthon v. Synthlabo, Kirin Amgen,* and *Yeda Research and Development* as well as the important Court of Appeal decisions in *Aerotel, Nova v. Mazooma,* and the *Da Vinci Code* case. We have also accommodated the growing body of case law at the EPO on morality exclusion to patentability. Additionally, we have taken account of the growing body of case law on trade marks and designs emanating from the Community trade mark and design offices, as well as the jurisprudence of the European Court of Human Rights in *von Hannover* and *Anheuser-Busch.* We have also tried to accommodate the expanding body of critical literature that has developed in the last couple of years (which has served to enrich and enliven many aspects of intellectual property law).

Perhaps the most important challenge relates to the decision as to the material that is included and excluded in an intellectual property law textbook. While there is a large amount of material that most people would expect to see in such a book, there are some areas where there is less agreement. This might be the case, for example, with geographical indications of origin, which we have dealt with in some depth. In part this is a reflection of the economic and cultural importance of this topic. Another reason for including this material is that geographical indications of origin may extend beyond food and agriculture to deal with other subject matter (such as indigenous creations). A related problem concerns the extent to which we should include material from 'outside' intellectual property law: a decision that depends on how we define intellectual property law in the first place.

In writing the third edition we have accumulated a number of debts. In particular we would like to thank Eamon Carew and Julian Moore for their valuable research assistance. We are also indebted to Michael Handler, Stephen Hubicki, Kim Weatherall, and Leanne Wiseman for reading and commenting on chapters. Their comments were invaluable. We would like to thank the staff at OUP (particularly Ruth Ballantyne) for their help and forbearance. We would like to express gratitude to Susi Paz for her valiant efforts at picture research, as well as Shirin Guild, Simon Malynicz, Gaenor Moore, Peter O'Byrne, Hamish Porter, John Swarbrick, Roger Wyand QC and Dirk Visser for either granting permission or helping us locate or obtain permission to use various images. Finally, and most importantly, we should pay tribute to Clair Milligan and Leanne Wiseman for their patience, tolerance, and on-going support.

CONTENTS

PART II   PATENTS

PART III THE LEGAL REGULATION OF DESIGNS

PART IV TRADE MARKS AND PASSING OFF

PART VI   LITIGATION AND REMEDIES

ABBREVIATIONS

AC	*Appeal Cases*
AIPC	*Australian Intellectual Property Cases*
AIPJ	*Australian Intellectual Property Journal*
ALJR	*Australian Law Journal Reports*
ALR	*Australian Law Reports*
Annand and Norman (1994)	R. Annand and H. Norman, *Blackstone's Guide to the Trade Marks Act 1994* (London: Blackstone, 1994)
Annand and Norman (1998)	R. Annand and H. Norman, *Blackstone's Guide to the Community Trade Mark* (London: Blackstone, 1998)
Aplin	T.F. Aplin, *Copyright Law in the Digital Society: The Challenges of Multimedia* (Hart, 2005)
App Cas	*Appeal Cases*
Arnold	R. Arnold, *Performers' Rights* (3rd edn., London: Sweet & Maxwell, 2004)
Art.	Article
ASA	Advertising Standards Authority
BCAP	British Code of Advertising, Sales Promotion and Direct Marketing
Beav	*Beavan's Reports*
Beier and Shricker	F.K. Beir and G. Shricker, *From GATT to TRIPS* (Weinheim: IIC/VCH, 1996)
Bently, Davis & Ginsburg	L. Bently, J. Davis and J. Ginsburg (eds.), *Trade Marks and Brands: An Interdisciplinary Critique* (Cambridge: CUP, 2008)
Berne	Berne Convention for the Protection of Literary and Artistic Works of 9 September 1886
Beverley-Smith	H. Beverley-Smith, *The Commercial Appropriation of Personality* (Cambridge: CUP, 2002)
Bing NC	*Bingham, New Cases*
Biotech. Dir.	Directive 98/44/EC of the European Parliament and of the Council of 6 July 1998 on the Legal Protection of Biotechnological Inventions
Brussels	Brussels Convention on Jurisdiction and Enforcement of Judgments in Civil and Commercial Matters, 1968
Brussels Reg.	EC Regulation 44/2001 of 22 December 2000 on Jurisdiction and the recognition and enforcement of Judgments in Civil and Commercial Matters
CA	Court of Appeal

CA 1911	Copyright Act 1911
CA 1956	Copyright Act 1956
CANZ	Court of Appeal of New Zealand
CBD	Convention on Biological Diversity (5 June 1992)
CDIR	Commission Regulation (EC) No. 2245/2002 of 21 October 2002 implementing Council Regulation (EC) No. 6/2002 on Community designs
CDPA	Copyright, Designs and Patents Act 1988
CDR	Community Design Regulation
Ch	*Chancery*
Ch App.	*Chancery Appeal*
Ch D	*Chancery Division*
Chip Dir.	Council Directive 87/54/EEC of 16 December 1986 on the legal protection of semiconductor products
CIPA	*Chartered Institute of Patent Agents' Guide to the Patents Act 1977* (5th edn., London: Sweet & Maxwell, 2007)
CIPAJ	*Journal of the Chartered Institute of Patent Agents*
CJJA	Civil Jurisdiction and Judgments Act 1982
CLR	*Commonwealth Law Reports*
CMLR	*Commonwealth Market Law Reports*
CMLRev	*Commonwealth Market Law Review*
Copinger	K. Garnett, G. Davies, and J. Rayner (eds.), *Copinger and Skone James on Copyright* (15th edn., London: Sweet & Maxwell, 2007)
Cornish and Llewellyn	W.R. Cornish and D. Llewellyn, *Intellectual Property* (6th edn., London: Sweet & Maxwell, 2007)
CPA	Civil Procedure Act 1998
CPC	Community Patent Convention
CPR	Civil Procedure Rules 1998
CPV	Community Plant Variety
CPVO	Community Plant Variety Office
CPVR	Council Regulation (EC), No. 2100/94 of 27 July 1994 on Community Plant Varieties
Craig and de Búrca	P. Craig and G. de Búrca, *E.U. Law: Text, Cases and Materials* (4th edn., Oxford: Oxford University Press, 2007)
Cr App. Rep.	*Criminal Appeal Reports*
Cro Jac	*Croke Jacob Reports*
CTMIR	Commission Regulation (EC), No. 2869/95 of 13 December 1995, implementing Council Regulation (EC), No. 40/94 on the Community Trade Mark
CTMR	Council Regulation (EC), No. 40/94 of 20 December 1993 on the Community Trade Mark

DACS	Design and Artistic Copyright Society
Database Dir.	Directive 96/9/EC of the European Parliament and of the Council of 11 March 1996 on the Legal Protection of Databases
Database Regs.	Copyright and Rights in Database Regulations 1997
Davison	M. Davison, *The Legal Protection of Databases* (Cambridge: CUP, 2003).
DBERR	Department for Business, Enterprise and Regulatory Reform
DCES	Department of Culture, Education and Sport
DCMS	Department for Culture, Media and Sport
Dean	R. Dean, *Law of Trade Secrets and Personal Secrets* (North Ryde, NSW: Law Books Co., 2002)
Derclaye	E. Derclaye, *The Legal Protection of Databases* (Edward Elgar, 2008)
Designs Dir.	Directive 98/71/EC of the European Parliament and of the Council of 13 October 1998 on the legal protection of designs
DIUS	Department of Innovation, Universities and Skills
DTI	Department of Trade and Industry (whose responsibilities have now devolved to the DBERR and DIUS)
Duration Dir.	Directive 2006/116/EC of the European Parliament and of the Council of 12 December 2006 on the term of protection of copyright and certain related rights (codified version) (repealing and replacing Council Directive 93/98/EEC of 29 October 1993 harmonizing the term of protection of copyright and certain related rights)
Duration Regs.	Duration of Copyright and Rights in Performances Regulations 1995
Dworkin and Taylor	G. Dworkin and R. Taylor, *Blackstone's Guide to the Copyright, Designs and Patents Act 1988* (London: Blackstone, 1989)
EBA	Enlarged Board of Appeal
EC	European Community
ECDR	*European Copyright and Design Reports*
ECHR	European Convention on Human Rights
ECJ	European Court of Justice
ECLR	*European Competition Law Review*
ECR	*European Court Reports*
EEA	European Economic Area
EHRR	*European Human Rights Reports*
EFTA	European Free Trade Association
EIPR	*European Intellectual Property Review*

Electronic Commerce Dir.	Directive 2000/31/EC of the European Parliament and of the Council of 8 June 2000 on certain legal aspects of information society services, in particular Electronic Commerce in the Internal Market
ELR	*European Law Review*
EMLR	*Entertainment and Media Law Reports*
Enforcement Dir.	Directive 2004/48/EC of the European Parliament and of the Council of 29 April 2004 on the enforcement of intellectual property rights
Ent LR	*Entertainment Law Review*
EPC	Convention on the Grant of European Patents, at Munich, 5 October 1973
EPC 2000	European Patent Convention, 2000
EPC Revision Act	Act Revising the Convention on the Grant of European Patents (EPC), Munich, 29 November 2000, MR/3/00 Rev. 1e
EPO	European Patent Office
EPOR	*European Patent Office Reports*
EPR	European Patent rules
ER	*English Reports*
ETMR	*European Trade Mark Reports*
Fawcett and Torremans	J. Fawcett and P. Torremans, *Intellectual Property and Private International Law* (Oxford: Clarendon Press, 1998)
FCA	Federal Court of Australia
Fellner	C. Fellner, *Industrial Design Law* (London: Sweet & Maxwell, 1995)
Firth	A. Firth, *Trade Marks: Law and Practice* (Bristol: Jordans, 2005)
Fiscor	M. Fiscor, *The Law of Copyright and the Internet* (Oxford: Oxford University Press, 2002)
Franzosi	M. Franzosi (ed.), *European Design Protection: Commentary to Directive and Regulation Proposals* (The Hague: Kluwer, 1996)
FSR	*Fleet Street Reports*
GATT	General Agreement on Tariffs and Trade
Gervais	D. Gervais, *The TRIPS Agreement* (2nd edn., London: Sweet & Maxwell, 2003)
GRUR	*Gewerblicher Rechtsschutz und Urheberrecht*
Gurry	F. Gurry, *Breach of Confidence* (Oxford: Clarendon Press, 1984)
Hague	Geneva Act of the Hague Agreement Concerning the International Deposit of Industrial Designs, 1999

H & Tw	*Hall and Twell's Chancery Reports*
Hansard	Hansard's Parliamentary Debates
Hare	*Hare's Chancery Reports*
HL	House of Lords
ICANN	Internet Corporation for Assigned Names and Numbers
ICR	*Industrial Court Reports*
IGR	Council Regulation No. 1383/2003 concerning Customs action against goods suspected of infringing certain intellectual property rights and the measures to be taken against goods found to have infringed such rights (Infringing Goods Regulation)
IIC	*International Review of Industrial Property and Copyright Law*
ILJ	*Industrial Law Journal*
Info. Soc. Dir.	Directive 2001/29/EC of the European Parliament and of the Council of 22 May 2001 on the harmonization of certain aspects of copyright and related rights in the information society
IPI	Intellectual Property Institute (formerly Common Law Institute of Intellectual Property)
IPJ	*Intellectual Property Journal*
IPQ	*Intellectual Property Quarterly*
IPR	*Intellectual Property Reports*
IR	*Irish Reports*
ITMA	Institute of Trade Mark Agents
IViR	Instituut voor Informatierecht (Institute for Information Law, University of Amsterdam)
JIPL	*Journal of Intellectual Property Law*
JIPLP	*Journal of Intellectual Property Law & Practice*
JPTOS	*Journal of the Patent and Trademark Office Society*
Jur	*Jurist*
Kamina	P. Kamina, *Film Copyright in the European Union* (Cambridge: CUP, 2000)
Kerly	D. Kitchin *et al.*, *Kerly's Law of Trade Marks and Trade Names* (14th edn., London: Sweet & Maxwell, 2005)
KB	*King's Bench*
Know How Block Exemption	Commission Regulation (EEC), No. 556/89 of 30 November 1988 on the Application of Article 85(3) of the Treaty to certain categories of Know-how Licensing
Laddie *et al.*	H. Laddie, P. Prescott, M. Vitoria, A Speck and L. Lane, *The Modern Law of Copyright* (3rd edn., London: Butterworths, 2000)

LJCh	*Law Journal, Chancery*
LJChD	*Law Journal, Chancery Division*
LQR	*Law Quarterly Review*
LR	*Law Reports*
LR Eq	*Law Reports (Equity)*
LT (NS)	*Law Times (New Series)*
Lugano	Lugano Convention of 16 September 1988
Mac & G	*MacNaghten and Gordon's Reports*
MacG CC	*MacGillivray's Copyright Cases*
Madrid	Madrid Agreement Concerning the International Registration of Marks of 14 April 1891
Madrid Prot.	Protocol Relating to the Madrid Agreement, adopted at Madrid on 27 June 1989
MCAD	Directive 2006/114/EC of the European Parliament and of the Council of 12 December 2006 concerning Misleading and Comparative Advertising (repealing Directive 97/55/EC)
MCPS	Mechanical-Copyright Protection Society
Michaels	A. Michaels, *A Practical Guide to the Law of Trade Marks* (2nd edn., London: Sweet & Maxwell, 1996)
MIP	*Managing Intellectual Property*
MLR	*Modern Law Review*
Morcom *et al.*	C. Morcom, A. Roughton, and J. Graham, *The Modern Law of Trade Marks* (London: Butterworths, 2000)
Musker	D. Musker, *Community Design Law: Principles and Practice* (London: Sweet & Maxwell, 2002)
OFT	Office of Fair Trading
OHIM	Office of Harmonization in the Internal Market
OJ C	*Official Journal of the European Community (C Series)*
OJ EPO	*Official Journal of the European Patent Office*
OJ L	*Official Journal of the European Community (L Series)*
OJ OHIM	*Official Journal of the Office of Harmonization in the Internal Market*
OJ Sp Ed	*Official Journal of the European Community (Special Edition)*
OPSI	Office of Public Sector Information
PA	Patents Act 1977
PA 1949	Patents Act 1949
PAC	Practice Amendment Circular (of the UK Trade Mark Registry)
Paris	Paris Convention for the Protection of Industrial Property of March 1883 (latest revision, Stockholm 1967, with 1979 amendments)
Paterson	G. Paterson, *The European Patent System: The Law and Practice of the EPC* (2nd edn., London: Sweet & Maxwell, 2007)

PA r.	Patent Rules 2007 (SI 2007/3291)
PCT	Patent Co-operation Treaty (1970)
PD	Practice Direction
PDO	Protected Designation of Origin
PGI	Protected Geographical Indication
Phonograms Treaty	Convention for the Protection of Producers of Phonograms against Unauthorized Duplication of Their Phonograms, Geneva, 29 October 1971
Piracy and Counterfeiting	Council Regulation 3842/86 of 1 December 1986 providing Regulation for measures to prohibit the release for free circulation of goods infringing certain intellectual property rights
PLR	Public Lending Right
PLT	WIPO Patent Treaty Law (2000)
PLRA	Public Lending Right Act 1979
PP	*Parliamentary Papers*
PPL	Phonogram Performance Ltd
Proposed UM Dir.	Amended Proposal for a European Parliament and Council Directive approximating the legal arrangements for the protection of inventions by Utility Model (12 Aug. 1999)
Protocol on Jurisdiction	Protocol on Jurisdiction and the Recognition of Decisions in respect to the Right to the Grant of a European Patent
Protocol on Litigation	Protocol to the Community Patent Convention on Litigation
PRS	Performing Right Society
PVA	Plant Varieties Act 1997
PVSA	Plant Varieties and Seeds Act 1964
PW	*Patent World*
PWms	*Peere Williams Chancery Reports*
QB	*Queens Bench*
QBD	*Queens Bench Division*
QdR	*Queensland Reports*
r.	rule
RCD	Registered Community Design
RDA	Registered Designs Act 1949
RDAT	Registered Designs Appeal Tribunal
RDR	Registered Design Rules
Recasting Copyright	Instituut voor Informatierecht (Institute for Information Law, University of Amsterdam) , *Recasting Copyright for the Knowledge Economy* (2006)
Reid	B. Reid, *A Practical Guide to Patent Law* (3rd edn., London: Sweet & Maxwell, 1999)

Reinbothe and von Lewinski (1993)	J. Reinbothe and S. von Lewinski, *The EC Directive on Rental and Lending Right and on Piracy* (London: Sweet & Maxwell, 1993)
Reinbothe and von Lewinski (2002)	J. Reinbothe and S. von Lewinski, *The WIPO Copyright Treaties* (London: Butterworths, 2002)
Related Rights Regs.	Copyright and Related Rights Regulations 1996
Rental Dir.	Directive 2006/115/EC of the European Parliament and of the Council of 12 December 2006 on rental right and lending right and on certain rights related to copyright in the field of intellectual property (codified version (replacing Council Directive 92/100/EEC of 19 November 1992 on rental and lending right and on certain rights related to copyright in the field of intellectual property)
Resale Right Dir.	Directive 2001/83/EC of 27 September 2001 on the resale right for the benefit of the author of an original work of art
Ricketson	S. Ricketson, *The Berne Convention for the Protection of Literary and Artistic Works* (London: Kluwer & QMW, 1987)
Ricketson & Ginsburg	S. Ricketson and J.C Ginsburg, *International Copyright and Neighbouring Rights: The Berne Convention and Beyond* (2nd edn., 2006)
RIDA	*Revue international du droit d'auteur*
Rome	International Convention for the Protection of Performers, Producers of Phonograms, and Broadcasting Organizations, Rome, 26 October 1961
RPC	*Report of Patent Cases*
Russell-Clarke	M. Howe (ed.), *Russell-Clarke on Industrial Designs* (7th edn., London: Sweet & Maxwell, 2005)
Satellite Conv.	Convention Relating to the Distribution by Programme Carrying Signals Transmitted by Satellite, Brussels, 21 May 1974
Satellite Dir.	Council Directive 93/98/EEC of 27 September 1993 on the coordination of certain rules concerning copyright and rights related to copyright applicable to satellite broadcasting and cable retransmission
SCCR	*Scottish Criminal Case Reports*
SCt	Supreme Court
Sherman and Bently	B. Sherman and L. Bently, *The Making of Modern Intellectual Property Law* (Cambridge: CUP, 1999)
Sherman and Strowel	B. Sherman and A. Strowel (eds.), *Of Authors and Origins: Essays on Copyright Law* (Oxford: Clarendon Press, 1994)
Singer and Stauder	R. Singer, *The European Patent Convention: A Commentary* (3rd edn., Cologne: Heymann, 2003)
Software Dir.	Council Directive 91/250/EEC of 14 May 1991 on the legal protection of computer programs
SPC	Supplementary Protection Certificate

SPC (MP) Reg.	Council Regulation (EEC), No. 1768/92 of 18 June 1992 concerning the creation of a supplementary protection certificate for medicinal products
SPC (PPP) Reg.	Council Regulation (EC), No. 1610/96 of the European Parliament and of the Council of 23 July 1996 concerning the creation of a supplementary protection certificate for plant protection products
Stamatoudi	I. Stamatoudi, *Copyright and Miultimedia Works* (Cambridge: CUP, 2002)
Stothers	C. Stothers, *Parallel Trade in Europe: Intellectual Property, Competition and Regulatory Law* (Hart, 2007)
Strasbourg	Strasbourg Convention on the Unification of Certain Points of Substantive Law on Patents for Inventions (1963)
Suthersanen	U. Suthersanen, *Design Law in Europe* (London: Sweet & Maxwell, 2000)
TBA	Technical Board of Appeal
TDA	Trade Descriptions Act 1968
Terrell	S. Thorley, R. Miller, G. Burkill, and C. Birss (eds.), *Terrell's Law of Patents* (16th edn., London: Sweet & Maxwell, 2006)
TEU	Treaty Establishing the European Union
The Treaty	Treaty Establishing the European Community
TLR	*Times Law Reports*
TLT	Trademark Law Treaty, signed 28 October 1994
TMA	Trade Marks Act 1994
TMA 1938	Trade Marks Act 1938
TM Dir.	Council Directive 89/104 of 21 December 1988 to approximate the laws of member states relating to trade marks
TMR	Trade Marks Rules 2000
TM Rep	*Trademark Reporter*
TMR Work Manual	*Trade Mark Registry Work Manual*
TRIPS	Agreement on Trade-related Aspects of Intellectual Property Rights 1994
Tritton	G. Tritton (ed.), *Intellectual Property in Europe* (3rd edn., London: Sweet & Maxwell, 2007)
TSG	Traditional Speciality Guaranteed
TTBER	Commission Regulation (EC) No. 772/2004 of 27 April 2004 on the application of Article 81(3) of the Treaty to categories of technology transfer agreements
TTR	Commission Regulation (EC) No. 240/96 of 31 January 1996 on the Application of Article 85(3) of the Treaty to certain categories of Technology Transfer Agreements
UCC	Universal Copyright Convention

UCD	Unregistered Community Design
UDR	Unregistered Design Right
UPOV	International Convention for the Protection of New Varieties of Plants of 2 December 1961 (latest revision 19 March 1991)
USPTO	United States Patent and Trademark Office
VRR	Commission Regulation (EC) No. 2790/99 of 22 December 1999 on the application of Article 81(3) of the Treaty of Categories of Vertical Agreements and Concerted Practices
Wadlow (2004)	C. Wadlow, *The Law of Passing Off* (3rd edn., London: Sweet & Maxwell, 2004)
Wadlow (1998)	C. Wadlow, *Enforcement of Intellectual Property in European and International* Law (London: Sweet & Maxwell, 1998)
Washington	Treaty on Intellectual Property in Respect of Integrated Circuits, Washington, DC, 26 May 1989
WCT	WIPO Copyright Treaty adopted by the Diplomatic Conference on 20 December 1996
Whitford Committee	Whitford Committee, *Report of the Committee on Copyright and Designs Law*, Cmnd. 6732 (London: HMSO, 1977)
WIPO	World Intellectual Property Organization
WLR	*Weekly Law Reports*
Worsdall and Clark	A. Worsdall and A. Clark, *Anti-Counterfeiting: A Practical Guide* (Bristol: Jordans, 1998)
WPPT	WIPO Performances and Phonograms Treaty adopted by the Diplomatic Conference on 20 December 1996
WTO	World Trade Organization

USEFUL WEB SITES

	htttp://www
Advertising Standards Authority	asa.org.uk
Chartered Institute of Patent Agents	cipa.org.uk
Competition Commission	competition-commission.org.uk
Community Plant Variety Office	cpvo.fr
Department for Business, Enterprise & Regulatory Reform	berr.gov.uk
Department of Culture, Media, and Sport	culture.gov.uk
Department for Environment, Food and Rural Affairs	defra.gov.uk
Department of Innovation, Universities and Skills	dius.gov.uk
European Commission	ec.europa.eu
European Court of Justice	curia.europa.eu
European Free Trade Association	efta.int
European Patent Office	epo.org
Her Majesty's Revenue and Customs	hmrc.gov.uk
House of Lords (judicial decisions)	parliament.the-stationery-office.co.uk
Institute of Trade Mark Attorneys	itma.org.uk
Office of Harmonization in the Internal Market	oami.europa.eu
Office of Public Sector Information	opsi.gov.uk
Parliamentary Debates	parliament.the-stationery-office.co.uk
The Patent Office (UK)	ipo.gov.uk
Performing Rights Society	mcps-prs-alliance.co.uk
Plant Varieties Office	defra.gov.uk.planth/pvs
Public Lending Right	plr.uk.com
UK Government	direct.gov.uk
UK Courts	courtservice.gov.uk
US Patent Office	uspto.gov
World Intellectual Property Organization	wipo.org
World Trade Organization	wto.org

LIST OF FIGURES

TABLE OF CASES

TABLE OF STATUTES

TABLE OF STATUTORY INSTRUMENTS

TABLE OF EU LEGISLATION

Regulations

TABLE OF FOREIGN STATUTES

TABLE OF INTERNATIONAL LEGISLATION

1

INTRODUCTION

CHAPTER CONTENTS

1 INTRODUCTION

Intellectual property law regulates the creation, use, and exploitation of mental or creative labour.[1] The term 'intellectual property' has been used for almost one hundred and fifty years to refer to the general area of law that encompasses copyright, patents, designs, and trade marks, as well as a host of related rights.[2] Intellectual property law creates property rights in a wide and diverse range of things from novels, computer programs, paintings, films, television broadcasts, and performances, through to dress designs, pharmaceuticals, genetically modified animals and plants. Intellectual property law also creates rights in the various insignia that are applied to goods and services from FUJITSU for computers to 'I CAN'T BELIEVE IT'S NOT BUTTER' for margarine. We are surrounded by and constantly interact with the subject matter of intellectual property law. For example, you are reading a copyright work bearing Oxford University Press's trade mark. You are probably sitting on a chair protected by design rights and marking the book with a pen the mechanism for which has, at some stage, been patented. Alternatively you may be typing notes into a computer, which no doubt has parts (such as the mouse) which are protected by patents and design rights (in the shape of the product as well as the semiconductor chip topographies inside).

While there are a number of important differences between the various forms of intellectual property, one factor that they share in common is that they establish property protection

---

[1] According to Art. 2, para. viii, WIPO Convention (1967) 'Intellectual property' includes 'the rights relating to—literary, artistic and scientific works—performances and performing artists, photographs and broadcasts—inventions in all fields of human endeavour—scientific discoveries—industrial designs—trade marks, service marks, and commercial names and designations—protection against unfair competition and all other rights resulting from intellectual activity in the industrial, scientific, literary or artistic fields'.

[2] See Sherman and Bently, 95–100.

over intangible things such as ideas, inventions, signs, and information. While there is a close relationship between intangible property and the tangible objects in which they are embodied, intellectual property rights are distinct and separate from property rights in tangible goods. For example, when a person posts a letter to someone, the personal property in the ink and parchment is transferred to the recipient. If the recipient is pleased with the letter, they can frame it and hang it on the wall; if they are unhappy with the letter they can burn it; or, if it is a love letter, they might store it away in which case it will pass under the recipient's will when they die. Despite the recipient having personal property rights in the letter as a physical object, the sender (as author) retains intellectual property rights in the letter.[3] The author will be the first owner of copyright in the letter, which will enable them to stop the recipient (or anyone else) from copying the letter or from posting it on the internet.

For many, the fact that intellectual property rights are separate from the physical objects in which they are embodied may be counter-intuitive. For example, if someone owns a recipe book, why should they not be able to photocopy a couple of recipes to send to a relative? Similarly, if someone owns an animal or plant, should they not be able to buy and sell seeds from the plant, or offspring of the animals? Or if someone purchases bottles of perfume in Singapore, should they not be able to sell them in the United Kingdom? One of the consequences of intellectual property rights being separate from property rights is that the legal answer to these questions might well be 'no'.[4] As rights over intangibles, intellectual property rights limit what the owners of personal property are able to do with the things which they own.

While the law has long granted property rights in intangibles, the law did not accept 'intellectual property' as a distinct and (relatively) non-controversial form of property until late in the eighteenth century.[5] In granting property status to intangibles the question arose as to how and where the boundary lines of the intangible property were to be determined. That is, once it was accepted that the law should grant property rights over intangibles, the question arose: how was the object of the property to be identified and its limits defined? While in real and personal property law, questions of this nature are answered by reference to the boundary posts and physical markers of the objects in question,[6] one of the defining features of intangible property is that these reference points do not exist. As a result, each area of intellectual property law has been forced to develop its own techniques to define the parameters of the intangible property. These include schemes of deposit and registration techniques of representation (such as the patent specification and claims), statutory rules and legal concepts such as the requirement of sufficiency of disclosure (in patent law),[7] and the originality requirement (in copyright law).[8]

One fact that will become apparent as we look at the various forms of intellectual property law is that they share a similar image of what means to 'create' (or produce), for example, a book,

---

[3] Commercial practices frequently operate in apparent ignorance of the distinction: see R. Deazley, 'Collecting Photographs, Copyrights and Cash' [2001] *EIPR* 551 (describing, and doubting, the legitimacy of certain claims to copyright ownership of photographs used by the press).

[4] J. Litman, 'Consumers and the Global Copyright Bargain' [1998] *IPQ* 139, 145. ('The copyright statute is a law that most people, at least in the United States, don't believe in, that is, they don't believe copyright law says what it says.')

[5] It was not called intellectual property until midway through the nineteenth century.

[6] And Latin maxims such as *cujus est solum, ejus usque ad coelum et ad inferos* (the owner of soil is presumed to own the airspace above and the matter below as far as the centre of the earth).

[7] Which effectively means that the property claimed must correspond to the invented subject matter: see Ch. 20.

[8] See Sherman and Bently, 25, 153–5, 185–93.

a design for a car, or a new type of pharmaceutical. More specifically, it is commonly assumed that it is an individual, rather than a god, a machine, a force of nature, or a muse that creates ideas, information, and technical principles. It is also assumed that the act of creation occurs when an individual exercises their mental labour to manipulate the underlying raw material.

Another fact that will become clear as we progress through the book is that intellectual property law is highly politicized. On the one hand there are groups who represent existing (or putative) right holders which have tended to argue that the existing laws provide inadequate protection: that, for example, the threshold for patent protection for genetically modified biological material is set too high, that copyright and patent protection need to be explicitly extended to cover multimedia works and software, that trade mark owners are not sufficiently protected against cyber squatters who acquire related domain names, and so on. At the other extreme, there are a range of groups who oppose stronger intellectual property protection: whether they be representatives of the developing world, consumers and users of intellectual property (such as home tapers, digital samplers, appropriation artists, 'netizens', and librarians), defenders of free speech, classical liberal economic theorists, competition lawyers, postmodern theorists, ecologists, or religious groups. While there is a tendency to caricature such debates about intellectual property as battles between good and evil, there are many shades of opinion between these extremes that deploy a diversity of more nuanced arguments.[9]

While anyone reading recent commentaries on music on the internet or the legal status of genetically modified plants and animals might be led to think otherwise, intellectual property law has a long and rich history. Despite this, intellectual property has only recently become part of the typical law school syllabus (although textbooks or treatises have existed since the middle of the nineteenth century). In part, the growing interest in intellectual property may be attributed to the fact that, in the last two decades or so, intellectual property law has come to be widely viewed as an area of primary economic and social importance.

The remainder of this chapter provides an introduction to some topics that impinge upon all areas of intellectual property law. After looking at some of the justifications that have been given for the grant of intellectual property rights, we explain the key international and regional structures that are central to an understanding of British intellectual property law.

2 JUSTIFICATIONS FOR INTELLECTUAL PROPERTY

Legal and political philosophers have often debated the status and legitimacy of intellectual property.[10] In so doing, philosophers have typically asked 'why should we grant intellectual property rights?' For philosophers, it is important that this question is answered, since we have a choice as to whether we should grant such rights. It is also important because the decision to grant property rights in intangibles impinges on traders, the press and media, and the public.[11]

---

[9] See, e.g. A. Thierer and C. Crews, *Copy Fights: The Future of Intellectual Property in the Information Age* (Washington DC: Cato Institute, 2002).

[10] For a useful collection, see A. Moore (ed.), *Intellectual Property: Moral, Legal and International Dilemmas* (1997).

[11] In *A v. B* [2003] *QB* 195, 205 para. 11 Lord Woolf CJ observed that 'any interference with the press has to be justified'. For emphasis on free speech, see P. Drahos, 'Decentring Communication: The Dark Side of Intellectual Property', in T. Campbell and W. Sidurski (eds.), *Freedom of Communication* (1994); J. Waldron, 'From Authors to Copiers: Individual Rights and Social Values in Intellectual Property' (1993) 68 *Chicago-Kent Law Review* 841. For emphasis on the relationship between intellectual properties, identity and alterity, see R. Coombe, *The Cultural Life of Intellectual Properties: Authorship, Appropriation and the Law* (1998).

Moreover, because the conventional arguments which justify the grant of private property rights in land and tangible resources are often premised on the scarcity or limited availability of such resources, and the impossibility of sharing, it seems especially important to justify the grant of exclusive rights over resources—ideas and information—that are not scarce and can be replicated without any direct detriment to the original possessor of the intangible (who continues to be able to use the idea or information). As we will see, philosophers have not always found intellectual property rights to be justified,[12] and there are now many commentators who doubt that all intellectual property rights are justified in the form they currently take.

The justifications that have been given for intellectual property tend to fall into one of two general categories. First, commentators often call upon ethical and moral arguments to justify intellectual property rights. For example, it is often said that copyright is justified because the law recognizes authors' natural or human rights over the products of their labour.[13] Similarly, trade mark protection is justified insofar as it prevents third parties from becoming unjustly enriched by 'reaping where they have not sown'.

Alternatively, commentators often rely upon instrumental justifications that focus on the fact that intellectual property induces or encourages desirable activities.[14] For example, the patent system is sometimes justified on the basis that it provides inventors with an incentive to invest in research and development of new products,[15] or an incentive to disclose valuable technical information to the public, which would otherwise have remained secret. Similarly, the trade mark system is justified because it encourages traders to manufacture and sell high-quality products. It also encourages them to provide information to the public about those attributes.[16] Instrumental arguments are typically premised on the position that without intellectual property protection there would be under-production of intellectual products. This

[12] A. Plant, 'The Economics of Copyright' (1934) *Economica* 167; S. Breyer, 'The Uneasy Case for Copyright: A Study of Copyright in Books, Photocopies and Computer Programs', 84 *Harvard Law Review* 281; R. Brown, 'Advertising and the Public Interest: The Legal Protection of Trade Symbols' (1948) 57 *Yale Law Journal* 1165 (on trade marks); N. Kinsella, 'Against Intellectual Property' (2002) 15 *Journal of Libertarian Studies* 1. Different theories may work better for different intellectual property rights: L. Paine, 'Trade Secrets and the Justifications of Intellectual Property: A Comment on Hettinger' (1990) 19 *Philosophy & Public Affairs* 247; *Sirena*, Case C–40/70 [1971] ECR 69 (the ECJ admitted that the interests protected by patents merited a higher degree of protection than trade marks.)

[13] Universal Declaration of Human Rights Art. 27(2); Article II–17 (3) of the draft European Constitution (18 Jul. 2003) CONV 850/03; Charter of Fundamental Rights of the European Union, (7 Dec. 2000), Art. 17. For a critical assessment of such claims, see P. Drahos, 'Intellectual Property and Human Rights' [1999] *IPQ* 349. On the theoretical basis of these claims, see J. Hughes, 'The Philosophy of Intellectual Property' (1988) 77 *Georgetown Law Review* 287 (exploring application of Locke and Hegel); A. Moore, *Intellectual Property and Information Control: Philosophical Foundations and Contemporary Issues* (2001) (rejecting utilitarian argument and favouring a version of Lockean theory); W. Gordon, 'Property Right in Self Expression' (1993) 102 *Yale Law Journal* 1533. On desert, see L. Becker, 'Deserving to Own Intellectual Property' (1993) 68 *Chicago-Kent Law Review* 609. The ethical justifications provide an important basis for the claims of indigenous peoples over their traditional knowledge: see, e.g. M. Spence, 'Which Intellectual Property Rights are Trade-Related?', in Francioni, F. and Scovazzi, M. (eds.), *Environment, Human Rights and International Trade* (2001), 279–80 (describing the claims to inclusion of such rights in the TRIPS framework as based on commutative justice).

[14] For an overview, see E. Hettinger, 'Justifying Intellectual Property Rights' (1989) 18 *Philosophy & Public Affairs* 31; F. Machlup and E. Penrose, 'The Patent Controversy in the Nineteenth Century' (1950) *Journal of Economic History* 1, 10 ff; T. Palmer, 'Are Patents and Copyrights Morally Justified?' (1990) 13 *Harvard Journal of Law and Public Policy* and reprinted in Thierer and Crews, *Copy Fights: The Future of Intellectual Property in the Information Age* (Washington DC: Cato Institute, 2002).

[15] For an example, see W. Landes and R. Posner, 'An Economic Analysis of Copyright Law' (1989) 18 *Journal of Legal Studies* 325.

[16] See, e.g. W. Landes and R. Posner, 'The Economics of Trademark Law' (1988) 78 *TM Rep* 267.

is because, while such products might be costly to create, once made available to the public they can often be readily copied. This means that (in the absence of rights giving exclusivity) a creator is likely to be undercut by competitors who have not incurred the costs of creation. The inability of the market to guarantee that an investor in research could recoup its investment is sometimes called 'market failure'.

A set of related, but distinct, economic theory argues that by transforming potentially valuable intangible artefacts into property rights, those artefacts are more likely to be exploited to their optimal extent. Such a theory (in contrast with theories of intellectual property rights as incentives to create or disclose), are not concerned with how the intangibles came into existence, and tend towards the protection of a broader range of subject matter, potentially in perpetuity. This 'neo-classical' economic theory would draw the limit of intellectual property protection at the point where it begins to inhibit efficient uses (that is, where the costs of transacting with a property holder start to prevent uses to which parties would agree were there no such costs).[17]

These justifications are examined in more detail in the introductory sections dealing with copyright, patents, and trade marks.[18]

3 INTERNATIONAL INFLUENCES

One of the defining characteristics of intellectual property rights is that they are national or territorial in nature. That is, ordinarily they do not operate outside the national territory where they are granted.[19] The territorial nature of intellectual property rights has long been a problem to rights holders whose works, inventions, and brands are the subject of transnational trade. Throughout the nineteenth century, a number of countries that saw themselves as net exporters of intellectual property began to explore ways of protecting their authors, designers, inventors, and trade mark owners in other jurisdictions. Initially, this was done by way of bilateral treaties, whereby two nations agreed to allow nationals of the other country to claim the protection of their respective laws. Towards the end of the nineteenth century a number of (largely European) countries entered into two multilateral arrangements: the Paris Convention for the Protection of Industrial Property of 1883 and the Berne Convention for the Protection of Literary and Artistic Works of 1886. While the detail of these treaties is left for later chapters, it is worth observing here that both treaties adopted as their central criterion for protection the principle of 'national treatment'. The principle of national treatment is fundamentally a rule of non-discrimination. This provides that a member state of the Paris and Berne Union (country A) must offer the same protection to the nationals of other member states (say country B) as country A gives to its own nationals. The beauty of the principle of national treatment is that it allows countries the autonomy to develop and enforce their own laws,[20] while meeting the demands for international protection. Effectively, national treatment is a mechanism of international protection without harmonization.

---

[17] Classic texts include: Landes & Posner, *The Economic Structure of Intellectual Property* (2003); E. Kitch, 'The Nature and Function of the Patent System', *Journal of Law & Economics* 265; W. Gordon, 'Fair Use as Market Failure: A Structural and Economic Analysis of the Betamax Case and Its Predecessors' (1982) 82 *Columbia Law Review* 1600. For a general discussion see W. Gordon and R. Watt (eds), *The Economics of Copyright: Developments in Research and Analysis* (2003).

[18] See below Chapters 2, 14 and Part IV.

[19] On the ability of UK courts to decide issues of infringement of foreign intellectual property rights, see Ch. 47.

[20] Although this is usual, it is not a necessary consequence of national treatment: see Ch. 47.

While the principle of national treatment provides rights owners with some protection in other jurisdictions, it only offers a partial solution. One problem that national treatment fails to address is that where country A requires registration as a prerequisite for protection, the right holder in country B must endure the time and cost of registration to protect their creations in country A. Since the end of the nineteenth century one of the goals of international intellectual property law has been to reduce the inconvenience caused by registration. In the copyright field, this was achieved by requiring members of the Berne Union to grant copyright protection without the need for formalities (such as registration). In the field of trade marks, a mechanism was developed under which a national trade mark owner could make an 'international registration' which would take effect almost automatically in designated countries.[21] A similar procedure for international application for patents was not developed until 1970.[22]

The expansion of international arrangements for the protection of intellectual property continued through the twentieth century and into the present one. Over this time, the Paris and Berne Conventions have been revised on a number of occasions, their membership has expanded (particularly as former colonies achieved independence), and a number of new treaties have been formulated. Most of these treaties have been developed and are supervised by the World Intellectual Property Organization (WIPO), which has its headquarters in Geneva.[23] It continues to be the main forum for the development of new intellectual property initiatives at an international level.

Early intellectual property treaties were largely established between countries with a shared interest in recognizing such rights (even if arrangements often implicated colonies which had quite different interests). For a long time, countries such as the USA, the USSR, and the People's Republic of China remained outside the treaty arrangements, often believing that as 'net consumers' of intellectual property, recognition of the rights of foreigners would work against their national economic interests. The persistent refusal of the USA to protect British copyright owners in the nineteenth century was a cause of great annoyance. While more acceptable arrangements were made in the twentieth century, the USA did not join the Berne Convention until 1988.

By the 1980s, the USA had realized that it was a net producer of intellectual property-based goods and, along with the EC and Japan, began to advocate for higher levels of intellectual property protection on a global basis. Frustrated by the difficulties encountered under the traditional treaty arrangements,[24] the developed countries began to employ tactics that were

---

[21] The Madrid Agreement concerning the International Registration of Marks 1891. (However, given that trade mark procedures remained a matter for national law, this system proved unattractive to some countries, including the UK.)

[22] The Patent Co-operation Treaty. Discussed at pp. 352–3, 373–4 below.

[23] WIPO, a specialized agency of the UN, was established by a treaty signed in Stockholm on 14 July 1967 (replacing 'BIRPI', the body which supervised the Berne and Paris Conventions). See K. Pfanner, 'World Intellectual Property Organization' (1979) 10 *IIC* 1. The most important treaty falling outside WIPO supervision is the Universal Copyright Convention of 1952, which operates under the auspices of UNESCO. K. Idris, 'WIPO and the Rule of Law in a Changing World' (1999) 61 *The Review* 11.

[24] The frustrations of the developed world can be traced back to 1967 with the Stockholm Protocol to the Berne Convention: H. Sacks, 'Crisis in International Copyright: The Protocol Regarding Developing Countries' (1969) *Journal of Business Law* 26. This was compounded by the failure to revise the Paris Convention between 1980 and 1984: K. Beier, 'One Hundred Years of International Cooperation: The Role of the Paris Convention in the Past, Present and Future' (1994) 15 *IIC* 1; Opinion 1/94 (1994) ECR I–5267, 5294. Yet more disappointment followed WIPO's failure to combat copyright piracy: see M. Blakeney, 'Intellectual Property in World Trade' (1995) 3 *International Trade Law Review* 76 (which provides a concise overview of the origins of TRIPS). See also K. Beier and G. Schricker (eds.), *GATT or WIPO?* (1996).

much more aggressive than had hitherto operated at WIPO.[25] More specifically, in the 1980s the US Government started to take advantage of its trading power to threaten trade sanctions against countries that did not offer sufficient protection to American intellectual property rights owners.[26] Frustrated by the experience of WIPO-controlled treaty negotiations, the USA also sought to bring intellectual property protection within the General Agreement on Tariffs and Trade system (GATT).

The GATT was formed after the Second World War with a view to stabilizing and liberalizing trade conditions on a worldwide basis. In 1986, a new round of negotiations begun which included 'Trade-Related Aspects of Intellectual Property Rights' (or TRIPS) on the agenda.[27] When compared with WIPO negotiations, the TRIPS negotiations had a number of advantages. First, they brought intellectual property rights within a broader framework, thus making clear to the parties that, although it may not have been in their interest to accept stronger intellectual property standards, these would be offset by other advantages elsewhere.[28] Second, as non-Governmental Organizations (NGOs) and other organizations are largely excluded from the treaty process, the GATT negotiations are conducted between countries in a more streamlined manner. The negotiations that began in 1986 were concluded in 1993,[29] and became part of the World Trade Organization agreement signed in Marrakesh in April 1994. There are 146 parties to the Agreement.[30]

The TRIPS Agreement covers all the main areas of intellectual property.[31] For the most part, it requires members of the WTO to recognize the existing standards of protection within the Berne and Paris Conventions.[32] It also demands substantive protection for 'neighbouring rights'

[25] See E. Uphoff, *Intellectual Property and US Relations with Indonesia, Malaysia, Singapore and Thailand* (1991). In addition, the US Semiconductor Chip Protection Act 1984 heralded a return of reciprocity, rather than national treatment, as a technique for recognition of foreign entitlements: non-US nationals could not obtain the benefit of the 1984 Act unless similar laws were in place in the claimant's country. Japan and the EC responded by enacting equivalent laws.

[26] Most notoriously, under 'Special 301' of the Omnibus Trade and Competitiveness Act of 1988, *Pub L*, No. 100–418, 102 *Stat* 1176–9 the US Trade Representative conducts an annual audit, placing countries which fail to give adequate and effective protection on a 'watch list', followed (currently in the case of the Ukraine) by sanctions (the withdrawal of trade privileges). For annual reports and current watch lists see http://www.ustr.gov. The European Community also applied retaliatory measures against countries with inadequate intellectual property protection, under Council Regulation (EEC) No. 2641/84 of 17 Sept. 1984 on the strengthening of the common commercial policy with regard in particular to protection against illicit commercial practices OJ L 252/1 and Council Regulation (EEC) No. 4257/88 of 19 Dec. 1988 applying generalized tariff preferences for 1989 in respect of certain industrial products originating in developing countries OJ L 375/1.

[27] See C. Wadlow, 'Including trade in counterfeit goods: the origins of TRIPS as a GATT anti-counterfeiting code' [2007] *IPQ* 350.

[28] P. Gerhart, 'Why Lawmaking for Global Intellectual Property is Unbalanced' [2000] *EIPR* 309.

[29] S. Sell, *Private Power, Public Law: The Globalization of Intellectual Property Rights* (2003).

[30] China became a party in December 2001.

[31] See Beier and Schricker (eds.), *GATT or WIPO?* (1996); D. Gervais, *The TRIPS Agreement—Drafting History and Analysis* (2nd edn. London, 2003); C. Arup, *The New WTO Agreements: Globalizing Law Through Services and Intellectual Property* (2002); P. Drahos, 'Global Property rights in Information: The story of TRIPS at the GATT' (1995) *Prometheus* 6; J. Reichman, 'Universal Minimum Standards of Intellectual Property Protection under the TRIPS Component of the WTO Agreement' (1995) 29 *The International Lawyer* 345. M. Spence, 'Which Intellectual Property Rights are Trade-Related?' in Francioni, F. and Scovazzi, M. (eds), *Environment, Human Rights and International Trade* (2001), 279–80 (attempting to locate a principled basis to justify the scope and content of TRIPS and permit its coherent development, and arguing that TRIPS Art. 7 fails to provide such a basis).

[32] TRIPS Art. 2(1), Art. 9.

to copyright,[33] trade marks,[34] geographical indications,[35] designs,[36] patents,[37] topographies of integrated circuits,[38] and undisclosed information.[39] Perhaps the most significant difference between TRIPS and the existing treaties is in the detailed provisions on enforcement of intellectual property rights in Part III. Prior to TRIPS matters of procedure, remedies, and criminal sanctions had largely been left to national law.

TRIPS has had an important impact on the general development of intellectual property law since it came into force on 1 January 1995.[40] As the procedures of enforcement through the International Court of Justice are cumbersome, little could be done where a country ratified but did not comply with an intellectual property treaty. However, as a result of TRIPS being part of the WTO Agreement, if a country fails to bring its laws into line with TRIPS, another member may complain to the WTO and set in motion a so-called 'dispute resolution procedure'.[41] This involves initial consultations between the parties, followed by the establishment of a panel of three experts that produces a report that the parties either accept or appeal. Where a successful complaint has been made against a nation, it is usually required that the relevant laws are amended so as to comply with the TRIPS Agreement,[42] though the possibility exists for the parties to the dispute to reach an alternative arrangement.[43] The consultation procedures have been invoked over twenty times, and—perhaps surprisingly—most of the disputes have arisen between developed countries,[44] rather than between developed and

---

[33] TRIPS Art. 14.

[34] TRIPS Arts 15–21. For a conclusion that the TRIPS agreement covers trade names, see *EC v. US*, WT/DS 176/AR.

[35] TRIPS Arts 22–4.   [36] TRIPS Arts 25–6.   [37] TRIPS Arts 27–34.

[38] TRIPS Arts 35–8.   [39] TRIPS Art. 39.

[40] Developed countries were granted a transitional period of one year, developing countries five years. The WTO has been called a 'global regulatory ratchet in place for intellectual property, which for the time being is being worked by a technocratic elite': P. Drahos, 'Intellectual Property and Human Rights' [1999] *IPQ* 349, 370. Although TRIPS has had little direct impact on UK law, in general because the standards embodied in the Agreement reflect pre-existing European standards, it has been frequently referred to in cases interpreting UK (and European) legislation: see, e.g. T–1173/97 *IBM/Computer program product* [1999] *OJEPO* 609 (referring to TRIPS Art. 27); *S. v. Havering Borough Council* (20 Nov. 2002), para. 11; *Libertel Groep BV v. Benelux MerkenBureau*, Case C–104/01 [2004] *FSR* (4) 65 (ECJ); *Nova Productions v. Mazooma Games* [2007] *EWCA Civ 219* (CA).

[41] TRIPS Arts 63–64; Understanding on Rules and Procedures Governing the Settlement of Disputes.

[42] Procedures exist for determining a time-scale, if necessary by way of arbitration.

[43] As occurred in *EC v. US*, WT/DS 160 (where, following Panel Report that US violated TRIPS Art. 13, the EC accepted compensation in lieu of change in US law). It has been observed that agreements of this sort enable those who are rich enough to buy themselves out of compliance with TRIPS standards, and that this, in turn, undermines the moral force of the TRIPS Agreement.

[44] See, e.g. *US v. Japan*, WT/DS 28 (retrospective rights for sound recordings); *US v. Portugal*, WT/DS 37 (patent term); *EC v. Japan*, WT/DS 42 (retrospective rights for sound recordings); *US v. Ireland*, WT/DS 82 (copyright enforcement); *US v. EC/Denmark*, WT/DS 83/1 (enforcement, provisional measures); *US v. Sweden*, WT/DS 86/1 (enforcement, provisional measures); *EC v. Canada*, WT/DS 114 ('regulatory review' and 'stockpiling' exceptions to pharmaceutical patents); *US v. EC/Greece*, WT/DS 124/1 (enforcement of film copyright); *US v. EC/Greece*; WT/DS 125/1 (enforcement of copyright in relation to Greek TV stations); *Canada v. EC*, WT/DS 153 (EC supplementary protection certificates breach TRIPS Art. 27 on non-discrimination between technologies); *EC v. US*, WT/DS 160 (public playing of music); *US v. EC*, WT/DS 174 (geographical indications, beer); *EC v. US*, WT/DS 176 (US legislation on Cuban confiscations); *US v. Canada*, WT/DS 179 (patent term); *Australia v. EC*, WT/DS 290 (geographical indications).

less-developed countries.[45] To date there have been a limited but growing number of disputes,[46] with even fewer appeals.[47] Although there are aspects of the process that might be thought to need improvement,[48] so far the enforcement machinery has been effective without any need to resort to trade sanctions.

Although TRIPS is the single most important development in international intellectual property law of the last thirty years, it does not appear to have permanently eclipsed the role of WIPO. Indeed, not long after the Marrakesh Agreement was signed, two new intellectual property treaties were formulated and agreed through WIPO: the 1996 WIPO Copyright Treaty and the 1996 WIPO Performances and Phonograms Treaty. These reincorporated the Berne-plus elements of TRIPS into an exclusively intellectual property environment, as well as adding new TRIPS-plus elements. Other WIPO initiatives, particularly in relation to traditional knowledge and standardization of patent law, will continue to play a significant role in international intellectual property law (albeit now in tandem with the WTO).

Although the intellectual property instruments that have been developed at the international level have occasionally recognized the peculiar needs of the developing and least-developed countries (most notably in terms of transitional periods),[49] the globalization of intellectual property standards has largely been a process whereby the wish-lists of various developed-world lobby groups are inscribed into public international law.[50] One notable exception to this is found in the 1992 Convention on Biological Diversity (CBD), which recognizes the rights of the (indigenous) peoples who preserve biological resources to share in the

---

[45] *US v. Pakistan*, WT/DS 36, *US v. India*, WT/DS 50, *EC v. India*, WT/DS 79 (all on protection of pharmaceutical patent rights pending full recognition); *US v. Argentina*, WT/DS 171 (pharmaceutical patents); *US v. Argentina*, WT/DS 196 (on patents/confidential test data); *US v. Brazil*, WT/DS 199 (local working of patents, compulsory licences); *Brazil v. US*, WT/DS 224 (discrimination in patents).

[46] For example see: *Brazil v. US,* WT/DS 224 (re US Patents Code); *Australia v. EC,* WT/DS 290 (Geographical Indications); *US v. EC* WT/DS 174 (Geographical Indications); *US v. India*, WT/DS 50 (holding that India failed to provide a suitable set of procedures regarding filing of patent applications relating to pharmaceuticals, and granting exclusive marketing rights, largely affirmed on appeal); *EC v. India*, WT/DS 79/1 (largely following WT/DS50), *EC v. Canada*, WT/DS 114 (holding that Canadian exception to patent protection allowing 'stockpiling' prior to expiry of patent term breached TRIPS, but finding 'regulatory review' exception compatible with TRIPS Art. 30); *US v. Canada*, WT/DS 170 (Canada's patent term of 17 years from grant violated TRIPS Art. 33, affirmed on appeal); *EC v. US*, WT/DS 160 (holding that 'business' exemption, but not 'home-style' exemption, to liability for public playing of music from broadcasts, violated TRIPS Art. 13); *EC v. US*, WT/DS 176 (US law on Cuban confiscations mostly related to ownership of trade marks, an issue not covered by TRIPS; largely affirmed on appeal).

[47] *US v. India*, WT/DS 50 (overturning Panel's finding on extent of requirements of TRIPS Art. 70.8, but finding India in violation nevertheless); *US v. Canada*, WT/DS 170 (affirming Panel's finding that Canada's patent term based on grant violated TRIPS Art. 33), *EC v. US*, WT/DS 176 (overturning a number of Panel findings, as regards scope of TRIPS, national treatment, and most favoured nation standard, but largely affirming that US law on Cuban confiscations concerned 'ownership' of trade marks, a matter for Member States).

[48] One problem is the possibility of successive actions by different complainants over identical issues, as occurred in *US v. India,* WT/DS50 and *EC v. India*, WT/DS 79. For general discussion of reform see D. Georgiev and K. van der Borght, *Reform and Development of the WTO Dispute Settlement System* (2006); Y. Taniguchi, A. Yanovich, J. Bohanes (eds), *The WTO in the Twenty-first Century: Dispute Settlement, Negotiations* (2007).

[49] TRIPS Arts 65–7.

[50] P. Gerhart, 'Why Lawmaking for Global Intellectual Property is Unbalanced' [2000] *EIPR* 309; D. Halbert, 'Intellectual Property Piracy: The Narrative Construction of Deviance' (1997) 10 *International Journal for the Semiotics of Law* 55. R. Sherwood, 'Why a Uniform Intellectual Property System Makes Sense for the World' in M. Wallerstein, M. Mogee, R. Schoen (eds.), *Global Dimensions of Intellectual Property Rights in Science and Technology* (1993).

benefits arising from the commercial exploitation thereof.[51] This has prompted further calls for greater protection for traditional intellectual resources of the developing world; notably plant culture, medicinal products, and indigenous folklore.[52] Recent years have also witnessed growing resistance to the wholesale imposition of IP standards on the developing world.[53] Most importantly, the Ministerial declaration at the Doha review of TRIPS in December 2001 acknowledged the primacy of the right to life and health over the protection of intellectual property rights.[54] Moreover, the UK government established a Commission on Intellectual Property Rights which investigated the relationship between intellectual property rights and development, health, and food security, and proposed that such considerations be integrated in national and international policy making.[55] While the acknowledgement of the different positions and interests of developing countries is a welcome development, a number of commentators have observed a parallel trend for further 'ratcheting up' of standards through bilateral trade negotiations (particularly between the USA and developing-world countries).[56] The progressive geographical extension of higher standards for intellectual property rights through such trade arrangements raises the spectre of further norm-setting in the multilateral arena. Indeed, ministers at the meeting in Doha agreed to negotiate the establishment of an international registration system for geographical indications of wines and spirits, and to provide higher levels of protection for names of agricultural products.[57] As with many recent proposals to reform multilateral treaties, these proposals have stalled.

One of the notable developments in recent years is the gradual shift away from multilateral treaties as the sole domain in which the aims of the standardization and harmonization of intellectual property are pursued. In addition to the well documented shift (or return) to bilateral treaties (which we discuss below), there have also been moves towards more subtle forms

---

[51] See pp. 355–6.

[52] See V. Shiva, *Protecting our Biological and Intellectual Heritage in the Age of Bio-piracy* (1996).

[53] See, e.g. V. Shiva, *Protect or Plunder? Understanding Intellectual Property Rights* (2001). For a more general exploration of the appropriateness of imposing western legal concepts on other cultures, see R. Burrell, 'A Case Study in Cultural Imperialism: The Imposition of Copyright on China by the West', in L. Bently and S. Maniatis, *Intellectual Property and Ethics: Perspective on Intellectual Property, Vol. iv* (1998).

[54] WTO, Declaration on the TRIPS Agreement and Public Health (20 Nov. 2001) WT/MIN(01)/DEC/2. See pp. 353–5.

[55] See Commission on Intellectual Property Rights, *Integrating Intellectual Property Rights and Development Policy* (2002). The Commission was established by the Secretary of State for International Development in 2001 to consider how intellectual property rights regimes could be designed to benefit developing countries, to reduce poverty and hunger, improve health and education, and ensure environmental sustainability. See also, Royal Society, *Keeping Science Open: The Effects of Intellectual Property Policy on the Conduct of Science* (2003) (recommending that developing countries should not be required to implement tranches of legislation until their level of development is such that the benefits of implementation outweigh the disadvantages, though without giving an indication as to *how* this could be calculated). For a defensive response to these reports, see S. Crespi, 'Intellectual Property Rights Under Siege' [2003] *EIPR* 242. See also C. May, 'Why IPRs are a Global Political Issue' [2003] *EIPR* 1.

[56] See, e.g. Commission on Intellectual Property Rights, *Integrating Intellectual Property Rights and Development Policy* (2002), 162–4. For a recent example, see Ch. 17 of the US–Chile Trade Agreement, requiring implementation in Chile of standards well above those in TRIPS. An EU–Chile Agreement, while less ambitious, also contains TRIPS-plus obligations: see Council Decision of 18 Nov. 2002 on the signature and provisional application of certain provisions of an Agreement establishing an association between the European Community and its member states, of the one part and the Republic of Chile, of the other part [2002] *OJ L* 352/1, esp. Art. 170. See more generally Peter Yu, 'Currents and Cross Current in the International Intellectual Property Regime' (2004) *Loyola LA Law Review* 323, Peter Drahos, 'BITs and BIPs—Bilateralism in Intellectual Property' (2001) *Journal of World IP* 791.

[57] See below at Ch. 43.

of harmonization, particularly in the standards applied in the different intellectual property offices throughout the world. As well as the standardization of examination practice (such as is being developed between the American, European, and Japanese patent offices), the fact that the US Patent Office has outsourced some of its patent examination work to patent offices in Australia and South Korea is likely to have a subtle but nonetheless important impact on patent standards.

4 REGIONAL INFLUENCES

If an understanding of some of the basic aspects of international intellectual property is important for students of UK intellectual property law, familiarity with European Union law is essential. This is because the majority of developments in UK intellectual property law over the last thirty years have had their origin in the European Community and, since the Maastricht Treaty came into force in 1993, the European Union. Moreover, any future legal developments are likely to stem from, or at least be directed through, the Community/Union.

The European (then 'Economic') Community was established by the Treaty of Rome 1957 (hereafter 'The Treaty'). In its initial conception, the Community focused on the goals of achieving a customs union, a single market, and avoiding the distortion of competition within that market.[58] The original Treaty has been amended and extended by the Treaty on European Union of Maastricht (hereafter 'TEU'),[59] the Treaty of Amsterdam, and most recently the Treaty of Nice.[60] The Amsterdam Treaty introduced a consolidated version of the Treaty establishing the European Community (hereafter 'EC'), operative from 1999.[61] Under the Treaty on European Union, the possibility exists for further forms of action at Community level, for example in the field of criminal law.[62] The Charter of Fundamental Rights of the European Union, proclaimed on 7 December 2000, is another possible influence on intellectual property

---

[58] Art. 2 EC (formerly Art. 2 of the Treaty) sets out the tasks of the Community as being to establish 'a common market and economic and monetary union' and 'by implementing common policies and activities...to promote throughout the Community a harmonious, balanced and sustainable development in economic activities'. Subsequent provisions explain that the Community must prohibit restrictions on the import or export of goods, remove obstacles to the free movement of goods, persons, services, and capital; introduce a system ensuring that competition in the internal market is not distorted. Art. 3 EC (formerly Art. 3 of the Treaty).

[59] The TEU is important for intellectual property rights partly through its provisions recognizing fundamental rights as guaranteed by the European Convention for the Protection of Human Rights and Fundamental Freedoms (Art. 6, TEU, formerly Art. F) and on police and judicial cooperation in criminal matters (Arts. 29–30 TEU, formerly Art. K.1).

[60] In force from 2003. Article II–17(3) of the draft European Constitution provides that 'intellectual property shall be protected'. (18 Jul. 2003) CONV 850/03.

[61] In the latter document, many of the important provisions were renumbered. In this textbook, following the lead of the European Court of Justice, we will refer to Articles of the Treaty of Amsterdam as Art. X EC, and refer to corresponding provisions in parentheses (formerly Art. X of the Treaty). In some cases even this format will be confusing, because some provisions of the initial Treaty of Rome were 'renumbered' by amendments in 1992. The most important of these for our purposes is Art. 12 (formerly Art. 6 of the Treaty (as amended), and prior to that Art. 7 of the Treaty) (non-discrimination).

[62] The 'third' pillar of the Treaty on European Union (Maastricht) covers 'justice and home affairs'. But see *Commission v. Council*, Case C–176/03 [2006] *All ER (EC)* 1, [2005] *ECR* I–7879 (ECJ) (striking down 'framework decision' under TEU because its object was environmental protection, a matter under the EC Treaty). This decision suggests that the EC can adopt criminal provisions under Art 95 EC. See Proposal for a European Parliament and Council Directive on criminal measures aimed at ensuring the enforcement of intellectual property rights {SEC(2005)848}/* COM/2005/0276 final—COD 2005/0127 */ (referring to Art. 95).

within Europe.[63] Despite the rejection by a number of member states of a new 'Constitutional Treaty' in 2005, many of the proposals in that treaty have made themselves into a new 'Reform Treaty' agreed at Lisbon in 2007.[64] This is currently awaiting ratification by member states. As far as intellectual property law is concerned, the Reform treaty contains a new special head of legislative power relating to Community Intellectual Property Rights.[65]

In its early years, European intervention in British intellectual property law largely came through two avenues. First, the judicial interpretation of the Treaty of Rome produced various doctrines that limited the operation of national intellectual property laws in the Community. In addition, the Commission also played a role in policing various competition law aspects of the Treaty that had an impact on intellectual property law. However, for the last twenty years or so, most of the important interventions have been legislative in nature. In particular, there have been moves to centralize the administration of intellectual property rights and to harmonize national laws. As a result, it is not possible to describe British intellectual property law in any sensible way without constant reference to various European Council and Parliament Directives and Regulations, to the decisions of the Court of Justice and the Court of First Instance (interpreting both the EC Treaty and various directives and regulations),[66] the regulations and decisions of the Commission, as well as various intellectual property-granting offices (such as the Office of Harmonization in the Internal Market and the Community Plant Variety Office). Indeed, a high-profile judicial figure has asked whether national intellectual property rights have become 'a moribund anachronism'.[67]

4.1 FREE MOVEMENT OF GOODS AND THE INTERNAL MARKET

In the 1970s and 1980s, much of the influence of European Community law on British intellectual property law was a consequence of the interpretation of Articles 28 and 30 EC (formerly Articles 30 and 36 of the Treaty). These two provisions reflect the desire to establish an 'internal market', that is a single European market with no internal frontiers or national barriers to trade. To this end, Article 28 EC (formerly Article 30 of the Treaty) prohibits 'quantitative

---

[63] See Craig and de Búrca, pp. 379–427. Note the influence of the European Union's Charter of Fundamental Rights on the Advocate General's opinion in *Netherlands v. European Parliament and Council*, Case C–377/98 [2001] *ECR* I–7079 (para. 197). On the legal status of the charter, see A. Menéndez, 'Chartering Europe: Legal status and Policy Implications of the Charter of Fundamental Rights of the European Union' (2002) 40 *Journal of Common Market Studies* 471. Presumably, the Charter may obtain legal status when directly referred to by legislation: see, e.g. Council Regulation (EC) No. 1/2003 of 16 Dec. 2002 on the implementation of the rules on competition laid down in Art. 81 and 82 of the Treaty [2003] *OJ L 1/1*), Recital 37.

[64] Signed 13 December 2007, *OJ C* 306.

[65] Lisbon Reform Treaty, inserting new Art. 97a mandating action establishing uniform intellectual property rights under the 'ordinary procedure.'

[66] The Court of Justice has jurisdiction to give preliminary rulings concerning the interpretation of the Treaty. Where any question arises before a court of tribunal of a member state then it may refer the question to the Court under Art. 234 EC (formerly Art. 177(2) of the Treaty). If the court or tribunal is one against whose decision there is no judicial remedy under national law, that court or tribunal must refer the matter to the Court of Justice.

[67] H. Laddie, 'National IPRS: A Moribund Anachronism in a Federal Europe?' [2001] *EIPR* 402, 407 (arguing that national intellectual property rights are an anachronism but regretting that they are not yet moribund, and advocating the adoption of Community-wide rights and Community courts, in particular to prevent forum shopping). See also W. Kingston, 'What Role Now for National Patent Offices?' [2003] *EIPR* 289.

restrictions' on trade and provisions 'having equivalent effect'.[68] While the use of intellectual property rights to prevent the importing of goods from one Community country into another would be a 'quantitative restriction', Article 30 permits such restrictions where they are necessary to protect industrial and commercial property. This is conditional on the fact that such restrictions do not 'constitute a means of arbitrary discrimination or a disguised restriction on trade between member states'.[69]

While Articles 28 and 30 EC appear to be contradictory, the two provisions were reconciled by permitting the maintenance and use of different national intellectual property laws, while simultaneously limiting the negative effects of the territorial nature of such rights through the so-called 'doctrine of exhaustion'.[70] Initially this was dressed up to appear as if it only invalidated the exercise of intellectual property rights, while preserving their existence (so as not to contravene Article 30).[71] Later, the concept of the existence of the right was refined in terms of its 'specific subject matter'[72] and the 'essential function' of the right. However clothed, the doctrine of exhaustion is best seen as a judicial and political compromise that allows the free movement of goods within the Community. This is despite the fact that national intellectual property rights enable intellectual property rights owners to interfere with the free movement of goods.

In a nutshell, the doctrine of exhaustion prohibits an intellectual property right owner from utilizing their rights to control the resale, import, or export of any goods that have been placed on the market in the Community by or with their consent. For example if A, who has acquired a patent in France and the United Kingdom over a particular machine, sells a machine in France, they cannot use their UK patent rights to prevent importing of the machine into the United Kingdom. This is based on the idea that the 'first sale' gives the intellectual property owner the reward that constitutes the 'specific subject matter'[73] of the right. It is irrelevant that the patentee expressly prohibited the purchaser from reselling the machine or exporting it. This is because it is the consent to first sale that is important.[74] As the doctrine of exhaustion

---

[68] Art. 49 EC (formerly Art. 59 of the Treaty) makes similar prohibition on restrictions on freedom to provide services.

[69] Note also Art. 295 EC (formerly Art. 222 of the Treaty).

[70] In this context, the national and territorial nature of the rights refers to the essential separateness and distinctiveness of each right—for example, the idea that a copyright owner in France and the UK has two separate French and UK copyrights. It was thought to follow from this that consent to distribution in France could in no way affect the exercise of the separate UK copyright. The doctrine of exhaustion does not change the distinctness of the two national rights (so, for example, each might be assigned separately to different persons). Rather, it limits the scope of each national law where the rights are in common control.

[71] H. Cohen Jehoram, 'The *Ideal Standard* Judgment: An Unheeded Warning' [1999] *IPQ* 114. The distinction between existence and exercise was developed in the context of Art. 81 EC (formerly Art. 85 of the Treaty) in *Etablissements Consten SARL and Grundig-Verkaufs-GmbH v. EEC Commission*, Case C–6/65 [1966] *ECR* 299; *Music Vertrieb Membran GmbH and K-tel International v. GEMA*, Joined Cases C–55 and C–7/80 [1981] *ECR* 147.

[72] In *Centrafarm BV and Adriaan De Peijper v. Sterling Drug*, Case C–15/74 [1974] *ECR* 1147 (Art. 30 derogations are limited to the purpose 'of safeguarding rights which constitute the specific subject matter of this property').

[73] *Centrafarm BV and Adriaan De Peijper v. Sterling Drug*, Case C–15/74 [1974] *ECR* 1147 (defining the specific subject matter of patents and trade marks). Note also the discussion of the concept by Advocate General Gulmann in *RTE and ITP v. EC Commission*, Joined Cases C–241/91 and C–242/91 [1995] *ECR* 808 (the 'Magill' Case).

[74] *Dansk Supermarked A/S v. Imerco A/S*, Case C–58/80 [1981] *ECR* 181.

facilitates the 'parallel importation' of goods within the Community, it operates to minimize price differentials for identical goods between countries in the Community.[75]

The doctrine of exhaustion of rights only applies to the right to control distribution (resale, export, or import). It does not apply to the right to rent, perform, or show a (copyright) work in public where the 'specific subject matter' of the right allows the owner to control each and every use (for it is through charging for each use that the essential function of the right is achieved).[76] The case law of the ECJ has elaborated this general principle in a range of subsequent cases. Rather than rehearse the detailed reasoning, the resulting principles can be summarized as follows:

(i)   The principle of exhaustion applies to all types of intellectual property.[77]

(ii)   Consent by the intellectual property right owner includes the consent of person or persons legally or economically dependent on the proprietor (e.g. a licensee or subsidiary).[78]

(iii)   Consent by the intellectual property right owner does *not* include the consent of a person who is an independent assignee of the right (or who happens to be the holder of a right that once had a 'common origin'). For example, the owner of copyright in countries A and B may assign the copyright in a particular work in country B. If the new owner of the right places works on the market in country B, the owner of copyright in country A (being independent) has not exhausted their rights in country A.[79] Although assignments of this nature will often be void as illegitimate agreements to divide up the market (and contrary to Article 81 EC),[80] where the assignments are valid the exception to the principle of exhaustion leaves open the possibility that intellectual property rights might restrict the free movement of goods. This can only be rectified by harmonized regimes (such as the Community trade mark) that forbid separate assignments of national rights.[81]

(iv)   National intellectual property rights may be used to prevent the further circulation of pirated, counterfeit, and other illicitly manufactured goods which by definition have not been placed on the market in the Community with the right holder's consent.

[75] *Deutsche Grammophon GmbH v. Metro GmbH*, Case C–78/70 [1971] *ECR* 487.

[76] *Warner Bros. v. Christiansen*, Case C–158/86 [1988] *ECR* 2605 (rental); *Coditel SA v. Cine Vog Films SA (No. 1)*, Case C–62/79 [1980] *ECR* 881 (public performance). For more nuanced interpretations of *Coditel*, see IViR, *Recasting Copyright for the Knowledge Economy* (2006), pp. 21–30, and T. Dreier, 'The Role of the ECJ for the Development of Copyright in the European Communities' (2007) 54 *Journal of Copyright Society USA* 183, 198–200.

[77] See, e.g. *Deutsche Grammophon GmbH v. Metro GmbH*, Case C–78/70 [1971] *ECR* 487; *Music Vertrieb Membran GmbH and K-tel International v. GEMA*, Joined Cases C–55 and Case C–57/80 [1981] *ECR* 147; *EMI Electrola GmbH v. Patricia Im-und Export*, Case C–341/87 [1989] *ECR* 79.

[78] *Deutsche Grammophon GmbH v. Metro GmbH*, Case C–78/70 [1971] *ECR* 487 (subsidiary); *Keurkoop BV v. Nancy Kean Gifts BV*, Case C–144/81 [1982] *ECR* 2853.

[79] *IHT International Heiztechnik v. Ideal-Standard*, Case C–9/93 [1994] 1 *ECR* I–2789. This reversed *Sirena*, Case C–40/70 [1971] *ECR* 3711 and *Hag I*, Case C–192/73 [1974] *ECR* 731.

[80] Whether the agreement is treated as market sharing will depend on the context, the commitments, the intention of the parties, and the consideration provided. See *Etablissements Consten SARL and Grundig-Verkaufs-GmbH v. EEC Commission*, Case C–58/64 [1966] *ECR* 299 (assignment void). cf. *IHT International Heiztechnik v. Ideal-Standard*, Case C–9/93 [1994] 1 *ECR* I–2789 (assignment had been prompted by the assignor's financial difficulties); *GSK Services Unlimited v. Commission*, Case T–168/01 [2006] *ECR* II–2969.

[81] H. Cohen Jehoram, 'The *Ideal Standard* Judgment: An Unheeded Warning' [1999] *IPQ* 114.

(v)   Where intellectual property rights subsist in country A but not in country B (where A and B are both in the Community), and goods are legitimately placed on the market by parties unconnected with the right holder in country B, the right owner has not consented to the marketing of those goods and as such will not have exhausted their rights. The right holder can therefore prevent import into and distribution of the goods in country A.[82]

(vi)   Where intellectual property rights subsist in country A but not in country B (where A and B are both in the Community), and goods are legitimately placed on the market by the right holder (or parties connected with the right holder) in country B, the right owner will have been taken to have consented to the marketing of those goods and so have exhausted their rights.[83]

(vii)   Where intellectual property rights subsist in country A but are subject to a compulsory licence (i.e. any person may exploit the intellectual property right on payment of a fee), the rights are *not* exhausted when goods are manufactured under such a licence. Here, the intellectual property right owner will be able to use national laws to prevent imports into country B.[84]

(viii) Where goods have been marketed in the EC by the intellectual property right holder (or with their consent), the right of the owner of the goods to resell might permit behaviour (such as advertising) that overrides other aspects of the proprietor's intellectual property rights.[85]

(viii) Where goods have been marketed in the EC by the intellectual property right holder (or with their consent), but the goods have subsequently been altered, a series of specific rules have been developed that define when a resale is legitimate. These are considered later, in the context of trade marks.[86]

(ix)   Where goods have been marketed *outside* the EC by the intellectual property right holder (or with their consent), the principle of exhaustion has no application. In the absence of harmonization, it is for member states (and where there has been harmonization, the ECJ) to determine the effects of such marketing.[87]

Although the doctrine of exhaustion of rights has reduced some of the disruption that national intellectual property laws pose to the internal market, it has not provided a complete solution.

---

[82] *EMI Electrola GmbH v. Patricia Im-und Export*, Case C–341/87 [1989] *ECR* 79. For the limits of this see *Commission v. French Republic*, Case C–23/99 [2000] *ECR* I–7653.

[83] *Merck & Co. v. Stephar BV & Exler*, Case C–187/80 [1981] *ECR* 2063 (marketing of drug in Italy when patent protection was not available); *Merck & Co. v. Primecrown*, Joined Cases C–267/95 and C–268/95 [1996] *ECR* I–6285 (affirming *Merck v. Stephar*).

[84] *Pharmon v. Hoechst*, Case C–19/84 [1985] *ECR* 2281 (import into the Netherlands of drugs manufactured under compulsory licence in the UK); *Music Vertrieb Membran GmbH and K-tel International v. GEMA*, Joined Cases C–55/80 and C–57/80 [1981] *ECR* 147. One problem with this effect is that it may undermine compulsory licences which are intended to induce voluntary licensing arrangements, since the latter (but not the former) will be treated as exhausting the intellectual property owner's rights.

[85] *Parfums Christian Dior SA v. Evora BV*, Case C–337/95 [1997] *ECR* I–6013; *Norwegian Government v. Astra Norge SA*, E1–98 [1999] 1 CMLR 860.

[86] See below at pp. 945–52.

[87] *EMI Records v. CBS United Kingdom*, Case C–51/75 [1976] *ECR* 811 (stopping import of copyright works from the US); *Polydor and RSO Records v. Harlequin Record Shops and Simons Records*, Case C–70/80 [1982] *ECR* 329 (stopping import of copyright works from EFTA countries); *Sebago and Ancienne Maison Dubois et fils SA v. GB-Unic SA*, Case C–173/98 [1999] *CMLR* 1317. See below at pp. 953–6.

This is because the national intellectual property laws of the member states can vary significantly. Since the principle of exhaustion comes into effect when the right owner consents to goods being placed on the market, that consent will not exist where a third party makes and distributes goods in a country where the right does not exist or has lapsed.[88] It is largely for this reason that the Commission set about to harmonize intellectual property laws in Europe.

4.2 COMPETITION RULES

The second way in which European initiatives have exerted an influence over British intellectual property law is through the rules on competition contained in Articles 81 and 82 EC (formerly Articles 85 and 86 of the Treaty). These provisions are designed to prevent anti-competitive agreements and practices, as well as abusive conduct by monopolies. These provisions impact on intellectual property law in a number of ways. Articles 81 and 82 EC are both couched as prohibitions and thus automatically render void arrangements between 'undertakings' which meet the specified criteria (or in the case of Article 81 are not exempted by Article 81(3)).[89] In certain cases, they also provide the basis for an action for damages,[90] a ground for applying to the Commission for a compulsory licence to exploit an intellectual property right,[91] and a defence (a so-called 'Euro-defence') to an action for infringement of intellectual property rights.[92] Articles 81 and 82 EC are both enforced by the European Commission, and from May 2004, by national competition authorities (in the United Kingdom, the Office of Fair Trading, and on appeal from a finding of infringement or rejecting a complaint, the Competition Appeal Tribunal).[93] If an undertaking is found to have been acting anti-competitively, the European Commission has the ability to impose serious fines, whether the behaviour was intentional or negligent.[94]

---

[88] *Bassett v. SACEM*, Case C–402/85 [1987] *ECR* 1747; *EMI Electrola GmbH v. Patricia Im-und Export*, Case C–341/87 [1989] ECR 79.

[89] Art. 81(2). This might be a significant penalty where a patentee has carefully calculated the terms of the licence, only for it later to be held to be void.

[90] In the UK, either before a Court, or the Competition Appeal Tribunal: Competition Act 1998, s. 47A (introduced by the Enterprise Act 2002, s. 18).

[91] *RTE and ITP v. EC Commission*, Joined Cases C–241/91 and C–242/91 [1995] *ECR* 808.

[92] Whether and, if so, when abuse can be used as a defence is a controversial issue. See *Chiron Corp. v. Organon Teknika* [1993] *FSR* 324; [1994] *FSR* 202; *Intel v. Via Technologies* [2003] *FSR* 574 (para. 115); *Sportswear Spa v. Stonestyle* [2007] (2) 33. Two other penalties are available in serious cases: criminal penalties as regards dishonest 'horizontal agreements' (Enterprise Act 2002, Part 6) and disqualification of directors (Enterprise Act 2002, s. 204).

[93] Council Regulation (EC) No. 1/2003 of 16 Dec. 2002 on the implementation of the rules on competition laid down in Art. 81 and 82 of the Treaty [2003] *OJ L* 1/1, Art. 5. This Regulation sees a 'modernization' and decentralization of the enforcement of European competition law, with the European Commission operating as part of a 'European Competition Network' of national authorities. In general, the European Commission will enforce cases involving practices or agreements that affect at least three member states.

[94] Council Regulation No. 17/62 of 6 Feb. 1962: First Regulation Implementing Arts. 85 and 86 of the Treaty *OJ Sp Ed* 1962 No. 204/62 p. 87, reg. 15(2) fines of up to 1 million Euro or 10% of turnover in the preceding business year. Council Regulation No. 1/2003, Art. 7 (empowering the Commission to impose behavioural or structural remedies which are 'proportionate' and necessary to bring the infringement to an end); Art. 23(2) (fines of up to 10% of turnover in the preceding business year); Art. 24 (periodic penalties of up to 5% of average daily turnover per day). Competition Act 1998 (giving OFT power to impose penalties of up to 10% turnover for up to 3 years).

Article 81 prohibits 'all agreements between undertakings…and concerted practices which may affect trade between member states and which have as their object or effect the prevention, restriction or distortion of competition'. As the term 'undertakings' has been interpreted liberally, Article 81 potentially applies to agreements concerning the licensing and assignment of intellectual property rights,[95] whether between competitors or parties at different levels of distribution (for example, exclusive distribution agreements). Article 81 goes on to outline certain practices, such as price fixing and market sharing, which will normally be prohibited. In other cases, a conclusion that the agreement has an anti-competitive effect depends on the actual conditions in which the agreement would function, including the economic contexts, the products covered by the agreement, and the structure of the market.[96]

Even though the Treaty is not meant to prejudice the rules in member states governing the system of property ownership,[97] the European Commission and the European Court of Justice have had little hesitation in applying Article 81(1) to agreements involving intellectual property rights. According to the Court, interference with intellectual property rights is justified on the basis that it 'does not affect the grant of those rights but only limits their exercise to the extent necessary to give effect to the prohibition under [Art. 81]'.[98] Article 81 also applies to institutions and arrangements for the collective administration of rights: a common feature of copyright exploitation.[99]

Given the potential breadth of Article 81, it is important to note that Article 81(3) allows for Article 81(1) to be 'declared inapplicable' in a number of circumstances.[100] Such exemptions must 'contribute to improving the production or distribution of goods or to promoting technical or economic progress, while allowing consumers a fair share of the resulting benefit'. The European Commission has issued a number of such 'block exemptions' in the form of Commission Regulations: the most important relate to 'technology transfer agreements', 'R&D agreements', and 'vertical agreements'.[101] These block exemptions enable operators to be confident that their agreements are exempt (though the benefit of a block exemption may be withdrawn as regards an individual agreement), and may also be treated as 'guidelines' even for agreements that fall outside the scope of the block exemption. In other situations, operators will have to form their own judgements as to whether agreements are exempt. (The

---

[95] For example, *Etablissements Consten SARL and Grundig- Verkaufs-GmbH v. EEC Commission*, Case C–583/64 [1966] *ECR* 299. (German manufacturer G appointed French company C as exclusive distributor in France. C had registration of GINT mark in France. The ECJ agreed with the Commission's view that the agreement (including the provision allowing C to register the mark in France) was contrary to Art. 85.) Minor agreements are excluded: Commission Notice on agreements of minor importance which do not fall within the meaning of Art. 81(1) EC [2001] *OJ C* 368/13 (agreements between firms who are not competitors as falling outside of Art. 81(1) if the market share held by each of the parties does not exceed 15% on any of the relevant markets affected by the agreement). See, generally, Stothers, Ch. 3.

[96] *European Night Services v. Commission*, T–374/94 [1998] *ECR* II–3141.

[97] Art. 295 EC (formerly Art. 222 of the Treaty).

[98] *Etablissements Consten SARL and Grundig-Verkaufs-GmbH v. EEC Commission*, Case C–58/64 [1966] *ECR* 299. Cf. *Panayiotou v. Sony Music Entertainment* [1994] *EMLR* 229.

[99] See below at pp. 274–7, 296–302.

[100] Regulation No. 19/65/EEC.

[101] Commission Regulation (EC) No 772/2004 on the application of Article 81(3) of the Treaty to categories of technology transfer agreements [2004] *OJ L* 123/11 (27 April 2004) (Technology Transfer Block Exemption: TTBER); VRR; see below at pp. 576–7, 968–9.

possibility for obtaining individual exemption through a notification system, which became an unacceptable administrative burden, has been abolished from May 2004.)[102]

Article 82 EC prohibits an undertaking from abusing a dominant position. This prohibition has primarily affected intellectual property law in two ways. First, it provides a basis for regulating collective organizations that administer intellectual property rights on behalf of owners and which occupy a dominant position in the market. To prevent abuse, organizations in a dominant position are only able to impose obligations and restrictions that are necessary to achieve their legitimate aims.[103] Second, Article 82 provides a remedy for misuse or abuse of intellectual property rights. On one reading of Article 82, it is possible to argue that, as intellectual property rights confer monopoly rights, they necessarily place owners in a dominant position for the market covered by the intellectual property right. On this basis, all activities carried on by intellectual property right holders would need to be scrutinized to ensure that they were not abusive. However, the European Court of Justice has declined to use Article 82 in this way. Instead, the Court has made it clear that ownership of an intellectual property right does not of itself confer dominance in a market. As a consequence, a refusal to license an intellectual property right only constitutes an abuse of a dominant position in exceptional circumstances.[104]

4.3 CENTRALIZATION AND HARMONIZATION

While the doctrine of exhaustion has reduced the impact of national intellectual property rights on the completion of the internal market, it has been unable to guarantee that barriers to trade would not arise where national laws differed in terms of substance or duration. Consequently, it soon became apparent that to achieve the holy grail of an internal market, some level of harmonization would be necessary. There are three relevant ways in which the Community is able to harmonize national laws.[105]

---

[102] Formerly, where there had been no notification to the Commission and an agreement fell outside the scope of a block exemption, the national court could not authorize an agreement: Regulation 17/62 of 6 Feb. 1962: First Regulation Implementing Arts. 85 and 86 of the Treaty *OJ Sp Ed* 1962, No. 204/62, 8, Art. 9. If faced with such a situation the court was forced to seek information from the Commission or refer the case to the ECJ. See Notice on Cooperation between National Courts and the Commission in Applying Arts. 85 and 86 EEC [1993] *OJ C* 39/6. However, the system of prior notification became unworkable, and has now been abolished. From 1 May 2004, Art. 81(3) is directly applicable by the courts of member states: Council Regulation No. 1/2003, Art. 1(2), Art. 6, Recital 4. The Commission may still produce block exemptions, may make decisions withdrawing the benefit of such exemptions in individual cases (Art. 29), or finding that Arts. 81 or 82 are inapplicable to individual cases (Art. 10).

[103] These are discussed below at pp. 298–9. *Re GEMA (No. 1)* [1971] CMLR D35; *Belgische Radio en Televise (BRT) v. SABAM*, Case C–127/73 [1974] *ECR* 313.

[104] Thus, it was not an abuse for a designer and manufacturer of automobiles to refuse to license its intellectual property rights to persons wishing to manufacture replacement parts for vehicles. *AB Volvo v. Erik Veng (UK)*, Case 238/87 [1988] *ECR* 6211; *CICRA v. Regie Nationale des Usines Renault*, Case C–53/87 [1988] *ECR* 6039. However, an abuse of dominant position was found where a broadcasting organization which generated programme schedules in which copyright was held to subsist, refused to license a newspaper to publish those schedules on a weekly rather than daily basis: *RTE and ITP v. EC Commission*, Joined Cases C–241/91 and C–242/91 [1995] *ECR* 808 (the 'Magill' Case). Subsequent decisions have sought to identify the basis to the Magill Case, but as yet have proved inconclusive: *Oscar Bronner v. Media Print*, Case C–7/97 [1998] *ECR* I–7791; *Tierce Ladbroke v. Commission*, Case T–504/93 [1997] *ECR* II–923; *IMS Health Inc v. Commission*, Case T–184/01R [2002] 4 *CMLR* 58; *NDC Health Corporation and NDC Health GmbH*, Case C–481/01P(R); *Microsoft v. Commission*, Case T–201/04 [2007] 5 *CMLR* (11) 846.

[105] See generally, Craig and de Búrca, Chs. 3 and 4.

The Council can issue directives for the approximation of the laws of member states 'as directly affect the establishing and function of the common market'.[106] Under this process a Commission issues a proposal and then consults with the European Parliament and Economic and Social Committee. To be passed, a proposal must be approved unanimously by the Council. The Council is also able to adopt measures (not just directives) 'for the approximation of the provisions laid down by law, regulation or administrative action in Member States which have as their object the establishment and functioning of the internal market'.[107] Typically, this process begins with a Commission proposal,[108] which must be approved by the Council and the European Parliament. As only a qualified majority of the Council must support the proposal it is not necessary to have the unanimous approval of all the member states. Third, if action by the Community is 'necessary to attain, in the course of the operation of the common market, one of the objectives of the Community, and this Treaty has not provided the necessary powers, the Council shall, acting unanimously on a proposal from the Commission after consulting the European Parliament, take the appropriate measures'.[109] This provision may only be used where no other provision of the Treaty gives the Community institutions the necessary power to act.[110] It has usually been the basis for the establishment of Community offices.[111]

Community involvement with intellectual property can be divided into four stages. In the 1970s, the focus of attention was on the establishment of a Community patent system, that is a system in which a single patent would be granted for the whole of the Community, enforceable in Community patent courts. To this end, in 1975 the Community Patent Convention was agreed to at an intergovernmental level between the (then nine) member states. However, the political will to introduce the scheme never materialized.[112] In part this was because in 1973 a separate instrument for the granting of patents, the European Patent Convention (EPC), had been agreed to between states (a number of which were then outside the EC). As such, there was little urgency to implement the distinct (though linked) Community patent. Despite attempts to revive the Treaty through a 1989 Protocol in Luxembourg,[113] it is only in the last couple of years that a real will for a single Community patent regime has emerged. This has taken shape in the form of a Commission proposal to introduce a Community patent by way of a Community Regulation.[114] In the meantime, the existence of the European Patent Convention has limited the ability of the Community to harmonize national patent laws.[115] The reason for this is that

---

[106] Art. 94 EC.

[107] Art. 95 EC (formerly Art. 100A of the Treaty). See *Netherlands v. European Parliament and Council*, Case C–377/98 [2002] *OJEPO* 231; [2002] *FSR* 575 (ECJ) paras. 13–29 (Biotech Directive was properly based on Art. 100A).

[108] The Protocol on the Application of the Principles of Subsidiarity and Proportionality states that the Community should legislate only to the extent necessary and that, in general, directives should be preferred to Regulations, and framework directives preferred to detailed measures (para. 6). It also requires the Commission to consult widely before proposing legislation (para. 9). Such consultation is usually by way of issuing Green Papers and holding meetings of 'interested parties'.

[109] Art. 308 (formerly Art. 235 of the Treaty).

[110] *Commission v. Council*, Case C–45/86 [1987] *ECR* 1493, para. 13.

[111] e.g. CTMR, Recital 4. In these cases the legislature is not harmonizing, but creating new rights: see Opinion 1/94 [1994] *ECR* I–5267 (para 59); Case C–377/98 (para 35).

[112] [1976] *OJ L* 17/43.

[113] Luxembourg Agreement of 15 Dec. 1989 relating to Community Patents (1989) *OJ L* 401/1.

[114] See below at p. 351. After the proposal stalled in 2004, it has, once again, been revived.

[115] Paradoxically, the Community's exclusive competence in the field of civil jurisdiction stands in the way of an inter-governmental agreement to simplify patent litigation: see A Arnull & R Jacob, 'European Patent Litigation: Out of the Impasse?' (2007) *EIPR* 209 (noting that member states cannot enter the proposed European

all member states are parties to and therefore bound by the EPC. At the same time, they cannot amend the Convention without the assent of the non-EC participants. In the two fields where Community action has taken place, the proposals have been made to appear as if they leave the EPC untouched. The two Regulations on Supplementary Protection Certificates are worded so as to avoid appearing to be extensions of the patent term.[116] Similarly, the Directive of the European Parliament and Council on the Legal Protection of Biotechnological Inventions, which attempts to harmonize patent law for biological inventions, is presented as a Directive to harmonize the 'interpretation' of existing provisions of the EPC, rather than amending or modifying those provisions.

In the 1980s, attention turned to the harmonization of trade mark law. The first part of a two-pronged strategy was to approximate national trade mark laws. This was eventually completed by way of a directive.[117] The second prong saw the establishment of a single office that granted Community trade marks enforceable in the courts of member states designated as Community Trade Mark Courts. The Community trade mark was introduced by way of a Council Regulation, and in 1996 the Office of Harmonization in the Internal Market was established in Alicante, Spain.[118] As the substantive rules of the Regulation are virtually identical to those of the Directive, appeals of decisions of the Office of Harmonization to the OHIM's Boards of Appeal, the Court of First Instance, and the ECJ offer valuable guidance to national authorities.

At the end of the 1980s, the third wave of harmonization began when the Commission set out to harmonize a number of aspects of copyright law.[119] The need for action arose because the different levels of copyright protection in different member states was seen to consti-tute a potential barrier to trade.[120] In contrast with the approach taken to trade marks, the Community passed a series of seven Directives each harmonizing particular aspects of copy-right law (especially relating to areas of technological change). In so doing, the Commission also aimed to set the standard of protection to be given to creators at a 'high level'.[121]

The 1990s also witnessed Community intervention in relation to a number of the so-called *sui generis* intellectual property rights. A Community Plant Variety Regulation established a Community Office in Angers, France. In contrast to the strategy in relation to trade marks, no harmonization directive was passed regulating national law.[122] A directive was also passed relating to the harmonization of the law relating to designs which was followed by a Regulation introducing a Community Registered Design (to be issued by the Office of Harmonization in the Internal Market), and a Community Unregistered Design Right.[123] The latter, available since April 2002, is the first Europe-wide, unitary right to be granted automatically, rather than after application to an office.[124]

Patent Litigation Agreement, but suggesting possible revision limiting it to institutional questions to avoid over-lap with Directive 2004/48 and Reg 44/2001).

[116] SPC (MP) Reg.; SPC (PPP) Reg.   [117] Trade Marks Directive.

[118] See below at pp. 781–2 and Chapter 35, Section 3.

[119] See below at Chapter 2, Section 7.

[120] It was also motivated by the prompting of the ECJ, e.g. in *EMI Electrola GmbH v. Patricia Im-und Export*, Case C–341/87 [1989] *ECR* 79.

[121] For example, Duration Dir. Recital 10.

[122] CPVR. See below at p. 593.

[123] See below at Section 4 of the Introduction to Part III.

[124] The Commission also put forward a proposal to harmonize the law on utility models which would have required member states to supplement patent protection with a system for issuing a second tier of rights for inventions. This proposal has been abandoned. See Bently and Sherman, 2nd edn., pp. 338–40.

Given the breadth of European intervention in intellectual property law, it is not surprising that a number of challenges have been made to particular European initiatives. In most cases, such challenges must be brought by national governments before the Court of Justice.[125] National courts do not have the power to declare acts of the Community institutions to be invalid.[126] If past experiences are much to go on, it seems that attempts to set aside Community legislation are unlikely to be successful.[127]

4.3.1 Implementation

In the UK, directives have been implemented through the introduction of new statutes (as with the Trade Marks Act 1994), or more commonly by amending existing statutes by way of statutory instrument.[128] When implementing directives, the UK government has tended to rewrite the (often abstract) provisions used in the directives into the language that is more commonly found in British statutes. Unfortunately, such rewriting can make interpretation doubly difficult, and a number of UK judges have made adverse comments about this practice.[129] Unlike the case with directives, regulations do not need to be implemented into national law to be effective.[130] However, where national procedures need to be established (as with the Regulations on Supplementary Protection Certificates), some action must necessarily follow.

If a government fails to implement a directive or implements it partially or tardily, the Commission may commence an action against that member state before the ECJ.[131] Moreover, pending implementation, a number of consequences may follow automatically.[132] First, in accordance with general principles of European law, the provision has a direct effect 'vertically' on state bodies, including rights-granting bodies such as the Patent Office or Trade Marks Registry. This direct effect only applies where the provision is clear and unconditional.[133] Second, the national courts must interpret existing national law in line with

---

[125] The *locus standi* rules mean that the applicant must normally be a member state or community institution rather than an individual. But in certain circumstances an individual may challenge EC legislation: see *Codorniu SA v. Council*, Case C–309/89 [1994] *ECR* 1853 (Spanish producers of sparkling wine, also owners of graphic trade mark 'Gran Cremant de Codorniu', successfully objected to regulation restricting legitimate use of '*cremant*' to wine made in France or Luxembourg).

[126] *Foto-Frost*, Case C–314/85 [1987] *ECR* 4199.

[127] *Spain v. The Council of the European Union*, Case C–350/92 [1995] *ECR* I–1985; *Metronome Music v. Music Point Hokamp GmbH*, Case C–200/96 [1998] *ECR* I–1953; *Netherlands v. European Parliament and Council*, Case C–377/98 [2002] *OJEPO* 231; [2002] *FSR* 575 (ECJ).

[128] European Communities Act 1972, s. 1(2).

[129] *Philips Electronics BV v. Remington Consumer Products* [1998] *RPC* 283; *British Horseracing Board v. William Hill* [2001] 2 *CMLR* 212, 225; *Apple Computer Inc.'s Design Application* [2002] *FSR* (38) 602, 603.

[130] Art. 249 EC (formerly Art. 189 of the Treaty).

[131] See, e.g. *Commission v. United Kingdom*, Case C–30/90 [1992] *ECR* I–829 (UK compulsory licence provisions incompatible with Treaty); and *Commission v. Ireland*, Case C–212/98 [1999] *ECR* I–8571 (failure of Republic of Ireland to implement the Satellite Directive); *Commission v. Ireland*, Case C–213/98 [2000] *ECDR* 201 (failure of Republic of Ireland to implement the Rental Directive); *Commission v. Ireland*, Case C–13/00 [2002] *ECR* I–2943; [2002] 2 *CMLR* 10 (failure of Ireland to implement the Paris Act of Berne and thus failure to fulfil its obligations under Art. 300(7) EC and Art. 5 of Protocol 28 of the European Economic Area of 2 May 1992).

[132] See Craig and de Búrca, 268–303.

[133] *NV Algamene Transport en Expeditie Onderrenning van Gend en Loos v. Nederlandse Administratie der Belastingens*, Case 26/62 [1963] *ECR* 1. These conditions have been whittled away, so the question may well now be whether the provision is capable of being applied by a court to a specific case: *H.J. Banks & Co. v. British Coal Corporation*, Case C–128/92 [1994] *ECR* I–1209, 1237 (Advocate General Gerven). For an example, see *Mister Long Trade Mark* [1998] *RPC* 401 (TM Dir. Art. 13).

the unimplemented provisions of a directive: a consequence sometimes referred to as 'indirect effect'.[134] Where this is not possible, individuals are not able to rely on the unimplemented provisions to bring an action against other private bodies: there is no 'horizontal' direct effect. While in these circumstances private individuals may not get the remedy they would have been entitled to if the directive had been implemented, they are not left without a course of action. This is because, if a private individual has suffered damage as a result of a government's failure to implement a directive, the member state may be required to compensate the individual. For this to occur, the claimant must show that the object of the directive was to create rights, that the scope of rights is identifiable, and that failure to introduce such rights caused the damage.[135]

4.3.2 Interpretation

When interpreting provisions that are intended to give effect to a European directive, not surprisingly the directive will be a critical aid to interpretation. For the uninitiated common lawyer, European directives may seem strange since they are often formulated in relatively vague language. In such cases, the provisions should be interpreted purposively.[136] While the text of the directive remains critical, particular attention should be given to the Recitals at the front of the directive, since these often provide specific examples explaining what a clause is intended to cover.

The material available to assist in the interpretation of a directive will be different from the material that is used to interpret British statutes. Whereas it is possible to look to Hansard when interpreting (purely) UK law, when considering the implementation of a European directive, what is said in the British Parliament will be of little assistance (except possibly as regards the implementation of optional aspects of European legislation).[137] Instead, attention must be paid to the European 'travaux préparatoires', such as Commission proposals.[138] In exceptional cases, it may be helpful to refer to the so-called 'Agreed Statements', that is to the minutes of what was agreed between the Commission and the Council.[139] Legislation is also to

---

[134] *Marleasing v. La Comercial Internacional de Alimentacion*, Case C–106/89 [1990] *ECR* I–4135; *Silhouette International Schmied GmbH & Co. KG v. Hartlauer Handegesellschaft mbH*, Case C–355/96 [1998] *ECR* I–4799; [1998] *CMLR* 953, 979; *Webb v. EMO Air Cargo* [1992] 2 *All ER* 43; [1995] 4 *All ER* 577.

[135] *Francovich v. Italian Republic*, Joined Cases C–6, and 9/90 [1991] *ECR* I–5357 (paras. 31–45); *R v. Secretary of State for Transport, ex p. Factortame* [1999] 3 *CMLR* 597.

[136] *Re Adidas AG*, Case C–223/98 [1999] 3 *CMLR* 895 (under Community law legislation is to be interpreted by reference to the wording taking into account the context and object of the legislation); *SA Société LTJ Diffusion v. SA Sadas* Case C–291/00 [2003] *ECR* I–02799 (AG, para. 18); *Ansul v. Ajax*, Case C–40/01 [2003] *ECR* I–2439, para. 26.

[137] *British Sugar v. Robertson* [1996] *RPC* 281, 292 (no room for the application of *Pepper v. Hart* or the *White Paper*). Cf. R. Burrell, H. Smith, and A. Coleman, 'Three-dimensional Trade Marks: Should the Directive be Reshaped?', in N. Dawson and A. Firth (eds.), *Trade Marks Retrospective: Perspectives in Intellectual Property*, vol. 7 (2000) 137, 160 n. 5.

[138] S. Schønberg and K. Frick, 'Finishing, Refining, polishing: on the use of *travaux préparatoires* as an aid to the interpretation of Community legislation' (2003) 28 *ELR* 149, 156–7 (observing that such documents have frequently been used in the interpretation of the regulations creating 'supplementary protection certificates' and on the registration of 'geographical indications.')

[139] Schønberg and Frick, 164–7. In relation to the TM Dir., *see Libertel Groep BV v. Benelux MerkenBureau*, Case C–104/01 [2004] *FSR* (4) 65 (para. 25) (ECJ) (noting that the Minutes specifically acknowledge that they should not be used in interpretation); *Heidelberger Bauchemie*, Case C–49/02 [2004] *ECR* I–6129, paras. 16–17; *Anheuser-Busch*, Case C–245/02 [2004] *ECR* I–10989 (ECJ, Grand Chamber) (paras. 78–80). For the general proposition that 'declarations recorded in minutes…cannot be used for the purposes of interpreting a provision of Community law where no reference is made to the content of the declaration in the wording of the

be interpreted in the light of any international agreements to which the Community is a party, including, importantly, the TRIPs Agreement.[140]

When interpreting British law implementing a directive, it may be important to take account of decisions of other European courts.[141] Occasionally decisions given by the courts of member states before the adoption of the directive may provide some indication of what the directive was intended to achieve. Where a directive is meant to correspond to pre-harmonized law in one jurisdiction, the decisions of that jurisdiction may carry special weight.[142] While the judgments of the courts of member states as to the meaning of a directive may be helpful, there is no obligation to follow the interpretation of the first court that happened to do so. Decisions of the courts of all member states are meant to be equally authoritative.

Ultimately, the question of the way a directive (or regulation) is to be interpreted is decided by the ECJ.[143] The Court is assisted by one of the eight Advocates General, who make reasoned submissions in order to assist the Court. The Advocate General's opinion may be a useful interpretative tool to resolve doubts over a decision of the ECJ. In some situations, particularly in relation to appeals from the Boards of Appeal of the OHIM, hearings are initially to the Court of First Instance (from whence appeals can be heard by the ECJ). Given the enormous workload of the ECJ, it seems likely (and desirable) that a specialist chamber of the Court of First Instance (with a limited possibility for further appeals to the ECJ) will be established sometime in the future. Until that time, the final word on the meaning of Community provisions is left to a tribunal that is clearly less than comfortable with intellectual property law.

4.4 EXTERNAL RELATIONS

Another way in which the European Community is involved in intellectual property law is through the role it plays in negotiating and signing treaties. The Community's treaty powers are set out in Article 133 EC (formerly Article 113 of the Treaty), as amended by the Treaty of Nice in 2003.[144] This gives the Community the exclusive power to enter into treaties with respect to common commercial policy, a notion which is expressly extended to the negotiation and

provision in question', see *VAG Sverige AB*, Case C–329/95 [1997] *ECR* I–2675 (para. 23) and *Antonissen*, Case C–292/89 [1991] *ECR* I–745, [1991] 2 *CMLR* 373 (para. 18). For British objections to use of such minutes where they are not public documents, see *Wagamama v. City Centre Restaurants* [1995] *FSR* 713, 725.

[140] *Heidelberger Bauchemie*, Case C–49/02 [2004] *ECR* 1–6129, paras. 19–21.

[141] For example in *Philips Electronics NV v. Remington Consumer Products* [1999] *RPC* 809, 820–1 reference was made to the Swedish decision in *Ide Line Aktiebolag AG v. Philips Electronics NV* [1997] *ETMR* 377; and in *Premier Brands UK v. Typhoon Europe* [2000] *FSR* 767 reference was made to a number of German decisions.

[142] But for them to do so there must be solid evidence of the relevant legislative intention: *Wagamama v. City Centre Restaurants* [1995] *FSR* 713, 725. In *British Horseracing Board v. William Hill* [2002] *ECDR* 41 the Court of Appeal acknowledged that a different understanding of the Database Directive from that of Laddie J at first instance prevailed in Scandinavian countries, and noted that the latter's understanding may be significant given the fact that the Directive was said to be influenced by the so-called 'Nordic catalogue rule'. The Court of Appeal therefore referred the case to the ECJ.

[143] One controversial issue concerns when 'interpretation' permitted under Art. 234 EC ends, and determination of facts—a matter for the national courts—begins. See, generally, Craig and de Búrca, 493–4, and in the context of intellectual property, *Arsenal v. Reed*, Case C–206/01 [2002] *ECR* I–10273; *Arsenal FC plc v. Reed (No. 2)* [2003] 1 *CMLR* 13; [2003] 1 *All ER* 137 (CA). On the UK courts' relationship with the ECJ, see B. Trimmer, 'An Increasingly Uneasy Relationship—the English Courts and the European Court of Justice in Trade Mark Disputes', [2008] *EIPR* 87.

[144] In a case concerning the powers of the Community to enter TRIPS, the European Court of Justice held that Art. 113 (as it then was) did not cover treaties relating to intellectual property rights, except insofar as they related to border measures, Opinion 1/94 [1994] *ECR* I–5267, 5316. The TRIPS Agreement was entered into by

conclusion of agreements relating to 'the commercial aspects of intellectual property'. Article 133(7) of the amended text continues to allow the Council, after consulting the Parliament, to enter into treaties relating to intellectual property.[145] To date the Community has entered into a number of intellectual property-related treaties. For example, the Community is now a party to TRIPS, the Madrid Protocol on international registration of trade marks, the WIPO Copyright Treaty and WIPO Performances and Phonograms Treaty,[146] as well as bilateral agreements with Morocco, Tunisia, and Australia for the protection of denominations of wine.[147] In October 2007, the European Commission announced that it would seek the authority of member states to begin negotiations of anti-counterfeiting trade agreements (with, inter alia, the US, Japan, Korea, Mexico, and New Zealand).

Although the United Kingdom has historically adopted a 'dualist' approach to international law (meaning that international treaties cannot be relied upon as a source of rights unless they have been implemented into national law), the Community's participation in international norms presents the possibility of such norms being relied upon directly in certain circumstances. While the European Court of Justice has been willing to interpret European Community legislation in the light of its treaty obligation,[148] the Court has yet to hold that any provisions in international treaties have direct effect.[149]

4.5 EUROPEAN ECONOMIC AREA

To understand intellectual property law in the United Kingdom, it is important to be familiar with the European Economic Area (EEA). This is an initiative entered into between the EC and certain satellite countries who are members of the European Free Trade Area (EFTA). In 1994, the majority of the countries then in EFTA decided to enter into a joint EC–EFTA initiative

---

the Community (under implied powers) and member states: Opinion 1/94 [1994] *ECR* I–5267. See generally Craig and de Búrca, 169–182.

[145] A. Dashwood, 'External Relations Provisions of the Amsterdam Treaty' (1998) 35 *CMLR* 119; P. Pescatore, 'Opinion 1/94 on Conclusion of the WTO Agreement: Is There an Escape from a Programmed Disaster?' (1999) 36 *CML Rev* 387.

[146] Council Decision 2000/278 of 16 Apr. 2000, [2000] *OJ* L89/6; Council Decision of 27 Oct 2003 approving accession of the European Community to the Protocol relating to the Madrid Agreement Concerning the International Registration of Marks [2003] *OJ L* 296/1; Council Decision of 18 Dec 2006 Approving accession to the Geneva Act of the Hague Agreement Concerning the International Registration of Industrial Designs *OJ* L 386/28 (29 Dec 2006).

[147] Under Art. 133. Council Regulation (EEC) No. 482/77 of 8 Mar. 1977 [1977] *OJ L* 65/1; Council Regulation (EEC) No. 3618/87 of 30 Nov. 1987 [1987] *OJ L* 3618/87; Council Decision 89/146/EEC of 12 Dec. 1988 [1989] *OJ* L 56/1.

[148] *Sociedad General de Autores y Editores de Espana (SGAE) v. Rafael Hotels SL,* Case C–306/05 [2006] *ECR* I–11519, para. 35 (ECJ) (interpreting the Information Society Directive in the light of the Berne Convention). More radically, in *Hermes,* Case C–53/96 [1998] *ECR* I–3603, the ECJ held that it should interpret TRIPs Art. 50(6) to assist the national court to determine its own obligations and 'to forestall future differences of interpretation'.

[149] *Dior,* Cases C–300/98 and C–392/98 [2000] *ECR* I–11307 (refusing to treat TRIPs Art. 50 as having 'direct effect'); *Develey Holding v. OHIM,* Case C–238/06P (ECJ 8th ch) (25 Oct 2007) (refusing to treat Art. 6*quinquies* of Paris as of direct applicability because the Community is not a party to the Convention; and holding that it was not indirectly applicable via TRIPs Art. 2, because TRIPs is not itself to be regarded as directly applicable). *Merck Genericos v. Merck & Co,* Case C–431/05 (11 Sept 2007) (holding that patent term, a subject dealt with in TRIPs, Art. 33, was primarily a matter of national competence, because of the limited harmonization in the patent field to date). Note Council Decision 94/800/EC of 22 Dec. 1994, Recital 11 ('whereas, by its nature, the Agreement Establishing the WTO, including the Annexes thereto, is not susceptible to being directly invoked in Community or Member State courts.')

and form the European Economic Area.[150] The countries that joined the EEA from EFTA undertook to join various international conventions,[151] to implement domestic provisions on the free movement of goods (similar to those in Articles 28 and 30 EC), on competition (equivalent to Articles 81 and 82), and a raft of EC directives (including those on trade marks and copyright).[152] These provisions are enforced by the 'EFTA Surveillance Authority' and the 'EFTA Court'.[153] In return, the EC agreed to extend its provisions to the EEA countries. As a result where the term 'Community' or 'common market' are used in provisions falling within the EEA, they refer to the territories of the contracting parties.[154] Moreover, the doctrine of exhaustion and the jurisprudence of the ECJ on Article 28 EC explicitly apply to goods placed on the market in the EEA.[155]

4.5.1 'Europe agreements'

Increasingly, 'European' intellectual property law is having an ever-expanding significance outside the EU. In part, this was promoted by the Treaty of Nice, which paved the way for a number of countries to join the Community on 1 May 2004.[156] In addition, the EC has entered into 'Europe Agreements' with so-called 'candidate countries'.[157] The agreements, which aim to establish a free-trade area, contain a number of provisions in relation to intellectual property.

The EC also operates a number of initiatives and has agreements with many satellite countries.[158] The EC has also entered into 'Euro-Med Association Agreements' with countries of the South and East Mediterranean,[159] 'Partnership and Co-operation Agreements' with countries in Eastern Europe and Central Asia,[160] and 'Stabilisation and Association Agreements' with Balkan states (such as Albania).[161]

Typically these agreements include prohibitions on 'quantitative restriction on imports and measures having equivalent effect', as well as competition provisions similar to Articles 81 and 82 EC. The agreements usually also require the contracting party to apply to become parties to

---

[150] Although the EFTA countries at one time included Austria, Finland, and Sweden, these have since acceded to the EC. The EFTA countries that are parties to the EEA are: Iceland, Norway, and Liechtenstein. The only remaining EFTA country, Switzerland, refused to join the EEA.

[151] Indeed member states agreed to adhere to these Conventions, and the Court ruled that Ireland had failed to do so in *Commission v. Ireland*, Case C–13/00 (19 Mar 2002) (ECJ).

[152] Agreement on the European Economic Area OJ L 001, 3 Jan. 1994, 3. See esp. Arts 11, 13, 53, 54. Subsequent instruments have updated the content of the obligations.

[153] See http://www.efta.int. There have been few decisions of the EFTA court of interest in intellectual property: *Mag Instrument v. California Trading Co.*, E2–97 [1998] 1 *CMLR* 331 discussed at p. 954 n. 151; *Paranova v. Merck*, E–3/02 [2003] *EFTA Court Reports* 101. See also E–10/02, *L'Oreal Norge SA v. Smart Club Norge SA* (pending) (requesting an interpretation of Art. 7 of the Trade Marks Directive).

[154] Para. 8 of Protocol 1 on Horizontal Adaptation to the EEA Agreement.

[155] Protocol 28 on Intellectual Property, Art. 2.

[156] Cyprus, The Czech Republic, Estonia, Hungary, Latvia, Lithuania, Malta, Poland, the Slovak Republic, Slovenia. Bulgaria and Romania joined on 1 Jan. 2008.

[157] Turkey, Croatia, and Former Yugoslav Republic of Macedonia. Note the Council Decision of 19 May 2003 on the principles, priorities, and immediate objectives and conditions contained in the Accession Partnership with Turkey, *OJ L* 145/40.

[158] As part of the so-called 'neighbourhood policy'. See e.g. Communication from the Commission to the European Council and Parliament on Strengthening the Neighbourhood Policy, COM (2006) 726 final.

[159] e.g. Tunisia, Morocco, Israel, Jordan, Egypt, and Syria. The Agreement with Egypt came into force on 1 June 2004. Article 37 and annex VI relate to IPRs, obliging the parties mostly in relation to the international treaties. There are plans for a Euro-Med free trade area by 2010.

[160] These include Armenia, Georgia, Russia, Moldova, and the Ukraine.

[161] EC–Albania Stabilization and Association Agreement, 22 May 2006, esp Arts 70, 73 and Annex V.

(or if already parties, to affirm their commitment to) various intellectual property treaties such as the European Patent Convention, the Union for the Protection of Plant Varieties, the Rome Convention, the Madrid Protocol, the Berne and Paris Conventions, the Madrid Agreement, and the Patent Cooperation Treaty. They also require states to implement the Community 'acquis' so as to approximate their laws on intellectual property with those of the EC. The implementation of these standards is monitored, and the Commission reports have frequently emphasized the importance of implementation both in law and in practice, in particular insisting on training law enforcement bodies and the judiciary on intellectual property matters.

4.6 NON-EUROPEAN UNION REGIONAL INITIATIVES

Finally, it is important to note that there are a number of European initiatives that are independent of the European Community/Union which relate to intellectual property law. One of the most important is the 1973 European Patent Convention (EPC). The EPC established a single central office for the granting of bundles of national patents in Munich. The EPC is a treaty independent of the European Union, and includes all the member states of the EU, the EEA, as well as a number of non-EEA countries such as Switzerland and Turkey.[162]

The Council of Europe, a political organization founded in 1949 comprising 45 European countries, has also had an impact on intellectual property. While the Council of Europe is largely concerned with the promotion of democracy and human rights, it has undertaken a number of initiatives in the field of intellectual property. The Council supervises certain treaties, including treaties on patents (relating to formalities required for patents, international classification of patents, and the Strasbourg Treaty on the Unification of certain points of substantive law on patents for inventions) and copyright (in particular requiring recognition of the rights of broadcasting organizations), and the protection of authors where their works are broadcast across frontiers.[163] The Council also makes certain recommendations to governments (for example on copyright law and reprography),[164] as well as being a forum for discussion.

The European Convention on Human Rights, a treaty signed in 1950 under the aegis of the Council of Europe, requires contracting parties to recognize certain rights such as fair trial (Article 6), privacy (Article 8), freedom of expression (Article 10), and property (Article 1 of the first Protocol). Alleged failures to comply with the Convention are justiciable before the European Court of Human Rights (Article 19). Until recently the impact of the Convention on British intellectual property law was limited to cases of breach of confidence and remedies. However, with the coming into force of the Human Rights Act 1998 in October 2000, arguments based on the Convention have become more frequent and the jurisprudence of the

---

[162] See p. 341 n. 29.

[163] For example the Convention on the Unification of Certain Points of Substantive Law on Patents for Inventions (1963) ETS No. 47 (the UK ratified the Convention which came into force in 1980); European Agreement on the Protection of Television Broadcasts (1960) ETS No. 34 and Protocol (1965) ETS No. 54, Additional Protocol (1974) ETS No. 81, and Additional Protocol (1985) ETS No. 113 (the UK ratified this Treaty in 1965; European Convention on Transfrontier Broadcasting (1989) ETS No. 132 (which the UK ratified in 1993) (defining, e.g. the act of broadcasting). With the stalling of the proposed WIPO Broadcasting Treaty, attention has turned in 2008 to the possibility of formulating a treaty within this forum.

[164] Recommendation no. R(90)11 of the Committee of Ministers to Member States on Principles Relating to Copyright Law Questions in the Field of Reprography (adopted by the Committee of Ministers on 25 Apr. 1990 at the 438th meeting of the Ministers' Deputies).

Court more relevant.[165] The Convention has, however, had some impact on the law of countries with more expansive intellectual property rights than those of the UK, particularly countries with broad laws against 'unfair' competition.[166]

One recent development is likely to prove particularly significant: in *Anheuser-Busch Inc. v Portugal*,[167] the Grand Chamber of the European Court of Human Rights held that a trade mark application was a 'possession' for the purposes of Article 1 of the first Protocol. The question was whether the Convention had been breached when the Portuguese Supreme Court held that Anheuser-Busch's trade mark application for BUDWEISER, made in 1981, was invalid on the basis of a Bilateral Treaty entered between Portugal and the Czech Republic in 1986, that is, five years *after* the trade mark application had been made. Having held that the application was a 'possession',[168] the majority found there was no undue deprivation, because the Supreme Court had been applying domestic law between parties in circumstances where the precise intent of the domestic law was in issue. This was not something that the Court felt was its place to judge. A much clearer and persuasive dissent (from Judges Caflisch and Cabral Barreto) carries the majority holding that a trade mark application is a possession to its logical conclusion: the 1986 Bilateral treaty, found to be retrospective, deprived Anheuser-Busch of its property and was not undertaken in the public interest or with compensation.[169] As the status of intellectual property rights as protected property is confirmed, policy makers will at the very least need to acquaint themselves with ECHR jurisprudence on when a 'deprivation' occurs, and in what circumstances such a taking is legitimate.[170]

---

[165] For arguments based on ECHR, Art. 6(2) (presumption of innocence), see the discussion of criminal liability for trade mark infringement in *R v. Johnstone* [2003] FSR (42) 748; for arguments based on ECHR, Art. 8 (privacy) see chs. 44–6; for arguments based on ECHR, Art. 10 (free expression), see, e.g. *Levi's v. Tesco* [2002] 3 CMLR 11; [2002] ETMR (95) 1153 (rejecting an argument for international exhaustion), *Ashdown v. Telegraph Group Ltd* [2001] 3 WLR 1368 (public interest defence to copyright); [2002] RPC 235; *Confetti Records v. Warner Music UK* [2003] EMLR (35) 790 (para. 161) (rejecting argument that ECHR Art. 10 requires a narrow reading of moral rights); *FCUK Trade Mark* [2007] RPC 1 (Arnold QC) (relevance of Art. 10 in assessment of the 'morality' objection to trade mark registration).

[166] *Hertel v. Switzerland*, Case 25181/94 (1999) 28 EHRR 534 (ECtHR) (application of Swiss unfair competition law to publication of research on health impact of microwaves breached ECHR, Art. 10); *Krone Verlag GmbH & Co Kg v. Austria*, Case 39069/97 (2006) 42 EHRR (28) 578 (application of Austrian unfair competition law against comparative advertiser breached ECHR, Art. 10).

[167] Application No 73049/01 (11 Jan 2007), [2007] EHRR (36) 830, [2007] ETMR (24) 343.

[168] [2007] EHRR (36) 830 (para 78), [2007] ETMR (24) 343, 364–5.

[169] [2007] ETMR (24) 343, 369–71.

[170] In general, a 'deprivation' must be lawful, in the public interest and strike a fair balance between the needs of the state and the rights of an individual. The latter balance, in all but exceptional cases, is only achieved by the payment of compensation.

PART I

COPYRIGHT

2

INTRODUCTION TO COPYRIGHT

CHAPTER CONTENTS

1 INTRODUCTION

In British legal parlance, 'copyright' is the term used to describe the area of intellectual property law that regulates the creation and use that is made of a range of cultural goods such as books, songs, films, and computer programs.[1] The intangible property protected by copyright law is distinctive in that it arises automatically and usually for the benefit of the author.[2] Various rights are conferred on the owner of copyright, including the right to copy the work and the right to perform the work in public.[3] ('Work' is the term used in British law to describe the various objects that are protected by copyright.) The rights vested in the owner are limited, notably in that they are not infringed when a person copies or performs a work that they have created themselves. The rights given to a copyright owner last for a considerable time: in many cases for 70 years after the death of the author of the work.[4] The basic framework of British copyright law is largely to be found in the Copyright, Designs and Patents Act 1988,[5] as amended, most significantly to implement European Community directives.

This chapter provides an outline of certain background matters that will make the following chapters easier to follow. We begin by looking at some of the concepts that we will encounter in the following chapters. We then turn to look at the history and functions of copyright law, as well as international and European influences on British copyright law.

---

[1] For an analysis of various other perspectives on copyright, see P. Goldstein, 'Copyright' (1990–1) 38 *Journal of the Copyright Society of the USA* 109.

[2] See Ch. 5.   [3] See Ch. 6.   [4] See Ch. 7.

[5] Certain related rights, such as the 'publication right' and the 'database right', are found in statutory instruments.

2 'COPYRIGHT' AND *DROIT D'AUTEUR*

Many factors shape the way we view British copyright law. To some, it may appear as an unnecessary restriction on their ability to express themselves. For others copyright law provides the means to protect investment and labour. More generally, the image we have of British copyright law is shaped by the way we think it relates to other legal regimes. On the one hand, British copyright law is often seen as a gift that was bequeathed to colonial countries. At the same time British copyright law (and its 'unruly colonial children') is seen to be distinct from the 'copyright law' that exists in other countries. Most famously, common law copyright is said to be distinct from and in many ways in opposition to the civil law *droit d'auteur* system (of France). While there is now a growing body of literature that questions the accuracy of these portrayals,[6] nonetheless these caricatures have had and undoubtedly will continue to have an impact on the way the law develops.

The common law copyright model is said to be primarily concerned with encouraging the production of new works.[7] This is reflected in copyright law's emphasis on economic right, such as the right to produce copies. Another factor that is held to typify the copyright model is its relative indifference to authors. This is said to be reflected in the fact that British law presumes that an employer is the first owner of works made by an employee, the paucity of legal restrictions on alienability, and the limited and half-hearted recognition of moral rights.[8] In contrast, the civil law *droit d'auteur* model is said to be more concerned with the natural rights of authors in their creations. This is reflected in the fact that the civil law model not only aims to secure the author's economic interests, but also aims to protect works against uses which are prejudicial to an author's spiritual interests (in particular through moral rights).

3 AUTHOR'S RIGHTS AND NEIGHBOURING RIGHTS

While British copyright law abandoned the formal distinction between different categories of work with the passage of the 1988 Act, nonetheless an informal distinction is still drawn between two general categories of subject matter. More especially, a distinction is drawn between what are known as 'authorial works' and 'entrepreneurial works' (or 'neighbouring rights'). This reflects the distinction drawn in many legal systems between 'author's rights' and 'neighbouring rights'. Author's rights refer to works created by 'authors' such as books, plays, music, art, and films. In contrast, neighbouring rights (which are sometimes called 'related rights' or '*droits voisins*') refer to 'works' created by 'entrepreneurs', such as sound recordings, broadcasts, cable programmes, and the typographical format of published editions. The rationale for differentiating between these two categories of subject matter lies in the facts that neighbouring (or entrepreneurial) rights are typically derivative, in the sense that they use or develop existing authorial works; that they are a product of technical and organizational skill rather than authorial skill; and that the rights are initially given, not to the human creator, but

---

[6] G. Davies, *Copyright and the Public Interest* (1994; 2nd edn, 2002); J. Ginsburg, 'A Tale of Two Copyrights: Literary Property in Revolutionary France and America', in Sherman and Strowel; A. Strowel, '*Droit d'Auteur* and Copyright: Between History and Nature', in Sherman and Strowel; Sherman and Bently, ch. 11; D. Vaver, 'The Copyright Mixture in a Mixed Legal System: Fit For Human Consumption?' [2002] *Juridical Review* 101.

[7] For a classic statement see A. Sterling, *World Copyright Law* (1999), para. 16.06.

[8] See below at pp. 127–31, Ch. 12 Section 2, and Ch. 10.

to the body or person that was financially and organizationally responsible for the production of the material.[9]

4 HISTORY

The history of copyright is a complex, subtle, and rich subject. Depending on one's interest it is possible to highlight many different themes and trends. For example, a history of copyright could look at the gradual expansion of the subject matter and the rights granted to owners, the role that copyright law plays in shaping the notion of authorship, or the impact that copyright has on particular cultural practices. Most histories of British copyright law tend to focus on the origins of copyright, which are usually traced back to the 1710 Statute of Anne, or occasionally to the practices developed in the sixteenth century to regulate the book trade.[10] In this section we limit ourselves to a brief chronological account of some of the more important political and legal events that frame and shape the current law.

While aspects of copyright law have a long history, copyright law did not take on its modern meaning as a discrete area of law that grants rights in works of literature and art until at least the mid-nineteenth century.[11] Moreover, it was not until the passage of the 1911 Copyright Act that copyright law was rationalized and codified into the type of modern, abstract, and forward-looking statute that concerns us here. The 1911 Act was also important insofar as it abolished common law copyright in unpublished works and also repealed the plethora of subject-specific statutes that existed at the time. In their place the 1911 Act established a single code which conferred copyright protection on a number of works (whether published or not, and including many previously unprotectable works such as works of architecture, sound recordings, and films).[12] In most cases, protection lasted for 50 years after the death of the author of the work.[13] At the same time, the 1911 Act abandoned all requirements concerning formalities (in particular the need for registration with the Stationers' Company). Infringement was also expanded to include translations and adaptation as well as reproductions 'in a material form'.[14]

---

[9] For a general discussion see W. Grosheide, 'Paradigms in Copyright Law' in Sherman and Strowel, 223 (identifying two extremes thus: 'one is the view that traditional copyright law must be purified and updated; the other is the notion that copyright is an integral part of intellectual property law, and that a more liberal and unorthodox approach to copyright law should be adopted').

[10] A. Birrell, *Seven Lectures on Copyright* (1898); Copinger, ch. 2; B. Kaplan, *An Unhurried View of Copyright* (1967), 1–25 L.-R. Patterson, *Copyright in Historical Perspective* (1968); D. Saunders, *Authorship and Copyright* (1992). For accounts of specific periods and moments, see M. Rose, *Authors and Owners* (1993); R. Deazley, *On the Origin of the Right to Copy: Charting the Movement of Copyright Law in Britain throughout the Eighteenth Century (1695–1775),* PhD (Queens University, Belfast, 2000); C. Seville, *Literary Copyright Reform in Early Victorian England* (1999); C. Seville, *Internationalisation of Copyright: Books, Buccaneers and the Black Flag* (2006). For a historiography, K. Bowrey, 'Who's Painting Copyright's History?' in D. McClean and K. Schubert, *Dear Images: Art, Culture and Copyright* (2002), 257. Primary sources and commentaries are available at http://www.copyrighthistory.org.

[11] See Sherman and Bently, 111–28; B. Sherman, 'Remembering and Forgetting: The Birth of Modern Copyright Law' (1995) 10 *IPJ* 1.

[12] Films were protected as 'photographs', without prejudice to copyright in the dramatic works embodied in films. Sound recordings were deemed to be musical works: Copyright Act (CA) 1911 s. 19.

[13] Literary, dramatic, musical, and artistic works other than photographs, which received a term of 50 years from making.

[14] CA 1911 s. 1(2).

Following a review by the Gregory Committee in 1952, the 1911 Copyright Act was replaced by the 1956 Copyright Act.[15] This extended the scope of copyright to encompass sound and television broadcasts, as well as typographical formats of published editions. Along with sound recordings and films (which were now recognized as having copyright in their own right), these new rights were placed in a special category in Part II of the 1956 Act.[16] The 1956 Act was amended on a number of occasions, primarily to take account of new technologies such as cable television and computer software.[17] A further periodic review by the Whitford Committee in 1977 proposed a general revision of the 1956 Act.[18] After further negotiations and refinement, these proposals led to the passage of the Copyright, Designs and Patents Act 1988.[19]

The 1988 Act substantially reorganized the statutory regime. In particular, it removed the distinction between 'Part I works' and 'Part II subject matter'. This was achieved by treating films, sound recordings, and broadcasts (along with the authorial works) within a single general category of 'copyright works'. In many cases, these changes were not intended to alter the substantive law.[20] However, the rights given to copyright owners were expanded significantly (notably by the introduction of a distribution right and a rental right). At the same time, the Copyright Tribunal was established to ensure that copyright owners did not exercise their rights in an anti-competitive manner.[21] The 1988 Act also introduced a new category of non-assignable 'moral rights' for authors.[22] Performers' rights, which were formerly dealt with under special Acts, were also included within the 1988 Act (where they are protected separately under Part II).[23] The 1988 Act also created a new automatic form of short-term protection for designs, known as the unregistered design right.[24]

Although the 1988 Act forms the basis of contemporary copyright law, it has been amended on a number of occasions since it came into force in August 1989. In most cases, these amendments were made to give effect to obligations imposed by European Community directives. As we will see, while the Community has stopped short of a wholesale approximation of copyright law, a series of specific interventions has altered the contents of the 1988 Act to such an extent that a recodification of national law would be desirable. In particular, two new rights related to copyright, which are currently found in statutory instruments (namely the database right and the publication right) could usefully be incorporated into the statutory regime, as could the meaning of 'information society service provider' (for which one has to consult an EC Directive and its annex).

5 JUSTIFICATIONS

The existence of copyright in a particular work restricts the uses that can be made of the work. For example, a person who purchases a book in which copyright subsists cannot legally photocopy the book. Similarly a person who buys a protected CD cannot legally rip the recordings

---

[15] Report of the Gregory Committee on the Law of Copyright (Cmnd. 8662, 1952).

[16] CA 1956 ss. 12–16.

[17] Cable and Broadcasting Act 1984 (adding cable programmes to protected subject matter); Copyright (Computer Software) Act 1985 (establishing copyright protection for computer programs). The Design Copyright Act 1968 sought to remedy certain problems in relation to copyright protection for designs.

[18] Report of the Committee on Copyright and Designs Law (Cmnd. 6732, 1977).

[19] See Green Paper, Reform of the Law relating to Copyright, Designs and Performers' Protection (Cmnd. 8302, 1981); Green Paper, Intellectual Property Rights and Innovation (Cmnd. 9117, 1983); White Paper, Intellectual Property and Innovation (Cmnd. 9712, 1986).

[20] CDPA s. 172.   [21] See below pp. 299–301.   [22] See Ch. 10.

[23] See below Ch. 13, Section 2.   [24] See Ch. 30.

from that CD for a friend to use on her mp3 player. As well as being inconvenient and/or expensive, copyright has the potential to inhibit the public's ability to communicate, to develop ideas, and produce new works. For example, in order for a person to parody a song it will normally be necessary for them to reproduce a substantial proportion of the lyrics and the music from the song. In the United Kingdom, this would usually require the permission of the copyright owner, who may be reluctant to grant permission in the circumstances.

Because copyright law has the potential to inhibit the way people interact with and use cultural objects, it is important that we constantly reassess its legitimacy. More specifically, we need to ask whether (and why) copyright is desirable. In this context it is important to note that not everyone thinks that copyright is a good thing.[25] In fact, with the advent of the internet, there are many who think that copyright unjustifiably stifles our ability to make the most of the new environment,[26] or that it impinges upon the public domain.[27] Others consider that, while some aspects of copyright are justifiable, others are not. Typically the argument is that copyright law has gone too far.[28] In response to these copyright sceptics or critics, five basic arguments are used to support the recognition (and further extension) of copyright: natural rights arguments, reward arguments, incentive arguments, neo-classical economics, and arguments from democracy.[29]

5.1 NATURAL RIGHTS

According to natural rights theorists, the reason why copyright protection is granted is not because we think that the public will benefit from copyright. Rather, copyright protection is granted because it is right and proper to do so. More specifically, it is right to recognize a property right in intellectual productions *because* such productions emanate from the mind of an individual author. For example, a poem is seen as the product of a poet's mind, their intellectual effort and inspiration. As such it should be seen as their property, and copying as equivalent to theft. Copyright is the positive law's realization of this self-evident, ethical precept. However, at this point, natural rights theorists divide as to exactly what it is about origination that entitles an author to protection. Some, particularly those associated with the European traditions, explain that works should be protected because (and insofar

---

[25] For an early example see the minority report of Sir Louis Mallet, *Report of the Royal Commission on Copyright*, C 2036 (1878) 24 PP. More recent attacks have been associated with the Austrian school of free-market liberal economics, e.g. A. Plant, 'The Economics of Copyright' (1934) *Economica* 167.

[26] In fact, it is commonly argued that widespread illegal copying on the internet can be explained by reference to the fact that the public is not persuaded by the rationales offered for copyright: J. Garon, 'Normative Copyright: A Conceptual Framework for Copyright Philosophy and Ethics' (2003) 88 *Cornell Law Review* 1278, 1283–5. However, other accounts of these practices are emerging: see L. Strahilevitz, 'Charismatic Code, Social Norms & the Emergence of Co-operation on the File-Swapping Networks' (2003) 89 *Virginia Law Rev* 505 (examining social psychology of peer-to-peer). For a review of consumer awareness in the EC, see Instituut voor Informatierecht (Institute for Information Law, University of Amsterdam—IViR), *Recasting Copyright for the Knowledge Economy* (2006), Ch 6.

[27] For a general discussion of the public domain see (2003) 66 *Law and Contemporary Problems* (Special Edition on the Public Domain); F.W. Grosheide and J.J. Brinkhof (eds), *Intellectual Property Law 2004: Articles on Crossing Borders between Traditional and Actual* (2005); B. Hugenholtz and L. Guibault (eds), *The Future of the Public Domain: Identifying the Commons in Information Law* (2006); C. Waelde and H. MacQueen (eds), *Intellectual Property: The Many Faces of the Public Domain* (2007).

[28] S. Trosow, 'The Illusive Search for Justificatory Theories: Copyright, Commodification and Capital', (2003) 16 *Canadian Journal of Law and Jurisprudence* 217.

[29] For an overview, see M. Spence, 'Justifying Copyright' in D. McLean and K. Schubert, *Dear Images: Art, Culture and Copyright*, 388 (2002).

as) they are the expressions of each particular author's personality.[30] On the assumption that a work created by an individual reflects the unique nature of them as an individual, the natural rights arguments require that we allow the creator to protect the work (from misattribution, modification, or unauthorized exploitation) because it is an extension of the persona of its creator. In the words of an ancient aphorism, 'to every cow its calf'. A second version of natural right theory, strongly represented in the US literature, has tended to found itself on labour. Drawing on Locke's idea that a person has a natural right over the products of their labour, it is argued that an author has a natural right over the productions of their intellectual labour.[31]

Critics of natural rights theories of copyright take a number of different positions. Some simply reject the idea of 'natural rights'. Others criticize the assumptions within the theory, for example that a natural right in labour justifies a natural right in the product of mixing labour and unowned resources. Some criticize the extension of natural rights theories to copyright, challenging the idea of individual creation of ideas, emphasizing the social (or 'intertextual') nature of writing and painting.[32] If works are seen less as the products of individual labour or personality, and more as reworkings of previous ideas and texts, the claim to ownership seems weak. Another critique questions why it is that a natural right in the products of one's labour should justify recognition of anything more than a right over the manuscript or immediate creation. A final argument criticizes natural rights theory on the ground that it provides no normative guidance as to the specific form of copyright law.[33]

5.2 REWARD

According to reward arguments, copyright protection is granted because we think it is fair to reward an author for the effort expended in creating a work and giving it to the public. Copyright is a legal expression of gratitude to an author for doing more than society expects or feels that they are obliged to do. In a sense, the grant of copyright is similar to the repayment of a debt. (Although the language of reward often appears when discussing the 'incentive' theory of copyright, it differs from incentive theory: in reward theory proper the reward is an end in itself, in incentive theory the reward is a means to an end.)

Critiques of reward theory tend to pose two questions. First, they ask, do the circumstances in which copyright protection is granted correspond to the circumstances in which people deserve rewards? One answer is that a reward is only deserved where someone has done something they felt was unpleasant and that they would not otherwise have done. If this is the case, copyright does seem to give far too many rewards. As we will see, copyright's threshold is set at a very low level and thus catches works which are created for their own sake such as letters, holiday photographs, and amateur paintings. Another account sees the reward as being

---

[30] For personality theory based on Hegel see J. Hughes, The 'Philosophy of Intellectual Property' (1988) 77 *Georgetown Law Journal* 287.

[31] On Locke and labour, see Hughes, ibid; A. Yen, 'Restoring the Natural Law: Copyright as Labour and Possession' (1990) 51 *Ohio State Law Journal* 517; W. Gordon, 'A Property Right in Self-Expression: Equality and Individualism in the Natural Law of Intellectual Property' (1993) 102 *Yale Law Journal* 1533.

[32] S. Shiffrin, 'Lockean Arguments for Private Intellectual Property', in S. Munzer (ed.), *New Essays in the Legal and Political Theory of Property* (2001) (disputing the idea that intellectual works are more susceptible to Lockean arguments than tangible objects); P. Drahos, *The Philosophy of Intellectual Property* (1996), ch. 3; Lior Zemer, *The Idea of Authorship in Copyright* (2006).

[33] J. Garon, 'Normative Copyright: A Conceptual Framework for Copyright Philosophy and Ethics' (2003) 88 *Cornell LR* 1278, 1299–1306.

deserved where the person invested labour (irrespective of their ulterior motives or the pleasure or pain of labouring).[34]

The second criticism questions the nature of the reward: why should a person be granted an exclusive right? There are other systems of reward (such as the MAN Booker Prize) that have fewer social and economic costs. The usual answer is that copyright allows the general public to determine who should be rewarded and the size of that reward: the more copies of a book that are purchased, or the more a record is played on the radio, the greater the financial reward that accrues to the copyright owner.[35] Consequently, a property right is often the best way to ensure that the reward is proportional to the public's appreciation of the work.

5.3 INCENTIVE-BASED THEORIES

In contrast to the natural rights and reward theories, the third argument for copyright is not based on ideas of what is right or fair to an author or creator. Rather, it is based on an idea of what is good for society or the public in general. The incentive argument presupposes that the production and public dissemination of cultural objects such as books, music, art, and films is an important and valuable activity. It also presupposes that, without copyright protection, the production and dissemination of cultural objects would not take place at an optimal level. The reason for this is that, while works are often very costly to produce, once published they can readily be copied. For example, while this textbook took a considerable amount of time and energy to write, once published, it can easily and cheaply be reproduced. Consequently, in the absence of copyright protection, a competitor could reproduce Bently and Sherman's *Intellectual Property Law* without having to recoup the expense of its initial production. In so doing they could undercut Oxford University Press. According to the incentive argument, if Bently, Sherman, and Oxford University Press were not given any legal protection, *Intellectual Property Law* would never have been written or published—and the world would have been a commensurably poorer place. The legal protection given by copyright is intended to rectify this 'market failure' by providing incentives that encourage the production and dissemination of works. In short, copyright provides a legal means by which those who invest time and labour in producing cultural and informational goods can be confident that they will be able not only to recoup that investment, but also to reap a profit proportional to the popularity of their work.[36]

Utilitarian arguments for copyright are commonly met with three criticisms. Some question whether an incentive is really necessary for much production, and certainly there are plenty of examples of practices of creation and dissemination of works that do not depend

[34] British copyright law has often employed a variant of reward theory. For example see *Designers Guild v. Williams* [2001] *FSR* 11, para. 2 (HL): Lord Bingham said that the 'law of copyright rests on a very clear principle: that anyone who by his or her own skill and labour creates an original work of whatever character shall, for a limited period, enjoy an exclusive right to copy that work. No one else may for a season reap what the copyright owner has sown.' See also *Walter v. Lane* [1900] *AC* 539, 545 *per* Earl of Halsbury LC (it would be a 'grievous injustice' if 'the law permitted one man to make profit and to appropriate to himself the labour, skill, and capital of another'), 551 (Lord Davey).

[35] Thus Bentham argued that 'an exclusive privilege is of all rewards the best proportioned, the most natural, and the least bothersome': *A Manual of Political Economy*, in J. Bowring (ed.), *The Works of Jeremy Bentham*, iii (1843) 31, 71.

[36] W. Landes and R. Posner, 'An Economic Analysis of Copyright Law' (1989) 18 *Journal of Legal Studies* 325; W. Gordon, 'An Inquiry into the Merits of Copyright: The Challenges of Consistency, Consent and Encouragement Theory' (1989) 41 *Stanford Law Review* 1343.

on the existence of copyright.[37] Others, admitting the need for an artificial incentive to rectify the market failure, question whether the grant of an exclusive property is the appropriate
incentive.[38] After all, exclusive properties impose costs on people who wish to use the work,
costs of policing rights and enforcement on owners, and transaction costs on those who seek
permissions.[39] In some cases, in fact, exclusive rights are replaced by payments from general taxation (as with the Public Lending Right discussed in Chapter 13), thus ensuring that
authors are provided with an incentive but that the costs associated with exclusive rights are
minimized. Even if we accept that exclusive rights are the optimal form of incentive, the third
problem with the utilitarian approach is deciding exactly what incentive is optimal. What
should a copyright owner be able to prevent another person from doing and for how long?

5.4 NEO-CLASSICAL ECONOMICS

If economic theory that sees copyright as an incentive to create or publish implies a rather
narrow right, an alternative economic theory, associated with neo-classical economics, would
justify protection of virtually all 'value'.[40] According to this school of thought, private ownership of resources is the juridical arrangement most conducive to optimal exploitation. In
contrast, common ownership or non-ownership is likely to lead to over-exploitation (the
so-called 'tragedy of the commons'). For example, it has been argued that failure to protect
sound recordings by copyright would lead to their over-use, so that the public interest in the
recording would tire, and their value diminish.[41] Accordingly, copyright protection should
only be limited where the transaction costs involved in locating and negotiating licence agreements would prevent the conclusion of optimal agreements. These theoretical positions have
not only featured in the arguments of scholars and treatise writers, and in the lobbying process,
but have even been adopted by some US courts.[42] However, the idea that copyright should be
unlimited in coverage, scope, and duration because this will promote optimal use of intellectual resources seems to neglect a fundamental characteristic of intellectual products, namely,
their 'non-rival nature'.[43] Fears about over-exploitation of physical resources, which (might)
make private ownership the most satisfactory allocative model, simply do not apply to cultural
resources: the more people who can get access to the works of Shakespeare, Mozart, and even
Jeremy Bentham, the better.

[37] S. Breyer, 'The Uneasy Case for Copyright: A Study of Copyright in Books, Photocopies and Computer
Progams' (1970) 84 *Harvard Law Review* 281 (emphasizing, in particular, the incentives provided by lead time,
and possible use of contractual methods such as subscription).

[38] R. Hurt and R. Schuchman, 'The Economic Rationale for Copyright' (1966) 56 *American Economic Review*
421 (suggesting private patronage and government support).

[39] See *Eldred v. Ashcroft* (2003) 123 S Ct 769, 804 ff (Breyer J in the US Supreme Court explaining the costs
imposed on the public from extension of the term of copyright). For an argument that copyright diminishes
diversity, see G. Pessach, 'Copyright Law as a Silencing Restriction on Non-Infringing Materials: Unveiling the
Scope of Copyright's Diversity Externalities' (2003) 76 *Southern California Law Review* 1067.

[40] For a concise, if unsympathetic, explanation, see N.W. Netanel, 'Copyright and a Democratic Civil Society'
(1996) 106 *Yale Law Journal* 283, 290, 306–7, 308–36.

[41] W. Landes and R. Posner, 'Indefinitely Renewable Copyright' (2003) 70 *University of Chicago Law
Review* 471.

[42] For example the US Supreme Court in *Harper & Row Publishers Inc v. Nation Enterprises* 471 US 539
(1985), where fair use was grounded in implied consent.

[43] For a compelling critique, see M. Lemley, 'Ex Ante versus Ex Post Justifications for Intellectual Property',
(2004) 71 *University of Chicago Law Review* 129.

5.5 DEMOCRATIC ARGUMENTS

In an important intervention in 1996, Neil Netanel has tried to justify copyright by reference to the 'democratic paradigm'.[44] Netanel sees copyright as 'fortifying our democratic institutions by promoting public education, self-reliant authorship, and robust debate. More precisely, this democratic paradigm views copyright law as a state measure designed to enhance the independent and pluralist character of civil society.' Copyright encourages greater production, but also, 'is designed to secure the qualitative condition for creative autonomy and expressive diversity'.

5.6 THE PLACE OF JUSTIFICATIONS

There is a large body of literature criticizing, developing, and refining these five justifications. There is not room here to recount and assess this literature further. Nevertheless, it is worth noting a number of points about the ways these theories are marshalled in support of legal arguments relating to copyright. It is often said that a natural rights-based justification for copyright inevitably produces a different conception of copyright from that which results from an incentive argument. More specifically, it is argued that a natural rights conception of copyright leads to longer and stronger protection for authors (and copyright owners) than an incentive-based conception. This is because a natural rights argument for copyright is assumed to result in a form of property that is perpetual and unqualified.[45] In contrast, an incentive-based argument only justifies the grant of the minimum level of protection necessary to induce the right holder to create and release the work. While there is an element of truth in these arguments, they should not be overstated. The reason for this is that the copyright law that operates in the United Kingdom today is a product of a range of different factors, only a few of which could be said to have been influenced by the justificatory theories.[46]

Although the various theories have relatively distinct philosophical pedigrees, when they have been employed in support of various claims little if any attention is given to such niceties. Instead, the five arguments are typically deployed side by side. In fact, in most cases where a claim is made for the legal protection of works not previously protected (such as television formats), or the expansion of the rights conferred by the law in respect of such works, one can reasonably anticipate that all five types of justification will be used. While it is understandable that lobby groups use (or abuse) the various justifications to further their ends, more problems arise when people begin to believe the rhetoric and assume that copyright law is determined and shaped by these philosophical ideals.[47]

[44] Neil Weinstock Netanel, 'Copyright and a Democratic Civil Society' (1996) 106 *Yale LJ* 283, 291.

[45] See *Millar v. Taylor* (1769) 4 Burr 2303, 98 ER 201, 218–22 (Aston J), 252 (Mansfield CJ).

[46] Most important is the prevailing understanding of the processes of 'authorship': where 'authorship' is understood in its 'romantic' sense as the outpouring of the soul, so that the resulting work is the unique product of its author, no doubt a natural right justification does lead to a maximalist conception of copyright. In contrast, where the processes of authorship are perceived as processes of a combination of existing texts, of *bricolage*, and collocation, a natural rights approach might only justify a short-term and highly qualified 'property' in the resulting work.

[47] J. Litman, *Digital Copyright* (2001) 77 ('in the ongoing negotiations among industry representatives, normative arguments about the nature of copyright show up as rhetorical flourishes, but, typically, change nobody's mind'); G. Austin, 'Copyright's Modest Ontology—Theory and Pragmatism in *Eldred v. Ashcroft*' (2003) 16 *Canadian Journal of Law & Jurisprudence* 163 ('the realities of intellectual property lawmaking are such that there are few instances where theory dictates the formulation and development of positive law').

6 INTERNATIONAL INFLUENCES

One of the constant themes in the history of British copyright law is that it has been influenced by foreign and international trends and developments. While the sources may have changed, contemporary law is no different.[48] There are a number of international treaties that impact upon British copyright law.[49] Here, we will limit ourselves to the five most significant treaties. These are the Berne Convention, the Rome Convention, TRIPS, the WIPO Copyright Treaty, and the WIPO Performances and Phonograms Treaty.

6.1 BERNE CONVENTION (1886–1971)

The most important international influence on the development of UK copyright has been the Berne Convention on the Protection of Literary and Artistic Works. The Berne Convention was drawn up in 1886 as a small treaty allowing for mutual recognition of rights amongst a few largely European countries. Since then, the treaty has been revised on a number of occasions,[50] and the membership expanded to 151 states.[51]

In its earliest form, there were two key provisions of the Berne Convention. The first was the adoption of the principle of national treatment. This meant that with certain exceptions a country of the Union should not discriminate between its own nationals and those of other countries of the Union.[52] For example, under the principle of national treatment, French law was obliged to confer the same rights on a British author as it conferred on French authors. In addition to the principle of national treatment, the Berne Convention has long required that the 'enjoyment and exercise' of copyright in the works of the Convention should not be 'subject to any formality'. This means that registration or notices cannot be made prerequisites for protection.[53] Because international protection is to be automatic, there is no need for international bureaucratic regimes to simplify registration processes.

Over time the Berne Convention has come to demand that members of the Union provide certain minimum standards of protection to copyright owners and authors. These include the right to reproduce the work,[54] to perform the work publicly,[55] to translate the

---

[48] Under the powers conferred by the International Copyright Act 1844 (7 & 8 Vict. c. 12) Britain had begun to build bilateral arrangements with other countries for mutual recognition of copyrights.

[49] Also important are the Universal Copyright Conventions (last revised at Paris in 1971); the Geneva Convention on Phonograms of 1971; and the Convention Relating to the Distribution of Programme-Carrying Signals Transmitted by Satellite, Brussels, 21 May 1974.

[50] The last revision was at Paris on 24 Jul. 1971, and amended on 28 Sept. 1979.

[51] As of 15 Oct. 2003. The Convention applies to all works in which copyright has not expired at the time of accession to the Convention: Berne Art. 18.

[52] Berne Art. 5(1). These are to be enjoyed by authors who are nationals of one of the countries of the Union, for their works, whether published or not; and authors who are not nationals of one of the countries of the Union, for their works first published in one of those countries: Berne Art. 3. The exceptions to national treatment relate to (i) copyright terms which exceed the Berne minimum, Art. 7(8); (ii) copyright in applied art; and (iii) *droit de suite,* Art. 14 *ter*(2).

[53] Berne Art. 5(2). For consideration as to whether the requirement for assertion of the right to attribution complies with this, see below at p. 246.

[54] Berne Art. 9 (countries to recognize the exclusive right to authorize the reproduction of works 'in any manner or form'); Art. 9(3) specifically states that a sound or visual recording is to be considered a reproduction.

[55] Berne Art. 11 (for dramatic, dramatico-musical, and musical works); Art. 11 *ter* (public recitation and communication of literary works).

work,[56] to adapt the work,[57] and to broadcast the work.[58] Members of the Union are also to give authors (rather than copyright owners) the moral rights of attribution and integrity.[59] In recognition of the need for the public to be able to utilize works without payment, there is limited scope for members of the Union to create exceptions.[60] In relation to the reproduction right, these exceptions must satisfy the so-called three-step test. This requires that all exceptions must be limited to certain special cases, not conflict with a normal exploitation of the work, and not unreasonably prejudice the legitimate interests of the author.[61] Moreover, protection is to last at least for the life of the author, plus 50 years thereafter.[62]

6.2 ROME CONVENTION (1961)

The coverage of the Berne Convention is limited to literary and artistic works, which include cinematographic works.[63] It does not include provisions for the protection of performers, producers of sound recordings, broadcasters, publishers, and many others. Despite several attempts to expand the coverage of the Berne Convention to include performers and sound recordings, these were resisted.[64] The various authors' societies opposed the inclusion of such works within the Berne Convention on the grounds that they are non-creative and derivative in character,[65] and that recognition of performers' rights might reduce the royalties available for authors.[66] Similar arguments were also used to oppose the introduction of sound recordings into Berne (though additional arguments were made that sound recordings are properly seen as industrial, not literary or artistic,[67] and that there are difficulties in identifying an author of a sound recording).[68]

Eventually, it became clear that international recognition of the rights of phonogram producers, performers, and broadcasters would need to be sought under a separate instrument. In 1961 an international agreement on these 'neighbouring rights' was reached at the

---

[56] Berne Arts. 8 and 11(2) (translation); Art. 12 (adaptations, arrangements, and other alterations); Art. 11 *ter* (2) (communication of translations).

[57] Berne Art. 12 (authorizing adaptations, arrangements, and other alterations of their works); Art. 14 (cinematographic adaptation).

[58] Berne Art. 11 *bis*.   [59] Berne Art. 6 *bis*. See Ch. 10.

[60] Minor exceptions are permitted in accordance with the understandings expressed at various conferences but these must be *de minimis*: see WTO Panel Report, WT/DS/16OR June 2000. Compulsory licences are permitted under Art. 11 *bis* (2) and Art. 13 (mechanical copying).

[61] Berne Art. 9(2). Note also Art. 10(2) (use by way of illustration in publications for teaching); Art. 10 *bis* (use for reporting current events).

[62] Berne Art. 7. Certain exceptions are possible relating to cinematographic works, pseudonymous and anonymous works (where a 50-year minimum operates), and photographic works and works of applied art insofar as they are protected as artistic works (where a minimum of 25 years operates).

[63] Berne Art. 14 *bis*.

[64] For example, at the Rome Revision in 1928. Opponents included France and Hungary: see Ricketson, paras. 15.40–54.

[65] So are translations, adaptations, and films, though these are protected under Berne.

[66] On the so-called 'cake theory' see Ricketson, paras. 15.52–3.

[67] Ricketson, para. 6.76 (arguing that explanation for inclusion of photographs and films but exclusion of sound recordings and broadcasts from Berne is best explained by the historical fact that, when claims to include the former were made, the idea of separate neighbouring rights regimes had not developed).

[68] The making of a recording is typically a collective exercise and protection is sought by corporate authors. However, so is the making of a film. For a comparative account, see G. Boytha, 'The Intellectual Property Status of Sound Recording' (1993) 24 *IIC* 295. Note, in particular, that the USA did not give protection at a Federal level until 1971, with the Sound Recording Amendment Act of 15 Oct. 1971.

Rome Convention[69] (which now has 76 signatories).[70] Like the Berne Convention, the central principle of the Rome Convention is national treatment: national treatment must be provided to performances that take place in a contracting state, or which are embodied on protected sound recordings, or carried by a protected broadcast; to sound recordings produced by nationals of a contracting state, fixed in a contracting state, or first published in a contracting state; and to broadcasts where the broadcasting organization is situated in a contracting state or the broadcast is transmitted from a contracting state.[71]

The Rome Convention also requires that phonogram producers, performers, and broadcasters be granted certain substantive rights. For performers these are relatively limited, being largely restricted to matters relating to 'bootlegging' (that is, the fixation of their unfixed performances without their consent), the broadcasting of their unfixed performances without their consent, and the duplication of any such recordings which have been made illicitly.[72] Notably, contracting states are not required to give performers rights to control the reproduction, distribution, or public communication of legitimately made recordings of their performances. (As a result there is no requirement, for example, that performers be paid when films are shown at a cinema.) The protection that is given is to last for 20 years from the first fixation of the performance or, if it has not been fixed, 20 years from the date when the performance took place.

Producers of phonograms and broadcasting organizations received better treatment. Producers of phonograms are to be granted the right to prevent the reproduction of those recordings for 20 years.[73] Broadcasting organizations are to be given exclusive rights, for a minimum of 20 years from when a broadcast took place, to authorize or prohibit the rebroadcasting of their broadcasts, the fixation of their broadcasts, and the reproduction of fixations of their broadcasts. Broadcasters were also given the right to control the showing of television broadcasts in places accessible to the public (against payment of an entrance fee).[74]

The three divergent interests that coexist in the Rome Convention gave rise to one further and important compromise. This was that contracting states are to confer a right to a *single* equitable remuneration when phonograms are broadcast or played in public.[75] This right to remuneration must be provided either to the performers whose performances are embodied on phonograms, or to the producers of phonograms, or both. This means that broadcasters, nightclubs, restaurants, etc. must pay a single fee to play sound recordings. It is left to the contracting states whether the beneficiary of the right is to be the performer, the phonogram producer, or both.

Contracting states are permitted to make these rights subject to defences as regards private use, news reporting, ephemeral recordings, and teaching and scientific research,[76] as well as the same kind of limitations as are provided for literary and artistic works under the Berne Convention.[77]

---

[69] International Convention for the Protection of Performers, Producers of Phonograms and Broadcasting Organisations.

[70] As of 15 Oct. 2003. Though significantly not the USA, as a result of its refusal to give broadcasting organizations copyright.

[71] Rome Art. 4 (performers); Art. 5 (phonograms); Art. 6 (broadcasts). National treatment is defined in Rome Art. 2.

[72] Rome Art. 7. Note also Art. 19.

[73] Rome Art. 10. If formalities are required, they are complied with by using the 'P' symbol: Rome Art. 11.

[74] Rome Art. 13; Art. 14, see Ricketson, paras. 15.41 ff.

[75] Rome Art. 12. This can be excluded under Art. 16.   [76] Rome Art. 15(1).   [77] Rome Art. 15(2).

6.3 TRIPS

The third important international development that impacts upon British copyright law is TRIPS.[78] There are a number of provisions in TRIPS that relate to copyright. The most important of these is that members must implement Articles 1–21 of the Berne Convention (but not Article 6 bis dealing with moral rights).[79] One of the consequences of this is that disputes over compliance with Berne can now be considered by the WTO.[80] While the TRIPS Agreement does not require member states to adhere to the Rome Convention, Article 14 of TRIPS contains substantively similar provisions to Rome (though the term of protection in such cases is substantially longer under TRIPS).[81]

In addition, the TRIPS Agreement contains certain 'Berne-plus' features, as regards various aspects of copyright. Some of these are responses to new technologies that have given rise to new sorts of work and new modes of distribution. For example, under TRIPS, protection must be given to computer programs as literary works within the Berne Convention;[82] and to compilations of data or other material which, by reason of the selection or arrangement of their contents, 'constitute intellectual creations'.[83] Reflecting the impact of new modes of distribution, members must (in most cases) give copyright owners the right to authorize rental of computer programs, cinematographic works, and phonograms.[84] Other provisions flow from more general concerns as to the nature of copyright protection. In particular, copyright is defined generally as covering 'expressions' and *not* ideas or methods.[85] Moreover, TRIPS requires that *all* limitations and exceptions (rather than the right to reproduction as in Berne) must satisfy the three-step test.[86]

6.4 WIPO COPYRIGHT TREATY (1996)

In December 1996, two treaties were agreed at Geneva: the WIPO Copyright Treaty and the WIPO Performances and Phonograms Treaty.[87] In part, these grew out of the frustration at the inability to produce a revised version of the Berne Convention and subsequent attempts to produce a 'Protocol' to the Berne Convention (possibly incorporating the rights of record producers and performers within a single treaty). Both treaties are intended to supplement the existing Conventions to reflect, in particular, technological changes and changes in practice.[88]

---

[78] See above at pp. 6–11.   [79] TRIPS Art. 9(1).

[80] As has occurred in the WTO Dispute Panel Report on US limitations on the public performance right. WT/DS160/R (15 Jun. 2000). According to TRIPS Art. 14(6) the provisions on neighbouring rights in performances and phonograms apply to existing works: the WTO Dispute Resolution procedure was used to induce Japan to comply with this requirement: WT/DS22 and WT/DS 48.

[81] TRIPS Art. 14. The term of protection for performers and producers of phonograms is extended to 50 years from fixation of the performance or the date of the performance: Art. 14(5). As regard broadcasts, Art. 14(3) requires that broadcasting organizations are to have various rights (to prohibit the fixation, reproduction of fixations and re-broadcasting of broadcasts, and communication to the public of the same), but a derogation provides that 'where Members do not grant such rights to broadcasting organizations, they shall provide owners of copyright in the subject matter of broadcasts with the possibility of preventing the above acts, subject to the provisions of the Berne Convention (1971)'.

[82] TRIPS Art. 10(1); see also, WCT Art. 4.   [83] TRIPS Art. 10(2).

[84] TRIPS Art. 11, Art. 14(4).   [85] TRIPS Art. 9(2).

[86] TRIPS Art. 13. For consideration of the relationship between Art. 13 and EC law, particularly Art. 82 EC, see *Microsoft v. Commission*, Case T-201/04, [2007] 5 CMLR (11) 846 (paras 794–803).

[87] Reinbothe and von Lewinski (2002); M. Ficsor, *Copyright and The Internet* (2002); D. Saunders and B. Sherman (eds.), *From Berne to Geneva* (1997).

[88] WCT Art. 1 defines the Treaty as a 'special agreement' within Art. 20 Berne.

For the most part, the WIPO Copyright Treaty (WCT), which came into force in 2002,[89] repeats many of the extensions effected in the TRIPS Agreement,[90] though importantly the WCT places them back under the supervision of the WIPO. Some of these are extended. For example, contracting parties must provide copyright owners with the exclusive right to distribute fixed copies that can be put into circulation as tangible objects.[91] In addition, contracting parties must provide copyright owners whose works are embodied in phonograms (not just those in computer programs or cinematographic works) with the exclusive right to authorize the commercial rentals of those fixed copies.[92]

The WCT also embodies three provisions that reflect the so-called 'digital agenda'. (In essence these are responses to concerns raised by copyright owners about new digital communication technologies.)[93] First, as part of the 'communication right', contracting parties must provide copyright owners with the exclusive rights to make their works available to the public in such a way that members may access the work from a place and at a time individually chosen by them.[94] (This is intended to cover, for example, the placing of a work on a web site that can be accessed by the public.) Second, contracting parties must provide adequate legal protection against the circumvention of 'effective technological measures' used by authors to protect their rights.[95] Third, contracting parties must provide adequate remedies to those who tamper with 'rights management information', that is information used to facilitate the identification or exploitation of those works.[96]

6.5 WIPO PERFORMANCES AND PHONOGRAMS TREATY (1996)

Although the WIPO Performances and Phonograms Treaty ('WPPT') was intended to supplement the Rome Convention, it only contains provisions relating to rights of performers and phonogram producers, and *not* broadcasters.[97] The WPPT upgrades the position of performers whose performances are embodied on phonograms. However, largely as a result of the resistance of the American film industry, it does little for actors. Under the WPPT, contracting parties must confer on all performers rights against bootlegging equivalent to those in the Rome Convention. This is upgraded from 'the possibility of preventing' to an exclusive right.[98] Performers in the music industry (whose performances have been 'fixed in phonograms') are to be given three extra rights. First, they are to be given rights to control various acts in relation to fixations of their performances, that is the reproduction, distribution, rental, and making

---

[89] There were 51 signatories and as of 28 May 2008 there were 65 ratifications.

[90] Art. 2 WCT is on a par with TRIPS Art. 9(2); Art. 4 WCT is on a par with TRIPS Art. 10(1); Art. 5 WCT is on a par with TRIPS Art. 10(2); Art. 10 WCT is on a par with TRIPS Art. 13; Art. 14 WCT is on a par with TRIPS Art. 41.

[91] WCT Art. 6; 'Agreed Statement' concerning Arts. 6 and 7.

[92] WCT Art. 7. Note the qualifications in Art. 7(2)–(3).

[93] The Preamble recognizes 'the profound impact of the development and convergence of information and communication technologies on the creation and use of literary and artistic works'. Note the Agreed Statement concerning WCT Art. 1(4) which defines reproduction to include the storage of a work in digital form in an electronic medium.

[94] WCT Art. 8. Note also the 'Agreed Statement' annexed to the treaty stating that the mere provision of physical facilities for enabling or making a communication does not in itself amount to a communication.

[95] WCT Art. 11.   [96] WCT Art. 12.

[97] The WPPT entered into force on 20 May 2002 (pursuant to Art. 29: 3 months after deposit by 30 states of their instruments of accession of ratification). There were 50 signatories and as of 28 May 2008 there were 70 ratifications to the WPPT.

[98] WPPT Art. 6.

available of copies of such fixations.[99] Second, where there is public performance or broadcasting of such fixations, contracting states are to ensure that performers receive a share in the remuneration that is paid.[100] Third, contracting states are to confer moral rights of attribution and integrity on the performers of 'live aural performances or performances fixed in phonograms'.[101] The upshot of this is that, while recording artists and musicians will get rights which are equivalent to those given to authors, actors (and other individuals whose performances are embodied in films/audiovisual works) will be confined to the right to prevent first fixation (etc.) without their consent.

The WPPT also extends the rights given to producers of phonograms. Contracting states are not only to confer on the producers of phonograms the right to control reproduction, but also the exclusive right to control the distribution, rental, and making available of copies of phonograms.[102] The WPPT also requires certain action for the benefit of *both* performers and phonogram producers. In particular, the WPPT replicates the three provisions of the WCT on the digital agenda, that is, the 'making available' right, the requirements relating to technological measures of protection, and the provisions on rights management information. The Treaty also provides that contracting states may only create exceptions and limitations to the rights of performers or phonogram producers if those limitations pass the three-step test.[103]

7 EUROPEAN INFLUENCES

In the last twenty years or so, European initiatives have had an important and growing impact on British copyright law.[104] This is because various European directives now prescribe in some detail when and in what manner member states must (and often may) recognize intellectual property rights in this field. As we saw in Chapter 1, the need for harmonizing legislation arose because, despite the efforts of the European Court of Justice (notably through the doctrine of exhaustion),[105] differences in national laws relating to copyright and related rights operate to produce barriers to trade within the internal market. Perhaps the clearest example of this was in the decision in *EMI Electrola GmbH v. Patricia Im-und Export*.[106] This grew out of the fact that because of differences in the terms of copyright in sound recordings in Germany and Denmark,[107] the sound recording rights in songs by Cliff Richard had expired in Denmark but not in Germany. Patricia attempted to import the records from Denmark (where the records were lawfully available) back into Germany. The European Court of Justice held that even though the copies were lawfully marketed in Denmark (because the copyright had expired there), the German right holder was entitled to prevent the importing of the recordings into Germany where copyright continued to subsist. This was because, as the

---

[99] WPPT Arts 7–10. [100] WPPT Art. 15.

[101] WPPT Art. 5. This was implemented in the UK by Performances (Moral Rights, etc.) Regulations 2006 SI 2006/18. See pp. 308–9 below.

[102] WPPT Arts 11–14. [103] WPPT Art. 16.

[104] For an outline of earlier Community activities, see J. Pardo, 'Highlights of the Origins of European Union Law on Copyright' [2001] *EIPR* 238.

[105] *Deutsche Grammophon v. Metro*, Case C–78/70 [1971] *ECR* 487.

[106] Case C341/87 [1989] *ECR* 79. See also *Warner Bros v. Christiansen*, Case C–158/86 [1988] *ECR* 2605 (rental right).

[107] Both countries granted terms of 25 years but from different starting dates, Denmark favouring fixation and Germany publication.

copyright owner had not consented to the marketing of those copies in Germany, they had not exhausted their rights. The Court observed that 'in the present state of the Community, characterized by an absence of harmonization, it is for national legislatures to specify the conditions and rules for such protection'. Such restrictions are justified by Article 30 EC (formerly Article 36 of the Treaty) if the period of protection is inseparably linked to the existence of the exclusive rights.

By the time of the *Patricia* decision, the Commission had already decided that, if the plan for an internal market free from barriers was to be made good, then certain aspects of copyright had to be harmonized. The first step in the harmonization programme was the publication of the Green Paper, *Copyright and the Challenge of Technology*.[108] This set out a basic plan to harmonize specific areas of copyright, particularly those relating to new technologies. Given that it was widely believed that national copyright traditions were very different, it was decided that the wholesale approximation of copyright law was impossible. In the light of comments on the Green Paper,[109] the Commission expanded its proposals in 1990.[110] The subsequent decade has seen the formulation and passage of a series of directives on software, cable and satellite broadcasting, rental and lending, and 'neighbouring rights', the duration of copyright, databases, the resale royalty right, and copyright in the 'information society'. While each of these directives concerned itself primarily with a specific aspect of copyright (that is, a specific type of subject matter or a specific right), the Directive on copyright in the Information Society concerned a series of rights and exceptions applicable to virtually all copyright works. Consequently, this directive is widely regarded as heralding a shift from 'vertical' harmonization to 'horizontal' harmonization. While we look at these directives at appropriate points in the following chapters, it may be useful to outline their key features here. Before doing so, it may be helpful to highlight some of the themes that are beginning to develop in the European legislation, some of which have been interpreted as representing a step towards a coherent European copyright policy.[111]

One notable trend is that the directives consistently distinguish between two categories of work: 'copyright' which means authorial works falling under the Berne Convention; and 'related rights' (specifically not 'neighbouring rights') which means various rights of performers, phonogram producers, the producers of the first fixations of films, and broadcasting organizations. The related rights given to producers of the first fixations of 'films' by various Directives are important in that they are not confined to audiovisual or cinematographic works, but also extend to other moving images (such as films of sporting events).

Another notable aspect of the directives concerns the way they manage the (supposed) differences between the different legal regimes (copyright and *droit d'auteur*). Given that the directives are largely the result of lobbying and horse-trading between interest groups and member states, it is not surprising that the end-results are a hybrid mix of concepts taken from both the *droit d'auteur* and copyright law.[112] For example, there is recognition of an unwaivable

---

[108] Interestingly, it had been the subject of discussion as early as 1980: S. von Lewinski, 'EC Proposal for Council Directive Harmonizing the Term of Protection of Copyright and Certain Related Rights' (1992) 23 *IIC* 785, n. 1.

[109] The Green Paper received a lukewarm reception. See A. Francon, 'Thoughts on the Green Paper' (1989) 139 *RIDA* 128; M. Moller, 'On the Subject of the Green Paper' (1989) 141 *RIDA* 22 (1989); G. Shricker, 'Harmonization of Copyright in the EEC' (1989) 20(4) *IIC* 466, 475.

[110] *Follow Up to the Green Paper,* 17 Jan. 1991 COM (90) 584 Final.

[111] H. Comte, 'The Rental Rights Directive: A Step towards a Copyright Europe' (1993) 158 *RIDA* 2.

[112] See, e.g. E. Derclaye, 'Software Copyright Protection: Can Europe Learn from American Case Law?' [2000] *EIPR* 7, 9–10; D. Vaver, 'The Copyright Mixture in a Mixed Legal System: Fit For Human Consumption?' (2002) *Juridical Review* 101 (largely defending the harmonization process against some of its critics).

right to 'equitable remuneration' for the authors of works which are the subject of rental and lending. This corresponds to similar (though more general) provisions in French and German law guaranteeing authors proportionate remuneration.[113] On the other hand (much to the disappointment of some French commentators), computer programs are recognized as literary works.[114] In addition, where a computer program is made by an employee in the course of employment, the economic rights are given to the employer, rather than to the employee.[115] In some ways, the form that the directives have adopted is a return, at least from the British perspective, to the openly hybrid nature of intellectual property statutes in the nineteenth century.

Another trend that is apparent is that, while the need for harmonization arose because variations in the law of member states posed a potential barrier to trade, the Commission has tended to harmonize 'upwards'. That is, the EC has tended to strengthen the protection given to copyright owners. The most obvious example of this was the decision to increase the term of copyright to the term of life plus 70 years which existed in Germany, rather than ask that the German term be reduced to life plus 50 years (which was the term then used by many member states). While the strengthening of protection has sometimes been explained in terms of legislative convenience, it also suggests that it is at least an implicit agenda that aims to maximize copyright protection. This can be detected in Recital 10 to the Duration Directive which says that 'these rights are fundamental to intellectual creation... their protection ensures the maintenance and development of creativity in the interests of authors, cultural industries, consumers and society as a whole'.[116] Another example of the strengthening of the position of right holders has been the progressive restriction of the defences or exceptions that member states are able to use in their laws.[117] This is particularly noticeable in the Database Directive where the option of a 'private use' defence is excluded when the database is in an electronic form, and when use in scientific research is confined to uses for 'non-commercial purposes'.

Another notable, and possibly growing, trend is that the directives adopted in the name of harmonization have only a very limited harmonizing effect. In fact, there are many situations where the directives tolerate a level of difference between the laws of member states. For example, in relation to subject matter, member states are expressly permitted to protect non-original photographs, and critical and scientific publications of works which have fallen into the public domain.[118] Although there is some degree of prescription, member states have flexibility as regards specifying who are the co-authors of cinematographic works.[119] Member states are sometimes permitted to confer greater rights on right holders than those specified in the directives,[120] and occasionally (as with the lending right) to derogate from the standards set by the directives.[121] There are also permissive clauses in relation to defences,[122] presumed transfer of rights,[123] and the kinds of collective licensing regime required.[124] The details of

---

[113] Rental Dir., Art. 5. [114] Software Dir., Art. 1. [115] Ibid, Art. 2(3).

[116] Duration Dir., Recital 10. [117] Rental Dir., Art. 10(1). [118] Duration Dir., Arts 5 and 6.

[119] Rental Dir., Art. 2(2); Duration Dir., Art. 2(1). As well as designating 'legal persons' as rights holders: Software Dir., Art. 2(1); Database Dir., Art. 4(1).

[120] Satellite Dir., Art. 6 (expressly permitting member states to provide more far-reaching broadcasting and communication rights than those mandated by Rental Dir., Art. 8).

[121] Rental Dir., Art. 5.

[122] Rental Dir., Art. 10; and the more restricted Database Dir., Art. 6(2); Info. Soc. Dir., Art. 5(2), (3).

[123] Rental Dir., Arts 2(6), (7).

[124] Rental Dir., Art. 8(2) (conditions as to sharing remuneration for broadcasting and public performance between performers and the producers of phonograms), Art. 13(9) (level of remuneration for rental); Satellite Dir., Art. 3(2), Art. 9(3), Art. 13.

'transitional provisions' are also left largely to member states.[125] Moreover, as the case law on transitional provisions in the Term Directive, and that on the concept of 'equitable remuneration' make clear, the harmonizing directives often offer loose, open-textured concepts around which member states must formulate specific rules, within certain limited parameters.

Another notable trend that is apparent from the directives is that the Commission is developing a series of conceptual solutions that may ultimately form the basis for a harmonized law. The most obvious example of this is in relation to the notion of originality, which we discuss in Chapter 4. By harmonizing the originality requirement in an identical manner for computer programs, photographs, and databases, the Commission has set up a single European standard, namely that works should only be protected where they are their author's 'own intellectual creations'.[126]

With these general points in mind, we now outline the main features of the seven Directives.

7.1 COMPUTER PROGRAMS DIRECTIVE (1991)

The first European initiative in the copyright field was the Computer Programs Directive, which had to be implemented by 1 January 1993.[127] The Computer Programs Directive addressed the question whether computer programs should be protected by copyright, patents, or a *sui generis* right. Fearing that the member states might have responded differently, the Commission sought a swift and unified response. After consulting with interested parties, it was decided that computer programs should be protected by copyright. This is reflected in the fact that the Directive requires member states to protect computer programs as literary works under the Berne Convention. To ensure that this operates as a matter of substance as well as form, the Directive also harmonized the criteria for protection. Prior to the Directive, there were wide divergences as to what member states required of computer programs before they could be regarded as original, with German law setting the definition of originality at a particularly high level. Ultimately, the Directive requires member states to protect computer programs as long as they are original in the sense that they are their author's own intellectual creation.

The Computer Programs Directive also goes some way to harmonizing the protection member states must give to computer programs. More specifically, the Directive requires member states to confer certain rights on the owners of copyright in computer programs, including the right to control temporary reproduction, the running and storage of the program, the translation or adaptation, distribution or rental of programs;[128] as well as certain liabilities for 'secondary infringers'.[129] The Directive also requires member states to recognize certain exceptions to the exclusive rights. Negotiations over these exceptions caused intense and acrimonious lobbying in Brussels. Ultimately, the Directive requires member states to enact four exceptions. The first concerns acts done by a lawful acquirer of a program which are necessitated by use of the program for its intended purpose; the second allows the making of back-up copies;

[125] Rental Dir., Art. 13(3)–(8); Satellite Dir., Art. 7; and Duration Dir., Art. 10(3), which was considered by the ECJ in *Butterfly Music SRL v. Carosello Edizioni Musicali e Discografiche SRL*, Case C–60/98 [1999] *ECDR* 1.

[126] Software Dir., Art. 1(3); Duration Dir., Art. 6, Recital 17; Database Dir., Art. 3(1). But note IViR, *Recasting Copyright*, pp. 36–7, suggesting that the test differs for photographs.

[127] Commission, *Report on the Implementation and Effects of the Directive in 2000*: COM (2000) 199 final.

[128] Ibid, Art. 4. See Ch. 6.   [129] Ibid, Art. 7. See Ch. 8.

the third permits the studying and testing of the program; the fourth, and most controversial, permits—in very limited circumstances—the decompilation of programs.[130]

One final provision of interest in the Computer Programs Directive concerns the way it allocates the ownership of copyright. In the case of programs that are made by employees in the course of their employment, the Directive requires member states to allocate the copyright in such programs to the employer.[131]

7.2 RENTAL DIRECTIVE (1992) (codified in 2006)

The Rental Directive is in two parts, the first dealing with the specific issues of rental and lending, the other dealing with related rights.[132] The second part comes as close to the codification of copyright as any of the European Directives. Most of the provisions in the Directive had to be implemented by 1 July 1994.[133]

Chapter 1 of the Directive was drafted in response to the increasing economic importance of home rental as a source of revenue for copyright owners. Some member states had decided to confer a rental right, and some had adopted provisions relating to the public lending of works. The Directive attempts to avoid the development of divergent approaches by harmonizing the law relating to rental and lending.[134] It requires member states to confer on authors (of works within the Berne Convention), performers, phonogram producers, and film producers the exclusive right to control the rental and lending of copies (or in the case of performers, fixations) of their works.[135] However, member states are given a number of options, sometimes in derogation from the exclusive rights. The most important of these is the option not to recognize an exclusive right to authorize 'public lending' if authors receive remuneration of some sort for such lending.[136] Member states may also exempt certain establishments from the payment of remuneration for lending.[137]

Chapter 1 of the Directive also includes some interesting provisions on the ownership of the rental right. The Directive recognized the need for creators to obtain an 'adequate income as a basis for further creative and artistic work'.[138] As a result, a fiercely debated provision requires member states to confer on authors and performers an 'unwaivable right to equitable remuneration' when copies of films or phonograms are rented.[139] In turn, it was decided that this required further definition of who is the author of a cinematographic or audiovisual work (a matter on which there are wide divergences under the laws of different countries).[140]

---

[130] Ibid, Arts. 5 and 6. See further Ch. 9.   [131] Ibid, Art. 2(3). See Ch. 5.

[132] The Rental Directive emerged in part in response to the European Court of Justice's decision in *Warner Bros. v. Christiansen,* Case C–158/86 [1988] *ECR* 2605. For background see Reinbothe and von Lewinski (1993).

[133] Rental Directive 92/100/EEC, Art. 13. On implementation, see Commission, *Report from the Commission to the Council etc on the Public Lending Right* COM (2002) 502 final (12 Sept. 2002).

[134] In *Metronome Music v. Music Point Hokamp GmbH,* Case C–200/96 [1998] *ECR* I–1953, 1978–80 (paras. 21–2), the ECJ held that the Directive was legitimate despite its impact on the freedom to pursue trade because it effected an objective of general interest pursued by the Community and did not constitute a disproportionate and intolerable interference impairing the very substance of freedom to pursue a trade.

[135] Rental Dir., Art. 1(1). Rental and lending are defined in Art. 2. See Ch. 6.

[136] Rental Dir., Art. 6(1). See below at pp. 221–2, 225, 328–9.

[137] Ibid, Art. 6(3). See below at p. 225.   [138] Ibid, Recital 5.

[139] Ibid, Art. 5. See below at p. 285.

[140] In the original proposal this was left as a matter for member states. The provision originated in an amendment to the proposed Directive by the European Parliament Committee on Culture.

The Directive requires that member states recognize that the 'principal director' is one of the authors of such a work.[141]

Chapter 2 of the Rental Directive requires member states to confer various rights on performers, producers of phonograms, broadcasters, and cable distributors (in addition to the rental and lending rights conferred by Article 2). *Performers* are to be given the exclusive right to authorize or prohibit the fixation,[142] broadcasting, or communication to the public of their unfixed performances.[143] They are also to be given the right to control the distribution of fixations of their performances.[144] Performers are also granted the right to share in the remuneration paid for the right to broadcast or play in public phonograms embodying their performances.[145] In turn, *phonogram producers* are to be given the exclusive right to authorize or prohibit the distribution of their phonograms.[146] They are also given a right to share in remuneration paid for the right to broadcast or play in public phonograms embodying their performances.[147] *Broadcasting organizations* are to be given the exclusive right to authorize or prohibit the fixation[148] of their unfixed broadcasts;[149] the distribution of fixations of their broadcasts; or the rebroadcasting or communication to the public of their broadcasts.[150]

Part 2 also requires member states to confer similar rights on the producers of first fixations of films. In the European schema, 'first fixations of films' is a category of related rights over and above the category of 'cinematographic and audiovisual works', which covers all fixations of moving images. A film of a football match, for example, would be a first fixation of a film, even though it might not be a cinematographic work. The producers of these fixations are to be granted the exclusive right to authorize or prohibit the distribution of their films.[151]

7.3 CABLE AND SATELLITE DIRECTIVE (1993)

The third European initiative, the Cable and Satellite Directive, was a response to technological developments. The Directive required member states (by 1 January 1995) to recognize that copyright and related rights include the right to authorize communication to the public by satellite.[152] The Directive does not harmonize these rights. Instead it requires member states 'to ensure that when programmes from other member states are retransmitted by cable in their territory the applicable copyright and related rights are observed'. The Directive indicates that the rights recognized must be full property rights and that statutory licensing schemes must be abolished by 31 December 1997. The Directive limits the ways in which the rights may be administered. The Directive requires that the right to grant or refuse authorization to a cable operator who wishes to retransmit a broadcast shall only be exercised through a collecting

---

[141] Rental Dir., Art. 2(2). Reiterated in Duration Dir., Art. 2(1). See below at pp. 123–5.

[142] Rental Dir., Art. 7(1). See below at pp. 306–8. The reproduction right was repealed and replaced by Info. Soc. Dir., Art. 2.

[143] Ibid, Art. 9(1).

[144] Ibid, Art. 9. See below at p. 307.

[145] Ibid, Art. 8(2). The ECJ has declined to give guidance on what amounts to equitable remuneration, leaving it to member states to determine, though seemingly reserving the right to say when member states get it wrong: *Stichting ter Exploitatie van Naburige Rechten (SENA) v. Nederlandse Omroep Stichting (NOS)*, Case C–245/00 [2003] *EMLR* 364. See below at pp. 307–8.

[146] Ibid, Art. 9.   [147] Ibid, Art. 8(2). See Ch. 6.   [148] Ibid, Art. 7(1).

[149] Ibid, Art. 8(1).   [150] Ibid, Art. 9(1)(d); Art. 8(3). See Ch. 6.

[151] Ibid, Art. 9(1)(d). For the problems UK law has with films, see below at Ch. 3, Sections 3 and 6.

[152] Satellite Directive, Arts 2 and 4. (It also permits member states to require 'collective administration' of some such rights, but only in the case of simulcasts of terrestrial broadcasts.)

society.[153] This does not apply, however, where the rights are owned by broadcasting organizations. The right of the broadcaster to prohibit retransmission of its own transmissions can be exercised independently.[154]

The most notable feature of the Directive concerns the definition of the place where the communication takes place. Prior to the Directive, different jurisdictions responded differently to the question of whether a satellite broadcast takes place in the country where the broadcast originated, the country from which the signals are sent, the satellite itself, or the countries where the signal can be received (this is known as the 'footprint'). Opting for the simplest solution, the Directive requires member states to treat a satellite broadcast as taking place where the signals are introduced (or 'injected'). This is the simplest solution because permissions to broadcast the various works to be included in a satellite broadcast are only required from the copyright owners in the country of introduction.[155]

7.4 DURATION DIRECTIVE (1993) (codified 2006)

The Duration Directive was adopted in response to the *Patricia* decision, which made it clear that varying terms of protection posed a hurdle to the completion of the internal market.[156] Prior to its adoption, most member states granted copyright protection for a period of 50 years after the author's death. However, some countries granted a 60-year *post mortem* term and Germany a 70-year term. Preferring to harmonize upwards, the Duration Directive required member states, by 1 July 1995, to grant a term of protection for copyright works (including original photographs) lasting for the life of the author plus 70 years.[157] In the case of cinematographic works, the duration is 70 years from the death of the principal director, author of the screenplay, author of the dialogue, and composer of music.[158] Terms of protection for related rights (including broadcasting organizations and film producers) are to be based on a fixed 50-year term.[159] However, where the country of origin of the work is a third country, and the author is not a Community national, these terms of protection are to be restricted so that the terms expire in the EEA no later than their date of expiry in their country of origin.[160] The Directive also requires member states to grant a new right, called the 'publication right', where previously unpublished works in which copyright has expired are published for the first time.[161]

7.5 DATABASE DIRECTIVE (1996)

The Database Directive, which member states were obliged to implement by 1 January 1998, attempts to harmonize the laws of copyright in the field of databases.[162] It also requires member states to introduce a new *sui generis* right in non-original databases. This was seen to

---

[153] Satellite Dir., Art. 9(2), Art. 10. For British implementation see CDPA s. 144A. Note the criticism of the German implementation which requires cable operators to pay right holders an equitable remuneration, thereby precluding the possibility of cable operators dealing with only broadcasting organizations, and broadcasting organizations dealing with the collecting society: COM (2002) 430 final (July 26, 2002) p. 5.

[154] Satellite Dir., Art. 10.　　　[155] Satellite Dir., Art. 1. See below at p. 150.

[156] See above at pp. 45–6, 161.

[157] Duration Dir., Art. 1. Original photographs are defined as those which are their author's own intellectual creation. Recital 16 of the codified version of the Directive suggests that this means the photograph must reflect the personality of the author. Member states may protect non-original photographs. See below at pp. 109–11.

[158] Ibid, Art. 2(2).　　　[159] Ibid, Art. 3. See below at p. 166.

[160] Prompting a rapid response from the United States.

[161] Duration Dir., Art. 4. See below at pp. 167–8.　　　[162] See Davison, Chs. 3 and 4.

be necessary to sustain investment in the production and exploitation of electronic databases equally throughout the Community. While digital technologies had enhanced the potential of databases, differences in national laws (particularly as to originality) meant that databases were probably only protected by copyright in a few member states. This presented the possibility of distortions within the internal market. The Directive attempts to remedy this problem by requiring member states to ensure that their copyright laws protect *some* databases. It also requires that member states introduce new *sui generis* rights to protect other databases (no matter how mundane the arrangement of the material). In a sense, the two-tiered system recognizes that copyright only protects the selection or arrangement of materials, whereas the database right protects the collection and verification of the materials themselves.

The Directive requires member states to grant copyright to 'original databases'. A 'database' is defined rather vaguely as a collection of independent works, data, or other materials arranged in a systematic or methodical way and individually accessible by electronic or other means.[163] A database is only original where 'by reason of the selection or arrangement of their contents' the database constitutes the author's own intellectual creation.[164]

Member states are to give the owner of copyright in a database the exclusive right to reproduce the database, to translate it, to adapt, arrange, or alter it, distribute it, and communicate it to the public.[165] Member states must provide a defence to the lawful user of a database who commits acts that are necessary to access the contents of the database and to use those contents normally.[166] A limited list of optional defences is also prescribed.[167]

The Directive also requires member states to introduce a new *sui generis* right (which is reviewed in Chapter 13). For the moment it is worth observing that the database right arises where the maker of a database has made a substantial investment in either the activities of obtaining, verifying, or presenting the contents of the database. The maker of such a database is to be granted a right to prevent extraction or reutilization of the whole or substantial parts of the database. In certain circumstances, they also prevent the systematic extraction and/or reutilization of insubstantial parts.[168] Member states may subject the database right to certain limited defences and exceptions as regards private use of non-electronic databases, use for illustration of teaching and in non-commercial scientific research, public security, and administrative or judicial procedures.[169] This right is to last for 15 years from completion of the database or its publication, and a new right can arise where there is a substantial new investment in an existing database.[170]

7.6 ELECTRONIC COMMERCE DIRECTIVE (2000)

The EC Directive on Certain Legal Aspects of Electronic Commerce in the Internal Market aims to promote electronic commerce within the European Union, that is the provision of goods and services online. As such, it encompasses matters such as electronic contracts, unsolicited communications, and codes of conduct which are outside the scope of this text. However, a number of Articles impact upon intellectual property more directly, probably the most important of which concern the liability of service providers. As we will see, important questions arise as to whether people who provide the infrastructure and facilities for electronic communications become liable for the actions of those to whom their services are

---

[163] Database Dir., Art. 1. See pp. 66–7.   [164] Ibid, Art. 3. See pp. 107–9.
[165] Ibid, Art. 5. See Ch. 6.   [166] Ibid, Art. 6(1). See p. 232.   [167] Ibid, Art. 6(2). See p. 207.
[168] Ibid, Art. 7.   [169] Database Dir., Art. 9.   [170] Ibid, Art. 10(3).

provided.[171] Articles 12–15 of the Directive differentiate between situations where services are mere conduits and where they are involved in caching and hosting. The E-Commerce Directive requires member states to provide that a mere conduit is not liable, except under a 'prohibitory injunction', for information transmitted on the network. Moreover, a provider shall not be liable for 'caching', that is the automatic, intermediate, and temporary storage of information, as long as it complies with a series of conditions. Finally, the Directive states that a provider shall not be liable for 'hosting', that is storage of information at the request of a recipient, so long as the provider does not have actual knowledge that the activity is illegal and, as regards claims for damages, is not aware of facts or circumstances from which illegal activity is apparent; or upon obtaining such knowledge or awareness, acts expeditiously to remove or disable access to the information.

7.7 INFORMATION SOCIETY DIRECTIVE (2001)

By far the most significant of the Community initiatives dealing with copyright is the Information Society Directive: often referred to as the Copyright Directive.[172] This Directive has its origin in the Green Paper, *Copyright in the Information Society*[173] and the 1996 *Follow Up*.[174] According to one commentator, it was 'one of the most intensively debated proposals in recent EU history'.[175] The Directive is intended to implement the two WIPO Treaties agreed in Geneva in 1996. However, the Directive goes much further in responding to the perceived changes brought about by digital technology to the environment in which copyright law operates. As Recital 5 says:

technological development has multiplied and diversified the vectors for creation, production and exploitation. While no new concepts for the protection of intellectual property are needed, the current law on copyright and related rights should be adapted and supplemented to respond adequately to economic realities such as new forms of exploitation.

As well as introducing a 'making available right' and controls over technological measures of protection and rights management information,[176] the Directive harmonizes the reproduction and distribution rights, and attempts to limit the number and scope of the exceptions

---

[171] See below at Ch. 6 Section 9.

[172] Even by the Commission itself: see Commission Staff Working Paper, *Digital Rights: Background, Systems, Assessment* SEC (2002) 197 (Brussels, 14 Feb. 2002) p. 4.

[173] COM (95) 382 final.

[174] COM (96) 568 final. For commentary, see L. Bently and R. Burrell, 'Copyright and the Information Society: A Matter of Timing as well as Content' (1997) 34 *Common Market Law Review* 1197. A Proposal was first issued by the Commission in 1997, an Amended Proposal in May 1999 COM (97) 628 final [1998] *OJ C* 108/6 (7 Apr. 1998); COM (1999) 628 final [1999] *OJ C* 180/6 (25 Jun. 1999). A Common Position was reached in Sept. 2000: Common Position (EC) No. 48/2000 [2000] *OJ C* 344/1 (1 Dec. 2000).

[175] M. Fallenbock, 'On the Technical Protection of Copyright: the Digital Millennium Copyright Act, the European Community Copyright Directive and Their Anticircumvention Provisions' (2002–3) 7 *International Journal of Commercial Law & Policy* 4, 80. See also M. Hart, 'The Copyright in the Information Society Directive: An Overview' [2002] *EIPR* 58 ('the number of interests engaged in active lobbying on this proposal has been striking'); B. Hugenholtz, 'Why the Copyright Directive is Unimportant and Possibly Invalid' [2000] *EIPR* 499 (describing 'the unprecedented lobbying, the bloodshed, the vilification, the media propaganda, and the constant hounding of EC and government officials').

[176] See Info. Soc. Dir., Recital 15, 61; Art. 6 (technological measures); Art. 7 (rights management information). See below, pp. 318–23, 327–8.

(or defences) that a national regime can operate.[177] The Directive was adopted on 22 May 2001 and had to be implemented by 22 December 2002. The UK complied with that obligation on 31 October 2003.[178]

7.8 RESALE RIGHTS DIRECTIVE (2001)

A number of European countries currently offer artists the right to participate in the resale value or profits from the resale of their works. This is known as the *droit de suite* or artist's resale royalty. In the 1990s, the Commission took the view that variations in national laws could affect the operation of the art market. To ensure that this did not happen, the Resale Rights Directive was introduced in 2001.[179] The UK, which has a substantial art market but no resale right, strongly resisted adoption of the Directive. While the UK was unable to prevent the Directive being adopted, it did succeed in diluting some of the provisions. The Directive had to be implemented by 2006. The Directive and its implementation is discussed further in Chapter 13.

8 THE FUTURE

Although the British copyright legislation has been amended on a number of occasions over the last 15 years, further reforms are already being discussed. In 2006, the Gowers Committee recommended certain amendments of British law with respect to exceptions and enforcement,[180] but concluded that no case had been made out to extend the term of copyright in sound recordings. In addition, it is to be hoped, though not expected, that Parliamentary time will be made available for the passage of a Copyright Act which incorporates previous amendments (thereby removing doubts that have been raised about their validity), places the publication right and database right within the statutory schema, and codifies the law so that it is more comprehensible. In an era where members of the public are more directly involved with works protected by copyright, copyright owners are increasingly dependent on the public's knowledge of, and compliance with, the law. Given this, it is even more pressing that the problems with the existing law be remedied.

8.1 INTERNATIONAL CHANGES

At the international level, WIPO has embarked on a number of initiatives that involve or relate to copyright law. The first area of activity is in relation to audiovisual performances: a topic that was largely excluded from the 1996 Copyright Treaties because of opposition from US-based interests.[181] A diplomatic conference was held in Geneva in December 2000 with a view to adopting either a treaty or a protocol to the WPPT. While the parties were in agreement about 19 of the 20 proposed paragraphs, they were unable to reach final

---

[177] Art. 5(2).

[178] The Copyright and Related Rights Regulations 2003, SI 2003/2498. France was the last Member State to introduce implementing legislation in August 2006. For a review of implementation see IViR, *Study on the Implementation and Effect in Member States' Laws of Directive 2001/29/EC on the Harmonisation of Certain aspects of Copyright and Related Rights in the Information Society* (Amsterdam, February 2007).

[179] See below at pp. 329–32.   [180] HM Treasury, *Gowers Review of Intellectual Property* (2006).

[181] Diplomatic Conference on the Protection of Audiovisual Performances, Fourth Session (Geneva, 8–20 Dec. 2000).

agreement.[182] In particular, they were unable to reach agreement as to whether the rights acquired by producers should arise by operation of law or by agreement. This issue was discussed at an ad hoc Informal Meeting on the Protection of Audiovisual Performances in Geneva in November 2003. To date there have no formal proposals for a diplomatic conference. As such, it seems that it may be some time before we see any movement in this area.

The second area where WIPO is active is in relation to indigenous culture.[183] In reflection of the fact that many indigenous cultures do not draw a rigid line between art and science in the way that Western cultures often do, WIPO's activities extend beyond copyright to include patents, trade marks, and other related rights. While many of the copyright-related problems have been resolved, there are still a number of issues that need resolution. These include community moral rights, fixation, duration, and ways of protecting against the usurpation of indigenous style.

Another area where WIPO is active is in relation to databases. When WIPO began work on copyright reform in the 1990s, there were plans for three treaties (dealing, respectively, with changes to copyright, performances and phonograms, and databases). However, only two of the three treaties were passed: the third proposed treaty on databases was left on the table.[184] Given the criticisms of the EU Database Directive and that the United States, despite concerted attempts, has been unable to produce legislation in this field,[185] it is unlikely that anything comparable to the original draft would be acceptable. The most likely outcome is a treaty that requires contracting parties to protect databases from misappropriation, but leaves the means of protection to member states.

The fourth area of possible international reform is in relation to copyright protection for broadcasting organizations.[186] This has been under consideration for a decade and various versions of a possible treaty text are in circulation. As with the other WIPO treaties, the initiative was prompted by a desire to update international copyright standards to bring them into line with the 'information age'. Even though much of the content of the proposed treaty echoes that which was adopted for copyright, sound recordings, and performers in the two 1996 Treaties, in the subsequent years opposition to copyright has grown. Coupled with real doubts over the best way to deal with internet services which are similar to broadcasting, it is by no means clear that the proposal will produce a treaty.[187]

8.2 EUROPEAN INITIATIVES

The European Commission has announced that it will introduce in 2008 a proposal for a Directive extending the copyright term in sound recordings.[188] The Commission is also

---

[182] S. von Lewinski, 'The WIPO Diplomatic Conference on Audiovisual Performances: A First Resume' [2001] *EIPR* 333; O. Morgan, 'The problem of the international protection of audiovisual performances' [2002] *IIC* 810–827; Ficsor 70–74, 668–700; Reinbothe and von Lewinski (2002), 469–86.

[183] See Ficsor, 76–8, 704–8.

[184] See Ficsor, 69–70, 701–2; Reinbothe and von Lewinski (2002), 486–94; Davison, 226–34.

[185] The Database Investment and Intellectual Property Antipiracy Bill of 1996, The Collections of Information Antipiracy Bill 1997, The Collections of Information Antipiracy Bill 1999, The Consumer and Investor Access to Information Bill of 1999, Database and Collections of Information Misappropriation Act 2003 (H.R. 3261). See Davison, ch. 5.

[186] See Ficsor, 74–6, 702–4.

[187] The Draft Non-Paper on the WIPO Treaty on the Protection of Broadcasting Organizations of March 8, 2007 is a very modest proposal indeed, proposing protection of broadcasting organizations' broadcasts for 20 years. There would be no obligation to grant 'rights' and the Treaty would expressly not cover web transmissions.

[188] IP/08/240 (Brussels, 14 Feb. 2008).

reviewing the issue of levies on copying equipment, and is alive to potential internal market aspects of this problem.[189] Some legislative initiative may prove necessary, though the issues are complex. The Commission is also reviewing issues of Europe-wide licensing, though any action in this field is likely to be through soft law.[190]

In the medium term, there are still some possible candidates for future harmonization: these include the moral rights, copyright contracts, and collective administration.[191] While many of the copyright reforms initiated by the Commission have proved to be difficult, it is likely that these remaining topics will be particularly problematic.[192] In part, this is because these are areas where the differences between different member states are most marked. They are also areas of copyright law which are closely intertwined with other areas of national law such as contract law and labour law. As such, reform will invariably be caught up in broader debates. Early studies on moral rights and copyright contracts indicate that there is little support for harmonization of these matters on the Continent, because of fears that the laws would be made less author-protective.[193] There are a number of other piecemeal issues that may be addressed in the future. For example, while certain works have to be recognized under the existing Directives, the Commission has not yet looked at the way works are defined more generally (including issues such as TV formats or protection of perfumes), nor at fixation. In addition, there has been only partial harmonization of 'originality' and 'qualification' (in the context of the resale royalty right).

There are always murmurings amongst the more ambitious or federally inclined about the possible codification of European copyright law. In its study for the European Commission, entitled *Recasting Copyright for the Knowledge Economy,* the Institute for Information Law at the University of Amsterdam has made a tentative proposal that long-term consideration be given to creation of a European Copyright Code, conferring a single, Europe-wide, indivisible copyright (and pre-empting any corresponding national rights). The proposed right would be created by Community Regulation and draw on the existing Directives and the jurisprudence of the ECJ. It would also fill in many of the gaps, but would not cover aspects of copyright

---

[189] E.C., *Fair Compensation for Acts of Private Copying* (Brussels, 14 Feb 2008).

[190] E.C., *Communication from the Commission to the Council, the European Parliament and the European Economic and Social Committee: The Management of Copyright and Related Rights in the Internal Market* COM(2004) 261 final (Brussels 16 Apr 2004); E.C., *Communication from the Commission to the European Parliament, the Council, the European Economic and Social Committee and the Committee of the Regions on Creative Content Online in the Single Market* (SEC(2007) 1710 (3 Jan 2008) COM(2007) 836 final. See also E.C., *Monitoring of the 2005 Music Online Recommendation,* (Brussels, 7 Feb 2008).

[191] Info. Soc. Dir., Recital 17 ('it is necessary, especially in the light of the requirements arising out of the digital environment, to ensure that collecting societies achieve a higher level of rationalisation and transparency with regard to compliance with competition rules'); Resale Rights Directive, Recital 28 ('Member States should ensure that collecting societies operate in a transparent and efficient manner').

[192] See, e.g. M. Walter, 'Updating and Consolidation of the *Acquis*: The Future of European Copyright', Report of the Commission meeting Santiago de Compostela, June 2002 (proposing harmonization of moral rights, as well as general application of the unwaivable right to equitable remuneration). But cf. IViR, *Recasting Copyright,* Ch. 7 advising against further harmonizing directives, and proposing immediate action through 'soft law' to clarify inconsistencies, and a longer-term project for a core Copyright Code through a regulation.

[193] A. Strowel, M. Salokannel, and E. Derclaye, *Moral Rights in the Context of the Exploitation of Works Through Digital Technology* (2000); B. Hugenholtz and L. Guibault, *Study in the Conditions Applicable to ContrACts Relating to Intellectual Property in the EU* (2002) (suggesting harmonization would be 'premature'). See also *Communication from the Commission to the Council, the European Parliament and the European Economic and Social Committee: The Management of Copyright and Related Rights in the Internal Market* COM(2004) 261 final (Brussels 16 Apr 2004), 13 (para 2.3) (given common ground there is no need for the time being to harmonize rules on copyright contracts).

that did not affect the operation of the internal market, or which reflected national cultural policy. The study thus suggests that moral rights, authorship, ownership, and supervision of collective administration would remain aspects of national law. In addition, lest such a Code introduce undue inflexibility, the study suggests that national legislatures be provided with some flexibility to introduce new exceptions or limitations. The potential advantages of such a change are self-evident. A code would be simpler, insofar as it consists of a single law, rather than a series of national laws. If drafted correctly, it would remove inconsistencies between the existing Directives. Such a code would also be more user-friendly insofar as it enabled rights to be enforced in a single action across Europe. Despite these attractions, it is unlikely that it will be introduced, at least in the near future. The Commission seems rather intent on adapting existing copyright law to market conditions through recommendations and less intervention-ist mechanisms. In the longer term, however, these ideas deserve fuller exploration.

3

SUBJECT MATTER

CHAPTER CONTENTS

1 INTRODUCTION

This chapter examines the subject matter protected by copyright law. In contrast with some other jurisdictions, where the subject matter protected by copyright is defined by statute in broad and open-ended terms,[1] the Copyright, Designs and Patents Act 1988 provides a detailed and exhaustive list of the types of creation protected by copyright law. In order for a creation to be protected by copyright it must fall within one of the following eight categories of work: (1) literary works, (2) dramatic works, (3) musical works, (4) artistic works, (5) films, (6) sound recordings, (7) broadcasts, (8) published editions (or typographical works).

Before looking at the categories of subject matter in more detail, it is necessary to make some preliminary points. The first is that, as the 1988 Act provides an exhaustive list of the protected subject matter, there is little opportunity for the courts to recognize new forms of subject matter, other than through the creative interpretation of the existing categories. The closed nature of the categories, especially when combined with the fact that the UK has no law of unfair competition, has meant that at times copyright has been 'stretched to give protection to creative talents and activities the protection of which was never in the contemplation...of those who from time to time have been responsible for the framing of the successive statutes'.[2] On other occasions, the fact that the list is exhaustive has led to the exclusion from UK copyright

---

[1] For example, French law protects '*toutes les oeuvres de l'esprit*': French Intellectual Property Code, 1992, Art. L–112–1. See also Berne, Art. 6. For a proposal to abandon classification of works, see A. Christie, 'Re-conceptualising Copyright in the Digital Era' [1995] *EIPR* 522, 525; 'A Proposal for Simplifying United Kingdom Copyright Law' [2001] *EIPR* 26.

[2] *CBS v. Ames Records* [1981] *RPC* 407, 417.

Fig. 3.1 The album cover of Oasis's *Be Here Now*
Source: Reproduced courtesy of Big Brother Recordings.

law of 'works' which would be protected in countries operating a non-exhaustive system.[3] This was graphically illustrated in the case of *Creation Records*. Here, as preparation in the production of the cover for Oasis's album *Be Here Now,* (see Fig. 3.1) Noel Gallagher arranged for a series of objects (a Rolls Royce, a motor bike, a clock) to be placed around a swimming pool. This collection of 'artistically' distributed objects was then photographed by the claimant, and the photograph used as the album cover. However, a photographer from the defendant newspaper was present, and also took a photograph of the scene. When the newspaper published this photograph, and offered to sell posters of the scene, the record company sought an interim injunction alleging infringement of its copyright. The claim based on copyright failed because the scene did not fall within the meaning of any of the (then) nine (now eight) categories of protected work: in particular, it was not an artistic work, nor a dramatic work.[4]

A notable feature of the 1988 Act is that all types of subject matter that are protected by copyright are called 'works'. This is in contrast to the 1956 Copyright Act where a distinction was drawn between Part I 'works' (literary, dramatic, musical, or artistic works) and Part II

---

[3] Some European countries have even protected perfumes by copyright: *Lancôme Parfums v. Kecofa* [2006] ECDR (26) 363 (Dutch Supreme Court); cf. *Bsiri-Barbir v. Haarmann & Reimer* [2006] ECDR (28) 380 (French Cour de Cassation). This clearly would not be possible under UK law. See C. Seville, 'Copyright in Perfume: Smelling a Rat' (2007) 66 *CLJ* 49; H. Cohen Jehoram [2006] *EIPR* 629.

[4] *Creation Records v. News Group* [1997] *EMLR* 444 (interim relief, however, was granted on the basis of breach of confidence. See below Chs. 44–6).

'subject matter' (sound recordings, films, broadcasts, and typographical arrangements). It is also in marked contrast to the position in civil law systems, such as in France, which distinguish between 'author's rights' (or *droits d'auteur*) and 'neighbouring rights' or entrepreneurial works (*droits voisins*). Author's rights typically cover literary, dramatic, musical, and artistic work, whereas neighbouring rights are afforded to sound recordings, broadcasts, and performers.[5] This distinction is also reflected in the International Conventions: with the 1886 Berne Convention protecting 'author's rights' and the 1961 Rome Convention protecting 'neighbouring rights'. Under EC law, 'neighbouring rights' are usually classed as 'related rights'. While the 1988 Act may have jettisoned the distinction between works and subject matter other than works, it should not be assumed that all works are treated the same. Indeed, as will become apparent in the following chapters, the conditions under which rights are granted differ, sometimes considerably, between different classes of work, as do the scope, nature, and duration of those rights. It is also important to note that, although British law may have abandoned the formal distinction between authorial works (literary, dramatic, musical, and artistic works) and entrepreneurial works (sound recordings, films, broadcasts, and typographical works),[6] nonetheless copyright law treats these two broad categories differently. While there are problems with this distinction, notably now that films occupy a space somewhere in between the two categories, it provides a useful way of describing the subject matter of copyright.

It should also be noted that the legal categories do not necessarily correspond to the objects commonly associated with copyright law. Instead, individual tangible objects may embody a number of different copyright works. For example, a book or newspaper might contain a literary work, an artistic work, and a typographical arrangement;[7] a song may consist of literary and musical works (the lyrics being a literary work); and a CD might contain a sound recording, a musical work, and a literary work. While the legal categories do not necessarily correspond to the objects protected by copyright, in most cases there have been few problems in matching a particular creative act to one of the protected categories. In some cases, however, the question has arisen as to whether it is possible for a particular creation to fall within two categories simultaneously. This question arose in *Electronic Technique v. Critchley,* where Laddie J was called upon to consider whether a circuit diagram could simultaneously be a literary work and an artistic work.[8] Laddie J said that, although it might be possible in theory to say that a single piece of creative effort may 'give rise to two or more copyrights in respect of the same creative effort', nonetheless 'there are compelling arguments that the author must be confined to one or the other of the possible categories'. However, other judges have taken a different view.[9] While it is still unclear whether the same creative effort can simultaneously give rise to both a literary work and an artistic work, in *Norowzian v. Arks (No. 2)* the Court of

---

[5] The division of subject matter into 'authorial' and 'entrepreneurial' works is based upon a belief that copyright for authors is the pure form and should not be conflated or equated with rights given in return for investment. See above, pp. 32–3.

[6] For example, as to the requirement for originality (see Ch. 4) or the concept of reproduction (see Ch. 6 Section 2 and p. 304).

[7] *The Newspaper Licensing Agency Ltd v. Marks and Spencer plc* [2003] 1 *AC* 551, 557; [2001] 3 *WLR* 390 (para. 4).

[8] [1997] *FSR* 401.

[9] *Anacon Corporation v. Environmental Research Technology* [1994] *FSR* 659 (Jacob J suggesting that a circuit diagram is both a literary and artistic work). Surely a poem in a particular shape could be an artistic work as well as a literary work: *Sandman v. Panasonic UK Ltd* [1998] *FSR* 651. See generally Copinger, para 3–04 pp. 51–3.

Appeal accepted that the maker of a film may simultaneously produce two copyright works: a film copyright in the fixation and a dramatic work in the 'cinematographic work'.[10]

With these general points in mind, we now turn to look at the eight types of work recognized by copyright law.

2 LITERARY WORKS

Literary works have been protected from unauthorized reproduction since at least 1710.[11] Literary works are defined in section 3(1) of the 1988 Act to mean 'any work, other than a dramatic or musical work, which is written, spoken or sung, and accordingly includes (a) a table or compilation (other than a database), (b) a computer program, (c) preparatory design material for a computer program, and (d) a database'.

It is important to note that literary works are not limited to works of literature, but include all works expressed in print or writing (other than dramatic or musical works).[12] It is also important to note that protection is not limited to words, but also includes things such as symbols and numerals. The scope of the subject matter protected as a literary work is enhanced by the fact that a work will be protected irrespective of the quality or style of the creation in question: copyright law does not pass judgment on the standard of the work. As a result, the types of thing that will be protected as a literary work include novels by Salman Rushdie, poems by Ted Hughes, lyrics by Courtney Love, as well as advertising slogans, railway timetables, and examination papers.[13] The fact that literary works include works that are spoken means that spontaneous conversations, interviews, and the like may also be protected (although, as we shall see, copyright does not subsist in a spoken work unless it is recorded).

For the most part, there have been few problems in deciding what is meant by a literary work. Where problems have arisen, the courts have tended to rely on the test set out in *Hollinrake v. Truswell* where it was said that, to qualify as a 'book' under the Literary Copyright Act 1842, the creation must afford 'either information and instruction, or pleasure, in the form of literary enjoyment'.[14] While this was not intended to provide a comprehensive or exhaustive definition,[15] it provides useful guidance as to where the boundaries of the category are to be drawn.

Most of the cases where the meaning of literary work has arisen have been concerned with works that afford information or instruction. These cases have made it clear that for a work to provide information or instruction, it must be capable of conveying an intelligible meaning.[16] In line with the principle that protection should not be dependent upon the quality of the work, the courts have been willing to accept a very low threshold when considering whether a work 'conveys an intelligible meaning'. For example, in one case it was accepted that sequences of letters set out

---

[10] [2000] *EMLR* 67.

[11] The Statute of Anne 1710 and the Literary Copyright Act 1842 used the term 'book'. However, since 1911 the statutes have referred to literary works.

[12] *University of London Press v. University Tutorial Press* [1916] 2 Ch 601.   [13] Ibid.

[14] (1894) 3 *Ch* 420. The Court of Appeal held that a cardboard sleeve chart (i.e. a representation of a sleeve designed for a lady's arm with certain scales or measurements on it, intended for practical use in dressmaking) was not a 'book' within the 1842 Act. Under the CDPA such a work would almost certainly be treated as an artistic work.

[15] *Apple Computer v. Computer Edge* [1984] *FSR* 481, 495 (Fed. Crt. Australia); Laddie *et al.*, para. 3.31.

[16] Ibid, 521 (Fed. Crt. Australia).

HERE'S HOW TO WIN THE
PRIZE OF A LIFETIME

● **THIS is your bonus chance to win £1 million. Just match your personal cash code on your card against the single line grid, from left to right IN ORDER. IF you have the perfect match you are in with a chance for that magical million.**

Fig. 3.2 The grids in *Express Newspapers v. Liverpool Daily Post*
Source: Courtesy of Express Newspapers.

in grids published in a newspaper provided information as to whether a reader had won or lost a bingo game and, as such, were literary works[17] (see Fig. 3.2). In order for a work to 'convey an intelligible meaning' it is not necessary that the work be understood by the general public; it is sufficient that the work is understood by a limited group with special knowledge. Thus a telegraphic code has been held to be a literary work, even though the words of the code were meaningless in themselves.[18] It has also been held that ciphers, mathematical tables, systems of shorthand, and Braille catalogues convey meaning and as such qualify as literary works.[19] One of the few situations where works have been held not to provide information or instruction is where the work is meaningless or gibberish.[20] Another situation where a work fails to provide information is where it is an invented name. For example, it was held that the word EXXON, which had been created to act as a company name, conveyed no information and hence was not protected as a literary work. (Although, as we will see, there may have been other grounds for this decision.)[21]

In contrast to informational works, there has been little discussion of what is meant by works that 'provide pleasure in the form of literary enjoyment'. The need for a work to provide literary enjoyment and pleasure seems to suggest a qualitative test. If so, it would run counter

---

[17] *Express Newspapers v. Liverpool Daily Post* [1985] 3 *All ER* 680.
[18] *D. P. Anderson v. Lieber Code Company* [1917] 2 *KB* 469.
[19] *Apple Computer v. Computer Edge* [1984] *FSR* 481, 521 (Fed. Crt. Australia).
[20] Ibid., 495 ('meaningless rubbish would plainly be excluded').
[21] *Exxon Corporation v. Exxon Insurance* [1982] *RPC* 69, 90.

to the widely accepted principle that the quality of the literary work is not to be taken into account when deciding whether a work should be protected.

With these general points in mind, we now turn to look in more detail at the types of thing that are protected as literary works. After looking at names and titles (which are not protected), we turn to look at tables and compilations, computer programs, preparatory material for computer programs, and databases.

2.1 NAMES, TRADE MARKS, AND TITLES

Despite the fact that names and titles are expressions in writing or print (and are often traded for substantial amounts of money), the UK (like most countries) refuses to protect them as literary works.[22] Thus, invented words such as EXXON (which had been invented by Esso Petroleum as a trade name),[23] titles of game shows such as *Opportunity Knocks*,[24] or song titles such as 'The Man Who Broke the Bank at Monte Carlo'[25] have been held not to be protected by copyright as literary works.

Two different reasons are used to account for the exclusion of names or titles from copyright. Sometimes, it is said, though not without some criticism,[26] that these matters are not 'literary works' at all. This is because although names and titles are in writing, they do not afford 'information, instruction or pleasure of a literary kind'. It was on this basis that the Court of Appeal held that EXXON was not a literary work.[27] In other cases, the tribunals focus on the fact that names and titles are not 'original'. That is, the courts refuse protection because the title is not the result of a substantial amount of labour, skill, and judgment, or is itself not 'substantial enough'. It was on this basis that *The Lawyer's Diary* and 'The Man Who Broke the Bank at Monte Carlo' were held to be unprotected.[28] This latter approach leaves room for the possibility that some creative titles might still qualify for copyright protection, particularly lengthy titles which are a product of substantial labour, skill, and judgment.[29]

There are a number of policy reasons why names and titles may be excluded from protection as literary works by copyright law. Perhaps the main reason for not protecting names and titles

[22] See R. Stone, 'Copyright Protection for Titles, Character Names and Catch-phrases in the Film and Television Industry' [1996] *Ent LR* 178. For related regimes see R. Stone, 'Titles, Character Names and Catch-phrases in the Film and Television Industry: Protection under the Trade Marks Act 1994 and Alternative Registration Systems' [1997] *Ent LR* 34.

[23] *Exxon Corp. v. Exxon Insurance* [1982] *RPC* 69.

[24] *Green v. Broadcasting Corporation of New Zealand* [1989] *RPC* 469, 472, 475, 490 (CA of New Zealand).

[25] *Francis Day and Hunter v. 20th Century Fox* [1940] *AC* 112 (copyright in the song 'The Man Who Broke the Bank at Monte Carlo' was not infringed by the performance of a motion picture of the same title). See also *Dick v. Yates* [1881] *Ch* 6 (no copyright in 'Splendid Misery').

[26] For criticisms of this rationale see Dworkin and Taylor, 21–2; J. Cullabine, 'Copyright in Short Phrases and Single Words' [1992] *EIPR* 205, 208.

[27] *Exxon Corp. v. Exxon Insurance* [1982] *RPC* 69.

[28] *Rose v. Information Services* [1987] *FSR* 254 Hoffmann J (there was too slight a degree of skill and labour); *Francis Day and Hunter v. 20th Century Fox* [1940] *AC* 112 (not substantial enough). In *Sinanide v. La Maison Kosmeo* (1924) LTR 365 protection was refused to the advertising slogan 'youthful appearances are social necessities, not luxuries' by reference to the principle *de minimis non curat lex*. Cf. *Weldon v. Dicks* [1878] *Ch* 247 ('Trial and Triumph' protected—but almost certainly no longer good law: see, Copinger, para. 21–20, 985 n. 98).

[29] In *Francis Day and Hunter v. 20th Century Fox* [1940] *AC* 112, the Privy Council indicated that, if a title was extensive and important enough, it might be possible to protect it. For cases of protection see *Lamb v. Evans* [1893] 1 *Ch* 218 (headings in trade directory protected) and *Shetland Times v. Dr Jonathan Wills* [1997] *FSR* 604 (arguable that newspaper headline of eight or so words ('Bid to save centre after council funding cock-up') was protected because it was designedly put together for the purpose of imparting information).

relates to the general inconvenience that would arise if someone was able to control the way certain words and phrases were used. It would be inconvenient—indeed absurd—if business commentators and political activists could not refer (e.g. in broadcasts, newspapers, or campaign literature) to the oil conglomerate by using the term EXXON without gaining permission in advance. Another reason for refusing protection to names and titles as literary works under copyright law is that it is unnecessary to do so, given that they are adequately protected by passing off, trade mark law,[30] and artistic copyright.[31]

2.2 TABLES AND COMPILATIONS (OTHER THAN DATABASES)

Section 3(1)(a) of the 1988 Act specifically states that literary work includes 'tables or compilations (other than a database)'.[32] As a part of the reforms made to accommodate the Database Directive, section 3 was amended as of 1 January 1998 to add the rider that 'tables and compilations' no longer includes databases. At the same time, the definition of literary work was amended so as specifically to recognize databases as a separate type of literary work.[33] The reason why databases were placed in a separate category was to enable the 1988 Act to impose a different requirement of originality on databases from that applied to tables and compilations.

Prior to these amendments, a wide range of subject matter had been protected as compilations. This included football pools coupons,[34] a leaflet conferring information about herbicides,[35] TV schedules,[36] directories listing the names and addresses of solicitors,[37] a compilation of computer programs,[38] a timetable index,[39] trade catalogues,[40] and street directories.[41] As we will see, a database is defined in very wide terms. As a result, it is possible that most if not all of the subject matter previously protected as compilations would now be

---

[30] The corollary of this is that, while a person is usually free (as far as copyright is concerned) to appropriate names and short titles, care must be taken to ensure that the use of such a title cannot be seen as passing-off or a trade mark infringement. The claimant in *Exxon* succeeded in its passing-off claim: [1982] *RPC* 69, 75 (Graham J), but nevertheless appealed on the copyright issue.

[31] *'Karo Step' Trade Mark* [1977] *RPC* 255 (a pictorial mark may be an artistic work); *Auvi Trade Mark* [1995] *FSR* 288 (High Court, Singapore); *Hutchinson Personal Communications Ltd v. Hook Advertising Ltd* [1996] *FSR* 549 (logo consisting of inverted 'R' with a dot assumed to be protected by copyright); *News Group v. Mirror Group* [1989] *FSR* 126 (masthead from *The Sun* newspaper).

[32] Berne, Art. 2(5) (collections of literary or artistic works); TRIPS, Art. 10(2); WCT, Art. 5 (compilations of data or material).

[33] CDPA s. 3(1)(d).

[34] *Ladbroke v. William Hill* [1964] 1 *All ER* 465, 471. Lord Evershed said that the coupon is 'a compilation in the sense that it is made up by putting together in writing (that is, in print) a number of individual items or components'. See also *Football League v. Littlewoods* [1959] *Ch* 637 (fixture lists); *Greyhound Services v. Wilf Gilbert (Staffs) Ltd* [1994] *FSR* 723 (advance programme of greyhound races).

[35] *Elanco v. Mandops* [1980] *RPC* 213.

[36] *Independent Television Publications v. Time Out* [1984] *FSR* 64.

[37] *Waterlow Directories v. Reed Information* [1992] *FSR* 409; *Waterlow Publishers v. Rose* [1995] *FSR* 207 (suggesting such a work might be protected even though it has no identifiable author). See also *Kelly v. Morris* (1866) *LR* 1 *Eq* 697.

[38] *Ibcos Computers v. Barclays Mercantile Highland Finance* [1994] *FSR* 275 (comprising 335 program files, 171 record layout files, and 46 screen layout files was held to be a compilation).

[39] *Blacklock v. Pearson* [1915] 2 *Ch* 376.   [40] *Purefoy v. Sykes Boxall* (1955) 72 *RPC* 89.

[41] *Kelly v. Morris* (1866) *LR* 1 *Eq* 697.

protected as databases.[42] If this is the case, it will leave little or no room for 'tables and compilations' in the future.[43]

2.3 COMPUTER PROGRAMS

After considerable debate at both national and international level over whether computer
programs should be regulated by copyright law, patent law, or by a *sui generis* regime, it was
decided in the 1980s that computer programs ought to be protected as literary works.[44] This
position is now well entrenched in European and international intellectual property law.[45] In
line with these trends, the 1988 Act protects computer programs as literary works.[46] While
the 1988 Act does not define what is meant by a computer program,[47] it is clear that it includes
source code,[48] assembly code, and object code. It is also clear that 'computer program' is
not synonymous with software. On this basis it has been held that the definition of computer program includes instructions permanently wired into an integrated circuit (that is,
firmware).[49]

2.4 PREPARATORY DESIGN MATERIAL FOR
COMPUTER PROGRAMS

To bring British law into conformity with the EC Software Directive, preparatory design
material for computer programs is now included within the general definition of literary
works.[50] It has been suggested that this is an inappropriate way of implementing the Directive
and that preparatory design material should be treated as part of a computer program.[51]

---

[42] For a systematic analysis, see E. Derclaye, 'Do sections 3 and 3A of the CDPA violate the Database Directive?
A Closer Look at the Definition of a Database in the UK and its Compatibility with European Law' [2002] *EIPR*
466 (suggesting that a shopping list is a collection which is not a database because it is not arranged systematically or methodically and that a table of contents in a book is a collection where the individual elements are not
'independent'. Derclaye also argues that, by affording protection to such 'near-databases', UK law is incompatible with the Directive.)

[43] Note, however, *IPC Media Ltd v. Highbury Leisure Ltd* [2005] *FSR* (20) 434, 441 where the claimant alleged
that the series of monthly magazines taken together constituted a database.

[44] The judiciary were willing to accept that software was protected under the CA 1956: *Gates v. Swift* [1982]
RPC 339–40; *Sega Enterprises v. Richards* [1983] *FSR* 73 ('assembly code' was a literary work); *Thrustcode v. WW
Computing* [1983] *FSR* 502 (literary copyright is capable of subsisting in a computer program).

[45] Software Dir.; TRIPS, Art. 10(1); WCT, Art. 4.

[46] CDPA s. 3(1)(b). The Copyright (Computer Software) Act 1985 had declared only that computer programs
were to be *considered* as literary works.

[47] WIPO model provisions on Protection of Computer Software (1978) defined computer program as a set
of instructions expressed in words, codes, schemes, or in any other form, which is capable, when incorporated
in a machine-readable medium, of causing a computer—an electronic or similar device having information-
processing capacities—to perform or achieve a particular task or result. See also Green Paper, *Copyright and
the Challenge of Technology* COM (88) 172 final, 170. A similarly vague definition has been adopted in the USA:
see Copyright Act 1976, 17 USC s. 101. (A 'computer program' is a 'set of statements or instructions to be used
directly or indirectly in a computer in order to bring about a certain result'.)

[48] *Ibcos Computers v. Barclays Mercantile Highland Finance* [1994] *FSR* 275.

[49] Software Dir., Recital 7.

[50] For background see ibid. For implementation, see Copyright (Computer Programs) Regulations 1992 (SI
1992/3233), operative from 1 Jan. 1993.

[51] Software Reg., reg. 3. For commentary, see S. Chalton, 'Implementation of the Software Directive in the
UK' [1993] *EIPR* 138, 140; A. Meijboom, in A. Meijboom and H. Jongen (eds.), *Software Protection in the EC*
(1993), 8.

2.5 DATABASES

As we mentioned earlier, in order to comply with the Database Directive the definition of literary works was amended from 1 January 1998 to introduce 'databases' as a distinct class of literary works.[52] A database is defined very broadly as 'a collection of independent works, data or other materials which (a) are arranged in a systematic or methodical way, and (b) are individually accessible by electronic or other means'. It seems that the definition is broad enough to cover most if not all of the material previously protected as tables and compilations (though preparatory documents suggest that the definition may exclude collections of three-dimensional objects).[53]

Some aspects of the definition of a database were explained by the European Court of Justice in *Fixtures Marketing Ltd v Organismos Prognostikon Agonon Podosfairou AE (OPAP)*.[54] The case concerned a claim by Fixtures Marketing to be the proprietor of database right in English football fixtures. The defendant organization, which used the fixtures in its betting games, asserted that the fixture lists were not 'databases' and the Athenian Court referred a number of questions to the ECJ. The Court considered that the notion of database was intended to have 'a wide scope, unencumbered by considerations of a formal, technical or material nature'. Consequently, there was no reason why a collection of sporting information should not be a database. As regards the prerequisite of 'independence', the Court said this required the con-stituent material to be 'separable from one another without their informative . . . or other value being affected',[55] and the Court intimated that this was true of individual fixtures, each of which had 'autonomous informative value' by providing 'interested third parties with relevant information'.[56] The Court also commented on the requirement that the materials be arranged in a 'systematic or methodical' manner so as to be individually accessible, and stated that this required either that there be technical means for searching or other means, such as an index, table of contents, plan, or classification, to allow retrieval.[57] The fixture lists, being organized chronologically, and within the chronology alphabetically, constituted just such an arrange-ment. Applying these definitions, the poems in a book of poems by the same poet would most likely be regarded as 'independent' and 'individually accessible' and thus constitute a database. It is more difficult to say whether the data on a map would be considered to be 'independent' or 'individually accessible'.

A database does not include a computer program used in the making or operation of data-bases accessible by electronic means,[58] or presumably a compilation of programs. It should be noted that a computer program might itself be or include a compilation of information and hence be a database as well. Insofar as a computer program incorporates parts that fall within the definition of a database, it seems that these components may be independently protected as databases (whether under copyright or the *sui generis* database right). For example, if program

---

[52] CDPA s. 3(1)(d).

[53] Explanatory Memorandum, Com (93) 464 final_SYN 393, 41. In *Football Association Premier League Ltd v. Panini UK Ltd* [2004] *FSR* (1) 1 (paras. 25, 29) Chadwick and Mummery LJJ suggested that an album for stickers of football players (the stickers being artistic works) was a compilation, but it is probably a database.

[54] Case C–444/02 [2005] 1 *CMLR* (16) 367.

[55] Ibid, para. 29. See also Derclaye [2002] *EIPR* 466, 469 (' "independent" means that an element makes sense by itself; its meaning does not depend on another element, another piece of information'); Davison, 72, suggest-ing that the element must have 'a stand-alone function to play in terms of informing or entertaining people'.

[56] Ibid, para 33.   [57] Ibid, para. 30.

[58] Database Dir., Art. 1(3). See also J. Reichman and P. Samuelson, 'Intellectual Property Rights in Data?' (1977) 50 *Vanderbilt Law Review* 51, 132.

interfaces can be characterized as databases, they may be protected by either copyright or the *sui generis* database right. The fact that a computer program may be protected both as a literary work and by the database right may have a number of important consequences. As the defences available in relation to the database right are less extensive than those offered by copyright, the overlap might undermine the defences to copyright infringement specially tailored for computer programs. In particular, it is possible that the copyright defence that allows decompilation of programs for the purpose of ascertaining interface information might be rendered redundant.

One question that has arisen in this context is the extent to which a multimedia work as a whole (as distinct from the sound, pictures, text, and moving images of which it is made up) can be protected as a database. While individual elements may be protected by copyright, the question has arisen as to whether all the elements combined together can be protected by copyright as a database.[59] While there are doubts about whether multimedia works could be protected as compilations (this was because it is unclear whether the protection afforded to compilations is confined to compilations of *information* or to compilations of *literary works*),[60] this problem does not arise in relation to databases. This is because databases are defined, seemingly without restriction to the type of material, as a collection of 'works data or other materials'. While it may seem odd that a compilation of artistic works or sound recordings is protected as a literary work,[61] this conclusion now seems unavoidable.[62]

3 DRAMATIC WORKS

The next general category of works that are protected by copyright is that of dramatic works. The 1988 Act does not define what a dramatic work is, except to state that it includes a work of dance or mime.[63] However, it is relatively clear that dramatic work includes the scenario or script for films, plays (written for the theatre, cinema, television, or radio),[64] and choreographic works.[65]

---

[59] See Stamatoudi, ch. 5.; T Aplin, *Copyright Law in the Digital Society* (Hart: 2005) ch. 3; S. Beutler, 'The Protection of Multimedia Products through the European Community's Directive on the Legal Protection of Databases' [1997] *Ent LR* 317 (treating the Directive as the main way of protecting multimedia works, and pointing out that the effectiveness of the Directive to protect multimedia works will be dependent upon its interpretation).

[60] See Stamatoudi, 75–8 (arguing that failure to do so would have meant non-compliance with Berne).

[61] See *Football Association Premier League Ltd v. Panini UK Ltd* [2004] *FSR* (1) 1 (para. 32) Mummery LJ (giving examples of compilations made up of artistic works); *Kalamazoo v. Compact Business Systems* (1985) 5 *IPR* 213. One effect could be that a compilation of sound recordings would achieve much longer protection under copyright as a database than a single sound recording.

[62] Stamatoudi's argument (at 98–102) that individual elements of a multimedia work cannot be regarded as 'individually accessible' unless items can be lifted out of the multimedia work (rather than merely be made to appear on the screen) is not sustainable in the light of the ECJ interpretation of that concept in *Fixtures Marketing v. OPAP* Case C-444/02 [2005] 1 *CMLR* (16) 367.

[63] CDPA s. 3(1).   [64] *Green v. BC New Zealand* [1989] *RPC* 469, 493.

[65] The fixation of such a work can be in writing 'or otherwise' and may accordingly be, for instance, on film. Where a dramatic work is recorded on a film, the film must contain the whole of the dramatic work in an unmodified state: *Norowzian v. Arks (No. 2)* [2000] *EMLR* 67 (dance recorded on film held unprotected because the film had been drastically edited, and so was no longer a recording of the dance).

For a creation to qualify as a 'dramatic work', it must be a 'work of action' that is 'capable of being performed'.[66] While the courts have not yet fully explored what is meant by a 'work of action', it is clear that it does not include static objects, sets, scenery, or costumes[67] (though these might be protected as artistic works).[68] It has been said that a film will usually be a dramatic work where there is 'cinematographic work' on the film.[69] In some limited circumstances a work of action might include sports such as gymnastics or synchronized swimming.[70]

The requirement that to be a dramatic work the subject matter must be 'capable of being performed' initially operated in a restrictive manner. In the *Hughie Green* case,[71] Green was the originator and producer of a talent show called *Opportunity Knocks*, a programme which followed a particular format: certain catchphrases were used, sponsors introduced contestants, and a 'clapometer' was used to measure audience reaction. Beyond this, the content of the show varied from show to show. The Broadcasting Corporation of New Zealand broadcast a television talent quest that was similar to *Opportunity Knocks* in that the title and catchphrases were the same. It also used a clapometer, as well as the idea of using sponsors to introduce contestants.[72] Green's action for copyright infringement against the Broadcasting Corporation of New Zealand failed, primarily because he was unable to show that the programme was a dramatic work. In part, this was because, when looked at as a whole, the show lacked the specificity or detail for it to be performed. In particular, the Privy Council said that the scripts only provided a general idea or concept of a talent quest, which was not capable of being protected. The Privy Council also held that the features of the programme that were repeated in each show (namely the format or style of the show) were not dramatic works. The reason for this was that a dramatic work must have sufficient unity for it to be capable of being performed.[73] On the facts it was held that the particular features which were repeated from show to show (the format) were unrelated to each other except as accessories to be used in the

---

[66] *Norowzian v. Arks (No. 2)* [2000] *EMLR* 67, 73 (CA).

[67] *Creation Records* [1997] *EMLR* 444 (finding no arguable case that a photo shoot is dramatic work, since scene was inherently static, having no movement, story, or action).

[68] See *Shelley Films v. Rex Features* [1994] *EMLR* 134 (seriously arguable that film set prepared for film *Mary Shelley's Frankenstein* was a work of artistic craftsmanship). Cf. *Creation Records*, ibid (no arguable cause of action that arranging objects for photo shoot for record sleeve was a work of artistic craftsmanship or collage, because the composition was intrinsically ephemeral and its continued existence was to be in the form of a photographic image).

[69] *Norowzian v. Arks (No. 2)* [2000] *EMLR* 67. (In the view of Buxton LJ such a construction went some way towards ensuring compliance with Art. 14 *bis* of the Berne Convention which specifies that a cinematographic work must be protected 'as an original work' and that the owner of copyright therein 'shall enjoy the same rights as the author of an original work'. Nourse LJ said he reached his conclusion without reference to the Convention.) One problem with defining the scope of 'dramatic work' by reference to 'cinematographic works' is that the latter seems to refer merely to a technique of production: see Stamatoudi, 133.

[70] Although a film of a sporting event may be a work of action, it is probably not an 'original' dramatic work, being a mere recording of actions. Kamina argues that in order to be a dramatic work, an audiovisual work must convey a story and therefore concludes that documentaries could be protected but doubts whether newsreels or television productions of sports matches would be: Kamina, 72–4.

[71] *Green v. BC New Zealand* [1989] *RPC* 469, 477 (scripts could not constitute dramatic works because they could not be acted or performed, which is the essence of drama) (CA of New Zealand); [1989] 2 *All ER* 1056 (Privy Council).

[72] *Green v. BC New Zealand* [1989] *RPC* 469, 478, 480, 493.

[73] Cf. *Ladbroke v. William Hill* [1964] 1 *All ER* 465 where copyright was held to exist in pools coupons even though the matches changed each week.

presentation of some other dramatic performance.[74] The requirement of 'unity' means that interactive video games are not 'dramatic works' since the sequence of images will not be the same from one play to another. Thus, in *Nova Productions Ltd v Mazooma Games*,[75] Kitchin J held that a computer game simulating billiards involved artistic works, and literary works, but not a dramatic work.

The failure of the Privy Council to protect television formats in the *Hughie Green* case prompted a number of (unsuccessful) attempts to have formats recognized by British law.[76] The proponents of format rights appealed to the usual moral and economic arguments to support their case. In particular it was argued that formats require creative input similar to that involved in existing copyright works. It was also argued that failure to protect formats is not only unjust, but also fails to provide sufficient incentives to television producers. Those opposed to format rights noted the problems of defining what a format is, the anti-competitive effects, and the costs of such rights, as well as the potential for nuisance litigation.[77] The opponents of format rights favour leaving the developers of formats to the remedies offered by passing off[78] and breach of confidence.[79]

While formats are not protected to the extent that some would like, the need for *sui generis* format protection is less pressing as a result of the Court of Appeal decision of *Norowzian v. Arks*.[80] This is because in this case the Court of Appeal liberally interpreted the requirement that a dramatic work must be 'capable of being performed' to include performances by artificial means, such as the playing of a film.[81] Consequently a cartoon may be a dramatic work. In this decision, the Court of Appeal was called upon to decide whether a Guinness advertisement (which featured an actor dancing while a pint of Guinness was being poured) had infringed copyright in an earlier film *Joy* (which the advertisement copied). To answer this question it was necessary to determine whether *Joy* was a dramatic work.[82] One of the notable features of *Joy* was that it utilized a particular editing technique known as jump-cutting (this is done by cutting segments out of the film to produce a series of artificial effects). One of the consequences of this was that the finished film contained a series of movements that could not be performed by an actor.[83] At first instance it was held that as the (artificial) dance shown on

---

[74] *Green v. Broadcasting Corporation of New Zealand* [1989] *RPC* 469, 477; [1988] 2 NZLR 490, 497 (New Zealand Court of Appeal); cf. *Television New Zealand v. Newsmonitor Services* [1994] 2 NZLR 91 (High Court of Auckland) (TV news programme made up of unscripted and unchoreographed interviews and discussions was not a dramatic work).

[75] [2006] *RPC* (14) 379 (paras 116–119).

[76] See 'Programme Formats: A Further Consultative Document' [1996] *Ent LR* 216; R. McD. Bridge and S. Lane, 'Programme Formats: The Write-In Vote' [1996] *Ent LR* 212. After the consultation exercise in 1996 a decision was made to neither support nor introduce legislation to give specific copyright protection to television and radio programme formats. There seem to be no plans to reconsider the matter. For an overview of case law and developments, see U. Klement, 'Protecting Television Show Formats under Copyright Law—New Developments in Common Law and Civil Law Countries' [2007] *EIPR* 52.

[77] Mr Mellor, Standing Committee F, IV Hansard, 8 Mar. 1990, cols. 1293–4.

[78] The New Zealand Court of Appeal unanimously rejected the claim as to passing-off because of lack of sufficient goodwill in New Zealand. *Green v. Broadcasting Corporation of New Zealand* [1989] *RPC* 469, 474, 480–1, 488–9. The British show had never been broadcast in New Zealand, and the goodwill relied on was that of former British residents living in New Zealand.

[79] Lord Sanderson of Bowden, Hansard (HL), 26 July 1990, cols. 1718–19.

[80] *Norowzian v. Arks (No. 2)* [2000] *EMLR* 67, 73.   [81] Ibid.

[82] Note that the argument on appeal was not that there was copyright in the dance as a dramatic work (recorded on film), but that the film was not merely a 'record' of a dramatic work but was itself a dramatic work: ibid.

[83] That is, the finished film owed as much to the editing technique as to the dance that was filmed.

the edited film could not be performed, the film did not embody a dramatic work. (If the film had shown all the movements of the actor it would have been protected.) However, on appeal it was held that the film itself was a dramatic work. The Court said that, as it was possible for the film to be played, it was therefore 'capable of being performed'.

4 MUSICAL WORKS

The next category of works protected under the 1988 Act is that of 'musical works'. A musical work is defined to mean 'a work consisting of music exclusive of any words or action intended to be sung, spoken or performed with the music'.[84] Thus, the words and the music of songs and similar works are treated as the subject matter of distinct copyrights. A song therefore consists of both a musical work and a literary work: the tune and lyrics respectively.

There has been very little discussion in the UK as to what is meant by 'music', though it is normally understood to include melody, harmony, and rhythm.[85] A recent exception to this is to be found in the case of *Sawkins v Hyperion Records*.[86] This case concerned the efforts of Sawkins in producing what are termed 'performing editions' of four of the works of the seventeenth-century composer Michel-Richard de Lalande. Sawkins' efforts included 'figuring of the bass', adding 'ornamentation', and performance directions. Hyperion, which made recordings of performances of the works of Lalande by musicians using Sawkins' scores, denied that by so doing it infringed copyright, arguing that Sawkins' contribution had not created an original *musical* work. One question was whether Sawkins' contributions could count as contributions to the music in circumstances where they did not involve alteration of the notes or melody. The Court of Appeal held that they could. Mummery LJ explained that the:

essence of music is combining sounds for listening to. Music is not the same as mere noise. The sound of music is intended to produce effects of some kind on the listener's emotions and intellect. The sounds may be produced by an organised performance on instruments played from a musical score, though that is not essential for the existence of the music or of copyright in it.

The defendant's argument mistakenly assumed that the *actual notes* were the only matter covered by musical copyright: according to the Court of Appeal, other elements that contributed *to the sound* as performed, such as tempo and performance practice indicators, were equally music.

Although the Court of Appeal explicitly excluded 'noise' from the scope of 'music', it said nothing about the controversial question of whether 'silence' can be music.[87] According to

---

84 CDPA s. 3(1). Sheet music was held to be covered by the term 'book' in the Statute of Anne: see *Bach v. Longman* (1777) 2 Cowp 623, but that merely conferred a right to print and reprint the music. See R. Rabin and S. Zohn, 'Arne, Handel, Walsh, and Music as Intellectual Property: Two Eighteenth-Century Lawsuits' (Apr. 1995) 120 *Journal of the Royal Musical Association* 112.

85 Some countries have defined music. For example, Canadian law formerly defined music as any combination of melody and harmony or either of them, printed or reduced to writing or otherwise graphically reproduced. This definition was described as 'unnecessarily limiting' in that it excluded elements such as rhythm and timbre from protection. In particular, such limited definitions may have negative effects for the protection of traditional music. See J. Collins, 'The Problem of Oral Copyright: The Case of Ghana' in S. Frith (ed.), *Music and Copyright* (1993), 149 (arguing that rhythm is an equal component with lyrics and melody in African music).

86 *Sawkins v. Hyperion Records* [2005] 1 *WLR* 3281; [2005] *RPC* (32) 808.

87 Saw, 'Protecting the Sound of Silence in 4' 33''' [2005] *EIPR* 467; Copinger, para 3–46, p. 82 ('it is doubtful that a passage of silence by itself is capable of being a musical work, even if claimed by the author or critics to be such.').

newspaper reports, a dispute over just such a work of 'silence' resulted in a settlement (and a six-figure payment for the rights to use the work!) The work in question was by the avant garde composer John Cage, who in the 1950s wrote a piece entitled *4′ 33″*, a work of silence. Apparently, the basis for the claim was that the classical–pop fusion group, the Planets, included 60 seconds of silence on its recording. A member of the group claimed that this was an improvement on Cage's effort—because they had achieved in 60 seconds what he accomplished in 273! The payment to Cage's publisher suggests, however, that the legal advisers to the Planets (and the group's record company) feared that a court would treat Cage's work as protected.[88]

5   ARTISTIC WORKS

The fourth category of works protected by copyright is artistic works.[89] The first artistic works protected by statute were 'engravings' (1735). These were followed by calico designs (1787), sculptures (1798 and 1814), drawings, paintings, and photographs (1862), and works of artistic craftsmanship (1911).[90] The various artistic works are now collected together in section 4(1) of the 1988 Act which contains a detailed list of the types of subject matter that are protectable as artistic works. These are divided into the following three categories:[91]

(i)   irrespective of artistic quality, a graphic work (including painting, drawing, diagram, map, chart or plan, engraving, etching, lithograph, woodcut, or similar work), a photograph (excluding a film), a sculpture, or a collage;

(ii) a work of architecture, being a building or fixed structure or a model therefor; or

(iii) a work of artistic craftsmanship.

5.1 GRAPHIC WORKS, PHOTOGRAPHS, SCULPTURES, AND COLLAGES

The first subcategory of artistic works, which is set out in section 4(1)(a), includes graphic works, photographs, sculptures, and collages. It is important to note that the material contained in section 4(1)(a) is protected irrespective of artistic quality. This ensures that once a creation falls within a particular category of works, copyright protection is not contingent on the work reaching a certain aesthetic standard. As a result, the task of having to decide what is good or bad art and all the associated problems are thus avoided.[92] More controversially, the decision that copyright law should not concern itself with the artistic quality of these types of

---

[88] *The Independent*, 22 June 2002.

[89] See S. Stokes, *Art and Copyright* (2001); A. Barron, 'Copyright, Art and Objecthood', 277 in D. McClean and K. Schubert (eds.), *Dear Images: Art, Copyright and Culture*, 331–51 (2002) (describing affinities between judicial approaches to defining art in technical materialist terms and those of modernist commentators, observing that this leads to a law which includes items which have no creativity and excludes ones which do, so that 'copyright law's conception of the artistic work now faces a crisis of credibility').

[90] The Engravings Act 1735 was amended by Acts in 1766 (7 Geo. 3 c. 38) and 1776 (17 Geo. 3 c. 57). The Sculpture Copyright Act 1798 was amended and expanded in 1814 (54 Geo. 3 c. 56); Fine Art Copyright Act 1862 (25 & 26 Vict. c. 68). On the latter, see L. Bently, 'Art and the Making of Modern Copyright Law', in McClean and Schubert, note 89 above, 331–51.

[91] CDPA s. 4(1).

[92] In *Burge v. Swarbrick* [2007] *HCA* 17; (2007) 234 *ALR* 204; 81 *ALJR* 950 (26 April 2007), para 63, the Australian High Court referred to 'the supposed terrors for judicial assessment of matters involving aesthetics'.

work has been used to expand the *types* of subject matter (as distinct from the *quality* of subject matter) protected as artistic works. While few would have problems with Marcel Duchamp's Readymades (for example, his famous urinal) being protected as an artistic work, more problems arise when objects exclusively used for industrial purposes to achieve commercial ends are protected as artistic works. For a period of time, a fear of making aesthetic judgements (when combined with a degree of formalism) led the courts to provide such protection. In recent years, however, the courts have been more willing to use a general sense of what is meant by art to limit the scope of protectable works.

5.1.1 Paintings

Graphic works are specifically defined in section 4(1)(a) to include 'paintings'. For the most part, there have been few problems in determining whether something is a 'painting' and thus whether it qualifies as an artistic work. One of the few situations where this was not the case was in *Merchandising v. Harpbond*,[93] where it was argued that the facial make-up of the pop star Adam Ant was a painting and thus protected by copyright. The Court of Appeal rejected this submission, Lawton LJ remarking that it was fantastic to suggest that make-up on anyone's face could possibly be a painting. He held that a painting required a surface and that Adam Ant's face did not qualify as such, noting that '[a] painting is not an *idea*: it is an object; and paint without a surface is not a painting' (see Fig. 3.3).[94]

The reasoning of Lawton LJ seems odd,[95] for it is difficult to see why Adam Ant's face is less of a surface than a piece of canvas. The decision could however be justified on the ground that a painting must be intended to be permanent. If so a tattoo would be protected, but dramatic or cosmetic make-up would not.[96] Equally, since the make-up in question consisted of two broad red lines round a light-blue line running from nose to jaw, it is arguable that the work did not satisfy the criteria of originality.[97] Alternatively, the decision could be seen as a case of merger of idea and expression (where no protection is granted).[98] At the end of the day, however, it seems that the reason why Adam Ant failed was because the traditional image of a painting as a framed canvas to be hung on a wall prevailed.

5.1.2 Drawings

The next type of subject protected as an artistic work under section 4(1)(a) is drawings. In addition to sketches of people and landscapes that we expect to be classified as drawings, protection has been granted to the drawing of a hand on a 'how to vote' card,[99] typeface design,[100] architects' plans (as distinct from actual buildings), and sketches for dress designs.[101] Because protection is granted 'irrespective of artistic quality', copyright in drawings has been widely used to protect industrial designs.[102] Thus drawings of exhaust pipes, boxes for storing kiwi fruit,

---

93 [1983] *FSR* 32.   94 Ibid, 46.   95 Copinger, para 3–55, p. 85 n40.

96 *J. & S. Davis (Holdings) v. Wright Health Group* [1988] *RPC* 403 may lend support to such a view. Cf. *Metix v. Maughan* [1997] *FSR* 718, 721.

97 Laddie *et al.*, paras. 4.20 and 4.37, favours the rationalization based on originality.

98 Cf. *Ibcos Computers v. Barclays Mercantile Highland Finance* [1994] *FSR* 275.

99 *Kenrick v. Lawrence* (1890) 25 *QBD* 99.

100 *Stephenson Blake & Co. v. Grant, Legros & Co.* (1916) 33 RPC 406.

101 *Bernstein v. Murray* [1981] RPC 303.

102 D. Booton, 'Framing Pictures: Defining Art in UK Copyright Law' [2003] *IPQ* 38 (criticizing the 'technical' approach of the courts to defining drawings, which focuses on how the artefact was made, and arguing that a distinguishing characteristic of literary works is that they are capable of being notated in a form which defines all the constitutive properties of such works, so that circuit diagrams, architects' plans, and engineering drawings are not artistic but literary).

Fig. 3.3 The defendant's poster in *Merchandising Corp v. Harpbond* (created by Mr. Langford)

and the like have been protected.[103] Importantly, such protection has frequently prevented the copying of the (three-dimensional) designed artefact itself. As we will see later, section 51 of the 1988 Act has reduced the significance of copyright in drawings for three-dimensional designs, other than in designs for artistic works.[104]

5.1.3 Engravings

Engravings were first protected by copyright in 1735. For the most part, the way the law has developed since then has provided few surprises: protection being granted to etchings, aquatints, woodcuts, lithographs, and the like. In the last twenty or so years, however, a range of somewhat surprising objects have been protected as engravings.[105] For example, in *Wham-O v. Lincoln Industries* the New Zealand Court of Appeal held that both the mould from which a frisbee was pressed and the frisbee itself were protected, because the mould was made by cutting onto a surface and so was an engraving, and the frisbee itself was a print from the engraving.[106] (see Fig. 3.4)

Despite subsequent doubts being expressed by the Australian Federal Court[107] about the reasoning in *Wham-O*, it was recently followed in *Hi-Tech Autoparts v. Towergate Two*

---

[103] *British Leyland v. Armstrong* [1986] *RPC* 279; *Plix Products v. Frank Winstone* [1986] *FSR* 92 (NZ).

[104] See below at Ch. 29 Section 3.

[105] In *James Arnold v. Miafern* [1980] *RPC* 397, it was held that the term engraving not only covered the articles made from a block but also the block itself. See also *Martin v. Polyplas* [1969] *NZLR* 1046 (coin is an engraving).

[106] [1985] *RPC* 127.

[107] *Greenfield Products v. Rover–Scott Bonnar* (1990) 17 *IPR* 417; (1991) 95 *ALR* 275 (Fed. Crt. Australia). Pincus J declined to hold that the drive mechanism of a lawnmower was an engraving, As Pincus J stated that 'engraving' does not cover shaping a piece of metal or wood on a lathe, but has to do with marking, cutting, or working the surface—typically the flat surface—of an object. In *Talk of the Town v. Hagstrom* (1991) 19 *IPR* 649, 655, Pincus J qualified the suggestion that an engraving must be on a two-dimensional surface.

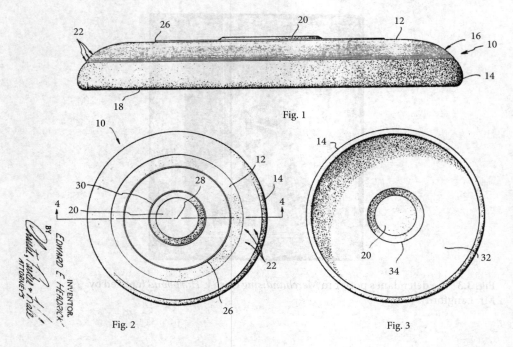

Fig. 3.4 Headrick's flying saucer
Source: Wham-O Manufacturing [1982] *RPC* 281, 296.

Ltd.[108] In that case Judge Christopher Floyd QC held that copies of the claimant's rubber floor mats for cars could not be sold by the defendant on the grounds that the moulds used in the production of the mats, and the mats themselves, were engravings. The moulds had been made by cutting a series of concentric circles, to a depth of 1/16th inch and a bevel angle of 45°, into flat plates. In so holding, the Judge placed particular emphasis on the fact that the statute requires engravings to be protected 'irrespective of their artistic quality'. Floyd J also rejected the defendant's argument that the plates were models for the purposes of sculpture rather than engravings, stating that he did not think it was possible to limit the skill and labour of the engraver to that only concerned with the flat surface, excluding work on the interior.

5.1.4 Photographs

Although photographs were protected by copyright shortly after photography was invented in the 1840s,[109] copyright law has never been completely comfortable with photographs,[110]

---

[108] *Hi-Tech Autoparts Ltd v. Towergate Two Ltd* [2002] *FSR* 254 (treating plates for the production of rubber mats as engravings); *Hi-Tech Autoparts Ltd v. Towergate Two Ltd (No. 2)* [2002] *FSR* 270 (treating rubber mats stamped from plates as engravings).

[109] 1862 Fine Art Copyright Act. See Ricketson, paras. 6.33–43 (protected under Berne since 1886, enumerated since 1948). In contrast, Edelman has described how French law was caught out by the emergence of photography in the mid-nineteenth century: B. Edelman, *Ownership of the Image* (1979); J. Gaines, *Contested Culture: The Image, the Voice and the Law* (1992), ch. 2.

[110] The question what was an 'original photograph' was treated as problematic in *Graves' Case* (1869) *LR* 4 *QB* 715 and the idea of the 'author' of a photograph was grappled with in *Nottage v. Jackson* (1883) 11 *QB* 627, 630 *per*

primarily because they seem to be ill-suited to the paradigm of the 'original' and the 'copy'.[111] Photographs are defined in the 1988 Act as 'a recording of light or other radiation on any medium on which an image is produced or from which an image may by any means be produced, and which is not part of a film'.[112] The definition is broad enough to include digital photographs (where there is no film). Individual frames from a film are not treated as photographs.[113]

5.1.5 Other Graphic Works

Other non-itemized works, such as computer screen icons and graphic user interfaces, are protected as artistic works. This is because these items fall within the inclusive definition of the subcategory 'graphic work'.[114] However, the dynamic effect created by a series of drawings is not protected as an artistic work.[115]

5.1.6 Sculpture

Sculptures were one of the earliest kinds of artistic work to be protected from reproduction. The recognition of copyright in sculptures in 1798 is notable because it took 'copyright' (insofar as such a concept existed at that time) out of the realm of printing (books, engravings, or calico printing) to cover reproduction more generally.

When most people think about sculptures, they might envisage a work by Henry Moore displayed in the Tate Gallery, or a statue of Queen Victoria in a town square. While it will come as no surprise to learn that these would qualify as sculptures, it might come as a surprise to learn that, for the purpose of copyright law, in *Wham-O Manufacturing v. Lincoln* the New Zealand Court of Appeal held that the wooden model which was used as a mould to make the frisbees was 'a sculpture'. However, the Court declined to hold that the frisbee itself was a sculpture, since it was created by injecting plastic into a mould and was thus not the expression of a sculptor's ideas.[116]

In recent years, the courts have construed the term sculpture more restrictively.[117] For example, in *Metix v. Maughan*[118] Laddie J said that 'sculpture' should be construed narrowly.[119]

Brett MR (holding that the author of the photograph was the person who was the effective cause of the picture, that is, the person who superintended the arrangement).

[111] K. Bowrey, 'Copyright, Photography and Computer Works—The Fiction of an Original Expression' (1995) 18 *University of New South Wales Law Journal* 278.

[112] CDPA s. 4(2). Whether something is a photograph may also be important because of CDPA s. 30(2) and CDPA s. 62.

[113] *Spelling Goldberg Productions v. BPC Publishing* [1981] *RPC* 283, 288, 297, 298, 300 (single frames from *Starsky and Hutch* were not photographs but part of a film under CA 1956). See Kamina, 92–4.

[114] *Navitaire Inc v. EasyJet Airline Co & Bulletproof Technologies Inc* [2006] *RPC* 111, 153 (para 98); *Nova Productions Ltd v. Mazooma Games* [2006] *RPC* (14) 379 (para 100).

[115] *Nova Productions Ltd v. Mazooma Games* [2007] *EWCA Civ* 219 (para 16) where Jacob LJ described the various subject categories listed in section 4 of the CDPA to be 'static, non-moving' and thus held that the effect produced from a series of drawings falls outside the scope of protection.

[116] *Wham-O v. Lincoln Industries* [1985] *RPC* 127, 157.

[117] In *J & S Davis (Holdings) v. Wright Health Group* [1988] *RPC* 403, it was held that a cast for dental impression trays was not a 'model or cast intended for the purposes of sculpture' since the cast was made in plasticine and was thus not intended to be permanent. *Metix v. Maughan* [1997] *FSR* 718, 721.

[118] [1997] *FSR* 718, 722.

[119] A similar interpretation of the term was adopted by Falconer J in *Breville Europe v. Thorn EMI* [1995] *FSR* 77, 94 when he said that the term 'sculpture' was to be given its ordinary dictionary meaning. Despite this, Falconer J concluded, rather surprisingly, that copyright would protect as sculptures scallop-shaped moulds that were used in toasted-sandwich makers.

He added that ordinary usage of the term refers to a three-dimensional work made by an artist's hand. Consequently, Laddie J held that the argument that moulds for making functional cartridges in the shape of double-barrelled syringes should be protected as sculptures had no prospect of success. Laddie J noted that none of the evidence indicated that the creator regarded himself, or was regarded by anyone else, as an artist.[120] While this aspect of Laddie J's reasoning has rightly been criticized because it contradicts the statutory requirement that sculpture be protected 'irrespective of artistic quality',[121] the judge's conclusion that the moulds were unprotected seems justified on the basis that the ordinary notion of sculpture requires that the maker be concerned with shape and appearance rather than just with achieving a precise functional effect.

While the legal understanding of 'sculpture' is by no means confined to the works of those who exhibit in art galleries, not all three-dimensional works exhibited in art galleries and attributed to artists will necessarily qualify as sculptures. In *Creation Records* (the Oasis record cover case—see Fig 3.1), Lloyd J held that the collection of a series of objects around a swimming pool was not itself a sculpture.[122] He explained that he could not see how 'the process of assembling these disparate objects together with the members of the group can be regarded as having anything in common with sculpture...No element in the composition has been carved, modelled or made in any of the other ways in which sculpture is made...'. This conclusion leaves unclear the position in relation to so-called *objets trouvés,* and other situations where artists 'create' artistic works from found material: famous examples being Duchamp's urinal, Carl André's bricks, Damien Hirst's shark, or Tracy Emin's bed.[123] It is by no means obvious that these fall within Laddie J's definition of sculpture as a three-dimensional work made by an artist's hand.

5.2 WORKS OF ARCHITECTURE

The second subcategory of artistic works listed in the Act is 'works of architecture': section 4(1)(b). A work of architecture is defined in the 1988 Act as a building or a model for a building.[124] In turn, a building is defined as including 'any fixed structure, and a part of a building or fixed structure'. It should be noted that copyright also exists in the architect's plans as drawings.

One question that has arisen is whether buildings include things such as greenhouses, Portakabins, and swimming pools that are built off-site.[125] The main obstacle to protection is that a building is defined as a *fixed* structure.[126] While this was apparently intended to

---

[120] Booton, 63 (noting, with approval, a convergence between Laddie J's approach and an 'institutional approach' to the definition of art).

[121] *Hi-Tech Autoparts v. Towergate Two Ltd* [2002] *FSR* 254 (para. 48) (Judge Floyd QC); Copinger, para 3–58, p. 90.

[122] *Creation Records v. News Group* [1997] *EMLR* 444.

[123] In *Creation Records*, Lloyd J referred to the issue of whether copyright subsisted in Carl André's bricks, by saying he would distinguish Mr Gallagher's composition as being 'ephemeral', that is, put together solely to be the subject matter of a number of photographs and disassembled as soon as those were taken. Perhaps Lloyd J was suggesting that a work of sculpture is a three-dimensional artefact *either* made by an artist's hand *or* intended to have a permanent existence as an object of art.

[124] CDPA s. 4(1)(b). Copyright protection for works of architecture was first introduced under the 1911 Act; most probably to give effect to the Berlin Revision of the Berne Convention. Ricketson, paras. 6.31–2.

[125] See also *Half Court Tennis* (1980) 53 *Federal Law Report* 240 (half-size tennis court made of concrete slab with posts was a work).

[126] CDPA s. 4(2) (but note the provision says 'building' *includes* 'any fixed structure').

prevent ships from being protected as works of architecture, the status of articles which are not fixed when they are created, but which are intended to be subsequently fixed or permanently placed, is unclear. In an Australian case, the Supreme Court of the Northern Territory held that a plug and mould used for manufacture of pre-cast fibreglass swimming pools were protected by copyright.[127] Explaining that there was no single test for what is a building, Mildren J said that a number of factors needed to be considered. These included the size of the structure, its proposed use, whether it is fixed or portable, and its degree of permanence. As a result he concluded that while neither the plug nor the mould were buildings, the pools were. This was despite the fact that the pools were manufactured off-site and were capable of being removed.

In contrast to other types of artistic work, there is no requirement that architectural works (and works of artistic craftsmanship) should be protected 'irrespective of artistic quality'. This seems to suggest that, when deciding whether subject matter qualifies as an architectural work (or as a work of artistic craftsmanship), we should consider whether the work is a work of architecture (or artistic craftsmanship); and if so, whether it is sufficiently artistic. While the courts have accepted that a work of artistic craftsmanship must by its very nature be sufficiently artistic to attract copyright, the position in relation to architectural works is less clear. If buildings are only protected if they are artistic, it is unlikely that designs for things such as swimming pools would be protected.[128] One factor that suggests that for a work to qualify as a work of architecture it must also be 'artistic' is that, in contrast to section 4(1)(a), there is no explicit statement that such works are to be protected 'irrespective of artistic quality'. However, this interpretation is difficult to reconcile with the legislative history. While under the 1911 Act a work of architecture had to satisfy a qualitative threshold in order to be protected, this criterion was removed under the 1956 Copyright Act. This would suggest that, under the 1988 Act, the legislature intended that there was no need for a work of architecture to be 'artistic' for it to be protected. Unfortunately, the Act is ambiguous.

5.3 WORKS OF ARTISTIC CRAFTSMANSHIP

The final category of artistic works listed in the Act is 'works of artistic craftsmanship': section 4(1)(c). The legislative origins of this category of work, which first appeared in the 1911 Copyright Act, are obscure.[129] Works of artistic craftsmanship cover creations such as handcrafted jewellery, tiles, pots, stained-glass windows, wrought-iron gates, hand-knitted jumpers, and crocheted doilies. In order for a work to fall within this category, it is necessary to show that the work is 'artistic' and that it is a work of 'craftsmanship'. We will deal with each in turn.

---

[127] *Darwin Fibreglass v. Kruhse Enterprises* (1998) 41 *IPR* 649.

[128] In *Darwin*, Mildren J assumed there is no requirement for artistry: ibid.

[129] In *George Hensher v. Restawile Upholstery (Lancs)* [1976] *AC* 64 Lord Simon said that 'when Parliament, in 1911, gave copyright protection to "works of artistic craftsmanship" it was extending to works of applied art the protection formerly restricted to works of the fine arts, and was doing so under the influence of the Arts and Crafts movement'. That movement, which dated from the 1860s and was led by William Morris, emphasized the importance of handicraft techniques in the applied or decorative arts, restoring the hand-craftsman to his creative role in society. However, Lord Simon argued that, given the context, the choice of the word 'craftsmanship' rather than 'handicraft' was a deliberate indication that the provision was not to be limited to handicraft or exclude products of machine production.

5.3.1 The requirement of 'artistic quality'

A work will only qualify as a work of artistic craftsmanship if it is 'artistic': that is, if it has an element of real artistic or aesthetic quality.[130] This approach is unusual in copyright law because it requires the courts to consider whether the work satisfies the qualitative threshold of being artistic. The question of what is meant by a work of *artistic* craftsmanship was discussed by the House of Lords in *Hensher v. Restawile Upholstery*.[131] As the defendants conceded that the claimant's prototype of a mass-market upholstered chair was a work of craftsmanship, the only question to be determined was whether the chair was a work of *artistic* craftsmanship. While all their Lordships agreed that the chair was not artistic, they all differed in their explanations as to why.

Lord Reid said that an object could be said to be artistic if a person gets 'pleasure or satisfaction...from contemplating it'. As a result, Lord Reid said that the test to decide whether a work was artistic was whether 'any substantial section of the public genuinely admires and values a thing for its appearance and gets pleasure or satisfaction, whether emotional or intellectual, from looking at it'. Lord Reid noted that 'looking nice appears to me to fall short of having artistic appeal'. While the author's intention that the resulting product is artistic might be important, Lord Reid indicated it was neither 'necessary [n]or conclusive'. Since there was no evidence that anyone regarded the furniture in issue as artistic, Lord Reid concluded that the prototype was not protected by copyright.

Lord Morris said that, in this context, the word 'artistic' required no interpretation. However, he acknowledged that as the question whether a particular artefact was artistic was a matter of personal judgment, courts might be faced with differences of opinion. Because of this, Lord Morris said that a court should look to see if there was a general consensus of opinion 'among those whose views command respect'. The views of the artist and the person acquiring the object might act as pointers as to whether something is artistic. However, the question was ultimately one for the court, guided by evidence (particularly of specialists). Since the most favourable thing that had been said about the prototype chair was that it was distinctive, Lord Morris was content to conclude that it was not artistic.

Lord Kilbrandon said the question whether something was a work of art depended on whether it had come into existence as the product of an author who was consciously concerned to produce a work of art. For Lord Kilbrandon, this must be judged from the work itself and the circumstances of its creation. A work did not become a work of art as a result of the opinions of critics, or the public at large. As a consequence, expert evidence was irrelevant. Instead, it was for the judge to determine whether the author had the 'desire to produce a thing of beauty which would have an artistic justification for its own existence'. Since in the case in hand the objective was to produce a commercially successful chair, it was not a work of artistic craftsmanship.

In deciding whether a craftwork was artistic, Viscount Dilhorne explained that this was really a question of fact for the court to answer. As such, he declined to elaborate much further on the meaning of artistic. He did say, however, that a work would not be artistic merely because there was originality of design, but that it could be artistic even if it was functional. While Viscount Dilhorne said that expert evidence and public opinion would be relevant, in the end it seems that he preferred to act on his own intuition as to what was a 'work of art'.

---

[130] *Cuisenaire v. Reed* [1963] VR 719, 730; *Hensher v. Restawile Upholstery (Lancs)* [1976] AC 64, 77, 78, 81, 85, 86, 96; *Merlet v. Mothercare plc* [1986] RPC 115 and *Bonz Group v. Cooke* [1994] 3 NZLR 216, 222.

[131] *George Hensher v. Restawile Upholstery (Lancs)* [1976] *AC* 64.

However, since no witness had described the chair as a work of art, he said that this was not even a borderline case: the prototype was not protected by copyright.

Lord Simon took a rather different approach from his colleagues, insofar as he emphasized that it was the craftsmanship rather than the work that must be artistic. Lord Simon also said that the fact that the work 'appeals to the eye of the beholder, giving him visual pleasure' was irrelevant. Examples of 'artistic craftsmen' included hand-painters of tiles, makers of stained-glass windows and wrought-iron gates, but not 'plumbers'. Lord Simon said that many craftsmen fell into an intermediate category: some of their products being the result of artistic craftsmanship, while others were the product of craftsmanship. In making the decision as to whether a particular object was created by a person who was an 'artist craftsman', Lord Simon took the view that 'the most cogent evidence is likely to be either from those who are themselves acknowledged artistic-craftsmen or from those who are concerned with the training of artist-craftsmen—in other words, expert evidence'. Lord Simon added, however, that the crucial question was 'the intent of the creator and its result'. Like the other Law Lords, he found the application of his test to the facts relatively easy: none of the experts had regarded the settee as exhibiting anything more than originality of design and appeal to the eye. The settee was an ordinary piece of furniture, and not an example of artistic craftsmanship.

Given the 'different and apparently irreconcilable' tests employed in *Hensher,* it is not surprising to find that there has been little consistency in subsequent case law as to the approach to be taken when assessing 'artistry'.

In *Merlet v. Mothercare,*[132] where Walton J had to decide whether a baby's cape made by Madame Merlet was a work of artistic craftsmanship, Walton J said that the majority in *Hensher* had held that the relevant question in determining whether a work was artistic was whether the object in question was a work of art.[133] However, given the warning not to exercise a value judgment, he concluded that in the first instance the question is whether the artist-craftsman intended to create a work of art. If the intention was present and the creator had not 'manifestly failed' in this regard, then the work was a work of art. As Madame Merlet had not set out to create a work of art, but instead had utilitarian considerations in mind (she hoped the cape would shield her son from the rigours of the climate when visiting her mother in the Scottish Highlands), Walton J concluded that the baby cape was not a work of artistic craftsmanship. In contrast, in *Vermaat v. Boncrest,* Evans-Lombe J seems to have declined to follow *Merlet* and instead adopted a new test which required that for a work to be artistic there had to be evidence of creativity.[134] The case concerned the design of a patchwork bedspread and whether this was a work of artistic craftsmanship. Evans-Lombe J referred approvingly to the view of the New Zealand High Court that the question whether a work was of artistic craftsmanship could not depend purely on the intention of the creator: the finished work must have some artistic quality in the sense of being produced by someone with creative ability and having aesthetic appeal.[135] Applying that test of artistry to the facts, the judge held that though the designs were 'pleasing to the eye' they did not exhibit the necessary requirement of creativity.

---

[132] *Merlet v. Mothercare* [1986] *RPC* 115. The Court of Appeal (at 129 ff) only considered issues relating to infringement of copyright in Mme Merlet's drawings.

[133] Ibid, 125–6 citing Viscount Dilhorne, Lord Simon, and Lord Kilbrandon.

[134] *Vermaat v. Boncrest* [2001] (5) *FSR* 49.   [135] *Bonz Group v. Cooke* [1994] 3 *NZLR* 216.

If the judgment in *Vermaat* undermined Walton J's attempt in *Merlet* to resolve the question of when a work of craftsmanship is 'artistic', yet more confusion has been created by the rather incoherent judgment of Rimer J in *Guild v. Eskandar*.[136] Here the question was whether the claimant's wide, square-shaped designs for a cardigan and sweater were works of artistic craftsmanship. (For an example of Shirin Guild's work from this period see Fig. 3.5).[137]

Initially, Rimer J purported to follow *Merlet*, and found that there was no evidence that the claimant regarded herself as an artist or intended to create a work of art: she chose the design because it appealed to her, and she therefore believed it would appeal to others. If he had been rigorously following *Merlet*, that should have been an end of the investigation. However, Rimer J went on to consider whether the garment 'can fairly be regarded as satisfying the aesthetic emotions of a substantial section of the public'.[138] (He may have done so purely out of deference to Lord Reid in *Hensher*, or just in case a different criterion was applied on appeal, but the case is unsatisfactory for failing to explain the reasons for this examination.) The judge took account of the conflicting expert evidence, but ultimately concluded the garments were not works of art. This was in spite of the fact they had been displayed in the Victoria & Albert Museum, Rimer J explaining that they were exhibited as examples of developments in fashion (rather than because anyone regards them as works of art).

Clearly, the decisions in *Vermaat* and *Guild* have done little to clarify when a work of craftsmanship is to be treated as artistic. Further guidance from a higher court would be welcome indeed.

5.3.2 The requirement of 'craftsmanship'

As well as showing that the work is artistic, it is also necessary to show that it is a work of 'craftsmanship'. In *Hensher v. Restawile* Lord Simon defined a work of craftsmanship as presupposing 'special training, skill and knowledge' for its production. He also said that it implied 'a manifestation of pride in sound workmanship'. A rather different definition was provided by Lord Reid, who referred to a work of craftmanship as 'a durable, useful handmade object'. Lord Reid seemed to suggest that if the defendant had not conceded that the prototype was a work of craftsmanship, he would not have been inclined to that view. This was because the prototype, which was a flimsy, temporary, knock-up which had subsequently been destroyed, was better described as a 'step in a commercial operation' with no value of its own rather than as a work of craftsmanship.[139] While wooden rods (used to teach addition and subtraction to children) have been held not to be products of craftsmanship,[140] knitting and tapestry-making have been held to be a craft;[141] and the baby's cape in *Merlet v. Mothercare* was said to be 'very much on the borderline'.[142]

---

[136] *Guild v. Eskandar* [2001] (38) *FSR* 645.

[137] This image shows items that were typical of Guild's style in 1996, but these were *not* exhibits in the case. See http://www.shiringuild.com for further details on this fashion designer.

[138] *Guild v. Eskandar* [2001] *FSR* (38) 645, 700.

[139] *George Hensher v. Restawile Upholstery (Lancs)* [1976] *AC* 64, 77.

[140] *Cuisenaire v. Reed* [1963] *VR* 719 (Supreme Court of Victoria); *Komesaroff v. Mickle* [1988] *RPC* 204, 210 (Supreme Court of Victoria) (while assembling picture windows and dispensing into them chosen amounts of selected sands, liquid, and a bubble-producing substance might be artistic, there was no craftsmanship in performing those acts).

[141] *Bonz Group v. Cooke* [1994] 3 *NZLR* 216 (NZ High Court) (a case approved by the English High Court in *Vermaat*, note 134 above).

[142] [1986] *RPC* 115, 122.

Fig. 3.5 Shirin Guild jumper
Source: Courtesy of the Victoria & Albert Museum.

One problem with the courts' failure to provide a helpful definition of craftsmanship is that it is unclear whether the work needs to be handmade to be protected. In *Hensher v. Restawile,* Lord Reid and Viscount Dilhorne suggested that craftsmanship implied that the work was handmade.[143] In contrast, Lord Simon said that 'craftsmanship' could not be limited to handicrafts, nor was the word 'artistic' incompatible with machine production.[144] The approach of Lord Simon was followed by the Federal Court of Australia in *Coogi Australia v. Hysport International.*[145] There, Drummond J held that the stitch structure of a fabric made up of different yarns (used to make jumpers), which was constructed in such a way as to produce a mixture of textured surfaces—some flat, some rolled, some protruding—was a work of artistic craftsmanship. Drummond J said that the way the designer had used the stitch structures and colour to produce an unusual textured and multi-coloured fabric meant that the design was artistic. This was so even though the design was mass-produced and had been formulated on a computer, rather than using traditional craft techniques.[146] As regards the issue of mass-production, Drummond J reviewed the authorities and found that he preferred Lord Simon's approach in *Hensher v. Restawile.* To hold otherwise, he said, would be to import a Luddite philosophy into copyright legislation which was enacted against a background of modern

---

[143] *George Hensher v. Restawile Upholstery (Lancs)* [1976] *AC* 64, 77 (Lord Reid), 84 (Viscount Dilhorne: made by hand and not mass-produced).

[144] Ibid, 90.

[145] (1999) 157 *ALR* 247 (Fed. Crt. of Australia). See also *Burge v. Swarbrick* [2007] *HCA* 17; (2007) 234 *ALR* 204; 81 *AJLR* 950 (26 April 2007), para. 60 (noting that something such as a 'plug' for a mass-produced boat could be a work of artistic craftsmanship).

[146] 'There is no necessary difference between a skilled person who makes an article with hand-held tools and a skilled person who uses those skills to set up and operate a machine which produces an article. Such an article can still be a work of craftsmanship even though the creator has used a highly sophisticated computer-controlled machine to produce it, if nevertheless it is a manifestation of the creator's skill with computer-controlled machinery, knowledge of materials and pride in workmanship.' For similar reasoning in relation to computer-related literary works, see Whitford J in *Express Newspapers v. Liverpool Daily Post* [1985] *FSR* 306.

industrial organization and was intended to regulate rights of value to persons in the area of activity. As Drummond J's approach presents a realistic and workable approach to this issue, hopefully it will be followed in the United Kingdom.[147]

Another aspect of the notion of artistic craftsmanship that has proved to be problematic is whether the requirements of artistic quality and craftsmanship must emanate from the same person. In *Burke v. Spicer's Dress Designs*[148] Clauson J suggested as much when he said that a woman's dress was not a work of artistic craftsmanship because the artistic element (the sketch of the dress) did not originate from the person who made the dress (the dressmaker).[149] However in *Bonz Group v. Cooke*[150] the New Zealand High Court held that hand-knitted woollen sweaters depicting dancing lambs and golfing kiwis was a work of artistic craftsmanship: the handknitters being craftspersons and the designer an artist. Tipping J observed that:

there are some passages in the authorities that suggest that it is essential that the same person both conceive and execute the work. For myself I do not regard that as being necessary. If two or more people combine to design and make the ultimate product I cannot see why that ultimate product should not be regarded as a work of artistic craftsmanship.[151]

While the rejection of the requirement that artistry and craftsmanship come from the same person is welcome, *Bonz Group v. Cooke* raises problems in determining who is the author of a work of artistic craftsmanship. Where a work is created by collaboration between artist and craftsperson, a court is likely to treat them as co-authors. However, in *Bonz* itself the court treated the company as the copyright owner, even though the craftspersons were unidentified outworkers (and thus possibly not even employees). Perhaps that was a case where the craftspeople were merely executing the detailed designs of the artist: if this is true, it seems strange that the existence of craftsmanship is a prerequisite for protection, but does not even confer a claim to co-authorship. Another possibility is that, in the absence of collaboration such as to give rise to co-authorship, the craftsperson is to be regarded as the author, since they give expression to the artistic ideas.

5.3.3 The Australian escape route

It is clear that the English courts have struggled with the interpretation of the notion of artistic craftsmanship. An indication as to how the problems can be avoided has recently been provided by the unanimous decision of Australia's highest court, the High Court, in *Burge v. Swarbrick*.[152] The question there was whether Swarbrick's design for a yacht, the JS 9000 (see Fig. 3.6), (in particular the hull and deck) mouldings, were works of artistic craftsmanship.

---

[147] The fact that a design is created without using traditional 'craftsmanship techniques', or is intended to be mass-produced, may be a factor. See e.g. *Guild v. Eskander* [2001] *FSR* (38) 645, 700 (finding sample garments, made both by machine and as prototypes for mass production, not to be works of craftsmanship) (not considered on appeal at [2003] *FSR* (3) 23).

[148] [1936] 1 *Ch* 400, 408.

[149] This approach is consistent with the views of Lord Simon in *George Hensher Ltd v. Restawile Upholstery (Lancs)* [1976] *AC* 64, to the effect that a work of artistic craftsmanship is the work of a person who is an 'artist-craftsman'.

[150] *Bonz Group v. Cooke* [1994] 3 *NZLR* 216 (High Court of New Zealand). See also *Spyrou v. Radley* [1975] *FSR* 455; *Bernstein v. Sydney Murray* [1981] *RPC* 303; *Merlet v. Mothercare* [1986] *RPC* 115, 123–4.

[151] *Bonz Group v. Cooke* [1994] 3 *NZLR* 216, 224 (High Court of New Zealand). This passage was approved and applied by Evans-Lombe J in *Vermaat v. Boncrest* [2001] *FSR* 49 (though he held that there was no sufficient 'creativity' to render the work one of artistic craftsmanship).

[152] [2007] *HCA* 17; (2007) 234 *ALR* 204; 81 *ALJR* 950 (26 April 2007).

Fig. 3.6 JS9000 yacht
Source: Courtesy of Mr John Swarbrick.

The High Court conducted a careful review of the history of the concept of 'artistic crafts-manship' noting its origins in the Copyright Act 1911 (which had been applied to Australia) and the interpretation thereof by Lord Simon in *Hensher v. Restawile*. By emphasizing the fact that it was only Lord Simon who had considered the meaning of the composite phrase,[153] the High Court avoided the difficulty of 'distilling a ratio decidendi' from the five judgments.[154] While refusing to provide 'any exhaustive and fully predictive identification of what can and cannot amount to a "work of artistic craftsmanship"', the Court concluded that the key factor that separates protected works of artistic craftsmanship from mere industrial designs is the significance of functional constraints.[155] With works of artistic craftsmanship there is considerable 'freedom of design choice' and thus scope for 'real or substantial artistic effort'. The intention of the designer could cast some light on this, and in his evidence Swarbrick had acknowledged that he sought to produce a 'well mannered, easily balanced boat that was fast'. However, in most cases the crucial evidence would be the views of experts, and here this confirmed that speed was the overriding consideration in the design of 'sports boats'.[156] Designing the JS 9000 therefore involved the application of principles of mathematics, physics, and engineering, rather than making something visually or aesthetically appealing. Thus, the plug and mouldings were not works of artistic craftsmanship.

Although the decision in *Burge v. Swarbrick* is based on legislation that now differs sub-stantially from that operating in the UK, there is much to be said for the clarity it brings to the notion of a work of artistic craftsmanship. Had the 'design freedom' test been applied in *Guild v. Eskander* or *Vermaat v. Boncrest,* one could imagine that a different result might well have been reached: both look like cases where the creator possessed and utilized the freedom avail-able in creating the design of clothes and bedspreads. Of course, other cases, such as *Hensher* itself or *Merlet v. Mothercare,* would require the court to face up to the difficult question as to

---

[153] According to the Court, 'craftsmanship' and 'aesthetic quality' are not distinct questions (para. 66).
[154] Ibid, paras 55–56.   [155] Ibid, paras. 82–84.
[156] See paras 63–65, noting the problems with such evidence, in particular that 'few alleged authors of works of artistic craftsmanship [will] be heard readily to admit the absence of any aesthetic element in their endeavours'.

how much design freedom would suffice to render a work one of artistic craftsmanship. The High Court was only willing to say that this was a question of 'fact and degree'.

6 FILMS

Moving pictures were first produced towards the end of the nineteenth century. Initially, films were only indirectly protected in the UK as series of photographs[157] or as dramatic works.[158] At an international level, films were gradually recognized as the subject matter of authors' rights protection.[159] UK law recognized cinematic 'films' as an independent category of subject matter in the 1956 Act,[160] conferring first ownership on 'the maker' thereof.[161] Under the 1988 Act, films are defined to mean a recording on any medium from which a moving image may be produced by any means.[162] This broad definition encompasses celluloid films and video recordings or disks, as long as they produce 'moving images'.[163] Multimedia products may sometimes be protected as films,[164] though it is has been doubted whether recordings which generate text, such as teletext, would be covered.[165]

The EC Duration and Rental Directives, which required directors to be recognized as authors, distinguishes between cinematographic works and related rights in mere fixations, so-called 'films', or 'videograms'.[166] This approach has not been followed in the UK where

---

[157] Films were registered as series of photographs at the Stationers' Company, as required under the Fine Art Copyright Act 1862, but from 1911 this became unnecessary.

[158] CA 1911, s. 35(1). For a systematic account, see Kamina, ch. 2. For theoretical reflections, see A. Barron, 'The Legal Properties of Film' (2004) 67 *MLR* 177.

[159] Article 14 of the Berlin Revision of Berne in 1908 required that cinematographic productions be protected as literary or artistic works if 'by the arrangement of the acting form or the combination of the incidents represented, the author has given the work a personal and original character'. Such works are now listed in Art. 2(1) of the Paris text, and assimilation is further provided in Art. 14 *bis*.

[160] CA 1956, s. 13. See more generally, M. Salokannel, 'Film Authorship in the Changing Audio-visual Environment', in Sherman and Strowel, ch. 3 (it was only with the rise of the notion of the 'director as author' (or *auteur*) that copyright law came to embrace films as copyright subject matter on a par with literary and artistic works).

[161] CA 1956, s. 13(4), (10) (defining maker in terms similar to the definition of producer in CDPA, s. 178). Prior to the amendments in 1996, copyright in films was treated in a similar manner to that in sound recordings and broadcasts, with the producer being designated as the sole 'author'. Films now have a hybrid status under CDPA s. 9(2)(ab) which gives the principal director joint authorship with the producer of films made on or after 1 July 1994.

[162] CDPA 5B(1). Cf. CA 1956, s. 13(10) and *Spelling Goldberg v. BPC Publishing* [1981] *RPC* 283 (stating that film has three characteristics: a sequence of images, recorded on material, capable of being shown as a moving picture).

[163] See Kamina, 88–91 (in particular, considering whether a computer program which produces images on a screen which can appear to move is a film, and arguing that there must be something in the nature of a pictorial work).

[164] M. Turner, 'Do the Old Legal Categories Fit the New Multimedia Products? A Multimedia CD–ROM as a Film' [1995] *EIPR* 107; Aplin, note 109 above, Ch. 3; T. Aplin, 'Not in Our Galaxy: Why Film Won't Rescue Multimedia' [1999] *EIPR* 633; Stamatoudi, ch. 6, esp. 126–51 (arguing that few multimedia products would be audiovisual works, since moving images rarely form the main element, and objecting in any case to the artificiality of interpreting a multimedia work as a recording which produces moving images); Kamina, 92 (suggesting that the definition of film as 'a recording' might afford protection to multimedia works in which moving images form only a limited part). Despite these criticisms, the biggest problem with relying on film copyright to protect multimedia works derives from the narrow scope of protection given by film copyright. In some cases, a multimedia work might be a dramatic work, and thus benefit from 'thick' protection: Kamina, 79.

[165] Stamatoudi, 111.   [166] See above p. 50; below at pp. 123–5.

the 1988 Act only acknowledges one copyright work, a film. Provisions are made for circumstances where there is no principal director, nor any author of screenplay, dialogue, or music.[167] Moreover, there is no requirement under UK copyright law that films be original, as is the case with literary, dramatic, musical, and artistic works. However, it has now been accepted that films which would be 'cinematographic works' under the Berne Convention are also 'dramatic works' under UK copyright law.[168]

The soundtrack accompanying a film is treated as part of the film. As we will see, there is no reason why such a soundtrack would not also qualify as a sound recording. This leads to a potential problem of overlap. Section 5B(3) clarifies the position by stating that (i) references to the showing of a film include playing the film soundtrack to accompany the film and (ii) references to playing a sound recording do not include playing the film soundtrack to accompany the film. Consequently if a cinema wished to show a film which included a soundtrack, the cinema would only need to obtain rights clearances from the owner of copyright in the film.[169] In contrast, where the soundtrack is played without the moving images, for example on a jukebox in a pub, it is only necessary to obtain the consent of the right holder in the sound recording of the soundtrack.[170]

7 SOUND RECORDINGS

Sound recordings were first given protection under the 1911 Copyright Act where they were protected as musical works.[171] It soon became apparent that sound recordings were fundamentally different from musical works. The change of attitude was summed up in *Gramophone Company v. Stephen Cawardine*[172] where Maugham J considered the creative contribution to the gramophone record 'Overture to the Black Domino'. He said:

[I]t is not in dispute that skill, both of a technical and of a musical kind is needed for the making of such a record as the one in question. The arrangement of the recording instruments in the building where the record is to be made, the building itself, the timing to fit the record, the production of the artistic effects...combine together to make an artistic record, which is very far from the mere production of a piece of music.[173]

These sentiments are now reflected in the 1988 Act, where sound recordings are defined to mean '(a) a recording of sounds, from which the sounds may be reproduced', or '(b) a recording of the whole or any part of a literary, dramatic or musical work, from which sounds reproducing the work or part may be produced, regardless of the medium on which the recording is made or the method by which the sounds are reproduced or produced'.[174] It thus covers vinyl records, tapes, compact discs, digital audiotapes, and MP3s which embody recordings. The

---

[167] CDPA s. 13B(9). For an argument that this fails to implement the Directives see P. Kamina, 'British Film Copyright and the Incorrect Implementation of the EC Copyright Directives' [1998] *Ent LR* 109.

[168] *Norowzian v. Arks (No. 2)* [2000] *EMLR* 67. For criticism, see T. Rivers, '*Norowzian* Revisited' [2000] *EIPR* 389 (arguing that the case creates problems identifying the author).

[169] See also P. Kamina, 'The Protection of Film Soundtracks under British Copyright after the Copyright Regulations 1995 and 1996' [1998] *Ent LR* 153.

[170] CDPA s. 5B(2)–(3).

[171] *Panayiotou v. Sony Music Entertainment* [1994] *EMLR* 229, 348 (brief history of recorded music). Gaines, note 109 above, has argued that the print-based concept of copyright had difficulties accommodating sounds. This was clearly not the case in the UK.

[172] [1934] 1 Ch 450.   [173] Ibid, 455.   [174] CDPA s. 5B(1).

definition also seems to encompass digital instructions embodied in electronic form which produce sounds. In a different legal context (that of licensing places of entertainment), it has been held that 'recorded sounds' can include CD–ROM embodiments of Musical Interface Digital Interface (MIDI) instructions (rather than data in wave form) which cause a sound module or synthesizer to generate sounds.[175]

As the definition of sound recording requires that there be 'sounds', it appears to exclude a single sound from protection (even though a considerable amount of production work may go into its recording).[176] Interesting questions have also arisen as to how the limits of a sound recording are to be determined. We review these issues when we look at copyright infringement.[177] Because sound recordings exist irrespective of the medium on which the sounds are recorded, a soundtrack of a film is a sound recording. However, the soundtrack of a film will also be treated as part of the film insofar as the soundtrack 'accompanies' the film.[178] The effect of this is that the public showing of a film and its soundtrack only requires the consent of the owner of copyright in the film.[179] In contrast, where the soundtrack is played without the moving images[180] this would only require the consent of the holder of rights in the sound recording.[181]

8 BROADCASTS

Broadcasts, whether of sounds or images, were first included as copyright works in the 1956 Copyright Act. Subsequently, they were deemed to be suitable subject matter for protection by neighbouring rights at the 1961 Rome Convention.[182] The decision to extend copyright protection to broadcasts marked an important change in copyright law. In contrast with art, literature, films, and recordings, a broadcast is essentially the provision of a service which involves a communication: it is not the creation of a thing, but an action. This is because broadcasts are not fixed or embodied (though they can be), they are ephemeral acts of communication. This means that a broadcast does not protect any fixed entity *per se*. Instead, what is protected are the signals which are transmitted. In a sense copyright law recognizes the value in the act of communication itself, as distinct from the content of what is being communicated.[183]

---

[175] *Sean Toye v. London Borough of Southwark* (2002) 166 JP 389.

[176] P. Theberge, 'Technology, Economy and Copyright reform in Canada', in S. Frith (ed.) *Music and Copyright* (1993), 53; S. Jones, 'Music and Copyright in the USA', in S. Frith (ed.) *Music and Copyright* (1993), 67.

[177] See Ch. 8, especially pp. 176–7, discussing *Hyperion Records v. Warner Bros* (1991, unreported).

[178] This gives effect to Duration Dir. Art. 3, which required that the term 'film' be defined as 'a cinematographic or audiovisual work or moving images, whether or not accompanied by sound'.

[179] CDPA s. 5B (3)(a).   [180] CDPA s. 5B(3)(b).

[181] Contrast the current position with the position under the 1988 Act as initially enacted where 'sound recordings' and 'films' were mutually exclusive. This meant that the showing of a film in public required the consent of both the copyright holder in the moving images and the copyright owner of the soundtrack.

[182] Rome, Art. 3(f), Art. 6, Art. 13, Art. 14, Art. 16(1)(b). TRIPS, Art. 14(3). The UK is also party to the European Agreement of 1960 on the Protection of Television Broadcasts. Broadcasts were not the subject of the recent WIPO Treaties.

[183] On the question of what amounts to a 'work' in this context, see the Australian High Court decision in *TCN Channel Nine v. Network Ten* [2004] *HCA* 14 (11 Mar. 2004), where the majority held that in the case of a broadcast the work is the individual programme transmitted.

Provision was made for protection of cable programmes from 1 January 1985.[184] This differentiated treatment was carried through into the 1988 Act, as enacted, which recognized two categories of subject matter: a 'broadcast', which referred to a wireless transmission, and cable programmes. This differentiation has been abandoned, as of 31 October 2003, with cable programmes being assimilated within a broadly defined concept of 'broadcast'. Doubts will almost certainly be expressed as to the validity of these amendments to the primary Act by way of delegated legislation: the following paragraphs, however, assume the changes are allowed to stand.[185]

In its amended form, a broadcast is defined as an 'electronic transmission of visual images, sounds, or other information which—(a) is transmitted for simultaneous reception by members of the public and is capable of being lawfully received by them, or (b) is transmitted at a time determined solely by the person making the transmission for presentation to members of the public'.[186] This definition merely requires that the transmission be 'electronic',[187] being indifferent otherwise as to the means of transmission, the route taken, or the form of the signals.[188] The definition therefore covers transmissions both by wire ('Cable TV') and wireless (e.g. 'free-to-air' broadcasts), terrestrial and satellite transmission, and analogue and digital broadcasts. By referring to the transmission of 'visual images, sound, or other information', the definition is also broad enough to cover systems which transmit different forms of content, such as radio, television, and other broadcasts (such as teletext). It also takes into account the forms of broadcasting which may be directly received by individuals or may be received by subscribers who obtain a decoder.[189]

While the definition of broadcast is deliberately broad, it was readily appreciated that this breadth was likely to confer protection on some subject matter for which it was neither needed nor desired.[190] Two alternative criteria limit the definition further: to constitute a broadcast

---

[184] Cable and Broadcasting Act 1984, s. 22, adding CA 1956, s. 14A. Although diffusion services existed in 1956, they merely relayed BBC and ITA broadcasts to subscribers in areas where the signals were weak.

[185] But see *Oakley Inc v. Animal Inc* [2006] *Ch* 337 (liberal interpretation of European Communities Act 1972, s. 2(2)). The Copyright Directorate viewed the changes as necessary to implement Info. Soc. Dir. Art. 3 (communication to the public right). However, while that justified altering CDPA s.20 on 'rights', it is not obvious how it justifies altering CDPA s. 6 which deals with works.

[186] CDPA s. 6(1) (as amended by Copyright and Related Rights Regulations 2003 SI 2003/2498, Reg. 4). Perhaps the amendments were influenced by the definition of broadcast contained in Directive 89/552/EEC *OJ L* 298/23 (17 Oct. 1989) Art. 1 ('"television broadcast" means the initial transmission by wire or over the air, including that by satellite, in unencoded or encoded form, of television programmes intended for reception by the public. It includes the communication of programmes between undertakings with a view to their being relayed to the public. It does not include communication services providing items of information or other messages on individual demand such as telecopying, electronic data banks and other similar services').

[187] Defined in CDPA s. 178 as 'actuated by electric, magnetic, electro-magnetic, electro-chemical or electro-mechanical energy'.

[188] The Copyright Directorate refers to this as a 'technologically neutral definition': *Consultation on UK Implementation of Directive 2001/29/EC on Copyright and Related Rights in the Information Society: An Analysis of Responses and Government Conclusions*, para. 3.6. The definition of wireless telegraphy in CDPA s. 178 had excluded transmission by microwave energy between terrestrial fixed points: the new definition of broadcast has no such exclusion.

[189] That is, any encrypted broadcast, whether terrestrial or by satellite relay, is 'lawfully' received if decoding equipment has been made available through the person transmitting it in encrypted form. CDPA s. 6(2).

[190] Copyright Directorate, *Consultation on UK Implementation of Directive 2001/29/EC: An Analysis of Responses and Government Conclusion*, para. 3.6 (explaining its attempt to exclude on-demand services from the definition of broadcast on the basis that the subject matter transmitted is usually protected under other headings).

the transmission must be 'for simultaneous reception by members of the public' (and capable of being lawfully received) or be made 'at a time determined solely by the person making the transmission for presentation to members of the public'. Moreover, a new section 6(1A) excludes from broadcasts 'any Internet transmission', though with three (not insubstantial) exceptions.

The limitation of broadcasts to transmissions *for* simultaneous reception 'by members of the public' excludes from protection transmissions between individuals, such as telephone calls, faxes, or e-mails, as well as transmissions on private networks (such as company 'intranets'): these are not for reception by members of the public. The requirement that the transmission be 'capable of lawful reception' reinforces the exclusion of private communications from the definition of broadcast, because the interception of such a transmission would be illegal under the Interception of Communications Act 1985.[191] The requirement for 'simultaneous reception', too, excludes transmissions where the individual recipient decides the time of the transmission, as with on-demand services,[192] or interactive database services (such as *Lexis* or *Westlaw*). The alternative criterion, that the transmission be at a time determined solely by the person making the transmission 'for presentation to members of the public', is designed to cover transmission for playing or showing, as where a football game is beamed back to the away team's stadium.[193] It also covers what is frequently referred to as 'narrow-casting': such as transmission to shops for presentation to the public.

The scope of the definition of broadcast is confined further by excluding 'any Internet transmission', but this exclusion is subject to three exceptions of its own. No definition is provided for an 'Internet transmission' but the better view is that the internet is not confined to the 'worldwide web'. E-mails to news groups and web sites therefore, are generally excluded from protection as 'broadcasts' (though they might be protected as literary or artistic works).[194] A non-interactive on-line database service (formerly thought to be a cable programme service, and its contents therefore protected as cable programmes)[195] would also be excluded. In contrast, an information service through telecommunications networks to subscribers to certain mobile phone services is probably a broadcast.

Having said that, the amendments have sought to keep broadcast protection for 'Internet transmissions of a conventional broadcast character' through three exceptions to the exclusion of 'Internet transmissions' from the definition of broadcasts. First, section 6(1A)(a) clarifies

---

[191] Rather surprisingly this might mean that foreign encrypted broadcasts, such as satellite broadcasts, where there is no authorized distribution of decoders in the UK, are unprotected because they are not capable of lawful reception in the UK. This would be a breach of Art. 6(1)(b) of the Rome Convention, and is best avoided by treating the definition as covering broadcasts which are capable of lawful reception in the country at which the signals are primarily targeted.

[192] Many web sites are probably not for 'simultaneous reception' in that the transmitter intends that the site can be accessed at any time the user desires. Is a web site which is updated on a daily basis, the new version being transmitted at 8 A.M. each morning, for 'simultaneous reception'? Probably it does not matter, as it is excluded under CDPA, s. 6(1A) as an internet transmission.

[193] Copyright Directorate, *Consultation on UK Implementation of Directive 2001/29/EC: An Analysis of Responses and Government Conclusion*, para. 3.9 (explaining requirement that timing be determined by the person making the transmission as designed to exclude on-demand services from the definition of broadcast).

[194] Ibid (explaining the exclusion as a response to user groups who were concerned that web sites would be protected and that exceptions, such as research and private study, would therefore be unavailable). In these respects, the decision in *Shetland Times v. Dr Jonathan Wills* [1997] *FSR* 604 that a web site is protected (then, as items included in a cable programme service) is no longer good law.

[195] *Dun & Bradstreet v. Typesetting Facilities* [1992] *FSR* 320.

that the exclusion of 'Internet transmissions' does not encompass 'a transmission taking place simultaneously on the Internet and by other means'. This means that web sites which transmit sounds and images simultaneously with broadcasts—all the BBC radio stations, for example, are accessible from the BBC's web site—remain protected broadcasts.

A second provision allows for broadcasts to include an internet transmission which is a 'concurrent transmission of a live event'. The term 'concurrent' implies that the internet transmission must occur at the same time as the 'live event', so would seem to cover internet transmission of a cricket match or sounds of a pop concert. The provision refers to transmission *of* a live event and so would not treat as a broadcast a transmission of *commentary* on a live event. News-group e-mails of progress at the latest international copyright convention would not be a broadcast, therefore; nor would the commentary on a football match (unless the commentary itself were treated as an event). Whether the courts will interpret 'live event' to cover transmissions of the *Big Brother* house (even where these were not being broadcast on TV), remains to be seen: an approach which refuses to discriminate will end up treating all live web-cam feeds into web sites as broadcasts.

A third saving indicates that an internet transmission is not excluded from the definition of broadcast if it is 'a transmission of recorded moving images or sounds forming part of a programme service offered by the person responsible for making the transmission, being a service in which programmes are transmitted at scheduled times determined by that person'. This means that a person who wishes to set up a conventional style of broadcast service, solely utilizing the internet to distribute the programme service, does gain protection for the broadcasts.

9 PUBLISHED EDITIONS

The final category of works that are protected by copyright is 'typographical arrangements of published editions'. This category of works was first introduced in the UK in 1956, and remains largely a peculiarity of the British, and British-influenced, copyright systems (having no corresponding international regime).[196] A 'published edition' means 'a published edition of the whole or any part of one or more literary, dramatic or musical works'.[197] In *Newspaper Licensing Agency v Marks & Spencer,* Lord Hoffmann held that 'the "edition" is the product, generally between covers, which the publisher offers to the public'.[198] In this context, the copyright in the published edition protects the typographical arrangement, that is, the overall appearance of the page or pages. This protects the publisher's skill and investment in typesetting, as well as the processes of design and selection that are reflected in the appearance of the text.[199] There is no requirement that the published edition must be a previously unpublished

---

[196] CA 1956 s. 15. See *Report of the Copyright Committee* (Cmd. 8662), paras. 306–10.

[197] CDPA s. 8(1). Cf. Art. 5 Duration Dir. which permits member states to create a publishers' right in critical and scientific works which have fallen into the public domain.

[198] *The Newspaper Licensing Agency Ltd v. Marks and Spencer plc* [2003] 1 *AC* 551, 558; [2001] 3 *WLR* 390 (Lord Hoffmann) (holding that whole newspaper was the 'edition').

[199] Ibid (para. 23) ('It is not the choice of a particular typeface, the precise number or width of the columns, the breadth of margins and the relationship of headlines and strap-lines to the other text, the number of articles on a page and the distribution of photographs and advertisements but the combination of all of these into pages which give the newspaper as a whole its distinctive appearance.... The particular fonts, columns, margins and so forth are only, so to speak, the typographical vocabulary in which the arrangement is expressed.')

work. It therefore covers modern editions of works in the public domain (such as the complete works of Shakespeare), and prohibits the reproduction of the layout (but not the work itself). It should be noted that the concept of reproduction of a typographical arrangement is extremely narrow, being restricted to facsimile reprography. Consequently, the reproduction of the material contained in a published work will not infringe this limited copyright where a different layout is employed. It has been suggested that typographical arrangements may also be protected as 'photographs'.[200]

[200] Laddie *et al.*, paras 9.4–5 (but observing that such a photograph may lack originality). See also J.A.L. Sterling and M.C.L Carpenter, *Copyright Law in the United Kingdom and the Rights of Performers, Authors and Composers in Europe* (1986), para. 244 (publishers have copyright in photographic plates used in printing process).

4

CRITERIA FOR PROTECTION

CHAPTER CONTENTS

1 INTRODUCTION

In order for a work to be protected by copyright, it is necessary to show that, as well as falling within one of the eight categories of work listed in the Act, the work also satisfies the particular requirements that are imposed on it. As we will see, the requirements that need to be complied with vary, sometimes considerably, between different categories of work.

(i) The *first* general requirement for copyright to subsist is that the work must be recorded in a material form. As we will see, this only applies to literary, dramatic, and musical works.

(ii) The *second* requirement that must be satisfied for protection to arise is that the work must be 'original'. It should be noted that this only applies to literary, dramatic, musical, and artistic works. In contrast, there is no need for entrepreneurial works (sound recordings, films, broadcasts, and typographical arrangements) to be 'original' for them to qualify for protection. Instead the 1988 Act declares that copyright only subsists to the extent that such works are not copied from previous works of the same sort.[1]

(iii) The *third* requirement that must be satisfied for a work to be protected, which applies to all works, is that it is necessary to show that the work is sufficiently connected to the UK to qualify for protection under UK law.

(iv) The *fourth* requirement is that the work is not excluded from protection on public policy grounds. Occasionally the courts have said that works which are immoral, blasphemous, or libellous, or which infringe copyright, will not be protected.

We will deal with each of these requirements in turn.

---

[1] CDPA ss. 5(2), 6(6), 7(6), 8(2).

2 RECORDED IN MATERIAL FORM

There is no requirement that a work be registered for copyright protection to arise. Instead, the right arises automatically. However, the 1988 Act provides that copyright does not subsist in literary, dramatic, or musical works 'unless and until' the works are 'recorded in writing or otherwise'.[2] This is usually referred to as the requirement that the work be recorded in a material form. The fixation or recording of creative ideas carries with it many benefits. Perhaps the most obvious legal benefits are evidential. While evidence that has not been recorded in some way is admissible, the law has always preferred evidence that is fixed (written, taped, or filmed) to oral evidence. The reduction of ideas to a material form also increases the probability that a work may continue to be accessible beyond the death of its author.

In many cases, there is no need for any special rules to be made to ensure that a work is recorded. The reason for this is that, in the case of artistic works,[3] works of artistic craftsmanship,[4] sound recordings, films, and published editions, expression ordinarily takes place in a recorded physical form. That is, it is impossible for someone to create, say, a sound recording or a film in a way in which it is not fixed. This is not the case, however, in relation to literary, dramatic, and musical works which can be expressed in ways in which they are not fixed or recorded: literary works can be spoken, musical works sung, and dramatic works performed. To remedy this, section 3(2) of the 1988 Act states that copyright does not subsist in literary, dramatic, or musical works unless and until they are recorded, in writing or otherwise (for example, on film).[5] Writing is defined to include any form of notation or code 'regardless of the method by which, or medium in or on which, it is recorded'.[6]

There is no requirement that broadcasts be fixed or embodied in any particular form. Thus, broadcasts are protected whether or not the Broadcasting Authority makes a permanent version of them. Arguably, the ephemeral nature of broadcasts makes them one of the most intangible of all forms of intellectual property.

The requirement that literary, dramatic, and musical works be recorded is rarely a serious impediment to copyright protection. The reason for this is that the fixation requirement will be satisfied even if the recording is carried out by someone other than the creator (with or without their permission),[7] whether the recorded form is in the claimant's hands, or has subsequently been destroyed.[8] Given that when someone infringes copyright they will normally have reproduced the work, and that parties unconnected with the creator can carry out the requisite recording, this means that in most cases the work will in fact have been recorded.

---

[2] CDPA s. 3. This is deemed to be the time when the work is 'made': CDPA s. 3(2).

[3] There is an area of uncertainty in the case of artistic works that are not fixed, such as a display of coloured lights. It could be argued that, since fixation is not specifically required by the CDPA for artistic works, such a display could be protected (though, *quaere* under what sub-category of CDPA s.4). If so, live televizing of the display would infringe. The point remains to be decided by the courts. It has been stated that an ice sculpture, though not permanent, is protected: *Metix v. Maughan* [1997] *FSR* 718, 721.

[4] But cf. *Komesaroff v. Mickle* [1988] *RPC* 204 (a device consisting of a mixture of sand, liquid, and bubble-producing substance did not qualify as a work of artistic craftsmanship).

[5] CDPA s. 3(2). This clarifies any doubts which may have existed under the 1956 Act that recording on tape was not sufficient.

[6] CDPA s. 178.   [7] CDPA s. 3(3).

[8] *Lucas v. Williams & Sons* [1892] 2 *QB* 113, 116; *Wham-O Manufacturing Co. v. Lincoln Industries* [1985] *RPC* 127, 142–5 (CANZ); *J & S Davis (Holdings) v. Wright Health Group* [1988] *RPC* 403, 409.

One question that has arisen in relation to the fixation requirement concerns works that change form (such as databases or works of kinetic art).[9] While works that continually change form may give rise to problems in other respects, it seems that as long as a work is recorded it will be protected, even though it may subsequently change form.

3 ORIGINALITY: LITERARY, DRAMATIC, MUSICAL, AND ARTISTIC WORKS

Perhaps the most well-known requirement that must be satisfied for copyright protection to arise is that the work be 'original'. It should be noted that this only applies to literary, dramatic, musical, and artistic works.[10] In contrast, there is no need for entrepreneurial works (sound recordings, films, broadcasts, and typographical arrangements) to be original for them to qualify for protection. Instead the 1988 Act declares that copyright only subsists to the extent that such works are not copied from previous works. (We look at this in the following section.)

While the originality requirement has been a general statutory requirement since 1911,[11] it is very difficult if not impossible to state with any precision what copyright law means when it demands that works be original. This uncertainty has been exacerbated by the fact that, as part of the harmonization of copyright law in Europe, a new concept—that of the *author's own intellectual creation*—is now used in the United Kingdom to determine the originality of databases, and arguably also computer programs and photographs. In what follows, therefore, we need to distinguish carefully between the traditional British conception of originality, and the European one.

While we will explore the differences between the British and European conceptions of originality below, both conceptions share a number of characteristics. In both British and European conceptions, 'originality' is concerned with the relationship between an author or creator and the work. That is, originality is not concerned with whether the work is inventive, novel, or unique.[12] While the novelty requirement in patent law focuses on the relationship between the invention and the state of the art, the originality examination is primarily concerned with the relationship between the creator and the work. When copyright says that a work must be original, this means that the author must have exercised the requisite intellectual qualities (in the British version *labour, skill, or effort,* in the European '*intellectual creation*') in producing the work.[13] More specifically, in determining whether a work is original, copyright

---

[9] In *Komesaroff,* note 4 above, King J held that a device consisting of a mixture of sand, liquid, and bubble-producing substance did not qualify as a work of artistic craftsmanship. The device, when moved, produced pretty patterns. King J held that: 'it must be possible to define the work of artistic craftsmanship on which she bases her action, and this can be done only by a reference to a static aspect of what has been referred to by counsel as a "work of kinetic art"'.

[10] CDPA s. 1(1).

[11] Though the requirement was introduced for paintings, drawings, and photographs by the Fine Art Copyright Act 1862.

[12] *University of London Press v. University Tutorial Press* [1916] 2 *Ch* 601; *Sawkins v. Hyperion* [2005] 1 *WLR* 3281, 3288 *per* Mummery LJ (para. 31) (originality does not require 'novelty, usefulness, inventiveness, aesthetic merit, quality or value. A work may be complete rubbish and utterly worthless, but copyright protection may be available for it...')

[13] Lord Reid in *Ladbroke v. William Hill* [1964] 1 *All ER* 465, 469.

law focuses on the input that the author contributed to the resulting work.[14] Consequently, a person who writes a film script based on an original story recounted by Homer in *The Odyssey* produces an 'original' work even though the story and characters have been widely known for thousands of years.[15]

The originality requirement sets a threshold that determines when material falling within the definition of literary, dramatic, musical, or artistic work is protected by copyright law.[16] Nevertheless, the policy basis for the threshold requirement has never been made clear. It certainly excludes from protection trivial works, the creation of which involves little labour, skill, or effort. As we will see, the European conception of originality may well set the threshold higher,[17] excluding works which are merely the product of labour alone.[18] The originality requirement also functions to limit the duration of protection by preventing existing works from being the subject of further copyright protection in the absence of some additional contribution. Since this function could be achieved by requiring that the work must not already exist (as is the case with entrepreneurial works), it seems that the originality requirement is intended to do something more. What this is, however, is unclear.

In addition to operating as a threshold, originality may be important in establishing whether a person has infringed copyright. This is because a person will not infringe copyright if they merely copy elements which are not original in the claimant's work. That is, deciding what is original in a claimant's work plays an important role in ascertaining whether a substantial part of a work has been taken by the defendant. (However, it should be noted that the fact that a person creates an original work does not mean that they are not infringing copyright in work they have drawn on.[19] This is because, as we see in Chapter 8, infringement depends on what a person has taken from a copyright work; the effort that such a person adds is irrelevant.)

3.1 THE BRITISH CONCEPTION OF ORIGINALITY

It would be foolish to claim that the case law developed since 1912 (or carried over from earlier jurisprudence) has defined clearly the circumstances in which a literary, dramatic, musical, or artistic work will be treated as original. Much of the case law seems inconsistent, and according

[14] To use Benjamin Kaplan's terminology in *An Unhurried View of Copyright* (1965), the test in copyright is psychological, whereas in patents it is historical.

[15] *Christoffer v. Poseidon Film Distributors* [2001] *ECDR* 481.

[16] Originality has also played an important role in deciding whether new classes of work (photography in the nineteenth century and more recently Aboriginal art) ought to be protected by copyright law. There is also a possibility that the growing judicial suspicion about the over-extension of copyright may mean that originality comes to be used as a way of restricting the scope of the subject matter protected by copyright law.

[17] Given that many such countries have an 'open' list of works protected by copyright, the 'originality' requirement does the job of delimiting the sphere of copyright in those countries (a role performed in the UK by the list of eight types of work in CDPA s. 1).

[18] See J. Ginsburg, 'Creation and Commercial Value: Copyright Protection of Works of Information' (1990) 90 *Columbia Law Review* 1865 (in the context of US law, doubting whether copyright should be confined to works exhibiting traces of personality, given the social value of works which are a product of 'sweat of the brow'.) But as regards databases in Europe, an attempt is made to meet this objection through the *sui generis* right: see Ch. 13.

[19] See *Wood v. Boosey* (1868) *LR* 3 *QB* 223, 229; *Redwood Music v. Chappell* [1982] *RPC* 109, 120; *ZYX Music GmbH v. King* [1995] 3 *All ER* 1, 9–11; cf. *Ashmore v. Douglas Home* [1987] *FSR* 553 (Judge Mervyn Davies denied copyright protection to part of a play which was derived from an existing copyright play on the grounds that the former was 'infringing material').

to one commentator 'the dividing line between original…works, and unoriginal…works, remains an uncertain and shifting one'.[20] In part these difficulties arise because originality 'must depend largely on the facts of the case and must in each case be very much a question of degree'.[21]

As we explained above, when British copyright says that a work must be original, this means that the author must have exercised the requisite *labour, skill, or judgment* in producing the work.[22] However, while the phrase 'labour, skill, or judgment' may be a useful label by which to describe the traditional British test of originality, it should be noted that it is a form of words that is not used with great precision (and thus should not be viewed as if it were a statutory phrase). Sometimes the courts use the phrase disjunctively, referring to labour, skill, *or* judgment,[23] sometimes cumulatively as labour, skill, *and* judgment.[24] On other occasions the words work, capital, effort, industry, time, knowledge, taste, ingenuity, experience, or investment are used.[25] This looseness may be criticized on the basis that it leaves the law uncertain, particularly as regards whether works which are only a product of labour (so called 'sweat-of-the-brow' works) are original. But the truth is that this is a question whose economic and legal importance has only become paramount with the advent of electronic databases. In the past, the distinction between labour and skill was less momentous (and, indeed, the line drawn between labour and skill was less obvious).

Before looking at the notion of originality in more detail, it will be helpful to make a few preliminary points.

3.1.1 Preliminary points

(i) The first point to note is that in most cases the requisite labour, skill, and effort that is needed for a work to be original will be exercised in the way the work is *expressed*: in the way the paint is applied, the words are chosen and ordered, ideas executed, or the clay moulded. That is, in assessing originality, British law is concerned with the originality of expression rather than ideas.[26]

(ii) However, while the originality with which we are concerned is originality of expression, the courts have accepted that the originality of a work may arise in the steps preceding the production of the work (in the *pre-expressive* stage).[27] That is, the labour that confers originality on a particular work may arise in the selection of the subject matter or the arrangement of the image that comes to be embodied in the painting. In other cases, such as with respect to literary compilations, the courts will consider the footwork involved in discovering the

---

[20] S. Ricketson, 'The Concept of Originality in Anglo-Australian Copyright Law' (1991) 9(2) *Copyright Reporter* 1.

[21] *Macmillan v. Cooper* (1923) 93 *LJPC* 113 (Lord Atkinson).

[22] *Ladbroke v. William Hill* [1964] 1 *All ER* 465, 469 (Lord Reid).   [23] *Ibid* 469 *per* Lord Reid.

[24] *Ibid* 473f *per* Lord Evershed; *Interlego v. Tyco* [1988] *RPC* 343, 371.

[25] *Ladbroke v. William Hill* [1964] 1 *All ER* 465, 475 *per* Lord Hodson ('work, labour and skill'); 478 *per* Lord Devlin ('skill, industry, or experience'); 480 *per* Lord Pearce ('labour or skill or ingenuity or expense'); *Macmillan v. Cooper*, note 21 above (Lord Atkinson) ('labour, skill and capital'); *Sawkins v. Hyperion* [2005] 1 *WLR* 3280, 3285 *per* Mummery LJ (para. 15) ('effort, skill and time').

[26] *University of London Press*, note 12 above.

[27] On another reading, three different factors have been taken into account: the relative importance of each depending on the subject matter in question. In certain situations, the courts have considered the *quality* of the labour. In other situations the courts have focused upon the *quantity* of labour that has been invested in the creation of the work. Where the labour is expended on an existing work, the courts have paid attention to the *effect* that the labour has on the underlying work.

information,[28] or the selection or choice of the materials that are later embodied in the work. This was made clear in *Ladbroke v. William Hill* where the question arose as to whether football pools coupons (which listed matches to be played and offered a variety of bets arranged in 16 categories) were original compilations.[29] On the basis that the expressive form of the coupons inevitably followed from the preceding commercial decisions as to the bets which should be offered, the appellants argued that the coupons were not original. The House of Lords rejected these claims.[30] According to Lord Reid, it was artificial to divide the inquiry up, on the one hand into the commercial decisions about which bets to offer and, on the other, the form and arrangement of the table. The selection of wagers and their presentation was so interconnected as to be inseparable. Consequently, when considering originality, it is inappropriate to dissect the labour, skill, and judgment into pre-expressive and expressive stages: both elements should be taken into account to determine whether the threshold had been reached.[31]

(iii) It is important to appreciate that the question of whether a work is original often depends on the particular cultural, social, and political context in which the judgment is made. In part this is because originality turns on the way the labour and the resulting work are perceived by the courts. One of the consequences of this is that what is seen as original may change over time. A good example of this is provided by photography. When invented in the 1840s, photography was seen as a non-creative (and non-original) mechanical process whereby images were produced by exposing chemically sensitive materials to light. In the late nineteenth century, however, photography came to be seen as an artistic activity. As a result, photographs came to be seen as creative and thus potentially original works.[32] Similar changes recently occurred in relation to the artistic works of Australian Aborigines.[33]

The historical specificity of the originality examination means that we must be careful as to the conclusions we draw from earlier decisions. This can be seen for example, if we look at the 1900 decision of *Walter v. Lane*.[34] In this case it was held that a newspaper report of an oral speech was protected by copyright because the reporter exercised considerable labour,

---

[28] For example in *Kelly v. Morris* (1866) 1 *Equity Cases* 697 the author 'needed to make time-consuming enquiries and to write down the results with painstaking accuracy'. Cf. *Sawkins* v. *Hyperion* [2005] 1 *WLR* 3280, 3291 (para 43) (time and effort spent discovering and retrieving original scores treated as irrelevant when deciding whether claimant had created original musical work).

[29] [1964] 1 *All ER* 465, 469 (Lord Reid); 477 (Lord Hodson); 479 (Lord Devlin); 481 (Lord Pearce). See also *Football League v. Littlewoods* [1959] *Ch* 637, 656; *Bookmakers' Afternoon v. Gilbert* [1994] *FSR* 723.

[30] Note, however, *Ladbroke v. William Hill* [1964] 1 *All ER* 465, *per* Lord Evershed, at 472, who considered the task of expressing the wagers a distinct one involving 'considerable skill, labour and judgment'.

[31] Two points are worth adding. The first is that there must be limits to the relevance of pre-expressive work. One such limit may be where pre-expressive work is provided by someone else, but is not sufficient to render that person a co-author. In these circumstances, such pre-expressive work cannot count towards the originality assessment. Another is where the pre-expressive labour is unconnected to the production of the work, as where a person selects products they are going to sell and then produces a catalogue. In such cases, it seems, pre-expressive work cannot contribute to the originality of the catalogue: *Purefoy Engineering v. Sykes Boxall & Co* (1955) 72 *RPC* 89. See also *Ladbroke v. William Hill*, [1964] 1 *All ER* 465, 477 *per* Lord Hodson; 479 *per* Lord Devlin (one of objects of pre-expressive labour should be production of work); 481 (Lord Pearce) ('if the work was done with no ultimate intention of a compilation'). The second point is that, to the extent that pre-expressive labour confers originality, so its appropriation may be infringement: see below, pp. 177–85.

[32] B. Edelman, *Ownership of the Image: Elements for a Marxist Theory of Law* (1979); J. Gaines, *Contested Culture: The Image, The Voice and the Law* (1992).

[33] See B. Sherman, 'From the Non-original to the Aboriginal', in Sherman and Strowel.

[34] *Walter v. Lane* [1900] *AC* 539. This was decided under the 1842 Act and there was no specific requirement of originality; it has been treated as being 'undeniably good law'. See *Express Newspapers v. News UK* [1990]

skill, and judgment in producing a verbatim transcript of the speech. (See Fig. 4.1.) More specifically, the court said that the reduction to writing of the words of a person who spoke quickly was an art requiring considerable training. It is possible that changes since 1900, notably the spread of simple tape-recorder technology, may mean that the transcription of a speech will no longer be treated as labour that gives rise to an original work.[35]

(iv) The next point to note is that the originality threshold has been set at a very <u>low level</u>. It may come as a surprise for some to learn that the courts have accepted as original such things as railway timetables and exam papers (which were drawn from the stock of knowledge common to mathematicians, produced quickly, and included questions similar to ones which had previously been asked by other examiners).[36] One of the consequences of the originality standard being set at a low level is that there have been relatively few instances where subject matter has been excluded on the basis that it was non-original. Most of the problems that have arisen have been in relation to tables and compilations, derivative works (that is, works which incorporate material copied from another source), and industrial designs.

3.1.2 Determining whether a work is original

As we explained above, when copyright says that a work must be original, this means that the author must have exercised the requisite *labour, skill, or effort* in producing the work. However, not all 'labour, skill, and judgment' will give rise to an original work. The problem facing us is to try and explain coherently when a work is original, and when it is not. In part these difficulties arise because the effort, skill, or judgment which is needed to confer originality on a work cannot be defined in precise terms. This is because originality 'must depend largely on the facts of the case and must in each case be very much a question of degree'.[37] As a result, it is very difficult to explain originality in terms of any overarching principles or rules. While a number of equally plausible accounts could be given of the British concept of originality,[38] perhaps the best approach is to look at originality in terms of the types of work in question. To this end we will look at the way the courts approach originality in relation to the following types of work:

(i) new works,

(ii) derivative works,

(iii) tables and compilations, and

(iv) computer-generated works.

FSR 359 (Browne-Wilkinson V-C); *Sawkins v. Hyperion* [2005] 1 *WLR* 3280, 3288 *per* Mummery LJ (para. 33); and Jacob LJ (para. 79).

[35] For a comparable argument that the labour, skill, and effort that was required to create a photographic reproduction of an art work was much greater in the 1860s than today, so that such a work should not necessarily be regarded as original today, see R. Deazley, 'Photographing Paintings in the Public Domain: A Response to Garnett' [2001] *EIPR* 179, 181.

[36] *University of London Press v. University Tutorial Press* [1916] 2 *Ch* 209. Although widely referred to, Peterson J's comment that the work 'should originate from the author' offers limited assistance when distinguishing between original and non-original works in the difficult cases of derivative works, compilations, and computer-generated works.

[37] *Macmillan v. Cooper* (1923) 93 *LJPC* 113 (Lord Atkinson).

[38] It may well be that there is no single British concept of originality, but that different tests apply to different categories of work, for example, that the originality requirement operates differently in relation to artistic work from the way it operates in relation to literary work. Indeed, in *Interlego v. Tyco Industries* [1989] *AC* 217 Lord Oliver said it would be 'palpably erroneous' to apply the test of originality developed in relation to literary compilations in *Ladbroke v. William Hill* [1964] 1 *All ER* 465, namely that originality was dependent upon the degree of skill, labour, and judgment involved in preparing the compilation, to art works.

3.1.3 New works

The first situation we wish to consider is where a 'new' work is created.[39] In particular we wish to consider the situation, for example, where inspired by a particular event a person sits down at their desk and writes a poem or a song. As in these circumstances the work clearly emanates from the author, there are unlikely to be any problems in showing originality. In the words of Peterson J in *University of London Press*, such works are original because they originate with the author and are not copied.[40]

The one exception to this principle is where the labour is trivial or insignificant and the result is trivial or insignificant. A possible example is the case of *Merchandising Corporation v. Harpbond*,[41] where face-paint was held unprotected by copyright. While (as we saw in the previous chapter) protection was refused on the rather unsatisfactory basis that the work was not a painting, the decision was justifiable on the basis that the work was a trivial outcome of an insignificant amount of labour.[42] Another example of a work held insufficiently original on the basis of insignificant labour involved the routine application of a formula to produce forecast dividends on greyhound races.[43] Yet other examples can be found in the case law on titles and advertising slogans, also discussed in Chapter 3. Titles, such as 'The Lawyer's Diary', involve too trivial an amount of labour to be regarded as original.[44]

However, in many cases the courts have been prepared to accept that even very simple works can be original. This was in effect the position in *British Northrop* where it was argued that drawings of things such as rivets, screws, studs, a bolt, and a length of wire lacked original-ity because they were too simple. In rejecting the argument, Megarry J said that he would be 'slow to exclude drawings from copyright on the mere score of simplicity' or on the basis that they were of elementary or commonplace objects.[45] This reluctance to exclude simple abstract works probably reflects a desire to ensure that works of abstract artists, such as Mark Rothko, which may be extremely simple, are regarded as original. Equally, even short poems such as haiku would be regarded as original.[46]

3.1.4 Derivative or copied works

The next type of creation that we wish to consider concerns the so-called derivative works, that is, works which were derived from or based upon existing works (whether or not they are protected by copyright). Obvious examples of such works are translations, abridgements, and new editions. Copyright law has long recognized that it is important that authors should be

---

[39] The distinction would doubtless be unsatisfactory to someone who views all works as derivatives, as 'inter-texts' which draw on and refer to existing works. While we accept that works are never created *de novo*, we have used the terms 'new works' and 'derivative works' as convenient labels with which to describe distinct judicial approaches taken to works which do not draw directly on the expressive form of existing works (new works) and those which do (derivative works).

[40] *University of London Press v. University Tutorial Press* [1916] 2 *Ch* 209.

[41] *Merchandising Corp. of America v. Harpbond* [1983] *FSR* 32.

[42] This may be what Lawton LJ meant when he said a 'painting is not an idea'.

[43] *Greyhound Services v. Wilf Gilbert (Staffs)* [1994] *FSR* 723.

[44] *Rose v. Information Services* [1987] *FSR* 254; *Sinanide v. La Maison Kosmeo* (1924) *LTR* 365. Perhaps the *Exxon Corp. v. Exxon Insurance* decision is explicable as a case where, even though the labour was extensive, the result was too trivial to be regarded as original.

[45] *British Northrop v. Texteam Blackburn* [1974] *RPC* 57, 68. See also *Karo Step Trade Mark* [1977] *RPC* 255, 273. An example of a non-original artistic work would be a straight line drawn with a ruler.

[46] In some cases, where the resulting work is regarded as sufficiently creative, the work may be very small: *Kipling v. Genatosan* (1917–23) *MacG CC* 203 (extract of four lines from poem 'If').

rewarded not just for creating new works, but also for building upon existing works. However, for a derivative work to be treated as original, copyright law seems to have imposed three hurdles. First, the labour expended must be of the right kind. Second, the effort must bring about a material change in the work. Third, that change must be of the right kind.

Before examining these, it is worth reiterating that copyright may subsist in a derivative work even though it might infringe copyright in the existing work.[47] That is, a derivative work may be both original and infringing. In such a situation, any copyright that is acquired in a derivative work will be distinct from and subordinate to the copyright in any prior original work which is incorporated into it. Provided that the original work is still apparent in the new version, both the maker of the new version and any third-party copier will need the licence of the owner of copyright in the original.

The labour must be of the right kind. As Lord Oliver said in *Interlego* 'only certain kinds of skill, labour and judgment confer originality'.[48] Consequently, a person may exercise a considerable amount of labour yet the resulting work will not be original if the labour is of the wrong kind. This would be the case, for example, where there is a direct or slavish copy of another work or where a work is photocopied.[49] While the tracing or copying of drawings, especially technical drawings, requires patience, skill, and labour, as Lord Oliver said in *Interlego,* 'copying *per se,* however much skill or labour may be devoted to the process, cannot make a work original'.[50] More specifically, he said a 'well-executed tracing is the result of much labour and skill but remains what it is, a tracing'.[51] It is clear that the reason why tracing and photocopying do not produce original works is not that there is no labour. Rather, it is that it is not the right type of labour.[52]

In some cases, the courts have suggested that for labour, skill, and judgment to be relevant it must not be mechanical or automatic, but must exhibit some 'individuality'. In *Macmillan v. Cooper* the Privy Council held that a reduction of Plutarch's *Life of Alexander* from 40,000 to 20,000 words so that it was suitable for use in schools was not original. An important factor in the finding that the selection was *not* original and thus not protected by copyright was that the process of selection was motivated by a desire to cut down the work so that it was merely shorter and more readily mastered and to exclude material which was of an indecent or indelicate character and unfit for schoolchildren.[53] To this end passages from the original were merely omitted at various points. Such a process did not require 'great knowledge, sound judgment, literary skill or taste to be brought to bear upon the translation'.[54] There had been effort expended in making the reduction, no doubt, but the Privy Council contrasted it with a (hypothetical) original abridgement, by explaining that the (hypothetical) process of

---

[47] *Redwood Music v. Chappell* [1982] *RPC* 109, 120; *ZYX Music GmbH v. King* [1995] *3 All ER* 1, 9–11.

[48] *Interlego AG v. Tyco Industries* [1989] *AC* 217, 268 (Lord Oliver).

[49] *British Northrop v. Texteam (Blackburn)* [1974] *RPC* 57, 68 (a drawing which is simply traced from another drawing is not an original artistic work); *Rexnold v. Ancon* [1983] *FSR* 662, 664 (improbable that copyright would be given to a mere tracing); *Davis (Holdings) v. Wright Health Group* [1988] *RPC* 403, 409 (casts made from models are not original) and 412 (tracing not original).

[50] *Interlego AG v. Tyco Industries* [1989] *AC* 217, 263.

[51] Ibid, 262 ('it takes great skill, judgment and labour to produce a good copy by painting or to produce an enlarged photograph from a positive print, but no one would reasonably contend that the copy painting or enlargement was an "original" artistic work in which the copier is entitled to claim copyright').

[52] *The Reject Shop v. Robert Manners* [1995] *FSR* 870, 876.

[53] However, the appellant had added marginal notes, an introduction, and a chronological table. The Privy Council held that these were well chosen, neatly condensed, sufficiently copious and accurate, and must have required literary skill, taste, labour, and judgment.

[54] *Macmillan v. Cooper* (1924) 40 *TLR* 186.

abridgement would have required some form of 'learning, judgment, literary taste and skill'.[55] That is, it lacked what the courts saw as the necessary skills to qualify for protection. Quoting from an early edition of Copinger's *Treatise on Copyright,* the Privy Council said that 'the act of abridgement is an exertion of the individuality employed in moulding and transfusing a large work into a small compass...Independent labour must be apparent, and the reduction of the size and work by copying some of its parts and omitting others' does not do this.[56] In contrast, the Privy Council said that the reduction of the *Life of Alexander* from 40,000 to 20,000 words was non-original because it lacked the 'exertion of the individuality employed in moulding and transforming a large work into a small compass'.

Macmillan v. Cooper seems to set a surprisingly demanding standard for the types of labour, skill, and judgment that are relevant. It can be contrasted with *Walter v. Lane* (though the Privy Council saw no inconsistency with that decision).[57] In that case it was held that a newspaper report of an oral speech given by Lord Rosebery, transcribed by a reporter from the talk, was protected by copyright (see Fig. 4.1).

This was because the reporter exercised considerable labour, skill, and judgment in producing a verbatim transcript of the speech. More specifically, the House of Lords said that the reduction to writing of the words of a person who spoke quickly was an art requiring considerable training.[58] Lord James of Hereford explained that 'from a general point of view a reporter's art represents more than mere transcribing or writing from dictation. To follow so as to take down the words of an ordinary speaker, and certainly of a rapid speaker, is an art requiring considerable training, and does not come within the knowledge of ordinary persons'.

One question that remains unanswered in this context is whether the digitization of a work (with no other changes) is sufficient to confer originality on the resulting work. For example, would the digital scanning of a novel or the creation of a digital database from non-digital sources give rise to an original work? Some commentators have suggested that the translation of a work into a digital format (in the case of a literary work, from a 'typographical character to numerical token')[59] may give rise to an original work. While there can be no doubt that the process of digitization does generate a product which is different, in the light of *Macmillan* it is doubtful whether the labour is of the sort which can render the outcome original.

The effort must bring about a material change in the work.   Second, labour, skill, and judgment must have been applied to existing materials so as to bring about a *material change* to the raw material. More specifically, the labour, skill, and capital must have imparted to the product 'some quality or character which the raw material did not possess, and which differentiates the product from the raw material'.[60] In so doing the law ensures that any copyright that is acquired in a derivative work is distinct from the original work that is incorporated into it.

---

[55] Ibid, 187.   [56] Ibid.

[57] *Walter v. Lane* [1900] *AC* 539. This was decided under the 1842 Act and there was no specific requirement of originality; it has been treated as being 'undeniably good law'. See *Express Newspapers v. News UK* [1990] *FSR* 359 (Browne-Wilkinson V-C); *Sawkins v. Hyperion* [2005] 1 *WLR* 3280, 3288 *per* Mummery LJ (para. 33); and Jacob LJ (para. 79).

[58] The court also noted that considerable skill had to be invested in learning shorthand and that judgment was exercised in deciding how to convert spoken words and performance to written sentences, with suitable grammar. On the skills of the journalist see *Walter v. Lane* [1900] *AC* 539, 551–2 (Lord Davey); 554 (Lord James of Hereford).

[59] Laddie *et al.*, para. 20.67 suggest that it was akin to the copyright protection given to the speechwriter in *Walter v. Lane*.

[60] *Macmillan v. Cooper* (1924) 40 *TLR* 186, 188; note 21 above (a passage described in *Interlego* as 'perhaps the most useful exegesis' on the issue of originality).

THE TIMES, FRIDAY, JUNE 26, 1896.

LORD ROSEBERY ON FREE LIBRARIES.

Yesterday afternoon the Earl of Rosebery opened a new free public library, named after its munificent donor, the Passmore Edwards Library, and erected as a memorial of Leigh Hunt and Charles Keene, at Uxbridge-road, near Shepherd's-bush-green, W. The special feature of this building is the complete supervision throughout all the departments from the librarian's counter, and to insure this advantage the several public rooms are divided by glazed screens. Ample light is provided everywhere, and the interior is bright and cheerful. The exterior has been designed in accordance with the English Renaissance style with bold cornices and handsome mullioned windows. The central gable is sculptured with a life-size group representing the "Shepherd in the Bush," suggested by the name of the district in which the library has been built. The librarian's house is on the first floor of the front buildings, and above are large storage rooms in connexion with the library. The architect was Mr. Maurice B. Adams, F.R.I.B.A., of Bedford-park, Chiswick. The cost of the building, exclusive of the site, has been rather more than £6,000. Lord Rosebery and Mr. Passmore Edwards were received on their arrival by the Library Commissioners, and conducted to the central room, where the chair was taken by Prebendary Snowden, chairman of the commissioners.

The CHAIRMAN, in opening the proceedings, explained that the site, which was peculiarly well adapted for the purpose of a public library, and which was very valuable, having an excellent building frontage, was a benefaction from the copyholders and the Ecclesiastical Commissioners, and when, after the refusal of the ratepayers to increase the library rate, those in favour of the library were almost in despair as to raising the necessary funds, Mr. Passmore Edwards came forward to their relief. (Cheers.) With noble, but not unaccustomed, generosity, he had erected that beautiful building, which was complete in all its arrangements as far as experience and skill could make it so. The chairman also made a reference to Lord Rosebery's literary achievements, and expressed the hope that he would present the library with a volume of his life of Pitt, inscribed with the author's autograph.

LORD ROSEBERY, who was received with loud cheers on rising to speak, said :—Mr. Chairman, Ladies, and Gentlemen,—I have much pleasure in declaring this library open. (Cheers.) I do that at the beginning and not at the end of what I have to say because I have observed almost invariably that public speakers whenever they have a formal duty to discharge and attempt to discharge it at the end of their speech forget to do so. (Laughter.) Now, Mr. Chairman, you have been very kind in the remarks that you have made. I shall cherish your reference to my little book which I had great pleasure in seeing on your shelves, but I will not accept your invitation to present the book to your library. In the first place, you already have a copy of it, which I do not think was at all worn out. (Laughter.) And in the second place, as it is sold I believe—although I have never bought a copy myself—at the ridiculously inadequate sum of 1s. 10d. (laughter), it is not at all a suitable offering for me to make to this library. I trust to find a more valuable book that I may leave as a memento of my visit here to-day. (Cheers.)

MR. PASSMORE EDWARDS.

But I have another duty to perform besides declaring this library open, it is that of proposing a vote of thanks to the generous donor of the building. (Cheers.) You have expressed a wish that I may have a long time before me to devote to literary pursuits. (Hear, hear.) I thought my neighbour on my right expressed a particularly fervent and enthusiastic assent to that sentiment. (Laughter.) I for my part have nothing to say in contravention of it. "Sweet are the uses of adversity," or what is called adversity, and it is difficult for those who are intrusted with the government of the country to come and open public libraries or perform functions of that kind ; and therefore you have reason to thank her Majesty's Opposition for their existence when it comes to any question of a function of this kind. But I am bound to say that even when I was in office, and when I was subject to the responsibilities and censures of office, I found time in the very first beginning of that period to go and open another library, founded of course, and given of course, by Mr. Passmore Edwards. (Cheers.) Now there is something about the permanence of pursuits in individuals which gives one a sense of the nothingness of time. We must all have known in our younger days some venerable ancestress or female relative who was occupied in some interminable piece of worsted work. (Laughter.) We went to school, we went on our travels, and we returned again and found that piece of worsted was still progressing (laughter), and I had something of the same feeling when I came here to-day and found Mr. Passmore Edwards still giving public libraries. (Cheers.) I do not know whether you remember the old story of the gambler who lost an enormous sum at Crockford's in the old days, and came out of that haunt with a generally vicious feeling against himself and the whole human race which he did not know how to vent. Looking opposite at White's Club-house he saw a gentleman kneeling against the stairs and tying his shoe lace. The gambler saw in him an object on which to vent his feeling, and, rushing up to the gentleman, he kicked him, and cried, " Bless you "—he did not say " Bless you," but in the presence of the chairman I will not quote the exact word he did use (laughter)—but he said, " Bless you, you are always tying up your shoe lace." (Laughter.) Well, I feel inclined to approach Mr. Passmore Edwards, not to kick him, but to say, " Bless you, you are always doing good." (Cheers.) Another word about Mr. Passmore Edwards. I am given to understand by those who are accustomed to commendation that it is not pleasant to be praised, in public at any rate, and therefore I think I shall best suit his feelings if I say nothing more on a subject which I could not adorn by eloquence, and which certainly does not need eloquence to recommend it.

OUTDOOR SPORTS IN ENGLAND.

But I think those who watch the growth of the free libraries system in this country, in spite of the almost persistent opposition of the ratepayers, have some cause to inquire, What object is it that these free libraries answer in our modern commonwealth ? I confess I have formed a very clear conviction on that head. I think no one can watch the progress of our nation without seeing the enormous predominance that is given everywhere to-day to outdoor sports. I welcome that tendency. I think it is a healthy and rational tendency, but of course it may be carried too far. What we do see in the tendency to outdoor sport at this time is that it weans the race from occupations that might be objectionable, and it is rearing a noble and muscular set of human beings ; and it subserves other objects which are not so immediately apparent. For instance, I take it the connexion between Australia and the mother country has been rendered closer than it would have been otherwise by the cricket contests which take place between the two countries ; and I am given to understand, though I

Fig. 4.1 One of the newspaper reports considered protected by copyright in *Walter v. Lane*

Source: The Times, Friday 26 June 1896, page 12.

In some situations, originality has been denied where the labours of a creator fail to bring about a <u>material change</u> in the resulting product. That is, while the efforts of the author might have led to a change in the resulting product, the change (and thus the labour) is not regarded as <u>sufficient</u> to confer originality on the resulting work. Conversely, where the change is material, the work will be original. This approach has been used to confer originality on new editions,[61] compilations, anthologies, translations,[62] adaptations of existing materials,[63] as well as arrangements of music,[64] and engravings. In all these cases, the labour of the author not only produced a change, it also produced what was taken to be a 'material change' in the raw material. The difficult question is deciding when such a transformation has occurred.

In *Interlego v. Tyco,* the Privy Council was called upon to decide whether there was copyright in drawings for the children's building blocks known as LEGOBRICKS.[65] After Lego's patents and designs in the bricks expired in 1975, Lego sought to retain its monopoly over the bricks by claiming that copyright existed in drawings produced in 1973. As these drawings were based upon earlier drawings, the question arose as to whether the alterations made in 1973 were sufficient to produce an original artistic work. The major differences between the drawings concerned the sharpening of the outer edges of the tubes in the brick, changes in tolerances, and increase in the radii on the outer edges of the knobs on the brick from 0.2 to 0.3 mm.

While the Privy Council recognized that these changes were technically significant and the result of considerable labour and expertise, they denied that there was copyright in the later drawings.[66] The mere fact that the drawing took skill and labour to produce did not necessarily mean that it was therefore an original drawing. As Lord Oliver explained, '[t]here must in addition be some element of material alteration or embellishment which suffices to make the totality of the work an original work'.[67]

This decision can be usefully contrasted with *Macmillan Publishers v. Thomas Reed Publications.*[68] The case turned on whether the preparation of a number of small, local charts

---

[61] *Black v. Murray* (1870) 9 *Macph* 341, 355. Lord Kinloch held that to create copyright in a new edition, alterations must be extensive and substantial; additional notes must be not superficial or colourable, but impart to the book a true and real value over and above that belonging to the text. Although as has been explained in the discussion of *Walter v. Lane,* there was no requirement of originality under the Literary Copyright Act 1842, decisions thereunder have often been cited in the context of works created after 1911.

[62] *Byrne v. Statist Co.* [1914] 1 *KB* 622; *Cummins v. Bond* [1927] 1 *Ch* 167.

[63] *Warwick Films v. Eisinger* [1969] 1 *Ch* 508 (book comprising large extracts from court transcripts was original because of editorial work, addition, and omission of material, etc.).

[64] *ZYX Music GmbH v. King* [1995] 3 *All ER* 1 (appeal dismissed: on other grounds [1997] *All ER* 129) (transformation) of ballad into disco or dance track was original arrangement). See R. Arnold, *Performers' Rights,* 240–53. But note *Hadley & Others v. Kemp* [1999] *EMLR* 589 (contributions of performers not relevant when assessing originality).

[65] *Interlego v. Tyco Industries* [1989] *AC* 217.

[66] Lord Oliver was happy to find that these drawings were not original. Otherwise, Lego would have been able to maintain a perpetual monopoly by continually revising the picture. This type of behaviour, he noted, had been disapproved of by the House of Lords in *Coca-Cola Co. Trade Mark Application* [1986] 1 *WLR* 695. It seems that Lord Oliver overlooked the fact that the pre-1973 works were not protected by copyright and therefore that a competitor was free to copy pre-1973 drawings (or models based on upon pre-1973 drawings).

[67] *Interlego v. Tyco Industries* [1989] *AC* 217. This leads to the rather bizarre conclusion that good reproductions are denied copyright but poor ones have sufficient visually significant variation. This was explicitly stated by Lord Oliver, ibid. For further discussion, see Laddie *et al.,* para. 4.42.

[68] [1993] *FSR* 455. Mummery J explained, 'on originality I find that this is a case where sufficient work and skill have been done; both in the creation of the simplified form of a work, showing the outline of the coast and geographical features, and in the compilation of selected information, such as depth soundings, geographical features, buoys and so on'.

that contained an outline of the coastline as well as relevant information (such as depth soundings, buoys, and geographical features) was original. More specifically, the question arose as to whether the charts were original, given that they were drawn from and based upon Admiralty charts. The High Court held that the labour used in producing the simplified charts involved the appropriate level of work and skill and transformed the charts sufficiently for the resulting work to be original.

It should also be noted that the requirement that the labour needs to produce a materially different work for it to be original is unnecessary where the same author produces a series of drawings or drafts.[69] As Nourse LJ explained:

What the Copyright Act requires is that the work should be the original work of its author. If, in the course of producing a finished drawing, the author produces one or more preliminary versions, the finished product does not cease to be his original work simply because he adopts it without much variation, or even if he simply copies it from an earlier version. Each drawing, having been made by him, each is his original work.[70]

In effect, the Court of Appeal indicated that no material change is required in situations where there are a series of drafts *by the same author*. It should be noted, however, that this exception to the rule that a derivative work must involve a material change if it is to be original has no application where there are different authors at each stage.[71]

The change must be of the right kind.   Another situation where an author may exercise a considerable amount of labour and the work not be original is where the type of labour used does not correspond to the type of work for which protection is sought. This can be seen in *Interlego*.[72] As noted, the major differences between the 1973 drawings and the earlier ones from which they were derived concerned the sharpening of the outer edges of the tubes in the brick, changes in tolerances, and increase in the radii on the outer edges of the knobs on the brick. Of the changes made, only the first was shown pictorially, the others by letters and figures. While the Privy Council recognized that these changes were technically significant they were not sufficient to render the work original because in the case of artistic works the change must be *visually significant*. That is, to confer copyright the skill and labour must produce a change which is relevant to the category of work in question. On the facts it was held that as the changes made to the drawings were primarily to the written specifications, this was not an alteration of visual significance.[73] As such, the drawings were not original. If this principle is applied in other contexts, it may have important ramifications for forms of appropriation art; that is where artists focus on the meaning rather than the visual appearance of the work.[74]

---

[69] Moreover, it has been held that, where a drawing was made from a three-dimensional functional design, such a drawing would be original if there was a continuous design process between the creation of the three-dimensional functional object and the subsequent creation of the two-dimensional drawing copying the three-dimensional object. *Murray Engineering v. Nicholas Cesare* (1997, unreported).

[70] *LA Gear v. Hi-Tech Sports* [1992] *FSR* 121, 136 (Nourse LJ).

[71] *Biotrading and Financing Oy v. Biohit* [1996] *FSR* 393, 395 (not sufficient merely to be owner of copyright in earlier drawings if later ones which are relied upon are not significantly different). Cf. *Rexnold v. Ancon* [1983] *FSR* 662 (summary judgment refused in similar circumstances).

[72] *Interlego v. Tyco Industries* [1989] *AC* 217.

[73] Ibid, 268 (Lord Oliver). Cf. *Interlego AG v. Croner Trading* 25 IPR 65 (Fed. Crt. Australia). Visually significant variations have been held to include changes of shape but not mere changes of scale: *Drayton Controls v. Honeywell Control Systems* [1992] *FSR* 245, 260.

[74] See B. Sherman, 'Appropriating the Postmodern: Copyright and the Challenge of the New' (1995) 4 *Social & Legal Studies* 31 and D. McClean and K. Schubert (eds.), *Dear Images: Art, Copyright and Culture,* (2002) 405;

The question whether the labour, skill and judgment was 'of the right kind' was considered by the Court of Appeal in *Sawkins v Hyperion*.[75] As will be recalled from chapter 3, the key question in this case was whether performing editions of musical works first composed in the seventeenth and eighteenth centuries were original musical works. It was argued by Hyperion that the reconstructed and edited scores were not original musical works, because Lionel Sawkins had added no new music over and above that in the original. While he had laboured to reconstruct the manuscripts and make them more user-friendly to today's performers, that did not involve labour, skill, or judgment of a musical sort. Mummery LJ agreed that some aspects of Sawkins' efforts 'such as time and labour spent on discovery or retrieval of the original scores and in their layout on the page' were irrelevant. However, labour, skill, and judgment in adding information that could potentially affect the totality of sounds produced by musicians were pertinent. On the facts, the work had sufficient aural and musical significance to attract copyright protection.

3.1.5 Tables and compilations (other than databases)

In this section, we consider the way in which the originality of tables and compilations has been approached. As we explained earlier, as a result of the Database Directive a new European standard of originality now applies for databases. The consequence of this is that the following analysis is now only applicable to a very narrow category of works, namely, tables and compilations (other than databases). However, the following analysis is helpful in two other respects. First, an understanding of the way the originality of tables and compilations has been dealt with in the past in the UK is helpful in understanding the nature of the changes effected by the Directive.[76] Second, and more importantly, the case law on originality of compilations indicates the confused approaches taken by the British courts.

Over time the courts have used two different and largely inconsistent approaches when determining whether tables and compilations are original. While the approaches are similar insofar as they focus upon the labour exercised in the creation of the work, they differ in terms of the *type* of labour that is needed for the work to be original. In some cases, originality arises through the application of the appropriate skill, labour, and effort in the creation of the work (the *quality* of the labour used in creation of the work). More controversially, originality can also arise through the application of a sufficient amount of routine labour (the *quantity* of the labour used in creation of the work). We will deal with each in turn.

Quality of the labour. The originality of tables and compilations may arise through the application of the appropriate skill, labour, and effort in the creation of the work (the *quality* of the labour used in creation of the work). It seems that the requisite labour may be employed either in the way the information to be included is *selected,* or in the way that it is *arranged.* For example, if we take the case of an edited collection, originality might arise as a result of the way the authors to be included in the volume are selected, or through the way the chapters are organized.

Given that tables and compilations are similar to derivative works (after all, a list is made up from existing materials), the comments made above about the originality of derivative works

P. Anderson, 'On the Legal Limits of Art' (1994) *Arts & Entertainment Law Review* 70.

[75] *Sawkins v. Hyperion* [2005] 1 *WLR* 3280.

[76] In addition, tables and compilations which are databases and which existed prior to 27 Mar. 1996 retain copyright if they passed the British test of originality then operative, even though they would now fail the European test: Database Regs, SI 1997/3032, reg. 29.

apply here. Looking at the question negatively, it seems that a table or compilation would not be original where the selection and arrangement is directly or slavishly copied from another work. Another situation where a compilation would lack originality is where the resulting work is a consequence of a mechanical, automatic, or formulaic process. The position would be the same where the material to be included in a compilation was selected automatically. In *Cramp v. Smythson,* Viscount Simon suggested that the making of a chronological list which is 'automatic and only requires painstaking accuracy' would not, of itself, be original.[77] The reason for this is that the making of a chronological list requires no element of 'taste or selection, judgment or ingenuity'.[78] On this basis it seems that where a list is organized alphabetically, it would not give rise to an original work (although originality might arise through the quantity of labour used in creating the compilation).

Quantity of the labour. In certain situations the courts have accepted that the mere exercise of a substantial amount of routine labour may give rise to an original work.[79] For example, where a compiler spends a considerable amount of time and effort creating a chronological list of television programmes or an alphabetically ordered list of lawyers,[80] the resulting work will be original. That is, even though in creating the table or compilation the author might not have exercised the appropriate quality of labour, nonetheless the work may still be original if the process of compilation involves a sufficient amount of (mundane) labour.

Where there is insufficient labour (and originality does not arise through the exercise of requisite qualitative skill, labour, and effort), the resulting work will not be original. For example, where the process of compilation involves little effort or judgment and the effect is commonplace, the work will not be treated as original. Thus the selection of seven tables at the front of a diary, consisting of things such as days and dates of the year, tables of weights and measures, and postal information,[81] was held by the House of Lords to be non-original. Similarly, in another case involving a local timetable showing a selection of trains to and from a particular town that was prepared from official railway timetables, the compilation was held to be non-original.[82] In these circumstances the difficult question is knowing how much labour needs to be exercised for the resulting work to be original.[83]

The willingness to accept that a substantial amount of routine labour may give rise to an original work is usually explained in terms of the fact that defendants ought not to be able to

[77] In relation to indisputable facts (such as when the sun rises or sets), it was said that there is 'no room for taste or judgment. There remains the element of choice as to what information should be given': all that a table can do is state the facts accurately: *Cramp v. Smythson* [1944] *AC* 329, 336 (Viscount Simon).

[78] *Football League v. Littlewoods* [1959] *Ch* 637, 654. Though in this case, Upjohn J *obiter* at 656 would have accepted that the expenditure of labour requiring painstaking hard work and accuracy would suffice.

[79] *Ladbroke v. William Hill* [1964] 1 *All ER* 465, 478 (Lord Devlin).

[80] *BBC v. Wireless League Gazette Publishing Co.* [1926] *Ch* 433; *Independent Television Publications v. Time Out* [1984] *FSR* 64; *Waterlow Directories v. Reed Information Services* [1992] *FSR* 409; *Dun & Bradstreet v. Typesetting Facilities* [1992] *FSR* 320. *Blacklock v. Pearson* [1915] 2 *Ch* 376 (list of railway stations in UK).

[81] *Cramp v. Smythson* [1944] *AC* 329 (Viscount Simon LC) ('commonplace information which is ordinarily useful and is…commonly found prefixed to diaries'). See also *Waylite Diary CC v. First National Bank* [1993] *EIPR* D–242 (no copyright in diary pages which lacked quality of individuality sufficient to distinguish the work from the merely commonplace).

[82] *Leslie v. Young* [1894] *AC* 335.

[83] See *Cramp v. Smythson* [1944] *AC* 329 *Greyhound Racing Association v. Shallis* [1923–8] *MacG CC* 370; *Total Information Processing Systems v. Daman* [1992] *FSR* 171 (linking of three computer programs was not a compilation). Cf. *Ibcos Computers v. Barclays Mercantile Highland Finance* [1994] *FSR* 275, 290.

avail themselves of the labour and expense which a claimant invested in the production of a work.[84] Instead of asking whether the work is original and thus protectable, where the courts have focused on the quantity of the labour involved in the creation of the work they have tended to start from the premise that any labour or effort that a claimant exerted in the production of work ought to be protected (so long as it reaches the requisite quantitative threshold). This is reflected in the maxim: 'what is worth copying is prima facie worth protecting'.[85] One issue that has yet to be answered in this context, to which we will return shortly, relates to the impact upon these decisions of the new standard of originality which is now to be applied to databases (namely, an author's own intellectual creation).

The position in the United Kingdom, where the exercise of non-creative labour can give rise to an original work, can be contrasted with the position in other jurisdictions such as Germany (where case law suggests that some minimal degree of creativity is required) and France (where originality is said to require 'the imprint of the author's personality' on the work, or an intellectual contribution). The UK position is also at odds with the position in the USA where, as the Supreme Court pointed out in the *Feist* decision, a work must have at least a minimal degree of creativity to be protected.[86] In relation to the question of the originality of a white-page telephone directory, the Supreme Court held that since facts were not created, the names and numbers were not themselves 'copyrightable'. Moreover, while the collection might have been original had the selection or arrangement involved some minimal creativity, as the directory in question had been selected by area and arranged alphabetically, it did not meet that minimum threshold.[87]

It should be noted that, in the UK, routine labour has only been used to confer originality on the resulting work in a limited number of situations. In particular, it has only been applied to a limited category of works: largely to tables and compilations of things such as maps, guidebooks, street directories, dictionaries, authors' works, and selections of poems.[88] More specifically, the cases which have accepted that originality can arise through the exercise of a sufficient degree of labour have tended to focus on the amount of labour exercised in the *selection* of materials to be included in tables and compilations: that is, they take place in the pre-expressive rather than the expressive stage.[89]

---

[84] *Weatherby and Sons v. International Horse Agency and Exchange* (1910) 2 *Ch* 297, 303–5; *Waterlow Directories v. Reed Information Systems* [1992] *FSR* 409.

[85] *University of London Press v. University Tutorial Press* [1916] 2 *Ch* 601 (Peterson J). This can be justified on the basis that, if a person copies an existing work, that person has demonstrated that the work incorporated skill or labour since otherwise it would not be worth copying. If the aphorism were taken at face value, it would prevent defendants from asserting that they were entitled to copy the claimant's work on the basis that it was not original.

[86] *Feist Publications v. Rural Telephone Service Co.*, 499 *US* 340 (1991).

[87] The *Feist* approach has been explicitly rejected in Australia, in *Desktop Marketing Systems Pty Ltd v. Telstra Corporation Ltd* (2002) 119 *FCR* 491, with the Federal Court of Australia affirming that laborious collection of data was sufficient to render the telephone directory an 'original literary work'. *Feist* has also been rejected in Canada, with the Supreme Court decision in CCH *Canadian Ltd v. Law Society of Upper Canada* [2004] *SCC* 13 (4 Mar. 2004) (holding that copyright subsisted in headnotes of judicial decisions) stating that imagination or creative spark was not a necessary element of originality but that skill and judgment was (para. 16). At the same time, however, the Supreme Court of Canada stated that labour alone would not usually suffice to demonstrate originality and that the skill and judgment required to produce the work must not be so trivial that it could be characterized as a purely mechanical exercise. The Supreme Court was opposed to granting copyright purely on the basis of labour so as to safeguard the 'public domain' and prevent authors from being overcompensated for their work.

[88] *Macmillan v. Cooper* (1924) 40 *TLR* 186, 189.   [89] *Cramp v. Smythson* [1994] *AC* 329, 330.

3.1.6 Computer-generated works

Prior to the passage of the 1988 Act, there was some uncertainty as to the status of computer-generated works; that is, of works created by translation programs, search engines, and the like. In part, the 1988 Act resolved this uncertainty by providing that a literary, dramatic, musical, or artistic work attracts copyright protection even where it has been generated by computer in circumstances where there was no human author.[90] While these changes were useful insofar as they clarified that creations generated by a computer could be classified as works, they said nothing about how the originality of such works was to be determined. The particular problem that arises with computer-generated works is that it is difficult to see how the existing criterion of originality, which focuses on the relationship between the author and the work, can be applied to computer-generated works which, by definition, have no readily identifiable author.[91]

Given that computer-generated works are protected where there is no human author, the question arises: what test for originality should be applied to such works? One possible test would be to ask whether the work was produced as a result of the independent acts of the computer. That is, is the work original in the sense that it was 'not copied'? Alternatively, a court might say that originality exists where the computer has produced a work which is different from previous works (i.e. it is novel). It has also been suggested that the courts ought to ask the hypothetical question: if the same work had been generated by a human author would it have required the exercise of a substantial amount of skill, labour, and effort? If yes, then the computer-generated work would be original.[92]

3.2 EUROPEAN ORIGINALITY: DATABASES, PHOTOGRAPHS, AND COMPUTER PROGRAMS

As we noted in Chapter 2, a process of partial harmonization of copyright law is taking place within Europe. The Software and Database Directives require that a computer program or database can only be protected by copyright where it is the 'author's own intellectual creation'.[93] A similar test was also introduced for photographs in the Duration Directive.[94]

3.2.1 Databases

In implementing the Database Directive, the UK Database Regulations explicitly amended the originality requirement of the Copyright, Designs and Patents Act 1988 in relation to databases to include the new criterion of the 'author's own intellectual creation'.[95] In particular, section 3A(2) says that 'a literary work consisting of a database is original if, and only if, by

---

[90] CDPA s. 9(3), 178. Cf. *Payen Components South Africa v. Bovic Gaskets* (1996) 33 IPR 406, 411 (Supreme Crt. of South Africa) (distinguishing between 'computer-generated' and 'computer-assisted' works).

[91] As regards computer-generated computer programs and databases, the EC standard should apply so that presumably no copyright protection is available.

[92] Laddie *et al.,* para. 20.63.

[93] Software Dir., Art. 1(3) ('a computer program shall be protected if it is original in the sense that it is the author's own intellectual creation. No other criteria shall be applied to determine its eligibility for protection': Database Dir., Art. 3(1)).

[94] It is arguable that this European standard is also required of photographs by Art. 6 of the Duration Dir., which states that photographs which are original in the sense that they are the author's own intellectual creation shall be protected in accordance with Art. 1. No other criteria shall be applied to determine their eligibility for protection.

[95] CDPA s. 3A(2), introduced by Database Regs. 1997, r. 6.

reason of the selection or arrangement of the contents of the database the database constitutes the author's own intellectual creation'.

The position in the United Kingdom under the revised law is similar to the old law in that the originality of the database may arise either through 'the selection' or through the 'arrangement' of the contents of the database. It should be noted, however, that the new criterion does not appear to permit a court to take account of the *creation* of information included in the database. Thus an organization which spends time carefully thinking about what television programmes to broadcast and at what times they should be broadcast will not obtain copyright protection for listings produced using a database. This is because the 'intellectual creation' lies not in the selection or arrangement of the contents, so much as in their creation. (In other words, the European standard seems to require a court to distinguish more rigorously than British courts have hitherto been accustomed, between pre-expressive and expressive aspects in the creation of a database.)

The extent to which the new law will differ also depends on the way 'an author's own intellectual creation' is interpreted by the courts. At present it is difficult to predict how this phrase will be interpreted. It has been widely assumed that the new EU standard is higher than the previous British standard of originality.[96] There is some suggestion that a quantitative criterion as well as this qualitative criterion of originality should apply.[97] However, someone familiar with the common law might find it difficult to see how the phrase differs from the words used by Peterson J in *University of London Press v. University Tutorial Press*.[98] There is some indication of the intended standard in Recital 17 of the Duration Directive. This explains that a photograph will be original 'if it is the author's own intellectual creation reflecting his personality'. Whether this will be used in relation to databases has yet to be seen.

While the courts may use the new standard as a way of rethinking the law in relation to originality, for the most part the new standard probably will not lead to different results. In particular, where the originality derives from the quality of the labour used in either the selection or the arrangement of the database, it is still likely to be regarded as an author's intellectual creation. The one area where the new definition may lead to a change is where originality arises through the mere exercise of routine labour; that is, where the *quantity* as distinct from the quality of the labour is used in the creation of the database. Where all an author has done is to exert a considerable amount of effort in the creation of a database, it is difficult to see how this, on its own, could be seen as an 'intellectual creation', especially one which reflects the author's personality. As a result it is possible that the previous decisions which accepted that the exertion of a sufficient amount of routine labour could confer originality on tables and compilations may no longer be good law for databases (though it might be for tables and compilations other than a database).[99] In a recent case in which the issue whether customer lists were protected by copyright arose (albeit as something of a side issue), Deputy Judge Fenwick

---

[96] Davison, 15–16.

[97] *British Horseracing Board v. William Hill* [2001] ECDR 257, 269 (Laddie J) (an inference from Database Dir., Recital 19 which states that the compilation of several recordings of musical performances on a CD does not meet the conditions for copyright protection).

[98] [1916] 2 *Ch* 601, 608. C. Millard, in H. Jongen and A. Meijboom (eds.), *Copyright Software Protection in the EC* (1993), 239. Because the phrase can be interpreted as requiring no change for any particular EC country, Karnell calls it a 'chimera': G. Karnell, 'European Originality: A Copyright Chimera', in *Intellectual Property and Information Law* (Kabel *et al.* ed., 1998), 201–9. While this may be true in the short term, the ECJ will eventually decide on the standard that prevails.

[99] As explained below, pp. 104–6, if this criterion is not met, the material data may be protected by a *sui generis* right.

said he was 'far from persuaded that the exercise of assembling a list of contact addresses' was original work.[100]

3.2.2 Computer programs

In implementing the Computer Programs Directive the government did not consider it necessary to amend the 1988 Act in relation to originality.[101] As was the case before the Directives, such works are protected if they are 'original'. The fact that no changes were made to the standard of originality for computer programs seems to suggest that it was thought that the position in the United Kingdom prior to the implementation of the Directives was already similar to the position required under the Directives. Nevertheless, the language of the 1988 Act should be construed as far as possible to be consistent with international obligations,[102] so the originality of computer programs in the United Kingdom should now be assessed in light of the EU standard of an author's own intellectual creation.

Accordingly, it seems that elements in a computer program which are dictated by the function the program is to perform or by economic necessity are probably not original.[103] To require computer programs to be demonstrated to be an author's own intellectual creation may also mean that commonplace routines used by programmers would not be protected.

3.2.3 Photographs

The position with respect to photographs is more complicated. This is for two reasons. First, the law on originality of photographs prior to the Directive was unclear. Second, even after the Directive, it is difficult to know whether the traditional British test of originality must be employed, or whether the Act implicitly adopts the European one.

Prior to the adoption of the Duration Directive, little judicial guidance had been given in the United Kingdom as regards the exact circumstances in which photographs would be regarded as original.[104] While there was little doubt that protection would be granted to more 'artistic' photographs (where there might be considerable effort in selection of the material to be photographed and the way the photograph is executed in terms of light, angle, exposure),[105] doubts existed over the originality of routine snapshots, as well as the originality of photographs of existing artistic works. Although, in *Graves' Case,* Blackburn J held that a photograph of an engraving of a painting was an 'original photograph' and therefore protected under the Fine Art Copyright Act 1862, doubts had been raised as to the usefulness of this case as an authority

---

[100] *Penwell Publishing* v. *Ornstein* [2007] *EWHC* 1570 (QB) (para. 107).

[101] Cf. Germany, which explicitly repeats the wording of the Directive: G. Schricker, 'Farewell to the "Level of Creativity" in German Copyright Law?' (1995) 26 *IIC* 41.

[102] *Von Colson and Kamann,* Case 14/83 [1984] *ECR* 1891.

[103] See G. Dworkin, 'Copyright Patents or *Sui Generis*: What Regime Best Suits Computer Programs?' in H. Hansen (ed.), *International Intellectual Property Law and Policy* (1996) 165, 168; J. Drexl, *What Is Protected in a Computer Program?* (1994), 96–7 (emphasizing that the European standard was a direct reaction to the German *Inkassoprogram* decision, and that the standard adopted is consistent with the copyright approach of treating originality as requiring the independent creation of an author, though not mere 'sweat of the brow').

[104] In *Graves' Case* (1869) *LR* 4 *QB* 715 Blackburn J held that a photograph of a painting was an 'original photograph' but noted the difficulty involved, explaining, '[t]he distinction between an original painting and its copy is well understood, but it is difficult to say what can be meant by an original photograph. All photographs are copies of some object.' It should be noted that, in contrast with the position in relation to protection of books under the Literary Copyright Act 1842, photographs, drawings, and paintings were only protected under the Fine Art Copyright Act 1862 if they were 'original'. *Graves' Case* therefore remains relevant.

[105] K. Bowrey, 'Copyright, Photography and Computer Works: The Fiction of an Original Expression' (1995) 18 *University of New South Wales Law Journal* 278.

today, given that the technological apparatus for taking photographs is so much more developed (and thus the act of taking photograph so much easier).[106]

As regards snapshots, no judicial guidance had been provided as to whether pointing a camera and pressing the button was sufficient 'labour, skill and effort' to justify protection. It was possible to claim that in such circumstances the photograph 'originated with the author' and so should be treated as original (applying the *University of London Press* case). Moreover, it was argued, if someone wished to copy a photograph, is that not sufficient reason to treat it as original? On the other hand, it is clear that copyright does not protect the products of trivial effort. What could be more trivial than a snapshot?

As regards photographs of existing works, doubt was cast on the usefulness of the authority in *Graves' Case* by *Interlego v. Tyco*. As we have seen, Lord Oliver was dismissive of the idea that labour in the process of copying could confer originality. If an artist gets no copyright by making a faithful copy of a painting, it was asked, how could a photographer be said to create an original work where they expended much less labour or skill in photographing a painting? On this basis, in the US case *The Bridgeman Art Library Ltd v. Corel Corp,* an American judge (Justice Kaplan) found that *under UK law* a photograph of a painting in the public domain is not entitled to copyright because it is not an original work.[107] The US decisions, which are not binding on UK courts, concluded that a photograph which attempted to duplicate another work was the equivalent of a photocopy, and thus is not protected by copyright because there is no visually significant embellishment to render the photograph an original work. However, it has been trenchantly argued that it is wrong to apply the dicta in *Interlego v. Tyco* in this way, and there would certainly be serious economic implications for museums and art galleries if this were ultimately found to be the law.[108] In *Antiquesportfolio. com v. Rodney Fitch & Co Ltd,*[109] it was held that copyright subsists in simple photographs of three-dimensional objects because the taking of such photographs involves judgment—the positioning of the object, the angle from which the picture is taken, the lighting, and the focus. It seems likely therefore that, despite *Interlego,* the British courts, applying the traditional originality test, would treat photographs of existing (albeit two-dimensional) paintings in the same way. The labour and skill of photography produces a material change in the work, by converting it from paint on canvas, to the flat representation of a photograph. In so doing, the photographer employs various skills, which can be described as more than skills in the mere process of copying.

The position after the Duration Directive is even more unclear. This is because the Directive itself allows for two courses of action, and it is unclear which of these courses the United Kingdom has taken. As mentioned, the Directive requires original photographs to be protected by copyright if they meet the European originality criterion (that is, they are their 'author's own intellectual creation'). However, the Directive allows member states to give protection to

---

[106] Deazley, 'Photographing Paintings in the Public Domain', 181.

[107] *The Bridgeman Art Library Ltd v. Corel Corp* (1998) 25 *F Supp* 2d 421, 36 *F Supp* 2d 191.

[108] See, e.g. K. Garnett, 'Copyright in Photographs' [2000] *EIPR* 229. Cf. Deazley, 'Photographing Paintings in the Public Domain (arguing that *Graves' Case* is inapplicable in the light of *Interlego*); S. Stokes, 'Graves' *Case* revisited in the USA—*The Bridgeman Art Library v. The Corel Corporation*' [2000] *Ent LR* 104; S. Stokes, 'Photographing Paintings in the Public Domain: A Response to Garnett' [2001] *EIPR* 354 (in fact, a response to Deazley, arguing for copyright in such works to protect the labour and skill of the photographer); R. Deazley, 'Copyright; Originality; Photographs; Works of Art' [2001] *EIPR* 601 (responding to Stokes); S. Stokes, 'Graves' *Case* and Copyright in Photographs: *Bridgman v. Corel*', in McClean and Schubert, 109.

[109] [2001] *FSR* 345; [2001] *ECDR* 51.

non-original photographs (i.e. ones which are non-original in the European sense). Insofar as the traditional (UK) standard of originality is lower than the (European) standard in Article 6(1) (and Recital 17) of the Duration Directive, this allows the United Kingdom to maintain its lower standard: that is, to protect photographs which are 'non-original' (in the European sense). The difficulty with interpreting the British law lies in the fact that the legislature said nothing about this issue when implementing the Directive. That is, after 1 January 1996, UK law only protects 'original' photographs, but it is unclear whether by that it means 'original' in the British sense or 'original' in the European sense.

As things stand, the most obvious way to interpret the originality requirement in the 1988 Act so that it complies with the Duration Directive with respect to photographs is to treat the word 'original' as referring to the European standard. That is, as requiring the photograph to be an author's own intellectual creation reflecting his or her personality. However, it is equally plausible to argue that the lack of any transitional provisions applying to photographs taken prior to January 1996 suggests that the old standard, i.e. the traditional British standard, is intended to apply. That is, that when UK law protects 'original' photographs it protects photographs that are original in the European sense, and takes advantage of the derogation also to protect photographs which are non-original in the European sense, but original in the British sense.

The conclusion matters. Under the Directive, an original photograph is one which is the author's own intellectual creation, 'reflecting his personality'. It seems unlikely that photographs of existing painting or sculptures (at least when done purely to produce a faithful impression of these artefacts) could be said to reflect a photographer's personality. However, as already noted, such photographs may well be original in the traditional British sense.

4 ENTREPRENEURIAL WORKS: 'NOT COPIED'

Unlike the case with literary, dramatic, musical, and artistic works, there is no requirement that films, sound recordings, broadcasts, or published editions be original. Instead, the 1988 Act provides that copyright does not subsist in a sound recording, a film, or a published edition to the extent that it is itself copied from a previous work of the same kind.[110] In relation to broadcasts, the Act provides that copyright does not subsist to the extent that it infringes copyright in another broadcast.[111] One of the consequences of this is that entrepreneurial works will be protected irrespective of whether or not the author exerted mental skill, labour, or effort in the creation of the work. This means that if a video recorder or tape recorder is turned on and left on a table, the resulting film or sound recording would be protected.[112]

It has been suggested that the reason why a lower standard is applied to entrepreneurial works than to authorial works relates to the nature of the rights which are granted.[113] In relation to authorial works, the scope of the rights is more expansive than with entrepreneurial works. As a result, it is more important that the law monitors the types of authorial work that are protected. Conversely, in the case of entrepreneurial works where protection is thin, there

---

[110] CDPA ss. 5A(2), 5B(4), 8(2).   [111] CDPA ss. 6(6).

[112] Kamina, 96–9 (the only films that benefit from the absence of an originality requirement are security camera recordings and fortuitous films).

[113] Laddie *et al.*, para. 6.13.

is less need to monitor the subject matter protected. This does not mean, however, that it is not necessary to regulate the types of subject matter protected as entrepreneurial works. In particular, to have allowed such works to be protected with no threshold requirement would have created the undesirable position that rights in entrepreneurial works could have continued in perpetuity. The reason for this is that, in the absence of some limitation, every time someone copied an entrepreneurial work they would have obtained a fresh copyright in the 'new' work. This problem is avoided in the 1988 Act by ensuring that entrepreneurial works are only protected to the extent that they are not copied.

For the most part these provisions are relatively straightforward. However, three issues remain unsettled. The first is whether a compilation of parts of sound recordings (such as a 'megamix') would be protected as a separate sound recording.[114] On one view, if the megamix is compiled from existing recordings, then nothing is protectable. The reason for this is that each existing element is excluded on the basis that it is copied from another sound recording. However, if such an approach were to be followed it would lead to the bizarre result that the absence of a notion of originality in respect of entrepreneurial works means the threshold of protection is higher than with respect to authorial works (where collections of materials are protected as databases, tables, and compilations).[115] Perhaps the better view is that a compilation of sound recordings ought to be protected as a sound recording, on the basis that the compilation is more than the sum of its parts.

The second question is whether, in the process of digitally remastering an old work, the resulting work would be protected. Where no change is made to the contents of the work, it is difficult to see how the digital version of the work could be protected by copyright, since the recording is copied from existing recording of sounds. Would the position be any different if, in the process of remastering an old recording, it was cleaned of unnecessary noise and interfering sound? It seems that the way this question will be answered depends on the way the phrase 'to the extent that' is construed.[116]

Another question that has arisen is whether the recent introduction of a provision to the effect that the producer and principal director are the creators of a film means that films are now to be treated as authorial rather than entrepreneurial works (or indeed as some sort of hybrid). In turn this might suggest that to be protected a film must be original.[117] Weighing against this, however, is the fact that the provisions dealing with duration provide that a film may lack a director yet still attract copyright.[118] Given this (and the express language used in the Act), it seems that films will not be subject to the originality requirement.

---

[114] P. Theberge, 'Technology, Economy and Copyright Reform in Canada', in S. Frith (ed.), *Music and Copyright* (1993), 53.

[115] It might be the case that a 'megamix' would indirectly create an original musical work or that the process of digitization creates an original literary work.

[116] Laddie *et al.,* para. 6.13 (sound recording); para. 7.30 (films); Kamina, 98–9 (noting that the film producers' copyright required under the Rental and Duration Directives refers to the *first* fixation).

[117] The existing understandings of the originality requirement developed from judicial interpretation of the notion of 'authorship' in a period when there was no express requirement of originality. See, e.g. *Walter v. Lane* [1900] *AC* 539.

[118] The Act specifically makes provision for circumstances where there is no principal director, author of screenplay, dialogue, or music, by limiting the copyright term to 50 years from the year in which the film was made. See CDPA s. 13B(9).

5 IS THE WORK 'QUALIFIED'?

In order for a work to be protected in the United Kingdom, it is necessary to show that the work is suitably 'qualified'.[119] That is, it is necessary to show that the work is sufficiently connected to the UK to qualify for protection under UK law. UK law withholds protection from works that fail to establish a sufficient connection to the United Kingdom. In essence, the requirement that the work be qualified helps to balance the protection offered to British authors in other jurisdictions against the protection given to foreign authors in the United Kingdom. Once a work qualifies, British law applies the principle of national treatment. That is, UK copyright law generally treats foreign works as it does those of British authors.[120]

5.1 CONNECTING FACTORS

The benefits of British copyright law have been extended to cover a vast array of works created by foreign authors or published in foreign countries.[121] Nevertheless, the task of determining whether a particular work is protected under British copyright law is remarkably complex. While in some situations this task may be avoided through the use of statutory presumptions,[122] in most situations it needs to be undertaken. Given that British law effectively provides universal protection, some regard the complexity of the task as unnecessary.[123]

There are three connecting factors which enable works to qualify for copyright protection (sections 154–6). These are by reference to (i) authorship, (ii) country of first publication, and (iii) place of transmission. A work qualifies if it satisfies *any* of these three factors.[124] Once a work qualifies for copyright protection, British copyright law does not usually discriminate between it and a work created by or first published in the United Kingdom.[125]

5.1.1 Qualification via authorship

Section 154(1) provides that a work qualifies for copyright protection if at the 'material time' the author of the work was a 'qualifying person'.[126]

In order for a work to qualify for protection, it is necessary that the author be connected to a relevant country at the 'material time'.[127] For unpublished literary, dramatic, musical, and

---

[119] For further details, see Copinger, paras 3–152 to 3–259, pp 135–181.

[120] But see pp. 162–3 for an exception to this concerning duration (applying shorter term in country of origin).

[121] In international parlance, these are referred to as the connecting factors, the *points d'attachement* or the *Anknupfungspunkt*.

[122] See *Microsoft Corp. v. Electro-wide* [1997] *FSR* 580, 594.

[123] Laddie *et al.*, paras. 5.10, 5.146–50.

[124] Where created before 1 Jun. 1957, a published work could be protected only on the basis of first publication and not by virtue of personal status: CA 1956, Sched. 7, para. 1.

[125] In the light of the requirements of the Duration Directive, the application of *the rule of the shorter term* to works which have as their country of origin a non-EEA state. CDPA ss. 12–14. This may have a more startling impact than has sometimes been assumed: see pp. 162–3.

[126] This may make determination of authorship important. In *Century Communications v. Mayfair Entertainment* [1993] *EMLR* 335 the court had to determine whether the author of a film made under restrictive conditions in China was a Hong Kong company that initiated and organized the making of the film, in which case the film qualified for protection under s. 154, or whether the author was the Chinese national carrying out the detailed making of the film, in which case the film did not qualify for copyright protection.

[127] CDPA s. 154(4).

artistic works, the 'material time' is the date when the work was made. Where the work has been published, it is the author's status at the date of first publication that is decisive; or, if the author died before publication, their status at the date of death.[128] By contrast, the material time for other types of copyright works does not change; qualification depends on the personal status of the 'author' of a sound recording or film at the time of its making or, for the organization broadcasting a transmission, at the date of transmission; and, for typographical format, it is the publisher at publication that is relevant.[129] Since a work may take a considerable time to make, section 154(4)(a) provides that, in the case of an unpublished literary, dramatic, musical or artistic work, the 'material time' is 'a substantial part of that period'. Rather oddly, no such provision exists for films.

To qualify under section 154, it is necessary to show that the author was a 'qualifying person'. There are three ways in which this can be achieved. First, a person will be a 'qualifying person' if they can show that they are a British citizen, national, or subject; a person within certain categories of the British Nationality Act 1981; or a person domiciled or resident in, or a body incorporated in, part of the United Kingdom.[130] The concepts of 'domicile' and 'residence' are not defined in the Act. It seems, however, that 'domicile' refers to the country where a person makes their permanent home. In contrast, the concept of 'residence' is more flexible, simply demanding some degree of continuous association with the country in question. A person can be a resident of more than one country, though a person will not be a resident if he or she is a casual visitor.[131]

Second, a person will qualify if they can show that they are an individual domiciled or resident in, or a body incorporated under the law of, a country to which the law has been 'extended'.[132] In this context it should be noted that 'extension' refers to the fact that Her Majesty by Order in Council is given the power to extend the 1988 Act to other territories, including the Isle of Man, the Channel Islands, and any colony.[133] Along with the power of 'application' (discussed below), 'extension' is a technique that is used to protect works that originate from outside the United Kingdom. While few such orders have been made under the 1988 Act (in relation to Guernsey and Bermuda),[134] orders made under the equivalent section of the 1956 Copyright Act continue to operate,[135] for example in the Falkland Islands.[136] The effect of such orders is not simply to provide protection in the UK for categories of work with a relevant connection to those countries: protection is also afforded in those countries to works protected in the United Kingdom.[137] As the power to extend the 1988 Act permits the extension to be 'subject to such exceptions and modifications as may be specified', each order needs to be considered individually.

---

[128] Ibid.   [129] CDPA s. 154(5).   [130] CDPA s. 154(1)(a).   [131] Laddie *et al.*, paras 5.60–1.

[132] CDPA s. 154(1)(b); British Nationality Act 1981, s. 51.   [133] CDPA s. 157.

[134] *Bermuda*, SI 2003/1517; *Guernsey*: SI 1989/1997. Orders extending the Act to *Gibraltar* (SI 2005/853) and the *Isle of Man* (SI 1990/1505, SI 1990/2293) were revoked and both are now countries to which the Act applies: Copyright and Performances (Application to Other Countries) Order, SI 2008/677, Sched.

[135] They continue to operate because of CDPA, Sched. 1, para. 36.

[136] *British Indian Ocean Territory*: SI 1984/541; SI 1987/2200; *British Virgin Islands*: SI 1962/2185; 1985/1988; *Cayman Islands*: SI 1965/2010; *Falkland Islands and Dependencies*: SI 1963/1037; 1987/2200; *Gibraltar*: SI 1960/847; 1985/1986; 1987/2200; *Montserrat*: SI 1965/1858; 1985/1987; 1987/2200 *St. Helena and Dependencies*: 1963/1038. Many Orders made in respect of other colonies which have become fully independent territories have been revoked. The Copyright (Status of Former Dependent Territories) Order, SI 1990/1512 lists territories to which the 1956 Act is deemed to have extended immediately before 1 Aug. 1989: Antigua, Dominica, Gambia, Guyana, Jamaica, Kiribati, Lesotho, St Christopher, Nevis, St Lucia, Swaziland, and Tuvalu. Pending revocation, these countries continue to be treated as qualifying, under previous extension orders.

[137] Laddie *et al.*, para. 5.82.

Third, a person will qualify if they can show that they are a citizen or subject of, and an individual domiciled or resident in, or a body incorporated under a law of, a country to which the Act has been 'applied'.[138] Section 159 empowers Her Majesty by Order in Council to 'apply' the copyright sections of the 1988 Act to other countries. This may be done so as to let either authors connected to such countries, works first published in such countries, or broadcasts sent from such countries qualify for protection in the United Kingdom. Moreover, such 'applications' may be subjected to such exceptions and modifications as are specified or confined to certain classes of cases specified in the Order. The power to make such Orders is restricted to 'Convention countries', other member states of the EEC, or to countries which give adequate protection to the owners of copyright in respect of the class of works to which the Order relates.[139] The latest version of the Order is the Copyright and Performances (Application to Other Countries) Order 2008.[140]

Where a work has been jointly authored, the work qualifies for copyright protection if any of the joint authors is qualified. However, the non-qualifying author is ignored when considering issues of first ownership[141] and duration.[142] Consequently, if one joint author qualifies and another does not, the qualifying owner alone will be first owner.[143] Similarly, copyright in a co-written literary work expires 70 years after the death of the last qualifying co-author.[144]

5.1.2 Qualification by first publication

A work may also qualify for protection if it is first published in the United Kingdom or in another country to which the Act has been 'extended' or 'applied'. (These concepts were discussed above.)[145] A work is published when copies of the work are issued to the public[146] or, in the case of literary, dramatic, musical, and artistic works, when the work is made available to the public through an electronic retrieval system.[147] It does not include: performing a literary, dramatic, or musical work; exhibiting an artistic work; issuing specified types of copies of such works;[148] playing or publicly showing a sound recording or film; or communicating to the public any work.[149]

---

[138] CDPA s. 154(1)(c).

[139] CDPA s. 159–60. Under CDPA s. 160, the Order may limit protection by virtue of first publication in respect of works from a country which does not adequately protect British works. The main example of such restrictions relate to sound recordings. According to the Copyright and Performances (Application to Other Countries) Order 2008, SI 2008/677, Sched. Column 3, the protection given to sound recordings varies between three categories of country: those merely parties to the WTO; those which are 'asterisked,' comprising Rome Convention countries and EC member states, to which a required connection results in *full* protection that includes the right to control public playing and communication to the public; and those marked by a 'hash' sign, being WPPT countries which are not also parties to the Rome Convention (most significantly, the USA), but to which a required connection results in *basic* protection, coupled with the right to control communication to the public other than broadcasting.

[140] SI 2008/677.   [141] Under CDPA s. 11.   [142] Under CDPA s. 12.

[143] But the non-qualifying author, it seems, can claim moral rights, and therefore should be named on the work, and the work should not be subjected to any derogatory treatment without their consent.

[144] CDPA s. 154(3).   [145] CDPA s. 155(1).   [146] CDPA s. 175.

[147] CDPA s. 175(1). There is also a definition of 'commercial publication': CDPA s. 175(2). Note also the differences in the concept of publication employed in relation to the 'publication right': see Related Rights Regulations, SI 1996/2967, r. 16.

[148] CDPA s. 175(4)(a)–(b). Publication of an artistic work does not include issuing copies of a film depicting such a work, nor copies of graphic works or photographs representing a sculpture, a work of artistic craftsmanship, or a work of architecture. However, the construction of a building is the equivalent of publishing the architectural work that it embodies: CDPA s. 175(3).

[149] CDPA s. 175(4). But an electronic retrieval system may still serve to publish literary, dramatic, musical, or artistic works even if it operates by way of broadcasting: CDPA s. 175(4)(a)(ii), (b)(iv).

If a work is to qualify for protection by publication, the publication must be authorized by the author.[150] The 1988 Act provides that publication does not include merely colourable publications which are not intended to satisfy the reasonable requirements of the public.[151] The threshold for protection is very low. At a minimum, if a work attracts no interest, the mere fact that a few copies have been made available for sale will suffice.[152] Publication takes place wherever the publisher invites the public to acquire copies[153] and may take the form of gift, hire, or sale.[154] Since publication consists in offering reproductions to the public, it seems that anything that amounts to a reproduction will suffice.[155]

To qualify for protection, the work must be published *first* in the United Kingdom or in another country to which the Act has been 'extended' or 'applied'. The fact that publication first occurs in a non-qualifying country will not matter, so long as that work is published within 30 days in the United Kingdom or in another country to which the Act has been 'extended' or 'applied'.[156] It should also be noted that films that have been released commercially under conditions of restricted distribution may well not have been published, since copies will not have been made available to the public.[157]

5.1.3 Qualification by place of transmission: broadcasts

A broadcast qualifies for protection if it is made or sent from a place in the United Kingdom, or a country to which the Act 'extends' or 'applies'.[158] In the case of satellite broadcasts, the broadcast is made where the signals are introduced.[159]

---

[150] CDPA s. 175(6) (no account shall be taken of any unauthorized act); s. 178 (defining unauthorized act where no copyright subsists). Joint authors are not specifically dealt with, but probably all must consent before a publication is authorized.

[151] CDPA s. 175(5).

[152] *Francis Day & Hunter v. Feldman* [1914] 2 *Ch* 728 (placing six copies of music in retail showroom was publication, so that the work attracted UK copyright protection). In contrast, in *Bodley Head v. Flegon* [1972] 1 *WLR* 680, Brightman J said he thought it unlikely that underground publication was enough since it intentionally disregarded the requirements of the public. That case concerned whether Solzhenitzyn's work *August 1914* had been published first in France or Russia. It was claimed (by the defendant) that publication had occurred in Russia illegally by way of *samizdat*. However, the court found no evidence to support the claim.

[153] In *British Northrop v. Texteam* [1974] *RPC* 57 Megarry J held that a work was issued to the public when reproductions of the work were put on offer to the public. That offer could be sale or gift. The place of first publication is where the offer is made, not where copies are received.

[154] Ibid.

[155] *Merchant Adventurers v. Grew* [1973] *RPC* 1; *British Northrop v. Texteam* [1974] *RPC* 57. Doubted in Laddie *et al.*, paras. 5.30–2.

[156] CDPA s. 155(3). A publication in the UK or any other country is not to be treated as other than first publication by reason only of earlier publication elsewhere if the latter occurred within a stated period of the former. For works published after the 1956 Act took effect, this period is 30 days; for those published before, it is 14 days (CDPA s. 155(3), Sched. 1, para. 35).

[157] Cf. *Bodley Head v. Flegon* [1972] 1 *WLR* 680.

[158] The Copyright and Performances (Application to Other Countries) Order 2008, SI 2008/677, specifies the countries to which the Act applies with respect to broadcasts in columns 4 & 5. Column 4, which relates to wireless broadcasts, distinguishes between, on the one hand, those made by persons or entities appropriately connected to Rome or EC countries, which receive 'full protection' and, on the other, those by parties thus connected to WTO countries, which benefit from a more modest regime of rights. Column 5 relates to non-wireless broadcasts and extends protection only to those made by persons or entities appropriately connected to other EC or EFTA countries.

[159] CDPA s. 156(1).

6 EXCLUDED SUBJECT MATTER

Although a work may be recorded in material form, be original, and be sufficiently connected to the United Kingdom, in some circumstances the courts may nonetheless refuse to recognize copyright for policy reasons. It appears that copyright protection will not be granted for obscene, blasphemous, or immoral works. This can be seen from *Glyn v. Weston Film Feature*[160] where Younger J refused to grant an injunction for infringement of copyright in the claimant's dramatic work, *Three Weeks,* which he described as a 'sensual adulterous intrigue' and condemned on the ground that it advocated 'free love'. Younger J said, 'it is clear that copyright cannot subsist in a work of a tendency so grossly immoral as this'.

For some time it had been thought that *Glyn* and the other cases where copyright had been denied to obscene, blasphemous, libellous, irreligious, or misleading works[161] were the products of less enlightened times and, as such, would no longer be followed.[162] However, in *A-G v. Guardian (No. 2)*[163] the House of Lords cited *Glyn* with approval. In that case Peter Wright, a former security services agent, had written a book (called *Spycatcher*) about the various operations of the service. Importantly, in writing the book Wright breached the duty of confidence he owed to the Crown. The House of Lords held that Wright would not be able to bring a copyright infringement action because of the 'disgraceful circumstances' in which the book was written.[164] As well as citing *Glyn* with approval, the Lords extended the scope of the immorality exclusion beyond the content of the work to include the circumstances in which the work was created.

While the House of Lords affirmed the continued existence of the public policy exclusion, there is still some doubt as to the exact effect of immorality. It is unclear whether it means that there is no copyright in the work at all,[165] or that equity will not enforce the copyright.[166] The way this question is answered might be important given that, if there is no copyright, presumably all contracts that purported to deal with the copyright would be void.

---

[160] [1916] 1 *Ch* 261.

[161] One difficulty with the *Glyn* decision is that it is by no means clear when a work is immoral. Generally the criminal law restricts circulation of obscene works—works which are likely to deprave and corrupt. Immorality appears to be a wider test. It is certainly difficult to believe that a work which advocated free love would today be denied copyright. In *Stephens v. Avery* [1988] *Ch* 449, in the context of breach of confidence, Browne-Wilkinson V-C stated that he thought the *Glyn* exception should not apply in the absence of public consensus that the work in question was immoral. In *Fraserside Holdings* v. *Venus* [2005] *FMCA* 997, the Federal Magistrates' Court of Australia was prepared to enforce copyright in 'adult films', explaining that the court should look at the attitudes taken towards the work both in Australia and overseas.

[162] In *Chaplin v. Frewin* (1966) 1 *Ch* 71 the Court of Appeal said that it thought the book in question was worthless from a literary point of view as well as being blasphemous but nowhere suggested that the work should for that reason be deprived of copyright. It thus appeared that the doctrine in *Glyn* could no longer be viewed as sound law.

[163] [1990] 1 *AC* 109.

[164] At the same time they appeared to take the view that the Crown had copyright in Wright's book or that Wright held copyright in the book on trust for the Crown. This is a little difficult to square with the proposition that there was no copyright in the work.

[165] In *Glyn,* Younger J said there was no copyright in the work.

[166] In *Spycatcher* the House of Lords simply stated that Wright would not be allowed to enforce his copyright. The assertions that Wright held copyright on trust or that copyright rested in the Crown suggests that the House of Lords may have interpreted *Glyn* as a case where the remedy of an injunction was withheld rather than copyright denied. See Copinger, para. 3–260, p. 181 (copyright subsists but will not be enforced) and, generally, A. Sims, 'The Denial of Copyright on Public Policy Grounds' [2008] *EIPR* 189.

The scope of the exclusion is also unclear. Although hitherto it has been concerned with matters such as sexual morality, the exclusion may also be a basis for declining to protect so-called 'malware', that is, software designed to appropriate sensitive information from a user's infected personal computer.

The effect of the public policy exclusions is somewhat paradoxical. As the denial of copyright to obscene works effectively places them in the public domain, this might increase the speed and breadth of circulation. If dissemination is deemed to be undesirable, the denial of copyright seems to be counter-productive.[167] (It may also stimulate public interest in the work.) Presumably, other reasons have motivated the courts. The approach taken by the courts is consistent with the view that the primary concern of copyright is to encourage creation rather than to control dissemination. Denying copyright will (supposedly) remove the incentive to produce obscene works.

As we have seen, a derivative work that infringes copyright in the work on which it is based can be original. In such circumstances the question arises as to whether an original but infringing work should be denied protection on grounds of public policy. With one or two exceptions,[168] the courts have generally been willing to enforce copyright in derivative works even though they infringe.[169] This has been explained on the basis that if protection were denied to such works it would lead to a substantial injustice. As Goff J said:

It is understandable that the owner of copyright should be entitled to restrain publication of an infringing work; but the idea that he should be entitled to reap the benefit of another's original work, by exploiting it, however extensive such work might be, however innocently it might have been made, offends against justice and common sense.[170]

---

[167] See *Fraserside* v. *Venus* [2005] *FMCA* 997, paras 39–42.

[168] e.g. *Ashmore* v. *Douglas Home* [1987] *FSR* 553. (Judge Mervyn Davies denied copyright protection to part of a play which was derived from an existing copyright play on the grounds that the former was 'infringing material'.)

[169] See *Wood* v. *Boosey* (1868) *LR* 3 *QB* 223, 229; *Chappell* v. *Redwood Music* [1982] *RPC* 109, 120; *ZYX Music, GmbH* v. *King* [1995] 3 *All ER* 1, 9–11; *Ludlow Music Inc.* v. *Williams* [2002] *FSR* (57) 868, 886 (paras. 39–40).

[170] *Chappell* v. *Redwood Music* [1982] *RPC* 109, 120.

5

AUTHORSHIP AND FIRST OWNERSHIP

CHAPTER CONTENTS

1 INTRODUCTION

A considerable amount has been written about authorship and the role it plays in copyright law. It has become clear from these discussions that the concept of authorship which operates in copyright law is not the same as is used in many other fields.[1] One explanation for this relates to the particular role that the author plays in copyright law. More specifically it is because, in copyright law, the author acts as a focal point around which many of the rules and concepts are organized. For example, as we have just seen, the status of the author helps to determine whether a work qualifies for protection. Where relevant, the labour that an author expends in creating a work will also influence whether the resulting work is original. In other situations, the duration of many types of work is determined by reference to the lifespan of the author. Similarly, the moral rights that are recognized in the United Kingdom attach to the author of the work in question.

In this chapter we explore two closely related themes. First, we look at the concept of authorship, as it is understood in copyright law. In turn, we look at one of the most important consequences that flow from being named as author of a work: namely, first ownership of copyright and the various exceptions to this general rule.

2 AUTHORSHIP

The author of a work is defined in the 1988 Act as the person who creates the work.[2] Special provisions deal with the situation where more than one person is involved in the creation

---

[1] Frequently it is more expansive, including those whose effort might not reach the creative levels of literary authorship. See, e.g. *Walter v. Lane* [1900] *AC* 539.

[2] CDPA s. 9(1). For comparative analysis, see J. Ginsburg, 'The Many Faces of Authorship: Legal and Interdisciplinary Perspectives' (2003) 52 *De Paul LR* 1063.

of a work.[3] While to describe the creator of a painting or a sculpture as an 'author' may jar, few problems arise in ascertaining who is the author of most literary, dramatic, musical, and artistic works.[4] This is because in relation to the traditional categories of literary, dramatic, musical, and artistic work there is a general consensus as to which of the various people involved in the production of a work is to be treated as the creator or author of it.

More problems arise, however, in relation to entrepreneurial works and computer-generated works. In part, this is because the concept of authorship does not sit comfortably with the way we tend to think about such works. That is, we do not normally think of a sound recording, a typographical arrangement, or a broadcast as having an author, even in the broad sense in which it is used in copyright law. In these circumstances, it is important to appreciate that the 'author' is an artificial construct, a legal fiction, which is used to allocate rights. This can be seen in the fact that, in relation to sound recordings, broadcasts, and typographical arrangements, the 'author' is (effectively) defined as the person who made the work possible (as distinct from the creator). In the case of a literary, dramatic, musical, or artistic work that is computer-generated (which by definition has no author) the 'author' is 'the person by whom the arrangements necessary for the creation of the work are undertaken.'[5]

In its dealings with entrepreneurial works, British copyright law has tended to concentrate on the person who made the arrangements necessary for the making of the work (the entrepreneur). In contrast, civil law systems have tended to focus on the persons who made creative contributions to the work. This difference has long been seen as an important point of contrast between the two systems.[6] As a result of attempts to harmonize copyright law in Europe, this difference is slowly being undermined. In part, this is because one of the consequences of the process of harmonization is that civil law conceptions of authorship have been introduced into British law.[7] A prelude to this occurred with moral rights, where the director was recognized as having a status equivalent to the author of a literary, dramatic, musical, or artistic work. More recently, the notion of the principal director as joint author of a film has also been introduced into UK law.[8] One of the consequences of these changes is that films now occupy a hybrid position in between authorial and entrepreneurial works.

One of the key differences between copyright and most other forms of intellectual property is that copyright protection arises automatically, without the need for formality or registration. While this may be advantageous to authors, it generates some unexpected problems. In particular, while with patents, registered designs, and trade marks the identity of the creator of the intellectual property and, in turn, the nature of the property are clarified by the process of registration, with copyright this has to be achieved by other means.[9]

The task of determining who is the author of a work is made easier because the 1988 Act sets out a series of statutory presumptions as to who is the author of a work. Section 104 provides that the name that appears on a literary, dramatic, musical, and artistic work as published, or

[3] See below at pp. 125–7.

[4] For consideration of the question whether an amanuensis is an author, see *Donoghue v. Allied Newspapers* [1938] 1 *Ch* 106. But note that a medium who transcribed messages from the spiritual world was author of the work: *Cummins v. Bond* [1927] 1 *Ch* 167 (Eve J held that the medium 'had exercised sufficient skill, labour and effort to justify being treated as author').

[5] CDPA s. 9(4), 178.

[6] A. Strowel, *Copyright et Droit d'Auteur: Convergences et Divergences* (1993) 320–89.

[7] Note, however, that under the 1911 Copyright Act, UK law conferred copyright in cinematographic works as 'dramatic works' to their authors, and after *Norowzian v. Arks (No. 2)* [2000] *EMLR* 67 this may again be the case. Civil law systems have, occasionally, treated the 'producer' as the author of a film: see Kamina, 132–3.

[8] CDPA s. 9.   [9] See Sherman and Bently, 182–5.

on the work when it is made, shall be presumed to be the author. Section 105 establishes similar presumptions with respect to sound recordings, films, and computer programs.[10] The upshot of these presumptions, which only operate in civil matters, is that the burden of proof is placed on the person claiming that someone other than the 'named' author is the true creator of the work in question.

2.1 AUTHORSHIP OF LITERARY, DRAMATIC, MUSICAL, AND ARTISTIC WORKS

The author of literary, dramatic, musical, or artistic work is the person who creates it.[11] No further guidance is given in the 1988 Act as to what this means. The only exception to this is to be found in section 3(2) which indicates that the author need not necessarily be the person who fixes or records the work (although this will usually be the case).[12] The lack of statutory guidance as to the way the author is to be construed in this context does not matter that much given that there are few problems in identifying who is the author of a literary, dramatic, musical, or artistic work.

Having said that, problems have occasionally arisen in determining whether a person involved in the production of a literary, dramatic, musical, or artistic work is to be regarded as an author (or creator). The way this question is answered is similar to the way the originality of a work is determined. Basically, in order for someone to be classified as an author, it is necessary for them to be able to show that the labour, skill, and judgment that they contributed to the work are of the *type* that is protected by copyright: that is, that they would be sufficient to confer originality on the relevant work.[13] The upshot of this is that it is unlikely that a stenographer, an amanuensis, or a person who merely photocopies or traces a work would ever be considered as an author.[14] This is because the labour expended in relation to the work fails to bring about a (material) change in the resulting work. However, if the person exercised a degree of creative labour in producing the work, even if only a very small amount, it is more likely that they will be treated as an author. This can be seen, for example, in *Cummins v. Bond*[15] where it was held that a spiritualist who produced 'automatic writing' dictated to her from beyond the grave at a seance was the author of the resulting work. As the spiritualist exercised great speed in writing down the messages, and used great skill in translating the spiritual communication given in an 'unknown tongue' into 'archaic English', it was held that she had exercised sufficient skill, labour, and effort to justify her being treated as author. Similarly, in *Walter v. Lane,* the House of Lords held that a reporter who took a shorthand report of a speech had exercised sufficient skill to be treated as author of the resulting report.[16]

Where the contribution made by someone is at an abstract level, such as the idea for a play, or a book, or a structure of a computer program, they are unlikely to be treated as an author of the resulting work. Thus, for example, the telling of a person's experiences to form the basis of a 'ghost-written' book is (without more) unlikely to render the narrator of the tales an author of the resulting book: rather, the ghost writer who determines the way the stories are expressed

---

[10] CDPA s. 105.   [11] CDPA s. 9(1).   [12] CDPA s. 3(2).

[13] As the type of labour that confers originality is the same as that which enables someone to be classified as an author, in copyright law terms, reference should be made to the earlier discussions on this topic.

[14] *Donoghue v. Allied Newspapers* [1938] 1 *Ch* 106.

[15] [1927] 1 *Ch* 167. See also *Leah v. Two Worlds Publishing* [1951] 1 *Ch* 393.   [16] [1900] *AC* 539.

will be regarded in law as the author.[17] The more specific the contribution, however, the more likely it is that the person in question will be treated as an author. Thus, at the opposite extreme to that of the ghost writer, in the case of a person who dictates text and punctuation to another who merely follows the instructions, UK law would regard the dictator rather than the amanuensis as the author.[18] In between the two extremes lies a host of possibilities. In one case it was held that a person who developed an idea for a house design that he had explained in detail (both verbally and through sketches) to a technical draftsman was joint author of the plans that the draftsmen subsequently produced.[19] Similarly, a political figure who dictated his memoirs to a friend, read every word, and altered parts of the manuscript was held to be joint author of the resulting book.[20]

As we saw in relation to the originality requirement, the mere fact that a person expended labour in the creation of a work will not necessarily mean that the resulting work is original (or that the person is an author) if it is the wrong type of labour. This means that, although a person may play an important role in the production process, they still might not be treated as an author. In the case of a book, for example, while the copy editor, the jacket designer, and the typesetter all play an important role in giving shape to the final product, they will not be treated as authors of the resulting literary work.[21] (Although it is possible to imagine situations where the efforts of a copy editor might be such that they might be treated as a joint author.) Similarly, while copyright law has few problems in categorizing the person who wrote a play as the author of the play, in one case it was held that a person who had suggested the title, the leading characters, a few catchwords, and the scenic effects for the play had not contributed sufficiently to the play to justify them being treated as a joint author.[22] In a more recent case, *Brighton v. Jones,*[23] Park J held that the suggestions made by a director to a playwright, prompted by problems with the script encountered during rehearsals, were not of the right kind to justify the director's claim to co-authorship. He said the director had failed to establish 'that the contributions which she made were contributions to the creation of the dramatic work rather than contributions to the interpretation and theatrical presentation of the dramatic work'.[24]

2.1.1 Computer-generated works

In the case of literary, dramatic, musical, or artistic works that have been computer-generated,[25] the creator is 'the person by whom the arrangements necessary for the creation of the work are undertaken.' While the meaning of this provision has yet to be tested, it seems that it might include the person who operates the computer, as well perhaps as the person who provides or has programmed the computer.[26]

---

[17] *Donoghue v. Allied Newspapers* [1938] 1 *Ch* 106 (reporter was author of stories about jockey Steve Donoghue's life).

[18] Ibid.   [19] *Cala Homes (South) v. Alfred McAlpine Homes East* [1995] FSR 818.

[20] *Heptulla v. Orient Longman* [1989] FSR 598 (Indian High Court).

[21] A technician expending skill and labour in testing software, detecting bugs, and providing information towards de-bugging was likened to a proof-reader and therefore was not a joint author since he did not contribute to the authorship of the software as such: *Fylde Microsystems v. Key Radio Systems* [1998] FSR 449.

[22] *Tate v. Thomas* [1921] 1 *Ch* 503.   [23] [2005] FSR (16) 288.   [24] Ibid, para. 56.

[25] The term is defined in CDPA s. 178 as referring to the situation where a work is created by a computer in circumstances such that there is no human author of the work. Where a work is created merely with the assistance of a computer, it is therefore clearly not a 'computer-generated work'.

[26] In *Express Newspapers v. Liverpool Daily Post* [1985] FSR 306 Whitford J held that the author of computer-generated bingo sheets was the programmer of the computer. It is not clear whether this would be the position under the 1988 Act. See above p. 62, Fig. 3.2.

2.1.2 Unknown authorship

In certain situations, it may not be possible to ascertain who is the author of a literary, dramatic, musical, or artistic work. This may be because the name of the author is not attached to the work and it is not possible to ascertain authorship by other means. In other cases, an author may wish that their works be published anonymously, under a false name or a pseudonym. As the author acts as the focal point around which many of the rules of copyright are organized, this creates a number of potential problems. To remedy this, the 1988 Act includes the notion of 'unknown authorship.' A work is a work of unknown authorship if the identity of the author is unknown and it is not possible for a person to ascertain his or her identity by reasonable inquiry.[27] While in this situation the author remains the first copyright owner, since it is impossible to know when the author of such a work died, the duration of copyright is limited to 70 years from the date when the work was first made available to the public (or 70 years from when the work is made, if it is not made available before the expiry of that period).[28]

2.2 ENTREPRENEURIAL WORKS: STATUTORY AUTHORS

As we mentioned earlier, authorship does not sit comfortably with the way we tend to think about entrepreneurial works. Any potential difficulties in having to identify who is the author of, say, a broadcast or a sound recording are resolved by section 9(2) which defines who is the author of each of the different entrepreneurial works.

2.2.1 Sound recordings: the producer

Section 9(2)(aa) provides that the author of a sound recording is the 'producer.'[29] In turn, the 'producer' is defined as the 'person by whom the arrangements necessary for the making of the sound recording are undertaken.'[30] In most cases, the 'producer' of a sound recording will be the record company. This may change, however, where a sound recording is produced cooperatively, or where non-traditional modes of distribution (such as the internet) are used. The question of what is meant by 'the producer' is discussed in more detail in the next section.

2.2.2 Films: the producer and the principal director

When the 1988 Act was enacted,[31] for the purposes of determining authorship, films were treated in a similar fashion to sound recordings: the author was defined as 'the person by

---

[27] CDPA s. 9(4), (5).   [28] CDPA s. 12(3).

[29] CDPA s. 9(2)(aa). This section, which took effect from 1 Dec. 1996, was introduced by the Copyright and Related Rights Regulations 1996 (SI 1996/2967). This replaced s. 9(2)(a) which stated that 'in the case of a sound recording or film, the person by whom the arrangements necessary for the making of the recording or film are undertaken.'

[30] For works made between 1 Jun. 1957 and 1 Aug. 1989, 'the person who owns the first record (disc, tape or roll) embodying the recording at the time the recording is made' (the maker) is the owner: CA 1956 s. 12(8). In relation to pre-1957 works, 'the owner of the original plate upon which the sound recording were recorded is deemed to be the author,' CA 1911 ss. 5(1), 19(1). Cf. Rome Convention, Art. 3(c); Geneva Convention, Art. 1(b) (both defining the producer of a phonogram as the person or the legal entity which first fixes the sounds of a performance or other sounds). WPPT Art 2(d) refers to 'the person or legal entity who or which takes the initiative and has the responsibility for the first fixation.'

[31] CDPA s. 9(2)(ab); the status of the authorship of a film will differ depending on the date when the film was made. Prior to the 1956 Act, films were not recognized as a distinct category of work, but the elements of the film (photographs, sound recording, and dramatic works) were protected instead (in much the same way as

whom the arrangements necessary for the making of the film are undertaken.' As had been the case under the 1956 Copyright Act, films were treated as entrepreneurial works. In order to bring UK law into line with the EU Duration Directive, the 1988 Act was amended. The upshot of this is that the authors of a film made on or after 1 July 1994 are the producer and the principal director of the film. The principal director and producer are treated as joint authors, except where they are the same person.[32] The recognition of the principal director as author of the film marks an important change in the way films are regarded by British copyright law, from being treated as a type of entrepreneurial work, to being treated as a hybrid of entrepreneurial and authorial works.

The 'principal director' is not defined in the 1988 Act. Some guidance as to what is meant by this term is provided by section 105(5), which states that, where a film bears a statement that a particular person was the director (or principal director) of the film, this shall be presumed to be correct until the contrary is proved.[33] Section 105(6) adds that, where a person is named as the director of a film, this shall be presumed to mean that he or she is the principal director.

The 'producer' of a film is defined as 'the person by whom the arrangements necessary for the making of the film are undertaken.'[34] This is the same definition as is used to describe the producer of a sound recording. The question whether a person is a 'producer' of a film or a sound recording is a question of fact.[35] For the most part, there will be few problems in determining who is the producer of a film or a sound recording. Most questions regarding the allocation of ownership of copyright will be dealt with contractually. Problems may arise, however, because the production of sound recordings and films frequently involves the input of a range of different people, many of whom may lay claim to having helped to organize and facilitate the making of the sound recording or the film. Although the term 'producer' is used to define who is the creator, it should be noted that the courts have emphasized that there is a distinction between someone who 'makes' a recording and someone who 'makes the arrangements for the production of a recording': it is the latter who is the author rather than the person who actually records or makes the sound recording or film (the person who operates the recording system).[36]

The notion of the 'producer' presupposes that at the core of the production process there is a person (or more often a company) that coordinates, controls, and organizes the production of the work.[37] It seems that to be a 'producer' a person must exercise some degree of direct

---

multimedia works are now). This position under the 1956 Act and under the 1988 Act, prior to the amendments in 1994, were the same. That is, the author of the film is 'the person by whom the arrangements necessary for the making of the film are undertaken.' However, films begun before 1 Jul. 1994, but completed thereafter are treated as made when completed: Related Rights Regs., r. 25(2). Furthermore, it is not an infringement of any right which the principal director has by virtue of these Regulations to do anything after commencement in pursuance of arrangements for the exploitation of a film made before 19 Nov. 1992: Related Right Regs., r. 36(2).

[32] CDPA ss. 9(2)(ab) and 10(1A).   [33] CDPA s. 105(5).

[34] CDPA s. 178. However, it is unclear whether the term 'principal director' will be treated as narrower than the term 'director' when used in relation to moral rights.

[35] *Beggars Banquet Records v. Carlton TV* [1993] *EMLR* 349, 361; *A & M Records v. Video Collection* [1995] *EMLR* 25, 29.

[36] *Adventure Films v. Tully* [1993] *EMLR* 376; *A & M Records* [1995] *EMLR* 25; *Bamgboye v. Reed* [2004] *EMLR* (5) 61, 84 (para. 77). Kamina says that the definition of producer 'certainly excludes purely creative contributors, including the film director': Kamina, 139.

[37] *See also Century Communications v. Mayfair Entertainment* [1993] *EMLR* 335 (film made under restrictive conditions in China was produced by organizer outside China). For examples of situations where it is difficult to say who, if anyone, is the 'producer' (home movies, wedding videos) see Kamina, 140.

(organizational) control over the process of production.[38] If a person operates at the periphery of the process, such as the person who merely commissions the making of the recording, or merely provides the finance for a film or a sound recording, he or she will not be regarded as a producer. If this were not the case, banks and other lending institutions would qualify as authors. However, provision of finance may be one of the organizational matters that, in combination with others, amount to a 'necessary arrangement.'[39]

2.2.3 Broadcasts

In the case of sound and television broadcasts, the author is the person who makes the broadcast.[40] Where a person receives and immediately retransmits a broadcast, the author is the maker of the original broadcast rather than the person who relays it.

2.2.4 Typographical arrangements

The author of a typographical arrangement of a published edition of a work is the publisher.[41]

2.3 JOINT AUTHORSHIP

Collaborative research and creation is often a fruitful and productive way for authors to work.[42] Copyright recognizes this mode of creation through the notion of joint authorship. A number of important consequences, such as the way the work can be exploited, flow from a work being jointly authored.[43] While joint authorship is normally associated with literary, dramatic, musical, and artistic works, it is possible for any work to be jointly authored. As we saw earlier, the 1988 Act specifically provides that films are treated as works of joint authorship between the principal director and the producer, unless those are the same person.[44] The 1988 Act also extends the concept of joint authorship to a broadcast 'where more than one person is taken as making the broadcast,' namely, those 'providing,' or taking 'responsibility' for the contents of the programme, and those making the 'arrangements necessary for its transmission'.[45] No special definition of joint authorship is applied to sound recordings, or published editions.

In cases other than those special circumstances where joint authorship is deemed, a general principle applies: a work is a work of joint authorship if it is 'a work produced by the collaboration of two or more authors in which the contribution of each author is not distinct from that of the other author or authors.' A work is one of joint authorship if it satisfies three conditions:

(i) First, it is necessary to show that each of the authors *contributed to the making of the work*. In order to render a person a joint author, the contribution must be 'significant' and

---

[38] *Adventure Films v. Tully* [1993] *EMLR* 376.

[39] Ibid. *Beggars Banquet Records v. Carlton TV* [1993] *EMLR* 349 (arguable claim that person who provided finance and arranged access to venue where event was filmed was a person who made arrangements); *Century Communications v. Mayfair Entertainment* [1993] *EMLR* 335 (person had undertaken the arrangements necessary for the production of the film when it initiated the making of the film, organized the activity necessary for making it, and paid for it).

[40] CDPA s. 9(2)(b).   [41] CDPA s. 9(2)(d).

[42] For a discussion of collaboration in the context of universities and the role of copyright, see A. Monotti (with S. Ricketson), *Universities and Intellectual Property: Ownership and Exploitation* (2003).

[43] A joint owner (or other co-owner of copyright) can sue an infringer independently and can also bring an action against another co-owner.

[44] CDPA ss. 9(2)(ab) and 10(1A). Note, however, that the general scheme applies to determine authorship, or co-authorship, of the 'dramatic work': on which, see Kamina, 141–53.

[45] CDPA s. 10(2), cross-referenced to s. 6(3).

'original'.[46] The requirement of originality is easily satisfied: this merely requires that the claimant came up with the contribution as a result of his own skill and effort.[47] The requirement that the contribution be 'significant' has proved more problematic.[48] The better view is that 'significant' here means 'substantial', or 'considerable', or 'non-trivial', rather than 'aesthetically important'.[49] While to be a joint author it is necessary for an author to have made a significant and original contribution to the work, joint authorship does not require that the respective contributions be in equal proportions.[50] However, it does require the contribution to be of the right kind: a contribution to the words of a song will normally give rise to joint authorship of the literary work, but not of the music; and a contribution to the 'performance' of a piece of music will not render the performer a co-author of the musical work.[51] Equally, a contribution to 'interpretation and theatrical presentation' is not to be regarded as a contribution to the creation of a dramatic work.[52]

(ii) The second requirement that must be satisfied for a work to be one of joint authorship is that the work must have been produced through a process of *collaboration* between the authors. This means that, when setting out to create a work, there must have been some common design, cooperation, or plan that united the authors (even if only in a very loose sense).[53] So long as the authors have a shared plan of some sort, there is no need for them to be in close proximity for them to collaborate. Indeed, it is possible for the collaboration to take place over long distances (a practice made much easier because of e-mail).[54] There is no additional requirement that the parties must have intended to create a work of joint authorship.[55] The upshot of this second requirement is that, although two people may work on the same project, unless there is a shared goal they will not be classified as joint authors. This means, for example, that where one person writes a poem and another person translates it into another language, the author of the original poem would not be a joint author of the

[46] *Godfrey v. Lees* [1995] *EMLR* 307, 325–8; *Hadley v. Kemp* [1999] *EMLR* 589; *Brighton v. Jones* [2005] *FSR* (16) 288, para.34. See also *Fylde Microsystems v. Key Radio Systems* [1998] *FSR* 449 (suggestions not sufficient); *Robin Ray v. Classic FM* [1998] *FSR* 622.

[47] *Locksley Brown v. Mcasso Music Production Ltd* [2005] *FSR* (40) 846 para. 42.

[48] One can contrast the decision of *Godfrey v. Lees* [1995] *EMLR* 307 (classically trained musician who acted as orchestral arranger for a rock band was held to be joint author of a number of arrangements which included orchestral passages linking the verses and choruses) with *Hadley v. Kemp* [1999] *EMLR* 589 (contribution of saxophonist, singer, and drummer insufficient to render them co-authors because contributions were just what one would have expected). See A. Barron 'Introduction: harmony or dissonance? Copyright concepts and musical practice,' (2006) 15 *Social and Legal Studies,* 25; L. Bently, 'Authorship of Popular Music in UK Copyright Law' (2008) *Information, Communication and Society*

[49] *Fisher v. Brooker and Onward Music Ltd* [2007] *FSR* (12) 255 (para. 46), where Blackburne J preferred to ask whether the claimant's contribution was 'non-trivial'.

[50] Joint authorship will usually be presumed to lead to equal shares, but this may be varied either by the court, where it feels comfortable evaluating the contributions (as in *Bamgboye v. Reed* [2004] *EMLR* (5) 61, 86 (para. 85) and *Fisher v. Brooker and Onward Music Ltd* [2007] *FSR* (12) 255 (Fisher, author of the organ solo for 'A Whiter Shade of Pale', was awarded a 40 per cent share)).or according to the agreement of the parties: *Beckingham v. Hodgens* [2003] *FSR* 238, 249 (equal shares); *Peter Hayes v. Phonogram Ltd et al.* [2003] *ECDR* (11) 110, 123 ff (agreement as to size of share).

[51] *Peter Hayes v. Phonogram Ltd et al* [2003] *ECDR* (11) 110, 128; *Hadley v. Kemp* [1999] *EMLR* 589, 643. See R. Arnold, 'Are Performers Authors?' [1999] *EIPR* 464. Expert evidence may need to be employed to assist the court in distinguishing between what is the work and what is performance: *Barrett v. Universal Island Records* [2006] *EWHC* 1009 (para 356).

[52] *Brighton v. Jones* [2005] *FSR* (16) 288, para. 56.

[53] *Levy v. Rutley* (1871) LR 6 CP 583; *Cala Homes (South) v. Alfred McAlpine Homes East* [1995] *FSR* 818, 835.

[54] *Cala Homes (South) v. Alfred McAlpine Homes East* [1995] *FSR* 818, 835.

[55] *Beckingham v. Hodgens* [2003] *FSR* 238, 249.

translation. Similarly, where a musician arranges an existing musical work, the author of the original musical piece would not be able to claim joint authorship over the subsequent work: instead, there would be separate copyrights in the two pieces.[56]

(iii) Third, for a work to be jointly authored the respective contributions must not be *distinct* or *separate* from each other. In more positive terms, this means that the contributions must merge to form an integrated whole (rather than a series of distinct works).[57] For example, if the contributions of two authors merged in such a way that no one author is able to point to a substantial part of the work and say 'that is mine,' the authors would be joint authors. If, however, one author wrote the first four chapters of a book and the other author wrote the remaining six chapters, instead of the resulting book being a joint work, the respective authors would have copyright in the particular chapters they wrote.[58] In relation to a more difficult set of facts, it has been held that, where one person added an introduction to the music of a song, this introduction was not 'distinct' because it was 'heavily dependent' on the rest of the tune and because, by itself, it would 'sound odd and lose meaning.'[59]

3 FIRST OWNERSHIP

Authorship and ownership have long been closely intertwined in copyright law. Indeed, one of the notable features of the 1710 Statute of Anne was that it recognized authors as first owners of the literary property they created. This basic formula is repeated in the 1988 Act which declares that the author of a work is the first owner of copyright.[60] The rule that copyright initially vests in the author is, however, subject to a number of exceptions. The first and most important concerns works made by employees.[61] Exceptions also exist in relation to Crown copyright, Parliamentary copyright, and to works created by officers of international organizations.[62] Judicially originated exceptions also exist where a work is created in breach of a fiduciary duty or in breach of confidence.

Before looking at these in more detail, it is important to note that, although the author is usually the first owner, it is possible for an author to assign his or her copyright to third parties. This means that the question of who is the copyright owner at any particular point of time will depend upon what has happened to the copyright since it was first created. Since valid agreements can be made in relation to the transfer of future copyright, it may be that, when copyright arises, the first owner of copyright under the statutory scheme is immediately divested of their rights in favour of an assignee. It is also important to note that, while the law

[56] *Chappell v. Redwood Music* [1981] *RPC* 337. Cf. *Godfrey v. Lees* [1995] *EMLR* 307, where the claimant who provided orchestral arrangements of Barclay James Harvest's existing songs was treated as a co-author; and *Beckingham v. Hodgens* [2003] *FSR* 238, where the session musician who added an introduction to the song 'Young at Heart' was held to own 50 per cent of the copyright in the new arrangement. It seems that, where the author of a song collaborates in a new arrangement thereof, they acquire co-ownership of the arrangement even where they contribute nothing new.

[57] In this respect, the British notion of co-authorship differs from that of the United States, Belgium, and France where separable but interdependent elements can form joint works, such as songs, operas, and motion pictures. In France, for example, the author of a novel which is used as the basis of an audiovisual work is treated as an author of the audiovisual work.

[58] CDPA s. 10(1).

[59] *Beckingham v. Hodgens* [2003] FSR 238, 248. In any case, the introductory fiddle music was repeated a number of times elsewhere in the arrangement. Cf. *Hadley v. Kemp* [1999] *EMLR* 589, where Park J suggested that a saxophone solo in the middle of Spandau Ballet's 'Gold' might be a distinct work.

[60] CDPA s. 11(1).   [61] CDPA s. 11(2).   [62] CDPA s. 11(3).

recognizes that a person other than the author may be first owner, the question of who is the author remains a distinct one (and an important one). A work made by an employee author, for example, has a duration dependent on the life of the author (i.e. the employee) even if first ownership vests in the employer. Equally, issues of qualification and moral rights are determined by reference to authorship (not first ownership).

3.1 WORKS CREATED BY EMPLOYEES

Section 11(2) of the 1988 Act provides that, in the absence of an agreement to the contrary, where a literary, dramatic, musical, or artistic work, or a film is made in the course of employment, the employer is the first owner of any copyright in the work.[63] While employees retain moral rights in the works they create, these are subject to a number of limitations.[64]

Critics have suggested that, by granting first ownership of works made by employees to employers, British law fails to provide creators with sufficient additional incentives to create. It is also said that British law also fails to acknowledge the natural rights which employee-authors have in their creations. In so doing, it is said that British law fails to follow the underlying rationales for copyright. In response to arguments of this sort, it is suggested that, while employers might not create works, they provide the facilities and materials that enable the act of creation to take place. In so doing, they make an important contribution to the production of new works. It is argued that granting first ownership to employers encourages employers to invest in the infrastructure that supports creators. As employers are often in a better position than employees to exploit the copyright in a work, it is also suggested that it makes more sense to give copyright to employers than to employees. Another argument in favour of giving ownership to employers is that, in the absence of a provision that formally granted first ownership to employers, employers would require employees to assign their copyright to them. As section 11(2) achieves what would otherwise happen in practice, it thus serves to reduce transaction costs. In response to the argument that, in granting first ownership to employers, employees are not properly rewarded for their creative efforts, it is suggested that employees are rewarded through other means, such as pay, continued employment, and promotion.[65]

However problematic may be the arguments in favour of granting first ownership of employee works to employers, they have dominated policy changes that have been made in this area. In particular, while under the Copyright Act 1956 employee journalists presumptively shared copyright with the newspapers, this 'anomaly' was removed in the 1988 Act.[66] As a result, under the current law copyright in all works made in the course of employment belongs to the employer (unless there is an agreement to the contrary).

For an employer to be first owner of copyright it is necessary to show that (i) the literary, dramatic, musical, artistic work, or film was made by an employee; (ii) the work was made in

---

[63] In the USA, related, but distinct principles operate in relation to so-called 'works made for hire.' On the history, see C. Fisk, 'Authors at Work: The Origins of the Work for Hire Doctrine' (2003) 15 *Yale Journal of Law & Humanities* 1.

[64] CDPA s. 79(3) and s. 82.

[65] The Whitford Committee considered whether a scheme should be implemented, such as that which exists under the Patents Act, providing for extra reward for particularly successful works.

[66] More specifically, under the previous law, copyright in a work made by an author in the course of employment by the daily or periodical press presumptively vested in the employer for purposes of its publication in the newspaper or periodical. CA 1956 s. 4(2).

the course of employment; and (iii) there is no agreement to the contrary.[67] We will deal with each of these in turn.

3.1.1 Who is an employee?

An employee is defined in the 1988 Act as a person who is employed under a contract of service or apprenticeship.[68] A contract of service is frequently distinguished from a contract for services. In general, it is easy to determine whether someone is an employee or not. However, there are many different sorts of work relationship, some of which are less easy to designate as employment relations. In such situations the courts tend to focus on whether there is the so-called 'irreducible minimum' necessary to give rise to an employment relation: namely 'mutuality of obligation' and 'control'. If these two factors are present the relationship might be one of employment: if they are not present, it is not. However, these factors are not of themselves conclusive. The court will examine all other relevant aspects and provisions to establish whether they are consistent with a contract of service.

(i) *'Mutuality of obligation'* In an employment relation the employer undertakes and is bound to provide work and pay, the employee to provide their labour. In other sorts of relationship there is not necessarily such mutuality. Consequently, if no such mutuality exists, there is no employment.[69] So, for example, an arrangement whereby an artist carries out work for an advertising agency will not amount to an employment relationship if the agency is free to offer any work to others, and the artist is free to refuse the work requested by the agency (for example where the artist is working on a job for another agency).

(ii) *Control.* The second aspect of the irreducible minimum is that one party (the employer) must be capable of exercising control over the other (the employee).[70] The more control one party is able to wield, the more likely it is that the parties are in an employment relationship. The control test is regarded as relevant even though there are many professions ('from surgeons to research scientists') where a person has a considerable amount of freedom, but nonetheless is ordinarily regarded as an employee. In these circumstances the courts have stressed that the question whether someone is an employee depends on whether there is 'sufficient framework of control'. Thus, even where a person is not under a great degree of supervision, they still may be an employee.[71]

If the irreducible minimum is present, the tribunal will then consider all other factors. One important, but not determinative consideration is the descriptions used (such as 'independent contractor'). Other factors which suggest that someone is not an employee include the fact that they have a great deal of responsibility, provide their own equipment, hire their own helpers, take financial risks, have other commitments, and have the opportunity of profiting from the tasks they perform.[72] The courts will also look at the way financial arrangements between the parties are organized as a way of determining whether someone is an employee. Factors which indicate that someone is an employee include the fact that they are paid wages; that income

---

[67] While the 1988 Act introduced changes on point, effective from 1 Aug. 1989, the initial ownership of copyright continues generally to be determined by the law in effect when the materials in question were made. CDPA, Sched. 1, para. 11.

[68] CDPA s. 178.   [69] *Carmichael v. National Power plc* [1999] 4 *All ER* 897 (HL).

[70] *Ready Mixed Concrete (South East) Ltd v. Minister of Pensions and National Insurance* [1968] 2 *QB* 497; *Montgomery v. Johnson Underwood* [2001] *ICR* 819.

[71] See *Stevenson Jordan v. McDonnell & Evans* (1952) 69 *RPC* 10, 22 (Denning LJ).

[72] *Robin Ray v. Classic FM* [1998] *FSR* 622.

tax deductions are made on the 'Pay-As-You-Earn' basis; and that both parties contribute to pension schemes and make National Insurance payments.[73]

3.1.2 Was the work made in the course of employment?

In order for an employer to be first owner of copyright, it is also necessary to show that the work was made in 'the course of the employment.' Even though an author is an employee, if the work was not created in the course of employment, the author retains ownership of copyright. The question whether a work has been made in the course of employment will depend on the particular circumstances of the case in hand.

An important factor which has influenced the courts when determining if a work has been made in the course of employment is whether the making of the work falls within the types of activity that an employer could reasonably expect or demand from an employer. In turn, this depends on the scope of the employee's duties. This can be seen, for example, in *Stevenson Jordan v. MacDonnell*,[74] where the question arose as to whether an accountant or his employer (a firm of management consultants) owned copyright in a series of public lectures the account-ant had given about the budgetary control of businesses. Morris LJ noted that the employer had paid the expenses of the lecturers, that the employee-accountant could have prepared the lectures in the company's time, used its library, had the lectures typed up by company sec-retaries, and that the lectures were a useful accessory to his contracted work.[75] Nonetheless, Morris LJ found that, since it was not shown that the accountant could have been *ordered* to write and deliver the lectures, they were not created in the course of his employment. As such, the copyright belonged to the employee rather than to the employer.

Similar reasoning was also applied in *Noah v. Shuba*.[76] This was a copyright infringement action in relation to a book called *A Guide to Hygienic Skin Piercing*, written by the claimant, Dr Noah. During the proceedings it was argued that when Dr Noah wrote the guide he was employed as a consultant epidemiologist at the Public Health Laboratory Service. As such, the copyright vested in his employer.[77] While there was no doubt that Dr Noah was an employee of the Public Health Laboratory, it was less clear as to whether the guide had been written in the course of his employment. Dr Noah discussed his work with colleagues, made use of the serv-ices of the Public Health Laboratory Service library, and had the manuscript typed up by his secretary. In addition, the guide was published by the Public Health Laboratory Service at its own expense. Nonetheless, Mummery J held that the guide had not been written in the course of Noah's employment. An important factor that influenced this decision was that Dr Noah had written the draft at home in the evenings and at weekends.

It should be pointed out that the mere fact that a work is made at home, or that the employee makes use of their personal resources, does not necessarily mean that it will fall outside the scope of the employee's duties. Ultimately, the question whether a work is made within the scope

---

[73] In *Lee Ting Sang v. Chung Chi Keung* [1990] 2 *AC* 374, the Privy Council approved of the 'indicia' approach in *Market Investigations v. Minister for Social Security* [1969] 2 *QB* 173, without referring to the 'irreducible minimum.' See also *Todd v. Adams and Chope* [2002] 2 *Lloyds Rep* 293 (CA, refusing to find an employment relationship where there was sharing of profits and losses of fishing trips).

[74] *Stevenson Jordan v. McDonald & Evans* (1952) 69 *RPC* 10. However, a journalist who wrote a confiden-tial memorandum to colleagues about a possible article was acting in the course of her employment: *Beloff v. Pressdram* [1973] 1 *All ER* 241.

[75] In *Byrne v. Statist* [1914] 1 *KB* 622, a journalist made a translation to be used in the newspaper in his own time: this was not in the course of his employment.

[76] [1991] *FSR* 14.   [77] *Noah v. Shuba* [1991] *FSR* 14.

of employment depends upon the contract of employment. This can be seen in *Missing Link Software v. Magee*,[78] where the question arose as to whether software written by an employee outside work time and on his own equipment was created in the course of his employment and thus copyright in it owned by his employer. The claimant company argued that, since they had employed the defendant to write programs of the kind in dispute, similar programs, even if written in his spare time, were created in the course of his employment. The court held that, although the employee had written the software in his own time and on his own equipment, nonetheless it was not unarguable that, as it fell within the scope of the tasks he was employed to carry out, the computer programs were created within the course of his employment.

3.1.3 Agreements to the contrary

Finally, it should be noted that the copyright in works made in the course of employment will not be treated as belonging to the employer where there is an agreement to the contrary. Such an agreement may be written or oral, express, or implied.[79]

In some cases, such agreements have been implied from custom. For example, in *Noah v. Shuba* Mummery J said that if the skin-piercing guide had been written in the course of Dr Noah's employment, he would nonetheless have implied a term into Dr Noah's contract that the copyright remained with the employee.[80] The reason for this was the Public Health Laboratory Service's long-standing practice of allowing its employees to act as if they owned copyright in their works: they allowed employees to assign copyright to publishers, claim royalties, and with respect to the case itself, did not assert that they owned copyright. This decision has important ramifications where employers allow employees to act as if they own copyright (whereas in fact they may not).

3.2 CROWN COPYRIGHT

Another exception to the general rule that the author is the first owner relates to works governed by Crown copyright. Where a work is made by an officer or servant of the Crown in the course of their duties,[81] copyright in the work belongs to the Crown and not to the author of the work.[82]

3.3 PARLIAMENTARY COPYRIGHT

Where a work is made under the direction or control of the House of Commons or the House of Lords, the respective House owns copyright therein.[83] Such Parliamentary copyright lasts for 50 years from the year in which the work was made. All Bills introduced into

---

[78] [1989] *FSR* 361.

[79] As we will see there is a general requirement that assignments of copyright be in writing. However, such formality is unnecessary with respect to the agreement reversing the presumption of initial ownership, which can be oral or implied. But to refer to a relationship as not being one of employment was not an implied agreement that copyright was to vest in the employee: *Robin Ray v. Classic FM* [1998] *FSR* 622.

[80] *Noah v. Shuba* [1991] *FSR* 14.   [81] CDPA ss. 163, 164.

[82] CDPA s. 163. It lasts for 125 years from when the work is made or 50 years from its commercial publication. Crown copyright also exists in all Acts of Parliament and Measures of the General Synod of the Church of England.

[83] CDPA s. 164. The Government of Wales Act 1998, Sched. 12, has added to this list: 'any sound recording, film, or live broadcast of the National Assembly for Wales which is made by or under the direction or control of the Assembly.'

Parliament attract Parliamentary copyright, but this ceases on Royal Assent, withdrawal, or rejection of the Bill.[84]

3.4 INTERNATIONAL ORGANIZATIONS

Where a literary, dramatic, musical, or artistic work is made by an officer or employee of an 'international organization',[85] the organization is the first owner of the resulting copyright.[86]

3.5 COMMISSIONED WORKS AND EQUITABLE ASSIGNMENT

Another exception to the general rule that the author is first owner arises, in limited circumstances, where a person commissions someone to make a work. Under the Copyright, Designs and Patents Act 1988, copyright in a commissioned work belongs to the author of the commissioned work.[87] However, in certain circumstances the courts may infer that an independent contractor is subject to an implied obligation to assign the copyright to the commissioner. This may give rise to a trust with respect to the copyright in the commissioned work, and render the commissioner the equitable owner. A good example is provided by *Griggs v. Raben Footwear,* where Griggs, distributors of DR. MARTEN'S AIRWAIR, in 1988 commissioned the advertising agency, Jordan, to produce a logo for it.[88] Evans, who did freelance work for Jordan, produced the logo and was paid at his standard rate of £15 an hour. Nothing was said about copyright in the logo. In 2002, Evans purported to assign copyright in the artistic work to Raben Footwear, an Australian competitor of Griggs. In response, Griggs brought an action seeking a declaration that it was beneficial owner of copyright, and an assignment of legal title. Peter Prescott QC, sitting as Deputy High Court judge, granted the relief sought. He held that, while Evans was the author, and first owner of the legal title, an agreement that copyright was to belong to Griggs was to be implied. Such an agreements was necessary to give business efficacy to the arrangement, under which it was clearly contemplated that Griggs would be able to use the logo and stop others from using it.[89] This could only be achieved if the implied agreement was to assign the copyright or give a perpetual exclusive licence (and the latter solution would be less convenient for Evans). The Court of Appeal affirmed.

---

[84] CDPA ss. 165–7.

[85] This means an organization the members of which include one or more states: CDPA s. 178.

[86] CDPA s. 168.

[87] Under the 1956 Act, a party commissioning a photograph, portrait, or engraving for value presumptively acquired copyright in that work: CA 1956 s. 4(3), Sched. 8, para. 1(a). When this position was changed in the 1988 Act, commissioners of photographers and films for private and domestic purposes were 'compensated' with the so-called 'moral' right of 'privacy': CDPA s. 85. The right covers issuing of copies of the work to the public, its exhibition in public, and its communication to the public.

[88] *R. Griggs Group v. Raben Footwear* [2004] *FSR* (31) 673; [2005] *FSR* (31) 706 (CA). This decision is remarkable in two respects. First, because the implied assignment is in favour of a third party, Griggs, rather than the design company, Jordan. The more orthodox (if artificial) view would be that there are two implied agreements: one between Jordan and Evans, and another between Griggs and Jordan. The distinction would have been important if, for example, Jordan had decided the logo supplied by Evans was unsuitable. Second, the agreement to assign is implied in this case even though Evans did not know of the use intended by Griggs, Evans thinking the use was for point-of-sale only. The judge seems to have ignored this on the ground that Evans was 'indifferent' to the use, and had he known he would have accepted the more extensive use without charging a different fee.

[89] Para. 57.

Implied agreements to assign have also been found where a choreographer undertook to arrange certain dances for the Russian ballet;[90] a design of a trade mark was produced;[91] a person upgraded a previous version of a computer program;[92] and a person arranged for the making of a sound recording.[93] These decisions amount to judicial variations of a clear legislative scheme. Clearly, the judges are looking at transactions after the event, and are motivated by gut feelings of justice to prevent opportunistic behaviour by creators. However, the impact of the decisions is to undermine a clear scheme which is designed both to achieve certainty in transactions and to protect authors. It does so by requiring parties to allocate ownership through written assignments and in so doing requires those acquiring rights to specify what they want, thus giving authors an opportunity to reflect upon whether they wish to transfer all those rights. Under that scheme, the penalty for those commissioners who fail to organize their legal rights properly, is that they risk having to bargain for them later. The courts, by repeatedly responding to their sense that rights should follow money, remove this 'penalty' and, with it, undermine the goals that the statutory scheme aims to achieve. The better view is that these cases should be confined to their specific facts.[94]

3.6 BREACH OF CONFIDENCE

It also seems that copyright in works that are created in breach of a fiduciary duty or in breach of confidence will be held on constructive trust for the person to whom the duty was owed.[95] The same may be true of works made 'in circumstances involving the invasion of legal or equitable rights of the [claimant] or breach of the obligation of the maker to the [claimant].'[96]

4 HARMONIZATION

Questions of authorship, and the position of employed authors, are matters on which there has been little harmonization. As we have already noted, the issue was tackled, but only partially, in relation to films, by stating that the director is to be regarded as one of the authors of a cinematographic work. The only other harmonization has been in respect of the position of

---

[90] *Massine v. De Basil* [1936–45] *MacG CC* 223. See also *Brighton v. Jones* [2005] *FSR* (16) 288 (paras 57–8) (contributions of director to play were made on behalf of theatre, and so director was unable to claim copyright therein).

[91] *Auvi Trade Mark* [1995] *FSR* 288; *R. Griggs Group v. Raben Footwear* (2 Dec. 2003) [2003] *EWHC* 2914.

[92] *Flanders v. Richardson* [1993] *FSR* 497, 516–19, Ferris J held that where a computer program was improved, in circumstances where there was an acceptance or understanding that the plaintiff owned all the rights in the program, the court would hold the plaintiff to be the copyright owner. (Ferris J relied on *Massine v. De Basil* [1936–45] *MacG CC* 223.)

[93] *A & M Records v. Video Collection* [1995] *EMLR* 25.

[94] For example, *Saphena Computing v. Allied Collection Agencies* [1995] *FSR* 616, distinguishing *Warner v. Gestetner* [1988] *EIPR* D–89.

[95] *A-G v. Guardian (No. 2)* [1990] *AC* 109, 263, 276. Insofar as the constructive trust analysis is adopted there is no obvious reason why the analysis should be restricted to cases of breach of duties owed to the Crown. See *Ultraframe UK v. Clayton (No. 2)* [2003] *EWCA Civ* 1805 (director held unregistered design rights on trust for company). See below at pp. 1064–5.

[96] *Australian Broadcasting Corp v. Lenah Game Meats Pty. Ltd* (2001) 208 *CLR* 199 *per* Gummow and Hayne JJ at paras. 101–2 and *per* Callinan J at para. 309.

authors who create computer programs while employed: the Computer Programs Directive requires that the employer exclusively shall be entitled to exercise all economic rights in programs so created. Although differences in the rules operated by member states may lead to different conclusions as to who is an author or owner of a particular copyright work, it seems unlikely that the Commission will attempt harmonization in the near future. This is because these rules raise thorny political issues which go well beyond the field of copyright, in particular touching on national traditions as regards labour relations.

6

NATURE OF THE RIGHTS

CHAPTER CONTENTS

1 INTRODUCTION

This chapter is concerned with the rights that the law confers on the copyright owner. The scope of these rights is important insofar as it determines the types of activity which, unless done with the copyright owner's consent, amount to an infringement of the owner's copyright.

One of the most consistent themes in the history of copyright law is that the types of activity that have fallen within the copyright owner's control have steadily expanded. For example, the 1710 Statute of Anne conferred on authors and proprietors of books the limited right to 'print and reprint' those books. In the early nineteenth century, the copyright owner's monopoly as regards musical and dramatic works was extended to cover not only the reprinting of the work, but also the public representation of the work. In 1911, the reproduction right was expanded from the right to print and reprint to the right to 'copy,' which included copying in different dimensions. The same reforms conferred the right to 'adapt' a work, that is, a right to prevent translation and conversion into dramatic forms of literary works and arrangements of musical works. With the advent of broadcasting, the copyright owner's right was interpreted as covering broadcasting, and in 1956 a specific broadcasting right was added to the copyright owner's rights. Since then, further rights to distribute, rent, and lend copies have also been added, and the 'broadcasting right' has been transformed into a right to communicate a work to the public.[1] While the copyright owner is able to control the use that can be made of the work in many circumstances, there are still some that do not fall within the owner's control. If we take the case of the rights in a book, for example, the copyright owner is not able, at least yet, to control reading, browsing, or resale of the book.

For the most part, the rights have developed in a piecemeal way in response to external pressures: notably to technological change. As well as producing a complicated and illogical system of rights, the cumulative and reactionary way in which the rights have developed has also led to a degree of overlap between them.[2] While the expansion of the rights granted to the copyright owner has continued with the implementation of the Information Society Directive,[3] there have been growing signs that members of the judiciary are becoming suspicious about the over-expansion of copyright and the dangers that this poses for users and consumers of copyright.[4] What effect this will have upon copyright infringement has yet to be seen, though it might mean that the tendency to interpret the rights in favour of copyright owners may decline.[5]

The primary rights that are currently granted to copyright owners are set out in sections 16–21 of the 1988 Act. Anyone who carries out any of these activities, or authorizes some-one else to carry out these activities, is liable for primary infringement. This will not be the case, however, if the defendant has the permission of the copyright owner or can show that the activity falls within one of the defences available to them. While the nature of the rights which are granted varies according to the type of work in question, these include the exclusive right to:

(i) copy the work (reproduction right);

(ii) issue copies of the work to the public (distribution right);

(iii) rent or lend the work to the public (rental or lending right);

(iv) perform, show, or play the work in public (public performance right);

(v) communicate the work to the public;

(vi) make an adaptation of the work, or do any of the above acts in relation to an adaptation (right of adaptation); or

(vii) authorize others to carry out any of these activities.

It should be noted that the particular rights that are granted to copyright owners vary depending on the type of work which is protected.[6] In particular, while the right of repro-duction and the right to issue copies of the work to the public exist in relation to all types of work, the other rights only apply to certain of them. For example, the performing right

---

[1] As from Oct. 31, 2003 as a result of Copyright and Related Rights Regulations 2003 SI 2003/2498 implementation of Info. Soc. Dir., Art. 3.

[2] For example, between the right of reproduction and the right of adaptation.

[3] Copyright and Related Rights Regulations 2003 SI 2003/2498.

[4] H. Laddie, 'Copyright: Over-Strength, Over-Regulated, Over-Rated?' [1996] 5 *EIPR* 253; A. Mason, 'Developments in the Law of Copyright and Public Access to Information' [1997] *EIPR* 636.

[5] On previous tendencies to interpret rights broadly in favour of authors see, e.g. *Gambart v. Ball* (1863) 14 *CB (NS)* 306; *Harms v. Martans* [1927] 1 *Ch* 526, 534; *Messager v. BBC* [1927] 2 *KB* 543, 548–9.

[6] The rights, as we will see, are ultimately divisible according to convenience. Thus terms such as 'mechanical rights' and 'synchronization rights' have no place in CDPA s. 16. The mechanical copyright refers to a musical copyright owner's right to make a sound recording and is simply an example of the reproduction right. The synchronization right refers to the right to incorporate a record into a film soundtrack.

Table 6.1 Rights

Works	To copy the work (s. 17)	To issue copies of the work to the public (s. 18)	To rent or lend the work (s. 18A)	To perform or show the work in public (s. 19)	To communicate the work to the public (s. 20)	To make an adaptation (s. 21)
Literary, dramatic, and musical	✓	✓	✓	✓	✓	✓
Artistic	✓	✓	✓ (but not building/ applied art)	NO	✓	NO
Film	✓	✓	✓	✓	✓	NO
Sound recordings	✓	✓	✓	✓	✓	NO
Broadcasts	✓	✓	NO	✓	✓	NO
Typographical	✓	✓	NO	NO	NO	NO

applies to all works except artistic works and typographical arrangements; the right to communicate the work to the public applies to all works except typographical arrangements; and the right to make an adaptation of a work only applies to literary, dramatic, or musical works. Care must be taken to check which rights a copyright owner is given by the 1988 Act.

One of the key features of the restricted activities found in sections 16–21 is that they are based on a notion of strict liability. This means that the state of mind of the defendant is not relevant when determining whether an infringement has taken place. As such, it does not matter if a defendant knew that the work was protected by copyright or that the claimant owned the work. Nor does it matter that the defendant incorrectly believed that they had permission to copy the work. All that matters, at least in relation to primary infringement, is that the defendant copied the claimant's work. It should be noted that while the defendant's innocence is not a relevant factor in determining whether they have infringed copyright, it may be relevant when damages are being determined.[7]

In addition to the primary rights set out in sections 16–21, the 1988 Act also provides copyright owners with the ability to protect against secondary infringements (sections 22–6). A defendant may be liable for secondary infringement if, in the commercial exploitation of copies or articles specifically adapted to make copies, the defendant knew or had reason to believe that the copies were or would be infringements when made.[8] We deal with secondary infringement in Chapter 8.[9]

---

[7] CDPA s. 97(1). See below at p. 1117.   [8] CDPA ss. 22–4, 27. See Laddie *et al.*, ch. 10.
[9] See below at Ch. 8, Section 6.

2 THE RIGHT TO COPY THE WORK: THE RIGHT OF REPRODUCTION

The first and best-known right given to copyright owners is the right to copy the work (section 17).[10] The right to copy the work is the oldest of the rights granted to owners of copyright. While the right applies to all works, the scope of the right varies depending on the type of work in question. Having said that, one factor that is common to all works is that infringement takes place whether the copy is permanent, transient, temporary, or incidental to some other use of the work.[11] This means a person will infringe (absent a defence) when they reproduce a copyright work on a computer screen, or store it in computer memory, as much as when they copy the work from disk to disk. Activities associated with the internet, such as 'framing' (taking material from one site and placing it on another, though reframed with the latter's get-up) will be straightforward cases of copying. So will unauthorized acts of up-loading on to sites, or down-loading from peer-to-peer systems like Napster. The problems posed by the internet for copyright holders are, in essence, ones of detection and enforcement rather than absence of liability.

2.1 LITERARY, DRAMATIC, MUSICAL, AND ARTISTIC WORKS

When the 1710 Statute of Anne first granted copyright to books, the right was limited to the right to print and reprint copies of those books. Within a relatively short period of time, it became clear that if the rights of the copyright owner were limited to situations where the work was copied identically, it would undermine the value of the property. It would fail, for example, to protect an owner against someone making minor changes to the work (thus rendering the 'copied' work non-identical). In order to protect against such uses, the scope of copyright protection was expanded to include non-identical or 'colourable' copying. Even so, the emergence of new practices of replication, use, and distribution of works (which were often but not always linked to new technologies) has repeatedly given rise to doubts about what amounts to a reproduction. Some of these doubts were resolved in a straightforward manner. For example, photographic reproduction was readily treated as equivalent to reprinting.[12] On other occasions, however, it has been more difficult to accommodate the new uses within the existing conceptions of reproduction. For example, at the turn of the twentieth century it was held that a phonographic record was not a copy of sheet music for the purposes of the Literary Copyright Act 1842.[13] Similarly, the courts have held that the making of *tableaux vivants* (which is the practice of performers dressing up as characters from paintings so as to produce a 'live version' of the painting), did not amount to an infringement of the copyright in the painting.[14]

---

[10] It is called the 'Crown right' in Reinbothe and von Lewinski (2002) 312. For an argument that it should be jettisoned, in favour of a general right to control commercial exploitation, see J. Litman, *Digital Copyright* (2001), 180 ff.

[11] CDPA s. 17(6). *R v. Higgs* [2008] *EWCA Civ* 1324 (para. 9) (RAM copies of computer games generated when game is played are infringing). See Information Society Directive, Arts. 2 and 5 (certain temporary acts are to be deemed to be non-infringing).

[12] For example, *Gambart v. Ball* (1863) 14 *CB (NS)* 306; *Boosey v. Whight* [1900] 1 *Ch* 122, 123.

[13] *Newmark v. The National Phonograph Company Ltd* (1907) 23 *TLR* 439.

[14] *Hanfstaengl v. Empire Palace* [1894] 2 *Ch* 1; but after 1911 see *Bradbury Agnew v. Day* (1916) 32 *TLR* 349.

The 1988 Act attempts to minimize these kind of difficulties by using a technologically neutral concept of reproduction. This is reflected in the fact that, in relation to literary, dramatic, musical, and artistic works, copying means 'reproducing the work in any material form.'[15] This means that, as well as protecting owners against identical copying of the work (such as where a book is reprinted), a defendant may still infringe where they make a non-identical copy of a literary, dramatic, musical, or artistic work. In these instances the question arises: how different from the 'original' work can a copy be and still infringe?

The 1988 Act provides some guidance in this matter. It states, for example, that reproduction includes storing the work in any medium by electronic means. This means that the storing of a work on a computer amounts to a reproduction in material form. In relation to artistic works, the 1988 Act indicates that a person will reproduce a work if there is a change of dimensions. This means that photographing a sculpture, and making a car exhaust pipe from a design drawing, will be reproductions.[16]

Beyond the specific examples listed in the 1988 Act, the question of how different a copied work can be from the 'original' work and still infringe is a question decided by the courts on the particular facts of the case. It is clear that a photocopy of a book,[17] an engraving of a painting, a painting of a photograph, and a sound recording of a song are (potentially) reproductions.[18] Beyond this, it is impossible to predict in advance the exact point at which the translation of a work from one format into another will be treated as a 'reproduction.' It seems highly likely that the conversion of a work into digital form—from symbols perceptible and understandable to the senses into series of ones and noughts—will be treated as a reproduction.[19]

While copyright owners are protected against change of form in a wide variety of situations, nonetheless there are limits to the scope of the protection. In particular, the courts have stated that, in order to infringe, the derived form must be 'objectively similar' to the copyright work.[20] The requirement of objective similarity means that, to infringe, the relevant part of the defendant's work must be a copy or representation of the whole or part of the original work.[21] The question of whether the defendant's work is objectively similar to the copyright work has arisen in two situations: both concerned with infringement of literary copyrights.

The first is where the copyright work consists of *instructions* how to make or do something. While literary copyright in the instructions will be infringed if the instructions are photocopied or are repeated in different words,[22] the copyright will not be infringed where someone follows the instructions. Thus a person will not infringe the literary copyright in a recipe if they follow the instructions and bake a cake to the recipe.[23] This is because what is protected is the literary effort in creating the recipe as a work of information and not the cake *per se*.

---

[15] CDPA s. 17(2).   [16] CDPA s. 17(3).

[17] *Norowzian v. Arks* [1998] *FSR* 394, 398 ('copying of a book is not restricted to simply photocopying the pages from the book but extends to writing the work, retyping it any form whatsoever, dictating it into a tape machine or any other means of reproducing the work in a material form').

[18] *Bauman v. Fussell* [1978] *RPC* 485. However, it has been held that where someone follows the instructions on a knitting pattern so as to make up a jumper this is not a reproduction. This was because the pattern and jumper were not objectively similar.

[19] *Autospin (Oil Seals) v. Beehive Spinning (A Firm)* [1995] *RPC* 683, 698. (If a literary work precisely defines the shape of an article, copyright may be infringed by making the article or copying it.)

[20] *Francis Day Hunter v. Bron* [1963] *Ch* 587, 623.

[21] *Brigid Foley v. Ellot* [1982] *RPC* 433 (Megarry VC).

[22] *Elanco v. Mandops* [1980] *RPC* 213. See also *M.S. Associates v. Power* [1988] *FSR* 242 (interlocutory proceeding for alleged infringement of computer program).

[23] *Davis (J. & S.) Holdings v. Wright Health Group* [1988] *RPC* 403, 414. *Autospin (Oil Seals) v. Beehive Spinning* [1995] *RPC* 683, 698.

Similarly, a person who knits clothes according to a knitting guide does not infringe copyright in the guide.[24]

The need for objective similarity is also important where the copyright work *describes* something. As with instructional works, the key issue here is: when is a description replicated? While copyright in the literary work will be infringed if the work is photocopied, the position is less clear where someone makes or uses the object that has been described in a two-dimensional format. The problem has become acute with developments in computer-aided design (CAD) which mean that it is now 'possible to define any shape in words and letters. Therefore a design in a drawing can be defined equally accurately in non-graphic notation. In fact many three-dimensional articles are now designed on computers. A literary work consisting of computer code therefore represents the three-dimensional article.'[25]

The question of the protection available to a descriptive literary work was considered by Pumfrey J in *Sandman v. Panasonic*.[26] This was a copyright infringement action brought in respect of two circuit diagrams that were included in an article published in the journal *Wireless World*. The claimant argued that the copyright that existed in the two-dimensional literary work was infringed when the deign was made into a three-dimensional circuit and incorporated into amplifiers, CD players, radio tuners, and cassette decks.

Pumfrey J began by noting that the chief problem confronting the claimant was Lord Oliver's comment in *Interlego* that protection for change of form from 2D to 3D was limited to artistic works. On the strength of this Pumfrey J said that there may appear to be 'no way out of this difficulty, if one accepts that a literary-work is two-dimensional.' Pumfrey J went on to say, however, that 'I suspect that the proper answer is that the circuit itself is a reproduction because it still contains all the literary content of the literary work, albeit in a form which would require analysis for it to be extracted.'[27] That is, Pumfrey J accepted that in certain circumstances a two-dimensional literary work that described something could be reproduced in a three-dimensional form.

Two points are pertinent here. The first is that it is necessary to distinguish between factual and non-factual descriptions. The reason for this is that it is much more likely that a (factual) description written by an engineer would be protected than a description written by a novelist or a poet. It is unlikely that the copyright in a novel that describes a particular scene will ever be infringed when someone draws it.[28] The second is that it seems that a literary work that describes something will only provide protection against a 'reproduction' of the work where the description is very detailed. Thus, someone may infringe where they make a three-dimensional article from a data file in a computer (a literary work) which *precisely defines* the shape of the article.[29] By limiting protection to situations where the object is precisely defined, this means that the problem of inhibiting creation in the same area is avoided.

2.2 SOUND RECORDINGS AND FILMS

The definition of 'reproduction' used in relation to films and sound recordings is narrower than in relation to literary, dramatic, musical, and artistic works. As we saw earlier,

---

[24] *Brigid Foley v. Ellot* [1982] *RPC* 433 ('there is no reproduction of the words and numerals in the knitting guides in the knitted garments produced by following the instructions'). *Autospin (Oil Seals) v. Beehive Spinning* [1995] *RPC* 683, 701. (No infringement of the claimant's charts for calculating the dimension of oil seals when using them to make such oil seals.)

[25] *Autospin (Oil Seals) v. Beehive Spinning* [1995] *RPC* 683, 698. [26] [1998] *FSR* 651. [27] Ibid.

[28] Laddie *et al.*, para. 7–38. [29] *Autospin (Oil Seals) v. Beehive Spinning* [1995] *RPC* 683, 701.

entrepreneurial works (which are seen as the products more of investment than of creativity) are given a 'thinner' protection than is given to authorial works.[30] This is reflected in the fact that the scope of the reproduction right is inextricably linked to the way the particular work is defined.[31] Sound recordings are defined as the 'recording of sounds from which the sounds may be reproduced'.[32] Consequently, what is protected in relation to sound recordings is not the content *per se*—the song, storyline, plot, or language—or the music or lyrics (which are protected, if at all, as authorial works). Instead, copyright protects the recording of these sounds.[33] Similarly, because a film is defined as a recording on a medium from which a moving image may be produced, the courts have held that film copyright protects the recording of the image (rather than the image itself).[34]

One of the consequences of reproduction being defined very narrowly is that copyright in a sound recording of a speech is not infringed where a person transcribes the speech. Similarly, copyright in a film is not infringed when somebody writes a description of the film, or stages a play replicating events in the film. Moreover, there is no reproduction where a person records contents of a similar nature or style to those embodied on the claimant's (film or sound) recording.[35] Likewise, the reshooting of a film sequence (in which not a single frame of the copyright film had been included) was held not to be a copy for the purpose of the 1988 Act.[36] This is the case even if the second film closely resembles and imitates the claimant's copyright film, or reproduces the essential features of that film.[37] Similarly, copyright in a sound recording is not infringed where a person remakes (or 'covers') the same song or records the same song performed in a similar style (a.k.a. 'sound-alikes').[38] However, it should be noted that, while an entrepreneurial copyright will not be infringed where a new recording of identical or similar sounds or images is made, this might infringe copyright in an underlying work such as the music, lyrics, or screenplay,[39] or violate some other intellectual property right.[40]

Having observed that the reproduction right in relation to films and sound recording is confined to the reproduction of the recording, it should be noted that the recording will be treated as having being reproduced even though the recording medium has changed (as long as the particular sounds or images embodied on the claimant's recording are replicated). For example, a reproduction occurs where a person makes a tape recording of a CD, records a film on a digital camcorder, or up-loads or down-loads a sound recording from the internet. Even though the Act does not specify that copying of a film or sound recording includes storing it by electronic means, the better view is that it does.[41]

---

[30] It is important to remember that the narrow protection given to entrepreneurial works is balanced by the fact that protection arises irrespective of whether or not the work is original.

[31] This is not the case with photographs, where the copyright extends to the content or arrangement, not just the 'recording': *Creation Records v. News Group Newspapers* [1997] *EMLR* 444, 450.

[32] CDPA s. 5A(1)(a).

[33] In the case of broadcasts the definitions refer to the transmission or sending of visual images, sounds, or *other information*; CDPA s. 6(1).

[34] CDPA s. 5B(1).   [35] *Norowzian v. Arks (No. 1)* [1998] *FSR* 394.   [36] Ibid, 400.

[37] Ibid, 398.   [38] Ibid, 394; *CBS Records v. Telemark* (1988) 79 *ALR* 604; (1987) 9 *IPR* 440.

[39] *Norowzian v. Arks (No. 1)* [1998] *FSR* 394.

[40] For example, by passing the recording off as the recording of the claimant. Cf. *Sim v. Heinz* [1959] 1 *WLR* 313; [1959] *RPC* 75 (CA).

[41] Copinger, paras. 7–70, p. 422.

2.3 BROADCASTS

The 1988 Act provides little guidance as to what it means to copy a broadcast. However, it is clear that the making of an audiotape of a radio broadcast or a videotape of any image forming part of a television broadcast would amount to a reproduction of the broadcast (as well as the contents of the broadcast, be they sound recordings, films, or other works). In contrast with some jurisdictions, UK law does not differentiate between the first fixation and other reproductions of broadcasts.[42] Following the logic of entrepreneurial copyright it seems that the reproduction of a broadcast only protects the information, sound, and images sent through particular signals. Thus, a person would not infringe if they summarized a broadcast, or described its contents. Similarly, the right to copy the broadcast would not be infringed if someone broadcast exactly the same sound recordings in the same order as was used by another broadcaster.

2.4 TYPOGRAPHICAL ARRANGEMENTS

The scope of the reproduction right in relation to typographical arrangements is very narrow. This is because copying of a typographical arrangement means making a facsimile copy of the arrangement.[43] Although 'facsimile' is defined to include enlargements and reductions,[44] it seems to be confined to reproduction by way of reprography, photocopies, digital scanning, faxing, and little more. Retyping a work in a different font is a sure way of avoiding infringement of copyright in the typographical arrangement.

3 ISSUING COPIES OF THE WORK TO THE PUBLIC: THE DISTRIBUTION RIGHT

The owner of copyright in all categories of work is given the right to issue copies of the work to the public (section 18). This is commonly known as the 'distribution right.'[45] Section 18 explains that issuing copies of a work to the public means:[46]

(a) the act of putting into circulation in the EEA copies not previously put into circulation in the EEA by or with the consent of the copyright owner; or

(b) the act of putting into circulation outside the EEA copies not previously put into circulation in the EEA or elsewhere.

The distribution right is given in respect of the issuing of each and every copy (including the original).[47] As such it needs to be distinguished from a right to make the works available to the public for the first time (that is a 'publication' or 'divulgation' right of the kind previously recognized in UK law). Essentially, the distribution right is a right to put each tangible copy (which

---

[42] Cf. Rental Rights Dir., Art. 6 (fixation), Art. 7 (reproduction of fixations).
[43] CDPA s. 17(5).   [44] CDPA s. 178.
[45] The 1988 Act has been amended twice in this regard to implement the Software Dir., Art. 4(c) and the Rental Rights Dir., Art. 9. No amendments were thought necessary to implement Database Dir., Art. 5(c) or Info. Soc. Dir., Art. 4 (which, in turn, implements WIPO Copyright Treaty, Art. 6).
[46] CDPA s. 18(1).   [47] CDPA s. 18(4).

has not previously been circulated) into commercial circulation.[48] Once particular copies are in circulation (at least where the first circulation was consensual), the right no longer operates in relation to those objects. As the right of distribution does not include 'any subsequent distribution,'[49] copyright owners cannot control resale.[50]

But what acts count as 'issuing' to the public? Sub-section 18(3) indicates that once a copy is in circulation subsequent acts of 'distribution, sale, hiring or loan of copies' or 'importation' do not infringe. On one reading, at least, this implies that putting into circulation includes not only sale and other transfers of articles but also import,[51] hire, and even loan. In *Peek & Cloppenburg*, it was suggested by a German court, in a reference to the ECJ, that distribution 'by sale or otherwise' (the words of article 4(1) of the Information Society Directive) could be interpreted to encompass display in a shop of an article for use by customers as well as display in a shop window.[52] However, such a broad interpretation of distribution (under UK or European law) presents the possibility that the distribution right duplicates the rental and lending rights, but is not subject to their exception and limitations.[53] The German interpretation was rejected by the ECJ which took the view that distribution required the transfer of ownership of the object embodying the work. Consequently, distribution includes the import, sale,[54] and gratuitous transfer of any tangible article embodying the work. Advocate-General Sharpston's Opinion uses different reasoning to reach a similar conclusion.[55]

---

[48] Info. Soc. Dir., Art. 4(1) refers to distribution 'by sale or otherwise,' whereas CDPA s. 18 refers to 'putting into circulation.' Info. Soc. Dir., Recital 28 indicates that distribution relates to distribution in the form of a 'tangible article'.

[49] CDPA s. 18(3)(a). The Rental Rights Dir., Art. 9(2) and the Software Dir., Art. 4(c) refer to exhaustion on 'first sale,' whereas Info. Soc. Dir., Art. 4(2) allows for exhaustion in cases of 'first sale or other transfer of ownership in the Community'.

[50] This corresponds with the idea of exhaustion of rights. Note, however, proposals for a resale royalty right: see Ch. 13.

[51] *Independiente Ltd v. Music Trading On-Line (HK) Ltd* [2007] *EWHC* 533 (Ch), [2007] *FSR* 525 (supplier of CDS was held to have put them into circulation even though the items were posted outside UK, the customer paid a price which included a postage and packaging component, and that according to the terms of the agreement, property passed when the credit card payment had been made and the individual item had been allocated to the customer. The claimants argued that delivery through the UK postal system was the defendant's act of putting the CDs into circulation, relying on s. 32(4) of the Sale of Goods Act 1979 which regulates the notion of delivery to consumers. Evans-Lombe J agreed with the claimant, distinguishing the House of Lords decision in *Sabaf SpA v. MFI Furniture* [2005] *RPC* 10, a patent case, where the consigner of goods (which were said to infringe the claimant's patent) from Italy to the UK was held not to be importers as having concerned sale between businesses in which the property passed when the goods were dispatched. But cf Copinger, para 7–80, p. 427 ('it is difficult to see how the mere act of importation could amount to putting copies into circulation'). However, it seems to us that the clear intention of the legislation is that copyright owners be entitled to prevent the import into the EEA of copies not previously put into circulation there, so that member states must interpret the distribution right as including importation.

[52] *Peek & Cloppenburg KG v. Cassina SpA*, Case C–456/06 (17 April 2008) (concerning copies of Le Corbusier-designed furniture that was not protected by copyright in Italy but was in Germany). It should be noted that if the same facts fell to be analysed under British, as opposed to German, law the articles would have been infringing copies and the display thereof secondary infringements under CDPA, s.24.

[53] For example, those in Rental Dir., Art 3(2) (non-application to buildings and works of applied art), Recital 10 (certain acts not treated as lending), and derogations permitted to member states under Art. 6.

[54] Possibly also an 'offer of sale': *KK Sony Computer Entertainment v. Pacific Game Technology Ltd* [2006] *EWHC* 2509 (Ch) (holding that the defendant, a Hong Kong-based company, had breached s. 18 (as well as infringed various trade mark rights and rights in registered designs) when it advertised on its web site the sale of PlayStation Consoles (which had been placed on the market by the claimant in Japan) and then dispatched a console to the claimant's agents in England).

[55] *Peek & Cloppenburg KG v. Cassina SpA*, Case C–456/06 (17 April 2008) para. 41.

Even if it is uncontroversial that issuing covers 'sale,' the point in the chain of distribution when a copy is issued 'to the public' is unclear.[56] On one view, a copy will be issued to the public (and thus require the copyright owner's authority) when it is first sold from a manufacturer to a wholesaler. Thereafter, further sales will not require authorization. On another view, a copy will be issued to the public when a copy reaches the hands of a member of the public. Under this approach, the relevant act would occur when the retailer sold a copy of the work to a consumer.[57] The wording of section 18 is ambiguous and can support either interpretation, though EC legislation (which section 18 is supposed to implement) suggests that distribution takes place on first sale or other transfer of ownership.

It is important to note that the distribution right incorporates certain geographical distinctions. In particular, the distribution right was drafted to recognize the principle of Community-wide exhaustion. That is, once tangible copies have been placed on the market in the EEA, a copyright owner cannot utilize national rights to prevent further circulation within the EEA.[58] Section 18 achieves Community exhaustion by deeming the act of issuing not to include 'any subsequent distribution, sale, hiring or loan of copies previously put into circulation . . . or any subsequent importation of such copies into the UK or another EEA State.'[59] Consequently, if a copy is put on the market in the Netherlands and then imported into and sold in the United Kingdom, the import to and sale in the United Kingdom do not infringe the issuing right. The corollary of Community-wide exhaustion was that there was no 'international exhaustion.'[60] This means that the distribution right can be used to prevent importing of copies of the work to the EEA. Consequently, the issuing right may be invoked to prevent the parallel import to the United Kingdom of copies marketed outside the EEA even though that marketing was by or with the consent of the relevant copyright owner.[61] So, for example, UK copyright owners were entitled to prevent a Hong Kong company from supplying CDs to UK-based consumers: the copyright-owners' rights were not exhausted through marketing in Hong Kong, and sending the CDs to UK consumers counted as placing copies in circulation in the UK.[62]

4 RENTAL AND LENDING RIGHTS

While subsequent distribution of copies of the work is not generally within the copyright-owner's control, the owner of copyright does have the right to control the rental and lending of

---

[56] J. Phillips and L. Bently, 'Copyright Issues: The Mysteries of Section 18' [1999] *EIPR* 132.

[57] Some member states recognise a *droit de destination*, the right to control the destination of the work.

[58] Info. Soc. Dir., Art. 4(2).   [59] CDPA s. 18(3).

[60] Info. Soc. Dir., Recital 28. This was confirmed (as a matter of EC law) by the ECJ in *Laserdisken ApS v. Kulturministeriet,* Case C–479/04 [2006] *ECR* I–8089, [2007] *CMLR* (6) 187.

[61] Issuing implicitly includes such 'importation' as a result of the proviso to s. 18(3)(b), which having excluded import into the UK or another EEA state from the concept of issuing, provides that the exclusion does not apply so far as the issuing concerned is issuing in the EEA of copies not previously put into circulation in the EEA by or with the consent of the copyright owner. Such liability for parallel import, in contrast with import as an act of secondary infringement, is not dependent on knowledge. This would apply, *a fortiori,* if the copies being imported from outside the EEA were infringing.

[62] *Independiente Ltd v. Music Trading On-Line* [2007] *EWHC* 533 (CA), [2007] *FSR* 525. See also *KK Sony Computer Entertainment v. Pacific Game Technology Ltd* [2006] *EWHC* 2509 (Ch) (the judgment concentrates on the ECJ's trade mark jurisprudence on exhaustion and concludes that Sony had not exhausted its right, before holding that the web site included an offer to sell which was targeted at the UK, and thus, fell to be treated as an offer for sale in the UK. The judge did not expressly address the trickier issue as to where sale (or issuing) took place, but the clear implication is that the goods were issued to the public in the UK.)

the work. When the 1988 Act was first enacted, it provided a limited right to control the rental of copies of sound recordings, films, and computer programs.[63] No such right was given in relation to literary, dramatic, musical, or artistic works. However, as a result of amendments implementing the Rental Rights Directive,[64] an owner of copyright in literary, dramatic, or musical works, and even artistic works (other than works of architecture or applied art),[65] is granted an exclusive right to rent and lend copies of such works to the public (section 18A). The rental right is not exhausted by the first sale of copies of the work.[66]

Rental and lending both involve the making of the original or a copy of a work available for use on terms that it will or may be returned.[67] The distinction between rental and lending is that the act of rental involves a commercial advantage, whereas lending does not. More specifically, rental is defined as making the work available 'for direct or indirect economic or commercial advantage.' In contrast, lending occurs where there is no such advantage.[68] It has been suggested that rental not only includes rentals of the sort familiarly operated by video-rental stores, but also where videos were lent to hotel guests. It has also been suggested that an organization will indirectly derive a 'commercial advantage' through sponsorship (for example with a commercially sponsored library such as that of the Wellcome Institute) and hence be involved in rental, not lending.[69]

Lending means 'making a copy of the work available for use, on terms that it will or may be returned, otherwise than for direct or indirect economic or commercial advantage, through an establishment which is accessible to the public.'[70] The right does not cover loans between private individuals. This is because lending is only prohibited when it is made 'through an establishment which is accessible to the public.' Lending does not become a rental, at least as regards loans between establishments accessible to the public, where payment does not go beyond what is necessary to cover the operating costs of the establishment.[71]

The Rental Rights Directive and the 1988 Act both contain a number of limitations to the rental and lending rights.[72] Neither covers the making available of a copy for public performance, playing or showing in public, or broadcast. As Recital 13 explains, where a cinema owner rents a film from a film distributor that is to be shown to the public, this falls outside the scope of the rental right.[73] The exclusion also seems to cover a variety of other commercial practices, such as the rental of jukeboxes and possibly also the rental of sheet music.

In a similar vein, neither rental nor lending covers situations where a work is made available for the purposes of exhibition in public. As a result, the owner of a painting does not need to

---

[63] Prior to that there was no rental right: see *CBS v. Ames* [1981] *RPC* 407, 428.

[64] See Reinbothe and von Lewinski (1993).

[65] Rental Dir., Art. 2(3). Apparently these were excluded because it was thought that the rental right would then cover rental of housing, cars, etc.

[66] *Metronome Music v. Music Point Hokamp GmbH,* Case C–200/96 [1998] ECR I–1953; *Foreningen Af Danske Videogramdistributorer v. Laserdisken,* Case C–61/97 [1999] 1 *CMLR* 1297.

[67] CDPA ss. 18A(2), 18A(6), 182C(2) (performers). Contrast the terms of Rental Dir., Art. 1 'making available for use, for a limited period of time.' Note that it only applies to material copies.

[68] Recital 16 of the Software Dir. defined 'rental' as the making available of a computer program for use, for a limited time, and for 'profit-making purposes'. During formulation of the Rental Rights Dir. this formula, along with others defining rental as making available 'against payment' were rejected.

[69] See Reinbothe and von Lewinski (1993), 40; cf. J. Griffiths, 'Copyright and Public Lending in the United Kingdom' [1997] *EIPR* 499.

[70] CDPA s. 18A(2)(b).   [71] CDPA s. 18A(5). Reflecting the Rental Rights Dir., Recital 14.

[72] Ibid, Recital 13.

[73] But this act was long ago held to amount to authorization of infringement: *Falcon v. Famous Players Film Co.* [1926] 2 *KB* 474.

seek permission from the copyright owner before lending the work to an art gallery for public display. Moreover, the rental and lending rights do not cover situations where a work is made available for on-the-spot reference. It has been suggested that this will exempt situations where magazines are made available in waiting rooms.[74] Finally, lending does not cover the making available of a work between establishments that are accessible to the public. This means that 'inter-library loans' are permissible.[75] Special exemptions apply to the lending of works by educational establishments,[76] and for the lending of *books* by public libraries (if the book is eligible to fall within the Public Lending Right Scheme).[77] In addition, copyright in *any work* is not infringed by the lending of copies of the work by a 'prescribed' library or archive that is not conducted for profit.[78]

5 THE RIGHT TO PERFORM, SHOW, OR PLAY THE WORK IN PUBLIC

The fourth right conferred on a copyright owner is the right to perform the work in public (section 19). This right, which is usually known as the 'performing right,' was first introduced by statute in 1833 to protect owners of copyright in dramatic works.[79] This was because, as the primary way dramatic works are exploited is by way of performance, if the protection given to dramatic works was limited to the reproduction right, this would have been inadequate. In order to be consistent, the performing right was also extended to musical works and literary works in general. Today, section 19(1) of the 1988 Act provides that performance of a work in public is an act restricted by the copyright in a literary, dramatic, or musical work; and section 19(3) states that the playing or showing of the work in public is an act restricted by the copyright in a sound recording, film, or broadcast. There is no performing right for artistic works (and hence no right to authorize the public exhibition of the work),[80] or for typographical arrangements.

'Performance' is defined to include the delivery of lectures, addresses, speeches, and sermons; as well as 'any mode of visual or acoustic presentation of a work, such as by means of a sound recording, film, or broadcast'.[81] It has been held that a performance of a musical work or sound recording takes place where it can be heard.[82] Presumably, a performance of a film takes place where it can be seen. Where the performance is live, it should be fairly obvious who is responsible for the performance. Where more artificial means of delivery are employed (for example where copyright-protected music embodied in a sound recording is played by way of a radio in a restaurant), the person who infringes is not the broadcaster,[83] or the person who supplied the radio apparatus. Rather it is the person who operates the radio.[84] It seems that it is

---

[74] See Griffiths [1997] *EIPR* 499, 500.   [75] CDPA s. 18A(4).   [76] CDPA s. 36A.

[77] CDPA s. 40A; Rental Rights Dir., Art. 5. This was the most hotly contested issue during the passage of the Directive. See Ch. 13.

[78] CDPA s. 40A(2).   [79] See *Russell v. Smith* (1848) 12 *QB* 217, 236.

[80] But see moral right of attribution. In *Hanfstaegl v. Empire Palace* [1894] 2 *Ch* 1 it was held that copyright was not infringed by performing an artistic work in the form of a *tableau vivant*. This may, however, be a reproduction: *Bradbury Agnew v. Day* (1916) 32 *TLR* 349.

[81] CDPA s. 19.

[82] *PRS v. Camelo* [1936] 3 *All ER* 557 (the playing of a radio in the defendant's lounge infringed the performing right in the songs played on the radio because the radio could be heard in the neighbouring restaurant).

[83] CDPA s. 19(4). Cf. *PRS v. Hammond's Bradford Brewery Co.* [1934] 1 *Ch* 121, 139.

[84] *PRS v. Hammond's Bradford Brewery Co.* [1934] 1 *Ch* 21 (a person performs a musical composition when they cause it to be heard); *Messenger v. BBC* [1927] 2 *KB* 543, 548.

a publican, rather than a customer, who operates a jukebox and is liable if the public perform-ance is not authorized.

In order to infringe, the performance must be carried on 'in public.' There are many situ-ations where it is clear that a performance is in public: a performance at the Brixton Academy, the Royal Albert Hall, a West End theatre or cinema, or in a public house would normally all be to the public. Beyond these examples, however, what is meant by 'in public' is less clear.[85] Over time, three different conceptions of the 'public' have been used in the case law.

In some cases the concept of the public is understood according to the character of the audience.[86] In this context a distinction is drawn between a section of the general public (which have no other unifying theme other than the desire to see the performance), and a group of people who share a private or domestic link. For example, the residents of a hospital or a nursing home are bound together by a link that distinguishes them from the general public, namely, that they reside at a particular location. Consequently, in *Duck v. Bates,*[87] the Court of Appeal held that copyright in the play *Our Boys* was not infringed when an amateur dramatic club performed it at Guy's Hospital for the entertainment of the nurses. This was because it was held to be a domestic performance, not a performance to which the public or any portion of the public was invited. Using a test of this sort, a performance in a shop,[88] before members of a club,[89] or in a hotel lounge[90] would be a performance to a 'section of the general public' (so long as anyone could enter the shop, join the club, or enter the hotel lounge). However, using the same test, it is unlikely that a performance at a dinner party,[91] or to students at a boarding school,[92] would be treated as a performance to a 'section of the general public.' In these cases, the audience is linked by personal connection, residence, or employment.

Another test that has occasionally been employed to determine whether a performance is in public effectively ignores the public or private nature of the performance and focuses, instead, on whether the performance is motivated by financial considerations.[93] If the performance is run for profit, it is likely to be 'in public'. The rationale for this is that otherwise the performer or organizer of the performance could be unjustly enriched by the performance (at the expense of the person who owned copyright in the works that were performed).[94] Thus, in *Harms v. Martans* the Court of Appeal held that performance of the musical work 'That Certain Feeling' at the Embassy Club to an audience of 150 members and 50 guests was a performance in public. Lord Hanworth MR suggested that the critical considerations were whether the defendants' activities were for profit;[95] who was admitted; and where the performance took place. Since the members paid a substantial subscription and an entrance fee, were the sorts of people who would pay to go to a public theatre to hear a performance, and the club paid the orchestra to perform, the performance was 'in public.'

[85] *Jennings v. Stephens* [1936] 1 *Ch* 469, 476, 481 (the words are probably incapable of precise definition); *Harms v. Martans* [1927] 1 *Ch* 526, 530. M. F. Makeen, *Copyright in a Global Information Society: The Scope of Copyright Protection under International, US, UK, and French Law* (Kluwer, 2000), 148 ('no problem in contem-porary copyright law appears to have been debated more extensively or intensely').

[86] *Jennings v. Stephens* [1936] 1 *Ch* 469, 476, 479; *PRS v. Harlequin* [1979] 2 *All ER* 828, 833.

[87] (1884) 13 *QBD* 843.   [88] *PRS v. Harlequin* [1979] 2 *All ER* 828.

[89] *Harms v. Martans* [1927] 1 *Ch* 526, 537 (emphasizing that there was an invitation to the general public to become members of the club).

[90] *PRS v. Hawthorns Hotel (Bournemouth)* [1933] *Ch* 855.   [91] *Jennings v. Stephens* [1936] 1 *Ch* 469, 481.

[92] Ibid, 483.   [93] *Harms v. Martans* [1927] 1 *Ch* 526, 532–3.

[94] Some statutory support for this approach can be found in the defence provided by CDPA s. 67 (as amended) and 72 as regards the *free* public showing of a broadcast.

[95] A factor treated as of minimal significance in *Ernest Turner Electrical Instruments v. PRS* [1943] 1 *Ch* 167, 173.

A third test has focused upon the copyright-owner's monopoly. Under this approach, a performance is 'in public' if it is made to or before 'the copyright owner's public.' This test, which first emerged in the 1930s in the judgments of Lord Greene MR, later came to be quite widely adopted. In *Jennings v. Stephens*[96] the performance of a play *The Rest Cure* by the members of a Woman's Institute without charge and without guests was held to be a performance in public. Greene LJ said:

[T]he expression 'in public' must be considered in relation to the owner of the copyright. If the audience considered in relation to the owner of the copyright may properly be described as the owner's 'public' or part of his 'public,' then in performing the work before that audience he would in my opinion be exercising the statutory right conferred upon him.[97]

This test has been used to hold that the playing of the BBC's music broadcasts to 600 workers in a factory infringed the performing right. The factory owner claimed that the audience was not a 'section of the public'—a reasonable view given that the common bond was work, not a desire to listen to music. However, Lord Greene MR held the performances were 'in public,' because to hold otherwise would have meant that the value of the monopoly given by the statute would have been substantially 'whittled down.'[98] This test seems difficult to justify, since it is surely the case that most copyright owners would want to extend their monopoly as widely as possible and would therefore claim that all performances were before their 'public.'[99]

While uncertainties exist over the relationship between the three tests,[100] it should be clear that, historically, the notion of public is defined expansively, so as to favour the copyright owner. For the moment, copyright owners and their collective representatives seem content with the limits set by the courts. These make it clear that performances in places which are open to the public (from hairdressers' salons to hotel lounges) are performances in public. The cases also make it clear that performances before substantial numbers of people not connected by family or domestic ties, will be in public. The consequences of the different approaches to defining the public now remain to be felt only in marginal cases (such as the case of playing music in the office of a small family firm, or at a wedding reception).

With regard to the infringement of the performing right, it is important to bear in mind that there are a number of related acts of secondary infringement. These are considered in Chapter 8.

6 THE RIGHT TO COMMUNICATE THE WORK TO THE PUBLIC

The exclusive right to communicate a work to the public arises with respect to literary, dramatic, musical, and artistic works, sound recordings,[101] films, and broadcasts.[102] The right, which was introduced to implement the EC Information Society Directive,[103] is distinguished

---

[96] [1936] 1 *Ch* 469.   [97] Ibid, 485.

[98] *Ernest Turner Electrical Instruments v. PRS* [1943] 1 *Ch* 167 (Lord Greene MR). For a contemporary equivalent, see *PRS v. Kwik-Fit Ltd* [2008] *ECDR* (2) 13 (para. 3) (OH CS).

[99] See *PRS v. Harlequin Record Shops* [1979] 2 *All ER* 828, 834.

[100] Indeed, the courts have rarely acknowledged that the tests applied vary or are incompatible.

[101] In the case of sound recordings, when exercised by a collecting society, the right consists only of an entitlement to equitable remuneration: ss. 135A–H.

[102] CDPA s. 20.

[103] Copyright and Related Rights Regulations 2003, SI 2003/2498 implementing Info. Soc. Dir., Art. 3, itself implementing WCT, Art. 8, WPPT Art. 14.

from public performance, or playing or showing in public (section 19), by the fact that the public is not present at the place where the communication originates.[104] So, converting sounds into electronic signals and broadcasting them so that they can be received and heard on a radio is a communication to the public (rather than a public performance). In contrast, operating the radio so the sounds can be heard in a public place would be public performance (but not communication to the public).[105]

In its British implementation, the communication right is confined to 'electronic communication,' and is said to include 'broadcasting' and 'making available.' While a broadcasting right has been expressly conferred on copyright owners in the United Kingdom since 1956, the 'making available' right has its roots in the WIPO Copyright Treaty of 1996. We consider each separately.

6.1 BROADCASTING

As we saw in Chapter 3, a 'broadcast' is defined as an electronic transmission of visual images, sounds, or other information for simultaneous reception by the public, or which is made for presentation to the public, but excludes 'internet transmissions'.[106] As we have already observed, this covers digital, analogue, terrestrial, and satellite transmissions, but not the placing of a work on a web site. The definition of broadcast covers the forms of satellite broadcasting which may be directly received by individuals or may be received by subscribers who obtain a decoder.[107] The relaying of a broadcast by reception and immediate retransmission constitutes a separate act of broadcasting.[108] Thus where a hotel relays television programmes to individual guest rooms, this of itself is a communication to the public.[109]

The person who makes a broadcast is either the person transmitting an item, such as a programme, where that person has responsibility for its contents, or the person providing the item for transmission who 'makes with the person transmitting it the arrangements necessary for its transmission.'[110]

---

[104] Info. Soc. Dir., Recital 23.

[105] The distinction between broadcasting and public performance has not always been maintained. Soon after the emergence of radio broadcasting in the 1920s, it was successfully argued that the BBC had infringed the 'performing right' when it broadcast a private performance that was capable of being received on wireless receivers: *Messager v. BBC* [1927] 2 *KB* 543, 548–9. Later, a specific 'broadcasting right' was conferred on copyright owners by the 1956 Act. This was retained in s. 20 of the CDPA, as enacted, and has been included, in amended form, in the new s. 20. Broadcasters are given immunity from liability for public performances that result from the broadcasts by CDPA s. 19(4). The relationship between 'communication in public' and 'communication to the public' is explored in comparative, historical context by Makeen, *Copyright in a Global Information Society: The Scope of Copyright Protection under International US, UK, and French Law* (2000).

[106] CDPA s. 6(1). The definition of broadcast is the same for infringement as that used to define broadcasts as works capable of being protected by copyright.

[107] That is, any encrypted broadcast, whether terrestrial or by satellite relay, is 'lawfully' received if decoding equipment has been made available through the person transmitting it in encrypted form: CDPA s. 6(2).

[108] CDPA s. 6(5)(a). However, special rules apply to retransmissions of broadcasts from another EEA member state: CDPA s. 144A. These provide that, aside from rights of broadcasting organizations with regard to their own transmissions, only collecting societies may exercise rights to authorize cable retransmissions of broadcast works. Where such arrangements have not been made, the licensing body is treated as mandated to exercise the right.

[109] *Sociedad General de Autores y Editores de Espana (SGAE) v. Rafael Hotels SL*, Case C–306/05 [2006] *ECR* I–11519.

[110] CDPA s. 6(3).

Because of the potential transnational nature of broadcasting, it has long been acknowledged that it is important to ascertain where a particular broadcast takes place.[111] A person wishing to make a broadcast needs to obtain consents from copyright holders of works included in the broadcast, but only as regards those copyrights that are operative in the territory in which the broadcast occurs. However, when a signal is sent or up-linked to a satellite (from place A) and is then beamed back to Earth over a large reception area or 'footprint' (places A, B, and C), there are at least two possible territories where the act of broadcasting might be thought to take place. On the one hand, it could be said that the broadcast occurs from the place from which the signal was sent (the emission or introduction theory). Alternatively, it might be thought that the broadcast occurs in the places where it is received (the reception or communication theory). In the face of conflicting national decisions on this issue, it became clear in the late 1980s that it was necessary to harmonize the law in this area. Two contrary concerns dominated the decision as to the choice of the place of broadcast. On the one hand, the simplest answer and the one that facilitated satellite broadcasting was that the country of broadcast was the country of up-link. However, it was feared that this would lead to satellite up-link facilities migrating to countries where copyright protection was weak, and that copyright owners would thus be best protected if consent was required in all countries where the signal could be received. In the end a compromise was reached. The country of introduction is treated as the relevant place only where the standard of copyright protection is satisfactory. Accordingly, section 6 of the 1988 Act defines the place of wireless broadcasting as the place where the broadcaster introduces programme-carrying signals into an uninterrupted chain of communication, including any satellite relay.[112]

6.2 THE RIGHT TO MAKE THE WORK AVAILABLE

The second element of the communication right is the exclusive right to make the work 'available... by electronic transmission in such a way that members of the public may access it from a place and at a time individually chosen by them.' In contrast to the broadcasting right, which is premised on the idea of simultaneous reception, 'making available' encompasses individual communications to persons who are members of 'the public.' A recital to the Information Society Directive explains that the right will cover interactive on-demand transmissions,[113] such as 'video-on-demand' services and so-called 'celestial jukeboxes.' But the new right should also be assumed to cover most internet transmissions (other than broadcasts) where a person places a work on a web site because members of the public can access the work 'from a place' (their terminal, whether it be in their office, home, or on their mobile telephone) and 'at a time' chosen by them.[114]

Although the infringing act is the making available and infringement only occurs as regards acts done in the UK, neither the Directive nor the British implementation explains *where* the

---

[111] See Makeen, *Copyright in a Global Information Society* (2000) ch. 4.

[112] CDPA s. 6(4). These provisions reflect amendments in the Rental Regs., to give effect to the Cable and Satellite Directive, chs. I and II. CDPA s. 6 is subject to the safeguard rules in CDPA s. 6A, which operates in cases of transmissions from places outside the EEA. The addition of the word 'wireless' was added by the 2003 Info. Soc. Regs., SI 2003/2498 reg. 4(c).

[113] Info. Soc. Dir., Recital 25.

[114] On which see Reinbothe and von Lewinski (2002) pp. 108–11. See also Irish Copyright and Related Rights Act 2000, s. 40(1)(a) (defining making available explicitly to include the making available of copies of works 'through the internet').

act takes place. In the simple case of a British person who subscribes to a British service provider utilizing peer-to-peer software, it seems clear that deploying the software so that others can access files will amount to making available in the UK (even if those who access the files are in many cases outside the UK).[115] A more difficult case is that of a person in the United States creating a video using copyright-protected material, uploading that material on to YOUTUBE, so that it can be accessed in the United Kingdom. Whether there is an infringement of UK copyright law may well depend on which acts are regarded as making the work available and where those acts are understood to occur. One candidate is the place where the individual uploads the work on to a web site, so that in this example there would be no infringement in the UK (though there might be in the USA). A second possibility is that the act of making available occurs wherever the server which permits access is located: in the case of YOUTUBE, probably the United States. A third possibility is that the act occurs in the place or places from which it can be accessed. This would mean that YOUTUBE would be making available all over the world. The fourth possibility is that the work is made available in the territory where the public at which the work is targeted is located. This difficult issue will need to be resolved.

A further issue that will need to be confronted before long is which ancillary acts constitute distinct infringing communications: for example, is hyper-linking to a work itself a 'making available,' and if so, do search engines make works available? Although it might be arguable that hyper-linking makes a work available to a new public (as, for example, where a link is made from an intranet onto the worldwide web), and thus might be seen as an act which the copyright owner should be empowered to control,[116] the better view is that the 'making available right' is not an appropriate mechanism by which to protect a content-holder's interest in controlling access to different audiences (or its different publics). Most hyper-linking simply makes it easier to locate (and, if desired, access) works which are already available to the public, and it would be unduly constraining to require all links to be authorized.[117] In those relatively rare situations where a link enables broader access to a site than was originally authorized by a content owner, the rules dealing with circumvention of access controls should provide ample protection. Where a person operated a web site with hyper-link to files which contained copyright-infringing material, the Federal Court of Australia has held that the hyper-link was not a 'making available' but was rather an 'authorization' to reproduce the material.[118]

6.3 'TO THE PUBLIC'

In *Sociedad General de Autores y Editores de Espana (SGAE) v Rafael Hotels SL*,[119] the ECJ elaborated on the concept of the public in the context of Article 3 of the Information Society

---

[115] *Polydor Ltd v. Brown* [2005] *EWHC* 3191 (finding 'making available' in the act of connecting computer to internet, where the computer is running peer-to-peer software and music files containing copies of the claimant's copyright works are placed in a shared directory).

[116] In *Shetland Times v. Wills* [1997] *FSR* 604 it was found to be arguable that a newspaper web site which was linked to another web site, had thereby included items (the headline of the article) in a cable-programme service. The basis for the decision has been swept away by the 2003 amendments.

[117] Litman, *Digital Copyright* p. 183 ('the public has always had, and should have, a right to cite'); A. Strowel and N. Ide, 'Liability with Regard to Hyperlinks' (2001) 24 *Columbia Journal of Law & the Arts* 403, 425; B. Allgrove & P. Ganley, 'Search engines, Data Aggregators and UK Copyright Law: A proposal' (2007) *EIPR* 227 (arguing for clarification through a specific defence).

[118] *Universal Music Australia v. Cooper* [2005] *FCA* (14 July 2005) (only the authorization matter was dealt with on appeal).

[119] Case C–306/05 (ECJ, 7 December 2006).

Directive. The case concerned the relaying of television signals to individual hotel rooms. The Court rejected the contention that the definition of 'public' was a matter for each member state, and, took the view that the right was to be interpreted broadly.[120] The Court did not provide a definition of 'the public,' but referred to the statement in an earlier decision in *Lagardere* (interpreting the Satellite and Cable Directive) that the term refers 'to an indeterminate number of potential viewers'. While guests might occupy individual rooms and so watch broadcasts in private, 'the private or public nature of the place where the communication takes place is immaterial'.[121] The hotel guests 'quickly succeed each other' so that 'they may be considered to be a public'. The 'cumulative effects' of making works available to this group 'could become very significant'. Moreover, the Court observed that the provision of access to broadcast was 'an additional service' provided by the hotel and 'profit-making'. Consequently, the Court concluded that the distribution of signals by cable to customers staying in its rooms was a 'communication to the public'. Probably it is safe to follow the Advocate General's approach when determining whether a communication is to the public, which considers the key factors to be the extent of the circle of potential recipients and its economic significance to the author, as well as the existence of economic benefit to the person making the communication (in the case in question, the hotelier). Economic benefit is clearly a relevant factor, but probably not a necessary condition, for a communication to be regarded as one 'to the public'.

7 THE RIGHT TO MAKE AN ADAPTATION OF THE WORK

The owner of copyright in literary, dramatic, or musical work is given the exclusive right to make an adaptation of the work.[122] The owner of copyright in artistic works, sound recordings, and films is not given an adaptation right. The adaptation right is restrictively defined and is not to be confused with a general right to control all derivative works, such as that recognized by copyright law in the USA.[123] The adaptation right includes the right to do any of the other restricted acts in relation to an adaptation, including the right to make an 'adaptation of an adaptation'.[124] Consequently it is not only a restricted act to make an adaptation, but also to reproduce an adaptation in any material form, issue copies of it to the public, perform it in public, or broadcast it. As it is not possible to draw a clear line between an adaptation and a reproduction, in many cases the same act might be both a reproduction and an adaptation.[125]

7.1 MEANING OF ADAPTATION

Adaptation is defined differently for literary works, dramatic works, computer programs, databases, and musical works. We must deal with each in turn. In relation to *literary or dramatic* works, adaptation means a translation (such as a translation into French), or a dramatization

---

[120] Para. 36 (relying on recital 23). While in much of what it said the Court seems to have followed the opinion of Advocate General Sharpston, the judgment lacks the same clarity as the opinion.

[121] Para. 50.

[122] Implementing, for the most part, Berne, Arts. 8 and 11(2) (translation); Art. 12 (adaptations, arrangements, and other alterations); Art. 11*ter*(2) (communication of translation).

[123] And in this respect seems narrower than Berne, Art. 12.   [124] CDPA s. 21(2).

[125] CDPA s. 21(6).

of a non-dramatic work (such as where a novel is turned into a screenplay or ballet or, after *Norowzian v. Arks*,[126] a film). The adaptation right in a literary or dramatic work will also be infringed where the story or action is conveyed wholly or mainly by means of pictures (such as a comic strip). As regards dramatic works, adaptation means a version of a dramatic work that is converted into a non-dramatic work (such as the conversion of a film into a novel). In relation to musical works, an adaptation is defined as an arrangement or transcription of the work.[127]

Although an adaptation is only made when it is recorded in writing or otherwise, the public performance or broadcasting of an adaptation will infringe even if at that stage the adaptation has not been recorded in writing or otherwise. Consequently, an amateur dramatic group whose public performance is based on a novel, will almost certainly infringe the adaptation right. This is because in so doing the group will have adapted the novel by converting it into a dramatic work. Equally, the broadcast of someone translating a text from a foreign language into English will infringe, even though the translator has not made a written version of the translation.

The adaptation right also applies to computer programs and databases. In relation to computer programs, an adaptation means an arrangement, or altered version of the program, or a translation of it.[128] In these circumstances, translation includes the conversion into or out of a computer language, or from a computer language into a different computer language or code.[129] In relation to databases, adaptation means an arrangement or altered version of the database or a translation of it.[130]

8 AUTHORIZATION

As well as being given the right to carry out the restricted activities, the copyright owner is also given the right to authorize others to do any of the restricted acts.[131] When this right was introduced in the Copyright Act 1911, it was said to be superfluous and tautologous: the exclusive right to do an act implicitly carried with it the right of authorization.[132] However, it soon became clear that the term 'authorize' extended the copyright-owner's rights to cover the acts of persons in some way associated or affiliated with an infringement. It was said that 'authorize' meant to sanction, countenance, or approve,[133] or alternatively, to grant or purport to grant to a third person the right to do an act.[134] The latter formulation has now received the approval of the House of Lords. In order to amount to authorization, the person to whom 'authority' has illegitimately been granted must in fact commit an infringing act.[135] However,

---

[126] [2000] *FSR* 363.

[127] *Francis Day & Hunter v. Bron* [1963] 1 *Ch* 587, 611 (adaptation and translation must be deliberate).

[128] CDPA s. 21(3)(ab).   [129] CDPA s. 21(4); Software Directive, Art. 4(b).

[130] CDPA s. 21(3)(ac); Database Dir., Art. 5(b).

[131] CDPA s. 16(2). Y. Gendreau, 'Authorization Revisited' (2001) 48 *Journal of the Copyright Society of the USA* 341. The 'authorization' right needs to be compared with the general principles of joint tortfeasance described in Ch. 47. Acts which are 'authorizations' will often also be acts which amount to joint tortfeasance, but there is such a degree of uncertainty surrounding the case law (particularly after the narrow interpretation given to authorization in *CBS v. Amstrad* [1988] 2 *All ER* 484) that it remains impossible to estimate how far the tort of authorization extends beyond joint tortfeasance.

[132] *Falcon v. Famous Players* [1926] 2 *KB* 474, 495–6; *PRS v. Ciryl Theatrical Syndicate* [1924] 1 *KB* 1, 12.

[133] *Falcon v. Famous Players* [1926] 2 *KB* 474, 491.   [134] Ibid.

[135] *Nelson v. Rye and Cocteau Records* [1996] *FSR* 313, 337.

the person giving the authorization (in contrast with the person to whom authority is given) need not be located in the UK.[136]

The concept of authorization has been applied in two distinct ways. First, it has been used to expand the network of potential liability beyond vicarious liability. This has typically occurred in relation to the performance of copyright works.[137] Given that performers often do not have a lot of money, copyright owners have attempted to sue the parties who hired the performers. While the principle of vicarious liability made this relatively straightforward where the performer was an employee,[138] copyright owners argued, for example, that where a person hired a band (which infringed copyright), the hirer was liable for 'authorizing' the infringing performance. These attempts proved to be relatively successful where the hirer was aware of the songs which the band would perform, or did nothing to control the repertoire performed. In both cases the hirer was deemed to have authorized the infringements.[139] However, where a warning was given to the performers and the infringements were by way of spontaneous encores of which the hirer had no prior knowledge, the mere hiring of the band was held not to be an authorization.[140] In one case, an attempt to make a managing director liable for authorizing the infringing performance of a band was unsuccessful where the director had taken no interest in the content of the performance and was out of the country when it took place.[141]

The concept of authorization has also been applied where a person manufactures or supplies equipment or other means that enable or facilitate infringement. In these circumstances copyright owners have argued that, where a person makes facilities available in the knowledge that they will probably be used to infringe, this is equivalent to 'authorizing' infringement. Thus it has been asserted that a person who supplies films to a cinema, who sells blank tapes to the public when renting out records,[142] makes photocopying equipment available in a library,[143] or manufactures tape-to-tape machines, should be treated as having authorized the resulting infringements. Today the same kind of arguments are being used in relation to the activities of those who make available file-sharing software, such as Grokster or KaZaa, as well as others who provide hyper-links to infringing material, or provide the internet locations of infringing material, for example, on aggregation sites or through search engines.[144]

The leading authority in the UK is *CBS Songs v. Amstrad*,[145] where the House of Lords defined the term 'authorize' restrictively. Amstrad manufactured and marketed a double-speed

[136] CDPA s. 16(2), in contrast with s. 16(1) is not explicitly confined to 'acts' of authorization within the UK: *ABKCO Music & Records Inc. v. Music Collection International* [1995] *RPC* 657.

[137] But note also, e.g. *Pensher Security Door Co. v. Sunderland CC* [2000] *RPC* 249, 278–9 (door designs).

[138] *PRS v. Mitchell & Booker (Palais de Danse)* [1924] 1 *KB* 762 (applying a 'control' test). For consideration of the issue where the act is playing a radio, see *PRS v. Kwik-Fit Group Ltd* [2008] *ECDR* (2) 13 (OH CS).

[139] *PRS v. Bradford Corporation* (1921) [1917–23] *MacG CC* 309, 312–13, 314. If the hirer specified particular songs were to be performed, and those performances infringed copyright, the case would be even stronger: see *Standen Engineering v. Spalding & Sons* [1984] *FSR* 554; *Pensher v. Sunderland CC* [2000] *RPC* 249, 278–9 (commissioner specifying infringing design).

[140] *PRS v. Bradford Corporation* [1917–23] *MacG CC* 309, 314.

[141] *PRS v. Ciryl Theatrical Syndicate* [1924] 1 *KB* 1.

[142] *CBS Inc v. Ames Records and Tapes* [1981] 2 *All ER* 812 (a record library which lent out records and sold cheap blank tapes did not infringe).

[143] *Moorhouse v. UNSW* [1976] *RPC* 151, 159 (High Court of Australia) (university authorized infringement of copyright by providing a self-service photocopying machine without adequate warning about copyright). Cf. *CCH Canadian Ltd. v. Law Society of Upper Canada* [2004] *SCC* 13.

[144] *Perfect 10 Inc v. Google Inc* 416 F.Supp.2d 828 (CD Cal 2006).   [145] [1988] 2 *All ER* 484.

twin-tape recorder, which was sold by Dixons. The advertisement which Lord Templeman described as 'hypocritical and disingenuous' boasted that the model 'now features hi-speed dubbing enabling you to make duplicate recordings from one cassette to another, record direct from any source and then make a copy and you can even make a copy of your favourite cassette.' An asterisk drew attention to a footnote warning that the recording and playback of certain material was only possible with permission. It also referred the user to the relevant legislation. The British Phonogram Industry (BPI), which represents various owners of copyright in musical and literary works and in sound recordings, claimed that Amstrad had authorized infringement of copyright in BPI's sound recordings.[146]

The House of Lords held that neither the sale of the equipment nor the advertisement thereof amounted to an authorization. Lord Templeman said that an authorization means a grant or purported grant, express or implied, of the right to do the act complained of.[147] The House of Lords held that, while the machinery enabled a person to copy lawfully or unlawfully, this did not constitute an authorization.[148] Lord Templeman said that it was crucial that the footnote had warned that certain types of copying required permission and that Amstrad did not have the authority to grant that permission. In short, the Lords held that there was no authorization because it was up to the operator whether to infringe or not: Amstrad in no way purported to possess the authority to give permission to copy records.

Two Australian cases have applied the concept of 'authorization' to the internet.[149] In *Universal Music Australia v Cooper*,[150] the Full Federal Court held that a web site, 'mp3s4free. net', which provided links to other locations from which sound recordings could be copied, was liable for authorizing infringement (by users in copying the recordings, and third parties in communicating them to such users). The site was structured so that third parties could add links and the creator of the web site, Cooper, was unable to prevent the addition of or edit these links. Nevertheless, the Court—adopting the broad interpretation of 'authorize' as 'countenance, sanction or approve'—found that Cooper had authorized infringement. The Court emphasized that it was Cooper's deliberate choice to establish the web site in this way, and therefore he could not claim thereafter to lack power to control the infringements he had enabled others to carry out.[151] The Court also noted that Cooper benefited financially from advertising a sponsorship of the site and took no steps to prevent infringement. A disclaimer regarding copyright law was dismissed as merely cosmetic. Overall, the Court concluded that by establishing the web site Cooper *invited* users and third parties to do acts that infringed copyright, and thereby authorized those infringements. What is more, the Court affirmed the judge's finding that the service provider which hosted Cooper's web site was also liable for authorization, since it knew of Cooper's site and did nothing to curtail its operation.

In *Universal Music et al v Sharman License Holdings Ltd*,[152] the Federal Court of Australia held that the marketing of KaZaa software which was used to infringe the

---

[146] Their Lordships also considered and rejected a number of related claims as to joint tortfeasance. See below at pp. 1075–6.

[147] [1988] 2 *All ER* 484, 493.   [148] Ibid, 492.

[149] Under s. 101(1A) of the Copyright Act 1968 (as amended by the Copyright Amendment (Digital Agenda) Act 2000—so as to specify certain relevant factors in the assessment of whether authorization occurs).

[150] [2006] FCAFC 187 (18 December 2006).

[151] See Kenny J at 148–9. According to Branson J, 'a person's power to prevent the doing of an act comprised in a copyright includes the person's power not to facilitate the doing of that act by, for example, making available to the public a technical capacity calculated to lead to the doing of that act'.

[152] [2005] *FCA* 1242 (5 September 2005). Apparently, the case is being appealed. For commentaries, see R. Giblin & M. Davison, 'KaZaa goes the way of Grokster: Authorization of Copyright Infringement

applicants' copyright amounted to authorization so to do.[153] Wilcox J reiterated that under Australian law, 'authorisation' meant to 'sanction, approve or countenance' an infringement, and that inactivity and indifference may be such as to lead a court to infer authorization.[154] Despite using notices telling users that Sharman did not condone copyright infringements, the judge held that there was evidence of positive acts encouraging infringement, coupled with a failure to use filtering software. He went on to say that Sharman was in fact in a position to control users' activities.[155]

Although these two cases both depended upon interpretation and application of the concept of authorization, they are of dubious direct relevance as indications of British law. This is for two reasons. The first is because a divergence had already emerged between the UK and Australian courts' interpretations of authorization: the House of Lords in *Amstrad* preferring a narrow test ('to grant or purport to grant authority to do an act') whereas the Australian High Court in *Moorhouse* preferred the broader notion of 'sanction, countenance or approve'.[156] In *Universal v. Cooper*, Kenny J specifically rejected Cooper's argument that authorization should be understood restrictively (*à la* Amstrad) as inconsistent with Australian authority.[157] Second, the Australian legislature seemed to give its explicit approval to the broad interpretation of authorization when in 2000 it amended the Australian copyright law to 'codify' the test by introducing a series of statutory factors which a court is to consider when deciding that there has been an authorization.[158]

What would the results in these cases be under UK law? The result of the *Cooper* decision might well have been the same: after all, the provision of links to infringing material seems as inevitably to produce infringement as the supply of films to a cinema, which was held to amount to authorization in *Falcon v. Famous Players*. It is more difficult to predict the result in the UK of a case with the same facts as *Sharman*. The restrictive interpretation of 'authorization' adopted in *Amstrad*, with its emphasis on control, might well lead to a conclusion that Sharman was not 'authorizing'.[159] As a result, a court might be inclined to resort to a general theory of tortious liability, following the approach of the US Supreme Court in *Grokster*.[160] In this case, the Supreme Court held providers of peer-to-peer software liable for 'inducing' infringements. The inducement lay not in the supply of software itself, since this had some non-infringing uses,[161] but rather in the manner in which the device had been distributed

via Peer-to-Peer Networks in Australia' (2006) *Australian Intellectual Property Journal, 53*; J. Ginsburg & S. Ricketson, 'Inducers and Authorisers: A Comparison of the US Supreme Court's Grokster Decision and the Australian Federal Court's KaZaa Ruling' (2006) 11 *Media and Arts Law Review;* G. Austin, 'Importing KaZaa—Exporting Grokster' (2006) 22 *Santa Clara Computer and High Tech Law Journal* 577.

[153] [2005] *FCA* 1242, para 420.   [154] Ibid, para 402.   [155] Ibid, para 414.

[156] See also *Australasian Performing Right Association Limited v. Jain* (1990) 26 *FCR* 53, 57–60. Gendreau has offered an explanation of this divergence in terms of the different approaches to secondary infringement in the respective legislation: Gendreau, 'Authorization Revisited', 350–1.

[157] [2006] FCAFC 187, para 140.

[158] The matters that must be taken into account include the following: '(a) the extent (if any) of the person's power to prevent the doing of the act concerned; (b) the nature of any relationship existing between the person and the person who did the act concerned; (c) whether the person took any other reasonable steps to prevent or avoid the doing of the act, including whether the person complied with any relevant industry codes of practice.'

[159] Though some would argue that filtering technology is now at a sufficient level of sophistication that 'control' exists, a positive requirement to filter might impose considerable costs and administrative burdens on amateur operations and emergent businesses.

[160] *Metro-Goldwyn-Mayer Studios Inc v. Grokster* 125 S Ct 2764 (2005).

[161] Ginsburg and Kennedy JJ and Rehnquist CJ doubted whether the non-infringing uses were substantial enough to bring the software within the 'staple article of commerce' concept.

'with the object of promoting its use to infringe copyright, as shown by clear expression or other affirmative steps taken to foster infringement'. English law has a similar principle of joint tortfeasance through inducement or procurement of a tort which might equally apply to such a situation.

9 LIABILITY OF INTERNET SERVICE PROVIDERS

One issue that has caused particular concern is the position of those who provide services and facilities that facilitate infringement on the internet.[162] These people, who effectively provide the hardware and infrastructure for the new information society, include multi-national enterprises who provide the cables for communication, as well as others who provide access to the web through local 'servers,' who run bulletin boards and web sites where others can post information, and who provide temporary access to the net at internet cafés. At one stage, it became fashionable to suggest that the difficulties with rights holders policing their own rights were so great that some of these service providers should incur liability where infringing material was found on sites which they controlled. The argument ran that these persons were in the best position to supervise and inspect their cyber premises, and like the owner of a place of entertainment, should be liable for infringements which occurred on their 'premises'.[163]

The European Commission decided to pre-empt the development of diverse national responses to these issues through a harmonizing Directive, but took the view that, since service providers could incur liability on a number of bases (defamation, copyright, obscenity, etc.), the issue fell outside the remit of the Information Society Directive. Instead, harmonization was provided for in Articles 12–15 of the EC Directive on Electronic Commerce, which required member states, by 17 January 2002, to confer an immunity on such providers except in certain limited situations.[164] These parallel, in large part, the so-called 'safe harbours' introduced into US law by the US Digital Millenium Copyright Act.[165]

British implementation took place in the Electronic Commerce (EC Directive) Regulations 2002.[166] For internet and related service providers, law adjacent to copyright law introduces three general immunities from liability, whether it be for the infringement of copyright or the

---

[162] WCT, Art. 8. Note also the 'Agreed Statement' annexed to the Treaty stating that the mere provision of physical facilities for enabling or making a communication does not in itself amount to a communication.

[163] Info. Soc. Dir., Recital 59. Indeed, as 'filtering technology' becomes more widely available, some people predict that the immunities granted to ISPs in the formative years of the internet will increasingly be pared back.

[164] Electronic Commerce Dir. The European Council Directive on Certain Legal Aspects of Electronic Commerce in the Internal Market is aimed generally at promoting electronic commerce within the European Union, that is the provision of goods and services on-line, and so encompasses many matters such as electronic contracts, unsolicited communications, codes of conduct, etc., outside the scope of this book.

[165] Online Copyright Infringement Liability Limitation Act, Title II of the Digital Millennium Copyright Act, Pub. L. No. 105–304, amending Ch. 5 of Title 17 USC. In contrast with the DMCA no provision is made for the benefit of information location tools. For commentaries, see A. Yen, 'Internet Service Provider Liability for Subscriber Copyright Infringement, Enterprise Liability and the First Amendment' (2000) 88 *Georgetown Law Journal* 1883. For comparisons, see V. McEvedy, 'The DMCA and the E-Commerce Directive' [2002] *EIPR* 65.

[166] Electronic Commerce (EC Directive) Regulations 2002, SI 2002/2013 in force on 21 Aug. 2002.

violation of any other right.[167] The immunities in all cases excuse liability for damages, for any other monetary remedy, and for any criminal sanction, but they do not prohibit injunctive relief.[168]

The beneficiaries of these immunities are so-called information-society service providers, that is, any service which is normally provided for remuneration, and which operates at a distance by electronic means, and at the individual request of a recipient of the services. It would cover, therefore, most commercial Internet Service Providers, but would not cover internet cafés, whose services are not provided at a distance. The immunities apply to 'mere conduits,' 'caching,' and 'hosting,' as follows.

9.1 MERE CONDUIT[169]

Where the service provided is the transmission in a communication network of information provided by a recipient of the service, or is the provision of access to a communication network, the service provider is exempted from liablity where it did not initiate the transmission, select the receiver of the transmission, and did not select or modify the information contained in the transmission.[170]

9.2 CACHING

Where the service provided is the transmission in a communication network of information provided by a recipient of the service, the service provider shall not be liable if the information is the subject of 'automatic, immediate and temporary storage' and if the following conditions are satisfied:

(i)   the service provider provides storage for the sole purpose of making more efficient onward transmission of the information to other recipients of the service upon their request;

(ii)   the service provider does not modify the information;

(iii) it complies with the conditions on access to the information;

(iv)   it complies with rules regarding the updating of the information;

(v)   it does not interfere with the lawful use of technology, widely recognized and used by the industry, to obtain data on the use of the information; and

(vi)   it acts expeditiously to remove or disable access to the information, so stored, upon obtaining actual knowledge of the fact that the information at the initial source of the transmission has been removed from the network, or access to it has been disabled, or a court has ordered such removal or disablement.[171]

---

167 Ibid.   168 Electronic Commerce Reg. 20(1)(b).
169 Cp. s. 512(a) of the US Copyright Act 1976 providing the 'conduit' safe harbour in US law. It defines a 'service provider' as 'an entity offering the transmission, routing or providing of connections for digital online communications, between or among points specified by a user, of material of the user's choosing, without modification to the content of the material sent or received'.
170 Electronic Commerce Reg. 17.
171 Electronic Commerce Reg. 18. Cf. s. 512(b) of the US Copyright Act 1976 (as introduced by the DMCA).

9.3 HOSTING

Where the service provided consists of storage of information provided by a recipient of the service, the service provider shall not be liable for storage where it has no actual knowledge of unlawful activity or information, and is not aware of facts or circumstances from which it would have been apparent to the service provider that the activity or information was unlawful; or, upon obtaining such knowledge or awareness, it acts expeditiously to remove or disable access to the information.[172]

9.4 INJUNCTIVE RELIEF

Section 97A of the 1988 Act (which implements Article 8 of the Information Society Directive) imposes an important counterweight to those immunities. This confers a power on the High Court to issue an injunction against a service provider where that person has actual knowledge of another person using their service to infringe copyright. In assessing whether the service provider has the appropriate knowledge, the Court is directed to take account of any notice received by the service provider under regulation 6(1)(c) of the Electronic Commerce Regulations 2002. Right holders are in a position to apply for an injunction against intermediaries whose services are used by a third party to infringe a copyright or related right. While the immunities given by the Electronic Commerce Directive prevent financial liability, if the service provider is informed of the illegal acts, thereafter it seems they must take action to stop them continuing or face injunctive relief.

---

[172] Electronic Commerce Reg. 19. Cf. s. 512(c) of the US Copyright Act 1976 (as introduced by the DMCA). Note the 'notice and take-down' and 'put-back' procedures.

7

DURATION OF COPYRIGHT

CHAPTER CONTENTS

1 INTRODUCTION

The question of the appropriate period of protection that ought to be granted to copyright works has long captured the attention of policy makers, legislatures, judges, and commentators. For example, the central question of the literary property debate of the eighteenth century was whether common law literary property protection should be perpetual.[1] Similar debates have arisen at many other times during the history of copyright law. While these debates have always been shaped by the particular circumstances under discussion, they are similar in that they have attempted to mediate between the private interests of owners and the interests of the public in ensuring access to creative works.[2] That is, they have attempted to coordinate and balance the various interests that coexist in copyright law. Another common feature of these debates is that, whenever the question of duration has arisen, the length of protection has

---

[1] That is, the debates preceding and surrounding *Millar v. Taylor* (1769) 98 *ER* 201; 4 *Burr* 2303 and *Donaldson v. Beckett* (1774) 2 *Brown's Prerogative Cases;* Cobbett's *Parliamentary History* xvii, 954. See, e.g. A. Birrell, *Seven Lectures on Copyright* (1898); B. Kaplan, *An Unhurried View of Copyright,* 1–25 (1967); L.-R. Patterson, *Copyright in Historical Perspective* (1968); M. Rose, *Authors and Owners* (1993); D. Saunders, *Authorship and Copyright* (1992); Sherman and Bently, ch. 1.

[2] For an overview of policy considerations, see S. Ricketson, 'The Copyright Term' (1992) 23 *IIC* 753. The arguments were extensively ventilated in the US literature surrounding *Eldred et al. v. Ashcroft* [2003] 123 *S Ct* 769 in which the US Supreme Court (Stevens J and Breyer J dissenting) held constitutional Congress's extension of copyright for extant works to life plus 70 years. Of the more startling contributions, see W. Landes and R. Posner, 'Indefinitely Renewable Copyright' (2003) 70 *University of Chicago LR* 471 (proposing a system of indefinitely renewable copyright, the requirement of renewal ensuring most works fall into the public domain, the possibility of indefinite renewal ensuring sufficient incentive to exploit the work). For a compelling critique of the 'neo-liberal economics' espoused by Landes and Posner, see M. Lemley, '*Ex Ante* versus *Ex Post* Justifications for Intellectual Property' (2004) 71 *University of Chicago LR* 129.

typically increased rather than decreased. For example, literary works were initially protected for 14 years under the 1710 Statute of Anne. After great debate, the 1842 Literary Copyright Act extended the term of copyright in books to 42 years, or the author's life plus 7 years.[3] In 1911, this was extended to life plus a 50-year term. As a result of the EU Duration Directive, the term of protection was recently increased to the life of the author plus 70 years.[4]

Before looking at duration in more detail, it is important to note a number of things. The first is that the period of protection changes depending on the type of work in question. This is a reflection of the fact that different interests and policy issues arise with different categories of work. The way in which the term of protection is calculated also differs depending on the type of work in question. In relation to most literary, dramatic, musical, and artistic works, copyright subsists throughout the life of the author, and for a fixed term (currently 70 years) that is calculated from when the author dies (*post mortem*). In the case of entrepreneurial works and certain types of authorial work (such as those of unknown authorship), the protection is a fixed term which is calculated from when the work is either *made* or *published*. The term is calculated from the end of the year in which a particular event occurs.[5]

Harmonization of copyright laws in Europe has had an important impact upon the duration of copyright in the United Kingdom. When the 1988 Act was first enacted, the length of protection for literary, dramatic, musical, and artistic works was for the life of the author plus 50 years. In relation to sound recordings, films, and broadcasts, the period of protection lasted for 50 years from the making of the work. The duration for typographical arrangements was limited to 25 years from the year in which the edition was first published.

As a result of the EU Duration Directive the length of protection for literary, dramatic, musical, and artistic works in the United Kingdom was increased as of 1 January 1996 to the life of the author plus 70 years.[6] The term of protection offered to films also changed as a result of the Directive. Under the 1988 Act (as enacted), where films were treated as entrepreneurial works, films were given a fixed term of protection. As a result of the move towards harmonization of copyright in Europe, films are now treated more as authorial works.[7] This is reflected in the fact that the period of protection offered to films now depends on the life of the principal director, author of the screenplay, author of the dialogue, and the composer of music specifically created for use in the work. No changes needed to be made to the erm for broadcasts,[8] or for typographical arrangements. Some minor changes have taken place in relation to sound recordings.[9]

---

[3] C. Seville, *Literary Copyright Reform in Early Victorian England* (1999).

[4] Duration Directive. See W. Chernaik and P. Parrinder (eds.), *Textual Monopolies* (1997); N. Dawson, 'Copyright in the European Union: Plundering the Public Domain' (1994) *Northern Ireland Legal Quarterly* 193; S. Lewinski, 'EC Proposal for Council Directive Harmonizing the Term of Protection of Copyright' (1992) 23 *IIC* 785; A. Silvestro, 'Towards EC Harmonization of the Term of Protection of Copyright and so-called Related Rights' [1993] *Ent LR* 73.

[5] CDPA s. 12(2). The Duration Directive expresses this as calculating matters 'from the first day of January of the year following the event which gives rise to them'. Duration Dir., Art. 8.

[6] Duration of Copyright and Rights in Performances Regulations 1995 (SI 1995/3297). The length of protection is greater than that which is required in the WIPO Copyright Treaty, Art. 1(4) and the TRIPS Agreement: Art. 9 TRIPS.

[7] In fact the position is more complicated. Art. 3(3) of the Directive also provides that the rights of the producer of first fixation of a film are to last 50 years after fixation or after the fixation was lawfully published. These are distinct from the rights of the owner of copyright in a cinematographic or audiovisual work.

[8] Duration Dir., Art. 3(4).

[9] The Copyright and Related Rights Regulations 2003 (SI 2003/2498) reg. 29 amends CDPA s. 13A(2) to implement the Information Society's amendment to the Duration Dir., Art 3(2). Transitional provisions are made by regs 30–39.

In implementing the Duration Directive, member states were required to apply the new terms to all works and subject matter that were protected in at least one member state on 1 July 1995. As it turned out, this meant that not only was the copyright in many works extended, but also that the copyright in some works which had previously expired had to be revived.[10] For example, the United Kingdom copyright in a work by a British author who died in 1935 and which had first been published in the United Kingdom, would have lapsed on 1 January 1986; but would have been revived from 1 January 1996, since the work would have been protected in Germany on 1 July 1995.[11] The Directive also obliged member states when implementing the reforms 'to adopt the necessary provisions to protect in particular acquired rights of third parties'.[12] Acts done pursuant to arrangements made before 1 July 1995 at a time when copyright did not subsist in the work are treated as not infringing any revived copyright in a work.[13] In all cases, the revived copyright is treated as 'licensed by the copyright owner, subject only to the payment of such reasonable royalty or other remuneration as may be agreed or determined in default of agreement by the Copyright Tribunal'.[14]

As well as extending the period of protection given to many works, as of 1 January 1996 the Duration Directive also changed the way duration is calculated for works originating from outside the EEA. Prior to the introduction of the Directive, British law provided the same level of protection to works published in the United Kingdom as those published elsewhere. This principle changed, however, under the Duration Directive which only requires that the extended period of protection be offered to works originating from within the EEA. The period of protection given to works of non-EEA origin, that is to works not originating in the EEA or without an EEA author, is the same as that which the work would receive in the country of origin.[15] That is, the Duration Directive is based on a notion of 'comparison of terms' rather than national treatment.[16] This means that, where a work is first published in Australia[17] and the author is not a national of an EEA state, the work is only protected in Europe for 50 years after the death of the author (because that is the duration of Australian copyright law).[18]

However, it has been observed that the implementation of the 'comparison of terms' rule in the United Kingdom may be more far-reaching than the Directive was generally thought to have intended.[19] This is because section 12(6) (like sections 13A(4), 13B(7), 14(3)) refers to the

---

[10] Duration of Copyright and Rights in Performances Regulations 1995 (SI 1995/3297), especially r. 17.

[11] *Land Hessen v. G. Ricordi & Co*, Case C–360/00 [2002] *ECR* I–5089 (ECJ).

[12] Duration Directive, Art. 10. See also Recitals 26 and 27. For discussion by the ECJ of the Italian transitional provisions see *Butterfly Music Srl v. Carosello Edizioni Musicali e Discografiche Srl* Case C–60/98 [1999] *ECR* I–3939, [2000] 1 CMLR 587 (holding that the Italian legislation satisfied the criterion of legality imposed by the Directive, and did not defeat the intention of the Directive. The ECJ approved the fact that those who had reproduced and marketed phonograms during the period when copyright had expired were permitted by the Italian provisions to continue distribution for three months after the copyright revived, the Court saying 'a provision of that kind, which must necessarily be transitional in order not to prevent the application of the new term of copyright and related rights on the date laid down by the Directive, that being the Directive's principal objective': para. 28. See J. Phillips, 'The Butterfly that Stamped' [1999] *Ent LR* 189; B. Lindner, 'Revival of Rights v. Protection of Acquired Rights' [2000] *EIPR* 133; L. Ubertazzi, 'The *Butterfly* Case or EC Term of Protection Directive and Transitional Law' [2000] 31 *IIC* 142.

[13] Duration of Copyright and Rights in Performances Regulations 1995 (SI 1995/3297). *Sweeney v. Macmillan Publishers Ltd* [2002] *RPC* (35) 651.

[14] Ibid, r. 23, r. 24.

[15] On what is a country of origin see CDPA s. 15A. In relation to sound recordings, and broadcasts, the Act refers to the author of a work being 'a national of an EEA state': CDPA s. 13A(4), s. 14(3).

[16] Duration Dir., Recital 22, Art. 7.   [17] CDPA s. 15A(2).   [18] CDPA s. 12 (6).

[19] As observed by Mustafa Safiyuddin, of Little & Co, Mumbai.

duration of copyright as being 'that to which the work is entitled' in the country of origin. A literal interpretation requires reference therefore not only to duration in the country of origin, but also to whether copyright subsists at all in that country: after all, if there is no copyright in the work in its country of origin, it is difficult to say the work is 'entitled' to copyright for any length of time. The impact would be to deny copyright to works which were unprotected in the country of origin, for example, because they fell outside any list of subject matter, or failed to reach that country's originality threshold. UK implementation, thus interpreted, would take the comparison of terms rule and transform it into something akin to a rule of reciprocity (and thus incompatible with the Berne Convention). The Directive, in contrast, states that copyright 'shall expire on the date of expiry of the protection granted in the country of origin.' The use of the term 'expiry' suggests that the rule is not directed at conditions of subsistence. The preferable view is that section 12(6) should be read as only dealing with expiry of term: in cases where works are not protected in the country of origin, but would meet British requirements for sub-sistence, the section should be understood as requiring British law to give such works protection until such time as protection of a work *of that sort* would expire in the country of origin.

2 LITERARY, DRAMATIC, MUSICAL, AND ARTISTIC WORKS

Subject to the exceptions listed below, copyright in a literary, dramatic, musical, or artistic work expires 70 years from the year in which the author of the work dies.[20] Thus, where an author of a book died in 1990, the copyright in the book would expire in 2060. If a literary, dra-matic, musical, or artistic work is jointly authored, the 70-year *post-mortem* term of copyright is calculated from the year in which the longest surviving author dies.[21]

In discussions about copyright duration, the question is often asked: why not have fixed terms for all works? A number of justifications have been given as to why the 'life-plus' term should be used to calculate the duration of authorial works. It has been suggested, admittedly without any real evidence, that since authors will be providing for their next of kin, the life-plus protection provides authors with incentives to create up until their death. Another explan-ation given as to why the life-plus formula is used is that it overcomes the problems that often arise in determining when a work was made or published. While the date of an author's death is easily ascertained from public records, it is often difficult to determine when something was created. A final reason for using the life-plus formula is that it avoids the complications that would otherwise arise in calculating duration when authors make revisions to a work during their lifetime. Under the life-plus test, all works fall into the public domain on the same date.

2.1 EXCEPTIONS TO THE TERM OF LIFE PLUS 70 YEARS

The general rule that the duration of literary, dramatic, musical, and artistic works is life plus 70 years is subject to the following exceptions: computer-generated works; Crown copyright;

---

[20] CDPA s. 12(2).

[21] CDPA ss. 3(1), 12(4). However, because copyright subject matter remains unharmonized, different European countries have different concepts of joint authorship in relation to 'songs'. In Britain, a song comprises two works, and the duration of copyright in lyrics and music must be calculated separately. For an overview of the European situation, see IViR, *Recasting Copyright for the Knowledge Economy* (2006), Ch. 4.

Parliamentary copyright and international organizations; artistic works used in designs; works of unknown authorship; unpublished works not in the public domain.[22]

2.1.1 Computer-generated works

Where a literary, dramatic, musical, or artistic work is computer-generated, the duration of protection lasts for 50 years from the end of the year when the work was made.[23]

2.1.2 Crown copyright

Crown copyright in a literary, dramatic, musical, or artistic work lasts for 125 years from the year in which the work was made. If the work is published commercially within 75 years from the year it was made, then copyright lasts for 50 years from the date it was commercially published.[24]

2.1.3 Parliamentary copyright and international organizations

Parliamentary copyright lasts for 50 years from the year in which the work was made.[25] Where an international organization is the first owner, copyright also lasts for 50 years from when the work was made.

2.1.4 Artistic works used in designs

Copyright in artistic works which have been used in designs of industrially produced articles lasts for 25 years from the year in which such articles are first legitimately marketed.

2.1.5 Works of unknown authorship

As we saw earlier, in certain situations it may not be possible to identify the author of a particular work. Given that, with works of unknown authorship, there is no identifiable author whose death can help set the duration of protection, copyright law is forced to use other trigger points to calculate duration. In these circumstances, the 1988 Act provides that copyright in a literary, dramatic, musical, or artistic work of unknown authorship lasts for 70 years calculated either from the year of creation or, if during that period the work is made available to the public, from the year it was made available.[26] If the author's name is disclosed before the 70-year term lapses and before the author's death, this disclosure will have the effect of extending the term of copyright to the author's life plus 70 years.[27]

2.1.6 Unpublished works not in the public domain

Section 17 of the 1911 Copyright Act conferred protection on unpublished literary, dramatic, and musical works, and engravings, for 50 years from the date of publication. This meant that

---

[22] Prior, perpetual copyrights under past law end in 2040. Contrast, however, the curious exception for J. M. Barrie's *Peter Pan*: CDPA, Sched. 1, para. 13, and Sched. 6, respectively.

[23] CDPA s. 12(7).

[24] CDPA ss. 163(3), 164, 165(3), 166(5). International organizations initially acquiring copyright in a work may enjoy it for 50 years from making or longer if specified by order: CDPA s. 168(3).

[25] CDPA s. 165(3).

[26] CDPA s. 12(3). The requisite 'making available to the public' includes the following acts if authorized: publishing, performing in public, and communicating the work to the public, in the case of literary, dramatic, and musical works; and exhibition in public, and inclusion in a film shown in public, or a communication to the public, in the case of artistic works: CDPA s. 12(5).

[27] CDPA s. 12(4). Before 1996, absent identification of an author, an anonymous or pseudonymous work obtained a term of 50 years from the year of first publication.

so long as the works remained unpublished the copyright term was unlimited. The 1988 Act removed this possibility by specifying that copyright in works which were unpublished at the author's death and remained so until 1 August 1989, was to last for a fixed period of 50 years from 1 January 1990, that is, until 31 December 2039.[28]

3 FILMS

Under the 1956 and 1988 Acts (as enacted), where films were treated as types of entrepreneurial work, protection was limited to 50 years, normally calculated from the year of release.[29] The Duration Directive required recognition of copyright in both the first fixation of a film for 50 years, and the 'cinematographic or audiovisual work' for which the term was to be 70 years from the year of the latest death among four categories of person: the principal director, the author of the screenplay, the author of the dialogue, or the composer of music specially created for and used in the film.[30] Subsequent British attempts at implementation rather unwisely ignored the distinction, preferring to extend the copyright in 'film'—the section 5B copyright—to 70 years from the death of these four persons.[31] Where the identity of these four people is unknown, the term of protection is 70 years from the year in which the film was made.[32] Alternatively, if during that period the film is made available to the public, copyright expires 70 years from the end of the year in which the film was first made available.[33] Foreseeing potential problems in identifying when such copyright expires, the Duration Regulations also introduced a new exception to allow a film to be copied at a time when it is reasonable to assume that copyright has expired.[34]

Not long after this attempted implementation, the Court of Appeal recognized that cinematographic works benefit from copyright not merely as films but also as dramatic works.[35] While this decision moved British law some way towards compliance with international and regional obligations, it also exposed further the oddness of the British attempt to give effect to the Duration Directive. This is because the term of copyright in the cinematographic work as a dramatic work is left to be determined by reference to the life of the 'author.' In British law, this might well include the director and authors of scripts for the film (as long as they do not exist before the film-making process) and possibly the editors or director of cinematography, but it is highly unlikely to include the composer of music. If normal principles were to be applied, the term of protection would be unlikely to be that required by Article 2(2). If the legislation

---

[28] CDPA, Sched. 1, para. 12(4). A work published after the author's death, but before 1 Aug. 1989, obtained a term of 50 years from publication: CDPA, Sched. 1, para. 12(2). Under the 1956 Act, a work unpublished at the author's death continued in copyright until 50 years after first publication: CA 1956, ss. 2(3), 3(4). In some cases, certain acts, such as performance in public, had the same effect as publication. For some works unpublished on 1 Aug. 1989, the relevant copyright will have been extended by the recent increase in the term of copyright. For example, if an author died in 1988 leaving unpublished manuscripts (which remained unpublished in 1990), the effect of the changes made in 1988 was that copyright lasted until 31 Dec. 2039. However, as a result of the increase in the duration of copyright to life plus 70 years copyright will be extended to 31 Dec. 2058.

[29] CDPA s. 13 (as enacted).   [30] Duration Dir., Art. 2(2).

[31] CDPA s. 13B(2). Each category may include more than one member, but unidentified members do not count: CDPA s. 13B(3), (10).

[32] CDPA s. 13B (4)(a), (10).

[33] CDPA s. 13B(4)(b), (10). The requisite 'making available to the public' includes the following acts if authorized: showing in public or communicating to the public: CDPA s. 13B(6).

[34] CDPA s. 66A.   [35] *Norowzian v. Arks (No. 2)* [2000] *FSR* 363.

is not amended, it is not unlikely that a court will be faced with the choice of applying these normal principles, and acknowledging failed implementation, or reading the term 'author' in this context as being open-textured enough to take its meaning from the Directive. Moreover, once a *post-mortem* term is acknowledged to exist in relation to the cinematographic work as a dramatic work, the wrong-headedness of extending the term of the section 5B film copyright is apparent. If the section 5B copyright is to reflect the Directive's demands in relation to related rights in the first fixation of a film, the period should be confined to 50 years from the making of the fixation.[36]

4 ENTREPRENEURIAL WORKS

As entrepreneurial works have no readily identifiable author, the period of protection is calculated using different trigger points.[37]

4.1 SOUND RECORDINGS

For sound recordings, copyright expires 50 years from the end of the year in which it is made. If during that period the sound recording was published, copyright expires 50 years from the year of such publication. If during the 50 years from making the work is not published but is made available to the public by being played in public or communicated to the public, copyright expires 50 years from the year of communication or playing in public.[38] The maximum duration of copyright in a sound recording thus appears to be 100 years (which should be available where a work is published or communicated to the public 50 years after its making).

4.2 BROADCASTS

The duration of broadcasts is 50 years from when the broadcast was first made.[39] Where the author of a broadcast is not a national of an EEA state, the duration of copyright is that to which the broadcast is entitled in the country of which the author is a national (provided that the period of protection does not exceed 50 years).[40]

4.3 TYPOGRAPHICAL ARRANGEMENTS

For typographical arrangements of published editions, copyright expires 25 years from the year of first publication.[41] This right should be distinguished from the publication right conferred on the publisher of a previously unpublished work in which copyright has expired, which also lasts for 25 years from publication.[42]

---

[36] Duration Dir., Art. 3(3). See Kamina, 123.

[37] For transitional provisions see CDPA, Sched. 1, paras. 12(2)(d)–(e), (5), (6).

[38] CDPA s. 13A(2) (as amended by SI 2003/2498, with transitional provisions in regs. 30–32, 36–9) implementing Duration Dir., Art. 3(2) (as amended by Info. Soc. Dir.). Note that an original collection of recordings would constitute a database and therefore be protected as a literary work.

[39] CDPA s. 14(2).   [40] CDPA s. 14(3).   [41] CDPA s. 15.

[42] Related Rights Reg. 16(6). See below at pp. 167–8.

5 MORAL RIGHTS

In the United Kingdom, moral rights of integrity and attribution subsist as long as copyright subsists.[43] The right to object to false attribution is less extensive, only lasting for 20 years after the author's death. In some other countries moral rights are capable of operating in perpetuity. The Duration Directive made no attempt to harmonize the duration of moral rights and was expressed to be without prejudice to them.[44]

6 PUBLICATION RIGHT IN WORKS IN WHICH COPYRIGHT HAS LAPSED

In order to give effect to Article 4 of the Duration Directive, a new property right equivalent to copyright, called a 'publication right', was introduced in the United Kingdom.[45] The right is granted without formality to any person who, after the expiry of copyright protection, publishes for the first time a previously unpublished literary, dramatic, musical, or artistic work or film. This new right lasts for 25 years from the end of the year in which the work was first published.

In order to have the right, a publisher must publish a public-domain literary, dramatic, musical, or artistic work or a film for the first time.[46] The right is only acquired where the work is previously unpublished. It should be noted that publication in this context has a special meaning.[47] When determining whether the work is previously unpublished, no account is to be taken of any unauthorized act done at a time when there is no copyright in the work. An unauthorized act means an act done without the consent of the owner of the physical medium in which the work is embodied or on which it is recorded.

The publication right that vests in the publisher is only available 'after the expiry' of copyright protection.[48] This means that the publication right is unlikely to be of great significance in the United Kingdom for some time. This is because of the dual effect of the changes made as regards unpublished works in the 1988 Act and the other changes made to the copyright term introduced to give effect to the Duration Directive. The effect of these transitional provisions is that the publication right is currently restricted to unpublished artistic works other than engravings.[49]

Another consequence of limiting the availability of the publication right to cases where copyright has expired is that it may exclude works in which copyright has never subsisted. Since the majority of existing unpublished works received statutory copyright protection in 1911, it will normally be possible to resolve the question of whether a work ever enjoyed

---

[43] See Ch. 10.   [44] Duration Dir., Art. 9.   [45] Related Rights Reg. 16.

[46] The publication right does not arise from the publication of a work in which Crown copyright or Parliamentary copyright subsisted: Related Rights Reg. 16(5).

[47] It includes any making available to the public and, in particular, includes the issue of copies to the public; making the work available by means of an electronic retrieval system; the rental or lending of copies of the work to the public; the performance, exhibition, or showing of the work in public; or communicating the work to the public: Related Rights Reg. 16 (as amended).

[48] Ibid.

[49] For an elaboration of the reasoning that leads to this conclusion, see Copinger, paras. 17–29 to 32.

copyright protection without too much difficulty (although problems exist in relation to artistic works). It seems that no statutory copyright existed in unpublished paintings, drawings, and photographs created before 1862 by an artist who died before 1855, nor in unpublished sculptures created prior to 1 July 1862.[50]

While the publication right may supplement existing rights given to publishers in their typographical arrangement of published editions, it differs from these rights in three regards. First, the publication right is only available for the first publication of a previously unpublished work. Second, while the new publication right may apply where the publication relates to an artistic work, the typographical arrangement right is not relevant in such circumstances. This is because the right in typographical arrangement is confined to 'a published edition of the whole or any part of one or more literary, dramatic or musical works'.[51] Third, the publication right is much more extensive than the right to prevent facsimile copying of a typographical arrangement.

A work qualifies for a publication right[52] only if the first publication occurs in the European Economic Area and the publisher of the work at the time of first publication is a national of an EEA state.[53] Publication has a more extended meaning than that discussed in relation to copyright. Where two or more people jointly publish a work, it is sufficient if any of them is a national of an EEA state. No provision is made for the extension of the publication right so as to recognize equivalent rights for foreign publishers, where the country of publication provides reciprocal rights to publishers in the EEA.[54]

7 REFORM PROPOSALS

The record industry and allied interests, particularly performers, have recently been campaigning for an extension of the term of copyright in sound recordings. The background to the campaign is the imminent lapse of sound recording copyright in material from the late 1950s and early 1960s, the heyday of rock 'n' roll and the early years of pop, when artists such as Elvis and the Beatles were performing. An argument is made that extension of copyright in the UK, and of necessity therefore in Europe, is needed because copyright protection of such recordings still exists under the law of the United States. Absent some sort of harmonization with the United States, there is a fear that artists will record with the more lucrative US market in mind, thus producing a sort of 'cultural distortion.' A second argument that is put is that it is unfair to treat sound recording producers and performers differently to creators of literary and artistic works, including cinematographic works. It is said to be particularly unfair that performers, such as Sir Cliff Richard, will find their income from their recording dries up during their lifetime.[55] Consequently, all copyright terms should be aligned at 'life plus 70' (or some equivalent, such as 95 years from publication or 120 years from creation). Thirdly, it is claimed by the record industry that investment in record production in any given year is linked to the previous year's income, so that once its income declines (as recordings go out of copyright) so will its investment. Finally, the record industry argues that increasing the term of copyright in sound recordings may induce greater investment in the production of sound recordings.

---

50 For background, see Sterling and Carpenter, para. 2A.01.   51 CDPA s. 8(1).
52 For general analysis of concepts relevant to protecting foreign claims, see above at Ch. 4, Section 5.
53 Related Rights Reg. 16(4).   54 Ibid.
55 The record industry has not campaigned, however, for longer performers' rights.

The record industry's arguments—particularly the economic ones—have been scrutinized and found to be unpersuasive by a number of independent bodies: the Centre of Intellectual Property and Information Law,[56] the Gowers Committee,[57] and the Institute for Information Law at the University of Amsterdam.[58] These reviews see increasing copyright term as imposing costs on consumers (and welfare generally by increasing so-called 'deadweight loss'),[59] without being likely to increase investment in the production of sound recordings in any significant way. The critical explanation as to why increasing term does not have a substantial effect on present incentives lies in the fact that the current value of money that might be raised in 50 years' time is a tiny fraction of the latter sum.

Not surprisingly, given the revenues that it would gain if it were to be successful in the pursuit of a longer term, the record industry is continuing to lobby national legislatures and the European Commission. The battle over copyright term remains, inevitably, one that will be fought in the political arena where economic rationality is only one weapon that will be deployed. At the time of writing, the record industry's efforts appear to have borne some fruit. On St Valentine's Day, 2008, the Internal Market Commissioner announced that he would be introducing legislation to increase the term of sound recordings to 95 years. The Commissioner claims he is doing so on the basis of the 'moral right' of performers 'to control the use of their work and earn a living from their performances'. Having said he can see no justification for performers being treated differently from authors (who get life plus 70 years), he nowhere explains why he proposes that the EC adopt the 95-year term (that the US confers on copyright owners in sound recordings, insofar as they are perceived as works for hire).[60] If the Commissioner really wanted to protect performers, the proposal would give them a life-long, inalienable right to remuneration from use of their performances, rather than giving the owners of copyright in sound recordings (the record industry) a fixed term.

[56] Centre for Intellectual Property and Information Law, *Review of the Economic Evidence relating to the Extension of the Term of Copyright in Sound Recordings* (2006).

[57] HM Treasury, *Gowers Review of Intellectual Property* (2006), Recommendation 3, paras 4.20–4.47, pp. 48–57.

[58] IViR, *Recasting Copyright*, Ch. 3. See also N. Helberger, N. Dufft, S. van Gompel, B. Hugenholtz, 'Never Forever: Why Extending the Term of Protection for Sound Recordings is a Bad Idea' [2008] *EIPR* 174.

[59] The deadweight loss is the loss caused to those who would have bought a record at the price it would sell for in a competitive market (without copyright) but who are not willing to pay the price established by the copyright owner and thus do not make the relevant purchase.

[60] IP/08/240 (Brussels, 14 Feb 2008).

8

INFRINGEMENT

CHAPTER CONTENTS

1 INTRODUCTION

The aim of this chapter is to explore copyright infringement. We begin by discussing 'primary' infringement, that is, the activities of those involved in infringing the copyright owner's exclusive rights (which we described in Chapter 6). We then discuss the statutory provisions which render accessories—whether before or after the act of primary infringement—liable for assisting in the making or distribution of infringing copies or the giving of infringing performances. These liabilities are referred to as 'secondary infringements'.

Before examining 'primary' infringement in detail, it is worth observing that, while there has been a great deal of norm setting in relation to the rights of the copyright owner, the question of what amounts to copyright infringement has not generally been the subject of much international or regional harmonization. The relevant tests for infringement have largely been developed locally, and for the most part by the judiciary.[1] Having acknowledged that British law on infringement has taken its own course, it is worth noting two recent developments. First, the rule that copyright does not protect ideas has found its way into both

---

[1] While infringement analysis in the UK may use concepts, such as 'substantiality' and 'idea–expression', similar to those used elsewhere, British applications of these concepts are distinct. Consequently, although case law from the United States has sometimes been referred to, the British courts have doubted its relevance. Contrast *John Richardson v. Flanders* [1993] *FSR* 497, 527 (Ferris J, finding useful US case law on infringement in relation to computer programs, especially the abstraction–filtration–comparison approach adopted in *Computer Associates v. Altai* (1993) 23 *IPR* 385); with *Ibcos Computers v. Barclays Mercantile Highland Finance* [1994] *FSR* 275, 289 (Jacob J, finding US case law unhelpful, and pointing out the different statutory basis for US decisions).

regional and international arrangements, and has been interpreted as a copyright 'maximum'.[2] Second, regional harmonization initiatives seem to require that copyright infringement be found to occur where 'any part'—as opposed to any 'substantial part'—of a work is reproduced.[3] Quite what impact, if any, these two developments will have on British case law is difficult to predict.[4]

2 PRIMARY INFRINGEMENT

In an action for primary infringement, the onus falls upon the claimant to show on the balance of probabilities that:

(i) the defendant carried out one of the activities which falls within the copyright owner's control;

(ii) the defendant's work was *derived* from the copyright work ('causal connection'); and

(iii) the restricted act was carried out in relation to the *work* or a *substantial part* thereof.[5]

3 RESTRICTED ACTIVITIES

The first question that needs to be asked in considering whether copyright in a work has been infringed is whether the defendant carried out one of the activities that falls within the copyright owner's rights. This topic was discussed in Chapter 6.

4 A 'CAUSAL CONNECTION'

The second matter that needs to be proved in order to establish infringement is that the defendant's work was *derived* from the claimant's work.[6] That is, it is necessary to show that there is a causal link between the work used by the defendant (i.e. reproduced, issued, rented, performed, communicated, or adapted) and the copyright work. This means that, unlike the

---

[2] TRIPS, Art. 9(2) (copyright protection shall extend to expressions and not to ideas, procedures, methods of operation, or mathematical conceptions as such); WCT, Art. 2. In *Nova Productions v. Mazooma* [2007] *EWCA Civ* 219, [2007] *RPC* 589, 602 (para. 38) Jacob LJ stated that TRIPS, though a minimum standards treaty, 'lays down a positive rule as to the point beyond which copyright protection may not go'. The Software Dir., Art 1(1) states that 'ideas and principles which underlie any element of a computer program...are not protected by copyright'. This, too, is an obligatory requirement, but has not been expressly implemented in the UK.

[3] Database Dir., Art. 5; Software Dir., Art. 4(a); Info. Soc. Dir., Art. 2(1). No alteration of the British statute was seen to be necessary.

[4] In *Nova Productions v. Mazooma* [2007] *EWCA Civ* 219, [2007] *RPC* 589, 602 Jacob LJ stated that the idea that there might be infringement by copying *insubstantial* parts was 'so absurd as to be assuredly wrong'. The question of substantiality will be reviewed by the ECJ in *Infopaq International AS v. Danske Dagblades Forening*, Case C–5/08 (pending) (whether 11 words from newspaper article is substantial part).

[5] CDPA s. 16(3).

[6] See e.g. *Autospin (Oil Seals) v. Beehive Spinning* [1995] *RPC* 683 (failure to show a causal chain); *Sawkins v. Hyperion* [2005] 1 *WLR* 3281, 3288 (para. 30). As we saw at p. 137 above the knowledge of the defendant is not important in determining whether an act of primary infringement has taken place, but see also Ch. 6 Section 9 above.

case with patents, copyright law does not protect a copyright owner against independent creation. It is important to note that it is not necessary for the defendant's work to be derived directly from the original of the work;[7] it is possible for a defendant to infringe where they base their work on a copy of the work. It is also important to note that it does not matter if the intermediate reproduction is itself a legitimate or a pirated copy.[8] This means, for example, that where a person copies a three-dimensional object (such as an exhaust pipe), they may infringe the copyright in the drawings on which the three-dimensional object was based, even though they have never seen those drawings.[9]

Whether a defendant's material was derived from a claimant's copyright work is a matter of fact, and it is for the claimant to persuade the tribunal that this has occurred. In order to do so, the claimant may use different forms of evidence. First, and most convincing, is direct evidence that the defendant utilized the claimant's work in producing their own. For example, an ex-employee may be able to give evidence that they were asked to produce something similar to the claimant's work; or a third party may have witnessed the appropriation. Indeed, a defendant may in some circumstances admit that they drew upon the claimant's work.

However, such direct evidence is often unavailable. In these circumstances, the courts have sometimes been willing to infer derivation.[10] In order to persuade a court to infer copying, a claimant will typically rely on similarities between the works, coupled with evidence that the defendant had access and opportunity to copy the copyright work. a court is likely to accept that there is a causal connection between the two works if the similarities are very numerous, or so individual,[11] that the possibility of their having been independently conceived by the defendant is implausible.[12] Even if the shared elements are less individual or numerous, an inference of derivation may be drawn where a claimant can positively demonstrate the defendant's familiarity with the copyright work.[13] Where such an inference of copying has been established by a claimant, the onus then shifts onto the defendant to prove that they created the work independently.[14] In order to do so, a defendant may claim that the similarities between the two works can be explained by factors other than copying. For example, a defendant may attempt to show that the similarities are attributable to the fact that the two works were inspired by the same source,[15] that both works were constrained by the functions

---

[7] CDPA s. 16(3)(b).   [8] CDPA s. 16(3).

[9] *British Leyland v. Armstong* [1986] *AC* 577 (production of replacement exhaust pipes for claimant's cars indirectly copied the claimant's original drawings).

[10] *IPC Media Ltd v. Highbury Leisure Ltd* [2005] *FSR* (20) 434, 443.

[11] *Billhöfer Maschinenfabrik GmbH v. Dixon & Co.* [1990] *FSR* 105, 123 (Hoffmann J, observing the paradox that it is 'the resemblances of inessentials, the small, redundant, even mistaken elements of the copyright work which carry the greatest weight' in proving derivation). See also *L.B. (Plastics) v. Swish Products* [1979] *FSR* 145, 159 (Lord Hailsham); *Ibcos Computers v. Barclays Mercantile Highland Finance* [1994] *FSR* 275, 298 (proving derivation via the inclusion in the defendant's program of spelling mistakes and redundant code from the claimant's program).

[12] *Designers Guild v. Russell Williams* [2000] 1 *WLR* 2416, 2425 *per* Lord Millett.

[13] At this stage, key factors include the relative age of the claimant's work, and how widely distributed it had been: *Francis Day & Hunter v. Bron* [1963] *Ch* 587 (where, on facts, derivation not established).

[14] *Designers Guild v. Russell Williams* [2000] 1 *WLR* 2416, 2425 *per* Lord Millett; *Ibcos Computers v. Barclays Mercantile Highland Finance* [1994] *FSR* 275, 297; *Stoddard International v. William Lomas Carpets* [2001] *FSR* 848, 857–8.

[15] *Harman Pictures v. Osborne* [1967] 1 *WLR* 723, 728 (plays about the Charge of the Light Brigade may have been created independently but in the absence of an express explanation by the defendant, Goff J granted an interim injunction).

they perform,[16] or, less plausibly, to chance.[17] Such claims are likely to be undermined by evidence that the defendant has been engaged in similar acts of copying on previous occasions.

This process of inference can be well illustrated by the House of Lords' decision in *Designers Guild v. Williams*.[18] The claimant had produced its fabric design, named *Ixia*, in 1994. The design was impressionistic in style, made up of roughly drawn pink and yellow stripes with flowers scattered haphazardly across them (see Fig. 8.1).

The fabric was made available in shops from September 1995. A year later the claimant discovered that the defendant was selling fabric with a design called *Marguerite*, also based on vertical stripes in alternating colours and with flowers and associated stalks and leaves scattered across the stripes (see Fig. 8.2).

There were, however, several differences between the two designs, and the defendant denied that *Marguerite* had been copied from *Ixia*, asserting that its designer had developed it from her own *Cherry Blossom* design. Nevertheless, Judge Lawrence Collins QC inferred from the evidence that *Marguerite* in fact had been derived from *Ixia*,[19] a finding which the

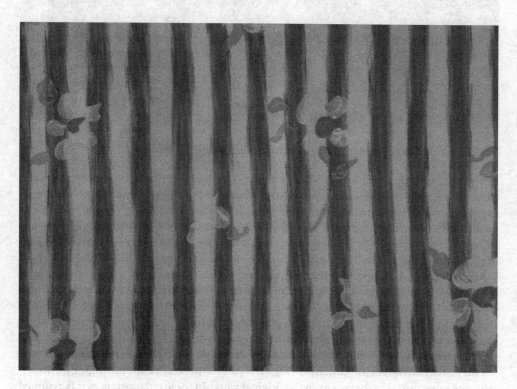

Fig. 8.1 The claimant's *Ixia* design, created by Helen Burke
Source: Courtesy of Designer's Guild.

---

[16] *Catnic Components v. Hill and Smith* [1982] *RPC* 183, 222 (CA, affirming Whitford J); *Kleeneze Ltd. v. D.R.G. (UK) Ltd* [1984] *FSR* 399, 401 (both designs relied on same concept, but beyond that similarities were attributable to functional considerations or were commonplace).

[17] *Francis Day v. Bron* [1963] *Ch* 587, 615–6 (*per* Willmer LJ, accepting similarities in two musical pieces were a result of coincidence).

[18] *Designers Guild v. Russell Williams* [2000] 1 *WLR* 2416.

[19] *Designers Guild v. Russell Williams* [1998] *FSR* 803.

Fig. 8.2 The defendant's *Marguerite* design, created by Jane Ibbotson

House of Lords approved. First, the judge found that there were seven similarities between the two designs.[20] Both designs were based on stripes with scattered flowers; both were in an impressionistic style, showing brushwork; in both the stripes had rough edges; in both the petals were executed in a similar way; in both the stripes showed through some of the petals; in each, the flower heads comprised a 'strong blob'; and in each the leaves were in two shades of green. The judge concluded that these similarities went 'far beyond the similarities which would be expected simply from both being based on an impressionistic style or from both being based on a combination of stripes and scattered flowers and leaves'. Second, the judge found that the designer of *Marguerite* had had an opportunity to copy *Ixia*, since she was at a trade fair in 1995 where the *Ixia* design was exhibited. Third, the judge rejected the defendant's own account of how she came to produce the *Marguerite* design, finding her story unconvincing. Consequently, he found that the defendant's design was derived from the claimant's.

One factor that has been useful in proving derivation is the fact that the infringing work contains the same mistakes that occur in the original work. In these circumstances it is assumed that the reason why the same mistakes appear in the two works is that they are copies of each other. Where works involve low levels of innate individuality, in order to assist in the task of proving derivation, copyright owners sometimes place incorrect or false information in their works. For example, the creators of a telephone directory might include a number of false names and addresses in the directory. Similarly, computer programs might contain lines of meaningless code. Where this incorrect or meaningless information appears in a defendant's

---

20   [1998] *FSR* 803, 815.

work, it is very difficult for them to argue that they created the work independently of the copyright work.[21]

In most cases, the process of copying will be a conscious act. In some cases, however, the courts have been willing to accept that the process of derivation may occur at a subconscious level.[22] While a defendant may honestly not recall having seen or heard the copyright work, the courts seem open to the argument that the defendant subconsciously copied from the copyright work. This is particularly the case in relation to songs, where catchy, even annoying, tunes embed themselves in the subconscious. The acceptance of subconscious copying provides the courts with a way of reconciling the implausibility of independent creation with the conflicting evidence of a defendant who claims that they cannot remember having any contact with the work.[23]

5 THE WORK OR A SUBSTANTIAL PART THEREOF?

The third and final question that needs to be asked in an infringement action is whether the restricted act has been carried out in relation to the *work* or a *substantial part* thereof. The basic approach was set out by Lord Millett in *Designers Guild*:[24]

Once the judge has found that the defendants' design incorporates features taken from the copyright work, the question is whether what has been taken constitutes all or a substantial part of the copyright work. This is a matter of impression, for whether the part taken is substantial must be determined by its quality rather than its quantity. It depends upon its importance to the copyright work. It does not depend upon its importance to the defendants' work, as I have already pointed out. The pirated part is considered on its own . . . and its importance to the copyright work assessed. There is no need to look at the infringing work for this purpose.

This question of substantiality is the most difficult aspect of copyright infringement. In principle, in order to answer this question it is necessary to ask two subsidiary questions:

(1) what is the work for the purposes of infringement; and

(2) has the defendant's utilized the whole of the claimant's work or a substantial part thereof?

---

[21] *Waterlow Directories v. Reed Information* [1992] *FSR* 409; *Waterlow Publishers v. Rose* [1995] *FSR* 207.

[22] *Francis Day v. Bron* [1963] *Ch* 587. According to Willmer LJ, at 614, to establish subconscious copying it must be shown that the composer of the offending work was familiar with the work alleged to have been copied. Cf. Upjohn LJ, at 621–2 (leaving undecided the issue of whether a different test applied for subconscious copying). In this case there was not sufficient material from which such an inference could be drawn. See also *E. Gomme Ltd v. Relaxateze* [1976] *RPC* 377 (requiring high degree of familiarity for subconscious copying); *Jones v. London Borough of Tower Hamlets* [2001] *RPC* (23) 407, 432.

[23] *Francis Day v. Bron* [1963] *Ch* 587, 619 (*per* Upjohn LJ). The decision of Wilberforce J at first instance is called 'a wise judgment' by Mummery LJ in *Baigent v. Random House* [2007] *EWCA Civ* 247, [2007] *FSR* 579 para. 122. See also *Jones v. Tower Hamlets* [2001] *RPC* (23) 407, 432; *Elanco Products v. Mandops* [1980] *RPC* 213, 227 (CA) (where similarities were so remarkable there must have been deliberate and conscious copying).

[24] *Designers Guild v. Williams* [2000] 1 *WLR* 2426, 2426.

5.1 WHAT IS THE WORK FOR THE PURPOSES OF INFRINGEMENT?

Logically, the first task that arises when determining whether the defendant has utilized the whole or a substantial part of the copyright work is to ascertain the limits of the copyright work. To determine what the work is, it is necessary first to determine the parameters of the work, and then to diistinguish the protected from non-protected elements of the work. We will deal with each of these in turn.[25]

5.1.1 What are the parameters of the work?

In many situations the parameters of the work will not be in dispute. This would be the case, for example, where a person photocopies all of a book, or they copy all of a computer program. Where a work is divisible into smaller elements the question may arise as to whether the 'parts' should be treated as separate and distinct works. If we take the case of a book, for example, while it is clear that the book as a whole is a copyright work, what of the chapters, pages, paragraphs, sentences, or words that are included in the book? The decision as to the size of the copyright work may have an important bearing on the outcome of an infringement action. The reason for this is that the question whether something is 'the whole or a substantial part' of something else depends on what it is being judged against. In this case, that something else is the copyright work.[26]

The question of how the parameters of the work are to be determined was considered by Judge Laddie QC in *Hyperion Records v. Warner Music*.[27] This was an application for summary judgment brought by Hyperion Records who owned copyright in a sound recording of the medieval chant, 'O Euchari'. The chant, which was 5 minutes 18 seconds long, appeared on the album *A Feather on the Breath of God*. Hyperion Records alleged that their copyright had been infringed when the electronic-pop band, The Beloved, copied (or sampled) eight notes from 'O Euchari' and incorporated them into their record 'Happiness'.

While it was clear that the song 'O Euchari' was a work, Hyperion Records argued that the eight notes sampled by The Beloved also formed a distinct copyright work in their own right.[28] If this was accepted, it would clearly have been an infringement, as 100 per cent of the 'work' would have been taken. Judge Laddie QC rejected the argument saying that 'I do not accept that all copyright works can be considered as a package of copyright works, consisting of the copyright in the whole and an infinite number of subdivisions of it'. He added that 'if the copyright owner is entitled to redefine his copyright work so as to match the size of the alleged

---

[25] The task of identifying the work is made easier because the claimants will specify in their statement of case the parameters of the work as well as the parts of the work that they believe have been infringed. While not definitive, this provides a useful starting point for demarcating the scope of the work.

[26] In the past, statutory definitions have helped give guidance as to the parameters of the work. For example, under the Literary Copyright Act 1842, 'book' was defined as 'every volume, part or division of a volume...separately published'. However, the abstract categories in CDPA s. 1(1) provide no such guidance. See also Sherman and Bently, 192–3 (explaining that for many intellectual property rights 'representative registration' helps define the parameters of the work, and noting this is not the case with copyright).

[27] *Hyperion Records v. Warner Music* (1991, unreported). See also, *Spelling Goldberg Productions v. BPC Publishing* [1981] *RPC* 283 (Buckley LJ); *Merchandising Corporation v. Harpbond* [1983] *FSR* 32, 39 (Walton J: it was not open to a claimant to select certain parts of a sketch and say each part had a separate copyright therein); *Coffey v. Warner/Chappell* [2005] *FSR* (34) 747.

[28] They also argued that the whole track was the work and that the defendant had reproduced a substantial part thereof.

infringement, there would never be a requirement for substantiality'. More specifically, Judge Laddie did not accept that it was legitimate 'to arbitrarily cut out of a large work that portion which has been allegedly copied and then to call that the copyright work'.[29] While Judge Laddie held that the eight notes sampled by The Beloved could not be treated as a separate work, this did not mean that in other circumstances a recording of eight notes could not be a copyright sound recording: it is possible that it could. The reason for this was that a particular aspect of a larger work might be treated as a separate work if it has a discrete, natural, or non-artificial shape. Thus, a day's footage on a film that is 'a discrete product of the film-maker's art' may be treated as a distinct work. Presumably the results of a recording session, as distinct from the final product, would also attract separate copyright protection.[30]

Judge Laddie's judgment provides us with some useful assistance in undertaking the (much neglected) task of defining the parameters of the work. In addition to focusing on whether a particular item can be seen as 'natural' or 'non-artificial', it seems that other relevant considerations would include: the intention of the creator; the level of interdependence or independence of the units concerned; and the commercial form in which the work is to be published or made available.[31] Given that one consequence of recognizing small units as discrete copyright works is potentially to increase the level of protection,[32] a useful starting point should be that, where a work has been published, the form in which the work is first issued is presumed to determine the parameters of the work.

5.1.2 The depth of protection

As we explained in Chapter 6, the protection given to entrepreneurial works is limited to the form in which the work is fixed (e.g. in the case of a film, the specific images; or in the cases of a sound recording, the specific sounds recorded). One of the consequences of this is that the only question that arises in relation to entrepreneurial works is whether a substantial part of a work has been taken. In relation to authorial works, however, the protection extends beyond the specific form in which the work is recorded to include other aspects of the work. For example, the protection afforded to a literary work, such as a novel, may extend beyond reproduction

[29] It is not always in the copyright-owner's interests to define the work in this way. Where a defendant has taken small helpings from a number of separate publications there may be benefits from asserting that the separate publications were in fact one. See, e.g. *PCR v. Dow Jones Telerate* [1998] *FSR* 170, 183 (Lloyd J rejecting claimant's argument that its two articles should be taken together for the purpose of determining whether a substantial part).

[30] Note the correspondence in the definition of sound recording with the notion of a musical work, in CDPA s. 5(1)(b). This may suggest that the parameters of a sound recording are defined by the parameters of a musical work: *The Newspaper Licensing Agency Ltd v. Marks and Spencer plc* [2003] *AC* 551, 557–8 (para. 11) *per* Lord Hoffmann (a sound recording of one musical work is by definition different from the recording of another, even if they are issued on the same CD).

[31] This will be the primary factor in relation to copyright in the typographical arrangement of a published edition: *The Newspaper Licensing Agency Ltd v. Marks and Spencer plc* [2003] *AC* 551 (HL). Here the issue was whether the copyright in the typographical arrangements in a number of the newspapers had been infringed by copying and distributing individual articles. As a result the House of Lords was called upon to consider whether the NLA had typographical copyright in each of the individual articles in the newspapers or only in each newspaper as a whole. The House of Lords held that 'the frame of reference for the term "published edition" is the language of the publishing trade' and therefore that 'the edition is the product, generally between covers, which the publisher offers to the public'. Thus, each edition of the newspaper rather than each article benefited from the typographical copyright.

[32] For an example of an exceptional case where it was in the interests of the claimant to define the parameters of the work expansively, so that the defendant's individually *de minimis* takings might be regarded as substantial, see *Electronic Techniques (Anglia) v. Critchley Components* [1997] *FSR* 401.

of the printed words on the page to include copying of the story line, plot, and characters that form part of the novel.

In some cases, the non-literal elements of the work may take the form of more abstract or general ways of describing the literal aspects of a work. As Mr Justice Learned Hand said in the well-known American decision in *Nichols v. Universal Pictures Corporation,* '[u]pon any work, and especially a play, a great number of patterns of increasing generality will fit equally well, as more and more of the incident is left out'.[33] Thus, at its most specific, a play may consist of the words of the script. At a more abstract level, it may consist of the plot or story line. The play may also be described very generally as a tragedy or a comedy. (It should be noted that the very general aspects of the work may not be protected on the basis that they are 'ideas'.) While thinking about a copyright work as if it consisted of a series of levels of abstraction may be useful in certain instances, in other situations the non-literal elements of a work cannot be described in these terms. In these cases the non-literal elements are better seen as aspects of a work that are not visible on looking at the surface of the work: this is particularly the case in relation to computer programs.[34] Given this, perhaps the best way to understand the scope of protection potentially available beyond the surface of the work is to provide some examples.

In relation to *literary and dramatic works,* as well as the words on the page (the literal aspect of the work), the non-literal elements of a novel or play (which may be protected by the copyright therein) may include the plot,[35] the story line,[36] as well as the incidents and themes.[37] While the issue has not really been addressed in the United Kingdom, it is less likely that the characters of a novel or play will be protected.[38] As we explain below, the non-literal elements of a literary work do not include the general ideas that may have informed or underpinned a work. In relation to *computer programs* copyright protection potentially extends beyond the object and source code of the program to include non-literal elements such as the structure or architecture of the program,[39] as well as the sequence of operations, functions, and interfaces that are used in the program.

There have been fewer decisions defining what is protected in relation to *musical works.* However, it seems that protection might include the melody, phrasing, or rhythm; the time; or the suggested orchestration, but not aspects such as timbre or pitch contour that can be said to be purely aspects of performance style.

The question of the scope of protection available for artistic works was considered in *Krisarts SA v. Briarfine.*[40] The defendants commissioned a Mrs Gardner to paint scenes and views such

---

[33] *Nichols v. Universal Pictures Corporation* (1930) 45 *F (2d)* 119, 121.

[34] Most literary copyright works involve both literal matter (the exact words of a novel or computer program) and varying levels of abstraction (more or less detailed plot of a novel, general structures of a computer program). *Ibcos Computers v. Barclays Mercantile Highland Finance* [1994] *FSR* 275, 302.

[35] *Harman Pictures v. Osborne* [1967] 1 *WLR* 723, 728; *Rees v. Melville* [1914] *MacG CC* 168; *Brighton v. Jones* [2005] *FSR* (16) 288 (paras. 63–6). In relation to literary works, the taking of a plot of a novel or play can certainly infringe—if the plot is a substantial part of the copyright work: *Designers Guild v. Williams* [2001] 1 *WLR* 2416; *Ibcos Computers v. Barclays Mercantile Highland Finance* [1994] FSR 275, 291.

[36] *Corelli v. Gray* (1913) 29 *TLR* 570; *Autospin (Oil Seals) v. Beehive Spinning* [1995] *RPC* 683, 697; *Kelly v. Cinema Houses* [1914] *MacG CC* 168.

[37] *Corelli* (1913) 29 *TLR* 570; *Rees v. Melville* [1914] *MacG CC* 168. Cf. *Norowzian v. Arks (No. 2)* [2000] *FSR* 67, 74, 76 (rhythm and pace, theme, and editing style were not subjects of copyright).

[38] *Kelly v. Cinema House* [1928–35] *MacG CC* 362, 368. For a review, see J. McCutcheon, 'Property in Literary Characters—Protection under Australian Copyright Law' [2007] *EIPR* 140.

[39] 'Architecture' may also be used to describe what Jacob J in *Ibcos Computers v. Barclays Mercantile Highland Finance* [1994] *FSR* 275, 292, 302 called program structure. *Cantor Fitzgerald International v. Tradition (UK)* [2000] *RPC* 95, 133–4. See generally, M. Shaw and D. Garlan, *Software Architecture: Perspectives on an Emerging Discipline* (1996).

[40] [1977] *FSR* 557.

as the Houses of Parliament with Westminster Bridge in the foreground, the Tower of London, Windsor Castle, and so on. In so doing they showed Mrs Gardner picture postcards of the scenes they wanted her to paint. The defendants also gave Mrs Gardner prints taken from M. Legendre's paintings. While there was no accusation of slavish copying, many of the paintings were made from the same view and the same angle as M. Legendre's paintings. As such, the question arose as to whether there was any copyright in the view or angle that a painter adopts. While Whitford J stressed that other painters should not be prevented from painting the same scenes, he did accept that there could be certain elements of the scenes that were 'distinctive' enough to warrant being protected.[41] As he said:

When one is considering a view of a very well-known subject like the Houses of Parliament with Westminster Bridge and part of the Embankment in the foreground, the features in which copyright is going to subsist are very often the choice of viewpoint, the exact balance of foreground features or features in the middle ground and features in the far ground, the figures which are introduced, possibly in the case of a river scene the craft on the river and so forth. It is in choices of this character that the person producing the artistic work makes his original contribution.[42]

In the light of this, Whitford J held that it was arguable that Mrs Gardner's use of M. Legendre's work was sufficiently substantial to amount to infringement of copyright. While it is highly unlikely that the style used by an artist could be protected (style being the equivalent of an idea), it has been suggested that if the 'feeling and artistic character' of the claimant's work has been taken infringement might have occurred.[43]

5.1.3 Distinguishing the protected parts from the non-protected parts

Although the scope of the work may extend well beyond its literal appearance, in most cases there will be certain parts of a work that are not protected. In order to ascertain whether infringement has occurred, therefore, it is necessary to distinguish the protected parts of the work from those parts that are not protected (which form part of what is sometimes called the 'public domain'). The reason for this is that, when deciding if a copyright work has been infringed, copyright law is only concerned with the protected parts of the work.[44] The problem is knowing how the line is to be drawn between the protected and non-protected parts of the work. Given the diverse nature of the subject matter protected by copyright, it is not surprising that the aspects of the work that are potentially protected vary considerably between the different categories of work.

Three principles are used to divide a work into the part that is protected by copyright law and the unprotected parts that are free to be used by all. The first flows from the fact that protection is only granted over the parts of a work that are relevant to the type of work in question. The second is that copyright law only provides protection over those parts of the work that ensure that the work is original. The third is that copyright does not protect the 'ideas' that lie behind or inform a work.

---

[41] While Whitford J was not willing to reach a final decision on copyright infringement, he was sympathetic to such a finding.

[42] [1977] *FSR* 557, 562.

[43] Copinger, para. 7–60 citing *Bauman v. Fussell* [1978] *RPC* 485; *Brooks v. Religious Tract Society* (1897) 45 *WR* 476.

[44] *Ladbroke (Football) v. William Hill (Football)* [1964] 1 *WLR* 273, 293 (Lord Pearce); *Warwick Film v. Eisenger* [1969] 1 *Ch* 508.

Irrelevant elements.   The only elements of a work that are protected are those which are relevant to the type of work in question.[45] This means that the way a work is classified may influence the aspects of a creation that are protected. For example, because there are two copyrights in a song, one relating to the lyrics and one to the music, a claim to infringement must be made out distinctly in relation to one or other. That is, evidence of copying of the music will not make an insubstantial taking of the lyrics any more substantial: it is simply not relevant to the claim.

For the most part, there are few problems in ascertaining which aspects of a particular creation are relevant to the type of work in question, though as we observed in Chapter 3, certain difficulties have arisen in distinguishing between literary and artistic aspects of functional works, such as circuit diagrams. Another situation where a strict distinction may prove unsatisfactory is in relation to maps: while strictly speaking maps are 'artistic works', the courts have, rightly, considered them not just visually but as compilations of information.[46]

Non-original elements.   Another factor that separates the public and the private elements of a copyright work is the requirement of originality (discussed in Chapter 4). This is because a person will only infringe if they appropriate a part of the work upon which an author's original skill and labour had been expended.[47] This means that the copying of an unoriginal part of the work is not an infringement.[48] This can be seen if we consider the situation where a person compiled a list of the names of Arsenal supporters living in Australia. If the originality of the compilation lay in the way the information was arranged, third parties would not be able to make use of the way the names were organized. They would, however, be able to make use of the information (if, for example, they scrambled the list). Alternatively, if the originality of the compilation stemmed from the selection of the material (but not its arrangement), third parties would not be able to make use of the information (although they would not be prevented from independently compiling the list themselves).

The correspondence between originality and what needs to be taken if a person is to be regarded as infringing can be seen in *Kenrick v. Lawrence*.[49] This case concerned the copyright protection available for a rudimentary drawing of a hand pointing to a square on a ballot paper to be used by illiterate voters. In considering this issue, the court said that 'the degree and kind of protection given must vary greatly with the character of the drawing, and that with such a drawing as we are dealing with the copyright must be confined to that which is special to the individual drawing over and above the idea—in other words, the copyright [in the case at hand] is...[of] extremely limited character'.[50] As such, while the court held that the drawing was protected by copyright, it also said that, as the level of skill, labour, and effort that was used in creating the work was minimal (it was a simple, functional work), nothing short of an exact

---

[45] *Cantor Fitzgerald International v. Tradition (UK)* [2000] *RPC* 95, 131.

[46] *Geographia Ltd v. Penguin Books Ltd* [1985] *FSR* 208.

[47] *Designers Guild v. Williams* [2000] 1 *WLR* 2416, 2431 (Lord Scott, approving as useful a test suggested by Laddie *et al.* asking whether the infringer incorporated a substantial part of the independent skill, labour, etc. contributed by the original author in creating the copyright work); *Cantor Fitzgerald International v. Tradition (UK)* [2000] *RPC* 95, 131 (copyright law protects the relevant skill and labour expended by the author on the creation of the work); *Autospin (Oil Seals) v. Beehive Spinning* [1995] *RPC* 683, 697; *Ibcos Computers v. Barclays Mercantile Highland Finance* [1994] *FSR* 275.

[48] *Ladbroke (Football) v. William Hill (Football)* [1964] 1 *WLR* 273, 293 (Lord Pearce); *Bowater Windows Ltd v. Aspen Windows Ltd* [1999] *FSR* 759, 781–2 (holding redrafted version of an 8-page sales ad not to infringe copyright in the document on which it was based because any literal similarity existed only in respect of aspects of the document which embodied a negligible amount of skill and labour and because no claim could be made to originality in the basis of the document); Laddie *et al.*, paras. 4.1, 8.35.

[49] (1890) 25 *QBD* 99.   [50] Ibid, 104.

literal reproduction of the drawing would constitute an infringement. The upshot of this is that, where the originality is thin, the scope of protection will be correspondingly thin. The principle that copyright protection is 'thinner' where the originality is 'thinner' may go some way to explain statements of courts that a copyist may legitimately take greater amounts of technical or historical material than would be permitted in the case of a work of fiction.[51]

It is important to recognize that a great deal of care needs to be taken when distinguishing between original and non-original aspects of a work. Although in some situations, the work as a whole can be dissected and non-original aspects ignored for the purposes of the infringement analysis, such 'dissection' carries with it a potential danger. This danger arises from the fact that originality can be provided not merely from labour and skill in the creation of new, original, material, but also from the collation or collection of existing, non-original, material. A process of dissection can cause a tribunal to overlook the creativity involved in such collation or arrangement. In other words, dissection may cause a tribunal incorrectly to treat the whole as merely the sum of its parts. However, if a defendant takes a number of elements from the claimant's work, each of which might individually be non-original, there may well nevertheless be a taking of a substantial part of the labour and skill involved in collating the material.[52] This can be seen from the different positions of the Court of Appeal and the House of Lords in *Designers' Guild v. Williams*. The Court of Appeal found that various elements of the claimant's design were unoriginal, and this led it to hold that the defendant had merely reproduced the idea of stripes and flowers, which was not a substantial part. As the House of Lords pointed out, in overturning this finding and reinstating the finding of the High Court, the error involved in this analysis was that the originality of the claimant's design lay in the composition of the design as a whole. As Lord Hoffmann stated, 'the exercise in dissection...dealt with the copied features piece-meal instead of considering, as the judge had done, their cumulative effect'. Likewise, Lord Scott described the approach whereby the constituent features of the rival designs were isolated from the whole and compared with one another as 'wrong in principle', because the claim related to altered copying of the claimant's design as a whole.[53]

Non-protection of ideas. Another factor which enables the public and the private elements of a work to be distinguished derives from the long-established principle that copyright protection is not granted to the ideas which are embodied in or which may have inspired the work.[54] In more positive terms this means that third parties are able to make whatever use they wish of the ideas that are contained in a copyright work. Thus it is not an infringement for someone to take the ideas or concepts 'behind' a painting, a book, or a computer program and incorporate them into their own work. In this context it is important to note that 'idea' is a shorthand

---

[51] *Ravenscroft v. Herbert* [1980] *RPC* 193, 205–6 (while the court based its view on a notion of implied licence, we prefer the view that copyright is 'thinner' in such cases).

[52] On the relationship between unoriginal works and the context in which they are taken see *Biotrading & Financing v. Biohit* [1998] *FSR* 109, 122.

[53] [2000] 1 *WLR* 2416, 2421 (Lord Hoffmann), 2434 (Lord Scott). See also *Baigent v. Random House* [2007] *EWCA Civ* 247, [2007] *FSR* 579, *per* Mummery LJ paras 127–129.

[54] The dangers of copyright protection of ideas were recognized in the eighteenth-century discussions of common law property, in particular *Millar v. Taylor* (1769) 98 *ER* 201; (1774) 2 *Bro PC* 129 and *Donaldson v. Beckett* (1774) Cobbett's *Parliamentary History* xvii, 954. The principle that there can be no copyright in an idea has been described at the highest level as 'trite law': *L.B. (Plastics) v. Swish Products* [1979] *FSR* 145, 160 (Lord Hailsham), 165 (Lord Salmon). The non-protection of ideas has been recognized in international treaties: see TRIPS Art. 9(2); WCT Art. 2; Software Dir., Art. 1(2).

expression that covers an array of different things such as the ideas which prompted the work (for example, to explore the impact of copyright law on artists); the subject matter of the work (for example, a book on intellectual property law);[55] or the general style in which the work is created (such as a cubist painting).[56]

Sometimes, the principle that copyright law does not protect ideas is referred to as the idea–expression dichotomy. This is usually taken to mean that what is protected is not an idea but its expression. Insofar as the dichotomy implies that copyright predominantly protects the mode of expression used by the author, rather than the ideas, the dichotomy is not inaccurate. It is unhelpful, however, in that it wrongly suggests that copyright protection is limited to the form or expression used by the author and that copyright does not protect against change of form nor against non-literal copying.[57] For, as we noted earlier, copyright law will protect many of the ideas expressed in a work. As Lord Hoffmann explained in the *Newspaper Licensing Agency* case, copyright infringement 'is sufficiently flexible to include the copying of ideas abstracted from a literary, dramatic, musical or artistic work, provided that their expression in the original work has involved sufficient of the relevant original skill and labour to attract copyright protection'.

In *Designers Guild v. Williams,* Lord Hoffmann reviewed the case law on idea and expression, and concluded that it supported two quite distinct propositions. The first is that a copyright work may express certain ideas which are not protected 'because they have no connection with the literary, dramatic, musical or artistic nature of the work'.[58] Lord Hoffmann said this would be the case with a literary work which described a system or invention. Although the work would be protected, copyright would not entitle the author to claim protection for their system or invention as such. He gave, as a specific example, the case of *Kleeneze Ltd v. DRG (UK),* in which Whitford J found there had been no infringement of copyright in the claimant's drawing of a letterbox draught-excluder, where the defendant had merely taken the concept of the draught-excluder.[59] The other proposition is that certain ideas expressed by a copyright work may not be protected because, although they are ideas of a literary, dramatic, or artistic nature, they are not original, or so commonplace as not to form a substantial part of the work. Lord Hoffmann gave the example of *Kenrick v. Lawrence,* which we have already discussed. In that case copyright subsisted in the drawing of a hand, but such copyright would not enable the copyright owner to object to other people drawing hands, if in so doing all that was reproduced was the idea. As Lord Hoffmann explained, '[a]t that level of abstraction, the idea, though expressed in the design, would not have represented sufficient of the author's skill and labour as to attract copyright protection'.

---

[55] *Kenrick v. Lawrence* (1890) 25 *QBD* 99, 102 ('mere choice of subject matter can rarely if ever confer upon the author of a drawing an exclusive right to represent the subject').

[56] *Norowzian v. Arks* [2000] *FSR* 67, 74, 76 (no copyright in film-editing style).

[57] For a warning about the use of this aphorism see *Designers Guild v. Williams* [2000] 1 *WLR* 2416, 2422 (Lord Hoffmann); *Ibcos Computers v. Barclays Mercantile Highland Finance* [1994] *FSR* 275 (Jacob J).

[58] *Designers Guild v. Williams* [2000] 1 *WLR* 2416, 2423. Discussed by Jacob LJ in *Nova Productions v. Mazooma* [2007] *EWCA Civ* 219, [2007] *RPC* 589, 601 (esp para 35).

[59] [1984] *FSR* 399. The example is problematic for a number of reasons. First, because Whitford J's judgment is couched mainly in terms of whether there had been 'copying'. Second, because the claimant's work had two components: Berry's idea and Snow's drawing which embodied the idea, and the decision merely found indirect copying of Berry's idea, not direct copying of Snow's labour. The case would stand better for the proposition that there cannot be copyright in ideas for new functional products (because there are public policy reasons for promoting competition in that domain, as well as a specific intellectual property regime, patents).

Lord Hoffmann's articulation of the rule that ideas are unprotected is helpful in that it recognizes that the vagueness of the concept of 'idea' is likely to lead to misinterpretation of the nature and scope of the exclusion. In fact, the exclusion is a relatively narrow one, and does not encompass everything that might be referred to, in common speech, as an idea. However, his attempt to pin down the rule that copyright is not infringed by the use of some ideas is open to the criticisms that it lacks clarity,[60] is incomplete,[61] and (by collapsing the rule on the non-protection of ideas into a rule on originality, rather than acknowledging its basis in public policy) might produce an unduly limited account of the exception. Failing to acknowledge that the rule is based in public policy suggests that if general ideas embody substantial labour and skill they will benefit from protection (unless they are 'unconnected' with the work). This would be a novel, and undesirable, outcome. The exclusion of 'ideas' from the scope of protection is an important judicial technique that is used to reconcile the divergent interests of copyright owners with those of users, creators, and the public more generally.[62] These interests include, but are by no means confined to: the public interest in ensuring that new works can be made dealing with the same topic, or subject matter;[63] the public interest in ensuring that copyright protection does not undermine the free use of functional ideas (other than those protected by designs);[64] the desirability of allowing multiple works using the same techniques of production (again subject to the limitation of patent law); the public interest in free expression; and particularly the free dissemination of political and economic ideas and historical facts.[65] The rule on non-protection of ideas is thus primarily directed at leaving free from

---

[60] In particular, his speech leaves unclear what kind of connections make ideas part of the protected elements.

[61] Lord Hoffmann's account seems to be incomplete, in that it omits techniques, methods, or style, matters which are usually considered unprotected: *Harman v. Osborne* [1967] 1 *WLR* 723, 728 ('there is no copyright in ideas or schemes or systems or methods: it is confined to their expression'); *Norowzian v. Arks* [2000] *FSR* 67, 74, 76 (no copyright in film-editing style); *Sawkins v. Hyperion* [2005] 1 *WLR* 3280, 3288 (para. 29) (copyright 'does not prevent use of the information, thoughts or emotions expressed in the copyright work'); *IPC Media v. Highbury Leisure Ltd* [2005] *FSR* (20) 434, 444 ('the law of copyright has never gone as far as to protect general themes, styles or ideas'); *Baigent v. Random House* [2007] *EWCA Civ* 247 (para 146) (no infringement to 'replicate or use items of information, facts, ideas, theories, arguments, themes and so on derived from the original copyright work').

[62] There is an abundance of US literature: W. Landes and R. Posner, 'An Economic Analysis of Copyright' (1989), 12 *J Legal Studies* 325 (explaining idea–expression dichotomy in terms of law and economics); A. Yen, 'Restoring the Natural Law: Copyright as Labour and Possession' (1990) 51 *Ohio State LJ* 517, 552 (arguing that the idea–expression dichotomy is informed by natural law doctrines of possession, which recognize certain things as being inherently incapable of possession and suggesting that copyright statutes should be interpreted correspondingly, so that copyright protects only 'the most concrete and obvious facets of a work'); A. Yen, 'A First Amendment Perspective on the Idea/Expression Dichotomy and Copyright in a Work's "Total Concept And Feel"' (1989) 38 *Emory LJ* 393 (emphasizing role and limitations of dichotomy in protecting freedom of speech); J. Litman, 'The Public Domain' (1990) 39 *Emory LJ* 965 (explaining the law's reluctance to protect ideas, information, short phrases, simple plots, themes, stock scenes, and utilitarian solutions to concrete problems on the ground that they are difficult to trace); S. Vaidhyanathan, *Copyright and Copywrongs: The Rise of Intellectual Property and How it Threatens Creativity* (2001) (arguing that the distinction has been steadily collapsing and that it is crucial that we rediscover, reinvent, and strengthen the idea–expression dichotomy).

[63] *Jones v. London Borough of Tower Hamlets* [2001] *RPC* (23) 407, 418–9. ('If the idea were protected at law that would prevent any subsequent person using that idea producing a variant. That would give the originator of the idea a very wide monopoly and not one contemplated by law.')

[64] *Kleeneze v. DRG (UK) Ltd* [1984] *FSR* 399 (permitting defendant to take idea of letterbox draught-excluder, and recognizing desirability of competition in production of articles which perform the same function).

[65] *Ashdown v. Telegraph Group Ltd* [2001] 3 *WLR* 1368, 1379; [2002] *RPC* 235 (Lord Phillips MR, discussing relation between copyright and freedom of expression, and noting that there will rarely be a conflict between them because 'only the form of the literary work is protected' so copyright does not normally prevent the

monopolization the building blocks of culture, communication, innovation, creativity, and expression.[66] It can be no surprise, then, that given the potential variety of influences, the application of the rule has been somewhat unpredictable. Moreover, in an era in which there is increased international norm setting in the definition of the rights of the copyright owner, the non-protection of ideas represents one of the few avenues by which the courts can take account of the individual circumstances and merits of particular decisions.

While *Designers Guild* might have heralded a narrow interpretation of copyright law's refusal to protect 'ideas', subsequent cases indicate that the lower courts prefer to take advantage of the flexibility that the 'idea–expression' dichotomy provides to dismiss speculative claims. In *Navitaire v EasyJet*,[67] the owner of copyright in source code brought an action against a former licensee who, having never seen the source code, tried to emulate the functional behaviour of the program. Pumfrey J found no infringement, stressing that the functional behaviour of a program was different from the plot of a novel (which might gain protection) and that policy weighed against protecting the 'business logic' of a program through copyright.[68] In *Nova Productions Ltd v Bell Fruit Games*,[69] Kitchin J held that similarities between video games were attributable to general ideas which had 'little to do with skill and effort' expended by the programmer. This was affirmed on appeal, Jacob LJ concluding that 'what was found to have inspired some aspects of the defendants' game is just too general to amount to a substantial part of the claimant's game'.[70] In *Baigent v Random House* (the da Vinci Code case),[71] Peter Smith J held that Dan Brown's book did not infringe copyright in Baigent and Leigh's *The Holy Blood and the Holy Grail*. In essence, Peter Smith J held that Brown had used HBHG (along with other books) but what was taken was facts and ideas at such a level of abstraction that there was no infringement.[72] In so holding, the judge observed that the line between idea and expression 'is to enable a fair balance to be struck between protecting the rights of the author and allowing literary development'.[73] The decision was affirmed on appeal, the Court unanimously agreeing that there was no reproduction of a substantial part of HBHG because that which was in *The da Vinci Code* was ideas rather than 'the form or manner in which ideas were expressed'.[74] Mummery LJ, in particular, emphasized that literary copyright does not give rights that enable persons 'to monopolise historical research or knowledge'.[75] A final example of a situation where the defendant was 'inspired' by the claimant's copyright work but was held not to have taken a substantial part is provided by the World Cup Willie case.[76] The claimant's work was the World Cup logo from 1966 comprising a lion in an England strip kicking a football. The defendant created a modernized version of a lion playing football for England. Although the defendant had copied the idea of a lion kicking a ball with its right foot, the postures were different (one leant back, the other forward), the angle of the faces differed (the plaintiff's drawing depicted the lion's face from the side, whereas the defendant's showed

---

publication of the information conveyed by the literary work. Understood in this way, the rule cannot be limited to the general or abstract ideas or facts).

[66] *Jones v. London Borough of Tower Hamlets* [2001] *RPC* (14) 379, 418–9 (referring to common stock of architectural ideas which everyone is free to use).

[67] [2006] *RPC* (3) 111.   [68] Ibid, 162 (para. 130).

[69] *Nova Productions v. Mazooma Games Ltd* [2006] *RPC* (14) 379.

[70] [2007] *EWCA* Civ 219, [2007] *RPC* 589, 603 para 44.

[71] [2006] *EWHC* 719 (7 April 2006), [2006] *FSR* (44) 893; (2007) *EWCA Civ* 247, [2007] *FSR* 579.

[72] [2006] *FSR* (44) 893, 952 (para. 266).

[73] [2006] *FSR* (44) 893, 926 (at para 153), 951 (at para 255). See also at 963 (para. 348).

[74] (2007) *EWCA Civ* 247, [2007] *FSR* 579, 618 (para. 92, 621 (para. 99) (*per* Lloyd LJ); 622–3 (para 105) (*per* Rix LJ); para 137, paras. 153–4 (*per* Mummery LJ).

[75] Ibid, at para. 156.   [76] *Jules Rimet Cup Ltd v. Football Association Ltd* [2008] *FSR* (10) 254.

the whole face). While the stylization was similar, the High Court concluded that all that had been reproduced was ideas rather than 'a substantial part of the original'.

5.2 HAS THE DEFENDANT TAKEN THE WHOLE OR A SUBSTANTIAL PART OF THE COPYRIGHT WORK?

Once the protected elements of the work have been identified, it is then possible to consider what the defendant has taken from the copyright work and ask whether the defendant has used the whole or a substantial part of the claimant's work.[77] Identical copying (that is, copying the totality of the claimant's work in an identical form—sometimes referred to as 'piracy') raises no analytical problems, and thus in the absence of an exception (on which see Chapter 9) a finding of infringement follows inevitably. Consequently, we say nothing further about such copying. Copyright law, however, has long recognized that protection ought not to be limited to situations where the defendant makes an exact copy of the work.[78] The reason for this is that, if copyright protection is limited to situations where identical copies of the work were used, plagiarists would be able to escape infringement simply by making minor variations to the copied work.[79] Copyright law therefore provides protection not just where the whole work has been copied but also where a defendant has used a substantial part of the protected aspects of the work. In extending protection from identical copying to copying of 'any substantial part' of a work, the law enables a copyright owner to control situations where a defendant takes *part of a work* (e.g. where half of a book is photocopied or a sample of a sound recording is copied); and where the defendant *changes the form of the work* (e.g. where a play is translated from English into Spanish, or is converted into a film).[80] This move from protecting only against identical copying to protecting partial copies or copies of the substance of a work, inevitably has required the courts to make difficult value judgements.

While it seems eminently defensible to protect a copyright work against 'colourable variations', the term 'substantial'—introduced for the first time in the 1911 Act—has allowed the courts to expand the scope of protection much further than the mere coverage of substantially competing works.[81] The term is one with a 'wide range of meanings' and the courts have preferred those at the lower end of the range.[82] This is not the place for an historical review of the case law, but it can be said that there has been a discernible shift towards allowing a copyright owner to control ever-smaller uses and re-uses of their works. In the not-too-distant past,

---

[77] As Lord Millett emphasized in *Designers Guild v. Williams* [2000] 1 *WLR* 2416, 2425, copyright infringement does not involve a work-for-work comparison. Rather, it is important to focus on what the defendant derived from the claimant's work.

[78] Thus, in the case of a book, as well as protecting the surface of the text (the printed words), copyright law also protects the intangible property that lies behind or, more accurately, is represented in the text.

[79] As should be clear, the circumstances in which someone infringes copyright are different from the circumstances in which someone might be regarded as a 'plagiarist'. For discussions of the distinction, see S. Green, 'Plagiarism, Norms, and the Limits of Theft Law: Some Observations on the Use of Criminal Sanctions in Enforcing Intellectual Property Rights' (2002) 54 *Hastings LJ* 167, 200–202; L. Stearns, 'Copywrong: Plagiarism, Process, Property and the Law' (1992) 80 *California LR* 513, 525 ff.

[80] These two situations are sometimes referred to as cases of 'fragmented literal similarity' and 'comprehensive non-literal similarity', or as 'literal copying' and 'altered copying'. See, e.g. *Designers Guild v. Williams* [2000] 1 *WLR* 2416, 2431 *per* Lord Scott, following Laddie *et al.*

[81] CDPA s. 16(3). The term 'substantial part' was first introduced in CA 1911 s. 1(2). The term had however been used in case law prior to 1911 (where taking was contrasted with 'fair use' of a work).

[82] *Newspaper Licensing Agency v. Marks & Spencer plc* [2001] *Ch* 257, 268 *per* Peter Gibson LJ (citing Lord Mustill in *R v. Monopolies and Mergers Commission, ex p South Yorkshire Transport Ltd* [1993] 1 *WLR* 23, 29); at 286–7, *per* Mance LJ.

the courts often took the view that a person would only infringe where the part taken was an essential, vital, or important part of the work.[83] In recent years, however, tribunals have being willing to find infringement as long as the defendant's use is not of an 'insignificant' part or *de minimis*.[84] Indeed, in an important speech by Lord Bingham (with whom all the other Lords agreed) in *Designers Guild*,[85] the concept of substantiality has been treated implicitly as leaving beyond the scope of the copyright-owner's monopoly only trivial, valueless, and insignificant elements of the work. More specifically, his Lordship explained section 16(3)'s reference to a substantial part as the law 'realistically recognising that no real injury is done to the copyright owner if no more than an insignificant part of the copyright work is copied'. In our view this tendency, to treat the test whether the defendant has used a substantial part as merely a test whether a taking is more than *de minimis,* involves an unjustified and undesirable extension of the copyright-holder's rights. We therefore proceed on the orthodox basis, that is that for a defendant to be held to have infringed it is necessary to show that they have used a substantial part of the claimant's copyright work, that is, an important part of that work.

5.2.1 When is a part important?

The question whether a restricted act carried out in relation to part of a work amounts to an infringement always depends on the facts of the case. In particular, the question whether a copyright work has been infringed depends primarily on the nature of the claimant's work, and on what has been taken by the defendant. While the evidential nature of the infringement inquiry means that each case will depend on its facts, it is possible to make some general comments about the way that importance is likely to be judged. In essence, the fate of a defendant depends on the relative *importance* of the part that is taken.[86]

Types of evidence.   While the question whether a part is substantial is decided by the courts,[87] in cases involving technical or esoteric subject matter they may rely on expert evidence from computer programmers, musicologists, choreographers, and other specialists as to the relative importance of the part.[88] At the end of the day, however, it is for the court to decide whether the part taken is important. Although the focus of the tribunal should be on whether the part taken was important to the copyright work, in reaching a determination a court will inevitably be influenced by the surrounding circumstances (including: the way the claimant's work was created; the nature of the work, for example, whether it is a work of information or fiction; the relationship between the parties, in particular, whether they are in competition; the conduct of the parties, in particular whether the defendant has copied merely to save itself expending

---

[83] *Hawkes & Sons v. Paramount Film Service* [1934] 1 *Ch D* 593, 606 (Slesser LJ) (where the defendant's broadcast of part of the claimant's song, while not prolonged, was held to be 'a substantial, vital and essential part').

[84] *Designers Guild v. Williams* [2000] 1 *WLR* 2416, 2418 (Lord Bingham). See also *Newspaper Licensing Agency v. Marks & Spencer plc* [2001] *Ch* 257, 268 *per* Peter Gibson LJ (substantiality describes something 'more than *de minimis*, something considerable in amount; that is, of an amount to make it worthy of consideration'); at 287, *per* Mance LJ (specifically rejecting argument that substantial part meant the 'essential part', saying it set the test too high).

[85] [2000] 1 *WLR* 2416, 2418.

[86] *Sillitoe v. McGraw-Hill Book Co. (UK)* [1983] *FSR* 545, 549–50; *Hawkes & Sons v. Paramount Film Service* [1934] 1 *Ch D* 593, 605–6 (CA).

[87] *Ibcos Computers v. Barclays Mercantile Highland Finance* [1994] *FSR* 275, note 1 above, 302.

[88] *Cantor Fitzgerald International v. Tradition (UK)* [2000] *RPC* 95. The evidence assists the court to form a view about the nature of the skill and labour involved in a particular work: *The Newspaper Licensing Agency v. Marks and Spencer plc* [2003] *AC* 551 (para. 21).

effort; the reason why the part was taken, for example, whether it has been used for the purposes of parody; and whether the use is degrading).[89] In addition, the tribunal is likely to be influenced by its understanding of the functions (and legitimacy) of copyright law,[90] and its general perceptions of the work and the part used.[91]

Importance to claimant's work.   The next point to note is that the relative importance of the part taken is judged in terms of its importance to the copyright work and not the defendant's work.[92] The reason for this is that the test imposed by the statute is whether the part used by the defendant is a substantial part of the *claimant's* copyright work, not whether it is a substantial part of the *defendant's* work.[93] This has two consequences. First, it means that it does not matter that the part taken forms an unimportant part of the defendant's work, nor that the defendant has expended considerable labour, skill, and effort themselves. The contributions of the defendant in transforming a copyright work have been regarded as largely irrelevant, the court preferring merely to attend to what the defendant has taken.[94] Translations and abridgements, however valuable, have for more than a century been regarded as infringements.[95] Equally, in the case of copying elements of an artistic work (as with that of *Ixia* by *Marguerite* in *Designer's Guild:* Figs. 8.1 and 8.2), it is a matter of no relevance to a finding of substantial taking that the defendant's work gives off an overall different impression than the claimant's. For the same reason (most) parodic uses of copyright works are regarded as infringements, irrespective of the parodist's skill or the social value accorded to parody.[96] The second consequence of focusing on whether the part is important to the claimant's work is that, if it is not, then in principle it does not matter whether the part is used repeatedly in the defendant's work (as often happens with the digital sampling of musical works).

[89] Laddie *et al.*, para. 4.55. But note the emphatic statements of Lloyd LJ in *Baigent v. Random House* [2007] *EWCA Civ* 247, [2007] *FSR* 579, 620 that the intention of the copier is 'irrelevant as a matter of law' (para. 95) and 'a red herring in modern English copyright law that...should not be invoked in the future' (para. 97).

[90] See R. Deazley, 'Copyright in the House of Lords' [2004] *IPQ* 121 (highlighting the Lockean underpinnings of the House of Lords judgment in *Designers Guild v. Williams*).

[91] This can be seen in the way data division of a program (which defines the nature and structure of the files used by the program) was construed. In *Total Information Processing* [1992] *FSR* 171, Judge Baker likened the data division to a table of contents of a book, which he said would be unlikely to be protected as part of a book. Cf. *Ibcos Computers v. Barclays Mercantile Highland Finance* [1994] *FSR* 275, 303.

[92] *Designers Guild v. Williams* [2000] 1 *WLR* 2416, 2420, 2426.

[93] *Warwick Films v. Eisinger* [1969] 1 *Ch* 508; *Hyperion Records v. Warner Music* (1991, unreported). (The 'importance of the copied part to the defendant's recording is a poor guide as to whether or not it is a substantial part of the work from which it was taken', particularly where the recordings were in different styles.)

[94] It was not always so: courts previously took into account any effort the defendant had made in transforming the work into another work: if a transformation was substantial, as with a translation or abridgement, there would be no finding of infringement, e.g. *Gyles v. Wilcox* (1741) 2 *Atk* 141.

[95] D. Vaver, 'Abridgments and Abstracts: Copyright Implications' [1995] *EIPR* 225. R. Burrell, 'Reining in Copyright Law: Is Fair Use the Answer?' [2001] *IPQ* 361, 365ff. (pointing out that even cases such as *Gyles v. Wilcox* can be seen as pro-copyright owner, given the statutory starting point).

[96] *Williamson Music v. Pearson* [1987] *FSR* 97, 107; *Schweppes v. Wellington* [1984] *FSR* 210 (suggesting that what the defendant added is irrelevant, so issue is whether defendant has taken a substantial part, which will usually be the case with parodies—though it was not so on the facts in *Williamson Music*). Cf. *Glyn v. Weston Feature Film* [1916] 1 *Ch* 261; *Joy Music v. Sunday Pictorial Newspapers* [1960] 2 *QB* 60 (both suggesting that the defendant's effort is relevant, and if sufficient, parodies are non-infringing). The killing-off of this 'nascent exception for parodies' is characterized by Burrell as 'cavalier': Burrell, ibid., 376. See also Laddie *et al.*, para. 3.142 and 4.62 (arguing that there is still room for the courts to indulge the parodist, and suggesting a test based on injury to the economic interests of the copyright owner); M. Spence, 'Intellectual Property and the Problem of Parody' (1998) 114 *LQR* 594; E. Gredley and S. Maniatis, 'Parody: A Fatal Attraction?' [1997] *EIPR* 339.

Substantiality a qualitative criterion.   While the use of the term 'substantial' suggests that importance should be judged in terms of the amount taken, the inquiry is as much concerned with the *quality* as the *quantity* of the part taken.[97] Indeed, in two recent decisions Lord Hoffmann went further, saying that the question of substantiality is a matter of quality *rather than* quantity.[98] So long as a part is qualitatively an important part of the work as a whole, even a very small part of a work may be a substantial part.

Assessing quality.   To say that the issue is one of quality leaves open how quality is to be determined. In *The Newspaper Licensing Agency Ltd. v. Marks and Spencer plc,* Lord Hoffmann provided some guidance, when he stated that the qualitatively important parts of a work were to be identified 'by reference to the reason why the work is given copyright protection'.[99] He explained that in the case of literary copyright, copyright is conferred (irrespective of literary merit) upon an original literary work, and it followed that the quality relevant for the purposes of substantiality is the 'literary originality' of that which has been copied.[100] In the case of an artistic work, Lord Hoffmann said, it is the 'artistic originality' of that which has been copied—which primarily relates to the visual significance of what has been copied.[101] In relation to typographical arrangements, it is the labour and skill invested in choosing the presentation and layout (as opposed to the particular words and images published in the edition) that are protected.[102] However, it is not always easy to determine exactly which labour and skill are 'relevant'. This is because each category of works accommodates a whole variety of different genres—'literary works' include novels and poems; tables and compilations, computer programs; 'artistic works' include realist and abstract paintings and drawings, as well as engineering drawings and maps, and so on—and in turn there are potentially a wide variety of types of relevant skill and labour.[103]

---

[97] *Ladbroke (Football) v. William Hill (Football)* [1964] 1 *WLR* 273, 276 (Lord Reid), 283 (Lord Evershed, not just physical amount but substantial significance).

[98] *The Newspaper Licensing Agency Ltd v. Marks and Spencer plc* [2003] 1 *AC* 551, 559 (para. 19); *Designers Guild v. Williams* [2000] 1 *WLR* 2416, 2422; see also *per* Lord Millett, 2426; *Ladbroke (Football) v. William Hill (Football)* [1964] 1 *WLR* 273, 288 *per* Lord Hodson; *L.B. (Plastics) v. Swish Products* [1979] *FSR* 145, 152 (Lord Wilberforce), 159 (Lord Hailsham).

[99] *The Newspaper Licensing Agency Ltd v. Marks and Spencer plc* [2003] 1 *AC* 551, 559. Later he reiterated that 'the purpose of the copyright is something which can be taken into account in deciding the kind of skill and labour which will attract protection'. Ascertaining Parliamentary intention was relatively easy in relation to 'typographical arrangements', but may be less easy in relation to other works.

[100] At times the courts come dangerously close to analysing quality in aesthetic terms, and thus breaching the 'principle of non-discrimination' which they attempt to apply in the context of determining subsistence. In *Chappell v. D.C. Thompson* [1928–35] *MacG CC* 467, where 4 lines were taken from a 20-line poem ('Her Name is Mary'), the importance of the part was judged in terms of its literary merit. The lines—'Her name is Mary/The sweetest name I know/And she's the one that I will love/For ever and a day'—were held not to be a substantial part of the poem. This can be contrasted with *Kipling v. Genatosan* [1917–23] *MacG CC* 203 where it was suggested that 4 lines which formed the crescendo of Kipling's 32-line poem 'If' were a substantial part of the poem.

[101] In *Billhöfer Maschinenfabrik v. T.H. Dixon & Co.* [1990] *FSR* 105, Hoffmann J (as he then was) said that the question of whether part of an artistic work is substantial depends upon the importance of the particular dimensions and spatial arrangements depicted.

[102] *The Newspaper Licensing Agency Ltd v. Marks and Spencer plc* [2003] 1 *AC* 55. However, it is not always easy to determine exactly which labour and skill is 'relevant' because each category of works accommodates a whole variety of different genres—'literary works' include novels and poems; tables and compilations, computer programs; 'artistic works' include realist and abstract paintings and drawings, as well as engineering drawings and maps; and so on. In turn there are potentially a wide variety of types of relevant skill and labour.

[103] *Baigent v. Random House* [2007] *EWCA Civ* 247, [2007] *FSR* 579 (para 145 *per* Mummery LJ).

Quality of entrepreneurial works.   It seems that the same approach is taken in assessing what amounts to a substantial part of an entrepreneurial work as in the case of any other work. a number of commentators had suggested that it was not possible to speak in a meaningful way about the 'important' part of an entrepreneurial work, contending that the quality of the entrepreneurial work will not change throughout the work.[104] For example, it was argued that, while a three-second sample that contains the 'hook' of a song may be an important part of a musical work, it does not necessarily follow from this that the way the three seconds were recorded will be any different from the way the rest of the song was recorded.[105] Indeed it is more likely that the quality of the sound recording will be the same throughout the recording than change from part to part. Following the decision of the House of Lords in *Newspaper Licensing Agency,* it is evident that the same general approach is taken *at least* in relation to typographical arrangements as in relation to literary, dramatic, musical, and artistic works. However, while the decision applied only to typographical arrangements, leaving the position in relation to sound recordings, films, and broadcasts undecided, the better view is that the House of Lords decision applies to all such works.

Photographs of films.   In assessing substantiality in relation to films, account needs to be taken of a special statutory provision. Section 17(4) of the 1988 Act states that copying in relation to a film or television broadcast includes making a photograph of the whole or any substantial part of *any image* forming part of the film or broadcast. This means that where someone takes a photograph of a single image from a film and reproduces it on a T-shirt, a poster, or a web site they could infringe (were that regarded as a substantial part).[106]

Importance to audience.   It is sometimes said that the importance of the part is judged from the point of view of the person to whom the work is addressed.[107] For example, in dealing with an infringement action brought in 1934 in relation to the copying of 28 bars from the well-known military march 'Colonel Bogey', the Court of Appeal concluded that the part was substantial because anyone hearing the part taken would recognize it.[108] It was also the part by which the march was chiefly known and the cause of its popularity. In *ITP v. Time Out,* the court held that, in copying part of the claimant's compilation of television and radio programmes, *Time Out* (a weekly listings magazine) reproduced a substantial part of the copyright work.[109] The court stressed that a key factor in finding that the part taken was important and thus substantial was that *Time Out* had concentrated on the peak viewing times and on the programmes which occurred at irregular times. In essence, *Time Out* took the parts of the TV listings that were of most value to users. A similar approach was adopted in *Express*

---

[104] Laddie *et al.,* paras. 7.59 (films), 9.20, 8.37 (broadcasts) (typographical arrangements). It had been suggested that in this context a 'substantial part' simply means any part of the work so long as it is not so small as to be trifling or insignificant: Laddie *et al.,* para. 7.59.

[105] Moreover, a substantial part of a newspaper protected by copyright as a 'literary work' may well not be a substantial part of the 'typographical arrangement': *Nationwide News v. Copyright Agency Ltd* (1996) 34 *IPR* 53, 71.

[106] See *R v. Higgs* [2008] *EWCA Crim* 1324, para. 9. Although the existence of this provision indicates that the legislature is happy, on occasions, that copyright protection extends to very small parts of work, it should be recognized, first, that this was done in response to the existence of a market for film stills for use in posters; and second, that the express provision only covers infringement by copying. The sub-section should not be read as a green light to those seeking to transform the meaning of 'substantial part' into 'non-*de minimis* part'.

[107] *Billhöfer Maschinenfabrik v. T. H. Dixon & Co.* [1990] *FSR* 105; *Francis Day & Hunter v. Bron* [1963] *Ch* 587, 623.

[108] *Hawkes & Sons v. Paramount Film Service* (1934) 1 *Ch D* 593, 609 (CA); *King Features v. Kleenman* [1941] *AC* 417.

[109] [1984] *FSR* 64, 74.

Newspapers. In considering whether the copying of the small sequences (two sequences of five letters and a twenty-five letter grid) from an original work of somewhere between 700 and 750 different sets of grids and five-letter sequences (which was used in a newspaper game), the court said that the part was substantial because it was 'the only part of the work that on that day will be any matter of consequence to anybody'.[110] (See Fig. 3.2.)

While this approach to the determination of the importance of a part is not necessarily wrong, it should be noted that it may be misleading. It is unobjectionable in those cases where the audience's view is founded on an appreciation of the relevant labour, skill, judgment, or craftsmanship that has gone into the work. For example, in the 'Colonel Bogey' case, the decision could as easily have been articulated in terms of the fact that the part taken was that which was most musically original. Similarly, although in the *Time Out* decision Whitford J emphasized that the parts were important because they related to the peak viewing times, his decision might have been justified by treating the taking of the 'irregular scheduling' as a substantial part because more skill and labour was required in scheduling the irregular programs than the regular ones: Whitford J had earlier treated the labour, skill, and judgment in choosing the programme times as well as compiling the list as 'relevant' to the literary originality of the schedules.

Focusing on audience evaluation or commercial importance is potentially misleading, however, because the audience to whom the work is addressed might be interested in parts of the works which involve little *relevant* labour, skill, or investment. The key inquiry is that stated by Lord Hoffmann: the importance of a part of a work is to be judged in terms of criteria that are relevant to the type of work in question. In contrast, the mere fact that part of a work becomes commercially significant or that there is a market for it should not matter when deciding whether the part is substantial. For example, if a closed-circuit camera in a fixed position records incidents in a car park, while the incidents or personalities recorded may hugely affect the commercial value of parts of the tape, they in no way affect the qualitative importance of any part for copyright purposes.[111] If we consider exactly what was the relevant labour, skill, and judgment invested by the creators in the *Express Newspapers* case, we might wonder whether the conclusion that there was infringement was properly justified on the ground that the particular day's grid was the most important part of the claimants' respective work.[112] It seems that the court, no doubt motivated by a desire to prevent 'unfair competition', stretched copyright too far.

Importance of ideas.   One of the chief difficulties caused by Lord Hoffmann's holding that the qualitatively important parts of a literary work were to be identified by reference to the 'literary originality' and the important parts of an artistic work by reference to 'artistic originality', is that the case law on 'originality' (described in Chapter 4) hardly comprises an uncontroversial

---

[110] *Express Newspapers v. Liverpool Daily Post & Echo* [1985] *FSR* 306, 311. See also *PCR v. Dow Jones Telerate* [1998] *FSR* 170.

[111] In the case of a sound recording, it seems on this basis it would be wrong to treat the part of which embodies the most distinctive, unusual, or catchy sounds as automatically representing the important part of the sound recording. This is because those parts may reflect, for example, the musical work, performance, and so on, rather than labour, skill, and judgment in creating the recording itself.

[112] Whitford J was of the view that a good deal of labour had gone into ensuring the grids produced enough winners to be attractive, but not so many as to render the game hopelessly uneconomic. In fact, the claimant had developed a computer program, and then checked that the grids were acceptable. Perhaps the case can be said to be one where there was a substantial taking from a quantitative point of view.

or settled body of law.[113] One key difficulty it raises is knowing to what extent labour, skill, and judgment in producing ideas, information, or making commercial decisions which precede the creation of the work itself can be treated as part of the 'literary or artistic originality'. In the context of determining originality, we saw that the House of Lords in *Ladbroke v. William Hill* had said that the court should not dissect labour, skill, and judgment in deciding what bets to offer from the labour, skill, and judgment in creating the coupon thereafter.[114] If this general proposition also carries weight when determining literary or artistic originality for the purpose of deciding whether a part is important and thus whether there is infringement, we are a short step away from concluding that the important parts of a copyright work may be those that incorporate the ideas or carry the information that have taken the most labour or skill to produce (rather than express).[115] And yet, in *Catnic v. Hill & Smith,* (in a passage which received the approval of the Privy Council in *Interlego v. Tyco*), Buckley LJ has said that importance may be judged by how far a part contributes to conveying information, but not to the importance of the information which it helps to convey. What is protected is the skill and labour devoted to making the work not the skill and labour devoted to developing some idea or invention communicated or depicted in the work.[116] In due course, the courts will be forced to confront this apparent conflict. If current trends persist, it is likely that they will reject the *Catnic* approach, which requires too subtle an analysis, and favour the stronger protection that application of *Ladbroke* would produce.

Functional importance. A similar difficulty has arisen in relation to determining the importance of parts of functional works. Here, the courts have held that, while a part may be important to the functioning of the work, if it is not also significant in terms of the originality of the work it will not be substantial. In the case of an artistic work this means that, while a part may be important to the functioning of a work, if it is not visually important then it will not be a substantial part. This can be seen, for example, in *Johnstone Safety v. Peter Cook* where the Court of Appeal had to consider whether a relatively small but functionally important feature of a sectional design of a plastic traffic cone which enabled the cones to be conveniently stacked was a substantial part of the drawing. Ralph Gibson LJ said that the fact that the feature was functionally important did not make it 'more potent' for demonstrating that a substantial part had been reproduced. As the feature had 'no substantial significance in the visual image of the artistic work' it was not a substantial part of the work.[117] Nevertheless, while 'functional importance' of a part is not the test, it does not follow that a part taken from an artistic work is only substantial if it is of visual significance to a layman. In the case of design drawings for a car exhaust system, the salient features were not to be assessed by the visitor observing the exhaust pipe mounted on a plinth at the Tate Gallery. Instead, they were to be judged by an engineer wanting to make an exhaust pipe to fit under a car.[118] Presumably, this person is in

---

[113] A further question is whether the European harmonization of originality in relation to computer programs, databases, and photographs (described at pp. 107–11) affects the substantiality inquiry.

[114] [1964] 1 *WLR* 273.

[115] *L.B. (Plastics) v. Swish* [1979] *FSR* 145, 163 (Lord Hailsham) (all information embodied in the design drawings could be considered when deciding if there was infringement).

[116] *Catnic Components v. Hill and Smith* [1982] *RPC* 183; *Interlego v. Tyco* [1989] *AC* 217, 265.

[117] *Johnstone Safety v. Peter Cook* [1990] *FSR* 161, 178. See also *Rose Plastics GmbH v. William Beckett & Co* [1989] *FSR* 113, 123 (substantial importance from point of view of operation was not same as substantial part of artistic work, which depended on visual significance).

[118] *Billhöfer Maschinenfabrik v. Dixon* [1990] *FSR* 105, 120.

the best position to assess the labour, skill, and judgment that the author has invested in the drawings in question.

The relation between functional importance and 'substantiality' has also arisen where a small part of a computer program is copied. In these circumstances it is sometimes pointed out that the program will not function or will not function properly without the part.[119] Given that 'every part of a computer program is essential to its performance' it has been suggested by some commentators that every part, however small, should be treated as a 'substantial part' of the program.[120] This approach has been rejected in the United Kingdom.[121] The reason for this is that it applies the wrong criterion to test whether the part is important.[122] While it may be clear that the functional importance of part of a computer program is not a relevant consideration when deciding whether the work has been infringed, it is not yet clear which aspects of a computer program will be relevant.

The part must itself be capable of being protected.   In some cases the courts have suggested that a part will not be substantial if the amount that is taken would not itself attract copyright.[123] This can be seen in *Francis Day & Hunter* where the owners of copyright in the song 'The Man Who Broke the Bank at Monte Carlo' brought an infringement action against a person who made a film of the same name. In response Lord Wright said that the 'copying which is complained of is the use of the title, and that is too unsubstantial on the facts of this case to constitute infringement'.[124] In other words, Lord Wright thought there was no copyright in the title by itself. a similar approach was adopted in the parody case of *Williamson Music v. Pearson* where the only parts left in the defendant's parody of the claimant's song 'There is Nothin' Like a Dame' were the words 'we got', which were repeated several times. Judge Baker QC held that the words were not a substantial part of the copyright work, noting that 'in themselves the words would not be copyright as a literary work'.[125] While the rule that a part will not be substantial if it would not itself attract copyright may be uncontroversial, it would be dangerous to infer from these cases a different proposition, namely, that if the amount taken could itself have constituted a protected work, then it necessarily follows that the amount taken is substantial.[126] Such a proposition would fail to take account of the importance of the part taken to the claimant's work as a whole: indeed, it would involve ignoring the rest of the claimant's work.

Repeated takings.   In certain situations the question has arisen as to whether the taking of an insubstantial part of the copyright work over a period of time amounts to the taking of a

---

[119] *Cantor Fitzgerald International v. Tradition (UK)* [2000] *RPC* 95, 130; *Ibcos Computers v. Barclays Mercantile Highland Finance* [1994] *FSR* 275.

[120] See *Data Access Corp v. Powerflex Services* (1999) 45 *IPR* 353 (HC of Australia) citing with approval *Cantor Fitzgerald International v. Tradition (UK)* [2000] *RPC* 95.

[121] *Cantor Fitzgerald International v. Tradition (UK)* [2000] *RPC* 95, 130.

[122] *Interlego v. Tyco* [1988] *RPC* 343 (PC); *Electronic Techniques Anglia v. Critchley Components* [1997] *FSR* 401.

[123] *Ladbroke (Football) v. William Hill (Football)* [1964] 1 *WLR* 273, 293 *per* Lord Pearce; *Designers Guild v. Williams* [2000] 1 *WLR* 2416, 2423 *per* Lord Hoffmann (second interpretation of idea–expression rule); *Merchandising Corp v. Harpbond* [1983] *FSR* 32, 47 *per* Lawton LJ; *IPC Media Ltd v. Highbury Leisure* [2005] *FSR* (20) 431, 443–4 (paras. 12–13).

[124] *Francis Day & Hunter v. 20th Century Fox* [1940] *AC* 112, 123–4.

[125] [1987] *FSR* 97, 107. After some early cases suggesting a different test for infringement by way of parody, this case confirmed that no special rules apply.

[126] Cf. Laddie *et al.*, para. 4.45 (arguing that if the part taken could have stood on its own as an original work, the defendant's work 'is a plagiarism').

substantial part of the work. This question arises in two situations. The first is where a defendant regularly takes insubstantial amounts from a *single copyright work*. For example, while students might not infringe the copyright in a 300-page textbook if they copied 5 pages, what of the situation where, over the course of an afternoon, the same student went to a photocopy machine 20 times and photocopied a different 5-page section each time? While the copying of 5 pages may not amount to an infringement, what of the copying of 100 pages? The second scenario is where copyright works are created regularly and the defendant consistently takes insubstantial amounts from different works. For example, would it be an infringement for an evening newspaper to reproduce regularly an insubstantial amount taken from daily financial reports of foreign markets that appeared in a morning paper?

As regards the first situation, that is where a defendant regularly takes insubstantial amounts from a *single copyright work,* the court in principle must decide whether there are a number of takings or only one: a person will infringe if the acts can reasonably be seen as a single act, and the cumulative taking is 'substantial'.[127] Relevant factors would presumably include whether the taking were used for the same purpose, and the time frame in which the activities took place. Beyond those limited situations where a series of acts could be interpreted as a single act, it seems the courts recognize a broader doctrine of 'repeated systematic copying from the same work'. Although Laddie J had observed that 'the concept of infringement by taking small and regular amounts was problematical',[128] the Court of Appeal in *Newspaper Licensing Agency v. Marks & Spencer plc* stated that such systematic copying could be infringement.[129] (The issue was not discussed in the House of Lords.) The Court of Appeal found support for its view from a case where a defendant was held to infringe copyright in the fixture lists for the football season, because it had copied a part of the list every two weeks.[130] Nevertheless, the comments in *NLA* were obiter, and the Court gave no indication as to when (or why) copying would be treated as 'systematic'.[131]

In contrast, where there is repeated copying of insubstantial parts from a series of the claimant's works there can be no finding of infringement (despite certain nineteenth-century cases to the contrary).[132] Dismissing those authorities on the basis of the different statutory terms, Peter Gibson LJ said, 'I do not understand how in logic what is an insubstantial part of a work can when aggregated to another insubstantial part of another work become a substantial part of the combined work'.[133] Here the only issue is whether in each case the claimant can show some use of a substantial part of the individual works.[134]

5.2.2 Judicial and practical responses to the complicated inquiry

Having set out a structured approach suited to a rigorous analysis of copyright infringement, we should conclude our discussion of primary infringement with three points.

---

[127] *Electronic Techniques Anglia v. Critchley Components* [1997] FSR 401, 410.   [128] Ibid.

[129] *Newspaper Licensing Agency v. Marks & Spencer plc* [2001] *Ch* 257, 269 (para. 33) *per* Peter Gibson LJ. See also 288–9 (para. 108) (Mance LJ).

[130] *Football League Ltd v. Littlewoods Pools Ltd* [1959] *Ch* 637 (whether such fixture lists would now be protected by copyright depends upon whether, as a result of the selection or arrangement, they could be said to be their author's own intellectual creation). Perhaps this would be the most satisfactory explanation for *Express Newspapers v. Liverpool Daily Post & Echo* [1985] FSR 306 (which, as we saw earlier, is otherwise problematical).

[131] Indeed, the fixture list case could have been an example of a single act, given that there was a preconceived course of action.

[132] *Cate v. Devon Constitutional Newspaper* (1889) 40 *Ch D* 500; *Trade Auxiliary v. Middlesborough* (1889) 40 *Ch D* 425. There is a possibility of infringing *sui generis* database right: see Ch. 13.

[133] *Newspaper Licensing Agency Components* [1997] FSR 401, 269, 288.

[134] *PCR v. Dow Jones Telerate* [1998] FSR 170, 183 (Lloyd J rejecting claimant's argument that its two articles and the defendant's three articles should be taken together for the purpose of determining whether a substantial part).

First, it should be noted that courts have not always been as rigorous or structured in their analyses as we suggest is necessary in the preceding account. In most cases, in fact, the court does not examine the nature of the claimant's work, rather taking for granted the boundaries of the work and that the work as a whole is protected. In these cases, the court will merely go straight to the second issue, the substantiality of the taking.[135] In yet other cases, the court will not even examine the second, substantiality, issue with any rigour. In some such cases, the court will utilize the 'rough practical test', that 'what is worth copying is worth protecting'.[136] This might be justified where there is an indication that the defendant has deliberately copied, from which the court can at least draw an inference that the defendant regarded the material it had appropriated as 'worth taking' and, therefore, embodying original skill and labour.[137] In other circumstances, in particular where the issue of derivation has been determined through a process of inference from multiple similarities between the defendant's material and the claimant's work, the court may simply regard further inquiry as superfluous. This was the view of the majority of the House of Lords in *Designers Guild*. For example, Lord Bingham there observed that 'while the finding of copying did not in theory conclude the issue of substantiality, on the facts here it was almost bound to do so'. Lord Millett, too, agreed that while the issues of copying and substantiality are treated as separate questions, in some circumstances, 'the answer to the first question will almost inevitably answer both, for if the similarities are sufficiently numerous or extensive to justify an inference of copying they are likely to be sufficiently substantial to satisfy this requirement also'.[138]

Second, as should be clear, the factual nature of the infringement inquiry means that it is often difficult to state in advance when a particular work may be infringed. This uncertainty is particularly problematic for bodies such as libraries who deal with copyright works on a day-to-day basis and who need to provide advice as to the types of use which are permissible. Faced with this uncertainty, it is not surprising that standards and protocols have been formulated in many industries that set out in a clear and readily quantifiable manner the type of copying that is permissible. Perhaps the best-known example is the rule of thumb that 10 per cent or one chapter of a book may be copied. Similar standards have also been formulated to deal with the digital sampling of musical works and are currently being

---

[135] *Ibcos Computers v. Barclays Mercantile Highland Finance* [1994] FSR 275.

[136] *University of London Press v. University Tutorial Press* [1916] 2 Ch 601, 610. In *Ladbroke (Football) v. William Hill (Football)* [1964] 1 WLR 273 the House of Lords misread Peterson J's dictum (which was directed at the issue of the originality of mathematics exams) and treated it as if it was concerned with substantial taking.

[137] As Laddie J said in *Autospin (Oil Seals) v. Beehive Spinning* [1995] RPC 683, a belief that taking was blatant led courts, sometimes with almost evangelical fervour, to apply the commandment 'thou shalt not steal'. The test has been criticized by the lower courts on the ground that, where the test is used, the tribunal relinquishes the task of asking whether the work has been infringed according to the rules of copyright law and focuses instead on the mere fact that the work has been copied. In so doing, all that a claimant has to show to establish infringement is that their work has been copied. For criticisms, see *Ibcos Computers v. Barclays Mercantile Highland Finance* [1994] FSR 275, 289 (Jacob J, test 'proves too much'); *Hyperion Records v. Warner Music* (1991, unreported) (Judge Laddie QC, saying test 'goes too far'); *Cantor Fitzgerald International v. Tradition (UK)* [2000] RPC 95, 131 (Pumfrey J, test 'proves too much').

[138] [2000] 1 WLR 2416, 2418 (Lord Bingham), 2426 (Lord Millett), 2435 (Lord Scott). Lord Scott put the proposition more forcefully still, stating that in cases of 'altered copying', '[i]f the similarities between the two works were sufficient to justify the inference that one had been copied from the other, there was, in my judgment, no further part for the concept of substantiality to play'. But cf. *Baigent v. Random House* [2007] EWCA Civ 247, [2007] FSR 579, in which an inference of copying was drawn, but this was held not to be substantial; and *Nova Productions v. Mazooma* [2007] EWCA Civ 219, [2007] RPC 589, 599 para 26 where Jacob LJ explained Lord Scott's dictum and denied that it established a general principle.

formulated in the multimedia industries. While these standards do not take account of the qualitative nature of infringement, they do provide an important and workable way of dealing with a difficult issue.

Third, and finally, as should be clear from the foregoing, the courts have recently interpreted the rules on primary infringement in a way that leaves little scope for unauthorized utilization of copyright-protected material. Those parts of a work which are not protected (as unoriginal, or as ideas) are defined increasingly narrowly. At the same time, the courts are willing to treat virtually any appropriation as substantial (and pay no attention to the way the material comes to be used). These trends reflect a widely-held judicial understanding of copyright law as intended to protect all contributions of labour, skill, and judgment. Copyright works are protected by the courts with a zeal that seems to reflect a belief that the work is the absolute, despotic dominion of the copyright owner. Yet, if we reflect on the dominant justification for copyright, namely that copyright is intended to provide the minimum incentive necessary to the production of new works, such an approach seems problematic.

6 SECONDARY INFRINGEMENT

In an attempt to inhibit the negative impact that illegal acts have upon copyright owners, copyright law recognizes that it is not enough merely to provide remedies against those who copy or perform the copyright work. Instead, copyright law recognizes that it is also necessary to provide owners with protection against those who aid and abet the primary infringer. Such accessorial infringement is known as *secondary infringement*.

There are two important differences between primary and secondary infringement. The first relates to the scope of protection. Primary infringement is concerned with people who are directly involved in the reproduction, performance, etc. of the copyright work. In contrast, secondary infringement is concerned with people in a commercial context who either deal with infringing copies, facilitate such copying, or facilitate public performance. The second difference between the two forms of infringement relates to the mental element that the defendant must exhibit in order to infringe. As we explain below, the state of mind of the defendant is not formally taken into account when deciding whether an act of primary infringement has occurred. In the case of secondary infringement, however, liability is dependent on the defendant knowing or having reason to believe that the activities in question are wrongful.[139]

6.1 TYPES OF SECONDARY INFRINGEMENT

Secondary infringement can be divided into two general categories. First, those who distribute or deal with infringing copies once they have been made; and second, those who facilitate copying by providing the equipment or means that enable the copying to take place.

6.1.1 The distribution of infringing copies

The first general category of secondary infringement is concerned with people who deal with infringing copies of the work in a commercial context. To this end, sections 22 and 23 of the

---

[139] CDPA ss. 22–4, 27. See Laddie *et al.*, ch. 19.

1988 Act provide that the copyright in a work is infringed by a person who without the licence of the copyright owner:

(i)   *imports* an infringing copy into the UK otherwise than for their private and domestic use,[140]

(ii) *possesses* an infringing copy in the course of business,[141]

(iii) *sells* or *lets for hire,* or offers or exposes for sale or hire an infringing copy,

(iv) in the course of business *exhibits* in public or distributes an infringing copy,[142] or

(v)   *distributes* an infringing copy, otherwise than in the course of a business, to such an extent as to affect prejudicially the copyright owner.

Section 27(2) provides that an article is an 'infringing copy' if its making constituted an infringement of the copyright in the work in question.[143] In the case of imported copies, infringing copy also includes 'notional infringements', that is copies which if they had been made in the United Kingdom would have infringed copyright at the time of making, or would have constituted a breach of an exclusive licence agreement relating to the work.[144] This provision has proved to be problematic.[145] Its significance has been reduced, however, by the extension of liability for primary infringement to include the issuing of copies, including the importing of copies from outside the EEA. Liability for secondary infringement by import remains important in cases of import from one EEA state to another: however, this right is subject to the Treaty of Rome and the principle of exhaustion.[146]

6.1.2 Providing the means for making infringing copies or performances

The second general category of secondary infringement is concerned with people who facilitate copying. This occurs, for example, where someone provides the equipment or the means that enables the copying to take place. There are a number of different situations where the provision of the means for making infringing copies or performances will amount to a secondary infringement.

Section 24(1) provides that a person is liable for infringement where they supply an article that is specifically designed or adapted for making copies of the copyright work. More specifically, section 24(1) provides that copyright in a work is infringed by a person who

---

[140] CDPA s. 22.

[141] Business is defined in CDPA s. 178 as including a 'trade or profession'. In *Pensher Security Doors v. Sunderland City Council* [2000] *RPC* 249, 280–2, Aldous LJ held that (i) the letting of flats by a local authority was a 'business activity', and (ii) the council possessed infringing copies (in the case, security doors which infringed the claimant's copyright in its design drawings) 'in the course of' that business even though there was no intention to distribute the infringing copies. This was because possession of the doors was an integral part of the business of letting the flats and thus not 'incidental' to the business.

[142] An art gallery carries on business even though certain paintings are not for sale: *Pensher,* ibid, 282.

[143] However, note the many situations in which the making of a copy is not infringing because of the existence of a defence, but the statute requires the copy be treated as an infringing copy when subsequently dealt with in specified ways: CDPA s. 27(6) referring to s. 32(5), s. 35(3), s. 36(5), s. 37(3), s. 56(2), s. 63(2), s. 68(4), and s. 141.

[144] CDPA s. 27(3), Sched. 1, para. 14(3).

[145] Described by Laddie *et al.*, para. 19.16 as 'far from straightforward'. One question that has been debated is who does the hypothetical making—the maker abroad, the importer, or someone else. See W. Rothnie, *Parallel Imports* (1993), 199–241. Laddie *et al.* argue that the identity of the maker is not in issue; what is in issue is the purpose which the import is intended to fill.

[146] CDPA s. 27(5). See above at pp. 12–16, 142–4.

without the licence of the copyright owner (a) makes, (b) imports into the United Kingdom, (c) possesses in the course of business, or (d) sells, or lets for hire, or offers or exposes for sale or hire *an article specifically designed or adapted for making copies of that work*.

It should be noted that section 24(1) states that the article must be *specifically* designed or adapted for the purpose of copying. This means that it is not enough that an article, such as a photocopier or a tape-to-tape recorder, has the potential to copy. Rather, for the section to operate the article must be specifically designed for the copying of a particular work. This would be the case, for example, where someone makes a template or a mould of a copyright work that is used to create infringing copies.

Special provisions are also made for people who *transmit the work* without the appropriate permission. Section 24(2) states that copyright in a work is infringed by a person who without licence transmits the work by means of a telecommunications system (such as a fax). It does not apply, however, to communications to the public. As with all forms of secondary infringement, infringement is dependent upon the defendant 'knowing or having reason to believe that infringing copies of the work will be made by means of the reception of the transmission in the UK or elsewhere'.

Where the copyright in a literary, dramatic, or musical work is infringed by a performance at a 'public place of entertainment',[147] any person who gave permission for that place to be used for the infringing performance is also liable for infringement. This does not apply, however, where the defendant gave permission on reasonable grounds that the performance would not be infringed.[148]

Special provisions also apply to those who facilitate an infringing performance. Section 26 deals with the situation where copyright is infringed by a public performance or by the playing or showing of the work in public by means of apparatus for (a) playing sound recordings, (b) showing films, or (c) receiving visual images or sounds conveyed by electronic means. In these situations, the following people will infringe:

(i) The person who *supplies the apparatus* which enables the act of primary infringement to take place is liable for infringement. This covers someone who supplies equipment to play records or show films. Infringement here is conditional on the fact that, where an apparatus is normally used in public, the defendant did not reasonably believe on reasonable grounds that it would be used to infringe copyright.[149]

(ii) An occupier of premises who gave permission for an apparatus to be brought on to the premises will be liable if they knew or had reason to believe that the apparatus was likely to be used to infringe copyright.[150]

(iii) a person who *supplies a copy* of a sound recording or a film will be liable if they knew or had reason to believe that the copy was likely to be used to infringe copyright.[151]

Finally, it should be noted that special rules, analogous to provisions on secondary infringement, apply where persons do various acts that facilitate access to or duplication of works that have been protected by technological measures. We deal with these in detail in Chapter 13. For the moment we merely need to note that these rights cover (i) acts which

---

[147] Defined in CDPA s. 25(2) to include premises occasionally used for public entertainment.
[148] CDPA s. 25(1).   [149] CDPA s. 26(2).
[150] CDPA s. 26(3). For a possible example, see *PRS v. Kwik-Fit Group Ltd* [2008] *ECDR* (2) 13 (OH CS).
[151] CDPA s. 26(4).

circumvent technological measures;[152] (ii) the manufacture and distribution of devices either 'primarily designed, produced, adapted . . . for the purpose of enabling and facilitating' circumvention, or 'promoted, advertised or marketed' for that purpose, and having 'only a limited commercially significant purpose or use other than to circumvent';[153] and (iii) the provision of services for the purpose of enabling or facilitating circumvention. Distinct, and narrower provisions apply where the measures protect computer programs.[154]

6.2   ACTUAL OR CONSTRUCTIVE KNOWLEDGE

One of the notable features of secondary infringement is that liability is dependent on the defendant 'knowing or having reason to believe' that the activities in question are wrongful. That is, liability is dependent on the defendant having either actual or constructive knowledge. The question of whether a defendant has the requisite knowledge is decided objectively.[155] As such, it does not matter that the defendant may not have believed that the act in question was wrongful. All that matters are the conclusions a reasonable person would have reached in the circumstances.

The question that needs to be asked is whether the defendant knew or had reason to believe that they were dealing with or helping to facilitate the creation of an 'infringing copy' of the copyright work. In answering this question, the courts have stressed that the defendant must be in a position where they are able to evaluate the information that is given to them.[156] This means that they must be given a reasonable period of time to consider the information.[157] It also means that the information that they are given must be sufficiently detailed as to the nature of the work in question: general allegations about infringement will not suffice.[158] The courts have also said that it is *not* enough for the facts to lead a reasonable person to suspect the relevant conclusion.[159] Although it will enhance the claimant's case where the defendant is supplied with a copy of, or given reasonable access to, the copyright work, the circumstances of the case may be such that the reasonable defendant could have 'known' about the wrongful nature of their activities without ever having seen the copyright work.[160]

---

[152] CDPA s. 296ZA.   [153] CDPA s. 296ZD.   [154] CDPA, s. 296(1).

[155] Cf. Laddie *et al.*, paras. 19.4 ff. (arguing that a subjective element is appropriate, at least in cases where the defendant is in possession of contradictory information).

[156] *LA Gear v. Hi-Tec Sports* [1992] *FSR* 121, 129 (action for infringement of copyright in the drawings of its shoes by import of infringing copies. Since the claimant had sent the defendants a letter and copies of the drawings, they had reason to believe these were infringing copies).

[157] The normal period is often 14 days. Cf. *Monsoon v. Indian Imports* [1993] *FSR* 486.

[158] *Hutchinson Personal Communications v. Hook Advertising* [1995] *FSR* 365; *Metix UK v. Maughan* [1997] *FSR* 718.

[159] *ZYX Music GmbH v. King* [1997] 2 *All ER* 129.

[160] *Pensher Security Doors v. Sunderland City Council* [2000] *RPC* 249.

9

DEFENCES

CHAPTER CONTENTS

1 INTRODUCTION

In this chapter we look at the exceptions that a defendant may rely upon when sued for infringement of copyright.[1] Most of these exceptions are found in Chapter III of Part 1 the 1988 Act (where they are referred to as permitted acts). As Laddie J said, Chapter III 'consists of a collection of provisions which define with extraordinary precision and rigidity the ambit of various exceptions to copyright protection'.[2] In addition to the exceptions in the 1988 Act the courts have also developed a number of common law defences that a defendant may rely upon when sued for infringement of copyright.

[1] See generally, R. Burrell & A. Coleman, *Copyright Exceptions: The Digital Impact* (2005).
[2] *Pro Sieben Media v. Carlton UK Television* [1997] *EMLR* 509.

The exceptions examined here provide that certain acts that might otherwise constitute an infringement of copyright do not incur liability. The exceptions only come into play once a claimant has established that copyright has been infringed. Where this occurs, the onus of proof falls on the defendant to prove that one of the exceptions applies.[3]

Given that the exceptions span a wide variety of activities, it is not surprising that they perform a number of different roles. In some cases, the exceptions promote and encourage the creation of works. This is particularly the case where the permitted use transforms the original work in some way. In other cases, the exceptions overcome the market failure that arises where an economically optimal use would not occur for one reason or other. This occurs, for example, where the dealing is so small that the transaction costs of formulating an agreement outweigh the value of any licence that might be negotiated between the parties.[4] In other cases the defences are intended to protect other non-copyright interests, such as the protection of privacy and free speech.[5] In yet other cases the exceptions prevent monopolies from being abused[6] and help to preserve material that is culturally and historically valuable.[7] Some of the defences encourage the parties to enter into collective licences.[8]

As the 1988 Act reminds us, the mere fact that an activity falls within one of the permitted acts does not mean that it does not contravene some other legal right,[9] an obvious example being breach of contract. In recent years questions have arisen as to whether the law should limit a person's ability to contract out of the exceptions.[10] So far, British copyright law has taken a piecemeal approach to these issues, and the various provisions which prevent contracting-out are examined in their particular contexts.[11] A related problem is that raised by the interface between the exceptions to copyright and technological measures of protection. If a person cannot take advantage of a defence because of the application of access or copy control mechanisms, can that person legally circumvent the measure in order to do so? So far, the UK legislature has answered this question with a clear 'no', leaving users deprived of the ability to utilize some of the exceptions with the possibility of applying to the Secretary of State. These provisions are reviewed in Chapter 13.[12]

For the most part, the exceptions to copyright protection available in the UK have largely been unaffected by international influences. Under the Berne Convention,[13] members of

---

[3] Rather surprisingly, given that the defences derogate from property rights, there does not appear to be any consistent process of interpreting copyright exemptions strictly against the defendant.

[4] W. Gordon, 'Fair Use as Market Failure' (1982) *Columbia LR* 1600. CDPA s. 30 (criticism or review), s. 59 (public recitation), ss. 57, 66A (difficulty locating author), s. 60 (abstracts), s. 74 (sub-titling), s. 35 (recording of broadcasts for education), s. 36 (educational copying).

[5] See, e.g. CDPA s. 29 (private study), s. 70 (home taping).

[6] CDPA s. 50B (decompilation), s. 73 (cable retransmission).

[7] CDPA s. 61 (folksongs), s. 75 (archives).

[8] CDPA s. 35 (recording of broadcasts for education), s. 36 (educational copying), s. 60 (copying of abstracts), s. 66 (compulsory licensing of lending of works), s. 74 (sub-titling for hard of hearing, etc), s. 143 (certification).

[9] CDPA s. 28(1).

[10] T. Vinje, 'A Brave New World of Technological Protection Systems: Will there be room for copyright?' [1996] *EIPR* 431; T. Heide, 'Copyright, Contract and the Legal Protection of Technological Measures: Not "The Old Fashioned Way": Providing a Rationale to the "Copyright Exceptions Interface"' (2003), 50 *Journal of the Copyright Society of the USA* 1001.

[11] CDPA s. 36(4), s. 50A, s. 50B, s. 296A(1)(a), s. 296A(1)(b), s. 296A(1)(c), s. 296B. Broadcasting Act 1996, s. 137. The more general issue about the relationship between contract and copyright is reviewed in Ch. 12.

[12] CDPA s. 297ZA, 297ZE; Info. Soc. Dir., Art. 6. See below pp. 321–3.

[13] As regards phonograms and broadcasts, see Rome, Art. 15(1).

the Union are permitted to create exceptions to the exclusive rights, in limited circumstances.[14] In particular, exceptions to the reproduction right must satisfy the so-called 'three-step test'.[15] According to this test, all exceptions must (i) be limited to certain special cases, (ii) not conflict with a normal exploitation of the work, and (iii) not unreasonably prejudice the legitimate interests of the author. As TRIPS requires that *all* limitations comply with the three-step test, the test has become more important.[16] Indeed, in a notable decision it was held by the Dispute Panel that a provision of US law which allowed certain establishments to play or show publicly works which were received from broadcasts violated the 'three-step test'.[17] Although the United States has not been able, as yet, to amend its law to comply with the Report, it has agreed to compensate European copyright holders for the losses they have incurred.[18] With the entry into force of the WIPO Treaties, the same test is to be applied to the additional rights required to be recognized, such as the distribution right and the right to make the work available to the public.[19] The WPPT extends the application of the 'three-step' test to the exceptions from rights in phonograms.[20]

The three-step test sets general parameters to the freedom of national legislatures to create exceptions: in contrast, European Community developments have had a more pronounced impact upon the copyright exceptions available in the UK. The Software, Databases, Rental and Information Society Directives require member states to operate certain exceptions,[21] and limit the circumstances in which other exceptions may be granted.[22] The Information Society Directive, in particular, contains one mandatory exception as regards transient or incidental acts of reproduction[23] and a huge list of optional defences, many covering the analogue environment.[24] The list is exhaustive: member states may not maintain any other exceptions.[25] The defences listed in the Directive are subject to the three-step test.[26]

---

[14] Minor exceptions are permitted in accordance with the understandings expressed at various conferences but these must be *de minimis*: see WTO Panel Report, *United States: Sec. 110(5) of the US Copyright Act* (15 June 2000) WT/DS160/R.

[15] Berne, Art. 9(2).   [16] TRIPS, Art. 13.

[17] The WTO Dispute Panel has assessed whether various provisions of US law passed the test and thus complied with Art. 13 TRIPS. WTO Panel Report, *US: Sec. 110(5)*, note 14 above. For commentary, see L. Helfer 'World Music on Stage: A Berne/TRIPS and Economic Analysis of the Fairness in Music Licensing Act' (2000) 80 *Boston University LR* 93; J. Ginsburg, 'Toward Supranational Copyright Law? The WTO Panel Decision' (2001) 187 *RIDA* 3; Bettina C. Goldmann, 'Victory for songwriters in WTO music royalties dispute between U.S. and EU—background of the conflict over the extension of copyright homestyle exemption' [2001] *IIC* 412–429.

[18] Richard Owens, 'TRIPS and the Fairness in Music Arbitration: the Repercussions' [2003] *EIPR* 49.

[19] WCT, Art. 10.

[20] WPPT, Art. 16. TRIPS, Art. 13 is not specific about exactly which rights to which it applies: in that it is part of 'section A', it might be thought also to be applicable to phonograms. However, because it comes before Art. 14(2), which requires members to give reproduction rights to phonogram producers, and this is qualified by Art. 14(6), the more obvious interpretation is that Art. 13 only affects Berne rights, and the Rental Right in Art. 11. See also Rome, Art. 15(2) (permitting certain exceptions).

[21] Software Dir, Arts 5 and 6; Database Dir, Art. 6.

[22] Rental Dir., Art. 10, especially At 10(3) (three-step test, added by Info. Soc. Dir., Art. 11); Software Dir., Arts. 5 and 6; Database Dir., Art. 6.

[23] See Sections 16 and 17 below.

[24] Info. Soc. Dir., Art. 5. Early proposals contained a very limited catalogue of exceptions, reflecting the limited concerns of the Directive with the 'information society'.

[25] See Info. Soc. Dir., Recital 32. The Directive divides the exceptions into two categories: five that relate to the reproduction right, and fifteen that relate to both the reproduction right and the communication right. Member states are also able to extend the exceptions to cover distribution of copies 'to the extent justified by the purpose of the authorized act of reproduction'. Defences relating to public performance, e.g. in CDPA s. 34, are unaffected.

[26] Ibid, Art. 5(5).

Finally, the European Convention on Human Rights, and the jurisprudence of the Strasbourg Court, appears to offer an important backdrop for the interpretation of a number of the defences (especially after the Human Rights Act 1998 came into force in October 2000).[27] As mentioned in Chapter 2, Article 10 of that Convention confers a freedom of expression, limitations to which must be 'necessary in a democratic society'. In *Ashdown v. Telegraph,* the Court of Appeal acknowledged that Article 10 considerations were to be taken into account, first, in the process of interpreting the existing exceptions; second, in the formulation of remedies; and third, if necessary, in the formulation of a judicial 'public interest' exception to copyright.[28]

2 FAIR DEALING

Of the various permitted acts in Chapter III, perhaps the most significant (in terms of their scope) are the fair-dealing defences that are found in sections 29 and 30.[29] These provide that a person will not be liable if they can show:

(i)   fair dealing for the purposes of research or private study—section 29(1) and (1C);

(ii) fair dealing for the purposes of criticism or review—section 30(1); or

(iii) fair dealing for the purpose of reporting current events—section 30(2).

Before looking at the three defences, we wish to make some general comments about fair dealing.

2.1 'DEALING'

It is important to note that all that is meant by dealing is that the defendant has made use of the work. Dealing does not imply that there has to be some sort of transaction between the parties.

2.2 PURPOSE

One of the notable features of UK copyright law is that fair dealing is only permitted for the purposes specifically listed in the 1988 Act. This means that the dealing must be fair for the purpose of research or private study, criticism or review, or the reporting of current events. As such, it is irrelevant that the use might be fair for a purpose not specified in the Act, or that it is fair in general. Thus, the fact that it might be impracticable for a commercial organization to circulate and distribute articles cut from a newspaper does not make the photocopying of the articles fair. Instead, it makes it a reason to seek an appropriate licence.[30] The restricted approach adopted in the UK should be contrasted with American copyright law which has a

---

[27] R. Burrell, 'Defending the Public Interest' [2000] *EIPR* 394. See more generally J. Griffiths & U. Suthersanen (eds.), *Copyright and Free Speech: Comparative and International Analyses* (2005).

[28] *Ashdown v. Telegraph Group Ltd* [2002] *Ch* 149, 167 [2001] 3 *WLR* 1368; [2002] *RPC* 235 (para. 46).

[29] These defences were first introduced in the CA 1911 s. 2(1)(a).

[30] *Newspaper Licensing Agency v. Marks & Spencer plc* [1999] *EMLR* 369 (para. 18).

general defence of *fair use* such that if the court is satisfied that the use is fair, then there will be no infringement.[31]

In thinking about whether an alleged infringer falls within one of the purposes listed in the 1988 Act, it is important to note two things. The *first* is that the courts have construed the specific purposes liberally.[32] As such, the first hurdle (namely that the dealing falls within one of the purposes in the 1988 Act) has been relatively easy to satisfy. The *second* point relates to the standpoint of interpretation that will be adopted when deciding the purpose for which the work was used. At first glance the language of the statute seems to suggest that the test for determining the purpose of the dealing should be decided according to the subjective intentions of the alleged infringer. However, as Aldous LJ pointed out in *Hyde Park*, when deciding the purpose of the dealing, it is not necessary 'for the court to put itself in the shoes of the infringer of the copyright'.[33] Instead, a more objective approach ought to be adopted. This ensures that the court does 'not give any encouragement to the notion that all that is required is for the user to have sincere belief, however misguided, that he or she is criticizing a work or reporting current affairs'.[34]

2.3 THE DEALING MUST BE FAIR

Once a defendant has shown that their dealing falls within one of the purposes listed in the 1988 Act, they must then show that the dealing was fair. The determination whether a dealing is fair is a question of degree and impression.[35] While it is not possible to provide precise guidelines as to when a dealing will be fair, it is possible to identify a number of factors that might influence the way this question is answered. It should be noted that the relative importance of each of these factors will vary according to the case in hand and the type of dealing in question. Moreover, now the Human Rights Act 1998 is in force, as Lord Phillips MR stated, '[i]t is…essential not to apply inflexibly tests based on precedent, but to bear in mind that considerations of public interest are paramount'.[36] Where 'freedom of expression' is affected, this may require the courts to place less weight than had previously been the case on factors such as whether the work was unpublished, or the commercial purpose of the dealing, and more weight on factors, not previously to the fore, such as the political importance of the contents of the copyright work, whether the subject matter is at the margins of copyright, and perhaps even how old the work is.[37]

2.3.1 Is the work unpublished?

Where the dealing takes place in relation to a work that has not been published or made widely available to the public, this will weigh against the dealing being fair. In fact, in the case

---

[31] Copyright Act 1976 (US) s. 107. For a careful argument that the restrictive approach of British law would not necessarily change were a fair-use defence adopted, see R. Burrell, 'Reining in Copyright Law: Is Fair Use the Answer?' [2001] *IPQ* 368.

[32] *Newspaper Licensing Agency v. Marks & Spencer plc* [2000] 4 *All ER* 239, 257 (Chadwick LJ) (CA). See also *Pro Sieben Media v. Carlton Television* [1999] *FSR* 610, 620; *Ashdown v. Telegraph Group Ltd* [2002] *Ch* 149, 172 (para. 64).

[33] *Hyde Park Residence v. Yelland* [2000] *EMLR* 363 (para. 21).   [34] *Pro Sieben*, note 32 above, 620.

[35] *Hubbard v. Vosper* [1972] 2 *QB* 84.   [36] *Ashdown*, note 32 above, 173 (para. 71).

[37] J. Griffiths, 'Copyright Law After *Ashdown*—Time to Deal Fairly with the Public' [2002] IPQ 240 (critical of Court of Appeal's recourse to existing case law establishing 'factors' on this basis): M. Birnhack, 'Acknowledging the Conflict Between Copyright Law and Freedom of Expression under the Human Rights Act' [2003] *Ent LR* 24, 33 (to similar effect). On the relation between the age of copyright and 'fair use' under US law, see J. Liu, 'Copyright and Time: A Proposal' (2002) 101 *Michigan Law Revieew* 409; J. Hughes, 'Fair Use Across Time' (2003) 50 *UCLA Law Review* 775.

of fair dealing for criticism or review, the defence is specified to be unavailable if the work has not been previously 'made available' to the public.[38] In other cases, particularly that of reporting current event, the fact that a work has not been published will certainly stand against a defendant.[39] In this respect, it is likely that the weight a court gives to the fact that a work is unpublished will vary according to the nature of the work in question: giving more weight in relation to private letters than it would for official reports that revealed matters of public importance.

2.3.2 How the work was obtained

The method by which the copyright material has been obtained has also been a factor in determining whether the dealing is fair.[40] It is less likely for a dealing to be fair if the dealing relates to a work that is leaked or stolen, or obtained by unauthorized access to a database, than a work that is obtained legitimately.[41]

2.3.3 The amount taken

The quantity and quality of what is taken will be a crucial factor in deciding whether a dealing is fair. As Lord Denning MR said in *Hubbard v. Vosper,* you 'must consider the number and extent of the extracts' and ask are 'they altogether too many and too long to be fair?'[42] This is because lengthy and numerous extracts, or extracts of the most important parts of a work, will reduce the expected returns to the copyright owner. By focusing on the quantity and quality of what is taken, the courts have recognized that fair dealing should not undermine the role copyright plays in encouraging creativity. In general, therefore, the defence will only apply where part of a work was taken. Nevertheless, the courts have acknowledged that, in some cases, such as where the work itself is short, it may be fair to reproduce the whole work.[43]

2.3.4 Use made of the work

Another factor that may influence the decisions as to whether a dealing is fair is the use that is made of the work in question. In some instances, it may be possible to reproduce someone else's work without comment or analysis and it be a fair use. However, a use is more likely to be fair if the defendant can show that they have added to or recontextualized the part taken. That is, a defendant will have a stronger case if they can show that the dealing was transformative.[44] This is particularly the case with fair dealing for criticism or review.

---

[38] CDPA s. 30(1), (1A) (as amended to give effect to Info. Soc Dir. Art. 5(3)(d)). Cf. Lord Denning, *Hubbard v. Vosper,* note 35 above, a result which would now have to be justified on the basis of the public interest.

[39] *Hyde Park Residence v. Yelland* [2000] *EMLR* 363, 378 (para. 34) *per* Aldous LJ (it is 'difficult to imagine that it could be fair dealing to use a work that had not been published nor circulated to persons for the purpose of…newspaper reporting'); *HRH the Prince of Wales v. Associated Newspapers* [2007] 3 *WLR* 222, 264 (para. 174 *per* Blackburne J), 288 (paras. 78–9 *per* Lord Phillips MR). But cf. *CCH Canadian v. Law Society of Upper Canada* [2004] *SCC* 13 (para. 58).

[40] *Beloff v. Pressdram* [1973] 1 *All ER* 241.

[41] Ibid; *The Controller of Her Majesty's Stationery Office, Ordnance Survey v. Green Amps Ltd* [2007] *EWHC* 2755 (Ch) (para. 54); *Queensland v. TCN Channel Nine* [1993] *IPR* 58 (Sup. Crt. of Qld.); *British Oxygen v. Liquid Air* [1925] 1 *Ch* 383. Cf. *Time Warner v. Channel 4* [1994] *EMLR* 1.

[42] *Hubbard v. Vosper* [1972] 2 *QB* 84.

[43] Ibid, 94–5, 98 (Megaw LJ) (example of a parishioner quoting an epitaph on a tombstone in the churchyard); *Sillitoe v. McGraw Hill* [1983] *FSR* 545; *Associated Newspapers Group v. News Group Newspapers* [1986] *RPC* 515, 520; cf. *Zamacois v. Douville* [1943] 2 *DLR* 257 where the Canadian Exchequer Court suggested that the copying of an entire work cannot qualify as fair dealing.

[44] *Newspaper Licensing Agency v. Marks & Spencer plc* [1999] *EMLR* 369, 380 (Lightman J).

It seems that the fact that a defendant derives a *commercial benefit* from the dealing will weigh against them when attempting to show that the dealing was fair. (Indeed, in the case of fair dealing for purposes of research, the defence only applies to research for a non-commercial purpose.)[45] As Chadwick LJ said in the Court of Appeal decision of *Newspaper Licensing Agency v. Marks & Spencer plc,* 'a dealing by a person with a copyright work for his own commercial advantage—and to the actual or potential commercial disadvantage of the copyright owner—is not to be regarded as a "fair dealing" unless there is some overriding element of public advantage which justifies the subordination of the rights of the copyright owner'.[46]

2.3.5 Motives for the dealing

Another factor that may influence the decision as to whether a use is fair relates to the motives of the alleged infringer.[47] The court must 'judge the fairness by the objective standard of whether a fair minded and honest person would have dealt with the copyright work in the manner' in question.[48] Thus, where a person acts dishonestly or for a motive that the court finds questionable (such as being primarily motivated by financial gain), it is likely to weigh against them. In contrast, if an alleged infringer can show that they were acting benevolently or were motivated by some altruistic or noble cause, this will increase the chances of their establishing that the dealing was fair.

2.3.6 Consequences of the dealing

Another factor that will influence the decision as to whether a dealing is fair relates to the impact that the dealing will have upon the market for the work. This is particularly important where the parties are in competition and the defendant's use of the work acts as a substitute for the purchase of the original work.[49] This would be the case, for example, if in criticizing it a defendant showed all of a film.

2.3.7 Could the purpose have been achieved by different means?

In some cases, the courts have asked whether the purpose could have been achieved in a manner that is less intrusive on the copyright holder's rights.[50] While there can be few objections to this test being used to determine whether a dealing is fair, problems may arise in the way it is applied by the courts. This can be seen in *Hyde Park Residence v. Yelland.* This case concerned an application for summary judgment against the *Sun* newspaper for publishing stills of Dodi Fayed and Diana, Princess of Wales, taken from security film, the copyright in which was owned by the claimant. The defendant argued that the stills revealed the times when Fayed and Diana were present at Villa Windsor and therefore exposed the falsehood of statements

---

[45] CDPA s. 29(1)(as amended, to give effect to Info. Soc. Dir., Art. 5(3)(a); Database Dir., Art. 6(2)(b)).

[46] Ibid. *Newspaper Licensing Agency v. Marks & Spencer plc* [2000] 4 *All ER* 239, 257 (Chadwick LJ) (CA).

[47] *Hyde Park Residence v. Yelland* [2000] *EMLR* 363, para. 36 (CA); *Pro Sieben Media v. Carlton Television* [1999] *FSR* 610, 614 (Walker LJ); *Beloff v. Pressdram* [1973] 1 *All ER* 241, 263.

[48] *Hyde Park Residence v. Yelland* [2000] *EMLR* 363, 379. Followed in *Newspaper Licensing Agency v. Marks & Spencer plc* [2000] 4 *All ER* 239, 250 (Gibson LJ) (CA).

[49] *Hubbard v. Vosper* [1972] 2 *QB* 84.

[50] *Newspaper Licensing Agency* [1999] *EMLR* 369, 382–3. Note also Info. Soc. Dir., Art. 5(3)(a), (c), (d) (limiting scope of exceptions for research, reproduction by the press, and criticism or review respectively, to 'the extent justified' by the non-commercial purpose, the 'informatory purpose', and the 'specific purpose'). Such an approach seems difficult to reconcile with ECHR-informed jurisprudence, which gives journalists leeway to determine what is necessary for a particular purpose: *Fressoz & Roire v. France* [2001] 31 *EHRR* 28, 60 (para. 54); *A v. B & C* [2002] 3 *WLR* 542 (para. 11).

made by Mohammed Al Fayed. At first instance it was argued that it was not necessary for the *Sun* to have published the images taken from the video. Instead, it was suggested that the same result could have been achieved via written word. In particular it was argued that the *Sun* could have interviewed the security guard and said that they had seen the photographs without actually publishing them. The Court of Appeal agreed. As Aldous LJ said, 'the information as to the timing of arrival and departure of Dodi and Princess Diana could have been given in the articles by the reporter in the *Sun* stating that he had seen the photographs which proved the Princess and Mr Dodi only stayed at the Villa for 28 minutes'.[51] In so doing, the Court of Appeal implied that the pictures were no more effective evidence than the written word.[52]

2.4 SUFFICIENT ACKNOWLEDGEMENT

In certain situations, for the fair dealing defence to apply the dealing must be accompanied by a 'sufficient acknowledgement'. In essence this means that the author and the work must be identified. It should be noted that sufficient acknowledgement is not required in all cases.

(i)   In relation to fair dealing for research for a non-commercial purpose or private study, sufficient acknowledgement is *only* required where the dealing relates to research, and acknowledgement is not impossible 'for reasons of practicality or otherwise'.[53]

(ii) In relation to fair dealing for criticism and review, sufficient acknowledgement is required for *all* works.[54]

(iii) In relation to the reporting of current events, sufficient acknowledgement is required for all works.[55] However, no acknowledgement is required in connection with the reporting of current events *by means of* a sound recording, film, or broadcast where this would be not impossible 'for reasons of practicality or otherwise'.[56]

Where required, the defendant must show that they have identified both the work *and* the author of the work.[57] A work can be identified by its title or by some other description.[58] The author can be identified by name, pseudonym, or by other means such as a photograph or a logo.[59] Whatever method is chosen, it must convey 'to a reasonably alert member of the relevant audience that the identified person is the author'.[60] It is important to note that it is the author and not the owner of the copyright work who must be identified.[61] There is no need for the author to be identified where a work is published anonymously or, in the case of an unpublished work, where it is not possible for a person to ascertain the identity of the author by reasonable inquiry. It seems that even in these cases the work still needs to be identified.

---

[51] *Hyde Park Residence v. Yelland* [2000] *EMLR* 363, 379.

[52] Mance LJ also said the interest 'in resolving general falsity did not require the misappropriation of the stills or their supply to the *Sun,* presumably for money or their publication by the *Sun*'. *Hyde Park Residence v. Yelland* [2000] *EMLR* 363, 392.

[53] CDPA s. 29(1), (1B) (as amended to give effect to Info. Soc. Dir. Art. 5(3)(c)).

[54] CDPA s. 30(1).   [55] CDPA s. 30(2). The exception does not apply to photographs.

[56] CDPA s. 30(3) (as amended to give effect to Info. Soc. Dir., Art. 5(3)(c)).

[57] CDPA s. 178.   [58] *Pro Sieben Media v. Carlton Television* [1999] *FSR* 610, 616.

[59] Ibid, 625. The logo of Pro Sieben, a stylized figure 7 (Sieben means seven in German) in the top right-hand corner of the broadcast images, was sufficient acknowledgement. Newspaper publishers need to be identified by the name of the newspaper that they publish: *Newspaper Licensing Agency* [1999] *EMLR* 369, 384.

[60] *Pro Sieben Media v. Carlton UK Television* [1997] *EMLR* 509, 597.

[61] *Express Newspapers v. Liverpool Daily Post* [1985] 3 *All ER* 680.

With these general points in mind, we now turn to consider each of the specific fair dealing defences.

3 FAIR DEALING FOR THE PURPOSES OF RESEARCH OR PRIVATE STUDY

Section 29(1) provides that fair dealing with a work for the purpose of non-commercial research or private study does not infringe copyright in the work. The defence applies where the dealing takes place with literary, dramatic, musical, and artistic works, as well as with the typographical formats of published works.[62] The exception does not apply where the dealing is with a broadcast, sound recording, or film.[63] The limited scope of the defence has been criticized because it 'fails to reflect the increasing importance of non-textual media for both study and research'.[64] The defence is also of limited application to computer programs.[65]

The rationale for this defence lies in the belief that research and study is necessary to generate new works. It also recognizes that non-commercial research and study does not normally interfere with the incentives and rewards that copyright provides to creators and owners. In effect, the defence helps to achieve copyright's goal of maximizing the production of works. The defence also takes account of the fact that dealings of this kind would often be difficult to detect.

In order for a defendant to rely upon the research or private study defence they must show (i) that the use made of the copyright work was for the purpose of non-commercial research or private study and (ii) that the dealing was 'fair'. In the case of research, the work and the author must be sufficiently acknowledged (with certain exceptions).

3.1 IS THE DEALING FOR THE 'PURPOSE OF RESEARCH OR PRIVATE STUDY'?

To fall within section 29(1), the defendant must show that the dealing was for the purpose of either research for a non-commercial purpose or private study. Private study is defined, in section 178, as not including any study which is directly or indirectly for a commercial purpose.[66] The provisions therefore cover most research or private study for academic purposes but will also potentially include situations where a person copies material to investigate their

---

[62] CDPA s 29(2) (in relation to the typographical copyright, the defence is available for all research, not just non-commercial research). The defence of fair dealing for private study is available in relation to databases, whether electronic or not, despite Database Dir., Art. 6(1).

[63] CDPA s. 29: *Pro Sieben Media v. Carlton UK Television* [1997] 1 *EMLR* 509.

[64] Copinger, para. 9–23, p. 484; Burrell & Coleman, *Copyright Exceptions: The Digital Impact* (2005), p. 116. It has been proposed in the *Gowers Review* that these limitations be removed and detailed aspects are considered in IPO, *Taking Forward the Gowers Review of Intellectual Property* (2008) 21–27.

[65] CDPA s. 29(4)–(4A) (excluding from the fair-dealing exceptions acts which are permitted in relation to computer programs under CDPA ss. 50B and 50BA).

[66] To give effect to the limitation in Info. Soc. Dir., Art. 5(b). The reference to 'indirect' seems particularly problematic: much study, even in schools, is intended to equip the student with skills or knowledge that improve their own commercial potential. Surely, it cannot have been intended that this would be regarded as 'indirectly' for a commercial purpose.

family history. In contrast, where a work (such as a database) is used in the market-testing of new drugs, or for a commercial training course, the defence would not apply. Much research, however, will occupy a difficult middle ground. In a recent case the High Court appears to have approved the test of whether it is contemplated that the research will ultimately be used for a purpose which has some commercial value.[67] Here, useful reference might also be made to Recital 42 of the Information Society Directive which indicates that the determination is to be by reference to the activity as such, rather than 'the organisational structure and the means of funding the establishment'. Research carried out in an independent school or a private university may be non-commercial, and, depending on its orientation, research in a publicly-funded university may be commercial.[68]

Prior to 2003, little turned on whether an activity was defined as research or private study. It seemed that the only difference between the two concepts was that research was seen as a process that is intended to lead towards a particular result (be it a conclusion, a decision, an answer to a problem, an article, or a book), whereas study might be 'for its own sake'. However, the distinction may now prove more important, as the defence will usually only apply to dealings for research where there is 'sufficient acknowledgement'. The terms must also be interpreted in the light of the Information Society Directive. In this context, it seems that the key difference between private study and research is that research may not be private. Private study can cover any private use, such as note-taking or photocopying from a book, whether it be for its own sake or with a goal in mind,[69] whereas 'research' seems to relate to the use of copyright material in papers, documents, talks, and other output which make arguments, observations, or draw conclusions. The research exception is intended to be available to justify the public communication or distribution of copyright material, as well as its reproduction. Indeed, the permitted exception in the Directive relates to 'use for the sole purpose of illustration for . . . scientific research'. It seems therefore that the use of quotations in a book or journal article can be dealings for research. However, not all public output is research. The book, paper, or article must have been researched: that is, it must be a product of systematic inquiry (as opposed, for example, to fiction).[70]

3.2 THE DEALING MUST BE 'FAIR'

The mere fact that a defendant can show that the work was used for private study or non-commercial research does not necessarily mean that the dealing will be exempt from liability. It is also necessary to show that the dealing was fair. As we explained earlier, a number of different factors will influence the decision as to whether a particular dealing is fair. In this context the most important are likely to be the amount taken,[71] whether the work is readily available, and the effect that the dealing has on the market for the original work.

---

[67] *The Controller of Her Majesty's Stationery Office, Ordnance Survey v. Green Amps Ltd* [2007] *EWHC* 2755 (Ch) (para. 23) (citing Copinger, para 9–28).

[68] Davison, pp. 79–80.

[69] Thus, private study would include situations where a student is preparing for a seminar, or photocopies material to assist in the writing of an essay, or where a person photocopies pages from various newspapers to study the form of a particular horse, or to help them decide what type of stove to buy.

[70] The Federal Court of Australia has said that research means 'a diligent and systematic inquiry or investigation into a subject': *De Garis v. Neville Jeffress Pidler* (1990) 18 *IPR* 292 (FCA).

[71] *Universities U.K. v. Copyright Licensing Agency Ltd.* [2002] *RPC* 693, 702 (para. 34) (student who photocopies an article or short passage from a book is likely to be involved in a 'fair' dealing, while a student who photocopies the whole of a textbook would not be).

3.3 SPECIAL CASES

3.3.1 Copying by third parties

In many cases, the person who does the copying will also be the person who carries out the research or study. Indeed, as a general rule, in order to come within the defence the dealing must be for defendant's *own* research or study. For example, a publisher cannot rely on the exception to justify reproducing parts of copyright-protected works in study guides.[72] However, in some circumstances, the defence is available even though the primary actor may not be the person engaged in the research. This might be the case, for example, where a research assistant or a librarian makes photocopies for academics or students. The 1988 Act recognizes that, for the defence to apply, it is not necessary for the activity that leads to the alleged infringement to be undertaken by the researcher or student. That is, it is possible for an agent to do the copying on behalf of the researcher or student. However, an important limitation to this possibility is imposed by section 29(3)(b).[73] This provides that copying by a person other than a researcher or student is not a fair dealing if the person doing the copying knows it will result in 'copies of substantially the same material being provided to more than one person at substantially the same time and for substantially the same purpose'.[74] This means that lecturers are unable to use the research or private study defence where they make multiple copies of a work for their students.

3.3.2 Limited application in relation to computer programs

As a result of changes introduced to implement the Software Directive, the research and private study defence is limited in relation to computer programs. Section 29(4) provides that it is not fair dealing (a) to convert a computer program expressed in a low-level language into a version expressed in a higher-level language or (b) incidentally in the course of so converting the program to copy it. Section 29(4) ensures that the decompilation of computer programs is taken outside the remit of the research and private study defence. Instead, defendants will have to resort to the more limited defence under section 50B (which is discussed below). Section 29(4A) similarly excludes from the scope of the defence the acts of observing, studying, and testing the functioning of a computer program in order to determine the ideas and principles which underlie it. Since the Software Directive requires such acts to be permitted irrespective of whether the acts are done for commercial purposes, it was decided to provide a special exemption in section 50BA, which we will return to later. It should be noted that the fair-dealing defence is available for other uses of computer programs.

3.4 SUFFICIENT ACKNOWLEDGEMENT

Where a dealing is for purposes of non-commercial research, it can only benefit from the exception if there is 'sufficient acknowledgement'.[75] However, this can be dispensed with where

---

[72] *Sillitoe v. McGraw Hill* [1983] *FSR* 545; *Longman Group v. Carrington Technical Institute* [1991] 2 *NZLR* 574 (CANZ).

[73] This should be read in conjunction with the education copying defences discussed below (especially CDPA s. 38) and the relevant collective licensing schemes (see section 9 below).

[74] CDPA s. 29(3). Cf. *Longman v. Carrington,* note 72 above.

[75] Reflecting, and in such implementation eliding, Database Dir. Art. 6(2)(b) ('as long as the source is indicated') and Info. Soc. Dir., Art. 5(3)(a) ('as long as the source, including the author's name, is indicated, unless this turns out to be impossible').

the acknowledgement is impossible for reasons of practicality or otherwise. As mentioned above, no such requirement is required as regards 'private study'. Although the exact distinction between research and private study will now require judicial articulation, the requirement for sufficient acknowledgement seems to take account of the fact that research output, whether papers or articles, is often circulated.

4   FAIR DEALING FOR CRITICISM OR REVIEW

Section 30(1) provides that fair dealing with any work for the purpose of criticism or review does not infringe the copyright in the work. This defence recognizes the value of criticism or review. It also recognizes that, for a person to critique someone's work, they will normally need to cite the author—something that authors might be reluctant to allow. The defence prevents copyright owners from using copyright to control who should review their works, when they may do so, and what parts of the work may be used.[76]

   In order to rely upon the defence, a defendant must show that (i) the dealing was for the purpose of criticism or review, (ii) the work had previously been made available to the public, (iii) the dealing was 'fair', and (iv) the dealing was accompanied by sufficient acknowledgement.

4.1   WAS THE DEALING FOR THE PURPOSE OF 'CRITICISM OR REVIEW'?

For a defendant to rely upon section 30(1), they must show that the dealing was for the purpose of criticism or review of the work, or of another work,[77] or the performance of a work. As we explained above, the courts take an objective approach when deciding the purpose for which the work was used. The courts have also said that criticism and review should be construed liberally.[78] Consequently, the criticism or review may be of the work as a whole or a single aspect of a work, the thought or philosophy underpinning a work,[79] or its social and moral implications.[80] Some decisions have seemed to suggest that the criticism or review need not be of a work at all. For example, where a television programme used extracts from Kubrick's film *A Clockwork Orange* to criticize the decision to withdraw the film from distribution, Henry LJ explained that this fell within the defence, which applied 'equally where the criticism is of the decision to withdraw from circulation a film in the public domain, and not just the film itself'.[81] In *Pro Sieben*, the Court of Appeal treated as justified the use of extracts from the claimant's television broadcast (which featured interviews with a woman who was pregnant with octuplets) even though the defendant's programme criticized the practices of 'cheque-book journalism' of which the claimant's programme was said to be an example, rather than the claimant's broadcast itself.[82] In

76 *Time Warner v. Channel 4* [1993] *EMLR* 1, 14; *Banier v. News Group Newspapers* [1997] *FSR* 812.
   77 *Beloff v. Pressdram* [1973] 1 *All ER* 241; *Associated Newspapers Group v. News Group Newspapers* [1986] *RPC* 515.
   78 *Newspaper Licensing Agency v. Marks & Spencers plc* [2000] 4 *All ER* 239, 257 (Chadwick LJ) (CA); *Pro Sieben Media v. Carlton Television* [1999] *FSR* 610, 620.
   79 *Hubbard v. Vosper* [1972] 2 *QB* 84, 94 ff.; *Time Warner v. Channel 4* [1994] *EMLR* 1, 15.
   80 *Pro Sieben Media v. Carlton Television* [1999] *FSR* 610, 621.
   81 *Time Warner v. Channel 4* [1994] *EMLR* 1, 15.
   82 *Pro Sieben Media AG v. Carlton UK Television Ltd. & Anor* [1999] *EMLR* 109. See *Fraser-Woodward v. BBC* [2005] *FSR* 762 (excusing the use of photographs in a broadcast which criticized relations between celebrities and newspapers).

some cases, however, the courts have been more fastidious in relation to the requirement that the criticism be of 'that or another work or of a performance of a work'.[83] In *Ashdown v. Telegraph,* for example, the exception was held not to justify the reproduction in the *Sunday Telegraph* of sections of Ashdown's memorandum of a meeting with Tony Blair where the gist of the article lay in criticizing the political event and actors described in the memorandum, rather than the existence, style, or other aspects of the memorandum.[84] If this narrow (though, on the basis of the statutory wording, hardly unjustified) reading of the exception takes root, defendants will be forced to rely on the other exceptions: an academic paper criticizing the Blair–Ashdown meeting might be able to claim fair dealing for research, and a newspaper account (being for commercial purposes) might be permitted as reporting current events or exceptionally disclosing matters in the public interest.

4.2 THE WORK MUST HAVE BEEN MADE AVAILABLE

The defence is only available where the work has been made available to the public. Making available is broadly defined to include the issuing of copies, making the work available by an electronic retrieval system, rental, or lending of copies to the public, the performance, exhibition playing, or showing of the work, and the communication to the public.[85] In *HRH the Prince of Wales v. Associated Newspapers* it was held that Prince Charles's 'Hong Kong journals' had not been made available to the public, even though they had been distributed to as many as 75 people, because the recipients understood that the work was being disclosed in confidence.[86]

4.3 WAS THE DEALING FAIR?

Once a defendant has shown that the dealing was for the purpose of criticism or review, they must then show that the dealing was fair. As we explained earlier, a number of different factors will influence the decision as to whether a particular dealing is fair. In this context the most important of these are likely to be the amount taken,[87] the effect on the market,[88] and the nature of the dealing.[89] When deciding whether a dealing for the purpose of criticism

---

[83] This limitation is not required by the Info. Soc. Dir., Art. 5(3)(d), where it is the 'quotations' that must relate to a work rather than the criticism or review, and it is hoped that when the legislature comes to recodify the 1988 Act, it seriously considers leaving the object of criticism or review at large.

[84] *Ashdown,* note 32 above, 171; [2002] *RPC* 235, 251.

[85] CDPA s. 30(1A) (added by SI 2003/2498 to give effect to Info. Soc. Dir., Art. 5(3)(d)). Since this requirement was included by delegated legislation under the European Communities Act 1972, it is difficult to see a justification for applying it to databases and computer programs (which were unaffected by the Info. Soc. Dir. (see Info. Soc. Dir., Art. 1)), or typographical arrangements. However, in the light of *Hyde Park v. Yelland* [2000] *EMLR* 363, 378 (para. 34) and *British Oxygen Liquid Air* [1925] 1 *Ch* 383, the addition of the requirement is unlikely to be of material significance.

[86] [2007] 3 WLR 222, 265 (para. 176 *per* Blackburne J).

[87] Rather oddly, the Info. Soc. Directive seems to require that the defence be confined to 'quotations', implying that paraphrasing or summarizing is outside its scope. Given that Art. 5(3)(d) is built around an idea of proportionality, it would seem sensible to interpret 'quotations' as covering 'quotations and other infringing uses'.

[88] *IPC Media Ltd. v. News Group Newspapers Ltd.* [2005] *FSR* 752 (copying for own competing commercial purpose unfair). Cf. *Pro Sieben Media AG v. Carlton UK Television Ltd & Anor* [1999] *EMLR* 109 (Court of Appeal) ('the degree to which the challenged use competes with exploitation of copyright by the copyright owner is a very important consideration, but not the only consideration').

[89] *Fraser-Woodward v. BBC* [2005] *FSR* 762 (inclusion of copyright photographs in broadcast was fair, taking into account the brief time for which the images were shown).

or review is fair, the courts have not tended to consider whether the criticism itself is fair.[90] Rather, they take account of whether the extent of the copying is fair to illustrate or support the criticism. As such, the criticism may be malicious, unbalanced, or motivated by insecurity without forfeiting the defence.[91] While this is likely to continue to be the general nature of the assessment, UK courts may now pay attention to the limitation in the Information Society Directive that the use be 'in accordance with fair practice, and to the extent required by the specific purpose'.

4.4 SUFFICIENT ACKNOWLEDGEMENT

The third and final factor that a defendant must show to fall within the criticism or review defence is that the dealing was accompanied by 'sufficient acknowledgement'. This is required for *all* works.[92] The issue of sufficient acknowledgement was discussed above.

4.5 PARODY

Where parodies breach the rule against substantial taking, it is necessary to consider whether such uses avoid liability through the 'fair dealing' exceptions, particularly those relating to criticism or review. The possibility was mooted in *Williamson Music v Pearson*,[93] but cases in other jurisdictions suggest that this role for the exception might be quite limited. Two particular problems have arisen.

First, restrictive interpretation of the concept of 'criticism' has made it difficult to predict whether it covers parody.[94] In the 1996 Canadian Federal Court case *Michelin v National Automobile, Aerospace, Transportation and General Workers Union of Canada* a trade union distributed literature deploying Michelin's famous Bibendum logo with his foot raised as if about to crush underfoot an unsuspecting Michelin worker.[95] The company sued, claiming violation of various trade marks and infringement of copyright. It failed on the trade mark issues, but succeeded on copyright. Teitelbaum J, having found that the image on the leaflet reproduced a substantial part of the original artistic work, held that the defence of 'fair dealing for criticism or review' was inapplicable. The judge said that the choice of the terms 'criticism and review' indicated a desire that parody not be treated as excepted and, in his view, exceptions to property rights were to be construed narrowly. While it is possible to take issue with each of these grounds, what seems most peculiar about Teitelbaum J's reasoning is the claim

---

[90] There is no need for the critical work to be representative of the original. *Time Warner v. Channel 4* [1994] *EMLR* 1, 12.

[91] *Pro Sieben Media v. Carlton Television* [1999] *FSR* 610, 619. In these circumstances an author's remedy for malicious and unjustified criticism lies in the law of defamation, not copyright.

[92] CDPA s. 30(1).

[93] *Williamson Music v. Pearson* [1987] *FSR* 97, 103. Paul Baker QC stated that the point 'does not arise in the present case, because that was not the purpose of the compilers of the advertisement.' Subsequent case law indicates that 'subjective' intention of the user is not determinative, and that 'for the purposes' of is equivalent to 'in the context of', a matter to be decided objectively.

[94] The Supreme Court of Israel, however, held that parody could be 'criticism' in *Geva v. Walt Disney Co*, PLA 2687/92, 48 PD (1) 251, para 38. See Wilkof, ISR–37, in Nimmer & Geller, *International Copyright Law and Practice* (2007). Unfortunately, the ground-breaking decision was not translated into English and, as a consequence, has failed to influence subsequent judicial interpretation of the concept of 'criticism and review'.

[95] *Cie Générale des Etablissements Michelin v. CAW Canada* (1996) 71 *CPR* (3d) 348 (Fed Ct of Canada, on Canadian Copyright Act, s. 27).

that criticism and parody are mutually exclusive notions, and thus that parody has never (and could never) 'figure as criticism'. While one can readily accept the judge's statement that 'criticism' is not synonymous with 'parody', as there can clearly be criticism that is not parodic, it by no means follows that no parody can be critical.[96]

Second, the requirement that the dealing give 'sufficient acknowledgement' to the author of the parodied or caricatured work can present a practical hurdle to the application of the exception to such uses. Although in the world of art and particularly that of the cartoonist, it has been common to designate works 'after x', in many other types of parody an explicit reference of this sort might seem inappropriate, even an admission of failure.[97] While it is arguable that, were the sufficient acknowledgement requirement given a broad construction it could be said that *implicit* recognition would be sufficient,[98] the possibility of 'implicit' acknowledgement was denied in the *Michelin* case. Teitelbaum J rejected outright the trade union arguments that, in cases of parody, there is no need for express mention of the source, because it is obvious. The judge observed that such a rule would lead to distinctions between cases where the parody was poorly executed and so the source not recognized and good parodies (where the source would be recognized and so there would be no infringement), as well as between cases of parodies of obscure works (where the parodied work could not be implicitly recognized) and parodies of famous works (where acknowledgement could be implicit). In his view, 'the law cannot permit such distinctions'. Moreover, the judge stated that the 'requirement to actively mention the source and author is there for a reason and not to be lightly skipped over'. Passive or implicit acknowledgement is insufficient.

The Gowers Review has recommended that UK law be amended to incorporate a defence in relation to parody, caricature, and pastiche (following the EC Directive on Copyright in the Information Society). Follow-up consultations,[99] on-going at the time of writing, are considering the appropriate breadth of such an exception. Should it apply to all works? Should it be limited to 'fair dealing' for parodic purposes? Should parodic uses in advertising be exempted? Should sufficient acknowledgement be required?

5 REPORTING OF CURRENT EVENTS

Section 30(2) provides that fair dealing with any work (other than a photograph)[100] for the purpose of reporting current events does not infringe the copyright in the work provided it is

---

[96] An Australian Federal court decision suggests that, whatever the position in relation to parody, the 'criticism or review' defence is available for satire: *TCN Channel Nine v. Network Ten* [2001] *FCA* 108, (2001) 108 *FCR* 235, (20 February 2001), Conti J (Federal Court of Australia); (2002) 118 *FCR* 417, [2002] *FCA* 146. The decisions of Conti J and the Full Federal Court are savagely criticized by Michael Handler in 'A Real Pea Souper: The Panel Case and the Development of the Fair Dealing Defences to Copyright Infringement in Australia' [2003] *Melbourne University LR* 15.

[97] Burrell and Coleman, at 61; Copinger (15th ed) para 9–41; Laddie *et al*, para 4.62 (explicit reference may be 'ponderous, heavy-handed and likely to undermine the deft touch of the satirist, as where one has to explain the point of a joke').

[98] Spence (2007), '*Rogers v Koons*: Copyright and the Problem of Artistic Appropriation', in D. McClean (ed.), *The Trials of Art* (2007) 213–234, 228.

[99] IPO, *Taking Forward the Gowers Review*, 31–36.

[100] This means that a newspaper is not able to take photographs from another paper and claim this defence. Hence the need to rely on the criticism or review defence in *Banier v. News Group Newspapers* [1997] *FSR* 812.

accompanied by a sufficient acknowledgement.[101] No acknowledgement is required, however, in connection with the reporting of current events by means of a sound recording, film, or broadcast where this would be impossible by reason of practicality or otherwise.[102]

As Gibson LJ explained, the reporting of current events defence aims to strike a 'balance between protection of rights of creative authors and the wider public interest (of which free speech is a very important ingredient)'.[103] In order to rely upon the defence, a defendant must show (i) that the dealing was for the purpose of reporting current events, (ii) that the dealing was 'fair', and (iii) that there was sufficient acknowledgement.[104] Before looking at these, it should be noted that contractual restrictions on what would otherwise fall within the defence of fair dealing for the purpose of reporting current events are void insofar as the restriction relates to the inclusion of visual images taken from a broadcast in another communication to the public.[105]

5.1 WAS THE DEALING FOR THE PURPOSE OF REPORTING A CURRENT EVENT?

As we explained above, the courts take an objective approach when deciding the purpose for which the work was used. The courts have also said that the reporting of current events should be construed liberally.[106]

To fall within the defence, the dealing must take place in relation to an event that is *current*. An event will be current if it deals with a contemporary issue. The older the issue, the less likely it is that it will be treated as having any currency. An event that took place some time ago may however be current if it is still under discussion. For example, in *Hyde Park* it was accepted, both at first instance and by the Court of Appeal (albeit grudgingly), that although the stills in the *Sun* were published more than a year after the visit by Fayed and Princess Diana to Villa Windsor, the events still had some currency. As Jacob J said, 'at the time of publication the events were still very much under discussion that it would pedantic to regard them as anything other than current'.[107]

For the defence to apply, a defendant must also show that the dealing took place in relation to an *event*.[108] It seems that certain matters by their very nature will be treated as events. Thus, matters of national or political importance (planned minimum wage proposals, a campaign about child labour, a case about alleged race bias at a rival establishment, or announcements

---

[101] Cf. CA 1911, s. 2(1)(a) which referred to fair dealing with any work for the purposes of newspaper summary. This became 'reporting current events' in CA 1956, s. 6(3).

[102] CDPA s. 30(3).

[103] *Newspaper Licensing Agency v. Marks & Spencer plc* [2000] 4 *All ER* 239, 249 (Gibson LJ) (CA).

[104] CDPA s. 30(2).   [105] Broadcasting Act 1996, s. 137 (as amended).

[106] The value placed on freedom of information and freedom of speech requires that gateway to be wide: *Newspaper Licensing Agency v. Marks & Spencer plc* [2000] 4 *All ER* 239, 382; *Ashdown v. Telegraph Group Ltd* [2002] *Ch* 149, 172.

[107] *Hyde Park Residence v. Yelland* [1999] *RPC* 655, 661. See also *Ashdown v. Telegraph Group Ltd* [2002] *Ch* 149, 172 (meeting between Ashdown and PM in October 1997 was an event that was 'a matter of current interest to the public' in Nov. 1999).

[108] The concept of 'current events' is narrower than 'news': *Newspaper Licensing Agency v. Marks & Spencer plc* [2000] 4 *All ER* 239, 382; cf. [2000] 4 *All ER* 239, 249 (Gibson LJ) (CA).

about the Euro[109]), as well as major sporting contests (the World Cup,[110] Wimbledon, or the Olympics) are likely to be events.[111]

In contrast, matters that are trivial, ephemeral, or immaterial will not be treated as events. For example, it has been said that comparisons of products such as wines, chicken Kiev, and taramasalata,[112] lifestyle articles on choice of underwear, and the times of television programmes were not current events.[113] The fact that a matter is currently of interest or in the press does not mean that it is a current event.[114] However interesting an article may be, the fact that it is reported in a newspaper does not necessarily make it a current event. Thus, it was suggested in the *NLA* decision that the mere fact that a fashion editor of a journal featured a Marks & Spencer garment did not make it a current event.[115]

While trivial or immaterial matters will not ordinarily be treated as events, it is possible for such matters to be transformed into an event through media coverage. This can be seen in *Pro Sieben,* where a matter that was otherwise of limited and ephemeral interest (here it was the sale to German television by a member of the public of an interview about a woman pregnant with octuplets)[116] was nonetheless treated as an 'event'. This was because the volume and intensity of the media coverage was sufficient to bring that coverage within the ambit of current events.

The material dealt with by the defendant must relate to or be relevant to the current event in question. This means that the defence will not cover any dealing that takes place separately from the current event in question. Thus, it was held that the *Daily Mail* newspaper was unable to rely on the death of the Duchess of Windsor to justify the republication of correspondence between the Duchess and her husband.[117] Similarly, in *Hyde Park,* the Court of Appeal held that the publication of the driveway stills that showed the arrival and departure times of Fayed and Princess Diana did not fall within the current events defence. This was because the material in question (the driveway stills) did not correlate with the event in question (the purpose being to expose the lies of Mohammed Al Fayed).[118]

The upshot of this is that while the publication of historical material is not ordinarily a current event,[119] old information may become relevant in response to some fresh event. As Walton J said:

[T]he publication of historical material, material that is strictly historical, may nonetheless be of urgent necessity in reporting current events. One has only to think, for example, of correspondence dealing with nuclear reactors that have just blown up or have had a core melt-down: that might date from a very considerable period previous to the event happening, but would be of a topical nature in order to enable a report of what actually happened to be properly prepared.[120]

---

[109] Ibid, 267 (Mance LJ) (CA). According to Lightman J, the event 'may be a matter of entirely local interest or of interest to few people': *Newspaper Licensing Agency v. Marks & Spencer plc* [2000] 4 *All ER* 239, 382 (para. 18).

[110] *British Broadcasting Corporation v. British Satellite Broadcasting* [1992] *Ch* 141.

[111] Chadwick LJ took a more subjective approach when he said the publication of an article which features comments that relate to or impact upon the appellant's products was an event: *Newspaper Licensing Agency v. Marks & Spencer plc* [2000] 4 *All ER* 239, 257 (CA).

[112] *Newspaper Licensing Agency* [1999] *EMLR* 369, 383.

[113] *Independent Television Publications v. Time Out* [1984] *FSR* 64.

[114] *Newspaper Licensing Agency* [1999] *EMLR* 369, 382.

[115] *Newspaper Licensing Agency* [2000] 4 *All ER* 239, 250 (Gibson LJ); 267 (Mance LJ) (CA).

[116] *Pro Sieben Media v. Carlton UK Television* [1999] *FSR* 610.

[117] *Associated Newspapers v. News Group Newspapers* [1986] *RPC* 515.

[118] The Court of Appeal looked to the relevant parts of the *Sun* to ascertain the perceived purpose of the use of the work. *Hyde Park v. Yelland* [2000] *EMLR* 363, 374, 379–80.

[119] *Ashdown v. Telegraph Group Ltd* [2002] *Ch* 149, 166–7 (para. 44).

[120] *Associated Newspapers v. News Group Newspapers* [1986] *RPC* 515.

5.2 WAS THE DEALING FAIR?

Once a defendant has shown that their dealing was for the purpose of reporting current events, they must then show that the dealing was fair. According to the Court of Appeal, the defence should be available 'where the public interest in learning of the very words written by the owner of the copyright is such that publication should not be inhibited by the chilling factor of having to pay damages or account of profits'.[121] Although a number of different factors will influence the decision as to whether a particular dealing is fair, including whether the work is published or unpublished,[122] the amount taken, and the motive for the dealing,[123] the most important is likely to be whether it is reasonably necessary to refer to the work in order to deal with the events in question.[124] It also seems that the courts will be influenced by what is taken to be normal behaviour in the circumstances. Thus, in the *World Cup* case, it was fair for the defendant to reshow the goals and match highlights, typically 30 seconds of a 90-minute match, even though these were clearly the most important extracts. This was because the sequences were the normal and obvious means of illustrating the news report.[125]

It has also been suggested that the commercial nature of a dealing will weigh against a defendant trying to establish that the dealing was fair. A more extreme view was taken by Mance LJ in the *NLA* decision. While he was not willing to express a final opinion on the matter,[126] Mance LJ had doubts about whether it was possible to extend the fair-dealing exception, which represents a public-interest exception to copyright, to the reporting of current events for private commercial purposes.[127] Such an approach is problematic in that it will greatly restrict the ability of commercial media to rely upon fair dealing. A more realistic approach was adopted by Jacob J in the first instance decision of *Hyde Park Residence v. Yelland*, where he held that the fact that the security guard and the *Sun* had both expected to make money from the publication of the pictures did not derogate from the fair-dealing justification.[128] As Jacob J said, the 'press often have to pay for information of public importance. And when they publish they will always expect to make money. They are not philanthropists.'[129]

---

[121] *Ashdown v. Telegraph Group Ltd* [2002] *Ch* 149, 173 (para. 69).

[122] *HRH the Prince of Wales v. Associated Newspapers* [2007] 3 *WLR* 222, 264, 287 (newspaper copying of Prince's travel journals not fair because obtained in breach of confidence and more than necessary for purpose of reporting current events).

[123] *Newspaper Licensing Agency v. Marks & Spencer* [2000] 4 *All ER* 239, 258 (Chadwick LJ) (CA).

[124] *Associated Newspapers Group v. News Group Newspapers* [1986] *RPC* 515, 519; *Hyde Park v. Yelland* [2000] *EMLR* 363, 393 (para. 78).

[125] Although the BBC and the BSB were in competition, Scott J did not think it to be important because 'highlights' of this nature do not really compete with a full-length live broadcast lasting 90 minutes.

[126] *Newspaper Licensing Agency v. Marks & Spencer* [2000] 4 *All ER* 239, 267 (Mance LJ) (CA).

[127] 'The rationalization that in a capitalist society all economic activity serves the public good does not avoid the distinctions'. Ibid.

[128] Cf. *Initial Services v. Putterill* [1968] 1 *QB* 396.

[129] *Hyde Park Residence v. Yelland* [1999] *RPC* 655, 663. The Court of Appeal overturned Jacob J's decision. While the Court of Appeal did not address the issue directly, the fact that the security guard and the *Sun* benefited financially from the dealing seems to have influenced the finding that the use was not fair. When combined with other factors, the Court of Appeal concluded that to 'describe what the *Sun* did as fair dealing is to give honour to dishonour': *Hyde Park Residence v. Yelland* [2000] *EMLR* 363, 379 (para. 40).

5.3 SUFFICIENT ACKNOWLEDGEMENT

The third and final factor that a defendant must show to fall within the defence is that the dealing was accompanied by 'sufficient acknowledgement' (which was discussed earlier).[130] This is required for all works to which the defence applies.[131] However, no acknowledgement is required in connection with the reporting of current events *by means* of a sound recording, film, or broadcast, where this would be 'impossible for reasons of practicality or otherwise'.[132]

6 INCIDENTAL USES

The urban landscape is full of works that are protected by copyright. Most city centres contain an array of murals, buildings, sculptures, and advertisements.[133] This creates a potential problem for photographers, film makers, broadcasters, painters, and the like who wish to represent that landscape. If a movie is filmed in a public place, it is highly likely that the final product will include a number of different copyright works. This gives rise to a potential problem in that the recording of these works is prima facie an infringement of copyright.[134]

To ensure that problems of this nature do not arise, section 31(1) provides that copyright in a work is not infringed by its 'incidental inclusion' in an artistic work, sound recording, film, or broadcast.[135] This means that a defence is available where a copyright work, such as a painting, is incidentally included in the background of another work, such as a film. Section 31(2) extends the defence to include the exploitation of works that incidentally include other works. This ensures that the showing, as distinct to the making, of a film does not infringe.

The question of when a work is 'incidentally included' in another work was considered in *Football Association Premier League Ltd v. Panini UK*.[136] There, the Premier League, its members, and Topps brought an action alleging that Panini had infringed copyright in their club emblems and the Premiership heraldic lion emblem by distributing stickers depicting well-known footballers, for purchase and collection in a book. Topps had obtained an exclusive licence from the claimant to use the emblems in this way, and Panini had lost out in the tendering process for the licence but nevertheless gone ahead and produced an 'unofficial' product. In Panini's product, most players were in club strip, with their club emblems and the Premiership heraldic lion emblem often visible. The defendant argued that the emblems were artistic works which were incidentally included in other artistic works (photographs). Peter Smith J rejected the defence, and this was affirmed by the Court of Appeal. There, the Court

---

[130] See above at p. 206.   [131] CDPA s. 30(2).   [132] CDPA s. 30(3).

[133] See also CDPA s. 62 (re public display of artistic works).

[134] For similar issues raised in the context of Canada's right to use one's own image, see *Aubry v. Éditions Vice Versa Inc* 157 *DLR* (4th) 577 (paras. 58–9).

[135] CDPA s. 31(1). For a discussion of the relationship between this section and its predecessors (CA 1956, s. 9(4) (works of architecture), s. 9(5)), see *Football Association Premier League Ltd v. Panini UK Ltd* [2004] *FSR* 1 *per* Chadwick LJ (paras. 19–20) (doubting whether linguistic differences would have any effect on the result in a particular case); but cf. Mummery LJ (para. 39). There is no defence of incidental inclusion in a web site, because internet transmissions fall outside the scope of the meaning of 'broadcast' in CDPA s. 8. However, the inclusion in a web site of a work which incidentally includes another work, and thus benefits from the exception in CDPA s. 31(1), will not infringe: CDPA s. 31(2).

[136] [2004] *FSR* 1. For commentary, see K. Garnett, 'Incidental Inclusion under s.31' [2003] *EIPR* 579.

of Appeal declined to define the term 'incidental',[137] Mummery LJ stating that the 'range of circumstances in which the word "incidental" is commonly used to describe a state of affairs is sufficiently clear to enable the courts to apply it to the ascertainable objective context of the particular infringing act in question'. The question whether the uses were incidental did not have to be determined at the time the photograph was taken, but rather when the sticker was created.[138] The question was why one work was included in another, and the court could take account of commercial as well as artistic or aesthetic reasons.[139] Given that the answer in the case was the self-evident one of producing 'something which would be attractive to a collector', in this case a player in their authentic club strip, the Court concluded that the inclusion of the emblem was 'essential to the object for which the image…was created' rather than incidental. In an earlier case the High Court held that by featuring the claimant's magazine, *Woman,* in a TV advertising campaign run for the defendant's own magazine, the defendant had infringed the claimant's artistic copyright in the masthead, the layout, and the photographs on the magazine cover. The defendant's argument that the use was incidental was rejected 'since the impact of the advertisement would be lost entirely if the front cover of *Woman* was not used. The inclusion of the copy of *Woman* was an essential and important feature of the advertisement. The impact could not be more obvious.'[140]

The defence will apply irrespective of whether a work is accidentally or deliberately included.[141] This is not the case, however, with musical works or lyrics (as well as a sound recording, or broadcast of a musical work or lyrics). The reason for this is that section 31(3) says that musical works or lyrics shall not be regarded as being incidentally included if they are deliberately included. This means that the defence is not available where a song is chosen for the background of a film, or a song from a radio is deliberately played in the background to a broadcast. Thus, if the makers of the police drama *The Bill* decide to have a scene where a character is listening to a radio playing a Rolling Stones' song, this is not an incidental inclusion. However, if a musical work is accidentally included in a live broadcast, this is within the defence. Thus, a broadcast of a football match that accidentally includes a sound recording played over the public address system falls squarely within the defence.[142]

---

[137] In contrast with Richard McCombe QC, sitting as Deputy High Court judge in *IPC Magazines v. MGN* [1998] *FSR* 431, 441 (a use was incidental if its inclusion was 'casual, inessential, subordinate, or merely background').

[138] This rather technical approach, requiring an assessment whether the inclusion is 'incidental' to be made for every act of infringement, undermines the value of CDPA s. 31(2). This implies that, if copyright in the emblems is not infringed by taking the photograph, it is not infringed by issuing copies of the photograph. However, the Court of Appeal decision suggests that this inference is incorrect: whether the inclusion is incidental must also be assessed when the commercial form of the copy (here the sticker) is determined.

[139] Cf. *IPC Magazines v. MGN* [1998] *FSR* 431, 441 where the judge suggested that the question whether a work was incidentally included does not depend on the user's intention, nor on the views of those who witness the use.

[140] Ibid. This was, evidently, a case of comparative advertising: the argument that it should therefore be permitted under the Comparative Advertising Directive was rejected at ibid, 447. But cf. *O2 Holdings v. Hutchison 3G Ltd* [2007] *RPC* (16) 407 (para. 45–47, para.55) (indicating that this question will have to be answered one day by the ECJ). See pp. 937–42 below.

[141] *Football Association Premier League Ltd* v. *Panini UK Ltd* [2004] *FSR* 1 (para. 24) (' "incidental" was not intended to mean "unintentional" '). However, the courts may well resort to the 'logic' that, if something was deliberately included, then it must be of more than 'incidental' significance.

[142] Laddie *et al.*, para. 2.161.

7 DISCLOSURE IN THE PUBLIC INTEREST

Despite the lack of any statutory provision on point,[143] a defendant may resist an action for copyright infringement—probably, though, only in very rare instances—on the grounds that the use in question is necessary 'in the public interest'. Although such a defence was recognized by the High Court in the 1970s and the Court of Appeal in the 1980s, the reasoning in those cases and thus the existence and scope of this defence has been heavily debated, both by courts and commentators, over the last few years.[144] In order to gain an appreciation of the uncertainty surrounding the existence and scope of the defence, it is necessary to pay close attention to three Court of Appeal decisions: *Lion Laboratories v. Evans, Hyde Park Residence v. Yelland,* and *Ashdown v Telegraph.*

In *Lion Laboratories v. Evans,*[145] the manufacturers of a breathalyser (the Lion Intoximeter) sought to prevent the defendant newspaper, the *Daily Express,* from publishing extracts of a confidential internal memorandum which cast doubt on the accuracy of the device. The defendant claimed that the public had an interest in knowing that the breathalyser might be faulty. They also said that the public interest should override the rights of the copyright owner. All three members of the Court of Appeal accepted that the public interest defence was available in an action for infringement of copyright. According to the Court of Appeal, if the alleged fault with the breathalyser was not investigated, a significant number of motorists could have been wrongly convicted of driving with excess alcohol. On the basis that there was a seriously arguable case that the disclosure was justified in the public interest, the Court refused to grant interim relief.

It will be recalled that *Hyde Park Residence v. Yelland* concerned an application for summary judgment against the *Sun* newspaper for publishing stills of Dodi Fayed and Diana, Princess of Wales, taken from security film, the copyright in which was owned by the claimant.[146] The defendant argued that the stills revealed the times when Fayed and the Princess were present at Villa Windsor and therefore exposed the falsehood of statements made by Mohammed Al Fayed. As such, the publication was in the public interest. The Court of Appeal found that there was no arguable defence. The Court did not consider that it was in the public interest to publish the stills to prove that Al Fayed's statements were false: the information could easily have been made available by the *Sun* without infringing the claimant's copyright. While the Court could have argued that the public interest defence did not succeed on the facts, the majority (Aldous LJ, with whom Stuart-Smith LJ agreed) said that there is no general public interest defence to an action for infringement of copyright in the UK (though this was not how *Ashdown,* a later case, interpreted Aldous LJ). He gave three reasons. First, on the basis that the statutory regime was exhaustive, Aldous LJ observed that no such defence is

[143] The validity of the common law defence recognized in case law under the 1956 Act seemed to have been accepted by CDPA s. 171(3) which says that nothing in the Act 'affects any rule of law preventing or restricting the enforcement of copyright, on grounds of public interest or otherwise'. This is confirmed by *Hansard,* which shows that Parliament intended to preserve a common law public interest defence. Lord Beaverbrook, 491 *Hansard,* HL, 8 Dec. 1987, col. 77. See Copinger (14th ed.), para. 22.48; Dworkin and Taylor, 81–2.

[144] See *Lion Laboratories v. Evans* [1985] *QB* 526 (esp. at 536 *per* Stephenson LJ and 550 *per* Griffiths LJ). *Beloff,* note 40 above is usually regarded as the first case to recognize the public interest defence for an infringement of copyright. There, drawing inspiration from the public interest defence in breach of confidence, Ungoed-Thomas J said that the 'public interest is a defence outside and independent of statutes, is not limited to copyright cases and is based on a general principle of common law'.

[145] [1985] *QB* 526.

[146] *Hyde Park Residence v. Yelland* [2000] *EMLR* 363, note 33 above. For criticism, see R. Burrell, 'Defending the Public Interest' [2000] *EIPR* 394.

recognized in the code. Second, he said the defence of disclosure of information in the public interest was inappropriate, because copyright restricts reproduction of the form of a work, not the information it contains. Third, Aldous LJ argued that the defence was incompatible with the Berne Convention.[147] In addition, Aldous LJ held that the reasoning in *Lion Laboratories* lacked any substantial basis in precedent.[148] In contrast, Mance LJ accepted that Parliament had intended, via section 171(3), that the courts should retain some discretion to refuse to enforce copyright on public interest grounds.

In *Ashdown v Telegraph*,[149] a differently constituted Court of Appeal rejected the approach of the majority in *Hyde Park,* preferring that of Mance LJ and referring with approval to *Lion Laboratories.* As we have seen, the *Ashdown* case concerned the publication in the *Sunday Telegraph* of sections of a secret memorandum written by the leader of the Liberal party, Paddy Ashdown, about a meeting that had taken place with Tony Blair concerning a possible pact between the Liberal Party and the Labour Party. Ashdown sought summary judgment, and the newspaper sought to justify its infringement on the basis of the public interest defence (the criticism defence having failed because there was no criticism of a work, and the current-events reporting defence because the use was not fair). Although the Court of Appeal rejected the *Sunday Telegraph*'s arguments on the facts,[150] it reviewed the law relating to the 'public interest defence' in the light of the Human Rights Act 1998. While the Court explained that copyright was not normally in conflict with freedom of expression, because copyright does not prevent the publication of information,[151] there could be such a conflict where expression required reproduction of specific text or images.[152] In such cases, if fair dealing and refusal of discretionary relief would not protect the public interest, a defendant could invoke the public interest defence, as developed by the common law and acknowledged by section 171(3) of the 1988 Act.[153]

In the absence of a decision of the House of Lords on this issue, the view favoured by the majority on the Court of Appeal over the three cases thus seems to be that a 'public interest' defence might justify an act otherwise infringing copyright. But in what circumstances? The Court of Appeal in *Lion Laboratories* failed to draw any distinction between the application of the public interest defence to a case of breach of confidence, and one based upon copyright. The Court was clear that the defence was not confined to cases of iniquity, but covered situations where there was 'just cause or excuse' for breaking confidence.[154] In *Hyde Park,* Mance LJ had declined to define the exact circumstances in which the defence would be available, but said that this discretion is much more limited than the defence recognized in breach of confidence

---

[147] Cf. Berne, Art. 17. See Ricketson, para. 9.72; Ricketson & Ginsburg, para. 13.88, pp. 842ff.

[148] Although Aldous LJ denied the existence of a public interest defence, he recognized that the courts do retain a power under their 'inherent jurisdiction' to refuse to enforce copyright where it offends against the 'policy of the law'. In effect, Aldous LJ sought to conflate the case law on 'public interest' with the general power of the courts to refuse to enforce copyright in scandalous, libelous, seditious, or blasphemous works employed in cases such as *Glyn v. Weston Feature Film Co.* [1916] 1 *Ch* 261 (immoral) and discussed at Ch. 4 Section 6 above. Thus, for Aldous LJ, the courts would refuse to enforce copyright on the basis that it would be against the 'policy of the law' where the work is scandalous, immoral, or contrary to family life; the work itself is injurious to public life, public health, and safety, or the administration of justice; or where a work incites or encourages others to act in a way which is injurious to public life, public health, and safety, or the administration of justice: *Hyde Park Residence v. Yelland* [2000] *EMLR* 363, 389.

[149] *Ashdown v. Telegraph Group Ltd* [2001] 3 *WLR* 1368; [2002] *RPC* 235 (Lord Phillips MR, Keene LJ, and Robert Walker LJ). For commentary, see R. Burrell, 'Reining in Copyright Law: Is Fair Use the Answer?' (2001) *IPQ* 368.

[150] Ibid, at para. 02.   [151] Ibid. [2002] *Ch* 149, 163 (para. 31).   [152] [2002] *Ch* 149, 166 (para. 39).

[153] Ibid. [2002] *Ch* 149, 164 (para. 34), 170–1 (paras. 58–9).

[154] See *Lion Laboratories v. Evans* [1985] *QB* 526, 538 (Stephenson LJ), 548 (O'Connor LJ); 550 (Giffiths LJ).

cases. According to Mance LJ, the countervailing public interest was of more limited scope in the case of copyright, given that it is a property right and regulated by statute.[155] The Court of Appeal in *Ashdown* said it agreed with Mance LJ that the circumstances in which the public interest may override copyright are not capable of precise categorization or definition, but indicated that the defence would only succeed in 'very rare' circumstances.[156] The more recent decisions therefore offer little assistance as to when the 'public interest defence' would apply, except to indicate that the circumstances are more limited than in cases of breach of confidence.

8 LIBRARY USES

The 1988 Act provides librarians with a number of defences.[157] Most of these apply only to prescribed, non-profit libraries, that is libraries prescribed by the Secretary of State, and the defences cover inter alia school, university, and local authority libraries.[158]

8.1 COPIES FOR RESEARCH OR PRIVATE STUDY

Librarians (from a prescribed, non-profit library) are permitted, in specified circumstances, to copy works in order to supply them to individuals at cost *and* for purposes of non-commercial research or private study.[159] In the case of articles, they may copy up to one article in an issue of a periodical.[160] In the case of published literary, dramatic, or musical works, they may copy no more than a reasonable proportion of the work.[161] In the case of unpublished works, librarians may make and supply single copies of a literary, dramatic, or musical work as long as the copyright owner had not prohibited copying thereof.[162] The requirement that the recipient satisfy the librarian or archivist that they require the copies for the purposes of research for a non-commercial purpose or private study, is likely to place librarians in a difficult position. For example, if a person requires copies because they are researching a topic for publication in a book (and they will receive royalties from the publisher), in the absence of guidance the librarian will have to determine whether this is for a 'commercial purpose'. The legislation fortunately provides that librarians may rely on signed declarations by any person requesting a copy.

---

[155] *Hyde Park v. Yelland* [2000] *EMLR* 363, 392. See R. Burrell, 'Defending the Public Interest' [2000] *EIPR* 394.

[156] *Hyde Park v. Yelland* [2000] *EMLR* 363 (Mance LJ); *Ashdown v. Telegraph Group Ltd* [2002] Ch 149, 170 (para. 59).

[157] CDPA ss. 37–44; Copyright (Librarians and Archivists) (Copying of Copyright Material) Regulations 1989 (SI 1989/1212). Different classes of library are prescribed by the Regulations in relation to different exemptions. Such exemptions are permitted by Info. Soc. Dir. Art. 5(2)(c) at least as they relate to 'specific acts of reproduction made by publicly accessible libraries, educational establishments or museums, or by archives, which are not for direct or indirect economic or commercial advantage'. For an extensive review of library exemptions under US law, see *The Section 108 Study Group Report* (March 2008) at <http://www.section108.gov>.

[158] CDPA s. 37(1)(a). See J. Griffiths, 'Copyright and Public Lending in the United Kingdom' [1997] *EIPR* 499, 501.

[159] The immunity conferred relates not just to copyright in the article, or literary, dramatic, or musical work, but also in any illustrations accompanying the work, and in the typographical arrangement.

[160] CDPS s. 38.

[161] CDPA s. 39. 'Prescribed library' means those specified in Part A, Sched. 1 to the Regulations. CDPA s. 40 qualifies s. 38 and s. 39 so that it cannot be used as a mechanism to facilitate multiple copying.

[162] The provisions in CDPA ss. 38–9 and s. 43 require the person requiring the copy to pay the cost price of its production.

8.2 LENDING OF WORKS

Special defences also exist where libraries lend copyright works. Section 40A provides that copyright in a work of any description is not infringed by the lending of a *book* by a *public library* if the book is eligible to be within the Public Lending Right Scheme.[163] The second defence that relates to the lending of works is found in section 40A(2). This states that no copyright in *any work* is infringed by the lending of copies of the work by a prescribed library or archive (other than a public library) that is not conducted for profit.

8.3 LIBRARY COPYING

Prescribed libraries are allowed to make copies of periodical articles, or the whole or part of a published edition of a literary, dramatic, or musical work, in order to supply another prescribed library.[164] Libraries are also able to copy from any item in order to preserve or replace material in a library's permanent collection without infringing copyright in any literary, dramatic, or musical work.[165]

9 EDUCATIONAL USES

The copying that takes place in educational institutions is governed by a complex web of provisions. In addition to the fair-dealing defences and the defences for library copying we have already looked at, the 1988 Act contains a number of defences that relate to the copying carried out by schools and other educational establishments (which includes universities and colleges of further education).[166]

9.1 COPYING FOR INSTRUCTION AND EXAMINATION

The 1988 Act contains a number of defences that relate to copying carried out for pedagogical purposes. Section 32(1) provides that copyright in a literary, dramatic, musical, or artistic work is not infringed if it is copied in the course of, or preparation for, instruction. This is subject to four provisos: that the copying is done by the person either giving or receiving the instruction (i.e. the teacher or student), that the instruction is for a non-commercial purpose,

---

[163] Rental Dir., Art. 5. On the uncertain scope of the provision see Griffiths, 'Copyright and Public Lending', 502.

[164] CDPA s. 41. This does not apply if at the time the copy is made the librarian knows or could reasonably ascertain the name and address of a person entitled to authorize the making of the copy: CDPA s. 41(2).

[165] CDPA s. 42. This applies to prescribed libraries and archives where the item is in the permanent collection and it is not reasonably practicable to purchase a copy for that purpose. It has been proposed in the *Gowers Review* that these exceptions be expanded beyond literary, dramatic, and musical works to cover e.g. films and sound recordings, to allow 'format shifting', and the making and retention of more than one copy. Detailed aspects are considered in IPO, *Taking Forward the Gowers Review,* 28–30.

[166] As specified by the Secretary of State under his powers under CDPA s. 174(1)(b); s. 174(3). 'School' is defined by reference to the Education Act 1996, the Education (Scotland Act) 1962 and the Education and Libraries (Northern Ireland) Order 1986 (SI 1986/59: NI 3). Universities, theological colleges, and various institutions providing further education are 'educational establishment(s)': Copyright (Educational Establishments) Order 2005 (SI 2005/223). These provisions have been extended to apply to teachers employed by a local authority to give instruction to pupils unable to attend an educational establishment: the Copyright (Application of Provisions relating to Educational Establishments to Teachers) (No. 2) Order 1989 (SI 1989/1067).

that the copying is *not* done by means of a reprographic process, and that the copying is accompanied by sufficient acknowledgement.[167] The defence applies whether the work in question is published or not, and there appears to be no limit on the quantity of copying. For example, this exception enables a student or a teacher to write out a whole poem, or extensive passages from a book, in longhand without fear of infringing copyright in the work. A second exception applies as regards copying of literary, dramatic, musical, or artistic works in slightly different circumstances. Section 32A provides that copyright in a literary, dramatic, musical, or artistic work is not infringed if it is copied in the course of, or preparation for, instruction but is subject to five provisos: that the work has been made available to the public,[168] that the copying is a fair dealing with the work, that the copying is done by the person either giving or receiving the instruction (i.e. the teacher or student), that the copying is not done by means of a reprographic process, and that the copying is accompanied by sufficient acknowledgement (but it is not a requirement that the instruction be for a non-commercial purpose). Both provisions appear to be of limited value since neither allows for 'reprographic' copying. This term is defined so broadly that it would almost certainly apply to digital copying carried out for the purpose of instruction.[169] Bizarrely, making (computer or projector) slides will likely involve copyright infringements (even though, because of an absence of relevant blanket licences, there will often be no simple way for educational institutions to obtain permission).

A related defence exists for copying done for film-making courses. Section 32(2) states that the 'copyright in a sound recording, film, or broadcast is not infringed by its being copied by making a film or film sound-track' in the course of, or in preparation for, instruction in the making of films or film soundtracks. This is subject to three conditions: that the person giving or receiving the instruction does the copying, that the copying is accompanied by sufficient acknowledgement, and that the instruction is for a non-commercial purpose.

A special defence applies to copying done for the purpose of preparing or giving examinations. Copyright is not infringed by anything done for the purposes of setting exam questions, communicating the questions to the candidates, or answering the questions, provided that the questions are accompanied by sufficient acknowledgement. The classic form of exam question, familiar to all law students, which comprises a quote followed by the instructions 'discuss critically', must therefore be attributed appropriately. This defence does not apply, however, to the making of a reprographic copy of a musical work to be used in an exam.[170]

9.2 COPYING SHORT PASSAGES IN ANTHOLOGIES AND COLLECTIONS

Section 33 provides that copyright is not infringed where a 'short passage' from a published literary or dramatic work is included in a collection that is intended for use in an educational establishment.[171] This is subject to the proviso that (i) the collection consists mainly of material in which no copyright subsists, (ii) the inclusion is acknowledged, and (iii) the inclusion does not involve more than two excerpts from copyright works of the same author in collections published by the same publisher over any period of five years. These restrictions greatly restrict

---

[167] CDPA s. 32(1) (as amended by SI 2003/2498, introducing the sufficient acknowledgement requirement (reflecting Art. 5(3)(a)) and the non-commercial purpose limitation reflecting Info. Soc. Dir. Art. 5(2)(c)). This does not apply to subsequent dealings (sale, hire, or offering for sale or hire or communicating to the public).

[168] As defined in CDPA s 30(1A).   [169] Reprographic copying is defined in CDPA s. 178.

[170] CDPA s. 32(3) (as amended by SI 2003/2498). On subsequent dealings with copies see CDPA s. 32(5).

[171] CDPA s. 33; CA 1956 s. 6(6); CA 1911 s. 2(1)(iv).

the utility of the defence.[172] The defence would be used, for example, to compile a collection of cases, many of which were out of copyright.

9.3 PERFORMING, PLAYING, OR SHOWING WORKS

A special defence exists to protect the performing, playing, or showing of literary, dramatic, or musical works before an audience consisting of teachers and pupils at an educational establishment.[173] Section 34(1) operates by deeming certain performances not to be public performances and hence not to be infringements of the performing right. To fall within the defence, the performance must be before an audience consisting of teachers and pupils at an educational establishment. The performance must be carried out either by a teacher, a pupil, or by any other person for the purposes of instruction. This will exempt performances, whether by students or outsiders, before students in a drama class. It does not cover pupil performances to audiences of parents.[174]

A similar defence exists with regard to the showing of films and broadcasts and the playing of sound recordings before an audience of teachers and pupils for the purposes of instruction.[175] While this would cover the showing of a documentary about the first Moon landing to a primary-school class, it presumably would not cover school film societies since they are for pleasure and not instruction. Both provisions appear to permit the use of material in (computer or projector) slide shows (though the making of the slides (involving reproduction), as well as the distribution of copies, or the making-available on-line would not fall within the exception).

9.4 RECORDING OF BROADCASTS

Section 35 provides that, in the absence of a 'certified licensing scheme',[176] educational establishments may make a recording of a broadcast, or a copy of such a recording, for the educational purposes of that establishment, provided that there is sufficient acknowledgement of the broadcast and the educational purposes are non-commercial.[177] As educational establishments have entered into a number of relevant certified licensing schemes, section 35 has little practical importance.[178] Nevertheless, the Gowers Review has proposed that the exception be expanded to allow the communication of broadcasts to distance learners (through secure 'virtual learning environments' and beyond 'broadcasts'. The detailed issues arising from these proposals are currently being reviewed.[179]

---

[172] The work from which the passage is taken must itself not be intended for use in an educational establishment, and no more than two excerpts from copyright works by the same author may be published in collections by the same publisher over any period of five years. Moreover, the collection in question must be described as being for use in educational establishments, must consist mainly of material in which no copyright subsists, and there must be a sufficient acknowledgement.

[173] CDPA s. 34(1).   [174] CDPA s. 34(3).

[175] CDPA s. 34(2). These are deemed not to be public performances.

[176] CDPA s. 143.   [177] CDPA s. 35(1).

[178] For example, Copyright (Certification of Licensing Scheme for Educational Recording of Broadcasts and Cable Programmes) (Educational Recording Agency Ltd.) Order 2005 (SI 2005/222); Copyright (Certification of Licensing Scheme for Educational Recording of Broadcasts) (Open University) Order 2003 (SI 2003/187).

[179] IPO, *Taking Forward the Gowers Review*, 9–11.

9.5 REPROGRAPHIC COPYING

Section 36 provides that, to the extent that licences are unavailable, educational establishments may reprographically copy 1 per cent of literary, dramatic, and musical works per quarter of a year for the purposes of instruction without infringing copyright.[180] The exception only operates where the copies are accompanied by sufficient acknowledgement (except where this would be impossible), and the instruction is for a non-commercial purpose. Again, the operation of the section 36 defence is limited as a result of the fact that educational establishments have entered into a number of relevant certified licensing schemes. The Gowers Review has proposed that the exception be expanded to take account of developments in instructional techniques in the 'digital age', including 'interactive whiteboards' and 'virtual learning environments'. The Review also suggested that the exception be extended to other media. The issues arising from the proposal are being reviewed by the IPO.[181]

9.6 LENDING OF COPIES

Copyright in a work is not infringed by the lending of copies of the work by an educational establishment.[182]

10 USES OF WORKS FOR THE HANDICAPPED

Two sets of provisions are designed to facilitate the making available of works to persons whose aural or visual senses are impaired.

10.1 MODIFICATION OF BROADCASTS FOR THOSE WITH POOR HEARING

Section 74 allows a designated body to make copies of broadcasts to provide subtitled or modified copies of broadcasts to people who are deaf, hard of hearing, or physically or mentally handicapped.[183] The making, supply, or lending of such copies does not infringe any copyright in the broadcasts or in any work included in them.[184] This defence does not apply, however, if there is a relevant certified licensing scheme in existence.[185]

10.2 MODIFICATIONS FOR BENEFIT OF THE VISUALLY-IMPAIRED

The Act permits the making of copies of commercially published literary, dramatic, musical, and artistic works, as well as of published editions, for the personal use of visually impaired persons.[186]

---

[180] CDPA s. 36. [181] IPO, *Taking Forward the Gowers Review*, 11–14.

[182] CDPA s. 36A was introduced into the 1988 Act by the Related Rights Reg. 11. See Rental Dir., Art. 5(3).

[183] CDPA s. 74; Copyright (Subtitling of Broadcasts and Cable Programmes) (Designated Body) Order 1989 (SI 1989/1013) (designating The National Subtitling Library for Deaf People). See Info. Soc. Dir., Art. 5(3)(b).

[184] CDPA s. 74(1). [185] CDPA s. 74(4) and s. 143.

[186] CDPA s. 31A (added by the Copyright (Visually Impaired Persons) Act 2002). The exception does not apply to copyright databases. It is subject to the following conditions: (i) the visually impaired person has lawful possession or use of a copy; (ii) the copy is not accessible to them because of their impairment; (iii) copies

In addition, in the absence of a licensing scheme notified to the Secretary of State,[187] an educational establishment, or a body not conducted for profit, is permitted to make and supply, other than for profit, accessible copies of commercially published literary, dramatic, musical, or artistic works, or of published editions, for the personal use of visually impaired persons.[188] Most obviously, this would include transliterations into braille, or the making and issue of recordings of spoken versions of those literary works.[189] The exemption does not apply if copies making the works accessible to visually impaired persons are already commercially available.[190]

11 PUBLIC ADMINISTRATION

The 1988 Act contains a number of defences that facilitate involvement in, and the dissemination of information about, public administration.[191] To this end the Act provides that copyright is not infringed by anything done for the purposes of Parliamentary or judicial proceedings,[192] or for proceedings of a Royal Commission or statutory inquiry.[193] This means that copyright is not infringed if a barrister digitally scans a case report, or a police officer photocopies a statement for use in a trial. The 1988 Act also provides that copyright is not infringed by anything done for the purposes of *reporting* such proceedings.[194] This means that law reports do not infringe copyright in the barristers' statements, a defendant's evidence, or a speech of a judge. It should be noted that these defences do not extend to the copying of the published reports of such proceedings.[195] As such, the defence does not apply, for example, to the photocopying of law reports.

Special defences also enable the copying of material that is open to public inspection pursuant to a statutory requirement (this would apply to material on the patents, designs, and trade

---

that would be accessible to them are not commercially available; (iv) the copy states it was made under s. 31A; (v) there is acknowledgement of author and title. A 'visually impaired person' is defined in CDPA s. 31F(9) as a person: (a) who is blind; (b) who has an impairment of visual function which cannot be improved, by the use of corrective lenses, to a level that would normally be acceptable for reading without a special level or kind of light; (c) who is unable through physical disability, to hold or manipulate a book; or (d) who is unable, through physical disability, to focus or move their eyes to the extent that would normally be acceptable for reading. For background, see Copyright Directorate, *Summary of Responses to the Consultative Exercise on a Possible Copyright Exception for the Benefit of Visually Impaired People that took place from February to May 2001* (2001). For commentary, see K. Garnett, 'The Copyright (Visually Impaired Persons) Act 2002' [2003] *EIPR* 522.

[187] CDPA s. 31D(1). The scheme must not be 'unreasonably restrictive'.

[188] CDPA s. 31B (added by the Copyright (Visually Impaired Persons) Act 2002). For background, see Copyright Directorate, *Summary of Responses to the Consultative Exercise*.

[189] CDPA s. 31B(2) states that the exemption does not apply 'if the master copy is of a musical work, or part of a musical work, and the making of an accessible copy would involve recording a performance of the work or part of it'. The exemption also does not apply if the work concerned is a database.

[190] CDPA s. 31B(3), (4).   [191] Info. Soc. Dir., Art. 5(3)(e).

[192] CDPA s. 45(1); CA 1956 ss. 6(4), 9(7), 13(6), 14(9), 14A(10).   [193] CDPA s. 46(2).

[194] CDPA ss. 45(2); 46(2). The latter, which relates to Royal Commissions and statutory inquiries, is limited to the reporting of any such proceedings held in *public*.

[195] This would include arbitration proceedings, *London & Leeds Estates v. Paribas (No. 2)* [1995] 1 *EGLR* 102, 106. Note also *A v. B* [2000] *EMLR* 1007 (refusing summary judgment in a case where defendant had copied pages from claimant's diary with a view to using them in divorce proceedings, even though those proceedings had not yet begun); *Vitof Ltd. v. Altoft* [2006] *EWHC* 1678; *Television New Zealand v. Newsmonitor Services* [1994] 2 *NZLR* 91, 100 (High Court of Auckland) (extends to situation where a work is required to be reproduced so that legal advisers can properly advise client whether or not it is appropriate to commence legal proceedings or to defend proceedings which are threatened).

mark registries);[196] to material that is communicated to the Crown in the course of public proceedings;[197] and, in certain circumstances, to material on public records.[198]

12 CULTURAL PRESERVATION

A number of defences aid in the preservation of cultural objects.[199] A designated non-profit organization may record a song and make copies available for non-commercial research or private study even though there is copyright in the words or music. This is subject to the proviso that the words are unpublished and are of unknown authorship.[200] In addition, where an article of culture or historical importance cannot lawfully be exported from the UK unless a copy of it is made and deposited in an appropriate library or archive, it is not an infringement to make that copy.[201] Finally, a recording of a broadcast of a designated class,[202] or a copy of such a recording, may be made for the purpose of being placed in an archive maintained by a designated body without thereby infringing any copyright in the broadcast or in any work included in it.[203]

13 EXCEPTIONS FOR ARTISTIC WORKS

A number of defences exist in relation to artworks. Given that artistic works protect a broad array of subject matter from paintings and sculpture through to typefaces and industrial designs, it not surprising that these defences are similarly eclectic. In addition to the defences listed below, it should be noted that a number of defences exist in relation to industrial designs. These are discussed in Chapter 29.[204]

13.1 REPRESENTATION OF WORKS ON PUBLIC DISPLAY

A special defence exists in relation to the representation of artistic works on public display.[205] Section 62 provides that copyright in (a) buildings and (b) sculptures, models for buildings, and works of artistic craftsmanship if permanently situated in a public place or in premises open to the public, may be represented in a graphic work, photographed, filmed, or broadcast with-

---

[196] CDPA s. 47.   [197] CDPA s. 48.

[198] CDPA ss. 47 and 49. CDPA s. 50 provides a defence for acts specifically authorized by an Act of Parliament.

[199] See above at Section 8 (ability of libraries to make copies for purposes of preservation).

[200] CDPA s. 61. The making of the recording must not infringe any other copyright and must not have been prohibited by any of the performers. For designated bodies, see Copyright (Recording of Folksongs for Archives (Designated Bodies) Order 1989 (SI 1989/1012).

[201] CDPA s. 44.

[202] All broadcasts other than encrypted transmissions and all cable programmes have been designated for this purpose.

[203] CDPA s. 75. The Copyright (Recording for Archives of Designated Class of Broadcasting and Cable Programmes) (Designated Bodies) Order 1993 (SI 1993/74).

[204] CDPA ss. 51–3. See below Ch. 29 Section 3.

[205] See also incidental use defence in CDPA s. 31 discussed at Section 6 above (but with CDPA s. 62 there is no need for the use to be incidental). Info. Soc. Dir. Art. 5(3)(h) permits member states to have an exception relating to 'use of works, such as works of architecture or sculpture, made to be located permanently in public places'.

out a licence. The defence also applies to subsequent dealings with the representation. Thus, a postcard of a sculpture in Trafalgar Square can be reproduced and distributed without infringing copyright in the sculpture. Similarly, a film of a new building could be made or broadcast without the consent of the owner of copyright in the building.[206] It seems that the defence applies to both private and public buildings. If so, this means that a company that was taking photographs of private homes to be stored on a database for use by real estate agents could rely upon the defence to avoid a claim for infringement of any copyright in the building.

One potential problem with the defence is that section 62 says that copyright in *such a work* is not infringed. As such the defence seemingly would not apply to any preliminary drawings or plans that were used to create the public work. If so, it greatly reduces the scope of the defence.[207]

13.2 ADVERTISEMENTS FOR SALE OF AN ARTISTIC WORK

Section 63 declares that it is not an infringement of copyright in an artistic work to copy it or to issue copies to the public in order to advertise the sale of the work. This means that it is permissible when selling a painting to take a photograph of the painting and to publish it in a catalogue. Section 63 serves to reconcile the conflict that may arise where the artistic work and the copyright in that work are owned by different parties. It does this by preventing the copyright owner from exercising their copyright so as to hinder the owner of the artistic work from selling it. It should be noted that subsequent uses of the copy, such as selling it, are not covered by the defence.[208] This means that the sale of a catalogue formerly used to advertise the sale of the work is prima facie an infringement of copyright.[209]

13.3 SUBSEQUENT WORKS BY THE SAME ARTIST

It is common practice for artists to build upon and develop earlier works they have created. A potential problem that arises for artists who sell the copyright in their works is that copyright owners may object to the artist continuing to work in the same style. Under general copyright principles, artists are able to develop the same ideas as long as they do not copy a substantial part of the expressive form of the earlier work. To ensure that owners of copyright in an earlier work are unable to stifle an artist's ability to work in the same style, section 64 adds that an artist is able to copy their earlier works, provided they do not repeat or imitate a work's main design.

13.4 RECONSTRUCTION OF BUILDINGS

Section 65 allows for the reconstruction of a building without infringement of any copyright in the building or in the original drawings or plans for it.[210] This ensures that an owner of a building is able to carry out repairs without having to seek the approval of the copyright owner.

---

[206] Though (as a consequence of amendments made by SI 2003/2498) while a film of a building could be placed on a web site without infringing (CDPA s. 62(3) referring to communications to the public of anything whose making was not an infringement), a direct live feed of images of the building would appear to fall outside the scope of the exception (CDPA s. 62(2) referring to broadcasts).

[207] Copinger, para. 9–169; Burrell & Coleman, note 1 above, 233.   [208] CDPA s. 63.

[209] Info. Soc. Dir., Art. 5(3)(j) permits member states to have an exception for such advertising 'to the extent necessary to promote the event, excluding any other commercial use'.

[210] CDPA s. 65; Info. Soc. Dir., Art. 5(3)(m).

13.5 USE OF TYPEFACES IN THE ORDINARY
COURSE OF PRINTING

A special defence exists where typefaces (which are protected as artistic works) are used in the ordinary course of printing. Section 54 provides that it is not an infringement of copyright in an artistic work consisting of the design of a typeface to use the typeface in the ordinary course of printing activities. The section also provides that it is not an infringement to possess or do anything in relation to the material produced by such a use.[211]

14 EXCEPTIONS FOR COMPUTER PROGRAMS

Special provisions in the 1988 Act, which follow from the Software Directive, govern how far it is permissible to copy and otherwise use computer programs without infringing. These defences ensure that a lawful user is able to make a back-up copy, to decompile a program for certain purposes, to study the program, and to adapt or copy the program where necessary for the lawful use of the program. The first three of these exceptions cannot be excluded or restricted by contract, and provisions attempting so to do are to be treated as null and void.[212] A report by the European Commission in 2000 on the implementation of the Software Directive concluded that overall the aims of the Directive had been achieved. The Commission did however make some comments about the way that the Directive had been implemented in the United Kingdom, which might require adjustment in the future.[213]

One issue that may impact upon the scope of the defences relates to the question of whether computer programs are seen as databases (and thus protected under the database right). As we alluded to in our discussion of the database right, if 'database' is defined broadly enough it may include computer programs. If so, this will impact upon the relevance of the copyright defences. This is because there are fewer defences available to a defendant in relation to infringement of the database right than are available for infringement of copyright.

14.1 MAKING BACK-UP COPIES

Section 50A(1) provides that it is not an infringement of copyright for a 'lawful user'[214] of a copy of a computer program to make any back-up copy of it, which is necessary for them to have for the purpose of their lawful use.[215] By enabling users to make back-up copies, it provides a form of insurance in case a computer program fails or is corrupted. Importantly

---

[211] CDPA s. 54. The typeface itself may be reproduced 25 years after the year of authorized marketing. CDPA s. 55. See J. Watts and F. Blakemore, 'Protection of Software Fonts in UK Law' [1995] 3 *EIPR* 133.

[212] CDPA s. 50A(3), s. 50BA(2), s. 50B(4), s. 296A(1), reflecting Software Dir., Art. 9(1), Recital 26.

[213] *Report from the Commission on the implementation and effects of Directive 91/250/EEC on the legal protection of computer programs*, COM (2000) 199 final (Brussels, 10 Apr. 2000), 12–14. The UK has since added CDPA s. 50BA which meets one of the Commission's criticisms.

[214] Defined as a person who has a right to use the program: CDPA s. 50A(2). In its Report on the Software Directive, the Commission said that 'lawful acquirer' (which was the term used in the Directive), meant a 'purchaser, licensee, renter or a person authorized to use the program on behalf of the above'. *Report on the implementation and effects of Directive 91/250/EEC*, 12.

[215] The Commission said that the notion of 'back-up' meant 'for security reasons' and that the result of the wording of Art. 5(2) was that only one copy is permitted. *Report on the implementation and effects of Directive 91/250/EEC*, 18.

section 50A(3) provides that any term or condition in an agreement that purports to prohibit or restrict an act that is permitted under section 50A is void.[216]

The scope of the defence will depend on when it is 'necessary' for a lawful user to make a back-up copy. It is likely that this will depend on factors such as the relative stability of the program (the more vulnerable the program the more the need for back-up), the environment in which the program operates, and the consequences of a program failing (it is more likely that a court will consider it necessary to make a back-up copy where the program is used for air traffic control or to assist in heart surgery than where it is a computer game). Indeed, in *Sony Computer Entertainment Inc. v. Owen* it was held that, when a person buys a computer game on a CD, it is not 'necessary' for that person to make a back-up copy of the disk.[217]

14.2 DECOMPILATION

One of the problems facing creators of computer programs is that they have to ensure that their creations can be used in conjunction with existing products and processes. In the same way in which a manufacturer of spare parts for cars needs to ensure that their products are the appropriate size and shape, so too producers of computer programs and devices used in conjunction with existing programs need to ensure that their products comply with the existing standards. While some of this information will be generic and widely available, some of it may be hidden in the program. For a producer to ensure that their creations are compatible (or inter-operable) with existing systems, they need to have access to the information that is hidden in the program. Some developers (most famously IBM) publish such information to encourage others to construct further application programs or add-on devices, whereas others license the information. In some circumstances, the only way in which the relevant information can be obtained is by decompiling or reverse engineering the program. The process of decompilation reduces the object code in the program to a form that approximates with the source code. The potential problem with this is that as decompilation involves intermediate copying of a program, it is prima facie an infringement of copyright.[218]

After considerable debate it was decided to include a defence for decompilation in the Software Directive.[219] This found its way into British law via section 50B. Before looking at the defence it should be noted that the parties cannot contract out of the decompilation defence.[220] It should also be noted that the importance of section 50B is reinforced by the fact that fair dealing for the purpose of research and study does not apply to the decompilation of computer programs.[221]

Section 50B provides that it is not an infringement of copyright for a lawful user of a copy of a computer program expressed in a low-level language to convert it into a higher-level language (that is, to 'decompile' it) *or* incidentally in the course of converting the program, to copy it. This is subject to the proviso that:

(a) it is necessary to decompile the program to obtain the information necessary to create an independent program which can be operated with the program decompiled, or with another program (the 'permitted' objective); *and*

---

[216] CDPA s. 50A(3), s. 296A.   [217] [2002] *EMLR* 742.
[218] See Copinger, para. 9–134, pp.540–1. S. Chalton, 'Implementation of the Software Directive in the UK' [1993] *EIPR* 138,
[219] Software Dir., Art. 6.   [220] CDPA ss. 50A(3), 50B(4), 50D(2).   [221] CDPA s. 29(4).

(b) the information obtained is not used for any purpose other than the permitted objective.

These conditions will be not be met, for example, where (i) the relevant information is readily available to the lawful user, (ii) the decompilation is not confined to acts necessary to achieve the permitted objective, (iii) the lawful user supplies the information to any person to whom it is not necessary to do so in order to achieve the permitted objective, or (iv) the lawful user uses the information to create a program which is substantially similar in its expression to the program decompiled, or to do any act restricted by copyright.[222]

In its *Report on the Implementation of the Software Directive*, the Commission was critical of the way Article 6 had been implemented in the United Kingdom. (Article 6 sets out the decompilation exception.) In particular, the Commission said there are four reasons why section 50B may be non-conforming. First, section 50B's use of 'lawful user' appears not to include a 'person authorized on behalf of the licensee or person having a right to use a copy of the program'. Second, while Article 6 mentions 'reproduction of the code and translation of its form', this has been implemented in section 50B as 'expressed in a low-level language to convert it into a higher-level language'. Third, there is no restriction in the UK to 'parts' of the decompiled program: instead section 50B is restricted to 'such acts as are necessary to achieve the permitted objective'. The final criticism is that the section 50B defence is not expressly subject to the three-step test (as is required under Article 6(3)).[223] It is possible that British courts could construe section 50B in such a way as to comply with many of the criticisms (if this was considered desirable).

14.3 OBSERVING, STUDYING, AND TESTING PROGRAMS

Section 50BA, introduced in October 2003,[224] implements Article 5(3) of the Software Directive, by providing that a lawful user of a copy of a program is not liable for infringement if, when carrying out an act they are entitled to do (such as to load, display, run, transmit, or store the program), that person observes, studies, or tests the functioning of the program in order to determine the ideas or principles which underlie any element of the program.

14.4 COPYING AND ADAPTING FOR LAWFUL USE

In the absence of contractual terms to the contrary, section 50C(1) allows a lawful user of a computer program to copy or adapt it if 'it is necessary for his lawful use'.[225] An example of a situation where it will be necessary to copy for a lawful use is given by section 50C(2). This says that it is not an infringement for a lawful user of a copy of a computer program to copy or adapt it for the purpose of correcting errors. Another obvious example is copying that occurs in the RAM of a computer that enables the program to run. In contrast, it has been held that a

---

[222] CDPA s. 50B(3).   [223] *Report on the implementation and effects of Directive 91/250/EEC*, 14.

[224] As noted earlier, these acts no longer fall to be treated as fair dealing under CDPA s. 29. The specific implementation of Software Dir., Art. 5(3) seems to have been required now that the notion of fair dealing for research and private study has been limited to non-commercial ends. See *Navitaire Inc. v. Easy Jet Airline Co. & BulletProof Technologies Inc.* [2006] *RPC* (3) 111 (para. 77).

[225] Note the contradictory provisions of Software Dir., Art. 5(1) and Recital 18 (stating that the acts of loading and running necessary for use of the program, and the act of correction of its errors, may not be prohibited by contract. This defence does not apply to the making of back-up copies (s. 50A), to the decompilation of programs (s. 50B), or to acts carried out to study or test the program (s. 50BA).

licence to use a computer game in Japan did not justify adaptation to circumvent copy protection so as to enable its use in the UK.[226] Given the limits of the licence to Japan, there was no lawful use in the UK.

15 EXCEPTIONS FOR DATABASES

Section 50D provides that it is not an infringement of copyright in a database for a person who has a right to use the database or any part of the database (whether under a licence to do any of the acts restricted by the copyright in the database or otherwise) to do, in the exercise of that right, anything which is necessary for the purposes of *access to* and *use of* the contents of the database or of that part of the database. This means that if, in the course of searching a database, the database is downloaded into the memory of a computer, this will not be an infringement. Although in situations where the copyright owner and the user are in a contractual relation (as a subscriber to *Lexis* would be) the user would have, at the very least, an implied licence covering these acts, this exception seems to operate in favour of others with a right to use the database, such as transferees of material copies of databases (e.g. the purchaser of a second-hand CD–ROM of the *Oxford English Dictionary*). It is important to bear in mind that fair dealing for the purposes of research and study is not available for databases. This increases the relative importance of the section 50D defence. As with the defences for the making of back-up copies and decompilation, it is not possible to contract out of the section 50D defence.[227]

16 EXCEPTIONS FOR WORKS IN ELECTRONIC FORM

Under section 56, if the purchaser of a work in electronic form (such as a computer program or an e-book) is entitled to make further copies or adaptations of the work, then unless there is an express stipulation to the contrary, so too is anyone to whom the ownership of the copy has been transferred. That is, the defence applies when a back-up copy is transferred if the original copy is no longer usable. Any copies remaining with the original purchaser after transfer are infringing.[228]

17 TEMPORARY TECHNOLOGY-DICTATED COPIES

In order to implement Article 5(1) of the Information Society Directive, a new defence was introduced in October 2003 relating to the temporary copying of copyright works other than programs or databases. This applies only if four conditions are met: (i) the copy must be transient or incidental; (ii) the making of the copy must be 'an integral and essential part of a

---

[226] *Sony Computer Entertainment Inc v. Owen* [2002] *EMLR* 742, 747. See B. Esler, 'Judas or Messiah? The Implications of the Mod Chip Cases for Copyright in an Electronic Age' (2003) *Hertfordshire Law Journal* 1.

[227] CDPA s. 50D(2). For speculation as to the scope of this exception and criticism, see Davison, 77–8.

[228] CDPA s. 56(2)–(3). See C. Millard in H. Jongen and A. Meijboom (eds.), *Copyright Software Protection in the EC* (1993), 224.

technological process'; (iii) the copying must take place to enable either transmission of the work in a network between third parties and an intermediary, or a lawful use of the work; and (iv) the temporary copy must have 'no independent economic significance'. Lawful use is defined to include uses 'authorised by the rightholder or not restricted by law'.[229] The provision appears to have been designed to allow 'caching',[230] that is the temporary storage of information in the user's computer or server which allows for speedier access to web sites.[231] Such activities are positively desirable, since they enable the 'web' to function speedily and efficiently, and seem to have no obvious impact on the economic interests of content holders. Nevertheless, while the provision may have been designed to exempt such acts (which otherwise might technically infringe the reproduction right in the content being stored),[232] the conditions imposed make it difficult to predict when (if at all) such acts will in fact be legitimate. First, the requirement that the reproduction be an 'integral and essential' part of a technological process raises a difficult hurdle. This is because, while digital transmission is more efficient if caching occurs, such transmission can occur without caching. Can it then be said that caching is 'integral and essential' rather than desirable?[233] Second, the requirement that the acts be of no 'independent economic significance' raises the question exactly how a defendant might prove that (as well as how a court is to determine whether) activities have any 'independent economic significance'.

18 DEFENCES FOR FILMS AND SOUND RECORDINGS

18.1 EXPIRY OF FILM COPYRIGHT

As we saw earlier, one of the changes brought about as a result of the Duration Directive is that copyright in films expires 70 years from the end of the calendar year in which occurs the death of the last of the following: the principal director, the author of the screenplay, the author of the dialogue, or the composer of any music specifically created.[234] One of the consequences of this is that it may be difficult to determine when copyright in a film actually expires. To ensure that this uncertainty does not unduly hinder subsequent uses of the film, section 66A provides that copyright in a film is not infringed if (i) it is not possible by reasonable inquiry to ascertain the identity of any of the relevant persons and (ii) that it is reasonable to assume that the copyright has expired *or* that the last relevant person has been dead for over 70 years.

---

[229] Info. Soc. Dir., Recital 33.

[230] Info. Soc. Dir., Recital 33. This seems to impose further conditions paralleling those set out in the E-commerce Directive. These are: first, that the intermediary does not modify the information; and second, that he does not interfere with the lawful use of technology, widely recognized and employed by industry, to obtain data on the use of information. The scope of Art 5(1) will be reviewed in *Infopaq International AS v. Danske Dagblades Forening*, Case C–5/08 (pending).

[231] See P.B. Hugenholtz, 'Caching and Copyright: The Right of Temporary Copying' [2000] *EIPR* 482, 483 (in particular focusing on 'proxy (web) caching' and 'client caching').

[232] But note P. B. Hugenholtz, 'Why the Copyright Directive is Unimportant and Possibly Invalid' [2000] *EIPR* 499, 501 ('a common sense interpretation of the reproduction right would have done the job [of exempting caching and browsing] as well, if not much better').

[233] See Hugenholtz, 'Caching and Copyright', 488–9.   [234] CDPA s. 13B(2). See Ch. 7 Section 3 above.

18.2 CHARITABLE USES OF SOUND RECORDINGS

Another exception operates in favour of non-profit, charitable organizations and permits those organizations to play sound recordings as part of the activities of, or for the benefit of, the organization without infringing copyright in the sound recording.[235] As a practical consequence, charitable organizations do not need to obtain licences from PPL (the collective body that deals with the public playing of sound recordings), but only from PRS (since the exception does not apply to copyright in the literary and musical works). Not surprisingly, this exception has long been a source of resentment to the record industry and performers' groups who see no reason why the revenues to which they would otherwise be entitled (and which other authors do get) should be compulsorily given to charity. Because of a belief that the exception in the form originally enacted in the 1988 Act fell foul of the 'three-step test', it has been made subject to a host of conditions.[236]

Firstly, the exception only applies if the organization is not established or conducted for profit, and its main objects are charitable or are otherwise concerned with the advancement of religion, education, or social welfare.[237] Secondly, the exception only applies if the sound recording is played by a person who is acting primarily and directly for the benefit of the organization and who is not acting with a view to gain. This means the exemption does not apply if the organization hires a disc jockey to choose and play the recordings. Thirdly, the exception only applies if the proceeds of any charge for admission to the place where the recording is to be heard are applied solely for the purposes of the organization. Finally, for the exemption to operate it is required that the proceeds from any goods sold by or on behalf of the organization (in the place where the sound recording is heard and when the recording is played) are applied solely for the purposes of the organization.[238] The effect of this last condition depends particularly on what is meant by 'good or services sold by, or on behalf of, the organisation'. If a charitable organization has a fund-raising event at which recorded music is played, but obtains the services of the local publican to serve drinks (and the publican keeps the profits from such sales), are the bar services provided 'on behalf of the organisation' so that the defence does not apply? Or are the services provided by and on behalf of the publican, with the paradoxical consequence that the exception applies? If the aim of the limitations is to restrict the operation of this defence to events where everybody involved gives their services and profits to the charity, it is likely that the publican who has been invited to sell drinks at the event (primarily for their own benefit), would be treated as acting 'on behalf of' the charity.

---

[235] CDPA s. 67(1) does not apply to musical works.

[236] The Info. Soc. Dir., Art. 11 amended the Rental Dir., Art. 10, by adding that limitations to the fixation, broadcasting, communication, and distribution rights are only applied in accordance with the three-step test. See also WPPT, Art. 16(2). It is not obvious why the three-step test led to the imposition of the new conditions. For example, why would the mere fact that the organization paid a professional disc jockey render the activities prejudicial to the legitimate interests of the 'rights holders', or mean that the use conflicts with 'normal exploitation'? The view seems to be that if anyone is paid or makes a private profit, then so should the record companies and performers. It should be noted, however, that the European Commission had issued a warning letter to the UK Government complaining that section 67 does not comply with Art 8(2) and 10 of the Rental Rights Dir: 'Internal Market: Infringement Proceedings Against France, Ireland, Luxembourg, Spain and the United Kingdom', IP/07/92 (27 June 2007).

[237] A local government authority was held to be neither an 'organization' similar to a club or society, nor an organization whose main object was the advancement of 'social welfare': *Phonographic Performance Ltd v. South Tyneside Metropolitan Borough Council* [2001] *RPC* 594 (exemption held not to cover playing sound recordings at fitness classes run by the local authority).

[238] CDPA s. 67(2).

19 BROADCASTS

Various acts are permitted in relation to the making, retransmission, and reception of broadcasts. In addition to the provisions we have already looked at in relation to archives,[239] education, and sub-titling for the hard of hearing,[240] the following defences may apply.

19.1 INCIDENTAL RECORDING FOR THE PURPOSE OF BROADCASTING

A person authorized to broadcast a work may make a recording of it for purposes of the broadcast.[241] This is subject to the requirement that the recording should not be used for any other purpose and should be destroyed within 28 days of first being used.[242] This ensures that any temporary copies that are made in the course of broadcasting will not infringe.

19.2 RECORDING FOR PURPOSES OF SUPERVISION

As part of the regulatory framework that governs the broadcasting industry, a number of organizations are given the task of supervising broadcast programmes. To ensure that these bodies are able to perform these tasks, the 1988 Act provides that supervisory bodies (in particular, after the Communications Act 2003, the unitary body, Ofcom) may make recordings of broadcasts for the purpose of controlling broadcasting.[243]

19.3 TIME SHIFTING

Section 70 provides for the much-debated time-shifting defence that allows for the private recording of broadcasts so that they may be watched at a later time. The making of a recording of a broadcast, in domestic premises for private and domestic use, solely in order to view it or listen to it at a more convenient time, does not infringe any copyright in the transmission, or of works included in the transmission.[244] This enables a person to video a programme to watch at a more convenient time or tape radio programmes so that they can be listened to later. Since broadcasts do not include most 'internet transmissions' this defence cannot be employed to justify private copying from web sites. Moreover, the limitation of the defence to recordings made 'in domestic premises' means it cannot justify acts of recording broadcasts in commercial establishments, such as the recording of simultaneous internet broadcasts in internet cafés.[245] Rather strangely, however, it means that, if a person tapes a radio programme on a

---

239 CDPA s. 75.   240 CDPA ss. 32(2), 34(2), 35.

241 CDPA s. 68; Info. Soc. Dir., Art. 5(2)(d); Rental Dir., Art. 10(1)(c); Berne, Art. 11*bis*(3).

242 See *Phonographic Performance v. AEI Rediffusion Music* [1998] *Ch* 187; [1997] *RPC* 729 (holding that the making of permanent recordings for the purpose of broadcast could not be treated as authorized under compulsory licence).

243 CDPA s. 69; Info. Soc. Dir., Art. 5(3)(e). Communications Act 2003, Sched. 17, para. 91(3).

244 CDPA s. 71. Presumably this is thought to be within Info. Soc. Dir., Art. 5(2)(b), and that under Recital 35 no compensation need be paid. The requirement that the recording be on domestic premises may have been intended to ensure compliance with the requirement that the reproduction not be for ends which are directly or indirectly commercial.

245 Even prior to the addition of this requirement by SI 2003/2498 it had been held that the exception did not justify the copying of such material by a commercial organization at the request of individuals, because the

cassette recorder situated in their office they will infringe, whereas they would not do so were they at home. In an era where it is increasingly important for the rules relating to copyright liability to make sense to the public, this different treatment seems regrettable.

19.4 FREE PUBLIC SHOWING OR PLAYING

Although running a radio or television in public normally infringes the public performance right in the broadcast, and any works therein, a special defence limits the scope of such liability where a broadcast is shown or played to a non-paying audience.[246] An audience will be paying if they have paid admission, *or* if goods or services are supplied at that place at prices which are substantially attributable to the facilities afforded for seeing or hearing the broadcast or programme, or at prices exceeding those usually charged there and which are partly attributable to those facilities.[247] So a wine bar wishing to offer a television for the benefit of customers, but which does not alter its prices, would fall within the exception, whereas a bar which charges an entry fee when broadcasts are being shown would not. The free-showing defence also covers the showing or playing of broadcasts to residents of hotels, inmates in prisons, patients in hospitals, and members of clubs; and covers free demonstrations of broadcast-receiving equipment, for example in shop windows.

The free-playing defence only applies to claims relating to infringement of copyright in the broadcast or any film included in it and, in certain specified situations, to the copyright in sound recordings. Permissions as regards other works included in the broadcast, for example music and lyrics of songs, will be required (so a PRS licence will be required).[248] In the case of sound recordings, the section distinguishes between two categories of recording. If they either are not recordings of music or songs (for example, recorded interviews with politicians), or are musical recordings of which the author is also the author of the broadcast (such as sound recordings created as theme music for the channel or to accompany a programme), it is not an infringement of the copyright in the recording to show in public a broadcast which includes the recording.[249] The exception however does not excuse any infringement of the copyright in other sound recordings i.e. those which are recordings of music and songs where the author of the recording is not the author of the music (termed 'excepted sound recordings'). These excepted sound recordings encompass most commercially-distributed popular and classical music, so that the general free-playing defence would not apply to sound recordings featured on the radio or *Top of the Pops*. For these 'excepted sound recordings', a much more limited exception exists as regards the free playing or showing of a broadcast which 'forms part of the activities of an organisation that is not established or conducted for profit'.[250]

---

copying was not for the 'private and domestic use' of the organization: *Sony Music Entertainment (UK) Ltd v. EasyInternetcafe Ltd.* [2003] *FSR* (48) 882 (paras. 40–1). For commentary, see K. Garnett, 'The *Easy Internet Café* Decision' [2003] *EIPR* 426.

[246] CDPA s. 72.

[247] CDPA s. 72(2)(b). Residents or inmates and the members of a club or society are not normally regarded as having paid for admission.

[248] Hence many electrical retailers allow the demonstration of television equipment with the sound off.

[249] CDPA s. 72(1A), introduced by SI 2003/2498 to implement Rental Dir., Art. 10(3). The EC Commission announced on 26 July 2001 that it had referred the question of whether the UK had failed to implement the Rental Directive to the European Court of Justice: the action may now be dropped.

[250] CDPA s. 72(1B)(a). A further exception applies where the broadcast is played for the purposes of repairing equipment for the reception of broadcasts, demonstrating that such repair has been carried out, or

So, while a wine bar or hotel will benefit from the broad free-playing defence as regards broadcasts and films included therein, a PPL licence will need to be obtained to cover the 'excepted sound recordings' included in the broadcast.[251] In contrast, the defence will extend to broadcasts which include excepted sound recordings where the broadcast is played to an NHS Hospital or government-owned prison, since these activities fall within both the broad free-playing defence and the narrower version of the defence which applies to excepted sound recordings.[252]

19.5 PHOTOGRAPHS OF TELEVISION BROADCASTS

The taking of a photograph of an image from a broadcast, in domestic premises for private and domestic use, is not an infringement of copyright in the broadcast or any film included in it.[253] The exception does not extend to photographs of artistic works included in TV broadcasts.[254]

19.6 RECEPTION AND RETRANSMISSION OF WIRELESS BROADCAST BY CABLE

A special defence in section 73 deals with the retransmission of wireless broadcasts by cable operators. The defence helps to ensure that people in areas where reception of the broadcast is very poor or restricted are able to get access to programmes.[255] The defence also takes account of the fact that certain cable operators are under a 'must carry' obligation.[256]

Section 73 applies where a wireless broadcast made from a place in the United Kingdom is received and immediately retransmitted by cable. Such retransmissions, in the absence of any exceptions, would infringe copyright in the broadcast and any works included therein.[257] However, retransmissions are often made merely to enable potential customers of a broadcast to obtain reception in areas where the signal is weak. In these cases, where there is no alteration of the transmission at all, it is difficult to see in what way the copyright owners in the works included in the broadcast are prejudiced by the act of retransmission (after all, they have been paid by the initial broadcaster). Consequently, the Act provides that copyright in any work included in the broadcast is not infringed when the broadcast is retransmitted by cable if and to the extent that the broadcast is made for reception in the area in which it is retransmitted by cable.[258] The broadcaster's permission is required, however, unless the

demonstrating such equipment. This is acceptable under Info. Soc. Dir., Art. 5(3)(l), and implicitly therefore under Rental Dir., Art. 10(2).

[251] CDPA ss. 128A–B requires that such licensing arrangements should be notified to the Secretary of State by a licensing body, before they come into effect, and the Secretary of State may refer the licence or scheme to the Copyright Tribunal.

[252] The government has indicated that it will consider modifications of this provision, and doubts have been raised as to the compatibility of the provision with the EC Rental Directive.

[253] CDPA s. 71. Justifiable, possibly under Info. Soc. Dir., Art. 5(2)(b) or Art. 5(3)(i).

[254] In these circumstances, it would be necessary to rely upon other defences (e.g. CDPA s. 31).

[255] Copinger, para. 9–207, pp. 574–5.

[256] Such obligations are imposed under the Communications Act 2003, s. 64. For the background see Copinger, para. 9–206, pp. 573–4.

[257] CDPA s. 20(1), s. 6(5A) (defining broadcast to include relaying by reception and immediate retransmission).

[258] CDPA s. 73(2). This seems to be the legal basis on which certain Internet retransmissions are being made by zattoo.com. However, where the making of a *broadcast* was an infringement of copyright in the work, the fact that the broadcast was retransmitted is to be taken into account in assessing damages for that infringement. Note also CDPA s. 73(9), empowering the Secretary of State to limit the operation of s. 73(3).

broadcast is part of a qualifying service (such as the BBC, or Channels 3, 4, or 5), and was made for reception in the area in which the retransmission is provided.[259]

Some other acts of transmission are obligatory under the Communications Act 2003. As it would be grossly unfair to make a person who is obliged to transmit a broadcast liable to the copyright owner, either in the broadcast, or the works contained therein, the Act exempts such a person from infringement. As regards copyright in the broadcast itself, retransmission is permitted if the retransmission takes place in pursuance of a 'relevant requirement' (whether the transmission extends beyond the intended broadcast area or not).[260] As regards copyright in the underlying works, retransmission in the same area as the broadcast is exempted by section 73(3). Where a cable retransmission goes beyond the area of reception of the broadcast, and the retransmission has been required under a 'relevant requirement', the Act provides that the retransmission of any work included in the broadcast is to be treated as licensed by the owner of copyright, subject to the payment of a reasonable royalty by the person making the broadcast.

20 MISCELLANEOUS DEFENCES

20.1 NOTES OR RECORDINGS OF SPOKEN WORDS

As a result of changes introduced by the 1988 Act, it is now possible for a person who makes a speech to have copyright in the speech. This innovation gave rise to a concern that speakers would be able to use the new copyright to restrict people who record speeches (such as journalists) from making use of their recordings. To avoid this, section 58 provides that the copyright that vests in a person who makes a speech cannot be used to restrict the use of recordings made of their speech for the purpose of reporting current events, or recordings made for communicating to the public the whole or part of the work.[261] For the defence to operate the recording must be a direct record of the spoken words, and the speaker must not have prohibited the recording of their speech.[262]

20.2 PUBLIC RECITATION

Section 59(1) provides that the reading or recitation in public by one person of a reasonable extract from a publicized literary or dramatic work does not infringe any copyright in the work so long as it is accompanied by a 'sufficient acknowledgement'.[263] Section 59(2) provides that copyright in a work is not infringed where a recording or recitation covered by section 59(1) is included in a sound recording, or communicated to the public.[264]

---

[259] CDPA s. 73(2)(b). Qualifying service means a regional or national Channel 3 service, Channel 4, 5, and S4C (both analogue and digital); the teletext service; and the television and teletext services of the BBC. CDPA s. 73(6).

[260] CDPA s. 73(2)(a).

[261] CDPA s. 58; cf. Info. Soc. Dir., Art. 5(3)(f) (which requires that the source, including the author's name, is indicated).

[262] CDPA s. 58.   [263] Defined in CDPA s. 178.

[264] As long as the recording or communication consists mainly of material in relation to which it is not necessary to rely on CDPA s. 59. CDPA s. 59(2) may be justified by reference to Info. Soc. Dir., Art. 5(3)(o) on the basis that recitation is an 'analogue use'.

20.3 ABSTRACTS

Where an article on a scientific or technical subject is published in a periodical accompanied by an abstract indicating the contents of the article, it is not an infringement of copyright in the abstract or in the article to copy the abstract or issue copies of it to the public.[265] This provision does not apply, however, if or to the extent that there is a relevant licensing scheme certified under section 143 of the Act.[266] As no licensing scheme has been established in this area, the defence plays an important role in ensuring the circulation of scientific information.

20.4 DIFFICULTIES WITH IDENTIFYING AUTHORS

Where works are of unknown authorship, a fixed term of copyright replaces the normal *post-mortem* term.[267] Similarly, in the case of films, where it is not possible to identify any of the persons by whom the calculation of the term of protection is normally made, a fixed term operates. In both situations the possibility arises that, while a user may rely on the fixed term, the author might later become known. If so, the longer conventional term would apply.[268] In order to ensure that this does not create problems, there is a defence to infringement where reasonable inquiry cannot ascertain the identity of any author of a work and it is reasonable to suppose that copyright has expired in the work.[269]

20.5 TIT-FOR-TAT COPYING

The courts have refused to enforce copyright because the claimant was involved in activities similar to the defendant. In *Express Newspapers v. News (UK)*, Browne-Wilkinson V-C refused to enforce the copyright owned by one newspaper against a competitor who copied a story. This was because the claimant newspaper had itself indulged in a similar act of appropriation.[270] The judge explained that the claimant should not be allowed to 'approbate and reprobate'. This is sometimes referred to as the tit-for-tat defence. It is probably better seen, however, as an exercise of the court's judgment as to the balance of convenience in proceedings for an interim injunction, or as an exercise of the equitable discretion to refuse injunctive relief where the claimant has unclean hands. It is not a defence to an action for damages.

20.6 RIGHT OF REPAIR

As part of the general jurisdiction to refuse to enforce copyright where it would contravene public policy, the courts have sometimes treated a person as having a right to repair their property even though to do so would be a direct or indirect reproduction of a copyright work.[271] This was taken furthest by the House of Lords in *British Leyland v. Armstrong*,[272] where it was

---

[265] CDPA s. 60(1). The retention of this defence might be justified on Info. Soc. Dir., Art. 5(3)(a) or (o) (for analogue uses).

[266] CDPA s. 60(2).   [267] CDPA s. 12(3).

[268] CDPA ss. 12(4); 13(4). Cf. CDPA 13(9) where there is no person.

[269] CDPA ss. 57, 66A. The retention of this defence might be justified under Info. Soc. Dir., Art. 5(3)(o) (though this is confined to analogue uses).

[270] [1990] *FSR* 359.

[271] See Info. Soc. Dir., Art. 5(3)(l) (allowing exceptions relating to use in relation to repair of equipment).

[272] [1986] *RPC* 279.

held that manufacturers were entitled to make spare parts for motor vehicles (even though to do so would be to indirectly reproduce the claimant's design drawings) so as to facilitate the repair of such vehicles. However, the defence enunciated in *British Leyland* has subsequently been qualified to such an extent that it is hard to imagine any situations where it might apply. In *Canon Kabushiki Kaisha*,[273] Lord Hoffmann said that for the defence to apply it must be plain and obvious that the circumstances are unfair to customers and that the monopoly is anti-competitive. Soon after that decision, the scope of the repair defence was further restricted in *Mars v. Teknowledge*.[274] There Jacob J held that the *British Leyland* defence could not be applied to claims for infringement of copyright in computer software or to rights in databases because those rights stemmed from exhaustive European statutory regimes.[275] The upshot of this is that the right of repair has effectively been abolished.[276]

21 REFORM PROPOSALS

The narrow scope of the exceptions to copyright law in the UK has attracted considerable criticism.[277] The *Gowers Review of Intellectual Property* has proposed that copyright exceptions be reformed to introduce more flexibility into UK law.[278] More specifically, it proposes that legislation be introduced to extend the exception for research and private study to all media; to amplify the library exception applicable to the archiving of material; and to expand the scope of the educational exceptions to encompass virtual learning environments. The *Review* also recommended the introduction of two new exceptions. One would exempt private copying through a narrow exception for format shifting, 'to allow consumers to make a copy of a work they legally own, so that they can make the work accessible in another format for playback on a device in their lawful possession'. Clearly, the primary aim of such an exception is to render it lawful for people to copy their own records and CDs and put the digital versions on their MP3 players. However, the exact formulation of the exception is likely to be heavily contested. The second 'new' exception (mentioned earlier) would permit caricature, parody, and pastiche. The government has begun further consultation on these matters, in order to flesh them out and determine their implications.[279] Any amendments to the Act are likely to be drafted specifically. Unfortunately, there is no plan to conduct any thorough-going rationalization of Chapter III of the Act. A broader suggestion in *Gowers,* to exempt all 'transformative uses' falling within the so-called three-step test, will be pursued (if at all) at the EU level.

At the regional level, the European Commission continues to review the matters of private copying and levies.[280] These issues are easily ignored by UK copyright scholars, because the UK has no private copying exception as such, and thus no levies.[281] Nevertheless, most member states have such provisions and the variations between them may ultimately draw the Commission to consider harmonization.

---

[273] [1997] *FSR* 817.   [274] [2000] *FSR* 138.

[275] Ibid (the defence was unlikely to succeed unless the court can be reasonably certain that no right-thinking member of society would quarrel with the result).

[276] See G. Llewellyn, 'Does Copyright Recognize a Right to Repair?' [1999] *EIPR* 596, 599.

[277] Burrell & Coleman, note 1 above.   [278] (HM Treasury, 2006) ch.4.

[279] IPO, *Taking Forward the Gowers Review,* 9–11.

[280] EC, *Fair Compensation for Acts of Private Copying* (Brussels, 14 Feb 2008).

[281] Although the UK Office does not at present intend to accompany the proposed 'format-shifting' exception with a levy, it may ultimately come to be questioned whether this complies with the Information Society Directive.

10

MORAL RIGHTS

CHAPTER CONTENTS

1 INTRODUCTION

Once a work qualifies for copyright protection two distinct categories of right may arise. In addition to the economic rights that are granted to the first owner of copyright, the 1988 Act also confers moral rights on the authors of certain works.[1]

Moral rights[2] protect an author's non-pecuniary or non-economic interests.[3] The 1988 Act provides authors and directors with the right to be named when a work is copied or communicated (the right of attribution), the right *not* to be named as the author of a work which one did not create (the right to object against false attribution), and the right to control the form of the work (the right of integrity). The moral rights recognized in the United Kingdom are more limited than the rights granted in some other jurisdictions where, for example, authors are provided with the right to publish or divulge a work, to correct the work, to object to the alteration or destruction of the original of a work, to object to excessive criticism of the work, and to withdraw a work from circulation on the ground that the author is no longer happy with it (because, for example, it no longer reflects the author's world view, or because the person to whom the economic rights in the work have been assigned has failed to exploit it).

---

[1] See E. Adeney, *The Moral Rights of Authors and Performers: An International and Comparative Analysis* (2006); W. Cornish, 'Moral Rights under the 1988 Act' [1989] *EIPR* 449; R. Durie, 'Moral Rights and the English Business Community' [1991] *Ent LR* 40; J. Ginsburg, 'Moral Rights in a Common Law System' [1990] 1 *Ent LR* 121; Copinger, ch. 11; Laddie *et al.*, ch. 27; P. Anderson and D. Saunders (eds.), *Moral Rights Protection in a Copyright System* (1992).

[2] The term 'moral rights' is derived from the French *droit moral*.

[3] Ginsburg, note 1 above, 121. This does not mean that they cannot be used to secure economic benefits. The estate of French painter Maurice Utrillo has benefited considerably from the grant of the right to use Utrillo's name in relation to certain paintings. See J. Merryman, 'The Moral Right of Maurice Utrillo' (1993) 43 *American Journal of Comparative Law* 445; A. Dietz, 'The Artist's Right of Integrity under Copyright Law: A Comparative Approach (1994) 25 *IIC* 177.

Infringement of a moral right in the United Kingdom is actionable as a breach of a statutory duty[4] and will result in an award of damages. The moral rights of integrity and attribution recognized under the 1988 Act last for the same time as the copyright in the relevant work. The right to object to false attribution is less extensive, only lasting for 20 years after the author's death.[5] After the author's death, moral rights usually are exercised by their heirs,[6] but in some countries may be enforced by executive bodies such as the Ministry for Culture.

The moral rights in the 1988 Act were introduced to give effect to Article 6*bis* of the Berne Convention,[7] which requires that members of the Union confer on authors the right of attribution and integrity.[8] More specifically, it states that:

Independently of the author's economic rights, and even after the transfer of the said rights, the author shall have the right to claim authorship of the work, and to object to any distortion, mutilation or other modification of, or other derogatory action in relation to, the said work, which would be prejudicial to his honour or reputation.

Instead of replicating Article 6*bis* verbatim, the British legislature chose to introduce a series of detailed statutory provisions, each of which contains a number of conditions, limitations, and exceptions.[9] This has led commentators to suggest that the manner in which Article 6 has been implemented in the United Kingdom is 'cynical, or at least half-hearted'.[10] Given that failure to give effect to Article 6*bis* does not represent a ground of objection to the World Trade Organization,[11] it is unlikely that much will come of these complaints.

While moral rights have received a considerable amount of support,[12] particularly from creators, they have also been subject to a degree of criticism.[13] At a general level, moral rights

---

[4] CDPA s. 103.

[5] UK law also describes a further right, that of privacy in photographs, as a 'moral right': CDPA s. 85. We consider this briefly in Ch. 6. Breach of confidence may provide something akin to a divulgation right: see, e.g. *Prince Albert v. Strange* (1848) 2 *De G & Smith* 652 (1849) 1 *MacG CC* 25 (preventing unauthorized disclosure of previously unpublished artwork on grounds of common law copyright and breach of confidence).

[6] The rights pass on death to the person nominated by testamentary disposition, or else to the person to whom copyright is being passed; otherwise they are to be exercised by personal representatives, CDPA s. 95(1). As an exception, the right against false attribution passes to the author's personal representatives: CDPA s. 95(5).

[7] While various moral rights existed in the UK prior to 1989, it was widely believed that the protection was not sufficient to meet the criteria in the Berne Convention. The Gregory Committee (1952), Cmnd. 8662, paras. 219–26 had been reluctant to introduce such rights in 1956, anticipating difficulties in their drafting. The Whitford Committee, Cmnd. 6732, paras. 51–7, impressed by the form of their implementation in Dutch law, recommended their adoption in 1977. See G. Dworkin, 'Moral Rights and the Common Law Countries' (1994) 5 *AIPJ* 5, 11; Adeney, ch.13.

[8] These were introduced at the Rome Conference in 1928. See Ricketson, paras. 8.92–8.116; Ricketson & Ginsburg, para. 3.28, p. 108, para. 10.07, pp. 590–94; Adeney, ch.6. Art. 6*bis* was in many ways a compromise. Durie tells us that the terms 'honour and reputation' were introduced in place of 'moral interests of the author' to satisfy objections of the common law jurisdictions. Most importantly, Art. 6(3) leaves Union countries free to determine the conditions under which the rights are exercised. Durie, 'Moral Rights and the English Business Community' [1990] *Ent LR* 40; Ricketson, para. 8.98; Ricketson & Ginsburg, para. 10.36, p. 614.

[9] CDPA ch. IV. The criticisms are that the provisions do not implement Berne; do not improve the position of authors; are, in practical terms, ineffective; and neglect the essential characteristics of moral rights.

[10] Ginsburg, 'Moral Rights in a Common Law System' [1990] *Ent LR* 121, 129.

[11] Cornish has suggested that the express recognition of moral rights might lay the foundation for less meagre treatment in future—particularly by penetrating judicial attitudes. Cornish, 'Moral Rights under the 1988 Act' [1989] EIPR 449.

[12] Although TRIPS requires member states to comply with Arts. 1 to 21 of Berne, it is notable that the agreement says that 'members shall not have rights or obligations under this Agreement in respect of the rights conferred under Art. 6*bis* of that Convention'.

[13] Dworkin, 'Moral Rights and the Common Law Countries' [1994] *AIPJ* 5, 34 (opposition to moral rights has at times bordered on the hysterical).

have been criticized for the fact that they are founded upon a romantic image of the author as an isolated creative genius who in creating a work imparts their personality upon the resulting work. Under this model, moral rights enable the author to maintain the 'indestructible creational bond' that exists between his or her personality and the work.[14] The notion of the romantic author, which became unfashionable in the second half of the twentieth century, has been criticized because it presents an unrealistic image of the process of authorship. In particular, it has been criticized for the fact that it fails to acknowledge the collaborative and inter-textual nature of the creative process.[15]

Another criticism made about moral rights focuses on what is perceived as their foreign or alien nature.[16] More specially, it has been suggested that moral rights, which have their origin in continental copyright systems,[17] cannot readily be absorbed or transplanted into a common law system.[18] Any attempt to do so will not only fail, it will also upset the existing copyright regimes.

Moral rights have also been criticized on the basis that they represent an unjustified legal intervention in the working of the free market. Such arguments highlight the fact that moral rights typically secure authors' interests at the expense of entrepreneurs, disseminators, and exploiters of copyright.[19] Given this, it is not surprising that, while authors' groups argue for further entrenchment of the rights (so that they are inalienable), the entrepreneurial interests lobby for further restrictions on the rights and their subjugation to voluntary market transactions.[20] Another criticism made of moral rights is that they prioritize private interests over the public interest. More specifically, it has been suggested that moral rights may inhibit the creation and dissemination of derivative creations, such as multimedia works and parodies.[21] For example, if an author was to use their moral right of integrity to prevent the publication

[14] Dietz, 'The Artist's Right of Integrity under Copyright Law' (1994) 25 *IIC* 177, 182.

[15] P. Jaszi, 'On the Author Effect: Contemporary Copyright and Collective Creativity' (1992) 10 *Cardozo Arts and Entertainment LJ* 293.

[16] For a discussion of tension along such 'comparative' lines, see I. Stamatoudi, 'Moral Rights of Authors in England: The Missing Emphasis on the Role of Creators' (1997) 4 *IPQ* 478. For similar concerns see the Gregory Report. For a less caricatured approach, see Dworkin, 'Moral Rights and the Common Law Countries' (1994) 5 *AIPJ* 5, 6.

[17] The earliest French cases based moral rights on contract. However, by the end of the nineteenth century the courts recognized an artist's moral rights in their own right. For the French and German histories, see D. Saunders, *Authorship and Copyright* (1992), chs. 3 and 4. For a recent statement of the position in France, P. Dulian, 'Moral Rights in France through Recent Case Law' (1990) 145 *RIDA* 126. For an exhaustive (if dated) account, S. Stromholm, *Le Droit Moral de L'Auteur en droit Allemand, Française et Scandinave* (1966).

[18] While historically, there have been those who have wished to confine copyright to the protection of an author's pecuniary interests, they have not in general succeeded. The Engravings Act of 1735, for example, was directed, in part, to protecting an engraver against 'base and mean' imitations. See *Gambart v. Ball* (1863) 14 *CB (NS)* 306; 143 *ER* 463 (submission that Engravings Act could not be relied on to prevent photography on grounds that the Act's sole purpose was protection of reputation and quality, which was not diminished in a photograph, was rejected).

[19] Moral rights have been characterized as limits on the 'right of the owner of the copyright to do what he likes with his own'. *Preston v. Raphael Tuck* [1926] *Ch* 667, 674.

[20] Dworkin, 'Moral Rights and the Common Law Countries' (1994) 5 *AIPJ* 5 36 argues for 'a fair balance between the genuine moral interests of the author and the genuine economic interests of those using and exploiting copyright works', but his employment of the language of balance does not take the analysis very far.

[21] G. Pessach, 'The Author's Moral Right of Integrity in Cyberspace—A Preliminary Normative Framework' (2003) 34 *IIC* 250 (proposing a 'liberal' approach to use of components of existing works in new digitized works by reference to whether the later work 'is identified as a work of the first author'); J. Gaster, 'Copyright and Neighbouring Rights in the European Information Society', in *Copyright in Multimedia: Papers from the Aslib Conference held on 19 July 1995* (1995).

of a parody of their work, this would conflict with the right to free expression, and thus with broader public interests.[22]

With these initial points in mind, we now turn to look at the moral rights which are recognized in the United Kingdom.

2 THE RIGHT OF ATTRIBUTION (OR PATERNITY)

The right of attribution or (as the statute prefers) the right of paternity is perhaps the best-known of all the moral rights recognized in the United Kingdom. In essence the right of attribution provides the creators of certain types of works with the right to be identified as the author of those works.[23] While the right of attribution cannot be assigned, as we will see, it can be waived. The moral right of attribution lasts for the same period of time as the copyright in the relevant work.

The right to be named as author of a work carries with it a number of symbolic, economic, and cultural consequences. The reason for this is that the name of the author performs a number of different roles: it facilitates the management of intellectual works (through indexes, catalogues, and bibliographies),[24] the channelling of royalties (for example from the Public Lending Right), the interpretation of the work (insofar as it provides a psychological or biographical history of the author), the celebration, reward, and sustenance of authorial talent or genius,[25] and the construction of the individual as the creator of an intellectual *oeuvre*. In many cases, the right to be named as author of a work will be unnecessary because it is in the interests of all the parties concerned in the exploitation of the work to attribute it. Where this is not the case, however, the right of attribution is potentially a very important right.

Before looking at the right of attribution in more detail, it should be noted that an author may be able to rely on a number of mechanisms other than the right of attribution to ensure that they are named as author. Publishing contracts, for example, will often contain terms dealing with attribution which may be enforced against a publisher[26] and possibly also against third parties who knowingly induce such breaches. In some circumstances, such a term might be implied into a contract.[27] The right to be named as author of a work may also be ensured by other means such as union power and industry standards.[28] The law of reverse passing-off might also be used to prevent another person from falsely claiming that they are the author of a work.

---

[22] See *Confetti Records v. Warner Music UK Ltd* [2003] *EMLR* (35) 790 (para. 161) (declining to 'read down' the integrity right to give effect to ECHR, Art. 10).

[23] Cf. the information protected by rules on 'rights-management information' discussed in Ch. 13. For a detailed exploration of the inter-relation between moral rights and protection of rights-management information, see J. Ginsburg, 'Have Moral Rights Come of (Digital) Age in the United States?' (2001) 19 *Cardozo Arts and Entertainment LJ* 9; S. Dusollier, 'Some Reflections on Copyright Management Information and Moral Rights' (2003) 25 *Columbia Journal of Law & the Arts* 377.

[24] See R. Chartier, 'Figures of the Author', in Sherman and Strowel.

[25] A link is frequently drawn between the right to be named and the ability to gain a reputation and make an income as an author or artist. See *Tolnay v. Criterion Film Productions* [1936] 2 *All ER* 1625.

[26] Ibid (breach of contractual stipulation to give author of a screenplay credit was held to give rise to claims for damages for loss of advertising and publicity which would enhance the author's reputation in the future).

[27] *Miller v. Cecil Film Ltd* [1937] 2 *All ER* 464 (implying term that credit should not be given to person other than the plaintiff author, but not implying a term that the plaintiff should be mentioned).

[28] See D. Read and D. Sandelson, 'Credit Where Credit's Due' [1990] *Ent LR* 42.

2.1 SUBSISTENCE OF THE RIGHT OF ATTRIBUTION

In order for the right of attribution to arise it is necessary to show two things. First, it is necessary to show that the work in question is the type of work to which the right applies. Second, it is also necessary for the right of attribution to have been asserted.[29] We will deal with each of these requirements in turn.

2.1.1 Relevant works

The right of attribution is only granted to the creators of a limited number of works. More specifically, the right is only recognized in relation to original literary, dramatic, musical, and artistic works, and in films. In the case of literary, dramatic, musical, and artistic works the right is granted to the author of the work. In the case of films, the right of attribution is granted to the director.[30]

Within these general categories, a number of specific types of work do not give rise to a right of attribution. The right of attribution does not arise in relation to works made for the purpose of reporting current events. Nor does it apply to contributions to a newspaper, magazine, or periodical, or an encyclopedia or similar work.[31] These exceptions, which are difficult to reconcile with the Berne Convention, reflect government concessions to the lobbying power of the newspaper and other publishing industries. The objections were informed by fears that the need to name the author of a work would interfere with the prompt delivery of news.[32] It was also feared that enabling an author of a news story to be named would undermine the image of the news as being objective and neutral.

The 1988 Act also states that the right of attribution does not apply to computer programs,[33] computer-generated works,[34] typefaces,[35] or works protected by Crown or similar copyright.[36] No satisfactory policy-based justification has been given for denying authors of computer programs or typefaces a right of attribution.

2.1.2 The requirement of assertion

The right of attribution does not arise until it has been asserted.[37] Even if it has been asserted, in an action for infringement of the attribution right the courts take into account any delay in asserting the right when considering remedies.[38] The imposition of the requirement of

---

[29] The requirement of assertion and the rules governing who is bound by an assertion have the effect that the attribution right occupies a grey area between property rights and rights *in personam*. In many cases, third parties will be bound by the attribution right whereas an author who was forced to rely on contract law might not succeed.

[30] For such works created prior to 1 Aug. 1989, see CDPA, Sched. 1, para. 23(2)–(3) (the right applies: except in the case of a film made before that date; and other works where the author died before that date; or where the author had assigned the copyright before that date).

[31] CDPA s. 79(6).   [32] Laddie *et al.*, para. 27.14; Copinger, para. 11–32, p. 642.

[33] TRIPS Art. 10 states that computer programs shall be protected as literary works under the Berne Convention. Thus while TRIPS Art. 9 does not require that members apply Art. 6*bis*, it seems (somewhat counter-intuitively) that Art. 10 requires that Art. 6*bis* be applied as regards computer programs.

[34] Perhaps on the ground that such works do not fall within Berne, that is, a Union for the protection of the rights of authors: Berne Art. 1.

[35] CDPA s. 79(2). Typefaces are probably within the scope of Art. 2(7), which requires members only to protect such works by copyright if they do not offer protection as designs and models. Typefaces also fall under the remit of the Vienna Convention.

[36] CDPA s. 79(7). Perhaps justified because of Berne Art. 2(4).

[37] CDPA s. 78(1).   [38] CDPA s. 78(5).

assertion is said to be justified because Article 6*bis* merely requires members of the Union to confer on authors the right 'to claim' authorship.[39] However, it has been suggested that such an interpretation is unsustainable given that Article 5(2) of the Berne Convention requires that an author's 'enjoyment and exercise of these rights shall not be subject to any formality'.[40] As the TRIPS Agreement does not require that Article 6*bis* of Berne be implemented, the merits of these arguments are unlikely to be tested before the WTO.[41]

In general, the right can be asserted in one of two ways. First, when copyright in a work is assigned, the author or director includes a statement that asserts their right to be identified.[42] Second, the right may be asserted by an instrument in writing signed by the author or director. The form of assertion has an important impact on the extent to which third parties are bound to comply with the right.[43] If the first mode of assertion is chosen, it binds the assignee and anyone claiming through them, whether or not they have notice of the assertion. If the second mechanism is employed, however, the assertion only binds those who have notice of the assertion. The former is consequently the more effective mode of assertion. There seems to be no reason why an author or director should not use both methods or make a number of assertions.

Two additional modes of assertion exist in relation to artistic works.[44] First, the right will have been asserted if the artist is identified on the original, copy, frame, mount, or other attachment when the artist or the first owner of copyright parts with possession of the original.[45] Such an assertion binds anyone into whose hands the original or copy comes (including borrowers and purchasers), whether or not the identification is still present or visible.[46] If the work is exhibited in public thereafter, the artist should be named.[47] Second, the right may be asserted by the inclusion of a specific statement to that effect in a licence that permits copies of the work to be made.[48] This kind of assertion binds the licensee and anyone into whose hands a copy made in pursuance of the licence comes, whether or not they have notice of the assertion.[49]

2.2 INFRINGEMENT

The attribution right provides that, when the work is dealt with in certain ways, authors and directors have the right to be identified as author of the work. In order for the right of attribution to be infringed, it is necessary to show that:

(i)   the author has not been properly identified;

(ii)   the work has been dealt with in circumstances where attribution is required; and

(iii) none of the defences or exceptions applies.

---

[39] The requirement of assertion also helps to overcome some of the problems that may arise in tracing authors, Laddie *et al.*, para. 27.10.

[40] See Ginsburg, 'Moral Rights in a Common Law System' [1996] *Ent LR* 121, 128.

[41] It has been argued that 'the assertion requirement will have to go when the legislation is amended and that such an amendment is already overdue'. Stamatoudi, note 16 above, 504.

[42] This may be difficult because the author need not be a party to such an assignment, for example, where they are not first owner. But, in such circumstances, if there is an assertion, it does not seem to matter that the author was not party to the assignment.

[43] CDPA s. 78.   [44] See 491 *Hansard* (HL) cols. 346–56.   [45] CDPA s. 78(3)(a).

[46] CDPA s. 78(4)(c).   [47] Described as 'ill-drafted' by Copinger, para. 11–23, 637.

[48] CDPA s. 78(2)–(3).   [49] CDPA s. 78(4)(d).

2.2.1 Nature of the identification

For the attribution right to be infringed, it is necessary to show that the author has not been properly identified as an author. Merely thanking a person for 'preparing materials' was held not to have identified his authorship.[50] In order to be properly identified, the name of the author must appear in or on each copy of the work in a clear and reasonably prominent manner.[51] Where it is not appropriate for the name of the author to appear on each copy of the work, the name must appear in a manner which is likely to bring their identity to the notice of a person acquiring a copy of the work.[52] So long as the name becomes apparent during its use, there does not seem to be any need for the author to be named in a way which can be ascertained prior to acquisition of the copy.[53] Thus, an author of a book might be named on the inside of the work. Where a performance, exhibition, showing, broadcast, or cable transmission is involved, the author has the right to be identified in a manner likely to bring their identity to the attention of a person seeing or hearing the communication. Where the relevant work is a building, the identification should be visible to persons entering or approaching the building.[54]

If, in asserting the right of attribution, the author specifies that a pseudonym, initials, or some other form of identification such as a symbol be used (as the Artist-formerly-known-as-Prince has required), then that form of identification should be adopted.[55] Otherwise any reasonable form of identification may be used. It is not clear whether the attribution right gives rise to a right of anonymity, which may be valuable in raising public curiosity about the work and in protecting the author from vilification or criticism. However, it seems unlikely from the wording of the provisions that if an author made it clear that they wanted the work to be published anonymously, that this would be treated as the particular form of identification that had to be used.

2.2.2 Circumstances where attribution is required

The right to be identified as author or director of a work only arises when the work is dealt with in certain ways. While the particular circumstances in which the right arises vary depending upon the type of work in question, in all cases the right applies whether the act is carried out in relation to the whole work or a substantial part thereof.

An author of *literary or dramatic work* has the right to be identified whenever copies of the work are published commercially, or the work is performed in public or broadcast.[56] This means, for example, that the author of a play has the right to be named when copies of the play are sold in bookshops or the play is performed in public. Similarly, the writer of a film script has the right to be named when videos are sold to the public, or the film is broadcast on television, (but not, it seems, on rental copies).[57] The right applies equally to adaptations of the work: so the author of a French novel has the right to be named on copies of an English translation.

Songwriters are treated slightly differently. The author of the music or lyrics of a song has the right to be named on commercial publication of copies of the song—such as the issue of songbooks, sound recordings, or films containing a recording of the song. However, the right of attribution given to the author of a song does not extend to circumstances where the song

---

[50] *Sawkins v. Hyperion Records* [2005] 1 *WLR* 3281.   [51] CDPA s. 77(7).   [52] CDPA s. 77(7)(a).
[53] Cf. Copinger, para. 11–17, p 634 (arguing that identification needs to be outwardly apparent).
[54] CDPA s. 77(7)(b).   [55] CDPA s. 77(8).   [56] CDPA s. 77(7)(a).
[57] Although the practice of renting copies of films in plain packaging is common, this does not depend upon the absence of a right of attribution in relation to rental: for in such cases, the director of a film, or the author of other works included therein, will usually be identified in the film credits.

is performed in public or broadcast.[58] This limitation, often dubbed the disc-jockey exception, was introduced so that disc jockeys and broadcasters would not have to name the songwriters when songs are played at discotheques or broadcast. It thus allows them to continue the current practice whereby only the name of the recording artist is mentioned.[59]

Where a right of attribution relates to an *artistic work,* the artist has the right to be identified where the work is published commercially, is exhibited in public, or where a visual image of it is broadcast or included in a cable transmission. If an artwork is filmed, the artist should be identified when copies of the film are issued to the public or if the film is shown in public. The 1988 Act also specifies that the creator of a building, sculpture, or work of artistic craftsmanship should be named where 'copies of a graphic work representing it, or of a photograph of it' are issued to the public.[60] The author of a work of architecture has the right to be identified on the building as constructed. If a series of buildings are made, however, the architect only needs to be identified on the first building to be constructed.

The director of a *film* has the right to be identified whenever the film is publicly shown, broadcast or included in a cable service. The director also has the right to be named on copies of the film, but not (it seems) where the films are rented.

2.2.3 Exceptions

A number of exceptions and qualifications are placed upon the scope of the right of attribution by the 1988 Act. The right of attribution is constrained by section 79(3) which provides that if the employer or copyright owner authorized reproduction, etc. of the work, then the right does not apply.[61] It has been suggested that this exception can be explained on the basis that, as an employer has paid for the creation of the work, they should have complete freedom to exploit it. It is also said that they should not be required to keep detailed records of who contributes to a collaborative work.[62] Insofar as the right of attribution plays a role in the establishment of an author's or artist's reputation, the link between authorship and livelihood is less important when the creator is employed.

The 1988 Act also provides that the right of attribution will not be infringed where the act in question amounts to fair dealing for the purpose of reporting current events by means of a sound recording, film, broadcast, or cable programme.[63] The 1988 Act also provides that the attribution right is not infringed where the work is incidentally included in an artistic work, sound recording, film, broadcast, or cable programme.[64] Exceptions also exist where the work is used for the purposes of examinations, Parliamentary or judicial proceedings, and government inquiries.[65]

---

[58] CDPA s. 77(2), (3).

[59] This was so even though there was no specific obligation to do so. However, WPPT, Art. 5 now confers moral rights on the performers of 'live aural performances or performances fixed in phonograms'.

[60] CDPA s. 77(4).   [61] CDPA s. 79(3).   [62] Laddie *et al.,* para. 27.12.

[63] CDPA s. 79(4)(a). This corresponds with CDPA s. 30(2)–(3), which require 'sufficient acknowledgement' in cases of fair dealing for reporting current events by other means, such as in newspapers. The effect is that the fair-dealing defences parallel the moral rights provisions: fair dealings where acknowledgement is required but not provided are likely to be infringements of both the copyright and the author's moral right.

[64] CDPA s. 79(4)(b).

[65] The right of attribution applies to cases which would not infringe copyright because they amount to cases of fair dealing for purposes of criticism or review. However, because a finding of fair dealing requires 'sufficient acknowledgement' of the author, most cases of fair dealing will not infringe the moral right of attribution. See also Adeney, para. 14.44, p. 401. These provisions relate to Berne Art. 10, which is intended to protect the author's attribution right: see Gregory Committee, para. 42.

Further exceptions to the right of attribution exist in relation to works that lie at the interface between design law and copyright law. The defences to infringement of copyright granted by sections 51 and 52 of the 1988 Act also apply to infringement of the attribution right. Consequently, if a person makes an article to a design document, there is no need to obtain the permission of the copyright owner, or to name the author of the design. This is also the case where 25 years has elapsed since an artistic work has been industrially applied. Such a time limitation fits awkwardly with the broader conception of moral rights as the personal rights of the artist.

2.2.4 Waiver

Finally, it should be noted that an author can waive his or her right of attribution.[66] Waiver of the right of attribution, which is relevant for activities such as 'ghost writing', is discussed in more detail below in the context of the integrity right.

3 THE RIGHT TO OBJECT TO FALSE ATTRIBUTION

The right to object to false attribution is the oldest of the United Kingdom's statutory moral rights.[67] Re-enacted in section 84 of the 1988 Act, this right is effectively the flip side of the attribution right: the right of attribution provides authors with the right to be named on works which they have created, whereas the right to object to false attribution provides individuals with the right *not* to be named on works which they have not created.[68] Unlike the right of attribution, the right to object to false attribution applies whether or not the claimant is an author. The right to object to false attribution applies to persons[69] wrongly named as the authors of literary, dramatic, musical, or artistic works, or as the directors of films.[70] The right of false attribution only lasts for 20 years after the death of the person who is falsely said to be the author.

The right is infringed by a person who issues copies of a work to the public, or exhibits in public an artistic work, on which there is a false attribution (rather than by the person who makes the false attribution). The right can also be infringed by a person who performs, broadcasts, or shows the work and who knows that the attribution is false. Section 84(5) also provides for infringement where certain commercial acts are done with the knowledge that the attribution is false.[71]

---

[66] CDPA s. 87(2).

[67] CDPA s. 84(6) re-enacts CA 1956, s. 43 which, in turn, was an expansion to literary, dramatic, and musical works of the Fine Art Copyright Act 1862, s. 7(4). Gregory Committee, para. 225. CDPA, Sched. 1, para. 22. The general transitional provision of the 1988 Act states that no act done before 1 Aug. 1989 is actionable as a violation of these moral rights, but preserves causes of action previously arising under s. 43 of the 1956 Act for violating the right against false attribution of authorship.

[68] For discussion of whether the Berne Convention implicitly requires recognition of such a right see Ricketson, para. 8.105; Ricketson & Ginsburg, para 10.19, p. 601 (suggesting Berne does not cover the case where an author is seeking to deny rather than establish their authorship).

[69] *Clark v. Associated Newspapers* [1998] 1 *All ER* 959, 964. According to Lightman J, the section confers a personal or civic right (at 965).

[70] The provision does not contain the usual exceptions for computer programs or computer-generated works, so that while the author of a program has no right to be named, a person who is not the author of a program has the right not to be named as its author.

[71] CDPA s. 84(5), (6) (possessing or dealing with a falsely attributed copy of the work in the course of business or, in the case of an artistic work, dealing with it in business as the unaltered work of the artist when in fact it was altered after leaving their possession, knowing or having reason to believe that there is false attribution).

Whether a work has been attributed to the wrong person depends on 'the single meaning which the... work conveys to the notional reasonable reader'.[72] There is no need for the complainant to prove that the attribution actually caused them any damage.[73] Examples of situations where the right has been violated include the attribution to a member of the public of a newspaper article written by a journalist but based on conversations between the two,[74] and a newspaper parody of a politician's diaries (see Fig. 10.1).[75]

In another decision, an author's work was held to be falsely attributed when it was attributed to the author after having been substantially added to by another person without their consent.[76] On this basis, it seems that a replica of a painting that included the signature of the original artist could be said to be falsely attributed, since the replica painting would not be solely made by the original artist.[77] In the case of artistic works, the right to object to false attribution is extended by a special provision to circumstances where the work has been altered, even if that alteration only amounts to deletion of part of the work. This would be the case, for example, where a detail is cut from a broader canvas and sold as an unaltered original.[78] The right would also be infringed where a black-and-white drawing was colourized.[79]

The right to object to false attribution of authorship is supplemented by various non-statutory causes of action, such as the action for passing off or defamation.[80] Under the former, a person can complain where a work is misrepresented as being by the claimant, when it is in fact the work of the defendant.[81] In *Ridge v. English Illustrated Magazine* the defendant published a story that they attributed to the plaintiff, a well-known author, which in fact had been written by a grocer's assistant from Bournemouth.[82] The court instructed the jury to find the publication to be defamatory if 'anyone reading the story would think that plaintiff was a mere commonplace scribbler'.[83]

---

[72] *Clark,* note 69 above, 968; also [1998] *RPC* 261.   [73] Ibid, 965.

[74] *Moore v. News of the World* [1972] 1 *QB* 441 (finding false attribution in a newspaper article entitled 'How my love for the Saint turned sour by Dorothy Squires', written in the first person by journalist on basis of conversations with Squires). It is not altogether clear whether the work was falsely attributed because Squires had not written the words, or because she had not spoken them. In the light of the changes in the 1988 Act, which confer copyright on spoken words, it seems that a verbatim account of a speech by a journalist should not be treated as having been falsely attributed to the speaker.

[75] *Clark v. Associated Newspapers* [1998] 1 *All ER* 959; [1998] *RPC* 261.

[76] *Noah v. Shuba* [1991] *FSR* 14 (finding no false attribution of 17 words added to passage extracted from the plaintiff's work, since these words did not constitute a work, but that there was false attribution of the extract as a whole as attributed solely to the plaintiff). In effect the plaintiff succeeded in protecting his right to endorse the defendant's services, and thus indicates a potential usefulness in the context of 'personality merchandising'.

[77] *Preston v. Raphael Tuck* [1926] *Ch* 667 (replica with no signature would not be falsely attributed).

[78] CDPA s. 84(6) (introduced in response to a complaint of this sort by the English painter Landseer). For discussion of the extent of such alterations see *Carlton Illustrators v. Coleman* [1911] 1 *KB* 771 (alteration must be material in the sense that it might affect the credit and reputation of the artist).

[79] Ibid (in a case where colour was taken to be a very important element).

[80] Indeed, Fine Art Copyright Act 1862, s. 7(4) was described as 'a kind of statutory prohibition against what is commonly known as a passing off of the goods of one person as the goods of another': *Carlton Illustrators*, note 78 above, 779.

[81] Passing off requires a claimant to demonstrate not merely a misrepresentation, but also the existence of goodwill and likelihood of damage. It is broader than s. 84 in that s. 84 relies on a single meaning, whereas a misrepresentation can be established in passing off in circumstances where a substantial or large number of consumers are likely to be misled. See *Clark v. Associated Newspaper* [1998] 1 *All ER* 959.

[82] *Ridge v. English Illustrated Magazine* [1911–16] *MacG CC* 91.

[83] See also *Marengo v. Daily Sketch* (1948) 65 *RPC* 242 (a cartoonist called KIM succeeded in a passing-off action against another cartoonist using the name KEM); *Samuelson v. Producers Distributing* [1932] 1 *Ch* 201 (passing off by giving film similar title to play).

Alan Clark's Secret Political Diary

On the historic day Tony Blair made his Commons debut as Prime Minister, Alan Clark found himself in the ignominious position of sitting on the Opposition benches. PETER BRADSHAW imagines how the great diarist would record the event

It's wonderful to be back in the old place

Tuesday 6th May
Albany

Well, the Tory political landscape is a smoking ruin.

But as the dawn comes up, and Blair's Messerschmitts drone away over the horizon, I am delighted to report that the smart shops and elegant terraces of Kensington and Chelsea are unscathed. The only vote I seem to have lost is that of Michael Winner, the film director, who cut up rather rough over my comments about his house in this Diary.

We are in a mess, though, and every revolting little BBC functionary and Guardian scribbler with a colleague or homosexual "partner" on the New Labour benches is gloating.

Little Major has mumbled something about the show being over and it being time to leave the stage. This apparently was a phrase he learned at his father's knee as the old boy, wearing smeared make-up and floppy-toed clown shoes, hid in his dressing room with the lights off while the angry audience demanded their money back.

We have now started a spastic "leadership contest", which has about as much political significance as the election of a refreshments secretary in a suburban golf club. Heseltine is *hors de combat*, and while he was delirious with pain-killers on his hospital bed, his lady wife Anne typed out his withdrawal statement, then gripped his writing hand and wrote out his signature underneath. I'm not sure how he took the news of his standing down.

Clarke is standing for the collaboration with Kohl faction, Michael Howard is running on his iron-fist-in-the-iron-glove ticket, apparently with fresh-faced, apple-cheeked young Hague as his supporter, an arrangement toasted over champagne earlier this evening.

No one seems to be begging *me* to stand.

◇　　◇　　◇

Wednesday 7th May
Albany
Morning

Hague has dumped.

His claque of admirers encouraged him to think of himself as the Young Pretender, and he is believing this publicity whole-heartedly. So the engagement is broken off.

Now Dorrell is courting the bore vote and Redwood's candidacy is gravely damaged by the support of The Times.

A complete shower. I am going to the Commons.

◇　　◇　　◇

House of Commons
Evening

Extraordinary.

In the Commons I saw what appeared to be a crocodile of schoolchildren in the Central Lobby, moving unimpeded into the Chamber. When I complained, someone explained that this was the New Labour intake, all polytechnic lecturers, media folk and trades union press officers, with their electronic pagers dutifully turned off, and the person at their head barking instructions was little Mandelson — although what *he* knows about Parliament could be written on the back of a stamp.

It is *marvellous* to be back in the House; I simply can't believe it has been five years, although it was *very* strange to see the sides reversed. I couldn't get used to the through-the-looking-glass effect — I felt dizzy and disorientated and had a slight nose bleed.

We were in opposition when I first arrived in '74, when Ted Heath was Leader and it was a disagreeable shock to see that he is *still here*, Sir Edward Heath, Father of the House, still pompous and slow-witted — visibly bridling when Gwyneth Dunwoody, in her speech proposing dear Betty Boothroyd as Speaker, called him "Mr" Heath.

Later I was strolling towards the Strangers Bar, whistling a lively air, when I came across a *very* pretty girl in tears. "What's the matter?" I asked. The dear little thing gulped and pouted and said: "It's my first day. I'm lost ... " I twinkled, like Alec d'Urberville. "Never mind," I said, proffering a hanky. "It's easy for a secretary to get lost on her first day." She turned on me, her beautiful eyes flashing angrily. "I am the New Labour Member for Watford!" she shouted, and ran off down the corridor.

But she still has my handkerchief — an excuse to get back in touch!

How have I existed out of this place?

Fig. 10.1 Alan Clark's Secret Political Diary: Evening Standard, May 1997
Source: Courtesy of the *Evening Standard*.

4 RIGHT OF INTEGRITY

The right of integrity is one of the most important of the innovations in the 1988 Act. The moral right of integrity lasts for the same time as the copyright in the relevant work. The right of integrity is the right to object to derogatory treatment of a work, or any part of it. The basis for this authorial prerogative is that the artist, through the act of creation, has embodied some element of their personality in the work, which ought to be protected from distortion or mutilation.[84] In some cases, this carries with it the corollary that the artist feels some degree of responsibility for the work.[85] The desire to protect the reputation of authors was also a factor used to support the right.

4.1 SUBSISTENCE OF THE RIGHT

As with the other moral rights recognized under the 1988 Act, the right of integrity is given to the author of a literary, dramatic, musical, or artistic work, and the director of a film.[86] It is not given to computer programs, nor to computer-generated works.[87] With respect to computer programs, the exclusion is justified on the basis that it might be necessary to alter, debug, improve, or modify a program to render it suitable to achieve its purpose.[88] The integrity right does not apply to a work made for the purpose of reporting current events,[89] to publications in newspapers, or collective works of reference such as encyclopedias.[90] In the latter case, the relevant publishers were keen to retain their power to edit or otherwise alter any submissions without having to consult contributing authors.[91]

4.2 INFRINGEMENT OF THE RIGHT

In order for the right of integrity to be infringed, an author or director must be able to show that:

(i)   there has been a 'derogatory treatment' of the work;

(ii) the work has been dealt with in circumstances where the author is protected from derogatory treatment;

---

[84] A. Dietz, 'The Artist's Right of Integrity under Copyright Law' (1994) 25 *IIC* 177, 181. See also B. Ong, 'Why Moral Rights Matter: Recognising the Intrinsic Value of Integrity Rights' (2003) 26 *Columbia JL & the Arts* 297.

[85] This is the case, for example, with Stanley Kubrick's reaction to copy-cat violence (and the resulting media coverage) that followed the release of the film he directed, *A Clockwork Orange* (1971).

[86] CDPA s. 80(1). For such works created prior to 1 Aug. 1989, see Sched. 1, para. 23(2)–(3) (the right applies: except in the case of a film made before that date; and other works where the author died before that date; or where the author had assigned the copyright before that date). Colourization of pre-1989 black-and-white films would not infringe the moral right of integrity. See Laddie *et al.*, para. 27.21. However, insofar as the film consists of photographs of which the director is the author, colourization might incur liability on the basis of 'false attribution' under CDPA s. 84(6). Cf. *Carlton Illustrators v. Coleman* [1911] 1 *KB* 77 (on Fine Art Copyright Act 1862, s. 7). This last caveat would not apply to films made after 1956.

[87] CDPA s. 81(2). See the discussion in relation to these exclusions from the right of attribution above as to whether this is compatible with Berne.

[88] Cf. Copinger, para. 11–50 p.649 (observing that inept alterations to a computer program which are still likely to be regarded as the work of the original author might be highly damaging to his reputation). The right of integrity for the author of a computer program is limited even in France: Dietz, 'The Artist's Right of Integrity under Copyright Law' (1994) 25 *IIC* 177, 184.

[89] CDPA s. 81(3).   [90] CDPA s. 81(4).   [91] See Copinger, para. 27–111ff. pp. 1423–4.

(iii) none of the exceptions apply; and

(iv) the right has not been waived or the action consented to by the author.

4.2.1 Derogatory treatment

In order for an author or director to show that the right of integrity has been breached, it is necessary to show that there has been a 'derogatory treatment' of their work. Before looking at the meaning of 'derogatory', it is necessary to explore what the Act means when it refers to a 'treatment' of the work.

Treatment. 'Treatment' of a work means any 'addition to, deletion from, alteration to or adaptation of the work'. The concept of the work that is employed here is that of an autonomous artefact, which is born out of, tied to, or related to neither other works, nor its environment. Moreover, the work has its own internal integrity or logic (a beginning, middle, and end; a foreground, middleground, and background; line, shade, colour).[92] For a treatment of the work to take place, it seems that the defendant must interfere with the internal structure of the work.[93] This idea of treatment, it seems, would cover a situation such as in *Noah v. Shuba*[94] where 17 words were added to the claimant author's medical guide. It would also cover situations where a portion of a painting was cut from its original canvas and exhibited; a song was chopped up and inserted into a megamix;[95] a drawing was reproduced in reduced size or recoloured;[96] or a black-and-white film 'colourized'.[97] In these cases the internal composition or structure of the work is changed.

The definition of treatment that is used in the United Kingdom is narrower than is employed in Article 6*bis* of the Berne Convention, which requires that the author be able to object to 'any...derogatory action' in relation to a work. The broader definition used in Berne seems to acknowledge that a treatment of a work can take place even though the composition or structure of the work is not altered. Importantly it suggests that a treatment of a work can take place where the meaning and significance of the work is affected. It has been suggested, for example, that the mere act of placing a work in a new context, such as the hanging of a religiously inspired artistic work alongside a piece of erotic art, probably would not amount to a treatment of a work under UK law. It would, however, amount to a treatment of the work under the Berne Convention.[98]

---

[92] *Pasterfield v. Denham* [1999] FSR 168, 180. This structural approach is evident in the interpretation of the concept of 'alteration' under the Fine Art Copyright Act 1862, s. 7(4) in *Carlton Illustrators v. Coleman* [1911] 1 KB 771 and *Preston v. Raphael Tuck* [1926] *Ch* 667.

[93] No indication is given as to the degree of significance to be attached to changing the 'meaning' rather than the structure, sequence, and organization of the work. Laddie *et al.*, para. 27.17 (actual physical treatment not as important as message).

[94] See note 76 above. [95] *Morrison v. Lightbond* [1993] *EMLR* 144.

[96] In *Tidy v. Trustees of the Natural History Museum* (1998) 39 IPR 501, 503 neither party disputed that a reduction was an alteration. Cases of alteration under Fine Art Copyright Act, s. 7(4) will be clear cases of 'treatment': *Carlton Illustrators v. Coleman* [1911] 1 KB 771 (colouring of drawing) and *Preston v. Raphael Tuck* [1926] *Ch* 667.

[97] *Huston v. Turner Entertainment* (1991) 23 *IIC* 702 (French Cour de Cassation) (injunction granted to prevent television broadcast of colourized version of *The Asphalt Jungle*). See B. Edelman, 'Applicable Legislation Regarding the Exploitation of Colourized Films' (1992) 23 *IIC* 629; J. Ginsburg, 'Colors in Conflicts' (1988) 36 *Journal of the Copyright Society USA* 810.

[98] Dworkin and Taylor (p. 97) argue that to put an artistic work in a pornographic exhibition would not be a treatment. See also Copinger, para 11–43, p. 647; Cornish and Llewelyn, para 12–75, p. 492; Adeney, para 14.63, p. 406 (referring to the 'treatment' concept as 'unexpectedly narrow' in that it does not cover 'non-transformational uses of the work, such as its use in a particular context').

In the absence of much case law, we can only speculate as to which of the following scenarios would be considered to be a 'treatment' under UK law: placing two written works side by side in a bound volume? Changing the title of a work? Placing a book in an offensive or vulgar dust jacket?[99] Placing a caption on the frame of a painting? Placing a caption beside a painting?[100] Placing a ribbon around the neck of a sculpture of a goose? Placing a sculpture designed for a particular location in a different location? Performing a song's lyrics to a different tune or adding different words to a song's music?[101] Performing a tragedy in a manner whereby it seems like a farce?[102] Adding recordings of the claimant's music to a film of which they did not approve?[103] Interrupting a film for advertising breaks?[104]

The type of activities that will be considered to be a 'treatment' is further restricted by the fact that treatment is defined to exclude translations of literary and dramatic works, and arrangements or transcriptions of musical works involving no more than a change of key or register.[105] It is unclear why moral rights are deemed to be inappropriate here. One rather implausible explanation is that such acts never affect the internal structural or composition of a work.[106] Another possible explanation is that these activities would amount to adaptations of the work and as such require the consent of the copyright owner.[107] However, it is clear that an inaccurate translation may have a negative impact upon an author of a literary work.[108] It may be that, in order to minimize the incompatibility between UK law and Article 6bis, the courts might treat an inaccurate or poor-quality translation as if it were not a 'translation' at all, thus falling outside the scope of the exclusion.[109]

'Derogatory'.   Once it has been shown that there has been a treatment of the work, it is then necessary to show that the treatment was 'derogatory'. Section 80(2)(b) of the 1988 Act states that a treatment is derogatory if it amounts to a 'distortion' or 'mutilation' of the work; or if it is otherwise prejudicial to the honour or reputation of the author.[110]

As yet there is little indication of what the 1988 Act means when it talks about the 'distortion' or 'mutilation' of a work.[111] There appears, however, to be a growing consensus that, in

---

[99] *Mosely v. Staley Paul & Co.* [1917–23] *MacG CC* 341 (where such action was held to be defamatory).

[100] *Pasterfield v. Denham* [1999] *FSR* 168, 180.

[101] In *Confetti Records v. Warner Music UK Ltd* [2003] *EMLR* (35) 790, the defendants had 'rapped' over the claimant's 'track' (which comprised an insistent instrumental beat accompanied by the vocal repetition of the word 'burning'). The defendant accepted that this was a treatment, but the judgment of Lewison J. leaves unstated what was 'treated'—the musical work by the addition of the rap, or the literary work comprising the repetition of a single word. A more thorough analysis would have been helpful.

[102] Ricketson, para. 8.107; Ricketson & Ginsburg, para. 10.22, p. 603.

[103] *Shostakovich v. Twentieth-Century Fox Film Corp* (1948) 80 *NYS (2d)* 575 (failed). Apparently the claim was successful in France: *Société le Chant de Monde v. 20th Century Fox* 1953 *DA* 1954 16 80 cited in Durie, 'Moral Rights and the English Business Community' [1991] *Ent LR* 40, 42.

[104] T. Collova, 'Les interruptions publicitaires lors de la diffusion de films à la television' (1990) 146 *RIDA* 124.

[105] CDPA s. 80(2)(a).

[106] See Dworkin, 'Moral Rights and the Common Law Countries' (1994) 5 *AIPJ* 22, 22.

[107] See P. Goldstein, 'Adaptation Rights and Moral Rights in the UK, the US and the Federal Republic of Germany' (1983) 14 *IIC* 43.

[108] See, e.g. the French case of *Leonide Zorine v. Le Lucernaire* [1987] *ECC* 54.

[109] There is authority that suggests that a 'translation' must be accurate: *Wood v. Chart* (1870) *LR* 10 *Eq* 193, 205; *Lauri v. Renad* [1892] 3 *Ch* 402.

[110] CDPA s. 80(1), (2).

[111] In *Tidy v. Natural History Museum* (1998) 39 *IPR* 501, 503 it was accepted that a reproduction in reduced size is not a mutilation.

order for a work to be distorted or mutilated, the action must be prejudicial to the honour or reputation of the author.[112]

The question what the phrase 'prejudicial to honour and reputation' means was considered in the Canadian case *Snow v. The Eaton Centre*.[113] Michael Snow, a sculptor of international repute, created a work entitled 'Flight-Stop' which he sold to a shopping complex in Toronto called the Eaton Centre. The work comprised 60 geese flying in formation. The Eaton Centre tied ribbons around the necks of the geese as a Christmas decoration. Snow argued that this was prejudicial to his honour and reputation (the Canadian Copyright Act being in similar terms to the British 1988 Act).[114] Snow was adamant that his naturalistic composition was made to look ridiculous by the addition of the red ribbons, which he likened to the addition of earrings to the Venus de Milo. Snow's views were shared by a number of well-respected artists and experts. Although the Eaton Centre produced another artist to deny the claim, the Ontario High Court ruled for Snow and ordered that the ribbons be removed. In so doing the court indicated that, so long as it was not irrational, the author's word on the matter would be sufficient. More specifically, O'Brien J said that the words 'prejudicial to honour and reputation' involved a certain subjective element or judgment on the part of the author, so long as it was reasonably arrived at.

In ascertaining what is meant by the phrase 'prejudicial to the honour or reputation of the author', as used in the 1988 Act, British courts have shown little inclination to follow the emphasis in the *Snow* case. In *Tidy v. Trustees of the Natural History Museum*,[115] the cartoonist Bill Tidy gave the gallery of the Natural History Museum the right to exhibit a series of black-and-white cartoons of dinosaurs that he had drawn. Tidy claimed that his right to integrity in the drawings had been violated when, in putting the cartoons in a book, the gallery reduced the size of the cartoons from 420 mm × 297 mm to 67 mm × 42 mm and added coloured back-grounds to the black-and-white originals. Tidy complained that the reduced cartoons had less visual impact, that the captions were unreadable, and that the process led to the inference that he had not bothered to redraw the cartoons so as to ensure that they were suitable for publication in a book. In the High Court, Rattee J refused Tidy's application for summary judgment for breach of his right of integrity, explaining that he was far from satisfied that the reductions amounted to a distortion of the drawings. The judge also suggested that, in order to find the gallery's treatment of the cartoons was prejudicial to Tidy's honour, it was necessary to have evidence as to how the public perceived the defendant's acts. Referring to *Snow*, Rattee J said

---

[112] *Confetti Records v. Warner Music UK Ltd* [2003] *EMLR* (35) 790 (para. 149–50); *Pasterfield v. Denham* [1999] *FSR* 168, 182; Adeney, pp.408–9; Laddie *et al.* (3rd edn.), para. 13.18; Copinger, para. 11–38, p. 644; Ricketson, para. 8.107 (otherwise concepts of distortion and mutilation could lead to problems because they appear to be 'highly subjective'). *Snow v. The Eaton Centre* (1982) 70 *CPR* (2d) 105 (Canada) ('I am satisfied that the ribbons do distort or modify the plaintiff's work and the plaintiff's concern that this will be prejudicial to his honour or reputation is reasonable under the circumstances'). If this is right, then it is possible that highly distorting treatments, such as parodies, which might not be prejudicial to the author's reputation, do not infringe the integrity right. An alternative view is that distortions and mutilations are to be treated as prejudicial *per se*, and that prejudice need only be proved for lesser cases of 'treatment'. In *Tidy v. Natural History Museum*, note 96 above, 504 the submission that the treatment was a 'distortion' was treated as an alternative to the submission that it was 'otherwise prejudicial'. The two views largely depend on differing interpretations of the words 'or otherwise', but also reflect disagreement as to interpretation of the Berne Convention itself: see Ricketson, para. 8.112, Ricketson & Ginsburg, para. 10.32, pp. 609–10, but note Adeney's categorical view that the qualification that the act must have a prejudicial effect on the honour or reputation of the author applies to distortions and mutilations: Adeney, para 6.52, 14.72.

[113] *Snow v. The Eaton Centre* (1982) 70 *CPR* (2d) 105 (Canada).

[114] Section 12(7) RSC 1970 c. C–30.

[115] *Tidy v. Trustees of the Natural History Museum* [1996] *EIPR* D–86; (1998) 39 *IPR* 501 (reductions of cartoons). See also Laddie *et al.*, para. 27.18 (court unlikely to treat author's own reaction as determinative).

that he would have to be satisfied that the view of the artist was one which is reasonably held, which 'inevitably involves the application of an objective test of reasonableness'.[116] Without further evidence, Rattee J said he could not see how he could draw such a conclusion.

A county court judge has recently gone further and argued that, for a treatment to be derogatory, 'what the plaintiff must establish is that the treatment accorded to his work is either a distortion or a mutilation that prejudices his honour or reputation as an artist. It is not sufficient that the author is himself aggrieved by what has occurred.'[117] Applying that test the judge took the view that certain colour variations between the original and the artwork in question (the design of a brochure), the omission of trivial matter, and the reduction in size were not derogatory. The judge added that, while the changes to peripheral matters were of the kind that 'could well be the subject of a Spot the Difference competition in a child's comic', it would be wrong to elevate such differences to a 'derogatory treatment'.

In a third UK case, *Confetti Records v. Warner Music UK Ltd*,[118] Lewison J held that the claimant, Andrew Alcee (a member of the 'Ant'ill Mob'), had not made out a sufficient case for a finding of derogatory treatment where his garage track 'Burnin'', which comprised an insistent instrumental beat accompanied by the vocal repetition of the word 'burning', had been superimposed with a rap by another garage act, 'The Heartless Crew' (the words of which were difficult to make out). The defendant accepted that this was a treatment, so the crucial issue was whether it was derogatory. The claimant had argued that it was, first, because the rap contained references to violence and drugs, by using phrases such as 'mish mish man', 'shizzle (or sizzle) my nizzle'; and 'string dem up one by one', which was, according to the claimant, an 'invitation to lynching'. Alternatively, it was argued that the rap affected the 'coherence of the original work'. Lewison J rejected the claimant's argument. First, he stated that the fact that the words were difficult to decipher militated against them being derogatory. Second, he noted that the meaning of the words, which he described as being 'in a foreign language', could only be determined by way of expert evidence, and no such evidence had been offered. Third, Lewison J took the view that 'string dem up' was not necessarily an 'invitation to lynching', and could be heard as merely advocating the return of capital punishment. Most importantly, however, he rejected the claimant's argument because he had failed to provide evidence of his honour or reputation. In the absence of such evidence, even by the complainant himself, the judge was not prepared to infer prejudice. Lewison J was confirmed in this view by the fact that the Ant'ill Mob itself utilized the imagery of gangsters. As regards the claim based upon the effect of the rap on the coherence of the song, Lewison J seems to have been strongly influenced by indications that the song was written as a background for rapping, and that the Ant'ill Mob's own mixes added rapping over the whole track.

Despite these decisions, it is still unclear how derogatory treatment will be construed in the UK. In particular, there is still some uncertainty as to whether the question whether a treatment is prejudicial to the honour or reputation of an author is to be judged from an objective or subjective standpoint. Under UK law one would expect that the notion of reputation used in this context would be similar to that which is employed in defamation law.[119] If this were the case, one would expect that the question whether or not conduct was prejudicial to an author's

---

[116] *Tidy v. Trustees of the Natural History Museum* [1996] *EIPR* D-86; (1998) 39 *IPR* 501.

[117] *Pasterfield v. Denham* [1999] *FSR* 168, 182.

[118] [2003] *EMLR* (35) 790.

[119] Ricketson, para. 8.110; Ricketson & Ginsburg, para. 10.27, p. 606, para. 10.09, pp. 592–3, para. 10.11, pp. 594–6 (explaining that these terms were preferred to the wider concept of 'moral or spiritual interest of the author').

reputation should be judged from the viewpoint of right-thinking members of society (that is, objectively).

While 'reputation' is a familiar concept in British law, the same cannot be said for 'honour'. If 'honour' is taken to refer to what a person thinks of themselves (and is thus similar to the Roman law concept of *dignitas*), it would seem that prejudice to honour might well involve a strong subjective element.[120] This distinction might be important where a defendant parodies the claimant's work in such a way that a member of the public would not believe the parody to be the claimant's work, so would be unlikely to find that the claimant's reputation was harmed.[121] Nonetheless, the claimant might feel offended.

4.2.2 Circumstances where the author is protected from derogatory treatment

The right of an author or a director to object to, or prevent, the derogatory treatment of their work only arises when the work or copies thereof are dealt with in certain ways (section 80). While these acts vary according to the category of work involved, basically they arise where someone communicates, disseminates, or otherwise renders the derogatory treatment available *to the public*. As a result of this requirement, the right to integrity is not a right to prevent destruction or spoliation of the work itself.[122]

In relation to *literary, dramatic, and musical works* the right to object to derogatory treatment may be invoked when a derogatory treatment of the work is published commercially, performed in public, or communicated to the public. It is also triggered when copies of a film or sound recording embodying the derogatory treatment are issued to the public.[123] In turn, with an *artistic work,* the right may be invoked against a person who publishes commercially or exhibits in public a derogatory treatment of the work. The right is also triggered where someone communicates to or shows in public a film including a visual image of a derogatory treatment of the work.[124] Further acts are specified in relation to works of architecture, sculpture, and works of artistic craftsmanship.[125] In relation to *films,* the right of integrity is infringed whenever a derogatory treatment of the film is shown in or communicated to the public, or when copies of a derogatory treatment of the film are issued to the public.[126]

In addition, it should be observed that certain acts may amount to a secondary infringement of the right of integrity.[127] This will occur where, in the course of business, a person possesses, sells or lets for hire, offers or exposes for sale or hire, exhibits in public, or distributes an article which they know or have reason to know, is an infringing article. In this context an infringing article means a work or a copy of a work which has been subjected to a derogatory treatment and has been, or is likely to be, the subject of any of the infringing acts in section 80. Secondary infringement only takes place if the dealing prejudicially affects the honour or reputation of the author. If the treatment itself is derogatory, it seems likely that the dissemination of the treatment will prejudice the honour or reputation of the author.

---

[120] Laddie *et al.,* para. 27.18 (honour refers to integrity as a human being). This is consistent with the Report of Michael Plaisant at the Brussels Conference revising Berne: see Ricketson, para. 8.110; Ricketson & Ginsburg, para. 10.27, p. 606.

[121] Copinger, para. 11–41, p. 646.

[122] Such a right has been accepted in the US Visual Artists Rights Act 1990. At the Brussels Revision of Berne, one of the *voeux* adopted said that countries introduce such a prohibition. See Ricketson, para. 8.109; Ricketson & Ginsburg, para. 10.26, pp. 605.

[123] CDPA s. 80(3)(a), (b). These are identical to the occasions on which an author has a right to be identified under CDPA s. 77(2): no differentiation is made for songs as in CDPA s. 77(3).

[124] CDPA s. 80(4)(a).   [125] CDPA s. 80(4)(c).   [126] CDPA s. 80(6).   [127] CDPA s. 83.

4.2.3 Exceptions and defences

A number of exceptions are placed upon the right of integrity by the 1988 Act. It is notable that there are no defences for fair dealing, nor for the design–copyright interface. Some commentators have therefore suggested that the defences are 'unduly narrow'.[128]

In the case of works created by employees,[129] the right of integrity does not apply to anything done by or with the authority of the copyright owner except in two particular situations.[130] The general rule, then, is that an employer can deal publicly with derogatory treatments of an employee's work. In these circumstances, the authorial prerogative gives way to the demands of the employer for control.[131] This means, for example, that artists who work for a design firm will not be able to use their right of integrity where their artworks are modified either by their employer or by other employees. Similarly, an employee who drafts a report will not be able to restrain publication of a version that is rewritten on behalf of the employer.

The exceptions to this general position relate to circumstances where the author/employee has been, or is to be, identified. Although the law privileges the needs of the employer and the copyright holder, those needs do not extend as far as continuing to name the employee where the work has been modified. Consequently, 'the right does not apply to anything done in relation to such a work by or with the authority of the copyright owner unless the author or director (a) is identified at the time of the relevant act, or (b) has previously been identified in or on published copies of the work'.[132] However, even in these cases, the right of integrity is not infringed if there is 'sufficient disclaimer'. That is, if there is a clear and reasonably prominent indication that the work has been subjected to treatment to which the author or director has not consented.[133]

There are also special defences to infringement of the moral right of integrity. In particular, the right is not infringed by anything done for the purpose of avoiding the commission of an offence (such as under the Obscene Publications Act 1959 or the Public Order Act 1986), complying with a duty imposed by or under an enactment, or in the case of the British Broadcasting Corporation 'avoiding the inclusion in a programme broadcast by them of anything which offends against good taste or decency or which is likely to encourage or incite crime or to lead to disorder or to be offensive to public feeling'.[134] In the case of a work of architecture, the right is limited. Where an architect is identified on a building which is subject to derogatory treatment, the architect is given the right to have their identification as architect removed from the building.[135]

4.2.4 Waiver

Although the moral right of integrity, like the other moral rights, cannot be assigned, section 87 of the 1988 Act ensures that they can be waived by way of agreement in writing. Such a waiver can be specific or general, and relate to existing or future works. It has been said that most 'objective observers would acknowledge that such wide waiver provisions, both in theory

---

128 Laddie *et al.*, para. 27.27.

129 CDPA s. 82. The same rules apply to works in which Crown or Parliamentary copyright subsist and works in which copyright originally vested in an international organization under CDPA s. 168.

130 The provision refers to the circumstance where works vested in the director's employer by virtue of CDPA s. 9(2)(a). The Copyright and Related Rights Regulations 1996 (SI 1996/2967) amended the provisions on film authorship and ownership without altering the reference in CDPA s. 82(1)(a).

131 Dworkin, note 7 above, 27, 'the exceptions and qualifications to moral rights... were attempts by the UK Government to modify... moral rights in the light of business reality'.

132 CDPA s. 82(2).   133 CDPA s. 178.   134 CDPA s. 81(6).   135 CDPA s. 80(5).

and in practice, erode significantly, indeed drive a coach and horses through the moral rights provisions'.[136] This is because the industries that exploit copyright works tend to oblige authors and artists to enter standard-form contracts which require them to waive the integrity rights. Even the requirement that waiver be in writing, which provides authors with some residual protection, is compromised by section 87(3) which states that the general law of contract and estoppel applies to informal waiver.

4.3 ALTERNATIVE AND RELATED FORMS OF RELIEF

If an argument based upon the moral right of integrity fails (or is dubious), an author may fall back on protection under common law or contract.[137] If a work is presented as being that of the author but has been substantially altered, that representation could be defamatory. Thus, in *Humphries v. Thompson*,[138] a newspaper which serialized a story, but changed the names of the characters and omitted and added other text, was found by the jury to have defamed the author by damaging her literary reputation. Similarly, in *Archbold v. Sweet*,[139] an author successfully claimed that his reputation had been injured by the publication of a further edition of his work that contained a number of errors. The new edition would have been understood by the public to have been prepared by the author.[140]

Similarly, there are many situations in which an author may be able to rely on contract rather than moral rights to object to derogatory treatment of their work. In *Frisby v. BBC*,[141] the claimant had written a play for the BBC, and the BBC deleted the line 'my friend Sylv' told me it was safe standing up...' on the ground that it was indecent.[142] The complex contractual arrangement prohibited the BBC from making 'structural' as opposed to 'minor' alterations to the script. The court decided the contract was a licence and considered whether the alteration was structural or minor. The claimant alleged that it was essential to and even the climax of the play. In contrast, the BBC claimed it was a minor deletion. Goff J granted the injunction, saying that the author 'prima facie would appear to be the best judge' of the significance of the line.

4.4 THE FUTURE: HARMONIZATION

In April 2000, the Commission published a report on moral rights which had been prepared for it by Alain Strowel, Marjut Salokannel, and Estelle Derclaye. The existing Directives have steered carefully clear of the hornets' nest that moral rights stirs up, particularly in the UK. Nonetheless, one would have thought that however politically difficult it may seem, there would be clear justification (in terms of the Internal Market) for activity in this sphere.[143] The

---

[136] Dworkin, note 7 above, 28. Durie, note 1 above, 40, 48, calls this 'the greatest compromise in the Act'.

[137] For a general review of the common law analogues to moral rights, see G. Dworkin, 'Moral Rights: The Shape of Things to Come' [1986] *EIPR* 329.

[138] [1905–1910] *MacG CC* 148. Interestingly, the jury rejected the defendant's arguments that any moral obloquy would attach to them, as publishers, rather than the author.

[139] [1832] 172 ER 947. See also *Springfield v. Thame* (1903) 89 *LT* 242.

[140] See also *Ridge v. English Illustrated Magazine* [1911–16] *MacG CC* 91 (where the defendant published a story attributed to the plaintiff, a well-known author, but in fact written by a grocer's assistant from Bournemouth, the judge instructed the jury to find defamation if 'any one reading the story would think that plaintiff was a mere commonplace scribbler').

[141] *Frisby v. BBC* [1967] *Ch* 932.

[142] The defence under CDPA s. 81(6)(c) means that claimant in *Frisby v. BBC* would still have to rely on contract.

[143] See L. Bently, *Between a Rock and A Hard Place* (2002).

Report, entitled *Moral rights in the context of the exploitation of works through digital technology,* reveals substantial differences in the detail of the laws of member states on moral rights, but little dissatisfaction with the lack of harmonization. In part, this reflects the similar (high) levels of moral right protection in most European countries. The Report also revealed that one of the reasons for the failure to press the Commission to undertake harmonization was fear that the effect of the legislative process would be to allow the influence of exploiters and the 'copyright countries' to lower the level of protection. Not all commentators share the view espoused by the study.[144]

---

[144] For example, M. Walter, 'Updating and Consolidation of the *Acquis*: The Future of European Copyright', Report of the Commission meeting at Santiago de Compostela, Jun. 2002 (proposing harmonization of moral rights). Cf. IViR, *Recasting Copyright for the Knowledge Economy* (2006), para. 7.3, p. 220.

11

EXPLOITATION AND USE OF COPYRIGHT

CHAPTER CONTENTS

1 INTRODUCTION

As we saw in Chapter 6, copyright law confers on the first owner of copyright certain exclusive rights over the exploitation of the work. These rights are capable of being exploited in a number of ways. Most obviously, the rights enable copyright owners to control the sale of both the original work and copies of the work. By selling copies of the work at an appropriate price, copyright owners can ensure they reap a reward sufficient to cover the costs of producing the work. This form of exploitation is most important where the market for the work is limited and the owner can easily be linked to a purchaser: as with sales of limited editions of engravings or prints by artists.

If copyright law only gave the author the right to exploit the work, its economic usefulness would be limited. Few authors have the financial ability, economic acumen, or the willingness to print and sell their own works. Consequently, the law treats copyright as a form of personal property that can be exploited in a number of ways, most importantly by being assigned or licensed.[1] This enables copyright to be transferred to those who can exploit it most profitably. Where this occurs the terms of the transfer agreement will determine how the profits are to be distributed. As we will see, such transfers are often arranged in advance of the creation of a work, for example, where an author enters into a publishing contract prior to writing a book. Moreover, since some works can be exploited in a variety of ways, there may be many assignments, licences, and sublicences. With new forms of exploitation, the web of transactions is becoming ever more complex.

[1] CDPA ss. 1 and 90(1).

One of the characteristics of the intangible property protected by copyright is that it has the potential to be used by a range of different people at the same time. For example, a sound recording can be played in numerous public places (such as pubs, shops, and discos) simultaneously. As works are increasingly exploited in this manner, the role of licensing in exploitation becomes ever more important. In some situations the copyright owner will be able to license the use of the work by the customer directly (for example where sale of software on a floppy disc includes a licence to make the immaterial copies necessary to run the program). In other cases, owner–user relations are mediated by an agency or collective management systems.

In this chapter, we look at the ways copyright can be exploited or transferred. After exploring the most important forms of exploitation, *viz.* assignment and licensing, we consider the transfer of copyright in the case of mortgages, bankruptcy, or death. In turn, we examine situations where the rights are exploited by way of compulsory licence. We also consider briefly techniques for exploiting works that rely on the use of technological protection measures, techniques which are becoming increasingly important in the digital environment. (These are examined in detail in Chapter 13.) Finally, we look to the important role that collecting societies play in copyright exploitation.

Before doing so, it is important to note that assignment, licence, or other transaction in relation to copyright is only effective if the purported assignor was able to enter the transaction. Consequently, it is important to ensure that the person entering the transaction is the owner, or is appropriately authorized by the owner.[2] In this respect it should be noted that, where there are joint proprietors, all of them must consent to any transaction (if it is to affect more than their own share).[3] Particular difficulties may arise in relation to transactions made by minors. These are only inviolable if made for the benefit of the minor. If not so made, on reaching majority, the minor can have such a transaction set aside.[4]

2 ASSIGNMENT

An assignment is a transfer of ownership of the copyright. As a result of an assignment, the assignee stands in the shoes of the assignor and is entitled to deal with the copyright as he or she pleases. Although an assignment may be for payment of a royalty (as well as for a fixed sum), the nature of the assignment means that, if the assignee transfers the copyright to a third party, the transferee takes free of the personal agreement to pay royalties.[5]

It is not necessary that all of the copyright be assigned.[6] In contrast with other types of property, where the tendency is to simplify transfers by limiting the ways in which the rights can be divided up, copyright law takes a liberal view of what may be assigned. In particular, copyright allows partial assignments by reference to 'times, territories and classes of conduct'.[7] For example, an agreement to write a book might include an exclusive grant of all rights. In turn, the publisher might parcel out the exploitation of the work by way of hardback, paperback, newspaper serialization, audiotape, reprography, electronic distribution, dramatization,

---

[2] *Beloff v. Pressdram* [1973] *RPC* 765.   [3] *Powell v. Head* (1879) 12 *Ch D* 686.

[4] *Chaplin v. Frewin (Publishers)* [1966] *Ch* 71.

[5] *Barker v. Stickney* [1919] 1 *KB* 121 (royalty clause not enforceable against subsequent assignees but only on the basis of contract against the initial assignee). See J. Adams, '*Barker v. Stickney* Revisited' [1998] *IPQ* 113 (arguing that the case was wrongly decided; in particular, that the agreement constituted a charge); Copinger, para. 5–69 (discussing role of the doctrine of mutual benefit and burden).

[6] CDPA s. 90(2).   [7] *Kervan Trading v. Aktas* (1987) 8 *IPR* 583, 587.

translation, as well as by being filmed.[8] Restrictions that are geographical in nature are subject to EC rules, so that agreements that are intended to divide up the Common Market will be prohibited.[9]

In order for an assignment to be valid, it must be in writing and signed by or on behalf of the assignor. It has been held that sufficient writing might be provided by an invoice or receipt.[10] The assignment should identify the work concerned with sufficient clarity that it can be ascertained, though the courts have admitted oral ('parol') evidence to assist in the process of identification.[11] No special form of words is required, so a transfer of 'all the partnership assets' will include a transfer of any copyright owned by the partnership.[12] Assignment of copyright is a distinct legal transaction and is not effected by mere sale or transfer of the work itself.[13] Thus, if a person sells an original painting or manuscript, this (of itself) only transfers the personal property right in the chattel: the copyright remains with its owner.[14] If a vendor wishes to transfer the copyright as well as the personal property in the chattel, this should be done explicitly.

Where an assignment is made orally, this will be ineffective *at law*. However, the general equitable rule that treats a failed attempt at a legal assignment as an oral contract to assign the interest will usually apply to attempted assignments of copyright. So long as there is valuable consideration, an oral contract of this nature will be specifically enforceable.[15] Where this occurs a prospective assignee will be treated as the immediate equitable owner.[16] While such an equitable owner may commence an action against an infringer and secure interlocutory relief, the legal owner needs to be joined as a party before final relief can be secured.[17]

A prospective copyright owner (usually an author) can also make assignments of future copyright. That is, they can assign the copyright in works not in existence at the time of the agreement.[18] This will be useful, for example, where a painting is commissioned, or where a music publishing agreement is entered into before a songwriter creates the songs. However, it seems that the assignment of future copyright only operates where the agreement is for valuable consideration, since it is only in these circumstances that the assignee would be 'entitled as against the whole world'.[19]

An assignment does not need to be registered to be valid. Priority is determined by reference to rules as to first-in-time and bona fide purchase. In the case of legal assignments, the first transfer in time has priority over claims deriving from subsequent purported transfers of the same rights. Assignments effective in equity will only be defeated at the hands of a later bona fide purchaser for value without notice of the earlier assignment.

---

[8] See further Copinger, paras. 27.15–16. For consideration of the limits of such parcelling see Copinger, para. 5.87.

[9] *IHT International Heiztechnik v. Ideal-Standard*, Case C–9/93 [1994] 1 *ECR* I–2789. It seems, geographical restrictions may not be imposed so as to subdivide the UK: Copinger, para. 5.92. Cf. *British Actors Film Co. v. Glover* [1918] 1 *KB* 299.

[10] *Savoury v. World of Golf* [1914] 2 *Ch* 566.

[11] Ibid. *Batjac Productions v. Simitar Entertainment* [1996] *FSR* 139, 146–7.

[12] *Murray v. King* [1986] *FSR* 116, 124, 128, 130, 134–5 (FCA).   [13] Cf. CDPA s. 93; CDPA s. 56.

[14] *Cooper v. Stephens* [1895] 1 *Ch* 567 (supply of electro blocks for printing of copyright drawings did not assign copyright).

[15] *Western Front v. Vestron* [1987] *FSR* 66, 78 (copyright a unique property).

[16] *Wilson v. Weiss* (1995) 31 *IPR* 423; *Ironside v. HMAG* [1988] *RPC* 197.

[17] *Batjac Productions v. Simitar Entertainment* [1996] *FSR* 139, 146–7.

[18] CDPA s. 91(1) (reversing *PRS v. London Theatre of Varieties* [1924] *AC* 1).

[19] Laddie *et al.*, para. 13.6.

2.1 PRESUMED TRANSFERS

Although transfer of ownership of copyright (or its component rights) is usually governed by contract, an important exception exists in relation to film production agreements. Where a contract concerning film production is concluded between an author and a film producer, the author is presumed to have transferred their *rental* right to the film producer.[20] The presumption only operates in relation to authors of literary, dramatic, musical, and artistic works, and therefore does not apply to the director of a film. Moreover, the presumption does not apply to the author of a screenplay, dialogue, or music specifically created for and used in a film.[21] The presumption is important in relation to the incorporation of existing works in films, for example where the author of a novel agrees to their work being made into a film, or a musical composer agrees to their work being used in a soundtrack. The presumption can be rebutted by an agreement to the contrary, which it seems can be express or implied.

3 VOLUNTARY LICENCES

The powers conferred on the copyright owner are most commonly employed by the copyright owner giving licences to particular individuals permitting them to carry out specified activities. At a basic level a licence is merely a permission to do an act that would otherwise be prohibited without the consent of the proprietor of the copyright.[22] A licence enables the licensee to use the work without infringing. So long as the use falls within the terms of the licence,[23] it gives the licensee an immunity from action by the copyright owner.

In contrast with an assignment (where the assignor relinquishes all interest in the copyright), the licensor retains an interest in the copyright. Indeed, no proprietary interest is passed under a licence,[24] though in most circumstances a licence is binding on successors in title of the original grantor of the licence.[25] While the essential nature of a licence is that it is a mere permission, copyright law has developed a sophisticated repertoire of ways whereby a work might be licensed.

Licences may take many forms: from a one-off permission through to an exclusive licence. Licences may be limited geographically, temporally, and in relation to specific modes of exploitation of the copyright work. A licence, even if non-exclusive, may (if the parties so choose) grant the licensee a right of action against infringers.[26] For the most part, the terms of a voluntary licence are up to the parties to choose. As such, terms will vary with the needs, capacities, and wishes of the parties.

---

[20] CDPA s. 93A. Implementing Rental Dir., Art. 2(6). See Copinger, para. 5.96.   [21] CDPA s. 93A(3).

[22] *British Actors Film Co. v. Glover* [1918] 1 *KB* 299; *Canon Kabushiki Kaisha v. Green Cartridge Co.* [1997] *AC* 728, 735.

[23] Where a licensee breaches the agreement the question arises whether there is an action merely for breach of contract or for infringement of copyright: if the act is outside the scope of the licence, it is an infringement; if the breach relates to a condition precedent for the licence, the action will also infringe (*Miller v. Cecil* [1937] 2 *All ER* 464); moreover, if the breach is sufficiently serious to amount to a repudiation of the contract, this may be accepted by the copyright owner and an action will lie for infringement of copyright as regards subsequent acts.

[24] *CBS v. Charmdale* [1980] *FSR* 289, 295.   [25] CDPA s. 90(4).

[26] CDPA s. 101A (added by SI 2003/2498).

3.1 EXCLUSIVE LICENCES

Of the different forms of licence, perhaps the most significant is the 'exclusive licence'. An exclusive licence is an agreement according to which a copyright owner permits the licensee to use the copyright work. At the same time, the copyright owner also promises that they will not grant any other licences and will not exploit the work themselves. The legal consequence of this is that the licence confers a right in respect of the copyright *work to the exclusion of all others including the licensor*.[27] In some ways it is the intangible property's equivalent of a 'lease'.[28]

While a bare licensee acquires the right not to be sued in relation to the acts set out in the licence, an exclusive licence confers on the licensee a 'statutory procedural status' that is equivalent to that of the proprietor.[29] One significant aspect of this status is that exclusive licensees can sue infringers without having to persuade the proprietor to take action on their behalf.[30] Section 101(1) of the Act declares that an exclusive licensee has the same rights and remedies in respect of matters occurring after the grant of the licence as they would have if the licence had been an assignment.[31] An exclusive licensee is given the same rights as a copyright owner and therefore has the right to bring proceedings in respect of any infringement of the copyright after the date of the licence agreement. Indeed, an action can be brought by both the copyright owner and an exclusive licensee: special provisions dealing with this situation are set out in section 102. Exclusive licences of legal interests in copyright have to be in writing and signed by or on behalf of the assignor[32] if the licensee wishes to take advantage of their statutory entitlement to sue for infringement.[33] This is in contrast to a non-exclusive licence, which may be made orally, or in writing; and might be contractual or gratuitous, express or implied.[34]

In practice, the grant of an exclusive licence can often be seen as equivalent to an assignment.[35] Consequently, publishers are often happy to be granted exclusive licences, rather than full assignments, by authors.[36] However, there are legal differences between an assignment and an exclusive licence. The first difference arises from the fact that an assignee becomes the copyright owner, whereas an exclusive licensee does not. One of the consequences of this is that the remedies available to the exclusive licensee are limited to those that arise in an action for breach of contract against the copyright owner.[37] The second difference is that the rights given to licensees are less certain and can be defeated at the hands of a purchaser in good faith for valuable consideration and without notice (actual or constructive) of the licence.[38] Third, an exclusive licensee may not always be able to grant a sublicence or transfer the benefit of their

---

[27] Cf. *Sega Enterprises v. Galaxy Electronics* (1998) 39 *IPR* 577.

[28] D. Vaver, 'The Exclusive Licence in Copyright' (1995) 9 *IPJ* 163, 165 (which also reviews the history of such licences).

[29] Copinger, para. 5.201.

[30] The copyright owner is made party to the proceedings, if necessary by joining it as a defendant. But note that a mere licensee may be able to bring an action under CDPA s. 101A if the infringing act was directly connected to a previous licensed act of the licensee, the licence is in writing signed by the copyright owners, and it expressly grants the right of action.

[31] Except that the exclusive licensee cannot sue the copyright owner for breach of copyright (though if the terms are breached, the copyright owner will be liable for breach of contract).

[32] CDPA s. 90(3).   [33] CDPA s. 101.   [34] *Godfrey v. Lees* [1995] *EMLR* 307.

[35] *R. Grigg v. Raben Footwear* [2003] *EWHC* 2914 para. 58; *Chaplin v. Frewin* [1966] *Ch* 71, 93.

[36] The Publishers' Association Code of Practice (revised and reissued 1997) recommends that in a publishing contract the author should normally retain copyright.

[37] *CBS v. Charmdale* [1980] *FSR* 289, 297.   [38] CDPA s. 90(4).

licence to a third party.[39] Fourth, the rights of an exclusive licensee may be limited by implied terms.[40] Finally, a copyright owner who wishes to permit another to exploit a work can retain better protection by giving an exclusive licence.[41]

In some situations it may be difficult to determine whether a copyright owner has assigned their copyright or merely granted an exclusive licence.[42] Whether a person is an exclusive licensee or an assignee is a matter of construction of the agreement. The question to be answered is whether there is evidence from which an intention to assign can be inferred. The way in which the parties describe the arrangement will be influential, but not conclusive. Use of terms such as 'grant', 'sole', and 'exclusive rights', and provisions on 'retransfer' if the copyright is not exploited, might indicate an assignment.[43] However, these descriptions may be ignored if the tenor of the agreement suggests that in substance there is an exclusive licence.[44] Occasionally, the courts have treated provisions concerning 'royalties' as suggesting that the arrangement is an exclusive licence rather than an assignment.[45] But in all cases the court should beware of linguistic formalism and infer the intention from all the circumstances of the case.[46]

3.2 CREATIVE COMMONS, FREE SOFTWARE, AND VIRAL LICENCES

While it has been extremely common hitherto for an author to grant an exclusive licence to an exploiter, such as a publishing company, the last decade has seen the rise in popularity of 'open access' modes of distributing works, that is, the use of standardized licences allowing for particular re-uses of works by any member of the public.[47]

The first popular version of such as licence was the so called 'General Public License' developed for use in relation to computer programs.[48] Given the manner in which computer programs build on existing programs it was immediately evident to a few of those involved that the need to obtain copyright permissions could become a significant impediment to software development. Richard Stallman of the Free Software Foundation conceived that one way to avoid this would to be to grant permission in advance permitting anyone to use and modify material, but making it a condition of use that subsequent developers make their software available on the same terms.[49] The GPL therefore has been said to be 'viral' in nature, in that

---

[39] Copinger, para. 5.196. Publishing contracts are generally non-assignable: see Laddie *et al.*, para. 14.23.

[40] For example, in *Frisby v. BBC* [1967] *Ch* 932 (in the case of a licence the courts will more readily imply a term limiting the right of the licensee to alter the work).

[41] *Barker v. Stickney* [1919] 1 *KB* 121.

[42] *Western Front v. Vestron* [1987] *FSR* 66, 75. Nevertheless the Supreme Court of Canada has called the distinction between an assignment and an exclusive licence 'important and meaningful': *Euro-Excellence Inc v. Kraft Canada Inc* (2007) *SCC* 37, para 85.

[43] *Jonathan Cape v. Consolidated Press* [1954] 3 *All ER* 253; *Messager v. BBC* [1929] *AC* 151; *British Actors Film Co. v. Glover* [1918] 1 *KB* 299, 308.

[44] *Messager v. BBC* [1929] *AC* 151.   [45] *Western Front v. Vestron* [1987] *FSR* 66, 75–6.   [46] Ibid, 76.

[47] S. Dusollier, 'Sharing Access to Intellectual Property Through Private Ordering' (2007) *Chicago-Kent Law Review* 1391.

[48] See <http://www.gnu.org>. There are three versions of the GPL. See M. O'Sullivan, 'The pluralistic, evolutionary, quasi-legal role of the GNU General public license in Free/Libre/Open Source Software' (2004) *EIPR* 340; T. Rychlicki [2008] *EIPR* 232.

[49] GPL (version 1) states that 'you may modify your copy or copies of the Program or any portion of it, and copy and distribute such modifications..., provided that you...cause the whole of any work that you distribute or publish, that in whole or in part contains the Program or any part thereof, either with or without modifications, to be licensed at no charge to all third parties under the terms of this General Public License.'

Fig. 11.1 Logo of the Creative Commons movement
Source: Courtesy of Creative Commons, <http://creativecommons.org>.

those who take advantage of the licences must subject their own work to the same conditions.[50] Developers are able to obtain remuneration by selling individual pieces of software, rather than extracting licence fees based on copyright. The GPL has proved to be an amazing success,[51] though doubts exist over the enforceability of 'viral' clauses.[52]

Following in the wake of the GPL, the 'Creative Commons' movement has attempted to develop similar standard open licences for other types of work.[53] In so doing, the Creative Commons movement has been forced to take account of different national legal systems, and currently it operates in 42 jurisdictions.

In contrast with the GPL, Creative Commons offers copyright owners a menu of licences: some allow re-use of a work only in unmodified form, some allow re-use only with attribution, some allow re-use only for non-commercial purposes; and some attempt to impose a 'share-alike' condition on users. As a result, a copyright owner has considerable flexibility, and the take-up of such licences has been very widespread. Nevertheless, it should be observed that the most commonly adopted licence is the 'attribution-non-commercial no derivative works' licence, which confers only the freedom to duplicate, distribute, play, or perform the work in an unmodified state, for non-commercial purposes and with attribution of authorship.[54]

While the use of both the GPL and the Creative Commons licences has become very widespread, these projects have not gone uncriticized, even by those who share similar ideological goals or desire similar practical results. Niva Elkin-Koren, for example, has emphasized the dangerous effect of 'open access' as constituting informational goods as property, and creators as owners.[55] In fact, recognizing the dependence of the Creative Commons licences on the existence of property right, one of the leaders of Creative Commons, Jamie Boyle, has

[50] The characterization of such contracts as viral is attributed to M.J. Radin, "Humans, Computers, and Binding Commitment" (2000) 75 *Ind. LJ* 1125. The term 'copyleft' is also frequently used to describe this feature of the GPL and other licences.

[51] 50,013 projects, 67% of projects listed in the SourceForge open source repository, are released under the GPL.

[52] A. Guadamuz Gonzalez, 'Viral Contracts or Unenforceable Document: Contractual Validity of Copyleft Licences' (2004) *EIPR* 331; cf. Westkamp [2008] *IPQ* 14.

[53] See <http://www.creativecommons.org>. See S. Dusollier, 'The Master's Tools v. the Master's House: Creative Commons v. Copyright' (2005) 29 *Col. J. L. A.* 271; M. Fox, T. Ciro and N. Duncan, 'Creative Commons: An Alternative, Web-Based, Copyright System' (2005) *Ent LR* 111.

[54] A. Chander and M. Sunder, 'The Romance of the Public Domain' (2004) 92 *Cal. LR* 1331, 1361–2.

[55] N. Elkin-Koren, 'What Contracts Cannot Do: The Limits of Private Ordering in Facilitating a Creative Commons' (2005) 74 *Fordham LR* 375, 398. The dependence of open access licensing on copyright was earlier emphasised by Dusollier: S. Dusollier, 'Open Source and Copyleft: Authorship Reconsidered' (2003) 26 *Col. J. L. A.* 281, 286–7, but she also argues that creative commons may bring about a shift in the notion of the author from the romantic author-as-owner who controls the meaning of a text, to the post-modern author as the 'founder of a discursivity': Dusollier, 'The Master's Tools' (2005), at 285–6.

advocated the extension of legal protection to non-original databases, so that such products can effectively come within the terms of creative commons share-alike licensing schemes. More practically, Severine Dusollier has called attention to a number of potential limitations to the effectiveness of viral contracts,[56] in order to remind those in the open access movement and beyond of the remaining importance of public law.

Others, more sympathetic to traditional avenues of copyright exploitation, have emphasized the dangers of ill-considered adoption of these licences by aspiring authors. While it may seem attractive for a young or naïve author to adopt an easy-to-use CC licence at a time when many others seem to be so doing, it is by no means obvious that such a move is in their best interests. Rather, only those with a clear idea as to how they will be able to turn a profit if their works become popular should throw away the mechanism that has traditionally secured rewards to successful writers or composers. From this perspective, creative commons licences are primarily useful tools for those who do not need remuneration *from copyright* (or at all).

3.3 IMPLIED LICENCES

In certain circumstances the court may see fit to imply a licence to use a copyright work. However, for the most part the courts have been reluctant to imply licences from the circumstances.[57] They have indicated that they will normally imply terms into a contract only in two situations. First, terms may be implied 'by law' where they are 'inherent in the nature of the contract'. Second, terms may be implied to fill gaps left in an agreement where it is necessary to provide 'business efficacy'.

In relation to terms implied by law, the court is primarily concerned with whether the contract falls into a particular class. However, that is not to say that the express terms are not important. This is because they may indicate that the parties did not intend the normal incidents of a particular class of contract to apply. The classes subject to such implied terms are not closed, and change with the necessities of the times. An Australian case has indicated that one such class of contracts concerns 'persons who prepared written material with the intention it should be used in a particular manner'.[58] The specific terms to be implied in this class then depend upon the 'particular purpose'. For example, where an architect provides a client with plans, the court might determine the purpose (and the extent of any licence) from the fee when viewed in the light of the standard professional fee scales operating.[59]

Where courts are implying terms for particular cases, they look at the existing express terms and the surrounding context. It has been said that for a term to be implied it must be reasonable and equitable, necessary to give business efficacy to the contract, obvious that it 'goes without saying', capable of clear expression, and must not contradict any express term of the contract.[60] In *Ray v. Classic FM,* Lightman J found that an expert in music who had been

---

[56] Dusollier emphasizes three limits: the definition as to when the viral effect occurs, the validity of the licence itself, and the compatibility of different licences. On the potential problems posed by revocation, see L.P. Loren, 'Building a Reliable Semicommons of Creative Works: Enforcement of Creative Commons Licenses and Limited Abandonment of Copyright' (2007) 14 *Geo. Mason LR* 271.

[57] *Philips Electronique v. BSB* [1995] *EMLR* 472, 481; *Cescinsky v. Routledge* [1916] 2 *KB* 325, 319.

[58] *Acohs v. RA Bashford Consulting* (1997) 37 IPR 542 (FCA).

[59] *Blair v. Osborne & Tompkins* [1971] 2 *QB* 78; *Stovin-Bradford v. Volpoint Properties* [1971] 1 *Ch* 1007. Note that *Ray v. Classic FM* [1998] *FSR* 622 treats these cases as ones where the terms are implied to give business efficacy to the agreement.

[60] *BP Refinery (Westernport) v. Hastings Shire Council* (1977) 16 *ALR* 363, 376 (Lord Simon of Glaisdale) approved in *Ray v. Classic FM.*

engaged by a radio station to catalogue its musical recordings had copyright in the catalogues produced. While the terms of his consultancy were silent as to copyright, the court held that the expert had granted an implied licence to the radio station to do certain things with the catalogues. The scope of the licence was limited to use of the material for the purpose of broadcasting in the United Kingdom. This meant that claimant's copyright was infringed where copies were made for the purpose of exploiting the database abroad.

In less formal circumstances (particularly those involving consumers) the courts have tended to react flexibly in deciding the nature and extent of any licence. For example, it seems that sale of an article to a consumer usually carries with it a licence to repair that article,[61] and sale of a knitting pattern might carry with it an implied licence to the effect that a person can make the pattern for domestic, but not commercial, purposes.[62] Where the licence is claimed by a competitor who could have entered formal contractual arrangements but neglected to do so, the courts have been reluctant to imply a licence.[63]

4 MORTGAGES

Like other forms of property, copyrights may be mortgaged, that is assigned as security for a debt.[64] This can be a useful technique that enables copyright owners to raise funds. It has proved to be particularly common where a work is extremely expensive to create, as in the film industry.[65] In this context, a mortgage is achieved by way of an assignment of the copyright by the copyright owner to the mortgagee (lender). This is subject to a condition that the copyright will be reassigned to the mortgagor when the debt is repaid (or, as the law describes this, on 'redemption'). In addition, it is important that the assignment reserves for the mortgagor a right to continue selling copies of the work. This is probably best achieved by reservation of an exclusive licence.[66] Alternatively, copyright can be used as security by way of a charge. While in these circumstance there is no assignment, the chargee gains certain rights over the copyright as security.[67] In the case of both forms of security, the transaction must be in writing and signed by the parties in order to be valid. A mortgage or charge by a company of its copyright must also be registered within 21 days of its creation with the Registrar of Companies, if it is not to be void against the liquidator or a creditor of the company.[68] It has been assumed that a mortgagee has the powers of proprietor and is therefore able to sue infringers,[69] even though, as a matter of practice, the borrower is in a better position to police infringements.

'Securitization' is the name given to a further way of raising money from copyright. Typically, securitization involves selling tranches of (that is, defined periods of entitlement

---

[61] *Solar Thomson v. Barton* [1977] *RPC* 537, 560–1; *Canon Kabushiki Kaisha v. Green Cartridge Co.* [1997] *AC* 728, 735. Cf. *Sony Entertainment Inc v. Owen* [2002] *EMLR* (34) 742, 747 (Jacob J holding that because a licence is territorial, a licensee must prove that a Japanese licence to use a computer game extended to the UK).

[62] *Patricia Roberts v. Candiwear* [1980] *FSR* 352.

[63] *Banier v. News Group* [1997] *FSR* 812; cf. *Express Newspapers v. News (UK)* [1990] *FSR* 359 (tit-for-tat defence).

[64] Copinger, para. 5–190.

[65] M. Henry, 'Mortgages and Charges over Films in the UK' [1992] *Ent LR* 115.

[66] On the importance and delicacy of the terms of the licence, see M. Antingham, 'Safe as Houses? Using Copyright Works as Security for Debt Finance' (Mar. 1998) 78 *Copyright World* 31, 32.

[67] Copinger, para. 5–193 seems to suggest that such a charge is equitable. While there is no definitional provision equivalent to PA s. 130, there seems no reason why it should not be legal.

[68] Companies Act 1985, ss. 395 and 396.   [69] Copinger, para. 5–191.

over) the rights to royalties accruing from bundles of copyrights: a well-known example being in relation to David Bowie's recordings. The reasons for creating these financial arrangements stem from the desire to exchange future possible income for immediate capital, which will facilitate reinvestment of that capital in new projects.[70]

5 TESTAMENTARY DISPOSITIONS

Because copyright is personal property, it is capable of passing on the death of the proprietor either by will or according to the rules applicable in cases of intestacy. In the case of the death of one co-proprietor, because they hold copyright as tenants in common (rather than as joint tenants), the share of the deceased co-owner passes along with the rest of their estate.[71] A presumption exists that, where a work is unpublished and a bequest is made of a document or other material thing containing the work, the bequest is to be construed as including the copyright in the work, insofar as the testator was the owner of the copyright immediately before their death.[72]

6 BANKRUPTCY

On bankruptcy, copyright passes to the trustee in bankruptcy by operation of law.[73] Where a court appoints a receiver to sell assets, both the appointment and subsequent sales by the receiver will involve transfers 'by operation of law' and therefore need not comply with the formal requirements.[74] Where copyright has been assigned in return for a royalty and the assignor subsequently becomes insolvent, that right also vests in the bankrupt's trustee in bankruptcy.[75]

7 COMPULSORY LICENCES

In general, if copyright owners choose not to allow others to exploit their rights then that is their prerogative.[76] However, in certain exceptional circumstances, the law will intervene to force the copyright owner to license the work and require the 'licensee' to pay a fee. The basis for such action varies, as do the conditions on which the law permits the copyright owner's wishes to be overridden. Provisions of this nature are called 'compulsory licences'. In jurisprudential terms, the grant of a compulsory licence converts a property rule into a liability rule.[77] Compulsory licences can arise either as a result of various provisions in the 1988 Act or through the general powers of the European Commission. We discuss these in turn.

---

[70] See A. Wilkinson, 'Securitization in the Music Industry' (Dec. 1998), 86 *Copyright World* 26.

[71] *Lauri v. Renad* [1892] 3 *Ch* 402, 412–13. Cf. Copinger, para. 5.165–6.

[72] CDPA s. 93 and Sched. 1, para. 30. Cf. *Re Dickens* [1935] 1 *Ch* 267.

[73] Laddie *et al.*, para. 12.13; Copinger, para. 5.71.

[74] *Murray v. King* [1986] *FSR* 116, 124, 130, 137 (FCA).   [75] *PRS v. Rowland* [1997] 3 *All ER* 336.

[76] *Oscar Bronner v. Mediaprint*, Case C–7/97 [1998] *ECR* I–7791, 7811 (AG, para. 56).

[77] See further R. Merges, 'Contracting into Liability Rules: Intellectual Property Rights and Collective Rights Organizations' (1996) 84 *California LR* 1293.

7.1 COMPULSORY LICENCES IN THE UNITED KINGDOM

Compulsory licences are only made available under British law in a small number of specifically defined circumstances. One reason why so few non-voluntary licences exist in the United Kingdom is because the international standards that the United Kingdom has committed itself to are generally incompatible with compulsory licensing. Although two provisions of the Berne Convention explicitly permit the national legislature to grant such licences,[78] the United Kingdom no longer takes advantages of these provisions. As regards rights in phonograms, the Rome Convention intimates that compulsory licences may only be imposed as regards the broadcasting or communication to the public of phonograms.[79]

Another reason for the limited circumstances in which compulsory licences are available is that they are generally seen as unsatisfactory when compared with full property rights. This is because, in contrast to exclusive property rights, the existence and terms of compulsory licences require some administrative procedure, which is costly and time-consuming when compared to free-market negotiations. Critics of the compulsory licence also complain that the value of a licence can only ever be determined accurately by negotiations in the marketplace. It is also argued that compulsory licences unfairly deprive the copyright holder of the most significant element of their rights, namely the right to bargain.

There are no common characteristics that explain the circumstances in which compulsory licences are granted.[80] In some cases they are granted in response to past practices of 'abuse', usually where that abuse either prevented the production of a product for which there was a clear demand, or where the evidence showed that the copyright holder had imposed unjustifiable restrictive conditions. This is true of the compulsory licence relating to the publication of television schedules,[81] which was introduced to end the practice by television companies of only licensing the publication of daily listings, so that they could reserve for their own subsidiaries the market for weekly guides.[82] After a Monopoly and Mergers Commission Report,[83] the Broadcasting Act 1990 introduced provisions entitling publishers, once certain conditions are satisfied, to reproduce that information.[84] On other occasions, compulsory licences are granted where changes in market conditions unduly strengthen the copyright owner's interest. This sort of consideration explains the introduction of compulsory licences where copyright had lapsed but has been revived by the Duration Regulations.[85]

---

[78] Berne Art. 11*bis*(2); Berne Art. 13 (aka the 'mechanical licence'). Berne Art. 17 is not intended to permit any general system of compulsory licences but to cover such things as the maintenance of public order and morality. See Ricketson, para. 9.72.

[79] Rome Art. 12. Note also Art. 15(2).   [80] For a full review, see Copinger, ch. 29.

[81] Broadcasting Act 1990, ss. 175, 176 and Sched. 17.   [82] *ITP v. Time Out* [1984] *FSR* 64.

[83] MMC, *The British Broadcasting Commission and Independent Television Publications: A Report on the Policies and Practices of the BBC and ITP of limiting the publication of advance programme information* (1995) (Cmnd. 9614).

[84] *News Group Newspapers v. ITP* [1993] *RPC* 173. From 1946 to 1990, the owners of copyright in sound recordings (through PPL) insisted that broadcasters should limit the amount of time that they spent playing their recordings (so called 'needle-time'). This was done to induce such broadcasters to employ their own musicians. A Monopoly and Mergers Commission Report concluded that these restrictions were an anti–competitive practice that adversely affected radio licensees and that it should be abandoned: MMC, *Collective Licensing: A report on certain practices in the collective licensing of public performances and broadcasting rights in sound recordings* (1988) (Cm. 530). In response, the Broadcasting Act 1990 introduced provisions making a compulsory licence available against a licensing body which imposes restrictions on either the total or the proportion of air-time in which such recordings can be played: CDPA ss. 135A to 135G. The terms of one such licence were settled in *The Association of Independent Radio Companies v. Phonographic Performance* [1994] *RPC* 143.

[85] Duration of Copyright and Rights in Performances Regulations 1995 (SI 1995/3297), r. 24(1).

7.2 COMPULSORY LICENCES ORDERED BY THE EC

Compulsory licences may also be made available by the European Commission if a copyright owner is found to have violated Article 82 EC (formerly Article 86 of the Treaty) which prohibits the 'abuse' of a 'dominant position'.[86] *RTE and Independent Television Publications v. Commission* (known as the 'Magill' case),[87] involved a battle between an Irish broadcaster (RTE) who produced copyright-protected television listings, but only licensed them on a daily basis (in order to reserve to themselves the market for weekly guides to their own programmes), and a person wishing to publish a comprehensive weekly guide. The Commission held this refusal to license the copyright to be an abuse of the dominant position of the broadcaster, and ordered the broadcasters to license the listings.[88] The Court of Justice affirmed the legality of the action by the Commission. The substantive basis of this power to intervene—which it should be noted is limited to exceptional circumstances—is discussed in Chapter 12.[89] As Microsoft has recently discovered, failure to comply with a Commission decision that it should grant a licence can result in a very substantial fine.[90]

8 TECHNOLOGICAL PROTECTION MEASURES

As already mentioned, copyright works have traditionally been exploited by the manufacture and sale of duplicated copies (where the processes of manufacturing and distribution have been controlled by the copyright owner). In light of the emergence of digital communication technologies, and digital reproduction, many copyright owners are concerned that continued use of such a traditional model of exploitation will expose them to undue levels of infringement. More specifically, there is a concern that if digital versions of works are made available, it will result in widespread unauthorized copying, particularly by individual users in private. Since these digital copies will be perfect, this is seen as a much greater threat than that previously posed by photocopiers, for example. Relying on copyright against widespread copying by individuals is not a realistic option. So copyright holders have sought techniques outside copyright to protect their interests: in particular through the use of so-called 'technological measures of protection'. That is, they have sought to make available works only when they have additional protection systems through technologies which prohibit access, encrypt, or control copying. A familiar example of such a technology is the encryption of satellite broadcast signals and the provision to authorized service subscribers of cards that enable the use of decoding technology. A second is the 'content scrambling system' used to protect DVDs and ensure they can only be used on authorized players with CSS descrambling software. A third example is that of the 'Series Copyright Management System' introduced in the 1980s by record companies which allowed for the making of first-generation but not second-generation copies of sounds embodied on Digital Audio Tape (DAT)—that is, copies of copies. The system worked by triggering a device fitted in electrical goods.

Technological measures are regarded as critically important for the so-called 'information society', because the feared duplication of works is thought likely to take place in private, and

---

[86] I. Goraere, *The Use and Abuse of Intellectual Property Rights* (1996), 135–50.

[87] [1995] 4 *CMLR* 18.   [88] *Magill TV Guide/ITP, BBC and RTE* (1989) *OJ L* 78/43.

[89] Note also *IMS Health v. Commission*, T–184/01 R [2002] 4 *CMLR* 58, where the Commission had also ordered a compulsory licence, but the CFI overturned the interim measure.

[90] €899 million: EC, Press Release IP/08/318 (Brussels, 27 Feb 2008).

thus be impossible to police. Technological measures provide an opportunity to police private uses, by forcing users to enter contractual arrangements before they can use or copy works. If users do not contact the copyright owner, they do not get a set of keys to open the technological locks. However, the potential for technological measures is much more than just operating to solve the problem of the digital shift in replication from public to private arenas. It poses the possibility of radical transformation in the way works are delivered. For example, in a technological fantasy world a person would not have to buy a whole book: they could just buy a copy of Chapter 1 and, if they liked it, then buy the rest (such a user need only spend £1 rather than £8 on all the books they buy and end up not liking). Similarly, technological measures might mean a person could buy a digital newspaper for a single read with the advantage that the proprietor would not need to set the price on the basis that other readers will look at the newspaper (and so will not buy their own copy). The potential of technological measures is to enable us all to get works delivered in the form we want, with costs to the user tailored more closely to the use of the work. Everybody should be better off.

The use of technological measures to support copyright, however, is not a complete answer to the problems of digital distribution and replication. This is because for every lock, there is some enthusiast willing to pick it. So those wishing to rely on technological measures have sought government support for the use of such measures through the passage of laws prohibiting circumvention of the measures. Governments—particularly the US Government and the European Commission—have been supportive.[91] They argue that, by providing protection now, copyright owners will be given appropriate incentives to develop such systems. If such legal protection were not provided, that investment is vulnerable to being undermined by the rapid spread of circumventing technology. So there has been felt to be a need to act immediately. The problem with formulating legal principles to prevent circumvention, however, is that it is the locking systems currently being used that are crude. Strong protection of crude systems carries two problems: it may give users of technological protection too much control (or control of public domain dimensions of content), and it provides developers with little reason to make the systems more sophisticated.[92]

The 1988 Act, as amended, contains a formidable array of civil and criminal provisions dealing with situations where a person facilitates access to works which the person concerned is not entitled to use or receive. Some of these relate to the circumvention of effective technological measures applied to copyright works other than computer programs, and are designed to implement Article 6 of the Information Society Directive.[93] Others, somewhat less prescriptive in scope, apply only to computer programs (and implement Article 7(1)(c) of the Software Directive). The third category, in sections 297–9, relate to reception of transmissions (and

---

[91] S. Dusollier, 'Technological Measures and Exceptions in the European Directive of 2001: An Empty Promise' (2003) 34 *IIC* 62. For an examination of the US provisions under the Digital Millennium Copyright Act 1998, see D. Nimmer, 'A Riff on Fair Use in the Digital Millennium Copyright Act' (2000) 148 *University of Pennsylvania Law Review* 673.

[92] Not surprisingly, therefore, the formulation of legislative provision in the Information Society Directive 'caused more controversy than any other in the Copyright Directive': M. Hart, 'The Copyright in the Information Society Directive: An Overview' [2002] *EIPR* 58, 61.

[93] CDPA s. 297ZA(1), (6); s. 296 ZD(1), (8) (copyright works (other than computer programs), performances, database right, publication right); Info. Soc. Dir., Recital 50 (without prejudice to Software Directive). In turn, Art. 6 implements Art. 11 of the WCT and Art. 18 of the WPPT. However, they go beyond the requirements of those treaties in breadth (since they apply also to broadcasting organizations, publication right, and *sui generis* database right), and—more importantly—depth. The Directive goes beyond acts of circumvention to cover devices and services which enable circumvention.

implement an EC Directive giving legal protection to services based on 'conditional access').[94] We consider these provisions in Chapter 13. Whether these provisions will give copyright owners the confidence to exploit works, particularly in electronic form, by utilizing technological protection, remains to be seen.

9 COLLECTING SOCIETIES

One of the central problems facing copyright owners who wish to exploit their works is how to monitor or police infringements. Where the main form of copyright was the book and the main mode of exploitation the sale of printed copies, this policing (typically undertaken by a publisher) was ad hoc and depended on monitoring activities in the marketplace. However, as copyright expanded to encompass a wider array of subject matter and (particularly ephemeral) uses, the problems of policing copyright have changed. One of the main mechanisms developed by copyright owners to monitor infringement has been collective systems of management and enforcement of rights, in particular, the 'collecting society'.[95]

Collective administration is a system whereby certain rights are administered for the benefit of authors and/or copyright owners. The organizations that administer the rights are empowered to authorize various specified uses of their members' works, normally by way of a licence.[96] The essential characteristic of these arrangements is that they are able to negotiate and act without individual consultation. In most cases the copyright owner assigns their rights to the society. Where this occurs the rights are pooled so as to create a repertoire of works at the disposal of potential users.

The main UK collecting societies are:

(i)   The Performing Right Society (PRS), formed in 1914, which administers as assignee the performing and broadcasting rights in music and song lyrics. PRS annual income from all sources is in the region of £200 million.[97]

(ii)   The Mechanical-Copyright Protection Society (MCPS), formed in 1924, which administers as agent the 'mechanical rights' in music and song lyrics, that is, the right to make a sound recording (part of the reproduction right).

(iii) Phonographic Performance Limited (PPL), formed in 1934, which administers as assignee the performing and broadcasting rights in sound recordings, and from 2007 (when it merged with PAMRA and AURA) has also represented performers.

(iv)   Video Performance Limited (VPL), which administers, as agent, the performing, and broadcasting rights in videos.

(v)   Authors' Licensing and Collecting Society (ALCS), formed in 1977, which, inter alia, collects fees for writers from the retransmission by cable of all terrestrial channels.

---

[94] Directive 98/84 EC of the European Parliament and of the Council of 20 Nov. 1998 on the Legal Protection of Services based on, or consisting of, Conditional Access.

[95] For commentary, see Copinger, ch. 28; Laddie et al., paras. 15.14–15.38.

[96] M. Freegard, 'Collective Administration' (1985), Copyright 443. A similar definition can be found in Satellite Dir., Art. 1(4). Note also the definition of 'licensing body' in CDPA s. 116(2).

[97] On the history of the PRS, see T. Ehrlich, Harmonious Alliance: A History of the Performing Right Society (1989). For details of the PRS see <http://www.prs.co.uk>.

(vi)   Copyright Licensing Agency (CLA), formed in 1982, represents authors' and publishers' licensing societies (including ALCS) with regard to reprographic reproduction. It enters blanket licences with educational authorities and universities.

(vii)   The Design and Artists' Copyright Society (DACS), formed in 1983, administers, as agents, the reproduction rights for painters, printmakers, sculptors, and photographers, as well as the new resale royalty right.

(viii)   Educational Recording Agency (ERA) and Open University Educational Enterprises, which license educational establishments to record off-air under schemes which have been certified.[98]

(ix)   Artists Collecting Society CIC, formed in 2006 to administer the resale royalty right (in competition with DACS).

9.1 ORGANIZATION

As collecting societies are private organizations that have emerged in response to particular commercial environments, there is no great uniformity to their organizational structures. Nevertheless, it is worth considering the different dimensions of some of the existing societies.

9.1.1 Membership terms

In terms of copyright owner–society relations, the relevant relationship will be determined in the membership agreement and the rules of the society. To ensure that each collecting society is capable of licensing the relevant right on behalf of the copyright owner, the owner has to assign the right to the society or appoint the society as its agent. The scope of any such assignment or agency will depend on the proposed function of the society. For example, a copyright owner joining the PRS is required to assign the 'small rights' relating to non-dramatic performances. The 'grand rights' relating to dramatic performances, which are not included, are administered by individual agreements. The rules of a society might also make provision for a member to assign rights in relation to works not in existence at the time of joining. A society may have different categories of membership (for example, author members and publisher members). As a member, a copyright owner will have power to vote at meetings and thus to influence the way the society operates. A collecting society will distribute any licensing revenues it collects in accordance with the rules of the society. Often this will involve some kind of sampling mechanism that enables the society to estimate the amount that each member is proportionally entitled to. Usually a society will first deduct its administration expenses. In some jurisdictions a portion of the revenue is used for 'cultural purposes' (for example to fund indigenous music culture in the country making the deduction) and for pension and welfare payments.[99] Provisions exist within the rules of a society specifying the circumstances in which a person may leave the society, which will usually require a substantial period of notice.

---

[98] CDPA s. 35; Copyright (Certification of Licensing Scheme for Educational Recording of Broadcasts) (Educational Recording Agency) Order 1990 (SI 1990/879, as amended by SI 1996/191), and Copyright (Certification of Licensing Scheme for Educational Recording of Broadcasts) (Open University) Order 2003 (SI 2003/187).

[99] See A. Harcourt, 'The Unlawful Deduction Levied upon UK Composers' Performing Rights Income' (Oct. 1996) 64 *Copyright World* 15 (criticizing the practice of European performing rights societies in deducting up to 10% of income in this way).

9.1.2 Licensing arrangements

The collecting societies enter into negotiations with copyright users, either as associations of users or on an individual basis. Negotiations with associations of users will often result in the establishment of tariffs.[100] Sometimes a society–user agreement will cover more than just a licence fee. Some associations of users will involve themselves in ensuring that licence fees are paid by their members, or help in other ways with the administration in return for a reduced tariff. Although the terms of licences will vary, it is common for collecting societies to grant a 'blanket' licence entitling users to use any work in the repertoire of the licensing body without restriction.[101]

9.2 ASSESSMENT

At a practical level, collecting societies are a convenient way of resolving some of the difficulties faced by copyright owners and users in reaching appropriate arrangements.[102] Collecting societies are useful insofar as they provide users with a focal point to locate and transact with copyright owners. Collecting societies reduce the 'transaction costs' that would otherwise exist in ascertaining and negotiating individual licences with individual copyright owners. This is particularly important where a user wishes to utilize a large number of copyright works, so that transacting on an individual basis would be time-consuming and costly.[103] Moreover, where the society grants a user a blanket licence, this offers users a degree of flexibility. For example, where a blanket licence is granted to a disco or a radio station, it means that they do not need to determine in advance the works they are going to play.

For the copyright owner, collective administration relieves an otherwise impossible burden of policing and enforcing rights. It also provides copyright owners with a bargaining power that they would not possess as individuals. Moreover, the possibility of collective administration has enabled owners to argue for the extension of rights in relation to subject matter that might not otherwise have been protected on the basis that it was unenforceable.

Probably the most interesting thing about collecting societies is the way in which their emergence represents a significant shift in the character of copyright. As Thomas Streeter has observed, with collective administration copyright loses much of its character as a property right exploited through distribution of copies bought and sold in the marketplace. Instead, copyright becomes more like the legal underpinning of an institutional bureaucracy that attempts to simulate a market through statistical mechanisms. Each copyright loses its individuality and the 'property form' is replaced by a liability form. In effect, collecting societies turn an author's property right into a right to receive welfare payments and a user's licence fee into a tax upon their activities.[104]

[100] For example, at sports grounds where music is played incidentally the PRS receives a rate of £1.56 per 1,000 persons admitted; whereas for pop concerts the PRS charges 3% of box-office receipts. See *BSB v. PRS* [1998] *RPC* 467 (para. 4.29).

[101] While the MCPS operates a blanket licence for re-recordings, first recording requires individual licensing: *BPI v. MCPS* [1993] *EMLR* 86, 139.

[102] G. Davies, 'The Public Interest in Collective Administration of Rights' (1989) *Copyright* 81.

[103] J. Fujitani, 'Controlling the Market Power of Performing Rights Societies: An Administrative Substitute for Antitrust Regulation' (1984) 72 *California LR* 103, 106 (breaking down the transaction costs in identifying and locating the copyright owner, obtaining the information necessary to negotiate a price, and transaction time costs).

[104] T. Streeter, 'Broadcast Copyright and the Bureaucratization of Property' (1992) 10 *Cardozo Art & Entertainment LJ* 567, 570, 576.

9.3 INTERNATIONAL DIMENSIONS

Although collecting societies tend to operate at the national level, they form part of a global network of collecting agencies. For example, while performing rights are administered in the UK by the PRS, there are equivalent societies in the USA (BMI, ASCAP), Australia (APRA), Germany (GEMA), France (SACEM), Belgium (SABAM), and so on. Typically, there will be 'reciprocal representation contracts' between national copyright management societies. Under these arrangements, one national society (A) undertakes, on a reciprocal basis, to manage the rights attached to the repertoire of a foreign society (B) within its sphere of operation, normally its national territory. The society (A) collects royalties on behalf of the foreign society (B), pursues infringers, takes any necessary proceedings in respect of infringement, and transfers sums collected to (B). Effectively, these agreements can mean that a particular national society controls within the territory the entire world repertory of works.

9.4 EUROPEAN DEVELOPMENTS

These national arrangements—under pressure from the Community authorities, as well as business pressures—are giving way to more flexible options. As markets for particular uses have become more and more transnational, attempts have been made to develop Community-wide licences (so that users do not have to get permission on a territory-by-territory basis). For such Community-wide licensing to be possible, the collecting Societies must agree that they can grant licences permitting uses outside their territories—so, for example, that GEMA can authorize web-casting in the UK or the PRS–MCPS can do the same for Germany. This sets the collecting societies up in competition with one another, which from one perspective could make them operate more efficiently. However, if collecting societies compete amongst themselves for users by reducing authors' (and copyright owners') remuneration, one might wonder whether the overall effect is in the public interest. One attempt to avoid this kind of competition was proposed by the music performing rights societies in an agreement that would have permitted all collecting societies to authorize Europe-wide licensing of public performance right, but would have required users to seek permission from their local society. The Commission doubted whether this was compatible with competition law, and has encouraged collecting societies to compete with one another.[105] A recent report claims there has been significant movement towards Europe-wide licensing.[106]

---

[105] EC, Commission Staff Working Document, *Impact Assessment Reforming Cross-Border Collective Management of Copyright and Related Rights For Legitimate On-line Music Services,* SEC (2005) 1254 (Brussels, 11 Oct. 2005) 9; EC, *Communication from the Commission to the Council, the European Parliament and the European Economic and Social Committee: The Management of Copyright and Related Rights in the Internal Market* COM(2004) 261 final (Brussels 16 Apr 2004) 6–9.

[106] See also EC, *Monitoring of the 2005 Music Online Recommendation,* (Brussels, 7 Feb 2008).

12

LIMITS ON EXPLOITATION

CHAPTER CONTENTS

1 INTRODUCTION

The terms and conditions under which a copyright work is transferred or exploited are usually determined contractually by the parties. In this chapter we look at the exceptional situations where the law controls the way those rights are exploited. We begin by looking at the various mechanisms that are used to regulate contracts between authors and entrepreneurs. We then go on to look at the impact that British and European competition law has on copyright owners' ability to exploit their copyright. In turn we look at the ways in which copyright contracts are regulated in respect to users of copyright. Finally, we look at the various controls that are imposed on collecting societies.

Before looking at these, it is important to note that there are many other restrictions placed on the owners' ability to exploit and use the copyright work that we will not look at here.[1] Although copyright is described as a 'property right' and therefore might be expected to give absolute dominion, copyright law operates as an exclusionary right: it prevents all parties (other than the copyright holder) from exploiting the work. Copyright, however, does not confer on the proprietor of the copyright any positive rights to make and sell copies of the work. Consequently, the copyright owner will be subject to the regulatory regimes in the field in question (relating for example to the showing of films or broadcasts), and criminal laws (such as obscenity or public order legislation). Another factor that may affect the ability of a copyright owner to exploit a work is the rights that exist in any underlying works. For example, where the owner of the copyright in an English translation of a French novel

---

[1] The moral rights of attribution and integrity operate as techniques of control over the manner in which a work is exploited, and thus are frequently akin to statutory implied contract terms. See Ch. 10.

wishes to exploit the copyright in the translation, it will be necessary for them to obtain the permission of the owner of copyright, if any, in the French novel that has been translated. With some copyright works, such as films or multimedia works, a whole host of prior right owners will have to be identified, approached, and persuaded to consent to the exploitation.[2] It should be noted that one joint owner may not exploit the work without the licence of the other owners.[3]

2 LIMITS ON AGREEMENTS BETWEEN AUTHORS AND ENTREPRENEURS

This section considers the extent to which UK law will interfere to regulate the terms of transactions between authors and entrepreneurs, either to protect the psychological link between the author and their work, or to protect an author's financial interests. A number of other jurisdictions, notably France and Germany, include within their copyright legislation provisions relating to the interpretation of copyright contracts. They also impose overriding terms that protect the financial interests of authors.[4] In the United Kingdom, there are very few provisions specifically directed at authors. The legal validity of such arrangements is generally dependent upon the law of contract, not the law of copyright. In the United Kingdom, the basic principle is that a contract freely entered into by an adult is binding. The court will not reopen the contract merely because the court thinks that the terms are unreasonable or unfair. The main way in which authors' interests are protected derives less from legal regulation than from collective processes such as union activity or the promotion of standard contracts like those formulated by the Society of Authors and the Writers' Guild.[5] Individual authors and artists are also better able to secure reasonable terms by the engagement of literary agents.[6]

Having said this, a contract entered into between an author and entrepreneurs may be regulated in a number of ways. On occasions the general contractual doctrines of undue influence and restraint of trade have been used to protect particularly vulnerable authors from the more egregious of practices. In other cases the courts may interfere with the sanctity of author–entrepreneur contracts where they are anti-competitive (either under domestic or European law). After looking at these, we will examine the specific terms that are implied by statute into certain contracts.

---

[2] Sometimes it will be impossible to trace the relevant copyright holders, in which case the exploiter might take out insurance, pay notional royalties into a fund, or simply take a risk. Cf. CDPA s. 190 (performers).

[3] CDPA s. 173(2); *Lauri v. Renad* [1892] 3 *Ch* 402; *Powell v. Head* (1879) 12 *Ch D* 686; *Cescinsky v. Routledge* [1916] 2 *KB* 325, 330.

[4] See L. Bently, *Between a Rock and a Hard Place* (2002); W. Cornish, 'The Author as Risk-Sharer' (2002) 26 *Columbia Journal of Law & the Arts* 1; G. D'Agostino, 'Copyright Treatment of Freelance Works in the Digital Era' (2002) 19 *Santa Clara Computer & High Technology Law Journal* 37; W. Nordemann, 'A Revolution of Copyright in Germany' 49 (2002) *Jurnal of the Copyright Society of the USA* 1041.

[5] Even here, however, competition law may limit collective self-help. In *Re: Royal Institute of British Architects*, Case ref GP/908 (March 2003), the OFT held that 'fee guidance' to its members infringed the Chapter 1 prohibition, though a collation of historical price trends did not.

[6] See D. De Freitas, 'Copyright Contracts: A Study of the Terms of Contracts for the Use of Works Protected by Copyright under the Legal System in Common Law Countries' [1991] *Copyright* 222. For an example, see B. Nyman, 'The Author–Publisher Agreement' [1995] *Ent LR* 127.

2.1 UNDUE INFLUENCE

If a disadvantageous bargain is the result of the exercise of undue influence the court may set the bargain aside. An extreme example would be where an author assigned copyright to a publisher because of threats made by the publisher. However, the court's power to interfere extends beyond those extreme scenarios to all situations where a 'person in a position of domination has used that position to obtain unfair advantage for himself, and so caused injury to the person relying on his authority or aid'.[7] For the courts to interfere in the sanctity of the contract, two elements need to be satisfied. *First,* it must be shown that the parties are in a relationship in which one person has influence over another. *Second,* it must be shown that the influence was used to bring about a 'manifestly disadvantageous transaction'.[8] If undue influence exists, the contract is then voidable, and copyright assigned thereunder may be revested in the author. It seems that since the contract is voidable (as opposed to void), contractual dealings with bona fide purchasers which take place before the contract is avoided will remain binding.

In order to have a contract set aside on the basis of undue influence, it must first be shown that the parties are in a relationship in which one person has influence over another. That is, it is necessary to demonstrate a 'dominating influence'. The most common situation where this occurs is where the parties are in a fiduciary relationship; that is, one of trust. Where the relationship between the parties is deemed by the court to be 'fiduciary', the existence of a dominating influence is presumed. In most cases of copyright assignments, for example a publishing agreement, such a fiduciary relationship is unlikely to exist because there will rarely be any pre-existing relationship. An example of an exception to this is provided by *Elton John v. James*.[9] There Elton John sought to avoid an agreement tying him and fellow songwriter Bernie Taupin to a publishing arrangement with James for six years. Nicholls J held that there was a 'dominating influence' even though the acquaintance of John, Taupin, and James was short before the publishing agreement was signed, because James 'really took charge', while the writers were young and eager and received no independent advice, reposing trust 'in a man of stature in the industry that he would treat them fairly'.

A similar position was reached in *O'Sullivan v. Management Agency*.[10] This decision arose as a result of the fact that a young and then unknown composer named Gilbert O'Sullivan entered into an exclusive management agreement with the defendant. The defendant operated through a number of companies with whom O'Sullivan entered into publishing and other agreements. O'Sullivan later sought a declaration that these contracts were void and unenforceable on the ground, inter alia, that they had been obtained by undue influence. Mars-Jones J held that the defendant was in a fiduciary position and thus the agreements were presumed to have been obtained by undue influence. The associated companies were equally subject to fiduciary obligations.[11] Although there was no pressure on O'Sullivan to execute the agreements that did not matter. As Fox LJ said, on appeal, '[t]he fiduciary relationship existed. The onus was then upon those asserting the validity of the agreements to show that they were the consequence of the free exercise of Mr O'Sullivan's will in the light of full information regarding the transaction. That has not been done. He had no independent advice about these matters at all'.[12]

---

[7] *National Westminster v. Morgan* [1985] 2 WLR 588, 599 (quoting Lord Shaw).

[8] The relationship need not be one of domination: *Goldworthy v. Brickell* [1987] *Ch* 378, 404–6.

[9] *Elton John v. James* (1985) [1991] *FSR* 397.   [10] [1985] *QB* 428.   [11] Ibid, 448 (Dunn LJ).

[12] On appeal, the central issue was to determine the appropriate remedy. Dunn, Fox, and Waller LJJ held that the court should try to achieve 'practical justice' and found that the assignments of the copyright should be set aside, the copyrights be returned to the author, and the manager be required to account for profits made from

In order to have a contract set aside on the basis of undue influence, it must also be shown that the dominating influence was used to bring about a transaction that was 'manifestly disadvantageous'. The problem that confronts authors and artists here is that in many cases their grievances are collective, rather than individual, in nature. Consequently, the possibility exists for an assignee or exclusive licensee to deny that there is disadvantage by referring to agreements with other authors and the practices of other entrepreneurs. It should be noted that this tactic does not always work. For example, in *Elton John v. James* some of the publishing agreements were found to be unfair even though James acted in a bona fide manner, imposing terms standard in the trade. In that case (as with the *O'Sullivan* decision), the court was influenced by the fact that the royalty under the contract was less than that paid to other 'unknown' artists.[13]

2.2 RESTRAINT OF TRADE

The second way in which vulnerable authors are protected is via the doctrine of 'restraint of trade'. As it suggests, this doctrine reflects a general policy of contract law that a person should be able to practise their trade.[14] Contracts that restrict this right will be scrutinized by the courts to ensure that they are justified.[15] In these circumstances the courts have said that the terms must be no more than is reasonably required to protect the legitimate interests of the promisee and the public interest.[16] This doctrine has been important in relation to long-term contracts that are common in the music industry.

The impact of the doctrine of restraint of trade can be seen in *Schroeder Music Publishing Co. v. Macaulay*,[17] where the House of Lords held that an agreement between a songwriter and a publisher was invalid because it was in restraint of trade. The agreement was in a standard form and required the songwriter to assign copyright in his works to the publisher. The most important factor was that the duration of the agreement was to be five years and, if the royalties for those years exceeded £5,000, a further five-year period. In effect, the songwriter was bound to the publisher for ten years. However, the publisher was under no obligation to exploit the songs. Lord Reid suggested that even if there was a term requiring the publisher to use its best endeavours to promote the composer's work, this would be of little use to the composer. He said, 'if no satisfactory positive undertaking by the publisher can be devised, it appears to me to be an unreasonable restraint to tie the composer for this period of years so that his work will be sterilized and he can earn nothing from his abilities as a composer if the publisher chooses not to publish'.[18] Only a clause permitting the composer to terminate the agreement could save it. Lord Diplock said that the doctrine of restraint of trade was part of a general jurisdiction to protect parties from unconscionable contracts. In these circumstances, the relevant question was whether the bargain was fair, that is, 'whether the restrictions are both reasonably necessary for the protection of the legitimate interests of the promisee and commensurate

---

them, but subject to deduction of a service fee for his contribution to the composer's success: ibid, 458–9, 466–9, 471–3. See, generally, J. Tatt, 'Music Publishing and Recording Contracts in Perspective' [1987] *EIPR* 132.

[13] *Elton John, v. James* (1985) [1991] *FSR* 397, 453.

[14] *Schroeder Music Publishing Co. v. Macaulay* [1974] 3 *All ER* 616, 621 (Lord Reid). See also below at pp. 1035–6.

[15] Certain categories may be excluded from the doctrine: *Esso Petroleum Co. v. Harper's Garage* [1968] *AC* 269; *Panayiotou v. Sony Music Entertainment* [1994] *EMLR* 229, 320.

[16] This is referred to as the 'Nordenfelt test' after *Nordenfelt v. Maxim Nordenfelt* [1894] *AC* 535.

[17] *Schroeder Music Publishing Co. v. Macaulay* [1974] 3 *All ER* 616.   [18] Ibid, 622.

with the benefits secured to the promisor under the contract'.[19] Lord Diplock's reliance on the broad notion of inequality of bargaining power, after receiving a positive reception,[20] has been largely ignored in subsequent cases which have preferred to rely on the more concrete doctrines of restraint of trade, rather than develop general principles of this sort.[21]

Another situation where restraint of trade has been used to protect an author is in *Zang Tumb Tuum v. Holly Johnson*,[22] which dealt with a publishing agreement and a recording agreement that the group Frankie Goes to Hollywood signed with Perfect and ZTT respectively. The publishing agreement was for five years and the recording agreement possibly for nine years. Soon after the group became successful, Holly Johnson left the group. ZTT tried to enforce a 'leaving member' clause in the recording contract and sought an injunction to restrain him from working for another record company. ZTT's action failed. Applying the doctrine of restraint of trade, the Court of Appeal set aside the recording contract and the publishing agreement. The Court was particularly influenced by the duration of the agreement: Dillon LJ said that 'stringent provisions such as many of those in the recording agreement may be justifiable in an agreement of short duration. But the onus must, in my judgment, be on the recording company to justify the length and the one-sidedness of the provisions as to its duration in this recording agreement'.[23] The Court held that ZTT had failed to justify the terms.

If, in the light of these cases, the doctrine of restraint of trade seems to offer substantial protection to authors and artists, it is important to observe the doctrine's limitations, which were highlighted in *Panayiotou v. Sony Music Entertainment*.[24] Panayiotou, a songwriter and singer who worked under the name George Michael, sought to have the recording agreement which he had entered into with Sony in 1988 set aside. The background to the agreement was relatively complicated. In 1982 as a member of the group Wham!, Michael signed an agreement with a record company called Innervision. After some initial success, the validity of the agreement was called into question. Subsequent legal proceedings were settled and in 1984 a new agreement was entered into between Wham! and Sony (who had been licensees of Innervision). This agreement placed Wham! under a potential obligation to record eight albums. When the group disbanded in 1986, Sony exercised its 'leaving member clause' which was to the effect that the 1984 agreement was to continue to bind Michael as an individual recording artist. After the success of Michael's first solo album (*Faith*), the 1984 agreement was renegotiated and replaced by a new agreement with Sony (the 1988 agreement). This also bound Michael, if the defendant so wished, to deliver a further eight albums and was to endure for fifteen years. As part of the renegotiation, Michael was given much improved financial terms. As a result of changes in the corporate structure of the defendant company, Michael became disenchanted and in 1992 sought to release himself from his obligations to Sony.

Parker J rejected Michael's claim that the 1988 agreement should be set aside. The main ground for rejecting George Michael's claim was that it was contrary to public policy to seek to reopen a previously compromised action, and that the 1984 agreement was such a compromise:[25] the 1988 agreement being based on the 1984 predecessor, was covered by the

---

[19] Ibid, 623.   [20] For example *Clifford Davis v. WEA Records* [1975] 1 *All ER* 237.

[21] *NatWest v. Morgan*, note 7 above (rejecting inequality of bargaining power and unconscionability) and *Union Eagle v. Golden Achievement* [1997] 2 *All ER* 215 (describing as 'beguiling heresy').

[22] *Zang Tumb Tuum v. Johnson* [1993] *EMLR* 61.   [23] Ibid, 73.

[24] *Panayiotou*, note 15 above. For criticism, see A. Coulthard, 'George Michael v. Sony Music: A Challenge to Artistic Freedom?' (1995) 58 *MLR* 731.

[25] For criticism of this aspect of the case, see Coulthard, ibid, 736 (pointing out that the action compromised by the 1984 agreement did not involve the defendant, and moreover that the 1984 agreement contained no express promise not to reopen the 1982 agreement).

same policy. However, aware that the case was likely to be appealed,[26] Parker J went on to consider whether, had there been no compromise, the 1988 agreement was an unreasonable restraint of trade. He found that the agreement was restrictive of trade,[27] but that the restraint was reasonable. Although not explicit, Parker J appears to have accepted that the restraint was necessary to protect the defendant's interests, not merely in recouping investment they had placed in Michael, but also the investment they generally made in young artists who turned out to be unsuccessful.[28] Moreover, the restraint was reasonable as regards Michael's interests given the generous remuneration which was to be promised to the artist: the length of the agreement was simply a product of Michael's success. Parker J added that, when Michael's obligations under the 1984 agreement were taken into consideration, the 1988 agreement hardly restrained Michael at all.[29]

The *Panayiotou* case makes it clear that there are limits to the operation of the doctrine of restraint of trade. However, it has not provided any clear markers as to how to determine where those limits are. More specifically, it is unclear what the legitimate interests of a recording or publishing company are, and how the decision is to be made that the obligation (for example, to produce eight albums, rather than three albums, or a five-year deal), is reasonable. Moreover, the case introduced a new limitation on the doctrine through Parker J's final reason for dismissing Michael's claim: Parker J found that Michael, by requesting an 'advance' from Sony in 1992 had affirmed the existence of the contract and could not thereafter argue that it should be set aside.[30] If this approach is followed,[31] authors, artists, and performers who seek to have lengthy or one-sided agreements set aside, will have to take great care to ensure they do not accept the benefit of the agreement after being informed of its potential unenforceability.

2.3 ANTI-COMPETITIVE CONTRACTS

A further ground on which a court might reopen an agreement between an artist and an entrepreneur is on the basis that it is anti-competitive. More specifically, a contract may be declared to be void by virtue of Article 81 EC (formerly Article 85 of the Treaty). As noted in Chapter 1, this renders void all agreements which affect trade between member states and which have the object or effect of distorting competition within the Common Market. The case of *RAI/ Unitel*[32] indicated that an exclusive contract with four opera singers for one operatic work was an agreement between 'undertakings' which might have an 'appreciable effect' on trade between member states and thus might be subject to Article 81. Although the Commission took the view that the agreement concerning the broadcast of the performance of *Don Carlos* at La Scala in Milan was subject to Article 81, the case was settled. As such, it remains unclear when such an agreement would be unlawful.

It seems possible that a contract between an author and an entrepreneur would fall outside the scope of Article 81 because the effect on competition might not be 'appreciable'. Alternatively, as with exclusive distribution agreements, the contract might be justifiable under

---

[26] In fact, no such appeal was heard.

[27] *Panayiotou v. Sony Music Entertainment* [1994] *EMLR* 229, 342. [28] Ibid, 361.

[29] Cf. *Watson v. Prager* [1993] *EMLR* 275. In fact, the 1988 agreement effectively required Michael to produce eight albums, not the six that would have been needed to meet his remaining obligations under the 1984 agreement.

[30] *Panayiotou v. Sony Music Entertainment* [1994] *EMLR* 229, 385–6.

[31] It has been in *Nicholl v. Ryder* [2000] *EMLR* 632. For arguments against the affirmation doctrine, see Coulthard, 'George Michael v. Sony Music', 741–3.

[32] [1978] *OJ L* 157/39; [1978] 3 *CMLR* 306; *12th Report on Competition Policy* 1982, para. 90.

Article 81(3).[33] An argument based on Article 81 was also raised but rejected in *Panayiotou v. Sony Music Entertainment*.[34] Parker J held that the 1988 agreement between Michael and Sony had no effect on trade between member states of the EU because the agreement operated 'worldwide',[35] that because the 1988 agreement replaced the 1984 agreement it in fact had no effect on trade at all,[36] and did not have the object or effect of restricting competition.[37] Moreover, because the agreement involved an assignment of copyright in the sound recordings to Sony, Parker J held that it fell within Article 295 (formerly Article 222 of the Treaty) which protects property. Whether any or all of these conclusions are satisfactory has been doubted. However, had the contrary conclusion been reached, that the agreement fell within Article 81(1), it is likely that the Commission would have been required to consider a deluge of individual applications for exemptions.

Three developments which have taken place since the *Panayiotou* case are worth noting. The first is the Commission Regulation on Vertical Restraints (discussed in Chapter 42), which makes available a block exemption from Article 81 for 'vertical agreements' including exclusive supply agreements.[38] This means that, even if an agreement falls within Article 81 EC, it is exempt as long as the market share of the purchaser is under 30 per cent.[39] However, while a publishing, recording, or songwriting contract would fall within the general definition of a 'vertical restraint' in the Regulation,[40] the Block Exemption does not apply where the *primary object* of the agreement concerns intellectual property.[41] We await a decision on whether the primary object of such an arrangement concerns intellectual property. This seems more likely with publishing than recording agreements. However, even if the Block Exemption does not apply, a restrictive agreement may be found exempt individually under Article 81(3).

The second significant development since the *Panayiotou* case is that section 2 of the Competition Act 1998 introduced a national provision (the so-called 'Chapter I prohibition') equivalent to Article 81.[42] It seems that an author or artist will be better served by the domestic provision, since it does not require that the applicant show that the contract had an adverse effect on trade between member states. This is because the Competition Act only requires that the agreement 'may affect trade within the United Kingdom'. There is no express requirement that this effect must be 'appreciable' or 'substantial' (though there is an immunity from fines for 'small agreements' and 'conduct of minor significance').[43] However, as with the European provision, most vertical agreements are exempt from section 2 unless the agreement has as its primary object terms relating to the assignment or use of intellectual property.[44]

---

[33] Article 81(3) is directly applicable from May 2004, and the old system which required 'prior notification' has been abandoned.

[34] [1994] *EMLR* 229. For a review of this see A. Coulthard, '*Panayiotou v. Sony Music Entertainment*' [1995] *Journal of Business Law* 414.

[35] [1994] *EMLR* 229, 416.   [36] Ibid, 420.   [37] Ibid, 425.

[38] If the market share of each is less than 15% such agreements will be minor agreements as falling outside of Art. 81(1): Notice on Agreements of Minor Importance [2001] *OJ C* 368/13. Below the threshold, the Commission considers that the competition authorities of member states should provide primary supervision.

[39] VRR, Art. 3. Assuming it has no 'hard core' terms.   [40] Ibid, Art. 2(1).   [41] Ibid, Art. 2(3).

[42] Competition Act 1998, s. 2. See J. Turner, 'The UK Competition Act 1998 and Private Rights' [1999] *EIPR* 181.

[43] Competition Act 1998, ss. 39 and 40; Competition Act 1998 (Small Agreements and Conduct of Minor Significance) Regulations 2000 (SI 2000/262). But the OFT takes the view that an agreement will have no appreciable effect on competition if the parties' combined share of the market does not exceed 25%.

[44] The Competition Act (Land and Vertical Restraints Exclusion) Order 2000 (SI 2000/310).

Third, and finally, it should be noted that, as from 1 May 2004, the effect of Regulation 1/2003 is to render Article 81(3) directly applicable by competition authorities and courts of member states. (Previously, such decisions could only be made by the European Commission.) This means that a finding that an exclusive recording agreement breaches Article 81 will not now produce the bureaucratic consequences (in terms of notifications) that it formerly would have entailed. This may make a court willing to abandon the reasoning employed in the *Panayiotou* case, treat exclusive recording arrangements as anti-competitive, but rely on its own assessment of Article 81(3) in deciding whether such arrangements improve the production of goods, while allowing consumers a fair share of the resulting benefit.

2.4 THE STATUTORY RIGHT TO EQUITABLE REMUNERATION

Although UK copyright law treats the terms of a contract as essentially a matter for voluntary negotiation, a significant exception has recently been introduced in relation to transfers of rental rights. This so-called 'unwaivable right to equitable remuneration' marks a first step in the transplanting of provisions protecting authors in countries such as France and Germany, via the process of European harmonization,[45] into UK copyright law. Section 93B of the 1988 Act specifies that where a person transfers the rental right 'concerning' a film or sound recording to the producer of the sound recording or film, 'he retains the right to equitable remuneration for rental'. The potential beneficiaries of the retained right are the authors of literary, dramatic, musical or artistic works, and the principal director of a film.[46]

The right applies whether the transfer is presumed under section 93A (or with performers, section 191F), or is voluntarily transferred. The right to remuneration cannot be excluded by agreement.[47] The remuneration is to be claimed from the person 'for the time being entitled to the rental right', and the relevant time is presumably the time of rental rather than of claim. The right can only be assigned to a collecting society, by testamentary transmission, or by operation of law (e.g. on bankruptcy). The amount deemed equitable is to be determined by agreement or, failing this, by the Copyright Tribunal. In determining what is equitable, the Tribunal is directed to take into account the importance of the contribution of the author or performer to the film or sound recording. Remuneration is not to be considered inequitable merely because it was paid by way of a single payment or at the time the rental right was transferred.[48]

2.5 HARMONIZATION?

As can be seen, with one or two exceptions, English law leaves authors free to make arrangements for the exploitation of their rights, and rarely interferes to protect authors against

---

[45] More specifically, the Rental Dir., Art. 4.

[46] CDPA s. 191G has the same effect as regards performers. It seems that CDPA s. 93B applies not just to circumstances where the work is incorporated in a film or sound recording (for example, the music used on a film) but also where the work is to be rented with the sound recording or film, such as might occur with artwork on a record sleeve. This conclusion is consistent with the expansive definition of author in CDPA s. 93B(1)(a) as covering authors of artistic works and the use in s. 93B(1) of 'concerning'. However, s. 93C(3) refers to the importance of the 'contribution...to' the sound recording or film.

[47] CDPA s. 93B(5).

[48] The right applies even where transfers were made pursuant to agreements made prior to 1 Jan. 1994, but only if the author asserted a claim to that effect between 1 Dec. 1996 and 1 Jan. 1997. See Related Rights Reg. 33(b).

decisions that are not in their long-term interests. In contrast, most member states have provisions regulating the terms and conditions of contracts between creators and exploiters. So far, the only harmonization in this area was the 'unwaivable equitable right of remuneration' conferred on authors and performers after the transfer of their rental rights. In 1992, this looked like this was going to be the first stage of a European copyright law that would protect authors from unfair contractual exploitation. But since then little has happened. In May 2002, a study by Hugenholtz and Guibault was published under the title *Study in the Conditions Applicable to Contracts Relating to Intellectual Property in the EU*.[49] The Report does not recommend harmonization. While it acknowledges that 'the demand expressed within some member states for a more adequate protection for creators against abusive contractual practices may indeed be quite justified', it offers little prospect of action at a European legislative level. The Report concludes instead that harmonization of the rules on copyright contracts would be premature. This, it says, is because: there has yet to be harmonization of other substantive copyright rules, such as rules on ownership and moral rights; there is no evidence of any impact of differences in national laws on the Internal Market; and European intervention must honour the principle of subsidiarity. The Report argues that 'the issues of copyright contract law are best addressed at the national level, since the national legislator is in the best position to reconcile the principles of copyright law, with those of contract law, labour law, and social law, while taking account of the relevant cultural considerations'. The Commission has held that differences between contractual rules are not significant enough to require harmonization—for the moment.[50]

3 COMPETITION LAW AND THE EXPLOITATION OF COPYRIGHT

In this section we look at the impact that UK and European competition law have on the copyright owner's ability to exploit copyright.

3.1 REFUSALS TO LICENCE

In general, copyright is regarded as a property right which its owner may use or not use as they wish: an author cannot normally be compelled to publish their private letters or manuscripts, nor are publishers required to keep their books 'in print'. Nevertheless, just as in exceptional circumstances competition law will require a property owner to make available an 'essential facility' to an economic operator,[51] so—exceptionally—competition law might require a copyright owner to license its rights to other traders.[52] The legal basis for this requirement is Article 82 EC (formerly Article 86 of the Treaty), which prohibits the 'abuse' of a 'dominant position'.[53] An operator holds a 'dominant position' when it holds a position

---

[49] ETD/2000/BS–3001/E/69.

[50] EC, *Communication from the Commission to the Council, the European Parliament and the European Economic and Social Committee: The Management of Copyright and Related Rights in the Internal Market* COM(2004) 261 final (Brussels 16 Apr 2004).

[51] *Commercial Solvents v. Commission,* Case 6 & 7/73 [1974] *ECR* 223.

[52] In so doing, competition law does not violate TRIPS because special provision is made in TRIPS, art 40(2): *Microsoft v. Commission,* Case T–201/04, [2007] 5 *CMLR* (11) 846, 1077 (para 1192).

[53] I. Goraere, *The Use and Abuse of Intellectual Property Rights* (1996), 135–50.

of economic strength which enables it to behave to an appreciable extent independently of its competitors, customers, and consumers.[54] Operators in a dominant position are regarded as having a 'special responsibility' not to allow their conduct to impair competition. If an operator in such a position fails to license its copyright, such refusal may be regarded as an abuse and can result not merely in the order of a compulsory licence, but also very substantial fines.[55]

The first case in which the ECJ affirmed the application of Article 82 to copyright was *RTE and Independent Television Publications v. Commission* (known as the 'Magill' case).[56] The decision in *Magill* arose from the practice whereby the Irish broadcasting organization (RTE), who owned copyright in its television schedules, refused to license newspapers to publish TV listings in a weekly format. The effect of this was that the only weekly guides available were those issued separately by RTE and the other broadcasting organizations (BBC and ITV). As such, if a viewer wanted to plan their television viewing for the week ahead, they would have to purchase all three magazines. Magill, who proposed to publish a comprehensive guide, claimed that the refusal to license contravened Article 82. The Commission agreed and ordered the defendant to license the listings.[57]

The Court of Justice held that the broadcasting organization held a dominant position in the market for weekly television magazines.[58] The Court of Justice also agreed that the refusal to license was an abuse. The Court observed that the refusal to license an intellectual property right 'cannot of itself constitute abuse of a dominant position' but that 'the exercise of an exclusive right by the proprietor may, in exceptional circumstances, involve abusive conduct'.[59] The Court agreed with the Court of First Instance that this was a case of abuse, because there was a specific, constant, and regular potential demand on the part of consumers for comprehensive weekly listings, which was going unmet because the appellants would offer only their own partial weekly guides. There was no 'justification' for this behaviour related either to broadcasting or to the publishing of television magazines. The consequence of the refusal to license was that the broadcasters reserved to themselves the secondary market in weekly television guides by excluding all competition from that market.

Parties in subsequent cases have sought to explore the scope of the *Magill* holding,[60] but so far the courts have managed to make determinations within its parameters. In *IMS*, for example, the ECJ indicated that it is 'sufficient' to constitute an abuse if these elements are present (leaving open the question whether all elements of *Magill* must be present).[61]

[54] *Compagnie Maritime Belge Transports and Others v. Commission*, Cases C–395 & 396/96 P [2000] *ECR* I–365 (para. 34).

[55] In the case of *Microsoft*, the Commission's 2004 Order imposed a fine of Euro 497 million: Decision 2007/53 relating to a proceeding pursuant to Art 82 EC and Art 54 of the EEA Agreement against Microsoft Corp (COMP/C–3.37.792–*Microsoft* ([2007] *OJ L* 32/23). The level of the fine was challenged by Microsoft before the CFI, but the Court affirmed: Case T–201/04, [2007] 5 *CMLR* (11) 846 (paras 1326–1367).

[56] [1995] 4 *CMLR* 18.   [57] *Magill TV Guide/ITP, BBC and RTE* (1989) *OJ L* 78/43.

[58] [1995] 4 *CMLR* 18, 718 (para. 50). The ECJ's reasoning on this point has also been treated as less than fully satisfactory: T. Vinje, 'The Final Word on *Magill*' [1995] *EIPR* 297, 299. Subsequent commentaries have suggested that one distinguishing feature of *Magill* was that the dominance of RTE, ITV, and the BBC was in the provision of broadcasting services.

[59] [1995] 4 *CMLR* 18, 718 (para. 50).

[60] The differences between the Commission and the CFI in the *IMS* case related to the very broad interpretation the Commission was taking on when an abuse would be found under Article 82. *IMS Health* [2002] *OJ L* 59/18; *IMS Health Inc v. Commission*, T–184/01 R [2002] 4 *CMLR* 58. Moreover, in the *Microsoft* case the Commission argued that the application of *Magill* did not require the presence of all the elements identified in *Magill*. Nevertheless, it argued, and the CFI found, that all those elements were present (para. 712).

[61] *IMS Health GmbH & Co OHG v. NDC Health GmbH & Co KG*, Case C–418/01 [2004] 4 *CMLR* (28) 1543 (para 38).

3.1.1 Indispensability

The first requirement is that the asset must be 'indispensable' for operation of another's business.[62] This means it must be impossible or at least unreasonably difficult for an undertaking to operate in the relevant market without a licence.[63] In *IMS Health,* IMS provided information to pharmaceutical firms about sales by wholesalers to pharmacies (which gave the firms an indication of doctors' prescribing habits and thus enabled the pharmaceutical companies to assess and respond to the effectiveness of their marketing to doctors). For privacy purposes, the data had to be collated from data relating to at least three pharmacies. With the assistance of pharmaceutical firms, over a number of years IMS had developed a geographical model for analysing the German pharmaceutical market—a so-called 'brick structure', comprising 1,860 segments, which it used from January 2000. IMS believed NDC was using the same brick structure and brought an action for copyright infringement. The Landgericht Frankfurt granted an interim injunction, but referred various questions concerning the application of Article 82 EC to the ECJ.[64] One issue was whether use of the brick structure was 'indispensable' to NDC's operations.[65] It was clear that the brick structure had been developed with the assistance of the pharmaceutical companies, and that there would likely be resistance (and costs) were they to adapt to a different basis for assessing data. In these circumstances, even were NDC to develop an alternative structure, it might 'be obliged to offer terms which are such as to rule out any economic viability of business on a scale comparable to that' of IDC. The ECJ advised that these factors were relevant to the national court's assessment of the 'indispensability' of using the brick structure for the provision of data services. In contrast, in *Tierce Ladbroke v. Commission,*[66] the proprietor of a chain of betting shops in Belgium complained that a refusal by the owner of rights in certain televised pictures of French horse races to allow retransmission in the applicant's betting shop amounted to a breach of Article 82 EC. The CFI held that, while the refusal to license the complainant was an exercise of power from a primary market (transmission of horse races) into a secondary market (betting shops), the refusal to license in no sense prevented the defendant from operating in the secondary market. The provision of pictures was not essential for the applicant's activity.

3.1.2 New Product

The second requirement, that of a new product, was also at issue in *IMS Health.*[67] A key question before the ECJ was whether it was necessary for NDC to establish that it was offering

---

[62] In *Microsoft v. Commission,* Case T–201/04 [2007] 5 *CMLR* (11) 846, much time was spent contesting exactly what interoperability information was required, Microsoft claiming that the Commission's orders in effect required disclosure that would enable its competitors to clone its products, and arguing that all that it should need to disclose was sufficient information to allow its competitors' products to connect with its system ('one-way' functionality). The Court of First Instance declined to overturn the Commission's ruling, agreeing that, for the competitors to remain viable, the information must be sufficient to enable 'two-way' functionality, and observing that the requirements imposed fell well short of requiring the revelation of source code or enabling cloning.

[63] Ibid, para. 28.

[64] In the light of the injunction, NDC sought a licence to use the 1,860-brick structure, offering an annual licence fee of about €5,000. When that was refused, NDC lodged a complaint with the Commission alleging an infringement of Article 82. The Commission adopted a decision ordering interim measures, on the basis that IMS was abusing its dominant position: [2002] OJ L59/18. The President of the CFI suspended the Commission's decision, because it had taken a very broad interpretation of *Magill: IMS Health Inc v. Commission,* T–184/01 R [2002] 4 *CMLR* 58.

[65] *IMS Health GmbH & Co OHG v. NDC Health GmbH & Co KG,* Case C–418/01 [2004] 4 *CMLR* (28) 1543.

[66] Case T–504/93 [1997] *ECR* II–923.

[67] *IMS Health GmbH & Co OHG v. NDC Health GmbH & Co KG,* Case C–418/01 [2004] 4 *CMLR* (28) 1543.

a 'new product' since, on the face of things, it appeared that NDC wanted to use the brick structure to compete with IMS in providing an identical service (pharmaceutical data services). The
Advocate General had noted that, in *Volvo v. Veng*,[68] the ECJ had declined to hold that a refusal
to license the manufacture of car spare parts was an abuse, owing to the fact that it was simply
proposed to produce duplicates.[69] The ECJ held that the refusal would only be an abuse where
a licensee did 'not intend to limit itself essentially to duplicating the goods or services already
offered on the secondary market by the owner of the copyright, but intends to produce new
goods or services not offered by the owner of the right and for which there is potential consumer demand'. The Court elaborated a little upon the requirement that there be an upstream
and downstream market. While acknowledging that this leveraging from one market into
another was an essential component in the *Magill* analysis, the ECJ admitted a certain artificiality was possible in constructing the upstream market—it did not have to be a market that
was actually offered. Thus, in the *IMS* case, the Court contemplated that the market for the
1,860-brick structure itself might be the primary market.

The 'new product' requirement was also discussed by the CFI n *Microsoft v Commission*.[70]
Here, the Court of First Instance was asked to review a Commission decision from 2004
fining Microsoft and ordering it to make available so-called 'interoperability information'
about its work-group server systems to interested parties. 'Work-group server systems' are
systems which connect PCs to each other, to common servers, and to printers so that they
can share files, share printers, and operate as efficient and secure networks.[71] Microsoft had
a 60 per cent share of the work-group server market, so was in a dominant position.[72] While
the Commission found that some information was available, it took the view that this was
not sufficient to enable competitors to remain viably on the market. The 13-member Grand
Chamber of the CFI therefore found that the refusal would prevent the appearance of a 'new
product' because the refusal to permit full interoperability would limit technical development.[73] Evidence indicated that consumers preferred various facets (reliability, security) of
the work-group server operating systems of Microsoft's competitors, and that the chief quality
associated with Microsoft's systems was their ability to interoperate.[74] In effect, people were
buying Microsoft's items primarily because they were locked in, when they would have preferred the technical features offered by Microsoft's competitors. The refusal of Microsoft to
make available relevant information was thus impeding 'innovation'.

3.1.3 Elimination of Competition

The third *Magill* requirement is that the refusal must be *likely to exclude all competition in
the secondary market*. In the *Microsoft* case, Microsoft argued that the continued existence
of competitors in the work-group server system market, namely Unix, Linux, and Novell,
indicated that the refusal to license the information had not eliminated competition in the
market. The Commission rejected that view and the CFI affirmed. The CFI stated that it
was not 'necessary to demonstrate that all competition on the market would be eliminated.
What matters,...is that the refusal at issue is liable to or is likely to, eliminate all effective

---

[68]   *AB Volvo v. Erik Veng (UK)*, Case 238/87 [1988] *ECR* 6211.
[69]   Case C–418/01 [2004] 4 *CMLR* (28) 1543, AG 65.   [70]   Case T–201/04 [2007] 5 *CMLR* (11) 846.
[71]   The CFI was asked by Microsoft to consider whether the Commission had formulated the relevant market
too narrowly, but the CFI found that it had not done so: ibid, (para. 531).
[72]   Of course, in this litigation even this was contested. The CFI findings are at ibid, paras. 555–8.
[73]   Para 647.   [74]   Paras 652, 407–12.

competition on the market.'[75] The existence of competitors with a marginal presence in niche markets was not evidence of effective competition.[76]

3.1.4 Objective Justification

The final *Magill* requirement is that the refusal must *not be justified* by objective considerations. In the *Microsoft* case, the CFI said that the burden of proving objective justification lies on the operator holding the dominant position.[77] It is evident that the existence of intellectual property rights (IPRs) is not itself a sufficient basis (otherwise Article 82 could never apply to IPRs).[78] In *Microsoft,* the Court of First Instance affirmed the Commission's view that the existence of secrets was not of itself a good reason to refuse to licence,[79] but would, it seems, have accepted as an objective justification a substantiated argument that the requirement to license would seriously have affected Microsoft's incentives to innovate.[80]

3.2 EXCESSIVE PRICING

The Competition provisions may also be applicable where a copyright (or database right) owner is willing to licence, but only at a price that is unacceptable to the user. Some such issues arose in *Attheraces Limited, Attheraces (UK) Limited v. The British Horseracing Board Limited, BHB Enterprises plc,* where the Court of Appeal considered whether the British Horseracing Board was guilty of 'excessive pricing', and thereby abusing its admittedly dominant position, in relation to its charges for supplying pre-race data to horse-racing broadcaster, Attheraces.[81] The Court of Appeal allowed an appeal from the judgment of Etherton J., who had held there was abuse. The Court recognized the difficulties with deciding the 'economic value of data', which was a preliminary to deciding whether BHB's pricing was excessive. The Court rejected Etherton J.'s approach of asking what the cost of creating the information was and allowing a reasonable profit on that cost. Instead the Court accepted that the value to the user might also be a relevant component of the 'economic value' of the data.[82]

3.3 TYING

If traders in a dominant position need to think carefully before refusing to license their copyright, they should also think carefully before giving away their copyright-protected software with their other products. In *Microsoft,*[83] the Commission held Microsoft had breached Article 82 EC by its bundling-in Windows Media Player with its operating system package.[84] The Commission had found that Microsoft was dominant in the operating system market, with a 90 per cent market share. During the early 1990s, it had offered (but not imposed) its competitor's media players (in particular that of RealNetworks) but from the end of the 1990s it had included its own audio-streaming software and stopped supporting the software of its competitors.[85] The CFI agreed with the Commission's analysis that there was abuse where (a) the tying (Windows OS) and tied (Media Player) products are two separate products; (b) the undertaking concerned is dominant in the market for the tying product; (c) customers are not

---

[75] Para. 563.   [76] Para. 563.   [77] Paras. 688, 697.
[78] Para. 690.   [79] Para. 693.   [80] Para. 701.
[81] [2007] *EWCA Civ* 38. (The case concerned supply of data, but was not based on database right.)
[82] Ibid, para 218.   [83] Case T-201/04 [2007] 5 *CMLR* (11) 846.   [84] Art 82(d).
[85] The history is neatly summarised at Case T–201/04 [2007] 5 *CMLR* (11) 846 (para. 837).

offered the choice of buying the tying product alone; (d) the practice forecloses competition (in the market for the tied product).[86]

The CFI held that the OS and the media player were, at the relevant time, two products. The fact that Microsoft bundled them together and was dominant in the operating system market—so that they appeared to be two parts of a single product—had to be ignored when making the assessment. Rather, the Court was persuaded that these were two products as a result of evidence that Microsoft sometimes offered Windows without Media Player, marketed Media Player separately, and that there was demand (from employers) for Windows without Media Player.[87] The second factor, Microsoft's dominance in the OS market, was not contested. As to the third factor, consumer choice, Microsoft argued that consumers got the Media Player for free and were able to install and use alternative media players.[88] Referring to Article 82(d), Microsoft argued that the circumstances were different from the classic case of abuse by tying, which involved imposing an additional obligation or expense (for example, an obligation to buy expensive nails to go with a nail gun). The Court rejected the arguments: just because there was no separate charge for Windows Media Player did not imply it was included gratis. Moreover, it found that it was not technically possible to remove Windows Media Player, and that the bundling provided consumers with an incentive to use the Windows Media Player 'at the expense of competing media players, notwithstanding that the latter are of better quality'.[89] Turning to the fourth element, the CFI affirmed the Commission's view that the sheer ubiquity of the Windows Media Player, which could not be removed from the operating systems with which it was installed, was likely to foreclose competition.[90] Given that most operating systems were pre-installed on PCs and laptops by 'original equipment manufacturers' (OEMs) (who were given no choice but to instal Windows Media Player), meant that OEMs and consumers were unlikely to choose to instal a second, non-Microsoft, media player. In fact, had Microsoft not adopted the bundling tactic, the Court suggested that there would have been real competition with the market leader from the 1990s, Real Player. Finally, the Court considered whether there was an objective justification for the behaviour, through efficiency gains that outweighed the harm from the anti-competitive action. The Court found the claimed technical efficiencies unsubstantiated. Microsoft therefore had rightly been fined by the Commission and ordered to offer its Windows operating system without the Media Player (though it was also permitted to continue to sell the package).

3.3 ANTI-COMPETITIVE CONTRACTUAL TERMS

The key provision of European competition law affecting copyright agreements is Article 81 EC (formerly Article 85 of the Treaty). This renders void all agreements which affect trade between member states and which have the object or effect of distorting competition within the Common Market. Nevertheless, certain agreements that provide benefits may be exempt. In contrast with the fields of technology licensing and vertical restraints, the Commission has been slow to develop block exemptions in the copyright field. The Technology Transfer Block exemption exempts certain agreements which deal with copyright,[91] but only where such agreement is 'ancillary' to a pure patent licensing or know-how licensing agreement, or to mixed patent and know-how licensing agreements. The Regulation on Vertical Restraints is

---

[86] Recital 794 of the Commission decision, set out at ibid (para. 842) and expressly adopted by the CFI (at para 859).

[87] Paras. 912–44.   [88] Paras. 951–2.   [89] Para. 971.   [90] Paras. 1036–7.   [91] TTR.

be of more general applicability: exempting many agreements relating to the distribution of copyright works (for example, the distribution of books or sound recordings).[92] However, as we noted earlier, the exemption does not apply where the primary object of the agreement is the assignment or use of IPRs. Therefore it will rarely be applicable to copyright licences, such as software licences. However, the exemptions made may provide an important guide to the thinking of the Commission on terms in such agreements.

As a result of the Competition Act 1998, UK regulation of copyright agreements parallels European competition law. Section 2 introduces the 'Chapter 1 prohibition', which is equivalent to Article 81 EC.[93] An agreement will be deemed to be exempt from the national prohibition if it is exempt from Article 81 EC under the Community's Technology Transfer Regulation or Vertical Agreements Regulation.[94]

With these general points in mind, we now look at the cumulative effect of the Chapter 1 prohibition and Article 81 EC on various terms that are used in copyright contracts.

3.3.1 Agreements Conferring Exclusive Territorial Rights

A copyright assignment or licence commonly includes terms guaranteeing the licensee the exclusive right to sell the work in a particular territory. For example, the licence may grant someone the exclusive right to sell paperback versions of a book in the United Kingdom, or to show a film in public in Belgium. It may also include an undertaking by the licensor not to put the work on the market in that territory and an undertaking by the licensee not to sell the work in the territories of other licensees. The inclusion of such a guarantee of exclusivity may be important to a licensee, who has to invest in the advertising or marketing of the work, and who needs to ensure that they have a reasonable degree of control in the relevant market.

In related situations, the Commission has recognized *both* the value of such terms *and* the threat posed by exclusive licensing to the achievement of the internal market. Consequently, the Commission treats exclusive agreements as legitimate, but simultaneously prohibits certain terms which it considers will have an unduly restrictive effect on the practices of parallel importers. Consequently, while the Commission allows terms which prohibit the active marketing of the work in the territory of another licensee, the agreement may not prohibit 'passive' sales.[95]

Where an exclusive territorial agreement covers the representation (or exhibition), as opposed to the distribution of copies of the work, it may also fall within Article 81 EC. In *Coditel (No. 2)*,[96] a French company granted a Belgian company the exclusive right to exhibit the film, *Le Boucher,* in Belgium for seven years. The French company later licensed a German broadcasting company to broadcast the film on German television. When it did so, Coditel, a Belgian cable operator, included the film in its Belgian service. The question referred to the

---

[92] VRR.

[93] Competition Act 1998, s. 2. See OFT, *Intellectual Property Rights: A Draft Competition Act 1998 Guideline,* OFT 418 (Nov. 2001).

[94] Competition Act 1998, s. 10 (parallel exemptions).

[95] TTR, Art. 1(2), Recital 15; VRR, Art. 4(b); See *Re BBC* [1976] *CMLR* D–89. An OFT investigation into the CD market found evidence of past anti–competitive agreements requiring retailers of CDs not to import cheaper CDs from mainland Europe, or offering favourable terms to those who did not do so: see OFT, Annual Report (2002–3), 61.

[96] *Coditel SA v. Cine Vog Films SA (No. 2),* Case 262/81 [1982] *ECR* 3381.

European Court of Justice was whether the exclusive exhibition agreement was prohibited by Article 81 (then Article 85 of the Treaty). The Court held that in general exclusive licences of this nature did not automatically fall within Article 81. However, the Court added that it might do so if the royalties exceeded a fair remuneration; if the agreement was excessively long; or if the exercise of the right was likely to distort competition within the Common Market.[97]

With the strong emphasis now placed on Europe-wide licensing and a European audio-visual area, it may well be that the authorities would want to revisit the *Coditel* holding that exclusive licences on a territorial basis do not automatically fall foul of Article 81 EC. The market has transformed massively since the 1980s, when national—often monopolistic or publicly-funded—television was the norm. The EC Cable and Satellite Broadcasting Directive attempted to limit the impact of territorially limited national rights by redefining the place of broadcast as the place of 'injection' of the programming material. It is quite foreseeable that attempts to maintain national exclusivity—for example by requiring those who supply decryption cards to do so solely on a territorial basis—might be regarded as illegitimately restricting competition. The matter has been raised before the English courts,[98] in a action between the FA and importers of equipment and cards that enabled people in the UK to watch Greek broadcasts. The defence's argument that the FA had breached Article 81 by requiring its Greek licensees to prevent the use of the cards outside Greece has survived a strike-out application. Ultimately, the matter will need to be decided by the ECJ.

3.3.2 Restrictive Field of Distribution Agreements

Where a work has a number of potential markets, a copyright owner may wish to limit the field in which the licensee exploits the work. For example, a copyright owner may wish to license a work for sale by a book club, separately from sale by retail outlets. Such agreements are akin to 'fields of use' limitations. Under the Vertical Restraints Regulation these would be restrictions of the customers to whom the buyer may sell the contract goods or services. These would not be exempt unless the restriction is confined to active sales to an exclusive customer group allocated by the supplier to another buyer. If a copyright owner has given general retail rights exclusively to one person and book club rights to another, a restriction preventing the book club owner from actively selling outside the club would be exempt from Article 81. The OFT seems to have taken a similar stance as regards the application of the Part I prohibition.[99]

3.3.3 Price Limitations

A copyright owner may wish to restrict the price at which the licensee sells a particular product. They might also require the licensee to specify to subsequent purchasers that they may not resell the product at anything other than a specified price. Although such agreements have traditionally been treated as being unlawful, rather surprisingly from 1956 until recently the UK law went out of its way to tolerate one such price-fixing arrangement in the form of the 'Net Book Agreement'. This was an agreement between members of the Publishers' Association to impose certain conditions on booksellers as regards the price at which certain books ('net books') could be sold.[100] However, in 1995 the majority of publishers decided to

---

[97] Ibid, 3401–2 (paras. 15, 17, 19).

[98] *The Football Association Premier League Ltd v. QC Leisure & Ors* [2008] *EWHC* 44 (Ch) (Barling J.).

[99] See OFT, *Intellectual Property Rights: A Draft Competition Act 1998 Guideline*, OFT 418 (Nov. 2001) (para. 2.21). Competition Act 1998, s. 10.

[100] *Re Net Book Agreement 1957* [1962] 1 *WLR* 1347.

abandon the net book system. As a result, the exemption previously afforded to the Agreement was removed.[101]

Under the Vertical Restraints Regulation attempts at resale price maintenance constitute 'hardcore' restrictions that prevent the block exemption from operating.[102] An individual assessment would therefore be necessary.[103] The domestic position is similar: a provision relating to minimum price maintenance which is, on its face, anti-competitive would need to be justified on the ground that it (a) improves the production or distribution of goods or promotes technical or economic progress and also (b) allows consumers 'a fair share of the resulting benefit.'[104]

3.3.4 Site licences

One of the characteristics of most digitized works is that users of the work will ordinarily infringe copyright (insofar as they make a temporary reproduction on their computer). As a result, licences are frequently needed to permit such use. In the cases of software, databases, and journals in electronic form, it has become common to limit permitted use to a particular location. The question arises whether such a restriction is anti-competitive. It has been argued that, inasmuch as site licences operate as caps on output, they are anti-competitive and fall within Article 81 EC. For example, if the effect of licensing software to one particular terminal restricts the productive use of that software, such a licence may fall within Article 81 EC. However, if a site licence is 'open' in the sense that it allows for expansion of output or has a clause allowing for further licences on commercial terms, then this objection does not operate.[105] Under the Technology Transfer Regulation,[106] restrictions on quantities of output will place agreement outside the block exemption.

4 REGULATION OF CONTRACTS FOR THE PROTECTION OF USERS

In this section, we consider the ways in which the law interferes with copyright contracts for the benefit of 'users'. By 'users' we primarily mean individual consumers who wish to utilize copyright-protected material. The idea of protecting users from unfair contracts imposed by copyright owners is a relatively new one. In part this has arisen because certain acts carried out by users have come to require the consent of copyright owners. In the past, a person who bought a book could do almost whatever they wished with the book without the need for further consent: the book could be read, lent to a friend, or sold to a charity shop without raising any potential liability. Today, as a result of technological developments, many similar acts (such as photocopying the book or reading an electronic version on screen) might now require permission. The second reason why contracts between copyright holders and users

---

[101] *Re Net Book Agreement 1957 (No. 4)* [1998] ICR 753.   [102] VRR, Art. 4(a).

[103] The European Court of Justice held the UK Net Book Agreement to fall within the then Art. 85 prohibition but said it might be justifiable under Art. 85(3), overturning the views of the Commission and Court of First Instance: *Re Net Book Agreements: Publishers' Association v. EC Commission*, Case C–360/92P [1996] *FSR* 33; [1996] *ICR* 121; [1995] *EMLR* 185 (ECJ); *Publishers' Association v. EC Commission* [1992] 4 *All ER* 70; [1992] *ICR* 842 (CFI).

[104] Competition Act 1998, ss. 4 (individual exemptions from Director General of Office of Fair Trading, 9 (criteria for exemption), 10 (parallel exemption).

[105] M. Dolmans and M. Odriozola, 'Site Licence, Right Licence? Site Licences under EC Competition Law' [1998] *ECLR* 493; cf. J. Townsend, 'The Case for Site Licences' [1999] *ECLR* 169.

[106] TTR Art. 3(5).

are becoming increasingly common is that new techniques of distribution, particularly digital dissemination, are removing intermediaries from the distribution process. A consumer who formerly would have bought a hard copy of a phonogram from a retailer can now be supplied with an equivalent digital version over the internet directly from the copyright holder. This direct contact allows the copyright owner to reinforce any rights they may have under copyright with obligations imposed as part of the contract they have with the owner.

The main concern in these circumstances is that click-through contracts will extend copyright owners' rights beyond their existing scope. Consequently, such licences might impose conditions for use of works in which copyright has lapsed, or in the case of software might prohibit the making of back-up copies or decompilation, or in other cases might prohibit criticism or review. As the use of electronic resources increases and such contracts become the norm, the 'delicate balance' between owners and users encapsulated in statutory copyright may be sacrificed.

Although the E-Commerce Directive specifies that 'electronic contracts' should be recognized as valid,[107] specific Directives nevertheless indicate that certain exemptions may not be overridden by contract law.[108] For example, the Software Directive allows certain acts, including the decompilation of computer programs. It also renders void contracts that attempt to restrict those rights.[109] A similar clause has been introduced to prevent contractual circumvention of defences to infringement of copyright in databases.[110] Moreover, the Information Society Directive explicitly takes on board concerns about oppressive use of technological measures to prevent access to material falling within copyright's carefully defined exceptions. Article 6(4) of the Information Society Directive provided for a strange, barely comprehensible, compromise.[111] This, and its UK implementation in section 297ZE of the 1988 Act, is reviewed in Chapter 13.

5 ORPHAN WORKS

One problem with exploiting copyright-protected material that has attracted increasing attention is that of so-called 'orphan works'.[112] An orphan work is one whose copyright owners (parents) either do not exist or cannot be located. Orphan works exist in part because there is no formal structure for registering copyrights and keeping track of ownership. In some cases the authors of works may not even appreciate that they have created something protected by copyright. In other cases, the ownership of copyright is impossible to trace, perhaps because a firm went bankrupt, or simply because the relatives of a deceased author cannot be identified. The fact that many works are protected by copyright but that owners are not easy to identify means that the market in copyright transactions is inefficient. It is inefficient because some transactions that would voluntarily occur—agreements to use copyright-protected material—are not occurring simply because the costs of locating the owner are greater than the value of

---

[107] Electronic Commerce Dir., Art. 9(1).   [108] Broadcasting Act 1996, s. 137.

[109] CDPA ss. 50A, 50B, 296A(1)(a), 296A(1)(b), 296A(1)(c).

[110] CDPA s. 296B. See also Database Reg. 19(2).

[111] Brian Esler has called this 'arguably the most obtuse and incoherent provision yet enacted by the EU in the touchy area of intellectual property harmonization'. See B. Esler. 'Technological Self-Help: Its Status under European Law and Implications for UK Law' at <http://www.bileta.ac.uk> (follow link from 2002 section of 'Conference Papers' page).

[112] For the deliberations of the U.S. Copyright Office, see Register of Copyrights, *Report on Orphan Works* (2006) at <http://www.copyright.gov/orphan/>. For more general discussion, see D.W.K. Khong, 'Orphan works, abandonware and the missing market for copyrighted goods' (2007) 15 *International Journal of Law & Information Technology* 54.

the transaction to the potential licensee. In other cases, users simply take a risk or utilize litigation insurance in case the copyright holder does appear.

The issue of orphan works has come on to the legislative agenda for two reasons. The first is that the potential problem is growing as copyright term is extended. The British Library has estimated that 40 per cent of all print works are orphan works.[113] The second is that digital technologies have given rise to new potential uses of such largely forgotten or valueless works, for example in digital archives, but also because they can now be made available profitably to niche markets. If such projects are not to be impeded by heavy costs investigating copyright owners, it is necessary to offer users some way of immunizing themselves from later liability. This could be done by providing some sort of limited defence or immunity from financial liability.

The US Copyright Office has proposed such a scheme, and the matter is being looked at in the UK and the EU. The *Gowers Review* recommended that such a provision be proposed to the European Commission,[114] giving some limited immunity from financial liability for those who have conducted a 'reasonable search' to locate the copyright owner, as well as (rather oddly) proposing a voluntary registration system for copyright. The IViR Study for the Internal Market division of the European Commission, entitled *Recasting Copyright for the Knowledge Economy*, for its part, recommended action initially at a national level, proposing that national authorities (in the UK, e.g. the IPO or Copyright Tribunal) have the capacity to grant licences to potential users of orphan works. It also suggested a bolder plan to establish some central European database of information relating to 'rights management', which would help alleviate the problem.[115] A 2006 Commission Recommendation on the digitization and on-line accessibility of cultural material and digital preservation also calls on member states to develop mechanisms for dealing with orphan works.[116] The Information Society and Media Directorate in the Commission is actively involved in trying to develop non-legislative measures for dealing with the issue, and with the help of a High Level Expert Group on Digital Libraries, has issued a model licensing agreement. While there is widespread recognition of the importance of this subject, it seems no-one is precisely sure whether action should be taken at national or European level, and if the latter, which arm of the Commission should have control.[117]

6 CONTROLLING COLLECTING SOCIETIES

In Chapter 11 we looked at the ways in which copyright owners exploit their rights by way of collective administration. While collective licensing can clearly be beneficial to both copyright owners and users, the existence of single bodies solely responsible for administering

---

[113] *Gowers Review*, para. 4.91.   [114] *Gowers Review*, para. 4.99.

[115] IViR, *Recasting Copyright for the Knowledge Economy*, ch.5.

[116] Commission Recommendation of August 24, 2006 on the digitisation and online accessibility of cultural material and digital preservation (2006/585/EC), *OJ L* 236/28, (31 Aug 2006) Recital 10. ('Licensing mechanisms in areas such as orphan works—that is to say, copyrighted works whose owners are difficult or even impossible to locate—and works that are out of print or distribution (audiovisual) can facilitate rights clearance and consequently digitisation efforts and subsequent online accessibility. Such mechanisms should therefore be encouraged in close cooperation with rightholders.')

[117] EC (DG Information Society and Media), *Communication from the Commission to the European Parliament, the Council, the European Economic and Social Committee and the Committee of the Regions on Creative Content Online in the Single Market* (SEC(2007) 1710 (3 Jan 2008) COM(2007) 836 final para 2.1 ('the Commission will closely monitor the implementation of the [2006] Recommendation and the need for further action at European level').

rights may also cause a number of problems. The problems posed are of two sorts: problems with members and problems with users. Problems with members typically occur because a copyright owner has little alternative to joining the society, which can thus impose restrictive terms. The second set of problems arises from the relations with users, who similarly have little alternative but to take a licence from the collecting society on whatever terms it chooses. Because of these problems collecting societies have been described (in terms similar to the atom bomb) as 'at once the most ingenious and the worst invention of mankind'.[118]

This section looks at how these problems have been recognized and regulated at a national and European level.[119] As we will see, although the Treaty imposes certain restrictions on the operation of collecting societies that will be investigated at a Community level, collective licensing is largely controlled at the national level. A number of the existing Directives highlight the need for collecting societies to meet certain standards of rationalization and transparency,[120] but none of the Directives propose anything of substance. In 2004, the Commission seemed to be very close to proposing legislation regulating all aspects of the establishment and operation of collecting societies.[121] The Communication concluded that 'abstaining from legislative action does not seem to be an option any more'.[122] Nevertheless, a year later the Commission decided that the best way to achieve community-wide licensing for music was through a recommendation under Article 211 EC,[123] and such an instrument was indeed issued.[124] Whether the Commission has completely abandoned its aims to harmonize the framework regulating other societies, or as regards other activities, remains to be seen. For the moment, the Internal Market arm of the Commission seems relatively content with the impact of the Recommendation.[125]

5.1 REGULATION OF MEMBER–SOCIETY RELATIONS

The terms of membership and control over the collecting society are a matter, first and foremost, for the rules of the society. If a large enough number of members object to these rules, they can be changed by consent. Equally, if a majority of the members are unhappy with the management of the society, control can be changed.[126]

---

[118] A. Bertrand, 'Performing Rights Societies: The Price is Right "French Style", or the SACEM Cases' [1992] *Ent LR* 147.

[119] For a proposal that there be an ombudsman to regulate these relations see T. Meredith, 'Dealing with Complaints against Collecting Societies' (1995) 13(2) *Copyright Reporter* 58.

[120] Info. Soc. Dir. Recital 17 ('it is necessary, especially in the light of the requirements arising out of the digital environment, to ensure that collecting societies achieve a higher level of rationalisation and transparency with regard to compliance with competition rules'); Resale Rights Dir., Recital 28 ('member states should ensure that collecting societies operate in a transparent and efficient manner').

[121] EC, *Communication from the Commission to the Council, the European Parliament and the European Economic and Social Committee: The Management of Copyright and Related Rights in the Internal Market* COM(2004) 261 final (Brussels 16 Apr 2004).

[122] Ibid, 19 (para. 3.6).

[123] EC, Commission Staff Working Document, *Impact Assessment Reforming Cross-Border Collective Management of Copyright and Related Rights For Legitimate On-line Music Services,* SEC (2005) 1254 (Brussels, 11 Oct. 2005) 13 (para. 1.5).

[124] Commission Recommendation of 18 May 2005 on collective cross-border management of copyright and related rights for legitimate on-line music services (2005/737/EC) *OJ L* 276/54 (21 Oct. 2005).

[125] See also EC, *Monitoring of the 2005 Music Online Recommendation,* (Brussels, 7 Feb 2008).

[126] Copinger, para. 28–27.

5.1.1 UK Competition Control

A powerful form of external control of society–member relations is provided by the UK competition authorities. As mentioned previously, the Competition Act contains prohibitions on agreements and concerted practices which restrict competition (the Part I prohibition) and 'abuse of a dominant position' (the so-called Part II prohibition). Since collecting societies occupy a dominant position in the market (the supply of services of administering particular rights) relations are apt to be scrutinized to ensure there is no abuse. In addition, under Part IV of the Enterprise Act 2002, the Office of Fair Trading is able (after conducting a preliminary informal investigation) to make a 'market investigation reference' to the Competition Commission where OFT has grounds for suspecting the features of a market prevent, restrict, or distort competition.[127] The Competition Commission must investigate, assess whether there is an adverse affect on competition, and report. As a result of such a finding, the Competition Commission may require that action be taken to remedy the adverse affect, and make orders or require undertakings to bring about appropriate changes.[128] In a previous investigation, under powers similar to those now granted by the Enterprise Act, the Monopoly and Mergers Commission (the predecessor of the Competition Commission) held that certain practices of the Performing Right Society were unsatisfactory and the Society agreed to amend its rules.[129] The *Gowers Review* invited the OFT to conduct another study of UK collecting societies 'to ensure the needs of all stakeholders are being met.'[130]

5.1.2 EC Competition Law

Another form of control over the rules of the society is to be found in Article 82 EC (formerly Article 86 of the Treaty). This prohibits the abuse by an undertaking of a dominant position. Most rights organizations constitute 'undertakings' and have a dominant position in the supply of relevant services to composers, authors, and publishers.[131] The critical issue is in what circumstances the terms constitute an abuse.

The balancing exercise required by Article 82 EC has been felt in four important aspects of society–member relations. *First,* it is clear that under European law societies may not discriminate on grounds of nationality, for example, by conferring associate status on foreign authors. All collecting societies must permit other nationals from the EU to join the society.[132] *Second,* the Commission has stated that the rules of collecting societies should ensure that no group of members obtains preferential treatment from revenue collected from the membership as a whole.[133] *Third,* in *Belgische Radio v. SABAM,*[134] the European Court of Justice held that abuse would occur if a society imposed obligations on members which were not absolutely necessary for the attainment of the society's objectives and which could encroach unfairly on members' freedoms.[135] A restriction imposed upon a member must be 'indispensable' to the operation of the society, and must restrict the member's freedom to dispose of their works no more than is absolutely necessary (the 'equity' test).[136] *Fourth,* societies are not permitted to impose unduly

---

[127] Enterprise Act 2002, s. 131.   [128] Enterprise Act 2002 s. 134(4)

[129] *Report on the Supply in the UK of the Services of Administering Performing Rights and Film Synchronization Rights* (1996) (Cmnd. 3147).

[130] *Gowers Review,* paras 5.63–7.

[131] For the opinion that such organizations are 'undertakings', see *Belgische Radio en Televisie v. SV SABAM,* Case 127/73 [1974] *ECR* 313, 322–3 (AG Mayras).

[132] *Re GEMA (No. 1)* [1971] *CMLR* D–35.   [133] *Re GEMA's Statutes (No. 2)* [1972] *CMLR* D–115.

[134] *Belgische Radio,* note 131 above.   [135] Ibid, 317 (para. 15).

[136] See *Re GEMA (No. 1)* [1971] *CMLR* D–35 (where the Commission held that it was an abuse for the German society to require the assignment of all categories of right). Similarly, in the context of complaints against the

lengthy notice periods. In *Belgische Radio v. SABAM,* the European Court of Justice observed that rules operated by SABAM, the Belgian society of authors and composers, allowing the society to retain rights for five years after a member withdrew, 'may appear an unfair condition', but left the specific determination of whether this was so to the national authority.[137]

5.1.3 The EC Recommendation on On-Line Music

The 2005 Commission Recommendation on On-line Licensing of Music reiterates many of these requirements in an official text directed at member states and economic operators.[138] With the aim of encouraging Community-wide licensing of music on-line, the Recommendation states that rights holders should have the right to appoint any body to manage their rights on a multiterritorial basis, implicitly requiring collective rights managers to accept members irrespective of the territory of the rights holder's residence.[139] The Recommendation calls for collective managers to administer the rights with 'the utmost diligence', and to permit rights holders to determine what rights to transfer, the territorial basis of any licensing, and to withdraw rights from the society.[140] It requires the managers to distribute income equitably, specifying any deductions that are for purposes other than management (e.g. for the support of cultural activities generally) and that there be no discrimination (for example against non-nationals).[141] The Recommendation calls on collective managers to account appropriately, and invites member states to establish governance and dispute mechanisms.[142]

5.2 REGULATION OF SOCIETY–USER RELATIONS

Another way in which collecting societies are regulated is in terms of their relationship with users of copyright. Here the problem is that most people wishing to use copyright works have no alternative but to seek a licence from a collecting society. This places the society in a strong bargaining position, which may enable it to dictate terms of use to the licensee. In the absence of regulatory control, the society might charge exorbitant fees, discriminate unfairly between different kinds of user, or require parties to acquire licenses over many more works than they want. In order to ensure that this monopoly power is not abused, there are both domestic and European regulatory controls.[143]

5.2.1 The Copyright Tribunal

The Copyright Tribunal (which replaced the Performing Right Tribunal in 1989) has wide-ranging powers to review licences and licensing schemes operated by collecting societies.[144]

PRS, the MMC recommended that further exceptions could be allowed to the exclusive assignments that PRS demanded of its members, in particular permitting them to collect their own live performance revenues. The MMC also found that the PRS did not have in place adequate systems for ensuring that the distribution of royalties was carried out equitably. It recommended that the PRS rectify these failings by publishing detailed accounts, as well as taking advice about its mechanisms of sampling and how changes in those mechanisms and distribution policies impact on members. *Report on the Supply in the UK of the Services of Administering Performing Rights and Film Synchronization Rights* (1996) (Cm. 3147) (paras. 2.119–2.121).

[137] *Belgische Radio,* note 131 above, 317 (para. 12), 325–6 (AG). See also *GEMA (No. 2),* note 133 above (Commission allowed three years' minimum membership).

[138] Commission Recommendation on collective cross-border management for on-line music services, note 124 above.

[139] Ibid, para. 3.   [140] Ibid, paras. 4–5.   [141] Ibid, paras. 10–12.   [142] Ibid, paras. 14–15.

[143] A 'market investigation' reference could also be made under the Enterprise Act 2002.

[144] Though, as is explained below, not every aspect of copyright is regulated by the Tribunal. See Related Rights Reg. 17(4); CDPA s. 205B; Database Regs., Sched. 2.

The Tribunal normally sits in panels of three, selected from a group of up to eight. While it has been said that the Tribunal carries out a 'useful and indeed necessary function', its procedures have been criticized as being costly and lengthy.[145] Reforms are under consideration.[146]

The Copyright Tribunal is primarily concerned with the operation of 'licensing bodies'. A licensing body is defined as a society or other organization that has as one of its main objects the negotiation or granting of copyright licences. A body is still a licensing body if it is an agent, as well as when it becomes the owner of copyright. This means, for example, that the MCPS (which operates as an agent) is within the jurisdiction of the Copyright Tribunal. However, a body is only a licensing body if its object is the granting of licences covering works of more than one author.[147]

The 1988 Act distinguishes between two kinds of activity involving a licensing body, namely 'licensing schemes' and one-off 'licences'. A licensing scheme is defined as any regime that specifies the circumstances and terms on which a licensing body is willing to grant licences.[148] The Tribunal can consider complaints by representative organizations concerning the terms of a proposed scheme;[149] or complaints by organizations or individuals with respect to a scheme in operation.[150] The Tribunal has wide powers: it may approve or vary schemes, hold that particular applicants should be granted licences under such schemes, or approve or vary the terms of particular licences.[151] The Tribunal will also hear disputes over which applicants for licences fall within the scheme,[152] as well as refusals to grant licences. The Tribunal may make an order declaring that the complainant is entitled to a licence. After the Tribunal makes an order, a scheme may be referred again by its operator, a claimant for a licence, or a representative organization.[153]

The criterion by which the Tribunal judges matters is one of 'reasonableness'. As such, its role is more than one of 'arbitration'.[154] Indeed, where there are several reasonable solutions, the Tribunal's job is to select whatever is the 'most reasonable'.[155] In considering whether to make an order the Tribunal is instructed to have regard to a number of factors, of which the most important is to ensure there is no 'unreasonable discrimination' between the scheme or licence in issue and comparable schemes or licences.[156] Apart from that, specific factors are to be considered in relation to different schemes.[157] For example, if the scheme concerns reprographic copying, the Tribunal is to have regard to the availability of published editions, the proportion of the work copied, and the nature of the use to which the copies will be put. In add-

---

[145] M. Freegard, 'Forty Years on: An Appraisal of the United Kingdom Copyright Tribunal, 1957–1997' (1998) 177 *RIDA* 3, 69, 63. See also *Universities UK v. Copyright Licensing Agency* [2002] *RPC* 693, 699 (para. 16) (explaining that the goal of the Tribunal is to prevent unreasonable terms from being imposed and stating that current perceptions of proceedings as 'extremely costly, intolerably lengthy and highly complex' undermine the objective of the Tribunal). In *BPI Ltd et al v. MCPS et al* (19 July 2007) the costs were some £12 million.

[146] IPO, *Review of the Copyright Tribunal* (2007).

[147] See D. Zeffman and J. Enser, 'The Impact of UK Competition Law on the Music Industry' [1993] *Ent LR* 67, 71 (licensing body arguably includes companies such as publishers).

[148] CDPA s. 117.   [149] CDPA s. 118.   [150] CDPA s. 119.   [151] CDPA ss. 118–20.

[152] CDPA s. 119. The Tribunal can make orders concerning matter excluded from a licensing scheme: *Universities UK*, note 145 above, 707 (para. 59) (interim decision that the Tribunal had jurisdiction to review handling of 'study pack' material which had been excluded from the scope of the licensing scheme).

[153] CDPA s. 120.

[154] *British Airways v. The PRS* [1998] *RPC* 581.   [155] *BPI v. MCPS* [1993] *EMLR* 86, 139; 22 *IPR* 325, 333.

[156] CDPA s. 129. Any discrimination should be 'logical': *BSB v. PRS* [1998] *RPC* 467, para. 5.4. Cf. Freegard, 'Forty Years On', 57 (comparisons rarely used as guides).

[157] CDPA ss. 130–5.

ition to the factors specifically listed in the 1988 Act, the Tribunal will also take account of factors indicated as relevant in EC Directives.[158]

In determining the reasonableness of licence fees, the Copyright Tribunal has often described its task as determining what a 'willing licensor and willing licensee' would have agreed.[159] The usual starting point for ascertaining what this might be is with previous agreements, which are evaluated by the Tribunal in the light of changed circumstances.[160] Because the Tribunal is directed to ensure that there is no unreasonable discrimination, it will often be presented with evidence of allegedly equivalent arrangements.[161] These may include arrangements by the same licensing body with other categories of user,[162] or arrangements by similarly positioned licensing bodies with the same licensees.[163] While evidence of schemes in other jurisdictions is frequently put forward, it has rarely been influential.[164] Other factors which are often treated as relevant include the extent of use, the size of the audience, and the user's revenue. Ultimately, calculating fees is not a process of mathematics, but one of 'judicial estimation'.[165]

5.2.2 Other avenues

A user who is dissatisfied with the terms of a licensing scheme or an individual licence from a collecting society might also be able to bring an action based upon either Article 81 or 82 EC (formerly Articles 85 and 86 of the Treaty),[166] or the two prohibitions contained in the domestic Competition Act 1998.[167]

Applying Articles 81 and 82 EC, the ECJ has provided national courts with general guidance on legitimate collecting society behaviour. In particular, in *Ministère Public v. Tournier*[168] it was argued that the arrangements between the French copyright management society SACEM and discotheques were prohibited under Articles 81 and 82 EC. In that case SACEM granted a blanket licence for its whole repertoire and charged discotheques according to a percentage of gross receipts. Some discotheque owners complained that the charges were excessive and that SACEM refused to grant licences for part of its repertoire, namely in relation to popular dance of Anglo-American origin. The public prosecutor brought criminal proceedings against Tournier, who was director of SACEM, for 'unfair trading'. As part of the action, certain questions were referred to the ECJ.

In relation to SACEM's refusal to license use of music from abroad separately, the Court noted that the parallel behaviour might amount to strong evidence of a concerted practice (contrary to Article 81). The Court added that it might be possible to account for the parallel behaviour on the grounds that direct licensing would require each society to establish its own management and monitoring system in other countries.[169] With regard to SACEM's decision to grant only blanket licences, the Court suggested that the test was one of 'necessity', that is

---

[158] *BSB v. PRS*, note 156 above (Satellite Dir., Recital 17).

[159] For example, *Working Men's Club v. PRS* [1992] *RPC* 227, 232.

[160] *BACTA v. PPL* [1992] *RPC* 149; *BPI v. MCPS* [1993] *EMLR* 86, 139.

[161] See *BPI Ltd et al v. MCPS et al* (19 July 2007).　　[162] *BACTA v. PPL* [1992] *RPC* 149.

[163] Ibid; *AIRC v. PPL* [1994] *RPC* 143.　　[164] *BA v. The PRS* [1998] *RPC* 581.

[165] *Universities UK v. Copyright Licensing Agency* [2002] *RPC* 693, 726 (para. 177).

[166] These prohibitions would also apply to society–society arrangements, such as reciprocal agreements. See Commission Decision of 8 Oct. 2002 relating to a proceeding under Art. 81 of the EC Treaty and Art. 53 of the EEA Agreement (Case no. COMP/C2/38.014—*IFPI 'Simulcasting'* (2003/300/EC) *OJ L* 107/58 (30 Apr. 2003) (granting exemption to reciprocal agreement permitting multiterritorial simulcasting).

[167] Competition Act 1998, s. 2 (Ch. 1 prohibition), s. 18 (Ch. 2 prohibition).

[168] *Ministère Public v. Tournier and Verney*, Case 395/87 [1989] *ECR* 2521.

[169] Ibid; also [1991] 4 *CMLR* 248.

whether the terms or practices were 'necessary' to safeguard the interests of authors, etc. This was a matter for national courts to determine.

With respect to the charges, the ECJ found that, if there exists an appreciable difference between the fees charged in one member state and those charged in other member states for the same services, such a discrepancy 'must be regarded as indicative of an abuse of dominant position'.[170] In such circumstances, the ECJ indicated that the burden of proof was effectively reversed. Where this occurs it would be for the relevant collecting society 'to justify the difference by reference to objective dissimilarities between the situation in the member state concerned and the situation prevailing in all the other member states'.[171]

With so-called 'modernization' of competition law and establishment of the European Competition Network, complaints about society–user relations are likely to be directed to national authorities. In the United Kingdom this would be to the courts or the OFT if Articles 81 and 82 are implicated, otherwise to the Copyright Tribunal.

5.2.3 The EC Recommendation on On-Line Music

The Recommendation also contains provisions bearing upon society–user relations.[172] The Recommendation calls on collective managers to inform users promptly of changes in the repertoire the manager represents, and calls on commercial users to inform collective managers of exactly which permissions they want.[173] Collective managers are required to grant licences to users on an objective basis and without discrimination.[174] The Recommendation calls on member states to establish mechanisms to regulate licensing conditions.[175]

---

[170] Ibid, 2577 (para. 38). In *Bassett v. SACEM*, Case 402/85 [1987] *ECR* 1747, 1769 (para. 19) the Court did observe that 'it is not impossible, however, that the amount of royalty...charged by the copyright management society may be such that [Art. 82] applies'.

[171] Case 395/87 [1989] *ECR* 2521, 2577 (para. 38).

[172] Commission Recommendation on collective cross-border management for on-line music services, note 124 above.

[173] Ibid, paras. 7–8.   [174] Ibid, para. 9.   [175] Ibid, para. 15.

13

RELATED RIGHTS: PERFORMERS' RIGHTS, DATABASE RIGHT, TECHNOLOGICAL PROTECTION MEASURES, RIGHTS MANAGEMENT INFORMATION, PUBLIC LENDING RIGHT, AND THE *DROIT DE SUITE*

CHAPTER CONTENTS

1 INTRODUCTION

If there is one characteristic that typifies the development of intellectual property law since the Second World War, it is the proliferation of new forms of intellectual property. In this chapter we outline a number of regimes which are related to but which fall outside of the remit of copyright law: performers' rights; database right; rights relating to technological protection measures and rights management information; public lending right; and the so-called *droit de suite,* or artist's resale royalty right.

2 PERFORMERS' RIGHTS

While the creative or cultural contributions made by people who play instruments, read poetry, and act in plays have long been valued, nonetheless performers have been poorly served by intellectual property law. Indeed, it was not until technological changes at the beginning of the twentieth century (notably the emergence of sound-recording technologies and radio broadcasting) threatened the livelihood of performers that the law intervened to protect performers. This occurred in 1925 when criminal sanctions were introduced to discourage people from abusing a performer's right to control the fixation and subsequent use of their performances.[1] The courts provided additional relief by allowing performers to bring civil suits for injunctions and damages for threatened breaches of the criminal law.[2] While it might have been expected that copyright law would have been expanded to accommodate performers, this was not the case. In part this was because the transitory nature of performances meant that they could not satisfy the requirement of material form that was widely considered to be a prerequisite for the subsistence of copyright. Another reason why performers were not protected by copyright was that they were considered to be subservient to the interests of the 'proper' rights holders: namely, authors, composers, and dramatists. While authors and composers create primary works, performers were seen to merely translate or interpret these works. In short, it was believed (at least by some) that performers were involved in acts that were less 'creative' than authors, graphic artists, and film directors. The second-rate status of performers was reflected in the decision that performers did not belong within the Berne Convention (along with the producers of phonograms and broadcasting organizations). Indeed it was not until the Rome Convention of 1961 that performers were recognized at the international level.[3] The rights given to performers have been expanded further in the WIPO Performances and Phonograms Treaty 1996.

Eventually, the lobbying efforts of performers paid off when the 1988 Act provided performers with the right to control the recording of live performances (and other related rights).[4] As the rights were not assignable, they are described as 'non-property' rights. The 1988 Act also provided producers with certain rights when they entered into exclusive contracts to record performers.[5] The scope of the protection given to performers was further expanded as a result of European harmonization. To bring UK law into line with the Rental Rights Directive, the 1988 Act was amended from 1 December 1996 to provide performers with fully assignable 'property rights' and certain 'rights to remuneration'. In a third significant development, Article 5 of the WIPO Performances and Phonograms Treaty required contracting parties to grant moral rights of attribution and integrity to performers),[6] and these have now been implemented in the UK. In all but two respects, namely duration and depth of protection,[7] these bring performers' protection to a level virtually equivalent to that of authors.

2.1 SUBSISTENCE

Protection is confined to dramatic performances (which include dance or mime), musical performances, readings and recitations of literary works, and also to 'a variety act or any similar presentation'.[8] This definition clearly encompasses much of what we would expect.

---

[1] Dramatic and Musical Performers' Protection Act 1925, consolidated and amended in the Performers' Protection Acts 1958 and 1972. See R. Arnold, *Performers' Rights* (3rd edn., 2004).

[2] *Rickless v. United Artists* [1987] *FSR* 362.   [3] See above at p. 42.

[4] The Act has been held to confer rights on performers, such as Jimi Hendrix, who were long dead: *Experience Hendrix LLC v. Purple Haze Records Ltd* [2007] *EWCA Civ* 501.

[5] CDPA ss. 180–4.   [6] See above at pp. 44–5.   [7] Performers are not protected against imitation.

[8] CDPA s. 180(2). The WPPT, Art. 2(a), defines performers as 'actors, singers, musicians, dancers and other persons who act, sing, deliver, declaim, play in, interpret, or otherwise perform literary or artistic works or expressions of folklore'.

Protection therefore arises for dramatic performances, such as the acting of a play in front of a live audience, or film script before a camera, or the performing of a ballet. It also arises where the performance is 'musical' as with the playing of a classical piece, such as Beethoven's Fifth Symphony by an orchestra, or the rendition of a pop song by a band.[9]

However, the definition is not without its ambiguities and apparent restrictions. First, there are ambiguities raised by the definition as to whether the work performed must exist before the performance takes place. The wording of section 180 of the CDPA suggests this need not be so for musical or dramatic works, since sub-section (2) refers to musical or dramatic performances. Thus unscripted and improvised musical and dramatic performances are almost certainly covered.[10] However, in the case of readings or recitations, the definition suggests that the literary work must be in existence prior to the performance. Consequently, a person who gives a spontaneous speech or an interview will not obtain protection as a performer. Presumably, a singer who sings a song gives a 'musical' performance, even though in copyright terminology there might only be a performance of a literary work. Another ambiguity relates to what constitutes a 'musical performance'. It is unclear whether the term covers the playing of the work from a recording, so that a disc jockey could be a performer. Finally, the definition of performance seems unduly restrictive. It seems that a performance of an 'artistic work'—by way of *tableaux vivant*, for example—is not included, unless such a performance can be classed as a 'variety act' or 'similar presentation'. (A broad interpretation may be desirable in order to ensure compliance with the UK's international obligations.) Owen Morgan has proposed a 'principled definition' of a performance as 'the transitory activity of a human individual that can be perceived without the aid of technology and that is intended as a form of communication to others for the purpose of entertainment, education or ritual'.[11]

Before moving on, it should be noted that international and regional treaties frequently distinguish between audiovisual performances and performances embodied on phonograms: indeed, international standards are directed primarily at the latter. While the reasons for the distinction are easy to understand (some parts of the film industry fearing that giving performers rights will potentially jeopardize a film company's ability to exploit a film), the distinction is not entirely satisfactory. This is because there is now a significant overlap and interchangeability between media, so, for example, that some performances start life as audiovisual before being recorded onto purely aural media, and some aural performances are later fixed on audiovisual media. The boundary lines are, not surprisingly, highly contested.

2.2 PERFORMERS, AND RELATED BENEFICIARIES

The beneficiary of the rights given in a performance is prima facie the performer (or performers).[12] Although performers are typically freelance workers rather than employees, a

---

[9] One may wonder whether performance of Cage's '4' 33"' constitutes a musical performance. See the earlier discussion at pp. 70–1 as to whether the piece is a 'musical work' for copyright purposes.

[10] Kamina, p. 350. Given that a 'dramatic work' is a 'work of action which is capable of being performed' it seems that a performance of a dramatic work requires action: performances lacking movement not being covered (unless they can be categorized as akin to 'variety acts').

[11] See O. Morgan, *International Protection of Performers' Rights* (2002), 27.

[12] The Act provides no indication as to the test for co-performance. For example, one might ask whether, if a band perform a song, there is: (a) one performance and multiple performers (as one might assume); or (b) multiple performances each given by the individual performer (guitarist, singer, drummer, which is not implausible given that each will be 'miked-up' individually, so that the contributions are technically separable); or (c) two performances (one a musical performance by the musicians, one a dramatic performance by the singer). Is

performer is entitled to performance rights *even if* they are employed.[13] Two issues are worth further consideration. The first concerns exactly who counts as a performer. The second concerns special provisions relating to the rights of those who are a party to exclusive recording agreements.

2.2.1 Main performers, ancillary performers, and other contributors

In contrast with some other jurisdictions, no attempt is made under UK law to exclude ancillary performers from the scope of protection.[14] This means that in practice care must be taken to deal contractually with all participants, session musicians as well as named artists, extras as well as star performers. A person present in the audience at a performance would not normally be regarded as 'giving' a performance, though in situations where a show depends upon active participation of members of the audience it is possible that a member of the audience might become a performer.[15] Although a director, or choreographer, or make-up artist may contribute significantly to the preparation of a performance, it cannot be said that they 'give' the performance. Consequently, they are left to their rights, if any, under copyright or contract law. The same is true for the organizer of a performance, such as a theatre or venue operator.

2.2.2 Exclusive recording contracts

Special provisions exist in the 1988 Act that relate to exclusive recording contracts. Section 185 defines an exclusive recording contract as 'a contract between a performer and another person under which that person is entitled to the exclusion of all other persons (including the performer) to make recordings of one or more of his performances with a view to their commercial exploitation'. If the person having such rights is a qualifying person, then they are granted rights similar to a performer's non-property rights. More specifically, their consent is required by anyone else wishing to make a recording. A party who is the beneficiary of an exclusive recording contract may commence an action for breach of statutory duty against a person who makes such a recording,[16] or who shows a wrongful recording in public or broadcasts it,[17] as well as against those dealing commercially in such illicit recordings.[18] While performers' non-property rights are not transferable, the person with an exclusive recording contract may assign rights under that contract.[19]

2.3 RIGHTS

There are four types of right available to protect performers: non-property rights, property rights, remuneration rights, and moral rights.

---

the issue one of separability of contribution, intention to integrate, or perception of integration? The answer might be important when determining whose consent is required to exploit elements or parts of the collective performance. The courts have consistently favoured the view that each performer gains rights in his or her own performance: *Bamgboye v. Reed* [2004] *EMLR* (5) 61; *Experience Hendrix v. Purple Haze Records Ltd.* [2005] *EMLR* (18) 417 (para. 21); *Bourne v. Davis* [2006] *EWHC* 1567 (para. 7).

[13] Arnold, *Performers' Rights*, ch. 3. Note that such performers are presumed employees under French law: see Kamina, p. 357.

[14] Cf. Art. L. 212 of the French Intellectual Property Code.

[15] Cf. Copyright Act 1968, s. 248A(2)(d) (Australia) (excluding 'a participation in a performance as a member of an audience').

[16] CDPA s. 186.   [17] CDPA s. 187.   [18] CDPA s. 188.   [19] CDPA s. 185(2), (3).

2.3.1 Non-property rights

A performer has the right to authorize the recording of a live performance. They also have the right to prevent the making of a recording of a live performance from a broadcast in which it has been included.[20] (These are the acts of 'bootlegging'.) Performers also have the right to prevent their live performances being broadcast. Prior to the mass distribution of fixed recordings, this right would have been very important. Where a recording has been made without the consent of a performer, their rights are infringed when the wrongfully recorded performance is shown or played in public, or communicated to the public. This right is only infringed where the defendant knew or had reason to believe the recording was made without the performer's consent.[21] This would cover the playing of obviously bootlegged recordings at discotheques or over the radio. Performers are also given the right to control the distribution of illicit recordings. These are recordings made, otherwise than for private purposes, without the consent of the performer or the person, if any, having recording rights.[22] Import and sale of illicit recordings is prohibited where the person knows or has reason to believe that the recording is illicit.[23]

All of these non-property rights are non-transmissible, except on death.[24] Infringement is actionable as a breach of statutory duty. A person may also be subject to criminal liability if they knowingly commit certain commercial acts in relation to illicit recordings.[25]

2.3.2 Property rights

Performers are also given property rights in their performances. These rights were introduced in order to implement the Rental Rights Directive.[26] The performer's property rights include the right to make copies of a recording of a qualifying performance, the right to issue copies of a recording to the public, the right to rent or lend copies, and the right to include the performance in an on-demand service.[27] The definitions of these three rights correspond to those of a copyright owner.[28] In contrast with the other rights given to performers, these property rights are transmissible. Any assignments made must be in writing and signed by the assignor.[29] In relation to film-production agreements, a performer is presumed, in the absence of an agreement to the contrary, to have transferred the rental right to the producer.[30]

2.3.3 Right of remuneration

Performers are also given two 'remuneration rights'. These were introduced in the process of implementing the Rental Rights Directive. The most important of these, at least financially, is the right to claim equitable remuneration from the owner of copyright in a *sound recording* (note, not an audiovisual work) of a qualifying performance, where the sound recording is played in public, or communicated to the public (other than by way of 'making available').[31] This

---

[20] CDPA s. 182. The limitation to the effect that these rights are not infringed if the recording is made for private and domestic purposes has been removed to implement the Info. Soc. Dir.: SI 2003/2498 Sched. 2.

[21] CDPA s. 183.   [22] CDPA s. 197.   [23] CDPA s. 184.   [24] CDPA s. 192A.

[25] CDPA s. 198. Illicit recording is defined in CDPA s. 197.

[26] See Ch. 2. The new regime applies to performances given before commencement: Related Rights Reg. 26(1).

[27] CDPA s. 191A and s. 182A–C, s. 182CA (as added by SI 2003/2498 r. 7). The Copyright Tribunal has an ultimate power to override a performer's right to consent, if they cannot be identified: CDPA s. 190, as amended. Prior to 1 Dec. 1996, the Tribunal had power to override refusal of consent if it was being unreasonably withheld.

[28] See Ch. 6.   [29] CDPA s. 191B.   [30] CDPA s. 191F.

[31] CDPA s. 182D (as amended by SI 2003/2498 r. 7). A sound recording is not played in public when a film in which the recording is incorporated is shown in public: CDPA s. 5B(3)(a). Cf. Kamina, pp. 356–7 n. 111.

right formalized the existing practice whereby recording companies made *ex gratia* payments to bodies representing musicians. Under the new regime, performers must claim their revenue that accrues in the United Kingdom from the collecting society that administers the performing and broadcasting rights on behalf of the owners of copyright sound recordings, namely Phonographic Performance Limited.[32] The second remuneration right is less important. This provides that where a performer has transferred their rental right concerning a sound recording or film to the producer, the performer retains the right to equitable remuneration for the rental of sound recordings or films.[33]

Both of the remuneration rights may only be assigned to a collecting society.[34] In the absence of a relevant agreement, the Copyright Tribunal may determine royalty rates.[35] As yet there have been no cases where the Tribunal has been asked to assess what an equitable remuneration should be. Although the concept of 'equitable remuneration' is a 'Community concept' it is one to be applied by national authorities, so each is left with a wide margin of appreciation, particularly as to determining relevant criteria. In the only decision to date, the ECJ has said that it was within this margin to calculate the money to be paid by a broadcaster by reference to the number of hours of phonograms broadcast; the viewing and listening densities; the tariffs used in respect of such uses of musical works; the tariffs used in other member states; and the amounts paid by other (commercial) stations.[36] The 'national court is therefore doing everything to ensure the best possible compliance with the provisions of Article 8(2)...assuring the equitable remuneration of performing artists and phonogram producers by giving preference to a contractual agreement based on objective criteria'.[37]

2.3.4 Moral Rights

Performers are granted the moral rights of attribution and integrity.[38] Like authors' moral rights, these rights are not assignable, but may be waived, and are transmissible on death.[39]

The right of attribution applies in relation to live performances, to live broadcasts of performances of all kinds, and to the distribution and communication to the public of performances fixed on sound recordings.[40] Performers have the rights to be so named that their identities are brought to the notice of the relevant public; however, where a performance is by a group, attribution to the group may be sufficient.[41] As with the moral right of attribution granted to authors, the right is not infringed unless it has first been asserted.[42] The right is subject to various exceptions, the most important being that the right does not apply where it is not 'reasonably practicable' to identify the performer or, as appropriate, the group; also, inter alia, it does not apply where the performance is for the purpose of reporting current events or where the performance is for the purpose of advertising any goods or services.[43]

---

[32] Until 2007, this was done via either PAMRA (the Performing Artists' Media Right Association) or AURA (Association of United Recording Artists), but in Jan 2007 these two organizations were merged into a reformed PPL (which previously had just represented record companies).

[33] CDPA s. 191G.   [34] CDPA s. 191G(2).   [35] CDPA ss. 182D(4), 191H.

[36] *Stichting ter Exploitatie van Naburige Rechten (SENA) v. Nederlandse Omroep Stichting (NOS)*, Case C–245/00 [2003] *EMLR* (17) 364.

[37] Ibid, para. 44.

[38] Performances (Moral Rights, etc.) Regulations 2006 SI 2006/18. For background, see Copyright Directorate, *Consultation Paper on Regulations Implementing Performers' Moral Rights in the U.K. Resulting from the WIPO Performances and Phonograms Treaty Obligations.*

[39] CDPA s. 205J(2) (waiver), 205L (non-assignability), 205M (transmission on death).

[40] CDPA s. 205C.   [41] CDPA s. 205C(3), (4).   [42] CDPA s 205D. On such assertion, see pp. 245–6.

[43] CDPA s. 205E.

The right of integrity applies in relation to live broadcasts of all qualifying performances, as well as to the playing or communication to the public of sound recordings embodying qualifying performances.[44] The performers have the right to object to any such performance insofar as it is subject to a distortion, mutilation, or other modification that is prejudicial to the reputation of the performer. Modifications 'consistent with normal editorial or production practice' are permitted, and other exceptions parallel those to author's moral rights.[45] The integrity right is also infringed by possession or distribution in the course of business of copies of a sound recording embodying a performance which has been so modified as to prejudice the reputation of the performer, but liability is dependent on a showing of *scienter*.[46]

2.4 DURATION, DEFENCES, AND REMEDIES

All performers' rights last for at least 50 years from the end of the year of the performance. However, if a recording incorporating the performance is released within this period,[47] the rights last for 50 years from the year of release.[48] Rights vested in a performer at the time of their death may only be exercised by a person specifically nominated in the performer's will or by their personal representative.[49]

Performers' rights are subject to a host of defences that, rather inconveniently, are contained in Schedule 2 to the 1988 Act. The defences parallel those for copyright and include fair dealing for criticism or review, fair dealing for reporting current events, incidental inclusion, as well as a range of educational and library defences. These are all discussed in Chapter 9, and the comments made there apply equally to performers (*mutatis mutandis*). One defence notable by its absence is the defence of fair dealing for research and private study. However, the defence applicable to recording broadcasts for the purpose of watching or listening to the broadcast at a later time also applies to any performance included in the broadcast.

Like copyright, the property and non-property rights are enforceable in civil and criminal actions. The usual remedies for breaches of statutory duty are available, namely injunctions, damages, or account of profits. The right owner may also prosecute for a range of statutory offences, seek orders which include delivery-up and disposal, and seize infringing articles from traders without premises. These remedies are discussed in Chapter 48.[50]

2.5 FOREIGN PERFORMANCES

Performances by foreign performers or performances that take place in foreign countries will be protected in the United Kingdom if the performance is 'qualifying'. A performance is a 'qualifying performance' if it is given by a 'qualifying individual' or takes place in a 'qualifying country'.[51] A 'qualifying individual' is a citizen of, or an individual resident in,

---

[44] CDPA s. 205F.   [45] CDPA s. 205G(3). On parallel exceptions to authors' moral rights, see Ch. 10.

[46] CDPA s. 205(H).

[47] CDPA s. 191(2). The requisite 'release' includes the following acts if authorized: publication, playing or showing in public, or communication to the public: CDPA s. 191(3). For further details on these rights, see Ch. 6.

[48] CDPA s. 191.   [49] CDPA s. 192.   [50] CDPA ss. 194–202.

[51] CDPA s. 181. Despite the use of the present tense in the legislation, once a country becomes a qualifying country or a person becomes a qualifying individual, the rights arise retrospectively in relation to past performances: see *Experience Hendrix LLC v. Purple Haze Records Ltd* [2007] EWCA Civ 501. Unfortunately, the relevant Order in Council did not contain any saving for vested rights or for those who have prepared arrangements on the assumption that no relevant performer's right operated. See Arnold, *Performers' Rights*, 68–9. The Orders which have operated since 1 May 2005 have rectified this anomaly.

a 'qualifying country'.[52] A 'qualifying country' is defined as the United Kingdom, another member state of the EEA, or a country 'designated ... as enjoying reciprocal protection' under section 208 of the 1988 Act.[53] Section 208 empowers Her Majesty to designate certain countries as qualifying countries by Order in Council: either countries party to a convention relating to performers' rights (namely the Rome Convention or TRIPS), or countries deemed to give 'adequate protection' to performances by British citizens, residents or taking place in the United Kingdom.[54]

Section 185, which confers equivalent rights on a person who is party to an exclusive recording contract, does so only if they or one of their licensees, is a 'qualifying person'. A 'qualifying person', is defined as a 'qualifying individual' or a body corporate sufficiently connected with a 'qualifying country'.[55]

2.6 REFORM OF DURATION

As mentioned in Chapter 7, the European Commission has announced that it intends to extend copyright in sound recordings to 95 years, particularly with a view to ensuring performers (in particular, session musicians) continue to receive royalties on recordings created in the 1950s and 1960s. Commissioner McCreevy has even promised that 20 per cent of receipts will be distributed amongst session musicians.

3 DATABASE RIGHT

Many different technologies organize and order information: encyclopedias, filing cabinets, and textbooks all play their role in placing information in a usable format. Databases are another obvious example. While databases have existed in one form or another for a very long time, digital technology has transformed and revitalized databases. In particular, the digital database has enabled the production of facilities that enable easy access to vast collections of information. Examples familiar to lawyers include LEXIS and WestLaw, as well as CD–ROMs such as the 'Index to legal periodicals'. The value of these facilities is the comprehensive nature of the information that they contain and the ease of access, rather than the way in which that information is ordered. While databases can cost a considerable amount of money to construct, they are readily copied. This makes them an ideal candidate for intellectual property protection.[56]

Faced with the fact that the level of protection varied, sometimes considerably, between member states,[57] the EC decided to harmonize the law that protected the effort that went into creating

---

[52] CDPA s. 206. For a general analysis of concepts relevant to protecting foreign claims see above at pp. 5–6 and Ch. 4 Section 5.

[53] There is no distinction drawn between 'extension' and 'application', though CDPA s. 208(5) allows Part II of the Act to be 'applied' to countries that in Part I are subject to 'extension'.

[54] Copyright and Performances (Application to Other Countries) Order 2008 (SI 2008/667).

[55] CDPA ss. 181, 185(3), 206(1).

[56] At least in economic theory: see Davison, 239 ff., with criticisms; E. Derclaye, *The Legal Protection of Databases: A Comparative Analysis* (2008) *Ch.* 1.

[57] Some, such as the UK and Ireland, would probably have protected most databases by copyright; others would have done so through 'unfair competition'; the Nordic countries had adopted a special form of protection for catalogues and a burning issue remains to what extent the Directive should be read as generalizing the latter position. On this, see Davison, 141.

databases.[58] Eventually these efforts took shape in the form of the Database Directive,[59] which was implemented into the United Kingdom on 1 January 1998, in the Database Regulations.[60] The Database Directive required member states to introduce a two-tier system of protection for databases. The first tier involves retaining copyright protection for databases that are 'original'.[61] This was discussed in Chapters 3 and 4. The Directive also requires member states to provide a second tier of protection by way of a new *sui generis* right known as the 'database right'. Database rights arise in relation to databases, including those that fail to reach the copyright's originality threshold.[62] The database right is separate from and in addition to any copyright protection that may exist in relation to a database. Although, this new database right was described as 'one of the least balanced and most potentially anti-competitive intellectual property rights ever created',[63] much of its apparent strength has been curtailed by the European Court of Justice in four decisions: *Fixtures Marketing v. Oy Veikkaus,*[64] *Fixtures Marketing v. Organismoa Prognostikon Agnon Podosfairou,*[65] *Fixtures Marketing v. Svenska,*[66] and *British Horseracing Board v. William Hill.*[67] The first three concerned whether there was database right in Premier League fixture lists, and the ECJ clearly indicated that there is not. *BHB* concerned cumulative lists of runners and riders in British horse races, and, following the ECJ's advice, this was held by the Court of Appeal not to be protected.[68]

3.1 SUBSISTENCE

The database right is a property right that subsists in a database whether made before or after 1 January 1998.[69] A 'database' is defined as 'a collection of independent works, data or other

[58] Complete uniformity has not been achieved because member states are able to retain unfair competition protection, and to diverge in implementing exceptions (Database Dir. Art 9, Art. 13). See Davison, 156–7. Note also Recital 52, which enables countries which have specific rules providing a right comparable to the *sui generis* right (presumably, the Nordic countries) to retain 'as far as the new right is concerned, the expectations traditionally specified by such rules'.

[59] See above at pp. 51–2. The legislative history of the Directive is explored in Davison, 50–68.

[60] Copyright and Rights in Databases Regulations 1997 (SI 1997/3032). For implementation in Europe, see Davison Ch. 5.

[61] Transitional provisions make it clear that databases which were already protected by copyright on 27 Mar. 1996, but which would not reach the standards required under the Directive, continue to enjoy protection until the end of the copyright term.

[62] Database Reg. 13(2) (reflecting Database Dir. Art. 7(4)) says that it is immaterial whether or not the database or any of its contents are copyright works. In the original proposal, a work which benefited from copyright would not have been able to benefit from database right: Davison, 81.

[63] J. Reichman and P. Samuelson, 'Intellectual Property Rights in Data?' 50 *Vanderbilt Law Review* 51, 81. Davison, 285, though less hysterical, is equally critical, saying the Directive has 'significant flaws in both its detail and overall design'.

[64] Case C–46/02 [2005] *ECDR* (2) 21.   [65] Case C–444/02 [2005] 1 *CMLR* (16) 367.

[66] Case C–338/02 [2005] *ECDR* (4) 43.   [67] Case C–203/02 [2005] 1 *CMLR* (15) 319.

[68] *British Horseracing Board v. William Hill* [2005] *RPC* 883. For commentaries on the cases, see T. Aplin, 'The ECJ elucidates the database right' (2005) *IPQ* 204; Derclaye, 'The Court of Justice interprets to database *sui generis* right for the first time' (2005) *ELR* 420; M. Davison & B. Hugenholtz, 'Football Fixtures, Horseraces and Spin Offs: the ECJ domesticates the database right' (2005) *EIPR* 113.

[69] Database Regs. 13(1), 27–8 (implementing Database Dir., Art. 14(3), Art 16). It is immaterial whether or not the database or any of its contents is a copyright work, so that there may be a database right where there is no copyright, or there may be both copyright and a database right. It may also be possible for a database to attract copyright but not the database right if the selection and arrangement renders the collection the author's own intellectual creation but there is not substantial 'human' investment in presenting the contents of the database. Nothing in these Regulations affects any agreement made before commencement; nor does any act done

materials that are arranged in a systematic or methodical way, and are individually accessible by electronic or other means'.[70] We reviewed the meaning of 'database' in Chapter 3, noting its potentially awesome breadth.

The database right only arises if there has been a substantial investment in obtaining, verifying, or presenting the contents of the database. 'Investment' includes any investment, whether of financial, human, or technical resources.[71] Investment may be 'substantial' in terms of quality, quantity, or a combination of both. The former refers to 'quantifiable resources', the latter 'to efforts which cannot be quantified, such as intellectual effort or energy'.[72] The ECJ did not comment on the Advocate General's view that the Directive requires an absolute lower threshold for investments worthy of protection as a sort of *de minimis* rule albeit at a low level: a high threshold level 'would undermine the intended purpose of the Directive, which was to create incentives for investment'.[73]

The act of 'obtaining' information is, it seems, to be distinguished from creating information: investment in creation is not relevant.[74] It is to be 'understood to refer to the resources used to seek out existing independent materials and collect them in the database, and not to the resources used for the creation as such of independent materials'.[75] So the investment in deciding which horses may run in a race was regarded as investment in the creation of data, and thus to be disregarded when assessing whether a collection of such material was a database that resulted from substantial investment.[76] Equally, the resources deployed to determine the football league fixtures was an investment in creating data rather than the database. Finding and collecting, verifying and presenting that existing data did not require 'any particular effort'.[77] In the same case, 'verification' was described as monitoring the accuracy of the materials when the database is created and during its operation. It does not include verification during the stage of creation of data.[78] In the three *Fixtures Marketing* references, Advocate General Stix-Hackl had observed that 'presentation' 'entails not only the presentation for users of the database, that is to say, the external format, but also the conceptual format, such as the structuring of the contents'.[79] The ECJ did not comment on this.

The basic term of protection is 15 years.[80] More specifically, the database right expires 15 years from the end of the calendar year in which the database was completed.[81] However,

---

either before or after commencement, in pursuance of an agreement made before commencement, amount to an infringement of the database right in a database.

[70] Database Reg. 12.

[71] Database Reg. 13; Database Dir., Recitals 7, 12, 39, 40 (right protects *any* investment and referring to various types). Note Derclaye, *Legal Protection*, 74 (arguing that databases created by the state are unprotected because the state does not 'invest').

[72] *Svenska*, Case C–338/02 [2005] *ECDR* (4) 43, para 28; *OPAP*, Case C–444/02 [2005] 1 *CMLR* (16) 367, para. 44; *Veikkaus*, Case C–46/02 [2005] *ECDR* (2) 21, para. 38.

[73] *Svenska*, AG Stix-Hackl, para. 39. See Derclaye, *Legal Protection*, 76–83 for a review of national case law.

[74] *BHB v. William Hill*, Case C–203/02 [2005] 1 *CMLR* (15) 319 (ECJ).

[75] *BHB*, Case C–203/02 [2005] 1 *CMLR* (15) 319 (ECJ), para. 31; *Svenska*, Case C–338/02 [2005] *ECDR* (4) 43, para. 24; *OPAP*, Case C–444/02 [2005] 1 *CMLR* (16) 367, para 40; *Veikkaus*, Case C–46/02 [2005] *ECDR* (2) 21, para. 34.

[76] *BHB*, Case C–203/02 [2005] 1 *CMLR* (15) 319 (ECJ), para. 38. *BHB v. William Hill* [2005] *RPC* 883 (CA) (applying the decision of the ECJ and holding the lists of runners and riders to be based on investment in creating the data, that is, the official list, rather than collecting and verifying existing data).

[77] *Svenska*, Case C–338/02 [2005] *ECDR* (4) 43, para. 36; *OPAP*, Case C–444/02 [2005] 1 *CMLR* (16) 367, para 49; *Veikkaus*, Case C–46/02 [2005] *ECDR* (2) 21, para 44.

[78] *BHB*, Case C–203/02 [2005] 1 *CMLR* (15) 319 (ECJ), para. 34; *Svenska*, Case C–338/02 [2005] *ECDR* (4) 43, para 27; *OPAP*, Case C–444/02 [2005] 1 *CMLR* (16) 367, para. 43.

[79] For example, *OPAP*, Case C–444/02 [2005] 1 *CMLR* (16) 367, AG's Opinion para. 78.

[80] Where the making of a database was completed on or after 1 Jan. 1983, the right begins to subsist in the database for the period of 15 years beginning on 1 Jan. 1998: Database Reg. 30.

[81] Database Reg. 17 (implementing Database Dir. Art. 10).

where a database is made available to the public before the end of the period of 15 years from when it was made, rights in the database expire 15 years from the end of the calendar year in which the database was first made available to the public. It is possible that a database right might subsist for 30 years (and thereafter be extended, as discussed below). Where copies of the database as published bear a label or a mark stating that the database was first published in a specified year, the label or mark shall be presumed to be correct until the contrary is proved.[82]

It is important to note that a new period of protection may be acquired for a database. For this to occur there must be a substantial change *to the contents* of the database.[83] This will include a substantial change resulting from the accumulation of successive additions, deletions, or alterations (so long as the changes constitute a substantial new investment in the database). In these circumstances the 'new' database qualifies for its own term of protection, but probably only as regards those contents that reflect the new substantial investment. In many cases, therefore, it will be legitimate to extract contents that are more than 15 years old from the database, even if the accuracy of those contents has been verified.[84] While the idea of giving a new period of protection to an updated database may seem no less justified than the idea of giving the authors of the third edition of a textbook copyright in the new edition, problems exist in relation to databases because many are subject to a process of continual updating. For example, in *British Horseracing Board,* the BHB database was constantly being updated so that 800,000 new records or changes to existing records were being made each year—that is over 2,000 a day. In these cases, which Laddie J has described as relating to 'dynamic databases', there are clear difficulties in deciding when a sufficient alteration of the contents will have occurred as to render the database a new, separate database.[85]

3.2 MAKERS AND OWNERS

The 'maker' of a database is the first owner of the database right.[86] Subject to an exception as regards employees, the maker of the database is the person who takes the initiative in obtaining, verifying, or presenting the contents of a database, and who assumes the risk of investing in that obtaining, verification, or presentation.[87] The implication of this is that the maker must take the initiative *and* the risk of the investment. If one person takes the risk and another person takes the initiative, joint making may occur. Where a database is made by an employee in the course of employment, unless otherwise stipulated, the employer is regarded as the maker of the database.[88]

---

[82] Database Reg. 22(3). Cf. Database Dir., Recital 53.

[83] Database Reg. 17(3); Database Dir., Art. 10(3); Recitals 54, 55.

[84] Derclaye, *The Legal Protection of Databases,* 141–2 (criticizing a comment in Bently & Sherman, *Intellectual Property Law* (2nd ed.) 300).

[85] *British Horseracing Board v. William Hill* [2001] *ECDR* 257, 283–285 (Laddie J); [2002] *ECDR* 41 (Court of Appeal). In the case of such a 'dynamic database', Laddie J noted that an 'attempt to split it into a series of discrete databases, besides being impossible to do, would not reflect reality'. He accordingly reasoned that, in that case, '[a]s new data are added, so the database's term of protection is constantly being renewed'. Nonetheless, he qualified this conclusion by opining that, if a person extracts old data from the database, that person is infringing only if the data were added to the database in the last 15 years.

[86] Database Reg. 15.   [87] Database Reg. 14; Database Dir., Recital 41.

[88] Database Reg. 14(2). Where a database is made by Her Majesty or by an officer or servant of the Crown in the course of his duties, Her Majesty shall be regarded as the maker of the database: Database Reg. 14(3). Where a database is made by, or under the direction or control of, the House of Commons or the House of Lords, the rule is varied: Database Reg. 14(4).

A number of presumptions simplify the task of proving ownership.[89] Where a name purporting to be that of the maker appears on copies of the database as published or on the database when it was made, the person whose name appeared is presumed to be the maker of the database and to have made it in an employment relationship. Where copies of the database as published bear a label or a mark naming a person as the maker of the database, the label or mark is presumed to be correct. Both presumptions are rebuttable.

The database right is an assignable property right, and sections 90–93 of the 1988 Act apply to the database right as they would to copyright works. It is also possible to license database rights, and licensing schemes and licensing bodies are subject to supervision in accordance with Schedule 2. The jurisdiction of the Copyright Tribunal has been extended accordingly.

3.3 INFRINGEMENT, RIGHTS, AND REMEDIES

The database right is infringed where a person, without the consent of the owner of the right, 'extracts' or 're-utilizes' all of, or a substantial part of, the contents of the database.[90] The owner of database right must prove that the alleged infringer has derived the material from the claimant's database, whether directly or indirectly.[91]

'Extraction' means the permanent or temporary transfer of those contents to another medium by any means or in any form. 'Re-utilization' means making those contents available to the public by any means. In *BHB* the ECJ indicated that the concepts must be interpreted in the light of the objective pursued by the Directive, namely promoting investment in the creation and maintenance of databases.[92] Consequently, the terms are defined widely, to refer to:

any act of appropriating and making available to the public, without the consent of the maker of the database, the results of his investment, thus depriving him of revenue which should have enabled him to redeem the cost of the investment.[93]

This might include indirect as well as direct extraction or re-utilization.[94] In the case in hand, the ECJ held that William Hill had extracted data (albeit indirectly) and reutilized those data by making them available to the public on its internet betting site.[95] The question whether there can be an extraction where a person consults a database and uses the results, rather than physically transferring them from one database to another, is currently awaiting an answer from the ECJ.[96]

The act must occur in relation to a 'substantial' part of the contents of the database. This means substantial in terms of quantity or quality or a combination of both. The ECJ in *BHB* held that this is assessed by reference to the investment in the creation of the database and the prejudice caused to that investment by the act of extracting or re-utilizing that part.[97] The

---

[89] Database Reg. 22(1).

[90] Davison, at 87, argues that, while these new terms give the impression that this is a new kind of right, the terms in fact 'refer to rights that already exist and are well known in copyright law': 'extraction' is really reproduction, and 're-utilization' a combination of distribution, rental, and communication to the public.

[91] As was the case in *BHB v. William Hill* [2001] *ECDR* 257, 271 *per* Laddie J; approved on appeal [2002] *ECDR* 41.

[92] Case C–203/02 [2005] 1 *CMLR* (15) 319, para. 46.   [93] Ibid, para. 51.

[94] Ibid, para. 52 (contradicting the opinion of Advocate General Stix-Hackl, at para AG 157).

[95] Ibid, para. 65.

[96] *Directmedia Publishing GmbH v. Albert-Ludwigs-Universität Freiburg and Professor Ulrich Knoop*, Case C–304/07 (on the meaning of extraction).

[97] Case C–203/02 [2005] 1 *CMLR* (15) 319, para. 69.

quantitative assessment compares the volume of data extracted to the volume of the whole contents of the database. However, an extraction/re-utilization of a part will also be substantial if it represents a significant part of the investment viewed qualitatively, that is, in terms of human, technical, or financial investment in obtaining, verification, or presentation of the database. The intrinsic value of the material taken is irrelevant.[98] So too is the investment in the creation of those data.[99]

Regulation 16(2) provides that the repeated and systematic extraction or re-utilization of insubstantial parts of the contents of a database may come to amount to the extraction or re-utilization of a substantial part of those contents. This will only be infringement where it comprises acts 'which conflict with a normal exploitation of that database or which unreasonably prejudice the legitimate interests of the maker of the database' (Database Directive, Article 7(5)). In the context of a database of information relating to horse races, Laddie J had held that the repeated use of information for betting services was the systematic extraction of parts of the claimant's 'dynamic database'.[100] However, the ECJ has taken the opposite view. The Regulation on insubstantial parts is 'to prevent circumvention of the prohibition in Article 7(1)'. The systematic and repeated uses must be such that they would lead to the reconstitution of a substantial part of the database, and thus cumulatively would seriously prejudice the investment made by the maker of the database.[101] In the ECJ's view, William Hill's uses were systematic and repeated but not infringing because there was 'no possibility that, through the cumulative effects of its acts, William Hill might reconstitute and make available the whole or a substantial part of the contents of the BHB database'.

One problem which has already been raised before the courts is the conflict between, on the one hand, these rights over the 'contents' of the database, and, on the other, the assertion made in the recitals to the Directive that these rights 'should not give rise to the creation of a new right in the works, data or other materials themselves': Database Directive, recital 46. What is the difference between a right over the contents of a database and a right over the data themselves? Rejecting an argument to the effect that all that is protected is the 'database-ness' of a collection of information, Laddie J has held that infringement of the right is not avoided by rearranging the contents of the database: according to Laddie J what is prohibited is certain kinds of use of 'parts of the contents' of the database. Taking a collection of data from the database is such an act: *British Horseracing Board v William Hill*.[102] However, it should be noted that, on appeal, the Court of Appeal referred the issue of the exact scope of protection to the ECJ.[103] The Advocate General recommended to the Court of Justice that protection not be limited to 'database-ness', referring to such views as 'fundamentally mistaken'.[104] The ECJ declined to determine this issue.[105]

The database right allows the maker to control the first sale, but not the subsequent distribution, of hard copies on which data is stored. Where a copy of a database has been sold within the EEA by, or with the consent of, the owner of the database right in the database, further sales within the EEA of that copy shall not constitute the extraction or re-utilization of the contents of the database. It is interesting that the right is only exhausted by 'sale' and not by other forms of transfer.[106] Consequently, the sale by a customer of gratuitously distributed copies of

---

[98] Ibid, paras. 72, 78; cf. Laddie J at first instance.   [99] Ibid, para. 79.

[100] *British Horseracing Board v. William Hill* [2001] *ECDR* 257.

[101] *BHB*, Case C–203/02 [2005] 1 *CMLR* (15) 319, paras. 86–7.

[102] *BHB v. William Hill* [2001] *ECDR* 257.

[103] *British Horseracing Board v. William Hill* [2002] *ECDR* 41 (CA).

[104] *BHB*, Case C–203/02 [2005] 1 *CMLR* (15) 319, AG para. 70.

[105] Ibid, para. 81.   [106] Database Reg. 12(3).

databases, such as British Telecom telephone directories, may infringe. Oddly, where there has been first sale of hard copies on which data are stored, the Regulations only permit resale and not other forms of transfer. The Regulations appear to suggest that the lawful buyer of a copy of a database cannot give it away, nor rent it.[107]

In relation to the remedies available for breach of the database right, the Database Regulations provide that equivalent provisions of the 1988 Act apply in relation to the database right and databases in which that right subsists, as they apply in relation to copyright and copyright works.[108]

3.4 EXCEPTIONS AND DEFENCES

3.4.1 Lawful use

A lawful user of a database which has been made available to the public in any manner is entitled to extract or re-utilize insubstantial parts of the contents of the database for any purpose.[109] This limitation may not be excluded by agreement.

3.4.2 Fair dealing

Where a database has been made available to the public in any manner, the database right is not infringed by a fair dealing with a substantial part of its contents if three conditions are satisfied: (i) if that part is extracted from the database by a person who is a lawful user of the database; (ii) if it is extracted for the purpose of illustration for teaching or research and not for any commercial purpose; and (iii) if the source is indicated.[110] In exempting pedagogical uses, this provision gives rise to the possibility that a person may infringe copyright in an original database, but not the database right in the component data.[111]

3.4.3 Public lending

An exception is also made for public lending.[112] For lending to be 'public' it must take place through an establishment which is accessible to the public. Such an establishment is permitted to charge borrowers an amount that does not go beyond what is necessary to cover the costs of the establishment.[113] However, permitting remote access is not deemed to constitute a lending.[114] Bizarrely, the exception for public lending does not apply to the making of a copy of a database available for on-the-spot reference use. Even if the lending is gratuitous and in a public establishment, the Regulations suggest that it may be an infringement.[115]

---

[107] Database Reg. 12(2).   [108] See Ch. 48.

[109] Database Reg. 19; Database Dir., Art. 8. The definition of 'lawful user' is problematic: see pp. 229, 331; Derclaye, *Legal Protection*, 120–26.

[110] Database Reg. 20(1); Database Dir., Art. 9(b). Criticized by the Royal Society as 'vague and unhelpful': Royal Society, *Keeping Science Open: The Effects of Intellectual Property on the Conduct of Science* (2003) para. 5.5.

[111] On fair dealing, see Ch. 9.   [112] Database Reg. 12(2); Database Dir., Art. 7(2).

[113] Database Reg. 12(3).

[114] Fourth Standing Committee on Delegated Legislation, 3 Dec. 1997, Minister of State, Dept. of Trade and Industry (Ian McCartney): 'On the question of libraries holding databases and making them available for remote access, we believe that is likely to count as an extraction or reutilization of the database's contents, and not as public lending. Public lending means that a copy of the database held by the library is lent out and is to be returned. Public lending is excluded from the scope of the database right, under Reg. 12(2).'

[115] Database Reg. 12(4).

3.4.4 Other defences

Defences also exist in relation to Parliamentary and judicial proceedings, Royal Commissions and statutory inquiries, material open to public inspection or on an Official Register, material communicated to the Crown in the course of public business, public records, and acts done under statutory authority.[116] The Regulations also provide a defence where the extraction or re-utilization occurs at a time when the identity of the maker could not be ascertained by reasonable inquiry, or in pursuance of arrangements made at a time when such identification was not possible. It must also be reasonable to assume that the database right has expired.[117] Competition law will also apply to database right in the same way as to other intellectual property rights.[118] This is considered in Chapter 12.

3.5 FOREIGN DATABASES

The database right will only subsist where, at the material time,[119] its maker was either: a national of an EEA state; habitually resident within the EEA; a body incorporated under the law of an EEA state; a body with its principal place of business or its registered office within the EEA; or a partnership or other unincorporated body which was formed under the law of an EEA state which, at that time, satisfied certain conditions.[120] Mark Davison has argued that these rules put the EC in breach of its obligations under Berne and TRIPS to provide national treatment. This is because, in Davison's view, the so called '*sui generis*' right is in substance a type of copyright: the criteria for acquisition of the right (in particular taking account of the quality of investment in the creation and arrangement of the database), the nature of the rights conferred, and the exceptions, all—he argues—have the characteristics of copyright.[121] If Davison is wrong, and the *sui generis* right is deemed to be an unfair competition right, there might equally be a violation of TRIPS and the Paris Convention, which requires countries of the Union to grant national treament as regards the protection of industrial property, including 'the repression of unfair competition'.[122]

3.6 ASSESSMENT

Although the Directive had been described by many as unduly protective, the ECJ cases have seriously curtailed the perceived excesses (by limiting the availability of protection of sole-source databases). In December 2005 the Commission issued an evaluation of the effect of the Directive and was disappointed to find that the number of databases created in 2004 had declined to pre-Directive levels.[123] The Commission then embarked on a stakeholder consultation,

---

[116] Database Regs., Sched. 1: these correspond to the provisions of CDPA ss. 45–50; Database Dir., Art. 9(c).

[117] Database Reg. 21(1).   [118] Database Dir., Recital 47.

[119] Database Reg. 18. The 'material time' means the time when the database was made, or, if the making extended over a period, a substantial part of that period.

[120] Database Reg. 18(2). The conditions are (a) that the body has its central administration or principal place of business within the EEA or (b) that the body has its registered office within the EEA and the body's operations are linked on an ongoing basis with the economy of an EEA state.

[121] Davison, 222–5. One unfortunate consequence of such a characterization is that the database right should last for a minimum term of 50 years *post mortem*.

[122] Paris, Art. 2(1), 1(2); TRIPS, Art. 2(1), Art. 3(1).

[123] DG Internal Market and Services Working Paper, *First Evaluation of Directive 96/9/EC on the legal protection of databases* (Brussels, 12 Dec 2005) (paras. 1.4, 4.23).

asking whether stakeholders favoured maintenance of the status quo, repeal of the whole Directive (including its copyright components), repeal of the *sui generis* database right, or modification of the latter right. Most respondents favoured reform of the right, but they were divided over whether the right should be strengthened or the exceptions broadened. The Commission has given no indication of its plans. In the meantime, three references have been made to the ECJ.[124] It seems we should look to the Court for further clarification of the Directive.

4 TECHNOLOGICAL PROTECTION MEASURES

As mentioned in Chapter 11, copyright owners have begun to exploit copyright-protected works using self-help mechanisms in the form of 'technological measures of protection'. As mentioned, this new mode of exploitation reflects real fears amongst the right holders that digital reproduction and communication technologies present the threat of such widespread private copying that copyright law by itself could not be relied upon to protect the investment involved in creating and publishing the work. Such technological protection measures include encryption and similar access controls, which encode works so that only those with legitimate keys can obtain access, and copy controls, which allow users access to works but operate to prevent the subsequent making of copies.

The use of technological measures to support copyright is reinforced by complex and extensive laws prohibiting circumvention of such measures. The reinforcement is by way of a mesh of overlapping civil and criminal actions. This complex topic deserves treatment separate from secondary infringement of copyright, but as 'related rights' for two reasons. First, because the measures are in many cases not limited to those applied to protect copyright works, but also protect performances, and *sui generis* database right. Second, because the civil rights of action are frequently conferred not only on the copyright holder who applies the measure to the work, but also on the person issuing copies to the public in protected form, and any other person with intellectual property rights in the technological measure employed.

The 1988 Act, as amended, contains three categories of provision dealing with situations where a person facilitates access to works which the person concerned is not entitled to use or receive. The first category, in sections 296ZA–ZF, relates to the circumvention of effective technological measures applied to copyright works other than computer programs, and is designed to implement Article 6 of the Information Society Directive.[125] The second category, which is found in section 296, applies only to computer programs (and is intended to implement Article 7(1)(c) of the Software Directive). The third category, in sections 297–9, relates to reception of transmissions (and is intended to implement an EC Directive giving legal protection to services based on 'conditional access').[126] Each needs to be considered in turn.

---

[124] *Verlag Schawe GmbH v. Sächsisches Druck-under Verlaghaus AG,* Case C–215/07 (on the status of official databases); *Directmedia,* note 96 above (on the meaning of extraction); *Apis Hristovich EOOD v. Lakorda ad,* Case C–545/07 (an array of questions on extraction and substantiality from Bulgaria).

[125] CDPA s. 297ZA(1), (6); s. 296 ZD(1), (8) (copyright works (other than computer programs), performances, database right, publication right); Info. Soc. Dir., Recital 50 (without prejudice to Software Dir.). In turn, Art. 6 implements Art. 11 of the WCT and Art. 18 of the WPPT. However, they go beyond the requirements of those treaties in breadth (since they apply also to broadcasting organizations, publication right, and *sui generis* database right), and—more importantly—depth. The Directive goes beyond acts of circumvention to cover devices and services which enable circumvention.

[126] Directive 98/84 EC of the European Parliament and of the Council of 20 Nov. 1998 on the Legal Protection of Services based on, or consisting of, Conditional Access, *OJ* 1998 *L* 320.

4.1 MEASURES APPLIED TO COPYRIGHT WORKS (OTHER THAN COMPUTER PROGRAMS)

Sections 296ZA–ZF are intended to implement Article 6 of the Information Society Directive which requires member states to provide 'adequate legal protection' against a number of activities in relation to the circumvention of 'effective technological measures'. Because those provisions are not supposed to affect the provisions in the Software Directive, we are here concerned with cases where effective technological measures have been applied to a copyright work other than a computer program.[127] Section 296ZF defines 'technological measures' as 'any technology, device or component that is designed, in the normal course of its operation, to protect a copyright work other than a computer program'.[128] A technological measure is 'effective' where the use of a protected work, etc. 'is controlled by the copyright owner through either (a) an access control or protection process such as encryption, scrambling or other transformation of the work, or (b) a copy control mechanism, which achieves the protection objective'.[129] This makes clear that the provisions apply both to access controls, such as encryption, and copy controls, such as SCMS. It remains unclear, however, whether they cover devices which monitor usage.[130] Following largely the schema of the Directive, the Act distinguishes between two sorts of objectionable behaviour: on the one hand, protection is given against the act of circumvention itself; on the other, protection is given against those who make or sell devices which enable circumvention, or supply services that achieve that end.

4.1.1 The act of circumvention

Section 296ZA gives specified persons civil rights of action where a person does anything which circumvents technological measures knowing or with reasonable grounds to know that they are pursuing that objective. The persons given the right to bring the action, who are described as having the same rights as a copyright owner has in respect of an infringement of copyright, are: the copyright owner of the work protected (or their exclusive licensee); and the person issuing copies of the work or communicating the work to the public in a form to which technological measures have been applied.[131] The *scienter* requirement means that users do not commit a wrong if they circumvent accidentally: it is only where a person knows or has reasonable grounds to know that they are trying to circumvent technological measures that they infringe. The wrong is only committed where a successful act of circumvention has taken place: mere attempts are not covered. The provision is inapplicable where a person circumvents a measure 'for the purposes of research into cryptography' unless by so doing 'or issuing information derived from that research, he affects prejudicially the rights of the copyright owner'.[132]

---

[127] CDPA s. 296ZA(1).

[128] CDPA s 296ZF. This largely echoes Info. Soc. Dir., Art. 6(3). However, there the definition is worded so as to relate to devices designed 'to prevent or restrict acts, in respect of works or other subject matter, which are not authorised' by the right holder. A device which merely discourages infringement, rather than physically preventing it, is not covered: *R v. Higgs* [2008] *EWCA Crim* 1324.

[129] CDPA s 298ZF(2), replication Info. Soc. Dir., Art. 6(3).

[130] L. Bygrave, 'The Technologisation of Copyright: Implications for Privacy and Related Interests' [2002] *EIPR* 51, 54–5. It is unclear whether the definition in Info. Soc. Dir., Art. 6(3) of 'effective' is exhaustive and so only covers access or copy controls, and, if it is, whether a system for monitoring usage is an 'access control or protection process'.

[131] CDPA s. 296ZA(3). Cf. the wider range of persons mentioned in s. 296ZD(2) and s. 296(2).

[132] CDPA s. 296ZA(2); Info. Soc. Dir., Recital 48. One may wonder whether circumvention ought not to be lawful where it is done in the public interest: e.g. where an employee circumvents a measure protecting

4.1.2 Facilitating circumvention

In addition to prohibiting the act of circumvention itself, civil and criminal measures provide protection against a host of related activities which facilitate such circumvention—including manufacture, import, distribution of devices, products, or components, or the provision of services.[133] The addition of criminal liability reflects the fact that these acts are regarded as the ones which seriously threaten the copyright holder's interests: after all, the general public does not have the time or means to break technological locks or controls. It is only with the assistance of commercially available circumvention devices or services that anti-circumvention is likely to become widespread.

There are two criminal provisions. The first applies to devices, products, or components 'primarily designed, produced or adapted for the purpose of enabling or facilitating the circumvention of effective technological measures'.[134] The limitation to devices 'primarily designed' for circumvention is important, and while it would cover forged smart cards for decrypting copyright-protected broadcasts, devices which serve legitimate purposes (such as general-purpose personal computers) fall outside its scope even if they can be used to avoid technological protection (as was notoriously the case with SCMS). A person commits an offence if they manufacture such a device for sale or hire, or distribute one in the course of business, or to such an extent as to affect prejudicially the copyright owner, unless they prove they did not know, and had no reasonable grounds for believing, that the device enabled or facilitated the circumvention of effective technological measures.[135] One peculiar feature of this offence is that, in a situation where a device is primarily designed for circumvention but can be used for other legitimate purposes, a person commits an offence by making and selling such devices even where they were genuinely making and selling them for legitimate purposes. In such a situation, the defence is of no assistance because, while they have good reason to believe the device will not be used to circumvent, they know it *could* be so used. The second criminal provision relates to a service, the purpose of which is to enable or facilitate the circumvention of effective technological measures. A person commits an offence if, in the course of business or to such an extent as to affect prejudicially the copyright owner, they provide, promote, advertise, or market such a service.[136] As with devices, it is a defence for the accused to show that they did not know, nor had reasonable grounds for believing, that the service enabled or facilitated circumvention. In both cases a further defence applies to acts of the intelligence services and law enforcement agencies.[137]

---

business records (e.g. bypasses a password control) in order to reveal the wrongful practices of their employer, or where a person wants to investigate the practices of those who design censorware (internet filters) to find out exactly what they are preventing us from accessing. A provision equivalent to CDPA s. 171(3) might provide this flexibility.

[133] Member states may also prohibit private possession of such devices: Info. Soc. Dir., Recital 49.

[134] CDPA s. 296ZB(1). See *R v. Higgs* [2008] *EWCA Crim* 1324.   [135] CDPA s. 296ZB(5).

[136] CDPA s. 296ZB(2). The reference to non-business activities which affect the copyright owner prejudicially goes beyond the requirements of the Directive and seems designed to cover making available on the internet of decryption code (as occurred in the US case of *Motion Picture Association of America v. Corley and 2600 Enterprises, Inc* 111 *F. Supp. 2d* 294 (SDNY) affd 273 *F.3d* 429 (2d cir, 2001)). See, e.g. N. Hanbridge, 'Protecting Right Holders Interests in the information society: Anti-Circumvention; Threats Post *Napster*; and DRM' [2001] *Ent LR* 223; B. Esler, 'Protecting the Protection: A Trans-Atlantic Analysis of the Emerging Right to Technological Self-Help' (2003) 43 *IDEA* 553. Although not in the Directive, the provision may well be justified because the former CDPA s. 296(2)(b) covered the situation where a person 'publishes information intended to enable or assist persons to circumvent copy-protection'.

[137] CDPA s. 296ZB(3).

The civil actions cover broader ground than the criminal ones (and, in contrast to the criminal provisions, apply *mutatis mutandis* to effective technological measures used in relation to performances, database right, and publication right).[138] As regards manufacture and distribution of devices (etc.), liability exists not just in relation to devices 'primarily designed, produced, adapted…for the purpose of enabling and facilitating' circumvention, but also to devices 'promoted, advertised or marketed' for that purpose and ones having 'only a limited commercially significant purpose or use other than to circumvent'.[139] As regards services, civil liability is in some respects more narrowly defined than criminal liability, being confined to the *provision* of services (as opposed to the advertising, promoting, and marketing of a service). Civil liability exists, most obviously, where the service is performed for the purpose of enabling or facilitating circumvention. However, civil liability also exists in two other circumstances: where the service provided is merely advertised or promoted for that purpose (even if the service does not achieve the advertised purpose!), and second, where a service is provided which has only a limited commercially significant purpose other than to circumvent (even, it seems, if it is provided for just such a non-circumventing use). Civil actions to enforce these provisions can be brought by a number of parties: the copyright owner, or their exclusive licensee; the person issuing copies of the work to the public or communicating to the public the work to which technological measures have been applied; and the owner, or exclusive licensee, of 'any intellectual property right in the effective technological measures'. There is no defence of ignorance, though damages may not be awarded against a defendant who demonstrates that they did not know, nor had reason to believe, that their acts enabled or facilitated an infringement of copyright.[140]

4.1.3 Attempts to avoid digital lock-up

When the proposals to expand the scope of protection of technological measures were being debated representatives of consumers vigorously articulated their fear that such provisions would facilitate digital lock-up of material which the public is currently entitled to access and use (without payment). Those fears related in part to the supply of works in the public domain (for example, the works of Shakespeare) in digital form but subject to technical measures: why, it was asked, should the public not be able to circumvent such measures to access what are, after all, works in the public domain? The fears also related to the use of technical measures to prevent uses that fall within existing copyright exceptions: in a world where works are protected by technical measures, and those measures are protected by law against circumvention, how are users to be able to access and copy works for research and private study, criticism and review, and so forth?

The first concern may seem to have been met through the definition of 'technological measure'. As already observed, 'technological measure' is defined as a technology designed in the normal course of its operation to protect a copyright work other than a computer program. Moreover, the provisions on civil liability for circumvention, or supplying devices or services that facilitate circumvention, only apply where 'effective technological measures have been applied to a copyright work other than a computer program'. While this may seem at

---

[138] CDPA s. 296ZD(8). s. 296 ZE(11).

[139] CDPA s. 296ZD. The wrongful acts are more broadly defined too: any manufacture, as opposed to manufacture for sale or hire; import, compared to import 'otherwise than for his private and domestic use'; any distribution, rather than distribution in the course of business; selling or hiring, or offering or advertising for sale or hire, rather than doing so in the course of business. Moreover, civil liability extends to the situation where a person has a device in their possession for commercial purposes.

[140] CDPA s. 296ZD(7).

first glance to protect the public against 'digital lock-up', in practice the result is likely to be quite different: this is because, if the measure protects at least one work, civil liability applies. Consequently, devices cannot be circulated, services provided, or acts of circumvention carried out where versions of public domain (i.e. unprotected) works protected by technological measures include *any* copyright material: liability will exist, for example, where a person circumvents a measure to access the complete works of Shakespeare, because the collection also contains a recently written introductory essay.[141]

In addition, one should note that the criminal provisions apply irrespective of the *particular* application of a technological measure. As long as the measure is 'designed' to protect a copyright work other than a computer program, criminal infringements occur in the circumstances which have been set out above. Imagine that an entrepreneur designs a technological measure to protect copyright works, but then decides to apply the measure to works in the public domain. The measure, even though now applied to such works, retains its quality of being designed to protect a copyright work. A person commits a criminal act by selling devices or advertising services to enable or facilitate the circumvention of such measures. The defence in section 296ZB(5) will not assist.

As regards the relationship between technological measures and exceptions to copyright, Article 6(4) of the Information Society Directive provides a strange, barely comprehensible, compromise.[142] The Community was caught in the tricky position of wanting to legislate to protect technological measures from circumvention, but without being in a position to understand fully the implications of such strong protection.[143] As things currently stand, it is impossible to predict how dependent consumers are going to be on digital delivery, or the extent to which consumers who previously relied on the limited scope of the rights conferred on copyright owners are going to be inconvenienced by such measures. Article 6(4) is intended to reassure the user community that the legislature will not stand by and let everything go horribly wrong. If technological measures start to impair user actions seriously, ways will be

[141] One issue worth noting here is whether the typographical arrangement right could apply to works in digital form: if so, it seems a person is not permitted to break into a technologically protected non-copyright literary work where there is a copyright typographical arrangement. For criticism of the equivalent US provisions, see J. Litman, *Digital Copyright* (2001), 183–4 (the public should have an affirmative right to gain access to, extract, use, and re-use ideas, facts, information, and other public domain material embodied in protected works. That affirmative right should include a limited privilege to circumvent any technological access controls for that purpose, and a privilege to reproduce, adapt, transmit, perform, or display so much of the protected expression as is required in order to gain access to the unprotected elements).

[142] Brian Esler has called this 'arguably the most obtuse and incoherent provision yet enacted by the EU in the touchy area of intellectual property harmonization'. B. Esler, 'Technological Self-Help: Its status under European Law and Its Implications for UK Law' (2002) <http://www.bileta.ac.uk> (follow link from 2002 section of 'Conference Papers' page).

[143] For thoughtful consideration of ways of protecting users see D. Burk and J. Cohen, 'Fair Use Infrastructure for Rights Management Systems' (2001) 15 *Harvard J Law & Tech* 41 (suggesting access/copying systems that allow fair use; third party-operated procedures such as key escrow—management of rights management keys by trusted third parties (but issues of whether identity of applicant should be revealed to the copyright holder); or both (condition enforcement on automatic fair use defaults)). The US law permits circumvention of access-control measures for certain narrowly-defined classes of works that are determined by the Librarian of Congress on the basis of hearings and findings of the Register of Copyrights every three years: 17 USC s. 1201(a)(1). There are six classes in the 2006 regulations: one concerns access for educational use in the classroom for film and media studies; another concerns the circumvention of malfunctioning devices used on software; a third concerns the need for archiving services to circumvent protection measures which have become obsolete in order to archive computer programs and video games; another case relates to circumvention of access controls which prevent the use of an e-book's read-aloud function, so as to enable blind users to take advantage of that facility; a fifth concerns programs in mobile telephones; and the final one concerns technological measures that compromise the security of personal computers.

found to sort out the problems. Pending review at the EU level (under Article 12(1), every three years), national authorities may (or indeed in some cases must) take action to release content from its technological chains. Article 6(4) also operates to indicate to content holders that they should develop technological measures with as much sophistication as is possible so that they can enable users to take advantage of limitations and exceptions traditionally recognized by copyright law. Article 6(4) of the Directive states that:

[n]otwithstanding the legal protection provided for by paragraph 1, in the absence of voluntary measures taken by rightholders, including agreements between rightholders and other parties concerned, Member States shall take appropriate measures to ensure that rightholders make available to the beneficiary of an exception or limitation provided for in national law in accordance with Article 5(2)(a), (2)(c), (2)(d), (2)(e), (3)(a), (3)(b), or 3(e) the means of benefiting from that exception or limitation, to the extent necessary to benefit from that exception or limitation and where that beneficiary has legal access to the protected work or subject-matter concerned.

The UK implemented Article 6(4) in section 297ZE of the 1988 Act.[144] This allows for complaints to be made to the Secretary of State where an effective technological measure prevents a person from carrying out a permitted act. The relevant permitted acts are listed in Schedule 5A.[145] It does not apply to copyright works that are made available on agreed contractual terms in such a way that members of the public may access them from a place and at a time individually chosen by them.[146] Given that this would cover most internet supply of works (where a person accesses a work from their own terminal at a time chosen by them), this exclusion may confine the scope of the complaint procedure to circumstances involving encrypted broadcasts or technologically-protected hard copies.[147] The Secretary of State is given wide powers to issue directions to ascertain whether voluntary measures are in place enabling such acts to be permitted, and if not, to ensure that the owner or exclusive licensee of the copyright work makes available to the complainant the means to carry out the permitted acts.[148] The order might be complied with by placing a copy lacking the technological measures at the disposal of the complainant; or possibly by giving the complainant access to a circumvention device. If the copyright owner fails to comply, the complainant is granted normal remedies for breach of statutory duty.[149]

4.2 COMPUTER SOFTWARE

Section 296 confers a civil right of action where a person does either of two specified acts which facilitate the circumvention of any 'technical device' which has been applied to a computer

---

[144] See *Gowers Review,* paras 4.104–4.108 (recommending that it be made easier to complain).

[145] The contents of the list are determined by Art. 6(4), though the logic is hard to fathom. Why is action to be taken only where some exceptions are impeded (photocopying, educational, ephemeral recordings for broadcasts, reproductions of broadcasts, teaching, disability, and public security) but not others, and particularly ones such as reproduction in the press, or criticism or review, that represent important public interests? Why is there an *obligation* to take action where some limitations are concerned but only an option where the private use exception in Art. 5(2)(b) is concerned? See T. Foged, 'US v. EU Anti-circumvention Legislation: Preserving the Public's Privileges in the Digital Age' [2002] *EIPR* 525, 537.

[146] CDPA s. 296ZF(9) implementing Info. Soc. Dir. Recital 53.

[147] M. Hart, 'The Copyright in the Information Society Directive: An Overview' [2002] *EIPR* 58, 63 ('as more and more music, film and other content become available on the Internet, this could be a very important qualification in relation to the ability of users to exercise exceptions'). This assumes that the courts accept that 'click-on' or other non-negotiable agreements make the works available on 'agreed contractual terms', and this is an assumption that will need to be tested.

[148] CDPA s. 296ZE(3).   [149] CDPA s. 296ZE(6).

program.[150] Technical device is defined as 'any device intended to prevent or restrict acts that are not authorised by the copyright owner of that computer program and are restricted by copyright'.[151] The right is conferred on three sets of persons: the owner of copyright in the computer program, or his exclusive licensee; the person issuing or communicating the program to the public; and the owner (or his exclusive licensee) of 'any intellectual property right' in the technical device.[152] The right is infringed by two specified acts: the manufacture, distribution, or possession for commercial purposes of 'any means the sole intended purpose of which is to facilitate the unauthorised removal or circumvention of the technical device'; or the publication of information intended to enable or assist persons to remove or circumvent the technical device.[153] In either case, liability is predicated on *scienter,* that is, there is only infringement where a person does the act 'knowing or having reason to believe it will be used to make infringing copies'.[154]

It is useful here to observe how much more limited are the provisions related to software than those applicable to other copyright works. First, there is only civil liability in relation to circumvention of software (subject to what was said above about the possible application of measures 'designed' for copyright works (other than computer programs) to other material including computer programs). Second, there is no liability for the act of circumventing devices protecting software. Third, as regards software, liability applies only in relation to any means 'the sole intended purpose of which' is to facilitate circumvention, whereas the Information Society provisions cover the much broader array of devices advertised for, or primarily designed for circumvention, or with only a limited commercially significant purpose other than circumvention. Fourth, liability in relation to the supply of devices to circumvent measures protecting software is predicated on a knowledge requirement that the person knows or has reason to believe the computer program will be used to make infringing copies: *scienter* is not relevant to section 296ZD except as part of a defence of innocence to an action for damages. Fifth, in relation to technological measures protecting software, no liability pertains to offering or carrying out circumvention services.[155] Although these differences might be taken to reflect a legislative awareness that too-strong control of technical measures applied to software might seriously limit access to and development of software, almost certainly they reflect a desire not to re-open the legislative compromise effected in the Software Directive of

---

[150] CDPA, s. 296(1).

[151] CDPA s. 296(6). This is narrower than the previous provision on 'copy protection' in that it does not encompass technical devices which are intended merely 'to impair the quality of copies made', but is broader in that it covers devices which would prevent *any act* which would infringe copyright, not just devices designed to prevent or restrict *copying* of a work.

[152] CDPA, s. 296(2). Formerly, the right was only given to the person issuing copies.

[153] The wording of the first act follows closely that in Software Dir. Art. 7(1)(c), and is consequently narrower that the previous CDPA s. 296(2)(a), which applied to 'any device or means specifically designed or adapted to circumvent the form of copy-protection employed'. The difference between 'specific design' and 'sole intended purpose' will be important if there is a second purpose.

[154] Infringing copies are made for these purposes when a computer is loaded into a console: *Sony Computer Entertainment v. Owen* [2002] *EMLR* 742; *R v. Higgs* [2008] *EWCA Crim* 1324. See also *Sony Entertainment v. Ball* [2004] *ECDR* (33) 323 (holding that: (i) infringing copies are limited to 'articles,' but an article containing a transient reproduction is an infringing copy (para. 15); (ii) where a person makes mod-chips for export these do not produce copies which infringe UK copyright law; but (iii) a copyright owner might nevertheless sue in the UK in relation to foreign infringements).

[155] While the general effect of this comparison is that technological measures receive much stronger protection outside the field of computer programs, it should be noted too that the safeguard provisions of s. 296ZE (implementing Art. 6(4) of the Info. Soc. Dir.) do not apply to computer programs and, in that minor respect, the provisions of s. 296 are stronger.

1991. Nevertheless, the existence of such stark differences in the scope of protection is likely to prompt those who own copyright in software to argue that the technological measures they employ simultaneously protect copyright software and other protected works, so that they too obtain the benefit of the generous protection granted by Article 6 of the Information Society Directive and section 296ZA–ZF of the 1988 Act.

4.3 TRANSMISSIONS

A third set of provisions deals with protection measures used in relation to transmissions. Although the 1988 Act, as enacted, contained some such provisions, they have been amended to implement the 'Conditional Access' Directive by the Conditional Access Regulations 2000.[156] These apply to broadcasts and 'information society services' which are encrypted and, inter alia, prevent unauthorized dealings in decoders. The definition of information society service is found in Council Directive 98/34/EC of June 22, 1998 laying down a procedure for the provision of information in the field of technical standards, and covers any service which is normally provided for remuneration and which operates at a distance by electronic means and at the individual request of a recipient of the services.[157]

4.3.1 Fraudulent reception

Section 297 imposes criminal liability for dishonestly receiving a programme included in a broadcasting service provided from a place in the United Kingdom. It must be proved that the recipient intended to avoid payment of any charge applicable to the reception of the programme. The provision has been applied to a publican who received signals of Premier League football games from a Greek satellite channel, Nova.[158] The programmes had been made by BSkyB at the football ground and sent to the Premier League in Chiswick, which encrypted and sent the images to Nova by satellite, which in turn uplinked the signals to its satellite (and on to its subscribers). The High Court said that the provision required the court to decide, first what was the 'programme', and thereafter from where the broadcasting service was provided. Here the programme was said to be the recording of the game, and its identity was not altered by adding Greek commentary and the Greek logo. The place from which the broadcasting service was provided was 'the point at which the initial transmission of the programme for ultimate reception to the public took place' i.e. the United Kingdom. Despite the fact that this was a judgment of the late Pumfrey LJ, a respected intellectual property specialist, one cannot help but observe that it feels like a rather strained construction (following extremely sophisticated submissions). In a criminal case, should not the words be given their more obvious meaning, even if this would mean that Ms Murphy's clearly dishonest behaviour went unpunished?

4.3.2 Unauthorized decoders[159]

Section 297A imposes criminal liability on those who supply 'unauthorized decoders' which decode encrypted transmissions so as to enable access to the transmission without payment

[156] Directive 98/84, note 126 above; Conditional Access Regulations 2000 (SI 2000/1175).

[157] Council Directive 98/34/EC of 22 June 1998 laying down a procedure for the provision of information in the field of technical standards, *OJ* 1998 *L* 204. The Directive excludes television and radio broadcasts from the definition, as well as providing an 'indicative list' of services which are not 'at a distance', 'by electronic means', nor 'at the individual request of a recipient', in Annex V.

[158] *Karen Murphy v. Media Protection Services Ltd* [2007] *EWHC* 3091 (Pumfrey LJ).

[159] CDPA s. 297A.

of the fee which the person making the transmission charges for access.[160] A transmission is defined as any programme included in a broadcasting service from a place within the UK or any other member state, or 'an information society service'. It therefore covers transmissions of encrypted television services (which as we saw in Chapters 3 and 6 do not include most 'on-demand' transmissions), and encrypted services providing video, music, or access to databases 'on demand', the latter falling squarely within the complex definition of 'information society service'. The wrongful acts include making, importing, distributing, selling, possessing (for commercial purposes), and advertising the sale or hire of unauthorized decoders, as well as installing, maintaining, and replacing for commercial purposes an unauthorized decoder. Obvious examples of such wrongs would include the unauthorized manufacture of 'digi-boxes', as well as re-enabling or extending the range of reception on old smart cards.[161]

4.3.3 Civil liabilities

Section 298 gives civil rights of action, akin to those of a copyright owner, to persons who charge for the reception of programmes included in a broadcasting service, send encrypted transmissions, or provide 'conditional access services'.[162] This would cover many of the existing satellite broadcasters, such as Sky, Film Four, etc. A 'conditional access service' is defined as a service providing conditional access technology, that is, any technical measure or arrangement whereby access to encrypted transmissions in an intelligible form is made conditional on previous individual authorization.[163]

A person covered by section 298 has the same rights as a copyright owner against a person who makes or trades in various ways in apparatus which is 'designed or adapted to enable or assist persons to access the programmes or other transmissions or circumvent conditional access technology related to the programmes or transmissions when they are not entitled to do so'.[164] This would seem to cover the situation where somebody made or sold fraudulent smart cards or decoders to enable reception of Sky channels by persons who were not subscribers, and the import of smart cards authorized for use abroad.[165] The rights also encompass a person who publishes any information calculated to enable or assist access.[166]

---

[160] CDPA s. 297A(4): a transmission is 'encrypted' when it is 'subjected to scrambling or the operation of cryptographic envelopes, electronic locks, passwords or any other analogous application'. A 'decoder' is defined as an apparatus designed or adapted to enable an encrypted transmission to be decoded. A decoder is unauthorized where it is designed or adapted to enable an encrypted transmission to be accessed in an intelligible form without payment of the fee which the person making the transmission charges for access.

[161] See, e.g. *R. v. Bridgeman & Butt* [1996] *FSR* 538 (re-enabling or extending the range of reception on old smart cards for Spain, where the transmitter did not supply the cards, violated CDPA s. 297A and thus involved a conspiracy to defraud).

[162] CDPA s. 298 (as amended by the Conditional Access Regulations). The rights only apply to transmissions 'from a place in the UK or any other member State'.

[163] CDPA ss. 298(7), 297A(4).

[164] CDPA ss. 298, 299. See *BBC Enterprises v. HI–Tech Xtravision* [1992] *RPC* 167 (manufacture in UK of decoders for sale abroad infringed s. 298: 'not entitled' meant 'not authorized').

[165] Though this may raise difficult issues concerning the free movement of goods and services. For a taste, see *The Football Association Premier League Ltd v. QC Leisure & Ors* [2008] *EWHC* 44 (Ch) (Barling J) (an action between FA and importers of equipment and cards that enabled persons in the UK to watch Greek broadcasts was met with a defence that the FA had breached Art 81 by requiring its Greek licensees to prevent the use of the cards outside Greece; the Court refused to strike out the defence, finding it to be arguable).

[166] CDPA s. 298, as amended by the Conditional Access Regulations, in order to implement Directive 98/84, *OJ* 1998, *L* 320.

4.3.4 Relationship with sections 296ZA–ZF

As we saw earlier a copyright owner and person communicating a work to the public have various rights under sections 296ZA and ZD where technological measures are applied to the work. These can operate cumulatively with the special transmission and conditional access provisions. For example, if a person instals a device enabling receipt of an encrypted transmission, they will violate section 296ZA if they knowingly circumvent a technological measure. They will also violate section 298(2)(a)(iii) if they instal, maintain, or replace for commercial purposes 'an apparatus designed or adapted to enable or assist persons to access the programmes or transmissions or circumvent conditional access technology…when they are not entitled to do so'. If someone distributes an unauthorized decoder, they will both be distributing 'a device…primarily designed…for the purpose of enabling the circumvention of those measures'—that is measures applied to the copyright-protected broadcast—and so violate section 297ZD(1)(b)(iii); and also be distributing an apparatus 'designed or adapted to enable or assist persons to access the programmes or transmissions or circumvent conditional access technology…when they are not entitled to do so'. In each situation, a careful analysis needs to be undertaken to decide which section is most suitable.

5 RIGHTS MANAGEMENT INFORMATION

Article 7 of the Information Society Directive has required the introduction of provisions protecting 'electronic rights management information'.[167] By 'rights management information' is meant any information provided by the copyright owner which identifies the work, the author, the copyright owner, the holder of any intellectual property rights, information about the terms and conditions of use of the work, or any numbers or codes that represent such information.[168] In effect, what we are concerned with is information equivalent to the copyright page of a book (author, publisher, ISBN, etc.) that is electronically attached to (typically being woven into the fabric of) a work which is distributed digitally. This is sometimes referred to as 'meta-data'.[169] The information falls within the scope of protection when it (or any of it) is associated with a copy of a work or appears in connection with the communication to the public of a work.[170] The provision also applies to the *sui generis* database right.

Although the phrase 'rights management information' may not sound very glamorous, the European Commission sees its protection as the key pre-requisite to an effective 'information society'.[171] This is essentially for two reasons. The first is that rights management

---

[167] For a discussion of the equivalent US provisions, see D. Nimmer, 'Puzzles of the Digital Millenium Copyright Act' 46 (1999) *Journal of the Copyright Society of the USA* 401.

[168] CDPA s. 296ZG(7). It is clear from this that protection extends to all sorts of information which is electronic rather than being limited to information about 'electronic rights'.

[169] Dusollier has questioned whether the definition of RMI would cover digital watermarks, because some do not contain 'identifying information': S. Dusollier, 'Some Reflections on Copyright Management Information and Moral Rights' (2003) 25 *Columbia-VLA Journal of Law & the Arts* 377. For speculation as to whether it covers personal data about users, see Bygrave, 'The Technologisation of Copyright', 55–6 (examining whether removal of personal data for the sake of individual privacy would give rise to liability).

[170] Info. Soc. Dir. Art. 7(2). It is unclear whether details that appear on a web site, but are not embedded in an aspect of it which is reproduced, would qualify as being 'associated with a copy of a work'.

[171] See Commission Staff Working Paper, *Digital Rights: Background, Systems, Assessment* SEC (2002) 197 (Brussels, 14 February 2002).

information is seen as having the potential to enable direct contracting between content holders and consumers, the 'metering' of uses of works, and enabling rights clearances more generally (for example, in relation to the production of multimedia works). It is thus seen as the lubricant that will keep the legal cogs of the internet turning. As Thomas Dreier has written, digital rights management 'clearly goes beyond mere protection against piracy and illegal copying. Rather,...[digital rights management] aims at implementing a technical structure which enables product and service differentiation together with, and on the basis of, price discrimination.'[172] Second, the Commission recognizes that works in digital form are 'plastic'. In other words, works in digital form are readily capable of modification and alteration. The protection of rights management information is needed to prevent the removal of various identifying insignia from works and to enable users to keep track of what the information is and where it comes from.

Section 296ZG provides the copyright owner, its exclusive licensee, and any person communicating or issuing work to the public,[173] with the ability to prevent the removal of rights management information and the further circulation of copies from which such information has been removed.[174] Liability is dependent in both cases on *scienter*. As regards removal or alteration, a person is liable where they 'knowingly and without authority' remove or alter meta-data in circumstances where that person 'knows or has reason to believe that by so doing [they are] inducing, enabling, facilitating or concealing an infringement of copyright'. Accidental removal of data is therefore permitted, as is deliberate removal of meta-data where a person has no reason to think there has been, is, or is likely to be an infringement. A researcher who deliberately deletes meta-data when making an electronic copy of material from an electronic source for purposes of their own non-commercial research or private study will not violate the section, therefore. As regards dealings in material that has been tampered with by the removal or alteration of meta-data, a person infringes where they 'knowingly and without authority' distribute, import for distribution, or communicate to the public, copies of such material where that person 'knows or has reason to believe that by so doing [they are] inducing, enabling, facilitating or concealing an infringement of copyright'. The provisions do not expressly prevent the publication of information on how to remove such information or the sale of devices which enable the removal of information, though the English legal system might regard this as joint tortfeasance.[175]

6 PUBLIC LENDING RIGHT

Although copyright in books enables authors to control (and seek compensation) where their works are copied, they have no right to prevent a range of people from reading the same book. Typically this occurs when books are repeatedly borrowed from a library. As borrowing reduces sales of a work, when it is carried out on a large scale (public libraries in England lend 600 million times a year), it can substantially reduce an author's expected income. To remedy these problems, a public lending right was established in the UK in 1979.[176] The Public Lending

---

172 Thomas Dreier in the Rights Management Report of the Commission meeting Santiago de Compostela, June 2002.

173 CDPA s. 296ZG(3)–(5).   174 Info. Soc. Dir., Art. 7; Cf. 17 USC s. 1202.

175 See below at Ch. 47 Section 3.

176 B. Brophy, *A Guide to Public Lending Right* (1983); J. Phillips, 'Public Lending: The Structure of a New Statutory Right' [1979] *EIPR* 187.

Rights Act 1979 provides a framework for the scheme which is contained in the Public Lending Right Scheme 1982.[177] This Scheme has been amended a number of times and its modern form is set out in a 1990 text.[178]

The public lending right scheme entitles authors to remuneration where their works are loaned by public libraries.[179] This is based on the principle that authors should be compensated for lost revenues since such loans are substitutes for sales. The public lending right does not provide authors with large sums of money. Basically, an author[180] may register their right to receive a share of up to £6,600 per annum from a government fund of £8 million.[181] The right persists for the same period as copyright.[182] To qualify for the scheme, authors must have their principal homes in a listed country (at present, EEA countries). The right only applies with respect to books, which must be 'printed and bound'. Musical scores are excluded.[183] The scheme is administered for the government by a Registrar of Public Lending Right. However, section 3(3) declares that the entitlement is to be 'dependent on, and its extent ascertainable by reference to, the number of occasions on which books are lent out from particular libraries'. Libraries thus have to provide information about the books they have loaned.

7 DROIT DE SUITE

The final right 'related' to copyright is the *droit de suite,* or as it is also known, the 'artist's resale royalty'.[184] The '*droit de suite*' (literally translated as the right to follow the work) enables artists to claim a portion of the price for which a work is resold. The idea is that an artist may sell a painting for a low price at a time when they are unknown, and have little bargaining power. In due course, if the artist's reputation develops, that painting can be resold for continually increasing sums. The *droit de suite* enables the artist to claim a proportion of the increased value. The right is seen as justifiable not only because it encourages creation, but also because the artist is conceived (through the authorial link) as responsible for the increase

---

[177] Public Lending Right Scheme 1982 (Commencement) Order 1982 (SI 1982/719); Public Lending Right Scheme (Increase of Limit) Order 2003 (SI 2003/839).

[178] SI 1990/2360. Since then there have been further alterations in the Public Lending Right Scheme (Commencement of Variation) Order 1992 (SI 1992/3049) (altering Art. 46(a) of scheme); 1991 (SI 1991/2618) (removing Art. 6(2)(b)); SI 2005/1519; SI 2005/3351. For fuller commentary, see Copinger, Ch. 19.

[179] A number of countries also recognize 'public lending rights'. See S. von Lewinski, 'Public Lending Right: General and Comparative Survey of the Existing System in Law and Practice' (1992) 154 *RIDA* 3: Denmark (1946), Norway (1947), Sweden (1955), Finland (1961), Iceland (1963), Netherlands (1971), Germany (1972), New Zealand (1973), Australia (1974), UK (1979), Canada (1986), and Israel (1986). These rights are not within the remit of the Berne Convention and vary considerably from place to place.

[180] Defined in Art. 4. Note that the author's name should appear on the title page or be entitled to a royalty from the publisher: Art. 4(2). NB while the right is assignable and devolves on death, only the author may apply to register a book. It has yet to be seen whether publishers will require its assignment to them or the payment over of any part of the moneys received.

[181] Public Lending Right Scheme (Increase of Limit) Order 2003 (SI 2003/839) and SI 2005/1519.

[182] Public Lending Right Scheme (Commencement) Order 1982 (SI 1982/719) as amended by Art. 20, Public Lending Right Scheme (Commencement of Variations) Order 1997 (SI 1997/1576); SI 1999/420 (excluding books which lack ISBNs).

[183] Eligible books are defined in Art. 6. Book means printed and bound publication but does not include books bearing corporate names, musical scores, and serial publications. The restriction to books of 32 pages has been removed.

[184] S. Stokes, *Artist's Resale Right (Droit de Suite): Law and Practice* (2006).

in value (economic success) of their works.[185] Consequently, although the right is essentially economic in nature, it is sometimes categorized as a 'moral right'. Because of its specific *sui generis* nature, we have included it in this chapter on related rights.

Until recently, no such artists' resale right was recognized in British copyright law.[186] However, as many European countries did so, and there was thought to be a potential impact on the internal market from the differences in national laws for modern artworks, the Resale Right Directive was adopted by the European Parliament and Council requiring all member states to introduce such a right.[187] Prior to its adoption, the proposed Directive was widely criticized, particularly from the perspective of the UK art market. One particular fear that was expressed was that the effect of harmonizing 'upwards' would be to drive sales of modern artworks out of Europe—to the auction houses of New York, where no such 'tax' will be imposed on the seller. (Apparently, when California created a *droit de suite,* Sotheby's closed its auction house there.) These criticisms and questions, however, did not prove persuasive, though the *droit de suite,* as adopted, is much more limited than that originally proposed and gives considerable leeway to member states as regards implementation. The Directive was implemented in the UK by a statutory instrument, operative from February 2006.[188] The British government, rather surprisingly, did not take advantage of all the flexibilities provided to implement the Directive in a minimal fashion.

The Directive applies to original works of art,[189] that is 'works of graphic or plastic art'. It does not apply to manuscripts of writers and composers.[190] The Directive includes within that definition works such as paintings, engravings, tapestries, ceramics, and photographs, and this implicitly suggests that the right is not available to designers of 'works of applied art'. The right will apply not merely to unique works but also to works produced in multiples, provided they are made by the artist or are copies considered to be original works of art which have been made in limited number by the artist or under their authority.[191]

---

[185] Cf. J. Merryman, 'The Proposed Generalisation of the Droit de Suite in the European Communities' [1997] *IPQ* 16, 22–3 (arguing that increases in value can be attributed to a variety of causes, including the work of critics, museums, dealers, collectors, and that the artist shares in their efforts through the increased value in any works they have retained).

[186] See, for previous British views, *Report of the Committee on Copyright and Designs Law,* Chap. 17 (Cmnd. 6732, 1977).

[187] Directive 2001/84/EC of the European Parliament and of the Council of 27 Sep. 2001 on the resale right for the benefit of the author of an original work of art, *OJ* 2002, *L* 272 (hereafter Resale Right Dir.). For commentaries, see J. Merryman, 'The Proposed Generalisation of the *Droit de Suite* in the European Communities' [1997] *IPQ* 16 (arguing that the premise on which the Commission operates, that the *droit de suite* is a 'good thing', is not sustainable, so harmonization requires its removal); D. Booton, 'A Critical Analysis of the European Commission's Proposal for a directive Harmonising the *Droit de Suite*' [1998] *IPQ* 165; S. Hughes, in L. Bently and S. Maniatis, *Intellectual Property and Ethics, Perspectives in Intellectual Property Vol. IV* (1998).

[188] Effective February 13, 2006. The Directive had an implementation date of 1 January 2006. See IPI, *A Study Into the Effect on the UK Art Market of the Introduction of the Artists Resale Royalty* (2008) (reporting no evidence of diversion of trade).

[189] The right will be applied to existing works still in copyright on 1 Jan. 2006, but only as regards sales after that date.

[190] Resale Right Dir., Recital 19. Presumably existing national regimes which extended resale royalties further will need to limit the operation of the right. This follows from the reasons for harmonization and more specifically from Recital 21 which states that 'the categories of work of art subject to the resale right should be harmonised'.

[191] Resale Right Dir., Art. 2; The Artist's Resale Right Regulations 2006 (SI 2006/346), Reg 4.

The Directive requires member states to confer the resale royalty right on the author of such a work.[192] The right is to last for the full term of copyright protection.[193] After death, the right passes with the author's estate.[194] The right is not assignable.[195] Royalties can only be collected through a 'collecting society', and provision is made for the administration of rights by a collecting society even without the holder's action.[196] The Design and Artistic Copyright Society has undertaken to administer the resale right, and in its first year collected over £1 million. At least one competitor has now emerged: the Artists Collecting Society.[197] Although the right applies to sales of existing works in which copyright subsists,[198] it may be exercised only by a person who is at the contract date a 'qualifying individual' or a charity. As regards 'individuals', they must be a national of an EEA state or of one of the 26 countries currently listed in Schedule 2 of the Regulations.[199]

The right operates only in relation to 'resales' of such works, that is, sales by persons to whom the tangible property in the embodiment of a work has already been transferred,[200] and only when such resale is effected by an art-market professional, such as salesrooms, galleries, and dealers.[201] It therefore seems to exclude transactions between individuals acting in their private capacity. A Recital in the Directive also makes clear that the right is not to apply to resales by persons acting in their private capacity to museums which are not-for-profit and are open to the public.[202] The royalty is payable by the seller, and the seller's agent, or if there is no such agent, either by the agent of the buyer, if there is one, or by the buyer.[203]

As regards calculation of the sum due it should be noted that member states may operate a threshold where the seller acquired the work directly from the author within three years of the resale, and the resale price is less than €10,000.[204] Recital 18 implies that this is confined

---

[192] See Resale Right Dir., Art. 6(1). The Artist's Resale Right Regulations define the term 'joint authors' in a different manner than for copyright: Reg. 5 (different from CDPA, s. 10). The name appearing on the work is presumed to be the author: Reg. 6.

[193] Resale Right Dir., Art. 8.   [194] See Resale Right Dir., Art. 6(1); Artist's Resale Right Reg. 9, 7(4).

[195] Artist's Resale Right Reg. 7. Nor is it chargeable nor waivable: Reg. 7(2), 8.

[196] Artist's Resale Right Regulations 2006, Reg. 14.

[197] See: <http://www.dacs.org.uk>; also: <http://www.artistscollectingsociety.org.uk>.

[198] Artist's Resale Right Reg. 16(1)(b).

[199] Foreign authors—that is, those from non-EU countries—may enjoy the right as long as authors from member states enjoy reciprocal treatment in the third countries concerned: Art. 7.; Artist's Resale Right Reg 10(3). The list comprises countries that offer reciprocal protection: Algeria, Brazil, Bulgaria, Burkina Faso, Chile, Congo, Costa Rica, Croatia, Ecuador, Guinea, Iraq, Ivory Coast, Laos, Madagascar, Mali, Monaco, Morocco, Peru, Philippines, Romania, Russian Federation, Senegal, Serbia and Montenegro, Tunisia, Turkey, and Uruguay. The list does not include the United States.

[200] Artist's Resale Right Reg. 3. 'Transfer of ownership by the author' is further defined as including transfer by testamentary disposition in accordance with the rules on intestacy, disposal by the author's personal representative, or disposal by an official receiver or trustee in bankruptcy: Reg. 3(5).

[201] Resale Right Dir., Art. 1. More specifically, the royalty is only applicable to resales where the buyer or seller, or the agent of the buyer or of the seller where the sale takes place through an agent, 'is acting in the course of a business of dealing in works of art': Artist's Resale Right Reg. 12(3)(a).

[202] Recital 18.

[203] Artist's Resale Right Reg. 13. Resale Right Dir. Art. 1(3). Recital 25 states that the seller 'is the person or undertaking on whole behalf the sale is concluded'. Note Resale Right Dir. Art. 1(4) (member states may provide that a buyer or intermediary shall 'alone be liable or shall share liability with the seller for payment of the royalty').

[204] Resale Right Dir., Art. 3(1). Member states may make the right available below that threshold so as to further the interests of young artists: Art. 3(2), Recital 16. Artist's Resale Right Regulations 2006, Reg. 12(3)(b). A sale price of €1,000 produces a royalty of a mere €40. No royalty is payable on a sale for less than €10,000 where the seller acquired the work directly from the author less than three years before the sale: Reg 12(4).

'to the particular situation of art galleries which acquire works directly from the author'. But the Article is not so restricted. Since the maximum such a seller would have to pay would be €500,[205] the utilization of this exemption would seem particularly mean-minded.

Under the Directive royalties are calculated on sales prices, net of tax.[206] The member states are given free rein in establishing a threshold (as long as it does not exceed €3,000) and setting royalty rates where the minimum threshold is lower than €3,000, as long as the rate is 4 per cent or above.[207] The United Kingdom, rather surprisingly (given its outright opposition to the Directive)—and controversially—elected to set a threshold of €1000 at 4 per cent. After that, the royalty rates are set by the Directive and the percentage decreases as the resale price increases: up to €50,000 the artist is to be entitled to 4 per cent;[208] between €50,000 and €200,000 3 per cent; for sales between €200,000 and €350,000, 1 per cent; for those fetching €350–500,000 a mere 0.5 per cent and for those exceeding €500,000 0.25 per cent. As if these sums were not measly enough—a sale for €1 million giving the artist €10,000 (exactly 1 per cent), there is a cap—so that the royalty may not exceed €12,500.[209] The rates are set so low in order to avoid the right having the effect of causing sales to relocate in order to circumvent the rules.[210] Provision is made for periodic review by the Commission.[211]

---

[205] In a state operating Art. 4(2).

[206] Resale Right Dir., Recital 20. This is in contrast to some member states, where authors were only entitled where the price of the work increased.

[207] Resale Right Dir., Art. 3, 4(3). The threshold may help to avoid disproportionately high collection and administration costs: Recital 22. However, member states may desire to provide royalties below €3,000 'to promote the interests of new artists'. The Recital notes that variations are unlikely to have a significant effect on the proper functioning of the internal market.

[208] Resale Right Dir., Art. 1(a), 1(2). If a member state elects, this figure can be set at 5 per cent. The UK chose 4 per cent.

[209] Resale Right Dir., Art. 4(2). Artist's Resale Right Regulations, Sched. 1. The rates are cumulative: 4% on the first €50,000; 3% on the next €150,000; 1% on the next €150,000; and 0.5% on the next €150,000. The right holder is entitled to 0.25% on any part of the sale price above €500,000. The maximum royalty would only be achieved on a net sale of €2.3 million.

[210] Resale Right Dir., Recitals 24 and 26.   [211] Resale Right Dir., Recital 26.

PART II

PATENTS

14

INTRODUCTION TO PATENTS

CHAPTER CONTENTS

1 INTRODUCTION

A patent is a limited monopoly that is granted in return for the disclosure of technical information. Under this Faustian pact, the applicant is required to disclose their invention so that it can be used (or worked) by a 'person skilled in the art'.[1] In return, the state (in the guise of the Patent Office) issues the applicant with a patent that gives them the exclusive right to control the way that their patented invention is exploited for a 20-year period.

While the protection provided by a patent, which is limited to 20 years, is not as long as the protection provided by copyright law or (possibly) trade mark registration, the rights granted are more extensive. The rights granted to the patent owner cover most commercial uses of the patented invention. In addition, the rights will be infringed irrespective of whether or not the defendant copied from the patented invention. In part, the breadth of the patent monopoly is offset by the fact that patents are only granted if an applicant complies with a relatively onerous registration process. Unlike copyright, which arises automatically on creation of the work, patents are only granted after the applicant satisfies the requirements of registration. Although the granting process may not be as onerous as some would like, it does impose a number of limits and safeguards on the types of invention that are patented, the scope of the monopoly granted, and the nature of the information that is disclosed in the patent. As such, rather than merely being seen as a prerequisite to grant, patent registration should be seen as a process in which policy goals are implemented and enforced.

Two bodies grant the patents that operate in the United Kingdom. The first and oldest granting authority is the UK Intellectual Property Office. (Until 2 April 2007, the Intellectual

---

[1] This is a notional person who has the requisite skill and knowledge appropriate to the type of invention in question.

Property Office was known as the UK Patent Office.) Patents granted by the UK Office only apply in the UK. A British patent cannot be infringed, for example, in Ireland or Germany. As of 1 June 1978, it is also possible to get a patent to protect inventions in the United Kingdom by applying to the European Patent Office (EPO). It should be noted that the EPO grants a bundle of national patents. That is, rather than granting a single pan-European patent, the EPO grants a series of national patents. While there are some subtle differences, once a patent has been granted by the EPO, it is treated as if it had been issued by the British Intellectual Property Office.

Applications for grant of a patent can be made directly to the British Intellectual Property Office or the European Patent Office. It is also possible to apply to these offices indirectly by way of an international filing under the Patent Cooperation Treaty (PCT). The European Patent Convention (EPC) has superseded the UK Intellectual Property Office as a source for applications for UK patents. As a result, the question has arisen as to whether there is much to be gained from retaining a national patent office.[2] In line with the fact that there are two routes by which a patent for the UK can be granted, there are also two (interrelated) legal regimes that need to be taken into account. These are set out in the European Patent Convention 2000 ('EPC 2000') and the Patents Act 1977 (which is modelled on the EPC). In addition, there are also two different sets of tribunals that adjudicate on patent disputes: the tribunals at the EPO and the traditional British judicial structure (with some amendments for specialist tribunals for patents).

2 HISTORY OF THE BRITISH PATENT SYSTEM UP UNTIL 1977

The passage of the Patents Act 1977 marked an important change in British patent law. As well as introducing procedural and substantive changes, it also saw Britain's entry into the European Patent Convention. While there are many important differences in the post-1977 law, in the following chapters we will encounter many concepts that predate the 1977 Act. For example, the image of the invention as the human intervention in nature that brings about a resulting physical change which underpins much contemporary jurisprudence, was well entrenched in British law by the mid-nineteenth century.

Insofar as patents can be seen as monopolies offered by the state as rewards, there are many historical antecedents. A notable example is the practice that came to prominence in sixteenth- and seventeenth-century Britain, where the Crown granted privileges to subjects in return for the subject carrying out some corresponding duty. Initially, these privileges were granted in letters patent, that is as 'an open letter' from the Crown to a subject (from which the term patent is derived). Unlike the present system, there were no formal checks or balances on the privileges granted by the Crown. As such, patents were frequently granted for activities that were already being performed by individuals. A famous example is the grant of a monopoly over the selling of playing cards.[3] Clearly, the grant of such a monopoly would have been detrimental to anyone who was already selling playing cards. As Crown grants of patents

---

[2] See W. Kingston, 'What role now for European National Patent Offices' [2003] *EIPR* 289; J. Phillips, 'Time to Close the Patent Office Doors?' [1990] *EIPR* 151.

[3] *Darcy v. Allin* (1602) 11 *Co Rep* 84b; 74 *ER* 1131.

increased over the course of the sixteenth and seventeenth centuries, so too did the criticism. Eventually, the Crown's right to grant such privileges was challenged in the courts.[4] It was also subject to Parliamentary intervention with the passage of the 1624 Statute of Monopolies, which imposed a general prohibition on the grant of patents by the Crown. While the Statute of Monopolies imposed a general prohibition on the grant of monopolies, an exception was made in section 6 where the grant related to 'a manner of new manufacture'. As well as limiting the circumstances in which a patent could be granted, the Statute also limited the duration of the patents for new manufacture to a period of 14 years. This period, which corresponded to two terms of apprenticeship, was based upon the idea that in return for the monopoly the patentee would teach the new 'art' to two sets of apprentices.

While patents have existed in one form or another for many centuries, the patent system that exists today is largely a creation of the nineteenth century. Indeed many aspects of the registration process as well as many of the legal concepts that we look at in subsequent chapters crystallized over this period.[5] One of the most important changes that took place over the course of the nineteenth century was that patents changed from primarily being a creature of Crown prerogative to become a creature of bureaucracy. Although some of the trappings of the patent system's early connection with the Crown remain, patents are better seen as the product of an administrative process than a form of Crown prerogative. The shift from Crown to administration was reinforced with the passage of the Patents Act 1977, which saw Britain enter the EPC. Another important yet often overlooked change that took place in the nineteenth century was the crystallization of patent *law*. Indeed, it was only after the publication of the first textbooks on patent law and the first series of judicial decisions to consider the validity and infringement of patents that a distinct and relatively coherent body of law came into existence.

Another important event that took place over the nineteenth century was that the emerging patent system was subject to a considerable amount of vocal and highly critical public scrutiny.[6] This scrutiny not only led to calls for the reform of patent law; but also in some cases to calls for the abolition of the whole patent system itself. Critics of the patent system said that it was unnecessarily complicated, technical, and obscure. They also said that, while applicants were able to benefit from the protection provided by the patent monopoly, the corresponding public interest in the disclosure of technical information was not being met. In part this was because in many cases the information disclosed in the patent was of limited practical value. Given the lack of control exercised over the nature and content of the information disclosed in the patent, key aspects of inventions often were not disclosed. As a result, third parties were often not able to work or practise the invention from the information that was disclosed in the patent. Even where the information disclosed in the patent was potentially valuable, it was often very difficult for third parties to locate the relevant information. This was attributed to a range of factors, from the fact that the titles of many patents did not match the subject matter of the invention, through to the fact that patent specifications were often not filed in a consistent or logical fashion. The criticisms of the patent system were also motivated by ideological concerns that focused on the monopolistic nature of the patents. Motivated by political economists, who

---

[4] Ibid; 77 ER 1260; *The Clothworkers of Ipswich Case* (1614) *Godb R* 252; 78 *ER* 14.

[5] See Sherman and Bently, 95–110.

[6] The patent controversy was also important insofar as it led to public discussions about the goals and functions of patent law (and intellectual property law more generally). See F. Machlup and E. Penrose, 'The Patent Controversy' (1950) 10 *Journal of Economic History* 1.

championed *laissez-faire* ideas that the government should only interfere in the operation of the market where it was absolutely necessary, patent monopolies were presented as unjustifiable inhibitions on the market that inhibited free trade. (This is in contrast with critics of the Crown grant of patents in the seventeenth century when monopolies were seen to be undesirable because of their association with the Stuart attempts to govern without Parliament.)

The criticisms made of the patent system had a long-standing impact on its shape and direction. Importantly, the shift away from patents being seen as a form of Crown prerogative opened the system up to the possibility of reform. Many of the objections to the existing patent laws were rectified in the Patents Designs and Trade Marks Act 1883 and by changes to Patent Office rules and guidelines. In turn many of the criticisms made of the registration process were met by a raft of administrative reforms. For example, the patent system was rationalized with the establishment of the Patent Office in 1852. In addition, patents were organized alphabetically and rules were introduced that helped to ensure that the titles of the patent corresponded to the patented invention. The growing practice of including a description of the invention in the patent application (now called the specification) was formalized. There was also more attention given to the form and nature of the information disclosed in the patent.

While many of the criticisms made of the patent system were met by legal and administrative reforms, nonetheless the criticisms made of the patent system continued to have an impact upon the way patents were viewed, long after the debates had ended. In part, this may explain why it was that from '1883 until after the end of the [Second World War], the courts tended to regard patent monopolies with some disfavour as being generally contrary to the public interest'.[7] It is interesting to contrast these attitudes with the approach after 1949, where 'the climate of opinion has changed. It is now generally recognized that it is in the public interest to encourage inventive genius. Accordingly the modern tendency of the courts has been to regard patent claims with considerably more favour than before.'[8] This trend has become even more marked in recent years as both UK courts and the EPO have grown increasingly inventive in their efforts to circumvent legislative obstacles to patent protection.

Another notable trend that developed over the nineteenth century was the growing influence that foreign patents systems had on the development of the British patent regime. As well as borrowing concepts from French and American patent law, aspects of the British registration process were modelled on foreign regimes. The second half of the nineteenth century also saw the growing internationalization of the patent system. These moves reached their peak with the signing of the 1883 Paris Convention[9] (which at the end of 2007 had 172 member countries).[10] One of the notable achievements of the Paris Convention was that it introduced the principle of national treatment. This is the principle that a convention country must treat the nationals of other signatory countries in the same way as it treats its own.[11] Another notable aspect of the Convention was that it provided that an application for a patent in one member state should not prejudice subsequent applications in other member states.[12] This is achieved by requiring the later application to be treated as having the priority date of the

---

[7] *Ethyl Corporation's Patent* [1972] *RPC* 169, 193 (Salmon LJ).   [8] Ibid.

[9] Bilateral arrangements that dealt with patent-related issues were entered into in the early nineteenth century. These were usually in the form of Treaties of Freedom, Commerce, and Navigation.

[10] See S. Ladas, *The International Protection of Industrial Property* (1930); E. Penrose, *The Economics of the International Patent System* (1951); *Asahi Kasei Kogyo* [1991] *RPC* 485, 532 (HL).

[11] Paris Art. 2.   [12] Ibid, Art. 4. The priority period is 12 months.

earlier application. It should be noted that the Paris Convention does not impose minimum standards of protection for patents, as the Berne Convention does for copyright.[13]

3 JUSTIFICATIONS FOR PATENTS

Over time, a number of different justifications have been given in support of the patent system. At times, the proponents of patent protection have emphasized the natural rights of inventors to the products of their mental labour.[14] Others have argued that justice demands that an inventor's contribution should be recognized by the grant of a reward.[15] While arguments of this ilk have occasionally been relied upon in discussing aspects of the patent system, they have not been as popular as the public interest rationales. Having said that, the current debates about how indigenous interests should best be accounted for in the patent system have seen a resurgence of interest in arguments about inherent rights and justice.

While commentators have occasionally drawn on natural rights in support of the grant of patents, the most common form of argument has concentrated on the public benefits that flow from the grant of patent monopolies. Although these arguments have changed over time, what they share in common is the basic idea that the public should only ever have to endure the harm caused by the grant of a patent if the public receives some corresponding benefit. These arguments have tended to dominate discussion of the function of the patent system since the nineteenth century.

Initially, the public interest in the patent system was said to flow from the fact that the patentee introduced a form of technology that had not previously been available in the United Kingdom. Often this simply involved the patentee importing information about a trade or a craft from another country. Over time, this rationale was replaced by the argument that the public benefit lay in the disclosure of the invention that occurred on publication of the patent application. That is, the justifications focused on the role that the patent system played in the generation and circulation of technical information. (This is often referred to as the 'information function' of the patent system.) In particular it is said that patents act as incentives to individuals or organizations to disclose information that might otherwise have remained secret.[16] Patents also encourage information to be disclosed in a way that is practically useful. At a more general level, the public interest in allowing patents is said to flow from the fact that the numerous patents that have been granted over time constitute a substantive and valuable database of technical and scientific information. The information function of the patent system was reinforced by the Patents Act 1977 and the EPC, which emphasized the need for the invention to be disclosed in such a way that it could readily be put into practice.[17] The value and effectiveness of the information was also bolstered by the publication of patent specifications on the internet.

While the primary focus of the patent system is on the disclosure of technical information for scientific and industrial reasons, the information that is collected at patent offices throughout the world is occasionally used for other purposes. For example, historians have used the patent

---

[13] Although Paris Art. 4*ter* requires mention of the inventor, Art. 4*quater* requires that patents are not refused on the ground that sale of the product is restricted in domestic law, Art. 5 restricts the ability to forfeit the patent and the availability of compulsory licences.

[14] Machlup and Penrose, 'The Patent Controversy', 11–17.   [15] Ibid, 17–21.

[16] See D. Davies, 'The Early History of the Patent Specification' (1934) 50 *LQR* 86.

[17] See below, Ch. 20 Sections 1 and 2.

system as an indicator of public attitudes towards different technologies.[18] More bizarrely, the fact that patent applications had been lodged for ovens for the burning of human corpses was used in a defamation action as evidence of the existence of gas chambers at Auschwitz.[19]

Patents have also been justified by the fact that they provide an incentive for the production of new inventions.[20] As Lord Oliver said in *Asahi* the 'underlying purpose of the patent system is the encouragement of improvements and innovation. In return for making known his improvement to the public the inventor receives the benefit of a period of monopoly during which he becomes entitled to prevent others from performing his invention except by his licence.'[21] More specifically, it is said that as patents provide the possibility for inventions to be exploited for a 20-year period, this means that investors will be more willing to fund research and development. In this sense, patents act as a vector that links scientific and technical research with commercial spheres.[22] Arguments of this nature have proved to be particularly important in situations where an invention can be readily ascertained (or reverse-engineered) from the product which is put on the market (and no other form of protection exists).

The fact that a product is patented is often used by retailers trying to gain a competitive advantage to show the innovative nature of their products. There is also a sense in which the fact that a product has been patented suggests that the product (or process) has been publicly sanctioned in some way or other. This has proved to be an important consideration in the ethical debates about whether patents should be granted for genetically modified humans, animals, and plants.

If we reflect upon the way that patent law has been viewed over the last century or so, a number of things stand out. The first notable feature is that the patent system has widely been seen, both by supporters and critics alike, as a system of regulation: that is, as a regime that modifies behaviour. While in some cases this is explicit; in most cases it is implicit in the way commentators talk about and think about patents.[23] Another notable and consistent trend has been that whenever commentators talk about the patent system in a *positive* sense, that is as a system that regulates and controls behaviour in a desirable way, they have almost always seen it as a tool to promote economic ends, such as the encouragement of new industries, research and development, or innovation.[24] In contrast, whenever non-economic factors such as health, human rights, the environment, or ethics are discussed, they have either been treated as

---

[18] T. O'Dell, *Inventions and Official Secrecy* (1994).

[19] *Irving v. Penguin Books* (11 Apr. 2000), para. 7.65 (QB). G. Reimann, *Patents for Hitler* (1945).

[20] Kitch emphasized the way in which the grant of patents could be analogized to the grant of mineral rights, giving the grantee an incentive to invest in the exploitation of the 'prospect'. See E. Kitch, 'An Economic Review of the Patent System' (1977) 20 *Journal of Law & Economics* 265.

[21] *Asahi*, note 10 above, 523 (Lord Oliver) (HL); Mansfield, 'Patents and Innovation: An Empirical Study' (1986) 32 *Managing Science* 173; *Esswein/Automatic programmer*, T579/88 [1991] EPOR 120, 125. See J. Aubrey, 'A Justification of the Patent System', in J. Phillips (ed.), *Patents in Perspective* (1985); A. Plant, 'The Economic Theory Concerning Patents for Inventions' [1934] *Economica* 30; C. Taylor and A. Silbertson, *The Economic Impact of Patents* (1973), chs. 2 and 14.

[22] The role that the patent system played in inducing the invention and implementation of new industrial practices has been widely but inconclusively debated. See C. MacLeod, *Inventing the Industrial Revolution* (1988); H. Dutton, *The Patent System and Inventive Activity during the Industrial Revolution: 1750–1852* (1986).

[23] Driven by a form of legal positivism that has long disappeared from most other areas of law, it is occasionally suggested that patent law does not regulate behaviour: rather, it merely grants property (or monopoly) rights in inventions. Invariably, however, the pretence of neutrality that underpins arguments of this nature disappears when commentators talk about the importance of patent protection in promoting technical innovation or investment in innovation.

[24] Occasionally, policy debates have also focused on the positive impact that patents have on the collection and distribution of technical information.

external (*negative*) constraints upon the core activities of the patent system, or as undesirable side effects that need to be mitigated.

While there is no denying the important role that patents play in macro-economic policy, there is no reason why the patent system, as a regulatory tool, should only be used in the pursuit of economic ends, nor any reason why 'external' factors such as the impact of technology on the environment or health should not fall within the core remit of the patent system. That is, there is no compelling reason why the various practices, rules, and concepts that have been developed and fine-tuned over the last couple of centuries or so should only be used for economic ends. Given that modern patent law already performs a number of sometimes surprising non-economic roles, this is not as alien a proposition as it might first appear. For those who require an older lineage, there are also many examples from pre-modern patent law where the grant of a patent was used by the Crown to achieve political and personal, rather than economic, ends. As we will see below, arguments of this nature are beginning to have an influence on patent law, particularly in relation to the use of biological inventions and the protection of indigenous knowledge.[25]

4   CURRENT LEGISLATIVE FRAMEWORK

The law that regulates the creation and use of patents that operate in the UK is a hybrid mixture of national, European, and international elements. In this section, we provide an introduction to the legislation, conventions, and treaties that we will encounter in subsequent chapters. We begin by looking at the most important regimes, namely the European Patent Convention and the Patents Act 1977. We then go on to look at the impact that the European Commission has had on patent law. After looking at the Community Patent Convention, we turn to look at some of the international treaties that have shaped British patent law. In particular, we look at the Patent Cooperation Treaty, TRIPS, and the Convention on Biological Diversity.[26]

4.1   THE EUROPEAN PATENT CONVENTION

The European Patent Convention (EPC) was signed in Munich in 1973 and came into operation on 1 June 1978.[27] The original convention, which we will refer to as the 'EPC 1973' was replaced by the European Patent Convention 2000 ('EPC 2000') on 17 December 2007.[28] The provisions of the EPC 2000 apply unless the transitional provisions provide otherwise for the applicability of the EPC 1973.

The EPC is based upon (and modified) the patent law of the various member states in force at the time. The EPC is an intergovernmental treaty that is distinct from the European Community. As such, membership extends beyond members of the EC. At the beginning of 2008, the EPC had 34 member states.[29]

---

[25] See below pp. 355–56, 388–90.

[26] There are a number of other regional patent agreements, most notably the Bangui Agreement, the Harare Protocol on Patents, and the Eurasian Patent Convention (Moscow, 1994).

[27] Work began on a European patent system in 1949 in the Council of Europe with the Longchambon plan. For background see K. Haertel, 'The Munich Diplomatic Conference on European Patent Law' (1973) 4 *IIC* 271. P. Braendli (1974) 4 *IIC* 402.

[28] See below at pp. 343–4.

[29] As of 1 Jan 2008, the 34 members were: Austria, Belgium, Bulgaria, Cyprus, Croatia, Czech Republic, Denmark, Estonia, Finland, France, Germany, Greece, Hungary, Iceland, Ireland, Italy, Latvia, Liechtenstein,

The EPC is primarily concerned with the granting of European patents.[30] This was facilitated by the establishment of the European Patent Office (EPO) in Munich, which acts as a centralized system for the grant of European patents. When an applicant wishes to protect their invention in a number of European countries, the EPO provides them with the benefit of a single application and search procedure, and a single grant of a bundle of national patents in each of the member states.[31]

Applications are made to the European Patent Office, which is based in Munich. The application is submitted to the Examining Division and appeals are made from there to the Technical or Legal Board of Appeal. In rare cases, the Boards of Appeal (or the President of the EPO) may refer legal matters to the Enlarged Board of Appeal.[32] While applications may be filed in any language,[33] if the application is not in an official language of the EPO (English, German, or French), the applicant is given two months to translate the application into an official language.[34] Upon grant, a European patent becomes a bundle of national patents that have effect in each of the member states for 20 years from the date of filing. The procedure for application to the EPO is similar to that at the UK Intellectual Property Office.[35]

When the EPC was being formulated, it was decided that for there to be an effective single granting process, it was necessary for the member states to harmonize the basic rules of patent law. This was particularly the case in relation to the rules on patentability and validity. As we will see, the tribunals at the EPO have had a substantial impact on this area of law. The EPC only provides a mechanism for the grant of national patents. As such, while the EPC is concerned with the validity of European patents, matters of infringement, enforcement, revocation, renewal, and litigation are exclusively dealt with by national law. One of the consequences of this is that a patent granted at the EPO for two countries might be interpreted differently in each country. In order to reduce the chances of problems of this nature from arising, the EPO examiners, national judges, and examiners meet annually. Further, a Protocol on the Interpretation of Article 69 of the EPC 2000 [Article 69 EPC 1973] provides guidance as to how patents should be interpreted.[36]

Lithuania, Luxembourg, Malta, Monaco, the Netherlands, Norway, Poland, Portugal, Romania, Slovenia, Slovak Republic, Spain, Sweden, Switzerland, Turkey, and the UK. In addition there are four extension states: Albania, Bosnia and Herzegovina, the former Yugoslav Republic of Macedonia, and Serbia.

[30] This has cast doubts over the independence of the Office. Interestingly, the European Parliament suggested that the EPO reconsider the practice whereby it 'obtains payments for the patents that it grants as this practice harms the public nature of the institution'. *Proposal for a Directive of the European Parliament and of the Council on the Patentability of Computer-implemented Inventions* COM (2002) 92 final, Recital 7b (introduced by European Parliament, Amendment 95).

[31] The second planned element of the European patent system, the Community Patent Convention (CPC), provided for the establishment of a Community-wide patent. It has not yet come into force and has been supplanted by the EC's plan for a Europe-wide patent. See below at p. 351.

[32] EPC 2000 Art 112a provides that decisions of the boards of appeal can be contested on limited grounds including fundamental procedural defects.

[33] EPC 2000 Art. 14(2), EPC 2000 r. 40.   [34] EPC 2000 r. 6(1), r 58.

[35] One important difference is that the EPC allows for third-party opposition to the grant during the nine months after publication of the details of the grant. Opposition is not possible under the UK system, but it is open to a person who objects to the patent to seek revocation on similar grounds.

[36] PA 125(3). See B. Sherman, 'Patent Claim Interpretation: The Impact of the Protocol on Interpretation' (1991) 54 *MLR* 499.

4.1.1 EPC 2000

Over the course of the 1990's, there were growing calls for the European Patent Convention to be changed to take account of the technological, political, and legal changes that had occurred since it was signed in 1973. To this end, a conference took place in Munich in November 2000 to discuss revision of the EPC.[37] The conference aimed to modernize the European patent system while maintaining the proven principles of substantive patent law and procedure. The conference also aimed to undertake a comprehensive review of the EPC in light of technical and legal developments, and over twenty years of practical experience. The conference also wanted to bring the EPC into line with TRIPS, the future Community patent, and the provisions of the (WIPO) Patent Law Treaty. In light of the leading political and legislative role that the European Union played in relation to the protection of biotechnological inventions, it was decided that it was inadvisable to open up parallel discussions in this area. It was also decided that further diplomatic conferences should be organized to consider the protection for computer programs and biotechnology inventions, as well as the changes required to implement the Community patent.

At the end of the conference, the member states of the EPC agreed to make a number of changes to the EPC.[38] The revised Convention, known as the 'EPC 2000', and new Implementing Regulations, were adopted by the EPO Administrative Council on 28 June 2001. The EPC 2000 and its Implementing Regulations came into force on 13 December 2007. In so doing the EPC 2000 replaced the EPC (1973). The new law applies to all European patent applications and to patents granted on the basis of this application which were filed after the EPC came into force. In certain situations, the EPC 2000 also applies to applications that were pending on 13 December 2007 and to patents that had already been granted by that date. Under the transitional provisions of the EPC 2000 most of the provisions of the new law will apply to applications lodged and patents granted prior to the EPC 2000 coming into force. In this section we provide an overview of some of the key features of the EPC 2000; we leave more detailed discussions (including the transitional arrangements) for the appropriate place in the text.

For the most part, the EPC 2000 did not bring about (or at least was not intended to bring about) many changes in the existing law. For example, Article 52(1) EPC 2000 does not make any substantial changes to the types of invention that were patentable under EPC 1973. Following Article 27(1) of TRIPS, EPC 2000 does however add a new phrase that 'European patents shall be granted for any invention, in all fields of technology'. Contrary to the Base Proposal for the Revision of the European Patent Convention, which proposed to delete '*computer programs as such*' from Article 52(2)(c),[39] the conference decided not to remove computer programs from the list of non-patentable inventions in Article 52(2) of the EPC 2000.[40] As such, the statutory position under the EPC 1973 remains unchanged. The provisions in the EPC 2000 in relation to novelty, inventive step, and the internal requirements for patentability are basically the same as in the EPC. The main change is that Article 54(4) EPC has been deleted. This means that the state of the art will include all previous European applications irrespective of their designation.

---

[37] The Administrative Council of the EPO launched the revision project in 1998.

[38] Act Revising the Convention on the Grant of European Patents (EPC) (Munich) (29 Nov. 2000) MR/3/00 Rev. 1e (hereafter EPC Revision Act).

[39] CA/1000/00e. Distributed by the German Federal Ministry of Justice on 27 June 2000. Diplomatic Conference 20–9 Nov. 2000.

[40] EPC 2000, Art. 52(2)(c) (which is identical to EPC 1973, Art. 52(2)(c)).

In other cases, existing provisions have been reworded to make them more transparent. For example, Article 52(4) EPC 1973 said that methods of treatment and diagnosis were lacking in industrial applicability and as such as excluded from patentability. In contrast, Article 53(c) EPC 2000 takes a more direct approach insofar as it simply says that such methods are excluded from patentability. In other cases, the text has been changed to ensure that the EPC 2000 reflects current practice. As such, while there may have been a change in the language of the Convention, this was not intended to bring about changes to the existing law. For example, Article 54(5) EPC 2000 expressly allows for claims to second and further medical uses of known substances or compositions without the need for such claims to be expressed as Swiss-type claims, as was previously the case. The EPC 2000 also clarifies and strengthens the extent of protection conferred by European patents by expressly including the doctrine of equivalents in the revised Protocol on Article 69 EPC 2000.[41]

One of the most notable changes brought about by the EPC 2000 is that it provides patent owners with the option of limiting the protection afforded by their patents in a central procedure before the EPO.[42] The existence of a centralized procedure for amendment means that proprietors no longer have to go through the national patent offices. It also means that should a patent as granted turn out to be invalid, it can be amended quickly. It was hoped that this would act as an incentive to amend incorrectly granted patents promptly and at a lower cost. Article 138 EPC 2000 also enables proprietors to amend patents granted by the EPO in national proceedings relating to a patent's validity. As we will see, this has ramifications for the judicial discretion that exists in UK patent law as to whether an amendment should be allowed.

The EPC 2000 also made a number of amendments that simplified the patent grant procedure before the EPO.[43] These changes were intended to provide greater legal certainty for applicants and patent owners. It is now possible, for example, to file patent applications in any language, since a translation into one of the official languages of the EPO will not be required until a later date. The EPC 2000 also aims to streamline the European grant procedure. Notably, it was decided that the search and examination parts of the patent application should be brought together. Previously, search and examination were carried out in a number of different locations. On the basis that, as the EPO's vast collection of search documentation were available through databases at all its duty stations, it has been decided that there is no longer any need to separate the two tasks. It was expected that this will lead to a 'significant increase in the productivity and efficiency of the EPO'. The EPC 2000 also made a number of other notable procedural changes. For example, in contrast to the EPC 1973 which requires applicants to designate the states in which they wish to be protected,[44] Article 79(1) EPC 2000 provides that all EPC states will be deemed to be designated at the date of filing. The EPC 2000 has also created a legal basis for special agreements to be made between the contracting states concerning the translation of European patents. It also provides for the introduction of a central court system for the enforcement of European patents, issues which are of importance for the Community patent proposed by the European Commission.[45] In addition, the EPC 2000 authorizes the Administrative Council to adapt the EPC to international treaties and European Community legislation.[46] Given the activity of the European Community in patent law, this may prove to be an important change.

---

[41] EPC 2000, Protocol on the Interpretation of Art. 69, Art. 2: EPC Revision Act, Art. 2, item 2.

[42] EPC 2000, Art 105 (a)–(c). See below at Ch. 16 Section 5.

[43] See, e.g. EPC 2000 Art. 15 ff; EPC 2000 Implementing Regulations. See also EPC Revision Act, Art. 1, items 27–43.

[44] See EPC 1973, Art. 79.   [45] EPC 2000, Art. 149a(1).   [46] EPC 2000, Art 149a (2).

4.1.2 The London Agreement

One of the long-standing problems confronting the European patent system is the cost of translation. Given the informational role played by patents and the problems that arise where European patents are granted for 34 member states (with over 23 different languages), it is not surprising that translation has been a key issue within the EPO. Many of these problems have been alleviated as a result of the London Agreement, which came into operation in the EU and the UK on 1 May 2008.

One of the reasons why translation proved to be so problematic under the EPC, and why the London Agreement was initiated in the first place, was that Article 65 EPC 2000 (as was the case under EPC 1973) allows member states to require the patent to be translated into the national language as a pre-requisite for validity.[47] Prior to 1 May 2008, for example, for a European patent (UK) not in English to be valid in the UK, the patent had to be translated into English within three months. As the number of member states proliferated, so too did the cost of translation. Given the expense of translation (estimated to be 40 per cent of overall patent costs, with an average cost of €3,800),[48] it is not surprising that it attracted a lot of attention. The concerns about translation cost were heighted by the fact that, as most patent litigation was said to be based on the 'authentic' text (published in English, German, or French) rather than the translated text, it was suggested that the national translations were redundant.[49] Given this, the contracting parties to the EPC decided to modify Article 65.[50] To this end, the London Agreement was adopted on 17 October 2000.[51] The Agreement came into force on 1 May 2008.

In order to reduce translation costs and thus the cost of patenting in Europe, Article 1(1) of the Agreement provides that signatory parties that share an official language with the EPO (namely, Austria, Belgium, France, Germany, Ireland, Luxembourg, Monaco, Switzerland, and the UK) must waive, wholly or partially, the requirement under Article 65 EPC 2000 that a patent be translated into their national language. Article 1(2) provides that member states that do not have English, French, or German as their official language must also dispense with the translation requirement (allowed under Article 65 EPC 2000). Article 1(3) does, however, allow these countries to require that, for a patent to be valid, the claims must be translated into the local language.[52] Under Article 2 of the Agreement, in the case of a patent dispute,

---

[47] EPC 2000 Art. 65.

[48] See EPO, 'The London Agreement' (14 Nov 2007), 1. In 1995 the cost of translation was estimated to be DM400 million per year.

[49] Interestingly, this does not take account of the informational value of the patents and what impact this might have, for example, in Portugal or Turkey. The EPO's response is to deny the value of the translation in providing information about new technologies, as they occur four or five years after filing. EPO, 'The London Agreement', 2.

[50] Previously the EPO had proposed that full translation be replaced with translation of an enhanced abstract European Patent Office, 'Cost of Patenting' (1995) 26 *IIC* 813; P. Braendli, 'The Future of the European Patent System' (1995) 26 *IIC* 813. This has generated further proposals, including only requiring translation of claims or some part of the description, or allowing further delays as to when the translation must take place. B. Pretnar, 'How to Reduce High Translation Costs to European Patents' [1996] *EIPR* 665; K. Heinonen, 'Translation of European Patents: Package Solution not the Answer' [1997] *EIPR* 220; E. Jeneral, 'Once More How to Reduce High Translation Costs of European Patents' [1997] *EIPR* 490; C. Lees, 'Translation: The Key Solution' [1997] *EIPR* 594. On the role of translation in the proposed Community Patent, see p. 344 above.

[51] The full title is: The Agreement on the application of Article 65 of the Convention on the Grant of European Patents made in London on 17th Oct. 2000.

[52] The Netherlands, Sweden and Denmark require that the claims be translated into their official languages. They will also require the description to be published in English.

the owner of the patent is required to supply a full translation of the patent to both the alleged infringer and the competent court.

The UK implemented Article 1(1) of the London Agreement as of 1 May 2008.[53] As a result, section 77(6) of the Patents Act 1977 no longer has effect in the UK. This means that European patents in French or German no longer have to be translated into English within three months of grant at the EPO for them to be valid in the UK. In line with Article 2 of the London Agreement, the rules of procedure before British courts and the Comptroller may require that the full text of the patent is translated into English.

4.2 PATENTS ACT 1977

The law that regulates the creation and use of patents in the United Kingdom is found in the Patents Act 1977, as amended.[54] As the bulk of the 1977 Act was based upon the EPC, the passage of the Act brought with it a number of substantive and procedural changes to British patent law. It also saw the United Kingdom's entry into the EPC.

Insofar as the provisions of the Patents Act 1977 are based on the EPC, the Act says that those provisions should be interpreted so as to give effect to the EPC and decisions made there-under.[55] The important task of ensuring that the UK law remains consistent with the law at the EPO has been recognized by the English courts in numerous cases.[56] Interestingly, the EPO has occasionally reciprocated by taking notice of the decisions of national offices and courts so as to avoid lack of uniformity in the law of the EPC countries.[57] Although there is no consist-ent pattern, pre-1977 decisions have not been treated as being wholly irrelevant when deciding questions under the 1977 Act. In some cases the courts have said that the 1977 Act swept away the old law.[58] In other cases, however, they have acknowledged that, as the intent of the EPC was to harmonize existing national rules, pre-1977 decisions are still important.[59] Despite this, as the jurisprudence at the EPO develops, it is clear that pre-1977 cases are becoming less important in the United Kingdom.

4.2.1 Reform of the Patents Act 1977

In November 2002, the UK Intellectual Property Office and the Department of Trade and Industry released a consultation paper that outlined a number of possible amendments to the Patents Act 1977.[60] While the aim of these changes was primarily to give effect to the EPC 2000, the consultation paper also suggested a number of other changes designed to improve the 1977 Act. The government's conclusions drawn from the consultation process were published in late 2003.[61] After a brief period of debate, the Patents Act received Royal Assent on 22 July 2004.

---

[53] Patents (Translations) Rules 2005 (SI 2005/682).

[54] This replaced the PA 1949.   [55] PA s. 130(7); PA s. 91(1).

[56] *Wyeth's Application* [1985] *RPC* 545; *Gale's Application* [1991] *RPC* 305, 322–3 (Nicholls LJ), 332 (Browne-Wilkinson V-C).

[57] *Wellcome Pigs* T116/85 [1989] *OJ EPO* 13, citing *Stafford Miller's Application* [1984] *FSR* 258; *ICI/Cleaning Plaque*, T290/86 [1991] *EPOR* 157 following *Oral Health Products (Halsteads) Application* [1977] *RPC* 612.

[58] *Unilever's Application* [1983] *RPC* 219; *Merrell Dow v. Norton Healthcare* [1996] *RPC* 76, 82; *Hallen v. Brabantia* [1990] *FSR* 134, 139.

[59] *Gale's Application* [1991] RPC 305.

[60] *Consultation Paper on the Proposed Patents Act (Amendments) Bill* (29 Nov. 2002).

[61] *Consultation on the Proposed Patents Act (Amendment) Bill: Summary of responses and the Government's conclusions* (13 Nov. 2003). See also Explanatory Notes to the Patents Bill (2004) (HL).

Many of the changes made by the Patents Act 2004 mirror those in the EPC 2000 (discussed above). The 1977 Act was amended to reflect the changes in the EPC 2000 by dealing with methods for treatment and diagnosis as exceptions to patentability under section 4A(1), rather than on the basis that they lacked industrial applicability, as had been the case previously.[62] Following Article 54(5) EPC 2000, the government also simplified and clarified the manner in which patent protection can be obtained for second and further medical uses. In particular, under the Patents Act 2004, claims to second or further medical uses of a known substance or composition are allowed whether or not they are drafted as Swiss-type claims.[63] This allows further medical use claims in the UK, while not precluding the possibility of Swiss-type claims.[64] The 1977 Act was also amended to reflect the fact that all applications for European patents form part of the state of the art under section 2(3).[65] The government's earlier proposal to amend section 1 of the 1977 Act to reflect the Article 52(1) EPC 2000 (particularly that inventions 'should be granted in all fields of technology') was not adopted in the 2004 Patents Act.[66]

A number of changes also relate to the amendment of patents. As well as recognizing the new centralized limitation process available under EPC 2000, the government changed the 1977 Act to remove a number of anomalies that previously existed in terms of when a patent may be amended.[67] The Patents Act 2004 also made a number of minor changes to the scheme developed to compensate employee-inventors.[68] It also clarified that co-owners have the ability to amend and revoke a patent if they act jointly.[69]

Infringement proceedings can only be brought before the comptroller if both parties agree that this should happen. In order to provide patentees (particularly small and medium-sized organizations) with an alternative dispute resolution process, the Consultation Paper suggested that the 1977 Act be changed to allow infringement proceeding to be brought before the comptroller at the request of one party. This proposal was not supported.[70] Instead, the 2004 Act amended the 1977 Act to give the comptroller a general power to undertake both post-grant re-examination of a patent and also to make declarations as to whether a particular patent has been infringed. This is to be a non-binding opinion of the Intellectual Property Office, rather than a legally binding decision. It was hoped that this will provide a fast, fair, and effective way of resolving disputes, as an alternative to formal litigation.[71] The Patent Office rules, which play a central role in many aspects of patent law in the UK, were overhauled and

---

[62] Patents Act 2004, cl. 1 (inserting new s. 4 A into the 1977 Act). See *Consultation on the Proposed Patents Act (Amendment) Bill: Summary of responses*, paras. 19–20; Explanatory Notes to the Patents Bill 2004, paras. 15–21.

[63] Patents Act 2004, cl. 1 (inserting new s. 4A(4) into the 1977 Act). See also *Consultation on the Proposed Patents Act (Amendment) Bill: Summary of responses*, paras. 25–27.

[64] *Consultation Paper on the Proposed Patents Act (Amendments) Bill* (29 Nov 2002), para. 26.

[65] *Consultation on the Proposed Patents Act (Amendment) Bill: Summary of responses*, para. 23–24.

[66] Ibid, para. 17. On the basis that the revised Protocal to Art. 69 would operate in the UK under the current arrangements, it was decided that it was not necessary to make any changes in this regard. Ibid, paras. 40–41.

[67] PA s. 75 was changed to allow amendment during any proceedings in which validity may be in issue. Responding to problem highlighted by Jacob J in *Norling v. Eez-Away* [1997] *RPC* 160.

[68] Patents Act 2004, cl. 10 (amending PA ss. 40–41) *Consultation on the Proposed Patents Act (Amendment) Bill: Summary of responses*, paras. 94–99; see also *Consultation Paper on the Proposed Patents Act (Amendments) Bill*, paras. 73–82.

[69] Patents Act 2004, cl. 9 (amending PA, s. 36). See also *Consultation on the Proposed Patents Act (Amendment) Bill: Summary of responses*, paras. 115–124 (co-owners would be able to contract out of this requirement).

[70] Patents Bill 2000, cl. 12 (inserting new PA s. 74A–B). See also *Consultation on the Proposed Patents Act (Amendment) Bill: Summary of responses*, paras. 115–124.

[71] Ibid, paras. 156–185. On the current position, see below p. 1085.

revised to modernize and simplify the patent process as well as improve patent litigation at the Office. The new rules, which are which are known as the 'Patent Rules 2007' came into force on 17 December 2007. All references to UK patent rules will be to the 2007 rules unless otherwise stated.[72]

4.3 THE COMMUNITY PATENT CONVENTION

As part of the plans for the establishment of a European patent system in the 1960s and the 1970s, it was decided that a dual system of protection should be introduced. The first element, which eventually emerged as the EPC, aimed to establish a centralized granting authority. The second part aimed to establish a single Community patent that was to be obtained by one central procedure and be binding in all member states. This came to be known as the Community Patent Convention (CPC), and was signed in Luxembourg in 1975.[73] One of the key advantages that is said to flow from the Community patent is that it would lead to a rationalization of patent administration and thus to a reduction in costs. Unlike the EPC, the CPC has never come into force. To a large extent, these initial plans have recently been superseded by EU moves to establish a single Community-wide patent.

Under the CPC, a patent application would be made to an office at the EPO. To facilitate this, two new departments would be established: the Administration Division to deal with the administrative matters such as transfers and renewals of patents; and the Revocation Division, to deal with applications to revoke Community patents. It is proposed that the system would offer a degree of flexibility, allowing an applicant to switch between EPC and CPC systems in early stages. A number of major problems emerged with the proposed system as regards languages and litigation. Under the 1975 Convention, it was proposed that an applicant would provide translations of claims in all (then eight) official languages. Under a 1989 revision to the CPC it was proposed that this translation be of the complete text, not just the claims, and be supplied within three months of publication. Where this is not complied with, the patent would be void. This proposal would make a Community patent much more costly and less attractive. There will therefore be little advantage to an applicant in a Community patent rather than a European patent. The advantages of the CPC would be limited to convenience and cheaper renewal fees.

The Community patent would offer the possibility of Europe-wide litigation and enforcement (as well as challenge) through a Community patent court. The jurisdiction of the 1975 Convention was to be divided between national courts and the Community court, the former dealing with scope of protection, and the latter with validity. This was rejected in 1989. Under the revised CPC, the validity of a patent would be challengeable either by application to the Revocation division, or in a counterclaim for revocation before a national community patent court. Appeal from either would lie to a (yet to be established) Community Patent Appeal Court (COPAC). Appeal from a national court on other issues (such as damages) would be to the national appeal court. COPAC would also make the final decisions on appeals from the Administration and Revocation divisions. The plan was for COPAC to be an independent

---

[72] Patent Rules 2007 (SI 2007/3291). For an outline of the changes in the way that hearings are conducted at the IP Office see *Tribunal Practice Notice* (TPN 6/2007).

[73] A. Krieger, 'The Luxembourg Convention on the Community Patent: A Challenge and a Duty' (1988) 19 *IIC* 143; V. Scordamaglia, 'The Common Appeal Court and the Future of the Community Patent' (1991) 22 *IIC* 334; V. Scordamaglia, 'The Common Appeal Court and the Future of the Community Patent following the Luxembourg Conference' (1991) 22 *IIC* 458.

organization attached to neither the EPO nor the ECJ. COPAC would not only be the appeal court but would also give preliminary rulings on the interpretation of the CPT, on request from national courts. With respect to remedies, the national rules of the contracting state where the infringement occurred would have to apply. These Conventions have not been ratified by all the member states and have never entered into force.

4.4 IMPACT OF THE EUROPEAN COMMUNITY

While the European Community has not been involved in the reform of patent law anywhere near as much as it has in relation to trade marks and copyright, the Commission has been active in two areas. These are in relation to the duration of patents (via the Supplementary Protection Certificates scheme) and biotechnological inventions.[74] In this context it is important to recall that the European Patent Convention, whose membership extends beyond the boundaries of the EC, is a separate and distinct treaty which operates outside the remit of the EC. The potential for overlap and conflict between the two regimes has been minimized by the fact that the two bodies have worked in tandem on many issues (which, given the membership overlap, is not that surprising).

The first area of patent law where the EC has intervened is in relation to the duration of patent protection. Faced with growing delays caused by the need for regulatory approval prior to marketing, patent owners argued that the time available for them to exploit their inventions was much shorter than the planned 20-year period.[75] To remedy this problem the EC introduced the so-called Supplementary Protection Certificates, which extend patent protection where it has not been possible for the patent proprietor to take full advantage of their patent rights over the period of the grant.[76] In particular, Supplementary Protection Certificates compensate the owner where they have not been able to market the patented product because of delays in seeking regulatory approval.[77] The effect of the basic patent can be extended for up to five years by this supplementary right. The right is characterized as a right distinct from patents in order to avoid the apparent conflict that would otherwise occur with the maximum term under Article 63 of the European Patent Convention. A challenge made by the Spanish Government to this regime in 1995 was dismissed by the European Court of Justice.[78] A corresponding scheme for Supplementary Protection Certificates has been introduced in the UK.[79]

A second area where the EC has intervened in the patent field is in respect of biotechnological inventions. After a decade of heated debate, the Biotechnology Directive was formally

[74] EU competition law also plays a key role in shaping British patent practice: see below at Ch. 23 Section 3.

[75] On the extent to which competitors may experiment prior to expiry of the patent, see below at pp. 564–5.

[76] Council Regulation (EEC) No. 1768/2 of 18 Jun. 1992 concerning the creation of a supplementary protection certificate for medicinal products; (1992) *OJ L* 182/1. Regulation (EC) No. 1610/96 of the European Parliament and of the Council of 23 Jul. 1996 concerning the creation of a supplementary protection certificate for plant protection products; (1996) *OJ L* 198/30–35.

[77] The relevant regulatory authorities include the Medicines Control Agency, the Veterinary Medicines Directorate, the European Agency for the Evaluation of Medicinal Products, and the Pesticides Safety Directorate.

[78] This was on the grounds that the Community did not have competence to legislate a new patent right, and that intervention could not be justified by reference to the need to harmonize laws for the internal market: *Spain v. Council of the European Union*, Case 350/92 [1995] *ECR* I–1985.

[79] See below at pp. 602–6.

adopted by the Council and the European Parliament on 6 July 1998.[80] The Biotechnology Directive deals with the patentability[81] and scope of protection conferred on biotechnological inventions.[82] As well as introducing special defences,[83] the Directive also establishes a scheme for compulsory licences and cross-licences to deal with the overlap between patent and plant variety protection.[84] In addition it also provides for the deposit of biological material.[85] The Directive has now been implemented in the United Kingdom.[86]

During the passage of the Directive, the question arose as to the nature of the relationship between the Biotechnology Directive and the EPC. What would a British court do, for example, if the EPC and the Directive were in conflict? Problems of this nature were resolved when the Administrative Council of the EPO incorporated the Biotechnology Directive into the Implementing Regulations of the EPC.[87] In so doing, the Administrative Council aligned the EPC with the provisions of the Biotechnology Directive. The Council also provided that the Directive should be used as a supplementary means of interpreting the EPC. As a result, the Recitals to the Directive can be taken into account where relevant.[88]

The controversial nature of the patenting of biotechnological inventions, which delayed the passage of the Directive for so long, has continued since it was passed. In addition to ongoing public criticism of biotechnological patents, in November 1998 the Dutch Government filed a challenge to the Biotechnology Directive in the European Court of Justice. While the ECJ rejected the Dutch challenge to the Directive,[89] there are still many critics of the ongoing expansion of patent law in the life sciences.[90]

4.5 PROPOSED EUROPEAN COMMUNITY CHANGES

There are currently a number of proposals for reform that have been put forward by the European Commission that will have an important impact upon patent law if and when they are finalized.[91] We look at the two proposals that have grown out of the *Green Paper on Innovation*.[92] In particular, we examine the plans for the establishment of a unitary patent valid throughout the EU, and the proposed Directive on patent protection for computer-implemented inventions.[93]

[80] EC Directive on the Legal Protection of Biotechnological Inventions 98/44/EC of 6 Jul. 1998; (1998) *OJ L* 213/13 (hereinafter Biotech. Dir.).

[81] Biotech. Dir., Arts. 1–7.   [82] Ibid, Arts. 8–10.   [83] Ibid, Art. 11.   [84] Ibid, Art. 12.

[85] Ibid, Arts. 13–14. It also deals with implementation and review procedures Arts. 15–18.

[86] Arts. 1–11 of the Directive were introduced into British law by Patents Regulations 2000 (SI 2000/2037) (in force 28 July 2000). Note also SI 2001/1412 and SI 2002/247.

[87] Administrative Council of the EPO 16 Jun. 1999 amending the Implementing Regulations of the EPC [1999] *OJ EPO* 437, 573 (in force from 1 Sept. 1999).

[88] British Group of AIPPI, 'Report Q 150: Patentability Requirements and Scope of Protection of Expressed Sequence Tags (ESTs): Single Nucleotide Polymorphisms (SNPs) and Entire Genomes' [2000] *EIPR* 39, 40.

[89] *Netherlands v. European Parliament,* Case C–377/98 [2001] *ECR* I–7079; [2002] *OJ EPO* 231; [2002] *FSR* 575 (ECJ) (Italy intervened in support of the Dutch, France intervened in support of the Council of the EC. For the challenge see [1998] *OJ C* 378/13). See A. Scott, 'The Dutch Challenge to the Bio-Patenting Directive' [1999] *EIPR* 212.

[90] See Commission on Intellectual Property Rights, *Integrating Intellectual Property Rights and Development Policy* (Sept. 2001); Nuffield Council on Bioethics, *The ethics of research related to healthcare in developing countries* (2001). See also G. Dutfield, *Intellectual Property Rights and the Life Sciences Industries* (2003).

[91] For an examination of the fate of the proposal for Utility model protection under the EU see Bently and Sherman, (2004), 338–40.

[92] COM (95) 382. The Green Paper also considers intervention into other areas of patent law, such as employees' inventions, the use of patent agents, and the recognition of professional qualifications.

[93] See O. Bossung, 'The Return of European Patent Law to the European Union' (1996) 27 *IIC* 287. Following the Commission's *Green Paper on Innovation* Dec. 1995, in Nov. 1996 the Commission issued an *Action Plan*

4.5.1 The Community patent

The goal of establishing a single European patent has been on the political agenda for over thirty years. Undeterred by the failings of the CPC, on 5 July 2000 the European Commission proposed the creation of a Community patent.[94] The possibility of a pan-European patent received a considerable boost on 3 March 2003 when EU Ministers agreed on the text of a Common Political Approach regarding the principles of the Community Patent.[95] The Common Approach sets out the main outlines of the system, including a centralized Community Court that would rule on disputes, the languages to be used, costs, the role of national patent offices, and the distribution of fees. The Common Political Approach was supported by the Council of Europe on 21 March 2003. Following the political agreement, a revised version of the Commission's draft Regulation was published in September 2003. The Commission has said that if the Community patent was introduced it would significantly lessen the burden on business and encourage innovation by making it cheaper to obtain a patent (by reducing translation costs). It is also meant to provide a clearer legal framework.

The planned Community patent offers an alternative for patent protection in Europe alongside the national and EPO systems. The Community patent would provide inventors with the option of obtaining a single patent valid throughout the European Union. However, if a Community patent was successfully challenged, it would fail in all EU member states. While applications are to be filed either in national patent offices or with the EPO in Munich, Community patents would only be issued by the EPO. The role of national patent offices is to be limited to a search at the applicant's request. Applications for a Community patent would have to be in one of three languages—English, French, or German—or in any other language together with a translation. Once granted, the patentee will have to translate all of the claims (but nothing else) into all Community languages. This would then be filed at the EPO. Community patents would coexist with the national and EPC patents giving inventors the option to choose the system that best suited their needs.

The Commission also proposes to create a new centralized Community tribunal called the Community Patent Court. The Community Patent Court is to be established in Luxembourg by 2010 as a panel attached to the ECJ Court of First Instance. Prior to this, member states are to designate a limited number of national courts to have jurisdiction in relation to Community Patent matters. When established, the Community Patent Court will have exclusive jurisdiction in relation to invalidity and infringement of Community patents, and actions relating to declaration of non-infringement, and be able to grant provisional measures. Disputes relating to contractual licensing and ownership of Community patents will be handled by national courts. After a period of four years with no progress, the Commission and Council seemed determined to make some headway with the Community Patent in 2008.

for Innovation in Europe, proposing three lines of action for tackling Europe's perceived 'innovation deficit'. Subsequent to this initiative, a Green Paper on the European Patent was adopted by the European Commission on 24 Jun. 1997, the main proposal of which concerns the option of converting patent law into a Community instrument. This was followed by Promoting innovation through patents: the follow up on the Community Patent and the Patent System in Europe [1999] OJ EPO 197.

[94] Proposal for a Council Regulation on the Community Patent COM (2000) 412 final Brussels (1 Aug. 2000). On the changes needed in the EPC to allow for a Community patent see: A Community policy for the realisation of the Community patent in the context of a revision of the European Patent Convention (7 May 2001) SEC (2001) 744; Commission Working Document on the Planned Community Patent Jurisdiction (30 Aug. 2002) COM (2002) 480 final.

[95] Council of the EU, Community Patent: Common Political Approach (7 Mar. 2003) 7159/03. See also N. Jones, 'European patents break free: Community patent becomes a reality' [2002] Bioscience Law Review 183.

4.5.2 Patentability of computer-implemented inventions

Another area where the Community has been active is in relation to computer-implemented inventions. After a period of consultation, which raised a number of questions about the scope, nature, and impact of patents for computer-related inventions,[96] the Commission published a proposal for a *Directive on the Patentability of Computer-Implemented Inventions* in February 2002.[97] The proposed Directive was rejected by the European Parliament in July 2005.[98] While many commentators took this as marking the end of the issue, the question of the patentability of computer-related inventions was reopened in 2007 by the EPO President who called for public discussion to fill the vacuum left by the rejection of the Directive.[99]

4.6 INTERNATIONAL TREATIES

As we mentioned earlier, international treaties have long played an important role in shaping aspects of British patent law. In addition to the Paris Convention (discussed above), the other treaties of note are the Patent Cooperation Treaty, TRIPS, and the Convention on Biological Diversity.

4.6.1 Patent Cooperation Treaty

The Patent Cooperation Treaty (PCT) was signed in 1970 and came into operation from 1978. The key feature of the Treaty is that it provides for a system of international application and preliminary examination procedure. The PCT has 138 contracting states.[100] The Patent Cooperation Treaty only provides for an international application and search: the authority to grant the patent remains with the national patent office.[101] The PCT provides a second route through which applications for patents that operate in the United Kingdom and the EPO can be made.

Under the PCT, an applicant can apply to an international office and get an international search and an international preliminary examination. Once this is carried out the application is sent to the designated national offices to decide whether to grant national patents. The centralized procedure is particularly useful for countries where the patent office is not capable of carrying out its own examination. The patent cooperation system is attractive because it reduces the fees payable and because of the lengthy period between the initial application to

---

[96] The EC launched a process of consultation on 19 Oct. 2000.

[97] *Proposal for a Directive of the European Parliament and of the Council on the Patentability of Computer-implemented Inventions* (hereinafter, Computer-Implemented Inventions Dir.) COM (2002) 92 final. The Council considered the proposal and reached a common position in Nov. 2002. See Committee on Legal Affairs and the Internal Market, *REPORt on the Proposal for a Directive* (18 Jun. 2003) FINAL A5–0238/2003 (McCarthy Report). For a discussion of the proposed Directive see L. Bently and B. Sherman, *Intellectual Property Law* (2nd edn), pp. 342–4.

[98] The Directive was rejected 648 to 14. For a more detailed analysis of the draft Directive see Bently and Sherman (2004), 342–4.

[99] Lucy Sherriff, 'Incoming President reopens software patent debate' (4 July 2007) *The Register* <http://www.theregister.co.uk/2007/07/04>.

[100] As of 1 Jan. 2008.

[101] The PCT was signed in Washington 1970; amended in 1979; modified in 1984. See K. Pfanner, 'The Patent Cooperation Treaty: An Introduction' (1979) *EIPR* 98; D. Perrott, 'The PCT in Use' [1982] *EIPR* 67; C. Everitt, 'Patent Cooperation Treaty (PCT)' (1984) 13 *CIPAJ* 383; Anon. 'Patent Cooperation Treaty (PCT) in 1992' (1993) 75 *JPTOS* 354; J. Cartiglia, 'The Patent Cooperation Treaty: A Rational Approach to International Patent Filing' (1994) 76 *JPTOS* 261; J. Anglehart, 'Extending the International Phase of PCT applications' (1995) 77 *JPTOS* 101. See below at pp. 372–4.

the international office and the time when that application is forwarded to the relevant national offices. The extra time, which varies between eight and eighteen months, gives applicants time to decide whether the invention is likely to be successful enough to warrant the translation costs that arise when the application is transferred to the national offices.

4.6.2 TRIPS

While TRIPS had a dramatic impact upon many developing countries, it had little direct impact upon European or British patent law.[102] Perhaps the most significant change brought about by TRIPS relates to the limits imposed on compulsory licences. The impact of TRIPS may increase, however, as the jurisprudence at the World Trade Organization takes shape. In an important decision in relation to the patenting of computer programs, the EPO Board of Appeal noted that as the EPO was not a signatory to TRIPS they were not bound by it. However, on the basis that TRIPS aimed at setting common standards the Board said that it acted as an indicator of modern trends.[103] As we will see shortly, the member states of TRIPS are currently in negotiations over the reform of TRIPS.

The member states of TRIPS are currently in the process of reviewing and updating the 1994 Agreement. Two areas of reform concern us here, namely patents and public health, and the patentability of plants and animal inventions.

One issue that has attracted a lot of attention in recent years is the extent to which patents restrict access to life-saving drugs. This problem came to a head when patentees threatened to challenge legislation in South Africa that would have allowed their patented medicines (for the treatment of HIV/AIDS) to be sold at a price lower than they would have liked. Triggered by the dispute in South Africa, the 4th WTO Ministerial Conference, held at Doha in November 2001, focused on access to patented medicines in developed and less-developed countries. The delegates noted that compulsory licences, which are allowed under TRIPS, offer a possible solution for countries, such as South Africa, that have the domestic capacity to manufacture medicines. However, Article 31(f) of TRIPS, which provides that medicines produced under compulsory licence must predominantly be for the domestic market, creates problems for countries that are unable to manufacture the patented medicines themselves. In particular, it means that it is not possible to manufacture a patented drug under compulsory licence in Country A, with the intention of exporting the drug to Country B. While the delegates at Doha agreed that this problem needed to be resolved, they were unable to decide on how this should be done.[104] After heated public debate, on 30 August 2003 the WTO member states agreed that developed and less-developed countries that do not have the domestic capacity to manufacture drugs should be able to import cheaper generic drugs made under compulsory licences in other countries.[105] That is, the member states agreed to allow countries to manufacture patented pharmaceutical products under compulsory licence for export to developing countries. The decision covers

---

[102] TRIPS Art. 2 requires members to comply with Arts. 1–12 of the Paris Convention (1967). In addition TRIPS Arts. 27–34 increases the level of standards: Art. 27 as regards patentability; Art. 28 rights; Art. 29 disclosure requirements; Art. 30 exceptions; Art. 31 authorized uses; Art. 33 requires a term of 20 years from filing date.

[103] *IBM/Computer programs*, T1173/97 [2000] *EPOR* 219, 224–5.

[104] WTO, *Declaration on the TRIPS Agreement and Public Health* (20 Nov. 2001) WT/MIN(01)/DEC/2. See C. Correa, 'Implications of the Doha Declaration on the TRIPS Agreement and Public Health' *WHO Health, Economics and Drugs EDM Series No. 12* (June 2002).

[105] WTO, *Implementation of para 6 of the Doha Declaration on the TRIPS Agreement and Public Health* (1 Sept. 2003) WT/L/540 (decision of the General Council of 30 Aug. 2003).

patented products and products made using patented processes in the pharmaceutical sector, including active ingredients and diagnostic kits. The WTO member governments agreed that the obligations under Article 31(f) were to be waived, at least until the Article is amended.

The second area of the Agreement currently under review in the TRIPS Council is Article 27.3(b). This provides a limited exception to the general rule that patents should be granted in all areas of technology in relation to plant and animal inventions. In particular, it provides that members may exclude from patentability plants and animals other than micro-organisms, and essentially biological processes for the production of plants or animals.[106] As part of the review process, a number of submissions have been made outlining the existing national patent protection for plants and animals, and also the plant variety protection. A number of countries have also made suggestions as to how Article 27.3(b) should be amended. These include discussions about whether patent applicants should be forced to disclose the origin of genetic materials and/or traditional knowledge used in the creation of their invention: the main debate here is the consequences of non-compliance.[107] At the same time, a group of African countries has argued that there should be a general ban on the patenting of any life forms (including animals, plants, and micro-organisms), and that farmers should have a general right to save seed. Given the divergence of views on the question of patenting life forms, it is not surprising that reform of Article 27.3(b) has progressed slowly. The slow progress can also be attributed to the fact that the review touches on a number of contentious issues, such as patent protection for indigenous knowledge, the relationship between intellectual property and the protection of biodiversity, and the way in which TRIPS and the CBD are to interact.[108] Given this, it is likely that the review of Article 27.3(b) may take some time.

The slow progress of the TRIPS review continued at the 5th WTO Ministerial Conference, which was held in Cancun (10–14 September 2003). While intellectual property issues were not at the forefront of the discussions, the meeting ended in a deadlock with the parties unable to reach agreement as to the next phase of the Doha negotiations. It is currently unclear how future negotiations will proceed. Given that developing countries have little to gain from the TRIPS review (with the possible exception of extending protection for geographical indications of origin), it seems that there is little impetus for them to break this stalemate. As a result we might expect to see a move away from multilateral treaties towards bilateral agreements (as is currently being favoured by the USA) in an attempt to extend the scope of patent protection beyond that permitted by TRIPS.

The only area where it seems that there might be some hope of change relates to compulsory licensing of patented medicines for export to developing countries. In late 2005, the WTO General Council decided that the 2003 Doha declaration should be permanently incorporated into the TRIPS Agreement.[109] To this end, a Protocol amending the TRIPS Agreement was

---

[106] TRIPS Art. 27.3(b) also requires members to provide for the protection of plant varieties either by patent, an effective *sui generis* system, or both.

[107] The EU has proposed that patent applicants disclose the origin of genetic material, with legal consequences outside the scope of patent law. Switzerland has proposed an amendment to WIPO's Patent Cooperation Treaty (and, by reference, WIPO's Patent Law Treaty) so that domestic laws ask patent applicants to disclose the origins of genetic resources and traditional knowledge. Failure to disclose could hold up a patent being granted, or affect its validity. In turn Brazil, Cuba, Ecuador, India, Peru, Thailand, and Venezuela want the TRIPS Agreement to be amended to make disclosure an obligation.

[108] The Doha Declaration says that in reviewing Art. 27.3(b) the TRIPS Council should look at the relationship between the TRIPS Agreement and the CBD; and the protection of traditional knowledge and folklore.

[109] General Council, 'Amendment of the TRIPS Agreement: Decision of 6 Dec 2005' (8 Dec 2005) Doc No WT/L/641.

produced which proposes that TRIPS be amended to include a new Article 31*bis* and a new Annex. The proposed amendments are very similar to the text of the 2003 Doha declaration. Under the proposed new changes, member countries will be able to grant compulsory licences to allow the manufacture and export of pharmaceuticals for public health reasons. This will be permitted where the importing country is a developing country which lacks the capacity to produce the relevant pharmaceuticals (the proposed new Annex sets out the criteria to be used to determine whether a country lacks capacity). Importing countries have an obligation to take reasonable measures to prevent re-exportation.

The proposed changes will only come into effect when two-thirds of the WTO membership accepts the amendment. As of January 2008, only 14 of the 151 member states have done so. This includes the EU,[110] the United States, Australia, Switzerland, China, and India. After one deadline was missed, the period for acceptance of the Protocol has been extended until 31 December 2009.[111] While it may be some time before the Doha declaration is formally embodied in the TRIPS Agreement, this has not stopped countries from using the provisions. The first and (as of January 2008) only notification of a compulsory licence being granted to allow a company to make a generic version of a patented medicine for export was made by Canada on 4 October 2007. The licence allows the Canadian company to manufacture the AIDS therapy drug TriAvir and export it to Rwanda.

4.6.3 The Convention on Biological Diversity (CBD)

The Convention on Biological Diversity (CBD) was signed in June 1992.[112] While the Convention was not directly concerned with patent standards, it heralds a new approach to the way biological resources are treated. The Convention provided developing countries with an opportunity to voice their unhappiness at the exploitation of indigenous resources by firms from the developed world. Of late, there have been numerous examples of situations where this has occurred: the neem tree traditionally used in India to make medicines and insecticides has been the subject of 37 patents in Europe and the USA;[113] there have been applications relating to the use of turmeric for treating wounds,[114] and inventions based on genetic material obtained from the Hagahai people, a small group in Papua New Guinea, have been patented. The Convention on Biological Diversity offers a potential basis to control the uses made of traditional knowledge. The preamble recognizes the close and traditional dependence of many indigenous and local communities embodying traditional lifestyles on biological resources. It also recognizes the desirability of sharing equitably the benefits arising from the use of traditional knowledge, innovations, and practices relevant to the conservation of biological diversity and the sustainable use of its components.

While the Convention may not have an immediate impact on patent law, it does represent a change of attitude towards the way natural resources are exploited which may impact upon the way patents are viewed. In particular it may help to undermine the pro-patent attitudes

---

[110] See below at pp. 583–4.

[111] Council for Trade-Related Aspects of Intellectual Property Rights, 'Annual Review of the Decision on the Implementation of Paragraph 6 of the Doha Declaration' (1 Nov. 2007) IP/C/46, para. 20–21.

[112] On 1 Jan 2008 there were 190 parties (168 signatures) to the Convention. The UK signed on 12 June 1992; the EC on 13 June 1992.

[113] S. Kadidal, 'Subject Matter Imperialism? Biodiversity, Foreign Prior Art and the Neem Patent Controversy' (1996) 37 *IDEA* 371; E. Da Casta de Silva [1995] *EIPR* 546; M. Huft, 'Indigenous and Drug Discovery Research: A Question of Intellectual Property Rights' (1995) 89 *Northwestern University Law Review* 1678.

[114] (26 Oct. 1996) *New Scientist,* 14.

that have dominated for the last forty or so years. The impetus provided by the Convention on Biological Diversity to reconsider the aims and functions of the patent system has been reinforced by the growing body of literature that questions the often taken-for-granted assumption that technological development is both desirable and neutral. In so doing, commentators have emphasized the adverse physical and psychological effects of technology on individuals, their relations with society (alienation), and the planet in general (environmental problems). Technology is also seen as having vastly altered the nature of political government and reduced individual autonomy (computer databases, surveillance devices). Some authors have called for the democratic control of technology, in particular arguing that some research and development should be prohibited (note, for example, the debate over the patenting of higher life-forms).

In recent years, the CBD has begun to impact upon patent law in a variety of ways, the most notable being the possibility of making 'prior informed consent' a condition of patentability. Debates about this and related issues have become intertwined with the ongoing review of the TRIPS Agreement being conducted by the TRIPS Council and with WIPO's discussions about the protection of indigenous knowledge.[115] We look at these issues in more detail below.

4.6.4 WIPO Patent Law Treaty

In the last decade or so, the World Intellectual Property Organization (WIPO) has been engaged in an ongoing programme of reform of international patent law. The first concrete outcome from this process was the Patent Law Treaty (PLT) which was completed in June 2000.[116] The PLT, which opened for signature on 2 June 2000, entered into force on 28 April 2005.[117] In essence the PLT is an international treaty that aims to simplify and streamline procedures for obtaining and maintaining a patent. It also aims to harmonize patent procedures relating to national and regional patent applications and the maintenance of patents.[118]

The PLT promises to reduce the cost of patent protection (as a result of changes such as national patent offices sharing the results of search and examination procedures) and to make the process more user-friendly and more widely accessible. The specific changes include: the use of standardized forms and simplified procedures that reduce the risk of error; cost reductions for inventors, applicants, and patent attorneys; elimination of cumbersome and complicated procedures; improved efficiency of patent offices and lower operating costs; possibility of introducing electronic filing of patent applications and related communications; standardization of patent formalities in all countries party to the PLT (including the incorporation of provisions under the Patent Cooperation Treaty); exceptions from mandatory representation; and the possibility of obtaining a filing date, even if the main part of the application (description) is filed in a foreign language.[119] Under the PLT, the requirements and procedures for national and regional patent applications, and those for Patent Cooperation Treaty international applications, will be harmonized. This will eventually lead to standardized formal requirements and streamlined procedures for all patent applications at both national and regional patent offices.[120]

---

[115] See above at pp. 388–90.   [116] WIPO, Patent Law Treaty (2 Jun. 2000) PT/DC/47.

[117] There were 107 signatories to the Final Act of the Diplomatic Conference (including the UK and the EPO) on 2 June 2000. The Treaty had been ratified by 17 countries as of 1 January 2008. The UK ratified the Treaty on 22 March 2006.

[118] For criticisms see R. Dreyfus and J. Reichman, 'Harmonizing Without Consensus: Critical Reflections on Drafting a Substantive Patent Law Treaty' (2007) 57 *Duke Law Journal* 85.

[119] WIPO Press Release PR/2000/222; WIPO, Patent Law Treaty (2 Jun. 2000) PT/DC/47.

[120] Consultation on proposed reforms to bring UK legislation into line with the WIPO Patent Law Treaty ended on 30 May 2003.

4.6.5 Global harmonization of substantive patent law

The next stage in WIPO reform of global patent law began in November 2000, when WIPO launched discussions on the harmonization of the substantive requirements of patent law.[121] These discussions go beyond the Patent Law Treaty of June 2000, which focused on the task of harmonizing the processes by which patents are granted, to consider substantive issues. It is hoped that by standardizing the rules on patentability this will mean that as applicants will not have to prepare totally different patent documents for different patent offices, the costs of patenting will decrease. It is also hoped that it will increase predictability about patentability of inventions.

Although the Patent Cooperation Treaty (PCT) contains some principles of substantive patent law, these are only taken into account at the international phase when an application is submitted under the PCT. PCT contracting states are free to apply any substantive conditions of patentability during the national phase of an international application. Importantly, it is at this stage that the national authorities make the important decision as to whether a patent should be granted. At present there are six basic legal principles under consideration by the Standing Committee on the Law of Patents. These are definitions of prior art, novelty, inventive step (non-obviousness), industrial applicability (utility), sufficiency of disclosure, and the structure and interpretation of claims. It is planned that a future meeting will consider 'first-to-file' versus 'first-to-invent', post-grant opposition, and time limits upon the publication of applications.[122]

---

[121] WIPO Standing Committee on the Law of Patents, 'Suggestions for the further development of international patent law' (25 Sept. 2000) SCP/4/2. Negotiators attended a meeting of the Standing Committee on the Law of Patents (SCP), which met 6–10 Nov. 2000. For the background see R. Petersen, 'Harmonization: a Way Forward' (1987) 16 *CIPAJ* 234; R. Petersen, 'Harmonization—or Backward' (1987) 17 *CIPAJ* 66; R. Petersen, 'Harmonization: Postponement' (1989) 18 *CIPAJ* 118, 293; R. Petersen, 'On to Harmonization' (1990) 19 *CIPAJ* 147; R. Petersen, 'Harmonization Again' (1990) 19 *CIPAJ* 356; J. Pagenberg, 'WIPO: Diplomatic Conference in the Hague on Harmonization of Patent Law' (1991) 22 *IIC* 682.

[122] Copies of SCP meeting documents are available from the WIPO web site: <http://www.wipo.int/activities>.

15

THE NATURE OF A PATENT

CHAPTER CONTENTS

1 INTRODUCTION

Patents have changed dramatically since they were first granted in England and Wales over four centuries ago. Initially, patents were crude documents, often only one or two sentences long. Since then, patents have become much more sophisticated, complex, and lengthy. As we will see in the next chapter, the process by which a patent is granted has also changed dramatically. A lot of care and attention has been given to the form and content of the patent. If there is a kind of symmetry or logic to the patent system, the content of the patent is the key to that process. As such, to understand many facets of patent law, it is important to have a good grasp of the nature and content of the patent. This chapter is intended to provide an introduction to the nature of the patent. In so doing we look at the different ways patents are described, the way patents are drafted, and the contents of a patent. To help get a sense of the nature of a patent, a patent for a relatively simple piece of technology is reproduced at the Online Resource Centre, <http://www.oxfordtextbooks.co.uk/bentlysherman3e>.

2 TYPES OF PATENT

Patents are described in a number of different ways in the United Kingdom. Most commonly, a patent is seen as a legal document that confers a 20-year monopoly on the patentee. Patents are also characterized in terms of the organization that grants them. As we saw earlier, the patents that operate in the United Kingdom are granted by two authorities: the UK Intellectual Property Office and the European Patent Office. The patents that operate in the United Kingdom are known either as British patents or European patents (UK). British patents are issued by the Intellectual Property Office and are subject to British law. European patents are issued by the EPO in Munich; a European patent (UK) is a patent issued by the European Patent Office which applies in the United Kingdom. Prior to the introduction of the EPC 2000, applicants had to designate the member states in which they wanted the patent to operate. In contrast, the EPC 2000 provides that all EPC states will be deemed to be designated as the country where the patent will operate at the date of filing.[1] While there are a number of differences between the two systems, once a European patent (UK) has been granted, it is treated as if it had been granted by the UK Intellectual Property Office.[2]

Another way of classifying patents is in terms of the subject matter that they protect. In some instances, patents are described by reference to the industry or branch of science to which the patented invention relates. So, for example, it is common to speak of chemical patents or biotechnology patents. In other cases, patents are classified according to the nature of the interest that is protected; whether it is a product patent, a process patent, or a product-by-process patent. These are looked at below.

3 DRAFTING OF PATENTS

The drafting of patents, which is normally undertaken by patent agents, is an important part of the patent process. It is also a complex and difficult task. In part, these difficulties can be attributed to the nature of the subject matter that is protected by patent law and to the fact that it is sometimes very difficult to explain particular forms of technology in the form demanded by patent law. In certain instances, notably in relation to biological inventions, patent law has been forced to develop specific rules and procedures to enable them to meet the requirements for patentability.

Another reason why patent drafting is often such a difficult process is that patents are at once technical, commercial, and legal documents. As such, they are written with a number of different purposes in mind. As we saw earlier, one of the rationales for the grant of patents is that they encourage the dissemination of technical and scientific information. In the hypothetical patent bargain which sees patents as if they were a contract between inventors and the state, the information contained in the application is treated as the 'consideration' for the grant of the monopoly.[3] As well as encouraging inventors to disclose information that mighht otherwise remain secret, the patent system also attempts to ensure that the information which is made public is recorded in a format that is usable. To this end, a series of detailed rules and procedures regulate the way the patents are drafted.[4] To take one example, patent law stipulates that the patent specification ought to disclose the invention in a manner which is clear enough and complete enough for the invention to be performed by a person skilled in the art.[5]

While the patent system encourages inventors to disclose their technical creations, it would be incorrect to conclude from this that patentees necessarily draft their patents according to the rules and procedures set down by the law. In some cases inventors may take out a patent, but attempt to manipulate the information in the patent application in a way which suits their

---

[1] EPC 2000 Art. 79(1) provides that all EPC states will be deemed to be designated as the country where the patent will operate at the date of filing (in contrast to Art. 79 EPC 1973, which required applicants to designate the states in which they wished the patent to operate).

[2] PA ss. 77–78; EPC 2000 Art. 64.

[3] 'This is the price which the inventor pays in return for his twenty-year monopoly'. *Mentor v. Hollister* [1993] *RPC* 7, 9. See also *Grant v. Raymond,* 31 *US* (6 *Pet*) 218, 247 (1832).

[4] For example PA r. 14–15, Parts 1–4 of Schedule 2; EPC 2000 r. 47.

[5] PA s. 14(3), r. 12(4); EPC 2000 Art. 83, r. 42, See below at Ch. 20, Sections 1 and 2.

own purposes. For example, as well as disclosing the invention applicants may draft their patent in such a way as to attract sponsorship, or to advertise the existence of their patent.[6]

Given that the information contained in a patent application may be used by an applicant's competitors, it is understandable that applicants may be tempted to provide only the minimum amount of information that is necessary for them to obtain a patent. While patentees may not be able to obscure their inventions in the way they once were, applicants are only required to disclose such details of the invention as to enable a person skilled in the art to make the invention. As a result, a patent might not reveal important features about the invention such as the cheapest or strongest starting materials.[7] This 'know-how' may provide the patentee with a strategic advantage over competitors that may be important when an invention is made available to the public. Ultimately, the degree to which applicants are able to draft patents for their own purposes depends upon how stringently the patent offices and the courts enforce the disclosure requirements.

Another factor that adds to the complexity of the drafting process relates to what has been called the infringement–validity dichotomy (or, as it is also known, the *Gillette* defence). As the scope of the monopoly is determined by what is claimed in the patent, the applicants may be tempted to claim more than they perhaps ought. At the same time, however, applicants need to be mindful of the fact that, if they draft claims too broadly, this increases the chance of the patent being declared invalid (primarily for lack of novelty). As matters of infringement and validity are heard in the same tribunal, the infringement–validity dichotomy helps to ensure that the scope of the patent monopoly corresponds to what was actually invented.

4 CONTENTS OF A PATENT

Patents in Britain and the EPO are made up of four key parts:

(i)   an abstract,[8]

(ii) a description of the invention,[9]

(iii) one or more claims,[10] and

(iv) any drawings referred to in the description or claims.[11]

Before looking at these in more detail, it is important to bear in mind a number of preliminary issues.

The various components of a patent perform a number of different roles. Some of these, such as the abstract, are used both for administrative purposes and as a way of advertising the existence of the patented invention. The description and claims, which form the core of the patent,

---

[6] In *Cartonneries de Thulin v. CTP White Knight* [2001] *RPC* 107, 116 Robert Walker LJ said patent attorneys in different industrial countries adopt perceptibly different approaches to drafting patent specifications: German (and other continental) draftsmen tend to a 'central' style which concentrates on the 'centre of gravity' of an invention: British (and still more, American) draftsman tend to a 'peripheral' style which seeks to delimit the boundaries of an invention.

[7] Although there is no requirement of good faith, note PA ss. 62(3) and 63(2).

[8] PA s. 14(2)(c), PA r. 15 ; EPC 2000 Art. 78(1)(e), EPC 2000 r. 47.

[9] PA s. 14(2)(b), PA r. 12(4)(a), Parts 1–4 of Schedule 2; EPC 2000 Art. 78(1)(b), EPC 2000 r 42.

[10] PA s. 14(2)(b) and PA r. 12; EPC 2000 Art. 78(1)(c). EPC 2000 r. 43.

[11] PA s. 14(2)(b), PA r. 12; EPC 2000 Art. 78(1)(d), EPC r. 46. Patent applications must also contain a request for the grant of a patent and designate the inventor.

respectively disclose the invention in a usable form and demarcate the scope of the monopoly. It is also important to note that the contents of a patent application differ somewhat from the patent itself. While the patent and the application for a patent both contain a description and claims, the main difference is that the patent application contains additional information—the request for grant. The request for grant, which is used for administrative purposes, normally includes the title of the invention (which clearly and concisely states the technical designation of the invention), as well as relevant biographical details of the applicants and patent agents (if used). As it is permissible to amend the patent application during and after the grant process, the final form that a patent takes may differ from the initial application. This process of amendment is examined in more detail later.[12]

While UK and European patents are very similar,[13] there are some differences that ought to be borne in mind. One of these relates to the language that is used to describe the components of the patent. More specifically, it relates to the fact that, while the core of a British patent is known as the 'specification' (which comprises a description of the invention, the claims, and any drawings referred to in the description or claims), the EPC and the PCT speak of the contents of a 'patent application' rather than of the specification.[14] Another difference between UK and European patents relates to the controls that are exercised over the form and content of the patent. While similar, in that both have to meet the statutory requirements for patentability, the rules of the EPC (but not the United Kingdom) provide detailed guidance as to the precise form that a patent should take. This is particularly the case in relation to the description and claims. With these initial points in mind, we can now turn to look at the contents of a patent in more detail.

4.1 THE ABSTRACT

The first element of a UK and EPO patent is the abstract.[15] This is a brief summary (usually around 150 words) of the more important technical features of the invention. Normally, an abstract contains the title of the invention, a concise summary of the matter contained in the specification, and an indication of the technical field to which the invention belongs. The relevant rules also provide that the abstract should outline the technical problem which the invention attempts to resolve, the gist of the solution to that problem, and the principal use or uses of the invention.[16]

Patent abstracts perform two main tasks. First, they are used by the patent offices as a search tool in the examination of other patent applications. To this end, the patent rules stipulate that abstracts ought to be drafted in such a way that they constitute an efficient instrument for searching in the particular technical field.[17] Abstracts, which are normally published around eighteen months after the application was filed, also alert third parties to the existence of the application. To ensure that abstracts are only used for these purposes, the Patents Act 1977

---

[12] See below at p. 385, Ch. 16 Section 5, Ch. 20 Section 4.

[13] European patents which designate the UK are treated as UK patents. PA s. 77.

[14] PA s. 14. See *Genentech's Patent* [1989] *RPC* 147, 197–9, 236–7, 261. A. White, 'The Function and Structure of Patent Claims' [1993] *EIPR* 243.

[15] PA s. 14(2)(c), PA r. 15; EPC 2000 Art. 78(1)(e), EPC 2000 r. 47.

[16] PA r. 15(3); EPC 2000 r. 47(2) (abstract may be amended by the Comptroller).

[17] EPC 2000 r. 47(5) requires that the abstract be drafted in such a way that it constitutes an efficient instrument for purposes of searching in the particular technical field, in particular by making it possible to assess whether there is a need to consult the specification (or patent application) itself.

and the EPC 2000 stipulate that the abstract can only be relied upon to provide 'technical information'.[18] One of the consequences of this is that, for patent law purposes, the abstract does not form part of the state of the art.[19] This avoids the potential problem of the abstract anticipating the patent and in so doing rendering it invalid for lack of novelty. The fact that the abstract is only used for 'technical' purposes also means that it cannot be used to influence the scope of the monopoly.[20]

4.2 THE DESCRIPTION

The next element of a patent is the description.[21] As with the abstract, the description plays an important role in ensuring that the information function of the patent system is performed. In many ways, descriptions are similar to scientific or technical papers: they explain what has been created, the problems that the invention solves, why it is important, and how the invention differs from what has been created before.[22]

In most cases, a description will begin with an account of the background to the invention.[23] In so doing, the description will summarize the prior art, usually referring to existing patents and other published documents. This information is used to understand the nature of the invention, for carrying out the search report, and for the purposes of examination.[24] Typically, a description will then disclose the invention as claimed.[25] This is usually done by outlining the technical problem that the invention attempts to solve and the solutions that it offers (which are often couched in terms of the advantages that the invention offers over the 'background art').[26] Following a brief introduction to any drawings that are used,[27] the description will normally provide a detailed account of how the invention is carried out.[28]

To ensure that the invention is disclosed in such a way that it is of practical use to people in the art, patent law imposes a number of constraints upon the way inventions are disclosed. At a general level, the application ought to describe the invention in a manner that is clear and complete enough for it to be performed by a person skilled in the art.[29] The description must

---

[18] PA s. 14(7); EPC 2000 Art. 85.

[19] This is explicit in EPC 2000 Art. 85 and implicit in PA s. 14(7).

[20] *Bull/Identification system,* T246/86 [1989] *OJ EPO* 199. (The TBA refused to allow an applicant to use an abstract which suggested that the apparatus was a credit card as a way of expanding the preliminary description and claims, which had not suggested that the apparatus could include a portable object.)

[21] PA s. 14(2)(b), PA r. 12(4)(a), Parts 1–4 of Schedule 2; EPC 2000 Art. 78(1)(b), EPC 2000 r 42, r. 49 Unlike the EPC, which provides detailed guidance as to the contents of the description, the Patents Act 1977 and the rules are silent as to the form that the description in a UK application ought to take.

[22] On the specification see R. Merges and R. Nelson, 'On the Complex Economics of Patent Scope' (1990) 90 *Columbia Law Review* 839, 844; G. Myers, 'From Discovery to Invention: The Writing and Re-writing of Two Patents' (1995) 25 *Social Studies of Science* 57.

[23] EPC 2000 r. 42(1)(b); *EPO Guidelines* C–II, 4.3–4.4. See *Sony/Television receivers,* T654/92 [2000] *EPOR* 148 (on the meaning of 'background art').

[24] EPC 2000 r. 42(1)(b).   [25] EPC 2000 r. 42(1)(c); *EPO Guidelines* C–II, 4.5–4.6.

[26] EPC 2000 r. 42(1)(c). For criticisms of EPC 1973 r. 27 (which is similar to EPC 2000 r 42(1)(c)) on the basis that it is ambiguous and uncertain see H. Ullrich, *Standards of Patentability for European Inventions: Should an Inventive Step Advance the Art?* (1977), 113.

[27] EPR 2000 r. 42(1)(d); *EPO Guidelines* C–II, 4.7.

[28] The patent should include a specific description of at least one detailed embodiment, often referred to as the preferred embodiments. Occasionally, this will be unnecesary: see *Toshiba/Semiconductor device,* T407/87 [1989] *EPOR* 470. EPC 2000 r.42(1)(f) adds that, where necessary, the applicant should state the way in which the invention is capable of industrial exploitation. *EPO Guidelines* C–II, 41.2.

[29] PA s. 14(3); EPC 2000 Art 83.

also support the claims.[30] If the patent fails to meet these criteria, it may later be declared invalid. These issues are dealt with in more detail later.[31]

4.2.1 Description of biological materials

One of the rationales for the inclusion of the description in a patent application is that it ensures that the public is able to access and make use of the invention that is disclosed in the application. This is based on the presupposition that it is possible to describe the invention, whether using words, figures, or diagrams, in such a way that third parties will be able to understand and make use of it. While this assumption holds true in relation to most technologies, it is not necessarily the case in relation to biological inventions. The reason for this is that, where an invention depends on the use of living materials such as micro-organisms or cultured cells, it may be impossible to describe the invention so that the public is able to make the invention.[32]

The EPC 2000[33] and the Patents Act 1977[34] attempt to address this problem by providing that, if an invention involves biological material which cannot be described in a way that enables the invention to be carried out by a person skilled in the art, the applicant must deposit a sample of this biological material at a 'recognized institution' (or depositary).[35] These issues were also addressed in the Biotechnology Directive.[36] The application must contain such relevant information as is available on the characteristics of the biological material.[37] In depositing a sample, the applicant is treated as consenting to the depositary making the sample available after publication of the application.[38] An applicant may require that, until the application has either been abandoned or patented, the deposit should only be released to experts who are only allowed to use the culture for experimental purposes.[39] Special rules also exist in relation to patent applications relating to nucleotide and amino acid sequences.[40]

4.3 THE CLAIMS

The next element of a patent is the claims.[41] While the purpose of the description is to ensure that the invention disclosed in the patent is of some practical use, the primary function of

[30] PA s. 14(5)(c); EPC 2000 Art. 84.   [31] See below at Ch. 20 Sections 1 and 2.

[32] In *American Cyanamid (Dann)'s Patent* [1971] *RPC* 425 the House of Lords held that there was no obligation on a patentee under the Patents Act 1949 to supply the micro-organism to the public. See generally, B. Hampar, 'Patenting of Recombinant DNA Technology: The Deposit Requirement' (1985) 67 *JPTOS* 569; V. Meyer, 'Problems and Issues in Depositing Micro-organisms for Patent Purposes' (1983) 65 *JPTOS* 455.

[33] EPC 2000 r. 31.

[34] PA s. 125A (introduced by CDPA, Sched. 5 para. 30).

[35] Recognized depositary institutions include all international depositaries under the 1977 Treaty on the International recognition of the Deposit of Micro-organisms (the Budapest Treaty) (modified 1980). This established minimum requirements for maintaining an international depositary for micro-organisms (UK joined 29 Dec. 1988). In January 2008, there were 68 member states with 37 International Depositary Authorities.

[36] Biotech. Directive Arts. 13–14; implemented in the UK by Patents (Amendment) Rules 2001, SI 2001/1412 (as of 6 July 2001).

[37] EPC 2000 r. 31(1)(b); PA s. 125A, PA r. 13 (1), Schedule 1 (2007 Patent Act Rules).

[38] EPC 2000 r. 31; PA r. 13 (1), Schedule 1 (2007 Patent Act Rules).

[39] EPC 2000 r. 32; PA r. 13 (1), Schedule 1, para 6–7 (2007 Patent Act Rules).

[40] EPC 2000 r. 30. See also 'Decision of the President of the EPO 2 Oct. 1998 concerning the presentation of nucleotide and amino acid sequences in patent applications and the filing of sequence listings' (1998) 11 *OJ EPO Supp. No. 2* 1. PA r. 13.

[41] PA s. 14(2)(b), PA r. 12; EPC 2000 Art. 78 (1)(c), EPC r. 43. The requirement for a claim was first introduced in the UK by the Patents, Designs and Trade Marks Act 1883 s. 5(5). However, the practice of including claims had been common from at least the 1830s. Claims are central to the operation of the European patent

the claims is to set out the scope of the legal protection conferred by the patent.[42] As such the claims play a key role in patent law.

Typically, a patent will consist of a number of claims that are arranged hierarchically.[43] Such patents will commence with a widely drawn 'principal' or 'generic' claim that defines the invention by setting out its distinctive technical features. General claims of this sort are often followed by a series of narrower dependent or subsidiary claims (which may refer back to earlier claims).[44] For example, the primary claim may be for a product (such as a contact lens) having a particular character (such as being made up of recycled plastic), whereas the dependent claims may limit the principal claim to certain quantitative parameters (such as minimum or maximum length).

One of the reasons why claims are arranged hierarchically is that this provides patentees with the flexibility to respond to any legal challenges which are made to the patent.[45] More specifically, if claims are arranged hierarchically, a challenge to the patent might lead only to the principal or broadest claim being severed, leaving behind the more narrowly drafted claims.[46] Confident in the knowledge that the validity of narrower claims are not dependent on the validity of the more general claims, patentees are able to draft claims more generously than they would otherwise be able to do. The rules under the EPC 2000 require that, where appropriate, claims ought to be in two parts.[47] The first, which is called the 'preamble', sets out the technical features of the invention which are necessary for the definition of the claimed subject matter, but which are already part of the prior art. This is followed by a 'characterizing portion' that sets out the novel technical features that the applicant wishes to protect.[48] The so-called characterizing portion of the claim is neither required nor forbidden in the United Kingdom.[49] In British patents, the final claim will often be an omnibus claim, that is a claim that largely mimics the way the invention is set out in the descriptions or the drawings.[50] While permissible in the United Kingdom, omnibus claims are generally not permitted in EPO applications.[51]

A notable feature of most patent claims is that they are difficult to understand, at least to the non-expert reader. This not surprising, given that patents are not written for the general

---

system: *Mobil/Friction-reducing additive*, G2/88 [1990] *OJ EPO* 93, 99; J. Kemp (ed.), *Patent Claim Drafting and Interpretation* (1983). On the history see *British United Shoe Machinery v. Fussell* (1908) 23 *RPC* 631, 650.

[42] PA s. 14(5); EPC 2000 Art. 84. Given that the claims define the scope of protection, the way the claims are interpreted is very important. See below at Ch. 22 Section 3. For an interesting examination of the typical nature of the claims (and how they might differ from the abstract) see *R (on the application of Knight) v. Comptroller-General of Patents, Trade Marks and Designs* [2007] *All ER* (D) 125.

[43] The number has to be reasonable having regard to the nature of the invention claimed. EPC 2000 r. 43(5). In *Oxy/Gel forming composition*, T246/91 [1995] *EPOR* 526, a patent with 157 claims violated EPC 1973 Art. 84 and EPC 1973 r. 29(5): 'patents should not be allowed to erect a legal maze or smokescreen in front of potential users of the inventions to which they lay claim'.

[44] *Hallen v. Brabantia* [1990] *FSR* 134, 140–1.   [45] Myers, 'From Discovery to Invention', 82.

[46] See *Van der Lely v. Bamfords* [1964] *RPC* 54, 73, 76 (CA); *Chiron v. Organon (No. 7)* [1994] *FSR* 458, 460–6.

[47] This provision, apparently put in to appease British interests, enables UK patents to be drafted according to the traditional British approach.

[48] EPC 2000 r. 43(1)(b), *EPO Guidelines* C–III: 2. In the USA there are three parts: the preamble, transition, and body. See R. Merges, *Patent Law and Policy* (1992), 12.

[49] *CIPA*, para. 14.22.

[50] *Raleigh Cycle v. Miller* (1948) 65 *RPC* 141; *Surface Silo v. Beal* [1960] *RPC* 154; *Deere v. Harrison McGregor & Guest* [1965] *RPC* 461.

[51] See *CIPA*, para. 14.26. *Bayer/Polyamide moulding composition*, T150/82 [1981] *OJ EPO* 431. In *Philips Electronics' Patent* [1987] *RPC* 244, the patentee was permitted to add an omnibus claim to a European patent (UK) on the grounds that it did not extend the scope of protection.

reader, but for the relevant person skilled in the art. As well as being written for specialists, the drafting and reading of claims builds upon well-established and sophisticated techniques and procedures that make them difficult for the uninitiated to understand. Another reason why the claims may be difficult to understand is that they often use expressions not ordinarily employed in everyday speech. For example, while most people commonly talk about 'mice', a claim may refer to 'non-human mammals'. Similarly a door handle may be called a 'rotatable actuating means'[52] and a train's sleeping car known as 'a communal vehicle for the dormitory accommodation of nocturnal viators'.[53] Moreover, while in other contexts the rules of grammar are used to make the language we use easier to understand, this is not so with patents, where claims are often made up of single lengthy, repetitive sentences.[54] Indeed, in one case an attempt to divide claims up into separate (shorter) phrases was considered to be ambiguous in scope.[55] One problem that has arisen is the number of claims incorporated in a patent. As part of their drafting strategy, some applications include a very large number of claims. To prevent this, the EPO has announced that from 1 April 2009, the fees charged will increase to €200 where a patent includes more than 15 claims and €500 where it includes more than 50 claims.[56]

4.3.1 Types of claim

Given that claims operate to demarcate and define the patented invention, they will always vary from case to case. Having said that, claims are usually grouped together on the basis either of the subject matter that is protected or the way the claims are formulated. While there are many different types of claim, such as Swiss claims, Markush claims, and novelty-of-use claims, in this section we wish to focus on some of the more common types.

   (i) *Product claims.* Product claims, which were the first type of patent to be recognized by British law, provide protection over physical entities or things (such as products, apparatuses, devices, and substances). Such a patent could be, for example, for a new type of contact lens or, as a patent agent might say, 'a new type of optical membrane being made up of at least one polymer and at least one solvent'.[57] Product claims or, as they are also known, claims for a product *per se,* confer protection over all uses of that product, no matter how the product was derived.[58] As we will see, this has been the subject of some controversy, particularly in relation to claims for gene patents.

---

[52] *Southco v. Dzus Fastener Europe* [1992] *RPC* 299.

[53] *Hookless Fastener v. GE Prentice* (CCA 2d, 1934) 68 F (2d) 940, 941. See also W. Woodward, 'Definiteness and Particularity in Patent Claims' (1948) 46 *Michigan LR* 755.

[54] 'The repetitiveness of the claims and the lack of any indication of the strategic links between them, is part of what makes them so hard for a non-lawyer to read'. Myers, 'From Discovery to Invention', 75. The technique of drafting claims in this way can have important implications for their interpretation: see *Glaverbel SA v. British Coal* [1995] *RPC* 255, 281.

[55] *Leonard's Application* [1966] *RPC* 269.

[56] EPO Decision CA/D 15/07. See also CA/D 16/07 (which increases fees, notably renewal fees, from 1 April 2008).

[57] *Advanced Semiconductor Products/Limiting feature,* T384/91 [1995] *EPOR* 97 [1994] *OJ EPO* 169.

[58] See *Mobil/Friction reducing additive,* note 41 above; *Telectronics/Pacer,* T82/93 [1996] *EPOR* 409; [1996] *OJ EPO* 274, 285. In *Moog/Change of category,* T378/86 [1988] *OJ EPO* 386 the EPO explained: '[The] division of patents into various categories (process or product) is legally important because the extent of protection depends to a crucial extent on the category selected, specific types of use being allocated to each category which in some cases differ substantially from each other. The difference in effect on the right conferred by a patent is the reason why it is at all justifiable to classify patents in categories'.

(ii) Process claims. In contrast process claims, which were recognized by patent law in the early part of the nineteenth century, protect activities or actions (such as methods, processes, or uses).[59] Such a patent would claim, for example, the particular method by which a contact lens is made (or, 'the method of making an optical membrane from a solution comprising at least one polymer and at least one solvent').[60] Sometimes a claim for a product *per se* will not be available because the product is already known in the field, and a claim for the process or use is therefore all that is possible.

(iii) Product-by-process claims. Beyond these two broad categories of claim, there is a range of hybrids.[61] A well-known example is the 'product-by-process' claim.[62] To continue with the example used above, a product-by-process patent might claim 'a contact lens made by a particular method'. Where a product already exists but a new process is devised for producing that product, it might be desirable to claim for both the process and the product produced by the process. It is important to bear in mind the Court of Appeal's reminder that 'it is not right to lump all claims which contain a process feature into a category called product-by-process claims... a patentee can define the monopoly claimed so as to disclaim products made by a particular process or only disclaim products which do not have the features of products made by a particular process. The two types of claims can be loosely called product-by-process claims, but to do so is likely to hide the differences between the two'.[63]

For many years product-by-process claims were viewed differently in the United Kingdom and at the EPO. As a result of the House of Lords' 2005 decision in *Kirin-Amgen*, however, the approach in the UK is now the same as at the EPO.[64] The Technical Board of Appeal at the EPO has consistently said that product-by-process claims are not recognized at the EPO, except where the 'product cannot be satisfactorily defined by reference to its composition, structure or other testable parameter'.[65] That is, product-by-process claims are only acceptable as 'a manner of claiming structurally indefinable product claims' or where a product cannot be satisfactorily defined by its features. In contrast, prior to *Kirin-Amgen*, British courts had expressly rejected the position at the EPO and said that, other than the general criteria for patentability, there were no limits either in the Patents Act 1977 or in the EPC as to how the monopoly is defined.[66] As such, there were no additional limits on when product-by-process claims were allowed in the United Kingdom.[67] Recognizing the need for consistency between

59 *Crane v. Price* (1842) 134 *ER* 239. See Sherman and Bently, 108.

60 *Advanced Semiconductor Products/Limiting Feature*, T–384/91 [1995] *EPOR* 97; [1994] *OJ EPO* 169.

61 'There are no rigid lines of demarcation between the various possible forms of claim'. *Mobil/Friction reducing additive*, note 41 above, 98–9. *IBM/Computer-related claims*, T410/96 [1999] *EPOR* 318.

62 *Ethylene Polymers/Montedison* T93/83 [1987] *EPOR* 144; *Eli Lilly/Antibiotic*, T161/86 [1987] *EPOR* 366.

63 *Kirin-Amgen v. Transkaryotic Therapies* [2003] *RPC* 3, para. 27 (Aldous LJ) (CA).

64 *Kirin-Amgen Inc v. Hoechst Marion Roussel* [2005] *RPC* 9 (HL), para 101.

65 *IFF/Claim categories*, T150/82 [1984] *OJ EPO* 309, para. 10–11. This decision was made in the knowledge of the different approach in the UK (para. 11).

66 *Kirin-Amgen v. Transkaryotic Therapies*, [2003] *RPC* 3, paras. 29–31 (Aldous LJ) (CA); upholding the finding of the Patents Court on this point in *Kirin-Amgen v. Roche Diagnostics* [2002] *RPC* 1, para. 296 ('as a matter of ordinary language, I find it impossible to construe a product-by-process claim... in an absolute sense as the Board apparently felt able to do in T219/83').

67 In essence the difference between the approach adopted at the EPO and the pre-*Kirin Amgen* approach turned on the way the invention was defined: the Board of Appeal placing more emphasis on the interaction of the process and the product as a separate entity. On one level the different approaches can be traced to different legal cultures (British compared to a more German approach). More specifically the difference can be traced to differences in the way the invention is characterized. In essence the crux of the difference is that the EPO sees

the approach adopted in the UK and that at the EPO, the House of Lords rejected previous British law and followed the approach at the EPO. The upshot of this is that, where a product is known, product-by-process claims are no longer accepted in the UK on the basis that they lack novelty.

Product-by-process claims remain useful at the EPO and in the United Kingdom where there is no other information available to define the product by reference to its composition, structure, or other testable parameter.[68] This is particularly the case in relation to certain biotechnological and chemical inventions, where the product-by-process claim offers the only way 'to define certain or macromolecular materials of unidentified or complex composition which have yet to be defined structurally'.[69]

(iv) Representative claims. It has long been accepted practice for patents to be granted for extremely large classes of objects. This is particularly the case in relation to chemical and bio-technological inventions where patents may claim hundreds of thousands and sometimes millions of compounds, DNA sequences, and the like.[70] If patentees were required to out-line every particular manifestation of their invention, it would make those patents unwieldy, cumbersome, and, in some cases, unworkable. Because of this, where a patent is for a class of compounds, it is not necessary for applicants to spell out each and every product or process covered by the patent,[71] nor to show that they have 'proved their application in every individual instance'.[72] Instead patentees are able to claim a broad range of products on the basis of a limited number of (representative) examples. This can be done, for example, through the use of functional language (particularly where the relevant features cannot be defined more precisely), the use of 'Markush' claims (where a claim refers to a chemical structure by means of symbols indicating substituent groups),[73] or the inclusion of a practical application of a theoretical principle or a formula. In other cases, a patent may include variations, analogues, or deemed equivalents that greatly expand the scope of the claims.[74]

Functional claims define the invention by reference to the function that the invention performs, or its purpose, rather than the structure or elements of the invention. That is, instead

the invention in terms of the relationship between the product and the process, whereas the UK tribunals seem to draw a clear divide between product and process. For example, at the EPO it has been said that 'the effect of a process manifests itself in the result, i.e. in the product in chemical cases together with all its internal characteristics': *Gelation/Exxon*, T119/82 [1984] *OJ EPO* 217. In a similar vein, 'the product is in consequence of the invention, without being the invention itself, which is rather the novel interaction represented by the process in such cases. Any attempt to claim the in itself non-inventive product by means of product-by-process claims is claiming the mere effects instead'. *IFF/Claim categories*, note 65 above, para. 10. As we will see below, this has important consequences when a patent is being examined for novelty. See below at pp. 477–8.

   [68] *IFF/Claim categories*, T–150/82 [1984] *OJ EPO* 309.

   [69] *EPO Guidelines* C–III, 4.12. The benefits of product-by-process claims are less important under the European Patent Convention since infringement of a process occurs where a person disposes of, uses, or imports any product obtained directly by means of that process. PA s. 60(1)(c); EPC 2000 Art. 64(2).

   [70] See K. Luzzatto, 'The Support and Breadth of Claims to New Classes of Chemical Compounds' (1989) *Patent World* 21.

   [71] *Biogen v. Medeva* [1997] *RPC* 1, 48 (Lord Hoffmann) (HL).

   [72] *Kirin-Amgin v. Transkaryotic Therapies*, [2003] *RPC* 31, 67 (Aldous LJ) (CA).

   [73] Named after US patent application 1,506,316 by Eugene Markush. See M. Franzosi, 'Markush Claims in Europe' [2003] *EIPR* 200.

   [74] For problems that may arise see *American Home Products v. Novartis Pharmaceuticals* [2001] *RPC* 159 (CA).

of specifying what the invention is, a functional claim outlines what the invention does. For example, instead of claiming a modified form of bacteria in terms of its elements or structure, the invention might be described functionally as a bacterium which eats pollution.[75] Functional claims are permissible so long as they provide instructions that are sufficiently clear for the expert to reduce them to practice without undue burden[76] and 'if from an objective point of view, such features cannot otherwise be defined more precisely without restricting the scope of the claim'.[77]

In some cases, patentees use functional claims because language and concepts are not available to describe the invention in any other way.[78] This is often the case with biotechnological inventions.[79] In other cases, patentees might use functional language because it offers them a strategic advantage over competitors. For example, in describing how two metal plates are attached, a patentee might use functional language and claim a 'means for attaching' instead of claiming a 'nut and bolt'. This has the advantage of preventing a competitor from getting round the claim by using a screw.

4.3.2 Regulating the form and content of claims

A number of different rules and procedures regulate the form that claims ought to take.[80] At a general level, the contents of the claims must comply with the substantive requirements for patentability: namely, subject matter, novelty, and non-obviousness. The claims must also define the matter for which protection is sought in terms of the technical features of the invention,[81] be clear and concise,[82] be supported by the description,[83] and relate to one invention, or a group of inventions that are so linked as to form a single inventive concept.[84] We look at these criteria in more detail later.[85]

4.4 DRAWINGS

The final component of a patent is the drawings. These provide a representation of the invention.[86] Along with the description, the drawings may be used to interpret the claims.[87] The

---

[75] See *Biogen v. Medeva*, note 71 above, where the claim was to a DNA molecule characterized by the way it was made (recombinant DNA) and what it did (display HBV antigen specificity).

[76] For US analogues, see *In re Donaldson* (1994) 16 *F.3d* 1189; K. Adamo, 'The Waiting at the Patent Bar is Over: the Supreme Court decides Hilton Davis' (1996) 78 *JPTOS* 367; R. Taylor, 'The Pitfalls of Functional Claims in the US' (June 1997) *MIP* 13.

[77] *Mycogen/Modifying plant cells*, T694/92 [1998] *EPOR* 114, 119; *EPO Guidelines* C–III, 4.7–4.9; *CIPA*, para. 14.24.

[78] The Technical Board of Appeal at the EPO said that the use of structural description of chemical compounds by means of Markush-style formulae, which was part of the standard toolkit of the skilled-person chemist, is the most concise means of defining a class of chemical compounds in a claim. *Bayer CropScience/Safeners*, T1020/98 [2003] *OJ EPO* 533, 540–1.

[79] *Genentech/Polypeptide expression*, T292/85 [1989] *EPOR* 1; [1989] *OJ EPO* 275.

[80] Beyond the requirements that are set out in the Patents Act 1977, British law provides no guidance as to the particular format that the claims ought to take. This is in marked contrast to the EPC, which provides detailed guidance as to the form and content that claims ought to follow.

[81] PA s. 14(5)(a); EPC 2000 Art. 84, EPC 2000 r. 43(1).

[82] PA s. 14(5)(b); EPC 2000 Art. 84.   [83] PA s. 14(5)(c); EPC 2000 Art. 84.

[84] PA s. 14(5)(d), PA r. 16; EPC 2000 Art. 82, EPC 2000 r. 44.   [85] See Ch. 20.

[86] PA s. 14(2)(b), PA r. 12(2), 18; EPC 2000 Art. 78(1)(d), EPC r. 46.   [87] PA s. 125(1).

patent office rules provide very detailed rules as to the nature and form of the drawings. These range from the quality of the paper,[88] the size of the margin,[89] and the use of shading,[90] through to the height of the letters or numerals used. The standardization of the way inventions are represented plays an important role in ensuring the usefulness of the information provided by the patentee.

[88] UK Manual of Patent Practice para. 14.27.
[89] Ibid, para. 14.28.   [90] Ibid, para. 14.30.

p.111 notice rules provide a very detailed outline as to the nature and format of the drawings. These
range from the quality of the paper, the size of the margins, and the use of shading, through
to the height of the letters or numerals used. Notwithstanding this, very few features are
more visible [this] a more important role than the various uses of the kind of information provided
by the patent.

16

PROCEDURE FOR GRANT
OF A PATENT

CHAPTER CONTENTS

1 INTRODUCTION

Unlike the position under copyright law where rights arise without formality, patents are only
granted after a series of formal procedures have been complied with. The process of registration plays a key role in defining many aspects of patent law and practice. In this chapter we
explore some of the key features of those processes. We begin by exploring some of the issues
that would-be applicants ought to consider when deciding whether to take out a patent to protect their inventions in the United Kingdom. We then follow the trajectory of a patent through
the administrative process from its inception as a patent application through to grant. In so
doing we discuss the British and European patent systems, the Patent Cooperation Treaty, and
how they intersect.

2 PRELIMINARY CONSIDERATIONS

2.1 DECIDING TO PATENT

A range of factors are taken into account when considering whether to patent an invention. A
potential applicant will need to consider the benefits that may flow from patenting. Perhaps
the most obvious benefit is that as a patent confers an exclusive right to make, use, and sell
the patented invention for a period of up to 20 years it provides the owner with associated
monopoly profits. It should be noted that the economic value derived from a patent will vary
according to the type of invention in question. For example, where competitors are able to

develop new ways of achieving the same result which fall outside the scope of the monopoly (this is known as inventing around the patent), the economic benefits are reduced. Another benefit associated with patenting flows from the fact that patenting translates inventions from the world of science and technology to the world of commerce. In so doing, patenting enables inventions to be included on the balance sheets of organizations and on the research returns of publicly-funded institutions. This may be particularly important in attracting funds to pay for research.

Other less obvious benefits flow from patenting. These include the esteem or symbolic capital that flow from being recognized as an inventor. Indeed in some cases it is the romantic appeal of becoming an inventor that encourages a person to enter into the patent system in the first place.[1] Another benefit of patenting is that it enables manufacturers to enhance the image of their goods. By advertising that their goods are patented, sellers are able to represent to consumers that they are buying cutting-edge technologies. There is also a sense in which the mere fact that something has been patented carries with it the belief that the product has public approval: this has been particularly important in relation to the patenting of life forms.

The benefits that flow from patenting need to be weighed against the associated costs. The financial costs of patenting include patent agent fees (possibly £150 per page), the administrative charges imposed by national and international institutions as a condition of grant,[2] and where a patent is sought in a non-English-speaking country, the costs of translation. A 2004 study commissioned by the EPO showed that the average cost of obtaining a patent directly at the EPO was €24,100.[3] Non-financial costs such as the time and effort involved in transforming a practical technical idea into the form required by the patent system also need to be taken into account. Another cost associated with patenting relates to the fact that the applicant must make their invention available to the public. While competitors may not be able to copy the patented invention, the disclosure of the invention makes it easier for them to invent around the patent. Another factor to be taken into account is whether the benefits that flow from patenting can be achieved through other means with fewer of the associated costs.[4] An important factor here is that an inventor (or owner) may be able to rely upon other techniques to protect their creations that do not require the invention to be disclosed to the public. These include contractual restrictions on the use or disclosure of the process, the law relating to breach of confidence, or to non-legal techniques such as secrecy. The problem with these techniques is that they carry with them the risk that, if the information is disclosed to the public (even if through a breach of contract or confidentiality), in most cases the invention becomes part of the public domain, free for all to use.[5] Another factor that may influence

---

[1] G. Myers, 'From Discovery to Invention: The Writing and Re-writing of Two Patents' (1995) 25 *Social Studies of Science* 57, 59.

[2] *Study on the Cost of Patenting in Europe,* prepared on behalf of the EPO by Roland Berger Market Research (2004); European Patent Office, 'Cost of Patenting in Europe' (1995) 26 *IIC* 650; M. Bednarek, 'Planning a Global Patent Strategy: where to get the most "Bang for your buck"' (1995) 77 *JPTOS* 381; S. Helfgott, 'Why Must Filing In Europe Be So Costly?' (1994) 76 *JPTOS* 787.

[3] This included: pre-filing expenditure excluding R&D (€6,240), internal cost of processing (€3,070), attorney fees (€4,930), translation of application and claims (€3,020), official EPO fees (€3,410), validation (€9,870). The cost of a Euro-PCT patent was €46,700. *Study on the Cost of Patenting in Europe,* ibid.

[4] There may be a danger of another person patenting the invention. This has occasionally prompted defensive patenting which, at one time, prompted a third of all applications in the USA: W. Davis (1947) 12 *Law & Contemporary Problems* 796, 799–800; W. Ericson and I. Freedman (1957) 26 *George Washington Law Review* 78.

[5] On the trade secret/patenting decision, see Munson (1996) 78 *JPTOS* 689.

the decision to seek a patent is the ease by which the details of the invention can be ascertained or reverse-engineered when the invention or the products thereof are made available to the public.

Given that the decision to patent is influenced by a range of factors, it is not surprising that patenting practices vary from industry to industry. For example, in the pharmaceutical industry, where research and development costs are high and the products are readily and cheaply copied, the patent process is commonly relied on to protect inventions. In other industries, such as in the aviation field where the expense of copying is very high, greater emphasis is placed on secrecy as a mode of protection.

2.2 ROLE OF PATENT AGENTS

It is common for decisions concerning patent applications to be made in consultation with a patent agent. Since emerging as a discrete profession during the nineteenth century,[6] patent agents have come to play a central role in the operation of the patent system. Under the EPC a new breed of expert, the European patent agent, has developed to deal with the intricacies of the European patent system.[7] Patent agents normally have knowledge of the law, the patent administration process, and a particular branch of science. As well as assisting in the drafting and processing of patents, patent agents also offer advice as to whether a patent should be taken out and where and how patents are best exploited. In some cases they are also able to litigate on behalf of patentees. In a sense, patent agents act as go-betweens who unite the technical–scientific domains with the legal and commercial. The patent system encourages the use of patent agents by penalizing the owners of poorly drafted patents. For example, where a patent is found to be partially valid, relief by way of damages, costs or expenses is only available where a claimant can show that the patent was framed in good faith and with reasonable skill and knowledge:[8] a matter which may be difficult for non-specialists to prove.

2.3 CHOICE OF ROUTES TO GRANT

Once the decision is made to protect an invention in the United Kingdom by patent, it is then necessary to decide the particular route to take to secure grant of the patent. In particular, it is necessary to decide whether to take out a British patent or a European patent (UK).[9] In turn,

---

[6] See D. Van Zyl Smit, 'Professional Patent Agents and the Development of the English Patent System' (1985) 13 *International Journal of Society and the Law* 79; H. Dutton, *The Patent System and Inventive Activity during the Industrial Revolution 1750–1852* (1984), ch. 5; F. Kittel, 'Register of Patent Agents: A Historical Review' (1986–7) 16 *CIPAJ* 195.

[7] See EPC 2000 Arts. 133–134a; L. Osterborg, 'The European Patent Attorney: A New Profession' (1994) 25 *IIC* 313.

[8] PA s. 63(2). See *General Tire v. Firestone Tyre* [1975] *RPC* 203, 269; *Hallen v. Brabantia* [1990] *FSR* 134, 143; *Chiron v. Organon Teknika (No. 7)* [1994] *FSR* 458. Good faith primarily depends on whether the patentee knew something detrimental to the patent, or which escaped the eye of the patent examiner. Reasonable skill and knowledge relates to the competence employed in framing the specification. See *Hoechst Celanese v. BP Chemicals* [1997] *FSR* 547. For criticisms of the provision see Jacob LJ in *Beheer BV v Berry Floor NV* [2005] *EWCA Civ* 1292 (CA), para 35 (it makes no sense to restrict the right to damages but not account of profits). Jacob also questioned whether the provisions comply with the Directive on the Enforcement of IP Rights (2004/48/EC).

[9] Applications to the EPO and UK IPO are alternatives, so a patentee cannot have patents via both mechanisms. To prevent this PA s. 73(2) requires the Comptroller to revoke a UK patent where there is a European patent (UK) for the same invention having the same priority date which was applied for by the same applicant.

it is necessary to decide whether to apply directly to the UK Intellectual Property Office or the EPO, or whether it would be better to make use of the application system provided by the Patent Cooperation Treaty.[10] The particular route which is chosen depends on a variety of factors: perhaps the most important are the countries where protection is desired.

When deciding whether to bring an application to the UK or the EPO, commercial and strategic considerations may come into play. From a commercial point of view, the primary variable is the fees charged by the respective patent offices. As the cost of an application to the EPO is greater than to the UK office, if an applicant only wishes to file in the United Kingdom or in a few countries it would be cheaper for them to apply to the respective national offices. There comes a point, however, where the cumulative cost of applying to several national offices will exceed the cost of a European application.[11]

Applicants may also be influenced by strategic considerations when they are considering whether to apply to the EPO or to national offices. An important factor relates to the fact that although the substantive law of the national systems and the EPC are largely the same, there are a number of other important differences.[12] In particular, while the EPC has a full examination system some national offices do not require examination at all,[13] some allow for deferred examination, some require patent agents to provide the examination service, while others will only reject applications on limited grounds (such as novelty).[14] Another factor that may influence the route that is taken is the relative vulnerability of the patent. In particular, while a national patent can only be challenged in national tribunals, the EPC allows for a central challenge to be made against a European patent (this takes the form of an 'opposition' to the grant which can be brought in the nine-month period after grant).[15] If a would-be-patentee believes that the application is likely to be challenged, the applicant might prefer to maximize the survival chances of their patent by registering in a range of national offices rather than risking the possibility of a successful central attack which would deprive the applicant of protection in all the designated states.

Similar factors will influence inventors when they are considering whether to apply directly to the UK Intellectual Property Office or the EPC, or whether they want to make use of the

---

Before revocation the patentee is given an opportunity to justify holding two patents: PA s. 73(3), amended by CDPA, Sched. 5, para. 19.

[10] There are four routes available to get a patent for the UK: directly to the UK Patent Office, indirectly to the UK Patent Office via the PCT, directly to the EPO, or indirectly to the EPO via the PCT. *AstraZeneca/Priorities from India* G2/02 and G3/02 [2004] *OJ EPO* 483 (not possible to claim priority for a European patent from first publication in India by way of TRIPS, as India was not a party to PCT).

[11] While translation costs have been a significant consideration in the decision whether to file for a European patent or a national patent, this should be less important after 1 May 2008, when the London Agreement became operational.

[12] Early versions of the EPC proposed a two-stage approach: a provisional grant which was only subject to formal examination and novelty report, followed by the possibility of confirmation as a final European patent within five years at the behest of applicant or a third party. G. Oudemans, *The Draft European Patent Convention* (1963), 53–60, 164–76.

[13] There is no examination in Belgium, the Netherlands, Switzerland, or Ireland. On the latter see *Rajan v. Minister for Industry and Commerce* [1988] 14 *FSR* 9; A. Parkes, 'The Irish Patent Act 1992' (1991–2) 21 *CIPAJ* 426.

[14] For example, the French Patent Office will not refuse on grounds of lack of inventive step: Law of 2 Jan. 1968, Art. 16, J. Schmidt-Szalewski, 'Non-obviousness as a requirement of patentability in French Law' (1992) 23 *IIC* 725. For Germany, see E. Fischer, 'The New German Patent Procedure: From the View of a Corporate Patent Department' (1971) 2 *IIC* 277.

[15] EPC 2000 Arts. 99–101.

international filing system provided by the Patent Cooperation Treaty (PCT).[16] While the PCT does not issue patents, it does provide an alternative starting point by which both UK and European patents (UK) can be obtained.[17] Under the PCT,[18] an international application can be made to the patent office of one of the contracting states, which is called the receiving office.[19] The application must contain:[20] a request, a description, at least one claim, drawings (where appropriate), and an abstract. Prior to 1 January 2004, applicants also had to designate the states in which protection is sought.[21] This is no longer necessary, however, as the filing of a request automatically applies in all contracting states to the PCT (unless the applicant specifies otherwise).[22] Applicants can apply to designated international offices for an international search[23] and an international preliminary examination to be carried out.[24] At this point, the applicant can shift to the designated national offices who will decide whether to grant national patents.[25] At this stage, the national office treats the application as if it has been filed in that office. Instead of going straight to the national stage, an applicant may ask for an international preliminary examination by an examining authority.[26] The examining authority issues an international preliminary examination report indicating whether the invention appears to meet international standards of novelty, inventive step, or industrial applicability.[27] It should be noted that the examination is merely advisory and not binding on designated countries.[28]

The procedures are useful for countries where the patent office is not capable of carrying out its own examination. Another factor in favour of the PCT is convenience. Rather than having to apply in each individual country, a single application can be submitted to a relevant PCT body. The PCT is also attractive because of the lengthy period between the initial application to the international office and the time when the application is forwarded to the relevant national offices when the expensive process of translation must be completed.

[16] See above at pp. 352–3. D. Perrott, 'The PCT in Use' [1982] *EIPR* 67; B. Bartels, 'Patent Cooperation Treaty: The Advantages for the Applicant in the UK' (1983) 13 *CIPAJ* 3; J. Cartiglia, 'The Patent Cooperation Treaty: A Rational Approach to International Patent Filing' (1994) 76 *JPTOS* 261; J. Anglehart, 'Extending the International Phase of PCT Applications' (1995) 77 *JPTOS* 101.

[17] This was signed in 1970 and came into operation from 1978. As of 1 Jan. 2008 there were 190 Parties (168 Signatures). PA s. 89 gives statutory effect to some of the Treaty's provisions.

[18] PCT Art. 3.

[19] The receiving office retains one copy of the application, transmits another to WIPO, and a third to an international search authority. The receiving office checks to ensure that a filing date should be granted (Art. 14) and that appropriate fees have been paid. The ISA conducts a search and reports its findings to WIPO: Art. 15 PCT. The application can then be amended within two months (PCT Art. 19, Regulations under the Patent Cooperation Treaty (7 Dec. 2006) (hereafter, PCT r.) 46) and it and the search report are then communicated to the patent offices of the designated states: PCT Art. 20. The application must be published after the expiry of 18 months from the priority date: PCT Art. 21 (2).

[20] PCT rr. 4–8.

[21] On the need to correct failure to designate during the international phase, see *Vapocure Technologies Application* [1990] *RPC* 1.

[22] PCT r. 53.7. For a discussion of changes to the filing of international applications as of 1 Jan. 2004, see PCT Newsletter no. 11/2003 (Nov. 2003).

[23] There are nine International Search Authorities.

[24] There are eight International Preliminary Examination Authorities.

[25] At 20 months after the priority date the national stage begins, by formally initiating prosecution in the designated states, filing translations, and paying fees as necessary.

[26] PCT Ch. II; PCT Art. 22 (revised by PCT Assembly on 3 Oct. 2001) (provides for a minimum period of 30 months within which the applicant must provide certain documents and fees). Implemented in the UK by Patent (Amendment) Rules 2002 (SI 2002/529) (1 Apr. 2002). See now PA r. 66.

[27] PCT Art. 35(2).   [28] PCT Art. 33.

3 FEATURES OF THE PATENT APPLICATION PROCESS

Before looking in detail at the procedures for grant of a patent, it may be helpful to highlight some of the key features of the UK and EPO patent application processes.[29]

3.1 THE REQUIREMENT OF REGISTRATION

Registration has long been a prerequisite for grant of a patent in the United Kingdom. In modern times, this is largely explained by reference to the type of monopoly that a patent confers. The decision to make patent protection dependent upon registration is said to result from the fact that patents confer an absolute monopoly that enables the patentee to prevent all others from practising the invention. This is the case even if the infringer developed the same invention independently from the patented invention. Consequently, as a matter of fairness it is necessary to have a register open to the public. This ensures that third parties are able to ascertain whether they are infringing someone else's rights. The process of filing also helps to establish the priority of the invention and is a prerequisite to systems of pre-grant examination such as those that operate in the UK and EPO.

3.2 FIRST-TO-FILE

Most patent systems, including the United Kingdom's and the EPC, operate on the basis that the first person to file an (acceptable) application for an invention should be granted a patent over the invention. The fact that patents are granted via a system of registration does not necessarily mean that the patent ought to be granted to the first person to file an application. In some other patent systems, notably the USA, a patent is granted to the first person to invent, rather than to the first person to file an application.[30]

While the first-to-file system may be incompatible with a regime of intellectual property predicated on natural rights, it avoids the need to consider difficult questions about who was the first person to have a particular idea or to reduce the idea to a working model (as occurs in first-to-invent systems).[31] Instead, the first-to-file system replaces such investigations with

---

[29] The Strasbourg Agreement concerning International Patent Classification 1971 (UK joined on 7 Oct. 1975) has led to a degree of uniformity in the presentation of patent documents. See A. Wittmann, R. Schiffels, and M. Hill, *Patent Documentation* (1979), 124–34.

[30] C. Macedo, 'First-to-file' (1990) 18 *AIPLA Quarterly Journal* 193. The USA now accepts provisional applications: see 'The same effect: United States Provisional Patent Applications and Paris Convention Priority Rights' (1996) 78 *JPTOS* 716. In 2007 The Patent Reform Bill of 2007 was introduced into US Congress and Senate in plans to shift the USA away from a first-to-invent to a first-to-file system.

[31] The preference for a first-to-file system, however, does not avoid all legal investigations into who was the 'inventor'. This is because inventors are entitled to be named on the patent, even if they are not the applicant: PA s. 13; EPC 2000 Art. 62, Art. 81. If the inventor is not designated, the application is treated as having been withdrawn: EPC 2000 Art. 90(3), Implementing Regulations to the Convention on the Grant of European Patents (2006) (hereafter, EPC 2000 r. 57. However, there is no investigation into the correctness of the designation. Where the inventor designated and the applicant are different persons the practice is to inform the inventor of the application, thereby enabling the inventor to raise any objection they may have. Procedures are also available for inventors to be omitted from published versions of the application if they wish: EPC 2000 r. 20(1).

an administrative practice that delivers rough but simple justice.[32] The first-to-file system is also justified on the basis that it provides inventors with an incentive to disclose (or a reward for having disclosed) the invention: the first applicant to disclose the invention obtains the patent.[33] As we will see, the adoption of a first-to-file system has certain consequences that need to be taken into account later in the grant process.[34]

3.3 EXAMINATION

Another notable feature of the patent application processes in the UK and the EPO is that applications are subject to a full examination.[35] That is, all applications are examined to ensure that they comply with the formalities of filing, as well as the requirements of subject matter, novelty, non-obviousness, and sufficiency.

For most of its long history, British patents were granted without examination. The question whether examination as a prerequisite for grant should be introduced into the UK was considered and rejected on a number of occasions during the nineteenth century.[36] One of the main arguments against examination was that it would have made the recognition of property rights subject to the discretion of government officials. Examination would also have added to the cost and time of obtaining a patent:[37] changes which would have run counter to the spirit of much nineteenth-century reform which aimed to simplify the system and to reduce the 'taxes' imposed on inventors.

After much deliberation, a limited system of examination was introduced into the United Kingdom in 1905.[38] An important factor which helped to support the case for examination was the finding of the 1901 Fry Committee that 40 per cent of the patents registered at the time were for inventions which had already been described in previous patents.[39] As these patents would not have withstood litigation, they were theoretically harmless. Nevertheless, it was believed that they deterred others from working in the same field. Moreover, the lack of examination brought the system into disrepute and undermined the trust placed in valid patents. For some, the prospect of an examination system sanctioned and controlled by the state was attractive because it would have created a legal (and thus a commercial) presumption that any patents which had been granted were valid. Another factor which supported the case for examination was that fears of arbitrary or self-seeking exercise of discretion on behalf of those in charge of the register had been allayed by a growing trust in bureaucracy: a trend which was cemented by the increased use of experts.[40]

---

[32] T. Nicolai, 'First-to-File vs. First-to-Invent: A Comparative Study Based on German and United States Patent Law' (1972) 3 *IIC* 103; W. Kingston, 'Is the United States Right about First-to-Invent?', [1992] *EIPR* 223; T. Roberts, 'Paper, Scissors, Stone' [1998] *EIPR* 89.

[33] For arguments for first-to-file see [no named author] 'Prior Art in Patent Law' (1959) 73 *Harvard LR* 369, 380.

[34] See below at Section 5, and Ch. 20 Section 4.   [35] G. Smith, 'Why Examine?' (1982) 12 *CIPAJ* 9.

[36] (1864) 29 *PP* 321; (1871) 10 *PP* 603; (1872) 11 *PP* 395.

[37] The most common criticism of examination today is delay. Many patent systems operate with time limits in an attempt to reduce such problems. In the UK, examination should occur not later than 4 years and 6 months from priority.

[38] Patents Act 1902. The Office began to search British patents in 1905.   [39] (1901) 23 *PP*.

[40] EPC 2000 Art. 113 gives an applicant whose patent has been refused an opportunity to comment. This is of fundamental importance for ensuring a fair procedure and reflects the generally accepted notion of a right to be heard. The examiner must give the grounds for refusal, that is, the essential reasoning, sufficient for the case to be properly understood. See *NEC/Opportunity to comment*, T951/92 [1996] *EPOR* 371; [1996] *OJ EPO* 53.

The limited examination system established in 1905 was maintained until the passing of the Patents Act 1977, when the current full examination system was introduced.[41] While the examination system currently forms an integral part of the British patent system, there may come a time where the United Kingdom may wish to follow other countries in the EPC who in the face of falling national applications have abandoned full examination as part of national procedure. If this were to happen, it would provide applicants with greater choice: the alternatives being an unexamined national patent or an examined European patent.

3.4 AMENDMENT

Another notable feature of the grant system is that applicants are able to alter or amend their initial application both during and after grant of the patent. The decision to give patentees the opportunity to amend their patent recognizes that the first-to-file system may encourage applicants to register without a full understanding of the invention or complete familiarity with the relevant prior art. It is also based on the fact that subsequent examination, either by the applicant or the Patent Office, may reveal the existence of a piece of prior art which requires the application to be reformulated to ensure its validity.[42] Similarly, an applicant may wish to amend the application as filed in light of subsequent experiments carried out on the invention. Where a patent is found to be partially valid,[43] it is desirable that the patent be amended by the deletion of the invalid claims which otherwise might remain as a potential nuisance to industry.[44] At the end of this chapter we look at the situations where applicants and patentees are able to amend and the restrictions that they operate under.

4 PROCEDURE FOR GRANT

The basic procedure for application for a patent to the UK Intellectual Property Office is roughly the same as at the European Patent Office. In this section we provide an overview of some of the more important features of those processes (see Fig. 16.1).

4.1 WHO IS ENTITLED TO APPLY FOR A PATENT?

There are virtually no restrictions on who may apply for a patent. In contrast with the rules relating to copyright and trade marks, there are no limitations as regards the nationality or residency of the applicant.[45] Where appropriate, an application for a patent may be made by two or more applicants. While anyone may apply for a patent, there are a number of restrictions placed on those who are entitled to be granted a patent. The issue of entitlement to grant is dealt with later.[46]

---

[41] Prior to the 1977 Act, examination was for patentability and novelty only. Examination for inventive step was introduced by the 1977 Act.

[42] G. Aggus, 'The Equities of Amendment' (1980–1) 10 *CIPAJ* 389. For the history of reissues in the USA, see K. Dood, 'Pursuing the Essence of Inventions: Reissuing Patents in the 19th Century' 32 (1991) *Technology & Culture* 999. For the history of 'intervening rights' see P. Federico, 'Intervening Rights in Patent Re-issues' (1962) 30 *George Washington Law Review* 603.

[43] PA s. 63(1).   [44] *Van der Lely v. Bamfords* [1964] *RPC* 54, 73–4 (Pearson LJ).

[45] PA s. 7(1); EPC 2000 Art. 58. Cf. Paris Art. 2(1) which requires members to provide the same protection as nationals receive to nationals of any other country in the Union. See also PCT Art. 9.

[46] See Ch. 21 below.

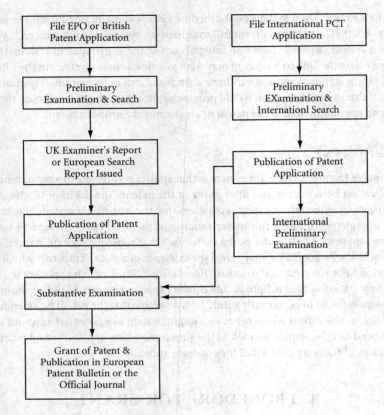

Fig. 16.1 Flowchart of a patent application

During the application process disputes over who is entitled to a patent that may subsequently be granted are dealt with differently, depending on whether it is a British or a European application.[47] For the purposes of proceedings before the EPO, it is assumed that the applicant is entitled to exercise the right to the European patent: issues about entitlement are determined elsewhere.[48] The EPO will only take account of the question of entitlement if a decision is made by an appropriate national court that a person other than the applicant is entitled to the patent.[49]

As with the EPC, an applicant for a British patent is presumed to be entitled to grant of the patent.[50] However, in contrast with the EPC the comptroller is able to consider issues of entitlement which are raised before grant.[51] If a person 'properly entitled' to a patent decides

---

[47] Under EPC 2000 Art. 60 the right to a European patent belongs to the inventor or his successor in title. The rights of employees depend on the law of the state in which they are mainly employed or, if that cannot be determined, that in which the employer has his place of business. See below at pp. 533–8.

[48] EPC 2000 Art. 60(3). See G. Le Tallec, 'The Protocol on Jurisdiction and the Recognition of Decisions in Respect of the Right to the Grant of a European Patent' (1985) 16 *IIC* 318; *Kirin-Amgen/Erythropoietin*, T412/93 [1995] *EPOR* 629 (questions of entitlement could not be considered in opposition proceedings).

[49] Three courses of action available: prosecution of the application in place of the applicant; filing of a new application; or a request that the application be refused: EPC 2000 Art. 61(1). See *Latchways/Unlawful applicant*, G3/92 [1995] *EPOR* 141.

[50] PA s. 7(4).   [51] PA s. 8. See T. Gold, 'Entitlement Disputes: A Case Review' [1990] *EIPR* 382.

to submit a new application, they may be able to use the wrongful applicant's priority date.[52] The comptroller of the UK Intellectual Property Office is given similar powers to determine entitlement where a patent has already been granted.[53]

4.2 FILING A PATENT APPLICATION

Applications for British patents are filed in Newport. The contents of all documents included in an application for a British patent must be in English or Welsh.[54] Applications for a European patent may be filed either with the European Patent Office in Munich or in The Hague, or with national patent offices in the contracting states.[55] Unlike the case under the EPC 1973 (where applications had to be in one of three official languages and the text of the patent had to be in that language), the EPC 2000 allows European patent applications to be filed in any language.[56] If the application is not made in an official language of the EPO (English, German, or French), the applicant is given two months to translate the application into an official language.[57]

Applicants at the UK Intellectual Property Office and the EPO are faced with the choice either of making a 'full application' or alternatively of taking advantage of the facility which allows for 'early filing'.[58] A full application for a patent must contain a request for grant of a patent, a description of the invention, one or more claims, any drawings referred to in the description or the claims, and an abstract.[59]

In order to provide applicants with greater flexibility, the patent systems provide that, instead of filing a full application, applicants are able to make an 'early filing'.[60] Early filing occurs where an applicant supplies an indication that a patent is sought, information identifying the applicant, and a description of the invention.[61] Essentially, early filing provides applicants with a twelve-month breathing-space in which they can decide whether they wish to pursue a patent, are able to carry out further experiments on the invention, look for investors, and further consider the countries in which they wish to seek patents. The applicant must file the claims and abstract within twelve months of the early filing (the so-called filing date) if an early application is not to lapse.[62] While early filing offers a breathing space 'for completion of the formalities and the interim preservation of priority', early filing was not intended 'to provide a cover for making improvements in the disclosed invention by bringing in new

---

[52] PA s. 8(3).

[53] PA s. 37. See *James Industries Patent* [1987] RPC 235 (applicant's claim for share of patent for net beds rejected in absence of contract evincing clear understanding that patent rights were to be shared); *Nippon* [1987] RPC 120; *Norris' Patent* [1988] RPC 159.

[54] PA r. 14(1).

[55] EPC 2000 Art. 75(1)(2). On designation costs see O. Bossung, 'The Return of European Patent Law to the European Union' (1996) 27 *IIC* 287, 296. On the international status see *Lenzing* [1997] RPC 245.

[56] EPC 2000 Art. 14(2), EPC 2000 r. 40.   [57] EPC 2000 r. 6(1), r 58.

[58] Patent application fees at the UK Patent Office were abolished from 1 Oct. 2000.

[59] PA s. 14(2); EPC 2000 Art. 78(1); PCT Arts. 3–7, PCT r. 3–8, 10, 11, 13, and 32; *A. C. Edwards v. Acme Signs* [1990] RPC 621, 642; see *Xerox/Amendments*, T133/85 [1988] *OJ EPO* 441, 448. Patent applications must also designate the inventor. PA s. 13, PA r. 10; EPC 2000 Art. 81, EPC 2000 rr. 19–21, *EPO Guidelines* A–III, 5.

[60] PA s. 15(1); EPC 2000 Art. 80, EPC 2000 r. 49; PCT Arts. 11 and 14(2), PCT r. 7, 14.1(b), 15.4(a), 16, and 20.2(a)(iii).

[61] It is no longer necessary for applications to the EPO to include one or more claims. EPC 2000 Rule 40(1); see also EPC 2000 Rule 57(c). PCT Art. 4(ii).

[62] See *Antiphon's Application* [1984] RPC 1, 9. On late submission of drawings see *VEB Kombinat Walzlager* [1987] RPC 405.

material not covered by the disclosure whilst preserving for it the priority conferred by the original filing date'.[63]

4.3 PRIORITY DATE OF THE APPLICATION

The initial application is important in that it sets in play the sequence of steps that may ultimately result in the grant of the patent. Irrespective of whether the filing is an early filing or a full application, filing is also important since it establishes the 'priority date' of the patent. In the absence of a claim to an earlier date, the priority date is the filing date of the application.[64] As we will see, the priority date is the date at which the novelty, inventiveness, and other aspects of the invention are assessed. As such it is often of critical importance for the validity of the patent. The priority date is of practical significance in several other ways. Firstly, because novelty is assessed as of the priority date, once the date is established an applicant is able to exploit their invention without fear of invalidating the patent. Second, applicants are able to use the priority date established by filing in the UK or EPO as the priority date for applications in other countries.

4.4 PRELIMINARY EXAMINATION AND SEARCH

The next formal step in the process of grant is the preliminary examination and search.[65] When the claims and abstract have been submitted, the applicant should request a preliminary examination and search.[66]

On preliminary examination the application is examined to see whether it complies with certain formal requirements.[67] These are that the application contains a request for grant, a description of the invention, one or more claims, any drawings referred to in the description or claim, and an abstract. In addition, the preliminary examination also ensures that the inventor(s) have been identified and that the application accords with other formalities (such as payment of fees).[68]

Applicants are alerted to any problems that may have been identified in the preliminary examination in a report which is issued to them.[69] Applicants are then given the opportunity to respond to the report or, if necessary, amend their application to overcome the problems. If an applicant fails to change their application in a manner that satisfies the respective patent offices, the application may be refused.

The examiner or (at the EPO) the Search Division also carry out a limited search of the existing literature for relevant prior art (that is, information similar to the invention in question).[70] The aim of the search is to identify the documents that may be used at the substantive examin-

---

[63] *Asahi Kaei Kogyo* [1991] *RPC* 485, 526 (HL) (Lord Oliver).

[64] PA s. 5, PA r. 6; EPC 2000 Arts. 87–9. An application for which a date of filing has been accorded under the PCT is treated as an application for a patent under the 1977 Act.

[65] PA s. 17, PA r. 23, 27; EPC 2000 Art. 90. PCT Arts. 14, 15, 17, and 18, PCT r. 26–30, 33, 37, 38, 40, and 43.

[66] PA s. 17(1). Under the EPC 2000, the search and examination stages of the application process were combined.

[67] The receiving office retains one copy of the application, transmits another to WIPO, and a third to an international search authority. The receiving office checks to ensure that a filing date should be granted and that appropriate fees have been paid. EPC 2000 Art. 90.

[68] PA r. 31; EPC r. 40, 55; EPO Guidelines A–II.   [69] PA r. 29; EPC 2000 r. 57.

[70] PA s. 17(1); EPC 2000 Art. 92, EPC 2000 r. 61–64.

ation stage when the application is examined for novelty and inventive step.[71] The applicant is informed of the findings of the search by way of an examiner's report or, as it is known at the EPO, the European search report.[72]

As well as identifying the documents that may be relied upon when the application is examined for novelty and inventive step, the application is also examined during the search stage to ensure that it relates to one invention or to a group of inventions which form a single inventive concept.[73] That is, it is examined to ensure it meets the requirement of 'unity of invention'.[74]

Where two or more inventions are claimed in the one application, the application will fail to comply with the requirement of unity of invention unless it can be shown that the inventions form a single inventive concept.[75] To do this it is necessary to show that the inventions share the same 'special technical features'. Special technical features are the features that define the contribution that each of the claimed inventions, considered as a whole, makes to the claimed advance over the prior art.[76] There are at least two reasons for limiting patent applications to a single inventive concept. The first is that patent protection should not be available to two inventions for the price of one. Second, and more importantly, to allow more than one inventive concept to be included in a single patent is likely to undermine the administrative systems for locating, identifying, and searching for patents.

If it is found that the application contains more than one invention, the search is limited to the first invention that is set out in the claims.[77] In the face of a finding that an application contains more than one patent, applicants may simply pursue a patent for one of the inventions. Alternatively, they may divide the initial application into two (or more) fresh applications. So long as additional fees are paid and no new material is added, they may use the priority date for the original application for the new applications.[78]

4.5 PUBLICATION

The next stage in the grant process is the publication of the patent application. The application will be published and made available for public inspection 18 months from the date of filing (or 'as soon as possible thereafter').[79] This process informs third parties that the application has been made. While third parties are not able to oppose the grant of a patent at this stage, they are able to make observations as to whether the patent should be granted.[80]

---

[71] PA s. 17(4)(5); EPC 2000 Art. 92, EPC 2000 r. 61(1).   [72] PA s. 17(5); EPC 2000 r. 65.

[73] PA ss. 14(5)(d), (6), s. 17(6), PA r. 17; EPC 2000 Art. 82, EPC 2000 r. 64.

[74] Lack of unity is not a ground for revocation. PA s. 26, PA r. 16. No EPC equivalent, but see EPC 2000 Art. 82.

[75] PA s. 14(5)(d) and s. 14(6), PA r. 16; EPC 2000 Art. 82, EPC 2000 r. 64.

[76] PA r. 16(2); EPC 2000 r. 44. Technical features 'are the physical features which are essential to the invention'. With respect to a product these are 'the physical parameters of the entity'. In relation to a process, the technical features are 'the physical steps which define such activity'. *Mobil Oil/Friction Reducing additive*, G2/88 [1990] *EPOR* 73; [1990] *OJ EPO* 93, 100. See also *May & Baker v. Boots* [1950] 67 *RPC* 23, 50; *Biogen v. Medeva* [1995] *RPC* 25, 92–3; *Bayer/Benzyl esters* [1983] *OJ EPO* 274; *Siemens/Unity*, G1/91 [1992] *OJ EPO* 253.

[77] *Hollister's Application* [1983] *RPC* 10; G2/92 [1993] *OJ EPO* 591.

[78] Failure to meet an objection of lack of unity is frequently remedied by the making of divisional applications. EPC 2000 r. 36; PA s. 18(3), PA r. 100.

[79] PA s. 16, PA r. 26; EPC 2000 Art. 93, EPC 2000 r. 67–70; PCT Arts. 21 and 29, PCT r. 9.1 and 48.

[80] PA s. 21, PA r. 33; EPC 2000 Art. 115, EPC 2000 r. 114.

The documents published in the UK and the EPO include the description, claims, and drawings (if any) that have been filed. In the United Kingdom, the publication must include the original claims, any amendments that have been made to the claims, as well as any new claims. The UK Intellectual Property Office is also given power not to publish parts of the application which are offensive or disparaging,[81] or which might be prejudicial to national security.[82] At the EPO, the abstract and (where available) the search report are also published.[83]

Publication is important for two reasons. First, since the act of publication discloses the invention to the public, an unwanted publication may prevent applicants from relying on other ways of protecting their invention (such as confidentiality). Similarly, once a patent application has been published, the application can no longer be resubmitted (whereas if the application is withdrawn prior to publication it is possible to make a later application).[84] Second, if the patent proceeds to grant, the date of publication is the date from which the patentee is able to sue for infringement of the patent. This is on the condition that the act would have infringed both the patent as granted and the claims in the form in which they were published.[85] In these circumstances, the patentee is only entitled to damages for infringement in the period between publication and grant.

As mentioned, a third party may respond to the publication of the application by submitting 'observations' to the Patent Office (at any time before grant).[86] Such observations should relate to whether the invention is a patentable invention.[87] Observations may be made by 'any person' and must be submitted in writing accompanied by appropriate reasons. The comptroller of the UK Intellectual Property Office is instructed to consider the observations, whereas the European Patent Office is merely required to communicate the observations to the proprietor who, in turn, is permitted to comment on them. If the EPO wishes, it can take account of such observations when examining the application.[88] In both fora, the party submitting the observations does not become party to the proceedings and so will not be asked to any hearing, nor made to pay the costs of any proceedings.

4.6 SUBSTANTIVE EXAMINATION

Once the requirements of preliminary examination and search have been satisfied, the next stage in the application process is the 'substantive examination'.[89] The applicant must request

---

[81] PA s. 16(2), PA r. 33.

[82] PA s. 22 (no EPC 2000 equivalent). PA s. 23 provides that British residents need prior written approval from the comptroller before they file applications outside the UK. This gives the office the opportunity to examine applications to see if the information is prejudicial to the defence of the realm or the safety of the public. If so, the office may prohibit or restrict publication.

[83] EPC 2000 r. 68(1).

[84] EPC 2000 Art. 128 specifies that the application prior to this point is confidential and may only be viewed by third parties with the consent of the applicant.

[85] PA s. 69(2); EPC 2000 Art. 67; PCT Art. 29.   [86] PA s. 21; EPC 2000 Art. 115.

[87] That is, matters covered in PA s. 21(1), s. 1; EPC 2000 Arts. 115, 52.   [88] EPC 2000 Art. 114.

[89] PA s. 18(1), PA r. 28–29; EPC 2000 Art. 94, EPC r. 70–71. Under the PCT, the national stage begins 20 months after the priority date by formally initiating prosecution in the designated states, filing translations, and paying fees as necessary. Instead of going straight into the national stage, an applicant may ask for an international preliminary examination by an examining authority (PCT Art. 31). This is dealt with in Chapter II of the Convention. This delays entry into the national systems for a further 10 months, so that entry is within 30 rather than 20 months of the priority date. The IPEA establishes an international preliminary examination report indicating whether the invention appears to meet international standards of novelty, inventive step, or industrial applicability (PCT Art. 35(2)). Such examination is merely advisory and not binding on designated countries: PCT Art. 33.

this within six months from the date of publication of the application, or (at the EPO) the publication of the search report.[90]

The purpose of the substantive examination is to ascertain whether the application complies with the requirements of the Patents Act 1977 or, in the case of the EPO, the European Patent Convention 2000.[91] Unlike the preliminary examination, which is mainly concerned with ensuring the presence of certain documents, during the substantive examination the application is scrutinized to ensure that it is valid in all aspects. In particular, the invention is examined to ensure that it does not consist of subject matter excluded from patentability, and that the invention is novel, involves an inventive step, and is industrially applicable. The substantive examination also ensures that the application has been sufficiently disclosed, and that the claims are concise and are supported by the description.

The substantive examination takes the form of a dialogue between the examiner and the applicant. After the examination has taken place the examiner draws up a report which outlines any objections to the application which have been identified. The report is supplied to the applicant who is given an opportunity to comment on the objections, often in the hope of persuading the examiner that any doubts they have about the application are ill-founded. Alternatively, the applicant may respond to the objections by amending the patent application.[92] If they think it necessary, the examiners may make or require further searches. Ultimately, the dialogue may lead to a hearing before the Senior Examiner in the United Kingdom or the full Examining Division of the EPO, and from there by way of appeal to the UK Patents Court or the Board of Appeal of the EPO.[93]

4.7 GRANT OF THE PATENT

If the respective patent office is not satisfied that the application satisfies the various requirements for grant, the application will be refused.[94] If the respective patent office is satisfied that all the necessary requirements have been satisfied, the patent will be granted.[95] The decision to grant a patent does not take effect until the date on which it is mentioned in the *Official Journal* (for a UK patent) or the *European Patent Bulletin* (for a European patent).[96] The protection afforded by a patent can last up to 20 years from the filing date.[97] Renewal fees must be paid after four years.[98] As we will see, the protection may extend beyond the 20-year period where a supplementary protection certificate is issued. The extent of protection conferred by a patent will be considered later.[99]

The date of the grant of a European patent is also the date of its transition from a European application to a bundle of separate national rights.[100] With the exception of opposition proceedings, questions of validity and infringement are thereafter considered at a national level.[101] Once granted, a European patent (UK) is given the same level of protection as those granted by

---

[90] PA r. 28(2); EPC 2000 r. 70(1). This distinction is not of great significance, given that in the UK an applicant should receive the search report before the date of 'early' publication.

[91] Substantive examinations of EPO applications are carried out in Munich, The Hague, and Berlin.

[92] PA s. 18(3); EPC 2000 Art. 94(3)(4), EPC 2000 r. 71; PCT Ch. II (preliminary examination).

[93] PA s. 97(1); EPC 2000 Art. 106–112a, EPC 2000 rr. 90–96. EPC 2000 Art 112a provides parties with the ability to petition for review by the Enlarged Board of Appeal in limited circumstances.

[94] PA s. 18(3); EPC 2000 Art. 97(2), *EPO Guidelines* C–VI, 7.6.   [95] PA s. 18(4); EPC 2000 Art. 97(1).

[96] PA s. 24(1); EPC 2000 Art. 97(3).   [97] PA s. 25; EPC 2000 Art. 63(1).

[98] The fees increase over time to ensure that the Registry does not become cluttered with useless patents.

[99] See Ch. 22 below.   [100] EPC 2000 Art. 64(1); PA s. 77.   [101] EPC 2000 Art. 64(3).

the national patent office.[102] As discussed above, it is no longer necessary to translate European patents in French or German into English within three months of grant at the EPO for them to be valid in the UK.[103]

4.8 REVOCATION

While the patent examination processes at the UK and European Patent Office are relatively rigorous, they are not conclusive. As such, it is possible for patents to be revoked after grant on a limited number of grounds. The grounds on which a patent may be revoked are set out in section 72 of the 1977 Act and Article 138 of the EPC 2000. These are that:

(i)   the invention is not a patentable invention;[104]

(ii) the patent was granted to a person who was not entitled to that patent;[105]

(iii) the specification of the patent does not disclose the invention clearly enough and completely enough for it to be performed by a person skilled in the art;[106] or

(iv) the material in the patent extends beyond the material in the application as filed (impermissible amendment).[107]

In addition, the UK Intellectual Property Office has limited power to revoke patents on its own initiative.[108]

One of the notable features of section 72 is that it says that 'any person' can apply to have a patent revoked. This has been taken to mean that there is no need for a person to have any interest, whether commercial or otherwise, in the outcome of proceedings to bring an action to revoke a patent.[109] Unlike the position under the Patents Act 1949, a person who has no interest in the revocation is nevertheless entitled to apply to have the patent revoked. As Jacob J said, 'Parliament purposively made patents vulnerable to attack from anyone'.[110]

4.9 OPPOSITION PROCEEDINGS AT THE EPO

While the grant of a European patent generally brings the European stage to an end, a central challenge can be made to the validity of the European patent in the nine-month period following grant of the patent.[111] This process, known as 'opposition', has a number of advantages over leaving decisions about the validity of patents exclusively to national offices or

---

[102] PA s. 77(1)(a).

[103] See above at p. 346. EPC 2000 Art. 97(1), r. 71(3), (7). Under PCT Art. 3 an international application can be made to a Patent Office of one of the contracting states, which is termed the receiving office. Rules 4–8 PCT set out the contents of a filing, i.e. a request, a description, at least one claim, drawings where appropriate, and an abstract. The application must designate the states in which protection is sought.

[104] PA s. 72(1)(a); EPC 2000 Art. 138(1)(a); Arts 52–7.

[105] PA s. 72(1)(b); EPC 2000 Art. 138(1)(e).   [106] PA s. 72(1)(c); EPC 2000 Art. 138(1)(b).

[107] PA s. 72(1)(d)–(e); EPC 2000 Art. 138(1)(c)-(d).   [108] PA s. 73.

[109] *Cairnstores v. Aktiebolaget Hassle* [2002] *FSR* 35 (there were circumstances where the commencement of revocation proceedings might amount to an abuse of process). See also *Indupack Genentech/Third party opposition*, G03/97 [2000] *EPOR* 8.

[110] *Oystertec's Patent* [2003] *RPC* 559, 563. Cf. PA 1949 ss. 14 and 32 (an applicant for revocation had to be a 'person interested').

[111] EPC 2000 Art. 99. See generally Bossung, 'The Return of European Patent Law to the European Union', 296.

courts. The most obvious advantage is cost: it is cheaper to launch or defend a single attack in one place rather than to engage in revocation proceedings in each of the countries where the patent was issued.

Any person may file a notice of opposition. For a period, it was common for the proprietor to file oppositions in order to make post-grant amendments (which otherwise would have to be made at national level).[112] This practice has now been curtailed.[113] Opposition has to be filed within nine months from grant and must be based on one of three grounds.[114] These are that:

(i) the subject matter of the European patent is not patentable under Articles 52–57 EPC 2000;[115]

(ii) the European patent does not disclose the invention in a manner sufficiently clear and complete for it to be carried out by a person skilled in the art;[116] or

(iii) the subject matter of the European patent extends beyond the content of the application as filed.[117]

Any opposition to a European patent is communicated to the patent proprietor who may contest the opposition, make observations and/or make amendments. The opposition proceedings will determine whether the patent should be revoked, maintained, or maintained in an amended form.[118] If the proceedings result in revocation, the patent is deemed, from its outset, not to have had any of the effects specified in the EPC.[119]

5 AMENDMENT

As we mentioned earlier, applicants are able to alter or amend their initial application both during and after grant of the patent. *Prior to grant,* applicants are able to amend their application where the examination reveals that the formal and substantive requirements are not complied with.[120] In addition, applicants have a general power to amend their application at any time before a patent is granted.[121] The ability to amend during grant is based on a belief that it would be unreasonable to expect applicants to be fully aware of all prior art at the point when they filed their application. This is especially the case given that the patent system provides for a search and examination at a later stage.

After a patent has been granted, the owner of a patent is also able to amend their patent.[122] In addition, the comptroller is able to instigate proceedings that may prompt such amendment.[123] Under the EPC 1973 post-grant amendment only occurred in opposition proceedings.[124]

---

[112] *Mobil Oil/Opposition by proprietor,* G1/84 [1985] *OJ EPO* 299; [1986] *EPOR* 39; *Mobil/Admissibility,* T550/88 [1992] *OJ EPO* 117; [1990] *EPOR* 391.

[113] *Peugeot & Citroen/Opposition by patent proprietor,* G9/93 [1995] *EPOR* 260.

[114] EPC 2000 Art. 100. The procedure for opposition is set out in EPC 2000 rr. 75–89.

[115] EPC 2000 Art. 100(a).   [116] EPC 2000 Art. 100(b), Art. 83.

[117] EPC 2000 Art. 100(c); Art. 123(2). The question whether it is possible to amend a claim by way of a disclaimer allowable under EPC Art. 123(2) was referred (from *Genetic System Corporation,* T451/99 [2003] *OJ EPO* 334) to the EBA and is being heard under cases numbers G1/03 and G2/03.

[118] EPC 2000 Art. 101.   [119] EPC 2000 Art. 68.

[120] PA s 18(3), PA r. 31; EPC 2000 Art. 123(1), EPC 2000 r. 137; PCT Ch. II (preliminary examination).

[121] PA s. 19(1), PA r. 3; EPC 2000 Art. 123(1); PCT Arts. 19 and 34(2)(b), PCT rr. 46 and 66.

[122] PA s. 27(1), s 72, s. 75. EPC 2000 Art. 105a–c.   [123] PA s. 73.

[124] *Advanced Semiconductor Products/Limited Feature* G1/93 [1994] *OJ EPO* 169. Amendments in opposition proceedings are only considered where they are appropriate and necessary, that is that they can fairly be said

Otherwise, such matters were for national law.[125] Under the EPC 2000, however, patent owners are given a general power to revoke or limit European patents after grant at the EPO.[126] Article 138(3) EPC 2000 also provides proprietors of European patents with the right to amend a patent in national proceedings relating to the patent's validity. As we will see, this has ramifications for the role of the judicial discretion to allow amendment. Under the procedures in the UK and EPO, the application to amend is advertised so that any person may oppose it within two months. If granted, the amendment is deemed to have taken effect from the grant of the patent. Since these provisions make no provision for circumstances where there are infringement proceedings and amendment is desired but validity is not in issue, they leave a lacuna in the legislative scheme.[127] This discrepancy is to be resolved by amending section 75 so as to allow patentees to propose amendments in the course of any proceedings.[128]

5.1 RESTRICTIONS ON AMENDMENT

In order to ensure that any amendments that are made comply with the overriding aims of the patent system,[129] a number of restrictions are placed on an owner's ability to amend their application/patent. The amended patent must comply with the requirements that have to be met by all patents. These include the requirements of subject matter, novelty, and inventive step. The amended claims must also be clear and concise, be supported by the description, and relate to one invention or group of inventions that are linked to form a single inventive concept.

There are a number of other provisions that restrict an owner's ability to amend either the application or the patent. Perhaps the most important of these, which we deal with in Chapter 20, strike at the validity of the patent. Under these provisions, if the amendment introduces subject matter that was not in the original application, or the amendment extends the scope of protection beyond the initial application, the amended patent is liable to be revoked.[130] In this section, we wish to focus on the situations where validity is not at stake.

---

to arise out of the grounds of opposition: *Mobil/Admissibility,* T550/88 [1992] *OJ EPO* 117; [1990] *EPOR* 391 397, For a discussion of the situations where amended claims will be allowed at the EPO see *Minnesota Mining and Manufacturing Company,* G/99 [2001] *OJ EPO* 381 (EBA); *Lubrizol Corporation,* T525/99 [2003] *OJ EPO* 452, 457–8.

[125] *Mobil/Admissibility,* T550/88 [1992] *OJ EPO* 117; [1990] *EPOR* 391, 394.

[126] EPC 2000, Art. 105a–105c. See also Art. 1, items 51, 62 of the Act Revising the Convention on the Grant of European Patents (EPC) (Munich) (29 Nov. 2000) MR/3/00 Rev 1e. It has been proposed that where a patent not in English is limited at the EPO, the UK will require a translation of the patent as granted, limited, or amended within a specific time before that limited patent can take effect in the UK. *Consultation on the proposed Patents Act (Amendment) Bill: Summary of responses and the Government's conclusions* (13 Nov. 2003), para. 32–33.

[127] *Norling v. Eez Away* [1997] *RPC* 160, 165. 'All this suggests that the sooner the whole procedure of amendment of a patent is rethought and provided for by an amended statute and rules the better. Preferably, so far as European patents are concerned, there should be one, effective and cheap, procedure'. In *Boston Scientific v. Palmaz* (unreported, 20 Mar. 2000), the Court of Appeal held that if the EPO had amended a patent 'after judgment in UK patent litigation, but before an appeal of that judgment is heard, the Court of Appeal must consider the patent as amended' [2000] *EIPR* N–115.

[128] It is proposed that PA s. 75 be changed to allow for amendment during any proceedings where validity *may* be put in issue, namely during any proceedings for infringement, groundless threats, declarations of non-infringement, revocation proceedings, or disputes over Crown use. See *Consultation on the proposed Patents Act (Amendment) Bill: Summary of responses,* paras. 153–155.

[129] R. Krasser, 'Possibilities of Amendment of Patent Claims during the Examination Procedure' (1992) 23 *IIC* 467, 471; Gunzel, *Staking Your Claim: Claiming Options and Disclosure Requirements in European Patent Practice* (1990), 29. A. Bubb, 'Implied Added Subject Matter, A Practitioner's View of History' (1991) *CIPAJ* 444.

[130] PA s. 72(1)(d) and (e), s. 76; EPC 2000 Art. 138(1)(c).

An important factor that limits the owner's ability to amend their application as filed arises from the fact that post-grant amendment is at the discretion of the comptroller and the courts.[131] The onus is on the patentee to establish that the amendment should be allowed.[132] As a result of changes made in 2004, when deciding whether to allow an amendment the courts and the Comptroller are directed to take account of 'any relevant principles applicable' under the EPC 2000.[133]

The courts have tended to use their discretion to deny amendments where the owner has not acted innocently. As Jacob J noted, '[n]o patent office is there for the purpose of enabling people deliberately to impose bogus monopolies on the public'.[134] There are two situations where the discretion has been exercised against the patentee. The first is where a patentee knowingly and deliberately obtained claims that were wider than justified by what was invented.[135] The second situation where discretion has not been exercised is where knowing of the doubtful validity of the patent, a patentee has been slow to take action to amend.[136] In *Raleigh Cycle v. Miller*[137] the House of Lords emphasized that a patentee who suspects a patent is too widely drawn should amend it promptly. If they do not, the discretion to amend will be refused. Lord Normand explained that 'the public interest is injured when invalid claims are persisted in so that inventors are illegitimately warned off an area ostensibly monopolised by the claims'. In this situation, patentees should either litigate or amend. However, if they choose to litigate, they should not be permitted to amend later. It is reasonable for a patentee to delay where they believed on reasonable grounds that the patent was valid.[138]

Another factor that regulates the way patents are amended arises from the fact that the courts may limit the damages that are awarded where an amended patent is infringed. There are two situations where this may occur. If an amended application expands the claims beyond that which was reasonable to expect from the application as it was initially published, the courts may limit the damages that are available to the patentee. The question whether the inference is reasonable is objective. As such, it does not matter what the defendant (subjectively)

---

[131] PA ss. 27(1); 75(1). EPC 2000 Art 105a. The Court of Appeal confirmed the general discretion of the courts to refuse post-grant amendments in the public interest under PA s. 75 in *Kimberly-Clark Worldwide v. Procter & Gamble* [2000] *RPC* 422, 435. In so doing it overturned Laddie J's decision in the Patents Courts in *Kimberly-Clark Worldwide v. Procter & Gamble* [2000] *RPC* 424. (Cf. *Palmaz's European Patent (UK)* [1999] RPC 47, 63–5 which distinguished Laddie J on this point.) For the application of the CA decision see *Oxford Gene Technology v. Affymetrix (No. 2)* [2001] *RPC* 310 (CA). See generally P. Cliffe, 'A Sorry Case of Making Amends' [2002] *EIPR* 277.

[132] *SKF v. Evans Medical* [1989] *FSR* 561, 569; *Chevron Research Company's Patent* [1970] *RPC* 580.

[133] PA s. 75(5).

[134] *Richardson-Vicks Patent* [1995] *RPC* 561. See also *Hallen v. Brabantia* (1990) *FSR* 134, 149; *Kimberly-Clark Worldwide v. Procter & Gamble* [2000] *RPC* 422, 435 (Aldous LJ) (CA).

[135] *ICI (Whyte's) Patent* [1978] *RPC* 11. In *Richardson-Vicks Patent* [1995] *RPC* 561, 568, Jacob J observed that there was little EPO jurisprudence as regards post-grant amendment in opposition proceedings. Nonetheless he assumed that if it was shown that an applicant had deliberately sought to patent an unjustifiably wide claim, the EPO would refuse leave to amend. Beyond this, however, Jacob J predicted that the EPO might allow a patent to be amended. Consequently, Jacob J held that, for purposes of consistency, nothing short of really blameworthy conduct by a patentee should act as bar to amendment in the UK. See also *Kimberly-Clark Worldwide v Procter & Gamble (No. 2)* [2001] *FSR* 339, 342–3.

[136] *SKF v. Evans* [1989] *FSR* 561, 577.   [137] (1950) 67 *RPC* 226.

[138] On some occasions the courts have suggested that delay is more justified where the patentee operates outside the UK. *Bristol Myers Company v. Manon Freres* [1973] *RPC* 836, 857; *Mabuchi Motor KK's Patent* [1996] *RPC* 387 (not blameworthy to delay when involved in worldwide litigation in which the UK was not an important country).

thought.[139] It has been suggested that this rule will apply where a defendant reasonably thought that no claim covering what they do would be supported by the description in the specification. Apart from that, it was seen as unlikely to have wide application.[140] Another factor that regulates the way patents are amended arises from the fact that, where a specification is amended, damages are only awarded prior to the date of the amendment if the court is satisfied that the specification as originally published was framed in good faith and with reasonable skill and knowledge.[141] In practice, it is rare for the courts to find that patents were not framed in these terms.

5.2 ERRORS AND CLERICAL MISTAKES

Instead of amending a patent, a patentee may seek to have the patent altered to correct errors and clerical mistakes.[142] Such corrections take effect retroactively. The ability to correct mistakes does not conflict with the general policy of protecting third parties which forbids amendments that extend the patent beyond the scope of the application as filed. The reason for this is that 'if the mistake was obvious, it cannot have misled'.[143]

If the request to correct a mistake concerns the description, claims, or drawings, the correction must be obvious. A correction will be obvious where it is immediately evident that nothing else would have been intended other than what is offered as the correction.[144] If there are any doubts, a correction cannot be made. A useful example of the limits imposed on a patentee's ability to correct mistakes can be seen in *PPG Industries Patent*.[145] In this case it was said that, faced with the proposition '2 + 2 = 5' a person might readily presume that this was obviously incorrect and that to correct the mistake the '5' should be changed to a '4'. However, as Dillon and Slade LJJ pointed out, since an alternative solution was to change one of the '2's to a '3', in the absence of an indication as to where the mistake lay, the correction was not obvious within the meaning of the Act.

6 REFORM

Another change that may take place in patent procedure relates to the information that applicants have to disclose in their patent application. While these changes are some way off, discussions are taking place at the national, community, and international level about the possibility of requiring inventors who draw upon or utilize genetic resources in the development of their inventions to disclose information in their patent application, such as the fact that they have prior informed consent to use the genetic resources. These discussions have been prompted by Article 15 of the CBD (which recognizes equitable benefit sharing for access providers) and

---

[139] *Unilever v. Chefaro* [1994] RPC 567, 592.

[140] Jacob J's reasoning, which was dependent on the assumption that there could be no revocation for broad unsupported claims, is now doubtful in the light of *Biogen v. Medeva* [1997] RPC 1 (HL).

[141] PA s. 62(3). See *General Tyre & Rubber v. Firestone Tyre & Rubber* [1975] RPC, 270 (CA); *Chiron v. Organon (No. 7)* [1994] FSR 458. PA s. 62(3) does not apply to an account of profits. *Codex Corporation v. Racal Milgo* [1983] RPC 369 (CA).

[142] PA s. 117(1), PA r. 105; EPC 2000 r. 139.

[143] *Holtite v. Jost* [1979] RPC 81, 91 (Lord Diplock). In *Correction Under Rule 88; G3/89* [1993] EPOR 376, it was held by the Enlarged Board of Appeal that, as a matter of construction of the EPC, the correction must not extend protection contrary to EPC 1973 Art. 123(2) (which is the same as EPC 2000 Art 123(2)).

[144] This was the position under PA 1949 s. 31(1): *Holtite v. Jost* [1979] RPC 81.

[145] [1987] RPC 469, 478, 483.

by Article 8(j) of the CBD (which encourages the equitable sharing of benefits arising from the use of indigenous knowledge).[146] The discussions have also been prompted by the growing concern about biopiracy and the general misuse of genetic resources in the biodiscovery process. The idea that applicants should be required to disclose information about their invention builds upon the idea that patent law has the potential to modify behaviour to promote good corporate and scientific conduct.[147] The fact that an organization might not be able to patent products derived from genetic resources, if they do not have the informed consent of the access provider in advance, will act as a powerful incentive for such organizations to ensure that they have the necessary prior consent. As we mentioned earlier, debates are at present taking place at the international level over whether or not prior informed consent should be incorporated into patent law, and if so, how.[148] Discussions are also taking place within Europe as to the best way in which the goals of the CBD might be achieved.[149] The issue of prior informed consent has already been recognized in Europe in the Biotechnology Directive, albeit only in the non-binding Recitals. In particular, Recital 27 encourages patent applications to include information on the geographical origin of biological material. In turn, Recital 55 requires member states to recognize Article 8(j) of the CBD when developing laws and regulations. To date these have had minimal impact on member states.[150] More recently, the Commission has suggested that there should be a debate over the unilateral development under EC law of 'a self-standing obligation for patent applicants to disclose the origin of genetic resources'.[151] This builds upon existing requirements that encourage disclosure of information, namely enabling disclosure, disclosure of relevant prior art for novelty examination, and the disclosure of the inventors.[152] The proposal by the Commission is fairly modest. Prior informed consent will not be treated as an additional or formal requirement for patentability. Rather, the Commission has suggested that failure to comply with the requirement for prior informed consent would carry consequences outside patent law. For example, it might prompt civil law claims for compensation or administrative sanctions (such as a fee for refusal to submit relevant information). The Commission is also looking at introducing a similar requirement for plant variety rights.[153]

As well as the above, the Commission has opened up discussions as to the position that it should adopt in international multilateral treaty negotiations about prior informed consent.[154] In this context, the Commission has said that it should be prepared to discuss prior informed consent as a formal condition for patentability, and not merely as a self-standing obligation. Here the options include the non-processing of patent applications until all the relevant information has been provided, and the invalidation and revocation of patents if the

---

[146] See also the *Bonn Guidelines on access and benefit sharing*, adopted at the Sixth Conference of the Parties to the CBD, (The Hague, 2002). These are voluntary provisions that act as a guide to the implementation of CBD Art. 1, 8 (j), 10(c), 15, 16, and 19.

[147] See B. Sherman, 'Regulating access and use of genetic resources: intellectual property law and biodiscovery' (2003) *EIPR* 301.

[148] Particularly at the CBD, the TRIPS Council, and at WIPO. See above at pp. 355–6.

[149] See also 'EC Thematic Report on Access and Benefit-Sharing', submitted to CBD Secretariat in Oct. 2002, available at <http://biodiversity-chm.eea.eu.int/>.

[150] A notable exception being Denmark. See G. van Overwalle, 'Belgium goes its own way on Biodiversity and Patents' [2002] *EIPR 233*.

[151] *The Implementation by the EC of the 'Bonn Guidelines' on access to genetic resources and benefit-sharing under the Convention on Biological Diversity* (19 Dec. 2003) COM (2003),18.

[152] Ibid, 17. The proposal also builds on a Concept Paper submitted by the EC to the TRIPS Council in Oct. 2003 on the relationship between TRIPS and the CBD.

[153] Ibid, 18.   [154] Ibid, 19.

applicant fraudulently disclosed incorrect information. As a way of assisting applicants, the Commission has suggested the use of certificates of origin. As we saw earlier, this issue has been taken up as part of the on-going reform of TRIPS. However, like many other recent proposed changes, it is unlikely that these proposals will ever be implemented.

While there are many questions that remain unanswered, there is a chance that prior informed consent might go some way to providing indigenous groups, as well as mega-biodiverse countries, with an equitable share of the benefits that flow from the use of their resources. Ironically, by encouraging the situation in which access providers will be entitled to a percentage of the patent royalties that flow from products developed from genetic resources, this adds to the problem of 'royalty stacking' that is causing so many problems in the life sciences. Unrealistic expectations about the value of the genetic resources have served to exacerbate this problem.

Another area where reform might be considered is examination. Here there are two issues that are currently attracting interest. The first relates to the rigour with which examinations are conducted. Some argue that, given the fact that the number of patent applications vastly exceeds the number of commercially significant inventions, it is a huge waste of resources to examine every application in detail. The most efficient approach, it is said, is to perform a cursory examination of all applications, and to review seriously the validity of any grant that has commercial significance.[155] As the validity of any commercially valuable patent will be subjected to a thorough review in any litigation, we should not bother to waste resources on pre-grant examination of patents. On the other hand, some argue that examination is important to protect the public, in particular small traders, from threats of patent litigation by well-resourced claimants on the basis of granted patents of dubious validity. Essentially, the argument is that even invalid patents can be used to chill activity of legitimate traders, or extort settlements from risk-averse or poorly financed potential defendants. A related problem is said to be the activity of 'patent trolls', that is commercial organisations that acquire patents specifically with a view to bringing actions in the hope of making money by forcing settlements.[156] Although the causes and effects of patent trolling are controversial, some argue that the impact has been made much worse by the practices of some Patent Offices in granting patents which rigorous examination would have shown related to subjects which lacked novelty or were obvious.

The second issue related to examination arises from increasing backlogs in the processing of applications. Filings at the EPO, for example, have quadrupled in the last 25 years to over 208,000 in 2006, leaving substantial backlogs. One possible solution that has been mooted is to farm out examinations to other countries, such as India or Korea, where they can be processed more cheaply and quickly. Another possible solution would be for the EPO examiners to rely on the decisions of other Offices. So, for example, a patent that passed examination at the US Office might be regarded as automatically registrable in Europe. The problem with such a proposal for 'mutual recognition' is that not all Offices apply the same standards. Substantive patent harmonization may need to be effected first.

---

[155] M. Lemley, 'Rational Ignorance at the Patent Office' (2001) 95 *Northwestern ULR* 1495; A. Jaffe & J. Lerner, *Innovation and its Discontents* (Princeton: Princeton University Press, 2007), ch. 7.

[156] For a discussion of the use of remedies to deal with the behaviour of trolls see M. Lemley & C. Shapiro, 'Patent Holdup and Royalty stacking', 85 *Texas Law Rev* 1991 (2007); John Golden, ' "Patent Trolls" and Patent Remedies' (2007) 85 *Texas Law Rev* 2111.

17

PATENTABLE SUBJECT MATTER

CHAPTER CONTENTS

1 INTRODUCTION

In the previous two chapters, we looked at the nature of a patent and the processes by which patents are granted. In this and the following three chapters we look at the factors that an invention must comply with to be patentable. These are that the invention:

(i)   consists of subject matter that is patentable (this chapter),

(ii) is new (Chapter 18),

(iii) involves an inventive step (Chapter 19), and

(iv) complies with the internal requirements of patentability (Chapter 20).

If an application fails to comply with any of these criteria, a patent will not be granted. If a patent has already been granted, non-compliance may mean that the patent is revoked. With these general points in mind, we now turn to look at the subject matter that is capable of being patented.

2 PATENTABLE SUBJECT MATTER

The task of having to decide the types of subject matter that ought to be patentable invariably generates conflict and uncertainty. This is because patent law inevitably finds itself dealing with technologies that it may not yet understand. It is also because the task of having to decide whether to grant property rights in a particular type of invention raises a complex mix of legal, cultural, political, and social questions. Over time a range of different factors has restricted the subject matter protected by patents. Perhaps the most important is the image of the invention as something concrete and physical which results from human intervention in nature.[1] A range of other more explicit policy factors has also limited the type of subject matter that is protected by patents.

The subject matter that is potentially patentable under the Patents Act 1977 and the EPC 2000 is regulated in five ways.

The first limitation is that to be patentable an invention must be capable of 'industrial application': section 1(1)(c), section 4/Article 52(1). While this is probably the least important of the five requirements, it has been important in relation to inventions involving naturally occurring substances.

The second restriction on patentable subject matter is found in section 4A(1) and Article 53. These provide that a patent shall not be granted for methods of medical and veterinary treatment.[2]

The third restriction on the subject matter protected by patents is set out in section 1(2) and Article 52(2)(3). In essence these provide a non-exhaustive list of things which are not regarded as inventions. If the subject matter of an application falls within the scope of these provisions, it will not be patentable.

The fourth general restriction on the subject matter excluded from patent protection is in paragraph 3(f) of Schedule A2 to the 1977 Act[3] and Article 53(b). These provide that a patent shall not be granted for 'any variety of animal or plant or any essentially biological process for the production of animals or plants, not being a microbiological process or the product of such a process'.

The fifth factor which restricts the subject matter protected by patent law is that patents are not granted for immoral inventions or inventions which are contrary to public policy: section 1(3)[4]/Article 53(a). While rarely used in the past, this exclusion has taken on a new significance in light of developments in biotechnology. A number of specific exclusions relating to immoral biological inventions are also contained in paragraph 3(a)–(d) of Schedule A2 to the 1977 Act and Rule 28 EPC 2000 (formerly Rule 23d EPC 1973).

We will look at each of these in turn.

3   INDUSTRIAL APPLICATION

In order for an invention to be patentable it must be capable of 'industrial application'.[5] This reflects the long-held view that patent protection should not be available for purely abstract or intellectual creations. The need to show industrial applicability also reflects the image of the patentable invention as having a concrete and technical character.[6]

---

[1] Sherman and Bently, 46, 150–7.

[2] Previously, methods of medical and veterinary treatment were excluded on the basis that they were not industrially applicable.

[3] This provision, which replaced PA s. 1(3)(b) (as enacted), was introduced by the Patents Regulations 2000 (SI 2000/2037) (in force 28 Jul. 2000).

[4] This provision, which replaced PA s. 1(3)(a) (as enacted), was introduced by the Patents Regulations 2000.

[5] PA s. 1(1)(c); EPC 2000 Art. 52(1).

[6] EPC 2000, Art. 52(1) provides that European patents 'shall be granted for any inventions *in all fields of technology,* provided that they are new, involve an inventive step and are susceptible of industrial application'.

An invention is capable of industrial application if it can be used or made in 'any kind of industry'.[7] Industry is construed in its widest sense, including activities whether or not for profit,[8] and expressly extends to include agriculture.[9] As such, the requirement that an invention be made or used in industry presents few problems. In a controversial decision, however, it was held that a private and personal activity (the application of a contraceptive composition to the cervix) was not industrial in character and thus not patentable.[10]

As well as being used or made in any kind of industry, for an invention to be industrially applicable, it is also necessary to show that it has a 'useful purpose'.[11] As the Patents Act 1977 and the EPC 2000 provide that inventions only need to be *susceptible* or *capable* of industrial application, this implies that there is no need to show actual use: it is enough to show that the invention has the *potential* to be used or made in industry. Where a product has been used (or put on the market), the commercial success of the product is not relevant when deciding industrial applicability.[12]

The requirement that inventions need to exhibit a useful purpose is particularly important in relation to biological research. The reason for this is that although researchers have been successful in locating and identifying new gene structures, so far they have been much less successful in ascertaining what many of these genes do.[13] While researchers have been able to identify the genes that make up the human genome, the role that many of these genes play remains unknown. Unless a useful purpose can be found for these genes, they will not be industrially applicable and, as such, not patentable.[14] This position is reinforced by the Biotechnology Directive insofar as it attempts to clarify the industrial applicability requirement in relation to biological inventions.[15] As the Recitals to the Directive explain, a mere

---

See Art. 1, item 17 of the Act Revising the Convention on the Grant of European Patents (EPC) (Munich) (29 Nov. 2000) MR/3/00 Rev. 1e; Base Proposal for the Revision of the European Patent Convention, CA/100/00 e (2000), 38. PA s. 1 was to be amended to reflect Art. 52(1) EPC 2000. *Consultation on the proposed Patents Act (Amendment) Bill: Summary of responses and the Government's conclusions* (13 Nov. 2003), para. 17. Despite earlier plans, this was not adopted in the Patents Act 2004.

[7] PA s. 4(1); EPC Art. 57. But not when the invention contravenes well-established natural laws: *Duckett v. Patent Office* [2005] *EWHC* 3140 (application for machine that contravened the principle of conservation of energy was rejected); *Thompson v. Comptroller General of Patents, Designs and Trade Marks* [2005] *EWHC* 3065 (invention which purported to contravene Newton's third law of motion was rejected); *Ward v. Comptroller-General* (unreported) (19 May 2000) (CA) (application for perpetual motion machine was rejected).

[8] *Chiron v. Murex (No. 12)* [1996] *RPC* 535, 607 (Morritt LJ).   [9] PA s. 4(1); EPC Art. 57.

[10] *British Technology Group/Contraceptive method,* T74/93 [1995] *EPOR* 279, 284. For criticisms of the decision see J. Pagenberg, 'Comment' (1996) 27 *IIC* 104.

[11] *Chiron v. Murex (No. 12)* [1996] *RPC* 535, 607 (Morritt LJ).

[12] *Harvard/Onco-mouse* [2003] *OJ EPO* 473, 494 (Opposition Division). (The fact that the transgenic mice were commercially unsuccessful was not relevant: all that mattered in this context was that they were on the market.)

[13] This problem has been exacerbated by the success of the human (and other) genome projects which attempt to identify the thousands of genes that comprise the genetic blueprint of biological entities. On which see T. Wilkie, *Perilous Knowledge* (1993); BMA, *Our Genetic Future: the Science and Ethics of Genetic Technology* (1992); P. Gannon, T. Guthrie, and G. Laurie, 'Patents, Morality and DNA: Should there be Intellectual Property Protection of the Human Genome Project' (1995) 1 *Medical Law International* 321; J. Straus, 'Patenting Human Genes in Europe: Past Developments and Prospects for the Future' (1995) 26 *IIC* 920.

[14] On the proposal for a probationary or interim patent pending discovery of the function of a gene sequence see M. Llewellyn, 'Industrial Applicability/Utility and Genetic Engineering: Current Practices in Europe and the United States' [1994] *EIPR* 473, 480.

[15] In *Icos Corporation/Seven transmembrane receptor* [2002] *OJ EPO* 293, 304 (para. 9), the Opposition Division said that the Recitals to the Biotech Dir. were relevant as supplementary rules of interpretation when examining European patent applications.

DNA sequence without any indication of function does not contain any technical information and is therefore not a patentable invention.[16] In relation to gene sequencing, the Biotechnology Directive and the Patents Act (as amended) specify that the industrial application of a sequenced or a partial sequence of a gene must be disclosed in the application.[17] Where a full or partial sequence of a gene is used to produce a protein or part of a protein, the subject matter will only satisfy the requirement of industrial applicability if the application specifies which protein is produced or the function that it performs.[18] For example it would be necessary to show a biological function (which would imply a therapeutic use), or that the sequence could be used as a genetic marker (which would imply a diagnostic use). The Opposition Division at the EPO applied this reasoning in *Icos Corporation* to deny patent protection for a purified and isolated polynucleotide encoding for the amino acid sequence of the V28 protein.[19] The specification in question listed a number of predicted uses for the claimed protein (in relation to 'immunological and inflammatory events'). The problem for the applicant, however, was that these uses were based on the *predicted* function of the protein as a receptor.[20] Importantly, the applicants were unable to show that the receptor was actually involved in any specific immunological and/or inflammatory events. The Opposition Division said that it was not enough for the application to disclose uses that were merely speculative.[21] Echoing (but not citing) the USPTO Guidelines,[22] the Opposition Division added that 'DNA sequences with indications of function which are not substantial, specific, and credible shall not be patentable inventions according to Article 52(1) EPC'.[23] On this basis, the Opposition Division said that the application lacked industrial applicability and, as such, was not patentable.

While critics who argue that gene patents are having a chilling impact on research will welcome this decision, others may find that it does not go far enough. In particular, it is now being suggested that the problem with patents over genes is that, while a patentee only has to disclose one specific use to show industrial applicability, once this threshold is satisfied they are given control over *all* uses of the patented gene: even those uses which they had not discovered or even imagined. The problem here is that there is a lack of symmetry between what is disclosed and what is protected. This has led some to argue that protection should be limited to what is

---

[16] Biotech. Dir., Recital 23.

[17] Ibid, Art. 5(3), Recital 22. PA s. 76A, and Sched. A2, para. 6, See also Administrative Council of the EPO 16 June 1999 amending the Implementing Regulations of the EPC, EPC Rule 23e(3) (1999) 7 *OJ EPO* 437 (which introduced the Biotech. Directive, Art. 5(3) into the EPC).

[18] S. Bostyn, 'The Patentability of Genetic Information Carriers' [1999] *IPQ* 1, 7–8; Straus, 'Patenting Human Genes in Europe', 934–5; O. Gandy, 'The EC Biotechnology Patent Directive: A More Ethical European Patent System?' (1998) 12 *World Intellectual Property Reports* 239. Biotech. Dir., Recital 24. See *Chiron v. Murex (No. 12)* [1996] FSR 153, 177 (claim to polypeptides invalid because the claim covered 'an almost infinite number of polypeptides which are useless for any known purpose').

[19] The UK Patent Office said that it will follow *Icos Corporation/Seven transmembrane receptor*, note 15 above. UK Patent Office, *Biotechnology Examination Guidelines* (Sept. 2002), para. 33–35.

[20] This was because the specification did not disclose any antibody substances which specially recognize V28 protein.

[21] This was based on Recital 23 of the Biotech. Dir. (which provides that 'a mere DNA sequence without indication of a function does not contain any technical information and is therefore not a patentable invention').

[22] The USPTO issued guidelines on the interpretation of the utility requirement under US patent law on 5 Jan. 2001. These state that for an invention to have requisite utility (which is similar to industrial application), there must be a 'specific, substantial and credible' use. The Guidelines are available at <http://www.uspto.gov/web/menu/utility.pdf>.

[23] *Icos Corporation/Seven transmembrane receptor* [2002] *OJ EPO* 293, 307 (para. 11(ii)).

actually disclosed in the application.[24] Despite its importance, this issue has not yet been given the attention that it clearly requires.

4 METHODS OF MEDICAL AND VETERINARY TREATMENT

The second category of subject matter excluded from patentability is inventions for methods of medical and veterinary treatment.[25] Such inventions are excluded to ensure that people who carry out medical or veterinary treatments are not inhibited by patents.[26] As the Enlarged Board noted, this helps to achieve the socio-ethical and public health goal that '[m]edical and veterinary practitioners should be free to take the actions they consider suited to diagnose illness by means of investigative methods'.[27] Prior to the EPC 2000, methods of medical and veterinary treatment were excluded on the basis that they were not capable of industrial application.[28] Under the EPC 2000, however, methods of treatment and diagnosis are now directly excluded from patentability under Article 53(c) EPC 2000 rather than on the basis that they were not capable of industrial application, as was the case previously. Article 53(c) EPC 2000 provides that 'a patent shall not be granted for methods of treatment of the human or animal body by surgery or therapy, and diagnostic methods practiced on the human or animal body'.[29] Similar changes were made in the UK to bring the Patents Act 1977 into line with EPC 2000: the exclusion now being found in section 4A of the Act.[30] On the basis that the changes brought about by EPC 2000 in this area were primarily editorial in nature, the Enlarged Board of Appeal has said that the 'actual legal position remains unchanged'.[31] Given this, the case law previously decided under EPC 1973 is still applicable.

4.1 METHODS

It is important to note that the exclusion is confined to *methods* of medical and veterinary treatment.[32] As such, it does not prevent the patenting of surgical, therapeutic, or diagnostic substances and compositions (such as drugs), or apparatuses or products (such as ECG machines, prosthetic ball and socket joints, or pacemakers).[33]

---

[24] See above at pp. 366–7.

[25] See generally, D. Thums, 'Patent Protection for Medical Treatment: A Distinction between Patent and Medical Law' (1996) 27 *IIC* 423; G. Burch, 'Ethical Considerations in the Patenting of Medical Processes' (1987) 65 *Texas Law Review* 1139 (under US law, methods of medical treatment are patentable).

[26] *Wellcome/Pigs I*, T116/85 [1989] *EPOR* 1; [1989] *OJ EPO* 13; *Telectronics/Pacer*, T82/93 [1996] EPOR 409; *See-Shell/Blood flow*, T182/90 [1994] EPOR 320. A technique that results in death of the animal does not fall within the exception.

[27] *Diagnostic methods* G 01/04 (2006) *OJ EPO* 334, 348 (EBA).

[28] PA s. 4(2)/EPC 1973 Art. 52(4) (both provisions have been repealed). TRIPS Art. 27(3) allows members to exclude from patentability diagnostic, therapeutic, and surgical methods for the treatment of humans or animals.

[29] While Art 53 EPC 2000 and PA s 4A are drafted (slightly) differently, it is unlikely that this will have any significant consequences.

[30] Patents Act 2004, cl. 1 (inserting a new s. 4A into the Patents Act 1977). See also *Consultation on the proposed Patent's Act (Amendment) Bill: Summary of responses*, paras. 19, 20. Minor changes were also made to bring the language in the 1977 Act closer to that used in EPC 2000.

[31] *Diagnostic methods*, G01/04 (2006) *OJ EPO* 334, 360 (EBA).   [32] PA s. 4A; EPC 2000 Art. 53(c).

[33] T712/93 [1998] *OJ EPO* (special edn.) 12; *Visx v. Nidek* [1999] *FSR* 405, 465.

4.2 SURGERY, THERAPY, OR DIAGNOSIS

For an invention to be caught by section 4A/Article 53(c), it must consist of a method of *surgery, therapy,* or *diagnosis*. In the past, when deciding whether an invention is for method of surgery, therapy, or diagnosis the tribunals have occasionally focused on the skill and knowledge that is needed for a person to use the method in question. Thus, if an activity needs to be carried out by or under the supervision of a doctor or a vet,[34] exercising medical or veterinary skills,[35] it was more likely to fall within the exclusion.[36] If the invention could be used by someone such as an engineer[37] or a farmer,[38] it was more likely to fall outside the scope of the exclusion. After the Enlarged Board of Appeal decision in *Diagnostic methods,*[39] this approach is no longer relevant. The reason for this is that the Board said that the decision as to whether an invention falls within the exclusion is not dependent on who carries out the method in question: 'whether or not a method is a diagnostic method within the meaning of [EPC 1973 Article 52(4); EPC 2000 Art 53(c)] should neither depend on the participation of a medical or veterinary practitioner, by being present or by bearing the responsibility, nor on the fact that all method steps can also, or only, be practiced by medicinal or non-medicinal support staff, the patient himself or herself or an automated system'.[40] (While these comments were made in relation to diagnostic methods, it is likely that the reasoning would also be applied to surgery and therapy.) This means that, while the skill and knowledge needed to perform an invention may provide a useful indication as to whether it is excluded, this is not definitive.[41] Instead, it is necessary to look at whether the invention in question falls with the definition of surgery, therapy, or diagnosis.[42]

(i) Surgery. 'Surgery' has been defined as the branch 'of medicine concerned with the healing of disease, accidental injury or bodily defects by operating on the living body'. It is said to include both 'conservative (non-invasive) procedures such as repositioning and the far more numerous operative (invasive) procedures using instruments'.[43] In recent years it has become clear that there are two inconsistent approaches to the way that surgery is defined.[44] While one line of decisions focused on the nature of the physical intervention itself, a second line of decisions concentrated on the *purpose* of the intervention. Under the first and older approach, the tribunals have looked at the nature of the intervention and whether this could be classified as 'surgery'. This approach is endorsed by the *EPO Guidelines* which state that surgery is defined by 'the nature of the treatment rather than the purpose'.[45] It has also been

---

[34] *Thompson/Cornea,* T24/91 [1995] *OJ EPO* 512.

[35] *Ultrafem/Feminine hygiene device,* T1165/97 (15 Feb. 2000), para. 4.3 (a device used to collect vaginal discharge was not a method of medical treatment, even though it was inserted and removed by a medically trained person or doctor. The problem was that there were no 'particular medical skills needed to position and remove the collector').

[36] Cf. *Cygnus/Device and method for sampling substances,* T964/99 [2002] *OJ EPO* 4, 17 ('it is immaterial that the claimed methods (for determining blood sugar levels) could be performed by a patient himself'. The invention was excluded under EPC Art. 52(4)).

[37] *Siemens/Flow measurement,* T2245/87 [1989] *OJ EPO* 171.

[38] *Wellcome/Pigs I,* T116/85 [1988] *EPOR* 1; [1998] *OJ EPO* 13.

[39] G01/04 [2006] *OJ EPO* 334 (EBA).   [40] Ibid, 355.

[41] *Baxter/Blood extraction method,* T329/94 [1998] *EPOR* 363, 366–7.

[42] Ibid, 367–8 (an invention of performing a method with the *technical* aim of facilitating blood flow towards a blood extraction point, was held to have no therapeutic purpose or effect and was thus not excluded).

[43] See-*Shell/Blood flow,* T182/90 [1994] *EPOR* 320, 323.

[44] The TBA recognized other approaches, including the risk of the activity, may be applied: *Medi-Physics/ Treatment by surgery,* T992/03 (2007) *OJ EPO* 557, 570.

[45] C–IV, 4.8.

applied in a series of decisions by the Technical Board of Appeal at the EPO.[46] It is also the approach that has been adopted in the UK.

In a second series of decisions, the EPO has moved beyond the nature of the intervention itself to focus on the *purpose* of the invention in question. In particular, this second line of decisions has focused on whether the physical intervention 'is suitable for maintaining or restoring health, the physical integrity of the physical well being of a person or animal'. The Enlarged Board of Appeal seemed to support this approach when it said (in obiter) that surgery 'includes any physical intervention on the human or animal body in which maintaining the life and health of the subject is of paramount importance'.[47] By emphasizing the purpose of the intervention rather than its nature, a distinction has been drawn between two different types of physical intervention in the body. The first, which falls within the definition of surgery, comprises those curative practices which aim to maintain or promote health. The second type of physical intervention, which does not qualify as surgery for the purposes of Article 53(c) EPC 2000, comprises interventions carried out for non-curative purposes. On the basis that surgery is limited to processes that give 'priority to maintaining life or health of the human or animal body on which they are performed', it does not include processes the end result of which is the death of living beings under treatment, either deliberately or incidentally.[48] In a similar vein, in the *General Hospital* decision, the Technical Board of Appeal said that surgical treatment aims at protecting curative activities. This means that the exception applies to activities aimed at maintaining and restoring the health, physical integrity, and physical well-being of a person (and also preventing diseases).[49] On this basis, it was held that surgical treatments[50] which were 'neither clearly suitable nor potentially suitable for maintaining or restoring the health, the physical integrity, or the physical well being of human beings or animals' did not fall with the exclusion in Article 52(4) EPC 1973 (Article 53(c) EPC 2000).[51] From this perspective, the Board concluded that an application that related to 'methods for hair-removal using optical radiation' (effectively applying optical radiation to a selected wavelength to damage the hairs and follicles without causing significant damage to the skin) was *not* excluded from patentability. While the invention involved 'a non-intentional physical intervention which [was] to be regarded as a surgical operation', it was not 'potentially suitable for maintaining or restoring the health, physical integrity, or physical well-being of a person or animal'. The purpose of the application was to improve the aesthetic appearance of the person treated rather than to cure the underlying malady. As such the Board held that the application did not fall within the remit of Article 53(c). Applying a similar logic, the Board also said that tattooing and piercing, whose only possible object was to beautify the human or animal body, would not fall foul of Art 53(c). This was not the case, however, in relation to breast enlargement or nose reconstructions, which could be used to restore the physical integrity of the body following, for example,

---

[46] See-Shell/Blood flow, T182/90 [1994] EPOR 320; Georgetown University/Pericardial access, T35/99 (2000) OJ EPO 447; Baxter/Blood extraction method, T329/94 [1998] EPOR 363 (focused on the use of surgical instruments).

[47] Diagnostic methods, G01/04 (2006) OJ EPO 334, 352 (EBA).

[48] Georgetown University/Pericardial access, T35/99 [2000] OJ EPO 447, 451.

[49] General Hospital Corp/Hair removal method, T383/03 (2005) OJ EPO 159, 165. (the same applies to activities performed on animals).

[50] The board also stressed that 'surgery' and 'treatment' could not be considered as two distinct requirements for the exclusion Ibid, 163. It did not matter if the medical profession referred to these activities as 'treatment by surgery'. Instead, what was important was whether the activity fell within the language and spirit of the exclusion.

[51] Ibid, 166.

breast cancer or a car accident.[52] The key difference is that the latter methods *are* potentially suitable for maintaining or restoring the health, physical integrity, or physical well-being of a person. This was in contrast to methods whose only application is for aesthetic purposes, which could not be used for medical reasons, and thus would be excluded under Article 53(c).

As the *UK Intellectual Property Office Guidelines* for medical inventions note, the second approach (as outlined in the *General Hospital* decision) is out of step with British practice. Following the 1983 UK decision in *Unilever (Davis' Application)*, which held that claims for a method of surgery should be refused regardless of their purpose, the UK Intellectual Property Office has decided not to follow the EPO in this regard.[53]

The nature of the conflict between the two lines of decisions at the EPO was recognized by the Technical Board of Appeal in *Medi-Physics,* where the question of the proper approach to be followed was referred to the Enlarged Board for consideration.[54] In so doing, the Technical Board raised the familiar complaint of purpose-bound tests, namely that the same physical activity may be used for different purposes.[55] Thus the injection of a medicament (such as Botox) for treating a disease would be excluded, whereas the injection of the same medicament for the purpose of reducing wrinkles would not (on the basis that it would be carried out for cosmetic rather than curative reasons). In this context, the operation of the exclusion will depend on the motive of the person administering the drug: which runs counter to the Enlarged Board's decision that it was important to focus on the nature of the activity itself, rather than on the type of person who delivers the activity and what their motive might have been.

(ii) Therapy. 'Therapy' has been interpreted broadly as the curing of a disease or malfunction of the human or animal body[56] and includes *prophylactic* treatments with a view to maintaining health by preventing ill effects that would otherwise arise.[57] It has also been held to include *curative* treatments that aim to cure diseases or bodily malfunctions that have already arisen.[58] On the basis that pregnancy and lice infestation are not diseases, inventions for methods of treatment that prevented pregnancies[59] or removed lice were not caught by the exclusion.[60] However, a method of immunizing against coccidiosis,[61] and another for controlling mange in pigs, were held to relate to diseases and, as such, were excluded as methods of treatment by therapy.[62] The exclusion of therapeutic methods applies irrespective of whether the disease or bodily malfunction that the invention seeks to prevent or cure is internal or

---

[52] Ibid, 167.

[53] UK Intellectual Property Office, *Examination Guidelines for Patent Applications relating to Medical Inventions in the UK Intellectual Property Office* (June 2007), 17 para 46. The Guidelines said that the type of activities in the *General Hospital* decision would 'not generally be considered to be surgical in nature under UK Intellectual Property Office practice'. Ibid.

[54] See 'Communication for the Enlarged Board of Appeal concerning case G/107' (2007) *OJ EPO* 360.

[55] To be considered in G 1/07. The Board also asked whether the exclusion could be avoided by omitting or disclaiming the step in question.

[56] *Diagnostic methods*, note 27 above, 352 (EBA).

[57] *Duphar/Pigs II*, T19/86 [1988] *EPOR* 241, [1989] *OJ EPO* 24.

[58] *Duphar/Pigs II*, ibid; *Unilever's (Davis) Application* [1983] *RPC* 219; *Salimen/Pigs III*, T58/87 [1989] *EPOR* 125; *Thompson/Cornea*, T24/91 (1996) 27 *IIC* 530; *Eisai/Second medical indication*, G5/83 [1979–85] B *EPOR* 241.

[59] *Schering's Application* [1971] *RPC* 337; *BTG/Contraceptive Method*, note 10 above. But a method of contraception which includes a therapeutic method will be unpatentable even where that therapy is only present to counteract the side-effects of the contraceptive method: *General Hospital/Contraceptive Methods*, T820/92 [1995] *EPOR* 446.

[60] *Salimen/Pigs III*, T58/87 [1989] *EPOR* 125.   [61] *Unilever's (Davis) Application* [1983] *RPC* 219.

[62] *Wellcome/Pigs I*, T116/85 [1988] *EPOR* 1; [1989] *OJ EPO* 13. Fatigue is not a disease: T469/94 (1998) *OJ EPO* 12.

external, and whether or not it is a temporary or a permanent infliction.[63] It also applies irrespective of the origin of the pain, discomfort, or incapacity that the therapy seeks to remedy.[64] Therapeutic methods (which are seen as being carried out for noble purposes) are often contrasted with cosmetic methods (which are carried out for less important reasons). As such, a method that leads to weight loss for the purpose of curing or preventing obesity would fall within the exclusion;[65] in contrast, a method for weight loss that is undertaken for cosmetic purposes would not and, as such, might be patentable.[66]

(iii) Diagnostic Methods. After some uncertainty, the nature and scope of the exclusion of diagnostic methods has been clarified by the decision of the Enlarged Board of Appeal in *Diagnostic methods.*[67] In this decision, the Enlarged Board said that methods of diagnosis typically consist of four subsidiary steps.[68] These are:

(1) *Examination:* involving the collection of data (recording the case history),

(2) *Comparison:* comparing this data with normal values,

(3) *Identification:* identifying any significant deviation from the norm (i.e. symptom), and

(4) *Diagnosis:* the 'deductive medical or veterinary decision phase' where the diagnosis for curative purposes is made (which represents a purely intellectual or non-technical exercise).

One of the questions that the Enlarged Board was asked to consider was whether to fall within the exclusion, an application only needed to include the fourth 'deductive stage' (narrow interpretation), or whether it had to include all four stages (broad interpretation). Drawing on a range of factors, the Enlarged Board adopted the narrow interpretation and said that to fall within the exclusion, *all* four steps needed to be present in an invention. (In so doing the Enlarged Board overturned the Technical Board's decision of *Cygnus*[69] and reinstated the earlier decision of *Bruker/Non-invasive measurement*[70]). The Board also said that no distinction should be drawn between essential method steps that have a diagnostic character and non-essential steps that do not.[71]

A general distinction is now drawn between the act of making a diagnosis (which involves using examination and data to reach a decision) and methods of data acquisition or data

---

[63] *Wellcome/Pigs I,* T116/85 [1988] *EPOR* 1.

[64] *Rorer/Dysmenorrhea,* T81/84 [1988] *EPOR* 297; [1988] *OJ EPO* 207.

[65] A method of treating plaque, since it inevitably had a beneficial effect, was held not patentable: *ICI/Cleaning plaque,* T290/86 [1991] *EPOR* 157.

[66] A cosmetic method is patentable unless it inevitably has a therapeutic effect. It was therefore possible to patent a method of dieting involving suppression of appetite, since the effect would not necessarily have been positive: *Du Pont/Appetite suppressant,* T144/83 [1987] *EPOR* 6; [1986] *OJ EPO* 301.

[67] *Diagnostic methods,* G01/04 [2006] *OJ EPO* 334, 352 (EBA).

[68] As the EBA noted, these four steps overlap. The main point is that a diagnostic method is a multi-step process.

[69] *Cygnus/Sampling substances,* T964/99 [2002] *OJ EPO* 4, 13. The invention, which monitored sugar levels from the skin thus avoiding the need for the pricking of fingers to collect blood, did not involve all the steps in medical diagnosis (it only provided information used to make a diagnosis). The Board rejected *Bruker* (see below) and held that the patent was a method of medical diagnosis and as such was excluded from patentability. Drawing upon the French text of the EPC, the Board in *Cygnus* said that the EPC 'does not favour an interpretation limiting the exception to patentability encompassing all steps required for reaching a medical diagnosis'. Ibid, 15. Instead the Board said that 'any medical activity concerning the gathering of information in the course of establishing a diagnosis qualifies as a diagnostic method'.

[70] *Bruker/Non-invasive measurement* T385/86 [1988] *EPOR* 357, para. 3.2–3.4 (for an invention to be classified as a non-patentable diagnostic method, *all* of the different steps had to present).

[71] *Diagnostic methods,* G01/04 [2006] *OJ EPO* 334, 356 (EBA).

processing (the results of which may subsequently be used in diagnosis). If an invention only provides interim or preliminary results (data or information), the invention will not be excluded from patent protection by Article 53(c).[72] Put differently, the exclusion will only apply where an invention makes it immediately possible to decide on a particular course of medical treatment. As a result, a method of taking a sample or determining internal temperature or pH would not in itself identify a condition and as such would not be classified as a diagnostic method. This means that many diagnostic methods will no longer be caught by the exclusion despite the express language of the EPC 2000 and the 1977 Act. It also means that common diagnostic procedures practised on the human body, such as percussion or palpitation, could, in principle, be patented because they do not constitute a complete diagnosis. The reasoning of the Enlarged Board has been applied in a subsequent decision which concerned methods for magnetic resonance imaging. On the basis that the invention only led to the acquisition of data, it was held that the invention was not a diagnostic method as defined in Article 52(4) EPC 1973 [now Article 53(c) EPC 2000].[73]

The approach adopted by the Enlarged Board in *Diagnostic methods* has been followed by the UK Intellectual Property Office. Given the willingness of judges in the UK to change British law to ensure that it mirrors the jurisprudence at the EPO, it is unlikely that British courts will deviate from the approach outlined in *Diagnostic methods*. By reading down the scope of the exclusion, it seems that the Enlarged Board may reopen concerns about the negative impact that patent law has upon health care and delivery (exemplified most famously by the patents granted to Myriad over both the genes that highlight the propensity to breast cancer and the diagnostic tests that use such genes). The Board has also raised interesting questions about the changing role of technology in the delivery of medical and veterinary care, and whether this should change the way we think about the role that patents play in these fields.

4.3 TREATMENT ON OR IN THE BODY

The third point to note is that the exclusion of methods of medical or veterinary treatment only applies to methods of treatment that are practised *on*[74] or *in*[75] the human or animal body. The ambit of this provision has been interpreted broadly to include 'any interaction with the human or animal body, necessitating the presence of the later'.[76] It has also been suggested that there is no need to show a specific type of interaction with the body. This means that the steps can either be invasive processes (which require physical contact with the body), or non-invasive ones that are practiced at 'a certain distance to it'.[77] The key factor is that the step requires interaction with the body. This means that exclusion does not apply to methods practised on substances that are removed from the body.[78] Thus, neither the treatment of blood for storage in a blood bank nor diagnostic testing of blood samples is excluded. Similarly, operations that occur at a cellular level (such as the incorporation of an oncogene into the fertilized egg of an animal) are

---

[72] *Bruker/Non-invasive measurement,* T385/86 [1988] *EPOR* 357. For criticisms see R. Moufang, 'Methods of medical treatment under Patent law' (1993) 24 *IIC* 18, 46–47.

[73] *Medi-physics/Treatment by Surgery,* T992/03 (2007) *OJ EPO* 557, 563.

[74] *Salimen/Pigs III,* T58/87 [1989] *EPOR* 125.

[75] *Siemens/Flow measurement* [1989] *EPOR* 241; T254/87 [1989] *OJ EPO* 171.

[76] *Diagnostic methods,* G01/04 (2006) *OJ EPO* 334, 357 (EBA).

[77] *Diagnostic methods,* G01/04 (2006) *OJ EPO* 334, 357 (EBA).

[78] The treatment of body tissues or fluids after removal from the body is not excluded: *EPO Guidelines* C–IV, 4.3.

not performed on or in the body.[79] In contrast, a treatment of blood by dialysis, where the blood is returned to the same body, would be excluded.[80] While an invention may interact with or relate to a human or animal body, it will only be excluded if it is classed as a form of treatment on the body. In line with this, the Technical Board of Appeal held that 'a method and apparatus for preventing piglets from suffocating' by blowing hot air under a mother pig to discourage piglets from going under her was patentable. While the invention protected the body, it was still patentable because the method was not practised *on* the body of the piglet.[81]

As we saw earlier, diagnostic methods typically consist of a number of steps, all of which much be present if an application is to fall within the ambit of the exclusion. While this is all well and good for the purposes of deciding whether an invention is a diagnostic method, it seems that a different approach is adopted when considering whether that diagnostic method is practised on or in the human or animal body. The reason for this is that some of the stages in a diagnostic method (particularly the final 'deductive phase') are intellectual exercises: they are carried out in the mind of the medical or veterinary practitioner. To get around the problems that this might pose, the Enlarged Board of Appeal said that the requirement that the invention be 'practised on or in the human or animal body' is only to be considered in relation to method steps of a *technical* nature. 'Thus, it does not apply to the diagnosis for curative purposes *stricto sensu*, i.e. the deductive decision phase, which as a purely intellectual exercise cannot be practiced on the human or animal body'.[82] It also seems that the requirement would not be applied where the data gathered is compared to normal values. The requirement that the invention needs to be practised on or in the human or animal body would be important, however, where a step in an invention is deemed to be technical. This might be the case, for example, where part of the diagnosis makes use of a computer program, is carried out *in vitro*, or in a laboratory.[83] In these cases, as the (technical) step is not practiced on the body it would not fall within the exclusion in Article 53(c) EPC 2000.

4.4 DIRECT TREATMENT

In order for a patent to fall within the therapeutic method exclusion, it is necessary to show that the invention constitutes a *direct* treatment by therapy. This means, for example, that while the programming of a pacemaker to control the way it uses energy undoubtedly has an indirect effect on the human body, this was held to be concerned more with improving an apparatus, than with health.[84] While it is difficult to draw the line between direct and indirect effects, a patent is more likely to fall within the exclusion if it can be shown that there is a 'corresponding functional link' between the invention and human or animal health.[85] That is, a method does not fall within Article 53(c) 'if there is no functional link and hence no physical causality between its constituent steps carried out in relation to a therapy device and the therapeutic effect produced on that body by that device'.[86] In a similar vein, it has been held that to

[79] *Harvard/Onco-mouse* [2003] *OJ EPO* 473, 491 (OD). It added that 'the incorporation of the oncogene into the genome is a method which is neither surgical nor therapeutic nor diagnostic in nature'.

[80] *EPO Guidelines*, C–IV, 4.8. See *Baxter/Blood extraction method*, T329/94 [1998] *EPOR* 363, 367.

[81] *Salimen/Pigs III*, T58/87 [1989] *EPOR* 125; *Thompson/Cornea*, T24/91 [1996] *EPOR* 19.

[82] *Diagnostic methods*, G01/04 [2006] *OJ EPO* 334, 356 (EBA).   [83] Ibid, 357 (EBA).

[84] *Ela Medical*, T789/96 [2002] *OJ EPO* 364, 369 (para. 2.2.2.1).   [85] Ibid, 369–70.

[86] *Siemens*, T245/87 [1989] *OJ EPO* 171 (para. 3.2.3).

fall within the exclusion, the invention must target a particular illness or disease,[87] and also provide a 'defined, real treatment' of a pathological condition.[88]

4.5 TWO OR MORE USES

So long as an application has a use which falls within the scope of section 4A/Article 53(c) it will be excluded. This is the case even if the invention has other uses that do not fall within the exclusion.[89] Thus, an application for a method of cleaning plaque from human teeth which had both an (excluded) therapeutic effect and a (non-excluded) cosmetic effect was excluded from patentability by Article 53(c) EPC 2000 on the basis that the application claimed a therapeutic treatment.[90] While the presence of a surgical step in a multi-step method for treatment of the human or animal body normally confers a surgical character on the method, there may be some cases where this is not the case.[91] On the basis that methods that have a destructive purpose do not fall within the aim of section 4A/Article 53(c) surgery is limited to processes that give 'priority to maintaining life or health of the human or animal body on which they are performed'.[92] As such, a process that has as its end result the death of a living thing (either deliberately or incidentally) will not be caught by the exclusion: even if the process involves a surgical step. Similarly, the fact that a chemical product has both a cosmetic and a therapeutic effect when used to treat the human or animal body does not render the cosmetic treatment unpatentable.[93]

4.6 LIMITS

While section 4(A)/Article 53(c) impose important limits on the types of medical and veterinary invention that may be patented, it would be wrong to assume that all medical and veterinary inventions are excluded from the scope of patent protection. The reason for this is that the potential scope of the exclusion is restricted by the fact that it must be read in light of section 4A(4)/Article 54(5). While we deal with this in more detail later,[94] it is enough to note that these provisions have been construed in such a way that they permit the patenting of uses of known substances for the *manufacture* of a medicament to treat a particular disease.[95] As we will see, while the so-called second medical use patents continue to undermine the scope of the exception for methods of medical and veterinary treatment, the question of whether an application relating merely to a new dosage regime is patentable remains controversial.

---

[87] *Sequus Pharmaceuticals*, T4/98 [2002] *OJ EPO* 139, 149–50.

[88] *Eli Lilly/Serotonin receptor*, T241/95 [2001] *OJ EPO* 103, 109 (para. 3.1.2); See also *Norsk Hydro*, T135/98 (20 Nov. 2002) (a feed mixture for optimally satisfying the nutritional requirements of farmed fish was not a medical treatment practised on an animal body).

[89] Unlike PA s. 1(2)/EPC Art. 52, the exclusion is not confined to methods of treatment 'as such'.

[90] *ICI/Cleaning plaque*, T209/86 [1991] *EPOR* 157; [1992] *OJ EPO* 414; *Du Pont/Appetite suppressant*, T144/83 [1986] *OJ EPO* 30; *General Hospital/Contraceptive methods*, T820/92 [1995] *EPOR* 446; *Meiji/Feeds*, T438/91 [1999] *EPOR* 452; *Telectronics/Pacer*, T82/93 [1996] *EPOR* 409 (if hybrid claims include a feature within the exception, the whole is unpatentable).

[91] *See-Shell/Blood flow*, T182/90 [1994] *EPOR* 320; *EPO Guidelines* C–IV, 4.3.

[92] *Georgetown University/Pericardial access*, T35/99 [2000] *OJ EPO* 447, 451. This is in contrast to processes whose end result is the death of living things 'under treatment' either deliberately or incidentally.

[93] *General Hospital Corp/Hair removal method*, T383/03 [2005] *OJ EPO* 159, 162.

[94] See below at pp. 479–80.

[95] *ICI/Cleaning plaque*, T209/86 [1991] *EPOR* 157; [1992] *OJ EPO* 414. For PA s. 2(6)/Art. 54(3) to operate, the use must fall within PA s. 4(2)/Art. 52(4): *Nycomed/Contrast agent for NMR Imaging*, T655/92 [1988] *EPOR* 206.

As section 4A(4)/Article 54(5) only apply to medical *methods* which use substances or compositions, the exclusion of methods of medical and veterinary treatment still applies where apparatuses and objects are used. The residual scope of the exclusion was reaffirmed by the Appeal Board of the EPO when it resisted attempts to extend the scope of Article 54(5) beyond the use of substances and compositions to include the surgical use of an instrument.[96]

5 EXCLUDED SUBJECT MATTER

Up until 1977, for a patent to be valid it was necessary to show a 'manner of new manufacture'. This phrase, which was first used in the 1624 Statute of Monopolies, proved to be a remarkably versatile and flexible tool which enabled patent law to adapt to and accommodate many of the technological and scientific changes that have taken place over the last two-and-a-half centuries. The passage of the Patents Act 1977 saw a dramatic change in the way in which British patent law determined what was patentable subject matter. The reason for this was that unlike previous legislation, neither the 1977 Act nor the EPC upon which it is based contains a definition of 'invention'.[97] Nor do they expressly require that applicants disclose an invention in order to be patentable. Instead, the 1977 Act and the EPC 2000 contain a non-exhaustive list[98] of creations which were deemed *not* to be inventions.[99] To this end section 1(2) (which is the equivalent of Article 52(2) EPC 2000) states:

It is hereby declared that the following (among other things) are not inventions for the purposes of this Act, that is to say, anything that consists of:

(a) a discovery, scientific theory or mathematical method;[100]

(b) a literary, dramatic, musical or artistic work or any other aesthetic creation whatsoever;

(c) a scheme, rule or method for performing a mental act, playing a game or doing business, or a program for a computer;

(d) the presentation of information;

but the foregoing provisions shall not prevent anything from being treated as an invention for the purposes of this Act only to the extent that a patent or application for a patent relates to that thing as such.

While the decision not to require the existence of an invention as an express requirement for patentability marked an important change in British patent practice, section 1(2) (and

---

[96] In response to an attempt to patent a second use of a surgical instrument, the Appeal Board said 'a surgical use of an instrument is not analogous to a therapeutic use (of a medicament)... since the former is not consumed in the application and could be repeatedly used for the same or even other purposes as well... medicaments on the other hand are expended in the process of use and thus have a once for all utility'. *Codman/Second surgical use*, T227/91 [1994] *OJ EPO* 491; [1995] *EPOR* 82.

[97] Under s. 101 of the Patents Act 1949 inventions were defined by the phrase 'manner of manufacture'.

[98] See *Lux Traffic v. Pike Signals* [1993] *RPC* 107, 137ff.; *Christian Franceries/Traffic regulations*, T16/83 [1988] *EPOR* 65.

[99] G. Kolle, 'The Patentable Invention in the EPC' (1974) 5 *IIC* 140, 144.

[100] For a discussion of 'mathematical methods' see *Citibank v. Comptroller General of Patents* [2006] *EWHC* 1676 (Ch), para 19 (concept did not merely operate at the rarefied atmosphere of calculus but also extended to 'lower levels': para 21).

Article 52) effectively codified the picture of the invention which had built up in Britain (and most other EPC countries) prior to 1977.[101]

On the face of it, the excluded categories of subject matter share little in common, other than the fact that they are unable to be patented.[102] It is clear, for example, that there is no single policy that unifies them: these vary from the fact that the subject matter is already protected by other forms of intellectual property (computer programs, literary, dramatic, musical, or artistic work, or any other aesthetic creations), through to the stifling effect that protection would have on research and development (discovery, scientific theory, or mathematical method). Lurking behind many of the categories of subject matter excluded from protection is an image of the invention as something that is concrete and technical in character. Whereas an invention leads to a practical concrete result, this is not the case with a discovery, a mathematical method, or a scientific theory. Neither is it the case with a scheme, rule, or method for performing a mental act, playing a game, or doing business, or the presentation of information: activities that are seen to be abstract and intellectual in nature and thus not patentable.

While most, but by no means all, of the material listed in section 1(2)/Article 52(2) is excluded because it is abstract and non-technical,[103] this is not the case with computer programs which were excluded because it was thought at the time the EPC was drafted that they were better protected by copyright law.[104] As we will see, a lot of time and effort has subsequently been expended attempting to undo this decision.[105]

5.1 AN INVENTION AS A POSITIVE REQUIREMENT FOR PATENTABILITY?

Despite the absence of any formal requirement to show the existence of an invention as a precondition for patentability, a number of recent decisions in the UK and the EPO have suggested that for an invention to be patentable it is necessary to show that the application discloses an invention.[106] In the UK, support for this view comes from the decision in *Genentech v. Wellcome,* where the Court of Appeal said that it was an essential requirement which 'must be satisfied before a patent can properly be granted... that the applicant has made an "invention"'.[107] The question of whether the existence of an invention was a prerequisite for patentability was touched upon in the House of Lords decision of *Biogen v. Medeva.* While Lord Mustill suggested that the requirement that there be an invention may be of relevance in the future, the question was left unanswered.[108] As such, the only issue that applicants currently

---

101 Because the exceptions were intended to harmonize existing laws, pre-1977 case law has been treated as of persuasive value when interpreting the exclusions: *Gale's Application* [1991] *RPC* 305. Over time pre-1977 decisions have been replaced by decisions of the EPO and other member states.

102 See J. Pila, 'Art. 52(2) of the Convention on the Grant of European Patents: what did the framers intend?' (2005) 36 *IIC* 755.

103 Cf Jacob LJ in *Aerotel v. Telco Holdings* [2007] 1 *All ER* 225, para 9.

104 Kolle, 'The Patentable Invention in the EPC', 147–8.

105 'Given the ubiquity of computers in modern life it is not surprising that the precise limitations of [PA s(1)2(c)] have given rise to difficulty'. *Autonomy Corporation v. Comptroller General* [2008] *EWHC* 146 (Pat).

106 *EPO Guidelines,* C–IV, 1.1, 2.2; EPC rr. 27 and 29.

107 *Genentech's Patent* [1989] *RPC* 147, 262 (Mustill LJ). Mustill LJ based his arguments on the wording of PA s. 1(2), EPC Art. 52 and the *EPO Guidelines* C–IV, 1.1, and 2.2.

108 *Biogen v. Medeva* [1997] *RPC* 1, 31 (Lord Mustill), cf. Lord Hoffmann, 42.

need to concern themselves with in this context is whether their invention falls within the scope of the subject matter excluded by section 1(2) and Article 52(2).[109]

6 IS THE INVENTION EXCLUDED BY SECTION 1(2)/ARTICLE 52(2)?

The question whether an invention is denied patent protection on the basis that it falls within one of the excluded categories listed in section 1(2)/Article 52(2) plays an important role in determining the types of invention protected by patents.[110] The law in this area is currently in a state of flux. In part this is an inevitable consequence of the fact that law has to pass judgment over complex and rapidly changing technologies. Another reason for the uncertainty is that this area of law has become caught up in a power struggle between the institutions of the European Union and the EPO as to who controls the future direction of patents in Europe. There is also an ongoing pressure for the threshold for patent protection to be lowered in Europe to ensure that it is on a par with that in the USA (where non-technical business methods are patentable). At the same time, there is a growing concern about the number of trivial patents that have been granted (particularly for computer-related inventions) and the breadth of many gene-based patents.

While all these factors have played their part in muddying the waters, perhaps the single most important reason for the complexity that we now face is because (at least) two different approaches are used when deciding whether an invention falls foul of section 1(2)/Article 52(2). The first approach, which is called the *Aerotel* or 'technical effect' approach, was set out by the Court of Appeal in *Aerotel v Telco Holdings*. This consists of a four-step test to be followed when determining whether an invention falls within one of the excluded categories. This approach is currently applied in the United Kingdom and is very similar to the approach that was used at the EPO until (around) 2000. The second approach, which we call the 'any hardware' approach, was first suggested by the Technical Board of Appeal in the *Pension Benefit Systems Partnership* decision.[111] While focusing on the patentability of a business method invention, the decision has broader consequences for the way section 1(2)/Article 52(2) is applied. Although the any hardware approach was followed in one Patent Office decision in the UK[112] and incorporated into the *EPO Guidelines for Examination*,[113] it was resoundingly rejected in *Aerotel* by the Court of Appeal, who reaffirmed the technical effect approach in the UK. In contrast, the approach adopted in *Pension Benefits* has been applied and expanded in subsequent decisions at the EPO.

---

[109] EPC Art. 52 is repeated in EPC 2000, Art. 53(2). There are no substantive changes to the patentable subject matter: Art. 1, item 17 EPC 2000.

[110] In some cases, British Courts have taken to using the text of Art. 52 EPC rather than that set out in PA s 1(2). For a discussion on this see *Aerotel v. Telco Holdings* [2007] 1 *All ER* 225, para 6.

[111] *Pension Benefit Systems Partnership*, T931/95 [2001] *OJ EPO* 441 (TBA).

[112] *John Edward Rose*, 0/075/01 (14 Feb. 2001) (Patent Office).

[113] See *EPO Guidelines* C–IV, 2; C–IV, 9.5 (amended as of 31 Aug. 2001). See 'Notice from EPO' [2001] *OJ EPO* 464.

6.1 LAW IN THE UK PRIOR TO AEROTEL

The approach adopted in the UK when applying section 1(2)/Article 52(2) is set out in the Court of Appeal decision in *Aerotel*. In outlining the new four-step approach, the Court stressed that it was consistent with earlier Court of Appeal decisions (notably *Merrill Lynch* and *Fujitsu*: both of which are discussed below).[114] While the Court of Appeal said that it was merely reformulating British law, the decision may yet have indirect and unexpected consequences in the way that its provisions are applied. In order to appreciate the test in *Aerotel*, it may be helpful to look first at the way that British courts approached section 1(2) prior to this case.

In the pre-*Aerotel* era the first task that was undertaken when deciding whether an invention fell within one of the excluded categories was to determine what was being claimed. In particular, it was necessary to construe the claims to identify the contribution made by the invention. Once the invention had been characterized, it was then possible to determine whether it fell within the scope of section 1(2)/Article 52(2). In situations where the invention clearly fell within one of the excluded categories, it would not be patentable. This can be seen, for example, in *Merrill Lynch's Application*[115] where the Court of Appeal was called upon to consider whether an automatic share-trading system which operated using a computer program fell within the scope of section 1(2)(c). While the invention had a computer program as one of its elements, the court said that since the invention needed to be looked at as a whole, this did not necessarily mean that the patent was invalid. Rather, what the court needed to ask was whether, viewed as a whole, the invention made a contribution in a field not excluded from patentability. Unfortunately for the applicants, the Court of Appeal found that the contribution made by the invention was limited to the field of business (explicitly excluded by section 1(2)(c)) and, as such, was unpatentable.[116]

Although in many situations it was relatively easy to determine whether an invention fell within the scope of section 1(2)/Article 5292), in some circumstances this was not the case. In the 20 or so years during which tribunals in the UK and the EPO (pre-*Pension Benefits*) have been thinking about how applications which are solely made up of excluded subject matter can be distinguished from inventions which happen to include as a component something such as a computer program and are therefore prima facie patentable, a somewhat surprising situation developed. This is that in determining whether an invention fell within the scope of section 1(2)/Article 52(2), the courts ignored the often difficult question whether the invention was, for example, a computer program or a mathematical method. Instead, they asked whether the invention-as-claimed was 'technical'. If the invention exhibited technical character, or the problem that it solved was technical,[117] this was taken to mean that it fell outside the scope of section 1(2)/Article 52(2).[118] Conversely, the absence of technical character was treated as virtual proof that the invention fell within the scope of section 1(2)/Article 52(2) and that it was therefore unpatentable. In a sense what happened, before *Aerotel* at least in difficult borderline cases, was that the negative criteria set out in section 1(2)/Article 52(2) were recast in more

---

[114] *Aerotel v. Telco Holdings* [2007] *All ER* 225, para 41–48.   [115] [1989] *RPC* 561 (CA).

[116] Ibid, 569.

[117] *IBM/Data processor network*, T6/83 [1990] *OJ EPO* 5; [1990] *EPOR* 91; *IBM/Computer-related invention*, T115/85 [1990] *EPOR* 107. The feature of using technical means for a purely non-technical purpose and/or for processing purely non-technical information does not necessarily confer technical character on any such individual steps of use or on the method as a whole: in fact, any activity in the non-technical branch of human culture involves physical entities and uses, to a greater or lesser extent, technical means.

[118] The mere occurrence of technical features in a claim is not enough: *Pension Benefit Systems Partnership*, T931/95 [2001] *OJ EPO* 441, 450 (TBA).

positive terms. This meant that for an invention to be patentable it was necessary to show that the invention exhibited technical character or, in other words, that it made a technical contribution to the art.

The introduction of technical character as a de facto non-statutory requirement for patentability owes its origin to an imaginative interpretation of Article 52 of the EPC. This stated that what the categories in Article 52(2) have in common is that they are non-technical, either because they are abstract (discoveries, scientific theories) or because they are clearly non-technical (aesthetic creations or presentations of information).[119] As Article 52(1) and (2) only exclude from protection those inventions which are non-technical, it is a short inductive leap to conclude from this that the term 'invention' relates to inventions of a technical nature. This conclusion was reinforced by the Rules and Guidelines of the EPC that clearly state that in order for an invention to be patentable it must be technical.[120]

The use of technical character as a way of determining whether an invention falls within the scope of the excluded subject matter is set out in the leading EPO decision of *Vicom*.[121] In deciding that an application which related to a method of digitally filtering images using a device called an operator matrix which aimed at producing enhanced images was patentable the Board stressed that even if the idea underlying an invention was a mathematical method, it could still be patentable if the invention as a whole made a technical contribution to the known art.[122]

While some initial doubts were raised in the United Kingdom about the use of technical character as a way of distinguishing inventions which are 'in reality' or 'in truth' patentable from those which are made up solely of excluded subject matter,[123] before *Aerotel* British courts followed the lead of the EPO and adopted technical character as a way of determining whether an invention fell within section 1(2).[124] This was highlighted in the Court of Appeal in *Merrill Lynch* when Fox LJ said:

[I]t cannot be permissible to patent an item excluded by section 1(2) under the guise of an article which contains that item—that is to say, in the case of a computer program, the patenting of a conventional computer containing that program. Something further is necessary. The nature of that addition is, I think, to be found in the *Vicom* case where it was stated 'Decisive is what technical contribution the invention makes to the known art'. There must, I think, be some technical advance on the prior art in the form of a new result.[125]

While Fox LJ's language differs in certain respects from the language of the Technical Board of Appeal, the Court of Appeal accepted that the presence of technical character was sufficient

---

[119] *Sternmheimer/Harmonic vibrations*, T366/87 [1989] *EPOR* 131.

[120] A patentable invention must relate to a technical field: EPC r. 27(1)(b); it must be concerned with a technical problem: EPC 2000 r. 43(1), and it must be characterized in the claims by means of technical features: EPC 2000 r. 43(1)9b). *EPO Guidelines* C–IV, 1.2(ii).

[121] *Vicom/Computer-related invention*, T208/84 [1987] *EPOR* 74; [1987] *OJ EPO* 14. Beyer 'Der Begriff der Information als Grundlage fur die Beeurtilung des technischen Charakters von programmbezogenen Erfindungen' [1990] *GRUR* 399.

[122] *Hitachi/Auction Method* T258/03 (2004) *OJ EPO* 575, 580 (the term invention is to be construed as 'subject matter having a technical character').

[123] *Wang Laboratories* [1991] *RPC* 463, 470; *Fujitsu's Application* [1996] *RPC* 511, 521. The Munich Diplomatic Conference on the establishment of the EPC abstained from limiting the concept of the invention by use of 'technical' as was earlier proposed: Kolle 'Patentable Inventions in the EPC', 145.

[124] Technical character has become decisive in determining whether or not a patent falls within the scope of s. 1(2). *CIPA*, para. 1.09.

[125] [1989] *RPC* 561, 569.

to show that an invention did not relate to a disqualified matter and, as such, that it was prima facie patentable.[126]

One of the main advantages of shifting attention towards the idea of technical character is that the courts are able to avoid the difficult task of having to define the subject matter listed in section 1(2)/Article 52(2), a task which is not only technically problematic but also one that changes in technology are likely to render obsolete. Indeed, one of the major problems with specific formulations such as section 1(2) and Article 52(2) is that because they are drafted in light of contemporary technologies, they are prone to obsolescence or, at least, convoluted interpretations.

Whatever advantages there may be in using technical character as a de facto requirement for determining whether an invention falls within the ambit of section 1(2)/Article 52(2), it still leaves us with the difficult task of having to formulate and understand what is meant by the term 'technical'. (As we will see, it is the difficulty in answering this question that led to adoption of the *Pension Benefits* approach at the EPO.) It is to this question that we now turn.

6.1.1 Determining whether an invention is technical

In the vast bulk of cases it is very easy to ascertain whether an invention is technical. This is because it is generally accepted that certain types of creation, such as those in the fields of mechanical engineering or organic chemistry, are technical and as such belong within the remit of patent law. This is made all the easier by the fact that applicants are required to specify the technical field into which their applications fall.

While in most circumstances it may be easy to determine whether an invention is technical, in some situations this is not the case.[127] Typically this arises in relation to creations which fall outside the currently accepted legal limits. This is presently the case with inventions in relation to financial systems, software-generating software, language processing, text editing, and computer programs. In these borderline cases, determining whether an invention is technical is often a difficult task. This problem was highlighted by the British Comptroller of Patents who complained that 'in practice it is often very difficult to determine whether a particular invention does as a matter of fact involve the sort of technical contribution or result alluded to in the cases'.[128] The difficulty of this task was borne out by the fact that while the legal studies which prompted the revision of the EPO guidelines were able to propose 'technical character' as one of the ways of determining whether subject matter was excluded from patentability, they were unable to provide a precise definition of what was meant by the term 'technical'.[129] Instead, they left the task of defining technology to the jurisprudence of the courts.

While the task of having to define what is meant by a technical creation may have been left to the respective courts, so far they have provided little direct guidance in this matter. In many cases where this issue has arisen, no indication is given as to how a decision was reached as to whether something was technical. In other cases, the tribunals have offered the equally unhelpful 'it depends on the facts of the case'.[130] Given that the fate of many inventions depends on the way technology is defined, it may be helpful to provide some guidance in this matter.

In determining whether an invention is technical, the courts have tended to fall back on the model of the invention that has long been employed in patent law.[131] This is one that sees

---

[126] *IBM/Document abstracting and retrieving*, T22/85 [1990] *OJ EPO* 12; [1990] *EPOR* 98, 103.

[127] See J. Thomas, 'An Epistemology of Appropriation: Patentable Subject Matter after *State Street Bank*' [2000] *IPQ* 27, 49 ff.

[128] *Fujitsu's Application* [1996] *RPC* 511, 521.   [129] WG/CP/I/1.

[130] *Wang Laboratories* [1991] *RPC* 463, 473. See also *Fujitsu's Application* [1997] *RPC* 608 (CA).

[131] See *NRDC's Application* [1961] *RPC* 134, 142; *Rote Taube* (1970) 1 *IIC* 136, 137–8.

the process of invention as the reduction of the abstract to the specific, or as a transformation from the general to the concrete, processes which are mediated by the inventor. In turn, this model distinguishes between creations that are abstract, intellectual, mental, undefined, and unpatentable, and those that are concrete, physical, tangible, and patentable.[132] Drawing upon this model of the invention, it has been held that an invention is technical and patentable if it provides or leads to a concrete, causal, or non-abstract result or change in things. When translated into the context of section 1(2)/Article 52(2), this means that if it can be shown that the invention brought about a tangible physical change, this is taken as virtual proof that the invention is technical and that it therefore falls outside the scope of the excluded categories.[133]

The use of physical change to determine whether an invention is technical can be seen in *Vicom* where the Board of Appeal explained how unpatentable mathematical methods could be distinguished from patentable inventions:

the fact that a mathematical method or a mathematical algorithm is carried out on numbers...and provides a result also in numerical form, the mathematical method or algorithm being only an *abstract* concept prescribing how to operate on numbers. No direct technical result is produced by the mathematical method as such. [While abstract creations are not patentable,] if a mathematical method is used in a technical process, that process is carried out on a physical entity (which may be a material object but equally an image stored as an electrical signal) by some technical means implementing the method and provides as its result a certain *change* in that entity.[134]

Although the approach followed in the United Kingdom was less consistent than at the EPO, there were a number of cases (pre-*Aerotel*) where the physical model of the invention was used to determine whether a patent fell within the scope of section 1(2).[135]

In a move that has important ramifications for many inventions, particularly in the field of information technology, the physical conception of technology has been interpreted very broadly at the EPO. This can be seen in the comment that 'physical entities' includes 'a real thing, i.e. an image, even if that thing was represented by an electrical signal'.[136] The wide definition given to physical entity can also be seen in the EPO decision of *Kock & Sterzel*. In this case, it was held that the fact that the invention controlled X-ray tubes in such a way as to ensure optimum exposure while at the same time minimizing the danger of overloading the tube was sufficient change for the application to be deemed technical.[137] Perhaps the best example of the way in which the meaning of 'physical entity' has been extended can be seen

---

[132] The 'invention must belong not to the field of abstractions or speculations, but to that of practical achievement. It must concern not an abstract principle but a conception which is implemented in industry'. *Christian Franceries/Traffic regulations*, T16/83 [1988] *EPOR* 65, 70.

[133] The following inventions were held to be unpatentable because they did not bring about a physical change: inventions for document abstracting (*IBM/Document abstracting and retrieving*, T22/85 [1990] *EPOR* 98); linguistic expression processing (*IBM/Text clarity processing*, T38/86 [1990] *EPOR* 606); a system for listing semantically related linguistic expressions (*IBM/Semantically related expressions*, T52/85 [1989] *EPOR* 454); method for automatically detecting and correcting contextual homophone errors in a text document (*IBM/Text processing*, T65/86 [1990] *EPOR* 181).

[134] *Vicom/Computer-related inventions*, T208/84 [1987] *EPOR* 74, 79.

[135] *Gale's Application* [1991] *RPC* 305 (CA).

[136] *IBM/Document abstracting and retrieving*, T22/85 [1990] *EPOR* 98, 105.

[137] *Kock & Sterzel/X-ray apparatus*, T26/86 [1988] *EPOR* 72; [1988] *OJ EPO* 14. See also *IBM/Computer-related invention*, T115/85 [1990] *EPOR* 107; and [1990] *OJ EPO* 30 (an invention which automatically gave visual indications of conditions prevailing in an apparatus or system was said to resolve a technical problem).

in *BBC/Colour television signal* where it was said that despite its transient character, as a TV signal could be detected by technical means it had a physical reality and therefore could not be considered to be an abstract entity.[138] As such, it was prima facie patentable.

6.2 THE AEROTEL TEST

In the UK, the approach that is currently adopted when considering whether an invention falls within the scope of section 1(2)/Article 52(2) was set out by the Court of Appeal in the decision of *Aerotel v Telco Holdings*.[139] In this case, the Court of Appeal said that to determine whether an invention falls within one of the excluded categories of subject matter, it was necessary to undertake four separate tasks. These are:

(i)   construe the claim,

(ii) identify the contribution,

(iii) ask whether the contribution falls within one of the excluded categories, and

(iv) check to see whether the invention is technical.

We will look at each of these in turn.

Step 1: Construe the claim

The first task that needs to be undertaken under the four-step test is that the claims need to be construed to determine the scope of the patented invention. While this may appear to be relatively inconsequential, it has proved to be crucially important in determining the validity of many patents.

One of the first questions that arose in relation to section 1(2)/Article 52(2) was what happens if an application contains a mixture of both excluded and permitted features? What should be done, for example, if an invention includes as one of its elements a discovery or a computer program which is expressly excluded under section 1(2)/Article 52(2) as well as other non-excluded elements? Initially, discussions in this area focused on the meaning that should be given to the proviso to section 1(2)/Article 52(2) which states that the listed exclusions only apply to the extent that the alleged invention relates to that thing *as such*. Given the ambiguous nature of the proviso, it is not surprising that it lent itself to a number of different and sometimes conflicting styles of interpretation.[140]

Despite initial doubts, courts in the UK and at the EPO (even after *Pension Benefits*) have come down in favour of what is known as the 'whole-contents' approach to interpretation.[141] In so doing they rejected the so-called 'contribution approach' (under which the courts only consider those aspects of the invention which were not excluded).[142] This means that when

---

[138] *BBC/Colour television signal*, T163/85 [1990] *EPOR* 599; [1990] *OJ EPO* (Suppl.) 19. On this basis the invention did not fall within EPC Art. 52(2)(d).

[139] *Aerotel v. Telco Holdings* [2007] 1 *All ER* 225, para 40. It should be noted that the Aerotel patent was subsequently held to be invalid.

[140] It was initially suggested that, when determining whether an invention falls within PA s. 1(2)/EPC Art. 52, the courts should separate the excluded and non-excluded elements of the application and focus only upon the non-excluded components. *Merrill Lynch's Application* [1988] *RPC* 1.

[141] In the UK see *Merrill Lynch's Application* [1989] *RPC* 561 (CA); *Genentech v. Wellcome* [1989] *RPC* 147, 204–14, 224 ff. At the EPO see *Vicom/Computer-related invention*, T208/84 [1987] *OJ EPO* 14; [1987] *EPOR* 74; *Kock & Sterzel/X-ray apparatus*, T26/86 [1988] *EPOR* 72; [1988] *OJ EPO* 19.

[142] See *Aerotel v. Telco Holdings* [2007] 1 *All ER* 225, para 26 (1), paras 32–37 where Jacob LJ said that there was a lot to be said for the contribution approach, but that he was bound by precedent to follow *Merrill Lynch et al.*

considering whether an invention falls foul of section 1(2)/Article 52(2), the courts disregard the fact that the invention has as one of its elements, say, a computer program or a discovery, and focuses instead on the invention *as a whole*. In so doing the courts have stressed that when determining whether an invention is patentable, it is not necessary to compare the non-technical and the technical elements of the invention. That is, it is irrelevant that an invention is made up of a mixture of technical and non-technical elements.[143]

Step 2: Identify the contribution

While the whole-contents approach offers guidance where a patent is made up of a mixture of excluded and non-excluded elements, it offers little assistance on the more general question of how the invention ought to be interpreted. In thinking about the nature of the invention a number of different approaches could have been adopted. The courts, for example, could have attempted to distil the essence or kernel of the invention from the claims themselves. One of the interesting features of the way the invention has been interpreted by courts in the UK and the EPO (pre-*Pension Benefits*) is that rather than attempting to identify the essential nature of the invention, they have focused on what the invention does. That is, when determining whether an invention falls within section 1(2)/Article 52(2) the courts have concentrated upon the *contribution* or *effect* that the invention has upon the known art (or knowledge in the area in question). This is now set out in the second step in the *Aerotel* test, where the court is required to identify the contribution made by the invention.

One of the problems that needs to be confronted when identifying the contribution made by an invention is that applicants may attempt to describe an invention which prima facie falls foul of section 1(2)/Article 52(2) in such a way that it appears to fall outside the scope of the excluded categories. Faced with the possibility of applicants dressing non-patentable inventions up in a way that makes them appear as if they are patentable, the courts have responded by ignoring the *form* of the claims and focusing instead on the *substance* of the invention.[144] In *Aerotel,* the Court of Appeal accepted that the test is an exercise in judgment, involving the problem to be solved, how the invention works, what its advantages are. They also said that the second step was best summed up by the question: what has the inventor really added to human knowledge?[145]

Step 3: Determine whether the contribution falls within the excluded subject matter

Once the contribution made by an invention has been identified, the court then needs to consider whether that contribution falls within any of the categories of excluded subject matter set out in section 1(2)/Article 52(2). The way that that this question is answered largely depends on the way that the specific forms of subject matter listed in section 1(2)/Article 52(2) are interpreted: something that we look at in more detail in the next section. In this context, we will limit ourselves to some general comments about the approach that is taken by the courts when deciding whether an invention falls within one of the excluded categories.

The first point to note about the third-stage test is that because of the uncertainty that existed about the rationales behind the excluded categories, the Court of Appeal said that the third step should be carried out without bias either in favour of or against exclusion. Instead, the task was simply to try and make sense of the provisions using the language used in the legislation.[146]

---

[143] *Kock & Sterzel/X-ray apparatus,* T26/86 [1988] *EPOR* 72; [1988] *OJ EPO* 1; *Pension Benefit Systems Partnership,* T931/95 [2001] *OJ EPO* 441, 450 (TBA); Cf. *IBM/Text clarity processing,* T38/86 [1990] *EPOR* 606.

[144] Ibid (Fox LJ); *IBM/Document abstracting and retrieving,* T22/85 [1990] *OJ EPO* 12; [1990] *EPOR* 98, 105.

[145] *Aerotel v. Telco Holdings* [2007] 1 *All ER* 225, paras 43–44.   [146] Ibid, para 21.

As we said above, in many cases it will be relatively easy to ascertain whether an invention falls within one of the excluded categories of subject matter. In some cases, however, it is difficult to predict whether a particular invention will fall within the ambit of section 1(2)/Article 52(2). It was this problem that led the courts to use 'technical effect' as a de facto test for deciding this aspect of patentability in the first place. Prior to *Aerotel*, British courts followed the approach of the EPO and used physical change as a way of determining whether an invention was 'technical' and thus whether it fell within excluded subject matter. One of the questions that arises post-*Aerotel* is whether a similar approach will now be followed when deciding the third step. Given the Court of Appeal's statement that it was merely reformulating rather than changing the existing law, it may be safe to assume that technical effect and physical change would still be used to decided whether an invention is excluded by section 1(2)/Article 52(2). Against this, however, is the fact that in reformulating the law the Court of Appeal downplayed the role that 'technical character' plays in determining whether an application is excluded. Instead of being used as a way of deciding whether an invention was excluded, technical character has been relegated to the role of a final cross-check in the four-step test.[147] The downplaying of 'technical effect' as a tool for determining whether an invention complied with section 1(2)/Article 52(2) coincided with the argument, initially made by Pumfrey J but followed by others, that the technical contribution test needed to be qualified. In part, this was prompted by the realization that the word 'technical' was inherently vague (which is not surprising given that it is meant to act as a proxy for the equally vague 'invention').[148] The potential change in the law was highlighted by Warren J in *IGT v Comptroller of Patents* who said that after *Aerotel* 'the issue of what is "technical" is of much less importance than in the past since that aspect ought to have been dealt with in looking at the third step. The ultimate question in each of the present applications is not whether a contribution is technical, but whether it lies in an excluded area.'[149] This view also found favour with Kitchin J in *Astron Clinica v Comptroller General of Patents* who said that '[t]aken together, the first three steps should provide the answer' as to whether an invention fell within the scope of section 1(2) 'with the important benefit that they avoid the vexed question of what is a relevant "technical" contribution'.[150] The idea that the technical character test and the corresponding use of physical change are not as important after *Aerotel* is also supported by Jacob LJ's argument in the case that the various forms of excluded subject matter are not united by the common theme that they are abstract and intellectual in nature which, as we saw above, was used to justify the technical contribution test in the first place.

Despite this, one of the notable features of the way that British courts have answered the third question in *Aerotel*—namely, does the contribution fall within section 1(2)/Article 52(2)—is that they have resorted to some, but not all, of the practices that had been used previously. In particular, while the courts have been careful not to ask does the invention exhibit 'technical character', they have relied upon physical change as a way of helping to determine whether an invention falls within one of the excluded categories. That is, the courts have skipped 'technical character' and gone directly to 'physical change' as a way of determining whether an invention falls within section 1(2)/Article 52(2). This can be seen, for example, in *Aerotel* where

---

[147] As Pumfrey J noted, although the test is sometimes called the 'technical effect approach', the word 'technical' does not appear until the fourth and final stage: *IGT v. Comptroller of Patents* [2007] *EWHC* 134, para 13.

[148] See, e.g. ibid, para 13; *CFPH LLC v. Comptroller-General of Patents, Designs, and Trade Marks* [2006] *RPC* 259 ('technical is 'a useful servant but a dangerous master'); *Aerotel v. Telco Holdings* [2007] 1 *All ER* 225, paras 121–24.

[149] [2007] *EWHC* 134, para 39. See also *Re Oneida Indian Nation's Application* [2007] *EWHC* 954 (Pat), para 9.

[150] *Astron Clinica v. Comptroller General of Patents* [2008] *EWHC* 85, para 45. (Pat).

one of the factors that seemed to sway the Court of Appeal in finding that the application for a new system for making telephone calls was not a method of doing business, was that the invention consisted of a 'new physical combination of hardware'.[151] A similar approach was adopted in *IGT v Comptroller of Patents,* where the Warren J rejected the application on the basis that there was no new physical combination of hardware: instead, the 'novelty lay in the computer program'.[152] Another example of the way that physical change has been used to help decide whether an invention falls within section 1(2)/Article 52(2) is *Cappellini v Comptroller of Patents.* While Pumfrey J stressed that he did not think that 'every result must be a physical article before the claim is allowed', he did reject a claim in the application in question on the basis that it was the 'pure manipulation of data without the production of any physical or real-world effect'.[153] Pumfrey J highlighted the important role that physical change plays in answering the third *Aerotel* question when he said: while a claim to an algorithm standing alone may be objectionable, this would not be the case if the claim was tethered to a physical article. Using the language of *Aerotel,* Pumfrey J said that 'there is no contribution lying outside excluded matter until the claim also covers the result of performing the claimed algorithm'.[154]

While the British courts post-*Aerotel* have embraced physical change as a guide to determine whether an invention falls within section 1(2)/Article 52(2), they have been careful to distance themselves from some of the more liberal readings at the EPO (which we discussed above). For example, in *Shopolotto.com's Application,* Pumfrey J cast doubt over the Technical Board's decision in *IBM/Computer Program II,*[155] which held that material technical effect was found 'only in computer once programmed with the claimed software'.[156] In so doing, Pumfrey J reinforced a more traditional (empirical) understanding of the invention that has long dominated in British patent law.

Step 4: Check whether the contribution is technical in nature

The fourth and final step that needs to undertaken under the *Aerotel* test is that the court needs to ask whether the contribution is technical in nature. As we explained above, in pre-*Aerotel* law technical effect was an integral part of any determination whether an invention fell within one of the excluded categories. It was something that went hand-in-hand with the examination, rather than something which was undertaken after the event. In explaining the operation of the four-step test, the Court of Appeal in *Aerotel* said that the fourth step might not be necessary because it should already have been covered by the third step (lending credence to the view that (relevant) 'technical' effect has a place to play in construing the meaning of the excluded categories). While some of the decisions applying *Aerotel* seemed to have slipped back into the 'old' approach under which the third and fourth steps were integrated (or lip service paid to the final task), it is too early to suggest that the third and fourth steps should be merged into a single test. In the meantime, it seems as if the approach that was adopted prior to *Aerotel* is still relevant. The only qualification that may need to be kept in mind is that the courts have begun to talk about the need for an invention to show *relevant* technical

---

[151] *Aerotel v. Telco Holdings* [2007] 1 *All ER* 225, para 40, 53. The fact that the invention involved the use of an apparatus was taken to show that the invention was technical. Ibid. *IGT v. Comptroller of Patents* [2007] *EWHC* 134, para 35.

[152] *IGT v. Comptroller of Patents* [2007] *EWHC* 134, para 35.

[153] *Cappellini v. Comptroller of Patents* [2007] *EWHC* 476, para 18. See also *Re Oneida Nation's Application* [2007] *EWHC* 954 (Pat), para 9.

[154] *Cappellini v. Comptroller of Patents* [2007] *EWHC* 476.   [155] T0935/97.

[156] *Shopolotto.com's Application* [2006] *RPC* 29, para 11.

effect. This has been promoted by the realization that as most computer-related inventions are technical in nature, if technical character was used as a shorthand for determining whether an invention fell within one of the excluded categories this would have meant that most inventions would have satisfied the subject matter requirement. Faced with this problem, Pumfrey J suggested that not all technical effects are relevant and in particular that where computer programs are under consideration, the fact that a computer with *ex hypothesi* a new program will be a new machine and so have a technical effect '...the technical effect to be identified had to be technical effect over and above that to expected from the mere loading of a program into a computer'.[157] In a similar vein, it was also said that in 'one sense computer programs are "technical" but they are also excluded from being inventions'.[158] The attempt to qualify the *type* of technical character needed to ensure that an invention does not fall within section 1(2)/Article 52(2) is an interesting development that needs to be watched in the future. While the EPO has taken a different course (to achieve a similar result), Pumfrey J's approach deals directly with the issue that has driven a lot of the law in this area, namely how to reconcile the fact that computer-related inventions are an essential form of technology with the fact that computer programs *as such* are explicitly excluded from the scope of protection.

6.3 THE 'ANY HARDWARE' APPROACH AT THE EPO

The second approach used to determine whether an invention falls within Article 52(2)/section 1(2), which is currently applied at the EPO, has been called (somewhat pejoratively) the 'any hardware' approach. This approach was developed by EPO Technical Board of Appeal in the decision of *Pension Benefits Systems Partnership*[159] and subsequently expanded in *Hitachi*.[160] Under the any hardware approach (in its expanded form), an invention will not be fall within any of the excluded categories in Article 52(2) if it embodies or is implemented by some technical means (such as a computer). This is the case even if the technical means is used in relation to a non-technical activity. In effect, under the any hardware approach, the tribunal will stand back from the invention—whether a method or an apparatus—and ask whether it can be classified as a form of technology (irrespective of whether it is novel or inventive): all that matters is that the invention makes use of, or embodies, some form of technology (or hardware).

The first key decision that outlined the any hardware approach was the *Pension Benefits* decision which was published in 2001. The patent at issue in *Pension Benefits* related to a computer-related invention that performed a number of different tasks that were necessary in running pension benefit schemes (such as calculating amounts payable and determining future assets). The patent included both method and apparatus claims for controlling a pension benefits system. The method claim (a method of controlling a pension benefits program by administering at least one subscriber employer account which is to receive periodic payments) was made up of a series of steps, including the provision of data, determining the average age of all employees,

---

[157] *Shopolotto.com's Application* [2006] *RPC* 29, para 9. See also *Cappellini v. Comptroller of Patents* [2007] *EWHC* 476, para 5 (noting that the Court of Appeal did not disprove of this statement). In *Re Oneida Indian Nation's Application* [2007] *EWHC* 954, para 13, it was said that Pumfrey J's statements were entirely consistent with the judgment in *Aerotel*.

[158] *Re Oneida Indian Nation's Application* [2007] *EWHC* 954, para 12 ('it does not follow, just because [a] system of gaming machines is technical, that everything they do (e.g. tracking and controlling the operation of the system) is technical *in the sense required*'.

[159] *Pension Benefit Systems Partnership*, T931/95 [2001] *OJ EPO* 441.

[160] *Hitachi/Auction Method*, T258/03 [2004] *OJ EPO* 575.

and so on. The apparatus claim was for a data processing means which was arranged to receive and process information to be used to control a pension benefits system.

The approach the Technical Board of Appeal adopted to the *method claim* in *Pension Benefits* was very similar to the approach previously adopted at the EPO and to the approach currently used in the United Kingdom. The Board began by noting that the question to be asked was whether the method claim represented a method of doing business as such. The Board then went on to characterize the invention, saying that all the features of the method claim were 'steps of processing and producing information having purely administrative, actuarial and/or financial character. Processing and producing such information are typical steps of business and economic methods'.[161] On this basis the Board concluded that the method claim was merely a method of doing business as such and was therefore excluded from patentability under Article 52(2)(c).[162] The mere fact that the invention operated on a computer did not turn the subject matter of the claim into an invention within the meaning of Article 52(1).[163] (As we will see, this aspect of *Pension Benefits* has been modified in *Hitachi*.)

While the Board found that the method claims fell foul of Article 52(2), this was not the case with the *apparatus claims*. The apparatus claims in question were for an apparatus consisting of a suitably programmed computer or system of computers. In considering whether the apparatus claims were patentable, the Board made a number of general comments. It began by noting that there are four basic requirements for patentability under the EPC, namely that there must be an invention, and that the invention must satisfy requirements for industrial applicability, novelty, and inventive step.[164] The Board also said that the basic test of whether there is an invention within the meaning of Article 52(2) is *separable and distinct* from the questions whether the subject matter is susceptible of industrial application, is new, and involves an inventive step.[165] The Board added that 'in addition to these basic requirements' the EPC and the Implementing Regulations implicitly contain the further requirement that the invention must be of technical character.[166]

The Board also considered the way that an invention should be characterized when deciding whether it complies with Article 52(2). In particular they looked at the 'contribution approach' recommended in the *EPO Guidelines for Examination* (which is basically the same as the approach used in the United Kingdom). These said that, when deciding whether an invention complied with Article 52, it was necessary to:

disregard the form or kind of claim and concentrate on its content in order to *identify the real contribution* which the subject matter claimed, considered as a whole, adds to the known art. If this contribution is not of a technical character, there is no invention within the meaning of Art 52(1).[167]

The Board said that there were a number of problems with the contribution approach.[168] The first and most general was that there 'is no basis in the EPC for distinguishing between "new features" of an invention and features of that invention which are known from the prior art

---

[161] *Pension Benefit Systems Partnership*, T931/95 [2001] *OJ EPO* 441, 449 (TBA).   [162] Ibid.
[163] Ibid.
[164] *EPO Guidelines* C–IV, 1.1 (The Guidelines were changed as of 31 Aug. 2001 to bring them into line with EPO case law on computer-related inventions.)
[165] *EPO Guidelines* C–IV, 1.2.
[166] *Pension Benefit Systems Partnership*, T931/95 [2001] *OJ EPO* 441, 454; following *EPO Guidelines* C–IV, 1.2.
[167] *EPO Guidelines* C–IV, 2.2 (emphasis added). The revised Guidelines have taken out the reference to the contribution made by the invention.
[168] The Board said that the distinction drawn between a method of doing business and an apparatus situated to perform such a method was justified by the fact that, while 'schemes, rules and methods' are non-patentable categories in the field of economy and business, the category of 'apparatus' in the sense of 'physical entity' or

when examining whether the invention concerned to be an invention within the meaning of Article 52(1) EPC'.[169] The contribution approach was also criticized because it failed to keep the Article 52(1) inquiry separate and distinct from the questions as to industrial applicability, novelty, and inventive step. The Board also said that the contribution approach confused the requirement of 'invention' with the requirements of 'novelty' and 'inventive step'.[170] Moreover, the Board believed that the contribution approach incorrectly imported issues relating to inventive step into the inquiry into whether a patent complied with Article 52(1).[171] As a result, the Board rejected the contribution approach saying that there 'is no basis in the EPC for applying this so-called contribution approach'.[172]

Rather than looking at the contribution made by the invention and determining whether this was technical, the Board focused on the *character* of the invention. That is, the Board attempted to distil the essence or kernel of the invention, rather than looking at what the invention did. On the facts the Board said that what was claimed was a computer system suitably programmed for use in a particular field. Once the invention had been characterized, the next question to be decided was whether the invention exhibited the requisite technical character. In answering this question, the Board said that 'a computer system suitably programmed for use in a particular field, even if that is the field of business and economy, has the character of a concrete apparatus in the sense of a physical entity, man-made for a utilitarian purpose'. Given that an invention is likely to have a technical character if it leads to or produces a physical change in things, it is not surprising that the Board said that an 'apparatus constituting a physical entity or concrete product suitable for performing or supporting an economic activity, is an invention within the meaning of Article 52(1) EPC'.[173] That is, unlike the situation with the method claim, the apparatus claim could not be classified as a method of doing business and, as such, did not fall foul of Article 52(1). (It is important to note that the patent was refused on the basis that it lacked inventive step.) The upshot of the reasoning in *Pension Benefits* was that where a claim is to a *method* which consists of an excluded category it is excluded, even if hardware is used to carry out the method. In contrast, a claim to *an apparatus* itself, being concrete, is not caught by Article 52(2).

The reasoning that was developed by the Technical Board of Appeal in *Pension Benefits* was applied and expanded in *Hitachi*.[174] The invention in *Hitachi* was an automatic auction method executed in a server computer. In essence the invention was for a method of carrying out a Dutch auction, that is an auction in which the seller starts at a high price which is lowered until a bid is received. As in *Pension Benefits,* the application included both a product and a method claim. The Technical Board of Appeal began by reaffirming that there was no basis in the EPC for applying the contribution approach when deciding whether an invention falls foul of Article 52 EPC.[175] The Board also said that as the reasoning used in *Pension Benefits* was independent of the category of the claim, it would be inconsistent to reject the contribution approach for

'product' is not mentioned in Article 52(2) EPC. *Pension Benefit Systems Partnership,* T931/95 [2001] *OJ EPO* 441, 452 (TBA).

[169] Ibid, 454 (TBA).

[170] The TBA cited the German Federal Court of Justice (BGH) decision of *Sprachanalyseeinrichtung (Speech Analysis Apparatus)* (11 May 2000) X ZB 15/98 [2002] *OJ EPO* 415. For further discussion see *Dell USA,* O/177/02 (24 Apr. 2002), para. 24 (Patent Office).

[171] The Board said that the contribution approach used to determine whether a patent complied with Art. 52(1) was 'so very closely related to examination with regard to the requirement of inventive step that the examining division decided in fact implicitly that there was lack of inventive step under Article 56 EPC'. *Pension Benefit Systems Partnership,* T931/95 [2001] *OJ EPO* 441, 455 (TBA).

[172] Ibid, 442.   [173] Ibid, 453.

[174] *Hitachi/Auction Method,* T258/03 [2004] *OJ EPO* 575.   [175] Ibid, 581–2.

apparatus claims, but not for method claims. On this basis, the Board held that '[i]n order to be consistent with the finding that the so-called contribution approach...is inappropriate for judging whether claimed subject-matter is an invention within the meaning of the Article 52(1) EPC there should be no need to further qualify the relevance of technical aspects of a method claim in order to determine the technical character of the method'. While in *Pension Benefits* the Board of Appeal had only been willing to apply the any hardware approach to apparatus claims (preferring to retain the contribution approach for the method claim), this was not the case in *Hitachi,* where the Board applied the any hardware approach to both apparatus *and* method claims.[176] That is, the Board concluded that a method involving a technical means is an invention within the meaning of Article 52(1). The upshot of *Hitachi,* which has been applied in subsequent decisions at the EPO,[177] is that (i) a claim to *hardware* is not caught by Article 52(2) and (ii) a claim to a *method* of using that hardware is also not excluded. This means that so long as a technical means such as a computer is used, the resulting invention will not fall foul of Article 52(1). This is the case even if the invention is for a purely non-technical purpose.[178]

There are a number of notable features of the any hardware approach. The first relates to the way the invention is to be characterized when determining whether it complies with Article 52(1). A key feature of the any hardware approach is the belief that it is not appropriate to look to the contribution made by the invention. Instead, the any hardware approach requires the tribunal to look to the character or essence of the invention: the contribution made by the invention is only looked at when novelty and inventive step are examined. One of the consequences of this is that under the any hardware approach, the tribunal is more concerned with categorizing the subject matter in question, than with asking whether the application has disclosed an invention.

As the Board noted in *Hitachi,* the broad interpretation given to the term 'invention' under the any hardware approach means that it will include activities which are so familiar that their technical character tends to be overlooked, such as the act of writing using pen and paper.[179] The breadth of the any hardware approach can be seen in the *Microsoft/Clipboard formats I* decision. The application in question, which was for a way of 'facilitating data exchange across different formats', consisted of both method claims and a claim to a program on a computer-readable medium. The Board said that the 'method was implemented in a computer and this amounted to a technical means sufficient to escape the prohibition in Article 52'. As Kitchin J said in *Astron Clinica,* 'the Board in *Microsoft/Clipboard formats* appears to have found that any program on a carrier has a technical character and so escapes the prohibition in Article 52'.[180] While the any hardware approach has meant that more applications are now able to satisfy Article 52, it does not mean that the applications will necessarily be patentable. While the any hardware approach has made it easier to satisfy the subject-matter threshold at the EPO, this does not mean that all inventions will necessarily cross the threshold. For example, in *Pitney Bowes/Undeliverable*

---

[176] In this sense, we see *Hitachi* as a continuation of the approach that was begun in *Pension Benefits.* Cf the comments by the UK Court of Appeal that these decisions are 'mutually contradictory'. *Aerotel v. Telco Holdings* [2007] 1 *All ER* 225, para 25 (CA).

[177] See, for example, *Man/Provision of product-specified data* [2007] *OJ EPO* 421, 427 (the claims in question did not bear scrutiny in light of *Pension Benefits,* T931/95 and *Hitachi,* T258/03); *Pitney Bowes/Undeliverable Mail,* T388/04 [2007] *OJ EPO* 16.

[178] As the Microsoft/data transfer with expanded clipboard formats. Simply ask whether there is a claim for something concrete e.g. an apparatus: if yes, the exclusion does not apply.

[179] *Hitachi/Auction Method,* T258/03 [2004] *OJ EPO* 575, 585.

[180] *Astron Clinica v. Comptroller General of Patents* [2008] *EWHC* 85.

Mail, an application for a method of responding by a mailer to notice from a postal service that a piece of mail was undeliverable was held to fall within Article 52(1). The telling factor in this case was that no technical means whatsoever were described in the application. The fact that the invention *might* have been implemented by an unspecified technical process was not enough to prevent the application from being excluded on the basis that it was for a method of doing business for the purposes of Article 52(2)(c).[181] Another reason why the any hardware approach does not necessarily mean that more inventions will now be patentable is because the invention still needs to be new, non-obvious, and susceptible to industrial application. One of the consequences of the any hardware approach is that it shifted the focus of attention at the EPO away from the inquiry whether a patent complies with Article 52(1) to the inquiry whether there is an inventive step (and arguably also novelty and industrial applicability).[182] This is spelt out clearly in the revised *EPO Guidelines* that say that when examining computer-related inventions, it may 'be more appropriate for the examiner to proceed directly to the questions of novelty and inventive step, without considering beforehand the question of technical character'. The shift towards inventive step is reinforced in the *EPO Guidelines* by the fact that when 'assessing whether there is an inventive step, the examiner must establish an objective technical problem. The solution of that problem constitutes the invention's technical contribution to the art. The presence of such technical information establishes that the claimed subject matter has a technical character and therefore is indeed an invention within the meaning of Art. 52(1)'.[183] The shift has also been confirmed in subsequent decisions at the EPO that have focused on inventive step rather than exclusion from patentability.[184]

While initial reactions in the United Kingdom were mixed,[185] in *Aerotel* the Court of Appeal clearly rejected the any hardware approach, suggesting that it 'must be wrong' and that it was 'not intellectually honest'.[186] Jacob LJ also said that *Pension Benefits*, and like-minded decisions at the EPO, were based on the mistaken assumption that the various categories of excluded subject matter were all limited to something abstract or intangible.[187] This reflects earlier criticisms of *Pension Benefits* that it runs contrary to a number of Court of Appeal decisions in the United Kingdom that had held that claims directed to a system (hardware or apparatus) did not avoid the terms of section 1(2).[188] The Board's decision was also criticized

---

[181] *Pitney Bowes/Undeliverable mail,* T388/04 [2007] *OJ EPO* 16, 23.

[182] The 'inference from *Pension Benefit*…is that lack of technical contribution might be a matter for inventive step rather than exclusion from patentability'. *Dell USA,* O/177/02 (24 Apr. 2002), para. 27 (M. Wilson) (Patent Office).

[183] *EPO Guidelines* C–IV, 2.3.

[184] *Comvik/Two identities,* T641/00 [2003] *OJ EPO* 352; *International Computers/Information modelling,* T49/99 (5 Mar. 2002).

[185] In one Patent Office decision, the *Pension Benefits* approach was used to decide whether an application for 'behaviour modification' fell within section 1(2). *John Edward Rose,* O/075/01 (14 Feb 2001) (as in *Pension Benefits,* the application was eventually excluded on the basis that it lacked inventive step). Cf *Pintos Global Service's Application,* O/171/01 (6 Apr. 2001) (Patent Office); *Hutchins' Application* [2002] *RPC* 264; *James Shanley,* O/422/02 (16 Oct. 2002) (Patent Office) which expressly rejected the *Pension Benefits* approach.

[186] *Aerotel v. Telco Holdings* [2007] 1 *All ER* 225, paras 27–29. Jacob LJ's arguments in this regard are far from convincing. In particular, it is difficult to imagine an application for an i-Pod loaded with a new piece of music being non-obvious. Interestingly, most of the criticisms of the EPO decisions are in relation to the way that they applied inventive step, rather than how they approach excluded subject matter.

[187] Ibid, para 30. Jacob LJ continued saying 'We have already observed that the categories are disparate with differing policies behind each. There is no reason to suppose there is some common factor (particularly abstractness) linking them. The *travaux prépatoires* at least confirm this'. Ibid.

[188] *Merrill Lynch's Application* [1989] *RPC* 561 (CA) (not possible to patent under the guise of an article which contains that item); *Fujitsu's Application* [1997] *RPC* 608 (CA) ('the fact that the invention was claimed

because it contradicts the established British view that questions of patentability should be decided as a matter of substance and not according to the actual form of the words.[189] Given that many of the applications excluded under section 1(2) via the *Aerotel* approach would be excluded under the any hardware approach because they lack inventive step, it is unlikely that the new approach will lead to different results.[190] This was reflected in Pumfrey J's comment that *Pension Benefits* was the correct result, but by the wrong approach.[191]

6.4 SUMMARY

The law in this area is far from clear. There are many problems, both in the way that the rules are applied and in the way that different approaches have been represented. Having said this, it is possible to make some general statements about the two approaches. The key difference between the approach that has been adopted in the UK and that at the EPO relates to the way that the 'invention' is construed. In essence, the any hardware approach differs from the approach adopted in the UK in two ways. The first is in terms of the way that the invention is characterized. While British courts look to the contribution made by the invention, this approach has been rejected at the EPO where the focus is on the nature of the invention. As the Technical Board of Appeal said, 'the technical character of an invention is an inherent attribute independent of the actual contribution of the invention to the state of the art'.[192] The second way in which the two approaches differ is in terms of the way that technical character is determined. Technical character may be implied at the EPO in at least three ways. These are (i) by the physical features of an entity, (ii) by the nature of the activity, or (iii) conferred on a non-technical activity by the use of a technical means.[193] While the UK courts have adopted the first two approaches, they have rejected the third.

That different approaches that have been adopted in the UK and the EPO is not desirable. Given that the President of the EPO rejected Jacob LJ's request that the question of how

---

as a method, a way of manufacture or an apparatus was irrelevant when the only invention claimed revolved around the use of a computer program'). Cf. 'a computer system suitably programmed for use in a particular field, even if that use, for example, the field of business and economy, has the character of a concrete apparatus, in the sense of a physical entity or product and is thus an invention within the meaning of Article 52(1)'. *EPO Guidelines* C–IV, 2.3.

[189] This has led the Patent Office to conclude on a number of occasions that it is bound to follow the contribution approach set out in UK courts, and not the approach advocated in *Pension Benefits*. See, e.g. *Hutchins' Application* [2002] *RPC* 264, 270 (Patent Office); *Pintos Global Application,* O/171/01 (6 Apr. 2001), paras. 20–29.

[190] The nature of the change brought about by *Pension Benefit,* and the impact it has on the way a patent is examined, can be seen in the Patent Office decision in *James Shanley,* where the contribution approach and the *Pension Benefits* approach were applied to the same facts. *James Shanley,* O/422/02 (16 Oct. 2002). The invention in question was for dismountable partitions for buildings (that included both flat and curved panels). Using the contribution approach, the Hearing Officer said that the contribution made by the invention was wholly aesthetic insofar as it was solely directed 'to altering appearances'. As the invention neither solved a technical problem nor made a contribution in a non-excluded field, the application was excluded by section 1(2)(b). The Hearing Officer then went on to consider how the invention would have fared under the *Pension Benefits* approach. After reviewing the Technical Board's decision, the Hearing Officer said that 'what is claimed is a partition for buildings, and since this, taken as a whole and without regard to whether or not any technical contribution is involved, manifestly has a technical character…I would have to find that what is claimed…is an invention under section 1(2)'. As the Officer was bound by UK decisions, he did not follow the *Pension Benefits* approach: ibid, para. 22. The interesting question here is whether the application would have satisfied the requirements of inventive step.

[191] *Cappellini v. Comptroller of Patents* [2007] *EWHC* 476, para 9.

[192] *Quest International/Odour Selection,* T619/02 [2007] *OJ EPO* 63, 84.

[193] *Hitachi/Auction Method,* T258/03 [2004] *OJ EPO* 575, 585.

Article 52(2) should be construed be referred to the Enlarged Board of Appeal, it seems unlikely that the EPO will change its approach in the future. The most immediate change brought about by the any hardware approach is in the way computer-related inventions are excluded from protection. It is possible that the new approach might lead to changes in the way applications are examined.[194] It will be interesting to see whether the any hardware approach and the approach outlined in *Aerotel* bring about any other changes. While there are many issues that are unclear, there is little doubt that this is a topic that needs to be followed closely.

7 SPECIFIC APPLICATIONS

Having looked at the general approaches that are taken to the question of whether an invention falls within the scope of section 1(2)/Article 52(2), we now look at a number of more specific problems that arise in relation to the scope of the protected subject matter. These are in relation to naturally occurring substances and discoveries; computer programs and computer-related inventions; methods of doing business; the presentation of information; and methods for performing a mental act. After looking at these specific applications, we will look at possible reforms, particularly in relation to computer programs and computer-related inventions.

When thinking about these specific forms of subject matter, it is important to keep in mind the different approaches that are taken in the UK and at the EPO. While the case law at the EPO prior to *Pension Benefits* is still important in the UK, the liberalization brought about by the 'any hardware' approach means that they may no longer be as important at the EPO. Moreover, while the different approaches have not had much of an impact, at least to date, in relation to discoveries and natural substances, they have played an important role in the way that the other forms of subject matter have been treated.

7.1 DISCOVERIES AND NATURAL SUBSTANCES

Advances in genetic engineering over the last few decades have enabled scientists to isolate and replicate a host of naturally occurring substances. Given the considerable investment that has been made in this research, it is not surprising that attempts have been made to patent the results of that research. In part, the extent to which this biological research is patentable depends on whether the resulting products and processes are treated as discoveries or inventions. The reason for this is that discoveries as such are excluded from the remit of patentable subject matter.[195] However, if it can be shown that when viewed as a whole, an application that incorporates a discovery brings about a technical change, it may be patentable. This means

---

[194] It has been suggested that one of the most valid complaints about computer programs and business method patents 'is that they are for inventions that [are] trivial or that they seek protection that is too broad for their scope'. Both of 'these issues—obviousness and insufficiency— ... get tested by the EPO before granting patent applications in other technologies, but in the case of applications for computer programs and business method patents, matters used never to get that far and discussion instead was limited to the rather sterile and philosophical issue of whether or not the alleged invention confers a "technical effect"'. T. Cook, 'Intellectual Property Protection for Computer Programs', *BCS Review* 2003.

[195] PA s. 1(2)(a); EPC 2000 Art. 52(2)(a). On attempts to protect discoveries see F. Neumeyer, 'Legal Protection of Scientific Discoveries' [1975] *Industrial Property* 348; K. Beier, 'Scientific Research, Patent Protection and Innovation' [1975] 6 *IIC* 367; E. Kitch, 'The Nature and Function of the Patent System' (1977) 20 *Journal of Law & Economics* 265, 288.

that if a person finds a new property of a known material or article, this will be treated as an unpatentable discovery. However, if that person puts the property to a practical use, the invention may be patentable. For example, the discovery that a known material is able to withstand mechanical shock would not be patentable. However, a railway sleeper made from that material could well be patentable.[196]

In thinking about the extent to which biological products and processes are patentable, it is important to bear in mind that patent law distinguishes between naturally occurring substances (unpatentable discoveries) and the products and processes which result from the human effort in isolating those substances from their natural environment (patentable inventions).[197] That is, a distinction is drawn between things that freely exist in nature (and can only be unearthed or discovered) and things that are artificial (and which contain the necessary degree of human intervention for the resulting product to be called an invention).[198]

Given this, the important question that we need to consider is: what is the difference between something that is 'natural' and thus unpatentable, and something that is 'artificial' and thus potentially patentable? More specifically, given that the act of discovery and the act of invention often both involve a considerable amount of time, effort, skill, and labour, we need to ask: what type of effort is needed for an activity to be described as an artificial invention as distinct from a natural unpatentable discovery? In answering these questions, it becomes apparent that the borders between discovery and invention are far more vague and problematic than they might seem at first glance. Perhaps the best way to think about the extent to which biological inventions are patentable is to look at the different types of patents that may be granted.[199]

(i) If a process is developed that enables a substance found in nature to be isolated and obtained from its surroundings, the *process* may be patentable.[200]

(ii) The finding of a *substance* freely occurring in nature is a mere discovery and, as such, is unpatentable. As the Opposition Division at the EPO explained this means that the 'discovery' of the Moon (when the Americans landed on it in 1969), the finding of a 5,000-year-old mummy in the Italian/Austrian Alps, or of a new animal, would not be patentable.[201] This is reflected in Article 5(1) of the Biotechnology Directive which says that the 'human body, at the various stages of its formation and development, and the simple discovery of one of its elements, including the sequence or partial sequence of a gene, cannot constitute a patentable discovery'. Similar provisions exist in the Patents Act 1977 and the EPC.[202]

---

[196] *EPO Guidelines* C–IV, 2.3.1. It is unclear whether the 'any hardware' approach will impact on the patentability of naturally occurring substances.

[197] See R. Whaite and N. Jones, 'Biotechnological Patents in Europe: The Draft Directive' [1989] *EIPR* 145, 149; A. White, 'The Patentability of Naturally Occurring Products' [1980] *EIPR* 37.

[198] For a different perspective on the issue of patenting of higher life forms see *Harvard College v. Canada (Commisioner of Patents)* [2002] *SCC* 76 (Supreme Ct of Canada) (rejecting an application to patent the genetically altered Onco-mouse).

[199] As yet there has been no case directly on this point in the UK. There is little reason to doubt that the position in the UK will be the same as that at the EPO. Cf. *Chiron v. Murex Diagnostics* [1996] *FSR* 153, 177.

[200] *EPO Guidelines* C–IV, 2.3.1.

[201] *Howard Florey/Relaxin,* T741/91 [1995] *EPOR* 541, 549. It is interesting to note that plant breeders' rights are available to those who 'discover' varieties, whether growing in the wild or occurring as a genetic variant, whether artificially induced or not: PVA, s. 4(3) and 4(6). Apparently the Braeburn apple was found in this way in 1952. See T. Boswell, *Hansard* (HC) (24 Jun. 1997) col. 717.

[202] See PA Sched. A2, para. 3(a) (introduced by Patents Regulations 2000 (SI 2000/2037)); EPC Rule 23(e)(1), Implementing Regulations to the EPC (introduced by [1999] *OJ EPO* 437).

(iii) If a natural substance that has been *isolated* from its surroundings can be properly characterized either by its structure, by the processes by which it is obtained, or by other parameters, the substance *per se* may be patentable. This means that, as long as 'something' is inside a human or animal body or a plant, it is a natural element and cannot be considered to be patentable. However, once this 'something' is isolated from the human or animal body or plant by means of a technical process, it becomes eligible for patent protection.[203] This is the case even if its structure is identical to that of a natural element, since the processes used to isolate the element are technical processes.[204] This can be seen in the *Relaxin* decision, which concerned claims relating to DNA sequences of a naturally occurring substance that relaxes the uterus during childbirth, which was obtained from the human ovary.[205] The Opposition Division of the EPO held that the invention was not a discovery and as such was not excluded from patentability. Following the *EPO Guidelines*, the Opposition Division said that, as the substance Relaxin had not previously been recognized, that a process had been developed to obtain Relaxin and the DNA which encoded it, that the products were characterized by their chemical structure, and that the products had a use, the claims were patentable under Article 52(2).

This position was affirmed in the Biotechnology Directive[206] and in equivalent provisions in the Patents Act 1977 and EPC 2000.[207] These provide that 'biological material that is isolated from its natural environment or produced by means of a technical process may be the subject of an invention even if it previously occurred in nature'.[208] More specifically, Article 5(2) of the Biotechnology Directive states that an element isolated from the human body or otherwise produced by means of a technical process, including the sequence or partial sequence of a gene, may constitute a patentable invention even if the structure of that element is identical to that of a natural element. Equivalent provisions have been introduced in the UK[209] and in the EPC 2000.[210]

This means that 'raw data' on the human genome (including the human DNA sequence and its variations:[211] human genes, partial gene sequences, the human body at various stages of its development) which are not isolated, purified, or somehow produced by a technical process, are not patentable.[212] However, if the genetic information (including the sequence or partial sequence

---

[203] See Biotech. Directive Recitals 21–2. Similar arguments apply for the *purification* of a naturally occurring substance.

[204] S. Sterrckx, 'Some Ethically Problematic Aspects of the Proposal for a Directive on the Legal Protection of Biotechnological Inventions' [1998] *EIPR* 123, 124–5; cf. S. Crespi, 'Biotechnology Patents: the Wicked Animal Must Defend Itself' [1995] *EIPR* 431, 432–3.

[205] (1996) 27 *IIC* 704, 705–6. See *Icos Corporation/Seven transmembrane receptor* [2002] *OJ EPO* 293, 307 para. 11(i) (Opposition Division) (while 'the V28 protein exists as a segment of the human genome and thus is a part of nature, the purified and isolated nucleic acid having that sequence does not exist in nature and thus cannot be discovered').

[206] Biotech. Dir. Art. 3(2).

[207] Para. 2 of Schedule A2, to the Patents Act 1977, introduced by Patents Regulations 2000 (SI 2000/2037), in force 28 July 2000.

[208] Biotech. Dir. Art. 3(2); PA Sched. A2, para. 2 (introduced by Patents Regulations 2000); EPC Rule 23c(a) Implementing Regulations to the EPC (introduced by [1999] *OJ EPO* 437).

[209] See PA Sched. A2, para. 5 (introduced by Patents Regulations 2000).

[210] EPC 2000 Rule 29(2).

[211] This was confirmed by the joint statement by Tony Blair and Bill Clinton, 'Joint Statement to ensure that discoveries for the human genome are used to advance human health', 14 Mar. 2000.

[212] See Bostyn, 'Patentability of Genetic Information Carriers' [1991] *IPQ* 1; Lord Hoffmann adopted a similar approach in *Kirin-Amgen v. Transkaryotic Therapies* [2005] *RPC* (9) 169, 195, 201 (paras. 76 and 109) when

of a gene) has been isolated from the human body or somehow produced by a technical process, it will potentially be patentable. For example, if we take the situation where a research team successfully isolates the gene responsible for migraines, while the underlying genetic information would be in the public domain, the technique used to isolate the gene (which may include complicated processes of identification, purification, and classification) would be patentable. On the basis that the isolated gene would not have been identified without the human intervention (*techne*), the isolated gene may be patented.[213] This would also be the case where an invention is for a transgenic plant or animal, which by definition do not exist in nature.[214]

The *Kirin-Amgen* decision, which involved Amgen's highly valuable patent for a method of producing erythropoietin (EPO), offers another useful example of the impact that the invention–discovery dichotomy has upon patentable subject matter. EPO is the hormone that promotes the production of red blood cells, and is particularly useful in the treatment of anaemia. Underlying the patent was Amgen's discovery and subsequent sequencing of the gene that produces EPO. Building on this discovery Amgen isolated and cloned the DNA sequence that produces EPO. The DNA sequence was then introduced into a host cell (Chinese hamster ovary cell), which was used to manufacture the EPO. At first instance Neuberger J said the claim was 'ultimately to the use of information first revealed in the patent, namely, the genetic code for EPO, for the purpose of expressing EPO cells by artificial manipulation of DNA. The essence of the invention was not the artificial manipulation but the use of the information'.[215] As a result, the technique used to manufacture the EPO was irrelevant. The Court of Appeal disagreed, saying that Neuberger J's definition was too broad. While the Court of Appeal had no doubt that the discovery and sequencing of the gene that produced EPO was at the heart of the invention, the Court said that the gene sequence *per se* could not be claimed as the invention because it existed in nature. Instead, the Court held that what was claimed was an exogenous DNA sequence suitable for expressing EPO when introduced into a host cell. The House of Lords agreed. While the decision did not directly focus on discovery as patentable subject matter, it is important insofar as it exemplifies the way that the non-patentability of naturally occurring substances can influence not only the subject matter that is patentable, but also the decision as to whether a patent has been infringed.[216]

While the patenting of processes used to isolate natural substances is relatively uncontroversial, the same cannot be said about the patenting of the substances that are isolated using those processes. In particular, doubts have been raised as to whether the act of isolation and characterization of a naturally occurring substance is really that different from the mere finding of the substance. As one commentator has noted 'even if a natural element is isolated from the body by technical means, this does not change the "naturalness" of the element (neither does a purification

---

he treated the information as to the make up of DNA as an unpatentable discovery. But cf. Jacob LJ, speaking for the Court of Appeal, in *Aerotel Ltd v. Telco Holdings Ltd* [2007] *RPC* (7) 117, 134 (para. 37) (doubting whether the revelation of the precise sequence of a piece of DNA, as opposed to its general existence, could be described as a discovery).

[213] The requirement that there be technical intervention is closely related to the requirement that the invention be non-obvious (*DSM NV's Patent* [2001] *RPC* 675, 709 (talking about obviousness over nature)) and also be industrially applicable (*Salk Institute for Biological Studies*, T338/00 (6 Nov. 2002).

[214] *Harvard/Onco-mouse* [2003] *OJ EPO* 473 (Opposition Division) ('transgenic animals of the present invention having an artificially inserted oncogene do not exist in nature as such but are the result of a technical intervention by man', at 491).

[215] *Kirin-Amgen v. Transkaryotic Therapies* [2002] *RPC* 187, 201 (Neuberger J).

[216] [2003] *RPC* (3) 31 (CA); [2005] *RPC* (9) 169, 195 (para. 76). See above at Ch. 22 Section 3.

of the element)'.[217] However valid these arguments may be, they have been outweighed by the policy goal outlined in the Biotechnology Directive that research aimed at obtaining and isolating elements valuable to medicinal production should be encouraged by the patent system.[218]

7.2 COMPUTER PROGRAMS AND COMPUTER-RELATED INVENTIONS

When the Patents Act 1977 and the EPC 1973 were enacted it was commonly thought that copyright law rather than patents would be the area of intellectual property law which would regulate the creation and use of computer programs. While copyright has been important in this process, one of the most notable changes that has taken place since 1977 is the growing role played by patent law in relation to computer programs and computer-related inventions. Given that computer programs are expressly excluded from patentability by section 1(2)(c)/Article 52(2)(c), it may come as a surprise to learn that many patents have already been granted for computer-related inventions.[219] Moreover, while it may have been assumed when the EPC was first drafted that copyright rather than patent law would regulate information-technology-based creations, since 1977 the trend has been towards more and more patent protection for computer-related inventions. As we will see, in certain circumstances there has also been a move towards allowing the patenting of computer programs. One of the last hurdles facing those who favour greater use of patents in the field of information technology is the fact that computer programs *as such* are expressly excluded from the scope of patentable subject matter.[220] In this section, we will look at the way that the law has developed in this area. In so doing we will look at the current position in the UK, which was similar to the position at the EPO prior to the adoption of the any hardware approach. We will then look at the standing of computer programs and computer-related inventions at the EPO.

7.2.1 United Kingdom

In this section we look at the current position in the UK. It is important to keep in mind that the case law at the EPO prior to *Pension Benefits* is still relevant in the UK. As such, in our analysis of the current UK position, we will make reference to the pre-*Pension Benefits* decisions from the EPO. It is also important to bear in mind that there is a possibility that the law in the UK after *Aerotel* may have changed the approach that British courts take toward this old case law: although, as we suggested above, this has not been borne out in the UK decisions that have applied *Aerotel* to date.

The approach that has been adopted towards the patenting of computer-related inventions in the UK has seen the courts consistently apply the general approach that was outlined above.

[217] Sterrckx, 'Some Ethically Problematic Aspects of the Proposal for a Biotech Directive', 123, 124–5. See also M. Davis, 'The Patenting of the Products of Nature' [1995] *Rutgers Computer and Technology Law Journal* 331; cf. Bostyn, 'Patentability of Genetic Information Carriers' [1999] *IPQ* 1, 3–4.

[218] Biotech. Dir., Recital 17.

[219] The Comptroller of the British Office reported on 2 Nov. 2000 that over 15 per cent of the patents granted by the British Patent Office have a software element. Interview with Alison Brimelow, *Patent Office News and Notices*, <http://www.patent.gov.uk/softpat/en/index.html>. The EPO has granted over 20,000 software-related patents, and it is said that objections are made in relation to fewer than 1 per cent of software-related applications. See I. Kober, 'Software Patents: An Essential Element of the European Patent System', *The Patent Office Conference on Software Patents* (<http://www/patent.gov.uk/softpat/en/index.html>).

[220] PA s. 1(2)(c); EPC 2000 Art. 52(2)(c).

One of the most important changes that led to the liberalization of the protection offered to computer-related inventions in the UK (and at the EPO pre-*Pension Benefits*) was the decision that an invention which included a computer program could be patentable so long as the invention as a whole was technical. The upshot of the acceptance of the whole contents approach was, as the Board of Appeal said in *Vicom,* that 'an invention which would be patentable in accordance with conventional patentability criteria should not be excluded from protection by the mere fact that for its implementation modern technical means in the form of a computer program are used'.[221] This approach was adopted and endorsed by a number of decisions in the UK, notably the Court of Appeal decisions of *Gale's Application* and *Merrill Lynch.*

While a computer program *per se* remains unpatentable in the UK, following the acceptance of the whole contents approach it is clear that applications which contain a computer program are prima facie patentable, so long as the invention as a whole makes a technical contribution to the art.[222] This can be seen, for example, in *Kearney*[223] where the Technical Board of Appeal held that a computer program that alerted machine operators when their machines needed to be repaired or a worn tool needed to be replaced solved a technical problem and as such was patentable subject matter. Similarly, in *Bosch* the Board of Appeal said that a device for monitoring computer components was technical because it considerably reduced 'the operating time of the computer component and thus undoubtedly improved the effectiveness of the device'.[224] Both of these decisions were followed in the UK.

In contrast, if it *cannot* be shown that an application that contains a computer program is technical, then it will not be patentable. This was the case, for example, in *Gale's Application* where the Court of Appeal decided that a ROM carrying a particular program was not distinguishable from the program itself and, as such, was unpatentable.[225] This was reinforced in *Fujitsu's Application*[226] where the Court of Appeal held that a computer-related invention that enabled chemists to produce digital models of hybrid chemicals was not patentable. The reason for this was that, while the invention saved chemists a considerable amount of time and effort (in that they did not have to undergo the laborious task of building models by hand), it did not produce a technical result. More specifically the Court of Appeal said that the invention only achieved something that had previously been possible albeit at a much faster speed and more conveniently than had previously been the case. On this basis, the Court of Appeal held that the invention was for a conventional computer operating in a conventional way and as such was not patentable.[227]

Following these decisions it was clear that an invention which included a computer program could be patentable so long as the invention as a whole was technical. With this question settled, the next question that arose for consideration was in relation to the exclusion of computer programs as such. The question of the scope of the exclusion of computer programs was considered in two decisions by the Technical Board of Appeal, both involving applications by IBM. The invention in the first decision *IBM/Computer programs* (T935/97) was a method

---

[221] *Vicom/Computer-related invention,* T208/84 [1987] *EPOR* 74; [1987] *OJ EPO* 14.

[222] This means that, if it can be shown that the subject matter makes a technical contribution to the known art, patentability would not be denied merely on the ground that a computer program is involved in its implementation.

[223] *Kearney/Computer-related invention,* T42/87 [1997] *EPOR* 236, 241.

[224] *Bosch/Electronic computer components,* T164/92 [1995] *EPOR* 585, 592. See generally J. Pila, 'Dispute over the Meaning of "invention" in Art 52(2) EPC: the patentability of Computer-Implemented Inventions in Europe' (2005) 36 *IIC* 173.

[225] *Gale's Application* [1991] *RPC* 305 (CA).   [226] *Fujitsu's Application* [1997] *RPC* 608.

[227] *Gale's Application* [1991] *RPC* 305.

for allowing information in a data-processing system that was displayed in one window to be altered if that window was obscured by another window. The application included claims for software in itself, and for software recorded in a computer-readable medium.[228] While some of the claims were accepted, the Examining Division refused the application insofar as it was directed to a computer-program product. The second *IBM* decision (T1173/97) related to 'resource recovery in a computer system'.[229] Again, the Examining Division rejected the application insofar as it claimed a computer-program product. In both cases the question for consideration related to the scope of the exclusion of computer program *as such*. The reasoning in both cases was identical.

The Board of Appeal began by noting that the language of Articles 52(2) and (3) showed that the legislators did not want to exclude all computer programs from patentability.[230] Instead, all that was excluded were computer programs *as such*. Drawing upon the logic that has been applied to Article 52(2) and (3) generally, the Board said that when the EPC referred to computer programs *as such*, it meant mere abstract creations, lacking in technical character. In more positive terms this meant that computer programs that had a technical character were potentially patentable.[231] In so doing, the Board distinguished between computer programs as such (which are not patentable) and computer programs that had a technical character (which are patentable).[232]

This gives rise to the question: when does a computer program have a technical character? As with all inventions, the requisite technical character may exist either in technical effects or in the solution to a technical problem. In addressing this question, the Board began by noting that a computer program cannot be assumed to have a technical character merely for the reason that it is a program for a computer. This means that *normal* 'physical modifications of the hardware (causing, for instance, the generation of electrical currents) deriving from the execution of the instructions given by programs for computers cannot *per se* constitute the technical character required for avoiding the exclusion of those programs'.[233] The Board added that such modifications were a common feature of all computer programs and therefore could not be used to distinguish programs with a technical character from programs 'as such'. Instead, the Board said that the technical character must be found elsewhere in the effects caused by the execution of the computer program by the hardware. That is, a computer program product could be patentable if it resulted in additional technical effects that went beyond the 'normal' physical interaction between the program (software) and the computer (hardware) on which it was run.

The Board also noted that computer program products only produced and showed an effect when the program concerned was made to run on a computer. The effect only shows in 'physical reality' when the program is being run. On the basis that there was no good reason to distinguish between a direct technical effect and the potential to produce a technical effect, the Board accepted that a computer program that had the potential to cause a predetermined further technical effect was in principle not excluded from patentability under Article 52(2) and (3).[234]

After reviewing the scope of protection for computer programs, the Board remitted both cases to the Examining Division to determine whether the applications complied with this

---

[228] *IBM/Computer programs*, T935/97 [1999] *EPOR* 301.

[229] *IBM/Computer programs*, T1173/97 [2000] *EPOR* 219.

[230] *IBM/Computer programs*, T935/97 [1999] *EPOR* 301, 309; T1173/97 [2000] *EPOR* 219, 226.

[231] They did so on the basis of EPC r. 27, 29. *IBM/Computer programs*, T1173/97 [2000] *EPOR* 219, 226.

[232] In so doing, the Board overturned *EPO Guidelines* C–IV 2.3 which state that a 'computer program by itself or as a record on a carrier is not patentable, irrespective of its content'. The Board also distinguished *ATT/System for generating code*, T204/93 (unreported, 29 Oct. 1993). *IBM/Computer programs*, T935/97 [1999] *EPOR* 301, 308.

[233] *IBM/Computer programs*, T935/97 [1999] *EPOR* 301, 310; T1173/97 [2000] *EPOR* 219, 227.

[234] *IBM/Computer programs*, T935/97 [1999] *EPOR* 301, 313; T1173/97 [2000] *EPOR* 219, 230.

reading of Article 52(2)(c). While it is clear that the *IBM* decisions mark a victory for the proponents of greater protection for information-technology-related inventions, ultimately the extent to which computer programs are patentable depends on how 'technical character' is construed. One factor that suggests that the exclusion will be read narrowly flows from the Board's comment that it does not make any difference for the purpose of the exclusion whether a computer program is claimed by itself or as a record on a carrier.[235] This means that so long as a computer program is technical, the medium in which it is recorded (the carrier) is irrelevant.[236] This would allow, for example, patents to be granted for software-implemented inventions distributed over the internet[237] and to computer-program products directly loadable into the internal memory of a digital computer.[238]

In order to ensure that practice at the UK Patent Office was consistent with the approach of the European Patent Office, in 1999 the UK Patent Office amended its practice guidelines to follow the *IBM* decisions.[239] The 1999 UK Patent Office *Practice Notice* provided that the British Patent Office would 'accept claims to computer programs, either in themselves or on a computer, provided that the program is such that when it is run on a computer it produces a technical effect which is more than would necessarily follow merely from the running of any program on a computer'.[240] (As we will see below, it has been suggested that the approach adopted in the 1999 *Practice Notice* reflects law in the UK after *Aerotel*).

While the law at the EPO may have changed after the *IBM* decisions, the law in the UK (which was reflected in the Patent Office *Practice Notice* from 1999) remained stable for a number of years, at least until the 2007 decision in *Aerotel*. As part of his wide-ranging judgment, Jacob LJ attempted to provide some guidance as to how 'computer program' was to be construed. Jacob LJ began by noting that there are two views about what was meant by a computer program. Under the first narrow view, which has been followed in post-*Pension Benefits* case law at the EPO, a computer program is the set of instructions as an abstract thing, albeit they could be written down on a piece of paper. The second wider view, which was adopted in pre-*Pension Benefits* case law at the EPO and in UK decisions (such as *Gale's Application*), sees a computer program as including the 'instructions on some medium (floppy disk, CD, or hard drive) which cause a computer to execute the program—a program that works'.[241] Jacob LJ came down in favour of the later wider view, arguing that to do otherwise would render the exclusion meaningless.[242] He also suggested that the framers of the EPC 'really meant to exclude computer programs in a practical and operable form. They meant to exclude real computer programs, not just an abstract series of instructions'.[243] In so doing, Jacob LJ appeared to

---

[235] *IBM/Computer programs*, T935/97 [1999] *EPOR* 301, 317; T1173/97 [2000] *EPOR* 219, 234.

[236] The Board said that if the 'computer program product comprises a computer-readable medium on which the program is stored, this medium only constitutes the physical support on which the program is saved and thus constitutes hardware'. *IBM/Computer programs*, T935/97 [1999] *EPOR* 301, 312; T1173/97 [2000] *EPOR* 219, 229.

[237] R. Hart, P. Holmes, and J. Reid, *The Economic Impact of Patentability of Computer Programs* (2000), 13.

[238] J. Lang, 'Patent Protection for e-Commerce Methods in Europe' [2000] *Computer and Telecommunications Law Review* 117, 119 (contrasting the IBM decisions with the US decision in *Re Beauregard*, 53 F.3d 1583 (Fed Cir 1995), which held that computer programs embodied in a tangible medium, such as floppy discs, are patentable). R. Hart, 'Computer Program-Related Patents' (1999) 15:3 *Computer Law and Security Report* 188, 189.

[239] PA s. 130(7); *Merrell Dow Pharmaceuticals v. Norton* [1996] *RPC* 76 (HL) (on the importance of unity of practice between UK Patent Office and EPO).

[240] Patent Office, *Practice Notice* [1999] RPC 563.

[241] *Aerotel v. Telco Holdings* [2007] 1 *All ER* 225, para 31.

[242] On this see *IGT v. Comptroller of Patents* [2007] *EWHC* 134, para 10 (the definition also included a program which was actually open on a computer and operational, and not simply a program sitting, stored, unopened on a hard drive).

[243] Ibid.

reaffirm British practice in this area. He also reinforced the divide that has opened up between the approach that is taken to section 1(2)/Article 52 in the UK and at the EPO.

While the Court of Appeal expressly said that it was reformulating rather than changing the law in this area, nonetheless following *Aerotel*, in November 2007 the UK Intellectual Property Office changed its practice in relation to the patenting of computer programs, and reverted to its old practice of rejecting all computer program claims.[244] The question whether the Intellectual Property Office's reading of *Aerotel* was correct was raised in the first instance decision on *Astron Clinica v Comptroller General of Patents*. In this case, Kitchin J considered whether *Aerotel* prohibited the patenting of all computer programs and, in particular, those which would have been considered under the old approach to make a conventional computer operate in a new way so as to deliver a relevant technical contribution.[245] For various reasons, Kitchin J said that he thought that the approach that had been adopted at the Intellectual Property Office after *Aerotel* was incorrect: instead, he inclined more to the approach that had been set out in the 1999 *Practice Notice*.

Kitchin J noted that the Court of Appeal in *Aerotel* had been critical of the EPO's adoption of the 'any hardware approach'. The Court of Appeal had also been critical of the practice of focusing on form rather than substance that had developed at the EPO (particularly in relation to the distinction that had been drawn between a program as a set of instructions and a program on a carrier). Nonetheless, Kitchin J did not see anything in the judgment that suggested that all computer programs were necessarily excluded. In particular, he said that there was nothing to suggest that the Court of Appeal had any doubts about the earlier *IBM* decisions. As Kitchin J said, the approach outlined in *Aerotel* was consistent with the reasoning of the Board of Appeal in the IBM decisions.[246] On the basis that the Court of Appeal had set out to re-order rather than change the test in *Merrill Lynch*, Kitchin J also said that the new approach should produce the same result as had been obtained under the old approach.[247] Applying the *Aerotel* test to a computer-related invention which produces a substantive technical contribution, Kitchin J said that the application of the second stage in *Aerotel* will identify that contribution, while the application of the third step will lead to the answer that the invention does not fall wholly within excluded matter. Importantly, Kitchin J said that the way that the *Aerotel* tests are answered would be the same 'irrespective of whether the invention is claimed in the form of a programmed computer, a method involving the use of that programmed computer, or the program itself'.[248] As Kitchin J said, the court in *Aerotel* concluded, as it had done in *Merrill Lynch* and *Gale*, 'that a computer program remained just that, whether in abstract form or embodied in a storage medium or in a computer'.[249] This meant that if 'a conventional computer programmed with...a new program is patentable because it is no longer a computer program as such then...the same reasoning must apply to the program itself. It is in the program that the technical advance truly lies'.[250] From this basis, Kitchin J concluded that 'where claims to a method performed by running a suitably programmed computer or to

---

[244] Intellectual Property Office, *Practice Notice* (2 Nov 2006). On this see *Astron Clinica v. Comptroller General of Patents* [2008] *EWHC* 85, para 46.

[245] *Astron Clinica v. Comptroller General of Patents* [2008] *EWHC* 85, para 46.

[246] They had also been followed by the 2007 Board of Appeal decision of *Tao Group Limited* (2007) T121/06.

[247] *Astron Clinica v. Comptroller General of Patents* [2008] *EWHC* 85, para 49. Kitchin J also said that the question of the patenting of computer programs did not arise in either *Aerotel* or Macrosson's inventions (para 47).

[248] Ibid, para 49.   [249] Ibid, para 41.   [250] Ibid.

a computer programmed to carry out the method are allowable, then, in principle, a claim to the program itself should also be allowable'.[251]

Following the clear statements by Kitchin J in *Astron Clinica,* in February 2008 the Intellectual Property Office issued a statement saying that it was going to replace aspects of the *Practice Notice* issued in November 2007.[252] While the original 2007 *Practice Notice* said that claims for computer programs or for programs on a carrier were not patentable, the 2008 revision, which came into operation on 7 February 2008, follows the approach in *Astron Clinica.* As a result of the 2008 revisions, the 2007 *Practice Notice* now says: so long as a claim to a computer program is drawn to reflect the features of the invention which would ensure the patentability of the method which the program is intended to carry out when it is run, examiners will no longer reject claims for a computer program or a program on a carrier. In so doing the change made to the 2007 *Practice Notice* not only applies the decision of Kitchin J, it also re-opens the door in the UK to the patenting of computer programs *per se.*[253]

Although British courts have adopted a more liberal approach to the patenting of computer programs than might have been envisaged when the 1977 Act was passed, nonetheless there are still some important limitations. While the extent to which computer-related inventions will be patentable always depends on the particular application in question, it can safely be said that in the UK an ordinary computer program used in a general-purpose computer would normally be unpatentable. The reason for this is that while the implementation of the program in a computer transforms mathematical values into electrical signals, the electrical signals amount to no more than a reproduction of information which would not be regarded as bringing about a technical effect.[254] It also seems clear that the mere inclusion of a program on a carrier is not enough to circumvent the exclusion: more is needed, such as a change in the speed with which the processor works.[255] This was reinforced in another post-*Aerotel* decision which concerned an invention for inventory management (that consisted of databases that contained both textual and pictorial information). In rejecting the application, the court said that 'the result is not a new combination of hardware as in *Aerotel.* Nor is [it] an improved computer or an improved display as in *Vicom.* The result is a computer of a known type operating according to a new program, albeit one which reduces the load on the processor and makes an economical use of the computer memory'.[256] On this basis the application was held to be a computer program and so excluded under section 1(2).

7.2.2 EPO

As we mentioned above, one of the consequences of the adoption of the any hardware approach at the EPO is that it is much easier for an invention to satisfy the subject matter requirement, whether for an apparatus or claim, than had previously been the case. Indeed, one commentator has suggested that Article 52 is now an insignificant bar to patentability, given that all that

[251] Ibid, para 50. Kitchin J said that he thought that the decision was consistent with *Re Oneida Indian Nation's Application* [2007] *EWCA* Civ 954 (Pat).

[252] Director of Patents, 'Patents Act 1977: Patentable Subject Matter' (7 February 2008).

[253] For a summary of the recent law and an example of a situation where claims were rejected see: *Autonomy Corporation v. Comptroller General* [2008] *EWHC* 146 (Pat).

[254] *Kock & Sterzel/X-ray apparatus,* T26/86 [1988] *EPOR* 72.

[255] Ibid, para 54. See also *Aerotel v. Telco Holdings* [2007] 1 *All ER* 225, para 92.

[256] *Raytheon v. Comptroller of Patents, Designs and Trade Marks* [2007] *EWHC* 1230.

is required to 'impart the requisite technical character to a claimed method is the specification of some technical means, however banal or well-known'.[257]

If an invention is implemented by a computer, it will be considered to use technical means and by that very token will be taken to have technical character.[258] This means that, so long as an invention makes use of, or is implemented by, a computer, it will fall outside the subject-matter exclusion. This can be seen in *Hitachi/Auction method,* where a method of using a memory (clipboard) on a computer was held to be an invention for the purposes of Article 52(1).[259] The liberal interpretation can also be seen in the *Microsoft/Clipboard formats I* decision.[260] The application in question, which was for a way of 'facilitating data exchange across different formats', consisted of both method claims and a claim for a program on a computer-readable medium. The Board said that the 'method was implemented in a computer and this amounted to a technical means sufficient to escape the prohibition in Article 52'. More specifically the Board said that 'a method implemented in a computer system represents a sequence of steps actually performed and achieving an effect'. Even though a method, in particular a method of operating a computer, may be put into practice with the help of a computer program, a claim relating to such a method does not claim a computer program as such.[261]

The any hardware approach has been extended beyond computer-implemented inventions in relation to the medium on which a computer program is supported. (Jacob LJ in *Aerotel* said that this presupposes that computer program is defined narrowly as an abstract set of instructions.) As the Technical Board of Appeal said in the *Microsoft/Clipboard formats I* decision, an invention will have technical character where it relates to a computer-readable medium (a technical product involving a carrier). That is, a computer-readable medium is a technical product and thus has technical character. This means that where a computer program enhances the internal operations of a computer it will have technical character: so long as it goes beyond the elementary interaction of hardware and software of data processing.[262]

7.3 METHODS OF DOING BUSINESS

The approach which has been used in the UK and at the EPO to determine whether an application is excluded on the basis that it consists of 'a method of doing business' under section 1(2)(c)/Article 52(2)(c) is much the same as has been used with the other areas of section 1(2)/Article 52.[263]

---

[257] David Booton, 'The Patentability of Computer-Implemented Inventions' (2007) IPQ 92, 102. J. Pila, 'Dispute over the Meaning of Invention in Art 52(2) EPC: The Patentability of Computer-Implemented Inventions in Europe' (2005) 36 *IIC* 173.

[258] *Infineon Technologies/Circuit simulation I,* T1227/05 (2007) *OJ EPO* 574, 581.

[259] T258/03 [2004] *OJ EPO* 575.

[260] *Microsoft/Clipboard formats I,* T0424/03 (23 Feb 2006), para 5.1.   [261] Ibid.

[262] Ibid; *IBM/Computer programs* [1999] *OJ EPO* 609. In *Astron Clinica,* Kitchen J said that the Board in *Microsoft/Clipboard formats* appears to have found that any program on a carrier has a technical character and so escapes the prohibition in Article 52'.

[263] See *Trilateral Report on Comparative Study on Business Method Related Inventions* (14 June 2000) for a summary of approaches at EPO and US and Japanese Patent Offices. H. Hanneman, 'The Patentability of "Methods of Doing Business"' [2000] *epi Information* 16; D. Booton and P. Mole 'The Action Freezes? The Draft Directive on the Patentability of Computer-implemented inventions' [2002] *IPQ 289*.

7.3.1 United Kingdom

The approach adopted in the UK (and at the EPO prior to *Pension Benefits*) is the same as the general approach discussed earlier. This can be seen in *Merrill Lynch's Application*[264] where the Court of Appeal held that an automatic share-trading system operated by a computer program was unpatentable because it merely amounted to a method of doing business. This has been confirmed by a UK Patent Office *Practice Notice*[265] and in a number of subsequent decisions.[266] A similar approach had been followed at the EPO. This can be seen in *Petterson/Queueing system*,[267] which concerned a patent for a system for handling customers queuing at a number of service points. The patent consisted of a turn-number allocating unit, an information unit, a selection unit, and a computer program that decided which particular turn-number was to be served at a particular service point. While the patent was rejected in Sweden, the Board of Appeal at the EPO held that the claimed apparatus was clearly technical in nature and thus patentable.[268] Although the invention was used in a business context, a telling factor in the Board's decision to uphold the validity of the patent was their finding that the essence of the invention lay in the way the elements of the system were combined.[269] More specifically, the validity of the patent was upheld because the problem that the invention solved related to the way the components of the system interacted: which was seen as a technical rather than a business problem.[270]

The Court of Appeal in *Aerotel* said that business-method exclusion was not limited to abstract matters. The Court also said that there was no need for an activity to be completed—for the cash register to ring—for it to fall within the exclusion.[271] On the basis that the information was to be used in the conduct of the business, it was held that the idea of presenting information to be used in undertaking inventories in a pictorial form was a method of doing

---

[264] *Merrill Lynch's Application* [1989] RPC 561; *Maghsordi's Application* (SRIS O/86/96); *Stockburger/Coded distinctive mark*, T51/84 [1986] EPOR 229.

[265] Patent Office Practice Notice, *Patents Act 1977: Interpreting section 1(2)* (24 Apr. 2002) [2002] RPC 40. (Stressing that technical contribution is the basis for deciding patentability and in so doing rejecting the view that 'some excluded things cannot be patentable even if a technical contribution is present'. This means that 'inventions which involve a technical contribution will not be refused a patent merely because they relate to business methods or mental acts'.)

[266] *Crawford v. Jones* [2005] EWHC 2417 (Pat). The following applications were refused at the UK Patent Office on the basis that they were business methods: web-based on-line user system for ordering computer equipment—*Dell USA*, O/432/01 (4 Oct. 2001); system for exchange of information between providers and enquirers—*Pintos Global Services*, O/171/01 (6 Apr. 2001); a system for automating the ordering of food in a cafeteria—*Fujitsu Ltd*, O/324/03 (23 Oct. 2003); method for allowing users to buy personalized financial products over the internet—*Accucard Ltd*, O/145/03 (29 May 2003); a computer system for handling conflicting demands for resources, such as booking of meeting rooms—*Fujitsu Ltd*, O/317/00 (23 Aug. 2000).

[267] T1002/92 [1995] *OJ EPO* 605; [1996] *EPOR* 1; See also *Texas Instruments/Language-understanding system*, T236/91 [2000] *EPOR* 156; *Fujitsu's Application* (23 Aug. 2000) (O/317/00).

[268] The possibility of patenting business method inventions received a boost as a result of the *Sohei* decision where the Technical Board of Appeal suggested that 'business' ought to be construed narrowly: *Sohei/General-purpose management system*, T769/92 [1996] *EPOR* 253, 258. *Sohei* 'is generally acknowledged to have adopted an even more software-friendly approach in assessing patentability'. Kober (President of the EPO), 'Software Patents'.

[269] *NAT/Bagging plant* [1993] *EPOR* 517 (claims were allowed for a computer method which involved weighing and bagging on the quayside material transported in bulk by ship, because it used technical equipment to achieve a technical end (the production of sealed weighed bags of materials)). See also *Pension Benefit Systems*, T931/95 [2001] *OJ EPO* 441 (TBA) (claim for method of controlling a pension administration system).

[270] *Sohei/General purpose management system*, T769/92 [1996] *EPOR* 253; *Pitney Bowes/System for processing mail*, T767/99 (13 March 2002) (TBA), para. 2.6.

[271] *Aerotel v. Telco Holdings* [2007] 1 *All ER* 225, paras 67–71.

business.[272] It has also been said that the mere fact that an invention provides financial gains is not enough for it to be classified as a method of doing business: otherwise, nearly all patents would fall within the exclusion.[273]

7.3.2 EPO

As we noted above, the fate of methods of doing business under the any hardware approach at the EPO was clearly spelt out in the *Pension Benefits* decision.[274] (It is important to note that the reasoning developed in *Pension Benefits* was extended to both apparatus and method claims.) Given that the corresponding patent application was granted in the United States, the decision also highlights the difference in approach between Europe and the USA in relation to patent protection for business-method inventions.[275]

7.4 THE PRESENTATION OF INFORMATION

The approach that has been used in the UK and the EPO to determine whether an invention consists of the presentation of information and thus falls foul of section 1(2)(d)/Article 52(2) (d) is similar to the approach that has been used in relation to the other categories of subject matter excluded from protection.[276]

7.4.1 United Kingdom

The approach that has been adopted in the UK (and at the EPO prior to *Pension Benefits*) in relation to the presentation of information can be seen in *Broselow/Measuring tape,* where the invention was for a method of ascertaining information about accident victims (such as drug dosage or defibrillation techniques). More specifically, the method involved an ambulance officer measuring the body length of the emergency victim using a particular tape, which provided information about how the patient was to be treated. Importantly this was done without the need for clinical expertise or reference to other sources. Highlighting the importance of the way the invention is construed, the Board of Appeal held that the 'co-relation between the measured length and the information on the tape measure results in the tape...becoming a

---

272 *Raytheon, v. Comptroller General of Patents, Designs and Trade Marks* [2007] *EWHC* 1230 (Pat), para 40. For more recent discussion see: *Autonomy Corporation v. The Comptroller General of Patents* [2008] *EWHC* 146 (Pat) (6 Feb. 2008).

273 *Quest International/Odour Selection,* T619/02 [2007] *OJ EPO* 63.

274 This is reflected in the *EPO Guidelines* which state that 'in relation to an apparatus claim which contains computers, computer networks or other conventional programmable apparatus or a program thereof, for carrying out at least some steps of a scheme, it is to be examined as a computer-related invention'. *EPO Guidelines,* C–IV.

275 A patent had been granted on the appellant's pension system in the US. See *Pension Benefit Systems,* note 111 above, 447 (para. iv). Despite the fact that the reasoning of the Board was said to be reminiscent of the USPTO's 1996 *Guidelines for the Examination of Computer-Related Inventions,* see M. Likhovski, 'Fighting the Patent Wars' [2001] *EIPR* 267, 270. In the USA, see *State Street Bank & Trust v. Signature Financial Group* 149 *F. 3d* 1368 (1998). The Federal Circuit Court of Appeals (23 Jul. 1998) said that 'since the 1952 Patent Act, business methods have been, and should have been, subject to the same legal requirements (utility, novelty, non-obviousness, disclosure) for patentability as applied to any other process or method' so that a patent application relating to the transformation of data, representing discrete dollar amounts, by a machine, through a series of mathematical calculations into a final share price, constitutes a practical application of a mathematical algorithm, formula or calculation, and is thus patentable subject matter. There is no exception for 'methods of doing business'.

276 See, e.g. *Texas Instruments/Language-understanding system,* T236/91 [2000] *EPOR* 156; See also *Hiroki Ashizawa,* O/235/03 (18 Aug. 2003) (Patent Office); *Crawford v. Jones* [2005] *EWHC* 2417 (application excluded on the basis that it was limited to display of information).

new gauge for directly measuring the patient treatment values'. Such a new gauge 'for directly measuring the patient values, is clearly technical in character'.[277]

When considering whether a patent is excluded under Article 52(2) and (3), the EPO drew a distinction between ordinary (cognitive) information, which is excluded by section 1(2)(d)/ Article 52(2)(d), and special (functional) information (which is not excluded).[278]

Ordinary cognitive information, which is the type of information excluded under section 1(2)(d)/Article 52(2)(d) as a presentation of information, includes subject matter that merely conveys cognitive or aesthetic content directly to a human.[279] In essence, ordinary cognitive information includes any representation of information that is characterized solely by the content of the information. This would include, for example, a TV signal solely characterized by the information *per se* (e.g. moving pictures, modulated upon a standard TV signal). Similarly, digital data that encode cognitive content (such as a picture) in a standard manner would also be excluded.[280] As the *EPO Guidelines* explain, a claim will be excluded where it is directed to the presentation of information *per se* (e.g. acoustic signals, spoken words), to information recorded on a carrier where the carrier (i.e. the book, the gramophone record, or magnetic computer tape) is characterized solely by the content being carried (the subject of the book, musical content, or data or programs), or to processes and apparatus for the presentation of information.[281] In all these cases, the key aspect of the invention is the content of the message.

In contrast, a patent for *functional information* (or data) does not fall within the scope of Article 52(2)(d). As with all inquiries into excluded subject matter, if it can be shown that the information carrier, or the process or apparatus for presenting the information, has a technical feature, the invention may be patentable. It is also possible that the arrangement or manner of representation, as compared with the content of the information itself, may be patentable. This would include instruments designed to measure information, or the use of a code to represent characters. In explaining what is meant by functional information, the EPO supported the view that information (in its special sense) must not be confused with meaning. In fact, two messages, one of which is heavily loaded with meaning and the other of which is pure nonsense, can be exactly equivalent from the information technology point of view. Information in communication theory relates not so much to what you do say, as to what you could say. That is, information is a measure of one's freedom of choice when one selects a message.[282]

---

[277] *Broselow/Measuring tape* T77/92 [1998] *EPOR* 266, 270. The Board added that 'the subject matter as a whole of a claim consisting of a mix of known technical elements and non-technical elements is not excluded from patentability under Art. 52(2) and (3) when the non-technical elements interact with the known technical elements in order to produce a technical effect'.

[278] The Board said that with the growth of information technology in the last half-century, information in its 'special sense had become much more important'. Nonetheless, the Board noted that the information mentioned in Art. 52(2)(d) was limited to information in the ordinary (cognitive sense): *Koninklijke Philips Electronics/Picture retrieval system*, T1194/97 [2000] *OJ EPO* 525, 541, para. 3.7.2.

[279] Ibid. The Board said that the only decision that appeared to have construed 'presentation of information' to include an aspect of the special sense of information was *Kock & Sterzal/X-ray apparatus*, T26/86 [1988] *EPOR* 72. The Board noted that *Kock & Sterzal* dealt with the exclusion of computer programs and as such was 'strictly obiter as far as Article 52(2)(d) is concerned': para. 3.7.4.

[280] In rejecting an application for a configuration for simultaneously displaying several images on a computer screen, the Technical Board of Appeal said that imparting information on events in a screen window merely drew attention to the content of the images and, as such, was not technical: T599/93 [1997] *OJ EPO* (special edn.) 14.

[281] *EPO Guidelines* C–IV, 2.

[282] *Koninklijke Philip's Electronics*, T1194/97 (15 Mar. 2000), para. 3.7.1, quoting from C. Shannon and W. Weaver, *The Mathematical Theory of Communication* (1949) [no page number provided].

Using this definition the Board of Appeal said that information in the special (non-excluded) sense includes physical interactions within and between machines that do not convey any humanly understandable meaning. They have also said that a TV signal solely characterized by the information *per se* (e.g. moving pictures, modulated upon a standard TV signal) would be an excluded presentation of information. In contrast, a TV signal defined in terms that included the technical features of the TV system in which it occurs has been held not to be a presentation of information.[283] In a similar fashion, the Board held that an invention that was defined in terms that inherently included the technical features of the system in which the record carrier operated was not excluded as a presentation of information.[284] In *Koninklijke* the Board said that the difference between (excluded) cognitive information and (non-excluded) functional data was illustrated by the fact that if the cognitive data or content were lost, the result would be a humanly meaningless picture, like snow on a TV screen. This would not have any effect whatsoever on the technical working of the system. In contrast, the loss of functional data would impair the technical operation of the system and might indeed bring the system to a halt.[285]

To date there has been no indication from British courts as to whether they will follow the approach that had developed at the EPO pre-*Pension Benefits*. The only guidance courts in the UK have provided is to note that this 'presentation of information' in section 1(2)(d) was not limited to the way that information is presented or expressed (the format, font etc), but also includes the provision of information. On this basis, it was held that an application for an advent calendar designed so that it could be used simultaneously by more than one person was excluded under section 1(2)(d).[286]

7.4.2 EPO

The approach adopted at the EPO under the any hardware approach in relation to 'presentations of information' has been consistent with the general approach outlined above. Thus, if an invention employs some technical means, it will not fall foul of Article 52(2)(d): even if the contribution made by the invention was limited to presentation of information. One of the consequences of the adoption of the any hardware approach is that the some of the earlier decisions at the EPO, which were based on the contribution test, will no longer be followed.[287] In *Hitachi/Auction Method,* the Technical Board of Appeal said that the *Guidelines* at the EPO were inconsistent with the approach outlined in *Pension Benefits* insofar as they say that 'devices such as visual displays, books, gramophone records, traffic signs and apparatus for said not to be patentable…if defined solely by the content of the information.[288] It seems clear that applications of this nature will now pass the subject-matter test in Article 52(2)(d) if they include some technical means: no matter how old, banal, or trivial.

---

[283] *BBC/Colour television signal,* T163/85 [1990] *EPOR* 599, 603; *OJ EPO* 379, 603.

[284] On the facts the Board held that the claim in question was not a presentation of information since it had functional data recorded thereon (in particular a data structure of picture line syntonization, line numbers, and addressees): *Koninklijke Philip's Electronics/Picture retrieval system,* T1194/97 (15 Mar. 2000). The Board followed *IBM/Computer programs,* T1173/97 [1999] *OJ EPO* 609.

[285] *Koninklijke Philip's Electronics,* T1194/97 (15 Mar. 2000).

[286] *Re Townsend's Patent Application* [2004] *EWHC* 482 (Pat).

[287] This can be seem, for example, in the decision of the Board in *Infineon Technologies/Circuit simulation I,* T1227/05 [2007] *OJ EPO* 574, 584–7 that the decisions of *IBM/Method for physical VLSI-chip design,* T453/91 (31 May 1994) and *International Computers/Information modelling,* T49/99 (5 Mar. 2002) were no longer to be followed.

[288] T258/03 [2004] *OJ EPO* 575, 583.

7.5 METHODS FOR PERFORMING A MENTAL ACT

While the approach that has been adopted at the UK (and at the EPO pre-*Pension Benefits*) and at the EPO (under the any hardware approach) has been fairly consistent, albeit somewhat confusing, this is not the case in relation to the exclusion of claims for methods for performing a mental act, which is to be found in section 1(2)(c)/Article 52(2)(c).

7.5.1 United Kingdom

The approach that has been adopted in the UK towards the exclusion of methods for performing mental acts has involved the application, at a general level, of the approach that was outlined above. The main difference is that there has been more attention given to what is meant by 'performing a mental act'. That is, the decisions have seemed to focus more on the statutory language, than on whether the invention is technical: which is one of the main advantages of the approach outlined in *Aerotel*. In line with this, it has been suggested that 'if a claim covers a method of arriving at a particular result by the exercise of rational process alone, then . . . it is a claim to a scheme, rule or method of performing a mental act'.[289] Beyond this, the approach that has been adopted in the UK and at the EPO prior to to *Pension Benefits* differs depending on the nature of the invention in question. This is particularly the case in relation to inventions in the field of text editing, artificial intelligence, and expert systems. While there is agreement between courts in the UK and the EPO (pre-*Pension Benefits*) in relation to many aspects of section 1(2)/Article 52(2), there are a number of differences in the way they have approached the exclusion of mental acts.

Text editing. In considering whether text-editing-based inventions are patentable, the EPO pre-*Pension Benefits* largely followed the line of thought used in relation to other areas of Article 52(2). This meant that if an application only related to the internal, linguistic elements of the text (which are seen as being non-technical), it fell foul of Article 52(2) and was thus unpatentable. This can be seen in *IBM/Text-clarity processing*[290] where the Technical Board of Appeal was called upon to decide whether an application for improving the clarity of texts was patentable. The invention in question was made up of a program that identified linguistic expressions that were difficult to understand. The program then offered alternative expressions that were easier to understand. An important factor in the decision that the invention was directed to text editing and, as such, that it was not patentable was that the inventive element of the application lay in the mental elements of the process: *viz.* in the process of identifying parts of texts that were difficult to understand and offering alternatives. Unfortunately for the applicants, the Board of Appeal found that the process by which these mental acts were placed in a format where they could be performed automatically by a computer only involved the routine straightforward application of conventional techniques. Given that the only contribution made by the application was in relation to the mental steps of the process and not (for example) in the way these steps were automatically carried out by computer, the Board declared that the application was invalid. A number of other text-editing applications have been rejected on

---

[289] *Cappellini v. Comptroller of Patents* [2007] *EWHC* 476; also [2007] *All ER* (D), para 8.

[290] *IBM/Text clarity processing*, note 133 above (application for a method for detecting and replacing incomprehensible expressions using conventional hardware and a dictionary); *IBM/External interface simulation*, T833/91 [1998] *EPOR* 431 (method of designing external interfaces for a computer application program excluded).

the basis that they use the same steps as mental processes and when automated merely employ conventional equipment ordinarily programmed.[291]

In contrast, if it can be shown that the contribution made by the application is technical and not merely linguistic in nature, then it was prima facie patentable. That is, if it can be shown that the application extends beyond text processing to provide a technical contribution or resolve some technical problem, then it will be patentable. A helpful example of this is provided by *IBM/Editable document form*,[292] which concerned an application for a method for transforming printer control items in word-processing documents from one format to another (which in turn allowed documents to be transferred from one text-processing format to another). Using the same logic that is used in relation to the other parts of Article 52(2), the Board of Appeal said that, in considering whether the application was valid, they needed to 'investigate whether the claim seen as a whole constitutes nothing more than a method for performing mental acts as such, albeit performed on a computer'. After reviewing the nature of the invention in question, the Board found that the application could not be described as a method for performing a mental act (nor as a computer program). The reason for this was that the invention was concerned above all with (printer) control items in the source document. Given that the ultimate purpose of these control items was the control of hardware, the Board said that the application had nothing to do with the linguistic meaning of the texts being processed. Rather, it represented features of the technical, internal working of that system.[293] As such, the application did not fall foul of Article 52(2)(c).

While there was a consistent line of authority in relation to text-editing-based inventions at the EPO (pre-*Pension Benefits),* as yet no pertinent decisions in this field have been heard in the UK. However, on the basis of the approach that has been adopted by British courts in relation to the patenting of expert systems (discussed below), there is good reason to doubt whether UK courts will follow the approach adopted at the EPO pre-*Pension Benefits* towards text-editing inventions.

Expert systems.   Although courts in the UK and at the EPO (pre-*Pension Benefits*) are largely in agreement that a patent will not be granted if the only contribution that the invention offers is mental (or intellectual), there is disagreement as to what is meant by a 'mental act'.[294] More specifically there is disagreement as to whether or not and, if so, in what circumstances a process which automatically performs a mental act will fall within the scope of section 1(2)(c)/Article 52(2)(c). This difference is most notable when the respective tribunals have considered the nature of patent protection available for expert systems.

While methods of performing mental acts *per se* remain unpatentable at the EPO, where technical means are used to carry out a method for performing a mental act, such a process *may* be patentable. Although these inventions may face difficulties in relation to obviousness

---

[291] *Siemens/Character form*, T158/88 [1992] *EPOR* 69 (methods for representing letters on a VDU was non-technical); *Beattie/Marker*, T603/89 [1992] *EPOR* 221 (apparatus for a method for learning how to play a keyboard instrument was non-technical). Abstracting a document (*IBM/Document abstracting & retrieving*, T22/85 [1990] *EPOR* 98); processing data set out in table form (T95/86); detecting linguistic expressions (*IBM/Text clarity processing*, T38/86 [1990] *EPOR* 606); detecting contextual homophone errors ('there' for 'their') (*IBM/Text processing*, T65/86 [1990] *EPOR* 181): were all held not patentable because they were 'mental acts'.

[292] T110/90 [1995] *EPOR* 185.

[293] They were said to be akin to the technical functions carried out in mechanical typewriters, such as carriage return, new page, and new paragraph.

[294] See D. Wells, 'Expert Systems, Mental Acts and Technical Effects' (1995) *CIPAJ* 129; C. Muse, 'Patented Personality' (1988) 4 *Computer High Technology Law Journal* 285.

and novelty, the EPO (pre-*Pension Benefits*) accepted that patents would not fall foul of Article 52(2)(c) if the invention viewed as a whole was technical.[295] Many of the activities which are carried out by a computer, such as object recognition or the checking of text for spelling mistakes, are tasks that can also be performed by humans. Nonetheless, the EPO pre-*Pension Benefits* had been willing to accept that activities carried out automatically by machine may be *qualitatively* different to similar activities carried out by humans. That is, while a computer and a human may perform the same task, when this task is carried out automatically by computer it might be done with such speed or accuracy that it is not the same as a functionally equivalent task performed by a human.[296]

In contrast, courts in the United Kingdom have consistently refused applications that amount to the automation of operations that could otherwise be performed by humans.[297] This means that inventions in the fields of expert systems,[298] pattern recognition systems,[299] or systems for rearranging conflicting demands for resources (such as room bookings)[300] will not be patentable in the United Kingdom. Somewhat bizarrely, this is the case even if the invention could not be carried out by the unaided human mind.[301] While the EPO (pre-*Pension Benefits*) had accepted that where a mental act is automatically performed by a computer the activity may change in such a way that it can no longer be seen as the performance of a mental act, in the United Kingdom such activities remain a method for performing a mental act. This is the case even when the computer carries out the process in a way that could not be mimicked by the human mind.[302] This point was reinforced by the Court of Appeal in *Fujitsu's Application* where it was held that the concept for performing a mental act should be construed widely to include all methods of the type performed mentally, even if the particular method in question would not be carried out by the human mind.[303] This was because a method 'remains a method for performing a mental act, whether a computer is used or not'. As Aldous LJ said, 'a method of solving a problem, such as advising a person whether he has acted tortiously, can be set out

---

[295] *Stockburger/Coded distinctive mark*, T51/84 [1986] *EPOR* 229.

[296] *IBM/Text clarity processing*, T38/86 [1990] *EPOR* 606. See the discussion on the EPO practice on text editing above at pp. 435–6. See also, D. Wells 'Patents for Software: the "Mental Act" Exclusion' [1993] *CIPAJ* 272, 273 (arguing that the UK Patent Office's decision in *Raytheon's Application* [1993] *RPC* 427 is 'completely at variance with the practice of the EPO'). For the position in Germany (following the approach at the EPO) see *Sprachanalyseeinrichtung (Language analysis device)* (BGH), X Z.B 15/98 [2002] *OJ EPO* 415.

[297] Claims for an inference processor forming the core of an expert system have been allowed in a hearing at the Patent Office. D. Wells, 'Expert Systems, Mental Acts and Technical Effects' [1995] *CIPAJ* 129.

[298] *Wang Laboratories* [1991] *RPC* 463 (expert system, comprising a conventional computer operating in the normal way with an expert system program the knowledge base of which was in the form of hierarchically defined terms and their definitions, was a mental act and was therefore excluded from protection).

[299] *Raytheon's Application* [1993] *RPC* 427 (patent for a method of 'pattern recognition and the matching of silhouettes, particularly those of ships' was rejected). In *Fujitsu's Application* [1996] *RPC* 511, the Court of Appeal refused an application directed to methods for modelling a synthetic crystal structure by combining images of two structures to display a third image representing a further crystal structure. In rejecting the application, the Court focused on the method claimed which 'left it to the operator to select what data to work on, how to work on it, and which results, if any results, to use'. The control left to the operator was such that the end product was largely determined by the personal skill of the operator. To have granted a patent over this would have meant that property rights were being granted (in substance) for a scheme or method of performing a mental act.

[300] *Fujitsu's Application*, O/317/00 (23 Aug. 2000) (Patent Office).

[301] *KK Toshiba* [1993] *IPD* 160 (19 Feb. 1993).

[302] *Fujitsu's Application* [1996] *RPC* 511, 518–19 (Patent Office).

[303] *Fujitsu's Application* [1997] *RPC* 608. The suggestion was made that the provision be limited to those acts that can be carried out by the human mind. This was rejected on the basis it would require the courts to engage in the extremely difficult task of deciding how the human mind actually works: ibid, 619–20.

on paper or incorporated into a computer program. The purpose is the same, to enable advice to be given, which appears to me to be a mental act'. Aldous LJ added that the 'method may well be different when a computer is used, but to my mind it still remains a method for performing a mental act, whether or not the computer program adopts steps that would not ordinarily be used by the human mind'.[304]

The current position in the United Kingdom is not only out of step with the approach adopted at the EPO pre-*Pension Benefits,* it is also out of step with the image of technology as the process of artificially reproducing that which already exists in nature. In part this can be attributed to a failure to recognize that while activities carried out by machines may be functionally equivalent to similar tasks performed by the human mind, this does not mean that the two are therefore necessarily equivalent. While computer-related inventions may perform tasks analogous to those carried out by humans, there must come a time when the analogy breaks down. That is, there is a point when a process which is carried out by a computer is so qualitatively different to a functionally equivalent process carried out by the human mind that the two events cannot be equated with each other: the question that is yet to be determined in the United Kingdom is where and how this line is to be drawn.

7.5.2 EPO

For the most part the approach adopted at the EPO under the any hardware approach in relation to methods for performing mental acts has been consistent with the general approach outlined above. This can be seen, for example in *Quest International/Odour Selection,* where the invention was directed to matching the tastes of the public to the design of perfumes. More specifically, it involved a 'perceptual evocation test' in which a person was presented with certain odours and with a target or priming stimulus of a visual or auditory nature. This was used to select an odour according to the response of the test subject. Insofar as the method in question involved physical activities ('activities in the physical world such as presenting test persons with odours and stimuli'), the Board held that the method did not constitute a mental act.[305] In this respect, the decision follows the any hardware approach. In other respects, however, the Board seemed to adopt some of the techniques that had been applied under the contribution approach. The Board also provided a detailed analysis of what is meant by 'methods for performing mental acts'. In particular, the Board said that the selection method used in the application relies on the test subject's 'implicit odour memory', that is, non-conscious associative recollections as opposed to explicit memory. They added that such 'perceptual processes (emotions, impressions, feelings etc) are psychological in nature and relate to—at least to a predetermined degree—subconscious processes that take place in the human mind, in contrast to the abstract nature of mental acts within the meaning of Article 52(2)(c)—are primarily based on cognitive, conceptual or intellectual processes conducted by the human mind.'[306] On this basis the Board said that not even the perceptual processes in the mind of the test subject constituted mental acts within the meaning of Article 52(2)(c). Given that this is the type of analysis promoted under the third stage of the *Aerotel* test, it will be interesting to see whether this reasoning is adopted in the UK.

---

[304] *Wang Laboratories' Application* [1991] *RPC* 463, 473; *Fujitsu's Application* [1997] *RPC* 620, 621 (CA). The comptroller adopted a similar approach to reject an application for a computerized system for resolving disputes for resources (such as room or flight bookings) according to certain priorities more easily accessible to users: *Fujitsu's Application,* O/317/00 (23 Aug. 2000), 11.

[305] *Quest International/Odour Selection,* T619/02 [2007] *OJ EPO* 63, 73.   [306] Ibid.

7.6 REFORM

The last three decades have seen a remarkable transformation in the way computer programs and computer-related inventions are dealt with under European law. From a situation where computer programs 'as such' were expressly excluded from patentability, approximately 15 per cent of all applications for patents received by the EPO[307] and the UK Patent Office relate to computer-implemented inventions.[308] The scope of protection available for computer-related inventions was enhanced by the fact that while computer programs *per se* have long been considered to be non-technical and thus outside the scope of patent law, this way of thinking about computer programs has recently been questioned. In particular, a number of decisions at the EPO have recast computer programs as technical creations.[309] This reconfiguration of computer programs has been particularly important in light of Article 27 of TRIPS which states that 'patents shall be available for any inventions, whether products or processes, in all fields of technology' and that 'patents shall be...enjoyable without discrimination as to...field of technology'.[310]

Notwithstanding (or possibly because of) these changes, there have been growing calls for reform of the scope of protection available for computer programs and computer-related inventions in Europe.[311] In part, these debates have been stimulated by changes in US patent law that facilitated the patenting of computer programs and business methods.[312] As well as setting a benchmark against which European law is judged, the liberalization of the level of protection in the USA also led to a flood of applications for computer-related inventions in Europe. In turn, these changes have led to the suggestion that the threshold for protection in Europe should be lowered to ensure that there is a level playing field between Europe and the USA. In response to such suggestions, a consortium of interests led by members of the open-source community have campaigned against greater protection.[313]

Despite the widespread calls for reform, to date there has been little change in the scope of protection for computer-implemented inventions in Europe. At best, there have been proposals for the law to be changed to make it clearer and more consistent. Notably, the American approach that protects business-method inventions has not found favour at the EPO, the UK Intellectual Property Office, or in any of the Community agencies responsible for legislative change in Europe. The preference for the status quo can be seen in the revision of the EPC

[307] *Report of the proposal for a directive of the European Parliament and of the Council on the patentability of computer-implemented inventions* (COM) (2002) 92) European Parliament (18 Jun. 2003).

[308] UK Patent Office, *Progress on Directive for Software Patents* (25 Sept. 2003) (15 per cent of 30,000 applications received each year).

[309] *Bosch/Electronic computer components*, T164/92 [1995] *EPOR* 585, 592.

[310] The Board of Appeal noted that, as the EPO was not a signatory to TRIPS, they were not bound by it. However, on the basis that TRIPS aimed at 'setting common standards and it acted as an indicator of modern trends, the Board noted that it was the clear intention of TRIPS not to exclude from patentability any inventions, in particular, not to exclude programs for computers': *IBM/Computer programs*, T1173/97 [2000] *EPOR* 219, 224–5.

[311] For problems associated with software patents see D. Haselden, 'The Practical Issues: A View from a Patent Office', *The Patent Office Conference on Software Patents* (<http://www.patent.gov.uk/softpat/en/index.html>). These include (i) practical problems of searching prior art given that there is no tradition of patenting software, (ii) lack of expertise, (iii) problems of breadth, and (iv) the problem of description.

[312] Prompted by changes in US Patent Office guidelines which expanded the scope of protection offered to computer programs in America. *USPTO Guidelines*, Jan. 1997. As long as it is novel, a computer program that causes a computer to function in a particular fashion would be protected. This is not the case in Europe.

[313] These include EuroLinux and the Association for the Promotion of Free Information Infrastructure (FFII).

that took place in 2000. While it was suggested that 'computer programs as such' be deleted from the subject matter excluded from patentable status in Article 52(2)(c),[314] delegates to the Diplomatic Conference voted against the proposal.[315] As a result, Article 52(2)(c) EPC 2000 replicates the exclusion of 'programs for computers' that was found in Article 52(2)(c) EPC 1973.

The UK government came out in support of the status quo. During a process of consultation in 2000, respondents were asked to what extent should computer programs and internet business methods be patentable. The resulting study found that, while there was no consensus about the extent to which software should be patentable,[316] there was support for the ongoing patentability of computer-related inventions with technical effect. It was also clear from the responses that the law in this area was unclear. This led the UK government to conclude that clarification was needed, particularly as to 'how to define the boundary defining when software is, and is not, part of a technological innovation, so that what is patentable will be clear in specific cases in the future'.[317] The consultation process also revealed that there was widespread opposition to patents for computer-implemented business methods that did not bring about some form of technological innovation.[318] This led the UK government to conclude that 'those who favour some form of patentability for business methods have not provided the necessary evidence that it would be likely to increase innovation. Unless and until that evidence is available, ways of doing business should remain unpatentable'.[319]

One of the consequences of the decision to retain the status quo in the revised EPC 2000 was that the debate on the patenting of computer-related inventions shifted to the European Commission and the European Parliament. After a period of consultation, which raised a number of questions about the scope, nature, and impact of patents for computer-related inventions,[320] the Commission's response took shape with the publication of the draft *Directive on the Patentability of Computer-Implemented Inventions* in February 2002.[321] With the possible exception of the exclusion of a 'patent claim to a computer program, either on its own or on a carrier',[322] the draft Directive does not expressly alter existing law. For example, business methods, algorithms, and non-technical computer-implemented inventions were also excluded from protection. However, given that the proposed Directive used concepts that are alien to British law, there was a chance that the Directive might have brought about a number of unexpected consequences. This is reinforced by the fact that, although the Directive was very short (it consisted of six Articles), it lacks a coherent structure.

---

[314] Distributed by the German Federal Ministry of Justice on 26 Jun. 2000 CA3sh1000/00.

[315] M. Delio, 'Europe Nixes Software Patents' (23 Nov. 2000) *Wired News*, at <http://www.wired.com>. Art. 1, item 17 of EPC 2000. As the explanatory remarks explained, the EPO Board of Appeal decisions, that computer programs producing a technical effect are patentable subject matter, meant that the 'current exception has become de facto obsolete'. Base Proposal for the Revision of the European Patent Convention, CA/100/00 e (2000), 37. It was also suggested that Art. 52(2) ought to be abolished altogether. This was not put forward to the Diplomatic Conference for Nov. 2000.

[316] See *Should patents be granted for computer software or ways of doing business?: The government conclusions* (March 2001), para. 11. Available at <http://www.patent.gov.uk/about/formal_consultations>.

[317] Ibid, para. 20.   [318] Ibid, para. 21.   [319] Ibid, para. 24.

[320] The EC launched a process of consultation on 19 Oct. 2000.

[321] *Proposal for a Directive on the Patentability of Computer-implemented Inventions* (hereinafter, Computer-Implemented Inventions Dir.). The Council considered the proposal and reached a common position in Nov. 2002. See Committee on Legal Affairs and the Internal Market, *Report on the Proposal for a Directive* (18 Jun. 2003) FINAL A5–0238/2003 (McCarthy Report). For a discussion of the proposed Directive see Bently and Sherman, 2nd edn), p. 423.

[322] Computer-Implemented Inventions Dir. Art 5(1a).

Faced with widespread criticisms of the Draft Directive, particularly from the open-source community, not unsurprisingly the proposed Directive was resoundly rejected by the European Parliament in July 2005.[323] While many commentators took this as marking the end of the issue, in 2007 the question of the patentability of computer-related inventions was reopened by the EPO President who has called for public discussion to fill the vacuum left by the rejection of the Directive.[324] In the meantime, it seems that the jurisprudence developed at the EPO and in the United Kingdom will continue to play a key role in the transformation of patent law in this area.

8   BIOLOGICAL SUBJECT MATTER

The fourth category of subject matter excluded from patent protection is set out in paragraph 3(f) of Schedule A2 of the Patents Act 1977[325] and Article 53(b) EPC 2000 (which is the same as Article 53(b) EPC 1973). These provide that a patent shall not be granted for 'any variety of animal or plant or any essentially biological process for the production of animals or plants, not being a microbiological process or other technical process or the product of such a process'.[326]

These provisions fall into two parts. First, they declare that patents should not be granted for 'animal varieties', 'plant varieties', and 'essentially biological processes'. The second part of paragraph 3(f)/Article 53(b) goes on to qualify and limit the subject matter which is excluded from patentability. As an exception to the exception, it provides that if an invention is 'a microbiological process or other technical process or the product of such a process', the invention may be patented.

Before looking at the exceptions, it might be useful to point out there is no general bar on the patenting of biological material or biotechnological inventions.[327] Indeed, as the EPC 2000 and the 1977 Act (as revised) make clear, an invention shall not be considered unpatentable solely on the ground that it concerns a product consisting of or containing biological material or a process which by which biological material is produced.[328] More specifically, the EPC 2000 and the 1977 Act explicitly state that it is possible to patent inventions for plants and

[323] The proposed Directive was rejected 648 to 14.

[324] Lucy Sherriff, 'Incoming President reopens software patent debate' (4 July 2007) *The Register* (<http://www.theregister.co.uk/2007/07/04>).

[325] Formerly PA s. 1(3)(b).

[326] The Biotech. Directive prompted the introduction of the phrase 'or other technical process'; Biotech. Dir. Art. 4(1); EPC Rule 23(b)(c), Implementing Regulations to the EPC (introduced by (1999) *OJ EPO* 437).

[327] TRIPS Art. 27(3) permits members to exclude 'plants and animals other than micro-organisms, and essentially biological processes for the production of plants or animals other than non-biological and microbiological processes'. EPC 2000, Art. 53 provides that European patents shall not be granted in respect of 'plant or animal varieties or essentially biological processes for the production of plants or animals: this provision shall not apply to microbiological processes or the products thereof'. See Art. 1, item 18 of EPC 2000. The Technical Board of Appeal said that when Art. 53(b) was drafted, 'the knowledge of the potential development in the field of biotechnology was rather limited'. *Lubrizol/Hybrid plants*, T320/87 [1990] *OJ EPO* 71. For a comparative study on the patentabilty of DNA fragments see *Trilateral Project B3b: Comparative Study on Biotechnology Patents* available at <http://www.epo.org> (1998). See also J. Funder 'Rethinking Patents for Plant Innovation' [1999] *EIPR* 551.

[328] PA Sched. A2, paras. 1(a)–(b); Biotech. Dir. Art. 3. *Harvard/Transgenic Animals*, T 315/03 (2006) *OJ EPO* 15, 78 (TBA) (Art. 53(b) only excludes a limited category of animals and not all animals).

animals, so long as they comply with the general requirements of patentability.[329] The exclusion under Article 53(b) is the denial of patents to the specified subject matter *per se*, rather than as under the morality exclusion in Article 53(a) (discussed below) 'which is to inventions covering such subject matter whose publication or exploitation must be measured by a moral or other standard'.[330]

8.1 ANIMAL VARIETIES

The first form of subject matter excluded from protection by paragraph 3(f) of Schedule A2 to the Patent Act 1977/Article 53(b) is 'animal varieties'.[331] While the exclusion of plant varieties is usually explained on the basis that when the EPC was drafted there was a ban on dual protection in UPOV, the fact that there is no equivalent treaty for animal varieties has led some to question why animal varieties were also excluded in the first place. In discussing the rationale for the animal variety exclusion, the Opposition Division at the EPO said that 'the most obvious reason for this must have been the intention or at least the keeping open of the possibility to create such a law for the protection of animal varieties later on'.[332] A more honest explanation for the exclusion of animal varieties is that they are simply 'not an appropriate subject matter'.[333] When Article 53(b) EPC 1973 was first drafted the potential scope of the animal variety exclusion was straightforward and uncontroversial. This has changed, however, as patent law has been forced to confront the developments in biotechnology that have taken place since then.

The meaning of 'animal variety' was considered at the EPO in the early 1990s in the *Onco-mouse* decisions. The claims in question related to a genetically modified non-human mammal (in particular a mouse), which had been modified so that it would be susceptible to cancer. The resulting products (the mice with cancer) were used in cancer research. At first instance, the Examining Division held that the exclusion not only covered groups of animals but animals in general. As such, the invention was for an unpatentable animal variety.[334] On appeal, the Technical Board of Appeal held that the Examining Division had misconstrued the exclusion, which being an exception to patentability, ought to be construed narrowly.[335] Importantly, the Board of Appeal said that Article 53(b) did not exclude animals in general. On this basis, the Board of Appeal remitted the matter to the Examining Division for reconsideration.

The Examining Division said that animal variety either meant a species or a subunit of a species. The Examining Division acknowledged that, while the terms of the Convention were not consistent—the English and French terms (animal varieties and *races animales*) meaning subunit of a species and the German term (*Tierarten*) meaning species—it was not necessary to decide which was the authoritative meaning for the Convention.[336] This was because the claims in question related to non-human mammals, a category that was neither a species nor a subunit of a species. (In zoological terms, mammals are of a higher taxonomic classification

---

[329] PA Sched. A2, para. 4, EPC 2000 Rule 27; Biotech. Dir. Art. 4(2).

[330] *Harvard/Transgenic Animals*, note 328 above, 56 (TBA). The reference to publication has been removed in Art 53(a) EPC 2000.

[331] Biotech. Dir. Art. 4(1)(a). V. Di Cerbo, 'Patentability of Animals' (1993) 24 *IIC* 788; U. Kinkeldey, 'The Patenting of Animals' (1993) 24 *IIC* 777.

[332] *Harvard/Onco-mouse* [2003] *OJ EPO* 473, 499 (Opposition Division).

[333] *Harvard/Onco-mouse* [1990] *EPOR* 4; [1989] *OJ EPO* 451 (Exam).

[334] Ibid, T19/90 [1990] *EPOR* 501 (TBA).   [335] Ibid. [1991] *EPOR* 525 (Exam).

[336] EPC Art. 177 (1) says that the English, French, and German versions of the EPC are equally authentic.

than species.) Consequently, the subject matter did not relate to an animal variety and as such was not excluded by Article 53(b).

The meaning of 'animal variety' was considered by the Technical Board of Appeal in its 2006 decision in *Harvard/Transgenic Animals* (which is effectively a rerun of the earlier *Onco-mouse* decisions). The Technical Board of Appeal began by noting that the Enlarged Board of Appeal's reasoning in relation to plant varieties in *Novartis* was applicable to the decision as to whether an invention fell within the animal variety exclusion.[337] In *Novartis* (which is discussed in the next section), the Board held that where a specific plant variety is not individually claimed, the claim will not be excluded from patentability under Article 53(b) EPC. This is the case even though it may embrace plant varieties.[338] While the Technical Board of Appeal accepted the reasoning of the Enlarged Board in *Novartis,* they were faced with the problem that the three official texts of the EPC use different taxonomic terms to refer to animals—the English speaks of 'animal varieties', the German uses 'animal species', while the French version refers to 'animal races'.[339] (This was in contrast to the way that plants are dealt with under Article 53(b), where all three official languages refer to 'plant varieties'.) As the Board said, the fact that the three official texts of the EPC used different taxonomic categories 'would lead to the absurd result that the outcome of an Article 53(b) objection depended on the language of the case'. (As species was of a higher taxonomic order, it offered the widest objections.)[340] Faced with this problem the Board said that a 'definition by reference to taxonomical rank would be consistent with the position in relation to plant varieties and in the interests of legal certainty'.[341] While the Board noted that the uncertainty created by these linguistic differences was undesirable, nonetheless the Board said that it was unnecessary to pursue the matter further. The reason for this was that the claim for 'transgenic rodents' was for a taxonomic category that was higher than 'species', 'variety', and 'race'. This meant that the patent would not have been caught by either the English, French, or German versions of Article 53(b). The upshot of the *Transgenic Animals* decision is that Article 53(b) 1973 (Article 53(b) EPC 2000) will only apply where a patent is for a single animal variety (species or race depending on the language of the EPC that is used). That is, it modified the reasoning of *Novartis* to take account of the different taxonomic terms used in the English, French, and German versions of the EPC. Until the problem is rectified, it will pose interesting challenges for those drafting animal patents.

As well as looking at the fate of the applicant's main request (which was for transgenic rodents), in the *Transgenic Animals* decision the Technical Board of Appeal also looked at whether Article 53(b) acted as a bar to the patentability of the auxiliary request, which was restricted to 'transgenic mice'. Following *Novartis,* the Board said that an objection under

---

[337] *Novartis/Transgenic plant* G1/98 [2000] *EPOR* 303, 319 (EBA). (Whereas 'G1/98 makes reference to plants and not to animals, its holding can also be transferred to the interpretation of the exclusion of animal varieties in Article 53(b)': *Harvard/Onco-mouse* [2003] *OJ EPO* 473, 499 (OD). *Harvard/Transgenic Animals,* T315/03 [2006] *OJ EPO* 15, 58 (TBA).

[338] The Opposition Division, who also adopted the reasoning in *Novartis,* said that this meant that, for a claim to be excluded because it was for an animal variety, the claim had to be for a variety *per se.* On this basis, the Opposition Division said that, as the invention was applicable to more than just varieties of mice, the patent was not excluded by Article 53(b).

[339] While the English text of the EPC refers to 'plant or animal varieties', the German text refers to 'plant varieties or animal species' (*Pflanzensorten oder Tierarten*), while the French text refers to 'plant varieties and animal races' (*les variétés végétales et les races animals*). The problems created by the fact that the three official texts use three different taxonomic terms—variety, species and races—was compounded by the way that Rule 23c EPC has been translated.

[340] *Harvard/Transgenic Animals,* T315/03 [2006] *OJ EPO* 15, 60 (TBA).   [341] Ibid, 58.

Article 53(b) would only arise if 'one or more claims of the request are to a taxonomic category at least as narrow as an animal species—the broadest of the three taxonomic categories excluded in the three language texts of Article 53(b) EPC'. As the auxiliary claims did not fall within these criteria, the Board held that the auxiliary request did not fail Article 53(b).[342]

8.2 PLANT VARIETIES

The second form of biological subject matter that is excluded from the scope of protection is 'plant varieties'.[343] The reason for the exclusion can be traced to the fact that the EPC was drafted in light of the International Convention for the Protection of New Varieties of Plants (UPOV): a regime established in 1961 to grant property rights in new plant varieties. In order to ensure that plant breeders were not able to obtain patent protection *and* plant variety protection, it was decided that the two conventions should be mutually exclusive: a person could be given either a *sui generis* plant breeder's right or patent protection, but not both.[344] Article 53(b) and section 1(3)(b) were drafted to give effect to this policy decision.[345] While the principle that the scope of the two regimes should be mutually exclusive was removed when UPOV was revised in 1991, nonetheless the exclusion of plant varieties still exists in both the EPC 2000 and the Patents Act 1977. Article 4(1) of the Biotechnology Directive confirms that plant varieties are not patentable. It also provides, as do the resulting changes to the 1977 Act and the changes to the Implementing Regulations to the EPC, that the concept of plant variety is to correspond to the definition used in Article 5 of the Community Plant Variety Regulation.[346]

One of the earliest decisions to consider the scope of the plant variety exclusion was *Ciba-Geigy's Application*.[347] The application in question claimed any plant-propagating material which had been chemically treated so as to make the material resistant to other agricultural chemicals. In deciding that the invention was not a 'plant variety', the Technical Board of Appeal held that plant varieties were 'limited to claims to individually characterized plants which would have the detailed taxonomy and the reproductive capacity which is required in general for a plant variety right'. The Board of Appeal also stressed that a defining feature of

---

[342] The Board rejected the argument that the transgenic mice constituted a new species (primarily on the basis that they had not seen any evidence to this effect).

[343] PA Sched. A2, para. 3(f); EPC Art. 53(b); Biotech. Dir. Art. 4(1)(a). For the position before the Patents Act 1977 see *Rau Gesellschaft* (1935) 52 *RPC* 362; *Lenard's Application* (1954) 71 *RPC* 190; *Commercial Solvents Case* (1926) 43 *RPC* 185; *Szuec's Case* [1956] *RPC* 25; *NRDC's Application* [1961] *RPC* 134; *Swift's Application* [1962] *RPC* 37. For an international overview see T. Roberts, 'Patenting Plants around the World' [1996] *EIPR* 531.

[344] UPOV Art. 2(1).

[345] Art. 53(b) EPC 1973 was intended to express a general intention to exclude patent protection for subject matter capable of protection within the UPOV convention. *Ciba-Geigy/Propagating material application*, T49/83 [1979–85] *C EPOR* 758; [1984] *OJ EPO* 112; *Plant Genetic Systems/Glutamine synthetase inhibitors* (1993) 24 *IIC* 618.

[346] A 'plant variety' has been defined to mean: 'a plant grouping within a single botanical taxon of the lowest known rank. This is subject to the proviso that the grouping can be (a) defined by the expression of the characteristics that result from the given genotype of combination of genotypes, and (b) can be distinguished from other plant groupings by the expression of at least one of the said characteristics, and (c) considered as a unit with regard to its suitability for being propagated unchanged'. PA Sched. A2, para. 11; Biotech. Dir. Art. 2(3); EPC Rule 23b(4)(a)—(c), Implementing Regulations to the EPC (introduced by (1999) *OJ EPO* 437).

[347] *Ciba-Geigy/Propagating material application*, T49/83 [1979–85] *C EPOR* 758; [1984] *OJ EPO* 112. Followed in *Lubrizol/Hybrid plants*, T320/87 [1990] *EPOR* 173; [1990] *OJ EPO* 71 ('the present hybrid seed and plants from such seed, lacking stability in some trait of the whole generation population, cannot be classified as plant varieties'); and *PGS/Glutamine synthetase inhibitors*, T356/93 [1995] *EPOR* 357 (practice is to allow claims directed to groups of plants larger than plant varieties if the invention is applicable to such larger plant groups.

a plant variety was that it contained certain features that distinguished the variety in question from other varieties. These distinguishing features needed to be stable enough so that the essential characteristics were passed on through subsequent generations. In so doing the Technical Board of Appeal highlighted the need for homogeneity between different generations. They also added that 'it is perfectly sufficient for the exclusion to be...restricted...to cases in which plants are characterized *precisely* by the genetically determined peculiarities of their natural phenotype'.[348]

On the facts, the Technical Board of Appeal held that claims for plant-propagating materials that had been chemically treated so as to make the material resistant to other agricultural chemicals were not claims to a 'plant variety'. The reason for this was that while plant breeding (which is a form of genetic modification) introduced a trait to plants that reappeared in subsequent generations, this did not occur with chemical treatment. As such, the Technical Board of Appeal held that the claims were not for plant varieties and thus not excluded from the scope of protection.

The next decision to consider the plant varieties exclusion was *Plant Genetic Systems*.[349] The claims in dispute related to plants, plant cells, and seeds that possessed a foreign gene which made them resistant to a type of herbicide. Given that modified plants were immune to the application of the weed-killer, farmers were able to spray (modified) crops safe in the knowledge that the weed-killer would only affect the unmodified weeds. Greenpeace objected to the application arguing, inter alia, that the material claimed was a plant variety and thus excluded by Article 53(b).

At first instance, the Opposition Division held that the claims were not restricted to a specifically defined narrow group of plants (such as a variety), but related to a much broader group of plants. As such, the claims were unobjectionable. In overturning this decision, the Board of Appeal acknowledged that 'the concept of plant variety under Article 53(b) refers to any plant grouping within a single botanical taxon [or classification] of the lowest known rank'. On this basis the Board said that plant cells as such, which modern technology allows to culture much like bacteria and yeasts, 'cannot be considered to fall under the definition of plant or of plant variety'.[350] Following *Ciba-Geigy* the Board stressed that stability and homogeneity were important factors in determining whether something was a plant variety. More specifically, the Board noted that a plant variety 'is characterized by at least one single transmissible characteristic distinguishing it from other plant groupings and which is sufficiently homogeneous and stable in its relevant characteristics'.[351]

While the Board of Appeal in *Plant Genetic Systems* agreed with much of the reasoning in *Ciba-Geigy,* it disagreed with the way the ambit of the exclusion had been interpreted. More specifically, while in *Ciba-Geigy* plant varieties were restricted 'to cases in which plants are characterized precisely by the genetically determined peculiarities of their natural phenotype', the Board of Appeal in *Plant Genetic Systems* adopted a more expansive reading of the exclusion. In particular, they were willing to extend the exclusion beyond claims that were specifically directed to or characterized as plant varieties, to include claims that encompassed or included a plant variety within their scope. On the facts, the Board of Appeal held that what was being claimed was based upon or derived from genetically engineered cells (and that the

---

[348] *Ciba Geigy/Propagating material application*, T49/83 [1979–85] *C EPOR* 758; [1984] *OJ EPO* 112, para. 4 (our emphasis).

[349] *PGS/Glutamine synthetase inhibitors*, T356/93 [1993] 24 *IIC* 618 (Opposition Division) [1995] *EPOR* 357; [1995] *OJ EPO* 545 (TBA); [1995] *OJ EPO* 545 (TBA).

[350] *PGS/Glutamine synthetase inhibitors* [1995] *EPOR* 357, 375 (TBA).   [351] Ibid.

application required the production of plant varieties to exemplify them). This meant that they were claiming rights over the plant varieties formed by those plants and seeds. As such, they were not patentable.

In summary, the Technical Board of Appeal held that while claims relating to plant cells are potentially patentable, claims which 'encompass' or are 'based on' a plant variety are not.[352] (This is subject to the rider that the resulting plants have a distinguishable characteristic that is stable and homogeneous.) Given that plant varieties are frequently used as the starting point for the production of genetically engineered plants,[353] this meant that in most cases plants produced as a result of genetic engineering would not have been patentable:[354] a decision which, if followed, would have had important ramifications for the plant-breeding industry.[355] Given this, it is not surprising that the PGS decision was subject to a considerable amount of criticism.[356]

Much of the cause for concern about the impact of the PGS decision of plant genetics has now been alleviated. This is because two subsequent events have effectively overturned the PGS decision. These are the Biotechnology Directive and the decision of the Enlarged Board of Appeal in Novartis.

Article 4(2) of the Biotechnology Directive provides that 'inventions which concern plants...shall be patentable if the technical feasibility of the invention is not confined to a particular plant...variety'.[357] Similar provisions have been introduced in the 1977 Act and the EPC 2000.[358] So long as a claim encompasses more than one variety it is potentially patentable. The upshot of the Biotechnology Directive is that claims to plants will be allowed even if they encompass a plant variety. However, claims specifically directed to particular plant varieties (which are protected by a separate regime) will not be protected. This would appear to require member states to accept claims to genetically modified plants (such as those in Plant Genetic Systems) as being patentable.

A similar position was reached by the Enlarged Board of Appeal of the EPO in Novartis[359] (which related to plants that were genetically modified to render them resistant to fungi). In

---

[352] On 'essentially derived variety', see Art. 14(5) UPOV.

[353] Most of the reaction was negative: U. Schatz, 'Patentability of Genetic Engineering Inventions in EPO Practice' (1998) 29 IIC 2; Roberts, 'Patenting Plants around the World', 534; A. Schrell, 'Are plants still patentable?' [1996] EIPR 242; M. Llewellyn, 'The Legal Protection of Biotechnological Inventions: An Alternative Approach' [1997] EIPR 115. Cf. M. Llewellyn, 'Article 53 Revisited: Greenpeace v. Plant Genetic Systems NV' [1995] EIPR 506.

[354] Schrell, 'Are Plants Still Patentable?' [1996] EIPR 242, 243.

[355] The President of the EPO, believing there to be a contradiction between PGS and Ciba Geigy (and also with the Onco-mouse decision), referred the matter to the Enlarged Board of Appeal. The Enlarged Board of Appeal refused to answer the question, which it ruled was improper because there was no conflict between the decisions. Inadmissible referral, G3/95 [1996] EPOR 505; [1996] OJ EPO 169 (EBA).

[356] As Bostyn explained, '[There] is a difference between a claim embracing a plant variety and a claim to a variety. Every claim to plants will embrace plant varieties, since a plant variety is a plant grouping of the lowest possible rank. When claiming a species, or even a higher rank, it will always embrace plant varieties: all Golden Delicious Apples (variety) are apples (species), but not all apples are Golden Delicious.' Bostyn, 'Patentability of Genetic Information Carriers', [1999] IPQ 1, 18. See also R. Crespi, 'Patents and Plant Variety Rights: Is there an Interface Problem?' (1992) 23 IIC 173.

[357] Biotech. Dir. Recital 29–32. Recital 31 states that 'a plant grouping which is characterized by a particular gene (and not its whole genome) is not covered by the protection of new varieties and is therefore not excluded from patentability even if it comprises new varieties of plants'.

[358] PA Sched. A2, para. 4; EPC Rule 23c(b), Implementing Regulations to the EPC (introduced by (1999) OJ EPO 437).

[359] Novartis/Transgenic plant (TBA), T1054/96 [1999] EPOR 123; [1998] OJ EPO (Special Edn.) 149; R. Nott, 'You Did It: The European Biotechnology Directive At Last' [1998] EIPR 347, 351.

relation to the plant variety exclusion, the Board found that 'a claim wherein specific plant varieties are not individually claimed is not excluded from patentability under Article 53(b), even though it may embrace plant varieties'.[360]

The Enlarged Board of Appeal noted that Article 53(b) serves to define the borderline between patent and plant variety protection. They also noted that the extent of the exclusion for patents is the obverse of the availability of plant variety rights[361] and that plant varieties are only granted for specific plant varieties (and not for technical teachings). On this basis the Enlarged Board of Appeal held that in 'the absence of the identification of a specific plant variety in a product claim, the subject matter of the claimed invention is not directed to a plant variety or varieties within the meaning of Article 53(b) EPC'.[362] In short, the Enlarged Board overturned the *PGS* decision and held that a claim that encompasses more than one variety is not excluded under Article 53(b). That is, the mere fact that a patent encompasses a plant variety will not mean that the invention falls within the exclusion. Instead the exclusion will operate only where the patent claims a plant variety *per se* (which should be protected by plant variety protection).

While the proponents of patent protection for plants will welcome the *Novartis* decision, it gives rise to a potential problem, similar to the problems that arose when the whole contents approach was first adopted in relation to the patenting of computer programs. This is the problem that patent claims will be dressed up to appear as if they do not fall within the exception.[363] While the jurisprudence on the patentability of computer programs may provide guidance in this area, the different rationales behind the exclusions means that the whole contents-technical effect approach cannot be directly imported into paragraph 3(f) of Schedule A2 to the Patents Act 1977/Article 53(b). It may, however, provide some useful insights into the potential problems that might arise.

8.3 ESSENTIALLY BIOLOGICAL PROCESSES

The third type of invention excluded from protection is those inventions which are regarded as 'essentially biological processes for the production of animals and plants'.[364] As with the exclusion of animal and plant varieties, the exclusion of essentially biological processes has been reconfirmed in the Biotechnology Directive,[365] and by corresponding changes made to the 1977 Act and to the EPC.[366] Three aspects of this exclusion are worth emphasizing.

First, as the exclusion only applies to processes, it has no application to a product claim or a product-by-process claim. Consequently, in the *Onco-mouse* litigation it was irrelevant to

[360] *Novartis/Transgenic plant*, G1/98 [2000] *EPOR* 303, 319 (EBA). The EBA gave the analogy with Art. 53(b) (morality) of a patent for a copying machine. The fact that the machine could be used for copying counterfeit notes would not mean that the machine was excluded since the improved properties could be used for other purposes. As we will see, this suggests a particular approach to morality that is not universally accepted.

[361] This was because 'inventions ineligible for protection under the plant-breeder's rights systems were intended to be patentable under the EPC provided they fulfilled the other requirements for patentability'.

[362] *Novartis/Transgenic plant*, G1/98 [2000] *EPOR* 303, 319 (EBA).

[363] *Novartis/Transgenic plant*, T1054/96 [1999] *EPOR* 123, 137 (TBA).

[364] Para. 3(f) of Schedule A2 to the Patents Act 1977/Article 53(b) EPC 2000. The Biotech. Dir. affirms that essentially biological processes for the production of plants or animals are not patentable. EPC 2000, Art. 53(b) provides that European patents shall not be granted in respect of 'plant or animal varieties or essentially biological processes for the production of plants or animal: this provision shall not apply to microbiological processes or the products thereof': Art. 1, item 18 of EPC 2000.

[365] Biotech. Dir. Art. 4(1)(b).   [366] PA Sched. A2, para. 3(f).

the patentability of the invention that the claims included circumstances where genetically modified rodents reproduced. The offspring of such an 'essentially biological process' (if sexual reproduction is such a process) were products and hence fell outside the exclusion.[367]

Second, the exclusion only applies where the process is for the 'production of animals or plants'. As such, the exclusion may not apply if the process results in the death or destruction of animals or plants.[368]

Third, the exclusion only applies where the process is 'essentially biological'. According to the Biotechnology Directive, a process for the production of plants and animals is said to be essentially biological if 'it consists entirely of natural phenomena such as crossing or selection'.[369] The key question that has arisen in this context is—how much human intervention is needed for a process that involves biological steps not to be classified as an essentially biological process?[370] This question was considered in *Lubrizol*,[371] where the Technical Board of Appeal had to decide whether a process of producing high-quality hybrids was excluded from patentability on the ground that it was 'essentially biological'. Drawing upon the image of the invention widely used in patent law, the Board of Appeal said the question of whether a claim was for an essentially biological process had to be 'judged on the basis of the essence of the invention taking into account the totality of human intervention and its impact on the result achieved'.[372] Turning to the facts of the case, the Board noted that the process in question was divided into a number of steps. First, parent plants were selected and crossed. The resulting hybrids were then evaluated and suitable hybrids selected. The parent plants of the chosen hybrids were then cloned. The crossing was then repeated. The Board held that while each step might be characterized as biological, the arrangement of steps *as a whole* represented an essential modification of known biological processes. On this basis, the Board of Appeal held that the process was not an essentially biological process and, as such, not excluded by Article 53(b).

The question of the degree of technical intervention needed for a process to fall outside the scope of the exclusion was also considered in the *Novartis* decisions. The Technical Board of Appeal said that to decide whether a process was 'essentially biological', the tribunal must make a value judgment about the extent to which a process should be non-biological before it loses the status of 'essentially biological'.[373] The Board added that there were three possible approaches that could be taken when answering this question.

---

[367] [1990] OJ EPO 476, 488.

[368] Cf. *NRDC's Application* [1961] *RPC* 134; *Swift's Application* [1962] *RPC* 37.

[369] Biotech. Dir. Art. 2(2).

[370] Earlier drafts of the Directive defined 'essentially biological' as 'a process in which human intervention consists in [no] more than selecting an available biological material and letting it perform an inherent biological function under natural conditions'; 'a process which, taken as a whole, does not exist in nature and is more than a mere production process shall be patentable'; and also 'a process which, taken as a whole, does not exist in nature and is more than mere breeding process'.

[371] *Lubrizol/Hybrid plant*, T320/87, [1990] *EPOR* 173; [1990] *OJ EPO* 71. (These were prior to the introduction of the definition.) See also *Ciba-Geigy/Propagating material application*, T49/83 [1984] *OJ EPO* 112 (propagating material not the result of essentially biological process where the process involved treatment with chemical agents); *Harvard/Onco-mouse* [1989] *OJ EPO* 451 (Exam) (process for producing transgenic mouse not essentially biological because it involved micro-injection); *Harvard/Onco-mouse*, T19/90 [1990] *EPOR* 501; [1990] *OJ EPO* 476, 488 (agreeing that micro-injection is not essentially biological and noting also that sexual reproduction is not necessarily essentially biological).

[372] *PGS/Glutamine synthetase inhibitors*, T356/93 [1995] *EPOR* 357. ('In the present case the impact of human intervention is decisive since the claimed plants and plant material only exist as a result of the process of the invention.')

[373] *Novartis/Transgenic plant*, T1054/96 [1999] *EPOR* 123, 134 (TBA).

(i) Under the first approach, an invention would be excluded if it included an aspect or step that was biological. To fall outside the exclusion, the claimed processes would have to be exclusively made up of non-biological process steps.[374]

(ii) The second approach, which was taken from *Lubrizol*, requires the tribunal to weigh up the overall degree of human intervention in the process.[375] Under this approach, the decision whether an invention was essentially biological would be made on the basis of the essence of the invention, taking into account the totality of human invention and its impact on the result received.

(iii) The third option, which was the most liberal, provides that the mere presence of a single artificial (or technical) element in the process might be enough to prevent its being classified as an essentially biological process.[376] The Technical Board of Appeal said that the third approach was reflected in Article 2(2) of the Biotechnology Directive.

Neither the Technical Board of Appeal nor the Enlarged Board of Appeal in *Novartis* provided any direct guidance as to which of these approaches was to be adopted.[377] Despite this, there is little doubt that purely biological processes—that is, processes where there is no human intervention—are essentially biological. Article 2(2) of the Biotechnology Directive offers a useful example of this, insofar as it provides that 'a process for the production of plants or animals is essentially biological if it consists entirely of natural phenomena, such as crossing or selection'.[378] This means that conventional breeding procedures would not be patentable. 'In contrast, where (human) technical intervention plays a significant part in determining or controlling the result it is desired to achieve, the process would not be excluded'.[379]

While these two extremes may be clear, one question that remains is whether processes that only have a trivial or minimal amount of human intervention will also be classified as essentially biological processes. In *Lubrizol*, the Board of Appeal said that while trivial interventions may mean that a process is not 'purely' biological, it does not mean that it is not essentially biological.[380] Such a process may therefore still be excluded. In contrast, it seems that the changes made to the EPC and the UK Patents Act in light of the Biotechnology Directive may suggest a different conclusion. This is because a process is defined as essentially biological if 'it consists *entirely* of natural phenomena such as crossing or selection'.[381]

Given that the definition of 'essentially biological process' contained in paragraph 11 of Schedule A2 does not say 'includes', but instead uses the word 'means', we can infer that if a process involves any technical intervention it would fall outside the exclusion from patentability in Article 53(b) and paragraph 3(f) of Schedule A2. This reading of the provision was supported by the Technical Board of Appeal in *Novartis*, when it said that the third approach (outlined above) was reflected in Article 2(2) of the Biotechnology Directive.

---

[374] Ibid. This was drawn from EPC 1973 Art. 52(4) re methods of treatment by surgery and therapy. See *General Hospital/Contraceptive method*, T820/94 [1995] *EPOR* 446.

[375] *Lubrizol/Hybrid plants*, T320/87 [1990] *EPOR* 173.

[376] *Novartis/Transgenic plant*, T1054/96 [1999] *EPOR* 123, 135 (TBA).

[377] *Novartis/Transgenic plant*, G01/98 [2000] *EPOR* 303, 321 (EBA).

[378] Similar provision are found in EPC 2000 Rule 26(5) (formerly Rule 23b(5), Implementing Regulations to the EPC (introduced by (1999) *OJ EPO* 437): PA Sched. A2, para. 11.

[379] *EPO Guidelines* C–V, 3.4.

[380] The Board said that 'the necessity for human intervention alone is not yet sufficient criterion for its not being "essentially biological". Human interference may only mean that the process is not "purely" biological process, without contributing anything beyond a trivial level.' *Lubrizol/Hybrid plants*, T320/87 [1990] *EPOR* 173, 178.

[381] Biotech. Dir. Art. 2(2); EPC 2000 Rule 26(5); PA Sched. A2, para. 11.

Despite or possibly because of this, there is still some uncertainty about the degree of human or technical intervention needed for a process to fall outside the scope of the exclusion. The problems in this area were highlighted in the 2007 decision in *Plant Bioscience/Broccoli* (T83/05).[382] The central claim of the application in question was for a method for the production of broccoli (Brassica). This consisted of a number of steps traditionally used in breeding including the crossing of specific species of broccoli and the subsequent selection of hybrids with certain defined features from those crosses. This was then followed by backcrossing and further selection. Importantly, the application also involved the use of molecular markers to help identify plants with the desired characteristics. It was argued in opposition that the subject matter of claim 1 was for an essentially biological process and as such it should be excluded under Article 53(b).

As part of its deliberations, the Technical Board of Appeal provided a general history of Article 53(b) noting that the drafters regarded 'biological' as being in opposition to 'technical' and that they had deliberately chosen the adverb 'essentially' to replace the narrower term 'purely'. The Board also noted that the drafters of the legislation intended that the exclusion apply to processes such as the selection or hybridization of existing varieties. This was the case even if, as 'a secondary feature, "technical" devices were involved (use of a particular type of instrument in a grafting process, or a special greenhouse in growing a plant)'.[383]

The Board also highlighted a number of problems with Rule 23b(5) EPC 1973 (which is now in EPC 2000 Rule 26(5)), which (as we saw above) provides that a 'process for the production of plants or animals is essentially biological if it consists entirely of natural phenomena such as crossing or selection'. The Board noted that EPC 1973 Rule 23(b)(5) says that processes will only be considered to be essentially biological where they consist *entirely* of biological processes for the production of plants. At the same time, the rule also says that crossing and selection, which clearly involve human (technical) intervention, are examples of natural phenomena. As the Board said, this seems to be contradictory to the extent that 'the systematic crossing and selection as carried out in traditional plant breeding would not occur in nature without the intervention of man'.[384] The Board then went on to say that Rule 23(b)(5) (EPC 2000 Rule 26(5)) suggests that Article 53(b) should be read narrowly. In particular, the Board said that Rule 23(b)(5) meant that a process which contains an additional feature of a technical nature would be outside the ambit of the process exclusion'.[385] This would not be the case, however, in relation to 'natural phenomena' (which covered crossing and selection by way of a legal fiction).[386] The Board of Appeal noted that on this reading of the exclusion, the use of molecular markers as part of a breeding process (which required the removal and *in vitro* analysis of plant tissues) would lead to the conclusion that the invention would fall outside the ambit of the exclusion. The Board also noted that this narrow reading of Article 53(b) would be contrary to the earlier decisions of *Lubrizol* and *PGS*.[387] Faced with the uncertainty about

---

382 [2007] *OJ EPO* 644.

383 Preliminary Draft Convention of the Council of Europe (Doc. EXP/Brev (61) 2 rev, p 26). Cited in *Plant Bioscience/Broccoli* [2007] *OJ EPO* 644.

384 *Plant Bioscience/Broccoli*, ibid, 660.   385 Ibid, 661.

386 The Board said that this did not reflect the approach that had been adopted by the boards of appeal prior to the introduction of the rule. See *Novartis/Transgenic plant (TBA)*, T1054/96 [1999] *EPOR* 123 (point 96).

387 For example in T315/03 the TBA cited Rule 23b(5) and concluded that it was self-evident that a process which included genetic manipulation did not consist entirely of natural phenomena and was therefore not excluded by Article 53(b) EPC. Cf *Novartis/Transgenic plant (TBA)*, T1054/96 [1999] *EPOR* 123 (point 3) On the apparent clash of these decisions see *Plant Bioscience/Broccoli* [2007] *OJ EPO* 664, 665.

the scope of Article 53(b), the Technical Board of Appeal in *Plant Bioscience/Broccoli* decided to refer the matter to the Enlarged Board for deliberation. In particular, the Technical Board of Appeal asked the Enlarged Board of Appeal to consider the question: 'Does a non-microbiological process for the production of plants which contains the steps of crossing and selecting plants escape the exclusion of Article 53(b) merely because it contains, as a further step or as part of any of the steps of crossing and selection, an additional feature of a technical nature?'[388] The Technical Board of Appeal also asked the Enlarged Board to identify the criteria that should be used to determine whether an invention fell within Article 53(b).[389] The outcome of this decision will hopefully provide important guidance on these vexed issues.[390]

8.4 MICROBIOLOGICAL OR TECHNICAL PROCESSES

As we saw earlier, the exclusion of animal varieties, plant varieties, and essentially biological processes from the scope of patentable subject matter is subject to the general qualification that the invention is not 'a microbiological process or other technical process or the product of such a process'.[391] If an invention is for a microbiological or technical process,[392] it will not be caught by the exclusion. In essence, the qualification restricts the subject matter excluded by paragraph 3(f) of Schedule A2/Article 53(b) to non-microbiological and non-technical processes. Given that the qualification restricts the scope of the subject matter excluded by paragraph 3(f)/Article 53(b), this means that if it was interpreted broadly it would greatly undermine the impact of the provision as a whole. If this were the case, it would increase the scope of biological subject matter that is patentable.

It should be noted that when the 1977 Act and the EPC 1973 were first enacted, the qualification was limited to 'a microbiological process or the product of such a process'. This was changed as a result of the Biotechnology Directive to apply to 'a microbiological process *or other technical process* or the product of such a process'.

The question of what is meant by a 'microbiological process' was considered in *Plant Genetic Systems*[393] where the Board of Appeal said that microbiological processes refers to processes in which micro-organisms or their parts are used to make or to modify products. They also said that it refers to processes where new micro-organisms are developed for specific uses. Products of microbiological processes encompass 'products which are made or modified by micro-organisms as well as new micro-organisms as such'. While cells and parts thereof were said to be microbiological, processes of genetic engineering were not.[394] The extension of the provision to include technical processes largely renders these issues obsolete.

When construing the qualification as enacted (that is, when it was limited to microbiological processes), most of the discussions focused on whether a process that was made up of

---

[388] *Plant Bioscience/Broccoli*, T83/05 [2007] *OJ EPO* 644.   [389] Ibid, p. 669.

[390] Third-party interventions on the matter before the Enlarged Board (G 2/07) closed at the end of 2007.

[391] PA Sched. A2, para. 3(f); EPC Rule 23c(c), Implementing Regulations to the EPC (introduced by [1999] *OJ EPO* 437). EPC 2000, Art. 53(b) only refers 'to microbiological processes or the products thereof'. See Art. 1, item 18 of EPC 2000. TRIPS only requires that micro-organisms, non-biological, and microbiological processes be patentable. It does not require that products of micro-biological processes be patentable. See also Teschemacher, 'Patentability of Micro-organisms *per se*' (1982) 13 *IIC* 27; Cadman, 'The Protection of Micro-organisms under European Patent Law' (1985) 16 *IIC* 311; Marterer, 'The Patentability of Micro Organisms *per se*' (1987) 18 *IIC* 666.

[392] A microbiological process is defined as 'any process involving or performed upon or resulting in microbiological material'. Biotech. Dir. Art. 2(2). EPC Rule 23b(6); PA Sched. A2, para. 11.

[393] *PGS/Glutamine synthetase inhibitors* (1993) 24 *IIC* 618 (Opposition Division); [1995] *OJ EPO* 545 (TBA).

[394] *PGS/Glutamine synthetase inhibitors* [1995] *OJ EPO* 545 (TBA).

a mixture of microbiological and technical steps fell within the qualification.[395] For example, when contemplating whether a process that involves a number of different steps is a microbiological process, the Board of Appeal in *PGS* said that a process was not a microbiological process simply because a microbiological step was involved. Instead, the process had to be judged as a whole. On the facts of the case, the Board said that while the introductory step of transforming plant cells or tissues with recombinant DNA *was* microbiological, subsequent steps of regeneration and transformation that played an important role in bringing about the final product were not microbiological processes. When viewed as a whole, the process was best described as a technical process that included a microbiological step, rather than a microbiological process (which would have justified the patenting of the process or a product of the process). As a consequence, the resulting plants were held not to be the product of a microbiological process within the meaning of Article 53(b) (as enacted).[396]

While *Plant Genetics Systems* provides us with some guidance as to the limits of the qualification, its precise scope remains unclear. It seems, however, that this may not matter too much. This is because the changes introduced to the exclusions so that they also include 'technical processes' means that the problems of the type discussed in *PGS* have largely been overcome. Given that genetic manipulation is undoubtedly a technical process, this appears to demand the patentability of genetically modified plants and animals.[397] As much of the research carried out in relation to biological subject matter involves a degree of human intervention, most of the processes will be captured by the qualification and thus fall outside the scope of the exclusions.[398] By increasing the scope of the qualification to section 1(3)(b)/Article 53(b), the changes initiated by the Biotechnology Directive will minimize the impact that the exclusion has upon the scope of patentable subject matter.

The scope of the subject matter excluded by paragraph 3(f) of Schedule A2 to the Patents Act 1977/Article 53(b) would have been further undermined if the approach suggested by the Technical Board of Appeal in *Plant Genetic Systems* had been followed. In that case, the Board suggested that a plant variety that was a product of a microbiological process would not have been caught by the exclusion and thus would have been patentable. This approach was rejected in *Novartis* when the Enlarged Board of Appeal said that the plant variety exclusion applied irrespective of how the plant varieties were produced. The mere fact that a plant variety was obtained by means of genetic engineering does not give the producers of such plant varieties a privileged position.[399] This reflects the position set out in Recital 32 of the Biotechnology Directive which says that 'if an invention consists only in genetically modifying a particular plant variety, and if a new plant variety is bred, it will still be excluded from patentability even

---

[395] The issue of how you ascertain whether a process with a number of steps is a microbiological process is similar to the question whether a process is 'essentially biological'.

[396] While the point was not discussed at length, it was suggested in *PGS/Glutamine synthetase inhibitors* [1995] *OJ EPO* 545 (TBA), that a microbiological process was a purer process (with less human intervention) than a process which was essentially biological.

[397] Earlier drafts of the Directive defined microbiological to mean 'a process carried out with the use of or performed upon or resulting in a micro-organism'; as 'a process consisting of a succession of steps' including 'at least one essential step of the process' which is microbiological; and as meaning 'a process involving or performed upon or resulting in microbiological material'. All were abandoned. See M. Llewelyn, 'The Patentability of Biological Material: Continuing Contradiction and Confusion' [2000] *EIPR* 191.

[398] Schrell, 'Are Plants Still Patentable?' [1996] *EIPR* 242, 243. O. Mills, *Biotechnological Inventions: Moral Restraints and Patent Law* (2005).

[399] *Novartis/Transgenic plant,* G01/98 [2000] *EPOR* 303, 321 (EBA). This is supported by Recital 32 of the Biotech. Dir.

if the genetic modification is the result not of an essentially biological process but of a biotechnological process'.

9 IMMORAL INVENTIONS

It is a long-standing principle of patent law that patents should not be granted for immoral inventions. Until recently, the principle was rarely invoked. However, as a result of developments in biotechnology and related attempts to patent the products of that research, in recent years ethical considerations have played a more prominent role in patent law. While these provisions are potentially applicable to all patentable subject matter, more detailed provisions have also been introduced in relation to biotechnological inventions. What is most striking about the interaction of patent law and ethics is how uncomfortable the relationship has been and the difficulties that it has produced.[400]

When the EPC and the 1977 Act were first drafted, the relevant statutory provisions in relation to immoral inventions were set out in section 1(3)(a) of the Act and Article 53(a) of the Convention.[401] Since then, the law in this area has undergone a number of important changes, notably to take account of the Biotechnology Directive.[402] When the Directive was first proposed, it made no reference to the morality of patenting. Over time, however, the Directive became a focal point for public concerns about the ethical and social dimensions of biotechnology generally, as well as specific concerns about the patenting of the products of such activities. In response, the proponents of patenting argued that the patent system was an inappropriate vehicle for dealing with concerns over morality. The reasons for this were said to be that the uses to be made of an invention are not clear at the application stage, that patent examiners are not qualified to deal with ethical questions, and most importantly because patents do not control whether or how an invention is exploited. Instead it was said that exploitation of biotechnological inventions was best controlled through other regulatory systems.[403] In the end, the Biotechnology Directive took a middle ground insofar as it provides that inventions shall be unpatentable where their commercial exploitation would be contrary to *ordre public* or morality.[404] The Biotechnology Directive also provided specific

---

[400] L. Bently and B. Sherman, 'The ethics of patenting: towards a transgenic patent system' (1995) 3 *Medical Law Review* 275.

[401] These are permitted by Art. 27(2) TRIPS which says that members may exclude: 'inventions, the prevention within their territory of the commercial exploitation of which is necessary to protect *ordre public* or morality, including to protect human, animal or plant life or health or to avoid serious prejudice to the environment, provided that such exclusion is not made merely because the exploitation is prohibited by domestic law'.

[402] It is likely that the Directive will bring about other changes. For example, Article 7 of the Directive states that the Commission's European Group on Ethics in Science and New Technologies is to evaluate all ethical aspects of biotechnology. While this is unlikely to have a direct impact on patenting, there is a possibility that it may influence attitudes towards ethical issues. This is reinforced by the fact that the Commission is obliged under the Biotechnology Directive to report annually to the European Parliament and Council on the implications of patent law in the field of biotechnology and genetic engineering: Biotech. Dir., Art. 16(3).

[403] For an overview of some of the regulatory regimes see J. Black, 'Regulation as Facilitation: Negotiating the Genetic Revolution' (1998) 61 *MLR* 621.

[404] This is mirrored in the new section 1(3) and, in turn, reflects Article 53 EPC (as enacted). Article 6(1) goes on to say that exploitation shall not be considered to be contrary to morality simply because it is prohibited by law or regulation. Similar provisions exist in the 1977 Act and the EPC 2000.

examples of types of invention that were unpatentable.[405] These are now mirrored in the 1977 Act[406] and the EPC 2000.[407]

The upshot of these changes is that there are effectively two different types of morality provision that may be applied. The first and more general is found in EPC 2000 Article 53(a)[408] and section 1(3).[409] These require an assessment 'as to whether or not exploitation of the invention in question would be contrary to morality or "*ordre public*"'.[410] The Technical Board of Appeal refers to these as the 'real' Article 53(a) objections. The second, more specific morality provisions are found in EPC 2000 Rule 28(a)–(d)[411]/Patent Act 1977 Schedule A2, paragraph 3(b)–(c).[412] These provide specific guidance as to when an invention will be excluded under Article 53(a)/section 1(3). EPC 2000 Rule 28 provides that

under Article 53(a), European patents shall not be granted in respect of biotechnological inventions which, in particular, concern the following:

(a) processes for cloning human beings;[413]

(b) processes for modifying the germ line genetic identity of human beings;[414]

(c) uses of human embryos for industrial or commercial purposes;[415]

(d) processes for modifying the genetic identity of animals which are likely to cause them suffering without any substantial medical benefit to man or animal, and also animals resulting from such processes.[416]

After looking at the general prohibition in Article 53(a)/section 1(3), we will look at each of these specific cases in turn. Before doing so it is important to note that if an application falls within any of the four types of invention, the application must ipso facto be denied a patent under Article 53(a) /section 1(3). In this situation there is no need to consider Article 53(a)/section 1(3) any further. However, if an application falls outside the four categories of invention, the application needs to be assessed to determine whether it falls within Article 53(a).[417] That is, a case

---

[405] Biotech Dir. Art 6(2).   [406] PA Sched. A2, paras. 3(b)–(e).

[407] EPC 2000 Rule 28 (which is the same as EPC 1973 Rule 23d:, Implementing Regulations to the EPC (introduced by [1999] *OJ EPO* 437). On the basis that Rules 23b to 23e EPC did not constitute a departure from previous law, it was held that they could be applied to matters that started prior to their enactment on 1 Sept. 1999: *Harvard/Onco-mouse* [2003] *OJ EPO* 473, 496 (Opposition Division).

[408] For the background, see Art. 1, item 18 of EPC 2000; Base Proposal for the Revision of the European Patent Convention CA/100/00 e (2000), 42.

[409] PA s. 1(3)(a) (as enacted) of the 1977 Act was replaced by a new section 1(3) in 2000. Patents Regulations 2000 (SI 2000/2037) (in force 28 Jul. 2000). The old section 1(3)(a) provided that a patent should not be granted for 'an invention the publication or exploitation of which would be generally expected to encourage offensive, immoral or anti-social behaviour'. In contrast, the new section 1(3) provides that a 'patent shall not be granted for an invention the commercial exploitation of which would be contrary to public policy or morality'. PA s. 1(4) states that for the purpose of s. 1(3) exploitation shall not be regarded as contrary to public policy or morality only because it is prohibited by law in force in the UK. This replicates the language in Biotech. Dir. Art. 6(1).

[410] Ibid, 51.   [411] Formerly EPC 1973 Rule 23(a)-(d).

[412] PA Sched. A2, para. 3(b)–(c); EPC Rule 23d (a)–(d); Biotech. Dir., Art. 6(1).

[413] EPC 2000 Rule 28(a) (formerly EPC 1973 Rule 23d(a), Implementing Regulations to the EPC (introduced by (1999) OJ EPO 437); PA Sched. A2, para. 3(b); Biotech. Dir., Art. 6(2)(a).

[414] EPC 2000 Rule 28(b) (formerly EPC 1973 Rule 23d(b)), Implementing Regulations to the EPC; PA Sched. A2, para. 3(c); Biotech. Dir., Art. 6(2)(b).

[415] EPC 2000 Rule 28(a) (formerly EPC 1973 Rule 23d(c)), Implementing Regulations to the EPC; PA Sched. A2, para. 3(d); Biotech. Dir., Art. 6(2)(c).

[416] EPC 2000 Rule 28(a) (formerly EPC 1973 Rule 23d(d)), Implementing Regulations to the EPC; PA Sched. A2, para. 3(e); Biotech. Dir., Art. 6(2)(d).

[417] *Harvard/Transgenic Animals*, T315/03 [2006] *OJ EPO* 15, 40.

not falling within Rule 28 EPC 2000 does not escape the operation of Article 53(a). The position is presumably the same in the UK.

9.1 INVENTIONS CONTRARY TO ORDRE PUBLIC OR MORALITY

Article 53(a) EPC 2000 provides that European patents 'shall not be granted in respect of inventions the commercial exploitation of which would be contrary to "*ordre public*" or morality…'. While the UK provisions have changed so that they are more closely aligned to the EPC than had previously been the case, the language in section 1(3) is slightly different in that it provides that 'a patent shall not be granted for an invention the commercial exploitation of which would be contrary to public policy or morality'.

The role and meaning of the morality exclusion under the EPC (as enacted) was first considered in the 1989 *Onco-mouse* decision.[418] The case concerned the patentability of mice that had been genetically modified so that they would develop cancer: a result that the applicants hoped would be useful in cancer research.[419] Initially, the Examining Division declined to consider Article 53(a), taking the view that it was inappropriate for people who were essentially qualified as technicians to consider such an issue.[420] On appeal, the Technical Board of Appeal took a very different view.[421] It observed that the genetic manipulation of mammalian animals is 'undeniably problematical in various respects', particularly in circumstances where the modifications 'necessarily cause suffering'.[422] Moreover, the release of the mice into the environment might 'entail unforeseeable and irreversible adverse effects'. Consequently, it was necessary to consider the application of Article 53(a).

The Technical Board of Appeal, remitting the case to the Examining Division for reconsideration,[423] explained that the application of Article 53(a) 'would seem to depend mainly on a careful weighing-up of the suffering of animals and possible risks to the environment on the one hand, and the invention's usefulness to mankind on the other'. Applying this utilitarian balancing test, the Examining Division held that the subject matter was patentable. It reasoned that finding a cure for cancer was a highly desirable end, and that the mouse would assist in achieving that end. In contrast, the Examining Division played down the harm caused by the invention. The Examining Division suggested that given that the research would take place anyway, and that it would require vast numbers of mice to locate some which had 'naturally' developed cancer, the invention produced a benefit to mouse-kind in that large numbers of healthy mice would no longer need to be bred and then destroyed.[424]

The utilitarian balancing test adopted in the *Onco-mouse* decision was applied in 1991 when the EPO warned the pharmaceutical company Upjohn that it would not accept an application to patent a mouse into which a gene had been introduced leading the mouse to lose its

[418] See V. Vossius, 'Patent Protection for Animals' [1990] *EIPR* 250; Dresser, 'Ethical and Legal Issues in Patenting New Animal Life', [1988] *Jurimetrics Journal* 399; U. Schatz, 'Patentability of Genetic Engineering Invention' (1998) 29 *IIC* 2; Manspeizer, 'The Cheshire Cat, the March Hare and the Harvard Mouse' (1991) 43 *Rutgers Law Review* 417.

[419] More accurately, of a mammal into which malignancy-creating genes had been introduced so that the mammal had an increased probability of developing tumours.

[420] [1989] *OJ EPO* 451 (Exam).   [421] *Harvard/Onco-mouse*, T19/90 [1990] *OJ EPO* 490 (TBA).

[422] Ibid. [1990] *EPOR* 501, 513 (para. 5). It has been suggested that the EPO was awaiting the outcome of the Directive before issuing a decision. See CIPA, *Briefing Paper Patentability of Animals* (May 1998) <http://www.cipa.org.uk/pages/info-papers-animals>.

[423] *Harvard/Onco-mouse* T19/90 [1990] *OJ EPO* 490 (TBA).

[424] *Harvard/Onco-mouse* T19/90 ([1991] *EPOR* 525 (Exam).

hair. In weighing up the benefit that flowed from the invention (the usefulness of the mice in experiments to cure hair loss) as against the harm suffered by the mice, the EPO asserted that the invention was immoral and thus would not be patentable.[425]

The next occasion on which the application of Article 53(a) was considered was by the Opposition Division in *Plant Genetic Systems*.[426] In this case, the opponents (Greenpeace) objected to the patent that had been granted for a genetically engineered plant (which rendered the plants resistant to herbicide) on the grounds that it was inherently immoral and that it created risks to the environment. Following the cost–benefit test suggested in *Onco-mouse*, the opponents argued that these risks should be balanced against the benefits likely to accrue from the invention. The Opposition Division refused to apply the utilitarian cost–benefit analysis. On the basis that the patent system was primarily concerned with technical considerations and that they were not competent or qualified to decide ethical issues, the Opposition Division believed that it should not be routinely involved in considering ethical questions. Instead, the Opposition Division said that it was only necessary to consider the exclusion where the invention would be universally regarded as outrageous and where there was an overwhelming consensus that no patent should be granted. That is, it was only necessary to consider ethical questions once a certain ethical threshold had been crossed. The upshot of this is that in most cases it would not be necessary to consider the morality of patents.

The *Plant Genetic Systems* decision highlights a further difficulty in relation to the immorality examination. In an attempt to apply the balancing test outlined in *Onco-mouse*, the Opposition Division was faced with the problem that it was unable to quantify the objections raised against the patent. This was compounded by the fact that no evidence was submitted to support these claims. Instead, the examiners were asked to determine the opposition on the basis of personal philosophy or conviction. The Opposition Division rejected such an approach on the basis that it would produce 'individualistic' or 'arbitrary' decisions. Moreover, even if it were possible to convert abstractly formulated objections into a more concrete format (for example, through the use of opinion poll evidence), the Opposition Division clung to the view that patent law should not be the forum in which such opinions should play a role.

The approach advocated in the *Plant Genetic Systems* decision was adopted by the Opposition Division in the *Relaxin* case.[427] This decision concerned an opposition by the Green Party to the Howard Florey Institute's patent for the DNA sequences of a naturally occurring substance, that relaxes the uterus during childbirth, which is obtained from the human ovary. The Green Party objected to the patent on three grounds. First, they argued that the use of pregnancy for profit was offensive to human dignity; second, that the applicant was involved in patenting life, an activity that was intrinsically immoral; and third, that such patenting was equivalent to slavery. In rejecting the Green Party's objections, the EPO noted that the tissue used in the research was donated during the course of necessary gynaecological operations and thus had not offended 'human dignity'. Moreover, the Opposition Division said that DNA was not 'life'. Rather, it was a 'chemical substance which carries genetic code'. The argument that the applicant was 'patenting life' was thus misconceived. Finally, the Opposition Division rejected the Green Party's assertion that such patenting was equivalent to slavery on the ground that such an assertion misunderstood the nature of a patent. This was because, according to the Opposition Division, a patent does not give the proprietor any rights over a human being: all a patent monopoly provides is the right to prevent someone from practising the same invention.

---

[425] *Independent* (2 Feb. 1992).   [426] [1993] 24 *IIC* 618.
[427] *Howard Florey/Relaxin*, T74/91 [1995] *EPOR* 541 (Op. Div.).

As with the *Plant Genetics* decision, the Opposition Division's decision in *Relaxin* further highlights the problems that confront patent law in accommodating ethical considerations. This was explicitly acknowledged in *Relaxin* when the Opposition Division said the question of whether 'human genes should be patented is a controversial issue on which many persons have strong opinions…the EPO is not the right institution to decide on fundamental ethical questions'.[428] The case also reveals the difficulties involved in translating the ethical concerns of the objectors into the language of patent law. Faced with a choice between a scientific understanding of DNA as a chemical substance and the social understanding of DNA as life, the former interpretation was preferred by the Opposition Division. This prioritization of the scientific view of genetic process over the Green Party's approach illustrates the depth of the conflict between the logic of ethical objections and those of patenting, at least as it is currently understood.

The next development in this area came with the decision of the Board of Appeal in *Plant Genetic Systems*[429] where the Technical Board of Appeal concluded that claims for genetically modified seeds did not contravene Article 53(a). Although this decision, which has attracted many critics,[430] represents a more flexible approach to the incorporation of ethics into patent law, it still highlights the uncertainty and ambiguity that exist in this relationship. The Board of Appeal said that the concept of morality under the EPC was built upon the belief that some behaviour is right and acceptable whereas other behaviour is wrong: a belief that was founded on norms deeply rooted in European society and civilization. Noting that patent offices exist 'at the crossroads between science and public policy', the Board of Appeal said that *ordre public* in Article 53(a) covers the protection of public security, the physical integrity of individuals as part of society, and protection of the environment. On this basis, the Board of Appeal said that, where the exploitation of an invention was likely to breach public peace or social order (for example, through acts of terrorism) or seriously prejudice the environment, the invention would be excluded from patentability under Article 53(a).[431]

The Technical Board of Appeal then attempted to clarify the way Article 53(a) was to be interpreted. As well as casting doubts on the value of opinion poll evidence, the Board said that the mere fact that the exploitation of a particular type of subject matter was permitted in some or all of the contracting states would not automatically influence the ethical status of that subject, at least in relation to its patentability. The Board observed that a balancing exercise was not the only way of assessing patentability, although it was useful in situations where actual damage and/or disadvantage existed. The Board added that although the morality provision is to be construed narrowly, it should not be disregarded. This is the case even if it is difficult to judge whether the claimed subject matter is contrary to *ordre public* or morality. Given the explicit wording of Article 53(a), it is difficult to see how they could have concluded otherwise.

The scope of Article 53(a) was also considered by the Technical Board of Appeal in its 2006 *Transgenic Animals* decision. In this case, which is the latest instalment in the ongoing *Oncomouse* saga, the Technical Board of Appeal was called on to consider whether a patent for transgenic rodents containing an additional cancer gene was excluded from patentability under Article 53. This was an appeal from the 2003 decision of the Opposition Division to maintain the patent in an amended form.[432]

---

[428] Ibid, 552.   [429] [1995] *OJ EPO* 545.

[430] Straus, 'Patenting Human Genes in Europe' (1995) 26 *IIC* 920.

[431] The *EPO Guidelines*, C–V, 3.1, gives the example of a letter-bomb.

[432] *Harvard/Onco-mouse* [2003] *OJ EPO* 473 (Opposition Division). In upholding the patent in an amended form, the Opposition Division set out what it saw to be the general principles underlying Article 53(a) EPC. In

The Technical Board of Appeal began by stressing that the words 'contrary to *ordre public* or morality' were not concerned with the morality of genetically manipulating a mouse, with the morality of the onco-mouse thereby produced, nor with the patenting of either the onco-mouse or the genetic manipulation method. Instead the Board stressed that the morality provisions were only concerned with the morality of the publication or exploitation of the onco-mouse or that method.[433] (It should be noted that the EPC 2000 no longer refers to the publication of the invention. Instead it is now limited to the commercial exploitation of the invention.)[434]

The Board reconfirmed that the balancing approach set out in the 1991 *Onco-mouse* decision (T 19/90) was the correct approach to be adopted when deciding whether an invention fell within a 'real' Article 53(a) assessment. The Board reiterated that, unlike the balancing test mandated under EPC Rule 23d(d) (now EPC 2000 Rule 28), the T19/90 test allowed a range of factors to be taken into account including harm to the environment, possible use of non-animal alternatives, possible threats to human evolution, and so on.[435] As we will see below, the applicant's main request—which claimed 'transgenic rodents' and thus embraced all animals within the taxonomic order *Rodentia* including rats, mice, squirrels, beavers, and porcupines—was rejected on the basis that it failed the balancing test required under Rule 23d(d) EPC 1973 (EPC 2000 Rule 28). Given this, the Board did not need to consider the fate of the main request under Article 53(a). Nonetheless, the Board said that the claims would have failed under the balancing test as set out in the *Onco-mouse* decision (T19/90). This was on the basis that the balancing test in conjunction with Article 53(a) was able to take account of more factors than were permissible under Rule 23d(d) EPC 1973 (EPC 2000 Rule 28). This meant that additional factors such as the degree of animal suffering and the availability of non-animal methods could also be taken into account. The Board said that, when these factors were added to the inevitable harm created by the invention and the fact that there was no evidence that the medical benefits from the invention applied to all rodents, it further tilted the balance against the acceptance of the request.[436]

The fate of the main request under Article 53(a) needs to be contrasted to that of the auxiliary request, which was limited to 'mice' rather than 'rodents'. While it was accepted that the auxiliary invention caused actual suffering to mice, the auxiliary request differed from the main application in that the applicant was able to show that the invention also produced actual medical benefits. As the Board said, this meant that 'no suffering was envisaged to any animals without a corresponding prospect of benefit'.[437] As such, the Board concluded that the auxiliary request passed the *Onco-mouse* (T19/90) test under Article 53(a). Interestingly, while the Board accepted that additional factors (such as harm to the environment) could be taken into account if they were able to be substantiated,[438] they were highly critical of the arguments

particular, they said that Article 53(a) would only ever apply in exceptional cases. They also said that, in assessing whether a patent fell foul of Article 53(a), they had no intention to apply 'extreme positions'. By this they meant they would not take account of possible abuses of the invention. the Opposition Division said that *ordre public* and morality had to be assessed 'primarily by looking at laws or regulations which are common to most of European countries because these laws and regulations are the best indicators about what is considered right or wrong in a society'.

[433] *Harvard/Transgenic Animals,* T315/03 [2006] *OJ EPO* 15, 29 (TBA). The Board also said that *ordre public* and morality may form the basis of separate objections.

[434] This brings the EPC into line with Art 27(2) TRIPS and Art 6(1) of the Biotech. Dir.

[435] *Harvard/Transgenic Animals,* T315/03 [2006] *OJ EPO* 15, 54.   [436] Ibid, 63.   [437] Ibid.

[438] Other factors, including the threat to evolution posed by the transgenic mice, the fact that the patent would have encouraged the use of transgenic mice in research, and the more general argument that genetically engineered mice were morally unacceptable to the public, were rejected. See ibid, 69–72

made by some of the opponents about the degree of suffering. This was rejected (presumably on the unsubstantiated moral basis) that it was distasteful even to attempt to draw a distinction between acceptable and unacceptable suffering.[439]

9.2 INVENTIONS DEEMED TO BE IMMORAL

In addition to the general morality provisions in Article 53(a)/section 1(3), there are a number of specific types of biological invention that are deemed to be immoral or contrary to *ordre public*. These are to be found in EPC 2000 Rule 28 (formerly EPC 1973 Rule 23d) and paragraph 3, Schedule A2 of the Patents Act 1977.[440]

9.2.1 Processes for cloning human beings

The first type of biological invention that is deemed to fall foul of Article 53(a)/section 1(3) is 'processes for cloning human beings'.[441] The exclusion of processes for human cloning reflects concerns about eugenics. Human cloning is defined as 'any process, including techniques of embryo splitting, designed to create a human being with the same nuclear genetic information as another living or deceased human being'.[442] It has been suggested that the scope of the exclusion will depend on how 'human being' is defined.[443] In particular, 'human being' may be defined in such a way as not to include human embryos and embryonic tissue. The UK Intellectual Property Office has said that human totipotent cells (which have the potential to develop into an entire human body) would not be patentable 'because the human body at the various stages of its formation and development is excluded from patentability'.[444] In contrast, the Office is willing to grant patents for human embryonic pluripotent stem cells (which arise from the division of totipotent cells but do not have the potential to develop into an entire human body). The fact that a number of reports from key scientific bodies, including The Royal Society and the Nuffield Council on Bioethics, supported embryonic stem-cell research, was taken as evidence that such research was not contrary to public policy or morality in the UK.[445] It should be noted that the EPO declared (on the basis of the 'old' law) that methods in a cloning process which fused human and pig cells were contrary to morality. As a consequence the applicants did not pursue the application any further.[446] As such, it seems that even if the cloning of human embryos was not caught by EPC 2000 Rule 28(a) (EPC 1973 Rule 23d(a)) it would fall under the general prohibition in Article 53(a).[447]

---

[439] Ibid, 67. The time at which a real Article 53(a) assessment was to be made was the effective date of the patent (namely either the filing or priority date), although later evidence may be taken into account so long as it is directed to the position at the relevant date.

[440] The TBA also said that the date at which the application should be assessed is the filing date or the priority date of the patent in question. *Harvard/Transgenic Animals*, ibid, 66 (TBA).

[441] EPC 2000 Rule 28(a) [EPC 1973 Rule 23d(a)]/Schedule A2, para 3(b) 1977 Act.

[442] Biotech. Dir., Recital 41. See also Biotech. Dir., Recital 40.

[443] Bostyn, 'Patentability of Genetic Information Carriers' [1999] *IPQ* 1, 11.

[444] UK Patent Office, *Practice Note: Inventions involving Human embryonic stem cells* (Apr. 2003), citing PA Sched. A2, para. 3(a).

[445] UK Patent Office, *Practice Note: Inventions involving Human embryonic stem cells* (Apr. 2003).

[446] Patent applications for the cloning of embryos (including human embryos) as well as mixed-species embryos from pigs and humans: reported on Yahoo.news, 27 Oct. 2000.

[447] Such activities may also be caught by Biotech. Dir. Art. 5; Rule 23e(1); PA Sched. A2, para. 3(a).

9.2.2 Processes for modifying the germ-line genetic identity of human beings

The second type of biological invention that is deemed to fall foul of Article 53(a)/section 1(3) are processes for modifying the germ line genetic identity of human beings 'processes for cloning human beings'.[448] The exclusion of processes that modify the germ-line genetic identity of human beings (a process that could alter the reproductive cells that are capable of transmitting genetic material to our descendants) also reflects concerns about eugenics. While somatic-cell gene therapy is not caught by the provisions, germ-cell-line therapy inventions are.[449] It has been suggested that the exclusion of all forms of germ-line therapy is an overreaction. More specifically, it has been said that, as it is conceivable that morally unobjectionable applications of germ-line therapy (for example, for inheritable diseases like cystic fibrosis) may arise in the future, the exclusion is 'retrograde and short-sighted'.[450] As Recital 42 of the Biotechnology Directive points out, the exclusion does not affect inventions for therapeutic or diagnostic purposes which are applied to the human embryo and are useful to it.

9.2.3 Uses of human embryos for industrial or commercial purpose

The third type of biological invention that is deemed to fall foul of Article 53(a)/section 1(3) is for 'uses of human embryos for industrial or commercial purpose'.[451] The exclusion of uses of human embryos for industrial or commercial purposes is relatively straightforward.[452] To a large extent, the scope of the exclusion will depend on what is meant by 'industrial' or 'commercial' purposes. The UK Intellectual Property Office has said that, as well as excluding uses of human embryos, patents will not be granted for processes of obtaining stem cells from human embryos.[453] As we mentioned above, the UK Intellectual Property Office has also said that while human totipotent cells are not patentable, they had no objections to the patenting of human embryonic pluripotent stem cells.

In one of the first decisions to consider the new provisions, the Opposition Division at the EPO held that the University of Edinburgh's controversial human embryo patent did not comply with EPC 1973 Rule 23d(c) (EPC 2000 Rule 28(c)).[454] The patent 'involved removing stem cells from human embryos, genetically manipulating these cells and cultivating genetically manipulated embryos from them'.[455] Many of the legal issues that arose in this case have been superseded by the Technical Board of Appeal decision in *Wisconsin Alumni Research Foundation/Stem cells*.[456] The application in this case was for a cell culture made from primate-embryonic stem cells. It was clear that the application covered human-embryonic stem cells.

---

[448] EPC 2000 Rule 28(b) [EPC 1973 Rule 23d(b)]/Schedule A2, para 3(c) 1977 Act.

[449] Bostyn, 'Patentability of Genetic Information Carriers' [1999] *IPQ* 1, 8. Bostyn offers the following definitions: 'somatic cell gene therapy applies to differentiated cells of the foetus, the child or the adult, such as cells of the liver, blood or other organs' (8, n. 36); 'germ line therapy applies to non-differentiated cells, such as gametes or the fertile egg, and implies that the genetic modification will be transmitted to the individual's offspring' (8, n. 37).

[450] Nott, 'You Did It' [1998] *EPIR* 347, 349; Llewellyn, 'Legal Protection of Biotechnological Inventions' [1997] *EPIR* 115, 122.

[451] EPC 2000 Rule 28(c) [EPC 1973 Rule 23d(c)]/Schedule A2, para 3(d) 1977 Act.

[452] EPC Rule 23d(c) Implementing Regulations to the EPC (introduced by [1999] *OJ EPO* 437); PA Sched. A2, para. 3(d); Biotech. Dir., Art. 6(2)(c).

[453] UK Patent Office, *Practice Note: Inventions involving Human embryonic stem cells* (Apr. 2003).

[454] Patent EP 695351, granted by EPO Dec. 1999. The patent was allowed to continue in an amended form by the Opposition Division (hearing date 22–24 Mar. 2002). See EPO press release, 'Edinburgh patent limited after European Patent Office opposition hearing' (24 Jul. 2002).

[455] After amendment, the patent no longer includes human or animal embryonic stem cells but still covers modified human and animal stem cells other than embryonic stem cells.

[456] T1374/04 [2007] *OJ EPO* 313 (TBA).

It was also clear that, to repeat the invention, the skilled person had to start from spare pre-implantation embryos, and that they had to destroy them in the process. Given the importance of the area, the Technical Board of Appeal has referred a number of questions to the Enlarged Board of Appeal for consideration.[457] The first question, which concerns the transitional arrangements for the Rules, is whether EPC 1973 Rule 23d(c) (EPC 2000 Rule 28(c)) applies to an application filed before the Rule came into force. The second question referred to the Enlarged Board concerns the way that the Rule should be interpreted. This question was prompted by the uncertainty that has arisen as to whether EPC 1973 Rule 23d(c) (EPC 2000 Rule 28(c)) should be construed narrowly (thereby only excluding from patentability applications whose claims are directed to the use of human embryos), or broadly (thereby extending the exclusion to products whose isolation necessitated the direct and unavoidable use of human embryos). The Technical Board effectively asked the Enlarged Board how this question should be answered in its second referral: 'Does Rule 23d(c) EPC forbid the patenting of claims directed to products (here human-embryonic stem cell cultures) which…at the filing date could be prepared exclusively by a method which necessarily involved the destruction of the human embryos from which the said products are derived?' The third question asked of the Enlarged Board of Appeal is whether Article 53(a) forbids the patenting of such claims? The issue at stake here is whether the balancing test set out in the *Onco-mouse* (T19/90) decision should be applied in relation to Rule 23d(c) (EPC 2000 Rule 28(c)). While the appellant had argued that it should, the Technical Board said that it had doubts whether, when it comes to human life, it would be 'ethically acceptable to make a decision by weighing the interests of human beings who could potentially benefit from the invention against a right (if any) of human embryos to get to life and of not being destroyed for the benefit of others'.[458] The fourth and final question referred to the Board is whether it makes any difference that 'after the filing date the same products could be obtained without having to recur to a method necessarily involving the destruction of human embryos?'[459] These are important and challenging questions which should assist in interpreting not only the scope of EPC 2000 Rule 28(c) (EPC 1973 Rule 23d(c)), but also of Article 53(a) more generally.

9.2.4 Processes for modifying the genetic identity of animals

The final category of inventions expressly excluded from protection is 'processes for modifying the genetic identity of animals which are likely to cause them suffering without any substantial medical benefit to man or animal, and also animals resulting from such processes'. These are to be found in EPC 2000 Rule 28(d) (EPC 1973 Rule 23d(d))/Schedule A2, para 3(e) 1977 Act.[460] The fact that the provision is limited to the modification of animals means that it will not impact upon animal cloning (such as Dolly the sheep).

In the 2006 decision in *Harvard/Transgenic Animals* the Technical Board of Appeal was called on to consider whether a patent for transgenic rodents containing an additional cancer gene was excluded from patentability under EPC 1973 Rule 23d(d) (EPC 2000 Rule 28(d)). In looking at this provision, the Board stressed that the balancing test in Rule 23d(d) only applies where suffering to animals is likely. This meant that a 'likelihood—but no more than a likelihood of such suffering is necessary to trigger the operation of Rule 23d(d).'[461] While the balancing test in EPC 1973 Rule 23d(d) (EPC 2000 Rule 28(d)) was based on the approach adopted

---

[457] The pending decision is G 2/06.   [458] *WARF/Stem cells*, T1374/04 [2007] *OJ EPO* 313, 338 (TBA).
[459] Ibid, 339.   [460] This corresponds to Article 6(2)(d) of the Biotech Directive.
[461] *Harvard/Transgenic Animals*, T315/03 [2006] *OJ EPO* 15, 40–41 (TBA).

in the *Onco-mouse* (T19/90) decision,[462] the tests differed. In particular, although the test in *Onco-mouse* balances the suffering of animals against 'usefulness to mankind', the test in Rule 23d(d) (EPC 2000 Rule 28(d)) balances the suffering of animals against 'substantial medical benefit to man or animal'. It is clear from this that the test in *Harvard/Transgenic Animals* was broader than the test that was developed in *Onco-mouse*. It was also clear that, if 'substantial medical benefit' is established for the purposes of Rule 23d(d), usefulness to mankind under *Onco-mouse* T 19/90 would also be established.[463]

The Board also said that EPC 1973 Rule 23d(d) (EPC 2000 Rule 28(d)) requires two matters to be evaluated. These are (i) whether animal suffering is likely; and (ii) whether likely substantial benefit has been established. While the criteria that need to be met may be different, the Board noted that the standard or level of proof to be applied in relation to the two integers of EPC 1973 Rule 23d(d) was the same.[464] Since only a likelihood of suffering needs be shown, other matters such as the degree of suffering or the availability of non-animal alternatives do need to be considered. Evidence need not be limited to that available at the filing or priority date, but evidence available thereafter must be directed to the position at that date.[465]

In applying the test set out in EPC Rule 23d(d) (EPC 2000 Rule 28(d)), the Board stressed that there needed to be a 'necessary correspondence between suffering and benefit'. This was based on the understanding that EPC Rule 23d(d) provided that a patent should only extend to those animals whose suffering was balanced by a medical benefit.[466] Taking a hypothetical example, the Board said, 'if likely suffering to both cats and lions was established, it would none the less be contrary to Rule 23d(d) EPC [1973] to allow claims which encompassed both cats and lions when the only established likely medical benefit arose in relation to the use of cats'.[467] The impact that the principal of correspondence is able to play in limiting the scope of what may be patented, which is reminiscent of the requirement for sufficiency of disclosure, is evident from the way that the main and auxiliary requests were dealt with by the Technical Board of Appeal in *Harvard/Transgenic Animals*. The main request considered by the Board was for 'transgenic rodents'. On the basis that the request embraced all animals within the taxonomic order *Rodentia*, the Board said that 'suffering will—and must—be present in the case of every such animal—not just mice but also squirrels, beavers, porcupines, and every other rodent'.[468] Applying this logic to the case in hand, the Board noted that no evidence had been produced that showed that there was a likelihood that a substantial medical benefit to man or animal would arise from applying the claimed process to all rodents, or indeed to any animals of the order *Rodentia* apart from mice. That is, there was no evidence that the medical benefits for cancer research that were meant to arise from the invention applied to all rodents. On this basis, the Board held that the likelihood of substantial medical benefit required by Rule 23d(d) had not been substantiated.[469] Given that animal suffering was 'not just a likelihood but an inevitable consequence of the very purpose of the patent', the Board concluded that the main request failed the balancing test of Rule 23d(d) and was therefore refused under Article 53(a) EPC.

The fate of the main request in *Harvard/Transgenic Animals* needs to be contrasted to that of the auxiliary request, which was limited to 'mice' rather than 'rodents'. As with the main request, the Board noted that one of the inevitable consequences of the invention was that it would cause harm and suffering to mice. In contrast to the main claim, however, the

---

462 Ibid.   463 Ibid, 42, 53–54.   464 Ibid, 62 (TBA).   465 Ibid, 50–51.
466 Ibid, 47.   467 Ibid.   468 Ibid.   469 Ibid, 63.

applicant was able to produce evidence that showed that the invention (as defined in the auxiliary request) did have medical benefits. On this basis, the Board said that the subject matter of the auxiliary claims (which were limited to transgenic mice) satisfied the test in Rule 23d(d) (EPC 2000 Rule 28(d)). The Board then went on to consider the fate of the auxiliary application under Article 53(a) proper which, as we saw above, was found not to apply to the claim for transgenic mice.

18

NOVELTY

CHAPTER CONTENTS

1 INTRODUCTION

Both the Patents Act 1977 and the EPC 2000 stipulate that for an invention to be patentable it must be 'new'.[1] An invention is said to be new if it does not form part of the 'state of the art'.[2] The 'state of the art' is defined very broadly to include all matter that is available anywhere in the world before the priority date of the invention. Where an invention is disclosed or 'anticipated' by the state of the art, a patent will not be granted or, if it has been granted (because the prior art escaped the attention of the Examiner), the patent is liable to be revoked.[3]

Novelty requires that the invention be *quantitatively* different from what has been disclosed previously; that is, that the technical information disclosed by the patent is not already available to the public. In this sense, novelty is different from the requirement that to be patentable an invention must have involved an inventive step (or be non-obvious), which is basically a *qualitative* examination to ascertain whether the contribution is creative enough to warrant a monopoly.

By ensuring that patents are not granted for products or processes which are already known, novelty helps to ensure that patents are not used to stop people from doing what they had already done before the patent was granted.[4] As we will see, this so-called right to work

---

[1] PA s. 1(1)(a); EPC 2000 Art. 52(1) [previously EPC 1973 Art. 52(1)].

[2] PA s. 2(1); EPC 2000 Art. 54(1) [previously EPC 1973 Art. 54(1)]. PA s. 130(7) provides that PA s. 2 is framed so as to have, as nearly as practicable, the same effect in the UK as the corresponding provisions of the EPC.

[3] PA s. 72(1)(a); EPC 2000 Art. 138(1)(a). Lack of novelty is a ground of opposition at the EPO under EPC 2000 Art. 100(a).

[4] Prior to the 1624 Statute of Monopolies, the Crown granted patents for activities which had already been carried out, one of the most infamous examples being for the buying and selling of playing cards. This meant that those who were already practising the activities could no longer continue to do so. Not surprisingly, such persons were aggrieved. See *Clothworkers of Ipswich Case* (1614) *Godb R* 252; 78 ER 147; *Darcy v. Allin* (1602) 74 *ER* 1131. In part, the 1624 Statute of Monopolies was introduced to overcome these problems.

argument has been modified as a result of changes in the way novelty is determined.[5] Another factor that is used to justify the novelty requirement relates to the overall rationale for the grant of patents.[6] More specifically, it is argued that the public is willing to pay the costs (or monopoly profits) of patenting if, and only if, they are able to get access to information that would not otherwise have been available to them. To adopt the contract analogy that is often used to justify and explain patents, novelty ensures that the inventor provides the consideration necessary to warrant the patent being granted in the first place.

While the Patents Act 1977 retains many of the basic principles and rationales that have long been a feature of British law on novelty, Britain's entry into the EPC introduced some important changes in the way the novelty requirement is applied in the United Kingdom. One of these relates to the fact that the 1977 Act and the EPC operate on the principle of 'objective novelty': that is, an attempt, where possible, to avoid subjective judgements (which are seen to lead to uncertainty).[7] Perhaps the clearest example of this is that both British and European patent law have adopted the principle of 'absolute novelty'.[8] This means that the novelty of an invention is judged against all the information which is available at the priority date of the invention; irrespective of where the information was released or the form that it was released in.[9]

Given the broad nature of the knowledge base against which the novelty of inventions is assessed, it is not surprising that it has been criticized on the basis that by allowing obscure materials to anticipate, absolute novelty produces harsh results. In its favour, however, absolute novelty is said to provide a 'bright line' test, thus 'avoiding subjectivity and most questions of degree'.[10] Given the sophisticated information tools that are currently available to researchers, there may be good reasons for providing disincentives to prevent the duplication of research that has already been carried out.[11] Another notable change in the post-1977 law is that in determining whether an invention is novel, the courts have placed increased attention on the information function of the patent system. As we will see, this has had important consequences for so-called secret or inherent uses and their ability to anticipate.

The task of determining whether an invention is novel can conveniently be broken down into three separate questions. These are:

(i)   What is the invention?

(ii)   What information is disclosed by the prior art?

(iii) In light of (i) and (ii), is the invention novel? That is, is the invention part of the state of the art?

---

[5] On the right to work see *Windsurfing International* [1995] *RPC* 59, 77; B. Reid, 'The Right to Work' [1982] *EIPR* 6. With respect to registered designs *Falk v. Jacobwitz* (1944) 61 *RPC* 116, 123.

[6] At the EPO, the purpose of the novelty requirement is to prevent the prior art from being repatented: *Bayer/Diastereomers*, T12/81 [1982] *OJ EPO* 296; [1979–85] *EPOR* B–308, 312; *Bayer/Amino acid derivatives*, T12/90 [1991] *EPOR* 312, 317.

[7] See *Genentech's Patent* [1989] *RPC* 147, 198, 203 (Purchas LJ) (CA).

[8] Strasbourg Convention Art. 4. France and Italy already had such a standard.

[9] This is wider than under pre-1977 law, especially as regards the requirement of worldwide novelty. In other ways it may be narrower since the pre-1977 condition 'having regard to what was known and used' had no specific requirement that the use make 'the invention' available to the public. Some countries require novelty within the territory, exclude old documents, or confine the state of the art to printed documents. For an argument in favour of a more 'realistic standard' see Note, 'Prior Art in the Patent Law' (1959) 73 *Harvard Law Review* 369.

[10] *Milliken Denmark AS v. Walk Off Mat* [1996] *FSR* 292.

[11] R. Merges, *Patent Law and Policy* (1992), 192–4 (examining the rationale behind the novelty doctrine from the point of view of its impact on search activities).

We will deal with each of these in turn. After doing so, we will look at three specific types of invention and the problems that have arisen when assessing their novelty.

2 WHAT IS THE INVENTION?

Before being in a position to determine whether an invention is new, it is first necessary to identify what the alleged invention is.[12] While the way an invention is characterized often plays a key role in shaping many aspects of the novelty examination and consequently the fate of many inventions,[13] it has received very little attention.

3 WHAT INFORMATION IS DISCLOSED
BY THE PRIOR ART?

Once the technical features of an invention have been identified, it is then necessary to ascertain the nature of the information that has been disclosed by the prior art. In order to do this it is first necessary to ask: what material forms part of the state of the art? Once this has been ascertained (and the prior art which is relevant to the invention in question has been identified), it is then possible to determine the nature of the information (or teaching) which is disclosed by the prior art.

3.1 WHAT IS THE STATE OF THE ART?

The state of the art is defined in extremely broad and inclusive terms to include all matter (whether a product, process, information about either, or anything else) which, at the priority date of the application in question, has been made available to the public (whether in the United Kingdom or elsewhere) by written or oral description, by use or in any other way.[14] There are a number of features of the way in which the state of the art is defined which should be borne in mind.

3.1.1 No geographical limits

There are no geographical limits on where the state of the art must be disclosed. As such, it includes information that is available *anywhere* in the world.

3.1.2 No restrictions on the mode of disclosure

Information will become part of the state of the art irrespective of the way in which it was made available to the public. Consequently, information may become part of the state of the art as a result of written descriptions (such as previously published patents[15] or journal articles),[16]

---

[12] *Merrell Dow Pharmaceuticals v. Norton* [1996] *RPC* 76, 82 (HL); *Evans Medical Patent* [1998] *RPC* 517.

[13] *Glaverbel v. British Coal* [1994] *RPC* 443; [1995] *RPC* 255 (CA); *CIPA*, para. 2.03.

[14] PA s. 2(2); EPC 2000 Art. 54(2).

[15] T877/98 [2001] OJ EPO Special Edition No. 3, 20 (a patent becomes part of the public domain on publication in the relevant Official Journal, not upon notification of the decision to grant).

[16] This includes a magazine available to the public one day before the priority date, but not a doctoral thesis which has been placed in a library archive and not yet been indexed: *Research Corporation/Publication*, T381/87 [1990] *OJ EPO* 213; [1989] *EPOR* 138. See also *Exxon Mobil*, T314/99 (21 Jun. 2001).

through past uses,[17] exhibitions, sales,[18] or by oral communications (although in the latter case difficult evidential questions may arise).[19] If the information is accessible, then its age, obscurity, duration, language, or location is irrelevant.[20] Similarly, there are no minimum requirements on how widely the information must be published for it to be disclosed. Thus, a single copy of a document, or the sale of a single item, will be sufficient for the information to become part of the state of the art.[21]

3.1.3 Potential rather than actual disclosure

Material is factually available (and part of the state of the art) if it is open to or capable of being accessed by the public. As such, there is no need to demonstrate that anyone *actually* had access to the information in question: all that matters is that if they had wanted to, they could have accessed the information.[22]

3.1.4 Priority date

Both the Patents Act 1977 and the EPC provide that the date at which the novelty is to be assessed is the 'priority date' of the invention in question.[23] The upshot of this is that the state of the art only includes information that is made available to the public *before* the priority date of the invention in question. While the priority date is normally the date on which an application was filed,[24] in some cases the priority date is earlier[25] (notably where an application is made in a Paris Convention country during the previous twelve months).

In contrast with some other patent regimes,[26] applicants for UK and European patents are not provided with a 'grace period', that is a period prior to filing in which they are able to practise their inventions.[27] Consequently, patents are frequently anticipated and thus rendered

---

[17] *Luchtenberg/Rear-view mirror,* T84/83 [1979–85] *EPOR* 793, 796. On previous use as prior art under the EPC see Castro (1996) 27 *IIC* 190; and under French law, see Mandelo (1996) 27 *IIC* 203.

[18] *Telemecanique/Power supply unit,* T482/89 [1993] *EPOR* 259; [1992] *OJ EPO* 646.

[19] *Hooper Trading/T-cell growth factor,* T877/90 [1993] *EPOR* 6. CIPA, para. 2.23. See also *University of Pennsylvania,* T1212/97 (22 Aug. 2001) (discussing the problems in interpreting the information provided by a lecture given to an audience of over 100 people).

[20] *Windsurfing International* [1995] *RPC* 59 (CA).

[21] *Fomento v. Mentmore* [1956] *RPC* 87. *Monsanto (Brignac's) Application* [1971] *RPC* 153, where a publication placed in the hands of salesmen was held to have been made available to the public, since there was no fetter on their use of that information. See also *Van Wonterghem,* T1022/99 (10 April 2001) (sale of object to a single customer). However, supply to a manufacturer is likely to be treated as in confidence: *Strix v. Otter* [1995] *RPC* 607, 633–4. It should be noted that supply will only make the invention available if it reveals it: *Pall Corp v. Commercial Hydraulics* [1990] *FSR* 329.

[22] *Japan Styrene Paper/Foam particles,* T444/88 [1993] *EPOR* 241. There is no requirement that a person be likely to examine the document: *Hoechst/Polyvinylester dispersion,* T93/89 [1992] *OJ EPO* 718; [1992] *EPOR* 155; *Woven Plastics v. British Ropes* [1970] *FSR* 47; *Harris v. Rothwell* (1887) 4 *RPC* 225.

[23] PA s. 2(1); EPC 2000 Art. 54(2). In the USA, the relevant date is the date when the invention was made.

[24] PA s. 5(1); EPC 2000 Rule 40.

[25] The law facilitates this by allowing for priority not only from full filing but also from early filing. PA s. 14–15; EPC 2000 Rule 40. On a situation where early PCT filing is claimed under EPC Arts. 87–88 [EPC 2000 Arts, 87–88] see *Requirement for claiming priority of same invention,* G/98 [2001] *OJ EPO* 413 (earlier priority could only be claimed from an earlier application if the skilled person could derive the subject matter of the later claim directly and unambiguously from the previous application as a whole).

[26] A grace period is provided by US law—35 USC section 102(b)—in which the applicant's own acts are deemed to fall outside the state of the art.

[27] For calls for grace periods, see WIPO H1/c.e./1/2 (15 May 1985); Lesser, (1987) *EIPR* 81. More recently the Intergovernmental Conference of Member States of the EPO called for the EPO to examine the conditions under

invalid for want of novelty as a result of the applicant's own acts and disclosures.[28] The priority date is thus important not just because it is the date at which novelty is assessed, but also because it is the date from when inventors are able to exploit their inventions without jeopardizing any potential patents.[29]

3.1.5 Material specifically included within the state of the art

While as a general rule patent law provides that the state of the art only includes material in the public domain before the priority date of the invention, an exception is made in relation to patent applications that are published after the priority date of the application in suit. More specifically, the relevant laws provide that in addition to the matter published before the priority date of the invention, the state of the art also includes applications for other patents that are published after the priority date of the invention in question, but nonetheless have a priority date earlier than the application in question.[30] The reason why the state of the art is (effectively) backdated in this way is to avoid the possibility of double patenting, that is, of patents being granted to different applicants for the same invention.[31] This potential problem is created by the fact that there is a time lag between the date of filing, which is normally the priority date, and the early publication of the application—when the application becomes part of the state of the art.

3.1.6 Material specifically excluded from the state of the art

There are two situations where material in the public domain is not taken into account when assessing novelty of inventions. The first is where the information was obtained unlawfully or was disclosed as a result of a breach of confidence.[32] In a sense this reaffirms the old principle that material is only available to the public if the recipient is free in law and equity to divulge

which a grace period should be introduced into the EPC. For expert opinions on this see at <http://www.epo.org>. See F. Blakemore, 'Grace Periods in European Patent Law' (Oct. 1998) *Patent World* 18.

[28] See *Fomento* [1956] *RPC* 87; *Lux Traffic Controls v. Pike Signals* [1993] *RPC* 107, 134–5; *Research Corporation/Publication*, T381/87 [1990] *OJ EPO* 213; [1989] *EPOR* 138.

[29] *Asahi Kasei Kogyo* [1991] *RPC* 485, 529 (Lord Oliver) (HL). In the USA, experimental use will not invalidate a patent even though the invention was in public use or on sale more than a year before the priority date.

[30] PA s. 2(3), s. 130(3); EPC 2000 Art. 54(3), Art. 87(4). The test for novelty under PA s. 2(3) is the same as under PA s. 2(2): *SmithKline Beecham plc's Patent* [2003] *RPC* 114, 120–22 (CA) and *Synthon BV v. SmithKline Beecham* [2002] *EWHC* 1172. EPC Art. 54(3) does not treat existing national rights as part of the state of the art, so that a European patent (UK) would be granted at the EPO but not in the UK where the existing national right would anticipate. See *Mobil/Admissibility*, T550/88 [1992] *OJ EPO* 117; [1990] *EPOR* 391 (construing the term 'European patent application' in EPC Art. 54(3) as excluding previous national applications, by reference to Arts. 93 and 139); *Woolard's Application* [2002] *RPC* 39; *Zbinden's Application* [2002] *RPC* 13 (discussing when a withdrawn application forms part of the state of the art). The EPC 2000 abolished EPC 1973 Art 54(4). The effect of this is that will be that the state of the art for a European application or patent now includes all previous European applications irrespective of their designation. The Patents Act 1977 was amended accordingly.

[31] The section, however, may not always avoid double patenting because the disclosure will only anticipate if it is enabling. See *Asahi Kasei Kogyo* [1991] *RPC* 485 (HL).

[32] PA s. 2(4)(a)(b); EPC 2000 Art. 55(1)(a) [EPC 1973 Art. 55(1)(a)]. Relevant examples include disclosure by employees (*Robert Bosch/Electrical machine*, T1085/92 [1996] *EPOR* 381); submission of an article to a refereed journal (*Research Corporation/Publication*, T381/87 [1989] *EPOR* 138); and disclosures at a meeting with a manufacturer (*Macor Marine Systems/Confidentiality agreement*, T830/90 [1994] *OJ EPO* 713; *Telecommunications/Antioxidant*, T173/83 [1987] *OJ EPO* 465; [1988] 3 *EPOR* 133). Cf. *Unilever/Deodorant Detergent*, T585/92 [1996] *OJ EPO* 129 (early publication by Brazilian Patent Office as a result of lamentable error was unfortunate and detrimental but not an evident abuse within Art. 55 since evident abuse required state of mind of abuser to be influenced by its specific relationship with the applicant, as with breach of confidentiality). On the timing of the disclosure see *University Patents/Materials and methods for herpes simplex virus vaccination*, G3/98 [2001] *OJ EPO* 62.

its contents.[33] The second situation where information is excluded from the state of the art is where the disclosure was due to or made in consequence of the inventor displaying the invention at an 'international exhibition'.[34]

It is important to note that the exclusions only apply to disclosures that are made in the six-month period immediately preceding the date of filing the claim for the invention in question.[35] Any disclosures that are made outside of this period will not be caught by the exceptions and will thus form part of the state of the art for the purposes of assessing novelty.

3.2 WHAT INFORMATION IS DISCLOSED BY THE PRIOR ART?

The information disclosed by the prior art is restricted to the information that a person skilled in the art is able to derive from the prior art in question.[36] In considering the way the prior art is interpreted by a person skilled in the art, it is useful to distinguish between situations where the relevant prior art consists of a document and where it is made up of a product.[37]

3.2.1 Interpreting documents

Documents are interpreted as if they were being read at the date of their publication,[38] and not the priority date of the invention or the date of trial. Given that the act of interpretation usually takes place after the date on which the document was published, it is important that documents are neither read retrospectively,[39] nor construed in light of events which have taken place since publication (notably the creation of the invention in question). The information available is that which a person skilled in the art would derive from reading the document in light of common general knowledge. In this respect the skilled person has a limited ability to extend the meaning of the document beyond that which would be provided by a literal reading.[40] In line with this, the person skilled in the art is able to correct obvious mistakes, inconsistencies, or errors that may exist in the documents.[41]

Another important rule of interpretation is that the information must be drawn from a single document. This means that it is not possible to combine together (or 'mosaic') separate items in the prior art. In a similar vein, it is not normally possible to combine elements from

[33] *Humpherson v. Syer* (1887) 4 *RPC* 407; *Bristol Myers Application* [1969] *RPC* 146; *James Industries' Application* [1987] *RPC* 235; T818/93 and T480/95 [1997] *OJ EPO* 20–21; *Robert Bosch/Electrical Machine*, note 32 above; *Research Foundation/Translation inhibitor*, T838/97 (14 Nov. 2001) (oral presentation of an invention to a conference of 100 experts, who were told that the information could not be used without specific authorization, was a private communication that did not form part of the public domain).

[34] PA s. 2(4)(c); EPC. 2000 Art 55(1)(b) [EPC 1973 Art. 55(1)(b)]. 'International exhibitions' are defined in PA s. 130 and Art. 55(1)(b) as relating to the Convention on International Exhibitions signed at Paris in 1928. See A. Serjeant 'International Exhibitions' (1985–6) 15 *CIPAJ* 319.

[35] PA s. 2(4) refers to the period preceding the application date. According to the EBA, under EPC Art. 55(1) the 'relevant date is the date of the actual filing of the European patent application; the date of priority is not to be taken into account in calculating this period'. *University Patents*, G3/98 [2001] *OJ EPO* 62 (EBA).

[36] See R. Jacob, 'Novelty of Use Claims' (1996) 27 *IIC* 170, 174.

[37] T270/89 in G. Keller, 'Summary of Some Recent Decisions at the EPO' [1993] *JPTOS* 237.

[38] *General Tire & Rubber v. Firestone Tyre & Rubber* [1972] *RPC* 457; *Minnesota Mining v. Bondina* [1973] *RPC* 491; *Tektronix/Scottky barrier diode* [1995] *EPOR* 384. Cf. questions of sufficiency of disclosure where documents are read at the priority date of the invention.

[39] *Rhone-Poulenc/Taxoids*, T77/97 [1998] *EPOR* 256.

[40] See *Bayer/Chimeric gene*, T890/02 [2005] *OJ EPO* 497.

[41] *Toshiba*, T26/85 [1990] *OJ EPO* 22; *Scanditronix/Radiation beam collimation*, T56/87 [1990] *OJ EPO* 188; [1990] *EPOR* 352; *ICI/Latex composition*, T77/87 [1990] *OJ EPO* 280; [1989] *EPOR* 246.

within a single document.[42] The only occasion where it is permissible to combine documents together is where a primary document inevitably leads to a second document; that is, where the person skilled in the art would read different documents as if they were one.[43]

3.2.2 Interpreting products

A number of special rules have been formulated to deal with situations where the prior art consists of a product, such as a drug or a machine that has been released on the market.[44] In circumstances where the product is the same as the invention, few problems arise. The task of interpretation becomes more problematic, however, where the technical information necessary to anticipate an invention is not immediately apparent from looking at the product, but can only be obtained if the product is analysed.[45]

It has long been recognized that the information disclosed by a product is not limited to the information that is immediately apparent from looking at the product. Importantly, the information available to the public also includes the information that a skilled person would be able to derive from the product if they analysed or examined it.[46] The person skilled in the art is able to make use of the analytical skills and techniques commonly available in the field before the priority date of the invention. This means that if the skilled person worked in a field in which reverse engineering was commonly practised, then a machine placed on sale would reveal all the information that a person skilled in the art would be able to obtain if they reverse-engineered the machine.

Any information that is obtained as a result of an analysis undertaken by a person skilled in the art must be obtained without undue burden or without the need to exercise any additional inventive effort.[47] If it were necessary for the person skilled in the art to embark on inventive or exploratory research to reveal the information in question, the information would not form part of the state of the art.

The amount of information that is revealed by an examination depends on the type of analysis undertaken.[48] This would vary with things such as the skills of the researchers in question, and the time and money spent on the examination.[49] Given this, the question has

---

[42] *Draco/Xanthines,* T7/86 [1985] *EPOR* 65; [1988] *OJ EPO* 381; *Scanditronix,* ibid.

[43] If the disclosure reveals one part of the product, and another disclosure another element, there is no anticipation: *Bayer/Diastereomers,* note 6 above. *Texaco/Reaction injection moulded elatomer,* T279/89 [1992] *EPOR* 294, 298; *Amoco Corporation/Alternative claims,* T153/85 [1988] *OJ EPO* 1; [1988] *EPOR* 116, 123; *ICI/Latex composition,* T77/87 [1990] *OJ EPO* 280; [1989] *EPOR* 246, 251.

[44] *Quantel v. Spaceward Microsystems* [1990] *RPC* 83.

[45] See L. Tournroth, 'Prior Use' (1997) 28 *IIC* 800, 800–1; Paterson, para. 10–07. In *Lux Traffic,* Aldous J distinguished between cases of prior use where the public had access to the invention and were able to handle it, and prior uses which allowed the public only to observe the object. The circumstances in which each would anticipate would differ, disclosure being much more likely in cases of handling. This, however, was not conclusive. In *Luchtenberg/Rear-view mirror,* T84/83 [1979–85] *EPOR* 793, 796, the TBA accepted that the use of a mirror attached to a car in public for six months might be revealed if all aspects were disclosed. Cf. *Pfennigabsatz* [1966] *GRUR* 484, 486.

[46] *Thomson/Electron tube,* T953/90 [1998] *EPOR* 415.

[47] *Availability to the Public Decision,* G1/92 [1993] *EPOR* 241; [1993] *OJ EPO* 277. Undue burden, however, seems to carry with it a subjective element. In *Packard/Liquid scintillatia,* T952/92 [1997] *EPOR* 457, the TBA argued that the reference to 'undue burden' in G1/92 was obiter and that the issue of burden in terms of time or work was irrelevant.

[48] It also depends on the general nature of the article: *Wesley Jessen Corp v. Coopervision* [2003] *RPC* 355, 384 (the skilled addressee would have 'all the information he might require' from a contact lens in the public domain, which was 'not a product of high technical sophistication').

[49] *Novartis/Erythro-compounds,* T990/96 [1998] *EPOR* 441; [1998] *OJ EPO* 489 (re disclosure for chemical compounds).

arisen as to whether limits should be placed on the type of (hypothetical) analysis that is undertaken. Following the principle of objective novelty, subjective factors such as the cost of carrying out the analysis or the time taken to find the relevant information are *not* taken into account when determining the nature of the information revealed by a product.[50] Neither is it necessary that there be particular reasons which prompted the skilled person to examine the composition of the product in the first place:[51] the question is *could* and not *would* the product be analysed by the person skilled in the art?

4 IS THE INVENTION NOVEL?

Once the invention under examination and the information disclosed by the prior art have been identified, it is then possible to determine whether the invention is new. In many cases, particularly where the prior art and the invention are identical or the prior art leads directly to the patented invention, it will be relatively easy to determine whether an invention has been made available to the public. This task becomes more problematic, however, where there is a gap between the prior art and the invention. The reason for this is that the same thing may be known by the public in a number of different ways: things may be described in terms of what they look like, how they are made, what they do, the problems they solve, what they are made of, how much they cost, and so on.[52] This gives rise to the question, how does a patent need to be described for it to be known by the public? Put differently, how specific must a disclosure be for an invention to be 'known' or 'made available' to the public?[53] For example, will a chemical invention be anticipated if the formula of the chemical structure of the invention is made available to the public?[54] Or is it necessary for the formula and the means by which the formula is implemented both to be available to the public?

After some uncertainty[55] it is now clear that an invention will lack novelty if, at its priority date, it has been 'made available' to the public.[56] Drawing upon the principle that patents should only be granted if the public has been provided with useful information, an invention

---

[50] *Packard/Liquid scintillatia*, T952/92 [1997] *EPOR* 457.

[51] *Availability to the Public Decision*, G1/92 [1993] *EPOR* 241.

[52] *Merrell Dow v. Norton*, note 12 above, 88 (HL). As Lord Hoffmann reminds us, this is essentially an epistemological question: what does it mean for the public to know something so that it can anticipate? The problem is that there is often a marked difference between something being 'known' by the general public, and being known for the purposes of patent law: hence Lord Hoffmann's comments about the specific epistemological basis of patent law. In a similar vein the TBA said 'the concept of novelty must not be given such a narrow interpretation that only what has already been described in the same terms is prejudicial to it…There are many ways of describing a substance': *Bayer/Diastereomers*, T12/81 [1979–85] *EPOR* B–308, 312; *Hoechst/Thiochloroformates*, T198/84 [1979–85] *C EPOR* 987; [1985] *OJ EPO* 209.

[53] While this question would have been relatively easy to answer if anticipation had been limited to circumstances where the disclosure and the invention were identical, it is not necessary that an invention be replicated exactly in the prior art, or that it be described in identical terms, for a disclosure to destroy novelty. A mere difference in wording or phraseology will not substantiate a claim to novelty. 'The term "made available" clearly goes beyond literal or diagrammatical description, and implies a communication, express or implicit, of technical information by other means as well. The inevitability of the outcome requires proof beyond reasonable doubt': *Allied Signal/Polyolefin fiber*, T793/93 [1996] *EPOR* 104, 109.

[54] Similarly, would a patent for quinine be anticipated by the fact that Amazonian Indians have known for some time that the spirit of the cinchona bark possessed certain qualities that made it good for treating fevers?

[55] See, e.g. *PLG Research v. Ardon International* [1993] *FSR* 197, 218.

[56] Available 'carries with it the idea that, for lack of novelty to be found, all the technical features of the claimed invention in combination must have been communicated to the public, or laid open for inspection'. *Mobil Oil/ Friction reducing additive*, G2/88 [1990] *EPOR* 73; *Chemie Linz/Reinforced channels*, T242/85 [1988] *EPOR* 77.

is said to have been made available to the public if there has been an *'enabling disclosure'*.[57] Following the House of Lords decision in *Synthon BV v SmithKline Beecham,* it is clear that 'enabling disclosure' consists of two separate requirements which need to be satisfied if an objection of lack of novelty is to succeed.[58] These are the requirements for *prior disclosure* and *enablement.* As Lord Hoffmann said in *Synthon,* it is important to keep in mind that disclosure and enablement are distinct concepts, each of which has to be satisfied and each of which has its own rules. He also stressed that there was a serious risk of confusion if the two concepts were not kept separate. Before looking at what is meant by 'disclosure' and 'enablement', it is important to note that in some situations the same disclosure may satisfy both requirements. As Lord Hoffmann said,

'the prior art description may be sufficient in itself to enable the ordinary skilled man, armed with general knowledge of the art, to perform the subject matter of the invention. Indeed, when the prior art is a product, the product itself, though dumb, may be enabling if it is "available to the public" and a person skilled in the art can discover its composition or internal structure without undue burden'.[59]

In other cases, however, different factors will be used to show disclosure and enablement. The difference between 'disclosure' and 'enablement' is clear from the facts in *Synthon.* The patent in question identified and claimed a crystalline chemical. The prior art contained both a description of such a product and a recipe for making it. If the skilled man tried to follow the recipe using his ordinary skill and knowledge he would have failed. The recipe as such was not enabling. But even without it, the skilled man would have been able, with a little trial and experiment, to make the described product. So the prior art satisfied both the 'necessary result' and the 'enablement' requirements.[60]

4.1 DISCLOSURE

The first point that must be established to show that a patent has been anticipated is that there has been a 'disclosure'. Under what is sometimes called the reverse-infringement test, prior art will disclose a patent if it reveals subject matter which, if performed, would necessarily (or inevitably) result in an infringement of the patent.[61] With disclosure, there is no room for experiment. While the person skilled in the art is permitted to draw upon the general knowledge common to the field, the prior art must place that person in a position where they are able to work the invention without the need for further information, or to engage in new experiments, or some other additional inventive activity.[62] As the Court of Appeal said in *General Tire,* the prior disclosure must have planted the flag on the invention. If it is an inevitable consequence of following the information disclosed in the prior art that the invention is made, the invention will have been disclosed.[63] If the instructions probably, normally, or only sometimes produce the product, however, there will be no anticipation.[64]

---

[57] The same requirement operates in Germany: *Fluoron* [1989] *IIC* 736.

[58] *Synthon BV v. SmithKline Beecham* [2006] *RPC* 10 (HL).

[59] Ibid, para 29 (citing *Availability to the Public* [1993] *EPOR* 241, para 1.4 (EBA)).

[60] See *Ferag AG v. Muller Martini Ltd* [2007] *EWCA Civ* 15, para 10.

[61] *Synthon* [2006] *RPC* 10, para. 22, 24 (HL).   [62] *Hills v. Evans* (1862) 31 *LJ Ch* 457; 45 *ER* 1195 (HL).

[63] See *Inhale Therapeutic Systems v. Quadrant Healthcare* [2002] *RPC* 419 (where Laddie J reviewed his earlier judgment in *Evans Medical Patent,* note 12 above); *SmithKline Beecham PLC's Patent (No. 2)* [2003] *RPC* 607, 631.

[64] On inevitable disclosure, see *General Tire v. Firestone* [1972] *RPC* 457, 458–6. Inevitably has been defined to mean in 99 cases out of 100 (*Fomento* [1956] *RPC* 87); 'tantamount to 100 per cent probability' (*Allied Signal/ Polyolefin fiber,* T793/93 [1996] *EPOR* 104). It seems that at the EPO the inevitability of the disclosure needs to be satisfied 'beyond all reasonable doubt': *Allied Signal,* ibid.

The question whether a disclosure enables the public to work an invention is decided objectively.[65] Drawing upon the principle that patent infringement does not require that a person needs to know that they are infringing, Lord Hoffmann said that knowledge does not play a role when determining whether there had been a disclosure. Instead, all that matters is that the subject matter described in the prior disclosure is capable of being performed and is such that if performed, it must result in the patent being infringed. This means that there is no need to show that a member of the public actually worked the invention, nor that they were aware of its existence. In these circumstances, there is no need for the person skilled in the art to know that they are producing the product in question: all that matters is that the prior art discloses information which, if followed, inevitably leads to the invention. To use the analogy often used in this context, 'if the recipe which inevitably produces the substance is part of the state of the art, so is the substance made by that recipe'.[66] It does not matter that the cook was ignorant of the fact that they were producing the product.

4.2 ENABLEMENT

The second point that needs to be demonstrated to show anticipation is that the disclosure was 'enabling'. A disclosure will be enabling and thus destroy novelty if the public is given sufficient information to enable the invention to be put into effect. That is, a disclosure will anticipate an invention if it enables the invention to be 'worked' or 'practised'.[67] Enablement means that the ordinary skilled person would have been able to perform the invention which satisfies the requirement for disclosure.[68] Lord Hoffmann said that the test for enablement of a prior disclosure for the purpose of anticipation was the same as the test for enablement for the purpose of sufficiency. This means that the authorities on sufficiency under section 72(1)(c) are applicable to enablement for the purposes of section 2(2) and (3).

As we saw above, for the purpose of disclosure, the prior art must reveal an invention which, if performed, would necessarily infringe the patent.[69] The disclosure must occur without further experiment or undue effort.[70] This is in contrast to the requirement for enablement where the person skilled in the art is assumed to be willing to make trial and error experiments to get it to work.[71] Another way in which 'disclosure' and 'enablement' differ is in terms of the role that the person skilled in the art plays. As Lord Hoffmann said, 'once the meanings of the prior disclosure and the patent have been determined, the disclosure is either of an invention which, if performed, would infringe the patent, or it is not. The person skilled in the art has no further role to play.' This is in contrast to the inquiry into whether the disclosure was enabling,

---

[65] *Merrell Dow v. Norton* [1996] *RPC* 76, 88, 89, 90. 'This does not affect the principle that the prior art directions or information that will inevitably result in the use of a patented process or creation of the patented product invalidates by anticipation'. Ibid. 90, 93. *Kaye v. Chubb* (1887) 4 *RPC* 289, 298.

[66] *Merrell Dow* above, 90. See also *CPC/Flavour concentrates decision,* T303/86 [1989] *EPOR* 95; *Bayer/Diastereomers* T12/81 [1979–83] EPOR B-308, 312; *Availability to the Public,* G1/92 [1993] *EPOR* 241.

[67] *Merrell Dow* above, 89. This reiterates the old idea that, in order for a method or use claim to be anticipated, the prior art must provide 'clear and unmistakable directions to do what the patentee claims to have invented': *Flour Oxidizing v. Carr* (1908) 25 *RPC* 428, 457.

[68] *Synthon* [2006] *RPC* 10, para 26 (HL).   [69] Ibid, para 30.

[70] On this see *SKB v. Apotex* [2005] *FSR* 23, where Jacob LJ criticized the practice of 'litigation chemistry', that is the use of contrived experimental repetitions of the prior art. See also *Mayne Pharma v. Debiopharm* [2006] *EWHC* 164 (Pat), para. 10–11.

[71] *Synthon* [2006] *RPC* 10, para 30 (HL).

where the 'question is no longer what the skilled person would think the disclosure meant but whether he would be able to work the invention which the court has held it to disclose'.[72]

It is very difficult to state with any precision the circumstances in which the prior art will enable an invention to be worked and thus be anticipated.[73] This is because the decision as to whether there has been an enabling disclosure always depends upon the facts of the case in question. That is, the information that is needed for an invention to be 'worked' always depends upon the particular invention under examination. As a result, it is impossible to specify in advance that to be novelty-destroying the prior art must adopt a particular format. It is impossible to predict, for example, the nature of the information that needs to be disclosed for a chemical compound to be worked or practised. This can be seen if we look at the various ways in which chemical compounds can be anticipated. For example, in *Asahi Kasei Kogyo*[74] the House of Lords held that the disclosure of the formula to a particular chemical compound did not anticipate a patent for that compound.[75] The reason for this was that for a skilled person to be in a position where they could work the invention in question, they not only needed to be given the chemical formulae but also the means by which the compound could be produced. While on the facts of *Asahi* the formulae may have been non-enabling, as Lord Oliver said there might 'be [other] cases where the means of producing the thing will be self evident to the man skilled in the art from the mere Recital of the formula of its composition'.[76] That is, there might be circumstances in which the disclosure of the formula to a chemical compound is sufficient to anticipate the compound. In other instances, in order to anticipate it might be necessary for the prior art to disclose not only the formulae and the means, but also details of the starting materials.[77]

4.3   SECRET OR INHERENT USE

One of the most important changes that has taken place with the shift to enabling disclosure is in relation to the issue of whether the existence of a previous secret or inherent use is enough to anticipate a subsequent patent. Basically, a secret or inherent use occurs where something is created, usually either accidentally or as an unknown by-product of some process, without the public knowing of its existence. While it was possible for a secret or inherent use to anticipate

---

[72] Ibid, para 32.

[73] As such, it is not very helpful to attempt to quantify the situations in which a patent can be anticipated. Cf. *Inhale v. Quadrant* [2002] *RPC* 21, 436; *SmithKline Beecham plc's Patent (No. 2)* [2003] *RPC* 607, 630–1 (suggesting that a claim can be anticipated in two ways: if the prior art describes something falling within its scope, and where the inevitable result of carrying out what is described in the prior art falls within the claims).

[74] See note 29 above.

[75] Drawing upon a series of cases decided under the Patents Act 1949 which utilized the reverse-infringement test (such as *Gyogyszeripari's Application* [1958] *RPC* 51), it was argued that, as the prior art disclosed the formulae of the chemical compound and there was an indication that the compound had actually been made, the chemical compound lacked novelty. This was the case irrespective of whether the chemical could have been made. In rejecting this line of argument (and in so doing finding that Asahi's patent had *not* been anticipated), the House of Lords stressed that, in order for a disclosure to destroy novelty, it needed to be 'enabling'. As such, the crucial question was whether the prior art provided sufficient information to enable the skilled person to make the chemical compound.

[76] [1991] *RPC* 485, 536.

[77] *ICI's Application/Herbicidal pyradine,* T206/83 [1986] 5 *EPOR* 23; [1987] *OJ EPO* 5. In other instances a chemical compound will not be 'known' unless the information disclosed in the prior art enables the compound to be prepared or, in the case of a naturally occurring compound, to be separated. *EPO Guidelines* C–IV, 7.3.

under the Patents Act 1949, this is no longer the case under the 1977 Act.[78] The position under the 1949 Act was set out in *Bristol-Myers' Application*,[79] where the question arose as to whether Bristol-Myers' patent for an ampicillin compound (an artificial antibiotic derived from penicillin) had been anticipated by the fact that before the priority date of the invention Beecham had made small quantities of the ampicillin. At the time the ampicillin was made, Beecham did not know about the invention, nor were they aware of its particular advantages. While the prior art conveyed no relevant information about the product to the general public, nonetheless the House of Lords held that the patent had been anticipated by the secret or uninformative use. The explanation for this was twofold. First, had the patent been granted, the patentees would have been able to stop another trader from doing what they had done before (the right to work doctrine); second, the test for anticipation was coextensive with the test for infringement. Given that for a defendant to infringe it was not necessary for them to have realized that what they were doing was an infringing act, such knowledge was therefore equally unnecessary when determining whether the invention was novel (the reverse-infringement test).

The question of the status of secret or inherent use under the Patents Act 1977 was considered by the House of Lords in *Merrell Dow v. Norton*.[80] This decision arose from the fact that in 1972 the claimant was granted a patent for the antihistamine terfenadine: a drug used in treating hay fever and other allergies. When terfenadine was taken by patients, it was transformed (or metabolized) in the body to produce a number of different products (metabolites). While terfenadine proved to be very effective in the treatment of hay fever, it had a number of unwanted side effects, notably it led to heart-related problems in some patients. As the initial patent was nearing the end of its duration, the claimant isolated and identified the particular metabolite that acted as an antihistamine. It was accepted that prior to this the specific metabolite that acted as an antihistamine had not been identified. In 1983, the claimant obtained a patent for the newly identified metabolite. More accurately, it obtained a patent for the making of the metabolite with the antihistamine effects within the human body. This carried with it the obvious advantage that while it was useful in the treatment of hay fever it did not have any of the side effects associated with terfenadine.

After grant of the patent for the metabolic acid, Merrell Dow (the claimant) brought an action against Norton claiming that by supplying terfenadine the defendant was facilitating the making of the patented metabolite, thus infringing the second patent.[81] The defendants counterclaimed arguing that the second patent had been anticipated by prior use. The argument for anticipation by use relied on the fact that terfenadine had been made available to and used by volunteers in clinical trials before the priority date of the patent. As the patented

---

[78] The Patents Act 1977 'introduced a substantial qualification into the old principle that a patent cannot be used to stop someone from doing what he has done before. If the previous use was uninformative, then subject to section 64 [which provides a defence for secret use before the priority date] it can': *Merrell Dow v. Norton* [1996] *RPC* 76, 86.

[79] [1975] *RPC* 127. Such an approach would mean that a previous secret use would anticipate a patent even if it were not clear how the invention worked. This is because such a use would give the public the benefit of the old invention even without their knowledge. Under the 1977 Act, it seems that there is nothing to prevent a person from concealing the use of their invention in this manner, though it has been suggested that in a clear case of fraud the Patent Office might decline to grant a patent. See H. Frost, 'Why Europe Needs a Sale Bar' [1996] *EIPR* 18; Jacob, 'Novelty of Use Claims'.

[80] *Merrell Dow v. Norton* [1996] *RPC* 76 (HL); I. Karet 'A Question of Epistemology' [1996] *EIPR* 97; see V. Vossius, C. Vossius, and T. Vossius, 'Prior Written Disclosure and Public Prior Use under German Law and the EPC' [1994] *EIPR* 130.

[81] This was on the basis it amounted to a contributory infringement under PA s. 60(2).

metabolite was produced in the livers of the volunteers when they took terfenadine, it was argued that the second patent had been anticipated and was thus invalid.

Lord Hoffmann said that, while under the Patents Act 1949 mere uninformative use of this kind would have invalidated the patent, this was no longer the case under the 1977 Act.[82] In rejecting the reverse-infringement test, Lord Hoffmann said that when deciding novelty the starting point was whether there had been an enabling disclosure of the claimed invention.[83] Importantly, Lord Hoffmann said that while an invention might have been in existence before the priority date through a secret or inherent use this was not sufficient in itself to destroy novelty. The reason for this was that 'the use of a product makes the invention part of the state of the art only insofar as that use makes available the necessary information'.[84] While the patented metabolite was inevitably produced in the body of the volunteers when they took terfenadine, this working of the invention was not as a result of information that had been made available to the public. The uninformative consumption of terfenadine, which secretly or inherently produced the metabolite, did not reveal or disclose information that would have allowed either the volunteers or the public more generally to make the metabolite in their bodies. On the basis that the use of terfenadine in the clinical trials conveyed no information that would have enabled anyone to work the invention (it was not enough that it had in fact been made), the House of Lords held that the prior use was not anticipatory.[85]

As Lord Hoffmann said in *Synthon,* problems of confusion between disclosure and enablement were acute in cases such as *Merrell Dow,* where the subject matter disclosed in the prior art is not the same as the claimed invention but, if performed, will necessarily infringe. 'To satisfy the requirement of disclosure it must be shown that there will necessarily be infringement of the patented invention. But the invention which must be enabled is the one disclosed by the prior art. It makes no sense to inquire as to whether the prior disclosure enables the skilled person to perform the patented invention, since *ex hypothesi* in such a case the skilled person will not even realise that he is doing so. Thus in *Merrell Dow* the question of enablement turned on whether the disclosure enabled the skilled man to make terfenadine and feed it to hay-fever sufferers, not on whether it enabled him to make the acid metabolite.'[86]

It should be pointed out that the invention in *Merrell Dow* was anticipated by the earlier patent. In the case of anticipation by use, the acts relied upon conveyed no information which would have enabled anyone to work the invention: that is, to make the acid metabolite in the body. In contrast, the earlier patent made information available to the public that enabled it to perform an act, the inevitable consequence of which was that the patented metabolite was produced. The terfenadine specification taught that the ingestion of terfenadine produced a chemical reaction in the body. For the purposes of working the invention in this form, this was a sufficient description of the making of the patented metabolite.

---

[82] As such *Bristol-Myer's Application* [1975] *RPC* 127 is no longer good law.

[83] 'The question to be decided is not what may have been "inherent" in what was made available (for example, by a prior written description or in what has previously been used (prior use). Rather it was what has been made available to the public'. *Mobil/Friction reducing additive,* G2/88 [1990] *EPOR* 73, 88.

[84] Lord Hoffmann emphasized that the invention, which was a piece of information, must have been made available to the public. *Merrell Dow v. Norton* [1996] *RPC* 76, 86.

[85] This rule applies whether the prior art is a previous application, a previous use, a description, or a set of instructions. The 'information deriving from a use is governed in principle by the same conditions as is information disclosed by oral or written description'. *Availability to the Public,* G1/92 [1993] *EPOR* 241, 243.

[86] *Merrell Dow v. Norton* [1996] *RPC* 76, para. 33.

4.4 PRODUCT-BY-PROCESS CLAIMS

As we saw earlier, product-by-process claims are only allowed at the EPO where it is impossible, or at least very difficult, to define the product in any other way.[87] The approach taken towards product-by-process claims manifests itself in the way that the novelty of such claims is assessed. At the EPO, a product-by-process claim will only be novel if the product itself is novel: novelty cannot be conferred by the process alone. That is, the EPO 'does not recognise that novelty can be conferred on a known substance by a novel process for producing that substance'.[88] This means that even if the process claimed is novel a product-by-process claim will be anticipated (and thus held to be invalid) unless the product itself is also novel.

The approach that has been adopted at the EPO is in contrast to the approach traditionally taken to product-by-process claims in the UK. While product-by-process claims are only permitted at the EPO in exceptional circumstances, they were traditionally allowed in the UK. The different approach taken towards product-by-process claims manifested itself in the way that the novelty of such claims were assessed in the UK and at the EPO. While the EPO has consistently refused to accept that the novelty of a product-by-process claim can arise from the novelty of the process used (i.e. it must flow from the novelty of the product), the approach traditionally followed in the UK was different. For example, the practice in the UK under the Patents Act 1949 and earlier was 'to treat the fact that a product was made by a new process as sufficient to distinguish it from an identical product which was already part of the state of the art'.[89] The difference between the traditional British approach and the approach adopted at the EPO was made clear when the UK Court of Appeal in *Kirin-Amgen* explicitly rejected the EPO approach saying that there was 'no reason why the limitation of claims to products produced by a process could not impart novelty...If a person invents a new method of extracting gold from rock, he can obtain a claim to the process and as Art 64(2) [EPC 1973, EPC 2000] makes clear, he can also monopolise the gold when produced directly by the process.'[90] That is, a product-by-process claim was valid in the UK provided the process itself was patentable. While this may have suggested that new monopolies could be established over old products (such as gold) every time a new process was invented, the protection only applied to products made by that process.

When *Kirin-Amgen* went on appeal to the House of Lords in 2005, the Lords overturned the Court of Appeal decision and in so doing brought British law into line with practice at the EPO. While Lord Hoffmann accepted that this meant a change in a practice that had existed in the UK for many years, he thought it was important that the UK should apply the same law as the EPO and other member states. In any case Lord Hoffmann did not think that the adoption of the EPO approach would have much practical importance since patentees could rely on the process claim and Article 64(2) to receive equivalent protection.[91] The upshot of the House of Lord decision is that a product-by-process claim, where the product is known, will be rejected on the basis that it is not novel. The UK Intellectual Property Office has accordingly changed

---

[87] This is where there is no chemical or biological means for distinguishing a product from the prior art.

[88] UK Patent Office, *Examination Guidelines for Patent Applications relating to Biotechnological Inventions* (Sept. 2002), para. 13; *Kirin-Amgen v. Transkaryotic Therapies* [2003] *RPC* 31, para. 296 (CA).

[89] *Kirin-Amgen v. Hoechst Marion Roussel* [2005] *RPC* 169 (HL), para 88.

[90] *Kirin-Amgen* [2003] *RPC* 31, para. 33 (CA). 'I can discern no reason in principle or in practice why a claim to a product made by a certain process could be invalid simply because the product is not novel, if the process is novel, so that a claim to a process would be valid.'

[91] *Kirin-Amgen* [2005] *RPC* 9, para 101. PA s 60(1)(c), which accords to Article 64(2) EPC 1973/2000, states that protection provided by a claim for a process extends to the product of that process.

its practice and now adopts the view that 'a claim to a product obtained or produced by a process is anticipated by any prior disclosure of that particular product *per se*, regardless of its method of production'.[92]

4.5 BIOTECHNOLOGIAL INVENTIONS

While a number of changes have been made to patent law to accommodate biotechnological inventions, for the most part these are treated in a similar manner to other types of invention. The test for novelty is no exception to this general rule: a biotechnological invention will only be anticipated and thus be invalid where there has been an enabling disclosure.[93] Despite this, questions sometimes arise where biotechnological inventions are based on natural materials. In this context it is important to note that a natural substance that has been isolated for the first time (such as a polynucleotide sequence) will not lack novelty because it was already present in nature (for example in the human genome). Here, patent law draws a distinction between the invention (the isolated 'artificial' polynucleotide) and the natural substance (the polynucleotide that exists in nature).[94] The artificial nature of the isolated substance provides the requisite difference between the prior art and the invention, necessary to ensure novelty.

5 THE DISCOVERY OF A NEW ADVANTAGE OF AN OLD THING USED IN AN OLD WAY

In this final section we move away from the general principles of novelty that have concerned us so far to concentrate on three specific types of invention and the problems that have arisen when assessing their novelty. In particular, we look at the novelty of inventions which relate to medical uses, non-medical uses, and so-called selection inventions.

For many years, the primary goal of the research carried out in many areas of science and technology was the creation of either new products or new uses of old things. On the whole, the fruits of this research have been well served by patent law. This can be seen in the fact that patent law has long recognized as being novel both the discovery of new things[95] (such as the discovery of aspirin) and the discovery of new ways of using old things[96] (such as the discovery that aspirin rubbed on the skin acts as an effective insect repellent).

In the last forty years or so, a number of changes have taken place in the type of research undertaken in various industries. These changes were motivated by a realization that in certain fields (notably in relation to pharmaceutical and biological inventions), the possibility of discovering new things or finding new uses for old things was decreasing. As a result, the focus of research shifted to concentrate on the discovery of new uses (or purposes) of old substances used in old ways. The problem that confronted researchers working in this way was that British

---

[92] UK Intellectual Property Office, *Examination Guidelines/Biotechnological Inventions*, para 14.

[93] See, e.g. *Asahi Kasei Kogyo* [1991] *RPC* 485; *Genentech's (Human Growth Hormone) Patent* [1989] *RPC* 613; UK Patent Office, *Biotechnology Guidelines* (Sept. 2002) paras. 8–11.

[94] *Howard Florey Institute's Application* T74/91 [1995] *OJ EPO* 388. See also D. Schertenleib, 'The Patentability and Protection of DNA-based Inventions in the EPO and the European Union' [2003] *EIPR* 125; EPO, USPTO, JPO Trilateral Project 24.1, *Biotechnology Comparative Study on Biotechnology Patent Practices*.

[95] Claims for a substance provide protection not only over the thing itself, but also over all subsequent uses.

[96] Typically, new uses are claimed as a 'new method of using the old article'.

patent law traditionally refused to recognize as being novel the discovery that an old thing, used in an old way, can have a new advantage. This would mean, for example, that if someone discovered that as well as being useful in the curing of headaches, the consumption of aspirin also thinned the blood (and was thus useful in preventing blood clots), they would be unable to patent the invention. The reason for this is that the traditional British approach treated a claim to a 'product for a particular use' as a claim to the product *per se,* so that the product would lack novelty even if it had previously been employed for a different purpose.[97] The problem that confronted this 'new' style of research was, in short, that patent law was not willing to recognize 'novelty of purpose' as a basis on which an invention could be patented.

One of the notable trends in recent years is the way in which this principle has slowly been undermined. One of the first areas where the general rule was relaxed was in relation to medical uses.[98] With the EPO leading the way and UK courts following, this was interpreted to include second and subsequent medical uses. While initially seen as an exception which left the general rule intact, the EPO and (arguably) now UK courts have recognized novelty of purpose irrespective of the field of technology.

5.1 NEW MEDICAL USES

As we saw earlier, when the EPC was being drafted it was decided that methods for treatment of the human or animal body should not be patentable.[99] While the pharmaceutical industry were able to patent new substances,[100] the proposed blanket exclusion of methods of medical treatment presented them with a problem.[101] The reason for this was that most of the research then being carried out was not into the creation of new substances or drugs. Rather, most of the research focused on the discovery of new uses for old substances, or of new benefits from old substances. As such, the exclusion of methods of medical treatment from the scope of patent protection would have had a dramatic impact upon medical research. To appease the interests of the pharmaceutical industry, special provisions to 'compensate' for the exclusion of methods of medical treatment were introduced. Initially these provisions were found in section 2(6) of the 1977 Act (as enacted) and Article 54(5) EPC 1973. As part of the reforms instigated by EPC 2000, the compensation provisions are now found in section 4A(3) of the 1977 Act and Article 54(4) EPC 2000. Section 4A(3) states that '[i]n the case of an invention consisting of a substance or composition for use in any such method, the fact that the substance or composition forms part of the state of the art shall not prevent the invention from being taken to be new if the use of the substance or composition in any such method does not form part of the state of the art'.[102]

---

[97] See *Adhesive Dry Mounting v. Trapp* (1910) 27 *RPC* 341; Jacob, 'Novelty of Use Claims', 173.

[98] It is arguable that selection patents, discussed below, were an early exception to the general rule about the non-patenting of novelty of purpose.

[99] PA s. 4(2); EPC Art. 52(4). See above at p. 395.

[100] PA s. 4(3) and EPC Art. 52(4) leave open the possibility of claims for new substances or compositions. Consequently, while it is not possible to obtain a patent for a method of preventing headaches involving the taking of aspirin, aspirin is patentable *per se.*

[101] When the EPC and the PA were enacted, the exclusion of methods of medical treatment was based on the fiction that they were not susceptible to industrial application. PA s. 4(2), EPC 1973 Art. 52(4). Under EPC 2000 and the revised UK Act, methods of medical treatment are directly excluded. PA 4A(1), EPC 2000 Art. 53(c).

[102] The old PA s. 2(6) was similar: 'the fact that an invention consisting of a substance or composition for use in a method of medical treatment forms part of the state of the art, shall not prevent the invention from being taken to be new, if the use of the substance or composition in any such method does not form part of the state of the art'.

Essentially, section 4A(3)/Article 54(4), which permit the patenting of new applications for old substances used in old ways (in a medical context), create a statutory exception to the traditional British view that the mere discovery of purpose could not confer novelty on an invention.[103] In essence the provisions confer novelty via the new purpose ('the new pharmaceutical use of a known substance'), even though 'the substance itself is known and comprises part of the state of the art'.[104]

5.1.1 Second and subsequent medical uses of a known product

When enacted, it was widely believed that section 2(6)/Article 54(5) (now section 4A(3)/ Article 54(4) EPC 2000) only applied to the discovery of the first medical use of known products: a position supported by a normal reading of the provisions. This reading would have meant that claims for second or further medical uses of products would have lacked novelty.

The question of the scope of Article 54(5) (now EPC 2000 Article 54(4)) was considered by the Enlarged Board of Appeal of the EPO in *Eisai/Second Medical Indication*.[105] Basing its arguments on the legislative history of the EPC and the principle that exceptions to patentability should be construed narrowly, the Board decided that as well as protecting first uses, Article 54(5) also applied to second and subsequent medical uses. The Enlarged Board of Appeal went on to say, however, that this was conditional on the fact that claims were drafted in a style known as the 'Swiss form of claims'. Basically this meant that the patent had to claim the 'use of a substance for the manufacture of a medicine for a specified new therapeutic use'.[106] This would mean that, for the discovery that the consumption of aspirin was useful in thinning the blood to be valid, the applicant would have to claim the 'use of aspirin in making a medicament for use in the prevention of blood clots'.[107]

One of the notable features of a Swiss claim is that it is directed at the *manufacture* of the known substance. This ensures that the invention is not excluded on the basis that it is a method of medical treatment under section 4(2)/Article 52(4).[108] At the same time, the novelty of a Swiss claim arises from the new therapeutic application (the drug and first medical use already being known).[109] As a result, the focus of the patent shifts so that the novelty of the invention is not in the known way the substance is used, nor in relation to the substance itself. Rather, the novelty of the invention is in the new therapeutic use (or purpose) which has been discovered. This is the case even 'where the process of manufacture does not differ from known processes using the same active ingredients'.[110]

This was apparently based on French law. Paterson, para. 9.61; R. Singer, *The European Patent Convention* (1995), 167; *Hoffmann–La Roche/Pyrrolidine derivatives*, T128/82 [1984] *OJ EPO* 164; [1979–85] *B EPOR* 591.

[103] See A. Benyamini, *Patent Infringement in the European Community* (1993), 80 ff.; G. Paterson, 'The Patentability of Further Uses of a Known Product under the EPC' (1991) *EIPR* 16; G. Paterson, 'Product Protection in Chemistry: How Important for the Protection of an Apparatus, Device or Substance Are Statements Made in a Patent as to their Purpose?' (1991) 22 *IIC* 852; G. Paterson, 'Novelty of Use Claims' (1996) 27 *IIC* 179; Jacob, 'Novelty of Use Claims'.

[104] A. Horton, 'Methods of Treatment and Second Medical Use' (Aug. 2000) *Patent World* 9.

[105] *Eisai*, G5/83 [1985] *OJ EPO* 64. See *EPO Guidelines* C–IV, 4.2.

[106] *Second Medical Indication: Switzerland* [1984] *OJ EPO* 581. See also Germany [1984] *OJ EPO* 26; Netherlands [1988] *OJ EPO* 405.

[107] Patents have been allowed where the novelty lay in the frequency of drug administration.

[108] As the Enlarged Board of Appeal said in *Eisai*, the Swiss-type of use claim is not prohibited by Art. 52(4) and is capable of industrial application': G5/83 [1985] *OJ EPO* 64.

[109] Horton, 'Methods of Treatment and Second Medical Use' (Aug. 2000) *Patent World* 9.

[110] Ibid. For a general discussion see *IGF-I–Genentech/Method of administration*, T1020/03 [2007] *OJ EPO* 204.

The status of second medical use patents in the United Kingdom was considered by the Patents Court sitting *in banc* in *Wyeth's Application*.[111] *Wyeth's Application* included three claims.[112] First, the application claimed 'a guanidine for use as an anti-diarrhoeal agent'. This was rejected on the ground that since a medical use of guanidine was already known, section 2(6) could not confer novelty on the application. Second, Wyeth claimed 'the use of guanidine in treating diarrhoea'. This was also rejected on the basis that this was essentially a claim to a method of medical treatment and, as such, that it was directly in conflict with section 4(2). Third, Wyeth claimed 'the use of a guanidine in the preparation of an anti-diarrhoeal agent for treating or preventing diarrhoea'. While this claim, which was drafted in the Swiss form, was refused by the examiner on the basis that it was inconsistent with existing UK case law, it was allowed on appeal by the Patents Court sitting *in banc*. In recognition of the need for the harmonization of patent law, the Patents Court followed the lead of the EPO and permitted the claims in the Swiss form. The finding in *Wyeth's Application* was confirmed, albeit somewhat reluctantly, by the Court of Appeal in *Bristol-Myers v. Squibb*.[113] Following this decision, it is clear that section 2(6) of the Patents Act 1977 includes second and subsequent medical uses that are drafted in the Swiss form.

Any doubts that there might have been about the standing of second and subsequent medical use claims[114] have been put beyond doubt as a result of changes made by EPC 2000. In order to promote certainty across member states, Article 54(5) EPC 2000 allows applicants to claim second and further medical uses of known substances or compositions, without having to make a Swiss-type claim.[115] Article 54(5) EPC 2000 has been replicated in the UK in section 4A(4) of the 1977 Act (as amended). The aim of Article 54(5) EPC 2000 and section 4A(4) of the 1977 Act was to eliminate any legal uncertainty over the patentability of further medical uses. In particular, the provisions aimed to put it beyond doubt that applicants were able to claim 'purpose-related product protection for each further new medical use of a substance or composition already known as a medicine'. One of the consequences of these changes is that applicants are able to claim second medical use inventions more directly. In contrast to the convoluted Swiss claim—'Use of [known substance X] for the manufacture of a medicament to treat [medical condition Y]'—applicants can now use a simpler and clearer form of second medical use claim in the form—'Substance X for treatment of disease Y'.[116] The aim of these new provisions is to codify case law in the UK, the EPO, and many other member states which has embraced the Swiss claims. The protection that is now available is said to be equivalent to that offered by the Swiss type of claim. Although the new provisions were not intended to change the law in any way, as with most statutory changes, there is always a chance that this may occur in the future.

---

[111] [1985] *RPC* 545.

[112] The patent in question in *Wyeth's Application* arose out of research carried out by Wyeth in relation to pharmaceuticals known as guanidines. While prior to this it was known that guanidines lowered blood pressure, Wyeth discovered that guanidines were also useful in treating and preventing diarrhoea: *Schering's Application* [1971] *RPC* 337.

[113] *Bristol-Myers Squibb v. Baker Norton Pharmaceuticals* [2001] *RPC* 1, 18, 24–6, Aldous LJ, para. 48; Buxton LJ, paras. 76–81. See also *Actavis UK v. Merck & Co* [2008] *EWCA Civ* 444 (21 May 2008).

[114] See, for example, Jacob J's comments about the 'artificial construct of a Swiss form claim': *Merck & Co's Patent* [2003] *FSR* 498, para 80.

[115] Art. 54(5) EPC 2000 applies to applications pending or filed after 17 Dec. 2007.

[116] UK Intellectual Property Office, 'Methods of Treatment or Diagnosis' *Patents Act 2004: Guidance Note No. 7*, para 7.

While Article 54(5) EPC 2000/section 4A(4) of the 1977 Act were not expected to lead to any changes in what is and is not patentable,[117] one question that arises is whether the cases that had developed in and around the Swiss claim will still be relevant. It seems clear, for example, that the cases where the Swiss claims were accepted (such as *Eisai* and *Wyeth's Application*) are mainly now of historical interest only. Beyond this, it is uncertain whether the law that focused on the elements of a Swiss claim, such as the need to show manufacture of a medicament, or that the claim disclosed a new therapeutic application, remains relevant.

As a result, the courts will now be more concerned with the limits of what can be done with Swiss form claims. For example, in *Actavis v. Merck* the Court of Appeal held that, under the pre-EPC 2000 law, Swiss form claims are allowable where the novelty is conferred by a new dosage regime or other form of administration of a substance. While this provides some help in understanding the limits of the Swiss claim, there are still many uncertainties, particularly about the law in this area under the EPC 2000. Hopefully, the current uncertainty about the scope of the new provisions will be clarified when the Enlarged Board of Appeals responds to the questions referred to it by the Technical Board of Appeal in *Kos Life Sciences* (T1319/04) about the scope of Swiss claims under Art 53(c) and 54(4) EPC 2000.[118]

5.2 NON-MEDICAL USES OF KNOWN PRODUCTS: NOVELTY-OF-PURPOSE PATENTS

Shortly after the scope of the medical use exception was clarified, the question arose as to whether patent law should also recognize novelty of purpose in non-medical fields.[119] That is, should patent law recognize the discovery of new applications for old substances used in old ways, irrespective of the field in which the invention was made? This question was particularly important given that a great deal of non-medical research is devoted to the discovery of new applications of known compounds.

The status of novelty-of-purpose patents under the EPC was considered by the Enlarged Board of Appeal in *Mobil/Friction reducing additive*.[120] This decision arose from Mobil's attempt to patent a substance for use as a friction-reducing additive in lubricating oils. The application was opposed by Chevron on the basis that the substance was already known, and was already being used to inhibit rust-formation in ferrous metals. In response Mobil applied to amend their application by limiting it to the use of the substance for reducing friction, saying that its usefulness for this purpose had not previously been known. The question that thus came to be considered by the Enlarged Board was whether the discovery of a new use of a known substance used in an old way could be patented.

The Enlarged Board of Appeal held that, while using an old substance in a new way to achieve a new purpose might be novel, the use of an old substance in an old way to achieve a new purpose would not. In the latter case, the only difference between the discovery and the old use was that it was carried out with a different purpose in mind: the applicant would be doing the same thing with the same substance. Given that on the facts of the case the same

---

[117] UK Intellectual Property Office, *Examination Guidelines for Patent Applications relating to Medical Inventions in the UK Intellectual Property Office* (June 2007), 5.

[118] *Actavis UK v. Merck* [2008] *EWCA Civ* 444 (CA) para. 31. *Kos Life Sciences,* T1319/04.

[119] See Paterson, 'Patentability of Further Uses'; Paterson, 'Product Protection in Chemistry'; Paterson, 'Novelty of Use Claims'; Jacob, 'Novelty of Use Claims'; C. Floyd, 'Novelty under the Patents Act 1977: The State of the Art after *Merrell Dow*' [1996] 9 *EIPR* 480.

[120] G2/88 [1990] *EPOR* 73. See also *Bayer's Application*, G6/88 [1990] *OJ EPO* 114.

substance (the additive) was used in the same way (for example, by pouring it into the engine), it might have been reasonable to presume that the attempt to patent its use as a friction reducer (when it was previously thought only to inhibit rust) would have failed. This was not the case.

The reason for this, as the Board of Appeal went on to say, was that a claim for the use of an old compound in an old way for a new purpose could be interpreted to include 'the function of achieving the new purpose (because this is the technical result)'.[121] In such a case, the fact that the substance achieved the new purpose would be an objective 'functional technical feature' of the invention, rather than something which only resided in the mind of the user. In relation to the case in hand, the Enlarged Board of Appeal said that the invention exhibited a functional technical feature in that the substance operated to reduce friction. As such, the Board held that claims for the use of a specified lubricant for the reduction of friction in engines were patentable, even though the lubricant had previously been used as a rust inhibitor. As a result of this decision, it is now clear that the discovery of a new purpose for an old thing used in an old way is potentially patentable at the EPO, irrespective of the technical field in which the invention takes place.[122]

As we will see, a number of criticisms have been made of the *Mobil* decision in the UK.[123] Nonetheless it is clear that in Britain it is now possible to patent the discovery of a new purpose for an old thing used in an old way.[124] Unlike pre-1977 law, the mere fact that an invention's sole point of novelty lies in the discovery of a new purpose no longer means that the application will automatically be disallowed.

The key feature of a novelty-of-purpose claim is the discovery that a known use of a known substance achieves a new purpose. The only aspect of the invention that is novel is the third element: *viz.* the discovery of the new purpose. The step that facilitated the acceptance of novelty-of-purpose patents was the decision that a previous secret use does not destroy the novelty of a patent. As we explained earlier, under British law before 1977 it was possible for a past secret use to anticipate a later patent. Under the old law, the discovery that a known substance used in a known way could be put to a hitherto unknown purpose would not have been patentable. This is because the new purpose would have been seen as inherent in the existing use of the known substance. The fact that the use was secret would not have affected the fate of the invention.

As we pointed out above, under existing law a previously secret use will no longer destroy the novelty of a later patent.[125] As the Enlarged Board said in *Mobil*, the 'question to be decided is what has been "made available to the public": the question is not what may have been "inherent" in what was made available'. 'Under the EPC, a hidden or secret use, because it has not been made available to the public, is not a ground of objection' to validity of a patent. As such,

---

[121] *Mobil/Friction reducing additive*, G2/88 [1990] *EPOR* 73.

[122] The Court of Appeal in *Bristol-Myers* said that a Swiss claim was based on a different logic to *Mobil*. *Ortho/Pharmaceutical prevention of skin atrophy*, T254/93 [1999] *EPOR* 1.

[123] See Floyd, 'Novelty under the Patents Act'; *CIPA*, para. 2.21; A. White, 'The Novelty Destroying Disclosure' [1990] *EIPR* 315; J. Lane, 'What Level of Protection is Required to Anticipate a Patented Invention by Prior Publication or Use' [1990] *EIPR* 462. These problems are particularly acute in the UK (and not at the EPO) because the EPO is only concerned with issues of validity, whereas British courts have to deal with both validity and infringement.

[124] *Bristol-Myers v. Baker Norton* [2001] *RPC* 1, 18, Aldous LJ, para. 49 noting that *Mobil* had been considered in some detail and applied by the House of Lords in *Merrell Dow* (admittedly on a different point). Aldous LJ said, 'it is unlikely that [the Court of Appeal] would conclude that [*Mobil*] was wrongly decided when the House of Lords did not so conclude'. See also Buxton LJ, para. 81.

[125] See above at pp. 474–6.

'the question of "inherency" does not arise' under the EPC (nor under the Patents Act 1977).[126] In so ruling this opened up the possibility for patent protection to be given to the discovery that a known substance used in a known way could be put to a new purpose. Once this step was taken, deciding the status of a discovery that a known substance used in a known way could be put to a new purpose is relatively straightforward. As the Enlarged Board of Appeal said in *Bayer*, the question to be decided in these circumstances, as with all inventions, is whether the invention has already been made available to the public.[127] This has been reflected in subsequent case law, which has focused on whether the purpose that has been discovered is actually new.[128]

In those cases where novelty-of-purpose patents have been accepted the applicant has been able to show that they have 'two distinctly different effects, two distinctly different applications or uses of the same substances, which can clearly be distinguished from each other'.[129] For example, in *Mobil* the patent was for the use of an additive as a lubricant, whereas the state of the art revealed use of the same additive as a rust inhibitor. Similarly in *Bayer* the patent application was directed to the use of a compound as a fungicide, whereas the state of the art described use of the same compound as an agent for influencing plant growth.[130] In both cases, the patent revealed that the known substance used in a known way could be put to a new purpose.

In contrast, in *Robertet/Deodorant compositions*, the patent was rejected on the basis that it lacked novelty. The applicants discovered that when used as an active ingredient in a deodorant composition, 'aromatic esters' can inhibit esterase-producing micro-organisms on the human skin. The prior art disclosed the use of aromatic esters as an active ingredient in deodorizing products. The Technical Board of Appeal rejected the application saying that all the patent did was disclose information about an existing purpose. That is, it was an ex post facto explanation of what had already taken place. While in *Mobil* and *Bayer* a new purpose had been discovered, all that had been disclosed in this case was more information about a known purpose. The application was merely more information or an explanation of a past event, rather than the discovery of a new purpose *per se*. As such, it was held not to be novel. A similar conclusion was reached in *Ortho Pharmaceuticals* where the Technical Board of Appeal said that 'the mere explanation of an effect obtained when using a compound in a known composition, even if the effect was not known to be due to this compound in the known composition, cannot confer novelty on a known process if the skilled person was aware of the occurrence of the desired effect'.[131]

The principles used to determine novelty in new-purpose patents are similar to those used for other types of invention. In other respects, however, notably in terms of the problems that arise when deciding whether a novelty-of-purpose patent has been infringed, they mark a more radical change of direction. We look at this issue in more detail in our discussions of patent infringement.[132]

---

[126] *Mobil/Friction reducing additive*, G2/88 [1990] *EPOR* 73, 88 (EBA).

[127] *Bayer/Plant growth regulating agent*, G6/88 [1990] *EPOR* 257, 265 (EBA).

[128] In many ways, the reasoning used in relation to new purpose is similar to that used in relation to second and subsequent medical uses. The main difference is that in this context there is no need to show manufacture.

[129] *Robertet/Deodorant compositions*, T892/94 [1999] *EPOR* 516, 526.

[130] *Bayer/Plant growth regulating agent*, G6/88 [1990] *EPOR* 257.

[131] *Ortho/Prevention of skin atrophy*, T254/93 [1999] *EPOR* 1, 8. This was reinforced by the fact that the specific purpose in question was also known (at 7).

[132] See above at pp. 550–2.

5.3 SELECTION PATENTS: GENERIC DISCLOSURE

The third area that we wish to focus on is the novelty of so-called selection patents. As with methods of medical treatment and novelty-of-purpose patents, selection patents developed in response to a particular problem. This arose from the fact that, in some fields such as organic chemistry, a researcher may discover that a particular combination of molecules produces certain results. In some instances, the researcher then extrapolates from this initial discovery to assert that the same qualities will be produced by a range of variants or homologues. This is referred to as a generic or general disclosure. In so doing, the researcher (potentially) discloses an extremely broad range of compounds.

Problems arise when it is subsequently discovered that some of the compounds which were outlined in the generic disclosure are particularly advantageous or have uses other than were initially envisaged. As the compounds have already been made available to the public, the previous generic disclosure appears to prevent subsequent claims being made for individual members of the group.[133] This led to the potential problem that if the generic disclosure was able to anticipate, it would act as a disincentive for further research to be carried out in relation to the materials already disclosed. The question that underpins the doctrine of selection patents is whether, and if so the extent to which, a previous generic disclosure anticipates subsequent inventions in the same field.

In the United Kingdom, the classic answer to this problem is provided by the 1930 decision of *IG Farbenindustrie*.[134] This decision concerned an application to revoke IG Farbenindustrie's patent for a process of manufacturing certain azo and aromatic amine dyestuffs. This was on the ground that in light of a prior disclosure in an expired patent, the invention lacked novelty. In response, IG Farbenindustrie claimed that there were potentially millions of combinations of azo and aromatic amine dyestuffs outlined in the expired patent. They also argued that the particular group of dyes that they had selected had peculiar and beneficial properties in that they withstood certain processing techniques required of cotton.[135] Maugham J said that if the compounds in question had previously been made, they would have lacked novelty. If the compounds had not been previously made, however, the patent might be valid if it could be shown that:

(i)   the selection was based on substantial advantage resulting from the use of selected members,

(ii) all members of the selected class possessed the advantage in question, and

(iii) if the selection was in respect of a quality of a special character, that it could fairly be said to be peculiar to the selected group.

While, on the facts, IG Farbenindustrie's patent was held to be invalid,[136] the decision helped to establish the principle that selection inventions are potentially patentable where it can be

---

[133] This is exacerbated by the fact that (at least until recently) patent law did not normally allow patents for discoveries of new advantages.

[134] (1930) 47 *RPC* 289, 322–3. See *Shell Refining and Marketing Patent (Revocation)* [1960] *RPC* 35, 52; P. Grubb, *Patents in Chemistry and Biotechnology* (1986), 132. While mechanical subject matter does not readily lend itself to the idea of selection, there have been a number of selection patents for mechanical inventions. See *Clyde Nail Russell* (1916) 33 *RPC* 291, 306 (Lord Parker); *Shell Refining and Marketing Patent (Revocation)* ibid, 54; *EI Du Pont de Nemours (Witsiepe's) Application* [1982] *FSR* 303, 314; *Hallen v. Brabantia* [1991] *RPC* 195.

[135] More specifically, the advantage claimed was 'fastness to kier boiling under pressure in caustic liquor'.

[136] This was because the dyestuffs claimed did not have the property which the applicant alleged.

shown that the 'inventiveness' of the application lies in a particular selection from a known field. Selection patents:

enable a valid patent to be obtained for the selection of a product or process from a range of known or obvious products or processes because of surprising and non-obvious advantages over the others…The selection must be based on a substantial advantage of special character. The selected member or class must have the advantage, and the specification must direct the mind of the skilled reader to the advantage of the selection from the class.[137]

Although Maugham J's judgment was approved in subsequent decisions,[138] a number of issues remain unclear.[139] Many of the uncertainties result from a failure to distinguish clearly between novelty and inventive step. Another reason for the confusion can be traced to the fact that while Maugham J expressly said that the three propositions outlined in his judgment were not meant to be exhaustive, nonetheless they have often been treated as if they were definitive guidelines as to when a selection invention will have been anticipated. Another problem is that it is often forgotten that selection patents are not limited to new uses; they apply, at least potentially, to the discovery of new substances, new uses for old substances, and new purposes for old substances used in old ways.[140]

Perhaps the greatest uncertainty that exists in relation to selection patents is whether the doctrine has any continued relevance under the Patents Act 1977. In light of recent changes—notably, the shift to enabling disclosure, the consequential move away from secret or inherent use, and the (apparent) acceptance of the discovery of new purposes as conferring novelty—there are good reasons for suggesting that it does not.

To argue that under British law the doctrine of selection patents should be jettisoned in favour of the more general rules about novelty is not as radical as it may first seem. This is because the issues which arise with selection patents are really no different from the question which Lord Hoffmann said underpinned the novelty examination more generally: *viz.* how specific must a disclosure be for an invention to be 'known' or 'made available' to the public? (The key difference is that with selection patents the question is rephrased to be: how specific must a generic or general disclosure be for it to destroy the novelty of a subsequent invention which incorporates the prior knowledge?) While Lord Hoffmann wisely answered that it always depends on the invention in question, the doctrine of selection patents has attempted the impossible and tried to stipulate in advance the type of disclosure that is needed to anticipate. Given the futility of this, it may be better if the novelty of selection patents were answered through the general rules about novelty.[141] If this approach were adopted, it would mean that a previous generic disclosure would only anticipate a selection invention if it was enabling: that is, if the disclosure placed a skilled person in a position from which they could 'work' the invention in question.

---

[137] *Boehringer Mannheim v. Genzyme* [1993] *FSR* 716.

[138] *Du Pont (Witsiepe's) Application* [1982] *FSR* 303, 309.

[139] It should be noted that there is some inconsistency in the EPO decisions in this area, e.g. *Pfizer/Penem*, T1042/92 [1995] *EPOR* 207 is inconsistent with *Sanofi/Enantiomer*, T658/91 [1996] *EPOR* 24.

[140] It is only if this is correct that selection patents provide obvious tactical advantages over patents for 'uses' that the EPO has recently recognized. Moreover, if this were not the case, the requirement demanded (particularly by the EPO) of novelty *per se* rather than mere novelty of use, would be unnecessarily stringent.

[141] In *IG Farbenindustrie* Maugham J argued that the rules applicable to 'selection patent' did not differ from the general rules of patent law: a view which was reaffirmed in *Shell Refining (Revocation)* [1960] *RPC* 35.

It appears that this is in fact the approach that has been adopted at the EPO, where the rules on selection patents have been treated as being consistent with, rather than an exception to, the general rules about novelty. In these circumstances a previous generic disclosure will anticipate a substance if it can be characterized as an enabling disclosure.[142] This can be seen, for example, in *Bayer/Diastereomers*:[143] a decision that concerned an application for the diastereomeric form of a compound which was useful in treating mycoses (fungal diseases such as ringworm). The problem that confronted the applicants was that a prior patent had disclosed a group of compounds including the compound in question, as well as the method by which the compound could be produced. The Technical Board of Appeal rejected the application on the basis that it was lacking in novelty. In so doing the Board held that the teaching of a prior document was not confined to the detailed information given in the examples of how the invention is carried out. Rather, it embraces any information in the claims and description enabling a person skilled in the art to carry out the invention. The Technical Board of Appeal stressed that the essential point is what a person skilled in the art could be expected to deduce from the earlier disclosure in carrying out the invention.

---

[142] *Sanofi/Enantiomer*, T658/91 [1996] *EPOR* 24. On the EPO see M. Vivian, 'Novelty and Selection Patents' (1989) 20 *IIC* 303.

[143] T12/81 [1982] *OJ EPO* 296; [1979–85] *EPOR* B-308.

19

INVENTIVE STEP

CHAPTER CONTENTS

1 INTRODUCTION

In this chapter we focus on the requirement that to be patentable an invention must involve an 'inventive step'.[1] An invention is said to involve an inventive step if it is not obvious to a person skilled in the art[2] (the terms inventive step and non-obviousness are used interchangeably).[3] The question whether an invention is obvious can arise during examination in the patent offices, where it is *ex parte*. It can also arise *inter partes* in opposition proceedings at the EPO, or in revocation proceedings before the comptroller or the courts. In each case, the onus is on the patent office, the opponent, or the party seeking revocation (as opposed to the applicant or patentee) to establish that the invention is obvious. While the inventive step requirement has long been a key element of patent law, it may become more important in the future. This is a result of changes that have taken place at the EPO, but not in the United Kingdom, in the way patentable subject matter is determined. As we explained in Chapter 17, as a result of the *Pension Benefits System* decision the Technical Board of Appeal has shifted the focus of attention away from subject matter to inventive step.[4] (The Board held that while the claim for an apparatus for controlling a pension benefits system was an invention for the purposes of Article 52(1) (now EPC 2000 Art 52(1)), it lacked inventive step and thus was not patentable.) While there is a close relationship between the two requirements (particularly as a result of

---

[1] PA s. 1(1)(b); EPC 2000 Art. 52(1) [EPC 1973 Art. 52(1)]; PCT Art. 33(3); TRIPS Art. 27(1). See generally, J. Bochnovic, *The Inventive Step* (1982); H. Ullrich, *Standards of Patentability for European Inventions* (1977).

[2] PA s. 3; EPC 2000 Art. 56 [EPC 1973 Art. 52(1)].

[3] However, a useful proposal (such as the idea to cover an umbrella with water-soluble textile) might be non-obvious but lack inventive step. R. Singer, *The European Patent Convention* (1995), 181, n. 1; *Exxon/Gelation*, T119/82 [1979–85] *EPOR* 566; [1984] *OJ EPO* 217.

[4] *Pension Benefits Systems Partnership/Controlling pension benefits systems,* T931/95 [2001] *OJ EPO* 413.

the focus on 'technical character' when determining subject matter), it is not clear what the consequences of this shift will be. It is, however, an important change that needs to be followed in the future.

As we will see, deciding where the line should be drawn between inventions that are obvious (or non-inventive) and those that are inventive (or non-obvious) is a difficult task. As well as being one of the most important requirements for patentability, inventive step is also one of the most problematic. Indeed, it has been said that inventive step is 'as fugitive, impalpable, wayward, and vague a phantom as exists in the whole paraphernalia of legal concepts'.[5] In part this is because the examination for inventive step is a factual inquiry: to this end it has frequently been dubbed a 'question of fact' or a 'jury question' (though juries have not sat in patent cases in the United Kingdom since 1883). The corollary of the factual nature of the inquiry is that precedents should be treated with caution, even those that involve decisions on the same invention. The evaluative nature of the inquiry also means that reasonable people can easily reach different conclusions: thus making it extremely difficult to predict the outcome of an obviousness attack or objection.[6] This has led to accusations of uncertainty and to the arbitrary use of discretion.[7] It also means that, on appeal, courts are often reluctant to overturn decisions of the lower courts.

While the novelty examination ensures that there is a quantitative difference between the invention and the state of the existing knowledge, non-obviousness ensures that this difference is of a quality deserving of patent protection.[8] By ensuring that patents are only granted for non-obvious inventions, the requirement for inventive step acts as a qualitative threshold which ensures that only meritorious inventions are granted protection. The need to show inventive step as a condition for patentability has been explained on the basis that 'if every slight difference in the application of a well-known thing was held to constitute a ground for a patent', it would lead to an unjustifiable interference with trade.[9] As the Court of Appeal said in *PLG Research v. Ardon International,* the 'philosophy behind the doctrine of obviousness is that the public should not be prevented from doing anything which was merely an obvious extension or workshop variation of what was already known at the priority date'.[10] In more positive terms, it has been suggested that the obviousness inquiry encourages people to carry out research that might not otherwise be undertaken. More specifically, the fact that patents are *not* granted for obvious inventions encourages speculative or risky research.[11]

---

[5]   *Harries v. Air King* 183 F 2d 158, 162 (1950) (Judge Learned Hand).

[6]   This 'contributes significantly both to the insecure commercial value of many patents and to the cost of litigating their validity'. W. Cornish, 'The Essential Criteria for Patentability', (1983) 14 *IIC* 765, 771.

[7]   Ullrich, *Standards of Patentability*, 37; J. Schmidt-Szalewski, 'Non Obviousness as a Requirement of Patentability in French Law' (1992) 23 *IIC* 725, 737.

[8]   While there has been a shift in the theoretical basis of the novelty requirement from a 'right to work' to an information-related understanding, such a shift has yet to be recognized in relation to inventive step.

[9]   *Harwood v. Great Northern Railway Co.* (1964–5) 11 *HLC* 654, 682 (Lord Westbury). See also *Elias v. Grovesend* (1890) 7 *RPC* 455, 467; *Brugger v. Medic Aid* [1996] *RPC* 635, 653; *VDO Adolf Schindling/Illuminating Device*, T324/94 [1997] *EPOR* 146, 153.

[10]   [1999] *FSR* 116, 136. See also *Philips (Bosgra's) Application* [1974] *RPC* 241 (emphasizing right to work); F. Scherer, *Industrial Market Structure and Economic Performance* (1980), 440.

[11]   R. Merges, *Patent Law and Policy* (1992), 411–21. *Société Technique de Pulvérisation STEP v. Emson* [1993] *RPC* 513. Cf. *Mölnlycke v. Procter & Gamble (No. 5)* [1994] *RPC* 49; Ullrich, *Standards of Patentability*, 103.

2 DETERMINING WHETHER AN
INVENTION IS OBVIOUS

In order to harmonize the divergent approaches to obviousness that had been adopted in the member states prior to the passage of the EPC, the European Patent Office set out to develop an approach to the assessment of inventive step that was objective, economical, and transparent. In so doing they also hoped to bring a degree of certainty to the area.[12] The technique that was chosen to achieve these ends is known as 'the problem-and-solution approach'.[13] This is based on an image of the invention as a solution to a problem. Accordingly, an inventive step is seen as 'a step from the technical problem to its solution'.[14] As such, rather than asking whether an invention is obvious, the European Patent Office asks whether the solution that an invention provides to the problem being addressed would have been obvious to the person skilled in the art. In more positive terms, this means that for an invention to be patentable, the solution must have been *not* obvious to the person skilled in the art at the priority date of the invention in question. There are a number of subsidiary steps that need to be undertaken when applying the problem-and-solution approach. In particular, it requires the tribunal to: ascertain the technical field of the invention (which is used, amongst other things, to determine the field of expertise of the person skilled in the art); and identify the closest prior art in the field; the technical problem which can be regarded as solved in relation to the closest prior art; and finally, whether the technical feature(s) which form the solution claimed could be derived by the skilled person in a manner obvious from the state of the art.[15]

Over the period that the problem-and-solution approach has been utilized at the EPO, it has proved to be a useful technique for determining inventive step. It is also one that was applied in nearly all situations. Despite this, aspects of the approach were called into question by the Technical Board of Appeal in *Alcan/Aluminium alloys*.[16] In this decision, the Board said that while it was often assumed that the problem-and-solution approach was applicable in all situations, it was better seen as one of many possible approaches that could be adopted when assessing inventive step. The Board said that there was no legal reason why all cases involving inventive step should be shoehorned into a single approach. In situations where the invention broke new ground, the test was inappropriate because there was no close prior art from which to formulate the problem. In these circumstances, the problem-and-solution approach was unnecessarily artificial. As this approach proceeds on the basis of a search that is made with actual knowledge of the invention, it also suffered from the fact that it was inherently based on hindsight.[17]

In a sense, what the Technical Board of Appeal did in *Alcan* was to align the problem-and-solution approach more closely with the types of research under consideration. By modifying (and narrowing) the circumstances in which the test may be applied, the Board has served to

---

[12] G. Knesch, 'Assesing Inventive Step in Examination and Opposition Proceedings at the EPO' (1994) *epi-Information* 95, 98.

[13] This was espoused in the first published decision of the TBA, *Bayer/Carbonless Copying*, T1/80 [1979–85] *B EPOR* 250.

[14] The problem-and-solution approach builds upon an image of research as an activity that sets out to solve particular problems. *ICI/Containers*, T26/81 [1979–85] *B EPOR* 362; [1982] *OJ EPO* 211.

[15] *Comvik/Two identities*, T641/00 [2003] *OJ EPO* 319, para. 5.   [16] T465/92 [1995] *EPOR* 501.

[17] For a general discussion of need to avoid hindsight see *Ferag v. Muller Martini* [2007] *EWCA Civ* 15, para. 13.

strengthen the test. Despite these criticisms, the problem-and-solution approach is still the chief way in which inventive step is determined at the EPO.

2.1 UNITED KINGDOM

Whatever the current state of the law at the EPO, English courts have largely remained isolated from and resistant to the adoption of the problem-and-solution approach.[18] Instead, when considering the way in which an invention is to be interpreted, they have relied on the approach set out in the *Windsurfing* decision.[19] In this decision, the Court of Appeal said that the court must begin by identifying the inventive concept embodied in the patent. The court should then identify the differences that exist between the cited prior art and the alleged invention. Finally, the court should ask whether, viewed without any knowledge of the alleged invention, those differences constitute steps that would have been obvious to the skilled man, or whether they required a degree of invention.[20] Recently, in the Court of Appeal decision in *Pozzoli*, Jacob LJ reordered and elaborated on the *Windsurfing* test. While judicial attempts to restructure well-established rules, such as those in *Windsurfing*, are often counter-productive, Jacob LJ's reformulation is useful; particularly insofar as it takes the question of what is the invention more seriously. Under the new approach, which is called the *Windsurfing/Pozzoli* approach, the court asks four questions. These are:

(i)   who is the notional 'person skilled in the art', identifying the relevant common general knowledge of that person;

(ii) what is the inventive concept of the claim or, if that cannot readily be identified, construe it;

(iii) what, if any, difference exists between the matter cited as forming 'part of the state' of the art and the inventive concept of the claim, or the claim as construed; and

(iv) viewed without any knowledge of the alleged invention as claimed, do those differences constitute steps which would have been obvious to the person skilled in the art, or do they require any degree of invention?[21]

The decision to use the approach set out in *Windsurfing* rather than the approach used at the EPO was reinforced by the fact that the problem-and-solution approach has been subject to a considerable degree of criticism in the UK.[22] As well as being criticized for its use of hindsight,[23] the test is also said to be unnecessarily artificial because many inventions are developed without

---

[18] Although these provisions are intended to be applied uniformly throughout the EPC states, inventive step appears to be an area where British courts have taken little notice of EPC precedents, and therefore in which harmonization seems at its most embryonic. *Hallen v. Brabantia* [1991] *RPC* 195, 212 (Slade LJ); *Hoechst Celanese v. BP Chemicals* [1997] *FSR* 547, 567, 572.

[19] *Windsurfing International v. Tabor Marine* [1985] *RPC* 59 (CA). Followed in *Lux Traffic v. Pike Signals* [1993] *RPC* 107; *Hallen v. Brabantia*, above; *Mannheim v. Genzyme* [1993] *FSR* 716, 724; *Mölnlycke (No. 5)* [1994] *RPC* 49, 115; *PLG Research* [1995] *FSR* 116; A. Griffiths, '*Windsurfing* and the Inventive Step' [1999] *IPQ* 160.

[20] For criticism see J. Claydon, 'The question of obviousness in the *Windsurfer* decision' [1985] *EIPR* 218. See *Unilever v. Chefaro* [1994] *RPC* 567, 580.

[21] *Pozzoli SPA v. BDMO SA* [2007] *EWCA Civ* 588 (CA), para 15–19. For further elaboration see Jacob LJ in *Nichia Corporation v. Argos* [2007] *EWCA Civ* 741, para 12.

[22] '[A]ttempts to force all questions of obviousness into a 'problem-solution' approach can lead to trouble, though often the test can be a helpful guide'. *Nichia*, ibid, para 22. Jacob LJ also noted that a similar view has been taken by the US Supreme Court in *KSR International v. Teleflex* 127 *SC* 1727, 167 *L. Ed. 2d* 705 (2007). A. White, 'The problem-and-solution approach to obviousness' [1986] *EIPR* 387; J. Beton, 'Vote of thanks to G. Szabo' (1987) 16 *CIPAJ* 361.

[23] Singer, *European Patent Convention*, 186; *Grehal/Shear*, T305/87 [1991] *EPOR* 389.

having a problem in mind. Perhaps the most important objection is that while the problem-and-solution approach is presented as being applicable to all types of research, there are situations where its use is inappropriate. While this approach is sensibly applied to the improvement of existing techniques, it is not easy to formulate a problem for many inventions, particularly in the chemical–pharmaceutical field.[24] As well as being difficult to apply in situations involving the discovery of a new application for an existing technique or product, it is said to be wholly inappropriate where an innovation satisfies a latent need which has never previously been expressed.[25] In the case of so-called 'problem inventions', where the solution becomes obvious once the problem has been formulated, the reformulation of the research undertaken in terms of problem and solution 'is equivalent to emptying the definition of the problem of any substance, and thereby depriving the problem-and-solution approach of any effectiveness'.[26]

In determining obviousness under the Patents Act 1977 British tribunals have tended to utilize the test set out in the *Windsurfer* decision rather than the problem-and-solution approach. In recent years, however, there has been a growing belief that the latter type of approach ought to be used in the United Kingdom.[27] In part this has been motivated by a realization that the two tests may not be as conceptually different as they first appeared,[28] by the fact that the EPO approach has precursors in UK patent law,[29] and because the *Alcan* decision goes some way towards resolving some of the criticisms which have been made of the approach adopted at the European Patent Office.[30] Perhaps the strongest support for the use of the problem-and-solution approach comes from the House of Lords' decision in *Biogen v. Medeva,* where Lord Hoffmann said that a 'proper statement of the inventive concept needs to include some express or implied reference to the problem which it required invention to overcome'.[31]

While it is important to keep in mind the different approaches that have been adopted at the UK and the EPO, there are enough similarities for them to be dealt with together. Perhaps the best starting point for thinking about whether an invention is obvious is with section 3 of the 1977 Act (EPC 2000 Article 56 [EPC 1973 Article 56]) which states that an invention is taken to involve an inventive step 'if it is not obvious to a person skilled in the art, having regard to any matter that forms part of the state of the art'. Stated in this way, the inquiry gives rise to three further questions. These are:

(i)   Who is the 'person skilled in the art' and what skills and knowledge do they have?

(ii) What is the 'invention' that is being examined?

(iii) What does it mean to say that something is 'non-obvious'?

We will deal with each in turn.

---

[24] F. Hagel and C. Menes, 'Making proper use of the problem–solution approach' [1995] *epi-Information* 14.

[25] *Rider/Simethicone Tablet,* T02/83 [1979–85] *C EPOR* 715.

[26] Hagel and Menes, 'Making proper use of the problem–solution approach', 16.

[27] P. Cole, 'Inventive Step: Meaning of the EPO Problem and Solutions Approach and Implications of the United Kingdom' [1998] *EIPR* 214, 271.

[28] *CIPA,* para. 3.02. Descriptions in UK patents often begin by setting out the background of the invention and then explain the particular problem that the invention solves.

[29] See Cole, 'Inventive Step', 267; *Sharp and Dohme v. Boots Pure Drug Company* (1928) 45 *RPC* 153, 173 (Sir Stafford Cripps). Beton, 'Vote of Thanks to G. Szabo'; S. Avery, 'Problem and Solution at the EPO: The Primary Consideration' (1984–5) 14 *CIPAJ* 166; G. Szabo, 'Questions on the Problem-and-solution approach to the Inventive Step' (1986–7) 16 *CIPAJ* 351.

[30] See *Haberman v. Jackel International* [1999] *FSR* 683, 683, 699–700; *Dyson Appliances v. Hoover* [2001] *RPC* 26, Patents Court, para. 153.

[31] [1997] *RPC* 1, 45.

3 PERSON SKILLED IN THE ART

As section 3 of the 1977 Act and Article 56 of the EPC 2000 make clear, obviousness is determined from the standpoint of the average person skilled in the art.[32] This means that, when considering whether an invention is obvious, the tribunal views the invention through the eyes of a notional interpreter equipped with the attributes, skills, background knowledge, and qualifications relevant to the field in which they work.[33] The objective nature of the inquiry means that the *actual* process by which the invention came about is irrelevant.[34] As such, it does not matter if an invention arose as a result of years of research by a team of leading experts, or as a chance result by an unskilled person. All that matters is whether the person skilled in the art would consider the invention to be non-obvious.[35]

The skills and qualifications of the person skilled in the art, as well as the resources and equipment that are available to them, vary according to the particular invention in question.[36] More specifically, the qualities of the skilled person depend on the technical field into which the invention falls. Determining the technical field of the invention is made easier by the fact that, at the EPO, the patent description should specify the technical field into which the invention falls.[37] Similarly, in the United Kingdom, the description begins with a short title that indicates the general subject matter of the invention. The choice of technical field is particularly important in situations where the invention is made up of a mixture of technical and non-technical features. This is particularly the case in relation to computer-related inventions and business-method patents. To date the tribunals have been careful to ensure that the person skilled in the art has expertise only in technical fields. For example, in *Comvik* (which concerned the invention of a new single-user identity card (SIM card) which dealt with the way charges for different types of mobile phone call were organized for digital mobile telephones)[38] the Technical Board of Appeal said that the 'skilled person will be an expert in a technical field. If the technical problem is concerned with a computer implementation of a business, actuarial or accountancy system, the skilled person will be someone in data processing, and not merely a businessman, actuary, or accountant.'[39] If the skills base of the expert was extended to include non-technical areas such as business or management skills, it would increase the

---

[32] Recently described as 'an assembly of nerds with different basic skills, all unimaginative'. *Rockwater v. Technip* [2004] *RPC* 46, para 7, 10. See also *Brugger v. Medic Aid* [1996] *RPC* 635, 653. See Bochnovic, *The Inventive Step*, 59; J. Pagenberg, 'The Evaluation of the "Inventive Step" in the European Patent System: More Objective Standards Needed' (1978) 9 *IIC* 1, 16–17; J. Tresansky, 'PHOSITA: The Ubiquitous and Enigmatic Person in Patent Law' (1991) 73 *JPTOS* 37.

[33] *Technograph Printed Circuits v. Mills & Rockley (Electronics)* [1972] *RPC* 346, 355 (Lord Reid); *Polymer Powders/Allied colloids*, T39/93 [1997] *OJ EPO* 134, 149; Pakuscher (1981) 12 *IIC* 816.

[34] *Hoechst Celanese v. BP*, note 18 above, 565; *BASF/Metal refining*, T24/81 [1979–85] *B EPOR* 354.

[35] For a summary of some of the attributes of the person skilled in the art see Jacob LJ in *Rockwater v. Technip*, note 34 above, para 6–12.

[36] *Genentech's Patents* [1989] *RPC* 147, 278 (Mustill LJ).

[37] EPC 2000 r. 42(1)(a), r. 47(2) [EPC r. 27(1)(a), r. 33(2); *Luminescent Security Fibres/Jalon*, T422/93 [1997] *OJ EPO* 24.

[38] 'The inventor's merits resided in realizing the economical and administrative problem for certain subscribers that distribution costs for various categories of calls within one and the same subscription causes extra work'. *Comvik/Two identities*, T641/00 [2003] *OJ EPO* 319, para. vi.

[39] *Comvik*, above, para. 7 (ingenuity of the invention occurred in non-technical fields, which could not contribute to inventive step).

494

PATENTS

patentability of business patents and other types of invention that are currently excluded from protection.[40]

The skills attributed to the person skilled in the art will vary depending on what is regarded as normal in the field in which they are deemed to operate. In some cases, the person skilled in the art may have a Ph.D. and a well-established research record;[41] in other cases they may have no formal academic qualifications and only have 'ordinary' skills.[42] While the person skilled in the art is normally an individual, in situations where research is carried out by groups of researchers, the court will adopt the standpoint of a notional research team.[43]

While the skill and qualities of the notional interpreter vary according to the art in question, one trait that is shared by skilled persons irrespective of the field in which they work is that they are uninventive.[44] It has also been said that the person skilled in the art is conservative in the sense that they would not go against established prejudices, try to enter into sacrosanct or unpredictable areas, or take incalculable risks.[45]

3.1 THE STATE OF THE ART

In considering whether an invention is obvious, the person skilled in the art has regard to any matter that forms part of the state of the art at the priority date of the invention.[46] With two notable exceptions, the state of the art in an obviousness examination is the same broad concept as is used in a novelty examination (which was discussed in Chapter 18 above).[47]

The first difference is that patent applications that have priority over the application in suit, but have not yet been published, are not included in the state of the art for the purposes of assessing inventive step.[48] The second difference is that, when considering whether an invention is non-obvious (but not whether it is novel), it is possible to combine together (or 'mosaic') information from different sources. The act of combining documents must be 'natural and logical'.[49] It must also be a process that an unimaginative skilled person would (as opposed to could) follow.[50] Documents that conflict or are unrelated cannot be combined to demonstrate obviousness.[51]

---

[40] *Pension Benefits Systems*, T931/95 [2001] *OJ EPO* 413 (assessment for inventive step was to be carried out from the point of view of a software developer or application programmer).

[41] *Genentech's Patent* [1989] *RPC* 147, 241 (Dillon LJ).

[42] *Dredge v. Parnell* (1899) 16 *RPC* 625, 628 (Lord Halsbury); cf. *Genentech's Patent*, above, 214 (Purchas LJ).

[43] *Genentech's Patent*, above, 278 (Mustill LJ); *Adolf Schindling/Illuminating device*, T324/94 [1997] *EPOR* 146.

[44] This has been questioned in relation to the field of biotechnology. *Genentech's Patent*, above, 214 (Purchas LJ) and 279–280 (Mustill LJ). See also *Technograph Printed Circuit*, [1972] *RPC* 346 (Lord Morris); *Polymer Powders/Allied colloids* T39/93 [1997] *OJ EPO* 134, 149.

[45] *Genentech/Expression in yeast*, T445/91 [1995] *OJ EPO* 684.

[46] This date might be critical. For example, in *Biogen v. Medeva* [1995] *RPC* 25 (CA) it was acknowledged that because recombinant DNA technology had developed so quickly, the invention would have been obvious by Dec. 1979. As such, it was critical whether Biogen could take advantage of an earlier priority date from Dec. 1978.

[47] See above Ch. 18 Sections 2 and 3.   [48] *BASF/Metal refining*, T24/81 [1979–85] *EPOR* B-354.

[49] *Phillip Morris/Tobacco lamina filler*, T323/90 [1996] *EPOR* 422, 430.

[50] *Technograph v. Mills & Rockley* [1972] *RPC* 346, 355.

[51] *Mobay/Nethylenebis*, T2/81 [1982] *OJ EPO* 394; [1979–85] *B EPOR* 265. See also *Discovision/Optical recording*, T239/85 [1997] *EPOR* 171.

The state of the art is made up of everything that is made available to the public before the date of filing: irrespective of the language of publication or how widely it has been circulated.[52] The potentially broad nature of the state of the art is restricted by the fact that the prior art is judged through the eyes of a person skilled in the art. On this basis the courts have accepted that a person skilled in a particular art may place greater emphasis on certain types of information than on others.[53] In more extreme cases, the fact that the person skilled in the art is able to evaluate the prior art may mean that certain types of information are discarded.[54]

The potentially broad nature of the state of the art is further restricted by the fact that the skilled person is only expected to have scrutinized the information available in their own or closely related fields. The impact that this has on the material available to the person skilled in the art can be seen in *Mobius/Pencil Sharpener*,[55] which concerned an application for a patent over a hand-operated pencil sharpener with a device that prevented pencil shavings from escaping. The application survived an obviousness attack on the basis of two pieces of prior art: one concerned with pencil sharpeners, the other with savings boxes. The Technical Board of Appeal held that, while the prior art concerning the pencil sharpener represented the closest prior art, it failed to suggest the answer employed in the invention and was thus of no relevance. Given the technological differences between the two fields, the prior art in relation to savings boxes was also of no relevance because it was not in a closely related or neighbouring field. Consequently, the person skilled in the art would not have utilized the solution set out in the prior art relating to the savings box.[56]

In addition to being confronted with relevant material from the state of the art, the person skilled in the art is also presumed to have the benefit of the 'common general knowledge' of the particular art or technical field in question.[57] As well as being a valuable source of information in its own right,[58] the common general knowledge is also important because it enables the notional interpreter to combine different pieces of prior art and to develop and build upon existing pieces of prior art (so long as they do not do anything inventive). The common general knowledge is also important because it acts as the basis from which documents are interpreted.

The sources from which the notional skilled addressee acquires their general knowledge vary depending on the nature of the technical field in question.[59] Frequently, the tribunal assumes that the common general knowledge is that which can be found in encyclopedias and standard dictionaries. Where this is the case, care must be taken to avoid a logical fallacy: common general knowledge will be in encyclopedias, but that does not mean that everything in

---

[52] *Blaschim/rearrangement reaction*, T597/92 [1996] *EPOR* 456; *Mitsoboshi/Endless power transmission*, T169/84 [1979–85] *B* EPOR 354; *Hoechst Celanese v. BP* [1997] *FSR* 547, 563.

[53] *PLG Research* [1994] *FSR* 116, 137: '[k]nowing of a piece of prior art is one thing; appreciating its significance to the solution to the problem in hand is another.'

[54] Cf. *Brugger v. Medic Aid* [1996] *RPC* 635, 653. The 'court should be wary of uncritical ageism in relation to prior art…The fact that a document is old does not, *per se*, mean that it cannot be a basis for an obviousness attack'.

[55] T176/84 [1986] *OJ EPO* 50; [1986] *EPOR* 117.

[56] *Kereber/Wire link bands*, T28/87 [1989] *OJ EPO* 383; [1989] *EPOR* 377. *Mobius* was distinguished in *Boeing/General technical knowledge*, T195/84 [1986] *OJ EPO* 121; [1986] *EPOR* 190.

[57] *Hoechst Celanese v. BP Chemicals* [1997] *FSR* 547, 563; *British Ore Concentration Syndicate v. Mineral Separation* (1909) 26 *RPC* 124, 138.

[58] Sometimes information may fail to ground an invalidity attack when viewed as part of the prior art but succeed in so doing once categorized as common general knowledge. See *Boeing/General technical knowledge*, above.

[59] *Beloit v. Valmet* [1997] *RPC* 489, 494 (Aldous LJ).

such works is common general knowledge.[60] Individual patent specifications are not normally regarded as forming part of the common general knowledge.[61] Scientific papers only become part of the general knowledge 'when it is generally known and accepted without question by the bulk of those who are engaged in the particular art'.[62] Usually, information that is common general knowledge will have been used in some capacity or other. The fact that a concept has not been used does not mean that it is necessarily excluded: only that it is unlikely to form part of the common general knowledge.[63]

4 WHAT IS THE 'INVENTION'?

As the Court of Appeal pointed out in the *Windsurfer* decision, when considering whether an invention is non-obvious the court must identify the inventive concept embodied in the patent.[64] As we saw in relation to patentable subject matter and novelty, the way an invention is interpreted may play an important role in determining whether it is patentable. This is also the case with inventive step. As Lord Hoffmann said, before you can apply the test for obviousness stated in section 3 of the Act and ask whether the invention involves an inventive step, 'you first have to decide what the invention is'.[65] As we explained earlier, one of the consequences of *Pension Benefits Systems* is that it places greater emphasis on the requirement that there must be an inventive step. In particular, it places more emphasis on the way that the invention is characterized, that is on the way the 'inventive concept' is determined.

At the EPO, the task of identifying the invention is achieved via the problem-and-solution approach. More specifically, based on an image of the invention as a solution to a problem, to identify the 'thing' that must be non-obvious, it is necessary to identify the particular problem that the invention addresses. As with most aspects of the obviousness inquiry, this is understood from an objective point of view at the priority date of the invention.[66] The task of having to identify the problem that the invention solves is made easier by the fact that the rules to the EPC provide that 'the description should disclose the invention as claimed in such terms that the technical problem (even if not expressly stated as such) and its solution can be understood'.[67]

While in many cases it is possible to rely upon the problem that is disclosed in the patent application, in some cases the patent application cannot be used to provide an objective statement of the problem.[68] In situations where the problem is not properly set out in the application,

---

[60] *Mars II/Glucomannan*, T112/92 [1994] *EPOR* 249.

[61] See *General Tire and Rubber v. Firestone Tyre & Rubber* [1972] *RPC* 457, 482.

[62] *British Acoustic Films v. Nettlefordfold Productions* (1936) 53 *RPC* 221, 250.

[63] *Beloit v. Valmet* [1997] *RPC* 489, 494 (Aldous LJ).

[64] *Windsurfing International* [1985] *RPC* 59. The importance of the way an invention is interpreted is illustrated in *Genentech's Patents* [1989] *RPC* 147. See also B. Reid, 'Biogen in the EPO: The Advantage of Scientific Understanding' [1995] 2 *EIPR* 98.

[65] *SABAF SpA v. MFI Furniture Centres* [2005] *RPC* 10, para 24 (HL). In particular, it was necessary to decide whether you were dealing with one or two or more inventions. The House of Lords said that it was not appropriate to combine separate inventions and then ask whether the combination would have been obvious: (para 28).

[66] The problem that the applicant is required to specify should be a technical as opposed to a commercial one: *Esswein/Automatic programmer*, T579/88 [1991] *EPOR* 120.

[67] EPC 2000 r. 42(1)(c), r. 47 [EPC 1973 r 27(1)(c)], r. 33(2)].

[68] The problem might need to be reformulated in the light of information revealed by the search report, or the documents relied upon in opposition or appeal proceedings, if these represent a closer state of the art than that

the problem may be reformulated by the EPO.[69] In these circumstances, the nature of the problem is determined from the differences between the closest prior art[70] and the invention (which is seen in terms of its effects rather than its structure).[71] This may refer to the need to achieve the same kind of result, an improved result (for example, a quicker, stronger, or cheaper result), or a different result than is achieved by the existing art.[72]

As we explained earlier, English courts have largely remained resistant to the problem-and-solution approach. While there has been criticism of the problem-and-solution approach in the United Kingdom, there has been little discussion of what alternative approach ought to be adopted. It seems that British tribunals distil the 'invention' from the specification (presumably read purposively from the perspective of the relevant person skilled in the art).[73] It is important to recall that in *Biogen v. Medeva* Lord Hoffmann said that a 'proper statement of the inventive concept needs to include some express or implied reference to the problem which it required invention to overcome'.[74] More pertinently, in *Cipla v. Glaxo,* Pumfrey J said that he was 'not persuaded that' the structured approach to obviousness at the EPO was 'substantially different from the *Windsurfing* approach subject to one qualification', namely that unlike the case in the UK, the EPO will only consider obviousness on the basis of the closest prior art.[75] Given the importance of this issue, it warrants more attention.

One question that arises in this context concerns the way inventions that are made up of a mixture of technical and non-technical features are to be characterized. While it is legitimate for there to be a mix of technical and non-technical features when deciding patentable subject matter under section 1(2)/Article 52(1),[76] this is *not* the case when deciding whether there is an inventive step. As the Technical Board of Appeal said in *Comvik,* non-technical factors are not relevant when deciding whether there was inventive step. This means that, where an invention consists of a mixture of technical and non-technical characters, the non-technical features should be ignored.[77] 'This approach, which is actually a method of construing the claim to determine the technical features of the claimed invention, allows separating the technical from the non-technical features of the claimed invention even if they are intermingled in a mixed type-claim.'[78] The exclusion of non-technical features (which echoes the approach currently taken to subject matter in the United Kingdom) has important consequences for the

originally mentioned. Similarly the technical problem might need to be reformulated in light of experiments which reveal that the claim is too broad. *Polymer Powders/Allied colloids*, T39/93 [1997] *OJ EPO* 134, 144 ff.

[69] *Phillips Petroleum/Passivation of Catalyst*, T155/85 [1988] *EPOR* 164, 169; *Sperry/Reformulation of the problem*, T13/84 [1986] *EPOR* 289.

[70] *IBM/Enclosure for data-processing apparatus*, T9/82 [1997] *EPOR* 303. *Bayer/Thermoplastic moulding composition*, T68/83 [1979–85] *C EPOR* 71; Knesch, 'Assessing Inventive Step' ('the crucial question is whether the man skilled in the art would really have chosen that document as the starting point').

[71] *Pegulan/Surface finish*, T495/91 [1995] *EPOR* 517.

[72] It seems this was derived from practices in Germany, but differs in that the EPO problem-and-solution approach is 'effects centred': *CIPA*, para. 3.21. On the approach in Germany see J. Pagenberg, 'Examination for Non-obviousness: A Critical Comment on German Patent Practice' (1981) 12 *IIC* 1.

[73] *Brugger v. Medic Aid* [1996] *RPC* 635, 656. (The inventive concept must be characterized in the light of the claims and must apply to all embodiments in the claim.)

[74] [1997] *RPC* 1, 45. Lord Hoffmann identified the 'inventive concept' differently at different stages of his analysis.

[75] [2004] *EWHC* 477, para 43–45

[76] *Kock & Sterzel/X-ray apparatus*, T26/86 [1988] *OJ EPO* 19.

[77] Non-technical meaning 'features relating to non-inventions within the meaning of Article 52(2)': *Comvik/ Two identities*, T641/00 [2003] *OJ EPO* 319, para. 4.

[78] Ibid, para. 7; following *Pension Benefits Systems*, T931/95 [2001] *OJ EPO* 413.

fate of computer-related inventions (particularly those in relation to business and economics). Given that, in many cases the real innovations will be in solving managerial or business problems rather than in relation to information technology *per se,* the exclusion of non-technical features means that the inventive step is judged against standard computer technology. As *Pension Benefits Systems* and *Comvik* showed, one of the consequences of this is that such inventions are now excluded at the EPO on the basis that they lack inventive step. While courts in the UK have been highly critical of the way that inventions are characterized for the purposes of an obviousness inquiry at the EPO, the approach outlined in *Comvik* and *Pension Benefits* has been adopted in subsequent decisions at the EPO.[79] This divergence in the way that the invention is construed for the purpose of deciding inventive step must be seen in conjunction with the different approaches to patentable subject matter discussed earlier.[80] When seen in this broader perspective, it seems that, while the tribunals in the UK and EPO may have adopted different approaches, in most cases they seem to lead to the same result.

5 IS THE INVENTION 'OBVIOUS'?

Once the person skilled in the art and the invention have been identified, it is then possible to consider whether the invention is non-obvious.[81] While the question whether an invention is non-obvious is widely regarded as one of the most difficult questions in a difficult area of law, in some ways it is not that different from other questions the courts are required to consider, such as whether a contractual term is fair, or whether evidence is relevant to an issue. In other ways, however, the task of determining whether a particular invention is non-obvious is not only different but also more problematic. One reason for this is that in patent law the tribunals are frequently required to pass judgment on complex and novel technologies. While in deciding whether a person acted negligently judges may be able to rely on their background experience and knowledge, there may be little to guide them when they are forced to consider, for example, the inventiveness of a genetic modification. These problems are exacerbated by the fact that questions about the obviousness of an invention may arise some time after the invention was made. It also means that the way that inventive step is determined will change as a technical field develops. For example, while in the 1980s the futuristic nature of molecular biology meant that the threshold for inventiveness was easily crossed, advances over the last decade or so mean that the criteria will be harder to satisfy. In particular, as more 'is known about the various genomes and the function of the constituent genes, the more difficult it will be to establish an inventive step for any isolated gene'.[82]

While ascertaining whether an invention is obvious is a difficult task, it is made easier by the fact that the question is asked from the perspective of the person skilled in the art. Although a non-specialist may find it difficult to assess whether an invention is obvious, a person who has knowledge of the area, particularly of what is regarded as normal progress in the field, will find it much easier to judge whether something is inventive. The task of determining whether an inventive step is present is also made easier by the fact that the courts invariably draw upon the

---

[79] *Hitachi/Auction method,* T258/03 [2004] *OJ EPO* 575, 583, 588; *Man/Provision of product-specific data,* T1242/04 [2007] *OJ EPO* 421, 430.

[80] *Aerotel v. Telco Holdings* [2007] 1 *All ER* 225, para. 27, 105–6, *Pozzoli* [2007] *EWCA Civ* 588, para 21.

[81] Where the problem-and-solution approach is followed this question becomes whether the solution that an invention provides to the problem being addressed would have been obvious to the person skilled in the art.

[82] UK Patent Office, *Biotechnology Guidelines* (Sept. 2002), 8–9.

evidence of experts. While experts are not able to take the place of the court in making the final decision as to whether an invention is obvious, they play an important role in providing the court with a sense of what would be normal in the field (and thus what would be unexpected and inventive).[83] However helpful these factors may be, it still leaves us with the question: what does it mean to say that an invention is obvious?[84]

5.1 THE MEANING OF 'INVENTIVE STEP'

One of the things that courts and commentators regularly agree on is that the qualitative and factual nature of the inquiry means that it is not possible to reduce obviousness to a precise verbal formula.[85] That is, it is not possible to define either 'inventive step' or 'non-obvious' in a meaningful or helpful way. While it may not be possible to formulate a test which enables us to predict with accuracy whether an invention will be regarded as obvious, it is possible to offer general guidance as to some of the factors which have shaped obviousness inquiries in the past.[86]

An important factor that has influenced decisions as to whether an invention is obvious is the extent to which the notional researcher would have had to exercise choice in the inventive process. In situations where there is no opportunity or need for an inventor to enter into and shape the research process—that is where there is 'no real choice' or 'the skilled man is in an inevitable "one-way street"'[87]—the invention is likely to be obvious. In these situations there is little or no scope for a researcher to act in a technically creative way. The converse of the need for choice is that there is a possibility that the research will fail. Where the research involves no risk or uncertainty, that is where the results are predictable or likely, the invention is more likely to be obvious and thus unpatentable.

In a sense, the focus on the degree of choice or control exercised by the notional inventor builds upon the idea of invention as a process whereby the inventor (as creator) engages with Nature to produce something new. More specifically, it builds upon a model of the invention as a process in which the inventor is actively involved with and ultimately shapes the final product. It presumes that there is a degree of human intervention in the production of the invention. In situations where there is no real need nor opportunity for a researcher to make decisions about the shape and nature of the research, there is no real potential for 'human intervention' and, as such, no inventiveness. This is the case, for example, where an invention results from the application of a known technique to a known problem, or where it was obvious to try the technique in question.[88] It is also the case where the person skilled in the art is 'directly led as a matter of course' to the invention.[89]

---

[83] *Hoechst Celanese v. BP* [1997] *FSR* 547, 563; *British Westinghouse v. Braulik* (1910) 27 *RPC* 209 (Fletcher Moulton LJ); *Brugger v. Medic Aid* [1996] *RPC* 635, 661.

[84] While the *Windsurfing* decision and the 'problem-and-solution approach' provide guidance as to how the invention is to be interpreted, they provide no assistance in determining whether an invention is obvious.

[85] *John Manville's Patent* [1967] *RPC* 479, 493 (Diplock LJ). Singer suggests 13 subtests: *The European Patent Convention*, 182–3.

[86] The inquiry was said to be based on a myriad of factors, which 'divide broadly into matters technical and matters historical'. *Saint-Gobain Pam SA v. Fusion Provida* [2004] *All ER* (D) 44, para 19.

[87] *Hallen v. Brabantia* [1991] *RPC* 195 (CA).

[88] For a discussion of obvious-to-try see *Generics (UK) v. H. Lundbeck* [2007] *RPC* 729, para 70ff; *Actavis v. Merck* [2007] *EWHC* 1311 (Ch), para 42.

[89] *Olin Mathieson v. Biorex* [1970] *RPC* 157.

The mere fact that the notional researcher must have exercised a degree of choice and control over the research process is not in itself enough for the final product to be non-obvious. Put differently, while the exercise of (mental) labour and effort is a necessary condition for an invention to be non-obvious, it is not a sufficient condition. In order for an invention to be non-obvious, it needs to be shown that the way the choice is exercised is technically creative: a notion which not only changes across technologies (both in terms of how it is expressed and also the amount of ingenuity involved), but also over time.

A number of different factors have been taken into account when determining whether an invention is technically creative. At a general level, a distinction is drawn (similar to the distinction drawn in copyright law between sweat of the brow and creativity) between the exercise of routine skills (where the results are non-patentable) and inventive skills (the results of which are). This is based upon the idea that inventions which are based on laboratory techniques, are routine, or which follow 'plainly or logically from the prior art'[90] do not contribute anything to 'the real advancement of the arts'[91] and, as such, are not worthy of protection.

The courts have also taken care to ensure that only *technical* factors are taken into account when determining inventive step. To this end, it was held that the fact that a particular route was not tried for some time because it was believed that the outcome would not get regulatory approval did not make it a route that was not 'obvious to try'.[92] Equally, while the activities of a manager or accountant might play an important role in shaping the research process, their input is not regarded as 'technical' and, as such, is not taken into account when deciding whether an invention is non-obvious.[93] This was exemplified in the *Pension Benefits Systems* decision where the Technical Board of Appeal said that 'the improvement envisaged by the invention', (which was for a computer apparatus for controlling a pension benefit system), 'is an essentially economic one, i.e. lies in the field of economy, which, therefore cannot contribute to inventive step'.[94] As such, the claimed subject matter lacked inventive step. While the level of inventiveness required must be more than the mere application of time, money, and effort,[95] the courts have acknowledged that 'in practice what is technically feasible is unlikely to be wholly isolated from what is commercially feasible'.[96] This means that in some cases commercial and technical considerations may be so inextricably linked that commercial factors may be relevant when considering whether a contribution is technical.[97]

---

[90] *EPO Guidelines* C–IV, 9. The Guidelines were devised largely by reference to German patent practice: Buhling (1978) *AIPLA Quarterly J* 61, 62.

[91] *Atlantic Works v. Brady*, 107 US 192 (1883) (Justice Bradley).

[92] *Richardson Vicks Patent* [1995] *RPC* 568, 579–80.

[93] *Genentech's Patent* [1989] *RPC* 147, 237 (Mustill LJ) (CA).

[94] *Pension Benefits Systems*, T931/95 [2001] *OJ EPO* 413, para. 7.

[95] *Wiederhold/Two component polyurethane lacquer*, T259/85 [1988] *EPOR* 209; *Medtronic/Defibrillator*, T348/86 [1988] *EPOR* 159; *American Cyanamid (Dann's) Patent* [1971] *RPC* 425, 451.

[96] *Ward Building v. Hodgson* SRIS/C/47/97 (23 May 1997) (Robert Walker J).

[97] If 'the intellectual horizon of practical research and innovation is in part set by the economic milieu, commercial realities cannot necessarily be divorced from the kinds of practical outcome which might occur to the law's skilled addressee as potentially worthwhile', *Dyson Appliances v. Hoover* [2002] *RPC* 465, 493 (Sedley LJ) (CA); (see also Arden LJ at 494–5). Applied by Aldous LJ in *Panduit v. Band-It* [2002] *EWCA Civ* 465, para. 49 (CA).

5.2 SPECIFIC APPLICATIONS

Given that decisions about the obviousness of an invention are closely linked to the facts of each case, it may be helpful to look at the way inventive step has been approached in a number of different circumstances.[98]

5.2.1 Technique or avenue for research

In some situations, the inventive step may lie in the technique or the avenue of research that is followed. In these circumstances an invention will be obvious if a person skilled in the art *would* (rather than *could*) have taken the route in question.[99]

The person skilled in the art is assumed to have tried all avenues that have a good prospect of producing valuable results.[100] Factors that might in reality mean that one route is tried before another—such as low cost, easy availability of starting materials, or the likely time before the outcome of an experiment is known—are ignored since they are not pertinent to whether or not the route is technically obvious. As Laddie J explained in *Brugger v. Medic Aid*, 'if a particular route is an obvious one to take or to try, it is not rendered any less obvious from a technical point of view merely because there are a number, and perhaps a large number, of other obvious routes as well'.[101] The position is the same if the route to an invention requires the person to take a succession of obvious steps.[102]

In order for a particular avenue of research to be obvious, there is no need for a researcher to be 100 per cent certain that the chosen route will lead to a particular result. Thus, 'a route may still be an obvious one to try even if it is not possible to be sure that taking it will produce success, or sufficient success to make it commercially worthwhile'.[103] All that needs to be shown for an invention to be obvious is that there was a reasonable expectation of success, or that there was an expectation that the avenue of research 'might well produce a useful desired result'.[104] In *John Manville's Patent* Diplock LJ said that an invention would be obvious if the 'person versed in the art would assess the likelihood of success as sufficient to warrant actual trial'.[105] The test of 'expectation of success' cannot be applied in all situations. While the test is useful where predictable methods are relied on to solve technical problems (e.g. methods of genetic engineering such as cloning and expressing DNA sequences), as the Technical Board of Appeal noted, the test is not useful where an invention depends on random techniques (such as mutagenesis). Where the outcome of a process depends on random events, luck, or chance, the Board said that it was not appropriate to attempt to evaluate the expectation of success. 'Under these circumstances, as for example in a lottery game, the expectation of success always

---

[98] For discussions focusing on biotechnological inventions see *Trilateral Project 24.1: Comparative Study on Biotechnology Patent Practices;* D. Schertenleib, 'The Patentability and protection of DNA-based Inventions in the EPO and the European Union' [2003] *EIPR* 125; UK Patent Office, *Examination Guidelines for Biotechnological Inventions* (Sept. 2002), para. 17–30.

[99] *Rider/Simethicone tablet,* T2/83 [1984] *OJ EPO* 265; *Genentech/Expression in yeast,* T455/91 [1996] *EPOR* 85.

[100] *American Cyanamid v. Ethicon* [1979] *RPC* 215, 266–67.   [101] [1996] *RPC* 635, 661.

[102] *VDO Adolf Schindling/Illuminating device,* T324/94 [1997] *EPOR.* The number of alternative routes may be relevant: if there is only one route, then even an unexpected result might be treated as being obvious: *Rider/simethicone,* T2/83 [1984] *OJ EPO* 265.

[103] *Brugger v. Medic Aid* [1996] *RPC* 635, 660.   [104] *Olin v. Mathieson Biorex* [1970] *RPC* 157, 187.

[105] [1967] *RPC* 479, followed under the 1977 Act in *Brugger v. Medic Aid* [1996] *RPC* 635, 661. *Chiron Corporation v. Murex Diagnostics* [1996] *RPC* 535, 557.

ranges irrationally from nil to high, so that it cannot be evaluated in a rational manner based on technical facts.'[106]

The inventiveness of a particular avenue of research can arise in a number of different ways.[107] In some fields an avenue of research will not be obvious to try because the person skilled in the art considers the whole field to be unpredictable.[108] In other circumstances, the inventive step might arise from the fact that the research overcomes 'prejudices in the art'.[109] That is, it breaks with current views about an area of research. The decision to follow a particular line of research may be inventive where it had previously been thought that the area was either exhausted or fruitless. Similarly, the decision to follow a line of research may be inventive where all recent developments have exploited a different avenue.[110] As the EPO Guidelines explain, as 'a general rule, there is inventive step if the prior art leads the person skilled in the art away from the procedure proposed by the invention. This applies in particular where a skilled person would not even consider carrying out experiments to determine whether these were alternatives to the known way of overcoming a real or imagined technical obstacle.'[111] Similarly, if a document in the prior art suggests that the route in question is unlikely to work, but the patentee successfully took the route, it is likely that the invention will be patentable. In this context it is important to keep in mind the comment by Lord Hoffmann that the mere fact that scientific opinion might have thought that something was 'perfectly useless' does not mean that practising it, or having the idea of making a preparation to do so, necessarily amounts to an inventive step. If this was allowed, it would lead to the paradoxical situation where 'anyone who adopted an obvious method for doing something which was widely practised, but the best scientific opinion thought was pointless, could obtain a patent.'[112]

A particular line of research will also be inventive where it would not have been pursued by the person skilled in the art. It is important to show, as well, that the research was selected for technical reasons: factors such as the cost of the research are not taken into account. In this context it is interesting to note that in *Biogen v. Medeva*[113] the evidence suggested that, whereas a person less skilled in the art might have regarded the route as being obvious, a person skilled in the art would consider it so beset by obstacles as not to be worth trying.[114]

5.2.2 Overcoming obstacles

In some cases, the ingenuity and skill needed for an invention to be non-obvious lies not so much in the identification of a research problem or in reaching the final goal. Instead, the invention arises in the way the obstacles and problems that arise en route to reaching the

---

[106] *DMS/Astaxanthin*, T737/96 (9 March 2000), para. 11. Patentees argued that there was no reasonable expectation of achieving the solution offered by the patent. This test was rejected by the Board because it was not possible to make reasonable predictions about the possibility of success because the success of the invention depended on chance events (mutagenesis).

[107] A distinction is drawn between an exercise of ingenuity and a voyage of discovery. See *Beechams Group (Amoxycillin) Application* [1980] *RPC* 261 (Buckley LJ) (CA).

[108] *Genentech/Expression in yeast*, T455/91 [1995] *OJ EPO* 684.

[109] Schmidt-Szalewski, 'Non-obviousness as a Requirement of Patentability in French Law', 735–6.

[110] If a particular route has not been considered for commercial reason, such a prejudice is irrelevant. See *Brugger v. Medic Aid* [1996] *RPC* 635.

[111] *EPO Guidelines* C–IV, Annexe 4; *Mobay/Nethylenebis*, T2/81 [1982] *OJ EPO* 394 (documents revealed a prejudice or general trend pointing away from the invention).

[112] *Ancare New Zealand Ltd's Patent* [2003] *RPC* 139, 143 (Lord Hoffmann); [2002] *UKPC* 8 (Privy Council).

[113] [1997] *RPC* 1. See also *Hoechst Celanese v. BP* [1997] *FSR* 547.

[114] *Raleigh Cycle v. Miller* (1946) 63 *RPC* 113; *Phillips Petroleum/Passivation of catalyst*, T155/85 [1989] *EPOR* 164.

final goal are overcome.[115] Where unforeseeable difficulties exist, the outcome will be non-obvious if the route chosen to overcome those difficulties is inventive.[116] However, where the obstacles are overcome through tenacity, sound technique, or trial and error, the outcome remains obvious.[117]

5.2.3 Selection of the problem

In some cases, the non-obvious nature of an invention may lie in the problem that has been selected, or in the selection of the goals to be pursued.[118] In situations where the inventiveness lies in the way the problem to be solved is chosen, for the resulting invention to be non-obvious the perception of the problem must be beyond the capability of the person skilled in the art.[119] In *Boeing/General technical knowledge*[120] the patent application related to a mechanism for extending a high-lift device (similar to a crane): the problem to be solved was how this could be done without using long cables. The solution developed by the applicant involved using short cables and pulleys. The Examining Division rejected the application on the basis of two pieces of prior art: one from the aircraft-engineering field, the other a patent application directed at no specific field. The Technical Board of Appeal stated that inventiveness could not be found in the perception of the problem since the overcoming of recognized drawbacks and the achievement of consequent improvements must be considered as the normal task of a skilled person.

5.2.4 Unexpected result

Another situation where the pursuit of an obvious route may result in a non-obvious invention is where the outcome is, in some important way, unexpected. If a route is obvious to try in response to a known problem, but the particular route chosen produces unexpected advantages, the result might be inventive. This is because the person skilled in the art would not associate the avenue of research with the final result.[121] Where the route taken merely produces a result of the sort that was expected, but more cheaply or efficiently, it is unlikely to be inventive.

5.3 SECONDARY EVIDENCE

While the question whether an invention is obvious is ultimately decided by the tribunals, at times they have been willing to accept so-called secondary evidence that supports a claim that an invention is non-obvious.[122] In effect, secondary evidence is evidence which acts as virtual proof that the invention involved an inventive step. That is, it provides a basis from which it can be inferred that the invention is non-obvious.

---

[115] *John Manville's Patent* [1967] *RPC* 479.   [116] *Unilever/Chymosin*, T386/94 [1997] *EPOR* 184, 194.

[117] *Genentech's Patent* [1989] *RPC* 147, 276 (Mustill LJ) (CA).

[118] *Beecham (Amoxycillin)* [1980] *RPC* 261. Buckley LJ said 'it will suffice if it is shown that it would appear to anyone skilled in the art but lacking in inventive capacity that to try the step or process would be worthwhile…Worthwhile to what end? It must, in my opinion, be shown to be worth trying in order to solve some recognized problem or meet some recognized need.' *Rider/Simethicone*, T2/83 [1984] *OJ EPO* 265.

[119] *Rider*, ibid. With problem inventions dangers of hindsight are particularly pronounced: *Bonzel v. Intervention (No. 3)* [1991] *RPC* 553.

[120] T195/84 [1986] *OJ EPO* 121.

[121] *Rider/Simethicone*, T2/83 [1984] *OJ EPO* 265. The discovery of a yet-unrecognized problem may give rise to patentable subject matter and, as an unexpected bonus, might be interpreted as a solution of a yet-unknown problem.

[122] See Bochnovic, *The Inventive Step*, 70; Singer, *The European Patent Convention*, 196–205.

While supporters of secondary evidence argue that it makes decision making simpler and adds a degree of realism to the inquiry,[123] there is a growing consensus of opinion against placing too much reliance on it.[124] As Laddie J warned, secondary evidence 'must not be permitted, by reason of its volume and complexity, to obscure the fact that it is no more than an aid in assessing the primary evidence'.[125] The growing suspicion about secondary evidence may reflect the fact that, with the increased specialization of the patent courts, the judges are happier to make technical judgements.[126] It also reflects a desire to keep the cost of patent litigation down: with secondary evidence seen as adding unnecessarily to the time and cost of litigation. With these general reservations in mind, we will now outline some of the forms of secondary evidence that have been used as proof of the non-obviousness of inventions.

5.3.1 Closeness to prior art

One factor that has been used to indicate that an invention is obvious is its proximity to the prior art. If, for example, an invention combines two documents from neighbouring fields, it is likely to be obvious. In a famous case, the Court of Appeal held that a design for a sausage machine that merely combined a better way of cutting sausages with an existing filler was obvious.[127] It would be possible, however, for elements from different areas to be combined in a non-obvious way. Similarly, where a patent application is for a 'new use' that is analogous to the existing known uses of the thing, it is unlikely to be inventive. The use of a substance to reduce friction when it was already known that the substance operated as a rust inhibitor was held not to be analogous.[128]

5.3.2 Comparative efforts

The efforts of researchers working in the same field as the inventor have also been used as evidence to support non-obviousness.[129] If a number of people working in the same field were pursuing the same goal, the fact that the inventor was the only person successfully to solve the problem might imply inventiveness. This is on the basis that the corresponding failure of others indicates that the solution was not obvious. On the other hand, if other researchers made the same invention shortly after the applicant, that might imply that the invention was obvious.[130]

The courts have emphasized that evidence of comparative effort should be treated with caution. In order to be of any value, the comparative inventors must have been working from the

---

[123] See Pagenberg, 'The "Inventive Step" in the European Patent System', 13; J. Pagenberg, 'Different Level of Inventive Step for German and European Patents? The Present Practice of Nullity Proceedings in Germany' (1991) 22 *IIC* 763, 764; E. Kitch, 'The Nature and Function of the Patent System' (1977) 20 *Journal of Law and Economics* 265, 283.

[124] *Glaverbel SA v. British Coal* [1995] *RPC* 255; *Hoechst Celanese v. BP* [1997] *FSR* 547, 566; R. Merges, 'Commercial Innovation and Patent Standards: Economic Perspectives on Innovation' (1988) 76 *California Law Review* 805.

[125] *Hoechst* above, 563 (echoing *Mölnlycke* [1994] *RPC* 49).

[126] Cf. A. Cambrosio, P. Keating, and M. MacKenzie, 'Scientific Practice in the Courtroom' (1990) 37 *Social Problems* 275.

[127] *Williams v. Nye* (1890) 7 *RPC* 62; Bochnovic, The *Inventive Step*, 76–8; *Man/Intermediate layer for reflector*, T06/80 [1979–85] *B EPOR* 266; Cole [1979] *EIPR* 316.

[128] *Mobil/Friction reducing additive*, T59/87 [1990] *EPOR* 514; *Mars II/Glucomannan*, T112/92 [1994] *EPOR* 249.

[129] *Lucas v. Gaedor* [1978] *RPC* 297; *Fichera v. Flogates* [1984] *RPC* 227; *Chiron v. Organon (No. 3)* [1994] *FSR* 202; *Mölnlycke (No. 5)* [1999] *RPC* 49; *General Tire v. Firestone Tyre* [1976] *RPC* 197, 203 (HL).

[130] *Windsurfing International* [1985] *RPC* 59, 73–4; *Beloit Technologies* [1995] *RPC* 705, 753; *Genentech's Patent* [1989] *RPC* 147, 221 (Purchas LJ).

same prior art as that cited in the non-obviousness inquiry. They must have been pursuing the same goal and working for some time. If different starting points were used, no inference can be drawn as to the obviousness of the invention from their relative activities. As Laddie J said, the fact that 'a particular researcher working from an unpleaded piece of prior art, arrived at the invention in suit is of no assistance to the court'.[131]

5.3.3 Long-felt want

A related form of evidence that is used to support claims for inventive step is evidence that the invention satisfies a 'long-felt want'. The logic of this is straightforward: if people had been trying to solve a particular problem for many years and the solution had been obvious, someone would already have invented it.[132] Given the existence of a long-felt want, the fact that no one had previously developed the invention means that the invention must have been non-obvious. While long-felt want may indicate inventiveness, there might be other reasons why a development was not made earlier.[133] As such, it is necessary to be careful when inferring non-obviousness from a long-felt want. The need must have been known about for some time; there must have been an interest in developing the field; and the materials and information that form the basis of the solution must have been known and available.[134]

5.3.4 Commercial success

In some situations, the fate of an invention after grant may provide evidence that suggests that the invention is non-obvious. For example, if an invention proves to be commercially successful, or is widely copied by or licensed to competitors, it might be inferred that the invention involved a leap beyond what previously existed. As Tomlin J said in *Parkes v. Cocker*:

When it has been found that the problem had awaited solution for many years and that the device is in fact novel and superior to what had gone before and has been widely used and indeed in preference to alternative devices, it is practically impossible to say that there is not present that scintilla of invention necessary to support the patent.[135]

Evidence about the fate of an invention after grant which is introduced to prove inventive step needs to be treated with caution.[136] This is because there may be a number of reasons other than the non-obvious nature of an invention that explain the reaction of the market or competitors to the invention. For example, a competitor might have taken out a licence from a patentee to avoid threats of litigation, rather than because they regarded the patentee's invention as based on a significant technical advance. Similarly, commercial success might be attributable to factors such as advertising, distribution, marketing, or business acumen rather than to technical advance. For evidence of the fate of an invention after grant to be of value, it must suggest a link between the success of the product and the product's patented features.[137]

---

[131] *Hoechst Celanese v. BP* [1997] *FSR* 547, 565.

[132] See *Brugger v. Medic Aid* [1996] *RPC* 635, 654; *Frisco-Findus/Frozen fish,* T90/89 [1991] *EPOR* 42; *Air Products/Removal of hydrogen sulphide,* T271/84 [1987] *OJ EPO* 405; [1987] *EPOR* 23.

[133] *Brugger,* above, 654–5.

[134] *BASF/Metal Refining* [1979–85] *B EPOR* 354. *VDO Adolf Schindling/Illuminating device,* T324/94 [1997] *EPOR* 146.

[135] (1929) 46 *RPC* 241, 248.

[136] *Longbottom v. Shaw* (1891) 8 *RPC* 333, 336 (Lord Herschell); *ICI/Fusecord,* T270/84 [1987] *EPOR* 357; *EPO Guidelines* C–IV, 9.9.

[137] Merges, 'Commercial Innovation and Patent Standards'; E. Walker, 'Objective Evidence of Non-Obviousness: The Elusive Nexus Requirement' (1987) 69 *JPTOS* 175, 236; Comment, 'Non-obviousness in Patent Law: A Question of Law or Fact' (1977) 18 *William & Mary Law Review* 612.

As a result, commercial success will rarely be of significance unless it can be shown that there is evidence of a previous need for a solution to the particular problem, that the relevant prior art had been published for some time, and, most importantly, that the commercial success was attributable to the technical features of the invention.[138] It has also been suggested that the ability to rely on commercial success depends on being able to isolate what it is that has contributed to the success. As such, it has been suggested that commercial success would only ever be applicable for simple inventions.[139]

5.3.5 The belief and conduct of the inventor

While the factual nature of the obviousness inquiry, which requires the court to pass judgment on the relative 'inventiveness' of the patent, may seem to suggest that the views of the inventor would be critical, as Jacob LJ said, such evidence, is at best secondary evidence, which much be kept firmly in place. This helps to protect against the inventor who 'may have thought that what he did was little short of, or actually [was], a work of genius—that he was a latter-day Edison'.[140]

[138] EPO Guidelines C–IV, 9.9; Raychem's Patent [1998] RPC 31.

[139] See Haberman v. Jackel [1999] FSR 683 (re the 'AnyWayUpCup'); Conor Medsystems v. Angiotech Pharmaceuticals [2007] RPC 487, paras 51–2. (The patent at issue in this decision can be examined at the Online Resource Centre, <http://www.oxfordtextbooks.co.uk/bentlysherman3e/>.)

[140] Nichia Corporation v. Argos [2007] EWCA Civ 741, 479, paras 13–43.

20

INTERNAL REQUIREMENTS
FOR PATENTABILITY

CHAPTER CONTENTS

1 INTRODUCTION

In this chapter, we turn our attention away from the external criteria for patentability (subject matter, novelty, and inventive step) to focus on the internal criteria for patentability (so named because they focus on the way the patent is drafted). The first is the requirement that the invention be disclosed in a manner that is clear and complete enough for it to be performed by a person skilled in the art.[1] Secondly, we look at the form and content of the claims. In particular, we look at the requirements that the claims be clear and concise, be supported by the description, and relate to one invention.[2] Finally, we look at the requirement that the patent must not be amended in such a way that it acquires additional subject matter or extends the protection conferred by the patent.[3]

2 SUFFICIENCY OF DISCLOSURE

In determining how the scope of protection is to be determined, patent law has had to juggle a number of conflicting demands. On the one hand, it is necessary to ensure that patents offer sufficient rewards to encourage organizations to become involved in the patent process in the first place. To do this, the protection must be robust enough to ensure that competitors are unable to circumvent the patent, for example, by making minor changes to the invention. It is also important that the scope of protection coincides with the invention as disclosed in the patent. As Aldous

---

[1] PA s. 14(3), s. 72(1)(c)/EPC 2000 Art. 83 [EPC 1973 Art. 83].
[2] PA s. 14(5)(c)/EPC 2000 Art. 84 [EPC 1973 Art. 84].
[3] PA s. 76(2)–(3)/EPC 2000 Rule 136(1)–(2) [EPC 1973 Art. 123(2)–(3)].

LJ said, 'I do not believe that the patent system should be used to enable a person to monopolise more than that which he has described in sufficient detail to amount to an enabling disclosure. If it was, it would stifle research.'[4] It is also important that the information disclosed in the patent is useful. It makes little sense to reward someone for disclosing their invention with a patent if a key element of the invention is missing, or if members of the public have to undertake additional or onerous research before they are in a position to reproduce the invention. In this section we look at one of the most important rules used to regulate the scope of patent protection and in so doing help to resolve such issues.[5] This is the requirement that the patent application disclose the invention in a manner that is clear enough and complete enough for it to be performed by a person skilled in the art:[6] which is usually referred to as the requirement for sufficiency of disclosure. Failure to comply with the requirement for sufficiency gives rise to an objection before grant, and is also a ground for revocation once a patent has been granted.[7]

In recent years there have been a number of attempts to categorize the sufficiency examination according to the nature of the disclosure and the type of invention in question.[8] However, the Court of Appeal in *Kirin-Amgen* dismissed these efforts, saying there is only one ground for sufficiency set out in the 1977 Act (and the EPC 2000): namely that the specification must enable the invention to be performed.[9] This means that the test for sufficiency is the same whether the claimed invention is a class of chemical compounds, a DNA sequence, or a simple mechanical invention. In all cases, the disclosure in the specification must enable a person skilled in the art to manufacture the invention.[10] In Lord Hoffmann's words, there must be an enabling disclosure. It is important to note that the information that has to be disclosed for a person skilled in the art to perform an invention always varies depending on the nature of the invention and the circumstances of the case.[11] In a recent case, Lord Hoffmann warned about drawing too much from *Biogen* suggesting instead that '*Biogen* is limited to the form of claim which the House of Lords was there considering and cannot be extended to an ordinary product claim in which the product is not defined by a class of processes of manufacture'. In some situations, the mere disclosure of a formula may be sufficient for the invention to be performed or worked.[12] In other cases, it may be necessary for both the formula and the starting materials (or means) to be disclosed before a person skilled in the art can put the invention into practice.

The question whether the invention has been adequately disclosed is assessed as of the date of filing.[13] While the onus of establishing that an invention has been sufficiently disclosed

---

[4] *American Home Products v. Novartis Pharmaceuticals* [2001] *RPC* 159, 179 (Aldous LJ) (CA).

[5] See B. Domeij, 'Patent Claim Scope: Initial and Follow-on Pharmaceutical Inventions' [2001] *EIPR* 326.

[6] PA s. 14(3), s. 72(1)(c)/EPC 2000 Art. 83 [EPC 1973 Art.83].

[7] PA s. 72(1)/EPC 2000 Art. 100 [EPC 1973 Art. 100].

[8] See Neuberger J's attempt to divide the insufficiency examination into 'classic insufficiency' (where the teaching of the patent does not support that which the teaching specifically purports to deliver) and *Biogen* insufficiency (where claims are cast more widely than the teaching of the patent enables): *Kirin-Amgen v. Roche Diagnostics* [2002] *RPC* 1, 82 (para. 300).

[9] *Kirin-Amgen v. Transkaryotic Therapies* [2003] *RPC* 31, 65 (Aldous LJ) (CA). H. Sheraton and A. Sharples, 'The Court of Appeal Puts *Biogen* Insufficiency Back Where it Belongs' [2002] *EIPR* 596. This issue was not addressed when the matter went to the House of Lords.

[10] *Biogen v. Medeva* [1997] *RPC* 1, 47 (Lord Hoffmann) (HL); *Asahi Kasei Kogyo* [1991] *RPC* 485, Lord Oliver, 536; Lord Jauncey of Tullichettle, 547 (HL); *Pharmacia Corporation v. Merck* [2002] *RPC* 775, 800 (Aldous LJ) (CA).

[11] *H. Lundbeck A/S v. Generics (UK) Ltd & Ors* [2008] *EWCA Civ* 311 (10 April 2008), para. 35. *Mentor Corporation v. Hollister* [1993] *RPC* 7, 12; *Mycogen/Modifying plant cells*, T694/92 [1998] *EPOR* 114, 120.

[12] *Merck/Starting Compounds*, T51/87 [1991] *OJ EPO* 177.

[13] *Biogen*, above, 53–4 (Lord Hoffmann) (HL); *Kirin-Amgen v. Transkaryotic Therapies*, above, 71 (Aldous LJ) (CA).

initially falls upon the applicant/patentee, at trial the obligation is on the defendant to establish that the claims were insufficient.[14] It is not enough for a defendant merely to allege that a patent has not been disclosed in a way that enables the invention to be performed by a person skilled in the art.[15] Instead, a patent can only be challenged on the basis that the invention is not sufficiently disclosed if there are 'serious doubts which are substantiated by verifiable facts'.[16] In the absence of evidence to this effect, the patent will be upheld.[17]

Sufficiency is decided by the court judged through the eyes of a person skilled in the art. As the Patents Act 1977 and the EPC 2000 make clear, the specification must be disclosed in such a way that it can be performed by *the person skilled in the art*. The notional skilled person employed in this context is similar to the notional interpreter used to assess inventive step. One difference is that, whereas for the purposes of evaluating inventive step the skilled person only has knowledge of the prior art, for the purpose of evaluating sufficiency of disclosure the skilled person has knowledge of the prior art *and* of the invention as disclosed.[18]

As the focus of the sufficiency requirement is on whether the *invention* has been disclosed, one of the first tasks that arises in this context is for the scope and nature of the invention to be ascertained. Once this is done, it is necessary to ask whether the invention-as-claimed is disclosed in a manner that is clear enough and complete enough for it to be performed or carried out by a person skilled in the art. This means, for example, that if an invention is a compound that reduces pain, the specification must contain sufficient information to enable compounds with that attribute to be manufactured.[19] Similarly, where the claims 'include a number of discrete methods or products, the patentee must enable the invention to be performed in respect of each of them'.[20] That is, the disclosure must enable the invention to be performed across the whole range of the products claimed.[21] If this cannot be done, the patent will be invalid.[22]

In recognition of the fact that many (if not most) patents require some degree of fine-tuning before they can be put into practice, the patent specification does not need to spell out every

[14] *Pharmacia v. Merck* [2002] *RPC* 775, 798 (Aldous LJ) (CA).

[15] PA s. 14(3), s. 72(1)(c)/EPC 2000 Art. 83 [EPC 1973 Art. 83].

[16] The mere fact that a claim is broad is not in itself a ground for considering the application as not complying with the requirement for sufficient disclosure in EPC Art. 83 [now EPC 2000 Art. 83]: *Harvard/Onco-mouse* T19/90 [1990] *OJ EPO* 476.

[17] T9182/89 [1991] *OJ EPO* 391.

[18] *Mycogen/Modifying plant cells,* T694/92 [1998] *EPOR* 114, 120. For the purposes of determining sufficiency of disclosure, the person skilled in the art is non-inventive, is able to make use of common general knowledge, and is able to perform non-inventive experiments. The notional interpreter 'is not to be expected to exercise any invention nor any prolonged research or inquiry or experiment. He must, however, be prepared to display a reasonable degree of skill and common knowledge of the art in making trials and to correct obvious errors in the specification if a means of correcting them can readily be found'. *Mentor v. Hollister* [1993] *RPC* 7, 13 (Lloyd LJ); *Valensi v. British Radio Corporation* [1973] *RPC* 337; *Edison & Swan Electric Light v. Holland* (1889) 6 *RPC* 243. While the skilled reader is presumed to have *access* to everything in the state of the art, this does not mean that they also have *knowledge* of everything in the state of the art. *EPO Guidelines* C–IV, 9.6.

[19] *Pharmacia v. Merck* [1997] *RPC* 1, 798 (Aldous LJ) (CA).

[20] *Biogen* [1997] *RPC* 1, 48 (Lord Hoffmann) (HL).

[21] *Exxon/Fuel oils,* T409/91 [1994] *EPOR* 149 (18 March 2003); *Unilever/detergents,* T435/91 (9 Mar. 1994); *Biogen,* ibid, 48 (the specification must enable the invention to be performed to the *full* extent of the monopoly claimed). See also *Evans Medical Patent* [1998] *RPC* 517, 562; *Chiron v. Organon (No. 12)* [1994] *FSR* 153, 184 (CA). Similarly, there has 'never been a requirement that all embodiments within the scope of the monopoly should have been tested. Sufficiency required the monopoly to match the contribution': *AHP v. Novartis* [2000] *RPC* 547, 567; A similar approach has been adopted at the EPO: *Exxon/Fuel Oils,* above.

[22] *Pharmacia v. Merck,* [1997] *RPC* 1, 800 (Aldous LJ) CA). (If the invention 'is a selection of certain compounds, in order to secure an advantage or disadvantage, the specification must contain sufficient information on how to make the compounds, and also describe the advantage or how to avoid the disadvantage').

specific detail necessary for an invention to be performed.[23] In line with this, it has been accepted that in putting an invention into practice, the skilled person is able to make use of common general knowledge,[24] engage in routine laboratory tests, correct obvious errors in the specification,[25] and does not have to be told what is self-evident.[26] There are, however, two important limitations on the types of activity that the person skilled in the art can legitimately be called upon to engage in when implementing the invention. The first is that if the person skilled in the art needs to use any inventive skill when putting the invention into practice, the invention will not have been disclosed sufficiently and, as such, will be invalid.[27] The second limitation is that the invention must be able to be reproduced without 'undue burden'.[28] Undue burden is a catch-all phrase that covers activities that the courts deem to be onerous.[29] This has been the case, for example, where the patent required the skilled person to undertake lengthy experiments before they are able to perform the invention,[30] or where the reproduction of the invention depended on a 'stroke of luck'.[31] Rejecting the argument that timescale should not be taken into account when assessing sufficiency, Jacob LJ said, 'patents are meant to teach people how to do things. If what is "taught" involves just too much to be reasonable for all the circumstances including the nature of the art, then the patent cannot be regarded as an "enabling disclosure". That is the basic concept behind the requirement of sufficiency and one that lies at the heart of patent law... The setting of a gigantic project, even if merely routine, will not do.'[32]

2.1 REPRESENTATIVE CLAIMS

As we explained earlier, it is accepted practice for patents to be granted for extremely large classes of compounds, DNA sequences, and the like.[33] This is particularly the case in relation

[23] *Valensi v. British Radio Corp* [1973] *RPC* 337, 375; *Mentor v. Hollister* [1993] *RPC* 7, 12.

[24] *Genentech/t-PA*, T923/92 [1996] *EPOR* 275, 302.

[25] *Air Products/Redox catalyst*, T171/84 [1986] *OJ EPO* 95; [1986] *EPOR* 210.

[26] *Biogen v. Medeva* [1995] *RPC* 1, 25, 98 (HL); *Chiron v. Organon (No. 12)* [1994] *FSR* 153, 185.

[27] *Mentor v. Hollister* [1993] *RPC* 7, 12; *Valensi v. British Radio Corp.*, [1973] *RPC* 337, 377; *Wacker-Chemie*, T931/91 (20 April 1993).

[28] *Unilever/Cleanser Composition*, T226/85 *EPOR* 18; [1988] *OJ EPO* 336 (17 March 1987).

[29] The 'whole subject-matter which is defined in the claim should be enabled without undue burden by the teaching of the patent specification': *Weyershauser/Cellulose*, T727/95 [2001] *OJ EPO* 1, para. 7; *Mycogen/Modifying plant cells*, T694/92 [1998] *EPOR* 114, 119 (where the Technical Board of Appeal said the 'claims need to provide instructions which are sufficiently clear for the skilled person to reduce them to practice without undue burden, i.e. with no more than a reasonable amount of experimentation and without applying inventive skill'). The person skilled in the art should not be called upon to make a prolonged study of matters that present some initial difficulty. *Valensi v. British Radio Corp.* [1973] *RPC* 337; *Badische Anilin v. Société Chimique* (1898) 15 *RPC* 359.

[30] *DSM NV's Patent* [2001] *RPC* 675, 712–716 (cloning, sequencing, and recombinant expression of the gene for phytsase from fungus, held to be extremely broad and unworkable because the skilled person would have had to depart from the patent, and to experiment over what may have been a long period of time to achieve the desired goal). *Icos Corporation/Seven transmembrane receptor* [2002] *OJ EPO* 293, 300 (Opposition Division) (disclosure of a predicted function of a protein in combination with a method of verification of this function was insufficient because the skilled person was required to test millons of available compounds). Cf. *Bayer CropScience/Safeners*, T1020/98 [2003] *OJ EPO* 533, 542 (the actual time taken was not relevant when deciding whether a claim could be performed if clear and concise).

[31] *Weyershause/ Cellulose*, T727/95 [2001] *OJ EPO* 1, para. 10.

[32] *Halliburton Energy Services v. Smith International (North Sea)* [2006] *EWCA Civ* 1715, paras 17–18.

[33] '[M]ost claims are generalizations from one or more particular examples. The extent of generalization permissible is a matter which the examiner must judge in each particular case in the light of the relevant prior art'. *EPO Guidelines* C–III 6.2. See K. Luzzatto, 'The Support and Breadth of claims to new classes of chemical compounds' (1989) *Patent World* 21.

to chemical and biotechnological inventions, where patents may claim hundreds of thousands (sometimes millions) of compounds. The test for whether a patent for a large class of compounds has been sufficiently disclosed is the same test as is used to examine a patent for a simple mechanical device. So long as the patent equips a person skilled in the art with the means to perform the invention without undue burden[34] or the need to use inventive skills,[35] the invention will be sufficiently disclosed. This is subject to the rider that the applicant must be able to show that the specification discloses a principle of general application that is shared by all members in the class. As Lord Hoffmann explained, if 'the invention discloses a principle capable of general application, the claims may be in correspondingly general terms'. This means that, if the patentee has disclosed something 'which is common to the class, he will be entitled to a patent for all products of that class...even though he has not made more than one or two of them'.[36]

The information needed for a patent over a class of compounds to be disclosed sufficiently differs depending on the type of invention in question. In some situations this might include details about the relationship between the chemical structure and the activities that the chemicals perform.[37] In other cases, knowledge of an appropriate DNA sequence might provide the skilled person with enough information to rework the invention.[38] Another example is offered by the *Genentech* decision where the applicants invented a general principle that enabled plasmids to control the expression of polypeptides in bacteria. As there was no reason to believe that the invention would not work equally well with any plasmid, bacterium, or polypeptide, the patent for more general claims was granted.[39] Problems arise, however, if the patentee is unable to show that there is something that unifies the general class. This would be the case, for example, where a patentee discovers 'a new product which has the beneficial effect but cannot demonstrate that there is a common principle by which that effect will be shared by other products of the same class[;] he will be entitled to a patent for that product but not for that class: even though some may turn out to have the same beneficial effect'.[40] In the absence of a unifying principle, the claim will be for a generalized description of a large number of compounds, rather than a true class.[41]

The criteria that a patentee must comply with to ensure that a patent over a class of compounds satisfies the sufficiency requirement are relatively clear. The same cannot be said, however, when the onus shifts to the defendant to show that such a patent is insufficient. In particular there are doubts about the evidence that a defendant needs to produce to show that a class of compounds has not been disclosed in a manner that is clear enough and complete enough for it to be made by a person skilled in the art. Is it enough, for example, if an opponent

---

[34] *Unilever/Cleanser composition*, T226/85 (17 Mar 1987).

[35] *Wacker-Chemie*, T931/91 (20 Apr. 1993).

[36] *Biogen v. Medeva* [1997] *RPC* 1, 49 (Lord Hoffmann) (HL). A principle of general application 'means an element of the claim which is stated in general terms. Such a claim is sufficiently enabled if one can reasonably expect the invention to work with anything that falls within the general term'. *Kirin-Amgen v. Hoechst Marion Roussel* [2005] *RPC* 169, para 112 (HL).

[37] See *Monsanto v. Merck* [2000] *RPC* 709, para. 7.

[38] *Weyershauser/Cellulose*, T727/95 [2001] *OJ EPO* 1.

[39] *Genentech/Polypeptide Expression*, T292/85 [1989] *EPOR* 1.

[40] *Biogen* [1997] *RPC* 1, 49 (Lord Hoffmann) (HL); *AHP v. Novartis* [2001] *RPC* 159, 176 (CA) Aldous LJ (CA); *Pharmacia v. Merck* [2002] *RPC* 775 (inability to point to any characteristic that unified an otherwise unpredictable class of chemical compounds meant that the claims were insufficient and thus invalid).

[41] *Monsanto v. Merck* [2000] *RPC* 709, para. 67; approved on appeal *Pharmacia v. Merck* [2002] *RPC*, 799 (CA). *Biogen* [1997] *RPC* 1, 47 (HL) ('may claim every way of achieving a result, when it enables only one way and it is possible to envisage other ways of achieving that result which makes no use of the invention') (drawing on *Genentech I/Polypeptide expression*, T292/85 [1989] *OJ EPO* 275).

shows that of a class of 1,000 compounds, 1 compound cannot be manufactured? If not one, how many?[42]

There is no easy answer to this question. In part, the answer will depend on the invention in question, the prior art in the field, and how developed the relevant discipline is.[43] Having said this, it is possible to make some general comments as to how insufficiency is calculated. The first and most straightforward point, which flows from the fact that the onus is on the defendant to show that claims are insufficient,[44] is that a patent will be upheld if the defendant fails to provide evidence showing that at least one of the claims cannot be performed.[45] The courts have also stressed that when carrying out experiments to test whether the invention is insufficient and thus invalid, the defendant should select representative samples, rather than samples that are likely to fail. This follows from the fact that the person skilled in the art will be motivated by a desire to succeed, not to fail.[46] The courts have also suggested that where a defendant introduces experimental evidence that casts doubts over the sufficiency of a patent, it may hinder the patentee's case if they do not provide experimental evidence to the contrary.[47]

2.2 BIOLOGICAL INVENTIONS

As we saw earlier, one of the problems that confronted applicants in their attempt to patent biological invention, whether it be new plants, micro-organisms, or the products of modern biotechnological research, was the concern that they would not be able to describe their new creations in such a way that the inventions would satisfy the requirement for sufficiency of disclosure. The reason for this is that where an invention depends on the use of living materials such as micro-organisms or cultured cells, it may be impossible to describe the invention so that the public is able to make the invention.[48] The EPC 2000[49] and the Patents Act 1977[50] attempt to address this problem by providing that if an invention involves biological material which cannot be described in a way that enables the invention to be carried out by a person skilled in the art, the applicant must deposit a sample of this biological material at a

---

[42] *Mycogen/Modifying plant cells,* T694/92 [1998] *EPOR* 114, 119 (the *essential* features of the claimed invention must be capable of being performed); *Exxon/Fuel Oils,* T409/91 [1994] *EPOR* 149; *Sumitomo/Vinyl chloride resins,* T14/83 [1984] *OJ EPO* 105; *Unilever/Stable bleaches* T226/85 [1989] *EPOR* 18.

[43] The tribunals seem to have taken a more relaxed approach in relation to biotechnological inventions than chemical inventions.

[44] *Kirin-Amgen v. Transkaryotic Therapies* [2003] *RPC* 31, 71 (Aldous LJ) (CA).

[45] The importance of this can be seen in *Kirin-Amgen* where the absence of any evidence from the defendant that a single DNA sequence could not be worked meant that the ground of insufficiency was not established. Allowance is made for situations where a few minor or marginal embodiments cannot be made to work: *Filtration/Fluid filter cleaning system,* T126/89 [1990] *EPOR* 292; *Sumitomo/Vinyl Chloride Resins,* above; T 79/88 [1992] *EPOR* 387.

[46] *British Thomson-Houston v. Corona Lamp Works* (1922) 39 *RPC* 49, 89; followed in *Kirin-Amgin v. Transkaryotic Therapies,* above, 70–71 (Aldous LJ) (CA).

[47] In *Pharmacia v. Merck* [2002] *RPC* 775, 806 (CA) Aldous LJ said, the 'patentees had ample opportunity to do experiments in reply to demonstrations that the compounds were not representative. They had equipment and the knowledge to do the experiments, but failed to do them.' *AgrEvo/Triazoles,* T939/92 [1996] *OJ EPO* 309, para. 2.5.4.

[48] In *American Cyanamid (Dann)'s Patent* [1971] *RPC* 425 the House of Lords held that there was no obligation on a patentee under the Patents Act 1949 to supply the micro-organism to the public. See generally, B. Hampar, 'Patenting of Recombinant DNA Technology: The Deposit Requirement' (1985) 67 *JPTOS* 569; V. Meyer, 'Problems and Issues in Depositing Micro-organisms for Patent Purposes' (1983) 65 *JPTOS* 455.

[49] EPC 2000 r. 31.   [50] PA s. 125A (introduced by CDPA, Sched. 5 para. 30).

'recognized institution' (or depositary).[51] These issues were also addressed in the Biotechnology Directive.[52] The application must contain such relevant information as is available on the characteristics of the biological material.[53] If an applicant intends to rely upon deposit as a way of satisfying the requirement for sufficiency of disclosure, it is important that the patent makes specific reference to the deposit: failure to do so may mean that the deposit cannot be relied upon.[54]

The extent to which an applicant needs to rely upon deposit to satisfy the requirement for sufficiency depends on the nature of the invention in question. The use of deposit is not mandated for biological invention: it is an option that may be relied upon if needed. While it is more likely traditionally bred plants will need to be deposited, this is not necessarily the case for many of the outcomes of molecular biology, which are able to be described in a way that enables the invention to be replicated by a person skilled in the art. This can be seen, for example, in the *Wisconsin Alumni Research Foundation / Stem cell* decision where the Technical Board of Appeal was called upon to consider whether, in the absence of a reference to a deposit and of specific examples, the description contained sufficient information to enable the skilled person to prepare the claimed human-embryonic stem-cell cultures without excessive burden or undue experimentation.[55] The Board accepted that the skilled person would have been in a position to prepare and grow human embryonic cell lines and, as such, that the invention complied with Article 83 (Article 83 EPC 2000).

3 CLAIMS

The claims play a crucial role in the patent system, not least because they define the scope of protection.[56] Given this, it is not surprising that there are a number of restrictions on how the claims are drafted. Here we focus on the requirements in section 14(5)(c)/Articles 82 and 84 that the claims must be clear and concise (clarity), be supported by the description, and relate to one invention or group of inventions. Before looking at these in more detail, it is necessary to make some comments about the consequences of non-compliance with these provisions.

As we mentioned earlier, non-compliance with the requirement for sufficiency of disclosure gives rise to an objection before grant.[57] It is also a ground for revocation after grant. This is because insufficiency is specifically listed as a ground for revocation in section 72(1).[58] One of the notable features of the revocation provisions is that they do not mention any of the criteria listed in section 14(5)(c) or its EPC equivalents as the basis on which a patent may be revoked. (As unity of invention has traditionally only ever arisen before grant, these discussions are limited to the requirements that the claims be 'clear and concise' and that they be

[51] Recognized depositary institutions include all international depositaries under the 1977 Treaty on the International recognition of the Deposit of Micro-organisms (the Budapest Treaty) (modified 1980). This established minimum requirements for maintaining an international depositary for microorganisms (UK joined 29 Dec. 1988). In January 2008, there were 68 member states with 37 International Depositary Authorities.

[52] Biotech. Directive Arts. 13–14; Implemented in the UK by Patents (Amendment) Rules 2001, SI 2001/1412 (as of 6 July 2001).

[53] EPC 2000 r. 31(1)(b); PA s. 125A, PA r. 13 (1), Schedule 1 (2007 Patent Act Rules).

[54] *Wisconsin Alumni Research Foundation/Stem cell*, T1374/04 [2007] *OJ EPO* 313, para 10.

[55] Ibid.   [56] PA s. 14(5)(a).   [57] PA s. 14(3)/EPC 2000 Art. 100 [EPC 1973 Art. 100].

[58] EPC 2000 Art. 100 (grounds for opposition); Art. 138 (grounds for revocation). [EPC 1973 Art. 83, 100].

'supported by the description'.)[59] On a strict reading, this suggests that while non-compliance with section 14(5)(c)/Articles 82 and 84 will be a basis on which a patent will not be granted, non-compliance is *not* a ground for revocation once a patent has been granted. This strict reading was followed when the matter first came before the courts in the UK, where it was held that while failure to comply with section 14(5)(c) could be objected to prior to grant, it was not a ground on which a patent could be challenged after grant.[60]

This question was revisited by the House of Lords in *Biogen v. Medeva* where Lord Hoffmann said that the 'substantive effect of section 14(5)(c), namely that the description should, together with the rest of the specification, constitute an enabling disclosure, is given effect by section 72(1)(c). There is accordingly no gap or illogicality in the scheme of the Act.'[61] A similar position was adopted at EPO where it was said that '[a]lthough Art. 84 is not open to objection under the terms of Art. 100 EPC [1973], it may nevertheless constitute a proper ground for revoking a patent if objections to either clarity or support arise out of amendments to the patent as granted'.[62] These rulings suggest that while failure to comply with Article 14(5)(c) is not a ground that could be *directly* argued against after grant, the requirements that the claims be 'clear and concise' and that they be 'supported by the description' could *indirectly* be taken into account when deciding insufficiency. In effect, it was suggested that the section 14(5)(c) requirements could be subsumed, after grant, within section 14(3)/Section 72(1).

This reading of *Biogen* was thrown into doubt by the Court of Appeal decision of *Kirin-Amgen* where the Court considered whether the section 14(5)(c) requirements could indirectly be taken into account via section 14(3) to revoke a patent. This was triggered by the argument that there were problems in the way claims had been drafted (namely, that there was no standard against which the named recombinant polypeptide could be tested). The Court of Appeal began by reiterating the line taken pre-*Biogen* that while clarity and support were relevant when assessing whether to grant a patent, they were not express grounds for revocation under section 72(1).[63] (The Court noted that this was also the position under the EPC.) Because of this, the only way in which the claims could have been revoked in the circumstances was on the basis that they were insufficient. Following *Biogen,* the Court of Appeal said that the test for whether claims were insufficient under section 72(1)(c) was whether the disclosure was enabling. On the facts, the Court said that while the claims may have lacked clarity, nonetheless the person skilled in the art could still implement the invention. That is, as the invention could be performed without undue effort, there had been an enabling disclosure. As such, the claims were not insufficient. The Court also said that they believed that the defendant's challenge was not an attack on the basis of insufficiency, rather it was 'an attack of lack of clarity dressed up to look like insufficiency'.[64] In relation to the suggestion that the section 14(5)(c) criteria of clarity and support might indirectly be raised to undermine a patent after grant, the Court of Appeal said that 'the fact that a claim is not clear or is not supported by the specification is likely to be irrelevant'.[65] They also added that '[w]e can see no reason to stretch s72(1)(c) to seek to cover

[59] *Siemens/Unity,* G1/91 [1992] *OJ EPO* 253 (lack of unity is not an issue in opposition or oppositional appeal proceedings).

[60] See *Genentech's Patent* [1989] *RPC* 147, 248 (CA); *Chiron v. Organon (No. 3)* [1994] *FSR* 202, 242 (Aldous J); *Chiron v. Organon (No. 12)* [1994] *FSR* 202, 178–9 (CA).

[61] *Biogen* [1997] *RPC* 1, 47 (Lord Hoffmann) (HL).

[62] *Mycogen/Modifying plant cells,* T694/92 [1998] *EPOR* 114, 119. Art 84 and 100 EPC 1973 are the same as under Art 84 and 100 EPC 2000.

[63] *Kirin-Amgen v. Transkaryotic Therapies* [2003] *RPC* 31, 69 (CA).   [64] Ibid.   [65] Ibid.

issues of lack of clarity of claiming as patentees will not be able to establish infringement of unclear claims'.[66]

The nature of the relationship between clarity and sufficiency, and the role that these concepts are able to play after grant, were also raised when *Kirin-Amgen* was heard by the House of Lords. Lord Hoffmann began by noting that at first instance the judge had held that lack of clarity had made the specification insufficient. He also noted that the Court of Appeal disagreed, saying that failure to specify which product the skilled person needed to use to make the invention was 'lack of clarity dressed up to look like insufficiency'. In reinstating the judge's finding at first instance that the claim in question was invalid for lack of sufficiency, Lord Hoffman said:

if the claims says that you must use an acid, and there is nothing in the specification or context to tell you which acid, and the invention will work with some acids but not with others but finding out which ones work will need extensive experiments, then that in my opinion is not merely lack of clarity; it is insufficiency. The lack of clarity does not merely create a fuzzy boundary between that which will work and that which will not. It makes it impossible to work the invention at all until one has found out what ingredient is needed.[67]

In so ruling, the House of Lords in *Kirin-Amgen* not only reinstated the decision at first instance, they also clarified that clarity and lack of support continue to have a role to play in deciding questions of validity after grant.

3.1 CLARITY

During the nineteenth century, when anti-patent feelings were at their peak, many patents were struck down because they contained trivial errors in grammar or spelling. While patent law is no longer as harsh as it once was, it still demands that the public should not be left in any doubt as to the subject matter covered by a particular patent. As the claims demarcate the scope of the monopoly, if the claims are unclear or inconcise the extent of protection cannot easily be discerned. This would lead to the undesirable situation that third parties would not be able to determine whether they were infringing the patent.[68] To ensure that this does not occur, patent law requires that the claims be clear and concise.[69] While clarity may not be an issue that can be used to challenge a patent after grant, it has been suggested that where a claim contains a vague and ambiguous term, it is less likely that the courts will find that there has been an infringement.[70] The requirement that the claims be clear and concise has been important in relation to structural and functional claims.[71]

Claims will be clear and concise if the skilled person is able to understand the language used.[72] The requirement that the claims be clear and concise applies to 'the choice of category

---

[66] Ibid.   [67] *Kirin-Amgen v. Hoechst Marion Roussel* [2005] *RPC* 9, paras 125–6 (HL).

[68] Another reason why the claims need to be clear and concise is because they will invariably be translated into another language. If a claim were not formulated in clear and precise terms, it would undermine the translation process and also cast doubts on 'foreign' patents.

[69] PA s. 14(5)(b); EPC 2000 Art. 84 [EPC 1973 Art 84]; EPC 2000 Rule 43 [EPC 1973 r. 29].

[70] *Albany/Pure terfenadine*, T728/98 [2001] *OJ EPO* 319, 325–6 (para. 3.1).

[71] P. Ford, 'Functional Claims' (1985) *IIC* 325; *Efamol/Pharmaceuticals compositions*, T139/85 [1987] *EPOR* 229. *Ciba-Geigy/Synergistic herbicides*, T68/85 [1987] *EPOR* 302; *General Hospital/Contraceptive*, T820/94 [1995] *EPOR* 446.

[72] *Strix Limited v. Otter Controls* [1995] *RPC* 607.

of claims, to the terminology and also to the number and order of the claims'.[73] While claims should be internally consistent and free from contradiction, most of the problems tend to arise as a result of the use of relative or imprecise terms. Where this occurs, the test is whether the skilled person would have had difficulty in understanding the language used when read in light of common general knowledge.[74] As the skilled addressee reads the claims, this means that words and phrases that might not be understood outside the field of the invention may still be clear and concise.

The mere fact that a claim is very broad or takes a long time to understand does not necessarily diminish its clarity. As the Technical Board of Appeal said, there is no basis in the Article 84 clarity requirement 'for objecting that a claim is not simple but complex and hence takes too long to understand, as complexity is not tantamount to lack of clarity of a claim'.[75] All that Article 84 requires is that the claims 'define the subject matter for which protection is sought clearly and unambiguously for the skilled person'.[76] In contrast to the requirement for sufficiency of disclosure (where length of time may impose an undue burden on the public), the actual time required to determine whether a given compound falls within the scope of a claim 'does not really matter as long as the claim itself is clear'.[77] In reaching this position the Board stressed that there was no justification for imposing quantitative criteria (such as the amount of time taken to understand a claim) on what is essentially a qualitative requirement that the claims be clear and concise.

The parameters of the invention may be defined by quantitative criteria (such as size, weight, volume, temperature) or qualitative criteria. While in most cases applicants will use precise measurements to define their inventions, applicants may confine their descriptions to general relationships between component parts where nothing turns on finite limits.[78] Relative terms such as thin, fat and slow are admissible, but only if they have a generally recognized meaning in the field. Where no unequivocal generally accepted meaning exists in the relevant art, this casts uncertainty over the subject matter covered by the claim. On this basis it was held that use of the term 'substantially pure' (the sole feature designated to distinguish the subject matter of a chemical invention), which had no clear and unequivocal meaning, meant the patent was unclear and thus not in conformity with Article 84.[79]

3.2 SUPPORTED BY THE DESCRIPTION

The second requirement imposed on the claims is that they 'must be supported by the description'.[80] This helps to ensure that there is a correlation between what is invented and what has been claimed. The requirement that the claims must be supported by the description reflects the 'general legal principle that the extent of the patent monopoly as defined in the claims, must correspond to the technical contribution to the art'.[81] The requirement that the claim be supported by the description plays an important role in ensuring that the scope of

---

[73] Singer and Stauder, 378.

[74] *Strix v. Otter* [1995] *RPC* 607; *ICI/Optical sensing apparatus*, T454/89 [1995] *EPOR* 600.

[75] *Bayer CropScience/Safeners*, T1020/98 [2003] *OJ EPO* 533, 542 (TBA). In relation to a Markush formula for a class of chemical compounds, the TBA held that simplicity of a claim is not a criterion for the granting of a patent under the EPC.

[76] Ibid, 542–3.   [77] Ibid, 542.   [78] *No-Fume v. Pitchford* (1935) 52 *RPC* 231.

[79] *Albany/ Pure terfenadine*, T728/98 [2001] *OJ EPO* 319, 329 (para. 3.3).

[80] PA s. 14(5)(c)/ EPC 2000 Art. 84 [EPC 1973 Art. 84].

[81] *CIRD Galderma*, T1129/97 [2001] *OJ EPO* 273, 287.

the protection provided to the patentee does not exceed or differ from the invention disclosed in the patent.[82] By ensuring that the claims (which shape the scope of the legal monopoly) are supported by the description (which provides the necessary technical information), patent law enables potential users to ascertain without undue burden or the need for inventive activity whether their planned commercial use is likely to infringe the patentee's monopoly.[83]

The approach that is used to decide whether the claims are supported by the description is similar to the approach that is used to decide whether the specification has been disclosed sufficiently.[84] As is the case with the requirement for sufficiency of disclosure, a description that outlines one way of performing the claimed invention may support broader claims. This would be the case, for example, 'where the disclosure of a new technique constitutes the essence of the invention and the description of one way of carrying it out enables the skilled person to obtain the same effect of the invention in a broad area by use of suitable variants of the component features'.[85] As with sufficiency of disclosure, a single embodiment can only ever justify a broader claim if the class as a whole shares a common principle.[86] In other cases, more technical details and more than one example may be necessary to support claims of a broad scope.[87]

One situation where claims may not be supported by the description is where the breadth of the claims extends beyond the technical contribution provided by the invention.[88] This might occur, for example, where the patent claims results that cannot be performed from the information in the claims. This would be the case where the patent claims the making of a wide class of products, but it only enables one of those products to be made and fails to disclose a principle that enables the other products to be made. Similarly, a patent may lack support where it claims every way of achieving a particular result but only enables one way of making the product, and it is possible to envisage other ways of achieving that result which do not make use of the invention.[89]

3.3 UNITY OF INVENTION

As well as being clear, concise, and supported by the description, claims must also relate 'to one invention or to a group of inventions which are linked as to form a single inventive concept'.[90] The requirement that there be unity of invention, which ensures that applications only contain a single invention or a single group of inventions, plays an important administrative role. It

---

[82] *Exxon/Fuel oils*, T409/91 [1994] *EPOR* 149, 154; *Mycogen/Modifying plant cells*, T649/92 [1998] *EPOR* 114, 118.

[83] *Oxy/Gel-forming composition*, T246/91 [1995] *EPOR* 526, 531.

[84] The phrase 'supported by matter disclosed' is also used in PA s. 5(2) (to establish whether priority from an earlier application is acceptable). A description would not support claims for the purpose of s. 14(5)(c) unless the specification contained sufficient material to constitute an enabling disclosure under s. 14(3). *Biogen* [1997] *RPC* 1, 47 (Lord Hoffmann) (HL); *Asahi Kasei Kogyo* [1981] *RPC* 485, 535–6 (Lord Oliver) (HL). A similar approach was adopted by the Technical Board of Appeal in *Mycogen/Modifying plant cells*, above, 119.

[85] *Mycogen*, ibid, 120.

[86] *Mölnlycke AB v. Procter & Gamble* [1992] *FSR* 549, 600 (Morritt J) based on *Genentech/Polypeptide Expression*, note 39 above and applied in *Chiron v. Organon (No. 3)* [1994] *FSR* 202, 241–2.

[87] This is the case where the achievement of a given technical effect by known techniques in different areas constitutes the essence of the invention and there are serious doubts as to whether the said effects can readily be obtained for the whole range of applications claimed; *Mycogen/Modifying plant cells*, above, 120. *Xerox/Amendments*, T133/85 [1988] *OJ EPO* 441, 448.

[88] *Biogen*, above, 50–1 (Lord Hoffmann) (HL) ('whether the claims cover other ways in which they might be delivered: ways that owe nothing to the teaching of the patent or any principle which it disclosed').

[89] *Mycogen/Modifying plant cells*, above, 120.

[90] PA s. 14(5)(d), PA r. 22; EPC 2000 Art. 82 [EPC 1973 Art. 82]; EPC 2000 r. 44 [EPC 1973 r. 30].

also helps to minimize some of the problems that might otherwise arise in the application of the substantive tests for patentability if a patent contained a number of distinct inventions.[91] For two or more inventions to appear in the same patent, there must be a single inventive concepts that links them together. This might occur, for example, if there was an expectation in the art that the various inventions will behave the same way. Importantly the unifying factor that links the different inventions must be an inventive concept and not some other feature of the invention.[92]

4 IMPROPER AMENDMENTS

The final internal requirement for patentability we look at here concerns the extent to which patents can be amended. As we saw earlier, a number of restrictions are placed on the way patents can be amended.[93] In this section we wish to concentrate on those amendments which throw the validity of the patent into doubt. There are two important limits on the way patents may be amended. The first is that an application must not be amended in such a way as to bring in subject matter that extends beyond the content of the application as filed. The second restriction is that amendments after grant must not extend the protection conferred by the patent.

The restrictions placed on the ability of patents to be amended have been criticized on the basis that the rules have been applied too rigorously.[94] It has been said that this denies legitimate inventors the protection they deserve, and encourages loose filing.[95] Another problem with the law in this area is that there has been very little discussion about the principles on which the restriction of amendment is based. As Staughton LJ observed:

[The] problem is not that the technology in this case is obscure or recondite, but that the law as to added matter is…A clear and precise test is not to be found in the Patents Act. Those who are engaged in the important business of inventing and manufacturers too, are to my mind entitled to more precise guidance as to how they should conduct their affairs. But they must seek it from Parliament, or from an international convention.[96]

4.1 RESTRICTIONS ON AMENDMENTS THAT ADD MATTER

The first limit is that an application must not be amended in such a way as to bring in subject matter that extends beyond the content of the application as filed.[97] Failure to comply with these

---

[91] *Exxon*, T314/99 (21 Jun. 2001) (three different embodiments covered by the claim did not belong to the same single general inventive concept. While lack of unity could not be raised in opposition, it was held that the inventiveness of the claim as a whole was denied in the event that only one of the embodiments was obvious).

[92] *Draenert/Single general inventive concept* W6/90 [1991] OJ EPO 438. For the problems this presents for gene patents see D. Schertenleib, 'The patentability and protection of DNA-base inventions in the EPO and the European Union' [2003] *EIPR* 125, 128–9.

[93] For a discussion on the role of disclaimers in amending patents at the EPO see *PPG/Disclaimer* G1/03 [2004] *OJ EPO* 413.

[94] *Protoned BV 's Application* [1983] *FSR* 110.

[95] R. Krasser, 'Possibilities of Amendment of Patent Claims during the Examination Procedure' (1992) 23 *IIC* 467, 471.

[96] *AC Edwards v. Acme Signs* [1992] *RPC* 131, 147 (CA).

[97] PA s. 76(2); EPC 2000 Art. 123(2) [EPC 1973 123(2)]; *EPO Guidelines* C–VI; CPC Art. 57(1). Despite obvious similarities, PA s. 76 is not listed in PA s. 130 (7) as being framed as to have as nearly as practicable the same

requirements opens the patent up to the possibility of revocation.[98] Consequently, applicants are confined by the scope of the description of the invention that is set out in the application. This ensures that patentees are not permitted to extend the patent so as to claim an invention developed after the priority date.[99] It also ensures, as the Technical Board of Appeal said, that applicants are not able to improve their position by adding subject matter not disclosed in the application as filed, giving them 'an unwarranted advantage and possibly being detrimental to the legal security of third parties relying on the contents of the application as filed'.[100]

While it is permissible for a patentee to claim the same invention in a different way, patentees are not able to amend their application so as to protect an inventive concept that was not disclosed in the original application.[101] The purpose of the restrictions on amendment is to stop patentees inserting information after filing which enables them to support their claims.[102] As Aldous LJ said, this means that if a feature was omitted from a claim which the specification had made clear was essential, or if a feature was added that had not been disclosed in the application as filed, the amendment would add matter.[103] It is permissible to add information which explains rather than expands the scope of the claims. In this situation the amendments 'harm no one and assist the public'.[104]

The basic issue is whether the amended patent contains any additional (technical) material that was not disclosed in the original application.[105] Basically this requires the tribunal to compare the application as filed (the description, any claims, or drawings,[106] but not the abstract[107] or priority documents) with the amended application to determine whether the amended application contains any additional matter.[108] As has been noted at the European Patent Office, the issues that arise here are conceptually similar to those that arise in relation to the requirement for novelty: in both cases the issue is whether something 'new' has been added. In the case of novelty, the invention must be new; in the case of amendment, the amended application must not contain anything new.[109] Under this approach the test is whether a skilled

---

effect as the corresponding provision of the Convention. Nevertheless, the UK courts have referred to EPO decision.

[98] *B & R Relay's Application* [1985] *RPC* 1; *Edwards v. Acme* [1990] *RPC* 621, 144 (Fox LJ) (CA). PA s. 72(1) (d) renders it a ground for revocation that the matter disclosed in the specification of the patent extends beyond that disclosed in the application as filed.

[99] *Edwards v. Acme*, above, 147 (Staughton LJ).

[100] *British Biotech/Heterocyclic compounds*, T684/96 [2000] *EPOR* 190, 197.

[101] *Southco v. Dzus Fastener Europe* [1990] *RPC* 587, 618. Consequently amendment of a claim from 'handle' to a 'rotatable actuating means' would be read as not extending the disclosure.

[102] *Vector Corporation v. Glatt Air Techniques* [2007] *EWCA Civ* 805; [2007] *All ER* (D) 297, para 3.

[103] *Texas Iron Works Patent* [2000] *RPC* 207, 246–7 (CA).   [104] *Vector v. Glatt,* above, para 3.

[105] 'Clearly the function of this provision is to prevent the addition of subject matter to a patent application after the date of filing. In contrast the reformulation of the same subject matter . . . would be permissible'. *Xerox/Amendments,* note 87 above, 449. *Milliken Denmark AS v. Walk Off Mats* [1996] *FSR* 292.

[106] *Amp/Connector*, T66/85 [1989] *EPOR* 283; [1989] *OJ EPO* 167; cf. *Sulzer/Hot gas cooler* [1990] *EPOR* 14; [1989] *OJ EPO* 441.

[107] *BULL/Identification System*, T246/86 [1989] *OJ EPO* 199. The documents are looked at through the eyes of the notional skilled addressee: *Siegfried Demel v. Jefferson* [1999] *FSR* 204, 214.

[108] *Bonzel v. Intervention (No. 3)* [1991] *RPC* 553, 574; *Molnlycke AB v. Procter & Gamble (No. 5)* [1994] *RPC* 49 (CA). Aldous J held that 'matter' included both structural features and inventive concepts: *Southco v. Dzus,* above, 616. However, this has proved to be controversial. see *Edwards v. Acme Signs* [1992] *RPC* 131, 144 (Fox LJ). For a more sympathetic reading see *Sara Lee Household & Body Care v. Johnson Wax* [2001] *FSR* 261 (Judge D. Young QC), following *Metal-Fren/Friction pad assembly,* T582/91 [1995] *EPOR* 574.

[109] *EPO Guidelines* C–VI, 5.4, 7.2, 9. *Shell/Lead Alloys,* T201/83 [1984] *OJ EPO* 401; *General Motors/Electrodes,* T194/84 [1990] *OJ EPO* 59, 65. It is different from the requirement that the claim be supported by the

person could derive any information in the amended patent that was not already in the application as filed.[110]

Unlike the position after grant, there is no reason *per se* to object to the broadening of the claims prior to grant.[111] This is because it is immaterial whether the amendment widens or narrows the monopoly claimed. The only restriction is the general one that prevents patentees from altering their claims in such a way that they claim a different invention from that which is disclosed in the application.[112] If the application as filed described the insertion of cancer genes in mice and flagged the potential application of the invention to other mammals, there is no reason why the claim should not be expanded to cover cats, dogs, or mammals in general.[113] The broadening of claims is legitimate as long as there is no new matter introduced. However, if the description as filed only mentioned mice, then such broadening of the claims would add subject matter and thus be invalid.[114]

A simple illustration of the way the courts determine whether the amendment has introduced additional matter is provided by *Ward's Application*,[115] which concerned an application for a patent for the packaging of flowerpots. The specification as filed referred to the packaging of a number of articles nested one within another. It also referred to nested flowerpots or similar containers. Subsequent amendments that added references to plant pot bases were objected to by the Examiner on the basis that they extended the content of the application. Mr Bridges in the Patent Office concurred, saying that the question was whether 'the amendment...resulted in the specification disclosing matter which extends beyond that disclosed in the specification as filed...matter must not be disclosed which extends, in the sense of enlarging upon the original disclosure, i.e. which increases the specificity or particularization of that disclosure'.[116] On the basis that plant pot bases are recognizably different from plant pots, the specification breached section 76(3)(a).[117]

While the question whether an amended application contains additional subject matter always depends on the facts of the case, it may be helpful to outline some of the more common scenarios that may arise. It is not normally possible to amend a patent application where the description was insufficient.[118] As Lord Hoffmann said in *Biogen v. Medeva* the application may not add new matter to make an insufficient application sufficient. At the EPO applicants are prohibited from removing matter from a claim which appeared to be essential in the original application.[119] This is because, if the feature that is being removed was essential in the original application, then the amended feature introduces novel subject matter.[120] The

---

description, since support may justify broadening where novelty would not: *Xerox/Amendments*, note 87 above, 450. In the UK, the courts have referred to the novelty test employed at the EPO as a useful test but one which should be applied with caution. *Edwards v. Acme*, note 98 above, 644.

[110] *British Biotech/Heterocyclic compounds*, T684/96 [2000] *EPOR* 190, 197; *Advanced Semi-Conductor Products*, G1/93 [1994] *OJ EPO* 541.

[111] *Spring Foam v. Playhut* [2000] *RPC* 327, 337–8.

[112] *Southco v. Dzus Fastener Europe* [1990] *RPC* 587, 615.

[113] Broadening is permissible where there is a basis for a claim lacking the feature in the application as filed: *Amp/Connector*, T66/85 [1989] *EPOR* 283.

[114] *Edwards v. Acme Signs* [1992] *RPC* 131.   [115] [1986] *RPC* 50.

[116] *Ward's Application,* ibid, 54.

[117] For a more structured approach see *European Central Bank v. Document Security Systems* [2007] *EWHC* 600 (Pat).

[118] *Edwards v. Acme Signs* [1992] *RPC* 131, 147 (Staughton LJ).

[119] This will be so if the feature was essential in the original disclosure, is indispensable in the light of the technical problem, or the removal requires other features to be modified. *ALZA/Infuser*, T514/88 [1990] *EPOR* 157, 161–2. Adopted in *Southco v. Dzus Fastner Europe* [1992] *RPC* 299, 324 (Nicholls LJ), 327 (Staughton LJ) (CA).

[120] See *ALZA/Infuser*, above, 161–2.

prohibition on removing essential features does not prevent an amendment that introduces an essential feature that was previously described as non-essential.[121]

Often a patentee may wish to narrow the ambit of the patent. This usually occurs where a search reveals that some of the examples of prior art fall within the claims as originally filed or where subsequent experimentation reveals that some of the examples listed in the claims as filed do not work. Here, an applicant may amend the claim by disclaiming the examples.[122] While increasing the specificity of a claim, for example by narrowing it from mammals to mice, does not generally introduce new matter, it should not automatically be assumed that this is the case. The reason for this is that if the narrowing of the claims adds a technical feature (or something inventive) it will not be permissible.[123] However, if the limitation merely excludes protection for part of the subject matter of the application as filed, this would not give any unwarranted advantages to the applicant and as such is prima facie allowed.

4.2 AMENDMENTS THAT EXTEND THE SCOPE OF PROTECTION

In recognition of the fact that third parties may modify their behaviour in light of the patent as published, restrictions are placed on the degree to which the scope of protection conferred by the patent can be altered after grant.[124] To this end section 76(3)/Article 123(3) provide that amendments after grant must not extend the protection conferred by the patent. That is, after the patent has been granted, a patentee may not amend the scope of the claims so as to extend the monopoly beyond that covered by the claims as granted.[125] Failure to comply with these provisions opens the amended patent up to the possibility of revocation.[126]

The limits imposed on amendments that extend the scope of the patent operate in a similar way to the prohibition on amendments that introduce additional subject matter (discussed above). The provisions will not operate where claims are narrowed.[127] Perhaps the most notable situation where amendments have been allowed under this head is where they contain changes to the types of claim employed.[128] Thus, it is normally permissible to amend a claim from

---

[121] *Hymo/Water-soluble polymer dispersion*, T583/93 [1997] *EPOR* 129. The rule against the removal of essential features may explain the criticized decision in *Protoned BV's Application* [1983] *FSR* 110. See D. Stanley, 'Euphemism v. Pragmatism of the Implication of Added Subject Matter' (1988) 17 *CIPAJ* 108; G. Dworkin 'Implied Added Subject Matter: An Academic Overview' (1990–1) 20 *CIPAJ* 340.

[122] *Sulzer/Hot gas cooler*, T170/87 [1989] *OJ EPD* 441; *Mölnlycke (No. 5)* [1994] *RPC* 49, 135.

[123] If a limiting feature is not disclosed in the application as filed or otherwise derivable therefrom it will violate EPC Art. 123(2) [Now EPC 2000 Art. 123(2)]. *Advanced Semiconductor/Limited features*, G1/93 [1995] *EPOR* 97; [1994] *OJ EPO* 541; [1995] *EPOR* 110, 114.

[124] *Leland/Light source*, T187/91 [1995] *EPOR* 199, 202–3.

[125] PA s. 76(3) says that no amendment of the specification of a patent shall be allowed under PA ss. 27(1), 73, or 74 if it results in the specification disclosing additional matter or extends the protection conferred by the patent. PA s. 72(1)(e) provides for the revocation of patents on the ground that the protection conferred by the patent has been extended by an amendment which should not have been allowed. EPC 2000 Art. 123(3) [EPC 1973 Art. 123(3)] makes it clear that amendments of claims after grant (unlike those before) must not extend the scope of protection. The acceptance of post-grant amendments is subject to the discretion of the comptroller or court, who have tended to employ that discretion to deny amendments to those whose behaviour is not perceived to have been innocent.

[126] While it would be possible to allow widening amendments that are prospective only, it might be thought that a person should be able to rely on the patent in its state as granted rather than to have to constantly check to see whether it has been altered.

[127] *Strix v. Otter* [1995] *RPC* 607; *Mobil/Friction reducing additive*, G2/88 [1990] *OJ EPO* 93, 100–1.

[128] In *Philips Electronic's Patent* [1987] *RPC* 244, the patentee was permitted to add an omnibus claim to a European patent (UK) on the ground that it did not extend the scope of protection.

a compound to a use, since the claim to a use is narrower than the claim to the compound. Amendments of this type commonly arise where the patent application has been drafted on the basis that the compound was new *per se,* whereas it turns out that the compound was already within the state of the art, but the use was not.[129]

[129] *Moog/Change of category,* T378/86 [1988] *OJ EPO* 386 (an amendment of a process claim to include a claim to the apparatus for carrying out the process was allowed); cf. *Telectronics/Cardiac pacer,* T82/93 [1996] *OJ EPO* 274, where change from a method of operating a device (a pacer) to the device itself was not allowed, because the latter claim extended the subject matter to cover the situation where the pacer was ready for use (not just when it was being used).

21

OWNERSHIP

1 INTRODUCTION

Ownership plays a key role in shaping the way the rights and responsibilities that flow from the grant of a patent are organized. The owner, or as the Patents Act 1977 prefers, the proprietor of a patent is able to exploit and control the use that is made of a patent.[1] They are also able to make decisions about when and the conditions under which a patent can be assigned, licensed, or mortgaged.[2] The owner of the patent is also the person who is able to sue for infringement.[3]

The question as to who is the owner of a patent is closely connected with the question who is entitled to be granted the patent. This is because the chain of ownership begins with the person entitled to grant of the patent: they are treated as first owner (or proprietor) of the patent. It is important to note at the outset that the right to be granted a patent, which is the central focus of this chapter, is primarily given to the inventor or joint inventors. This presumption may be overridden in a number of situations: notably in relation to employee inventions and where the right to the patent has been transferred to a third party.

While a particular individual or group of individuals might *initially* have been given the right to be granted the patent, it does not necessarily follow from this that they will also be the owner of the patent. One reason for this is that the person entitled to grant of the patent may have assigned his or her rights in the patent to someone else. Alternatively, the patent may have been transferred to a third party as a result of death or insolvency. Consequently, in ascertaining ownership it is necessary to discover who was initially entitled to the grant of the patent, and thereafter, whether there has been an effective transfer of the patent to another person.

---

[1] 'Proprietor' is not defined in the 1977 Act.

[2] Under the 1977 Act, applications for a patent are also capable of being owned.

[3] The Patents Act 2004 amended PA s. 36(3) to clarify that co-owners are able to seek, amend, and revoke a patent if they act jointly, and have not contracted out of this requirement. See further: *Consultation on the proposed Patents Act (Amendment) Bill: Summary of responses and the Government's conclusions* (13 Nov. 2003), para. 115–124.

2 ENTITLEMENT TO GRANT

Given the consequences that flow from the ownership of a patent, it is not surprising that disputes often arise over who is properly entitled to be granted a particular patent. Questions about who is properly entitled to be granted a patent can arise both during and after the grant of a patent, and may even be heard prospectively, that is before any application has been made for a patent. In practice, however, most disputes tend to be heard after the patent has been granted.[4]

When the EPC was being drafted it was decided that matters relating to the ownership of patents were better dealt with by the national courts or tribunals, than by the EPC.[5] As a result, the European Patent Office has only a limited procedural role in determining disputes over entitlement.[6] The upshot of this is that while the processes by which patents are granted in the UK and the EPO are very similar, the procedures by which a UK patent and a European patent (UK) may be challenged are somewhat different. As such, we will deal with them separately.

2.1 UK PATENTS

The starting point for determining who is properly entitled to the grant of a British patent is set out in section 7(4).[7] This creates a rebuttable presumption that the patent applicant is the person who is entitled to be granted the patent. The grounds on which this presumption may be rebutted, which we deal with below,[8] are set out in section 7(2). If none of these grounds can be established, the applicant will be treated as the proprietor of the patent. The significance of the presumption should not be underestimated. This is because, as the evidence about entitlement is often inconclusive,[9] the presumption frequently operates to maintain the status quo.[10]

Prior to the grant of a patent for an invention, anyone may refer to the comptroller the question whether they are entitled to be granted (alone or with other persons) a patent for that

---

[4] This is because, if an issue is raised during the application under PA s. 8(1), but has not been determined by the time of grant, the dispute is usually continued as if it were a dispute as to the entitlement of a granted patent (that is, as if it were a PA s. 37 application). See PA s. 9; *Goddin & Rennie's Application* [1996] *RPC* 141.

[5] This was because disputes about entitlement potentially raise questions about legal personality, contract, equity, and labour law, rather than patent law.

[6] This issue was recently reopened in the *EC Green Paper on the Community Patent* where, after noting that the application of these different rules has an impact on research work and management, it asked respondents to indicate whether 'existing differences between member states laws on employees' inventions impacted on innovation and employment conditions and/or the freedom to provide services and/or the conditions of competition? Are they such as to justify harmonization at Community level?' See also Commission, *Comparative Study of Employees' Inventions Law in Member States of the European Communities* (1977).

[7] In answering the question who is the proprietor of the patent, a useful starting point is with the patent itself. This is because PA s. 13(2) provides that anyone who makes an application must state who the inventor is or, if the inventor is not applying, indicate on what basis they are applying. See T. Gold, 'Entitlement Disputes: A Case Review' [1990] *EIPR* 382.

[8] See above at pp. 377–9 and below at Section 3.

[9] In part, this is because it is often difficult to determine the precise point in time and the circumstances in which an invention was created. The reason for this is, as Lord Wilberforce said, that 'it is often difficult to fix the point or points in a continuous line of discovery at which an invention has been made'. *Beecham Group v. Bristol Laboratories International* [1978] *RPC* 521, 567.

[10] On the importance of the presumption see *Staeng's Patent* [1996] *RPC* 183; *Viziball's Application* [1988] *RPC* 213.

invention.[11] They may also ask the comptroller to determine whether they have or would have any rights in or under any patent so granted. While these issues will normally be referred to the comptroller, if the comptroller considers that the question involves matters that would be better dealt with by the court, the comptroller may refer the matter to the courts for consideration.[12]

The question who is properly entitled to a UK patent may also be raised after grant. Any person claiming a proprietary interest in a patent may ask the comptroller to clarify who is the true proprietor of the patent, whether the patent should have been granted to the person to whom it was granted, or whether any right in or under the patent should be transferred or granted to another person.[13]

2.1.1 Possible remedies

Where it has been decided that the wrong person has applied for a patent or a patent has been granted to the wrong person, the comptroller has a number of options available. In deciding what action to take, it has been said that the main aim should be 'to reach a solution which would provide a reasonable opportunity for the patent to be exploited should there be a demand for it':[14] a goal which reflects a desire to see that the invention enters the commercial domain, rather than a concern with recognizing entitlements.

Where a successful entitlement challenge has been made in relation to a patent application, the comptroller can refuse, amend, or transfer the application.[15] If the application is refused and the person properly entitled to apply decides to submit a new application, they may be able to avail themselves of the wrongful applicant's priority date.[16] Comptrollers also have jurisdiction to reach more creative solutions. For example, they may grant the patent to one co-inventor, but order that the other co-inventor be given a non-exclusive, non-assignable licence, perhaps with payment of a royalty.

Where a patent has been granted, an order may be made directing that the person referring the issue to the tribunal shall be listed as the proprietor of the patent. Alternatively, the comptroller may grant a licence to the claimant or revoke the patent on the ground that it was granted to the wrong person.[17] If it is decided that the patent should be revoked, the comptroller may order that the person who made the application (or their successor in title) may make a new application for a patent. It is important to note that no order may be made to transfer the patent or permit the reapplication if the reference was made two years from the date of the

---

[11] PA s. 8(1).   [12] PA s. 37(8).

[13] PA s. 37(1). See *Paxman v. Hughes* [2005] *All ER* (D) 255 (Comptroller has wide discretion to grant licences to third parties), *Hughes v. Paxman* [2007] *RPC* 34 (Comptroller has the jurisdiction to grant licence under s 37(1) on the application of one co-proprietor).

[14] *Goddin & Rennie's Application* [1996] *RPC* 141. The factors that were considered relevant in this case included whether either of the joint inventors wished to exploit the patent themselves, and the feasibility of their agreeing to license third parties.

[15] PA s. 8(2)(c). PA s. 8(2)(a) suggests that, where it is decided that the referent was the sole inventor, it will probably be ordered that the application shall proceed in the name of that person. Alternatively, if it is found that the invention was made jointly, the likely order is that the application proceed jointly.

[16] PA s. 8(3).

[17] That is, to a person not entitled under PA s. 7(2) or PA s. 36. PA s. 72(1)(b); EPC 2000 Art. 138 (1)(e). While lack of entitlement is a ground of revocation, it appears that the right to demand revocation is only available to a person 'initially entitled' to the patent, and not to someone to whom that right has been transferred. *Dolphin Showers and Brueton v. Farmiloe* [1989] *FSR* 1; *Henry Brothers v. Ministry of Defence* [1997] *RPC* 693. It remains unclear whether a declaration under PA s. 37 is required prior to an action for revocation under PA s. 72.

grant. This exclusion does not apply, however, if the proprietor of the patent knew that they were not entitled to the patent.[18]

2.2 EUROPEAN PATENTS (UK)

As we mentioned above, the European Patent Office only has a limited procedural role in determining disputes over entitlement. For the purposes of proceedings before the EPO, the applicant is deemed to be entitled to exercise the European patent, leaving issues of entitlement to be determined in national fora. As a result, the EPO only takes account of questions of entitlement if a decision has been made by an appropriate national court to the effect that a person other than the applicant is entitled to the patent. This means that questions relating to the ownership of European patents (UK)[19] both before and after grant[20] *may* be heard by the British comptroller[21] or courts.[22]

In order to prevent a proliferation of ownership proceedings in different member states (and to prevent forum shopping), a Protocol to the EPC was formulated (The Protocol on Jurisdiction and Recognition in Respect of the Right to a Grant of a European Patent).[23] The Protocol provides that questions about entitlement are only to be heard by one member state. The Protocol also establishes rules to determine the nation which has jurisdiction to hear ownership disputes.[24] In the absence of an agreement between the claimant and the applicant stating the jurisdiction which is to operate, the Protocol provides that questions about entitlement are to be determined by the tribunals (and the law) of the country of which the applicant is resident (or has their place of business). If the applicant is from outside the EPC, ownership is decided by the tribunal of the country of the claimant.[25] Consequently, a UK court would decline to hear a case concerning a dispute between a French claimant and a German applicant, or between a British claimant and a French applicant. It would, however, consider disputes between a German claimant and a British applicant, and between a British claimant and an American applicant.

2.2.1 Possible remedies

Once a national tribunal has made a determination as to entitlement, the EPO will take appropriate action. In these circumstances, Article 61 of the EPC provides that three courses of

---

[18] Protection for third parties in these situations is offered by PA ss. 37(6)–(7), 38(1), 38(3)–(4).

[19] PA s. 12(1); s. 77(1)(b). See *Norris's Patent* [1988] *RPC* 159; *Canning's US Application* [1992] *RPC* 459 (re international patent applications). *Kirin-Amgen/Erythropoietin*, T412/93 [1995] *EPOR* 629 (questions of entitlement could not be considered in opposition proceedings).

[20] It seems that the issue of jurisdiction will be determined in accordance with the general rules of the Brussels Convention and that Art. 16(4), which requires issues relating to the validity and registration of patents to be dealt with by the tribunals of the country from which the patent issued, has no applicability. See *Duijnstee v. Goderbauer* [1985] *FSR* 221; [1985] 1 *CMLR* 220.

[21] PA s. 37(8). For a discussion of the principles by which the Comptroller should exercise the discretion conferred by PA s. 12(20 see *Luxim Corporation* [2007] *EWHC* 1624.

[22] PA s. 82 provides for rules as to UK jurisdiction over disputes as to ownership of European patents. See *Kakkar v. Szelke* [1989] *FSR* 225.

[23] 5 Oct 1973.

[24] It also provided for the recognition of their decisions by other member states. See G. Le Tallac, 'The Protocol on Jurisdiction and the Recognition of Decisions in Respect of the Right to the Grant of a European Patent (Protocol on Recognition)' (1985) 16 *IIC* 318, 356.

[25] These are reflected in PA ss. 82 and 83.

action are available: prosecution of the application in the applicant's home state, the filing of a new application, or a request that the application be refused.[26]

3 DETERMINING WHO IS ENTITLED TO GRANT

While the Patents Act 1977 provides that anyone is entitled to apply for a patent,[27] section 7(2) goes on to say that patents should only be granted to a limited category of persons.[28] These provisions are the basis on which issues of entitlement are determined. As Lord Hoffmann said in *Yeda*, section 7(2) and section 7(3) provide an exhaustive code for determining who is entitled to the grant of a patent.[29] This means that the question whether a person is entitled to grant is solely dependent on them being able to show that they had been the actual inventor. In so ruling, the House of Lords rejected the argument that to prove entitlement, it was not enough for a person (A) to show that they and not the person (B) named on the patent were the actual inventor. In particular, the House of Lords rejected Jacob LJ's comment in *Markem* that '[A] must be able to show that in some way B was not entitled to apply for the patent, either at all or alone. It follows that A must invoke some other rule of law'—typically by virtue of contract or breach of confidence—'to establish his entitlement—that which gives him title, wholly or in part, to B's application'.[30] The upshot of *Yeda* is that the decision as to whether a person is properly entitled to grant of a patent turns solely on precisely who came up with the inventive concept: a question we look at shortly.

The starting point for determining issues of entitlement and ownership is section 7(2)(a). This provides that the right to be granted a patent is *primarily* given to the inventor or joint inventors. This focus upon the inventor follows the common practice whereby the creator is accorded the privileged status of first owner of intellectual property rights. Although the process of invention is frequently presented as being less creative than the production of literary or artistic works, patent law bears many of the marks of the romantic author. It is, at the very least, based on a model of an individual inventor; a matter emphasized in the 1977 Act by the requirement that the inventor be the 'actual deviser' of the invention.[31]

The assumption that the inventor is the person who is properly entitled to grant of the patent can be overridden in two situations. The first of these is set out in section 7(2)(b). This states that the presumption in favour of the inventor as owner does not apply where it can be established that at the time the invention was made, another person was entitled to the invention by virtue of (i) any enactment or rule of law, (ii) any foreign law, treaty, or international convention, or (iii) an enforceable term of any agreement entered into with the inventor before the making of

---

[26] *Latchways/Unlawful applicant*, G3/92 [1995] *EPOR* 141.   [27] PA s. 7(1).

[28] As we saw earlier, PA s. 7(4) creates a rebuttable presumption that the person who applies for a patent is the person who is entitled to grant of a patent. The grounds on which this presumption may be rebutted are set out in PA s. 7(2), which exhaustively sets out the parties to whom a patent may be granted.

[29] *Rhone-Poulenc Rorer International Holdings v. Yeda Research and Development Co Ltd* [2007] *UKHL* 42, [2007] *All ER* (D) 373 (HL), para 18.

[30] *Markem Corp v. Zipher* [2005] *RPC* 31 (para 79) (CA). For similar statements by Jacobs LJ (which were also expressly rejected by the House of Lords in *Yeda*) see *University of Southampton's applications* [2006] *RPC* 21, para 8 (CA).

[31] PA s. 7(3).

the invention. Although the precise meaning of the section is unclear,[32] it is widely accepted that it deals with employee inventions caught by section 39.

The second situation where the presumption in favour of the inventor as owner is overridden is set out in section 7(2)(c). This states that a patent may be granted to 'the successor or successors in title of any persons or persons mentioned in section 7(2)(a) or (b)'. This provision allows for the rights in the invention to be transferred to third parties. In all cases, it is important to note that in certain situations the registered proprietor may be able to rely upon the equitable rules of proprietary estoppel to prevent or limit the transfer of a patent under section 7(2).[33]

While section 7(2) potentially covers a broad array of situations, in practice questions relating to entitlement to grant tend to fall into two general areas: (i) inventors and joint inventors; and (ii) employee inventions. We will deal with each of these in turn.

3.1 INVENTORS AND JOINT INVENTORS

Being named as the inventor or joint inventor of a new product or process often carries with it a number of rewards. In addition to the kudos which is associated with being named as the creator of a new invention,[34] a lot flows from the presumption that patents are granted *primarily* to the inventor or joint inventors.[35] Given this, it is not surprising that the tribunals are often called upon to decide who is properly entitled to be named as inventor or joint inventor of a given invention.[36] Problems in this field tend to group together in two areas.

The first arises where someone claims that they and not the named inventor are the 'actual deviser' of the patented invention.[37] Problems also arise where an individual claims that their contribution to the invention has not been properly recognized.[38] In both situations, the courts are required to identify the 'inventive' elements of the invention. In turn, the courts are required to consider whether the claimant was responsible for the development of some

---

[32] Rather oddly it would not appear to cover the position of an employee who was a joint inventor with someone who was not also an employee, since the employer would not then be a person who, at the time of the making of the invention, was entitled to the *whole* of the property. It might have been assumed that such an anomaly would have been capable of being rectified by the use of express agreements between those concerned. However, the clause entitling a person to a patent as a result of being the beneficiary of 'an enforceable agreement entered into with the inventor before the making of the invention' is uncertain in scope too. See *Goddin & Rennie's Application* [1996] *RPC* 141. Because the provision excludes from its remit 'equitable interests', it is arguable that it would not cover a contractual agreement made prior to invention that a person was to assign their rights, because such an agreement creates a mere equitable right to the patent. However, such a pedantic interpretation seems to render redundant the provision relating to agreements, as well as to contradict the obviously desirable policy of encouraging the formation of such agreements allocating ownership.

[33] See *Yeda* [2007] *UKHL* 42; [2007] *All ER* (D) 373, para 22.

[34] Inventors are entitled to be named on the patent, even if they are not entitled to the patent: PA s. 13; EPC 2000 Arts. 62 and 81 [EPC 1973 Art. 62 and 81]. If the inventor is not designated, the application is treated as having been withdrawn, EPC 2000 Art. 90(5), EPC 2000 r. 60 [EPC 1973 Art. 91].

[35] PA s. 7(2)(a); EPC 2000 Art. 60(1). For a useful overview of the steps involved in determining whether parties were jointly entitled to an application see *Minnesota Mining and Manufacturing Companies' International Patent Application* [2003] *RPC* 28.

[36] See *IDA v. University of Southampton* [2006] *EWCA Civ* 145 (CA) (noting that there has been a recent rash of entitlement cases before the Comptroller and that these cases were particularly apt for mediation: para 44).

[37] 'Inventor' is defined in PA s. 7(3) to mean the 'actual deviser' of the invention. Joint inventors are construed accordingly.

[38] PA s. 10. For the application of PA s 7 see *Cinpres Gas Injection v. Melea* [2008] *EWCA Civ* 9 (CA). On US law, see W. Fritz Fasse, 'The Muddy Metaphysics of Joint Inventorship: Cleaning Up after the 1984 Amendments to 35 USC' (1992) 5 *Harvard Journal of Law & Technology* 153.

or all of those elements.[39] In some cases, the courts have been willing to divide an invention up into parts: allocating responsibility for different claims to different inventors. In a recent case the court emphasized that the appropriate way to determine who was the inventor was not to divide up the elements of a claim and ask who devised each; rather, it was necessary to interpret the claim so as to ascertain the essential inventive concept and then determine who contributed that concept.[40]

3.1.1 What is an inventive contribution?

In order to determine whether someone is entitled to be called an 'inventor' or 'joint inventor' under the 1977 Act, it is necessary to know what has been invented.[41] The courts have stressed that a person will not be regarded as an inventor merely because they have contributed to the claims: instead, to qualify as an inventor, a person needs to show that they have contributed to the 'inventive concept'.[42] As Lord Hoffmann explained in *Yeda,* the reason why it was not enough for someone to show that they had contributed to the claims was because the claims might include non-patentable integers derived from the prior art. The task of determining whether someone has contributed an inventive concept is a difficulty one, not least because the process of invention is often a complex process. As Lord Hoffmann went on to say, in some cases, the complexity can be attributed to the fact that 'the inventive concept is a relationship of discontinuity between the claimed invention and the prior art. Inventors themselves will often not know exactly where it lies.'[43] While certain contributions—such as the posing of the problem to be solved or the answering of those problems—are usually treated as being inventive, other contributions—such as the supply of the test tubes used in the experiments—would usually be regarded as being non-inventive. In between these two extremes there are a range of other types of contribution which are more difficult to categorize. The question that arises here is which of the various contributions that are made to the production of an invention ought to be recognized as being inventive (or technically creative) and which ought not.[44] This is a particularly complex issue, not least because what is considered to be inventive not only changes over time,[45] it also changes between different areas of science and technology.[46] Given

---

[39] For an analysis of this in the USA see *Mueller Brass v. Reading Industries* 352 *F. Supp.* 1357 at 1372–3. (ED Pa 1972), aff'd without opinion, 487 *F 2d* 1395 (3d Cir. 1973).

[40] *Henry Brothers v. Ministry of Defence* [1997] *RPC* 693.

[41] Ibid. [1999] *RPC* 442, 449 (Robert Walker LJ) (CA) (observing, at 452, that the 'whole question of co-ownership called for clarification').

[42] *GE Healthcare v. Perkin Elmer* [2006] *EWHC* 214 (Pat), para 146. 'The task of the court is to identify the inventive concept of the patent or application and identify who devised it': *Stanelco Fibre Optics v. Biopress Technology* [2005] *RPC* 319, para 12. See also Lord Hoffmann, *Yeda* [2007] *UKHL* 42, para 20.

[43] *Yeda* [2007] *UKHL* 42, para 20.

[44] The task of determining who is the inventor or joint inventor is similar to the non-obviousness inquiry. However, in contrast with the non-obviousness inquiry, which is determined 'objectively', the idea of inventorship carries a 'subjective' component. This arises because the inquiry can be undertaken even when no application has been made for a patent: PA s. 8(1)(a). See *Viziball's Application* [1988] *RPC* 213; *Goddin & Rennie's Application* [1996] *RPC* 141.

[45] For example, it is no longer possible to obtain a patent (as it was for a long time) merely for being the 'importer' of an invention. *Edgeberry v. Stephens* (1691) 1 *WPC* 35; 1 Hayward's Patent Cases 117.

[46] The question who should be recognized as creators in intellectual property law is an important and often contentious issue. Over time, the law has witnessed many occasions where interest groups have attempted to argue that they are creative enough to warrant the protection offered by intellectual property law. While these struggles may not be as visible in patent law as in other areas of intellectual property law, patent law is no exception to this general statement.

this, and that the definition of inventor offered in the Patents Act offers little guidance in this regard,[47] perhaps the best way to approach this issue is by example.

It is commonly accepted that where a person has done something that helps to solve a particular problem or answer a particular question, this will be regarded as an inventive contribution. As such, if it can be shown that an individual has done something that helps to solve a problem, it is likely that they will be treated as an inventor or joint inventor. While the answering of a problem is, in some ways, the archetypal inventive contribution, it is by no means the only type of contribution that is recognized as being inventive. For example, the perfection or improvement of a solution may also be regarded as an inventive contribution. Improvement of an existing device or process might itself provide for a patentable invention, in which case one would expect the patent to belong to the person who made the improvements (irrespective of the ownership of the starting invention). However, in practice the process of devising a patent may incorporate a series of elements, some of which are mere improvements of an initial breakthrough. In those circumstances, the question arises as to whether these later contributions are sufficient for their author to become a joint inventor.[48]

The generation of the idea or avenue for research, that is the formulation of the problem to be addressed, has also been treated as being inventive.[49] For example, in *Staeng's Patent,*[50] it was held that a person (A) was a joint inventor of a new method of securing electric cables, where it was unlikely that the main inventor (B) would have turned his mind to the question without having been prompted (by A). In this case, the Patent Office was influenced by the fact that the principal inventor, who did not work in the field, was only alerted to the possibility of the improvement by A.

In other cases, however, the mere posing of a question to be answered (or the recognition of the problem to be solved) will *not* be treated as an inventive contribution. The reason for this is that in some circumstances, particularly in the biotechnology industry, particular goals are commonly known (this is illustrated by the fact that a number of different companies often pursue the same goal).[51] In these circumstances, the decision to pursue a particular goal is unlikely to be treated as being sufficiently creative for it to be recognized as an inventive contribution.

3.1.2 What is a non-inventive contribution?

In the same way in which certain types of contribution are normally considered to be inventive, there are other types of contribution that are not. Thus where a party has only contributed 'unnecessary detail' to an invention, they will not be treated as an inventor.[52] It also seems that managerial and entrepreneurial contributions, such as the provision of money, facilities,

---

[47] Inventor is defined in PA s. 7(3) as the 'actual deviser'.

[48] In *Allen v. Rawson* (1845) 1 *CB* 551; 135 *ER* 656, Earle J said that, where a person collaborated in the elaboration of a 'main principle' and in so doing made valuable accessory discoveries, these were the property of the inventor of the original principle. The applicability and scope of this principle is, however, unclear. *Goddin & Rennie's Application* [1996] *RPC* 141.

[49] It was said in *Staeng's Patent* [1996] *RPC* 183, 189 that 'blowing the fire, rather than igniting it' can be sufficient for the contributor to be considered as the 'deviser' of the resulting invention.

[50] [1996] *RPC* 183. Under German law, the formula for calculating compensation for use of employee inventions gives equal weighting to those who 'elucidate' the problem and those who 'devise' the solution. See V. Schmied-Kowarzik, 'Employee Inventions under German Law' (1972) 54 *JPTOS* 807.

[51] See *Genentech v. Wellcome* [1989] *RPC* 147 (CA).

[52] *IDA v. University of Southampton* [2006] *EWCA Civ* 145 (CA), para 39.

materials, support staff, and the like, will not be regarded as inventive contributions (although the provider of such contributions may obtain the right to apply for a patent).[53]

Another type of contribution that seems to be excluded from what may be labelled as an inventive contribution is the supply of crucial starting materials.[54] In a celebrated American case, doctors at the UCLA Medical Center extracted a cell line from the spleen of the patient (and plaintiff) John Moore who was being treated for hairy-cell leukemia. The cell line formed the basis of an invention that was subsequently patented by the university. The Supreme Court of California held that Moore had no proprietary interests in the invention (or patent).[55] More specifically, the court held that he had no property rights in either the genetic information encoded in his cells or the cells themselves. In so ruling the court noted that everyone's genetic material contains information for the manufacture of lymphokines, and as a result that Moore's cell line was 'no more unique to Moore than the number of vertebrae in the spine'. The court contrasted the mundane nature of the source materials with the skills of the researchers, noting that the 'adaptation and growth of human tissues and cells in culture is difficult—often considered an art'. From the view of one commentator, the case illustrates the pervasive influence of the 'author construct' which leads intellectual property law to privilege certain kinds of contribution: the material basis of intellectual property is disregarded, while the researchers who manipulate that material are prioritized.[56]

A related issue arises in relation to bioprospecting. This is the practice whereby pharmaceutical firms, typically from the developed world, employ the knowledge of indigenous groups to identify the medicinal properties of local plants which are then sythentically reproduced. Perhaps one of the best-known examples of this is the US patent, which has subsequently been revoked, directed to the medicinal application of turmeric in wound healing (a practice that has been known about in India for centuries).[57] In an attempt to argue that indigenous peoples should be compensated for the use that is made of their knowledge, the question has been raised as to whether the contribution of indigenous knowledge (such as the identification of starting materials) ought to be recognized as an 'inventive' contribution to the resulting synthetic drugs. As the law is currently formulated, it seems that the provision of information is unlikely to amount to co-inventorship.[58] The main reason for this is that the contribution of knowledge about a plant's whereabouts or uses, especially where the information is already in

[53] *Morgan v. Hirsch*, 728 F 2d 1449, 1452 (Fed. Cir. 1984) (claimant confused entrepreneurship with inventorship); *3M International Patent Application* [2003] *RPC* 28, 556 (a party whose contribution was to identify or to draw attention to some prior art could qualify as an inventor in the appropriate circumstances).

[54] Cf. in the novelty examination, where the fact that prior art fails to disclose the starting materials may mean that the prior art does not destroy novelty. See above at pp. 474–6.

[55] *Moore v. Regents of the University of California*, 793 P 2d 479 (Cal 1990), cert denied, 111 S. Ct. 1388 (1991). It was accepted that Moore had a cause of action for breach of fiduciary duty or lack of informed consent. For some of the many commentaries see T. Dillon, 'Source Compensation for Tissues and Cells used in Biotechnical Research: Why a Source Shouldn't Share in the Profits' (1989) 64 *Notre Dame Law Review* 628; B. Edelman, 'L'Homme aux cellules d'or' (1989) 34 *Recueil Dalloz Sirey* 225; B. Edelman, 'Le Recherche biomedicale dans l'économie de Marché' (1991) 30 *Recueil Dalloz Sirey* 203; B. Hoffmaster, 'From the Sacred to the Profane' (1992) 7 *IPJ* 115.

[56] J. Boyle, 'A Theory of Law and Information: Copyright, Spleens, Blackmail, and Insider Trading' (1992) 80 *California Law Review* 1413, 1516.

[57] See M. Uniyal, 'Trade: Biopirates Stake Claim to Southern Knowledge', Inter Press Service, 29 Aug. 1996.

[58] M. Huft, 'Indigenous Peoples and Drug Discovery Research: A Question of Intellectual Property Rights' (1995) 89 *Northwestern University Law Review* 1678, 1728; M. Blakeney, 'Access to Genetic Resources: The View from the South' (1997) 3 *Bioscience Law Review* 94, 99.

the public domain,[59] is unlikely to be seen as an essential part of the structure and composition of a synthetically produced drug. As a result, many now accept that the goal of providing proper rewards to indigenous communities is better served by other means (such as by the international recognition of a *sui generis* right or by mandated contractual benefit-sharing arrangements).

In order for a contribution to an invention to rise to the level of joint inventorship, the contribution must be concrete and specific rather than vague or general.[60] Having said this, the courts have said that to qualify as an inventor, there was no need for a person to show that they have, to use the American concept, brought about 'a reduction to practice'. Thus, it was said that a person who comes up with and communicates an idea consisting of all of the elements in the claim, 'even though it is just an idea at that stage', will normally be treated as an inventor.[61] In contrast, if an inventor instructs an assistant or employee to carry out specific tests, it is unlikely that the assistant will be treated as a joint inventor. This is because the carrying-out of instructions is likely to be seen as a process of execution rather than creation. For the purposes of determining ownership between employers and employees, a person who merely contributes advice or other assistance in the making of an invention is not an inventor.[62] Outside the employer–employee context, such contributions are also likely to be treated as non-inventive unless it can be shown that the advice or assistance was in some way inventive.[63] It is also clear that if a person's contribution is limited to applying common general knowledge, their contribution will not be regarded as inventive.[64]

While there has been little guidance as to the amount of mental labour that a person must contribute to an invention for them to qualify as a joint inventor, there may be grounds for arguing that, where a person only makes a minor contribution to an invention, they should not be treated as a joint inventor. The reason for this is that joint inventors are sometimes able to control the ability of the other joint inventors to obtain or maintain a patent:[65] a power that might not be justified if the contribution is particularly small.[66] It should also be noted that in contrast with copyright law,[67] there is no explicit requirement in patent law that for a person to be recognized as a co-inventor, the parties must have collaborated. Having said this, it is clear that where two persons independently create the same invention, they will not be treated as co-inventors: the first to file is the person entitled to the patent.[68]

---

[59] Whether because the information is known within the community or because it has been documented by ethnobiologists. The classic anti-malarial drug, quinine, is derived from the bark of South American cinchona trees, the extract from which was first used to treat fever by the indigenous peoples of Peru in the eighteenth century. See Huft, 'Indigenous Peoples and Drug Discovery Research', 1700. See the observations of Lord Hoffmann in *Merrell Dow v. Norton* [1996] *RPC* 76, 88.

[60] It has been suggested that the 'conceptual specificity of a person's contribution' is a critical factor in deciding whether or not they are joint inventor. See R. Harris, 'Conceptual Specificity as a Factor in Determination of Inventorship' (1985) 67 *JPTOS* 315. *Garrett v. United States, 422 F 2d* 874, 881 (Ct Cl 1970).

[61] *Stanelco v. Biopress* [2005] *RPC* 319, para 14.

[62] PA s. 43(4). *Allen v. Rawson* (1845) 1 *CB* 551; 135 *ER* 656; *Smith's Patent* (1905) 22 *RPC* 57.

[63] *Staeng's Patent* [1996] *RPC* 183.

[64] *IDA v. University of Southampton* [2006] *EWCA Civ* 145 (CA), para 35.   [65] PA s. 36.

[66] A co-inventor who refuses to apply for a patent can have any such patent that has been granted to a co-inventor revoked.

[67] CDPA s. 11.

[68] The other inventor being left with such *in personam* defences as they can establish.

3.2 EMPLOYEE INVENTIONS

Although the romantic image of the amateur inventor plays an important role in shaping the way we think about patent law, it has long been recognized that many inventions are made by professional researchers who are employed to invent, often by large corporations:[69] a situation which has expanded rapidly with the growth of so-called big science in the last fifty years or so.[70] Patent law recognizes the financial interests of such employers by providing that in certain circumstances it will be the employer rather than the employee who will be the owner of inventions made by employees. In this way, patent law retains the romantic model of the inventor in name, but allocates the important monopoly rights to the commercial interests that support and maintain the research.[71]

When the EPC was being drafted it was decided that questions relating to ownership of employee inventions were a matter which was better dealt with by national laws rather than the EPC.[72] While the EPC (as with the CPC and the PCT) makes no provision in relation to employee inventions, when the Patents Act 1977 was drafted, the (then) Labour Government took the opportunity to regulate the position of employee inventors. In so doing they effectively codified an area which, prior to the enactment of the Act, was primarily dealt with by case law.[73]

There are two notable features of the Patents Act 1977 relating to employee inventions. The first, which is the focus of the remainder of this chapter, is that sections 39–43 of the Patents Act provide detailed guidance as to the way in which ownership disputes between employers and employees should be determined. The second notable feature of the Patents Act, which is dealt with in Chapter 23, is that employees are provided with a right of fair reimbursement (or compensation) where their inventions belong to their employers.

In deciding whether an invention made in the course of employment should belong to the employee or the employer, patent law had to balance a range of competing interests. On the one hand, a desire to protect and promote freedom of labour, particularly for activities carried on outside the scope of employment, lent support to those who favoured employee ownership. These arguments were supported by the long-standing principle that the inventor is the first owner of a patent. Mitigating against this, however, was the powerful and ultimately more

---

[69] Cf. S. Cherensky, 'A Penny for Their Thoughts: Employee-Inventors, Preinvention Assignment Agreements, Property, and Personhood' (1993) 81 *California Law Review* 595; J. Hughes, 'The Personality Interest of Artists and Inventors in Intellectual Property' (1998) 16 *Cardozo Arts & Entertainment LJ* 81.

[70] See P. Galison and B. Hevly (eds.), *Big Science: The Growth of Large Scale Research* (1992).

[71] For a comparative position see H. Parker, 'Reform for Rights of Employed Inventors' (1984) *Southern California Law Review* 603, 615ff.; Schmied-Kowarzik, 'Employee Inventions under German Law'; J. Joviczyk, 'Employee Inventions' (1989) 20 *IIC* 847.

[72] As such, national laws are free to determine ownership issues between employer and employee. All the EPC 2000 does is specify which national law should operate. *EC Green Paper on the Community Patent* (1997) COM (97) 314 final, para. 4.3 (explaining that there are great differences between member states' rules governing inventions by employees: that in some member states the question is dealt with in general terms by patent law (e.g. in France and the UK); in others a specific law has been enacted, as in Germany and Sweden. Other laws distinguish between 'permanent', 'temporary', and 'occasional' inventive roles, with different rules for determining ownership of the patent in each case. Other laws, such as the German Act, contain a long series of provisions relating to the remuneration of employees with an inventive role and lay down the precise method for calculating additional remuneration.)

[73] PA ss. 39–43 only apply to inventions made after 1 Jun. 1978. J. Phillips and M. Hoolahan, *Employee Inventions in the UK* (1982); W. Cornish, 'Rights in Employee Inventions: The UK Position' (1990) 21 *IIC* 290; W. Cornish, 'Rights in University Inventions' [1992] *EIPR* 13.

influential argument that where someone is employed to do something (such as invent), the employer and not the employee should be the owner of the resulting products (or inventions).

Disputes between employers and employees over who is entitled to apply for a patent, or if a patent has already been granted who is the rightful initial owner of the patent, are governed by section 39 of the 1977 Act. Following the common law position, the 1977 Act provides that an invention belongs to an employer in two situations.[74] Employee inventions that fall outside these two categories belong to the employee.[75]

The first situation where an employee invention belongs to the employer is where the invention was made in the course of the employee's normal or specifically assigned duties *and* the invention was made in circumstances where an invention might reasonably have been expected to have resulted from the carrying-out of those duties: section 39(1)(a).

The second situation where an employee invention belongs to an employer is set out in section 39(1)(b). This provides that in certain circumstances an employee's position and status within an organization will be such that they will be taken to be under a 'special obligation to further the interests of the employer's undertaking'. Thus, where an employee occupies a senior managerial or administrative position, any inventions that they produce belong to their employer.

3.2.1 Employer ownership of employee inventions

Before looking at the way ownership of employee inventions is allocated under the Patents Act 1977, it is necessary to take account of a number of preliminary points.

(i) Made in the course of employment. In order for section 39 to come into play, it is necessary to show that the invention was made by an 'employee' who was 'mainly employed' in the United Kingdom.[76] For the most part, showing that an invention was made in the course of employment is unlikely to present any major difficulties. Problems may arise, however, in situations where inventions are made by consultants, academics, visitors to universities, students, researchers on secondment, home-workers, and company directors.[77] While 'employee' and 'employer' are both defined in section 130 of the Act, this provides little guidance in these grey areas. In order to determine whether a particular inventor is in an employment relationship, a range of different factors are taken into account.[78] These include the relevent National Insurance and tax arrangements, the way the relationship is described by the parties, the provision of materials, as well as the control and responsibility that is exercised by the parties in question.

(ii) 'Inventions'. Another notable feature of section 39 is that it refers to 'inventions' rather than to 'patented inventions' (or some similar phrase). One of the consequences of this is that the section will operate to resolve issues of ownership irrespective of whether a patent

---

[74] PA s. 39(1)(a)(b). As the sections are not necessarily mutually exclusive, an employee may be caught by either subsection (a) or (b): *Memco-Med's Patent* [1992] RPC 403, 406.

[75] PA s. 39(2). PA s. 39(3), which was introduced by the CDPA, provides that where an employee is entitled to the patent, they may 'use material in support of the application in which the employer owns copyright or design.' For the common law position in the USA see *United States v. Dubilier Condenser Corp.,* 289 US 178 (1933), amended by 289 US 706 (1933).

[76] PA s. 43(2).

[77] See *CIPA,* para. 39.06. B. Sherman, 'Governing Science: Patents and Public Sector Research in the United Kingdom' (1995) 26 IIC 15.

[78] *O'Kelly v. Trusthouse Forte* [1984] QB 90; *Lee Ting Sang v. Chung Chi-Keung* [1990] 2 AC 374 (PC); *CIPA,* para. 39.06. For a discussion on equivalent provisions in copyright, see above Ch. 5 Section 3.

application has been filed or a patent granted. It has also been suggested that the fact that the section refers to inventions may mean that the section extends beyond patentable subject matter to include things such as suggestion schemes.[79]

(iii) Onus of proof. While evidential and procedural matters are often overlooked in discussions about patent law, decisions relating to the onus and standard of proof play an important role in shaping the way patent law operates in practice. Although the standard of proof in this context is clear enough—it is the civil standard of balance of probabilities—there is some uncertainty as to whether the onus of proof falls upon the employer or the employee. Given that the inventor is presumed to be the owner of the patent and that section 39 provides exceptions to this, it would seem reasonable to expect that the onus of proof falls upon the employer to establish that a particular employee invention belongs to them as a result of section 39(1)(a) or (b). Mitigating against this, however, is the fact that in a number of cases the comptroller has presumed that the onus of proof falls upon the person who is putting the question of entitlement in issue.[80] As this approach concentrates on the person who makes the application, rather than on the relative bargaining powers of the parties, if it is not an untenable position then it certainly is an undesirable position.[81]

(iv) It is not possible to diminish the rights of employees by contract. In order to protect an employee whose inferior bargaining position may lead them to sign their statutory rights to their employer, section 42 of the 1977 Act provides that any term in a contract of employment[82] which diminishes the rights of an employee in any invention shall be unenforceable against the employee.[83] The scope of the section is limited by the fact that it does not apply in relation to an employee's duty of confidentiality.[84] It is also limited in that section 42 does not seem to prohibit contracts dealing with inventions created after an employee leaves employment.[85] The reason for this is that while such contracts may appear to fall within the terms of section 42, the section probably has no application because the inventions will have been made when the inventor was no longer in employment.[86] The exact scope of the provision, and the degree to which it modifies the common law rules in this area, remain unclear.

With these initial points in mind, we now turn to look in more detail at the two situations in which employee inventions will belong to an employer.

---

[79] In other contexts it has been held that 'invention' encompasses unpatentable subject matter: *Viziball's Application* [1988] *RPC* 213.

[80] *Staeng's Patent* [1996] *RPC* 183; *Viziball's Application*, above.

[81] *CIPA*, para. 39.07. In *Greater Glasgow Health Board's Application* [1996] *RPC* 207, where an employee agreed to allow the employer to proceed with a patent application pending a decision, Jacob J said that it would be unfortunate if anything turned on the question of onus of proof.

[82] The provisions apply to contracts of employment, as well as to contracts made between employees and third parties either at the request of the employer or in pursuance of the employee's contract of employment. The section applies both to contracts made before and after the 1977 Act came into force.

[83] PA s. 42(2).

[84] On the question of employee's duty to disclose inventions and its relationship with PA s. 44, see *CIPA*, para. 42.02. More generally see J. Turner, 'Pre-invention Assignment Agreement Breach: A Practical Alternative to Specific Performance or Unqualified Injunction' (1997) 5 *JIPL* 631.

[85] In the USA these are called 'holdover' or 'trailer clauses'. See Hershovitz, 'Unhitching the Trailer Clause: The Rights of Inventive Employees and Their Employers' (1995) 3 *JIPL* 187.

[86] Even if these were not invalidated by s. 42, they would be subject to the doctrine of restraint of trade. See *Electrolux v. Hudson* [1977] *FSR* 312.

3.2.2 Persons employed to invent

The first situation where an employee invention belongs to an employer is set out in section 39(1)(a). This provides that an invention made by an employee will belong to their employer if the invention was made in the course of the employee's normal or specifically assigned duties *and* the circumstances in which the invention was made were such that 'an invention might reasonably have been expected to result from the carrying out of those duties'.

(i) Scope of an employee's duties. In order to determine whether an employee invention belongs to the employer by virtue of section 39(1)(a), it is necessary to determine the scope and nature of an employee's duties. It is then necessary to ascertain whether the invention was made by the employee carrying out those duties.

The job description and the contract of employment are often used as a way of determining the precise nature of an employee's normal duties.[87] There has also been a willingness to look beyond the formal legal arrangement of the contract of employment to the activities that are *actually* undertaken by the employee.[88] Once the scope of an employee's normal duties has been ascertained it is relatively easy to determine whether an employee has been assigned any additional duties.

Once the duties of the employee have been ascertained it is necessary to determine whether the invention was made 'in the course of those duties'. The factors to be considered include when and where the invention was made, the facilities used by the employee, and the relationship between the invention and the field in which the employer operates.[89] So long as it can be shown that the activity in question falls within the general scope of employment, this is unlikely to present any major problems.

(ii) Duties which can be expected to result in an invention. As well as establishing that the invention was made in the course of an employee's normal or special duties, the second limb of section 39(1)(a) provides that it is also necessary to show that the invention was made in circumstances where an invention might reasonably have been expected to result from the carrying-out of such duties.

One of the notable aspects of the second limb of section 39(1)(a) is that it requires that *the* invention be made in circumstances where *an* invention might reasonably be expected to result from the carrying-out of the employee's duties. The question what is meant by 'an invention' in this context was considered by Falconer J in *Harris's Patent* where he said that 'an invention' did not mean *any* invention, nor did it mean 'the precise invention that was made'.[90] While Falconer J's comments are useful in telling us what the phrase does not mean, it offers little positive guidance as to what it does mean.[91] One possibility is that it

---

[87] *Staeng's Patent* [1996] *RPC* 183, 198 (the job description will normally be decisive).

[88] *LIFFE Administration and Management v. Pinkava* [2007] *RPC* 667 (CA), stressing that, while the employment contract was an important starting point, the duties of an employee often evolved over time. In *Harris's Application* [1985] *RPC* 19, there was no evidence as to the contract of employment and Falconer J looked at what was actually done. See also *Greater Glasgow* [1996] *RPC* 207, 222. It should be noted, that most of the cases begin, at least as a starting point, with the job description.

[89] In *Staeng's Patent*, note 10 above, it was suggested that any invention that was useful to the employer would automatically fall within the employee's duties, cf. *Greater Glasgow* [1996] *RPC* 207, 222. See P. Chandler, 'Employee's Inventions: Inventorship and Ownership' [1997] *EIPR* 262.

[90] *Harris's Application*, above, 29.

[91] In this context it is interesting to note that PA s. 40(7) speaks of 'inventions of the same description'. In *Harris*, above, 29 Falconer J said that the phrase an 'invention might reasonably have been expected to result

could be construed to mean an invention of the same description or type as the invention in suit.[92]

An important factor which is often relied upon when deciding whether there was an expectation that the carrying-out of the employee's duties would lead to an invention is the extent to which the employee was engaged to invent or design.[93] Inventions that are made by an employee whose duties are limited to mechanical, routine, or non-creative tasks will ordinarily remain with the employee.[94] This can be seen in *Harris's Patent*:[95] an ownership dispute between Reiss, who manufactured valves under licence from Sistag, and Harris, who worked as a manager for Reiss. The particular issue in dispute was whether Reiss or Harris owned rights in a valve, invented by Harris, which controlled the flow of dust through ducts. A number of factors led the court to its finding that the invention belonged to Harris. These included the fact that Harris's normal duties were limited to the non-inventive tasks of sales and after-sales service. Importantly, in dealing with customer problems, Harris's role was limited to non-creative or routine application of known engineering practices. The fact that Reiss had no research laboratory, was not involved in research and development, and always referred major technical problems to Sistag for solution, reinforced the conclusion that Harris had not been employed to design or invent. Indeed, when Harris made suggestions to Reiss as to how the valves could be improved, Reiss turned them down. Given that it was not part of the employer's business to solve design problems in valves, it could hardly have been a part of Harris's duties.[96]

Where a person is employed to invent or design, there will ordinarily be an expectation that the carrying-out of the employee's duties would lead to an invention and, as such, that any inventions which are made will belong to their employer. This is the case even if the creative aspect of an employee's duties only forms a small part of an employee's overall duties. For example, in *Staeng's Patent*[97] it was held that while an employee was primarily engaged in marketing, the fact that his job description also assigned to him the creative role of using discussions with customers to generate ideas for new products, as well as thinking of novel uses for existing products, meant that any inventions he made belonged to his employer. As yet, it is unclear how small the creative contribution of an employee's duties needs to be for section 39(1)(a) not to apply.

3.2.3 Special obligations

The second situation in which an invention made by an employee will belong to his or her employer is set out in section 39(1)(b). While section 39(1)(a) primarily deals with people who are employed to invent or design, section 39(1)(b) is concerned with inventions which are made by managerial or administrative employees. More specifically, section 39(1)(b) provides

from the carrying out of the duties' refers to 'an invention which achieves, or contributes to achieving, whatever was the aim or object to which the employee's efforts in carrying out his duties'.

[92] Another aspect of PA s. 39 that is unclear is that the section provides that the invention must be made in cicumstances where it might reasonably be 'expected'. It is unclear who it is that ought to expect the invention, whether the invention ought to be expected by the employee, the employer, or, most probably, an objective third party.

[93] Presumably, the status of the employee, a factor normally limited to PA s. 39(1)(b), would influence whether an invention would be 'expected'. It was said in *Greater Glasgow* [1996] *RPC* 207, that this was to be judged in terms of the circumstances in which the invention in suit was made and not the general circumstances of employment.

[94] Ibid, 222. It was said that a duty to treat patients did not impose a general duty to invent new ways of diagnosing and treating patients.

[95] [1985] *RPC* 19.   [96] Ibid, 32.   [97] [1996] *RPC* 183.

that in certain circumstances an employee's position within an organization is such that they are deemed to be under a special obligation to further the interests of their employer. While the normal or special duties of an employee may not require them to invent or design, this is overidden by the fact that their seniority effectively places them under a legal obligation not to compete with the firm.[98] This fiduciary principle, which is embodied in section 39(1)(b), means that if an employee who occupies a senior position within an organization produces an invention and it can be shown that the invention was made in the course of the duties of the employee, the invention will belong to the employer.

Whether an employee is under a 'special obligation' largely depends upon the position that the employee occupies within an organization and the responsibilities that flow from that position. Employees who occupy senior positions, such as senior executives, directors, and managers, are treated as alter egos of their employers and are, as such, under a 'special obligation to further the interests of the employer's undertaking'.[99] In contrast, fewer obligations are imposed on less senior employees, such as sales managers or marketing managers.[100] The difficult issue here is deciding at what point within the hierarchy of an organization section 39(1)(b) ceases to apply: how junior must an employee be for them to retain the inventions which they produce?

We are able to gain some guidance as to where this line is to be drawn if we compare *Harris's Patent,* where the employee was held not to be under a special obligation, with *Staeng* where section 39(1)(b) applied. As we saw earlier, *Harris's Patent* turned on the question of whether an invention made by Harris belonged to Harris, as employee, or Reiss, as employer. As well as failing under section 39(1)(a), section 39(1)(b) was also held not to apply. This was because while Harris was called a manager, when the court looked at what Harris actually did, it found that he had no power to hire, fire, or agree holiday dates, he never attended board meetings (even when his department was being discussed), and had limited financial control. As such, the court found that Harris did not owe a 'special obligation' to his employer. Rather, they found that he was only under an obligation to do the best that he could to effect sales of the valves and related customer after-care service. Consequently, the court concluded that as Harris was not under a special obligation, the invention in question belonged to Harris. In contrast, in *Staeng's* case the employee operated at a very senior level: he attended board meetings; often acted in a similar capacity to the directors; had some control over budgetary matters (such as the product range); was party to the company's profit-bonus scheme; and had discretion whether to solve problems himself or to pass them on to others. From this basis, the court concluded that Staeng was under a special obligation under section 39(1)(b). As such, the invention he made belonged to his employer.

---

[98] In many circumstances this implied duty of good faith meant that an employee was under a duty to assign the patent to the employer: *Patchett v. Sterling* [1955] *RPC* 50; *British Syphon v. Homeword* [1956] *RPC* 330. The statutory rule may be more strict than the common-law position: on which see *Worthington Pumping Engine Company v. Moore* (1903) 20 *RPC* 41.

[99] Ibid, 46. It was said in *Harris's Application* [1985] *RPC* 19 that pre-1977 cases offered guidance as to the extent and nature of an employee's obligations to further the interest of his employer's undertakings.

[100] *Harris,* above, 37–8.

22

INFRINGEMENT

CHAPTER CONTENTS

1 INTRODUCTION

Patent infringement is a notoriously complex area of law.[1] In part this is a consequence of the evidential nature of the inquiry, a fact that often makes it difficult to generalize beyond the particular case in hand. Another factor that has added to this complexity (but simultaneously enhanced the effectiveness of the patent system) is that it has long been accepted that the scope of the patent monopoly should not be limited to situations where the infringing act takes place in relation to a product or process which is exactly the same as the patented invention. While extending the scope of the monopoly beyond a strict reading of the claims may have satisfied the law's desire to protect the equity of the patent, it generated a new question: how broadly can the patent be read? Similarly, when it was agreed that not all of an invention needed to be taken for a patent to be infringed, the question arose: how much of the invention needs to be taken? The difficulties that these questions generate further accentuate the problems that arise in understanding patent infringement.[2]

The complexity of the topic is also a consequence of Britain's entry into the European Patent Convention. When the EPC 1973 was drafted it was decided that questions about the infringement of patents issued by the EPO were better dealt with by national courts.[3] Nonetheless, the close relationship between validity and infringement has meant that decisions at the EPO (particularly in relation to novelty) have impacted on the British law of infringement. These

---

[1] It is also potentially a very costly process. In one case it was suggested that it cost £250,000 for a two-day trial in the county court and about £112,000 for the Court of Appeal: *Warheit v. Olympia Tools* [2003] *FSR* 6.

[2] See A. Benyamini, *Patent Infringement in the European Community* (1993).

[3] Infringement proceedings can be also brought before the comptroller so long as both parties consent: PA s. 61(3). The suggestion that the 1977 Act be amended to remove the need for the consent of both parties was not adopted in the proposals for reform of the 1977 Act. See *Consultation on the proposed Patents Act (Amendment) Bill: Summary of responses and the Government's conclusions* (13 Nov. 2003), para. 115–124.

transitions have proved to be all the more problematic because of the absence of a common tribunal dealing with infringement. To some extent, the uncertain nature of a patent infringement or at least some aspects thereof, have been clarified by the House of Lords decision on patent infringement under the 1977 Act.

Despite its complex and often uncertain nature, determining patent infringement can be separated into three tasks.

(i) First, it is necessary to determine the types of activity that constitute an infringement.

(ii) Second, it is necessary to ascertain whether the activity complained of falls within the scope of the patent monopoly.

(iii) Third, it needs to be determined whether the defendant is able to make use of any of the defences that are available to them.

Each of these tasks will be dealt with in turn.

2 TYPES OF INFRINGING ACTIVITY

It is important to note at the outset that patent law draws a general distinction between direct and indirect infringement. The main difference between them is that direct infringement involves some immediate engagement with the patented product or process,[4] whereas indirect infringement applies where a person facilitates the act of infringement:[5] in effect a patent law version of aiding and abetting. Before looking at direct and indirect infringement in more detail, it is important to note that to infringe the activity must be carried out without the consent of the patentee (i.e. the activity must not be covered by licence);[6] occur within the UK;[7] and take place during the duration of the patent.[8]

2.1 DIRECT INFRINGEMENT

For a patentee to succeed in an infringement action they must show on the balance of probabilities that the defendant performed one of the activities that falls within the patent owner's control.[9] The primary rights given to a patent owner are set out in section 60(1). As we will see, section 60(1) covers a wide array of activities from the making or using of a product or a process, through to the sale or import of the product. As a result, most if not all of the commercially valuable activities are within the owner's control.

The rights given to an owner differ depending on whether the patent is for a product, a process, or a product obtained directly from a process. It is important to note that, with the exception of the situation where an infringer uses a process or 'offers a process for use' under section 60(1)(b), direct infringement takes place irrespective of the knowledge of the defendant. This

---

[4] PA s. 60(1).

[5] PA s. 60(2); CPC Art. 26. The Patents Act also contains provisions in relation to contributory infringement.

[6] See below at pp. 572–3.

[7] The UK includes the Isle of Man and the territorial waters of the UK, PA s. 132(2)(3).

[8] A patentee may only sue with respect to acts that occur after publication of the application and then only if the patent has been granted. PA s. 62(3) introduces certain qualifications where the patent application is amended after publication. PA s. 62(2) deals with the position where the patentee fails to renew the patent promptly. For considerations of duration and supplementary protection certificates see below at pp. 602–6.

[9] PA s. 60(1)–(2); CPC Arts. 25–8.

means that liability is absolute in relation to a patent for a product, or where a product has been obtained directly from a patented process. As such, there is no need for a patentee to show that the defendants knew that they were infringing. In these cases, independent, accidental, or unintentional creation of the same invention will infringe.

2.2 PATENT FOR A PRODUCT

The owner of a patent for a *product* is given the right to make, dispose of, offer to dispose of, use, import, or keep the product, whether for disposal or otherwise.[10] It is important to note that in this context liability is absolute: the knowledge of the defendant is not relevant when deciding whether they have carried out one of the activities within the owner's control. While intention to infringe is not relevant to the determination of liability, *mens rea* might play a significant role in relation to the remedy granted by the court.[11]

Three different rationales are usually given to explain why patent liability is absolute.[12] The first and most general is that the principle is necessary to allow patentees full enjoyment of their monopoly rights.[13] This is often said to be more pressing because of the onerous nature of the validity requirements imposed on patent applicants. When thinking about assertions of this nature, it is important to remember that property rights are never absolute and that the rights recognized in patents are no exception to this.[14] For example, patents are limited in terms of duration, scope of operation, subject matter, and types of activity that are protected. As such, there is little, if anything, in this argument that demands that infringement be absolute.

The second argument in favour of the principle that the intention of the defendant is irrelevant can be traced to the so-called reverse-infringement test which is sometimes used to determine whether an invention is novel.[15] Under this test, which is based on a belief that the novelty examination is a mirror of the test for infringement, the court asks the following hypothetical question: if the disclosure was made or took place after grant, would it have infringed the patent (if granted)? If yes, then the disclosure is anticipatory.[16] The next step in the argument is to remind us that when considering whether information in the public domain anticipates an invention, the intention of the person who made that information public is irrelevant (that is, novelty is decided objectively). On the basis that novelty and infringement are mirrors of each other and that novelty is determined objectively, it is therefore suggested that infringement should also be decided objectively. While the reverse-infringement test was approved in the

---

[10] PA s. 60(1)(a).   [11] PA s. 62(1). See further below Ch. 48 Section 5.

[12] The following cases are usually cited in support: *Proctor v. Bennis* (1887) *RPC* 333, 356–7 (no real justification given); *Curtis v. Platt* (1863) 3 *Ch D* 135 at 140n; *Valensi v. BRC* [1972] *FSR* 273, 306 (adds nothing); *Stead v. Anderson* (1847) 2 *WPC* 151, 156; *Wight v. Hitchcock* (1870) *LR* 37, 47 (argument based on a version of parallel importing: 'if the law were otherwise...another might by merely crossing the Channel, and manufacturing abroad, and selling for far less than the original price...wholly deprive the patentee of the benefit of the invention'); *Walton v. Lavater* (1860) 8 *CB (NS)* 162, 186; 29 *LJ (CP)* 275, 279; *Betts v. Neilson* (1865) 34 *LJ (Ch)* 537; *Elmslie v. Boursier* (1869–70) *Law Rep 9 Eq* 217.

[13] *Lishman v. Erom Roche* (1996) 68 *CPR (3d)* 72 at 77 (FCTD).

[14] R. Gordon, 'Paradoxical Property', in J. Brewer and S. Staves (eds.), *Early Modern Conceptions of Property* (1995), 95. '[P]atents do not create wholly controlled monopolies. They confer on their owners the narrower benefit of exclusive commercial exploitation for a duration limited to twenty years. Even during the currency of the patent, members of the public are free to conduct experiments on the patented invention'. Lord Irvine of Lairg, 'The Law: An Engine for Trade' (2001) 64 *MLR* 333.

[15] See, e.g. *Robert Alfred Young and Robert Neilson v. Rosenthal* (1884) *RPC* 29, 31–33.

[16] The classic statement is provided by Sachs LJ in *General Tire & Rubber v. Firestone Tyre & Rubber* [1972] *RPC* 457, 485–6.

United Kingdom in a number of decisions under the Patents Act 1977,[17] it has become clear that it is no longer the test to be applied to determine whether an invention is novel.[18] Instead of determining novelty by asking whether, if the disclosure had been made after grant, it would infringe the patent (if granted?), the focus of the 'new' law is much more upon novelty in its own right. In any case, while the test may have brought conceptual clarity to the novelty examination, it offers little real guidance when considering whether intention should be a factor taken into account when deciding infringement.

The third argument in support of the principle that the intention of the defendant is irrelevant in deciding infringement focuses on the existence of the patent register and the information function performed by the patent system more generally. Here, the potential harm that third parties might endure as a result of infringement being absolute is said to be mitigated by the fact that as part of the patent process, the invention is made available to the public. More specifically, it is argued that as information about the patented invention is in the public domain, third parties are able to access the information and subsequently alter their behaviour (or licence the patent), and thus avoid infringing the patent. While this rationale *might* carry some weight in relation to mechanical inventions, it is not as easily applied to biological inventions. This is because the rationale for strict liability is based on an image of the invention as something inert, static, and (largely) immutable. In the case of mechanical inventions (where it is the behaviour of the defendant that determines whether they infringe), would-be defendants are able to modify their conduct to ensure that they do not do so. However, in the case of biological inventions, which are dynamic and active, there may be very little (if anything) that a defendant can do to avoid infringing. Given that the infringement might be traced to the action of the invention (rather than the defendant), this may be the case even if the defendant had known about the patented invention.

The potential problems that arise in relation to biological inventions were highlighted by the Canadian decision of *Monsanto v. Schmeiser*,[19] where a farmer was successfully sued for infringing Monsanto's patent for glyphosate-resistant plants, when patented plants were found growing on his property. Importantly, it was held that the principle of strict liability meant that it did not matter whether the defendant farmer had planted the infringing plants, or whether, as he claimed, the plants were there as a result of conduct outside his control (including cross-field breeding by wind or insects; seed blown from passing trucks with loose tarpaulins; seed dropped from farm equipment; and seed that had escaped when a neighbour dropped a bag of Monsanto's seed from his truck): all that mattered was that there had been an unauthorized use of the patented invention. The decision is important since it highlights the possibility of, and some of the problems associated with, what could be called passive infringement of biological inventions. This is the fact that farmers, through no fault of their own, may be liable for patent infringement when a patented plant 'invades' their property and cross-pollinates with one of their plants. (Similar problems could arise with genetically modified animals.) The possibility of passive infringement has important ramifications for the traditional farming practice whereby seeds saved from one year's harvest are used to sow crops in the following year. Even if this does not occur, the mere possibility of passive infringement of biological inventions will increase the pressure on farmers to obtain licences to use patented inventions of this nature. It is, however, a problem that could easily be remedied through the introduction of a defence for passive infringement.

---

[17] See, e.g. *PLG Research v. Ardon International* [1993] *FSR* 197, 218.
[18] Arguably, the test never did state the law accurately since the carrying-out of instructions which might (rather than inevitably would) lead to the invention was not thought to be an anticipation, though clearly on some occasions after grant it would amount to infringement.
[19] *Monsanto v. Schmeiser* [2004] 1 *SCR* 902, 2004 *SCC* 34 (Supreme Crt. of Canada).

2.2.1 The right to make the product

Perhaps the most important right given to the owner of a patent for a product is the exclusive right to 'make' the product. Few problems have arisen in determining what is meant by the right to make a product. One exception to this is where the defendant repairs or modifies the patented product. Patent law has long recognized that purchasers of patented products should be able to repair and modify those products. As Lord Hoffmann said in the *United Wire* decision, 'repair is one of the concepts (like modifying or adapting) which shares a boundary with "making" but does not trespass on its territory'. He added that 'as a matter of ordinary language, the notions of making and repair may well overlap. But for the purposes of the statute, they are mutually exclusive. The owner's right to repair is not an independent right conferred upon him by licence, express or implied. It is a residual right, forming part of the right to do whatever does not amount to making the product.'[20] At the same time, however, patent law has been keen to ensure that while a person who obtains a patented product is able to repair or modify the product, they may not go so far as to make the product anew.[21] In these circumstances, the question arises: how much of a product is a person able to repair or modify before they infringe the owner's right to make the product? That is, when does the legitimate act of repair or modification switch to become the illegitimate making of the patented product?

The way these questions are answered depends upon the circumstances of the case under consideration. It seems that both quantitative factors, such as the amount of the product that is repaired, and qualitative considerations, such as the relative importance of the part of the patented product that has been repaired, are likely to be taken into account.[22] It is less likely for a court to hold that a person has made a patented product when they have repaired an immaterial part of a product.[23] For example, if a patented product related to the invention of a pool table with a novel coin-operating system, it would almost certainly be legitimate for a person to replace the cloth on the pool table. It would probably not be legitimate, however, for them to replace an old coin-operating system with a new one, since it is likely that this would be an essential component of the invention.[24] Where purchasers of a patented article are entitled to repair the product, they 'must be entitled to carry out what is a genuine repair whether it is economical to do so or not, and whether the part repaired or replaced in the course of what is truly a repair is crucial to the function of the patented article or not'.[25] It also seems that, if the repaired article does not work as well or as safely as the original product, this will not affect the decision as to whether the repair is legitimate.[26]

2.2.2 The right to dispose of the product

Another important right given to the owner of a product patent is the right to sell (or vend) the product. The right to sell, which is part of the general right to dispose of the invention,[27]

---

[20] *United Wire v. Screen Repair Services* [2000] 4 *All ER* 353 (HL). Prior to this decision, the right to repair had sometimes been based on the idea of implied licence: *Solar Thomson Engineering v. Barton* [1977] *RPC* 537, 555; *British Leyland v. Armstrong* [1986] *RPC* 279, 358, 361–2 (Lord Bridge). Cf. *Canon v. Green Cartridge Co.* [1997] *FSR* 817, 822; *Hazell Grove v. Euro League Leisure* [1995] *RPC* 529, 537–41.

[21] *Solar Thompson,* above; *Sirdar Rubber v. Wallington Weston* (1907) 24 *RPC* 537 (Lord Halsbury); *BL v. Armstrong*, above, 376.

[22] *Sirdar Rubber,* ibid.   [23] *United Wire v. Screen Repairs,* above.

[24] *Hazell Grove,* above.   [25] *Solar Thompson v. Barton,* above, 555 (Buckley LJ).

[26] Ibid, 556–7 (Buckley LJ). *Dellareed v. Delkin Developments* [1988] *FSR* 329; approved in *Hazell Grove,* above, 541.

[27] *Gerber Garment v. Lectra* [1995] *RPC* 383. To be an infringing act an 'offer to dispose' must be made in the UK and propose disposal within the UK: *Kalman v. PCL Packaging* [1982] *FSR* 406. For issues relating to joint tortfeasance where the joint tortfeasor is located outside the jurisdiction, service out of the jurisdiction, and actions for infringement of foreign patents see below at pp. 1075–6.

includes the sale of individual articles.[28] It also applies where the patented product is sold to people who intend to use the article in non-infringing activities (such as sale to a person who intends to use the article for experimental purposes).[29] A patent owner's right to dispose of a product will be infringed where a person supplies the product in kit form. As with all infringement actions, the kit must fall within the scope of the claims.[30] If the kit partially falls outside the claims, a patentee will have to rely on indirect or contributory infringement to prevent sale of the kits.[31] These matters are discussed below.[32]

Implied licences and exhaustion.   A patent owner's ability to control the way patented products are disposed of is limited by the common-law doctrine of implied licence and the doctrine of exhaustion as developed under Community law. According to the doctrine of implied licence, in the absence of any limitation to the contrary, where the patentee sells a patented product, the patentee is unable to rely on the patent to prevent the resale of the article. This is because the sale of a product carries with it an implied licence to keep, use, and resell the product.[33] However, where there is an express limitation, it will bind those who receive the goods with notice of the limitation: unless the limitation contravenes Article 28 or 81 EC (formerly Articles 30 and 85 of the Treaty of Rome).

Under the doctrine of exhaustion,[34] a patentee is unable to use a patent to prevent the further disposal of an article that has been placed on the market in the EEA with the patentee's consent.[35] Consequently, an express limitation on further disposal of a patented article will contravene Article 28 and thus be void if it prevents import into or resale in another member state.[36] However, such a limitation might enable a UK patentee to prevent export to Australia, or perhaps further disposal within the United Kingdom.[37]

2.2.3 The right to import the product

The patentee has the right to control the import of products that fall within the scope of the product. It seems that where the patented product is passively imported (that is, where the patented product is of no importance as far as any question of carriage is concerned), the patent

---

[28] *Hadley Industries v. Metal Sections and Metsec* (UK) (unreported, 13 Nov. 1998)(Patents Court).

[29] *Hoffman La Roche v. Harris Pharmaceuticals* [1977] *FSR* 200 (under the PA 1949).

[30] *Rotocrop v. Genbourne* [1982] *FSR* 241; *Furr v. CD Truline (Building Products)* [1985] *FSR* 553, 565. Benyamini, *Patent Infringement in the EC,* 68–74 (suggesting that kits are dealt with as direct infringements unless they lack one or more essential elements).

[31] *Rotocrop,* above, 258–9.   [32] See below at p. 554.

[33] *Betts v. Willmott* (1871) 2 *Ch LR* 6; *Incandescent Gas Light Co. v. Cantelo* (1895) 12 *RPC* 262; *National Photograph Co. of Australia v. Menck* [1911] *AC* 336. While the common law has tended to adopt an implied licence approach, there is some evidence that this case law may be being reinterpreted as part of an 'exhaustion-of-rights' principle like that found within European law. In *Canon v. Green Cartridge* Lord Hoffmann said that the notion of 'a general implied licence to use the patented product at all, which is sometimes used to explain why mere user does not infringe the patentee's monopoly…is perhaps better regarded as a consequence of the exhaustion of the patentee's rights in respect of the particular article when it is sold', [1997] *FSR* 817, 822.

[34] See above at pp. 12–16.

[35] The doctrine of exhaustion has been held inapplicable to products made under a compulsory licence: *Merck v. Stephar,* Case C–187/80 [1981] *ECR* 2063 (ECJ).

[36] If the CPC comes into force, PA s. 60(4) will come into effect (see CPC Art. 81). On the scope of PA s. 60(4) see *Dellareed v. Delkin,* [1988] *FSR* 329, 347.

[37] *Roussel Uclaf SA v. Hockley International* [1996] *RPC* 441 (for a limited licence applied to sales of a patented product outside the EEA to be effective, notice of it must be brought to the attention of every person down the chain of supply).

will not be infringed.[38] As Tomlin J said, 'I cannot think…that the employment of a patented cutting blow-pipe or a patented hammer in the manufacture of some part of a locomotive would necessarily render the importation of the locomotive an infringement'.[39] A person will infringe where they deal with the patented product in the course of trade or for the purposes of profit.[40] As an importer must have a legal and beneficial interest in the infringing goods, foreign parties will not infringe where they transfer their interests in the infringing object outside the UK (although they might be liable as a joint tortfeasor).[41] As with the right to dispose of the product, the patentee's right to prevent import is limited by the common law principle of implied consent and by the doctrine of Community exhaustion.

2.2.4 The right to keep the product

The patentee's monopoly also includes situations where an infringer keeps the product, whether for disposal or otherwise. The scope of this right was considered in *SKF v. Harbottle*,[42] where the court was called upon to decide whether the storage of a product in a London warehouse fell within the meaning of 'keep' in section 60(1). This decision arose from the fact that British Airways, who were in the process of transporting an antihistamine drug called Cimetidine from Italy to Nigeria, stored 20 kg. of the drug in a warehouse in London. While the drug was being stored, a patent infringement action was brought by the UK patentees (SKF) against the owner and importer of the drug, Harbottle. British Airways were joined as co-defendants in the infringement action on the basis that they had infringed the owner's right to keep the product. Finding in favour of British Airways, the court held that the act of passively storing a patented drug in a warehouse in London could not be construed as the 'keeping of a product' within the meaning of section 60(1). While declining to arrive at a definitive meaning of the term 'keep', the court was strongly influenced by the 'very much more limited' terms employed in Article 29(a) of the Community Patent Convention, where the equivalent wording refers to 'stocking' a patented product. On this basis it was said that 'keep' implied 'keeping in stock' rather than acting as a custodian.

Despite the approach adopted in the *Harbottle* decision, a broader interpretation of the right to keep a product was adopted in *McDonald v. Graham*.[43] In this case, the patentee asserted that the defendant (a marketing consultant who had been introduced to the patentee) who retained certain articles (and later made them available to a third party) had infringed their right to 'keep' the patented product. In response, the defendants argued that the materials had not been kept 'for disposal or otherwise'. The Court of Appeal held that the defendant had kept the product 'in the sense of keeping them in stock for the purposes of his business in order to make use of them as and when it would be beneficial to him to do so'.[44] As such, the patent had been infringed.

In circumstances where the patentee has placed the product on the market, a person will be free from liability under the implied licence theory. However, if no such licence is implied, liability for mere possession or use is absolute (irrespective of knowledge or intent).

---

[38] See *SABAF SpA v. MFI Furniture Centres* [2005] *RPC* 10, para 40–46 (HL) (on the definition of 'importer').

[39] *Wilderman v. Berk* (1925) 42 *RPC* 79, 88.

[40] This is the case irrespective of whether the ultimate destination is the UK or elsewhere: *Hoffmann-La Roche v. Harris Pharmaceuticals* [1977] *FSR* 200 (under the PA 1949).

[41] *SABAF v. Meneghetti* [2003] *RPC* 264, 284–5 (CA). As the Italian defendants passed legal title in the 'infringing' article (that was subsequently imported into the UK) to another party in Italy, it could not be said that they imported the goods into the UK, although they did organize and pay for the haulage of the articles. In so doing the Court of Appeal expressly disregarded *Waterford Wedgwood v. David Nagli* [1988] *FSR* 92 (re-import under Trade Marks Act 1994).

[42] [1980] *RPC* 363; M. Howe, 'Infringing Goods and the Warehouseman' [1979] *EIPR* 287.

[43] [1994] *RPC* 407.   [44] Ibid, 431.

2.2.5 Scope of protection for biotechnological inventions

In the lead-up to the Biotechnology Directive[45] questions arose about the scope of protection for biotechnological inventions. The issues were dealt with by Articles 8–10 of the Directive. The Patents Act 1977 has been amended to take account of these provisions.[46] The scope of protection of product patents for biological material is dealt with in Articles 8(1) and 9 of the Directive.

Article 8(1) provides that the protection conferred by a patent on biological material (possessing specific characteristics) extends to any biological material derived from that biological material by propagation or multiplication in an identical or divergent form. This would apply, for example, to inventions for herbicide-resistant plants and genetically manipulated animals.[47] For the derivative biological material to be covered by the patent it must possess the same characteristics as the patented biological material. This means that a patent for a genetically modified animal would extend to include future generations (so long as they retain the 'specific characteristics' of the 'original' animal).[48]

Article 9 (which is mirrored in the United Kingdom in paragraph 9 of Schedule A2 to the Patents Act 1977)[49] deals with the scope of protection for a product that contains genetic information. More specifically, it provides that the protection conferred on a patent containing or consisting of genetic information shall extend to all material, save as provided in Article 5(1),[50] in which the product is incorporated and in which the genetic information is contained or performs its function.

In recent years, there has been a growing concern about the nature of the protection granted to biotech inventions, particularly in relation to product patents granted for genes, DNA sequences, and the like. The main problem with product patents in this context is that they give the patentee control over subsequent uses of the product, even for uses that they did not envisage or know about. For example if a research team discovered that the ABC gene caused acne, it might be possible for them to obtain a product patent over the isolated ABC gene. If another research team subsequently discovered that the ABC gene also played a role in the development of skin cancer, this would be covered by the earlier product patent. One objection to a situation such as this is that the reward granted to the patentee outweighs the benefits that flow from their disclosure. Another related problem is that product patents may stifle research into new uses of a patented product. While special defences have been introduced to minimize the impact of product patents for biological inventions,[51] many commentators believe that further action is necessary. One solution that has been suggested is that the scope of protection for gene patents should be limited to the use that is actually disclosed in the patent.[52] To continue with the example mentioned above, this would mean that the initial patent would be granted for the ABC gene only insofar as it triggers acne. In this situation, the protection reflects the disclosure. The more limited protection also means that the patent would not act as a disincentive for others to look for other uses of the ABC gene. It has been suggested that this proposal is supported by Recital 25 of the EC Biotechnology Directive insofar as it limits product claims

---

[45] See above at pp. 349–50.

[46] Patents Regulations 2000 (SI 2000/2037). Arts. 8–10 are said to be declaratory of existing law.

[47] S. Bostyn, 'The Patentabilty of Genetic Information Carriers' [1999] *IPQ* 1, 28.   [48] Ibid.

[49] Introduced by Patents Regulations 2000 (SI 2000/2037) (in force 28 Jul. 2000).

[50] Biotech. Dir. Art. 5(1)/PA Sched. A2, para. 3(a), states that the human body at the various stages of its formation and development, and the elements thereof (including gene sequences), cannot be patented.

[51] See below at pp. 567–8.

[52] See D. Schertenleib, 'The patentability and protection of DNA-based inventions' [2003] *EIPR* 125, 136–8; A. White, 'Gene and Compound *Per Se* Claims: An Appropriate Reward?' [2001] 6 *Bioscience Law Review* 239; P. Jacobs and G. Van Overwalle, 'Gene Patents: a different approach' [2001] *EIPR* 505.

to the parts of the product which are essential to the invention, that is, it restricts the scope of DNA-product patents based on their disclosed function.[53] Another more radical suggestion, which harps back to the way chemical inventions were treated in the early part of the twentieth century, is to limit gene patents to process claims. That is, product production would simply not be available for gene-based inventions.

2.3 PATENTS FOR A PROCESS

The owner of a patent for a process is given the right to use the process or to offer it for use in the UK.[54] This is subject to the proviso that the right is only infringed where it can be shown that the defendant knew, or it would have been obvious to a reasonable person in the circumstances, that the unauthorized use of the process would be an infringement of the patent. It is important to note that in contrast with the rights given to owners of patents for products (discussed above) and the rights given to patents for products derived from processes (discussed below), liability for infringement of a patent for a process is *not* absolute. That is, liability depends upon the owner proving that the defendant knew, or that it would have been obvious to a reasonable person in the circumstances, that the unauthorized use of a process would be an infringement of the patent. In essence the owner of a patent for a process is given the right to practise the invention or to put the invention into effect. For the most part, there have been few problems in interpreting this provision (although discovering how a defendant makes a particular product may be one).[55] Problems may arise, however, in relation to patents for novelty-of-use claims, which are discussed below.

2.3.1 Direct products of patented processes

It has long been accepted that where a patent is granted over a process the protection includes both the process in question and the products that flow from that process. This principle is now to be found in section 60(1)(c) of the Patents Act 1977, which provides that a person infringes a process patent if they dispose of, offer to dispose of, use, import, or keep any product derived from that process.[56] This protection is particularly important where no claim has been made to a product as such. It is also important where the process is carried on outside the United Kingdom and a product derived from that process is imported into the United Kingdom.[57] As we have already looked at the way these terms are construed, there is no need to examine them again.

The protection given to process patents is potentially very wide. In part this is because, where a range of different products flow from a single process, all of the products fall within the remit of the patent. It is also because the scope of protection not only includes the products that flow from the process, but also the products that are based upon the products which flow from the process: if you like, the derivatives of the derivative. To ensure that the scope of the monopoly is kept within justifiable limits, an important restriction is placed on the products that are protectable by process patents. This has been done by stipulating that for protection to arise, there must be a direct *relationship* between the process and the product in question.[58]

---

[53] Where the claimed DNA sequences 'overlap only in parts which are not essential to the invention, each sequence will be considered as an independent sequence in patent law terms'. Schertenleib, 'DNA-based Inventions', 136

[54] PA s. 60(1)(b).

[55] For some of the problems that arise in proving infringement of a process patent where the process is carried out overseas see *Nutrinova Nutrition Specialties & Food Ingredients v. Sanchem UK* [2001] *FSR* 797.

[56] CPC Art. 25(c); EPC 2000 Art. 64(2) [EPC 1973 Art. 64(2)].

[57] *CIPA*, para. 60.06.

[58] PA s. 60(1)(c). For the common-law position see *Saccharin Corp v. Anglo Continental Chemical* (1900) 17 *RPC* 307.

The question of what is meant by a 'direct' relationship was considered by the Court of Appeal in *Pioneer Electronics v. Warner Music*.[59] This action arose when the claimant argued that their process patent for a method of manufacturing compact discs had been infringed after the defendants imported into the United Kingdom optical discs that were a by-product of the patented process. While there was no doubt that the imported discs had been derived from the patented invention, it was unclear whether there was a 'direct' relationship between the process patent and the imported discs.

After considering the way equivalent provisions were interpreted in other European jurisdictions, the Court of Appeal concluded that 'directly' meant 'without intermediary'. More specifically, Nourse LJ said that when the Patents Act 1977 stipulated that for protection to arise there had to be a direct relationship between the process and product, this meant that there were no material or important steps that intervened between the process and the product in question. In situations where material and important steps did intervene, the process patent could not be used to control the use that was made of the product. This situation would only change if it could be shown that the intervening steps were immaterial or trivial.

The process patent for the production of the master discs was not infringed when the final discs were imported into the United Kingdom. The reason for this was that a number of important and material steps separated the product from the process. A key factor in the finding of non-infringement was that the production of the master discs was only an initial stage in the production of the final optical discs. The master discs were used to produce 'mothers' which in turn were converted into 'sons', which subsequently acted as the basis from which the moulding of the final discs took place. While the patented invention may have acted as a platform that aided in the production of the final discs, because there were a number of important and material steps that separated them, there was not a direct relationship and thus no infringement. The requirement that there be a direct relationship is in accord with the general logic of patent law. While a product may draw upon a process patent, if the product only comes into existence as a result of material steps that occur outside the process, the products are no longer derivative; they are new products that warrant separate patent protection. If patentees were able to regulate the use that was made of such products, this would extend the ambit of the monopoly beyond the scope of the invention disclosed in the patent.[60]

The question of what is meant by a direct relationship was also considered in *Monsanto v Cargill*.[61] In this case Monsanto argued that, by importing into the UK a cargo of soybean meal produced in Argentina, Cargill had infringed Monsanto's patent for Round Up Ready soybeans: the main claim being for 'a method of producing genetically transformed plants'. There was no doubt that the soybean meal imported into the UK (or at least a substantial part of it) was produced from Round Up Ready soybeans in Argentina. In deciding whether the method claims in the patent had been infringed, the court had to consider whether the soybean meal had been 'directly obtained' from the process in question under section 60(1)(c). Pumfrey J said that the phrase 'directly obtained by means of the process' means the 'immediate product of the process, or where the patented process is an intermediate stage in the manufacture of some ultimate product, that product, but only if the product of the intermediate process retains its identity'.[62] Following *Pioneer Electronics v. Warner Music*, Pumfrey J said that a

---

[59] [1997] *RPC* 757 (CA). See H. Hurdle, 'What is the Direct Product of a Patented Process?' [1997] *EIPR* 322; F. Russell and H. Hurdle, 'What is the Direct Product of a Patented Process?' [1995] *EIPR* 249.

[60] If a 'patentee wants appropriate cover . . . they should secure a product-by-process claim.' *Banks Committee*, para. 297.

[61] *Monsanto Technology LLC v. Cargill International SA* [2008] *FSR* 7, paras 34–35.

[62] Ibid.

product that is derived from a patented process will be directly obtained so long as the product retains its essential characteristics. However, where a product has 'lost its identity and become something else' it will not be directly obtained. As Pumfrey J noted, intermediate processes in chemical cases often suffer this fate.

In considering whether the method claim in Monsanto's patent had been infringed by the importing of the soybean meal, Pumfrey J said that the method claim consisted of the isolation and insertion of a recombinant DNA molecule with prescribed characteristics into the genome of a plant cell. The DNA molecule was inserted into one original plant, which was named and identified in the patent as the parent of all Round Up Ready plants in Argentina. Pumfrey J noted that the transformation of the original plant had occurred many generations ago and that since then soybeans had been grown by seedsmen or retained by farmers for planting. After some generations, the harvested beans were processed into the meal that had been imported in the UK. Pumfrey J was willing to accept that all the Round Up Ready soybean plants in Argentina were lineal descendents of the original plant and also that the 'huge mountain of soybean meal' could be described as the ultimate product of the original transformation of the parent plant. Pumfrey J was unable to accept, however, that the soy meal was the ultimate product of the original transformation of the parent plant: a phrase which he reserved for the original transformed plant. On this basis, Pumfrey J held that the imported soybean meal was not 'directly obtained' for the purposes of section 60(1)(c) and as such did not infringe. In so doing Pumfrey J rejected Monsanto's argument that the product retained its essential characteristics when it was made into meal. In rejecting the hereditary nature of the relationship between the Round Up Ready sequence (as inserted in the parent plant) and the soybean meal, Pumfrey J said that Monsanto's argument confused the 'informational content of what passed between the generations (the Round Up Ready genomic sequence) with the product, which is just soybean meal with no special intrinsic characteristics from one of the generations of plants'.[63] As well as clarifying what it means for a product to be directly obtained, the decision is also important in that it provides some insight into the approach that courts in the UK may take towards the infringement of biological inventions.

2.3.2 Direct products of biotechnological processes

The question of the scope of protection for patents for biotechnological processes is dealt with in Article 8(2) of the Biotechnology Directive. A similar provision now exists in the Patents Act 1977 as a result of amendments made in July 2000.[64] These provide that:

[T]he protection conferred by a patent on a process that enables a biological material to be produced possessing specific characteristics as a result of the invention shall extend to biological material directly obtained through that process and to any other biological material derived from the directly obtained biological material through propagation or multiplication in an identical or divergent form and possessing those same characteristics.

As with the protection given to product patents for biological materials, the derived material must possess the same characteristics as the 'original' material. It should be noted that the protection under Article 8(2)/paragraph 8 of Schedule A2 to the Patents Act 1977[65] is limited to material 'directly obtained' from the patented process. It seems that 'directly obtained' would be construed in a way similar to how 'direct' relationship was construed in *Monsanto v Cargill*[66] and *Pioneer Electronics v. Warner Music*[67] (discussed above).

---

[63] Ibid, para 38.   [64] Patents Regulations 2000 (SI 2000/2037) (in force 28 July 2000).
[65] Introduced by Patents Regulations 2000.   [66] *Monsanto v. Cargill* [2007] *EWHC* 2257, paras 34–35.
[67] [1997] *RPC* 757 (CA).

2.4 NOVELTY-OF-USE CLAIMS

For the most part, when determining whether a defendant has carried out one of the activities within the patentee's control the key question is the way the language of the patent is construed. One situation where problems may arise, however, is in relation to patents for a new use of a known substance used in an old way, which have been recognized at the EPO and in the United Kingdom.

The decision to accept novelty-of-purpose patents has met with considerable resistance in the United Kingdom.[68] As Lord Hoffmann said in *Merrell Dow*, the Board's decision in *Mobil* has been criticized on the 'ground that a patent for an old product used in an old way for a new purpose makes it difficult to apply the traditional UK doctrine of infringement'.[69] The problem with novelty-of-use claims is that it may be difficult to ascertain when a product is being used in the relevant way. Unless use claims are confined to uses of products that are distinct, it seems that a patentee of an invention that consists of a new use must demonstrate that the infringer intended to produce the particular effect.[70]

The reason why the recognition of use claims is incompatible with the traditional UK doctrine of infringement can be traced to the fact that the infringement of a patent turns exclusively on the physical conduct of the defendant. A person will infringe if, for example, they manufacture or sell the patented invention without permission. In so doing, the alleged infringer's state of mind is irrelevant; it does not matter whether the alleged infringer knew that they were dealing with the patented product. In most cases, this presents few problems. For example, because claims to a new use of an old thing will be physically different from previous uses of the same thing, the earlier use can continue to be performed without it infringing the subsequent patent. Problems may arise, however, in relation to novelty-of-use patents. This is because for infringement purposes the discovery that a known product used in a known way can be put to a new purpose is physically identical to the previous use: the only difference between the two uses being in the mind of the user. Given that the physical acts protected by a novelty-of-purpose patent would be the same as the steps taken during the previous use, when someone uses an old substance in an old way, there is no obvious way of telling whether they are using the substance to achieve the old purpose, or whether they are using the substance to achieve the new purpose. As Lord Hoffmann said:

liability for infringement is, as I have said, absolute. It depends upon whether the act in question falls within the claims and pays no attention to the alleged infringer's state of mind. But this doctrine may be difficult to apply to a patent for the use of a known substance in a known way for a new purpose. How does one tell whether the person putting the additive into his engine is legitimately using it to inhibit rust or infringing by using it to reduce friction?[71]

---

[68] To 'hold that every new use of an old composition may be the subject of a patent upon the composition would lead to endless confusion and go far to destroy the benefits of our patent laws': *In re Thuau* 135 *F 2d* 344 (CCPA 1943).

[69] *Merrell Dow Pharmaceuticals v. Norton* [1996] *RPC* 76, 92 (HL). In *Mobil* it was said that the analogous problems concerning infringement would arise in relation to second and subsequent medical uses. *Mobil/ Friction reducing additive*, G2/88 [1990] *EPOR* 73, 89.

[70] For consideration of the position of the supplier of the substance see indirect infringement below at pp. 552–5.

[71] *Merrell Dow v. Norton* [1996] *RPC* 76, 92 (HL). See also *Bristol-Myers Squibb v. Baker Norton Pharmeucticals* [2001] *RPC* 1, 18 (CA), para. 49 (Aldous LJ said that it was unlikely that the Court of Appeal would suggest that *Mobil* was wrongly decided when the House of Lords 'did not so conclude').

The problem raised by novelty-of-purpose patents is that while the only feature which enables a novelty-of-purpose patent to be distinguished from the previous use is the purpose for which it is used (which exists in the mind of the user), the purpose of the alleged infringer is not taken into account when determining whether a patent has been infringed: all that matters is whether the physical act of infringement has taken place. The consequence of this is that a patent granted for the discovery of a new purpose of an old thing used in an old way could prevent someone from doing what they had done before: thus denying the user their previous right to work.[72]

While it has been suggested that these problems are based on an artificial distinction,[73] the inherent conflict between the physical nature of infringement and the mental nature of novelty-of-purpose patents gives rise to real problems in the United Kingdom which will need to be resolved if such patents are allowed. If novelty-of-purpose patents are not to impinge upon the legitimate (existing) activities of others,[74] it may be necessary to limit the scope of the monopoly (possibly to the making, using, and commercial supply of the thing for the specified use) or to modify the defence of prior use.[75]

2.5 INDIRECT INFRINGEMENT

In addition to the prohibited activities set out in section 60(1), the Patents Act 1977 also provides that a patent is infringed where a person contributes to, but does not directly take part in, the infringement.[76] This is particularly important where the maker or user is difficult to detect (for example where the manufacture or use occurs in private), or they are not worth suing. Section 60(2) states that a person infringes a patent where they supply or offer to supply any means relating to an essential element of the invention for putting the invention into effect. Thus, a patent for a glue which is produced by combining two chemicals A and B may be infringed by a person who supplies either A or B to a person who then manufactures the glue.[77] The question of what it means for an on-line invention to be put into effect in the United Kingdom was recently considered by the Court of Appeal. The patent in question was for a gaming system consisting of a host computer, terminal computers, and software that operates the system. The invention enabled end-users on terminal computers to engage in interactive gaming with the host computer. The defendant, William Hill, operated an on-line gaming system for punters in the UK. British punters were supplied with a computer program (either

---

[72] 'New use patents raise vexing questions about the patentee's right to prevent others from selling the old compound': *Dawson Chemical Co. v. Rohm & Haas Co.*, 448 US 176 (1980).

[73] Paterson, para. 10–31.

[74] In response to arguments of this type, the Enlarged Board of Appeal offered the following unhelpful advice: 'there is a clear distinction between the protection which is conferred and the rights which are conferred by a European patent'. While the 'protection conferred by a patent is determined by the terms of the claims (Art. 69(1) EPC [1973]) and in particular by the categories of such claims and their technical features… [i]n contrast, the rights conferred on the proprietor of a European patent (Art. 64(1) EPC [1973] [EPC 2000 Art. 64(1)]) are the legal rights… [conferred] upon the proprietor'. *Mobil/Friction reducing additive*, G2/88 [1990] *EPOR* 73, 80–1.

[75] See below at pp. 565–7.

[76] PA s. 60(2); CPC 26(1). *Dow Chemical v. Spence Bryson* [1982] *FSR* 598, 628–30 (inducing or procuring infringement by persuading infringer to adopt process, teaching how to operate it). See below Ch. 47 Section 3.

[77] The policy of expanding the patentee's monopoly to cover contributory infringement seems to conflict with the policy underpinning the rules preventing a patentee from requiring licensees to utilize particular suppliers. On these see below at pp. 576–7. The connection is recognized in US jurisprudence where the Supreme Court has observed that the 'doctrines of contributory infringement and patent misuse have long and interrelated histories': *Dawson Chemical Co. v. Rohm & Haas Co.*, 448 US 176 (1980).

via CD or downloaded from the net) that transformed their computer into a terminal computer of the defendant's system. The claimants argued that when the defendant's system was in use it infringed their patent. The defendant argued that it did not infringe the patent because its host computer was located abroad and not in the United Kingdom (in Antigua and then in Curaçao in the Netherlands Antilles). Aldous LJ said that it was 'not straining the word "use" to conclude that the UK punter will use the claimed gaming system in the UK, even if the host computer is located in, say, Antigua'.[78] Focusing on the way the end-user related to the invention, Aldous LJ said that a punter who uses the William Hill system would be using the whole system as if it was in the United Kingdom. The punter will in substance use the host computer in the United Kingdom, it being irrelevant to him where it is situated. Aldous LJ concluded that in supplying the computer program in the United Kingdom, the defendant intended to put the invention into effect in the United Kingdom and as such infringed the claimant's patent.[79]

A person will also indirectly infringe where they supply a number of the essential components of a patented invention. This would occur, for example, where a patent is for an oil lamp (which is made up of a vessel holding the oil, a burner and wick, an outer glass container, and a chimney) and the defendant supplied all of the parts other than the chimney.[80]

For indirect infringement to take place, three criteria must be satisfied. First, the proprietor of the patent must establish that the means supplied by the defendant relate to an essential element of the invention.[81] Second, the supplier must know, or it must be obvious to a reasonable person in the circumstances, that the means are both 'suitable' for and are 'intended' to be used in putting the invention into effect.[82] The imposition of a knowledge requirement, which is construed objectively, ensures that parties who do not knowingly benefit from the misuse of a patent are not caught as indirect infringers. Third, in recognition of the fact that there might be legitimate reasons why a person supplies or offers to supply something that enables the means for putting the invention into effect, section 60(3) provides that the supply of a staple commercial product will not constitute an indirect infringement under section 60(2).[83] The meaning of 'staple commercial product' is not clear, though it might be assumed that it covers basic products that are readily available.[84] The staple commercial product exemption does not apply where the product is specifically supplied for the purpose of *inducing* an infringement.[85]

2.5.1 Novelty-of-use claims

Given the difficulty in establishing direct liability in relation to new-use patents (discussed earlier), indirect liability may take on a greater significance. Taking the example of a patent for the use of a substance in oil as a lubricant, where it was previously known that the substance inhibited rust, it would seem that a defendant would infringe if they supplied the oil to persons and advertised it as a lubricant. However, a person would not infringe if they continued to supply the oil as a rust inhibitor. While it might be known that the oil could be used as a lubricant, it would be difficult to prove that the defendant 'intended' that the oil be used in this way (as is required under section 60(2)). In these circumstances, secondary factors may be helpful, such as the documentation that accompanies the product, which might indicate the way the

---

[78] *Menashe Business Mercantile v. William Hill Organization* [2003] *RPC* 575, 584–5 (CA); upholding Jacob J's decision ([2002] *RPC* 951), but for different reasons.

[79] Ibid.   [80] See *Wallace v. Holmes*, 29 *F Cas* 74 (No. 17, 100) (CC Conn 1871).

[81] *Hazell Grove* [1995] *RPC* 529 , 541.

[82] For the pre-1977 position see *Dunlop v. Moseley* (1904) 21 *RPC* 274.

[83] In *Pavel v. Sony* SRIS CC/14/93 the Patents County Court defined staple commercial product as meaning 'products of regular kind needed daily and generally available'.

[84] Benyamini, *Patent Infringement in the EC*, 234–5.

[85] *Furr v. Truline (Building Products)* [1985] *FSR* 553, 565.

product was expected to be used.[86] It would be more difficult to determine whether a defendant indirectly infringes where they supplied the oil saying that it acted both as a rust inhibitor and a friction reducer. The liability of the defendant is also uncertain when they supplied the oil saying it acted as a rust inhibitor, where it was widely known that the oil could also be used to reduce friction. In these circumstances, the likelihood of the user using the oil as a lubricant is high but not certain. Jacob J, who has expressed doubts about the role of novelty-of-use claims, has called for these issues to be considered in detail by the European Patent Office whenever it gives further consideration to claims for uses.[87] So far, these pleas have fallen on deaf ears.

2.6 ADDITIONAL LIABILITY

In addition to the rights set out in sections 60(1) and 60(2), patentees are also able to make use of a limited number of provisions that exist outside the Patents Act 1977. These provisions will be particularly important where a party acts in such a way as to undermine the value of a patent, yet the activities fall outside of the scope of section 60(1) or (2).

Perhaps the most important non-statutory mechanism available to a patent owner is the concept of joint tortfeasance.[88] This provides that, even if a party does not fall within the scope of section 60, the patentee can enjoin the third party as a joint tortfeasor if it can be shown that they have acted in a 'common design' with a party who is liable for a statutory tort of infringement under section 60 (and that they jointly inflicted damage on a patentee).[89] For a party to be liable as a joint tortfeasor, they must be 'so involved in the commission of the tort as to make himself liable for the tort'.[90]

It has also been suggested that the law of restitution provides patentees with an additional ground on which to found liability. More specifically, it has been argued that independently of the rights set out in the Patents Act, the law also recognizes unjust enrichment as a separate cause of action. Proposals of this type were considered and rejected in *Union Carbide Corporation v. BP Chemicals* where Jacob J said that the law of restitution could *not* be used to supplement the law of patents to the extent of providing a cause of action for unjust enrichment.[91] Jacob J did say, however, that there might be cases where the strict rights set out in section 61 of the 1977 Act might not limit what a court could do in furtherance of the policy of patent law: what this policy is and what it might mean in this context was left unclear.

3 SCOPE OF PROTECTION

Once it is clear that a defendant has carried out one of the activities listed in section 60, it is then necessary to consider whether in so doing they fell within the scope of the patent. This requires the court to compare the patented invention with the defendant's alleged infringing process or device. Where the two are identical, the defendant will clearly infringe. Similarly,

---

[86] It has been said that German case law supports the view that in this form there is direct infringement, either because a use claim is seen as primarily a product claim and this amounts to sale of the product, or because such an act is an offering of a process for use: see Benyamini, *Patent Infringement in the EC*, 84–90 (advocating direct infringement approach). See further A. Horton, 'Methods of Treatment and Second Medical Use' (Aug. 2000) *Patent World* 9, 12.

[87] *Bristol-Myers Squibb v. Baker Norton Pharmaceuticals* [1999] *RPC* 253, 280.

[88] See, *CIPA*, para. 60.24.   [89] See further below at p. 1076.

[90] *Celem SA v. Alcon Electronics* [2006] *EWHC* 3042 (Pat), para 33.   [91] [1998] *FSR* 1.

where the claimant's invention and the alleged infringing product are very different, there will be no infringement. It is also clear that a defendant will infringe where they incorporate the patented invention into a larger process or product. This is the case even if the addition improves upon the patented invention. It is also clear that the defendant will infringe where they supply a patented product in parts or in kit form.[92] A defendant will not infringe, however, if the consumer needs to exercise inventive skill in putting the kit together.

While these situations are relatively unproblematic, problems arise where there is only a slight difference between the patented invention and the defendant's alleged infringing product. This would be the case, for example, where rather than adding to the patented invention a defendant alters or omits to include part of the patented invention in their product or process and on this basis argues that their invention falls outside the scope of the monopoly.[93] Problems also arise where a defendant changes one aspect of an invention, or where they use a different means to reach the same end result as the patented invention. In these situations, the decision as to whether a defendant infringes largely turns on the way the scope of protection is determined.[94]

3.1 DETERMINING THE SCOPE OF PROTECTION

The starting point for determining the scope of protection is section 125 of the Patents Act, which corresponds to Article 69 of EPC 2000 [formerly Article 69 EPC 1973].[95] This provides that the extent of the protection conferred by a patent shall be 'taken to be that specified in a claim of the specification of the application or patent, as the case may be, as interpreted by the description and any drawings contained in that specification'. Over time, a number of rules have been developed that influence the way patent claims are interpreted. The more important of these provide that a patent specification must be read as a whole; that the description and drawings shall be used to interpret the claims;[96] that the claims must be interpreted as part of the entire document;[97] and that the court can hear expert evidence on the meaning of technical terms.[98] The patent document is read from the point of view of a person skilled in the art and is understood according to the common general knowledge available at the time of its publication.[99] Controversially, the prosecution history, that is information exchanged

---

[92] *Rotocrop* [1982] *FSR* 241.

[93] A related situation arises where a defendant supplies most but not all of the patented invention in kit form.

[94] For a summary of the approach to be taken in construing patent claims see *Mayne v. Pharmacia* [2005] *EWCA Civ* 137, para 5 (which is a restatement of the summary made by Jacob LJ in *Rockwater v. Technip France SA* [2004] *RPC* 6, para 41), following the qualified approval of *Rockwater* by Lord Hoffmann in *Kirin-Amgen v. Hoechst Marion Roussel* [2005] *RPC* 169.

[95] While the 1973 version said that the scope of protection 'shall be determined by the terms of the claims', Article 69(a) EPC 2000 simply says that the scope 'shall be determined by the claims'.

[96] PA s. 125; EPC 2000 Art. 69 [EPC 1973 Art. 69]. In *Rosedale v. Carlton Tyre* [1960] *RPC* 59 the Court of Appeal used the drawings and descriptions in determining that 'holes' did not have to be round.

[97] *EMI v. Lissen* (1939) 56 *RPC* 23; *Glaverbel SA v. British Coal Corporation* [1995] *RPC* 255, 269. The statement of the problem which the invention is intended to solve may be particularly influential: *Minnesota Mining & Manufacturing Co. v. Plastus Kreativ AB* [1997] *RPC* 737 (CA); *SEB v. De'Longhi* [2002] *EWHC* 1556, para. 2 (when one encounters a word of degree, the problem is to ascertain its function in the claim so as to obtain a handle on its meaning).

[98] *Glaverbel*, above, 269 (Staughton LJ).

[99] *Hoechst Celanese Corporation v. BP Chemicals* [1999] *FSR* 319 (Aldous LJ). On common general knowledge, see *Beloit Technolgies v. Valmet Paper Machinery* [1997] *RPC* 489, 494.

between the applicant and the Patent Office during the grant of the patent, has also been used to interpret the claims.[100]

While a variety of different factors are taken into account when determining the scope of protection provided by a patent, four things stand out. These are Lord Diplock's judgment in *Catnic v. Hill and Smith,* the Protocol on the Interpretation of Article 69, Hoffmann J's judgment in *Improver v Remington* and the House of Lords decision in *Kirin-Amgen* – the first such decision to look at infringement under the 1977 Act. We will look at each in turn.

3.1.1 *Catnic v. Hill and Smith*

In order to understand the way patents have been interpreted under the Patents Act 1977, it is necessary to examine the 1982 House of Lords decision of *Catnic v. Hill and Smith* where Lord Diplock argued that a patent specification should be given a *purposive* rather than a literal construction.[101] Although *Catnic* was decided under the Patents Act 1949, it has been decided not only that Lord Diplock's rejection of the literal mode of interpretation and its replacement by a purposive style of interpretation is still relevant under the 1977 Act, but also that the purposive approach to interpretation is the correct approach to be adopted under the Protocol on the Interpretation of Article 69 of the European Patent Convention.[102] The ongoing importance of Lord Diplock's judgment was reinforced by Hoffmann J's 1990 decision in *Improver v. Remington,* which builds upon Lord Diplock's judgment. It was also reconfirmed by Lord Hoffmann's clear statement that the '*Catnic* principle of construction is... precisely in accordance with the Protocol'.[103]

In *Catnic* the House of Lords was called upon to decide whether in manufacturing steel lintels the defendants had infringed the claimant's patent for galvanized-steel lintels. (A lintel is a load-bearing beam that spans open spaces such as doors and windows in cavity walls.) While it was evident that the defendant's lintel and the patented invention (see Fig. 22.1) were very similar, one issue remained unclear. This arose from the fact that while the patent specified that the rear side of the lintel should be 'vertical', the defendant's lintel (see Fig. 22.2) was at an angle of 84 degrees. In order to determine whether the claimant's patent had been

[100] In *Kirin-Amgen Inc v. Hoechst Marion Roussel Ltd* [2005] *RPC* (9) 169, 187 (para. 35) Lord Hoffmann indicated that the British courts generally do not look at so called 'prosecution history': 'The courts of the United Kingdom, the Netherlands and Germany certainly discourage, if they do not actually prohibit, use of the patent office file in aid of construction. There are good reasons: the meaning of the patent should not change according to whether or not the person skilled in the art has access to the file and in any case life is too short for the limited assistance which it can provide.' Despite such an authority, counter-examples exist: *Furr v. CD Truline (Building Products)* [1985] *FSR* 553, 560–4; *Rohm and Haas v. Collag* [2002] *FSR* 445, 457–8 (letter to EPO held to contain objective information that was of assistance in resolving aspects of the specification that were unclear); *Wesley Jessen v. Coopervison* [2003] *RPC* 355, 382 (prosecution history at the EPO, which showed that application was changed from pattern to dots to avoid prior art, was used to limit 'dots' to mean 'small roundish marks' and nothing else). Cf. *Glaverbel v. British Coal (No. 2)* [1993] *RPC* 90. For the position of prosecution history estoppel in the US see *Festo Corporation v. Shoketsu Kinzouku Kogyo KK,* 535 *US* 722 (2002); [2003] *FSR* 10 (patentee bound by representations made at US patent office).

[101] [1982] *RPC* 183, 241 (HL).

[102] In *PLG Research v. Ardon* [1993] *FSR* 197, 309, the Court of Appeal argued that *Catnic* was no longer good law under the 1977 Act. However, the promotion of Aldous LJ to the Appeal Court led to an immediate reversal of this view. This has been confirmed in a range of subsqent decision. See, e.g. *Kastner v. Rizla* [1995] *RPC* 585, 594; *Beloit v. Valmet* [1997] *RPC* 489; *3M v. Plastus* [1997] *RPC* 737 (CA); *Codex v. Racal-Milgo* [1983] *RPC* 369 (CA); *Anchor Building v. Redland Roof Tiles* [1990] *RPC* 283 (CA); cf. J. Turner, 'Purposive Construction: Seven Reasons Why *Catnic* is Wrong' [1999] *EIPR* 531 (but, see the critical response by M. Franzosi, 'In Defence of *Catnic*' [2000] *EIPR* 242).

[103] *Kirin-Amgen v. Hoechst Marion Roussel* [2005] *RPC* 9, para. 48.

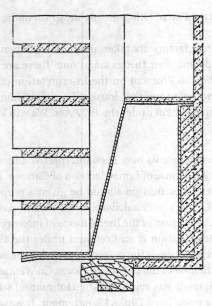

Fig. 22.1 Claimant's lintel

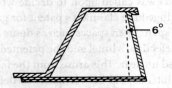

Fig. 22.2 Defendant's lintel

infringed, the House of Lords had to decide whether a claim that specified that the rear support be vertical encompassed a lintel whose rear support was not precisely vertical.

While a literal reading of the claims would have limited the claimant's patent to lintels at 90 degrees (and thus to a finding of non-infringement), Lord Diplock said that the patent ought to be construed *purposively*. A purposive interpretation demands that the claims be read through the eyes of the person skilled in the art, and that the purpose or function of the invention be borne in mind when the patent is interpreted.[104] This meant that when deciding whether 'vertical' included lintels at an 84-degree angle, the person skilled in the art would take into account the function or purpose of the invention. On reading the patent, it was decided that the person skilled in the art would have understood that the reason why the patent specified that the rear support member was to be 'vertical' related to the load-bearing capacity of the lintel. An important factor in the finding that the patent had been infringed was that a 6-degree movement away from 90 degrees only led to a 0.6 per cent reduction in the load-bearing capacity of the lintel. This meant that the defendant's lintel effectively performed the same purpose or function as the claimant's lintel.

[104] *Kastner v. Rizla* [1995] *RPC* 585.

It is often assumed that purposive interpretation offers greater protection to patentees than a more literal reading of the claims may provide and, in turn, that the two styles of interpretation are opposites. However, this is not necessarily the case.[105] The reason for this is that while the use of a purposive style of interpretation often means that the scope of the monopoly is broader than that which would arise if the claims were interpreted literally, purposive interpretation does not necessarily require that the claims be read broadly or indeed in the patentee's favour. All that the purposive approach requires is that the court interpret patents through the eyes of the person skilled in the art, while taking into account the purpose of the invention. Nothing more, nothing less. How broadly claims will be read in any particular case *always* depends on the approach undertaken by the person skilled in the art in the case in hand which, in turn, is influenced by the purpose of the invention and the way the claims are drafted.[106]

The potentially limiting nature of the purposive interpretation was highlighted in *Catnic* when Lord Diplock said that there may be good reasons why a person skilled in the art reads the patent claims literally, thus restricting the scope of the monopoly.[107] The most obvious reason why a patentee might have intended that the primary meaning of the claim should be strictly understood is because of the existence of some closely related prior art which would anticipate (and thus invalidate) the patent if it was construed broadly. Another reason why the person skilled in the art might think the patentee intended to confine the scope of the claims relates to the language or types of parameter used by the patentee. Where specific numerical ranges or technical terms (such as 'helical spring') are used, a person skilled in the art might be inclined to think the choice of wording was deliberate.[108]

3.1.2 The Protocol on Interpretation of Article 69 EPC

One of the problems that confronted the drafters of the EPC 1973 was that some member states, notably the United Kingdom and Germany, approached the task of interpreting patent claims differently. While the British were said to favour a strict, literal reading of the claims, it was suggested that in Germany the claims simply acted as a guide for determining the scope of protection. Given the potentially important role that claim interpretation plays in determining the scope of protection, if these different styles of interpretation were allowed to continue under the EPC, it would have undermined the aim of a standardized pan-European patent system. In an attempt to overcome these (perceived) differences and to harmonize the way patents are interpreted across member states, the Protocol on Interpretation of Article 69 of the EPC 1973 was introduced to provide guidance as to how patent claims should be interpreted.[109] The Protocol was replicated in EPC 2000 in a slightly modified form.[110]

There are three notable features of the Protocol under EPC 2000. The first is that it stipulates the standpoint of interpretation that should *not* be adopted when interpreting a patent. In particular, it says that the courts should not read the claims literally. The Protocol also says

---

[105] See *Kirin-Amgen v. Hoechst Marion Roussel* [2005] *RPC* 9, paras 34–5; *3M v. Plastus* [1997] *RPC* 737, 747; *Auchinloss v. Agricultural and Veterinary Supplies* [1997] *RPC* 649.

[106] See above at pp. 365–8.

[107] *Catnic v. Hill & Smith* [1982] *RPC* 183. See also *3M v. Plastus* [1997] *RPC* 737, 747.

[108] *Improver Corp. v. Remington* [1989] *RPC* 69 where Hoffmann J interpreted the term 'helical spring' to be one which would be understood by a person skilled in the art as being confined so that it did not include a functional equivalent made out of rubber.

[109] On the Protocol generally see B. Sherman, 'Patent Claim Interpretation: The Impact of the Protocol on Interpretation' (1991) 54 *MLR* 499. Proposed new Protocol on the Interpretation of Art. 69: Art. 2, item 2 of the Act Revising the Convention on the Grant of European Patents (EPC) (Munich) (29 Nov. 2000) MR/3/00 Rev 1e.

[110] The new Protocol includes, in Art. 2, provision in relation to equivalents.

that the claims should not be used as a mere guide to interpretation. Instead it says, somewhat cryptically, that the courts should adopt a position in between these extremes.[111] The second, more positive feature of the Protocol is that it says that the courts should interpret the claims in a way that combines a fair protection for the patentee with a reasonable degree of certainty for third parties.[112] The third notable feature of the Protocol, which we look at below, is that it explicitly allows for the doctrine of equivalents.[113]

3.1.3 *Improver v. Remington*

Alongside *Catnic,* the most influential decision on patent infringement in the United Kingdom is Hoffmann J's judgment in *Improver Corporation v. Remington Consumer Products.*[114] The patent in issue in this case was for a device designed to remove body hair known as the 'Epilady'. The Epilady consisted of a helical spring attached to an electronic motor which, when activated, expanded and contracted. When applied to the skin, hairs were caught in the spring (as it closed) and then pulled out as the spring contracted. The defendant's product, evocatively called the 'Smooth & Silky', also removed body hair. In contrast to the helical spring used in the Epilady, the Smooth & Silky used a piece of rubber that had a series of small slits cut into it to capture and pull out hair. In finding that the claimant's patent had not been infringed, Hoffmann J. said that Lord Diplock's judgment in *Catnic* could be reduced to three questions (known as the *Improver* questions).[115] These are:

(i)   does the variant have a material effect on the way the invention works? If yes, the variant is outside the claim. If no:

(ii) would this (i.e. that the variant has no material effect) have been obvious to a reader skilled in the art at the date of the publication of the patent? If no, the variant is outside the claim. If yes:

(iii) would a reader skilled in the art nevertheless have understood from the language of the claim that strict compliance with the primary meaning was an essential requirement of the invention? If yes, the variant is outside the claim.[116]

The first *Improver* question requires the court to identify the difference (or variation) between the patented invention and the alleged infringing product. In *Improver* this was the use of a rubber tube rather than a helical spring. Once this is done, the court must then ascertain whether the variation had a material impact on the way the invention works. Two key concepts underpin the first *Improver* question. The first is that it 'envisages that the claim has wider ambit than the literal meaning of the words, so as to give fair protection for the patentee'.[117] That is, it encourages a non-literal reading of the claims. (If the scope of protection was limited to that which was provided by a literal reading of the claims, any variation would mean that there was no infringement.) At the same time, the question harks back to a long-standing rule in British patent law that it is not necessary for every element of a patented invention to be taken for it to be infringed. Rather, for an infringement to take place, a defendant must take all of the *material* or *essential* elements of

---

[111] Art. 1, Protocol on the Interpretation of Article 69 EPC 2000.

[112] On the background see *American Home Products v. Novartis Pharmaceuticals* [2000] *RPC* 547, 557.

[113] Art. 2, *Protocol on the Interpretation of Article 69 EPC 2000.*   [114] [1990] *FSR* 181, 189.

[115] These questions have been called the '*Improver* Questions', the 'Protocol Questions' (*Wheatley v. Drillsafe* [2001] *RPC* 133, 142 (CA) (Aldous LJ)) and 'the Questions' (*Kirin-Amgen v. Transkaryotic Therapies* [2002] *RPC* 187, 194–5 (Neuberger J). To avoid confusion we will refer to them as the *Improver* Questions.

[116] *Improver* [1990] *FSR* 181.   [117] *Wheatley v. Drillsafe* [2001] *RPC* 133, 142, Aldous LJ.

the invention.[118] Correspondingly, the fact that a defendant fails to take an immaterial or non-essential part of the patented invention will not allow them to escape liability for infringement. This ensures that patentees' interests are not undermined by defendants who dress up infringing inventions to appear as if they fall outside the scope of the patent monopoly.[119]

If the court finds that the variant has a material effect on the way the invention works this is the end of the matter: there is no infringement. However, if the court finds that the variant does not have a material effect on the way the invention works, the court then goes on to ask the hypothetical question: would this (i.e. that the variant has no material effect) have been obvious to a reader skilled in the art at the date of the publication of the patent?[120] If no, the variant is outside the claim. To secure a reasonable degree of certainty for third parties, the second question imposes limits on the non-literal reading encouraged by the first question. One issue that has arisen when applying this question is the level of knowledge that should be imputed to the skilled person. Should they, for example, be told that the defendant's invention works? Or should the skilled person simply be presented with the invention, with no additional explanations or instructions? The way this issue is resolved is important, since the more information given to the skilled person, the more likely it is that they would conclude that it was obvious that the variant did not have a material effect on the way the invention worked. In *Kirin-Amgen* the Court of Appeal proceeded on the basis that the skilled addressee would know about the existence of the alleged infringing product, but would not know whether it worked or that it had a material effect on the way the invention works.[121]

The third and final *Improver* question requires the court to ask whether a reader skilled in the art would have understood from the language of the claim that strict compliance with the primary meaning was an essential requirement of the invention. If so, the variation is outside the claim. This is the clearest and most straightforward of the three *Improver* questions. As Lord Diplock explained in *Catnic*, there are a number of reasons why patentees might want to have their claims read strictly: the most obvious being the desire to avoid some prior art that would otherwise anticipate the patent. In this sense, it provides fairness to the patentee and also a degree of certainty for third parties.[122]

---

[118] There has been little discussion about how the material elements of the invention are to be determined. Presumably, the courts ought to construe the patent purposively from the perspective of a reasonable person skilled in the art. The terms 'essence', 'pith and marrow', 'substantial', 'material', and 'essential' have been used interchangeably. All boil down to the same point, that for an infringement action to be successful, it is necessary for the essence or core of a patented invention to be 'taken'. See *Clark v. Adie* (1877) 2 *App Cas* 315 (Lord Cairns).

[119] Albeit the question is turned inside out. Instead of stating that the material aspects of an invention must be taken for there to be an infringement, the first *Improver* Question requires the court to find that the variant does not have a material effect on the way the invention works. This is supported by Arden LJ's comment that the 'variant must be immaterial, obvious, and consistent with the language of the patent'. *Pharmacia v. Merck* [2002] *RPC* 775, 830 (CA).

[120] Hoffmann J followed *Catnic* [1982] *RPC* 183, 243, and said that the second question was to be judged as of the date when the specification was published. However, this was not followed in *American Home Products v. Novartis Pharmaceuticals* [2001] *RPC* 159, 172 (CA) (date of the patent). Similarly in *Kirin-Amgen v. Transkaryotic Therapies* [2003] *RPC* 31 (CA), the court looked at evidence from the filing date of the patent. See H. Dunlop, 'Court of Appeal Gets to Grips with the Protocol' [2003] *EIPR* 342, 349 (arguing that the 'second question is judged at the filing date of the application (or the priority date if this is claimed and relied upon)').

[121] *Kirin-Amgen* [2003] *RPC* 31, 63 (CA) For a similar approach pre-*Amgen*, see *Owen Mumford v. Novo Nordisk*, O/261/02. On this see Dunlop [2003] *EIPR* 342, 348 ff (person skilled in the art should not be provided with a working example as that would tip the balance in favour of a 'yes' answer).

[122] Dunlop, above, 345.

3.1.4 Kirin-Amgen

There is little doubt that *Catnic* and the *Improver* questions play an important role in patent claim interpretation. Despite this the rules, or more specifically the way that they have been applied, have been subject to growing criticism. In the 2005 House of Lords decision of *Kirin-Amgen* Lord Hoffmann summed up many of the concerns about the way that *Catnic* has been applied when he said that there is a tendency to regard the expression 'purposive interpretation' as 'a vague description of some kind of divination which mysteriously penetrates beneath the language of the specification'.[123] Lord Hoffmann was also critical of the way that the *Improver* decision had been used, suggesting that 'the cases show a tendency for counsel to treat the Protocol questions as legal rules rather than guides which will in appropriate cases help to decide what the skilled man would understand the patentee to mean'.[124] This is part of a more widespread concern about the way that the *Improver* (or Protocol) questions have been applied. For example, while the courts have tended to favour the *Improver* questions when determining whether a patent has been infringed,[125] the tests are applied inconsistently.[126] For example while Aldous LJ may have used the *Improver* questions fairly consistently, in other cases the *Improver* questions have been applied, but then 'checked' against the principles laid down in the Protocol.[127] In other situations the courts have jettisoned *Catnic* and the *Improver* questions and simply relied on first impressions.[128] In other cases, the courts have looked to the essence or core of the invention as the basis for determining infringement.

While *Catnic* and *Improver* often provide useful guidance when thinking about whether a patent for a mechanical invention has been infringed, they are less helpful when it comes to the infringement of complex chemical and biotechnological inventions.[129] Where a patent for a mechanical invention such as a door lintel or a hair removal device is infringed, there are unlikely to be any doubts about the parameters of either the invention or the alleged infringing device. In these situations, the main question is whether they are the 'same'. This is not the case, however, with complex biotechnological and chemical inventions. One of the main problems, particularly with the *Improver* questions, is that they do not provide any guidance as to how the patented invention or the defendant's 'product' are to be characterized. Instead, the *Improver* questions take these as givens, focusing instead on the difference between the two. While it may be relatively easy to characterize the claimant's invention and the defendant's alleged infringing device where mechanical inventions are involved, this is often not the case with complex technologies. As Laddie J explained, this is because 'precision is not always possible: either because the language is incapable of defining the boundary or because the technology has not developed sufficiently for the boundary to be identified'.[130] Lord Hoffmann made similar but more specific comments about the *Improver* questions in *Kirin-Amgen*. In particular he said that, insofar as the questions require a court to decide what is meant by a 'primary,

---

[123] *Kirin-Amgen v. Hoechst Marion Roussel* [2005] *RPC* 9, para 33 (HL).

[124] Ibid, para 52.

[125] *Monsanto v. Merck* [2000] *RPC* 709, 782 (Pumfrey J); *Wheatley v. Drillsafe* [2001] *RPC* 133, 144 (Aldous LJ).

[126] For problems in the application of the *Improver* test, see *Wheatley*, above; *Consafe Engineering v. Emtunga* [1999] *RPC* 154, 160–1; *Kastner v. Rizla* [1995] *RPC* 585, 595 (suggesting that the court should lean away from over rigid application of the *Improver* test).

[127] *Pharmacia v. Merck* [2002] *RPC* 775, 830 (Arden LJ).

[128] *Wheatley v. Drillsafe*, above, 151 (Sedley LJ).

[129] See G. Thomson and L. Kempton. 'Construction Issues in Pharmaceutical and Biotech Cases' [2002] *EIPR* 591; P. Cole 'Pioneering Pays—Or Does It?' [2000] *EIPR* 534, 540.

[130] *AHP v. Novartis* [2000] *RPC* 547, 558 (Laddie J).

literal or acontextual meaning', they assume that the author used words strictly in accordance with their conventional meanings. While this assumption may be appropriate when dealing with figures, measurements, angles and the like, as Lord Hoffmann said, this was not the case (as in *Kirin-Amgen*) where the case turned on the way that the invention was defined.[131]

Problems of this nature led some commentators to suggest that the *Improver* questions should 'be reserved for the types of cases from whence they came, namely those involving mechanical variants'.[132] While it is not clear whether the role played by the *Improver*/Protocol questions will be restricted to mechanical inventions, following the House of Lords in *Kirin-Amgen* it is clear that the *Improver* questions should not be applied mechanistically,[133] nor necessarily in all cases.[134] It is also clear that they should not be used as a de facto test for determining the scope of protection. Instead, it is important to keep in mind that they are 'no more than aids to assist to arrive at the proper construction'[135] that should only be used where they assist the court in deciding the key question: what is the scope of the claims?

As Lord Hoffmann said in *Kirin-Amgen*, the key question to ask was: 'what would a person skilled in the art have understood the patentee to have used the language of the claim to mean... [e]verything else, including the Protocol [*Improver*] questions, was only guidance to a judge trying to answer that question'.[136] The type of approach that should be taken to the interpretation of claims is exemplified by *Pharmacia v. Merck*, which involved infringement in relation to the complex chemical compound rapamycin. While the decision was made before *Kirin-Amgen*, it reflects the type of approach that Lord Hoffmann recommended. In *Pharmacia v. Merck* Aldous LJ said that he found it difficult to apply the *Improver* questions to a 'claim in which every term is unambiguous and devoid of any question of degree... but which would nonetheless be read as necessarily involving the presence of other species not mentioned... It is the nature of class claims that not every member of every class will be exemplified and described.'[137] As a result, Aldous LJ accepted that this was not a situation where the *Improver* questions could be used without modification. Instead he said that the Court had no alternative but to seek the middle way required by the Protocol by considering what would be fair for the patentee and whether that would unfairly impinge upon the required certainty for the public.[138] In *Kirin-Amgen* itself, which concerned a patent for the production of erythropoietin (EPO), the key question was whether the patent covered the defendant's use of 'gene activation' to produce EPO. It was claimed that the defendant infringed claim 26, which referred to expression in a 'host cell', but the defendant argued that the reference to 'host cell' indicated that the genetic coding material must have originated outside the cell, whereas its technique activated genetic coding matter already within the cell. Lord Hoffmann, interpreting the claim from the standpoint of the person skilled in the art, agreed with the defendant's construction. As a result, there was no need to apply the so-called 'Protocol' or 'Improver' questions. It will be interesting to see whether the courts follow Lord

---

[131] *Kirin-Amgen v. Hoechst Marion Roussel* [2005] *RPC* 9, para 66.

[132] Thomson and Kempton [2002] *EIPR* 591, 595.

[133] On this see Lord Hoffmann, *Kirin-Amgen v. Hoechst Marion Roussel* above, para 52.

[134] *Kirin-Amgen v. TKT* [2002] *RPC* 187, 202 (Neuberger J).

[135] *Wheatley v. Drillsafe* [2001] *RPC* 133, 156 (Mance LJ).

[136] Ibid. As Lord Hoffmann said in *Kirin-Amgen*, the only compulsory factor to be taken into account when determining the extent of protection conferred by a European patent: namely the rules as set out in Article 69 of EPC [2000] and its protocol.

[137] *Monsanto v. Merck* [2000] *RPC* 709 (approved on appeal in *Pharmacia v. Merck* [2002] *RPC* 775, 796 (Aldous LJ)).

[138] *Pharmacia*, above, 796 (Aldous LJ).

Hoffmann's lead, or whether they resort, as they have done so often in the past, to a more literal reading of the claims.

3.2 REPLACEMENT OF PART OF AN INVENTION WITH AN EQUIVALENT PART

It is well settled that for there to be an infringement, the defendant must deal with all the material elements of the invention. One issue that was uncertain for many years under the 1977 Act was whether a person will infringe where they replace a material element of an invention with something that is functionally equivalent. Prior to the passage of the Patents Act 1977, under the so-called doctrine of equivalents, the courts held that elements of an invention were the same not just when they were identical, but also when they were functionally equivalent.[139] This means that 'there may be infringement even if the accused product falls outside the meaning of the words of the claim when understood in context'.[140] As Thomas Webster wrote in 1851, 'the question is, whether that which may have been done, though different in form and configuration, is not a geometrical, mechanical or chemical equivalent; whether, though the form be changed, the same result be not attained'.[141]

Despite its long tradition, doubts have been raised as to whether the doctrine of equivalents is still applicable under the 1977 Act. The reason given for this is that neither Article 69 of the EPC 1973[142] nor the Protocol (under EPC 1973) made any specific reference to the doctrine of equivalents.[143] While this is undoubtedly the case, it is wrong to assume from this that the doctrine of equivalents therefore had no place in British law. Rather, following the widely shared view that a purposive style of interpretation is the approach that ought to be adopted under the Protocol, the question whether the doctrine of equivalents has any continued relevance under the 1977 Act ought to be decided purposively on the facts of individual cases. This means that whether the replacement of a part of an invention with something that is functionally equivalent constitutes an infringement ought to depend on the way the person skilled in the art views the patent in question.[144] Such an approach would not only be consistent with the current jurisprudence in other EPC countries, by focusing upon the function or purpose that invention is to perform (which is what the doctrine of equivalents demands), it also would follow the spirit rather than the letter of the Protocol: the very point that Lord Diplock was making in the *Catnic* decision.

In many ways, it seemed that the uncertainty about the status of the doctrine of equivalents were answered by the EPC 2000. In affirming the continued role of the doctrine of equivalents, Article 2 of the Protocol on Interpretation of Article 69 in the EPC 2000 reads that for 'the purposes of determining the extent of protection conferred by a European patent, due account

---

[139] See *Kirin-Amgen v. Hoechst Marion Roussel* [2005] *RPC* 9, para 36ff; *Van der Lely v. Bamfords* [1963] *RPC* 61 (HL); *Rodi & Weinenberger v. Showell* [1969] RPC 367 (HL); *Beecham Group v. Bristol Laboratories* [1978] *RPC* 153.

[140] *Celltech* [2003] *FSR* 433, 436 (Jacob J); see generally M. Franzosi, 'Equivalence in Europe' [2003] *EIPR* 237.

[141] T. Webster, *The Subject Matter of Letters Patent for Inventions and the Registration of Designs* (1851), 83.

[142] PA s. 125.

[143] *Beloit Technolgies v. Valmet Paper Machinery* [1995] *RPC* 705, 720; *Celltech,* above, 436 (no express provision in Europe for doctrine of equivalents).

[144] In *Eli Lilly v. Novopharm* [1966] *RPC* 1, 21 the Federal Court of Canada said that, as the court was entitled to adopt a purposive approach in construing the claims and the essential parts thereof, this obviated the need to resort to the doctrine of equivalents.

shall be taken of any element which is equivalent to an element specified in the claims'.[145] As a result, it seemed clear that the doctrine of equivalents needs to be taken into account when deciding whether a patent has been infringed.

Any hope that the EPC 2000 might have resolved the uncertainty about the status of 'equivalents' under British law has been quashed by the House of Lord's decision in *Kirin-Amgen*, where Lord Hoffmann said that the amendment changes nothing: the provision only makes it clear that equivalents need to be considered, not that there is a 'doctrine of equivalents' allowing a court to extend protection beyond that covered in the claims (as interpreted by the person skilled in the art). As Lord Hoffmann said 'It seems to me that both the doctrine of equivalents in the United States and the pith and marrow doctrine in the United Kingdom were born of despair. Since the *Catnic* case we have article 69 which, firmly shuts the door on any doctrine which extends protection outside the claims. I cannot say that I am sorry because...American patent litigants pay dearly for results which are no more just or predictable than could be achieved by simply reading the claims.'

Of course, Lord Hoffmann's views on the impact of the changes in the EPC 2000 were *obiter*, and in an appropriate case we expect that a patentee will try and argue that the inclusion of the reference to equivalents in the amended Protocol is intended to prompt a change in judicial practice in member states.

4 DEFENCES TO PROCEEDINGS FOR INFRINGEMENT

Once the claimant has proved that the defendant has performed an activity that falls within the scope of the patent monopoly, the obligation then shifts to the defendant to show that the activity is exempted from liability by one of the defences to patent infringement that are available. There has been surprisingly little discussion about the defences to patent infringement actions and the policies that inform them.[146] At a general level, the exceptions balance the interests of patentees against the interests of other groups, such as competitors, previous users, traders, users, non-profit-making bodies, as well as teaching and research establishments. In some cases, the defences operate to overcome the market failure that occurs where a patentee declines to license a socially beneficial use because of the transaction costs involved. With these general points in mind, we now turn to look at some of the more important defences that may exempt a defendant from liability.

4.1 PRIVATE NON-COMMERCIAL USES

Section 60(5)(a) provides that acts that are done privately *and* for non-commercial purposes do not infringe.[147] The private use exception is usually explained on the basis that while private uses may increase scientific knowledge and thus be socially beneficial, high transaction

---

[145] Proposed new Protocol on the Interpretation of Art. 69: Art. 2, item 2 of EPC 2000. M. Fisher, 'New Protocol, Same old Story? Patent Claim construction in 2007' (2008) *IPQ* 133.

[146] D. Gilat, *Experimental Use and Patents* (1995); R. Eisenberg, 'Patents and the Progress of Science: Exclusive Rights and Experimental Use' (1989) 56 *University of Chicago LR* 1017; J. Karp, 'Experimental Use as Patent Infringement' (1991) 100 *Yale LJ* 2169.

[147] CPC Art. 31.

costs may mean that they are unlikely to be licensed.[148] Another factor in favour of the defence
is that private non-commercial uses do not pose much of a threat to the patent monopoly.
While private uses need not be secret or confidential, they must be 'for the person's own use'.[149]
Where an activity has both commercial and non-commercial benefits, it is necessary to ascertain the subjective intention of the user. If the infringer was motivated by commercial interests, the defence would not apply. However, if the subjective purposes were non-commercial,
the defendant could rely on the immunity. This is the case even if the resulting information
has a commercial benefit.[150]

4.2 EXPERIMENTAL USES

Section 60(5)(b) provides immunity for acts done for experimental purposes relating to the
subject matter of the invention.[151] This defence gives effect to a number of related policies, the
most obvious is that the patent monopoly should not be allowed to inhibit scientific developments. It is likely that the experimental-use defence will become increasingly important
as patenting (especially in relation to biotechnology) enters the traditional domains of 'pure'
scientific research carried out within the universities.[152]

To a large extent, the scope of the defence depends on the way 'experimental purpose' is
defined.[153] If it can be shown that the purpose of the activity was to discover something unknown
or to test a hypothesis, it would be regarded as an experiment.[154] An act will also be experimental where a person is attempting to discover whether the patented invention works.[155] This
may occur, for example, where a party is thinking whether to license a patent or they believe
that the patent is invalid on grounds of insufficiency. Given the public interest in determining
whether a monopoly has been validly granted it is desirable that competitors undertake this
kind of policing task. In the absence of an experimental-use defence, such acts might require
the licence of the patentee, which in the circumstances may not be forthcoming.[156]

If the purpose of the activity is to prove something that is already known, to demonstrate to
a third party that the product works in the way the maker claims, or to obtain official approval

---

[148] See Gilat, *Experimental Use and Patents*, 25. The US courts have occasionally employed the principle of *de
minimis non curat lex*. See, e.g. *Finney v. United States* 188 *USPQ* 33 (CCTD 1975).

[149] *SKF Laboratories v. Evans Medical* [1989] *FSR* 513, 518; *McDonald v. Graham* [1994] *RPC* 407.

[150] *SKF v. Evans* above.

[151] CPC Art. 27(b). See W. Cornish, 'Experimental Use of Patented Inventions in European Community
States' (1998) 29 *IIC* 735. T. Cook, *A European Perspective as to the Extent to which Experimental Use and Certain
Other Defences to Patent Infringement Apply to Differing Types of Research* (2006).

[152] E. Barash, 'Experimental Uses, Patents and Scientific Progress' (1997) 91 *Northwestern University Law
Review* 667 (recommending expansion of experimental-use defence for non-profit research).

[153] The 'purposes for which tests or trials are carried out may in some cases be mixed and in some cases may
be difficult to discern'. *Monsanto v. Stauffer Chemical* [1985] *RPC* 515, 542 (Dillon LJ) (CA).

[154] Ibid, 515.

[155] The decision of the Supreme Court of Canada in *Micro-Chemicals v. Smith Kline and French InterAmerican*
(1971) 25 *DLR* 79, 89 (that use by a defendant to establish that it could manufacture a quality product in accordance with the specification was not an infringement) was explicitly approved by Dillon LJ in *Monsanto v. Stauffer*,
above, 538. Trials directed to discovering whether something which is known to work in certain conditions will
work in different conditions could fairly be regarded as experiments: above, 542; Gilat, *Experimental Use and
Patents*, 20.

[156] The situation is analogous to the criticism-or-review defence in copyright law, which is based on the idea
that criticism would be stifled if the law were to require a prospective critic to obtain a licence from the copyright
owner before criticizing the work.

for a product,[157] these would not be regarded as acts done for experimental purposes.[158] In one case it was held that trials that were carried out to obtain safety clearances, and to gather information to support an attempt to gain approval for a new use of a patented product (to be used once the patent had expired), were for commercial rather than scientific purposes.[159] While the issue has yet to be considered in any detail, it seems that if there is a commercial motive behind the experimental use that it is more likely to fall outside the scope of the exception.[160] This question will undoubtedly become more pressing given the growing trend for public sector agencies that have traditionally relied upon the defence, such as universities, to commercialize their research results.[161] So far, there has been no consideration given to the question whether a person who tests an invention to improve it, to invent around the patent, or to invent something else, falls within the defence.[162] However, the German Supreme Court has held that experiments to discover the most appropriate form that a patented product should take to alleviate a specific disease fell within the experimental-use defence under German law.[163]

Once it has been shown that a use has been carried out for an experimental purpose, it is then necessary to show that the experiment relates to the subject matter of the patent.[164] This means, for example, that a person who wished to test a cure for cancer they had developed by applying it to a genetically modified mouse could not rely on the defence against a claim by the patentee of the mouse. If the law were otherwise, the patentees of diagnostic test kits would never receive any remuneration because all uses of the kit would be experimental.[165] Where a researcher wishes to use patented processes or products to test other subject matter, they would need to obtain a licence.[166]

In addition to the experimental use defence, researchers may also be able to rely on the more specific, but related, medical regulatory use defence. This newer defence, which is set out in the Medicines (Marketing Authorisations etc) Amendment Regulations[167] provides a defence for

---

[157] *Auchinloss v. Agricultural and Veterinary Supplies* [1999] *RPC* 397, 405.

[158] *Monsanto v. Stauffer* [1985] *RPC* 515, 542 (CA).

[159] Ibid, 515; *Auchinloss* [1997] *RPC* 649; [1999] *RPC* 397 (CA). Another situation where a person may wish to rely on the defence is where they test someone else's patented invention for the purposes of obtaining regulatory approval, either by providing data or samples to the relevant authority. In *Upjohn v. Kerfoot* [1988] *FSR* 1, Whitford J held that the mere application for a marketing authorization in respect of a medicinal product, even when accompanied by test results, did not constitute an infringement of the patent since it did not amount to use of the patent. In the USA such samples are permitted under the Drug Price Competition and Patent Term Restoration Act 1984, 35 USC s. 271. The EU argued that a similar Canadian provision, which permits making and stockpiling of the drug up to six months prior to the expiry of the patent, contravened TRIPS. The matter was referred to the WTO: 12 Nov. 1998. See 'Canada: Patent Protection of Pharmaceutical Products (Report of the panel)' (17 Mar. 2000) WT/DS114/R.

[160] *Inhale Therapeutic Systems v. Quadrant Healthcare* [2002] *RPC* 419, 463.

[161] For the approach taken in the USA in this situation see *Madey v. Duke University* 64 USPQ 2d 1737 (Fed. Cir. 2002) (Duke University could not rely on experimental-use defence because of the commercial nature of the University inter alia).

[162] *McDonald v. Graham* [1994] *RPC* 407 ('no doubt the defendant would be right to submit that supplying a patented article to a designer with a request that he design a non-infringing equivalent would be, in principle, an unobjectionable use of the article if the article were a "franked" article, but the defendant used infringing articles which he was well aware were not supposed to be in his possession at the material time').

[163] *Klinische Versuche (Clinical trials) II* [1998] *RPC* 423, s. 11(2) of the German Patent Act. See P. Tauchner, 'Experimental Use Exemption in Germany' (Dec. 1997) *Patent World* 23.

[164] In *Auchincloss*, above 402, 406 (CA), Aldous LJ said the 'subject matter' of the invention must be ascertained from the patent as a whole.

[165] *SKF v. Evans* [1989] *FSR* 513, 523.   [166] *Monsanto v. Stauffer* [1985] *RPC* 515, 522.

[167] SI 2005/2759 reg. 60(5)(i).

an act done in conducting a study, test or trial which aims to produce medicinal products for either human[168] or veterinary use.[169]

4.3 PRIOR USE

As we saw earlier, one of the changes brought about by the 1977 Act was that novelty was redefined to exclude inventions that had been 'made available to the public'. As a result, secret third-party use does not destroy novelty.[170] One of the consequences of this is that the rights conferred by a patent might cover secret activities carried out by a third party prior to grant.[171] In recognition that it would be wrong if patents were allowed to be used to prevent a person from carrying on an activity that they were doing prior to grant (the so-called right-to-work doctrine), section 64(1) provides previous users with a personal defence.[172]

There are a number of points to note about the defence. The first is that it only applies where the previous acts were committed in the United Kingdom (or possibly the EEA).[173] Given that the novelty standard is worldwide, this raises the possibility that a person carrying out an activity in Japan which is then patented by another person in the United Kingdom, will not be able to practise the invention in the United Kingdom.

It is also important to note that the defence is only available where the acts were carried out in good faith. Although the notion of good faith has yet to be interpreted by the courts, this might prevent a member of a research team from relying on the prior-use defence where they left the research team contrary to an understanding between them. Similarly, if a former employee was preparing to use trade secrets obtained while in employment to compete with their ex-employer, the ex-employee would not be able to rely on the preparatory acts as a defence to patent infringement actions.[174]

The defence is only available where the defendant has done the acts or, before the priority date of the patent, made 'serious and effective preparations' to do an act which would be infringing if it was carried out after the grant of the patent. It has been said that the preparations 'must be so advanced as to be about to result in the infringing act being done'.[175] The defence allows a past user to continue to do the same act after the patent has been granted. While it is

---

[168] Paras. 1–4. of Art. 10 of Directive 2001/83/EC.

[169] Paras. 1–5 of Art. 13 of Directive 2001/82/EC.

[170] This reinforces the policy that the patent should be granted to the first to file and disclose the invention rather than the first to invent. See P. Hubert, 'The Prior User Right of H.R. 400: A Careful Balancing of Competing Interests' (1998) 14 *Computer & High Tech Law Journal* 189; Symposium (1996) 36 *IDEA* 345.

[171] Art. 4(B) of the Paris Convention leaves such matters to the domestic legislation of contracting states. See R. Rohrback, 'Prior User Rights: Roses or Thorns?' (1993) 2 *University of Baltimore IP Journal* 1; N. Marterer, 'The Prior User's Right' (1990) 21 *IIC* 521; A. Monotti, 'Balancing the Rights of the Patentee and Prior User of an Invention: The Australian Experience' [1997] *EIPR* 351.

[172] *Helitune v. Stewart Hughes* [1991] *FSR* 171, 206.

[173] The latter modification may be required to prevent the provision being contrary to Art. 28 EC (formerly Art. 30 of the Treaty), as interpreted in *EC Commission v. United Kingdom*, Case C–30/90 [1993] *RPC* 283; [1992] 2 *CMLR* 709; [1992] *ECR* I–829. There is no Community harmonization of this issue. See L. Osterborg, 'Towards a Harmonized Prior User Right within the Common Market Patent System' (1981) 12 *IIC* 447; J. Neukom, 'A Prior Use Right for the Community Patent Convention' [1990] *EIPR* 165; 'A Prior Use Right for the Community Patent Convention: An Update' [1991] *EIPR* 139.

[174] Subject to the 'springboard principle', the action for breach of confidence might not be available once the employee's patent is published, so it is important that the ex-employee cannot rely on the s. 64 defence. See below at pp. 1016–17.

[175] *Lubrizol Corporation v. Esso Petroleum* [1998] *RPC* 727, 770 (CA); *Helitune* [1991] *FSR* 171 (serious and effective preparations required more than general research into the same field).

not necessary for a defendant to show unbroken use, they must show a clear link or a 'chain of causation' between the previous use and the infringing use.[176] As the past-secret-use defence is a personal defence, the continued use must be by the same person (or partner). The exact scope of the act is therefore crucial. The defence is not available to a defendant who does a thing that is wholly different in nature. This would mean, for example, where the previous use was in relation to a process, the previous user would not be able to use the defence in relation to acts carried out (after grant) in relation to products of the process.[177] It is important to note that some variation is allowed between the previous use and the alleged infringing act:[178] the difficult question is, how much of a variation is possible?

If the act or preparations were done in the course of business, the previous user has the right to authorize the doing of the act by their business partners at that time. They also have the right to assign that right or to transmit it on death to any person who acquires the part of the business in the course of which the act was done or the preparations were made.[179] Importantly, the defence does not extend to include licensees.[180]

4.4 DEFENCES FOR BIOTECHNOLOGICAL INVENTIONS

As a part of the regime dealing with biotechnological inventions, three new defences to the infringement of patents for biotechnological inventions have been formulated. These are set out in Articles 10 and 11 of the Biotechnology Directive and in changes made to the Patents Act 1977 by the Patents Regulations 2000.

4.4.1 Exhaustion of biological patents

Article 10/paragraph 10 of Schedule A2 of the 1977 Act provide that the protection conferred by a patent[181] shall not extend to biological material obtained from the propagation or multiplication of biological material placed on the market by the owner of the patent (or with his consent), where the multiplication or propagation necessarily results from the application for which the biological material was marketed. This is subject to the proviso that the material obtained is not subsequently used for other types of propagation or multiplication.

In effect Article 10 introduces a specific form of exhaustion for biological patents. For the patent rights to be exhausted under Article 10, it is necessary to establish that the multiplication or propagation (which potentially infringes the patent) is 'an incident of what might be called the true purpose of the sale'.[182] The upshot of this is that a person who used a patented yeast to make beer would prima facie infringe the patent in the yeast. This is because the process of making the beer necessarily involves the multiplication of the yeast. However, if the patented yeast were sold in a home-brew shop for the purpose of beer making, Article 10 (and its British equivalent) would provide the defendant with a 'defence'. Nonetheless, if the defendant propagated the yeast and offered it for sale, the defence would not apply.[183] The defence will allow farmers to sow a patented seed, and to harvest and sell the resulting crop (for example, to

---

[176] *Hadley Industries v. Metal Sections* (13 Nov. 1998) (unreported) (Patents Court).   [177] Ibid.

[178] *Helitune v. Stewart Hughes* [1991] *FSR* 171, 206; *Lubrizol v. Esso Petroleum* [1992] *RPC* 281, 295; ibid [1998] *RPC* 727 (CA).

[179] PA s. 64(2) provides an equivalent to exhaustion when a previous user disposes of the product. The person who acquires the product is entitled to deal with the product in the same way as if it had been disposed of by a sole registered proprietor.

[180] PA s. 64(3).

[181] As set out in Biotech. Dir. Arts. 8 and 9; PA Sched. A2, paras. 7, 8, 9. These were discussed above at pp. 546–7.

[182] See Bostyn, 'Patentability of Genetic Information Carriers' [1999] *IPQ* 1, 30.   [183] Ibid.

sell the wheat for flour). They would not be permitted, however, to sell the seed to other farmers for the purpose of propagating new crops.[184]

4.4.2 Farmers' privilege

In the debates surrounding the Biotechnology Directive, one of the fears raised was that patent protection of biological inventions would have a negative impact on traditional farming practices. In particular, it was feared that patent protection would mean that farmers would not be able to use the seeds that they harvested from their crops to resow in future, nor would they be able to breed patented animals. The potential problem was that sowing and breeding carried out in relation to a patented product would infringe. To remedy problems of this sort, Article 11(1) and (2) of the Biotechnology Directive provide farmers with specific defences. These provisions have been mirrored in sections 60(5)(g) and 60(5)(h) of the 1977 Patent Act, introduced in July 2000.

Section 60(5)(g) provides a defence where a farmer uses the product of their harvest for propagation or multiplication by them on their farm, after there has been a sale or other form of commercialization of plant-propagating material to the farmer by the patent owner for agricultural use. In effect the defence enables farmers to save seeds from one year's crop to sow crops in the following year. The defence in section 60(5)(g) only applies to the plant species and groups set out in paragraph 2 of Schedule A1 to the Patents Act 1977. This covers various types of fodder plants, cereals, potatoes, and oil and fibre plants. In situations where a farmer successfully relies on the defence in section 60(5)(g), the farmer must pay the relevant rights holder equitable remuneration.[185] The remuneration must be 'sensibly lower than the amount charged for the production of the protected material of the same variety on the same area with the holder's authority'.[186] The need to pay equitable remuneration does not arise if a farmer can prove that they are a 'small farmer'.[187] Where requested, the rights holder and the farmer must supply each other with certain information.[188] The use of the defence is subject to a number of other restrictions (such as ability of the farmer to move protected material from their farm).

Section 60(5)(h) provides farmers with a defence in relation to the breeding of animals. More specifically, it provides that 'the use of an animal or animal reproductive material by a farmer for an agricultural purpose...of breeding stock or other animal reproductive material which constitutes or contains the patented invention' is non-infringing. The farmer's defence for the breeding of animals is potentially very broad. In part, the scope of the defence will depend on how the phrase 'use for an agricultural purpose' is construed. The Act tells us that 'use for an agricultural purpose' includes situations where the animal or animal reproductive material is made available for the purposes of pursuing the farmer's agricultural activity. However, it does not include 'sale within the framework, or for the purposes of a commercial reproduction activity'.[189]

It will be interesting to see what impact these defences have upon farming practices. It will also be interesting to see how the biotechnology industry responds to these defences. It has

---

[184] R. Nott, 'You Did It: The European Biotechnology Directive at Last' [1998] *EIPR* 347, 349.

[185] PA Sched. A1, para. 3(1) (introduced by Patents Regulations 2000).

[186] PA Sched. A1, para. 3(3) (introduced by Patents Regulations 2000) says that a remuneration will be sensibly lower if it would be 'sensibly lower within the meaning of Art. 14(3) third indent of the Council Regulation on Community plant variety rights'.

[187] PA Sched. A1, paras. 4(1)–(2) (introduced by Patents Regulations 2000). A 'small farmer' is defined via Art. 14(3) third indent of the Council Regulation on Community plant variety rights.

[188] PA Sched. A1, paras. 5–11 (introduced by Patents Regulations 2000).

[189] PA s. 60(6B)(a)(b). Sale is defined to include any other form of commercialization: PA s. 60(6C).

been suggested that defences such as those provided in section 60(5)(g)(h) may act as a stimulus for the development of techniques such as terminator genes or special hybrids that operate to ensure that seeds will not regerminate.[190]

4.5 MISCELLANEOUS DEFENCES

A number of other exceptions to infringement exist. Section 74(1)(a) expressly provides that the validity of a patent may be put in issue by way of a defence to proceedings for infringement. This is the most commonly used defence: an alleged infringer will normally argue that the patent is invalid because the invention lacks novelty or is obvious. A particular example of this is the so-called *Gillette* defence, where a defendant attempts to demonstrate that the infringing activity was being carried out in public before the priority date of the patent, thus forcing the patentee either to require the patent to be interpreted so as to exclude the activity, or to accept that the patent covers the activity and is therefore invalid (for want of novelty).

A defence is available where a person in a pharmacy makes an extempore preparation of a medicine in accordance with a prescription.[191] A defence also exists where products or processes are used on ships, aircraft, hovercraft, or vehicles that have temporarily or accidentally entered UK airspace or waters.[192] The Crown has a broad immunity from infringing the exclusive rights of patentees.[193] The Crown may use an invention without obtaining a licence in advance, so long as it pays compensation. More specifically, the defence permits 'any government department and any person authorized in writing by a government department' to do certain acts[194] in return for which the department must provide payment,[195] including 'compensation' for loss of profits.[196] In some cases, the doctrines of exhaustion of rights and implied licence, reviewed above, also (effectively) provide defences to accusations of infringement.

Prior to the passage of the Competition Act 1998, section 44 provided a defence where a patentee imposed a requirement on a licensee 'to acquire from the licensor or his nominee, or prohibit him from acquiring from any specified person, or from acquiring except from the licensor or his nominee, anything other than the product which is the patented invention or (if it is a process) other than any product obtained directly by means of the process or to which the process has been applied'. The defence was available to any person against whom the licensor brought an infringement action.[197] Section 44, which was widely criticized, has now been repealed by the 1998 Competition Act.[198]

---

[190] Nott, 'You Did It' [1998] EIPR 347, 349 n. 27.

[191] PA s. 60(5)(c).

[192] PA s. 60(5)(d)(e). See *Stena Rederi v. Irish Ferries* [2003] *RPC* 668 (CA). A ship that sailed between Dublin and Holyhead in the UK three or four times a day (each visit the ship was in UK waters for about three hours), was held to have temporarily entered the UK. Here 'temporarily' meant 'transient' or 'for a limited period of time', rather than the frequency of the visits. See further R. Sharma and H. Forrest, 'A Lifeline for Infringing Ships' [2003] *EIPR* 430.

[193] PA s. 55.   [194] Listed in PA s. 55(1)(a)–(e).

[195] PA s. 55(4). An exception, where no royalty need be paid, operates under PA s. 55(3).

[196] PA s. 57A.   [197] PA s. 44(3).

[198] See SI 2000/311 for transitional provisions.

23

EXPLOITATION

CHAPTER CONTENTS

1 INTRODUCTION

As forms of personal property,[1] patents and patent applications may be assigned, licensed, or mortgaged, and they may devolve by operation of law (notably through death or bankruptcy).[2] One of the consequences of this is that patents have become part of the commercial currency; they can be traded, exploited, and included on the balance sheet of companies. As such, instead of being seen as a peripheral aspect of the patent system, patent exploitation is better seen as a central component. Following similar developments in copyright, there have been various attempts to use the exploitation of patents to create a more open and free flowing science commons, particulary for biotechnological research.[3]

The terms and conditions that control the way patents are exploited are usually determined contractually by the parties: patent law merely provides a framework within which parties are able to manoeuvre. Where parties have agreed upon the way a patent is to be exploited, the law has been reluctant to interfere with the sanctity of the contract. There are some situations, however, where this is not the case. Apart from the general vitiating factors of contract law (such as unreasonable restraint of trade), special provisions exist in the Patents Act 1977 in relation to co-owners,[4] employee inventions, and (at least until recently) certain types of contractual term. Competition law, both domestic and European, also places important limits upon the nature and content of transactions entered into by a patentee. In recognition of the fact that non-use of a patent may produce undesirable consequences, in certain situations the law may order a patent owner to grant a licence to work the invention. Where this occurs, it is often necessary for the tribunal to set the rates of remuneration that should be paid to the proprietor.

---

[1] PA s. 30(1).   [2] PA s. 30(3).

[3] J. Hope, *Bio Bazaar: Biotechnolagy and the Open Space Revoluation* (2008); S. Dusollier, 'Sharing Access to Intellectual Property Through Private Ordering' (2007) 82 *Chic-Kent LR* 1391.   [4] PA s. 36(3), (7).

This chapter is divided into four parts. First, we consider the various ways patents may be exploited. We then look at some of the limits that are imposed on the way patents are exploited to minimize any possible anti-competitive effects. We then examine situations where compulsory licences are available (for example, where a patent is not used or is under-used). Finally, we look at the compensation payable where the patent is used via a compulsory licence, as well as when an employer or the Crown uses the invention.

2 MODES OF EXPLOITATION

In this section, we examine some of the ways in which patents are exploited. After considering the situation where patentees exploit the patent themselves, we look at some of the more common forms of voluntary uses: *viz.* assignment and licence. We then turn to consider situations where the patent is exploited by way of a compulsory licence or a licence as of right.

2.1 EXPLOITATION BY THE OWNER

In many cases, the owner of a patent may decide to manufacture or use the patented invention himself. While in most cases self-exploitation presents few legal problems, difficulties may arise when the patent is owned by a number of different parties. The most significant issue that arises here is whether one co-owner is able to practise the invention without the consent of the other co-owners. In some cases, the conditions of use will be dealt with contractually between the parties. As well as setting out the way each of the co-owners is able to exploit the patent, ideally such a contract should also specify the obligations that the parties have to each other. In situations where there is no contract between co-owners of a patent,[5] the Patents Act 1977 declares that each of the co-owners is 'entitled to operate under the patent themselves'.[6] That is, each owner is permitted to use and benefit from their undivided share of the patent. This means that a joint owner with a one per cent interest can work the patent on their own to the detriment of the other owners. The possibility for opportunistic behaviour that this presents is limited by the fact that a joint owner cannot license others to use the patent without the permission of the other co-owners.[7]

2.2 ASSIGNMENT

A common way in which patented products and processes are exploited is for the owner to assign their interests to another party. An assignment is a transfer of ownership of the patent (or application). As a result of an assignment, an assignee stands in the shoes of the assignor and is entitled to deal with the patent as they see fit. In contrast to a licence (where the licensor

---

[5] A patent may be co-owned where the invention is a product of joint inventorship, or as a result of dealings with a patent that was initially solely owned, such as an assignment to two persons.

[6] PA s. 36. The Patents Act 2004 amended PA s. 36(3) to clarify that co-owners are able to seek, amend, and revoke a patent if they act jointly, and have not contracted out of this requirement. Disputes between co-owners may be resolved via PA s. 37. See R. Merges and L. Locke, 'Co-Ownership of Patents: A Comparative and Economic View' (1990) 72 *JPTOS* 586.

[7] *Henry Brothers v. Ministry of Defence* [1997] *RPC* 693. Cf. M. Anderson, 'Applying Traditional Property Laws to Intellectual Property Transactions' [1995] *EIPR* 236, 240.

retains an interest in the patent), once a patentee has assigned the patent they no longer have any interest in or responsibility to maintain the patent.[8]

For an assignment to be valid, it must be in writing and signed by or on behalf of all the parties to the transaction.[9] Where the patent or application is owned by more than one party, for the assignment to be valid, all of the co-owners must consent to the assignment.[10] While assignments need not be registered to be valid, certain advantages flow from registration: these are reviewed below.[11]

2.3 VOLUNTARY LICENCES

Another common way in which patents are exploited is by licence. A licence provides a party with permission to do an act that would otherwise be prohibited. Licences may be made orally or in writing,[12] and may be express or implied.[13] Where a patent is owned jointly, all of the co-owners must provide their consent for the licence to be valid.[14] In contrast with an assignment, no proprietary interest is passed under a licence.[15]

Licences may take many forms: from a one-off permission through to an exclusive licence. One important example of a non-exclusive licence is that which patent holders who participate in standard-setting arrangements (particularly in the information and communication technologies sector) give to users of such standards allowing use of the patent on 'fair, reasonable and non-discriminatory terms' (FRAND). One example would be the mobile telephone standards established by the European Telecommunication Standardization Institute (ETSI), which requires participants to disclosure and licensing on FRAND terms of any patented technologies they possess before ETSI will consider the adoption of that technology as part of a standard. Another emerging licensing practice is the grant of 'open licences' allowing subsequent researchers to use patented material on condition that they apply similar terms to any improvements. One example of such a licence is that offered in the field of agricultural biotechnology called the Biological Innovation for Open Society (BiOS) agreement. An exclusive licence is an agreement under which the owner of a patent not only grants the licensee permission to use the patented technology, they also promise that they will not grant any other licences, nor will they exploit the technology themselves. The legal consequence of this is that an exclusive licence confers rights upon the licensee to the exclusion of all others, including the licensor.[16]

---

[8] It seems that an assignor comes under a personal disability in that they may not challenge the validity of the assigned patent: *Chambers v. Crichley* (1864) 33 *Beav* 374 (assignor prohibited from challenging validity of patent on basis of non-derogation from grant). But see A. Robertson, 'Is the Licensee Estoppel Rule Still Good Law? Was It Ever?' [1991] *EIPR* 373.

[9] PA s. 30(6). Differently worded but largely equivalent provisions for Scotland are set out in PA s. 31. An oral assignment might take effect as an agreement to assign and be enforceable in equity: *Stewart v. Case* (1891) 8 *RPC* 259; (1892) 9 *RPC* 9.

[10] PA s. 36(3), (7). For a situation in which the Patent Office ordered an assignment of a patent where one of seven co-owners was opposed to the agreement, see *Florey's Patent* [1962] *RPC* 186.

[11] See below at pp. 573–4.   [12] *Crossley v. Dixon* (1863) 10 *HLC* 293.

[13] See *Morton-Norwich v. Intercen and United Chemicals* [1981] *FSR* 337. A voluntary and exclusive licence is granted 'under' and not 'in' a patent—therefore PA s. 30(6) does not apply: *Instituform v. Inliner* [1992] *RPC* 83; *CIPA*, para. 30.05.

[14] PA s. 36(3), (7).

[15] *Allen & Hanbury v. Generics* [1986] *RPC* 203, 246. A licence itself can be dealt with: PA s. 30(4)(a).

[16] Cf. *Peaudouce SA v. Kimberly-Clark* [1996] *FSR* 680, 690–1.

While the grant of an exclusive licence is very similar to an assignment,[17] an exclusive licence does not need be made in writing.[18] Indeed, as with other licences, an exclusive licence may be made orally or in writing,[19] and may be express or implied.[20] While a 'bare licensee' acquires the right not to be sued in relation to the acts set out in the licence, an exclusive licence confers powers on the licensee that are equivalent to those of the proprietor. Undoubtedly the most significant of these is that exclusive licensees can sue infringers in their own right: they do not need to persuade the proprietor to take action on their behalf.[21]

2.4 MORTGAGES

Like other forms of property, patents may be mortgaged (or assigned as security for a debt).[22] This can be a useful technique to enable patentees to raise the funds necessary to exploit the patented invention. In this context, a mortgage is achieved by way of an assignment of the patent by the patentee–mortgagor to the mortgagee–lender. This is subject to a condition that the patent will be reassigned to the mortgagor when the debt is repaid (or as the law says, on redemption). It is important that the assignment reserves for the mortgagor a right to continue practising the invention. This is probably best achieved by the reservation of an exclusive licence. Alternatively, a patent can be used as security by way of a legal charge, in which case there is no assignment.[23] In this case, the chargee gains certain rights over the patent as security.

In order to be valid, a mortgage must be in writing and signed by the parties.[24] Where there are joint proprietors, all of them must consent to the mortgage.[25] A mortgage need not be registered to be valid, but there are advantages to registration: these are reviewed below.

2.5 TESTAMENTARY DISPOSITIONS

Because a patent is personal property, it is capable of passing on the death of the proprietor either by will or via the rules of intestacy. Because co-owners hold patents as tenants in common (rather than as joint tenants),[26] if a co-proprietor dies their share passes along with the rest of his or her estate, rather than accruing to the other co-owners. In devolving the patent, the personal representative must sign a written consent.[27]

---

[17] There are a number of differences between an assignment and an exclusive licence. For example, while an assignment of a patent must be in writing, an assignment of an exclusive licence need not: *Instituform*, note 13 above. In addition, note the weak position of the exclusive licensee in relation to the compulsory licence-of-right provisions operating in relation to the extension of patent terms: *Kaken Pharmaceutical Patent* [1990] *RPC* 72.

[18] Cf. the position in relation to copyright: CDPA s. 92 (exclusive licences must be in writing). *Morton-Norwich*, note 13 above.

[19] *Crossley v. Dixon* (1863) 10 *HLC* 293.   [20] *Morton-Norwich* [1981] *FSR* 337.

[21] PA s. 67. The proprietor is made party to the proceedings, if necessary by joining them as a defendant.

[22] A mortgage includes a charge for securing money or money's worth: PA s. 130(1). See M. Bezant and R. Punt, *The Use of Intellectual Property as Security for Debt Finance* (1997); D. Townend, *Using Intellectual Property as Security* (1996); M. Henry, 'Mortgages of Intellectual Property in the United Kingdom' [1992] *EIPR* 158.

[23] Charges are included within the definition of mortgage in PA s. 130.

[24] PA s. 30(6).   [25] PA s. 36(3).

[26] On an attempt to alter this (which failed) see *Florey's Patent* [1962] *RPC* 72.   [27] PA s. 30(6)(b).

2.6 REGISTRATION OF INTERESTS AND TRANSACTIONS

There is no need for transactions to be registered in order to be valid. Nonetheless, the Patents Act provides that assignments, mortgages, licences, sub-licences, and certain equitable interests may be registered.[28] While non-registration will not affect the validity of transactions made in relation to a patent, there are two reasons why a transaction should be registered.

The first is that registration gives the registrant priority against anyone who has an earlier unregistered right, subject to the proviso that the registrant had no notice of the earlier right.[29] In so doing, registration helps to allocate priorities between the parties who have interests in a patent. The act of registration enables a person with an interest to secure priority over those who engage in subsequent transactions. The effect of this can be illustrated as follows:

(i)   On 1 July 2008 X assigns their patent to Y. On 1 August 2008 X licenses the patent to Z. At the time of the licence, Y had not registered the assignment, nor did Z have any knowledge of the assignment to Y. On being informed by Y of their interest, Z registered its licence on 1 September 2008. In this case, Y is bound by Z's licence.

(ii)   On 1 July 2008 X grants an exclusive licence to Y, which Y duly registers on 15 July 2008. On 1 August, X grants another licence to Z. Y can sue Z if Z attempts to exercise the 'rights' they were purportedly granted.

(iii) X grants a mortgage of her patent to Y. Z, who was aware that Y has not registered the mortgage, obtains an exclusive licence from X which they immediately register. Y's mortgage binds Z.

The second reason why registration is advisable is that, in the case of assignments and exclusive licences, non-registration may affect a party's right to costs.[30] This is because a proprietor or exclusive licensee who does not register within six months of the transaction cannot claim costs in relation to actions for infringements which occurred in the period prior to registration.[31] Given that an infringement action might relate to acts of a defendant that occur during a period extending both before and after registration, courts will be faced with some difficult questions of apportionment.

2.7 LICENCES OF RIGHT

A patentee who is willing to license the technology to all comers may take advantage of the facility to enter on the register that licences are to be available as of right.[32] Once an endorsement 'licences of right' is entered on the register, anyone is able to apply for a licence and establish the scope of the licence they desire (whether it be to manufacture, sell, or import the invention). There are two reasons why a patentee might want to render a patent subject to licences as of right. First, the endorsement of a patent 'licences of right' acts as an advertisement that

---

[28] PA ss. 32–3.

[29] The relevant date to assess whether the registrant knew of the right is the date at which the later registrant acquired their interest. Both the fact of registration and the knowledge of the party are assessed at the time of the transaction (which is registered), not the date of registration.

[30] A previous incarnation of the section, which prevented the patentee from claiming damages or an account of profits for the relevant period, was described as intended to protect infringers: *Mölnlycke AB v. Procter & Gamble* [1992] *FSR* 549, 606–10.   [31] PA s. 68.

[32] On the history see *Allen & Hanbury v. Generics* [1986] *RPC* 203, 246.

the owner of the patent is willing to grant licences to parties who wish to exploit the invention. Second, such an endorsement halves the renewal fees payable.

One of the consequences of making licences available as of right is that the patentee is no longer able to dictate who can exercise the patent, nor control the terms of such licences. The terms of any licence are set by the parties, or if they cannot agree, by the comptroller. The courts have accepted that they have a wide discretion in the determination of terms.[33] When deciding the terms under which the licences should be exercised, the courts have taken into account the guidelines provided for the grant of compulsory licences.[34] A patentee who has previously rendered a patent subject to 'licences of right' can apply to the comptroller for cancellation of the entry. If accepted, the patentee must repay the balance of the renewal fees owing. Applications to remove the entry may be opposed.[35]

2.8 COMPULSORY LICENCES

The final mode of exploitation worth noting is the compulsory licence. A compulsory licence is a licence compulsorily imposed on the patentee. In contrast to a licence of right, which is usually initiated voluntarily, the decision as to whether a compulsory licence should be granted and if so the terms on which it is to be granted, is made by the relevant tribunals. We deal with the situations where compulsory licences may be granted in more detail below.[36]

3 LIMITS ON EXPLOITATION

A number of limits are also imposed on the ability of the patent owner to exploit the invention. When a patent owner exploits an invention, they must comply with the general laws and regulations. These require respect for the rights of other patentees, as well as compliance with health and safety laws, environmental regulation, product liability, and criminal laws.[37] While these non-economic restrictions on patent exploitation should not be neglected, our particular concern here is with the potentially anti-competitive effects of patent exploitation. There are three areas of law which minimize the potential for patent misuse. These are British patent law, British competition law, and EC competition law.

3.1 BRITISH PATENT LAW

For most of its long history patent law has used various techniques to minimize the potential for abuse that the monopoly conferred. These have included rules prohibiting the use of certain terms in patent licences,[38] as well as provisions permitting the use of patented inventions by third parties where the patent was being under-used or misused by the patentee. Despite this long tradition, it was recently decided that it was more appropriate for the potential abuse of patents to be regulated by competition law than by patent law. This farming-out of patent

---

[33] *Cabot Safety Corp's Patent* [1992] RPC 39. In that case the tribunal made decisions about who the licence should be granted to.

[34] PA s. 50; e.g. *Smith Kline & French Laboratories (Cimetidine) Patents* [1990] *RPC* 203, 250.

[35] PA s. 47.   [36] See below at pp. 577–84.   [37] Biotech. Dir., Recital 14.

[38] PA ss. 44 and 45 (now repealed).

regulation took place when the draconian provisions of sections 44 and 45 were repealed by section 70 of the Competition Act 1998.

3.2 BRITISH COMPETITION LAW

The introduction of the Competition Act 1998 marked an important change in the way British law regulated anti-competitive behaviour.[39] The Act establishes a system that parallels European competition law. It does this by enacting a prohibition (the 'Chapter 1 prohibition') that is equivalent to Article 81 EC (formerly Article 85 of the Treaty). Section 2 of the Competition Act prohibits agreements that may affect trade within the UK and have as their object or effect the prevention, restriction, or distortion of competition within the UK.[40] An agreement will not be caught by section 2 if it falls within any individual exemption, or under a 'block exemption' that may be made under section 6.[41] While the details of the British exemptions to section 2 have yet to be finalized, an agreement is deemed to be exempt from the national prohibition if it is exempt from the Community prohibition. This is also the case with licences that fall within the terms of the EC Technology Transfer Block Exemption, but which are not subject to Article 81 EC because they do not affect trade between EC member states.[42]

3.3 EC COMPETITION LAW

The key provision of European competition law affecting patent licences and exploitation agreements is Article 81 EC. This provides that all agreements which affect trade between member states, and which have the object or effect of distorting competition within the common market, shall be void.[43] However, under certain conditions, agreements falling within Article 81(1) may be exempt from Article 81 as a result of Article 81(3). Whether a transaction is exempt depends either on an individual assessment (now made by the tribunal ex post) or, attenatively, whether the transaction falls within the scope of block exemption.[44] The most important 'block exemption' for patent licences is the Technology Transfer Block Exemption Regulation (TTBER) which entered into force on 1 May 2004.[45] To assist corporations in the interpretation of the new block exemption, the Commission published *Guidelines on the*

---

[39] S. Rose, A. Clark, and M. Burdon, 'A New UK Competition Law: More Restrictions on Restrictions' (Jan. 1997) *Patent World* 27.

[40] Conduct that amounts to the abuse of a dominant position in a market within the UK of a part thereof is also prohibited: The Chapter II prohibition.

[41] Competition Act 1998, ss. 4–11.

[42] Ibid, s. 10. See Office of Fair Trading, *Intellectual Property Rights: A Draft Competition Act 1998 Guideline* (Nov 2001), 18 n. 2. (Revised draft Guidelines have yet to be published.)

[43] A licence term was held to be 'incompatible with EC Art. 81 if it sought to regulate the commercial market by controlling not only what was made with the licensed technology but also the use which was made of it thereafter'. *Intel Technologies v. Via Technologies* [2003] *FSR* 574, 600 (Morritt VC).

[44] From 1 May 2004, organizations must determine for themselves whether their agreements come within the Block Exemptions: Council Regulation No. 1/2002 of 16 December 2002 on the implementation of the rules on competition laid down in Articles 81 and 82 of the Treaty (2003) *OJ L*/1.

[45] See M. Hansen and O. Shah, 'The new EU Technology Transfer Regime' (2004) *ECLR* 1. For background see Draft Commission Regulation on the application of Article 81(3) of the Treaty to categories of technology transfer agreements. This grew out of the *EC Technology Transfer Block Exemption Evaluation Report* (Dec. 2001).

application of Article 81 EC to technology transfer agreements.[46] The TTBER replaces the 1996 block exemption Regulation, which adopted a more prescriptive approach. Although the effect of the TTBER on patent licences is considered in detail in specialist texts, we will briefly outline its scope and application to a few typical patent licence terms.[47]

The first aspect of the TTBER worth observing is its scope. Unlike the 1996 Regulation, which applied to patent licensing, know-how licensing agreements, and to mixed patent and know-how licensing agreements, a 'technology transfer agreement' is defined under the TTBER to include agreements that relate to patents, know-how, and software copyright.[48] Although the primary target of the Regulation is licences, it also applies to licences that are dressed up as assignments.[49] In many ways the TTBER follows the logic of the 1996 Regulation insofar as it declares that technology transfer agreements are to be exempt from the Article 81(1) prohibition.[50] One of the changes brought about by the new block exemption is that the Commission will no longer provide parties with specific exemptions for particular agreements: instead, the parties will have to judge for themselves whether they comply with the relevant provisions. A notable feature of the TTBER is that it treats agreements differently depending on whether the parties are 'competing undertakings' or 'non-competing undertakings'. Competing undertakings are defined as undertakings that compete on the relevant technology market and/or the relevant product market.[51] Other undertakings are dealt with on the basis that they are non-competing. Another notable feature of the Regulation is that it imposes a threshold that parties must not cross if they are to benefit from the block exemption. In particular, it says that if the combined market share of the parties exceeds 20 per cent for competing undertakings and 30 per cent for non-competing undertakings, the agreement will fall outside the scope of the immunity conferred by the block exemption.[52] Failure to remain below these market ceilings does not mean that agreements are illegal *per se*. Rather, it simply means that their compliance with Article 81(3) EC has to be judged on a case-by-case basis.

While the TTBER does not contain a White List of permitted terms, it does contain a series of 'hardcore restrictions' (Black List).[53] If an agreement contains a clause that has been black-listed, it will fall outside the scope of the block exemption and thus carry the risk that the agreement (or at least part thereof) is void. An activity not covered by the hardcore restriction is exempted. Any provision not covered by one of the hardcore restrictions will be covered by the 'safe harbour' provisions. Different standards apply depending on whether the parties to an agreement are in competition with each other. For 'competing undertakings' the black-listed terms include those that restrict a party's ability to set prices, limit output or sales, allocate markets or customers, or restrict the licensee's ability to exploit its own technology or carry out research and development.[54] For 'non-competing undertakings' the black-listed terms include those that restrict a party's ability to set prices, restrict the territory in which or the customers to whom the licensee may sell, or restrict sales to end-users.[55]

---

[46] *Guidelines on the application of Article 81 EC to technology transfer agreements* (27 April 2004). OJEU (2004/C 101/02).

[47] See V. Korah, *Intellectual property rights and the EC competition rules* (2006).

[48] Technology Transfer Block Exemption Regulation, Art. 1(b).

[49] Ibid, Recital 9.　　[50] Ibid, Art. 2.

[51] Ibid, Art 1(1)(j) (which also defines 'relevant technology market' and 'relevant product market').

[52] Ibid, Art. 3.　　[53] Ibid, Art. 4–5.　　[54] Ibid, Art. 4(1).　　[55] Ibid, Art. 4(2).

4 LIMITS ON NON-EXPLOITATION: COMPULSORY LICENCES

Another way in which patents can be misused is if the owner uses the patent to prevent the product from being manufactured or demand for the product is being met from some other source. In contrast with trade mark law, there is no obligation on a patentee to work or intend to exploit the invention. However, provisions exist in the form of compulsory licences that permit people other than the patent owner to exploit the invention in situations where the patentee is either unable or unwilling to do so.[56]

Compulsory licensing provisions were first introduced into British patent law at the end of the nineteenth century. These were motivated by a fear that large (often foreign) organizations that were in a dominant market position might buy up patents and decline to exploit them. There was also a concern that technical progress might be impeded by the holder of a basic patent who refused to license people to make improvements to patented inventions. In addition, there was a perceived risk that patents might be used to prevent the adequate supply of essentials, such as food or medicine. While few applications are made for compulsory licences, it would be wrong to conclude from this that the provisions are of little effect. This is because the threat of such licences being granted may stimulate the patentee into working or voluntarily licensing the patent. Compulsory licences have become a topic of debate recently, primarily as a result of discussions at the WTO about access to medicines in developing countries. As we saw earlier, the WTO member states agreed in August 2003 to allow pharmaceutical products to be produced under compulsory licence for export to developing countries.[57] Following the introduction of the new EU regulation giving effect to the Doha declaration,[58] in 2007 the UK government changed national legislation to allow the granting of compulsory licences for patented medicines to allow export to countries with public health problems.[59]

Under the Paris Convention, Union members are able to provide for compulsory licences 'to prevent the abuses which might result from the exercise of the exclusive rights conferred by the patent, for example, failure to work'.[60] The restrictions placed upon the granting of compulsory licences were greatly increased by Article 31 of TRIPS. British law on compulsory licences was amended in 1999 to take account of TRIPS.[61] As we will see, these changes have restricted the circumstances in which compulsory licences are available. One of the changes brought about by the TRIPS amendments is that the grounds on which a compulsory licence will be granted depend on whether the patent is owned by a WTO proprietor.

The Act distinguishes between five general situations where compulsory licences can be granted. These are: first, the various grounds set out in section 48 (which in turn distinguishes between patents with WTO owners and patents with non-WTO owners); second, following a report of the Competition Commission; third for Crown use; fourth, in relation to biotechnological inventions; and fifth, for licences granted on public health grounds. Before looking at these in more detail it is necessary to make some preliminary comments.

---

[56] See, e.g. C. Fauver, Comment, 'Compulsory Patent Licensing in the US: An Idea Whose Time Has Come' (1988) 8 *Northwestern Journal of International Law & Business* 666.

[57] See above at pp. 353–5.   [58] See below at pp. 583–4.

[59] UK Patent Office, *TRIPS and Essential Medicines* (17 Nov. 2003).   [60] Paris, Arts. 5A(2) and 5(4).

[61] Patents and Trade Marks (WTO) Regulations 1999 (SI 1999/1899) (in force 29 Jul. 1999).

4.1 COMPULSORY LICENCES UNDER SECTION 48

The general conditions under which a compulsory licence may be issued are set out in section 48 of the 1977 Act (as amended). As we mentioned above, the Patents Act 1977 was recently amended to take account of provisions in TRIPS in relation to compulsory licences. One of the consequences of these changes is that a different approach is taken depending on whether a WTO proprietor or a non-WTO proprietor owns the patent. As we will see, the grounds on which compulsory licences will be granted are more onerous in the case of WTO owners than non-WTO owners.[62] Given the number of countries in the WTO, it is unlikely that the more generous provisions will be used very often.

In both cases, a compulsory licence granted under section 48 is not available until three years after the grant of the patent.[63] This gives patentees a reasonable amount of time to exploit the invention or to arrange for others to do so.[64]

4.1.1 WTO proprietors

The relevant grounds on which a compulsory licence will be granted in relation to a patent owned by a WTO proprietor are set in section 48A. Before looking at the grounds on which such a licence will be granted, it is important to note that as with all compulsory licences, the onus is on the applicant for a licence to establish a prima facie case that the grounds relied upon apply.[65] It is also important to note that a compulsory licence (for a WTO patent) will not be granted unless the applicant has made efforts to obtain a licence from the proprietor on reasonable commercial terms and conditions, and they can establish that their efforts have not been successful within a reasonable period.[66] In addition, compulsory licences are not available if the patented invention is in the field of semiconductor technology.[67]

The grounds for grant are as follows:

(i)   The first ground on which a compulsory licence may be granted is where demand in the UK for a patented product is not being met on reasonable terms.[68]

(ii) A compulsory licence may be granted where the owner's failure to license a patent on reasonable terms has a blocking effect on later improvements.[69] The comptroller must be satisfied that the proprietor of the patent for the later invention is 'able and willing to grant to the proprietor of the patent concerned and his licensees a licence under the patent for the other invention on reasonable terms'.[70]

---

[62] A proprietor is a WTO proprietor if they are a national of, or domiciled in, a country that is a member of the World Trade Organization; or they have a real and effective industrial or commercial establishment in such a country: PA s. 48(5)(a)(b).

[63] PA s. 48(1) (as amended by SI 1999/1899). See PA s. 48B(2).

[64] Paris Art. 5. In some cases, three years may be too little so the comptroller may reject an application for compulsory licences if it is considered that the patentee ought to be given more time in which to attempt to exploit the patent themselves.

[65] *Monsanto's CCP Patent* [1990] *FSR* 93, 98.   [66] PA s. 48A(2).

[67] PA s. 48A(3).   [68] PA s. 48A(1)(a).

[69] PA s. 48A(1)(b)(i). It may be possible in such cases to claim that licences should be made available by the European Commission to prevent abuse of a dominant position contrary to Art. 82 EC. Laddie J's suggestion in *Philips Electronics v. Ingman* [1998] 2 *CMLR* 1185 that *Magill* might have no application to patents was rejected in *Intel v. Via* [2003] *FSR* 574. See above at pp. 16–18, 272.

[70] PA s. 48A(4).

(iii) A compulsory licence may also be granted where the owner's failure to license a patent on reasonable terms unfairly prejudices the 'establishment or development of commercial or industrial activities in the UK'.[71]

(iv) The next situation where a compulsory licence may be ordered focuses on the conditions imposed on the grant of licences under the patent, or on the disposal or use of the patented product, or on the use of the patented process. A compulsory patent may be granted where it can be shown that, as a consequences of these limitations, the manufacture, use, or disposal of materials not protected by the patent, or the establishment or development of industrial activities in the United Kingdom, is unfairly prejudiced.[72]

The power vested in the comptroller to grant a compulsory licence under section 48 is a discretionary power: section 50 provides a list of 'purposes' and 'factors' that the comptroller ought to take into account when exercising this discretion.[73] The recognized purposes are that:

- it is in the public interest to work an invention in the United Kingdom;
- an invention should be worked 'without undue delay' and 'to the fullest extent that is reasonably practicable';
- the patentee should receive 'reasonable remuneration having regard to the nature of the invention'; and
- the interests of the person who has worked the invention ought not to be unfairly prejudiced.

The factors which the comptroller is directed to take into account include the nature of the invention, the time which has elapsed since the grant of the patent, and the measures taken by the proprietor or exclusive licensee to make full use of the patent.

The grant of a compulsory licence in relation to a patent with a WTO owner is subject to the further restrictions that the licence should:[74]

- not be exclusive;
- not be assigned except to a person to whom there is also assigned the part of the enterprise that enjoys the use of the patented invention, or the part of the goodwill that belongs to that part;
- predominantly be for the supply of the market in the United Kingdom;
- include conditions entitling the proprietor of the patent concerned to remuneration adequate in the circumstances of the case, taking into account the economic value of the licence; and
- be limited in scope and in duration to the purpose for which the licence was granted.

In addition, the Act provides that compulsory licences should not be assigned except to a person to whom the patent for the other invention is also assigned.[75]

---

[71] PA s. 48 A(1)(b)(ii).   [72] PA s. 48A(1)(c).

[73] *Monsanto's CCP Patent*, [1990] *FSR* 93, 97.

[74] PA s. 48A(6)(a)–(e). TRIPS, Art. 31. See M. Blakeney, *Trade-Related Aspects of Intellectual Property: A Concise Guide* (1996), 88–93.

[75] PA s. 48A(5).

4.1.2 Compulsory licences in relation to non-WTO owners

In the case of an application for a compulsory licence made in respect of a patent whose proprietor is not a WTO proprietor,[76] the relevant grounds are set out in section 48B of the 1977 Act.[77]

(i) The first ground on which a compulsory licence may be granted is where the patented invention is not being commercially worked in the United Kingdom, or is not being worked to the fullest extent that is reasonably practicable.[78] A compulsory licence will not be granted under this head if the patented invention is being commercially worked in a country that is a member state of the WTO, and demand in the United Kingdom is being met by import from that country.[79]

(ii) A compulsory licence may also be granted where the demand for a patented product in the UK is not being met on reasonable terms, or is being met to a substantial extent by import from a country which is *not* a member state of the WTO.[80]

(iii) A compulsory licence may also be granted where the patented invention is prevented or hindered from being commercially worked in the United Kingdom by the import (from a country which is not a member state) of a patented product, a product obtained directly by means of a patented process, or to which the process has been applied.[81]

(iv) A compulsory licence may also be granted where the owner's failure to license a patent on reasonable terms means:

  • a market for the export of any patented product made in the United Kingdom is not being supplied,[82] or

  • the working or efficient working in the United Kingdom of any other patented invention which makes a substantial contribution to the art is prevented or hindered,[83] or

  • it unfairly prejudices the establishment or development of commercial or industrial activities in the United Kingdom.[84]

(v) The next situation where a compulsory licence may be ordered focuses on the conditions imposed on the grant of licences under the patent, or on the disposal or use of the patented product, or on the use of the patented process. A compulsory patent

---

[76] A proprietor is a WTO proprietor if they are a national of, or domiciled in, a country that is a member of the World Trade Organization; or they have a real and effective industrial or commercial establishment in such a country: PA s. 48(5)(a)(b).

[77] For discussions under the law prior to the 1999 amendments see *Penn Engineering & Manufacturing Corp. Patent* [1973] *RPC* 233; *Monsanto's CCP Patent* [1990] *FSR* 93, 100.

[78] PA s. 48B(1)(a).   [79] PA s. 48B(3).

[80] PA s. 48B(1)(b). These changes overcome the problem identified in *EC v. UK and Italy,* Case C–30/90 [1993] *RPC* 283. See M. Hodgson, 'Changes to UK Compulsory Patent Licensing Laws' [1992] *EIPR* 214.

[81] PA s. 48B(c).

[82] PA s. 48B(d)(i). This is subject to the proviso that a compulsory licence granted under this head should not contain such provisions as appear to the comptroller to be expedient for restricting the countries in which any product concerned may be disposed of or used by the licensee: PA s. 48B(4).

[83] PA s. 48B(1)(d)(ii). The comptroller must be satisfied that the proprietor of the patent for the other invention is able and willing to grant to the proprietor of the patent concerned and their licensees a licence under the patent for the other invention on reasonable terms: PA s. 48B(5).

[84] PA s. 48B(1)(d)(iii).

may be granted where it can be shown that, as a consequence of these limitations, the manufacture, use, or disposal of materials not protected by the patent, or the establishment or development of industrial activities in the United Kingdom, is unfairly prejudiced.[85]

In deciding whether to grant a patent the comptroller must take into account the factors set out in section 50. The only additional limit in relation to non-WTO-owned patents arises where an application is made on the ground that the patented invention is not being commercially worked in the United Kingdom, or is not being so worked to the fullest extent that is reasonably practicable. In these cases, if for any reason there has been insufficient time since the publication of the patent to enable the invention to be so worked, the application may be adjourned by the comptroller for a period to allow the invention to be so worked.

4.2 COMPETITION COMMISSION

The third situation where compulsory licences may be made available is where a report of the Competition Commission has concluded that an undesirable monopolistic situation exists or an anti-competitive practice is operating against the public interest.[86] The provision gives the appropriate Minister the power to respond to the report by applying to the comptroller to have the patent endorsed as a licence as of right. The application may be opposed.

4.3 CROWN USE

A special form of compulsory licence exists for the benefit of the Crown.[87] The elaborate provisions contained in sections 55 to 59 entitle any government department and any person authorized in writing by a government department to do certain acts[88] in return for which the department must provide payment[89] (including 'compensation for loss of profits').[90] In contrast with the compulsory licences described above, there is no requirement that the department needs to apply to the comptroller (or any other authority) before acting.[91] The Crown use of a patent is only legitimate where it is done by or with authorization of 'a government department',[92] and 'for the services of the Crown'. This is defined to include the supply of anything for foreign defence purposes, the production of specified drugs and medicines, and certain purposes relating to the production or use of atomic energy.[93] Disputes relating to the exercise, terms, or payment for Crown uses are referrable to the court.[94]

---

[85] PA s. 48B(1)(e).   [86] PA s. 51; see TRIPS Arts. 8, 31(k), 40.

[87] For background see *Pfizer Corporation v. Ministry of Health* [1965] *AC* 512.

[88] Listed in PA s. 55(1)(a)–(e).

[89] PA s. 55(4). An exception where no royalty needs to be paid operates under section 55(3). Payment may have to be made to others: see *Patchett's Patent* [1963] *RPC* 90.

[90] PA s. 57A.

[91] There is a duty to inform the proprietor that the department is using the invention.

[92] With recent trends to roll back the state, determining what is a government department is not always easy. In many cases, consultation of relevant legislation may be of assistance. See *Dory v. Sheffield Health Authority* [1991] *FSR* 221.

[93] PA s. 56(2).   [94] PA s. 58.

4.4 BIOTECHNOLOGICAL INVENTIONS

One of the features of the packages of reforms initiated by the Biotechnology Directive is that it introduces a new regime for compulsory licensing and cross-licensing of biotechnological inventions. In essence the new scheme attempts to manage the inter-relationship between patent protection for biological inventions and plant variety protection. A similar scheme was introduced into the United Kingdom as of 1 March 2002 by the Patents and Plant Variety Rights (Compulsory Licensing) Regulations 2002.[95]

The 2002 Regulations introduce two new forms of compulsory licence in the UK. The first of these is set out in Regulation 3.[96] This provides that where a person is unable to acquire or exploit a plant breeder's rights or a Community plant variety right without infringing a prior patent, they are able to apply to the Comptroller of Patents for a non-exclusive compulsory licence to use the invention. This is subject to the requirement that the applicant pay an appropriate royalty and that the holder of the patent be entitled to a cross-licence to use the protected variety on reasonable terms.[97] In order for a compulsory licence to be granted under Regulation 3, the applicant must show that they have applied unsuccessfully to the holder of the patent to obtain a licence. They must also show that the new plant variety in which they wish to acquire or exploit the plant breeder's rights or Community plant variety right 'constitutes significant technical progress of considerable economic interest in relation to the invention protected by the patent'.[98] It seems that the latter requirement may impose considerable limitations on the grant of compulsory licences for biotechnological inventions. In part, this will depend on how the '*significant* technical progress' and '*considerable* economic interest' are interpreted.

The second compulsory licence is set out in Regulation 11.[99] This provides that, where the holder of a patent for a biotechnological invention is unable to exploit the invention without infringing prior plant breeders' rights, the patent owner is able to apply to the Controller of Plant Variety Rights for a non-exclusive compulsory licence to use the protected plant variety.[100] This is subject to the requirement that the patent owner pay an appropriate royalty and that the holder of the plant breeder's rights be entitled to a cross-licence to use the patented invention on reasonable terms.[101] For a compulsory licence to be granted under Regulation 11, the applicant must show that they made an unsuccessful application to the holder of the patent or plant variety right to obtain a licence. As with the compulsory patent licence, an applicant for a compulsory plant variety licence is subject to the onerous requirement that the biotechnological invention protected by the patent 'constitutes significant technical progress of considerable economic interest in relation to the plant variety protected by the prior plant breeders' rights'.[102] It seems that this second requirement may impose considerable limitations on the grant of compulsory licences for biotechnological inventions.

In relation to prior Community Plant Variety Rights that restrict the ability of patentees to exploit their invention in the United Kingdom, the patentee must first apply to the Community Plant Variety Office for a 'compulsory exploitation right'.[103] Where such a right is granted to a patentee for a biotechnological invention who could not otherwise exploit their invention in

---

[95] SI 2002/247.   [96] Based on Biotech. Dir. Art. 12(1).

[97] Patents and Plant Variety Rights (Compulsory Licensing) Regulations 2002 (SI 2002/247), Reg. 7(1)–(5).

[98] Ibid, Reg. 3(2)(c); Biotech. Dir. Art. 12(3)(a).   [99] Biotech. Dir., Art. 12(2).

[100] The applicant must also comply with the Plant Breeders' Regulations established under Reg. 23.

[101] Patents and Plant Variety Rights (Compulsory Licensing) Regulations 2002, Reg. 11(1); 11(2)(b).

[102] Ibid, Reg. 11(c). Biotech. Dir., Art. 12(3)(a)(b).   [103] Dir. 98/44/EC, Art. 12(3).

the UK without infringing the prior Community plant variety right, the patentee is entitled to apply to the Comptroller of Patents for a cross-licence to use their biotechnological invention in the United Kingdom.[104]

4.5 COMPULSORY LICENCES FOR PUBLIC HEALTH

In order to follow through on commitments made at the Doha round of TRIPS to minimize the negative impact of patent law on access to medicines in developing countries, in 2006 the EU introduced a new Regulation that allows for the compulsory licensing of patents relating to the manufacture of pharmaceutical products for export to countries with public health problems.[105] In effect this allows for the grant of compulsory licences in relation to patents, and supplementary protection certificates for the sale and manufacture of pharmaceutical products intended for export to 'eligible importing countries in need of such products to address public health problems'.[106] To be 'eligible' a country must either be regarded by the UN as a least-developed country, have notified the Council for TRIPs of its intention to use the system as an importer, or be listed by the OECD as a low-income country.[107] To accommodate these changes in the UK, section 128A was introduced into the 1977 Act as of 17 December 2007.[108]

5 COMPENSATION FOR USE

In the vast bulk of cases, the amount that is paid for the use of a patent is largely left to the market and the negotiating skills of the parties. In a number of exceptional circumstances, however, the comptroller or court may be called upon to determine the amount payable for use of the patent. The question of the compensation payable arises in relation to employer use of employee inventions, compulsory licences, licences of right, and Crown use. In each case the tribunal has to make difficult qualitative judgments about the value of the patent, and how the profits that have been or might be made are to be allocated. In due course, international agreements may require that the contributions of indigenous groups are compensated where their knowledge and resources are used to develop pharmaceuticals.[109]

5.1 COMPENSATION FOR EMPLOYER USE

While the fate of a creator's relationship with his or her creations is normally left to the vagaries of contract law and the negotiating skills of the creator, intellectual property law occasionally recognizes that creators have residual interests in their creations.[110] One of the most notable examples of this is found in sections 40(1) and 40(2) of the Patents Act which provide employee-

[104] Patents and Plant Variety Rights (Compulsory Licensing) Regulations 2002, Reg. 15.

[105] Regulation (EC) No 816/2006 (17 May 2006) *OJ L* 157 (9 June 2006) p. l.

[106] Ibid, Art. 1.   [107] Ibid, Art 4(a)–(c).

[108] The Patents (Compulsory Licensing and Supplementary Protection Certificates) Regulations 2007 (SI 2007/3293).

[109] Convention on Biological Diversity, Art. 15(7).

[110] The most obvious examples are to be found in copyright law, where the creator's personality interests are protected by moral rights, and their financial interests by the *droit de suite* and unwaivable rights to remuneration.

inventors with a statutory right to compensation where their inventions are exploited by their employer.[111] The compensation provisions apply when an invention made by an employee is owned by the employer by virtue of section 39(1)(a) or (b) and it can be shown that the patented invention is of outstanding benefit to the employer.[112] The compensation provisions also apply where an employee-invention has been assigned to or exclusively licensed by the employer and it can be shown that the remuneration that the employee received from the transaction was inadequate. In both these situations, inventors have a statutory right of compensation.[113] Awards for compensation will only be made if it is 'just' to do so.[114]

While these provisions may appear to provide employee-inventors with a potentially valuable source of income, they have been construed in such a way as to provide little direct benefit to employees. Whether the compensation scheme provides indirect benefits to employees, for example acting as an impetus for the introduction of in-house compensation schemes, is another matter.[115]

Applications for compensation can be made to the comptroller or the court during the life of the patent and up to one year after the patent has expired. In recognition of the fact that the fate of a patented invention may change over time, if an initial application for compensation is rejected, employees can reapply for compensation at a later stage.[116] After some initial uncertainty,[117] it is now clear that the onus of proving that the patent is of outstanding benefit to the employer falls upon the employee.[118]

In order to protect employees, the 1977 Act provides that contractual terms which attempt to undermine the employee's right to compensation are unenforceable.[119] In recognition of the fact that unequal bargaining power might be mitigated by collective action, provision is made for collectively bargained schemes to override the individual claim machinery. Thus section 40(3) states that any employee who is a member of a trade union which has a 'relevant collective agreement' with the employer is unable to bring a claim for compensation.[120] For the provision to apply, the collective agreement must provide for the payment of compensation in respect of inventions of the same description as made by the employee.[121]

5.1.1 Compensation where an invention automatically belongs to employer

The first situation where employees are entitled to apply for compensation is set out in section 40(1). This states that, where an employee has made an invention belonging to the employer via section 39(1), the employee may be entitled to compensation. For an award for compensation to be made, the employee must show (i) that the invention *or* the patent for it is of benefit to the employer, (ii) that the benefit is outstanding, and (iii) that it is *just* that the employee be awarded compensation. We will deal with each of these in turn.

'The invention or the patent is of benefit to the employer'.   As a result of changes made in 2004, the benefit that flows to the employer can come either from the invention or the patent that is taken out for the invention in question.[122] Extending the remit of the section beyond

---

[111] See A. Chandler, 'Employee Inventions: Outstanding Compensation?' (1992) *Journal of Business Law* 300; K. Wotherspoon, 'Employee Inventions Revisited' (1993) 22 *ILJ* 119, 131; J. Hughes, 'The Personality Interest of Artists and Inventors in Intellectual Property' (1998) 16 *Cardozo Arts & Entertainment LJ* 81, 138.

[112] PA s. 40(1).   [113] PA s. 40.   [114] PA ss. 40(1) and 40(2)(d).

[115] The regime places an onus on an employer to keep detailed records. PA s. 59(2) specifies that personnel records of inventors should be kept for at least one year after the patent has ceased to have effect.

[116] PA s. 41(7).   [117] Cf. *GEC Avionics' Patent* [1992] *RPC* 107, 112.

[118] *Memco-Med's Patent* [1992] *RPC* 403.   [119] PA s. 42(2).   [120] PA ss. 40(3) and 40(6).

[121] PA s. 40(3).   [122] Patent Act 2004, s. 10.

benefits that are derived from a patent (which was the way that section 40(1) was originally drafted) broadens the scope of the provision. To date, there has been little to suggest that employee-inventors have derived much from the new provisions.

Determining the level of benefit that an employer has derived from an invention or a patent of it[123] is a complex task.[124] The process of calculation is made somewhat easier as a result of 'benefit' having been construed to mean 'money or money's worth'.[125] This means that non-financial benefits such as the kudos and prestige that flow from a patent are excluded from the equation. In calculating the benefit that flows to an employer from a patent, it is important to note that only *actual* rather than *potential* or *future* benefits are taken into account.[126] This point was emphasized by the examiner in *British Steel's Patent*,[127] when he said that while the benefits that were expected to flow from a patent were relevant when considering whether an award was 'just', they were not relevant when deciding whether the benefit from the patent was outstanding.[128] The examiner also declined to consider any benefits that might have accrued had the employer exploited the invention to its full potential. This was said not to have been germane in the circumstances because the relevant benefit was actual rather than potential.

Over time, a number of guiding principles have been developed to assist the tribunal when calculating the benefit. For example, in *Memco-Med's Patent*,[129] the court said it was useful 'to examine what the employer's position would have been if the patent had never been granted, in comparison with the actual position'.[130] It has also been suggested that the courts should speculate as to what an employee would have paid an independent contractor for the invention.[131] The benefit derived from the patent is not diminished by the possibility that a different invention might have produced a similar benefit, though this might have some bearing on whether the tribunal considers the benefit to be outstanding.[132]

However helpful these principles may be, the courts have tended to rely upon more concrete information when calculating benefit. Thus, where a licence has been granted for use of the patent, the licence fee or assignment income is taken as an indication of the patent's benefit to the employer.[133] Where a patent has been included on the balance sheet of an organization, this would presumably also provide a similar basis from which the benefits could be calculated. Another important piece of information that has been used to determine benefit is the employer's sales figures. This is particularly relevant where employers exploit or manufacture the patented invention themselves.[134] While sales figures, licence fees, and the like provide a useful basis from which to calculate the benefit that an employer has derived from a patent, they cannot be relied upon to provide an exact figure. The reason for this is that while the existence of a patent over a manufactured product will frequently influence sales, the number of products sold (as with the licence or assignment fees which are paid for use of the patent)

---

[123] The calculation may take into account the benefits received under foreign patents and equivalent rights (such as utility models): PA s. 43(4); *GEC Avionics' Patent* [1992] *RPC* 107, 111.

[124] On the importance of foreign patents see ibid; *British Steel's Patent* [1992] *RPC* 117, 121.

[125] PA s. 43(7).

[126] Future benefits can only be taken into account when they may reasonably be expected to come about. In *GEC Avionics' Patent*, note 117 above, 115 'options' were held to be too tentative.

[127] [1992] *RPC* 117.   [128] Ibid, 127.   [129] [1992] *RPC* 403.   [130] Ibid, 413.

[131] See *British Steel's Patent*, above, 128.   [132] Ibid, 127.

[133] *GEC Avionics' Patent* [1992] *RPC* 107, 108.

[134] The particular problem that arises in these situations is that there is no readily identifiable benchmark against which benefit can be measured.

may be a consequence of a range of factors—such as the advertising and marketing campaigns used to sell the product.[135]

Given that sales figures and licence fees may be influenced by an array of factors other than the patented invention, when they are being used to calculate benefit it is necessary to isolate the *net* benefits that flow from the patent to the employer from any other contributing factors. *British Steel's Patent*[136] offers another useful example of the care that needs to be taken when calculating the net benefit that flows to an employer from a patent. The particular accounting problem that arose in this case stemmed from the fact that a number of technical obstacles had to be overcome before the patented invention could be put into practice. In this situation, the examiner accepted that in calculating the net benefit that flowed to the employer, it was necessary to subtract the costs that the employer had incurred in moving the invention from its initial conception to a practical profitable reality.

The care that needs to be taken in using sales figures as a indicator of benefit was also highlighted in *Memco-Med's Patent,*[137] where Aldous J was called upon to resolve a remuneration dispute over a patented invention which detected when someone was near lift doors and prevented the doors from closing on them. In response to the argument that high sales of the patented detection device was evidence that the employer had derived high levels of benefit from the patent, the court found that the high sales were attributable more to the price and quality of the product and to the fact that the manufacturer had a long and established relationship with the purchaser than to the patent itself.[138] From this basis, the court concluded that the benefit that flowed to the employer from the patent was minimal.

Is the benefit 'outstanding'?   Once the level of benefit that an employer has derived from a patent has been calculated, it is then necessary to determine whether it is 'outstanding'. It has been suggested that the reason why compensation is only awarded where the benefit is outstanding is that the employees who would be making a claim under section 40(1) would already have received some remuneration for the invention in their salary package.[139] While 'outstanding' is not defined in the Act, it has been likened to 'significant or substantial' and said to require something out of the ordinary.[140] In *GEC Avionics' Patent*[141] an application for compensation was rejected on the ground that although the patent conferred some benefit, the employer achieved similar benefits in relation to products not involving the invention.

Whether a patent is of outstanding benefit to an employer depends on the circumstances of the case in question. The only guidance that the Act provides is that the 'size and nature of the employer's undertakings' ought to be taken into account when determining whether a patent is of outstanding benefit.[142] The provision has been interpreted in such a way that where an employee works for a large corporation, it is virtually impossible for that employee to produce anything which could be classified as 'outstanding'.[143] For example, in *GEC Avionics* the patent enabled the employer to secure a $72 million contract, with a $10 million profit.

---

[135] Whether an employer can circumvent the provision by deciding not to patent but utilize other form of protection such as confidentiality agreements remains unclear. PA s. 43(4) defines 'references to a patent' as covering 'a patent or other protection': arguably including confidentiality.

[136] [1992] *RPC* 117.   [137] [1992] *RPC* 403.

[138] Ibid, 417. There is a presumption that sales from non-patented goods are not attributable in any way to the patent. *GEC Avionics' Patent* [1992] *RPC* 107, 114.

[139] Ibid, 115.

[140] In *British Steel's Patent* [1992] *RPC* 117, 122 the examiner suggested that the term implied a 'superlative'. See also *Memco-Med's Patent* [1992] *RPC* 403, 414.

[141] [1992] *RPC* 107.   [142] PA s. 40(1).   [143] *British Steel's Patent*, above.

However, because GEC had entered into contracts of a similar size not involving the invention, the examiner held that the patent did not provide any outstanding benefit to the employer.[144]

Given that the benefit is looked at in relation to the size of the activities of the employer, it is important to ascertain the scope of the relevant undertaking. While it has been said that the size of the employer's undertakings could be either the whole or a division of the employer's business,[145] the reported decisions have not provided any guidance as to how this issue is to be resolved. Nevertheless, the consequences are clear. In *British Steel's Patent* an employee-inventor claimed compensation in relation to a patent taken out by his employer for a valve which had been described in the employer's publicity and the press as revolutionary and vital cost-saving technology. While the employee asserted that the employer had benefited from the patent to the tune of £5 million per year, the employee was only able to prove a benefit of between £100,000 and £500,000 per year. In any case the court rejected the application on the ground it was not outstanding. In so doing, the comptroller defined the undertaking as the undivided totality of British Steel's operation. Thus neither the proven benefit[146] nor the claimed benefit were outstanding when compared with British Steel's turnover of £4,900 million and a profit of £593 million.[147]

Is it just that compensation should be awarded? For compensation to be awarded, as well as establishing that the patent is of outstanding benefit to the employer, employees must also show that it is 'just' that they be awarded compensation.[148] The decision as to whether an award for compensation is just is based on the same factors as are taken into account when deciding whether the patent provides the employer with an outstanding benefit. As a result, it is difficult to imagine situations where a patent is of outstanding benefit to the employer and it is not also just for the employee to receive compensation. It may be that the requirement that the award ought to be just enables the tribunal to make more qualitative judgments. For example, where an employee works for a small firm and is already well compensated under their contract of employment, the tribunal may consider that a further award would place an unfair burden upon the employer.[149] The requirement that the award be just may also be used as a way of introducing general equitable principles to reject applications where the employee acted in a way that is contrary to their duty of fidelity.[150]

5.1.2 Compensation where an employee-invention has been assigned to an employer

The second situation where an award for compensation may be made to an employee is set out in section 40(2). This provides that additional compensation may be paid where the initial entitlement to an invention lay with an employee but the employee assigned or licensed the invention to the employer. The employee must demonstrate that the remuneration for the transaction is inadequate in comparison with the remuneration derived by the employer from the patent. They must also show that it is just that additional compensation be paid.

---

[144] *GEC Avionics' Patent* [1992] RPC 117, 115.   [145] *Memco-Med's Patent* [1992] RPC 403, 414.

[146] The proven benefit in money or money's worth to the employer of the patented invention represented no more than 0.01% of turnover or 0.08% of profits. Even on the most favourable interpretation of the facts, the benefit was not even equivalent to 1%.

[147] *British Steel's Patent* [1992] RPC 117, 126. In *Garrison's Patent* (SRIS O/44/97) a benefit of 2–3% of the total turnover of a small company manufacturing snooker cues was held not to be outstanding.

[148] PA s. 40(1).

[149] In *Memco-Med's Patent* [1992] RPC 403, 411 it was said that because of the duties of the employee 'it would need some quite exceptional benefits to flow from the patent for it to be just that an award should be made'.

[150] See *CIPA*, para. 40.04.

To determine whether compensation is payable under section 40(2), it is necessary to ascertain the benefit that the employee derived from the contract with their employer and the benefit the employer derived from the patent. Once these two figures have been calculated, it is then necessary to determine whether the remuneration was adequate. This appears to require the court to estimate what remuneration might have been achieved in a market transaction between a willing seller and purchaser. However, given that an employee who makes an application under section 40(2) will have had an opportunity to bargain with their employer, it is unlikely that the tribunal will hold that remuneration is inadequate in circumstances where it would not treat the benefit as outstanding.

5.1.3 Calculating the amount of compensation

Once it has been decided that compensation should be awarded to the employee, the question arises: how much? Section 41(1) directs that the award should secure for the employee a 'fair share' of the benefit that the employer has derived. Compensation may be awarded as a lump sum or in periodic payments.[151] There is a power to vary the amount at a later stage.[152] In determining the compensation to be awarded, the court or comptroller is directed to take account of an array of factors.[153] In *British Steel* the examiner said that the question was similar to the question that arose when determining the royalty payable in licence-of-right proceedings. The relevant considerations included the size of the benefit that had been and was likely to be derived from the patent, and the salary and awards that the employee had already received. In *British Steel* these would have included a £10,000 *ex gratia* payment from British Steel and an MBE. In other cases, the tribunal might take account of the contribution made by other people, such as co-inventors, other employees, and the employer.

5.2 COMPENSATION FOR COMPULSORY LICENCES AND LICENCES AS OF RIGHT

Another situation where the tribunals may be called upon to determine the compensation that ought to be paid for the exploitation of a patent is where the patent is subject to a compulsory licence or a licence as of right. In these circumstances, the principal goal is to ensure that the owner of the patent receives reasonable remuneration for the use that is made of the invention.[154]

Three techniques have been used to reach an appropriate sum. These are commonly referred to as the 'comparable-royalties', 'costs', and 'profits-available' approaches. The comparable-royalties test is regarded as 'by far the best and surest approach'.[155] It involves utilizing evidence from comparable licences to estimate what would have been agreed by the parties. The kinds of evidence used will vary from evidence relating to standard royalty rates for patented products in a particular field,[156] through to the actual examples of licence agreements voluntarily entered into by the patentee. In deciding whether a situation is comparable, the most important factor is the nature of the patentee's invention: if the patentee's invention is unusual, and the comparator licence covered the same invention, it is likely to offer a useful comparison (although it may be necessary to make adjustments in relation to market size and other

---

[151] PA s. 41(6).   [152] PA s. 41(7), (9)–(11).   [153] PA s. 41(4)–(5).
[154] *SKF Cimetidine* [1990] *RPC* 203, 236 (CA).   [155] Ibid.
[156] *Cabot Safety* [1992] *RPC* 39, 61; *Chiron Corp v. Murex Diagnostics (No. 13)* [1996] *FSR* 578.

terms in the licence).[157] If the invention is unusual, and the licence that is used as a basis for comparison relates to a different product, it is likely to be of little value (even if the size of the market is similar).[158]

Where no comparable licence exists, the terms are calculated by the so-called 'costs approach'.[159] Under this approach the tribunal tries to assess the value of the patent in terms of a return on costs. This involves an examination of the patentee's expenditure on research and development, promotional expenditure, and an appropriate annual increase. The idea behind this approach is that the patentee should receive a fair and reasonable return for their financial outlay. Once the costs have been calculated, it is necessary to determine what an appropriate increase would be. This may be done by looking at the average annual return that the patentee makes on other inventions.[160]

The third approach, which is called the 'profits available approach' is used as a last resort.[161] The approach requires the tribunal to determine the profit the applicant will make (if licensed) and then to divide the available profits between the patentee and the licensee. One problem with this approach is that it will often be difficult to decide how to split the profits.[162] It has been said that the profits-available approach is particularly dubious because it gets matters the wrong way round. It 'makes the licensee's reasonable remuneration the measure of what is an appropriate royalty instead of the patentee's reasonable remuneration'.[163] There is also a danger that it might leave the patentee with no royalty at all.[164] Despite these problems, it has been acknowledged that 'some assistance may often be derived from looking at what are the expected profits, if only as a cross-check on the end result'.[165]

5.3 COMPENSATION FOR CROWN USE OF PATENTS

Where an invention is used for the services of the Crown, the government department concerned is required to inform the proprietor of the patent and negotiate to pay such terms as may be agreed. In the absence of an agreed rate, the matter is determined by the courts who, following the approach taken in compulsory licence proceedings, attempt to second-guess what a willing licensor and licensee would have agreed.[166] At the very minimum, given Article 31 of TRIPS, the court should give the patentee adequate remuneration taking into account the economic value of the authorization. The Patents Act 1977 says that the patentee should be awarded compensation to cover 'loss of profit' that is 'any loss resulting from his not being awarded a contract to supply the patented product, or…to perform the patented process or supply a thing made by means of the patented process'.[167] In determining the loss, the court takes account of the profit which would have been made on such a contract and the extent to which any manufacturing or other capacity was under-used.[168]

---

[157] *Cabot Safety,* above.
[158] *Research Corp's (Carboplatin) Patent* [1990] *RPC* 663, 701.
[159] See *Geigy SA's Patent* [1964] *RPC* 391; *SKF Cimetidine* [1990] *RPC* 203, 253.
[160] Where the outcome of comparison and PA s. 41 are in conflict, the comparability figure is generally preferred. *American Cyanamid Co.'s (Fenbufen) Patent* [1990] *RPC* 309.
[161] *SKF Cimetidine* [1990] *RPC* 203, 244 (Nichols LJ).
[162] *American Cyanamid Fenbufen* [1990] *RPC* 309, 338; *SKF Cimetidine*, above, 230; *Cabot Safety,* 63.
[163] *SKF Cimetidine* [1992] *RPC* 39 above, 244.   [164] *Research Corp Carboplatin* [1990] *RPC* 663, 700.
[165] *SKF Cimetidine*, above 257.   [166] *Patchett's Patent* [1967] *RPC* 237, 247, 253.
[167] PA s. 57A. Reversing the Court of Appeal decision in *Patchett's Patent*, above, 246, 250, 257.
[168] PA s. 57A(3).

24

RIGHTS RELATED TO PATENTS

CHAPTER CONTENTS

1 INTRODUCTION

In this chapter we examine two areas of law that are related to, but do not traditionally form part of, patent law. The first and oldest of the two regimes is the system of plant variety protection. This gives protection to the breeders of new varieties of plant. We then go on to look at supplementary protection certificates that currently operate in the United Kingdom to extend the length of patent protection. In essence the supplementary protection certificate scheme was introduced to compensate owners for time lost while they were waiting to get regulatory approval to market their patented products.

2 PLANT VARIETIES

While the value of new plant varieties has long been recognized in the United Kingdom, a system of protection was only introduced in 1964. (In contrast a system of protection existed in the USA from 1930.)[1] In part this was because of the belief that the development of new varieties was part and parcel of traditional farming practices rather than a distinct activity of breeders (that required separate protection). Moreover, for much of the twentieth century, the leading breeders' organizations were publicly funded institutions that did not prioritize intellectual property protection.[2] However, during the Second World War the desire

---

[1] See B. Greengrass, 'The 1991 Act of the UPOV Convention' [1991] *EIPR* 466; M. Llewelyn, 'The Legal Protection of Plant Varieties in the European Union: A Policy of Consensus or Confusion?' [1997] 2 *Bioscience Law Review* 50; M. Llewelyn, 'European Plant Variety Protection: A Reactionary Time' [1999] *Bioscience Law Review* 211.

[2] See P. Palladino, 'Science, Technology, and the Economy: Plant Breeding in Great Britain, 1920–1970' (1996) 49 *Economic History Review* 116 (reporting that 83 per cent of wheat grown by British farmers in the 1990s was derived from seeds grown in publicly financed plant-breeding centres).

to improve agricultural yields became a matter of national significance. In addition, by the 1950s it had become clear that the few private seed firms that operated in the United Kingdom were losing ground to foreign competitors: the lack of property protection was seen as one possible cause.[3]

The production of successful varieties is thought to be highly desirable insofar as it increases yields, resistance to pests and disease, and the sheer number and diversity of varieties.[4] While the breeding of new varieties takes a considerable amount of time and is often very costly,[5] once a variety is made available to the public it can readily be duplicated.[6] Indeed, one of the features of plant varieties is that they produce their own reproductive material. Consequently, it was thought that it would be 'equitable to give plant breeders the opportunity of a fair reward for their work, effort, and investment in breeding, and to grant them protection against unauthor-ized exploitation'. It was also intended 'to provide plant breeders with an incentive to produce improved varieties of a wide selection of plant species to the benefit of farmers, growers, and private gardeners'.[7]

However, in the same way in which agriculture was long seen as being non-industrial (and thus outside the remit of patent law), so too the results of plant breeding were not thought to be appropriate subject matter for patent protection. In part this was because, prior to acceptance of Mendelian theories of genetics, the production of varieties was seen more as an art than a scientifically informed activity.[8] This was reinforced by the fact that there were technical problems in describing plant varieties in a way that met the requirements of patent law. However, the most significant reason why plant varieties were thought to be inappropriate subject matter for patent protection was that new plant varieties were unlikely to satisfy the inventiveness threshold of patents: most breeds were obvious. Consequently, it was decided that the protection needed could best be provided by a *sui generis* system tailored to the char-acteristics of plant varieties and the needs of breeders, growers, and traders.

The United Kingdom first adopted a system of plant variety protection in 1964. This was in response to the *Report of the Committee on Transactions in Seeds*[9] and to the International Convention for the Protection of New Varieties of Plants (UPOV), originally formulated in 1961.[10] The Plant Varieties and Seeds Act 1964 was substantially amended in 1978 and 1991 to take into account revisions in UPOV.[11] In 1997 it was repealed and replaced by the Plant

---

[3] See Palladino, ibid, 131 (another alleged cause was lack of capital).

[4] See the benefits listed by the British Association of Plant Breeders, cited in G. Dworkin, 'The Plant Varieties Act 1983' [1983] *EIPR* 270, n. 3; Palladino, ibid (describing a doubling in yields of cereals and potatoes and attrib-uting half of this gain to genetic improvements).

[5] For a discussion of the costs of production of a variety of barley see *Golden Promise Spring Barley* [1981] FSR 562. A successful variety might take between 8 and 20 years to develop: A. Lansley, *Hansard* (HC) 24 Jun. 1997, col. 711.

[6] CPVR, Recital 5. For criticism of plant variety rights, particularly from a developing country perspec-tive, see P. Mooney, *Seeds of the Earth: A Private or Public Resource?* (1979); S. Verma, 'TRIPS and Plant Variety Protection in Developing Countries' [1995] *EIPR* 281; V. Shiva, 'The Seed of Our Future' (1996) 4 *Development Journal*. For a defence against some of these attacks, see Dworkin, 'The Plant Varieties Act 1983', 271.

[7] Dworkin, ibid.

[8] Many of these themes are explored in P. Palladino, 'Between Craft and Science: Plant Breeding, Mendelian Genetics, and British Universities 1900–1920' (1993) 34 *Technology and Culture* 300.

[9] (1960) Cmnd. 1092. See P. Murphy, 'Plant Breeders' Rights in the United Kingdom' [1979] *EIPR* 236; M. Llewelyn, 'The Legal Protection of Biotechnological Inventions: An Alternative Approach' [1997] *EIPR* 115, 117.

[10] UPOV had 54 members as of 10 Nov. 2003. For a discussion of the early history see UPOV, *The First Twenty-Five Years of the International Convention for the Protection of New Varieties of Plant* (1986).

[11] UPOV was also modified on 10 Nov. 1972, and revised in 1978. The 1991 version came into force in Apr. 1998. For commentary, see B. Greengrass, 'UPOV and the Protection of Plant Breeders—Past Developments, Future

Varieties Act.[12] In 1994 the European Community adopted a Community Plant Variety Regulation which made it possible, from 27 April 1995, for breeders to apply for a single Community-wide right for varieties.[13] Community plant variety rights have uniform effect within the territory of the Community.[14] The grant of a Community right leads to the suspension of any equivalent national rights that may exist.[15] As the international, regional, and national systems are in similar terms, we will look at them together.

2.1 PROCEDURE FOR GRANT

As with patents, plant variety rights arise as a result of a process of registration. The initial application is made to a relevant granting authority: either the UK Plant Variety Rights Office in Cambridge, or the Community Plant Variety Office in Angers in France.[16] Anyone may apply for national rights irrespective of their nationality. However, a person may only apply for a Community right where they are a national of, or domiciled in, a country which is a member of UPOV.[17] As well as identifying the botanical taxon, the applicant must also provide the name of the breeder, a provisional designation for the variety, a technical description of the variety, the geographical origin of the variety, details of any previous commercialization of the variety, and information about applications made in respect of the variety.[18] In some cases a colour photograph of the variety must also be supplied. An applicant must select a name for the variety.[19] Provision is made for objections by third parties.[20] Fees are payable.[21]

The Office will examine the application in three stages. First, there is a formal examination.[22] This is followed by a substantive examination whereby the Office examines the application to

Perspectives' (1989) 20 *IIC* 622; Llewelyn, 'Legal Protection of Biotechnological Inventions', 119; N. Byrne, *Commentary on the Substantive Law of the UPOV* (1991).

[12] In force 8 May 1998: Plant Varieties Act 1997 (Commencement) Order 1998 (SI 1998/1028); Plant Breeders' Rights Regulations 1998 (SI 1998/1027). The four major changes are: that the regime extends to all genera and species; that the rules on previous exploitation are liberalized to allow market testing; a simplified system of rights pending grant; breeder's rights are strengthened. The plant breeders' regime falls under the control of the Dept. for Environment, Food, and Rural Affairs (formerly known as the Ministry of Agriculture, Fisheries and Food) rather than the Dept. of Trade and Industry. For an introductory guide see, MAFF, *UK Plant Breeders' Rights Handbook 1998*. The 1964 Act had previously been amended by the Plant Varieties Act 1983 which was intended to enable UK ratification of the 1978 Revision of UPOV.

[13] See M. Llewelyn and M. Adcock, *European Plant Intellectual Property* (2006); P. van der Kooij, *Introduction to the EC Regulation on Plant Variety Protection* (1997).

[14] CPVR, Art. 2.

[15] CPVR, Art. 92; PVA s. 11(3). The Regulation is otherwise 'without prejudice' to the rights of member states to grant national rights. While there is no 'approximation Directive', the common need to satisfy the requirements of UPOV and good sense have produced a high level of harmonization. Most countries in the Community have a parallel national system with the exception of Greece and Luxembourg.

[16] <http://www.cpvo.fr>. Neither system is heavily used: in 1994 there were 582 UK applications and 419 grants of PVRs, and 238 applications and 139 grants in 1998; in 1998 there were 1,835 Community PVR applications, and 1,491 issued CPVRs. See 'Statistics' (1999) 86 *Plant Variety Protection* 8. By 2007 the number of applications at the Community Plant Variety Office had increased to 2,977 and the grants to 2,616: Community Plant Variety Office, *Annual Report 2007* (2008).

[17] CPVR, Art. 12. The Commission may extend qualification to nationals and domiciliaries of other countries which provide corresponding protection.

[18] PVA s. 3(2); CPVR Art. 50.   [19] PVA s. 18(2)(a); CPVR, Art. 50(3).   [20] CPVR, Art. 59.

[21] The Plant Breeders' Rights (Fees) (Amendment) Regulations 1999 (SI 1999/1089). The application fee is £275, but the tests fees and renewal fees vary according to the species involved—for example, tests are £745 for cereals, but only £120 for roses; renewals are £435 for cereals and £70 for roses.

[22] CPVR, Art. 53.

ensure that it relates to appropriate subject matter (that is, a variety), that the variety is new, and that the applicant is the person entitled to plant breeders' rights.[23] The Office also considers the suitability of the name proposed for the variety, and takes account of a host of considerations, including previous registrations.[24] The third stage is the technical examination of the characteristics of the variety. At this stage, the Office examines the application to ensure that the variety is distinct, uniform, and stable.[25] These requirements are sometimes referred to as the 'DUS'.[26] An applicant must supply propagating material that the Office can use to test DUS by planting and growing the variety.[27] The tests may be carried out at more than one site. In most cases DUS tests will take between one and three years.[28] As a result, it may be some years between application and grant.[29] Indeed, the crop is grown throughout the period of the monopoly and if it becomes apparent that the variety does not satisfy the requirements of the Act grant is liable to be revoked.[30]

2.2 SUBJECT MATTER

All three systems of plant variety protection cover varieties of 'all plant genera and species' from ornamental roses, to vines, potatoes, and wheat.[31] Section 1(3) of the Plant Variety Act 1997 defines a variety as:

a plant grouping within a single botanical taxon of the lowest known rank, which grouping...can be (a) defined by the expression of the characteristics resulting from a given genotype or combination of genotypes, (b) distinguished from any other plant grouping by the expression of at least one of those characteristics, and (c) considered as a unit with regard to its suitability for being propagated unchanged.[32]

A botanical 'taxon' means a 'group' of plants: the requirements that it be of the lowest known rank is to make it clear that protection could not be granted for a 'family', 'genus', or 'species', which are groups higher in the taxonomical classification system.[33]

---

[23] Ibid, Art. 54.   [24] Ibid, Art. 63.   [25] UPOV, Art. 5; CPVR, Art. 6; PVA s. 4(2).

[26] CPVR, Art. 55.

[27] For the UK, this work is mainly carried out by the National Institute of Agricultural Botany (NIAB), the Scottish Agricultural Science Agency (SASA), and the Dept. of Agriculture for Northern Ireland (DANI). See also UPOV, Art. 12; CPVR, Arts. 53–5.

[28] Usually one year for ornamentals, three for herbage varieties and trees, and two years for other species.

[29] Provisional protection is provided: UPOV, Art. 13; CPVR, Art. 95; PVA s. 5(1). The fact that a plant variety right has been tested in other UPOV member states (Australia, New Zealand, USA, and South Africa) did not oblige the Community Office to accept the test reports. This was on the basis that the 'Community system is independent—and different from their systems'. Community Plant Variety Office, Case A 003/2003, para 1. (*Probril Rosa L*).

[30] CPVR, Arts. 20–1; PVA ss. 21–2.

[31] CPVR, Art. 5 (all botanical genera and species, including, inter alia, hybrids between genera and species); PVA s. 1(2).

[32] CPVR, Art. 5(2); PVA s. 1(3). See further *Van Den Bout and Ten Hoopen,* A1/2002 (CPVO Board of Appeal) (1 Apr. 2003), 5.

[33] A wild rose is in the species '*carolina*', which is in the genus '*rosa*', which is in the family '*rosaceae*', which is in the order '*rosales*', which is in the class 'dicotyledons', which is in the subphylum '*angiospermae*', which is in the phylum '*spermatophyta*' which finally is in the kingdom 'plants'.

2.3 VALIDITY

In order to be protected the variety must be 'new'. It is also necessary for the variety to be 'distinct', 'uniform', and 'stable'.[34]

2.3.1 Novelty

The requirement that the variety be new is nowhere near as onerous as the worldwide novelty requirement in patent law. A variety is new if there has been no sale or disposal of propagating or harvested material within the territory (under the Plant Variety Act, the UK, or in the case of the Community Plant Variety Regulation, the Community) more than one year prior to the application. The novelty of a variety may also be lost if there has been a sale or disposal outside the relevant territory, in the case of trees and vines, more than six years before the application date; for other plants, more than four years prior to the application date.[35]

Three features of the novelty requirement should be noted. The *first* is that novelty is not lost by previous use (for example, growth) of the variety, but only by previous sale or disposal. As such, a plant can be grown in someone's garden for years prior to application and an application still succeed. In part this reflects the desire to reward the discovery as much as the breeding of new varieties. Indeed, it seems that the applicant can still obtain a plant variety right even if they have given away propagating or harvested material, as long as this was not 'for the purposes of exploiting the variety'. The *second* notable feature is that the novelty provisions allow for substantial 'grace periods'. That is, they allow for periods in which the applicant can commercialize the plant prior to grant without prejudicing the application. As a result, a person can sell vines outside the UK for up to six years before they need apply for a plant variety right. *Third*, and perhaps most significantly, the only disposals or sales to be taken into account when considering the novelty of a particular variety are those *by the applicant themselves or with their consent*.[36] Sales of material by third parties who have independently developed the same variety will not render the variety lacking in novelty. In such circumstances, priorities are accorded to the first to apply.[37] However, no protection is given to the independent developer via prior user's rights. In such circumstances a monopoly may be granted to a person over an activity or trade which someone else was doing already.

2.3.2 Distinct, uniform, and stable

As well as being novel, to be the subject of plant breeders' rights the variety must also be 'distinct', 'uniform', and 'stable'.[38] These are sometimes referred to as the 'DUS' or 'agro-technical' requirements.

A variety is *distinct* if it is 'clearly distinguishable by one or more characteristics which are capable of a precise description from any other variety whose existence is a matter of common knowledge at the time of application'.[39] Distinctiveness may arise through visible differences in outward appearance, such as height, size of leaves, leaf colour, or in the ears of cereals.

---

[34] UPOV, Art. 5; CPVR, Art. 6; PVA s. 4(2).

[35] UPOV, Art. 6; CPVR, Art. 10; PVA Sched. 2, para. 4. *Case 001/2007 (Cowichan)* (farm catalogues offering to make a plant available to the public for fruiting trials was held to commercial disposal).

[36] See A. Christie, 'The Novelty Requirement in Plant Breeders' Rights' (1988) 19 *IIC* 646. Cf. van der Kooij, *Introduction to the CPVR*, 15.

[37] PVA Sched. 2, Part II, para. 5.   [38] UPOV, Art. 5; CPVR, Art. 6; PVA s. 4(2).

[39] UPOV, Art. 7; CPVR, Art. 7 (clearly distinguishable by reference to the expression of characteristics that results from a particular genotype or combination of genotypes); PVA Sched. 2, para. 1.

It may also arise through physiological differences associated with the variety's particular chemical or biological structure, such as resistance to disease,[40] or ability to withstand certain conditions.[41] Any difference will suffice:[42] there is no need for the distinguishing feature to confer any particular aesthetic or economic advantage. Distinctness is a comparative test and may require the claimed variety to be compared with similar varieties. The variety must only be compared with 'other' varieties and not with examples of 'itself'.[43] In practice, the comparison is made with the varieties of the same species in the Office's 'reference collection'. The reference collection is made up of those varieties for which rights already exist or are being sought. The types of characteristic and the extent of the deviation necessary for a variety to be distinct will vary with the grouping concerned. Moreover, the characteristics needed for a variety to be distinct may be different for each comparison (for example variety A might differ from variety B by being higher, but differ from variety C by being hardier).[44]

A variety is *uniform* if 'it is sufficiently uniform in those characteristics' which make it distinct.[45] This means that nearly all examples of the variety must bear the characteristics that make the plant distinct. During the early stages of the breeding process, a proportion of the plants grown may not bear the relevant characteristics. Where this is the case, it may be necessary to undertake further breeding to eradicate deviant strains. However, there comes a point where uniformity requires effort that is out of proportion to the improvement in uniformity gained by the removal of deviants. Consequently, it is not necessary for a variety to be completely uniform. This means that a variety will still be uniform even if a few of the plants that are grown do not exhibit the critical characteristics. To this end, the Plant Variety Office has stated that a variety is sufficiently uniform if there is:

the degree of uniformity a capable breeder skilled in the art can reasonably be expected to achieve having regard generally to the nature of plant material and more particularly to the biological possibilities of the species in which he is working including its mode of reproduction, and to any special features of the variety under consideration.[46]

A variety is *stable* if the characteristics that make it distinct 'remain unchanged after repeated propagation'.[47] The idea is that while a first generation might be distinct and uniform, when a second generation is grown a large number of deviants appear (due to residual 'heterozygosity'). This requires an assessment to be made of the inherent capability of the variety to remain true to its original characteristics. As with the testing of uniformity, deviants that appear as a result of pollination by nearby crops are ignored.

---

[40] *Maris Druid: Spring Barley* [1968] *FSR* 559 (resistance to mildew accepted as a characteristic).

[41] Under the 1964 Act these two types of distinctiveness were referred to as 'morphological' and 'physiological'.

[42] It seems that a mere modification of genetic structure which is not revealed or expressed in the variety will not make it distinct: van der Kooij, *Introduction to the CVPR*, 16.

[43] See Christie, 'The Novelty Requirement in Plant Breeders' Rights', 651–4; cf. van der Kooij, *Introduction to the CVPR*, 16.

[44] For an illustration (though under the differently worded provision in the 1964 Act), see *Daehnfeldt v. Controller of Plant Varieties* [1976] *FSR* 95.

[45] UPOV, Art. 8; CPVR, Art. 8; PVA Sched. 2, para. 2. For an example illustrating the difficulties of determining uniformity in tests where variants can arise through 'out-pollination' from nearby crops and spontaneous mutants see *Moulin Winter Wheat* [1985] *FSR* 283.

[46] *Zephyr: Spring Barley* [1976] *FSR* 576, 579.

[47] UPOV, Art. 9; CPVR, Art. 9; PVA Sch. 2, para. 3.

2.4 OWNERSHIP

The person entitled to the grant of plant breeders' rights is the person who breeds the plant variety, or discovers and develops it.[48] As the Board of Appeal at the Community Office said, '"breeding"…does not necessarily imply inventing something totally new but includes the planting, selection and growing on of pre-existing material and its development into a finished variety.'[49] In a different decision, the Board also said that 'discover' means that 'somebody comes across a variety either by search or chance, being conscious of the fact that it is a new variety, which was unknown to him before and which in his opinion is unknown to other persons as well'.[50] Where the breeding, discovery, and development occur in the course of a person's employment, the employer is presumed to be the person entitled to grant of the plant breeder's rights.[51] Plant breeder's rights are property rights and as such are assignable, though the statute forbids a separate assignment of rights in the protected variety and rights in 'dependent' varieties. The Community right cannot be assigned other than for the Community as a whole. Where this occurs the assignment must be in writing and should be entered in the Register kept by the Community Plant Variety Office.[52]

2.5 DURATION

The duration of rights varies with the type of plant concerned: UPOV requires members to provide a minimum duration of 20 years for most plants and a minimum of 25 years for trees and vines.[53] However, the European and UK systems go further than these minima, protecting potatoes, trees, and vines for 30 years, and other genera and species for 25 years.[54] Throughout the period for which the grant operates rights holders should ensure they are in a position to produce propagating material to the Office.[55] A national right will become ineffective on grant of a Community right for the same variety.[56]

2.6 RIGHTS AND INFRINGEMENT

A valid plant breeder's right gives the proprietor (initially, the breeder or discoverer) a number of rights.[57] While these rights are primarily in relation to the commercialization of propagating material, they may also apply to harvested material and to derivative varieties.[58] The rights given to breeders are more limited than in the cases of patentees.[59] Moreover, it should be noted that, as with other intellectual property rights, these are negative. It is also important to

---

[48] PVA s. 4(3); UPOV, Art. 1(iv); CPVR, Art. 11(1). The fact that rights are available to 'discoverers' has sometimes proved controversial: see Dworkin, 'The Plant Varieties Act 1983', 272.

[49] *Sakata Seed Corporation*, A017/2002 (3 Apr. 2003) (CPVO Board of Appeal), 8–9.

[50] Case A 001/2004 (*Canna Phasion*), 6. Thus, 'it was possible that one and the same variety is discovered by two or more persons independently, on different moments on the same spot, or on different spots'. Ibid.

[51] PVA s. 4(4); UPOV, Art. 1(iv). As far as the CPVR is concerned entitlement shall be determined in accordance with the national law applicable to the employment relationship in the context of which the variety was bred, or discovered and developed.

[52] CPVR, Arts. 2 and 23(2).   [53] UPOV, Art. 19.

[54] CPVR, Art. 19; Council Regulation (EC) 2470/96 of 17 Dec. 1996 (extending protection for a further five years for potatoes); PVA s. 11.

[55] PVA s. 16.   [56] CPVR, Art. 92(1).

[57] CPVR, Art. 11; PVA s. 4(3)–(5). The rights are assignable: CPVR, Art. 23; PVA s. 12.

[58] UPOV, Art. 14; CPVR, Art. 13; PVA ss. 6–7.   [59] 1960 Committee, para. 141.

note that, with the exception of ornamentals and fruit, the breeder must gain relevant regulatory approval before a variety is marketed.[60]

2.6.1 Propagating material

The fundamental right conferred on a proprietor of a plant breeder's right is the exclusive right to authorize certain acts in relation to 'propagating material' (which is referred to in the 1997 Act as 'reproductive material',[61] and as 'variety constituents' in the Community Regulation). In particular, a plant breeder is given the right to produce or reproduce the material; to 'condition' the material for the purposes of propagation; and to sell, offer for sale, stock, export, or import the material.[62] While propagating material is not defined, it includes seeds for sowing, seed potatoes, seedlings, bulbs, rhizomes, grafts, and the like. The nature of plant material and breeding technology is such that a variety can be propagated from a much wider array of plant material than has traditionally been the case, including material such as cut blooms. Consequently, material will be treated as propagating material if it is intended to be used as a propagating material. Obviously, a person will infringe the fundamental right if, for example, they sell seeds, produce cuttings, or import bulbs. However, if such a person (who has legitimately grown the plant) sells beans for canning, grain for milling, or blooms or rose bushes for personal use, and these are subsequently used for propagation, it is unlikely that the vendor will be liable. In these cases, the user will be liable because they will have reproduced or 'conditioned' the material for the purposes of propagation.

2.6.2 Harvested material

In most cases the rights conferred in relation to the exploitation of propagating material also apply to harvested material obtained through the *unauthorized* use of propagating material (for example, crops of wheat from unauthorized seed). Harvested material is defined to include entire plants and parts of plants.[63] As such it will encompass things such as cut blooms from flowers.[64] An exception to this right arises where, prior to harvest, the rights holder has had a reasonable opportunity to exercise their rights in relation to the unauthorized use of the propagating material.[65]

The plant breeder's rights also extend to any product that is made directly from such harvested material (such as flour made from wheat) which falls within the categories prescribed by the Ministers.[66] Certain procedures and presumptions operate to assist the holder of plant breeder's rights in proving that harvested material and products made directly from such

---

[60] They must pass tests of value for cultivation and use, that is of yield, quality, and disease resistance. Once this is done, the variety is entered on the National List: Seeds (National Lists of Varieties) Regulations 1982 (no seed of the major agricultural and vegetable species may be marketed in the UK unless the variety is on a UK National List or the EC Common Catalogue). See J. Harvey, 'UK Plant Breeders' Rights and the European Seed Regime' (1990) *Patent World* 22.

[61] For a discussion of definitional problems, see G. Dworkin, 'Plant Breeders' Rights: The Scope of United Kingdom Protection' [1982] *EIPR* 11, 12.

[62] PVA s. 6; UPOV, Art. 14(1)(a); CPVR, Art. 13(2). Though these rights are limited within EC law: *Re the Plant Royalty Bureau* [1979] *FSR* 644 (Commission investigation on restriction of exports).

[63] PVA s. 6(6)(b).   [64] The Scheme under Sched. 3 to the 1964 Act has been abolished.

[65] PVA s. 6(3).

[66] PVA s. 6(4). The provision only applies if no relevant consent has been gained in relation to dealing with the propagating material, and the right holder has not had a reasonable opportunity to enforce those rights—for example, where the wheat was produced in a country which did not recognize plant breeders' rights. It will also only operate as regards varieties prescribed in regulations by the Ministers. For background, see J. Rooker (Minister of State, MAFF) *Hansard* (HC) 24 June 1997, cols. 692–4.

material were obtained through unauthorized use of propagating material. The right holder may issue an information notice to a defendant requesting certain information as to the source of specified material. If the recipient fails to provide the relevant information within a particular time, the material is presumed to have been obtained by way of an unauthorized use.[67]

2.6.3 Derivative varieties

The plant breeder's rights extend beyond the registered variety to cover varieties that are 'dependent' on the protected variety. Dependent varieties include varieties whose production requires the repeated use of the protected variety, as well as 'essentially derived' varieties.[68] A variety is deemed to be 'essentially derived' where it is predominantly derived from the initial variety. In addition, the variety must retain the expression of the essential characteristics that result from the genotype of the initial variety, and at the same time be clearly distinguishable from the initial variety.

2.6.4 Naming rights

Registration is conditional on the applicant providing a suitable name for the variety. This prevents the confusion that would otherwise arise if a number of different names were used to describe the same variety.[69] Once approved, anyone who sells or markets propagating material is obliged to use that name. This duty, breach of which is punishable under criminal law,[70] applies to the proprietor as much as to the public at large.[71] The duty subsists indefinitely, that is, even after expiry of plant breeders' rights.[72] The proprietor of a British plant variety right is also able to control the wrongful use of that name. As a result, the right holder may bring an action against anyone who uses the name of a protected variety in marketing material of a *different* variety within the same class, or uses a name so nearly resembling the registered name so as to be likely to deceive or cause confusion.[73]

2.7 EXCEPTIONS

One important feature of the plant variety system is the careful way in which the competing interests of developers, users, and other interested parties have been accommodated through the use of exceptions and compulsory licences.[74] UPOV permits members of the Union to impose various restrictions on the operation of the monopoly.[75]

There are certain limitations that parallel those in the EPC. Acts done privately and for non-commercial purposes, and acts done for experimental purposes, are not infringing.[76] Moreover, acts done for the purpose of breeding, or discovering and developing other varieties do not infringe plant breeders' rights. There are also the customary rules relating to

---

[67] PVA ss. 14–15. Plant Breeders' Rights (Information Notices) (Extension to European Community Plant Variety Rights) Regulations 1998 (SI 1998/1023).

[68] PVA s. 7; UPOV, Art. 14(5); CPVR, Art. 13(5). On essential derivation, see J. Rooker, *Hansard* (HC) 24 June 1997, cols. 693–4. J. Sanderson, 'Essential Derivation, Law and the Limits of Science' (2006) 24 *Law in Context* 34.

[69] M.-C. Piatti and M. Jouffray, 'Plant Variety Names in National and International Law' [1984] *EIPR* 283.

[70] PVA s. 19. Failure to use the name is a crime punishable by a fine. See also UPOV, Art. 20(7).

[71] UPOV, Art. 20; CPVR, Art. 63. For a discussion of CPVR Art 63(3) see Case A 4/2004 *(Ginpent)*, 5–8.

[72] UPOV, Art. 20(7).   [73] PVA s. 20(2).

[74] Users are represented largely through the National Farmers Union. The breeders are represented by the British Society of Plant Breeders.

[75] UPOV, Art. 17.   [76] CPVR, Art. 15; PVA s. 8.

Community exhaustion of rights where material is 'disposed of to others by the holder or with his consent'.[77]

As regards certain varieties,[78] farmers are authorized to use 'in the field, on their own holding' the product of a harvest which they have obtained by planting a variety. Small farmers are permitted to use such saved seed without payment, whereas others must provide equitable remuneration.[79] Remuneration is required in relation to lists of fodder plants (such as vetch and clover), cereals, potatoes, as well as oil and fibre plants such as rape.[80]

2.8 COMPULSORY LICENCES

Compulsory licences may be granted by the controller in certain circumstances two years after grant of plant breeder's rights.[81] The first condition is that the holder of a plant breeder's right has either unreasonably refused to grant a licence or has proposed an unreasonable term for such a licence.[82] It has been said that this is a heavy burden to discharge.[83] The controller must also be satisfied that such licences are needed to ensure that the variety is available to the public at reasonable prices, is widely distributed (though not necessarily that demand is fully met),[84] or is maintained in quality. The applicant must be intending to exploit the rights and be in a position to do so.[85] The controller sets the terms of the licence as he thinks fit, having regard to the desirability of securing reasonable remuneration to the plant breeder, but the licence must not be an exclusive licence. The controller can require the plant breeder to supply propagating material to the holder of the licence.

As we saw above, a new regime for compulsory licensing and cross-licensing of biological innovations was introduced into the United Kingdom in 2002. In essence the new scheme attempts to manage the inter-relationship between patent protection for biological inventions and plant variety protection.[86]

2.9 RELATIONSHIP TO THE PATENT SYSTEM

The plant breeders' rights system was initiated because of the belief that plant varieties fell outside the types of creation that were traditionally considered to be patentable.[87] Nonetheless,

---

[77] CPVR, Art. 16; PVA s. 10.

[78] CPVR, Art. 14(2); PVA s. 9. On the importance of these sorts of provisions for developing countries, see Verma, 'TRIPS and Plant Variety Protection in Developing Countries' [1995] EIPR 281, 286.

[79] CPVR, Art. 14(3); PVA s. 9(3)–(4). Small farmers are further defined. Plant Breeders' Rights (Farm Saved Seed) (Specified Information) Regulations 1998 (SI 1998/1026).

[80] CPVR, Art. 14; Art. 29; Commission Regulation 1768/95 of 24 Jul. 1995. Collections of remuneration for farm saved seed began in autumn 1996.

[81] CPVR, Art. 29 (compulsory exploitation rights); PVA s. 17; Plant Breeders' Rights Regulations 1998 (SI 1998/1027) Reg. 10 (compulsory licences operate only two years after grant). Cama Wheat [1968] FSR 639, 643 (explaining that plant breeder should have complete control at the first introduction of a variety when seed supplies may be limited and demand uncertain).

[82] PVA s. 17(1).   [83] Cama Wheat, above, 644.

[84] Ibid, 645 (where the breeder's licensees supplied 2,000 tons of seed, a refusal to license the applicant to sell 30 tons did not result in the seed not being 'widely distributed').

[85] PVA s. 17(2)(b)–(c).

[86] Patents and Plant Variety Rights (Compulsory Licensing) Regulations 2002 SI 2002/247. See above at pp. 582–3.

[87] Most importantly, it was seen not as being capable of meeting the requirements of sufficient disclosure. For an international overview, see T. Roberts, 'Patenting Plants Around the World' [1996] EIPR 531.

when the EPC was formulated, a specific exclusion was placed in the definition of patentable subject matter to avoid the possibility of dual protection.[88] For most of the history of the operation of the EPC it was thought that the patent and plant variety systems were mutually exclusive. Indeed the 1961 version of the UPOV seemed to require that members allow either patenting or *sui generis* protection, but not both.[89]

However, developments in techniques for modifying plants, such as somatic cell hybridization and genetic engineering more generally, have thrown the relationship of mutual exclusivity into doubt. This has been reinforced by the fact that biotechnology companies have attempted to use the patent system to obtain protection for their innovations (for example claims directed to plant cell strains, or to groups of plants at a taxonomical level higher than a 'variety').[90] Such attempts increase the possibility of overlap with the plant breeders' system. As a result of the 1991 revision of the UPOV, the patent and plant variety systems are no longer mutually exclusive.[91] As such, this increased the possibility for overlap between the regimes. Since the patent system allows for stronger (though not longer) protection, the possibility of overlap has resulted in increased attempts to obtain patent protection for plant-related products.[92] Some commentators have called for the removal from the EPC of the exclusions relating to plant varieties, thereby leaving choice between the patent and plant breeders' regime to the applicant.[93] However, others have asserted that the scope of breeder's rights regimes should be extended and developed to protect plant biological material more generally.[94] At the same time, frustration with what are seen as overly broad exceptions in the plant breeders' rights systems has led some breeders to resort to technological measures, such as the controversial terminator technology (that renders plants sterile), to protect their research. The use of genetic use restriction technologies (GURTs) poses a direct threat to the plant variety systems. While plant variety rights are only granted to botanical innovations that satisfy certain criteria, are limited in time, and provide a number of exceptions to protect breeders and farmers, this is not the case with genetically-based protection regimes. Although it may be some time before genetic use restriction technologies are put to work, they are likely to shape the way intellectual property deals with biological inventions in the future.

---

[88] Art. 53(b) EPC. *Ciba-Geigy/Propagating material application,* T49/83 [1979–85] C EPOR 758; [1984] OJ EPO 112. (The legislator did not wish to afford patent protection under the EPC to plant varieties within 1961 Convention.) *Plant Genetic Systems/Glutamine synthetase inhibitors* (1993) 24 *IIC* 618 ('the purpose of Art. 53(b) EPC ... is to draw an appropriate dividing line between plant variety and patent law ... It is ... important that no grey area in which protection is not given exists between the above two systems').

[89] UPOV, 1961 Art. 2(1).   [90] See above Ch. 17 Section 8.

[91] Recital 8 states that the definition of plant variety is not intended to alter definitions applicable in relation to other intellectual property rights, especially in the patent field.

[92] A. Christie, 'Patents for Plant Innovation' [1989] *EIPR* 394; S. Crespi, 'Patents and Plant Variety Rights: Is there an Interface Problem?' (1992) 23 *IIC* 168; Llewelyn, 'Legal Protection of Biotechnological Inventions', 117; J. Funder, 'Rethinking Patents for Plant Innovation' [1999] *EIPR* 551.

[93] J. Straus, 'AIPPI and the Protection of Inventions in Plants: Past Developments, Future Perspectives' (1989) 20 *IIC* 600; in *Plant Variety Rights: An Outmoded Impediment? A Seminar Report* (1998), T. Cook argues that the 'option' to protect plants by *sui generis* rights in TRIPS Art. 27(3), should be removed.

[94] Greengrass, 'UPOV and the Protection of Plant Breeders'; M. Llewelyn, 'The Patentability of Biological Material: Continuing Contradiction and Confusion' [2000] *EIPR* 191, and *Plant Variety Rights: An Outmoded Impediment? A Seminar Report* (1998).

3 SUPPLEMENTARY PROTECTION CERTIFICATES

Supplementary protection certificates (SPCs) are intellectual property rights that are based on and are similar in nature to patents. SPCs operate to extend patent protection where it has not been possible for the patent proprietor to take full advantage of their patent rights over the period of the grant. In particular, they compensate owners who have not been able to market the patented product because of delays in obtaining regulatory approval.[95] The need for additional protection arose because, since the 1970s, the systems for regulatory approval have become more rigorous and lengthy. For example, in 1990 the average period for approval of medicines was twelve years. Such delays may erode the time in which the patent owner is able to market their inventions under the protection of the patent monopoly.

Following a Proposal by the Commission in 1990 (which has proved to be an important document in interpreting the legislation),[96] two Council Regulations were passed creating new rights related to patents for 'medicinal products' and 'plant protection products'.[97] The right is characterized as a right distinct from patents in order to avoid the apparent conflict that would otherwise occur with the maximum term under Article 63 of the European Patent Convention.

Because SPCs operate at the interface between the patent system and the system for regulatory approval, the availability, scope, and duration of protection is defined by concepts drawn from each system, coupled with the key hybrid concept of a 'product'. More specifically, under the systems for regulatory approval, approval is granted to the marketing of highly specifically defined products: 'medicinal products' or 'plant protection products'. These are usually defined by reference to their chemical or other ingredients and, for example, by their physical form or intended mode of delivery.[98] In contrast, a patent is likely to be much broader in its coverage, extending perhaps to a chemical *per se* or combination of chemicals, a method of production, or—at its narrowest—a new medical use of a known product. The effect of this is that a single patent may cover a range of individual medicinal or plant protection products. The key mediating concept between these two regimes is 'the product' (which is the 'active substance' for a plant protection product, or the 'ingredient' in the case of medicinal products, for which

---

95 The relevant regulatory authorities are the Medicines Control Agency, the Veterinary Medicines Directorate, the European Agency for the Evaluation of Medicinal Products, and the Pesticides Safety Directorate.

96 The USA introduced 'patent term restoration' in 1984 and Japan in 1987. In 1991 France and Italy introduced so-called 'certificates of complementary protection': see P. Kolker, 'The Supplementary Protection Certificate: The European Solution to Patent Term Restoration' [1997] *IPQ* 249. For a review of the operation of the SPC system, see D. Culey, Extending Rewords for Innovative Drug Development—A Report on Supplementry Certificates for Pharmaceutical Products (London: IPI, 2007).

97 Council Regulation (EEC) No. 1768/92 of 18 June 1992 concerning the creation of a supplementary protection certificate for medicinal products (*OJ* 1992 *L* 182/1) (hereafter the SPC(MP) Reg). Regulation (EC) no. 1610/96 of the European Parliament and of the Council of 23 Jul. 1996 concerning the creation of a supplementary protection certificate for plant protection products (*OJ* 1986 *L* 198/30–5). (Hereafter the SPC (PPP) Reg.) The Spanish unsuccessfully challenged Regulation 1768/92 on the grounds that the Community did not have competence to legislate a new patent right, and that intervention could not be justified by reference to the need to harmonize laws for the internal market: *Spain v. Council of the European Union*, Case 350/92 [1995] *ECR* I–1985, [1996] *FSR* 73. Note also the Canadian complaint, WTO/DS 153.

98 SPC(MP) Reg. Art. 1(a); SPC(PPP) Reg. Art. 1(1).

approval was gained).[99] For example, if marketing approval was sought for 'aspirin in 500-mg. tablet form to be sold in packets of not more than sixteen tablets', the 'active ingredient' would be aspirin. In most cases the product includes derivatives, such as salts or esters.

3.1 AVAILABILITY

In order to receive an SPC, a person must apply to the national patent office and not the EPO.[100] The application must be made within six months of receipt of authorization to market the medicinal or plant protection product.[101] At the time of application, the applicant must be the proprietor of a basic patent that is in force. Applications lodged outside the six-month period[102] will not be accepted.[103] Taking into account third-party observations,[104] the Intellectual Property Office assesses whether an SPC should be granted (that is, whether the patent covers the product,[105] and whether appropriate authorizations exist):[106] there is no reinvestigation of the validity of the patent. It should be noted that the relevant authorization must be the *first* authorization.[107] This means that if a patent is granted for a new process of making an old product, an existing authorization relating to the old product will probably mean that no certificate will be available.[108] The first authorization must be a marketing authorization in accordance with the relevant EC Directives and not some other authorization required by national law (such as is required to determine the pricing of medicines).[109] For pharmaceutical products the relevant Directive is the EC Directive on Medicinal Products for Human Use.[110] For veterinary products, it is the Directive relating to veterinary medical products.[111]

If a patentee applies for an SPC but is unable to submit the appropriate marketing authorization (for example, because it was granted to the patentee's licensee and that person refuses

[99] SPC(MP) Reg. Art. 1(b) (defining product); SPC(PPP) Reg. Art. 1(8) (defining product), Art. 1(3) (defining active substance), Art. 1(2) (defining substances).

[100] From 17 Dec 2007 this is done by virtue of PA s. 128B, Schedule 4A (introduced by The Patents (Compulsory Licensing and Supplementary Protection Certificates) Regulations 2007 (SI 2007 No. 3293)) and Patent Rules 2007 (SI 2007/3291), r. 116(1)–(5). See generally, UK Intellectual Property Office, *Supplementary Protection Certificates for Medicinal Products and Plant Protection Products: A Guide for Applicants* (Dec 2007).

[101] SPC(MP) Reg. Art. 7; SPC(PPP) Reg. Art. 7; *Yamannouchi Pharmaceuticals v. Comptroller-General* [1997] RPC 844 (ECJ). A valid authorization does not include a mere authorization of clinical trials: *British Technology Group SPC Application* [1997] RPC 118.

[102] Calculated from the date of grant of authorization and not the date of publication of grant in the relevant *Official Gazette*: *Abbott Laboratories' SPC Application* (25 Jul. 2002) O/302/02 (Patent Office).

[103] *Hässle AB v. Ratiopharm,* Case C–127/00 (11 Dec. 2003) paras. 80–89 (ECJ). 'Where a mistake has been committed regarding the date of first marketing authorisation in the Community...the certificate must be declared invalid' (para. 89).

[104] Art. 18(2); *BASF AG's SPC Application* [2000] RPC 1. Documents are usually open to public inspection within 14 days of being filed. Observations should be made in writing.

[105] If a patent is granted for a combination of ingredients but a certificate relates to one of the ingredients only, no certificate should be granted: *Centacor SPC Appn.* [1996] RPC 118. Whether a patent for a product would cover its salts or esters will be a matter of interpretation of the patent claims, applying principles explained at pp. 554–63: see *Takeda Chemical Industry's Application* [2003] EWHC 649 (Pat).

[106] *BTG SPC Application* [1997] RPC 844 (ECJ) (refusing an SPC because no relevant authorization).

[107] SPC(MP) Reg. Art. 3(d); SPC(PPP) Reg. Art. 3(1)(d).

[108] *BASF AG's SPC Application* [2000] RPC 1 (an attempt to claim that the certificate related to a different product which necessarily had certain impurities resulting from the particular patent process was rejected).

[109] *Hässle v. Ratiopharm,* above, paras. 58–59 (ECJ).

[110] 2001/83/EC [2001] *OJ L* 311/119 (which repealed and replaced EC Directive 65/65/EEC).

[111] 2001/82/EC [2001] *OJ L* 311/1 (which repealed and replaced EC Directive 81/851/EEC).

to cooperate), the Intellectual Property Office may contact the relevant authority.[112] However, the Office will first require the applicant to provide evidence of their inability to supply the authorization, as well as *Official Gazette* information that will enable the Office to verify the identity of the product and the date of authorization.[113] Once an SPC is granted, the relevant authority may demand an annual fee to maintain it in force. In the United Kingdom these fees are £600 for the first year, rising by £100 per year to a fee of £1,000 for the fifth (which must be paid in one instalment).[114]

An SPC will not be granted where it extends beyond the scope of the underlying patent. This is because, as Jacob J said, the SPC system is 'not a system for providing protection for different monopolies'.[115] Thus an application for an SPC for a combination of two active ingredients was rejected because the patent only covered one of the ingredients.[116] In certain circumstances, there may be more than one basic patent relating to a particular product.[117] This can be seen, for example, if we take the situation where A applied in 1990 for a patent for substance X and B applied in 1993 for a patent for use of substance X in making a pharmaceutical preparation for use in thinning blood. If authorization was given to B to market the pharmaceutical preparation in 2000, A would be entitled to a certificate lasting five years and B a certificate lasting two years (see Section 3.4 below for how these periods are calculated). However, the mere existence of a second patent will not of itself justify the grant of a certificate. If, in the same example, A had received authorization to market the substance as a cure for headaches in 1996, A would be entitled to a certificate for one year, but B would not be entitled to any certificate. This is because the authorization in 2000 was not the first authorization relating to the product. The existence of B's 1993 patent is of no special significance.

3.2 SUBJECT MATTER

The protection provided by an SPC extends to the 'product' covered by the authorization and any use of the product as a medicinal (etc.) product that has been authorized before expiry of the SPC.[118] The product is defined as the 'active substance' (in the case of plant protection) or the 'ingredient' (in the case of medicinal products) for which approval was gained.[119] For example, if A applies for a patent for aspirin on 1 January 1990 and was granted marketing authorization for sale of aspirin in tablet form as a treatment for headaches on 1 January 1996, and A then obtained an SPC, the SPC would not only cover sale in tablet form, but also any

---

[112] *Biogen v. Smith Kline Beecham Biologicals SA* [1997] *RPC* 833.

[113] See the Patent Office, *Supplementary Protection Certificates for Medicinal Products and Plant Protection Products: A Guide for Applicants* (1997), para. SPM 8.04.1.

[114] SPC(MP) Reg. Art. 12; SPC(PPP) Reg. Art. 12; Patents Rules 2007, r. 116(4)(b), Patents (Fees) Rules 2007, r. 6(2).

[115] *Takeda Chemical* [2003] *EWHC* 649, para. 12 (Pat).

[116] Ibid, para. 11–12. Jacob J. rejected an attempt to use a version of the reverse infringement test to determine whether a patent covers a 'product' saying that 'the fact that the combination might infringe the…patent simply because one componenet infringes is irrelevant'. (para. 12).

[117] If a patent holder has more than one patent for the same product, he should not be able to obtain more than one certificate for that product: *Takeda Chemical Industries Application* (31 May 2002) O/229/02 (Patent Office) (interpreting the statement from the ECJ that under 'Article 3(c) of the Regulation…only one certificate may be granted for each basic patent': *Biogen v. SKB,* above, 843 (ECJ)).

[118] SPC(MP) Reg. Art. 4; SPC(PPP) Reg. Art. 4. The product is the 'active substance' (for a plant protection product) or 'ingredient' (in the medicinal product) for which approval was gained.

[119] SPC(MP) Reg. Art. 1(b) (defining product); SPC(PPP) Reg. Art. 1(8) (defining product), Art. 1(3) (defining active substance), Art. 1(2) (defining substances).

subsequent authorizations of the same product which were obtained before the expiry of the patent in 2010. Thus, if A later gets marketing authorization for sale of aspirin in capsule form as a treatment for headaches in 1999, the SPC that would operate from 2010 to 2011 would also cover that use. It is clear that 'product' means the active ingredient or combination of 'active ingredients' or 'active substance' of a medicinal (etc) product.[120] This means that the concept of a 'product' cannot include the therapeutic use of an active ingredient protected by a basic patent.[121]

The scope of the SPC is not confined to the specific product for which authorization was first secured. The SPC is capable of covering the product mentioned in the marketing authorization 'in any of the forms enjoying the protection of the basic patent'.[122] As the European Court of Justice said in the *Farmitalia* decision, if an SPC were only able to protect the product in the specific form stated in the marketing authorization, this would mean that 'any competitor would be able, after the basic patent had expired, to apply for and in some circumstances, obtain marketing authorization for [a different version] of the same ingredient, formerly protected by that patent'. If this were permitted, it would allow 'medicinal products which were in principle therapeutically equivalent to that protected by the certificate to compete with the latter. The result would be to frustrate the purpose of [SPCs] which is to ensure the holder of the basic patent of exclusivity on the market during a given period extending beyond the period of the validity of the basic patent.'[123] In the *BASF* decision, the ECJ said that, in the case of plant protection products, the product is the active substance including any impurity inevitably resulting from the manufacturing process.[124] The ECJ also added that two plant protection products containing the same active substance in different concentrations were identical products for the purposes of the Regulations.[125]

3.3 LIMITS

The rights granted under an SPC are subject to the same limitations and obligations as applied to the basic patent.[126] An SPC will therefore be subject to licences of right if the patent would have been subject to such a licence prior to its expiry.[127]

3.4 DURATION

The SPC comes into operation at the expiry of the patent. This is subject to the requirement that the patent is maintained until the end of its potential term.[128] If the patent is permitted to lapse, is declared to be invalid, or is revoked, the SPC will not come into effect. The duration of an SPC will vary depending on the length of time it took to receive regulatory approval. The

---

[120] *Massachusetts Institute of Technology,* Case C–431/04, (2006/C 165/14) [2006] *ECR* I–4089, paras. 19, 21, 23, and 24.

[121] *Yissum Research and Development Company,* Case C–202/05 [2007] *ECR* I–2839, (2007/C 96/33), paras. 16–20.

[122] *Farmitalia Carlo Erba SRL's SPC Application,* Case C–392/97 [2000] *RPC* 580, 586.

[123] Ibid, 584.

[124] *BASF v. Bureau voor de Industriële Eigendom,* Case C–258/99 [2002] *RPC* 9, para. 28–29 (products with different levels of purity were the same for the purposes of calculating date of first authorization).

[125] Ibid.   [126] SPC(MP) Reg. Art. 5; SPC(PPP) Reg. Art. 5.

[127] PA s 128B, Schedule 4A, para. 1(2); *Research Corps SPC* [1994] *RPC* 667. On terms, see *Research Corps SPC (No. 2)* [1996] *RPC* 320.

[128] SPC(MP) Reg. Art. 13; SPC(PPP) Reg. Art. 13.

maximum period for an SPC is five years. The period is ascertained by calculating the difference between the date of application for the basic patent and the date of the grant of the first authorization, less five years. This means that, if a patent application was made in 1988 and authorization was granted in 1997, the relevant certificate should last for four years. However, as there is a maximum duration of five years, if the authorization was granted in 2000 the duration of the SPC would be five years. The average term of the SPCs granted in the UK in 2000 was just over three years.[129]

The duration of the SPC is formulated in a way to ensure harmonization within Europe as to the date of *expiry* of all national SPCs. Consequently, although for the purposes of an application the relevant authorization is the first national authorization, for the purposes of calculating the duration of the SPC, the relevant authorization is the first Community authorization.[130] For example, if A applies for a patent for aspirin on 1 January 1993 and gets marketing authorization for the sale of aspirin in the UK on 1 January 2000, but had already received marketing authorization in Portugal on 1 January 1999, the UK SPC will only last for one year. If national regulatory procedures are particularly quick in other member states, SPCs may not be available in the UK to compensate owners for the loss of the opportunity to exploit the patent in the UK. To a number of commentators, this is unfair since the patent owner suffers delays but gets no compensation.[131]

In calculating the duration of the SPC, it does not matter that the first authorization was for a different mode of delivery or a different use. For example, if A applies for a patent on 1 January 1993, and receives authorization for use in animals on 1 January 1999 and for use in humans on 1 January 2001, the relevant certificate would only subsist for one year. No separate certificate would be issued based on the later authorization.[132]

Amendments effected to encourage investigation into diseases affecting children can lead to a six month addition to the certificate (even where no paediatric indication is achieved).[133]

3.5 REFORM

The Commission announced in June 2008 that it was considering codification of the regulations relating to supplementary protection certificates.[134]

---

[129] B. Domeij, *Pharmaceutical Patents in Europe* (2000), 268.

[130] This would include relevant EEA authorizations, for example, in Iceland, Norway, and Liechtenstein. The question of the status of the first authorization as the basis for calculating duration was considered by ECJ in *Novartis* (C–207/03) (21 April 2005) (referral from *Novartis AG and University College London's SPC Application* (12 Feb. 2003) O/044/03).

[131] Domeij, *Pharmaceutical Patents in Europe*, 273.   [132] *Farmitalia Case*, C–392/97 [1996] *RPC* 111.

[133] Regulation (EC) No. 1901/2006 of the European Parliament and of the Council of 12 December 2006 on medicinal products for paediatric use, *OJ L* 378/1 (27 Dec 2006), Arts. 7, 8, 36, 52.

[134] COM(2008) 369 final (Brussels, 17 June 2008).

PART III
THE LEGAL REGULATION
OF DESIGNS

1 INTRODUCTION

Designs play an important but often neglected part in our lives. As well as influencing the appearance of the clothes we wear, the shape of the chairs we sit in, and the surfboards we ride, design also influences the decisions we make as consumers: why it is that we choose one tooth-brush over another?[1] The practice of design covers a variety of domains.[2] These range from industrial design,[3] urban planning, graphic design, and stage design through to costume design, fashion design, product design, and packaging design. In reflection of this diversity, the role played by design varies greatly. In some cases, an object may be designed for frivolous or trivial reasons; in other cases, the way an object is designed may play an important role in how effectively the designed article works. Whatever role design performs, it is widely recognized to be a time-consuming, costly, and valuable activity. Given that the art of designing is concerned with the nature and appearance of objects, one of the notable aspects of designing is that the results are readily copied. Not surprisingly, therefore, intellectual property protection plays an important role in regulating the creation and use of designs.

---

[1] For emphasis in legal commentaries on designs as marketing instruments, see: A Kur, 'The Green Paper's Design Approach—What's Wrong with It' [1993] *EIPR* 374, 376; F.-K. Beier, 'Protection for Spare Parts in the Proposals for a European Design Law' (1994) 25 *IIC* 840, 841.

[2] V. Papanek, *Design for the Real World: Human Ecology and Social Change* (1984) 3–4, defines design as 'the planning and patterning of any act towards a desired, foreseeable end.'

[3] C. Woodring, 'A Designer's View on the Scope of Intellectual Property Protection' (1996) 24 *American Intellectual Property Law Association Quarterly Journal* 309 (defining industrial design as 'the professional service of creating and developing concepts and specification that optimize the function, value, and appearance of products and systems for the mutual benefit of user and manufacturer').

Over time a number of different areas of intellectual property such as trade marks,[4] passing off,[5] and the law of breach of confidence[6] have been used to protect designs. In the next six chapters, we concentrate on those areas of intellectual property law more commonly used to protect designs. These are: the registered design system established by the Registered Designs Act 1949; the registered and unregistered rights recently made available at a Community level; copyright protection provided by the Copyright, Designs and Patents Act 1988; and the 'unregistered design right' protection which was set up by Part III of the latter. As we will see, the existence of five systems of protection renders design law surprisingly and unnecessarily complex.

2 THE NORMATIVE BASIS OF DESIGN PROTECTION

It is a notable feature of the commentary on the legal protection of designs that there is very little consideration of the justification for granting protection to designs.[7] Rather, it is assumed that the general arguments which justify the protection of works by copyright or inventions by patents, whether based on instrumental philosophies or ethical beliefs, are equally applicable to designs.

These assumptions are, no doubt, often warranted: the design process involves investment of time and money,[8] and successful designs can be (and are) readily copied. Those who favour ethical arguments of a 'reap–sow' type would argue that design protection is required to prevent a second-comer reaping where they have not sown. Those who cling to the utilitarian approach[9] would argue that protection is necessary to provide sufficient incentives for such investment.[10] However, it is notable that historically only rarely has the legal protection of

---

[4] *Philips Electronics BV v. Remington Consumer Products* [1998] *RPC* 283. It seems that, in the light of harmonization, words can be protected as designs and this raises the issue of the relation of design law to trade mark law, and practical questions as to whether a person is better off registering a logo as a design (or relying on unregistered design right in a logo) rather than a trade mark: Musker, 14; C.-H. Massa and A. Strowel, 'Community Design: Cinderella Revamped' [2003] *EIPR* 68, 77. Indeed, it might be noted that the effect of the *Arsenal* litigation (see pp. 922–3), led to an increase in the number of UK design registrations. On the extent to which overlap between the new designs law and trade marks should be seen as a concern, see A. Kur. 'Protection of Graphical User Interfaces under European Design Legislation' (2003) 34 *IIC* 50, 60–2 (arguing that these concerns are exaggerated, and observing that the possibility of such overlap has long existed in Germany without raising problems).

[5] *Benchairs v. Chair Centre* [1974] RPC 429. But cf. *Hodgkinson & Corby and Roho v. Wards Mobility Services* [1995] *FSR* 169.

[6] For recent examples, see *Carflow Products v. Linwood Securities* [1996] FSR 424; *Valeo Vision SA v. Flexible Lamps* [1995] *RPC* 205.

[7] J. Lahore, 'The Protection of Functional Designs: The Amended Proposal for a European Designs Directive' (1997) 1 IPQ 128, 132 (registering surprise at lack of analysis of benefits of design protection).

[8] Apparently the development costs for the outer appearance of the Ford Sierra in the 1980s amounted to $140 million, or 20 per cent of the total cost: M. Levin, 'Recent Developments in Nordic Design Protection' (1988) 19 *IIC* 606.

[9] *Electronic Techniques (Anglia) v. Critchley Components* [1997] FSR 401, 418.

[10] CDR, Recital 7 states that 'enhanced protection for industrial design not only promotes the contribution of individual designers to the sum of Community excellence in the field, but also encourages innovation and development of new products and investment in their production'. *In the Matter of Morton's Design* (1900) 17 *RPC* 117, 121 Farwell J (the purpose of the design portion of the Act is the same as the patent portion of it); *Allen West & Co. v. British Westinghouse Electric & Manufacturing Co.* (1916) 33 RPC 157, 162 (design protection was said to be 'primarily to advance our industries and keep them at a high level of competitive progress'); *Dart Industries v. Décor Corporation* (1989) 15 IPR 403.

designs been justified by reference to the natural rights of individual designers in their creations. This reflects a commonly held assumption that designs are less creative than artistic works because designing is subject to a number of inevitable constraints.[11] For example, the potential scope for the design of a table is constrained by our existing idea of a table, the functions it must perform, the need for it to be comfortable, its cost, and the possibilities presented by available materials.[12]

3 THE BRITISH HISTORY

While the story of how designs came to be protected by five different systems of protection is a long and important one, we must deal with it here only in outline.

The story starts in 1839,[13] when out of a desire to improve the aesthetic quality of industrially manufactured goods, Parliament introduced a registered design system.[14] Under this system, if an applicant submitted representations of a new and original design for an article of manufacture, the law would grant a monopoly over the design for up to three years. This registration system seemed to operate successfully for the rest of the century, with many thousands of designs being registered.[15] Insofar as there were problems with the design system, they largely concerned the relationship between the design system and the patent system in the protection of useful mechanical devices, and these problems seemed to disappear with improvements in the administration of the patent system.

However, at the turn of the twentieth century, just as the use of the registered design system reached its peak, issues came to be raised as to the relationship between it and the copyright system. These questions, in large part, arose as copyright law was expanded and rationalized to give effect to the Berlin revision of the Berne Convention of 1908. These reforms presented not only the possibility of the protection of many designs by copyright law for the first time, especially on the basis of the design drawings that were artistic works, but simultaneously threatened the viability of the registration system. This was because copyright offered a system of protection which was automatic (no longer requiring registration), potentially longer, and (in some respects) stronger.

The initial response of the legislature was to attempt to draw a boundary between designs which required registration and artistic works (such as works of artistic craftsmanship) which

[11] R. Denicola, 'Applied Art and Industrial Design' (1983) *Minnesota Law Review* 707, 741–3, and n. 165; J. Reichman, 'Design Protection in Domestic and Foreign Copyright Law' [1983] *Duke Law Journal* 1143, 1160, 1220–1, 1235.

[12] Moreover, there is a tendency to place greater emphasis on the potential social costs that the legal protection of designs cause to competitors of the proprietors of such right. As designs are applied to 'articles', it is feared that any impediments placed on the reproduction of the design will also interfere with free competition for the article itself. One commentator describes this as the 'two-market conundrum' that arises because designs operate to render articles desirable both as (useful) articles and as attractive objects: Reichman, ibid.

[13] Prior to this the Calico Printers Acts 1787 (27 Geo. 3. c. 23) and 1794 (34 Geo. 3 c. 23) conferred protection upon new and original patterns for linens, cotton, calico, and muslins *automatically*.

[14] Copyright of Designs (Registration) Act 1839 (2 Vict. c. 17). While design law was one of the first areas of modern intellectual property law to take shape, over time it has been eclipsed by copyright and patent law. This has led to the (inaccurate) claim that designs law is the stepchild of patents and copyright. See Sherman and Bently, chs. 3, 4, 163–6, 210–12.

[15] L. Bently, 'Requiem for Registration? Reflections on the History of the UK Registered Design System', in A. Firth (ed.), *Perspectives in Intellectual Property: Vol. i. The Prehistory and Development of Intellectual Property* (1997), 1.

were protected under the copyright system. As a result, the Copyright Act 1911 included a provision excluding from copyright protection works which were 'capable' of being registered as designs and which were intended to be used as the basis for multiplication by an industrial process. Later statutes employed different techniques to regulate the boundary. In one way or another, all of these proved to be unsatisfactory. Perhaps the most bizarre consequence of (at least) the last such attempt to establish a boundary was that designs which were unregistrable because they were 'dictated by function', were given greater protection than registrable designs. Such protection was widely referred to as 'industrial copyright'.

In response to these failings, the Copyright, Designs and Patents Act 1988 fashioned a new 'design–copyright interface'. It did so by modifying the Registered Designs Act 1949 so that registration was confined to aesthetic designs, adding important defences to copyright infringement (sections 51 and 52), and establishing a new unregistered design right regime.

4 INTERNATIONAL FAILINGS

While the United Kingdom pursued its own ideas as how best to protect designs, other countries took different approaches. Some placed emphasis on copyright, others on unfair competition law, others on registration.[16] There was little consensus, and consequently few international norms could be agreed. The Paris Convention contains provisions on national treatment and the priority dates of design applications, but nothing of substance on registered design protection.[17] The Berne Convention is only a little more prescriptive. While 'applied art' is included in the subject matter covered by the Convention,[18] countries of the Union are given free rein with regard to the scope of protection and to whether any formalities may be required.[19] The only specific requirement in relation to designs in the Berne Convention is that if special protection is not granted, then such works shall be protected as 'artistic works'. Even the TRIPS Agreement has only two articles on designs.[20] Design laws were allowed to vary on a national basis.

Not surprisingly these variations in national design protection laws were quickly understood to present a problem for the EC and in particular the internal market.[21] In 1991,[22] the

---

[16] Reichman, 'Design Protection in Domestic and Foreign Copyright Law'; H. Cohen Jehoram, 'Designs Law in Continental Europe and Their Relation to Copyright Law' [1981] *EIPR* 235; C. Fellner, *The Future of Legal Protection for Industrial Design* (1985), ch. 6.

[17] Paris, Arts. 2 and 4C(1). Indeed, until the Lisbon revision of 1958 the Convention did not even require countries of the Union to protect industrial designs: Paris Art. 5*quinquies*. This does not specify how protection is to be conferred, so that compliance may be achieved through copyright or unfair competition rather than *sui generis* designs law.

[18] Berne, Art. 2.

[19] Berne, Art. 2(7). Under Berne Art. (7)(4) applied art should be protected for a minimum period of 25 years.

[20] TRIPS, Arts. 25 and 26. This requires members to provide protection for independently created industrial designs that are new or original. More specifically, it provides that the owner of a protected industrial design shall have the right to prevent third parties from making, selling, or importing articles bearing or embodying the design for at least ten years. Certain limited exceptions are permitted. See Gervais, paras. 2.240–2.250, 211–17; A. Kur, 'TRIPS and Design Protection' in Beier and Shricker.

[21] *Keurkoop BV v. Nancy Kean Gifts BV,* Case 144/81 [1982] *ECR* 2853; *Consorzio Italiano della Componentistica de Ricambio per Autoveicoli & Maxivar v. Regie Nationale des Usines Renault,* Case 53/87 [1988] *ECR* 6039; *AB Volvo v. Erik Veng (UK),* Case 238/87 [1988] *ECR* 6211.

[22] Green Paper on the Legal Protection of Industrial Design (III/F/5131/91–EN, Brussels, June 1991) (hereafter, EC Green Paper).

Commission issued a Green Paper laying out a scheme by which to begin to tackle the problems raised by the enormous variation in national designs laws.[23] The Green Paper was notable for its advocacy of a 'designs' approach—treating designs as a distinct field of law rather than a branch or extension of copyright or patents. The Green Paper advocated a three-pronged approach, of the sort finally adopted, involving harmonization of national registered designs law, the establishment of a Community Registered Design System, and the introduction of a Community Unregistered Design Right. It seemed that, from the start, this would require the passage of two pieces of Community legislation, namely a directive to harmonize national law and a regulation to establish the two Community-wide rights. Following consultation, two Proposals were published.[24] The Commission decided to start with the directive, it being understood that the regulation—where relevant—would be in the same substantive terms. Following criticisms of the initial proposal, in particular in the European Parliament, an amended Proposal for a Directive was published in 1996.[25] Although there were a number of significant amendments for designs generally, the whole legislative process was dogged by the issue of the appropriate form of protection for car spare parts. Ultimately, as is explained in Chapter 26, differences could not be resolved. Consequently, in the so-called 'Standstill Plus' compromise, the Directive left the question to member states. Once the Directive was adopted in July 1998, the Commission's focus returned to the Regulation. Amended proposals were published in 1999 and 2000, and the Regulation was adopted in December 2001.

The Directive attempts to harmonize the features of national registered design systems which most obviously affect the functioning of the internal market.[26] It refers to this as being not 'full-scale' harmonization but rather 'limited' approximation.[27] Harmonization is required in relation to the 'conditions for obtaining registration', the rights of the design owner, the term of protection, and grounds on which the registration can be invalidated.[28] In contrast, issues of procedure and remedies are left to member states.[29] The Directive also allows member states to protect designs by other regimes such as through national unregistered design rights, or through competition law.[30] The Directive requires that member states do not treat the existence of registered design protection as pre-empting protection by copyright, a regime referred to as 'cumulation of copyright'.[31] The Directive was supposed to be implemented by 28 October 2001, and the British government did so by amending the Registered Designs Act 1949 from 9 December 2001.[32]

The Regulation on the Community Design, 6/2002 of 12 December 2001, established a Community-wide system of registered design protection with a Community Design Office

[23] For useful accounts of national laws prior to harmonization, see B. Gray and E. Bouzalas, *Industrial Design Rights: An International Perspective* (2001).

[24] For commentaries see: A. Horton, 'European Designs Law and the Spare Parts Dilemma: The Proposed Regulation and Directive' [1994] *EIPR* 52; Beier, 'Protection for Spare Parts'.

[25] For commentaries see G. Dinwoodie, 'Federalized Functionalism: The Future of Design Protection in the European Union' (1996) 24 *American Intellectual Property Law Association Quarterly Journal* 611; Lahore, 'Protection of Functional Designs'; H. Speyart, 'The Grand Design' [1997] *EIPR* 603.

[26] Designs Dir., Recitals 1, 2, 3.   [27] Designs Dir., Recitals 1, 3, 5.

[28] Designs Dir., Recitals 9; 10; Recitals 17, 21.   [29] Designs Dir., Recitals 5, 6.

[30] Designs Dir., Art. 16, Recital 7; CDR Recital 31.   [31] Designs Dir., Art. 17, Recital 8; CDR Recital 32.

[32] Perhaps not surprisingly (though no doubt rather annoyingly), the UK legislature has implemented the Directive into UK law by way of statutory instrument, and on occasions decided to alter the wording. We can be relatively certain that the UK courts will ignore these modifications and rely where appropriate on the Directive itself. Even the Patent Office has been irritated by the re-drafting: Designs Practice Notice, DPN 1/03 'Component Part of complex product visible in normal use' (7 Jan. 2003).

(Office for Harmonization in the Internal Market). This became operational on 1 April 2003.[33] Like the Community Trade Mark, the vision which drives the Registered Community Design is the replacement of national design systems (which, even if harmonized, present the possibility of national rights owned by different persons) with a unified system for obtaining a Community design to which uniform protection is given with uniform effect throughout the entire territory of the Community.[34] The Registered Community Design is acquired by application to the OHIM, but there is no substantive examination. The Registered Community Design can last for up to 25 years, and confers an 'absolute monopoly' on the proprietor. The validity of the designs will be able to be challenged either in proceedings at the Community Design Office,[35] or by way of defence to an infringement action in a Community Design Court.[36]

The Registered Community Design is supplemented by the Unregistered Community Design Right, available under the Community Design Regulation since 7 March 2002.[37] The Unregistered Community Design Right is intended to provide short-term protection for those industries (such as clothing manufacture) where registration is inappropriate: primarily because designs are only of value for a short period.[38] The Unregistered Community Design (UCD) is also intended to provide protection during the period in which a proprietor decides whether the design is worth registering.

The Unregistered Community Design Right is automatically obtainable on the making-available in the Community of a design which is novel and has an 'individual character'.[39] The protection lasts for three years from such making-available.[40] Unlike the Registered Community Design, the protection given by the UCD right is merely a protection against copying. The right will be enforced by action in a national Community Design Court. It is at this stage that the validity of the right may be challenged.

5   CUMULATIVE EFFECT

The effect of the combination of British and European law is to create a system of design protection which is multi-layered, complex, and lacking in logic. Cornish calls it an 'absurd maze'.[41] The British approach, adopted in 1988, of confining registered designs to visually attractive designs, while leaving unregistered design right for functional three-dimensional designs, has been modified in part (so as to comply with the Directive), but the implications of the modifications

---

[33] The substantive provisions are aligned with those in the Directive: CDR, Recital 9. The constitutional validity of the Registered Designs Regulations 2001 (which implemented the Directive in the UK) was upheld by the Court of Appeal in *Oakley Inc v. Animal Ltd and Others* [2006] *Ch* 337 (CA), See M. Howe, 'Oakley Inc v Animal Ltd: Designs create a constitutional mess' (2006) 28(3) *EIPR* 192.

[34] CDR, Recital 1.   [35] CDR, Art. 25.   [36] CDR, Arts. 24, 25.

[37] The aim of the Unregistered Community Design Right is to strengthen the competitive position of European industries (not to complete the internal market): EC Green Paper, 4.3.9.

[38] J. Reichman, 'Design Protection and the New Technologies: The US Experience in a Transnational Perspective' (1989) 19 *University of Baltimore Law Review* 6, 23.

[39] It is the first Community-wide right to be available automatically.

[40] V. Saez, 'The Unregistered Community Design' [2002] *EIPR* 585, 588 (thereby avoiding problems with using creation as the key date).

[41] 6th edn., para. 15–52, 598.

to the scheme as a whole have not been acknowledged. The effect is to create a national scheme which affords registered protection to virtually all new designs, and unregistered protection to most three-dimensional designs that are not commonplace, with the possibility of copyright protection for designs for three-dimensional artistic works, patterns, and surface decoration. On top of that national scheme, we now have two further layers of Community protection, covering designs of all types, either by way of registration (and lasting for up to 25 years) or arising automatically on publication of the design (and lasting three years thereafter). To summarize, there are currently five different ways in which a design may be protected. These are via:

(i)   UK registered design

(ii) Registered Community Design Right

(iii) Unregistered Community Design Right

(iv) copyright protection of design drawings for artistic works (such as sculptures), two-dimensional designs, and surface decoration, and

(v)   UK unregistered design right.

The task ahead is therefore daunting. In the first instance, we need to understand this highly complex body of law, to explore its limits, and expose its (many) problems. The European legislature, unfortunately, has left much to be elaborated by the ECJ. But, beyond merely scrutinizing the various sets of rules, we must consider what reforms would be appropriate, in the hope that at some stage Parliamentary time can be found for reform. Given that the British legislature only has limited room for manoeuvre, simplification of rules in this area, irrespective of their substantive merits, may for once be treated as a worthy end in itself. The most obvious, and hopefully least controversial, reform would be the modification of UK registered-design rules, such as those on entitlement, and procedures which are unharmonized, so as to make them consistent with those operated by the OHIM. Ultimately, abolition of the domestic registration system would at least remove one layer from the edifice,[42] and abolition of the UK's *sui generis* unregistered design right another. The latter experiment which targeted 'functional designs', now 15 years old, is by no means a proven success, and the new Community and harmonized regimes offer short-term, automatic protection for such designs. The Community legislature could also assist in clearing up this mess, first by resolving the 'spare parts' issue (a task which is currently under way[43]) and second by harmonizing the conditions and scope of protection of designs by copyright.

6 PLAN OF DISCUSSION

Since the substantive provisions of the harmonization Directive and the Community Design Regulation are virtually identical, we intend to treat the three systems—the UK registered design, the Registered Community Design, and the Unregistered Community Design— together over the next four chapters. Consequently, in the next chapter we look at the registration systems. In Chapter 26, we examine the meaning of 'design' employed in the Directive

---

[42] Unfortunately, abolition of the national registration system is not permitted by the Directive which requires member states 'to protect designs by registration': Design Dir. Art. 3.

[43] See below at pp. 674–7.

and the Regulation. In Chapter 27 we explore the concepts of 'novelty', 'individual character', and other aspects of validity. In Chapter 28, we consider who is entitled to apply for a design registration, the rules relating to ownership, and proprietary aspects. We also look at infringement and exceptions—again for the three harmonized systems. We then move on to consider the two other main forms of protection of designs in the United Kingdom which have not been the subject of harmonization. In Chapter 29, we examine UK copyright law, as it applies to designs. In Chapter 30, we look at the UK's unregistered design right.

25

ACQUIRING REGISTERED DESIGN PROTECTION IN THE UNITED KINGDOM AND THE EUROPEAN COMMUNITY

CHAPTER CONTENTS

1 INTRODUCTION

This chapter is concerned with the procedure by which design protection is acquired in the United Kingdom and Europe. The chapter, therefore, is not concerned with the systems of design protection where rights arise without formality—namely copyright, UK unregistered design right, and unregistered Community designs. Rather, it is concerned with the decision whether to register a design, as well as the process and function of registration. Although these matters are of practical importance, and might therefore be assumed to be equally unglamorous topics of discussion, we think that they are, or in due course will prove to be, critical to understanding design law generally. This is because the distinction between procedure and substance is in many ways a false one. Most obviously, the procedure by which design protection is acquired is the procedure by which the 'design' for which protection is sought is identified. It is through this bureaucratic process that the property in question is defined. And so the characteristics of the procedure have a direct bearing on the substance of design protection.

2   THE DECISION TO REGISTER

The decision whether to register a design will be primarily a question of business strategy.[1] The critical issue will be whether the advantages provided by the registration system over the protection afforded by the law automatically (through unregistered Community design, unregistered national design right in the United Kingdom, national copyright, or other rights (most importantly unfair competition)), are so attractive as to outweigh the disadvantages of registration. The assessment of these matters will vary depending upon the type of design in question, the amount expended in the creation of the design and the importance of monopoly protection, the likelihood of a competitor independently creating a similar design,[2] the geographical extent of its potential market, and so on. In recent years, registration has been attractive to the electronics and furniture industries.[3] Other industries which formerly relied heavily on design registration, such as the textile design sector, are likely to be satisfied with the systems of unregistered rights now available.[4] Another factor that may lead a person to register a design is that it might help them secure financial backing.

The registered systems are generally regarded as conferring three benefits on the design proprietor. First, it is thought that registration provides some degree of certainty such as to justify further investment in exploitation of a design. The certainty largely derives from the fact of filing, and the manner in which this establishes priority over later designs.[5] In some cases, where national procedures involve search and examination for novelty, registration can provide a registrant with confidence that their design is valid and not infringing any other previously published designs. However, such systems are now in the minority.[6] (As we will see, from 1 October 2006 the UK registry no longer undertakes examination for novelty or individual character.)[7] The second advantage of registration is that the rights conferred on the proprietor tend to be stronger than unregistered rights. This is true of the European harmonized national systems, and the Community Design. Unregistered rights (copyright, the Unregistered Community Design, or the UK unregistered design right) are only infringed where the user of the design has copied the design. The registered rights give monopolies that enable the proprietor to object to use of designs even if they were independently created.[8] A third advantage is that the registered system potentially provides protection for 25 years, whereas the unregistered design rights tend to be shorter: Unregistered Community Design only lasts for 3 years, while the UK unregistered design right lasts 10 years from marketing. (The exception is copyright which, to the extent that it can protect designs, also lasts for 25 years.)

---

[1] For some empirical work, see *Prospective Study about the Design Registration Demand at a European Union Level: Executive Summary,* on the OHIM's web site. Although we set out some factors that would be taken into account by someone deciding whether to register or not, often there will be an established practice in a particular sector.

[2] This question is much disputed. The EC Green Paper, para. 4.3.9, sees the risk of independent creation as slight.

[3] In 2002, the classes with the largest numbers of applications to the UK register were: packages (1,228); furnishing (1,121); recording/communication (1,079) and games, toys, sports goods (775). The most prominent users were Ty Inc. (135), Sony (91), Nike (67), Nokia (65), and Black & Decker (64).

[4] Especially in the light of the House of Lords decision in *Designers Guild v. Williams* [2000] 1 *WLR* 2416.

[5] EC Green Paper, para. 6.2.4.2, p. 83.

[6] EC Green Paper, para. 2.3.4, p. 17.

[7] Section 1A RDA was repealed by Regulation Reform (Registered Designs) Order 2006.

[8] EC Green Paper, para. 6.4.2–4, pp. 86–7.

So a designer or design owner will only be able to assess whether the automatic systems of protection are sufficient by carefully considering the likelihood that the design will be copied, the likelihood that someone will independently create a similar design, the difficulty of proving copying, the intended (and likely) markets for the design, and the likely longevity of the design. If automatic protection is deemed wanting, the design proprietor will need to consider whether the advantages of registration are sufficient to justify the expenditure in time and money required by registration. As we will see, much has been done, particularly at the OHIM, to make the system cheap and administratively attractive. The expense of registering a design is nothing like the expense associated with patenting.

3 APPLYING TO REGISTER IN THE UNITED KINGDOM

Although the Designs Directive harmonized the salient substantive features of the design registration systems in member states, it left procedure to national law. As we have already intimated, this may well result in significant divergences in the sorts of protection that can be acquired in different member states, and thus undermine, to some extent, the goal of harmonization. It certainly will affect decisions as to whether to apply for a bundle of national registrations, a single Community registration, or a combination of national registrations with a Community registration. Important differences might include: how the systems define the protected design (whether by reference to a deposit or specimen, to graphic representations, and to what extent the procedures allow for written delimitations of protection); whether the systems allow for single applications to relate to multiple designs;[9] whether the systems allow registrations in secret, or deferral of publication, and with what consequences;[10] whether the systems permit applications relating to designs which do not identify a product; how the systems define priority; whether the systems provide for substantive examination, and if so, as to which potential grounds of objection;[11] whether the systems carry out a search of existing designs, and how rigorous such a search is; whether the systems demand declarations by the applicant to the effect that they believe the design to be new and have individual character, or that they intend to apply the designs to products; and whether the system provides an opportunity for opposition.[12]

---

[9] Prior to harmonization Benelux and Germany would allow applications containing up to 50 designs, while France and Italy permitted up to 100. In contrast, the UK required each application to relate to a single article or set of articles.

[10] Prior to European harmonization, many countries allowed for deferral though the periods differed: in Scandinavia deferral was for 6 months only, in the Benelux for 12 months, in Austria for 18 months, and in France for 3 years.

[11] Article 14 of the Swedish Act No. 2002: 570 amending the Design Protection Act 1970: 485 (requiring examination as to whether the application relates to a design, whether the design is immoral or a misuse of a protected emblem, proprietorship, classification, representations). Prior to harmonization, some form of substantive examination took place in Austria, Portugal, and Scandinavia: see Suthersanen, 327; 337, 357.

[12] Article 18 of Swedish Act No. 2002: 570: 485 (allowing opposition for two months).

3.1 THE APPLICATION

In the United Kingdom, the registration process was modified on implementation of the Directive so as to reduce differences between the national process and that at the OHIM.[13] Section 1(1) of the Registered Designs Act 1949 states that '[a] design may...be registered under this Act on the making of an application for registration'. To bring UK registration into line with Community practice, from 1 October 2006 applicants are able to incorporate any number of new designs into a single application (in contrast with previous practice which limited applicants to one design per application).[14] The application should be made by the person claiming to be the owner of the design to the Design Registry in the Patent Office,[15] and include two identical representations of the design (including, if desired, an explanatory description), a statement as to the product to which the design is to be applied, and (if desired) a 'partial disclaimer' identifying the features of the appearance for which protection is sought. The applicant, or their representative, should also sign a declaration to the effect that 'the owner believes that the design is new and has individual character'. The fee is £60 per application, except in the case of designs for lace and certain textile patterns where it is £35. The cost of applying to register additional designs in the same application (which is now allowed in the UK) is £40 per additional design.

3.2 THE REPRESENTATIONS

Undoubtedly, the most significant parts of the application are the 'representations' of the design or 'specimens',[16] and any partial disclaimer which indicates that the design is the appearance of only part of a product.[17] The representations can be conceived as the positive claims, from which the disclaimer excludes matter, so that in combination they define the property. The interaction between representations and disclaimer is thus likely to play a key role in determining whether a design is validly registered and whether it is infringed.

The procedural rules which control the representations play an important role in defining the limits of what can be registered as a design. In the next chapter we will consider whether the definition of design in Article 1 of the Directive, by referring to 'appearance', confines designs to visual appearance. The better view, we believe, is that as a matter of substantive law, the Directive does not limit 'appearance' to the visual: the touch and feel of a designed item may also form an element meriting protection. Although Recital 11 of the Directive speaks of protection 'for those design features of a product, in whole or in part, which are shown visibly in an application', it does not require that protected features be solely or fully comprehended and appreciated from the visible representation. In order for the representations to define positively a property that is not itself visible, the UK rules permit the inclusion of a 'brief description explaining the representation' on the front of the first sheet only of each representation or

---

[13] In particular, 'statements of novelty' have been abolished, as has the requirement that the applicant specify an 'article' to which the design was to be applied. Substantive examination based on a previous search had been removed in 1999 even before harmonization made it desirable.

[14] Regulatory Reform (Registered Design) Order 2006 changed the RDA to allow for multiple applications.

[15] RDA s. 3(2). If unregistered design right subsists, the applicant should be that person.

[16] It is for the Registrar to decide whether specimens are acceptable, by reference, amongst other things, to ease of mounting: RDR r. 21.

[17] RDR r. 15 (partial disclaimer), r. 17 (representations). It should be noted that the register may be rectified under RDR r. 20, and if a design has been declared partially invalid, such a declaration should appear on the register.

specimen.[18] This can be used to specify the material from which the design is made, to identify a colour (for example using the Pantone system),[19] or dimensions, if they are important. In a German case, decided before harmonization, a description was utilized to explain that bright appearance of the stand for a lampshade resulted from illumination from within.[20] Such descriptions should also be permitted under UK practice.

Although these descriptions are important, for the most part they concern marginal cases. A much more important element in the system is the 'partial disclaimer'. Such partial disclaimer should appear on the representations, and so should be available to the public.[21] There seems no reason why the partial disclaimer should not identify a part of the designed product by stating, for example, 'protection is sought for the head of the toothbrush, the handle being disclaimed'.[22] Alternatively, especially in cases where the representation comprises a photograph of the finished designed product, it may be appropriate to disclaim some aspects of appearance of the whole product (such as 'protection is sought for the shape of the toothbrush, the materials, colours, words and patterns being disclaimed'), or a particular aspect of part of the product (such as 'protection is sought for the shape and texture, but not colour, of the handle of the toothbrush').

If there is no disclaimer, it is expected that a tribunal will treat the full contents of the representation as comprising the design.[23] While this would mean that the design might be found to be novel, it might render it easy for a competitor to avoid infringement by altering or adding some features so as to give a different overall impression (while perhaps still taking the features that embodied the registered proprietor's primary design investment). Imagine, for example, that an application relates to a toothbrush and the design investment went into developing a bend in the brush. The applicant submitted a photographic representation of the brush, including multicoloured bristles, coloured plastic stem, and COLGATE logo, but failed to disclaim the colours, the bristles, logo, or the colour of the stem. A competitor could foreseeably reproduce the bend in the brush, apply a different logo, make the brush out of blue plastic with white bristles, and thus make a product which creates a different 'overall impression' on an informed user. (Of course, in an extreme case it might be that the bend would be such a striking feature that even the competitor's version would be regarded as creating the same overall impression.)

3.3 IDENTIFICATION OF THE PRODUCT

Although the applicant for a registration in the United Kingdom will have been obliged to identify a product to which it is intended to apply the design,[24] the exact significance of this should be made clear. In principle, design protection is not limited to the particular product in relation to which registration is effected, and as a corollary a design may lack novelty in the face of the design of a different product.[25] The specification of the product, then, is merely

[18] Note to Form 2A which adds that 'any such description shall not be taken to limit the scope of protection conferred by registration of a design'.

[19] Verbal techniques could also usefully clarify colour as 'subtle shades of colour do not photograph or reproduce well': Musker, 15.

[20] F.-K. Beier and P. Katzenberger, 'Letter from the Federal Republic of Germany' [1975] *Industrial Property* 246 (describing a German case where this was permitted).

[21] RDA s. 22(1); RDR r. 15(2), r. 67.

[22] Designs Practice Note 2/03 ('Applying to register part of a product', Jan. 2003).

[23] As was the former practice: *Kestos v. Kempat and Vivien Fitch Kemp* (1935) 53 *RPC* 139, 150.

[24] RDR r. 14.   [25] RDR r. 14(3).

procedural,[26] its role being to enable classification, searching and so on, and supposedly without any substantive consequences. Thus, if a person designs a motif for use on wallpaper, and identifies the product as wallpaper, the protection granted by registration is in no way limited to wallpaper: the use of the motif by a third party on curtain fabric and duvet covers infringes. Equally, we can anticipate that a design for a 'whistling kettle' might be rejected in the face on an identical design for a 'kettle', or possibly that a toy car might be found to infringe the registered design covering the full-scale automobile. However, there are obvious *substantive* limits to the principle of the 'irrelevance of the product': it is unlikely that a registered design for the shape of a chair would be infringed by its use on the shape of a table, because an informed user would be unlikely to find that the two designs gave the same impression. Where the appearance of the product and the nature of the product have an inseparable connection, the product will matter. Nevertheless, it is not the identification of the product in the application form that has a substantive effect in such cases.

3.4 GROUNDS FOR REFUSAL AND EXAMINATION

A design included in an application can only be refused on certain specified grounds.[27] In order to bring the UK system into line with OHIM practice, from 1 October 2006 the grounds for refusal have been greatly restricted.[28] The Registrar *may* refuse to register a design if the application fails to comply with rules made under the Act,[29] and they *must* do so if the application has not been made by the person claiming to be the proprietor of the design and, where relevant, the owner of UK unregistered design right.[30] In addition, the Register *must* refuse an application if it does not comply with the definition of design,[31] if the design is dictated by function,[32] is contrary to public policy or morality,[33] or if the application is for an emblem mentioned in Schedule A1 of the Registered Designs Act 1949.[34] The Registrar *no longer* has the power to refuse registration on the grounds that something is not a design, or because the design lacks novelty or individual character. As a result of these changes, from 1 October 2006 the Registrar will no longer examine applications for novelty and individual character (as had been past practice), effectively ending substantive examination in the UK.

3.5 REGISTRATION AND PUBLICATION

On registration, the applicant is issued with a certificate and the design is open to inspection.[35] Registration gives the proprietor the exclusive rights set out in section 7, and described in

---

[26] It is also financial, since designs for lace and textile products are cheaper, and will affect whether the designs can be inspected.

[27] RDA s. 3A (as amended).

[28] RDA s 1A was repealed by the Regulation Reform (Registered Designs) Order 2006.

[29] RDA s. 3A(2). In many cases, refusal can be avoided and the Registrar can ask the applicant to amend the application. Section 1(1) of the Registered Designs Act 1949 refers to applications to register 'a design' and, in stark contrast with the approach of the OHIM, the UK Registry operates a rule of one design per application. If an applicant mistakenly submits an application relating to more than one design, the examiner may raise a 'Divide-Out' request, under s. 3B(3), leaving the original application as a 'parent' and treating additional designs as 'child' applications. Designs Practice Note 3/03 ('Divide Outs', 21 March, 2003).

[30] RDA s. 3A(3); s. 3(2)(3); s. 14.   [31] RDA s. 3A(4)(a) and s. 1(2).

[32] RDA s. 3A(4) and s. 1C.   [33] RDA s. 3A(4) and s. 1D.

[34] RDA s. 3A(4)(c) and Schedule 1A.

[35] RDA s. 18, s. 22 (as amended); RDR r. 67.

Chapter 28. Registration is treated as being made as of the date of application (despite a typical three-month processing period).[36] As part of the reform of design law that took place in 2006, the Registrar is now required to open all new designs to public inspection[37] (thus ending the previous practice which limited public access in relation to registered designs for textiles, wallpaper, or lace for 2–3 years).[38] Under the new regime, all applicants are able to defer publication for 12 months.

4 APPLYING TO REGISTER AT OHIM

Protection by way of Registered Community Design is acquired by application to the Office of Harmonization in the Internal Market at Alicante or indirectly through the offices of member states.[39] The procedure is governed by the Regulation itself, and the Implementing Regulations, but these are supplemented by the OHIM's *Examination Guidelines—Community Designs*. From 1 January 2008, applicants will also be able to make use of the international registration system for industrial designs (established under the Hague Agreement and administered by WIPO) to obtain registration of a Community Design.[40]

4.1 THE APPLICATION

The application, which must be signed, should include a request for registration, the name and address of the applicant (and their representative, if one is used), a representation of the design, indication of products in relation to which the design is intended to be used,[41] any relevant declaration of priority, and a specification regarding languages.[42] The application *may* also include a description, a request for deferment of publication, an indication as to classification, and citation of the designer.[43] Of these elements, the most important are the representation of the design suitable for reproduction,[44] and the description. If an application fails to include necessary data the Office will not accord a filing date.[45]

4.2 THE REPRESENTATIONS

The representation 'shall consist of a graphic or photographic reproduction of the design in black and white or colour'.[46] (In contrast with the United Kingdom, where the Registrar may accept specimens which can be mounted in the register, specimens can only be accepted at OHIM for registrations for which deferred publication is requested, since the process of publication

---

[36] RDA s. 3C.   [37] RDA s. 22(1).

[38] RDA s. 22(2) (repealed by Regulatory Reform (Registered Designs) Order 2006); RDR r. 69.

[39] CDR, Art. 35(1); The Community Design (Fees) Regulations 2002, (SI 2002/2942). (UK charge of £15). M. Schlotelburg, 'The Community Design: First Experience with Registrations' [2003] *EIPR* 383.

[40] The Hague Agreement allows applicants to make a single application to WIPO for a number of countries.

[41] CDR, Art. 36(2), CDIR, Art. 1(d). The indication of product should indicate clearly the nature of the product and OHIM requests applicants to utilize the 'Euro-Locarno List', which takes Locarno's 32 classes and elaborates in the region of 4–5,000 products: CDIR, Art. 1(d).

[42] The application can be made in any of the official languages of the Community, but must specify a second language from one of the five languages of the Office (Spanish, German, French, English, Italian).

[43] CDIR, Art. 1(2).   [44] CDR, Art. 36(1)(c) CDIR, Art. 1(c).

[45] CDIR, Art. 10.   [46] CDIR, Art. 4.

in the *Community Designs Bulletin* by definition demands that the design be represented.)[47] Each representation must consist of at least one 'view' and may involve a maximum of seven views.[48] The *Guidelines* point out that, since the representation is the means to specify the features of design for which protection is sought, 'it is of the utmost importance that it is clear and complete and that nothing regarding the design is left to conjecture'. The *Guidelines* further suggest techniques for delimiting the representation: dotted lines, for example, to indicate elements for which no protection is sought, 'boundaries' or 'colouring' (of black and white representations) to identify features for which protection is sought.[49] An official at the OHIM has even stated that 'the selection of the means for representing a design is equivalent to the drafting of the claims in a patent: including features means claiming them'.[50] Thus the choice of the representations is up to the applicant: it is for the applicant to ensure that the features for which protection is sought can be distinguished clearly (though it is possible that, in some extreme cases, as where the representations are obscured during fax transmission,[51] the application might not be given a filing date, or possibly would be rejected on the ground it does not disclose a design).

The representation should only cover one design. Where registration is for a repeating pattern, 'the representation of the design shall show the complete pattern and a sufficient portion of the repeating surface'.[52] Where registration consists of a 'typographic typeface', the representation should include the complete alphabet, all the arabic numerals, as well as five lines of text.[53]

The representation may also contain a single description per design not exceeding 100 words explaining the representation of the design or specimen.[54] However, this should not refer to novelty, individual character, or the technical value of the design. The description at the OHIM seems to be usable both positively to explain some aspect of the representation, and negatively to disclaim features for which protection is not desired. A description might say, for example, that 'features depicted in broken lines are not claimed'; or 'protection is sought for the encircled features'.[55] (A distinct facility is provided for 'partial disclaimers' to be added after registration.)[56]

4.3 MULTIPLE DESIGNS

In order to make the system as cheap and attractive as possible, particularly to those industries producing large numbers of short-lived designs,[57] several designs may be combined in one application.[58] Multiple applications are permitted so long as the designs are intended to be applied to products within the same class of the Locarno Convention, and even that restriction

---

[47] Alternatively, a specimen can be supplied (but only in relation to two-dimensional designs, and where publication is deferred): CDIR, Art. 5(1). This facility seems to be made available to those who need time deciding whether to proceed to full registration, and presumably the submission of a specimen is regarded as minimizing the costs of securing protection to such undecided designers.

[48] CDIR, Art. 4(2).

[49] Examination Guidelines, para. 11.4.

[50] Schlotelburg, 'The Community Design', 385.

[51] Examination Guidelines, para. 4.6.2.

[52] CDIR, Art. 4(3).   [53] CDIR, Art. 4(4).

[54] CDIR, Art. 1(2)(a); CDR, Art. 36(3a); EC Green Paper, para. 8.6.7, p. 110.

[55] Schlotelburg, 'The Community Design', 385.

[56] CDIR, Art. 18.   [57] CDR, Recital 25.

[58] CDR, Art. 37, Recital 25; CDIR, Art. 2; EC Green Paper, para. 4.3. 15, p. 49; para. 8.7.1, 110–11.

does not apply in the case of ornamentation.[59] Where an application includes a number of designs, the application may be divided.[60] The maximum per application is 999, and the highest, so far, is around 300. The process of using a single application for multiple designs has proved to be very popular, with the overall average being 6.6 designs per application.[61]

4.4 DEFERRED PUBLICATION

Provision exists for the registration of secret designs, where the application can remain unpublished for 30 months.[62] This is seen as desirable because publication can 'destroy or jeopardise the success of a commercial operation involving the design'.[63] The OHIM deferred publication procedure, which is available in relation to all designs, can occur earlier if the applicant requests.[64] In cases where deferred publication is sought, an applicant does not have to prepare representations and may prefer to submit five copies of a specimen of each design (though these must be two-dimensional if they are to comply with practical requirements).[65] A request for deferment is required, and a small fee has to be paid (€40), followed by the normal publication fee (€120) when the design is finally published. Protection during the period of deferred publication, however, is limited to situations where the design proprietor can prove that there was copying of the design.

4.5 THE DESIGNER'S ATTRIBUTION

Another feature of the Community system worth noting is the designer's 'moral' right of attribution: the designer (or the design team) has the right to be 'cited as such before the Office and in the register'.[66] It is rather strange that the procedural rules then state that the application may—but need not—mention the designer.[67] Possibly, this may be to enable the designer to remain anonymous, if they so wish. However, the effect is to leave unstated exactly how issues of citation are to be resolved.[68] Pending the formulation of specific rules by the Commission, existing legal procedures will need to be employed. In the case of a designer who has not been named by the legitimate proprietor, the most obvious way to enforce their right would be to bring an action against the OHIM. Conflicts between teams and individuals would probably need to be resolved before national Community Design Courts, seeking a declaration as to who possesses the Article 18 right. Such a declaration could then be the basis of a further

---

[59] CDIR, Art. 2(2). The Examination Guidelines, para. 8.3, state that 'ornamentation' is 'an additional and decorative element capable of being applied to the surface of a variety of products without affecting their contours'.

[60] CDIR, Art. 10(3).

[61] Statistics of Community Designs 2006, SSC07 (5/3/2007), 1.

[62] CDR, Art. 50; CDIR, Art. 1(2)(b).

[63] CDR, Recital 26; EC Green Paper, para. 8.11.3, 115.

[64] CDIR, Art. 15–16; EC Green Paper, para. 8.11.1, 115 (explaining that deferred publication is desirable in automobile industry as well as textile industry).

[65] CDIR, Art. 5.

[66] CDR, Art. 18. However, If the design is a result of teamwork, the citation of the team may replace that of the individual designers.

[67] CDIR, Art. 1(2)(d).

[68] Musker, 119–20 (describing the change in wording of Art. 18 from the designer having 'the right *vis-à-vis* the applicant' to having 'the right, in the same way as the applicant…').

action against the OHIM. These procedural difficulties remove much of the significance of the designer's Article 18 right.

4.6 EXAMINATION

The Office does not conduct a substantive examination (e.g. as to subject matter, novelty, or individual character).[69] This is to minimize the procedural burdens on the applicant, supposedly to render protection cheaper and readily available to all.[70] The idea is that examination is difficult, expensive, and inconclusive, and it is better that the validity of a given design be decided on the basis of an *inter partes* dispute (and thus only over those designs with a significant market value).[71] Nevertheless if, on formal examination, the Office 'notices' that the design does not satisfy the definition of design in Article 3a or is contrary to public policy or accepted principles of morality, it shall notify the applicant and, if the applicant fails to remedy the objection, refuse the application.[72] The Office, however, cannot refuse obviously old designs.[73]

4.7 REGISTRATION AND PUBLICATION

As long as the application meets the formal requirements, the Office is obliged to register the design and (except in cases of deferred publication) publish it in the *Community Design Bulletin*.[74] The published design registration includes the representations, indication of product, and name of designer, but not any description lodged with application.[75]

5 WHICH AVENUE TO CHOOSE?

The Registered Community Design and UK registered design rights can exist cumulatively,[76] or as alternatives. If only one form of registration is wanted, the Registered Community Design may be preferred to a UK registered design (and other national rights) for a number of reasons: because it is a Community-wide right, because it is cheaper,[77] because it is administratively more convenient (for example, because of the possibility of making a single application with multiple designs), because it is available without substantive examination, or because it offers the benefits of deferred publication. However, in some circumstances the UK registered design

---

[69] CDIR, Art. 11. A formal examination is conducted: CDR, Art. 45, CDIR, Art. 10.

[70] CDR, Recitals 18, 24. Explanatory Memorandum to the Proposal for a Regulation, para. 8.7 ('rapid and uncostly registration'); Musker, 173.

[71] EC Green Paper, para. 2.3.4, p. 17; para. 4.3.10–11, pp. 48–9; Posner in Franzosi (ed.) at 30. A suggestion that the OHIM provide a optional examination facility was not taken up: EC Green Paper, para. 8.9.1, 112.

[72] CDR, Art. 47; CDIR, Art. 11. The Examination Guidelines state that 'compliance with the definition of a design is subject to examination. Failure to comply with the definition constitute[s] a ground for non-registrability…Whether the product is actually made or used, or can be made or used, in an industrial or handicraft manner, shall not be examined.'

[73] Musker, 177 (noting no basis on which to refuse obviously old designs, or ones owned by others).

[74] CDR, Arts. 48, 49, and 73; CDIR, Art. 13.

[75] CDIR, Art. 14.   [76] CDR, Art. 95.

[77] OHIM charges a fee of €230 for registration, €120 for publication; in the case of multiple applications the basic fee must be paid only for the first design—thereafter for the seconnd to tenth design the fee is halved (to €115) and if the application contains 11 or more designs the registration fee is reduced to €50. In the UK the fee is £60 per application (except if the design is for lace or consists substantially of stripes or checks to be applied to textiles, in which case it is £35).

may be preferable to the Registered Community Design. This might be because only local protection is desired. In some countries—but not the United Kingdom—local protection may also be preferred because it enables the proprietor to obtain a registration for, and protection over, spare parts. Many of the reasons for choosing the UK system over the Community scheme which have existed in the past—notably the benefits of substantive examination and, for the textile industries, the United Kingdom's (temporarily) closed register (with full monopoly rights)—no longer exist. Not surprisingly, since the differences between the UK and OHIM systems do not offer substantial advantages to UK registrations, the opening of the OHIM for registration of Community designs in April 2003 prompted a notable decline in the number of UK applications. According to the UK Registry, the total numbers of applications are down 40 per cent and foreign applicants have halved.[78] Since it was opened, the number of application at OHIM have steadily increased, with nearly 18,000 applications in 2006. The changes made to the UK design system in 2006 are only likely to see this trend continue.

---

[78] Total UK design applications for 2002 numbered 9,505, and there were 9,192 registrations. By 2005, the number of designs registered had dropped below 4,000. For analysis of UK registered design applications from 1989–2005 see, *Gowers Review of Intellectual Property* (2006), 43.

26

THE COMMUNITY CONCEPT OF DESIGN

CHAPTER CONTENTS

1 INTRODUCTION

Prior to harmonization initiatives (and with one or two exceptions, most notably the Scandinavian countries), most European countries set a low threshold that needed to be satisfied for a design to be protected—only asking that the design meet some standard of local novelty.[1] An advantage of a low threshold is that it allows protection for different designs. However, a serious disadvantage of making protection easily available is that the protection conferred is necessarily very limited. If design protection is permitted at a low threshold and protection is strong, this could lead to unwarranted interference with the developers of subsequent designs. To prevent this, it has been common to match a low threshold with weak rights. Such an approach is frustrating for the developers of highly innovative designs as it means they will often be unable to establish infringement.[2]

The EC Green Paper had proposed to reinvigorate design protection by establishing a scheme which set the threshold at a higher level.[3] The Commission initially planned to give protection to fewer designs, and proposed that the protection that was granted was to be worth having.[4] In the Green Paper it was proposed that designs should only be protected if they possessed 'distinguishing character'.[5] After consultation it was accepted that the idea was impractical and the requirement of distinguishing character was likely to cause confusion with trade marks—the

---

[1] EC Green Paper, para. 2.3.7, 18. See Franzosi in Franzosi (ed.), 46; Levin in Franzosi (ed.), 64–5.

[2] Levin in Franzosi (ed.), 67. It was a common complaint that, prior to harmonization, the UK registered design system rarely produced a monopoly worth having.

[3] Fellner, para. 6.017. Cf. Franzosi in Franzosi (ed.) 58–9 (a halfway standard).

[4] EC Green Paper, para. 5.5.6.3; Official Commentary on Regulation in Franzosi (ed.), 56.

[5] Even in the EC Green Paper, the Commission proposed that this was to be assessed using a limited prior art. More specifically, it specialized circle: if 'not known to the circles specialised in the sector concerned' and 'through the overall impression it displays in the eyes of the relevant public, it distinguishes itself from any other design known to such circles'.

terms (in English, at least) being unfortunately similar to the concept of distinctive character in Article 3(1)(b) of the Trade Marks Directive.[6] Moreover, in the course of consultation (and indeed during the legislative process),[7] it came to be accepted that a high threshold would not work well for some industries, such as textiles.[8] In order to accommodate the differing needs of design industries and the cyclical nature of fashion, a new formula was employed. In order to be registered as a national or Community design, or to receive protection as an unregistered Community design, a design had to satisfy six criteria. These are that:

(i) there is a protectable design;

(ii) the design must be 'new';

(iii) the design must have 'individual character';

(iv) the design is visible in use (for parts of complex products);

(v) the applicant or right holder is entitled to the design; and

(vi) the design does not conflict with earlier relevant rights (which include earlier design applications, trade mark rights, copyright, and rights relating to certain types of emblem).

In this chapter we focus on the first of these criteria, namely that there must be a protectable design. We then turn, in chapter 27, to look at novelty, individual character, the visibility requirement, whether an applicant or rights holder was entitled to grant, as well as conflict with earlier rights. Finally, we look at entitlement to grant in chapter 28 as a part of the general discussion about ownership and exploitation.

Prior to October 2006, although the substantive 'grounds for invalidity' were the same for the Community design regimes and the United Kingdom's registered design system, the time at which these grounds could be raised differed. In particular, while the validity of the Community registered design could only be raised after grant, the British national regime drew a distinction between a narrow category of 'grounds of refusal' (which included novelty, individual character, and conflict with protected emblems—but not conflict with other earlier rights) and the broader category of 'grounds of invalidity' (which could be raised after grant). In October 2006, the UK ended substantive examination of designs.[9] In so doing, UK practice was brought into line with the registration of Community designs. One of the consequences of this is that it increased the importance of the post-grant challenges to the validity of designs. As a result, an application, whether for a Registered Community Design or a UK registered design, cannot be refused for want of novelty or individual character: these issues can only be addressed either in invalidity proceedings (before the OHIM) or as a counterclaim in proceedings for infringement (whether in a Community Design Court or a British court). In the case of unregistered Community design, jurisdiction to determine invalidity is confined to

---

[6] Franzosi in Franzosi (ed.), 59 n. 50; Levin in Franzosi (ed.), p. 68 (the change 'has its real grounds in a translation problem', noting that the German word *Eigenart* remains).

[7] The threshold included in the original proposal to the effect that the design must 'differ significantly' from previous designs was further reduced by removal of the adverb 'significantly' in the European Parliament: see Musker, 30. Note, however, that Designs Dir., Recital 13 left in 'differs clearly'—Musker explains that 'a small difference may be "clear" but not "significant"' (Musker, 31).

[8] Posner in Franzosi (ed.), 6; Franzosi in Franzosi (ed.), 62. The Scandinavians favoured a high threshold. The automobile industry was opposed to such a standard: F.-K. Beier, 'Protection for Spare Parts in the Proposals for a European Design Law' (1994) 25 *IIC* 840, 852–5.

[9] RDA s. 11ZA(1), s. 11ZB.

Community Design Courts, whether on an application for a declaration of invalidity or as a counterclaim to an infringement action.[10]

1.1 WHAT IS A PROTECTABLE DESIGN?

The scope of the design system is delimited at the most fundamental level through the definition of what is a protectable design.[11] Following the commencement of the Directive and Regulation, the definition of a registrable design at national and Community levels and, indeed, the definition of design for the purposes of Unregistered Community Design Right, are identical. This definition of a protectable design is exceedingly broad—broader than many of the definitions of design in the existing laws of member states.[12] Article 1(a) of the Directive defines a design as:

the appearance of the whole or part of a product resulting from the features of, in particular, the lines, contour, colours, shape, texture and/or materials of the product itself and/or its ornamentation.[13]

In turn Article 1(b) defines a 'product' as:

any industrial or handicraft item, including inter alia parts intended to be assembled into a complex product, packaging, get ups, graphic symbols and typographical typefaces, but excluding computer programs.[14]

These two definitions need to be considered in detail, before going on to examine certain mandatory exclusions from the concept of protectable design.

2 APPEARANCE

The definition of design focuses on 'appearance'.[15] Despite the fact that this directs attention to the way a product looks, it is clear that there is no requirement that the design be attractive, decorative, or ornamental: functional and aesthetic designs are equally protectable.[16] The definition of design provides a non-exhaustive list of characteristics that can produce appearance: these include lines, contours, shape, texture, or materials. This is a broad list and covers most aspects of conventional graphic design, industrial design, product and packaging design,

---

[10] CDR, Art. 24, Art. 25. Pending designation of such courts, the matter could be dealt with in the High Court or Patents County Court.

[11] If an application for a UK registration does not relate to a design, it should be refused: RDA s. 1A(1)(a). If it comes to be registered such a design can be declared invalid: RDA s. 11ZA(1). In the case of an application to register a Community Design, the fact that the design does not 'correspond to the definition under Article 3(a)' constitutes a ground for non-registrability: CDR, Art. 47(1)(a). It is also a ground for invalidity, under CDR, Art. 25(1)(a), and this can be raised against registered and unregistered Community designs.

[12] Previous British law (RDA, as amended by the CDPA 1988) had defined designs as 'features of shape, configuration, pattern or ornament applied to an article by an industrial process, being features which in the finished article appeal to and are judged by the eye'. It also required that the article be one for which appearance was material, that is persons acquiring the article took appearance into account when deciding which article to acquire.

[13] Designs Dir., Art. 1(a); CDR, Art. 3(a); RDA s. 1(2).

[14] Designs Dir., Art. 1(b); RDA s. 1(3); CDR, Art. 3(b).

[15] As opposed to the idea or overall concept: EC Green Paper, paras. 5.4.3.1–4, pp. 58–9.

[16] No aesthetic criteria are applicable: Designs Dir., Recital 14; CDR, Recital 10. *Explanatory Memorandum to the Proposal for a Regulation*, para. 8.2; Levin in Franzosi (ed.), p. 83.

and fashion design. In the case of a mobile phone, for example, it would include the overall shape, the arrangement of buttons, the positioning of the earpiece and screen, the colour of the screen, the lettering, and the numbering. In the case of an item of clothing, such as a shirt, it would include collar size, the proportions, the pattern, embroidered features (such as buttonholes), and potentially also the colours. The breadth of the definition attempts to reflect the breadth of designing activities.[17] As there is no indication otherwise, the internal features of products (other than complex products, which are discussed further below) may be protected as long as the features can be represented.[18]

Despite the obvious breadth of the definition of design, a number of issues will, no doubt, require a formal decision of the European Court of Justice before they can be regarded as fully settled.[19] One such issue is the degree to which the term 'appearance' implies that only the visual aspects of designs are protected. In other words, the question arises: to what extent does design encompass (and thus protect) the use of particular materials, textures, smells, and sounds that are perceived by senses other than the eye? It is possible to understand the term 'appearance' as limited to the visual,[20] and such a construction seems to be consistent both with the requirement in Recital 11 that protection corresponds to the features 'shown *visibly* in an application'[21] and the requirement in Recital 13 that the design only be protected if it has individual character, a determination to be made by reference to an 'informed user *viewing* the design'. However, while designs will rarely cover purely non-visual features, it was not the Commission's initial intention that the definition be limited to aspects perceptible by the eye.[22] While it does not seem possible to include sounds or smells within the notion of appearance (and the Commission had never intended that it would be),[23] references in Article 1 to texture and materials imply that touch may be an important attribute of a design, so that—for example—a conventional style of clothing might be protected when made in a new material with a distinct texture (such as Lycra was only a few years ago).[24] Equally, the weight and flexibility of materials might be an important part of the design.

3 PRODUCT

The definition of design refers to the appearance of 'a product'. 'Product' is defined, exhaustively, as any industrial or handicraft 'item'. There is no further definition of 'item' (or the adjectives industrial or handicraft), except that the Directive and Regulation include an exemplary

---

[17] Franzosi in Franzosi (ed.), p. 40 ('as neutral and broad as possible in order to cover any marketing value attached to the form or shape of a product').

[18] Patent Office, *Legal Protection of Designs: A Consultation Paper on the Implementation in the United Kingdom of EC Directive 98/71/EC* (12 Feb. 2001), 4, para. 3 (giving example of the inside of a suitcase).

[19] 'It goes without saying that a colour in itself or a material as such are not eligible for protection' ('Official Commentary of Proposal for Regulation' in Franzosi (ed.), 36).

[20] Musker, 12 (questionable whether the word is appropriate to any sense other than sight). The equivalent terms in the Directive are 'l'apparence d'un produit' (French), 'la apariencia' (Spanish), 'l'aspetto' (Italian) and 'Erscheinungsform' (German).

[21] This provision was included as part of a compromise justifying rejection of Parliamentary amendments that designs were only to protect 'outwardly visible' features: see H. Speyart, 'The Grand Design' [1997] *EIPR* 603, 605–6. See above pp. 618–19.

[22] EC Green Paper, para. 5.4.7.2 (referring to the texture of textiles).

[23] EC Green Paper, para. 8.9.2.

[24] Franzosi in Franzosi (ed.), 41 ('all those...elements of the product which may be perceived by the human eye or by touch').

list of items such as packaging, get-up, and graphic symbols, and exclude computer programs. Although the definition of product is therefore very broad, covering items such as clothes, fabric, furniture, electrical goods, and motor vehicles, there are likely to be controversies in a number of difficult cases which we must now examine.

3.1 'PRODUCTS' TYPICALLY ASSOCIATED WITH COPYRIGHT

First, the question arises whether a painting, drawing, or building is a product within the meaning of the Directive and Regulation. If so, then it seems as if certain works typically protected by copyright might also be protectable as designs—either through national or Community registration, or automatically (by unregistered Community design) after being made available to the public.[25] In turn, this creates the possibility of an absolute monopoly over the design for up to 25 years.

For a painting to obtain protection it would have to be seen to be a 'handicraft item'. Would a painting be regarded as an 'item'? Under old British case law on registered designs, where the definition of registrable design included 'pattern and ornament...applied to an article', it was held that the article had to have a distinct existence from the design: so that a design of a football pools coupon was not registrable because the design *was* the article.[26] The Community definition of protectable design, however, requires no such distinction to be made, as is clear from the inclusion of 'graphic symbols' in the list of examples of items. Thus it seems that a painting or canvas can be an item. Is a painting an 'industrial or handicraft item'? Presumably, it could be argued that a painting is neither, because painting is art rather than handicraft. While this would mean that the definition of design excluded the design of a painting and hence would preclude the duplication by design law of protection conferred by copyright, there is little doubt that tribunals are going to feel some discomfort in drawing a boundary between art and handicraft.

A related question is whether architectural designs relate to the appearance of a 'product'? Again the issue is whether 'industrial or handicraft item' includes buildings. Under old case law, it had been held that the process of building was not an 'industrial process' so that a design for a petrol filling station was unregistrable.[27] If followed, this would suggest that such items were not 'industrial items' and thus not products. This would also seem to be consistent with the definition of infringement in the Directive, which implies that the Directive and Regulation had portability in mind.[28] However, it should be observed that other commentators have taken a different view, arguing that environmental designs, whether interior or exterior, are protectable.[29] If deemed relevant, as might be the case (given that it has been specially designed for classification of designs by the OHIM), the Euro-Locarno Classification system includes houses, buildings, and buildings (transportable) in class 25—Building Units and Construction Elements.

---

[25] One could also protect such works when copyright has lapsed if they have previously not been widely published.

[26] *Re Littlewood's Pools* (1949) 66 *RPC* 309. British law also excluded many items from the definition of article, and thus from the design regime, through the Registered Designs Rules, r. 26 (relating to articles of primarily a literary or artistic character).

[27] *Collier & Co.'s Application* (1939) 54 *RPC* 253.

[28] Musker, 18.

[29] C.-H. Massa and A. Strowel, 'Community Design: Cinderella Revamped' [2003] *EIPR* 68, 71 (giving examples of amusement parks and gardens).

Article 1(b) specifically excludes one category of copyright subject matter—'computer programs'—from the definition of a product.[30] Consequently, the appearance *of* a computer program cannot constitute a design capable of a national or Community registration. Determining what this exclusion covers may prove tricky. One obvious construction is that the appearance of the computer program is the appearance of the source or object code and thus that this, and possibly preparatory design material, is not capable of protection. Such a construction would exclude from design protection the sort of material covered by copyright under the Software Directive, and has been favoured by a number of commentators. However, such a construction would not exclude from protection the effects of running the program in a computer: the user interface or images that appear on the computer screen might be protected individually or in the overall appearance.[31] Indeed, Article 1(b) of the Directive refers to 'graphic symbols' as products and it is widely accepted that this would include computer icons.[32] Insofar as such matters can be reduced to an appropriate form to meet the procedural requirements of national or Community law, it may be possible to register certain aspects of web design. However, it will probably be impossible to represent dynamic effects and sound effects visibly in the application.[33]

3.2 CORPOREAL AND BIOLOGICAL PRODUCTS

In an era where there is widespread interest in medical and cosmetic design of the human body, it might be asked whether designs for body parts, tattoos, and genetically modified animals (such as a scarlet-coloured cat) can be protected. The Euro-Locarno Convention includes artificial eyes, limbs, and teeth in class 24, and hairpieces in class 28, suggesting that the appearance of prosthetics and wigs constitute designs. As such, there seems little reason not to treat these as 'industrial items'. Tattoos are probably not designs since it is unlikely that the courts would think it acceptable to call the human body an 'industrial or handicraft item'. (However, were a tattoo design registered as a painting (if this is possible), it might be an infringement of registered design right to apply the image to a body, as this might amount to using the design.)[34] It is too early to say whether animals can be regarded as 'industrial items'. The European Patent Convention, in defining when an invention is 'capable of industrial application', talks of the use 'in any kind of industry, including agriculture', which might support an argument in favour of the protection of such artefacts by designs law.

[30] At one stage, the Commission said this was because computer programs 'cannot be designed': *Explanatory Memorandum to the 1993 Proposal for a Council Regulation on the Legal Protection of Designs* (III/F/5576/92–EN) in Franzosi (ed.), p. 36. Franzosi disagreed stating that '[i]n reality this is not completely correct' (p. 43). However, it should be noted that the document continues by saying '[it] may be useful, however, to state explicitly that the copyright protection provided under the umbrella of the aforementioned Directive cannot be supplemented or reinforced by a protection of the "look and feel" of a computer program by way of design protection'.

[31] See Patent Office, *Legal Protection of Designs*, 4, para. 4 (stating that the exclusion covers the programs themselves, i.e. the lines of code and the functionality); Musker, 16 ('the exclusion of screen displays seems either unnecessary or harmful' so that the scope of the exclusion should be confined to what is protected by copyright); A. Kur, 'Protection of Graphical User Interfaces under European Design Legislation' (2003) 34 *IIC* 50 (arguing that the exclusion may apply to the visual appearance generated by a computer program in its entirety, but not to individual graphic elements).

[32] M. Schlotelburg, 'The Community Design: First Experience with Registrations' [2003] *EIPR* 383, 386 (describing registrations at the OHIM No. 4213, No. 211, 286, 310).

[33] Musker, 17. See above pp. 618–19, 621–2.

[34] But note the private and non-commercial use defence: Designs Dir., Art. 13(1), RDA s. 7A(2), CDR, Art. 20(1).

3.3 CHIP PRODUCTS

Finally, it is worth noting that designs comprising the topographies of semiconductor chips are within the Community definition of design. Member states must therefore protect topographies by registered design. Topographies are also protectable by Registered Community Designs and automatically by Unregistered Community Design Right. This raises difficulties because member states are already obliged by the 1986 Chip Directive to give protection to topographies which are the result of the creator's own intellectual effort and are not commonplace. As if this mandatory accumulation of modes of protection was not inconvenient enough, the registered design system has important variations from those operating under the Chip Directive. For example, where the Chip Directive works on the basis of reciprocity, national treatment principles apply to registered designs under the Paris Convention.[35] Similarly, the rules on ownership of the rights are different.[36] Thankfully, it seems unlikely that the chip industry will take advantage of these provisions.

3.4 COMPLEX PRODUCTS

As indicated, the Directive requires member states to allow for the registration of designs of 'parts intended to be assembled into a complex product'.[37] A 'complex product' is defined as 'a product which is composed of multiple components which can be replaced permitting disassembly and reassembly of the product'.[38] The meaning of this phrase has further significance because such parts are required to reach a special standard (of novelty and individual character) before they can be protected. It is also important because they subject to special (as yet unharmonized) limitations.[39] The term 'complex product' is intended to cover motor vehicles, and to allow the registration of components for such vehicles in limited circumstances. Quite what the term 'complex product' covers beyond this is less clear. Many products are made up of a number of parts which can be disassembled and reassembled: tables can often be dismantled, as can book-cases, stereos, mobile phones, and so on. Whether these were all intended to fall within Article 1(c) is doubted by the United Kingdom Designs Registry which has suggested a 'more practical' and appropriate 'definition' of a complex product:

a product containing a multiplicity, or such a number of, components that it becomes technically complex, and one for which some of the components will need maintenance, service or repair during the life of the complex product. This will usually be a product with mechanical/electrical/electronic features such as a motor car.[40]

---

[35] Cf. Chip Dir., Recital 6 (on the extension of protection to persons outside the Community). See below pp. 707–8.

[36] Chip Dir., Art. 3(2) (allowing, but not requiring, member states to allocate ownership to employer 'where a topography is created in the course of the creator's employment', or to a commissioner); CDR Art. 14(3) (allocating ownership to employer, but only where 'developed by an employee in the execution of his duties or following the instructions given by his employer'.) Given that topographies might also be protected by patents, utility models, or copyright, the domain seems to be absurdly over-regulated.

[37] Designs Dir., Art. 1(b); RDA s. 1(3); CDR, Art. 3(b). As a result, it seems that the rule in *R v. RDAT, ex p Ford* [1995] *RPC* 167 has been reversed.

[38] Designs Dir., Art. 1(c); RDA s. 1(3); CDR, Art. 3(c). The British implementation of Art. 1(c) of the Directive, contained in s. 1(3) of the amended Act, redefined 'complex product' to mean 'a product which is composed of at least two replaceable component parts permitting disassembly and reassembly of the product'.

[39] Designs Dir., Art. 3(3); Art. 14; RDA s. 1B(10), s. 7A(5); CDR, Art. 4(2), Art. 110.

[40] Designs Practice Notice, DPN 1/03 'Component Part of complex product visible in normal use' (7 January 2003).

The definition of 'complex product' raises a further definitional issue, namely: what is a 'component part'? More specifically, does a component include a part which is exhausted and disposed of, such as a printer cartridge? The United Kingdom Designs Registry has indicated that consumable items which are intended to be 'used up' are not 'component parts': it prefers the test that, absent the part, the item would not be seen as a complete product.[41] A laser printer would be seen as a complete product without its cartridge (though it would not function), so the cartridge is not a component part (though the printer may be a complex product). However, the Design Registry advises that '[p]arts which are not "used up" in the same sense as consumables but which might require replacement from time to time in order to enhance the performance of the complex product (e.g. parts of engines such as spark plugs) are considered to be component parts and so may face objections to registration'. The Design Registry's definition is of only very limited authority, and its formulation and/or application is difficult to support. To say that a part is only a component if, absent the part, the item would not be seen as a complete product raises the question as to when an item would be seen as a complete product: is a car a complete product without its hubcaps, tyres, wing-mirrors, fenders, seats, fanbelt, or spark plug?

The question also arises whether, when the Article defines a product as 'any industrial or handicraft item', it excludes the possibility of protection for combinations of more than one item. For example, is design protection available for a suite of furniture or a kitchen design (comprising multiple units)? It is clear that one could register each unit—'including...parts intended to be assembled into a complex product'—and it is implicit that if they form a 'complex product' the totality can be registered. But what if the whole is not a 'complex product'? The Commission, in its Green Paper, contemplated registration of kitchen designs, though it is unclear whether this would be considered as a complex product under Article 1(c).[42] Probably, the critical question is whether the combination of items results in something which can itself be fairly called 'an item'. This, in turn, will depend on whether the component elements are attached or linked to one another, whether the design value of the whole is greater than the sum of its parts, and whether there is a distinct market for the combination.[43] If the totality can be called an item, it should be registrable.

4 EXCLUSIONS

There are three mandatory exclusions from the very broad definition of 'design'.[44] The first relates to features dictated by function; the second to interfaces; and the third to designs which are contrary to morality. We need to examine each in turn.

---

[41] Ibid. Cf. Suthersanen, 40 (toner cartridge for photocopying machine assumed to be component).

[42] Green Paper, para. 5.4.14.2, p. 67.

[43] Former German law had required that there be 'unity of design' before such combinations could be protected: see *Bernhard Pflug GmbH v. Interlübke KG*, Case 1 ZR 35/73 (1976) *IIC* 270 (where the Bundesgerichtshof held that furniture belonging to a 'furniture program' could be protected in its entirety. The ensemble comprised a bed, chest of drawers, shelf units, and corner elements which were intended to be used together, and regarded by the public as a unity.)

[44] If an application for a UK registration is confined to excluded matter, it should be refused: RDA s. 1A(1)(b); s. 1C–D. If it comes to be registered such a design can be declared invalid: RDA s. 11ZA(1). In the case of an application to register a Community Design, the fact that the design is contrary to public policy or accepted principles of morality constitutes one of only two grounds for non-registrability: CDR, Art. 47(1)(b). The other exclusions can only be raised as grounds for invalidity, under CDR, Art. 25(1)(b), against both registered and unregistered Community designs.

4.1 FUNCTIONAL FEATURES

Article 7 of the Designs Directive states that a design right 'shall not subsist in features of appearance of a product which are solely dictated by its technical function'.[45] Recital 13 of the Directive explains that this exclusion is designed to prevent technological innovation being hampered.[46] It is notable that the Article does not say that these features are not designs. Instead it says that design right shall not subsist in such features. The effect of this is that it may be possible to register (or obtain protection for) a design which includes functional features, unless the design only comprises such elements. If a design includes functional features falling within Article 7, these are not taken into account for the purposes of assessing novelty or individual character.[47] In addition, there is no infringement of design right where a person reproduces these features (because no design right subsists in relation to them).

4.1.1 Technical function

Although the exclusion relates to features dictated by technical function, no further guidance is given as to the meaning of 'technical'.[48] The term 'technical', however, has become a key concept in European patent law.[49] The exclusion of technical features appears to achieve three related goals. First, by preventing the protection of features necessary to achieve a technical function, the Directive leaves protection of those features to patent law (and, where they exist, utility models).[50] It thereby prevents applicants from attempting to gain protection for such features at lower cost, and without having to comply with standards of inventiveness demanded by patent law.[51] Second, by leaving such features unprotected, the law enables different people to reproduce and utilize features of shape which are necessary to achieve a particular function. In so doing it ensures that there is potential for competition in functional products. Third, the exclusion recognizes that, in a situation where a shape is dictated by function, a designer exercises no design freedom and contributes no relevant design effort, and so should not benefit from design right.[52] If such a person makes a contribution, it is not as a designer but as an inventor.[53]

4.1.2 Mandatory or causative?

The key question is what sort of relationship is indicated by the metaphorical language that the features be 'solely dictated' by technical function.[54] According to one reading (the so-called 'mandatory approach'), a design will be 'dictated' by technical function in situations where

---

[45] RDA s. 1C(1); CDR Art. 8(1).   [46] CDR, Recital 10.

[47] Designs Dir., Recital 14 and CDR, Recital 10.

[48] This limitation was probably required because TRIPS, Art. 25(1) only permits members to provide that protection shall not extend to 'designs dictated essentially by technical or functional considerations'.

[49] See pp. 408–10. Massa and Strowel, 'Cinderella Revamped', 72 ('technical function' may extend further to cover 'economic or marketing constraints'); Beier, 'Protection for Spare Parts', 851 (contrasting technical function with aesthetic functionality).

[50] EC Green Paper, para. 5.4.6.1.

[51] Beier, 'Protection for Spare Parts', 851 ('design protection…finds its natural limits when it comes to technical–functional features for which no design alternative exists').

[52] EC Green Paper, para. 5.4.6.2.

[53] Musker is opposed to the exclusion altogether, seeing little harm in protecting technical contributions by a broad design law: Musker, 41–3.

[54] The French language version refers to 'les caractéristiques de l'apparence d'un produit qui sont exclusivement imposé par sa fonction technique'; the German to 'die ausschließlich durch dessen technische Funktion bedingt sind'.

the designer was unable to exercise any control whatsoever over the final shape of the article. In other words, a design is only dictated by function if the precise shape of the article could perform the function. If the designer can demonstrate that other products achieving the same function have different designs, that is, that a number of forms are able to carry out the function, then (according to the mandatory approach) the form is *not* dictated by the function. According to the so-called 'causative approach', a design is dictated by function if it has been created purely with functional considerations in mind (even if the function could be performed by other shapes). Under the causative approach, a design is protectable if there is any feature which was not caused or prompted by the technical function the designer had in mind. After some uncertainty,[55] the courts, both in the UK[56] and at OHIM,[57] have come down in favour of the mandatory approach when interpreting Article 8(1). In the UK this was made clear by the English Court of Appeal in *Landor & Hawa International Ltd v. Azure Designs Ltd*,[58] where the court had to consider whether the design of rigid or shell suitcases which were fitted with an expandable section (that enabled the size of the suitcase to be increased) fell within the ambit of Article 8(1). In deciding whether the claimant's design for an expandable suitcase was solely dictated by the technical function and thus excluded, the Court of Appeal asked whether the design was 'driven without options'. That is, the court looked at whether in creating the design in question, the designer exercised a degree of choice. On the facts of the case, the court found that as the designer had exercised choice in many aspects of the design (including 'the spatial position of the constituent elements (big piping/zip/normal piping, zip/big piping) and the presence of the piping elements themselves'), this introduced 'an essentially non-functional and even capricious element to the final appearance of the ensemble'.[59] As such, the design was not excluded on the basis that it was solely dictated by function.

4.2 INTERCONNECTIONS

The second exclusion contained in the Designs Directive relates to interconnections. Article 7(2) states that a design right 'shall not subsist in features of appearance of a product which must necessarily be reproduced in their exact form and dimensions in order to permit the product in which the design is incorporated or to which it is applied to be mechanically connected to or placed in, around or against another product so that either product may perform its function'. This has been described as 'one of the most important basic principles of the protection system'.[60] The reasoning behind the exclusion seems to be that while the harmonized definition of design includes the appearance of 'parts' of products, features which enable mechanical parts to be connected together should not be protected because such protection might enable the proprietor of a design for a particular article to prevent competition in a

---

[55] Massa and Strowel, 'Cinderella Revamped', 72. It appears to have been accepted by the British Registry: Designs Practice Notice, DPN 5/03 'Designs Dictated by Their Technical Function' (18 Aug. 2003). For discussion of the arguments in favour of the mandatory approach see Bently and Sherman, 2nd edition.

[56] *Bailey (t/a Elite Anglian Products) v. Haynes (t/a RAGS)* [2007] *FSR* 10, para. 75 (Art. 8(1) is to be construed narrowly as only applying in situations where the design is the only design by which the product in question could function).

[57] *Linder Recyclingtech GmbH* Decision of the Invalidity Division (3/4/2007), *ICD* 3150, para 20 (the design was not excluded on the basis of CDR Art. 8(1) on the basis that the technical function of the design 'may be achieved by alternative arrangements').

[58] [2006)] *ECDR* (31) 413.

[59] *Landor & Hawa International v. Azure Design* [2007] *FSR* 9, para. 32 (citing Hon Judge Fysh QC).

[60] Posner in Franzosi (ed.), 29.

secondary market.[61] For example, protection of the design of the external ports of a laptop could operate to allow the designer to control the sale of electronic mice; protection of the design of the parts of a laser printer could operate to allow the designer to control the sale of printer cartridges; design rights over coffee machines could enable the designer to control sale of sachets of coffee needed to utilize the machine; and the protection of the design of a personal organizer might prevent competition in the sale of refill pages for the organizer.

As such, the provision is similar to the 'must-fit' exclusion recognized in the British law of unregistered design right (which we discuss further in Chapter 30).[62] However, given differences in wording, it seems unlikely that the case law on the 'must-fit' exclusion will be of much assistance in the application of Article 7(2) of the Designs Directive. First, while the British exclusion excludes features which 'enable' connections, Article 7 sets a more taxing requirement before the exclusion comes into play: the features 'must *necessarily* be reproduced in their *exact* form and dimensions'.[63] Where the shape of a designed artefact merely influences the shape of another product, for example where one must fit inside another but need not correspond exactly to the internal dimensions, the European exclusion would not come into play. Second, the European provision is confined to features which must be reproduced so that the design-protected product can be '*mechanically* connected to, or placed in, around or against another product'. The Recitals to the Directive and Regulation reiterate that the exclusion is targeted at 'mechanical fittings', but do not clarify whether the adverb 'mechanically' applies where the product is 'placed in, around or against' another product (or whether 'placement' might be regarded, necessarily, as 'mechanical').[64] While the connection of an exhaust pipe to the chassis of a car might be regarded as a classic example of a 'mechanical' fitting, it is less clear that the fitting of a lampshade to a table lamp, a filter to a coffee maker, or a candle to a candelabrum, would be regarded as 'mechanical'.[65] Given that the term 'mechanical' is often used in contrast to 'electrical', the possibility also arises that electrical fittings can be the subject of design protection, though the distinction has nothing to recommend it on policy grounds. Third, the only interconnections covered by the exclusion in Article 7(2) are those that relate to other products, i.e. 'industrial or handicraft items', and certainly would not cover interconnections to parts of the human body, (as the British must-fit exclusion has done).

4.2.1 Modular products

The interconnections exclusion is subject to an express derogation. Article 7(3) states that notwithstanding the interconnections exclusion, 'design right shall . . . subsist in a design serving the purpose of allowing multiple assembly or connection of mutually interchangeable products within a modular system'.[66] Recital 15 purports to justify the saving on the basis that 'the

---

[61] Designs Dir., Recital 14, and CDR, Recital 10, state that 'the interoperability of products of different makes should not be hindered by extending protection to the design of mechanical fittings'. See also EC Green Paper, para. 5.4.10.1, p. 63.

[62] CDPA s. 213(3)(b). 'Design right does not subsist in . . . features of shape and configuration of an article which . . . enable the article to be connected to, or placed in, around or against another article so that either article may perform its function'. See below pp. 692–4.

[63] Though in one case the British court held that 'enablement' required such a level of exactitude: see *Amoena v. Trulife*, discussed at p. 693.

[64] The limitation of the exclusion to mechanical connection was not in the initial proposal in the EC Green Paper.

[65] Cf. R. Durie, 'European Community Design Law', in B. Gray and E. Bouzalas (eds.) *Industrial Design Rights: An International Perspective* (2001), 75, 91 (giving example of TV set and stand as a mechanical interface).

[66] RDA s. 1C(3), CDR, Art. 8(2), Recital 11.

mechanical fittings of modular products may nevertheless constitute an important element of the innovative characteristics of modular products and present a major marketing asset and therefore should be eligible for protection'. The real explanation for the exclusion is that it was a product of lobbying by the Danish government, keen that the key features of LEGO bricks should remain protectable (though, since LEGO, with its stud and tube coupling system, has been available to the public since 1958, there can be very few regimes where the basic design protection has not lapsed). Other examples of modular design system include MECCANO construction sets, modular seating systems, and shelving arrangements.[67]

4.3 DESIGNS WHICH ARE CONTRARY TO MORALITY OR PUBLIC POLICY

According to Article 8 of the Directive, 'design right shall not subsist in a design which is contrary to public policy or to accepted principles of morality'. This exclusion corresponds to equivalent provisions in European patent and trade mark law, and previous provisions under many national design systems.[68] Importantly, this operates both as a ground for refusal of registration (both at national and Community levels), as well as a ground for invalidity.[69] While the appearance of objects is not a domain in which morals are heavily implicated, it has been suggested that a textile design which utilized a swastika,[70] or a functional design for landmines or man-traps, might fall within the exclusion.[71] Given that the Directive 'does not constitute a harmonization of national concepts of public policy or accepted principles of morality', one can expect that some designs would be considered immoral in some countries but not others. One would not expect many such designs to be excluded from protection in the United Kingdom. In a pre-harmonization case, *Masterman's Design,* which concerned an application to register a design for a male Highlander doll which, when its sporran was lifted, revealed its genitals, the court (on appeal) allowed the registration (see Fig. 26.1).

Aldous J stated that the test was not whether a section of the public would be offended. Instead, he said that the test was whether the moral principles of right-thinking members of the public would think it very wrong for the law to grant protection.[72]

---

[67] Patent Office, *Legal Protection of Designs*, 10, para. 24.

[68] Prior to amendment to implement the Directive, RDA s. 43(1) had stated that nothing in the Act should be construed as 'authorising or requiring the Registrar to register a design the use of which would, in his opinion, be contrary to law or morality'.

[69] RDA s. 1A(1)(b); s. 1D, s. 11ZA(1); CDR, Art. 47(1)(b), Art. 25(1)(b).

[70] EC Green Paper, para. 8.9.2. A swastika on the packaging of a board game about the Second World War would presumably not cause any offence.

[71] Musker, 52 (design of landmines).

[72] [1991] *RPC* 89, 103–104.

Fig. 26.1 Front view of the doll in *Masterman's Design*
Source: Courtesy of Keith Beresford.

27

GROUNDS FOR INVALIDITY: NOVELTY, INDIVIDUAL CHARACTER, AND RELATIVE GROUNDS

CHAPTER CONTENTS

1 INTRODUCTION

In this chapter we look at some of the key criteria that a design—whether a national registered design, a registered Community design, or an unregistered Community design—must comply with in order to be valid.[1] These are that the:

(i) design is 'new';

(ii) design has 'individual character';

(iii) design is visible in use (only for parts of complex products);

(iv) applicant or the right holder is entitled to the protected design; and

(v) design does not conflict with earlier relevant rights (which include earlier design applications, trade mark rights, copyright, and rights relating to certain types of emblem).

We will look at each of these in turn.

---

[1] Designs Dir., Art. 11 (listing four mandatory grounds, and three optional ones); RDA s. 3A (grounds for refusal), s. 11ZA (grounds for invalidity), Sched. A1 (emblems); CDR, Art. 25 (listing seven grounds of invalidity).

2 NOVELTY

The requirement of novelty is one common to most registered design systems, though its exact meaning can vary.[2] Under the definitions in the Directive and Regulation, a design is new if no identical design, or no design whose features differ only in immaterial details, has been made available to the public before the date of application (or in the case of Unregistered Community Designs, the date on which the design was first made available to the public).[3] This is an 'historical' or objective test, requiring that the design be compared with a body of existing material. As such, it can be contrasted with copyright's originality test which is a 'psychological' or 'subjective' test, in that its focus is the relationship between the creator and the creation. In order to assess whether a design is new we need to ask three questions: first, what is the design? Second, what material is the design to be compared with—in patent jargon, what is the state of the art? And third, what difference must exist between the design and the state of the art before a design can be described as new?

2.1 WHAT IS THE DESIGN?

In many cases, the preliminary question 'what is the design?' is likely to be important in deciding whether the design is novel. As we saw, the Designs Directive defines a design as *the appearance* of the whole or part of a product. In the case of national registered designs, it seems likely that the design will be treated as that which the applicant identifies in the application for registration. In the United Kingdom, the critical documents will be the two representations or specimens, and any partial disclaimer which indicates that the design is the appearance of part only of a product.[4] If there is no such disclaimer, it is expected that the tribunal will treat the full contents of the representation as comprising the design.[5] In addition, it should be noted that functional features and mechanical interconnections excluded from protection under Article 7 of the Directive are not to be considered when assessing novelty or individual character.[6]

In the case of a Registered Community Design, the scope of the design will similarly be deduced from the application/registration. This will include representations, an indication of the products in which the design is intended to be incorporated, and, if the applicant submits one, a 'description' not exceeding 100 words explaining the representation of the design or the specimen.[7] Although Article 1(2)(a) of the Implementing Regulations states that the description 'shall not contain statements as to the purported novelty or individual character of the

---

[2] EC Green Paper, para. 2.3.7, p. 18.

[3] RDA s. 1B(2); Designs Dir., Art. 4; CDR, Art. 5(2). If priority is claimed, the relevant date is the priority date.

[4] RDR r. 15 (partial disclaimer), r. 17 (representations). It should be noted that the register may be rectified under RDR r. 20, and if a design has been declared partially invalid, such a declaration should appear on the register.

[5] As was the former practice: *Kestos v. Kempat and Vivien Fitch Kemp* (1935) 53 *RPC* 139, 150.

[6] Designs Dir., Recital 14.

[7] Such statements are not published in the *Community Designs Bulletin*: CDIR, Art. 14(2)(d), and need not even be included in the register: CDIR, Art. 69(2)(o) but a person wishing to challenge the validity of the design can inspect the file under CDIR, r. 74, or request the Office to communicate the description to them under r. 75. The statement will no doubt be in the language of filing, which can be any of the official languages of the Community, but will have been translated, under CDR Art. 98(2) into one of the five languages of the office.

design or its technical value', the description may well prove to be useful in ascertaining the design for which protection is sought. (Rather than saying 'the novel part of the design is the pattern', the applicant should say 'the design for which protection is sought is the pattern, the shape of the teapot being disclaimed'.)[8] Article 18(2) of the Implementing Regulations also allows for maintenance of a design in an amended form by way of a 'partial disclaimer, not exceeding 100 words by the holder' or by an entry in the Register of a court decision or a 'Decision by the office declaring the partial invalidity of the design right' and such a partial disclaimer will also be relevant when working out exactly what the design comprises.[9]

In the case of Unregistered Community Designs, none of these bureaucratic aids are available to assist the court in identifying the design in question. As already noted the issue of the novelty of Unregistered Community Designs can only arise before a Community Design Court, either in infringement proceedings or invalidity proceedings. In such cases it seems that the Court will have to examine the appearance of the article in issue both as a whole, and as its discrete parts, to determine whether the design is novel and has individual character. Doubtless, in the case of an infringement action, the procedural rules of the member state in which the action is commenced will require the claimant to identify the design which they allege has been infringed. In principle, however, there seems no reason why a person should not claim a collection of features as a design, as well as each of the features individually.

2.2 WHAT IS THE STATE OF THE ART?

Once the design has been identified, it is necessary to ascertain what exactly makes up the state of the art. Since the state of the art changes as new designs are published, it is crucial to work out the relevant date on which the state of the art is assessed.

2.2.1 The date as of which the state of the art should be assessed

British and Community registrations. Similar rules apply to both Community and national registrations. A design application (or registration) is to be assessed for novelty as against designs made available to the public before the filing date for the application for registration or, if priority is claimed, the date of priority.[10] The most important mechanism for claiming priority relates to a claim based on an earlier application to a 'Convention country', made not more than six months before the UK filing.[11] In the case of a Community application, priority may also be claimed from an earlier exhibition. However, in contrast to the British position, the Regulation allows an applicant to claim priority from the date of disclosure at an officially

---

[8] Musker, 156–8, with useful examples.

[9] Musker, 157: 'disclaimers are allowed after an invalidity action and it would therefore seem sensible to allow them on filing, to forestall unnecessary invalidity actions...However, disclaimers may not be acceptable as "statements", or may be ineffective, in view of paragraph 6.'

[10] Design Dir., Art. 4; RDA s. 14; CDR, Art. 38 (date of filing), Art. 41 (right of priority). For speculation as to whether priority might be claimed from a patent application, see Musker, 169. For the Community position, see CDR, Arts. 41–44; CDIR, Art. 8. On exhibition priority see CDIR, Art. 9.

[11] RDA s. 14(1). The convention countries are identified by way of an Order in Council under RDA s. 13. See Designs (Convention Countries) Order 1994 (SI 1994/3219) (listing 129 countries) and amended by SI 1995/2988 (adding 10 Paris accessions, and 20 WTO countries) and SI 2000/1561 (adding 12 further countries). As regards CDRs, a six-month priority is accorded to applications for design right or for utility model protection made in a state which is party to the Paris Convention, the WTO Agreement, or which accords an equivalent right of priority.

recognized international exhibition.[12] Since there are very few such exhibitions, the difference in the approaches taken by the UK Designs Registry and OHIM are unlikely to prove of great significance.[13]

Unregistered Community designs.   In the case of Unregistered Community Designs, novelty is assessed from the date on which the design for which protection is claimed has 'first been made available to the public'.[14] (This is also the date from which the three-year term of protection commences). The act of 'making available to the public' covers publication, exhibition, use in trade, or any other disclosure but does not include disclosures made under conditions of confidentiality, or disclosures which could not reasonably have become known in the normal course of business to the circles specialized in the sector concerned.[15] This is sometimes referred to as the 'safeguard clause', but in the context of unregistered Community designs its impact will not really be to 'safeguard' the right holder: indeed, there may be circumstances in which an owner of a putative unregistered Community design right, who has no Community-wide protection between creation of the design and its 'making-available', may wish to argue that the design has been 'made available to the public' in the Community. Moreover, the safeguard clause may leave a design disclosed outside the Community vulnerable to appropriation within it, because there will be no unregistered Community design.[16]

2.2.2 The contents of the state of the art

The state of the art comprises all designs made available to the public before the relevant date, but is then subject to a series of exceptions. A design is deemed to have been made available to the public 'if it has been published following registration or otherwise, or exhibited, used in trade or otherwise disclosed'.[17] Taken alone this would create a state of the art comparable to that used in patent law, that is without geographical or temporal limits. Although, as is explained below, the effects are limited by the 'safeguard clause', it is important to bear this starting point in mind, particularly since the scope of the safeguard clause is as yet unclear. An important question will be whether the clarifying list 'published, exhibited, used in trade or otherwise disclosed' is to be regarded as a synonym for 'made available to the public', or merely as exemplifying some ways in which a design might be 'made available'. For example, it is unclear from the wording used whether a design only forms part of the state of the art if it has been exhibited in, or disclosed to, the public, or whether *any* exhibition or disclosure will suffice: including a private exhibition or disclosure. Other aspects of the harmonized law support the latter construction: in particular, the exclusion of confidential disclosure (discussed below) would not be necessary if disclosure meant 'disclosure to the public'.

As has already been suggested, although the legislation starts by defining the state of the art extremely broadly, it then excludes certain matters, namely: disclosures that derive from

---

[12] CDR, Art. 44.

[13] As we will see, in both the UK and at the OHIM, the exposure of a design at an exhibition by the applicant or with his consent in the 12 months preceding an application will not invalidate an application, because of the grace period. The inability to claim priority from the exhibition is only of significance if a third party who independently develops the design tries to register in the period between exhibition and application. Such cases are likely to be quite rare.

[14] CDR, Art. 5(1)(a).   [15] CDR, Art. 7.

[16] C.-H. Massa and A. Strowel, 'Community Design: Cinderella Revamped' [2003] *EIPR* 68, 74; V. Saez, 'The Unregistered Community Design' [2002] *EIPR* 585, 588 (discussing whether protection only arises on publications anywhere that can be accessed from the Community, or whether there must be publication within the territory of the Community, and finding different language versions of CDR, Art. 11 inconclusive).

[17] Design Dir., Art. 6; RDA s. 1B(5)(a); CDR, Art. 7(1).

obscure events (the 'safeguard clause'); disclosures that are confidential; disclosures that are a consequence of a breach of confidence; and disclosures by the applicant within the grace period.[18] We will deal with each in turn.

The safeguard clause. A design will not form part of the state of the art if it 'could not reasonably have become known in the normal course of business to the circles specialised in the sector concerned, operating within the Community, before the date of filing of the application for registration, or if priority is claimed, the date of priority'.[19] This is a 'safeguard clause', aimed at preventing a design from being unregistrable on the basis of previous obscure disclosures. It had been feared that a broadly defined state of the art might lead to claims of invalidity based on the citation of obscure prior art, such as that in museums. In principle, the safeguard clause applies to a wide range of obscure disclosures: these could be very old disclosures, or geographically remote disclosures, or disclosures to a very narrowly defined group of people. In positive terms, the safeguard clause allows for the protection of designs which, while previously disclosed as a matter of objective fact, have been lost or have not been available to the design market within the Community. In negative terms, the provision enables monopolies to be granted over designs which quite simply, are not really new, and possibly are not even original in a copyright sense.[20]

The precise impact of the 'safeguard clause' is difficult to predict, not least because its wording presents a number of ambiguities.[21] Presumably the onus of proving that a disclosure could not reasonably have been known falls upon the design proprietor, defending a design's alleged invalidity in the face of a disclosure presented by the applicant. The inquiry can be broken down into four elements.

First, we need to identify the 'event' in issue, that is, the event which is said to disclose the design. It should be noted that the safeguard clause does not ask whether 'the design' could reasonably have become known, but whether 'the event', i.e. the exhibition, use in trade, or other disclosure could reasonably have become known.

Second, we need to identify the 'sector' that we are concerned with. In many cases this will be unproblematic, as the disclosure and the design the novelty of which is in issue will relate to the same sector (for example, where a design for a chair had been disclosed at an exhibition in Japan and the issue was whether a similar design registered at the OHIM after the exhibition was novel). However, it is easy to foresee more complex situations: where the earlier design was a painting exhibited in a small art gallery and the later design is an application of a similar image to a teapot, is the relevant design sector here 'painters' or 'ceramic designers'? Some commentators have argued that the sector 'concerned' must be the sector to which the earlier design belongs (here, painters),[22] while others have argued that the sector will be

---

[18] Design Dir., Art. 6; RDA s. 1B(6); CDR, Art. 7.

[19] Design Dir., Art. 6(1); RDA s. 1B(6)(a); CDR, Art. 7(1). This is a reversal of the Max Planck Institute's original proposal of a relative novelty requirement according to which designs were assessed against other products 'made accessible to interested business circles in the EC'.

[20] In TRIPS terms this seems unproblematic, because TRIPS, Art. 25 merely requires members to protect designs which are new or original, but does not say that members should not protect designs which are neither new nor original! See Tritton (2nd edn.) ('just permissible as the agreement can be argued to be permissive in this respect'); Musker, 23–4 (if one takes TRIPS as mandating particular requirements 'one would struggle to find any country in compliance with TRIPS').

[21] The wording seems to originate in German and Benelux law: EC Green Paper, para. 2.3.7.

[22] Musker notes that, if a design is well known in one sector but unknown in another, and the latter sector is regarded as the relevant one for the safeguard clause, the design can be registered in the latter, but the scope of

determined by the prior art in question. Yet another approach was raised in the Green Paper which suggested that the relevant sector was that of the goods to which the design is intended to be applied.[23] The question of how the relevant sector is to be determined was discussed by the Court of Appeal in *Green Lane Products,* where said it was held that 'the relevant sector is the sector that consists of or includes the sector of the alleged prior art. It is not limited to the sector specified in the application for registration.'[24]

Once we have identified the relevant sector, we then need to identify 'the circles specialised in the sector concerned, operating within the Community'. It has been said that 'the circle' extends beyond designers to include all individuals who conduct trade in relation to products in that sector including those who design, make, advertise, market, distribute, or sell such products in the course of trade in the Community.[25] A further unresolved question is whether we are concerned with the persons 'currently' specialized in the sector, that is at the priority date (or in the case of an Unregistered Community Design Right, the date of disclosure). The better view is that this must be so: if we are to give effect to the aim of excluding very old designs from the relevant prior art,[26] then the fact that the design could reasonably have become known to those specialized in the sector concerned, operating in the Community long before the date of filing, must be irrelevant. The best way to achieve this is to treat the term 'operating' as meaning 'currently active in design'.

Once we have identified the circles specialized in the sector we then need to work out the sector's habits as regards searching for past designs. The question whether something could have 'reasonably' become known 'in the normal course of business' is reminiscent of tests for 'constructive knowledge' in relation to transactions in land, where a person is deemed to have knowledge of those interests which a reasonable conveyancer would have discovered. The question here is what would we expect a reasonable designer in this sector to look at in the routine course of business. Although what is normal for one sector will not necessarily be normal for another, the most obvious resources which we might expect a reasonable designer to know about include trade publications, either relating to design in general, or the sector specifically, or perhaps to a number of sectors including the sector concerned; trade fairs, either relating to design in general or the sector specifically, or perhaps to a number of sectors including the sector concerned; designs for products being sold on the High Street, and through retail outlets specializing in products for the sector. It must be doubtful whether reasonable designers would in fact check the OHIM, the international register held by WIPO under the Hague Union, or search national registries as part of 'the normal course of business' (as opposed to prior to applying), though it is easy to anticipate a tribunal wanting to treat such disclosures as outside the scope of the safeguard clause.[27]

---

protection would cover the former. Subject to any right-to-work defence, the later registration could prevent the continued exploitation of the earlier design. Musker observes that this cannot have been the legislature's intention, and so concludes that the relevant sector must be that of the earlier design: see Musker, 36.

[23] EC Green Paper, para. 5.5.5.1, p. 70.

[24] *Green Lane Products v. PMS International Group Limited* [2008] *EWCA Civ* 358 (CA), paras 10 & 11.

[25] *Green Lane Products v. PMS International Group Limited* [2007] *EWHC* 1712 (Pat), para. 34. EC Green Paper, para. 5.5.5.2 ('the specialists, designers, merchants, and manufacturers operating in the sector concerned'). Upheld by the Court of Appeal, above, paras 10 and 11.

[26] EC Green Paper, para. 5.5.5.2, pp. 70–1 ('if the design is unknown to them, then it should be eligible for protection even if an identical design has existed in the past and has completely vanished from the collective memory'); Musker, 37.

[27] Suthersanen asserts 'this must include all published Community registered and unregistered designs' (p. 43).

As will be apparent from the foregoing discussion, quite what comes to be excluded by the 'safeguard clause' is unclear. To return to the issues canvassed in the previous section, depending on how the provision is interpreted, it may have the effect of transforming the broad, objective novelty notion into a peculiar and complex form of local novelty.[28]

Confidential disclosure. The provisions dealing with confidential disclosures are more straightforward. A disclosure made under conditions of confidentiality will *not* make the design available to the public.[29] One potential difficulty, however, is that the legislation is silent as to when conditions of confidentiality will exist. The law of confidence has hitherto been treated as a matter of national law.[30]

Disclosures in breach of confidence. A related, but distinct, exclusion from the 'state of the art' applies 'if a design for which protection is claimed...has been made available to the public as a consequence of an abuse in relation to the designer or his successor in title'.[31] The most obvious example of such an abuse would be a breach of confidence: for instance, where an employee publishes the design. This exclusion is subject to the limitation that the disclosure must have taken place in the twelve months preceding the priority date.

Grace period. The most important of the exclusions from the 'state of the art' is the grace period. This excludes from consideration the designer's own disclosures in the twelve-month period preceding the priority date.[32] The purpose of the grace period is to allow applicants to test their designs in the marketplace before deciding whether to register.[33] It should be noted that the grace period applies to disclosures not just by the designer but also by their successor in title, 'or a third person as a result of information provided or action taken by the designer or his successor in title'.[34] The reference to disclosures by 'a third person *as a result of* information provided or *action* taken by the designer', is ambiguous. It may be interpreted to encompass the activities of a third party who copies a design made available by the designer and places imitations (or variations) on the market. The third party disclosure may be said to be 'as a result of' the action of the designer, in that it could not have occurred without the designer's disclosure. A narrower and more natural construction of the terms 'as a result of action' might confine the limitation to disclosures which have been initiated or authorized by the designer, for example publication by authorized advertisers or exhibition by distributors. While this latter interpretation might seem to raise serious doubts over the usefulness of the grace period, it should not be forgotten that the state of the art is defined elsewhere to exclude disclosures that have been made 'as a consequence of an abuse in relation to the designer'. If a third party has made available illegitimate or unauthorized copies of the design, these are made available as a consequence of 'an abuse', the abuse being an infringement of the designer's Unregistered Community Design Right.

---

[28] Musker, 61 ('parochial novelty').

[29] Designs Dir., Art. 6; RDA s. 1B(6)(b); CDR, Art. 7.

[30] British law has failed to decide, conclusively, whether implicit obligations of confidentiality are to be assessed by subjective or objective criteria: see below pp. 1027–8.

[31] Designs Dir., Art. 6(3); RDA s. 1B(6)(e); CDR, Art. 7(3).

[32] Designs Dir., Art. 6(2), RDA s. 1B(6)(c)–(d), CDR, Art. 7(2)(b). Musker refers to this as creating 'a regrettably long period of uncertainty for competitors' (para. 38). Existing national laws had sometimes been even more generous: see French Intellectual Property Code, Art. L.511–6 (no time limit). However, Germany had given six months only.

[33] CDR Recital 20; EC Green Paper, para. 4.3.2–6, pp. 45–6.

[34] RDA s. 1(b), (6)(d); Designs Dir., Art. 6(2)(a); CDR, Art. 7(2)(a).

While the grace period has been widely welcomed, at least two limitations are worth observing. The first is that the grace period merely exempts designers' own action from invalidating their own later application for registration—it does not backdate the application to the time of initial disclosure, nor establish priority over an independent design. Consequently, a design application by A will still be invalidated by disclosures of identical designs by third parties in the twelve months between A's first disclosure and application for registration. The second limitation is that the grace period only seems to be applicable to disclosures of 'a design for which protection is claimed'. On a literal reading, this would be highly unfortunate for an applicant who had been market-testing a design that differed—either in immaterial details or in material details which were nonetheless insufficient to create a different overall impression on an informed user: in these cases it must have been the legislative intention that the designer's own (or authorized) actions would not invalidate a later application (albeit for a non-identical design). Such a result could be achieved, albeit artificially, by saying the 'design for which protection is claimed' is that in the representations *and all others which would create the same overall impression on an informed user.* A designer could then argue that, insofar as his own previously disclosed variations would infringe the Community Registered Design if published by a third party after the date of registration, they are 'designs for which protection is claimed'.

2.3 IDENTITY

Once we have ascertained the state of the art, we need to decide whether the design for which registration is sought is novel. Article 4 of the Directive states that a design is new if no identical design has been made available to the public before the priority date. 'Identity' is a concept which purports to have an absolute and objective quality, requiring that the design for which protection is sought be exactly the same as that previously disclosed to the public.[35] Article 4 of the Directive indicates that designs are identical if their features only differ in 'immaterial details'.[36] If ascertaining identity had been relatively unproblematic, the notion of 'immateriality' is less so. In the many challenges to the validity of Community registered designs that have been raised to date, the Invalidity Division has adopted a very strict approach, requiring almost exact similarity between the registered design and the prior art for the design to be declared invalid. The legislation does not explain to whom the differences must be immaterial, and the other provisions of the Directive point to a number of candidates—the designer, design expert, consumer, 'informed user', 'relevant circles'. No doubt, the issue will rarely arise, and variations from previously disclosed designs will either be material to all those persons, or to none of them. But there might be variations of detail that a design expert might notice, which a consumer would not.[37] And there might be minor differences of appearance that might be regarded by the designer as crucially important, which are of no consequence to a consumer. Whatever questions identity and immateriality raise, nearly all commentators agree that they are unlikely to prove to be significant. For these commentators, the novelty investigation will almost always be rendered insignificant by the more exacting inquiry into individual character.[38] The same might be said of the two criteria of novelty and non-obviousness in

[35] Levin in Franzosi (ed.), 67, 69 (a 'strict and narrow concept' ... 'just no predecessors').

[36] Rather strangely, the Green Paper contrasts this with a 'creative independent development': EC Green Paper, para. 5.5.5.4, p. 71.

[37] EC Green Paper, para. 5.5.5.3, p. 71.

[38] Franzosi in Franzosi (ed.) ('all products having an individual character are necessarily also new'); Levin in Franzosi (ed.), 69 (to same effect); H. Speyart, 'The Grand Design' [1997] *EIPR* 603, 607–8; Tritton, 394 (since it

patent law, but there the lesser standard has retained its importance for the very reason that it enables the tribunal to bypass the difficult qualitative assessment of 'inventive step'. It may be that the novelty inquiry has a similar attraction in design invalidity actions.

Importantly, when undertaking the novelty examination we are comparing the *appearance* of the two disclosures not their function, nor (at least in most cases) the products to which the appearance is applied. In making the assessment, we should recall that appearance can include not just lines, contours, and shape but also colours, texture, and materials. The appearance of a red plastic teapot may therefore not be identical to a red crockery teapot, even if the shape and size are identical; an orange-coloured leather football of standard size may not be identical to a conventional white-lacquered leather football of the same size; and a miniature version of Arsenal's Highbury football stadium, however detailed and true to life, might well not be identical in appearance merely because of the different dimensions. The issue is whether the appearance is precisely the same. In these cases, novelty will often depend on the way that the design is represented. This can be seen for example in two related cases before the Invalidity Division which concerned the novelty of a registered design for a sponge which consisted of a thick white layer and a thin yellow layer. In one decision, where the design was represented in colour, it was held that the design was novel.[39] In contrast, in another decision it was held that the design for the same sponge, this time represented in black and white, lacked novelty.[40] In both cases, the prior art was the same: the fate of the designs turned on the way that they were represented.

3 INDIVIDUAL CHARACTER

As well as being novel, to be valid a design must possess 'individual character'.[41] The test of individual character is whether 'the overall impression [the design] produces on the informed user differs from the overall impression produced on such a user by any design which has been made available to the public'.[42] This has been described as 'the overall dominant and decisive criterion',[43] and is the most difficult aspect of any design to judge.[44]

Questions have been raised about whether the requirement for individual character is consistent with Community obligations under TRIPS, which obliges members to provide protection of 'independently created industrial designs that are new or original'. This is because at first blush 'individual character' looks like an additional and therefore illegitimate hurdle.

is likely narrower than individual character its exact ambit is likely to be of little legal significance); Massa and Strowel, 'Cinderella Revamped', 73. Cf. Musker, 27–8.

[39] *Bümag v. Procter & Gamble* (15/5/06) ICD 1741 (also held to have individual character).

[40] Ibid, 1758 (also lacked individual character).

[41] Designs Dir., Art. 3(2); RDA s. 11ZA(1)(b); CDR, Art. 4(1). Recital 9 of the Directive explains that the needs of the internal market require the adoption of 'a unitary definition of the notion of design and of the requirements as to novelty and individual character with which registered design rights must comply'. In the other four official languages of the Office individual character is: 'présente un caractère individuel'; 'carácter singular'; 'un carattere individuale'; 'Eigenart'.

[42] Designs Dir., Art. 5.

[43] Levin in Franzosi (ed.), 69. There are some potential precursors in national law: the French Intellectual Property Code, Art. L.511–3 allowed design registration where 'any industrial article...differs from similar articles, either by a distinctive and recognisable configuration affording it novelty or by one or more external effects giving it an individual and new appearance', though apparently the jurisprudence has been inconsistent. See Suthersanen, p. 165. Musker refers to the German requirement of *Eigentümlichkeit*, under its old design law, but notes that this is not the term used in the Directive, where *Eigenart* is used: Musker, 29–30.

[44] Designs Practice Note 4/03 ('Requirement of Novelty and Individual Character', 24 Jun. 2003) ('a much broader and more difficult test than the simple novelty test').

One attempt to justify the individual character standard argues that 'individual character' can be equated with the independent creation standard,[45] though this is unconvincing. A preferable approach is to see 'individual character' as being equivalent to 'significant difference': Article 25 of TRIPS permits members to provide that 'designs are not new or original if they do not significantly differ from known designs or combinations of known design features'. Viewed in this manner, TRIPS can also help us to define the limits of the 'individual character' inquiry.

The question whether a design has individual character can be broken down into distinct parts: (i) what is the design? (discussed previously) (ii) who is the informed user? and (iii) does the design have individual character? We will look at each in turn.

3.1 WHO IS THE INFORMED USER?

The 'informed user' is a fictitious character new to the law.[46] The informed user plays a key role in design law. As well as setting the bench mark for deciding individual character and infringement, the informed user is also used when deciding whether an application was in conflict with earlier rights. It seems that *informed* user was chosen in preference to the 'real consumer' (who might be too ready to see individual character),[47] and the expert (who might be too knowledgeable and unable to appreciate the development for what it is).[48] The informed user has been described as 'a connoisseur, yet not an initiate'.[49] It is clear that informed users are to be treated as distinct figures in their own right: they are different both to the 'person skilled in the art' in patent law (whose 'nerd-like' attributes were said to be too technical)[50] and also to the 'average consumer' in trade mark law.[51]

The informed user is deemed to be familiar with the existing design corpus,[52] the nature of the product to which the design is applied or in which it is incorporated, the industrial sector to which it belongs, and the designer's degree of freedom in developing the design.[53] The informed user has been described as a regular user of articles of the same sort as the registered design.[54] The notion of 'design freedom' is unexplained, but seems to refer to the various

[45] Suthersanen, 437 n. 65 ('arguably, the concept of "individual character" under the EC designs law may be a re-formulation of the "independently created" criterion').

[46] In the other four official languages of the Office: 'l'utilisateur averti'; 'usuario informado'; 'utilizatore informato'; 'informierten Benutzer'. The Green Paper had originally proposed a test of distinctive character to be determined by the relevant public or ordinary consumer: EC Green Paper, para. 5.5.6.2, p. 72.

[47] The user may be but is not necessarily the end-consumer. In the case of the internal aspect of an electrical fitting, like a light switch, the informed user would be an electrician rather than a householder. *Woodhouse UK Plc v. Architectural Lighting Systems* [2006] *ECDR* 11; *Eredu v. Arrmet* (OHIM ref: ICD 024: 27 April 2004, a bar stool).

[48] Levin in Franzosi (ed.), 67, 70 ('the main quality of an informed user is on the one hand that he knows and understands the type of products in question, and on the other that he is not a design specialist'.)

[49] Massa and Strowel, 'Cinderella Revamped', 71.

[50] *Woodhouse,* above, para. 50. This would require the notional interpreter to be the notional designer, not user: *Procter & Gamble Company v. Reckitt Benckiser* [2007] *EWCA Civ* 936 (CA), 15 (Jacob LJ).

[51] Ibid, para. 24–26.

[52] It seems this can be done both individually and collectively. Article 5 of the Directive talks about a comparison with 'any' design which has been made available, but Recital 13 indicates that these are not merely to be viewed individually, since it refers to the impression made on the informed user 'by the existing design corpus'. (This may mean that the informed user would be unimpressed by a combination of existing designs, for example, taking two existing floral motifs and combining them.) See Musker, 31.

[53] CDR, Recital 14.   [54] *Woodhouse,* above, para. 50.

constraints a designer would be under when developing the appearance of a product,[55] including constraints created by the fact that the product needs to perform a particular function,[56] as well as constraints imposed by market expectations, the cost of materials, existing designs, and ergonomics.[57]

3.2 DOES THE DESIGN HAVE INDIVIDUAL CHARACTER?

Once we have identified (i) the notional informed user and (ii) what they would know about the existing design corpus, the next step in the inquiry is to ask in light of this whether the design has individual character? To do this, the informed user will be presumed to compare the registered design with existing designs. While 'individual character' might suggest that the test is whether the design has a 'personality' of its own, this is not what is required by the definition: instead it merely focuses on the difference between the impression made by the registered design and that made by existing designs. Ultimately, the decision as to whether a design has individual character is a factual question that will depend on the circumstances of the case. Having said this, it is possible to give some general guidance as to how this issue might be addressed.

(i) *What standard is to be applied?* Given that the test for individual character is a comparative test, the question arises: how different does a design have to be for it to have individual character? Article 5(1) states that a design has 'individual character' if the overall impression that the design produces on the informed user *differs* from the overall impression produced on such users by designs which have previously been made available to the public. Recital 13, however, suggests that a higher standard should be imposed: namely that the impression given by the design must *'clearly differ'* from the impression produced on them by the 'existing design corpus'.[58] The history of the legislation suggests that the difference need not be 'significant'.[59] The question of the standard that must be satisfied for a design to have individual character was considered by Jacob LJ in the Court of Appeal decision of *Procter & Gamble*. While it is often presumed that the test for individual character is the same standard as for infringement of a design, Jacob LJ drew a distinction between the standard to be imposed in depending on whether the question was asked in relation to validity or infringement. Noting that the requirement in Recital 13, that the overall impression of the design *clearly differ* from that produced by the existing designs corpus, is framed around the 'requirement of registrability', Jacob LJ said:

it is one thing to restrict the grant of a monopoly right to designs which are shown 'clearly' to differ from the existing design corpus. That makes sense—you need clear blue water between the registered design and the prior art otherwise there is a real risk that design monopolies will or may interfere with routine, ordinary minor every-day design modifications—what patent lawyers would call 'mere workshop modifications'. But no such policy applies to the scope of protection. It is sufficient to avoid

---

[55] RDA s. 1B(4); Designs Dir., Art. 5(2) says 'developing' not 'creating'. As Musker points out, the Directive is ambiguous as to whether the important issue is how much design freedom there really is, and how much there appears to be to the informed user. See Musker, 32 ('only rarely will users have a true idea of the freedom available to the designer').

[56] *Procter & Gamble* [2007] *EWCA Civ* 936, para. 29 (CA).

[57] A broad range of 'constraints' on a designer's freedom was contemplated by the EC Green Paper, para. 5.5.8.3, 74.

[58] Designs Dir., Recital 13.

[59] The Official Commentary on the Regulation contrasted such a difference in impression, with an impression of *déjà vu*.

infringement if the accused product is of a design which produces a 'different overall impression'. There is no policy requirement that the difference be 'clear'. If a design differs, that is enough—an informed user can discriminate.[60]

While we will return to look at the consequences of this for design infringement in chapter 28, for the purposes of validity[61] it should be noted that when deciding whether a design had individual character, Jacob LJ favoured the strict approach that required there to be a *'clear differ-ence'* between the informed users' impression of the registered design and that gained from the existing design corpus. It should be noted that although the standard to be applied when deciding whether a design has individual character may be higher than that which is applied in an infringement action, this does not mean that other aspects of the inquiries, such as who is the informed user, how the comparison is to be made and so on, also differ: in all these situations, the law should be the same.

(ii) *When is the decision made?* One issue that has arisen in the cases is the question of the time at which or, more accurately, the way in which the comparison is to be made. This was prompted by the suggestion that the test to be applied when deciding whether a registered design has individual character is the test of 'imperfect recollection' (taken from trade mark law). More specifically, it was suggested that the question to ask was: if the informed user saw the design in question and later saw a previously disclosed design, would the informed user think that they were the same design? The role that might be played by the 'imperfect recol-lection' test in designs law was considered by Jacob LJ in *Procter & Gamble.* Jacob LJ began by noting that the informed user's familiarity with the design corpus means that the user has experience of similar articles. As such, they will be 'reasonably discriminatory'. This means that the informed user is not the same as the average consumer of trade mark law.[62] While Jacob LJ was not willing to say that the imperfect recollection test had no part to play in decid-ing individual character, he did say that it could not be decisive.[63] In particular, he said that what matters is what strikes the mind of the informed user *when* the design is carefully viewed, not what sticks in his mind *after* it has been carefully viewed.[64] Jacob LJ also said that while the test of imperfect recollection makes sense in trade mark law, where the main rationale for the protection is to prevent consumer confusion or deception, this was not the case with design protection. Instead, the point of protecting a design is to protect that design *as a design.* What matters is the overall impression created by the design: will the informed user 'buy it, consider it, or appreciate it for its *individual character?* That involves the user looking at the article, not half-remembering it.'[65]

(iii) *Need to focus on the appearance of the design.* It is important to keep in mind that when examining the designs for individual character, the informed user will focus on the appear-ance of the designs.[66] As such, the informed user is not concerned with the motivations of the

---

[60] *Procter & Gamble* [2007] *EWCA Civ* 936, para. 19 (CA).

[61] Jacob LJ's comments about 'registrability' apply equally to validity.

[62] Citing with approval the Higher Provisional Court in Vienna (in corresponding action involving Procter & Gamble) that 'the informed user will…have more extensive knowledge than an average consumer in posses-sion of average information, awareness and understanding…in particular he will be open to design issues and be fairly familiar with them' (6 December 2006). *Procter & Gamble,* above, para. 26.

[63] Such a test may be helpful at least in clarifying that the informed user is not involved in a side-by-side comparison, which would have a tendency to focus on detail.

[64] *Procter & Gamble,* above, para. 22–25.   [65] Ibid, para. 27.

[66] Cf the Austrian Court in *Procter & Gamble* (cited with approval by Jacob LJ in *Procter & Gamble*) where the court noted that the Febreze sprayer fits the hand differently to the Airwick sprayer (at para. 61, CA).

appellant,[67] how the design features were formed,[68] or how the designed article behaves:[69] all that matters is the overall impression given by the appearance of the designs in question.

(iv) *From what perspective should the design be viewed?* Yet another question about how the informed user would compare the designs in question was raised in *Woodhouse v Architectural Lighting Systems:* an infringement action concerning the design for street lights which were typically some 8–10 metres off the ground. As part of the judgment, the question arose: should the comparison be side-by-side or from a distance? Also, should the designs be viewed at night or during the day? Rejecting the way that the designs were actually sold as the basis by which the designs should be evaluated, the court said that the informed user would have in mind the visual impact of the street light *in situ*—during the daytime and a little distance from the base of the pole upon which the light is suspended.[70]

(v) *What part of the design needs to be compared?* When informed users compare the design in question with the existing design corpus, they are interested in 'overall impression'. Here, overall impression is to be contrasted with the idea of detailed dissection.[71] The notion of 'over-all impression' can be apt to mislead, however, and it is helpful to remind ourselves that the design can be the appearance of the whole or part of a product, and also that design protection exists irrespective of the product to which the design is applied. Given this it is not surprising that one issue that has arisen in this context is the specificity at which the comparison between the designs should be made. As Jacob LJ said, the 'level of generality to which the court must descend is important', given that, the more general the level of comparison, the more likely it is that the design will lack individual character (although this may not be the case with very novel designs). While the decisions to date have not (and arguably never could) develop a general rule—other than to say that the 'appropriate level of generality is that which would be taken by the notional informed user'[72]—it is possible to break the approaches down

(a) *Design as a whole:* the first and most straightforward approach is where the informed user looks at the design as a whole. This approach is typically used where the design is relatively simple[73] or where the design is very different to existing designs.

---

[67] *Pepsico v. Grupo Promer Mon-Graphic* (Case R 1003/2005–3; 27 Oct 2006: Decision of Third Board of Appeal), para. 25 (fact that the appellant was acting in bad faith and copied the design was irrelevant: the question is not whether the design was copied, but whether they produce the same overall impression).

[68] *HK Ruokatalo Group Oyj v. Heinonen* (OHIM ref: ICD 1964; 12 Sept 2006, 'meat foodstuffs') (it did not matter that the stripes on the surface of the meat were formed by grooves and ridges pressed into the raw meat (as was the case with the CRD) or whether the stripes were burnt onto the surface of the meat by frying them in a pan with ridges. The informed user was not concerned with how the stripes were formed: what mattered was that the resulting surface pattern was the same.

[69] The behaviour of dolls in use was not part of the appearance of the product and thus not to be taken into account in the assessment of the overall product: *Aktiebolaget Design Rubens Sweden v. Advikatefirnab Vinge KB* (OHIM ref: ICD 461; 20 Dec 2005; 'dolls'), para. 11.

[70] *Woodhouse* [2006] *ECDR* 11, para. 52.

[71] The EC from the start proposed that the threshold be determined by 'a synthetic approach, letting the design act on him as a whole and comparing this impression with the one produced by a similar design': EC Green Paper, para. 5.5.8.2, p. 73.

[72] In *Procter & Gamble* the Court of Appeal said that it was too general to say that the overall impression of the registered design is 'a canister fitted with a trigger spray device on the top': instead a more detailed inquiry was required. *Procter & Gamble* [2007] *EWCA Civ* 936, para. 35 (vii).

[73] *Mars UK v. Paragon Products* (OHM ref: ICD 1410; 29 Aug. 2006) (five-sided star configuration for animal foodstuff was different to four-sided star configuration of the same size).

(b) *Dominant features:* a second approach sees informed users shift their attention away from the design as a whole to focus on the 'dominant', 'characteristic',[74] 'main', or 'basic'[75] features of the design. Thus, in deciding that a design for go-karts had individual character, the informed user focused on the dominant features of the design: namely, the 'face' at the front side of the vehicle (which only appeared on the registered design).[76] A similar approach was adopted in a decision concerning the validity of a design for stools, where it was held that, when assessing the overall impression of a stool of the type registered, the informed user would focus their attention on the shape of the seat and the back of the stool since these are the features which are essential to or characteristics of stools.[77]

The subsidiary question of how we are to determine whether a feature of a design is dominant is very much dependent on the specific facts of the case and how the informed user would view the design. Given the importance of appearance in design law, it is not surprising that the decisions to date have focused on visual appearance. Thus in one case the fact that most of the differing features on an 'inverter generator' were situated in the darker parts of the generator led the Invalidity Division to conclude that the differences 'did not influence the overall impression of the informed user like the . . . visible elements in the brighter parts in the middle of the housing'.[78] In other cases the informed user has been influenced by the relative size of the distinguishing features and their relative impact of those parts on the overall impression of the design. Thus in comparing portable barbecues, the Invalidity Division discounted the fact that the registered design had wheels on its legs while the prior art did not, primarily on the basis of the relatively small size of the wheels compared to the design as a whole. While the registered design was novel, it lacked individual character.[79] Similarly when considering whether a design for a stool had individual character, the Invalidity Division focused on the seat and the back of the stool on the basis that they were the features with the largest surface area and as such were 'the visibly most important features'.[80] It also seems that the eye of the informed user will be drawn to aspects of a design, depending on the function that the designed product is meant to perform. Thus, when considering whether a design for tea packaging had individual character in comparison to the existing design corpus, it was held that informed users would focus their attention on the 'significant front sides of the tea packaging' as this was where the relevant information about the tea was to be found.[81]

(c) *Novel features:* a third approach, which has been used in many decisions to date, sees the informed user shift away from the design as a whole to focus on the novel features of the design. In many cases, this has also meant that the informed user will focus on

[74] *Honda Giken Kogyo v. Pross* (OHIM ref: ICD 2178 3 April 2007, 'inverter generators'), para. 17.

[75] *J. Wagner v. Weiss* (OHIM ref: 3168, 15 May 2007: 'outdoor lighting') para. 16.

[76] *Pavel Blata v. Campbell* (OHIM ref: ICD 2715; 27 April 2007: 'go-karts'), para. 17. The decision of the Invalidity Division that the design had individual character was reinforced by minor differences such as position of exhaust pipe, colour of front brakes, stamp of wheel, and front bumper. A photograph of the go-karts can be seen in the case report.

[77] *Eredu v. Consultores Urizar* (OHIM ref: ICD 24; 24 April 2004, 'stools'). The main difference between the registered design and the relevant was in respect of the foot rest and the back support.

[78] *Honda v. Pross*, above, para. 17. A photograph of the generator can be seen in the case report.

[79] *Cinders Barbecues v. Russell Gee* (OHIM ref: ICD 2160; 20 February 2007, 'barbecues'), para. 17. A photograph of the barbecues can be seen in the case report.

[80] *Eredu*, above. A photograph of the stool can be seen in the case report.

[81] *Beata Holdrowicz Panaceum v. Kaczmarczyk* (OHIM ref: ICD 2210; 14 March 2003; 'packaging for foodstuffs'), para. 14.

non-essential features of the design (although there is no reason why the novel features of a design will necessarily also be non-essential). This approach has been favoured in situations where the freedom of the designer in creating the new design was limited. In situations where a design field is cluttered with existing designs, the designer was constrained by functional constraints, or market expectation of how the design should look is demanding, the focus of the informed user will shift away from the common features of the design to look in more detail at its 'novel' features.[82] This can be seen, for example, in the OHIM Board of Appeal decision in *Pepsico*. In assessing whether the design for 'promotional metal plates (or toy) for games' (known as tazos or rappers) had individual character, the Board said that it was necessary to disregard all those elements of the design that 'are totally banal and common to all examples of the type of product in question'. Drawing on an example of design for cars, the Board said that 'two designs do not produce the same overall impression simply because they have four wheels, headlamps, red lights at the back, a windscreen... and so forth. The informed user will automatically discard such features when apprising the overall impression caused by two designs and will concentrate on features that *are arbitrary or different from the norm*'.[83] In most cases, this will mean that the informed user will focus on the non-essential features of the design[84] although, ultimately, the informed user will focus on those aspects of the design (if any) where the designer was able to express themselves and in so doing imbue the design with 'individual character'. This means that in situations where a designer has little opportunity to express themselves (that is, where they have little design freedom), even relatively small differences will suffice to create a different overall impression. (It should be noted that the scope of protection available is also correspondingly limited.) Thus, in relation to the design of the promotional toy, the Board said that the paradigm for this type of product is a small flat or nearly flat disk on which coloured images can be printed. Often the disc will be curved towards the centre, so that a noise can be made if a child's finger presses the centre of the disc. A rapper that does not possess these characteristics is unlikely to be accepted in the market place. A designer working within these constraints has little design freedom. In this situation, even a relatively small difference (as in this case) will suffice to create a different overall impression.[85]

The impact that this has on the way that individual character is assessed is evident in the series of OHIM decisions in relation to designs of bike wheels. On the basis of the functional limitations facing the designer of bike wheels and the high number of existing designs,[86] it was held that the informed user would appreciate that the designer would not be able to exercise much

[82] In the converse situation, there is a tendency to look at the design as a whole.

[83] *Pepsico v. Promer*, Case R 1003/2005–3, 27 Oct. 2006, para. 19. (emphasis added). *Armet SRL's Design: Application for declaration of invalidity by Eredu* (OHIM Cancellation Division: [2004] *ECDR* 24, para. 17) (the informed user 'will pay more attention to similarities of non-necessary features and dissimilarities of necessary ones').

[84] *Equipamientos y Materiales Deportivos v. Marcas* (OHIM ref 2087 19 Sept 2006, 'metal hooks'). (Thus in a decision in relation to the validity of a design for metal hooks, the the informed user would pay greater attention to the non-essential elements than the essential elements).

[85] *Pepsico v. Promer,* above, para. 20. A photograph of the rapper can be seen in the case report.

[86] Specifically that the degree of freedom that the designer is able to exercise is limited by the 'requirement that such a wheel has to be laced with the spokes between the hub and the rim in order to support the rim and transfer the weight of the rider to the rim' (para. 27). A photograph of the wheels can be seen in the case reports.

freedom when creating a new shape for a wheel. On this basis it was said that 'the informed user will pay more attention to the features where the designer was not limited in his creativity, such as the pattern of distribution of the spokes around the hub and between the hub and the rim, including... the distances and angles among the spokes, the angles among the spokes and the hub flange and among the spokes and the rim, the limitations on the freedom' and so on. Focusing on these features of the designs (the distribution of the spokes), the Invalidity Division held that the design had individual character and was thus valid.[87]

4 COMPONENT PARTS OF COMPLEX PRODUCTS: VISIBILITY IN USE

We have already observed that the European reforms were forged amidst heavy lobbying by the automobile manufacturing industry on the one side, and the spare parts manufacturers on the other. As we saw in Chapter 26, one of the outcomes of this messy compromise was that 'interconnections' are excluded from design protection. A further element—the 'visibility in use' requirement—was also imposed under the rubric of 'novelty and individual character'.[88] Article 3(3) of the Directive states that a design:

applied to or incorporated in a product which constitutes a component part of a complex product shall only be considered to be new and to have individual character (a) if the component part, once it has been incorporated into the complex product, remains visible during normal use of the latter, and (b) to the extent that those visible features of the component part fulfil in themselves the requirements as to novelty and individual character.

Article 3(4) defines 'normal use' as 'use by the end-user, excluding maintenance, servicing, or repair work'.[89] The idea behind this definition was to exclude so-called 'under-the-bonnet' spare parts from the remit of design protection.[90]

The exclusion only applies to the component part of a complex product. The meaning of these terms (component part, complex product) was discussed in Chapter 26. To be protectable, the component part must remain visible 'during normal use' of the complex product.[91] Normal use is defined as meaning use by the 'end-user' and specifically excludes maintenance, servicing, or repair work. This clarification gives substance to the exclusion, which might otherwise be undermined by the claim that normal users include car and bike enthusiasts who

---

[87] *Rodi Comercial SA v. Soldatini Andrea* (OHIM ref: ICD 27; 30 Aug 2005, 'wheels for bicycles'), para. 27.

[88] Designs Dir., Art. 3(3); CDR, Art. 4(2); RDA s. 1B(8).

[89] RDA s. 1B(9); CDR Art. 4(3). Recital 12: 'those component parts which are not visible during normal use of a product, or to those features of such part which are not visible when the part is mounted, or which would not, in themselves, fulfil the requirements as to novelty and individual character; whereas features of design which are excluded from protection for these reasons should not be taken into consideration for the purpose of assessing whether other features of the design fulfil the requirements for protection'. On the legislative history, see Posner in Franzosi (ed.), p. 7.

[90] See Speyart, 'The Grand Design', 609; G. Dinwoodie, 'Federalized Functionalism: The Future of Design Protection in the European Union' (1996) 24 *American Intellectual Property Law Association Quarterly Journal* 611, 680.

[91] *Lindner Recyclingtech v. Grunecker et al* (OHIM ref: ICD 3150; 3 April 2007; 'chaff cutters') (chaff cutters which were part of shredding machines were not caught by the visibility requirement because the cutter was visible during shredding, not necessarily by the person introducing the material, but by any other looking into the opening for reasons such as controlling the amount of material not yet processed: para. 15).

spend their weekends dismantling, cleaning, fine-tuning, and reassembling their vehicles. We can infer that normal use would include getting into and out of a vehicle, putting things in the boot, as well as driving (or being a passenger).[92] Changing the oil or fanbelt, or adjusting the points, are almost certainly maintenance. The protectable parts of a car would thus be the internal features such as the seats, gearstick, handbrake, steering wheel, and rear-view mirrors; the external features such as the bonnet, boot, doors, hubcaps, wipers, and wing-mirrors. The designs for things such as exhaust pipes and radiators (which are only rarely seen, for example, when the car is being repaired), will not be registrable.[93] If a part is visible in use, those parts must be novel and have individual character to be protectable.

5 RELATIVE GROUNDS FOR INVALIDITY

The Directive contains a number of other grounds for refusal or invalidity which we have yet to discuss. Two of these are mandatory, three optional. We can call these 'relative grounds for invalidity' because they concern conflicts between the rights of the putative design proprietor and other competing claims. The 'relative' nature of these grounds for objection is reflected in the fact that the Directive regulates who is entitled to rely on them.[94]

5.1 THE APPLICANT OR THE RIGHTHOLDER IS NOT ENTITLED TO THE DESIGN RIGHT

The Directive requires that design registrations be treated as invalid 'if the applicant for or the holder of the design right is not entitled to it under the law of the Member State concerned'.[95] This ground may only be invoked by the person who is so entitled.[96] As we will see in the next chapter, the Directive says nothing about ownership of designs, leaving these matters to national law. In the United Kingdom, ownership in the first instance vests in the designer, or his or her employer or commissioner. The British implemented the relative ground for refusal or invalidity in two ways. Firstly, if an application is made to the UK Registry by a person who does not 'claim to be' the proprietor of the design and, where relevant, the owner of a UK unregistered design right, the Registrar is required to refuse the application.[97] Secondly, a registration may be declared invalid on the ground that the registered proprietor is not the proprietor of the design.[98] In normal circumstances, however, the person properly entitled is much more likely to seek rectification of the register, so that they are entered thereon as the proprietor.[99]

The Community Design Regulation implements the same ground for objection purely as a ground for invalidity. Before applying, the person truly entitled must previously have

---

[92] Franzosi states that normal use includes the time of purchase (Franzosi in Franzosi (ed.), p. 48), though purchasers often carry out more thorough inspections at these moments than during 'normal use'.

[93] Speyart, 'The Grand Design', 609 argues that the exclusion is unnecessary, for such designs will be functional or made up of interconnections.

[94] Design Dir., Art. 11(5)–(6).   [95] Design Dir., Art. 11(1)(c).

[96] Design Dir., Art. 11(3).

[97] RDA ss. 3A(3), 3(2), and 3(3). Rather oddly, given the wording of the Directive, this is not dependent upon the real design owner objecting.

[98] RDA s. 11ZA(2).   [99] RDA s. 20.

obtained a court decision to that effect. This should be done in a national court, usually in the jurisdiction where the registered proprietor is domiciled.

5.2 CONFLICTS WITH EXISTING DESIGNS

The Directive requires member states to refuse registrations or to treat them as invalid in cases where 'the design is in conflict with a prior design which has been made available to the public after the date of filing of the application or if priority is claimed, the date of priority, and which is protected from a date prior to the said date by a registered Community design or an application for a registered Community design or by a design right of the Member State concerned, or by an application for such a right'. This ground can be invoked by the applicant for, or the holder of, the conflicting right, or if the member state elects, the appropriate authority of the member state on its own initiative.[100] Essentially, the conflicts provision requires member states to operate a 'first-to-file' system to determine priority between registrants in cases where the earlier application was not published by the priority date of the later application. The earlier application might not have been published by the time of the later application for a number of reasons: because the earlier application was outside the Community but was the basis of a later application to a national registry of a member state (or the OHIM) claiming priority;[101] or because there was deferred publication of the earlier Community registration. The fact that the Directive is satisfied that this ground would only be capable of being invoked by the right holder implies that the policy behind this ground of invalidity is not to avoid 'double design registration' in cases where two individuals come up with similar designs in close succession. Indeed, the effect of the provision leaves it open to member states to decide whether to allow two (or more) such proprietors to have rights over identical designs.

The UK Registered Designs Act 1949 implements the conflicts as a ground for invalidity which can only be invoked by the registered proprietor or applicant.[102] The relevant earlier designs are ones 'protected by virtue of a registration under this Act or the Community Design Regulation or an application for such registration'. It does not include, as it might have done,[103] earlier UK unregistered designs published after the date of application. There is a 'conflict' where the later registration lacks novelty or individual character when compared with such a design.

In contrast, the Community Design Regulation only recognizes conflict with a previous design as the basis of an invalidity action.[104] Like the United Kingdom, it limits the relevant earlier designs to earlier Community applications and registrations, and earlier applications and registrations for a 'registered design right of a Member State'.[105] If the invalidity action is before the OHIM, the only person who is permitted to invoke this ground is the applicant for or holder of the earlier right. If the invalidity action is before a Community Design Court on

---

[100] Design Dir., Art. 11(1)(d), (4), (6).

[101] For example A applies in USA on 1 Jan. 2003; B applies for registration of an identical design in the UK on 1 May 2003; A applies in UK on 31 May, claiming priority from its earlier US registration, and that application is published on 15 August 2003. In such circumstances B's application is in conflict with A's, and A's is earlier. So A has a ground for invalidity. A's is a prior design; has been made available after B's filing; but is protected from before.

[102] RDA ss. 11ZA(1), ZB(3)–(4).

[103] EC Green Paper, para. 6.5.2.2, p. 92.

[104] See, e.g., *Servicios de Distribucion e Investigacion v. Sola* (OHIM ref: ICD 396 20 Sept 2005, 'radio receivers'); *Burberry v. Duran-Corretjer & Partners* (ICD 1568, 8 February 2006, 'ornamentation for fabrics').

[105] CDR, Art. 25(1)(d).

the basis of a counterclaim in infringement proceedings, it seems the appropriate authority of the member state may invoke the ground on its own initiative.

5.3 CONFLICTS WITH DISTINCTIVE SIGNS

The Directive also permits member states to refuse registration of a design, or treat the design as invalid, 'if a distinctive sign is used in a subsequent design, and Community law or the law of the member state concerned governing that sign confers on the right holder of the sign the right to prohibit such use'.[106] This ground may only be invoked by the holder of the conflicting right. The UK has elected to include this in the grounds for invalidity,[107] as does the Community Design Regulation.[108] These provisions cover conflicts with trade mark rights. Thus, if a person tries to register the design of a football shirt with a purple body, yellow collar, orange arms, and blue cuffs, and bearing the Arsenal club crest (being a registered trade mark for clothing), such a registration could be declared invalid (even though in other respects it would be novel and have individual character). One problem which will need to be resolved is that the law of trade marks normally only prohibits use of a mark on goods which are the same or similar to those for which the mark has been registered, whereas under the harmonized law of designs a registration for one product covers use of the design on all others. In considering whether an earlier right holder has the 'right to prohibit the use of the sign', one question that the courts will have to decide is whether we are only concerned with the application of the distinctive sign to the goods which the design applicant has identified in its statement of product goods, or whether we need to assume that the design applicant will apply the design to all goods[109]

As well as basing an attack on registered trade marks, an earlier right holder may be able to rely on analogous regimes protecting 'distinctive signs',[110] which could include passing-off and possibly PDOs and PGIs. In some circumstances this ground may be capable of being used by famous personalities to prevent the registration of designs for merchandise bearing their name, signature, or image. This is important, since no other ground of objection seems to be available.[111]

5.4 CONFLICTS WITH EARLIER COPYRIGHT PROTECTED WORKS

The Directive permits member states to refuse registration of a design, or treat it as invalid, 'if the design constitutes an unauthorised use of a work protected under the copyright law of a Member State'.[112] This ground may only be invoked by the 'holder' of the copyright. The United

---

[106] Designs Dir., Art. 11(2)(a).   [107] RDA s. 11ZA(3).

[108] CDR, Art. 25(1)(e), (3).

[109] *Schwan-Stabilo v. Grunecker et al* (OHIM ref: ICD 2426; 24 Aug 2006, 'instruments of writing'); *Zellweger Analytics Design: application of Hee Jung Kim for cancellation* (Case 1477, 1 March 2006) [2006] *ECDR* 17, para. 16. *Zygmunt Piotrowski v. Compagnie Gervais Danone* (Case R 267/2007–3, 18 Sept 2007, Decision of the Third Board of Appeal), para. 22 (a trade mark owner is able to prevent use of the design if it is used 'in respect of goods or services which are identical to those for which the mark is registered).

[110] Whether all signs which are registered as trade marks, being not exclusively 'descriptive' or 'devoid of distinctive character', can be said to be 'distinctive signs' will, no doubt, have to be resolved in due course.

[111] Cf. Art. 4(4)(b) of the Swedish Act No. 2002: 570 amending the Design Protection Act 1970: 485. which states that design right shall not subsist if the design 'contains, without authorization, another person's portrait or anything that can be perceived as another person's family name, artistic name or similar name, unless the portrait or the name obviously relates to a person who is long deceased'.

[112] Designs Dir. Art. 11(2)(a).

Kingdom has elected to include this in the grounds for invalidity,[113] as does the Community Design Regulation.[114] An obvious example where this would occur is where a design for a T-shirt was based upon an unpublished painting.[115]

5.5 CONFLICTS WITH PROTECTED BADGES

Finally, the Directive gives member states the option of refusing the registration of designs which constitute improper uses of items listed in Article 6*ter* of the Paris Convention as well as 'badges, emblems and escutcheons... which are of particular public interest in the Member State concerned'.[116] Article 6*ter* requires countries of the Paris Union to refuse or invalidate the registration of trade marks which are or contain prohibited emblems: armorial bearings, flags and other state emblems, official signs and hallmarks of countries of the Union, or inter-governmental organizations. With the exception of flags, these insignia have to be notified to WIPO. The Directive allows for this ground to be raised by 'the person or entity concerned by the use' (such as an official representative of the state concerned) or, if a member state so chooses, an 'appropriate authority' of the member state may invoke this ground *ex officio*.[117]

The United Kingdom has treated this as a ground for refusal,[118] as well as invalidity.[119] Schedule A1 elaborates the emblems concerned. The domestic ones include Royal Arms, the Crown, 'a representation of Her Majesty or any member of the Royal Family', the Union Jack, flags of the home nations, and coats of arms granted by the Crown. The Community Regulation treats conflicts with protected badges as a ground for invalidity.

---

[113] RDA s. 11ZA(4). This refers to the 'owner' of copyright, which almost certainly would be taken to include exclusive licensees: CDPA s. 101(2); but not the owner of moral rights. It is expected that other countries will interpret the 'holder' of the right to include the author.

[114] CDR, Art. 25(1)(f), (3).

[115] If the painting was well known the design would probably lack novelty, though this depends upon whether a painting is a design, that is, 'the appearance of a product'.

[116] Designs Dir., Art. 11(2).   [117] Designs Dir., Art. 11(6).

[118] RDA s. 3A(4)(c); Sched. A1.

[119] RDA s. 11ZA(1). The application may be made by 'any person concerned by the use': s. 11ZB(2).

28

THE RIGHTS OF A PROPRIETOR OF A UK REGISTERED DESIGN, A REGISTERED COMMUNITY DESIGN, AND AN UNREGISTERED COMMUNITY DESIGN

CHAPTER CONTENTS

This chapter deals with two issues in relation to the harmonized and Community regimes. First, we identify the 'design proprietor'. This involves an examination of two sets of rules: those relating to initial entitlement and those relating to transfers. Second, we examine the rights which the law grants to the design proprietor, and the exceptions to those rights (sometimes referred to as defences).

1 INITIAL ENTITLEMENT

As we indicated in the introduction to this Part, the 'designer' plays a peripheral role in the discussions justifying the legal protection of designs. Given this, it is not surprising that the same can be said of the significance of the designer for the law itself.[1] There are two main reasons for this marginalization of the designer. The first is that the activity of designing is seen as less creative than that of authorship: a designer is seen as being constrained—by the market, by the laws of physics, by the needs of man, and by fashion.[2] The design is thus seen as having a significantly less intimate relationship with the personality of a designer.[3] The second reason is that

---

[1] 87 per cent of companies have their own design departments: *Prospective Study about the Design Registration Demand at the European Union Level: Executive Summary* (on the OHIM web site), 7.

[2] The Design Directive and CDR specifically acknowledge that the designer's freedom may be limited: see Design Dir., Art. 5(2), Art. 9(2), Recital 13; CDR, Art. 6(2), Art 10(2), Recital 14.

[3] Indeed, the designer is referred to as 'developing' rather than 'creating' a design: Design Dir., Recital 13; CDR, Art. 14(2), Recital 14. The requirement of 'creation', however, is employed in framing an exception to the

the activity of designing is rarely an activity of an individual: usually a designer will be part of a team, will be given a design brief, and asked to suggest a number of possible solutions. A design which reaches the marketplace will often be the product of many individuals not just one, and the role of the draughtsman in the design process may by no means be the most significant.[4] As a consequence, the law has tended to concern itself with ensuring that design protection meets the needs of 'industries' as opposed to individuals.[5] It has also focused on designs rather than designers. In this sense the law is concerned with designs as an asset and their effects in the market, rather than the protection of those involved in the design process.[6] This can be seen in the fact that protection commences either from making available (for Unregistered Community Design) or registration (national registered designs and Registered Community Design), rather than creation of a design; the absence of moral rights for designers (or in the case of the right to be named on the register, the practical impossibility of using such a right);[7] the fact that duration is not linked to the life of the author; and the relatively insignificant position of the designer in determining entitlement. It is to this last issue that we now turn.

The Directive does not deal with the question of who is entitled to a national registered design, so this remains a matter of national law. In the pre-harmonization era, most European countries awarded the rights to the designer or their employer, but the rules differed in their exact details (for example whether all designs created by an employee in the course of employment belonged to the employer or only those which could be expected to result from the employee carrying out their duties). Consequently, registered design rights in country A might vest in the designer, while in country B they belonged to the designer's employer. Harmonization would thus have reduced the potential for national design rights to vest in different undertakings—a situation which, as we have seen, can produce barriers to the free movement of goods made to particular designs. However, it was probably thought unlikely that such barriers would arise in practice, because subtle differences in the national laws of member states could (and would) be rectified by express contractual dealings between the designer and their employer. For example, an employer wanting to obtain protection in a number of European countries through national registration could readily enter into an agreement with the designer assigning (or affirming the employer's ownership of) worldwide rights.

1.1 ENTITLEMENT UNDER THE UK REGISTERED DESIGNS ACT 1949

In most circumstances the initial owner of a UK registered design (or as the Act prefers, the 'original proprietor') is the designer, that is the author of the design.[8] To this general principle there are two exceptions: first, where a design is created by an employee in the course of

---

Unregistered Community Design: see CDR, Art. 19(2). And cf. the French version, which uses the terms 'le créateur' and 'l'élaboration du dessin ou modèle'.

[4] CDR, Recital 7 does recognize the role of individual designers, but sees the more significant benefit from 'enhanced protection for industrial designs' as the encouragement of 'innovation and the development of new products and investment in their production'. The CDR explicitly refers to teamwork: CDR Art. 18.

[5] CDR, Recitals 8, 15. Though CDR Recital 24 contemplates that the Community system might be used by individual designers.

[6] Design Dir., Recital 15, CDR, Recital 11, both attribute the need to protect design features of modular products by reference to the fact that such features 'present a major marketing asset'.

[7] EC Green Paper, para. 7.1.4 stating that a moral right 'hardly appears to be desirable and probably also not practical'.

[8] RDA s. 2(1).

employment, the employer is treated as the original proprietor;[9] second, where a design is made in pursuance of a commission for money or money's worth, the person commissioning the design is treated as the original proprietor.[10] If a third party (A) commissions a company (B) to produce a design, and the design is created by an employee (C) of company (B), the proprietor of the design is the commissioner (A) rather than the employer (B).[11]

The author of a design is defined as 'the person who creates it'.[12] The person who creates a design is the person who gives the design its specific form and appearance.[13] There is case law, albeit prior to harmonization, which suggests that a person is not a creator if all they have done is to bring a design into the United Kingdom from overseas (despite the fact that it may be 'new' in the Community).[14] Nor is a person who is given the right to register,[15] or the exclusive right to distribute a design in the United Kingdom, a creator.[16]

If a person who does not claim to be the proprietor of the design applies for registration, the Registrar will refuse to register the application.[17] In addition, an application will only be permitted if it is made by a person 'claiming to be the design right owner'.[18] This means that where a design is for shape or configuration, the applicant must also claim to be the owner of unregistered design rights which exist in the design. This provision attempts to ensure that unregistered and registered design rights are vested in the same person. An application may be made for the registration to be declared invalid where registration has been made by a person who is not entitled to do so.[19] Alternatively, a court may order the register to be rectified by changing the name of the registered proprietor.[20]

1.2 ENTITLEMENT: THE COMMUNITY PROVISIONS

The rules as to entitlement to Registered and Unregistered Community Designs indicate that the rights should vest in the designer or their successor in title.[21] There is no further guidance as to who is the 'designer'. However, it is clear that the first person to disclose a design to

---

[9] RDA s. 2 (1B), 44; *Coffey's Registered Designs* [1982] *FSR* 227 (suggesting that the employer is only first proprietor where employment carries with it a duty to make the design for the benefit of the employer).

[10] RDA s. 2(1A). Where a person requests a design, and agreement is that the designer will have exclusive distribution in some places, the commissioner is the proprietor: *Breville Europe v. Thorn EMI Domestic Appliances* [1995] *FSR* 77.

[11] RDA s. 2(1B).

[12] RDA s. 2(3). RDA s. 2(4) defines the author of a computer-generated design as 'the person by whom the arrangements necessary for the creation of the design are made'.

[13] *A. Pressler & Co v. Gartside & Co.* (1933) 50 *RPC* 240 (Luxmoore J).

[14] *Lazarus v. Charles* (1873) *LR* 16 *Eq* 117 (importer not entitled to register under s. 5 of the 1842 Act). Cf. *Barker v. Associated Manufacturers (Gowns and Mantles)* (1933) 50 *RPC* 332, 337 (possible to obtain registration of a design which was used by the Ancient Egyptians six thousand years ago, if it had not been previously used in the UK).

[15] *Jewitt v. Eckardt* (1878) 8 *Ch D* 404; *Re Guiterman's Registered Design* (1886) 55 *LJ Ch D* 309.

[16] In *Neville v. Bennett* (1898) 15 *RPC* 412, it was held that, where one person selected an idea for a design from existing Persian designs, which was then rendered into a workable design by someone else, they were joint designers. This suggests that the process of selecting the basic design was considered a relevant act of creation, a proposition which seems difficult to reconcile with the 'import' cases.

[17] RDA s. 3A(3).   [18] RDA s. 3(2).

[19] RDA s. 11ZA(2) ('the proprietor of the design objecting'—the action can be brought by 'the person able to make an objection': s. 11ZB(5)).

[20] RDA s. 20(1A)(c). Section 20(1) refers to rectification 'by the making of any entry therein or the variation or deletion of any entry therein'.

[21] CDR, Art. 14(1).

the public is not, for that reason, the designer. Provision is made for the designer (or person entitled) to make a claim as to ownership of an unregistered Community design which has been 'disclosed or claimed by...a person who is not entitled to it'. The Regulation recognizes the possibility of joint design.

Where a design is 'developed by an employee in the execution of his duties or following instructions given by his employer, the right to the Community design shall vest in the employer, unless otherwise agreed or specified under national law'.[22] Four points should be noted about this provision. *First,* in contrast to the UK provision which ascribes rights to an employer where a design 'is created by an employee in the course of employment', the Community provision refers to both 'the execution of his duties' and 'following instructions'. The difference can be seen through the example of a situation where a person is employed as an administrator, but the employer specifically requests the employee to design the cover of a brochure. It seems that under UK law the employee might be the owner, as the design was not created 'in the course of' employment'.[23] However, if the Community provisions apply the employer would be the owner since the design was made 'following instructions given by his employer'. Although it is not easy to think of many situations which would fall within one provision but not the other, the divergence in terminology is unfortunate.[24] *Second,* in its UK form no provision is made for 'agreements to the contrary'.[25] In contrast, the Regulation allows for variation from the provision 'where it is agreed or specified under national law'. Such an agreement would not necessarily have to comply with the rules on formalities for transfer, just those for agreements. *Third,* the reference in the Regulation to specification under national law seems to enable member states to have their own rules about the allocation of rights to designs made by employees, and for these to override the Community rules. *Fourth,* the Community rules say nothing about commissioners, and thus leave the initial rights with the designer: a commissioner who wishes to own design rights must secure their prospective rights by assignment.

The person in whose name a Community Registered Design is registered 'shall be deemed to be the person entitled'.[26] Although this is put in categorical terms, it is obviously a presumption that can be rebutted. Provision is explicitly made for claims to be recognized as 'the legitimate holder of the Community design' and for the change in ownership to be entered in the Register.[27] In the absence of a provision giving the Office power to decide, the matter must be for the relevant national courts, with jurisdiction governed by the Brussels Convention.[28] The effect is that the action should usually be brought in the state where the defendant, the current proprietor, is domiciled.[29] The Regulation does, however, provide a limitation period

---

[22] CDR, Art. 14(3). The designer has a right to be named on the register: CDR, Art. 18, unless waived, under CDR, Art. 36(3)(e).

[23] Possibly, the design would be treated as having been commissioned.

[24] It is copied from the Software Directive: EC Green Paper, 7.2.3 para. 97.

[25] This leaves unclear whether the normal rules on transfer must be complied with if an employee is to be made owner. If a court sees the rule on employers as a statutory variation of the orthodox rule that the designer is the owner, it may take the view that the retention of the rights in the design by the designer is not a 'transfer', and so need not comply with the normal formalities. However, if a court wishes to emphasize the evidential importance of the transfer formalities, it may insist that any variation from the statutory rule is a transfer. See *Ultraframe,* an unregistered design right case below at p. 669 n. 8.

[26] CDR, Art. 17.

[27] CDR, Art. 15. Third parties whose activities are affected by such changes in the register are protected by the availability of licences upon reasonable terms: CDR, Art. 16.

[28] CDR, Art. 79.

[29] This would follow from *Duijnstee,* Case C–288/92 [1985] 1 *CMLR* 220; *FSR* 221.

for such actions. In general, incorrect ascription of rights can be rectified for up to three years following the publication of the Registered Community Design. However, this limitation is inapplicable where the registrant has acted in bad faith. Alternatively, a Community design may be declared invalid 'if, by virtue of a court decision, the right holder is not entitled to the Community design under Article 14'.[30]

The effect of these differences is to create a possible distinction between the person entitled under national design law and a person entitled to the Community Design rights—and thus to produce two different right holders with equivalent rights. For example, in the UK the commissioner of a design will be entitled to national design rights,[31] but under the Community regime such rights would belong to the designer.[32] In relation to the registered design regimes, it appears that the first party to apply for a national (or Community) registration will be able to invalidate the later applicant's Community (or national) registration.[33] If this is right, the problem of duplicating rights at national and Community level in the hands of different proprietors is likely to be confined to the situation where national registered designs and Unregistered Community Designs overlap.

2 ASSIGNMENT AND LICENCES

2.1 ASSIGNMENT AND LICENCES: THE UK PROVISIONS

The proprietor of a design may assign or mortgage the design, or licence others to make articles bearing it.[34] An assignment should be made in writing, as should a licence.[35] No provision exists for the assignment of future designs, and it is probably necessary for the original proprietor to register as such and then execute the relevant dealing.[36] An offer of exclusivity in distribution is not an assignment, because it is not a grant of the 'right to apply' the design to a product.[37] Neither an exclusive licensee nor the sole distributor of a design has a right of action against an infringer: this right belongs to the proprietor alone.[38]

2.1.1 Registration of transactions

Information concerning assignments and other transactions of registered designs is maintained at the UK Design Registry.[39] Any person who becomes entitled to an interest in a registered design should apply to the Registrar to have their interests entered on the register.[40] The interests which can be entered include assignments, mortgages, co-ownership, and licences, but not beneficial interests relating to trusts.[41] A strong incentive exists to register such a transaction: any document in respect of which no entry has been made in the register may not be admitted as evidence of such title 'unless the court otherwise directs'.[42] Moreover, a transferee

---

[30] CDR, Art. 25(1)(c).   [31] RDA s. 2(1A).   [32] CDR, Art. 14(1).

[33] Designs Dir., Art. 11(1)(d), CDR, Art. 25(1)(d). This assumes that the tribunal treats such a situation as one of 'conflict' between designs, whereas it could be characterized as a conflict in the rules of ownership—there being only one design.

[34] RDA s. 19.   [35] *Jewitt v. Eckardt* (1878) 8 *Ch D* 404.   [36] Ibid.

[37] *Leary Trading Co's Designs* [1991] *RPC* 609.

[38] *Oren & Tiny Love v. Red Box Toy Factory* [1999] *FSR* 785, 800 (speculating as to whether an exclusive licensee could be registered as a proprietor); *Woolley v. Broad* [1892] 9 *RPC* 208.

[39] RDA s. 17(1)(b).   [40] RDA s. 19(1).

[41] RDA s. 17(2).   [42] RDA s. 19(5).

of a registered design will take subject to any interests which have been registered:[43] the position in relation to unregistered interests, it seems, being governed by the general law. There are two notable effects here: first, licences, being interests which would not bind a purchaser under the general law (being non-proprietary), acquire a proprietary character as a consequence of registration; second, equitable interests—such as an equitable charge on the design—will bind a purchaser with notice but, in the absence of registration, not one without notice.

2.2 ASSIGNMENT AND LICENCES: COMMUNITY PROVISIONS

Community design rights are unitary, so can only be transferred for the whole Community.[44] While the Regulation does not establish the rules relating to transfers, leaving those to member states, it does provide a scheme for deciding which member states' rules apply. The basic rule is that national laws of the member state in which the holder has their seat or domicile apply. So if a design proprietor is British and assigns the Unregistered Community Design to a French citizen, the laws governing the transaction are the UK's rules. If the French owner assigns the design to a Spaniard, the rules that operate are French.

2.2.1 Registration

In the case of Registered Community Designs, an additional requirement is that the transfer be entered in the register. Pending such entry, the successor in title may not invoke the rights 'arising from the registration of' the Community design.[45] The same is true of grants of Registered Community Designs as security.[46]

2.2.2 Licences

A licence may be granted for the whole or part of the Community.[47] Any licence relating to part of the Community will need to be scrutinized to ensure it does not breach Article 81 EC (formerly Art. 85 of the Treaty). Licences may be exclusive or non-exclusive: an exclusive licensee may bring proceedings for infringement but a licensee needs the consent of the proprietor to do so. Licences can be entered in the register. The effect of this is likely to depend on the law of the member state of the proprietor,[48] but registration may well be a prerequisite for the licence to bind a third party transferee of the Community Registered Design. This would be so in the case of a transfer governed by British law.[49]

3 DURATION

Because the breadth of subject matter covered by design registration is so wide, calculating an optimal period of protection is inevitably difficult. Some designs will be the product of huge investment, others of quite trivial efforts. Some designs will have a very brief commercial life, whereas others—design 'classics'—might last for much longer.[50] Moreover, there will be a stronger public interest in freedom to make some, particularly more functional, designs than others.

---

[43] RDA s. 19(4).   [44] CDR, Art. 27.   [45] CDR, Art. 28(b).
[46] CDR, Art. 29.   [47] CDR, Art. 32.   [48] See CDR, Art. 33.
[49] RDA s. 19(4). A court might direct otherwise to prevent the statute being used as an instrument of fraud.
[50] EC Green Paper, paras. 4.3.16–4.3.18, 50–51; para. 6.3, 83.

The Directive harmonized the duration of national registered design right at 25 years, specifying that this be granted in periods of five years from the date of filing.[51] Recital 17 referred to this 'unification' of the term of protection as fundamental to the smooth functioning of the internal market. However, it is worth noting that—in contrast to the position in relation to copyright where harmonization was 'upwards', the 25-year period was not the longest provided under existing law—France had previously protected registered designs for 50 years.[52] The 25-year period probably was presented as a suitable compromise, and one for which the Commission could claim some international consensus (an easier course than justifying the term by reference to economic or philosophical argument):[53] the term corresponds to the minimum period of copyright protection for works of applied art under the Berne Convention.[54] The same term was adopted in the Regulation for Registered Community Designs.

Unregistered Community Designs are protected for a much shorter term: three years from the date on which the design was first made available to the public within the Community.[55] The period was chosen by the Commission in preference to the two-year term which had been suggested by the Max Planck Institute.[56] Apparently, it 'was considered almost unanimously to be a reasonable compromise'.[57] It is notable that the period starts irrespective of whether the making available was lawful: thus disclosures in breach of confidence or as a consequence of industrial espionage or theft can cause an Unregistered Community Design Right to come into operation. It is foreseeable, given the short period of protection, that litigation may often turn on the issue of when protection commenced (and hence lapsed). It will be for the claimant to prove subsistence of unregistered Community design and thus to demonstrate when the design was first made available within the Community.

4 RIGHTS OF THE DESIGN PROPRIETOR

The rights given to the proprietor of national registered designs, Registered Community Designs, and Unregistered Community Designs are couched in similar terms. Article 9 of the Directive and Article 10 of the Regulation deal with 'scope of protection'. In turn, Article 12 of the Directive and Article 19 of the Regulation deal with the rights conferred by design right.

4.1 THE RIGHTS CONFERRED

The rights conferred on the proprietor are the rights 'to use [the design] and to prevent a third party not having his consent from using it'. Use is specified as covering, in particular, 'the making, offering, putting on the market, importing, exporting or using of a product in which the design is incorporated or to which it is applied, or stocking such a product for those purposes'.[58]

---

[51] Designs Dir., Art. 10.

[52] IP Code L 513(1). Benelux had 15 years; Germany 20; UK 25; Italy, single period of 15 years; Scandinavia 15; Austria 15; Spain 20; Portugal 25.

[53] CDR, Recital 16 refers to the term as 'corresponding to the foreseeable market life of their products'.

[54] TRIPS, Art. 26(3) requires only a 10-year term.   [55] CDR, Art. 11.

[56] EC Green Paper, para. 6.3.1.2, 84. The Commission wanted the UCD to be valuable to industries which follow a policy of changing their designs after a limited number of years.

[57] Franzosi in Franzosi (ed.), 101.

[58] Designs Dir., Art. 12; RDA s. 7(1); CDR, Art. 19.

4.1.1 Beyond the product

As we saw in Chapter 26, the definition of design refers to the appearance of a product, a notion that is broadly defined to include such things as graphic symbols. Just as a design requires there to be a product, so too infringement only occurs where a person deals with or uses a product. However, the infringer's use need not be of the same product as the designer's. That is, infringement is not confined to dealings with the same product to which the design had been applied (or that is mentioned in the registration process). Instead, the rights are infringed by the use of *a product*—that is, any product—in which the design is incorporated or to which it is applied. So, a wallpaper design might be infringed by making curtains bearing a similar pattern, and a design for a car by making a toy version of it.[59] This is a dramatic change for UK registered designs law, which formerly confined the scope of infringing uses to use of substantially the same design on the article for which the design had been registered.[60] As such, it makes registration much more attractive and saves design proprietors from having to register a design for articles to which they do not intend to apply the design, but to which they suspect competitors might apply their design.[61]

One problem raised by the legal separation of the design from its use in relation to a particular product, relates to the treatment of 'books' (and other communications media) as products. It seems safe to proceed on the assumption that books constitute 'industrial or handicraft items' and so are products: otherwise the regime would fail to protect designs of book covers. But if this is the case, designs law may now be a potential tool of censorship. For example, if a design has been registered for a cartoon figure to be applied to wallpaper, the depiction of the design in a book may constitute a 'use' of the design by its application to a product. Although, as we will see, a 'citation' defence exists, it is subject to certain limitations (in particular it may only apply to acts of reproduction, not distribution) and so may not adequately protect free speech interests. It would be preferable for tribunals to interpret the statute so as to avoid having to look for such an exception in the first place.

4.1.2 The meaning of 'use'

Pending the elaboration of case law on the relevant provisions, there is little to be said about the itemized infringing acts, though useful guidance may be found in the jurisprudence relating to similar terms in the Community Patent Convention which have found their way into national laws.[62] However, the fact that the list of activities which count as 'use' is non-exhaustive is likely to reduce the significance of the definition of the itemized acts. For example, it may be that the list includes marketing a complete kit which when made up constitutes the design on the basis that this is 'putting on the market, ... *a product* ... to which [the design] is applied'. If not, such an activity is likely to be deemed infringing on the basis that it is 'use' of the design, even though it is a form of use which has not been explicitly particularized.[63]

---

[59] See J. Wessel, 'Germany: Registered Designs' [1996] *EIPR* D200 (discussing *BMW v. Carrera*, unreported).

[60] *Best Products v. Woolworth & Co* [1964] *RPC* 226; *Bourjis v. British Home Stores* (1951) 68 *RPC* 280.

[61] See J. Phillips in Franzosi (ed.), 94.

[62] See p. 543. The UK provisions formerly covered 'exposing for sale or hire' rather than offering, because such exposure fell short of an offer: see Fellner, para. 5.151. Although this has been deleted, the same act will almost certainly be covered, either as 'stocking' or 'use'.

[63] Formerly such acts were explicitly dealt with by RDA s. 7(4), with 'kit' being defined as 'a complete or substantially complete set of components intended to be assembled into an article'. Would the sale of a computer program which enabled a printer to employ a particular design-protected font be treated as use of a product in which the design is incorporated? The answer seems to be that such 'indirect use' is not covered by the harmonized and Community regimes, though it might well be by national rules on joint tortfeasance: for the UK, see p. 1075. See Ohlgart in Franzosi (ed.), 137–8.

A more interesting consequence of the fact that the list is non-exhaustive is that it means that the scope of the concept of use is vague. An important question will be whether 'use' is to be limited to activities of the same sort (*ejusdem generis*) as those listed, which relate to the manufacture and distribution of *products*. The better view is that it should be so limited, especially given the broad definition of design so that it can now encompass subject matter previously the preserve of copyright and trade mark law. For example, if a cartoon character has been registered as a design, one may ask whether it is used when the cartoon is broadcast for reception on television (or used on a web site)? In Spain, prior to the harmonization Directive, the broadcasting of a design was held non-infringing,[64] and such a conclusion under the harmonized and Community regimes would be welcome. Recital 21 of the Regulation states that the right 'should also extend to trade in products embodying infringing designs', and supports a view that the meaning of 'use' is to be confined to 'trade in products'.[65] On this basis use would not cover broadcasting.

4.1.3 Absolute Monopolies

As regards registered national designs and Community designs, the protection conferred is 'absolute': the rights are full exclusive rights like those conferred by patents, rather than qualified rights of the sort given by copyright, that only control the use of reproductions of the registered designs. The Commission was of the view that the right must be 'an efficient and strong right, sought after by industry'.[66] The effect is that the proprietor of a registered design need not be concerned with whether the defendant copied the design or arrived at the design independently.

4.1.4 Qualified monopolies: Unregistered Community Designs and cases of deferred publication

However, two qualifications to this general proposition need to be recognized. The rights conferred by Unregistered Community Designs and the rights conferred by Registered Community Designs which have yet to be published are confined to the situation where the defendant's use results from copying the protected design.[67] This reflects the belief that it would be wrong to stop somebody using a design which they developed in circumstances where they could not have ascertained from a central register that the design was protected.[68] In the absence of such a published source from which a user could be placed on notice of earlier rights, a person should only be prevented from using a design if they can be shown to have derived that design from the claimant. Copying will, no doubt, be for the design proprietor to prove on the balance of probabilities and it will be for a given Community Design Court to rely on its own rules of evidence.[69] In the UK, in the copyright and unregistered design context, courts

---

[64] Cf. *Heirs to Eduardo MS v. Television Espanola en Canarias SA* discussed by L. Gimeno, 'Spain: Design Right' [1997] *EIPR* D 216.

[65] The definition of design, however, indicates clearly that the appearance of graphic symbols is to be protected. In this respect, confining use to use on material products, rather than immaterial media such as the web, seems unduly limiting. The effect of this narrow construction is also to exclude web design from the field of designs law.

[66] EC Green Paper, para. 6.4.4. The CDR, Recital 21 states that such a right 'is consistent with its greater legal certainty'. The position before harmonization had not been uniform. Whilst most countries conferred a full monopoly, some, such as Germany, required derivation to be proved. See Suthersanen, 201.

[67] CDR, Art. 19(2), (3). It had been proposed that liability should turn on bad faith, but this was rejected. See Musker, 122; V. Saez, 'The Unregistered Community Design' [2002] *EIPR* 585, 586–7.

[68] Though this would be the case in the UK for secret designs.

[69] Cf. Ohlgart in Franzosi (ed.), 121–2, arguing that the rules as to evidence in such cases are Community rules.

have been willing to infer copying from the circumstances by focusing on similarities between the designs, evidence of the defendant's access to the claimant's work, and the plausibility of independent creation. Article 19 elaborates that use 'shall not be deemed to result from copying the protected design if it results from an independent work of creation by a designer who may reasonably be thought not to be familiar with the design made available to the public by the holder': it is difficult to imagine that without this provision a court would have concluded that copying had taken place.

Although the Regulation clearly imposes a requirement of 'copying' for Unregistered Community Designs and the rights conferred by Registered Community Designs which have yet to be published, it is silent on two further matters. First, it does not state whether such copying can be indirect as well as direct. Second, it does not state whether a person who sells a product to which the design has been applied is liable for infringement even though the person was ignorant of the fact that the product carried a design which had been copied from a protected design. On a literal reading, in both situations, 'the contested use results from copying the protected design' and falls outside the clause clarifying when a use 'shall not be deemed to result from copying'. Nevertheless, it does seem harsh to hold a secondary infringer liable in the absence of any *mens rea,* and at least one commentator has asserted that the relevant Article can be interpreted in accordance with general principles to avoid such an outcome.[70]

4.2 SCOPE

Under the harmonized and Community regimes, the scope of protection conferred is defined as including 'any design which does not produce on the informed user a different overall impression'.[71] The court should structure its assessment by first identifying the claimant's and defendant's designs. The court should then place itself in the shoes of the 'informed user'. Third, the court should ensure that the 'informed user' is apprised of the 'degree of freedom of the author in creating his design'.[72] Finally, the court should compare the designs. The second and third stages were considered in the context of our discussions of novelty in Chapter 27. It is to the first and last stages that we now turn our attention.

4.2.1 What is being compared?

The first matter is to determine what is being compared. Here the problem is identifying the relevant features of the claimant's design and the defendant's product. This task will differ depending upon whether the relevant right is registered (a national registered design or Registered Community Design) or unregistered (in the case of the Unregistered Community Design).

In the case of registered designs, the claimant's design will be defined by reference to the representations. It should be recalled that Recital 11 of the Directive indicates that protection corresponds to the features 'shown *visibly* in an application', so it is likely that a tribunal will start by considering the design's visual appearance. However, the relevant court can take into account the description or any partial disclaimers, insofar as they are permitted under national or Community schemes.[73] It must also exclude from consideration features which

---

[70] Ohlgart in Franzosi (ed.), 124–6; Musker, 122.

[71] Designs Dir., Art. 9(1); RDA s. 7(1); CDR, Art. 10(1). Cf. TRIPS, Art. 26, requiring that protection extend to use of a design which 'is a copy, or substantially a copy, of the protected design'.

[72] Designs Dir., Art. 9(2); RDA s. 7(3); CDR, Art. 10(2).

[73] RDA s. 7(4).

cannot benefit from design protection: features dictated by function, and interconnections excluded by Article 7(2) of the Directive.

It should be recalled that the protection sought, both in the UK and at the OHIM, might be for part of an article or even for some aspects only of a design. In contrast, the defendant's design has to be ascertained by examining the particular uses which are alleged to infringe. Where the claimant has claimed the design for the total appearance of a product and the defendant has used exactly the same design on the same product, the comparison will be straightforward. But it will be less straightforward where the claimant's design is for part of a product, or where a defendant's design differs or is used on a different product.

Where a design proprietor has only registered part of a product or part of a design then it seems that, when comparing the defendant's use with the claimant's registration, matter added by the defendant which is of a sort specifically not claimed by the claimant must be ignored. To return to an example used in Chapter 26 of the design of a bend in a toothbrush, where the registration disclaimed colour, writing, and patterning and only sought protection for the shape of the bend. Presumably, the comparison must be 'part' for 'part', so the fact that the defendant's use is in different colours, or bears strikingly different patterning, is irrelevant (even if these would cause it to create a different overall impression). These additions or differences might justify the defendant registering a new design (for the additions individually or in combination with the shape), but would not be taken into account when deciding whether the shape of the bend was identical or produced a different overall impression on an informed user. The comparison to be made is only between the shapes of the bends.

One consequence of the 'part'-for-'part' comparison is that a design which solely claims shape will only be infringed by making a product (or dealing with a product made) to that shape. This means that a design for a three-dimensional product, such as the design of an automobile, would not be infringed by use on two-dimensional products, such as posters or table mats. Here the defendant is guilty of 'use' by sale of an article *depicting* a design, but not 'putting on the market...of a product...to which [the design] is applied'. The design, that is the shape, has not been 'applied' to the poster or table mat. (For the same reason, a book featuring images of such designs will not infringe, though, as we already observed, this may not be the case if the designer claimed not just shape but also features of colour, line, or pattern.)

In the case of Unregistered Community Designs, the tribunal will not have the benefit of the bureaucratic mechanisms used in defining the product. In such cases, no doubt the tribunal will initially be involved in comparing the designs as a whole. But given the definition of design as 'the appearance of the whole or part of a product', that should not be the end of the inquiry. Indeed, a claimant should be entitled to claim Unregistered Community Design as regards not merely the whole design of the whole product, but also any single feature of the design of the whole product, or design for part of the product, or combination of features that are sufficient to render the claimed matter new and having individual character. In such cases, the comparison that the tribunal must make is likely to be determined by claimants' delineation of their claim according to procedural rules of the particular jurisdiction. In England and Wales, a claimant would be required to set out the design elements claimed in their statement of case, which would then be treated by the court in a similar manner to the bureaucratic delineation of the design in the register.

4.2.2 The comparison

It is difficult to predict how the various tribunals will operate in relation to the comparison of designs. Although Recital 11 of the Directive indicates that protection is conferred for the features 'shown *visibly* in an application', so it is likely that a tribunal will start by considering the design's visual appearance, that does not appear to exhaust the inquiry. At least on one reading (where the 'and' is disjunctive), the Recital goes on to indicate that other features are protected which are at least 'made available to the public by way of publication or consultation of the relevant file' (that is, by reference also to the description). Bearing in mind the broad definition of design to include the 'texture and/or materials of the product itself', and that the test is one of 'overall impression', the better view is that the comparison is not merely visual. As such, the court should consider the overall effect or impact of the design.

When making the comparison, the court, adopting the mantle of the informed user, takes into consideration the 'degree of freedom of the designer in developing his design'.[74] In the context of acquisition/validity, an equivalent consideration enabled the tribunal to be generous to the designer by treating minor variations in a highly constrained field as conferring individual character. In the context of infringement, most commentators have similarly assumed that the effect is to limit the protection of features in a crowded field to virtually identical features.[75] That would certainly make sense if we were to take into account the design freedom of the defendant, or the design freedom in the field in question: after all, if they have made a design which varies from the claimant's they have achieved as much as the first designer. However, when Article 9(2) says, in the context of 'scope of protection', that we are to consider the degree of freedom *of the designer in developing his design,* we could reasonably infer that the relevant freedom is that of the design proprietor and that the Directive requires the court to give strong protection to a designer who developed a new design in a highly constrained field. While this latter construction seems to accord better with the language, it has little to recommend it in principle. From a principled perspective, the levels of protection should correspond to the level of difference: in a heavily constrained field where design activity is limited, protection should also be highly limited.

In general, the informed user is required to assess whether the designs being compared produce a 'different overall impression'. It seems that the test of difference is closely related to the test of individual character, which is defined in much the same way. In other words, we can infer that, if the defendant's design has 'individual character' compared with the claimant's, as regards the relevant features being compared, it can be said not to infringe. However, the Directive refers the informed user to certain factors in the context of the assessment of individual character which are not mentioned in relation to the scope of protection. More specifically, it will be recalled that the informed user is to have regard to the existing design corpus, the product, and the industrial sector.[76] Will these be taken into account in assessing infringement? The answer to this will be directly relevant to deciding to what extent the comparison is not merely between the paper representation of the claimant's design and the defendant's product, but is also to take account of the difference between the claimant's design and the existing state of the art. Under many national laws prior to harmonization such considerations were relevant. Put positively, such a test would state that the greater the accomplishment, the greater the scope of protection.[77] Used negatively, such a test would lead defendants to argue that their designs were highly similar to designs available before the priority date of the claimant's design.

---

[74] Designs Dir. Art. 9(2); RDA s. 7(3); CDR Art. 10(2).
[75] For an example, see the *Danish nappy case* [1990] *EIPR* D–196.
[76] Designs Dir., Recital 13.
[77] In German law this was referred to as *Abstandläre.*

4.2.3 The persistent problem of the relevance of the product

Although protection is not limited to the product for which the design was registered, there are substantive limits to the principle of the 'irrelevance of the product'. This is particularly the case where the design comprises the shape of a three-dimensional item. In such cases, the design and product will be so inseparable that use of a similar design for a different product will usually fail to produce the same overall impression on the informed user. This can be seen if we consider two designs which are intended to be complementary, such as a dining table and a sideboard. Each may be made out of similar materials (say, oak), use simple lines, and give off a chunky though not inelegant appearance: yet it would be difficult for an informed user in such a situation to say the two designs produced the same 'overall impression', because one design has drawers and cupboards, as well as door handles, whereas the other has a flat top and four legs. The designs may be in the same 'style', but the *appearance* of the two products will differ. Where the appearance of the product and the nature of the product have an inseparable connection, the product will matter.[78]

5 EXCEPTIONS AND DEFENCES

The Directive and Regulation provide for, and the UK Act implements, certain 'limitations of the rights conferred' by the national design right or Community design.[79] Three of these relate specifically to ships and aircraft and need not be discussed.[80] Three others merit at least a brief discussion. Article 13(1) of the Directive states that:

[t]he rights conferred by a design right upon registration shall not be exercised in respect of:

(a) acts done privately and for non-commercial purposes;

(b) acts done for experimental purposes;

(c) acts of reproduction for the purposes of making citations or of teaching provided that such acts are compatible with fair trade practice and do not unduly prejudice the normal exploitation of the design, and that mention is made of the source.[81]

The Directive and Regulation also contain provisions on 'exhaustion' of rights, and the repair of complex products, and the UK Act and Regulation contain some other specific limitations. We will look at all these in turn.

---

[78] However, the former Benelux position that a change in the function of the product will take it outside the scope of protection, even if appearance is the same, can no longer be good law. In one case it was held that the design of a toy car, which included pedals, was not infringed when used as the immobile casement for a stool in a barber's shop. This is surely a classic case of use of an identical design on a different product.

[79] TRIPS, Art. 26(2) permits 'limited exceptions ... provided that such exceptions do not unreasonably conflict with the normal exploitation of protected industrial designs and do not unreasonably prejudice the legitimate interests of the owner of the protected design, taking account of the legitimate interests of third parties'.

[80] Designs Dir., Art. 13(2); RDA s. 7A(2)(d)–(f); CDR, Art. 20(2).

[81] Designs Dir., Art. 13(1); RDA s. 7A(2)(a)–(c), (3); CDR, Art. 20(1). The curious phrasing in terms of a prohibition on exercise of the rights is difficult to account for, and has not been adopted in the UK implementation.

5.1 ACTS DONE PRIVATELY AND FOR NON-COMMERCIAL PURPOSES

Designs law has traditionally been concerned with uses of designs in trade.[82] However, since the delineation of rights does not confine their scope to commercial uses, such non-trade activities are excluded by way of a limitation.[83] The meaning of 'private' and 'non-commercial' were discussed in relation to section 60(5)(a) of the Patents Act 1977,[84] and there is no reason to suppose that a different construction will be placed on the exception to national registered design or Community designs (whether Registered or Unregistered Community Designs).

5.2 ACTS DONE FOR EXPERIMENTAL PURPOSES

This defence corresponds to the exception available under section 60(5)(b) of the Patents Act 1977, and the case law interpreting that will provide useful guidance on the scope of this limitation.[85] Given that harmonized and Community designs law can protect designs informed by functional considerations (but not those features 'dictated by function'), the inclusion of such a defence seems warranted,[86] though its use may be rare. Imagine, for example a company trying to discover the optimal shape of a car chassis in terms of air resistance. The company might create five designs for testing, one of which falls within the design proprietor's protection. Such tests would be non-infringing.

5.3 ACTS OF REPRODUCTION FOR CITATION AND TEACHING

The exception relating to citation and teaching is not derived from existing patent law, and warrants more detailed discussion. The limitation seems to recognize that the breadth of the new law (particularly the wide definition of design, coupled with the principle of the irrelevance of the product and the wide ambit of the notion of use) presents the possibility of design protection inhibiting a wide range of activities which were hitherto only subject to copyright law.

The citation limitation may prove to be of greater significance than has hitherto been recognized.[87] As we have seen as regards three-dimensional designs, the reproduction of the design in a book or newspaper will rarely, if ever, amount to infringement. However, it is not possible to be nearly so confident about the reproduction of designs comprising other features. For example, a cartoon character or logo may be protected as a Community or national design, and this may give the design proprietor the right to prevent the sale of products, such as books and newspapers, to which the design is applied. The citation defence allows such uses in the specified circumstances (namely that such acts are compatible with fair trade practice, do not unduly prejudice the normal exploitation of the design, and that mention is made of the

[82] EC Green Paper, para. 6.4.7.2.

[83] TRIPS, Art. 26(1) only requires rights to be granted over acts which are undertaken for commercial purposes.

[84] See pp. 563–4 above.

[85] See pp. 563–4 above. One difference worth observing between the Patents Act provision and that in relation to designs is that the exempted experimental purposes are not restricted to ones relating to the 'subject matter' of the design: in principle, a design may be employed for experiments that do not relate to the design itself.

[86] Cf. Ohlgart in Franzosi (ed.), 143 ('there is no reason for a design-developer to base his design work on somebody else's protected design').

[87] The French terms *illustration*, and German *Zitierung*, confirm a broad understanding of citation as quotation or illustration.

source). A book about cartoons, logos, or a company that makes the products or the designer thereof (e.g. a book about Terence Conran or Phillip Starck), might be able to reproduce the designs in the book.

The teaching limitation exempts reproduction for the purposes of teaching. A school teacher of carpentry or metalwork may want to demonstrate how to produce certain design-protected features, and this exception makes such acts non-infringing. Equally, a teacher of intellectual property law might want to reproduce logos as part of the process of teaching when a design or figurative trade mark is infringed. The defence is likely to be more important in schools of art and design.[88] There seems no reason, however, for confining 'teaching' to the activities of educational establishments, so it might also include demonstrations for apprentices in the private sector.

Having established the potential importance of the defence, it is important to recognize its limitations. First, it is confined to 'acts of reproduction'. On one construction, dealings in products involving reproductions are not covered. This would seem to be unobjectionable, as there is no reason to allow a teacher or student to sell the designed product. Despite this, the limitation to reproductions could seriously undermine the citation defence. Perhaps, one way round this is to interpret the prohibition on the design proprietor exercising rights 'in respect of' reproductions broadly, so that selling a book featuring a reproduction of a design is seen as an activity 'in respect of' the act of reproduction.[89] Although broad interpretations of the limitation on rights are not usually acceptable under European intellectual property law, such an interpretation seems justified here, given that the defence is subject to further limitations, to which we should now turn.

The defence is subject to a rather strange version of the three-step test which we have already encountered in the Berne Convention, and extended through TRIPS to designs and patents. However, in contrast to the TRIPS requirement that the limitation does not 'unreasonably conflict with the normal exploitation' or 'unreasonably prejudice the legitimate interests of the owner', the conditions imposed are that the acts are 'compatible with fair trade practice', and 'do not unduly prejudice the normal exploitation of the design'. Moreover, a third condition, that 'mention is made of the source' is also added. This has been described as the grant of 'a moral right of paternity on the Community design holder'.[90] It is not clear whether 'the source' might not be regarded as the manufacturer or the designer rather than the design proprietor. A cautious user might be best advised to mention all three!

5.4 EXHAUSTION

Although 'importation' is specifically included in the list of prohibited uses, Community exhaustion applies under the Directive, and as regards Community designs under the Regulation.[91] This is Community exhaustion only, and occurs when the product has been 'put on the market in the Community by the holder of the Community design or with his consent'. Presumably, the implication is that member states may not provide for international exhaustion, because such a provision would undermine the internal-market objectives of the Directive. For discussion of the merits of such a position see Chapter 41.

---

[88] EC Green Paper, para. 6.4.7.3.

[89] Ohlgart in Franzosi (ed.), 144 favours a broad construction to cover any form of use of the protected design.

[90] Ohlgart in Franzosi (ed.), 144.

[91] Design Dir., Art. 15; RDA s. 7A(4); CDR, Art. 21.

5.5 A UK-ONLY LIMITATION: ACTS COMMITTED BEFORE THE GRANT OF THE CERTIFICATE OF REGISTRATION

As regards UK registered designs, a limitation applies to acts committed before the date of grant of the registered design. The date of registration, from which the first five-year monopoly commences, is the application date.[92] However, since such applications are not open for inspection until registration, it was thought unfair to permit a design proprietor to sue as regards acts occurring between application and registration. (This is strange, given the contrary position in trade mark and patent law.) Such a limitation is not clearly permissible under the Directive, though one commentator has suggested that member states are free to provide for defences (and since the Community Design Regulation contains a prior use defence which is not provided for in the Directive, this may be correct).[93] Certainly, the impact of this defence will be of little significance, given that most registrations occur within three months of the application, and if the design has been made available to the public, the design proprietor will be able to rely on Unregistered Community Designs (and, if not, may be able to rely on copyright or the UK's unregistered design right).

5.6 A UK-ONLY LIMITATION: CROWN USE

Although there is nothing in the Directive permitting it,[94] the UK has retained certain provisions relating to 'Crown use'.[95] This permits any Government department and any person authorized in writing by such a department to use a UK registered design 'for the services of the Crown'. A classic example might be the use of a design for a gun, nuclear missile, or mask suitable for use in the case of an attack with chemical or biological weapons. Compensation should be paid to the design proprietor or exclusive licensee, on the basis of lost profits.[96] If the sum cannot be agreed, it may be determined by a court.[97] From 1 October 2005, the Regulations also allow for Crown use of Community Designs (with a similar scheme for compensation as for UK registered design).[98]

5.7 OPTIONAL EXCLUSIONS: SPARE PARTS

The exclusions on complex products, interconnections, and functionality go some way toward ensuring that many spare parts will not be protected (and thus that competition in the production of such spares is possible). However, it is clear that designs for things such as car doors or hubcaps, where the designs are visible in use but not dictated by function, or designed to enable objects to be connected together, will often fall outside those exclusions, and so are in principle protected. The European legislature was unable to formulate an acceptable set of laws relating to spare parts that would allow their manufacture for the purposes of ensuring competition in the spare-parts market. However, a compromise was reached to the effect that the

---

[92] RDA s. 3C(1).

[93] Musker, 67. As we will see, the Commission is still working to harmonize the market in spare parts.

[94] Nevertheless, the Community Regulation implies, by recognizing a similar derogation, that the provisions of the Directive are not exhaustive on such matters: see CDR Art. 23 (which allows member states to permit use of Community design by or for the government but only to the extent that the use is 'necessary for essential defence or security needs').

[95] RDA s. 12, Sched. 1.   [96] Sched. 1, para. 2A.   [97] Sched. 1, para. 3.

[98] Community Designs Regulations 2005, Schedule 5 (Regulation 5). For an overview of the fate of spare parts in the UK see *Dyson v. Qualtex* [2006] *RPC* 31, para 3ff (CA).

existing laws in member states should be maintained or possibly 'liberalized', pending further work by the Commission.[99]

Article 14 of the Directive therefore states that

Member States shall maintain in force their existing legal provisions relating to the use of the design of a component part used for the purpose of the repair of a complex product so as to restore its original appearance and shall introduce changes to those provisions only if the purpose is to liberalize the market for such parts.[100]

The 'standstill-plus' or 'freeze-plus' provision (as this is sometimes known) is strangely worded and difficult to understand. The limitation to 'use of the design' does not mean that the design-protected component must already have been in existence, and all we are concerned with is the act of repair—after all, the act of repair would seldom amount to a 'making' of a complex product. Rather, the term 'use' here means 'making, offering, putting on the market, importing, exporting or using': so 'use of the design of a component part used for the purpose of the repair' includes manufacture of component parts for repair. The upshot of this is, as Jacob LJ bemoaned in *Dyson v. Hoover,* that there is 'no general rule about what can and cannot be done about spare parts within Europe'.[101]

A more perplexing issue is whether a legal provision *relates to the use* of the design of a component part *for repair* only if the provision is formulated in terms of an exception to the design-owner's rights, or possibly as a positive user's right, or whether a national provision can legitimately comprise an exclusion from the scope of protection altogether.[102] Two readings are possible. According to the narrow reading, the limitation of Article 14 to parts that are to be made, sold, or used *for repair* implies that such designs are still to be protected as regards *other uses* (for example in construction of the complex product). Moreover, in its requirement that such repair be 'so as to restore [the complex product's] original appearance', the Directive seems to have in mind the bespoke manufacture of a component part for a particular damaged or non-functioning complex product. According to a broader reading, in the reference to 'liberalization of the market' for such parts, the Directive implies that member states may exclude such parts from protection altogether, as it is difficult to see how a market in products can be created which limits how they might be used. Perhaps the ECJ, if called on to interpret the limits of what is acceptable under Article 14, will accept a middle-ground position. However artificial it may be, one such position is that a member state may be permitted to provide third

---

[99] Designs Dir., Recital 19. Article 18 of the Directive required the Commission to submit an analysis of the consequences of the provisions of the Directive for Community industry by 2004 and to propose any necessary changes by 2005. As we will see, the Commission is still working to harmonize the market in spare parts.

[100] The Council had previously sought to allow a 'free for all', i.e. giving the member states carte blanche to introduce or change national legal provisions in this area. See H. Speyart, 'The Grand Design' [1997] *EIPR* 603, 609. Parliament had wanted a harmonized system of fair and reasonable remuneration for right holders covering any use of the design of a component part in the repair of a complex product.

[101] [2006] *RPC* (31) 769, 776 (para. 4).

[102] Apparently, Denmark has interpreted the standstill by retaining its old 15-year term for such component parts. If it is correct that a provision *relates to use for repair* if its scope goes beyond, but would cover, such uses, then perhaps British implementation by removal of the 'must-match' exception breached Art. 14, which requires member states to maintain in force the provisions and introduce changes only to liberalize the market. The Patent Office had commented that, given the designs of such parts could not be registered, there was 'no possibility of greater liberalisation and consequently no possibility of change': Patent Office, *Legal Protection of Designs: A Consultation Paper on the Implementation in the United Kingdom of EC Directive 98/71/EC* (12 Feb. 2001), 17, para. 47 (concluding that the existing exclusion would merely be reframed using the terminology of the Directive).

parties with freedom to manufacture component parts in anticipation of a market for them, as long as any such parts are issued to the public in packaging that specifically indicates that the parts are only to be used for repair of certain identified complex products (or to trade channels which can reasonably be anticipated to use the parts in this way).

The British implementation, assuming (probably correctly) that absolute exclusions were not permitted under the Directive, deleted the previous exclusion of so-called 'must-match' features,[103] and instead inserted an exception or defence in section 7A(5) of the amended Act. This states that the right in a registered design of a component part (which may be used for the purpose of the repair of a complex product so as to restore its original appearance) is not infringed by the use for that purpose of any design protected by the registration. Section 7(2) indicates that use for these purposes includes making and putting on the market a product in which the design is incorporated.[104]

The Regulation contains a provision which is differently worded, but probably has a similar effect. Article 110 states that 'protection as a Community design shall not exist for a design which constitutes a component part of a complex product used...for the purpose of the repair of that complex product so as to restore its original appearance'.[105]

After the adoption of the Directive, the Commission consulted with manufacturers of original parts and spare parts, with the aim of arriving at a voluntary agreement which provided fair and reasonable remuneration.[106] Given that, in the words of the Commission, the parties were completely opposed, it is not surprising that the voluntary agreement failed. In light of this breakdown, the Commission undertook a study on the possible options for harmonizing the after-markets in spare parts.[107] While the study focused on the automotive sector, the subsequent proposals will apply to any sector where replacement and repair of complex products occurs. Drawing upon this study, the Commission decided that 'the option to exclude design protection in the aftermarket for spare parts is the only effective one to achieve an internal market'.[108] To this end, in 2004 the Commission proposed that Article 14 of the Directive be amended so as to introduce what is in effect a right of repair. If adopted the new Article 14(1) will provide that 'protection as a design shall not exist for a design which constitutes a component part of a complex product...for the purposes of repair of that complex product so as to restore its original appearance'. To alleviate concerns about quality control and safety, member states would also be obliged to ensure that consumers were duly informed about the origin of spare parts. While the proposal to end design protection for spare parts has been subject to considerable criticism, in November 2007 the Commission's proposal received the unanimous

---

[103] RDA s.1(1)(b)(ii), prior to amendment, excluded from protection 'features of shape and configuration of an article which are dependent upon the appearance of another article of which the article is intended by the author of the design to form an integral part'. Such an exclusion continues to exist for UK unregistered design right under CDPA s. 213(3)(b)(ii) and is discussed in Ch. 30, pp. 694–6 below.

[104] While this is a genuine attempt at compliance, it is difficult to see how it can be said to 'liberalize' the market.

[105] See F.-K. Beier, 'Protection for Spare Parts in the Proposals for a European Design Law' (1994) 25 *IIC* 840, 868–9 (considering whether the limitation to three years in a previous proposal was compatible with TRIPS).

[106] Parliament finally accepted the Council's request that this provision should not be incorporated into the text after receiving assurances from Commissioner Mario Monti that the Commission would issue a declaration referring to such a consultation exercise and that this would appear in the *Official Journal* along with the text of the directive.

[107] *Proposal for Directive of the European Parliament and the Council amending Directive 98/71/ERC on the legal protection of designs* COM(2004) 582 final (14 Sept. 2004), 6–7.

[108] Ibid, 7. See J. Strauss 'Design Protection for Spare Parts Gone in Europe?' (2005) 27(11) *EIPR* 391.

approval of the Legal Affairs Committee. Given the fate of earlier proposals, it seems that there are still a number of important obstacles that need to be overcome before it is adopted.

5.8 A COMMUNITY-ONLY LIMITATION: PRIOR USE

Article 22 of the Regulation confers a right for a third party to continue activities which they were doing, or preparing to do, before the priority date.[109] This provision, which parallels section 64 of the Patents Act 1977, recognizes that a person who has secretly been using a design would be unfairly prejudiced by the grant of monopoly rights over that design to someone else. To benefit from the right, the user must establish that before the priority date 'he has in good faith commenced use within the Community, or has made serious and effective preparations to that end'. The 'user right' is inapplicable if the design being used has been copied from the Registered Community Design.[110] The right allows the previous user to 'exploit the design for the purpose for which its use had been effected, or for which serious and effective preparations had been made', before the priority date. The previous user therefore will not be able to expand its activities into other arenas, for example by applying the design to new articles. The right is a personal right, in the sense that it cannot be exploited by way of licensing, and can only be transferred as part of the business.

---

[109] CDR, Recital 23. At least the Benelux had such rule prior to harmonization.
[110] Though if varied sufficiently such a copied design might not infringe.

29

COPYRIGHT PROTECTION FOR DESIGNS

CHAPTER CONTENTS

1 INTRODUCTION

The fourth regime that can be employed for the protection of designs is copyright law. The relationship between designs and copyright has been the focus of a great deal of attention for the last hundred years, and different countries have attempted to draw lines between the two forms of protection in a number of different of ways. France, classically, allowed for cumulation of design protection with that offered by copyright under the so-called theory of 'unity of art'. In contrast, Italy attempted to make the two regimes mutually exclusive. Although the British position varied through the twentieth century, the 1988 Act sought to limit the operation of copyright in much of the design field, particularly that of three-dimensional design, covered by the new 'unregistered design right'.

Community harmonization of designs only partially dealt with the interface between designs and copyright. While Article 17 of the Directive and Article 96(2) of the Regulation require member states to adopt a policy of cumulation of copyright, they leave it to member states to determine 'the extent to which, and the conditions under which, such protection is conferred, including the level of originality required.' This failure to harmonize the degree of protection afforded to designs through the copyright law of member states inevitably detracts from the goal of harmonization, and has rightly been criticized.[1] The United Kingdom has been permitted to retain its existing laws which only affect 'the extent to which, and the conditions under which' copyright protection is conferred. In this chapter, we initially set out the ways in which copyright might be available for designs, before examining the way in which this protection is limited through the defences contained in sections 51–3 of the Copyright (etc.) Act 1988.

---

[1] L. Bently, 'The Shape of Things to Come: European Design Law', in P. Coughlan (ed.), *European Initiatives in Intellectual Property* (1993), 63, 86–7; Suthersanen, 77–80; Musker, 80 ('requiring copyright protection, yet not harmonizing it, is a curious strategy').

2 SUBSISTENCE OF COPYRIGHT IN DESIGNS

Copyright can provide protection for designs by two routes: either directly, by protecting the form and decoration of articles as artistic works (in particular as sculptures, engravings, or works of artistic craftsmanship); or indirectly, through the protection copyright confers on the author of a preliminary document on which a design is based. In the latter situation the design document will normally be protected as a graphic work but may be protected, exceptionally, as a literary work.

2.1 PROTECTION OF THE DESIGN ARTICLE AS AN ARTISTIC WORK

In order for an article embodying a design to qualify for copyright protection as an artistic work it must fall within the terms of section 4 of the 1988 Act.[2] The most obvious ways in which designs might be protected are as engravings, sculptures, or works of artistic craftsmanship. In each case, only some designs will fall within the category and hence get copyright protection, and exactly which designs will do so is very difficult to predict with any precision.

2.1.1 As an engraving

In some cases it will be possible to argue that features of surface decoration (even functional ones) amount to engravings. Indeed, as we saw in Chapter 3, in *Wham-O v. Lincoln Industries,*[3] the New Zealand Court of Appeal held that both the mould from which a frisbee was pressed and the frisbee itself were engravings. However, we cannot assume from this decision that all surface designs will be protected by copyright as engravings.[4] For example, the Australian Federal Court declined to hold the drive mechanism of a lawnmower to be an engraving. This was on the basis that no consideration of policy or other approach 'could justify straining the English language so far as to call the moulds engravings'.

2.1.2 As a sculpture

Many designs for the shape of three-dimensional artefacts will be susceptible to protection by copyright as 'sculptures'. In *Breville Europe v. Thorn EMI Domestic Appliances*[5] Falconer J held that scallop-shaped moulds for toasted sandwich makers were sculptures; and in *Wham-O,* the Court of Appeal of New Zealand held that a wooden model prototype for a plastic frisbee was a sculpture. However, not all designed artefacts will be sculptures. For example, the plastic frisbees which were created by injecting plastic into a mould were said not to be sculptures. Moreover, Laddie J has recently signalled that the term 'sculpture' will not be construed broadly so as to encompass designs for products where the main considerations are achieving a functional effect: in *Metix UK v. G.H. Maughan*[6] Laddie J said that to constitute a sculpture, the maker must be concerned with shape and appearance rather than just with achieving a precise functional effect.

---

[2] CDPA s. 4.   [3] [1985] *RPC* 127.

[4] *Greenfield Products v. Rover–Scott Bonnar* (1990) 17 *IPR* 417 (FCA, Pincus J) (the term engraving has to do with marking, cutting, or working the surface, usually the flat surface, of an object).

[5] [1995] *FSR* 77, 94.   [6] [1997] *FSR* 718, 722 (Laddie J).

2.1.3 As a work of 'artistic craftsmanship'

Designs may also be protected by copyright if they are taken to be 'works of artistic craftsmanship'.[7] Although in *Hensher v. Restawile*,[8] the House of Lords rejected a claim that the prototype of an upholstered chair was a work of artistic craftsmanship, a significant body of designed artefacts may nevertheless fall within the category. In this respect, it should be observed that the decision admits that a work can be a work of artistic craftsmanship even though it is a utilitarian article. More significantly, despite *Hensher*, there is room to argue that a work may qualify as a work of artistic craftsmanship even though it is intended to be mass-produced. Although Lord Reid and Viscount Dilhorne suggested that craftsmanship implied 'hand made',[9] Lord Simon concluded that 'craftsmanship' in the statutory phrase cannot be limited to handicraft; nor is the word 'artistic' incompatible with machine production.[10]

2.2 INDIRECT PROTECTION

Although some designs will benefit from copyright protection as artistic works, many more will be able to benefit from copyright protection indirectly, that is through the copyright in the documents which were prepared in the process of devising the finished design. These may be drawings or literary works.

2.2.1 Design drawings

Copyright protection for designs may also arise through the creation of preliminary drawings for the design; that is, through the creation of two-dimensional graphic works on which the final article is based. As these works are protected irrespective of artistic quality, this is the most common way in which copyright is used to protect designs for articles. As copyright protection extends to three-dimensional reproductions of two-dimensional works, and also includes indirect as well as direct reproductions, a person who replicates a three-dimensional design will infringe the rights in the two-dimensional drawing. For example, if copyright exists in a drawing for an exhaust pipe or a LEGO brick, reproduction of the manufactured exhaust pipe or LEGO brick would infringe (subject to what will be said later).[11]

2.2.2 Protection of designs as literary works

Copyright law may also protect certain design documents as 'literary works'. This is the case, for example, in relation to a knitting pattern which describes a series of stitches to be employed to create a pullover of a particular pattern. The protection offered by copyright in this context is very limited. While the copyright owner is able to control reproduction of the pattern, the owner is probably not able to prevent the production of pullovers made to the pattern. The reason for this is that, as the pattern and the pullover are not objectively (or visually) similar (as is required to establish infringement of copyright), these are not reproductions.[12] While the courts have sometimes suggested that infringement of copyright in literary works ought to be

---

7 CDPA s. 4(1)(c).

8 *George Hensher v. Restawhile Upholstery* [1976] *AC* 64.

9 Ibid 77 (Lord Reid); 84 (Viscount Dilhorne).

10 Ibid, 90. *Coogi Australia v. Hysport International* (1998) 41 *IPR* 593 (FCA).

11 See, classically, *British Leyland v. Armstrong* [1986] *RPC* 279.

12 *Brigid Foley v. Ellott* [1982] *RPC* 433 (Sir Robert Megarry VC) (referring to the guide as comprising 'words and numerals'). But cf. *Autospin (Oil Seals) v. Beehive Spinning* [1995] *RPC* 683.

expanded,[13] as yet there have been no circumstances in which a court has held that a written description of a design has been reproduced by the making of articles embodying the design.

3 LIMITATIONS ON THE USE OF COPYRIGHT

Although copyright protection for designs had been limited judicially (through the requirement for originality,[14] the idea–expression dichotomy, and occasionally through the application of public policy considerations),[15] for the last 20 years there has been a widely-held view that copyright protection is inappropriate in much of the design field.[16] This view is commonly based upon an image of copyright law as being concerned with higher works of art (a difficult premise to support if one recalls the myriad of subject matter which copyright protects). Operating from the assumption that copyright law is intended to protect works of art and literature, the case law that extended copyright protection to design drawings for industrial objects (such as exhaust pipes) was subjected to a considerable amount of criticism. For example, in *Franklin Machinery v. Albany Farm Centre* Thomas J in the High Court of New Zealand remarked that:

the law relating to copyright has got quite out of hand…It is probable that a law historically developed to protect artistic works was never suitable for application in the field of industrial design in the first place…Copyright has now invaded the field of technical drawing in a manner which has been dramatic. The most banal of industrial or technical drawings, which involve little more originality than that which accompanies many routine domestic tasks, has come to attract an aggressive claim to copyright protection. Frequently, the monopoly protection which the statute confers is out of all proportion to the degree of originality involved in producing the copyright work. All this is unnecessary.[17]

Similar sentiments informed the radical amendments introduced by the 1988 Act. In short, it was decided that further restrictions should be made of the use that can be made of copyright protection of designs. To this end, sections 51–3 of the 1988 Act introduced a series of defences which minimize the role of copyright, particularly as regards the protection of *three-dimensional designs* (which are now, usually, protected by the tailor-made unregistered design right).[18]

3.1 SECTION 51

Section 51 of the 1988 Act states that copyright is not infringed by making an article from a design document or a model which records or embodies a design where the design is for 'anything other than an artistic work or a typeface'. The upshot of this is that copyright in a blueprint for a three-dimensional industrial design (such as an exhaust pipe) will not be infringed where a person makes articles (here exhaust pipes) that embody the drawing. The

---

[13] See above at pp. 139–40.   [14] *Interlego v. Tyco* [1988] *RPC* 343.

[15] *British Leyland v. Armstrong* [1986] *RPC* 279; *Canon Kabushiki Kaisha v. Green Cartridge Company* [1997] *FSR* 817.

[16] In particular it was thought that copyright protection is too long, and too strong (in that it protects against reproduction of even small parts of works, if the part is 'substantial').

[17] (1991) 23 *IPR* 649.

[18] *Mackie Designs v. Behringer Specialised Studio Equipment (UK)* [1999] *RPC* 717, 723 (intention of the legislature that copyright protection be removed from 'ordinary functional commercial articles').

section provides immunity from copyright liability because the blueprint is a 'design document', and the exhaust pipes are 'articles made to the design' or copies thereof.

Section 51, however, is not intended to remove all protection from such design drawings. Rather, by limiting the role of copyright in relation to three-dimensional designs (as we will see in Chapter 30), section 51 opens up a corresponding space for the operation of unregistered design right. This is because, according to section 236, if the making of an article to a design drawing is an infringement of copyright, then it is not an infringement of unregistered design right.[19] However, if there is a defence to infringement of copyright in the design document, there *may be* an infringement of unregistered design right. Judicial interpretation of section 51 will consequently be critical in defining the relative roles of copyright and unregistered design right in the protection of designs: if the defence is construed broadly, then unregistered design right has a greater role; if the defence is construed narrowly, then the role of copyright dominates.[20]

There are three critical elements to the operation of section 51. First, there must be a 'design document'. Second, the design document must be 'for something other than an artistic work'. Third, the defence only applies where the defendant has made an article to the design or copied an article made to the design. We consider each in turn.

3.1.1 Design documents

Section 51 only applies where there is either a 'design document' or a 'model recording or embodying a design'. A 'design document' means 'a record of a design, whether in the form of a drawing, a written description, a photograph, data stored in a computer or otherwise'.[21] It covers design documents which are both literary and graphic works.

It should be noted that in this context 'design' has a particular and restricted meaning. Design means 'any aspect of the shape or configuration (whether internal or external) of the whole or part of an article, other than surface decoration'. Thus, the exception does not affect copyright in any decorative feature that will be applied in two dimensions to industrial articles.[22] It does, however, affect three-dimensional applications embodying the shape or configuration of an article. The term 'configuration' has also been held to encompass the arrangement of features (resistors, diodes, etc.) on a circuit diagram.[23] As we will see, this definition corresponds to the definition of 'design' used for the purposes of unregistered design right. It is unclear how important is the intention of the designer in determining whether the

---

[19] *Mark Wilkinson Furniture v. Woodcraft Designs (Radcliffe)* [1998] *FSR* 63, 65 (copyright and unregistered design right described as mutually exclusive); cf. *Lambretta Clothing Co. Ltd v. Teddy Smith (UK)* [2003] *RPC* 728, 744 (paras. 60–68) (Etherton J) (discussing how CDPA s. 51 demarcates the relationship between copyright and unregistered design right, but observing that it seeks to achieve more than that, and refusing to accept propositions in *Wilkinson v. Woodcraft*).

[20] *Mackie v. Behringer* [1999] *RPC* 717, 723 (approving broad construction of 'design' so as to ensure protection by design right not copyright).

[21] CDPA s. 51(3).

[22] On the meaning of surface decoration, see *Mark Wilkinson Furniture,* above, discussed in the context of unregistered design right below at pp. 689–90. But cf. *Lambretta Clothing,* above (copying of design for sweater, including colourways, protected by s. 51 defence); cf. *Flashing Badge Co v. Groves* [2007] *EWHC* 1372 (examining CA decision in *Lambretta Clothing* and concluding that s. 51 defence inapplicable to design for surface decoration of flashing badges).

[23] *Mackie v. Behringer,* above, 722–3.

contents of a document constitute a 'design'. While still unsettled, it seems that something is only a 'design' if it is intended by its creator, at the outset, to be a 'design'.[24]

Section 51 also applies to 'models', that is three-dimensional prototypes: so, for example, the wooden prototype for a frisbee could not be relied upon to claim copyright infringement in the reproduction of mass-produced frisbees.

3.1.2 'For something other than an artistic work'

Section 51 only applies where the design or model 'is for something other than an artistic work or a typeface'. Consequently, there is no defence where the design document or model embodies a design 'for an artistic work'. This means, for example, that a sketch of the sitter for a portrait-sculpture or a plan for a building will not be caught by the defence, since they are designs for artistic works.[25]

The section once again raises the question of what is an artistic work. Section 4(1) states that artistic work means a graphic work, photograph, sculpture, work of architecture, or work of artistic craftsmanship. This means that a design drawing for a chair will be a design for an artistic work, if the chair is treated as a work of artistic craftsmanship. Moreover, given that the 1988 Act protects 'sculptures' and 'engravings' as artistic works irrespective of any artistic quality, it is uncertain which industrial objects would fall within these concepts.

3.1.3 Making articles to the design (or copying articles)

The section 51 defence only applies where a person makes an article that corresponds to the 'design' or where a person makes 'a copy' of 'an article made to the design'. The upshot of this is that the section appears to allow a person to make articles (such as exhaust pipes) to the design; or to copy an article (such as an exhaust pipe) which has been made to the design. The defence does not apply, however, where a person merely photocopies a design document: this remains an infringement of copyright.[26]

It has been suggested that the section 51 defence also provides a defence to a person who makes a two-dimensional copy of a (three-dimensional) article that has been made to a design document. In *BBC Worldwide v. Pally Screen Printing*[27] the BBC brought an action for infringement of copyright in the children's television characters, the Teletubbies. These characters were played by actors wearing costumes, and the defendants sold T-shirts bearing pictures of children's television characters. The claimant sought summary judgment, asserting infringement of copyright in the drawings upon which the characters' costumes were based. The defendants sought to resist summary judgment on the basis that there was an arguable defence under section 51. While the defendants admitted that they had derived the characters from the television broadcast (and thus, indirectly, from the documents) they alleged that the T-shirts were copies (albeit in two dimensions) of the costumes which, in turn, were articles made to design drawings. Laddie J said that while he did not find the defendants' case 'terribly attractive', it was arguable. Summary judgment was consequently refused.[28]

---

[24] *BBC Worldwide v. Pally Screen Printing* [1998] *FSR* 665, 672 (design must have been for something other than an artistic work from the outset).

[25] Ibid, 672 (emphasizing that if the drawings of the Teletubbies had been prototypes for a cartoon series the s. 51 defence could not have applied).

[26] *Lambretta Clothing* [2003] *RPC* 728 (para. 65) (Etherton J).

[27] [1998] *FSR* 665, 672.

[28] Affirmed in *Mackie v. Behringer* [1999] *RPC* 717, 723–4.

3.2 SECTION 52: ARTISTIC WORKS USED IN INDUSTRIAL PRODUCTION

Section 52 is intended to limit the term of copyright to 25 years as regards artistic works which are used as the basis for designs which are put into mass-production. In so doing, section 52 is intended to prevent copyright from providing a longer term of protection for industrially exploited designs than would be gained via registration. As such, its purpose is to regulate the boundary between the copyright system and the registered designs regimes.

3.2.1 When the defence applies

The section 52 defence only arises where the artistic work has been exploited (by or with the licence of the copyright owner) by making 'by an industrial process' and marketing articles that are copies of the work. An article is made by an industrial process if more than 50 articles are made (whether or not by hand), all of which are copies.[29] Certain articles do not fall within the scope of the section. These are specified in an Order.[30] These excluded articles, which are of an 'essentially literary and artistic character', are:

(i) works of sculpture, other than casts or models used or intended to be used as models or patterns to be multiplied by any industrial process;

(ii) wall plaques, medals, and medallions; and

(iii) printed matter primarily of a literary or artistic character, including book jackets, calendars, certificates, coupons, dress-making patterns, greeting cards, labels, leaflets, maps, plans, playing cards, postcards, stamps, trade advertisements, trade forms and cards, transfers, and similar articles.

Thus, even if these items are duplicated more than 50 times, they fall outside the defence (and hence retain the full 70-year *post-mortem* copyright term). Consequently, an artistic work which is used as a design for a book jacket remains protected for the full term, but a label for a paint tin is subject to the defence.[31] According to the Order, sculptures retain full protection (even if they are used in an industrial process) only for so long as they are not 'used or intended to be used' in 'any industrial process'. Given that the purpose of the Order is to identify articles of an essentially artistic character, it should be understood to exclude a sculpture from the operation of section 52 even where the sculpture is multiplied on a large scale (for example, with a bust of Beethoven). In contrast, section 52 can be assumed to have been intended to apply to the case of a frisbee, the prototype for which is a sculpture, but the final form of which is merely an industrially-produced artefact; and to the use of a sculpture as the base of a mass-produced table lamp. Paragraph 3(1)(a) of the Order should therefore be interpreted as applying to works of sculpture, other than any sculpture which is employed (or only ever intended to be employed) as an element of, or the basis for, a design for a mass-produced article (which is not itself a sculpture).

---

[29] CDPA s. 52(4)(a); Copyright (Industrial Process and Excluded Articles) (No. 2) Order 1989 (SI 1989/1070).

[30] CDPA s. 52(4)(b); Copyright (Industrial Process, etc) Order 1989.

[31] *Gary Fearns t/a Autopaint International v. Anglo-Dutch Paint and Chemical Co Ltd* [2007] *EWHC* 955 (Ch) (labels for paint tins were not articles of primary literary and artistic character).

3.2.2 The scope of the defence

Section 52 operates to reduce the duration of copyright to 25 years from the first legitimate marketing of articles that are copies of the copyright work. It does this by providing a defence to an action for copyright infringement.[32] The defence is similar in its operation to section 51. However, because the defence is in addition to section 51, it will apply most importantly where section 51 would not. That is, it applies to designs for two-dimensional aspects of an article, where a work was not initially *intended* to be a *design,* or where the work was initially a design for an artistic work which was subsequently exploited.

The defence in section 52 permits a person, in the specified circumstances, to make articles of any description which correspond to the artistic work. This means that if the artistic work has been applied to teapots, after 25 years from the first marketing of the teapots it will no longer be an infringement of copyright to apply the same work to pillow cases. However, the defence leaves the copyright intact where the design is applied to things other than articles: so after 25 years of marketing the teapot, it is still an infringement to photograph the artistic work (in its unapplied state). Anything may, however, be done in relation to an article to which the artistic work has been applied without infringing copyright in the work.

3.3 SECTION 53 (ACTS DONE ON THE BASIS OF RIGHTS IN THE REGISTERED DESIGN)

Section 53 deals with the situation where the ownership of copyright and the proprietorship of a registered design are vested in different people. This may occur through voluntary transactions or as a result of the fact that the principles by which ownership of copyright are determined differ from those relating to registered designs. Section 53 effectively provides a defence to a person who relies on permission from the registered design proprietor, but has failed to gain the authorization of the copyright owner. More specifically, section 53 states that copyright in an artistic work is not infringed by anything done 'pursuant to an assignment or licence' made by the proprietor of the registered design. The idea behind the section is to protect a person who transacts with the registered proprietor by giving that person immunity from copyright infringement.

The defence is qualified, however. It only applies where the person claiming the immunity has acted in good faith in reliance upon the registration and without notice of proceedings for cancellation or rectification of the design (if they exist). In normal circumstances the registered design displaces the copyright as far as third parties need be concerned. As soon as the legitimacy of the registration becomes questionable, however, the copyright regains its force. The acts of the registered proprietor do not fall within the scope of the defence.

---

[32] CDPA s. 52(2). The author's moral right of integrity is left intact, while CDPA s. 79(4)(f) denies the author the right of paternity.

30

UNREGISTERED DESIGN RIGHT

CHAPTER CONTENTS

1 INTRODUCTION

The fifth way in which designs may be protected is via the United Kingdom's unregistered design system. This was established under Part III of the Copyright Designs and Patents Act 1988,[1] as part of the reconceptualization of the way that designs were protected in Britain. Prior to 1988, the boundary between the UK registered design system and the copyright system was placed under pressure as a result of the decision that non-registrable designs—such as the design of car exhaust pipes—could be protected by copyright (so-called 'industrial copyright'). In an attempt to remedy the bizarre situation whereby unattractive designs obtained copyright protection but attractive ones would not, the unregistered design right was introduced to provide short-term, automatic protection to functional designs.[2] In so doing, the new right was meant to provide 'limited protection against unfair misappropriation of time skill and effort expended by the author of the design in the creation of the work'.[3] Consequently, it was decided to limit the registered system to designs for articles for which appearance

---

[1] *Guild v. Eskandar* [2003] *FSR* (3) 23 (para. 8) ('a new, wholly statutory right.') The right was modeled on principles enunciated in the European Council Directive of Dec. 1986 on the Legal Protection of Semiconductor Chips upon which the 1987 Semiconductor Products (Protection of Topography) Regulations were based. See A. Christie, *Integrated Circuits and Their Contents: International Protection* (1995), ch. 4.

[2] *A. Fulton Co. Ltd v. Totes Isotoner (UK) Ltd* [2003] *RPC* (27) 499 (para. 71) ('a medley of political and practical compromise…')

[3] *Farmers Build v. Carier Bulk Materials Handling* [1999] *RPC* 461, 480 *per* Mummery LJ. In *Landor and Hawa International Ltd v. Azure Designs Ltd* [2006] *ECDR* (31) 413 (para. 11), Neuberger LJ described the function of the system as the rewarding of 'imagination and inventiveness'.

mattered, and copyright to the protection of two-dimensional designs or designs for artistic works. As we noted in the previous chapter, the protection given to the proprietor of an unregistered design is intended to dovetail with the protection conferred by the copyright systems in respect of design drawings for three-dimensional designs.

The logic of that division has been undermined both by the harmonization of European registered design law, which covers functional as well as aesthetic designs, and by the establishment of the Unregistered Community Design, which covers a broader field than the United Kingdom's unregistered design right, albeit for a shorter term. While academics and policy makers might raise questions about whether there are any good reasons for maintaining the UK unregistered design right, a knowledge of this *sui generis* right remains essential for understanding the current law of designs. It may also provide valuable lessons for the Community rights.

2 SUBSISTENCE OF THE UNREGISTERED DESIGN RIGHT

As with copyright, unregistered design right arises automatically on creation of a design. An important preliminary step in any litigation in respect of an unregistered design right is that the 'claimant must identify with precision each and every "design" he relies upon'.[4] Given that the unregistered design right is intentionally flexible (as is the Unregistered Community Design Right), insofar as the proprietor is able to trim the right to match what they believe a defendant has copied,[5] if the right is not to be abused the courts will need to develop rules to ensure that that there is a level of correspondence between what is created and what is 'claimed'.

In order to establish the existence of an unregistered design right it is necessary to show (i) that there is a design (ii) which falls outside the exclusions from design right, (iii) which is 'original', and (iv) which qualifies for protection in the United Kingdom. We will deal with each requirement in turn.[6]

2.1 'A DESIGN'

In order for a design to be protected by unregistered design right, it is necessary to show that there is a 'design'. In this context, 'design' means 'the design of any aspect of the shape or configuration (whether internal or external) of the whole or part of any article'.[7]

The subject matter of UK unregistered design right is more limited than that of the harmonized registered design systems, insofar as the UK unregistered design rights do not protect most two-dimensional features.[8] In many other respects, however, the subject matter of

---

[4] *Dyson v. Qualtex* [2006] *RPC* (31) 769, para. 62.

[5] *Bailey (t/a Elite Anglian Products) v. Haynes (t/a RAGS)* [2007] *FSR* 10, para. 18.

[6] See *Dyson v. Qualtex*, above, 779 (para. 14) where Jacob LJ is scathing in his criticism of section 213 which he describes as having only one virtue, its brevity. In other respects it is badly drafted and there is no clear indication of what is intended.

[7] RDA s. 1(2).

[8] The courts have speculated as to whether 'configuration', in contrast to shape, is not confined to three-dimensional characteristics. See *Mackie Designs v. Behringer Specialised Studio Equipment (UK)* [1999] *RPC* 717, 722–3 (holding that 'configuration' should be broadly construed to cover circuit diagrams); *Baby Dan SA v. Brevi* [1999] *FSR* 377, 383 ('configuration' implies some form of arrangement of elements, e.g. the ribbing

unregistered design right is as broad as under registered designs. In particular, it should be noted that an unregistered design right will protect designs which are not aesthetic: in fact, there is no requirement that the design features be visible to the naked eye. In one case it was held that detailed dimensions as to the shape of contact lenses could be a design despite the fact that the lenses would appear identical to any normal observer and could only be distinguished with the aid of sophisticated measuring equipment.[9] The definition of designs for the UK unregistered design right also extends to designs which are purely functional.[10] One of the leading cases, for example, concerned the internal features of a farming machine used to separate the solid and liquid parts of slurry.[11]

A key feature of the definition of design is that it only applies to the *shape or configuration* of articles (or parts thereof). 'Shape and configuration' has the same meaning for unregistered designs as it does for registered designs.[12] It is clear that this does not limit designs to three-dimensional shapes: as Jacob LJ said, 'you can have 2D features of shape or configuration, e.g. one produced by cutting one out from a piece of paper'.[13] There is no reason why a design should 'not subsist in what people would ordinarily call a flat or 2-dimensional thing—for instance a new design for a doily would have shape and could in principle have UDR in it'.[14] Having said this, the courts have also made it clear that patterns (such as a patchwork quilt) and an article coloured in a novel way would not fall within the definition of 'shape' or 'configuration' and as such would not be protected.[15]

Unregistered design rights protect designs for 'articles'. The term is not defined further, but needs to be contrasted with the concept of 'products' utilized in the registered regimes.[16] Unregistered design rights not only apply to designs for whole articles, they also apply to designs for parts of articles. This means that an article may embody a number of different designs. In the case of a teapot, for example, an unregistered design right could reside in the shape of the whole pot, or in a part such as the spout, the handle, or the lid.[17] The main limitation on this is that the design must be of *an aspect* of the whole or part of the article: which has been taken to mean a 'discernible or recognisable' part of the article.[18]

---

arrangement of a hot-water bottle); *Lambretta Clothing Co. Ltd v. Teddy Smith (UK) & Next Retail plc* [2003] *RPC* 728 (Etherton J) (para. 48) (there is nothing to suggest that configuration is not confined to three-dimensional aspects of an article); *Dyson v. Qualtex* [2006] *RPC* (31) 769, 793 (para. 74) (cutting pattern out of piece of paper is 'configuration'). It was held that design right did not protect stitching on mobile phone cases: *Parker v. Tidball* [1997] *FSR* 680, 696. But cf. *A. Fulton Co. Ltd v. Grant Barnett & Co. Ltd* [2001] *RPC* (16) 257, 280 *per* Park J (para. 78) (stitching on case for umbrella treated as protected in case where it produced accentuated rectangular character).

[9] *Ocular Sciences v. Aspect Vision Care* [1997] *RPC* 289; *Fulton v. Totes*, note 2 above (para. 30) ('unregistered design right extends beyond the visually appreciable to other aspects of the design of an article').

[10] *A. Fulton Co. Ltd v. Grant Barnett & Co. Ltd* [2001] *RPC* (16) 257, 270 *per* Park J (para. 34).

[11] *Farmers Build* [1999] *RPC* 461. See also *Dyson v. Qualtex*, above, 781 para. 26 ('UDR can subsist in aspects of detail').

[12] *Lambretta Clothing v. Teddy Smith* [2005] *RPC* 6, para. 15.

[13] *Dyson v. Qualtex*, above, para. 74.

[14] *Lambretta v Smith* [2005] *RPC* 6, para. 24.

[15] Thus in *Lambretta*, ibid, para. 29, it was held that mere choice of different colours for a standard track top was not an aspect of 'shape or configuration'.

[16] It is possible that the shape and configuration of buildings may be protected by unregistered design rights. For similar argument as to whether buildings are 'products' in relation to the harmonized definition of designs, see p. 630.

[17] *Ocular Sciences v. Aspect Vision Care* [1997] *RPC* 289, 422; *A. Fulton Co. Ltd v. Totes Isotoner (UK) Ltd* [2004] *RPC* 16 (CA) (part of a cloth case for portable umbrella).

[18] *Dyson v. Qualtex*, above, para. 23. A photograph of the Dyson wand can be seen in the case report.

2.2 EXCLUSIONS

In order for a design to be protected by unregistered design right it is necessary to ensure that it does not fall within the list of excluded features contained in section 213. This provides that the unregistered design right does not subsist in 'surface decoration', 'methods or principles of construction', or features which 'must fit' or 'must match'.[19]

2.2.1 Surface decoration

Section 213(3)(c) provides that the unregistered design right does not subsist in features of 'surface decoration'. As Jacob LJ explained in *Dyson v. Qualtex*, the exclusion of 'surface decoration' is related to its inclusion within 'ordinary' copyright law.[20] This led Jacob LJ to suggest that the exclusion is confined to 'that which can fairly be described as a decorated surface'.[21] It is clear that surface decoration would cover the application of colour in two dimensions (such as stripes on a shirt),[22] but is not confined to two-dimensional features (strictly defined). This means, for example, that surface decoration would include both the situation where 'a surface is covered with a thin layer and where the decoration, like in Brighton rock, runs throughout the article'.[23] In some situations 'surface decoration' may be three-dimensional: there is no need for it be 'essentially flat'. As such it includes both 'decoration lying on the surface of the article (for example, a painted finish) and decorative features of the surface itself (for example, beading or engraving)'. Consequently, in *Mark Wilkinson Furniture v. Woodcraft Designs (Radcliffe)*, Jonathan Parker J held that the painted finish, V-grooves, and cockbeading on the kitchen furniture the claimant had created was surface decoration and thus not protectable.[24] Other features, such as cornices, quadrants, and handle were not, and as such were protected by unregistered design right (see Fig. 30.1).

In other cases, three-dimensional features may not be regarded as decoration, but as part of the overall shape and configuration: ultimately, the court has to make a value judgement. So, in *A. Fulton v. Grant Barnett*[25] Park J took the view that, although stitching on the seams of a rectangular umbrella case existed 'in a small third dimension', it was an aspect of shape which was not excluded as surface decoration because it gave that case its 'box-like character'. On

---

[19] An initial problem with the drafting of s. 213 should be observed. This arises from the fact that while the nature of unregistered design rights and the way in which these rights are infringed are defined in relation to 'designs', the exclusions relate to 'design rights'. A literal construction of s. 213 would produce the nonsensical result that it would be possible for an infringement to take place in relation to subject matter excluded from the scope of protection: *Mark Wilkinson Furniture v. Woodcraft Designs (Radcliffe)* [1998] FSR 63. This problem has been avoided in relation to the exclusion of 'surface decoration'. This was done by incorporating the exclusion of 'surface decoration' into the meaning of 'design'. Ibid., 72 (relying on the definition of design in CDPA s. 51(3)). It is hoped that similar strategies can be applied to the other exclusions. The reasoning employed in *Mark Wilkinson Furniture* would not resolve the problem for must-fit or must-match features.

[20] *Dyson v. Qualtex* [2006] RPC (31) 769, 793–4 para. 76. Although there may be rare situations where a design may fall between the gaps of the two regimes: ibid.

[21] *Dyson*, ibid, 793–4 para. 81.

[22] *Lambretta v. Smith* [2005] RPC 6, para. 30 (CA) (over-arm stripes on sleeves of track top were surface decoration; mere juxtaposition of colours, not 'configuration').

[23] Ibid, para. 30 (CA).

[24] [1998] FSR 63, 73. Cited with approval by Jacob LJ in *Lambretta v. Smith* [2005] RPC 6, para. 31. See also *Jo Y Jo v. Matalan Retail* [2000] ECDR 178 (embroidery on ladies' garments was surface decoration but other aspects of knitted cardigans, such as the choice of knit or fabric and edging, were not).

[25] [2004] RPC 16, 280 (paras. 78–9). See also, *Christopher Tasker's Design Right References* [2001] RPC 39 (features must be decorative).

Fig. 30.1 The plaintiff's kitchen
Source: Courtesy of Mark Wilkinson Furniture.

the basis that the unregistered design right was developed to protect functional designs, it has been suggested that surface features which have 'significant function' would not be excluded on the basis that they were surface decoration. On this basis the Court of Appeal in *Dyson* held that as the ribbing on the handle of a vacuum cleaner functioned to provide grip, it was not excluded as surface decoration (see Fig. 30.2).

In situations where a design feature is both functional *and* decorative, the courts have said that a subsidiary functional purpose does not take the design aspect out of the exemption if the primary purpose is surface decoration. As Mann LJ said in *Dyson* this will limit the scope of the exception. This is because, if an item of decoration has a functional purpose, 'it will be difficult to say that functional purpose is sufficiently subsidiary to make the feature surface decoration…I think that the subsidiary purpose of beading that is used to conceal a join can also fairly be described as decorative'.[26]

---

[26] *Dyson v. Qualtex* [2006] *RPC* (31) 769, para. 38. For a situation where a design with both a decorative and functional feature was held to be surface decoration see *Helmet Integrated Systems v. Mitchell Tunnard* [2006] *FSR* 41, para. 99–101 (re the scalloping on the visor of a fire fighter's helmet).

Fig. 30.2 Dyson

Source: Courtesy of Dyson, <http://www.dyson.com>.

2.2.2 Methods of construction

Section 213(3)(a) provides that unregistered design right does not subsist in 'a method or prin-ciple of construction'.[27] The provision, which is to be construed narrowly, does not preclude a design from being protected merely because it has a functional purpose.[28] The exclusion of methods of construction from the remit of protection, which has its origins in now-repealed British registered designs law, confines design protection to shape, rather than the ideas or principles underlying a shape. In so doing it ensures that protection does not exist in the method by which a shape is produced, as opposed to the shape itself.[29] That is, it ensures that designers are not able to obtain patent-style protection over the way that articles of a particu-lar style are made.[30] The application of the exclusion can be seen in *A. Fulton Co. Ltd v. Grant Barnett,* which concerned a claim to unregistered design right in rectangular umbrella cases, where the rectangular shape was created in part by the use of stitching. While Park J accepted that the stitching used in making the umbrella cases was a technique, he was happy to pro-tect the shape produced by that method. Accordingly, it appears that the exclusion only bites where the protection of the shape would itself prevent others using the method—that is, where the use of a method can result in only one shape or configuration.[31] In contrast, in *Bailey (t/a Elite Anglian Products) v. Haynes (t/a R.A.G.S.),* Fysh J held that a claim for infringement of unregistered design right in the shape of stitching of micromesh bags for fishing bait failed

[27] CDPA s 213(3)(a).

[28] *Landor & Hawa International Ltd. v. Azure Designs Ltd.* [2007] *FSR* 9, para. 10 (CA).

[29] *Landor & Hawa International Ltd. v. Azure Designs Ltd.* [2006] *FSR* (22) 427, 433 (PCC); [2006] *ECDR* (31) 413 (CA) (para. 10) (explaining that, while the language was 'a little opaque', it would be wrong in principle to attempt to define it further as opposed to applying it, but leaving unclear whether a shape which was the best way of achieving a function would be excluded from protection). Decision upheld on appeal.

[30] *Bailey v. Haynes* [2007] *FSR* 10, para. 62,

[31] *Fulton v. Grant Barnett* [2001] *RPC* (16) 257, 278 (para. 70). Cf. *Parker v. Tidball* [1997] *FSR* 680, 696, where the claimant claimed design right in mobile phone cases, the judge excluded stitching in seams as a method of construction. Copinger, para. 13–55 sees the different results as attributable to the fact that in *Fulton* the seam was intended to produce a design feature, whereas in *Parker* the seam was an unintended result of a method of construction. Perhaps it would be easier simply to regard the remarks in *Parker* as obiter, the stitching not being shape or configuration.

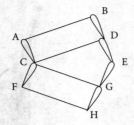

The 1cm Design, showing how it is made of the repeats;

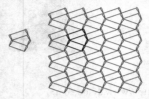

Fig. 30.3 Micromesh bags
Source: Bailey and Anor v. Haines & Ors [2006] *EWPCC* 5 (2 October 2006).

because the claim related to a method of construction.[32] The judge seems to have been influenced by the fact that there were no dimensional limitations on the pattern of threads being claimed. (See Fig. 30.3).

2.2.3 Must-fit

Section 213(3)(b)(i) of the 1988 Act provides that the 'design right does not subsist in...features of shape or configuration of an article which...enable the article to be connected to, or placed in, around or against, another article so that either article may perform its function'. This is known as the 'must-fit' exclusion (although the courts have stressed that it is important to apply the statutory language, rather than the language of the epithet).[33] This exclusion (along with the 'must-match' exclusion) is intended to minimize the significance of the unregistered design right in the protection of spare parts (particularly for automobiles). It has been said that the exclusion should be interpreted 'purposively' and 'should not be given a breadth which would take it far beyond what it was intended to achieve'.[34] There are a number of notable aspects of the exclusion.

(i) The article. The first is that the exclusion specifies that designs are excluded to the extent that they enable an article to be connected (etc.) to another 'article'. In this context, article has been interpreted very broadly as being synonymous with the word 'thing'.[35] Following from this, it has been held that article not only includes machines and objects, it also includes the human body. Thus, it has been held that the aspects of the shape of contact lenses which enable the lenses to fit the eyes of their users, or the aspects of the shape of a mobile telephone that enable it to fit the hand of a person holding it, fall outside the scope of the unregistered design right.[36]

---

[32] [2007] *FSR* (10) 199.   [33] See *Dyson v. Qualtex* [2006] *RPC* (31) 769, para. 27.

[34] *Fulton v. Grant Barnett* [2001] *RPC* (16) 257, 278 (para. 73).

[35] *Ocular Sciences* [1997] *RPC* 289, 425.

[36] Ibid, 425–8; *Parker v. Tidball* [1997] *FSR* 680, 697; *Dyson v. Qualtex*, above, 782 (para. 28). For criticism, see L. Bently and A. Coulthard, 'From the Commonplace to the Interface: Five Cases on Unregistered Design Right' [1997] *EIPR* 401.

(ii) Integrated parts. Where two articles are joined together to make a single article, it has been held that the 'must-fit' exception not only applies to the parts as separate articles, but also to the interfaces that become elements of the integrated whole.[37] However, this view has the potential to produce odd results (apparently, for example, that there would be no unregistered design right in the wing of an aeroplane). Consequently, in *Baby Dan v. Brevi,* Judge David Young QC preferred the view that when units are assembled unregistered design right may subsist in the whole; whereas when design right is asserted in the parts, protection is confined to parts of the design other than the must-fit features.[38]

(iii) No need for designer to have intention to fit. The must-fit exclusion operates where the shape of an article enables it to be attached or connected to another article. In assessing whether an article must fit another article, the designer's intention is irrelevant. The reason for this is, according to Laddie J, because 'the subsection does not require that the designer should know that the features enable the interface, it is sufficient if they do so in fact'.[39]

(iv) Closeness of fit. Features are only excluded as must-fit features if they 'enable' one article to fit with another article.[40] Perhaps the most important question is how closely shapes need to correspond to each other for the feature of one article to be said to enable it to be connected to another.[41]

In *Amoena v. Trulife*[42] Judge Sumption QC suggested that the provision should be read very narrowly. In particular, he said that the must-fit exclusion was 'concerned with a...precise correspondence between two articles, as with a rigid plug and socket, where the functional requirement that one article should fit in or against another displaces original design work'. Consequently, the design of breast prostheses was not excluded under the 'must-fit' exception, because while the prostheses were shaped so that they fitted into bras, the shape of the bra would only *influence* rather than *determine* the details of the design: the prostheses were highly flexible and compliant so that they would fit a number of different bras. However, other High Court decisions have taken a different approach, suggesting instead that features may fall within the must-fit exclusion even though other shapes might do equally well. For example, in *Ocular Sciences,* Laddie J said

[t]here is...nothing in the provision which requires the feature to be the only one which would achieve the proper interface. If a number of designs are possible each of which enables the two articles to be fitted together in a way which allowed one or other or both to perform its function, each falls within the statutory exclusion:[43]

---

[37] *Electronic Techniques (Anglia) v. Critchley Components* [1997] *FSR* 401, 417–19.

[38] [1999] *FSR* 377, 382.

[39] *Ocular Sciences* [1997] *RPC* 289, 424–8 (features of the claimants' lenses were excluded even though they were chosen without the fit requirement in mind).

[40] The term can be contrasted with three related notions: the notion in the must-match exclusion that the appearance of one article must be 'dependent' on that of another, and the two exclusions in the registered design arena of features 'dictated' by function, and features which 'must necessarily be reproduced in their exact form and dimensions' to enable functional connection to another product. See below at pp. 694–6, and above at pp. 634–37. Elements which enables parts to fit together to 'look nicer' are not within the exception: *Ultraframe v. Fielding* [2003] *RPC* (23) 435, 460 (para. 80).

[41] For a discussion about whether parts need to touch and how this issue applies to the must-fit exemption see *Dyson v. Qualtex,* [2006] *RPC* (31) 769, para. 37–38.

[42] Unreported, 25 May 1995, Jonathan Sumption QC, Deputy Judge of Ch. Div., SRIS C/72/95; *Fulton v. Grant Barnett,* note 8 above, 279 (para. 75) (emphasizing importance of exactness, so that a rectangular umbrella case was not excluded because it had to accommodate a rectangular umbrella handle: 'any case of the same approximate dimensions would do that').

[43] *Ocular Sciences,* above, 424–8.

Consequently, Laddie J held that the diameter of the claimant's soft contact lenses was not protected because evidence showed it enabled the lenses to fit onto the eyeball. This approach was approved in *Parker v. Tidball* by Judge Englehart QC, where he held that features of mobile phone casings which permitted use of the phone while inside the case, were excluded on the basis that they were must-fit features. This was despite the fact that the function that the shape performed could have been achieved by a number of other designs.[44]

(v) *Enabling an article to perform its function.* The must-fit exclusion only applies to features of shape or configuration which enable the article to be connected to, or placed in, around, or against, another article *so that either article may perform its function.* Applying this provision, the Court of Appeal in *Dyson* held that insofar as holes in the handle of the wand of a vacuum cleaner (so-called 'bleed holes') enabled the handle to be placed against a flat surface (e.g. a stair carpet), the holes allowed the handle to perform its function as a vacuum-cleaner handle. As such, the bleed holes fell within the exception and thus were not protected.[45]

2.2.4 Must-match

Section 213(3)(b)(ii) of the 1988 Act excludes from unregistered design right features of shape or configuration of an article which are dependent upon the appearance of another article of which the article is intended by the designer to form an integral part.[46] As with the must-fit exclusion, the idea behind this exclusion was to limit the protection afforded to spare parts, particularly for automobiles.

(i) *Appearance.* The must-match exclusion is only concerned with the *appearance* of objects. This is to be contrasted with the must-fit provision, which concerns the interconnection of parts so that either can perform their *function.* If we consider a classic example such as a car door, there will probably be both must-fit and must-match features: the must-fit features will enable the door to fit into the chassis and the handle to fit onto the door; the must-match features will relate to the general shape of the door, in particular any styling features which must match the rest of the car in order to be of an acceptable appearance.

(ii) *'Dependent' upon the appearance of another article.* The must-match exclusion only operates where designs are 'dependent' upon the appearance of another article. The fact that designs are aesthetically linked to (or dependent upon) the appearance of the article as a whole lies at the heart of the rationale for the must-match exclusion.

A part will be dependent and thus unprotected if it is *not* possible for it to be replaced with a different part without radically altering the appearance or the identity of the vehicle as a whole. A Mercedes-Benz with a Volkswagen roof is no longer a Mercedes-Benz but a cannibalized mismatch. Where the owner of a complete article is obliged to replace a worn, damaged, or missing component with an identical component to maintain the appearance of the article, the part will be dependent. Where a part is dependent, the maker of the spare part has to produce a part which looks exactly like the original or it is unsaleable. They have no design freedom. Consequently, it is likely that parts such as the main body panels, doors, bonnet lids, and so forth will be treated as being 'dependent' on the appearance of the car as a whole.[47]

---

[44] Note 8 above, 694. Cf *Dyson v. Qualtex* [2006] *RPC* (31) 769, para. 29 where Jacob LJ said that 'the actual decision may be questionable'.

[45] *Dyson v. Qualtex* above, paras 42–43.

[46] Prior to reform of the registered design system, the must-match exclusion also operated in that context: see Bently & Sherman (1st edn.), 590–2.

[47] See *In Re Ford Motor Co. & Iveco Fiat SpA* [1993] *RPC* 399 (a pre-harmonization registered designs case). The question was not considered by the House of Lords: *R v. Registered Designs Appear Tribunal, ex p Ford*

In contrast, a part will be independent and therefore protected if it can be replaced by a part with a different shape and configuration in such a way that it does not alter the appearance of the article as a whole. If it is possible to a substitute part with another part of different shape and configuration, while leaving the general shape and appearance of the vehicle unaffected, the part will not be dependent. One of the defining aspects of an independent part is that while it (necessarily) contributes to the appearance of the vehicle, it is *subsidiary* to the overall shape. That is, it can be replaced without 'radically altering' the appearance of the vehicle (or article) as a whole. As Jacob LJ said in *Dyson v. Qualtex,* 'if there is, as a practical matter, design freedom for the part, then there is no dependency'.[48]

For example, a steering wheel may be replaced with an alternative wheel of a sportier design while leaving the general appearance of the vehicle unchanged. Likewise, an owner might choose to substitute seats with more comfortable seats. Although the owner of a car might wish the component to blend in with the general style of the vehicle, such items would *not* be dependent on the appearance of another article. This reflects the goal of the section which was to 'protect spare parts to the extent that they have features of shape and configuration which do not have to be copied in order to fit or to match aesthetically'.[49]

(iii) 'Dependence' does not require the other article to exist. The must-match exclusion only prevents protection of those features of an article which must match those of another article. It is also clear that one shape can be dependent upon another article even though the latter may not yet exist. The provision requires the court to assume the existence of another article and decide whether the shape or configuration of the article depicted in the design is dependent on the appearance of that other article.[50]

(iv) Defining the 'other' article. Another notable aspect of the must-match exclusion is that design features are only excluded where they are dependent on the shape of 'another article'. This gives rise to the difficult question of what is meant by 'another article': an issue which was discussed under the old law of registered designs in *In re Ford Motor Co. & Iveco Fiat SpA*.[51] In the case, it was agreed that there were basically two ways of construing the phrase in the context of a part for a car. First, 'another article' could mean the vehicle as a whole, minus the part in question:[52] this is the so-called 'n–1' approach. Alternatively, 'another article' could mean the whole car, including the part in question. While the decision is not altogether clear (nor convincing in its reasoning), the Registered Design Appeal Tribunal ultimately favoured the latter approach.[53] On appeal, the High Court confirmed that in relation to spare parts, 'other article' meant the vehicle as a whole.[54]

(v) Integral part. The exclusion only operates where the features relate to an article which forms an 'integral part' of another article. A part is integral if it is essential to the overall design or look and feel of the article. As such, it excludes inessential parts (the extras) such as a tool kit

---

[1995] *RPC* 167. For unregistered design right cases, see: *Fulton v. Grant Barnett,* note 8 above, 279–80 (particular shape of umbrella case claimed by claimant held not dependent on shape of umbrella); *Ultraframe UK Ltd v. Fielding,* note 40 above, 460 (para. 79) (parts of conservatory roof assembly system which gave 'consistent theme' were not 'dependent').

[48] *Dyson v. Qualtex* [2006] *RPC* (31) 769, 789 para. 63.
[49] 494 *Hansard* (HL), 1 Mar. 1988, col. 110 (Lord Beaverbrook).
[50] *Valeo Vision SA v. Flexible Lamps* [1995] *RPC* 205 (a registered design case).
[51] Note 47 above.   [52] Ibid, 411.   [53] Ibid, 412, 420.
[54] In *Dyson v. Qualtex* [2005] *RPC* 19, Mann J also rejected the n-1 approach stating that, as a matter of logic, if 'article 1 is intended by the designer to form an "integral part" of article 2, then article 2 must comprise article 1' (para. 55).

or a car jack. As most articles or parts of articles that are non-integral will also be independent, it seems that it adds little to the scope of the provision.

The provision is important, however, insofar as it helps to clarify that although a particular item may not stand alone, this does not necessarily mean, therefore, that in addition the item forms part of another article. While articles such as cups and saucers or knives and forks may fit together, this does not necessarily mean that they fall within the scope of the exclusion.[55] For example, while an article such as a cup might need to match a saucer, it is unlikely that the designer would have intended the cup to form an 'integral part' of the saucer.

In order for an article to be treated as an integral part of another article, the designed article in question must be subservient to the appearance of the other article. As such, where the articles play an equal part in the overall product, the design will not fall within the scope of the exclusion. This can be seen, for example, in relation to a unit in a range of kitchen cupboards which was held not to be an article that formed an integral part of another article. Instead, it was seen as one of a 'series of matching articles none of which forms an integral part of another'.[56]

2.3 ORIGINALITY

Unregistered design rights only subsist in 'original' designs. A design is not 'original' if, at the time of its creation, it is 'commonplace in the design field in question'.[57] Deciding whether a design is original involves two stages. First, it is necessary to decide whether the design is original in the copyright sense. That is, in the sense that the design originated with the designer and was not slavishly copied from an existing design.[58] Second, if the tribunal is satisfied that the design is original, it is then necessary to determine if the design is 'commonplace in the field in question'.

The concept of 'commonplace designs' is peculiar to this right. In *Farmers Build v. Carier Bulk* the Court of Appeal said that it would be wrong to attempt any further definition of what 'commonplace' meant.[59] Rather, it preferred to look at the term in the light of its legislative history and purpose. Given that unregistered design right is intended to protect functional designs, only provides relatively weak protection, and includes safeguards excluding the protection of spare parts, Mummery LJ concluded that it would be wrong to interpret 'commonplaceness' broadly. Instead he said that its purpose was 'to guard against situations in which even short-term protection for functional designs would create practical difficulties'.[60] Consequently, once it is shown that the design was not copied, all that is required is that the design must be different in some respects from other designs so that it can be fairly and reasonably described as not commonplace. This second inquiry itself has three stages.

The first stage is to decide what is the *design field*. This is an important stage of the inquiry, because the broader the design field, the more likely it is that a particular design will be held to be commonplace. It has been suggested that the courts should adopt a reasonably broad

---

[55] [1993] *RPC* 399, 419.

[56] *Mark Wilkinson Furniture* [1998] *FSR* 63, 73.   [57] CDPA s. 213(4).

[58] *Farmers Build* [1999] *RPC* 461, 481. *Fulton v. Grant Barnett* [2001] *RPC* (16) 257, 272 *per* Park J (para. 42) (must have been consciously designed rather than arising accidentally). Cf. *Guild v. Eskandar* [2003] *FSR* (3) 23 (paras. 44–56) (recognizing that accidental feature could contribute to originality of design because it was perpetuated on purpose, but holding in the circumstances that the design lacked originality).

[59] *Farmers Build*, above, 479. *Dyson v. Qualtex* [2006] *RPC* 769, 799, para. 98 ('a far from easy concept').

[60] *Farmers Build*, above, 481; *Scholes Windows v. Magnet* [2000] *FSR* 432, 443; *Fulton v. Grant Barnett*, above, 273 (para. 50) (commonplace to be interpreted narrowly rather than widely).

approach when deciding what the appropriate design field is.[61] What matters is the type of design with which 'a notional designer of the article concerned would be familiar'.[62] A similar approach was adopted by the Court of Appeal in *Scholes Windows v. Magnet*.[63] In this case the defendant argued that the claimant's design for decoratively-shaped window frames made in unplasticated PVC was commonplace. The defendant said the assessment of whether a design was commonplace should be made by considering traditional window designs for wooden frames. The claimant disputed this, arguing that the design field was 'PVC window design'. The Court of Appeal rejected that view. It said that, while the words 'design field' bear their 'ordinary and natural meaning', the bounds of which are issues 'of fact and degree', the definition of 'design' in this context relates to shape and configuration, rather than materials or the nature and purpose of the article. Consequently the design field is not to be defined by reference to limitations of this sort. In the case in hand, therefore, the design field was that of window frames generally.[64]

The second stage of the inquiry requires the court to examine the design of other articles in the same field including any allegedly infringing articles. When considering this issue, it is important to bear in mind that a design which is commonplace in a design field will 'be ready to hand', rather than something that 'has to be hunted for and found at the last minute'.[65] The Court of Appeal in *Scholes* emphasized that the court should be concerned with those designs in the field at the time of creation of the design in issue.[66] This may include old designs, even if they are no longer available for purchase, if such designs were still available to be viewed by designers and interested members of the public. Consequently, the claimant's design in *Scholes* was to be considered in the light of the continued presence of Victorian sash windows in the built environment in 1994 (the date of creation of the claimant's design).[67] Other decisions have suggested that the issue of 'commonplaceness' is concerned primarily, and possibly exclusively, with designs which were available in the United Kingdom. As a result, designs only available in foreign countries or in other ways 'obscure' are unlikely to be taken into account.[68]

---

[61] *Lambretta v. Smith* [2005] *RPC* 6, para. 45.

[62] Ibid, para. 30. This is similar to the reading that is given to 'design field in question' in the Semiconductor Products Directive 87/54 (which is where the phrase was taken from). Ibid, para. 46.

[63] [2002] *ECDR* (20) 196; [2002] *FSR* (10) 172. See also, *Ultraframe (UK) v. Eurocell Building Plastics* [2005] *RPC* 36, para. 54 ff (what matters is the kind of material which would be well known to designers of articles of the type in question).

[64] In a case concerning designs of kitchen cabinets, the court held that the design field was 'fitted kitchen furniture' rather than 'cabinetry generally' because kitchen furniture was 'a discrete design field, with its own particular problems and characteristics': *Mark Wilkinson Furniture* [1998] *FSR* 63, 74. Presumably, *L. Woolley Jewellers Ltd v. A & A Jewellery Ltd* [2003] *FSR* (15) 255 (treating design field as '*coin-mounted* jewellery design') and *Spraymiser Ltd & Snell v. Wrightway Marketing Ltd* [2000] *ECDR* 349, 363 (defining field as 'the design of *wooden configurable* figures of the human form') defined the field too narrowly.

[65] *Ultraframe v. Eurocell*, above, 60.

[66] *Scholes Windows*, above, 205 (esp. para. 45).

[67] Old designs will not necessarily remain present in the field: whereas sash windows have a long life, umbrellas break and are quickly thrown away: *Fulton v. Totes* [2003] *RPC* (27) 499, 526 (para. 83).

[68] *Fulton v. Grant Barnett* [2001] *RPC* 257, 273 (para. 52) (an obscure piece of prior art does not render commonplace) (para. 52); *Fulton v. Totes*, above (paras. 73, 78) (Australian and Japanese examples irrelevant: this is not a novelty inquiry) (Judge Michael Fysh QC). Judgment upheld on appeal: *A. Fulton v. Totes Isotoner* [2004] *RPC* 16 (CA) Cf. *Guild v. Eskandar Ltd* [2001] *FSR* (38) 645 (Rimer J) (design field described as 'global one of ladies' luxury fashion' as opposed to the 'sensual/philosopher' market proposed by the defendant); *Spraymiser* [2000] *ECDR* 349, 364 (comparison with design from United States).

Third, the court should examine the design in question to determine how similar it is to designs in the same field.[69] The closer the similarities, the more likely it is that the design will be commonplace.[70] This is because if different designers have independently come up with similar designs, but each is given protection, practical difficulties of proof of copying and enforcement arise. These are precisely the difficulties which the requirement (that the design not be commonplace) was meant to avoid. If, however, there are aspects of the claimant's design which are not to be found in the field in question, the design is probably not commonplace.[71]

Obviously, 'commonplaceness' is a question of fact on which little further guidance can be provided. However, two observations are worth making. The first relates to the question whether a collection of commonplace designs can give rise to design that is protected. In what has been described as the legal form of *Gestalt*—in which the whole is more than the sum of its individual parts—it has been held that the unregistered design right can exist in 'an assembly of individual commonplace parts'.[72] The second is that the test for whether a design is commonplace seems to operate more harshly against decorative designs than against functional ones. This is because in the case of decorative designs, there is likely to be a larger reservoir of existing designs in the field. This can be seen by comparing *Farmers Build* with the *Scholes Windows* case. In *Farmers Build,* the Court of Appeal held various components of the slurry separator (such as the hopper design), as well as the combination of elements, to be original and protected. In part this was because slurry separators were relatively new machines, and there were not many comparators. Consequently, the (albeit visually unexceptional) functional differences between some of the claimant's parts and those of comparators meant that the claimant's design was not commonplace.[73] In *Scholes Windows,* however, the claimant's design was in the crowded field of window frame design where the requirement that the design should not be commonplace posed more of a hurdle.[74] The design—a design of a PVC window frame which was intended to evoke a traditional Victorian sash window—was held to be similar to existing window designs and not to be sufficiently different to lift it out of the ordinary run of such designs.[75]

2.4 QUALIFICATION

The unregistered design right is only available in a design which meets one of the following criteria:[76] (i) the designer is a 'qualifying person', namely a citizen or subject of, or an

---

[69] The court usually looks at the designs through the eyes of the customer: *Fulton v. Totes* [2003] *RPC* (27) 499, 509; *Scholes Windows* [2002] *ECDR* (20) 196, 206 (paras. 49–50) (expressly rejecting suggestion that comparison should be from the point of view of a designer who is an expert in the field).

[70] Though where similarities which existed between a design and one already in the field were a result of the fact that both designs were modelled on the human form, the court held the later design was not commonplace, because of differences in the detail of the features: *Spraymiser*, note 64 above.

[71] For a discussion of the fate of well-known designs in this context see *Dyson v. Qualtex* [2006] *RPC* 769, para. 100 ff.

[72] *Ultraframe v. Eurocell* [2005] *RPC* 36, paras 64–66.

[73] [1999] *RPC* 461, 484.

[74] [2000] *FSR* 432; affirmed on appeal [2002] *ECDR* (20) 196, 205.

[75] Ibid, 442. *Sales v. Stromberg* [2006] *FSR* (7) 89, para. 58 (design of decorative pendants, though simple geometric shapes common in rock art and 'native American culture', was original and not commonplace in field of complementary medical devices including one which were ornamental and decorative devices).

[76] CDPA s. 218. However, if the design was created in pursuance of a commission or in the course of employment, then it must qualify by that route or by first marketing.

individual habitually resident in, a 'qualifying country', that is the United Kingdom, the EC, a country to which the relevant Part of the 1988 Act 'extends', or a 'designated country'; (ii) the designer has been commissioned by or is employed by such a 'qualifying person';[77] or (iii) the design has been first marketed by a 'qualifying person' in the United Kingdom, the EC, or a country to which the Part 'extends'.[78] Because of the limited scope of these provisions, many foreign designs will not qualify for protection in the United Kingdom.[79]

3 OWNERSHIP

The unregistered design right initially vests in the designer (subject to two exceptions).[80] The designer is the person who creates the design.[81] The case law has yet to develop, though it seems that neither a person who provides an idea for a product,[82] nor a person who merely executes instructions, will be regarded as a creator.[83] As with copyright, it seems that the creator is the person who gives the expressive form—the shape and configuration—to the design.[84]

The two exceptions to the general principle of first ownership relate to (i) designs created in pursuance of a commission—which are owned by the commissioner,[85] and (ii) designs created in the course of employment—which are owned by the employer.[86] As Laddie J has explained '[a]s a rough and ready rule of thumb, if designs are created and paid for by another, the statutory rights under the Act should belong to that other'.[87] The rules on ownership of rights in commissioned designs are different from those in copyright law, so that copyright in design drawings may vest in one person (the designer) and the unregistered design right in the design embodied therein in another (the commissioner).[88]

---

[77] CDPA s. 219. A design which was commissioned or made in the course of employment cannot qualify via the s. 218 route (designer a 'qualifying individual').

[78] CDPA s. 255 allows for orders 'extending' the Part of the Act to the Channel Islands, the Isle of Man, or any colony, while CDPA s. 256 allows for orders to be made 'designating' countries as enjoying reciprocal protection. See Design Right (Reciprocal Protection) Order 1989 (SI 1989/1294) (designating countries such as Anguilla, Bermuda, Hong Kong, and New Zealand).

[79] *Mackie v. Behringer* [1999] *RPC* 717, 724.

[80] CDPA s. 215(1).   [81] CDPA s. 214.

[82] *Spraymiser* [2000] *ECDR* 349 (person who provided the idea of an articulated, reconfigurable, wooden figure that could be put to various uses (e.g. a magazine rack or plant stand) was not the designer); *Novum (Overseas) Ltd v. Iceland Foods plc* (30 Jan. 2002) (customer's views were important but customer was not designer).

[83] *Fulton v. Grant Barnett* [2001] *RPC* 257 (mould makers or stitchers working pursuant to instructions held not to be designers).

[84] *Spraymiser*, above (the designer was the person who developed the wooden figure (albeit with assistance of a person who was commissioned to help him), and who knew precisely how he wanted the figure to look); *Novum v. Iceland* (30 Jan. 2002) (designer 'responsible in significant part for design').

[85] CDPA s. 215(2); s. 263. See *Spraymiser*, ibid, 365 (where a person did not charge to create a prototype in the hope of being remunerated from the process of mass production, the design was nevertheless made for money's worth).

[86] CDPA s. 215(3). *Ultraframe UK Ltd v. Fielding* [2004] *RPC* 24 (CA) (managing director not employee, or commissioned, but held unregistered design rights on trust for company under fiduciary principles); *Fulton v. Grant Barnett*, note 8 above, 281 (director of the claimant company was held to be an employee).

[87] *Ultraframe UK Ltd v. Fielding* [2003] *RPC* (23) 435, 449 (para. 43). (followed *in Intercase UK v. Time Computers Ltd* [2004] *ECDR* 8. But cf. the reasoning of the CA in *Ultraframe* [2003] *RPC* 24.

[88] *APPS v. Weldtite Products Ltd* [2001] *FSR* 703, 730.

4 DURATION

The unregistered design right lasts for 15 years from creation[89] or, if the design was 'made available' within 5 years of creation, 10 years from the date of such marketing.[90] The maximum period of protection is therefore 15 years. The dual system of protection means that designers have a reasonable period in which to interest manufacturers or purchasers, before they market the design.[91] The right is subject to licences of right 'in the last five years of the design right term'.[92]

5 INFRINGEMENT

5.1 RIGHTS

The owner of an unregistered design right in a design has the exclusive right to reproduce the design for commercial purposes, inter alia by making articles to that design.[93] Reproduction of a design by making articles to that design is defined to mean 'copying the design so as to produce articles exactly or substantially to that design',[94] or making a design document recording the design for the purpose of enabling such articles to be made. The owner of an unregistered design right also has an 'authorization right', that is the right to authorize someone else to do any of the acts.[95] Since this is likely to be treated in the same way as the concept of 'authorization' in copyright law, the reader is referred back to Chapter 6.

The owner of an unregistered design right can also object to various acts of secondary infringement. These concern commercial dealings with infringing articles: importing infringing articles into the UK, possessing such articles for commercial purposes, as well as selling such articles, and exposing them for sale. These will often be of great importance in this context, as the primary act will frequently take place abroad (where labour and material costs are lower). As with secondary infringement of copyright, there is a *mens rea* requirement: namely, that the alleged infringer 'knows or has reason to believe' the article is infringing.[96] The concept of 'reason to believe' has been interpreted in the same way as the equivalent copyright provisions,[97] and, as before, the reader is referred back to Chapter 8 for further analysis.

---

[89] More specifically, from the end of the year in which the design was 'first recorded in a design document, or an article was first made to the design, whichever first occurred'.

[90] CDPA s. 216(1). *Dyson v. Qualtex* [2006] *RPC* 769, 802–3 (CA) (Jacob LJ complaining that 'the provision is not well-thought out' but affirming Mann J's view that something can only be made available if it exists, so advanced orders would not necessarily suffice).

[91] Fellner, paras. 3.046–3.053.

[92] CDPA s. 237. For an application of the licence of right and some of the complications that arise see: *NIC Instruments Licence of Right (Design Right) Application* [2005] *RPC* 1. This has potential ramifications for assessing damages: see CDPA s 239. On this see Neuberger LJ in *Ultraframe v. Eurocell* [2005] *RPC* 36, para. 103 ff (CA).

[93] CDPA s. 226(1). [94] CDPA s. 226(2). [95] CDPA s. 226(3).

[96] CDPA s. 233(2) limits the damages in a situation where the defendant acquired the infringing goods innocently. The test of innocent acquisition, as defined in s. 233(3), was said to be 'an objective test'. *Badge Sales v. PMS International Group Ltd* [2006] *FSR* 1, para. 8.

[97] *Baby Dan* [1999] *FSR* 377, 392; *Fulton v. Grant Barnett* [2001] *RPC* 257 (knowledge of the existence of a registered design); *Fulton v. Totes* [2003] *RPC* (27) 499, 530–1 (inference of knowledge based on knowledge of Fulton's action against Barnett in separate litigation).

Once it is clear that the defendant's activities fall within the scope of the protected rights, it is necessary to show that there has been 'substantive' infringement. The three key elements of substantive infringement are (i) derivation; (ii) so as to produce articles; (iii) which are substantially similar in design.

5.2 DERIVATION

In order for an unregistered design right to be infringed it must be copied. As a result, in order to show infringement it is necessary to demonstrate a causal connection between the two designs. It is not enough to show that the designs are similar. In some cases this will be unproblematic: there will be direct proof of copying. Often this will be where the alleged infringer was formerly supplied by the claimant of the design right, but decided (for whatever reason) to start manufacturing similar designs.[98] Occasionally, there will be evidence that the defendant's designer used the claimant's design as 'inspiration'.[99] However, in many cases there will be no direct proof of derivation, and proof of 'copying' will depend on proving 'access' and 'similarity'.[100] This can be seen in *Amoena v. Trulife*, where the defendant began to market PVC breast prostheses similar to ones which the claimant had been selling over the previous year. Jonathan Sumption QC dismissed Amoena's allegation of infringement of unregistered design right on the ground that it had failed to prove that Trulife had copied the design. Although the defendant would have had access to the claimant's product, and produced a similar product comparatively swiftly, Judge Sumption said he was unable to infer copying merely from the fact that the form of the designs was the same. The reason for this was because a number of design constraints limited the range of possible forms the design could take. As such, it was reasonable to conclude that the similarity could be explained on grounds other than copying. In designing breast prostheses a designer needed to emulate the appearance of a breast in a bra, the shape and size of scarring left by a mastectomy, as well as surgical practices. The judge concluded that 'designers pursuing similar objectives determined by bra design, surgical practice and stocking requirements are quite likely to arrive at designs which have a great deal in common'. While such similarities might have been the result of copying coupled with the deliberate introduction of differences, the two designs were not so similar that this was the only explanation or even the most inherently probable. The degree of similarity was capable of being explained on the basis that two designers had independently sought to achieve the result suggested to them, by the design of the bra and the location of the scars produced by current surgical methods.

5.3 SO AS TO PRODUCE 'ARTICLES'

In order to infringe an unregistered design right it is necessary to show that the defendant copied the design so as to produce *articles* exactly or substantially similar to the protected

---

[98] *Baby Dan* [1999] *FSR* 377, 387 (where the defendant's design retained certain functional features of the claimant's design, even though in the defendant's design these features were not necessary to achieve the function); *Parker v. Tidball* [1997] *FSR* 680; *Farmers Build* [1999] *RPC* 461, 466.

[99] It has been suggested that similar fact evidence, that is evidence of a defendant having mimicked a claimant's products a number of times in the past, may be of some use in deciding infringement (although the court stressed that such evidence would only be of minor probative value and would require wide-ranging investigations). *Mattel Inc v. Woodbro (Distributors) Ltd* [2004] *FSR* 12, paras. 14, 21–22.

[100] Ibid, 481. Compare *Fulton v. Grant Barnett* [2001] *RPC* 257 (inference of copying by manufacturer in Taiwan drawn from multiplicity of similarities), with *Guild v. Eskandar* [2003] *FSR* 23 (no copying proven).

design. Two questions arise in relation to this requirement. First, is there infringement where a defendant uses the design on different articles? Second, in the case of designs for parts of articles, is the comparison to be made between the parts themselves or between the part claimed and the whole of the defendant's alleged infringement?

5.3.1 Application to different articles

As with Registered and Unregistered Community Designs, and the new harmonized national registered design,[101] it seems that unregistered design right will be infringed where a substantially similar design is used on other articles. In *Electronic Techniques v. Critchley Components* Laddie J said that since unregistered design rights are 'presumably intended to reward and encourage design effort, it seems unlikely that the effort should only be protected and rewarded if the infringer happens to use the design on precisely the same type of article'.[102] However, Laddie J added an important qualification to the general proposition that unregistered design right is infringed by use of the design on other articles. He said that this did not mean that the nature of the defendant's article was irrelevant:

It may be that a design applied to certain articles has a different impact to the same design applied to other articles. In such cases it may well be that the design, in the context of other features of shape and configuration of the article itself, may be viewed differently to the same or a similar design in a different context.[103]

5.3.2 The test with partial designs

The definition of infringement as involving the use of the claimant's design in relation to 'articles' rather than to parts of articles has posed particular problems where the claimant's design is for part of an article. The reason for this is that although the design right subsists in 'the design of any aspect of the shape or configuration...of the whole or part of any article', infringement occurs where the defendant is shown to have copied 'the design so as to produce *articles* exactly or substantially to that design'. The statutory provisions thus seem to be inconsistent. In *Parker v. Tidball*, Englehart J attempted to resolve the conflict explaining that:

in a case where a design of part of an article is reproduced in part of an allegedly infringing article, one should ask oneself what by way of comparative design would be suggested to the interested observer but to do so in the light of the entirety of the allegedly infringing article, not just by confining attention to the corresponding parts. Moreover, the inquiry is directed to substantial, not necessarily exact, correspondence.[104]

5.4 SUBSTANTIAL SIMILARITY

In order to infringe an unregistered design right, it must be shown that the defendant copied the design so as to produce articles that are exactly the same as or *substantially similar* to the claimant's design.[105] This is a somewhat different test from that for copyright infringement, where (as we saw in Chapter 8) the focus is on whether the defendant has reproduced a

---

[101] See above at pp. 665–8, 671.
[102] *Electronic Techniques v. Critchley* [1997] *FSR* 401, 418.
[103] See above p. 671.
[104] *Parker v. Tidball* [1997] *FSR* 680, 691. Cf. *Dyson v. Qualtex* [2006] *RPC* 769, 802 (paras 113–14) (seeming to suggest the comparison is of relevant parts).
[105] CDPA s. 226(2).

'substantial part' of the claimant's work. In the case of designs, we are concerned with overall similarity, not just appropriation of part.[106]

In cases where the design is for the appearance of an article, the question whether the designs are the same is to be determined through the eyes of the relevant customer.[107] Substantial similarity is a matter of overall impression, and as such the courts often find it difficult to explain why they have reached a particular conclusion.[108] In one case, it was suggested that the question is whether a consumer looking at the two designs side by side would say they are made to substantially the same design.[109] However, a visual test is inappropriate where the design features lie in details that cannot be seen by the eye. It will be recalled that in *Ocular Sciences*, Laddie J accepted the claimant's argument that each of their lenses, though differing from their neighbours only in fine dimensional details, might constitute a separate design. Indeed, Laddie J observed that the designs were protectable despite the fact that a member of the public would not be able to distinguish the design of one lens in a particular range from another in the same range by mere visual inspection. If such protection is to be meaningful, the question whether copying is exactly or substantially to the same design should not simply be a question of visual similarity.

A visual test is also inappropriate where the features of shape or configuration that are protected by unregistered design right are functional.[110] In those circumstances the question should be whether the defendant's design embodies a form which is similar (taking into account the way the form operates to achieve the function). Although it was not necessary to decide the point, this was the kind of approach taken by Pumfrey J in his discussion in *Mackie Designs* of what would amount to infringement of unregistered design right in a circuit board.[111] The question of similarity would not be one of visual comparison of the shapes and colours from the point of view of someone unversed in electronics but a comparison through the eyes of someone versed in electronics, and interested in the functioning of the circuit, of the units, their order, and interconnections.

6 DEFENCES: RELATIONSHIP BETWEEN UNREGISTERED DESIGN RIGHT AND COPYRIGHT

Section 236 of the 1988 Act states that 'it is not an infringement of design right in the design to do anything which is an infringement of copyright in that work'.[112] Consequently, to the extent that there is dual protection, copyright pre-empts unregistered design right. However, as we seen, section 51 severely limits the impact of copyright protection in this area. This is because where copyright and unregistered design rights both exist, section 51 provides a defence so that making an article to the design does not infringe copyright, but might nevertheless still infringe unregistered design right. An exhaust pipe produced indirectly from

[106] *L. Woolley Jewellers* [2003] *FSR* (15) 255, 261.
[107] *Mark Wilkinson Furniture* [1998] *FSR* 63, 75; *Fulton v. Totes* [2003] *RPC* (27) 499, 528.
[108] *Ultraframe UK Ltd v. Fielding* [2003] *RPC* (23) 435, 462 (para. 85).
[109] *Fulton v. Grant Barnett* [2001] *RPC* 257, 283.
[110] Cf. *C. & H. Engineering v. Klucznik* [1992] *FSR* 421, 428 (applying visual test to functional design).
[111] *Mackie v. Behringer* [1999] *RPC* 717, 723; *Mark Wilkinson Furniture*, above, 75.
[112] CDPA s. 236.

design drawings would not infringe copyright in those drawings. It would, however, infringe unregistered design right as regards those features of the exhaust pipe which are not excluded as 'must-fit' or 'must-match' features.[113]

7 SYNTHESIS

The legal protection of designs is a complicated matter. As a result, it may be helpful to conclude with some simple examples.

Example 1. A has designed a double-barrelled syringe, which he marketed. It is registered as a design in the UK and at the OHIM. A similar syringe has subsequently appeared on the UK market where it is being sold by X.

First, we should consider the validity of A's national or Registered Community Designs. Both regimes afford protection to the 'appearance of…a product'.[114] One question will be whether the features are 'solely dictated by its technical function',[115] though as mentioned it is thought this will apply only rarely. Parts of the handle might be excluded as 'mechanical interconnections':[116] where an exact fit is required with the plunger. A more difficult hurdle will be whether the design is new and has individual character.[117]

On the assumption that the registrations are valid, we would need to decide whether X infringes. X is using a design by selling articles bearing it.[118] There is no need to prove that the design was copied. The critical issue will be whether X's design produces a different overall impression on an informed user: if it does there is no infringement.[119]

If A can prove copying he will also be able to rely on Unregistered Community Design Right at least for the period of three years from when the design was made available.[120]

A will not be able to rely on copyright. The syringe is not itself an artistic work.[121] The drawings, if any exist, are designs for something 'other than an artistic work'. It is not an infringement to make articles to the design or copy articles made to the design.[122]

A may be able, however, to rely on unregistered design right. This protection would arise automatically as regards features of shape and configuration.[123] Surface decoration (such as the measure) would not be protected. Parts of the handle might be excluded on the grounds that it must fit both the syringe barrel and, possibly, the hand of the user.[124] If the shape is 'not commonplace', it may be protected.[125] (It is conceivable that the syringe might lack 'individual character' and yet be not commonplace.) Assuming the syringe is protected, A will need to prove X is dealing in 'infringing articles': that is, articles made without A's permission, by copying A's design (directly or indirectly), and which are articles made substantially to the design.[126] Whether the articles are 'substantially to [the] design' is a matter of impression and

---

[113] However, where a design comprises surface decoration as well as configuration, the division of the creative elements amongst two forms of protection may have undesirable effects: *Jo Y Jo v. Matalan* [2000] *ECDR* 178, 200.

[114] Designs Dir., Art. 1(a); CDR, Art. 3(a); RDA s. 1(2).

[115] Designs Dir., Art. 7; RDA s. 1C(1); CDR, Art. 8.   [116] Designs Dir., Art. 7(2).

[117] Designs Dir., Art. 3(2); RDA s. 1B; CDR, Art. 4.

[118] Designs Dir., Art. 12; RDA s. 7(1); CDR, Art. 19.

[119] Designs Dir., Art. 9; RDA s. 7; CDR, Art. 10.   [120] CDR, Art. 11.

[121] CDPA s. 4. It is not a sculpture: *Metix v. Maughan* [1997] *FSR* 718.

[122] CDPA s. 51.   [123] CDPA s. 213.

[124] CDPA s. 213(3)(b)(i); *Ocular Sciences* [1997] *RPC* 289.   [125] CDPA s. 213(4).

[126] CDPA s. 228 (defining infringing article), s. 226.

only in a few cases would the result differ from that based on the registered design. A will also need to prove that X is either a primary infringer, or knows or has reason to believe the articles are infringing articles. The defence in section 236 will not apply because making articles to the design is not an infringement of copyright.

Example 2. B has designed a steering wheel for a new car and has retained his preliminary drawings. The steering wheel is of a conventional circular design and characterized by having four radiating spokes in the shape of a 'CND' sign. B is about to commence production.

B may be able to obtain a national or Registered Community Design for the shape of the steering wheel. The design relates to the appearance of a product, which includes 'parts intended to be assembled into complex products'.[127] The main question will be whether the design is new and has individual character. For parts to be used in complex products, the Community-based regimes require the part to be visible in use: this should not be a problem for steering wheels.[128] The fact that the design is known as a CND symbol might be thought to raise issues of novelty. However, the design of the symbol is two-dimensional, whereas the three-dimensional version is different—it will have spatial presence, texture, and weight. The design would almost certainly produce, on an informed user, a different impression to, say, a sticker. However, a registration might be declared invalid as an infringement of copyright.[129] Pending an application for registration, B benefits from the grace period for twelve months, and if B chooses not to register, from the Unregistered Community Design Right for three years from making the design available.

B will be able to rely on copyright in any design drawings. However, such copyright will not enable B to prevent anybody replicating the steering wheel.[130]

B will be able to rely on unregistered design right insofar as the steering wheel is a shape, which is original and not commonplace. Design right will not protect must-fit nor must-match features.

Example 3. C has developed a design for a door handle shaped like an eagle's head. C has original drawings and preliminary clay models.

C could register the design at a national or Community level, and will also have protection automatically (for three years from making available the design) by virtue of Unregistered Community Design Right. There may be issues as to whether the door handle is new and has individual character.

C could rely on copyright protection in the drawings and the clay model, if the latter were treated as a 'model for the purposes of sculpture'.[131] If the handle is mass-produced it is unlikely to be treated as a sculpture.[132] It could nevertheless be a work of artistic craftsmanship.[133] The extent of copyright protection will depend on the application of section 51 of the 1988 Act. If the design is a work of artistic craftsmanship, full protection would apply—either based on direct infringement of the work, or indirect infringement via the sculpture or drawings. If the door handle is an artistic work, then the design drawing is a design document for an artistic work: thus, the section 51 defence does not apply. If the door handle is not an artistic work, the question arises whether the drawings, on which the sculpture was based, are designs for an

---

[127] Designs Dir., Art. 1(b); RDA s. 1(3); CDR, Art. 3(c).

[128] Design Dir., Art. 3(3); CDR, Art. 4(2); RDA s. 1B(8).

[129] Designs Dir., Art. 11(2)(a); RDA s. 11ZA(4); CDR, Art. 25(I)(f).   [130] CDPA s. 51.

[131] Cf. *J. & S. Davis (Holdings) v. Wright Health Group* [1988] *RPC* 403.

[132] *Wham-O Manufacturing v. Lincoln* [1985] *RPC* 127.

[133] *Coogi Australia v. Hysport International* (1998) 41 *IPR* 593 (FCA).

artistic work; or whether they will be treated as designs for the door handle (a non-artistic work).

C could also attempt to rely on unregistered design right as regards the shape of the handles. However, according to section 236 of the 1988 Act, there will be no infringement of unregistered design right insofar as there is an infringement of copyright. The operation of unregistered design right is only significant, therefore, if there is no infringement of copyright.

Example 4. D, an artist, produces an abstract painting (in the style of Mondrian) which is widely exhibited. It is later applied by E to ties, with D's consent. Y has now made trays bearing the painting.

E can apply to register the design for the tie at national or Community level. The application relates to the appearance of a product. The first issue that will need to be addressed is whether the design of the tie is new, given the existence of the painting. The Community-based regime provides no clear answer: whether an identical design has been made available depends first on whether the painting itself counts as a design. Is a painting the appearance of 'a product', namely the canvas?[134] Assuming the painting is a design, has it been made available? Making available includes exhibition, so it seems the painting has been made available.[135] Is the design of the tie identical to the design of the painting? Would the change in size, texture, and possibly colours (as well as the very nature of the product) be such that the design of the tie differs only in 'immaterial details'?[136] Does the design have individual character? If not, can the use of the artistic work within the previous twelve months be ignored on the basis of the grace period?[137] Here the hurdle is that the painting was made available by D, rather than the design of the tie by E—a situation which does not fall easily into the exclusion.

If the painting is not a design, it would seem that the design for the tie is a new design. This would mean that E would obtain monopoly rights as regards use of the tie on any product. E consequently could bring an action against Y, and the issue would be whether the design produced a different overall impression on an informed user. Would the design on a tray give a different impression from the design on a tie? If E had registered the design without D's permission, D could invalidate the registration on the ground that it infringed E's copyright.[138] This ground would not, however, be available to Y.

D can rely, as against E or Y, on copyright in the painting. This is infringed where anybody applies the work to an artefact, because that amounts to reproduction of the work.[139] Section 51 has no application (because the painting was not a design 'for' anything: it was simply an artistic work).[140] However, if D permitted E to sell the tie bearing the design, after 25 years from marketing of the tie, it would no longer be an infringing act to apply the design to the tray.[141] It is difficult to see how E could claim any copyright in the tie.

Neither D nor E can rely on unregistered design right. The design is not a shape.[142]

Example 5. F, an artist, creates an abstract sculpture which is exhibited in Holland Park. Z is thinking of selling paperweights in a similar shape.

---

[134] RDA s.1(B)(2); Designs Dir., Art. 4; CDR, Art. 5(2).

[135] RDA s 1B(5)(a); Designs Dir., Art. 6; CDR, Art. 7(1).

[136] RDA s. 1B(2); Designs Dir., Art. 4; CDR, Art. 5(2).

[137] RDA s. 1B(6); Designs Dir., Art. 6(2); CDR, Art .7(2)(b).

[138] RDA s. 11ZA(4); Designs Dir., Art. 11(2)(a); CDR, Art. 25(1)(f), (3).   [139] CDPA s. 17.

[140] In any case, the painting is not a 'design', a term which relates to shape and configuration.

[141] CDPA s. 52.   [142] CDPA s. 213.

F may attempt to register the design of the sculpture at national or Community level. The critical question will be whether a sculpture is a product, that is, 'an industrial or handicraft item'.[143] It seems improbable that the Registry, OHIM, or the courts will refuse to register such things, but they will require that F specify a product (and identify its place in the Euro-Locarno Convention).[144] If this has occurred, Z's use of a similar design will infringe if the resemblance is such that it does not produce a different overall impression.

F could rely on copyright, a sculpture being one of the 'artistic works' enumerated in section 4 of the CDPA, and protected 'irrespective of artistic quality'. F will thus be able to bring an action against Z on the ground that Z has infringed by reproducing the sculpture, or issuing copies of it to the public.[145] However, F will need to prove that Z made the paperweights by copying the sculpture. If Z bought the paperweights from a third party, F will need to prove that the paperweights are copies of the sculpture, and that Z knew or ought reasonably to have been aware that these were infringing copies.[146]

F may have unregistered design right, if the sculpture is treated as the design of the shape of an article. However, F will not be able to use unregistered design right against Z because of section 236: 'it is not an infringement of design right in the design to do anything which is an infringement of the copyright in that work'.

Example 6. *G has produced a photograph and proposes to make birthday cards bearing the image.*

G can register, either nationally or at OHIM. The design relates to the appearance of a product, and will obtain protection for up to 25 years. It will also benefit from Unregistered Community Design Right for three years from the first making-available of the design.

G cannot rely on UK unregistered design right: there is no shape or configuration.

G can rely on copyright. The photograph is an original artistic work. Section 51 does not apply. Application to a greetings card will not affect the duration of protection: the article is excluded from the operation of section 52.[147]

8 SEMICONDUCTOR TOPOGRAPHIES

A special form of legal protection based on unregistered design right has been created to afford protection for the layouts of semiconductor chips (which are colloquially known as 'computer or silicon chips'). This section briefly explains this *sui generis* right.[148]

---

[143] RDA s. 1(B)(2); Designs Dir., Art. 4; CDR, Art. 5(2).   [144] RDA s. 3(2).

[145] CDPA s. 17, s.18. If F permits the exploitation of the sculpture by the making of more than 50 articles (which are copies of the sculpture) and their marketing, F's ability to restrain further uses of the sculpture after 25 years from such marketing may be compromised: s. 52(2). Although Copyright (Industrial Process and Excluded Articles) (No 2) Order 1989 (SI 1989/1070), para. 3(1)(a) excludes 'sculptures' from the operation of CDPA s. 52, it does so only for sculptures 'other than casts or models used or intended to be used as models or patterns to be multiplied by any industrial process'. The better view is that F's copyright is unaffected if F sells multiple copies of the sculpture as a sculpture, but CDPA s. 52 comes into play if F permits the sale of articles modelled on the sculpture.

[146] CDPA s. 23.

[147] CDPA s. 52(4)(b); Copyright (Industrial Process, etc) (No. 2) Order 1989, para. 3(1)(c) (excluding 'greetings cards').

[148] As noted in Ch. 26, chips are also now protectable by Registered Community Design, national registered design, and Unregistered Community Design Right.

When protection was first thought desirable for the designs of such chips, it was widely assumed in the USA that copyright protection would not be available (or if available would not be adequate) given that the design of such chips is essentially functional. As a result, in 1984 the USA passed a Semiconductor Chip Protection Act introducing a *sui generis* protection regime. Because the USA was only prepared to recognize the claims of foreign designers of semiconductor chips where the country of origin recognized the rights of US chip designers, the EC decided to adopt an equivalent system of protection. Consequently, in December 1986, an EC Directive was adopted requiring member states to bring into effect protection for semiconductor topographies.[149] In the UK, this was effected initially by the Semiconductor (Protection of Topography) Regulations 1987,[150] an instrument which was later repealed and replaced by the Design Right (Semiconductor Topographies) Regulations 1989.[151]

8.1 THE UK SCHEME

Semiconductor topographies are now protected in the United Kingdom as unregistered designs, with certain modifications. Protection is afforded to the pattern or patterns fixed, or intended to be fixed, in or upon a layer or layers of a semiconductor product. A semiconductor product is defined as 'an article the purpose, or one of the purposes, of which is the performance of an electronic function and which consists of two or more layers, at least one of which is composed of semi-conducting material and in or upon one or more of which is fixed a pattern appertaining to that or another function'. The prerequisite of design right protection, that the design be 'original' and 'not commonplace', applies equally to topographies. Protection is provided against copying, but there is a defence for private reproduction for non-commercial aims and generous provision is made for reverse engineering.[152]

Only a restricted range of foreign claims qualify relative to semiconductor topographies.[153] While the concept of 'qualifying country' is confined to the United Kingdom or another EEA member state, the notion of 'qualifying person' includes citizens, subjects, habitual residents, and bodies corporate listed in Schedule 1 to the Regulations. Consequently, if a design for a topography is commissioned by a 'qualifying person' who is also the first owner of design right, or is created by a designer who is a 'qualifying person',[154] or the first marketing of a topography is by a 'qualifying person' in Europe, the design qualifies for protection in the United Kingdom. The countries listed include Australia, the USA, Japan, and others.[155]

---

[149] Council Directive 87/54/EEC of 16 Dec. 1986 on the legal protection of semiconductor products, *OJ L* 24/36.

[150] SI 1987/1497.

[151] SI 1989/1100 (hereinafter Semiconductor Regs.).

[152] Semiconductor Reg. 8. Cf. Software Dir., Arts. 4 and 6.   [153] Semiconductor Reg. 4.

[154] The commissioner/employer and the designer routes are mutually exclusive, so that a commissioner or employer who is not a 'qualifying person' cannot claim the benefit of the designer being a 'qualifying individual'. Rather, if the commissioner or employer was first owner, it must be qualified; however, if the designer was first owner pursuant to an agreement to that effect, then the designer must qualify.

[155] For a lengthier exposition of these very complex requirements, see Christie, *Integrated Circuits and their Contents*, 67–71.

PART IV

TRADE MARKS AND PASSING OFF

1 INTRODUCTION

This part of the book is concerned with two related forms of intellectual property: namely, the common law of passing-off and the statutory regime which protects registered trade marks found in the Trade Marks Act 1994. These regimes regulate certain signs or symbols, usually words or pictures,[1] when used in trade in connection with particular goods or services. Classic (or infamous) examples include MARLBORO for cigarettes, APPLE for computers, the 'golden arches' in the shape of an M for restaurant services, and the 'swoosh' or rounded tick symbol for (NIKE) sports clothing. These two legal regimes transform signs into forms of property. In so doing, they enable the proprietors to prevent other traders from using the signs on the same or similar goods or services. Both forms of legal protection are available simultaneously. Under the law of passing off, the sign must have been used in trade so as to have acquired a reputation. In the case of the statutory regime, the sign must have been registered, either at the UK Trade Mark Registry or at the Community Trade Mark Office (called the OHIM). These forms of legal protection underpin the enormous value of some of these brands. In August 2007, the brand valuation agency Interbrand calculated that 100 brands are now worth over US$3 billion each, the most valuable, COCA-COLA and MICROSOFT, being worth in the region of $65 and $58 billion each.[2]

---

[1] Marks are often referred to according to the nature of the sign. A word mark is a registration of a word alone (irrespective of its depiction). A figurative mark is usually made up of a visual image, such as a picture. Marks which have both figurative and verbal elements are commonly referred to as 'composite marks'. As we will see, there are new possibilities to register 'three-dimensional marks', 'colour marks', and 'sensory marks' (such as sounds or smells).

[2] See <http://interbrand.com>.

31

INTRODUCTION TO PASSING OFF
AND TRADE MARKS

CHAPTER CONTENTS

This chapter has three aims. First, it provides a brief history of the development of the law in this area. Second, it considers the ways in which legal protection of signs and symbols are justified. Third, the chapter provides an introduction to the international and regional background that informs and constrains this area of the law in the United Kingdom.

1 HISTORY

Most accounts of the history of trade marks tend to focus on two intertwined themes. One is a history of the social practices and understandings attached to the activity of applying marks to goods; the other is a positivist history of trade marks law. These two histories are often conflated in a way which suggests that the law inevitably evolves with, or ought to reflect the changes in, the nature and function of marks.[1] While acknowledging that many developments in trade marks law have been made in response to changes in the functions that marks perform, we would prefer to keep the histories separate to avoid any implication that a change in the function of marks requires us to alter (typically expand the scope of legal protection afforded by) trade marks law.

---

[1] F. Schechter, *The Historical Foundations of the Law Relating to Trade Marks* (1925); G. Ruston, 'On the Origin of Trade-Marks' (1955) 45 *TM Rep* 127 (tracing 6,000 years of use); T. Drescher, 'The Transformation and Evolution of Trademarks—From Signals to Symbols to Myth' (1992) 82 *TM Rep* 301, 309–321. *Scandecor Development AB v. Scandecor Marketing AB* [2002] *FSR* (7) 122, 128–138 (Lord Nicholls).

1.1 HISTORY OF MARKS

In the earliest times traders applied marks to their good to indicate ownership. These are called proprietary or possessory marks. For example, farmers commonly branded cattle and ear-marked sheep as a way of identifying their livestock. In a similar way, merchants also marked their goods before shipment so that in the event of a shipwreck, any surviving merchandise could be identified and retrieved. From medieval times marks were used for a slightly different purpose within guild structures. Guilds were trade organizations that had control over who could make certain goods or provide certain services. They were also concerned to ensure that the goods were of a satisfactory quality. In order to be able to identify the source of unsatisfactory goods, the guilds required their members to apply identifying marks or signs to the goods.[2]

With the demise of the guilds, it was no longer obligatory for traders to apply particular marks or signs to goods. However, with the growth of regional (as opposed to local) trading and the rise of factory production that accompanied the Industrial Revolution, many traders continued to apply their marks to the goods they manufactured.[3] Moreover, with the growth of mass media and the reading public, traders started to advertise their goods by reference to these marks.[4] In turn, purchasers of goods started to rely on the signs the goods bore as truthful indications of the source of the goods. Importantly, they began to use them to assist their purchasing decisions. Over time, as consumers started to realize that some marks indicated a particular manufacturer, and in turn goods of a certain standard, the nature of the mark changed from being a source of liability to become an indicator of quality.

Another important change in the role played by marks took place around the beginning of the twentieth century. During this period trade marks changed from being indicators of origin (and thus signs from which consumers could assume consistency of quality) to become valuable assets in their own right.[5] Thus it is said that some marks, by virtue of their distinctiveness or appeal, were able to convey some sort of emotional allure to potential consumers. Literally the sign attracted custom, not as a result of some idea or assumption of origin or quality, but as a result of so-called 'advertising' quality.[6] Indeed, the mark *itself* (reinforced by advertising) gave rise to a desire for the product that was distinct from a desire based on a belief that the product would be of a particular quality. The trade mark served more as a marketing tool and less as a means of identifying a product's source or sponsorship. This change in the function of trade marks has been described as a transformation from 'signals' to 'symbols'.[7] As signals, trade marks trigger an automatic response and serve to identify the maker of the product. In contrast, as 'symbols' trade marks evoke a broader set of associations and meanings. Here they are used to identify the product or to give the product an identity. In so doing 'the mark

---

[2] P. Mollerup, *Marks of Excellence: The History and Taxonomy of Trademarks* (1997) 15–42; S. Diamond, 'The Historical Development of Trademarks' (1975) 65 *TM Rep* 265, 272.

[3] B. Pattishall, 'Trade Marks and the Monopoly Phobia' (1952) 42 *TM Rep* 588, 590–1.

[4] Diamond, 'Historical Development of Trademarks', 281 (with increased advertising came the increased use of trade marks in their modern function as identifiers of the source of the goods).

[5] *Eastman Photographic Material Co. v. John Griffith Cycle Corporation* (1898) 15 *RPC* 105.

[6] Brown identified three elements to the 'advertising' or 'persuasive' function: that which results from the distillation of associations, allure, etc. by advertising in the trade mark; that which results from previous experience by consumers of goods bearing the same mark; and that which results from the inherent attractiveness of the mark. R. Brown, 'Advertising and the Public Interest: The Legal Protection of Trade Symbols' (1948) 57 *Yale Law Journal* 1165, 1189.

[7] Drescher, 'Transformation and Evolution of Trademarks'.

became a symbol, a poetic device, a name designed to conjure up product attributes whether real or imagined'.[8]

More recently, trade marks have taken on new roles.[9] In one commentator's words, marks have come to take on a 'mythical status'.[10] In their mythical form trade marks help to provide consumers with an identity—for example, as a FERRARI or VOLVO driver, or BUDWEISER or BUDVAR drinker. When the consumer purchases a product bearing a mark they purchase an 'experience envelope' which helps to construct their identity. This conception of the trade mark as myth is illustrated by books such as *American Psycho* where the attributes of the characters are conveyed through descriptions of their use of particular trade-marked products.[11] The conception of trade mark as 'myth' can be seen in the increased attention given to 'brands'. While the definition of brands varies in both marketing and legal analysis,[12] it normally extends beyond a word or device mark to encompass the personality, style, or aura associated with a particular product. For those who would have us believe in the ontological status of brands, COCA-COLA is more than a product, a reputation for quality and a mark. Instead, it is an image and a way of life that is instituted through the presentation, marketing, advertising, and packaging, (as well as the production) of the product.[13]

1.2 HISTORY OF THE LEGAL PROTECTION OF MARKS

The history of the legal protection of trade marks has been less well charted than most areas of intellectual property, and the early developments are particularly obscure. It seems that the courts first began to protect 'marks' at the behest of traders in the sixteenth century. Acknowledging that such signs operated as an indication of source, the courts held that, if another trader were allowed to use the same sign, this would allow a fraud to be committed on the public. Initially, protection was provided by the Common Law Courts through the action for deceit.[14] The idea was, that if a trader had already used a mark, the deliberate use of the same mark by another trader would amount to a form of deceit. Not much later, the Courts of Chancery used the action for 'passing-off' to protect a trader who had developed a reputation or 'goodwill' through use of a particular sign or symbol. (This included the protection against innocent misrepresentations.) The passing-off action is still available today.[15] In reflection of its origins in the common law of deceit, passing-off always required a trader to establish that there had been a misrepresentation which deceived consumers. In effect this meant that the action was always concerned with confusion as to source. Even though the scope of the

---

[8] Ibid, 338.

[9] R. Dreyfuss, 'Expressive Genericity: Trademarks as Language in The Pepsi Generation' (1990) 65 *Notre Dame Law Review* 397, 397–8, also describes how trade marks are the emerging *lingua franca*: 'with a sufficient command of these terms, one can make oneself understood the world over, and in the process, enjoy the comforts of home'.

[10] Drescher, 'Transformation and Evolution of Trademarks'.

[11] B. Ellis, *American Psycho* (Random House, 1991).

[12] J. Davis, 'The Value of Trade Marks: Economic Assets and Cultural Icons' in Y. Gendreau (ed.), *Intellectual Property: Bridging Aesthetics and Economics—Propriete intellectuelle: Entre l'art et l'argent* (Montreal: Editions Themis, 2006) 97–125.

[13] J. Litman, 'Breakfast with Batman: The Public Interest in the Advertising Age' (1999) 108 *Yale Law Journal* 1717 (describing product 'atmospherics').

[14] On the early role of the Star Chamber, see Schechter, pp 126–7.

[15] For an analysis of the US history, see R. Bone, 'Hunting Goodwill: A History of the Concept of Goodwill in Trademark Law' (2006) 86 *Boston University Law Review* 549; Mark McKenna, 'The Normative Foundation of Trademark Law' (2007) 82 *Notre Dame Law Review* 1839.

passing-off action has since expanded, the action has never been severed from its origins in the law of deceit. This has meant that the action has not developed into a general action for misappropriation of intangible value or unfair competition of the type recognized by other European legal systems.

A system for registration of marks was first introduced in 1875.[16] The impetus for this came more from foreign sources than from domestic pressure. With increasing interest in international recognition of industrial property rights, foreign traders were unconvinced that British law provided them with the same level of protection against the misuse of their signs that foreign laws afforded to British traders in similar circumstances. Although the main impetus for the adoption of a registration system was to meet foreign concerns, the system that was adopted largely formalized the passing-off action. The system allowed for the registration of a limited range of marks that the Registry subjected to examination prior to their entry on the Register.[17]

Trade mark registration brought with it a number of benefits. The most obvious was that it reduced the difficulties of proving goodwill and distinctiveness that arose in a passing-off action.[18] In addition, registration brought with it the possibility of a sign being protected prior to use. Other advantages of registered trade marks over passing-off developed later: most notably, when the 1938 Act permitted the assignment of marks separately from the goodwill of the business.[19] Despite this, passing-off remained valuable insofar as the criteria of registrability were restrictive, the process of registration was inappropriate or unnecessarily onerous, and the rights granted were broader.[20]

Perhaps the most vexed question that has arisen has been that of determining the appropriate scope of protection. In reflection of its relationship with passing-off, the Trade Marks Act 1875 worked on the assumption that trade marks operated to indicate origin.[21] However, as we just observed, around the beginning of the twentieth century marks began to function in other ways, notably as a silent 'salesman' that could sell products irrespective of consumer understandings about origin or associated quality. The recognition of the changed function of trade marks was soon coupled with a claim that trade mark proprietors *deserved* stronger protection to reflect the new ways marks were being understood. One of the most important advocates for greater protection was Frank Schechter, who is also the leading historian of trade marks.

Schechter radically asserted that modern trade marks law should have a single rational basis.[22] More specifically, Schechter proposed that 'the preservation of the uniqueness of a

[16] L. Bently, 'The Making of Modern Trade Marks Law: The Construction of the Legal Concept of Trade Mark (1860–1880) in Bently, Davids & Ginsburg, *Trade Marks and Brands: An Interdisciplinary Critique* (2008).

[17] Although the position was not initially completely clear from TMA 1875 s. 10, it was soon accepted that the registered trade-marks system was a statutory supplement to the common law doctrine of passing off: *Great Tower v. Langford* (1888) 5 *RPC* 66; *Faulder v. Rushton* (1903) 20 *RPC* 477. It is clear today that protection is cumulative: TMA s. 2; *Interlotto v. Camelot Group plc* [2004] *RPC* (8) 171, Laddie J, [2004] *RPC* (9) 186 (CA).

[18] *Spalding v. Gamage* (1915) 32 *RPC* 273 (the difficulty of proving distinctiveness was 'one of the evils sought to be remedied by the Trade Marks Act 1875').

[19] TMA 1938 s. 22. Reviewed in *Scandecor Development AB v. Scandecor Marketing AB* [2002] *FSR* (7) 122, 134–138 (Lord Nicholls).

[20] M. Shúilleabháin, 'Common Law Protection of Trade Marks—The Continuing Relevance of Passing Off' (2003) 34(7) *IIC* 722.

[21] TMA 1875 s. 10.

[22] F. Schechter, 'The Rational Basis of Trade Mark Protection' (1927) 40 *Harvard Law Review* 813, 831. Schechter would have confined his proposal for stronger protection to coined, invented, or other unique marks. See S. Stadler, 'The Wages of Ubiquity in Trademark Law' (2003) 88 *Iowa Law Review* 731 (emphasising the limited nature of Schechter's vision, and observing that it is trade mark owners themselves who most frequently dilute their own marks.).

trade mark should constitute the only rational basis for its protection'.[23] For Schechter (and his cohort of followers), marks should be protected as a species of property. Importantly this would mean that the owner would be protected when they were used on dissimilar goods as well as similar goods. Schechter argued that trade marks law was no longer adequate if it was wedded to a prerequisite of consumer confusion. The reason for this was that:

the real injury in all such cases ... is the gradual whittling away or dispersion of the identity and hold upon the public mind of the mark or name by its use upon non-competing goods. The more distinctive or unique the mark, the deeper its impress upon the public consciousness, and the greater its need for its protection against vitiation or dissociation from the particular product in connection with which it has been used.[24]

Schechter's article soon became 'a talisman to members of the trademark bar who [sought] to expand the protection available to their clients'.[25] In fact, its impact was not confined to the Bar. Today, many commentators treat the subsequent period as one in which Schechter's insights have come to fruition. In particular, the arguments he made for expansion have gradually been acknowledged and implemented (even if in a much distorted fashion) in national law. Notable examples include the expansion of the rights given to a trade mark proprietor to include 'dilution' (that is, certain uses of marks on *dissimilar* goods, even where consumers appreciate there is no connection); the recognition of signs as assets;[26] the gradual abandonment of various restrictions on dealings with marks;[27] and the introduction of extended infringement provisions in the Trade Marks Act 1994.

2 THE COSTS OF TRADE MARKS

One of the major charges against the protection of trade marks is that trade marks are monopolies and that monopolies are inefficient.[28] In most situations the characterization of trade marks as monopolies is unhelpful. As one commentator has noted, '[m]onopoly is merely an ugly word used by people to put a curse on any kind of property they do not like'.[29] In any case, trade marks are not properly treated as monopolies. This is because, in contrast with patent, design rights, and copyright, a trade mark does not normally give exclusive control over the sale of particular goods or services. Rather, it merely provides control over the use of the sign in connection with goods or services. Trade marks do not create monopolies, unless the sign is

---

[23] Ibid.

[24] Most modern commentators argue that the three functions sit side by side rather than that the origin and quality functions are subsumed in the advertising function: e.g. Diamond, 'Historical Development of Trademarks', 289–90; J. Lunsford, 'Consumers and Trademarks: The Function of Trademarks in the Market Place' (1974) 64 *TM Rep* 75.

[25] J. Swann and T. Davis, 'Dilution: An Idea Whose Time Has Gone. Brand Equity as Protectable Property, the New/Old Paradigm' (1994) 84 *TM Rep* 267, 285.

[26] *Lego v. Lemelstrich* [1983] FSR 155; *Mirage Studios v. Counter-Feat Clothing* [1991] FSR 145. See below at pp. 876–8, 962–7.

[27] With increasingly less attention being paid to the role of the consumer: J. Davis, 'To Protect or Serve? European Trade Mark Law and the Decline of the Public Interest' [2003] *EIPR* 180 (arguing that emphasis on 'indication of origin' and 'advertising' functions have minimized extent of focus on consumer interest).

[28] E. Chamberlain, cited in N. Economides, 'The Economics of Trademarks' (1988) 78 *TM Rep* 523, 532.

[29] E. Rogers, 'The Social Value of Trade Marks and Brands' (1947) 37 *TM Rep* 249, 249.

treated in combination with the goods or services as a product in its own right.[30] As one commentator pointed out, a trade mark 'quite simply, is not a monopoly in the underlying good, and no product market has ever been defined as narrowly as a single brand'.[31]

Even if the charge that a trade mark is a monopoly has little to be said for it, that does not mean that trade marks law does not impose certain costs which require justification. Indeed, the grant of exclusive rights over certain signs has a number of social costs.[32] Probably the most obvious is that it restricts other people (most importantly other traders) from using the same or a similar sign. As the scope of the subject matter of trade mark rights has expanded to cover shapes, to avoid infringement a trader may need to design different packaging or shapes for goods. As the rights conferred by trade mark law expand, the costs increase for traders, even if they are not trading in the same or a similar field: costs of developing suitable marks, searching registers, and where necessary negotiating with owners of related marks. This is particularly so for new entrants.

To a large extent the way in which the 'harm' caused by trade marks is evaluated depends on the way signs and language are viewed. If we take the view that the number of suitable signs is infinite and the inherent value of all signs is fairly consistent, then the cost of adopting a different sign from one already used or protected by another trader should not be that great. If, however, we take the view that some signs are better than others and that the pool of available marks is limited, then the costs to other traders of one trader being granted ownership of a particular mark may be significant. As the better marks are used up, a trader will have to invest more and more money in establishing and building suitable associations with their signs. Business practices suggest that many traders consider that the choice of trade symbols is an important one and that some signs are better than others. This explains why firms such as Exxon spend so much time and money developing their marks. It also explains why so many marks are selected for their 'suggestive' or 'allusive' qualities.[33]

More expansive trade mark protection, which gives a trade mark holder the ability to control non-trade mark uses or uses of similar marks in relation to dissimilar goods, imposes further costs. Some such regulations may even restrict free speech.[34] To the extent that the law confers power over words and symbols, it places the ability to make and control meaning in private hands to some degree. As Rosemary Coombe has observed, intellectual property law enables 'the commodification of symbols, imagery and text'. This enables trade mark owners to control both 'the sign's circulation and its connotations'. As such, intellectual property laws 'play a fundamental role in determining what discourses circulate in the public realm and achieve

---

[30] See, e.g. P. Behrendt, 'Trademarks and Monopolies: Historical and Conceptual Foundations' (1961) 51 TM Rep 853.

[31] Swann and Davis, 'Dilution: Brand Equity as Protectable Property', 272. Brand premiums are rationalized as mere returns on reputation or investment in advertising.

[32] W. Landes and R. Posner, 'The Economics of Trademark Law' (1988) 78 TM Rep 267, 268–9 (referring, inter alia, to the costs of transferring marks, enforcing them, and from the restriction on others from using similar marks).

[33] See J. Cross, 'Language and the Law: The Special Role of Trade Marks, Trade Names and other Trade Emblems' (1997) 76 Nebraska Law Review 95 (arguing that trade marks potentially operate to communicate four distinguishable messages: the 'denominative' message that the product came from a particular source; the 'associative' message that the goods are the same as those previously experienced by the consumer; the 'descriptive' message that the goods are of a certain quality or type; and the 'allusive' message, one which obliquely suggests some quality or association).

[34] And thus raise issues under ECHR Art. 10: see WWF-World Wide Fund For Nature v. World Wrestling Federation Inc [2004] FSR (10) 161 (para. 65) (CA).

dominance, and how these "languages" are spoken, while providing both enabling conditions and limiting obstacles for those who seek to construct identities and compel recognition'.[35]

3 JUSTIFICATIONS FOR THE LEGAL PROTECTION OF TRADE MARKS

In this section, we ask the question: why should we protect trade marks? In contrast with commentaries on copyright and patents, this topic has received relatively little attention. One possible reason for this is that the negative impact of trade mark rights is less obvious. Another reason is that for much of the last fifty years the flourishing of brands has been equated with the success of capitalism (in terms of increasing consumer choice).[36] Indeed, to some commentators the benefits of trade marks (and thus their legal protection) are self-evident. In a remarkable post-war commentary, it was said that 'the faith in trade marks is a phenomenon that the social sciences, some day, will describe as one of the greatest contributions of all time to social harmony and social progress'. Moreover, trade marks 'transform mental confusion into mental harmony and…convert social distrust into mutual understanding'.[37] However, such blind faith in the value of trade marks is difficult to sustain and the time is ripe for a more open and critical examination of the justifications for protecting trade marks.[38]

A number of different rationales have been used to justify trade mark protection. As we will see, there have been few problems in justifying the protection given to signs and symbols insofar as they operate as indicators of origin (to identify the origin or ownership of goods to which the mark is affixed), or as guarantees of quality (to signify that all goods bearing the mark are of a certain quality).[39] However, more problems have arisen in justifying the extensive protection that is currently granted to marks.

3.1 CREATIVITY

The arguments which are used to justify copyright, designs, and patents, which focus on the protection of labour and personality (whether as recognition of a right, as a reward, or as an incentive) are difficult to apply to trade marks. This is because, while some trade marks may be invented, novelty is not a prerequisite to protection. These differences have not prevented some commentators from trying to extend the idea of 'creation' to encompass trade marks. This has been done by claiming that a trader creates goodwill as much as an author creates a work, that a trade mark must be created to be protected in the sense of being either invented, or by virtue of the fact that a new association has been created between the mark and a product, that is, a new meaning. Nevertheless, attempts to justify trade marks or goodwill as creations are weak, in

---

[35] R. Coombe, 'Tactics of Appropriation and the Politics of Recognition in Late Modern Democracies' (1993) 21 *Political Theory* 411, 414–5.

[36] 'Brand names, then, are the keystone of a competitive economy, an economy where every man is encouraged to do the best he can, and the public is the judge of whether or not he succeeds, because by branding his goods people will know that they came from him': Rogers, 'Social Value of Trade Marks and Brands', 253.

[37] H. Link, 'The Social Significance of Trademarks' (1948) 38 *TM Rep* 622, 623, 625.

[38] For example N. Klein, *No Logo: Taking Aim at the Brand Bullies* (2000); R. Coombe, *The Cultural Life of Intellectual Properties* (1998).

[39] E. Hamak, 'The Quality Assurance Function of Trademarks' (1975) 65 *TM Rep* 318, 319.

part because, while the associations between the mark and a source of goodwill may be instigated and nurtured by the trader, they are as much created by the customers and the public.

Perhaps the most plausible argument made along these lines sees trade marks as a reward for investment. This argument was summed up by Justice Breyer of the US Supreme Court when he said trade marks law helps 'to assure a producer that it (and not an imitating competitor) will reap the financial, reputation-related rewards associated with a desirable product'. In so doing trade marks law thereby encourages 'the production of quality products...and simultaneously discourages those who hope to sell inferior products by capitalising on a consumer's inability quickly to evaluate the quality of an item offered for sale. It is the source-distinguishing quality...that permits it to serve these basic purposes'.[40]

3.2 INFORMATION

Perhaps the most convincing arguments for the protection of trade signs is that they operate in the public interest insofar as they increase the supply of information to consumers and thereby increase the efficiency of the market. These arguments highlight the fact that trade marks are a shorthand way of communicating information that purchasers need in order to make informed purchasing choices. By 'preventing others from copying a source-identifying mark' trade marks law reduces 'the customer's costs of shopping and making purchasing decisions...for it quickly and easily assures a potential customer that this item—the item with this mark—is made by the same producer as other similarly marked items that he or she liked (or disliked) in the past'.[41]

The information provided by trade marks is particularly important in relation to goods that a consumer cannot judge merely through inspection. (These are known as 'experience goods'.) Where the quality and/or variety of goods is not readily apparent, trade marks enable consumers to choose the product with the desired features. Trade marks also encourage firms to maintain consistent quality and variety standards and to compete over a wide quality and variety. Consequently, it has been said that the 'primary reason for the existence and protection of trade marks is that they facilitate and enhance consumer decisions and...they create incentives for firms to produce products of desirable qualities even when these are not observable before purchase'.[42]

In some respects, it is impossible when assessing the protection of trade marks to divorce considerations about trade marks from considerations about advertising. This is because '[t]rade symbols are a species of advertising: their special characteristics are brevity and continuity in use, both of which are essential to their symbolic function'.[43] If trade marks function as a vehicle for advertising, one obvious question is whether we value advertising.[44] In a very

---

[40] *Qualitex v. Jacobson Products* 115 S Ct 1300 (1995).

[41] Ibid (Justice Breyer). In situations where the information relates to health or safety, the public interest in ensuring its accuracy is telling: see *S. v. London Borough of Havering* (20 Nov. 2002) (para. 11).

[42] Economides, 'Economics of Trademarks', 525–6. Landes and Posner call this the 'economizing function': Landes and Posner, 'Economics of Trademark Law', 270. See also A. Griffiths, 'The Law and Economics of Trade Marks' in Bently, Davis & Ginsburg Ch 11; J. Aldred, 'The Economic Rationale for Trade Marks: An Economist's Critique', ibid, ch 12.

[43] Brown, 'Advertising and the Public Interest', 1185.

[44] During the middle of the twentieth century economists were extremely sceptical about advertising. A view was taken that advertising persuaded consumers to accept or choose the wrong products and that it promoted allegiances that went beyond the superiority of the product. A. Greenbaum, 'Trademarks Attacked' (1968) 58 *TM Rep* 443.

influential article, American academic Ralph Brown tied the legitimacy of trade mark protection to advertising.[45] He said that 'advertising depends on the remote manipulation of symbols, most importantly of symbols directed at a mass audience through mass media or imprinted on mass-produced goods. The essence of these symbols is distilled in the devices variously called trade marks, trade names, brand names or brand symbols'. Importantly, Brown drew a distinction between what he called informational and persuasive advertising.[46] 'From the point of view of the economic purist, imparting information is the only useful function of advertising.'[47] However, most advertising was 'persuasive advertising' and was socially unjustifiable. This was because it added costs and effectively insulated traders from competition. 'By differentiating their products in order to carve out a separate market in which demand, price, and output can be manipulated ... The main drive of advertising is to facilitate this latter form of control.' Brown was sceptical about the idea that in buying brands consumers were buying the associations, intangible allure, etc. Given his negative view of persuasive advertising, Brown argued that the task of the courts in trade marks cases was to 'pick out, from the tangle of claims, facts and doctrines they are set to unravel, the threads of informative advertising, and to ignore the persuasive'.[48]

Brown argued that in addition to being justified insofar as they were used to indicate source and quality, trade mark protection was also justified where it supports the informational aspect of advertising. For Brown, the advertising or persuasive function of marks is 'of dubious social utility. There seems little reason why the courts should recognize or protect interests deriving from it.'[49] He considered likelihood of confusion to be the 'universal judicial touchstone'.[50] Because persuasive rather than informational advertising can lead to distortion of incentives in a competitive economy,[51] in order to justify a corresponding extension of protection, these costs need to be shown to be worth sacrificing to some greater goal.

3.3 ETHICAL JUSTIFICATIONS

Ethical arguments have also been used to justify the trade mark regime. The main ethical argument for the protection of trade marks is based on the idea of fairness or justice. In particular, it is said that persons should not be permitted 'to reap where they have not sown'. More specifically, it is said that by adopting 'someone else's mark, a person is taking advantage of the goodwill generated by the original trade mark owner'. Through this agricultural metaphor, the justification for protecting trade marks is linked to the broader arenas of the protection of traders against 'unfair competition' and 'unjust enrichment'.[52]

While classic cases where a trader uses someone else's trade mark on identical goods are clearly objectionable under the principle that a person should not reap where they have not sown, the principle has also been used to justify more extensive protection. For example, it is said that one objection to 'comparative advertising' is that even though it does not confuse consumers, it takes advantage of the reputation that the earlier trader has built up. Similarly,

[45] Brown, 'Advertising and the Public Interest'.

[46] See S. Haan, 'The Persuasion Route of the Law: Advertising and Legal Persuasion' (2000) 100 *Columbia Law Review* 1281 (describing the shift from informative/cognitive advertising to affective, symbolic, emotional, non-rational techniques of persuasion, and discussing the implication of this shift for legal advocacy).

[47] Brown, 'Advertising and the Public Interest', 1168.

[48] Ibid, 1184.   [49] Ibid, 1190.   [50] Ibid, 1195.

[51] Economides, 'Economics of Trademarks', 533.

[52] A. Kamperman Sanders, *Unfair Competition Law: The Protection of Intellectual and Industrial Creativity* (1997).

one of the objections which are made to marks being used on dissimilar goods (for example the ROLLS ROYCE café) is that it takes advantage of the repute of the earlier mark.

Problems arise from such attempts to use the principle that a person should not reap where they have not sown to justify more extensive forms of protection. The first problem is that it is not always easy to determine what the trade mark owner has sown: the mere selection of signs and symbols from the public domain seems a meagre basis on which to found such a claim (especially against a trader who is not aware that a mark may be registered). Also, it is not obvious that we should necessarily treat the associations that develop in the minds of the public as something of value which the trade mark owner has nurtured.[53] Second, it is often unclear whether another person is reaping from the cultivated soil of the trade mark owner or has obtained their fruits from the uncultivated commons. Although the causal link can be substantiated in cases of misrepresentation leading to confusion, it is difficult to justify protection where consumers are not 'confused'.[54] Third and more generally, the law does not penalize every case of reaping without sowing (for example, copying an unpatented business idea). As such, the onus falls on the advocates of the reap–sow principle to provide guidance as to the other factors that trigger the legal operation of the principle.[55]

Other ethical arguments have also been used to justify trade mark protection.[56] For example, it is sometimes argued that the misuse of trade marks is justified by reference to moral norms which treat 'truth-telling' as a core 'good' (rather than as necessary for the maintenance of efficient markets).[57] Under this approach, it is argued that the law ought to allow a person who suffers harm as a result of lying to bring an action against the liar. Misrepresentations of the source of goods are equivalent to lying or deception and are simply 'wrong'.[58] While arguments of this sort would justify a law of trade marks and passing off in some form, they would not appear to justify the protection of one trade mark owner against the innocent adopter of a mark, nor against uses which the public would not understand as indicating a business connection with the owner. As such, it would only support a very narrowly confined law of trade marks.[59]

Another ethical argument that could justify broader protection has recently been proffered by Michael Spence.[60] He has argued that justifications for protecting freedom of expression, grounded in notions of autonomy, might be used to explain why third parties should not be permitted to use trade marks in certain ways. Spence draws an analogy between misuse of trade marks and 'compelled' speech: if a person uses someone else's trade mark on goods (or in any way), that use implicates the expressive autonomy of the trade mark owner insofar as the

---

[53] M. Spence, 'Passing Off and the Misappropriation of Valuable Intangibles' (1996) 112 *LQR* 472, 479–80.

[54] Ibid, 472.

[55] For discussion of the extent to which Lockean arguments can justify trade mark protection see Scott, Oliver and Ley Pineda, 'Trade Marks as Property: A Philosophical Perspective' in Bently, Davis & Ginsburg (eds.) Ch. 13.

[56] W. Howarth, 'Are Trademarks Necessary?' (1970) 60 *TM Rep* 228 (legal protection of trade marks is really a means of directing and enforcing business morality).

[57] Cf. Cross, 'Language and the Law', 111 (the law's role is to control deception and thereby facilitate market communication).

[58] Pattishall, 'Trade Marks and the Monopoly Phobia', 600 (trade mark infringement is a sister of forgery, fraud, counterfeiting).

[59] Spence, 'Passing Off and the Misappropriation of Valuable Intangibles', 480 (arguing that norms concerning truth telling explain the existing limits of passing off).

[60] M. Spence, 'The Mark as Expression/The Mark as Property' (2005) 58 *Current Legal Problems* 491; 'An Alternative Approach to Dilution Protection: A Response to Scott, Oliver & Ley Pineda' in Bently, Davis & Ginsburg (eds.) ch. 14.

third party's speech is understood as communicating a message from the trade mark owner (e.g. 'I made these goods').[61] What is useful about Spence's argument is that both trade mark owner and user might be viewed as having claims grounded in speech rights, the conflicting interests thus being rendered 'commensurable'. However, while this kind of balancing is the sort of activity that the judiciary have already been compelled to undertake in the context of the protection of privacy, it is hard to imagine either judges or traders supporting such a radical rethinking of trade mark principles.

4 INTERNATIONAL AND REGIONAL DIMENSIONS

Trade marks have always been connected to particular geographical conditions. Indeed, in some sense, the need for legal recognition of marks arose with the decline of the local economy, which meant that consumers became dissociated from the source of the goods.[62] It is not surprising therefore that further changes in the geographical aspects of trade have prompted alterations in trade mark law. These have largely taken two forms. First, growth in international trade led to the establishment of international systems of registration, thereby enabling traders to gain protection swiftly and cheaply in all relevant markets. Second, changes in international trade prompted the establishment of international minimum standards of protection.

4.1 INTERNATIONAL REGISTRATION

Traders who operate on more than a local level will wish to protect their marks on a transnational basis. Various mechanisms have been developed to assist in this regard. The earliest of these was the Paris Convention of 1883 that requires members to apply the principle of national treatment. That is, it requires members to treat foreign nationals of contracting states as they would their own nationals.[63] This ensures the possibility for foreign protection of trade marks. This is further facilitiated by provisions which give registrants in one country a short period of priority,[64] and provisions obliging national offices to register any trade mark which has been registered in its country of origin.[65]

While the Paris Convention was of some assistance to transnational traders, it failed to create a mechanism for the international application for marks. However, the Madrid Agreement on the International Registration of Marks of 1891 and the Madrid Protocol of 1989 provide just such mechanisms. Under these arrangements, after making a 'home registration' or 'home application', an individual or company may apply to the Bureau of the World Intellectual Property Organization for an international registration. The Bureau passes the application on to relevant national trade mark offices. If the office of the contracting party does not refuse the application within a limited time, it is treated as registered. The simplification of the process of international registration has obvious advantages for trade mark owners. While the United Kingdom long resisted invitations to join the Madrid Agreement[66] (mainly on the ground that

---

[61] Spence calls this the 'freedom from compulsion to subsidise a message with which the person from whom the subsidy is sought chooses not to be associated.'

[62] B. Paster, 'Trade-Marks: Their Early History' (1969) 59 *TM Rep* 551, 551–2 ('the need for trademarks is a product of man's complex commercial society').

[63] Paris, Art. 2. The Trademark Law Treaty, signed on 28 Oct. 1994, is a limited agreement relating mostly to subject matter and prosecution procedure.

[64] Paris, Art. 4.   [65] Paris, Art. 6*quinquies*: the *telle-quelle* obligation.

[66] The UK has now acceded to the Madrid Agreement by way of the Protocol. See below.

the Agreement worked unfavourably against those who first registered in the United Kingdom where examination of all applications is required), the United Kingdom is now a party to the Protocol.[67]

While the Madrid Agreement and Protocol provide useful simplified mechanisms for obtaining national registrations, they necessarily result in the proprietor holding a portfolio of national marks each of which needs to be managed, licensed, and enforced separately. In contrast, the Community trade mark, which became fully operational on 1 April 1996, confers on a trade mark owner a single legal right that operates throughout the European Community.[68] Such rights are acquired by the filing of a single application for a Community trade mark with the Office for Harmonization in the Internal Market (Trade Marks and Designs) (the OHIM), which is located at Alicante (Spain). As of February 2008, the OHIM had received over 650,000 applications and has registered over 440,000 marks.[69] The Community registration system has also been linked to the Madrid Protocol: international applications can be based on Community marks, and the applicants under the Madrid Protocol can themselves designate the Community.

4.2 INTERNATIONAL STANDARDS

There has been relatively little action, either at the international or regional level, on the protection of *unregistered* marks. In part, this can be explained by the fact that, if a business operates on a transnational level, it typically will have the resources to protect its interests via registration. As a result, the protection of unregistered marks tends to be a matter of concern only for small enterprises and, as a consequence, has not prompted activities at the diplomatic level. Moreover, the forms and conditions for protection of unregistered marks vary widely, very much reflecting local legal principles. (In the United Kingdom the main form of protection is through the judge-made law of passing off.)

That said, the geographical expansion in the operations of many businesses has given rise to a form of opportunism, against which international action has been taken. More specifically, the Paris Convention has been revised to prevent the pre-emptive adoption of such marks by interlopers in countries where the 'proprietor' has not yet commenced marketing. Article 6*bis* of the Paris Convention imposes an obligation to recognize and protect well-known marks even where they have not been registered.[70] The concept of well-known marks (as distinct from distinctive marks, marks with a reputation, and famous marks) is left undefined, and has been contested.[71] Article 16(2) of TRIPS indicates that, in assessing whether a mark is well-known, members shall take account of the knowledge of the trade mark in the relevant sector of the public, including knowledge in the member concerned which has been obtained as a result of the promotion of the trade mark. UK law only recently gave effect to its obligation to recognize a special category of 'well-known trade marks'.[72] This is examined further in Chapter 34.

Second, and more generally, parties to the Convention are obliged to provide effective protection against unfair competition.[73] Article 10*bis* of the Paris Convention obliges member countries to assure 'effective protection against unfair competition' which, in turn, is defined

---

[67] See below at pp. 801–3.   [68] Annand and Norman (1998).

[69] See below at pp. 795–800.   [70] Paris, Art. 6. See TMA s. 52(2).

[71] F. Mostert, 'Well-Known and Famous Marks: Is Harmony Possible in the Global Village?' (1996) 86 *TM Rep* 103, 115 ff.; A. Kur, 'Well-Known Marks, Highly Renowned Marks and Marks Having a High Reputation: What's it All About?' (1992) 23 *IIC* 218; M. Blakeney, 'Well-Known Marks' [1994] *EIPR* 481.

[72] TMA s. 56. See below at p. 742.   [73] Paris, Art. 10*bis*.

as any 'act of competition contrary to honest practices in industrial or commercial matters'.[74] UK law has not expressly implemented this provision, presumably on the assumption that the existing rules relating to registered trade marks, passing-off, and malicious falsehood already deal adequately with it.

In relation to registered marks, the TRIPS Agreement provides by far the most detailed international prescription of the substantive rules relating to their protection. Article 15 defines the protectable subject matter expansively, to include, for example, service marks.[75] It also prohibits discrimination as to registrability based on the nature of the goods and services to which a trade mark is to be applied. Article 16 requires recognition of certain rights, in particular over the use of an identical or similar mark on identical or similar goods or services where such use would result in a likelihood of confusion (though not extending to dilution).[76] Articles 17 and 18 provide, respectively, for limited exceptions to the rights conferred by a trade mark, and for the potentially indefinite registration of marks on the basis of renewable terms each of a minimum of seven years. Article 19 limits the circumstances in which registrations may be revoked for non-use, and Article 21 prohibits the compulsory licensing of marks.[77] The significance of these standards for UK law is mainly in the restrictions that they place on potential future developments.

4.3 REGIONAL HARMONIZATION

It is impossible to understand current UK law without reference to regional harmonization matters. The most significant of these is the EC Trade Marks Directive. As we explained in Chapter 1, disparities in the trade mark laws of individual member states (which gave trade mark owners different rights in different circumstances) were thought to impede the free movement of goods, and freedom to provide services, and to distort competition within the Common Market.[78] In response, the Trade Marks Directive was designed to approximate 'those national provisions of law which most directly affect the functioning of the internal market'.[79] The Directive therefore harmonized the general 'conditions for obtaining and continuing to hold a registered trade mark' and the rights conferred by a trade mark.[80] In certain areas, however, it was decided that harmonization was not necessary. Consequently, member states are given discretion to decide whether to adopt certain of the rules provided for in the Directive. For example, there are certain optional grounds for refusing to register or invalidating a trade mark.[81] The Directive also leaves to the member states matters such as the procedure concerning the registration, revocation, and invalidity of trade marks.[82]

[74] Art. 39 of TRIPS requires member states to protect undisclosed information under Art. 10(2) of the Paris Convention.

[75] Paris, Art. 6*sexies* only contained a wish to that effect. D. Gervais, 'The TRIPS Agreement: Interpretation and Implementation' [1999] 21 *EIPR* 3. See also TLT Art. 15.

[76] TRIPS, Art. 16 (likelihood of confusion).   [77] TRIPS Art. 21.

[78] TM Dir., Recital 3 (aim not 'to undertake full-scale approximation of the trade mark laws of the member states').

[79] TM Dir., Recital 3.

[80] Ibid, Recital 7, Arts. 5, 6, and 7. See *David West, trading as Eastenders v. Fuller Smith* [2003] *FSR* (44) 816 (para. 69) *per* Arden LJ ('if King Canute had been a trade mark agent, the waters of Community law...would surely have overwhelmed him by now').

[81] TM Dir., Arts. 3(2) and 4(4); Art. 5(2). These optional provisions must be implemented in full or not at all: *Adidas-Salomon AG and Adidas Benelux BV v. Fitnessworld,* Case C–408/01 [2004] 1 *CMLR* (4) 448 (para. 20) (ECJ).

[82] TM Dir., Recitals 4–6.

In addition to the Trade Marks Directive, it is also important to be aware of four other EC initiatives in the general field. Firstly, a Directive on Misleading and Comparative Advertising harmonizes the circumstances where comparative advertising is permissible.[83] Secondly, the Community adopted an important Regulation on enforcement, which is discussed (alongside similar rules relating to other intellectual property rights) in Chapter 48. Thirdly, the Community adopted a Directive on Unfair Competitive Practices, though this is restricted to business-to-consumer practices. Quite what impact it will have,[84] and whether it will be a prelude to full harmonization of unfair competition law as it affects business, is difficult to predict.[85] Finally, the Community has a number of related initiatives dealing with the protection of 'designations of origin' (PDOs) and 'geographical indications' (PGIs) for wines, spirits, agricultural products, and food. These are considered in Chapter 43.

5 THE FUTURE

UK trade marks law has undergone dramatic change in the last 20 years: notably as a result of having implemented the Trade Marks Directive in the 1994 Act, and the entry into force of the Community Trade Mark Regulation. It should not be supposed, however, that intellectual property lawyers can simply sit back and slowly familiarize themselves with these rules. New pressures are constantly demanding judicial or legislative responses.

The wider recognition of brands has provided further fuel for those with expansionist tendencies. In addition to advocating protection against use of similar marks even where there is no confusion, arguments have been made for the subject matter to be expanded, for owners to be given broader control over imitation (especially in relation to 'look-alikes' and 'me-toos'), and for the relaxation of controls over licensing. Some commentators have argued that 'the positive associations that comprise a brand—a brand's equity—can rise to the level of a property right entitled separately to protection irrespective of confusion or the existence of a dilution statute'.[86] The *Gowers Committee* recommended that this area be kept under review.[87]

The advent of electronic commerce and the possibility of direct sales of goods over the internet has brought with it new questions for trade marks. Initially, questions arose about the relationship between trade marks and domain names. This issue attracted a lot of attention, both at the national and international level, and UK law has responded to these pressures through existing legal regimes, rather than attempting to promulgate new statutes. Where a domain name is used to trade in the same sphere as an existing trade mark owner, the courts have found little difficulty in employing the laws of passing off and registered trade marks.[88] Moreover, these laws have often been applied somewhat generously to enable existing

---

[83] See below at pp. 937–41.

[84] It is in the process of being implemented in the UK.: the Consumer Protection from Unfair Trading Regulations, SI 2008/TBA, implementing the Directive in the UK were laid before Parliament in March 2008 and will come in to force on 26 May 2008. See <http://www.berr.gov.uk>

[85] Directive 2005/29/EC of the European Parliament and of the Council of 11 May 2005 concerning unfair business-to-consumer commercial practices in the internal market and amending Council Directive 84/450/EEC, Directives 97/7/EC, 98/27/EC and 2002/65/EC of the European Parliament and of the Council and Regulation (EC) No 2006/2004 of the European Parliament and of the Council.

[86] Swann and Davis, 'Dilution: Brand Equity as Protectable Property'.

[87] *Gowers Review* (paras 5.82–88).

[88] See below at pp. 766–7, 922. There are, of course, real problems about jurisdiction where a foreign trader uses a similar name on a web site run from overseas and who targets a different market.

businesses to prevent opportunistic 'cyber-squatting'.[89] There has also been an international response of an interesting sort: the establishment of a code (ICANN) and a system of dispute resolution administered by WIPO.[90] Although the issue of domain names has not gone away, new questions are now testing legal systems round the globe: questions whether trade marks are infringed when used in metatags, banner ads, pop-ups and the search systems that control the placement of adverts on computer screens (but do not appear in the ads themselves).

[89] See below at pp. 766–7.   [90] See below at pp. 1098–9.

32

PASSING OFF

CHAPTER CONTENTS

1 INTRODUCTION

The oldest of the modern legal regimes for the protection of trade symbols is the action for passing off.[1] In essence the action allows trader A to prevent a competitor B from passing their goods off as if they were A's. Lord Langdale MR summed up the rationale for the passing-off action in *Perry v. Truefitt*[2] when he said:

A man is not to sell his own goods under the pretence that they are the goods of another man; he cannot be permitted to practise such a deception, nor to use the means which contribute to that end. He cannot therefore be allowed to use names, marks, letters or other indicia, by which he may induce purchasers to believe, that the goods which he is selling are the manufacture of another person.[3]

While the early history of passing-off is unclear,[4] it is widely thought that an action of this sort was first recognized in the Elizabethan case of *JG v. Samford*.[5] It is also generally acknowledged that the common law roots of the action are found in the torts of deceit and misrepresentation,[6] with the strictures of the common law action being mollified in a number of Chancery cases in the early nineteenth century.[7] The modern or classic formulation of the action (usually

---

[1] The pre-modern regimes included guild regulation, heraldry, and cutlers' marks: see Sherman and Bently, 166–8.

[2] (1842) 6 Beav 66; 49 ER 749.   [3] Ibid, 752.

[4] W. Morison, 'Unfair Competition and Passing Off' (1956) 2 *Sydney Law Review*. 50, 53; *Henderson v. Radio Corporation Pty* (1960) [1969] *RPC* 218, 236.

[5] First cited as a precedent in *Southern v. How* (1617) *Cro Jac* 468, 79 *ER* 400. See the discussion in F. Schechter, *The Historical Foundations of the Law Relating to Trade Marks* (1925) 10.

[6] For example, *Sykes v. Sykes* (1824) 3 *B & C* 543; 107 *ER* 834. For arguments that there remains a common law action based on fraud, without a requirement of goodwill, see Gummow J in *10th Cantanae Pty v. Shoshama Pty* (1989) 10 *IPR* 289; *ConAgra Inc. v. McCain Foods (Australia) Pty* (1992) 23 *IPR* 193.

[7] In particular Equity judges abandoned the requirement of bad faith in *Millington v. Fox* (1838) 3 *My & Cr* 338, 40 *ER* 956.

classified as a tort) emerged in the second half of the nineteenth century. In its classic form, the basis of the action was the existence of a 'misrepresentation'. Typically, a misrepresentation occurs where a person says or does something that suggests, incorrectly, that the goods or services they are selling are the goods or services of the claimant. In order to justify injunctive relief, the courts believed that it was necessary for the action to be based on a property right. For some time it was suggested that this property right was located in the name or symbol employed.[8] This approach was rejected in the early twentieth century when it was said that the basis of equitable intervention was the property in 'goodwill'.[9] The concept of goodwill, which will be examined in detail below, remains a prerequisite for a successful passing-off action today.

It is important to recognize that the modern action, if it can be called a single action,[10] has moved beyond the classic case.[11] Indeed, as a result of adapting to changes in the commercial environment, the tort now extends beyond the sale of goods to cover services; beyond pretences concerning the origin of goods to cover pretences concerning their quality; and beyond simple pretences that the goods are those of another trader, to cover pretences that the goods have been licensed by another trader.[12] As a result, the tort continues to play a central role in the legal regulation of trade behaviour.[13] The common law nature of the action also gives it a flexibility that makes it attractive in situations that are not covered by the statutory regimes. This is particularly important where business practices change and the legislature is slow to respond.[14]

With these developments it has become increasingly difficult to state the law of passing off with any clarity or precision. Indeed, it has been said that the law 'contains sufficient nooks and crannies to make it difficult to formulate any satisfactory definition in short form'.[15] The difficulty in formulating a precise and accurate statement of the law has not been made any easier by the fact that the most recent authoritative statements of the law, which are found in the House of Lords' decisions in *Warnink v. Townend* (sometimes called the 'Advocaat'

---

[8] L. Bently, 'From Communication to Thing' in G. Dinwoodie & M. Janis, *A Handbook of Contemporary Trade Mark Law* (2008).

[9] *Spalding v. Gamage* (1915) 32 *RPC* 273, 284.

[10] J. Phillips and A. Coleman, 'Passing Off and the Common Field of Activity' (1985) 101 *LQR* 242, 244–5, have argued that passing-off is better seen as a family of actions each with particular characteristics. Despite the strength of this argument, the courts have continued to treat passing-off as a unitary action, only occasionally distinguishing 'classic' passing-off, from 'extended' passing-off. See, e.g. *Chocosuisse Union des Fabricants Suisses de Chocolat v. Cadbury* [1998] *RPC* 117, 127 (distinguishing between 'extended' and 'classic' passing-off and describing question of whether it is the same tort as 'a matter of semantics'). Note also *British Diabetic Association v. Diabetic Society* [1996] *FSR* 1, 11 *per* Robert Walker J (warning against assumption that principles from one set of facts can be applied to very different facts).

[11] *Arsenal FC plc v. Reed (No. 2)* [2003] *RPC* (39) 696 (para. 70) *per* Aldous LJ.

[12] However, the law of passing-off has not expanded into a tort of unfair competition. See below Ch. 34 Section 3.

[13] *Cadbury Schweppes Pty v. Pub Squash Co.* [1981] *RPC* 429, 490 *per* Lord Scarman (the tort 'is no longer anchored in its early nineteenth-century formulation'). But cf. *Hogan v. Koala Dundee* (1988) 12 *IPR* 508, 517 (Pincus J, Federal Court of Australia) (little progress in English law beyond the traditional notion of passing-off). See also M. Shúilleabháin, 'Common Law Protection of Trade Marks—The Continuing Relevance of Passing Off' (2003) 34(7) *IIC* 722.

[14] Passing-off also operates as a basis for relief where a trader has failed to register a mark. The law relating to passing-off also retains a role within the registered trade mark system. As will be seen at pp. 889–90 it is not possible for a person to register a sign as a trade mark if the use of that sign would amount to passing-off.

[15] *ConAgra v. McCain Foods (Australia) Pty* (1992) 23 *IPR* 193, 247 (FCA).

decision),[16] and *Reckitt & Colman v. Borden* (the 'Jif'lemon decision), are in very different terms.[17] Having said that, it is possible to formulate a general statement as to the elements of the action. In order to succeed in an action for passing off, a claimant must establish that:

(i)   the claimant has 'goodwill' (see below),

(ii)   the defendant made a 'misrepresentation' that is likely to deceive the public (Chapter 33), and

(iii)   the misrepresentation damages the goodwill of the claimant (Chapter 34).

Before turning to examine goodwill in more detail, two caveats are in order. The first is that each of the three elements must be shown to have existed or occurred at the time when the conduct to which the claimant objects took place (as opposed, for example, to the time of proceedings).[18] The second point to note is that the three elements are inter-related. As a result, the same facts may be important in proving goodwill, deception, and/or damage. Consequently, the courts may dismiss an action for lack of misrepresentation where it might as easily involve a lack of goodwill.[19] The inter-relationship is also important because developments in one area, such as misrepresentation, may impact on another area, such as damages. This can be seen, for example, with the recent recognition of dilution as a form of damage, which has thrown into doubt the need for the defendant's misrepresentation to cause confusion or deception.[20]

2 GOODWILL

The first factor that needs to be proved to establish an action for passing off is goodwill.[21] The mere fact that consumers are confused about the source of a product or service is not enough for a trader to bring a successful passing-off action against another trader with whom their products are being confused.[22] Before a trader is able to bring an action, they must show that they have goodwill in relation to the product or service in question.

---

[16] *Erven Warnink BV v. Townend (J.) & Sons* [1979] *AC* 731. The case contains two different formulations of the requirements for the action. Lord Diplock, at 742, laid down five 'characteristics' that must be present to create a valid cause of action in passing-off: (i) a misrepresentation (ii) made by a trader in the course of trade (iii) to prospective customers of his or ultimate consumers of goods or services supplied by him (iv) which is calculated to injure the business or goodwill of another trader (in the sense that this is a reasonably foreseeable consequence), and (v) which causes actual damage to a business or goodwill of the trader by whom the action is brought or (in a *quia timet* action) will probably do so. Lord Fraser at ibid, 755–6, also set out five requirements: (i) that the claimant's business consists of, or includes, selling in England a class of goods to which the particular trade name applies; (ii) that the class of goods is clearly defined, and that in the minds of the public, or a section of the public, in England, the trade name distinguishes that class from other similar goods; (iii) that, because of the reputation of the goods, there is a goodwill attached to the name; (iv) that the claimant, as a member of the class of those who sell the goods, is the owner of goodwill in England which is of substantial value; (v) that he has suffered, or is really likely to suffer, substantial damage to his property in the goodwill by reason of the defendant selling goods which are falsely described by the trade name to which the goodwill is attached.

[17] In *Reckitt & Colman Products v. Borden* [1990] 1 *WLR* 491, 499, Lord Oliver reduced the elements of the action to three: reputation, deception, and damage.

[18] *J.C. Penney v. Penneys* [1975] *FSR* 367; *Barnsley Brewery Co. v. RBNB* [1997] *FSR* 462, 470; *Chocosuisse Union des Fabricants Suisse de Chocolat v. Cadbury* [1999] *RPC* 826, 836, 846; *Interlotto (UK) Ltd v. Camelot Group plc* [2004] *RPC* (8) 171 Laddie J; [2004] *RPC* (9) 186 (CA) (at para. 7).

[19] For example *Chivers & Sons v. Chivers & Co.* (1900) 17 *RPC* 420.

[20] *Harrods v. Harrodian School* [1996] *RPC* 697.

[21] *Star Industrial Co. v. Yap Kwee Kor* [1976] *FSR* 217, 223; *Warnink v. Townend* [1979] *AC* 731, 742, 755–6.

[22] *HFC Bank v. Midland Bank* [2000] *FSR* 176, 182–3.

Goodwill is a form of intangible property that is easy to describe, but difficult to define. It is the ineffable thing, the magnetism that leads customers to return to the same business or buy the same brand. In *IRC v. Muller & Co.'s Margarine,* Lord Macnaghten said:

[goodwill] is the benefit and advantage of the good name, reputation, and connection of a business. It is the attractive force that brings in custom. It is the one thing which distinguishes an old-established business from a new business at its first start. The goodwill of a business must emanate from a particular centre or source. However widely or extended or diffused its influence may be, goodwill is worth nothing unless it has power of attraction sufficient to bring customers home to the source from which it emanates. Goodwill is composed of a variety of elements. It differs in its composition in different trades and in different businesses in the same trade. One element may preponderate here and another element there.[23]

As Lord Macnaghten stressed, for goodwill to exist, there must be some 'causative' impact upon customer behaviour. Goodwill is the attractive force which 'brings in' custom. The goodwill must have a 'power of attraction sufficient to bring customers home to the source from which it emanates'. One consequence of this is that just because a trader has started business does not necessarily mean that there will be goodwill. This is because consumers might use the business, purchase the goods or services, because it is conveniently located, or just because it is there. Rather, for goodwill to exist, customers must be buying the goods or using the services as a result of the reputation that they have developed.[24]

2.1 MANIFESTATIONS OF GOODWILL

The law of passing-off is concerned with goodwill when it manifests itself in certain ways. Passing-off is usually concerned with the signs or 'badges' that are understood as indicating that a product or service emanates from a particular trade source. These 'badges' can take a variety of forms. Typically, passing-off is concerned with the goodwill that arises in relation to the name, symbol, or logo that has been employed by a trader and thus has come to be associated with the business. For example, it is clear that there is goodwill associated with the name 'Marks & Spencer', and the Nike 'swoosh' or tick. In these situations, the law is relatively straightforward. However, the courts have recognized that goodwill may arise in a number of other situations. These include goodwill associated with the packaging, get-up, or trade dress of products, and advertising style. In this section, we will limit our discussions to some of the less straightforward situations.

2.1.1 Goodwill in descriptive words

While goodwill is typically developed through the use of words, such as NIKE, MARLBORO, or ROLLS-ROYCE, to distinguish one trader's goods or services from those of its competitors, in some circumstances goodwill may come to be associated with words which initially were capable of being understood as descriptive of the goods themselves.[25] For example, FRUIT

---

[23] [1901] *AC* 217, 224 (Lord Macnaghten). Although a tax case, it has been frequently employed in passing-off cases and the Court of Appeal has said that 'no one, judge or jurist, has yet improved' on it as a description: *Scandecor Development AB v. Scandecor Marketing AB* [1999] *FSR* 26, 41.

[24] *HFC Bank v. Midland Bank* [2000] *FSR* 176, 183.

[25] In between the category of invented or coined words and descriptive words, are many allusive or quasi-descriptive terms. The courts will be willing to protect these terms soon after they are used in trade: see e.g. *Phones4U Ltd v. Phone4u.co.uk Internet Ltd* [2006] *EWCA Civ* 244; [2007] *RPC* (5) (paras 24–25, 30–34) (first

PASTILLES might be taken to be a description of a product delivered in pastille form which tastes of or is made from fruit. However, most children (and adults) in the United Kingdom will understand the words as indicating a particular brand of sweet confectionary, in fact made by Rowntree's. Consequently, such words have become the manifestation of the goodwill that Rowntree's own in the sweets. (Other familiar examples include TREETS (no longer designating a special indulgence but a confectionary made by Cadbury's) and EVIAN (no longer designating a place but instead a brand of water).

While it is possible for a descriptive term to become associated with a claimant, the courts are extremely reluctant to allow a person to obtain a monopoly in descriptive words.[26] In part, this is because policy considerations favour allowing other traders to make use of words that are part of the common stock-in-trade. It is also because in relation to descriptive words, it will be more difficult for a trader to show that the words indicate source, rather than what they ordinarily describe. In short, the more descriptive the words of the goods or services which the trader sells, the more difficult it will be to establish the existence of goodwill attaching to those words.

For a trader to show that they have goodwill in a descriptive word, they need to show that the word has become 'distinctive in fact' or has taken on a 'secondary meaning'.[27] This can be seen, for example, in *Reddaway v. Banham*,[28] where the House of Lords acknowledged that the claimant's use of the term CAMEL HAIR to describe their belts had acquired a secondary meaning. Other examples of (largely) descriptive words that acquired secondary meaning include: OVEN CHIPS for potato chips to be cooked in the oven rather than fried;[29] FLAKED OATMEAL;[30] MALTED MILK;[31] and MOTHERCARE for clothing for expectant mothers and children.[32]

For a trader to show that they have goodwill in a descriptive word, the trader needs to demonstrate that the words have acquired a secondary meaning not only of goods or services of that description, but also specifically of the goods or services of which they are the source.[33] It is also necessary to show that descriptive terms are distinctive of one source.[34] Thus, where two publishers are competing to launch magazines with a title such as *Leisure News,* it is unlikely that either will be able to bring a passing-off action until the magazine has been in the marketplace for a sufficient period of time to build up a public association between the name and a particular source.[35] As Farwell J said, the name should 'have to the whole of the trade and to all persons who have any knowledge of the article in question the sole meaning sought to be attached to it by the plaintiffs—that is to say, the original primary meaning must have been

---

instance judge had wrongly held there was no goodwill in PHONES4U because it was descriptive, even though turnover was £42 million and it held 19 per cent of the market); *Knight v. Beyond Properties Pty Ltd* [2007] *FSR* (34) 813 (goodwill in MYTHBUSTERS for children's books as a result of sales in thousands).

[26] *Spalding v. Gamage* (1915) 32 *RPC* 273, 284; *Cellular Clothing Co. v. Maxton & Murray* [1899] *AC* 326, 339.

[27] See Wadlow (2004), para. 8.61, 623–24. Acquisition of secondary meaning is discussed in the context of registered marks at pp. 840–6.

[28] [1896] *AC* 199.   [29] *McCain International v. County Fair Foods* [1981] *RPC* 69.

[30] *Parsons v. Gillespie* [1898] *AC* 239 (PC).

[31] *Horlick's Malted Milk Co. v. Summerskill* (1916) 33 *RPC* 108.

[32] *Mothercare v. Penguin Books* [1988] *RPC* 113, 115.

[33] Secondary meaning is essential not just where the name describes the product, but also where it embodies a reference to quality. For example, THE HIT FACTORY was descriptive of a quality of the claimant's recording studio and in the absence of a demonstration of secondary meaning could not form the basis of a passing-off action: *Peter Waterman v. CBS* [1993] *EMLR* 27.

[34] Ibid.   [35] *Marcus Publishing v. Leisure News* [1990] *RPC* 576, 584.

eliminated from the dictionary of persons who deal in this article in the trade and all other persons whom it may concern to know it'.[36]

In proving secondary meaning, it will be common for a claimant to submit evidence of things such as the length of use and the amount of money spent on advertising.[37] It will certainly be easier to find that a name is distinctive and thus protected where a trader has used the name separately rather than in conjunction with another sign that designates source.[38] Moreover, distinctiveness will be acquired more readily if the sign is not exclusively descriptive, as was the case with FARM FLUID for farm disinfectant.[39] A trader may acquire secondary meaning in a descriptive phrase through public adoption rather than their own action.[40] In these cases, the most important evidence is evidence of the trade or public. On the whole, the association must be in the mind of the general public, so that it is not normally legitimate 'to slice the public into parts'.[41]

Similar principles apply to geographic words and personal names. In general the adoption of a geographic term or a personal name will not prevent another trader from using the same designation.[42] In certain circumstances, however, secondary meaning can attach to such signs. For example, in *Montgomery v. Thompson*[43] the claimant had operated a brewery in the small town of Stone in Staffordshire for over a hundred years. Over time, its beer had become widely known as STONE ALE. The defendant, who had recently established a brewery in Stone, was prevented from using the term STONE to describe its beer.[44] Similarly, it was held by the Court of Appeal that the term SWISS CHOCOLATE had come to be understood by a significant section of the public to mean and mean only chocolate made in Switzerland, and that this was understood as being of a particular quality.[45]

Words, once distinctive, may later lose their ability to indicate source. In such cases, a passing-off action will no longer be available. A classic example is LINOLEUM, which is the name used for a floor covering made of solidified oil. The floor covering had been the subject of a patent, and during that time the claimant was its only manufacturer. After expiry of the patent other manufacturers began to make and sell the floor covering under the name LINOLEUM. Fry J refused to prevent competitors using this term, on the basis that it had become generic. That is, the public had begun to use the term to refer to the product generally, without connoting the source of manufacture.[46]

---

[36] *Chivers v. Chivers* (1900) 17 *RPC* 420, 430 (Farwell J) (in the context of personal names); Wadlow (2004), paras. 8.61–72, 623–632.

[37] Such factors, of themselves, will not give rise to recognition. Advertisement distinguished from trade is nothing: *Chivers*, ibid, 431 Farwell J (describing the act of advertising as an atrocious disfigurement of the fairest landscape in the kingdom); *Burberrys v. Cording* (1909) 26 *RPC* 693 (slip-on).

[38] *McCain v. County Fair* [1981] *RPC* 69 (OVEN CHIPS used with McCain's). See more generally at pp. 844–6.

[39] *Antec International v. South Western Chicks (Warren)* [1997] *FSR* 278; [1998] *FSR* 738, 743–4.

[40] *Edge & Sons v. Gallon & Son* [1900] *RPC* 557; *Waterman v. CBS* [1993] *EMLR* 27.

[41] Ibid. (rejecting arguments that it was sufficient that the claimant's recording studio was known as THE HIT FACTORY to popular music press and 'non-pompous end of market' when other sectors treated the phrase as referring to others).

[42] *Chivers v. Chivers* (1900) 17 *RPC* 420.   [43] [1891] *AC* 217.

[44] See also *My Kinda Town v. Soll* [1983] *RPC* 407 (CHICAGO pizza); *CPC (United Kingdom) v. Keenan* [1986] *FSR* 527 (OXFORD marmalade, OXBRIDGE marmalade).

[45] *Chocosuisse v. Cadbury* [1999] *RPC* 826, 832.

[46] *Linoleum Manufacturing Co. v. Nairn* (1878) 7 *Ch D* 834, 836.

Fig. 32.1 Jif Lemon

2.1.2 Goodwill associated with packaging, get-up, and trade dress

A person may acquire goodwill through use of particular packaging or 'get-up' for their products.[47] For example, in *Reckitt & Colman*[48] the claimant sold lemon juice in plastic containers that resembled a lemon in size, shape, and colour (see figure 32.1 below). The House of Lords held that, in using plastic lemons that were very similar to the claimant's, the defendant had passed its juice off as the claimant's. This was because the claimant had succeeded in persuading the public that lemon juice sold in plastic lemon-sized containers had been manufactured by it.

The protection that passing-off provides over trade dress, get-up, and the packaging of goods is particularly important where consumers identify products by their external features rather than by words. This will be the case where goods are sold in foreign-language markets (such as China) where little attention is likely to be paid to the words,[49] or where the goods are sold to people who are illiterate.[50] Get-up is also more likely to be an identifying feature in the case of common household goods,[51] rather than goods which are bought under professional supervision.[52]

In order to establish that the claimant has goodwill associated with the get-up or packaging of a product (and thus that copying of it may amount to passing off), a claimant must be able to prove that the public recognizes that the get-up is distinctive of the claimant's goods or services.[53] In practice, a claimant may experience a number of difficulties in establishing such an association, particularly where the claim relates to the shape rather than the packaging of a product. More specifically, it may be difficult to show that consumers care at all about the

---

[47] J. Evans, 'Passing Off and the Problem of Product Simulation' (1968) 31 *MLR* 642; Wadlow (2004), paras. 8.122–150, 670–93; *Edge v. Nicholls* [1911] *AC* 693 (washing soap sold in a calico bag with a stick attached). For the possibility of design protection for the shapes of articles and limitations of such protection see at pp. 628–9, 632–3, 634–7, 654–5, 674–6, 681–3, 687–96.

[48] [1990] *RPC* 341, 406.

[49] *Modus Vivendi v. Keen (World Marketing)* [1996] *EIPR* D–82 (sale of butane gas by defendant in similar get-up in China); *Johnston v. Orr Ewing* (1882) 7 *App Cas* 219, 225.

[50] *Edge v. Nicholls* [1911] *AC* 693.   [51] *United Biscuits (UK) v. Asda Stores* [1997] *RPC* 513.

[52] *Hodgkinson & Corby v. Wards Mobility Services* [1995] *FSR* 169.

[53] However, while it is clear that imitation of get-up or packaging may constitute a misrepresentation, this does not mean that in all cases it will do so: *Reckitt & Colman* [1990] *RPC* 341, 406.

trade origin of a product. Moreover, it may be difficult to establish that consumers understand functional features of a product as indicating source.

The need to show that the public regard a particular feature of a product as indicating source will prove particularly difficult where the product feature in question performs some function. While there is no public policy exception to the passing-off action for 'functional features' and no requirement that features of get-up be 'capricious',[54] it will be very difficult for a trader to demonstrate that the public view functional or non-capricious features of an article as indicating source. As Jacob J said in *Hodgkinson & Corby v. Wards Mobility Services*,[55] the claimant must prove a misrepresentation which will be hard where there is no manifest badge of trade origin. This is because people tend to buy things for what they are and what they do, rather than out of interest in their origin. Accordingly, Jacob J found that a defendant who produced cushions which were used to help alleviate bed sores, had not passed themselves off as the claimant's. This was the case even though the claimant's cushions were memorable and striking, and the defendant's cushions were similar in appearance.

2.1.3 Advertising style

A trader may also attempt to establish that they have goodwill associated with particular advertising techniques or slogans, and thus that a defendant is liable for passing off as a result of using techniques or slogans that are similar to those which are used by the claimant. In *Cadbury Schweppes v. Pub Squash*,[56] the claimant produced a lemon-flavoured soft drink called SOLO. As a part of its marketing campaign in Australia, the claimant launched a series of television advertisements which featured 'ruggedly masculine and adventurous men' drinking SOLO. The defendant promoted their lemon-flavoured soft drink with a similar campaign. While the Privy Council rejected the passing-off claim, Lord Scarman said that there was no reason *in principle* why the claimant could not have acquired goodwill associated with a particular advertising style. The reason for this was that:[57]

the tort is no longer anchored as in the early nineteenth-century formulation to the name or trade mark of a product or business. It is wide enough to encompass other descriptive material, such as slogans or visual images, which radio, television or newspaper advertising campaigns can lead the market to associate with the plaintiff's product, provided always that such descriptive material has become part of the goodwill of the product.[58]

While the Privy Council recognized that passing-off may protect a claimant's advertising campaign, it seems that claimants will have difficulties in demonstrating that the public associates a specific style of advertising with a particular source.[59]

2.1.4 Use of image, likeness, or voice

Finally, it is worth observing that, in principle, there is no reason why goodwill might not also arise through the use of a celebrity's image,[60] likeness, or voice.[61] Whether this is the case will

---

[54] *Hodgkinson v. Wards* [1995] FSR 169, 177. However, the House of Lords in *Reckitt*, ibid, 416, did indicate that such imitation of get-up might not amount to a misrepresentation when it was the only way to present the product. Lord Oliver noted that the association of the plastic shape with the claimant arose because 'there is nothing in the nature of the product sold which inherently requires it to be sold in the particular format'.

[55] *Hodgkinson*, ibid.   [56] *Cadbury Schweppes v. Pub Squash* [1981] RPC 429.

[57] Ibid, 490.   [58] Ibid.

[59] For further consideration of advertisements, see the cases discussed by Wadlow (2004), para. 8.186, 721–23.

[60] *Henderson v. Radio Corporation* (1960) [1969] RPC 218.   [61] *Sim v. H.J. Heinz Co.* [1959] 1 WLR 313.

always be a question of fact. In particular it will depend on whether the public believe that there is a relevant connection between the celebrity and the goods or services in issue. It should be noted that, unlike the position in many continental jurisdictions[62] and in several states in the USA,[63] British law does not recognize a general right of publicity or personality.[64]

2.2   A 'TRADER OPERATING IN TRADE'

As we indicated earlier, in order to demonstrate goodwill, a claimant must be a trader and operate in trade. We will look at each of these in turn.

2.2.1   The claimant must be a 'trader'

For a claimant to be in a position to show that they have the goodwill necessary to sustain a passing-off action, they must show that they are engaged in a very general sense in a business or commercial activity. The upshot of this is that the action is not available where one person changes their name to that of another, or calls their cat, boat, or house by the same name as their neighbour (however inconvenient or confusing that may be).

For the most part, the requirement that the claimant be in a trade has presented few problems. This is because the courts have been quite generous when deciding whether someone is engaged in business.[65] For example, the courts have recognized authors,[66] performers,[67] unincorporated associations,[68] and charities[69] as businesses that potentially give rise to goodwill.

The courts have only occasionally rejected a claimant's claim to passing off because of a lack of business status. One situation where a passing-off action was denied was in *Kean v. McGivan*[70] where the claimant claimed the exclusive right to the name Social Democratic Party. The Court of Appeal refused relief on the basis that the claimant was involved in a non-commercial activity. This was because the claimant was a small northern-based political party whose engagement in commercial activities was limited to the hiring of halls for meetings. If the claimant had been one of the major political parties who receive and spend large sums of money, however, the court might well have held that they were engaged in a trade. It should be

---

[62]   W. Van Caenegem, 'Different Approaches to the Problem of Celebrities against Unauthorized Use of Their Image in Advertising' [1990] *EIPR* 452.

[63]   O. Goodenough, 'The Price of Fame: The Development of the Right of Publicity in the United States' [1992] *EIPR* 55, 90.

[64]   Beverley-Smith, Ohly and Lucas-Schloetter, in their book, *Privacy, Property and Personality: Civil Law Perspectives on Commercial Appropriation*, (2005) 222–3 have argued that *Von Hannover* may require recognition of a right to identity. 'Following the ECHR's reasoning, Article 8 of the Convention arguably imposes an obligation on the member states to protect individuals against any misappropriation of their personal indicia in advertising or merchandising. A free speech defence will only be available in exceptional cases.' The authors argue that the jurisprudence 'will inevitably force English law to confront the issue of how best to develop a remedy for appropriation of personality', 225. See below pp. 1057–60.

[65]   'The word "trade" is widely interpreted': *Kean v. McGivan* [1982] *FSR* 119, 120 (Ackner LJ).

[66]   *Alan Clark v. Associated Newspapers* [1998] *RPC* 261, 269.

[67]   *Henderson v. Radio Corporation* (1960) [1969] *RPC* 218; cf. *Kaye v. Robertson* [1991] *FSR* 62 (Kaye, an actor, not a trader in relation to story about accident).

[68]   *British Legion v. British Legion Club (Street)* (1931) 63 *RPC* 555, 562.

[69]   *British Diabetic Association* [1996] *FSR* 1, 5.

[70]   [1982] *FSR* 119. The defendants were a high-profile breakaway group from the Labour Party, known as the 'Gang of Four'. In due course, the defendants' Social Democrats merged with the Liberal Party to form the Liberal Democrats.

noted, too, that the decision in *Kean v. McGivan* has been treated as doubtful, in the light of earlier authorities that were not cited to the court.[71]

A further situation in which the requirement that the claimant be a trader has proved problematic is where an action for passing off is brought by a trade association. If the trade association does not manufacture or sell any particular product, it will be unable to bring a passing-off action against a defendant who has merely passed off its products as those of the members of the trade association.[72] However, where a trade association organized exhibitions, it could own goodwill through its members which would form the basis for an action in passing-off: in such a case the action would have to be commenced by a member of the association acting in a representative capacity.[73]

2.2.2 The claimant must be trading

Once it has been shown that a claimant is engaged in a trade activity, there will usually be few problems in establishing that they have the goodwill necessary to sustain a passing-off action. Traders, however, have experienced problems in establishing goodwill in three situations. These are before they have started trading, after trading has ended, and where the trader is situated overseas. We will deal with each in turn.

Pre-trading goodwill. Given that goodwill 'has no independent existence apart from the business to which it is attached',[74] difficult questions arise when a person is setting up a business. In these circumstances the question may arise: at what point can a person claim to have goodwill? Is there any way in which a trader who is about to launch their business, and who has spent time and money on advertising and marketing, can prevent a competitor from taking advantage of their pre-launch publicity?

The traditional position is that before a passing-off action can be brought, trading must actually have commenced.[75] This can be seen, for example, in *Maxwell v. Hogg.*[76] Maxwell proposed to launch a magazine called BELGRAVIA in October 1866. As a part of the pre-launch publicity, in August and September of 1866 Maxwell advertised the forthcoming launch of BELGRAVIA in a magazine run by Hogg. On 25 September 1866, Hogg issued a magazine also called BELGRAVIA. Despite noting that this was hardly fair and candid dealing, the court held that Maxwell could not restrain Hogg from using the same name. This was because a declaration of intention to use a name did not secure any protection.

In contrast, where there has been substantial pre-launch publicity, claimants have occasionally succeeded in gaining interim relief prior to the launch of their products. In *Allen v. Brown Watson,*[77] the publisher of a book entitled *My Life and Loves by Frank Harris,* which had been widely advertised prior to publication, was granted an interim injunction against the

---

[71] In particular, *Holy Apostolic & Catholic Church of the East (Assyrian) Australia New South Wales Parish Association and others v. Attorney-General (New South Wales)* [1989] 18 *NSWLR* 291, 294 (Court of Appeal of New South Wales).

[72] A trade consortium may sue in its own name but cannot bring a representative action: *Consorzio del Prosciutto di Parma v. Marks & Spencer* [1991] *RPC* 351. See also *Chocosuisse v. Cadbury* [1999] *RPC* 826, 843–4. The Court of Appeal did acknowledge, however, that it might be convenient if a trade association could sue on behalf of its members in such circumstances.

[73] *Artistic Upholstery v. Art Forma (Furniture)* [1999] 4 *All ER* 277, 286–7.

[74] *Star Industrial v. Yap Kwee Kor* [1976] *FSR* 217, 223; *IRC v. Muller* [1901] *AC* 217, 223.

[75] The period of time and the types of activity that are needed to generate goodwill will vary from case to case: *Stannard v. Reay* [1967] *RPC* 589 (3 weeks' trade under the name MR CHIPPY was sufficient to establish goodwill on the Isle of Wight).

[76] (1867) *LR 2 Ch App* 307.   [77] [1965] *RPC* 191.

defendant who proposed to publish an abridged version also called *My Life and Loves by Frank Harris*.[78] Similarly, in *BBC v. Talbot Motor Co.*, the BBC had publicized their forthcoming traffic information service named CARFAX, which required motorists to have special car radios fitted or conventional ones adapted. The BBC was granted an interim injunction preventing the defendant from selling spare parts for vehicles under the name CARFAX. Sir Robert Megarry V-C noted that '[a]lthough that scheme has not yet been launched, that does not prevent the BBC from having built up goodwill in it which is entitled to protection'.[79] While these authorities represent individual victories based on pre-launch publicity, they have not established conclusively that the courts will recognize goodwill prior to trading. In part this is because the cases were interim,[80] aspects of the reasoning are unconvincing,[81] and neither really turned on a demonstration of goodwill.[82]

Later authorities, which have adopted a more hard-line approach, have acknowledged that, while pre-launch advertising and publicity assists in the acquisition of goodwill, it is necessary for a trader to have customers for them to demonstrate that they have goodwill. This can be seen, for example, in *My Kinda Bones v. Dr Pepper's Stove Co.*[83] where the claimant's claim to goodwill was based exclusively on pre-launch publicity. While the court refused to strike out the claimant's action on the ground that their case was not 'manifestedly unarguable',[84] nonetheless Slade J said that he thought that the claimant's prospects of success were very doubtful. The reason for this was that there was a requirement that 'a substantial number of customers or potential customers must at least have had the opportunity to assess the merits of those goods or services for themselves'. Slade J added that customers 'will not have sufficient opportunity to do this until the goods or services are actually on the market'.[85]

While it might be inappropriate to protect a trader who has only made preparations to launch a product, fewer objections can be made about a trader being able to rely on passing-off where they have engaged in widespread pre-launch advertising. This is because in these circumstances competitors are likely to be aware of the claimant's intention to use the name in a business context. Consumers are also more likely to expect a product with specific associations.

While the law in this area is unclear, it is important to note that even if there is no pre-launch goodwill, if goods or services are placed on the market after extensive preparatory publicity, goodwill may well be generated after a very short time.[86] It is also important to recognize that different businesses have different relationships with their customers. For example, the launch of a radio programme requires very little, if any, active involvement by the public. Finally, it is worth noting that other jurisdictions have been more flexible in recognizing the rights of traders based upon pre-launch publicity than has been the case in the United Kingdom.[87]

---

[78] However, the claimant's book had been published by the time of the hearing.

[79] [1981] *FSR* 228, 233.

[80] But in *BBC v. Talbot*, ibid the court was considering the parties' prospects of success, not merely whether there was a serious question to be tried.

[81] For example *BBC v. Talbot*, ibid may have misunderstood *Allen v. Brown Watson* [1965] *RPC* 191. See Wadlow (2004), para. 3.61, 149–50.

[82] Wadlow (2004) explains that 'in reality, neither *Allen v. Brown Watson*, ibid nor *BBC v. Talbot*, ibid actually turned on the existence of goodwill' because both Allen and the BBC had long-established businesses: para. 3.61, 149–50.

[83] [1984] *FSR* 289 (concerning restaurants selling spare ribs, both to be called 'rib shack').

[84] Ibid, 303. *BBC v. Talbot* meant it was not impossible to argue the case.

[85] Ibid, 299. See also *Marcus Publishing v. Leisure News* [1990] *RPC* 576.   [86] *My Kinda Bones*, ibid.

[87] *Pontiac Marina Private v. Cdl. Hotels International* [1998] *FSR* 839, 861 (Court of Appeal for Singapore); *Turner v. General Motors* (1929) 42 *CLR* 352 (Australia); *Windmere Corp. v. Charlescraft Corp.* (1989) 23 *CPR* (3d) 60 (Canada).

Goodwill after trading ends.   Given that goodwill is directly linked to the existence of a business, it follows that once a business ceases to trade that the goodwill starts to wither away.[88] As Lord Macnaghten said in *Commissioners of Inland Revenue v. Muller & Co.'s Margarine,* goodwill 'cannot subsist by itself. It must be attached to a business. Destroy the business and the goodwill perishes with it.'[89] Nevertheless, in recognition of the commercial reality that businesses may recede, change hands, or close temporarily, the courts have held that goodwill is an asset that does not dissipate immediately a business ceases to operate. As a result, when trading stops 'elements remain which may perhaps be gathered up and revived again'. Whether goodwill continues to exist depends on two matters: first, whether the public retains relevant associations between the sign and a particular trader; and whether there is evidence of an intent to resume the business.

In contrast with the law relating to registered marks which adopts a rule that the mark is revocable after five years, [90] the continued survival of repute (without the support of a business) will simply depend on the facts. Relevant factors include the extent of the original reputation, the existence of continuing promotion or other activities, the nature of the goods, and the nature of the mark.[91] If the extent of the goodwill was small, it will likely wither quickly;[92] whereas if there was nationwide familiarity with a trade mark, the reputation may remain for many decades.[93] Moreover, it may be that some goods remain in the public eye, as where films or television programmes are re-shown, records played,[94] or vintage cars are repaired and restored.

The trader must intend to resume business. This may be evident from the trader's acts or a court may infer such an intention from the fact that trading was brought to an end by outside forces.[95] In *Ad-Lib Club v. Granville,*[96] for example, the claimant was forced to shut its nightclub ('The Ad-Lib Club') because of noise problems. Pennycuick V-C granted an interlocutory injunction against the defendant who four years later announced that they were going to open a disco under the same name. This was because the public still associated the name with the club and, as the claimant had been seeking an alternative venue since the club had closed, there was no reason to think they had abandoned the business. In the recent World Cup Willie case, Deputy Judge Roger Wyand QC held that even though the FA had not used the World Cup Willie device for 40 years, and had allowed its trade mark registrations to lapse, the circumstances did not indicate that the FA had no intention to resume use of the sign. The sign related to the World Cup, so the FA was not able to comtemplate its re-use until it became a realistic

---

[88] Wadlow (2004), paras. 3.178–81, 232–234.   [89] [1901] *AC* 217, 224.

[90] In the context of registered marks, five years' non-use, without due cause, is treated as a ground for revocation: see pp. Ch. 39, Section 2.

[91] *Knight v. Beyond Properties* [2007] *FSR* (34) 813 (para. 68); *Jules Rimet Cup Ltd.v. Football Association Ltd* [2007] *EWHC* 2376 (Ch); [2008] *FSR* (10).

[92] *Knight,* ibid (author of Mythbuster books had goodwill in 1996 but by 2003 this was not more than trivial).

[93] *Jules Rimet Cup* [2007] *EWHC* 2376 (Ch); [2008] *FSR* (10) (FA retained goodwill in mascot device from 1966 World Cup despite 40 years of inactivity).

[94] Compare with *Knight v. Beyond Properties* [2007] *FSR* (34) 813 (rejecting argument that children's books 'remain on the shelves') *Sutherland v. V2 Music Ltd* [2002] *EMLR* (28) 568 (funk band using name LIBERTY, which was reasonably well-known in mid-1990s, retained sufficient goodwill so that pop group formed in 2001 under same name was passing itself off).

[95] *A. Levey v. Henderson Kenton (Holdings)* [1974] *RPC* 617 (closure for two years of claimant's department store, because of fire, coupled with notices saying that reopening, held to maintain goodwill).

[96] [1971] *FSR* 1; [1972] *RPC* 673.

prospect that England would host the event again. If a trader has assigned their goodwill to a third party, that is taken to be an indication that they did not intend to resume business.[97]

Foreign traders. The next situation where questions about the existence of goodwill arise is in relation to foreign traders.[98] Where a business located in a foreign country acquires an international reputation, this may lead the foreign trader to set up business in the United Kingdom. In this case, the UK-based business will normally have goodwill. In many situations, however, something short of this may occur. For example, the foreign business may merely have an agent in the United Kingdom, or may only respond to orders taken directly from customers in the United Kingdom. Alternatively, the only connection that a trader may have with England and Wales is that they have a reputation, but no place of business or customers to speak of. In these circumstances, the question arises: can a foreign trader rely on passing-off to protect their interests in the United Kingdom? The case law, which is by no means conclusive, appears to distinguish between three situations. We will deal with each in turn.

(i) Evidence of business activity. If the claimant can demonstrate a trading link with the United Kingdom, they will normally succeed in establishing goodwill. The courts have been generous when considering whether a foreign trader has a sufficient trade presence and, consequentially, goodwill in the UK. It is clear that there is no need to have a registered business in the United Kingdom. The generous approach taken by the courts can be seen, for example, in *Sheraton*.[99] In this case, the claimant company, which ran a chain of high-class hotels, but at the time had none in England, was granted an interim injunction to prevent the defendant from using the name, 'Sheraton Motels'. The court held that, although at the time the claimant did not have any hotels in the United Kingdom, the fact that bookings for their hotels abroad were frequently made both through an office which Sheraton maintained in London, and through travel agencies, was sufficient to entitle them to relief.

(ii) No business activity, but customers. The second situation where a foreign trader may attempt to claim goodwill is where they have customers in the United Kingdom.[100] The law on this point is unclear. On the one hand there is a line of cases that suggest that for a foreign trader to establish goodwill in the United Kingdom, they must show *both* that they have customers *and* that they carry on business in the United Kingdom. This can be seen in the *Crazy Horse* decision.[101] In this case, the claimant was proprietor of the CRAZY HORSE SALOON in Paris. The defendant opened a place of the same name in London. Pennycuick J refused to grant an interlocutory injunction to restrain the defendant from using the CRAZY HORSE SALOON name in London. While the claimant had distributed leaflets in England advertising the saloon, there was no evidence that there were English customers of the Paris saloon (at least in the sense of persons who made bookings in the United Kingdom). The judge explained that 'a trader cannot acquire goodwill in this country without some sort of user in this country. His user may take many forms and in certain cases very slight activities have been held to suffice... I do not think that the mere sending into this country by a foreign trader of advertisements advertising his establishment abroad could fairly be treated as a user in this country.'[102]

---

[97] *Star Industrial v. Yap Kwee Kor* [1976] *FSR* 256 (PC).

[98] For consideration of the extent to which a UK claimant can sue for passing-off committed abroad, see pp. 1089–97.

[99] *Sheraton Corporation v. Sheraton Motels* [1964] *RPC* 202.

[100] There is some authority to the effect that this is insufficient to justify a passing-off action, but the preponderance of authority now appears to be to the contrary.

[101] *Bernadin v. Pavilion* [1967] *RPC* 581.   [102] Ibid, 584.

The *Crazy Horse* decision has been criticized by commentators and distinguished by the courts in the so-called 'soft line' of cases.[103] In this second line of cases, it was held that, if a foreign business can demonstrate that they have customers in the United Kingdom (other than foreign customers who have merely moved here),[104] it is likely that the court will treat this as sufficient to establish goodwill. That is, it is not necessary for them to also establish that they carry on business in the United Kingdom (in any formal sense). For example, in *Athlete's Foot Marketing Association Inc. v. Cobra Sports,* an American retailer selling shoes under the name ATHLETE'S FOOT sought to prevent a UK business from using the same name. While the American firm had a reputation in the United Kingdom at the relevant time, they had not yet conducted business in the United Kingdom. Moreover, the claimant was unable to demonstrate that a single person in England and Wales had purchased their shoes. In considering whether the claimant had goodwill, Walton J said 'it does not matter that the plaintiffs are not at present actually carrying on business in this country, provided they have customers here'. The reason for this was that:

no trader can complain of passing off as against him in any territory…in which he has no customers, nobody who is in a trade relation with him. This will normally…be expressed by saying that he does not carry on any trade in that particular country (obviously, for present purposes, England and Wales) but the inwardness of it will be that he has no customers in that country: no people who buy his goods or make use of his services (as the case may be) there.[105]

Given that the claimant had no customers in the United Kingdom, the court held that they did not have the goodwill necessary to sustain the passing-off action.

Perhaps the most formidable critique of the approach adopted in the *Crazy Horse* decision is in *Peter Waterman v. CBS.*[106] Here, CBS was proposing to refurbish studios in London and call them THE HIT FACTORY. The claimant, who ran a recording business nicknamed THE HIT FACTORY, brought an action to stop CBS from using the same name. Based on the running of a recording studio in New York which was called THE HIT FACTORY, CBS responded by arguing that it had goodwill in the UK that was at the very least concurrent with any goodwill of the claimant. Browne-Wilkinson V-C held that the claimant failed to establish the distinctiveness of THE HIT FACTORY and, as such, consideration of the defendant's position was unnecessary. Nevertheless, Browne-Wilkinson V-C went on to review the authorities on the issue of whether the English courts will protect a foreign trader in the United Kingdom.

Browne-Wilkinson V-C began by noting that the essence of goodwill is the ability to attract customers and potential customers to do business with the owner of the goodwill. Consequently, any interference with the trader's customers is an interference with their

---

[103] The terms 'hard' and 'soft' were characterizations used in *Athlete's Foot* [1980] *RPC* 343, 349. See also *Baskin-Robbins Ice Cream v. Gutman* [1976] *FSR* 545, 548 and *Maxim's v. Dye* [1978] 2 *All ER* 55, 59.

[104] Customers on US forces bases who bought Budweiser beer from PX stores were excluded from consideration in *Anheuser-Busch v. Budejovicky Budvar Narodni Podnik* [1984] *FSR* 413 even though sales numbered 65 million per annum. However, in *Jian Tools for Sales v. Roderick Manhattan Group* [1995] *FSR* 924 Knox J treated as relevant customers resident in the UK who had been influenced by foreign advertising and ordered goods from the US business: these were customers on the open market. But note the Trade Mark Registry's approach in cases under TMA s. 5(4): *In re Speciality Retail Group's Application (Suit Express)* (5 Apr. 2000) *SRIS* O/124/00 (para. 42) ('it is doubtful whether an overseas retail outlet that UK residents have used casually whilst on business or holiday abroad can be said to be in business here merely because those customers returned here after doing business with the retailer whilst abroad').

[105] [1980] *RPC* 343, 350. See also *SA des Anciens Etablissements Panhard et Levassor v. Panhard Levassor Motor Co.* (1901) 18 *RPC* 405.

[106] [1993] *EMLR* 27.

goodwill. Browne-Wilkinson V-C added that, prior to the *Crazy Horse* decision, there was nothing in the authorities inconsistent with that view. For the Vice-Chancellor, that case law merely required the use of the name and the presence of customers in this country. To the extent that the *Crazy Horse* decision required that the trader had conducted some business (however slight) in England and Wales, Browne-Wilkinson V-C said that the case was wrongly decided.[107] The judge took the view that the presence of customers in this country was sufficient to constitute the carrying-on of business here. This is the case whether or not there is a place of business in England and Wales, or services are provided there. On this basis, Browne-Wilkinson V-C held that, since the defendant's New York recording studio had *a substantial number* of customers in England, they would have been entitled to protect their name in the United Kingdom against third parties.

(iii) Mere reputation. The third situation where the question arises whether a foreign trader has goodwill in the United Kingdom is where the claimant merely has a reputation, but no customers as such in the United Kingdom. This might be the case where there is 'spill-over' advertising or where the product becomes known through films, television, or via the internet.[108] Given that it is necessary for a foreign trader to have customers in the United Kingdom for them to establish goodwill (or on a more extreme view, customers and business), it would seem reasonable to assume that, where a foreign trader merely has a reputation in the United Kingdom, they would not be able to prove that they had the goodwill necessary to sustain a passing-off action.

The case law on this point is unclear. On the one hand, there is authority that supports the conclusion that a foreign trader who only has a reputation in the United Kingdom may nonetheless still be able to show that they have goodwill. Indirect (and inconclusive) support for this comes from the cases dealing with pre-trading goodwill, which were discussed above.[109] More direct support for this approach comes from the 1976 decision in *Maxim's v. Dye*. The claimant in this case was the world-famous restaurant in Paris known as MAXIM'S. In 1970, the defendant opened a restaurant in Norwich also called MAXIM'S. In considering whether the claimants were entitled to protect their reputation, although they were not running any business in England, Graham J held that the claimant did have sufficient goodwill to bring a passing-off action. After noting that globalization was making the 'world grow smaller', Graham J said that the true legal position was that the 'existence and extent of the claimants'... goodwill [in their business] in every case is one of fact however it may be proved and whatever it is based on'.[110] Graham J added that the claimants' existing goodwill in this country, 'which is derived from and is based on a foreign business... may be regarded as prospective but none the less real in relation to any future business which may be later set up by the plaintiff in this country'.[111]

In another line of decisions, however, the UK courts have made it clear that, where a trader only has a reputation in the United Kingdom, they will *not* have the goodwill necessary to justify an action for passing off.[112] This can be seen, for example, in the *Budweiser* case.[113] In

---

[107] For Browne-Wilkinson V-C if the foreign trader uses their name for the purposes of trade in the UK, the piracy of that name is an actionable wrong wherever the goodwill is located. Browne-Wilkinson V-C acknowledged that there is binding authority to the effect that the basis of claim must be a goodwill situated in England.

[108] *In re Readmans Ltd's Application (luxor)* (30 Jan. 2002) SRIS O/039/02 (mere existence of internet site accessible from UK does not give rise to goodwill).

[109] See pp. 735–6.

[110] *Maxim's v. Dye* [1978] 2 *All ER* 55, 59 quoting from *Baskin-Robbins*, note 103 above, 548.

[111] *Maxim's*, ibid, 60.

[112] *Athlete's Foot* [1980] RPC 343; *Jian Tools v. Roderick Manhattan Group* [1995] FSR 924.

[113] *Anheuser-Busch v. Budvar* [1984] FSR 413.

this decision Anheuser-Busch, an American company who manufactured BUDWEISER beer, sued the Czech brewers, Budejovicky Budvar, for passing off. The Czech brewers began selling their boutique beer in England under the name BUDWEISER BUDVAR in 1973.[114] While at this time the claimant's sales of BUDWEISER were confined to stores on American Air Force bases, the beer was widely known throughout the United Kingdom. The Court of Appeal rejected the claimant's claim on the basis that there was no goodwill in the United Kingdom. As the beer sold on the Air Force bases was not available for general purchase, the court held that these sales were to be ignored.[115] In rejecting the action, the court supported the view that mere reputation alone would not justify an action for passing off.

The requirement that for a foreign trader to have goodwill they must be able to show that they have customers in the United Kingdom has been criticized by those who consider the geographical division of goodwill to be out of step with the commercial reality of globalized trade.[116] Support for this criticism comes from the fact that a number of comparable jurisdictions have recognized the international character of goodwill. The Full Federal Court of Australia in *ConAgra v. McCain Foods (Australia)*[117] has perhaps gone the furthest in this regard. In this case, Lockhart J said that the 'real question is whether the owner of the goods has established a sufficient reputation with respect to his goods within the particular country in order to acquire a sufficient level of consumer knowledge of the product and attraction for it to provide custom which, if lost, would likely result in damage to him. This is essentially a question of fact'.[118]

In the *Peter Waterman v. CBS* case, Browne-Wilkinson V-C commented on the need for passing-off to be adapted to modern business environments in this way:

The changes in the second half of the twentieth century are far more fundamental than those in nineteenth-century England. They have produced worldwide marks, worldwide goodwill and brought separate markets into competition with the other. Radio and television with their attendant advertising cross national frontiers. Electronic communication via satellite produces virtually instant communication between all markets. In terms of travel time, New York by air is as close as Aberdeen by rail. This has led to the development of the international reputation in certain names, particularly in the service fields, for example Sheraton Hotels, Budget Rent A Car...In my view, the law will fail if it does not try to meet the challenge thrown up by trading patterns which cross national and jurisdictional boundaries due to a change in technical achievement.[119]

Despite these comments and his liberal interpretation of the case law, the Vice Chancellor was not prepared to abandon the requirement that, to establish goodwill, a foreign trader must have customers in the United Kingdom. This reluctance to allow an action based merely on reputation may have been grounded in a fear that if such a prerequisite was abandoned it would enable claimants with an international reputation to enforce a worldwide monopoly without any guarantee that they will ever expand into the domestic market.[120] In addition, it has been

---

[114] Budweis is the old German name of the town in which the Czech beer is brewed.

[115] In *Anheuser-Busch v. Budvar* [1984] *FSR* 413, 462, Oliver LJ defined the question as 'how far is it an essential ingredient of a successful claim in passing off that the plaintiff should have established in this country a business in which his goods or services are sold to the general public on the open market?'.

[116] A. Coleman, 'Protection of Foreign Business Names and Marks Under the Tort of Passing-off' [1986] *LS* 70, 76; F. Mostert, 'Is Goodwill Territorial or International?' [1989] *EIPR* 440.

[117] *ConAgra v. McCain* (1992) 23 *IPR* 193, 234.   [118] Ibid, 34.

[119] *Waterman v. CBS* [1993] *EMLR* 27.

[120] In Australia, this objection has been met by emphasizing the need for a claimant to show damage, diversion of trade that it is about to commence, or the tarnishment of reputation: *ConAgra v. McCain* (1992) 23 *IPR* 193, 235.

pointed out that too-ready recognition of rights of foreign traders may render it difficult for domestic traders to find marks which can be lawfully used in the United Kingdom.[121]

(iv) Well-known marks. Whatever the criticisms and prospects for further development, the Trade Marks Act 1994 provides foreign traders who lack local goodwill with a potential remedy.[122] Section 56, which gives effect to Article 6*bis* of the Paris Convention,[123] states that:

[t]he proprietor of a trade mark which is entitled to protection under the Paris Convention as a well-known trade mark is entitled to restrain by injunction the use in the United Kingdom of a trade mark which, or the essential part of which, is identical or similar to his mark, in relation to identical or similar goods or services, where the use is likely to cause confusion.

Importantly, this provision applies to a proprietor of a 'well-known' trade mark 'whether or not that person carries on business, or has any goodwill, in the United Kingdom'. (In fact, if the proprietor is a national of the United Kingdom, they will not benefit from the provision.)[124] The key limitation in section 56 is not goodwill. Rather, it is whether the mark is 'well-known'. It seems that a number of considerations will be taken into account when deciding whether a mark is well-known. These include trade recognition and public recognition in the United Kingdom;[125] the inherent distinctiveness of the mark; the duration and extent of any use (whether in the United Kingdom or neighbouring territories), or promotion or advertising (especially in territories covered by the same media); sales made abroad to British residents (e.g. those on holiday); and the value of the goodwill.[126] It seems that this evidence must point to a high level of recognition amongst the relevant consumers in the United Kingdom. In *General Motors v. Yplon SA,* the Advocate General described the protection afforded to well-known marks under the Paris Convention as 'exceptional' and therefore concluded that it 'would not be surprising...if the requirement of being well-known imposed a relatively high standard for a mark to benefit from such exceptional protection'.[127]

---

[121] *In re Tara Jarmon's Application (Tara Jarmon)* (7 Sept. 1999) (para. 36) *SRIS* O/311/99.

[122] This remedy is less attractive than passing-off in three obvious respects: firstly, TMA s. 56 is only available if the mark is 'well known'; second, s. 56 results only in injunctive relief rather than compensation or restitution; third, s. 56 does not extend to dissimilar goods, whereas passing-off might. Note, however, that many of the limitations on registrability of trade marks (e.g. s. 3(2)), and statutory defences to infringement of registered marks (TMA ss. 11–12), do not appear to apply to the s. 56 action.

[123] Trademark Law Treaty, Art. 16 and TRIPS, Art. 16(2) require application of Paris Art. 6*bis* to service marks.

[124] See TMA s. 55(1)(b); *Jules Rimet Cup Ltd v. Football Association Ltd* [2008] *ECDR* (4) 43 (Wyand QC) (para. 73). Nor need the proprietor of a well-known mark have registered the mark in a Convention country: *In re Sharif's Application (Advanced Health Products)* (23 Mar. 2000) (para. 52) *SRIS* O/112/00.

[125] Art. 16(2) of TRIPS requires that account be taken of the knowledge of the trade mark in the relevant sector of the public, including knowledge that has been obtained as a result of the promotion of the trade mark. The *WIPO Joint Recommendation Concerning Provisions on the Protection of Well Known Marks* refers to (i) the degree of knowledge or recognition of the mark in the relevant sector of the public; (ii) the duration, extent and geographical area of any use of the mark; (iii) the duration, extent and geographical area of any promotion, advertising, and publicity; (iv) the duration and geographical area of any registrations; (v) previous recognition by authorities of the well-known status of the mark; (vi) the value associated with the mark.

[126] For an example of such an assessment at the OHIM, see *Maurice Emram v. Guccio Gucci SpA,* Case R 620/2006–2 (3 Sept 2007) (OHIM 2d BA).

[127] Case C–375/97 1999] *ECR* I–5421 (para. 33) (Advocate General Jacobs). A mark is only 'well known' 'in a Member state' if it is well known in a substantial part of that state, as opposed to just in a city or its surrounding area: *Alfredo Nieto Nuño v. Leonci Monlleó Franquet,* Case C–328/06 (22 November 2007) *ECJ* (2d Ch).

3 THE SCOPE OF GOODWILL

Once it has been decided that the claimant has goodwill, the next question to consider is its scope. This is an important question because it may influence whether the defendant's representation amounts to passing off.[128] While similar inquiries take place with other forms of intellectual property, there is one important difference, which relates to the territorial scope of the property. For example, when considering whether a patent has been infringed, the question of the geographical scope of the protection is not an issue. This is because the patent operates throughout the whole of the United Kingdom. This is not the case, however, in relation to an action for passing off where the territorial or geographical scope of the goodwill must first be ascertained. Despite the apparent dominance of nationwide firms and franchises, there are many businesses that only trade in a small and relatively confined area. In these circumstances, the way the physical limits of the goodwill are determined may be crucial to the success or otherwise of a passing-off action.[129]

4 OWNERSHIP OF GOODWILL

In principle, the owner of goodwill is the business that generates it. While goodwill will normally be owned by a single trader or business, the courts have recognized that a group of traders may share goodwill in a name or feature of a product that they have in common. Where the singularity of a product is shared by a group of traders (normally in a specific region), they may share goodwill in the identifying feature: the name, image, logo, etc. The courts have recognized shared goodwill in relation to champagne,[130] sherry,[131] whisky,[132] advocaat, and Swiss chocolate.[133]

Problems arise, however, where a number of different people, companies, or businesses cooperate in the making and distribution of a product. In these circumstances, the courts are forced to decide whether the goodwill is individually or jointly owned and, if so, by whom. The difficulties in deciding how the ownership of goodwill is to be ascribed have become all the more problematic with the expansion of international trade, the globalization of markets, and the growth of multinational corporations.[134] In such cases it is common for a firm in one country to expand into another through a subsidiary, distributor, agent, or licensee. In the absence of a carefully formulated contract dealing with the relationships between the parties, difficult questions can arise as to ownership of the goodwill generated by the actions of the local distributor and foreign supplier. This is especially the case when the arrangements between the parties end. This can be see, for example, in *Scandecor Development v. Scandecor Marketing*.[135] In this case a Swedish art-poster business founded in the 1960s was rearranged

---

[128] *Associated Newspapers Ltd v. Express Newspapers* [2003] *FSR* (51) (para. 23) (considering whether repute of THE MAIL was limited to papers which were sold, or whether it extended to free papers).

[129] *Evans v. Eradicure* [1972] *RPC* 808; *Levey v. Henderson-Kenton* [1974] *RPC* 617; *Associated Newspapers*, ibid (para. 29) (a trader's reputation in Birmingham might be different from that in London).

[130] *Bollinger v. Costa Brava Wine Co.* [1960] *Ch* 262; *Taittinger v. Allbev* [1994] 4 *All ER* 75 (champagne companies able to prevent use of elderflower champagne).

[131] *Vine Products v. Mackenzie* [1969] *RPC* 1.

[132] *John Walker & Sons v. Henry Ost* [1970] 2 *All ER* 106.

[133] *Chocosuisse v. Cadbury* [1998] *RPC* 117.   [134] *Scandecor* [1999] *FSR* 26, 38–9 (CA).

[135] Ibid. [1998] *FSR* 500; [1999] *FSR* 26 (not considered by the House of Lords).

so that a subsidiary, Scandecor Marketing (the defendant), had responsibility for marketing the claimant's products in the United Kingdom. The claimant supplied poster products for sale. The defendants also sold ancillary products, such as calendars and cards, not supplied by the claimant, and over which they had no control. The defendant's marketing occasionally referred to the fact that they were connected with the world's largest poster company. In the 1980s the claimant was taken over. The new owners terminated the agreement with the defendant. After further negotiations failed, the claimant demanded that the defendant stop using the SCANDECOR mark.

At first instance, Lloyd J held that the goodwill was shared between the claimant and defendant, effectively finding two different, yet connected, forms of goodwill: a distributor's goodwill and a publisher's goodwill. The Court of Appeal rejected that view, holding instead that the goodwill belonged to the defendant. The Court of Appeal observed that where the goodwill originates from a common source overseas, but then expands and is developed by different companies in different territories, it is necessary to analyse the effect of the changes occurring from time to time in the control and ownership of the businesses which generate the goodwill.[136] Reviewing that history, the Court of Appeal noted that the contact with customers had been largely through the defendant. They also denied that there was any 'rule of law or presumption of fact that the goodwill generated by the trading activities of a wholly owned subsidiary company belongs to the parent company'.[137] Instead, 'what matters is who retailers identified as the person carrying out the trading activities in the local territory'.[138] In this respect the Court of Appeal placed less emphasis than Lloyd J had done on the fact that the defendant had occasionally referred to the international scope of its activities. The evidence showed that the customers treated the supplier, that is the defendant, as being more significant than the publisher.

4.1 GOODWILL AS PROPERTY

Goodwill is a form of property that is transmissible by assignment, on death, or by operation of law.[139] There are no formalities laid down for assignment of goodwill *inter vivos*. However, it is relatively settled that goodwill cannot be assigned in 'gross', that is separately from the business to which it is attached.[140]

---

[136] The Court of Appeal in *Scandecor* [1999] *FSR* 26, 42 accepted that, in an appropriate case, it is legally and factually possible for a business based overseas to acquire goodwill in this country by the supply of its products or services through a subsidiary, agent, or licensee. Whether or not that occurs must depend on the facts of the particular case. Cf. *Habib Bank v. Habib Bank AG Zurich* [1981] 2 *All ER* 650 (international parent may retain international goodwill); *Gromax Plasticulture v. Don & Low Nonwovens* [1999] *RPC* 367.

[137] *Scandecor* [1999] *FSR* 26, 43.   [138] Ibid, 45.

[139] *Artistic Upholstery v. Art Forma (Furniture)* [1999] 4 *All ER* 277, 286 (goodwill is property in context of assignment, nationalization, bankruptcy; and can be owned by unincorporated association through its members). In some circumstances where the relationship is purely personal, as with a barrister or conductor, goodwill will be regarded as inalienable: see *Newman v Adlem* [2006] *FSR* (16) 253 (para. 26) (Jacob LJ) (holding the rule inapplicable to the goodwill of a funeral director).

[140] *Barnsley Brewery Co v. RBNB* [1997] *FSR* 462, 469.

33

MISREPRESENTATION

1 INTRODUCTION

The second element of the passing-off action, which we consider in this chapter, is the misrepresentation.[1] Historically, the need for a misrepresentation, which is one of the factors that distinguishes passing-off from a law of unfair competition, is explained by the fact that the passing-off action grew out of the common law action for deceit.[2] Typically, a misrepresentation occurs where the defendant says or does something that indicates (expressly or impliedly) that the defendant's goods or services derive from (or are otherwise economically connected with) the claimant. Initially, liability for passing off was limited to situations where the defendant's actions gave rise to the suggestion that their goods or services had come from the claimant; that is, that there was confusion as to the source of the goods. Over time, however, the action has expanded to include representations that relate to the quality of the goods or services, and to representations that suggest that there is a connection between the claimant and the defendant.

This chapter is divided into four parts. First, we consider the type of conduct that forms the basis of the defendant's misrepresentation. Second, we look at the types of suggestion that are actionable. Third, we look at the requirement that, for a statement to be a misrepresentation, it must be likely to cause confusion. Fourth, we note that a passing-off action can be brought, not only against a person who carries out the misrepresentation, but also against someone who provides the means that enables the misrepresentation to occur.

---

[1] In *Spalding v. Gamage* (1915) 32 *RPC* 273, 284, Lord Parker referred to false representation by the defendant as 'the basis of a passing-off action'.

[2] See J. Phillips and A. Coleman, 'Passing-off and the Common Field of Activity' (1985) 101 *LQR* 242, 243 for a comparison of passing-off with deceit.

2 NATURE OF THE DEFENDANT'S REPRESENTATION

There are no formal restrictions on the types of representation that are actionable. Indeed, as Lord Parker said in *Spalding v. Gamage,* it is 'impossible to enumerate or classify all the possible ways in which a [trader] may make the...representation relied upon'.[3] So long as the representation confuses the public in a relevant way, the means by which this comes about is irrelevant. Having said this, it may be helpful to consider some of the more important points about the types of conduct that might constitute a misrepresentation.

2.1 DEFENDANT'S STATE OF MIND

In deciding whether a misrepresentation has taken place, the key concern is with the *consequences* of the defendant's actions and the effect that these have upon the public, rather than the state of the defendant's mind. As such, to succeed in a passing-off action, there is no need for the misrepresentation to be conscious, deliberate, intentional, or fraudulent.[4] It also does not matter whether the misrepresentation was made deliberately or innocently. Similarly, the fact that a statement is true does not matter, so long as the defendant's actions/representations generate the requisite confusion in the mind of the public.

The misrepresentation is actionable even if it is unintentional, or can be explained on what seem like legitimate grounds.[5] For example, if a person trades under their own name they might still be passing their goods off as those of the claimant.[6] For example, in *Parker Knoll v. Knoll International*[7] the defendant, Hans Knoll, established a furniture manufacturing business that he called KNOLL INTERNATIONAL. Another firm of furniture makers, established by the defendant's uncle, already traded as PARKER KNOLL. Despite dicta to the effect that individuals have a 'natural and inherent right' to use their own name,[8] the House of Lords denied that a person was entitled to use their own name to indicate that their goods are the goods of another. Consequently, their Lordships granted an injunction.[9] Given that there is no defence where a person uses their own name, it is not surprising that there is no defence where someone changes their name or uses a nickname.[10]

2.2 FORM OF THE MISREPRESENTATION

The courts have been very flexible in deciding whether a defendant has made the requisite misrepresentation. The flexible nature of the misrepresentation is reflected in the fact that the

---

[3] *Spalding v. Gamage*, note 1 above, 284.

[4] *HFC Bank plc v. Midland Bank* plc [2000] *FSR* 176, 181. But there are advantages for a claimant who can show that use was deliberate: *Irvine v Talksport* [2002] *FSR* 943.

[5] *Montgomery v. Thompson* [1891] *AC* 217, 220.

[6] G. Kodilinye, 'Passing-off and the Use of Personal Names' (1975) 26 *Northern Ireland Legal Quarterly* 177; Wadlow (2004) paras. 9.63–9.80, 764–76.

[7] [1962] *RPC* 265; *NAD Electronics Inc v. NAD Computer Systems* [1997] *FSR* 380, 392; *Reed Executive v. Reed Business Information* [2004] *RPC* 767 (paras 109–112).

[8] *Marengo v. Daily Sketch* (1948) 65 *RPC* 242.

[9] Kodilinye, 'Passing-off and the Use of Personal Names', preferring Lord Denning's dissenting speech to those of the majority, argues that the case 'far from laying down any coherent principles, seems to have thrown the law into even greater confusion'.

[10] *Biba Group v. Biba Boutique* [1980] *RPC* 413, 420.

misrepresentation can arise through the use of words or actions. We will look at each of these in turn.

(i) Words. The commonest form of misrepresentation involves the use of words, whether oral or written. In some cases this will occur where the defendant makes a statement that links them either explicitly or implicitly to the claimant. Often, the defendant will use a name that is identical or very similar to the trade name used by the claimant. Thus in *Taittinger v. All Bev*,[11] the Court of Appeal held that, by calling their drink ELDERFLOWER CHAMPAGNE, the defendants had made a misrepresentation that they were part of the group of champagne producers. One of the consequences of the fact that words are able to form the basis of a misrepresentation is that passing-off may prevent a person from calling their book, film, record, or band by the same name or title as is used by someone else.[12]

(ii) Action. In some cases the relevant misrepresentation may be implied from the action of the defendant. Perhaps the clearest example of this is where the defendant manufactures their goods to look like the claimant's. It will also occur if a customer asks a trader to supply them with someone else's goods, but the trader instead supplies the customer with their own goods: this would be an actionable misrepresentation.[13] Indeed, in some circumstances where a trader knows that a consumer is susceptible to a particular understanding concerning the origin of goods or services,[14] that trader must 'take such care as will prevent his chosen marketing method from conveying any misrepresentation to the effect that there is such a connection'.[15] A misrepresentation can also occur where the defendant places their product in close proximity to the claimant's. For example, in *Associated Press v. Insert Media*[16] the court held that, by inserting advertisements inside the claimant's newspaper after the paper had been delivered to newsagents, the defendant passed the inserts off as if they were the claimant's. The position might have been different, however, if the two products had only been delivered at the same time. It does not seem likely that, where products are placed side by side on a supermarket shelf, this would amount to a misrepresentation.

Another situation where the action of a defendant may give rise to an actionable misrepresentation is in relation to the adoption of domain names used on the internet. This can be seen in *British Telecommunications v. One In A Million*[17] which was one of the earliest British cases to deal with the practice of cyber squatting. The defendant in this case was a dealer in internet domain names and had secured domain name registration for prestigious names such as

---

[11] [1993] *FSR* 641.

[12] Wadlow (2004), 8.96–8.111, 651–62; R. Stone, 'Titles, Character Names and Catch Phrases in the Film and Television Industry: Protection under the Law of Passing-off' (1996) 7 *Ent LR* 263.

[13] *Bovril v. Bodega Co Ltd* (1916) 33 *RPC* 153 (supplying OXO when customer requested BOVRIL); *Bristol Conservatories v. Conservatories Custom Built* [1989] *RPC* 455; *LEEC v. Morquip* (7 Feb. 1996) [1996] *EIPR* D–176 (speculating on the possible significance of body language in forming the misrepresentation)'; *BSB Group plc v. Sky Home Services Ltd* [2007] *FSR* (14) 321.

[14] For example, where one trader has previously had a monopoly over the goods and the junior trader is one of the first competitors.

[15] *BSB v. Sky Home Services* [2007] *FSR* (14) 321 (para. 82) (where the defendant was offering warranty contracts relating to Sky equipment in circumstances where it was aware that many consumers considered it was authorized to do so by Sky).

[16] [1991] *FSR* 380.

[17] [1998] 4 *All ER* 476. For criticism, see M. Elmslie, 'The *One in a Million* Case' [1998] *Ent LR* 283, 284 (questioning the conclusion reached that no evidence of how users view the register was given in the case). See also *French Connection v. Sutton* [2000] *ETMR* 341.

virgin.com and tandy.com. These were registered without the consent of the organization who owned the goodwill in those names. The defendant's aim was either to sell the names they registered to the owners of the goodwill (using the blocking effect of the registration to negotiate for a better price),[18] or to sell them to other people (such as collectors). The Court of Appeal held that the act of registering names such as marksandspencer.co.uk amounted to an actionable misrepresentation. This was particularly the case where the name denoted a particular trader and no one else. Aldous LJ explained that the 'placing on a register of a distinctive name such as "marksandspencer" makes a representation to persons who consult the register that the registrant is connected or associated with the name registered and thus the owner of the goodwill in the name'.[19] This decision, which is not without its critics, has important ramifications for the legal regulation of the internet.[20]

3   WHAT TYPE OF SUGGESTIVE CONDUCT IS ACTIONABLE?

In the previous section we looked at the various forms of conduct that constitute misrepresentation. In this section we turn to look at the *consequences* that flow from that conduct. In so doing, it is important to note that, in order to promote the sale of their products or services, a trader might act or make statements that are suggestive of a number of things. For example, a defendant might act in such a way that the public comes to believe that their products are cheaper than the claimant's, or that they are better for the environment. They might also suggest that their goods are very suitable to be used in connection with the claimant's. Equally, a trader might suggest that their goods are similar to or better than the claimant's. While the defendant's conduct in each of these cases may harm the claimant, this does not mean that they will succeed in a passing-off action. This is because passing-off only protects against certain types of suggestion. In this section we examine the types of suggestion that are actionable.

3.1   MISREPRESENTATION AS TO SOURCE

The traditional form of misrepresentation occurs where the defendant's actions give rise to a suggestion that the defendant's goods or services are those of the claimant. That is, the defendant somehow suggests that the claimant is the 'source' of their goods.[21] Such a misrepresentation is objectionable because it confuses the public and attempts to ride on the back of the claimant's reputation.

A misrepresentation as to source occurs, for example, where the defendant suggests that they are the manufacturer, marketer, or retailer of the product. It also occurs where the defendant uses a word or name that the public associates with the claimant's business. In both these situations the defendant's conduct gives rise to the suggestion that their goods emanate from the

---

[18] For example, the defendants offered to sell the domain name burgerking.co.uk to BURGER KING for £25,000.

[19] *One in a Million* [1998] 4 *All ER* 476, 497.

[20] *Phones4U Ltd v. Phone4u.co.uk Internet Ltd* [2006] *EWCA Civ* 244, [2007] *RPC* (5); *Tesco Stores Ltd v. Elogicom Ltd* [2006] *EWHC* 403 (Ch); [2007] FSR (4) 83. See the discussion of ICANN at pp. 1098–9 below.

[21] It is irrelevant that the customers are not actually familiar with the source: *Birmingham Vinegar Brewery v. Powell* [1897] AC 710, 715; *Edge v. Nicholls* [1911] AC 693; *United Biscuits (UK) v. Asda Stores* [1997] RPC 513. This is referred to as the 'anonymous source' doctrine.

claimant. The representation may also give rise to a suggestion that the goods or services of the claimant and the defendant are related. For example, in *Kimberley Clark v. Fort Sterling*,[22] as a part of the defendant's campaign to promote the NOUVELLE toilet roll, the defendant offered to placate customers who had brought NOUVELLE but were dissatisfied with it, by replacing NOUVELLE with ANDREX toilet paper. The claimant, who owned the goodwill in ANDREX, objected. The court held the offer to be a misrepresentation because it was likely to lead purchasers into thinking that NOUVELLE was a product from the ANDREX stable, or that ANDREX was in some way behind the promotion.

3.2 MISREPRESENTATION AS TO QUALITY

The courts have also recognized that a misrepresentation may occur where a defendant makes a representation about the quality of the claimant's goods. The objection here is not that the defendant is riding on the back of the claimant's reputation (although this may occur), so much as to the negative impact that the defendant's actions have upon the claimant's goodwill. This can be seen in *Spalding v. Gamage*.[23] In this case, the claimant, who manufactured and sold footballs, brought a passing-off action against the defendants, who had obtained some of the claimant's old disused stock and sold them as if they were new and improved footballs. Lord Parker held that this was a misrepresentation. The reason for this was that:

[the] proposition that no one has the right to represent his goods as the goods of somebody else must, I think...involve as a corollary the further proposition, that no one, who has in his hands the goods of another of a particular class or quality, has a right to represent these goods to be the goods of that other of a different quality or belonging to a different class.[24]

The extension of the passing-off action to include representations about the quality of the claimant's goods may enable a trader to control the parallel importing of their goods. This has been particularly important where a trader places goods of one quality on a foreign market under a particular sign and goods of a different quality on the UK market under the same sign. In these circumstances, the trader may be able to use passing-off to prevent goods marketed abroad from being imported into the United Kingdom. In *Colgate-Palmolive v. Markwell Finance*,[25] the claimants were all members of an international group of companies which marketed toothpaste in different countries. While the external appearance of the toothpaste tube that was sold in different countries was very similar (the mark and get-up were the same), the quality of the contents varied from country to country. For example, the COLGATE toothpaste sold in Brazil was of a lower quality than that which was available in the UK. This was because the Brazilian toothpaste used a number of cheaper raw materials, such as local chalk, instead of the preferred ingredients which were used in the United Kingdom. Colgate UK, a wholly owned subsidiary of Colgate US, instigated an action to prevent Markwell from importing into the United Kingdom lower-quality COLGATE toothpaste which had been sold in Brazil. Markwell argued that Colgate UK had no right to rely upon the reputation for superior quality toothpaste that it had in the United Kingdom, when the COLGATE trade marks and the get-up were used as worldwide presentation for different quality toothpaste. Markwell also argued that Colgate US must have foreseen that different quality toothpaste would circulate around the world. In effect what Markwell argued was that it was Colgate, and not Markwell, that had made the relevant misrepresentation.

---

[22] [1997] *FSR* 877.   [23] (1915) 32 *RPC* 273.   [24] Ibid, 284.   [25] [1989] *RPC* 497.

Applying *Spalding v. Gamage,* the Court of Appeal held that traders who placed the same mark on distinct classes of articles were entitled to bring a passing-off action against a person who resold the inferior goods in circumstances which constituted a false representation that the goods were of the superior class and thereby damaged the trader's reputation.[26] Given that the defendant had made a misrepresentation to consumers in the United Kingdom as to the character and quality of the Brazilian toothpaste, it was irrelevant that the goods were originally produced and sold by a subsidiary of Colgate US.

Another situation where the courts have recognized misrepresentation of the quality of goods is in relation to the so-called 'extended form' of passing off, which was first recognized by Danckwerts J in *Bollinger v. Costa Brava Wine Co.*[27] As we explained earlier, this case recognized that a class or group of traders may share goodwill in a name (or some other indicator) that is distinctive of a particular class of goods. In particular, it was recognized that champagne producers who made sparkling wine with grapes from the Champagne region of France using the *champenois* process had goodwill in the 'champagne'. It was also recognized that individual members of the class of traders are able to bring an action against anyone who uses the distinctive name in relation to products of a different quality. On this basis, French champagne houses have been able to stop other traders who do not make drinks with those characteristics, for example, producers of the drinks SPANISH CHAMPAGNE or ELDERFLOWER CHAMPAGNE, from using the term 'champagne'.[28] The House of Lords approved this line of authority in *Warnink v. Townend.* In so doing they granted relief to a producer of an egg-based alcoholic drink ADVOCAAT.[29] The action has subsequently been used by the producers of PARMA HAM (albeit unsuccessfully) and SWISS CHOCOLATE.[30] The specifics of the action, which has a number of idiosyncratic characteristics, are considered below.[31]

3.3 MISREPRESENTATION THAT THE CLAIMANT HAS CONTROL OR RESPONSIBILITY OVER THE GOODS OR SERVICES

The courts have also recognized that a misrepresentation may occur where the defendant's conduct gives rise to the suggestion that the claimant has some type of control or responsibility over their goods or services. In *British Legion v. British Legion Club (Street)*[32] Farwell J held that an organization formed to assist First World War veterans called the 'British Legion' could rely on passing-off to prevent the words 'British Legion Club (Street)' from being used to describe a local social club. This was because members of the public would have thought that the social club was 'either a Branch of the plaintiff association, or at any rate that it was a club in some way amalgamated with or under the supervision of the plaintiff association for which the plaintiff association had in some way made itself responsible'.[33]

---

[26] Ibid, 514 (Slade LJ), 529 (Lloyd LJ). Cf. *Champagne Heidsieck v. Buxton* [1930] 1 *Ch* 330 which was distinguished, at 513, because on the facts resale in *Colgate* carried with it a misrepresentation as to quality.

[27] *Bollinger v. Costa Brava Wine Co.* [1960] *RPC* 16. See above at p. 743.

[28] *Taittinger v. Allbev* [1993] *FSR* 641 (elderflower champagne). But not BABYCHAM: *H.P. Bulmer and Showerings v. J. Bollinger SA* [1978] *RPC* 79.

[29] *Erven Warnink BV v. Townend (J.) & Sons (Hull)* [1979] *AC* 731, 742.

[30] *Consorzio del Prosciutto di Parma v. Marks & Spencer* [1991] *RPC* 351 and *Consorzio del Prosciutto di Parma v. Asda Stores* [1988] *FSR* 697 (parma ham); *Chocosuisse Union des Fabricants Suisses de Chocolat v. Cadbury* [1999] *RPC* 826.

[31] See below at pp. 743–7.   [32] (1931) 63 *RPC* 555.   [33] Ibid, 564.

It should be noted that the mere fact that a defendant suggests that they are somehow connected to the claimant will not necessarily amount to passing off. This is because the connection will only be relevant if the defendant's misrepresentation suggests that the claimant has some type of control or responsibility over the goods or services in question. The nature of the connection that is necessary to sustain a misrepresentation was considered in *Harrods v. Harrodian School.*[34] In this case, the famous London department store was refused an injunction to prevent a preparatory school known as 'The Harrodian Club', which was built on the site of the former Harrod's club, from calling itself the 'Harrodian School'.[35] (Harrods claimed that Harrodian was the adjectival form of Harrods.) In the Court of Appeal Millett LJ explained that:

the relevant connection must be one by which the plaintiffs would be taken by the public to have made themselves responsible for the quality of the defendant's goods or services...It is not in my opinion sufficient to demonstrate that there must be a connection of some kind between the defendant and the plaintiff, if it is not a connection which would lead the public to suppose that the plaintiff has made himself responsible for the quality of the defendant's goods or services. A belief that the plaintiff has sponsored or given financial support to the defendant will not ordinarily give the public that impression.[36]

The *Harrods* decision places an important limit on the scope of passing-off, particularly in relation to sponsorship.[37] For example, it seems that if a trader was to adopt the logo of the Diana Memorial Fund, this would not amount to passing off. This is because the public would most probably take this to mean that the trader has made a donation to the Diana Fund, rather than that the Fund had any control over the trader's business.[38]

3.3.1 Personality merchandising

The expansion of passing-off to include situations where the defendant makes a representation that the claimant has some type of control or responsibility over their goods or services helps to ensure that the action continues to be relevant in the modern commercial environment. It has also given rise to the possibility that celebrities may be able to utilize passing-off to control the use that is made of their images or other personal indicia. This is potentially very important given that personality merchandizing, that is the practice whereby celebrities use their names and images to endorse and associate themselves with products and services, has become a common feature of modern marketing and that, at present, UK law refuses to recognize a right of personality.[39]

Despite the flexible nature of the passing-off action it has provided, at best, minimal protection against traders who appropriate aspects of someone else's personality.[40] In *Lyngstrad*

[34] [1996] *RPC* 697; H. Carty, 'Passing-off at the Crossroads' [1996] *EIPR* 629, taking the view that Millett LJ's restrictive approach is less in line with existing authorities than Sir Michael Kerr's dissenting judgment.

[35] In so doing, the Court of Appeal criticized *Bulmer v. Bollinger* [1978] *RPC* 79, 117 (Goff LJ) where it was said that the connection must 'lead people to accept them on the faith of the plaintiff's reputation'.

[36] [1996] *RPC* 697, 712–13.   [37] *Irvine v. Talksport* [2002] *FSR* 943.

[38] B. Isaac, 'Merchandising or Fundraising? Trade Marks and the Diana, Princess of Wales Memorial Fund' [1998] *EIPR* 44 (use of Diana logo not an indication of source but rather an indication that the user has given the fund financial support).

[39] H. Beverley-Smith, *The Commercial Appropriation of Personality* (2002). On protection of non-pecuniary or dignitary interests through the law of confidence, see pp. 1006–7.

[40] For other impediments, in particular, the difficulty with demonstrating damage, see below at pp. 769–71.

v. Annabas Products,[41] the pop group ABBA complained that the defendant was selling paraphernalia that bore the name and image of the group. Refusing to grant relief, Oliver J said that he did not think anyone could reasonably imagine that the pop stars had given their approval for the paraphernalia. He also added that the defendants were not doing 'anything more than catering for a popular demand among teenagers for effigies of their idols'.[42]

The courts in Australia have adopted a more generous approach to the application of passing-off to personality and character merchandising. For example, in *Henderson v. Radio Corporation,*[43] the defendants reproduced a picture of the claimants, who were ballroom dancers, on one of their record covers. The Supreme Court of New South Wales held that in so doing the defendants had made a misrepresentation that there was a 'connection' between the claimants and the defendants. This was because 'the class of persons for whom the record was primarily intended would probably believe that the picture of the respondents on the cover indicated their recommendation or approval of the record'.[44]

An even more liberal approach was adopted by the Federal Court of Australia in *Hogan v. Koala Dundee*[45] where Pincus J said that it was no longer necessary to show misrepresentation to prove passing off. In this case the claimant, who was the writer and star of the film *Crocodile Dundee,* brought an action against two tourist shops which sold clothing, hats, and T-shirts that were 'of a particularly Australian nature'. The basis of the claimant's complaint was that the defendants had used the name DUNDEE and had also used an image of a koala bear which, like the hero in the claimant's film *Crocodile Dundee,* was dressed in a sleeveless shirt, wore a bush hat with teeth in the band, and carried a knife. The Federal Court of Australia granted the claimant relief, denying that there was a need for a misrepresentation. The Court grounded the decision on the basis of 'wrongful appropriation of a reputation, or, more widely wrongful association of goods with an image properly belonging to an applicant'.[46]

However, in a second *Crocodile Dundee* case, *Hogan v. Pacific Dunlop,*[47] the full Federal Court reverted to the conventional position that to succeed in a passing-off action the claimant must show that there has been a misrepresentation. Here, the claimant advertised shoes by reference to a particular scene (the knife scene) in the film *Crocodile Dundee.* The Federal Court of Australia said that there was a misrepresentation 'involving use of the image or indicium in question to convey a representation of a commercial connection between the plaintiff and the goods and services of the defendant, which connection does not exist'.[48]

English cases have stuck to the view that passing off requires a misrepresentation. They have also held that while the public does not need to believe that the personality made the goods or services, the public must have thought that the personality endorsed them. As a result, while labelling a product with the words 'official' or 'approved by' a particular personality would probably be treated as a misrepresentation, the unauthorized use of a celebrity's image on an advertisement might or might not.[49] In a similar vein, in the *Elvis Presley* decision Laddie J said that the public would not assume that the use of the words ELVIS, ELVIS PRESLEY, or the signature ELVISLY YOURS on toiletries and perfumes indicated any connection with Elvis's estate. This was because, when people buy such articles, they probably do not care one way or the other who made, sold, or licensed them. Similarly, it has been said that persons purchasing stickers showing the Spice Girls are unlikely to believe that the stickers were published by the band, or that the quality of the stickers was authorized by them. This was because the traders

[41] [1977] *FSR* 62.   [42] Ibid.   [43] [1969] *RPC* 218.   [44] Ibid, 232.
[45] (1988) 12 *IPR* 508.   [46] Ibid, 520.   [47] (1989) 12 *IPR* 225.
[48] Gummow J, at first instance.   [49] *Elvis Presley Trade Marks* [1997] *RPC* 543, 558.

who supplied the merchandise were merely responding to a demand 'for effigies and quotes of today's idols'.[50]

Although it has been regarded by some as marking a shift in judicial attitudes to personality merchandising, the decision of Laddie J. in *Irvine v. Talksport* probably is nothing of the sort.[51] In this case the famous Formula 1 racing driver brought an action against Talksport for using his image on a promotional brochure (used to attract advertising for the radio station). The brochure comprised a picture of Irvine, which had been modified so that he was listening to a radio bearing the Talksport logo. Irvine brought an action for passing off, and Laddie J found in his favour. Laddie J reviewed the cases on personalities and passing off, and held that they indicated that a person might be able to utilize passing-off to prevent a misrepresentation by a trader that its products or services had been endorsed by the personality. (In so doing the judge made it clear that endorsement was a narrower notion than merchandising.) On the facts in front of him, Laddie J found that Talksport's brochure had given the impression that Irvine endorsed the radio station. In particular, Laddie J was impressed by evidence from an associate of Irvine to the effect that he sought a free radio from the racing driver, an act which indicated that he believed Irvine had done a deal with the radio station. The Court of Appeal affirmed Laddie J's decision, emphasizing, in particular, that the actual image of Irvine listening to the radio gave an impression of endorsement.[52] At best, the case indicates that British courts will be sympathetic to any unauthorized use of a personality's image or likeness which wrongfully implies endorsement of a trader's products.

3.3.2 Misrepresentations in character merchandising

Character merchandising involves the application of images of cartoon and other fictional characters to merchandise. While the Australian approach has not been followed in the UK in relation to personality merchandising, it has been more enthusiastically applied to character merchandising. For example, in *Mirage Studios v. Counter-Feat Clothing*[53] the defendants were found liable for passing off when they applied the claimant's characters, the Teenage Ninja Mutant Turtles, to their clothing. Browne-Wilkinson V-C explained that 'the critical evidence in this case was that a substantial number of the buying public now expects and knows that where a famous cartoon or television character is reproduced on goods, that reproduction is the result of a licence granted by the owner of the copyright or owner of other rights in the character'.[54] As a result, he concluded that sale of the merchandise involved two misrepresentations. First, a (mis)representation to the public that the goods were 'genuine' (i.e. that the drawings were the drawings of the claimants). Second, a misrepresentation that the goods were licensed.[55] Browne-Wilkinson V-C went on to say that he regarded the Australian authorities as 'sound'.[56]

---

[50] *Halliwell v. Panini SpA* (6 Jun. 1997) Lightman J, echoing *Lyngstrad v. Annabas Products* [1977] *FSR* 62 and refusing the claimant an *ex parte* injunction demanding no further sale of the albums without a disclaimer.

[51] Note 4 above. The case for the shift is attractively made by H. Carty, 'Advertising, Publicity Rights and English Law' (2004) *IPQ* 209–254, 240 (describing the case as 'a radical re-alignment of the tort, at least where image rights are concerned.')

[52] *Irvine v. Talksport* [2003] *FSR* 619 (CA).

[53] [1991] *FSR* 145.   [54] Ibid, 155.

[55] The reference to 'genuineness' was interpreted by Laddie J as perhaps referring to the creator of the character, or his successors: *Elvis Presley* [1997] *RPC* 543, 553.

[56] The authorities did not, however, include the two *Dundee* cases. For a comparison of English and Australian law, see S. Burley, 'Passing-off and Character Merchandising' [1991] *EIPR* 227, 228.

While the *Ninja Turtle* case has received a mixed reaction,[57] the indications are that the English courts will treat the decision as being limited to its particular facts.[58] As we have seen, the decision has not been extended to personality merchandizing cases. Nor does it appear to extend to the use of names, as opposed to the use of copyright images.[59] This is because, in the case, the judge distinguished a number of authorities on the ground that they were concerned with the licensing of names in which no copyright subsists, rather than the copyright material.[60] Moreover, even where the merchandising is protected by copyright, the courts have subsequently indicated that, to succeed in a passing-off action, the claimant must show that the public understood that the goods were licensed *and* that they bought the merchandise on that basis. This can be seen in *BBC Worldwide v. Pally Screen Printing*.[61] The BBC owned copyright and merchandising rights to the popular children's characters known as the Teletubbies. The defendants printed pictures of the Teletubbies on various items such as T-shirts. In response to the BBC's action for passing off, Laddie J explained that to succeed:

the plaintiffs will need to show that they have built up the necessary reputation so that members of the public would look at this type of artwork and consider it to represent the plaintiffs or products made with the plaintiffs' approval. It seems to me that it is quite possible that members of the public will look at T-shirts bearing this artwork and think no more than it is artwork bearing illustrations of well-known television characters without having any regard whatsoever to the source of supply and without having any regard as to whether or not these T-shirts were put out with the sanction of or under the aegis of the plaintiffs.

Laddie J refused to grant the BBC summary judgment against the defendants because it was 'not unforeseeable' that the defendants might succeed.

3.4 REVERSE PASSING OFF

Reverse or inverse passing off is the name given to the situation where a trader tries to claim the benefit of another trader's goods or service to enhance their own reputation.[62] In the classic passing-off action, the defendant's misrepresentation gives rise to a suggestion that the defendant's goods or services are those of the claimant. However, with reverse passing off the defendant's misrepresentation gives rise to the suggestion that the defendant is the source of the claimant's goods or services (or is somehow responsible for the quality of the claimant's goods or services). That is, instead of the defendant pretending that their goods are the claimant's, the defendant claims the claimant's goods as their own.

It is not clear whether reverse passing off amounts to an actionable wrong.[63] In principle, it depends on whether the standard requirements of the 'classic trinity' are met. The problem here is in establishing misrepresentation and damage. If a person merely resells the goods of

---

[57] Wadlow (2005), para. 7.123, p. 507, is critical of the decision. More approving sentiments can be found elsewhere: J. Holyoak, 'United Kingdom Character Rights and Merchandising Rights Today' [1993] *Journal of Business Law* 444, 451 (in general arguing that character merchandising is now adequately protected).

[58] *Elvis Presley* [1997] *RPC* 543, 553.

[59] *Nice and Safe Attitude v. Piers Flook* [1997] *FSR* 14, 21.

[60] e.g. *Wombles v. Womble Skips* [1977] *RPC* 99; *Tavener Rutledge v. Trexapalm* [1975] *FSR* 179. He also asserted that *Lyngstrad v. Annabas Products* [1977] *FSR* 62 could be distinguished on that basis.

[61] [1998] *FSR* 665, 674.

[62] J. Cross, 'Giving Credit Where Credit Is Due: Revisiting the Doctrine of Reverse Passing-off in Trademark Law' (1997) 72 *Washington Law Review* 709–73.

[63] H. Carty, 'Inverse Passing-off: A Suitable Addition to Passing-off?' [1993] *EIPR* 370.

another trader, this will not usually amount to a misrepresentation. This is the case even if they have added a new sign to the goods. Moreover, given that the claimant-manufacturer will have already placed the goods on the market, it is difficult to see where the damage lies. Although a defendant may derive benefit where they resell the goods, this does not in itself harm the manufacturer. In some circumstances, however, the activities of the reseller may cross into the realm of passing-off. A good example of this is where a person represents the claimant's goods as their own, but subsequently supplies their own goods. For example, in *Bristol Conservatories v. Conservatories Custom Built*,[64] both the claimant and the defendant were engaged in the business of designing and selling conservatories. The defendant's salesmen showed potential customers photographs of the claimant's conservatories. In so doing, they led customers to believe that they were examples of their own design and craftsmanship. The defendant's application to strike out the statement of claim as disclosing no reasonable cause of action was successful at first instance. This decision, however, was overturned by the Court of Appeal. The Court of Appeal held that the defendant had made a misrepresentation that their goods were of the same quality as the claimant's. They added that, as the claimant's goodwill was 'asserted and demonstrated as the photographs were shown', it did not matter that the customer might not have known of the claimant. The damage caused was the diversion of sales from the claimant to the defendant. The Court of Appeal took the view that it did not matter that there was no confusion, because the misrepresentation 'left no room for confusion'. Whether it is helpful to categorize the case as one of reverse passing off is a matter of debate.[65]

3.5 COMPARATIVE ADVERTISING

'Comparative advertising' is the term used to describe advertisements where the goods or services of one trader are compared with the goods or services of another trader. To show the advertiser's wares in a favourable light, comparative advertisements usually emphasize differences in things such as price, value, durability, or quality.[66] The question whether a person engaged in comparative advertising is liable for passing-off depends on the nature of the comparison. In some situations the comparison will not be treated as a misrepresentation. For example, in *Bulmer v. Bollinger*,[67] Goff LJ said that there is no actionable passing off 'if one says that one's goods are very suitable to be used in connection with the plaintiffs'. Equally for a defendant to say that their goods are similar to or better than the claimant's does not amount to passing off.

In other circumstances, however, comparative advertising may be treated as a misrepresentation. For example, in *McDonald's Hamburgers v. Burger King*[68] Burger King advertised its hamburgers in the London Underground with the slogan 'It's Not Just Big Mac'. Opinion poll evidence indicated that members of the public treated these as advertisements for a Burger King hamburger called 'Big Mac', or as an improved version thereof. The evidence also indicated that people were likely to respond to the advertisement by going to Burger King restaurants

---

[64] [1989] *RPC* 455, 464–5. See also *Boehringer Ingelheim KG v. Swingward Ltd* (5 Mar. 2004) [2004] *EWCA Civ* 129 (paras. 55–8).

[65] Wadlow (2004), para. 7.144, 524 (not a nominate tort in its own right but a further example of an actionable misrepresentation to which the normal principles apply); J. Drysdale and M. Silverleaf, *Passing-off: Law and Practice* (1995), para. 4.14 (doubting that the concept of reverse passing-off is of any value).

[66] For the position of comparative advertising under the registered trade marks regime, and non-legal regulation, see below at pp. 928, 937–41.

[67] [1978] *RPC* 79, 117.   [68] [1986] *FSR* 45.

and ordering a 'Big Mac'. Consequently, Whitford J held that the advertisement was a misrepresentation. In *Kimberley Clark v. Fort Sterling*[69] the defendant promoted its NOUVELLE toilet roll with an offer to placate dissatisfied customers by replacing their NOUVELLE with ANDREX toilet roll. The NOUVELLE packaging said prominently 'Softness guaranteed (or we'll exchange it for Andrex ®)', the claimant, who owned the ANDREX brand, claimed that the defendant's promotion amounted to passing off. The court agreed, holding that this was a misrepresentation because it was likely to induce purchasers into thinking that NOUVELLE was another product 'from the Andrex stable or that ANDREX is in some way behind the promotion'.

4 IS THE MISREPRESENTATION DECEPTIVE?

As we explained earlier, in deciding whether a misrepresentation has taken place the key concern is not with the state of the defendant's mind. Instead it is with the *consequences* of the defendant's actions and the effect that these have upon the public. In particular, the claimant must show that the defendant's actions either have confused or are likely to confuse the public or a substantial part thereof. That is, to succeed in a passing-off action, the claimant must show that the defendant's misrepresentation is *deceptive*.[70] The question whether the misrepresentation is deceptive is a question of fact that requires the court to predict how the public will interpret the defendant's actions.[71] It does not matter that the defendant's representation is true, honest, or legitimate if it deceives the public. Equally, it does not matter if the defendant uses their own name, a relevant geographical name, or a descriptive term, if it was used in a way that was deceptive.[72]

In deciding whether the misrepresentation is deceptive, a number of different questions may arise. While the nature and relative importance of each will vary from case to case, these include: who must be deceived? how many people must be deceived? and, when must the deception occur? After looking at these we will consider the types of evidence that may be used by the courts in this context. We will then look at some of the factors that may be taken into account in deciding whether the misrepresentation is deceptive.

4.1 WHO MUST BE DECEIVED?

The question whether the misrepresentation operates to deceive the public is largely looked at by the courts through the eyes of the general public.[73] However, where the goods or services are not marketed to the general public, the court considers the impact that the misrepresentation has upon that part of the public for whom the product or services were intended. Although there are dicta to the effect that the appropriate part of the public is the defendant's customers, the better view is that the 'relevant public' should vary according to the type of misrepresentation being alleged. Thus, where the allegation is that the defendant has made a misrepresentation which suggests that the claimant is the source of their goods and that the goods

---

[69] [1997] *FSR* 877.

[70] *Phones4U* [2006] *EWCA Civ* 244 (Jacob LJ, contrasting 'confusion' and 'deception'; *Hodgkinson & Corby v. Wards Mobility Services* [1995] *FSR* 169, 175; *Nice and Safe v. Flook* [1997] *FSR* 14, 20; *Barnsley Brewery Company v. RBNB* [1997] *FSR* 462, 467 (confusion but no deception).

[71] This is a 'jury question': *Harrods v. Harrodian School* [1996] *RPC* 697, 717; *Neutrogena Corporation v. Golden* [1996] *RPC* 473, 482.

[72] *Montgomery v. Thompson* [1891] *AC* 217, 220.   [73] *Marengo v. Daily Sketch* (1948) 65 *RPC* 242, 250.

of the claimant and the defendant are similar, the court would consider the impact that the misrepresentation has upon the claimant's customers. Where the parties' goods or services are different, so that some other type of connection is being alleged, the court will focus on customers who are familiar with the claimant's activities, but who are in the market for goods and services of the defendant. This kind of approach was adopted in *Harrods v. Harrodian School*[74] where the relevant public was described by Millett LJ as 'affluent members of the middle class who live in London, shop at Harrods and wish to send their children to fee-paying schools'.

The attributes and skills of the notional customer will vary depending on the facts in question.[75] Indeed as Lord Oliver said in *Reckitt & Colman,* the 'customers have to be taken as they are found'.[76] In some cases, the relevant public might be quite discerning. For example, in a decision involving a passing-off action between two banks, it was said that 'potential customers wishing to borrow large sums of money from a bank could reasonably be expected to pay rather more attention to the details of the entity with whom they were doing or seeking to do business'.[77] In other situations, however, the notional customer might be careless and uninterested: as with supermarket shoppers who apparently spend less than ten seconds examining each purchase. A defendant cannot escape liability by arguing that customers would not have been misled if they were 'more literate, careful, perspicacious, wary or prudent'.[78] While the attributes and skills of the notional customer may vary depending on the facts in question, the court will not take account of situations where the notional customer does not care one way or another about the goods they are buying.[79] If customers are indifferent to the goods they are purchasing, a claimant will be unable to show that the defendant's misrepresentation was deceptive. This is because in these circumstances the misrepresentation has no impact upon the relevant consumers.[80]

4.2 HOW MANY PEOPLE MUST BE DECEIVED?

The next question to consider is how many people must be deceived. It is clear that for an action to succeed it is not necessary for a claimant to show that *all* of the consumers in the relevant section of the public were deceived by the misrepresentation. As Jacob J said, 'there is passing off even if most of the people are not fooled most of the time but enough are for enough of the time'. But what is enough? The courts' response to this has been that a 'substantial' part of the public must be confused. As Falconer J said in *Lego,* passing off only arises if there is a 'real risk that a substantial number of persons among the relevant sections of the public will in fact believe that there is a business connection between the plaintiff and the defendant'.[81]

---

[74] [1996] *RPC* 697, 716.   [75] *Reckitt & Colman (Products) v. Borden* [1990] *RPC* 341, 423.

[76] Ibid., 415–16.   [77] *HFC Bank v. Midland Bank* [2000] *FSR* 176, 185.

[78] *Reckitt & Colman v. Borden* [1990] *RPC* 341, 415–16; *Clark v. Associated Newspapers* [1998] *RPC* 261, 271.

[79] As Lightman J said in *Clark,* ibid, 271 'no claim lies if they are indifferent or careless as to who is the author'. See also *Politechnika Ipari Szovetzkezet v. Dallas Print Transfers* [1982] *FSR* 529.

[80] This explains Foster J's exclusion from consideration of a 'moron in a hurry': *Morning Star Co-Operative Society v. Express Newspapers* [1979] *FSR* 113. See also *Newsweek v. BBC* [1979] *RPC* 441, 447. (The test is whether ordinary, sensible members of the public would be confused. It is not sufficient that the only confusion would be to a very small unobservant section of society.) The Court of Appeal has recently employed the touchstone of the notional consumer developed in European trade marks law, that is confusion is to be assessed from the point of vew of the consumer who is reasonably well-informed, reasonably observant and reasonably circumspect: *Asprey & Garrard v. WRA (Guns) Ltd* [2002] *FSR* 487 (para. 35).

[81] *Reed Executive v. Reed Business Information* [2004] *RPC* 767, 797 (para. 111); *Phones4U* [2006] *EWCA Civ* 244 (para. 17); *Lego v. Lemelstrich* [1983] *FSR* 155, 188; *Knight v. Beyond Properties Pty Ltd* [2007] *FSR* (34) 813 (para. 80).

This, in turn, gives rise to the further question: what is meant by a 'substantial' part of the relevant group? There is no clear answer to this question. For the most part, the courts have defined the term negatively. Thus, it is clear that 'substantial' does not mean either a large proportion or a majority of the public.[82] For example in the *Chocosuisse* case, the number of persons confused into thinking a chocolate bar called SWISS CHALET was made from Swiss chocolate was smaller than those who had not been deceived. Nevertheless, this was substantial enough to amount to passing off.[83] The Court of Appeal has said that references to 'more than *de minimis*' and 'above a trivial level', which had been used in some cases, were best avoided.[84] Beyond these comments, the courts have been unwilling to give much guidance as to what 'substantial' entails.

4.3 WHEN MUST THE DECEPTION OCCUR?

One issue that remains largely unexplored in English law relates to the question: at what point of time must the public be misled? The way this question is answered depends on the facts of the case. In most cases the answer is straightforward: the confusion must occur at the time of purchase. This can be seen in *Bostik v. Sellotape GB*.[85] The claimant in this case manufactured and sold a blue reusable adhesive called BLU-TAK. To compete with the claimant, the defendants launched a blue-coloured adhesive called SELLOTAK that was sold in a similar sized wallet to BLU-TAK. Except for being approximately the same size, the competing products were 'wholly different in appearance'. As a result the claim for passing off rested entirely on the colour of the tack. The court held that the defendants had not passed their product off as BLU-TAK when they sold blue adhesive putty. The reason for this was that the defendant's blue adhesive putty was not visible at the point of sale.

In other cases, the relevant time to consider whether consumers were deceived is the point in time at which the product is consumed or used, rather than when it is purchased. For example, in relation to an action for passing off brought in relation to the authorship of a newspaper story, it was said that the relevant time to consider whether the public is confused is when the person reads the story, rather than when the newspaper was purchased.[86] Post-sale confusion may also be significant in other environments. This may be the case, for example, with designer goods such as clothes or kitchen equipment, where the manufacturer's label is often visible long after purchase.[87]

One question which remains unresolved is whether there is passing off where a defendant's misrepresentation causes immediate confusion, but that confusion vanishes by the time at which the consumer makes the decision whether to purchase the defendant's goods or engage the defendant's services. This will be a realistic scenario as regards transactions which are

---

[82] *Neutrogena v. Golden* [1996] *RPC* 473 (claimant had only 0.25 per cent of the market but it was held that a substantial number of members of the public would be misled into thinking the defendant's products were those of the claimant).

[83] *Chocosuisse v. Cadbury* [1999] *RPC* 826, 143; affirmed by the Court of Appeal on the basis that the conclusion was not one which could be regarded as 'perverse': ibid, 838.

[84] *Neutrogena v. Golden* [1996] *RPC* 473, 494.

[85] [1994] *RPC* 556. See also *Julius Sämaan Ltd v. Tetrosyl Ltd* [2006] *FSR* (42) 849 (para. 118) (Kitchin J) (no passing-off where christmas tree-shaped air freshener was sold in different packaging and at higher price than claimant's pine tree).

[86] *Clark v. Associated Newspapers* [1998] *RPC* 261, 271; *Marengo v. Daily Sketch* (1948) 65 *RPC* 242, 250.

[87] *Chelsea Man Menswear v. Chelsea Girl* [1987] *RPC* 189, 204 (Slade LJ, when considering risk of damage, observed that labelled garments can readily move about the country with their wearers).

prefaced by lengthy formalities, etc. such as those involving financial services. In *HFC Bank v. Midland Bank,* it seemed that a number of customers had gone to Midland because it was using a name, HSBC, similar to HFC, but that in no case did a customer do business with Midland without having been disabused of the error. Lloyd J accepted that to amount to passing off the deception must be more than momentary or inconsequential,[88] but beyond that declined to venture a view.[89] Even if such deception was treated as sufficient to give rise to passing off, it remains necessary for a claimant to show a likelihood of damage. In *Knight v. Beyond Properties,*[90] Richards J considered that there was no deception where the defendant called its television programme 'Mythbusters'. The claimant had written and sold children's books under the name MYTHBUSTERS, and the judge acknowledged that some people who had read the books might initially have wondered whether the programme was from the same source. However, he did not think that the initial confusion (which would have quickly been dispelled by the content of the programmes, which were directed at 'lads and dads') was such as to cause the claimant any damage.

4.4 EVIDENCE OF CONFUSION

While the question whether there is a likelihood of confusion is ultimately decided by the court,[91] the courts frequently do so on the basis of evidence introduced by the parties. Three types of evidence are commonly used, usually in combination: evidence of actual confusion, expert evidence, and survey evidence.

While there is no requirement that to succeed in a passing-off action the claimant must show evidence of actual deception, evidence that people have actually been misled will be highly significant.[92] The lack of such evidence may also be probative, but only where the products have been on the market for some time.[93] If after a lengthy period of time there is no evidence of actual confusion, this will weigh against a claimant, primarily because it suggests that there is no confusion.[94] However, before inferring a lack of confusion from this, it is important to note that a lack of evidence of confusion might arise for other reasons. For example, it may simply be because the relevant consumers have not been found or are not willing to come forward.

The courts have also been willing to accept expert evidence in relation to matters that the court is ignorant about and needs to be informed. Often this involves information about the particular trade involved and includes evidence of things such as the class of people, how the goods are displayed or purchased, the numbers sold,[95] and the amount of attention average shoppers give to the appearance of products at the point of purchase.[96] Thus, in deciding

---

[88] See also *Newsweek v. BBC* [1979] *RPC* 441, 449.

[89] *HFC Bank v. Midland Bank* [2000] *FSR* 176, 186, 202. Cf *Phones4U* [2006] *EWCA Civ* 244 (para. 21) (*HFC* was a case 'on its facts').

[90] [2007] *FSR* (34) 813 (paras 80–84).

[91] *North Cheshire & Manchester Brewery v. Manchester Brewery* [1899] *AC* 83, 86; *Mothercare v. Penguin Books* [1988] *RPC* 113, 116. The court must not surrender its own independent judgment to any witness or number of witnesses: see *Spalding v. Gamage* (1915) 32 *RPC* 273, 286–7 *per* Lord Parker. But note that it is the court's (rather than the judge's personal) judgment as to whether it would be deceived that is relevant: *Chocosuisse Union des Fabricants Suisses de Chocolat v. Cadbury* [1998] *RPC* 117, 136.

[92] *Harrods v. Harrodian School* [1996] *RPC* 697, 716.

[93] *Phones4U* [2006] *EWCA Civ* 244 (paras. 41–47).

[94] *Kimberley Clark,* note 22 above, 887–9. See also *Antec International v. South-Western Chicks (Warren)* [1998] *FSR* 738, 745.

[95] *Slazenger & Sons v. Feltham & Co.* (1889) 6 *RPC* 531, 534.

[96] *Kimberley Clark* [1997] *FSR* 877, 884.

whether the public was deceived into thinking that a chocolate bar called SWISS CHALET was made from Swiss chocolate, the Court of Appeal made extensive use of the expert evidence of the person responsible for selecting products (notably the chocolate) for Marks & Spencer.[97] In another decision, the court went so far as to admit expert evidence as to whether consumers were likely to be deceived. Although this is the very question that the court itself must determine, and therefore one on which evidence is not normally admitted, Browne-Wilkinson V-C saw no good reason why the court should not be assisted by experts in making that judgment.[98]

It is also commonplace for the courts to admit and rely upon survey evidence when deciding whether the public is deceived by the misrepresentation.[99] Although costly, surveys save the court from the obvious alternative, namely, a lengthy parade of witnesses.[100] The courts have been careful to scrutinize the nature of the survey. To this end, the courts frequently hear evidence from experts criticizing the methodology of the survey undertaken. The courts also scrutinize the survey to take account of issues such as who was interviewed, the questions asked, and whether or not the interviewees were prompted.[101]

4.5 FACTORS TO BE TAKEN INTO ACCOUNT IN DECIDING WHETHER THE MISREPRESENTATION IS DECEPTIVE

In deciding whether a defendant's misrepresentation is deceptive, the court will take a number of factors into consideration. These include the:

(i)   strength of the public's association with the claimant's sign,

(ii)   similarity of the defendant's sign,

(iii)   proximity of the claimant's and defendant's fields of business,

(iv)   the location of the claimant's and defendant's businesses,

(v)   the characteristics of the market,

(vi)   intention of the defendant,

(vii)   whether the defendant has made a disclaimer, and

(viii) whether the defendant is attempting a parody or satire.

We will consider these in turn. It is important to note that the relative importance of each of these will vary according to the facts in question and that the various factors are often closely interrelated.

4.5.1 The strength of the claimant's sign

One factor that will influence a court when deciding whether a misrepresentation is deceptive is the relative strength of the claimant's sign. If the claimant's mark is highly distinctive, the

---

[97] *Chocosuisse v. Cadbury* [1999] *RPC* 826, 836.

[98] *Guccio Gucci SpA v. Paolo Gucci* [1991] *FSR* 89, 91; *Sodastream v. Thorn Cascade Co.* [1982] *RPC* 459, 468.

[99] It seems that the problem of survey evidence being excluded because it is hearsay has been avoided. This has been done by treating surveys as situations which do not involve proof of the truth of the opinion stated, so much as its existence: *Lego v. Lemelstrich* [1983] FSR 155, 178–9. See, e.g. Wadlow (2004), para. 10.28–10.34, pp. 809–812. In any case, hearsay evidence is admissible in civil cases: Civil Evidence Act 1995, s. 1.

[100] *Pontiac Marina Private v. Cdl. Hotels International* [1998] *FSR* 839.

[101] *Mothercare v. Penguin* [1988] *RPC* 113, 117 *per* Dillon LJ. Even when flawed some courts sometimes still find surveys to be 'qualitatively valuable', though others find surveys unhelpful. *Kimberley Clark* [1997] *FSR* 877, 886–7.

courts are more likely to find that the use of similar marks in a different field of trading is likely to cause confusion. The classic example of this is provided by the *Lego* case, where it was held that the claimant's mark LEGO for children's toys was so strong that confusion resulted from use of the name on coloured plastic garden equipment.[102]

Where a mark or sign is less distinctive, slight differences between the claimant's and the defendant's marks, or between their fields of trading, may mean that there is no passing off. Where a claimant has adopted a descriptive word as a mark, a defendant may be able to avoid passing off by changing the word slightly.[103] Thus, where a claimant used the term FURNITURELAND, the court refused to hold a furniture retailer liable for passing-off for using the name FURNITURE CITY.[104] In contrast, BUSINESSPLAN BUILDER for software was held to be sufficiently similar to BIZPLAN BUILDER to constitute passing off. This was because BIZPLAN BUILDER was not wholly descriptive, the words 'Biz' and 'Business' were virtually interchangeable, and the capital 'p' and the style of script were common to both.[105]

4.5.2 The similarity of the signs

Another factor that may influence the court when considering whether a misrepresentation deceives the public is the similarity of the signs. It is important to note that the approach adopted by the courts in deciding whether the signs are similar always depends on the facts in hand. As such, the points below should be treated as providing no more than general guidance.

In deciding whether two signs are similar enough to cause confusion, the marks are rarely looked at side-by-side. Instead, the courts tend to ask the hypothetical question: if a person saw the signs separately, would they mistake the defendant's product for that of the claimant's? When deciding whether signs are similar, the courts also tend to look at the signs as a whole and in the context in which they are used. The impact that this has upon the scope of passing-off can be seen, for example, in *Wagamama v. City Centre Restaurants.* The claimant in this case ran a chain of Japanese restaurants called WAGAMAMA. Laddie J held that the defendant was liable for passing off when the defendant used the name RAJAMAMA for their chain of Indian restaurants. The judge was influenced by the similar form (the shared second half) of the word which might give an impression of similarity and connection. This was important in an area where it was common for recommendations to be made orally and where recollections were imperfect.[106]

The fact that signs are looked at as a whole has important ramifications where only part of the claimant's sign or mark is appropriated. Where this occurs, the likelihood of there being passing off depends on the relative distinctiveness of the element that is different. It also depends on the importance that consumers place on the part when purchasing the product in question. For example, where the distinctive feature of the claimant's get-up for water bottles was that the bottles were cobalt blue and were made in a particular shape, it was held that the defendant was not liable for passing off when they sold water in cobalt-blue bottles of a very different shape.[107] This can be usefully contrasted with *Reckitt & Colman* which, as we saw

---

[102] *Lego v. Lemelstrich* [1983] *FSR* 155, 187; *Antec International v. South-Western Chicks (Warren)* [1998] *FSR* 738, 747.

[103] *Office Cleaning Services v. Westminster Window and General Cleaners* (1946) 63 *RPC* 39.

[104] *Furnitureland v. Harris* [1989] *FSR* 536, 539–40; *Associated Newspapers Ltd v. Express Newspapers* [2003] *FSR* (51) (THE MAIL and THE LONDON EVENING MAIL).

[105] *Jian Tools for Sales v. Roderick Manhattan Group* [1995] *FSR* 924.

[106] [1995] *FSR* 713; *Neutrogena v. Golden* [1996] *RPC* 473.

[107] *Ty Nant Spring Water v. Simon Feeney Associates* (28 Apr. 1998) Scott VC refusing interlocutory injunction where both used bottles of the same colour (cobalt blue).

earlier, was a passing-off action in relation to the get-up of lemon-juice containers. While the shape, colour, and size of the two containers were the same, the labels on the two products were different. Nonetheless, the courts held that there had been passing off. This was because the labels were only a minor part of the get-up and not an element to which a customer would pay particular regard.[108]

In judging the similarity of signs, the courts sometimes emphasize the 'idea of the mark'. That is, they do not focus on the detail of the mark so much as the general idea that it conveys. For example, in one case the shared idea of 'seabirds' was a significant factor in holding that the defendant had passed its PUFFIN biscuits off as those of the claimant, who sold their biscuits under the name PENGUIN. Given the type of audience in question and the similarity of the get-up, the court held that a substantial number of customers would have been deceived into incorrectly thinking that the biscuits were produced by the same manufacturer.[109]

4.5.3 The proximity of the claimant's and the defendant's fields of business

For some time it was thought that, to succeed in a passing-off action, the claimant and defendant had to share 'a common field of activity'. Thus where a radio presenter's name was used for a breakfast cereal it was held that there was no passing off. This was because the fields of radio presentation and the sale of breakfast cereals did not overlap.[110] However, even at its inception, the need to show a common field of activity was difficult to reconcile with a number of earlier decisions.[111] It has since been reinterpreted,[112] diluted,[113] and ultimately declared to be heretical.[114] If a claimant can demonstrate a misrepresentation and likelihood of damage to their goodwill, they will succeed: there is no additional requirement that they need to establish a common field of activity.

Having said this, it is clear that the ability to demonstrate a 'common field of activity' will greatly assist a claimant's action for passing off. This is because, if two traders share a common field of activity, it will be easier for a court to hold that there is a misrepresentation that is likely to deceive the public and thus cause damage to the claimant.[115] Indeed, the abandonment of the requirement for a common field of activity has meant that a comparison of the trade activities of the parties is a factor that is taken into account in determining the likelihood of deception. The similarity of the fields also interacts with other factors such as the distinctiveness of the claimant's sign.

The courts have adopted a liberal approach when deciding whether the claimant and defendant operate in same field. For example, in one decision the use of CARFAX for spare parts for

---

[108] *Reckitt & Colman v. Borden* [1990] *RPC* 341, 423.

[109] *United Biscuits v. Asda* [1997] *RPC* 513.

[110] *McCulloch v. May* (1948) 65 *RPC* 58.

[111] For example, *Eastman Photographic Materials Co. v. John Griffiths Cycle Corporation* (1898) 15 *RPC* 105 (cameras and bicycles); *Walter v. Ashton* [1902] 2 *Ch* 282 (*The Times* newspaper and bicycles). As argued by Philips and Coleman, 'Passing Off and the Common Field of Activity' (1985) 101 *LQR* 242 and accepted by Millett LJ in *Harrods v. Harrodian School* [1996] *RPC* 697, 714.

[112] In the Abba case, *Lyngstrad* [1977] *FSR* 62, Oliver J interpreted *McCulloch* as merely requiring a 'real possibility of confusion'.

[113] *Lego v. Lemelstrich* [1983] *FSR* 155.

[114] *Mirage v. Counter-Feat* [1991] *FSR* 145, 157 Browne-Wilkinson V-C (referring to the common field of activity theory as discredited); *Harrods v. Harrodian School* [1996] *RPC* 697; *Irvine v. Talksport* [2002] *FSR* 943.

[115] *Nice and Safe v. Flook* [2002] *FSR* 943, 21 (Robert Walker J) 'the *Lego* case, though it illustrates a relaxation of the common field of activity concept does not mark its extinction. It must still be very relevant to the likelihood of deception.' *Oasis Stores' Trade Mark Application* [1998] *RPC* 631, 644 (where the fields of activity are far apart the burden of establishing a likelihood of confusion or deception will be significantly greater).

motor vehicles was held to be likely to amount to passing off, given the claimant's plans to launch a traffic information service under the same name.[116] Similarly, a claimant who used the name MARIGOLD for household rubber gloves was granted an injunction to prevent the defendant from using the mark on toilet tissue. The court was confident that a customer or, more specifically a 'housewife' who was familiar with the claimant's gloves, would expect toilet roll sold under the same name to be a product of the same business.[117] In a trade mark case, however, the Registry took the view that the owner of the EVER READY mark for batteries would not be able to succeed in a passing-off action against a person who used the same words for condoms.[118] Consequently, the mark was registrable for condoms.

4.5.4 The location of the claimant's and defendant's businesses

Goodwill is recognized as being local, and, in principle, there is no actionable misrepresentation where a person uses the sign in a different geographical area. This can be seen from the recent case of *Bignell v. Just Employment Law Ltd.*[119] Here the claimant was a solicitor specializing in employment law who had practised for about ten years in Guildford under the name JUST EMPLOYMENT. The defendant was a Scottish company, incorporated in 2004 as Just Employment Law Ltd. (JEL). When the defendant ran a radio campaign on Capital Radio, a number of listeners contacted Bignell's office on the assumption that it was his firm's advertisement, where upon he sued JEL alleging passing off. There was no evidence of anyone contacting the defendant in the belief that it had anything to do with the claimant's firm. Deputy Judge Engelhart QC dismissed the claim, finding that Bignell's goodwill was inherently local.[120] The claim for passing off failed as there was no actual damage, only some confusion, which was to be expected from two such similar names. However, the court left open the possibility that incidental passing off might occur if JEL were to open an office and solicit work near Guildford.

4.5.5 The characteristics of the market

In deciding whether a misrepresentation is deceptive the courts take account of 'the background of the type of market in which the goods are sold, the manner in which they are sold, and the habits and characteristics of purchasers in that market'.[121]

The characteristics of the market have a particularly pronounced impact on decisions as to whether two signs are similar. Where consumers are well-informed or particularly attentive to detail,[122] small differences between signs may be sufficient to avoid a finding of deception. For example, the defendant's use of *Mother care/Other care* as a title for their book was held not to be a misrepresentation that the book was connected with the shop MOTHERCARE. As Bingham LJ explained, the claimant's lettering was not employed, the words were not spelled as one word, the Penguin mark was liberally used on the books, and no one who was familiar with the claimant's literary output could see any similarity of style, content, or format. Bingham LJ added that reasonably literate people would not see the title as an indication that the contents bore any reference to the claimant.[123] The better the consumer's memory for detail, the closer the marks must be to cause deception.

---

[116] *BBC v. Talbot* [1981] *FSR* 228.   [117] *LRC v. Lila Edets* [1972] *FSR* 479.
[118] *Oasis Stores' Trade Mark Application* [1998] *RPC* 631 (in the context of TMA s. 5(4)).
[119] [2007] *EWHC* 2203 (Ch); [2008] *FSR* 125.   [120] Ibid, 145–47.
[121] *Reckitt & Colman v. Borden* [1990] *RPC* 341, 415–16.
[122] Although evidence as to consumer behaviour might reveal that even with élite goods consumers are oddly inattentive: *Guccio Gucci v. Gucci* [1991] *FSR* 89.
[123] *Mothercare v. Penguin* [1988] *RPC* 113, 121–2.

Ultimately, the level of detail remembered by the consumer will depend on the goods or services in question. While there may be exceptions, the courts do not normally assume that consumers have a perfect memory of the goods in question. Instead, they tend to assume that the notional consumers have a vague and hazy memory of the goods or services. That is, it is often assumed that consumers have 'imperfect recollection'. Consequently, where a defendant adds laudatory or commonplace words such as 'International' or 'Super' to a name, this will not mean that they will be able to escape liability.[124] The reason for this is that, while the addition of the prefix may mean that the signs are not identical, nonetheless they may be similar enough to deceive a consumer with a hazy and imperfect memory.

It is usually assumed that consumers pay little attention to detail in purchasing cheap necessities in supermarkets.[125] It will also usually be assumed that non-English-speaking audiences will pay little attention to verbal or textual, as opposed to visual references.[126]

4.5.6 The intention of the defendant

It is well established that it is not a prerequisite to liability that the claimant be able to show that the defendant intended to pass their goods off as those of the claimant.[127] However, it will assist a claimant if they can show that a defendant has acted fraudulently.[128] In these circumstances the likelihood of deception is more readily inferred. This is because the defendant is assumed to have achieved their goal.[129] Occasionally, a similar attitude has been taken to a defendant who makes a conscious decision to live dangerously and use a sign as close to that of the claimant as is legally possible.[130]

4.5.7 Disclaimers

Because the representation is to be viewed in context, it is sometimes possible for a defendant to correct any misunderstandings that their actions may potentially create.[131] For example, a defendant was able to avoid what would otherwise have been passing off by placing the word 'sliced' in front of the claimant's distinctive designation 'Parma ham'. This was held to be sufficient to counteract the alleged misrepresentation.[132]

It is a question of fact whether a defendant succeeds in correcting any misunderstandings the public may have as a result of their misrepresentation.[133] The relative effectiveness of a disclaimer depends on a number of things. To be effective a disclaimer must be as 'bold, precise and compelling as the trade description itself and must be as effectively brought to the notice of any person to whom the goods may be supplied'.[134] In effect, the disclaimer must

---

[124] *Pontiac Marina* [1998] *FSR* 839 (CA of Singapore); *Antec International* [1998] *FSR* 738, 745.

[125] *Kimberley Clark* [1997] *FSR* 877, 884.

[126] *Modus Vivendi v. Keen (World Marketing)* [1996] *EIPR* D–82.

[127] *Chocosuisse v. Cadbury* [1998] *RPC* 117, 137.

[128] *Burberrys v. Cording* (1909) 26 *RPC* 693, 701.

[129] *Slazenger v. Feltham* (1889) 6 *RPC* 531, 538; *Irvine v. Talksport*, note 4 above. In *Parker Knoll v. Knoll International* [1962] *RPC* 265, 290 Lord Devlin questioned the basis of the rule stating that 'it is not easy to see why the defendant's own estimate of the effect of his representation should be worth more than anybody else's. It seems probable that the rule is steeped in history rather than in logic'. *Slazenger* was recently applied by the Court of Appeal in *L'Oreal v. Bellure* [2008] *ETMR* (1) 1.

[130] *United Biscuits v. Asda* [1997] *RPC* 513.   [131] *Chivers v. Chivers* (1900) 17 *RPC* 420.

[132] *Consorzio Parma v. Marks & Spencer* [1991] *RPC* 351, 371 (Nourse LJ); 374 (Balcombe LJ); 379 (Leggatt LJ).

[133] The public can be surprisingly easily confused, for example, by confusing 'elderflower champagne' with champagne: *Taittinger v. Allbev* [1993] *FSR* 641.

[134] *Norman v. Bennett* [1974] 1 *WLR* 1229, 1232 (a case on the Trade Descriptions Act 1968); *Clark v. Associated Newspapers* [1998] *RPC* 261, 272.

negate the misrepresentation. The precise form that the disclaimer needs to take will depend upon the nature of the misrepresentation. In the old case of *Edge v. Nicholls*,[135] the claimants produced distinctive calico bags. The defendants produced a calico bag with a similar get-up to the claimant's, to which they added a label saying NICHOLLS. The disclaimer was ineffective because the consumers of the goods (being the 'poorer classes') relied on the get-up, rather than the name of the product.

The point in time when the disclaimer is communicated to the consumer will also influence whether or not it is effective. As a general rule the disclaimer must reach the relevant consumer before the misrepresentation brings about the requisite damage. Thus, a disclaimer will be ineffective where customers have already been lured into examining the defendant's product as a result of the defendant's use of the claimant's name. Another example of a situation where the importance of the timing of the disclaimer is exemplified is in *Associated Newspapers v. Insert Media*.[136] It will be recalled that, by placing advertising inserts inside the claimant's newspaper without their permission or knowledge, the defendants were held to be liable for passing off. In response, the defendants indicated that they would be prepared to include on their inserts a statement to the effect that the material did not appear with the approval or knowledge of the newspaper publishers. Browne-Wilkinson V-C said this would not nullify the misrepresentation. The reason for this was that the:

inclusion in the insert of a disclaimer of that kind would be most unlikely to come to the attention of a person reading the advertisement contained on the insert. It is just inappropriate in this field for the matter to be corrected by a disclaimer which is unlikely to come to the attention of the reader and may well confuse him further if it does come to his attention.[137]

A disclaimer may also fail for the simple reason that it is likely to become detached from the misrepresentation and as a result will be unable to nullify the misrepresentation.[138]

4.5.8 Parody

One area where special considerations may apply is where the defendant sets out to parody or satirize the claimant's goods or services (or some more general target).[139] In these cases, the owner of the goods that have been parodied may bring a passing-off action. The key problem here is that for a parody or satire to be effective the audience needs to understand that the defendant's aim is to ridicule the original. If a parody is effective, there will normally be no misunderstanding and hence no possibility of confusion. This can be seen from *Miss World v. James St Productions*.[140] The claimants in this case, who were the proprietors of goodwill in the 'Miss World' beauty contest, sought to prevent the showing of a film *Miss Alternative World*, which was described as a spoof of the Miss World pageant with sado-masochistic over-tones. The Court of Appeal declined to intervene on the ground that there was no danger that ordinary members of the public would be confused.

However, any confidence that parody will not amount to passing off must now be shaken by the *Alan Clark* case.[141] It will be recalled that in this decision the politician and author Alan Clark wished to prevent the *Evening Standard* from publishing a satirical column called 'Alan

---

[135] [1911] *AC* 693.   [136] [1991] 3 *All ER* 535.   [137] Ibid, 542.

[138] In *Reckitt & Colman v. Borden* [1990] *RPC* 341, 423 (*per* Lord Jauncey) the label was not effective to prevent misrepresentation because it would easily be detached from the product.

[139] For consideration of parody in the context of copyright and trade-mark infringements see Chs. 8 and 36. For reflections, see M. Spence, 'Intellectual Property and the Problem of Parody' (1998) 114 *LQR* 594.

[140] [1981] *FSR* 309.   [141] *Clark v. Associated Newspapers* [1998] *RPC* 261.

Clark's Secret Diaries' that bore Clark's name and photograph. (See Fig. 10.1, p. 251 above.) The main issue was whether Clark could establish that there had been a misrepresentation or a 'false attribution'.[142] In turn this required Clark to establish that a substantial number of readers of the *Evening Standard* had been or were likely to have been misled in a manner which was more than momentary and inconsequential. Looking at the column and having regard to the evidence of the witnesses, Lightman J held that a substantial body of readers would be misled. The counter-messages (or disclaimers) which appeared on the column, such as the use of the word 'secret' and the statement that 'Peter Bradshaw imagines how the great diarist might record', were said not to be sufficiently forthright to counteract the suggestion that the claimant was the author of the column. As one commentator rightly observed as a result of this decision, '[t]he author of even the most obvious parody cannot assume that his work is [not] a misrepresentation under the law of passing off'.[143]

5 PROVIDING DECEPTIVE MEANS OR INSTRUMENTS OF FRAUD

It is important to note that an action for passing off can not only be brought against a person who carries out the act of misrepresentation, but also against someone who provides the means or facilities which enable the passing-off to take place in the first place. This can be seen, for example, in *Lever v. Goodwin*,[144] where the claimant sought relief against a defendant who had been selling soap in a similar get-up. In the circumstances, while consumers might have been deceived by the similarity of the get-up, the defendants did not sell the soap directly to the public. Instead, they only sold the soap to retail buyers who, in turn, sold the soap to members of the public. The problem for the claimant was that the retailers were not deceived about the origin of the goods: they knew exactly what they were purchasing. The defendants argued that, as they did not sell the soap directly to the public, and as the retailers were not confused, they were not liable for passing off. Chitty J, whose judgment was approved on appeal, denied that a defendant could escape liability in this way. What a manufacturer did in these circumstances, he explained, was to put 'an instrument of fraud' into the retailer's hands. In these circumstances it was necessary to ask, have the defendants 'knowingly put into the hands of the shopman...the means of deceiving the ultimate purchaser'?[145] On the facts, he found that they had.

A more recent example of this variant of the passing-off action is provided by the *One In A Million* decision.[146] In this case, the Court of Appeal held that persons who registered and dealt in internet domain names such as marksandspencer.co.uk were likely to be restrained.

---

[142] Clark also based his claim on CDPA s. 84 (false attribution of authorship). On this see p. 250 above. It is interesting to note that the constituents of false attribution in s. 84 were treated as different from those under the law of passing-off, with s. 84 requiring consideration.

[143] See Spence, 'Intellectual Property and the Problem of Parody', 599.

[144] (1887) 4 *RPC* 492, 498.   [145] Ibid.

[146] [1998] 4 *All ER* 476. For criticism of the reasoning see Elmslie, 'The *One in a Million* Case', 285; and C. Thorne and S. Bennet, 'Domain Names—internet Warehousing: Has Protection of Well-Known Names on the internet Gone Too Far?' [1998] *EIPR* 468 (referring to *One in a Million* as 'a policy decision rather than a straight application of the law of passing-off'); Carty, 'Passing-off and Instruments of Deception' [2003] *EIPR* 188 (arguing that the doctrine requires (i) circulation of (ii) an instrument (iii) calculated to deceive, and that in *One in a Million* there simply was no instrument of deception. Carty prefers the view that the decision is to be justified as

This was on the basis that they were 'equipped with or intending to equip another with an instrument of fraud'.[147] Aldous LJ said that a 'name which will, by reason of its similarity to the name of another, inherently lead to passing-off is an instrument of fraud'.[148] Even if a name does not inherently lead to passing off, Aldous LJ said that it may nevertheless be an instrument of fraud. In deciding whether this is the case, the court should consider 'the similarity of the names, the intention of the defendant, the type of trade and all the surrounding circumstances'.[149] Aldous LJ added that if the court concluded 'that the name was produced to enable passing off, is adapted to be used for passing off, and, if used, is likely to be fraudulently used, an injunction will be appropriate'.[150]

On the facts it was held that the domain names in question were 'instruments of fraud'. This was because any 'realistic use of them as domain names would result in passing off'.[151] As the value of the names lay in the threat that they would be used in a fraudulent way, the court held that the 'registrations were... made for the purpose of appropriating the respondent's property, their goodwill, and with an intention of threatening dishonest use by them or another'.[152]

In contrast, in *French Connection v. Sutton*[153] Rattee J refused to grant summary judgment to French Connection (UK) against a defendant who had registered FCUK.COM. The judge reasoned that (in contrast to the examples in *One in a Million*) the defendant might succeed in establishing a defence at trial, namely, that the domain name was not registered with a view to passing off, but was registered for 'use by himself of what he thought would be a useful internet and E-mail name'. According to Rattee J, this was not an 'incredible' argument, because the letters FCUK were widely used by internet users as an alternative to the word 'fuck', usually to access sites containing pornographic material. As is clear from this, much will turn on when a court is willing to infer potential legitimate use of the name. In particular, it is not easy to predict whether a so-called 'typo squatter', who registers a name that is similar to that of a well known business (e.g. tescp.com) in the hope of attracting visitors who mistype (e.g. tesco.com), will face liability under the 'instruments of fraud' doctrine. The registrant might intend to collect revenue by forwarding such traffic to Tesco's own site, or may have other goals.

a case of threatened passing-off, or threatening to authorize another's passing-off.) However, the case has been followed: *Phones4U* [2006] *EWCA Civ* 244 (para. 27) (CA); *Tesco v. Elogicom* [2006] *EWHC* 403 (paras. 41–50).

[147] *One in a Million* [1998] 4 *All ER* 476, 493.

[148] Ibid.   [149] Ibid.   [150] Ibid.   [151] Ibid, 497.

[152] Ibid, 498. See also *Reality Group v. Chance* [2002] *FSR* (13) (where claimant sought to stop defendant's alleged 'blocking registration' of a CTM, Patten J referred to *One in a Million* when refusing to strike out).

[153] [2000] *ETMR* 341. For other cases where passing-off has been used to prevent use of web sites in trade see *Easyjet Airline Co v. Dainty* [2002] *FSR* (6) 111 and *Bonnier Media v. Smith (GL)* [2002] *ETMR* (86) 1050.

34

DAMAGE

CHAPTER CONTENTS

The third and final element that a claimant must prove to sustain a passing-off action is that they have suffered, or are likely to suffer, damage as a result of the defendant's misrepresentation.[1] After looking at the third limb of the passing-off action, we turn away from the classic passing-off action to consider the notion of extended passing off and then unfair competition.

1 HEADS OF DAMAGE

There are four types of damage that have been recognized by the courts in connection with misrepresentation. These are loss of existing trade and profits, loss of potential trade and profits, damage to reputation, and dilution.[2] In each case, there must be more than trivial or minimal damage.[3] Where the damage to reputation relates to future losses, the damage must also be reasonably foreseeable.[4]

1.1 LOSS OF EXISTING TRADE AND PROFIT

One of the most common forms of damage is where the misrepresentation diverts trade and thus profit from the claimant to the defendant. This will occur where the misrepresentation generates confusion about the source or origin of the goods or services. In this situation, the damage is self-evident: it is the loss of profit on the sale of goods or services that the claimant suffers. This type of damage will only occur where the claimant and the defendant deal in similar goods or services or operate in similar fields.

---

[1] A requirement of damage is specified in both Lord Diplock and Lord Fraser's fifth 'probanda': *Erven Warnink v. Townend* ([1979] *AC* 731, 742, 756) and the third branch of Lord Oliver's classic trinity.

[2] Wadlow (2004), Ch. 4; H. Carty, 'Heads of Damage in Passing Off' [1996] *EIPR* 487.

[3] Lord Fraser's reference, at *Warnink* [1979] *AC* 731, 756, to 'substantial' damage was reinterpreted in this way by Peter Gibson LJ in *Taittinger SA v. Allbev* [1993] *FSR* 641, 664.

[4] Not 'hypothetical' or 'far-fetched': *Mothercare v. Penguin Books* [1988] *RPC* 113, 116.

1.2 LOSS OF POTENTIAL TRADE AND PROFIT

The courts have also recognized that a claimant may incur damage where the misrepresentation leads to a loss of future profit. This will occur, for example, where a defendant trades in a field or geographical area into which the claimant intends to expand in the future. In this situation the damage suffered arises through the potential trade that is lost rather than the existing trade that is diverted.[5]

Importantly, the loss of potential profits includes the loss of a chance to expand into a new field. This can be seen, for example, in *Lego v. Lemelstrich,* which was an action brought by Lego, the well-known manufacturer of children's building blocks, against Lemelstrich who sold brightly coloured plastic garden sprinklers marketed under the name, LEGO. On the basis that Lego's reputation extended beyond children's toys to include garden sprinklers, Falconer J found that the defendant's use of the LEGO name in relation to garden equipment was likely to damage Lego's goodwill. Given that the LEGO goodwill extended to garden equipment, the claimant would have had the potential to use their name to operate in the field of garden equipment or to have licensed or franchised other traders in that field.[6]

1.3 LOSS OF LICENSING REVENUES

Loss of future profit may also include situations where the defendant's conduct undermines the claimant's ability to license their own mark and thus brings about a loss of potential licensing revenues. The recognition of the loss of future licensing revenue as a relevant form of damage may enable celebrities to use passing-off to prevent the misappropriation of their image or personality. (Without this form of damage, celebrities face the problem that if they had not already licensed their image, they would have difficulties in proving the requisite damage.) In *Mirage Studios v. Counter-Feat Clothing,*[7] Browne-Wilkinson V-C held that the creators of the *Teenage Mutant Ninja Turtles* (fictitious cartoon characters), suffered damage when the defendant licensed others to reproduce the cartoon characters on clothing. This was because they would lose the royalties that would otherwise have been paid to them to use the images. This line of reasoning has been criticized on the basis of its circularity.[8] The reasoning is said to be circular because a person is only entitled to licensing revenue if they have the legal ability to control the use that is made of their image (etc.). In turn, this only arises where the unauthorized use amounts to passing off. While this criticism may be technically correct, it overlooks the fact that parties may enter into licensing schemes even though there is no legal requirement to do so.[9] Despite doubts about the impact of passing-off on character and personality merchandising, it remains a profitable business. As long as the courts only recognize damage through loss of royalties where licensing is likely to take place, it is difficult to see that the circularity objection carries much force.

This must be contrasted with *Stringfellow v. McCain.*[10] The defendant in the case manufactured a new brand of long, thin oven-ready chips called STRINGFELLOWS. The television advertisements for the defendant's chips featured a choreographed disco number set in a kitchen, with a boy and his two sisters singing 'Stringfellows from McCains'. The claimant was the

---

[5] *LRC v. Lila Edets* [1973] *RPC* 560 (use on toilet tissue of same name, in a similar style, as claimant used for household gloves and nappies caused damage because claimant was planning to move into the field).

[6] *Lego v. Lemelstrich* [1983] *FSR* 155, 194. See also *Dunhill v. Sunoptic* [1979] *FSR* 337.

[7] [1991] *FSR* 145.   [8] Carty, 'Heads of Damage in Passing Off', 490.

[9] Wadlow (2004), para. 4.38, pp. 264–6.   [10] [1984] *RPC* 501.

owner of a well-known nightclub called STRINGFELLOW's. The London nightclub consisted of a restaurant and a discotheque: the latter being described in the decision as a place 'where people move their bodies in strange ways to even stranger music'.[11] The claimant argued that the defendant's misrepresentation was likely to prejudice their future chances of exploiting the goodwill associated with the name STRINGFELLOW's. The court refused to grant relief on the ground that it was unlikely that the misrepresentation would cause Stringfellow any damage. While Stringfellow might have been able to exploit his name (for example through the establishment of franchises), Slade LJ did not find that the television advert prejudiced his ability to do so. In part, Slade LJ was influenced by the fact that there was no evidence that Stringfellow had any intention to exploit his name. Stephenson LJ said that in a case such as this there must be clear and cogent proof of actual damage or real likelihood of damage. Along with Slade LJ, he said that where there is a tenuous overlap between the fields of activity of the protagonists, he doubted whether damage in the form of loss of future franchising or merchandising revenue was ever recoverable.[12]

1.4 DAMAGE TO REPUTATION

The courts have also recognized that damage may occur where the misrepresentation has a negative impact on the claimant's reputation.[13] This form of damage is particularly important where the misrepresentation is made in respect of non-competing goods or services. While the claimant may not lose any trade, the misrepresentation may nonetheless have a negative impact upon the claimant's reputation. This is particularly so where the claimant deals in high-quality goods or services. As we explained above, damage from loss of existing or potential trade arises where the public is confused about the origin of the goods or services. In contrast, damage to reputation arises where the defendant's misrepresentation leads the public to believe that the goods or services of the claimant and the defendant are somehow related. The resulting damage arises from the negative impact that this has upon the claimant's reputation. As Warrington LJ explained in *Ewing v. Buttercup Margarine Co.,* to 'induce the belief that my business is a branch of another man's business may do that other man damage in various ways. The quality of goods I sell, the kind of business I do, the credit or otherwise which I enjoy are all things which may injure the other man who is assumed wrongly to be associated with me'.[14]

Another example of the way reputation may be damaged is offered by *Associated Newspapers v. Insert Media*.[15] The claimants in this case were the publishers of two national newspapers. The defendant arranged with retail newsagents to have advertising materials inserted into the papers, without the publisher's knowledge or consent. The Court of Appeal held that, since there was a real risk that the newspapers would be thought to be responsible for the accuracy and honesty of the inserts, there was an obvious, appreciable risk of loss of goodwill and reputation by the publishers.

One situation where damage to reputation may be important is where the claimant deals in high-quality goods and the defendant acts in a way that undermines that reputation. This

---

[11] Ibid, 504.　　　[12] Ibid, 546–7.

[13] But cf. *Harrods v. Harrodian School* [1996] RPC 697, 718: 'damage to reputation without damage to goodwill is not sufficient to support an action for passing off', so that even if the School had a poor reputation it would not rub off on the department store.

[14] [1917] 2 *Ch* 1, 14. Applied by Laddie J. in *Associated Newspapers v. Express Newspapers* [2003] FSR (51) (para. 46); and by Mann J. in *Sir Robert McAlpine Ltd v. Alfred McAlpine plc* [2004] RPC (36) 711 (paras 4–45).

[15] [1991] FSR 380.

would be the case, for example, where the defendant trades under the same name as the claimant, but in a market in which the claimant would never operate. In these circumstances, the defendant's misrepresentation would not impact upon the claimant's sales. The reason for this is that the claimant would never have made the sales in the first place. Nonetheless, the courts have recognized that the defendant's conduct may damage the claimant's reputation. This can be seen, for example, in *Annabel's Berkeley Square v. Schock*[16] where a well-known London club called 'Annabel's' was granted relief to prevent the defendant from trading as 'Annabel's Escort Agency'. The court accepted that the defendant's use of the name 'Annabel's' could have tarnished and thus undermined the claimant's reputation.

Another situation where a misrepresentation may damage a claimant's reputation is in relation to the unauthorized use of the name, image, or likeness of a celebrity. Where the name or image of a celebrity is used without permission, and the celebrity can show that the public (incorrectly) thought that they had endorsed the use of their image, this may damage the celebrity's reputation. This would be the case, for example, where the picture of a sports star who has a reputation for healthy living is used to advertise a brand of cigarettes. Damage to reputation may also be important in relation to character merchandising. For example, in *Mirage Studios v. Counter-Feat Clothing,*[17] the claimants brought an action against the defendant for licensing the reproduction of images of *Ninja Turtles* on T-shirts and clothing. Browne-Wilkinson V-C said that, since the public 'associates the goods with the creator of the characters, the depreciation of the image by fixing the Turtle picture to inferior goods and inferior materials may seriously reduce the value of the licensing right'.[18] A similar approach was adopted by the Supreme Court of New South Wales in *Henderson v. Radio Corporation.*[19] It will be recalled that in this case the unauthorized use of a photograph of two ballroom dancers on a record cover was held to be a misrepresentation that the dancers had endorsed the product. On the basis that the 'wrongful appropriation of another's professional or business reputation is an injury in itself', the Court found that the misrepresentation had caused the requisite damage. This was because it had deprived the dancers of the right to bestow recommendations at will.[20] Whether this is really a case of damage to reputation or a loss of an opportunity to profit is questionable.

1.5 DILUTION

The final form of damage recognized by the courts is where the misrepresentation dilutes the claimant's goodwill. This occurs where the defendant's misrepresentation causes the claimant's sign to become familiar or commonplace and, as a result, undermines the ability of the sign to summon up particular goods or values. That is, the defendant's misrepresentation dilutes the pulling power or goodwill of the claimant's sign. Importantly, this applies where the public is not confused about the source or origin of the goods or where it is unlikely that the reputation will be damaged.

The notion of damage through dilution was acknowledged in English law in *Taittinger v. Allbev.*[21] The claimant was a member of a group of producers from the Champagne district who made a naturally sparkling wine, which had long been known in the United Kingdom

---

[16] [1972] *RPC* 838. See also *British Medical Assn. v. Marsh* (1931) 48 *RPC* 565.

[17] [1991] *FSR* 145, 156.   [18] Ibid.   [19] [1969] *RPC* 218.   [20] Ibid, 236.

[21] A number of earlier cases had referred to a trader's interest in maintaining the exclusivity of their signs: *Lego v. Lemelstrich* [1983] *FSR* 155; *Dalgety Spillers Food v. Food Brokers* [1994] *FSR* 504; *Peter Waterman v. CBS* [1993] *EMLR* 27.

as 'champagne'. Notably, the claimant's champagne was produced by a process of double fermentation from grapes grown in the Champagne district. The claimant brought an action
against the producer of a non-alcoholic sparkling beverage called ELDERFLOWER CHAMPAGNE
that was produced in England. At first instance, it was held that the claimants had goodwill in
'champagne' and that the labelling of the defendant's product amounted to a misrepresentation. However, the court found that, while a small number of people might be confused by
the defendant's misrepresentation, the claimant had not established that there was any real
likelihood of serious damage if the defendant continued to sell their product as ELDERFLOWER
CHAMPAGNE.

On appeal, the Court of Appeal overturned the first instance decision, finding that the
defendant was liable for passing off. While the Court of Appeal agreed with the judge's findings
at first instance in relation to goodwill and misrepresentation, it disagreed as to the question
of damage. In particular, the Court of Appeal held that the defendant's use of 'champagne' had
caused the requisite damage to sustain a passing-off action. Importantly, the Court of Appeal
found that the relevant injury to the champagne house's goodwill occurred under a head of
damage not considered at first instance. The damage arose from the fact that there would
have been blurring or erosion of the uniqueness associated with the name 'Champagne' which
would have debased the claimant's reputation. The use of the name champagne for the elderflower drink brought about 'a gradual debasement, dilution or erosion of what is distinctive'.[22]
This was because, as Cross J explained in another context:

if people were allowed to call sparkling wine not produced in Champagne 'Champagne' even
though preceded by an adjective denoting the country of origin, the distinction between genuine
Champagne and 'champagne-type' wines produced elsewhere would become blurred; that the word
'Champagne' would come gradually to mean no more than 'sparkling wine' and that part of the
plaintiff's goodwill which consisted in the name would be diluted and gradually destroyed.[23]

The explicit recognition of dilution as a form of damage was greeted enthusiastically by many
commentators, especially in light of similar extensions in trade mark law.[24] However, the status of dilution as a head of damage in passing off has subsequently been thrown into doubt
by *Harrods v. Harrodian School*.[25] In this decision, Millett LJ said that, while 'erosion of the
distinctiveness of a brand name has been recognized as a form of damage to the goodwill of the
business with which the name is connected in a number of cases, particularly in Australia and
New Zealand…unless care is taken this could mark an unacceptable extension of the tort of
passing off'.[26] Millett LJ also said that he had problems with an action based on confusion that
recognized a distinct head of damage that did not depend on confusion.[27] On the facts, Millett
LJ held that it was highly unlikely that, as a result of the defendant's activities, the Harrods
name would lose its distinctiveness or become a generic term to refer to shops that sold luxury
goods. As such, the passing-off action failed.[28]

As a result of the *Harrods* decision there is now some uncertainty over the extent to
which dilution will be recognized as a distinct head of damage. One view treats dilution

---

[22] *Taittinger v. Allbev* [1993] *FSR* 641, 670, 674, 678 ('singularity and exclusiveness of the description
Champagne').

[23] *Vine Products v. Mackenzie* [1969] *RPC* 1, 23.

[24] TMA s. 10(3) discussed below at pp. 876–89.   [25] [1996] *RPC* 697.

[26] Ibid, 715–16.   [27] See Wadlow (2004), para. 4.20, pp. 252–54.

[28] Sir Michael Kerr, in a dissenting judgment, applied the dilution doctrine from *Taittinger*.

as an appropriate form of damage only in extended passing-off cases.[29] Other authorities, however, have been willing to accept dilution in the context of classic passing off. In *British Telecommunications v. One In A Million*[30] the Court of Appeal held that persons who registered and dealt in internet domain names, such as marksandspencer.co.uk, were liable for passing off. This was because 'registration of the domain name including the words Marks & Spencer is an erosion of the exclusive goodwill in the name which damages or is likely to damage Marks & Spencer'.[31] Similarly in *Sir Robert McAlpine Ltd v. Alfred McAlpine plc*,[32] Mann J held that the defendant was guilty of passing off when it decided to rebrand itself as MCALPINE. While the two McAlpine forms had been long established as 'Robert McAlpine' and 'Alfred McAlpine' and shared goodwill in the 'McAlpine' name, the decision to use the surname by itself would blur the distinctive character of Sir Robert McAlpine's mark. 'Once the prefix goes', the judge explained, 'there is scope for a greater amount of elbowing (or blurring, or diminishing, or erosion . . . , to which Robert has not consented.'

2 EXTENDED PASSING OFF

As should be clear by now, the classic passing-off action contains a host of subcategories and subrules. The courts have developed one variant, known as 'extended passing off', that deserves special attention. The extended form of passing-off was first recognized by Danckwerts J in the *Bollinger* decision,[33] in which the claimants, who were Champagne producers, brought a successful action to prevent the defendant calling its product 'Spanish champagne'. The action for extended passing off represents a radical departure from the classic form, which is based on misrepresentation as to source.[34] As Laddie J said in *Chocosuisse,* although extended passing off grew from passing-off roots, it displays marked differences from the classic form of the cause of action.[35] These differences are best looked at in terms of the three elements of the action: goodwill, misrepresentation, and damage.

2.1 GOODWILL

The first point to note about extended passing off is that it recognizes that a class or group of traders may share goodwill in a name (or some other indicator) that is distinctive of a particular class of goods, such as 'advocaat', 'Champagne', or 'Scotch whisky'. This can be seen, for example, in the *Bollinger* decision,[36] where the claimants were members of a group of producers

[29] *Chocosuisse Union des Fabricants Suisses de Chocolat v. Cadbury* [1998] *RPC* 117, 127 (damage by dilution only in case of famous yet descriptive marks). Carty, 'Heads of Damage in Passing Off' advocates caution in extending the heads of damage. See also H. Carty, 'Passing Off at the Crossroads' [1996] *EIPR* 629, 631; H. Carty, 'Dilution and Passing Off: Cause for Concern' (1996) 112 *LQR* 632.

[30] [1998] 4 *All ER* 476, 497. See also, *Pontiac Marina Private v. Cdl. Hotels International* [1998] *FSR* 839 ('anything which dilutes the distinctiveness of MILLENNIA causes damage').

[31] [1998] 4 *All ER* 476, 497.   [32] [2004] *RPC* (36) 711 (paras 43, 49).

[33] *Bollinger v. Costa Brava Wine Co.* [1960] *RPC* 16.

[34] See S. Naresh, 'Passing Off, Goodwill and False Advertising: New Wine in Old Bottles' (1986) 45 *Cambridge Law Journal* 97, 98.

[35] [1998] *RPC* 117, 124; on appeal, [1999] *RPC* 826, 830, Chadwick LJ focused on two differences—the shared nature of the goodwill; and the fact that the class of traders was capable of continued expansion.

[36] *Bollinger v. Costa Brava Wine* [1960] *RPC* 16, See also *Vine Products v. Mackenzie* [1969] *RPC* 1 (sherry—wine produced by the solera process in the province of Jerez de la Fontera in Spain); *John Walker & Sons v. Henry Ost* [1970] *RPC* 489 (Scotch whisky—blended whisky distilled, but not necessarily blended, in Scotland);

from the Champagne district in France who made a naturally sparkling wine, which had long been known in the United Kingdom as 'Champagne'. The claimants's Champagne was produced by a process of double fermentation from grapes grown in the Champagne district. The claimants brought a passing-off action against the defendant for selling a product called 'Spanish champagne'. They did so on the basis that, as the defendant's drink was made in Spain and/or from grapes grown in Spain, it did not qualify to be called 'Champagne'. Danckwerts J reviewed the cases concerning geographical expressions as trade descriptions and the cases on shared goodwill. He said that passing-off would restrain a trader who sought to attach to their product a name or description with which they have no natural association, 'so as to make use of the reputation and goodwill which has been gained by a product genuinely indicated by the name or description'.[37] Danckwerts J added that it did not matter 'that the persons truly entitled to describe their goods by the name and description are a class producing goods in a certain locality, and not merely one individual'. In essence, the court recognized that the claimants, along with the other members of the class, had the requisite goodwill in the name 'Champagne'. This was because the name—CHAMPAGNE—indicated a sparkling wine that came from the Champagne district in France, was made by a particular method, and from grapes sourced from the Champagne region. As such, Champagne had a distinctive reputation which could only be used by producers from that region.

The extended form of passing-off was approved and elaborated on in *Warnink v. Townend*.[38] In this decision the House of Lords held that extended passing off was not confined to drinks, nor to indications of geographical origin. Instead, the action applied equally where any product had a particular characteristic or quality. In this case the claimant produced 'advocaat', a drink manufactured from eggs and a spirit called brandewijn. The defendant sold its drink, made out of eggs and wine, under the name 'advocaat'. The House of Lords held that this amounted to passing off. Previous case law had been confined to cases where a particular product had been manufactured in a particular way using ingredients from a particular geographical source, such as Champagne or Scotch whisky.[39] In *Warnink*, no such geographical connection was claimed. Instead, the claimant based its case on the association that existed between the name—*viz.* 'advocaat'—and a particular product with particular ingredients—*viz.* a drink manufactured from eggs and brandewijn.

Lord Fraser said that it was not necessary that the class of traders should be defined by reference to the locality in which the product was produced. Instead, the crucial thing was that the name was distinctive of a particular class of goods. He added that the name must have a 'definite meaning' so that its use in relation to a different product was a misrepresentation.[40] In a similar vein Lord Diplock said the name must denote 'a product endowed with recognizable qualities which distinguish it from others of inferior reputation that compete with it in the same market'.[41]

Lord Fraser's sentiment that the crucial thing in relation to extended passing off was that the name was distinctive of a particular class of goods was echoed in *Chocosuisse v. Cadbury*,[42] where Laddie J recognized that the Swiss Chocolate Industry Association had collective

---

Taittinger v. Allbev [1993] *FSR* 641 (champagne); *Consorzio del Prosciutto di Parma v. Marks & Spencer* [1991] *RPC* 351; *Consorzio del Prosciutto di Parma v. Asda Stores* [1988] *FSR* 697 (Parma ham).

[37] *Bollinger*, ibid, 31–2.   [38] [1979] *AC* 731.

[39] For example, in the *Bollinger* case 'champagne' was taken to refer to a drink made from grapes from the Champagne region which was produced by the champenois process. In *Walker v. Ost* [1970] *RPC* 489, 'Scotch whisky' referred to a blended whisky where the ingredients were all whiskies distilled in Scotland.

[40] *Warnink* [1979] *AC* 731, 754.   [41] Ibid, 744.   [42] [1998] *RPC* 117.

goodwill in the term 'Swiss chocolate'. The Swiss body argued that by introducing a chocolate product called SWISS CHALET, Cadbury had made a misrepresentation to the public that the product was made of Swiss chocolate. Laddie J (whose judgment was affirmed by the Court of Appeal) said that, for a claimant to succeed, it was necessary for them to show that 'a significant part of the public took the words "Swiss chocolate" to indicate a particular group of products having a discrete reputation as a group'. On the evidence, he held it had: a significant part of the public understood the words 'Swiss chocolate' to denote a group of products of distinctive reputation for quality. The fact that the public could not define what those distinctive features were, was of little relevance.[43]

In many ways, the concept of goodwill recognized in extended passing off is similar to that recognized in the so-called 'classic' action. In both cases, to establish goodwill a claimant must establish that the name in question is distinctive. The shared goodwill that underpins the extended passing-off action is similar to goodwill that is jointly owned by a number of parties. There are, however, a number of differences. Where classic goodwill is owned jointly, each owner cannot prevent other owners from using the particular sign. All joint owners, however, may prevent others from using the sign. By contrast, the goodwill recognized by extended passing off differs in that other traders may participate in the shared goodwill without the consent of existing owners.[44]

In determining whether a claimant has the requisite goodwill to bring an extended passing-off action, a distinction is drawn between establishing the distinctiveness of the descriptive term in the minds of the public and establishing who is entitled to use the term. This distinction was brought out clearly in the *Chocosuisse* decision.[45] Acknowledging that different manufacturers who called their chocolate 'Swiss chocolate' employed very different recipes, the Court of Appeal said that this did not prevent them from collectively acquiring a reputation for quality. Equally, it did not matter that the public did not know or appreciate the identifying characteristics of the class.[46] All that was required was that the designation 'Swiss chocolate' was taken by a significant section of the public to indicate a particular group of products (chocolate made in Switzerland) having a discrete reputation distinct from other chocolate.[47]

Despite the assistance provided by the *Chocosuisse* case, a number of issues are unclear in relation to the operation of collective goodwill. One issue that is uncertain relates to the question: how extensive must the trade of an individual be for them to participate in the collective goodwill? That is, what does an individual trader need to do to establish that they are a member of a class? According to *Warnink v. Townend,* the mere fact that a person has begun to trade in relation to a particular product does not mean that they are therefore entitled to share in the extended goodwill. As Lord Diplock noted:

As respects subsequent additions to the class, mere entry on to the market would not give any right of action for passing off; the new entrant must have himself used the descriptive term long enough on the market in connection with his own goods and have traded successfully enough to have built up a goodwill for his business.[48]

    [43] [1998] *RPC* 117, 133. See also *H.P. Bulmer and Showerings v. J. Bollinger SA* [1978] *RPC* 79, 119.

    [44] As Lord Diplock noted in *Warnink* [1979] *AC* 731, 744, the size of the class of traders will influence the scope of the goodwill.

    [45] [1998] *RPC* 117 (Laddie J); [1999] *RPC* 826 (CA). See also *Bulmer v. Bollinger* [1978] *RPC* 79, 119.

    [46] [1999] *RPC* 826, 849.   [47] Ibid, 832.

    [48] [1979] *AC* 731, 744. Lord Fraser ibid, 754, said '[a] new trader who begins to sell the genuine product would become a member of the class when he had become well enough established to have acquired a substantial right of property in the goodwill attached to the name'.

This requirement has recently been doubted at first instance in *Chocosuisse*.[49] There, Laddie J said that the courts would allow a joint action by new users without inquiring into how extensive their trade has been. The Court of Appeal made no comment on this issue when affirming Laddie J's decision.

A second question that remains unclear is exactly how the courts are to define the class of persons who are to participate in the goodwill. In many cases this will be uncontroversial, because the reputation will have arisen in relation to a discrete class of traders who are themselves subject to regulatory control. However, the potential for difficulty of definition can be seen from the *Chocosuisse* case. There, the claimants had proposed a definition of the class based on the recipes used to manufacture Swiss chocolate.[50] However, Laddie J rejected this on the ground that it excluded a number of those who were already using the designation and were represented by the Association. Instead, Laddie J took the defining feature of 'Swiss chocolate' to be that the chocolate was made in Switzerland, according to Swiss food regulations. However, on appeal, the Court of Appeal held that the group of traders entitled to use the goodwill was that identified by the claimant, that is, those who made chocolate in Switzerland, other than those who made chocolate with vegetable fat as an ingredient.[51] Since none of the claimants supplied a product with such added fat, nor wished to do so, Chadwick LJ said he saw no reason to define the product in less precise terms. Since, on either view, Cadbury's chocolate was not entitled to share in the goodwill (as it was made in England), the finding did not matter. However, had the dispute been with a Swiss producer of chocolate who added vegetable matter, the court would have been called on to locate its own basis for defining the product.

A third question relates to the extent to which the participants in the shared goodwill can themselves decide to modify the criteria by which the class is defined. If the majority of Champagne makers decided to abandon the double fermentation process, perhaps because it was discovered to be unhealthy, would they then be able to exclude others, who continued to do so, from using the term 'Champagne'?

2.2 MISREPRESENTATION

In establishing misrepresentation in an extended passing-off action, the critical factor is what the public understands by the way the name is used. As with classic passing off, this is a question of fact. Although extended passing off and classic passing off both require the claimant to show that there has been a misrepresentation, there are important differences between the way this is approached in the two actions. In relation to extended passing off, 'protection is given to a name or word that has come to mean a particular product rather than a product from a particular trader'.[52] It follows from this that the descriptiveness of the term will not be sufficient to defeat the action. Moreover, there will be no misrepresentation if the defendant uses the distinctive term accurately. Rather, the misrepresentation 'lies in marketing the goods in a way which will lead a significant section of the public to think that those goods have some attribute or attributes which they do not truly possess'.[53] Another difference relates to the use that the owner of the goodwill can make of the distinctive name. In conventional passing off a trader can change the quality of the goods or services that they offer under a particular sign.

[49] *Chocosuisse v. Cadbury* [1998] RPC 117.
[50] Ibid, 133–5.　　　[51] [1999] RPC 826, 840.
[52] *Chocosuisse v. Cadbury* [1998] RPC 117, 125. See also [1999] RPC 826, 832.
[53] [1999] RPC 826, 837.

However, in extended passing off an existing user is not able to use the 'sign' on products for which it is not a correct designation.[54] Thus an individual Champagne producer would not be able to use 'champagne' to describe another product. Each trader within the class, however, is able to use their own trade name in association with the distinctive name shared by the class of traders. This will not prejudice their right to share in the goodwill associated with the product. Thus, there is no problem with Bollinger using its name in association with Champagne, nor with Warninck using its name in relation to advocaat.

2.3 DAMAGE

A final feature of the extended form of passing-off worth observing is the treatment of damage. The most relevant form of damage is the reduction of the distinctiveness of the descriptive term, that is *dilution*. While doubts have been raised about the ongoing relevance of dilution in the classic passing-off action, it seems that it will continue to operate in relation to extended passing off.[55] While likelihood of damage remains a prerequisite of extended passing off, it is not essential for a claimant to demonstrate that they would have been damaged individually.[56]

2.4 ACTIONS RELATED TO EXTENDED PASSING-OFF

It is worth observing that the use that is made of names that designate the geographical origin or quality of goods is regulated by a number of regimes other than passing-off. For example, a person's ability to use an incorrect designation of origin or quality may lead to criminal liability under consumer protection laws such as the Consumer Protection from Unfair Trading Regulations 2008 (and formerly Trade Descriptions Act 1968.[57] The European Community has also adopted a number of Council Regulations dealing with geographical 'designations of origin' (PDOs) and 'geographical indications' (PGIs) for wines, spirits, agricultural products, and food. These are discussed in Chapter 43.

Finally, it is worth noting that marks that designate the geographical origin or quality of goods can be registered in the United Kingdom as 'certification' or 'collective' trade marks,[58] or as Community Collective marks.[59] Certification marks indicate that the goods or services

---

[54] The points are all drawn from Laddie J's analysis in *Chocosuisse v. Cadbury* [1998] *RPC* 117, 124–6.

[55] Ibid, 126–7, 143.   [56] *Warnink* [1979] *AC* 731, 756.

[57] In general, these do not impose statutory duties which give rise to civil liability: *Bollinger v. Costa Brava Wine* [1960] *RPC* 16, 34 (claim under the Merchandise Marks Acts 1887–1953). Consumer Protection from Unfair Trading Regs 2008, SI 2008/TBA, reg. 3 (unfair practices include misleading action), reg. 5(2)(a) (misleading action defined as action that contains false information likely to mislead average consumer as to matter in reg. 5(4)); reg. 5(4) (relevant misleading information includes information as to 'main characteristics' of the product), reg. 5(5)(p) (main characteristics includes geographic origin). Note also reg. 5(3)(a) (misleading by using distinguishing marks of competitor).

[58] Certification marks are permitted, but not required, under the TM Dir., Art. 15. The British system, which dates back to 1902, is found in s. 50 of the Trade Marks Act 1994 and Sched. 2 to that Act. For overviews, see Kerly (2005), Ch 11; J. Belson, 'Certification Marks, Guarantees and Trust' [2002] 24(7) *EIPR* 340–352; N. Dawson, *Certification Trade Marks: Law and Practice* (1988); Annand and Norman (1994), ch. 13. Collective marks are also permitted, but not required, under the TM Dir, Art. 15. The UK's collective mark system is relatively new, having been established in s. 49 of the Trade Marks Act 1994 and Sched. 1. See generally Kerly (2005), Ch 11. For British procedures, see *The Trade Mark Registry's Work Manual*, ch. 13.

[59] CTMR Art. 64. See Annand and Norman (1998), ch. 11. There is no Community certification mark.

meet certain standards.[60] This mechanism has been used to protect products such as 'Stilton' cheese.[61] In turn, Collective marks serve to distinguish the goods or services of the members of relevant associations.

3 UNFAIR COMPETITION

In the final part of the chapter, we consider the principles of unfair competition and their relevance in the United Kingdom. Many countries have granted protection well beyond the confines of passing-off under the more general rubric of unfair competition law. At its broadest, unfair competition provides general, open-textured rules against competitive acts that contravene trade mores. For example, the 1909 German Act Against Unfair Competition declares that 'anyone who for the purpose of competition commits acts in the course of trade that infringe good mores, is liable to incur injunctions or damages'.[62] It should be noted that generalized rules of this nature are not confined to civil law jurisdictions: the USA has recognized a notion of unfair competition through its case law.[63]

The notion of unfair competition law is enshrined in international conventions. Notably, Article 10*bis* of the Paris Convention obliges member countries to assure 'effective protection against unfair competition' which, in turn, is defined as any 'act of competition contrary to honest practices in industrial or commercial matters'. Article 10*bis*(3) then specifies three particular acts that will be treated as being unfair. These are:

1. all acts of such a nature as to create confusion by any means whatever with the establishment, the goods, or the industrial or commercial activities, of a competitor;

2. false allegations in the course of trade of such a nature as to discredit the establishment, the goods, or the industrial or commercial activities, of a competitor;

3. indications or allegations the use of which in the course of trade is liable to mislead the public as to the nature, the manufacturing process, the characteristics, the suitability for their purpose, or the quantity, of the goods.[64]

In some countries, the protection offered by unfair competition extends beyond the level specified in the international provisions to include dilution of another trader's indications (a form of 'free riding'), slavish imitation, and misleading advertising.[65]

---

[60] TMA s. 50.   [61] *Stilton Trade Mark* [1967] *RPC* 173.

[62] *Gesetz gegen den unlauteren Wettbewerb—UWG*. See W. Rowland, 'Unfair Competition in West Germany' (1968) 58 *TM Rep* 853; Knight, 'Unfair Competition: A Comparative Study of Its Role in Common Law and Civil Systems' (1978) 53 *Tulane Law Review* 164; A. Kamperman Sanders, *Unfair Competition Law: The Protection of Intellectual and Industrial Creativity* (1997) ch. 1; P. Kaufman, *Passing Off and Misappropriation (IIC Studies, Vol. ix)* (1986) (discussing Netherlands, West Germany, France, and the USA).

[63] The earliest recognition of a general doctrine of unfair competition in the USA occurred in the famous Supreme Court decision in *International News Service v. Associated Press, 248 US* 215 (1918). The doctrine has been characterized as having had a 'sickly growth'. See J. Adams, 'Unfair Competition: Why a Need is Unmet' [1992] *EIPR* 259.

[64] Wadlow (2004), Ch. 2 (reviewing history of Paris, Art. 10*bis*, and considering the impact of TRIPS).

[65] WIPO, *Protection against Unfair Competition* (WIPO Pubn. 725(E)) (1994).

3.1 UNFAIR COMPETITION FOR THE UNITED KINGDOM?

During the 1970s and 1980s, courts in the United Kingdom were developing passing-off in a way that looked as if it was evolving into a general tort of wrongful trading.[66] In particular, the developments associated with extended passing off were seen by many as heralding the judicial recognition of unfair competition. For example, in *Vine Products*,[67] Cross J said that the Spanish champagne case was not a passing-off action, but a 'new fangled tort called unfair competition'. Moreover, in *Warnink v. Townend* Lord Diplock characterized passing-off, along with conspiracy to injure a person in their trade and slander of title, as separate labels that had been attached to particular forms of 'unfair trading'. He also noted that the forms of unfair trading 'will alter with the ways in which trade is carried on and business reputation and good-will acquired'.[68]

While it seemed in the 1970s and 1980s that British law was on the verge of acknowledging a general action for unfair competition,[69] the judicial tendency was subsequently reversed.[70] In *Cadbury Schweppes v. Pub Squash*[71] the Privy Council made it clear that there is no cause of action for misappropriation as such.[72] There, it will be recalled, relief was denied to the claimant against the defendant who had imitated aspects of the claimant's advertising campaign for its SOLO soft drink. This was despite the fact that the court acknowledged that the defendant had set out in a deliberate and calculated fashion to take advantage of the claimant's past efforts. Lord Scarman explained that the claimant had failed to establish a misrepresentation. He also added that, while passing-off was a developing body of law,

[it] is only if the plaintiff can establish that a defendant has invaded his 'intangible property right' in his product by misappropriating descriptions which have become recognized by the market as distinctive of the product that the law will permit competition to be restricted. Any other approach would encourage monopoly. The new, small man would increasingly find his entry into an existing market obstructed by the large traders already well known as operating in it.[73]

The implications of the case were that the courts had gone far enough in *Warnink v. Townend* and that the Lords were not interested in developing passing-off into a tort of unfair competition.[74]

The approach taken by the Privy Council was echoed by a strong judgment of the Court of Appeal in *L'Oreal SA v. Bellure,* a case where the defendant was selling smell-alike perfumes

---

[66] For the position before that, see W. Morison, 'Unfair Competition at Common Law' (1951–3) 2 *University of Western Australia Law Review* 34; W. Cornish, 'Unfair Competition: A Progress Report' (1972) 12 *Journal of the Society for the Public Teachers of Law* 126.

[67] *Vine Products v. Mackenzie* [1969] *RPC* 1, 28.   [68] [1979] *AC* 731, 740.

[69] G. Dworkin, 'Unfair Competition: Is the Common Law Developing a New Tort?' (1979) *EIPR* 295, 244.

[70] Kamperman Sanders, *Unfair Competition Law,* 202.

[71] [1981] *RPC* 429.

[72] The lack of clarity, if any, arises from the Privy Council's decision not to consider the 'unfair competition' argument which the claimant had raised, on the grounds that it had been 'withdrawn'. See G. Dworkin, 'Passing Off and Unfair Competition: An Opportunity Missed' (1981) 44 *MLR* 564, 567 (optimistically saying that it was not clear what decision might have been reached on this point—but the tenor is enough to suggest the Privy Council was not about to develop such a tort).

[73] [1981] *RPC* 429, 496.

[74] J. Adams, 'Is There a Tort of Unfair Competition? The Legal Protection of Advertising Campaigns and Merchandising' [1985] *Journal of Business Law* 26, 32; J. Lahore, 'The *Pub Squash* Case. Legal Theft or Free Competition?' [1981] *EIPR* 54; S. Ricketson, 'Reaping without Sowing: Unfair Competition and Intellectual Property Rights in Anglo-Australian Law [1984] *University of New South Wales Law Journal* 1, 30.

in packaging which, by adopting some of the features of the fine fragrance brand packaging, indicated to consumers that the smells were equivalent.[75] Having struggled with its trade mark infringement claims and failed in its passing-off argument, the claimant tried to persuade the Court that this was a form of unfair competition that the law should prohibit. Jacob LJ was unimpressed, and indicated he considered recognition of such a rule unnecessary, undesirable, and inappropriate. It was unnecessary, because the UK's international obligations under Article 10bis of the Paris Convention required no more than a prohibition on deceptive conduct.[76] It was undesirable because it is a basic rule that 'competition is not only lawful but the mainspring of the economy'. There are real difficulties in formulating a clear and rational line between that which is fair.[77] Such a tort would be of 'wholly uncertain scope' and 'let the genie out of the bottle'.[78] Moreover it was inappropriate for the courts to legislate in this way, at least at the level of the Court of Appeal.[79] The legislature has formulated narrow exceptions to the principle that competition is desirable in the form of patents, copyright, trade marks, and designs. It is 'not for the judges to step in and legislate into existence new categories of intellectual property rights'.[80]

While much ink has been spilled debating the merits of unfair competition law, it seems unlikely that British judges are going to develop the existing regimes into a generalized action for unfair competition. Moreover, the domestic legislature has signalled a reticence about legislating in this field, either generally or in response to specific issues (such as look-alike brands).[81] As this is an area of law on which it will be difficult to reach commonly agreed principles, European harmonization also appears unlikely in the near future, though in the longer term European harmonization of consumer protection law may pave the way for the introduction of a parallel regime of business regulation.[82] For the time being, then, those who complain about unfair competitive practices will have to continue to bring their grievances within existing causes of action.

[75] [2008] ETMR (1) 1.

[76] Ibid (para. 147). 'Moreover, even if the United Kingdom is in derogation, it has been so for over 80 years without complaint. It is not a matter for the judges.'

[77] Ibid (para. 140).   [78] Ibid (para. 160).

[79] Ibid (para. 159).   [80] Ibid (para. 141).

[81] For example, Copyright and Designs Bill 2000. See Hansard (HL) (17 Mar. 2000), cols. 1885 ff. But the Gowers Review (paras 5.82–88) was supportive of brand owners who object to copy-cat packaging, and asked the Government to monitor changes and, if they are found to be ineffective, to consult on appropriate changes.

[82] The Unfair Commercial Practices Directive requires member states to prohibit certain forms of commercial practice, but is concerned explicitly with business-to-consumer, rather than business-to-business, practices. Nevertheless, recital 8 states that 'the Commission should carefully examine the need for Community action in the field of unfair competition beyond the remit of this Directive and, if necessary, make a legislative proposal to cover these other aspects of unfair competition'.

35

TRADE MARK REGISTRATION

CHAPTER CONTENTS

1 INTRODUCTION

In this chapter we look at the process by which registered trade marks come into being. While registering a trade mark is a costly and time-consuming process, it confers on the proprietor certain exclusive rights to use a particular sign in relation to specified commercial activities. In contrast with the law of passing-off, registration enables traders to protect their marks before they are put on the market. Registration is also advantageous in that, once a mark is registered, there is a presumption, though not a guarantee, that the registration is valid. A third advantage to registering a trade mark is that it reduces the possibility of disputes, and confers on the trade mark proprietor increased certainty, because the registration determines the scope of the property protected as a trade mark. The process of registration attempts to delineate what sign is protected and in which commercial spheres it is to be protected. The Register, which is open to the public, also acts as an important source of information.[1]

There are three possible routes UK traders might take to register a trade mark: national, Community, or international. A national registration system for trade marks has existed in the United Kingdom since 1875. The UK registry, which is based in Newport in Wales, provides successful applicants with rights in the United Kingdom in relation to the sign as registered. Registration at the Community level involves a single application to the Office for Harmonization in the Internal Market (OHIM) which is based in Alicante in Spain. A successful application to the OHIM results in the grant of a single trade mark which operates

---

[1] TMA s. 63(3)(a). For a sceptical view of the benefits of registration, see R. Burrell, 'Trade Mark Bureaucracies' in G. Dinwoodie & M. Janis, *Trademark Law and Theory: A Handbook of Contemporary Research* (Cheltenham: Edward Elgar, 2008) ch. 4.

throughout the Community.[2] A person can apply for both a Community Trade Mark and a national registration, and (in contrast with the position in relation to European Patents (UK), the grant of which leads to the revocation of an equivalent domestic patent) both, if granted, may subsist.

In contrast to registration at a national or community level, the international filing systems merely facilitate the acquisition of national marks. International registration, which is administered by the International Bureau of WIPO at Geneva, will be carried out either under the Madrid Agreement or the Madrid Protocol. The main advantage of the international system is administrative: instead of traders having to file separate applications in the countries where they would like protection, the international system enables traders to obtain protection in a number of different jurisdictions via a single application.

While there has been a degree of standardization of trade mark procedure at both the regional and international levels there are many important differences between the three regimes. In particular, although the procedures and documentation needed for national, regional, or international applications are similar, there are significant variations in the way applications are examined.[3]

2 REGISTRATION IN THE UNITED KINGDOM

A registration system for trade marks was introduced in the United Kingdom in 1875. Earlier attempts to introduce a registration system had been resisted on the basis that it would have been complicated, expensive, and unnecessary.[4] Eventually, the benefits of registration were seen to outweigh the potential disadvantages. In particular, it was thought that a registration system would help to reduce the difficulties that traders faced in proving reputation (which was necessary to sustain an action for passing off). It was also thought that a trade mark registry would enable third parties to discover whether other traders had claimed the right to use a particular sign and, where necessary, to locate the proprietor of the sign. The introduction of a registration system also helped to relieve the pressure that foreign powers were exerting on the British government to introduce a registration system for trade marks.

It is common for applicants to use trade mark attorneys in the drafting and processing of applications. While trade mark agents (as they used to be called) emerged in the United

---

[2] With the expansion of the Community by ten new states on 1 May 2004 and the further expansion to encompass Bulgaria and Rumania from 1 Jan 2008, the protection afforded by existing applications and registrations was automatically extended to cover the new territories. Transitional arrangements clarify that earlier rights in those states cannot be relied upon to found objections to the validity of a Community mark granted before (or, the case of Bulgaria and Rumania one year before) accession. However, the proprietors of such existing rights in accession states are permitted to continue using such signs and are rendered immune from liability for infringing the Community Trade Marks. For a useful explanation, see Communication No. 5/03 of the President of the Office of 16 October 2003 concerning the enlargement of the European Union in 2004 and see Communication No. 2/06 of the President of the Office of 19 June 2006 concerning the enlargement of the European Union in 2007.

[3] For example under the TM Dir., Recital 5, procedural matters are left to member states. Despite this, the ECJ has been happy to rule on what is 'graphic representation', on the need for a full *a priori* examination on absolute grounds, as well as the inappropriateness of certain types of disclaimer: see *Ralf Sieckmann v. Deutsches Patent-und Markenamt*, Case C–273/00 [2002] *ECR* I–11737; *Koninklijke KPN Nederland NV v. Benelux-Merkenbureau*, Case C–363/99 [2004] *ECR* I–1619.

[4] See, e.g. W. Hindmarch, giving evidence to the Select Committee on Trade Marks Bill and Merchandize Marks Bill, Report, Proceedings and Minutes of Evidence (1862) 12 *PP*; A. Ryland, *Trade Marks. Registration Essential to Successful Litigation* (1862).

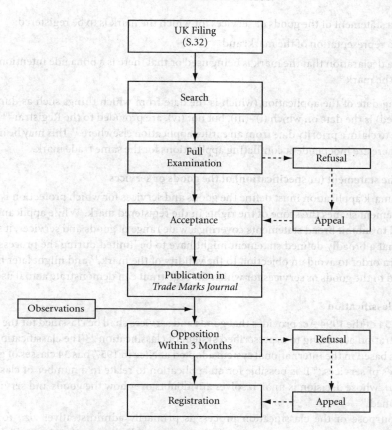

Fig. 35.1 Registering a trade mark in the UK

Kingdom late in the nineteenth century, the professional association that governs them, the Institute of Trade Mark Attorneys, was not formed until 1934.[5] While few restrictions were placed on who could act as a trade mark attorney until recently, the Trade Marks Act 1994 now places limits on the use of the title 'registered trade mark agent'.[6]

The registration process in the United Kingdom can be divided into four stages: (i) the filing of the application, (ii) examination, (iii) publication, observation, and opposition, and (iv) registration (see Fig. 35.1).

2.1 FILING OF THE APPLICATION

Any person (natural or legal) can apply for the registration of a trade mark.[7] Section 32 of the 1994 Act provides that an application for a trade mark must contain:[8]

(i) a request for registration, including the name and address of the applicant;

---

[5] It has a web site at <http://www.itma.org.uk>.
[6] TMA ss. 82–6. Kerly, ch. 22, 756–61.
[7] Since there is now only a single UK Register, there is no need to specify whether registration is sought in 'Part A' or 'Part B' as was required prior to 1994. Transitional provisions are contained in TMA, Sched. 3.
[8] TMA s. 32.

    (ii)   a statement of the goods or services for which the mark is to be registered;

    (iii) a representation of the mark; and

    (iv) a declaration that the mark is being used or that there is a bona fide intention to use the mark.[9]

The filing date of the application (which is the date from which things such as duration are calculated) is the date on which (i)–(iii), but not (iv), are provided to the Registrar.[10] It may be possible to claim a priority date from an earlier application elsewhere.[11] This may be important where there are independent conflicting applications for the same trade mark.

2.1.1 The statement (or specification) of the goods or services

A trade mark application must define the goods and services for which protection is sought.[12] The statement shapes the scope of the rights in the registered mark. While applicants may be tempted to submit broad statements covering a wide range of goods and services, it should be noted that a broadly defined statement might have to be limited during the process of registration in order to avoid an objection to the validity of the mark,[13] and might later have to be confined to the goods or services for which the registrant can demonstrate actual use.[14]

2.1.2 Classification

Section 34 of the 1994 Act provides that goods and services shall be classified for the purposes of registration according to a 'prescribed system of classification'.[15] The classification system, which is based in the international system adopted at Nice in 1957, has 34 classes of goods and 11 classes of services.[16] It is possible for an application to relate to a number of classes.[17] The Registrar, whose decision is final, resolves any doubts over how the goods and services are to be classified.[18]

The purpose of the classification process is primarily administrative: *viz.*, to facilitate searching for earlier competing marks.[19] In contrast with the specification, which helps to define the boundaries of trade mark protection, the way in which a mark is classified does not ordinarily impact upon substantive matters such as the scope of the rights given to the trade mark owner. Thus, the fact that a mark is used by a competitor on goods or services in a different class from those of the registered proprietor does not necessarily mean that it is not being used on 'identical' or 'similar' goods or services (which is the test for infringement). Having said that, there are some situations where the way a mark is classified *might* impact on the scope of the proprietor's rights. This will be the case where, in their statement of the goods

---

   [9] TMA s. 32(3).

  [10] TMA s. 33. See *Ty Nant Spring Water* [2000] *RPC* 55, 60–1.

  [11] TMA s. 35, TMR r. 6; Paris Art., 4(A)(1), 4(C)(1) (6 months).

  [12] For the relevance of TMA s. 3(6) that applications should be made in good faith, see below at pp. 790, 851–3. But cf. OHIM practice which permits extremely broad registrations, and regulates undue scope through the provisions on revocation for non-use.

  [13] See, e.g. *Mister Long Trade Mark* [1998] *RPC* 401, 407.

  [14] On revocation for non-use, and the processes for recalibrating a broad specification, see ch 39.

  [15] TMA s. 34; TMR r. 7; Sched 3.

  [16] From 1 Jan. 2002 (prior to which there were only eight classes of services).

  [17] TMR r. 8.

  [18] See *Cal-U-Test Trade Mark* [1967] *FSR* 39, 44. Note also PAC 4/00, *Classification of On-Line and Internet Services and Associated Goods: UK Practice as at Feb. 2000*.

  [19] *Cal-U-Test*, ibid, 45; *Carless Capek & Leonard v. Pilmore-Bedford & Sons* (1928) 45 *RPC* 205.

and services, an applicant makes reference to the classes used at the Registry:[20] that is, where applicants tie the list of goods or services claimed to the bureaucratic categories used at the Trade Mark Registry.

2.1.3 Representation of the sign

The trade mark applicant is also required to provide a representation of the sign, and before an application is accepted that representation must be 'adequate'.[21] This reflects the fact that the trade mark registration system is built around a notion of 'representative registration'.[22] That is, rather than depositing an actual sample of the mark, applicants are required to deposit a representation of the mark.[23] This representative registration has a number of rationales (as well as having some significant effects).[24] One function of the representation (which might be called the 'property' function, and is analogous to the role of patent claims) is to define the scope of the trade mark owner's rights and delineate with a degree of precision exactly what sign is protected. A second function of graphic representation (which might be called the 'information function') is to enable publicity to be given to the fact that an applicant is seeking registration, the publicity being provided by publication in the *Trade Marks Journal*. In particular, it helps to ensure that third parties are able to search the register, to ascertain things such as the scope of existing marks, and to determine whether a fresh application conflicts with earlier marks. A third and related function of the graphic representation requirement (which might be called the 'administrative function') is to make the bureaucratic dealing with the sign, its classification and comparison with other signs, more manageable.

While each of these functions demands different things, in effect, for a graphic representation to be adequate it must achieve all three goals. As the ECJ held in *Ralf Sieckmann*, a graphic representation is one which utilizes images, lines, or characters. In order to render a sign registrable as a trade mark the graphic representation must be clear, precise, self-contained, easily accessible, intelligible, durable, and objective.[25] (These are known as the *Sieckmann* criteria.) While the *Sieckmann* case is useful in that it articulates criteria which a graphic representation must meet, it remains difficult to say in particular situations whether a representation is *sufficiently* stable, durable, objective, or intelligible to satisfy the criteria. It seems that a representation is not sufficiently intelligible if it is only intelligible to a few, or to a limited section of the population (as for example, with a chemical formula). In the *Libertel* case, reviewed below, Advocate General Léger indicated that a representation was sufficiently accessible and intelligible if it did not require excessive efforts to be taken for the public to understand

---

[20] See also *GE Trade Mark* [1969] *RPC* 418, 458 ('electrical apparatus (included in this class)' did not cover switches, not because they were not electrical but because switches had never been treated as falling within the class); *Avnet v. Isoact* [1998] *FSR* 16 (examining the relationship between the list and 'classification'); and *Altecnic's Trade Mark Application* [2002] *RPC* (34) 639 (tribunal employing class when interpreting scope of ambiguously worded specification).

[21] The furnishing of a representation of the mark is one of the few elements necessary to obtain a filing date. The applicant is given two months to remedy any inadequacies.

[22] Sherman and Bently, 180–93. See M. Handler and R. Burrell, 'Making Sense of Trade Mark Law' (2003) *IPQ* 388.

[23] The Community system employs a more restrictive interpretation of what counts as 'graphic representation'. CTMIR r. 3(2) specifies that when a mark is not a word mark but a three-dimensional, colour, or other type of mark, a 'reproduction' of the mark must be submitted on a sheet of paper.

[24] *Ralf Sieckmann v. Deutsches Patent-und Markenamt*, Case C–273/00 [2002] *ECR* I–11737 (paras. 48–9).

[25] These were described by the OHIM Board of Appeal as 'high standards': *Metro-Goldwyn-Mayer Lion Corp*, R781/1999–4 [2004] *ETMR* (34) 480 (para. 20).

it.[26] Moreover, in *Shield*, the court noted that accessibility and intelligibility did not require 'immediate' intelligibility, but only that intelligibility be 'easy', so that a music score would suffice as a representation of sound.[27]

There are a number of different techniques that applicants may use to represent their marks graphically. These include words and images (such as line drawings and photographs). With the vast majority of marks, the process of graphic representation is straightforward: 'word marks' are written, and device or 'figurative' marks are represented by pictures.[28] However, difficulties arise because, as we will see, since the Trade Marks Act 1994 liberalized the definition of marks it is now possible to register various 'exotic' marks, such as sounds, shapes, colours, smells, gestures, etc., and in these cases graphic representation can be more problematic. The particular mode of description that is used will vary according to the type of mark in question.

Shapes. It has been held that a verbal description of a shape or packaging—such as 'vacuum packing' or 'a chewy sweet on a stick'—will rarely ever be satisfactory[29] because it will not convey the precise appearance of the sign:[30] rather, design drawings or photographs will be necessary.[31] The problems that arise where an applicant simply relies upon words to represent more unusual marks can be seen in *Swizzels Matlow's Trade Mark Application*,[32] where an application to register a shape mark was rejected. In the application, the description of the mark read: '[t]he trade mark consists of a chewy sweet on a stick for non-medicated confectionery'. The Trade Mark Registry rejected the application, primarily on the basis that it was neither possible nor practicable for anyone inspecting the register to determine what the trade mark was from the description. More specifically, the Registry found that the representation failed to define the mark with sufficient precision so that infringement rights could be determined. This was because the words 'chewy', 'sweets', and 'sticks' could be interpreted very widely and, in combination, covered 'an infinite variety of marks'. Moreover, the description could not stand in place of the mark without the benefit of supporting material, namely, samples of the goods. In the language of *Sieckmann*, the description was not 'self-contained'.

Colours. One area where trade marks law has long had problems is in relation to colour marks. Indeed, the reason why colour marks initially were not registrable was because the technology did not exist to enable colour marks to be reprinted in the *Trade Mark Journal*.[33]

---

[26] *Libertel Groep BV v. Benelux-Merkenbureau*, Case C–104/01 [2003] *ECR* I–3793, [2005] 2 *CMLR* (45) 1097, [2004] *FSR* (4) 65, para. 71 (AG).

[27] *Shield Mark BV v. Joost Kist*, Case C–283/01 [2003] *ECR* I–14313, [2005] 1 *CMLR* (41) 1046 (para. 63) (ECJ).

[28] Colour is presumed not to be an element of a trade mark unless the application contains a statement to that effect and specifies the colour: TMR r. 5(3); CTMIR r. 3(5). Similar rules operate under Madrid Art. 3 and Madrid Prot. Art. 3(3).

[29] The IPO has issued a practice amendment notice indicating that verbal descriptions alone will not be accepted because 'it is not...possible to represent a shape [as opposed to a design concept] in words alone': see PAN 3/07, *Shapes/Representations of the goods* (issued 13 June 2007). UK tribunals had previously allowed for the possibility that a verbal description might be satisfactory, (cp. *Swizzels Matlow's Trade Mark Application (Love Hearts)* [1999] *RPC* 879, 884–5; *In re Telecom Plus plc's Trade Mark Application* (4 Apr. 2003) *SRIS* O/187/03 (Geoffrey Hobbs QC)).

[30] *Antoni & Alison's Application/Vacuum Packing*, R4.97–2 [1998] *OJ OHIM* 3/180 [1998] *ETMR* 460.

[31] Likewise, an application which includes a representation of a three-dimensional image will not be treated as relating to the three-dimensional form unless the application contains a statement to that effect: TMR r. 5(2); CTMIR r. 3(4).

[32] [1998] *RPC* 244.   [33] See Sherman and Bently, 190.

In *LibertelGroep BV v Benelux-Merkenbureau*,[34] the ECJ considered the extent to which trade marks comprising a single colour could be registered. In this case the applicant had sought to register the colour orange for telephone books in class 9 and telecommunication services in classes 35–8. While the Court clearly accepted that simple colours could be represented graphically, it stated that an assessment was required in the light of the facts of the case and the mode of representation proposed by the applicant, as to whether the seven *Sieckmann* criteria would be met. The Court held that a mere sample of a colour would not satisfy those requirements, because the exact shade of colour on paper cannot be protected from the effects of the passage of time. Equally, the Court said that a verbal description would not normally satisfy the conditions.[35] However, the Court reiterated that it was necessary to decide whether a given description was satisfactory on the particular facts.[36] Finally, the Court noted that a designation using an internationally recognized identification code *might* be considered to constitute a graphic representation, adding that such codes are precise and stable.[37] Moreover, the use of a sample, verbal description, and international code—in combination—*might* satisfy the seven *Sieckmann* criteria.[38]

Libertel clearly prohibits member states from operating a *per se* exclusion of simple colours from registrability.[39] More seriously, however, the decision may be read as precluding the operation of procedural rules specifying that only certain forms of graphic representation are adequate. For example, while the regulations implementing the Community Trade Mark Regulation specify that an applicant who wants to register a colour mark submits a 'reproduction', the OHIM has now 'recommended' that applicants add a reference to an international code.[40] Similarly, while the UK previously treated samples of colours as acceptable,[41] following *Libertel,* colour samples on paper are no longer treated as graphic representations, but a written description coupled with the relevant code from an internationally recognized colour identification system will be regarded as acceptable.[42] Other applications are to be assessed on their facts to decide whether the applicant has graphically represented the sign in such a way

---

[34] Note 26 above. The Advocate General's opinion is reported at [2003] *ETMR* (41) 508.

[35] See also *Orange Personal Communication Services/Orange,* R7/97–3 [1998] *OJ OHIM* 5/640 (description 'too imprecise'); *TMR Work Manual,* ch. 6, para. 2.3.5 (description 'too vague').

[36] A British tribunal held that a scientific description would not do, in a pre-*Sieckmann* case, because the representation did not provide a sufficiently 'immediate' idea of the mark: *Ty Nant Spring Water* [2000] *RPC* 55, 59 ('a blue bottle of optical characteristics such that if its wall thickness is 3mm the bottle has, in air, a dominant wavelength of 472–4 nanometres, a purity of 44–48%, an optical brightness of 28–32%'). 'Immediacy' is not a requirement in *Sieckmann,* but this case could easily have been decided on the basis that the criteria used were not sufficiently intelligible (as with the chemical formula in *Sieckmann* itself).

[37] The Advocate General had suggested that the effort demanded of the applicant to look up the code was not 'excessive'. He said that, except in cases where the collection is difficult to access, such a code reference permits a user to know, clearly and without ambiguity, what is the mark: *Libertel Groep BV v. Benelux-Merkenbureau,* Case C–104/01 [2003] *ECR* I–3793; [2005] 2 *CMLR* (45) 1097 (para. 72) (AG).

[38] Ibid (paras. 28–38) (ECJ).

[39] The Advocate General observed that the practices of member states varied, some (such as Germany) permitting such registrations, others (such as Portugal) not: ibid, para. 57 (AG). On the practices of member states, see C. Schulze, 'Registering Colour Trade Marks in the European Union' [2003] *EIPR* 55.

[40] Commission Regulation (EC) No. 2868/95 of 13 December 1995, implementing Council Regulation (E) 40/94, r. 3(2). See Communication No. 6/03 of the President of the Office of 10 November 2003 recommending that applications relating to colour include a designation from an internationally recognized identification code while simultaneously observing that some shades might not be catered for by such coding systems.

[41] UK Trade Marks Registry, PAC 2/00 (1 March 2000).

[42] PAN 3/03 *Libertel—Graphical Representation of Colour Marks Filing Requirements* (23 Oct. 2003). This practice is reiterated in PAN 2/07, *Graphical representation* (issued 25 May 2007).

as to satisfy the *Sieckmann* criteria. One may wonder whether the ECJ has not moved too far into the domain of national procedure.[43]

In *Heidelberger Bauchemie*,[44] the ECJ addressed the related issue of the graphic representation of two colours. The reference concerned an application to register blue and yellow for various goods including adhesives, solvents, and paints, the application indicating that the colours would be used 'in every conceivable form'. The ECJ held that, in the case of a sign consisting of two or more colours, designated in the abstract and without contours, a graphic representation would only be sufficiently clear and precise if the application specified that the colours would be 'systematically arranged by associating the colours concerned in a predetermined and uniform way'. In contrast, the Court said that the mere juxtaposition of two or more colours, without shape or contours, or a reference to two or more colours 'in every conceivable form' did not exhibit the qualities of precision and uniformity. The Court thereby indicated that the application in question would not satisfy the requirements of Article 2 of the Directive. In contrast, it seems that an application will succeed if it specifies the colours and explains their distribution on the product and in relation to each other—for example, by stating that the colour blue, comprising 50 per cent of the surface area, runs horizontally above the colour red, forming a striped whole.[45] However, the description and reproduction must correspond: the Board of Appeal of the OHIM refused an application relating to purple and white, explaining that, while the representation might have appeared to indicate how the colours purple and white would be distributed on the various products, the written description indicated that there would be no such clarity.[46]

Smells. After a period of uncertainty in which the OHIM rather surprisingly held that a verbal description of a smell was sufficient,[47] in *Ralf Sieckmann* the ECJ has indicated that a smell will not be adequately graphically represented by a verbal description because it will not be 'sufficiently precise'. Sieckmann had sought to register the smell of cinnamon as a trade mark in Germany, and as well as providing a verbal description had also attempted to represent the mark by way of a chemical formula and a sample. The ECJ also indicated that these other mechanisms would not meet the requirements of the Directive: a deposit of a sample is not a graphic representation, but in any case would not be sufficiently durable or stable; and a chemical formula (though probably a representation of a chemical rather than an odour) would not be sufficiently intelligible, clear, or precise. While the Court has not ruled out the possibility of there ever being an acceptable graphic representation of a smell,[48] other possible techniques—such as through chromatography or so-called 'digital noses'—would not seem to satisfy the requirement of intelligibility. Even accepting a degree of variation between different countries and fora in the application of concepts such as 'intelligibility', it is unlikely that there will be many (if any) national or Community marks granted for smells.[49]

---

[43] Cf. Recital 5 of the Directive which reads 'whereas Member States also remain free to fix the provisions of procedure concerning the registration, the revocation and the invalidity of trade marks acquired by registration'.

[44] Case C–49/02, [2004] *ECR* I–6129.

[45] PAN 2/07, citing CTM No 2177566.

[46] *Mars Inc/Purple and white*, R1004/2006–2 (13 December 2006).

[47] *Vennootschhap Onder Firma Senta/The Smell of Freshly Cut Grass*, R156/1998–2 [1999] *ETMR* 429.

[48] *Eden SARL v. OHIM*, Case T–305/04 [2005] *ECR* II–4705, [2006] *ETMR* (14) 181 para. 28. Cf. *Sieckmann*, Case C–273/00 [2002] *ECR* I–11737 (para. 44) (AG).

[49] *Eden SARL*, ibid para. 33 ('smell of ripe strawberries' plus image of strawberry not sufficiently precise nor unequivocal given that evidence established that different strawberry varieties give off different smells). But note para. 28, where the CFI suggests that in some cases of smells a description might be sufficient.

Sounds. In *Shield Mark BV v. Joost Kist,* the Court considered the application of the graphic representation requirement to sounds. The case concerned two marks: the first nine notes of the melody for Beethoven's 'Für Elise' and the crowing of a cock, both for advice and services in the field of intellectual property and marketing. The applicant had used musical notation (including the instructions to be played on the piano), onomatopoeic representation (kuke-lekuuuuuu) as well as a verbal description 'the crowing of a cock'. The Hoge Raad asked the Court whether such marks were registrable as trade marks and, if so, whether the require-ment of graphic representation of a sound was met by: a note bar, a description in words, a voice picture or sonogram, a sound carrier, a digital recording that can be listened to via the internet, or a combination of these.[50] The Court stated that a score which comprised a stave with a clef, musical notes, and rests whose form indicates relative values and, where necessary, accidentals (sharp, flat, etc.) would satisfy the seven *Sieckmann* requirements.[51] This was so even though not everyone can read music: the requirements is 'intelligibility', not 'immedi-ate intelligibility'.[52] In contrast, the mere verbal description of sounds (of the type involved in the case) lacked clarity and precision.[53] The Court held that onomatopoeic representation was problematic for two reasons: first because 'there is a lack of consistency' between the onomato-poeia itself and the sound; second, because perceptions of an onomatopoeia are individual (and hence subjective) or at least culturally determined (in English, for example, such a sound would be represented as 'cock-a-doodle-doo'). Consequently, 'a simple onomatopoeia cannot without more constitute a graphical representation of the sound or noise of which it purports to be a phonetic description'. Although the Court declined to comment on whether a digital recording or a sonogram would suffice,[54] the Board of Appeal of the OHIM has indicated that sound spectrograms or sonograms which depict pitch, progression over time, and volume, may constitute an appropriate way of representing sounds such as the 'roar of a lion'. The Board thought that the fact that a person needs a certain amount of training before they could read a sonogram was no impediment, observing that the same is true of musical notation.[55] However, a later Board of Appeal at OHIM has expressly taken a contradictory position, hold-ing that a sound spectrogram of Tarzan's yell was not a sufficient graphic representation.[56] The latter decision is certainly more faithful to the *Sieckmann* and *Shield* rulings, holding the spectrogram to be neither self-contained (as it needs technical means to concert into sound) nor easily accessible.

Tastes. Following the earlier facilitative case law of the OHIM as regards registration of smells, Eli Lilly applied to register the taste of artificial strawberry in respect of pharmaceuti-cals. This application was initially rejected on the ground that the mere verbal description was

---

[50] *Shield Mark*, Case C–283/01 [2003] *ECR* I–14313.

[51] Cf. Advocate General (requiring score to specify the notes, the key, the tempo, and instruments). See also *MGM Lion Corp*, note 25 above (para. 21). This was British practice even before *Shield*: PAC 2/00 *Acceptable Forms of Graphic Representation*, para. 19; *Guidelines concerning Proceedings before the Office for Harmonization in the Internal Market*, Part B, 8.2.

[52] Para. 63 (ECJ); para. 40 (AG).

[53] Para. 59 (ECJ). Note the qualification that in another case a description might be sufficient.

[54] Para. 54 (ECJ).

[55] *MGM Lion Corp*, R781/1999–4 [2004] *ETMR* (34) 480 (para. 21). See also *Hexal Aktiengesellschaft*, Case R 295/2005–4 (8 Sept 2005) (German only).

[56] *Edgar Rice Burroughs, Inc.*, Case R 708/2006–4 (27 Sep 2007) (para. 19) (stating that the comments in the MGM case were obiter and expressly dissenting). For comment, see S. Yarvorsky, 'Ministry of Sound—the OHIM and the Tarzan Yell' [2008] *Ent LR* 63 (noting that a separate application for the yell, utilizing musical notation, was successful).

not sufficiently precise, but ultimately the examiner based her objection on lack of distinctiveness. Rejecting an appeal, the OHIM Board of Appeal affirmed the examiner's finding that the taste was not distinctive but added that, following *Sieckmann,* a verbal description would not be acceptable as a graphic representation of a gustatory sign.[57]

2.1.4 Bona fide intention to use

A UK application must also contain a declaration that the mark is being used or that there is a bona fide intention to use the mark.[58] According to section 3(6), a trade mark shall not be registered if or to the extent that the application is made in bad faith.[59] While we examine this ground of invalidity in detail later,[60] the declaration operates to warn the applicant that the UK Trade Marks Register is only intended to confer rights on persons who genuinely intend to use the particular mark in trade: it is not to be used for bogus applications in order to get in the way of opponents, blocking registrations, or ghost registrations.[61] In addition, the UK Registry has used the objection to induce applicants to restrict the specifications to a more limited range of goods and services. Although the Registry makes less use of section 3(6) to limit specifications than it did when the 1994 Act first came into force, so as to bring the UK approach more closely into line with that at the OHIM, it will refuse to accept very broad applications such as those 'for all goods or services' in a particular class as well as to applications for 'machines' in class 7, or 'electrical apparatus' in class 9.[62]

2.1.5 Series of marks

It is possible to register a series of marks in a single registration, thereby saving expense.[63] A 'series of marks' is defined as 'a number of trade marks that resemble each other as to their material particulars and differ only as to matters of a non-distinctive character not substantially affecting the identity of the trade mark'. The application should include a separate representation of each mark in the series.[64] Individual marks may be deleted from the series at any time.

2.2 EXAMINATION

Once the filing process has been completed, the Registrar conducts a search[65] and an examination of the application[66] to ensure that the proposed mark satisfies various requirements

---

[57] *Eli Lilly/The Taste of Artificial Strawberry flavour,* R120/2001–2 (4 Aug. 2003). Tastes have been rejected in the US, but for different reasons: see *Perk Scientific, Inc v. Ever Scientific, Inc.* 77 USPQ 2d 1412 (ED Pa. 2005), *In re N.V. Organon,* 79 USPQ 2d 1639 (TTAB 2006). See further, J.C. Ginsburg, '"See Me, Feel Me, Touch Me, Hea[r] Me" (and maybe smell and taste me too): I Am a Trademark—A U.S. Perspective', in Bently, Davis & Ginsburg (eds), *Trade Marks and Brands: An Interdisciplinary Critique* (2008) Ch. 4.

[58] TMA s. 32(3). This is not required by the OHIM.

[59] Pursuant to optional provision in Art. 3(2)(d) of the Directive; there is no corresponding provision in the CTMR Art. 26. But note Art. 51(1)(b).

[60] See below at pp. 851–5.   [61] See *Origins v. Origin Clothing* [1995] *FSR* 280, 285 (Jacob J).

[62] PAN 5/06, *Wide and vague specifications* (issued 12 April 2006), basing the objection on r. 8(2)(b) and repeating much of what was previously in *Classification: Examination of wide specifications and objections under Section 3(6) of the Act,* PAN 8/02 (19 Jun. 2002).

[63] TMA s. 41. The practice is explained in PAN 1/03 *Applications to Register a Series of Trade Marks,* following the decision of the Appointed Person in *Logica's Trade Marks* (5 Mar. 2003) *SRIS O/068/03* (holding that LOGICA followed by various domain name suffixes did not resemble each other as to their material particulars). See also *In re Digeo Broadband Inc's Trade Marks* [2004] *RPC* (32) 639 *SRIS O/305/03* (DIGEO plus domain name suffixes not a series).

[64] TMR r. 21(1).   [65] TMA s. 33(2).   [66] TMA s. 33.

set out in the Act. In particular the Registrar will ensure that the application complies with section 1(1), and that none of the absolute grounds for refusal apply.[67] Since October 1 2007, the Registrar will not object to registration on 'relative grounds.'[68] The ECJ has indicated that this examination of the absolute grounds is to be taken seriously.[69] The applicant is required to respond and, if they fail to do so, the application will be refused.[70] In some situations, where the objection only pertains to some of the goods or services to which the application relates, a process of reformulation of the specification is called for. So, for example, an application which relates to motor vehicles and bicycles might be objectionable in relation only to motor vehicles. Reformulation may be done by the applicant voluntarily, or by the Registrar., though the extent to which the Registrar can impose different wording is controversial.[71]

If the Registrar has no valid objections to the application, it will be *accepted.* The Registrar does not have a general discretion to reject applications: if an application satisfies the requirements set out in the Act, it must be accepted.[72] Acceptance of the application is not the same as registration. It merely marks the end of the *ex parte* procedure: registration only occurs after the period for opposition has elapsed.

2.3 PUBLICATION, OBSERVATIONS, AND OPPOSITION

Once an application has been accepted by the Registrar, it is published in the *Trade Marks Journal.*[73] In the three-month period following publication, there is an opportunity for third parties to comment on the application. This will either take the form of 'observations' on, or 'oppositions' to, the application. Any person may make observations to the UK Registry which are forwarded to the applicant.[74] It seems that third-party observations may prompt the UK Registry to reconsider the registrability of an application. Alternatively, a proprietor of an earlier mark or right may formally oppose the registration.[75] This must be lodged within three months of the publication of the application and should specify the grounds for opposition. Where an opposition is made, it sets in play a procedural process which is structured to

---

[67] In addition (and in contrast to the OHIM), the Registrar may object to the application on the basis that the applicant does not have a bona fide intention to use the mark.

[68] Trade Mark (Relative Grounds) Order 2007, SI 2007/1976 (made under TMA s. 8) bringing UK procedure into line with that at the OHIM. For background, see Patent Office, *Future of Official Examination on Relative Grounds* (2001).

[69] *Libertel,* Case C–104/01 [2003] *ECR* I–3793; [2005] 2 *CMLR* (45) 1097, paras. 58–9; *Henkel KgaA v. OHIM,* Joined Cases C–468/01P to C–472/01P [2004] *ECR* I–5089, [2004] *ETMR* (87) 1157 (paras. 51–2) (AG Colomer) (stating, in the context of the CTM, that the examination 'must not be brief, but must be stringent and thorough in order to prevent marks from being improperly registered'); *Nichols v. Registrar of Trade Marks,* Case C–404/02 [2004] *ECR* I–8499 (paras. 51–2) (AG Colomer) (repeating himself, in context of Directive and national procedures).

[70] TMA s. 37(4); *Postperfect Trade Mark* [1998] *RPC* 255.

[71] *Citybond Trade Mark* [2007] *RPC* (13) 301 (Appointed Person, Hobbs QC); *Sensornet Ltd's Trade Mark Application* [2007] *RPC* (10) 185.

[72] White Paper, *Reform of Trade Marks Law,* Cm. 1203 (1990) para. 3.11 ('administrative discretion is...out of place in a modern trade mark law').

[73] TMA s. 38; TMR r. 12, r. 65; TMA s. 67(2) prohibits the Registrar from publishing details prior to publication. Publication will render a proprietor vulnerable to potential cyber squatters, so proprietors should be advised to acquire all relevant domain names before this point.

[74] TMR r. 15. At the OHIM, observations may be made by 'any natural or legal person and any group or body representing manufacturers, producers, suppliers of services, traders, or consumers'.

[75] TMA s. 34(2). The original TMA s. 38(2), which states that any person may oppose, must be read in the light of Trade Mark (Relative Grounds) Order 2007, SI 2007/1976 reg. 2.

encourage the parties to reach an amicable settlement, but failing such, may lead to a hearing and a determination by the Registrar.[76]

2.4 CHANGING THE APPLICATION AS FILED

While applicants should take great care in the way applications are drafted, for a variety of reasons, an applicant may wish to make alterations to the application as filed. This may be in response to the results of the examination, to third-party observations and oppositions, or to changes in circumstances. There are a number of ways in which an application may be changed: the most common being by way of amendment, division, merger, or disclaimer.[77] Before looking at these, it should be noted that many of these changes, such as amendment, may occur either before or after grant. Other techniques, such as disclaimers, may be included in the initial application or added later.

2.4.1 Pre-grant amendment

Section 39 provides that that an applicant may amend the application, at any time, in such a way as to restrict the goods or services covered by the application. Applications may also be amended to correct the name or address of the applicant;[78] to alter errors of wording or copying; or to correct obvious mistakes.[79] Such amendments are only permissible where they do not substantially affect the identity of the mark or extend the goods or services covered by the application.[80] So, for example, it was stated in the POLO case that it is permissible to limit an application for 'sugar confectionery' to one for 'mint-flavoured compressed confectionery'[81] However, the Court of Appeal held that in the case of shape registrations, where the identity of the goods and the mark may be linked, it is not permissible to attempt to amend the *mark* being registered by amending the *goods* for which registration is sought. So it was not permissible to amend a shape mark by adding a reference to the colour and size of the goods.[82] An amendment that affects the representation or specification must be published and an opportunity provided for objections.[83]

2.4.2 Division

It is also possible for an applicant to transform a single application into several 'divisional applications'.[84] At any time before registration an applicant may request that their application be divided into two or more separate applications, with each relating to different goods or services.[85] The main reason for dividing an application up in this way is to isolate the problematic parts of an application. In so doing, it increases the chances of the uncontroversial parts being

---

[76] TMR r. 13.   [77] TMA s. 37(3).

[78] TMA s. 39(2). According to a Practice Notice, the Registry takes the view that correcting the name of a proprietor is a serious matter. On changing classes, see PAC 2/99 *Adding a class or classes to an application.*

[79] CTMR Art. 44. See *Blueco/Blue Water,* R117/1998–1 [1999] *ETMR* 394.

[80] The Court of Appeal has held that an amendment to change the classification was impermissible: *Altecnic's Application* [2002] *RPC* (34) 639.

[81] *Nestlé Trade Mark* [2005] *RPC* (5) 77 (para. 40).   [82] Ibid (para. 41).

[83] TMA s. 39(3); TMR r. 18. A request to restrict a specification may not be made conditionally: *Sensornet,* note 71 above (paras 64–65), following CFI authorities on CTMR, Art. 44 such as *Ellos v OHIM,* Case T–219/00 [2002] *ECR* II–753 at paras 58–63.

[84] TMA s. 41; TMR r. 19.

[85] On the timing of the application to divide, see *Sensornet* [2007] *RPC* (10) 185 (paras 60–63); *Oka Direct Ltd's Trade Mark Application* (O/43/06).

registered. Divided applications have the same filing date as the original application. Where division occurs after the application has been published, any objections to the original application apply to each of the divisional applications.

2.4.3 Merger

A corresponding facility exists for the *merger* of separate applications. Applicants will normally merge marks to simplify a trade mark portfolio and to save on fees. Merger only occurs if the applications are for the same mark, and have the same application date, and the same proprietor.[86] If two or more marks have already been registered, those registrations can also be merged so long as they are in respect of the same trade mark. If one of the registrations is subject to a disclaimer or limitation, the merged registration is restricted accordingly. Similarly, if they bear different dates, the date applicable for the merged registration is the latest date.

2.5 DISCLAIMERS

Section 13 of the 1994 Act enables applicants (or the proprietor) to disclaim any right to the exclusive use of specified elements of the trade mark. Applicants are also able to agree that the rights conferred by the registration shall be subject to a specified territorial or other limitation.[87] Where the registration of a trade mark is subject to a disclaimer or limitation, the rights conferred on the proprietor are restricted accordingly.[88] Use of disclaimers may assist an applicant in overcoming a potential objection to registration,[89] but will not enable the applicant to alter the nature of the mark that is registered. Thus an attempt to limit the (three-dimensional) sign in an application relating to confectionery by restricting its size and colour was held by the Court of Appeal not to be a disclaimer of any *right*.[90]

The practices relating to disclaimers expose the limitations of the registration system as an effective mechanism for defining the boundaries of intangible property rights. The courts have recognized that disclaimers are of limited value because they only appear on the Register and do not follow goods into the market.[91] Consequently, because consumers and competitors would normally be unaware that aspects of a mark had been disclaimed, often a disclaimer will not save a mark from objection.[92] The ECJ stated in *Postkantoor* that national registries may not accept marks 'subject to the condition that they do not possess a particular characteristic', such as allowing PENGUIN for 'books (other than books about penguins)'. This was said to be because third parties would not be aware of the condition, and might refrain from selling goods under the mark.[93] In applying this principle, the Intellectual Property Office

---

[86] TMR r. 20.

[87] The Registrar cannot impose a disclaimer: *Patron Calvert Cordon Bleu* [1996] *RPC* 94, 103.

[88] *General Cigar Co Inc v. Partagas y Cia SA* [2005] *FSR* (45) 960 (considering effect in opposition proceedings); *Phones4U Ltd v. Phone4u.co.uk Internet Ltd* [2006] *EWCA Civ* 244, [2007] *RPC* (5).

[89] For example, *Diamond T* (1921) 38 *RPC* 373; *Laura Ashley's Trade Mark* [1990] *RPC* 539, 549.

[90] *Nestlé* [2005] *RPC* (5) 77 (the POLO case).

[91] *Granada Trade Mark* [1979] *RPC* 303, 308.

[92] Moreover, in composite marks the disclaimer may mean that it is no infringement to use just the disclaimed component, but the disclaimed component is still one element of the composite whole: *Granada*, ibid, 306. Consequently matter which is disclaimed is not necessarily disregarded when questions of possible confusion are being decided. Cf. *Paco/Paco Life in Colour* [2000] *RPC* 451, 467.

[93] *KPN Nederland*, Case C–363/99 [2004] *ECR* I–1619 (para. 115). See *Patak (Spices) Ltd's Application*, Case R 746/2005–4 (OHIM BA) [2007] *ETMR* (3) 66 (paras 24–25); *Croom's Trade Mark Application* [2005] *RPC* (2) 23, paras 27–29. Cp. *Ford-Werke's Application* (1955) 72 *RPC* 191, 195 (the Registrar 'should not register a mark

draws a subtle distinction between conditions relating to a particular characteristic (which are unacceptable) and exclusions of subcategories (which are deemed acceptable). Thus, it is possible to register TUTANKHAMUN for 'books (other than historical or archaeological books)', because these are exclusions of discrete 'subcategories' rather than exclusions relating to goods not possessing a particular characteristic.[94] Philosophers would doubtless be amused.

2.6 REGISTRATION

In the absence of an effective opposition, the Registrar should register the trade mark.[95] The registration is then published in the *Trade Marks Journal*.[96] The date of registration of the trade mark is deemed to be the date of filing the application.[97] This is the date from which matters such as duration are calculated[98] and the rights of the proprietor are enforceable against third parties.[99] While registration in the United Kingdom lasts for ten years, trade marks may be renewed for further ten-year periods.[100] One characteristic which distinguishes trade marks from other forms of intellectual property is that there is no maximum period of protection. So long as they are renewed, potentially trade marks can last forever. As with patents and designs, the reason why renewal is required is to ensure that the only marks which are on the Register are those in which proprietors have some interest.[101] Proprietors are normally provided with some leeway for late renewal[102] and, in certain circumstances, are able to restore lapsed registrations.[103] Generally alteration of registered marks is not permitted.[104] The Registrar, however, may allow the proprietor's name or address to be altered. This is only permissible where the alteration does not 'substantially affect the identity of the mark'.[105]

2.7 THE TRADE MARK SYMBOL

Although the trade mark symbols ™ and ® are used widely, there is no legal requirement that proprietors use these symbols to indicate that a mark has been registered. Criminal liability does however exist for anyone who uses these marks, the word 'registered', or any other word or symbol which suggests that a mark is registered when, in fact, it is not.[106]

2.8 VALIDITY AND REVOCATION

Once a mark is registered there is a presumption, though not a guarantee, that the registration is valid.[107] As with all forms of registered intellectual property, it is possible for trade marks to

---

under conditions in which there would exist such a strong probability that the rights of the registered proprietor would be misconceived by the public'.)

[94] *Manual of Trade Mark Practice,* Ch 3, section 48.

[95] TMA s. 40.   [96] TMR r. 16.   [97] TMA s. 40(3).

[98] TMA s. 42. But note TMA s. 46(1)(a) calculating period of non-use from 'the date of completion of the registration procedure'.

[99] TMA s. 9(3) explains that the rights have effect from the date of registration, i.e. filing, but no infringement proceedings may be begun before the date on which the mark is in fact registered, and no criminal liability is incurred for acts done before the date of publication of the registration. This has no parallel in the TM Dir.: see *Interlotto UK Ltd v. Camelot plc* [2004] *RPC* (9) 186 (paras 19–20).

[100] TMA s. 42; CTMR Art. 47; Madrid Prot. Art. 7(1).

[101] TMA s. 43(2); TMR r. 27.   [102] TMA s. 43(3).

[103] TMA s. 43(5); TMR r. 30.   [104] TMA s. 44.

[105] TMA s. 64; TMR r. 38.   [106] TMA s. 95. See below at p. 1129.   [107] TMA s. 72.

be withdrawn after they have been registered. This may be because the mark should not have been registered in the first place, or because changes in circumstances mean that it should no longer be registered. The grounds on which a registered mark may be challenged by third parties are set out in sections 46 and 47 of the 1994 Act. Section 46(1) sets out the grounds on which a mark may be *revoked*. A trade mark registration may be revoked where it has not been used for five years, where as a result of the way it has been used it has lost its distinctiveness, or where as a result of the way it has been used the further use of the mark has become likely to 'mislead the public'. In addition a mark which should never have been registered can be declared invalid under section 47. A registration will be liable to be declared invalid where it should not have been registered on absolute grounds because of a potential objection under section 3 (for example because it lacks distinctiveness) and where relative grounds for refusal existed under section 5. These issues are dealt with in later chapters.

3 REGISTRATION OF COMMUNITY TRADE MARKS

Registration at the Community level involves the filing of a single application with the Office of Harmonization in the Internal Market (OHIM) which is based in Alicante in Spain.[108] The OHIM began receiving applications on 1 April 1996.[109] In contrast with the procedure for European patents (where the EPO issues a series of national patents), a successful application to the OHIM results in the grant of a single trade mark which operates for the whole of the European Community.[110] The main benefit of the Community system is that it enables traders to protect their marks throughout the Community on the basis of a single application, rather than having to file separate applications in each of the member states.

While the procedure at the OHIM differs in certain respects from the procedure at the UK Office, there is close similarity between the two regimes. As is the case with the UK Registry, traders who wish to have their signs protected as Community Trade Marks often rely upon the expert advice of trade mark agents. Legal representation before the OHIM is more strictly prescribed than in the United Kingdom. Although legal representation is not required in all cases,[111] businesses that are not domiciled and do not have their principal place of business in the Community must be represented before the OHIM. Representation before the OHIM can only be undertaken by a legal practitioner qualified in a member state or a professional representative recognized by the OHIM.[112] To be duly recognized, a representative must be a national of a member state with a place of business in the Community. In addition, they must be entitled to act as an agent before the trade marks office of the member state in which that business is located.[113]

---

[108] CTMR Art. 2.
[109] Strictly speaking, that was the date of opening and applications could be submitted from 1 Jan. 1996.
[110] CTMR Art. 1(2).   [111] CTMR Art. 88(1).
[112] CTMR Art. 89.   [113] CTMR Art. 89(2).

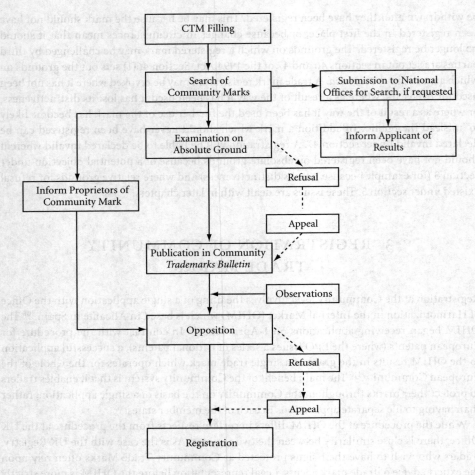

Fig. 35.2 Registering a Community Trade Mark

3.1 THE APPLICATION

The application for a Community Trade Mark, which can be made by anyone, [114] may be made directly to the OHIM in Alicante or to a national Registry, which is obliged to forward the application to the OHIM within two weeks (see Fig. 35.2).[115]

An application for a Community Trade Mark may be filed in any of the official languages of the Community. The applicant should also specify a second language in which opposition proceedings may be conducted. As in the United Kingdom, an application for a Community

---

[114] Prior to 2004, only a limited class of people was able to apply for a Community Trade Mark under the CTMR Art. 5 (as enacted). To apply for a Community Trade Mark, a person must be a national of, or domiciled in an EC state, or a country which is party to Paris or WTO, or be a national of a state which accords reciprocal protection. This was regarded as imposing an 'excessively complex exercise' and was therefore abolished by Council Regulation amending Regulation (EC) No. 40/9 on the Community Trade Mark No. 422/2004 of 19 Feb. 2004 *OJ L* 70/1.

[115] CTMR Art. 25(2). There were 641,658 applications between 1996 and December 2007, with 426,221 registrations.

Trade Mark must include a request for registration; the name and address of the applicant; a list of the goods or services for which the mark is to be registered; and a representation of the mark.[116] The date of filing is the date on which these documents are furnished to the OHIM. As in the United Kingdom, it may be possible to claim a priority date from an earlier application elsewhere.[117]

Three slight differences are worth observing. First, as regards the goods or services for which a mark is registrable, it seems that the OHIM is more generous, permitting applications, for example, relating to 'all goods in class x'. Second, and related, there is no requirement that an applicant state that they intend to use the marks. Third, practices as to graphic representation differ slightly. These have already been discussed.

3.2 SENIORITY AT OHIM

Applicants who seek registration of a Community Trade Mark may claim the seniority of earlier national registrations of the same mark of which they are the proprietor.[118] Seniority can be claimed either before or after registration of the Community Trade Mark.[119] To apply for seniority, an applicant must be able to show that the earlier national mark is for the same sign, the same goods and services, and has the same proprietor as the Community Trade Mark.[120]

The effect of a seniority claim is that, even though the national registration ceases to exist (because of lack of renewal or because it was surrendered),[121] the proprietor of the Community Trade Mark continues to have the same rights as if the national mark had continued to be registered.[122] Effectively, it allows the Community Trade Mark owner to let the national registration lapse without being prejudiced in any way.[123] As the Board of Appeal at the OHIM said, seniority is a useful way of encouraging proprietors of national marks to use the Community system and thereby consolidate the management of their national marks.[124] As a result of its popularity, problems have occurred in processing seniority claims and many have been let through without formal examination.[125]

3.3 EXAMINATION

Once the filing process has been completed the application is then examined. Initial examination at the OHIM is restricted to an inquiry as to whether the application complies with the

---

[116] CTMR Art. 26; CTMIR r. 1.

[117] CTMR Arts. 29–31. Communication No. 10/99 of the President of the Office of 8 Dec. 1999.

[118] CTMR Art. 34.   [119] CTMR Art. 35.

[120] CTMR Art. 34(1) (so called 'triple-identity rule'). The OHIM only examines the question of identity of signs: Communication No. 2/00 of the President of the Office of 25 Feb. 2000 concerning the examination of seniority claims. On identity of signs, see *International Business Machines Corp/Thinkpad*, R10/1998–2 (15 Jul. 1998) para. 15. On identity of the specification, see Communication No. 1/97 of the President of the Office of 17 June 1997 concerning the examination of seniority claims. On identity of proprietorship see *BatMark, Inc/ Viceroy* R 5/97–1 [1998] *ETMR* 449.

[121] *Allied Telesyn Inc v. Rapier 1 Ltd* (13 Jun 2007).

[122] There is no obligation on the Community office to treat the Community mark as valid just because seniority is claimed for an identical national mark: *Develey Holdings GmbH v. OHIM*, T–129/04 [2006] *ETMR* (85) 1190.

[123] CTMR Art. 34(2).   [124] *BatMark* R 5/97–1 [1998] *ETMR* 449, 455–6.

[125] Examination of seniority claims which was suspended has now resumed, but is confined to comparison of marks: Communication No. 2/00 of the President.

absolute grounds for refusal.[126] The absolute grounds for refusal will apply to the mark across the whole Community, even if they only arise in one member state.[127] Where the application fails to comply with the absolute grounds for refusal, the application may be amended or withdrawn.[128] The Office may request that the applicant disclaim any exclusive right in a particular element.[129]

While the OHIM does not examine applications to see if the relative grounds for refusal apply, it does provide third parties (and applicants) with some assistance. In particular, the OHIM searches the Community Register for similar marks and, if requested to do so by the applicant, asks member states to do the same.[130] These national searches are returned to the OHIM within three months and a cumulative search report is dispatched to the applicant. The results of the OHIM's search is also sent to the owners of any rival registrations that are found. The search, however, does not lead to an examination on relative grounds. Instead, it is left up to the holders of prior rights to bring opposition proceedings[131] or, if the mark has been registered, cancellation proceedings.[132]

3.4 PUBLICATION, OBSERVATIONS, AND OPPOSITION

Once an application has successfully been examined, it will then be published in the *Community Trade Marks Bulletin*.[133] Publication takes place one month after the applicant is provided with the search report. At the same time, the application file, which is previously closed, is opened up for public inspection.[134]

Following publication, there is an opportunity for third parties to make 'observations' on and 'opposition' to the proposed registration of the application. While a Community Trade Mark covers the whole Community, a single objection to the application can result in the entire application being refused. Third parties may make 'observations' explaining why the trade mark should not be registered under Article 7 (which are the absolute grounds for refusal). Although the Regulation states that the observations are to be communicated to the applicant 'who may comment on them', the OHIM has indicated that, where observations raise serious doubts about registrability, the Office will re-examine the application.[135]

---

[126] CTMR Art. 38; CTMIR r. 11. Absolute grounds are set out in CTMR Art. 7(1). One difference between the CTM and UK law, is that the UK will examine whether the application is in bad faith, whereas under the CTMR this is only a ground for invalidity (not refusal).

[127] CTMR Art. 7(2).

[128] CTMR Art. 38(3), Art. 44; CTMIR r. 13.

[129] CTMR Art. 38(2). *Cahill May Roberts's Application for a Declaration of Invalidity/Medicine Shoppe International's Trade Mark*, C 172734/1 [2000] *ETMR* 794, 780.

[130] CTMR Art. 39 (as amended by Regulation amending Regulation (EC) No. 40/9 on the Community Trade Mark No. 422/2004 of 19 Feb. 2004). Request to national authorities was previously automatic, but some national authorities (Italy, France, and Germany) did not do searches and the quality of the others varied enormously. See UK Patent Office, *A Consultation Paper on the European Commission's Regulation Amending Regulation (EC) No. 40/94 on the Community Trade Mark* (April 2003).

[131] CTMR Art. 42.   [132] CTMR Art. 52.

[133] CTMR Art. 40; CTMR Art. 85.

[134] Prior to publication, the file cannot be inspected without an applicant's consent: CTMR Art. 84.

[135] CTMR Art. 41(2); Communication No. 1/00 of the President of the Office of 25 Feb. 2000 concerning observations under Article 41 of the Community Trade Mark Regulation. *Durferrit GmbH v. OHIM*, T-244/0 [2003] *ECR* II–1589, [2004] *ETMR* (32) (para. 73). For an example, see *Wine Oh! LLC's Application*, R 1074/2005–4 [2006] *ETMR* (95) 1319 (observations relating to deceptive nature of mark).

Within three months of publication, the application may be *opposed* on relative grounds.[136] As in the UK, only a limited set of persons is entitled to bring opposition proceedings, namely the proprietors of earlier trade marks and their licensees, the proprietors of trade marks, and the proprietors of earlier marks or signs.[137] Once an opposition is accepted the OHIM notifies the applicant and a 'cooling-off' period of up to 24 months ensues. If the parties have not resolved the conflict (for example through a delimitation agreement allowing the registration), the 'adversarial' process begins. The opponent will be asked to substantiate the existence of an earlier right and, where this consists of a mark granted more than five years previously, the applicant may request the opponent prove use of its mark. In response, the applicant is entitled to make observations on the opponent's evidence and grounds of opposition. Ultimately, the matters are decided by the OHIM. In contrast to the process in the United Kingdom, oral hearings will only occur rarely. While it was anticipated that oppositions at the OHIM would be very common, it seems that they only affect about one-fifth of all applications.[138] Most oppositions are resolved in the cooling-off period, with only about one-third leading to an office decision.[139]

If an application to the OHIM is rejected or withdrawn, it may be converted back into a series of national applications which retain the filing date used at the OHIM.[140] Conversion is not possible, however, in those member states where the grounds for refusal of the Community Trade Mark relate to that state.[141] As with UK applications, it is possible for applications for a Community Trade Mark to be changed or amended after they have been lodged. While the way this is done at the OHIM is similar to the techniques used in the United Kingdom,[142] one important difference is that, whereas disclaimers are used voluntarily by UK applicants, they are imposed (or rather 'requested') by the OHIM 'as a condition' of registration.[143] Despite this, the examination guidelines at the OHIM suggest that disclaimers will be used infrequently.[144]

3.5 REGISTRATION

In the absence of an effective opposition, the mark will be registered.[145] The date of registration is the filing date, which is the date from which matters such as duration are calculated.[146] As regards the Community Trade Mark, a proprietor is only entitled to 'reasonable compensation' for acts occurring between publication of the application and publication of the registration.[147] Registration at the OHIM lasts for ten years.[148] A Community Trade Mark may be renewed for further periods of ten years.[149] Alteration of registered marks is generally not permitted.[150] As

---

[136] For analysis of the grounds, see Ch. 38. The opposition must be in one of the languages of the Office: English, French, German, Italian, Spanish. See F. Gevers and D. Tatham, 'Opposition Procedure in the Community Trade Mark System' [1998] *EIPR* 22.

[137] CTMR Art. 42.

[138] As of Dec 2007, OHIM had published 554,554 applications and there had been 124,844 oppositions.

[139] As of Dec 2007, 82, 417 oppositions had been resolved, 24,224 by decision and 58,193 by some other means.

[140] CTMR Art. 108; CTMIR r. 44.   [141] CTMR Art. 108(2)(b).

[142] CTMR Art. 38(3), Art. 44.   [143] CTMIR r. 1(3).

[144] OHIM Guidelines, para. 8.13.1. On the new possibilities for division of CTM applications: see Council Regulation No. 422/2004 of 19 Feb. 2004.

[145] CTMR Art. 45; CTMIR r. 23.   [146] CTMR Art. 46.

[147] CTMR Art. 9(3). *See Interlotto,* note 99 above (para. 21).

[148] CTMR Art. 46.   [149] CTMR Art. 47.   [150] CTMR Art. 48; CTMIR r. 25.

in the United Kingdom, it is possible for a Community Trade Mark to be revoked or declared invalid after it has been registered—and this may occur either as a counterclaim in proceedings in a Community Trade Mark court, or by application to the Cancellation Division of the OHIM.[151]

4 INTERNATIONAL FILING

The third way in which traders in the UK are able to protect their marks is via the international filing systems established under the 1891 Madrid Agreement and the 1989 Madrid Protocol. It should be noted at the outset that international registration does not lead to something such as an 'international mark', so much as facilitate the acquisition of national marks. The main advantage of international registration is that, instead of trade mark holders having to file a series of applications in each of the jurisdictions where they would like protection, they are able to obtain protection in a range of jurisdictions with a single application.

4.1 THE MADRID AGREEMENT

The oldest international filing system is the 1891 Madrid Agreement.[152] Under the Agreement—to which the United Kingdom is *not* a party—it is possible to register a trade mark at a national level and then to apply to have the mark recognized by the WIPO in Geneva as an 'international registration'. Despite being over 100 years old, only a relatively small number of countries have signed up to the Agreement.[153]

To apply for international registration, the applicant must have a trade mark registered in its country of origin, which must be a contracting state of the Agreement. Applications must be in French and include: the name and address of the applicant; information about the registration in the country of origin; a reproduction of the mark; and a statement of the goods and services to which the mark is applied.[154] The application should also nominate the countries of the Agreement where the applicant wishes the mark to be protected.[155] The Madrid Agreement can only be used by a person or business that has headquarters or a real and effective establishment in a country that is a party to the Agreement. Given that the United Kingdom is not a party to the Madrid Agreement, UK businesses will only be able to take advantage of the system where they have a base outside the United Kingdom.[156]

Once the national office of the country of origin is satisfied that the application is complete, it sends the international application to the International Bureau in Geneva. On receiving the international application, the International Bureau examines the application to ensure that it complies with various formalities: there is no substantive examination of the application. An application that satisfies the procedural requirements is immediately registered.[157] The registration date is the date when the International Bureau receives the completed application.

---

[151] *Cahill May Roberts* Case C–172734/1 [2000] *ETMR* 794 (Cancellation Division of same status as Examining Division).

[152] Madrid Agreement Concerning the International Registration of Marks of 14 Apr. 1891.

[153] The Madrid Agreement covers only 56 countries. The USA and Japan are not members.

[154] Madrid, Art. 3(2).   [155] Madrid, Art. 3*bis*.

[156] G. Souter, 'The Rights of Nationals of Non-Madrid Union Countries to Own International Registrations' [1995] *EIPR* 333.

[157] Madrid, Art. 3(4).

The International Bureau then sends applications to the National Offices nominated by the applicant. Article 4 of the Agreement provides that, from the date of the international registration, the application is to be treated in each of the designated countries as if it had been filed directly at that country's national office.[158] Upon receipt of the international registration, the national offices have the opportunity to reject the application. Registration under the Madrid Agreement lasts for 20 years and is renewable for further 20-year periods.[159]

One of the major problems with the Madrid Agreement is that it provides for the possibility of a 'central attack'.[160] This means that if, within five years from the date of international registration, the mark is declared invalid or otherwise lost in the country of origin, *all* the national registrations that are based upon it are also lost. At the end of the five-year period, the opportunity for central attack ends. From this point, the non-country of origin registrations are not dependent upon the fate of the mark in the country of origin.

4.2 THE MADRID PROTOCOL

The Madrid Protocol[161] was established in 1989 to provide an alternative mechanism to the Madrid Agreement for the international filing of marks. In particular, it was hoped to overcome some of the perceived shortcomings of the Agreement that have led to the membership being so small.[162] Given that there are currently 82 parties to the Protocol (as distinct from 56 to the Agreement), the Protocol has been a success, at least in this regard. While the Protocol and the Agreement are similar there are, as we will see, some important differences. The United Kingdom became a party to the Madrid Protocol on 1 December 1995[163] and the Protocol became operational on 1 April 1996. The European Community joined with effect from 1 October 2004.[164] The system established under the Protocol is run by WIPO in Geneva.

4.2.1 Application

In order to apply for international registration for a mark under the Protocol, an application for registration must have been made in a country party to the Protocol.[165] The existing registration or application provides the 'national basis' which grounds the Protocol application. Applications for international registration are filed in the office where the national basis was

---

[158] Madrid, Art. 4.   [159] Madrid, Arts. 6–7(1).   [160] Madrid, Art. 6.

[161] Protocol Relating to the Madrid Agreement Concerning the International Registration of Marks (as signed at Madrid on 28 June 1989).

[162] I. Kaufman, 'Madrid Agreement: Will Reform Proposals Attract more Members?' [1990] *EIPR* 407; G. Kunze, 'The Madrid System for the International Registration of Marks as Applied under the Protocol' [1994] *EIPR* 223. For an assessment, see E. McDermott, 'Measuring the Merits of Madrid', [2008] 177 *Managing Intellectual Property* 62.

[163] In order to give effect to its obligations under the Protocol, the UK has passed delegated legislation in the form of the Trade Marks (International Registration) Order (SI 1996/714, as amended by SI 2000/138).

[164] The Madrid Protocol allows for accession by intergovernmental organizations: Madrid, Art. 14. The authority to join was conferred by Council Decision of 27 October 2003 approving the Accession off the European Community to the Protocol Relating to the Madrid agreement Concerning the International Registration of Marks, Adopted at Madrid on 27 June 1989, *OJ L* 296/20 (14 November 2003). This act was accompanied by a Council Regulation (EC) No 1992/2003 of 27 October 2003 amending regulation No 40/94 on the Community Trade Mark to give effect to the Accession of the European Community to the Protocol to the Madrid Agreement, *OJ L* 296/1, adding Title XIII to the CTMR, and later Commission Regulation (EC) No 782/2004 of 26 April 2004 amending Regulation (EC) No 2868/95 on the accession of the European Community to the Madrid Protocol, *OJ L* 123/88.

[165] Madrid, Art. 2(1).

filed:[166] the WIPO will not accept applications that are filed directly with it.[167] For British traders, this would normally be the UK Trade Mark Office. International applications governed exclusively by the Protocol may be in either English or French (the office of origin, however, may restrict the applicant's choice to one of these languages).

An international application can also be based upon an application or a registration at an 'intergovernmental organization',[168] and a Council Decision has now enabled the OHIM to take advantage of this possibility.[169] Since the autumn of 2004, both applicants and holders of Community Trade Marks have been able to apply for international protection of their marks through the filing of an international application under the Protocol. Conversely, holders of international registrations under the Madrid Protocol can apply for protection of their marks as a Community Trade Mark.[170]

The national office or OHIM examines the international application to ensure that the international application corresponds to the basic application or registration, that is, it is for the same mark, has the same owner as, and covers the same goods and services as the 'basic application'.[171] An application for international registration must also designate the countries in which the mark is to be protected. Although this should be done at the application stage, further countries may subsequently be added.[172]

Once it is satisfied that the formalities have been complied with, the national office will then forward the application to WIPO which examines the application to ensure that it complies with the Protocol. Once it is satisfied that an application is in order, the International Bureau then places the mark on the International Register of Trade Marks, advertises the mark, and passes on details of an application to each of the designated countries listed in the application.[173] As with the Madrid Agreement, the application is treated in each of the designated countries as if it had been filed directly at that country's national office.[174] Each designated country then examines the application against its own criteria for registration.[175] Any refusal can only be based on the grounds which would apply under the Paris Convention.[176]

Countries normally have up to twelve months to notify the WIPO of any objections.[177] However, in accordance with a special provision, the United Kingdom has declared that the time limit to notify a refusal of protection is eighteen months.[178] Where a refusal to protect results from an opposition to the granting of protection, such refusal may be notified after the expiry of the eighteen-month time limit. Such a refusal is notified to WIPO which then sends notification of the refusal to the international registrant, who is able to contest, amend, and appeal the decision.[179] Where a Registry fails to notify WIPO of a decision to refuse registration within the relevant time limit, the mark is deemed to be protected as if it had been registered by the authorities of that country.[180]

Registration under the Protocol lasts for ten years,[181] with the possibility of being renewed for further ten-year periods.[182] Where a mark that is the subject of a national or regional

---

[166] On fees, see ibid, Art. 8.   [167] Ibid, Art. 2(2).   [168] Ibid, Art. 14(1)(b).
[169] Council Decision *OJ L* 296/1 adding Title XIII to the CTMR; Council Regulation No. 1992/2003.
[170] CTMR (as amended), Art. 146.
[171] Madrid, Art. 3(1). CTMIR, r. 103.   [172] Ibid, Art. 3*bis.*
[173] Ibid, Art. 3(2). WIPO advertises an applicant's mark in the WIPO *Gazette of International Marks.*
[174] Madrid, Art. 4.
[175] In the case of OHIM, the CTMR (as amended), Art. 149 provides for examination on absolute grounds.
[176] Madrid, Art. 5(1).   [177] Ibid, Art. 5(2).
[178] Ibid, Art. 5(2)(b)–(c).   [179] Ibid, Art. 5(6).   [180] Ibid, Art. 4(1)(a).
[181] Ibid, Art. 6(1).   [182] Ibid, Art. 7(1).

registration is the subject of a later international registration and both registrations stand in the name of the same person, the international registration is deemed to replace the national or regional registration, without prejudice to any rights acquired by virtue of the latter.[183] This occurs only if all the goods and services listed in the national or regional registration are also listed in the international registration in respect of the said contracting party. Rights in all the countries can then be renewed by a single transaction.

4.2.2 Central attack

Under the Madrid Agreement, the fate of the international registration (and all the subsidiary registrations made under it) depends on the fate of the trade mark registered in the country of origin: if it is lost, all the other registrations are also lost. While an international registration under the Protocol is vulnerable to a central attack (most obviously where the basic application is refused by the national authority),[184] the consequences of a successful attack are not as drastic as they are under the Agreement. As we saw above, a successful attack under the Agreement means that all of the national registrations made in pursuance of the international registration are also lost. Where a central attack is successful under the Protocol, however, it is possible to transform the international registration into a series of national or regional applications.[185] Under this provision, if within three months of cancellation the person who was the holder of the international registration files an application for the registration of the same mark with the office of any of the designated territories, that application shall be treated as if it had been filed on the date of the international registration. This only takes place, however, if the goods and services listed in the application correspond to the list of goods and services contained in the international registration. The fresh application must comply with the requirements of the applicable law.

5 DECIDING WHICH ROUTE TO TAKE

Because of the interaction between these systems an applicant is faced with a complex array of possible avenues through which he can acquire trade mark protection. The most obvious of the existing routes are as follows:

   (i)   application directly to the United Kingdom;

  (ii)   application to a Paris Convention country, then to the United Kingdom;[186]

 (iii)   application to the OHIM leading to a CTM;

 (iv)   application to a Paris Convention country, then to the OHIM;

  (v)   application to a Paris Convention country, then international registration designating the UK;

 (vi)   application to a Paris Convention country, then international registration designating the OHIM; or

(vii)   application to the OHIM followed by an international application.[187]

---

[183] Ibid, Art. 4*bis*.   [184] Ibid, Art. 6(3).   [185] Ibid, Art. 9*quinquies*.

[186] Under the 'telle quelle' provision contained in Paris Art. 6*quinquies*, a member of the Paris Convention is obliged to accept for registration any trade mark which has been duly registered in its country of origin.

[187] From 1 October 2004.

Decisions to register, and the choice of routes, are likely to involve commercial judgements as to the likely markets in which protection is desired compared with the cost of obtaining registrations for such territories. Probably the most significant factor determining choice of application process is the cost. If trade mark protection is required in several countries, it may be cheaper to use the Community Trade Mark or the Madrid Protocol than to make national applications in each country.[188] As well as savings in office fees, associated savings can be achieved by using the Madrid Protocol in terms of lower costs of trade mark agents. There are also obvious advantages to the OHIM or Madrid in terms of the simplicity of completing the OHIM or Madrid forms rather than numerous national forms in various national languages. One of the advantages with the regional and international systems lies in the fact that they avoid the obligations to submit applications in the language of each country where protection is sought. Moreover, in the long term, maintenance of regional or international marks will be easier, requiring only one renewal at each instead of several. Finally, the application of the substantive or procedural law might be perceived as being more favourable at the OHIM than in the local Registry.[189]

That is not to suggest there may not be reasons (especially for small enterprises) to use national registration systems.[190] It may be difficult to find appropriate marks to operate in all countries: trade mark lawyers love to tell anecdotes about word marks adopted in one country and transported to another without considering what the mark suggests in that territory. Moreover, it is foreseeable that valid marks will be harder to obtain at the OHIM than in some national registries, given the broader field in which the mark has to operate. Words which are distinctive in the United Kingdom may lack distinctiveness at the Community level (for example, because the word is a description in a foreign language or indicates a geographical origin). In addition, the number of similar marks in use or already registered, which form the potential basis for opposition, is likely to be substantially greater for Community marks than for national marks. One consequence of this will be that those who are seeking protection quickly might prefer to seek national registrations, rather than begin with a filing to the OHIM, because of the substantial risk that the mark will be rejected or prove invalid at the Community level.

---

[188] The basic application fee for CTM is €900 and the registration fee is €850. The cost of designating the EC in an international application is 2,855 Swiss francs, which is something like €1,772 or £1,315. The UK national fee is £200.

[189] OHIM permits broad specifications, and is more accepting of geographic marks, and marks comprising surnames.

[190] Ibid.

36

SUBJECT MATTER

CHAPTER CONTENTS

1 INTRODUCTION

The first requirement that a sign must satisfy to be validly registered or, if it is already registered, to ensure that it is not subsequently declared invalid, is that it must comply with the definition of a trade mark in section 1(1)/Article 4 CTMR. In particular, it is necessary to show that there is:

(i) a sign

(ii) which can be represented graphically, and

(iii) which is capable of distinguishing the goods or services of one undertaking from those of other undertakings.

Failure to comply with any of these requirements means that the sign will not be registered (this is one of the absolute grounds for refusal set out in section 3(1)(a). Alternatively, if a mark is incorrectly registered, the registration of the mark may be declared invalid under section 47(1).

Before looking at these three elements in more detail, it is important to recall that the requirement that the sign must possess the qualities of a trade mark that are set out in section 1(1)/Article 4 CTMR, is only the first of three general limitations which are placed on what can be registered as a trade mark. In addition, it is also necessary to ensure that the mark is not excluded by one of the absolute grounds for refusal found in section 3/Article 7 CTMR.[1] It is also necessary to show that the mark is not excluded by any of the relative grounds for refusal found in section 5/Article 8 CTMR.[2]

---

[1] See Ch. 37. [2] See Ch. 38.

2 WHAT IS A SIGN?

For a trade mark to be validly registered it is necessary to show that it consists of a 'sign'. No statutory definition is given as to what is meant by this term. Indeed, one of the notable features of the current law is that there are very few *a priori* restrictions placed on what may be registered as a trade mark.[3] The starting point for considering what may be protected as a sign is section 1, which provides a non-exhaustive list of the types of signs that may be protected as trade marks. These include words (including personal names), designs, letters, numerals, or the shape of goods or their packaging. Although all the matters referred to in section 1 of the Act are visually perceptible, the ECJ has held that the concept of a sign is not limited to visually perceptible matter: as a result, both sounds and smells have been held to fall within the notion of a sign.[4] Given this holding, it may be that the scope of trade marks extends even to encompass gestures or tastes.

The more open style of approach adopted under the new trade mark regime has been welcomed by trade mark owners. It has also been welcomed for the fact that, by increasing the features of products which may indicate source, it benefits consumers from different cultural backgrounds and with varying standards of literacy.[5] Some, however, have questioned whether the potential problems that are raised by some of the more exotic marks are justified by the benefits that they confer on their owners.[6]

Although it is clear that the concept of a 'sign' is broad, it is not without limits. In two cases the ECJ has indicated that attempts to register must be refused if the subject was not a 'sign' for the purposes of trade mark law. The first occasion related to an attempt to register a combination of colours (blue and yellow) howsoever they were applied to articles or packaging. The ECJ held that, while a colour *could be* a sign, it was not necessarily so: in many situations colour is simply a property or characteristic of a thing.[7] According to the ECJ, in order to prevent trade mark law being used by one trader to obtain an unfair advantage over other traders, an applicant for a colour mark must establish that the colour in question is seen as a 'sign'. Unfortunately, the ECJ provided little guidance on how an applicant was to establish (or an office assess) the semiotic status of a colour or colour combination. If the requirement is that the applicant must show that consumers see the colour combination as indicating origin, the requirement seems to add nothing over the demand that the mark be not devoid of distinctive character. The second case, *Dyson Ltd v. Registrar of Trade Marks*,[8] concerned an attempt to register as a trade mark the idea of having a transparent collection bin on a vacuum cleaner. According to the ECJ, this was a mere property of the product, and the protection of anything so unspecific would provide an unfair advantage to the trader who registered it, because he

---

[3] The new definition of what constitutes a trade mark is to be contrasted with the restrictive definition formerly found in TMA 1938, s. 68.

[4] *Ralf Sieckmann v. Deutsches Patent-und Markenamt,* Case C–273/00 [2002] *ECR* I–11737 (paras. 43–4); *Shield Mark BV v. Joost Kist,* Case C–283/01, [2003] *ECR* I–14313; [2005] 1 *CMLR* (41) 1046.

[5] G. Dinwoodie, 'Reconceptualising the Inherent Distinctiveness of Product Design Trade Dress' (1997) 75(2) *North Carolina Law Review* 471, 561.

[6] B. Elias, 'Do Scents Signify Source—An Argument against Trade Mark Protection for Fragrances' (1992) 82 *TM Rep.* 475 (arguing such extension is misguided).

[7] *Heidelberger Bauchemie,* Case C–49/02 [2004] *ECR* I–6129. Similar remarks had been made in *Libertel Groep BV v. Benelux-Merkenbureau,* Case C–104/01 [2004] *FSR* (4) 65 (para. 27).

[8] Case C–321/03, [2007] 2 *CMLR* (44) 303. See PAN 7/07 (20 July 2007). A photograph of the bin can be seen in the case report and also at Figure 30.2, p. 691.

would be able to prevent other manufacturers selling vacuum cleaners with transparent collection bins. This application, therefore (the ECJ said) did not relate to a 'sign'. While the result in the latter case seems correct, the reasoning seems somewhat problematic.[9]

2.1 LIMITS ON THE REGISTRATION OF SHAPES

While, in extending trade mark protection to the shape of goods, trade mark law took account of the realities of consumer buying habits, it also gave rise to a problem: that trade mark rights could operate to limit competition in ways which were contrary to the public interest. In order to avoid such undesirable effects, section 3(2)/CTMR Article 7(1)(e)[10] provide a 'preliminary obstacle' to registration,[11] namely that a sign shall not be registered as a trade mark if it consists exclusively of a shape which:

(i)   results from the nature of the goods themselves;

(ii)   is necessary to obtain a technical result; or

(iii) gives substantial value to the goods.

These objections cannot be overcome by showing that the sign is recognized as distinctive. The ECJ thus stated that if the shape of certain trousers (having an oval kneepad and two lines of sloping stitching from hip height to crotch height) gave substantial value to the goods, and so was unregisterable, it was of no consequence—for trade mark law—that consumers would recognize the shape and understand it as indicating that G-Star had made the trousers.[12]

It should be noted at the outset that the precise scope of much of section 3(2) remains unclear. So far, only section 3(2)(b) has been the subject of detailed consideration by the ECJ (in *Philips Electronics v. Remington*), and that decision raised as many questions as it answered. In due course, we will hopefully know more about the scope of the exclusions.

To be excluded the sign must consist 'exclusively' of an excluded 'natural, functional or ornamental' shape.[13] In *Philips Electronics v. Remington*,[14] the ECJ reinterpreted this by asking

---

[9] It is not clear when a trade mark gives an 'unfair advantage' nor what this has to do with whether the subject matter is a 'sign'. It may be that the real objection in both cases is that the applicant is applying for a category of signs, and that the trade mark system requires an individual application be made in relation to each. Would there have been any possible objection to Dyson applying to register the transparent bin of a particular model of a vacuum cleaner?

[10] TM Dir. Art. 3(1)(e). Cf. TRIPS Art. 15(1).

[11] *Koninklijke Philips Electronics NV v. Remington Consumer Products*, Case 299/99 [2002] *ECR* I–5475; [2002] 2 *CMLR* 5.

[12] *Benetton v. G-Star*, Case C–371/06 [2008] *ETMR* (5) 104.

[13] See ibid. para. 16 (AG Colomer); *Linde AG, Windward Industries, Rado Watch Co Ltd*, Joined Cases C–53/01, 54/01, C–55/01 [2003] *RPC* (45) 803 para. 29 (AG Colomer). Although s. 3 refers to shape rather than 'packaging', the ECJ has held that it applies to packaging of products which have no intrinsic shape of their own (such as liquids or granules): *Henkel's Application*, Case C–218/01 [2004] *ECR* I–1725, [2005] *ETMR* 569 (paras. 35, 37) (concerning a bottle for liquid detergent). In *Dyson v. Registrar of Trade Marks* Case C–321/03 [2007] 2 *CMLR* (44) 303, 319–322 (paras 76–102) (Advocate General Léger), the Advocate General argued that the provision of Art. 3(1)(e) of the Directive would apply even to an attempt to register the transparent bin of a vacuum cleaner, even though this was not obviously a 'shape'. The English Court of Appeal has held that the shape exclusions do not operate in relation to two-dimensional device marks representing excluded three-dimensional shapes: *Koninklijke Philips Electronics NV v. Remington Consumer Products* [2006] *FSR* (30) 537 (paras. 94–100); but cf. *Philips v. Remington* [1998] *RPC* 283, 290 (Jacob J); *Julius Sämaan Ltd v. Tetrosyl Ltd* [2006] *FSR* (42) 849 (para. 93) (Kitchin J).

[14] *Koninklijke Philips v. Remington*, Case 299/19 [2002] *ECR* I–5475; [2002] 2 *CMRL* 5.

instead 'what are the essential (functional) characteristics of the shape for which registration is sought?'[15] If the essential characteristics of the shape fall within the exclusions, so does the mark for which registration is sought. The effect of this is that the addition of trivial features to a shape which is otherwise excluded will not render the sign registrable.[16] In determining which characteristics are 'essential' and which are 'trivial' the Court of Appeal has suggested that the question be assessed from the point of view of the average consumer of the goods concerned.[17] In that case, which concerned the design for an electric razor, the Court emphasized the impact of the mark on the *eye* of the average consumer. The Court held that the judge had been entitled to hold, on the facts, that the 'clover leaf' feature of the design was an aspect which consumers might well overlook, and was thus not an essential feature. Having so held, the presence of such features could not affect the overall decision as to whether the shape for which registration was sought was excluded.

2.1.1 Where the shape results from the nature of the goods themselves

Section 3(2)(a)/Article 7(1)(e)(i) CTMR provide that a sign shall not be registered where it consists exclusively of a shape which results from the nature of the goods themselves. While the need to identify the nature of the goods may create a number of difficulties,[18] the logic of the section is relatively straightforward. If the shape results from the nature of the goods, the shape cannot possibly distinguish the product of one trader from another: any trader who sells goods of that type would necessarily have to use the same shape. They would have no choice as to the shape that the product took. To allow the registration of 'basic shapes' or 'shapes which are indispensable to the manufacture or distribution of products'[19] would greatly inhibit the ability of competitors working in the same field. It would also permit traders to control the respective goods themselves.[20] This would be the case, for example, where a trade mark was given for the round shape of balls.

What are the 'goods themselves'?   One question that is raised by the exclusion is what is meant by the phrase, 'the goods themselves'? The way this question is answered is important, given that the more narrowly the 'goods themselves' is defined, the more likely it is that the shape will correspond to the goods in question and thus be excluded. The question of what is meant by the 'goods themselves' was considered in *Philips v. Remington* both at first instance and by

---

[15] *Koninklijke Philips v. Remington* [2006] *FSR* (30) 537 para. 36 (CA); [2005] *FSR* (17) 35 Rimer J para. 28 (common ground that the inclusion of the word 'functional' in paras 83, 84 and 86 in the phrase 'essential functional features' was an error on the part of the ECJ).

[16] Advocate General Colomer has also advocated the use of a similar notion in the context of the distinctiveness exclusions: *Koninklijke KPN Nederland NV v. Benelux-Merkenbureaus,* Case C–363/99 [2005] 2 *CMLR* (10) 184, 209 paras. 70–74; *DKV Deutsche Krankenversicherung v. OHIM,* Case C–104/00 P [2002] *ECR* I–7561 (paras. 51–54), explaining that 'I do so in order to make it clear that a shape that simply incorporates an arbitrary element that is negligible from a functional point of view cannot escape the prohibition'.

[17] *Koninklijke Philips v. Remington* [2006] *FSR* (30) 537 para. 36 (CA). At first instance, Rimer J had said he regarded it as 'unfortunate' that the ECJ had failed to offer guidance on this matter: [2005] *FSR* (17) 35 Rimer J para. 31. In *Lego Juris A/S v. Mega Brands Inc,* Case R 856/2004–G [2007] *ETMR* (11) 169, the Grand Board of Appeal of the OHIM, the red colour of a Lego brick was regarded as not being an essential characteristic of the trade mark (so that the application to register the shape and colour of the brick was rejected). The case is on appeal to the CFI, T270/06.

[18] The provisions presuppose that the goods have certain, almost platonic, essential characteristics which cannot be protected.

[19] Annand and Norman (1998), 44.

[20] *Philips Electronics NV v. Remington Consumer Products* [1999] *RPC* 809, 820.

the Court of Appeal,[21] where the issue was whether the shape of a three-headed rotary shaver fell within the scope of section 3(2)(a). (see Fig. 36.1a on p. 812 below.)

At first instance, Jacob J said that it was possible for the 'goods themselves' to be defined either as 'three-headed rotary shavers', 'electrical shavers', 'mechanical shavers', or 'shavers' as such. While the way the goods were classified provided a useful starting point for determining what the 'goods themselves' were, Jacob J stressed that the question was not to be decided merely by reference to the way the applicant had categorized the goods in their specification. Rather, it was necessary to ask 'what are the goods as a practical business matter?' The answer to this question depended on how the goods were viewed as articles of commerce.[22] On the facts, Jacob J concluded that the goods were 'electrical shavers', since in business practice they were viewed as a single type of commercial article.

While agreeing with Jacob J that the goods in question were electrical shavers, the Court of Appeal placed more reliance on the way the mark was classified than on the way the goods were viewed as articles of commerce. As Aldous LJ said, 'the words the goods refer to the goods in respect of which the trade mark is registered. Those are the goods which it must be capable of distinguishing and in respect of which the proprietor obtains, on registration, the exclusive right to use the trade mark.'[23] However, Aldous LJ added the caveat that the 'purpose of the subsection is to prevent traders monopolizing shapes of particular goods and that cannot be defeated by the skill of the applicant when selecting the class of goods for which registration is sought'.[24]

When does a shape 'result from' the nature of the goods? The next question to ask is when does the shape *result from* the nature of the goods? It seems that the exclusion will only apply where the designer of a product has no real or effective choice as to the shape that the product can take. This can be seen in *Philips v. Remington,* where an important factor in the Court of Appeal's decision that the shape of the razor did not fall foul of section 3(2)(a) was the fact that there were a number of different ways in which the shape of a three-headed razor could have been designed. As there were a number of shapes other than the one in question that a three-headed electric shaver could have taken, this meant that the shape 'did not result from the nature of the goods themselves' (i.e. electric shavers). As Aldous LJ explained, the reason why the trade mark was not excluded by section 3(2)(a) was that there 'is no one shape, let alone that depicted in the trade mark, which results from the nature of such shavers'.[25] Consequently, it seems that if the applicant can demonstrate there are other shapes of the same goods on the market, no objection under section 3(2)(a) will be sustainable. In *Procter & Gamble v. OHIM,* the CFI held that a waisted bone shape was, in principle, registrable for soaps explaining that the fact that there are other shapes of soap bar in the trade without those features showed that the shape did not result from the nature of the goods.[26]

While it is clear that a shape which is dictated by the nature of the goods will fall foul of section 3(2)(a), it is not yet clear what degree of correlation there must be between the nature of the goods and the resulting shape. It is important to note that, if the exclusion only applied in situations where there is no alternative shape that a product could realistically take, this would greatly limit the ambit of section 3(2)(a). Indeed, as Aldous LJ said in *Philips v. Remington,* it is difficult to envisage shapes which would fall within the scope of the section, 'except those that

---

[21] Ibid; also [1998] *RPC* 283.   [22] Ibid [1998] *RPC* 283, 305.   [23] [1999] *RPC* 809, 820.

[24] Ibid. See also *Procter & Gamble Co. v. OHIM,* Case T–122/99 [2000] 2 *CMLR* 303 (although specification for 'soaps in class 3', goods themselves were 'soap bars').

[25] *Philips v. Remington* [1999] *RPC* 809, 820.   [26] Case T–122/99 [2000] 2 *CMLR* 303.

are produced in nature, such as bananas'.[27] In this overly narrow formulation,[28] it is only in nature that shape and goods have the appropriate causative link. The interpretation of 'nature' as 'biological' stands in contrast to the preferable position of the Registry which, recognizing that 'goods' are culturally constituted artefacts, has tended to focus on whether there is a 'normal' or conventional shape of the goods.[29] At least the shape of manufactured artefacts such as a football or a rugby ball must surely fall within the exception.

2.1.2 Where the shape is necessary to obtain a technical result

The second limitation on the types of shape that can be registered as trade marks is set out in section 3(2)(b)/Article 7(1)(e)(ii) CTMR.[30] These provide that a sign shall not be registered where it consists exclusively of a shape which is necessary to obtain a technical result. In many ways section 3(2)(b) is very similar to section 3(2)(a). In *Philips v. Remington,* the ECJ explained that the rationale for the exclusion was to leave unaffected by trade mark rights 'technical solutions or functional characteristics of a product which a user is likely to seek in the products of competitors'. In turn, the exclusion would ensure that trade marks did not become obstacles 'preventing competitors from freely offering for sale products incorporating such technical solutions or functional characteristics'.[31] The Court also noted that the exclusion would also prevent individuals from using registration 'to acquire or perpetuate exclusive rights relating to technical solutions'.[32] Given this rationale, which the English Court of Appeal subsequently dubbed the 'functionality principle',[33] it seems that the ECJ does not see the concept of 'technical result' as limited to the meaning given to it in patent law. Instead, it interpreted 'technical result' as broadly including any desirable functional aspect of a shape. Consequently, the exclusion should encompass shapes which facilitate convenient storage or transportation of the goods, or which provide the purchaser with other 'convenience features'.

When is a shape 'necessary' to achieve a technical result?   The key issue in relation to section 3(2)(b)/Article 7(1)(e)(ii) is when is a shape *necessary* to achieve a technical result? Ultimately, the impact that the section has upon what may be registrable as a trade mark depends on how this question is answered.

In *Philips v Remington,*[34] the reference arose from an action brought by Philips against its competitor Remington to prevent the latter from selling three-headed rotary shavers. Philips had developed the shaver in 1966, and in 1985 had successfully registered a graphic

[27] *Philips v. Remington* [1999] *RPC* 809, 820. See also *Société de Produits Nestlé SA v. Unilever plc.* [2003] *ETMR* (53) 681, 688 (paras. 14–15) (Jacob J, who seemed to be of the view that section 3(2)(a) is limited to 'naturally occurring shapes rather than artificially created shapes' such as that of VIENNETTA ice cream). The case was settled, so the initial reference (Case C–7/03) was never heard by the ECJ.

[28] See R. Burrell, H. Beverley Smith and A. Coleman, 'Three Dimensional Trade Marks: Should the Directive be Reshaped?' in N. Dawson and A. Firth, *Trade Marks Retrospective: Perspectives on Intellectual Property, Vol. vii* (2000) 139, 165 (describing this as interpreting the exclusion out of existence).

[29] *TMR Work Manual,* ch. 6, s. 8, 174.   [30] TM Dir., Art. 3(1)(e).

[31] *Koninklijke Philips v. Remington,* Case 299/99 [2002] *ECR* I–5475 (para. 78).

[32] Ibid (para. 82).

[33] *Koninklijke Philips v. Remington* [2006] *FSR* (30) 537, para. 36 (CA). 'The restrictions on registration incorporate the functionality principle and govern its application...competition factors explain the restrictions. The purpose of the restrictions is to prevent shape marks from extending trade mark protection beyond an indication of the origin of the goods to conferring on the proprietor a monopoly in the goods themselves. This rationale for the absolute unregistrability of the functional shape of goods exercises a potent influence on the interpretation and application of the statutory provisions.'

[34] *Koninklijke Philips v. Remington,* Case 299/99 [2002] *ECR* I–5475.

representation of the shaver-head as a trade mark.[35] In 1995 Philips brought an action against Remington claiming infringement of this trade mark. Philips argued that because the function that the razor was to perform (*viz.* providing a close and effective shave) could be achieved by shapes other than that shown in the representation, the shape did not fall foul of section 3(2)(b). More generally, Philips argued that 'provided the trade mark owner can show that some other shape will also do the job, their sign will not fall within this exclusion no matter how functional it may be'. That is, if it were possible for the same result to be achieved by a different shape, then the shape in question would not fall within the exclusion.[36] Jacob J found for Remington, and on appeal the Court of Appeal formulated a number of questions on which it required guidance from the ECJ. In particular, the Court asked whether the restriction relating to shapes necessary to achieve a technical result could 'be overcome by establishing that there are other shapes which can obtain the same technical result' or, if not, what test was to be applied.

The ECJ interpreted the exclusion in question as intended to preclude the registration of shapes:

whose essential characteristics perform a technical function, with the result that the exclusivity inherent in the trade mark right would limit the possibility of competitors supplying a product incorporating such a function or at least limit their freedom of choice in regard to the technical solution they wish to adopt.[37]

The ECJ added that the exclusion applies where the essential characteristics of the shape 'perform a technical function and were chosen to fulfil that function'.[38] Finally, the Court stated that the mere existence of other shapes which could achieve the same technical result is not of itself sufficient to overcome this ground for refusal.[39] Given the choice between treating 'necessary' as describing a mandatory relationship between technical result and shape (i.e. that the shape is the only one that could perform the function), and the broader interpretation of 'necessary' as indicative of a causal relationship, the ECJ chose the latter.[40]

While the ECJ in *Philips* made it clear that the mere possibility that more than one shape can achieve a technical function will not render a shape registrable, it provided little guidance as to what evidence is relevant when deciding whether a shape is 'attributable to a technical result?' The inconsistent language used by the Court suggests that subsequent tribunals should form an overall conclusion taking account of a variety of perspectives. In particular: first, whether the shape actually achieves a technical result (a *sine qua non* to the operation of the exception); second, whether the shape was chosen by the designer to do so; third, whether the shape is one of a limited number that a competitor could use to achieve the function.[41] When the ECJ's answers were referred back to the UK Courts the trade mark was held to be invalid in

---

[35] The registration was made under the UK's Trade Marks Act 1938. When this Act was replaced by the Trade Marks Act 1994, the registration became a valid registration under that Act.

[36] As was accepted by the Swedish court in *Ide Line Aktiebolag AG v. Philips Electronics NV* [1997] *ETMR* 377.

[37] Case 299/99 [2002] *ECR* I–5475 (para. 79).   [38] Ibid (para. 80).   [39] Ibid (para. 81).

[40] The jargon is adapted from that of G. Dinwoodie, 'Federalized Functionalism: The Future of Design Protection in the European Union' (1996) 24 *American Intellectual Property Law Association Quarterly Journal* 611. While this clarification is helpful, ascertaining when the ECJ considers a shape to be attributable to a technical result is more difficult. If there are 50 shapes that could conceivably achieve the same technical result, then presumably the exclusion will not come into play: but what if there is a choice of only ten or five, or three?

[41] The Grand Board of Appeal of the OHIM has held that the existence of a prior patent is practically irrefutable evidence that the shape that is the subject of the trade mark is functional: *Lego Juris*, Case R856/2004–G [2007]

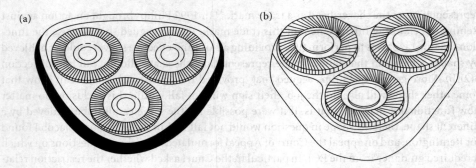

Fig. 36.1 (a) Philips three-headed electric shaver mark at issue in *Philips v. Remington*,
[1998] *RPC* 283 (H.Ct.), [1999] *RPC* 809 (CA), and Case 299/99 [2003] *ECR* I–5475 (ECJ).
(b) The clover-leaf design at issue in *Koninlijke Philips Electronics NV v. Remington
Consumer Products* [2006] *FSR* (30) 537 (CA)
Source: Courtesy of Koninklijke Philips Electronics NV.

the light of section 3(2)(b) of the Act.[42] Unfortunately, there is no reasoned judgment explaining exactly why.

In a subsequent case between Philips and Remington over the shape of a new version of Philips' three-headed electric shaver (see Fig. 36.1b),[43] the relevant shape was a 'clover leaf' and this was also held to be unregistrable.

At first instance, Rimer J reviewed the judgment of the ECJ in the earlier *Philips* case and concluded that, despite some oddities in the language of the judgment,[44] the Court had intended to endorse the views of the English Court of Appeal (which had made the reference). Armed with this insight, Rimer J held first that the ECJ had made a mistake when it repeatedly stated that the question was whether the 'essential *functional* features' were attributable to function. Such statements were tautological, and the question was whether the 'essential features' of the shape were attributable to function. Second, Rimer J took the view that the 'clover-leaf' design was not an essential feature of the shape, but even if it was, that it was attributable to function. In so holding he found that the ECJ had not intended that the question whether a sign was attributable to function should be determined from the subjective viewpoint of the designer. The designer's view would be relevant but not determinative.[45] Third, Rimer J rejected Philips' argument that if aesthetic considerations had also been relevant when designing the faceplate of the shaver the shape was not 'solely' or 'only' attributable to function. Rimer J's findings were approved on appeal. The Court of Appeal emphasized the purpose of the exclusion, drawing heavily from the US idea of 'functionality'. Pragmatically, the Appeal Court said that when applying the exclusion the shape was to be looked at as a whole. Consequently, given that the

---

ETMR (11) 169 (para 40), citing *TrafFix Devices Inc. v. Marketing Displays Inc*, 532 *US* 23 (2001) (US S Ct). The case is on appeal to the CFI, T270/06.

[42] *Koninklijke Philips v. Remington* [2006] *FSR* (30) 537, para. 6 (CA).

[43] Ibid (CA). A picture of the shaver can be seen in the case report.

[44] *Koninklijke Philips v. Remington* [2005] *FSR* (17) 325, 344 (para. 26) (Rimer J referred to a 'lack of uniformity of expression' in a number of 'somewhat repetitious paragraphs').

[45] Ibid, 344 (para. 32). As the report indicates, the Court heard evidence from Mr Nagelkerke who claimed to have modified the design of the clover leaf for aesthetic reasons (para. 54), but there was no evidence from the original designers (para. 127). The Court of Appeal affirmed Rimer J's decision without commenting on that particular passage.

clover leaf was a mere embellishment the judge had been correct to conclude that the overall 'effect or impression' was that the shape was in substance functional. The Court also carefully reviewed the evidence on the functionality of the lower face plate, which it agreed functioned to provide a smooth, effective, and comfortable shave.[46]

2.1.3 Where the shape gives substantial value to the goods

The third restriction placed on the types of shape that may be registered as trade marks is found in section 3(2)(c)/Article 7(1)(e)(iii) CTMR. These provide that a sign shall not be registered where it consists exclusively of a shape which gives substantial value to the goods.[47] The first point to note about the exclusion is that the value attributable to the shape in its operation *as a trade mark* should not be taken into account when considering whether it falls within the scope of section 3(2)(c). As Jacob J said in *Philips v. Remington*,[48] good trade marks add value to goods—that is one of the things they are for. So one must not take this exclusion too literally. This means, for example, that while the ROLLS-ROYCE grille adds value to a Rolls-Royce, it does so primarily because it signifies ROLLS-ROYCE and not because of its inherent shape. As such, it would not fall foul of section 3(2)(c).

Section 3(2)(c) therefore excludes shapes which exclusively add some sort of non-trade mark value to the goods. The question of the type of non-trade mark value that section 3(2)(c) is concerned with was considered by the Court of Appeal in *Philips v. Remington*. In overruling Jacob J on this point, the Court of Appeal said that section 3(2)(c):

> was aimed at preventing a trader from monopolizing by way of a trade mark registration shapes which added a substantial value to the goods over other shapes, e.g. a lampshade, a telephone designed to appeal to the eye. Such designs should be protected as registered designs or the like protection, not by trade mark registration… There may be overlap between [section 3(2)(c)] and [section 3(2)(b)] which excludes shapes necessary to obtain a technical result, but the purpose is different. The latter is intended to exclude functional shapes and the former aesthetic-type shapes. Thus the fact that the technical result of a shape is excellent and therefore the article can command a high price does not mean that it is excluded from registration by subsection (c).[49]

The decisive question is therefore whether the shape performs a trade mark function, or whether the contribution the shape provides (i.e. its value) is limited to aesthetic considerations, such as enhancing the beauty of the product in a way that does not function as a trade mark.[50] This means, for example, that 'goods which are purchased *primarily* because of the eye appeal of the shape—such as the shape of novelty soap, or the shape of an ornament or figurine for those goods—will fall foul of this provision'.[51] A good example of a shape which would give value of this sort to the goods is the shape of the famous lemon squeezer ('The Juicy Salif') designed by Philip Starck, where the squeezer component is suspended between three long legs to give the appearance of a space ship.

---

[46] *Koninklijke Philips v. Remington* [2006] *FSR* (30) 537 (CA).

[47] The section has been described as 'difficult territory': *Re Dualit's Trade Mark Application* [1999] *RPC* 890, 903.

[48] *Philips v. Remington* [1998] *RPC* 283; approved on appeal [1999] *RPC* 809, 822. See also *Julius Sämaan*, note 13 above (para. 100) (Kitchin J).

[49] *Philips v. Remington* [1999] *RPC* 809, 822. Note also a German Supreme Court decision in 2007 to similar effect in relation to the bonnets of BMW cars.

[50] *Nestlé v. Unilever* [2003] *ETMR* (53) 681, 686 (para. 8) (strongly arguable that shape of VIENNETTA ice cream adds aesthetic value to the product).

[51] *TMR Work Manual*, ch. 6, s. 8, 175–6.

One way to test whether a shape gives value to a product is to compare the price of the product made to the relevant shape with the price of an equivalent product which is not made to that shape. Thus, to determine the value of the shape of the COKE bottle, one could compare the price of a can of Coke with the price of a bottle of Coke (discounting the comparative cost of glass and aluminium). Such an approach was taken by the Amsterdam Court of Appeal, where it was held that differences in price between two crackers which were of equivalent taste and cost the same to manufacture could be attributed to the differences in the shape.[52] While the market offers one way of determining the value of the shape, there will be some situations where the courts will need to rely on other techniques to ascertain the value that the shape provides to the goods.

The question whether the value provided by the shape is *substantial* is a question of degree. As Aldous LJ said, this 'requires a comparison . . . to be made between the shape sought to be registered and shapes of equivalent articles. It is only if the shape sought to be registered has, in relative terms, substantial value that it will be excluded from registration'.[53] It seems that in the normal run of things a container will seldom give substantial value to a product. If the position were otherwise, the provision would exclude many shapes even though they operate to indicate source.

3 CAPABLE OF BEING REPRESENTED GRAPHICALLY

The second general hurdle that must be met for a trade mark to be validly registered under section 1(1)/Article 4 is that the sign must be 'capable of being represented graphically'. This requirement was discussed in the previous chapter (at pp. 787–90).

4 CAPACITY TO DISTINGUISH

The third and final hurdle that must be met for a trade mark to be validly registered under section 1(1)/Article 4 is that the sign must be 'capable of distinguishing the goods or services of one undertaking from the goods or services of another'. Corresponding to this, section 3(1)(a) provides that failure to comply with any of the requirements of section 1(1) is one of the absolute grounds under which a sign will not be registered.

Following the passage of the 1994 Act,[54] the British courts spent a great deal of effort trying to define 'capacity to distinguish' in a way that would both give it meaning but avoid it undermining the other substantive requirements relating to distinctiveness (which we examine in the next chapter). In particular, the courts sought to make sense of the inter-relationship between the requirement that a sign be 'capable of distinguishing' and the exclusion in section 3(1)(b) relating to marks which are 'devoid of distinctive character'. The goal was to resolve the seeming conundrum raised by the statute which seemed to presuppose the possibility of a sign

---

[52] *Bacony* [1989] *NJ* 835. See also *Julius Sämaan* [2006] *FSR* (42) 849 (para. 103) (Kitchin J) (comparing price of claimant's tree-shaped air freshener with other fresheners and concluding value of claimant's freshener was primarily attributable to its repute as a trade mark).

[53] *Philips v. Remington* [1999] *RPC* 809, 822.

[54] Bently and Sherman, 1st edn. (2001) pp. 769–73.

which was simultaneously 'capable of distinguishing' and 'devoid of distinctive character'. The judicial efforts produced a series of inconsistent decisions, and impossible tests.[55] Thankfully, in *Philips v. Remington*,[56] the ECJ has made it clear that these efforts were unnecessary.

As already noted, the reference arose from an action brought by Philips against its competitor Remington to prevent the latter from selling three-headed rotary shavers. The Court of Appeal held that the requirement that a sign be 'capable of distinguishing' the goods of one trader from those of another was a preliminary requirement. As such the court needed to consider this matter before examining whether the mark was 'devoid of distinctive character'. On the facts the Court of Appeal held that the three-headed rotary shaver failed the test. This was because the Court considered that a sign needed to have some 'capricious addition' to render it capable of distinguishing. A sign with such a capricious alteration could pass the first step (i.e. be capable of distinguishing), but fail the second (i.e. be devoid of distinctive character). The ECJ held that there was no 'capricious alteration' test in European law.[57] Second, the ECJ made it clear that if a sign was in fact distinctive (either by nature or by use) then it would be treated by definition as 'capable of distinguishing' the goods of one undertaking from those of others.[58] More specifically, 'there is no category of marks which is not excluded from registration by Article 3(1)(b), (c), and (d) and Article 3(3) thereof on the ground that such marks are incapable of distinguishing the goods of the proprietor of the mark from those of other undertakings'.

The ECJ seems to have said that Articles 2/3(1)(a) and 3(1)(b)–(d) of the Directive need to be 'read together'. Each provides flavour to the other. Article 3(1)(a) 'is intended essentially to exclude from registration signs which are not generally capable of being a trade mark'.[59] In this respect it is 'like the rule laid down by Article 3(1)(b), (c), (d)'.[60] The three specific exclusions are elaborations of the basic requirement of capacity to distinguish. If a mark is devoid of distinctive character, it lacks capacity to distinguish; if a sign is descriptive it lacks capacity to distinguish, and so forth. But Article 3(1)(a) does not 'constitute a separate ground for refusing registration in connection with lack of distinctiveness'.[61]

5 THE PROTECTION OF RETAIL SERVICES AS SERVICE MARKS

Service marks, that is, signs which are used in connection with the provision of services, first became registrable in the UK as a result of the Trade Marks (Amendment) Act 1984. Service marks are treated in the same way as trade marks by the 1994 Act. This enables the providers of professional, financial, commercial, or personal services to obtain the same statutory protection for their goodwill as is given to the manufacturers and sellers of goods.

---

[55] In *Dyson v. Registrar of Trade Marks* [2003] *ETMR* (77) 937, 945 (para. 16) Patten J described the problem as having been caused by 'an over-zealous devotion to definition'.

[56] *Koninklijke Philips v. Remington*, Case 299/99 [2002] *ECR* I–5475.

[57] Ibid (paras. 41–46).   [58] Ibid (para. 39).   [59] Ibid (para. 37).

[60] Ibid (para. 38). It has been argued that this decision still leaves room for an understanding of s. 1 as concerned with whether a sign has capacity to distinguish in the abstract, whereas s. 3(1)(b)–(d) concerns whether a sign is distinctive for the particular goods or services for which registration is sought: D. Keeling, 'About Kinetic Watches, Easy Banking and Nappies that Keep A Baby Dry' [2003] *IPQ* 131, 134–6. *Sat. 1 v. OHIM*, Case C–329/02 P [2004] *ECR* I–8317 (AG Jacobs) (para. 16–17).

[61] *Koninklijke Philips v. Remington*, Case 299/99 [2002] *ECR* I–5475 (para. 46).

One question that has arisen in this context is whether a service mark can be protected for 'retail services'. Prior to the Trade Mark Act 1994, the Court of Appeal held in *Re Dee Corporation's Application,*[62] that service marks could not be registered for 'retail services' under the (1984 amendments to the) 1938 Act: a retailer by definition sells goods (rather than services). Although the substantive provisions were largely unchanged in the 1994 Act, and there was nothing explicitly in either the Directive or Regulation to suggest a different policy, the ECJ has now held conclusively that member states must provide for the possibility of registering marks in relation to retail services. In *Praktiker Bau-und Heimwerkermärkte AG,*[63] the applicant had sought to register PRAKTIKER in Germany for 'retail trade in building, home improvement and gardening goods for the do-it-yourself sector'. The Bundespatentgericht referred various questions to the ECJ relating to registration for retail services. The ECJ held that there was nothing in the Directive that required the concept of 'services' to be restrictively defined, and noted that retail trade included the selection of goods, as well as the provision of services 'aimed at inducing the consumer to conclude transactions with the trader rather than a competitor'. In so holding, the Court took into account the fact that registrations for retail services were allowed at the OHIM and in many member states.[64] The Court also held that objections to such registration being of undue breadth could largely be accommodated by judicious application of the 'global assessment' of likelihood on confusion in relation to relative grounds for refusal or infringement. Consequently, a specification would be acceptable in principle if it used general words such as 'bringing together a variety of goods, enabling customers to conveniently view and purchase those goods' as long as the goods or type of goods to which the service related was specified. The UK Office, which had already reacted to OHIM practice by permitting registration,[65] has altered its practice to give effect to the decision of the Court.[66]

---

[62] [1990] *RPC* 159.

[63] Case C–418/02 [2005] *ECR* I–5873; [2006] 3 *CMLR* (29) 830.

[64] *Giacomelli Sport SpA,* R46/1998–2 [2000] *ETMR* 271 (Board of Appeal at the OHIM allowed a registration of a figurative mark for 'Bringing together for the benefit of others, of a variety of goods . . . to enable consumers to view and buy the products' in class 35, which encompasses advertising, business management, business administration, and office functions).

[65] From September 2000, the UK Registry allowed applications related to services where the sector was specified: PAC 13/00, reported *Change of Practice on Retail Services* [2001] *RPC* (2) 33.

[66] PAN 6/05, *Examination and classification practice about retail service* (issued 11 Nov. 2005). See also Communication No 7/05 of the President of the OHIM.

37

ABSOLUTE GROUNDS FOR REFUSAL

CHAPTER CONTENTS

1 INTRODUCTION

In this chapter, we explore what are commonly referred to as the 'absolute' grounds for refusing to register a trade mark. The absolute grounds for refusal are set out in section 3 of the 1994 Act (Article 3 of the Directive and Article 7 of the Regulation). The 'absolute grounds' share two key characteristics. First, with one or two exceptions, the term 'absolute' indicates that the ground for objection relates to the sign itself, rather than the rights of individual third parties. For this reason, absolute grounds for refusal concern matters which can be scrutinized easily by the various offices without reference to third parties.[1] Second, the 'absolute' grounds for refusal are grounds which give effect to a 'public' or 'general' interest (although the public interest underpinning each ground may vary).[2] One consequence of this is that, if a sign is registered that should have been refused on absolute grounds, any person may bring proceedings to have the mark declared invalid.[3]

The absolute grounds for refusal can conveniently be grouped into three general categories. The first is concerned with whether the sign falls within the statutory definition of a trade mark found in sections 1(1) and 3(1)(a) and (2). The second category of grounds, each of which

---

[1] This is the chief contrast with 'relative' grounds, discussed in Ch. 38. An absolute ground cannot, in general, be overcome by demonstrating the 'consent' of the rightholder to registration. For exceptions, relating to state emblems and, possibly, geographical indications, see below pp. 851, 855–6.

[2] *Sat. 1 Satellitenfersehen GmbH v. OHIM,* Case C–329/02 P [2004] *ECR* I–8317, [2005] 1 *CMLR* (57) 1546 (para. 25) ('The general interest to be taken into consideration when examining each of those grounds for refusal may or even must reflect different considerations according to the ground for refusal in question').

[3] TMA s. 47. Lack of distinctiveness is a ground for invalidity. A registered mark may be challenged at any stage by any person, by application to the UK Registrar or before the Cancellation Division at OHIM (CTMR Art. 55), or as a counterclaim to an action based on a national or Community mark (CTMR Arts. 51, 92, and 96).

is contained in section 3(1)(b)–(d), excludes from registrability marks that are non-distinctive, descriptive, and generic. The third and more eclectic category, which covers the absolute grounds for refusal set out in section 3(3)–(6), provides that trade marks shall not be registered if they are contrary to public policy or morality, if they are likely to deceive the public, if they are prohibited by law, or if the application was made in bad faith. Special provisions also exist for specially protected emblems.

We will deal with each of these general categories in turn.

2 SUBJECT MATTER

Section 3(1)(a) provides that a sign which does not satisfy the requirements of a trade mark as set out in section 1(1)(a) will not be registrable. The types of sign that are potentially registrable are further restricted by section 3(2) which provides special rules in relation to the registration of shapes as trade marks. As these topics were dealt with in Chapter 36, it is not necessary to look at them again here.

3 NON-DISTINCTIVE MARKS

The second category of absolute grounds for validity relates to what can be described as non-distinctive, descriptive, or generic marks. More specifically, section 3(1)(b)–(d) and Article 7(1)(b)–(d) of the Regulation provide that the following trade marks shall *not* be registered:[4]

(b) trade marks which are devoid of any distinctive character;

(c) trade marks which consist exclusively of signs or indications which may serve, in trade, to designate the kind, quality, quantity, intended purpose, value, geographical origin, or the time of production of the goods or of the rendering of the service, or other characteristics of the goods or service;

(d) trade marks which consist exclusively of signs or indications which have become customary in the current language or in the bona fide and established practices of the trade.

As each ground represents a separate basis for refusal (or invalidity), to be valid a mark must not fall within any of the three grounds. While each provision has a distinct sphere of operation, they will often be applied cumulatively.[5] That is, a mark will often be rejected on the basis of more than one ground. In many cases the tribunals have said that a mark which is descriptive falls within section 3(1)(c), and as a result, also lacks distinctive character and is

---

[4] This language, taken directly from the Directive, is, in turn, derived from Paris, Art. 6*quinquies* (2). See also TRIPS, Art. 15(2).

[5] *Linde AG, Winward Industries, Rado Watch Co Ltd,* Joined Cases C–53/01 C–54/01 C–55/01, [2003] *ECR* I–3161, [2005] 2 *CMLR* (44) 1073 (paras. 45, 67); *Campina Melkunie BU v. Benelux Merkenbureau*, Case C–265/00 [2004] *ECR* I–1699; [2005] 2 *CMLR* (9) 171 (para. 18); *Merz & Krell GmbH*, Case C–517/99 [2001] *ECR* I–6959; [2002] *ETMR* (21) 231 (para. 35); *DKV Deutsche Krankenversicherung v. OHIM*, Case C–104/00 P [2002] *ECR* I–7561 (each ground for refusal is 'independent of the others, and must be considered separately. That does not preclude the same sign in practice being caught by more than one category') (AG Colomer, para. 40); *Wrigley v. OHIM (Doublemint)* Case C–191/01P [2003] *ECR* I–12447; [2005] 3 *CMLR* 585 (AG Jacobs, para. 53); *Société des Produits Nestlé SA v. Mars UK Ltd* [2003] *ETMR* (101) 1235, 1250 (para. 42) (Mummery LJ) (although the grounds overlap, they are independent grounds and have to be separately examined).

thus excluded under section 3(1)(b). In contrast, a sign which is not descriptive may well lack distinctive character, and thus be excluded under section 3(1)(b) even though it is not excluded under section 3(1)(b).

Sub-sections 3(1)(b)–(d) are all subject to a proviso, namely, that a sign which falls within any of the provisions (i.e. is non-distinctive, descriptive, or generic) is not to be treated as invalid if, as a result of use, it has 'acquired distinctive character'. In other words, the objections in section 3(1)(b)–(d) apply to the 'inherent' characteristics of the sign, and can be overcome if the sign comes to be understood by consumers as in fact communicating that the particular goods or services in relation to which the sign is used come from one particular trade origin. Sometimes this distinction between inherent and acquired characteristics of a sign is likened to the characteristics which an individual has from 'nature' and those they acquire as a result of 'nurture'. A word perceived by consumers as intrinsically empty or meaningless (such as ANDREX or NOXEMA) will be innately distinctive from its 'nature', whereas a descriptive word (DOUBLEMINT for mint chewing gum, or OPTIONS for insurance services), will only acquire 'distinctive character', if at all, if there has been such use as to educate the public that the sign operates to distinguish the goods of one undertaking from those of another.

3.1 GENERAL APPROACH

3.1.1 What is the mark?

In order to decide whether a sign is excluded under section 3(1)(b)–(d) it is first necessary to decide what the sign is. In many ways this is straightforward: we have seen that the sign is that for which registration is sought. This task is made somewhat easier by the fact that the applicant has to submit documentation identifying the mark, and indicating whether protection is sought as a word mark, a figurative mark, a colour mark, or a three-dimensional mark.

3.1.2 The average consumer

In making the necessary predictive assessment, the relevant class from whose perspective the sign must be assessed has been defined as comprising the average consumers of the category of goods.[6] In turn, the relevant consumer has been construed as 'reasonably well-informed and reasonably observant and circumspect'.[7] Although the consumer is assumed to be reasonably observant, the cases make clear that levels of attentiveness vary from sector to sector: the general consumer's level of attentiveness in relation to everyday goods is lower than for expensive goods.[8]

In the case of national marks, the average consumer has the characteristics of a British person: whether marks in a foreign language will be treated as registrable or as descriptive will

[6] The 'average consumer' is a pivotal figure in trade mark law, akin to the 'person skilled in the art' in patent law. For discussion of the historical origins of the 'average consumer', see J. Davis, 'Locating the Average Consumer: His Judicial Origins, Intellectual Influences and Current Role in European Trade Mark Law' (2005) *Intellectual Property Quarterly* 183.

[7] *Linde et al*, note 5 above (para. 41); *Société des Produits Nestle SA v. Mars UK Ltd ('Have a Break')* [2004] *FSR* (2) 16 (para. 23); *Bach Flower Remedies v. Healing Herbs* [2000] *RPC* 513. One issue that may fall to be determined is whether the average consumer is confined to those likely to purchase an article, or those likely to confront the mark: see *Procter & Gamble v. OHIM*, Case C–107/03P (23 Sept 2004) (para. 41) (where the Court held that on the facts the issue was moot because the two categories of person were the same).

[8] Cf. *Henkel KgaA v. OHIM*, Joined Cases C–456/01P and C–457/01P [2004] *ECR* I–5089; *Procter & Gamble v. OHIM*, Joined Cases C–473/01 P and C–474/01 P [2004] *ECR* I–5173 (para. 62).

depend on whether the average consumer is likely to understand the meaning of the sign. In turn this will depend on the extent to which the mark is recognized in its original language, how widely the language is spoken in the United Kingdom, how familiar the word is, and how common it is for foreign words to be used in that trade.[9] Even though this proposition could lead to division in the Internal Market, the ECJ has given its imprimatur in a case where the German word for mattresses—MATRATZEN—had been registered in Spain for mattresses![10] In contrast, Article 7(2) of the Community Trade Marks Regulation provides that the exclusions 'shall apply notwithstanding that the grounds for non-registrability obtain in only part of the Community'. OLUT would thus be unregistrable as a Community mark for alcoholic beverages, given that OLUT means beer in Finnish.[11]

The tribunal must interpret the sign in the application as the notional consumer would. This process of interpretation will take into account so-called normal and fair use, including use on packaging and in advertising. Thus the assessment takes account of the possibility that the mark will normally be used not only in its represented form, but also orally. Consequently the mark will be interpreted in terms of the overall impression it makes on the average consumer—orally, conceptually, and visually. In the past, British tribunals would operate a general rule that a word that was 'phonetically equivalent' to an unregistrable word was itself unregistrable. It seems today that there is no concrete rule. Rather, the Registrar must consider the impression that is produced by the variant aurally and visually, taking account of the goods or services.[12] In situations where purchasers are attentive, and purchase is rarely done orally, a visual variation of a descriptive word (such as KA for cars) may render a sign registrable (even though the sign is phonetically equivalent to a description).[13] However, where the goods are of the sort that are purchased orally, or advertised on the radio or television, mere visual alterations, such as misspellings, of otherwise non-distinctive marks are unlikely to render the sign registrable.

It is important to note in this respect that the sign will normally be viewed as a whole: a sign will not be rejected just because parts of the sign lack distinctiveness or are descriptive or customary in the trade.[14] Nevertheless, consumers may ignore certain elements, which they regard as trivial or insignificant. Equally, consumers may readily expand abbreviated forms into their full unabbreviated form.[15] Another situation where the tribunal will have to assess

---

[9] *IPO, PAN 1/07*—Foreign descriptive use: interpretation of the internet and Registrability of non-English words *(25 May 2007).*

[10] *Matratzen Concord AG v. Hukla Germany SA,* Case C–421/04, [2006] *ECR* I–2303; *House of Donuts International v. OHIM,* Joined Cases T 333–334/04, [2007] *ETMR* (53) 877 (CFI) (DONUTS not lacking distinctiveness in Spain). Contrast the much stricter US position: *Otokoyama Co Ltd v. Wine of Japan Import Inc,* 175 *F. 3d* 266 (2nd Cir 1999).

[11] With the expansion of the Community in 2004 and 2007, the potential for such objections increased. Note, however, that while existing registrations are automatically extended to these countries, absolute grounds for refusal under Art. 7 (or invalidity based on Art. 51) do not operate where such grounds became applicable merely because of the accession of a new member state CTMR Art. 159a (as amended).

[12] *Koninklijke KPN Nederland NV v. Benelux-Merkenbureau,* Case C–363/99 [2004] *ECR* I–1619; [2005] 3 *WLR* 649, [2005] 2 *CMLR* (10) 184 (para. 99); *Campina* Case C–265/00 [2004] *ECR* I–1699 (para. 40).

[13] Trade Mark Registry, *Manual of Trade Mark Practice,* Ch 3, section 26.

[14] *Procter & Gamble Co v. OHIM (Baby Dry),* Case C–383/99 P, [2001] *ECR* I–6251; *Campina,* Case C–265/00 [2004] *ECR* I–1699 (para. 37); *DKV v. OHIM* Case C–104/00 P [2002] *ECR* I–1561 (para. 24); *Procter & Gamble v. OHIM,* Joined Cases C–468/01 P to C–472/01 P [2004] *ECR* I–5141; *Mag Instrument Inc v. OHIM,* Case C–136/02 P, [2004] *ECR* I–9165; *Bio-Id AG v. OHIM,* Case C–37/03P [2005] *ECR* I–7975.

[15] *Bio-Id,* ibid (affirming holding BIO-ID to be devoid of distinctive character, being an abbreviation of biometric identification for software based identification systems).

how the 'reasonably circumspect' consumer interprets a sign is where an applicant combines, shortens, or telescopes two (or more) unregistrable terms. Although consumers tend to interpret signs as a whole rather than dismembering them into their component parts, certain obvious combinations or abbreviations may immediately be translated back into their (non-registrable parts). Thus, EUROLAMB would immediately be interpreted as EUROPEAN LAMB and thus, being descriptive, be unregistrable.

3.1.3 Assessment

Distinctiveness is assessed by the Registrar or OHIM at the time of examination, or in response to observations.[16] Distinctiveness is assessed as of the date of application.[17] Where an application is made and it is held that the sign lacks distinctiveness for certain goods but not others, it should be refused only as regards the goods for which it lacks distinctiveness.[18] In deciding whether a sign is excluded, the tribunal should taken account of all relevant facts and circumstances, including (where pertinent) opinion poll evidence.[19]

Ultimately, the assessment is one of fact. This has at least three consequences. First, care must be taken about making broad generalizations on the basis of previous decisions. It also means that it is not possible to formulate with any precision general rules about whether types of mark will be distinctive. A second consequence of the factual nature of the distinctiveness inquiry is that it is a subject on which different minds may well take different views. In *Doublemint,* Advocate General Jacobs indicated that, in many situations, 'an element of subjective judgment' will be required in order to determine whether a sign is within the exclusions.[20] Third, the factual assessment in each individual case means that evidence of similar registrations at the Registry itself, or that the sign has been regarded as registrable elsewhere, will be of limited value. Although the ECJ has yet to confirm the approach,[21] the Court of First Instance (CFI) and English courts have emphasized that each application must be assessed on its merits by the relevant registry,[22] however much inconsistency this may appear to produce.[23] British courts have gone one step further and said that evidence about 'other

---

[16] TMA s. 37 (examination); s. 38(3) (observations). In the UK absolute objections can be raised in opposition proceedings by any person: TMA s. 38(2).

[17] *eCopy Inc. v. OHIM,* T–247/01 [2002] *ECR* II–5301 (CFI); *BIC SA v. OHIM,* Case T–262/04, [2005] *ECR* II–5959 (CFI, 3d ch) (para. 66); *Imagination Technologies Ltd v. OHIM,* Case T–461/04 [2008] *ETMR* (10) 196 (paras 77–78) (on appeal on this point, Case C–452/07P). Cf. *Henkel v. OHIM,* note 8 above; *Procter & Gamble v. OHIM,* Case C–107/03 P (23 Sept. 2004) (paras. 42–4) where Advocate General Colomer suggested that distinctiveness should be assessed at the dates both of application and of registration, so that a sign distinctive at the filing date should be refused if it has lost its distinctiveness by the date of registration.

[18] TM Dir. Art. 13; CTMR Art. 38(1); *KPN Nederland NV,* Case C–363/99 [2004] *ECR* I–1619 (paras. 112–17).

[19] *KPN Nederland,* ibid (paras. 33–7).

[20] *Wrigley (Doublemint),* note 5 above (paras. 56–7) (AG Jacobs); *Nichols plc v. Registrar of Trade Marks,* Case C–404/02 [2004] *ECR* I–8499 (para. 34) (AG Colomer).

[21] So far, the ECJ has only stated that a decision in respect of the registrability of a particular mark in one member state is irrelevant when another member state is considering registration of the same mark for similar goods: *KPN Nederland NV,* Case C–363/99 [2004] *ECR* I–1619 (para. 43). In *Sat. 1 v. OHIM,* Case C–329/02 P [2004] *ECR* I–8317, [2005] 1 *CMLR* (57) 1546, Advocate General Jacobs (at para. 51) approved the approach of the CFI.

[22] *Sykes Enterprises Inc. v. OHIM (Real People, Real Solutions),* T–130/0 [2002] *ECR* II–5179 (para. 31) (Office is not bound by its own previous decisions); *Streamserve Inc. v. OHIM* T–106/00 [2002] *ECR* II–723 (paras. 66–69); *Metso Paper Automation Oy v. OHIM,* Case T–19/04 [2007] *ETMR* (2) 55 (paras 30–34); *Golf USA, Inc v. OHIM,* Case T–230/05 (6 Mar 2007) (para. 58–64).

[23] For criticism that this fails to respect EU principles of non-discrimination and equal treatment, see D. Keeling, 'About Kinetic Watches, Easy Banking and Nappies that Keep a Baby Dry: A Review of Recent European Case Law on Absolute Grounds For Refusal to Register Trade Marks' [2003] *IPQ* 131, 158–160.

marks on the Register is in principle irrelevant when considering a trade mark tendered for registration'.[24]

With these general principles in mind, we now turn to examine in detail the exclusions relating to signs which are intrinsically or innately lacking distinctiveness, are descriptive, or customary. After looking at these three heads, we then turn to consider how signs can be shown to have acquired distinctive character through use?

3.2 DEVOID OF DISTINCTIVE CHARACTER

Section 3(1)(b)/Article 7(1)(b) CTMR provide that trade marks which are devoid of any distinctive character shall not be registered. The primary function of this exclusion is to exclude marks which do not even perform the 'distinguishing function'.[25] As the ECJ stated in *Linde, Winward & Rado*, distinctive character means 'for all trade marks, that the mark must be capable of identifying the product as originating from a particular undertaking, and thus distinguishing it from other undertakings'.[26] The focus is therefore on how the trade mark would be perceived by the relevant public, which consists of average consumers of the goods or services in question.[27] The focus of the tribunal is on the anticipated performance of the mark in relation to the goods or services for which it is proposed to be used and guess what the relevant class of consumers would understand from the sign. To avoid rejection under section 3(1)(b) the tribunal must conclude that the sign will be perceived as an indication that goods or services come from a single source, in other words, as a 'badge of trade origin'. Consumers will readily recognize words, such as NOXEMA (for shaving cream) or APPLE (for sound recordings), which have no relation to the goods, as indicating origin, and equally will see logos as having the same function. It is more difficult to predict whether consumers would see colours, shapes, slogans, and the like as indicating origin.

Article 3(1)(b) excludes those signs which the average consumer 'does not identify as reliably indicating the commercial origin of the product'.[28] Consequently, the provision excludes from registration those signs which would not be perceived to communicate any message (because they would just be treated as part of the goods, or the appearance thereof),[29] and those which while perceived as conveying information are not perceived as indicating information as to trade source (for example, where the sign is seen as a product number or perhaps as a slogan urging a person to do something). According to the ECJ,[30] 'it suffices that the trade mark should enable the relevant public to identify the origin of the goods or services protected thereby and to distinguish them from those of other undertakings'. There is no requirement that the sign be inventive, imaginative, unusual, or linguistically or artistically creative, or that it differ from those 'which from the point of view of the relevant public are commonly used in trade in connection with the presentation of goods or services or in respect of which they could

---

[24] *British Sugar v. James Robertson & Sons* [1996] *RPC* 281, 305; *AD2000 Trade Mark* [1997] *RPC* 168.

[25] *Bio-ID,* Case C–37/03 P [2005] *ECR* I–7975 (paras. 61–63) (CFI ruling on CTMR Art. 7(1)(b) had wrongly taken into account the public interest relevant under Article 7(1)(c)). In the second edition we argued that this public interest was also relevant to Article 7(1)(b). See Bently & Sherman (2nd edn.) p. 816. If a mark which is descriptive under Art. 7(1)(c) is necessarily devoid of distinctive character under article 7(1)(b) (on which, see *Campina,* Case C–265/00 [2004] *ECR* I–1699 (para. 19)), is it logical to say that the public interest underpinning Article 7(1)(c) is not relevant under Article 7(1)(b)?

[26] *Linde et al,* Joined Cases C–53/01, C–54/01 and C–55/01 [2003] *ECR* I–3161; [2005] 2 *CMLR* (44) 1073 (para. 47).

[27] *KPN Nederland NV,* Case C–363/99 [2004] *ECR* I–1619 (para. 34).

[28] *Nichols v. Registrar,* Case C–404/02 [2004] *ECR* I–8499 (para. 43).

[29] *Libertel Groep BV v. Benelux-Merkenbureau,* Case C–104/01 [2003] *ETMR* (63) 807; [2004] *FSR* (4) 65.

[30] *Sat. 1 v. OHIM* Case C–329/02 P [2004] *ECR* I–8317, [2005] 1 *CMLR* (57) 1546 (para. 41).

be used in that way'.[31] Signs are excluded only if they are 'devoid' of distinctive character: the tribunals have indicated that a minimal degree of distinctive character suffices for the absolute ground not to apply.[32]

Although the courts have repeatedly indicated that the same tests are applicable to all marks, whether words, pictures, shapes, or colours, it is useful to look at the way the tribunals deal with these different types of sign. This is because 'the perception of the relevant section of the public is not necessarily the same for exotic marks, such as colours or shapes, as for words or figurative devices which bear no relation to the appearance of the goods.'[33] Moreover, in its application to marks such as colours, section 3(1)(b) has been interpreted as requiring the tribunal to consider not just how the sign would be perceived by the average consumer of the goods, but also whether giving a single trader a monopoly over the sign would confer an unjustified competitive advantage on the applicant. The courts, however, have indicated that such considerations of 'public' or 'general interest' are not relevant in the case of words, names, slogans or shapes.[34] How far these kinds of consideration extend to other sorts of sign is controversial.[35]

3.2.1 Simple signs: letters, numbers, and grammatical signs

In most cases single letters, numbers, and grammatical signs will be treated as 'devoid of distinctive character'.[36] This is because consumers would not be able to assume that such signs indicated one particular source. Even in these cases, however, the question of whether the sign lacks distinctive character must be assessed on the facts. The Registry and the courts should consider carefully how relevant consumers of the particular goods or services would react to the specific sign. More specifically, the tribunal should consider whether the sign would be taken to indicate catalogue numbers, sizes, model numbers, date of production, etc., as opposed to being understood to be a trade mark.[37] The same is true of combinations, though in general the longer the combination, the more likely it would be thought to be a trade mark.

3.2.2 Colour marks

Simple colour marks are likely to be treated as devoid of distinctive character.[38] This is because in the case of colours the sign forms part of 'the look of the goods', and consumers are not in

---

[31] Ibid (para. 36).

[32] *Sat. 1 Satellitenfersehen GmbH v. OHIM*, T 323/00 [2002] *ECR* II–2839 (para. 35) (not discussed in appeal); *Henkel KgaA v. OHIM*, Case T–393/02, [2004] *ECR* II–4115 (CFI 4th Ch) (para. 42); *Nestlé v. Mars* [2003] *ETMR* (101) 1235 (para. 23) ('if the mark for which registration is sought is distinctive in the relevant sense *to any extent* then its registration is not precluded by s. 3(1)(b)'). The OHIM has said if there is 1 or 2 per cent distinctive character, the sign is not 'devoid'. In fact, the Boards of Appeal at the OHIM seems to have a narrower understanding of 'devoid' than the British Registry and courts.

[33] *Viking-Umwelttechnik GmbH v. OHIM*, T–16/00 [2002] *ECR* II–3715 (para. 27).

[34] *Henkel v. OHIM*, Joined Cases C–456/01P and C–457/01P [2004] *ECR* I–5089; *Procter & Gamble v. OHIM*, Joined Cases C–473/01P and C–474/01P [2004] *ECR* I–5173 (para. 78); *Sat. 1 v. OHIM*, Case C–329/02 P [2004] *ECR* I–8317, [2005] 1 *CMLR* (57) 1546 (para. 36); *Nichols v. Registrar*, Case C–404/02 [2004] *ECR* I–8499 (paras. 42–6) (AG Colomer). The issue appears now to be before the ECJ: *Bild.T-Online.de AG & Co. KG v. President of the German Patent- und Markenamt*, Case C–39/08 (pending).

[35] *In Re Bongrain's Application* [2005] *RPC* (14) 306 (Jacob LJ, para. 24) (refusing to accept that the 'depletion' public interest is confined to colour marks).

[36] *IPO, PAN 10/06—Letter and numeral marks (25 May 2006).*

[37] *Caterham Car Sales & Coachworks's Application/Numeral 7*, R 63/1999–3 [2000] *ETMR* 14, 19 (use of '7' on car would be taken to be model number). Cf. *Crucible Materials Co/440V*, R136/2000–3 (18 Nov. 2002) (OHIM BA) (440V registrable for metals).

[38] *Libertel*, Case C–104/01 [2003] *ETMR* (63) 807; [2004] *FSR* (4) 65.

the habit of assuming the origin of goods merely from the colour of packaging. Consequently, the ECJ in *Libertel* observed that '[a] colour *per se* is not normally inherently capable of distinguishing the goods of a particular undertaking'.[39] In addition, the ECJ has recognized that there is a strong public interest in favour of keeping colours free. This is because the number of colours actually available is limited and so a small number of trade mark registrations could exhaust the entire range of the colours available (an understanding sometimes referred to as 'colour depletion theory'). Exclusive trade mark rights over any such colour would potentially create 'an unjustified competitive advantage for a single trader'.[40] Consequently, in the case of a colour *per se*, 'distinctiveness without any prior use is inconceivable save in exceptional circumstances, and particularly where the number of goods or services for which the mark is claimed is very restricted and the relevant market very specific'.[41] Prior to the judgment in *Libertel*, the CFI had allowed registration of a shade of orange in relation to 'technical and business consultancy services in the area of plant cultivation, in particular the seed sector' in class 42.[42] This exceptional decision may be justified given the relatively narrow scope of the specification to which the mark related.

3.2.3 Shapes

Another area where the exclusion relating to marks that are 'devoid of distinctive character' may have an important impact is in relation to shape marks. Although the courts have repeatedly stated that the same test is applicable to shape marks as it applied to word or device marks, because consumer perception of such marks is different, the result of applying the tests will not necessarily be the same.[43] This is because the relevant consumers are unlikely to think of a shape as communicating at all, let alone being indicative of a particular trader's goods.[44] Consequently, the vast majority of such applications are refused.

In the case of shapes, an assessment of whether the shape is registrable requires an appraisal of whether the shape 'significantly departs from the norm or customs of the sector and thereby fulfils its essential original function'.[45] In turn this requires, first, an assessment as to whether there is anything unusual or idiosyncratic about the shape such that the relevant consumer would notice it and remember it; and then, if there is such individuality, an assessment as to whether the consumer would think of the shape as indicative of source, rather than being merely functional or decorative. The results of this assessment may change as practices change,

---

[39] Ibid, (para. 65).   [40] Ibid (paras. 54–5).   [41] Ibid (para. 66).

[42] *KWS Saat AG v. OHIM*, T–173/00 [2002] *ECR* II 3843(CFI) (rejecting registration of a shade of orange for installations for drying seeds, agricultural, horticultural, and forestry products, etc. but allowed in relation to 'technical and business consultancy services in the area of plant cultivation, in particular the seed sector' in class 42. The CFI took the view that 'a colour does not attach to the service itself, services by nature having no colour, nor does it confer any substantive value'. The ECJ affirmed the decision to reject the colour mark for the various goods, Case 447/02P [2004] *ECR* I–10107).

[43] *Linde et al*, Joined Cases C–53/01, C–54/01 and C–55/01 [2003] *ECR* I–3161; [2005] 2 *CMLR* (44) 1073 (paras. 42, 46, 49); *Glaverbel v. OHIM (Patterned Glass)*, Case C–445/02P [2004] *ECR* I–6267; *KWS Saat*, ibid, Case C–447/02P (para. 78).

[44] See e.g. *Henkel* C–218/01 [2004] *ECR* I–1725 (para. 52); ibid, Joined Cases C–456/01 P and C–457/01 P [2004] *ECR* I–5089 (para.38); *August Storck KG v. OHIM*, Case C–24/05 P [2006] *ECR* I–5677, (para. 25). Whether the public distinguishes goods by reference to shapes is a question of fact: the public, apparently, are used to identifying vehicles by reference to the design of the grille: *Daimler Chrysler Corp v. OHIM* Case T–128/01, [2003] *ECR* II–701 para. 42. Where the onus lies is somewhat unclear: it seems that the Office may 'infer' that consumers do not normally see certain sorts of sign as an indication of origin and in such cases 'it is for the applicant for a trade mark to show that consumers' habits on the relevant market are different': *Unilever NV v. OHIM*, T–194/01 [2003] ECR II–383 (para. 48).

[45] *Henkel*, C–218/01 [2004] *ECR* I–1725 (para. 49); *Henkel v. OHIM*, Joined Cases C–456/01 P and C–457/01 P [2004] *ECR* I–5089 (para. 39); *Mag Instrument*, Case C–136/02 P [2004] *ECR* I–9165. (para. 32) ('the more closely the shape…resembles the shape most likely to be taken by the product, the greater the likelihood of the shape being devoid of distinctive character').

Fig. 37.1 Werther's Originals
Source: Courtesy of August Storck KG

and with them consumer perceptions and expectations. Moreover, they may vary from sector to sector: a particular shape could be perceived as a trade mark in one field, but not in another.

The test of 'significant departure' is designed to ensure that consumers of the goods can perceive the difference between the shape in question and other shapes.[46] Basic geometric shapes will not be noticed by consumers and so will not perform the distinguishing function. Nor will shapes that are not readily differentiable from those ordinarily used in trade.[47] In one case, the ECJ affirmed the CFI decision that the brown colour and shape of WERTHER'S ORIGINALS (see Fig. 37.1) was not a significant departure from those commonly used. The Court said the mark comprised 'a combination of presentational features which come naturally to mind and which are typical of the goods in question, that it is a variation of certain basic shapes commonly used in the confectionery sector'. Given that the alleged differences are not 'readily perceptible', it agreed that the shape in question cannot be sufficiently distinguished from other shapes commonly used for sweets and that it does not enable the relevant public to distinguish immediately and with certainty the appellant's sweets from those of another commercial origin.[48]

Even if a shape is a significant departure from those ordinarily used in the sector, it does not follow that it is registrable. The shape must be one that the average consumer would view as indicating trade origin.[49] If average consumers would see a shape as just there to 'do a job',[50]

---

[46] A 'significant departure' is different, and it seems a lower threshold, from 'a marked difference': *August Storck*, Case C–24/05 P [2006] *ECR* I–5677 (para. 28).

[47] In *Procter & Gamble v. OHIM*, T–63/01 [2002] *ECR* II–5255 *(Soap Bar Shape)*, a bar shaped as a rectangular parallelepiped with rounded edges for soap was not registrable. The CFI explained that the claimed shape was only a slight variation on the shapes commonly used for soaps and so would not enable the relevant public 'to distinguish *immediately and with certainty* the applicant's soap from those having a different trade origin' (para. 43).

[48] *August Storck*, Case C–24/05 P [2006] *ECR* I–5677 (para. 25). See also *Wim de Waele v. OHIM*, Case T–15/05 (31 May 2006) (twisted shape of sausage not unusual, so lacked distinctiveness).

[49] *Bongrain's Application* [2005] *RPC* (14) 306 (CA); *Betafence Ltd. v. Registrar of Trade Marks* [2005] *EWHC* 1353 (Ch.) (Deputy Judge Floyd QC).

[50] In *Philips v. Remington* [1999] *RPC* 809, 819 the Court of Appeal said that the primary meaning of the three-headed rotary shaver was 'a three-headed rotary shaver of the design shown' and there was no evidence that it had any other meaning.

Fig. 37.2 The MAG-LITE® flashlight
Source: Courtesy of Mag Instruments Inc.

or as merely decorative, they are less likely to think of the shape as indicating source.[51] So, the Court of Appeal has refused registration for a floral shape, comprising six lobes, for cheese (Saint Albray);[52] the ECJ affirmed that the attractive, well-designed cylindrical shape of a MAG-LITE® torch would not function as an indicator of origin (Fig. 37.2);[53] and neither would an abstract design comprising countless tiny strokes for application to the surface of glass products (showers, windows, etc.) (Fig. 37.3).[54] In the cheese case, Jacob LJ explained that an average consumer would 'be astonished to be told that one of the shapes was a trade mark. Consumers do not expect to eat trade marks or part of them.'[55] In the *Mag* case, the ECJ explained that 'the fact that goods benefit from a high quality of design does not necessarily mean that a mark consisting of the three-dimensional shape of those goods enables *ab initio* those goods to be distinguished from those of other undertakings'.[56] In a rare counter-example, the CFI allowed registration concerned the distinctive shape of the grille of a jeep, explaining that consumers had come to understand car grilles as signs of origin, so the applicant's grille could serve as a trade mark (see Fig. 37.4).[57] More recently, the CFI annulled a decision of the examiner that the shape of a speaker was devoid of distinctive character: in the view of the CFI the shape was different from the customary shapes of loudspeakers and was characterized by specific and arbitrary features that would retain the attention of the average consumer.[58]

---

[51] *Procter & Gamble (Soap Bar Shape),* T–63/01 [2002] *ECR* II–5255 (even if the sign was sufficiently idiosyncratic to 'hold the consumer's attention' that would not of itself make the shape possess distinctive character. This is because, according to the CFI, the shape would be 'primarily interpreted as a functional feature making the soap easier to grip or as an aesthetic finish'.)

[52] *Bongrain's Application* [2005] *RPC* (14) 306 (CA). A picture of the cheese can be seen in the case report.

[53] *Mag Instrument,* Case C–136/02 P [2004] *ECR* I–9165. However, the three-dimensional shape of the MAG-LITE® flashlight was awarded a CTM registration on the ground of 'acquired distinctiveness'.

[54] *Glaverbel (Patterned Glass),* Case C–445/02 P [2004] *ECR* I–6267.

[55] *Bongrain's Application* [2005] *RPC* (14) 306 para. 29.

[56] *Mag Instrument* [2005] *RPC* (14) 306 (para. 68).

[57] *DaimlerChrysler (Grille)* Case T–128/01 [2003] *ECR* II–701.

[58] *Bang & Olufsen v. OHIM,* Case T–460/05 (10 Oct 2007) (CFI, 3rd Ch).

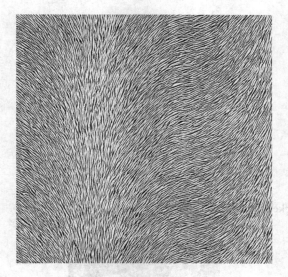

Fig. 37.3 Glaverbel's 'Chinchilla' design for glass
Source: Courtesy of AGC Flatglass.

Fig. 37.4 The jeep design, held to possess distinctive character in *Chrysler Corp v. OHIM*

3.2.4 Get-up and trade dress

Although it is not possible to say that the overall packaging of a product ('get-up' or 'trade dress') can never be inherently distinctive,[59] in most cases these matters will be devoid of distinctive character.[60] This is for the simple reason that (as with shapes) average consumers do not treat the majority of packaging or get-up as indicating source. Rather, they treat packaging as comprising protective material which has decorative, attractive, or eye-catching features. In part, this is a matter of current social practice—consumers have long been invited to focus on the literature on packaging as indicating source: as a result, the overall look of the get-up is ignored, at least in this regard.

In *Proctor & Gamble v. Registrar of Trade Marks,* Robert Walker LJ confirmed the rejection by the Registrar of applications for registration in Class 3 of a three-dimensional bottle bearing a label for floor-cleaning products. The hearing officer described the application as having

[59] According to Robert Walker LJ, 'get-up' is 'a convenient (though imprecise) expression for the characteristic style of a product which may be produced by the use of colouring, typography, materials, finishing and all other elements—apart from the text itself—that go into modern commercial design'. *Procter & Gamble v. Registrar of Trade Marks* [1999] *RPC* 673, 676.

[60] Examining authorities should also assess whether packaging is descriptive and thus contravenes section 3(1)(c): *Henkel,* C–218/01 [2004] *ECR* I–1725 (para. 44) (ECJ).

Fig. 37.5 Long-necked bottle with lemon in spout

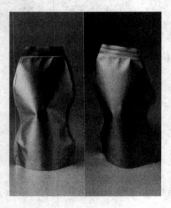

Fig. 37.6 Deutsche 'Si-Si' pouches
Source: Courtesy of Grünecker, Kinkeldey, Stockmair & Schwannhäusser.

three component parts, namely, the shape of the bottle, the pattern on the label, and the colours applied to both. Having concluded that none of the three components was individually distinctive, the hearing officer found that the combination was lacking in distinctiveness.[61] Affirming the Registry's conclusion, Robert Walker LJ emphasized that, in order to overcome an objection based on section 3(1)(b), the applicant's trade mark must *readily* distinguish the applicant's product, and that where a close examination was required to identify differences the get-up was not distinctive.

The ECJ and the CFI have been faced with a steady trickle of appeals from refusals of the OHIM to register get-up on the ground that it is lacking in distinctiveness. In one case, the ECJ affirmed that the CFI had not erred in law when it found that the shape of a long-necked bottle with a piece of lemon placed in the spout was not distinctive of beer (see Fig. 37.5). The CFI had found that this was a common way of presenting beer for consumption and, given that consumers paid little attention, the combination would not be viewed as

---

[61] *Procter & Gamble v. Registrar* [1999] *RPC* 673, 680 *per* Robert Walker LJ. See also *S.M. Jaleel's Trade Mark Application* [2000] *RPC* 471 (Appointed Person assessing shape of 'Chubby' bottle as 'visually unsurprising' and therefore lacking inherent distinctiveness).

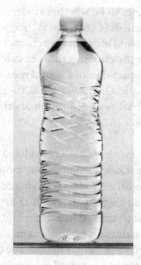

Fig. 37.7 The bottle design in *Nestlé Waters France v. OHIM*
Source: Courtesy of Nestlé Waters.

indicating source.[62] In another case, the ECJ affirmed that no error existed in the CFI's decision that stand-up pouches for packaging fruit juices and fruit drinks were not distinctive (see figure 37.6).[63]

In contrast, in *Nestlé Waters France v. OHIM (Bottle shape)*, the CFI allowed the registration of the shape of a bottle for non-alcoholic beverages.[64] (See Fig. 37.7.) The CFI took the view that, because of repeated attempts over a number of years by various traders to educate consumers into treating bottle shapes as trade marks, the average consumer is now 'quite capable of perceiving the shape of the packaging of the goods as an indication of commercial origin' if the shape possessed characteristics which are sufficient to hold their attention. The CFI reversed the OHIM's view that the bottle was commonplace, finding that the whole formed a design 'which is striking and easy to remember'. It was a combination capable of holding the public's attention and distinguishing the goods from those with a different commercial origin. As a result, the mark had a minimum degree of distinctiveness and fell outside Article 7(1)(b) of the Regulation (see figure 37.7).

Similarly, in *Henkel KgaA v. OHIM*,[65] the CFI overturned the OHIM BA's finding that a container resembling the shape of an upturned pear with flattened sides and coloured white and transparent, lacked distinctive character for washing liquids and detergents. The CFI found that the combination of elements had a 'truly individual character', commenting on its flat character and crystal shape.

---

[62] *Eurocermex SA v. OHIM,* Case C–286/04P[2005] *ECR* I–5797 (Corona beer) affirming Case T–399/02 [2004] *ECR* II–1391. Though not the original image submitted by Eurocermex, this photograph gives an idea of what Eurocermex was trying to register.

[63] *Deutsche Sisi-Werke GmbH & Co Betriebs KG v. OHIM,* Case C–173/04P [2006] *ECR* I–551.

[64] T–305/02 [2003] *ECR* II–5207 (para. 40).

[65] Case T–393/02 [2004] *ECR* II–4115. A picture of the container can be seen in the case report.

The touchstone, therefore, appears to be whether traders in the sector have educated consumers to view packaging as indicative of commercial origin. If this has been achieved, then whether particular packaging is devoid of distinctive character is likely to turn on whether the get-up is sufficiently noticeable in the circumstances to catch the attention of consumers. If this is not the case, as where a compact disc of a sound recording is suddenly sold in unusual packaging, the position is problematic. On the one hand, the packaging will be memorable. On the other, it is unlikely to be perceived as an indication of origin.

3.2.5 Names and signatures

Traditionally under UK law, surnames have been considered non-distinctive and thus unregistrable.[66] In part the decision to exclude surnames was motivated by the inconvenience that the grant of a right would cause to other traders who shared the same name. The courts also stressed that third parties who made legitimate use of their names ought not to be forced to rely on a defence equivalent to that contained in section 11(2).[67] However, under the 1994 Act there is no *a priori* exclusion of surnames, or personal names, and the question of registrability is determined by the same standards as for other marks. The question in any given case will be whether the average consumer of the goods would assume that the name operates to indicate one particular manufacturer or supplier. In making this assessment, the ECJ has indicated in *Nichols's Trade Mark Application* that an examining authority tribunal may not use *general* criteria, such as predetermined rules about how common the name is (for example, a rule that if the name appears more than 500 times in the London telephone directory it should not be registered).[68] Moreover, the ECJ was clear that the 'unfair advantage' obtained by the first person to register a name over other traders who might wish to use it, is irrelevant.[69] However, commonness may be relevant to the consumer's likely appreciation of the *specific* name as an indication of origin of the *specific* goods.[70]

The removal of the traditional rules for determining registrability of surnames has left something of a void which has not yet been filled with much guidance from subsequent decisions. However, the Appointed Person has provided some useful insights in *Oska's Ltd's Trade Mark Application*.[71] In the course of opposition proceedings it was necessary to assess the distinctiveness of the opponent's earlier mark, MORGAN for clothing. Following the guidance of the ECJ, Richard Arnold QC took into consideration the commonness of the name 'Morgan', the frequency with which names were used in the clothing trade, and the number of traders in the clothing field, and concluded that the average consumer would regard the surname as devoid of distinctive character. Before the average consumer would consider a common surname in the clothing trade as an indication of source, he or she would expect the addition of a forename (as with Paul Smith or Ted Baker).

One peculiarity should be noted here: the full name of a famous personality may well be devoid of distinctive character. In *Elvis Presley Trade Mark*,[72] the Court of Appeal refused to

---

[66] *Elvis Presley Trade Marks* [1997] *RPC* 543, 558.

[67] *Cadbury Bros's Appn.* (1915) 32 *RPC* 9, 12.

[68] *Nichols v. Registrar,* Case C–404/02 [2004] *ECR* I–8499, [2005] 1 *WLR* 1418 (para. 25–6). The registration of the mark Nichols for vending machines was subsequently confirmed on 26 May 2006: TM 2241893.

[69] Ibid [2005] 1 *WLR* 1418 (para. 31). The ECJ referred to the defence contained in Art. 6(1)(a).

[70] Advocate-General Colomer, para. 46; *Oska's Ltd's Trade Mark Application* [2005] *RPC* (20) 525 (paras 27–8) *per* Richard Arnold QC.

[71] Ibid.

[72] *Elvis Presley Trade Marks* [1999] *RPC* 567 and [1997] *RPC* 543, 558. See also *Corsair Toiletries's Appn. (Opposition by Jane Austen Memorial Trust)* [1999] *ETMR* 1038 (JANE AUSTEN lacked distinctiveness for

allow registration of ELVIS and ELVIS PRESLEY for toiletries, perfumes, cosmetics, and soaps. It had been argued by the applicants that, as a result of changes in public awareness about character merchandising, consumers seeing the name ELVIS would assume that the product to which it was attached was 'genuine'. That is, they would assume that the goods originated from Elvis's estate or from someone with rights granted by the estate. Laddie J was not willing to accept that this was an accurate portrayal of how the general public thought about the way the names of celebrities were used, and the Court of Appeal affirmed that view: people treat a name as part of the product which they are purchasing not as a feature that distinguishes the goods of one trader from those of another. For consumers, the goods are memorabilia or mementos of which the name is an essential component, rather than being a different class of consumable commercial goods which people purchased because they came from a specific trader.[73]

In those cases where a name itself lacks distinctiveness, registration may nevertheless be obtained where an application is for the name in conjunction with a device or represented in a special or particular manner so that the whole is distinctive. Perhaps the most obvious example of this is where the name takes the form of a person's signature. Signatures were specifically treated as registrable under the 1938 Act because they were seen as 'a substantially unique and frequently highly distorted way of writing the author's name. They are in a sense a private graphic tied to one person'. Under the 1994 Act a 'signature' may be registrable even if it is not written in a distinctive graphic style—a simple cursive rendition of Elvis's signature 'Elvis A. Presley' would probably be distinctive.[74] This may be the case even if the signature is not authentic.[75]

3.2.6 Slogans

As we will see, slogans will often be unregistrable because they are descriptive.[76] However, even if the slogan is not exclusively descriptive, it may lack distinctive character. In *Nestlé v. Mars UK*,[77] the Court of Appeal was asked to consider the inherent registrability of HAVE A BREAK for confectionery. An attempt to register the same sign had failed under the 1938 Act,[78] and an application under the new law met with the same result. The Court of Appeal agreed with the approach and conclusions of the hearing officer, that the slogan would readily be understood as 'an origin-neutral invitation to consume a snack...whether the use is in an advertisement or on the packaging of the product'. The CFI rejected REAL PEOPLE, REAL SOLUTIONS for technical support services in the computer industry on the grounds that the slogan would be perceived merely as promotional, and SAFTETY 1ST for bicycles, car seats, and children's play equipment on the basis that this would be perceived as a general slogan that safety is a priority, not as an

---

toiletries); *Executrices of the Estate of Diana, Princess of Wales's Application* [2001] *ETMR* (25) 254 (Mr A James) (DIANA, PRINCESS OF WALES devoid of distinctive character).

[73] *Presley*, ibid, 585. Although the case was decided under the 1938 Act the reasoning, relating to an issue of fact, seems applicable under the 1994 Act.

[74] Ibid. *In re Applications by the Estate of the Late Diana, Princess of Wales* (25 Jan. 2002) (Mr. A. James) (Diana signature registrable, signatures being 'a unique sign of authenticity').

[75] *Elvis Presley Trade Marks*, ibid, 586 (though note that it was presumed to be authentic at 576; and was refused on relative grounds, 587).

[76] So, for example, VOM URSPRUNG HER VOLLKOMMEN was refused by OHIM for beer on the grounds that its meaning (perfect at the point of origin) was descriptive and the CFI affirmed: *RheinfelsQuellen H. Hovelmann GmbH & Co. KG v. OHIM,* Case T–28/06 (6 Nov 2007).

[77] *Nestlé v. Mars* [2003] *ETMR* (101) 1235 (CA).

[78] *Have a Break Trade Mark* [1993] *RPC* 217.

indication of origin.[79] In contrast, the CFI indicated that OHIM had been wrong to refuse registration of DAS PRINZIP DER BEQUEMLICHKEIT (meaning 'the principle of comfort') for tools, furniture, and a vehicle on the grounds that it was unimaginative and unsurprising.[80] The ECJ affirmed, but also criticized the CFI's suggestion that a slogan would only be excluded under Article 7(1)(b) of the CTMR if it was a term 'commonly used in business communications and, in particular, in advertising'. Rather, the Court affirmed that the sole question was whether the slogan would be perceived as an indication of trade origin. However, importantly, it noted that, while the average consumer might not regard an advertising slogan as an indication of origin, there were no specific requirements that slogans had to meet.[81]

3.3 DESCRIPTIVE MARKS

The second category of marks excluded from registration relates to what may be called 'descriptive marks'. More specifically, section 3(1)(c)/Article 7(1)(c) CTMR excludes from registration trade marks which consist *exclusively* of signs or indications which may serve, in trade, to designate the (i) kind, quality, quantity, (ii) intended purpose, (iii) value, (iv) geographical origin, (v) the time of production of the goods or of the rendering of the service, or (vi) other characteristics of the goods or service.

3.3.1 Function of section 3(1)(c): the requirement for Availability

Whereas section 3(1)(b) is largely aimed at ensuring that the only signs which are registered are ones that could be perceived as trade marks section 3(1)(c) has an additional purpose (which we can call the 'protective function'), namely, to minimize the negative impact that the grant of trade marks may have upon traders working in the same or related fields. If trade marks law permitted one trader to obtain property protection over descriptive or generic marks it could have a dramatic impact upon other traders. For example, if one greengrocer was given trade mark protection over the word ORANGE or FRUIT (for oranges), it would interfere with the ability of other greengrocers to convey information about their goods or services. That is, where there are a limited number of possible ways of describing or presenting one's goods, the provision of legal monopolies over such signs might enable one trader to keep other traders completely out of the market.[82] The ECJ calls this 'the requirement of availability'.[83]

The first occasion on which the European Court of Justice considered Article 3(1)(c) of the Trade Marks Directive was in *Windsurfing Chiemsee v. Attenberger*.[84] In this case, the question before the ECJ was whether the word CHIEMSEE, the name of a lake in Bavaria, could be a trade mark for sports clothing or whether such a mark fell within Article 3(1)(c) of the Directive. More specifically, the ECJ was asked to consider whether the application of Article 3(1)(c)

---

[79] *Sykes Enterprises (Real People, Real Solutions)*, T–130/0 [2002] *ECR* II–5179 (paras. 28, 30) (not descriptive, but devoid of distinctive character); *Dorel Juvenile Group, Inc. v. OHIM,* Case T–88/06 (24 Jan 2008) (on appeal, Case C–131/088).

[80] *OHIM v. Erpo Möbelwerk GmbH,* Case C–64/02 P [2004] *ECR* I–10031. UK Practice is explained in PAN 1/06 *Slogans* (5 Jan 2006).

[81] Ibid, para. 35 (the authorities may take account of the fact that average consumers are not in the habit of making assumptions about the origin of products on the basis of such slogans.)

[82] Although the protective function is usually talked about in terms of the needs or desires of other traders, it can equally be expressed in terms of a trader's rights to free commercial expression: see P.N. Leval, 'Trademark: Champion of Free Speech', 27 *Columbia Journal of Law & Arts* 187 (2004).

[83] *Adidas AG & ors v. Marca Mode CV & ors,* Case C–102/07 (10 Apr 2008) (para. 23); (A.G. Colomer, 16 Jan 2008, paras 27–45).

[84] Joined Cases C–108/97 and C–109/97 [1999] *ECR* I–2779.

depends on whether there is a 'real, current, or serious need to leave the sign or indication free'. In answering this question, the Court acknowledged that one of the aims of Article 3(1)(c) of the Directive was to protect the public interest by keeping descriptive signs or indications free for use by all traders.[85] The Court observed:

Article 3(1)(c) of the Directive pursues an aim which is in the public interest, namely that descriptive signs or indications relating to the categories of goods or services in respect of which registration is applied for may be freely used by all, including as collective marks or as part of complex or graphic marks. Article 3(1)(c) therefore prevents such signs and indications from being reserved to one undertaking alone because they have been registered as trade marks. [It continued:] As regards, more particularly, signs or indications which may serve to designate the geographical origin of the categories of goods in relation to which registration of the mark is applied for, especially geographical names, it is in the public interest that they remain available, not least because they may be an indication of the quality and other characteristics of the categories of goods concerned, and may also, in various ways influence consumer tastes by, for instance, associating the goods with a place that may give rise to a favourable response.

The view that section 3(1)(c) must be understood in the light of this public interest has, with one notorious exception,[86] been reiterated on many occasions.[87]

3.3.2 General

To avoid objection under section 3(1)(c) the applicant will need to establish that the sign is not used (and is unlikely to be used in the future) as a description of the characteristics of the goods or services. Consequently, invented words such as MARANTZ (for hi-fi equipment), or PEPSI (for drinks), are likely to be registrable, because it is unlikely that traders could use them descriptively or that consumers would perceive them to be anything other than an indication of origin. In contrast, TREAT would be understood as describing the fact that the product was especially good, and EUROLAMB would be understood as usable in describing the fact that the product was a particular type of meat from a particular place. In between these extremes is a huge array of signs, not wholly descriptive but partly suggestive of a product quality: in such cases the tribunal will have to make a judgment as to how consumers will interpret the sign.

3.3.3 Exclusively

Trade marks are only excluded from registration by section 3(1)(c) if they consist *exclusively* of signs which characterize the goods and services. This means that the mark *as a whole* must be descriptive for it to be excluded. The converse of this is that, if it can be shown that part of a mark is non-descriptive, then it will fall outside the remit of the section, as long as that part is not *de minimis*. Thus, marks that are made up of descriptive and non-descriptive matter may be protected. In the famous *Baby Dry* case (where the ECJ held the words BABY DRY not exclusively descriptive of diapers) the ECJ suggested that 'any perceptible difference' between the applicant's sign and a descriptive term or terms is 'apt to confer distinctive character

---

85 [1999] *ECR* I–2779, I–2824 (para. 30).

86 *Procter & Gamble v. OHIM (Baby Dry)*, Case C–383/99 P [2001] *ECR* I–6251, [2002] *ETMR* (3) 22.

87 *Wrigley (Doublemint)*, Case C–191/01 P [2003] *ECR* I–12447 (AG); *Linde et al*, Joined Cases C–53/01, C–54/01 and C–55/01 [2003] *ECR* I–3161; [2005] 2 *CMLR* (44) 1073 (para. 73); *Campina*, Case C–265/00 [2004] *ECR* I–1699 (paras. 34–6); *KPN Nederland NV*, Case C–363/99 [2004] *ECR* I–1619; *Deutsche SiSi*, Case C–173/04 P [2006] *ECR* I–551 (para. 62); *OHIM v. Celltech R&D Ltd*, Case C–273/05 P, [2007] *ETMR* (52) 843 (para. 75). In *Golf USA*, Case T–230/05 (6 Mar. 2007) (paras 33–34), the CFI indicated that a mark should not be registered if this would 'chill' use of its descriptive components by competitors.

on the combination enabling it to be registered as a trade mark'. In *Campina Melkunie BV v. Benelux-Merkenbureau,* the ECJ stated that the mere combination of elements which are each descriptive will not normally create a neologism which is registrable. Rather there must be some 'unusual variation, in particular to syntax or meaning' which produces an impression on the relevant consumer of something which is 'sufficiently far removed from that produced by the mere combination of meanings lent by the elements of which it is composed, with the result that the word is more than the sum of its parts'.[88] The application of this test would leave the words BABY DRY as registrable for nappies, while rendering BIO-MILD and DOUBLEMINT unregistrable for natural yoghurt and chewing gum (respectively). In the former the words BABY and DRY each alluded to the function of diapers, but because of 'the syntactically unusual juxtaposition' it was not a familiar expression for designating nappies nor describing their essential characteristics. The phrase was a 'lexical invention, bestowing distinctive power on the mark so formed'.[89] In the latter, the subtraction of the space left the sign as no more than a designation of the characteristic of its being mint-flavoured.[90]

3.3.4 Multiple meanings

The requirement of 'exclusivity' does not mean that a sign is only excluded if all possible meanings of a sign fall within the exclusion. Consider, for example, a word with two or more meanings such as PEN (referring to a writing implement, a female swan, and a small enclosure for animals). In assessing whether PEN would be registrable for writing implements, the tribunal should not be content simply to find that there is one signification—that of a female swan—which is not excluded. If that were the case, then the existence of a single obscure meaning would render the mark not exclusively descriptive (and hence registrable). In *Doublemint,* the CFI indicated that a sign is only descriptive if it enables the public 'immediately and without further reflection to detect a description of the characteristics of the relevant goods':[91] it thus held that the ambiguity in the types of mintiness (spearmint, peppermint) and the notion of doubling (the types or strength) rendered DOUBLEMINT registrable. On appeal, the ECJ rejected that approach, stating that a sign is excluded from registration if 'at least one of its possible meanings designates a characteristic of the goods concerned'.[92] Following the reasoning of the Advocate General, the test in Article 7(1)(c) is not whether the sign is 'exclusively descriptive' but rather whether the trade mark consists exclusively of signs or indications which may have a descriptive capacity. The mere existence of another, non-descriptive meaning, is irrelevant.

---

[88] *Campina,* Case C–265/00 [2004] *ECR* I–1699; see also *KPN Nederland NV,* Case C–363/99 [2004] *ECR* I–1619.

[89] *Websphere Trade Mark* [2004] *FSR* (39) 796 (para. 50) (WEBSPHERE more than sum of parts 'web' and 'sphere' for computer programs). *Easynet Group plc v. Easygroup IP Licensing Ltd* [2007] *RPC* (6) 107 (Mann J) (denying there are special rules for juxtapositions and treating the question as purely one of deciding whether the mark 'as a whole' was descriptive or devoid of distinctive character. Consequently refusing to overturn examiner's decision to allow 'easy.com' for various goods and services including books, financial services and hairdressing.) On the latter, cf. *Jupitermedia Corp. v. OHIM,* R 211/2006–4 (11 Dec 2006) (internet.com unregistrable).

[90] The CFI has held that PURE DIGITAL, PAPERLAB and GOLF USA were insufficiently different from their unregistrable component parts: *Imagination Technologies,* Case T–461/04 [2008] *ETMR* (10) 196 (para. 33–36, 55–59) (the components being 'pure' and 'digital' for cameras and video equipment) (on appeal, Case C–452/07P); *Metso Paper Automation,* Case T–19/04 [2007] *ETMR* (2) 55 (paras 30–34) ('paper' and 'laboratory' for equipment for testing paper); *Golf USA,* Case T–230/05 (6 Mar. 2007) (para. 50) (the juxtaposition of GOLF and USA for sports clothes did not conform to linguistic rules, it equally did not involve linguistic error and was not more than the sum of its parts).

[91] According to the Advocate General in *Wrigley (Doublemint),* Case C–191/01 P [2003] *ECR* I–12447: [2003] *ETMR* (88) 1068 (para. 41).

[92] *Streamserve,* T–106/00 [2002] *ECR* II–723 (para. 42).

3.3.5 'May serve': the element of futurity

Article 3(1)(c) of the Directive excludes from registration trade marks which consist of signs or indications *which may serve*, in trade, to designate the characteristics of the goods or service. The requirement that the tribunal should consider not just the current use of a term, but also its future associations, was recognized by the ECJ in *Windsurfing*, where the Court said that the relevant tribunal was to ask whether there was 'an association in the mind of the relevant class of persons between the geographic name and the category of goods in question', or where there was none at the relevant date (i.e. the date of application) 'whether it is reasonable to assume that such an association may be established in the future'.[93] In contrast, the ECJ in *Baby Dry* formulated a test based around descriptions in 'current parlance'. Any doubt cast by this on the *Windsurfing* approach has been removed by the *Doublemint* decision. There the ECJ stated that for the exclusion in Article 7(1)(c) of the CTMR to operate it is not necessary for the sign in question to actually be in use as a description of the goods or their characteristics: it is sufficient 'that such signs could be used for such purposes'.[94] The test therefore has an element of 'futurity' about it.

3.3.6 Broad specifications and disclaimers

A final general point worth noting is that, when considering whether a sign is excluded, the tribunal should consider it in relation to each and every category of goods included in the specification. In many cases, a sign will be excluded only in relation to some categories of goods or services and not others. However, an application will be refused registration if it is descriptive of the characteristics of any of the goods or services in a specific category of the specification. So if an application relates to ORANGE for 'beverages', it will be refused registration on the grounds that it is descriptive (of orange-flavoured drinks) even though it would not be descriptive of apple-flavoured drinks.[95] In some cases, an applicant may be able to avoid such an objection by amending the application to 'apple drinks' but not, it seems, to 'beverages (other than those made from, coloured, or flavoured orange)'.

3.3.7 Any Characteristic of the Goods or Services

In the *Postkantoor* case the ECJ has indicated that a sign falls within Article 3(1)(c) if it is capable of being used to designate the characteristics of goods or services, even if the characteristic in question is of peripheral significance to the goods in question. Thus STINKY might be unregistrable for weedkillers, even though the most important characteristic of a weedkiller is whether it is effective in killing weeds.[96] It certainly should not be understood as presenting a purely abstract test, but rather should be considered in the context of the existing market and foreseeable developments therein.

---

[93] *Windsurfing*, Joined Cases C–108/97 and C–109/97 [1999] *ECR* I–2779; *Sat.1 v. OHIM (Sat.2)*, Case C–329/02 P [2004] *ECR* I–8317, [2005] 1 *CMLR* (57) 1546 (para. 37) ('or in connection with which there exists, at the very least, concrete evidence justifying the conclusion that they are capable of being used in that manner').

[94] *Wrigley (Doublemint)*, Case C–191/01 P [2003] *ECR* I–12447 (para. 32) (ECJ).

[95] *DaimlerChrysler AG v. OHIM* T–355/00 [2003] *ETMR* (87) 1050 (where TELE AID was found descriptive of repair services for automobiles even though that category could include some situations not involving distance; but finding the words not descriptive of electrical devices for transferring data because use of such devices in remote assistance was one of many possible areas of use).

[96] *KPN Nederland NV*, Case C–363/99 [2004] *ECR* I–1619 (para. 102).

3.3.8 Must the Association Be 'Specific and Direct'?

The CFI requires that for a sign to be descriptive the association between sign and goods/
services be 'sufficiently specific and direct to show that that sign enables the relevant public to
identify those goods and services immediately'.[97] The effect of this is that vague references to
the character of the goods, via laudatory epithets, may not be excluded under this provision
(though they might nevertheless be under section 3(1)(b) or 3(1)(d)). So, for example, the CFI
treated ULTRAPLUS as registrable for ovenware, and the English Court of Appeal held that
E.S.B. (an abbreviation of EXTRA STRONG BITTER) was protectable for bitter beer.[98] The test
has not yet received the endorsement of the European Court of Justice, and in some ways,
seems at odds with the general approach taken by the Court in *Doublemint* and *Postkantoor*.
In *Doublemint*, in particular, Advocate General Jacobs had offered three guidelines as to when
marks might be descriptive, one of which related to the 'specificity' and the second the 'immediacy' of the meaning conveyed by the sign in relation to the goods.[99] However, the ECJ gave
no hint that it found them to be useful, and (as we noted in the previous paragraph) in fact
explicitly rejected the third (the significance of the characteristic in the purchases of the goods/
services) in *Postkantoor*. Moreover, the Appointed Person, Geoffrey Hobbs QC, has said he has
'misgivings' about such a narrow interpretation. In the view of the Appointed Person, signs
such as BEST EVER or SERIOUSLY GOOD should be regarded as excluded descriptions.[100]

3.3.9 Marks that are not Words

Although section 3(1)(c) is most frequently applied to word marks, there is no reason why it
should not also be applied to pictures, shapes, colours, and other exotic marks. In joined cases
Linde AG, Winward Industries & Rado Watch Co Ltd,[101] the applicants sought to register three-
dimensional marks comprising the shape of a forklift truck, a torch, and a watch. The ECJ held
that Article 3(1)(c) of the Directive was equally applicable to shape marks. Although the Court
did not provide any examples, two obvious ones are the bone shape of BONIO dog biscuits,

---

[97] For example, *DKV Krankenversicherung AG v. OHIM* (Eurohealth), Case T–359/99 [2001] *ECR* II–1645
(paras 35 & 36); *DaimlerChrysler*, T–355/00 [2003] *ETMR* (87) 1050: [2002] *IP & T* 928 (Tele Aid) (para. 28);
Deutsche Post Euro Express GmbH v. OHIM, Case T–334/03 [2006] *ETMR* (52) 653 (para. 25); *PTV Planung
Transport Verkehr AG v. OHIM*, Case T–302/03 (10 Oct 2006) (para. 40); *Golf USA*, Case T–230/05 (6 Mar. 2007)
(para. 28); *Imagination Technologies*, note 17 above; *Hovelmann*, Case T–28/06 (6 Nov. 2007) (para. 31).

[98] *Dart Industries Inc v. OHIM*, T–360/00 [2002] *ECR* II–3867 (UltraPlus) (para. 27) ('when an undertaking
extols, indirectly and in an abstract manner, the excellence of its products by way of a sign such as "UltraPlus",
yet without directly and immediately informing the consumer of one of the qualities or specific characteristics
of the ovenware, it is a case of evocation and not designation'); *West (Eastenders) v. Fuller Smith & Turner* [2003]
FSR (44) 816 (though the case was based on an application of *Baby Dry* and may need reviewing in the light of
Doublemint).

[99] *Wrigley (Doublemint)*, Case C–191/01 P [2003] *ECR* I–12447 (AG paras. 61ff) First, the 'more factual and
objective' the way in which a term relates to a product, service, or one of its characteristics, the more likely it is
to be unregistrable; the 'more imaginative and subjective', the more likely to be registrable. Second, the more
immediately the meaning is perceived, the more likely it is to be unregistrable. Here the contrast is between
terms which are ordinary, definite, and down-to-earth and those that require the skills of a cryptic-crossword
enthusiast to detect any connection. Third, the tribunal should take into account the significance of the characteristic in relation to the product (or service). He contrasted characteristics which were essential or central to a
product, as flavour would be for chewing gum, with 'purely incidental or arbitrary' characteristics (for example
the shape or colour of chewing gum). If a designation related to the former, it would be unregistrable, if the latter
the case for refusing registration would be weaker.

[100] *In re Interactive Intelligence Inc's Application*, Case O/325/07 (30 Oct 2007) (holding that DELIBERATELY
INNOVATIVE for computer programs was not within section 3(1)(c) but was excluded by section 3(1)(b).)

[101] *Linde et al*, Joined Cases C–53/01, C–54/01 and C–55/01 [2003] *ECR* I–3161; [2005] 2 *CMLR* (44) 1073.

and the plastic lemon shape used by Reckitt's for their JIF lemon juice (See Fig. 32.1, p. 731). In one case where the descriptiveness of a shape was contested, the Court held that the shape of a pine tree was not inherently descriptive of pine-scented air freshener.[102]

3.3.10 Excluded significations

With these general points in mind, we now turn to look at the categories of descriptive mark excluded by section 3(1)(c).

(i) *Kind, quality, or quantity.* The first group of marks excluded from registrability are those which consist exclusively of signs which may serve to designate the 'kind, quality, or quantity' of goods and services. Undoubtedly, the greatest problem faced by a tribunal in this context is that of distinguishing between unregistrable terms or descriptions, and registrable allusions or suggestions. The CFI has recently affirmed OHIM findings that BASICS is descriptive of paint,[103] GOLF USA of sports clothing,[104] MAP&GUIDE of computer software,[105] TEK (the French and Italian word for teak) of metal shelves,[106] but that EUROPREMIUM is not descriptive of packaging.[107]

(ii) *Intended purpose.* A mark which describes what the product does, suggests what the consumer is to do with the product, or outlines what happens when the product is consumed will not be registrable. Consequently, for example, PAPERLAB was held descriptive of the intended purpose of 'computer equipment and measuring installations for surveying and testing of paper'.[108]

(iii) *Value.* Trade marks which consist exclusively of signs that refer to the value of the goods or services will not be registrable. The reason for this is that consumers are unlikely to treat references to value as indications of origin. The provision also ensures that other traders are free to use common words and expressions to refer to things such as price and value. On this basis, signs such as CHEAP, ECONOMY, PREMIUM, or BEST BUY would lack inherent distinctiveness, but could of course acquire distinctiveness through use (as with BUDGET for car-hire services.)

(iv) *Geographical origin.* While trade mark law has long been reluctant to grant protection to signs that consist of geographical names and places,[109] not every sign that happens also to be the name of a stream, village, lake, mountain, or other geographical reference will be unregistrable. The precise application of the exclusion depends on careful consideration of what the average consumers of the goods or services would be likely to understand from their naming. In *Windsurfing Chiemsee*, the question was whether the word CHIEMSEE, the largest lake in Bavaria, could be a trade mark for sports clothing or whether such a mark fell within Article 3(1)(c) of the Directive.[110] The ECJ said that the tribunal must assess whether a

---

[102] *Julius Sämaan Ltd v. Tetrosyl Ltd* [2006] *FSR* (42) 849 (paras. 39–40) (Kitchin J).

[103] *Colart/Americas Inc v. OHIM*, Case T–164/06 (12 Sep 2007).

[104] *Golf USA*, Case T–230/05 (6 Mar. 2007).   [105] *PTV Planung*, Case T–302/03 (10 Oct. 2006).

[106] *Tegometall International AG v. OHIM*, Case T–458/05 (20 Nov 2007) (since they could be given the appearance of teak).

[107] *Deutsche Post Euro Express*, Case T–334/03 [2006] *ETMR* (52) 653 (para. 25). The case relies heavily on the discredited parts of *Baby-Dry*.

[108] *Metso Paper Automation*, Case T–19/04 [2007] *ETMR* (2) 55.

[109] As Lord Simonds LC said, a manufacturer 'is not to claim for his own a territory, whether country, county, or town, which may in the future if it is not now, be the seat of manufacture of goods similar to his own': *Yorkshire Copper Work's Trade Mark Application* (1954) 71 *RPC* 150, 154.

[110] Joined Cases C–108/97 and C–109/97 [1999] *ECR* I–2779.

geographical name designates a place which is currently associated in the mind of the relevant class of persons with the category of goods concerned, or whether it is reasonable to assume that such an association may be established in the future.[111] As the ECJ explained, the exclusion does not necessarily preclude the registration of geographical names which are unknown to the relevant class of persons—or at least unknown as the designation of a geographical location—or of names in respect of which, because of the type of place they designate (say, a mountain or lake), such persons are unlikely to believe that the category of goods concerned originates there.[112]

If there is an established connection between the place and the products in question—as with Cuba for cigars, Sheffield for steel, Frankfurt for financial services, or Silicon Valley for computers[113]—registration will normally be refused. In the *Windsurfing Chiemsee* case, the ECJ observed that the connection was not necessarily confined to a belief that the goods were *manufactured* in a particular place but 'might depend on other ties, such as the fact that the goods were conceived and designed in the geographical location concerned'.[114] For example, an application to register SAVILE ROW for spectacle frames was refused because of the proximity that spectacles had to the goods for which Savile Row in London is famous (namely, tailors' services), both being fashion items.[115]

One key factor in deciding whether a sign of geographical origin should be excluded is the size of the place, since this affects how consumers are likely to understand the sign (and, in turn, whether other traders are likely to want to use it).[116] The larger the place, the more likely it is that another trader would wish to use the name. Hence the reluctance to register EUROLAMB for meat,[117] or NORDIC for buildings and building materials,[118] and the willingness to register TOTTENHAM for various goods (all relating to Tottenham Hotspur Football Club).[119]

Where no connection exists between place and the products in issue, such as with TENERIFE for boiler plates, MONTE ROSA for cigarettes, SWEDISH FORMULA for cosmetics, the signs will be registrable.[120] Even the names of sizeable places may be registrable if there is no realistic connection with the goods concerned: an example that has often been given is that of NORTH POLE for bananas.[121]

(v) The time of production of the goods or the time of rendering of the services. Marks such as 24 HOURS (for restaurant services), SUNDAY (for newspapers) or SUMMERTIME for travel agency services would be inherently unregistrable as descriptive of the time of production or rendering of the goods or services.

(vi) Other characteristics. The final part of section 3(1)(c) excludes signs which exclusively serve to designate 'other characteristics' of the goods or service.[122] In *OHIM v. Zapf Creation*, Advocate General Jacobs advised the ECJ to annul the CFI's finding that NEW-BORN BABY was not excluded from registration for toys and accessories for dolls under Article 7(1)(c) of the

[111] Ibid, 2824–5 (paras. 29–31).   [112] Ibid, 2825 (para. 33).
[113] In the US, this is referred to as the 'goods/place association.'
[114] Joined Cases C–108/97 and C–109/97 [1999] *ECR* I–2779, 2826 (para. 36).
[115] *Savile Row Trade Mark* [1998] RPC 155.
[116] See *Manual of Trade Mark Practice*, ch. 3, s. 35.
[117] *Eurolamb Trade Mark* [1997] RPC 279.
[118] *Nordic Sauna Ltd's Trade Mark Application* [2002] ETMR (18) 210 (Thorley QC).
[119] *Tottenham Trade Mark* (6 Jan. 2003) (Appointed Person, Prof. Annand).
[120] *Crosfield* (1909) 26 RPC 837, 856; *Procter & Gamble/Swedish Formula* R 85/98–2 [1999] ETMR 559.
[121] *British Sugar v. Robertson* [1996] RPC 281; *Yorkshire Copper* (1954) 71 RPC 150, 154, 156.
[122] This is not included in Paris, Art. 6*quinquies*(B)(2), and thus may fall to be construed *ejusdem generis*.

Regulation.[123] While the Advocate General agreed that NEW-BORN BABY was not a description of toys, he considered that the word-combination was unregistrable because it was a reference to the 'characteristics' of the goods, namely that the toys represented or looked like new-born babies.[124] In *Linkin Park LLC's Application*,[125] the Appointed Person held that LINKIN PARK, the name of a pop band, was unregistrable for posters, because the term was descriptive of posters of the band (which consumers would doubtless refer to as 'Linkin Park posters'). He rejected an argument that 'other characteristics' is confined to the 'measurable properties' rather than the 'information content' of the goods. Finally, in *Score Draw Ltd. v. Finch*,[126] Mann J. held that the 'CBD' device was so associated with the Brazilian football team that it could be said to designate the characteristics of goods bearing the device—Brazilian football shirts, boots etc.

3.4 CUSTOMARY AND GENERIC MARKS

Section 3(1)(d)/Article 7(1)(d) CTMR provide that 'trade marks which consist *exclusively* of signs or indications which have become customary in the current language or in the bona fide and established practices of the trade' shall not be registrable.[127] Although it has been stated by the ECJ that the reason for this exclusion is that such signs are 'incapable of distinguishing' the goods or services of one undertaking from those of another,[128] it should be noted that the section is especially concerned with the languages and practices 'of the trade'. In the view of Advocates-General Colomer and Jacobs, the so-called 'requirement of availability'/'protective function' also underpins this exclusion: signs which are customary in the trade are ones which other traders should be free to use.[129] However, in contrast to the operation of the protective function under section 3(1)(c), the terms of section 3(1)(d) refer to the meaning that has developed by the time of registration. Consequently, the possibility of the sign becoming a designation in the future is not relevant.

While the scope of the section has yet to be fully explored, it seems that it will cover so-called 'generic' marks. A mark, particularly a name mark, is generic if, even though when it was first adopted it was distinctive, over time it has come to designate a genus or type of product rather than a particular product originating from a particular source. Well-known examples include LINOLEUM, YO-YO, ASPIRIN, and CELLOPHANE. One of the features of a generic mark is that it is no longer capable of distinguishing the goods or services of different traders. Where a word

---

[123] Case C–498/01 P [2004] *ECR* I–11349 (AG).

[124] It is notable that he considered that this was an essential characteristics of the goods (a contrast with the ECJ decision in *Postkantoor*, which indicated that the commercial significance of a characteristic was irrelevant when deciding whether it was excluded).

[125] O/035/05 [2006] *ETMR* (74) 1017 (Appointed Person, Arnold QC) (para. 44).

[126] [2007] *FSR* (20) 508. The Court had already found that the device was devoid of distinctive character.

[127] The terms of this category are not dissimilar to those of TMA s. 46 on revocation (on which see below at pp. 907–9), though the differences are worthy of note. This ground covers not merely names but all marks, and applies where the mark is customary in the 'current language' (which arguably may not be confined to trade). For the view that there are two exclusions in section 3(1)(d), one relating to customary language and another to custom in the bona fide practices of the trade, see *Stash Trade Mark* BL O 281/04 (para. 30) (Appointed Person, Prof. Annand). Customary usage must relate to usage in the UK: Case O/348/99 reported in (2000) *CIPAJ* 34.

[128] See *Merz & Krell,* Case C–517/99 [2001] *ECR* I–6959.

[129] *Nichols v. Registrar,* Case C–404/02 [2004] *ECR* I–8499 (AG para. 43); *Sat. 1 v. OHIM,* Case C–329/02 P [2004] *ECR* I–8317, [2005] 1 *CMLR* (57) 1546, (AG para. 21–23). In the United States, these interests are regarded as over-riding so that a sign that is generic is unable to become a trade mark: *Abercrombie & Fitch Co. v. Hunting World Inc,* 537 *F2d* 4 (2nd Cir. 1976).

comes to describe a class of products, it can no longer be relied upon to separate the products in the class from each other. In *Alcon Inc v OHIM,* the ECJ held that the CFI had not erred in law when it found that BSS was unregistrable for sterile solutions for ophthalmic surgery. The CFI had found that ophthalmologists and ophthalmic surgeons practising in the EU would have understood BSS as an abbreviation for 'buffered saline solution': scientific dictionaries and articles used the abbreviation and many companies marketed products under designations containing BSS. The ECJ held that there was no error in deciding that the relevant public (for assessing whether the sign was customary) was the specialist medical public, nor in its assessment of the facts.

Quite what is covered by section 3(1)(d) beyond 'generic' marks is less than clear. In *Merz & Krell,*[130] the German Registry had rejected an application to register BRAVO for writing implements and the Bundespatentsgericht referred a question to the ECJ on the scope of Article 3(1)(d) of the Directive. Essentially, it wanted to know whether in the case of terms, like BRAVO, (which were used purely as terms of praise, or as incitements to purchase, or in advertising), there was a requirement that before they fell within Article 3(1)(d) they had to be understood by the trade *as descriptions of specific goods and services.* The ECJ answered that the application of the provision needed to be considered in relation to the mark and goods or services concerned.[131] However, the exclusion was not confined to terms which *described* the properties or characteristics of the goods or services covered by them: the exclusion covered signs which 'designate' the characteristics of the goods or services. The ECJ failed, however, to elaborate on the distinction between a description and a designation. It seems that designation involves a looser association with the goods or services than description.[132] The ECJ also said that, while the term need not describe the goods (as under Article 3(1)(c)), the mere use of the term in advertising did not of itself indicate that the term 'designated' the goods concerned.[133]

Section 3(1)(d) may occasionally exclude pictorial marks. In *RFU & Nike v. Cotton Traders,* a registration by the Rugby Football Union of an image of a rose for clothing was held to be invalid. Evidence of sales of shirts bearing a rose crest by undertakings not associated with the RFU indicated that it was customary to associate the rose with the England rugby team. Consequently, the sign was customary and not distinctive of the goods of the RFU.[134]

3.5 USED MARKS: ACQUIRED DISTINCTIVENESS

So far in our discussions of section 3(1)(b)–(d), we have been concerned with whether marks are inherently registrable. That is, we have been looking at marks in their 'natural' or unused

---

[130] Case C–517/99 [2001] *ECR* I–6959 (paras. 36–40).   [131] Ibid, (para. 29).

[132] At AG paras 48–50, Advocate General Colomer drew a distinction between Art. 3(1)(c), which he saw as concerned with 'description' by *direct* reference to characteristics, and Art. 3(1)(d) which was not so confined and did not specify the degree of association that must exist between the sign and the goods/services. The Advocate General, in fact, had suggested how such a conclusion would play out on the facts. In his view, Bravo—a mere expression of enthusiasm—would be registrable for typewriters but not for sports clothing or services, because in the sporting field the tern is 'habitually used' and, in bullfighting, it even refers to a characteristic of a fighting bull.

[133] Prior to *Bravo*, the OHIM excluded laudatory words, such as 'best', 'perfect', 'supreme', or 'superfine' under Art. 7(1)(d) on the basis that they are customary in the trade.

[134] [2002] *ETMR* (76) 861, 876 (Lloyd J). But in *Score Draw v. Finch* [2007] *FSR* (20) 508 (para. 45), Mann J said that the use of yellow and green or the CBD device on Brazilian football shirts was not a matter of trade custom but one of commercial necessity, and thus fell outside section 3(1)(d), though registration was invalidated under section 3(1)(b) and (c).)

state. In this section we turn to look at the ways in which an inherently unregistrable mark can become registrable through use.

As we mentioned earlier, while a mark may be inherently unregistrable because it is non-distinctive, descriptive, or generic, it is possible for it become registrable through use. As the proviso to section 3 under the 1994 Act states, 'a trade mark shall not be refused registration…if, before the date of application for registration, it has in fact acquired a distinctive character as a result of the use made of it'. Similarly, section 47(1) provides that a mark which is wrongly entered into the Register (because it lacks inherent distinctiveness) shall not be declared to be invalid where the mark has acquired distinctiveness after registration. The result of these provisions is that, even if a mark is inherently lacking indistinctiveness, it is now possible to register the mark if it does *in fact* become distinctive.

Consequently, the only question that needs to be asked where a mark has been used is: has the mark in fact acquired a distinctive character?[135] The inquiry in relation to used marks is exclusively concerned with customer perception (i.e. the 'distinguishing function'): the 'protective function' (the needs of other traders) is irrelevant.[136] As a result, consumer recognition becomes the litmus test for whether a mark is registrable.[137] The primary goal is to minimize consumer confusion by preventing other traders from using a similar mark. To succeed in a claim that a mark has become registrable through use, an applicant must be able to show that, irrespective of how the mark was perceived in its natural state, it now operates as a trade mark. That is, an applicant must be able to show that the primary significance of the word or sign indicates a source rather than, for example, merely describing or praising the product. The sign must have acquired 'secondary meaning'. In *Windsurfing*,[138] the ECJ explained that an unregistrable name (in that case a geographical one) 'may be registered as a trade mark if, following the use which has been made of it, it has come to identify the product in respect of which registration is applied for as originating from a particular undertaking and thus to distinguish that product from goods of other undertakings'. In effect, the trader must be able to show that they have appropriated the word and given it a new meaning. In this sense all that the law is doing is recognizing what has already happened in practice.[139]

3.5.1 Displacement of the primary meaning

While the various authorities make it clear that to be registrable a sign must have become distinctive, there is less guidance as to the nature of the relationship between the old and new meanings. At the most extreme some authorities seem to suggest that the new trade mark

[135] Note that it is not necessary to know the identity of the source, only that the product or service comes from a single source: see, e.g. *Messiah From Scratch Trade Mark* [2000] *RPC* 44, 51 (para. 30) (Appointed Person, Thorley QC). This is sometimes termed the 'anonymous source doctrine'.

[136] *Windsurfing*, Joined Cases C–108/97 and C–109/97 [1999] *ECR* I–2779, 2829 (para. 48); *Audi Ag v. OHIM*, T–16/02 (3 Dec. 2003) (para. 50). The competitive needs of traders are accommodated, if at all, through the few exclusions as regards shape marks and the defences to infringement contained in TMA s. 11.

[137] The ability for marks to become registrable through use which is provided for under the 1994 Act is in marked contrast to the position under the 1938 Act, where it was held that certain marks could never become registrable irrespective of how distinctive they were 'in fact': *York TM* [1984] *RPC* 231.

[138] Joined Cases C–108/97 and C–109/97 [1999] *ECR* I–2779.

[139] In *Koninklijke Philips Electronics NV v. Remington Consumer Products*, Case C–299/99 [2002] *ECR* I–5475, the ECJ stated that the tribunal is to assess acquired distinctiveness 'in the light of the presumed expectations of an average consumer of the category of goods or services in question, who is reasonably well-informed and reasonably observant and circumspect'. This seems strange because acquired distinctiveness is normally a factual inquiry, rather than one dependent on a legal construct. Nevertheless, it is a way of screening out the views of real people who are either very attentive or very inattentive (the famous 'moron in a hurry').

meaning must have completely replaced the original meaning. This seems to be what Jacob J required in *Philips v. Remington*[140] when he said that 'unless the word, when used for the goods concerned, has in practice displaced its ordinary meaning, it will not properly denote the trader's goods and none other'.[141] However, to require that there be nothing left of the original meaning in any circumstances would be going too far (and, indeed would be inconsistent with the idea that allusive marks will be registrable as long as the immediate impression given to consumers is not exclusively descriptive).[142] Other authorities acknowledge that it is possible for a sign to become distinctive even though the 'primary meaning' still exists. For example, in *Windsurfing Chiemsee*, the ECJ explained that, where a geographical name has come to identify the product as originating from a particular undertaking and thus to distinguish that product from goods of other undertakings, the geographical designation 'has gained a new significance and its connotation, no longer *purely descriptive*, justifies its registration as a trade mark'.[143] The critical displacement of meaning is that which operates when the sign is used in relation to the particular goods or services and the question is whether in such a situation the average consumer of the product immediately understands the sign as referring to source. In *Bach Flower Remedies*,[144] the Court of Appeal explained that a mark would not have acquired 'distinctive character' where the meaning to consumers remained ambiguous.[145]

3.5.2 Numerical extent of recognition

It is clear that, for an unregistrable mark to become registrable, it is necessary for consumers to think about the sign as an indication of origin. One question that arises is how widespread must the consumer recognition be? In *Windsurfing*, the ECJ said that the question is whether 'the relevant class of persons, or at least a *significant proportion* thereof', identify goods as originating from a particular undertaking because of the trade mark.[146] The ECJ made it clear that it is not possible to say whether a mark is distinctive by reference to predetermined percentages. This is because the evidence that is needed to support a claim that a mark has become registrable through use (or where wrongly registered that it deserves to stay on the register) depends on how descriptive (etc.) the mark is in its 'natural' state. Thus, if the objections to the word are not strong, then it is likely that less evidence of acquired distinctiveness will be required. However, the more descriptive a mark is, the more convincing must be the evidence of acquired distinctiveness. In *Windsurfing*, the ECJ said that, where a geographical name is

---

[140] [1998] *RPC* 283.

[141] Having said this a distinctive mark may contain other messages, such as suggestions or allusions as to quality or origin. As long as these are not deceptive, and thus contrary to TMA s. 3(3)(b), registration may proceed. See below at pp. 849–51.

[142] *West (Eastenders)* [2003] *FSR* (44) 816, 841 (para. 68) (Arden LJ); Kerly, paras. 7–103 to 112, 179 to 183.

[143] Joined Cases C–108/97 and C–109/97 [1999] *ECR* I–2779, 2829 (para. 47); *Messiah From Scratch,* [2000] *RPC* 44, 51 (para. 30) (Appointed Person, Thorley QC).

[144] [2000] *RPC* 513.

[145] See also *Ty Nant Spring Water's Application*, R5/1999–3 [1999] *ETMR* 974, 980 (para. 26) (sign must have an unequivocal, certain, and definitive meaning in the minds of the relevant consumers). In *Société des Produits Nestlé SA v. Unilever (Viennetta)* [2003] *ETMR* (53) 681, 697, Jacob J held that the shape of an ice cream had not acquired distinctiveness where some consumers thought other shapes were also by Viennetta. But the fact that consumers associate another mark incorrectly with a particular trader, does not mean that trader should not be able to protect the signs which consumers correctly associate with it.

[146] Joined Cases C–108/97 and C–109/97 [1999] *ECR* I–2779, 2830 (para. 52); *Koninklijke Philips v. Remington,* Case C–299/99 [2002] *ECR* I–5475 (para. 65) (substantial portion of the relevant class). *Bovemij Verzekeringen NV v. Benelux-Merkenbureau,* Case C–108/05, (7 Sept 2006) ECJ (1st Ch).

very well known, it can acquire distinctive character only if there has been long-standing and intensive use of the mark by the undertaking applying for registration.[147]

In *British Sugar v. Robertson*,[148] Jacob J had to decide whether the term TREAT, which was by its nature laudatory, had become registrable through use. Jacob J explained that the question whether the sign had acquired a sufficiently distinctive character was a question of degree. In particular he said that, with laudatory, descriptive, or common words, it was necessary to produce evidence of compelling rather than extensive use. More specifically, Jacob J said that for a mark that was inherently non-distinctive to be registrable, it must have come to be recognized by a substantial majority of people. For Jacob J, if 90 per cent of people took the word to be a trade mark this would have been enough to say it had a 'distinctive character'. However, in this case, British Sugar's claim that 60 per cent of the public recognized TREAT as a designation of source was not sufficient.

3.5.3 Geographical extent of recognition

In respect of the Community Trade Mark, interesting issues have arisen as to the geographical dimensions of acquired distinctiveness. Does the law merely require that a 'significant proportion' of European citizens see the mark as indicating trade origin? So far, the courts have distinguished between word marks and other marks. We look at each in turn.

Where a 'word mark' is inherently descriptive, this will usually relate to certain particular languages: to return to an earlier example, OLUT is descriptive of beer in Finnish but not in English. In such situations, the jurisprudence currently demands a showing of acquired distinctiveness in all the territories where the sign is inherently descriptive—in this example, Finland.[149] In *Ford Motor's Application/Options*,[150] the applicant sought to register OPTIONS for (inter alia) insurance services. When the examiner objected that the sign was devoid of distinctive character in French and English, the applicant filed evidence of use in a number of countries, including the United Kingdom, but not France. The applicant asserted that acquired distinctiveness in the United Kingdom was sufficient to establish distinctiveness in a substantial part of the European Community, and that was all that was required under Article 7(3) of the CTMR. However, the CFI, affirming the opinion of the OHIM refusing registration, held that in order to be accepted for registration a sign must possess distinctive character throughout the Community. Since the mark lacked distinctiveness in France, it was not registrable as a Community mark.[151] This seems like a sensible and pragmatic response, but doubtless requires numerous details to be considered further: for example, where a mark is descriptive in English, is it necessary to show acquired distinctiveness in Malta and Cyprus, as well as the UK and Republic of Ireland? If so, it may be onerous for trade mark applicants and may lead to further reliance on national marks (with all the problems for the internal market that this may present).[152] However, if a sign is descriptive in Malta, and there is no acquired distinctiveness there, why should traders be prevented from using the description by allowing a registration reflecting distinctiveness acquired elsewhere?

[147] Joined Cases C–108/97 and C–109/97 [1999] *ECR* I–2779, 2830 (para. 50). [148] [1996] *RPC* 281.

[149] *Ford Motor Company, v. OHIM*, Case T–91/99 [2000] 2 *CMLR* 276 (CFI).

[150] Ibid. See also *Audi v. OHIM (TDI)*, T–16/02 (3 Dec. 2003) (paras. 52, 60, 66).

[151] *Ford v. OHIM*, Case T–91/99 [2000] 2 *CMLR* 276, 281 (para. 24).

[152] In other areas, for example the transitional rules on acceding states, the convenience of Community harmony has been privileged over the needs of traders to describe their goods: Community marks are deemed to extend to the new territories and cannot be invalidated on the basis that they are descriptive in the languages spoken in these countries.

Where the marks are not words, it is probable that the inherent qualities of the sign are perceived identically throughout the Community (or so, at least, the CFI has said).[153] Consequently, in *Glaverbel v OHIM*,[154] it was stated that acquired distinctiveness must be proved for the whole Community. The CFI affirmed that in relation to the application for chinchilla glass (see fig 37.3), which was inherently devoid of distinctive character, it was insufficient to provide evidence of acquired distinctiveness in only 10 of the (then) 15 states. This was the position the ECJ took in the *Storck* (sweet wrapper) decision.[155] In contrast, in *BIC SA, v OHIM*,[156] the CFI stated that such proof must be produced in respect of 'a substantial part' of the Community. On the facts, despite substantial use of the lighter shape, the evidence failed to establish that it was seen as a trade mark, and the geographical extent of the recognition was thus moot. While the test in *BIC* may seem more realistic, at least to trade mark applicants, it raises the question of what constitutes a 'substantial part' of the Community. The OHIM had suggested an assessment by reference to 'the regions', but the CFI provided no guidance on how to determine what was a substantial or significant part of the Community. The *Glaverbel* case has been appealed.[157]

3.5.4 The relevant consumers

On general principles, distinctiveness needs to be acquired across the full range of goods or services for which registration is sought. The fact that a descriptive sign acquires distinctiveness for some goods does not lead to the conclusion that it is registrable for other goods. This principle may cause problems where a mark is used in relation to goods or services targeted at a niche market, because the sign might come to be known by an élite, but not by the mass of consumers of goods of the relevant type. For example in *Salvatore Ferragamo Italia SpA*,[158] the applicant sought registration of a bow which it had used on its shoes for the previous 20 years. While there was plenty of evidence of use, and of advertising in elite magazines, it was by no means evident that ordinary purchasers of shoes would have been familiar with the mark. However, it would be at odds with the aims of trade mark law to have confined the applicant's specification to 'luxury' shoes, since clearly one of aims of giving protection would be to allow a proprietor to prevent others using the sign (here the bow) on cheap versions of the product. As it was, the OHIM held that the mark had acquired distinctiveness, likening it to marks such as ROLEX and ROLLS-ROYCE. The implication seems to be that the Board thought that the bow had in fact become familiar not just to the elite purchasers of luxury shoes, but the broader public. As such, the decision leaves unclear the trickier situation where evidence shows the mark to be known *only* to the elite customers.

3.5.5 Types of supporting evidence

A number of different types of evidence may be used to support a claim for registrability through use. In *Windsurfing Chiemsee*,[159] the ECJ listed the following considerations: the market share held by the mark; how intensive, geographically widespread, and long-standing use

---

[153] *BIC SA*, Case T–262/04 [2005] *ECR* II–5959 (para. 68) (CFI); *Glaverbel v. OHIM*, Case T–141/06 (12 Sept 2007) (para. 36) (CFI).

[154] *Glaverbel*, ibid.

[155] *August Storck*, Case C–24/05 P [2006] *ECR* I–5677 (sweet wrapper) (paras. 81–6).

[156] *BIC SA*, Case T–262/04 [2005] *ECR* II–5959.

[157] *AGC Flat Glass Europe (formerly Glaverbel) v. OHIM*, Case C–513/07 P (pending) (arguing that what is required is a 'synthetic' assessment across the Community as a whole, rather than in each and every state).

[158] R254/1999–1 (14 Apr. 2000).

[159] Joined Cases C–108/97 and C–109/97 [1999] *ECR* I–2779, 2830 (para. 51).

of the mark has been; the amount invested by the undertaking in promoting the mark; the proportion of the relevant class of persons who, because of the mark, identify goods as originating from a particular undertaking; and statements from chambers of commerce and industry or other trade and professional associations.[160]

Evidence of use. Acquired distinctiveness must be proved 'on the basis of specific and reliable data'.[161] A tribunal may take into account evidence of the length of time the product has been on the market, the volume of the goods marketed, or the extent of services provided. Such evidence might be supplied by way of statutory declarations. Typically, examples of uses on packaging, marketing, and advertising, as well as details of expenditure will also be submitted. However, the critical evidence concerns the impact of such activities. Consequently, the CFI has observed that 'initiatives by the proprietor are to be taken into consideration insofar as they produce objective results in terms of the perception of the sign amongst the relevant public'. In the absence of evidence of the impact of a proprietor's actions, a tribunal will be reluctant to infer acquired distinctive character.[162]

In order for a mark to become registrable through use, it is necessary to show that the public has come to think of the sign as designating origin. In order for that to occur the applicant must have used the sign as a mark.[163] The ECJ has made clear that there is no need for the sign to be used alone—other trade marks may also be present. Thus a slogan on a product (e.g. HAVE A BREAK) might acquire distinctive character though it had only been used when accompanied by a registered mark (KIT KAT) in the phrase HAVE A BREAK...HAVE A KIT KAT.[164] Equally, a shape might acquire distinctive character though it is accompanied by a verbal mark.[165]

Particular problems have arisen when attempting to show that a shape has acquired distinctiveness through use. In *Philips v. Remington*[166] the ECJ was asked for guidance as to whether a sign could acquire distinctiveness where a trader had been the only supplier of particular goods to the market. Philips had previously been the only seller of three-headed shavers, and there was evidence that as a consequence the public associated the shape with Philips. The potential problem with taking this evidence as indicative of distinctiveness lay in the fact that Philips had previously operated a monopoly, so that it had not been possible to ascertain how consumers would have understood the three-headed shape if it had been presented to them by traders other than Philips. The ECJ acknowledged that extensive use of the shape '*may be* sufficient to give the sign a distinctive character', but hinted that it might be difficult to

---

[160] One of the factors is stated to be the proportion of the relevant class of persons who, because of the mark, identify goods as originating from a particular undertaking' (para. 51). However, in our view this is not really a 'factor', so much as the essence of the inquiry (see para. 52). Consequently, we think it is more helpful to distinguish, as patent law does in its non-obviousness inquiry, between 'primary' and 'secondary' evidence. See *Glaverbel,* Case T–141/06 (12 Sept. 2007) (para. 41).

[161] *Koninklijke Philips v. Remington,* Case C–299/99 [2002] *ECR* I–5475; *PC Connection Inc's Appn,* R194/1998–3 [2000] *ETMR* 362 (OHIM BA).

[162] *Alcon Inc. v. OHIM,* Case T–237/01 (5 Mar. 2003) (para. 55) affirmed on appeal, Case C–192/03, [2005] *ETMR* (69) 860.

[163] *Koninklijke Philips v. Remington,* Case C–299/99 [2002] *ECR* I–5475 (para. 64) ('as a result of use of the mark *as a trade mark,* and thus as a result of the nature and effect of it'); *Nestlé,* Case C–353/03 [2005] *ECR* I–6135 (para. 26). This means the sign must be used 'for the purpose of the identification by the relevant class of persons of the product or service as originating from a given undertaking': *Nestlé,* para. 29.

[164] *Nestlé,* ibid. The mark—which had been the subject of several contested applications over many years—was finally registered in July 2006, TM 2015684.

[165] *August Storck,* Case C–24/05 P [2006] *ECR* I–5677 (para. 59).

[166] *Koninklijke Philips v. Remington,* Case C–299/99 [2002] *ECR* I–5475.

demonstrate that a substantial portion of the relevant class of persons associated the shape with a specific trader or believed that goods of that shape come from the trader. Because distinctiveness can only be acquired as a result of use of the mark *as a trade mark,* it seems that, on the facts of *Philips,* the mark had not acquired distinctiveness. While there may have been evidence of 'familiarity' with the shape, and even 'association' of the shape with Philips, it seems unlikely that this derived from use of the three-head shape *as a trade mark.* Subsequent cases have confirmed the practical difficulties standing in the way of proving acquired distinctiveness through use. 'Secondary evidence' through demonstrations of expenditure on advertising or the extent of market share are less probative than in other cases, because they rarely indicate that the public recognizes the shape as a trade mark, rather than liking the shape for its aesthetic or functional attributes. On the other hand, advertising which urges consumers to 'look for' a particular feature, will have some probative value in establishing that such a feature has acquired trade mark significance.[167]

Advertising expenditure. Although the ECJ specifically stated that tribunals may take account of the amount invested by the undertaking in promoting the mark, British courts have been more sceptical as to the value of matters such as advertising expenditure or evidence of sales success as indicators of acquired distinctiveness. This is because evidence of use will not inevitably lead to a finding of distinctiveness *through* use. As Jacob J said in *British Sugar v. Robertson,*[168] it is not the extent of promotional efforts that is crucial so much as the effect on consumers. Consequently, evidence that the word TREAT had been used for five years did not, on its own, demonstrate that the mark had become a badge of trade origin.

Evidence of the trade. Moreover, although the ECJ also refers to the relevance of 'statements from chambers of commerce and industry or other trade and professional associations', UK courts have treated these as of only marginal significance.[169] The reason for this is that the relevant class of persons is not trade buyers, but the average customer of the product.[170]

Consumer surveys. Since the inquiry is focused upon consumer attitudes to the sign, direct evidence from consumers and consumer surveys will most likely prove to be of value. The ECJ has stated that in this context 'Community law does not preclude the competent authority, where it has particular difficulty in that connection, from having recourse, under the conditions laid down by its own national law, to an opinion poll as guidance for its judgment'.[171] Under UK law, opinion polls are accepted but must be scrutinized with considerable care.[172]

4 OTHER ABSOLUTE GROUNDS FOR INVALIDITY

The third and more eclectic category of absolute grounds for refusal is set out in section 3(3)–(6) of the 1994 Act. These provide that trade marks shall not be registered if they are contrary

---

[167] PAN 6/07—*Evidence of acquired distinctiveness through use* (17 July 2007).

[168] [1996] *RPC* 281. See also *L & D SA v. OHIM,* Case C–488/06P (AG Sharpston, 13 Mar 2008) (para. 86) (some evidence must be presented that the mark in issue is actually perceived as linking the products which bear it with a particular undertaking and such evidence cannot come solely from data such as market share and advertising investment or duration of use).

[169] Recognition of those in the trade will not, of itself, suffice: *Wickes's Trade Mark Application* [1998] *RPC* 698.

[170] *Re Dualit* [1999] *RPC* 890, 898 (para. 33).

[171] *Windsurfing,* Joined Cases C–108/97 and C–109/97 [1999] *ECR* I–2779, 2830 (para. 53).

[172] *Nestlé v. Unilever,* [2003] *ETMR* (53) 681 (para. 22).

to public policy or morality, if they are likely to deceive the public, if they are prohibited by law, or if the application was made in bad faith. Particular provisions also exist for specially protected emblems.

4.1 PUBLIC POLICY AND MORALITY

Section 3(3)(a) provides that a trade mark shall not be registered if it is contrary to public policy or to accepted principles of morality.[173] The two exceptions relate to the intrinsic qualities of the sign, rather than the manner in which it is used.[174]

4.1.1 Morality

Rather like the corresponding ground for invalidity in the European Patent Convention, this provision has generated a rather inconsistent case law, particularly with respect to the application of the notion of 'morality'.[175] The Registry and the OHIM seem to have made matters all the more confusing by trying to interpret the notion in the light of Article 10 of the ECHR, and permissible exceptions thereto.[176] In our view, the implications for 'free speech' of refusal to register a trade mark are negligible, and these considerations irrelevant.[177] However, the topic is one which would benefit from the authoritative views of a higher tribunal.[178]

In the UK, the question of morality has come before the Appointed Person four times. The test, which has repeatedly been mentioned as helpful in distinguishing cases of mere bad taste (which can be registered) from those that contravene principles of morality, has been said to be whether use of the sign would 'justifiably cause outrage or would be subject of justifiable censure as being likely significantly to undermine current religious, family or social values'.[179] Despite the apparently high threshold, the test has been applied to reach the surprising

---

[173] Note also that a trade mark which contains a representation of one of the flags of the countries of the UK, the use of which would be 'grossly offensive', shall not be registered: TMA s. 4(2).

[174] *Durferrit GmbH v. OHIM, Kolene Corp Intervening*, Case T–224/01 [2003] *ECR* II–1589 (para. 76) (Art. 7(1)(f) 'does not cover the situation if the trade mark applicant acts in bad faith' since it refers to 'the intrinsic qualities of the mark claimed and not to circumstances relating to the conduct of the person applying for the mark'). See also *Sportwetten GmbH Gera v. OHIM, Intertops Sportwetten GmbH Intervening*, Case T–140/02 [2005] *ECR* II–3247 (paras 27–29).

[175] For a lengthy account of the US case law, see T. Davis, 'Registration of Scandalous, Immoral and Disparaging Matter under Section 2(a) of the Lanham Act: Can One Man's Vulgarity Be Another's Registered Trademark?' (1993) 83 *TM Rep* 863.

[176] *In re Basic Trademark SA's Application* [2005] *RPC* (25) 611 (Hobbs QC) (para. 26); *FCUK Trade Mark* [2007] *RPC* 1 (Arnold QC) (para. 60) ('registration should be refused only where this is justified by a pressing social need and is proportionate to the legitimate aim pursued. Furthermore, any real doubt as to the applicability of the objection should be resolved by upholding the right to freedom of expression and thus by permitting the registration'.)

[177] J. Griffiths, 'Is There a Right to an Immoral Trade Mark?', in P. Torremans (ed), *Intellectual Property and Human Rights* (2008, forthcoming) (reviewing the cases in detail and arguing that the myth that Art. 10 is relevant to these circumstances is 'worth dispelling'.)

[178] Advocate General Colomer has suggested that BABY KILLER would be unregistrable on this ground for a pharmaceutical abortifacient: *Koninklijke Philips v. Remington*, Case C–299/99 [2002] *ECR* I–5475 (para. 18) (AG Colomer).

[179] *Ghazilian's Application* [2002] *RPC* (33) 628. Simon Thorley QC there suggested that a mark might be rejected if it would cause a high degree of outrage to a small section of the community, or a lower level of outrage to a larger section.

conclusions that TINY PENIS,[180] JESUS,[181] and FOOK (all for, inter alia, clothing) were 'contrary to accepted principles of morality',[182] while FCUK (for jewellery) was not.[183] TINY PENIS was held to be unregistrable for clothes because (according to Simon Thorley QC) use of the words would undermine an important social value, namely, that anatomical terms for parts of the genitalia should be retained for serious (educational) use and not tainted by 'use as a smutty trade mark for clothing'.[184] JESUS was rejected for clothing and other goods because 'branding which employs words or images of religious significance can quite easily have a seriously troubling effect on people whose religious beliefs it impinges upon and others who adhere to the view that religious beliefs should be treated with respect in a civilised society'.[185] FOOK was rejected because it was the phonetic equivalent of 'fuck', the use of which would apparently cause 'justifiable outrage' when used on clothing (despite its frequent use in football stadia),[186] but FCUK was acceptable because, even though it could be used to evoke the swear word, it was not a phonetic or visual equivalent of 'fuck'.[187] In reaching the latter conclusion, Richard Arnold QC seems to have been particularly influenced by the fact that other regulatory authorities (such as the ASA and Ofcom) had allowed use of FCUK, and that 16 million articles of FCUK-branded clothing had been sold.

The OHIM has also struggled to apply the corresponding provision of the CTMR.[188] For example, the OHIM Board of Appeal accepted DICK AND FANNY as registrable for clothing: this was merely in poor taste, having a 'rather smutty flavour'. The Board was particularly taken by the fact that the words 'merely designate things' rather than proclaiming an opinion, inciting behaviour, or conveying an insult.[189] In contrast, the Grand Board rejected SCREW YOU for sunglasses, clothing, and beverages (but not sex toys and condoms).[190] Recognising that 'screw' was a slightly less offensive profanity than 'fuck', the Board nevertheless held that 'a substantial number of citizens with a normal level of sensitivity and tolerance would be upset by regular commercial exposure to the term'.[191] The sign therefore should not be registered for the goods that, in normal use, would be exposed to the general population, including children. However, as sex toys are normally sold in specialist shops, 'a more relaxed attitude'

---

[180] Ibid.

[181] *Basic Trademark* [2005] *RPC* (25) 611 (Hobbs QC). Registration was sought for various goods in Classes 3, 9, 14, 16, 18, 24, 25 and 28.

[182] *Scranage's Trade Mark Application* (O/182/05) (24 Jun 2005) (Kitchin QC).

[183] *FCUK* [2007] *RPC* 1 (Arnold QC).

[184] The reasoning is therefore consistent with the result at the OHIM in *Dick Lexic/Dick & Fanny*, R111/2002–4 (25 Mar. 2003), since DICK and FANNY are not proper anatomical terms for genitalia. But Thorley QC's conclusions were doubted in *FCUK*, ibid (Arnold QC) (para. 61) (doubting that the social value to which he appealed is a generally accepted moral principle.)

[185] *Basic Trademark* [2005] *RPC* (25) 611 (Hobbs QC). Would the decision have been different if the Church of England or Jesus College, Cambridge had been the applicant? If so, why should this make a difference? The Grand Board of OHIM has suggested that cases of religious offence might best be dealt with under the heading of 'public policy' rather than 'morality': *Application of Kenneth (trading as Screw You)*, Case R 495/2005–G, [2007] *ETMR* (7) 111 (OHIM, Grand Board) (para. 20) ('signs which severely offend the religious sensitivities of a substantial group of the population are also best kept off the register, if not for moral reasons, at least for reasons of public policy, namely the risk of causing public disorder').

[186] In *Scranage's Trade Mark,* (O/182/05) (24 June 2005) Kitchin QC, at para. 11, said its use would be 'deeply offensive and insulting to many people'.

[187] In *FCUK* [2007] *RPC* 1, Arnold QC at para. 74 notes the widespread use of 'fuck.'

[188] CTMR, Art. 7(1)(f). Though the OHIM's examination guidelines, para. 8.7, provide as examples of signs that should be rejected swearwords, or images that are racist or blasphemous.

[189] *Dick Lexic,* R 111/2002–4 (25 Mar. 2003) (for various goods in Classes 9, 16 and 25).

[190] *Kenneth,* Case R 495/2000–G [2007] *ETMR* (7) 111 (OHIM, Grand Board).   [191] Para. 26.

was appropriate, and the sign was registrable. More strangely, perhaps, the Board held that a person who is 'sufficiently interested in [condoms] to notice the trade marks under which they are sold is unlikely to be offended by a term with crude sexual connotations'. The OHIM BA also accepted REVA, a slang Finnish term for female genitalia, as registrable for electric cars because, in that context, it carried no rude or disrespectful message.[192]

4.1.2 Public policy

The exclusion relating to 'public policy' has been invoked less frequently. According to the OHIM, 'obviously malevolent racial and cultural slurs, whether by word or pictorial representation, should not be allowed on a trade mark register'.[193] It also includes promoting illegal activity, for example, by glamourizing drug taking or terrorism. The exclusion is not concerned with economic grounds for objection, such as the effect that registration would have on competition.[194]

4.2 DECEPTIVE MARKS

Section 3(3)(b) states that a trade mark shall not be registered if it is 'of such a nature as to deceive the public (for instance as to the nature, quality or geographical origin of the goods or service)'.[195] This prohibition tends to be applied to marks which, though distinctive, contain some kind of suggestion or allusion that is inaccurate. This is likely to be assessed from the viewpoint of the consumer who is reasonably well-informed, observant, and circumspect.[196] The risk of deception must be a real one, and relate to the mark itself (as opposed to the way it is used). In *Elizabeth Emanuel*,[197] the opponent was a well-known designer of wedding clothes, Elizabeth Emanuel. Although she had assigned her business to a third party (including a trade mark application), she later opposed registration of the mark ELIZABETH EMANUEL on the absolute ground that its nature was such as to deceive the public into believing that the clothes sold by the trade mark owner were of her design. The Examiner refused the opposition and, on appeal, the Appointed Person referred several questions to the ECJ. According to the ECJ, the ground for refusal (and the corresponding ground for opposition) requires 'the existence of actual deceit or of a sufficiently serious risk that the consumer will be deceived'.[198] The Court denied that the assignment of the mark, of itself (as opposed to how the proprietor utilized it) gave rise to such a serious risk of deception. Even if the average consumer 'might be influenced in his act of purchasing a garment bearing the trade mark 'ELIZABETH EMANUEL' by imagining that the appellant in the main proceedings was involved in the design of that garment', there was no deception because the 'characteristics and the qualities of that garment remain guaranteed by the undertaking which owns the trade mark'. Although the questions referred, and

---

[192] *Reva Electric Car Co. (PVT) Ltd.* Case R 558/2006–2 (18 July 2006) (OHIM BA).

[193] *Kenneth* Case R 495/2005–G [2007] *ETMR* (7) 111 (para. 19–20). Note also, *Falcon Sporting Goods/BIN LADEN*, Case R 176/2004–2 (29 Sep 2004), (in Spanish) initially appealed under T–487/04.

[194] *Philips v. Remington*, Case C–299/99 [2002] *ECR* I–5475.

[195] CTMR Art. 7(1)(g); TM Dir. Art. 3(1)(g). See below at pp. 911–3.

[196] Consequently, mere advertising 'puff', as lawyers call it, as was present in the application KENCO THE REAL COFFEE EXPERTS, will not be misleading: *Kraft Jacobs Suchard Ltd's Application; Opposition by Nestlé UK* [2001] *ETMR* (54) 585 (the opponent's liking to think of themselves as the real experts).

[197] *Elizabeth Florence Emanuel v. Continental Shelf 128 Ltd*, Case C–259/04, [2006] *ECR* I–3089 ECJ (3d Chamber).

[198] Ibid, para. 47 citing *Consorzio per la Tutela del Formaggio Gorgonzola v. Kaserei Champignon Hofmeister GmbH*, Case C–87/97 [1999] *ECR* I–1301 (para. 41).

answers give by the ECJ, related to a rather specific set of circumstances (and accordingly leave some questions to be decided on another occasion),[199] the case appears to set a high threshold for the ground for refusal to apply.

The exclusion has been applied to signs which misleadingly suggest official approval and to signs that suggest goods are made out of particular materials,[200] or come from particular locations. The UK Registry refused an application for a collective mark, CHARTERED FINANCIAL ANALYST (for financial services), reasoning that the sign gave the impression to the average consumer that the users of the mark are members of a professional organization of the sort that benefits from a Royal charter.[201] The OHIM Board rejected an appeal from a decision refusing registration of TITAN (which means 'titanium' in German, Swedish, and Danish) for building units made of non-metallic materials, and of WINE OH! for (inter alia) beverages.[202] The term TITAN was misleading because consumers could be led into taking an interest in the products on the basis of an indication that they were made of titanium.[203] The term WINE was misleading for water, and the addition of 'OH!' merely emphasized this. The Board was not able to assume that the misleading connotation would be corrected as a result of the nature of the packaging of the water. In contrast, if the misdescription is obvious and is such that it would immediately be corrected on further observations by the consumer, such misdescriptions will not render the sign invalid.

Another situation in which a trade mark may be refused is if it gives rise to a real, but inaccurate, expectation that the goods come from a particular locality. For example, an application to register MCL PARFUMS DE PARIS for toiletries including perfumes was refused by the UK Registry, on the grounds that the mark created an expectation that the perfume would be manufactured in Paris, so that (if it was not) the trade mark would deceive the public not only as to the geographic origin of the goods but also as to their nature and quality.[204] Similarly the OHIM refused to register ARCADIA for wine, Arcadia being a Greek region known for wine: the name was either descriptive of geographical origin or, if limited as proposed by the applicant to cover only Italian wines, misleading because the wines did not come from Arcadia.[205] The refusal of signs involving geographical mis-descriptions parallels the role of section 3(4) discussed in Chapter 43 below. However, the circumstances in which the owner of a protected

---

[199] In particular, the questions/answers were confined to the case where the trade mark came to be assigned with goodwill of the business, leaving open the possibility of a different conclusion in cases of assignment or licensing 'in gross'. For comment, see R. Moscona, 'What really Matters? The Designer's Name or the Name on the Label?' (2007) 29(4) EIPR 152.

[200] Elizabeth Emanuel, Case C–259/04 [2006] ECR I–3089 (AG, para. 58). In his Opinion (at AG, para. 58), Advocate General Colomer referred, approvingly, to an old UK case in which the invented word 'Orlwoola' was refused registration for textile, saying 'its sound was almost identical to 'all wool', giving the public the impression that articles had been made using wool when, in fact, they contained only cotton.' The old UK case was Joseph Crosfield & Son [1910] 1 Ch 130.

[201] CFA Institute's Application; Opposition of the Chartered Insurance Institute, Case O/315/06, [2007] ETMR (76) 1253. In International Star Registry of Illinois/International Star Registry, R468/1999–1 (4 Apr. 2001) the OHIM Board of Appeal refused registration of INTERNATIONAL STAR REGISTRY for goods and services related to the recording of data on the ground that it appeared to create the impression that the names given to stars enjoyed some sort of official status.

[202] Wine Oh! LLC's Application, R 1074/2005–4 [2006] ETMR (95) 1319.

[203] Portakabin Ltd/Titan R789/2001–3 (23 Jan. 2002) (OHIM BA). Cf. Lord Corp/Metaljacket, R314/2002–1 (23 Oct. 2002) (ambiguous mark METALJACKET for non-metallic coatings for metals not misleading).

[204] Madgecourt's Application; Opposition by Federation des Industries de la Parfumerie [2000] ETMR 825.

[205] Enotria Holdings/Arcadia, R246/1999–1 (27 Mar. 2000).

designation of origin can object to use of that designation or a similar one, may be broader than the situations in which a mark will be treated as misleading.[206]

4.3 MARKS PROHIBITED BY LAW

Section 3(4) provides that 'a trade mark shall not be registered if or to the extent that its use is prohibited in the United Kingdom by any enactment or rule of law or by any provision of Community law.' Thus a mark will not be registered if it is unlawful under statutes such as the Geneva Conventions Act 1957 (protecting symbols of the Red Cross), Trade Descriptions Act 1968, Plant Varieties Act 1997, or the Hallmarking Act 1973. The illegality must be intrinsic or inherent in the mark, rather than in the goods for which its use is proposed.[207] The reference to Community law prevents the registration of 'protected designations of origin' and 'geographical indications' for wines, spirits, agricultural products, and food.[208]

4.4 BAD FAITH

According to section 3(6), a trade mark shall not be registered, if or to the extent that the application is made in bad faith.[209] The courts, tribunals, and offices have struggled to find a satisfactory definition of 'bad faith', in particular whether it is a question of conscious dishonesty, or whether it is to be decided by reference to objective standards.[210] Ultimately, the Court of Appeal has decided to align the definition in trade mark law with that in operating in other areas of civil liability, particularly so-called 'knowing assistance' in breach of trust.[211] This

---

[206] Under Regulation (EC) No 510/2006 of 20 March 2006 on the Protection of Geographical Indications and Designations of Origin for Agricultural Products and Foodstuffs OJ L 93/12 (repealing and replacing Regulation 2081/92), Art. 13, protection of PDOs and PGIs extends to any 'evocation', but an evocation will not, of itself, be misleading. *Gorgonzola v. Kaserei Champignon Hofmeister*, Case C–87/97 [1999] *ECR* I–1301.

[207] Paris Convention, Art. 7; *Arthur Fairest's Appn.* (1951) 68 *RPC* 197 (Lloyd Jacob J).

[208] See Ch. 43. See, e.g. *Re Mezzacorona Trade Mark* [2004] *RPC* (26) 537 (CA); *Consorzio per la tutela del formaggio Grana Padano, & Italian Republic, v. OHIM and Biraghi SpA*, Case T–291/03, [2008] *ETMR* (3) 57 (CFI 4th Ch). CTMR Article 7 (1)(j), added by Council Regulation (EC) No 3288/94 of 22 December 1994 amending Regulation (EC) No 40/94 on the Community trade mark for the implementation of the agreements concluded in the framework of the Uruguay Round, requires that trade marks be refused 'for wines which contain or consist of a geographical indication identifying wines or for spirits which contain or consist of a geographical indication identifying spirits with respect to such wines or spirits not having that origin'. See, e.g. *René Barbier SA/Duque de Villena*, R1220/2000–2 [2003] OJ OHIM 1927. CTMR Article 7(1)(k), added by Council Regulation (EC) No 422/2004 of 19 February 2004 amending Regulation (EC) No 40/94 on the Community trade mark, prohibits registration of marks which contain or consist of a designation of origin or a geographical indication registered in accordance with Regulation (EEC) No 2081/92 (now Regulation (EC) No 510/2006) when they correspond to one of the situations covered by Article 13 of the said Regulation.

[209] Pursuant to optional provision in TM Dir. Art. 3(2)(d). CTMR, Art. 51 (registration liable to be declared invalid where application was made in bad faith). For a review of case law across Europe, see S. Middlemiss and J. Phillips, 'Bad Faith in European Trade Mark Law and Practice' [2003] *EIPR* 397.

[210] *Gromax Plasticulture v. Don & Low Nonwovens* [1999] *RPC* 367, 379 (the concept of bad faith is to be understood as requiring 'dishonesty' or at most 'conduct falling short of acceptable commercial behaviour'); *Knoll AG's Trade Mark* [2003] *RPC* (10) 175, 182 (para. 27) (Neuberger J); *Nestlé v. Unilever (Viennetta)* [2003] *ETMR* (53) 681 (para. 7) (Jacob J) (using trade mark registration to extend patent monopoly 'miles from bad faith'); *R v. Reef Trade Mark* [2002] *RPC* (19) 387 (Pumfrey J) (applicant's conduct must be reprehensible). For broader views: *Road Tech. Computer Systems v. Unison Software UK* [1996] *FSR* 805; *Postperfect Trade Mark* [1998] *RPC* 255; *Artistic Upholstery v. Art Forma (Furniture)* [1999] 4 *All ER* 277, 290.

[211] *Harrison v. Teton Valley Trading Co* [2005] *FSR* (10). The case was heavily criticized by Richard Arnold QC, sitting as Appointed Person in *Robert McBride Ltd.'s Application* [2005] *ETMR* (85) 990 (paras 27–31).

definition requires first an inquiry into what the applicant actually knew, and then an assessment as to whether a reasonable person would regard the applicant's behaviour, given that knowledge, as 'conduct falling short of acceptable commercial behaviour'.[212] The views of the applicant as to whether its behaviour is dishonest are of no consequence, the issue is whether the act of applying for the registration was dishonest as judged by the 'ordinary standards of honest people'.[213] In many respects this is a broad test that the courts have applied to a wide range of situations. Although this has been said to be consistent with the approach of the OHIM, such an approach has introduced issues of priority between competing claims into the Registrar's determination of absolute objections—thus muddying the distinction between absolute and relative grounds for refusal and, arguably, making redundant certain specific provisions in the Act.[214]

The cases can be placed in three categories: where there is no intention to use the mark, where there is an abuse of a relationship, and where the applicant was aware that a third party had some sort of claim to the goodwill in the mark.

4.4.1 No intention to use the mark

The first situation where a mark may be refused because it was applied for in bad faith is where the applicant had no intention of using the mark in trade. Such applications are said to be in 'bad faith' because the applicant declares, under section 32(3), that the trade mark is being used or that the applicant has a bona fide intention to use the mark in relation to those goods or services. If there is no such intention, the declaration is dishonest and the dishonesty taints the application.[215]

The most obvious situation of lack of intent to use occurs where a person applies to register a mark with the intent either of preventing a competitor registering the mark or selling (or 'trafficking in') the registered right. So for example, where an antique dealer realized that DEMON ALE was an anagram of 'lemonade' and applied to register DEMON ALE as a mark, with a view to selling the mark and with no intention of brewing, the Appointed Person held that the application was in bad faith.[216] The requirement that a person should intend to use the sign means that an application is likely to be refused where a person applies to register a sign at a time when they are clearly unable to use that sign for the goods or services in question. For

However, he has subsequently observed in *Target Fixings v. Brutt* [2007] *RPC* (19) 462 that much of the force of the criticisms has been removed by the clarification of Prof. Annand QC in *Ajit Weekly Trade Mark* [2006] *RPC* (25) 633. The point made by Arden LJ in *Harrison*, at para. 40, and reiterated by Arnold QC at in *Robert McBride*, at para. 30, that 'good faith' is a European concept whose meaning must be found in the 'language, scheme and structure' of the Directive, remains significant: ultimately it will be the ECJ that determines the meaning of TMD Art. 3(2)(d) and CTMR Art. 51(1)(b).

[212] *Ajit Weekly*, ibid (Appointed Person, Ruth Annand); *Target Fixings,* ibid.

[213] *Ajit Weekly*, ibid (para. 41); *Jules Rimet Cup Ltd v. Football Association Ltd* [2008] *ECDR* (4) 43, 65 (para. 94) (Deputy Judge Wyand QC).

[214] For example TMA, s. 60, which states that an application for registration of a trade mark by an agent or representative of a person who is the proprietor of the mark in a Convention country is to be refused if that proprietor opposes the application. See also Art. 6*bis* of the Paris Convention; CTMR Art. 8(3). It is clear from *Target Fixings,* note 211 above that it is frequently easier to establish bad faith than that the applicant was an agent of the 'real trade mark owner'.

[215] *Demon Ale Trade Mark* [2000] *RPC* 345; *In re Ferrero SPA's Trade Marks (Kinder)*, O/279/03 [2004] *RPC* (29) 253 (Kitchin QC) (para. 25). Cf. *Knoll AG*, note 210 above, 185 (paras 33–4) (Neuberger J) (warning against relying on the s. 32(3) declaration on the basis that the requirement 'may be inconsistent with the Directive'). See also *Robert McBride* [2005] *ETMR* (85) 990 (paras 18–19).

[216] Ibid.

example, in *Mickey Dees (Nightclub) Trade Mark*,[217] Michael Dyer, an employee at a nightclub called 'Mickey Dees', was held to have lacked good faith when he registered the words MICKEY DEES for nightclub services. Given that the applicant did not own any nightclub, he could not show any realistic intent to provide nightclub services. However, the registration was allowed to stand as regards the provision of singing and musician services by an entertainer, because the applicant could intend in good faith to carry on such a trade.

As well as regulating the 'stockpiling' and 'trafficking' in marks,[218] the requirement of good faith can be used to prevent the registration of 'ghost marks', that is, the registration of marks that are similar to an unregistrable mark which the trader is in fact using. A famous example, from pre-1994 case law, was the illegitimate registration of NERIT for cigarettes, when the applicant really intended to use the mark MERIT but realised it would not be accepted for registration (as it lacks distinctiveness).[219] However, where an applicant intended to use a three-dimensional mark and registered a two-dimensional device comprising an image of the mark, the Appointed Person held that the applicant had not lacked good faith because, in some circumstances, use of the shape could count in fact as use of the two-dimensional mark.[220]

A person may also be held to have registered a mark with no bona fide intention to use it where the specification of goods and services is unduly broad. Nevertheless, the UK courts have emphasized that merely drafting a specification broadly will not mean that the application is in bad faith: to say one intends to use a mark, for example for pharmaceutical substances, where one intends to use the mark only in relation to a specific category of pharmaceutical products is not sufficient to warrant a finding of bad faith.[221] Consequently, a line is drawn between excessively wide specifications, and ones which merely provide room for some possible brand extension. As a matter of routine, the Registry objects only to specifications in the form of 'all goods/services in class X', claims to 'machines', 'electrical apparatus', and 'services that cannot be classified in other classes'.[222] The British practice should be contrasted with that of the OHIM, which declined to cancel broad registrations on the ground of bad faith in the *Trillium* decision.[223]

4.4.2 Abuses of Relationships

The second situation where an applicant may be held to lack good faith is where, in applying for the mark, they are knowingly abusing a relationship with a third party. The most obvious example of such abuse of a relationship is where the registration would give rise to a breach of trust or contract between them. This might be the case where the applicant is an employee or an agent, a partner or former partner or co-venturer. If the applicant is aware that his or her behaviour is wrongful in law,[224] then an honest person would likely regard that behaviour as

---

[217] *Mickey Dees (Nightclub) Trade Mark* [1998] *RPC* 359. Cf. *R. v. Reef* [2002] *RPC* (19) 387, 395 (para. 12) (Pumfrey J) (where claim that application was in bad faith because the applicant intended decorative use only, rather than trade mark use, was rejected because proposed use was 'at worst equivocal').

[218] *In re Ferrero* [2004] *RPC* (29) 253 (Kitchin QC) (para. 25) (a case of stockpiling of KINDER- related marks).

[219] *Imperial Group v. Philip Morris & Co.* [1982] *FSR* 72.

[220] *Robert McBride* [2005] *ETMR* (85) 990.

[221] *Knoll AG* [2003] *RPC* (10) 175, 182 (para. 27) (Neuberger J). Cf. *Betty's Kitchen Coronation Street Trade Mark* [2000] *RPC* 825 (finding application to have been in bad faith because no intention to use all four words together as a single mark, and only used on some of goods).

[222] IPO, *Manual of Trade Mark Practice*, Ch. 3, section 40 (the basis is TMR, r. 8(2)(b)).

[223] OHIM Cancellation division, 53447/03 discussed in *Robert McBride* [2005] *ETMR* (85) 990 (para. 20).

[224] But note *Johnson Pump Aktiebolag (publ.) v. Johnson Pump (UK) Ltd*, Case R 225/2006–1 (31 May 2007) (OHIM BA) (para. 34) (a breach of contract does not necessarily constitute an act of bad faith).

'conduct falling short of acceptable commercial behaviour'.[225] However, an application may be treated as in bad faith where the abuse falls short of a breach of a legal relationship, for example where the parties were in pre-contractual negotiations as to a licensing arrangement and, when this fell through, the disappointed licensee registered the mark.[226]

4.4.3 Knowledge of third-party claims

Another situation where an application may be rejected on the basis that it was made in bad faith is where a party attempts to register a mark when it knows that a third party has some better claim to the reputation or goodwill attaching to the sign.[227]

In *Ajit Weekly Trade Mark*,[228] a trade mark had been granted for a Punjabi word (meaning 'invincible') in relation to printed matter. The owner of a Punjabi newspaper of the same name, which had sold in India since 1959, and was a 'household name' in the Punjab, applied to have the mark cancelled on the grounds that the application had been made in bad faith. The examiner concluded that the proprietor of the mark had known of the Punjabi paper and its reputation, and that use of the mark in the UK would confuse the substantial Punjabi community present in the UK. The Appointed Person affirmed the decision, holding that (as a matter of law) it was unnecessary to show that the applicant thought what he was doing was dishonest, and that the Examining Officer had been entitled to reach a conclusion that an honest person would regard such behaviour as 'conduct falling below acceptable standards'. In *Jules Rimet Cup Ltd v Football Association Ltd.*, the applicant sought to register an image of a lion in the English football strip, the World Cup logo from 1966, known as 'World Cup Willie'. Before doing so, it had approached the FA to find out whether it still held rights in the mark, and had done searches and employed a trade mark attorney. As a consequence, it believed itself entitled to use the image of 'World Cup Willie'. Nevertheless, as it was knowingly taking advantage of the FA's residual goodwill, Deputy Judge Wyand QC held that the application was not in good faith and that the FA's opposition should succeed.[229]

As can be seen, the application of the absolute ground may overlap with, or even outflank, relative ground objections based on section 5(4) of the Act.[230] Insofar as it outflanks the relative

---

[225] *Target Fixings* [2007] *RPC* (19) 462; *Mary Wilson Enterprises Inc's Trade Mark Application* [2003] *EMLR* (14) 259 (bad faith application to register THE SUPREMES contrary to agreement with Motown Records); *Saxon Trade Mark* [2003] *FSR* (39) 704 (bad faith application by former member of heavy metal band to register SAXON which Laddie J considered to be a partnership asset); *Mickey Dees,* note 217 above (manager of nightclub could not have claimed in good faith to be the owner of the sign for nightclub services, possibly a breach of his duty of fidelity); *Mix FM Black Mix Trade Mark*, O/084/00 (2000) *CIPAJ* 403 (former producer of BBC radio show acted in bad faith when he applied to register programme name MIX FM BLACK MIX); *Gromax Plasticulture* [1999] *RPC* 367 (bad faith on part of distributor not established).

[226] *John Arthur Slater v. Prime Restaurant Holdings, Inc.*, Case R 582/2003–4 (13 Dec 2004) (OHIM BA) (concerning the sign EAST SIDE MARIOS registered in US and Canada).

[227] The ECJ will provide clarification of some of these issues in response to a reference from the Oberster Gerichshof (Austria) in *Chocoladefabriken Lindt & Sprüngli AG v. Franz Hauswirth GmbH*, Case C–529/07.

[228] [2006] *RPC* (25) 633. In *Kundry SA's Application: Opposition by the President and Fellows of Harvard College*, [1998] *ETMR* 178 (rejecting JARVARD for clothing, on the basis that the application was an attempt to make use of the opponent's reputation associated with the word 'Harvard').

[229] [2008] *ECDR* (4) 43 (Deputy Judge Wyand QC).

[230] Given that passing off does not depend upon the existence of any fraudulent intention, the law requires that the claimant show goodwill in the UK: see ch. 32. However, even where there is no goodwill in the UK, a trade mark application that seeks deliberately to take advantage of the reputation of a foreign business will be regarded as in bad faith.

grounds, the Registry will prevent registration of marks in circumstances where possibly there might not be grounds to prohibit use of the same sign. One practically important consequence of this is that, on such reasoning, an applicant might be treated as lacking good faith where he or she applies to register a sign incorporating the name or image of a well-known person without their agreement.[231]

4.5 SPECIAL EMBLEMS

Section 4 excludes from registration trade marks that consist of or contain 'specially protected emblems'.[232]

Section 4(1) precludes registration of signs that include symbolic elements connected to the Crown. These include emblems such as the Royal Arms, the Royal crown, and flags. The exclusion also covers any representation of any member of the Royal Family, or any other sign suggesting that the applicant has Royal patronage).

Section 4(2) excludes various national flags—the Union Jack and the flags of the various British nations. Here the criterion is that their use would be misleading or grossly offensive.

Section 4(3) has a similar exclusion for international emblems and flags that are protected under section 57 and 58 of the Act.[233] Sections 57 and 58 contain a similar list of excluded emblems, flags, etc. for other Convention countries. Applying the equivalent provision of the CTMR, the CFI held that an application relating to a flag containing a circle of twelve stars was unregistrable for computer programs, and arranging conferences, in the light of the EC's own flag, which it described, in heraldic terms as 'on a field azure a circle of 12 mullets or, their points not touching'.[234] Whatever the 'geometric' differences, the Court ruled, the two signs were to be compared 'from a heraldic point of view', and, as the applicant had not specified colour, from such a perspective it was an unregistrable imitation.[235]

Section 4(4) restricts registration of marks that include coats of arms, subjecting trade marks to the rules of the law of arms.

---

[231] *TMR Work Manual*, ch. 6, para. 9.11. The argument was unsuccessful in *Farley's Application* [2002] *ETMR* (30) 336 (TM Registry) (PQASSO for printed matter and training related to quality assurance).

[232] For general consideration of this under-studied topic, see R. Coombe, 'Tactics of Appropriation and the Politics of Recognition in Late Modern Democracies' (1993) 21 *Political Theory* 411.

[233] In accordance with Art. 6*ter* of the Paris Convention, TRIPS Art. 15(2); CTMR, Art. 7(1)(h).

[234] *Concept—Anlagen u. Geräte nach 'GMP' für Produktion u. Labor GmbH v. OHIM,* Case T–127/02 ('ECA') [2004] *ECR* II–1113.

[235] In this case the interpretation of the heraldic description, a verbal description, has more in common with patent interpretation than traditional trade mark infringement analysis. In other cases, the Board of Appeal of the OHIM has tended to compare the visual appearance of the signs: *Maple Skate BV*, Case R 503/2006–2 (16 Jun. 2006) (OHIM BA) (application for red maple leaf with word 'maple' rejected in the light of Canada's national flag); *Sovereign Military Hospitaller Order of Saint Joan of Jerusalem of Rhodes and of Malta*, Case R 1444/2005–2 (28 Jun. 2006) (OHIM BA) (application by ancient charity for shield mark for charitable, medical, and religious services accepted, despite featuring 'Maltese cross' that was on protected hallmark and shipping flag, because objections based on 'signs and hallmarks indicating control and warranty' only apply where the contested mark is intended for use on goods of a different kind). Note also *Cruz Roja Española*, R 315/2006–1 (28 Jun. 2007) (OHIM BA) (affirming refusal to cancel figuration mark for car spare parts which included orange cross, on the basis that it was not similar enough to the Red Cross's symbol, and so did not breach CTMR, Art. 7(1)(i)). The Red Cross symbol is protected in UK law under the Geneva Conventions Act 1957, and an objection would fall under TMA s. 3(4).

Section 4(5) also prohibits the registration of marks which consist of or contain a 'controlled representation' under the Olympic Symbol (Protection) Act 1995 (as amended by the London Olympic Games and Paralympic Games Act 2006). These controlled representations include the Olympic and Paralympic symbols, mottos, and various protected words (Olympics, Paralympics, Olympiad, Olympian *et al*). These words and symbols are controlled by the Olympic Association. Obviously, the temptation to register marks including such references will increase as 2012 approaches.

38

RELATIVE GROUNDS FOR REFUSAL

CHAPTER CONTENTS

1   INTRODUCTION

In this chapter, we explore the relative grounds for refusing to register a trade mark. The relative grounds for refusal, which are set out section 5(1)–(4) of the 1994 Act and Article 8 of the CTMR, are important insofar as they provide grounds on which an application to register a mark can be opposed, and, in the case of a successful opposition, refused.[1] They are also important because they can form the basis for an application to have a mark which has been registered declared invalid.[2]

The relative grounds for refusal fall into two general categories: those concerned with 'earlier trade marks' (sections 5(1)–(3) and Article 8(1) and (5) of the CTMR); and those concerned with 'earlier rights' (section 5(4) and Articles 8(4) and 52(2) of the CTMR). We deal with each in turn.

---

[1] Until Oct 1, 2007 (Trade Mark (Relative Grounds) Order 2007 (SI 2007/1976), The Trade Marks (Amendment) Rules 2007 (SI 2007/2076)), the UK Registry actually examined on relative grounds: former TMA, s. 37. Since that date the Registry searches and informs applicant of possible clashes and the earlier mark holder about the application: SI 2007/1976 r. 4, TM Rules, r. 11A. It is up to the earlier trade mark holder to bring opposition proceedings. The UK practice is thus now aligned with that at OHIM.

[2] TMA s. 47(2)(a), (b); CTMR Art. 51.

2   RELATIVE GROUNDS IN RELATION TO EARLIER TRADE MARKS

The relative grounds for refusal in relation to earlier trade marks are found in sections 5(1)–(3) and Articles 8(1) and (5) of the CTMR. These provide that a trade mark shall not be registered if, when compared with an earlier mark, it is found that:

(i)   the marks are identical *and* the goods or services are identical: section 5(1)/Article 8(1)(a);

(ii)   the marks are identical, *and* the goods or services are similar, *and* there is a likelihood of confusion, which includes the likelihood of association, with the earlier mark: section 5(2)(a)/Article 8(1)(b);

(iii)   the marks are similar, *and* the goods or services are either identical or similar, *and* there is a likelihood of confusion, which includes the likelihood of association, between the marks: section 5(2)(b)/Article 8(1)(b); or

(iv)   the marks are either identical or similar, the earlier trade mark has a reputation, and use of the applicant's mark would take unfair advantage of, or be detrimental to, the distinctive character or the repute of the earlier trade mark: section 5(3)/Article 8(5).

These relative grounds for refusal mirror the provisions dealing with trade mark infringement. In particular, sections 5(1), 5(2), and 5(3) correspond to sections 10(1), 10(2), and 10(3), which deal with trade mark infringement. Effectively, these relative grounds for refusal enable the owner of an earlier mark (A) to prevent the registration of a sign by another (B) where the use of that sign would infringe the rights of the earlier mark owner (A). As well as being sensible and convenient, one of the consequences of this symmetry is that much of the case law on infringement is relevant to the relative grounds for refusal.[3] As such, in this chapter we draw upon trade mark infringement cases where relevant.

2.1   PRELIMINARY QUESTIONS

Considering whether a mark falls foul of section 5(1)–(3)/Article 8(1) and (5), it is always necessary to consider three preliminary questions. These are:

(i)   what is an 'earlier trade mark'?

(ii)   does the opponent (or applicant for cancellation) have an appropriate interest on which to base a challenge?

(iii)   has the earlier mark been used?

2.1.1   What is an earlier trade mark?

In the United Kingdom, the definition of earlier trade mark is quite complex. In essence, it covers earlier UK trade marks, earlier international trade marks (designating the EC or UK), and earlier Community marks. The provisions make it clear that the concept of 'earlier trade marks' includes 'earlier trade mark applications' with priority over the application under scrutiny. They also make it clear that earlier trade marks include earlier 'well-known' marks which

---

[3]   *SA Société LTJ Diffusion v. SA Sadas,* Case C–291/00 [2003] *ECR* I–02799 (para. 43) (ECJ), (para. 19)(AG).

are protected under the Paris Convention, even though these marks may not have been registered. The concept of a 'well-known mark' was discussed in chapter 34. The specific list of earlier marks is as follows:

- a registered British mark, a Community trade mark, or an international trade mark (UK or EC) (i.e. a mark registered under the Madrid Protocol designating the United Kingdom or EC),[4] which has a priority date earlier than the trade mark in question[5]—section 6(1)(a);

- a Community trade mark or international trade mark (EC) which has a valid claim to seniority from an earlier registered trade mark or international trade mark (UK)[6]—section 6(1)(b);

- registered trade mark or international mark (UK) which had been converted from a Community Trade Mark or international trade mark (EC) which itself had a valid claim to seniority from an earlier registered trade mark or international mark (UK) and accordingly has the same claim to seniority[7]—section 6(1)(ba);

- an application for a mark which, when registered, would be an earlier trade mark[8]—section 6(2); and

- a trade mark which is entitled to protection as a well-known trade mark—section 6(1)(c).[9]

If the registration of a mark falling within the first two categories, (sections 6(1)(a) or (b)) has lapsed, the mark can form the basis of an objection for a period of one year after expiry. However, this will not be the case if the Registrar is satisfied that there was no bona fide use of the mark during the two years immediately preceding expiry.[10]

In relation to oppositions brought against Community trade marks, the definition of earlier marks is both narrower and wider than that applicable in the UK. Under the CTMR 'earlier trade marks' include not only Community trade marks, and international trade marks specifying the Community (under the Madrid Protocol), but also all trade marks registered in *any* member state, at the Benelux Trade Mark Office, and international registrations under the Madrid Agreement and the Madrid Protocol nominating a member state.[11] Thus they include registrations in other member states—which could not be the basis for an opposition to a UK mark. The important consequence of this is that, in many circumstances, marks will be capable of being registered in national registries, but not at the OHIM. The CTMR also permits oppositions on the basis of earlier well-known marks. Here, however, the provision is narrower in one respect than the UK provision. This is because the ability of the owner of an earlier well-known mark to oppose registration in relation to dissimilar goods or services is confined to situations where the mark has been *registered*.[12] No such limitation appears to exist under the UK Act (though this might well be as a result of an oversight).

---

[4] TMA s. 53.   [5] TMA s. 51.   [6] TMA s. 6(1)(b). See above at pp. XXX–Y.

[7] TMA s. 6(1)(ba).   [8] TMA s. 6(2).

[9] TMA s. 56(1) (as amended by the Patents and Trade Marks (WTO) Regulations 1999 (SI 1999/1899)). See above at p. 742. *Paco/Paco Life in Colour Trade Marks* [2000] *RPC* 451.

[10] TMA s. 6(3). The concept of genuine use is explored at some length at pp. 899–901 in the context of revocation.

[11] CTMR Art. 8(2).

[12] CTMR Art. 8(5); TRIPS Art. 16(3); *Mühlens GmbH & Co. KG, v. OHIM and Minoronzoni Srl*, Case T–150/04, (11 July 2007) (CFI 2d Ch).

2.1.1 Does the opponent (or applicant for cancellation) have an appropriate interest on which to base a challenge?

An opposition (or application for cancellation) on relative grounds can only be commenced by a person who has a relevant interest in an earlier mark.[13] Neither the Office nor third parties may object if the same or a similar mark is registered for the same or similar goods—however much confusion this might produce. In the case of opposition to a UK registration it is only the proprietor of the earlier trade mark who can bring proceedings.[14] In contrast, a cancellation action can be brought by the proprietor, or a licensee of an earlier mark (or in the case of a certification mark, an authorized user). This latter position is perhaps most easily explained by the fact that a cancellation action may be by way of a counterclaim to infringement: it would be unfair were it not possible for a licensee of the earlier trade mark who is accused of infringing a later mark to be able to challenge that mark. At the OHIM, opposition (or an application for cancellation based on an earlier trade mark) may be brought by the proprietor or a licensee authorized by the proprietor.[15]

2.1.2 Has the earlier trade mark been used?

Where an applicant for a mark is faced with an opposition on relative grounds on the basis of an earlier trade mark registered more than five years previously, the applicant can demand that the opponent produces evidence of use of the trade mark in the previous five years or proper reasons for non-use. If the opponent fails to do so, the opposition will be rejected.[16] This requirement reflects the fact that a trade mark may be revoked if it has not been used for five years, and so an application should not be prevented by opposition based on a mark that itself could be revoked. The issue of revocation and the jurisprudence on when a mark is to be regarded as having been 'used' are discussed in chapter 39.

2.2 DOUBLE IDENTITY: SECTION 5(1)/ARTICLE 8(1)(A)

The first relative ground for refusal, the so-called 'double identity' ground,[17] is found in section 5(1) and Article 8(1)(a) of the CTMR.[18] This provides that a trade mark shall not be registered if it is identical to an earlier trade mark *and* the goods or services to which the trade mark application relates are identical to the goods or services for which the earlier trade mark is protected. As earlier trade marks are protected unconditionally as against a later application to register an identical mark for identical goods and services, there is no need to prove confusion.[19]

In considering whether a mark falls foul of section 5(1)(a)/Article 8(1)(a), two questions arise:

(i)   when are marks 'identical'? and

(ii) when are the goods and services 'identical'?

---

[13] The Trade Marks (Relative Grounds) Order 2007, (SI 2007/1976), reg. 2 (opposition); reg. 5.

[14] Given the powers that can be conferred on a licensee to bring infringement actions under TMA ss 3–31, it seems strange that the power to oppose a later registration should be limited in this way.

[15] CTMR Art. 42, Art. 55(1)(b).

[16] TMA s. 6A(2)–(7) (introduced by the Trade Marks (Proof of Use etc) Regulations 2004, (SI 2004/946)); CTMR Art. 43(2).

[17] Hobbs QC in *In re Direct Wines Application,* O-306–03 (13 Oct. 2003) (para. 13).

[18] For an exhaustive review, see A. Griffiths, 'The Trade Mark Monopoly: An Analysis of the Core Zone of absolute Protection under Art. 591)(a)' (2007) *IPQ* 312.

[19] The rationale for this is that confusion will necessarily result: TRIPS, Art. 16(1); TM Dir., Recital 10; Griffiths, 'The Trade Mark Monopoly', at 317 ff.

2.2.1 Are the marks identical?

The first question to ask in relation to section 5(1)/Article 8(1)(a) is: are the marks identical? In answering this question, it is necessary to compare the representation of the earlier trade mark contained in the registration certificate with the trade mark which has been applied for (or, in the case of infringement, that being used by the defendant).[20] In contrast with the position on infringement,[21] where the court has to decide on the parameters of the defendant's sign, in the context of assessing relative grounds of validity the comparison is between the earlier trade mark (as registered) and the sign in the applicant's application. The two marks are considered as a whole: nothing in the applicant's mark is ignored.

While few problems are likely to arise in determining whether marks are identical, one particular issue warrants consideration, that is, whether marks that are slightly different may nonetheless still be treated as being identical. While specific provisions exist which prevent a mark that is similar to an earlier mark from being registered, the reason why owners of earlier marks might wish to argue their case under section 5(1)/Article 8(1)(a) is that, unlike the other relevant relative grounds, there is no need to prove confusion. Given this, it would seem reasonable for the courts to construe section 5(1)/Article 8(1)(a) narrowly. Applying such a logic, in *SA Société LTJ Diffusion v. SA Sadas*, the ECJ[22] concluded that the criterion 'must be interpreted strictly. The very definition of identity implies that the two elements should be the same in all respects'.[23] The Court then elaborated that there is identity where a sign reproduces 'without any modification or addition, all the elements constituting the [trade mark]'.[24] However, it qualified this strict interpretation by observing that the test is to be applied from the viewpoint of the average consumer, and that such a person will usually assess two signs globally, looking at the overall impression. Consequently 'insignificant differences between the sign and the trade mark may go unnoticed by the average consumer'. The existence of such 'insignificant differences', then, would not cause the signs to be lacking in identity. It is a question of fact whether consumers would see differences as significant: applying the test, Lewison J has held that consumers of computer software would not notice the difference between WEBSPHERE and WEB-SPHERE;[25] but Hart J held that KCS HERR VOSS was not identical to HERR-VOSS.[26]

2.2.2 When are goods or services identical?

The second element that must be proved for a mark to fall foul of section 5(1)/Article 8(1)(a) is that the goods or services to which the application relates must be identical with the goods or

---

[20] Disclaimed matter in the earlier trade mark will usually be ignored: *Torremar Trade Mark* [2003] *RPC* (4) 89, 98 (para. 29); *Paco Life in Colour*, note 9 above; *The European v. The Economist Newspaper* [1998] *FSR* 283, 289; *General Cigar Co Inc v. Partagas y Cia SA* [2005] *FSR* (45) 960 (Collins J). Cf. *Chantilly Polo Club Device/ Beverly Hills Polo Club Device*, R714/2000–1 (10 May 2001) (disclaimer does not affect assessment of confusing similarity); *Phones4U Ltd v. Phone4u.co.uk Internet Ltd* [2006] *EWCA Civ* 244, [2007] *RPC* (5).

[21] See pp. 917–18.

[22] *Soc. LTJ Diffusion v. Sadas,* Case C–291/00 [2003] *ECR* I–02799. In *Sadas SA v. OHIM,* Case T–346/04 [2006] *ETMR* (27) 329, the CFI upheld the opposition to registering ARTHUR ET FELICIE based on ARTHUR, both for clothes, on the basis that the similarities were sufficient that there was a likelihood of confusion.

[23] Ibid, para. 50.   [24] Ibid, para. 51.

[25] *Websphere Trade Mark* [2004] *FSR* (39) 796.

[26] *Blue IP Inc v. KCS Herr-Voss Ltd* [2004] *EWHC* 97 (Ch) (para 49) (referring to the test laid down by the ECJ as 'a very strict interpretation of identicality'). Note also *Bayer Cropscience SA v. Agropharm* [2004] *EWHC* 1661 (Ch) (Patten J) (issue whether PATRIOT C and PATRIOT P were identical to PATRIOT not suitable for summary judgment).

services for which the earlier mark is protected.[27] If the category of goods or services protected by an earlier trade mark is broader than, but includes, the category of goods or services to which the application relates, then the applicant's goods are identical with those of the earlier mark. So, if an earlier trade mark relates to 'broadcasting services', a later application relating to radio broadcasting services would be understood as being identical.[28] Equally, if the specifications of the trade mark applicant overlap with those of the earlier trade mark owner/opponent, those goods within the overlap will be regarded as identical.[29]

While the specification of goods or services for which the earlier mark is registered is the starting point for determining whether goods or services are identical, in some cases the language of the trade mark specification may need to be interpreted.[30] So, for example, courts may have to decide whether 'vermin' include insects,[31] or whether 'cosmetics' includes 'skin-lightening cream'.[32] As Jacob J explained, instead of construing the words literally, 'when it comes to construing a word used in a trade mark specification, one is concerned with how the product is, as a practical matter, regarded for the purposes of trade'.[33]

2.3 CONFUSING SIMILARITIES: SECTION 5(2)/ARTICLE 8(1)(B)

According to section 5(2)/Article 8(1)(b) (which correspond to Article 4(1)(b) of the Directive) a trade mark shall not be registered where it is:

(i)   identical or similar to an earlier trade mark;

(ii) to be registered for goods or services similar to those for which the earlier trade mark is protected; *and*

(iii) there exists a likelihood of confusion on the part of the public, which includes the likelihood of association with the earlier trade mark.

In considering whether a mark falls foul of section 5(2)/Article 8(1)(b), a number of questions arise. We have already considered what is meant by an 'earlier trade mark' and the situations where marks and services will be 'identical'. As such, it remains only to consider when goods or services are 'similar', when marks are 'similar', and what is meant by 'likelihood of confusion'.

---

[27] It is important to note that the section refers to the goods or services *protected by* the earlier trade mark. This language was chosen to ensure that the section covered well-known marks (which may not have been registered). In the case of other earlier marks, the use of the term 'protected' introduces an unfortunate ambiguity. This is because, while one would have expected the comparison to be between the goods or services identified in the specifications, there is a possibility that the goods or services 'protected by' a registered mark might extend beyond those that are identified in the specification.

[28] *Discovery Communications v. Discovery* [2000] *ETMR* 516 (need to assume normal and fair use across whole of specification).

[29] *Galileo Trade Mark* [2005] *RPC* (22) 569 (Appointed Person, Professor Annand).

[30] The interpretation of the specification is done as of the date of registration/filing: *Reed Executive plc v. Reed Business Information Ltd* [2004] *RPC* (40) 767 (para. 46) (Jacob LJ).

[31] *Bayer Cropscience v. Agropharm* [2004] *EWHC* 1661 (Ch).

[32] *British Sugar plc v. James Robertson & Sons* [1996] *RPC* 281, 289. See also *Omega SA v. Omega Engineering Inc* [2003] *FSR* (49) 893 (para. 4); *Beautimatic International v. Mitchell International Pharmaceuticals* [1999] *ETMR* 912, 921 ('skin-lightening cream' and 'dry-skin lotion' were identical to earlier trade registration relating to 'toilet preparations and cosmetics'); *Associated Newspapers v. Express Newspapers* [2003] *FSR* (51) Laddie J (para. 66) (newspapers 'for sale in England and Wales' not identical to 'free newspapers').

[33] *British Sugar*, ibid.

Before looking at these in more detail, it is important to note that, in *Canon Kabushiki Kaisha v. Metro-Goldwyn-Mayer*,[34] the European Court of Justice said the various elements of Article 4(1)(b) of the Directive are interdependent. This means that difficulties in proving one of the requirements may be offset by the way one of the other requirements is met. For example, low levels of similarity between goods might be offset by a high degree of similarity between marks. This has been called the 'interdependency principle'.[35] In other cases, however, the ECJ has indicated that the requirements—similarity of marks, similarity of goods, and a likelihood of confusion—are cumulative.[36] There are circumstances, therefore, where a tribunal is correct to reject an opposition (or find infringement) on the ground purely that the signs (or goods) are dissimilar—so dissimilar, at least, that there could be no confusion even were the goods (or signs) identical and the mark highly distinctive.[37] The seemingly contradictory approaches ('interdependence' and 'cumulation') are reconciled by saying that the interdependence of the factors only falls to be assessed once a 'minimum level' of similarity of marks or a 'slight' similarity of goods/services has been reached.[38]

2.3.1 Similarity of marks

The case law provides voluminous guidance on when marks will be treated as similar.[39] However, the starting point is *Sabel v. Puma,* where the ECJ laid down a basic framework that has been followed ever since—the so-called 'global appreciation' approach.[40] According to this approach the tribunal should compare the marks as a whole, in the way an average consumer would see them. As the ECJ observed, the average consumer *normally* perceives a mark as a whole and does not proceed to analyse its various details.[41] Consequently, attention should be paid particularly to the dominant and distinctive components of the mark. The tribunal should examine the degree of aural, visual, or conceptual similarity between the marks. In so doing, the tribunal will take into account the inherent or acquired distinctiveness of the mark.[42] One of the consequences of looking at the marks as a whole is that the courts will not necessarily examine the marks in too much detail.

Visual, aural, and conceptual similarity. The marks should be assessed from the point of view of their visual, aural, and conceptual similarities. Typically, tribunals consider each in turn,

---

[34] Case C–39/97 [1999] 1 *CMLR* 77, 95. See also *Marca Mode CV v. Adidas AG,* Case C–425/98 [2000] 2 *CMLR* 1061, 1084.

[35] *Julian James' Application; Opposition of Smart GmbH* [2005] *ETMR* (93) 1096 (Appointed Person, Richard Arnold QC).

[36] *Vedial v. OHIM,* Case C–106/03 [2004] *ECR* I–9573 (para 51); *Il Ponte Finanzaria v. OHIM,* Case C–234/06P [2008] *ETMR* (13) 242 (paras. 48–50); *El Corte Ingles SA v. OHIM,* Case T–443/05 [2007] *ETMR* (81) 1340 (para. 40) (CFI, extended composition) (if there is a 'slight' similarity between goods, the tribunal should apply the interdependence test); *Assembled Investments (Pty) Ltd v. OHIM,* Case T–105/05 [2007] (unreported) (para. 27).

[37] *Vedial,* ibid (para 51); *Bunker & Bkr v. OHIM,* Case T–423/04 [2005] *ECR* II–4035 (para. 77); *Il Ponte Finanzaria,* ibid (paras. 48–50); *El Corte Ingles,* ibid (para. 40).

[38] *Esure Insurance Ltd v. Direct Line Insurance Plc* [2007] *EWHC* 1557 (Ch) (para. 46).

[39] The Court's approach has been said to be similar to German *Prägetheorie: Medion AG v. Thomson Multimedia Sales Germany & Austria GmbH,* Case C–120/04 [2005] *ECR* I–8551 (AG para 33) (Advocate General Jacobs).

[40] *Sabel BV v. Puma AG, Rudolf Dassler Sport,* Case C–251/95 [1997] *ECR* I–6191, I–6224 (hereafter *Sabel v. Puma*).

[41] Ibid (para. 23).

[42] Ibid (para. 23). On disclaimed matter see fn 17.

before reaching an overall conclusion. In so doing, they have observed that a trade-off can occur: visual and conceptual differences, for example, can offset aural similarities.[43]

Although the marks are compared as a whole, emphasis is placed on the 'dominant' components. The tribunals therefore struggle, particularly in the case of composite marks, to identify which are the dominant elements. In much of the case law there is a tendency to emphasize the textual elements.[44] So, in *Claudia Oberhauser v. OHIM*,[45] an application for the word mark FIFTIES for denim clothing was successfully opposed because of similarities with the opponent's composite mark, registered for clothing, including words MISS FIFTIES in its lower part. Likewise, in *Matratzen Concord GmbH v. OHIM*,[46] the earlier word mark MATRATZEN was a successful basis for opposition to registration of a composite mark, comprising MATRATZEN MARKT CONCORD and including a figure carrying a mattress, because the word Matratzen was found to be the dominant feature of the applicant's composite mark. However, without casting doubt on these decisions, the ECJ has provided a reminder that the assessment is a global one. In *Shaker de Laudato v Limiñana y Botella*, an applicant for a composite mark for alcoholic beverages which included the word LIMONCELLO above an image of a plate decorated with six lemons, was opposed by the owner of the Spanish word mark LIMONCHELO, also relating to goods in class 33.[47] The CFI had held that the signs were dissimilar because of the dominance of the dish feature in the applicant's mark, a feature which was absent in the opponent's. (This finding was itself surprising, given the general tendency to emphasize verbal components.) The ECJ overturned this finding, reminding the Court that the assessment was a global one, and could not be conducted by comparing only one element. It is only where all other aspects are negligible that the assessment can be carried out on the basis solely of the dominant element.

The relative importance of each sort of similarity will vary with the circumstances in hand, in particular the goods and the types of mark. In the case of certain kinds of goods, such as clothes or furniture, visual similarity between the marks in issue will be the most important form of similarity.[48] In contrast, it has been said that wine marks will be perceived 'verbally';[49] with restaurant services (where word-of-mouth recommendation is highly important), it is likely that phonetic similarity will be a key.[50] Each case is therefore to be viewed in its own context. However, the ECJ has ruled that, in an appropriate case, mere aural similarity may make marks so similar as to be likely to cause confusion.[51] In the case of device marks (as well

---

[43] *Il Ponte Finanzaria*, Case C–234/06 P [2008] *ETMR* (13) 242 (para. 34); *Ruiz Picasso v. OHIM*, Case C–361/04 P [2006] *ECR* I–643 (para 20); *Mühlens v. OHIM*, Case C–206/04P [2006] *ECR* I–2717 (para. 35); *T.I.M.E. Art v. OHIM*, Case C–171/06 [2007] *ETMR* (38) 635 (para. 49) (conceptual differences did not offset aural and visual similarities between QUANTUM and QUANTIÈME).

[44] On the basis that 'words "speak louder" than devices': *Oasis Stores' Trade Mark Application* [1998] *RPC* 631, 644. For an obligatory counter-example, see *Vedial*, Case C–106/03 [2004] *ECR* I–9573 (ECJ said CFI made no error in finding the word mark SAINT-HUBERT-41 was dissimilar to a composite mark of a chef and the word HUBERT); *Plus v. OHIM*, Case T–34/04 [2005] *ECR* II–2401.

[45] T–104/01 [2002] *ECR* II–4359 (esp. para. 47).

[46] T–6/01 [2002] *ECR* II–4335.

[47] *Shaker de L. Laudato & C. Sas v. Limiñana y Botella, SL*, Case C–334/05 P (12 June 2007) (ECJ).

[48] *Inter-Ikea Systems BV v. OHIM*, T–112/06 (16 Jan 2008) (CFI) (para. 79); *Phillips–Van Heusen Corp. v. OHIM*, T–292/01 [2003] *ECR* II–4335 (para. 55) (BASS for footwear and clothing permitted despite opposition by owner of PASH for clothing made of leather, in part because aural similarities of little significance in clothing sector); cf. *Claudia Oberhauser*, Case T–104/01 [2002] *ECR* II–4359 (esp. para. 48) (in context of clothing CFI dismissive of figurative elements of sign, which would be interpreted as decorative features).

[49] *Castellani SpA v. OHIM*, T–149/06 (29 Nov. 2007) (para. 53).

[50] *Mystery Drinks GmbH v. OHIM*, T–99/01 [2004] *ETMR* (18) 217 (para. 48).

[51] *Lloyd Schuhfabrik Meyer v. Klijsen Handel BV*, Case C–342/97 [1999] 2 *CMLR* 1343. For an example, see *Mystery Drinks*, ibid (figurative mark MYSTERY with stylized M and MIXERY were neither conceptually nor

as three-dimensional marks), visual similarity will usually be the most important factor,[52] and in the case of sound marks, clearly, the inquiry will depend chiefly on aural similarity.

In the case of word marks, a determination of visual similarity typically involves looking at the length of the marks; their structure (whether there are the same number of words); and whether the same letters are used. The courts also bear in mind that consumers may not be able to remember a mark perfectly (this is called the notion of 'imperfect recollection'). The average consumer only rarely has the chance to make a direct comparison between marks, and so must place his trust in the 'imperfect picture of them that he has kept in his mind'.[53] In many cases this means that, while at first glance two marks may appear to be dissimilar, when the possibility of imperfect recollection is taken into account, the marks may in fact be similar. While the courts have used the notion of imperfect recollection to expand the ambit of protection given to earlier marks, they are always mindful of the need for the marks to be similar.

When comparing marks aurally, tribunals have tended to carry out a quantitative assessment: do the two signs have more syllables in common than not? For example, the CFI held that GIORGIO AIRE was not aurally similar to MISS GIORGI because only one syllable out of four was the same;[54] whereas MYSTERY and MIXERY were treated as similar.[55] In a short word, a slight variation may be sufficient to render the marks dissimilar: for example BASS and PASH were treated as dissimilar by the CFI,[56] though in a different case it held ILS to be similar to ELS.[57] In assessing similarity, the tribunal will typically be more influenced by the first than the last syllable. So the CFI treated BUD and BUDMEN, SUN and SUNPLUS, as similar, and the English High Court held VIAGRA and VIAGRENE to be similar.[58] Consistently with this logic, the CFI held words with common endings—NUTRIDE and TUFFTRIDE, ASTERIX and STARIX— not to be similar.[59] In other cases, similarity of the first syllable has proved insufficient to establish similarity, (for example, it was held by the CFI that GIORGI LINE was not similar to GIORGIO AIRE, and by the UK Registry that POLACLIP was not similar to POLAROID).[60] Despite emphasis on the first part, the CFI also has held LA MER confusingly similar to LABORATOIRES

visually similar, but were aurally similar, and in the field of beverages this was sufficient). But note *Mühlens v. OHIM*, Case C–206/04 P [2006] *ECR* I–2717 (ECJ holding CFI made no mistake in finding no similarity between ZIRH and SIR despite finding of aural similarity).

[52] *Julius Sämaan Ltd v. Tetrosyl Ltd* [2006] *FSR* (42) 849 (para. 54) (Kitchin J).

[53] *Lloyd Schuhfabrik*, Case C–342/97 [1999] 2 *CMLR* 1343, 1358–9 (paras. 22–6).

[54] *Laboratorios RTB, SL v. OHIM*, T–156/01 [2003] *ECR* II–2789 (para. 77).

[55] *Mystery Drinks*, T–99/01 [2004] *ETMR* (18) 217 (figurative mark MYSTERY with stylized M refused registration for non-alcoholic beverages in the face of earlier registration of MIXERY for beer).

[56] *Phillips–Van Heusen*, T–292/01 [2003] *ECR* II–4335 (para. 50). For further examples, see *Inter-Ikea Systems*, T–112/06 (16 Jan 2008) (CFI) (IDEA and IKEA); *Grether AG v. OHIM*, Case T–167/05 (13 June 2007) (FENNEL and FENJAL); *Ruiz-Picasso v. OHIM*, T–185/02 [2004] *ECR* II–1739 (PICARO and PICASSO); *In re Rosco Clothing's Application* (18 Jun. 2003) (Thorley QC) (FUTTI and FUZZI not similar).

[57] *Institut für Lernsysteme GmbH v. OHIM*, T–388/00 [2002] *ECR* II–4301 (earlier figurative mark including letters ILS similar to applicant's ELS, and together created a likelihood of confusion).

[58] *José Alejando SL v. OHIM*, T–129/01 [2003] *ECR* II–2251 (para. 49); *Sunplus Technology Ltd v. OHIM*, T–38/04 (15 Nov. 2007) (CFI); *Pfizer v. Eurofood Link (UK)* [2000] *ETMR* 187.

[59] *Durferrit GmbH v. OHIM*, T–224/01 [2003] *ECR* II–1589; *Les Éditions Albert René v. OHIM*, T–311/01 [2003] *ECR* II–4625 (esp. para. 56); *Phillips–Van Heusen*, T–292/01 [2003] *ECR* II–4335 (para. 50) (BASS not similar to PASH); *In re Bayer AG's Application* (XAROCID) SRIS O/140/03 (12 May 2003) (TARGOCID and XAROCID not sufficiently similar, though a 'near miss').

[60] *Laboratorios RTB*, T–156/01 [2003] *ECR* II–2789 (GIORGI was not thought particularly distinctive for perfumes); *Polaclip Trade Mark* [1999] *RPC* 282, 289 (the Registrar accepting that the 'pola' element would be understood as a reference to the polarizing effect of reducing glare).

DE LA MER (both in closely related goods in the cosmetics area),[61] and the Appointed Person affirmed a Registry decision that FELENDIL and PLENDIL were similar for pharmaceuticals.[62] These counter-examples are a useful reminder that the rulings are fact-specific, so previous decisions are helpful only to provide a sense of the standards being applied: they have virtually no value as precedents.

Because similarity is assessed conceptually as well as visually and phonetically, in thinking about whether marks are similar, it is necessary to take account of the ideas that lie behind or inform the earlier mark. The important role that non-visual features may play in deciding whether marks are similar can be seen in *Sir Terence Conran v. Mean Fiddler Holdings*.[63] Sir Terence, who had registered the word ZINC in respect of planning, design, and interior design of restaurants, brought an action for summary judgment against the defendant who had opened a wine bar called the ZINCBAR (with the letters ZN located on one side of the facia on the premises). In granting relief, Robert Walker J explained that the chemical symbol for the element zinc, 'Zn' (as well as 'ZN'), in addition to phonetic equivalents such as sinc and sync, were similar to ZINC.[64] In other situations, conceptual dissimilarity, as for example where one mark has a meaning but its comparator does not, may counteract aural or visual similarity.[65]

Distinctiveness. The question of whether marks are similar will often be dependent on the inherent or acquired distinctiveness of the mark (for the goods or services for which it is registered).[66] This has a number of effects.[67]

First, the less distinctive the earlier trade mark, the less literal or visual alteration is necessary to ensure that the later mark is not similar. For example, the CFI comparing two words CASTELLANI and CASTELLUCA for wine from the point of view of a German consumer found the two marks to be dissimilar, because the 'castel' element is a common descriptive component in wine names and the applicant's suffix 'luca' would be seen as the Italian name and thus

---

[61] *La Mer Technology Inc. v. OHIM*, T–418/03 [2008] *ETMR* (9) 169; *Julian James; Opposition of Smart*, note 35 above (Appointed Person, Richard Arnold QC) (CARSMART similar to SMART, both for cars, in part because while 'car' was at beginning it was descriptive).

[62] *Ratiopharm GmbH's Trade Mark Application* [2007] *RPC* (28) 630 (Appointed Person, Geoffrey Hobbs QC).

[63] [1997] *FSR* 856.

[64] See also *Fountain Trade Mark* [1999] RPC 490, 495 (FONT FOUNTAIN and FOUNTAIN both used in relation to computer hardware and peripheral devices alluded 'to the idea or image of a gushing jet or spray of water').

[65] *Phillips–Van Heusen*, T–292/01 [2003] *ECR* II–4335 (BASS not similar to PASH, despite visual and aural similarities, because the former was understandable as a musical reference, whereas the latter either had no meaning or referred to a German dice game).

[66] *Picasso v. OHIM*, T–104/01 [2002] *ECR* II–4359 (ECJ, 1st Ch) (PICASSO was highly distinctive for painting but not for cars).

[67] The status of some of these propositions, that is whether they are legal rules, presumptions of fact, or merely guidelines, has been a matter of dispute. Given the ECJ's role, particularly on references from member states, it has been assumed that some statements must be propositions of law. In *Reed Executive plc v. Reed Business Information Ltd* [2003] *RPC* (12) 207, 241 (para. 103), when referring to the ECJ's statements as regards the relevance of distinctiveness to a finding of likelihood of confusion, Pumfrey J stated: 'This is a very surprising proposition (and perhaps only a presumption of fact, since this cannot be a legal issue), since normally it is easier to distinguish a well-known mark from others close to it. But it seems to make more sense when one comes to consider device marks.' On appeal, Jacob LJ said he agreed with Pumfrey J's questioning of these propositions: note 30 above (para. 83).

sufficient to differentiate the marks.[68] In *Reed Executive plc v. Reed Business Information Ltd,*[69] Jacob LJ stated that 'where a mark is descriptive small differences may suffice to avoid confusion', giving an illustration from the law of passing-off concerning the terms OFFICE CLEANING ASSOCIATION and OFFICE CLEANING SERVICES. Where the distinctiveness of the earlier trade mark is very low, the later mark will have to be in close proximity for it to be similar, as with THERMAWEAR and THERMAWARM.[70] The same principle applies to common names which intrinsically have a low level of distinctiveness.[71]

Second, if the earlier mark is highly distinctive, then a mark that has been substantially modified might nonetheless still be similar.[72] In *De Cordova v. Vick Chemical Co.,*[73] the claimant was the proprietor of a device mark consisting of the words VICKS VAPORUB SALVE and a triangle with the words VICKS CHEMICAL COMPANY printed on the sides. They were also owners of a word mark, VAPORUB. The Privy Council held that the appellant had infringed the first of the claimant's marks by importing and marketing jars of ointment under the name KARSOTE VAPOUR RUB. Lord Radcliffe explained that VAPORUB was (at least at the time of registration) a fancy word, and evidence established that the public treated VAPORUB as being synonymous with VICKS VAPORUB.[74] As VAPORUB was an essential feature, or a material or substantial element, of the trade mark, the marks were similar.

Third, the chance of there being a likelihood of confusion on the basis of the ideas (or concepts) that underlie a mark is particularly influenced by the distinctiveness of the earlier mark:[75] in *Sabel v. Puma,* which concerned two images of bounding felines, the ECJ suggested that *if* the earlier mark was well known by the public and/or the image of the puma was imaginative, mere conceptual similarity might be sufficient to give rise to a finding of a likelihood of confusion (see Fig. 38.1 below).[76]

Fourth, although the comparison is to be made between the particular mark registered and the sign applied for,[77] the relevance of acquired distinctiveness may permit the tribunal to consider the earlier mark in the context of a 'family of marks'. Most readers will be familiar with

---

[68] *Castellani,* T–149/06 (29 Nov 2007). However, the ECJ has held that the so-called 'requirement of availability' is irrelevant to the determination of similarity between marks, goods, or likelihood of confusion: *Adidas Ag & ors v. Marca Mode CV & ors,* Case C–102/07 (10 Apr 2008).

[69] [2004] *RPC* (40) 767.

[70] See *Thermawear v. Vedonis* [1982] *RPC* 44, 55–6 (VENDONIS THERMAWARM similar to claimant's registered mark THERMAWEAR for underwear); *Associated Newspapers v. Express* [2003] *FSR* (51) (para. 73) (LONDON EVENING MAIL not sufficiently similar to THE MAIL ON SUNDAY, but EVENING MAIL was similar).

[71] *Reed Executive* [2004] *RPC* (40) 767 (para 86) (common surnames). See also *Laboratorios RTB* T–156/01 [2003] *ECR* II–2789 (para. 81) (GIORGIO AIRE not similar to GIORGI LINE because the common components were not distinctive given the prevalence of Italian names in the perfumery market).

[72] *Sabel v. Puma,* Case C–251/95 [1997] *ECR* I–6191 (para. 24); *Lloyd Schuhfabrik,* Case C–342/7 [1999] 2 *CMLR* 1343, 1357–8 (paras. 21–2); *Canon KK v. MGM,* Case C–39/97 [1999] 1 *CMLR* 77, 95 (paras. 17–18). The UK courts, while acknowledging the status of the Court making these statements, has frequently described it as a 'presumption of fact', and thus not a substitute for a proper analysis. Some famous signs, such as David Beckham or Coca-Cola are so famous that no one would think Dave Beckham or Roco-Cola was similar. See, e.g. *Kundry SA's Application* [1998] *ETMR* 178, 185 (JARVARD not similar to HARVARD even given the latter's reputation); *Albert René v. OHIM,* T–311/01 [2003] *ECR* II–4625 (esp. para. 58) (where fame of earlier mark ASTERIX meant it was extremely unlikely that there could be any confusion by use of the word STARIX); *Vedial,* Case C–106/03 [2004] *ECR* I–9573 (fame of SAINT-HUBERT-41 Mark could not alter the global assessment of likelihood of confusion given the finding that the sign was visually, aurally, and conceptually dissimilar to a composite mark of a chef and the word HUBERT).

[73] (1951) 68 *RPC* 103.

[74] Ibid, 106. Approved in *Wagamama v. City Centre Restaurants* [1995] *FSR* 713, 733.

[75] *Sabel v. Puma,* Case C–251/95 [1997] *ECR* I–6191 (para. 24).

[76] Ibid (para. 25).   [77] *Ener-Cap* [1999] *RPC* 362.

Puma

Sabel

Fig. 38.1 *Sabel v. Puma case*

the range of 'easy' services EASYJET (an airline), EASYINTERNET (internet cafés), etc. provided by what was the 'Easy' group. On the assumption that these are registered as trade marks, it might be that the existence of a 'family' allows each mark (the inherent distinctiveness of which is weak) to reinforce each other and gain a broader scope of protection than they would otherwise have. This might mean that an application by a third party for EASYBANK would be refused. The ECJ, in *Il Ponte Finanzaria SpA*,[78] has affirmed that the existence of a family of marks is a relevant factor when assessing similarity, though emphasized at the same time that the status of being a 'family' can only be conferred on marks that have been used in such a way that they would be recognized in the market as a family. Merely registering a series of marks will not confer this added strength.[79]

Deviation from the Global Approach. Having adopted the 'global approach' the ECJ found itself with a difficult case: what to do with a later mark which added a well-known 'house mark' or company name to an earlier registered mark, for example, where the owner of a weak mark, say SENSATIONS for crisps, is confronted with an application for WALKERS SENSATIONS, where WALKERS is a highly distinctive component of the later mark. Applying a 'global appreciation' that focuses on the 'dominant distinctive' components in such a case a tribunal would likely find the marks lacking in similarity, and thus would be a licence to big firms to swamp the goodwill engendered by smaller proprietors. Rather than accept the injustice that would arise from strict application of the global appreciation approach, the ECJ has added a qualification for cases where elements of a mark retain some 'independent distinctive role' in a later

---

[78] Case C–234/06 P [2008] *ETMR* (13) 242. See also *Citybond Trade Mark* [2007] *RPC* (13) 301 (para 44) (Appointed Person, Geoffrey Hobbs QC).
[79] Case C–234/06P [2008] *ETMR* (13) 242, paras. 63–64.

'composite mark'. In *Medion AG v Thomson Multimedia Sales*,[80] the ECJ has stated that, in such cases, at least where there is identity of goods or services, it suffices that 'because the earlier mark still has an independent distinctive role, the origin of the goods or services covered by the composite sign is attributed by the public also to the owner of that mark'.[81] While it is easy to understand the motivation behind this approach, one cannot help but wonder whether this does not drive the proverbial 'coach and horses' through the global appreciation test.

2.3.2 When are goods or services similar?

The question of whether goods or services are similar depends on the facts of the case. When deciding whether a trade mark application falls foul of one of the relative grounds for refusal, the comparison is normally between the goods or services for which the earlier mark has been registered and the goods or services to which the application relates. This is largely a paper exercise. (However, in an infringement action the court will usually compare the defendant's goods as they have actually been used with the goods in the claimant's specification. This requires the court to interpret the specification and then to characterize the defendant's goods or services to see if they fall within the specification.)

In *Canon Kabushiki Kaisha v. Pathé Communications,* the Japanese company, Canon, opposed MGM's registration of the sign CANNON for films in the German Trade Mark Registry. The opposition was based upon Canon's registration of CANON for 'still and motion picture cameras and projectors, television filming and recording devices, etc'. The German Bundespatentgericht held that the goods were not similar. On appeal, the Bundesgerichtshof asked the ECJ for a preliminary ruling on the interpretation of Article 4(1)(b) of the Directive (which is the equivalent of section 5(2)(a)/Article 8(1)(b)). In response, the ECJ explained that, when the tribunal assesses the similarity of the goods or services concerned, 'all the relevant factors relating to those goods and services themselves should be taken into account. Those factors include, inter alia, their nature, their end-users, and their method of use and whether they are in competition with each other or are complementary.'[82] The methods by which the goods are distributed may also be a pertinent factor.[83] Moreover (and in contradiction to the approach that had been taken in the UK courts), the tribunal should also take into account 'the distinctive character of the earlier trade mark, and in particular its reputation' when determining whether the similarity 'between the goods or services covered by the two trade marks is sufficient to give rise to the likelihood of confusion'.[84] In an infringement scenario, the tribunal might also have relevant evidence of how the defendant has marketed its goods.[85]

British Sugar v. Robertson illustrates how the courts have applied the factors in the case of a non-distinctive mark (namely TREAT). There the question was whether a sweet syrup to be

---

[80] *Medion v. Thomson,* Case C–120/04 [2005] ECR I–8551. Rather than deviate from the established 'global appreciation' approach, Advocate General Jacobs would have left the unfortunate holder of the earlier mark to whatever remedies existed under national unfair competition law.

[81] Ibid, para. 36.

[82] *Canon KK v. MGM,* Case C–39/97 [1999] 1 *CMLR* 77, 95 (para. 17).

[83] *Ampafrance SA v. OHIM,* Case T–164/03 [2005] *ECR* II–1401 (para 53); *El Corte Ingles,* T–443/05 [2007] *ETMR* (81) 1340 (para. 43) (CFI, extended composition.)

[84] See J. Palm, '*Canon, Waterford*...How the Issue of similarity of Goods should be Determined in the Field of Trade Mark Law', [2007] *EIPR* 475.

[85] Case C–39/97 [1999] 1 *CMLR* 77, 95 (para. 18). In *Pfizer v. Eurofood* [2000] *ETMR* 187, Deputy Judge Simon Thorley QC came to the conclusion that a herbal beverage sold as VIAGRENE was similar to the claimant's pharmaceutical product, VIAGRA. The court was influenced particularly by the defendant's marketing of the beverage as potentially stimulating the libido of its drinkers, so that, like VIAGRA, VIAGRENE would enhance a person's love life.

poured over desserts was similar to a sweet-flavoured spread. Jacob J concluded that the goods were not similar,[86] explaining that the goods were used differently (the spread could be used on desserts but generally would not be); were not in direct competition; were located in different places in supermarkets (the spread with jams, the dessert sauce with desserts); were physically different (the spread was more viscous than the sauce); and were treated differently by market researchers. In contrast, in *Balmoral Trade Mark,* whisky and wine were held to be similar goods: although the two products have very different producers, it is common to find them being bought and sold by the same merchants, and sold through the same outlets.[87]

It is clear that the fact that goods or services are registered in different classes does not inevitably mean that they are not similar. For example, the CFI held that the development of correspondence courses was similar to educational textbooks and printed materials.[88] The fact that the signs relate to different classes is irrelevant because the way the goods or services are classified is an administrative matter, whereas the question whether goods or services are similar is an issue for substantive law.[89] It is also clear that, if an earlier trade mark relates to goods whereas the applicant's mark relates to services, they may nonetheless still be similar (and vice versa).[90] In one case, an application for the sign BALMORAL for wines was rejected because of the existence of an earlier trade mark BALMORAL for bar services.[91]

Although application of the *Canon* test has generally proved unproblematic, one question that has raised concern is the application of the 'complementarity' factor. The basic idea seems straightforward: consumers of some goods under a particular mark (say KENZO for clothes) might believe complementary goods (say shoes, scent, or bath towels) sold under the same (or a similar) mark are made under the authority of the trade mark holder, whereas such a connection might not be made in relation to non-complementing goods (say hair-dryers or fridges). Nevertheless, the Court of First Instance has tried to formulate a notion of 'aesthetic complementarity' that is unduly exacting. In *Sergio Rossi SpA,*[92] the CFI held women's footwear were not similar to women's bags, in part because they were not aesthetically complementary. The Court explained 'the applicant has failed to demonstrate,...that this aesthetic or subjective complementary nature has reached the stage of a true aesthetic necessity in the sense that consumers would think it unusual or shocking to carry a bag which does not perfectly match

---

[86] [1996] *RPC* 281, 297. From a European perspective it seems this was 'a very narrow construction': A. Kur, 'Harmonization of Trade Mark Law in Europe—An Overview' (1997) 28 *IIC* 1, 22. Contrast, in particular, *Vedial SA v. OHIM,* T–110/01 (CFI) [2002] *ECR* II–5275 (edible fats were similar to vinegars and sauces, inter alia, because they are offered for sale on the same shelves) (not discussed on appeal, Case C–106/03 [2004] *ECR* I–9573); and *Pedro Díaz v. OHIM,* T–85/02 [2003] *ECR* II–4835 (condensed milk and cheese held similar because they are in the same family of 'milk products' so consumers might think they both come from the same enterprise).

[87] *Balmoral Trade Mark* [1999] *RPC* 297, 302. Note also *Thomson Holidays v. Norwegian Cruise Lines* [2003] *RPC* (32) 586 (CA).

[88] *Institut für Lernsysteme,* T–388/00 [2002] *ECR* II–4301.

[89] *El Corte Ingles,* T–443/05 [2007] *ETMR* (81) 1340 (para. 38) (CFI, extended composition.)

[90] The characterization of a defendant's activities may be such that it can be said that he is using the sign in relation to both goods *and* services. For example, a garage which advertises that it repairs BMW vehicles can be seen as using the sign BMW in relation both to cars and repairing services: *Bayerische Motorenwerke AG v. Ronald Karel Deenik,* Case C–63/97 [1999] 1 *CMLR* 1099, 1122–23 (paras. 38–42). However, the cases where use in relation to services is simultaneously regarded as use in relation to goods is limited to situations where there is a 'specific and indissociable link' between the products and services: *Adam Opel AG v. Autec,* Case C–48/05 [2007] *ETMR* (33) 500 (paras. 27–28).

[91] *Balmoral,* [1999] *RPC* 297, 301.

[92] *Sergio Rossi SpA v. OHIM,* Sissi Rossi, Case T–169/03 [2005] *ECR* II–685.

their shoes.'[93] In *Muhlens v OHIM,* a similarly constituted Second Chamber of the Court held that perfume and clothes were not similar, though the test was put in terms of requiring consumers to regard one as 'indispensable or important' for the use of the other.[94] This seems a strange conclusion given the very widespread practice among *haute couture* clothing designers such as Dior, Chanel, Alexander MacQueen, Issey Miyake or Jean-Paul Gautier of also producing quality perfumes. The very same day a CFI composed of five (rather than the usual three) judges held bags and clothes sufficiently complementary to be regarded as similar.[95] Although it cited the same test as the second Chamber did in *Muhlens* (a test derived from OHIM guidelines), in *El Corte Ingles SA v. OHIM* the extended Fourth Chamber seemed much more open to the idea that consumers might draw connections between goods because they are searching for aesthetic harmony. It was this that would lead consumers perhaps to consider that the origin of the goods would be economically linked. In the absence of an ECJ decision, the latter view seems most consistent with the general idea of a fact-sensitive 'global appreciation' required by the Court.

2.3.3 Likelihood of confusion

The final, and critical, element that has to be shown for a mark to fall foul of section 5(2)/Article 8(1)(b) is that (as a result of the similarities) there is 'a likelihood of confusion on the part of the public, which includes the likelihood of association with the earlier trade mark'.

Standpoint of interpretation: who must be confused?   The likelihood of confusion is considered from the point of view of the average consumer of the products concerned, comparing the marks as a whole. As the ECJ observed in *Sabel v. Puma,*[96] 'the average consumer of the type of goods or services in question plays a decisive role in the global appreciation of the likelihood of confusion'. Community law thus applies its own understanding of the consumer, rather than focusing on actual consumers (who might be ignorant or uninterested). In subsequent decisions the ECJ has said that the average consumer is 'reasonably well informed' and 'reasonably observant and circumspect'.[97] There is no confusion if only a minority of particularly inattentive consumers might possibly be confused.[98] However, these are the default characteristics of the 'average consumer' and the tribunals accept that the characteristics of the average consumer of the goods may vary with the sector concerned. For example, consumers purchasing cars take more care than those buying sweets.[99] In some circumstances, where consumers are advised (e.g. by medical professionals), they may be particularly attentive and thus unlikely to confuse superficially similar marks.[100] Beyond this, however, there has been as yet little discussion of the characteristics that ought to be attributed to the average consumer.

---

[93] Ibid, para. 62.

[94] *Mühlens v. OHIM,* Case T–150/04 (11 July 2007) (CFI, 2d Ch). Note also *Assembled Investments,* note 36 above (para. 34) (wine and glassware not complementary and thus no similarity of goods).

[95] *El Corte Ingles,* T–443/05 [2007] *ETMR* (81) 1340 (para. 38) (CFI, extended composition.)

[96] *Sabel v. Puma,* Case C–251/95 [1997] *ECR* I–6191 (para. 23).

[97] *Lloyd Shuhfabrik,* Case C–342/7 [1999] 2 *CMLR* 1343, 1358 (para. 26).

[98] See also *Marca Mode,* Case C–425/98 [2000] 2 *CMLR* 1061 (para. 30) (Advocate General); *Reed Executive* [2004] *RPC* (40) 767 (para. 82) (approach guards against 'too "nanny" a view of protection').

[99] *Picasso v. OHIM,* T–104/01 [2002] *ECR* II–4359 (ECJ, 1st Ch) (paras. 23, 39); *Reed Executive* [2004] *RPC* (40) 767, 241 (para. 103) (Pumfrey J: 'a 50 pence purchase in the station kiosk will involve different considerations from a once-in-a-lifetime expenditure of £50,000') approved by Jacob LJ at [2004] *RPC* (40) 767 (para. 78).

[100] In *Alcon Inc. v. OHIM,* Case C–412/05 P, [2007] *ETMR* (68) 1072 (ECJ 3rd Ch), an application for TRAVATAN in respect of 'ophthalmic pharmaceutical products' was confronted with an opposition based on TRIVASTAN for 'pharmaceutical, veterinary and hygiene products'. The ECJ found that the CFI was not wrong to include

What must the public be confused about?   The next question to consider is what is meant by 'likelihood of confusion' in section 5(2)/Article 8(1)(b)? In its 'classic' form, consumers must be confused about the source or origin of the goods or services—that is, they must be confused as to the designer, manufacturer, selector, or supplier of the goods or services. In other words, classic confusion is concerned with the situation where consumers believe that the goods or services emanate from one organization, but they, in fact, come from a different independent organization. This classic form of confusion has been extended to accommodate broader understandings of the source of goods or services. Consequently, a person will be confused for the purposes of section 5(2) if they incorrectly assume that there is some broader kind of *economic connection* between the users of marks,[101] for example, that the goods are being provided by a subsidiary or licensee of the trade mark owner.[102] Confusion might also arise if the use of a sign leads consumers to believe that a person's repair business is 'authorized' by the trade mark owner.[103]

In considering whether there is a likelihood of confusion, the tribunals must consider whether there is a genuine and properly substantiated likelihood of confusion:[104] it is not enough that confusion is hypothetical and remote.[105] The term 'likelihood' indicates probability rather than possibility.[106] However, it should be noted that while the English version of the Directive refers to 'likelihood', the other language versions use the terms 'risk' or 'danger'. In *Marca Mode* the Advocate General suggested that little would turn on these different terminologies and, giving judgment, the ECJ indicated that the mere inability to rule out the possibility of confusion was not sufficient.[107] Although the ECJ has yet to indicate exactly what proportion of the relevant public must be confused, Jacob J (as he then was) has boldly asserted that for trade mark infringement 'it is enough if a significant proportion of the public, exercising reasonable care, is confused'.[108]

Is 'mere association' confusion?   Perhaps the most hotly contested issue immediately following the adoption and implementation of the Directive was the question what Article 4(1)(b) of the Directive/section 5(2) meant in indicating that 'likelihood of confusion includes the likelihood of association with the earlier trade mark'? In particular, the debate focused on the question whether likelihood of association is a separate ground for objection, that proprietors of an earlier mark can rely on to oppose a later application, even where they cannot demonstrate a

---

healthcare professionals *and* end-consumers in assessment and to find likelihood of confusion on the part of end-users in spite of advice of healthcare professionals. In *Armour Pharmaceutical Co (Galzin/Calsyn)*, Case T–483/04, (17 Oct 2006), the CFI held that the level of attention of the average consumer of pharmaceutical preparations must be determined on a case-by-case basis, depending particularly on the therapeutic indications of the goods in question. Where medicinal products are subject to medical prescription the level of attention will generally be higher than average: *Ratiopharm's Trade Mark*, note 62 above (para 18) (Appointed Person, Geoffrey Hobbs QC) (in the case of prescription medicines the only relevant consumers are medical professionals).

[101] *Canon KK v. MGM*, Case C–39/97 [1999] 1 *CMLR* 77. See also, *Souza Cruz SA v. Hollywood SAS (Hollywood/Hollywood)* R283/1999–3 [2002] *ETMR* (64) 705 (para. 44) (belief in business link between proprietors, as subsidiary or association, or a contractual relationship such as a licence, sponsorship, franchise or group).

[102] *Durferrit*, T–224/01 [2003] *ECR* II–1589 (para. 62) (CFI).

[103] Opinion of Advocate General Jacobs in *BMW v. Deenik*, Case C–63/97 [1999] 1 *CMLR* 1099, 1111–12 (para. 45).

[104] *Lloyd Schuhfabrik*, Case C–342/7 [1999] 2 *CMLR* 1343, 1358 (para. 24).

[105] Ibid, 1357 (para. 20).

[106] *Peintures Du Lauragaise's Appn.*, O/430/99 (Appointed Person) (2000) *CIPAJ* 188.

[107] *Marca Mode*, Case C–425/98 [2000] 2 *CMLR* 1061, 1084 (paras. 40–2).

[108] *Société de Produits Nestlé SA v. Unilever plc* [2003] *ETMR* 681, 692 (para. 30).

likelihood of confusion as to origin.[109] The proponents of the view that mere association would suffice suggested that the provision needed to be construed via the Directive, through the EC Council Minutes,[110] and back to its origins in European law, particularly to Benelux trade mark law. When section 5(2)(a) is interpreted purposively, it is said to lead to the conclusion that a mark could be rejected in situations where there was merely a conceptual association between marks, even though consumers might not have been confused.[111]

The issue came before the European Court of Justice in *Sabel v. Puma*,[112] a reference from the German Bundesgerichtshof. Sabel had applied to the German Registry to register for leather products and clothing a picture mark of a 'bounding feline' with the word SABEL beneath it. Puma opposed the application on the basis that they were the proprietors of an earlier pictorial mark that had been registered in Germany for 'leather and imitation leather, goods made therefrom (bags) and articles of clothing' (see Fig. 38.1).

It was common ground that Puma's mark was not particularly well known (this was not the familiar Puma mark used on sportswear). While the Bundesgerichtshof provisionally considered that no likelihood of confusion existed between the two marks, they sought to ascertain from the ECJ the importance to be given to the idea or concept that the image conveys (in the present case, a 'bounding feline') in determining the likelihood of confusion. More generally, they asked the ECJ to consider whether, in the absence of likelihood of confusion, a mark nonetheless could still be refused under Article 4(1)(b)/section 5(2) merely on the basis of the conceptual association that the public might make between the two marks. The question, in short, was whether a mark could be refused on the basis that there was a likelihood of association but no likelihood of confusion between the marks.

After considering submissions from a number of member states, and particularly influenced by the fact that the tenth Recital to the Directive states that 'likelihood of confusion . . . constitutes the specific condition for such protection', the European Court of Justice held 'that the concept of likelihood of association is *not* an alternative to that of likelihood of confusion, but serves to define its scope'.

Although, the ECJ's conclusion was relatively clear in its tenor,[113] the proponents of the argument that association might constitute a distinct basis for opposition (or infringement) took heart from paragraph 24 of the judgment where the Court said that, in the case of a particularly distinctive mark, it is not impossible that the conceptual similarity resulting from the fact that two marks use images with analogous semantic content might give rise to a likelihood of confusion.[114] However, following the ECJ decision in *Marca Mode*, it has been made crystal clear that paragraph 24 in no sense tempers the fundamental principle that the mere existence of association will not suffice in the absence of genuine and substantiated likelihood of

---

[109] The debate flared particularly intensely around the decision in *Wagamama*. See, e.g. P. Prescott, 'Has the Benelux Trade Mark Law been Written into the Directive?' [1997] *EIPR* 99; P. Harris, 'UK Trade Mark Law: Are You Confused?' [1995] *EIPR* 601; A. Kamperman Sanders, 'Back to the Dark Ages of Trade Mark Law' [1996] *EIPR* 3 and 'The Return to Wagamama' [1996] *EIPR* 521.

[110] C. Gielen, 'European Trade Mark Legislation: The Statements' [1996] *EIPR* 83; (1996) 5 *OJ OHIM* 607.

[111] For example, C. Gielen, 'Harmonization of Trade Mark Law in Europe: The First Trade Mark Harmonization Directive' [1992] *EIPR* 262, 266–7; C. Gielen, 'Likelihood of Association: What Does it Mean?' (Feb. 1996) *Trademark World* 20; A. Kamperman Sanders, 'Some Frequently Asked Questions Concerning the Trade Marks Act 1994' [1995] *EIPR* 67, 69–70; Annand and Norman (1994), 154–6.

[112] Case C–251/95 [1997] *ECR* I–6191.

[113] A. Carboni, 'Confusion Clarified' [1998] *EIPR* 107; C. Pickering, *Trade Marks in Theory and Practice* (1998), 23–24.

[114] C. Gielen, 'A Benelux Perspective' [1998] *EIPR* 109.

confusion. In particular, the existence of a likelihood of association between two marks does not give rise to a presumption of confusion.[115]

Post-Sale Confusion.   One topic on which there has been some discussion is the extent to which the views of consumers who see the product away from the point of sale are relevant to a determination of 'likelihood of confusion'.[116] When discussing issues such as distinctiveness and trade mark 'use', the ECJ has indicated that the familiarity with a mark in the post-sale environment can either confer acquired distinctiveness, or jeopardize the sign's ability to function as a mark.[117] So, in *Arsenal*, the Court held that use of the mark ARSENAL on football scarves was a use likely to jeopardize the essential function of the mark, even though, at the time of selling the goods, a sign informed consumers that the goods were not official goods manufactured under the control of the football club. This was said to be because those who saw the sign away from the point of sale might believe the scarves in fact came from the football club. In the context of likelihood of confusion, however, a stricter approach seems to have been taken in the *Picasso* decision. Here, the owners of the PICASSO mark for cars objected to registration at OHIM of the mark PICARO for cars. The OHIM and CFI rejected the opposition, and the opponent appealed to the ECJ claiming that the CFI had been wrong to treat the average consumer as particularly attentive, and thus to conclude that the marks lacked similarity, because many consumers would see the PICARO car after sale and at such times would be much less attentive. The ECJ, following the opinion of Advocate General Colomer,[118] rejected the submission. In so doing it distinguished *Arsenal* as a case that did not concern likelihood of confusion and where it had not been intended to establish a general rule, particularly one that would conflict with the many authorities that define the 'average consumer.'

Proving confusion.   The question whether consumers are likely to be confused is an issue that is to be decided by the tribunal. As Sir Raymond Evershed MR said in *Electrolux Limited v. Electrix Limited*,[119] the question whether a mark is likely to be confused with another mark is 'a matter upon which the judge must make up his mind and which he, and he alone, must decide. He cannot, as it is said, abdicate the decision in that matter to witnesses before him'.[120]

The nature of the inquiry into whether there is a likelihood of confusion will vary depending on whether the mark has been used. Normally (although not necessarily), where the relative grounds are heard by the Registrar the mark will not have been used, thus there will be no evidence of actual confusion. In contrast, where it is argued that a mark should be declared invalid after registration because it falls foul of a relative ground for refusal, it is highly likely (as with an infringement action) that the mark will have been used and thus there ought to be evidence of actual confusion.

In the absence of evidence, the tribunal makes an intuitive and speculative judgment about whether there is a likelihood of confusion. In so doing, the tribunals assume that the marks are used in a normal and fair way. The reason for assuming normal and fair use is that:

---

[115] *Marca Mode,* Case C–425/98 [2000] 2 *CMLR* 1061, 1084 (paras. 40–2).

[116] For discussion, see P O'Byrne & B. Allgrove, 'Post-Sale Confusion' (2007) *JIPLP* 315 (arguing that post-sale confusion is not irrelevant, but will not of itself justify a finding of likelihood of confusion).

[117] Note 43 above.

[118] The Advocate General (at para 54) observed, in regard to *Arsenal,* that 'the Court simply used the post-sale confusion argument to confirm that there was a breach of trade mark rights...Furthermore, most writers do not accept that post-sale confusion is relevant when analyzing the likelihood of confusion.'

[119] (1954) 71 *RPC* 23, 31.

[120] Ibid, 3; *The European v. The Economist* [1998] *FSR* 283, 291.

[unless] one assumes notional use of the earlier mark, the answer to the question of whether a later trade mark gives rise to a likelihood of confusion on the part of the public will always be no. If the public have never seen the earlier mark the later mark cannot cause confusion. Thus it is necessary to assume use of the earlier mark (and the later mark) when considering the likelihood of confusion.[121]

In situations where the mark has been used, the courts will usually be able to draw on different forms of evidence to help them decide whether there is confusion. For example, the tribunal might be informed by evidence of actual confusion where the applicant has used the mark prior to the application, or in a post-grant application for a declaration of invalidity. A claimant will be in a strong position if they can produce testimony of a reasonably prudent purchaser who was in fact confused, or provide examples of conduct probative of actual confusion (such as telephone calls to the registered proprietor about the defendant's goods or services,[122] or misdirected letters).

In some cases, the absence of evidence of actual confusion *may* also be probative. For example, in *Baywatch* the judge was strongly influenced by the fact that there was no evidence that the public had confused the BAYWATCH series with the BABEWATCH adult channel series.[123] It should be noted that an inability to produce evidence of confusion is not always fatal to an action.[124] This is because there may be extraneous reasons that explain the absence of confusion. These include the possibility that the market conditions are such that actual instances of confusion are unlikely,[125] and the possibility that the confusion has been so complete that customers are not conscious of their mistakes.[126] In other cases, the appropriate evidence may simply be too difficult to obtain.

The courts are also likely to be faced with expert evidence. The extent to which such evidence is admissible is unclear. It has long been held that expert evidence must not relate to the key question of whether the use is confusing. Instead, it should be confined to factual explanations of things such as how the trade is structured. However, doubt was thrown on this in *Guccio Gucci SpA v. Paolo Gucci*[127] when Sir Nicolas Browne-Wilkinson V-C said that the court may rely on evidence from experts where the court requires specialist knowledge. This was because it is 'the function of the expert to instruct and inform the court as to those things which the court would otherwise not know'.[128] The Vice-Chancellor said that, where the case concerns an area of which the judge is ignorant (in this case Browne-Wilkinson V-C

---

[121] *React and Device Trade Mark* [1999] *RPC* 529, 532; *Reed Executive* [2004] *RPC* (40) 767 *per* Jacob LJ (paras. 80–81).

[122] The evidence of calls to the claimant's office did not demonstrate confusion, partly because it was not clear why the callers had called and when the caller was told that they were speaking to *The European* newspaper, they knew that this was not the same as *European Voice* and hung up.

[123] *Baywatch Productions v. Home Video Channel* [1997] *FSR* 22 (an infringement case).

[124] See *Ratiopharm's Trade Mark* [2007] *RPC* (28) 630 (Appointed Person, Geoffrey Hobbs QC); *Phones 4U Ltd* [2006] *EWCA* Civ 244, [2007] *RPC* (5); *Sadas SA v. OHIM* Case T–346/04 [2006] *ETMR* (27) 329. In *The European v. The Economist* [1998] *FSR* 283, 291 Millett LJ observed the '[a]bsence of evidence of actual confusion is rarely significant, especially in a trade mark case where it may be due to differences extraneous to the plaintiff's registered trade mark'.

[125] As where the purchase of washing soap was rationed, but detergent could be bought freely: *Lever Bros., Port Sunlight v. Sunniwite Products* (1949) 66 *RPC* 84, 91.

[126] *Sämaan v. Tetrosyl* [2006] *FSR* (42) 849 (para. 58) (Kitchin J) (holding confusion between claimant's pine-tree-shaped air-freshener and defendant's Christmas tree version, even though there was no evidence of actual confusion).

[127] [1991] *FSR* 89.   [128] Ibid, 91.

had little knowledge of the designer-label market), it was legitimate to produce evidence of the likelihood of confusion from experts.[129]

While this approach was largely approved in *The European v. The Economist Newspaper*,[130] doubts were raised about the admissibility of expert evidence on the critical question whether the marks were confusingly similar. At first instance, Rattee J was presented with evidence from people in the newspaper trade (including two editors and a former editor of national newspapers) that members of the public were likely to be confused into thinking that THE EUROPEAN and EUROPEAN VOICE were associated (or that the latter was a supplement of the former). The Court of Appeal said that this evidence was almost entirely inadmissible. This was because it related to the question whether the marks were confusingly similar, rather than explaining the 'special features of [the] market of which the judge may otherwise be ignorant'.[131] It is therefore unclear the extent to which Browne-Wilkinson V-C's view that trade evidence is admissible in areas with which a judge is unfamiliar, *even* if it pertains to the issue of confusing similarity,[132] remains good law.

Parties sometimes lead survey evidence as to whether marks are confusingly similar, though this can be very expensive to collect. The courts have not been consistent in their assessment of the relevance or weight to be given to such evidence. It should be noted that the rules of evidence apply in application proceedings before the Registrar as much as in the courts.[133] A particular problem that arises in relation to survey evidence is that it may be excluded on the basis that it is hearsay.[134] If proper procedures are followed, however, survey evidence is normally not excluded because it is hearsay. The fate of the evidence often depends on the nature of the survey, and the courts are conscious of the difficulties in formulating, executing, and interpreting such surveys.[135] However, a survey can be a useful mechanism to locate actual consumers, whose evidence may help the court or tribunal.[136]

2.4 PROTECTION OF NON-ORIGIN FUNCTIONS: SECTION 5(3)/ARTICLE 8(5)

The third absolute ground for refusal is found in section 5(3)/Article 8(5) CTMR. Section 5(3), which implements the optional Article 4(4)(a) of the Directive.[137] The section recognizes that the value of a trade mark may lie not simply in its ability to indicate source, but also in 'the

---

[129] Ibid.

[130] [1998] FSR 283. See also, *George Ballantine v. Ballantyne Stewart* [1959] RPC 273 (witness may explain how the business is conducted and practices of trader or customers).

[131] *The European*, [1998] FSR 283, 291 *per* Millett LJ.

[132] *Guccio Gucci*, note 127 above, 91.

[133] Registrar's Practice Direction of 20 Jun. 1995 [1995] RPC 381, following *St Trudo's Trade Mark* [1995] RPC 350.

[134] *Oasis Stores* [1998] RPC 631, 637.

[135] See, for example, *Imperial Group plc v. Philip Morris* [1984] RPC 293, 310; *Citybond Trade Mark* [2007] RPC (13) 301 (Appointed Person, Geoffrey Hobbs QC). The courts have been sceptical about other techniques used to measure confusion. These have been treated as largely irrelevant to a determination that (it is said) is concerned with the realities of the marketplace. See, e.g. *Laura Ashley v. Coloroll* [1987] RPC 1, 10ff. (rejecting evidence obtained by using 'tachistoscope').

[136] *Sämaan v. Tetrosyl* [2006] FSR (42) 849 (para. 58) (Kitchin J).

[137] *General Motors Corporation v. Yplon*, Case C–375/97 [1999] 3 CMLR 427, 443 (para. 29).

image conveyed by the trade mark', its so-called 'advertising function'.[138] As the CFI has stated in *Sigla SA v. OHIM*,[139] as well as operating as an indication of trade origin

a mark also acts as a means of conveying other messages concerning ... for example, luxury, lifestyle, exclusivity, adventure, youth. To that effect the mark has an inherent economic value which is independent of and separate from that of the goods and services for which it is registered. The messages in question which are conveyed inter alia by a mark with a reputation or which are associated with it confer on that mark a significant value which deserves protection, particularly because, in most cases, the reputation of a mark is the result of considerable effort and investment on the part of its proprietor.[140]

Section 5(3) introduces protection for this 'advertising function' by protecting the mark against various forms of use, including 'dilution'.[141] The protection encompasses: the prevention of unjust enrichment where a trader takes unfair advantage of the repute of the mark; the erosion of a mark's distinctiveness by its use on the goods of another (what is referred to as 'blurring'); and also the related concept of 'tarnishment', whereby the repute or goodwill associated with a mark becomes tainted by its use in connection with products of an unsavoury quality, or as a consequence of being portrayed in an unwholesome context. We will return to these concepts in the course of this chapter.

Section 5(3)/Article 8(5) provide that a trade mark will not be registered where:

(a) the later mark is identical with or similar to an earlier mark;

(b) the earlier trade mark has a reputation in the United Kingdom, or in the case of a Community trade mark, in the European Community;

(c) the use of the later mark must either take unfair advantage of, or be detrimental to, the distinctive character or the repute of the earlier trade mark; and

(d) the use of the later mark is without due cause.

While we have already addressed the issue of what qualifies as an earlier trade mark, it is worth observing that, as regards Community registrations, an opposition under Article 8(5) which is based on an earlier 'well-known' mark can only be brought if that mark has been registered.[142] The section requires consideration of the following issues:

(i) when does a mark have reputation?

(ii) when is a mark similar to an 'earlier trade mark'?

(iii) when will use of a mark (a) take unfair advantage of, or (b) be detrimental to the distinctive character or reputation of the mark?

(iv) when is a mark used with 'due cause'?

---

[138] *Ferrero SpA v. Kinder are Learning Centers Inc. (Kinder Care Device/Kinder)*, R1004/2000–1 (20 Oct. 2003) (para. 24); *Souza Cruz SA v. Hollywood*, R283/1999–3 [2002] *ETMR* (64) 705 (paras. 64–7).

[139] Case T–215/03 [2007] *ETMR* (79) 1296 (para. 35).

[140] For a description of these as 'atmospherics' see J. Litman, 'Breakfast with Batman: The Public Interest in the Advertising Age', 108 *Yale Law Journal* 1717 (1999).

[141] T. Martino, *Trademark Dilution* (1996), ch. 12. The doctrine of dilution is, however, often said to have its inspiration in cases such as *Eastman Photographic Materials Co. v. John Griffiths Cycle Corporation* (1898) 15 *RPC* 105 (KODAK confusing on bicycles); and *Hack's Application* (1914) 58 *RPC* 91 (proprietor of BLACK MAGIC registered for chocolates succeeded in opposing an application to register the same mark for 'laxatives other than laxatives made with chocolate').

[142] See *Mülhens*, Case T–150/04 (11 July 2007) (CFI, 2d Ch).

In his opinion in *General Motors Corporation v. Yplon*,[143] Advocate General Jacobs emphasized that in applying Article 5(2) it was important to give full weight to each of the elements. Before looking at these it might be worth observing two critical features of section 5(3), which distinguish it from section 5(2). The first feature is that there is no requirement for the earlier trade mark holder to prove a likelihood of confusion. After some early UK decisions suggesting that is necessary to demonstrate a likelihood of confusion for an application to be rejected under section 5(3)/Article 8(5),[144] the European Court of Justice has indicated repeatedly that confusion is not a prerequisite to liability under Article 5(2) of the Directive (the infringement counterpart to Article 4(4)(a)).[145] For example, in *Adidas-Salomon AG and Adidas Benelux BV v. Fitnessworld*, the ECJ has stated that 'unlike Article 5(1)(b) of the Directive, which is designed to apply only if there exists a likelihood of confusion on the part of the public, Article 5(2) of the Directive establishes, for the benefit of trade marks with a reputation, a form of protection whose implementation does not require the existence of such a likelihood'. The second feature is that section 5(3) applies even though the goods are dissimilar. Whereas section 5(1) operates where goods are identical, and 5(2) where they are dissimilar, section 5(3) may apply where the goods are identical, similar, or even dissimilar.[146]

2.4.1 Reputation

The first requirement that must be satisfied for a mark to fall foul of section 5(3)/Article 8(5) is that it has to be shown that the earlier trade mark has a 'reputation in the UK or in the case of a Community trade mark, in the European Community'. The concept of reputation is thus a threshold which must be crossed before the whole provision comes into play. Given this pivotal role, it is important that clear guidance be offered as to what the concept entails. In *General Motors Corporation v. Yplon*,[147] the Court of Justice was asked to provide such guidance. The reference was prompted by an application by General Motors, the proprietor of the sign CHEVY for motor vehicles, to restrain Yplon from using the identical sign for detergents. The Court stated that 'reputation' involved some kind of knowledge threshold, so that 'a mark would have a reputation where it was known by a significant part of the public concerned by the products or services covered by the trade mark'.[148] It was only when there was a 'sufficient degree of knowledge of the mark that the public, when confronted with the later trade mark may possibly make an association between the two trade marks, even when used for non-similar products or services, and that the trade mark may consequently be damaged'.[149] The Court also said that a realistic assessment of whether a mark had a reputation should be determined on the basis of a number of different criteria. These included 'the market share held by the trade mark,

---

[143] *Yplon*, Case C–375/97 [1999] 3 *CMLR* 427, 437 (para. 42) (AG). In *Ferroro GmbH v. Duplo (Duplo/Duplo)*, R802/1999–1 (5 Jun. 2000) (para. 17) (as well as on numerous subsequent occasions), the OHIM Board of Appeal described the protection of marks in relation to dissimilar goods as 'an exception to one of the fundamental principles of European trade mark law. The relevant provisions must therefore be interpreted strictly.'

[144] *BASF v. CEP* [1996] *ETMR* 51; *Baywatch v. Home Video*, [1997] *FSR* 22.

[145] *Sabel v. Puma*, Case C–251/95 [1997] *ECR* I–6191 (para. 20–1, 48); *Marca Mode*, Case C–425/98 [2000] 2 *CMLR* 1061, 1083 (para. 36); *Yplon*, Case C–375/97 [1999] 3 *CMLR* 427.

[146] As originally drafted the relative ground for refusal applied where 'a trade mark is to be registered for goods which are *not similar* to those for which the earlier trade mark is protected'. However, in *Davidoff & Cie SA v. Gofkid*, Case C–292/00 [2003] *ECR* I–389 the ECJ held that the provision also applied where the goods or services of the parties were similar (or identical). The act was amended to reflect the case law. In *Intel Corp v. Intelmark* [2007] *EWCA Civ* 431; [2007] *RPC* (35) 846 (para. 13), Jacob LJ referred to the amendment as 'pointless.' For background, see Bently & Sherman, 2nd ed, 868–70.

[147] Case C–375/97 [1999] 3 *CMLR* 427.   [148] Ibid, 442 (para. 22).   [149] Ibid, 442–3 (para. 23).

the intensity, geographical extent, and duration of its use, and the size of the investment made by the undertaking in promoting it'.[150]

In *Yplon* the Court of Justice seems to be making clear that the threshold for reputation is a relatively low one. The criteria cited by the Court echo those used in *Windsurfing* in relation to acquired distinctiveness. It appears from the judgment that the test is primarily quantitative, in the sense that the mark must be known, i.e. that a significant number of consumers must be familiar with the mark. The Advocate General in *Yplon* indicated that this was a lower threshold than that required for a mark to be 'well known', when he said 'although the concept of a well-known mark is itself not clearly defined, a mark with "reputation" need not be as well known as a well-known mark'.[151] While in its judgment, however, the Court of Justice did not explicitly consider the relationship between the concepts of 'reputation' and being 'well known', there is nothing to suggest it intended to contradict the Advocate General's analysis.

One possible problem with treating the concept of 'reputation' as purely 'quantitative' derives from the fact that the concept plays a second role in this context: 'reputation' is also one of the two 'interests' (along with 'distinctive character') that the provision seeks to protect from damage or unfair appropriation. As we will see in a moment, in that context damage to reputation has been seen largely in terms of 'tarnishment' (that is denigration of the mark's good reputation). This implies that reputation has a qualitative dimension: it is hard to think what damage to reputation would be, where reputation is understood as purely quantitative. This might suggest, as others have said, that reputation refers to a qualitative criterion that has been described as 'symbolic character'.[152] However, a short answer to this apparent inconsistency might be that 'good reputation' is merely a subset of reputation: so that any mark that has 'reputation' meets the threshold, but 'detriment to reputation' can only affect those marks that have developed a good reputation.[153]

One interesting question that is as yet unresolved relates to the geographic scope of reputation required for a Community trade mark. In the case of national marks, in *Yplon* the ECJ has said while the reputation must exist in the member state, it need not exist throughout the territory: it is sufficient if the reputation exists in a substantial part of it. However, in the case of Community marks, the issue is not straightforward. One possibility is that reputation need only exist in one member state: if this is the case a trade mark owner will get broad protection in countries where the mark does not even have a reputation. Another possibility is that reputation will need to be shown in the whole Community, or (by analogy with *Yplon*) a substantial part of it (as was held by the CFI in *Aktieselkabet af 21 November 2001 v. OHIM—TDK Kabushiki Kaisha).*[154] The problem with setting this as a requirement is that an opponent is in a much better position where it has a national mark (which can be used to oppose a CTM), than where it has a Community mark. Given the internal market goal that underpins the CTMR as an entity, it would be strange if such an advantage was held to exist in relation to national marks. One solution to this conundrum would be to set different geographic criteria

---

[150] Ibid, 443 (para. 27).

[151] Ibid, 434–5, 436 (Advocate General, paras. 32, 33, and 37). See *Albert Rene v. OHIM*, Case C–16/06P (Opinion of Advocate General Trstenjak, 29 Nov 2007, para 83) (commenting that it was not easy to distinguish 'well-known marks' from those with a 'reputation').

[152] A. Kur, 'Well-known Marks, Highly Renowned Marks and Marks Having A (High) Reputation: What's it All About?' (1992) 23 *IIC* 218.

[153] *Sigla v. OHIM*, Case T–215/03 [2007] *ETMR* (79) 1296 (para. 35).

[154] T–477/04 (6 Feb 2007). Note however that the opposition there was based on a Community trade mark and 35 national marks!

when considering whether an earlier mark has a reputation in opposition proceedings and in infringement proceedings: for the former, an applicant need only show reputation in a member state, whereas in infringement proceedings a reputation throughout the Community must be established. However, it seems highly unlikely that such an approach would be adopted: after all, the same wording appears in Article 5(2) as in Article 9(2) of the CTMR. The matter is before the ECJ on reference from Austria in *Pago Intl v. Tirolmich*,[155] and it will be interesting to see how it resolves the conundrum.

2.4.2 Similarity of Marks

The second requirement is that the marks be identical or similar. We have already considered these ideas in the context of section 5(1) and (2). While the general approach is much the same, it is worth observing that a finding of similarity or dissimilarity of marks in a case under 5(2) does not necessarily mean those marks are similar/dissimilar for the purpose of section 5(3).[156] This is because the concept of 'similarity' is interpreted in the light of the purpose of each provision. So, while a tribunal must look at the marks as a whole, taking into account their dominant and distinctive components, and is required to assess similarity from a visual, aural, and conceptual viewpoint,[157] what it is looking for under section 5(3) is not the same as what it is looking for under section 5(2). Whereas under section 5(2) the tribunal is asking whether the marks are 'confusingly similar', under section 5(3) the tribunal must assess whether the marks are sufficiently similar that the average consumer will *make a link* between them.[158] As the ECJ observed in *Adidas v Fitnessworld*, '[i]t is sufficient for the degree of similarity between the mark with a reputation and the sign to have the effect that the relevant section of the public *establishes a link* between the sign and the mark'.

What exactly is the 'link' that is required to establish that the marks are similar? Unfortunately, the ECJ has provided limited guidance. In *Adidas* itself, the Court indicated that where a sign is perceived purely as decorative, no such link would exist. Beyond that limited example, the matter is one for speculation. However, the English Court of Appeal has referred the matter to the ECJ in *Intel Corp v. CPM UK Ltd*,[159] a case in which Intel, the owner of the unique, invented, and highly renowned mark INTEL for microprocessor chips, sought a declaration that a registration of INTELMARK for marketing services be declared invalid. According to the High Court, a consumer seeing INTELMARK would think of INTEL, but would not necessarily believe there was any trade connection. Is such a 'bringing to mind' sufficient to trigger section 5(3)? Jacob LJ held that the answer to that question was not clear and so referred the matter to the ECJ. He said that he himself did not think a calling to mind was enough but that it would be sufficient were the average consumer to think there was a trade connection between the two traders (for example that Intelmark was licensed by Intel). He added that it might possibly be sufficient if the average consumer wondered whether such a link existed, though he was not persuaded that anything short of that would suffice.[160]

---

[155] Case C–301/07 (pending).

[156] Cf *Gateway, Inc v. OHIM*, T–434/05 (having held ACTIVY MEDIA GATEWAY was not similar to GATEWAY for purposes of Art. 8(1) CTMR, it followed that the marks were not similar for art 8(5)); *Esure v. Direct Line*, note 38 above (para. 78). Note also *Red Bull v. OHIM*, Case T–165/07 (pending appeal from OHIM BA decision in R 147/2005–4).

[157] *Adidas-Salomon AG and Adidas Benelux BV v. Fitnessworld*, Case C–408/01 [2004] 1 *CMLR* (4) 448 (paras. 27–31).

[158] Ibid (paras. 27–31).   [159] [2007] *EWCA Civ* 431; [2007] *RPC* (35) 846.

[160] The case is pending as Case C–252/07.

Fig. 38.2 MIRACLE packaging, L'Oreal

Fig. 38.3 MIRACLE bottle, L'Oreal

In *L'Oreal v Bellure*,[161] Jacob LJ reiterated his view that the link must be such as to affect 'the economic behaviour of consumers', in a case relating to the packaging of various smell-alike perfumes. The claimant had registrations relating to certain names (including TRÉSOR and MIRACLE) and for various forms of bottle and packaging. The issue arose whether the defendant's packaging of its imitation smells was 'similar' and whether the names COFFRET D'OR and PINK WONDER were similar to the name marks (see Figs 38.2–4).

Lewison J had found that some of the packaging was similar (e.g. the old packaging of LA VALEUR was similar to that of TRÉSOR and the bottle for the PINK WONDER perfume was similar to the MIRACLE BOTTLE), but in other cases (e.g. the PINK WONDER and MIRACLE boxes) it was

---

[161] [2007] *EWCA Civ* 968; [2008] *ETMR* (1) 1.

Fig. 38.4 PINK WONDER
Source: Courtesy of Baker & McKenzie.

not. Both parties appealed. The Court of Appeal rejected the defendant's appeal, noting with seeming approval that the judge had considered the appearance of the products, the intention of the designers, and the public reaction. Where the packaging was intended to convey the message 'this is a bit like', the Court agreed that it is 'a small step' for a tribunal to conclude that the designer succeeded (and thus that the signs were similar enough to create a link).[162] The claimant's appeal complained that Lewison J had been wrong to compare the registered sign with the defendant's mark, and to ignore other aspects of the defendant's marketing which imitated the marketing by the claimant. MIRACLE had been advertised on television using clouds, and the PINK WONDER box used cloud images. Jacob LJ rejected this, saying that the 'global appreciation test does not amount to the proposition that once a registered mark is used in marketing anything extraneous to the mark used in marketing comes in too—as though it formed part of the registered mark'.[163] Finally, the Court also affirmed the finding that the word marks were not sufficiently similar to create a 'link'; while in French there was 'some similarity at a high level of generality' between COFFRET D'OR and LA VALEUR this would have been lost on the average British consumer. The claim that there was sufficient similarity between MIRACLE and PINK WONDER to establish a link was described as 'near fantastic.'

Although the exact nature of the 'link' awaits clarification by the ECJ, it seems relatively clear that assessing whether there is sufficient similarity to give rise to a link will depend on a global appreciation of the marks. Clearly, a link is more likely to be established where marks are identical. Where marks are not identical, similarity will depend on appreciation of the dominant components of the earlier and later marks. In cases concerning the SPA mark, with a reputation in Benelux for mineral water, the OHIM BA has held there would be a link with SPALINE, MINERAL SPA and LIFE SPA but not with SPAGO: in the former cases the additional features ('line', 'mineral', 'life') were highly descriptive, so the link would be formed whereas in

---

[162] [2008] *ETMR* (1) 1, 31 (para 97): referring to *Slazenger v. Feltham* (1889) 6 RPC 531, 538 (Lindley LJ).
[163] *L'Oreal*, ibid, 33 (para 110).

the case of SPAGO the 'spa' element was absorbed in what would appear as an invented word.[164] The SPALINE case is being appealed to the CFI.[165] On appeal, L'Oreal is arguing that 'spa' would be understood by consumers of soap as a reference to water and bathing so no link would be made with the claimant's bottled drinking water.[166] Having adopted a descriptive dictionary word as its mark, the opponent should not be able to prevent others from using the same descriptive connotation in their marks.[167] Certainly it is easier to establish a link where the earlier mark is unique or invented, than when it has some dictionary meaning. Another factor that may be relevant in deciding whether a link is likely is the degree of similarity of goods or services.[168] Without the link there can be none of the 'cross-pollination' needed to transfer value to the applicant (or defendant).

2.4.3 Unfair advantage or detriment

The third requirement that must be met for a mark to fall foul of section 5(3) is that it must be shown that the use of the later mark *either*:

(i)   takes unfair advantage of the earlier trade mark;

(ii)   is detrimental to the distinctive character of the earlier trade mark; *or*

(iii) is detrimental to the reputation of the earlier trade mark.

The provision is not intended to prevent *any* use of a mark with a reputation: it is essential in any case that the opponent establish that use of a similar mark would have one of these three effects.[169] Because the analysis will often be prospective (the later mark not having been used), the opponent will need to establish prima facie evidence of future risk which is not hypothetical.[170] We will deal with each of these in turn.

Unfair advantage.   One way in which section 5(3)/Article 8(5) can be invoked is by showing that the use would take 'unfair advantage' of the earlier mark. According to one set of authorities, this is intended to enable a trade mark owner to prevent another trader from registering (or using) a similar mark when to do so would involve a free ride on the reputation of the

---

[164] *L'Oreal v. S.A. Spa Monople*, R 415/2005–1 (18 Oct 2006) (on appeal); *Mühlens GmbH v. S.A. Spa Monopole*, Case R 825/2004–2 (11 Jan 2006); *Primavera Life GmbH v. S.A. Spa Monopole*, R 1136/2006- (19 June 2007) (LIFE SPA); *De Francesco Import v. S.A. Spa Monopole*, R 1285/2006–2 (13 Sept 2007) (SPAGO). In *S.A. Spa Monople v. California Acrylic Industries Inc* Case R 710/2006–2 (20 April 2007) the BA found 'a low degree of similarity' between SPA and CAL SPA (for bath tubs).

[165] *L'Oreal v. OHIM–Spa*, Case T 21/07 (on appeal from OHIM BA decision R 415/2005–1). As is *Spago*, as T–438/07 (pending).

[166] But in *Spa Monopole v. OHIM–Spa finders* Case T–67/04 [2005] ECR II–1825 the CFI said that the parties had rightly agreed that SPA for mineral water was similar to Spa-finders (for travel agency services).

[167] This reasoning might equally apply to surnames: *Harman International Industries v. OHIM*, Case T–212/07 (pending appeal from OHIM BA decision R0502/2006–1 that no link between Becker and Barbara Becker, both in Class 9).

[168] *Souza Cruz v. Hollywood*, R283/1999–3 [2002] ETMR (64) 705 (para. 82); *Audi-Med Trade Mark* [1998] RPC 863, 874 (reputation would not easily transfer from cars to deafness aids).

[169] *Spa finders*, Case T–67/04 [2005] ECR II–1825, para 40; *Sigla SA v. OHIM*, Case T–215/03 [2007] ETMR (79) 1296, para 46.

[170] *Spa finders*, ibid (para 40); *Sigla*, ibid (para 46); *Antarctica Srl v. OHIM- The NASDAQ Stock Market*, Case T–47/06 (10 May 2007) (para. 54) (such a conclusion can be drawn from 'logical deductions resulting from an analysis of the probabilities and by taking account of the usual practices in the relevant commercial sector as well as all the other circumstances of the case'); *Esure v. Direct Line* [2007] EWHC 1557 (Ch) (para 116).

earlier mark.[171] The principle underpinning this ground for objection seems thus to be one of unjust enrichment, with the tribunals often referring to the unfairness as being the 'parasitic' nature of the advantage.[172]

However, in *L'Oreal v. Bellure* Jacob LJ questioned whether mere enrichment was enough, suggesting that an 'advantage' might not be regarded as 'unfair' unless it involved harming or damaging the trade mark owner. In that case Jacob LJ was confronted with a situation where the use on a replica of similar packaging and names to the claimant's fine fragrances would not be likely to cause the trade mark owner any damage, because no one intending to buy high-price perfume (retailing at £60 or more in exclusive outlets) would buy a replica from a market stall for £4. There was no confusion and no damage (tarnishment or blurring) to the trade mark owner. Nevertheless, it was also clear that the use of the trade marks on the replica goods would give the defendant an advantage: consumers would understand it as indicating that the perfume smelled like that of the claimant—and thus give it an edge in the market as against other replica perfume makers. Unconvinced that a mere advantage of that nature would necessarily be 'unfair' even if it would benefit the user of the material, Jacob LJ referred the matter to the ECJ. The case is pending.

To date most of the case law on 'unfair advantage' has concerned the question whether the later user will take advantage of the reputation at all (leaving the issue of unfairness pretty much uninterrogated). In establishing that use of the mark will *take advantage* the opponent will need to identify how value will transfer from one mark to the later mark. This will be easiest to do where the earlier mark is unusual, has a high reputation, the later mark is identical, and the goods are connected in some way.[173] In *Aktieselkabet af 21 November 2001 v. OHIM*,[174] for example, the CFI held that the opponent, owner of the Community Mark TDK for tapes, was justified in its objection to the registration of TDK for clothing. The evidence established that the opponent had a substantial reputation developed over decades. Because the opponent had used TDK on clothes at sponsorship events, albeit to promote its tapes, the CFI took the view that the use of the mark by the applicant on clothes would lead to the perception that clothing was manufactured by, or under licence from, the opponent.[175] The CFI stated that this was in itself sufficient to constitute prima facie evidence of a future risk of the applicant taking of unfair advantage of the reputation of the earlier marks.[176] The CFI has even gone to some lengths to find a connection between the applicant and the opponent's goods in a case of an applicant seeking to register NASDAQ for bicycle helmets.[177] The NASDAQ mark was

---

[171] *Adidas v. Fitnessworld*, Case C–408/01 [2004] 1 *CMLR* (4) 448 (para. 39) (AG); *Spa finders*, Case T–67/04 [2005] *ECR* II–1825, (para. 51); *Mango Sport v. Diknak*, Case R 308/2003–1 [2005] *ETMR* (5) (para 19); *Ferrero SpA v. Kinder*, R1004/2000 (20 Oct 2003) (para. 26).

[172] But cf. *Verimark v. BMW AG* [2007] *FSR* 803 (S Ct of App, SA) (advantage not unfair).

[173] Indeed, it has been suggested that unfair advantage might be assumed in certain cases: *Esure v. Direct Line*, [2007] *EWHC* 1557 (Ch) (para. 121) (citing *Sigla* (para. 48)).

[174] T–477/07 (6 Feb 2007).

[175] *Citybond Trade Mark* [2007] *RPC* (13) 301 (Appointed Person, Geoffrey Hobbs QC) (para 47 CITYBOND would take unfair advantage of CITIBANK because it would give rise to a likelihood of confusion).

[176] Similarly, in *Marie Claire Album v. Marie Claire*, R-530/2004–2 (6 Mar 2006) (on appeal, T–0148/06), the OHIM Board of Appeal held that a registration of MARIE CLAIRE for bathing suits would take unfair advantage of the opponent's MARIE CLAIRE mark for magazines. The marks were identical, so the link would be strong, and the goods were inter-related in that the applicant's goods were the sort of goods discussed and advertised in the opponent's magazine. See also *Mülhens GmbH v. The Hearst Corpn. (Cosmopolitan Cosmetics/Cosmopolitan)*, R552/2000–4 (26 Jul. 2001) (COSMOPOLITAN COSMETICS for cosmetics would be likely to take unfair advantage of COSMOPOLITAN for women's magazines).

[177] *NASDAQ*, T-47/06 (10 May 2007).

exceptionally distinctive, and well known for a stock exchange price- providing service, and the choice by the applicant seemed designed purely to take a ride on the opponent's image of 'modernity'.

Despite the rather strained reasoning in *Nasdaq*, it is clear that not every case where a sign used is identical to one with repute will necessarily transfer advantage, particularly if the goods are unrelated or the consumers associate the sign with other attributes. For example, in *Sigla v. OHIM*, the CFI said there was no reason for the Court to think that the reputation of VIPS for self-service restaurants would transfer to the applicant were it permitted to use the same sign for computer programming services intended for hotels and restaurants. The qualities of 'speed', 'availability', and 'youth' typically associated with fast food would not transfer to the costly, specialist service provided by the applicant.[178]

On the other hand, in some cases, reputation will transfer to marks that are not identical, if there is a logical or conceptual connection. In *Miss World Ltd v. Channel Four Television Corp*,[179] for example, Pumfrey J granted an injunction against the defendant who was planning to broadcast a programme called 'Mr Miss World' about a trans-sexual beauty pageant. The marks were similar, but the addition of 'Mr' left the sign MISS WORLD intact, and the judge held that this would take unfair advantage of the claimant's MISS WORLD mark, registered for beauty pageants. Similarly, the OHIM BA found unfair advantage when SPA was sought to be registered for soap as SPA LINE, LIFE SPA and MINERAL SPA: the repute of the SPA mark for mineral water, with its reputation for purity and its association with health, could transfer to soaps and cosmetics. The tribunals were influenced by the fact that some water sellers have also sold water for cosmetic purposes.[180] However, if the later mark contains some distinctive component, that will make it more difficult to establish that advantage has been taken of the earlier mark. In *Spa Monopole*, the CFI said that the use of the mark SPA-FINDERS would not take unfair advantage of the distinctive character or the repute of the mark SPA (registered for mineral water). There was no evidence that the reputation of the mark SPA would in any way transfer to the travel agency.

Detrimental to the distinctive character of the earlier mark. Another option available for an opponent is to show that the use of the later mark would be detrimental to the distinctive character of the earlier mark. This is usually referred to as 'dilution' or 'blurring'.[181] Dilution has been described as:

the gradual whittling away or dispersion of the identity and hold upon the public mind of the mark or name by its use upon non-competing goods. The more distinctive or unique the mark, the deeper is its impress upon the public consciousness, and the greater its need for protection against vitiation or dissociation from the particular product in connection with which it has been used.[182]

The rationale for this is that the use of the mark on different goods may erode the distinctiveness of the earlier mark. That is, the unauthorized use on similar or dissimilar products may undermine an established trade mark's uniqueness and thus its selling power and 'commercial

---

[178] Case T–215/03 [2007] *ETMR* (79) 1296 (paras. 73–4).

[179] [2007] *FSR* (30) 754.

[180] *L'Oreal v. Spa*, Case R415/2005–1 (18 Oct 2006) (on appeal); *Mühlens v. Spa*, Case R825/2004–2 (11 Jan 2006); *Primavera v. Spa*, Case R1136/2006–(19 June 2007) (LIFE SPA); *De Francesco v. Spa*, Case R1285/2006–2 (13 Sept 2007) (SPAGO). In *Spa v. California Acrylic*, Case R720/2006–2 (20 Apr 2007) the BA found 'a low degree of similarity' between SPA and CAL SPA (for bath tubs).

[181] *Premier Brands UK v. Typhoon Europe* [2000] *FSR* 767, 787 (blurring occurs where the distinctiveness of a mark is eroded); *DaimlerChrysler AG v. Alavi* [2001] *RPC* (42) 813 (para. 88); *Adidas v. Fitnessworld*, Case C–408/01 [2004] 1 *CMLR* (4) 448 (para. 37) (AG); *Souza Cruz v. Hollywood*, R283/1999–3 [2002] *ETMR* (64) 705 (para. 105).

[182] F. Schechter, 'The Rational Basis of Trademark Protection' (1927) 40 *Harvard Law Review* 813, 825.

magnetism'. As Schechter said, 'if you allow Rolls-Royce Restaurants, and Rolls-Royce cafe-
terias, and Rolls-Royce pants and Rolls-Royce candy, in ten years you will not have the Rolls-
Royce mark any more'.[183]

While the idea of damage to distinctiveness has an intuitive appeal and has been accepted by
the Advocate General,[184] and the CFI, it is nonetheless controversial. According to Pumfrey J,
'[i]t raises difficult conceptual issues'.[185] Indeed, there are many who deny that, in the absence
of confusion or tarnishment, any real or verifiable damage would occur, for example, if the
ROLLS-ROYCE mark were used for restaurants.[186] These difficulties of proof mean that tribunals
prefer to rely on the 'unfair advantage' ground rather than that of dilution (though this trend
may alter once we receive a more rigorous analysis of when advantage is 'unfairly' taken of the
distinctiveness or repute of an earlier mark).

In *Intel Corp v. CPM UK Ltd*,[187] the question arose whether a registration of INTELMARK for
marketing services would be detrimental to the distinctive character of the INTEL mark registered for microprocessor chips. Jacob LJ referred the question to the ECJ, seeking advice as
to whether the criterion only applied to a 'unique mark', whether a first conflicting use would
suffice to establish detriment, and whether the requirement was only satisfied if the economic
behaviour of the consumer would be affected. Jacob LJ himself said that he thought there
must be a 'real and tangible' prospect of harm, and whether this would be so required a global
appreciation. He offered up a non-exhaustive list of seven factors which he said ought to be
considered: these included the inherent distinctiveness and reputation of the earlier mark, an
assessment of the impact of use of the later mark on the pulling power of the earlier mark for
its goods or services, and whether the user of the later mark is likely to get a real commercial
advantage.[188]

Pending further clarification, it is clear that it will be easier to show dilution where the claim-
ant/opponent's mark is invented or unique, and the applicant's sign is identical. In the *Nasdaq*
case, for example, the OHIM BA did not hesitate in finding that the use of an identical mark
for cycle helmets would dilute the 'distinctive and attractive character' of NASDAQ for services
involving the provision of stock-price quotations.[189] Where the earlier mark is not inherently
distinctive—or has some other meaning or reference—it will be much more difficult to establish dilution. For example, in *Sigla v. OHIM*,[190] the owner of the mark VIPS for self-service
restaurants opposed registration of VIPS for 'computer programming relating to hotel services,
restaurants, cafes'. The CFI held that there was no risk of dilution. In so holding, the Court was
particularly influenced by two factors: first, the fact that V.I.P. is widely used to refer to a 'very
important person', so that the average consumer would more likely think of that meaning than

---

[183] Hearings before the House Committee on Patents, 72nd Cong., 1st Sess. 15 (1932) cited, inter alia, in
Martino, *Trademark Dilution*. cf. Tushnet, 86, *Texas LR* 507 (2008) (a compelling critique).

[184] *Adidas v. Fitnessworld*, Case C–408/01 [2004] 1 *CMLR* (4) 448 (para. 37) (AG Jacobs); *Marca Mode,* Case
C–425/98 [2000] 2 *CMLR* 1061, 707, (para. 44), where the Advocate General describes dilution as 'the blurring of
the distinctiveness of a mark such that it is no longer capable of arousing immediate association with the goods
for which it is registered and used'.

[185] *DaimlerChrysler AG v. Alavi*, [2001] *RPC* (42) 813, 844 (para. 93). According to Neuberger J, one must be
careful of applying the concept of dilution 'too blindly': *Premier Brands v. Typhoon* [2000] *FSR* 767, 802.

[186] Martino, *Trademark Dilution*, ch. 8. Certainly, it is not obvious that such use would mean that the mark
would no longer exist for cars: *Intel Corp* [2007] *EWCA Civ* 431 (para 32) (Jacob LJ).

[187] *Intel*, ibid.   [188] Ibid, 855 (para 36).

[189] On appeal, *NASDAQ*, Case T–47/06 (10 May 2007), the CFI decided the case purely by reference to 'unfair
advantage'.

[190] *Sigla SA v. OHIM*, Case T–215/03 [2007] *ETMR* (79) 1296.

of the opponent's fast-food restaurants.[191] Second, the CFI noted that the use of the applicant's mark would be among a very narrow section of the public. The risk of dispersion of the identity of the earlier mark was thus quite limited. If the junior mark contains additions or alterations, blurring may be difficult to establish.[192] Both this factor, and the alternative meaning of 'spa', led the CFI to hold that the use of SPA-FINDERS would not dilute the distinctive character of SPA, a mark with a reputation in Belgium for mineral waters.[193] However, differences in marks may be less significant with device marks: it has been held that the distinctiveness of a device mark (a telephone on wheels) was damaged by the applicant's mark comprising a mouse on wheels (both for insurance services),[194] and that the distinctiveness of a fir-tree shape for air fresheners was damaged by the defendant's air freshener in the shape of a Christmas tree.[195]

Damage to reputation. The third option for an opponent is to show that the use of the later mark would be detrimental to the repute of the earlier mark. Damage to reputation, which is often called degradation or 'tarnishment', exists if the subsequent use reflects badly on, sullies, or debases the earlier mark.[196] The owner of the earlier trade mark must establish that the negative association will be real, not fanciful. This involves not merely substantiating the existence of a particular image in the earlier mark, but also the way in which the later mark will bring about the damage.[197] There are two obvious ways in which tarnishment might occur.

The first is where the proposed use on the applicant's goods would reflect badly on the opponent's reputation. This would be the case where the mark is to be used on ineffective goods,[198] but there might equally be damage to reputation where there is some other negative association with goods—or, as it is sometimes called, 'antagonism' between the goods. So, in a classic pre-harmonization example (referred to with approval in some post-harmonization case law), the Benelux Court held that KLAREIN for detergent would tarnish CLAERYN for gin because 'no one likes to be reminded of a detergent when drinking their favourite tipple'.[199] Trade mark owners commonly object to association with sexual products or services, and the tribunals are

---

[191] '[T]he risk of dilution appears, in principle, to be lower if the earlier mark consists of a term which, because of a meaning inherent in it, is very common and frequently used, irrespective of the earlier mark consisting of the term at issue.'

[192] In cases of similar marks, such as TYPHOO and TYPHOON, blurring is even more difficult to establish: *Premier Brands,* [2000] *FSR* 767, 802.

[193] *Spa finders,* Case T–67/04 [2005] *ECR* II–1825. The Court denied that there would be detriment, because 'the term "spa" is frequently used to designate, for example, the Belgian town of Spa and the Belgian racing circuit of Spa-Francorchamps or, in general, places for hydrotherapy such as hammams or saunas'.

[194] *Esure v. Direct Line* [2006] *FSR* (42) 849 (para. 122).

[195] *Sämaan v. Tetrosyl* [2000] *FSR* 767 (para. 83) (Kitchin J).

[196] *Adidas v. Fitnessworld,* Case C–408/01 [2004] 1 *CMLR* (4) 448 (para. 38) (AG Jacobs); *Premier Brands,* [2000] *FSR* 767, 798 (Neuberger J referring to tarnishing, where the attraction and the capacity of the mark to stimulate the desire to buy is impaired). See Martino, *Trademark Dilution,* 60–3 (describing this as the judicially favoured facet of dilution, but arguing that 'tarnishment' is doctrinally confused).

[197] For example in *DaimlerChrysler v. Alavi,* [2001] *RPC* (42) 813, 844 (para. 94), the defendant's use of MERC on its shop web site, which had links to skinhead sites, was not detrimental to the repute of the claimant for high quality engineering, because nothing would actually 'rub off' on the MERC or MERCEDES sign.

[198] An example of this form of 'tarnishment' was found to occur where INTEL, a mark associated with high technology, was used on unsophisticated goods: *Sihra's Trade Mark Application* [2003] *RPC* (44) 789.

[199] *Colgate Palmolive v. Lucas Bols Claeryn/Klarein* (1976) *IIC* 420. This case was referred to with seeming approval in *Adidas v. Fitnessworld,* Case C–408/01 [2004] 1 *CMLR* (4) 448 (para. 38) (AG Jacobs); *British Sugar v. Robertson* [1996] *RPC* 281, 295; *Premier Brands,* [2000] *FSR* 767, 787.

generally sympathetic. In *C.A. Sheimer (M.) Sdn Bhd's Trade Mark Application*,[200] for example, the Appointed Person allowed VISA International's opposition to the applicant's mark VISA for condoms on the ground that it would 'burden VISA International's own use of its earlier registered mark with connotations of birth control and sexual hygiene that would alter perceptions of the mark negatively from the point of view of a provider of financial services... VISA International should not have to carry the burden of advertising condoms and prophylactics at the same time as it promotes its own services.'[201] Other 'antagonisms' might exist between goods associated with health, and cigarettes or alcohol.[202] However, the CFI has held that there was no antagonism between mineral water and travel agency services such that the use of SPA-FINDERS for a travel agency would harm SPA for mineral water;[203] or between self-service restaurants and hotel computer systems such that the use of VIPS for the latter would tarnish the mark VIPS for the former.[204]

The second circumstance where tarnishment could occur is where the *later mark* modifies the earlier sign in a way that is denigratory. Perhaps the most obvious example would be the modification of Coca Cola in its familiar cursive script to Cocaine—a modification which might tarnish the image of Coca Cola by suggesting it contains cocaine. In the infringement context, there are numerous examples from other jurisdictions of potential tarnishing modifications (and uses) of marks: of the Barbie doll being placed in a liquidizer or on a barbeque,[205] or the Carling Black Label mark being modified, in the same font, as Carling Black Labour to suggest the company had been involved in exploitative practices.[206] However, fewer examples exist in the context of opposition on relative grounds. In *Premier Brands* Neuberger J held that the mark TYPHOO was not tarnished by the use of TYPHOON on kitchenware, because it was unlikely that this would trigger an unfortunate connection with the destructive force of typhoons.[207]

2.5 WITHOUT 'DUE CAUSE'

Once an opponent has established that its earlier mark has a reputation, and that use of the applicant's mark will take unfair advantage of, or be detrimental to, the earlier mark, the obligation then falls upon the applicant to show that the use would not be 'without due cause'.[208]

---

[200] [2000] *RPC* 484, 506–7.

[201] Cf. *Oasis Stores* [1998] *RPC* 631 (the Registry registered the EVER READY mark for contraceptives, despite an opposition by the owner of a similar mark for batteries).

[202] In *Souza Cruz v. Hollywood*, R283/1999–3 [2002] *ETMR* (64) 705 (para. 85–6), the OHIM Board of Appeal found that the reputation of the proprietor's mark HOLLYWOOD for chewing gum, which had an image of 'health, dynamism and youth', would have suffered if the applicant were permitted to register the same mark for tobacco. The Board explained that 'no worse association can be imagined for a confectionery manufacturer than one with products capable of causing death'; *Inlima SL's Application; Opposition by Adidas AG* [2000] *ETMR* 325, 336 (Adidas's three-stripe mark would be tarnished by its use in connection with alcohol). Cf. *Spa Monopole v. OHIM–De Francesco Import*, Case T–438/07 (CFI pending, Spa opposition to SpagO for goods in class 33 (including alcoholic beverages) was rejected by OHIM. On appeal, Spa argues that antagonism exists.)

[203] *Spa finders*, Case T–67/04 [2005] *ECR* II–1825.

[204] *Sigla SA v. OHIM*, Case T–215/03 [2007] *ETMR* (79) 1296 (paras. 66–67).

[205] *Mattel Inc v. Walking Mountain Productions*, 353 *F* 3d 792, 809 (9th Cir, 2003).

[206] *South African Breweries v. Laugh It Off* [2005] *FSR* (30) 686 (SCA SA). The decision was overturned on appeal by the Constitutional Court applying freedom of expression doctrine: [2005] *ZACC* 7, [2006] (1) *SA* 144 (CC).

[207] *Premier Brands* [2000] *FSR* 767, 799–801.   [208] Ibid, 792.

While some individual instances of use might be justifiable (particularly in relation to an action for infringement),[209] it is difficult to imagine many situations where registration of a mark would be justifiable in the face of evidence that it takes unfair advantage of, or is detrimental to the distinctive character or reputation of the mark. In *Premier Brands UK v. Typhoon Europe*,[210] Neuberger J held that the phrase 'without due cause' required an applicant (or in the case of an alleged infringer, the defendant) to show some justifiable reason for using its sign in relation to its goods even though this was unfair or detrimental to the earlier mark. The decision to select a particular mark in good faith would not justify its registration (or continued use). Consequently, assuming TEL's use of TYPHOON for kitchenware took unfair advantage of the claimant's registered mark TYPHOO, the fact that TEL selected the sign in good faith did not mean its use was with 'due cause'. This was, in part, because TEL had failed to conduct searches. The OHIM seems to have imposed an even more onerous test of 'due cause'. In the *Hollywood* case, the OHIM Board of Appeal indicated that an earlier mark is only used with due cause where it can be shown that the applicant is 'obliged to use the sign in question, such that, notwithstanding the detriment caused to the proprietor of the earlier trade mark, the applicant cannot reasonably be required to abstain from using the trade mark, or that the applicant has a specific right to use the sign'.[211] Mere suitability, or existing use elsewhere, is not 'due cause'.

3 RELATIVE GROUNDS IN RELATION TO EARLIER RIGHTS

In addition to refusal on the basis of earlier trade marks, a mark may also be rejected on the basis that it conflicts with 'earlier rights'. The relative grounds for refusal in relation to *earlier rights* are found in sections 5(4)(a) and 5(4)(b), and Articles 8(4) of the CTMR respectively.[212] These provide that a trade mark shall not be registered where the use of the applicant's mark would be restrained under the law of passing-off—section 5(4)(a)/Article 8(4)—or by some other right, such as copyright—section 5(4)(b)/Article 52(2). We consider each in turn.

3.1 UNREGISTERED MARKS

Section 5(4)(a) provides that a trade mark shall not be registered if, or to the extent that, its use in the United Kingdom is liable to be prevented by virtue of any rule of law (in particular, the law of passing-off) protecting an unregistered trade mark or other sign used in the course of trade. It seems this section is intended to implement Article 4(4)(b) of the Directive, though that provision uses the narrower language of 'rights to a non-registered trade mark'.[213]

---

[209] One example of a situation where a mark might be used without due cause is where there has been long-standing use. See *In re St. Leonard Motors Ltd's Application* (6 Aug. 1999) (TM Registry).

[210] [2000] *FSR* 767, 789–92. In the context of infringement, it may be that ownership of a registered mark (albeit one that is the subject of a pending invalidity action) may be 'due cause': *Pebble Beach Co. v. Lombard Brands* [2003] *ETMR* (21) 252 267–8 (para. 30).

[211] *Souza Cruz v. Hollywood*, R283/1999–3 [2002] *ETMR* (64) 705 (para. 85–6). This is very similar to the approach taken by the Benelux court in *Claeryn/Klarein* (1976) *IIC* 420. See also *Mülhens v. Hearst Corp*, R552/2000–4 (26 July 2001) (para. 18).

[212] CTMR, Art. 52(2) recognizes the equivalent relative ground for invalidity.

[213] *Wild Child Trade Mark* [1998] *RPC* 455, 457. See also CTMR, Art. 8(4).

Section 5(4)(a) will cover passing off,[214] if the requisites of goodwill, misrepresentation, and likely damage can be established.[215] The burden of proving the existence of the earlier right falls upon the opponent. In this context it is important to note that 'in an action for passing off the likelihood of misrepresentation and the prospect of damage to goodwill must be sufficiently real and substantial to warrant the intervention of the court'.[216] Although it may be more costly and time-consuming to base an opposition on section 5(4) rather than 5(2), there may be advantages from so doing in that the court may focus more upon how the mark has been used by the opponent, and understood by the public.

In the case of Community Trade Marks, the owners of rights in unregistered marks may only oppose registration if the sign is 'of more than mere local significance'.[217] The threshold appears to be quite high. In *Compass Publishing*, the owners of a CTM for COMPASS brought an infringement action against the defendant who was using the mark COMPASS LOGISTICS for management consultancy services. The defendant counterclaimed, arguing that the CTM was invalid because of its earlier rights. This was based on the fact that the defendant had begun trading under the name Compass Logistics a few months prior to the CTM application. Laddie J rejected the defendant's argument on the basis that its rights were not of more than 'mere local significance'. Given the internal market aims underpinning the creation of unitary Community Trade Mark rights, Laddie J took the view that objections based on insignificant rights should be kept to a minimum.[218] As Community law provided immunity from any action by the CTM holder,[219] Laddie J decided to construe 'local' from a European perspective: a right was local if it did not relate to the whole or a substantial part of the Community. Compass Logistics's rights were not of more than local significance in the UK market, let alone the EU.[220]

---

[214] Note *Interlotto (UK) v. Camelot Group plc* [2004] *RPC* 186 (CA) (even if opponent cannot establish a relative ground of refusal as of the date of the application, the opposition should succeed if the opponent can establish it before the date of registration).

[215] See Chs. 32–4 above. On the difficulties with assessing this on paper, see *R v. Reef Trade Mark* [2002] *RPC* (19) 387 (paras. 27–28).

[216] *Corgi Trade Mark* [1999] *RPC* 549, 557.

[217] CTMR, Art. 8(4). Cf. *Saxon Trade Mark* [2003] *FSR* (39) 704 (Laddie J) (para. 32) (trader in Plymouth using same name as trader in Manchester, where trades do not compete because of their geographical separation, can prevent registration by the latter of the mark as a trade mark, because the latter's 'normal and fair use' would include use in Plymouth).

[218] At para. 44 Laddie observed that 'in a market of over 400 million people in 25 States, there are likely to be a myriad of minor unregistered rights in trade marks and signs. If all of these could invalidate later CTMs, the objective of securing Community wide trade mark rights would be frustrated in many, if not most, cases.'

[219] CTMR Art 107(3). Indeed the holder of an earlier right can oppose use by the later CTM holder of its mark in the territory of the local right: CTMR, Art 107(1).

[220] *Paddy Kehoe v. Williams-Sonoma Inc,* R 212/2005–4 (OHIM 4th BA, 7 June 2007), (use of POTTERY BARN in two villages of mere local significance); *Kabushiki Kaisha Yoshida, trading as Yoshida & Co., Ltd. v. Porter International Co., Ltd,* Case R 73/2006–4 (OHIM 4th BA) (19 November 2007) (sales of 275 bags, each retailing at £200, from Browns in South Molton St, of mere local significance). See also *Gill v. Frankie Goes to Hollywood Ltd* [2008] *ETMR* (4) 77 (in dispute over FRANKIE GOES TO HOLLYWOOD rights of band-members were regarded as of more than mere local significance because of the band's success in the UK and Europe in the 1980s).

3.2 COPYRIGHT, DESIGN RIGHT, AND REGISTERED DESIGN RIGHT

Section 5(4)(b) states that a trade mark shall not be registered if, or to the extent that, its use in the United Kingdom is liable to be prevented 'by virtue of any earlier right...in particular by virtue of the law of copyright, design right or registered designs'. This provision is permitted by, but does not take complete advantage of, Article 4(4)(c) of the Directive.[221] In contrast, there is no provision for opposition on this ground at the OHIM. Article 52(2) of the CTMR, however, does recognize conflict with earlier rights as a ground of invalidity.

If someone owns copyright in the design of a device, the effect of section 5(4)(b) is that the applicant cannot obtain protection for the device as a trade mark without their consent. For example, in *Karo Step Trade Mark*,[222] an applicant succeeded in having a registered proprietor's device mark cancelled on the basis that they owned artistic copyright in the mark.[223] Similarly, in *Oscar Trade Mark*[224] the Academy of Motion Pictures successfully opposed the registration of a device mark comprising a silhouette of the famous Oscar statue given out at the annual Academy Awards. Graham J held that the statue was protected by copyright as a sculpture and that the silhouette device had been copied from it.[225] It should be recalled that, because single invented words and short phrases do not ordinarily provide information, instruction, or literary pleasure they are not usually protected by copyright as literary works.[226] Therefore section 5(2)(b) will not enable the creator of a word or short phrase to prevent someone else from using the word or short phrase as a trade mark.[227]

3.3 UNAUTHORIZED REGISTRATION BY AGENT

An application for registration of a trade mark by an agent or representative of a person who is the proprietor of the mark in a Convention country is to be refused if that proprietor opposes the application.[228] The CFI has explained that this provision is intended to prevent the former agent from unjustly benefiting from the knowledge and experience of its principal.[229] The opponent must establish that it is the proprietor of a mark in a Convention country, that the applicant is (or was) its 'agent or representative', and that the application was not 'authorized'.[230]

---

[221] In particular, there is no ground for objection in UK law based on a person's right to 'names' or 'personal portrayal' because such rights have not received recognition as doctrines separate from passing off.

[222] [1977] RPC 255. The device must in fact amount to an infringement: *Jules Rimet Cup Ltd. v. Football Association Ltd* [2008] *ECDR* (4) 43 (Deputy Judge Wyand QC) (the applicant's device, though based on the claimant's copyright-protected World Cup Willie lion character, did not reproduce a substantial part of the copyright work).

[223] *Karo Step*, ibid, 273. See also *Hutchinson Personal Communications v. Hook Advertising* [1996] *FSR* 549; *Team Lotus Ventures's Application; Opposition of Group Lotus* [1999] *ETMR* 669.

[224] *Oscar Trade Mark* [1980] *FSR* 429.

[225] Ibid, 439, 440.

[226] See above at pp. 63–4.

[227] But see TMA s. 3(6), discussed at pp. 851–5 above.

[228] TMA s. 60. See also Art. 6*septies* of the Paris Convention; CTMR Art. 8(3).

[229] *DEF-TEC Defense Technology GmbH, v. OHIM and Defense Technology Corporation of America*, Case T–6/05, (6 September 2006) (CFI) (para.38).

[230] As regards the final element, the CFI has said the consent must be 'clear, specific and unconditional': *DEF-TEC*, ibid (para.38).

Where an agent applies for a trade mark using a corporate front, it may be necessary for the examiner to 'pierce the corporate veil' in order to revel the true agency relationship.[231] It has been observed that it is frequently easier to establish bad faith than that the applicant was an agent of the 'real trade mark owner'.[232]

[231] *KK Yoshida v. Porter*, Case R73/2006–4 (OHIM 4th BA) (19 Nov. 2007) (on the facts this proved unnecessary).

[232] *Target Fixings v. Brutt* [2007] *RPC* (19) 462 (para 101).

39

REVOCATION

1 INTRODUCTION

In spite of the examination process, the trade mark register is not a guarantee of the validity of trade marks.[1] There are two reasons why a mark might be removed from the register. The first is if it is held to be *invalid*. The grounds for invalidity are set out in section 47 of the 1994 Act and Articles 51–2 of the CTMR. These provide that a mark may be declared to be invalid on the basis that it was registered in breach of one of the absolute or relative grounds for refusal: topics which were dealt with earlier.[2]

The second reason why a mark might be removed from the register, which is the focus of this chapter, is if it is 'revoked'. There are four grounds for revocation and these are found in section 46 and Article 50 of the CTMR (which largely correspond to the provisions in Articles 10 and 12 of the Directive). Section 46/Article 50 provide that a mark may be revoked (in relation to all or some of the goods and services in respect of which it is registered)[3] on the ground that:

(i)   the trade mark has not been used for five years following the date of completion of the registration (*non-use*);

(ii) use of the trade mark has been suspended for an uninterrupted period of five years;

(iii) the trade mark has become the 'common name in the trade' (*generic*); or

(iv) the trade mark has been used in such a way that it is liable to mislead the public (*deceptive*).

---

[1] TMA s. 70.

[2] See Chs. 36–8. TMA s. 47(6) provides that, where the registration of a trade mark is declared invalid to any extent, the registration shall to that extent be deemed never to have been made.

[3] TMA s. 46(5); CTMR, Art. 50(2).

Section 7(4) of the Act provides that an application for revocation may be made by any person, and may be made either to the Registrar or to the court.[4] The onus of proving that a mark should be revoked falls upon the party seeking revocation of the mark.[5] In relation to revocation for non-use, however, section 100 modifies the general position by stating that the proprietor must show the use that has been made of the registered mark.[6] It should be noted that, while the section appears to confer a discretion on the Registrar to leave an otherwise revocable mark on the register (but not to remove a mark which is not revocable), the better view is that no such discretion exists.[7]

With these general points in mind, we now consider the grounds on which a registered mark may be revoked. It is convenient to deal with the two non-use grounds together.

2 NON-USE

The first ground on which a mark may be revoked is on the basis of 'non-use'. Revocation for non-use reflects the notion, also found in the law of passing-off, that protection for marks is justified as a result of their use.[8] As the ninth Recital to the Community Trade Mark Regulation explains, 'there is no justification for protecting earlier trade marks except where the marks are actually used'. It is only by virtue of use that marks come to communicate information to consumers, and thus operate in a way which merits legal protection.[9] Consequently, if a mark is not put into use within a reasonable period of registration, or use comes to be suspended, there is no good reason for preventing another trader from adopting that mark. Revocation for non-use helps to ensure that such unused marks, as well as marks which have been registered and used but use of which has ceased,[10] can be removed from the register so that other traders can safely use similar, as well as identical, marks.[11] Revocation for non-use also ensures that opportunistic stockpiling of good marks is fruitless.[12]

---

[4] As regards CTMs, an application for revocation may be made either directly to the Cancellation Division of the OHIM or by way of counterclaim to an action for infringement: CTMR, Arts. 50(1) and 95(1). Non-use can also be put in issue in opposition proceedings at the OHIM: CTMR, Art. 43(2).

[5] TMA s. 72. Nevertheless, it was held in *Softa Trade Mark* [1996] *RPC* 457 that where the registered proprietor entered no defence, prima facie, the application to remove is valid.

[6] Reversing *Nodoz Trade Mark* [1962] *RPC* 1, 5. But there is no equivalent in the CTMR: see Annand and Norman (1998), 142.

[7] *Premier Brands UK v. Typhoon Europe* [2000] *FSR* 767, 811.

[8] *Invermont Trade Mark* [1997] *RPC* 125; *Cabanas Havana (Device) Trade Mark* [2000] *RPC* 26, 34. TM Dir. Recital 8 refers to a desire to reduce the number of registered marks.

[9] See S. Carter, 'The Trouble with Trademark' (1989–90) 99 *Yale Law Journal* 759 (arguing that the protection of marks that convey no information to consumers carries significant, but rarely mentioned, costs by depleting market language and raising substantial barriers to entry).

[10] Jacob J graphically referred to these signs as 'abandoned vessels in the shipping lanes of trade': *Re Laboratories Goëmar SA* [2002] *ETMR* 34. See also Mummery LJ in *La Mer Technology v. Laboratoires Goëmar SA* [2006] *FSR* (5) 49 (para. 14) ('the evident purpose of the power of revocation for non-use is to prevent the Register from being cluttered up with unused marks, which would obstruct later traders wishing to use the marks and would create unnecessary conflict and confusion between the registered trade marks of traders and manufacturers of goods').

[11] Given that the OHIM allows applications for very broad specifications, revocation is likely to play a very significant role in restricting the rights of trade mark proprietors within appropriate confines.

[12] As we saw in Ch. 37, the UK treats applications without intent to use the mark as made in bad faith, contrary to section 3(6), and thus treats any resulting registration as liable to be held invalid. However, 'bad faith' can be difficult to establish in cases of 'greedy' rather than dishonest applications, and s. 46 is better suited to

2.1 THE RELEVANT PERIOD OF NON-USE

As indicated, there are two distinct types of non-use. The first ground for non-use is set out in section 46(1)(a)/Article 50(1)(a),[13] which provides that a trade mark may be revoked on the basis that 'within the period of five years following the date of completion of the registration procedure it has not been put to genuine use in the United Kingdom, by the proprietor or with his consent, in relation to the goods or services for which it is registered, and there are no proper reasons for non-use'.[14] In order for a mark to be revoked under section 46(1)(a), it is necessary to show that in the five-year period after registration the mark has not been put to genuine use.[15] The fact that the non-use must be for a five-year period recognizes that the registrant should be given a reasonably lengthy period of time in which to arrange the use of the mark.

The second ground of revocation for non-use is found in section 46(1)(b). This states that a mark may also be revoked where 'use has been suspended for an uninterrupted period of five years, and there are no proper reasons for non-use'. In order for a mark to be revoked on this ground, it is necessary to show that use of the mark has been suspended for an uninterrupted period of five years.[16] The fact that the non-use must be for a five-year period recognizes that the goodwill built up from the use of a mark does not immediately disappear when the owner stops using the mark.[17]

A mark will not be revoked on the basis of non-use if use is commenced or resumed after the expiry of the five-year period and before the application for revocation is made.[18] Section 46(3) goes on to say, however, that the commencement or resumption of use is to be disregarded if it takes place 'within the period of three months before the making of the application'. This provision will not apply, however, 'where preparations for the commencement or resumption began before the proprietor became aware that the application might be made'. The three-month cut-off period operates to prevent trade mark proprietors who have not used the mark from defeating an application for revocation for non-use by (re)-commencing use as soon as they get wind of the interest of the applicant. Thus applicants are theoretically able to write to the proprietor before they apply to have a mark revoked and ask whether there has been any use of the mark. In so doing, they will be safe in the knowledge that, although their inquiry may prompt the trade mark proprietor to use the mark, this will not defeat their application for non-use.

---

dealing with such cases. While sometimes revocation for non-use has also been said to reflect a public interest in maintaining the register as a reflection of enforceable marks (see, e.g. *Imperial Group v. Philip Morris* [1982] *FSR* 72, 84), the truth is that neither the national or Community registers come close to mirroring the enforceable marks. Cf. D. Vaver, 'Summary Expungement of Registered Trade Marks on the Ground of Non-Use' (1983) 21 *Osgoode Hall Law Journal* 17, 23 (discussing Canadian trade marks law).

[13] TM Dir. Art. 10(1). For the international standards limiting such powers, see Paris, Art. 5C; TRIPS, Art. 19.

[14] This has been interpreted as five years from the day after registration so that the earliest date of revocation for a mark registered on 9 February 1999 was 10 February 2006: *Valent Biosciences Trade Mark* [2007] *RPC* (34) 829.

[15] TM Dir. Art. 12. On the issue as to whether the Directive defined the precise dates, see *Armin Häupl v. Lidl Stiftung & Co. KG,* Case C–246/05, [2007] *ETMR* (61) 997 (ECJ).

[16] TMA, s. 46.

[17] Note the corresponding rules in relation to passing off at pp. 737–8 above.

[18] TMA s. 46(3). But the ECJ has recognized that use after this period may be of relevance when assessing the extent to which use during the relevant period was genuine: *La Mer Technology Inc. v. Laboratoires Goëmar SA,* Case C–259/02 [2004] *ECR* I–1159 (para. 31).

One question that has arisen is whether it was possible to register the same mark twice. If so, the further question arises: how does this impact on the five-year non-use rule? In *Origins Natural Resources v. Origin Clothing*[19] the claimant, who had taken an assignment of a mark registered for various clothes in Class 25, applied to register the same mark for a wider range of clothes. The defendant argued that this should not be allowed because it would undermine the five-year non-use rule. Jacob J disagreed, saying:

if a man were to keep registering the same mark with no genuine intention of using it then he would lose his mark...If, on the other hand, a man had registered a mark with a bona fide intention to use it and found himself unable to use it for a number of years so that the mark was removable...but he still had genuine plans to use the mark then I see no reason why he should not apply again.[20]

2.2 WHAT IS USE OF THE MARK?

The next question to ask in relation to section 46(1)(a)–(b)/Article 50(1)(a) is what is meant by 'use' of the mark. One preliminary point to note is that not all uses of a trade mark which would infringe (if made by a third party) amount to use for the purposes of defending an application for revocation.

2.2.1 Use

The most obvious way a registered proprietor will be able to show use is by demonstrating sales of articles that are marked with the sign. Other uses, such as advertising, may also be sufficient (as long as they are in connection with the anticipated sale of products bearing, or provision of services under the mark). Preparatory acts, such as gearing up a business to launch a product, are probably insufficient at least if they are internal to the trade mark owner's organization.[21] Similarly, negotiations between businesses referring to possible licensing of a mark do not count as use of the mark for the purposes of section 46.[22] In *Ansul BV v. Ajax Brandbeveiliging BV*, the Court indicated that what is required is:

use of the mark on the market for the goods or services protected by that mark and not just internal use by the undertaking concerned...Use of the mark must therefore relate to goods or services already marketed or about to be marketed and for which preparations by the undertaking to secure customers are under way, particularly in the form of advertising campaigns.[23]

One interesting question that may need to be decided in due course is whether 'oral use' is relevant. Under section 103(2) of the Act use is said to include 'use...otherwise than by means of a graphic representation'. This would suggest that oral use might suffice,[24] but in *Anheuser-Busch v. Bedejovicky Budvar* Deputy Judge Simon Thorley QC said that whether oral use by customers counts as use for section 46(1) 'raised complex questions of trade mark law'.[25]

---

[19] [1995] FSR 280.   [20] Ibid, 284.
[21] Cf. *Hermes Trade Mark* [1982] RPC 425.
[22] *Philosophy Inc v. Ferretti Studios* [2003] RPC (15) 287, 295–6 (paras. 18, 21) (Peter Gibson LJ). If this does count as use, it is not 'genuine use'.
[23] Case C–40/01 [2003] ECR I–2439; [2003] RPC (40) 717 (para. 37).
[24] *Ensure Plus Trade Mark* (26 Sept. 2002) (para. 39) (TM Registry); Kerly para. 9–51.
[25] [2002] RPC (38) 748 (para. 51). See also *Second Skin Trade Mark* [2002] ETMR (CN3) 326 (TMR) (even if oral use would suffice, mere use by customers would not).

2.2.2 Use as a trade mark

It seems that 'use' must be 'as a trade mark' in the sense of indicating trade origin of the goods or services in question. In *Animated Music Ltd's Trade Mark*,[26] the Registry revoked the registration of the mark NELLIE THE ELEPHANT even though the proprietor had been able to show some use of the sign on brochures and invoices relating to the licensing of cartoons. The Registry found that the evidence was at best evidence of use of the sign as the title of the cartoon or name of the character, not use 'as a trade mark', that is, to indicate the trade origin of any of the services. It follows from the case law that use of marks to decorate products—or which would be understood (by the average consumer) in that way will not amount to 'genuine use'. Similarly, use as a corporate name will not, of itself, justify maintenance of the mark.[27] Equally, evidence of use of a mark on the top of invoices, with addresses, etc. does not of itself prove genuine use.[28]

2.2.3 Use via associated marks

Trade mark owners might wish to modify their trade marks in accordance with changing fashions and styles. As long as the changes do not alter the distinctive character of the mark, the use of the modified mark will be recognized as use of the registered mark (unless the modified version is registered in its own right).[29] Section 46(2) explains that 'use of a trade mark includes use in a form differing in elements which do not alter the distinctive character of the mark in the form in which it was registered'.[30] According to Lord Walker in *Anheuser-Busch v. Bedejovicky Budvar*,[31] it is for the tribunal first to ascertain the points of difference between the mark as used and the mark as registered. Having done this, the tribunal should ask whether the differences alter the distinctive character of the mark as registered. The distinctive character in issue is what makes the mark 'in some degree striking and memorable'. This is judged from the point of view of the Registrar (rather than the average consumer), who is concerned with 'the mark's likely impact on the average consumer'.[32]

The question whether a change to a mark alters the distinctive character of that mark is one of 'first impression' (and thus one which an appeal court should be reluctant to overturn).[33] Much will depend upon the type of mark (whether a word or device mark), the way the mark is typically used and understood (whether visually, aurally, or conceptually), and the way the mark is varied. To change the distinctive character of the mark, it is necessary to alter the identity or individuality of the mark.[34] In the case of short or simple marks, or marks with

---

[26] [2004] *ETMR* (79) 1076.

[27] For example *Magrinya v. Sportsmania (MANIA/Sportsmania figurative mark)* OHIM Opp. Div. Decision No. 1042/2001 (25 Apr. 2001). But note the ECJ's comments, albeit in the context of infringement, that while use as a trade name is not necessarily use as a trade mark, certain uses of a trade name might be: *Céline SARL v. Céline SA*, Case C–17/06 [2007] *ETMR* (80) 1320. This was applied by the Registry in *Kim Trade Mark*, O/004/08 (9 Jan 2008).

[28] *Carlisle Corp v. Ibertrade Management Corp SL*, R791/2000–1 (13 Dec. 2001) para. 22; *Orient Express Trade Mark* [1996] *RPC* 25, 42. In *Euromarket Designs Inc v. Peters* [2000] *ETMR* 1025 (para. 56), Jacob J stated that use as a shop name was not use in relation to goods.

[29] *Il Ponte Finanziaria SpA, v. OHIM*, Case C–234/06 P [2008] *ETMR* (13) 242 (ECJ, 4th Ch), (para. 86).

[30] TM Dir., Art. 10.

[31] *Anheuser-Busch v. Bedejovicky Budvar* [2003] *RPC* (25) 477, 490 (para. 41).

[32] Ibid. Sir Martin Nourse said that the Registrar's failure to apply the right test would not have affected his view of the mark because the Registrar 'would necessarily have to view the matter through the eyes of the average consumer'.

[33] Ibid.

[34] The ECJ talks about 'a slightly different form': *Il Ponte Finanziaria*, Case C–234/06 P [2008] *ETMR* (13) 242 (ECJ, 4th Ch), (para. 86).

very little distinctive character, a slight modification may mean that use will not sustain the registration. So, for example, the CFI has held that the mark J. GIORGI was not used on invoices which bore the terms GIORGI, MISS GIORGI or GIORGI LINE because the distinctive character of the J. GIORGI mark was affected by such uses.[35] ('Giorgi' was viewed as a common name and so of low inherent distinctiveness.) In contrast, in the case of a word and device mark, substantial alteration to the device may have little impact if the average consumer sees the word as dominating the mark. This was the case in the *Budweiser* case where a registration of BUDWEISER BUDBRÄU in a stylised form was successfully maintained by relying on use of the words in block capitals as a circular surround to a device consisting of a castle and shield.[36] Similar reasoning almost certainly explains the CFI's decision that variations in the style of QUANTIÈME (capitalization, modifying and underlining the 'Q') did not alter the distinctive character of the mark for watches.[37]

Under the 1938 Act, the UK tribunals were keen to prevent the maintenance of 'ghost marks', a technique used to provide indirect protection to non-registrable marks. This may occur where a person discovers that for one reason or another, they cannot register the mark they wish to trade under. One option in these circumstances is for the trader to trade under the unregistrable mark and at the same time attempt to register a similar mark. Based upon the fact that trade mark protection includes marks which are similar, the trader would hope to be able to use the registered mark indirectly to protect the mark that they are actually trading under. So, in one case where it was impossible to register HUGGERS as a mark for clothing (the term describing the closeness-of-fit) the trader registered HUGGARS. In due course, the question arose as to whether use of HUGGERS could justify maintenance of the HUGGARS mark.[38] While noting there was no phonetic distinction, Mummery J observed that, as much of the use of the mark was visual, it should be regarded primarily in such a context. Moreover, the concept suggested by the marks differed substantially with HUGGERS easily associated with clothing and HUGGARS less obviously so. Consequently, altering a single letter of a word was held to have substantially affected its identity, so that the HUGGARS mark was revoked.[39]

2.2.4 Use by a licensee

According to section 46(1)(a)–(b)/Article 50(1)(a) the use must be by the proprietor or with *their consent*.[40] It will be for the proprietor of a mark to demonstrate consent, though a tribunal may infer this from the fact that the proprietor has evidence of use by a third party.[41] In

---

[35] *Laboratorios RTB, SL v. OHIM*, T–156/01 [2003] *ECR* II–2789 (para. 44).

[36] The Registrar accepted that the use of the words in this way was use of the mark in a form which did not alter its distinctive character, because the average consumer would view the graphic as use of the words (the underlining and different fonts not detracting from, or adding anything to, 'the central message'.) In the Court of Appeal, Sir Martin Nourse observed that the Registrar had legitimately found that 'the words have a dominance which reduces to insignificance the other recognisable elements'. Lord Walker said that if it had been for him to decide he would have taken a view more like that of the judge than the Registrar: but since the Registry had not erred in principle, it was not for the High Court or the Court of Appeal to replace the Registrar's assessment with its own.

[37] *Devinlec Développement Innovations Leclerc SA v. OHIM,* T–147/03 [2006] *ECR* II–11 (appealed on a different ground and aff'd, as Case C–171/06 P (15 March 2007)).

[38] *Huggars Trade Mark* [1979] *FSR* 310. See also *Imperial v. Philip Morris* [1982] *FSR* 72 where a registration of NERIT as a ghost mark for MERIT, an unregistrable, laudatory mark, was revoked for lack of a bona fide intent to use.

[39] *Arnold Trade Mark, O/474/01; Dialog Trade Mark, O/084//02.*

[40] TM Dir. Art. 10(3); TRIPS, Art. 19(2).

[41] *The Sunrider Corp v. OHIM*, Case C–486/04P [2006] *ECR* I–4237 (ECJ).

Hebrew University of Jerusalem v. Continental Shelf 128 Ltd (Einstein),[42] the applicant sought revocation of the mark EINSTEIN for clothing on the basis that it had not been used between 1999 and 2004. The proprietor provided a statement by a sales executive from a different company, Hornby Street Ltd, that it had used the mark on swing tags, sew-in labels and invoices. Hornby Street Ltd was described as a sister company of the proprietor, but no further evidence of a connection was given. While the examiner accepted that the evidence established use, he held that the proprietor had not shown the use was *with its consent.* This was because in his view what was required was not mere consent but some level of control. On appeal, the Appointed Person, Geoffrey Hobbs QC, conducted a thorough analysis of the history of the Directive to conclude that there was no requirement that the proprietor control the quality of the goods sold under the sign, so long as it has consented to the use, that is, that there existed an economic link between the proprietor and the user. Here, the common ownership of the two firms was sufficient.

2.3 GENUINE USE

For a mark to remain on the register, it is necessary to show that it has been put to genuine use in the UK (or, in the case of a Community mark, in the Community).[43] Two understandings of 'genuine use' have been employed in the case law.[44] According to the first understanding, any use which is not artificial, fictitious, or merely to retain the mark will suffice. In contrast, the second view of 'genuineness' of use, demands real substantial use in the marketplace, such as to bring the mark to the attention of consumers. Sometimes these tests are articulated in terms of the subjective genuineness of the use (where the test is whether there was honest intent) and objective genuineness (where the test is ordinary commercial standards).[45] The key difference is that, if the test is honest use, it can be *de minimis* (though it is also possible that substantial use in a trade mark protection programme might be disregarded); in contrast, for objective genuineness, there must be substantial use (though what is 'substantial' will vary from sector to sector).[46]

Despite a few decisions in which the 'objective' approach seems to have been taken by the CFI, it is now clear that the ECJ has adopted a test which is much closer to the 'subjective approach'.[47] In *Ansul BV v. Ajax Brandbeveiliging BV,*[48] Ansul had registered the mark MINI-MAX in the Benelux 1971 for fire extinguishers and associated products. However, it had not

---

[42] *Einstein Trade Mark* [2007] RPC (23) 539.

[43] As well as 'genuine', different language versions of CTMR Art. 50 talk about use which is 'sérieux', 'ernsthaft', 'effetivo/seriamente', 'efectivo', 'serio', 'normaal', 'reel' or 'verkligt' (in French, German, Italian, Spanish, Potuguese, Dutch, Danish, and Swedish). The Italian text uses the term 'effectivo' in relation to Art. 50, and 'seriamente' for Art. 43(2).

[44] L. Bently and R. Burrell, 'The Requirement of Trade Mark Use', (2002) 13 *Australian Intellectual Property Journal* 181; L. Bently, 'Use and the Community Trade Mark: What is its Role? What Should it be?', Paper delivered at Fordham University, April 2002.

[45] *Gerber Trade Marks* [2003] RPC (34) 637, 641 (Auld LJ) (a 1938 Act case).

[46] In assessing genuineness, assessment should be from the point of view of the average consumer and regard should be had to the expectations of the public as to the manner in which they are marketed and their points of sale: *Tiffany & Co/Emballages Mixtes et Plastique Sarl*, R1018/2000–3 (3 Dec. 2002).

[47] *Harrison v. Kabushiki Kaisha Fernandes,* T–39/01 [2002] *ECR* II–5233; *Jean M. Goulbourn v. OHIM,* T–174/01 [2004] *ETMR* (16) 190; *RTB v. OHIM,* T–156/01 [2003] *ECR* II–2789. All three cases were concerned with CTMR Art. 43(2).

[48] Case C–40/01 [2003] *ECR* I–2439.

sold any extinguishers since 1989. Nevertheless, Ansul had sold component parts for the extinguishers, repaired and maintained them, and used the mark MINIMAX on invoices in relation to such services. A German company called Minimax GmbH had made and sold fire extinguishers and had owned a German registration for MINIMAX for 50 years. In 1994, Ajax, a subsidiary of the German company, began to use the MINIMAX trade mark in the Netherlands. Ajax sought revocation of Ansul's 1971 registration, and Ansul sought an injunction against Ajax to prevent it using the MINIMAX mark in the Benelux countries. The outcome of the case depended on whether Ansul's mark had been put to genuine use in the period after 1989, when it had been used in relation to components and repairs. The referring court wanted to know whether this could be a genuine use.

The ECJ stated that the notion of genuine use required a uniform interpretation throughout the Community. It said that token use, serving solely to attempt to preserve rights, was not genuine use.[49] Genuine use must be consistent with the essential function of a trade mark, to guarantee the identity of the origin of goods or services to the consumer. It concluded that such use required 'use of the mark on the market for the goods or services protected by that mark and not just internal use by the undertaking concerned...Use of the mark must therefore relate to goods or services already marketed or about to be marketed and for which preparations by the undertaking to secure customers are under way, particularly in the form of advertising campaigns'.[50] Moreover, the Court observed that when assessing whether use was genuine it was necessary to take account of all the facts and circumstances to decide whether 'the commercial exploitation of the mark is real, in particular whether such use is warranted in the economic sector concerned to maintain or create a share in the market for the goods or services protected by the mark'.[51] Use of a mark need not always be quantitatively significant for it to be genuine. Finally, the Court indicated that use in relation to components or after-sales services could be use which 'related to' goods, even though the goods for which the mark was registered were no longer being sold. The Court declined to say anything about the specific case between Ansul and Ajax, pointing out that this was a matter for the national courts.

Although some aspects of the ECJ judgment are a little vague, further clarification was offered in response to a reference from the UK. In *Re Laboratories Goemar SA*, the question was whether there was 'genuine use' sufficient to resist a section 46 revocation of the sign LABORATOIRE DE LA MER for cosmetics containing marine products.[52] The proprietor was a small French company specializing in seaweed products and the applicant for revocation, Huber Laboratories, intended to launch a huge range of skin-care products under the LA MER name. The proprietor had made sales worth only £800 to a Scottish agent. There was no suggestion that the use by Goemar was 'token', that is, merely for the purpose of maintaining the mark on the register. Jacob J referred a number of issues to the European Court of Justice. The ECJ responded that even minimal use (not quantitatively significant) can qualify as genuine 'on condition that it is deemed to be justified, in the economic sector concerned, for the purpose of preserving or creating market share for the goods or services protected by the mark'. That requires an assessment by the national court, on the facts in front of it. In certain cases, the criterion might be met by use of a mark by a single client, but it would have to appear that the operation had 'a genuine commercial justification for the proprietor of the mark'. However, the need for such an assessment on the facts precludes any *a priori*, abstract, quantitative threshold.[53]

---

[49] Ibid, para. 36.   [50] Ibid, para. 37.   [51] Ibid, para. 38.   [52] *Re Goëmar* [2006] *FSR* (5) 49.
[53] *La Mer v. Goëmar*, Case C–259/02 [2004] *ECR* I–1159 (paras. 21–7).

Armed with the advice of the ECJ, Blackburne J held that the sales were not sufficient to constitute genuine use. However, on appeal, the Court of Appeal reversed.[54] The Court of Appeal said the use could not be considered 'internal': the Scottish agent was an independent entity and not, for example, a subsidiary of Goemar. Goemar was genuinely trying to sell its goods, that is to gain a share in the market. The fact that it had not been particularly successful, and that the goods had not reached the attention of consumers, was irrelevant. It was enough that there was a genuine attempt to sell goods bearing the mark. The Court of Appeal warned that any other approach would have amounted to setting a quantitative threshold (contrary to the ECJ's view). Neuberger LJ (now Lord Neuberger) indicated that an approach that required the courts and offices to assess whether use was substantial would be difficult, expensive, and time-consuming to apply.[55]

The ECJ had stated that genuine use requires use that is warranted in the marketplace to maintain or establish market share. This criterion, which requires the assessor to take account the kind of goods concerned and not to decide mechanically by reference to predetermined percentages, could easily have been understood as requiring some substantial presence. In contrast, the Court of Appeal has interpreted *Ansul* and *Goemar* as merely requiring use as a trade mark that is neither token nor purely internal. This position had already been advocated by the Appointed Person, the Irish Patents Office,[56] and it looks likely to remain the standard at least for the foreseeable future.[57] However, one might doubt whether the judicial selection of a test that is easy to apply over one which requires the proprietor to prove a substantial presence in the market place is the right one from a policy perspective. After all, a trade mark proprietor is given a five year period of exclusivity in which to establish usage. If the proprietor cannot show that it has made an impression on the market by then, ought it really be allowed to retain its registration?

2.4 USE IN RELATION TO THE GOODS OR SERVICES FOR WHICH THE MARK IS REGISTERED

To ensure that a mark is not revoked because of non-use, the mark must be used 'in relation to the goods or services for which the mark is registered'. In general, therefore, use in relation to similar goods is *not* use in relation to the goods for which the mark is registered. However, it seem there may be use *in relation to* the goods or services for which the mark is registered, when the proprietor applies the marks either on parts to be used in the repair of the goods for which the sign is registered, or in connection with services involving repair or maintenance of the goods.[58]

A related problem arises if a proprietor uses the registered mark on promotional goods such as T-shirts: does this amount to use *in relation to* T-shirts or only in relation to the goods

---

[54] *Laboratoires Goëmar SA v. La Mer Technology Inc* [2005] *EWCA Civ* 978.

[55] Ibid, para. 46.

[56] *Police Trade Mark* [2004] *RPC* (35) 693 (Richard Arnold QC); *Stefcom SPA's Trade Mark; Application for Revocation by Travel Hurry Projects Ltd* [2005] *ETMR* (82) 960.

[57] See also *MFE Marienfelde GmbH v. OHIM*, Case T–334/01 [2006] *ETMR* (9) 88; *La Mer Technology, Inc., v. OHIM*, Case T–418/03, [2008] *ETMR* (9) 169, where the CFI viewed minimal use as sufficient in relation to the relevant goods.

[58] *Ansul v. Ajax*, Case C–40/01 [2003] *ECR* I–2439, and [2005] 2 *CMLR* (36) 901 (paras. 41–42). This perhaps reflects an inclination to interpret the requirement of use more generously in relation to marks that have been used and retain residual goodwill than to marks for which a substantial goodwill has never been established.

which are being promoted? This is probably a question of fact, the answer being dependent on how the average consumer would perceive the use.[59] It should be observed however that such use could be seen as both use in relation to T-shirts and the goods promoted on the shirt. In *Premier Brands UK v. Typhoon Europe,* the proprietor of the TY.PHOO mark for domestic utensils and containers resisted revocation by claiming it had used the mark on tea canisters, biscuit barrels, etc. Neuberger J said that although the public would understand the use as promoting TYPHOO tea, it did not follow that the public would not *also* assume that the goods had been marketed by or with the approval of the makers of TYPHOO tea.[60]

2.5 PLACE OF USE

In relation to British marks, the relevant use must take place in the UK. An advertisement released in a foreign jurisdiction may also constitute use, so long as the advertisement is available in the United Kingdom. For example, in *Elle Trade Marks*[61] the proprietor of the mark ELLE for soap and perfume sought to rely on the fact that soaps and other cosmetics branded with ELLE had been offered for sale in the French edition of a well-known woman's magazine of which the appellants were also proprietors. It was accepted that the French edition was sold in the United Kingdom and that it contained an advertisement for ELLE soap which could be obtained by readers in Britain either by going to Paris or by ordering it by phone. Although there was no evidence of actual sale, Lloyd J held that this was a genuine use within the relevant class of goods. In contrast, mere use on an internet site is not use in the United Kingdom: as the Registrar, Mr Salthouse, has said, were the position otherwise 'the simple creation of a web site would provide use in every country in the world on the basis that it could be accessed globally'.[62] It seems that in such cases what is required is evidence of a site targeting customers in the United Kingdom.[63]

A special provision of a trade mark includes situations where the mark is affixed to goods or to the packaging of goods in the UK solely for export.[64] This has been interpreted broadly as including the situation whether the proprietor attaches the mark to goods in the UK and transfers them to a foreign subsidiary, rather than just to circumstances where export is made to an independent business abroad.[65] If this is right, the provision must be understood as an exception to the general requirement that the use be other than internal to the proprietor's organization.

---

[59] In *Henrique & Oliveira v. Twelve Islands Shipping (Malibu device/coconut tree device)* Decision No. 374/2001 (14 Feb. 2001) the OHIM Opposition Division held that the disposal of clothing bearing the Malibu mark was use in relation to drinks not use in relation to clothing. In so finding it noted that the clothing was distributed at promotional events and that the MALIBU trade mark appeared in the label of the neck of the garment so that the shirts would be perceived by consumers as promoting a brand for a drink rather distinguishing a particular clothing manufacturer from its competitors. See also *Young v. Medici* [2004] *FSR* (19) 383 (Jacob J) para. 3 (no use for boxes and packaging by selling trade marked goods in packaging).

[60] [2000] *FSR* 767. See also *Elle Trade Marks* [1997] *FSR* 529. (Where a women's magazine called ELLE gave away complimentary samples of perfumes bearing the name of another manufacturer, MONSOON, the magazine was unable to resist an application for revocation of the mark ELLE which had also been registered for perfumes. Lloyd J explained that 'the mark was used, if in any context at all other than the magazine, in relation to the promotion of the event and not the particular goods to be used or offered in connection with the event').

[61] *Elle,* ibid. Cf. below at p. 919.

[62] *Platinum Trade Mark,* O/133/01 (15 Mar. 2001) (para. 35).

[63] *Euromarket Designs v. Peters* [2000] *ETMR* 1025.

[64] TMA s. 46(2). Cf. below at pp. 920–1.

[65] *Imaginarium Trade Mark* [2004] *RPC* (30) 594 (TM Registry).

In relation to Community marks, the relevant use must be in the Community. It is unclear whether this requires use in more than one country: a Council and Commission Minute had suggested that use in one country would suffice, but leading commentators have questioned whether this should be followed.[66] Such Minutes are non-binding, and the ECJ has ignored them already (in relation, for example, to marks for retail services). Nevertheless, the OHIM has recognized use in the UK as justifying maintenance of a Community mark,[67] and the OHIM web site cites this as one of ten reasons to use the CTM system.[68] However, along with others, we are not certain that use in one state should be allowed to justify maintenance of Community-wide rights. Indeed, the provision in Article 108(2)(a), which allows for conversion of a revoked Community mark into marks operative in member states where use has occurred seems to imply that use in one member state would not suffice.

2.6 PROPER REASONS FOR NON-USE

Section 46(1)(a)–(b)/Article 50(1)(a) provide that failure to use a mark will not affect the fate of the mark if there are 'proper reasons for non-use'.[69] The ECJ has interpreted this in a manner which is difficult for a proprietor to rely on. *Armin Häupl v. Lidl Stiftung & Co. KG* concerned an Austrian mark, LE CHEF DE CUISINE, owned by the German supermarket chain Lidl.[70] Lidl had faced bureaucratic obstacles in opening its supermarkets in Austria, and after five years had elapsed, Häupl sought revocation. In response to various questions from the Austrian Supreme Patent and Trade mark Adjudication Tribunal, the ECJ indicated that, in order to rely on the proviso, a proprietor would need to demonstrate that (i) the obstacle must have arisen independently of the will of the proprietor, (ii) there must be a direct relationship between the obstacle and the failure to use the trade mark and (iii) the obstacle must be such as to make the use of the mark impossible or unreasonable. We examine each element in turn.

2.6.1 Circumstances Arising Independently of the Will of the Proprietor

The ECJ interpreted the notion of 'proper reasons' in the light of Article 19 of the TRIPS Agreement,[71] This states that '[c]ircumstances arising independently of the will of the owner of the trademark which constitute an obstacle to the use of the trademark, ... shall be recognised as valid reasons for non-use'. While Article 19 tells a tribunal about certain circumstances which shall be treated as 'proper reasons for non-use' the ECJ has gone further than this, and indicated that these are the only reasons which will be regarded as proper.[72]

---

[66] Cornish and Llewelyn (5th edn.), 693, in contrast, argues that use should be in more than one member state.

[67] *Fotiadis's Trade Mark; Application by Plato Learning Inc for a declaration of invalidity* [2007] *ETMR* (73) 1222 (para. 21); *ILG Ltd v. Crunch Fitness International Ltd,* R1168/2005–4 [2008] *ETMR* (17) 329 (para. 11) (citing Agreed Statement).

[68] OHIM's 'Ten Good reasons for Using the Community Trade Mark', reason no. 6 (obligation of use which is easy to meet). <http://www.oami.europa.eu>.

[69] Under the 1938 Act a similar exclusion was made where non-use was attributable to 'special circumstances in the trade'.

[70] *Häupl v. Lidl,* Case C–246/05 [2007] *ETMR* (61) 997 (ECJ).

[71] TRIPS, Art. 19 states that 'circumstances arising independently of the will of the owner of the trademark which constitute an obstacle to the use of the trademark, such as import restrictions or other government requirements for goods or services protected by the trademark, shall be recognised as valid reasons for non-use'.

[72] *Häupl v. Lidl,* Case C–246/05 [2007] *ETMR* (61) 997 (ECJ).

The idea of an obstacle arising 'independently of the will of the proprietor' is capable of being interpreted more or less broadly. It could be taken to refer only to matters wholly outside the proprietor's control, or more broadly to cover all matters which the proprietor has not 'willed.' While classic examples of such obstacles are 'import restrictions or other government requirements',[73] it is not obvious that one would say that other circumstances, such as a lack of resources, financial problems, lack of staff, marketing problems, difficulties in perfecting technology, are ones that a proprietor 'wills'.[74] Probably, however, the tribunals will continue to apply similar standards to those applicable before the *Häupl* judgment. Accordingly, these latter kinds of difficulty are regarded as not being 'independent of the will of the proprietor' because they are matters which are 'within the businessman's own control', for which the businessman should plan accordingly.[75] The CFI has stated that 'the concept of proper reasons...must be considered to refer essentially to circumstances unconnected with the trade mark owner which prohibit him from using the mark, rather than to circumstances associated with the commercial difficulties he is experiencing'.[76]

2.6.2 A Sufficiently Direct Relationship Between the Obstacle and the Mark

For the 'proper reasons' proviso to operate, the ECJ requires there to be a direct relationship between the obstacle and the use of the mark. Bureaucratic obstacles in gaining building permits for supermarkets, it is implied by the Court in *Häupl,* did not have a sufficiently direct relationship with the use of the mark LE CHEF DE CUISINE on foodstuffs (the goods or services for which it is registered).[77] In contrast, a sufficiently direct relationship would exist, for example, where use of a particular name for the goods was dependent on obtaining authorization from a regulatory authority (such as the European Medicines Evaluation Agency). If the concept of obstacles arising 'independently of the will' is interpreted broadly to include matters such as lack of resources or financial problems, there is probably an insufficient connection between these circumstances and the use of a specific mark on specific goods for these to ever count as a proper reason for non-use.[78]

---

[73] TRIPS, Art. 19. *Alza Corpn. v. Almirall-Prodesfarma SA (Viadur/Diadur),* R745/2001–2(9 July 2003); *Invermont Trade Mark* [1997] *RPC* 125, 130 (non-use said to be justified under the 1994 Act to include 'delays occasioned by some unavoidable regulatory requirement, such as the approval of a medicine'). External obstacles to use need not be ones imposed by the state: the UK Registry held that there were proper reasons for non-use of TEAM LOTUS where the proprietor had applied for but been refused entry to Formula 1 racing: *Team Lotus Trade Mark* (29 May 2003) (TM Registry).

[74] *Ercros SA v. Banco Akros SpA (Ercros/Akros),* Decision No. 3500/2002 (29 Nov. 2002) (Opposition Division).

[75] *Invermont Trade Mark,* note 8 above. Similarly, in *Philosophy v. Ferretti* [2003] *RPC* (15) 287, 298 (para. 25) (CA), the Court of Appeal has stated that: '[a] proprietor who does nothing for most of the five-year period and then embarks on a procedure known to be lengthy but intended to lead to goods bearing the mark being produced for sale cannot...say that the ordinary commercial delays in producing a new product bearing the mark amounted to proper reasons for non-use for the five year period'.

[76] *RTB v. OHIM,* T–156/01 [2003] *ECR* II–2789 (para. 41).

[77] *Häupl v. Lidl,* Case C–246/05 [2007] *ETMR* (61) 997 (ECJ) (para. 52). The ECJ refers with approval to the statements of Advocate General Colomer in his opinion, para. 79.

[78] *Anglian Mode Trade Mark SRIS,* O/181/00 (19 May 2000) 'economic downturns, the cyclical nature of some industries, exchange rate movements, interest rate variations and the like...constitute part of the normal range of risks that must be accepted as part and parcel of running a business...they do not constitute a proper reason for non-use of a trade mark over an extended period of time'.

2.6.3 Rendering Use Impossible or Unreasonable

The ECJ has noted that many circumstances arising independently of the will of the owner should only hinder preparation for use of the mark rather than prevent its use. As a consequence these will not suffice to justify non-use and bring the proprietor within the proviso. To do this, the obstacle should make the use of the mark impossible or at least unreasonable. The ECJ has said that, where an obstacle seriously jeopardizes 'the appropriate use of the mark, its proprietor cannot reasonably be required to use it nonetheless.'[79]

Cases of 'impossibility' will be rare. In most cases the question will be whether the obstacle is one to which the trade mark proprietor should respond flexibly to ensure the mark is used (or lose it), or one which justifies retention of the mark until the impediment evaporates. This will be a fact-specific inquiry.[80] The tribunal can examine the proprietor's existing corporate strategy (and the amount invested in it), any goodwill already achieved by the proprietor, the likely duration of the obstacle,[81] alternative strategies available to the owner (such as using the mark in a different form),[82] or licensing others to use the mark. The ECJ has stated that 'the proprietor cannot reasonably be required to sell its goods in the sales outlets of its competitors'.[83] In one UK case it was held that non-use of a mark for cigarettes was not justified where health regulations merely limited the tar content of cigarettes, because such regulations did not prevent use of the mark on cigarettes in general.[84] In contrast, in another, the court found that failure to perfect the technology for manufacturing certain sweets was a proper reason for non-use of the mark MAGIC BALL.[85] Both cases were pre-*Häupl,* and now careful consideration is required as to whether it it would be reasonable to require the proprietor in either case to have used the mark K-2 on low-tar cigarettes or MAGIC BALL on other confectionery.

Proper reasons for non-use may pertain, of course, to only a part of the specification. In such a case, a tribunal may permit the registration to be maintained for those goods or services where non-use was justified. For example, in the *Team Lotus* case, the proprietor's registration was for 'advertising services in Class 35', but its efforts had (unsuccessfully) been directed towards gaining entry for its team to the Formula 1 motor-racing championships: if successful, advertising activities would have followed as a matter of course. The Trade Marks Registry accepted that the peculiar barriers were a proper reason for non-use in relation to advertising in connection with Formula 1, though they would not have justified non-use for advertising in general or advertising related to motor racing. The Registry allowed maintenance of the mark

---

[79] *Häupl v. Lidl,* Case C–246/05 [2007] *ETMR* (61) 997 (ECJ) (para. 53). Cf. *RTB v. OHIM,* T–156/01 [2003] *ECR* II–2789 (para. 41) ('the concept of proper reasons...must be considered to refer essentially to circumstances...*which prohibit* [the trade mark owner] from using the mark...') (CFI).

[80] *Häupl v. Lidl,* ibid (para. 54).

[81] If it transpires that the circumstances which the trade mark proprietor claim justify non-use are not temporary, and may continue indefinitely (as with the US trade embargo on Cuba which was first imposed in 1962), those circumstances lose their capacity to justify non-use because they come to be 'the normal conditions in the trade': *Cabanas Habana* [2000] *RPC* 26, 33.

[82] Ibid, 33 (where use of the mark in a modified form, by removing the word HABANA, was treated as relevant. M Foley said 'if as it stated, it is necessary to judge matters in a business sense, it is in my view wholly appropriate to take into account reasonable alternatives that may have enabled the mark to be used, if those alternatives are commercially viable or established practice in trade').

[83] *Häupl v. Lidl,* Case C–246/05 [2007] *ETMR* (61) 997 (ECJ) (para. 53).

[84] *K-2 Trade Mark* [2000] *RPC* 413, 421.

[85] *Magic Ball Trade Mark* [2000] *RPC* 439 (Park J) (holding there were proper reasons for non-use of the proprietor's MAGIC BALL mark where a satisfactory system for manufacturing the product had been subject to delays).

but only in relation to advertising services included in Class 35, 'all relating to Formula One motor racing'.[86]

2.7 REWRITING THE SPECIFICATION

More difficult questions arise where the proprietor can demonstrate use (or proper reasons for non-use) for part only of the goods or services of the specification. If the Registry is to limit the scope of the registration there arise issues of characterization of the goods for which the sign has actually been used. In many cases this should be straightforward: for example there may be a registration for clothing and drinks, but only use in relation to drinks, so the mark is struck off for clothing. But what if there is a registration for alcoholic drinks, but use only in relation to whisky? Should the specification be rewritten? Should it limit the party to whisky? or malt whisky? or Scottish single malt whisky? The question is significant, not least because the specification defines the core of the trade mark owner's rights with respect to which, if any, use of an identical mark is prohibited (without any need to establish likelihood of confusion).

This problem initially prompted a division amongst the opinions of some of the United Kingdom's High Court intellectual property judges, some being willing to rewrite the specification,[87] while others were only prepared to eliminate items from the proprietor's existing list.[88] In *Thomson Holidays v. Norwegian Cruise Line,* the Court of Appeal has now expressed its approval of the former approach.[89] In that case the proprietor's mark was FREE-STYLE for arrangement and booking of travel tours and cruises. It had only used the mark in relation to package holidays for young groups (akin to 18–30 holidays) though some holidays included skiing. Aldous LJ held that it was for the court or tribunal to look at the actual use by the proprietor and to arrive at a 'fair specification' having regard to that use. In determining what was fair the tribunal should 'limit the specification so that it reflects the circumstances of the particular trade and the way the public would perceive the use'. One useful approach is to ask how the average consumer would describe the proprietor's use. In the particular case, Aldous LJ rejected suggestions that the proprietor's use would be described as 'land-based holidays', or 'holidays excluding cruises', and decided to limit the specification to 'package holidays'.[90]

The CFI, in *Reckitt Benckiser,*[91] has taken a rather different approach. In this case, an opposition was based on a registration of the mark ALADDIN for 'polish for metals', but the opponent was only able to prove use in relation to 'magic cotton', that is, cotton impregnated with a

---

[86] *Team Lotus Trade Mark,* (29 May 2003).

[87] *Daimler v. Alavi* [2001] *RPC* 813; *Decon Laboratories Ltd v. Fred Baker Scientific Ltd* [2001] *RPC* 17 (Pumfrey J.); *Minerva Trade Mark* [2000] *FSR* 734 (Jacob J).

[88] *Premier Brands v. Typhoon* [2000] *FSR* 767 (Neuberger J).

[89] [2003] RPC (32) 586. See also *Young v. Medici* [2004] FSR (19) 383 (Jacob J) ('the whole exercise consists in the end of forming a value judgment as to the appropriate specification having regard to the use which has been made').

[90] For other examples, see *Young v. Medici,* ibid (Jacob J) (holding that clothing is a fair description and refusing to confine the specification to 'casual clothing' or 'surf-type clothing'); *David West (trading as Eastenders) v. Fuller Smith & Turner* [2003] FSR (44) 816 (limit from beer to bitter beer); *Associated Newspapers v. Express Newspapers* [2003] FSR (51) (para. 62) (rejecting argument that THE MAIL had only been used for national Sunday newspapers for sale so should be restricted to such—existing specification 'newspapers for sale' was satisfactory).

[91] Case T–126/03, [2006] *ETMR* (50) 620. See also *Mundipharma AG v. OHIM,* Case T–256/04 (13 Feb. 2007).

polishing agent. The Court considered what was the breadth of a specification that would correspond to such use, distinguishing between 'coherent categories' and 'sub-categories', which 'cannot be divided other than in an arbitrary manner'. If use is demonstrated in relation to one commercial variant in a sub-category which cannot be divided other than arbitrarily, that use justifies retention of the trade mark for the sub-category itself. In making this assessment, the CFI paid particular regard to the categories and sub-categories of the Nice Agreement, concluding that 'polish for metals' was a 'particularly precise and narrowly defined sub-category' of the Nice list which mentioned 'cleaning, polishing, scouring and abrasive preparations'. Consequently, there was no justification for defining it further, by reference to the use of impregnated cotton. One might question whether the CFI is correct in relying on the Nice Agreement in this way. While the UK's Appointed Person has adopted some of the concepts deployed by the CFI,[92] and the different approaches will rarely, if ever, affect the outcome, we prefer the approach of the English Court of Appeal which utilizes the 'average consumer', to one which treats the Nice categories as representing some universal logic.[93]

3 GENERIC MARKS

The second reason why a mark may be revoked is because it has become generic. That is, it may have come to designate a genus or type of product rather than a particular product from a particular source.[94] As section 46(1)(c)/Article 50(1)(b) says, a mark may be revoked on the ground 'that in consequence of the acts or inactivity of the proprietor, it has become the common name in the trade for a product or service for which it is registered'. Examples of marks that have become generic include GRAMOPHONE,[95] LINOLEUM,[96] SHREDDED WHEAT,[97] and BACH FLOWER REMEDIES.

It has been argued that the revocation of generic marks is not justifiable. For example, Pendleton has suggested that the arguments for expunging generic marks seem 'weak but rarely examined'.[98] Moreover, he argues that the rule is 'an open invitation to commercial sharp practice through campaigns by a competitor to render a successful mark generic'. In contrast, others have suggested that, while the arguments for the revocation of generic trade marks may not have been articulated well,[99] consumers and competitors would be harmed if generic marks were allowed to stay on the register. This is because, where a mark has become generic, it loses its capacity to distinguish one trader's goods or services from those of another.

---

[92] *WISI Trade Mark* [2006] *RPC* (22) 580, 584–587 (Appointed Person, Hobbs QC) (elaborating principles and arguing that fair protection is to be achieved by identifying and defining not the particular examples of use, but the particular categories of goods they should realistically be taken to exemplify); *Datasphere Trade Mark* [2006] *RPC* (23) 590 (Appointed Person, Hobbs QC).

[93] The Agreement is designed for administrative classification, rather than defining property rights. See pp. 784–5.

[94] TM Dir. Art. 12(2)(a).   [95] [1910] 2 *Ch* 423.

[96] (1878) 7 Ch D 834 (passing off: no misrepresentation by use of generic term to describe goods).

[97] (1940) 57 *RPC* 137.

[98] M. Pendleton, 'Excising Consumer Protection—The Key to Reforming Trade Mark Law' (1992) 3 *AIPJ* 110, 116.

[99] R. Folsom and L. Teply, 'Trademarked Generic Words' (1980) 89 *Yale Law Journal* 1323, 1326 (suggesting that the courts and others 'have long relied on broad assumptions and generalisations that do not satisfactorily articulate the harm caused by trade-marked generic words').

The harm to consumers lies in the possible responses that a seller would give if consumers asked for the trade-marked product by its generic name. If consumers are only offered the trade mark owner's version of the product, consumers are not being offered the full range of prices, qualities, etc. that are available.

Another problem that arises where a mark becomes generic is that competitors are not legally able to use the term that most consumers use to refer to the product. While competitors may be able to develop alternative names for the product, explain the situation to the consumer, or take licences from the trade mark holder, these are potentially ineffective and costly.[100]

3.1 NAME

For a mark to be revoked on the basis that it has become generic, it is necessary to show that it has become the common *name* in the trade for a product or service for which it is registered.[101] Although marks that become generic are often name marks, the restriction of the scope of section 46(1)(c)/Article 50(1)(b) to 'names' seems unnecessary and unsatisfactory. This is because it is possible to imagine situations where what is generic does not involve words: where the initially arbitrary use of a certain colour on a pharmaceutical comes to be taken as indicating its nature, or the shape of a bottle as indicating the type of contents, or (through the standardization of technology) aspects of computer-user interfaces, such as icons, might become generic. In fact, a recent reference to the ECJ concerned the potential for the stitching on the pockets of denim jeans to be seen as generic—though no point seems to have been raised about whether such a sign could sensibly be described as a 'name'.[102] In these cases, the same policy concerns exist as with words, and revocation should be available. Hopefully, therefore, the ECJ will offer a broad construction of the clause (as its case law has done with other aspects of this ground of revocation).

3.2 COMMON IN THE 'TRADE'

The wording of section 46(1)(c)/Article 50(1)(b) suggests that the name must have become common in the *trade*—rather than amongst the public. Numerous examples show that this is an important distinction, because trade mark owners, by aggressive policing, can ensure traders continue to appreciate the trade mark significance of signs (such as gramophone or aspirin) even though consumers have come to see them as generic. However, in *Bjornkulla v. Procordia*,[103] the ECJ held that in most cases the assessment was to be undertaken from the point of view of consumers. The case concerned the mark BÖSTONGURKA registered in Sweden by Procordia for pickled gherkins. Evidence before the Swedish Courts showed that consumers

---

[100] Folsom and Teply argue that the question whether a mark is generic should be decided by reference to any harm that may be caused. On this basis, the question would be whether 'the challenged mark substantially increases ultimate consumer search costs or raises real entry barriers to new firms'. Folsom and Teply, ibid, 1352.

[101] Although the statutory text refers to the sign becoming *the* common name in the trade, it has been held to suffice if it has become *a* common name for the goods: *Hormel Foods Corp. v. Antilles Landscape Investment NV* [2005] *RPC* (28) 657, 700 (para. 167).

[102] *Levi Strauss & Co v. Casucci SpA*, Case C–145/05 [2006] *ECR* I–3703, [2007] *FSR* (8) 170 (ECJ). Cf. *Julius Sämaan Ltd v. Tetrosyl Ltd* [2006] *FSR* (42) 849 (para. 113) (Kitchin J) ('there must be considerable doubt as to whether this provision could ever apply to device marks').

[103] *Björnekulla Fruktindustrier Aktiebolag v. Pocodia Food Aktiebolag*, Case C–371/02 [2004] *ECR* I–5791, [2005] 3 *CMLR* (16) 429.

saw the sign as descriptive of the goods, but traders (grocers and stall holders) appreciated that it indicated the gherkins of a particular manufacturer, Procordia. The Court stated that both Articles 3 and 12 of the Directive reflected the need for a mark to perform the function of indicating origin in order to be placed on, or be permitted to remain on, the register.[104] The Court thus held that the matter should normally be interpreted from the viewpoint of consumers or end-users rather than those of the trade.[105] Nevertheless, as ever fearful of laying down categorical rules, the Court provided for the possibility of exceptional situations where 'features of the product market' meant their perception of the trade mark must also be considered.[106] Although it did not provide any examples, one circumstance where this might be the case is in relation to prescription pharmaceuticals, where the influence of medical professionals on the choice of drug could make them the relevant class when assessing whether the drug has become generic.

3.3 THE REQUIREMENT OF FAULT

Even if a mark has become the common name in the trade for a product or service for which it is registered, the mark will only be revoked if it has become generic as 'a consequence of the acts or inactivity' of the proprietor. The ECJ has referred to this as a 'requirement of vigilant conduct'.[107] This requirement means that the proprietor must not only abstain from using a mark in a way that causes it to become generic (for example, using the mark as a description of the product in their own advertising or labelling) but must also take action to ensure that other operators do not jeopardize the distinctiveness of the mark, for example, by bringing infringement proceedings.[108] Beyond bringing infringement actions against traders, the exact steps that owners need to take are less clear. The Community Trade Mark Regulation provides the trade mark owner with an express power to have the trade mark status of certain words recognized in dictionaries and encyclopedias, though there is no corresponding provision in UK law (and it seems doubtful whether such use would fall within current understandings of infringement).[109] There are, of course, non-legal steps a trader can take to try and maintain the perception of their signs as trade marks: many have explicitly used advertising to inform consumers and ask them not to use the trade mark as a verb ('to xerox' or to 'hoover') or noun ('lego' or 'lycra') but to use it as a proper adjective (Lego bricks, Xerox copiers, or Lycra fibre), accompanied by a ® or ™ (see Fig. 39.1).

---

[104] In so doing, the Court in *Björnekulla* implicitly suggests it is appropriate to adopt a broad reading of this ground for revocation, so that it potentially encompasses any situation where a sign has lost its capacity to distinguish.

[105] *Björnekulla*, Case C–371/02 [2004] *ECR* I–5791, [2005] 3 *CMLR* (16) 429, paras. 23–24.

[106] Ibid, para 25.

[107] *Levi Strauss v. Casucci*, Case C–145/05 [2006] *ECR* I–3703, [2007] *FSR* (8) 170 (paras 30–31) (ECJ). The act/inactivity of the proprietor must be 'a' cause of the mark becoming generic, but need not be the only cause: *Hormel Foods*, note 101 above, 700 (paras. 171–2).

[108] *Levi Strauss*, ibid (para 34) (ECJ); *Hormel Foods*, ibid (SPAMBUSTERS generic because owner had not policed its use, whereas SPAM was not so because it had been subject to policing).

[109] See the material on trade mark use in ch. 40, and that on the exceptions in ch. 41. There is an important, and yet underexplored, inter-relationship between these three legal spheres. If a competitor uses a sign descriptively with the deliberate intent of genericizing the mark, as in *Stix Products, Inc v. United Merchants and Manufacturers, Inc*, 295 F Supp 479 (SDNY 1968) will the trade mark owner be able to stop this on the ground that the use 'jeopardises one of the essential functions of the mark' (i.e. its distinctiveness) even though no consumers are likely to be deceived, and so is prima facie infringement, and is outside the descriptiveness defence in TMA s. 11(2)(b) on the ground that the use contrary to honest practices?

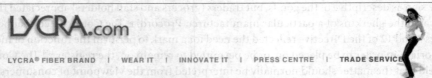

Fig. 39.1 Screenshot from Lycra.com

Source: Reproduced from <http://www.lycra.com/en/services/trademark-protection-campaign.htm>.

In the light of the *Bjornkulla* holding, the courts will need to decide to what extent 'the requirement of vigilant conduct' requires trade mark proprietors to take these kinds of step, so as to prevent consumers seeing the sign as generic.[110]

The ECJ explains the requirement of 'vigilant conduct' as a component in the balancing of the interests of the proprietor with those of other economic operators. In certain respects it is difficult to understand the policy underpinning the requirement. Firstly it is not clear why any mark that lacks or has lost distinctive character should be allowed to remain on the register. Second, some commentators argue that money spent on policing is wasted and should be a factor in support of, rather than against, revocation.[111] This is because 'from an economic perspective, such measures normally do not stimulate demand for a firm's product and are therefore economically inefficient'.[112] However, the requirement of policing might be justified on the basis of the general principle that property should not be lost without acquiescence on the part of the owner.

4 MISLEADING USES

The third reason why a mark may be revoked is on the basis that it has been used in a way which misleads the public. To this end, section 46(1)(d)/Article 50(1)(c) CTMR says that a mark may be revoked where:

in consequence of the use made of it by the proprietor or with his consent in relation to goods or services for which it is registered, it is liable to mislead the public, particularly as to the nature, quality, or geographical origin of the goods or services.[113]

Section 46(1)(d) corresponds to the absolute ground of refusal in section 3(3)(b), but recognizes that changes might occur after registration which mean that the mark becomes misleading.

4.1 REQUIREMENT OF FAULT

In order for a mark to be revoked under section 46(1)(d), the mark must have become misleading *either* as a result of the acts of the proprietor *or* as a result of acts done with their consent.[114] Given that a mark can become misleading as a result of the conduct of third parties, it is good counsel for trade mark owners to include provisions in their licence agreements which ensure that the licensee does not misuse the mark in a way which might jeopardize the mark's viability.

4.2 MISLEAD THE PUBLIC

In order for a mark to be revoked under section 46(1)(d), it must be shown that the use misleads the public, particularly as to the nature, quality, or geographical origin of the goods or

---

[110] See also Austrian Supreme Court, Case No. 4 Ob 269/01 (*'Walkman'*) (Jan. 29, 2002) (2003) IIC 966 (holding WALKMAN to be generic because there was no other term available to describe the portable cassette player) and *Jenken v. Creeks*, Paris Court of Appeal (Cour d'appel), Case No. 04/03753 ('Vintage'), (20 April 2005) (2006) IIC 347 (VINTAGE generic for clothing).

[111] Folsom and Teply, 1354.   [112] Ibid.

[113] TM Dir. Art. 12(2)(b). See above at pp. 849–51.

[114] In *Bostitch Trade Mark* [1963] *RPC* 183, the licensee had begun selling certain articles of his own manufacture without the permission of the trade mark owner. Such actions would not be such as to render the proprietor's mark liable to be expunged.

services. The ECJ has held that, for the ground to apply, there must evidence of 'the existence of actual deceit or of a sufficiently serious risk that the consumer will be deceived'.[115]

A mark may become misleading, for example, where a garment made entirely of wool, to which the mark ORLWOOLA is affixed, is subsequently manufactured with other materials (e.g. nylon): the connotation of an homogeneous woollen garment arising from the verbal pronunciation of the mark ('all wool' with a meaningless suffix) is misleading as to the true nature of the goods.[116] A mark may also be misleading where a proprietor alters the geographical location of their business in such a way that a mark that was formerly suggestive of origin becomes deceptive. However, in thinking about the situations where a use may be misleading, it should be borne in mind that a trade mark proprietor is perfectly entitled to change the quality of its goods or services without informing the consumer, is perfectly entitled to move geographical locations or change the sources from which it gains its resources, and is perfectly entitled to assign the mark to a third party or license it to others.[117]

One question that arises in this context is whether a use which misleads the public as to the *trade origin of the goods* or services constitutes a misuse for the purposes of section 46(1)(d). If so, this gives rise to the further question whether the very act of licensing a mark would justify removal under section 46(1)(d).[118] In *Elizabeth Emanuel,* a famous designer who had assigned her business and mark ELIZABETH EMANUEL to a third party sought revocation of that mark on the grounds that consumers believed that she had been involved in designing the garments sold under the mark. The ECJ was not persuaded that this fell within the purview of the section. This was because the mark had been assigned and the goods were in fact manufactured by or under the control of the owner of the mark. Consequently, the mark continued to carry out its function of indicating trade origin. Even if the average consumer imagined Elizabeth Emanuel was personally involved in the design process, this was not misleading as to the nature or quality of the goods.

The exact reasoning is a little opaque, and it is possibly worth teasing out some possibilities. The ECJ could be saying that the legal reality is that trade marks may comprise personal names, these may be legally assigned or licensed, and if so, the mark cannot be of itself misleading, even if consumers believe the individual is involved in production and their role has a significant impact on the quality or value of the goods. Alternatively, the case might just be about what the average consumer would understand in the light of the legal reality. That is, the 'average consumer' is reasonably well informed about trade mark law, and knows that

---

[115] Case C–259/04, para. 47 citing *Gorgonzola v. Kaserei Champignon Hofmeister GmbH,* Case C–87/97 [1999] *ECR* I–1301 (para. 41).

[116] *Orlwoola Trade Mark* (1909) 26 *RPC* 683.

[117] In *Bostitch,* [1963] *RPC* 183, 197, Lloyd Jacob J. famously observed that

> There is nothing in the Trade Marks Act or in the principles of trade mark law which have been developed thereunder which requires a proprietor of a registered trade mark to refrain from introducing modifications or variations in the goods to which he applies his mark or in the manner in which they reach the market. If he should find it convenient to transfer manufacture from one locality to another, or procure his supplies from sub-contractors, or arrange for assembly of completed articles by someone of his choice in lieu of doing it himself, these and a vast number of other changes in procedure are his sole concern. His mark only becomes vulnerable in this connection if he permits its use in a manner that is calculated to deceive or cause confusion.

Although this test may no longer be formulated in exactly the correct way, the sentiments remain relevant.

[118] It has been argued that 'although misleading trade origin is not listed...the wording...could be interpreted to include such deception...uncontrolled use will still render the mark deceptive as to trade origin (and so "liable to mislead the public")'. H. Norman, 'Trade Mark Licences in the UK' [1994] *EIPR* 154, 158.

a trade mark only signals that the goods have been made with the consent of the trade mark proprietor. Thirdly, the case could be saying that misunderstandings as to trade origin are not relevant when assessing this ground for revocation, which is concerned with the nature, quality, or geographic origin of the goods. This leaves open the question whether trade origin can affect the perceived qualities or nature of the goods. Fourthly, the Court could be saying that 'imagining a person is involved' is different from real deceit. While this might leave open the possibility of a trade mark comprising a personal name being deceitful, it is difficult to think of exactly when: one wonders whether the assignment by a visual artist of a mark comprising his signature for paintings and sculptures would be an example.

Although the *Elizabeth Emanuel* case indicates that revocation is not possible on this basis where there has been an assignment with goodwill, the logic probably extends further to encompass assignments in gross and licensing of a mark without any exercise of quality control. These questions were considered by the House of Lords in *Scandecor Developments AB v. Scandecor Marketing AB*.[119] In that case, an international group of companies operated in a way that afforded a degree of autonomy to its subsidiaries. While the international company held the marks, the local companies dealt with retailers. When one of the subsidiaries was sold off and the parent company refused to continue to license the mark to it, the (former) subsidiary argued (in a counterclaim to the claimant's action for infringement) that, by allowing the defendant to affix the trade mark to its goods, the claimant had allowed the trade marks to become deceptive. More specifically, it was argued that the mark had come to acquire distinctiveness in relation to the defendant's, rather than the claimant's, goods. As trade marks operate as indications of origin, the defendant therefore asserted that the claimant's mark had become misleading and should be revoked. The House of Lords held that it was not possible to reach a conclusion in the case without first receiving guidance from the ECJ. In particular, the House asked whether use of a mark by a bare licensee (i.e. without quality control being exercised by the trade mark owner) necessarily renders a trade mark liable to mislead. However, the case was settled before the ECJ was able to provide any guidance, so an understanding of the current law must deduced, for the moment, from the decision of the House. Lord Nicholls was clear that in his view such use was not inherently liable to mislead, at least during the term of any such exclusive licence. However, at the end of the licence, whether the trade mark would become misleading would depend on how the respective parties operated, in particular whether the former licensee carried on trading in the relevant goods or services. If customers of the former licensee associated goods bearing the mark, incorrectly, with the former licensee the mark will have become deceptive. Whether it does so, according to Lord Nicholls, is a question of fact. The ECJ's decision in *Elizabeth Emanuel* is consistent with this position.

5 EFFECT OF REVOCATION

Section 46(6) states that the rights of the proprietor cease to have effect from the date of application for revocation or if the registrar or court is satisfied that the grounds for revocation existed at an earlier date, that date.[120] If a party wants revocation to take effect from a date earlier than the date of application for revocation, it should explicitly allege that the grounds

---

[119] [2002] *FSR* (7) 122.
[120] *K-2 Trade Mark*, note 84 above (revocation from end of five-year period following completion of registration procedure).

for revocation existed at the earlier date.[121] The importance of this can be seen in *Riveria Trade Mark*.[122] There the mark RIVERIA, registered as of 1973, was the successful basis of an invalidity objection to a registration of FRANCO'S RIVERIA CONE which had been registered as of 2000. Just over a month later, RIVERIA was held to be revocable for non-use, with effect from May 2001 (the date of application for revocation). The later revocation, however, was unable to affect the earlier holding as to the validity of FRANCO'S RIVERIA CONE. Had revocation been sought with earlier effect, however, the position might have been different.

Where a person began using trade mark at a time when it was not revocable, but it later became so, no injunctive relief may be awarded. Instead, the trade mark proprietor will be limited to financial remedies of damages and an account of profits.[123]

---

[121] *Omega SA v. Omega Engineering Inc* [2003] FSR (49) 893, 896 (Jacob J); *Datasphere Trade Mark* [2006] RPC (23) 590 (Appointed Person, Hobbs QC). Note also *WISI Trade Mark*, note 92 above (revocation granted from five-year period following completion of registration procedure in a case where the question of use at any time since registration had been addressed).

[122] [2003] RPC (50) 883.

[123] *Levi Strauss v. Casucci*, Case C–145/05 [2006] ECR I–3703, [2007] FSR (8) 170, para 36.

40

INFRINGEMENT

1 INTRODUCTION

One of the most remarkable aspects in the recent development of trade mark law has been the expansion in the scope of the rights conferred on the proprietor. In the United States, a leading commentator has talked of equivalent developments as 'the death of common sense'.[1] Indeed, the rights granted to the owners of registered trade marks have expanded to such an extent that it could be said that they now confer a form of quasi-copyright protection which protects traders rather than consumers.

The rights of the owner of a British trade mark are set out in sections 9 and 10 of the 1994 Act and the rights conferred on the owner of a Community Trade Mark (which are largely the same as those given to UK trade mark owners) in Article 9 of the CTMR.[2] Community Trade Marks are enforced in national courts which have been designated as 'Community Trade Mark Courts'.[3] When dealing with the infringement of a Community Trade Mark, the national courts apply the Community Trade Mark Regulation supplemented where appropriate by national law.[4] When sitting as a Community Trade Mark Court, national courts are invested with the jurisdiction to grant relief in the territory of any member state.[5] Where an alleged infringement takes place in different member states, the appropriate forum is determined by jurisdictional rules which are similar to those operating under the Brussels Convention. Normally, it will be the state of the defendant's domicile.[6]

---

[1] Mark Lemley, 'The Modern Lanham Act and the Death of Common Sense' 108 *Yale Law Journal* 1687.

[2] These provisions apply equally to marks that were registered under the 1938 Act. See Sched. 3, para. 4, subject to certain savings as regards 'existing uses'. Sections 9–10 need to be read with sections 11–13, though these are discussed in Ch. 41.

[3] The Community Trade Mark Regulations 2006, SI 2006/1027 r. 12 (in England, the High Court (Chancery Division), or the Patents County Court, or certain specified county courts).

[4] CTMR, Art. 97.   [5] CTMR, Art. 99(2).

[6] CTMR, Art. 93. These matters are considered in detail at Ch. 47, Section 9.

While trade mark infringement proceedings will normally be brought by the owner of the mark,[7] it is also possible for an action to be brought by an exclusive licensee.[8] Where licensees are not entitled to bring proceedings in their own right, they are usually able to call on the proprietor to take proceedings on their behalf.[9]

Proceedings to enforce a trade mark may be brought as soon as a mark is registered. It should be noted that the rights of the proprietor are enforceable against third parties with regard to acts done after the date of registration (which is the date of filing).[10] The rights continue for ten years from registration[11] and may be renewed, possibly indefinitely, for further ten-year periods.[12] Similar principles apply in relation to Community Trade Marks, with the exception that the proprietors of Community Trade Marks are only entitled to 'reasonable compensation' for acts that occur between publication of the application and registration.[13]

2 INFRINGING ACTS

The circumstances in which a mark may be infringed are set out in sections 10(1)–(3) and Article 9 of the CTMR. Before looking at the circumstances in which a trade mark may be infringed, it is important to note that to infringe there is no requirement for knowledge, intention, or derivation on the part of the defendant. This is because, as with patents and registered designs, liability for trade mark infringement is strict: the monopoly is an 'absolute' one. Moreover, and in contrast with passing-off, there is no need for a trade mark owner to demonstrate damage. Indeed, a trade mark owner is able to commence an action for infringement even though the mark has not been used. It is also important to note section 10(1)–(3) clearly provide that, in order to infringe, it must be shown that the defendant used the mark 'in the course of trade'. We discuss the meaning of this phrase below.

In order to determine whether a trade mark has been infringed, it is necessary to compare the registered mark with the alleged infringing sign. The circumstances in which a mark may be infringed are set out in sections 10(1)–(3). These are where:

(i)   the marks are identical *and* the goods or services are identical: section 10(1)/Article 9(1)(a);

(ii) the marks are identical, *and* the goods or services are similar, *and* there is a likelihood of confusion, which includes the likelihood of association, with the registered mark: section 10(2)(a)/Article 9(1)(b);

---

[7]   A co-proprietor may bring an action but must join other co-proprietors either as co-plaintiffs or defendants: TMA s. 23(5). A co-proprietor will not normally be liable for infringement: TMA s. 23(1).

[8]   TMA s. 31 (where provision is made to that effect in the licence). No provisions are made under the Directive, and national laws take diverging approaches: A. Kur, 'Harmonization of the Trade Mark Laws in Europe—An Overview' (1997) 28 *IIC* 1.

[9]   TMA s. 30; CTMR, Art. 22.

[10]   TMA s. 9(3). No criminal liability can be incurred for acts done before the date of publication of the registration.

[11]   TMA s. 42.

[12]   TMA s. 43 deals with renewal. Six months after expiry of the mark, if there has been failure to renew it, the mark is removed from the register. Nevertheless TMR r. 30 permits restoration of the mark on application within six months of removal.

[13]   CTMR Art. 9(3).

(iii) the marks are similar, *and* the goods or services are either identical or similar, *and* there is a likelihood of confusion, which includes the likelihood of association, between the marks: section 10(2)(b)/Article 9(1)(b);

(iv) the marks are either identical or similar, the registered trade mark has a reputation in the United Kingdom, and use of the defendant's mark would take unfair advantage of, or be detrimental to, the distinctive character or the reputation of the registered trade mark: section 10(3)/Article 9(1)(c).

The grounds for infringement in section 10(1)–(3) mirror the relative grounds for refusal in section 5(1)–(3). One of the consequences of this is that a mark will fall foul of the relative grounds for refusal in exactly the same circumstances in which use of the later mark would amount to an infringement under section 10(1)–(3). Another consequence of the fact that the relative grounds for refusal mirror the provisions dealing with infringement is that the concepts used when deciding whether a mark has been infringed are the same as are used when deciding whether a mark falls within one of the relative grounds for refusal. As we have already looked in Chapter 38 at the concepts that arise in deciding whether a mark will be refused on relative grounds, it is not necessary to look at them again here. However, two key differences exist between an action for infringement and the relative grounds for refusal: the first relates to the need to identify the defendant's mark (a task that, in the context of relative grounds for validity, the applicant for the later mark carries out); the second difference is that, to establish infringement, it is necessary to show that the mark was 'used in the course of trade'. We treat each in turn.

3   WHAT IS THE DEFENDANT'S SIGN?

In determining whether a person infringes a registered trade mark it is necessary to compare the sign as registered with the sign used by the defendant. The question exactly what the defendant's sign is becomes of most importance when considering section 10(1)—the 'double identity' provision: if the marks and goods/services are identical, then a defendant will infringe irrespective of any confusion. However, determining exactly what the defendant's sign is can prove problematic.[14]

In *LTJ Diffusion*, the owners of a figurative mark including the word ARTHUR in handwritten form for clothes brought infringement proceedings against a company selling children's clothing under the name ARTHUR ET FÉLICIE. The French court sought clarification as to whether Article 5(1)(a) covers only identical reproduction without addition, or can extend to reproduction of the sign with added matter. The ECJ, in stating that there is identity where a sign reproduces 'without any modification *or addition*, all the elements constituting the [trade mark]',[15] seems to imply that there is no doctrine of 'added matter' or 'ineffective addition'. Although the Court's decision provides no specific guidance as to whether the defendant's sign was ARTHUR or ARTHUR ET FÉLICIE, the clear implication is that it is to be regarded as the latter.[16]

---

[14] Disclaimed matter in the earlier trade mark will usually be ignored: *Saville Perfume v. June Perfect and F.W. Woolworth* (1941) 58 *RPC* 147; *The European v. The Economist Newspaper* [1998] *FSR* 283, 289.

[15] Ibid, para. 51.

[16] *Reed Executive plc v. Reed Business Information* [2004] *RPC* (40) 767 (para 33).

While the *LTJ Diffusion* case indicates that member states are not free to ignore added matter, it gives virtually no guidance on the critical question how a tribunal is to identify the parameters of the defendant's mark. If we consider simple examples of signs featured in advertising or on packaging, it will be very rare for the sign to appear by itself, without any other material (slogans, images, colouring, decoration, ingredients, instructions, etc.). Nevertheless the mere proximity of other material surely does not mean that a defendant's use of a sign is not identical. Consequently some rules or practices will need to be adopted to help tribunals to decide the limits of the defendant's sign. Perhaps the most plausible guide is that a tribunal will only be justified in ignoring extraneous matter if, in the eyes of the average consumer, it would not be regarded as being part of the sign. One factor would be whether the matter is visually or syntactically interlinked so as to be perceived as part of a single visual or semiotic entity (for example, the use of the same font might suggest words form part of a single sign, the use of different fonts suggesting the opposite). So, REED BUSINESS INFORMATION in capitals might be regarded as a single semiotic entity (for trade mark purposes) whereas REED Business Information (with only REED in capitals) might be taken to be use of REED as the sign.[17] Another factor is whether the element is perceived as functioning in a distinct way: this might be the case if the extraneous matter were regarded as having no trade mark significance, for example, where it is regarded as a list of ingredients or instructions, or a description or designation of the product. Thus in the case of a person using the words PALMOLIVE SOAP in advertising, a tribunal may treat the word 'soap' as a description rather than as part of the mark.[18] However, the combination RITZPOKER.NET involved the sign RITZPOKER which was not identical to RITZ.[19] The prefix component of an e-mail address has been held to be distinct, so that herr-voss@kcs-industry.com was held to be use of a sign identical to the claimant's registered mark HERR VOSS.[20]

Where it is unclear whether consumers would consider an element to be outside the mark, the 'strict' approach in *LTJ* suggests that the tribunal should treat the mark as a whole, and the comparison should be under section 10(2) not section 10(1). If the rationale for section 10(1) is to improve simplicity of decision making, its application should be confined to obvious cases: complex tests of 'identity', with commensurably protracted debate, are inappropriate.

4 USED IN THE COURSE OF TRADE

In order to infringe, the mark must be *used in the course of trade*. This is a prerequisite for *all* of the grounds for infringement in section 10(1)–(3)/Article 9.

In order to sustain an action for infringement of a British trade mark, the infringing act must take place in the United Kingdom.[21] For the most part, this is relatively straightforward. One difficulty that should be noted concerns the situation where an advertisement shown

---

[17] Ibid (para 33).

[18] Ibid (para. 37). See also *Compass Publishing v. Compass Logistics* [2004] *EWHC* 520 (Ch) (para 21)(COMPASS LOGISTICS not identical to COMPASS, but 'at Compass logistics are king' would have been).

[19] *Ellerman Investments Ltd, The Ritz Hotel Casino Ltd v. Elizabeth C–Vanci* [2006] *EWHC* 1442 (Ch) (Deputy Judge Richard Harvey QC) (para 10).

[20] *Blue IP Inc v. KCS Herr-Voss Ltd* [2004] *EWHC* 97 (Ch) (para 53). In *Antoni Fields v. Klaus Kobec Ltd* [2006] *EWHC* 350(Ch) (paras. 68–72), Deputy Judge Sheldon QC has held that Klaus Kobec Limited and klauskobec. com were identical to KLAUS KOBEC, but that klauskobecrugby.com was not.

[21] TMA s. 9(1). And the Isle of Man: TMA s. 108(2).

outside the United Kingdom spills into Britain. This problem is likely to be particularly difficult in relation to internet advertising, as a result of which foreign sellers can be accessed from
the United Kingdom. Although such uses might appear *per se* to constitute a use in the United
Kingdom, Jacob J has indicated that he considers a *per se* rule to be inappropriate. In each case,
'there must be an enquiry as to what the purpose and effect of the advertisement in question
is'.[22] Consequently, an advertisement by an Irish shop, in a magazine with circulation in the
United Kingdom as well as the Republic of Ireland, was held not to infringe the claimant's UK
trade mark, either because it was not in 'use' in the United Kingdom or because it was not in
use in the course of trade in the United Kingdom. Similarly, the shop's Irish web site did not
infringe the claimant's mark, merely because the site could be visited by internet users from
the United Kingdom. However, had the Irish shop targeted UK customers, provided prices in
sterling, or offered international sales and distribution, Jacob J might have held that there was
use in the course of trade in the United Kingdom.

A second difficulty relates to the situation where packaging bearing another's mark is made
in the United Kingdom, though the goods are intended to be used in trade overseas. It seems
that a person will infringe where, in the United Kingdom, they apply a registered mark to
goods, or to packaging for goods which are packaged in the United Kingdom,[23] because in
those circumstances the mark is used 'in relation' to the goods. However, a mark is not used
'in relation to goods' where it is merely applied to packaging materials, and the goods are to be
packaged outside the United Kingdom.[24] In that case there is no use in relation to the claimant's goods in the United Kingdom.

The fact that the use must take place 'in the course of trade' serves to restrict the scope of
protection given to trade mark owners. In so doing, it helps to minimize the impact that trade
marks have upon non-commercial uses that are made of the sign. In thinking about whether a
mark has been used in the course of trade, a number of questions arise. These are:

(i)   what kinds of use are covered?

(ii)   what is meant by 'in the course of trade'?

(iii) does use of a sign require use as a trade mark?

4.1 KINDS OF USE

The starting point for considering what is meant by 'use in the course of trade' is section 10(4)/
Article 9(2), which provides a non-exhaustive list of the situations where a person uses a sign.[25]
These are where someone:

(a)   affixes the sign to the goods or to the packaging thereof;

(b)   offers or exposes goods for sale, puts them on the market or stocks them for these purposes
       under the sign, or offers or supplies services under the sign;

(c)   imports or exports goods under the sign; or

(d)   uses the sign on business papers or in advertising.

---

[22] *Euromarket Designs Incorporated v. Peters & Anor* [2001] *FSR* 288.

[23] *George Ballantine v. Ballantyne Stewart* [1959] *RPC* 273, 279 (no need for confusion to occur in UK as long
as wrongful act occurs in jurisdiction).

[24] TMA s. 10(5), as interpreted in *Beautimatic International v. Mitchell International Pharmaceuticals and
Alexir Packaging* [1999] *ETMR* 912, 919–20.

[25] TM Dir., Art. 5(3); CTMR, Art. 9(2).

4.1.1 Where the sign is affixed to goods

Section 10(4)(a)/Article 9(2)(a) provides that a sign is used where it is affixed to the goods or the packaging thereof. This is probably the most common form of trade mark infringement. This would occur, for example, where a counterfeiter places scented liquid in bottles to which they have attached the CHANEL label.[26] In order to affix a sign to goods, it seems that the defendant must engage in some positive act, such as stamping, engraving, or gluing a label onto the goods. To 'affix a sign', the mark must be used directly rather than indirectly on the goods; it is not enough if a mark incidentally appears on the defendant's goods. This can be seen in *Trebor v. Football Association*,[27] an infringement action involving the Football Association's 'three lions' logo. The action arose when a sweet manufacturer, Trebor, included photographs of footballers in packets of sweets it sold. The Football Association argued that, as some of the footballers were wearing the English team strip, which had the three lions logo attached to it, this amounted to an infringement of its mark. In dismissing the action, Rattee J explained that Trebor was 'not even arguably using the logo, as such, in any real sense of the word "uses", and [was] certainly not…using it as a sign in respect of its cards'. Rattee J added that it was 'unreal' to suggest that Trebor was affixing the English football logo to its cards, and therefore to goods, within the meaning of section 10(4)(a).[28] Whether this reasoning will be extended to situations where a mark is deliberately used in the background, such as where a model in a pornographic magazine wears a T-shirt with the M&M logo on it, has yet to be determined. As this would not be an incidental or accidental use, it would most probably fall within section 10(4)/Article 9(2)(a).

Affixing a trade mark owner's mark to packaging but not to goods is not an infringement under section 10(4)(a), but falls under section 10(5). This states that a person who applies the mark to 'material intended to be used for labelling or packaging goods, as business paper or for advertising goods or services' is liable for any infringing use of the material. Unlike an action for primary infringement, where knowledge is not a relevant factor, secondary infringement under section 10(5) only arises where the person who applied the mark 'knew or had reason to believe that the application of the mark was not duly authorized by the proprietor or a licensee'.[29]

4.1.2 Use 'under the sign'

Section 10(4)(b)/Article 9(2)(b) provides that a person uses a sign where they offer or expose goods for sale, put them on the market or stock them for these purposes 'under the sign', or offer or supply services 'under the sign'. Section 10(4)(c)/Article 9(2)(c) adds that a sign is also 'used' when someone imports or exports goods under the sign. The key concept in section 10(4)(b) and (c) is that the goods are dealt with *under the sign*. This suggests that, although a sign may not be physically attached to the goods in question, a sign may nonetheless still be

---

[26] Although such use does not of itself affect the essential function of the trade mark, Judge Prescott QC has explained that its purpose 'is precautionary: it intends to prevent the mischief—the deception of consumers—by destroying it in the egg'. See *Glaxo Group v. Dowelhurst* [2004] *ETMR* (39) 528, 551 (para. 97).

[27] [1997] *FSR* 211.

[28] In *Condé Nast Publications v. Luxottica (UK)* [1998] 41 *IPR* 505 (Federal Court of Australia), Master Moncaster rejected a broad interpretation of Rattee J's decision, confining it to cases where there was no act of 'affixing' the sign to the goods.

[29] The knowledge requirement is in similar terms to that employed in the context of copyright. See *Beautimatic International*, note 24 above and, more generally. See p. 198.

'used' where it is placed in proximity to, or is connected with, the goods. This would be the case, for example, where it is sold from a place which is called by the sign.

One question that arises here is whether section 10(4)(b)/Article 9(2)(b) would apply in situations where a consumer specifically asks for a product by a particular trade name, but is supplied with a competing product. This would be the case, for example, where in response to a request for a particular brand of pharmaceutical, such as the painkiller NUROFEN, customers were provided with the generic product IBUPROFEN. While this would undermine the value of the mark, it is unlikely that this would be treated as a situation where a mark was sold 'under a sign' for the purposes of section 10(4)(b)/Article 9(2)(b).

Although the situations where goods are used under a sign are potentially very wide, the scope of section 10(4)(b)/Article 9(2)(b) is limited by the fact that the defendant must play a direct and positive role in ensuring that a connection is drawn between the sign and the goods in question. It is not enough that the connection is incidental or accidental. This can be seen, for example, in *Trebor v. Football Association*,[30] where the decision that the sweet manufacturer had not put 'the cards on the market under the sign comprising the England logo within section 10(4)(b)' was influenced by the fact that the inclusion of the sign on the card was not a direct consequence of the manufacturer's actions. That is, the sign was there because the player was wearing the shirt when the photograph was taken, rather than being a direct result of the defendant's actions. In these circumstances it is more accurate to say that the goods were sold *with*, rather than *under*, the sign. On this basis, it seems that if a photograph of a cricketer with the trade mark of the team sponsor on their shirt appeared on the cover of a book, this would not amount to a 'use' of the mark under section 10(4)(b)/Article 9(2)(b).

4.1.3 Import or export

Section 10(4)(c) states that a sign is also 'used' when someone imports or exports goods under the sign.[31] This provision is important because it means that a trade mark owner can prevent the importing of goods which bear the mark into the United Kingdom. As we will see, this right can sometimes be used even where those goods have been marketed elsewhere with the trade mark owner's consent. The consequence of this is that a trade mark owner is empowered through this right to divide up markets on a territorial basis (and thus, possibly, to set prices differently for each territory). However, while a person need not have title to the goods to be treated as an importer,[32] merely transporting a product bearing a trade mark through a territory (i.e. where the destination is somewhere else) is not an infringing use.[33]

4.1.4 Use on business papers or in advertising

Section 10(4)(d)/Article 9(2)(d) provides that a person uses a sign where they 'use the sign on business papers or in advertising'. It seems that 'use on business papers' covers things such as use on letterheads, envelopes, and invoices.[34] Whether such uses are 'in relation to goods' will depend on whether they refer to the goods (as opposed, for example, merely to the packaging).[35]

---

[30] [1997] *FSR* 211.   [31] CTMR, Art. 9(2)(c)

[32] *Miller Brewing Co. v. The Mersey Docks and Harbour Co.* [2004] *FSR* (5) 81, 98 (para. 68) (where person ordered goods, organized a letter of credit to pay for them, and had intended to take delivery).

[33] *Class International v. Colgate Palmolive*, C–405/03 [2005] *ECR* 1–8735 (introducing goods physically into the EC for transit to third countries is not import); *Eli Lilly & Co v. 8PM Chemist Ltd* [2008] *EWCA Civ* 24 (drugs being transported from Turkey to the US, via Slough, England, were not imported into EU).

[34] *Broad v. Graham (No. 2)* [1969] *RPC* 295, 298; *Cheetah Trade Mark* [1993] *FSR* 263; *Beautimatic International*, [1999] *ETMR* 912, 925 (invoices).

[35] Ibid, 927.

As section 103(2) provides that reference to use of a trade mark includes use otherwise than by means of a graphic representation, this means that oral offers and oral advertisements also fall within the notion of use. It remains to be seen whether section 10(4)(d) also encompasses the use of 'meta-tags' to attract people to a particular web site.[36]

One of the notable features of section 10(4)(d)/Article 9(2)(b) is that, unlike the other examples listed in section 10(4)/Article 9(2), the section makes no mention of the goods. This means, for example, that where someone uses a sign on an advertising billboard they will infringe, even though the goods are not pictured. In these circumstances, it seems that it is only necessary for the advert to 'relate to' goods of a relevant kind. This would probably be the case where a trade mark for cigarettes is used in an anti-smoking campaign.[37]

4.1.5 Use on the Internet

Use on web sites will almost certainly count as use within section 10(4). This may be because there is an offer of goods 'under the sign', or use 'in advertising', or simply because this is a use of the same sort as those contained in the illustrative list provided by section 10(4), Article 6(3) of the Directive and Article 11(2) of the CTMR. Use as a domain name is also likely to be regarded as use within section 10(4).[38]

4.2 IN THE COURSE OF TRADE

In order to infringe the sign must be used 'in the course of trade'.[39] As 'trade' is defined to include 'any business or profession',[40] presumably it would not cover social or domestic uses. Indeed, in *Arsenal v. Reed,* the ECJ stated that a sign had been used in the course of trade where it had been used 'in the context of commercial activity with a view to economic advantage and not as a private matter'.[41] It remains to be seen whether use by public bodies, such as those responsible for health education, will amount to a trade use.[42] It also remains unclear whether use of a sign in art or music, as with Warhol's famous depictions of Campbell's soup cans or pop group Aqua's use of the mark BARBIE in its song 'Barbie Girl', would constitute use 'in the course of trade'. In *Arsenal v. Reed,* Advocate General Colomer suggested that such uses would

[36] *Reed Executive plc v. Reed Business Information Ltd* [2003] *RPC* (12) 207 (Pumfrey J) ('the concept of use is wide enough to cover invisible use in meta-tags which is invisible in the search results') overturned on appeal, note 16 above (para 149) (Jacob LJ, uncertain); *Roadtech v. Mandata* (2000) *CIPAJ* 346.

[37] *Gallaher (Dublin) v. Health Education Bureau* [1982] *FSR* 464.

[38] See, e.g. *BT v. One in a Million* [1999] 1 *WLR* 903 (a case of cyber squatting, where the CA held there to be a threatened infringement: even if use was not for the same goods or services, there would be liability under TMA s. 10(3)); *Bonnier Media v. Smith* [2002] *ETMR* (86) 1050; 1069–70 (where D was proposing to use web site with very similar name to provide similar services); *Musical Fidelity v. Vickers (David)* (8 May 2002) (Rimer J) (para. 22) (claimant, proprietor of mark MUSICAL FIDELITY for audio equipment granted summary judgment against defendant hI–fi seller who advertised business on the web via the domain name www.musicalfidelity. co.uk (a portal to his own site)). See also *Tesco v. Elogicom* [2007] *FSR* (4) 83. For discussion of cyber squatting in the context of passing off, see pp. 766–7. For discussion of dispute resolution outside the court system, see pp. 1098–9.

[39] TM Dir. Art. 5(1); CTMR Art. 9(1).   [40] TMA s. 103(1).

[41] Case C–206/01 [2002] *ECR* I–10273; [2003] *Ch* 454; [2003] 3 *WLR* 450; [2003] 1 *CMLR* (12) 345 para. 40. See also *Céline SARL v. Céline SA,* Case C–17/06 [2007] *ETMR* (80) 1320 (ECJ Grnd Ch) (para. 17); *Rxworks Ltd. v. Dr Paul Hunter (trading as Connect Computers)* [2007] *EWHC* 3061 (Ch) (para. 21).

[42] *Gallaher v. HEB* [1982] *FSR* 464 (argument that use in an antI–smoking educational campaign was not 'in the course of trade' rejected because the words 'in the course of trade' were not then present in the definition of the exclusive rights of a trade mark proprietor).

not be 'in the course of trade', but given that the ECJ subsequently suggested that uses which are in the context of commercial activity with a view to economic advantage are 'in the course of trade', it seems that these artistic uses would be in the course of trade. Whether they would infringe would depend upon whether they affected one of the essential functions of the mark, and whether they were covered by a defence under section 11.[43]

In *Rxworks Ltd v. Dr Paul Hunter*,[44] Hunter was owner of the mark vet.oval and accused Rxworks of supplying computer systems that contained the mark. Daniel Alexander QC, sitting as Deputy Judge, considered whether use on the system was infringing. He noted that use did not need to be visible at the point of sale to infringe. However, he was considerably more circumspect about whether use by the vets when they ran the program would infringe. The judge said he would have held that this was not use in the course of trade.

One question that arises in this context is whether the inclusion of a trade mark in a dictionary or an encyclopedia amounts to a use in 'the course of trade'. While this may appear to be a contrived or inconsequential question, trade mark owners are often very keen to control such uses. This is because when a mark appears in a dictionary or an encyclopedia, it increases the chance of the mark being used to refer to a product, rather than as a brand of the product. In so doing, it increases the chance of a mark being removed from the Register because it has become generic. While the inclusion of a trade mark in dictionaries and encyclopedias was not treated as being a use in the course of trade under the 1938 Act,[45] the position under the 1994 Act is unclear. The Community Trade Mark Regulation has recognized trade mark proprietors' interests by providing them with the specific right to have such works indicate that the mark is a registered mark.[46]

4.3 USE AS A MARK?

The use of a sign as a trade mark, that is to indicate origin, will constitute a relevant use. However, some controversy and uncertainty surrounds the question whether, and if so which, other uses should constitute infringements. According to the ECJ, whether other uses will infringe depends upon whether the use affects or is liable to affect the functions of the trade mark, 'in particular its essential function of guaranteeing to consumers the origin of the goods'.[47] Unfortunately, the ECJ has yet to tell us exactly what functions of a trade mark are protected under the harmonized European regime. Relevant factors in determining whether there has been use that will jeopardize the essential function of the mark include 'the nature of the sign, its meaning, the context of its use including, possibly, scale'.[48] These matters are to be viewed from the point of view of the average consumer.

---

[43] Case C–206/01 [2002] *ECR* I–10273; [2003] *Ch* 454; [2003] 3 *WLR* 450; [2003] 1 *CMLR* (12) 345 para. 40 (ECJ). See also *Travelex Global and Financial Services Ltd. & Interpayment Services Ltd. v. Commission*, Case T–195/00 [2003] *ECR* II–1677 (paras. 93–104) (dismissing an action alleging infringement of the claimant's trade mark by the Commission's activities in promoting the Euro, on the basis that the use of the Euro symbol was not use in the course of trade in this sense).

[44] [2007] *EWHC* 3061 (Ch) (Ch).

[45] *M. Ravok (Weatherwear) v. National Press* (1955) 72 *RPC* 110 (mistaken reference in directory of brands to person who was not the manufacturer did not infringe).

[46] CTMR Art. 10.

[47] *Arsenal v. Reed*, Case C–206/01 [2002] *ECR* I–10273; [2003] *Ch* 454; [2003] 3 *WLR* 450; [2003] 1 *CMLR* (12) 345; [2003] *RPC* (9) 144, para. 51; O_2 *(UK) Ltd v. Hutchison 3G UK Ltd*, Case C–533/06 (12 June 2008) (para. 57).

[48] *Rxworks*, [2007] *EWHC* 3061 (Ch) (Ch).

The question which uses implicate the essential function of the mark—which Advocate General Mengozzi has described as 'bristling with difficulties'[49]—has arisen in a variety of different factual circumstances. We look at each in turn.

4.3.1 Use as a Description

Certain uses of registered trade marks for purely descriptive purposes are non-infringing because they do not jeopardize the essential function of the mark.[50] In *Hölterhoff v. Freiesleben*,[51] the trade mark owner of the words SPIRIT SUN and CONTEXT CUT for 'precious stones for further processing as jewellery' had brought an action alleging infringement by Hölterhoff as a result of certain commercial dealings in which he had been asked to cut diamonds in the shape of SPIRIT SUN. The dealings were oral, and neither the customer nor the jeweller considered the term SPIRIT SUN to indicate that the goods came from the claimant. The European Court of Justice, in a decision focused on the specific facts that underpinned the reference (so that it was not necessary to 'discuss further what constitutes the use of a trade mark'[52]), held that:

Article 5(1) is to be interpreted as meaning that the proprietor of a trade mark cannot rely on his exclusive right where a third party, in the course of commercial negotiations, reveals the origin of goods which he has produced himself and uses the sign in question solely to denote the particular characteristics of the goods he is offering for sale so that there can be no question of the trade mark used being perceived as a sign indicative of origin.

In another case where a mark was used descriptively as the name of an internal domain in a computer system, and as such was unlikely to be encountered to a significant extent, the High Court held that there was no use that would be likely to jeopardize the claimant's mark's ability to indicate origin.[53]

4.3.2 Use to Indicate Loyalty

In contrast, even though use of a registered mark on clothing was not understood as indicating origin (but rather to indicate that the wearer supported a particular sports team), it has been treated as likely to affect the essential function of the mark to indicate that clothing bearing it came from the trade mark owner.

In *Arsenal FC plc v. Matthew Reed*,[54] Arsenal FC, which owned the trade mark for ARSENAL in respect of clothing and footwear, brought an action for infringement against a stall holder, Reed, who sold scarves bearing the mark from a stall located outside Arsenal's ground. The evidence indicated that the marks were not perceived by purchasers as indicating that the goods were made or supplied by the club: rather they were seen as badges of support, loyalty, or affiliation, used to indicate that those who possessed them supported Arsenal FC. On a reference to the ECJ, the Court indicated that the exercise of a trade mark owner's right was confined to cases in which a third party's use of the sign affects or is liable to affect the functions of the trade mark, in particular its essential function of guaranteeing to consumers the origin of the goods.[55] The Court then went on to make some observations on the case itself. It noted that the use of the sign takes place in the context of sales to consumers 'and is obviously not

---

[49] *O₂ Holdings Limited & O₂ (UK) Limited v. Hutchison 3G UK Limited*, Case C–533/06 (Opinion of AG Mengozzi, 31 Jan 2008) (para. 28).
[50] *Arsenal v. Reed* [2003] *RPC* (9) 144.
[51] Case C–2/00 [2002] *ECR* I–4187; [2002] *FSR* (52) 802; [2002] *ETMR* (79) 917.   [52] Ibid, para. 17.
[53] *Rxworks* [2007] *EWHC* 3061 (Ch) (Ch) (Deputy Judge, Daniel Alexander QC).
[54] Case C–206/01 [2002] *ECR* I–10273; [2003] *Ch* 454; [2003] 3 *WLR* 450; [2003] 1 *CMLR* (12) 345.
[55] Ibid, para. 51.

Fig. 40.1 Opel corporate logo
Source: Courtesy of Opel.

intended for purely descriptive purposes'.[56] The use was 'such as to create the impression that there is a material link in the course of trade between the goods concerned and the trade mark proprietor'.[57] This was so, even if the initial consumers were not confused because 'some consumers, in particular if they come across the goods after they have been sold... and taken away from the stall... may interpret the sign as designating Arsenal FC as the undertaking of origin of the goods'.[58] So the use was liable to jeopardize the guarantee of origin which constitutes the essential function of the mark.[59] Interpreting the ECJ's judgment, the Court of Appeal held that Reed had infringed Arsenal's trade mark.[60] According to the Court of Appeal, unchecked, non-descriptive use would damage the trade mark because it 'can no longer guarantee origin'. The 'wider and more extensive the use, the less likely the trade marks would be able to perform their function'.

4.3.3 Use on Replicas

In *Adam Opel AG v. Autec AG*,[61] the well-known car manufacturer Opel had registrations of its logo (see Fig. 40.1) for cars and toys. The defendant sold remote-controlled scale models of the Opel Astra V8 Coupé bearing the Opel logo on its radiator grille. Opel sued and the Landgericht Nürnberg-Fürth asked the ECJ for a ruling as to whether such use infringes Article 5(1) of the Directive in circumstances where consumers are used to scale models and accord importance to absolute fidelity, so that viewing the toy they would appreciate that it was a reduced-scale version of the Opel car. The ECJ responded that, as long as consumers did not think the toys came from Opel or an economically linked undertaking, then the use did not affect the essential function of the mark.[62]

Although *Arsenal* had acknowledged that some uses of a claimant's mark on another's goods might not affect the essential function, this case provides an illustration of where that is the case. Indeed, it raises the possibility that even on some football merchandise—for example, replica shirts where consumers expect them to be the same as those worn by the players and to include the relevant crests and logos—there will be no infringement.

---

[56] Ibid, para. 55.   [57] Ibid, para. 56.   [58] Ibid, para. 58.   [59] Ibid, para. 62.
[60] *Arsenal FC plc v. Reed (No. 2)* [2003] 3 *All ER* 865 reversing Laddie J's judgment [2003] 1 *CMLR* 13; [2003] 1 *All ER* 137. See also *Dyer v. Gallacher* [2007] *JC* 125 (use of Rangers FC name and logo on scarves and bags was not 'descriptive' of the characteristics and was liable to jeopardize the ability of the marks to guarantee origin.)
[61] *Adam Opel AG v. Autec AG,* Case C–48/05 [2007] *ETMR* (33) 500.
[62] Ibid, para. 24

4.3.4 Use to Identify Performers

According to the House of Lords in *R v. Johnstone,* it will be a question of fact whether use of registered marks to identify the performers on CDs or similar items constitutes a use that is liable to jeopardize the essential function of the mark.[63] This case concerned a criminal action against a bootlegger, who had made and sold recordings of (inter alia) a performance of Bon Jovi. It was alleged that by using the words Bon Jovi on the CDs, the defendant had infringed the trade mark BON JOVI. Having held that criminal infringement required that there be civil infringement, the House of Lords found that, on its reading of the ECJ's judgment in *Arsenal,* this required that the defendant had used the mark as a trade mark. According to Lord Nicholls, 'non-trade mark use is not within section 10(1)–(3)'.[64] More specifically, Lord Nicholls stated,[65]

the exclusive rights granted to the proprietor of a registered trade mark are limited to use of a mark likely to be taken as an indication of trade origin. Use of this character is an essential pre-requisite to infringement. Use of a mark in a manner not indicative of trade origin of goods or services does not encroach upon the proprietor's monopoly rights.

Whether a use constitutes use to indicate origin is, according to their Lordships, a question of fact ('of a fairly complex sort').[66] In most cases deciding whether a use indicates source will be relatively straightforward. However, this was not so with the facts in front of the House, concerning indications as to who performed on the bootleg recordings: such use might be purely descriptive of the contents of the disc and nothing more, or might indicate origin. The House did not have to decide whether there had been trade mark use (for Johnstone had not been allowed by the trial judge to substantiate this submission, so his conviction was unsafe). However, Lord Walker suggested some factors which might be relevant: the prominence of the mark, use of other marks, the terms and prominence of any disclaimer, and any other matters 'going to the alleged infringer's good faith and honesty'.[67]

4.3.5 Use as a Trade Name

In two cases, the European Court of Justice has been asked to consider whether use as a trade name is a use which infringes Article 5(1) of the Directive.

The first case concerned an action by Anheuser-Busch, owner of the BUDWEISER mark for beer, against its Czech trade rival, which was importing its BUDVAR beer into Finland.[68] The defendant's beer bore the BUDVAR mark but also stated below the trade mark, and in considerably smaller lettering, that the product had been 'brewed and bottled by the brewery Budweiser Budvar national enterprise'. The ECJ was referred questions specifically on the interpretation of Article 16 of the TRIPs Agreement, but answered that national law needed to be interpreted to give effect to both that provision and Article 5 of the Directive. In essence, the Court said

---

[63] [2003] 1 *WLR* 1736; [2003] 3 *All ER* 884; [2003] *FSR* (42) 748.

[64] Ibid, [2003] *FSR* (42) 748 para. 17.

[65] Ibid, 755 para. 13. Although the House seems to require trade mark use, the better view is that it did not intend to deviate from the stance of the ECJ: see *Rxworks* [2007] *EWHC* 3061 (Ch) (Ch) (para. 59).

[66] *Johnstone* [2003] *FSR* (42) 748, 778 para. 87 (*per* Lord Walker).

[67] The reference to 'good faith and honesty' seems odd in the context of determining whether use indicates origin as opposed to the distinct defence of descriptive use under TMA s. 11(2)(b). Unfortunately, the distinction between the two issues is elided in *Johnstone*: Lord Nicholls, at 755 (para. 8) stating that ss. 9–13 'comprise a *fasciculus* of sections setting out the effect of a registered trade mark'.

[68] *Anheuser-Busch,* Case C–245/02 [2004] *ECR* I–10989 (ECJ, Grand Chamber).

that the question was one for the national authority to assess, having regard to the way in which the average consumer of the goods would perceive the sign. The key question, as with *Arsenal,* was said to be whether the sign would be perceived in a way which would compromise the essential function of Anheuser-Busch's mark. However, rather curiously, it noted that if the sign was not being used to 'distinguish the goods or services of one undertaking' from those of another, then liability fell to be assessed on the basis of national law (in particular, whether the national law had taken advantage of Article 5(5) of the Directive).[69]

In *Céline SARL,* the Cour d'Appel of Nancy referred a question to the Court as to whether use of a sign as a company name, shop name, or trade name infringed trade marks under Article 5(1) of the directive. [70] The reference arose in a case in which the claimant Céline SA relied on its registered mark CÉLINE for clothes to bring an action against the operator of a clothes shop in Nancy trading under the name 'Céline'. The ECJ advised that use as a trade name was not of itself use within Article 5, for that required use to distinguish the goods or services of the user from those of other traders. However, the Court recognized that a shop might use a trade name in a way that was perceived as distinguishing the goods of the shop from those of other traders. In such a case, the use would be infringing. If the use was not to distinguish the defendant's goods or services from those of other traders, liability would turn on whether national law had taken advantage of Article 5(5) of the Directive.

Although the UK has not taken advantage of Article 5(5) of the Directive, it has enacted provisions governing the registration of company names which may produce a similar effect. Section 69 of the Companies Act 2006 allows persons to object to the registration of a company name which is 'the same' as a name associated with the applicant in which he has 'goodwill' (which is defined as including 'reputation of any description'), or which is 'sufficiently similar' to such a name that its use in the United Kingdom would be 'likely to mislead by suggesting a connection between the company and the applicant'. Objections fall to be heard by a Company Names Adjudicator.[71] By preventing the registration of company names that are likely to be confused with (used) trade marks, the trade mark owner can go some way to ensuring that use of its trade mark as a trade name does not take place.

4.3.6 Use in meta-tags and keyword advertising on the Internet

A wide-range of internet advertising practices have raised difficult questions in relation to trade mark use. One such practice is 'meta-tagging', that is embedding competitors' trade marks in one's own website in order to attract those who search for that trade mark to one's site.[72] Another is the practice of the operators of search engines guaranteeing to particular traders that their website will appear in response to use of certain search terms, including search terms comprising the trade marks of third parties. This practice is particularly associated with Google's *AdWord* program.[73] Yet another is the use of software that causes pop-up adverts to appear in response to particular prompts. In the United States, these practices have generated a good deal of case law, much of it turning on the controversial question whether

---

[69] Ibid, para. 64.

[70] *Céline v. Céline,* Case C–17/06 [2007] *ETMR* (80) 1320 (ECJ Grnd Ch). For commentary, see T. Scourfield, 'A Tale of Two Célines' [2008] *EIPR* 71.

[71] *Céline,* ibid (ECJ Grnd Ch).

[72] Most search engines today no longer rely on meta data.

[73] *Google France v. Louis Vuitton Malletier,* Paris Court of Appeal (Cour d'Appel) 4th Division, Section A (28 June 2006) (2007) *IIC* 117. On 20 May 2008, the Cour de Cassation referred the matter to the ECJ.

there is a trade mark use requirement and, if so, what it involves.[74] In the United Kingdom, the only case to date concerned the use of the word REED to prompt the generation of 'banner ads' and as 'meta-tags'. The Court of Appeal held that, as the defendant's services were not identical to the claimant's, the uses fell to be assessed under section 10(2). In the case of the banner advertisement which appeared in response to use of REED, there was no use of REED in the advertisement itself and no likelihood of confusion. Jacob LJ noted, however, that had this been a case under section 10(1), the key issue would have been whether there was 'use in the course of trade'. He expressed doubts as to whether such use would be within the realm of trade mark rights, noting that the use was invisible and as part of an interaction with a computer.[75] Jacob LJ also considered that the use of REED in meta-tags was non-infringing, again because the search results allayed any possibility of confusion. (In fact, the claimant's site appeared first in the results.) He declined to explain what his conclusion would have been had the case been one of 'double identity' under section 10(1), but again observed that there might be difficulties with regarding use in meta-tags as relevant 'use'.[76]

4.3.7 Comparative advertising

Does use in comparative advertising, for example to show that the advertiser's goods or services are cheaper or better value than those of the trade mark owner, constitute 'use' for the purposes of Article 5(1)? In *O₂ Holdings v. Hutchison 3G Ltd* and *L'Oreal v. Bellure,* Jacob LJ asked the ECJ precisely this question. In the first case, the claimants objected to an imitation of *O₂*'s bubble advertisement in order to promote Hutchison's mobile phone services.[77] The defendant argued that this was a descriptive use of the proprietor's sign to describe its own goods, and did not implicate the essential function of that mark. Jacob LJ said he was 'clear that the position is not clear', referred the question to the Court, and offered his own opinion—that such use was not infringing.[78] In *L'Oreal v Bellure,*[79] the defendant was selling cheap, smell-alike perfumes and had created a 'comparison chart' to inform traders exactly which branded perfumes the defendant was imitating. The trade mark proprietors objected to the use of their names (TRÉSOR, ANAÏS ANAÏS etc) in the tables. The Court of Appeal found that there would be no confusion, but that the defendant would benefit from its ability to promote its products in that manner. It asked the ECJ whether, in these circumstances, there was use liable to jeopardize the essential function of the mark.[80]

The ECJ has now issued its judgment in *O₂ v. Hutchison 3G.*[81] Declining to follow the Opinion of Advocate General Mengozzi (who had said it was unnecessary to decide whether use in comparative advertising was use for the purposes of Article 5 of the Directive), the ECJ held that such use *may* constitute trade mark infringing use. Because the facts in *O₂* concerned use of similar (rather than identical) marks, the ECJ said that whether there was an infringing use depended on whether there was use in respect of goods or services which are similar, which was 'liable to affect the essential function of the trade mark', which it identified as guaranteeing origin. As Hutchison used the O₂ bubbles as part of an advertisement that distinguished its telecommunication services from O₂'s there was relevant use in relation to identical services, but as there was no likelihood of confusion, it was not a use that would affect the essential

---

[74] S. Dogan & M. Lemley, 'Trademark and Consumer Search Costs on the Internet', (2004) 41 *Houston Law Review* 777; G. Dinwoodie & M. Janis, 'Confusion Over Use: Contextualism in Trademark Law' (2007) 99 *Iowa Law Review.*

[75] *Reed Executive v. Reed Business Information* [2004] *RPC* (40) 767, para 142,

[76] Ibid.   [77] [2007] *RPC* (16) 407.   [78] Ibid, para 33.

[79] [2008] *ETMR* (1) 1.   [80] Ibid.   [81] Case C–533/06 (12 June 2008).

function. The ECJ indicated that a use that was likely to confuse would not benefit from the immunity provided by the Misleading and Comparative Advertising Directive 2006/114/EC (MCAD), because it would breach one of the conditions on which that immunity was based. The decision indicates that there would be no liability under Article 5(1)(a) of the Directive/ section 10(1) of the Act were the use to satisfy the eight conditions of the MCAD, but does little to clarify whether there could be an infringement under Article 5(1)(a) in the absence of a likelihood of confusion.

4.4 USE AS A MARK IN DILUTION CASES?

One matter that remains somewhat uncertain is how the requirement that a use be liable to jeopardize the essential function of a trade mark plays out in cases where the basis of the action is section 10(3)—blurring, free riding, or tarnishment.[82] On the one hand, the term 'using' appears in both Article 5(1) (infringement in cases of identity and confusing similarity) and Article 5(2) (infringement by dilution) of the Directive, giving no hint that it could have a different meaning or scope in each case. Likewise, in the case of Community marks the term 'using' appears once in the preamble to Article 9(1), which then defines the scope of the rights in (a) double identity, (b) confusing similarity, and (c) dilution. The structures of the laws therefore suggest that the same requirement for use applies in both cases. On the other hand, the Court has left open the possibility that a trade mark might have functions other than to indicate origin (though it has yet to explain what these are), and it may be that it has been leaving open the possibility that these functions are the ones jeopardized in case of use of a mark that takes advantage or is detrimental to the distinctive character or reputation of the mark. In *Adam Opel AG v. Autec AG*,[83] the Opel logo (see Fig. 40.1) was registered for both toys and motor vehicles but had a reputation for motor vehicles. In giving the German court guidance to help it determine whether Autec had infringed by using the Opel logo on replica toys, the Court went out of its way to consider the significance of Article 5(2) of the Directive. In stark contrast to the advice it gave on Article 5(1)—i.e. that to infringe, Autec's use must be such as to jeopardize the essential function of the mark—the Court implied that *any use* that achieved one of the effects mentioned under Article 5(2) (i.e. conferred an unjustified advantage on Autec, or tarnished or blurred the distinctiveness of Opel's mark) would infringe. There is apparently no extra requirement that the use 'jeopardize the essential function' of the mark. Having said that, it must be questionable whether the Court was fully alive to the implications of such a holding, given that this question was not one which the German court had referred, nor one on which the Advocate General had given an opinion, and very possibly one on which neither the parties, nor the UK or French governments, nor the Commission, had made observations.

---

[82] See I. Simon, 'Embellishment: Trade Mark Use Triumph or Decorative Disaster?' [2006] *EIPR* 321 (arguing that the matter is undecided, and favouring the view that 'trade mark use should not be required.)

[83] *Opel v. Autec*, Case C–48/05 [2007] *ETMR* (33) 500. See *Verimark v. BMW AG* [2007] *FSR* (33) 803, 811 (Sth. African Sup. Ct. of App.) ('trade mark use' not a necessary requirement but one which may affect the assessment of 'unfair advantage').

5 SECONDARY INFRINGEMENT

In addition to the various forms of primary infringement set out in sections 10(1)–(3), trade mark owners are also given protection against forms of secondary or indirect infringement. Section 10(5) provides that a person who applies the mark to 'material intended to be used for labelling or packaging goods, as business paper or for advertising goods or services' is liable for any infringing use of the material. Unlike an action for primary infringement where knowledge is not a relevant factor, secondary infringement under section 10(5) only arises where the person who applied the mark 'knew or had reason to believe that the application of the mark was not duly authorized by the proprietor or a licensee'.[84] Defendants may also indirectly infringe the rights in a trade mark where they act as a joint tortfeasor. This may prove relevant in cases involving, for example, sales on E-bay facilitating the auction of infringing goods. The notion of joint tortfeasance is reviewed in Chapter 47.

---

[84] The knowledge requirement is in similar terms to that employed in the context of copyright. See Ch. 8.

41

TRADE MARK DEFENCES

CHAPTER CONTENTS

1 INTRODUCTION

In this chapter we explore the various defences that are available to a person who has been charged with trade mark infringement. While the defences to trade mark infringement have always been important, the expansion in the scope of protection in trade marks provided in the 1994 Act means that defendants are likely to try and rely much more frequently on the defences provided.[1] It should be noted that a common tactic for a defendant who is accused of infringement is to assert that the claimant's registered right was invalidly registered or that it ought to be revoked.[2] These issues have been considered in Chapters 36–9.

2 USE OF A REGISTERED MARK

The first defence to a claim of infringement of a UK trade mark is set out in section 11(1). This provides that a trade mark is not infringed by the use of another registered trade mark in relation to goods or services for which the latter mark is registered. In effect, section 11(1) provides

---

[1] The debate over the appropriate test for distinctiveness, explained at Ch. 37, has been informed by different views as to the scope and usefulness of the defences: see, especially, *Procter & Gamble v. OHIM (Baby Dry)* Case C–383/99 P [2001] *ECR* I–6251; *Wrigley v. OHIM (Doublemint)* Case C–191/01P, [2003] *ETMR* (88) 1068 (AG); *Nichols plc's Trade Mark* [2003] *RPC* (16) 301, 305–6.

[2] Note also CTMR Art. 95(3) providing a limited defence short of a counterclaim for revocation or invalidity.

that registration gives a defence to an action for infringement. This is in contrast to the situation in copyright law where a person can simultaneously exploit their own work and infringe someone else's. The immunity conferred by registration acts as an incentive for traders to apply for trade mark registration.

Where a defendant relies on the section 11(1) defence, the claimant will usually respond by challenging the validity of the registered mark under section 47(6). The ability of the claimant to nullify the section 11(1) defence by challenging the validity of the defendant's registration may be restricted if the claimant has acquiesced in the use of the later trade mark. This is because, where the owner of an earlier trade mark has knowingly acquiesced in the use of the mark for a continuous period of five years, section 48 of the 1994 Act provides that they lose the ability to apply for a declaration that the registration is invalid, or to oppose the use of the mark.[3] Unless the defendant's registration was in bad faith, where a claimant has acquiesced in the use of the later mark they lose the ability to counteract the section 11(1) defence.

3 USE OF NAME OR ADDRESS

In contrast with the law of passing-off,[4] trade mark law provides a defence to a claim of infringement where a person uses their own name. Section 11(2)(a) (or, with respect to Community marks Article 12(a) of the CTMR) provides that a registered trade mark is not infringed by 'the use by a person of his own name or address'.[5] As with all of the defences in section 11(2), this is subject to the proviso that the use is 'in accordance with honest practices in industrial or commercial matters'.[6]

In *Anheuser-Busch,* the owner of the BUDWEISER mark for beer sued its Czech trade rival, which was importing its BUDVAR beer into Finland.[7] The defendant's beer bore the BUDVAR mark but also stated below the trade mark, and in considerably smaller lettering, that the product had been 'brewed and bottled by the brewery Budweiser Budvar national enterprise'. The ECJ provided guidance on the interpretation of Article 6(1)(a) of the Directive which, in its view, was necessary for the Finnish court to dispose of the case. Most significantly, the Court held that the defence was not confined to personal names.[8] This was in spite of a Council and Commission Minute which had stated that the exception was so limited. The ECJ noted that these Minutes were non-binding, and that there was nothing in the text of the Directive to suggest such a limitation. While this resolved the most important question about the scope of the exception, which had existed since its enactment, doubt still remains over whether the section

---

[3] TM Dir., Art. 9.

[4] *Joseph Rodgers v. W.N. Rodgers* (1924) 41 *RPC* 277; *Baume v. Moore* [1958] *Ch* 907 (passing off but no trade mark infringement); *Parker Knoll v. Knoll International* [1962] *RPC* 265 (passing off but no trade mark infringement); *Biba Group v. Biba Boutique* [1980] *RPC* 413 (whatever the general position there is no defence to passing off if defendant uses first name or nickname); *NAD Electronics Inc. v. NAD Computer Systems* [1997] *FSR* 380, 392.

[5] See also TM Dir., Art. 6(a). Goldberg, 'The Right to Use One's Own Name in Business' (1984) 32 *Names (Journal of the American Name Society)* 156 (explaining transition in US cases from sacred right to own name, to recognition of public interest in avoiding confusion, so that current law tends to take a compromise position of requiring a defendant to use its full name or a disclaimer to minimize potential confusion).

[6] The wording of the proviso derives from Paris, Art. 10 *bis.*

[7] *Anheuser-Busch v. Budvar,* Case C–245/02 [2004] *ECR* I–10989 (*ECJ,* Grand Chamber) (paras. 75–84).

[8] Thus confirming the view of Lord Nicholls in *Scandecor Developments AB v. Scandecor Marketing AB* [2002] *FSR* (7) 122 (para. 54).

11(2)(a) defence would apply to the use of a nickname.[9] Following the approach of the ECJ, it might be arguable that, because the Directive does nothing to suggest that nicknames are not covered, we should assume that they are.

The Court also gave some indications as to when such use would be in accordance with honest practice in industrial and commercial matters. It said that this criterion was essentially similar to that contained in Article 17 of TRIPs and referred to a duty to act fairly towards the trade mark owner. In considering whether such 'unfair competition' existed, the Court cited three key factors. The first is the extent to which consumers would understand the use of the trade name as implying a link with the trade mark owner. This will doubtless depend on exactly how the defendant has displayed its name, and how observant the average consumer is likely to be. Presumably, the greater the level of confusion, the more likely that the use will be regarded as infringing. The second factor was the extent to which the defendant was aware, or ought to have been aware, that the consumer would consider there to be a link.[10] If it is obvious to the defendant that such a conclusion would be drawn by consumers, then most likely the use will not be regarded as honest. Finally, the Court suggested that the tribunal would need to take account of whether the trade mark had a reputation from which the third party might profit. Of course, the Court left it to the national authority to apply these factors to the facts in hand.

4 DESCRIPTIVE USES

The next defence to an action for trade mark infringement is set out in section 11(2)(b) (and, for Community marks, Article 12(b) of the CTMR).[11] This provides that a registered trade mark is not infringed where the mark is used to indicate the kind, quality, quantity, intended purpose, value, geographical origin, time of production (goods) or of rendering (services), or other characteristics of goods or services.[12] This is subject to the proviso that the use is in accordance with honest practice in industrial or commercial matters. If a descriptive term becomes registrable because it has acquired a secondary meaning, the section 11(2)(b) defence ensures that the rights conferred on the proprietor do not restrict other traders from using the same word or sign to describe goods or services. That is, the defence limits the extent to which a descriptive word can be taken from the public domain.

The section 11(2)(b) defence applies in situations where traders use the trade mark to describe their own goods, for example where, in the face of the trade mark BABY DRY registered for diapers, a competitor advertises its own nappies with the slogan 'guaranteed to keep your baby

---

[9] In *NAD v. NAD* [1997] *FSR* 380, Ferris J doubted that Hossain Afkami Aghda could rely on the defence to use the NAD sign on the basis that he was commonly known as Nader Aghda or Nad. In *Premier Luggage & Bags Ltd v. Premier Company (UK) Ltd* [2003] *FSR* (5) 69, 88–9 (para. 44) the Court of Appeal held that use of the terms 'Premier Luggage' and 'Premier Luggage Company' fell outside the defence, given the firm's name was 'The Premier Company (UK) Ltd'. Dropping the 'Ltd' alone would probably not have jeopardized the availability of the defence: see *Scandecor Developments AB v. Scandecor Marketing Ltd* [1998] *FSR* 500, 521–2 *per* Lloyd J; *Daimler Chrysler AG v. Alavi* [2001] *RPC* (42) 813, 846 (para. 100).

[10] The ECJ seems here to deal with some matters which were of concern to Jacob LJ in *Reed Executive plc v. Reed Business Information Ltd.* [2004] *RPC* (40) 767 (para. 131).

[11] See also TM Dir., Art. 6(b).

[12] The equivalent 'fair use' defence in the USA, Lanham Act (1946) s. 33(b)(4), is available only in actions involving descriptive terms and only when the term is used in its descriptive sense.

dry'.[13] It also applies where a person uses the mark to describe the claimant's goods (as with 'PAMPERS soak up twice as much liquid as BABY DRY' or 'COFFRET D'OR smells like TRÉSOR, but at one-tenth of the price').[14] It had been held that the defence could not apply where the defendant used the mark as a trade mark in relation to their own goods.[15] However, in *Gerolsteiner Brunnen GmbH & Co. v. Putsch GmbH,* a three-judge chamber of the ECJ held that use of a sign could fall within the defence if the use was as an indication of geographical origin (even if the sign also filled the role of indicating trade origin). In that case, the claimant had registered GERRI for mineral water and brought an action against the defendant for selling bottled water bearing the mark KERRY SPRING. On the assumption that there was such aural similarity between the marks as to create a likelihood of confusion, the Bundesgerichtshof asked the ECJ whether Article 6(1)(b) of the Directive could apply where a trader used the sign 'as a trade mark'. Although the judgment is hardly explicit in its answer, the ECJ seems to have accepted that the sign KERRY SPRING was an indication of geographical origin within Article 6(1)(b), even though it was also being used as a mark. The fact that a sign is used additionally as a mark is a factor pertinent to the assessment whether the use is in accordance with honest practice, rather than whether the sign indicated geographical origin.[16]

Given the broad reading of the descriptive use defence in *Gerolsteiner,* it came as a surprise that the Court adopted a rather restrictive approach in *Adam Opel AG v. Autec AG.*[17] As will be recalled, in this case the well-known car manufacturer Opel had registrations of its logo (see Fig. 40.1) for cars and toys, and brought an action against Autec which featured the Opel logo on its replica toys. The defendant asserted that this could be regarded as use to describe the goods, i.e. to indicate the goods were replicas of cars made by Opel. The ECJ indicated that Article 6(1)(b) of the Directive could not be stretched to exempt such uses (if indeed they fell within Article 5 of the Directive). The Court stated bluntly that '[t]he affixing of a sign which is identical to a trade mark registered, inter alia, in respect of motor vehicles to scale models of that make of vehicle in order to reproduce those vehicles faithfully is not intended to provide an indication as to a characteristic of those scale models, but is merely an element in the faithful reproduction of the original vehicles'.[18] It therefore contradicted Advocate General Colomer's views that such use should be within the exception. Unfortunately, it is simply unclear why the use of the logo is not regarded by the ECJ as a use which indicates that the toy is a replica of the Opel car.

A descriptive use will only provide a defence if it is in accordance with 'honest practices in industrial and commercial matters'. In *Gerolsteiner,* the ECJ stated that this expresses 'a duty

---

[13] *British Sugar v. James Robertson & Sons* [1996] *RPC* 281.

[14] For example, in comparative advertising: *British Sugar,* ibid, 298; *O₂ Holdings v. Hutchison 3G Ltd* [2007] *RPC* (16) 407 (para 55); *L'Oreal v. Bellure* [2008] *ETMR* (1) 1 (para. 50). In *PAG Ltd v. Hawk-Woods Ltd* [2002] *FSR* (46) 723 where the defendant was selling reconditioned batteries originally supplied by the claimant the defence failed because the goods were no longer appropriately described as the goods of the proprietor.

[15] *The European v. The Economist Newspaper* [1998] *FSR* 283, 291–2; *British Sugar,* ibid, 299; *BA v. Ryanair* [2001] *FSR* (32) 541, 548 (para. 20); *Discovery Communications Inc. v. Discovery FM* [2000] *ETMR* 516, 521. But cf. *Beautimatic International v. Mitchell International Pharmaceuticals and Alexir Packaging* [1999] *ETMR* 912, 930 (there may be exceptions in the case of semI–descriptive marks).

[16] Case C–100/02 [2004] *ECR* I–691 (ECJ, 5th Ch.). No reference was made to dicta in *Windsurfing Chiemsee* Case C–108 & 109/97 [1999] *ECR* I–2779 (para. 28).

[17] *Adam Opel AG v. Autec AG,* Case C–48/05 [2007] *ETMR* (33) 500. Note also the ECJ judgment in *Adidas AG & ors v. Marca Mode CV & ors,* Case C–102/07 (10 Apr 2008) (confirming that decorative use of two stripes would not fall within the scope of the exception).

[18] Ibid, para. 44.

to act fairly in relation to the legitimate interests of the trade mark owner'.[19] Even though use is 'as a trade mark', or may cause confusion, of itself this will not necessarily render the use to be other than in accordance with honest practice. Rather, an 'overall assessment' needs to be made, and this will include an examination of the get-up used by the parties to determine whether the use of the indication of geographical origin 'might be regarded as unfairly competing with the proprietor of the trade mark'. As with the other defences under Article 6(1) of the Directive/Article 12 of the CTMR, relevant factors will be the extent of any confusion, whether the defendant realized or ought to have realized its use would cause a link to be made between its operation and those of the trade mark owner, the reputation of the trade mark owner, and whether the use was likely to have any negative impact on that reputation or take unfair advantage of it.

In the case of a use in a comparative advertisement, the requirement of 'honest practices' has been said to require application of the Misleading and Comparative Advertising Directive (discussed below).[20] A comparative advertisement that complies with the conditions of Article 4 of that Directive will be regarded ipso facto as in accordance with honest practices. One that does not comply, will not be treated as honest.

5 USE TO INDICATE THE INTENDED PURPOSE OF A PRODUCT OR SERVICE

Section 11(2)(c)/Article 12(c) of the CTMR provides that a registered trade mark is not infringed where the defendant finds it necessary to use the mark to indicate the intended purpose of a product or service (in particular, as accessories or spare parts).[21] This is subject to the proviso that the use must be in accordance with honest practice in industrial or commercial matters. In effect, this defence recognizes that, while a trader may not be formally linked to the trade mark owner, they might find it necessary to refer to the trade mark as a part of the normal course of their trade. This would occur, for example, where a trader sells spare parts for a particular type of product.[22] In these circumstances, the trader will wish to inform consumers that the parts fit particular products. The most efficient way this can be done is by referring to the trade mark for that product. Another situation where it will be necessary to use a trade mark in the course of trade is where a trader repairs a particular brand of goods (such as SONY televisions). If trade mark owners were able to control such uses, they would unfairly restrict trade. As the ECJ said, the defence in Article 6(1)(c) of the Directive seeks to reconcile the 'fundamental interests of trade mark protection with those of the free movement of goods and freedom to provide services'.[23]

---

[19] *Gerolsteiner,* Case C–100/02 [2004] *ECR* I–691 (para. 24).

[20] *O₂ v. Hutchison* [2007] *RPC* (16) 407 (CA) (para. 56).

[21] See also TM Dir., Art. 6(c). This would also count as comparative advertising within that Directive: *Toshiba Europe GmbH v. Katun Germany GmbH,* Case C–112/99 [2002] 3 *CMLR* (7) 164, paras. 32–40, since it implicitly states that the two products have equivalent technical features. As we will see, the ECJ has increasingly used the conditions from Article 4 of the Misleading and Comparative Advertising Directive to define the notion of 'honest practices' under Art. 6(1)(c).

[22] *PAG v. Hawk-Woods* [2002] *FSR* (46) 723, 729 (Pumfrey J) (reconditioning of batteries might have justified use of language such as 'suitable for apparatus equipped with PAG LOKS' but would not justify retaining the word PAG LOKS on batteries when resold).

[23] *Bayerische Motorenwerke AG and BMW Nederland BV v. Deenik,* Case C–63/97 [1999] 1 *CMLR* 1099, 1127 (para. 64).

The nature of this defence was considered by the ECJ in *BMW v. Deenik*.[24] The defendant in this action ran a garage that specialized in repairing and maintaining BMW cars. Notably, he was not a part of the official BMW dealer network. BMW claimed that, when the defendant described himself as specializing in the repair and maintenance of BMWs, he made unlawful use of the BMW mark. The ECJ disagreed, explaining that in these circumstances the defendant could rely on the defence in Article 6(1)(c) of the Directive. This was because the defendant could not communicate the fact that he repaired and maintained BMW cars without using the BMW mark.[25] In relation to the question whether the use was *necessary* to indicate the intended purpose, the ECJ said that 'if an independent trader carries out the maintenance and repair of BMW cars or is in fact a specialist in the field, that fact cannot in practice be communicated to his customers without using the BMW mark'.[26]

The ECJ revisited the question of the scope of this exception in *Gillette*.[27] In this case the claimant, Gillette, had registered trade marks for the words GILLETTE and SENSOR for razors. The defendant was selling blades under its mark PARASON FLEXOR, with a sticker on the packaging stating that 'all PARASON FLEXOR and GILLETTE SENSOR handles are compatible with this blade'. When Gillette sought to prevent this, the Finnish courts were uncertain as to whether the blades constituted 'spare parts', and therefore referred the matter to the ECJ. The ECJ responded by observing that the scope of the exception was not limited to spare parts and accessories, which were simply examples of possible intended uses of goods that would likely fall within the exception. The Court therefore stated it was unnecessary to decide whether blades were accessories or spare parts. Instead the key issue was whether it was 'necessary' to refer to the Gillette marks to indicate the intended purpose of the blades. The court helpfully explained that this would only be so were it necessary to use the trade mark to provide the public with comprehensible and complete information about the intended purpose of the product (including its compatibility). Having given a generally broad definition of the scope, the Court gave a rather narrow interpretation of 'necessary' when it stated that this meant use of the claimant's trade mark must be the only way of conveying the relevant information. Consequently, where technical standards and other norms are available which are well understood by the public, it would not be necessary to use the claimant's trade mark to convey full information about compatibility. Armed with this advice, the Helsinki Supreme Court held that the reference to Gillette was indeed 'necessary'.[28]

When will such uses be 'in accordance with honest practices in industrial and commercial matters'? In *BMW*,[29] the Court said that a use would be contrary to honest practice where it gave rise to the impression that there is a commercial connection between the trader and the trade mark owner.[30] That is, the trader must not use the mark in a way that suggests that the trader's business is affiliated with the trade mark owner's business. The ECJ said that this was a question of fact to be decided by national courts.[31] The ECJ added that, if there is no risk that the public will be led to believe that there is a commercial connection between the trader and the trade mark proprietor, the mere fact that the trader derived an advantage from using the mark (for example because the advertisements lend an aura of quality to their business) would

---

[24] Ibid, 1099.   [25] Ibid, 1125–6 (para. 54).

[26] Ibid, 1113–14 (Advocate General para. 54), 1126 (para. 60).

[27] *Gillette Co v. L.A–Laboratories Ltd Oy*, Case C–288/03 [2005] 2 *CMLR* (62) 1540 (paras 24–39).

[28] *Gillette Co v. L.A.-Laboratories Ltd Oy*, [2007] *ETMR* (17) 235 (Supreme Court, Helsinki).

[29] *BMW v. Deenik*, Case C–63/97 [1999] 1 *CMLR* 1099, 1127 (para. 63).

[30] Ibid, 1125, 1127 (paras. 52 and 64).   [31] Ibid, 1126 (para. 55).

not of itself mean that the use was dishonest.[32] In *Gillette*,[33] the Court reaffirmed the relevance of these two considerations, but added three further factors. It said first that the use would not be in accordance with honest practice if it denigrated or discredited the trade mark. Second, it added that use would not be regarded as in accordance with honest practice if it presented the goods of the user as replicas or imitations of those of the trade mark owner. The court also indicated that a further consideration would be whether the defendant represented its goods as being of the same quality as those of the trade mark owner: were the defendant to suggest such an equivalence incorrectly, the use would likely not be in accordance with honest practice. These factors seem to have been drawn from the Directive on Misleading and Comparative Advertising. The court usefully went on to point out that, in deciding whether use of a trade mark was in accordance with honest practice, the tribunal would need to examine the overall presentation of the goods (or advertising of the services) by the defendant, the extent to which the defendant's signs were readily distinguishable from those of the trade mark owner, and all the effort made by the defendant to ensure the consumer distinguished its product from those of the trade mark owner. When the case returned to Helsinki to be decided, the Finnish Supreme Court held that the use by LA Laboratories was in accordance with honest practice.[34]

6 COMPARATIVE ADVERTISING

Comparative advertising is the term used to describe advertisements where the goods or services of one trader are compared with the goods or services of another trader.[35] To show the advertiser's wares in a favourable light, comparative advertisements usually emphasize differences in things such as price, value, durability, or quality. In so doing, advertisers often refer to the competitor's products or services by their trade mark. The EC has created specific regulations—the Directive on Misleading and Comparative Advertising (MCAD)[36]—dealing with the circumstances in which comparative advertising is permissible, and those in which it should be prevented.[37] However, the exact relationship between these rules and those relating to trade marks is rather unclear.[38]

---

[32] Ibid, 1125 (para. 53). The Düsseldorf Court of Appeals has given an enlightening decision allowing a seller of Mercedes cars to use its device mark, the famous three pronged star, in advertising: *Mercedes Star* (5 Jul. 2001) (2003) 34 *IIC* 438.

[33] *Gillette v. L.A.*, Case C–288/03 [2005] 2 *CMLR* (62) 1540 (paras 40–49). For criticism, see P.-J. Yap [2008] *EIPR* 286.

[34] *Gillette v. L.A.* [2007] *ETMR* (17) 235 (Supreme Court, Helsinki).

[35] See A. Ohly and M. Spence, *The Law of Comparative Advertising* (2000).

[36] Directive 2006/114/EC of the European Parliament and of the Council of 12 December 2006 concerning Misleading and Comparative Advertising *OJ L* 376/21 (27 Dec 2006) (repealing Directive 97/55/EC) (in force from 12 Dec 2007).

[37] The Directive amends Directive 94/450/EEC. Prior to that the laws of member states varied dramatically: comparative advertising was basically permitted in Ireland, Austria, and Switzerland but was illegal in Italy, Germany, and Benelux. These differences were perceived as obstacles to the free movement of goods. For background, see Ohly and Spence, *The Law of Comparative Advertising*; *O₂ v. Hutchison*, [2007] *RPC* (16) 407 (CA) (para. 40–41). For a review of national provisions before harmonization, see T. Bedewig, 'The Regulation Of Comparative Advertising In The European Union', (1994) 9 *Tulane European and Civil Law Forum* 179.

[38] The curious provision in TMA s.10(6) is now being treated by the UK courts as redundant. For example, in *O₂ v. Hutchison,* ibid (para 58) Jacob LJ describes section 10(6) as 'a pointless provision' which 'should be repealed as an unnecessary distraction in an already complicated branch of the law'). For the case law on this, see Bently & Sherman (2d ed) pp. 917–20.

In principle, the Directive requires member states to permit comparative advertising,[39] but does so only if the advertisement satisfies the eight conditions specified in Article 4. These are that:

(a) it is not misleading according to Articles 2(b), 3, and 8(1) (these oblige member states to provide a minimum of protection against 'misleading' advertising though leave that concept undefined);[40]

(b) it compares goods or services meeting the same needs or intended for the same purpose;[41]

(c) it objectively compares one or more material, relevant, verifiable, and representative features of those goods and services, which may include price;[42]

(d) it does not discredit or denigrate the trade marks, trade names, other distinguishing marks, goods, services, activities, or circumstances of a competitor;[43]

(e) for products with designation of origin, it relates in each case to products with the same designation;[44]

(f) it does not take unfair advantage of the reputation of a trade mark, trade name, or other distinguishing marks of a competitor or of the designation of origin of competing products;[45]

(g) it does not present goods or services as imitations or replicas of goods or services bearing a protected trade mark or trade name;[46]

---

[39] Article 2a defines 'comparative advertising' as 'any advertising which explicitly or by implication identifies a competitor or goods or services offered by a competitor'. See *De Landtsheer Emmanuel SA v. Comité Interprofessionnel du Vin de Champagne, Veuve Clicquot Ponsardin SA,* Case C–381/05 (ECJ, 1st Ch) [2007] 2 *CMLR* (43) 1146 (comparison with a group of products, such as champagne, could indirectly identify goods of a competitor, but for an advertisement to fall within the provision it must compare goods or services with those of a 'competitor').

[40] See *Pippig Augenoptik GmbH & Co. KG v. Hartlauer Handelsgesellschaft mbH,* Case C–44/01 [2004] *ETMR* (5) 65 (para. 53) (failure to state the brand sold by the competitor may render the comparison misleading where the brand might significantly affect the buyer's choice and the comparison concern products whose brand names differ considerably in the extent to which they are known); (para. 65) (there is no need for the goods to come from the same distribution channel); *Lidl Belgium GmbH & Co KG v. Etablissementen Franz Colruyt NV,* Case C–356/04 [2006] *ECR* I–8501 (ECJ, Gd ch). Ohly and Spence, *The Law of Comparative Advertising,* 60–1.

[41] *Emmanuel v. Veuve Clicquot,* Case C–381/05 (ECJ, 1st Ch) (explaining relationship between this requirement and the definition of comparative advertsing, that itself requires comparison with a competitor). See also, *Lidl Belgium,* ibid (esp. paras 28, 34, 36) (in the case of a supermarket, this could include a comparison involving a sample of goods).

[42] *Lidl Belgium,* ibid (paras 47, 49, 61) ('objective' comparison of a sample of products does not require that every single product compared be listed in the advertisement as long as every product compared is capable of being identified from the advert); (paras 70–74) (where the data justifying the claim is not contained in the advertisement the 'verifiability' requirement means that the advertiser must make it available to the target audience so that they, or third parties, can verify the truth of the claims).

[43] See *Pippig,* Case C–44/01 [2004] *ETMR* (S) 65 (para. 80) (comparing prices cannot do so, and inclusion of another trader's logo is permissible for purposes of such comparison).

[44] Though products outside a designation can be compared with ones within: *Emmanuel v. Veuve Clicquot,* Case C–381/05 (ECJ, 1st Ch).

[45] See *Toshiba v. Katun,* Case C–112/99 [2002] 3 *CMLR* (7) 164 (giving guidance for national court to help it determine whether product numbers were 'distinguishing marks'; and indicating that a trader would take unfair advantage if the advert gave the public the false impression of a relationship between the advertiser and the trade mark owner); *Pippig,* note 40 above (para. 84) (can use competitor's name, reproduce logo and picture of shopfront). Note the pending reference in *L'Oreal v. Bellure* [2008] *ETMR* (1) 1.

[46] In *L'Oreal,* ibid the Court of Appeal has referred a question to the ECJ on the interpretation of this factor in the context of smell-alike perfumes. The Court has asked whether stating that one perfume smells like another involves presenting the perfume as an imitation or replica?

and

    (h) it does not create confusion among traders, between the advertiser and a competitor or between the advertiser's trade marks, trade names, other distinguishing marks, goods or services and those of a competitor.

These conditions are to be interpreted in the sense most favourable to the comparative advertiser.[47] Member states are to ensure that 'adequate and effective' means exist to combat misleading advertising and enforce compliance with the rules on comparative advertising 'in the interests of traders and competitors'. Such means are to include the taking of legal action.

The UK implements its obligations under the Directive through a patchwork of provisions.[48] One of the most important of these is the British Code of Advertising, Sales Promotion and Direct Marketing (BCA), which was drafted by the Committee on Advertising Practice (CAP) and is administered by the Advertising Standards Authority (ASA).[49] The British Code of Advertising establishes what is primarily a self-regulatory system, and was drawn up by representatives from relevant trade and professional bodies. The Code applies to advertisements in newspapers and other printed publications, cinema and video commercials, and promotions.[50]

The British Code of Advertising permits comparative advertising so long as the comparisons comply with the terms of MCAD.[51] Conformity with these requirements is assessed according to the advertisement's probable impact, taken as a whole and in context. The impact that an advertisement has will depend on the audience, the medium, the nature of the product, and any additional material distributed to consumers at the time.[52] Before releasing an advertisement, advertisers must have documentary evidence to prove all claims, whether direct or implied, that are capable of being objectively substantiated.[53] The adequacy of this evidence will be judged against whether it supports both the detailed claims and the overall impression created by the advertisement.

The ASA investigates complaints against advertisements and promotions in non-broadcast media.[54] The ASA may request that a company withdraw or amend its advertisements or promotions.[55] The judgment of the ASA Council on interpretation of the Code is final, though there is some provision for appeal. A number of sanctions exist to counteract advertisements and promotions that conflict with the Code. The media may deny access to space, the publication of a ruling on the ASA's web site may generate adverse publicity, trading sanctions may be imposed or recognition revoked by the advertiser's, promoter's, or agency's professional association, and financial incentives provided by trade, professional, or media organizations may be withdrawn.[56]

---

[47] *Toshiba v. Katun*, Case C–112/99 [2002] 3 *CMLR* (7) 164, para. 37.

[48] See D. Fitzgerald, 'Self Regulation of Comparative Advertising in the UK' [1997] *Ent LR* 250; Ohly and Spence, *The Law of Comparative Advertising*, 6–7, 97–101. Note also the role of passing-off and malicious falsehood: though in general there has been a reluctance to intervene, the latter cause of action requiring as it does proof of malice. Indeed, in *Cable & Wireless v. British Telecommunications* [1998] *FSR* 383 Jacob J queried what a claim based on malicious falsehood could add to one based on trade mark infringement. See also *BA v. Ryanair* [2001] *FSR* (32) 541 (paras. 9–14).

[49] This is now in its 11th edition (2003). This can be accessed at the ASA web site: <http://www.asa.org.uk>.

[50] BCA, para. 1.1.

[51] Ibid, paras. 18.1–5, 20.1–2 and 21.2 (corresponding with the 8 conditions of Article 4).

[52] Ibid, para. 1.4b.   [53] Ibid, para. 3.1.

[54] Ibid, paras. 60.4, 60.6, 60.28 ff. Complaints are normally not pursued if the point at issue is the subject of simultaneous legal action: BCA, para. 60.32.

[55] Ibid, para. 61.1 ff.   [56] BCA, para. 61.1–9.

The self-regulatory system is reinforced by the Control of Misleading Advertisements Regulations 1988.[57] Under these Regulations, if a misleading advertisement or promotion continues to appear after the Council has ruled against it, the ASA can refer the matter to the Office of Fair Trading which can seek an undertaking from anyone responsible for commissioning, preparing, or disseminating it, that it will be discontinued. If this is not given or is not honoured, the Office of Fair Trading can seek an injunction from the courts to prevent its further appearance.[58]

Since late 2004, the Committee of Advertising Practice (CAP) has operated similar codes in relation to broadcast commercials (which are the primary responsibility of Ofcom).[59] There are two codes, one dealing with radio broadcasting and the other with television. Each incorporates, either in its terms or in notes, the criteria from the MCAD. Also, radio and television advertisements are usually cleared in advance by the Radio Advertising Clearance Centre and Clearcast. As with the non-broadcast regulation, complaints for breach of the Codes can be made to the Advertising Standards Authority. A broadcaster who fails to heed the Codes can be referred by the Advertising Standards Authority to Ofcom, which has powers, if necessary, to revoke the licences.

The MCAD only refers to trade mark law in its recitals. Recitals 13–15 note the rights granted to trade mark owners under the Directive, and recognize that in some cases it may be 'indispensable' for a trader to use a trade mark in their comparative advertisement. Recital 15 makes clear that such use 'does not breach the exclusive right in cases where it complies with the conditions laid down in this Directive, the intended target being solely to distinguish between them and thus to highlight differences objectively'. Thus, it seems, a comparative advertisement which uses a trade mark to identify the goods with which comparison is made will be regarded as non-infringing. What is left unclear is why this is so—whether it is because the use falls outside Article 5 of the Trade Marks Directive, or falls within an exception in Article 6 or for some other reason. What is also unclear is whether a use of another's trade mark which does not comply with the MCAD automatically infringes that person's trade mark rights. English courts have proceeded on the basis that a comparative advertiser who utilizes a mark within the terms of the Directive will not be liable for infringing either because there is no 'use' that is liable to affect the essential function of the mark or because of the defence for descriptive use in Article 6(b).[60] However, in O_2 *Holdings v Hutchison 3G Ltd*,[61] the ECJ indicated that a trade mark owner can rely on its trade mark rights to prevent unfair comparative advertising if the use implicates the trade mark proprietor's rights as generally understood (at least if the use causes confusion as to origin). However, if the use complies with the eight conditions of the MCAD, a *sui generis* immunity excuses the comparative advertiser from any liability.

---

[57] Control of Misleading Advertising Regulations 1988 (SI 1988/915) (as amended by the Control of Misleading Advertisements (Comparative Advertising) Regulations 2000 (SI 2000/914)).

[58] The OFT may also utilize the Stop Now Orders (EC Directive) Regulations 2001 (SI 2001/1422).

[59] Ofcom took over the duties of the Radio Authority, Broadcasting Standards Commission, and Independent Television Commission at the end of 2003, and was given responsibility in relation to misleading and comparative advertising by the Control of Misleading Advertisements (Amendment) Regulations 2003 (SI 2003/383). It has subcontracted its job of setting the relevant standards (Communications Act 2003, s. 319) to the Broadcast Committee of Advertising Practice Limited (BCAP) and its powers in relation to handling complaints (Communications Act 2003, s. 325) to the Advertising Standards Authority (Broadcast) Limited (ASA(B)). See Contracting Out (Functions Relating to Broadcast Advertising) and Specification of Relevant Functions Order 2004, SI 2004/1975.

[60] O_2 v. *Hutchison* [2007] *RPC* (16) 407 (CA); *L'Oreal v. Bellure* [2008] *ETMR* (1) 1.

[61] O_2, ibid.

Assuming that the MCAD provides a *sui generis* defence to trade mark infringement, in *O₂ v Hutchison*[62] the question was raised whether, in addition to the eight conditions in Article 4 (then Article 3(a)), the recitals imposed a further condition of 'indispensability'. It will be recalled that in this case the defendant had advertised its mobile phone service using bubble imagery similar to that for which the claimant had a registered mark (in relation to telecommunication services). It was argued by the claimant that, to be permissible under the Directive, the use of a trade mark in a comparative advertisement must be 'indispensable', and that while it might have been necessary for Hutchison to refer to O₂, it was not necessary for it to use the bubble marks. Consequently, use of the imagery took 'unfair advantage' of the trade mark. Jacob LJ said that, while he considered there was no such requirement, the matter was not clear and must be referred to the European Court of Justice. Advocate General Mengozzi's opinion is that there is no such requirement for 'indispensability'.[63] Reviewing the case law on (what was) Article 3(a)(g) of the CAD (and is now Article 4(g) of the MCAD), the Advocate General found no hint of any such requirement. The Court did not deal with this question in its judgment of 12 June 2008.

7 LOCAL USES

Section 11(3) provides that a UK registered trade mark is not infringed by the use in a particular locality of an earlier right which only applies in that locality.[64] An earlier right applies in a locality 'if, or to the extent that, its use in that locality is protected by virtue of any rule of law (in particular, the law of passing off)'. The defence only arises if the use of the earlier right began before both the use and the registration of the claimant's mark. It should be noted that it is not necessary to show that the defendant could have brought an action for passing off. Since the courts seldom provide injunctive relief confined to a particular locality, it seems that, if defendants can bring themselves within this section, then the defence may apply throughout the United Kingdom.

The relationship between local uses and Community trade marks is complex. While the Regulation does not have an equivalent to the earlier rights defence contained in national law, Article 106 allows the owner of any earlier right to rely on national law against the Community Trade Mark owner.[65] Thus, the owner of a national mark who has not opposed the grant of a Community mark[66] may utilize its national rights in national fora to prevent use of that Community mark (including, presumably an action for infringement against it). This is subject, however, to the principle of acquiescence: that is, five years of continuous use by the owner of the Community Trade Mark in the member state where the earlier right operates.[67] These

[62] Ibid.

[63] Case C–533/06 *O₂ v. Hutchison* (31 Jan 2008) (para. 43).

[64] TMA s. 11(3). This reflects TM Dir. Art. 6(2). In *Daimler Chrysler v. Alavi* [2001] *RPC* (42) 813, 848 (para. 107) Pumfrey J stated that he had difficulty in understanding the difference between marks of merely local significance and non-local marks.

[65] As defined in CTMR, Art. 8. However, while this excludes mere local rights, CTMR, Art. 107 provides similar protection for earlier rights which only apply to a particular locality, which presumably encompasses earlier rights of mere local significance: the law of the member state concerned may be utilized to prevent use of the Community mark in the territory in question.

[66] As we saw at p. 890, according to CTMR Art. 8(4) use of rights of no more than mere local significance cannot prevent registration on relative grounds.

[67] CTMR, Art. 53(2).

provisions are of increasing importance since the expansion of the Community from 15 to 25 states in 2004 and to 27 in 2008. While existing registrations of Community marks will automatically apply to the twelve new territories, Article 106 will operate to protect those who previously were operating in those territories from the otherwise potentially devastating effect of such automatic extension.

8 EXHAUSTION

Traditionally, trade marks have been territorial in nature, so that a proprietor may own distinct rights in different territories. Typically, those rights have included the right to prevent the import of goods bearing the mark into the territory where the rights apply.[68] This led to the situation where the owner of a trade mark was able to use the rights in territory (A) to prevent the import of goods from another territory (B). This was the case *even where* the goods had been put on the market in territory (B) with the consent of the owner. In practice, there are a number of reasons why the import of goods from one country to another may be desirable. The most obvious is where the price of the goods is cheaper in one territory (B) than another (A), or where demand in the second territory (A) is not being met. At first glance, it seems that if import was permitted, it would be to the advantage of all concerned. The public in territory (A) would benefit from cheaper products, while the trade mark owner's interests would be satisfied by sale in country (B). However, first impressions give way to more complex realities. This is because trade mark owners may have good reasons for wishing to divide markets up and to prevent parallel imports.[69] Given that it may be difficult to distinguish between legitimate and counterfeit goods at the border, parallel importing may also weaken the trade mark owner's capacity to prevent the import of counterfeit goods.

8.1 DEVELOPMENT OF THE BASIC RULES

Prior to the adoption of the Directive, the European Court of Justice developed a series of sophisticated rules which detailed the situations where the owner of a national trade mark for country (A) could prevent goods put on the market elsewhere in the Community (B) from being distributed in country (A).[70] Since Article 7 of the Directive and section 12 of the 1994 Act embody the notion of exhaustion developed under the case law, it is worth noting the basic features of that case law.

The jurisprudence that developed prior to the passage of the Directive recognized the conflicting demands of Articles 30 and 36 of the Treaty of Rome. Under Article 30 of the Treaty (now Article 28 EC), 'quantitative restrictions on imports or measures having equivalent effect' are prohibited. However, under Article 36 of the Treaty (now Article 30 EC), prohibitions or restrictions on imports between member states are permissible if they can be justified

---

[68] TMA s. 10(4)(c); CTMR Art. 9(2)(c); TM Dir. Art. 5(3)(c).

[69] In the case of pharmaceuticals, the price differentials are largely the result of the fact that regulatory mechanisms for price setting differ on a national basis. If parallel importing were always possible, effectively the trade mark owner would have to live with the lowest price set by any of the national authorities. On the legality of controlling markets by restricting supply, see *Bayer AG v. Commission*, T–41/96 [2001] *All ER (EC)* 1 (CFI), Joined Cases C–2/01 P and C–3/01 P (6 Jan. 2004) and Section 8.2.5 below.

[70] See Ch. 1 esp. at pp. 12–16. See generally C. Stothers, *Parallel Trade in Europe: Intellectual Property, Competition and Regulatory Law* (2007); T. Hays, *Parallel Imports* (2003).

on grounds of the protection of industrial and commercial property. This is on the proviso that they do not constitute a means of arbitrary discrimination or a disguised restriction on trade between member states.

As we observed in Chapter 1, in striking a compromise between the demands of the internal market and national industrial property rights,[71] the European Court of Justice recognized the principle of exhaustion of rights, where the goods were placed on the market under a trade mark with the consent of the trade mark proprietor.[72] On the other hand, in order to ensure that trade marks continue to function as indicators of origin and as guarantors of quality to the consumer,[73] the European Court of Justice also said that the rights were not exhausted where the trade mark owner had a legitimate reason for opposing further circulation of the goods.[74]

The principle of exhaustion represents a compromise between a respect for national rights and an attempt to ensure that those rights are not used to restrict trade across borders. To reach this compromise, the jurisprudence relies on the notion of the 'specific subject matter' of a trade mark. In the Community's view, the essential purpose of a trade mark is to guarantee that the owner has the exclusive right to use that mark for the product for the first time. The trade mark owner can therefore prevent competitors from taking unfair advantage of the status and reputation of the trade mark by selling products illegally bearing the mark. However, once the goods are placed on the market with the proprietor's consent, the trade mark has done its job. As such, the 'specific subject matter' of the trade mark is exhausted. Exhaustion means that trade mark rights cannot be used to prevent further trade in the goods. This is subject to the proviso that the owner of the mark may be able to control further use of the mark where that use implicates some other aspect of the specific subject matter protected by the trade mark right.

This jurisprudence on exhaustion of rights was carried over into Article 7(1) of the Directive[75] and section 12(1) of the 1994 Act.[76] This provides that a 'registered trade mark is not infringed by use of the trade mark in relation to goods which have been put on the

[71] *Bristol-Myers Squibb v. Paranova A/S and C. H. Boehringer Sohn, Boehringer Ingelheim KG and Boehringer Ingelheim A/S v. Paranova A/S, and Bayer Aktiengesellschaft and Bayer Danmark A/S v. Paranova A/S,* Joined Cases C–427/93 and C–429/93 [1996] ECR I–3457, I–3528 (para. 31) (hereafter *Bristol-Myers Squibb v. Paranova*).

[72] The principle of exhaustion applies where the same person owns the mark in the country of import and export. It also applies where the parties are economically linked, for example as subsidiaries of the same group: *Centrafarm BV and Adriaan De Peijper v. Sterling Drug,* Case C–15/74 [1974] *ECR* 1147. However, economic linkage does not cover the situation where an assignment of the trade mark rights has occurred: *IHT Internationale Heiztechnik v. Ideal Standard,* Case C–9/93 [1994] *ECR* I–2789, I–1850–1 (paras. 43–5). The doctrine of common origin recognized in *Hag I, Van Zuylen Freres v. Hag AG,* Case 192/73 [1974] *ECR* 731 can now be regarded as otiose: Case C–10/89 *CNL-Sucal v. Hag (Hag II)* Case C–10/89 [1990] *ECR* I–3711, I–3759 (para. 19). But note that a reference has been made to the ECJ as to whether there would be exhaustion where a licensee of a trade mark places goods on the market in breach of the licence: *Copad SA v. Christian Dior Couture SA,* Case C–59/08 (pending).

[73] See e.g. *Hoffmann-La Roche v. Centrafarm,* Case 102/77 [1978] *ECR* 1139 (para. 7); *Pfizer v. Eurim-Pharm,* Case 1/81 [1981] *ECR* 2913, 2925–6 (para. 7); *Hag* II, ibid, I–3758 (para. 14); and *IHT Internationale Heiztechnik,* ibid, 2847 (para. 33).

[74] See *Hoffmann-La Roche,* ibid; *Centrafarm v. American Home Products Corporation,* Case 3/78 [1978] *ECR* 1823.

[75] *Bristol-Myers,* Joined Cases C–427/93 and C–429/93 [1996] *ECR* I–3457, I–3528, 3529 (rejecting argument that exhaustion under TM Dir. Art. 7 only permitted the resale of goods, not repackaging and thus represented a change from the existing ECJ jurisprudence).

[76] CTMR Art. 13. To the extent that TM Dir. Art. 7 is narrowly drafted, Arts. 28 and 30 EC operate as previously: see *Pharmacia & Upjohn SA v. Paranova,* Case C–379/97 [2000] 1 *CMLR* 51, 81 (para. 28).

market in the European Economic Area under that trade mark by the proprietor, or with his consent'.[77] As with the pre-Directive jurisprudence, the principle of exhaustion found in Article 7(1) and section 12(1) is subject to the general rider that in certain circumstances the rights of the owner will not be exhausted. As Article 7(2) says 'Paragraph 1 shall not apply where there exist legitimate reasons for the proprietor to oppose further commercialisation of the goods, especially where the condition of the goods is changed or impaired after they have been put on the market'.[78]

8.2 LEGITIMATE REASONS TO PREVENT FURTHER DEALINGS IN GOODS BEARING THE MARK

Trade mark owners are only able to utilize their rights to prevent further dealings in goods bearing their mark which have been placed on the market, when there are 'legitimate reasons' to do so. The mere fact that the further dealing is to another trader's advantage is not a legitimate reason for the trade mark owner to prevent the use from taking place. There are a number of situations where a trade mark owner may have a legitimate reason to oppose further dealings in goods bearing the mark. These include situations where the goods are altered or repacked, or where the mark is altered, or where the goods or services are advertised. We will consider each in turn.

8.2.1 Altering the goods

One situation where a trade mark owner has a legitimate reason to oppose further dealings in a mark is where the condition of the goods has changed or been impaired after they have been put on the market. For example, a trader which manufactures and sells video-game consoles under a particular registered mark in France, may wish to prevent another trader from exporting the console from France to the United Kingdom, opening the packaging, adding adaptors to enable the console to work in the United Kingdom, and selling the repackaged goods. The trade mark owner may have a legitimate reason to object to the resale of such goods, for example, if the adaptor is of a different standard to that which the trader would supply in the authorized UK packages—at least where the repackaged goods do not clearly indicate the origin of the adaptors.[79] If the owner was unable to control such acts, the role that the mark plays in enabling the trade mark proprietor to control the quality of products placed on the market under the mark would be undermined.

---

[77] Although TM Dir. Art. 7(1) refers to marketing in the Community, the principle of the exhaustion of rights was extended for certain purposes to the EEA. See Ch. 1. For consideration of when goods are placed on the market, see *Peak Holding AB v. Axolin-Elinor ABR*, Case C–16/03 [2004] *ECR* I–11313 (sales which allow the TM proprietor to realise the economic value of the trade mark exhaust, whereas merely importing or offering for sale does not).

[78] TMA s. 12(2) is slightly different in its wording: 'sub-section 12(1) does not apply where there are legitimate reasons for the proprietor to oppose further dealings in the goods'. The main difference is that while s. 12(2) allows trade mark owners to oppose 'further dealings' with goods bearing their mark where there are legitimate reasons to do so, Art. 7 refers to further 'commercialization of goods'. It seems that the difference in language does not affect the scope of the provisions. Both terms encompass the import, resale, and advertising of goods bearing the trade mark.

[79] *Sony Computer Entertainments v. Tesco Stores* [2000] *ETMR* 104.

8.2.2 Repackaging

Another situation where a trade mark owner may have a legitimate reason to control further dealings is where the goods are repackaged.[80] In *Bristol-Myers v. Paranova*[81] Bristol-Myers marketed pharmaceutical products in various member states. It was the owner of certain trade marks for those pharmaceuticals in Denmark. Paranova purchased products sold by Bristol-Myers in member states, such as Greece and the United Kingdom, where the prices were relatively low, and then imported them into Denmark. The pharmaceuticals had originally been marketed as tablets in blister packs, flasks, phials, and ampoules. For the purposes of sale in Denmark, Paranova repackaged all the pharmaceuticals in new external packaging. In so doing, Paranova gave the pharmaceuticals a uniform appearance, namely, white with coloured stripes corresponding to the colours of the manufacturers' original packaging. The new packaging displayed the respective trade marks of the manufacturer (*viz.* Bristol-Myers). It also included statements that the products had been manufactured by Bristol-Myers and were imported and repackaged by Paranova. Bristol-Myers claimed that the import infringed various trade marks that they had registered in Denmark. The matter was referred to the ECJ for consideration.

The ECJ began by noting that Article 7(1) provides that owners of a trade mark cannot rely on their rights in the mark to prevent the importing or marketing of a product which has been put on the market in another member state by them or with their consent. The Court went on to point out that derogations from the fundamental principle of free movement of goods are only permitted in order to safeguard the rights which constitute the specific subject matter of that property.

With respect to repackaging of goods bearing the trade mark, the ECJ said that 'account must be taken of the essential function of the trade mark, which is to guarantee to the consumer or end user the identity of the trade-marked product's origin by enabling him to distinguish it without any risk of confusion from products of different origin'. That guarantee of origin means that consumers or end-users can be certain that the original condition of a trade-marked product offered to them has not been interfered with or affected by a third party.[82] The specific subject matter of a trade mark includes the right to oppose any use of the trade mark that was liable to impair the role it played in guaranteeing the origin of the goods. In particular, the ECJ said that the owner should be able to ensure that the product has not been interfered with in such a way as to affect the original condition of the product. As a result, the ECJ said that the trade mark owner could prevent the parallel import of repackaged goods. The upshot of this was that a trade mark proprietor may rely on their rights to prevent the parallel import of a product put on the market in another member state, where the importer has repackaged the product in new packaging to which the trade mark has been reaffixed. (Although Laddie J has questioned the logic of a rule which allows a trade mark owner to prevent parallel importing of goods where there s no identifiable damage

---

[80] See Stothers, 74–103; P. Koutrakos, 'In Search of a Common Vocabulary in Free Movement of Goods: The Example of Repackaging Pharmaceuticals' [2003] *ELR* 53; N. Gross and L. Harrold, 'Fighting for Pharmaceutical Profits' [2002] *EIPR* 497; C. Stothers, 'Are Parallel Imports Bad Medicine? Repackaging of Trade-Marked Pharmaceuticals within the EU' [2002] *ECLR* 417; D. McCann, 'Parallel Imports and Repackaging of Pharmaceutical Products' [2002] *International Company & Commercial Law Review* 363.

[81] Joined Cases C–427/93 and C–429/93 [1996] *ECR* I–3457, I–3528. Consequently Art. 7 applied to repackaging, not simply resale.

[82] Ibid, 3532–3 (para. 47).

to the trade mark,[83] the position was reaffirmed by the ECJ in *Boehringer Ingelheim KG v. Springward (No. 1).*[84]

The ECJ, in *Bristol Myers*, acknowledged that this may create problems insofar as it enables owners to exercise their rights in a way that constitutes a disguised restriction upon the free movement of goods under Article 30 EC (formerly Article 36 of the Treaty). To ensure that this did not occur, the ECJ said that the owner could *not* prevent the parallel import of repackaged goods where the use of the trade mark right by the owner contributes to the artificial partitioning of the markets between member states. In so doing, the ECJ limited the scope of the trade mark owner's rights.

To ensure that this derogation from the owner's rights did not adversely affect the subject matter of the trade mark, the ECJ said that parallel importing of repackaged goods is only permissible where the parallel importer satisfies certain conditions. These are that:

(i)   the repackaging does not adversely affect the original condition of the product;

(ii)   the parallel importer complies with certain obligations as to labelling and provision of samples; and

(iii) the quality of the repackaging does not adversely impact on the reputation of the mark.[85]

After looking at the question of what is meant by 'artificial partitioning of the market', we will look at each of the three conditions imposed on the parallel importer.

Artificial partitioning of the markets between member states   Repackaging by a parallel importer is only justified where and insofar as it is necessary to avoid artificial partitioning of the market.[86] The test for whether there has been an 'artificial partitioning' of the market is decided by objective standards. This means that the importer does not need to show that the trade mark owner deliberately intended to partition the markets between member states. The ECJ said that partitioning is artificial if it cannot be justified by the need to safeguard the essential function of the trade mark. In other words, the power of the trade mark owner should only be limited insofar as the repackaging undertaken by the importer is *necessary* to market the product in the member state of import.[87]

---

[83] *Glaxo Group v. Dowelhurst (No. 2)* [2000] *FSR* 529, 564 (Laddie J would require the trade mark owner to prove confusion or damage to the reputation of the trade mark).

[84] *Boehringer Ingelheim KG, Boehringer Ingelheim Pharma KG v. Springward Ltd,* Case 143/00 and *Merck, Sharp & Dohme GmbH v. Paranova Pharmazeutica Handels GmbH,* Case 443/99 [2003] *Ch* 27; [2002] 3 *WLR* 1697; [2002] All ER (EC) 581; [2002] *ETMR* (80) 933; [2002] *FSR* (61) 970 (para. 30) (repackaging *by its very nature* puts at risk the guarantee of origin, and therefore is prejudicial to the specific subject matter of the mark *irrespective of the actual effects* of the repackaging by the parallel importer). In his judgment at [2003] *ETMR* (89) 1078 (para. 20), Laddie J has called this 'an irrebuttable presumption that repackaging [is] prejudicial to the specific subject matter of the mark'.

[85] Joined Cases C–427/93 and C–429/93 [1996] *ECR* I–3457, I–3528, 3533–4 (para. 54).

[86] Ibid, 3535 (para. 56); *Frits Loendersloot, trading as F. Loendersloot Internationale Expeditie v. George Ballantine & Son,* Case C–349/95 [1997] *ECR* I–6227, 6255 (para. 29). But cf. *Glaxo v. Dowelhurst (No. 2)* [2000] *FSR* 529, 564, 571, 576–7 where Laddie J argued that the issue of necessity only arises if the use damages the specific subject matter of the trade mark.

[87] 'The trade mark proprietor's opposition to the repackaging is not justified if it hinders effective access of the imported product to the market of that state': *Boehringer Ingelhem v. Swingward,* note 84 above, para. 46 (ECJ). See D. Dryden and S. Middlemiss, 'Parallel Importation of Repackaged Goods: Is "Necessity" Really Necessary?' [2003] *Journal of Business Law* 82.

One situation where repackaging would be justified is where the goods are marketed in a different packaging in one member state from that used in another member state. In this situation, the goods may not be able to be sold in the second member state unless they are repackaged. In these circumstances reliance on a trade mark to prevent repackaging would contribute to the partitioning of markets between member states (even if that were not the deliberate intention of the rights owner).[88] For example, if a whisky was marketed as 'pure whisky' in one country, but regulations in another member state meant that the whisky could not be described as 'pure', it would be necessary to remove the word 'pure' from the packaging before the product could be imported into the latter state.[89]

Equally, a trade mark owner cannot oppose the repackaging of a product where the size of the original packet cannot be marketed in the importing member state.[90] This would occur, for example, where the size of the packaging was dictated by national regulations. It is unclear whether consumer familiarity with one size or type of packaging would justify the need for repackaging. In *Bristol-Myers* the ECJ made it clear that a 'need' to repackage may exist even where a number of different types of packaging are used in the importing state. This is so even if this includes the form of packaging in which the goods in question have been marketed.[91] The reason for this is that 'partitioning of the markets would exist if the importer were able to sell the product in only part of his market'.[92] This suggests that repackaging may be justified in response to consumer practices, in the same way as it is justified so as to meet national regulations on packaging. In *Boehringer Ingelheim (No. 1)*,[93] the ECJ indicated that, while consumer resistance would not always constitute an impediment to effective market access such as to render repackaging necessary, it might do so. More specifically, it stated 'there may exist on a market, or on a substantial part of it, such strong resistance from a significant proportion of consumers to relabelled pharmaceutical products that there must be held to be a hindrance to effective market access'.[94]

The question of necessity is a threshold question. This was made clear by the ECJ when it answered a second reference from the Court of Appeal in *Boehringer Ingelheim (No. 2)*.[95] In that case at first instance Laddie J had conducted a meticulous examination of all aspects of the defendant's repackaging to determine whether it had done the 'minimum necessary' to achieve access to the market. The Court of Appeal doubted that such an exercise was required, and referred a series of questions to the ECJ. The ECJ decided, as the EFTA Court had earlier,[96] that the 'necessity' requirement 'is directed solely at the fact of repackaging not at the manner

---

[88] *Bristol-Myers*, Joined Cases C–427/93 and C–429/93 [1996] *ECR* I–3457, I–3528, 3536 (para. 57).

[89] *Frits Loendersloot v. George Ballantine & Son*, Case C–349/95 [1997] *ECR* I–6227, 6260 (para. 45).

[90] *Bristol-Myers*, Joined Cases C–427/93 and C–429/93 [1996] *ECR* I–3457, I–3528, 3534–5 (para. 53). This is a matter of fact for the national tribunal to determine: *Aventis Pharma Deutschland GmbH v. Kohlpharma GmbH and MTK Vertbriebs-GmbH*, Case C–43/00 [2002] 3 *CMLR* 24; [2003] *ETMR* 11 (where claimants sold insulin in Germany in packs of ten cartridges of 3ml and in France in five cartridges of 3 ml and the defendant imported packages from France to sell in Germany, where they were repackaged as tens, the Advocate General said that 'if the only possible "retail units" in which Insuman cartridges...could be marketed in Germany were [in packs of ten]...[s]uch repackaging would accordingly be unequivocally necessary'. Whether they were the only retail units which could enable the defendants to access the German market or whether selling five-packs would have done this, was a matter to be assessed by the national court).

[91] Ibid, para. 54.   [92] Ibid, para. 54.

[93] *Boehringer Ingelheim v. Springward*, Case 443/99 [2003] *Ch* 27; [2002] 3 *WLR* 1697; [2002] *All ER (EC)* 581; [2002] *ETMR* (80) 933; [2002] *FSR* (61) 970 (para. 30).

[94] Ibid, paras. 51–2. This was consistent with Advocate General Jacobs's opinion, 12 Jul. 2001, paras. 117–9.

[95] *Boehringer Ingelheim v. Swingward Ltd;* Case C–348/04 [2007] 2 *CMLR* (52) 1445.

[96] *Paranova AS v. Merck*, Case E-3/02 (8 Jul. 2003).

and style of repackaging'.[97] Details of the repackaging need only be scrutinized when assessing whether there has been compliance with the other conditions.

Whether the original condition of the product is adversely affected   As we have noted, Article 7(2)/section 12(2) allow trade mark owners to prevent the sale of repackaged goods 'where the condition of the goods is changed or impaired'. This impacts on repackaging cases through the requirement that the repackaging must not affect the condition of the goods. If the repackaging is carried out in such a way that it does not affect the original condition of the product inside the packaging, the ability of the trade mark to function as an indication of origin is safeguarded. If the goods are altered, however, then the essential function of the trade mark would be compromised if the trade mark owner was not permitted to prohibit further circulation of the altered goods.[98]

Consequently, a trade mark owner may oppose any repackaging of their goods which involves either a risk that the product inside the package might be tampered with, or that the original condition of their goods is adversely affected.[99] This is sometimes referred to as the doctrine of 'adverse effects'. In order to constitute a legitimate reason for a trade mark owner to oppose further commercialization of goods that have been repackaged, the risks of adverse effects must be *real*. The hypothetical risk of isolated error will not do. An example is this provided by *Bristol-Myers* where it was argued that the repackaging of blister packs might affect the condition of the drugs. It was suggested that combining blister packs with different use-by dates into single sets might lead to the sale of products which might have been stored for too long. The Court of Justice did not consider this to be a real risk.

To determine whether the repackaging adversely affects the original condition of the product, both the nature of the product and the method of repackaging must be taken into account. Parallel importation is permissible where the repackaging only affects the external layer leaving the inner packaging intact, or where the repackaging is carried out under the supervision of a public authority to ensure that the product remains intact. Similarly, the addition of accurate information by the repackager will not constitute a legitimate reason to oppose the further circulation of the goods.[100]

The ECJ has recognized that the original condition of the product inside the packaging might be indirectly affected where the repackaged product omits important information, or gives inaccurate information about the nature, composition, effect, use, or storage of the product.[101]

The parallel importer must comply with certain obligations   The decision that trade mark owners may not rely on their rights to oppose the marketing of products repackaged by an importer where this leads to artificial partitioning of the market is essential to ensure the free movement of goods. To protect the owner against misuse, the ECJ said that parallel importing of repackaged goods ought to be recognized only insofar as the importer complies with certain requirements.[102]

---

[97] *Boehringer Ingelheim v. Swingward*, Case C–348/04 [2007] 2 *CMLR* (52) 1445 (para. 38).

[98] *Frits Loendersloot v. George Ballantine & Son*, Case C–349/95 [1997] *ECR* I–6227, 6255 (para. 28).

[99] *Bristol-Myers*, Joined Cases C–427/93 and C–429/93 [1996] *ECR* I–3457, I–3528, 3536 (para. 59).

[100] Ibid, 3537 (para. 66); *Phytheron International SA v. Jean Bourdon SA*, Case C–352/95 [1997] *ECR* I–1729, I–1748 (para. 23).

[101] *Bristol-Myers*, Joined Cases C–427/93 and C–429/93 [1996] *ECR* I–3457, I–3528, 3538 (para. 65).

[102] Ibid, 3533 (para. 49).

Since it is in the trade mark owner's interest that consumers or end-users should not be led to believe that the owner is responsible for the repackaging, the ECJ said that the packaging should indicate both who manufactured the product,[103] and who repackaged it. That indication must be clearly shown on the repackaged product,[104] and be printed in such a way as to be understood by a person with normal eyesight, exercising a normal degree of attentiveness.[105] It is not necessary that a statement be made that the repackaging was carried out without the authorization of the trade mark owner.[106] In the *Playstation* case,[107] it was said that the statement 'this product has been opened to fit an adaptor to enable it to be used in the UK three-pin power sockets and to include an optional RFU adaptor repacked for Tesco Stores UK' was probably insufficient to discharge the onus on the importer/seller of dispelling any impression that the trade mark owner was responsible for it.

The ECJ also said that the trade mark owner must be given advance notice that the repackaged product is being put on sale.[108] The owner may also require that they be supplied with a specimen of the repackaged product before it goes on sale. This enables the owner to check that the repackaging does not affect the original condition of the product or damage the reputation of the trade mark. This also affords trade mark owners with a better opportunity to protect themselves against counterfeiting.[109]

In *Frits Loendersloot v. George Ballantine,* which concerned the relabelling of alcoholic drinks, the ECJ suggested that, while in the case of pharmaceuticals it was necessary for a parallel importer to comply with the requirements set out in *Bristol-Myers,* it might not be necessary to do so in the case of other goods.[110] The Court agreed that the various requirements were intended to reflect the legitimate interests of the trade mark owner with regard to pharmaceutical products. In the case of the parallel import of alcohol, the interests of the trade mark owner, particularly to combat counterfeiting, only required that the relabeller/importer provide them with advance notice that the relabelled products are to be put on sale.

In order for marketing of repackaged trade-marked goods to be permissible, the trade mark owner must be given notice, and provided with samples of the proposed packaging. In *Glaxo,* Laddie J had taken the view that, in the case of pharmaceutical marketing, this notice did not have to be provided directly by the parallel importer: it was sufficient if the Medical Controls Agency informed the trade mark owner.[111] The ECJ, agreeing with Advocate General Jacobs,[112] did not accept Laddie J's view. Rather, the Court said it is incumbent on the parallel importer itself to give notice.[113] Moreover, whereas Laddie J had suggested that a period of two–three days' notice would suffice, the ECJ preferred a longer time-frame. Having observed that the requirement for a period of notice and the requirement for samples were designed to enable the proprietor to protect its legitimate interests, the ECJ said that the notice period must provide the proprietor with 'a reasonable time to react to the intended repackaging'. The

---

[103] *Pfizer v. Eurim-Pharm,* Case 1/81 [1081] *ECR* 2913, 2926–7 (para. 11); *Bristol-Myers,* Joined Cases C–427/93 and C–429/93 [1996] *ECR* I–3457, I–3528, 3540 (para. 74).

[104] *Hoffmann-La Roche,* Case 102/77 [1978] *ECR* 1139, 1165 (para. 12); *Pfizer,* ibid, 2926–7 (para. 11); *Bristol-Myers,* Joined Cases C–427/93 and C–429/93 [1996] *ECR* I–3457, I–3528, 3539 (para. 71).

[105] Ibid (para. 71).   [106] Ibid (para. 72).

[107] *Sony v. Tesco,* [2000] *ETMR* 104, 109.

[108] *Hoffmann-La Roche,* Case 102/77 [1978] *ECR* 1139, 1165 (para. 12).

[109] *Bristol-Myers,* Joined Cases C–427/93 and C–429/93 [1996] *ECR* I–3457, I–3528, 3540–1 (para. 77).

[110] *Frits Loendersloot v. George Ballantine & Son,* Case C–349/95 [1997] *ECR* I–6227, 6261 (para. 48).

[111] [2000] FSR 529, 583–4, 586.

[112] Case C–143/00 Advocate General Jacobs, 12 Jul. 2001, paras. 131–3.

[113] Ibid, para. 64 (ECJ).

Advocate General had suggested three–four weeks, but the Court indicated that, on the evidence before it, were a sample provided along with the notice, a period of fifteen working days would be a reasonable time.[114] In *Boehringer Ingelheim (No. 2)*,[115] the ECJ indicated that it was for national authorities to provide proportionate and effective sanction for failure to comply with the requirement for notice, and that the trade mark owner's right to prevent importing of repackaged goods where no notice had been given was no different from its right to oppose 'spurious goods'.

Quality of packaging   Another factor that may influence whether a parallel importer falls outside Article 7(2)/section 12(2) relates to the standard of repackaging. In *Bristol-Myers*,[116] the ECJ recognized 'the possibility that the reputation of the trade mark and thus of its owner may nevertheless suffer from an inappropriate presentation of the repackaged product'.[117] This is particularly the case where the repackaging is defective, untidy, or poor quality. As such, the ECJ acknowledged that poor presentation might constitute a legitimate reason for the trade mark owner to object to the further circulation of the goods. The ECJ saw this as an element of the 'specific subject-matter' of the trade mark right.[118] However, the Court said that, when assessing whether the presentation of the repackaged product is liable to damage the reputation of the trade mark, it is necessary to take account of the nature of the product and its market.[119] In the case of pharmaceutical products that are marketed directly to the public, packaging could be crucial in maintaining or inspiring public confidence in the quality and integrity of the product. In these cases, defective, poor-quality, or untidy packaging could damage the trade mark's reputation.[120] However, where a pharmaceutical is sold to hospitals, the presentation of the product will be of little importance.[121] In the intermediate situation, where the product is sold on prescription through pharmacies, presentation may be important to consumers even though some degree of confidence in the quality of the product would flow from the fact that the products were only sold on prescription.[122]

In *Boehringer Ingelheim (No. 2)*,[123] the ECJ indicated that the condition that the reputation of the trade mark owner not be damaged was not limited to cases where the packaging is defective, of poor quality, or untidy.[124] Rather, the national court had to determine whether the trade mark owner's reputation would be damaged in cases of 'de-branding' (where, in repackaging, the parallel importer removes many of the manufacturer's trade marks) and 'co-branding' (where the parallel importer adds its own brand). On its return to the Court of Appeal,[125] Jacob LJ held that the question was one of fact—whether there is damage depends on how the co-branding or de-branding is done. Referring to the facts as originally found by Laddie J, the Court concluded that neither the co-branding nor the de-branding did any damage to the reputation of the claimants' marks.[126]

---

[114]   Ibid, para. 67 (ECJ). In *Glaxo v. Dowelhurst*, [2000] FSR 529, Laddie J favoured a period of 7 days for cases of relabelling, but this was overturned on appeal: [2004] *EWCA Civ* 129 (para. 127).

[115]   *Boehringer Ingelheim v. Swingward*, Case C–348/04 [2007] 2 *CMLR* (52) 1445 (para. 59).

[116]   *Bristol-Myers*, Joined Cases C–427/93 and C–429/93 [1996] *ECR* I–3457, I–3528, 3540 (para. 75); *Frits Loendersloot v. George Ballantine & Son*, Case C–349/95 [1997] *ECR* I–6227, 6255 (para. 29).

[117]   *Bristol-Myers*, 3540 (para. 75).   [118]   Ibid.

[119]   Ibid.   [120]   Ibid (para 76).   [121]   Ibid (para. 77).   [122]   Ibid.

[123]   *Boehringer Ingelheim v. Swingward*, Case C–348/04 [2007] 2 *CMLR* (52) 1445 (para. 38).

[124]   Ibid, (para. 41).

[125]   *Boehringer Ingelheim v. Swingward Ltd* [2008] *EWCA Civ* 83 (21 Feb 2008).

[126]   The case was not resolved, however, because of a pending reference to the ECJ in *Wellcome v. Paranova*, Case C–276/05, *OJ* 2005 C217/29.

8.2.3 Rebranding

Another situation where the trade mark owner may have a legitimate reason to restrict further dealings of goods bearing their trade mark arises where the parallel importer alters the mark. This issue was discussed by the ECJ in *Pharmacia & Upjohn v. Paranova*. This action arose from Upjohn marketing an antibiotic called clindamycin throughout the Community. Upjohn used the trade mark DALACIN in Denmark, Germany, and Spain, and the trade mark DALACINE in France. Paranova bought clindamycin capsules in France, which had been put on the market there by Upjohn under the DALACINE trade mark. Paranova bought the clindamycin with the intention of reselling the antibiotic in Denmark. In importing the drug into Denmark, Paranova sold it under the different name of DALACIN, the mark that Upjohn used in Denmark. As part of a trade mark infringement action brought by Upjohn against Paranova, the question arose as to whether Paranova could reaffix the mark in this manner. The issue was referred to the Court of Justice.[127]

The ECJ said that there is no 'objective difference between reaffixing a trade mark after repackaging and replacing the original trade mark by another which is capable of justifying the artificial partitioning being applied differently in each of these cases'.[128] As such, the question whether a parallel importer could reaffix trade marks was to be decided by the same principles that were set out in the *Bristol-Myers* decision. The ECJ noted that the trade mark rights in the importing state may allow the proprietor of the trade mark to prevent the mark being replaced. They also noted that the rights of the trade mark owner cannot be used, however, where they give rise to an artificial partitioning of the market between member states. The ECJ said that the question whether there had been an artificial partitioning of the market was to be decided in the way set out in *Bristol-Myers*. As such, the ECJ said that, to justify reaffixing a trade mark as Paranova had done, the parallel importer needs to be able to show that the circumstances prevailing at the time of marketing were such that it was objectively necessary for them to replace the original trade mark to ensure that the product in question could be placed on the market by the parallel importer. In so doing the ECJ made it clear that the suggestion that had been made in *American Home Products,* that to justify reaffixing the mark the parallel importer had to prove that the owner had a subjective intention to divide up the market, was not correct.[129]

While the question whether the relevant circumstances existed to justify rebranding was to be decided by national courts, the ECJ said that the 'condition of necessity' would be satisfied if, for example, consumer protection legislation prohibited use of the mark, or use of the mark was not allowed because it was misleading (here language differences between member states become important).[130] The ECJ added that the requisite 'conditions of necessity' did not exist, however, if the replacement of the trade mark was 'explicable solely by the parallel importer's attempt to secure a commercial advantage'.[131]

---

[127] Case C–379/97 [2000] 1 *CMLR* 51.   [128] Ibid, 82 (para. 37).

[129] *Centrafarm v. AHP,* Case 3/78 [1978] *ECR* 1823, 1841–2 (paras 21–3) (suggesting some subjective action to partition by the trade mark owner is required).

[130] Case C–379/97 [2000] 1 *CMLR* 51, 83 (para. 43). For cases before the German Supreme Court, see (2003) 34(5) *IIC* 559 (zantec/zantic).

[131] Ibid (para. 44).

8.2.4 Advertising the goods

Another situation where the trade mark owner may have a legitimate reason to restrict further dealings in relation to goods bearing their trade mark is where the goods are advertised. The situations where the owner may have legitimate reasons to restrict such advertisements were discussed by the ECJ in *Christian Dior v. Evora*.[132] Evora operated a chain of chemist shops in the Netherlands. While not officially appointed as an official distributor of Christian Dior products, the Evora shops sold Dior perfumes (such as DUNE and FAHRENHEIT) obtained by means of parallel imports. When Evora advertised that it was selling Dior products, Dior claimed that Evora had thereby infringed Dior's trade marks associated with the perfumes.

The ECJ said that the proprietor is able to object to such advertising if there are 'legitimate reasons' for doing so. The ECJ held that the damage done to the reputation of a trade mark through subsequent advertising may in principle be a legitimate reason within Article 7(2) to allow the proprietor to oppose further commercialization of goods which have been put on the market in the Community by them or with their consent.[133] After referring to the case law concerning the repackaging of trade-marked goods, the ECJ said that:

a balance must be struck between the legitimate interest of the trade mark owner in being protected against resellers using his trade mark for advertising in a manner which could damage the reputation of the trade mark and the reseller's legitimate interest in being able to resell the goods in question by using advertising methods which are customary in his sector of trade.[134]

In the case of prestigious luxury goods, resellers must endeavour to prevent their advertising from affecting the value of the trade mark by detracting from the allure and prestigious image of the goods in question, and from their aura of luxury.[135] However, if the reseller is merely employing techniques that are customarily used for goods of the kind but not necessarily of the same quality in issue, then an objection to such advertising is only legitimate if it '*seriously damages* the reputation of the trade mark'.[136] The Court suggested that this would occur if, in advertising goods bearing the mark, the trade mark was placed in a context which seriously detracted from the image which the trade mark owner had succeeded in creating around his or her trade mark.[137]

8.2.5 Competition Law: Parallel imports and Article 82

Given the rule on exhaustion within Europe, some pharmaceutical firms have sought to limit parallel trade by restricting the supply of drugs in low-priced markets. In *Syfait & Ors v. Glaxo Smith Kline plc*,[138] it was argued that the refusal of GSK to supply Greek wholesalers with more serevent than it regarded as necessary to meet demand in that market was an abuse of a dominant position. GSK argued that, given the regulatory context, in particular the fixing of drug prices in Greece, all it was doing was protecting its legitimate commercial interests: were it obliged to supply the Greek wholesalers, the ultimate effect would be that it would have to

---

[132] *Parfums Christian Dior SA v. Evora BV*, C–337/95 [1997] *ECR* I–6013. See Stothers, pp. 71–4.

[133] Ibid, 6048 (para. 43).   [134] Ibid, 6049 (para. 44).

[135] Ibid (para. 45).   [136] Ibid.

[137] Ibid, 6050 (para. 47). In *BMW v. Deenik*, Case C–63/97 [1999] 1 *CMLR* 1099, 1127 (para. 64) the ECJ added that, if there is no risk that the public will be led to believe that there is a commercial connection between the trader and the trade mark proprietor, the mere fact that the trader derived an advantage from using the mark (for example because the advertisements lend an aura of quality to their business) would not of itself mean that the use was dishonest.

[138] Case C–53/03 (31 May 2005). See Stothers, pp. 254–62.

supply the whole European market at the price set by the Greek authorities. The Greek competition authority referred several questions to the ECJ. Advocate General Jacobs, in a bold opinion, suggested that, while refusal to supply within the EU that was motivated by a desire to limit parallel imports would ordinarily amount to an abuse of a dominant position, it would not always do so. Whether such a refusal was an abuse needed to be assessed in its regulatory context, particularly having regard to the effect on consumers and purchasers. AG Jacobs clearly thought that the facts revealed a special situation where abuse should not be found. However, the ECJ declined to deal with the substantive issue, instead holding that the Greek competition authority was not a body that could make references. The Court, however, is being pressed to answer the question in Joined Cases C–468 to 78/06.[139]

8.3 PARALLEL IMPORT OF TRADE-MARKED GOODS AND COPYRIGHT IN LABELS

While a parallel importer may be entitled to relabel goods for resale, the question may arise as to whether the proprietor can prevent import by relying on any copyright they have in the label. Since the parallel importer would presumably reproduce and issue copies of such labels, there is a prima facie infringement of copyright.[140] Nevertheless, a different approach has been taken in relation to labels. This can be seen in *Christian Dior v. Evora*[141] where Christian Dior sought to rely on its copyright in the picture marks to prevent Evora from reproducing their marks on advertising leaflets. The ECJ held that in these circumstances 'the protection conferred by copyright as regards the reproduction of protected works in a reseller's advertising may not...be broader than that which is conferred on a trade mark owner in the same circumstances'.[142] The ECJ added that the holder of copyright may not oppose the use of a trade mark by a reseller who habitually markets articles of the same kind but not necessarily of the same quality as the protected goods unless it is established that the use of those goods seriously damages their reputation.[143]

8.4 INTERNATIONAL EXHAUSTION

The scope of Article 7 of the Trade Marks Directive and section 12 of the 1994 Act is confined to products placed on the market in the EEA.[144] It does not matter that the product bearing the mark has been manufactured in a non-member country if it has been lawfully put on the market in the member state from which it has been imported by the owner of the mark or with their consent.[145] Article 7 gives no explicit guidance as to what happens if the product is

---

[139] *Sot. Lelos kai Sia EE v. GlaxoSmithKline Anonimi Emporiki Viomikhaniki Etairia Farmakeftikon Proionton*, Case C–468/06 (pending).

[140] Moreover, the normal jurisprudence of the ECJ would protect those rights as forming the 'specific subject matter' of copyright. See Ch. 1.

[141] *Dior SA v. Evora BV*, Case C–337/95 [1997] *ECR* I–6013.

[142] Ibid, 6053 (para. 58).   [143] Ibid (para. 59).

[144] Since the rules differ so dramatically, it is important to know when goods are placed on the market in the EEA and when outside it. In *Glaxo Group v. Dowelhurst Ltd* [2004] *ETMR* (39) 528 Judge Prescott QC held that trade-marked anti–retroviral drugs had been placed on the market in the Community where they were sold and delivered to a party in France so that property had passed, even though there was an understanding that the purchaser was to resell them in Africa—'whether the transaction is wholesale or retail is irrelevant'.

[145] *Phytheron v. Bourdon*, Case C–352/95 [1997] *ECR* I–1729, I–1748, 1748 (para. 21).

imported from outside the EEA and has not yet been placed on the market in the EEA with the consent of the trade mark owner. It is to this issue that we now turn.

8.4.1 Background

Prior to the passage of the Directive, the question of international exhaustion was a matter for individual member states.[146] The Commission's original proposal would have imposed international exhaustion. That is, trade mark owners would not have been permitted to oppose the resale of products which had been put on the market with their consent anywhere in the world.[147] The Commission subsequently changed its view, and its amended proposal explicitly limited the exhaustion principle to goods that had been put on the market 'in the Community'.[148] This left unclear the position in relation to goods placed on the market outside the Community.[149]

8.4.2 *Silhouette v. Hartlauer*

This issue was addressed in *Silhouette International v. Hartlauer,*[150] where the ECJ was called upon to decide whether the principle of international exhaustion applied under the Directive.[151] Silhouette manufactured high-quality fashion spectacles which it distributed worldwide under the trade mark SILHOUETTE. The claimant was the registered proprietor for the mark in Austria and many other countries. Silhouette sold an out-of-date range of frames to a firm in Bulgaria. The defendant, Hartlauer, acquired the out-of-date frames from the Bulgarian firm and then imported them into Austria for resale.[152] Silhouette sought an order prohibiting Hartlauer from marketing the spectacles in Austria under its trade mark. They did this on the basis that the frames had not been put on the market in the EEA by it or with its consent. As such, they had not exhausted their trade mark rights. Silhouette argued that the Directive provides that such rights can be exhausted only by reason of marketing within the EEA.

The Supreme Court of Austria sought a ruling from the ECJ as to whether Community law requires member states to provide for exhaustion only when the goods have been marketed in the EEA, or whether member states may (or perhaps must) provide for exhaustion when the

---

[146] *EMI Records v. CBS United Kingdom,* Case 51/75 [1976] *ECR* 811, 845 (case law under Arts. 28–30 EC (formerly Arts. 30–6 of the Treaty) could not be transposed to imports from third countries).

[147] [1980] OJ C 351/80 Art. 6; for the Explanatory Memorandum, see COM(80) 635 final. Stothers, pp. 335–6.

[148] COM (84) 470 final of 31 Jul. 1984; [1985] *OJ C* 351, 4. Stothers, pp. 336–7. In *Silhouette International Schied v. Hartlauer Handelsgesellschaft,* Case C–355/96 [1998] 2 *CMLR* 953, 966 (para. 47) the Advocate General stated that 'no doubt considerations of commercial policy and concern about the possible lack of reciprocity were among the reasons why the provision for international exhaustion which featured in the Commission's original proposal was not maintained'.

[149] See citations in N. Shea, 'Does the First Trade Marks Directive Allow International Exhaustion of Rights?' [1995] *EIPR* 463, n. 6. Advocates of international exhaustion include F.-K. Beier, 'Industrial Property and the Free-Movement of Goods in the Internal European Market' (1990) 21 *IIC* 131; J. Rasmussen, 'The Principle of Exhaustion of Trade Mark Rights Pursuant to Directive 89/104 (and Regulation 40/94)' [1995] *EIPR* 174.

[150] Note 146 above. For commentary: A. Carboni, 'Cases about Spectacles and Torches: Now, Can We See the Light?' [1998] *EIPR* 471; Stothers, pp. 342–4.

[151] The question had already been decided differently by the EFTA court in *Mag Instrument v. California Trading Company Norway* [1998] 1 *CMLR* 331, Case E–2/97 (para. 28) where the court concluded that it was for each of the EFTA states to decide whether to introduce or maintain the principle of international exhaustion with regard to goods originating outside the EEA.

[152] See T. Hays and P. Hansen, '*Silhouette* is not the Proper Case Upon which to Decide the Parallel Importation Question' [1998] *EIPR* 277 (detailing factual background and arguing the case was one of re-importing).

goods have been marketed in a third country. Reaching the opposite conclusion to the EFTA court, the ECJ rejected the argument that the Directive left the member states free to provide for exhaustion in their national law. In the light of the first and ninth Recitals, the ECJ said that Articles 5 to 7 of the Directive must be construed as 'embodying a complete harmonization of the rules relating to the rights conferred by a trade mark'.[153] A single rule was also necessary to safeguard the functioning of the internal market. Given the terms of Article 7, the only plausible harmonized rule was that member states are obliged to confer on trade mark owners the ability to prevent imports of trade-marked goods from outside the EEA (even where the same trade mark owner has consented to that marketing).[154]

8.4.3 Consent

Although *Silhouette* made clear that member states were not to apply rules of international exhaustion, it took another ECJ decision to clarify the next logical question: what amounts to consent to import goods into the European Economic Area? In *Zino Davidoff*,[155] Laddie J asserted that even though, in principle, the trade mark owner has the right to stop importation into the EEA of goods not previously marketed in the EEA by or with his consent, this right cannot be used where the trade mark owner had consented to such import: and, remarkably, he held that, at least under English law, consent existed where the proprietor 'has agreed, expressly or otherwise to such entry, or he has, directly or otherwise, placed the goods in the hands of a third party under conditions which give the third party a right to distribute and onward sell them without restriction'. In effect, in the absence of full and explicit restrictions being imposed on the purchasers at the time of purchase, according to Laddie J a trade mark owner is treated as impliedly consenting to further distribution of those goods (including their import into the EEA). On the facts of the case, placing goods on the market in Singapore was sufficient consent to their import into the EEA.

The ECJ, following the logic of *Silhouette*, rejected Laddie J's approach.[156] First, it held that it was implicit from the Directive that there must be a harmonized concept of consent in this context.[157] Second, the ECJ held that consent need not be express but could be implied. Nevertheless, that consent must indicate an intention to renounce one's right to object to the import of the item into the EEA unequivocally.[158] Consequently, while in some cases consent could be inferred from facts and circumstances prior to, simultaneous with, or subsequent to the placing of goods on the market outside the EEA, consent could not be implied from the failure to express positively that goods were not to be imported into the EEA, or from silence. In effect, it will be very difficult for a parallel importer to persuade a court that consent exists in the absence of evidence of express agreement. One example might be a situation where the

---

[153] *Silhouette*, Case C–355/96 [1998] 2 *CMLR* 953, 977 (para. 25).

[154] The decision of the Court of Justice received a mixed response. It was variously described as 'a welcome relief for trade mark owners' and as bad news for consumers: C. Steele, 'Fortress Europe for Trade Mark Owners' (1998) (Aug.) *Trademark World* 14, 16.

[155] *Zino Davidoff v. A. & G. Imports* [1999] 3 *All ER* 711.

[156] Joined Cases C–414/99 and C–416/99 [2002] *Ch* 109; [2001] *ECR* I–8691; [2002] 1 *CMLR* 1. For commentaries, see Stothers, pp. 345–7; P. Dryberg and G.T. Petursson, 'What is Consent? A Note on Davidoff and Levi Strauss' (2002) 27 ELR 464 (generally approving of the decision); T. Aplin, 'The Scope of Consent in Article 7(1) of the Trade Marks Directive' (2002) 61 CLJ 531; N. Gross, 'Trade Mark Exhaustion: The Final Chapter' [2002] *EIPR* 93 (describing the decision as a clear victory for brand-owners); D. Kalley, '*Levi Strauss v. Tesco*: At A Difficult, Juncture of Competition, IP and Free Trade Policies' [2002] *ECLR* 193 (criticizing the narrow reasoning of the Court, especially its failure to consider competition and trade issues).

[157] Ibid, para. 43.   [158] Ibid, para. 45.

trade mark owner has known about and facilitated, but not objected to, a practice of importing trade-marked goods into the EEA.[159]

8.4.4 Proving consent

The *Davidoff* decision seemed to imply that a trader operating within the EEA who is faced with an allegation that the goods have been imported from outside the EEA, must be able to show that a trade mark proprietor has consented to the circulation of goods in the EEA. In *van Doren + Q GmbH v. lifestyle + sportswear Handelsgesellschaft mbH*,[160] the ECJ indicated that the issue of the onus of proof was one for member states, but that the national rule should not itself inhibit the free movement of goods within the EEA. Here, Stüssy Inc, a company based in California, owned the mark STÜSSYS for clothes and Van Doren were the exclusive distributors of the STÜSSY clothes for Germany. Lifestyle was selling STÜSSY clothes in Germany, and Van Doren claimed there was trade mark infringement. Van Doren alleged the goods came from the United States, whereas Lifestyle alleged it had sourced them in the EEA (so that the trade mark rights were exhausted), but refused to name its suppliers. Under German law it was for the defendant to prove exhaustion, though the Appeal Court had sought to place some onus on the claimant. The Bundesgerichtshof therefore asked the ECJ whether Article 28 EC required there to be an exception to the rule that the full burden of proof fall on the defendant. First, the Court held that the German rule of evidence is consistent with Community law, including Articles 5 and 7 of the Directive. However, the Court qualified this by stating that such a rule of evidence might need to be qualified where its application might lead to 'a real risk of partitioning of national markets'. In such circumstances, Article 28 EC requires the rule of evidence to be qualified, and instead, a national court should divide up the different matters to be proved. More specifically, the onus would first fall on the proprietor of the mark to prove that the goods were first marketed outside the EEA. It would then be for the parallel importer to prove consent to subsequent import of the products.

The ECJ gave an example of a situation where there could be such a risk of partitioning as to qualify the general approach, that is, where European marketing is by way of an exclusive distribution system. In such cases, the effect of requiring the parallel importer to prove consent is tantamount to requiring it to reveal its sources (and hence expose the breaches in the trade mark owner's exclusive distribution system). Such exposure would enable the trade mark proprietor to remove its leaky distributor from the supply chain and thus prevent the parallel importer from continuing to obtain supplies in this way. In such cases, therefore, the ECJ

[159] The courts have found implied consent in two cases: *Corporation Habanos SA v. Mastercigars* [2007] *EWCA Civ* 176 (trade mark owner supplied Cuban shops with cigars which were sold to defendant, who obtained permission to export) and *Honda Motor Co v. Naseem* [2008] *EWHC* 338 (Ch). But cf *Roche Products Ltd v. Kent Pharmaceutical* [2006] *EWCA Civ* 1775 (no consent when goods placed on market in Dominican Republic even though they bore the 'CE' mark, indicating regulatory approval had been granted for marketing in Europe); *Quiksilver v. Robertson* [2005] *FSR* (8) 126 (clothing manufactured in Turkey for sale to former Soviet republics had made way into EEA without consent of claimant); *Sony v. Nuplayer* [2006] *FSR* (9) 126 (prohibiting sale by D of game consoles sourced in Japan and sold from website). See also *Levi Strauss v. Tesco* [2002] 3 *CMLR* 11; [2002] *ETMR* (95) 1153 (Pumfrey J took the view that the rule against international exhaustion, though controversial, was a justifiable limitation on the right of private property in the public or general interest and was not a disproportionate or intolerable restriction on that right. Pumfrey J also thought the argument based on freedom of expression was 'devoid of any substance'. Finally, he found the argument that Art. 7 of the Directive conflicted with the Treaty to be 'hopeless'.)

[160] Case C–244/00 [2003] 2 *CMLR* (6) 203; [2003] *ETMR* (75) 922. The importance of this issue was highlighted by Thomas Hays: T. Hays, 'The Burden of Proof in Parallel Importation Cases' [2002] *EIPR* 353.

requires the trade mark proprietor to prove that the goods were marketed outside the EEA. It might do so by referring to batch numbers, or other characteristics which demonstrate that first marketing was outside the EEA.

8.4.5 Competition rules

Finally, it should be noted that there are certain unresolved issues concerning the inter-relationship between European trade mark policy and European competition law, particularly Article 81 EC. The relevance of the latter was made clear by the ECJ in the *Javico v. Yves St Laurent* decision.[161] There, Yves St Laurent sought to terminate a distribution contract with Javico under which Javico undertook to sell products only in Russia and the Ukraine, because it had been discovered that some of the products had found their way to the United Kingdom. The Cour d'Appel of Versailles sought the advice of the ECJ as to whether such a contract might be prohibited by Article 81. The ECJ held that the agreement had as its object the restriction of competition, so the key question was whether it was capable of affecting trade between member states. If the agreement specifically prohibited imports into the EEA, it would have as its object the restriction of competition in the EEA and would be likely to be void. However, here the contract specified there were to be no sales outside the territory (whether to the EEA or not). Consequently, the Court said the question was what was the 'effect' of the agreement. This involved assessing the economic context, particularly the relative position and import-ance of the parties on the market in question. However, if the effects were insignificant, the contract would be outside the prohibition and hence valid. If the Community market is oli-gopolistic, or the price differentials are significant, it is necessary to examine the likely impact of the disputed contract. If the market outside the Community is relatively small compared to that within the Community, the impact is likely to be insignificant. However, assessing such matters is the task of national courts.

While, in *Silhouette,* the ECJ has clearly indicated trade marks law should enable a proprietor to keep legitimate goods first marketed outside the EEA out of the market, when examining competition policy the ECJ in *Javico* has suggested that agreements which prohibit marketing in the EEA are contrary to Article 81 EC (formerly Article 85 of the Treaty). The two policies are in conflict, and the likely reconciliation is through a limited application of *Javico.* In any case, *Davidoff* reduces the likely application of *Javico* for two reasons: first, because the def-inition of consent (and onus of proof issues) means that the trade mark proprietor need not support his trade mark rights through contractual prohibitions on import into the EEA, and so can avoid Article 81 (which applies to agreements rather than unilateral acts).[162] Second, because even if a contract selling goods outside the EEA obliges the purchaser not to resell within the EEA, it is arguable that such a clause has no effect on competition over and above that attributable to the proprietor's rights under trade marks law.[163]

8.4.6 Reform?

Following the *Silhouette* decision, the European Commission raised the question of reform of the rules relating to international exhaustion. It commissioned a study of the economic

---

[161] *Javico International and Javico AG v. Yves St Laurent Parfums SA,* Case C–306/96 [1998] *ECR* I–1983.

[162] T. Heide, 'Trade Marks and Competition Law after Davidoff' [2003] *EIPR* 163; 'End of the Road for International Exhaustion?' [2003] (July) *Managing Intellectual Property* 94.

[163] Commission Staff Working Paper, *Possible abuses of trade mark rights within the EU in the context of Community Exhaustion,* SEC (2003) 575 (21 May 2003) (finding current legal position to be satisfactory).

effects of changing to international exhaustion, which, in turn, indicated that the issues were complex (there might be effects not just on pricing, but also on matters such as product quality or after-sales services), but that the price benefits to consumers of changing the regime would probably be limited (in some sectors up to 2 per cent).[164] The Commission then consulted widely with member states and interested parties, mooting various possible options, such as having international exhaustion only for certain products (for example, excluding pharmaceuticals and sound recordings).[165] However, in May 2000, Commissioner Bolkestein informed the ministers at a meeting of the Internal Market Council that the Commission did not propose any action in this field.

9   OTHER DEFENCES: TRANSITIONAL AND GENERAL

The proprietor of an existing trade mark registered under the Trade Marks Act 1938 is given the benefit of the extended rights contained in sections 9 to 12 of the 1994 Act. Transitional provisions in Schedule 3, paragraph 4(2) state that it is not an infringement of such a mark 'to continue after commencement any use which did not amount to infringement of the existing registered mark under the old law'. Insofar as the rights contained in sections 9 and 10 are broader, or the defences contained in sections 11 and 12 are narrower, care must be taken as regards continued use of old marks. For example, a person who continues to use a mark for dissimilar goods, who would now be liable under section 10(3), is able to continue such use after 31 October 1994. The defendant must demonstrate continuous use, though a small hiatus in a long use may be ignored.[166] The defence is not confined to precisely the same use, but will not cover uses which are 'different in kind': thus non-infringing use of a mark in advertising prior to 1994 was held not to justify use on a web site after 1997.[167]

---

[164] National Economic Research Associates/SJ Berwin, *The Economic Consequences of the Choice of Regime of Exhaustion in the Area of Trade Marks* (Final Report for DG XV of the European Commission) (Feb. 1999).

[165] Select Committee on Trade and Industry, 8th Report, *Trade Marks, Fakes and Consumers* (8 Jul. 1999).

[166] *Daimler Chrysler v. Alavi* [2001] *RPC* (42) 813, 845 (paras. 96–8).

[167] Ibid.

42

EXPLOITATION AND USE OF
TRADE MARKS

CHAPTER CONTENTS

1 INTRODUCTION

Given that the law of registered trade marks developed from the law of passing-off, it is not surprising that it has long carried with it limitations derived from the law of passing-off. One such limitation is that passing-off does not protect property in the mark. Instead, it protects traders against misrepresentations affecting a distinct proprietary interest, namely, 'goodwill'. While this limitation has gradually been removed from the law of registered trade marks (trade marks are now treated as forms of property in their own right),[1] the law relating to the exploitation of trade marks has yet to embrace wholeheartedly the idea that a trade mark is an asset over which its proprietor should have full control.[2] Although it is now common practice for trade marks to be included on the balance sheet of companies,[3] the law still imposes a number of restrictions on the use that can be made of marks. We begin this chapter by looking at the ownership of trade marks, focusing in particular on the problems that arise in relation to co-ownership. After going on to look at the ways in which trade marks can be exploited, we will focus on the limitations placed on the uses that can be made of a trade mark.

Before examining these matters in more detail, it is worth observing that, while the exploitation of British trade marks is governed by the Trade Marks Act 1994, the Community Trade

---

[1] TMA s. 22 (personal property); CTMR, Art. 16 (an object of property). For a history of the same trend in the USA, see L. Johnston, 'Drifting Towards Trademark Rights in Gross' (1985) 85 *TM Rep* 19.

[2] The White Paper, *Reform of Trade Marks Law*, Cm. 1203, paras. 4.34–39 seemed to indicate acceptance of the view that it is in the proprietor's best interests that the mark is fully and properly exploited, and thus that legal regulation or restriction of such actions should be kept to a minimum. K. Lupton, 'Trade Marks as Property' (1991) 2 *Australian Intellectual Property Journal* 29.

[3] B. Sherman and M. Power, 'Law, Accounting and the Emergent Positivity of Intangible Property' (1994) 3 *Social and Legal Studies* 477. P. Cussons, 'Trade Marks on the Balance Sheet', in D. Campbell, H. Harmeling, E. Keyzer (eds.), *Trademarks: Legal and Business Aspects* (1994), 235.

Mark Regulation only sets out a partial code for dealing with Community marks. In the absence of harmonized Community laws on transfers, assignments, security interests, testamentary dispositions, and insolvency, the drafters of the Regulation decided that the most appropriate approach would be for transactions in relation to Community Trade Marks to be governed by the laws of the most closely connected member state. As a result, transactions of Community marks will normally be dealt with by the laws of the country in which the proprietor has their seat or domicile on the relevant date.[4]

2 OWNERSHIP

2.1 PROPRIETORSHIP

The owner of a trade mark is the person who registers it.[5] In contrast with patent law, which recognizes the concept of the 'inventor' and 'person entitled' as entities which have an existence prior to (and thus independently of) the application for a patent, the 1994 Act does not recognize that a trade mark may have a proprietor before an application is made. In short, the Act treats the first person to register as the proprietor; and the only proprietor is the registered proprietor. Where there is competition as to who should be entitled to a trade mark, those disputes are decided by reference to the relative grounds for invalidity, and by the requirement that all applications be made in good faith.

2.2 CO-OWNERSHIP

One potential problem which arises in the exploitation of a trade mark is when the mark is owned by two or more parties. In these circumstances, the question arises as to whether one co-owner can utilize the trade mark without the consent of other co-owners. Where there is no contract between two or more co-owners of a trade mark, the Trade Marks Act 1994 declares that each of the co-owners is 'entitled to an equal undivided share in the registered trade mark'.[6] This means that each owner is permitted 'by himself or his agents, to do for his own benefit and without the consent of or the need to account to the other or others, any act which would otherwise amount to an infringement of the registered trade mark'.[7] The power and immunity given to each co-proprietor is limited because, without the consent of the other co-owner(s), the joint owner cannot license others to use the trade mark.[8]

Two points are worth noting about the co-ownership of trade marks. The first is that the position with regard to co-ownership of Community marks is unclear. Article 16 refers to 'joint' proprietorship, which has been taken by some to be a reference to the fact that they hold as joint tenants rather than as tenants in common.[9] However, since the aim of Article 16 is to determine the national laws under which dealings in a mark fall to be assessed, the better view

---

[4] CTMR, Art. 16(1). See also Art. 20(2) (levy of execution). Cf. Art. 21(1) (applicable rules on bankruptcy are to be those of the state in which proceedings are first brought).

[5] In fact, an application is itself regarded as an object of property which can be transferred and has value, and is even protected as property under the European Convention on Human Rights. See *Anheuser-Busch v Portugal*, Appn No 73049/01 (11 Jan 2007), [2007] *EHRR* (36) 830, [2007] *ETMR* (24) 343.

[6] TMA s. 23.   [7] TMA s. 23(3).   [8] TMA s. 23(4).

[9] Annand and Norman (1998), 237.

is that, if the first-named joint proprietor is from the United Kingdom, the UK provisions on joint ownership apply. That is, the joint proprietors are deemed to be tenants in common.

The second point is that co-ownership of trade marks presents the possibility of two distinct traders using the same mark simultaneously in relation to the same categories of goods. Although this is unlikely in the normal course of events, such a situation is quite plausible where, for example, when a partnership breaks down: a disgruntled co-owner might use the same mark on goods of a lower quality. With formerly related but now unrelated businesses selling goods under the same sign, the rules on co-ownership are likely to create confusion in the marketplace.[10] Given that this is exactly the sort of confusion which trade marks law is designed to prevent, it might be questioned why the Trade Marks Act 1994 preferred this form of co-ownership. Perhaps it was foreseen that, because such fragmented use of the same sign might render the mark liable to revocation, the co-owners were likely to reach a solution that minimized consumer confusion and thus protect the mark.[11]

3 MODES OF EXPLOITATION

Trade marks and trade mark applications can be exploited in a number of different ways.[12] Perhaps the most common technique is for owners to exploit the mark themselves. Trade marks may also be assigned, licensed, mortgaged, or devolve by operation of law (notably through death or bankruptcy).[13] We will look at each in turn.

3.1 SELF-EXPLOITATION

One of the most common ways trade marks are used is for the owner to exploit the mark themselves. Often this will involve the owner making the goods, applying the mark, and selling the goods. While trade mark owners may do all of these acts themselves, they often use third parties. For example, a trade mark owner will use goods manufactured by someone else, a 'contract manufacturer', to which they apply their marks. In these circumstances, the mark is not used to indicate that the goods were manufactured by the trade mark owner. Instead, the mark indicates that the goods were selected and approved by the trade mark owner.[14] By and large, such relationships are not problematic. However, if they break down, for example, through bankruptcy or failure to meet contractual stipulations, difficulties may arise in determining whether parties other than the trade mark owner can sell the goods that have been marked with the trade mark proprietor's consent.[15]

Trade mark proprietors use a number of strategies when placing their goods on the market. In many instances, they will be happy for the goods to reach the market by any means. In other

---

[10] J. T. McCarthy, 'Joint Ownership of a Trademark' (1983) 73 *TM Rep* 1.

[11] For other criticisms of the provision on tenancy in common, see Annand and Norman (1994), 189–90.

[12] For a discussion of the many issues that may arise in the exploitation of trade marks, see N. Wilkof, *Trade Mark Licensing* (2005).

[13] TMA s. 24(1); CTMR Art. 21 (bankruptcy).

[14] Indeed, Millett J has noted that a trade mark owner 'may have the components made by one company, assembled by another, the trade mark affixed by a third and the goods marketed by a fourth'. *Accurist Watches v. King* [1992] *FSR* 80, 88.

[15] As in *Accurist Watches,* ibid (sale by manufacturer in exercise of retention of title clause); Wilkof, *Trade Mark Licensing*, ch. 8.

cases, however, to maintain the allure of the product they may wish to restrict distribution to particular persons. This is the case with perfumes, which many manufacturers have deemed unsuitable for sale in certain kinds of outlet, such as supermarkets.[16]

Once the goods are on the market in the EEA, the rights of the trade mark owner are exhausted. Usually, therefore distributors of the trade-marked goods do not need permission to sell goods bearing the mark. A trade mark owner may, however, wish to control certain uses of the mark by such a distributor. As we noted in Chapter 41, there will be limitations on the ways in which the distributor may use the mark in advertising, and as regards any alteration of the goods.

3.2 ASSIGNMENT

An assignment is a transfer of ownership of the trade mark (or application). As a result of an assignment, the assignee stands in the shoes of the assignor and is entitled to deal with the trade mark as they please. In contrast with a licence where the licensor retains an interest in the trade mark, once a trade mark owner has assigned the trade mark they no longer have any interest in, or responsibility to maintain, the trade mark.[17]

Assignments of trade marks can occur without any corresponding transfer of business or goodwill.[18] This is a critical difference between passing-off and registered trade marks. An owner of an unregistered mark can only assign the benefit of the mark by assigning the goodwill of the business with which it has been used. This common-law distrust of the trading in marks reflects the understanding that marks are protected because they operate in the consumers' eyes as indications of source. Following this logic, if assignments were allowed it would create confusion as to the source of the goods or services. With registered trade marks being treated more and more as assets, this rationale for restricting assignments carries less weight.

An assignment can be made in part or in a limited manner. A national trade mark may be assigned in relation to part of the goods and services for which the mark is registered, limited in the manner of its use,[19] or geographically (subject to compliance with the Treaty of Rome).[20] In contrast, a Community trade mark must be dealt with 'in its entirety, and for the whole area of the Community'.[21]

In order for an assignment to be valid, it must be in writing and signed by the assignor. In the case of a Community mark, the assignment must be signed by all the parties to the transaction.[22] In situations where the trade mark or application is owned by more than one party, each co-owner can only assign their share and then only if the others consent to such an assignment.[23] It follows that a full assignment of a mark would require the cooperation and signatures of all co-owners. While the assignment does not need to be registered to be effective, there are a number of advantages that follow from registration: these are reviewed below. With respect to the assignment of Community marks, the OHIM is obliged not to register any transfer which is likely to mislead the public as to the nature, quality, or geographical origin of the goods or services in respect of which it is registered. In contrast, the UK Registry has relinquished even a minimal supervisory role.[24]

[16] Wilkof., ch. 7.   [17] TMA s. 24; CTMR, Art. 24.

[18] TMA s. 24(1); CTMR, Art. 17. The change was first brought about in the UK by TMA 1938, s. 22.

[19] TMA s. 24(2).   [20] TMA s. 24(2)(b).   [21] CTMR, Art. 16(1).

[22] TMA s. 24(3) (must be signed by assignor); CTMR, Art. 17(3) (must be signed by parties to the contract).

[23] TMA s. 23(4).

[24] For refusal of transfer to be justified such deception must be clear from the transfer documents. Moreover, the OHIM should accept the transfer insofar as the transferee agrees to limit registration of the Community

3.3 VOLUNTARY LICENCES

Another common mode of exploitation is for a trade mark owner to grant a licence which enables others to carry out specified activities in relation to the mark. The licensing of trade marks, which facilitates merchandising, franchising, and distribution agreements more generally, is at the heart of a multi-billion pound industry,[25] that 'pervades the way…goods and services are distributed, marketed and sold, both domestically and internationally'.[26] At a basic level, a licence is merely a permission to do an act that would otherwise be prohibited without the consent of the trade mark owner. A licence enables the licensee to use the trade mark for specified goods or services without infringing. So long as the use falls within the terms of the licence, the licensee is immune from an action by the trade mark owner.[27] For the most part, the terms of a voluntary licence are up to the parties to determine and thus will depend on the needs, capacities, and wishes of the parties.[28]

However, under trade mark law a licence amounts to much more than a mere permission to use a mark. In the absence of an agreement to the contrary, a trade mark licence binds a successor in title to the grantor's interest.[29] In addition, the 1994 Act enables a licensee of a trade mark to enforce their rights against third parties.[30] Given the almost proprietary nature of a trade mark licence,[31] it is not surprising that the law requires the licence to be in writing for it to be 'effective'.[32] A licence need not be registered to be valid as against the licensor, but there are several advantages from registration, which are discussed below.[33]

Licences may take many forms: from a one-off permission through to an exclusive licence. Licences[34] (even of Community Trade Marks) may be limited geographically,[35] temporally, in relation to particular goods or services, or as to manner of use.[36]

Of the different forms of licence, perhaps the most significant (in terms of law, at least), is the 'exclusive licence'. An exclusive licence is an agreement according to which the registered proprietor of a trade mark not only confers permission on the licensee to use the trade mark, but also promises that they will not grant any other licences and that they will not exploit the mark themselves.[37] The legal consequence of this is that an exclusive licence confers a right in respect of the trade mark *to the exclusion of all others including the licensor*. In some ways it is the intangible property's equivalent to a 'lease'.[38]

---

mark to goods or services in respect of which it is registered: CTMR, Art. 17(4). In addition, under Art. 17(2) of the Regulation a presumption exists that a transfer of the whole of an undertaking includes the transfer of the Community Trade Mark.

[25] G. Battersby and C. Grimes, 'Merchandising Revisted' (1986) 76 *TM Rep* 271, 275.

[26] Wilkof, *Trade Mark Licensing*, 1.

[27] *Sport International v. Inter Footwear* [1984] 2 *All ER* 321.

[28] If provision is made for such action, the law recognizes that a licensee may grant sublicences. TMA s. 28(4).

[29] TMA s. 28(3); CTMR Art. 23(1). But note Art. 23(2).   [30] TMA s. 30; CTMR Art. 22(3).

[31] See Wilkof, *Trade Mark Licensing*, ch. 12. For discussion of the distinction between licences and proprietary interests in the context of relief from forfeiture see esp. paras. 12.43–55, 278–84.

[32] TMA s. 28(2). Presumably the law will continue to recognize implied licences and oral consents, as well as to apply the traditional principles relating to estoppel.

[33] Where there are joint proprietors, all of them must consent to any licence: TMA s. 23(4)(a).

[34] TMA 28(1)(b); TM Dir. Art. 8(1); CTMR Art. 22(1).

[35] TMA s. 28(1)(b); CTMR Art. 22(1).   [36] TMA s. 28(1).

[37] TMA s. 29(1). See *Scandecor International v. Scandecor Marketing* [2002] *FSR* 122 (para. 14).

[38] For an analogy between a franchise agreement and a lease of 'goodwill' see *Kall-Kwik Printing (UK) v. Frank Clarence Rush* [1996] *FSR* 114.

An exclusive licence confers powers on the licensee that are equivalent to those of an assignee.[39] Undoubtedly the most significant aspect of this is that, unlike a mere licensee,[40] an exclusive licensee can sue infringers without having to persuade the proprietor to take action on their behalf.[41] An exclusive licensee is given the same rights as an assignee and therefore has the right to bring proceedings in respect of any infringement that occurs after the date of the licence agreement. Indeed, an action can be brought by both the trade mark proprietor and an exclusive licensee.[42] The statute provides guidance where concurrent rights exist.[43]

Although the law distinguishes between bare, contractual, and exclusive licences, commercial dealings are less precise in the way the term 'licence' is used. Indeed it has been said that 'both business executives and lawyers use the word "licence" indiscriminately and conclude agreements they call "licences" when no licence is really necessary'.[44] From a commercial point of view, it is possible to characterize licences and similar arrangements in a more functional manner as product trade mark licences, franchise agreements, and distributorship agreements.[45]

Under a 'product trade mark licence', the licensee will manufacture the product and be permitted to apply the mark to it. This often occurs with character merchandising, and also with the manufacture of many products (such as soft drinks, where the trade mark owner supplies the syrup but the licensee makes up, bottles, and sells the drink). Product trade mark licences are also often linked to licences of patents and technology.

It has been said that franchising accounts for a third of the United Kingdom retail turnover.[46] Under a franchise agreement, the franchisor provides the framework within which the franchisee operates. While the nature of the agreement varies from case to case, the franchisor effectively provides the shell within which the business operates. The franchisor may provide things such as the corporate image (including the mark), the advertising, training, premises, know-how, and support service.[47] Familiar examples of franchises include PRONUPTIA's wedding attire, KALL-KWIK photocopying shops, and PIERRE VICTOIRE restaurants.[48]

A 'distribution agreement' is merely a means by which a producer regulates how their goods reach the market.[49] Although distribution agreements are not usually trade mark licences, such agreements may include clauses requiring the distributor to sell the goods under the producer's trade mark in a manner specified by the producer. Alternatively, they may require a licensee to use particular distributor's marks.[50] In order to protect the reputation of the brand, a supplier may restrict distribution to certain specialist shops: a recent example has been the refusal of perfume manufacturers to supply supermarkets.

---

[39] TMA s. 31(1).   [40] For the position of a mere licensee, see TMA s. 28(2)–(5).
[41] TMA s. 31(1).   [42] TMA s. 31(2).   [43] TMA s. 31(4)–(8).

[44] R. Joliet, 'Trademark Licensing Agreements under the EEC Law of Competition' (1983–4) 5 *Northwestern Journal of International Law and Business* 755, 765.

[45] Ibid, 765–6.

[46] M. Abell, 'Clouds on the Horizon for Franchisors in the EU' (1998) (Aug.) *Trademark World* 34.

[47] *Kall-Kwik v. Rush* [1996] *FSR* 114.

[48] Franchises have been subdivided into three categories: 'service franchise agreements' which concern the supply of services (e.g. KALL-KWIK); 'production' or 'industrial franchise agreements' which concern the manufacturing of goods; and 'distribution franchise agreements', which involve the sale of goods (e.g. PRONUPTIA).

[49] In some circumstances, distribution franchises can share many facets of distribution agreements. Joliet, 'Trademark Licensing Agreements under the EEC Law of Competition', 764–5.

[50] *Consten & Grundig v. EC Commission*, Case C–56/64 [1966] *CMLR* 418.

3.4 MORTGAGES

Like other forms of property, trade marks may be used as security for a debt.[51] This can be a useful technique to enable the proprietors of trade marks to raise funds. One form of such security is the legal mortgage, which involves an assignment of the trade mark by the trade mark owner (mortgagor–borrower) to the mortgagee–lender. This is subject to a condition that the trade mark will be reassigned to the mortgagor when the debt is repaid (or as the law says 'on redemption'). It is important that the assignment reserves for the mortgagor a right to continue using the trade mark. This is probably best achieved by reservation of an exclusive licence.[52] An alternative form of security is to subject the trade mark to a 'charge',[53] in which case there is no assignment. Instead, the chargee gains certain rights over the trade mark. In the case of both forms of security, to be valid the transaction must be in writing and signed by the parties.[54] Where there are joint proprietors, all of them must consent to the grant of a security interest.[55] While such an interest need not be registered to be valid, there are advantages from registration which are reviewed below.

3.5 TESTAMENTARY DISPOSITIONS

Because a trade mark is personal property, it is capable of passing on the death of the proprietor either by will or according to the rules applicable in cases of intestacy. In the case of the death of one co-owner, because they hold the trade mark as tenants in common (rather than as joint tenants),[56] the share of the deceased co-owner passes along with the rest of its estate rather than accruing to the other co-owners. In devolving the trade mark, the personal representative must sign a written assent. It appears that a Community Trade Mark will pass in accordance with the laws of the country in which the proprietor was domiciled at their death.[57]

3.6 REGISTRATION OF INTERESTS AND TRANSACTIONS

We observed earlier that trade mark registration performs a number of different functions.[58] It helps to overcome difficulties in proving the existence of goodwill, allocates priorities between competing traders wishing to secure rights over a particular trade mark, and acts as a repository of information which alerts third parties who might independently wish to use the same or a similar mark about the proprietor's rights. While in the past another, perhaps the chief, concern of registration (particularly of trade mark licences) was to restrict trafficking in marks (and thus to protect consumers from deception), under the 1994 Act the supervisory role of the Registrar has been reduced to virtually nothing. As a result, registration is now primarily concerned with providing public information and securing priorities between competing rights holders, or as the White Paper put it, with 'legal transparency'.[59]

Although legal transparency might be an admirable goal, because there is no statutory obligation to register marks or transactions therewith, and indeed transactions are valid in

---

[51] TMA s. 24(4); CTMR, Art. 19(1). See further: Morcom *et al.*, para. 11.1; C. Smith, 'Trade Marks as Collateral in the United Kingdom', in Campbell, Harmeling, and Keyzer (eds.), *Trademarks: Legal and Business Aspects*, 247.

[52] Ibid, 250–2 (advising that the legal mortgage technique be avoided).

[53] TMA s. 24(5).   [54] TMA s. 24(3)–(5).   [55] TMA s. 23(4).

[56] TMA s. 23(1).   [57] CTMR, Art. 1(a).   [58] See above at p. 781.

[59] White Paper, *Reform of Trade Marks Law*, Cm. 1203, para. 4.38.

the absence of registration, the register cannot be said to operate as a 'mirror' of legal rights over commercial signs in the way the Land Registration system purports to be a reflection of proprietary rights over real property. Nevertheless, the usefulness of the Register is ensured because of the existence of incentives for parties to transactions in marks to enter them on the Register. This is because, as unregistered transactions are vulnerable to later dealings, it is highly advisable to register them immediately.[60] Registrable transactions are listed in section 25(2) as assignments, the making of assents, the granting of securities, and the grant of licences.[61] Notice of trusts may not be registered.[62]

While similar transactions may be registered on the UK Register and at the OHIM, the consequences of failing to register a transaction differ between the two regimes. As such, they will be considered separately. Registration of transactions with regards to UK marks at the UK office has three distinct effects. First, registration ensures that the interest of the registrant survives further inconsistent transactions in relation to the mark. More specifically, section 25(3) states that an unregistered transaction is 'ineffective' as against a person acquiring a conflicting interest in or under the mark in ignorance of it.[63] Second, as regards licences, registration enables the licensee to acquire the full scope of available rights and remedies.[64] Third, costs in an unsuccessful infringement action are withheld from assignees and licensees who do not register promptly, that is within six months of the transaction, as regards any acts of infringement that occur prior to registration.[65]

According to the Community Trade Mark Regulation, similar consequences flow from non-registration of transactions affecting Community marks. Article 23 states that transfers, grants of security, and licences of Community marks shall only have effect *vis-à-vis* third parties after entry in the Register, unless that third party knew of the relevant transaction at the date on which they acquired their interest. The effect of levies of execution and bankruptcy on third parties are matters for the law of the relevant member states.

A special incentive to register is placed on transferees of Community marks. According to Article 17(6), as long as the transfer has not been entered in the OHIM, the successor may not invoke the rights arising from registration of the Community Trade Mark. It is important to note that the OHIM must not register any transfer that is likely to mislead or deceive the public as to the nature, quality, or geographical origin of the goods or services in respect of which it is registered.[66] For refusal of a transfer to be justified, the deception must be clear from the transfer documents. Moreover, the OHIM should accept the transfer insofar as the transferee agrees to limit the registration of the Community mark to goods or services in respect of which it is registered.

---

[60] See Wilkof, *Trade Mark Licensing*, chs. 3 and 4.

[61] The Community Trade Mark Regulation provides that on request of one of the parties the following shall be entered on the register and published: a transfer, security, levy of execution, licence (or transfer thereof): CTMR, Arts. 17(5), 19(2), 20(3), 21(2), 22(5).

[62] TMA s. 26.

[63] The effect of this can be illustrated as follows: A assigns the trade mark to B on 1 Jul. 1998, and A then licenses the trade mark to C on 1 Aug. 1998; B had not registered the assignment, and C had no knowledge of it on 1 Aug. B is bound by C's licence. See Wilkof, *Trade Mark Licensing*, 58.

[64] TMA s. 25(3)(b).

[65] TMA s. 25(4) as amended by SI 2006/1028, Sch. 2, para. 17. This corresponds to PA s. 68, discussed above at pp. 573–4.

[66] CTMR Art. 17(4).

3.7 COMPULSORY LICENCES

In contrast with other areas of intellectual property law such as designs, copyright, and patents, there are no compulsory licences in relation to trade marks.[67]

4 LIMITS ON EXPLOITATION

The terms and conditions under which a trade mark is exploited are usually determined contractually by the parties: the Trade Marks Act 1994 merely provides a shell within which parties are able to manoeuvre. Where parties have agreed upon the way a trade mark is to be exploited, the law has been loath to substitute its view of what should have been agreed. Having said this, as with all forms of intellectual property law, the power conferred by trade mark law on a proprietor is limited in a number of ways.

The restrictions imposed by British trade mark law are changing. Whereas the law previously imposed a number of impediments on the licensing of marks, after the liberalization effected by the 1994 Act, the major restriction on licensing arises through the operation of the revocation provisions contained in section 46.[68] This is because if the terms or extent of the licensing (or assignment) are such that the mark becomes deceptive, the registration may be revoked. As a result, in exploiting a trade mark, the proprietor should take care to ensure the mark does not become deceptive or generic. In order to avoid the mark becoming deceptive, trade mark owners would be wise to include quality control provisions in any licences they grant, and to operate some sort of monitoring policy to ensure that those standards are complied with.

Another important limitation placed on the use that can be made of a trade mark is provided by UK and European competition law. In the next section we outline the general nature of these regulations, before considering the ways in which these regimes treat a selection of commonly used trade mark licence terms.

4.1 EC COMPETITION LAW

The key provision of European competition law affecting trade mark licences and exploitation agreements is Article 81 EC (formerly Article 85 of the EC Treaty). This renders void all agreements that affect trade between member states and which have the object or effect of preventing, restricting, or distorting competition within the Common Market. The issue of whether an element in an agreement 'restricts trade' is usually looked at by the Commission in terms of whether it restricts the activities of the parties to the agreement (or third parties) to an 'appreciable extent'.[69]

---

[67] But note *Der Grüne Punkt–Duales System Deutschland AG v. Commission*, T–151/01R (15 Nov. 2001) (Commission order allowing use of collective mark) (on appeal to the ECJ on this and other issues, Case C–385/07 P).

[68] See at pp. 911–13.

[69] This is often called 'freedom of action theory' and has been widely criticized as casting the prohibition too broadly. The Court e.g. in *Javico v. Yves Saint Laurent*, Case C–306/96 [1998] *ECR* I–1983 (paras. 23–6), has tended to look at the effect in the market, and has treated a number of agreements as falling outside Art. 81(1) because they are objectively necessary for particular kinds of transactions. For discussion, see N. Green, 'Article 85 of the EC Treaty in Perspective: Stretching Jurisdiction, Narrowing the Concept of a Restriction and Plugging a Few Gaps' [1988] *ECLR* 190; H. P. Lugard, 'Vertical Restraints under EC Law: A Horizontal

For minor agreements, the Commission has issued a Notice on Agreements of Minor Importance, which treats agreements between firms who are not competitors as falling outside of Article 81(1) if the market share held by each of the parties does not exceed 15 per cent on any of the relevant markets affected by the agreement. This does not apply, however, where those agreements contain provisions relating to resale price-fixing or territorial protection.[70]

Even if an agreement falls within the Article 81 EC (formerly Article 85 ECT) prohibition, it may nonetheless fall within one of the block exemptions issued by the Commission. The two block exemptions that are relevant relate to:

(i)   technology transfer agreements (Block Exemption 772/2004);[71]

(ii) vertical agreements (Block Exemption 2790/1999).[72]

We have considered the Technology Transfer Regulation in Chapter 22. Here it should be noted that the Technology Transfer Regulation only applies where trade marks are ancillary to the main purpose of the agreement, namely, the licensing of patents or know-how.[73] If trade marks are a central component, the agreement cannot fall within the Block Exemption.[74] However, much more important for trade mark licences is the Commission Regulation 2790/99 on the application of Article 81(3) of the Treaty to Categories of Vertical Agreements and Concerted Practices.[75] The idea behind this block exemption is that vertical restraints often have positive consequences by increasing interbrand competition and are only anti-competitive in limited circumstances such as where the supplier has a high level of market power. Consequently, the Regulation provides for the exemption of many agreements where the market share of the supplier is under 30 per cent.[76] Nevertheless, even some agreements between small undertakings will not be exempt where they include provisions on the 'hard core' list (for example, price-fixing and strict territorial restraints): these are prohibited in all agreements.[77]

The Regulation applies to vertical agreements, which are defined as agreements or concerted practices entered into between two or more undertakings each of which operates, for

---

Approach' [1996] 17 *ECLR* 166. The Commission seems to be signalling a change towards a less formalistic approach: see R. Whish, 'Regulation 2790/99: The Commission's "New Style" Block Exemption for Vertical Agreements' (2000) 37 *CMLR* 887, 889–90.

[70] [2001] *OJ C* 368/13. Below the threshold, the Commission considers that the competition authorities of member states should provide primary supervision.

[71] Regulation 240/96 of 31 Jan. 1996 on the Application of Art. 85(3) of the Treaty to certain categories of Technology transfer agreements. See above at pp. 576–7.

[72] Commission Regulation 2790/99 on the application of Article 81(3) of the Treaty to Categories of Vertical Agreements and Concerted Practices.

[73] TTR Art. 1.

[74] *Moosehead/Whitbread* [1990] *OJ L* 100/36 (where the agreement was held to fall outside the Know How Block Exemption because the trade mark licence was central to the agreement). See R. Subiotto, '*Moosehead/Whitbread*: Industrial Franchises and No-Challenge Clauses Relating to Licensed Trade Marks under EEC Competition Law' [1990] 11 *ECLR* 226.

[75] This was adopted on 22 Dec. 1999 and entered into force on 1 Jun. 2000, replacing the previous Block Exemptions on Distribution (Regulation 1983/83 [1983] *OJ L* 173/1), and Franchising (Regulation 4087/88i [1988] *OJ L* 359/46) which had lapsed in May 2000. The Regulation will expire on 31 May 2010. Note also the Commission's Guidelines on Vertical Restraints 2000/C 291/1 (*OJ* 13 Oct. 2000). For a review, see R. Whish, 'Regulation 2790/99: The Commission's "New Style" Block Exemption for Vertical Agreements' (2000) 37 *CMLR* 887.

[76] VRR Art. 3. In the case of an 'exclusive supply obligation' the relevant share is that of the purchaser. Under VRR Art. 8 the Commission may withdraw the benefit of the block exemption where 50 per cent of the market is covered by similar agreements.

[77] VRR Art. 4. Where an agreement includes a term under Art. 5, these can be severed.

the purposes of the agreement, at a different level of the production or distribution chain, and relating to the conditions under which the parties may purchase, sell, or resell certain goods or services.[78] However, while it is explained that this covers agreements containing provisions which relate to the assignment to the buyer or use by the buyer of intellectual property rights, those provisions must be directly related to the use, sale, or resale of goods or services by the buyer or its customers. However, the Block Exemption does not apply if those provisions relating to intellectual property constitute the primary object of such agreement.[79] It should be noted, then, from the outset that the Block Exemption does not cover many trade mark transactions: it does not cover assignments, nor such things as merchandising arrangements.[80] However, for the most part it will be potentially applicable to franchising and distribution agreements, where trade mark issues often arise, but the provisions are directly related to the use, sale, or resale of goods or services.[81]

If the agreement constitutes a vertical restraint, does not contain a forbidden ('hard core') term, and does not fall outside the market share limitation, then the agreement is exempt. This is so irrespective of the other terms of the agreement: the exemption works on the basis that anything not forbidden is permitted. If, on the other hand, the Block Exemption does not apply, a restrictive agreement may be contrary to Article 81.[82]

4.2 UK COMPETITION LAW

British competition law is made up of a complex mixture of common law principles restricting the terms that may legitimately be imposed in contracts, such as the doctrine of restraint of trade, and statutory interventions, of which the most important is the Competition Act 1998. This Act establishes a system that parallels European competition law, by enacting a provision equivalent to Article 81 EC (formerly Article 85 of the Treaty).[83] An agreement may be regarded as falling outside the prohibition under section 9 (which parallels Article 81(3) EC) without any need for prior notification or exemption. Nevertheless, an agreement will be deemed to be exempt from the national prohibition if it is exempt from the Community prohibition.[84]

4.3 COMMONLY USED TRADE MARK LICENCE TERMS

In this section, we look at terms which are commonly used in trade mark licence agreements and the approach that competition law takes towards them.

4.3.1 Exclusivity

A trade mark licence commonly includes terms guaranteeing the licensee the exclusive right to sell the goods or provide the services under the mark in a particular territory, such as the

---

[78] VRR Art. 2(1).   [79] VRR Art. 2(3).

[80] Guidelines on Vertical Restraints, para. 32. But, at para. 43, the Commission intimates such agreements would be treated in a similar way.

[81] Guidelines on Vertical Restraints, paras. 42–4 (on franchising).

[82] There is no longer a system of notification.

[83] Competition Act 1998, s. 2. See OFT, *Vertical Agreements* OFT 419a (Apr 2004).

[84] Competition Act 1998, s. 10 (parallel exemptions). But note *Days Medical Aids v. Pihsiang Machinery* [2004] *EWHC* 44 (Comm.) (raising doubts about applicability of common law restraint of trade doctrine, over and above EC competition law, to distribution agreements).

United Kingdom. It may also include associated undertakings by the licensor not to put the goods on the market under the same mark in that territory, or compete with the licensee by providing the same services. In turn, the licensee may undertake not to sell goods bearing the mark in territories of other licensees.[85] The inclusion of a guarantee of exclusivity may be important to a licensee who has to make a considerable investment in the establishment of production facilities (in the case of trade mark product licences) or retail outlets (in the case of distribution or service franchisees). In these cases the licensee may wish to ensure that they have a reasonable degree of control over the relevant market. In the absence of exclusivity, the licensee would not only be exposed to competition that exists in the market in the goods or services, but also to competition from others dealing in goods or services bearing the brand name, and (not surprisingly) may prefer not to risk such investment. Consequently, exclusivity agreements may encourage the production and dissemination of goods and services with the mark into the market—and thus foster competition. Simultaneously, exclusive licences cause little detriment to third parties because the trade mark owner had such exclusivity as a result of the ownership of the trade mark. On the other hand, exclusive licensing—by dividing up territories—may have serious detrimental effects on the achievement of the internal market.

The Block Exemption on Vertical Restraints recognizes a compromise position. Article 4(b) states that the exemption will not be available where the object of the agreement is 'the restriction of the territory into which, or of the customers to whom, the buyer may sell the contract goods and services'. However, it is permissible to impose a restriction on active sales into 'the exclusive territory or to an exclusive consumer group reserved to the supplier or allocated by the supplier to another buyer where such a restriction does not limit sales by the customers of the buyer'. The key distinction is thus between 'passive' and 'active' sales, that is, between sales that are a response to customer action, and sales that involve the trader actively approaching the customer.[86] The basic idea underpinning the various exemptions is that an agreement is only exempt if the prohibition is limited to active selling outside the territory.

4.3.2 Manufacturing standards

To ensure that certain standards are maintained, a trade mark proprietor who is either involved in franchising or licensing others to manufacture and sell goods to which a mark is applied, will often wish to impose conditions on the manufacture or operation of the licensee's business.[87] Since one of the functions of a mark is to guarantee quality, such clauses are readily justified and, in general, are not treated as restrictions on trade. However, because such clauses might require the licensee to purchase ingredients, components, or other material from certain limited sources, such obligations may look like anti-competitive tie-ins. Nevertheless, the competition authorities have treated such clauses with less severity than they have in respect to patent agreements that include tie-ins.[88]

If such clauses are caught by Article 81, the Block Exemption on Vertical Restraints appears to permit them as long as they are not too long in duration or too extensive in scope. Article 5(a) excludes from the Block Exemption 'any direct or indirect non-compete obligation, the duration of which is indefinite or exceeds five years'. Article 1 defines 'non-compete' obligations as

---

[85] Joliet, 'Trademark Licensing Agreements under the EEC Law of Competition', 789–90 distinguishes between territorial licences, exclusive territorial licences, and territorial sales restrictions.

[86] Guidelines on Vertical Restraints, para. 50 (advertising and internet selling are treated as passive).

[87] Joliet, 'Trademark Licensing Agreements under the EEC Law of Competition', 779–85.

[88] OFT, *Intellectual Property Rights: A Draft Competition Act 1998 Guideline* OFT 418 (Nov. 2001) (paras. 2.25–7).

including 'any obligation on the buyer to purchase from the supplier or from an undertaking designated by the supplier more than 80 per cent of the buyer's total purchases of the contract goods or services and their substitutes on the relevant market'. Consequently, in many cases such clauses will be permissible.

4.3.3 Non-competition

A trade mark owner may be keen to prevent licensees from selling other goods. In *Campari* the Commission approved such a clause on the ground that it would ensure that licensees focused on selling the licensed product. The Commission said that although such clauses in patent licences might be objectionable on the basis that they constituted barriers to technical and economic progress, such a prohibition in trade mark licences 'makes for improved distribution of the relevant product in the same way as do exclusive distribution agreements'.

Trade mark owners might also wish to protect their interests by prohibiting licensees from competing in the same goods after termination of the licence. This is particularly desirable where the licence of the trade mark has been part of a deal involving trade secrets. It may be equally desirable to protect the trade mark owner's goodwill. Under the Block Exemption, it seems such restrictions are permitted in limited circumstances. First, the restriction must not exceed one year, it must be confined to sales of competing goods or services from the point of sale at which the buyer operated during the contract period, and the restriction must be indispensable to protect 'know-how' transferred from the supplier to the buyer.[89]

In domestic law such matters are also governed by the doctrine of restraint of trade which requires restraints to be reasonable having regard to the legitimate interests of the parties and the public interest. In *Kall-Kwik Printing (UK) v. Rush*,[90] a franchise agreement for a photocopying shop contained a restraint not to engage directly or indirectly in any business competitive with the business of the franchisor. It also said that the restraint operated within a ten-mile radius of the premises of any franchisee of the franchisor for two years after termination. During the term of the franchise, the franchisee set up a competing shop a short distance from the franchised premises. The court held that the clause was too widely drawn geographically. This was because since the franchisor had 191 franchisees, the effect of the clause would have been tantamount to a nationwide prohibition. However, the judge construed the clause as being confined to businesses competitive with that of the business and this allowed him to uphold it. Judge Cooke said he considered the two-year period to be reasonable.[91]

4.3.4 No-challenge clauses

Trade mark licence agreements often include undertakings prohibiting the licensee from challenging the validity of the registration. These are known as 'no-challenge clauses'. These are not dealt with in the Block Exemption, and are probably permissible. In *Moosehead/Whitbread*,[92] a no-challenge clause was upheld in the context of a trade mark licence between the Canadian beer manufacturer and its UK licensee. A distinction was drawn in the case between obligations not to contest the validity of the registration and no-challenge clauses concerned with

---

[89] VRR Art. 5(b). This obligation is without prejudice to the possibility of imposing a restriction which is unlimited in time on the use and disclosure of know-how which has not entered the public domain.

[90] [1996] *FSR* 114.

[91] See also *Kall-Kwik (UK) v. Bell* [1994] *FSR* 674 (18 months not unreasonable restraint); *Prontaprint v. London Litho* [1987] *FSR* 315 (3 years).

[92] Commission Decision of 23 Mar. 1990, *Moosehead/Whitbread* [1990] *OJ L* 100/36 and [1991] 4 CMLR 391. See Subiotto, '*Moosehead/Whitbread*'.

the ownership of the mark. Clauses preventing the licensee from challenging ownership did not contravene Article 85 of the EC Treaty (now Article 81 EC), because, according to the Commission, they did not restrict competition. However, a clause preventing the challenge to the validity of the mark might be a restriction within Article 81. In the case itself, the Commission held that as the obligation related to both, it did not constitute an appreciable restriction on competition. In the main this was because the MOOSEHEAD mark was new to the market. We will return to the question of no-challenge clauses in the context of trade mark delimitation agreements which are discussed below.

4.3.5 Price restrictions

A trade mark owner may wish to restrict the price at which the licensee sells the trade-marked product. Such restrictions are treated as anti-competitive under Article 81(1) EC, and exemptions are not possible under Article 81(3) unless the agreement allows consumers a fair share of resulting benefit. Unsurprisingly, such terms fall in the 'hard core' prohibited terms, which if present prevent an agreement from benefiting from the block exemption on vertical restraints.[93] Nevertheless, it is possible for an agreement to contain price recommendations. Similarly, under the Competition Act 1998 agreements which 'directly or indirectly fix purchase or selling prices' are specifically referred to as examples of prohibited agreements under section 2(2)(a).

4.4 TRADE MARK DELIMITATION AGREEMENTS

In the previous section we examined the application of competition regulations to various common clauses in vertical arrangements relating to trade marks, that is to agreements which operate down the chain from manufacturer to consumer, such as those between trade mark owner and franchisee or distributor. We now need briefly to consider horizontal arrangements, that is arrangements at the same level of distribution between competing manufacturers/trade mark owners. These are generally treated as much more likely to be anti-competitive. Our interest in them extends as far as 'consent agreements' or 'trade mark delimitation agreements'. Trade mark delimitation agreements are contracts between owners of similar marks which are intended to settle conflicts (or potential conflicts) between them.[94] While these arrangements may not be licences at all, because they contain many terms similar to those found in licence agreements which are regulated by competition law, we will consider them in this section.[95]

There seem to be a number of typical ways of resolving such conflicts:

(i) by agreeing that only one party may use the mark, so that the other must adopt a new mark;

(ii) by agreeing that one party will use the mark only in one field, and the other in a distinct field, so as to avoid the possibility of overlap;

(iii) by agreeing that one party will use the mark in a particular geographical area, and the other in a different one; and

(iv) by agreeing that each will only use the mark with specified get-up, so that consumer confusion is minimized.

---

[93] VRR Art. 4(a).

[94] See generally Wilkof, *Trade Mark Licensing*, ch. 9; M. Fawlk, 'Trademark Delimitation Agreements under Article 85 of the Treaty of Rome' (1992) 82 *TM Rep* 223.

[95] Joliet, 'Trademark Licensing Agreements under the EEC Law of Competition', 765.

The contents of trade mark delimitation agreements will vary, but in each case will need to be scrutinized under both European and domestic law. As regards European competition law, the key provision is Article 81 EC. The Commission and the Court of Justice have indicated that such settlement agreements may be acceptable because by resolving protracted litigation between the parties, they eliminate restraints on competition and the internal market that conflicting rights under national laws might cause.[96] The Commission has indicated, however, that in forging the compromise the enterprises should try and reach the least restrictive solution possible.[97]

If the agreement restricts competition or produces market sharing it will contravene Article 81(1). Whether the agreement restricts competition has been said largely to depend on the use to which the mark was previously being put. In *BAT Cigaretten-Fabrik GmbH v. EEC*,[98] for example, an agreement restraining a Dutch competitor of BAT from using its TOLTECS mark in Germany was an unlawful restraint, because BAT's DORCET mark was dormant (or unused). Where, however, the party who submits to the restraint has not used the mark (or was not utilizing it to a significant extent), the Commission has taken the view that assignment of that mark to the other party will not amount to a restriction on the assignor's ability to compete.[99] Indeed, the Commission seems to take the view that an unused mark has no value and a person can simply choose a different mark for their goods or services.

However, in most cases of conflict both parties will have been using their marks to some extent. As indicated, the Commission then favours the least restrictive solution. If conflict can be avoided by the parties merely agreeing to utilize different 'get-up', that is likely to be treated as outside Article 81.[100] Alternatively, it may be that the conflict can be settled by assigning one mark to one party and a different mark to another. Although the effect will be to force the party to re-establish goodwill under other marks and this may have a restrictive effect bringing it within Article 81, such an arrangement might be acceptable if there is a transitional phasing-out and/or the party is allowed to continue using the name as a trade name. It seems that the Commission has looked least favourably on agreements that give different parties use of the mark in different parts of the Common Market.[101] It also has indicated that it disapproves of widely drawn or lengthy 'no-challenge' clauses.[102]

As regards UK law, trade mark delimitation agreements have heretofore been treated as enforceable commercial contracts. The only ground for objection that seems to have been raised in the case law is restraint of trade. While in principle this would require a person imposing a restraint to demonstrate it is reasonable, according to the Court of Appeal in *WWF–World Wide Fund for Nature v. World Wrestling Federation Entertainment Inc* there is a presumption that the restraint represents a reasonable division of their interests. Consequently, the defendant must show that the restraint is unreasonable, for example, by demonstrating there was no goodwill to justify the restraint.[103] In *Apple Corp. Ltd. v. Apple Computer Inc*,[104] when

---

[96] *BAT Cigaretten-Fabrik v. EEC* [1985] *FSR* 533, 541 (para. 33).

[97] Commission Decision 78/193/EEC of 23 Dec. 1977 relating to a proceeding under Article 85 (Penney's) [1978] *FSR* 385, 395.

[98] [1985] *FSR* 533.

[99] Commission Decision 78/193/EEC, Penney's [1978] *FSR* 385, 396.

[100] Penney's, ibid.

[101] *Sirdar/Phildar* [1975] 1 *CMLR D* 93; *Community v. Syntex/Synthelabo* [1990] *FSR* 529.

[102] *BAT Cigaretten-Fabrik* [1985] *FSR* 533. In other cases more flexibility has been shown: Commission Decision 78/193/EEC, Penney's [1978] *FSR* 385, 396–7 (acceptable if under five years).

[103] [2004] *FSR* (10) 161. See also *Fenchurch Environmental Group Ltd v. Bactiguard AG* [2007] *RPC* (31) 701 (Registry).

[104] [1991] 3 *CMLR* 49.

considering various difficult procedural questions concerning litigation over a consent agreement, the Court of Appeal held that restraints contained in such agreements were legitimate only where they were necessary to protect the legitimate interests of the parties. The ownership of registered marks would not of itself justify such an agreement: rather the restraint would be justified only where it was necessary to protect the goodwill of the restrainer. As a consequence, such a restraint would be justified only where the mark had been used. The Court of Appeal observed that the approach under Article 85 of the EC Treaty (now Article 81 EC) and under the common law were largely similar.[105]

---

[105] Such an agreement may include a no-challenge clause: *Apple Corp v. Apple Computer Inc* [1992] *FSR* 431. For subsequent litigation over the scope of the delimitation, see *Apple Corp. Ltd v. Apple Computer Inc* [2006] *EWHC* 996 (Ch); [2006] *Info TLR* 9 (Ch D).

43

GEOGRAPHICAL INDICATIONS
OF ORIGIN

CHAPTER CONTENTS

1 INTRODUCTION

Over time, the EU has introduced a raft of measures to control the way agricultural products are described and labelled. These vary from laws regulating the marketing standards for olive oil[1] and the labelling of beef products,[2] through to complicated laws that regulate the description, designation, presentation, and protection of wines.[3] In this chapter we look at two specific regimes that form part of this overarching legal framework. First, we look at the scheme developed by the EU to regulate geographical designations.[4] These are the names that are used to describe foods and other agricultural products that originate from particular geographic areas. Some well-known regional products include Kalamata Olives, Feta Cheese, and Parma Ham. Second, we briefly look at the schemes developed by the EU to protect the names of traditional foods and recipes.

---

[1] Regulation 2815/98 concerning marketing standards for olive oil [1998] *OJ L* 349, 56 (regulates designations of origin on the labelling and packaging of virgin and extra virgin olive oils).

[2] Regulation 1760/2000 establishing a system for the identification and registration of bovine animals and regarding the labelling of beef and beef products [2000] *OJ L* 204, Recital 31, Art. 16(6).

[3] Regulation 1493/1999 on the common organization of the market in wine [1999] *OJ L* 179; Regulation 753/2002 laying down certain rules for applying Regulation 1493/1999 as regards the description, designation, presentation and protection of certain wine sector products [2002] *OJ L* 118; Regulation 1607/2000 laying down detailed rules for implementing Regulation 1493/1999 [2000] *OJ L* 185.

[4] Regulation 2081/92 on the protection of geographical indications and designations of origin for agricultural products and foodstuffs [1992] *OJ L* 208/1. (Hereafter, GI Regulation (2081/92)).

While it may seem, depending on one's age, as if Elizabeth David or Jamie Oliver invented geographical or traditional designations, in fact they have a very old lineage.[5] This is especially the case in countries such as Spain, France, Italy, Portugal, and (to a lesser extent) Germany. Given the important role that food and agricultural products play in all cultures, it is not surprising that special legal regimes have long been used to regulate geographical designations. For example, special legislation existed in fourteenth-century France to protect Roquefort Cheese. Over time a number of different legal regimes have been used to regulate geographical designations. In common law countries, the names of agricultural products and foodstuffs have been protected by passing-off, trade marks, and certification marks.[6] While civil law countries have relied on collective marks and unfair competition, they have also developed more specialized regimes, such as appellations of origin, to regulate the use that is made of agricultural names. Civil law countries have also entered into a series of bilateral and (occasionally) multilateral treaties that recognize rights in the names given to wines, cheeses, olive oils, and other agricultural products. More recently, the EU has introduced a series of Regulations to standardize the protection available for regional and traditional food names within Europe.

One of the questions that sometimes arises in discussions about the legal regimes that regulate geographical designations is their status as a form of intellectual property. While the Paris Convention expressly includes agriculture within its remit,[7] there are still some who doubt whether the laws covering geographical designations properly belong within intellectual property law. In Europe, there is little doubt that this is the case, given that both the European Court of Justice and the House of Lords have explicitly acknowledged that the geographic designations protected under European law are forms of intellectual property.[8] The laws regulating geographic designations also share a number of conceptual similarities with other areas of intellectual property.[9] For example, they share with certification and collective marks the idea that rights are controlled by groups or collectives, rather than individuals. As we will see below, one of the defining features of protected designations of origin and appellations of origin is that they presuppose an exclusive link between product and place. As with the idea of the unique expression of the author or the novelty of patented inventions, the 'uniqueness' of the intangible property ensures that the granting of property rights does not jeopardize the rights of third parties.

In this chapter, we focus on the names given to agricultural products and foodstuffs. However, it is important to note that geographic designations potentially apply to all products. This has led to the interesting suggestion that indigenous creations could be protected via a style of law modelled on geographic designations. This is an interesting possibility since it recognizes both collective rights, and a connection between 'product' and 'place', which are so important for many indigenous groups.

---

[5] See D. Gangjee, 'Melton Mowbray and the GI Pie in the Sky: Exploring Cartographies of Protection' (2006) 3 *IPQ* 291.

[6] See N. Dawson, 'The Parma Ham Case: Trade Descriptions and Passing Off—Shortcomings of English Law' [1991] *EIPR* 487; F. Gevers, 'Geographical Names and Signs Used as Trade Marks' [1990] *EIPR* 285.

[7] Art. 1(3) Paris Convention (industrial property shall apply not only to industry and commerce proper, but also to agriculture and to manufactured or natural products, for example, wines, grain, tobacco leaf, fruit, cattle, minerals, mineral waters, beer, flowers, and flour).

[8] Lord Hoffmann said in *Consorzio del Prosciutto di Parma v. Asda Stores Ltd* [2002] *FSR* 3, 38, para. 6 (HL) 'a PDO is a form of intellectual property right'.

[9] See D. Gangjee, 'Geographical Indications and Human Rights' in P. Torremans (ed) *Intellectual Property and Human Rights* (2008).

1.1 TYPES OF PROTECTION

There are subtle and often important differences between the various forms of legal protection that have been adopted to protect the names given to agricultural products and foodstuffs. While the enactment of European legislation regulating the naming of wines, spirits, and agricultural products has gone some way towards alleviating this problem in Europe, widely different approaches are still adopted elsewhere. The failure of the WTO negotiations in Cancùn, combined with the hostile reception that greeted the EU proposal to extend the level of protection required under TRIPS, suggests that this situation is likely to continue for some time in the future. Given this it may be helpful to define some of the key terms used in this area.

An *indication of source*—which is also known as an *indication of provenance* or as a *simple or qualified geographical indication of origin*—is the most general of the terms used to describe geographical designations.[10] A defining feature of an indication of source is that it connects a product to a particular geographical location: there is no requirement that there be any correlation between the characteristics or quality of a product and the place that the product originated from. Instead, an indication of source simply informs consumers that the product bearing the sign comes from a particular place, region, or country.[11] As a result, 'indication of source' is broader than both appellations of origin and geographical indications.

Another term used to describe geographical designations is *geographical indication of origin* (*GI*). Article 22(1) of TRIPS defines geographical indications as 'indications, which identify a good as originating in the territory of a Member, or a region or locality in that territory, where a given quality, reputation or other characteristic of the good is essentially attributable to its geographical origin'.[12]

An *appellation of origin* is a specific type of geographical indication.[13] An appellation of origin is the 'geographic name of a country, region, or locality, which serves to designate a product originating therein, the quality or characteristics of which are due exclusively or essentially due to the geographical environment, including natural and human factors'.[14] The defining feature of an appellation of origin is that the 'product for which an appellation of origin is used must have a quality and characteristics which are due exclusively or essentially to its geographic environment'.[15]

An indication of source is the most general of these three modes of protection: it simply signals that a product originates from a particular geographic location (e.g. French perfume). In contrast, geographical indications of origin and appellations of origin both require that the geographic location must imbue the product with particular traits or characteristics. Where they differ is in terms of the nature of the relationship and the types of trait that they recognize. In particular, with an appellation of origin the quality or characteristics of the product must be exclusively or essentially due to the geographical environment. That is, there must be a link between product and place. In contrast, geographical indications of origin extend beyond the

---

[10] Used in the Paris Convention and the Madrid Agreement for the Repression of False or Deceptive Indications of Source of Goods of 1891.

[11] See *Exportur*, Case C–3/91 [1992] 1 *ECR* 5529, para. 11; *Jacques Pistre*, Case C–321 to 324/94 [1977] *CMLR* 565, 587 (ECJ).

[12] For previous attempts to define geographical indications see WIPO, GEO/c.e./I/2; General Assembly of the International Vine and Wine Office, *Resolution* ECO 2/92.

[13] Derived from the French *appellation d'origine*.

[14] Art. 2, Lisbon Agreement for the Protection of Appellations of Origin and their International Registration of 1958. See below at pp. 979–80.

[15] For comparisons see Gevers, 'Geographical Names and Signs used as Trade Marks'.

quality of the product to include 'reputation or other characteristic of the good'. By shifting the focus beyond the strict connection of product to place, it subtly changes the nature of the protected interest away from something which mirrors the model of creation used in patents, copyright, and design law, to something more akin to that used in trade mark law.[16]

As part of its ongoing reform of agricultural policy in Europe, the EU has passed a series of laws that regulate geographic designations. In so doing, the EU introduced a number of new terms into the legal lexicon. The first is the *protected designation of origin* or PDO.[17] This is the term used to describe a designation of origin that has been registered under the 2006 EU Regulation on the protection of geographical indications and designations of origin for agricultural products and foodstuffs (hereinafter the 'GI Regulation').[18] In this context a 'designation of origin' is defined as the name of a region, a specific place, or, in exceptional cases, a country used to describe an agricultural product or foodstuff. To qualify as a PDO, the named product must originate in that region, specific place, or country. It is also necessary to show that the quality or characteristics of the product are 'essentially or exclusively due to a particular geographical environment with its inherent natural and human factors' and that the production, processing, and preparation take place in the defined geographical area.

Another new term introduced by the EU is *protected geographical indication* or PGI. This is the term that is used to describe a designation of origin that has been registered under the GI Regulation. Geographical indications are defined as the name of a region, a specific place or, in exceptional cases, a country used to describe an agricultural product or foodstuff. To qualify for protection, a geographical indication must originate in that region, specific place, or country. The product or foodstuff must also possess a specific quality, reputation, or other characteristic attributable to that geographical origin. It is also necessary to show that the production, processing, or preparation takes place in the defined geographical area.[19]

The third term introduced by the EU is the so-called *traditional speciality guaranteed* (TSG). This is the term given to traditional foods and recipes registered under the Traditional Specialties Regulations of 20 March 2006.[20] Specific character means 'the features or set of features which distinguishes an agricultural product or a foodstuff clearly from other similar products or foodstuffs belonging to the same category'. For a name to be registered as a traditional speciality guaranteed it must be specific, express the specific character of the foodstuff or product, and be traditional or established by custom.[21] As well as granting rights over use of the registered name, registration as a certificate of special character also enables producers to use the designation *Traditional Speciality Guaranteed* (*TSG*) and the accompanying logo (see Fig. 43.1 below).

---

[16] On the different models of creation used in intellectual property (other than trade marks) see Sherman and Bently, 166–172.

[17] This is the translation of *Appellation d'Origine Contrôlée* (AOC).

[18] EU Regulation 510/2006 of 20 March 2006 2 on the protection of geographical indications and designations of origin for agricultural products and foodstuffs [2006] *OJ L* 109. The 2006 Regulation replaced EU Regulation 2081/92 of 14 Jul. 1992 on the protection of geographical indications and designations of origin for agricultural products and foodstuffs [1992] *OJ L* 208/1.

[19] Ibid, Art. 2.1(a)(b) (previously 1992 GI Regulation Art. 2(2)(b)).

[20] Regulation 509/2006 of 20 March 2006 on agricultural products and foodstuffs as traditional specialities guaranteed (2006) *OJ L* 93/1 ('Traditional Specialties Regulations 509/2006'). This replaced Regulation 2082/92 of 14 Jul. 1992 on certificates of specific character for agricultural products and foodstuffs [1992] *OJ L* 201/9.

[21] Ibid, Art. 2(1).

1.2 INTERNATIONAL TREATIES

In this section we look at some of the more important of the international treaties that impact upon the legal regulation of geographic designations.[22]

1.2.1 Paris Convention for the Protection of Industrial Property

The 1883 Paris Convention provides for limited protection over geographical designations. Article 1(2) provides that the protection of industrial property has as its purpose, inter alia, indications of source or appellations of origin. Article 10(1), read in conjunction with Article 9, provides for the seizure of goods on import where there is 'direct or indirect use of a false indication of the source of the goods'. These provisions are limited to false indications: they make no reference to the situation where a term is translated, or where the name is accompanied by words such as 'type', 'like' or 'style'. It has been argued that use of a false indication of source may constitute an act of unfair competition covered by Article 10*bis* (2)(3).

1.2.2 Madrid Agreement for the Repression of False or Misleading Indications of Source on Goods

The Madrid Agreement for the Repression of False or Misleading Indications of Source on Goods (the Madrid Agreement), finalized in Madrid in 1891, aims to protect consumers against false indications of source.[23] The Agreement requires seizure or import prohibition of all goods bearing a false or misleading indication. The question whether an indication has become generic is decided by member states, with the exception of regional appellations for wine, which cannot be declared to be generic.

The primary aim of the Madrid Agreement is to protect consumers from being misled. To this end, the Madrid Agreement was designed to cover all false indications of source, irrespective of the intention of the user. When the Madrid Agreement was drafted, this was particularly important given that, prior to the Lisbon revision of the Paris Convention in 1958, Article 10 of the Paris Convention only protected indications of source if there was fraudulent intent. However, with the Lisbon revision in 1958, Article 10 of Paris Convention now protects indications of source without the need to show fraud. As a result, the continuing need for the Madrid Agreement was thrown into doubt.[24]

1.2.3 Lisbon Agreement for the Protection of Appellations of Origin and their International Registration

The Lisbon Agreement for the Protection of Appellations of Origin and their International Registration (the Lisbon Agreement), which was concluded on 31 October 1958,[25] establishes an international system for the protection of appellations of origin.[26] The Agreement defines an appellation of origin as 'geographic name of a country, region, or locality, which serves

---

[22] There are a number of other treaties. See, e.g. 1951 Stresa Convention on Designations of Origin for Cheese.

[23] 14 April 1891, revised in Washington 2 Jun. 1911, The Hague (6 Nov. 1925), London (2 Jun. 1934), Lisbon (31 Oct. 1958), Additional Act of Stockholm (14 Jul. 1967). There are currently 35 members of Madrid, including the UK, France, and Germany.

[24] See M. Leaffer, *International Treaties on Intellectual Property* (1990), 270.

[25] Revised in Stockholm on 14 Jul. 1967 (amended 28 Sept. 1979). There are currently 23 members.

[26] The bulk of these were for French wines. M. Hopperger, 'International Protection of Geographical Indications: The Present Situation and Prospects for Future Developments' (1999) *WIPO Symposium: South Africa*, 15.

to designate a product originating therein, the quality or characteristics of which are due exclusively or essentially due to the geographical environment, including natural and human factors'.[27]

Article 1 of the Lisbon Agreement provides that member states must protect the appellations of origin of other member states that are registered at WIPO. For a name to be placed on the international register administered by WIPO, an appellation of origin must first be protected in its country of origin. An application for registration at WIPO can only be made by the relevant administrative agencies in the member states, who act on behalf of the group who 'owns' the appellation. The appellation is published and member states are notified of the registration. Upon notification, member states have twelve months to make a declaration that they are unable to protect the appellation. If no declaration is made, the member state must protect the appellation of origin, so long as it is protected in its country of origin.

The Lisbon Agreement requires member states to provide protection against misleading use of a protected appellation of origin. While the Madrid Agreement was primarily concerned with the protection of consumers, the Lisbon Agreement also protects producers against misuse, even where consumers may not be deceived about the nature or origin of the product.[28] More specifically, the Lisbon Agreement requires member states to protect against usurpation or imitation, even if the true origin of the product is indicated (e.g. Cornish clotted cream made in Queensland), or if the appellation is translated or accompanied by terms such as 'kind', 'type', 'make', or 'imitation'.[29]

1.2.4 TRIPS

Perhaps the most important international treaty in this area, not the least because of its broad membership, is the 1994 TRIPS Agreement. TRIPS requires member states to provide legal means for interested parties to prevent (i) the use of any means in the designation or presentation of an item that indicates or suggests that it originates in a geographic area other than the true place of origin in a manner that misleads the public as to the geographical origin of the item; or (ii) any use that constitutes an act of unfair competition within the meaning of Article 10*bis* of the Paris Convention (1967). As we saw earlier, geographic indications are defined as 'indications, which identify a good as originating in the territory of a Member, or a region or locality in that territory, where a given quality, reputation or other characteristic of the good is essentially attributable to its geographical origin'.[30] It is important to note that TRIPS applies to all products, and not just agricultural products or foodstuffs.

A notable feature of the TRIPS Agreement is that it provides for higher levels of protection for wines and spirits than for other agricultural products. In particular, Article 23 requires member states to provide protection even where the true origin of the goods is indicated, the geographical indication is used in translation, or is accompanied by expression such as 'kind', 'type', 'style', 'imitation', or the like. It is also requires member states to determine the status of homonymous names. Article 23(4) also provides that the TRIPS Council should undertake negotiations for the establishment of a multilateral system of notification and registration for wines. Article 24 sets out certain exceptions (for example in relation to overlap between geographical indications and trade marks).

Despite protests from the United States and other WTO members, at the 2001 WTO Ministerial Conference in Doha, a group of WTO members, led by the EU, succeeded in

---

[27] Lisbon Agreement, Art. 2.
[28] See Leaffer, *International Treaties on Intellectual Property*, 278.
[29] Lisbon Agreement, Art. 3.   [30] TRIPS, Art. 22(1).

increasing the likelihood that the current regime of geographical indication protection would be revised.[31] In particular, the Doha Declaration set a mandate for the negotiation of a multilateral system of notification and registrations of geographical indications for wines and spirits, and the possibility of extending the higher level of protection currently given to wines and spirits under Article 23 TRIPS to all agricultural products.[32] In a sense, what was being proposed was that TRIPS should adopt the approach currently adopted in Europe as a global standard. It was also decided that the deadline for completing the negotiations was the Fifth Ministerial Conference to be held in Cancún in 2003.[33]

These proposals to amend TRIPS met with a degree of hostility, particularly from ex-British colonies who have little to gain (at least directly) from these changes. The hostility was exacerbated by the fact that in the lead-up to the Ministerial Conference in Cancún, the EU put forward a list of 40 names that were to be given absolute protection. Given this divergence of opinion among WTO members (there is a dispute over whether there was even a mandate to launch negotiations on extension), it was not possible to reach a consensus on this issue at the Ministerial Conference of Cancún. As such, it may be some time before the proposed extension of TRIPS takes place (if at all).[34] As we will see, the WTO dispute settlement provisions have been used successfully against the EU in relation to aspects of the 1992 GI Regulation.

1.2.5 Bilateral agreements

The EU has entered into a number of bilateral agreements to protect agricultural products and foodstuffs. For example, the EU has negotiated treaties with Australia (wine),[35] Chile (wines, spirit drinks, and aromatized drinks),[36] and Mexico (spirits).[37] Given the limited membership of the international treaties regulating geographic designation, and the impasse in the TRIPS negotiations at Cancún, the EU may now look more closely at bilateral agreements as a way of protecting European products in other jurisdictions.

2 GEOGRAPHICAL DESIGNATIONS FOR AGRICULTURAL PRODUCTS AND FOODSTUFFS

In this section, we look at the legal framework established by the EU to regulate regional food specialities. More specifically, we look at the system for the protection of geographical food names which is governed by the 2006 Regulation on the Protection of Geographical Indications and Designations of Origin for Agricultural Products and Foodstuffs ('GI Regulation').

---

[31] See WTO Ministerial Conference, Ministerial Declaration, WT/MIN(01)/DEC/1 (20 Nov. 2001), available at <http://www.wto.org>.

[32] Ibid, paras. 12 and 18.

[33] WTO Doc TN/C/M/1 (14 Feb. 2002), in particular 4 and para. 9–12.

[34] Australia has launched a dispute against Europe at the WTO in relation to the way geographical indications are protected in Europe: *Australia v. Europe* WTO DS/290.

[35] Australia–EU Agreement (concerning the conclusion of an Agreement between the European Community and Australia on trade in wine) 94/184/EC (31 Mar. 1994) *OJ L* 086, 1.

[36] EU–Chile Association Agreement (30 Dec. 2002) *OJ L* 352, 3.

[37] EU–Mexico Agreement (on mutual recognition and protection of designations for spirits and drinks) 97/361/EC (11 Jun. 1997) *OJ L* 152, 15.

Protection for geographical indications and designations of origin at the EU level was first conferred in 1993 by the 1992 GI Regulation.[38] As part of an ongoing dispute that the EU has been having, a complaint was made by the USA and Australia to the WTO Dispute Settlement Body that aspects of the 1992 GI Regulation were in breach of TRIPS.[39] Finding in favour of the USA and Australia, the Panel said that the 1992 GI Regulation did not provide national treatment to non-European WTO members because registration of a GI from a country outside the EU was contingent on the government of that country adopting a system of reciprocal GI protection. The Panel also said that the requirement for government-monitored inspection structures under the 1992 Regulation discriminated against foreign nationals. Following the Panel decision, in 2006 the Council adopted a new GI Regulation (510/2006) which repealed and replaced the 1992 Regulation. The main difference between the 1992 and 2006 Regulations is that protection under the 2006 Regulation is extended to foreign geographical indications, irrespective of whether the foreign government provides reciprocal protection. Foreign parties with an interest in a geographical indication are also now able to apply directly to the Commission, rather than having first to register with a national government. Beyond these changes, the 2006 Regulation is similar to its 1992 predecessor.

Two types of designation are protected under the 2006 GI Regulation. The first is 'designations of origin', which are called protected designations of origin (PDO) once they are registered.[40] A designation of origin is defined as the name of a region, a specific place or, in exceptional cases, a country used to describe an agricultural product or foodstuff. To qualify for protection as a PDO, the named product must originate in the defined region, specific place, or country. It is also necessary to show that the quality or characteristics of the named product are essentially or exclusively due to a particular geographical environment with its inherent natural and human factors. It is also necessary to show that the production, processing, and preparation take place in the defined geographical area.[41] A number of different product names have been registered as PDOs in the United Kingdom. These include Cornish clotted cream, West Country farmhouse Cheddar cheese, Jersey Royal potatoes, Shetland lamb, and white Stilton.[42] Some other well known PDOs include Roquefort cheese (France), Gorgonzola (Italy), Feta (Greece), Camembert de Normandie (France), Kalamata olives (Greece), Chianti Classico olive oil (Italy), and Prosciutto de Parma (Italy).

The second type of designation protected by the GI Regulation is known as 'geographical indications'. Once a geographical indication is registered, it is known as a 'protected geographical indication' (or PGI). Geographical indications are defined as the name of a region, specific place, or, in exceptional cases, a country, used to describe an agricultural product or foodstuff. To qualify for protection a geographical indication must originate in that region, specific place, or country. The product or foodstuff needs to possess a specific quality, reputation, or other

---

[38] GI Regulation (2081/92) The Regulation was amended in an attempt to ensure the procedure for obtaining Community GIs was available to producers from third countries Regulation 535/97 of 17 March 1997 and Regulation No 692/2003 of 8 April 2003. See B. Schwab, 'The Protection of Geographical Indications in the European Economic Community' [1995] *EIPR* 242.

[39] *US v EC* WT/DS174; *Australia v. EC*, WTO DS/290. See M. Handler, 'The WTO Geographical Indications Dispute' (2006) 69 MLR 70; M. Handler , 'The EU's Geographical Indications Agenda and its Potential Impact on Australia' (2004) 15 *Australian Intellectual Property Journal* 173.

[40] This is the translation of *Appellation d'Origine Contrôlée* (AOC).

[41] GI Regulation 510/2006, Art. 2(1) (formerly GI Regulation (2081/92), Art. 2(2)(a)).

[42] Other British PDOs include Orkney beef; Orkney lamb; Blue Stilton cheese; Beacon Fell Lancashire cheese; Swaledale cheese; Swaledale ewe's cheese; Bonchester cheese; Buxton cheese; Dovedale cheese; and Single Gloucester.

characteristic attributable to that geographical origin and the production. It is also necessary to show *either* that the production, processing, *or* preparation takes place in the defined geographical area.[43] A number of different geographical names have been registered as PGIs in the United Kingdom. These include Newcastle Brown Ale, Rutland bitter, Whitstable oysters, Scottish beef, and Welsh lamb.[44]

As Lord Hoffmann said, 'a PGI is similar to a PDO except that the causal link between the place of origin and the quality of the product may be a matter of reputation rather than verifiable fact'.[45] Another difference is that, while the production, processing, and preparation of a PDO *all* need to take place in the named geographic area, with a PGI it is only necessary for the production, processing, *or* preparation to take place in the named area. Yet another difference is that, while PDOs accommodate traditional non-geographic designations, no such provision is made in the case of PGIs (see p. 993 below).

As with most legal regimes, the GI Regulation performs a number of different roles. On one level it aims to ensure that consumers are able to rely upon the names of goods as indicators of the quality of the items they are purchasing. This enables consumers to purchase quality products with guarantees as to the methods of production and origin. The GI Regulation also performs an educative role, insofar as it informs consumers about the origin and quality of agricultural products. Surveys of consumer purchasing practices carried out by the EU in 1995 and 1998 suggest that the Regulation is delivering on at least some of these aims. These surveys showed that consumers had some knowledge of the scheme, and that they were willing to pay more for products bearing the PDO/PGI label. This was particularly the case with older, wealthier consumers, who were more likely to purchase protected regional products.[46] The surveys also found that people were more likely to purchase products from the area in which they lived.

The GI Regulation also aims to protect producers against piracy and unfair competition. In so doing it aims to encourage investment in the production of quality local products. This is reflected in the fact that registered names are protected even where consumers are not misled about the origin of the goods. Another important and often overlooked feature of the GI Regulation is that it helps to promote and protect agricultural heritage in Europe. Indeed, as the European Parliament said, designations of origin 'form part of a rich national heritage, which must be preserved'.[47] While the scheme has not been as popular in the UK as in some other member states,[48] it has generated interest in regional and traditional foods in the UK.[49]

---

[43] GI Regulation 510/2006, Art. 2(1).

[44] The other PGIs are Scottish lamb; Welsh beef; Teviotdale cheese; Dorset Blue cheese; Exmoor Blue cheese; Herefordshire cider; Herefordshire perry; Worcestershire cider; Worcestershire perry; Gloucestershire cider; Gloucestershire perry; Kentish ale; and Kentish strong ale.

[45] *Consorzio Parma v. Asda* [2002] *FSR* 3, 44, para. 8.

[46] See DEFRA, 'Protecting Food Names: Guidance on EC Regulations' (2006) available from <http://www.defra.gov.uk/foodrin/foodname>.

[47] This was a motivating factor in the early discussions. See *Motion for a Resolution on Protecting Community productions of cheeses with designations of origin*, EEC Parliamentary Session Documents, PE 128 390/Fin (28 Apr. 1989) (withdrawn). See M. Kolia, 'Monopolising Names: EEC Proposals on the Protection of Trade Descriptions of Foodstuffs' [1992] *EIPR* 233, 234.

[48] Of the 570 or so names registered by March 2002, only 33 products originated from the UK. 'Food Quality: Commission proposes better protection for geographical names', IP/02/422 (15 Mar. 2002). The full list of protected names is available at <http://ec.europa.eu/agriculture/qual/en/lbbaa_en.htm>.

[49] L. Mason with C. Brown, *Traditional Foods of Britain: An Inventory* (1999) (part of a Europe-wide initiative to list foods and food products produced in one place for three generations or more).

At a more general level, the Regulation forms part of the Community's Agricultural Policy.[50] More specifically, it is designed to encourage the diversification of agricultural production and promote products having certain characteristics to the benefit of the rural economy, particularly small farmers in disadvantaged, outlying, and upland areas.[51] The development of distinctive products is particularly important given the rapid market liberalization that is taking place in the agricultural sector.[52]

While the scheme has attracted a lot of support, it is not without its critics. For example it has been suggested that, insofar as the Regulation allows product names to be used as 'protective devices',[53] it introduces significant new 'barriers to compositional and processing innovation'.[54] In particular 'competing manufacturers offering costs or nutritional advantages will be required to overcome the special benefits' of registration.[55] While the GI Regulation allows for the protection of new designations, to date most of the names registered are from established producers. This has led to critics to complain that the Regulation is not, as is claimed, an attempt to re-orientate European agriculture. Rather, it is 'an effort to agree to mutually acceptable allocation of monopolies to each Member State in accordance with the interests which it represents'.[56]

2.1 REGISTRATION

For a name to be protected as a designation of origin or as a geographical indication, it must be registered. Once a name is registered, it is automatically protected in all member states. It also enables parties who comply with the relevant rules to use the appropriate EU logo (see Figure 43.1 below). From 1 May 2009, 'Protected Designation of Origin', or 'Protected Geographical Indication' and/or the appropriate logo associated with the designation must appear on the product label.[57] When the GI Regulation was first passed, a name could be registered using one of two routes: either the 'normal registration process' under Article 5, or the Article 17 'accelerated (or simplified) process'. As we will see, the accelerated process was abolished in 2003. However, names that were previously registered under the accelerated process continue to receive the same levels of protection as they received previously.[58]

2.1.1 Who can apply for registration?

Applications for registration may be made by groups of producers or processors. A group is defined as 'any association, irrespective of its legal form or composition, of producers and/or

---

[50] It is also part of a suite of laws regulating the naming of foods. See C. Lister, 'The Naming of Foods: The European Community's Rules for Non-Brand Food Product Names' [1993] ELR 179.

[51] See *Opinion of the Committee of the Regions on the Protection of geographical indications and designations of origin for agricultural products and foodstuffs*, Opinion COR/2001/58 (14 Nov. 2001). The romantic notion of the 'farmer' is evoked here in much the same way as the 'author' is used in copyright law.

[52] *Opinion of the Economic and Social Committee on the Proposal for a Council Regulation amending Regulation No. 2081/92* COM (2002) 139 final—2002/0066 (17 Jul. 2002), para. 2.10.

[53] See Lister, 'The Naming of Foods', 201.

[54] Ibid.   [55] Ibid.

[56] See Kolia, 'Monopolising Names', 238. The comments made about the Commission's policy on the quality of food, namely that it is '[g]uided by parochialism, sentiment or fading memories of childhood pleasures', might also apply here. See Lister, 'The Naming of Foods', 200.

[57] GI Regulation 510/2006, Art. 8(2).

[58] Regulation 692/2003 (8 Apr. 2003), Art. 1(15).

processors working with the same agricultural product or foodstuff'.[59] Individuals are also able to apply for registration so long as they comply with the procedures established under Article 15.[60] Groups or individuals are only able to apply for registration in respect of agricultural products and foodstuffs that they 'produce or obtain'.[61]

Special provisions are made for the fact that geographical areas may not coincide with geopolitical borders. While the scheme envisages that applicants will ordinarily be from one member state, groups or individuals in different member states are able to lodge a joint application where the geographical area extends beyond a single member state.[62] Unless a decision was 'tainted by manifest error' it is for national courts, rather than the European Court of Justice, to rule on the lawfulness of an application for a protected designation, such as the way geographical boundaries are drawn.[63]

2.1.2 The product specification

One of the central elements of the scheme established under the GI Regulation is the 'product specification'. The specification performs a number of different roles. During the registration process, it sets out the information that is used to determine whether a name should be protected. Once a name is registered, the specification, which contains a detailed definition of the protected product, sets out the standards that producers and processors must comply with if they wish to use the protected name. As a corollary, the specification also helps to delineate the scope of protection. That is, it provides the basis for ascertaining the scope of the intangible interest conferred by registration.[64]

Article 4(2) provides a non-exhaustive list of the information that needs to be included in a product specification. In particular the product specification must contain information about:

- the name of the agricultural product or foodstuff, including the designation of origin or the geographical indication;

- a description of the agricultural product or foodstuff including the raw materials, principal physical, chemical, microbiological, and/or organoleptic characteristics;[65]

- the definition of the geographical area;[66]

- evidence that the agricultural product or the foodstuff originates in the named geographical area;[67]

- a description of the method of obtaining the agricultural product or foodstuff and, if appropriate, the authentic and unvarying local methods, as well as information concerning

---

[59] GI Regulation 510/2006, Art. 5(1) (previously GI Regulation (2081/92), Art. 5(1)).

[60] Ibid. Applications can be made with another member state or with a third country that complies with the procedure set out in Art. 15 (as amended).

[61] Within the meaning of GI Regulation 510/2006, Art. 2(1) and 5(2) (previously GI Regulation 2081/92, Art. 2(2)(a) or (b) and Art. 5(2)).

[62] GI Regulation 2081/92, Art. 5(5) (inserted by Regulation 692/2003 Art. 1(3)).

[63] See *Carl Kuhne (and Others) v. Jutro Konservenfabrik*, Case C–269/99 [2001] *ECR* I–9517 (ECJ) (the decision as to where boundaries were to be drawn in relation to the PGI Spreewald gherkins was not a matter for the ECJ but for the German courts).

[64] *Consorzio del Prosciutto di Parma v. Asda* Case C–108/01 [2003] *ECR* I–5121, paras. 46–7 (ECJ).

[65] Organoleptic is an effect or impression produced by any substance on the organs, or the organism as a whole.

[66] GI Regulation 510/2006, Art. 2(4) (previously GI Regulation 2081/92, Art. 2(4)).

[67] Ibid, Art. 2(1)(a) or (b).

the packaging, if the group making the request determines and justifies that the packaging must take place in the limited geographical area to safeguard quality, ensure traceability, or ensure control;[68]

- details showing the link with the geographical environment or the geographical origin;[69]
- any specific labelling details; and
- any other requirements laid down by the Community and/or national law.

2.1.3 Normal registration

There are a number of steps that must be undertaken for an agricultural product or foodstuff name to gain protection under the normal registration process. Applicants must submit an application form and a product specification to the relevant national agency.[70] The application form is then examined by that national agency to see whether it is 'justified' in light of the criteria for protection.[71] If approved, the application and supporting documentation are submitted to the Commission for final approval. The Commission then undertakes a formal examination of the application to determine whether it includes all the particulars provided for in Article 4. If the Commission decides that the name qualifies for protection, a summary sheet is published in the *Official Journal of the European Communities*.[72] Once the summary of the specification is published in the *Official Journal*, third parties have six months in which they are able to object to the registration on the basis that the name does not comply with criteria for protection in Article 2.[73] If an acceptable solution is found, the 'summary sheet' for the product is republished in the *Official Journal* to confirm that the product is registered. If unresolved, the matter is passed to the EU Regulatory Committee to decide whether the name ought to be registered taking account of 'traditional fair practice' and the 'actual likelihood of confusion'.[74] If no valid objections are made to the proposed registration, the name of the group and the relevant inspection agency are entered into the *Register of Protected Designations of Origin and Protected Geographical Indications,* which is kept by the Commission.[75] The Commission then publishes the names entered in the Register in the *Official Journal*. Once registered, the product name is automatically protected in all member states.

---

[68] Ibid, Art. 4(2)(e).   [69] Ibid, Art. 2(1)(a) or (b).

[70] Ibid, Art. 5(2)–(4). From 1 April 2006 the responsibilities for handling of applications made under the EU protected food name scheme within England transferred from Defra to 'Food From Britain'.

[71] GI Regulation 510/2006, Art. 5(4).

[72] This includes the name and address of the applicant, the name of the product, the main points of the application, references to the national provisions governing the preparation, production, or manufacture of the product, and, if necessary, the reasons for the decision: GI Regulation 510/2006, Art. 6(2). As we will see, the fact that a summary of the specification, rather than full specification, is published has cast some doubt over the validity of the scheme.

[73] Third parties are able to object to the registration on the basis that the name does not comply with conditions/criteria for protection in GI Regulation 510/2006, Arts. 2, 7(1). See *La Conqueste v. Commission,* T215/00 [2001] *ECR* II-181 (CFI), paras. 44–47.

[74] GI Regulation 510/2006, Art. 7(5).

[75] Ibid, Art. 7(6), GI Regulation Implementing Regulations Art 7(6). The method used by the Commission to enter names into the register was established by Regulation 2400/96 on the entry of certain names in the Register of protected designations of origin and protected geographical indications provided for in Council Regulation 2081/92 on the protection of geographical indications and designations of origin for agricultural products and foodstuffs (17 Dec. 1996) *OJ L* 327, 11.

2.1.4 Accelerated registration

In addition to the normal registration process established under Article 5, the 1992 GI Regulation (as enacted) also provided for a fast-track or accelerated registration process.[76] The aim of the accelerated procedure was to ensure that names that had been protected in member states prior to the enactment of the GI Regulation were registered at the Community level. It was also meant to encourage the rapid harmonization of the national legal systems of the member states.

As we mentioned above, the accelerated registration process established under Article 17 was abolished in 2003.[77] However, this did not affect the validity of the names that had previously been registered under the accelerated process. The main reason why the accelerated process was abolished was because it did not provide for a right of objection, which was said to be 'an essential requirement for protecting acquired rights and preventing injury on registration' and for legal security and transparency.[78]

For a name to be registered under the accelerated process, member states had to notify the Commission of the names they wished to have protected. To be eligible for registration, it was necessary to show that the name was already protected in the member state or, where protection was not available, that the name was established by usage. So long as the names complied with the requirements for protection, they were subsequently entered onto the Register.[79] Unlike the situation where a name is registered under the normal process, there was no opportunity for third parties to object to the registration where the accelerated process was used. Another important difference between the two modes of registration relates to the information disclosed during the registration process. As we saw before, under the normal registration process, a summary of the specification is published in the *Official Journal*.[80] In contrast, the only information published in the *Official Journal* under the accelerated process was the protected name, the type of product or foodstuff to which the name attaches, the member state that forwarded the application, the type of protection granted (PDO or PGI), and details of the relevant inspection body.[81]

The limited nature of the information published under the accelerated process was the subject of two recent European Court of Justice decisions. The first of these was *Consorzio del Prosciutto di Parma v. Asda*.[82] The applicants in the case, the Consorzio del Prosciutto di Parma (the 'Consorzio'), is an association of producers of Parma ham. The Consorzio supervises and enforces rules and regulations promulgated under Italian law concerning the production and marketing of Parma ham. The Consorzio made use of the accelerated registration process and applied to have 'Prosciutto di Parma' registered as a PDO. After the Italian government sent the name to the Commission, 'Prosciutto di Parma' was registered as a PDO on 21 June 1996.[83] The only information published in the *Official Journal* was the fact that the name had been registered. Details of the inspection structures were published in the *Official*

---

[76] See 'Communication to Traders involved with designations of origin and geographical indications for agricultural products and foodstuffs concerning the simplified procedures as laid down in Article 17 of Council Regulation (EEC) No. 2081/92' (9 Oct. 1993) *OJ C* 273.

[77] Regulation 692/2003, Art. 1(15) (8 Apr. 2003).

[78] Ibid, Recital 13.   [79] GI Regulation 2081/92, Arts. 2 and 4.

[80] Ibid, Art. 17(2): deleted by Regulation 692/2003, Art. 1(15).

[81] See Annex to Regulation 1107/96 (12 Jun. 1996) on the registration of Geographical Indications and Designations of Origin under the procedure laid down in Article 17 of Council Regulation (EEC) No. 2081/92 (21 Jun. 1996), *OJ L* 148, (as amended).

[82] Case C–108/01 [2003] *ECR* I–5121 (ECJ).   [83] Regulation 1107/96.

Journal in October 1996.[84] In contrast, the specification—an 84-page document in Italian—contained detailed information about the conditions that had to be complied with before anyone could use the name 'Prosciutto di Parma'. Amongst other things, the specification said that if ham was sliced and in sold in packets, to be called 'Prosciutto di Parma', the slicing and packaging had to take place in the geographical area (a topic to which we return below).

The dispute arose when a UK-based company, Hygrade, purchased Parma ham (which is the English translation of Prosciutto di Parma) from an Italian member of the Consorzio. The ham had been boned, but not sliced. There was no dispute that the hams were properly made and authentic. Problems arose, however, when Hygrade sliced the ham in the United Kingdom, placed it into packets, and then sold it to the British supermarket chain, Asda. The ham was then sold in Asda's supermarkets, where the packet bore the phrase 'ASDA: A taste of Italy' and 'PARMA HAM Genuine Italian Parma Ham'. The back of the packet read 'PARMA HAM. All authentic Asda continental meats are made by traditional methods to guarantee their authentic flavour and quality' and 'produced in Italy, packed in the UK for Asda Stores'. The Consorzio brought an action under the GI Regulation to prevent Asda from calling the ham that had been sliced in the United Kingdom 'Parma ham'. In response Asda argued that they were not bound by the terms of the specification since the relevant conditions had not been disclosed in an appropriate manner.

After losing at first instance and in the Court of Appeal, the Consorzio appealed to the House of Lords, who referred a number of questions to the ECJ. In particular, the Lords asked whether Asda was bound by the terms of the specification, given that the conditions that the Consorzio were attempting to rely upon were not readily available to the public.[85] Importantly, nothing was published in official EU publications which said that the name could only be used where the ham was sliced and packaged in the defined geographical area. The ECJ accepted this argument and held that Asda were not bound by the specification. The ECJ said that, while the GI Regulation was directly applicable in member states, 'the requirement of legal certainty means that Community rules must enable those concerned to know precisely the extent of the obligations which they impose of them'.[86] The problem with accelerated registration was that it did not provide for the publication of either the specification or extracts from the specification. Instead, all that is published under the accelerated procedure was the protected name, the type of product or foodstuff to which the name attaches, the member state who forwarded the application, the type protection granted (PDO or PGI), and details of the relevant inspection body. This meant that third parties were not in a position readily to access information which (potentially) affected them. This was made worse by the fact that translations of the Italian specification were not generally available.[87] As a result of this lack of transparency, third parties could not reasonably ascertain what their legal obligations were. Given this, the ECJ said that the conditions set out in the product specification 'could not be relied on against economic operators, as it was not brought to their attention by adequate publicity in Community legislation'.[88] That is, Asda were able to slice and package ham in the United Kingdom and sell it as 'Prosciutto di Parma' or as Parma ham.

---

[84] This simply referred to, and gave the address of, the Consorzio.

[85] Apparently, the specification was not readily available in English.

[86] *Consorzio Parma v. Asda*, Case C–108/01 [2003] *ECR* I–5121, para. 89 (ECJ) citing *UK v. Commission* Case C–209/96 [1998] *ECR* I–5655, para. 35.

[87] *Consorzio Parma v. Asda* [2002] *FSR* 3, 61 para. 79 (Lord Scott) (HL).

[88] Ibid, para. 99. See also *Société Ravil v. Bellon Import*, Case C–469/00 [2003] *ECR* I–5053, para. 97 (ECJ).

Similar issues were also raised by the ECJ in the *Ravil* decision, which concerned the grating of 'Gran Padano' cheese (which had been registered under the accelerated process) outside the nominated geographical area. The specification said, inter alia, that the name GRAN PADANO could only be used where the cheese was grated in the nominated geographical area. While the ECJ accepted that, in principle, protection did mean that the name could only be used where the cheese was grated in the defined area, this could not be relied upon against 'economic operators as it was not brought to their knowledge by adequate publicity in Community legislation'.[89]

These decisions have important consequences for names that have been registered under the fast-track process. In particular, the ECJ rulings suggest that, while the names may still be valid, they cannot be enforced against third parties.[90] One way in which the problem could be resolved is if summary specifications of the names registered under the accelerated process were published in the *Official Journal* (or some equivalent forum). In the meantime, there must be serious doubts over the effectiveness of the names registered under the accelerated process. While the Court said that the issues raised in the decisions touch 'the very essence of the legislation and call into question the entire registration system laid down by Regulation 2081/92',[91] given the nature of the information published under the normal registration process, it is unlikely that the ECJ decisions will have any impact on names registered under the normal process.[92]

2.2 CRITERIA FOR PROTECTION

There are a number of different criteria that must be satisfied for a name of an agricultural product or foodstuff to be registered as a geographical indication or a designation of origin. When thinking about the threshold that must be passed for a name to be registered, it is helpful to distinguish between criteria relating to the 'name', and criteria that apply to the 'agricultural product or foodstuff' to which the name applies. We will look at each of these in turn.

2.2.1 Limitation on names

There are a number of restrictions that are placed on the types of name that are registrable under the Regulation.

(i) Geographic names. The first point to note is that the GI Regulation only applies to geographic names,[93] which are defined as names of regions, specific places, or in exceptional cases, countries (the latter was introduced to accommodate very small countries such as Luxembourg).[94] As such, it would not be possible to register the name of a member state (France), nor a fictitious or invented name. Similarly, where numbers were added to a geographical designation to distinguish mineral waters from the same area, the names were rejected on the

---

[89] *Ravil*, ibid, para. 104 (ECJ).

[90] Although the matter was not dealt with explicitly, it seems that the 'knowledge' was viewed objectively.

[91] *Consorzio Parma v. Asda*, Case C–108/01 [2003] *ECR* I–5121, para. 84 (ECJ).

[92] Many of these problems would have been overcome if the suggestion to establish a databank of applications and names registered, including the relevant product specifications, had been adopted. See Committee on Agricultural and Rural Development, *Report on the proposal for a Council Regulation amending Regulation 2081* COM (2002) 139 C5–0178/2002–2002/0066(CNS) *Final*, amendment 14, 14.

[93] It has been said that this refers to 'homogeneous areas': *Italian Republic v. Commission*, C–99/99 (14 Dec. 2000).

[94] Advocate General Jacobs, *Commission v. Germany*, Case C–325/00 [2003] 1 *CMLR* 1.

basis that they were not 'geographical names'.[95] Article 2(2) creates an exception to the general rule that only geographic name are registrable. In particular, it provides that traditional non-geographical names designating an agricultural product or foodstuff originating in a region or a specific place, shall be considered to be a designation of origin.[96] For example 'Feta', which is derived from the Latin and means 'to slice', does not designate a geographic place. Nonetheless it was said to be prima facie registrable under Article 2(3) as a traditional non-geographic name.[97]

(ii) Non-generic names. A name will be not be registered as a protected designation where it is generic.[98] The name of an agricultural product or foodstuff is generic where it has become the common name of, or the term commonly used to describe, an agricultural product or food-stuff.[99] That is, a name is generic where it designates the product *as such* without, in the view of the public, involving any reference to the geographic origin of the product.[100] This is the case even though the name originally related to the place or region where the product or foodstuff was originally produced or marketed. On this basis names such as Cheddar, Brie, Camembert, Edam, Emmentaler, and Gouda would be generic and thus unregistrable.[101] While it is not possible to register names that are generic *per se,* it is possible to register a geographical name that incorporates a generic name.[102] For example, Cheddar is a generic form of hard cheese and as such would not be eligible to be registered either as a PDO or PGI. Nonetheless, West Country farmhouse Cheddar cheese has been registered as a PDO.[103]

---

[95] The names were Dauner Quelle I, Dauner Quelle II, and Dauner Quelle III. See Recitals 1–4, Regulation 1285/2001 (28 Jun. 2001) rejecting a list of applications for the registration of designations communicated under Art. 17, GI Regulation 2081/92.

[96] GI Regulation 510/2006, Art. 2(2). It also adds that 'the quality or characteristics of which are essentially or exclusively due to a particular geographical environment with its inherent natural and human factors, and the production, processing and preparation of which take place in the defined geographical area'.

[97] Cf. Advocate General La Pergola, *Denmark v. Community,* Joined Cases C–289/96, C–293/96 and C–299/96 [1999] *ECR* I–1541, para. 7 (arguing, on substantive grounds, that Feta should not have been registered). The question of the status of Feta was considered and held not to be generic in *Germany v Commission of the European Communities,* Joined Cases C–465/02 and C–466/0 (2006) *OJ C* 86(1); [2005] *ECR* I–09115. See generally D. Gangjee, 'Say Cheese: A Sharper Image of Generic Use through the Lens of *Feta*' [2007] *EIPR* 172.

[98] GI Regulation 510/2006, Art. 3(1).

[99] See *Denmark v. Commission,* Joined Cases C–289/96, C–293/96 and C–299/96 [1999] *ECR* I–1541. Marketing of a cheese in France labelled as 'parmesan' which did not comply with the specification for the PDO PARMIGANO REGGIANO (registered by Italy under the accelerated Art. 17 process). The German government argued that 'parmesan' was generic insofar as it had become the common name for a foodstuff. The ECJ said that Germany had not provided sufficient evidence to conclude that Parmesan was generic. See also Opinion of Advocate General Ruiz-Jarabo Colomer in *Canadane Cheese Trading v. Kouri,* Case C–317/95 [1997] *ECR* I–4681.

[100] *Denmark v. Community,* ibid, para. 36.

[101] As was required by GI Regulation 2081/92, Art. 3(3), a non-exhaustive indicative list of the names of agricultural products and foodstuffs regarded as generic was presented by the Commission in 1996. However, it was not passed. See Proposal for a Council Decision drawing up a non-exhaustive, indicative list of the names of agricultural products and foodstuffs regarded as being generic, as provided for in Article 3(3) of Council regulation No. 2081/92 COM/96/0038/FINAL (6 Mar. 1996), not published in the *OJ*. This included Brie, Camembert, Cheddar, Edam, Emmentaler, and Gouda. See *Denmark v. Community,* ibid, para. 44.

[102] In *Denmark v. Community,* ibid, the ECJ stressed that all of the factors had to be taken into account.

[103] The Registration of 'Feta', which had been registered to Greece under Regulation 1107/96, was annulled because the Commission had not taken account of all the factors listed in Article 3(1) when deciding whether the name should be registered. *Denmark v. Community,* ibid, para. 103. Feta was reinstated as a PDO by the Commission on 14 Oct. 2002 by Regulation 1829/2002 Amending the Annex to Regulation 2081/92 with regard to the name 'Feta' [2002] OJ L 277. This decision was upheld in *Germany v Commission,* Joined Cases C–465/02 and C–466/0 (2006) *OJ C* 86(1); [2005] *ECR* I–09115. (Feta was not generic).

A range of factors must be taken into account when deciding the essentially evidential question whether a name has become generic.[104] These include the situation in the member state in which the name originates and in areas where the product is consumed; the situation in other member states; and relevant national and Community laws. Once a name is registered, it cannot become generic.[105]

(iii) Homonymous names. Special rules exist in relation to the registration of homonyms of names that are already registered:[106] that is, names that are spelt or pronounced in the same way. While there is no guidance as to the degree of similarity that is needed for these rules to apply, the Recitals to the 2003 amendments speak of geographical names that are 'entirely or partially homonymous'.[107]

A homonymous name that meets the requirements of the Regulation can be registered, so long as there is a clear distinction (in practice) between the name on the register and the (subsequent) homonymous name. However, if a homonymous name misleads the public into believing that products come from another territory, it will not be registered. This is the case even if the name is used accurately for the territory in question.[108] In deciding whether a homonymous name will be registered, the Regulation says that it is necessary to have 'regard to the need to treat the producers equitably and not to mislead consumers',[109] as well as taking into account local and traditional usage and the actual risk of confusion.

(iv) Plant or animal names. A name that conflicts with the name of a plant variety or an animal breed which is likely to mislead the public as to the 'true origin' of the product may not be registered.[110]

(v) Trade marks. As we will see, special rules were developed to prevent the dual protection of geographic names under both the GI Regulation and as a trade mark. A designation of origin or geographical indication will not be registered where, in the light of a trade mark's reputation, renown, and the length of time it has been used, registration is liable to mislead consumers as to the true identity of the product.[111]

2.3 AGRICULTURAL PRODUCTS OR FOODSTUFFS

There are also a number of restrictions placed on the types of agricultural product and foodstuff that can be protected under the GI Regulation.

2.3.1 Subject matter
The first and most general restriction is that the GI Regulation only applies to certain agricultural products and foodstuffs. More specifically the Regulation only applies to three general categories of product and foodstuff.[112] The first is agricultural products intended for human

---

[104] For a consideration of the type of evidence that may be used see *Consorzio per la tutela del formaggio Grana Padano v OHIM*, Case T–291/03 (2007) *OJ C* 247/23; [2008] ETMR 3; ('grana' was not generic); *Germany v Commission*, ibid .

[105] GI Regulation 2081/92, Art. 13(2).

[106] See Proposal for a Council Regulation amending Regulation (EEC) 2081/92 on the protection of geographical indications and designations of origin for agricultural products and foodstuffs COM(2002) 139 Final *OJ* C 181 E (30 Jul. 2002).

[107] Regulation 692/2003 (8 Apr. 2003), Recital 4.   [108] GI Regulation 510/2006, Art. 3(3)(a).

[109] Ibid., Art. 3(3)(b).   [110] Ibid., Art. 3(2).   [111] Ibid., Art. 3(4).

[112] Ibid., Art. 1(1). The Commission may amend Annex I and II of the Regulation with the assistance of a Regulatory Committee. Art. 1(1) (as amended).

consumption.[113] The second comprises the foodstuffs listed in Annex I to the GI Regulation. These are beer, beverages made from plant extracts, bread, pastry, cakes, confectionery and other bakers' wares, natural gums and resins, mustard paste, and pasta. The third and final group is the agricultural products listed in Annex II to the GI Regulation. These are hay, essential oils (e.g. lavender oil), cork, cochineal (a raw product of animal origin),[114] flowers and ornamental plants,[115] wool, wicker, and scutched flax.

The GI Regulation does not apply to wines (with the exception of wine vinegars), or to spirits (which are governed by specific legislation).[116] When the GI Regulation was first enacted it applied to names of mineral and spring water. However, as a result of problems such as the use of identical names for different waters, and the use of invented names,[117] the GI Regulation was amended to exclude mineral and spring waters from the types of product that are protectable.[118]

2.3.2 The product or foodstuff must originate from the named place

To qualify for protection, the agricultural product or foodstuff must originate from the named geographical area; be it a region, specific place, or country.[119] That is, a name will not be protected where the product comes from outside the geographic area. An exception is made to the requirement that the agricultural product or foodstuff must originate from the named geographic area in the case of 'raw materials' (which are defined as live animals, meat, and milk).[120] In particular, where the raw materials of a product originate from a geographic area that is larger than or different to the processing area, the product name may still be protected. For this to occur, the production area of the raw materials must be limited; there have to be special conditions for the production of the raw materials; and inspection arrangements need to be in place to ensure that these conditions are adhered to.[121] It is also necessary to show that the designation in question had been recognized as a designation of origin in the country of origin prior to 1 May 2004.[122]

2.3.3 Quality or character of the product or foodstuff

For a name to be protected under the GI Regulation, it is necessary to show that the nominated geographic area imbues products from that region with certain characteristics or traits. The requirement that there must be a link between product and place means that an abstract and general name, such as 'Mountain', which transcends geographic areas, would not qualify for protection since there is no link between the quality or characteristics of the product and its specific geographical origin.[123] Similarly, the fact that a product or foodstuff is closely linked to a country's traditional gastronomy, as distinct from a geographic area, would not, of itself, show the necessary connection to place.[124]

---

[113] These are listed in Annex I to the Treaty establishing the European Economic Community.

[114] Regulation 1068/97 *OJ L* 156 (13 Jun. 1997).

[115] Regulation 2796/2000 *OJ L* 324 (21 Dec. 2000).   [116] Regulation 510/2006, Art. 1(1).

[117] See Recitals 1–4, Regulation 1285/2001. Germany applied to have 314 names registered under the accelerated Art. 17 process: 125 of the names were not designations of origin, 15 names which included 'numbers' to distinguish names of the same designation were rejected because they were not geographic names.

[118] Names of mineral and spring waters already registered will continue in force until 31 December 2013. Regulation 692/2003, Art. 2, (8 Apr. 2003) amending Regulation 2081/92 on the protection of geographical indications and designations of origin for agricultural products and foodstuffs.

[119] GI Regulation 510/2006, Art. 2(1).   [120] Ibid, Art. 2(3).

[121] Ibid.   [122] Ibid.   [123] *Jacques Pistre*, Cases C–321 to 324/94 [1977] *CMLR* 565, 587 (ECJ).

[124] Opinion of Advocate General La Pergola, *Consorzio per la Tutela del Formaggio Gorgonzola v. Kaserei Champiognon Hofmeister*, Case C–87/97 [1999] *ECR* I–1301, para. 9.

The nature of the relationship between product and place necessary for a name to be registered is different for designations of origin (PDOs) than for geographic indications (PGIs). In relation to *designations of origin,* it is necessary to show that 'the quality or characteristics of the product are essentially or exclusively due to a particular geographical environment with its inherent natural and human factors'.[125] As Advocate General La Pergola said, 'the relationship between product and territory must be *exclusive,* in the sense that the product must have been conceived of, developed, and established exclusively in that area and nowhere else. Only this exclusive relationship justifies the grant of a collective monopoly: [p]recisely by virtue of the place where they are established'.[126] In contrast, for a name to qualify as a *geographical indication,* it is only necessary to show that the product which the name refers to 'possesses a specific quality, reputation, or other characteristics attributable to that geographical origin'.[127]

2.3.4 Place of production

Another factor that must be satisfied for a name to be registered relates to the place where the named agricultural product or foodstuff is produced. Again, different standards apply depending on whether a name is to be registered as a PDO or a PGI. In relation to *designations of origin,* the production, processing, *and* preparation all need to take place in the named geographic area.[128] In contrast, to be protected as a *geographical indication* it is only necessary for the production, and/or processing, and/or preparation to take place in the defined geographic area.[129]

2.4 EXPLOITATION

One of the distinguishing features of the scheme established under the GI Regulation is that it does not confer the right to use a registered name on either particular individuals or a specific group. Rather, it confers the right to use the registered name and the relevant logo on *any* undertaking whose products meet the prescribed geographic and qualitative requirements.[130] That is, the right is not addressed to specific producers, but to an abstract group.[131] This means that producers who were not part of the original application are able to use a protected name, so long as their products conform to the registered specification.[132] It also means that the interest in a protected name cannot be licensed or assigned to a third party (especially outside the nominated geographic area). While, in theory, the Regulation might enable anyone to use a registered name if they comply with the specification, in practice agricultural cooperatives, cartels of producers, or state interests may impose restrictions on the ability of third parties to produce or process agricultural products and foodstuffs.[133]

---

[125] GI Regulation 510/2006, Art. 2(1)(a).

[126] Opinion of Advocate General La Pergola, *Consorzio Gorgonzola v. Hofmeister,* Case C–87/97 [1999] *ECR* I–1301, para. 7.

[127] GI Regulation 510/2006, Art. 2(1)(b).

[128] Ibid, Art. 2(1)(a).   [129] Ibid, Art. 2(1)(b).

[130] *La Conqueste,* T215/00 [2001] *ECR* II–181, para. 32 (CFI).   [131] Ibid, paras. 32–33.

[132] To be eligible to use a protected designation of origin (PDO) or a protected geographic indication (PGI), an agricultural product or foodstuff must comply with the specification: GI Regulation 510/2006, Arts. 4(1).

[133] See Kolia, 'Monopolising Names'.

2.5 INFRINGEMENT

In this section we look at the situations where a registered name will be infringed (or misused). In particular, we consider who is entitled to sue in case of abuse, the scope of protection, and the situations where the name will be infringed.

2.5.1 Who is entitled to sue?

One of the defining characteristics of the regime established under the GI Regulation is that there is no 'owner' *per se*. Rather, anyone who complies with the specification is eligible to use the name. It is clear that producers and processors using a registered name are able to sue to prevent abuses. One question that has arisen is whether organizations formed to represent producers are also entitled to sue to protect a registered name. While there has yet to be a clear ruling on the matter, it seems that representative organizations might not be able to bring a representative action on behalf of their members.[134] Nonetheless, they might be able to sue if they can establish that they had sufficient interest in their own right. An organization might be able to do this if they could show that their membership would drop or their reputation would suffer if they did not attempt to protect a name used by their members.[135] In the meantime, if a representative organization wished to sue to protect a registered name, to avoid any doubts it would be advisable for them to join a producer or processor to the action.

2.5.2 Scope of protection

The starting point for ascertaining the scope of protection available for a PDO/PGI is the product specification. While the specification helps to delineate the scope of the intangible property protected by the GI Regulation, the mere fact that something is included in a specification does not mean that it is automatically protected. This is because the only matters within a specification that are relevant are those that impact upon the quality of the product. This is important given, as Lord Hoffmann said, that the product specification is a 'discursive document', meaning that it contains information that is not intended to be enforceable.[136] For example the 84-page specification submitted in support of the registration of PROSCIUTTO DI PARMA as a PDO included information on the history of the pig in the Po Valley, details about breeding and slaughtering, as well as how the ham was to be cured, stored, and sliced.

In other registration-based intellectual property regimes, such as patents and trade marks, one of the key issues in an infringement action is how the registered documents are to be interpreted. For example, in patent law a lot of attention is given to whether the claims should be read literally, purposively, and so on. Less problematic, but equally important, is the question of the types of activity that fall within the owner's exclusive control. In relation to names registered under the GI Regulation such issues are dealt with by Article 13. This sets out both the types of activity that infringe, and also how the underlying property interest is to be construed. While there will undoubtedly be situations where the courts are called upon to decide how a name should be interpreted or whether products are the same, most of these issues are dealt with by Article 13.

---

[134] See *Consorzio del Prosciutto di Parma v. Marks and Spencer* [1990] *FSR* 530, 536.

[135] See *Consorzio del Prosciutto di Parma v. Marks and Spencer* [1991] *RPC* 351, 368 (CA) ('the Consortium did have sufficient interest of its own to protect in passing-off proceedings'... 'the prevention of the reductions in its membership, both present and future, which would or might result from a perception among producers that it was not doing its best to further their interests', *per* Nourse LJ).

[136] See Lord Hoffmann, *Consorzio Parma v. Asda* [2002] *FSR* 3, 49 para. 29 (HL).

Registered names are protected against any direct or indirect commercial use in respect of products not covered by the registration.[137] This is subject to the proviso that the products are 'comparable' to the registered product, or using the name exploits the reputation of the protected name. Registered names are also protected against any 'misuse, imitation, or evocation'.[138] This is the case even if the true origin of the product is indicated (Cornish clotted cream made in Spain); the name is translated; or the name is accompanied by an expression such as 'style', 'type', 'method', 'as produced in', 'imitation', or something similar. A name is 'evoked' where the term used to designate a product incorporates part of a protected designation, so that 'when a consumer is confronted with the name of a product, the image triggered in his mind is that of the product whose designation is protected'.[139] As the ECJ said, it 'is possible for a protected designation of origin to be evoked where there no likelihood of confusion between the products concerned'. This was the case 'even where no Community protection extends to the parts of the designation which are echoed in the term or terms in issue'.[140] On this basis, the ECJ held that the name GORGONZOLA (which was a protected designation) was evoked, and thus infringed, where the phonetically and visually similar name *Cambozola* was used in relation to a soft blue cheese that looked like Gorgonzola.[141]

Article 13(1)(c), which focuses on the product to which the name attaches, provides that registered names are protected against 'any other false or misleading indication of the provenance, origin, nature or essential qualities of the product, on the inner or outer packaging, advertising material or documents relating to the product concerned, and the packaging of the product in a container liable to convey a false impression as to its origin'.[142] Finally, registered names are also protected against 'any other practice liable to mislead the public as to the true origin of the product'.[143]

Secondary uses of agricultural products   One issue that has attracted a lot of attention is whether registration confers protection over what might be called secondary uses of an agricultural product. While it might be acceptable for a specification to stipulate that a name can only be used if the product was grown and processed in the nominated geographic area, is it also acceptable for the specification to stipulate that secondary activities—such as grating, slicing, bottling, or packaging of products—must also be carried out in the region? Is it acceptable, for example, for a specification to state that the name PARMA HAM can only be used in relation to sliced ham where the slicing takes place in the nominated geographic area? What about the slicing of ham in a delicatessen, a restaurant, or at home? Put differently, at what point in the food chain are the rights in a name exhausted?

The question of whether protection should extend to secondary uses was considered by the ECJ in the *Parma Ham* and the *Ravil* decisions. In both cases, the ECJ's starting point was to note that secondary activities carried out in relation to agricultural products have the potential to harm the quality and thus the reputation of the designation of origin.[144] That is, the ECJ

---

[137] GI Regulation 510/2006, Art. 13(1)(a).

[138] Ibid, Art. 13(1)(b). Where a registered name contains within it a generic name, the use of the generic name is not contrary to Art. 13(1)(a)(b).

[139] Opinion of Advocate General La Pergola, *Consorzio Gorgonzola v. Hofmeister*, Case C–87/97 [1999] *ECR* I–1301, para. 25.

[140] Ibid, para. 26.

[141] Ibid, para. 27. In a similar vein, it was held that 'Parmesan' would appear in principle to constitute an evocation of the PDO 'Parmigiano Reggiano'. *Commission v. Germany*, Case C–132/05 (28 June 2007) (para 40).

[142] GI Regulation 510/2006, Art. 13(1)(c).   [143] Ibid, Art. 13(1)(d).

[144] In *Consorzio del Prosciutto di Parma v. Asda*, Case C–108/01 (25 Apr. 2002) and *Ravil*, Case C–469/00 [2003] *ECR* I–5053, Advocate General Alber was not willing to extend the scope of protection to secondary

accepted that the grating of cheese,[145] and the slicing and packaging of ham, had the potential to impact upon the quality of the final product. They also added that, if controls were not exercised over the way the particular activity was carried out, consumers would have no guarantee of the quality of the product other than the word of the retailer. It might also undermine the reputation of the protected name. Given this, the ECJ held that the requirement that secondary activities be carried out in the region was justifiable, so long as they were required to protect or preserve the quality of the agricultural product or foodstuff. In both cases the ECJ found that the requirement that the secondary activity (the slicing of the ham and the grating of the cheese) be carried out in the nominated geographic area was necessary to ensure the quality of the products in question.

One situation where quality is at issue is where the transportation of a product outside a region creates risks to the quality and thus the reputation of the product. Where wine is transported in bulk, which is required if the wine is to be bottled outside the region, this increases the risk of oxidization.[146] The quality of the wine might also be affected by variations in temperature that arise during transportation. Similar problems might arise where delays between the picking and processing of a fruit undermine the quality of the end product (as with olive oil).[147]

Any remaining doubts there might have been about whether registration covers secondary activities was resolved when the GI Regulation was amended in 2003 to state that producer groups are able to indicate in their specifications that packaging shall take place solely in the defined geographical area. ('Packaging' refers to the operations needed to prepare the product for sale, such as bottling or canning).[148] Echoing the reasoning of the ECJ, the GI Regulation says that this can only be done where it is necessary 'to safeguard quality, ensure traceability, or ensure control'.[149]

2.6 MONITORING AND ENFORCEMENT

WTO member states are required to implement objective and impartial inspection structures to monitor products and foodstuffs that are registered.[150] Applicants are required to nominate an independent inspection body, who will undertake regular inspections of their registered products to ensure that the requirements of the specification are being met. Inspection costs are borne by the producers using the protected name. The nominated inspection body

---

factors such as packaging and grating, focusing instead on the 'uniqueness' of the product in relation to the environment in which it was produced.

[145] *Ravil,* ibid (ECJ).

[146] See *Belgium v. Spain,* Case C–388/95 [2000] *ECR* I–3123 (re-bottling of Rioja wine).

[147] A more difficult situation arises, however, where it is technically feasible for the secondary activities to be carried on outside the nominated geographical area. The ECJ has consistently said that controls undertaken outside the geographical area provide fewer guarantees as to the quality and authenticity than those carried on within the nominated geographic area. They have also said that it was not reasonable to expect producers to have to monitor and supervise the way their products were prepared throughout the Community.

[148] Opinion of the Economic and Social Committee on the Proposal for a Council Regulation amending Regulation 2081/92 COM (2002) 139 final–2002/0066 (17 Jul. 2002), para. 2.6.

[149] GI Regulation 2081/92, Art. 4(2)(e). The later part of the Article dealing with packaging was introduced by Art. 1(2) Regulation 692/2003. In the *Parma ham* decision, the Lords accepted that protection would not extend to the slicing of ham in restaurants and delicatessens, as this was not something that a specification ought to be able to control. See Lord Scott of Foscote, *Consorzio Parma v. Asda* [2002] *FSR* 3, 62 para. 85 (HL).

[150] GI Regulation 2081/92, Art. 10(1).

can either be a public body (such as a local Trading Standards Office or an Environmental Health Department), or a private body (who must comply with the appropriate standards).[151] In the UK, the task of enforcement has been delegated to the Trading Standards Services under Article 10(1) of the GI Regulation.[152] If an inspection body finds that a producer is not complying with the registered specification, they are obliged to ensure that the GI Regulation is complied with.[153]

2.7 AMENDMENT AND CANCELLATION

There are two situations where the Commission is able to amend or cancel a registration. First, the Commission is given a general power to amend a specification to take account of matters such as scientific and technical developments, or to redefine a geographic area.[154] The second situation is if 'a condition laid down in a product specification is not being met'. This process is triggered when one member state complains to the member state who made the original application that a specification is not being complied with. If there are repeated irregularities or the member states cannot reach agreement, the matter is referred to the Commission, who after examination takes 'the necessary steps' including 'cancellation of the registration'.[155] Notification of the cancellation of a name is published in the *Official Journal*.

2.8 REMEDIES

While other member states have implemented legislation setting out the penalties and remedies where a registered name is infringed, to date no such legislation has been introduced in the United Kingdom. In the absence of specific provisions, applicants would need to rely on common law/equitable remedies.[156] This might include an injunction, an action for breach of statutory duty, or some equivalent order. An interesting development relates to the possibility of cross-border injunctions to enforce and protect names registered under the Regulations. In one decision, an Italian court (the Court of Bolzano) granted injunctive relief against defendants residing outside Italy (but within the EU). This was done on the basis that the GI Regulation was directly and immediately applicable in all member states. The Court also said that, as infringing acts would be sanctioned equally by courts in the defendant's country, this gives rise to rights directly enforceable against any EU citizen.[157]

---

[151] European Standard EN 45011.

[152] *Consorzio del Prosciutto di Parma v. Asda* [1998] *FSR* 697, 709.

[153] GI Regulation 510/2006, Art. 10(4). *Consorzio Parma v. Asda*, ibid, 709. An action for infringement might be brought under existing legislation such as ss. 14 and 15 of the Food Safety Act 1990, the Food Labelling Regulations 1999 (SI 1996/1499) or the Consumer Protection from Unfair Trading Regulations 2008 (SI 2008/1277), Regs 5(5)(p), 5(4)(b), 5(2)(a), 3(4)(a), 3(1). See *Consorzio Parma v. Asda,* ibid, 709.

[154] GI Regulation 510/2006, Art. 9(1). This occurs at the request of a member state. However the language suggests that other grounds would be considered.

[155] Ibid, Art. 12. See also GI Regulation Implementing Rules, Art. 17.

[156] Lord Hoffmann said that enforcement depends on the fact that Art. 8 of the 1992 GI Regulation [Art. 8(2) 2006 Regulation] lays down a clear rule and upon a general principle that the courts of the member states are obliged to provide remedies to enforce community rights. *Consorzio Parma v. Asda* [2002] *FSR* 3, 48 para. 25 (HL).

[157] *Consorzio per promozione dello Speck dell'Alto Adige* (28 Apr. 1998) (unreported). See Societa Italiana Brevetti, 'Geographical Indications of Origin: Cross-Border Injunctions May Come in Handy' [2000] *EIPR* N 31–32.

2.9 RELATION WITH OTHER REGIMES

Member states are able to maintain national protection of communicated names until such time as a decision on registration has been taken.[158] Once a name has been registered at the Community level, national rules cease to apply.[159] In some situations, the Commission may allow an existing (unregistered) name to coexist with an identical registered name for a period not exceeding 15 years. For this to occur, it must be shown that the identical unregistered name has been used consistently and equitably for at least 25 years prior to the entry into force of the GI Regulation (i.e. 26 July 1993); that the unregistered name has never been used to profit from the reputation of the registered name; and that the public has not been nor could be misled as to the true origin of the product. It is also necessary to show that the problems resulting from the use of the identical names were raised before the name was registered. The ongoing use of an identical unregistered name will only be allowed 'where the country of origin is clearly and visibly indicated on the label'.[160] The GI Regulation does not preclude member states from entering into bilateral agreements with non-member countries,[161] or from protecting 'simple' or 'qualified' geographical indications of source under national laws.[162]

A name cannot be registered as a PDO or a PGI if, in good faith, a similar trade mark already exists, has been applied for, or established by use, which, because of its reputation and renown or the length of time it has been used, might lead to confusion as to the true identity of the product.[163] Conversely, a name that has been registered as a designation of origin or a geographical indication under Regulation 510/2006 cannot subsequently be registered as a trade mark so long as the product to which the name attaches is the same. It is also necessary to show that, if the name was registered as a trade mark. it would fall within the scope of the protection offered to the PDO or PGI.[164]

3 TRADITIONAL SPECIALITIES GUARANTEED

In this section we turn our attention away from geographical designations to look at the EU scheme designed to protect the names of traditional foods and recipes. The laws that operate in

---

[158] *Commission of the EC v. French Republic,* Case C–6/02 [2003] *ECR* I-2389.

[159] *Consorzio Gorgonzola v. Hofmeister,* note 124 above. See also *Consorzio Parma v. Asda* [2002] *FSR* 3, 47–48 para. 22–23 (Lord Hoffmann) (HL).

[160] GI Regulation 510/2006, Art. 13(4).

[161] *Budejovicky Budvar v. Rudolf Ammersin,* Case C–216/01 (2004) *OJ C* 7/6; [2005] *CMLR* 56 (ECJ).

[162] Where there is no link between provenance and quality or reputation. *Schutzverband gegen Unwesen in der Wirtschaft v. Warsteiner Brauerei Haus Cramer,* Case C–312/98 (7 Nov. 2002), para. 40–47; Opinion of Advocate General Jacobs, ibid (25 May 2000), para. 35; *Jacques Pistre,* Cases C–321 to 324/94 [1977] *CMLR* 565.

[163] Section 3(1)(c) of the Trade Marks Act 1994 says that trade marks that consist exclusively of signs or designations which serve to indicate geographical origin should not be registered. See above pp. 837–8.

[164] On relationship with domain names see WIPO document SCT/2/9, para. 115; Hopperger, 'International Protection of Geographical Indications', 17.

GI Regulation 510/2006 Art. 14. The date at which conflict is judged is the date of submission of the application for registration (instead of the date of notice conferring the right as was initially the case. Ibid Art. 14(2).) For the position in Australia, see S. Stern, 'The Overlap Between Geographical Indications and Trade Marks in Australia' (2002) 2 *Melbourne Journal of International Law* 224.

Fig. 43.1 PDO, PGI, and TSG logos

this area are found in the Traditional Specialties Regulations of 20 March 2006.[165] As with the 2006 GI Regulation discussed above, this scheme repealed and replaced the Traditional Foods Regulation, which came into force on 24 July 1993.[166] Unlike the situation with protected designations of origin and protected geographical indications, there is no need to establish a link between the named product and the nominated geographical area to qualify for protection as a certificate of specific character. Instead, registration depends on a product having traditional features or characteristics. To date, the scheme has not proved to be very popular. 'Traditional Farmfresh Turkey' is the only product so far to receive protection as a certificate of specific character in the United Kingdom.[167] Other products that have been protected as certificates of specific character include Mozzarella (cheese) and Jamon Serrano (meat). Names that are registered as certificates of special character are able to use the description 'Traditional speciality guaranteed' (TSG) and the accompanying logo (see Fig. 43.1).

3.1 REGISTRATION

For a name to be protected as a certificate of special character, it must be registered. Unlike the case with the registration of PGIs and PDOs, it is only possible for a group to apply to register a certificate of special character.[168] As part of this process, the group must submit a product specification that contains the name of the product, a description of the method of production and the product (including traditional characteristics, raw materials, and ingredients), and details of the inspection procedures that will be used.[169] The application for registration is submitted to the competent authority in the member state.[170] After examination, the application is sent to the Commission who, in turn, sends a translation of the application to the other member states. The Commission also publishes the main points of the application in the *Official Journal*.[171] Third parties have five months from the date of publication to object to the proposed registration. If no one objects to the proposed registration, the name is entered

---

[165] Regulation 509/2006 of 20 March 2006 on agricultural products and foodstuffs as traditional specialities guaranteed ('Traditional Specialties Regulations 509/2006').

[166] Traditional Foods Regulation (2082/92) of 14 Jul. 1992 on certificates of specific character for agricultural products and foodstuffs [1992] *OJ L* 208, which came into force on 24 Jul. 1993.

[167] It might apply to products such as Worcestershire sauce.

[168] Group is defined in the Traditional Specialties Regulations 509/2006, Art. 2(1)(d).

[169] Ibid, Art. 6.

[170] In the UK this is the same as for PGIs and PDOs. See above p. 986.

[171] Traditional Specialties Regulations 509/2006, Art. 8(2).

into the Register of Certificates of Specific Character.[172] Once registered a certificate of special character can be amended or cancelled.[173] Where an objection is made, it is initially up to the relevant member states to resolve the matter 'amicably'. Failing that, the matter is sent to the Commission for resolution.[174] In order to safeguard established rights, the Traditional Foods Regulation provides that, if there are any valid formal objections to the application by third parties who are shown to be economically disadvantaged, the scope of protection may be limited. In these cases, registration will only confer rights to use the Community symbol and the description 'traditional speciality guaranteed'. However, it will not confer exclusive use of the name.[175]

3.2 CRITERIA FOR PROTECTION

To qualify for a certificate of special character, a name must be both specific[176] and also 'express the specific character of the agricultural product or foodstuff'.[177] It is also necessary for the name to be 'traditional'. In this sense it must comply with any relevant national provisions or be established by custom.[178] A name will not be registered if it is protected by the GI Regulation, or if it merely refers to claims of a general nature used for a set of agricultural products or foodstuffs (or to those provided by specific Community legislation).[179] Names that are misleading will not be registered. This would be the case where the name refers to obvious characteristics of the product, or does not correspond to the specification, or to consumer expectations about the characteristics of the product.

Certificates of specific character are granted for two classes of agricultural product and foodstuff. The first is the agricultural products intended for human consumption listed in Annex II to the Treaty establishing the EU.[180] The second is the foodstuffs listed in the Annex to the Traditional Foods Regulation. These are beer; chocolate and other food preparations containing cocoa; confectionery, bread, pastry, cakes, biscuits, and other baker's wares; pasta, whether or not cooked or stuffed; pre-cooked meals; prepared condiment sauces; soups or broths; beverages made from plant extracts; and ice cream and sorbets.[181]

To qualify for protection, the product or foodstuff must have a 'specific character'. That is, it must exhibit features that clearly distinguish it from similar products or foodstuffs.[182] To be eligible for registration, agricultural products and foodstuffs must be produced using traditional raw materials. Alternatively, they must be characterized by a traditional composition or a mode of production and/or processing that reflects a traditional type of production and/or processing.[183] To qualify for a certificate of special character, the product or foodstuff must comply with a product specification.[184] It is also necessary for inspection structures to be in place that ensure that products comply with the specification.[185]

---

[172] Ibid, Art. 3.   [173] Ibid, Arts. 10, 11.   [174] Ibid, Arts. 9(5), 18.   [175] Ibid, Art. 13(2).

[176] Such as pumpernickel or haggis (examples given by DEFRA).

[177] Traditional Specialties Regulations 509/2006, Art. 4(2)(a) (corn-fed chicken).

[178] Ibid, Art. 4(3).   [179] Ibid.

[180] These were initially listed in Annex I to the Treaty establishing the European Economic Community.

[181] Traditional Specialties Regulations 509/2006, Art. 1(1) and Annex.

[182] Ibid, Art. 2(1)(a).   [183] Ibid, Art. 4(1).

[184] Ibid, Art. 6(1).   [185] Ibid, Arts. 14–15.

3.3 SCOPE OF PROTECTION

Producers who comply with the product specification have the exclusive use of the name, the description 'traditional speciality guaranteed', and the accompanying logo. Registered names are protected against any practice liable to mislead the public, and against any misuse or misleading use of the registered name. However, if parties who are economically disadvantaged object to the application, applicants can ask for limited protection. In these circumstances producers will only be able to use the Community symbol and the indication 'traditional speciality guaranteed'. They will not have exclusive use of the name.

PART V

CONFIDENTIAL INFORMATION

1 INTRODUCTION

Up until now, the law has refused to recognize a property right in ideas or information. Nevertheless, people who generate ideas or have in their control previously undisclosed information will have the ability to prevent others from using or disclosing those ideas or that information if they can demonstrate that the latter are bound by an obligation. The common law of breach of confidence determines when such obligations exist. Because the action is largely concerned with the imposition of obligations, as long as the idea or information is (and remains) secret, there are few restrictions placed on the type of subject matter that can be protected. Accordingly, the action for breach of confidence is broad-ranging and has been used in relation to personal, commercial, and technical information, as well as trade secrets, know-how, and information about the government. As Keene LJ said, 'breach of confidence is a developing area of the law, the boundaries of which are not immutable but may change to reflect changes in society, technology and business practice'.[1]

Because the action is so broad-ranging, it performs a number of different roles and protects a variety of interests. Insofar as the action provides a space in which ideas can be tested and developed without fear of appropriation, it enables organizations to invest in and carry out research (and thus operates as an important supplement to the statutory intellectual property regimes).[2] In some cases, confidentiality encourages information to be disclosed to a small

---

[1] *Douglas v. Hello!* [2001] QB 967, 1011 para. 165 (CA); [2001] *EMLR* 199, 251.

[2] The action presents the possibility of a person gaining some limited protection as regards intellectual creations which for some reason are not covered by statutory regimes, e.g. business ideas: *Wheatley v. Bell* [1984] *FSR* 16. For empirical evidence of a growing use of secrecy as a means of protecting inventions, see W. Cohen, R. Nelson and J. Walsh, *Protecting their Intellectual Assets: Appropriability Conditions and why U.S. Manufacturing Firms patent (or not)* NBER Working Paper w7552 (Feb. 2000). For a sceptical view of the justifications for protecting trade secrets, see R. Bone, 'A New Look at Trade Secret Law: Doctrine in Search of a Justification' (1998) 86 *California Law Review* 241 (arguing that 'there is no such thing as a normatively autonomous body of trade secret law. Rather, trade secret law is merely a collection of other legal norms—contract, fraud, and the like—united only by the fact that they are used to protect secret information. Neither the fact that a trade secret is information nor the fact that it is a secret provides a convincing reason to impose liability for a non-consensual taking. Trade secret law is in this sense parasitic: it depends on a host theory for normative support.')

circle of confidants. More often, however, the action operates to restrict disclosure[3] in order to protect individual autonomy, personality, and privacy.[4] By encouraging respect for agreements, it also promotes fair competition.[5] As such, breach of confidence has done some of the work that unfair competition law does in other legal systems.[6] Breach of confidence also performs many of the tasks performed by a general right of privacy.

The origins of the breach of confidence action are obscure. Recent work has highlighted two possible genealogies. The first traces the action to a series of eighteenth-century decisions dealing with common law copyright in unpublished works,[7] where rights over undisclosed information were first recognized.[8] A second history, espoused by Megarry J in *Coco v. Clark*,[9] traces the action back to the sixteenth century when, in speaking about the general jurisdiction of the Court of Chancery (or conscience), Sir Thomas More said 'three things are to be helped in conscience; Fraud, Accident and things of confidence'. Although it is not possible to trace a line of cases back that far, a number of modern commentators have adopted the corresponding view that the action for breach of confidence is an application of a broader notion of good faith.[10] While the origins of the action may be obscure, it is clear that by the mid-nineteenth century the courts had developed a series of principles that were relied upon to protect what we now call confidential information. For example, in the 1849 decision in *Prince Albert v. Strange,* Lord Cottenham LC ordered that publication of a catalogue describing Prince Albert's etchings be restrained, noting that 'this case by no means depends solely upon the question of property, for a breach of trust, confidence, or contract would itself entitle the plaintiff to an injunction'.[11]

1.1 INTERNATIONAL INFLUENCES

Until recently the action for breach of confidence has largely fallen outside the remit of international treaties. This situation changed, however, as a result of the fact that the 1994 TRIPS Agreement requires members to afford protection to those who lawfully control 'undisclosed information'.[12] More specifically, Article 39 of TRIPS states that, in the course of providing protection against unfair competition (as required by Article 10*bis* of the Paris Convention), members shall provide natural and legal persons with the possibility of preventing information lawfully within their control from being disclosed to, acquired by, or used by others without their consent in a manner contrary to honest commercial practice. Article 39 requires information to be protected if it is secret, has commercial value because it is secret, and has been

---

[3] E. Hettinger, 'Justifications for Intellectual Property' (1989) 19 *Philosophy and Public Affairs* 31.

[4] L. Paine, 'Trade Secrets and the Justifications of Intellectual Property: A Comment on Hettinger' (1991) 20 *Philosophy and Public Affairs* 247.

[5] *Interfirm Comparison v. Law Society of NSW* [1977] *RPC* 137.

[6] See J. Reichman, 'Legal Hybrids between Patent and Copyright Paradigms' (1994) 94 *Columbia Law Review* 2432.

[7] G. Hammond, 'The Origins of the Equitable Duty of Confidence' (1979) 8 *Anglo-American Law Review* 71; S. Ricketson, 'Confidential Information—A New Proprietary Interest?' (1977–8) 11 *Melbourne University Law Review* 223, 233–5.

[8] But this was limited to unpublished ideas which were in recorded form, either in manuscript or otherwise: *Abernethy v. Hutchinson* (1824) 1 *H & Tw* 28; 47 ER 1313.

[9] [1969] *RPC* 41; *Fraser v. Evans* [1969] *QB* 349.   [10] *Seager v. Copydex (No. 1)* [1967] 2 *All ER* 415.

[11] (1849) 2 *De G & Sm* 652; 64 ER 293 (Knight Bruce LJ); (1849) 1 *Mac & G* 25; 41 ER 1171.

[12] See R. Krasser, 'The Protection of Trade Secrets in the TRIPS Agreement', in Beier and Shricker, 216–25.

subject to reasonable steps to keep it secret.[13] Although British law probably complies with Article 39, where there is doubt (such as in relation to the obligations of third parties) Article 39 may influence the way the case law is interpreted.

1.2 DOCTRINAL BASIS OF THE ACTION

One issue that has preoccupied commentators over the last few decades is the doctrinal basis for the action.[14] In particular, commentators have discussed whether breach of confidence has its roots in contract, tort, property, or equity.[15] While these debates may appear to be sterile, the decision as to the appropriate doctrinal basis of the action may have important consequences when it comes to matters such as conflicts of laws and limitation periods.[16] It has also been said that the failure to identify a single doctrinal or conceptual basis for the action is the reason why so many aspects of the action are unclear. In particular, the conceptual uncertainty is said to be the reason why there is confusion about the liability of third-party recipients, strangers, bona fide purchasers of information, and the remedies which are available to a confider.[17]

Instead of attempting to locate an assumed but ever-elusive doctrinal basis for breach of confidence, a preferable option is to treat breach of confidence as a separate cause of action in its own right.[18] This approach, which has found support in Canadian courts,[19] would mean that the action was not dependent upon a particular jurisdictional basis. The advantage of seeing breach of confidence as a *sui generis* action is that the courts would not be hidebound by particular conventions or models. As such, they could tailor rules to the circumstances as and when they present themselves.

It may also be more fruitful to consider whether the existing law could be reorganized so as to make it more comprehensible, predictable, or just. One possibility would be to divide breach of confidence into several related actions. In so doing the courts could better attune the rules to the interests involved and thereby provide greater clarity and certainty. Such an approach would recognize that different rules apply to different types of information; notably personal,[20] commercial,[21] or government information. This could take place along lines similar to the changes that took place in the United States during the last century.[22]

---

[13] The question whether Argentinean law provides appropriate protection for undisclosed test data submitted for marketing approval under TRIPS, Art. 39.3 is one of the issues raised in dispute at the WTO: *US v. Argentina* WTO DS/171.

[14] As one commentator has put it, '[t]he action for breach of confidence is something of an orphan. Various theories have been advanced about the correct jurisprudential foundation but no consensus is yet apparent.' J. McDougall, 'The Relationship of Confidence', in D. Waters (ed.), *Equity, Fiduciaries and Trusts* (1993), 157.

[15] Gurry, 23–62.   [16] See pp. 1090, 1124. See also Wallow [2008] *EIPR* 269.

[17] G. Jones, 'Restitution of Benefits Obtained in Breach of Another's Confidence' (1970) 86 *LQR* 463, 463; A. Weinrib, 'Information as Property' (1988) 28 *University of Toronto Law Journal* 117, 136.

[18] Gurry, 25–8, 58–61.

[19] *LAC Minerals v. International Corona Presource* [1990] *FSR* 441, 495 (Sopinka J, Supreme Court of Canada); *Cadbury Schweppes v. FBI Foods* [2000] *FSR* 491, 504–6 (Supreme Court of Canada).

[20] R. Wacks, *Personal Information* (1989) 131–2 explains how failure to differentiate in the way proposed leads to strained development of the rules relating to breach of confidence.

[21] J. Stedman, 'Trade Secrets' (1962) 23 *Ohio State Law Journal* 4, 26 (bemoaning the lack of a considered and articulate trade secret policy that can serve as a sure guide in deciding whether protection in any given situation should be granted or denied).

[22] This followed from the famous article on privacy by S. Warren and L. Brandeis, 'The Right to Privacy' (1890) 4 *Harvard Law Review* 193.

1.3 BREACH OF CONFIDENCE AND PRIVATE INFORMATION

While breach of confidence performs many, but not all,[23] of the tasks that might otherwise be performed by a tort of privacy,[24] there have long been calls for the introduction of such a tort into British law.[25] While for a long time these calls fell on deaf ears, following the introduction of the Human Rights Act 1998, the courts began to give effect to the requirement, contained in Article 8 of the European Convention on Human Rights, that persons be afforded the 'right to respect for his private and family life, his home and his correspondence'. As Sedley LJ said, 'we have reached a point at which it can be said with confidence that the law recognises and will appropriately protect a right of personal privacy'.[26] The prospects of British law recognizing a general tort of privacy, at least one developed by the courts, received a serious setback in the recent House of Lords decision in *Wainwright v. Home Office* where, after speaking critically about a general right to privacy, Lord Hoffmann rejected 'the invitation to declare that since at the latest 1950 there has been a previously unknown tort of invasion of privacy'.[27] As such, the question whether there was a high-level principle of invasion of privacy 'would have to wait another day'.[28] Lord Hoffmann's comments in *Wainwright* were confirmed by the House of Lords in *Campbell v. MGN*. While the Lords may not have agreed on how the law was to be applied, they were in agreement that there was 'no over-arching, all-embracing cause of action for "invasion of privacy"'.[29]

While there are still some areas of private life that the British courts are not willing to protect, it is clear that over the last decade there has been a remarkable change in the role that the breach of confidence action plays in protecting private information. In developing the law of confidentiality so as to protect personal information, the courts have modified the traditional requirements of the action. There are two changes that should be noted. The first is that the courts have imposed obligations of confidentiality and non-disclosure on recipients of private information where there is no relationship between the parties.[30] This is the case

---

[23] *Peck v. UK* (2003) 36 *EHRR* (41) 719 (ECHR) (British law of confidence at that time did not provide adequate remedy where a party had been filmed using a CCTV camera); cf. *Earl Spencer v. UK* (1998) 25 *EHRR* CD 105 (law of confidence provided adequate remedy to restrain the publication of private information).

[24] See *Duchess of Argyll v. Duke of Argyll* [1967] 2 *Ch* 302; *Stephens v. Avery* [1988] *Ch* 499; cf. *Kaye v. Robertson* [1991] *FSR* 62.

[25] See generally G. Phillipson, 'Transforming Breach of Confidence? Towards a common law right of privacy under the Human Rights Act' [2003] *MLR* 726; M. Richardson, 'Whither Breach of Confidence: A right of privacy for Australia?' [2002] *Melbourne University Law Review* 20; R. Singh and J. Strachan, 'The Right to Privacy in English Law' [2002] *European Human Rights LR* 129; T. Aplin, 'Breach of Confidence and Privacy: the Impact of the Human Rights Act' [2002] *Intellectual Property Forum* 26; T. Pinto [2007] *Ent LR* 170.

[26] *Douglas v. Hello!* [2001] *QB* 967, 997 para. 110 (CA). See also *Campbell v. MGN* [2003] *QB* 633, 663, paras. 69–70 (CA) (describing the process as 'shoehorning' and expressing preference for description as breach of privacy rather than breach of confidence).

[27] *Wainwright v. Home Office* [2003] *UKHL* 53; [2003] *All ER* 279, para. 35 (favouring specific legislative remedies rather than a general tort of privacy).

[28] Ibid, para. 30. See also *McKennitt v. Ash* [2008] *QB* 73, para 8.

[29] *Campbell v. MGM* [2004] 2 *AC* 457, 464, para 11 (*per* Lord Nicholls).

[30] At a greater level of detail, it is possible to say that recognition of privacy through the law of confidence has involved the following changes: (i) protection now extends to 'private' information that might not have been regarded as confidential; (ii) protection may exist even though the private information is widely known; (iii) there is no need to establish an existing relationship of confidence; (iv) there is no need for a claimant to prove damage; (v) a claimant may recover for emotional distress. For an insightful analysis of whether the scope of the 'tort of misuse of private information' extends, or should be extended, to corporate as well as individual claimants, see T. Aplin, in P. Torremans (ed.), *Intellectual Property and Human Rights* (2008).

even where the recipient acquired the personal information from legitimate public sources. As Lord Nicholls said in *Campbell v. Mirror Group Newspapers*, 'this cause of action has now firmly shaken off the limiting constraint of the need for an initial confidential relationship. In so doing it has changed its nature...Now the law imposes a "duty of confidence" whenever a person receives information he knows or ought to know is fairly and reasonably to be regarded as confidential.'[31] The second change that has occurred is that the courts have firmly embodied Articles 8 and 10 of the European Convention on Human Rights at the heart of the action. Indeed, as Lord Woolf said, Articles 8 and 10 are not merely of persuasive or parallel effect, but 'are the very content of the domestic tort that the English court has to enforce'.[32] As we will see, Articles 8 and 10 play a central role in all aspects of the action for disclosure of private information. As well as providing guidance as to whether there is a right to be protected, in deciding whether to grant relief the courts routinely balance the impact that the disclosure will have on private life (Article 8) against the impact that non-disclosure might have on the defendant's freedom of expression (Article 10).

The application of the breach of confidence action to private information has, in the words of Buxton LJ, created a 'feeling of discomfort'[33] amongst lawyers. In part this is because the use of the label 'breach of confidence' is misleading. The reason for this is that the confidence label 'harks back to a time when the cause of action was based on improper use of information disclosed by one person to another in confidence'.[34] But now the action applies where there is no 'disclosure' of confidential information or any relationship of trust or reliance. Another reason for the discomfort is that information about an 'individual's private life would not, in ordinary usage, be called "confidential". The more natural description today is that such information is private. The essence of the tort is better encapsulated now as misuse of private information.'[35] The feeling of 'discomfort' created by the shoehorning of the protection for private information into the traditional action for breach of confidence leads to the question: should the right be treated as a separate action? While there are many good reasons for doing so,[36] the protection against the misuse of private information shares many features with the traditional action. As such, we have kept the action for misuse of private information as a part of the general law of breach of confidence.[37] To do this, we have had to modify the language used and the way that some of the material is organized. While some may see this as a burden, it highlights the dynamic nature of breach of confidence and the capacity of the courts to adapt it to new demands and expectations.[38]

---

[31] *Campbell v. MGN* [2004] 2 *AC* 457, 464, para 13–14 (Lord Nicholls).

[32] *A v. B* [2003] *QB* 195, para 4; *McKennitt v. Ash*, note 28 above, para 11. But cf. *Douglas v. Hello!* [2008] 1 *AC* 1, 47–48, 72 (para 118) *per* Lord Hoffmann; (para. 255) *per* Lord Nicholls (both treating traditional breach of confidence and the privacy-informed action as distinct and, it seems, potentially cumulative in a case concerned with information about a person's personal life).

[33] *McKennitt v. Ash*, ibid, para 8 (iii).

[34] *Campbell v. MGN* [2004] 2 *AC* 457, para 13–14 (*per* Lord Nicholls).

[35] Ibid, para 14 (*per* Lord Nicholls).

[36] As Keene LJ said in *Douglas v. Hello!* in relation to private information, breach of confidence has 'developed into something different from the commercial and employment relationships with which confidentiality is mainly concerned'. *Douglas v. Hello!* [2001] *QB* 967, 1012 para. 166 (CA). For an overview see below pp. 1053–60.

[37] The precise relationship between the traditional action and the privacy variant has yet to be clarified in an authoritative manner, with different judges taking different views. For an academic's analysis, see T. Aplin, 'The relationship between breach of confidence and the "tort of misuse of private information"' [2007] *Kings Law Journal* 329–336.

[38] Ibid, para 14 (*per* Lord Nicholls). See *McKennitt v. Ash* [2008] *QB* 73, para. 8 (iv).

1.4 DATA PROTECTION LEGISLATION

A discussion of the protection of personal confidential information cannot be seriously conducted without reference to the Data Protection Act 1998, which controls the way information about living identifiable persons is used. This became clear after *Campbell v. MGN* where, as well as relying on the common law action for breach of confidence, Naomi Campbell also sought relief under the Data Protection Act 1998.[39] While the action did not succeed in *Campbell,* it highlights an alternative cause of action that may be, and indeed has been, employed in other situations where a person's image has been used without their permission.

The Data Protection Act contains eight data protection principles. These state that data must be: processed fairly and lawfully; obtained and used for only specified and lawful purposes; adequate, relevant and not excessive; accurate, and where necessary, kept up to date; kept for no longer than necessary; processed in accordance with individuals' rights (as defined); kept secure; and transferred only to countries that offer adequate data protection.[40]

2 ELEMENTS OF THE ACTION

However confused the details of the law relating to breach of confidence may be, its basic traditional framework is now well established. According to the seminal case of *Coco v. Clark,* in order to establish a claim for breach of confidence, the claimant must show that:

(i)   the information is capable of being protected;

(ii) the defendant owes the claimant an obligation to keep the information confidential; and

(iii) the defendant used the information in a way that breached that duty.[41]

Once these three points have been proved, a defendant may raise a defence, the most significant being that the disclosure was justified in the public interest.

In the next three chapters we will explore the elements of breach of confidence in more detail. Thus, in Chapter 44 we look at the type of information that is capable of being protected by the action. In Chapter 45, we look at the situations where a duty of confidence arises between the parties. In Chapter 46, after looking at whether the duty of confidence has been breached, we examine the defences to breach. We finish by looking at the remedies available.

---

[39] [2003] 1 *All ER* 224, para. 72–138. Also applied in *Douglas v. Hello! (No. 3)* [2003] 3 *All ER* 996, paras. 230–39 (no defence to compensation). See generally M. Tugendhat, 'The Data Protection Act and the Media' [2000] *Yearbook of Copyright and Media Law* 135.

[40] See *Murray v. Express Newspapers* [2007] *EMLR* (22) 583, para 69 ff.

[41] *Coco v. Clark* [1969] *RPC* 41. It is important to note that there is a degree of fluidity in its application. For example, faced with similar facts, one court might justify its conclusion on the ground that the defendant is not under a duty, while another court would accept that the defendant was under a duty of confidentiality, but either limit the duty so as not to cover the defendant's conduct or provide a defence.

44

IS THE INFORMATION CAPABLE OF
BEING PROTECTED?

CHAPTER CONTENTS

1 INTRODUCTION

The first factor that must be shown in a breach of confidence action is that the information is capable of being protected. Before being in a position to do this, it is necessary to identify the information in issue. As O'Connor J said, 'it was essential that the claimant should make it absolutely clear and certain what it was that he alleged to be confidential [and] which he sought to protect'.[1] This is not an inquiry into the quality of the information *per se,* so much as a preliminary examination as to whether the information has been identified in such a way that the action can proceed. As such, it is akin to the question of what is a work in copyright law.

If a claimant does not identify the information in sufficient detail, their action may be struck out on the basis that it is speculative and an abuse of process.[2] Failure to identify the information may also lead the court to refuse to grant an injunction. For example, in *Suhner v. Transradio* the claimants gave the defendant 246 drawings saying that about 100 of the documents contained confidential drawings and that part of the information in the other 146 documents was confidential. The court refused to grant an injunction primarily because 'it was very difficult to know precisely what information it is which the plaintiffs say is confidential'.[3] Laddie J

---

[1] *PA Thomas v. Mould* [1968] QB 913, 922. See also *Ocular Sciences v. Aspect Vision* [1997] RPC 289, 359–69; *CMI-Centers for Medical Innovation v. Phytopharm* [1999] FSR 235, 243.

[2] *John Zinc v. Lloyds Bank* [1975] RPC 385; *Inline Logistics v. UCI Logistics* [2002] RPC 611, 620, para. 29; *The Gadget Shop v. The Bug.Com* [2001] FSR 383, 405 (need to identify confidential information with precision so that the defendant can know the allegation against him).

[3] *Suhner v. Transradio* [1967] RPC 329, 334.

reiterated this position in the *Ocular Sciences*[4] decision where he said that the claimant should give full and proper particulars of all confidential information that he intended to rely upon. The reason for this was that unless the confidential information was properly identified, the injunction might be of uncertain scope and difficult to enforce. The absence of 'proper particulars of claim' could also compromise defendants' ability to defend themselves. On this basis Laddie J said that, if the claimant failed to give proper particulars, it was open to the court to infer that the purpose of the litigation was harassment rather than the protection of the claimant's rights. On this basis the action could be struck out as an abuse of process.[5]

With the exception of trivial or immoral information, no restrictions are placed on the *subject matter* that is protected by breach of confidence. As a result, the action has been used to protect a variety of subject matter: the idea for a new type of 'carpet grip';[6] a concept for a new television programme;[7] the genetic structure of a nectarine tree;[8] medical lectures;[9] customer lists; marital secrets;[10] the cultural and religious secrets of an Aboriginal Community;[11] and a report by the Department of Education on employment conditions.[12]

Information is protected irrespective of the *format* in which it appears. Thus, the action applies equally to information when embodied in writing,[13] drawings,[14] photographs,[15] goods or products, or where it has been disclosed orally.[16] It is also clear that the information does not need to be fixed or in a permanent form. As such, the information may be written, oral, encrypted, embodied in physical objects (whether it be the genetic code of a tree or the design of a product), or take shape as a formula, a plan, or a sketch.

While there are very few restrictions placed on the subject matter that is capable of being protected and the format that the information needs to take, there are four limitations placed on the *type* of information that may be protected under the action. These are where the information is trivial, immoral, vague, or in the public domain. We will deal with each in turn.

2 TRIVIAL INFORMATION

The first limit placed on the type of information that is protected by breach of confidence is that the courts may not protect information that is trivial. In *Coco v. Clark* Megarry J said he doubted 'whether equity would intervene unless the circumstances are of sufficient gravity; equity ought not to be invoked to protect trivial tittle-tattle, however confidential'.[17] In the context of trade secrets, the courts have occasionally suggested that, to be protectable an idea must be economically valuable or 'commercially attractive'. The trivia exception has had little impact upon the information protected by breach of confidence. This is because the courts have been reluctant to label information as trivial. The potential scope of the exception is

---

[4] *Ocular Sciences* [1997] *RPC* 289, 359.

[5] Ibid, 359. But cf. *Douglas v. Hello!* [2008] 1 AC 1 (where the House of Lords was prepared to protect *all* photographic images of the wedding.)

[6] *Seager v. Copydex (No. 1)* [1967] 2 *All ER* 415.   [7] *Fraser v. Thames TV* [1983] 2 *All ER* 101.

[8] *Franklin v. Giddins* [1978] *Qd R* 72.   [9] *Abernethy v. Hutchison* (1824) 1 *H & Tw* 28; 47 *ER* 1313.

[10] *Argyll v. Argyll* [1967] *Ch* 302.   [11] *Foster v. Mountford* [1978] *FSR* 582.

[12] *Director General of Education v. Public Services Association of New South Wales* (1985) 4 *IPR* 552.

[13] *Interfirm Comparison (Aust.) Pty. v. Law Society of New South Wales* [1975] 2 *NSWLR* 104.

[14] *Saltman Engineering v. Campbell Engineering* (1948) 65 *RPC* 203; *Inline Logistics* [2002] *RPC* 611.

[15] *Hellewell v. Chief Constable of Derbyshire* [1995] 1 *WLR* 804; *Douglas v. Hello!* [2008] 1 *AC* 1; *Campbell v. MGN* [2004] 2 *AC* 457 (HL); *Theakston v. MGN* [2003] *EMLR* 398; [2002] *EWHC* 137 (QB).

[16] *Fraser v. Thames* [1983] 2 *All ER* 101.   [17] [1969] *RPC* 41, 48.

further restricted by the fact that it has been suggested that it would never apply to government information. The reason for this is that it is impossible for the court to determine whether such information is important or not.[18] As part of the new approach adopted in relation to personal information, in *Mills v. MGN* the court held that the address of Heather Mills (model and then-wife of Paul McCartney) was protectable despite the 'relatively trivial character of the information'.[19] The willingness of the courts to exclude trivial information can also be seen from the Court of Appeal decision in *McKennitt v Ash*. This was an action brought by the Canadian folk singer Loreena McKennitt to prevent publication of a tell-all book published by an ex-friend. McKennitt's main claim was that the book revealed personal and private details that she was entitled to keep secret. While some of the information in the book was able to be protected,[20] Buxton LJ accepted that there was a category of cases (such as the trivial information in the book about matters such as a shopping trip to Italy), which involved innocuous, unimportant, and unremarkable events, which although private in one sense do not necessarily qualify for protection. However, there is no 'specific guidance (and probably cannot be) as to where precisely this line should be drawn'.[21] Indeed, it is worth noting that Lord Walker, dissenting in *Douglas v. Hello!*, seems almost to have been prepared to dismiss the action on the ground that the information which the *Hello!* photographs revealed about the Douglas/Zeta-Jones wedding could not be said to be anything other than trivial. Clearly, the majority did not take the same view, even though Baroness Hale emphasized the importance of the triviality in restricting the scope of the breach of confidence action in the post-*Spycatcher* era.[22]

3 IMMORAL INFORMATION

It also seems that the courts will not enforce obligations of confidentiality relating to matters that are grossly immoral.[23] However, in the absence of a generally accepted code of morality the courts have said that they should be extremely careful about castigating certain types of behaviour on the basis that it is immoral.[24] As such, as with the trivia exclusion, it seems that the exclusion of immoral information will have little impact upon the information protected by the action.

[18] *Attorney-General v. Guardian Newspapers* [1990] *AC* 109, 269 (Lord Griffiths). Cf. Lord Goff (recognizing exclusion but limiting it to trivia of the most humdrum kind).

[19] *Mills v. News Group Newspapers* [2001] *EMLR* 957 (when considering whether the information should be disclosed, the trivial nature of the information was weighed against the serious risk that stalkers posed if the address was disclosed).

[20] *McKennitt v. Ash* [2007] *EMLR* 113 (injunctive relief was granted in relation to information such as the claimant's personal and sexual relationships, her feelings after the death of her fiancé, and matters relating to her health and diet).

[21] *Murray v Express Newspapers* [2007] *EWHC* 1908 (Ch), para 59.

[22] *Douglas v. Hello!* [2008] 1 *AC* 1, 81–3 (paras. 287–91ff) (clearly Lord Walker also thought that *Creation Records* was wrongly decided and that the collection of objects around the swimming pool in that photograph was pure trivia); cf. ibid, 87 para. 307 (Baroness Hale) (no principled reason why photographic images of wedding should not be protected). For criticism of the majority on this point, see C. Michalos, '*Douglas v Hello*: the final frontier', [2007] *Ent LR* 241.

[23] Following from decisions in copyright law: see pp. 117–18. cf *M v. Secretary of State for Work and Pensions* [2006] *AC* 91, para 83 (interference with private life had to be of some seriousness before Art. 8 was engaged').

[24] *Stephens v. Avery* [1988] 2 *All ER* 477, 480–1.

4 INFORMATION THAT IS VAGUE

In many cases, the information protected by breach of confidence is detailed and specific. Information of this nature presents few problems. Thus, detailed plans of a prototype engine shown by an inventor to a manufacturer or a detailed formula for a new pharmaceutical may be protected. However, breach of confidence also applies to more general ideas and concepts such as a proposal for a new television series. The problem here is that if a claimant was able to impose confidentiality on very general ideas, this might enable them to impose unjustifiable burdens on anyone who received the information in confidence. To protect against this, the courts have said that the law will not protect information that is vague or general. More specifically, the courts have said that an aspiration or a desirable goal, the flavour of which can be captured in the phrase 'wouldn't it be great if...', would not be protected by the action.[25] Instead, such information is in the public domain, free to be used by all. It should be noted that the courts have been careful to stress that vagueness and simplicity are not the same thing.[26]

The exclusion of vague information can be seen in *De Maudsley v. Palumbo*.[27] The claimant in this case argued that the defendants, who ran the dance club called the Ministry of Sound, had appropriated his ideas for a new type of dance club that the claimant had told the defendant about at a dinner party. The claimant's idea for the new dance club consisted of five features. These were that the club would legally be open all night; be very large and fitted out in hi-tech industrial warehouse style; incorporate separate areas for drinking, dancing, and socializing; have an enclosed dance area where the sound quality would be high; and employ top-quality disc jockeys. Knox J held that all five features of the claimant's ideas were 'individually too vague' and thus not protectable. With the exception of the idea that the club would be legally open all night, he also said that the ideas were not novel. A similar approach was adopted in *Secton v. Delawood*.[28] In this case the claimant company, which was involved in developing methods of separating oil and water, brought an action to prevent the defendants, who were former employees, from working in the same field. The court refused to grant relief, holding that a bare goal, purpose, or possibility, a mere speculative idea, was not capable of being protected as a trade secret.

While general ideas may not be protected by breach of confidence, this does not mean that all ideas or concepts are therefore excluded. Indeed, one of the notable features of the action is that, unlike other areas of intellectual property such as copyright, breach of confidence provides protection over some of the more abstract aspects of the creative process. As with similar inquiries in other areas of intellectual property law, the difficult question is determining where and how the boundary is to be drawn between detailed information (which is clearly protectable) and very general ideas (which are not).

In thinking about where the dividing line is to be drawn, the courts have said that to be protected a concept or idea must be 'sufficiently developed to be capable of being realized'.[29]

---

[25] *De Maudsley v. Palumbo* [1996] *FSR* 447, 456.

[26] Ibid, 456; *Cranleigh Precision Engineering v. Bryant* [1965] 1 *WLR* 1293, 1309, 1310.　　　　[27] Ibid.

[28] *Secton Pty v. Delawood Pty* (1991) 21 *IPR* 136, 155 (Supreme Court of Victoria). See also *Intelsec Systems v. Grechi-Cini* [1999] 4 *All ER* 11, 31 (suggestion that flame detection could be developed as well as smoke detection was too vague to be capable of protection as a trade secret). Cf. the simple idea developed into the finished business plan in *Wheatley v. Bell* [1984] *FSR* 16.

[29] These requirements trace their origin to the comments of Harris J in the Supreme Court of Victoria in *Talbot v. General Television Corp.* [1981] *RPC* 1.

That is, it is necessary to go beyond simply identifying a desirable goal and to show a 'considerable degree of particularity in a definitive product'.[30] This can be seen, for example, in *Fraser v. Thames TV,* which concerned an idea for a TV series about the formation of a female rock group and the subsequent experiences of the members. Hirst J said 'that to be capable of protection the idea must be sufficiently developed, so that it would be seen to be a concept that has at least some attractiveness for a television programme and which is capable of being realised in actuality'. Similarly, in *Talbot v. General Television,* it was held that a new concept for a TV series was protectable because it was 'capable of being realized in actuality'.[31] The requirement that the idea must be capable of being realized 'as an actuality' has been taken to mean that the idea was capable of being transformed into 'a finished product in the relevant medium'.[32]

Perhaps the best way to get a sense of the level of detail needed for an idea to be protected is to look at the way the issue has been construed in the cases. We have already seen above how in *Palumbo* the claimant's ideas for a new dance club were held to be too vague to be protected. In contrast, in *Talbot* the court held that the proposal for a new television programme was sufficiently developed to be the subject of confidence. In this case, the claimant approached the defendant with an idea for a TV series about real-life millionaires. While the claimant subsequently sent the defendant a more detailed outline, this did not add very much of substance to the initial idea.[33] As such, it seems that the general proposal for a new type of programme involving real-life millionaires would have been protected in its own right. In effect this is what transpired in *Fraser v. Thames TV* where it was held that the claimant's concept for an idea for a TV series about the formation of a female rock group was specific enough to be protected.

The level of detail required for an idea or concept to be protectable varies depending on the case in hand. Speaking about the level of detail needed for a proposal for a television programme to be protected, Hirst J said 'I do not think that' the requirement of actuality 'necessitates in every case a full synopsis. In some cases the nature of the idea may require extensive development of this kind in order to meet the criteria. But in others the criteria may be met by short unelaborated statement of an idea.'[34] One factor that will influence the level of specificity required is the way information is normally treated in the industry in question. Thus, in *Fraser v. Thames TV* Hirst J said that the fact that it was normal practice in the theatre, television, and film industries to treat general proposals for new programmes as if they were protected was an important factor in his reaching the conclusion that the information was in fact protected.[35]

In some cases, the courts have suggested that the test for whether an idea or concept is sufficiently developed to be protectable is to consider whether the idea or concept is 'attractive'.[36] However, as Knox J pointed out in *Palumbo,* this requirement 'doesn't advance things much because if the element is missing it is hardly likely to be appropriated'.[37] The flip side of this is that if a defendant uses the information this would be proof of its attractiveness. As such, the relative attractiveness of the information adds little to the inquiry.

---

[30] *De Maudsley v. Palumbo* [1996] *FSR* 447. *Sales v. Stromberg* [2006] *FSR* (7) 89, 110 (designs of decorative pendants, though simple geometric shapes, were confidential).

[31] *Talbot v. General TV* [1981] *RPC* 1, 9.

[32] *De Maudsley v. Palumbo* [1996] *FSR* 447. Knox J distinguished between a 'mental product', that could be protected, and a mere 'aspiration', which could not.

[33] *Fraser v. Thames* [1983] 2 *All ER* 101, 121.   [34] Ibid.   [35] Ibid, 121–2.

[36] *Talbot v. General TV* [1981] *RPC* 1, 9.

[37] *De Maudsley v. Palumbo* [1996] *FSR* 447, Knox J. This requirement seems similar to the one that information is not 'trivial'.

5 INFORMATION IN THE PUBLIC DOMAIN

One of the most important restrictions placed on the information that is protected by breach of confidence is that the action does not apply to material that is in the public domain. As Laddie J said '[p]rima facie, information that is in the public domain is not capable of being treated as confidential'.[38] The upshot of this is that, however confidential the circumstances of communication, 'there can be no breach of confidence in revealing to others something which is already common knowledge'.[39] In more positive terms, this means that to be protected the information must be relatively secret.

The notion of public domain has a different meaning in relation to breach of confidence than it does in other areas of intellectual property law. Before looking at what is meant by the public domain in this context, it should be noted that the status of the information is a question of fact, not intention. Consequently, information is still capable of being protected even though the confider intended the information to be published, but failed to do this.[40] Conversely, if material is in the public domain, it does not matter that the confider intended, but failed, to keep the information secret.[41]

5.1 'RELATIVE SECRECY'

In patent law a single disclosure to one person is sufficient to place the information in the public domain and thus to destroy the novelty of an invention. In contrast, breach of confidence is built around a notion of 'relative secrecy'. In essence this means that it is possible for a number of people to know about the 'secret' and the information still not be in the public domain. The upshot of this is that the fact that information has been disclosed to a number of people does not necessarily mean that the information is incapable of being treated as confidential. For example, in *Prince Albert v. Strange*[42] the court held that while Prince Albert had disclosed details of his engravings to friends and relatives, this did not destroy the confidentiality that existed in the information.

The crucial question is how widespread must the information be for it to lose its status as a secret and for it to fall into the public domain? The degree of publication required before secrecy is lost depends on a range of different factors. These include the type of information; the section of the public who have an interest in knowing about the information;[43] the domain in which the information was published; the degree of publication within that domain; the form in which the information is published; and the vigour with which the information is

---

[38] *CMI v. Phytopharm* [1999] *FSR* 235, 255. See also *A-G v. Guardian* [1990] *AC* 109, 282.

[39] *Coco v. Clark* [1969] *RPC* 41, 47.

[40] A mere intention to publish in due course should not deprive information of its confidential status, despite the Court of Appeal's decision in *Times v. Mirror Group* [1993] *EMLR* 443. The Court of Appeal decision in *Times* is irreconcilable with the House of Lords position in *Douglas v Hello!* [2008] 1 *AC* 1 that the photographic information was confidential even though the magazine intended to publish it.

[41] It is clear that if the confider publishes the information, the obligation comes to an end: *Mustad v. Allcock and Dosen* (1928) [1963] 3 *All ER* 416.

[42] (1849) 2 *DeG & Sm* 652; 64 *ER* 293 (Knight Bruce LJ); (1849) 1 *Mac & G* 25; 41 *ER* 1171 (Cottenham LC).

[43] In *Ryan v. Capital Leasing* (High Court of Ireland, 2 Apr. 1993) it was said that the public domain means that 'the information is well known to that section of the public which has an interest in knowing the information'. See P. Lavery, 'Secrecy, Springboards and the Public Domain' [1998] *EIPR* 93.

likely to be pursued within that domain.[44] It is important to note that a partial disclosure only deprives that part of the information disclosed of its confidentiality.[45] The House of Lords in *Douglas v Hello!* was divided over precisely the question whether the information that had been confidential remained so after publication of the authorized photographs by *OK!* According to Lord Nicholls, once the claimant had published its photos (an action which was expedited so as to limit the impact of *Hello!*'s revelation) there was nothing really left that was confidential in the defendant's photographs. In contrast, the majority took a broader view. The content of the photographs was not equivalent to a verbal description of the event: each photograph was a separate piece of information. As Lord Brown explained '[t]he secret consists no less of each and every visual image of the wedding than of the wedding as a whole'.[46] Disclosure of some photographs of the wedding, therefore, did not deprive other photographs of their 'quality of confidence'.

A personal secret might be of interest to many more people than a trade secret, which is only likely to be of interest to competitors. Thus, a court may treat personal information as being relatively secret even though a lot of people know about it.[47] This arose in *Franchi v. Franchi*[48] where the court was called upon to consider whether information was still confidential after it had been published in a patent specification in Belgium, but before it had been published in the United Kingdom. It was held that the fact that the information was in the public domain in another country might be relevant when considering whether the information was confidential in the United Kingdom. The court also held that because patent agents were in the habit of inspecting foreign specifications, the information was in the public domain. As internet use grows, it will be increasingly difficult for a claimant to establish that information known in one place is confidential elsewhere.[49]

Another factor that may useful in indicating whether information remains confidential is the extent to which further publication would harm the claimant. In some cases, the requirement of harm and the finding that the information is confidential have operated as alternative grounds. This can be seen, for example, in the *Spycatcher* decision. Peter Wright, who was under an obligation of confidentiality as a member of the Security Services, wrote a book called *Spycatcher*. The book was published in Australia, Ireland, and the USA. The *Sunday Times* began to serialize the book in England and the *Guardian/Observer* sought to repeat the story. The Attorney General sought an injunction to prevent publication. Lord Keith said that the continued serialization of the book would not be a breach of confidence. This was because it would not have caused any further damage to the government.[50]

---

[44] Dean, 123–9.

[45] *House of Spring Gardens v. Point Blank* [1983] *FSR* 213, 255; *Attorney-General v. Times Newspapers* [2001] 1 *WLR* 885, 892–3 (CA).

[46] [2008] 1 *AC* 1, 73 (para 257) *per* Lord Nicholls; 48–9 (para 122) *per* Lord Hoffmann; 94 (para 329) *per* Lord Brown.

[47] *HRH Prince of Wales v. Associated Newspapers* [2007] 3 *WLR* 222; *G v. Day* [1982] 1 *NSWLR* 24 (ephemeral revelation on TV did not deprive information of confidential status).

[48] [1967] *RPC* 149.

[49] 'The truth of the matter is that in the contemporary world of electronics and jumbo jets news anywhere is news everywhere': *Attorney-General v. Guardian Newspapers* [1987] 1 *WLR* 1248, 1269 *per* Browne-Wilkinson V-C. Cf. *Attorney-General v. Turnaround Distributors* [1989] *FSR* 169 (publication of book in Ireland did not render it unarguable that the book was confidential in the UK)—a pre-*Spycatcher* case.

[50] *Attorney-General v. Guardian* [1990] *AC* 109, 260. Lord Keith said that in relation to government secrets, it was necessary to show that there was a public interest in restraining disclosure and that, given that no harm would occur, this was absent.

5.2 THE SPRINGBOARD DOCTRINE

One situation where the breach of confidence action may provide protection over information that is in the public domain is where one party uses information that they have obtained in confidence to steal a march on competitors. This issue is dealt with by the so-called springboard doctrine. In essence the doctrine aims to ensure that a person who breaches a duty of confidence is not able to benefit from the breach. As Lord Denning said in *Seager v. Copydex,*[51] a person who obtained the information from a private source should not be in a better position than someone who went to the public source. The effect of the doctrine is to prevent a person who obtained the information from a private source from getting a head start without paying for it. As Roxburgh J said in *Terrapin v. Builders' Supply Co.*:

a person who has obtained information in confidence is not allowed to use it as a springboard for activities detrimental to the person who made the confidential communication, and a springboard it remains even when all the features have been published or can be ascertained by actual inspection by any member of the public.[52]

The claimants in this case manufactured prefabricated portable buildings. As part of a joint venture the claimants gave the defendants detailed technical information about the prefabricated buildings. When the relationship broke down and the defendants continued to manufacture the buildings, the claimants sued for breach of confidence. The defendants claimed that the information was no longer capable of being protected by breach of confidence. This was because the claimants had sold buildings to members of the public (which could be dismantled to reveal the details) and also published a brochure that disclosed the technical details of the buildings. In short, they argued that, as the information was now in the public domain, it was no longer capable of being protected. Roxburgh J held that, to obtain information equivalent to that initially given to the defendant, the defendant would have had to dismantle a portable building and construct tests. The initial information gave the confidant a head start over a member of the public. Under the springboard doctrine, the defendants were to be placed under a special disability to ensure that they did not get a head start over competitors.

The springboard doctrine attempts to prevent a person from using any special information they may have obtained in confidence from gaining an advantage over others who would have had to obtain the information by other means (such as reverse engineering the publicly available embodiment of the information).[53] The doctrine serves two policies. It promotes the integrity of confidential relations by minimizing any benefits that can be gained by a confidant

---

[51] *Seager v. Copydex* [1967] 2 *All ER* 415, 417. See also *Schering Chemicals v. Falkman* [1982] *QB* 1, 15–16 (*per* Denning MR, dissenting).

[52] [1967] *RPC* 375, 391. See also *Saltman* (1948) 65 *RPC* 203 (the defendant could have taken the leather punch to pieces and constructed drawings, but had not done so, and thus was liable). For criticism of the springboard doctrine on the basis of its inconsistency with the rule that once in the public domain the confidence ceases to exist, see Buxton LJ in *EPI Environmental Technologies v. Symphony Plastic Technologies* [2006] *EWCA Civ* 3; [2006] 1 *WLR* 495 Note (stating that the decision did not address any issues of law or practice 'calling for report').

[53] The law could reach the same result if it recognized that a recipe or formula might still be 'relatively secret' even though products made to the recipe are on the market and are such that they can be analysed to ascertain the secret recipe. However, recent case law suggests that such information is no longer confidential: *Mars v. Teknowledge* [2000] *FSR* 138. But cf. *Murray v. Yorkshire Fund Managers* [1998] 1 *WLR* 951, 960, *per* Nourse LJ: 'in my view the springboard principle can have no application where, as here, the information has ceased to be confidential'.

utilizing information obtained in confidence. It also promotes fair relations between potential competitors.[54]

The springboard doctrine has a number of important features. The first is that the restrictions imposed on private information do not last forever.[55] In *Potters Ballotini v. Weston Baker*[56] Lord Denning explained that '[a]lthough a man must not use such information as a springboard to get a start over others, nevertheless the springboard does not last forever. If he does use it, a time may come when so much has happened that he can no longer be restrained.' Accordingly, the appropriate remedy was to restrict the confidant from using the information for a limited time. The appropriate period is calculated by reference to the time that it would take to discover the information from legitimate public sources.[57] The second feature of the action is that because of the difficulties in calculating the duration of the confidant's head start and the problems of enforcing it by way of injunction, the courts have indicated that they prefer to give monetary rather than injunctive relief.[58]

So far, we have focused on situations where a person acquires information in confidence that could *later* be located from public sources. However, the springboard doctrine has also been extended to situations where the confidential information was itself collated from public sources (rather than where private information has been disclosed to the public in a different form).[59] In *Roger Bullivant v. Ellis,*[60] the defendant had taken a copy of the list of customers from his employer during the course of his employment. While each of the names could have been acquired from public domain sources such as professional and trade directories, Falconer J granted an injunction to prevent the defendant from taking unfair advantage of the information. The Court of Appeal allowed the appeal and discharged the injunction saying that such an injunction should not normally extend beyond the period for which the unfair advantage is expected to continue.[61]

5.3 ENCRYPTED INFORMATION

Another situation where questions about the status of information arise is where information is encrypted. What is the effect of disclosing information in an encrypted form? If a person places encrypted information in the public domain, does this mean that the information is secret and potentially protectable? Or does it mean that the information is published and thus not protectable?

The question of whether the encrypted information that is in the public domain is capable of being protected by the law of confidentiality was considered in *Mars v. Teknowledge*.[62] The claimants in the case designed and manufactured coin-receiving and -changing mechanisms (which are used in vending machines). The mechanisms included 'discriminators' that function to determine the authenticity and denomination of a coin fed into the machine. One of the

---

[54] *Aquaculture v. New Zealand Mussel Co.* (1985) 5 *IPR* 353, 383 ('a principle, founded on the concept of fairness'). Dean, 143 describes the springboard doctrine 'as close to a de facto doctrine of unfair competition as Anglo-American courts have come'.

[55] *Sun Valley Foods v. John Philip Vincent* [2002] *FSR* 82 (application for springboard relief rejected because the advantage the defendants received from the misuse of the information was ephemeral and short term in nature).

[56] [1977] *RPC* 202.

[57] If reverse engineering is not a possibility, the springboard metaphor is inappropriate: *Electro Cad Australia v. Mejati RCS SDN BHD* [1999] *FSR* 291, 307.

[58] *Coco v. Clark* [1969] *RPC* 41, 47.   [59] But cf. *Schering v. Falkman* [1982] *QB* 1.

[60] [1987] *FSR* 172.   [61] Ibid, 184.   [62] [2000] *FSR* 138.

problems with the discriminators was that whenever there was a change in the coinage, they had to be reprogrammed. The claimants developed a new discriminator (called the 'Cashflow') which had the ability to be reprogrammed for new coin data. Cashflow consisted of 'a data layout, a serial communications protocol and an encryption system to make it difficult for third parties to find out by reverse engineering how to recalibrate (reprogram) the Cashflow discriminator'. Importantly, none of this information was published directly by the claimants. The defendant had broken the encryption system and reverse-engineered the Cashflow discriminator. The claimants brought an action arguing, inter alia, that the defendant's activities by way of reverse engineering amounted to a breach of confidence.

Jacob J held that the encrypted information in the Cashflow machine did not have the necessary quality of confidence. After noting that the machine was freely available on the market,[63] Jacob J said that '[a]nyone with the necessary skill to de-crypt had access to the information. The fact that only a few have those skills is...neither here nor there. Anyone can acquire the skills and, anyway, a buyer is free to go to a man who has them.'[64] On this basis, Jacob J concluded that as the information had been published, it was not capable of being protected.

The courts have adopted a similar approach in situations where the information is embodied in an object in the public domain that can only be accessed through reverse engineering.[65] The cases have suggested that where information is embodied (or hidden) in a machine or a product which is in the public domain, the information is also in the public domain and thus not capable of being protected. The upshot of this is that information will be treated as having been published and thus in the public domain, even though it can only be accessed through a process of decryption or reverse engineering.

These decisions, if followed, will restrict the use that can be made of the breach of confidence action to regulate information on the internet. Given that genetic information in biological matter is 'in the public domain', these decisions may also have important ramifications for the use of the action in respect of biotechnological inventions. It would not be very difficult, however, for a court to use the notion of 'relative secrecy', to reach a different conclusion.[66]

5.4 PUBLIC INFORMATION THAT BECOMES SECRET

In patent law, the standard for deciding whether information is in the public domain is absolute. This means that once information is in the public domain it can never become secret. In contrast, with the breach of confidence action the test for whether information is in the public domain is more flexible. As a result, the status of information may change over time. This means that it is possible for information that is in the public domain to become secret. This may occur because the public forgets the information, or because the individuals that make up the relevant public change. For example, in *Schering Chemicals v. Falkman*[67] details had been widely publicized between 1975 and 1978 that a drug called PRIMODOS, which Schering manufactured for use as a pregnancy test, had damaged unborn children. In order to improve its

---

[63] For consideration of the situation where the product has been hired rather than sold, so the product is not 'freely available', see *K.S. Paul (Printing Machinery) v. Southern Instruments (Communications)* [1964] *RPC* 118 (in accordance with a hiring agreement, the claimant supplied a telephone-answering machine to the defendant, but with a specific obligation not to interfere with it. In breach of that the defendant allowed another to remove it and examine it. The court granted an interim injunction).

[64] *Mars v. Teknowledge* [2000] *FSR* 138, 149.   [65] *Saltman* (1948) 65 *RPC* 203.

[66] Cf. *Ackroyds v. Islington Plastics* [1962] *RPC* 97, 104 (if what is in the public domain needs reverse engineering, that information ought to be treated as relatively secret).

[67] [1982] *QB* 1.

image, which had been damaged by the adverse publicity, Schering engaged a public relations firm, Falkman, to train its staff in the handling of television interviews in relation to the drug. One of Falkman's employees approached Thames TV with a view to making a documentary about Schering and PRIMODOS. Even though the information upon which the programme was based could have been derived from public sources, the Court of Appeal granted Schering an injunction on the grounds of a breach of confidence. Shaw LJ stated that 'to revive the recollection of matters which may be detrimental or prejudicial... is not to be condoned because the facts are already known and linger in the memories of others'.[68]

5.5 DISCLOSURE BY THE CONFIDANT

For some time, it was thought that, where information had entered the public domain as a result of a breach of confidence, this did not affect the status of the information. While the information may have been *public knowledge,* the fact that the information entered the public domain wrongfully meant that it was not *public property.*[69] This meant that the information remained confidential in spite of the fact that it was widely available. Others argued that, once information was in the public domain, it was not capable of being protected by the action. This was the case even where disclosure arose through a breach of confidence.

Most of the confusion as to whether information disclosed through a breach of confidence is still capable of being protected by the action was resolved in *Spycatcher.*[70] In this decision, the House of Lords held that once information was in the public domain, the courts could not restrain further publication.[71]

Even though information that enters the public domain via a breach of confidence is not capable of being protected by the action, this does not mean that the confidant is thereby absolved of liability. In these circumstances, the confidant has clearly committed a wrong and will be subject to the regular remedies for breach of confidence. Some cases have referred to the provision of remedies against the confidant in these circumstances as 'the springboard doctrine'.[72] The idea being that a person who obtained information in confidence is not allowed to use it as a springboard for activities detrimental to the person who made the confidential communication. We prefer to reserve the springboard metaphor for a different category of cases (which were discussed above). We will look at the remedies against an errant confidant when we look at remedies for breach of confidence later.

5.6 COMPILATIONS OF INFORMATION THAT IS IN THE PUBLIC DOMAIN

While information that is in the public domain will not be protected by the breach of confidence action, a distinction is drawn between such information (which is not protected) and information that builds upon such information (which may be protected). It is clear that, where someone

---

[68] Ibid, 28.

[69] *Cranleigh Precision Engineering v. Bryant* [1964] 3 *All ER* 289 and *Speed Seal Products v. Paddington* [1986] *FSR* 309 appeared to support the proposition that a confider could not be released from an obligation of confidentiality by their own acts.

[70] *Attorney-General v. Guardian* [1990] *AC* 109. For commentary, see G. Jones, 'Breach of Confidence—after *Spycatcher*' (1990) 42 *Current Legal Problems* 48; Dean, 161–2.

[71] Lord Goff held that once information was widely available there could be no obligation respecting it. This was because the subject matter of the obligation had vanished.

[72] *Ocular Sciences* [1997] *RPC* 289, 399.

collects, arranges, or elaborates on elements that are already in the public domain, the resulting information is capable of being protected.[73] As Lord Greene MR said in *Saltman Engineering*,[74] 'it is perfectly possible to have a confidential document...which is the result of work done by the maker on materials which may be available for the use of anybody'. He added that 'what makes it confidential is the fact that the maker of the document has used his brain and thus produced a result which can only be produced by somebody who goes through the same process'. In a similar vein, Megarry J said in *Coco v. Clark* that 'something constructed solely from materials in the public domain may possess the necessary quality of confidentiality...But whether it is described as originality or novelty or ingenuity or otherwise, I think there must be some produce of the human brain which suffices to confer a confidential nature upon the information'.[75]

It is clear that not all acts of compilation will produce results that are capable of being protected. Indeed, as Knox J has said, 'a combination of features which were not individually novel does not automatically become novel by being added together'.[76] The status of compilations of information that is in the public domain was considered in *Ocular Sciences v. Aspect Vision*.[77] In this case, the claimant asserted that a booklet that contained a compendium of the detailed dimensions of the claimant's range of contact lenses was confidential. This was the case even though each of the lenses had been put on the market. The claimant argued that to obtain even a small amount of the information contained in the booklet a lens manufacturer would need to analyse thousands of lenses, a process that would take considerable time and effort. Laddie J said that he had great doubts as to whether 'a mere mechanical collection of data which is in the public domain' could be confidential.[78] He added that *Saltman* and *Coco* do not establish that the compilation of information in the public domain is always enough to confer confidentiality. While valuable and novel ideas could be produced by the judicious selection and combination of a number of items which are separately in the public domain, and such ideas would be capable of being the subject of an obligation of confidence, they would only be such if they were the 'product of the skill of the human brain'. In contrast, Laddie J said that a 'mere non-selective list of publicly available information should not be treated as confidential even if putting it together involves some time and effort. No relevant skill is employed.'[79]

As is the case with the copyright protection for facts, the difficult question is knowing the type and level of labour that needs to be exerted on material in the public domain for the resulting information to be capable of being protected.[80] While this topic has attracted very little attention, it seems that the threshold for protection is low.[81] This can be seen in *Talbot*,[82] where the court was called upon to decide whether a proposal for a television programme about real-life millionaires was capable of being protected by the action. While similar television programmes had already been made, the court held that the claimant's programme had a 'commercial twist' or a 'particular slant' that distinguished it from previous programmes. The unique feature of the proposal was that as part of the programme successful [sic] millionaires, such as Alan Bond and Neil Diamond, were to give the recipe for their success.

---

[73] TRIPS, Art. 39(2) requires protection to be granted only where information is 'secret in the sense that it is not, as a body or in the precise configuration and assembly of its components, generally known among or readily accessible to persons within the circles that normally deal with the kind of information in question'.

[74] (1948) 65 *RPC* 203, 215.   [75] [1969] *RPC* 41, 47.

[76] *De Maudsley v. Palumbo* [1996] *FSR* 447, 459.

[77] [1997] *RPC* 289.   [78] Ibid, 374.   [79] Ibid, 375.

[80] See pp. 99–103. Note also that the springboard notion may limit relief in such cases.

[81] In *International Scientific Communications v. Pattison* [1979] *FSR* 429, 434 *per* Goulding J ('the lists with which I am concerned embodied enough labour of composition, experience of the trade, and practical utility to fall into the class of confidential trade information').

[82] *Talbot v. General TV* [1981] *RPC* 1, 9. See also *Fraser v. Thames* [1983] 2 *All ER* 101.

5.7 CONFIDENTIAL INFORMATION ABOUT PUBLIC INFORMATION?

The account so far has left at least one issue unexplained. This relates to the level of protection to be afforded to private information about public information. In *Cranleigh Precision Engineering v. Bryan*[83] the defendant had been managing director of the claimant firm, which manufactured swimming pools made according to a patent owned by the company. In the course of his employment, the defendant learned of the previous grant of a patent for similar swimming pools. Instead of informing the claimant, the defendant set up a rival business and purchased the patent. The claimant sought an injunction to restrain the defendant from making use of information received in his capacity as managing director, in particular 'the knowledge of the possible effect to and on the [claimant] of the existence and publication of the specification'. Roskill J granted an injunction preventing the defendant from making use of the patent.[84] In so doing, Roskill J rejected the defendant's argument that, because the information related to a patent that was in the public domain, the information in question was also in the public domain.

Although *Cranleigh* was initially interpreted as supporting the proposition that confiders could not be released from an obligation of confidentiality by their own acts,[85] subsequent case law has rejected this approach. How then are we to explain the result in *Cranleigh?* If we ignore the easy option of arguing that it was wrongly decided, two alternative ways of explaining the decision present themselves. According to the first view, the defendant was under a fiduciary duty that meant that, instead of taking advantage of the opportunity for himself, he should have exploited the patent for his employer. *Cranleigh* can also be explained as a case concerning confidential private information about public information. While information about the patent was in the public domain, the impact (and thus the value) of the patent depended on private information that the defendant had acquired through his employment with the claimants. As such, what was protected here was not the information disclosed in the patent *per se*, so much as the information about the consequences and importance of the patent to the defendant, which depended on information that was not in the public domain.[86]

6 NOVEL AND ORIGINAL INFORMATION?

One of the key differences between breach of confidence and the statutory forms of intellectual property relates to the qualitative restrictions placed upon the intangible property that is protected. For example, novelty and non-obviousness play a key role in limiting the inventions that are patentable. Similar restrictions exist in all the other areas we have covered in this book. With the exception of information that is vague, or in the public domain, there are few restrictions imposed on the information that is protected. In a number of recent cases, however, the courts have begun to use language that suggests that they are working towards the imposition of some type of qualitative restriction upon the type of information protected by

---

[83] [1964] 3 *All ER* 289.

[84] More specifically, 'from overtly making use of their acquisition of [the patent] or any licence granted in respect thereof in support of or in connection with sales...etc. of above-ground swimming-pools in competition with the plaintiff's above-ground swimming-pools': ibid, 303.

[85] See *Speed Seal* [1986] *FSR* 309 (claim to injunctive relief might be justified where facts alleged that confidant had himself published the confidential designs for couplings).

[86] [1965] 1 *WLR* 1293, 1312–14.

the action. For example, in *Coulthard v. Disco Mix*,[87] the High Court held that information relating to the techniques the defendant used for creating mega-mixes was not confidential. The technique involved the defendant listing the recordings, identifying the beat and key of each song, and then mixing the songs together in an order that enabled them to be blended smoothly. Judge Sher QC doubted that information about the techniques used by the claimant in creating mega-mixes would be protected. The reason for this was that the techniques were 'pretty obvious once one is setting out to create a beat-mix'.[88] In other contexts, the courts have also spoken of the need for information to be *original* and *novel*. For example, in *De Maudsley v. Palumbo*[89] Knox J said that, with the exception of the idea that the club would be legally open all night, the ideas were not novel.[90] The courts have also used novelty and originality as a way of gauging whether information that builds upon material in the public domain is capable of being protected.

It is difficult to know what to make of these statements. In part this is because the language of the decisions is unclear. Another problem is that most of the comments were *obiter* with little, if anything, turning on them. For the most part, it seems that such criteria seem to be most appropriate in relation to trade secrets and commercial information. The requirements seem superfluous in relation to personal information: there seems to be little that could be gained from asking whether information about a person's sexual preferences is 'obvious' or 'novel'.

In thinking about the potential relevance of novelty and related criteria to the information that is capable of being protected by breach of confidence, it is helpful to ask what purpose could they serve? That is, what is to be gained from looking at breach of confidence in this way? Unlike the situation with patents, the obligation of confidentiality only applies to those who are in a confidential relationship with the claimant. As such, the consequence of protecting information that is not novel is much more limited than with patents. Having said that, problems could still arise if protection was given over information that was not novel. For example, in the absence of any restrictions as to the need for novelty (or obviousness), what would happen if a person approached a publisher and said, in confidence, 'I have an idea to write a textbook on intellectual property law'? In the absence of a novelty requirement, there is a possibility that the publisher could be prevented from commissioning other authors from working in the area.[91] This consequence seems particularly undesirable where there are only very few people who have the potential to exploit a particular idea (here, legal publishers). Whether the novelty (etc.) requirement is intended to meet such concerns, and, if it is, the degree to which the law succeeds in protecting the public from such restraints, is far from clear.

7 PRIVATE INFORMATION

As mentioned earlier, the English courts have sought to adapt the action for breach of confidence to give effect to the obligation under Article 8 of the European Convention on Human Rights to provide a right to respect for a person's private life. To do so, the courts have extended

87 [1999] 2 *All ER* 457.
88 Ibid, 474. (The claimant had not argued that the idea of a mega-mix was confidential.)
89 *De Maudsley v. Palumbo* [1996] *FSR* 447.
90 Ibid, 456 (the idea 'must contain some significant element of originality').
91 Though the publisher would not be prevented from going ahead with an identical proposal independently put forward by another author.

the action to cover some information which is to be regarded as 'private' but which the legal system would not have traditionally treated as confidential. The test adopted in *Campbell v. Mirror Group Newspapers* for determining whether information is protected is whether the claimant has a 'reasonable expectation of privacy'. Three points are worth observing about this test.

First, if a person has a reasonable expectation of privacy, information is to be protected even though it might otherwise have been considered trivial. As Lord Walker explained in *Douglas v Hello!*, the argument that information is trivial or anodyne carries much less weight in a case concerned with facts about an individual's private life 'which he or she reasonably expects to be kept confidential'.[92]

Second, even if information is so widely disclosed that it would not be regarded as confidential, it may still retain its private character.[93] Consequently, courts may enjoin the further publication of private information, even though its dissemination is already widespread. This was recognized both by the House of Lords in *Campbell v. MGN*, when it enjoined further publication of photographs of Naomi Campbell leaving a meeting of Narcotics Anonymous, and by the Court of Appeal in *Douglas v. Hello!*, when it granted Douglas and Zeta-Jones injunctive relief preventing further publication of unauthorized photographs of their wedding.[94]

Third, there remain troublesome questions as to the extent to which any photograph of a public figure in a public place comprises 'private' information (even though it would be difficult to think of such information as confidential). To date, the UK courts have indicated that such images are only private if they contain something embarrassing or offensive. A picture of a celebrity 'popping to the shops' is not to be regarded as private. In contrast, the European Court of Human Rights, in its famous *von Hannover* decision, seems to suggest that all photographic images of a person (other than a public figure performing public duties) are to be regarded as 'private'. There it was held that the German courts had erred when they failed to prevent publication of images of Princess Caroline of Monaco doing acts as quotidian as eating an ice cream and riding a horse.[95] Presumably, as the ECHR's jurisprudence develops, the House of Lords may need to revisit the threshold applicable under UK law.

Fourth, while the question of whether a person has a reasonable expectation of privacy will always depend on the particular circumstances, the Court of Appeal has provided a useful checklist of considerations. In *Murray v. Express Newspapers*,[96] when holding that the infant child of a famous figure (J.K. Rowling) had a reasonable expectation of privacy even when out in public, Sir Anthony Clarke MR set out a series of factors that a tribunal should consider. These included the attributes of the claimant (whether a child or an adult), the nature of the activity in which the claimant was engaged (public duties, recreation etc.), the place where the claimant was, the nature and purpose of the intrusion, whether the observer was aware of the absence of consent from the claimant, the effect on the claimant, and how the information came into the hands of the publisher.

---

[92] [2008] 1 *AC* 1, para 291.   [93] Ibid, para. 255 (*per* Lord Nicholls).

[94] *Campbell v. MGN* [2004] 2 *AC* 457; *Douglas v Hello!* [2006] *QB* 125, 162 (para 105) (CA) ('there will be a fresh intrusion of privacy when each additional viewer sees the photograph and even when one who has seen a previous publication of the photograph is confronted by a fresh publication of it').

[95] *Von Hannover v. Germany* [2005] *EHRR* 1.

[96] [2008] *EWCA Civ* 446 (7 May 2008).

45

OBLIGATION OF CONFIDENCE

CHAPTER CONTENTS

1 INTRODUCTION

The second element that must be proved in a breach of confidence action is that the defendant was under a legal (as opposed merely to a moral) obligation of confidentiality.[1] While the rights recognized by copyright, patents, designs, and trade marks apply against anyone who deals with the intangible property within the relevant jurisdiction, traditionally the breach of confidence action only applies to those who receive information in confidence. As we will see, a different position now holds in relation to private information. In describing the situations where an obligation of confidentiality will arise, it is common practice to focus on the nature of the relationship between the parties. In following this model, we look at the duties that arise where the parties are in a direct relationship, where there is an indirect relationship, and where there is no relationship between the parties. We then look at the duties that arise when the parties are in an employment relationship and the special duties owed by statutory bodies who gather information.

2 DIRECT RELATIONSHIP

The first and most straightforward situation where a duty of confidence may arise is where the parties are in a direct relationship with each other. In these circumstances a duty of confidence may arise contractually, as a result of the type of relationship that exists between the parties, or because of the way the information is communicated. We will deal with each in turn.

---

[1] See *Attorney-General v. Jonathan Cape* [1976] QB 752; *Malone v. Metropolitan Police Commissioner* [1979] Ch 344.

2.1 CONTRACTUAL PROVISIONS AS TO CONFIDENTIALITY

A person may be under a contractual obligation not to use or disclose information. The contractual conditions of confidentiality may be express or implied.[2] Express obligations typically arise in employment contracts (which we look at later) and in the licensing of know-how. The relationship between banker and customer is an example of a situation where an obligation of confidentiality will normally be implied into the contract.[3]

2.2 INTRINSIC NATURE OF THE RELATIONSHIP

In some cases, an obligation of confidentiality arises as a result of the type of the relationship that exists between parties. More specifically, an obligation of confidentiality might exist as part of a fiduciary relationship that exists between the parties. A 'fiduciary relationship' is an equitable relationship in which one party has a duty to act for the benefit of another,[4] and arises, for example, between doctor and patient; priest and penitent; solicitor and client; husband and wife;[5] and trustee and beneficiary.[6] It is unclear whether the duty also applies to other types of personal relationship,[7] particularly to transient or commercial sexual relationships.[8]

The manner in which the law of confidence and the law of fiduciaries inter-relate is unclear.[9] Some courts and commentators have suggested that all confidential obligations are examples of fiduciary obligations.[10] However, such conflation seems inappropriate given that a number of persons normally subject to obligations of confidentiality (such as employees)[11] are not normally treated as fiduciaries.[12] It would seem preferable, at least for the sake of clarity, to keep the notions of 'fiduciaries' and 'confidences' distinct. In any case, the pressure to merge the two categories may well diminish if the courts accept that the remedy of a constructive trust is available for a breach of confidence, rather than only for a breach of fiduciary duty.[13]

---

[2] However an express confidentiality agreement may be void. In the case of software, for example, a click-wrap restriction prohibiting decompilation may be void. See p. 295.

[3] *Tournier v. National & Provincial Bank* [1924] 1 *KB* 461.

[4] See *Bristol and West Building Society v. Mothew* [1998] *Ch* 1, 18.

[5] *Argyll v. Argyll* [1967] *Ch* 302.   [6] *Boardman v. Phipps* [1967] 2 *AC* 46.

[7] See *M. & N. Mackenzie v. News Group Newspapers* (18 Jan. 1988) (a homosexual relationship did not give rise to a duty of confidence). But cf. *Stephens v. Avery* [1988] 2 *All ER* 477; *Barrymore v. News Group Newspapers* [1997] *FSR* 600, 602 (disclosures in all personal relationships fall within 'limited purpose' test, and hence are confidential).

[8] *Theakston v. MGN* [2002] *EMLR* 398, 419 para 64. In part, this will depend on the nature of the relationship (sex within marriage giving rise to different obligations than transient or commercial sexual relations). While the position is not clear, in some cases the courts have said that it is not inherent in the nature of a sexual relationship that anything that transpires within it is confidential. See below at pp. 1056–7.

[9] For a thorough review see D. Klinck, 'Things of Confidence: Loyalty, Secrecy and Fiduciary Obligations' (1990) 54 *Saskatchewan Law Review* 73 (a confidant is a type of fiduciary). Cf. G. Hammond, 'Is Breach of Confidence Properly Analysed in Fiduciary Terms?' (1979) 25 *McGill Law Journal* 244; J. Glover, 'Is Breach of Confidence a Fiduciary Wrong?' (2001) 21(4) *LS* 594 (stressing importance of keeping breach of confidence and the law of fiduciaries separate). See also Gurry, 158–62; Dean, 21 (the debate is 'largely sterile').

[10] *Schering v. Falkman* [1982] 1 *QB* 1, 27; *Attorney-General v. Blake* [1998] 1 *All ER* 833, 843 (not discussed by the House of Lords); *Ocular Sciences v. Aspect Vision* [1997] *RPC* 289, 413.

[11] *Balston v. Headline Filters* [1990] *FSR* 385. But cf. *A-G v. Blake*, ibid, 842 (employees are fiduciaries).

[12] *Indata Equipment Supplies v. ACL* [1998] *FSR* 248, 256, 262, 264 (breach of confidence despite lack of fiduciary relationship); following Sopinka J in *LAC Minerals v. International Corona Resources* [1990] *FSR* 441.

[13] See pp. 1064–5 below.

2.3 FROM THE MANNER OF COMMUNICATION

In some cases, an obligation of confidence may arise from the way the information is communicated between the parties.[14] In these circumstances, the test for whether there is a duty of confidence is to ask, would a reasonable recipient have realized that the information was given to them in confidence? As Megarry J said in *Coco v. Clark*:[15]

it seems to me that if the circumstances are such that any reasonable man standing in the shoes of the recipient of the information would have realized that upon reasonable grounds the information was being given to him in confidence, then this should suffice to impose upon him the equitable obligation of confidence.

The question whether a reasonable person would consider the information to have been communicated to them in confidence always depends on the facts of the case. Perhaps the most straightforward situation is where a party makes an *express* statement that the information is confidential. In these circumstances a defendant would find it very difficult to show that a reasonable confidant would not think that they were under an obligation of confidence.[16]

An obligation of confidence may also be *inferred* from the circumstances in question. When considering whether a reasonable person would infer that the information was confidential from the circumstances, the courts will take account of commonly held views, usages, and practices of the industry or trade in question. The way the parties understand their moral obligations may also be relevant.[17] While the question whether the reasonable person would infer that the information is confidential always depends on the facts in hand, it may be helpful to outline some examples.

(i) Normal conversation. Where a person blurts out information in public, no obligation of confidentiality would arise.[18] Equally, where information is disclosed in an informal, social setting, normally no obligation would arise.[19]

(ii) Disclosures for a limited purpose. In most instances, where a person reveals information to someone for a limited purpose this will give rise to an obligation that the information should only be used for that purpose.[20] This is because, where information is supplied for a specific purpose, the reasonable confidant would readily infer that the information should not be used for another purpose. This is sometimes referred to as the 'limited purpose' test. There may be circumstances, however, where this is not the case. In particular, where the information could be protected by copyright, patent, or design protection a reasonable recipient might not assume that the information was given to them under an obligation of confidence.[21]

---

14 For example in *Seager v. Copydex* [1967] 2 *All ER* 415.

15 *Coco v. A. N. Clark (Engineers)* [1969] *RPC* 41, 48.

16 *Stephens v. Avery* [1988] 2 *All ER* 477 (where the plaintiff expressly declared that the information was to 'go no further'). But if the stipulation is unreasonable an obligation might not arise: *Dunsford and Elliott v. Johnson* [1978] *FSR* 143, 148; *Yates Circuit Foil Co. v. Electrofoils* [1976] *FSR* 345, 380.

17 *Fraser v. Thames TV* [1983] 2 *All ER* 101, 121–2; *De Maudsley v. Palumbo* [1996] *FSR* 447, 457. Cf. *Carflow Products (UK) v. Linwood Securities (Birmingham)* [1996] *FSR* 424.

18 *Coco v. Clark* [1969] *RPC* 41, 48.   19 *De Maudsley v. Palumbo* [1996] *FSR* 447, 458.

20 *Ackroyds London v. Islington Plastics* [1962] *RPC* 97 (supply of plastic moulding tool for use in manufacture of 'swizzle sticks' (used to stir cocktails) not to be used for other purposes); *Barrymore v. News Group* [1997] *FSR* 600, 602 (disclosure of information in a personal relationship was 'for the relationship and not for a wider purpose').

21 *Carflow v. Linwood* [1996] *FSR* 424.

(iii) Encrypted material. Until recently little attention has been given to the question whether a person who receives encrypted information is thereby placed under a duty of confidence. The question here is whether a reasonable confidant who received encrypted information would take the fact that the information had been encrypted to mean that there was a duty of confidence in relation to the information. For example, would a person who visited an electronic bulletin board that contained encrypted information (which was only readily available via password) thereby be placed under a duty of confidence in relation to that information? In order to answer these questions positively, it would be necessary to treat the fact that the information was encrypted as equivalent to a sign saying 'confidential—you may not remove the encryption'. Similar questions also arise where information is embodied in a machine or a product and can only be obtained through reverse engineering.

One of the few decisions to consider issues of this nature was *Mars v. Teknowledge*.[22] As we saw earlier,[23] this was a breach of confidence action brought in relation to encrypted information embodied in the coin-receiving and -changing mechanisms used in vending machines. The question arose as to whether a person buying a machine that contained the encrypted information was under an implied duty of confidentiality in relation to the information. In effect the question was whether a reasonable recipient would consider the fact that the information had been encrypted to mean that they were under an obligation of confidentiality in relation to the information. Applying the reasonable person test, Jacob J said that the information embodied in the machine was *not* obviously confidential. More specifically Jacob J said:

I cannot see why the mere fact of encryption makes that which is encrypted confidential or why anyone who de-crypts something in code, should necessarily be taken to be receiving information in confidence. He will appreciate that the source of the information did not want him to have access, but that is all.[24]

It is possible, however, that the circumstances of communication might be such that the reasonable confidant might assume that the information was given to them in confidence. The question whether the fact of encryption gives rise to an implied duty of confidence is similar to the situation where someone uses other forms of technology (such as a fence) to protect the information. If this analogy is accepted, Jacob J's reasoning here is at odds with *Franklin v. Giddens*. As we will see, in this decision a duty of confidence was implied from the conduct of the defendant when he stole a branch that contained confidential genetic information from a nectarine tree in the claimant's orchard.

2.3.1 A subjective standard?

While in most cases the courts have favoured the objective standard of the reasonable-person test, in some cases the courts have taken into account the subjective expectations of the parties. For example, in *Schering Chemicals v. Falkman* Shaw LJ said that an obligation of confidence would be imposed in circumstances where the information 'is regarded by the giver and recognised by the recipient as confidential'.[25] In *Carflow Products v. Linwood Securities*[26] the question arose as to whether the demonstration of a car-lock device took place in circumstances

---

[22] [2000] *FSR* 138.   [23] See above at pp. 1017–18.   [24] *Mars* [2000] *FSR* 138, 150.

[25] Cf. *De Maudsley v. Palumbo* [1996] *FSR* 447, 458.

[26] [1996] *FSR* 424. See J. Phillips, 'Opportunity Knox' (1997) 1 *IPQ* 134 (pointing out that *De Maudsley v. Palumbo*, ibid, in preferring an objective test, is more consistent with existing authorities than *Carflow v. Linwood*).

of confidence. Jacob J acknowledged that there were two possible approaches to determining whether an obligation arose. The court could *either* examine what the parties thought they were doing, *or* focus on what a reasonable person would have thought the parties were doing. According to Jacob J, the key difference between the two approaches is that the former takes into account the subjective unspoken views of the parties. While such subjective views would not be relevant in relation to decisions concerning the making of a contract, however, because 'equity looks at the conscience of the individual', subjective views were relevant in relation to the equitable obligation of confidence.

Jacob J acknowledged that on the facts of *Carflow* it did not matter whether the problem was approached using a subjective or objective test. In other cases, however, the different tests (or some permutation thereof) might lead to different results. As such, it would be helpful to have some clarification as to which of the two approaches should be applied.

3 THIRD-PARTY RECIPIENTS

One of the most difficult issues that arises in this area of law concerns if and when parties outside an initial confider–confidant relationship will be bound by a duty of confidence.[27] More specifically, if a person owing an obligation of confidence discloses confidential information to a third party, what factors determine when that third party will be treated as being subject to an obligation not to use or disclose the information?[28]

In deciding whether a third-party recipient is under a duty of confidence, the courts have said that a third party who lacks good faith is bound by an equitable obligation of confidence. Sometimes this principle is said to 'derive' from the doctrine that 'it is equitable fraud in a third party knowingly to assist in breach of trust, confidence or contract by another'.[29] On other occasions, the courts have rejected the suggestion that third-party liability should be decided by analogy to traditional trust rules concerning the liability of those involved in a breach of trust.[30] Rather, the question whether a third-party recipient is bound by a duty depends on the circumstances of the case.[31] While this should be borne in mind, we will outline some of the more important factual situations that may arise.

(i) An indirect recipient of the information who is aware of its confidential status will normally be bound by a duty of confidence. In *Spycatcher*, Lord Keith said '[i]t is a general rule of law that a third party who comes into possession of confidential information which he knows to be such, may come under a duty not to pass it on to anyone else'.[32] Thankfully, there has been

---

[27] J. Stuckey, 'The Liability of Innocent Third Parties Implicated in Another's Breach of Confidence' (1981) 4 *University of New South Wales Law Journal* 73; S. Ricketson, 'Confidential Information: A New Proprietary Interest?' (1977–8) 11 *Melbourne University Law Review* 223, 244–5.

[28] If a third party has actively sought the information, it may be that they will have committed the tort of inducing breach of contract: see *British Industrial Plastics v. Ferguson* [1940] 1 *All ER* 479.

[29] *Campbell v. MGN* [2003] *QB* 633, 662 para. 66 (CA) (citing Toulson and Phipps, *Confidentiality* (1996)). For criticisms of *Campbell* see R. Arnold, 'Circumstances Importing an Obligation of Confidence' (2003) 119 *LQR* 193.

[30] *Valeo Vision Sociét Anonyme v. Flexible Lamps* [1995] *RPC* 205; *Wheatley v. Bell* [1984] *FSR* 16. Cf. *AG v. Guardian Newspapers* [1987] 1 *WLR* 1248, 1264 *per* Browne-Wilkinson V-C ('equitable property'); *Morison v. Moat* (1851) *Hare* 241; 68 *ER* 492).

[31] W. Cornish, 'Protection of Confidential Information in English Law' (1975) 6 *IIC* 43, 53.

[32] *Attorney-General v. Guardian Newspapers (No. 2)* [1990] *AC* 109, 260 (Lord Keith), 268 (Lord Griffiths).

none of the precise discussion of levels of knowledge that give rise to a duty, though it seems a duty should be imposed on any person who was grossly negligent in failing to know that a breach of confidence was involved.[33] However, it has been said that a recipient would not be bound if they were careless, naïve, or stupid, or merely knew of an assertion that a breach of confidence had occurred.[34]

(ii) If a person receives information innocently, but subsequently discovers that the information is confidential, they will be bound by a duty of confidence.[35] For example, in *English & American v. Herbert Smith*,[36] the papers of the counsel acting for the claimants in an action pending in the Commercial Court were mistakenly sent to the solicitors for the other side, Herbert Smith. The solicitors, who were the first defendants in this case, realized the mistake but were instructed by their clients to inspect the papers. The claimant sought an interim injunction preventing the solicitors from using information derived from the privileged documents. Browne-Wilkinson V-C granted the injunction on the ground that it did not matter whether the defendants were innocent when they received the documents, given that later use of the information was unconscionable.

(iii) It seems that the courts might grant an injunction, but not damages against a bona fide purchaser.[37] In *Valeo Vision Sociét Anonyme v. Flexible Lamps*[38] Valeo, who designed and manufactured lights for cars, disclosed details of the design to M. In turn, M revealed details of the lights to the defendant who produced similar lights. Valeo sued the defendant for breach of confidence. Aldous J held that the information was confidential and that, despite being a bona fide purchaser, the defendant was subject to a duty of confidentiality. In so doing Aldous J drew a distinction between a duty that will give rise to injunctive relief and one that would result in an award of damages. Aldous J indicated that while, when deciding whether to grant injunctive relief, the bona fide purchaser rule was too narrow, in order to get damages the conscience of the defendant had to be affected. On the facts, the plaintiff failed to establish that the defendant knew that the information they used 'was the confidential property of the plaintiff nor did it know that it should not be used without the plaintiff's consent'.[39]

(iv) Little attention has been given to the question whether a third-party recipient of information is under an obligation when the information is communicated to them by a person who is not bound by an obligation of confidence. Insofar as the duty may arise as a consequence of the knowledge of the defendant, it is foreseeable that an innocent party might communicate information to a third party who would be aware of the significance of the information. In some cases, the courts have been willing to assume that a third party is bound without investigating the position of the communicator. For example, in *Prince Albert v. Strange*,[40] it was held that a third party who proposed to publish the catalogue of Prince Albert's etchings was under an obligation of confidence. This was the case even though no evidence was available as to how

---

[33] See fn. to Art. 39 TRIPS. Note also *A-G v. Guardian (No. 2)*, ibid, 281–2 (knowledge includes circumstances where the confidant has deliberately closed his eyes to the obvious); *Thomas v. Pearce* [2000] *FSR* 718 (awareness or willingness to turn a blind eye).

[34] Ibid, 721; *Fraser v. Thames* [1983] 2 *All ER* 101; see also *Union Carbide v. Naturin* [1987] *FSR* 538, 549.

[35] *Stephenson Jordan & Harrison v. MacDonald & Evans* (1951) 68 *RPC* 190; (1952) 69 *RPC* 10; *Hoechst v. Chemiculture* [1993] *FSR* 270; *Cadbury Schweppes v. FBI Foods* [2000] *FSR* 491, 504 (Supreme Court of Canada). Cf. *Fractionated Cane Technology v. Ruiz-Avila* [1988] 7 *Qd R* 610.

[36] [1988] *FSR* 232.   [37] *Wheatley v. Bell* [1984] *FSR* 16.   [38] [1995] *RPC* 205.   [39] Ibid, 226.

[40] (1849) 2 *De G & Sm* 652; 64 ER 293 (Knight Bruce LJ); (1849) 1 *Mac & G* 25; 41 ER 1171 (Cottenham LC). See also *Times v. Mirror Group Newspapers* [1993] *EMLR* 443.

he came by the material.[41] However, this and related cases can be explained on the basis that the courts assumed that the information had been communicated by a wrongdoer.

4 WHERE THERE IS NO RELATIONSHIP BETWEEN THE PARTIES: STRANGERS

A person may come by confidential information without having it imparted to them by the confidant, or by a person owing an obligation of confidence.[42] For example, a burglar might uncover confidential files, or a member of the public might find a confidential document in the street. In some cases, it is possible for a duty of confidence to arise even though there is no relationship between the parties.

Until recently the case law dealing with the question as to whether (and, if so, when) a stranger comes under an obligation of confidentiality was unclear. The recent House of Lords decision in *Douglas v. Hello!* has clarified the matter to a large extent. Prior to this there were two competing views as to when a stranger receiving information was to be treated as owing a duty of confidence. The first focused on the conduct of the stranger in acquiring the information. Here the courts looked at whether the stranger had *acted illegally*. The second line of cases focused on whether the stranger *knew* that the information was confidential. As we will see, the courts have been willing to impose an obligation of confidentiality on recipients of information, even where they were not in any relationship with the claimant and where the information was acquired legitimately. It is this latter approach, based on knowledge and conscionability, that was adopted by their Lordships in *Douglas v. Hello!*

4.1 THE WAY THE INFORMATION WAS OBTAINED

In the early cases, the courts focused on the conduct of the person who acquired the information. More specifically, the courts have looked at whether the stranger has acted illegally: if strangers acted illegally they come under an obligation, if strangers acted legally they do not. This can be seen by contrasting two cases of telephone tapping: *Malone v. Commissioner of Metropolitan Police*[43] and *Francome v. Mirror Group Newspapers*.[44] In the first case, the police tapped a telephone line and as a result prosecuted the claimant for handling stolen goods. The claimant sued the police for breach of confidence.[45] The court held that the police did not come under an obligation of confidentiality. Megarry V-C said it 'seems to me that a person who utters confidential information must accept the risk of any unknown overhearing that is inherent in the circumstances of communication'. Deliberate tapping was one such risk and,

---

[41] Similarly, in *Times v. MGN*, ibid, the court assumed that the *Daily Mirror* came under an obligation of confidence with regard to the manuscript of Margaret Thatcher's *Diaries*, even though the source of the copy was undisclosed.

[42] G. Wei, 'Surreptitious Takings of Confidential Information' (1992) 12 *LS* 302; M. Richardson, 'Breach of Confidence, Surreptitiously or Accidentally Obtained Information and Privacy: Theory Versus Law' (1994) 19 *Melbourne University Law Review* 673.

[43] [1979] *Ch* 344.   [44] [1984] 1 *WLR* 892.

[45] Other claims were based on privacy, property, and human rights. The case prompted an application to the European Court of Human Rights—*Malone v. United Kingdom* (1984) 7 *EHRR* 14—and the government responded to criticism therein with the Interception of Communications Act 1985.

as such, no obligation of confidentiality arose.[46] In contrast, in *Francome*[47] it was a private investigator investigating breaches of Jockey Club rules (rather than the police) who illegally tapped the phone conversation of a jockey. The jockey concerned sought an interim injunction to prevent disclosure of the information. The Court of Appeal distinguished *Malone* and held that in these circumstances there was a serious question to be tried. Fox LJ noted that *Malone* was concerned with a case of authorized tapping rather than, as with the case in hand, with illegal tapping by private persons. He also observed that '[i]t must be questionable whether the user of a telephone can be regarded as accepting the risk of that in the same way as, for example, he accepts the risk that his conversation may be overheard in consequence of the accidents and imperfections of the telephone system itself'.[48]

The different conclusions in *Francome* and *Malone* seem to depend on a distinction between a person who obtains information lawfully—who does not come under an obligation—and a person who obtains information unlawfully, who is subject to a duty of confidence. It seems that this position needs to be refined in the light of recent decisions concerned with the question what is meant by a person acting 'legally' where the information was acquired under statutory powers. While we look at this in more detail later in the chapter, it should be noted here that the courts have held that such information may only be used for the purposes for which the powers are conferred.[49] These cases suggest that the police in *Malone* were under an obligation of confidentiality not to use the information for purposes other than those for which their powers existed. Use of the information in prosecuting the claimant for handling stolen goods was clearly furthering those purposes and as such was permissible. Consequently, where a stranger sets out to acquire information they come under a limited obligation when the acquisition is based on legal authority, and under a broader obligation when it is illegal.

4.2 KNOWLEDGE OF THE STRANGER

In a second line of cases, instead of focusing on whether the stranger acted illegally, the courts have looked at whether the stranger had *knowledge* that the information was confidential. In *Attorney-General v. Guardian (No. 2)*, Lord Goff said:

I start with the broad general principle (which I do not intend in any way to be definitive) that a duty of confidence arises when confidential information comes to the knowledge of a person (the confidant) in circumstances where he has notice, or is held to have agreed, that the information is confidential, with the effect that it would be just in all the circumstances that he should be precluded from disclosing the information to others...I have expressed the circumstances in which the duty arises in broad terms,...to include certain situations, beloved of law teachers—where an obviously confidential document is wafted by an electric fan out of a window into a crowded street, or where an obviously confidential document, such as a private diary, is dropped in a public place, and is then picked up by a passer-by.[50]

According to Lord Goff the key factor is not whether the stranger is acting illegally. Rather, it is whether the stranger knows that the information is private or confidential. As such, the question is whether 'anything reasonably leads the observer to realize that what he or she observes is confidential'.[51] This question arose in *Shelley Films v. Rex Features*[52] where the claimant,

---

[46] *Malone v. MPC* [1979] *Ch* 344, 376.   [47] [1984] 1 *WLR* 892.   [48] Ibid, 900.

[49] *Marcel v. Commissioner PM* [1992] 2 *WLR* 50; *Hoechst v. Chemiculture* [1993] *FSR* 270.

[50] [1990] *AC* 109, 281–2.

[51] Richardson, 'Breach of Confidence', 699.   [52] *Shelley Films v. Rex Features* [1994] *EMLR* 134.

who was producer of the film *Frankenstein,* sought to restrain the defendant, a photographic agency, from publishing copies of a photograph of Robert De Niro, which had been taken without authority by a stranger during filming. The defendant argued that neither they nor the photographer were under a duty of confidence. Judge Mann QC held that there was a 'serious question to be tried'. He noted that the photographer was not an invitee on the film set and that it could be assumed that he saw the signs at the entrance to the film studios and on the film set that said 'Absolutely No Photography—All Films will be confiscated' and 'No Admittance—Access to Authorized Persons only'. Judge Mann QC said that it was impossible not to conclude that this might have fixed the photographer with knowledge that the claimant regarded the information as confidential. One of the interesting things about this decision, especially when compared with *Francome,* is that instead of emphasizing the illegality of the means by which the photograph was taken, the judge focused on the fact that the photographer had knowledge that the claimant considered the images to be confidential. A similar approach has been adopted in the recent cases dealing with personal information.

The decision of the House of Lords in *Douglas v. Hello!* conclusively demonstrates that strangers can come under an obligation of confidence. In this case *Hello!* had received the images of the Zeta-Jones/Douglas wedding from a *paparazzo* photographer, Mr Thorpe, who had not been invited to the wedding. From various notices, however, it was clear that both he and *Hello!* must have been aware that the wedding was regarded as confidential (as photographs were to be published exclusively by *OK!*). Affirming the analysis of Lindsay J at first instance, Lord Hoffmann (with whom Lords Brown and Baroness Hale agreed) had no doubt that Thorpe came under an obligation of confidentiality which was binding upon *Hello!* Douglas and Zeta-Jones had made it clear that there was to be no unauthorized photography, and had taken steps to exclude the uninvited and preclude the taking of photographs. The rationale provided by Lindsay J, and seemingly adopted by their Lordships, was that Thorpe came under an obligation not because he was present illegally, but because he knew the event was regarded as confidential. As for *Hello!*, he explained that its 'conscience' was tainted and its actions lacked good faith, again because of its knowledge that the event was subject to an exclusive publication agreement with *OK!*[53]

4.3 TO WHOM IS THE OBLIGATION OWED?

Another question of significance which arose in *Douglas v. Hello!* was the question to whom the obligation was owed. This question arose because the appeal was brought by *OK!* against *Hello!*, Douglas and Zeta-Jones having been satisfied by their victory, on Article 8 grounds, in the Court of Appeal. There, the Court had held that any obligation of confidence was owed to Douglas/Zeta Jones and that the agreement they had entered with *OK!* had failed to transfer the benefit of any obligations to it. Indeed, Lord Phillips MR had gone so far as to say that the benefit of an obligation of confidence is not assignable. On appeal, the key issue was whether the obligations owed by Thorpe and *Hello!* were obligations owed to *OK!* The majority held that they were, though Lord Hoffmann's reasoning is far from transparent. He explained that the point 'of which one should never lose sight is that *OK!* had paid £1 million for the benefit of the obligation of confidence imposed upon all present at the wedding in respect of any photographs of the wedding. . . . Unless there is some conceptual or policy reason why they should

---

53 [2008] 1 *AC* 1, 46–7 (paras 113–115) (*per* Lord Hoffmann).

not have the benefit of that obligation, I cannot see why they were not entitled to enforce it.'[54] What is strange about Lord Hoffmann's reasoning is that it leaves unclear the precise legal mechanism by which an obligation came to be owed to *OK!*, as opposed to Douglas and Zeta-Jones. At one level, the implication is that any licensee of confidential information can bring an action against someone who uses that information in breach of confidence (at least if the latter person was aware that the licence or sharing arrangement existed). Lord Walker rightly observed that, rather surprisingly, this would place a licensee of confidential information in a stronger legal position than licensees of other intellectual property rights.

5 PRIVATE INFORMATION

A number of changes have taken place in the way the breach of confidence action is applied to personal and private information. One of the most important is that it is 'no longer a necessary element of the cause of the action that the [personal] information arises from a confidential relationship'.[55] As Sedley LJ said in *Douglas v. Hello!*, the 'law no longer needs to construct an artificial relationship of confidentiality between intruder and victim: it can recognize privacy itself as a legal principle drawn from the fundamental value of personal autonomy'.[56] In *Wainwright v. Home Office*, Lord Hoffmann said that Sedley LJ's remarks suggested that, 'in relation to the publication of personal information obtained by intrusion, the common law breach of confidence has reached the point at which a confidential relationship has become unnecessary'.[57] This has been extended beyond information obtained by intruders to include personal information generally.

A defendant will be under an obligation of confidentiality when the person publishing the information 'knows or ought to know that there is a reasonable expectation that the information in question will be kept confidential'.[58] That is, the law imposes a "duty of confidence" whenever a person receives information he knows or ought to know is fairly and reasonably to be regarded as confidential'.[59] The new test, which was adopted by the House of Lords in *Campbell* and followed in subsequent decisions in the UK, provides relatively clear guidance as to when an obligation of confidence will arise.[60] The courts have stressed that the decision as to whether a person has a reasonable expectation of privacy needs to be kept separate from issues of proportionality (which are better dealt with when determining breach). Instead, the primary focus has been 'on the nature of the information, because it is the recipient's perception of its confidential nature that imposes the obligation on him'.[61]

---

[54] Ibid, 47 (para. 117).   [55] *Mills v. MGN* [2001] *EWHC* 412 (Ch), para. 26.

[56] *Douglas v. Hello!* [2001] 2 *WLR* 992, 10255 para. 125–26 (Sedley LJ); cf. Brookes LJ, para. 95; Keene LJ, paras. 165–7.

[57] *Wainwright v. Home Office* [2003] *UKHL* 53; [2003] *All ER* 279, para. 20 (HL) While Lord Hoffmann said that this did not give rise to a separate tort of privacy, he did not say anything to suggest that he disagreed with this change. See further *Wainwright v. UK* (2007) 44 *EHRR* 40 (ECHR) (strip search held to be violation of Art. 8)

[58] *Campbell v. MGN* [2004] 2 *AC* 457 (HL), para 135 (Baroness Hale). The Lords rejected the test of Gleeson CJ in *ABC v. Lenah Game Meats* that 'disclosure or observation would be highly offensive to a reasonable person of ordinary expectations' (2001) 185 *ALR* 1, 13 para 42.

[59] *Campbell v. MGN*, ibid, para 13–14.   [60] Ibid, para 137 (Baroness Hale of Richmond).

[61] *McKennitt v. Ash* [2006] *EWCA Civ* 1714 (CA), para 15, citing Lord Goff in *A-G v. Guardian (No. 2)* [1990] *AC* 109, 218.

One of the consequences of the adoption of this approach is that decisions about whether private information is able to be disclosed depend not just on the threshold questions of whether the claimant has a reasonable expectation of privacy and whether the defendant was (or ought to have been) aware of this, but as often on whether or not the defendant has a good reason for disclosing the information. More specifically, in many of the recent cases, the courts have concentrated on whether the obligation is trumped by other interests (such as freedom of expression). We look at these issues below.[62]

6 EMPLOYEES

As we mentioned earlier, special considerations apply in relation to the application of the breach of confidence action between employer and employee. As different obligations are imposed on an employee during employment than after the employment relationship has ended, we will deal with each separately.

6.1 DURING THE COURSE OF EMPLOYMENT

6.1.1 Express duties during employment

In many cases, the contract of employment will include express provisions dealing with the nature and scope of the duty of confidence owed by the employee to the employer. During the period of employment, the courts will enforce the express terms of the contract.[63] Any express terms imposing a duty of confidentiality upon the employee (it is rare for an employer to be under equivalent duty) are subject to the general rules of contract.

6.1.2 Implied duties during employment

While a contract might not contain express clauses imposing a duty of confidentiality upon an employee, this does not mean that employees will not be bound by a duty of confidence. This is because in some cases the courts may imply a duty of confidence into the employment relationship. The courts have said that employees are under an implied duty of fidelity to their employers.[64] The duty of fidelity will prevent employees from disclosing information and from competing with their employers. According to the Court of Appeal,

[t]he employer is entitled to the single-minded loyalty of their employee. That employee must act in good faith; they must not make a profit out of their trust; they must not place themselves in a position where their duty and their interest may conflict; they may not act for their own benefit or the benefit of a third party without the informed consent of their employer.[65]

---

[62] See pp. 1053–60. Where the parties are in a relationship, traditional criteria are still used to decide whether private information is to be treated as confidential. Thus in *A v. B* [2003] QB 195, 207 (para. 11) (guidelines ix–x) the Court of Appeal held that 'a duty of confidence will arise whenever the party subject to the duty is in a situation where he either knows or ought to know that the other person can reasonably expect his privacy to be protected'. This could be express or conferred. It can arise where there is an intrusion, bugging, or the use of surveillance techniques.

[63] But note the Public Interest Disclosure Act 1998, s. 1, introducing the Employment Rights Act 1996 s. 43J (agreement void insofar as it purports to preclude a worker from making a protected disclosure).

[64] *Robb v. Green* [1895] 2 QB 315, 320; *Thomas Marshall v. Guinle* [1979] 1 Ch 227.

[65] *Attorney-General v. Blake* [1998] 1 All ER 833 (not considered by HL on appeal). See esp. *Hivac v. Park Royal Scientific Instruments* [1946] Ch 169.

The courts have sometimes imposed more onerous obligations on more senior employees, primarily because of the fiduciary duty that they owe to their employer.[66]

6.2 AFTER EMPLOYMENT

Once the employment relationship has ended different considerations apply. On the one hand, employers have an interest in controlling the use that an employee is able to make of information they acquired during the course of their employment. At the same time, this has been balanced against the fact that it would be unfair to enable employers to prohibit an employee from working in the same area again. This would effectively be the result if employers were able to control more generic skills that an employee might have gained during the course of their employment. If an employer repudiates the contract, it is unclear whether confidentiality obligations survive at all.[67]

6.2.1 Express obligations after employment: restraint of trade

In order to protect themselves, employers may include in their contract of employment a clause, usually referred to as a restrictive covenant, to the effect that the employee will not work in the same industry for a specified period after leaving employment.[68] While acknowledging the importance of such clauses, the law also recognizes that employees should be free to make use of the personal skills, knowledge, experiences, and abilities gained in the course of their employment.[69] The courts have attempted to navigate these conflicting goals through the doctrine of restraint of trade.[70] In essence this provides that a restrictive covenant will be struck down if the obligations go beyond what is reasonably necessary to protect the employer's interests. More specifically, a restraint of trade clause will only be enforceable if it is appropriately limited as to time,[71] geographical coverage,[72] and the scope of activities.[73]

The operation of the doctrine can be seen from *Mont v. Mills*.[74] In this case, the defendant had been employed in the paper tissue industry for 20 years. He left the claimant company and

---

[66] *Balston v. Headline Filters* [1990] *FSR* 385; *Helmut Integrated Systems Ltd v. Tunnard* [2007] *IRLR* 126; *Crowson Fabrics Ltd v. Rider* [2007] *EWHC* 2942 (Ch) (paras 77–85).

[67] See *Campbell v. Frisbee* [2002] *EMLR* 31 (arguable defence that obligations did not survive the breach, so summary judgment was inappropriate); *Rock Refrigerator Ltd v. Jones* [1977] 1 *All ER* 1; *General Billposting Company Ltd v. Atkinson* [1909] *AC* 118 (restrictive covenants unenforceable)

[68] An obligation specifically not to disclose trade secrets will rarely provide satisfactory protection: *Littlewoods Organisation v. Harris* [1978] 1 *All ER* 1026.

[69] *Herbert Morris v. Saxelby* [1916] *AC* 688; *Attwood v. Lamont* [1920] 3 *KB* 571.

[70] See above, pp. 281–3. The doctrine is alleged to date back to *Dier's Case* (1414) 2 *Hen. V* 5, pl. 26, but its modern form derives from *Mitchel v. Reynolds* (1711) 1 *P. Wms.* 181 which has been described as the 'carta' of the law. See N.H. Moller, *Voluntary Covenants in Restraint of Trade* (1925) 5.

[71] *Herbert Morris* [1916] *AC* 688 (seven years too long). But in *Attorney-General v. Blake* [2000] 3 *WLR* 625, 647 Lord Hobhouse said a lifelong obligation on a member of the Intelligence Service not to divulge any official information gained as a result of his employment was justified and thus not an unlawful restraint of trade.

[72] *Commercial Plastics v. Vincent* [1964] 3 *All ER* 546 (in absence of geographic limitation the restraints will be read as worldwide, in which case they will usually be void); *Lansing Linde v. Kerr* [1991] 1 *All ER* 418, 426 (facts would justify restraint in western Europe only).

[73] *Fellowes v. Fisher* [1976] *QB* 122, 129 (restrictive covenant purporting to restrain conveyancing clerk on one-year contract from working in 'legal profession' in districts of Walthamstow and Chingford for five years was too broad in scope, in geographic coverage and in duration). Cf. *Poly Lina v. Finch* [1995] *FSR* 751 (clause prohibiting defendant from engaging in any trade or business which was in competition with the plaintiff for one year held to be valid).

[74] [1993] *FSR* 577. See also *Thomas v. Farr* [2007] *EWCA Civ* 118.

signed a severance agreement, under which he received a large sum of money. The agreement also said that the defendant was required not to join another company in the tissue industry for one year. The defendant failed to honour this promise and became joint managing director of a competitor, whereupon the claimant sought an injunction. The Court of Appeal held that the severance agreement was unenforceable on the basis that it was an unjustifiable restraint of trade. This was because the undertaking was not limited as regards geographical area or the nature of the activities to which it applied. The court declined to construe the clause in favour of the employee: for to do so provided employers with no incentive to impose restraints in appropriately limited terms.[75] Simon Brown LJ noted that the fact that the company had paid the ex-employee during the period of restraint did not prevent the agreement from being unenforceable. The law's concern was not merely that all persons should be able to earn a living. If that were the only policy, the law would permit an employer to buy restraint. Rather, Simon Brown LJ argued that '[p]ublic policy clearly has regard to the public interest in competition and in the proper use of an employee's skills'.[76]

'Garden Leave'   The level of duty owed by employees to their employers differs markedly depending on whether or not they are employed.[77] If a company wishes to restrain an employee from entering into similar employment, the most effective mechanism is to retain them as an employee.[78] This is often done by placing employees on 'garden leave'. This occurs where an employee remains as a paid employee for a specified period of time, during which they are not required to attend work or carry out normal duties. In contrast with post-employment provisions, 'garden leave' agreements are not normally subject to the doctrine of restraint of trade: they are enforceable. Even so, questions remain as to what remedy is appropriate to enforce the contract.[79] In *GFI Group v. Egglestone*,[80] where an employee was required to give 20 weeks' notice, the court granted an injunction to prevent the employee from working for a competitor for three months after he had given notice of resignation. Here, the court was influenced by the high pay the employee received and the fact that the agreement had been negotiated between the parties (rather than imposed by the employer). Although the courts recognize employees' interest in exercising their skills, a 'garden leave' agreement will be enforced if failure to do this would harm the employer. The courts have suggested that an employer can utilize both a 'garden leave' agreement and a restrictive covenant, though the existence of the 'garden leave' agreement may be taken into account when determining the reasonableness of the restrictive covenant.[81]

6.2.2 Implied obligations after employment

In the absence of an express duty of confidence in the contract of employment, the courts may imply certain limited obligations on the use that ex-employees can make of information acquired during the course of their employment. In a normal business context,[82] the obligations imposed are primarily limited to the use that can be made of trade secrets.

---

[75] Ibid, 585. *Lansing Linde* [1991] 1 *All ER* 418, 429.   [76] *Mont v. Mills* [1993] *FSR* 577, 587.
[77] In some cases prompting an innocent employer to refuse to accept a repudiatory breach of contract by the employee: *Thomas Marshall* [1979] 1 *Ch* 227 (Megarry V-C).
[78] *Balston v. Headline Filters* [1990] *FSR* 385, 416.
[79] *Credit Suisse Asset Management v. Armstrong* [1996] *ICR* 882, 892–4.   [80] [1994] *FSR* 535.
[81] *Credit Suisse v. Armstrong* [1996] *ICR* 882 (but that does not mean that there is automatic set-off of garden leave period when considering reasonableness of a post-term covenant).
[82] Cf. *A-G v. Blake* [1998] 1 *All ER* 833 (in Secret Service context duty of confidence survives as long as the information remains confidential).

The classic authority on the position of ex-employees is *Faccenda Chicken v. Fowler*.[83] In this case the claimant, who sold fresh chickens from refrigerated vans, attempted to prevent a former employee from participating in a competing venture. The claimant argued that in so doing the ex-employee was utilizing confidential information concerning the customers, prices, products sold, and so forth. As the ex-employee's contract contained no restrictive covenant, the Court of Appeal was called upon to decide the scope of implied post-employment obligations. The Court of Appeal held that an ex-employee's obligations were confined to 'trade secrets', which include things such as chemical formulae,[84] secret manufacturing processes,[85] designs and special methods of construction,[86] and 'other information of a sufficiently high degree of confidentiality to amount to a trade secret'.[87]

In *Faccenda*, the Court of Appeal said that, in deciding whether information amounts to a trade secret, the court should consider four factors. The *first* is the nature of the employment. Under this heading the court would consider things such as how near the employee is to the 'inner counsel' of the employer. This is because information only made available to trusted employees is more likely to constitute a trade secret than information disclosed to shop-floor workers. The *second* factor to consider is the nature of the information. To be capable of protection the information must be defined with some degree of precision. Protection will not be available for general business methods and practices.[88] It has been said that just because the information is technical does not mean that it relates to trade secrets. If an employee is an expert or specialist, their general skill and knowledge might extend into the field of formulae, blends, or chemical processes.[89] The *third* factor to consider is whether the employer impressed on the employee the confidentiality of the information. If information was specifically designated as a trade secret by the employer, it is more likely to be treated as such by the courts. However, the courts have noted that 'it would be unrealistic to expect a small and informal organization to adopt the same business disciplines as a larger and more bureaucratic concern'.[90] In the case of small businesses, the courts may treat information as a trade secret even though the employer did not identify it as such. The *fourth* and final consideration taken into account when assessing whether information is a trade secret is whether the information can easily be isolated from other information (such as the employee's own stock of knowledge, skill, and expertise) which the employee is free to use or disclose.[91]

One issue which remains undecided is whether the obligations implied into an employment contract for the post-employment period change when an ex-employee intends to disclose rather than use the information. Because the policy considerations that restrict implied, post-employment obligations to trade secrets aim to promote the mobility of labour and socially productive use of skills it seems that the courts will be less generous to an ex-employee who sells information or exposes it gratuitously.[92]

---

[83] *Faccenda Chicken v. Fowler* [1987] 1 *Ch* 117.

[84] *Amber Size & Chemical Co. v. Menzel* [1913] 2 *Ch* 239.   [85] *Herbert Morris* [1916] AC 688, 701.

[86] *Reid and Sigrist v. Moss and Mechanism* (1932) 49 *RPC* 461.

[87] *Printers & Finishers v. Holloway* [1965] *RPC* 239, 253; *Faccenda Chicken* [1987] 1 *Ch* 117, 136.

[88] *Lancashire Fire v. S. & A. Lyons* [1996] *FSR* 629, 668; *Aveley/Cybervox v. Boman and Sign Electronic Signal* [1975] *FSR* 139; *Searle & Co. v. Celltech* [1982] *FSR* 92.

[89] *Ocular Sciences* [1997] *RPC* 289, 385 Laddie J (court should guard against imposing more stringent restraints on more technical employees).

[90] *Lancashire Fire* [1996] *FSR* 629, 668.   [91] *Printers and Finishers v. Holloway* [1965] *RPC* 239.

[92] *Faccenda Chicken v. Fowler* [1986] 3 *WLR* 288, 301; *United Indigo Chemical Co. Ltd v. Robinson* (1932) 49 *RPC* 178, 187; *Brooks v. Olysager Orms* [1998] *IRLR* 590.

7 STATUTORY OBLIGATIONS
AND PUBLIC BODIES

Obligations of confidentiality can be imposed by statute.[93] Where a statute permits a public body to acquire information, the statutory body is under a duty of confidentiality to use the information only to satisfy the statutory purpose. In *Marcel v. Commissioner of Police of the Metropolis*,[94] as part of a criminal investigation concerning a property development in the London Docklands, the police obtained information from the claimant under powers conferred by the Police and Criminal Evidence Act 1984. The police disclosed the information to a third party, who was bringing a civil action related to the property developments against Marcel (the claimant in this case). The claimant objected to the police's revelation of the information. The Court of Appeal held that public officers who exercise such powers for public purposes come under a duty of confidentiality which prevents them from using the information for other purposes without the consent of the confider. The powers to seize and retain are conferred for the better performance of public functions by public bodies and cannot be used to take information available to private individuals for their private purposes. The purpose for which the information can be used is a matter of statutory interpretation. As Sir Christopher Slade explained in *Marcel,* the only purposes for which the information could be used were those contemplated by the relevant legislation. However, on the facts, these were defined broadly as including purposes 'reasonably incidental' to the investigation and prosecution of crime: matters that he was happy to label as 'police purposes'.

Another example of the obligation of confidence that may be imposed on a statutory body is provided by *Hoechst v. Chemiculture*.[95] Here, Morritt J took a broad view of the purpose of the powers conferred by the Food and Environmental Protection Act 1985. Using these powers, the Health and Safety Executive obtained information from the defendant. The Executive subsequently disclosed the information to the claimant who, in turn, used the information in support of an Anton Piller application as regards trade mark infringement against the defendants.[96] Morritt J recognized that the Health and Safety Executive was under an obligation of confidentiality. However, he took the view that the claimant's action for trade mark infringement achieved similar purposes to the Act. This was because the claimant had been licensed to sell the herbicide by the Health and Safety Executive and the containers it used had been approved. The defendant, who had not been licensed to use the herbicide, was using the claimant's mark CHEETAH on containers different from those of the claimant.

---

[93] These may be expressly stated in the statute, as for example in the Consumer Credit Act 1974, s. 174; Building Societies Act 1986, s. 53; Competition Act 1998, s. 55 (each making disclosure of information gained using specified powers a criminal offence).

[94] [1992] 2 *WLR* 50; *Hellewell v. Chief Constable of Derbyshire* [1995] 1 *WLR* 804; *Bunn v. BBC* [1998] 3 *All ER* 552, 556.

[95] [1993] *FSR* 270. Note also, *R v. Licensing Authority, ex p Smith Kline & French Laboratories Ltd.* [1989] *FSR* 440, 446.

[96] See below at p. 1079 for further explanation as to Anton Piller/seizure orders.

46

BREACH, DEFENCES, PRIVATE INFORMATION, AND REMEDIES

CHAPTER CONTENTS

1 INTRODUCTION

In this chapter, we complete our examination of the breach of confidence action. After looking at the third factor that a claimant must show to sustain an action, namely that the obligation of confidence has been breached, we look at the defences that a defendant may rely upon to escape liability. Finally, we look at the remedies available where a duty of confidence has been breached.

2 HAS THE OBLIGATION OF CONFIDENCE BEEN BREACHED?

The third and final factor that must be shown to establish breach of confidence is that the obligation of confidence has been breached.

2.1 THE SCOPE OF THE OBLIGATION

In order to determine whether the duty of confidence has been breached it is first necessary to determine the scope of the obligation. At its most general, the duty of confidence prohibits the use and disclosure of the confidential information. While the scope of the obligation may restrict use and disclosure, it does not apply to the acquisition of information.[1] This may mean

---

[1] See also *R v. Layton* (*The Times*, 3 Mar. 1993) (industrial espionage not a crime). See V. Tunkel, 'Industrial espionage: What Can the Law Do?' [1993] *Denning Law Journal* 99; Law Commission Consultation Paper No. 150, Pt. VII.

that British law fails to comply with Article 39 of TRIPS which speaks of the disclosure, *acquisition,* or use of information.

While the scope of the action *potentially* extends to any use or disclosure of the information, the scope of the obligations that are *actually* imposed upon an individual always depends on the facts of the case. In some circumstances, the obligation may provide that the confidential information should not be used or disclosed in any circumstances. In other situations, the confidant may only use the information for limited purposes, or for a limited period of time. Despite its importance, the question how the scope of the obligation is determined has received very little attention.

Perhaps the most straightforward situation is where the obligation arises as a result of an *express* term in a contract or an express obligation in equity.[2] In these situations, the scope of the obligation depends on the way the relevant provisions are interpreted. The task of determining the scope of the obligation becomes more difficult where the obligation is *implied* into a contract or imposed by equity. Presumably, in these cases the scope of the obligation would depend on the views of the reasonable person in the circumstances.

One area that warrants special attention is where the scope of the obligation arises via the so-called 'limited purpose test'.[3] As we saw earlier, where information is imparted for a limited purpose, this may give rise to an obligation of confidence. Where information is supplied for a specific purpose, one can readily infer that the information should not be used for another purpose. In these circumstances, if the information is used for any purpose other than the limited one for which the information was imparted there may be a breach. In many cases, it will be clear from the circumstances that the confidant actually knew that the information being disclosed to them was only to be used for a restricted purpose. In other cases, the scope of the obligation is determined by the objective standard of what the confidant *ought* to have known. This can be seen from the Australian decision in *Smith Kline & French v. Department of Community Health.*[4] In this case the pharmaceutical company SK&F applied to the Australian Department of Community Services and Health for permission to market certain drugs. As part of the application process, SK&F supplied the Department with information concerning the drug. The Department of Community Services later proposed to use that information to decide whether it should authorize a different company to sell a related drug. SK&F argued that in so doing the Department had breached the duty of confidence owed to them. The reason for this was that SK&F had only disclosed the information to the Department for one specific purpose: namely, to enable their drug to be approved. The court refused the claimant's application for an injunction. The Federal Court said that the scope of the obligation was not to be determined by the subjective views of the confider (here SK&F). Instead, it was to be decided by the objective standard of what the confidant knew or ought reasonably to have known in the circumstances. As such, the question to be considered was whether the relevant officers of the Department ought to have known that the data furnished by SK&F was disclosed for a limited purpose (thus excluding the Department's practice of using the data to evaluate other applications).

In so ruling the Court suggested that a number of factors should be taken into account when determining the scope of the obligation. These include whether the information was supplied gratuitously or for a consideration; whether there were any past practices that gave rise to an

---

[2] See Gurry, 116.   [3] See above at pp. 1026–7.

[4] [1990] *FSR* 617, 647; 20 *IPR* 643. For the equivalent UK decision, see *R v. Licensing Authority, ex p Smith Kline & French Laboratories* [1989] *FSR* 440, 446 (obligation of confidence interpreted as of limited scope).

understanding that the use was limited; how sensitive the information was; whether the confider had any interest in the purpose for which the information was to be used; and whether the confider expressly warned the confidant against a particular disclosure or use of the information.

On the facts, the Federal Court held that the scope of the obligation did not restrict the Department's use of the information to the SK&F application. Two factors influenced the Court in deciding that the equitable obligation had not been breached. The first was that previous practices (SK&F themselves had submitted other applications where the Department relied upon information supplied earlier by SK&F) meant that 'it went without saying that the Department would look back at data that had already been submitted'.[5] The second factor was that the court stressed that, in determining the scope of the obligation, it was necessary to 'have regard to the effect of the legal framework within which the parties were dealing'. The Court added that it would 'be slow to attribute to a regulatory authority knowledge that a party dealing with it expected it to act in a manner which would inhibit it in the exercise of its legal powers and obligations'.[6]

The question of the way in which the scope of the obligation should be determined was also considered by the Court of Appeal in *Source Informatics*. In this case Source collected information about doctors' prescribing habits and patterns, which it then sold to pharmaceutical companies so that they could market their products more effectively. In return for a fee, pharmacists collated the relevant information from the prescription forms that had been completed by doctors and forwarded it to Source. Importantly, the information sent to Source did not include the name of the patients. The Department of Health issued a policy document that said that this process amounted to a breach of patient confidentiality. Source brought an action for judicial review challenging the Department's policy. In particular, they argued 'that disclosure by doctors or pharmacists to a third party of anonymous information (that is information from which the identity of the patients may not be determined), does not constitute a breach of confidentiality'. At first instance, the Department's policy was upheld. However, the Court of Appeal overturned the decision.[7]

Simon Brown LJ began by noting that, while the reasonable person test was useful in determining whether there is a duty of confidence, it does not give guidance as to the scope of the obligation of confidentiality. In considering how the scope of the obligation was to be determined Simon Brown LJ said that 'the touchstone by which to judge the scope of [the confidant's] duty and whether or not it has been fulfilled or breached is his own conscience, no more and no less'. On the facts this meant it was necessary to ask 'would a reasonable pharmacist's conscience be troubled by the proposed use to be made of patients' prescriptions? Would he think that by entering Source's scheme he was breaking his customers' confidence, making unconscientious use of the information they provide?'[8] If the language used here is stripped bare, the test proposed is the same objective standard as put forward in *Smith Kline & French*.

Given this, it would be reasonable to assume that Simon Brown LJ would then have gone on to consider what the reasonable pharmacist knew or ought reasonably to have known in the circumstances.[9] Instead of adopting such an approach, Simon Brown LJ turned to focus on the type of information in question. In particular, he said that, in relation to personal information, 'the concern of the law is to protect the confider's personal privacy'. Simon Brown LJ went

[5] Ibid, 646.   [6] Ibid, 647.

[7] *R v. Department of Health, ex p Source Informatics* [2000] 1 *All ER* 786 (CA).   [8] Ibid, 796 (CA).

[9] *S.K. & F. v. Department of Community Services and Health* (1991) 99 *ALR* 679, 691. Followed in *ex p Source Informatics* [2000] 1 *All ER* 786, 793 (CA).

on to say that the 'patient [has] no property in the information and no right to control its use provided only and always that his privacy is not put at risk'.[10] Using the language of rights, the Court held that the scope of the obligation was limited to uses that would affect the confider's personal privacy. On the facts, the Court of Appeal held that, as the information had been used anonymously, the patient's privacy was safeguarded. The reasonable pharmacist's conscience ought not to have been troubled. As such, there was no breach of confidence. Despite the gesture towards the use of an objective standard of the reasonable pharmacist, the Court of Appeal relied more on the *a priori* language of rights (the patient's right of privacy) than on what a reasonable pharmacist would have concluded from the circumstances.[11]

One area where problems may arise is where a number of people jointly generate information and one party later wants to develop it, but the others do not. For the most part this question is decided in terms of the nature of the relationship between the parties. This can be seen in *Murray v. Yorkshire Fund Managers*.[12] In this case, a group of businessmen (including the claimant) developed a plan to take over an ailing business. While the financial backers were happy with the remainder of the team, they refused to work with the claimant. The claimant brought an action for breach of confidence arguing that confidential information was disclosed to the defendant for the limited purpose of deciding whether the financier should invest in the venture disclosed in the business plan.[13] Rejecting this approach, Nourse LJ observed that there had never been a binding agreement that all the members would continue to participate in the project, so that any of them could have withdrawn. He therefore concluded that the confidential information came into being for the purpose of facilitating the project and was best viewed as 'an adjunct of a relationship'. It followed that when the claimant was excluded from the relationship, he lost the ability to control how the information was used.

The Court of Appeal decision should not be taken to be endorsing a view that one of several 'owners' of confidential information may use or exploit that information without the approval of the other 'co-owners'.[14] Such a rule would raise complicated questions about who generated and contributed what information, and when such information came to be 'co-owned'.[15] Rather, the Court of Appeal appears to have been attempting to produce a solution based on the expectations of the parties. This is also a sensible approach, in that if a different conclusion had been reached, it would have led to the unacceptable position where one member of a team could prohibit the remaining members from using the information. If an individual member of a team has problems with the way jointly developed information is to be used, they should deal with it contractually at the outset of the arrangement.

2.2 HAS THE OBLIGATION BEEN BREACHED?

Once the scope of the obligation has been ascertained, it is then possible to consider whether the obligation has been breached. This is primarily a factual question. Before looking at this in more detail, it is important to note three things.

---

[10] Ibid, 797 (CA).

[11] The Court of Appeal might have reached the same conclusion had they looked at the conclusions a reasonable pharmacist would have reached from the circumstances.

[12] [1998] 1 *WLR* 951.

[13] In *Murray*, ibid, 960 Schiemann LJ observed that 'insofar as [the plaintiff] submitted that the recipient of confidential information is not ever entitled to use it for his own benefit, that submission is clearly too wide'.

[14] Cf. *Heyl-Dia v. Edmunds* (1899) 81 *LT* 579 (drawing analogy between co-ownership of trade secrets and co-ownership of patent).

[15] Moreover, if the rule was applied (for example) to marital secrets, it would be a licence to 'kiss and tell'.

2.2.1 Derivation

The first is that, in order for a breach of confidence to occur, the information used by the defendant must have been *derived* from the confider's information and not from some other source. If the information has been independently generated, there is no breach. In *CMI-Centers v. Phytopharm*, Laddie J noted that there are three ways of proving that a defendant has used the confidential information.[16]

(i) The first is to show *direct evidence* of derivation. This would stem, for example, from an employee of the defendant who had seen the information being copied and then used.

(ii) The second way of proving derivation is *indirect*. For example, if the protected information contained a 'significant fingerprint',[17] and the defendant's use bore the same fingerprint, the court would infer that the defendant derived its product (etc.) from the claimant. For example, the defendant's product might have dimensions, a design, composition, or behaviour which is only to be found in the claimant's product, and which is consistent with use of the information and inconsistent with use of non-contaminated sources. Laddie J also said that it might be possible to show that the defendant has gone to all the same suppliers and customers as the claimant and that it would be 'highly unlikely that the same group would have been approached had the defendant been working from uncontaminated sources'.[18]

(iii) Third, a claimant may be able to 'persuade the court that the defendant could not have got to the position they have with the speed he has had he simply started from legitimate sources and worked everything out for himself'.[19]

2.2.2 The defendant's state of mind

The second general point to note is that the defendant's state of mind is not relevant when determining breach.[20] There is no need for a claimant to show that the breach was conscious or deliberate. Thus, it does not matter if the defendant acted in good faith, did not know that the information was confidential, or used the information accidentally[21] or subconsciously.[22]

2.2.3 Breach and damage?

The third point to note is that it remains unclear whether, for a disclosure to be actionable, claimants must show that they were harmed by the disclosure. That is, the question has arisen whether damage is an essential part of the action. The way this question is answered depends on the type of information in question. It also depends on how 'damage' and 'harm' are defined.[23]

---

[16] *CMI-Centers for Medical Innovation v. Phytopharm* [1999] *FSR* 235, 257–8.

[17] Ibid. In *Berkeley Administration v. McClelland* [1990] *FSR* 505, 528 the judge was satisfied that a defendant's figures were so similar to the claimant's that they must have been derived.

[18] *CMI v. Phytopharm*, ibid, 258; *Talbot v. General Television Corp* [1981] *RPC* 1, 17.

[19] *CMI v. Phytopharm*, ibid, 257–8.

[20] But *mens rea* is often a component when establishing the defendant's obligation. See above, pp. 1026–8, 1031–2.

[21] A confidant cannot escape liability by arguing that the disclosure was accidental: *Weld-Blundell v. Stephens* [1919] 1 *KB* 520.

[22] *Seager v. Copydex* [1967] 2 *All ER* 415; *Talbot v. GTV* [1981] *RPC* 1, 17.

[23] *Attorney-General v. Guardian Newspapers* [1990] *AC* 109, 281–2 (Lord Goff).

In the case of *government secrets* the Crown must demonstrate a public interest in restraining disclosure.[24] In *Attorney General v. Guardian (No. 2)*,[25] Lord Keith refused the government's claim to an injunction on the ground that it was necessary for the government to prove damage from the continued publication of *Spycatcher,* and it could prove none.

While there has been little discussion of this issue in other areas, it seems that it is only necessary to show harm in relation to government secrets. In the case of *personal secrets,* there is no need to prove damage. As the Court of Appeal said in *McKennitt v. Ash,* in relation to an action for violation of private information, there was no need to show detriment beyond the fact that there had been an invasion of the claimant's private life. This was followed in *Pauline Bluck v. The Information Commissioner,* where the Information Tribunal said that if 'disclosure would be contrary to an individual's expectation of maintaining confidentiality in respect of private information, then the absence of detriment... is not a necessary ingredient of the cause of action'.[26] A similar approach was suggested in *Spycatcher,* when Lord Keith said that there is no need to prove detriment, so that a person ought to be able to prevent a breach of a personal confidence which shows them in a good light, for example one which revealed that the confider had given large sums to charity.[27] It has even been said in relation to commercial information that detriment was 'not an essential constituent of a claim for a breach of confidence'. The Court of Appeal added that if detriment is a requirement the diversion of business opportunities could amount to a detriment to the person imparting the confidential information.[28]

Has the confidential information been misused?   For the most part, the question whether confidential information has been misused is relatively straightforward. Thus, if someone who is given an unpublished manuscript in confidence is told not to use or disclose it and they publish the manuscript, they will be in breach. Having said that, there are a number of unclear areas which warrant attention.

Where the information used or disclosed is different   Where the information used or disclosed by the defendant is identical (or very similar) to the confidential information, few problems arise in determining breach. If the action were limited to identical uses, it would enable a defendant to avoid liability by changing the information slightly. To ensure that this does not occur, the law has long recognized that the information used or disclosed by the defendant need not be identical to the confidential information. It is clear, for example, that the information can appear in another format and still breach. Thus, a change of language or a product built to a plan may be actionable. As is the case with all forms of intellectual property, the difficult question is determining how different the information can be and there still be a breach. Here the courts need to consider the interests of both the confider and the person making the disclosure. It seems clear that the way this question is answered will change depending on the nature of the information in question. Thus, where the information is personal in nature, it seems that the level of 'similarity' required need not be great. Here, what matters is the substance of the message. In the case of technical trade secrets, however, in order to avoid hampering competition, the courts may be less willing to construe the scope of protection as broadly.

---

[24] *Lord Advocate v. The Scotsman Publications Ltd* [1989] *FSR* 580.
[25] *Attorney-General v. Guardian* [1990] *AC* 109, 260 (Lord Keith).
[26] *Bluck v. Information Commissioner* (2007) *WL* 4266111 [2008] *WTLR* 1, para 15.
[27] Ibid, 256; *Coco v. A.N. Clark* [1969] *RPC* 41.
[28] *Federal Bank of the Middle East v. Hadkinson* [2000] 2 *All ER* 395, 413–14.

Partial uses   One situation where questions about the similarity of the information arise is where the defendant only uses part of the confidential information. In this situation, the information ultimately used is different from the information that was originally disclosed by the claimant. The case law has not considered this issue in much detail. It seems, however, that the answer will vary with the circumstances of the case. If the claimant's confidential information is the product of a lot of work, a defendant might infringe if they use a part of the information.[29] However, if the confidential information was the product of very little effort, it is likely that there will only be a breach of confidence if all (or most) of the information was used. An approach of this nature was supported by the Court of Appeal in *Source Informatics* when Simon Brown LJ agreed with the comment that 'a confidant will be liable for breach of his duty if he misuses *only part* of the confidential information which has been disclosed to him, provided that the misuse relates to a *material* part of the information'.[30]

The question whether partial use of information could constitute a breach was considered in *De Maudsley v. Palumbo*.[31] As we saw earlier,[32] this was a breach of confidence action brought in relation to an idea for a nightclub (which was rejected because the information was too vague). The court suggested that to breach the defendant would have needed to have used substantially the same idea. The defendant had only adopted two of the five features of the claimant's idea for a nightclub (namely that the club was to be open all night and have separate dancing areas). Knox J held that (in these circumstances) partial use would not be sufficient to constitute an unauthorized use for the purposes of breach of confidence. The judge also took into account that the defendant had added a number of important features, such as the idea that the club would not sell alcohol and that admission would be limited to those over 21.

Where the defendant alters the confidential information   Another situation where questions about the nature of the breach arise is where the defendant adds to or alters the confidential information. In these cases, the information ultimately used or disclosed is different from the information that was originally disclosed by the claimant. In *Ocular Sciences*, Laddie J took the view that it was a question of fact whether the use of a derived product should be treated as a use of the information employed in its creation.[33] He said:

It is not every derived product, process or business which should be treated as a camouflaged embodiment of the confidential information and not all ongoing exploitation of such products, processes or business should be treated as continued use of the information. It must be a matter of degree whether the extent and importance of the use of the confidential information is such that continued exploitation of the derived matter should be viewed as continued use of the information.[34]

It seems that similar reasoning would apply in other situations where the information used by the defendant is different from the information that was originally disclosed by the claimant. Following similar logic, the courts held that information about etchings was replicated when it appeared in a catalogue containing descriptions of those etchings.[35] In another case, it was held that information about the processes for making sausage casings was used by the import of sausage casings which had been bought from a manufacturer who had wrongfully used that

---

[29] *Amber Size v. Menzel* [1913] 2 *Ch* 239, 248 ('material part of the plaintiff's secret method').

[30] Gurry, 258, quoted with approval in *ex p Source Informatics* [2000] 1 *All ER* 786, 796 (CA).

[31] [1996] *FSR* 447.   [32] See above at p. 1012.   [33] [1997] *RPC* 289.   [34] Ibid, 404.

[35] *Prince Albert v. Strange* (1849) 2 *DeG & Sm* 652; 64 *ER* 293 (Knight Bruce LJ); (1849) 1 *Mac & G* 25; 41 *ER* 1171 (Cottenham LC).

information.[36] However, it has been held that the use of a confidential computer program did not justify broader relief relating to the defendant's business, which had benefited from previous use of the program. The problem here was that there was no evidence that the program made any significant contribution to the business.[37]

Non-action   One question that has yet to be considered is whether non-action amounts to a use. Would it be a breach of confidence if on the strength of confidential information a person decided *not* to act in a particular way? For example, if someone was told confidential information that showed that the value of a building that they were planning to buy was about to decrease, would they be liable for breach if on the basis of the information they decided not to buy the building? While this issue has not been addressed directly, Lord Hoffmann noted in relation to the Data Protection Act 1984 that a 'person who refrains from entering a field with a notice saying "Beware of the Bull" is using the information obtained from the notice'.[38] Whether similar reasoning would be used in relation to breach of confidence is unclear. If the courts were willing to treat failure to act as an actionable use, it would be necessary for a claimant to demonstrate that the defendant had previously set upon a particular course of conduct from which they subsequently withdrew. In the example above, a claimant would need to show that the defendant had set out to purchase the building and that the reason why they subsequently decided not to purchase it was because of the confidential information and not some other reason.

3 DEFENCES

Once it is established that a defendant has breached their obligation of confidentiality, the only way they can escape liability is if they can show that they fall within one of the defences which are available to them. These include consent or authorization to use the information, disclosure in the public interest, as well as a number of other equitable and statutory immunities. We examine these in turn.

3.1 CONSENT OR AUTHORIZATION

If a defendant is able to show that the claimant consented to or authorized the use of the information, they will be exempt from breach. Consent to the use or disclosure of information can arise through an express licence, or from a release from liability. An express licence might be contractual in nature, as with a technology-licensing agreement,[39] or gratuitous.[40] Consent or authorization might also be implied from the circumstances. The courts have suggested that special considerations apply in relation to consent given in relation to medical information.

---

[36] *Union Carbide Corp. v. Naturin Ltd.* [1987] *FSR* 538, 547.

[37] *Ocular Sciences* [1997] *RPC* 289, 403.   [38] *R v. Brown (Gregory)* [1996] *AC* 543.

[39] One question which has proved to be problematic is that of determining the position of the parties when the agreement comes to an end: *Torrington Manufacturing Co. v. Smith* [1966] *RPC* 285 (once agreement terminated there was no right to continue to use the confidential information); *Regina Glass Fibre v. Schuller* [1972] *RPC* 229 (continued right to use information even after licence agreement terminated).

[40] *C v. C* [1946] 1 *All ER* 562 (doctor did not breach confidence when patient asked him to reveal information about her venereal disease to third party).

3.2 PUBLIC INTEREST DEFENCE

The most important defence available to a defendant is the public interest defence. This provides defendants with the opportunity to escape liability for breach if they can establish that the disclosure is justified in the public interest. As Lord Phillips said 'the right of confidentiality, whether or not founded in contract is not absolute. That right must give way where it is in the public interest that the confidential information shall be made public.'[41] The origin of the defence lies in the dicta of Wood V-C in the 1856 decision in *Gartside v. Outram*.[42] In that case the claimant, who carried on business as woolbrokers, brought an action to restrain the defendant, an ex-employee, from communicating information about their business dealings. The defendant asserted that the claimant had been defrauding its customers using falsified business records. Wood V-C held that, if the defendant made out the case pleaded by him, he would have 'a very good case for resisting this injunction'.[43] He said that:

there is no confidence as to the disclosure of iniquity. You cannot make me the confidant of a crime or a fraud, and be entitled to close up my lips upon any secret which you have the audacity to disclose to me relating to any fraudulent intention on your part: such a confidence cannot exist.[44]

Although Wood V-C's comments suggest that the public interest is not so much a defence as a reason why the court will not recognize an obligation of confidence in the first place, case law since the 1960s has treated public interest as a defence in its own right. For example, in *Initial Services v. Putterill*[45] the defendant had been employed as a sales manager by the claimant company, a firm of launderers. The defendant resigned and revealed documents to the *Daily Mail* exposing the claimant's price fixing. After the *Daily Mail* published articles about the price fixing, the claimant brought an action for breach of confidence. In response, the ex-employee argued that the disclosure was in the public interest because it revealed that the claimants were parties to a price-fixing agreement contrary to the Restrictive Trade Practices Act 1956. The claimant's action failed. Salmon and Winn LJJ applied the iniquity rule, but widened it to include improper trade practices. This was on the ground that 'what was iniquity in 1856 differed from what was iniquity in 1967'.[46] Lord Denning suggested a different test altogether. This was that the defence was not limited to crime or fraud. Instead, it covered any misconduct of such a nature that it is in the public interest to disclose.[47] Lord Denning reasserted this view in *Fraser v. Evans*,[48] when he said that iniquity is merely an example of a 'just cause or excuse' for breaking a breach of confidence. More recently, the courts have incorporated the generalized public interest defence into a balancing process. For example, in *Spycatcher*, Lord Goff explained that:

although the basis of the law's protection of confidence is a public interest that confidences should be preserved and protected by law, nevertheless that public interest may be outweighed by some other countervailing public interest which favours disclosure.[49]

---

[41] *Campbell v. Frisbee* [2002] *EMLR* 31, para. 23. See also *Douglas v. Hello!* [2008] 1 *AC* 1, 75 (para. 272 *per* Lord Walker); 87 (para. 307 *per* Baroness Hale) (contrasting public interest in disclosure with private interest in secrecy).

[42] (1856) 26 *LJ (NS) Ch* 113; 5 WR 35; 3 *Jur (NS)* 39, 28 *LT (OS)* 120. The judgment was delivered *extempore* and the reports vary.

[43] 26 *LJ (NS) Ch* 113, 116.   [44] Ibid, 114.   [45] [1968] 1 *QB* 396.   [46] Ibid, 410.

[47] Ibid, 405.   [48] [1969] 1 *QB* 349.

[49] *Attorney-General v. Guardian* [1990] *AC* 109, 282. See also Lord Griffiths at 269.

Because many of the limitations to the action for breach of confidence have been modified in relation to personal information, the courts have been willing to widen the exceptions.[50] Certainly, some of the limitations of the standard public interest test seem to have been modified, particularly those relating to disclosure to a responsible authority. For example, in *A v. B*, Lord Woolf MR spoke of the public having an understandable and legitimate interest in being told information, an interest which should be taken into account even though it could not really be called a 'public interest'.[51]

The tendency of British courts to treat matters of public interest as a general defence was criticized by Gummow J in the Federal Court of Australia on the basis that it was 'picturesque but somewhat imprecise'.[52] He argued that *Gartside v. Outram* did not establish a defence. Instead, Gummow J said that it was better explained either as a case where the contractual obligation implied by the court did not extend to the information concerned, or where the court withheld equitable relief on the grounds of 'unclean hands'. In *Smith Kline & French v. Department of Community Health*,[53] Gummow J continued to criticize the English public interest defence on the basis that it had been constructed out of inadequate historical and doctrinal materials. Moreover, it was 'not so much a rule of law as an invitation to judicial idiosyncrasy'. In contrast, Gummow J asserted that equitable principles are best developed by reference to what conscionable behaviour demands of the defendant. Whatever validity Gummow J's criticisms may have, it is clear that, where a defendant discloses information in the public interest, British law provides them with a possible defence to escape liability. Having said that, the Court of Appeal cited Gummow J's comments about the defence being a call to 'judicial idiosyncrasy' as a reason for confining the public interest defence within strict limits.[54]

3.2.1 What is the public interest?

While it is impossible to delimit the types of circumstances in which a particular disclosure will be in the public interest, a number of different factors are taken into account when deciding whether the disclosure is in the public interest.[55]

The nature of the information   A key factor to be considered will be the nature of the information. If a disclosure relates to misdeeds of a serious nature and importance to the country, then it is likely to be justified as being 'in the public interest'.[56] Disclosure relating to a criminal offence, civil actions,[57] a failure to comply with a legal obligation, a miscarriage of justice, behaviour likely to endanger health or safety, or damage the environment are obvious examples of cases where disclosure might be justified. Although the public interest defence is defined broadly, it does not permit the unauthorized disclosure of information that is merely

---

[50] *Theakston v. MGN* [2002] *EMLR* 398, 420, paras. 66–7.

[51] [2002] *EMLR* 371, [2002] 3 *WLR* 542, (guideline xii). In so doing, he seems to have been edging towards the broader defences available under the US Restatement.

[52] *Corrs Pavey Whiting & Byrne v. Collector of Customs (Vic)* (1987) 14 *FCR* 434, 451–8 (FCA).

[53] [1989] *FSR* 617, 663.   [54] *Ex p Source Informatics* [2000] 1 *All ER* 786, 800 (CA).

[55] These factors are reflected in the provisions of the Public Interest Disclosure Act 1998, which protects employees from action by employers as regards 'protected disclosures'. A different definition is provided by the *Press Complaints Code of Practice*: see *A v. B* [2003] *QB* 195, 208 (guideline xiv).

[56] *Beloff v. Pressdram* [1973] 1 *All ER* 241, 260. This is not to say that iniquity always justifies disclosure: *Bunn v. BBC* [1998] 3 *All ER* 552.

[57] *Frankson v. Home Office* [2003] 1 *WLR* 1952 (information obtained during criminal investigations into assaults by prison officers could be disclosed as part of the prisoner's civil action against the prison officers).

'interesting to the public'.[58] In this context, the law draws a distinction between matters which affect the moral, political, medical, or material welfare of the public (or a section thereof), *and* the public's entertainment, curiosity, or amusement.

Having said this, the courts have been willing to permit the disclosure of confidential information in the public interest where it serves to correct a false image that a person has created about themselves. As said the House of Lords made clear in *Campbell v. MGN*, where a public figure makes untrue statements as to their private life, the press will normally be entitled to put the record straight: particularly where they have courted rather than shunned publicity.[59] This can be seen, for example, in *Woodward v. Hutchins* where the Court of Appeal held that disclosure by their former press agent of the private activities of a group of pop stars (including Tom Jones and Engelbert Humperdink) was justifiable where they had falsely represented to the public that they were clean-living.[60] According to Lord Denning, if the image which a public figure fostered was 'not a true image, it is in the public interest that it should be corrected'. This was because in these cases 'it is a question of balancing the public interest in maintaining the confidence against the public interest in knowing the truth'.[61] While there have been doubts cast over the ongoing relevance of *Woodward v. Hutchins,* it has been followed in a number of decisions.[62] This can be seen, for example, in *Theakston v. MGN,* an action brought by Theakston, a 31-year-old presenter for *Top of the Pops*, to suppress publication of the fact that he had had sex with a number of prostitutes in a brothel in London.[63] In allowing the publication, the Court of Appeal noted that Theakston had courted publicity and willingly placed information in the public domain about his sexual and personal relations. This was done 'so as to create and project an image calculated to enhance his fame, popularity and reputation as a man physically and sexually attractive to many women'. Citing *Woodward v. Hutchins* with approval the court said that this meant that he could not complain if the publicity given to his sexual activities was less favourable in this instance.

The consequences of non-disclosure   A disclosure may be justified as being in the public interest, even though it does not reveal wrongful behaviour or misconduct,[64] for example where the disclosure will protect public health or safety.[65] In *Lion Laboratories* the court held that it was legitimate for the press to disclose confidential internal papers that suggested that an alcohol-measuring machine was faulty. (The machine was used to test whether drivers were guilty of driving under the influence of alcohol.) The disclosure was justified because, if the information had remained concealed, the life and liberty of an unascertainable number of persons might have been affected. Revelation in the press was justified because disclosure to the police might not have been adequate.[66]

---

[58] *Lion Laboratories v. Evans* [1985] *QB* 526, 537.

[59] *Campbell v. MGN* [2004] 2 *AC* 457 (HL), 467, para. 24 (*per* Lord Nicholls), 474–5, para. 58 (*per* Lord Hoffmann), 479, para. 82 (*per* Lord Hope), 500, paras. 151–2 (*per* Baroness Hale).

[60] *Woodward v. Hutchins* [1977] 1 *WLR* 760, 763.   [61] Ibid, 764.

[62] *Campbell v. MGN* [2003] *QB* 633, 658, paras. 40–41 (publication of information about the internationally famous model Naomi Campbell's attendance at Narcotics Anonymous was justified because she had painted a false picture of herself, had re-branded herself as a reformed and stable individual who did not take drugs). The House of Lords did not refer to *Woodward*, though it accepted the general principle.

[63] *Theakston*, [2002] *EMLR* 398.

[64] *Malone v. Metropolitan Police Commissioner* [1979] *Ch* 344, 362 (Megarry V-C) ('there may be cases where there is no misconduct or misdeed but yet there is a just cause or excuse for breaking confidence').

[65] *Hubbard v. Vosper* [1972] 2 *QB* 84.

[66] See also *W v. Egdell* [1990] 2 *WLR* 47; *Schering Chemicals v. Falkman* [1982] 1 *QB* 1 (Shaw LJ would allow disclosure where the subject matter 'is something which is inimical to the public interest or threatens public safety').

The type of obligation   Another factor that is likely to play a significant role in determining whether a disclosure is permissible is the type of obligation involved. It seems that the courts will treat some obligations as more absolute than others. For example, a disclosure by a priest or doctor could rarely be justified in the public interest.[67] In a rare case, the Court of Appeal held that a psychiatrist was justified in breaching the obligation of confidence he owed to a patient who had been interned under the Mental Health Act, by alerting the Home Office to the patient's interests in firearms and explosives. This was vital information, directly relevant to public safety.[68] The courts have also suggested that they will give more weight to obligations that arise through agreement than through other means. For example, in *Campbell v. Frisbee* it was said that 'a duty of confidentiality that has been expressly assumed under a contract [arguably] carries more weight, when balanced against the restriction of the right of freedom of expression, than a duty of confidentiality that is not buttressed by express agreement'.[69]

The beliefs of the confidant   Because the public interest defence covers any situation where there is 'just cause or excuse' for breaking a confidence, the court is not confined to considering whether the information is *in fact* real misconduct. Instead, the court can also take into account whether the confidant believed on reasonable grounds that revelation was required in the public interest.[70] That is, according to the broader 'just cause' characterization of the defence, a disclosure may be justified where the confidant reasonably believed they were disclosing an iniquity, even if it turns out that they were wrong.[71] For example, in *Malone v. Metropolitan Police Commissioner*[72] it was held that, if the police owed a duty of confidentiality, nevertheless there was a reasonable suspicion of iniquity such as to justify the disclosure.

The party to whom the information was disclosed   Another factor that will influence whether a disclosure is justified is the party to whom the information is disclosed.[73] It may be legitimate to disclose information to one body, but not another. For example, while a disclosure is likely to be justified if it is made to a responsible body,[74] it is less likely to be justified if it is disclosed to the general public via a newspaper. As the Court of Appeal emphasized in *Lion Laboratories*, newspapers must take special care not to confuse the public interest with their own interest in increasing circulation. Thus, if the confidence relates to a crime, for a disclosure to be justified it should normally be made to the police.[75] In *Francome v. Mirror Group Newspapers*, an interim

---

[67] *X Health Authority v. Y* [1988] *RPC* 379, 395 (confidentiality was vital to secure public as well as private health, so that the interest in non-disclosure outweighed the interest in disclosure).

[68] *W v. Egdell* [1990] 2 *WLR* 47.

[69] *Campbell v. Frisbee* [2002] *EMLR* 31, para 22. See R. Arnold, 'The protection of confidential information in the human rights era: two aspects' [2007] *JIPLP* 599–608 (questioning significance of express contractual obligation).

[70] *Fraser v. Evans* [1969] 1 *All ER* 8.   [71] Y. Cripps, *Disclosure in the Public Interest* (1994), 25–6.

[72] [1979] *Ch* 344, 377. See also *Woolgar v. Chief Constable of Sussex Police* [2000] 1 *WLR* 25, 36.

[73] The Employment Rights Act 1986 allows for disclosures to employers, prescribed bodies, and 'in other cases'. In the latter case, the person to whom the information is revealed is a significant factor in assessing whether a disclosure is 'qualifying': ss. 43G(3)(a), 43H(2). *R v. Plymouth City Council* [2002] 1 *WLR* 2583, 2599, para. 50 (confidential information about why C had been put into guardianship under the Mental Health Act 1983 could be released to psychiatric and social work experts to advise in a challenge to the order); *Jockey Club v. Buffham* [2003] *QB* 462, 475–79 (disclosure of information by ex-employee that showed corruption within Jockey Club allowed. Judge took account of fact that Jockey Club was a public authority and the good conduct of the party (BBC *Panorama*)).

[74] *Imutran v. Uncaged Campaigns* [2002] *FSR* 21, 28 (no restriction on disclosure of confidential information about treatment of animals in xenotransplantation factory to specialist bodies with relevant responsibility).

[75] *Initial Services* [1968] 1 *QB* 396, 405–6.

injunction was granted preventing disclosure in a newspaper of conversations which were alleged to reveal that Johnny Francome had breached Jockey Club regulations and possibly committed criminal offences. The main basis of the decision appears to have been that disclosure to the Jockey Club would have sufficed: there was no need for full newspaper disclosure.[76] While the courts have been wary about using the public interest defence to justify publication in a newspaper, in some cases publication in the press might be justified.[77]

Other factors   A number of other factors may influence the court in determining whether disclosure is in the public interest. For example, in *Francome,* the court took account of the manner in which the information was acquired.[78] Another relevant factor is whether the person claiming the defence received remuneration for the disclosure.[79] While receipt of remuneration does not preclude the operation of the defence,[80] it may indicate that a defendant confused their own interests with that of the public.[81] Finally, it seems that the extent to which the information is already publicly available may impact on the operation of the public interest defence. If the information is not very confidential, disclosure may be justified even if there is only a low level of public interest.

Public and private interests   Typically, the public interest defence is characterized as the balancing of one public interest against another. The idea that it might involve a balancing of public interest against a private interest was rejected in *W v. Egdell* where the relevant private interest was that of the confider.[82] It has yet to be seen, however, whether the courts might accept a defence of disclosure in the private interests of the person to whom the disclosure was made. For example, if a doctor who knew that a patient had a contagious disease disclosed that information to a person in a sexual relationship with the patient, the court might be tempted to develop a defence of justified disclosure in the private interest.[83]

A related question is whether disclosure can be justified by reference to the confider's own interests. For example, is a doctor justified in revealing information about treatment of a child to the child's parents? While in *Gillick* the majority of the House of Lords held that doctors did not have a duty to inform parents about the advice they had given to their children (here in relation to contraception), the Lords did not express any view on whether, if doctors did so, they would be in breach.[84] Lord Templeman, dissenting, was clear that 'confidentiality owed

---

[76] [1984] 1 WLR 892, 899 (Lord Donaldson MR).

[77] For example, *Lion Laboratories* [1985] *QB* 526, 553. See also *Cork v. McVicar* (*The Times,* 31 Oct. 1984) (disclosure to the press might be in the public interest where the information disclosed concerned police corruption and therefore disclosure to police might not suffice).

[78] *Francome* [1984] 1 *WLR* 892 (rejecting the defence in a case where the information had been acquired criminally, in breach of the Wireless Telegraphy Act 1949). In contrast, the court will not do so if all the defendant has done is break a promise that will not weigh materially against a public interest defence: *Cork v. McVicar,* note 77 above, Scott J. See also Employment Rights Act 1986, s. 43B(3) (not a qualifying disclosure if person commits an offence by making it).

[79] *Initial Services* [1968] 1 *QB* 396, 406 (Lord Denning MR observing that 'it is a great evil when people purvey scandalous information for reward').

[80] *Hubbard v. Vosper* [1972] 2 *QB* 84; *Church of Scientology v. Kaufman* [1973] *RPC* 627, 635. Cf. Employment Rights Act 1986, ss. 43G(c), 43H(1)(c) (not a qualifying disclosure if person makes disclosure for personal gain).

[81] *Schering v. Falkman* [1982] 1 *QB* 1, 39.   [82] [1990] 2 *WLR* 47, 485.

[83] D. Caswell, 'Disclosure by a Physician of AIDS-related Patient Information: An Ethical and Legal Dilemma' (1989) 68 *Canadian Bar Review* 225.

[84] *Gillick v. West Norfolk & Wisbech HA* [1985] 3 *All ER* 402, 410–13.

to an infant is not breached by disclosure to a parent responsible to that infant if the doctor considers that such disclosure is necessary in the interests of the infant'.[85]

3.3 FREEDOM OF EXPRESSION

One of the factors that the courts take into account in deciding whether to grant relief for breach of confidence is the right to freedom of expression provided for in Article 10 of the European Convention of Human Rights. This right, which is directly applicable as between the parties to private litigation,[86] operates independently of the public interest defence.[87] As the Court of Appeal said, interference with the right has to be justified 'even where there was no identifiable special public interest in the material in question being published, since the existence of a free press was desirable in itself'.[88] While freedom of expression is valuable as a counterforce to privacy, the courts have been at pains to point out that it is not an 'ace of trumps'.[89] That is, freedom of speech is not paramount and must be balanced against other interests.[90]

3.4 MISCELLANEOUS IMMUNITIES

A defendant may also be immune from a breach of confidence action where they have revealed information pursuant to a statutory obligation or a court order.[91] Another way in which a defendant might be able to escape liability is via the equitable principle that, for a claimant to bring an action in equity, they must have 'clean hands'.[92] For the claimant's conduct to be relevant, 'it must have an immediate and necessary relation to the equity sued for'.[93] In *Lennon v. News Group*,[94] John Lennon sought to restrain his former wife, Cynthia, from publishing details of their married life in a newspaper article called 'I saw the man I loved turn into a snake'. The Court of Appeal affirmed the decision of Bristow J not to grant the injunction. The Court was influenced by the fact that newspaper articles written by the Lennons' chauffeur and by John Lennon himself, which had discussed 'their most intimate affairs', had already

---

[85] Ibid, 434.

[86] *Douglas v. Hello!* [2001] 2 *WLR* 992, 1027, para. 133 (Sedley LJ) (CA). *Response Handling v. BBC* (2008) *SLT* 51 (OH) (genuine and strong public interest in exploring the extent to which lapses in security at a call centre might contribute to back account fraud was sufficient to allow an undercover journalist to disclose information obtained under a contractual obligation of confidence: applying s 12(3) Human Rights Act 1998).

[87] *Theakston* [2002] *EMLR* 398, para. 70 (the apparent attempt by defendant to blackmail the claimant did not remove her right to freedom of expression nor her right to seek publication).

[88] See *A v. B* [2003] *QB* 195, 205 (CA); *Douglas v. Hello!* [2001] 2 *WLR* 992, 1027, para. 133 (Sedley LJ) (when deciding whether to grant an injunction the court should have regard to the availability of the material).

[89] *Douglas v. Hello! (No. 3)* [2003] 3 *All ER* 996, para. 185.

[90] *Imutran* [2002] *FSR* 21, 28, para. 17.

[91] Examples include the Criminal Justice Act 1988, s. 98 (where a person discloses to a constable a belief that property is the proceeds of a crime, that disclosure is not to be treated as a breach of any restriction upon disclosure of information imposed by contract).

[92] See *Hubbard v. Vosper* [1972] 2 *QB* 84, 101 (Megaw LJ) (refusing injunctive relief because of the deplorable means that the claimant used to protect its confidential information); *Church of Scientology v. Kaufman*, note 80 above.

[93] *Besant v. Wood* (1879) 12 *Ch D* 605. Moreover, a claimant will not be disentitled to an equitable remedy if the acts are not of the same kind or degree: *Duchess of Argyll v. Duke of Argyll* [1967] *Ch* 302 (granting relief in spite of claimant's wrongdoing because the defendant's behaviour was of altogether a different order of perfidy).

[94] [1978] *FSR* 573.

been published. According to Lord Denning, this put their relationship in the public domain. As such, neither could restrain the other.

4 PRIVATE INFORMATION

4.1 PROTECTION FOR PRIVATE INFORMATION

There has been a proliferation of cases in recent years where the modified breach of confidence action has been used to protect private information. The decision as to whether private information has been violated involves two steps. The first question to ask is: what is the scope of the right to private life? Once this has been clarified, the next question to ask is whether the interference with that right is justified.

What is the scope of the right of private life?   The first question that must be asked in this context is whether the information is private in the sense that it is in principle protected by Article 8.[95] Article 8 provides that:

(1) Everyone has the right to respect for his private and family life, his home and his correspondence.

(2) There shall be no interference by a public authority with the exercise of this right except such as is in accordance with the law and is necessary in a democratic society in the interests of national security, public safety or the economic well-being of the country, for the prevention of disorder or crime, for the protection of health or morals, or for the protection of the rights and freedoms of others.

As we explained earlier, 'the touchstone of private life is whether in respect of the disclosed facts the person in question had a reasonable expectation of privacy'.[96] 'The mind that has to be examined is not [that] of the reader in general, but [that] of the person who is affected by the publicity… The question is what a reasonable person of ordinary sensibilities would feel if she was placed in the same position as the claimant and faced with the same publicity.'[97]

For the most part, the courts have not had many difficulties in determining whether information is private. This is the case, for example, with information about a person's health, their personal relationships, their finances, as well as their name or image.[98] It was common ground in *Campbell,* for example, that all of the categories of information at issue potentially qualified for protection under Article 8. These were information about (i) Ms Campbell's drug addiction, (ii) that she was receiving treatment, (iii) that this was at Narcotics Anonymous, (iv) the details of the treatment (length and frequency of treatment), and (v) the visual portrayal of her leaving a Narcotics Anonymous meeting with other addicts. While, as we will see, the House of Lords may not have been willing to protect all these different types of information, they were willing to recognize that the information was private and thus potentially able to be protected.

---

[95] *McKennitt v. Ash* [2008] *QB* 73, para. 11. 'If no, that is the end of the case.'

[96] *Campbell* [2004] 2 *AC* 457, 466, para. 21 (Lord Nicholls). See above p. 1023.

[97] Ibid, 484, para. 99 (*per* Lord Hope). In *Campbell*, this meant that to determine whether the breach was objectionable, it was necessary to put oneself into the shoes of a reasonable person who is in need of that treatment: see ibid, 481–3 (Lord Hope).

[98] According to the Court of Appeal, it will usually be obvious whether a person's private life is involved; *A v. B* [2003] *QB* 195, 206, para. 11 (guideline vii) (CA); *Campbell v. MGN* [2003] *QB* 633, 660, para. 51 (CA).

While ascertaining that the private life of ordinary citizens has not created any real problems, this is not the case with celebrities and public figures. The problems have manifested in two ways. The first relates to the question how the law should deal with private information that is commercialized. What should the law do, for example, where the image rights to a celebrity wedding (Michael Douglas and Catherine Zeta Jones) are pre-sold for a considerable amount of money? Should the wedding be treated as a commercial secret, a private event, or as 'a hybrid kind in which by reason of it having become a commodity, elements that would otherwise have been merely private become commercial'?[99] The Court of Appeal's response to this question was that there 'was no reason in principle why equity should not protect the opportunity to profit from confidential information about oneself in the same circumstance that it protects the opportunity to profit from confidential information in the nature of a trade secret'.[100] That is, the fact that information is commodified did not affect its ability to be protected as private information. The second problem area, which we look at below, relates to the scope of protection that ought to be given to public figures in a public places. In essence, the question here is how much control should a public figure have over images that are taken of them in a public place?

Is the interference justifiable?   Once the information is identified as 'private', the court must then balance the claimant's interest in keeping the information private against the countervailing interest of the recipient in publishing it.[101] That is, once it has been shown that information is private, the next question to ask is whether 'in all the circumstances, must the interest of the owner of the private information yield to the right of freedom of expression conferred on the publisher by Article 10?'[102] Article 10 provides that:

(1) Everyone has the right to freedom of expression. This right shall include freedom to hold opinions and to receive and impart information and ideas without interference by public authority and regardless of frontiers. This article shall not prevent States from requiring the licensing of broadcasting, television or cinema enterprises.

(2) The exercise of these freedoms, since it carries with it duties and responsibilities, may be subject to such formalities, conditions, restrictions or penalties as are prescribed by law and are necessary in a democratic society, in the interests of national security, territorial integrity or public safety, for the prevention of disorder or crime, for the protection of health or morals, for the protection of the reputation or the rights of others, for preventing the disclosure of information received in confidence, or for maintaining the authority and impartiality of the judiciary.

As Lord Woolf said in *A v. B*, 'the manner in which the two articles operate is entirely different'. Article 8, which provides respect for private and family life, 'operates so as to extend the areas in which an action for breach of confidence can provide protection for privacy. It requires a generous approach to situations in which privacy is to be protected.' In contrast, Article 10 'operates in the opposite direction. This is because it protects freedom of expression and to achieve this it is necessary to restrict the area in which remedies are available for breach of confidence.'[103] In balancing these competing interests, it has been held that the 'restrictions

---

99   *Douglas v. Hello! (No. 3)* [2003] 3 *All ER* 996, para. 227.

100   *Douglas v. Hello!* [2006] *QB* 125, para. 13.

101   *Campbell* [2004] 2 *AC* 457, 496, para. 137 (Baroness Hale of Richmond).

102   *McKennitt v. Ash* [2006] *EWCA Civ* 1714 (CA), para 11.   103   *A v. B* [2003] QB 195, 203 (CA).

which the courts impose on the Article 10 right must be rational, fair and not arbitrary, and they must impair the right no more than is necessary'.[104]

The task of balancing the competing interests in Articles 8 and 10 essentially involves a factual inquiry.[105] One of the consequences of this is that appeal courts will only interfere with a trial judge's assessment of the balance between Article 8 and 10 when there has been an error of principle.[106] Another consequence of the factual nature of the inquiry is that it operates as a vehicle for policy-type issues. Following *Campbell* and *von Hannover* (see below), it is clear that the pendulum has swung in favour of private information and away from the protection of freedom of the press. While the factual nature of the inquiry means that it is difficult, if not impossible, to provide detailed guidance as to how and where the line will be drawn, it is possible to highlight some of the factors that have influenced the courts in balancing the competing interests.[107]

'Putting the record straight'   In some situations the conduct of the claimant plays a role in determining whether it is permissible to disclose information about them. This is particularly the case in situations where a person has actively courted publicity about their private life. Here, the question arises: should the celebrity be able to prevent disclosure of personal information that undermines the public image of themselves that they have cultivated? The key consideration here is whether the law is protecting the private sphere or whether non-disclosure is sought to protect a valuable 'brand'. This issue was addressed in the House of Lords decision in *Campbell* v. *MGN,* which was an action brought by the supermodel, Naomi Campbell, in response to the publication of newspaper stories and related photographs about her attendance at Narcotics Anonymous meetings. The House of Lords held that Naomi Campbell's 'public lies' that she did not use drugs precluded her from preventing the press from disclosing that this was untrue. 'Public disclosure that contrary to her assertions she did in fact take drugs and had a serious drug problem was not disclosure of private information...where a public figure chooses to present a false image and make untrue pronouncements about his or her life, the press will normally be entitled to put the record straight'.[108] While the press is able to disclose information that 'puts the record straight', the fact that a person has revealed or discussed some information about their private life does not mean that they have a greatly reduced expectation of privacy in relation to other information about their private life.[109]

Impact on the claimant   Another factor which the courts have taken into account when deciding whether to protect private information is the impact that the disclosure might have on the claimant. Given the decision that it was permissible to disclose information about her drug addiction to the public, the question in *Campbell* was whether the disclosure of additional information relating to her attendance at Narcotics Anonymous could be protected by Article 8. The majority held that, while the press was able to 'put the record straight' about Campbell's comments about her (lack of) drug use, information about the treatment which she

---

[104] *Campbell* [2004] 2 *AC* 457 (HL), 490, para. 115 (Lord Hope).

[105] The values underlying Articles 8 and 10 are not confined to disputes between individuals and public authorities. ibid, 465, para 18 (Lord Nicholls).

[106] On this see *McKennitt v. Ash* [2006] *EWCA Civ* 1714, para 45.

[107] *Theakston* [2002] *EMLR* 398, 418, para. 58.

[108] *Campbell* [2004] 2 *AC* 457 (HL), 467, para. 24 (Lord Nicholls), 479, para. 82 (Lord Hope).

[109] *McKennitt v. Ash* [2006] *EWCA Civ* 1714, para. 19.

was receiving ought to be treated differently.[110] While the minority downplayed the importance of the disclosure, the majority felt that the information about Campbell's treatment at Narcotics Anonymous was equivalent to the disclosure of treatment of a medical condition. As Lord Hope of Craighead said, 'there are few areas of the life of an individual that are more in need of protection on the grounds of privacy than the combating of addiction to alcohol or drugs'.[111] Importantly, the majority felt that there was a chance that the disclosure might undermine and disrupt Campbell's treatment. The Lords also noted that recovering addicts were particularly vulnerable and that an assurance of privacy was an essential part of the treatment.[112] On this basis the Lords upheld Campbell's claims. A similar approach was adopted in *Peck v. UK* where it was held by the European Court of Human Rights that widespread publication of a photograph which revealed a person in a situation of humiliation or severe embarrassment was an infringement of the right to respect for private life.[113]

Nature of the information   The approach that is adopted towards private information may also differ depending on the nature of the information in question. The more intimate the aspects of private life which are being interfered with, the more serious must be the reasons for doing so. This has led courts to suggest that political expression is to be treated differently to private information.[114] In some situations, the courts have also downplayed the importance that should be given to information that may be morally questionable. For example, in one case it was held that, while correspondence between two parties on private matters were 'a prime candidate for protection', where the 'letters contained unsolicited expressions of love from a married man to a married woman and…a semi-serious proposal to pay her husband a large sum for her release', it was held that it was not reasonable to expect that the facts disclosed would be kept private.[115]

Degree of disclosure   In some situations the extent of disclosure may weigh in favour of a claimant attempting to protect private information. This can be seen in *Peck v. UK,* where the European Court of Human Rights held that an embarrassing moment involving Peck which was filmed on CCTV and repeatedly broadcast on television was an invasion of Peck's right to privacy. Here, 'the relevant moment was viewed to an extent which far exceeded any exposure to a passer-by or to a security observation and to a degree surpassing that which the applicant could possibly have foreseen when he walked' in the public street.[116] In this situation, the artificiality of the disclosure—which meant that it was much greater than what could ordinarily be expected in a public place—combined with the embarrassing content, led the court to decide that the disclosure had violated Peck's right to privacy.

Nature of the relationship   The courts have also focused on the nature of the relationship that exists between the parties in determining the scope of a duty of confidentiality. This is particularly the case in relation to shared personal information generated by intimate relationships.[117]

---

[110] The minority held that the additional information was of such an unremarkable and inconsequential nature that it could not be protected. *Campbell* [2004] 2 *AC* 457 (HL), 467, para. 26 (Lord Nicholls).

[111] Ibid, 479, para. 81 (Lord Hope).

[112] Ibid, 481, para. 90 (Lord Hope), 499, para. 146 (Baroness Hale).

[113] *Peck v. United Kingdom* (2003) 36 *EHRR* 719. In *Campbell,* ibid, 478, para. 75 Lord Hoffmann said that the widespread publication of a photograph of someone which reveals them to be in a situation of humiliation or severe embarrassment, even if taken in a public place, may be an infringement of personal information.

[114] *Campbell* [2004] 2 *AC* 457 (HL), 490, para. 117 (Lord Hope), citing *Dudgeon v. UK* [1981] *EHRR* 149, para. 52.

[115] *Maccaba v. Lichtenstein* [2004] *EWCA* 1579.   [116] *Peck* (2003) 36 *EHRR* 719.

[117] *A v. B* [2003] *QB* 195, 204, para. 11 (guidelines).

In this situation, the courts have emphasized the stability of the relationship as a factor that shapes the strength of the obligation: the more stable the relationship, the greater will be the significance that is attached to it.[118] At one extreme are marital relationships of duration and stability, where the scope of the obligation will be the strongest. At the other extreme are one-night stands or visits to prostitutes which represent the 'outer limits of what is confidential'.[119] In these circumstances, in the Court of Appeal's words, the scope of the obligation will be 'modest'.[120] In an approach reminiscent of the fiduciary duty that underpins the traditional action, it has been held that a higher standard is expected of people such as headmasters, clergy, politicians, senior civil servants, surgeons, and journalists.[121] The same level of care might also be expected where a person acts as a role model in some way or another.

Matters of public interest   An important factor that is taken into account when balancing the competing rights of an individual against the more general rights of freedom of expression is the purpose of the disclosure.[122] In *von Hannover v. Germany,* the European Court of Human Rights said that the decisive factor in balancing the protection of private life against freedom of expression was the contribution that published photos and articles make to a debate of general interest.[123] This action grew out of a complaint made by Princess Caroline of Monaco about a number of photographs that had been taken of her in public places and subsequently published in a number of German magazines. These included images of Princess Caroline eating at a restaurant, shopping, and playing sport. Additional photographs showed Princess Caroline at the Monte Carlo Beach Club dressed in a swimsuit and towel, tripping over and falling down. In relation to the publication of the photographs, the Court said, the 'public does not have a legitimate interest in knowing where the applicant is and how she behaves in her private life'.[124] A similar principle was adopted in *Green Corns v. Claverley Group* where, in granting an injunction to prevent a local newspaper from disclosing the addresses of care homes for troubled children, the court said that, while the public interest in debating how children in need should be cared for was a question of the highest public interest, the injunction would

---

[118] Ibid (guideline xi).

[119] *Theakston* [2002] *EMLR* 398, para. 61. The lower the degree of confidentiality, the less likely it will be that an injunction will be granted.

[120] Ibid, para. 57 ('the very concept of a relationship for the purposes of confidentiality is simply inapplicable to such transitory or commercial sexual relations'). Cf. Jack J who said that the law should afford the protection of confidentiality within marriage and, in the context of modern sexual relations, it should be no different with relationships outside marriage: *A v. B* [2001] 1 *WLR* 2341, 2354, para. 56 (focusing on the nature of the informa-tion rather than the nature of the relationship). See also *A v. B* [2003] *QB* 195, 217, para. 45 (CA), where a married professional footballer attempted to suppress publication of the fact that he had had casual affairs with C and D. While the court (reluctantly) accepted that C owed A a duty of confidentiality, they said that 'the degree of confidentiality to which A was entitled to was very modest'. This was because '[r]elationships of the sort which A had with C and D are not the categories of relationship which the courts should be astute to protect': ibid, para. 45.

[121] *McKennitt v. Ash* [2006] *EWCA Civ* 1714, para 65 (CA).

[122] See *HRH Prince of Wales v. Associated Newspaper* [2007] 3 *WLR* 222 (interference with Art. 8 by publica-tion of information taken from Prince Charles' journal records outweighed the significance of the interference with Art 10).

[123] *Von Hannover v. Germany* [2005] *EHRR* 1, para. 76 (ECHR).

[124] Cf the concurring opinions of Judge Cabral Barreto: 'the applicant is a public figure and the public does have a right to be informed about her life' (but still found Art 8 was violated); and Judge Zupancic (public figures must expect some degree of intrusion): ibid.

not prevent debate.[125] The court added that there was no public interest in the publication of specific addresses; but only a series of private interests of those living nearby. In this situation, the court held that Article 10 interests did not outweigh the right to privacy that existed in relation to home addresses in accordance with Article 8.[126]

The obligations may change over time   While a duty of confidence in respect of private information can survive the death of the individual to whom the duty was owed,[127] the nature and scope of that duty may change over time. For example, while an injunction to prevent publication of an account by President Mitterrand's doctor of his relationship with Mitterrand was held not to be in violation of Article 10 when Mitterrand was alive, the situation changed after Mitterrand's death. As the European Court of Human Rights said, the ongoing prohibition on distribution was no longer justified nine-and-a-half months after President Mitterrand's death. This was because 'the more remote the date of the President's death became, the more this factor declined in importance and the more the public interest in the debate concerning his two seven-year terms of office outweighed the imperatives of protecting the rights of others and medical secrecy'.[128]

Scope of protection for public figures in public places   One area where the courts have had some difficulty in determining how the right to private information should be balanced against freedom of expression is in relation to public figures in public places. The high water mark for protection of public figures in public places is the decision in *von Hannover* where the European Court of Human Rights restated the rights and expectations of public figures with regard to their private lives. The German Federal Constitutional Court said that, as a leading figure in contemporary society, Princess Carolina had to tolerate the publication of photographs of herself in a public place, even if they showed her in scenes of daily life, rather than in official duties.

The European Court of Human Rights unanimously held that the publications had been a violation of Article 8. This was based on the fact that in certain situations a person has a legitimate expectation of protection for his or her private life.[129] That is, 'there is a zone of interaction of a person with others, even in a public context, which may fall within the scope of private life'.[130] In reaching this decision, the European Court of Human Rights drew a distinction between celebrities and people engaged in official public business. As the Court said:

a fundamental distinction needs to be drawn between reporting facts—even controversial ones—capable of contributing to a debate in a democratic society relating to politicians in the exercise of their functions, for example, and reporting details of the private life of an individual who, as in this case, does not exercise official functions. While in the former case the press exercises its vital role of 'watchdog' in a democracy by contributing to imparting information and ideas on matters of public interest it does not do so in the latter case.[131]

---

[125] While the need to disseminate information about Naomi Campbell's drug addiction was of a lower order than the need to disseminate information on other subjects such as political information the degree of latitude given to the journalists was reduced but not excluded altogether. *Campbell* [2004] 2 *AC* 457, 468, para 29. (Lord Nicholls). Note, however, that the majority held that the newspaper had gone too far in including the images of Campbell with the report.

[126] *Green Corns v. Claverley Group* [2005] *EWHC* 958.

[127] *Bluck v. Information Commissioner* (2007) WL 4266111, [2008] *WTLR* 1, para 17. The tribunal also held that in this situation the breach would be actionable by personal representatives of the deceased (ibid, para 30).

[128] *Editions Plon v. France* [2006] *EHRR* 36, paras. 51–54 (ECHR).

[129] *Von Hannover* [2005] *EHRR* 1, para. 51 (ECHR).   [130] Ibid, para. 50.   [131] Ibid, para. 63.

The Court said that the decisive factor in balancing the protection of private life against free-dom of expression lies in the contribution that the published photographs and articles make to a debate of general interest.[132] In this case, the court said that the public does not have a legitimate interest in knowing where the applicant is and how she behaves in her private life. The Court also said that the photographs in question did not 'come within the sphere of any political or public debate because the published photos and accompanying commentar-ies relate exclusively to details of the applicant's private life'.[133] The Court also noted that new communication technologies increased the need for the courts to be extra vigilant to protect private life.

The question of the protection to be afforded to public figures when they undertake activ-ities in a public space under British law was addressed by Patten J in *Murray v. Express Newspapers*.[134] This was an action to prevent publication of a photograph taken of J.K. Rowling and her husband pushing their son in a pram down a public street in Edinburgh. The photo-graph, which was taken through a long-range lens, showed the infant's face in profile. While the action was brought by the parents on behalf of their infant son, as Patten J said the action was 'something of a test case designed to establish the right of persons in the public eye (such as the claimant's mother) to protection from intrusion into parts of their private or family life even when they consist of activities conducted in a public place'.[135] The question that the court had to consider was the degree of protection which someone who is well known and of public interest is entitled to in respect of their private life.

As Patten J said, it was generally accepted following *Campbell* that protection in the UK was limited to information of a personal or embarrassing kind. In contrast, the European Court of Human Rights had taken a much wider view of what should be regarded as falling within the scope of an individual's private life for the purpose of Article 8.[136] This was clear from *von Hannover,* which recognized that an individual whose life and activities are of public inter-est may have a legitimate expectation of privacy in relation to private family and personal activities which are not in themselves either embarrassing or intimate in a sexual or medical sense.[137] The Court in *von Hannover* also made it clear that the disclosure of information could not be justified as a legitimate exercise of the right to freedom of expression where the sole purpose of the publication is to satisfy readers' curiosity, rather than to contribute to a debate on or raising of an issue of general public interest or importance.[138] As Patten J said in *Murray,* if this approach was followed in the UK it would 'herald a revolution in Britain's journalistic culture'.[139]

In thinking about the scope of protection that ought to be afforded to public celebrities in public places, Patten J looked at the decision of Eady J in *John v. Associated Newspapers*[140] (which was decided before the Court of Appeal decision in *McKennitt*). This was an action to prevent publication of an innocuous photograph of Elton John wearing a tracksuit and a baseball cap taken in a street outside his London home. Eady J began by noting the comment

---

[132] Ibid, para. 76.   [133] Ibid, para. 64 (ECHR).

[134] *Murray v. Express Newspapers* [2007] *EWHC* 1908 (Ch).   [135] Ibid, para 6.

[136] In *Sciacca v. Italy* [2006] *EHRR* 20, para 29, the European Court of Human Rights said that 'the concept of private life includes elements relating to a person's right to their picture and that the publication of a photograph falls within the scope of private life'.

[137] *Murray v. Express Newspapers* [2007] *EWHC* 1908, para 47.   [138] Ibid.

[139] M. Tugendhat and I. Christie, *The Law of Privacy and the Media* (2006) (2nd edn Supp), para 6.52. Cited with approval in ibid, para 47.

[140] [2006] *EMLR* 722.

of Baroness Hale (among the majority) in *Campbell* that 'there is nothing essentially private about how Naomi Campbell looks when she pops out to the shops for a bottle of milk...nor can [that information] be expected to damage her private life'.[141] On the basis that the photograph of Elton John was a 'popping out for a pint of milk case', Eady J refused to grant an injunction. This was on the basis that Elton John could not have a reasonable expectation of privacy in respect of the information conveyed by the photograph. In relation to *von Hannover,* Eady J said that an important factor in that case was the element of harassment, which was absent in relation to the photographs taken of Elton John.

After reviewing *John v. Associated Newspapers,* Patten J said that he disagreed with Eady J's reasoning, saying that he did not believe *von Hannover* could be isolated in the way that Eady J had suggested. Instead, Patten J decided to follow the approach of the Court of Appeal in *McKennitt v. Ash* where Lord Buxton LJ said that there 'is little doubt that *von Hannover* extends the reach of Article 8 beyond what had previously been understood'.[142] Buxton LJ added, 'it is far from clear that the House of Lords that decided *Campbell* would have handled *von Hannover* in the same way as did the European Court of Human Rights'. In part this was based on the fact that '[v]ery extensive arguments and discussion' were 'required before Ms Campbell was able to enjoin the publication of photographs of her[self] in the public street, and then only because of their connexion with her medical condition'.[143] Given this, it is not surprising that in *Murray v. Express Newspapers* Patten J said that *von Hannover* appeared to be in conflict with existing British case law.[144] On the basis that he was bound to follow the decision of the House of Lords, Patten J adopted the reasoning in *Campbell.* In so doing he drew a distinction between a situation where a person was engaged in family or sporting activities and a situation where they were engaged in something as simple as going to the shop to buy milk. The first type of activity was clearly part of a person's private recreation time intended to be enjoyed in the company of family and friends: publicity on the *von Hannover* test is intrusive and can adversely affect such social activities.

On the basis that routine acts such as a visit to a shop or a ride on a bus should not attract a reasonable expectation of privacy, Patten J rejected Murray's application to prevent publication of the photograph of her family walking in the street. This was on the basis that there was nothing untoward or undignified about the photographs of an ordinary street scene:[145] they certainly did not contain any of the additional elements that featured in *Campbell.*

The Court of Appeal allowed Murray's appeal, taking the view that there was an arguable case that her child had a reasonable expectation of privacy.[146] The Court recognised the apparent inconsistency between *von Hannover* and *Campbell,* but held that a person could have a reasonable expectation of privacy when carrying out routine activities. Much depended on the facts, and here Rowling had shielded the child from publicity. Patten J had been wrong to strike out the claim.

---

[141] *Campbell* [2004] 2 *AC* 457 (HL), para. 154.

[142] *McKennitt v. Ash* [2006] *EWCA Civ* 1714, para. 37.

[143] Ibid, para. 39.

[144] 'The width of the rights given to the media by *A v. B*' [2005] *EWHC* 1651 'cannot be reconciled with *von Hannover*'. *McKennitt v. Ash* [2006] *EWCA Civ* 1714, para. 61.

[145] *Murray v. Express Newspapers* [2007] *EWHC* 1908.

[146] [2008] *EWCA Civ* 446 (7 May 2008)

5 REMEDIES

In this final section we look at the more important remedies that may be granted where there has been a finding of breach. While we examine intellectual property remedies more generally elsewhere,[147] in this section we wish to highlight the peculiar considerations that arise in relation to breach of confidence.

5.1 INTERIM RELIEF

The primary remedy that a claimant is likely to pursue in a breach of confidence action is an interim injunction to restrain use or disclosure of the information.[148] In other areas of intellectual property law, the test for whether an injunction should be granted is that outlined in *American Cyanamid*. In essence, this provides that, once a claimant has established that there is a serious question to be tried, then the court will exercise its discretion to grant or withhold interim relief on the basis of the 'balance of convenience'. (We review its application in greater detail in Chapter 48.) While this test is widely used in other areas of intellectual property, as we will see in some circumstances the courts have decided not to apply this test in breach of confidence actions. This is particularly the case in relation to personal information where the courts have said that the threshold for injunction is higher than *American Cyanamid*.[149] In *A v. B* the Court of Appeal put forward a set of guidelines for dealing with interim applications in privacy cases.[150] Essentially, the guidelines advocate a balancing of the facts rather than a technical approach to the law.[151] When thinking about the grant of injunctive relief in this context, it is important to take account of the House of Lords decision in *Cream Holdings v. Banerjee,*[152] particularly in terms of the way in which section 12(3) of the Human Rights Act 1998 modified the threshold test for injunctive relief set out in *American Cyanamid*. This issue is discussed in detail below.[153]

5.1.1 Interim relief restraining publication

Where the defendant proposes to publish the information, the claim for injunctive relief is normally directed at preserving the confidential nature of the information. If the *American Cyanamid* test were applied it would almost always lead to the grant of injunctive relief.[154] This is because the balance of convenience almost always favours restraint in order to ensure that the information concerned retains its confidential quality until trial. However, such automatic grant of interim relief raises serious questions about freedom of expression. To avoid this, the

---

[147] See Ch. 47. It is by no means clear whether the action for breach of confidence is to be regarded as relating to 'intellectual property' and thus subject to interpretation in the light of the EC Enforcement Directive.

[148] See *Douglas v. Hello! (No 8)* [2005] *EWCA Civ* 595, para. 25.

[149] *Douglas v. Hello!* [2001] 2 *WLR* 992, 1028, para. 136 (Sedley LJ) (CA).

[150] *A v. B* [2003] *QB* 195, 204–10, para. 11 (CA).

[151] Ibid, 210, para. 12. The court has jurisdiction to grant an injunction against the world: *Venables v. News Group Newspapers* [2001] 2 *WLR* 1038 (not applied in *Mills v. MGN* [2001] *EWHC* 412 (Ch), para. 37).

[152] *Cream Holdings v. Banerjee* [2004] *UKHL* 44 (HL). [153] See below pp. 1104–5.

[154] *Attorney-General v. Newspaper Publishing* [1988] *Ch* 333, 358 *per* Sir John Donaldson MR; Robertson and Nicol, *Media Law* (1992), 192.

courts have been wary about using the *American Cyanamid* test in these circumstances, preferring to pay greater attention to the merits of the parties' claims.[155]

Section 12(3) of the Human Rights Act 1998 now confirms that where the relief impinges upon freedom of expression a claimant must show that there is more than a serious question to be tried. Section 12(3) provides that, where a court is considering whether to grant relief which might affect the exercise of the right to freedom of expression, no relief should be granted which will restrain publication prior to trial 'unless the court is satisfied that the applicant is likely to establish that publication should not be allowed'. Courts are also instructed to take account of the extent to which the material has or is about to become available to the public; and whether it is, or would be, in the public interest for the material to be published.[156] The tribunal is also instructed to take into account 'any relevant privacy code'.

5.1.2 Interim relief restraining use

Where injunctive relief is being sought to prevent *use* of confidential information, different considerations operate. Interim relief restraining use prevents wrongdoers from benefiting from their wrongful acts or from continuing to inflict damage on the claimant. Often, also, the grant of an injunction restricting use operates to restrain manufacture, sale, and competition. The stakes, therefore, can be very high. Where the effect of injunctive relief is likely to be that no trial will ever take place, the courts have taken it upon themselves to consider the strength of the parties' cases before deciding whether to grant interim relief.

The courts have also been reluctant to apply the *American Cyanamid* test in restraint of trade cases, on the basis that it might interfere with a person's right to trade.[157] The rejection of the *American Cyanamid* test is sometimes said to be justified on the ground that, in the absence of a speedy trial, matters are resolved by interim relief. For example, in *Lansing v. Kerr*,[158] where trial would not take place before a twelve-month restraint clause had expired, the Court of Appeal declined to apply the *American Cyanamid* test. Instead, the court looked at the parties' chances of success. Since the express restraint, though temporary, was worldwide, the judge considered it would be unlikely that it would be enforceable. The Court of Appeal held that such a consideration was appropriate. In contrast, where a speedy trial was pending and the restraint in question was two years, the Court of Appeal has used the *American Cyanamid* test to grant an interim injunction preventing a former employee from taking up a post at a competitor firm.[159]

5.1.3 Permanent injunctions (and delivery up)

If a claimant succeeds in establishing a breach of confidence at trial, they are prima facie entitled to injunctive relief.[160] Nevertheless, claimants are not entitled as of right to an injunction. As the courts retain discretion as to whether to grant the injunction, if there are special or

---

[155] *Hubbard v. Vosper* [1972] 2 QB 84, 96, 98; *Cambridge Nutrition v. BBC* [1990] 3 *All ER* 523; *Times v. Mirror Group* [1993] *EMLR* 443.

[156] Human Rights Act 1998, s. 12(4). See J. Griffiths, 'The Human Rights Act 1998, s. 12: Press Freedom over Privacy?' [1999] *Ent LR* 36. The injunctions granted in the *Spycatcher* litigation were reviewed by the European Court of Human Rights in *The Observer and The Guardian v. United Kingdom* (1991) 14 *EHRR* 153.

[157] *Fellowes v. Fisher* [1976] QB 122, 133 (*per* Lord Denning, arguing that *Cyanamid* does not apply to restraint of trade cases), 138, 142 (*per* Browne LJ and Sir John Pennycuick, taking *Cyanamid* approach but looking at the strength of the parties' cases when assessing the balance of convenience).

[158] [1991] 1 *All ER* 418; *Credit Suisse First Boston v. Lister* [1998] *EWCA Civ* 1551.

[159] *Lawrence David v. Ashton* [1991] 1 *All ER* 385.   [160] *Ocular Sciences* [1997] *RPC* 289, 410.

exceptional factors the court may refuse to do so. This would be the case, for example, if the effect of a permanent injunction would be oppressive, or out of all proportion to the value of the information used.[161] It is important that any injunction granted be formulated in specific terms.[162] As an adjunct to an injunction, a court may require the defendant to deliver up material containing confidential information for destruction.[163] This remedy is dealt with in Chapter 48.

5.2 DAMAGES

Specific problems have arisen in relation to financial remedies for breach of confidence as a result of the confusion as to the juridical nature of the obligation. Where the obligation of confidentiality is contractual, the promisee will usually be entitled to damages for breach of contract under normal contractual principles. However, doubts have been raised as to whether damages are available for breach of an equitable duty of confidentiality.[164] This was because only common law courts, rather than equity, awarded damages. Instead, it is said that if the claimant desires a financial remedy in a Court of Equity it should be in the form of an account of profits. Despite these doubts, the courts have awarded damages even though the obligation was equitable.[165] In some cases, the basis for doing so has been attributed to a 'beneficent construction of Lord Cairns's Act' which enables a court to grant damages 'in lieu of' an injunction.[166]

It has been said that the measure of damages for breach of confidence should be tortious, reflecting loss to the claimant.[167] In *Seager v. Copydex (No. 2)*[168] the Court of Appeal held that damages were to be assessed by reference to the market value of the information. This has been subsequently said to be one, but not the only, way of assessing damages.[169] Other techniques for the assessment of damages are by way of fair remuneration for a licence, loss of profit the

---

[161] Ibid, 410–11.   [162] *Potters Ballotini v. Weston Baker* [1977] *RPC* 202.

[163] *Peter Pan v. Corsets Silhouette* [1963] 3 *All ER* 402 (order to deliver up for destruction of bras which the defendant had manufactured with the use of confidential information); but cf. *Ocular Sciences* [1997] *RPC* 289, 410 (delivery up refused in relation to all documents needed for the running of its business and defendants' plant, equipment, or products).

[164] *Nichrotherm Electrical Co. v. Percy & G. A. Harvey & Co. (London)* [1957] *RPC* 207, 213–14.

[165] *Seager v. Copydex* [1967] 2 *All ER* 415.

[166] Chancery Amendment Act 1858 (21 & 22 Vict. c. 27); *Attorney-General v. Guardian* [1990] *AC* 109, 286 (Lord Goff); *Malone v. MPC,* note 64 above, 360 (only remedy is account where no injunction would issue). But see *Cadbury Schweppes v. FBI Foods* [2000] *FSR* 491, 516 (Supreme Court of Canada) (damages were not dependent on Lord Cairns's Act and accepting that the action was '*sui generis*').

[167] *Indata Equipment Supplies v. ACL* [1998] *FSR* 248, 261, 264. Cf. J. Beatson, 'Damages for breach of confidence' (1991) 107 *LQR* 209, 211 (remedy should be restitutionary: either profit attributable to breach or saving made by defendant); R. Plibersek, 'Assessment of Damages for Breach of Confidence in England and Australia' [1991] *EIPR* 283 (arguing that damages for breach of the equitable obligation of confidence should be assessed on a 'restitutionary' basis: giving a claimant sufficient to restore him to the same position he would have been in if the breach of duty had not occurred); P. Birks, 'The Remedies for Abuse of Confidential Information' [1990] *LMCLQ* 460 (compensatory and restitutionary damages should be available, but the choice should not merely be a matter of discretion: rather the restitutionary remedy should only be available where there is a strong need to buttress the practice of good faith in bargaining).

[168] [1967] 2 *All ER* 415.

[169] *Talbot v. GTV* [1981] *RPC* 1, 22; *Aquaculture v. New Zealand Mussel* (1985) 5 *IPR* 353 (NZ High Court); [1990] 3 *NZLR* (NZ CA); *Gorne v. Scales* [2006] *EWCA Civ* 311 (para. 74).

claimant would have gained,[170] or depreciation in the value of the right to have the information kept confidential.[171] It has been suggested that in calculating damages the courts are able to take account of distress and injury to feelings,[172] and might also award exemplary damages for breach.[173]

5.3 ACCOUNT OF PROFITS

In general, a claimant relying on an equitable duty of confidence is entitled to an account of profits for the wrongful use or disclosure of confidential information. This restitutionary remedy also appears to be available in cases where the obligation of confidence is contractual.[174] In either case, similar problems of computation arise as for other intellectual property claims.[175] A court may deduct from the profits made by the defendant an allowance for the skill and expertise he or she deployed. The rule requiring an election between either damages or an account of the profits is no longer strictly applied to infringements occurring after 29 April 2006. Instead, 'lost profit' is one of the factors that the courts take into account when determining damages.[176]

5.4 CONSTRUCTIVE TRUSTS

One feature that distinguishes the law of breach of confidence from other areas of intellectual property law is that constructive trust is a possible remedy. If a confider succeeds in a claim for breach of confidence, the court might order that property derived from the breach is held by the confidant on trust for the confider. The effect of this may be to enable a claimant to obtain priority over general creditors, to recover profits-from-profits made by the defendant, to obtain compound interest, and to bring an action outside the normal (contractual) limitation periods.[177]

The first signs that the remedy of the constructive trust may be available against an errant confidant appeared in the *Spycatcher* case where various of the Law Lords suggested that Peter Wright held copyright on constructive trust for the Crown.[178] Although emanating from the House of Lords, these views were *obiter,* were expressed without the benefit of any argument from Wright, and might easily have been interpreted as being confined to the narrow situa-

---

[170] *Dawson & Mason Ltd. v. Potter* [1986] 1 *All ER* 418; *Cadbury v. FBI* [2000] *FSR* 491, 513–14, 517 (Supreme Court of Canada) (damages for lost opportunity).

[171] In *Talbot v. GTV* [1981] *RPC* 1, 31–3, damages were assessed as the loss of the chance to make the television series which at best could have made the plaintiff a A$160,000 profit: the court awarded him A$15,000.

[172] *Peck* (2003) 36 *EHRR* 719, paras 117–20; *Cornelius v. de Taranto* [2001] *EMLR* 329; *Campbell* [2003] *QB* 633 (CA).

[173] *Aquaculture* (1985) 5 *IPR* 353, 301; *Hello! v. Douglas (No. 3)* [2003] 3 *All ER* 996, para. 273; See also *Legislating the Criminal Code: Misuse of Trade Secrets,* No. 150 para. 3.34 (no authority supporting award of exemplary damages for breach of confidence). And see generally pp. 1120–1 below.

[174] *Peter Pan Manufacturing Corporation v. Corsets Silhouette* [1963] 3 *All ER* 402; *Attorney-General v. Blake* [2000] 3 *WLR* 625, 641 (Lord Nicholls).

[175] See pp. 1122–3 below.   [176] *Bluscope Steel v. Kelly* (2007) *FCA* 517.

[177] Though this latter advantage seems doubtful in the light of *Coulthard v. DMC* [1999] 2 *All ER* 457, 477–80. See also Tang Hang Wu, 'Confidence and the Constructive Trust' (2003) 23 *LS* 135 (doubting whether such ancillary effects are justified in cases of confidentiality); M. Conaglen, 'Thinking about proprietary remedies for breach of confidence' (2008) *IPQ* 82 (exploring whether there is a principled basis for awarding proprietary relief in breach of confidence cases).

[178] [1990] *AC* 109, 139 (Scott J), 211 (Dillon LJ), 286 (Lord Goff).

tion where the confidant was also a fiduciary. However, in *LAC Minerals*[179] the majority in the Supreme Court of Canada held that it was appropriate to impose a constructive trust over land which the defendant had bought after he had been told in confidence that it might be gold-bearing. More recently, in *Ocular Sciences v. Aspect Vision*, Laddie J accepted that a constructive trust might be available where there was an existing fiduciary relationship, and that there would usually be such a relationship where there existed a confidential obligation.[180] This reasoning, which has much in common with that of Wilson J in *LAC Minerals*,[181] paves the way for the availability of constructive trusts in almost all cases of breach of confidence. This should not be taken to mean, however, that this remedy should be granted in all cases.

Other cases have cast doubt over whether the constructive trust is a remedy that is available in an action for breach of confidence. For example, in *Attorney-General v. Blake*,[182] Scott V-C said that existing case law would have precluded a finding of constructive trust in the case before him, where there was a breach of confidence but no existing fiduciary relationship. On appeal, Lord Woolf MR appears to have agreed that a constructive trust was an inappropriate remedy for breach of a contractual duty of confidentiality.[183] Although the House of Lords did not consider this issue explicitly, it seems clear from their approach that they did not consider a constructive trust to be an appropriate remedy for breach of contract.[184]

Whether the constructive trust is only available for breach of an existing fiduciary duty or for all breaches of confidence, it is clear that it will rarely be the appropriate form of relief.[185] In determining whether a proprietary remedy is appropriate, the court must look at the circumstances of the case and the effects of imposing a constructive trust. A constructive trust should only be awarded if there is reason to grant to the claimant the additional rights that flow from recognition of a right of property.

In *LAC Minerals*, La Forest J imposed a constructive trust on the grounds that, but for the actions of the defendant in misusing confidential information and thereby acquiring the Williams property, that property would have been acquired by the claimant. The defendant intercepted the claimant's efforts to obtain a specific and unique property that it would otherwise have acquired. The defendant was enriched by the acquisition of an asset that, but for the actions of that party, would have been acquired by the claimant. In contrast, in *Ocular Sciences*[186] Laddie J refused the claim for the imposition of a constructive trust over a part of the defendant's business and assets. This was because there was no question of the diversion of assets from the claimant, and because the contamination, which was 'small and technically inconsequential', only affected a fraction of the business. In relation to the latter point Laddie J noted that there would likely be difficulties in imposing a constructive trust over part of the business. In *United Pan-Europe Communications NV v. Deutsche Bank AG*,[187] the Court of Appeal held that a constructive trust might be available as a remedy for breach of confidence even if the breach was only 'relevant' to the acquisition made.

---

[179] [1990] *FSR* 441, 445, 452; 497 Sopinka J (dissenting recognized that the remedy would be available in very special circumstances).

[180] [1997] *RPC* 289, 413–14.   [181] [1990] *FSR* 441, 444.   [182] [1996] 3 *WLR* 741.

[183] [1998] 1 *All ER* 833, 842.   [184] [1963] 3 *All ER* 402.

[185] *LAC Minerals* [1990] *FSR* 441, 474, 497. Cf. Birks, 'The Remedies for Abuse of Confidential Information' (criticizing use of constructive trust for breach of confidence).

[186] [1997] *RPC* 289, 411–16.   [187] [2000] 2 *BCLC* 461 (CA).

5.5 CRIMINAL LAW

In English law, taking confidential information is not theft.[188] Section 1 of the Theft Act 1968 defines theft as the 'dishonest appropriation of property belonging to another with the intention of permanently depriving the other of it'. While section 4 says that property includes 'other intangible property', it has been held in a number of cases that for these purposes information is not intangible property. In *Oxford v. Moss*,[189] an undergraduate at Liverpool University obtained the proofs of an examination paper before the exam. After reading the exam, the student returned the paper, but 'retained' the information. Smith J held that this did not amount to theft. This was because information was not property and because there was no intention to deprive the university of the information. While it might be possible in certain situations to treat specific breaches of confidence as carrying criminal liability on other grounds, these all carry limitations.[190]

A number of calls have been made for the criminalization of the act of misappropriating trade secrets,[191] and the Law Commission have responded by issuing a consultation paper (No. 150).[192] The paper provisionally concluded that the case for criminal offences of trade secret misuse is a strong one, basing that view primarily on the close analogy between trade secrets and property 'in the strict sense', and on the economic importance of protecting business investment.[193] The paper reviewed the practical problems of legislating: in particular, difficulties associated with reaching a satisfactory definition of the concept of 'trade secrets'. The Law Commission said it wanted to ensure that all misuses of trade secrets which were criminalized would be breaches of confidence at civil law, but made it clear that it did not wish to criminalize all acts which would incur civil liability under the present law. Views were sought, in particular, about the definition of trade secret, whether errant employees should be subject to criminal liability, and the appropriate scope of a public interest defence.[194] It seems that the consultation exercise has been abandoned, and that the Law Commission is no longer pursuing the question.

---

[188] See A. Coleman, *The Legal Protection of Trade Secrets* (1992), ch. 7.

[189] (1979) 68 *Cr App R* 183.

[190] If two people steal a trade secret, this may constitute conspiracy to defraud: *R v. Lloyd* [1985] *QB* 29; [1985] 3 *WLR* 30. Other criminal charges may be available under the Prevention of Corruption Act 1906 and s. 1 of the Computer Misuse Act 1990, which creates the offence of gaining unauthorized access to data held on a computer.

[191] For example, Coleman, *The Legal Protection of Trade Secrets*, 93 (criminal law needed to stigmatize conduct, and afford adequate deterrent).

[192] For a review, see J. Hull, 'Stealing Secrets: A Review of the Law Commission's Consultation Paper on the Misuse of Trade Secrets' (1998) 4 *IPQ* 422.

[193] Law Commission, *Legislating the Criminal Code: Misuse of Trade Secrets,* Consultation Paper No. 150 (1997), para. 3.1.

[194] For the Law Commission's provisional proposal, outlining specific purposes for disclosure which are in the public interest, but without prejudice to the generality of the defence, see ibid, para. 6.54.

PART VI

LITIGATION AND REMEDIES

1 INTRODUCTION

It is sometimes said that intellectual property rights are only as good as the procedures and remedies by which they are enforced. While we would not necessarily subscribe wholly to that view, it is useful insofar as it highlights the importance of the so-called adjectival aspects of intellectual property law: that is, the rules of evidence, procedure, litigation, and remedies. The history of the adjectival aspects of intellectual property law is as old and complex as the history of the substantive law. Indeed, many developments in the substantive law have been influenced and shaped by changes in evidence, procedure, remedies, and litigation. In the following two chapters we wish to provide an introduction to these aspects of intellectual property law.

Until recently, the rules and practices that regulate litigation, procedure, and remedies have developed on a national basis, largely unaffected by international standards.[1] There are, for example, only a few references in the Berne[2] and Paris Conventions[3] to matters of enforcement. As a result of recent changes in European and international intellectual property law, the relative insularity of the adjectival aspects of British intellectual property law has ended.

Largely at the behest of the industrialized nations seeking to ensure that their rights are adequately enforced in developing countries, the extent of international norm setting has started to expand. Probably the most significant change at the international level is that matters relating to enforcement are comprehensively dealt with by Part III of TRIPS.[4] This requires that members ensure that enforcement procedures are available so that intellectual-property-right holders can take effective action against infringers. More specifically, the law of the member state must enable remedies to be obtained *expeditiously* so that imminent infringements can be prevented. Members are also required to provide remedies that are severe enough to deter further infringements. Procedures should be fair, equitable, and only as complicated, costly, or lengthy as is necessary.[5] TRIPS provides further details in relation to civil procedures, remedies, provisional measures, border measures, and criminal liability.

---

[1] Cf. *Coflexip v. Stolt Comex Seaway* [1999] FSR 473, 487–9.

[2] Berne Art. 16 (obligation to seize unlawful copies); Art. 13(3).

[3] Paris Art. 9 (seizure on import of goods unlawfully bearing a trade mark); Art. 6*bis*(1) and Art. 6*septies*(2) (injunctive relief for wrongful use of well known mark).

[4] T. Dreier, 'TRIPS and the Enforcement of Intellectual Property Rights', in Beier and Shricker, 248.

[5] TRIPS, Art. 41.

As the standards required are expressed in terms of particular purposes or goals (such as that the procedures must not be unduly costly) it may be difficult to assess whether national procedures and remedies satisfy the international standards. Indeed, the vague manner in which the effects are enunciated means that they are unlikely to be enforced at the WTO.[6]

Following the lead of TRIPS, the WIPO Copyright Treaty and the WIPO Performances and Phonograms Treaty also require contracting parties to have enforcement procedures in place which provide effective action against acts of infringement covered by the Treaties. These include expeditious remedies to prevent infringement and remedies which deter further infringement.[7] In addition, contracting states are required to provide 'effective legal remedies' for violation of Berne, TRIPS, and components of the WIPO Treaties dealing with the digital agenda.[8]

While these changes mark an important shift in direction for international intellectual property law, for the most part they have had little impact upon British law. This has not been the case, however, with the changes that have taken place at the European level. In considering the impact of European initiatives on procedural and remedial matters, we need to distinguish between intellectual property rights at the Community level and Community rules relating to the enforcement of national rights. We deal with these in turn.

The development of Community intellectual property rights—currently Community trade marks and plant varieties, registered and unregistered design rights, but one day possibly to include Community Patents—has brought with it a degree of Community regulation of the procedures by which rights are enforced. The most obvious impact is that member states must designate particular domestic courts as 'Community courts'. These are courts where actions to enforce Community rights, and in some circumstances, actions for declaration of invalidity are brought.[9] While matters of procedure and, with some exceptions, remedies are left to the law of the relevant member state,[10] the right to injunctions in relation to Community rights is governed by Community law: injunctive relief will be granted unless there are special reasons to the contrary.[11] Moreover, Community courts have general jurisdiction to grant provisional measures (including protective ones, such as interim injunctions) that operate in all contracting states.[12] Perhaps the most dramatic changes will occur if the Community Patent comes into force, or there is agreement on a European Patent Litigation system or a European Patent Court—though these proposals remain some way from being realized.

The procedures and enforcement of *national* intellectual property rights has also been the focus of attention at the European level. Three matters are worth mentioning at this stage. First, the European Union has adopted a Regulation governing jurisdiction and recognition of judgments (based on the Brussels Convention).[13] These provisions are examined in more detail in Chapter 47. The European Union has also adopted measures that regulate the

---

[6] See M. Blakeney, *Trade-Related Aspects of Intellectual Property Rights: A Concise Guide* (1996).

[7] WCT Art. 14; WPPT Art. 23.

[8] Technological measures: WCT Art. 11; WPPT Art. 18; rights management information: WPPT Arts 12 and 19.

[9] CDR Arts. 80–87; CTMR Arts. 91–2.

[10] In the case of procedure, the forum, and in the case of remedies, those available in the country where the infringement takes place. CDR Art. 88; CTMR Art. 97.

[11] Protocol on Litigation Art. 35(1); CTMR Art. 98; CDR Art. 89; *Nokia Corp v. Wardell*, Case C–316/05 [2007] 1 *CMLR* (37) 1167.

[12] CTMR Art. 93; CDR Art. 90; Protocol on litigation Art. 14.

[13] Council Regulation 44/2001 of 22 Dec. 2000 on Jurisdiction and Recognition and Enforcement of Judgments (2001) *OJ L* I2/1).

external borders of the Community.[14] More specifically, the Council set in place mechanisms that ensure that goods which infringe intellectual property rights can be retained by customs authorities when they are introduced into or exported from the Community.[15] These are discussed in Chapter 48. The third matter that should be noted relates to the EU involvement in the reform of litigation and remedies that has been developed in an attempt to control piracy. In a follow-up to the 1998 Green Paper on counterfeiting and piracy,[16] the Commission launched an 'action plan' to combat piracy in the Community.[17] This resulted in the so-called Enforcement Directive.[18] In part, the Directive was motivated by a concern that different member states had different rules on enforcement leading some to argue that some countries were softer on piracy than others. While the Commission's chief motivation in enacting the Directive was to minimize the effects of these disparities on the internal market, the Commission also wanted to strengthen remedies to counter piracy. The Directive cherry-picked legal remedies and procedures from a host of different states, and directed member states to make the full panoply available to its judicial authorities. The Enforcement Directive (as enacted) was considerably different from the initial draft. In part this was a consequence of the strong responses that the draft Directive elicited. While some rights-holder groups argued that the initial draft did not go far enough,[19] others criticized the draft. As well as questioning whether the Directive was needed to complete the internal market,[20] it was also said that there was no evidence to support the claim that pirates and counterfeiters were moving their operations to places where the remedial laws were weaker. Critics also asked whether the proposed Directive, which largely involved conferring powers on judicial authorities, would be capable of harmonizing enforcement across the EU (which surely requires the application of like remedies to like cases). Opponents also criticized the substance of the initial Directive, in which matters of human rights (privacy, right to a fair hearing) found little place.[21] Without harmonization of these basic rights, procedures, and protections, statements in the draft Directive (such as that the procedures should be 'fair and equitable') were thought to be worryingly vague.

To ensure that it was adopted before the enlargement of the Community in 2004, the European Commission, Parliament, and Council approved an amended version of the Directive. In order to assure the passage of the Directive, various aspects of the initial proposal were changed. Notably, the provisions that detailed who could bring proceedings were emasculated by the addition of the qualification 'as far as is permitted by the applicable law'. The provisions on criminal sanctions were deleted because of doubts over the Legislature's competence to deal with them in such a Directive. Even the harmonized rules on damages were

---

[14] On the basis of Art. 133 EC (formerly Art. 113 of the Treaty).

[15] Council Regulation No. 1383/2003 which came into force in July 2004 (hereafter IGR) (replacing Council Regulation 3295/95 of 22 Dec. 1994 (as amended by Council Regulation 241/99 of 25 Jan. 1999)).

[16] COM(98) 569 final.

[17] *Communication from the Commission to the Council, the European Parliament and the Economic and Social Committee* (Brussels, 17 Nov. 2000) COM (2000) 789.

[18] Directive 2004/48/EC of the European Parliament and of the Council of 29 April 2004 on the enforcement of intellectual property rights.

[19] S. Coombes, 'Piracy Report Reveals Startling Figures' [2004] *Ent LR* 28, 29.

[20] W. Cornish, J. Drexl, R. Hilty, A. Kur, 'Procedure and Remedies for Enforcing IPRs; the EC's proposed Directive' [2003] *EIPR*; J. Drexl, R. Hilty, A. Kur, 'Proposal for a Directive on Measures and Procedures to Ensure the Enforcement of IPRs—A First Statement' (2003) 34 *IIC* 530.

[21] The Charter of Fundamental Rights is not, as yet, a legally significant document for the EU (whatever Recital 32 may imply), and while the ECHR might be regarded as part of the general background of legal principles shared by all EU countries its systematic application is only now taking place in the UK after the Human Rights Act 1998.

made more palatable by the deletion of the proposed penal elements. The amended Directive required some changes to British intellectual property law, but nothing as drastic as would have been required had the initial proposal been adopted. The necessary changes to British law were introduced by the Intellectual Property (Enforcements) Regulations 2006, which came into effect on 29 April 2006.[22] While we will look at the impact of the Directive where relevant in the next two chapters, it is worth highlighting a few of the key provisions. Much of the Directive sets out to harmonize remedies which are familiar to a British lawyer. For example, Article 7 requires member states to empower the judicial authorities to grant orders akin to *Anton Piller* orders; Article 8 requires member states to confer powers to right holders to apply for disclosure orders (akin to our *Norwich Pharmacal* orders); Article 9 requires member states to make available interim relief, and provides for orders akin to *Mareva* injunctions. Article 10 requires the possibility to issue orders to dispose of infringing goods outside the channels of commerce, without any compensation being due, as well as orders for destruction of infringing goods. Article 11 provides for injunctive relief (subject to a qualification, via Article 12, that where pecuniary damages would suffice an injunction may be refused but only if the defendant had acted unintentionally and without negligence, and the grant of injunctive relief would cause him or her disproportionate harm). Article 13 deals with damages. The Directive also contains a raft of less familiar but no less far-reaching remedies.[23] Notably, Article 10 requires member states to provide a remedy of an order to 'recall' of infringing goods, at the infringer's expense.

---

[22] SI 2006/1028 and The Civil Procedure (Amendment No.4) Rules 2005, SI 2005/3515 (introducing rr 25.1(p) (on lodging of guarantees) and 25.2 (on the need to commence proceedings in order to maintain interim injunctive relief).

[23] Article 5 would entitle 'rights management and professional defence bodies' to seek the benefit of the measures and proceedings established by the Directive.

47

LITIGATION

CHAPTER CONTENTS

1 INTRODUCTION

While many improvements have taken place since Charles Dickens lampooned the archaic patent system of the mid-nineteenth century, nonetheless intellectual property litigation remains an expensive and time-consuming process.[1] In part this can be explained by the technical nature of intellectual property (especially in patent cases); by the role that experts play; and by the fact that infringement actions are frequently countered by claims for the invalidity of the intellectual property right. This chapter provides an overview of some of the more important aspects of intellectual property litigation.

---

[1] See J. Phillips, *Charles Dickens and the Poor Man's Tale of a Patent* (1984); M. Lubbock, 'Access to Justice: The Woolf Report' [1997] *EIPR* 385 (a patent action which would cost £600,000 in England might cost as little as £40,000 in Germany). Fewer patents are being litigated in England and Wales than previously, with the number of cases reaching trial per year being in single figures. It is unclear whether this represents a reaction of litigants to the cost of litigation in the UK, or a preference for the substantive findings of other courts (the English judges perhaps being seen as more likely to strike down patents), or is testament to the success of recent attempts to induce parties to settle out of court. Some attempt to reduce the cost of litigation has been made through the Civil Procedure Rules (Part 44(3)), which enable courts to deviate from the assumption that costs follow the result, so that decision on costs can now be made on an issue-by-issue basis: see *AEI Rediffusion Music v. Phonographic Performance* [1999] 1 *WLR* 1507, 1522; *McGhan Medical UK v. Nagor* [2002] *FSR* (9) 162; *Stena Rederi AB v. Irish Ferries (No. 2)* [2003] *RPC* (37) 681. Note also the possibility of seeking an opinion from the Patent Office on the validity or infringement of a patent for a mere £200.

2   WHO CAN BRING PROCEEDINGS?

Most intellectual property proceedings are concerned with the infringement of rights. In some cases, however, would-be defendants might want reassurance that their proposed activities will not infringe. In these circumstances, a person may be able to apply to the court for a declaration that their activities are non-infringing.

2.1   ACTION FOR INFRINGEMENT

Usually it is the rights holder as defined in the relevant legislation who is able to bring an action for infringement. In certain situations, however, other parties are able to litigate to protect their interests. For example, in some cases equitable owners are able to bring an action where their intellectual property rights have been breached or infringed. To do so, they must join the legal owner before final judgment can be given.[2] A co-owner can also bring an action for infringement.[3] While exclusive licensees are usually able to bring an action for infringement,[4] the question whether a licensee of a sign is able to bring a passing-off action depends on the circumstances.[5] In some cases, the courts have allowed representative actions to be brought, notably by trade associations such as the British Phonographic Industry.[6] Representative actions are allowed where there is a common interest and a common grievance so that the remedy sought will be of benefit to all those who are represented. In cases of criminal infringement, the police and other relevant public authorities, such as the local Weights and Measures Authority, may be empowered to take action.[7]

---

[2] *Columbia Pictures Industries v. Robinson* [1988] *FSR* 531, 547; *Batjac Productions v. Simitar Entertainment* [1996] *FSR* 139, 149–52.

[3] PA s. 66(2); TMA s. 23(5) (but must join all other co-owners to proceedings, other than for interim relief); CDPA s. 173(2), *Cescinsky v. Routledge* [1916] 2 *KB* 325; CDPA s. 259 (references to designer to be treated as references to all designers). In the case of patents and trade marks, acts done or authorized by another co-owner may not amount to an infringement: PA s. 36; TMA s. 23(3).

[4] PA s. 67; RDA, s. 15C, s. 24F (introduced by Intellectual Property (Enforcements) Regulations 2006, (SI 2006/1028)). See *Bondax Carpets v. Advanced Carpet Tiles* [1993] *FSR* 162, 163; CDPA s. 101, s. 191L; TMA s. 31 (if the exclusive licence specifically grants the right to bring proceedings); Council Regulation (EC) 6/2002 on Community Design Art. 32 (3) (exclusive licensee can bring action if proprietor, having been given notice to do so, does not himself bring proceedings within an appropriate period); Council Regulation 40/94 (20 Dec. 1993) on the Community Trade Mark, Art 22(3). The position of a bare licensee is more varied: normally a bare licensee cannot bring an action. But cf. TMA s. 30(3) (if proprietor refuses to bring proceedings 'in respect of any matter which affects his interests' the licensee may do so). As a result of changes introduced by the Copyright and Related Rights Regulations 2003 (SI 2498/2003), a non-exclusive licensee can bring an action for infringement of copyright if the infringing act was 'directly connected' to a previously licensed act by a licensee, and the licence expressly grants a right of action and is in writing signed by the copyright owner: CDPA s. 101A. Richard Arnold QC has highlighted the surprising flexibility demonstrated in *Douglas v Hello!* [2008] 1 *AC* 1 as to the right of action of a licensee of confidential information against a person acting in breach of confidence: R. Arnold, 'Confidence in Exclusives: *Douglas v Hello!* in the House of Lords' [2007] *EIPR* 339, 343.

[5] *Scandecor Developments v. Scandecor Marketing* [1998] *FSR* 500 (CA).

[6] *CBS Songs v. Amstrad* [1988] *RPC* 567.

[7] The Trade Descriptions Act 1968 also creates certain offences, discussed in Ch. 48, which the Trading Standards Departments enforce.

2.2 DECLARATION OF NON-INFRINGEMENT

Given the cost and uncertainty of intellectual property litigation, it may be important for someone who plans to invest a lot of money in a particular activity to find out whether the proposed conduct is non-infringing.[8] One option is to seek legal advice.[9] In some cases, would-be defendants are able to apply to the court for a declaration that their activities are non-infringing. A declaration of non-infringement can be made either under the court's general powers or (in relation to potential patent infringements) under the powers provided by the Patents Act 1977. We will look at each in turn.

For a court to grant a declaration of non-infringement under its general powers, it must be satisfied that the possibility of infringement is real and not theoretical. The court must also be satisfied that the applicant has a real interest in seeking the declaration and that there is a proper 'contradictor', that is, a defendant who has a true interest in opposing the claim.[10] This means that declarations of non-infringement will only be granted where legal rights have been contested or, more specifically, where the right holder has already made a claim against the applicant for the declaration.[11] As a result, declarations of non-infringement will only rarely be available.[12] Where granted, the declarations will be in narrow terms: the courts being unwilling to make broad declarations, such as the 'patent is, and has at all times, been invalid', without the benefit of a full trial.[13]

In addition to the general power the courts have to make declarations of non-infringement, the Patents Act 1977 contains specific statutory provisions that empower the courts to make declarations of non-infringement in relation to potential infringements of patents.[14] The provisions recognize the burdensome nature of patent litigation. In order to provide certainty to potential competitors and to facilitate investment, section 71 of the Patents Act 1977 enables applicants to apply to the court or the Comptroller for a declaration that certain acts do not constitute an infringement of the patent. This is the case even though no claim has been made against the applicant.[15] Declarations will only be made where it can be shown that the person has applied in writing to the proprietor for a written acknowledgement that they are not infringing and the proprietor has refused or failed to provide an acknowledgement.[16] The onus

---

[8] *Research in Motion (UK) Ltd v. Visto Corp* [2008] *EWCA Civ* 153 (para. 7). See P. Young, *Declaratory Orders* (1984) chs. 2 and 7; A. Hudson, 'Declaratory Judgments: Theoretical Cases and the Reality of the Dispute' (1977) 3 *Dalhousie Law Journal* 706.

[9] In the context of registered rights would-be defendants may also apply to have the right revoked or declared invalid. We have dealt with this in the relevant chapters.

[10] *Russian Commercial and Industrial Bank v. British Bank of Foreign Trade* [1921] 2 *AC* 438, 448; *Point Solutions v. Focus Business Solution* [2006] *FSR* (31) 567 (regarding infringement of copyright in software).

[11] On the relationship between declarations of non-infringement and the appropriate scope of an injunction, see *Coflexip v. Stolt Comex Seaway* [1999] *FSR* 473, 484.

[12] Where the applicant has already begun to take the relevant action (such as manufacture, import, or sale) and an intellectual property right holder has objected to that action, the court will consider the grant of a declaration more readily. Even then, the remedy is discretionary and so will only be granted in 'appropriate circumstances to settle appropriate questions': *Biogen v. Medeva* [1993] *RPC* 475, 489.

[13] *Lever Fabergé Ltd v. Colgate Palmolive* [2006] *FSR* 19.

[14] PA s. 71. The section does not prevent a person applying under the inherent jurisdiction, but it appears that it is not possible to put the validity of the patent in issue when seeking a declaration under the inherent jurisdiction, because of PA s. 74. On the limits see *Organon Teknika v. F. Hoffmann-La Roche AG* [1996] *FSR* 383.

[15] *Plastus Kreativ v. Minesota Mining and Manufacturing Co.* [1995] *RPC* 438, 442.

[16] On the need for specificity in the applicant's description of the activities about which they want a declaration see *MMD Design & Consultancy* [1989] *RPC* 131, 135; *Wollard's Patent* [1989] *RPC* 141. There is 'an interesting point of law' as to whether a court should ever entertain an application which is 'hypothetical': *Apotex Europe v. Beecham Group plc* [2003] *EWHC* 1395 (6 Jun. 2003) (para. 12) (Laddie J).

of proof lies on the party seeking the declaration.[17] When a declaration is issued, patentees are estopped from later claiming that the matters in the declaration constitute an infringement of the patent.[18]

3 WHO CAN BE SUED?

There are a number of parties who may be sued for infringement or breach of intellectual property rights. In deciding who should be sued, claimants will be guided by a range of factors. These include pragmatic concerns such as the convenience of suing a central party rather than a range of disparate infringers (a manufacturer rather than a retailer, or an Internet Service Provider rather than a person who posts or receives information). In other cases the relative financial stability of the parties may determine who is sued.

3.1 PRIMARY INFRINGERS

The most obvious person to sue is the primary infringer, that is the person directly responsible for the infringement or breach. We have dealt with the circumstances in which such persons will be liable in each of the infringement chapters.[19]

3.2 SECONDARY AND INDIRECT INFRINGERS

Most intellectual property regimes extend the scope of liability from immediate infringers such as manufacturers, importers, or vendors of infringing goods to include parties who facilitate, authorize, or induce infringement. Often these are referred to as secondary infringers. In most instances, to be liable, secondary or indirect infringers must have known, or it must have been obvious to a reasonable person, that they were facilitating, authorizing, or inducing the infringement. As with primary infringers, the special provisions relating to secondary infringers have been considered in the earlier chapters on infringement.

3.3 EMPLOYERS

The general tortious rule that the employer will be vicariously liable when an employee commits an infringing act in the course of their employment applies as much to intellectual property rights as to other torts. Where the wrong is equitable the position is not so clear. It is difficult to see, however, why an employer should not be just as liable for a breach of an equitable duty of confidentiality by an employee as they are for a breach of any other obligation.[20]

---

[17] *Rohm & Haas & Co. v. Collag* [2001] *FSR* 426. The court has a discretion, and so will take into account whether the application is timely, and whether it imposes unfair burdens on the patentee: *Apotex v. Beecham*, ibid (Laddie J).

[18] In some European countries, the declaration of non-infringement has been used as a 'torpedo' by defendants to pre-empt a claimant's selection of a different jurisdiction. For example, a defendant who anticipates being sued in Germany might bring an action for a declaration of non-infringement in a more sympathetic country: see, e.g. Franzosi [2000] *EIPR* N142; *Research in Motion (UK) Ltd v. Visto Corp* [2008] *EWCA Civ* 153. On jurisdictional issues, see section 9 below.

[19] See Chs. 6, 8, 13, 22, 28, 30, 40, and 46.   [20] *AGIP (Africa) v. Jackson* [1992] 4 *All ER* 385, 408.

3.4 JOINT TORTFEASORS

It is also possible to bring an action against a party where they are acting as a joint tortfeasor. A person will be liable as a joint tortfeasor where they are connected with or somehow associated with the infringement. It is important to note that not every connection is sufficient to render an associated person a joint tortfeasor.[21] In particular, mere assistance in the commission of a tort (knowing or otherwise) will not suffice to make a person civilly liable as a joint tortfeasor. Rather, the test for a joint tortfeasor is that 'each person has made the infringing acts his own'.[22] The situations where a party will be liable as a joint tortfeasor fall into two (overlapping) categories.[23] The first concerns the situation where one party intends and procures, or *induces*, the commission of the tort; the second, the situation where two or more persons joined in a *common design* pursuant to which the tort was committed.[24] We deal with each in turn.

3.4.1 Inducement

A person will be liable where they induce the infringement. An extreme example of this is where a person controls the operations of another (such as a company), which is merely that person's tool or 'cat's paw', and the other (the company) infringes: in such a case the moving spirit of the company may be found to have induced its acts.[25] Similarly, if a person sells an article in kit form with instructions, and that article, when constructed, infringes the claimant's copyright, the seller will be a joint tortfeasor with the person who puts the kit together, because they have *induced* that infringement.[26] In contrast, while people who sell an article knowing that it is going to be used to infringe may assist infringement, they will not be treated as having induced the infringement. For example, in *CBS Songs v. Amstrad*[27] the House of Lords was asked to consider whether, in selling a high-speed tape-to-tape recorder which the manufacturer and vendor knew was likely to be used to infringe copyright in sound recordings, the supplier was a joint tortfeasor. The House of Lords held that, because the supplier did not have control over how purchasers used the tape recorders, nor had they asked

---

[21] See *Credit Lyonnaise v. Export Credit Guarantee Department* [1998] 1 *Lloyds LR* 19, 44 (appealed on a different issue to the House of Lords [1999] 2 *WLR* 540); *Lancashire Fires v. SA Lyons* [1996] *FSR* 629, 675 (CA) (same principles apply to determine liability for breach of confidence). Cf. *Evans v. Spritebrand* [1985] *FSR* 267 (distinguishing between strict liability torts and those dependent on *mens rea*); *MCA Records Inc. v. Charly Records* [2002] *FSR* (26) 401 (para. 51) (hinting that there might be principles of joint tortfeasance specific to intellectual property). For discussion of joint tortfeasance in the context of passing off, see H. Carty, 'Passing Off and Instruments of Deception: The Need for Clarity' [2003] *EIPR* 188.

[22] *SABAF SpA v. MFI Furniture* [2003] *RPC* (14) 264 (para. 58).

[23] *Unilever v. Gillette (UK)* [1989] *RPC* 583, 608 (where Mustill LJ left it open as to whether these were just two aspects of a single way of infringing, but noted that procurement might lead to a common design and hence fall under both heads). Cp. *MCA Records* [2002] *FSR* (26) 401, 424 (paras. 51, 52) using the language 'intends and procures and shares a common design that infringement takes place'.

[24] *Unilever*, ibid, 608.

[25] Normally, directors are not liable for tortious acts done by servants of a company unless they are privy to the act, that is, they ordered or procured it: *PRS v. Ciryl Theatrical Syndicate* [1924] 1 *KB* 1, 14–15. If a director is acting constitutionally, only rarely can he be said to have procured the acts of the company (since, in principle, he has acted for it): *MCA Records* [2002] *FSR* (26) 401, 423–4 (para. 49). There is authority that, for directors to be liable as joint tortfeasors, they must have directed that an act be carried out knowing that it would be tortious: *Canon Kabushiki Kaisha v. Green Cartridge Co.* [1996] *FSR* 874, 894 (Hong Kong Court of Appeal); *White Horse Distillers v. Gregson Associates* [1984] *RPC* 61, 91.

[26] *Rotocrop International v. Genbourne* [1982] *FSR* 241, 259.   [27] [1988] *RPC* 500, 606.

purchasers to use the tape recorder in a particular way, the supplier was not a joint tortfeasor with purchasers who made illegal recordings.

3.4.2 Common design

Where a group of people share a 'common design' (a plan or a purpose), and one of the group commits a tort while carrying out the common design, the other members will be liable as joint tortfeasors.[28] Although one member of the group commits the tort, it is treated as if it was committed on behalf of and in concert with the other members of the group. For parties to operate in a common design it is not necessary for the secondary party to have mapped out a plan with the primary offender:[29] tacit agreement will suffice.[30] The common design need not be to infringe if the agreed action leads to an infringement.[31] Also, it does not matter whether or not the parties knew they were infringing.[32] The fact that a parent company has financial control of a subsidiary is not enough of a connection to constitute a common design. The parent company must be shown to have 'taken part' in the primary act.[33] Equally, under this head directors will only be liable for acts of the company where they and the company 'joined together in concerted action to secure that [the infringing] acts were done'.[34]

4 OBTAINING AND PRESERVING EVIDENCE

Often intellectual-property-right holders find out about infringement by chance.[35] For example, an employee or representative might stumble across an infringing article while on holiday, or a dissatisfied customer might complain to the right holder that the goods made by the infringer are faulty. Intellectual-property-rights owners also have more systematic ways of discovering infringements. In particular, collecting societies and trade associations such as the British Phonograph Industry's Anti-Piracy Unit, the Federation against Copyright Theft (which polices video piracy),[36] and the Federation against Software Theft (which monitors software infringement) play an important role in identifying and policing infringement.

---

[28] *Morton-Norwich Products v. Intercen* [1978] *RPC* 501, 512, 515 (where Dutch company supplied English firm with drug which infringed the claimant's patent, the Dutch company was a joint tortfeasor even though it had committed no act in the UK).

[29] A joint marketing agreement by which the supplier of infringing goods also provides demonstration machines, literature, and advertising material and training might be indicative of sufficient cooperation between the parties to constitute a common design: *Puschner v. Tom Palmer (Scotland)* [1989] *RPC* 430. But mere supply does not amount to a common design: *SABAF v. MFI* [2003] *RPC* (14) 264 (para. 59).

[30] *Unilever v. Gillette* [1989] *RPC* 583, 609. See also *Lubrizol v. Esso Petroleum (No. 1)* [1992] *RPC* 281.

[31] *Unilever*, ibid, 609; *Ravenscroft v. Herbert* [1980] *RPC* 193, 210 (contract between author and publisher whereby publisher was bound to publish constituted common design so author was also liable for act of publishing work).

[32] For example, that they believed the goods had been put on the market with the consent of the holder of the intellectual property right: *Morton-Norwich* [1978] *RPC* 501, 515.

[33] *Unilever v. Chefaro Proprietaries* [1994] *FSR* 135, 138; *Napp Pharmaceutical Group v. Asta Medica* [1999] *FSR* 370; *Coin Controls v. Suzo* [1997] *FSR* 660, 666; *The Mead Corporation v. Riverwood Multiple Packaging* [1997] *FSR* 484.

[34] *MCA Records* [2002] *FSR* (26) 401, 424 (para. 53).

[35] B. Olson *et al*, 'The 10 Things Every Practitioner should Know about Anti-Counterfeiting and Anti-Piracy Protection' (2007) 7 *Journal of High Tech. Law* 106.

[36] See *R v. Alpha Holbrough* (7 Nov. 2002) (para. 4) (CA).

Once right holders discover that their rights are being infringed, a number of options are available. For example, they can sue for infringement or attempt to settle out of court. Whichever route is chosen it is usually prudent and often necessary for them to gather the relevant evidence. The evidence that is needed will vary according to the facts in hand, and may include evidence that an infringement has taken place, the details of the parties involved, and the extent of infringement. In some cases, evidence of infringement is obtained by ambushing or entrapping the defendant. For example, a legal practitioner might pose as a bona fide customer of a person selling infringing products or service. Such actions, which are called 'trap orders', often involve a degree of deception by the person collecting the evidence. Despite this, the courts have not objected to evidence obtained in this way, nor have claimants relying on such evidence been treated as lacking 'clean hands'.[37] Instead, the courts have left the probity of such techniques to be regulated by the appropriate professional bodies. Copyright owners and anyone whom they authorize are also given the power to seize and detain infringing copies without first obtaining a court order.[38] To protect the expectations of property owners and the public more generally, the availability of such self-help mechanisms is limited.

Another important source of evidence derives from the fact that intellectual-property-right holders are able to obtain a court order requiring a person to reveal information relevant to the action.[39] This may include the names and addresses of relevant parties, the dates and quantities imported, and the source of goods or materials.[40] Orders for discovery are particularly useful in that they enable right holders to trace the channels through which infringing goods are distributed.[41] The traditional, so-called *Norwich Pharmacal* order continues to be available,[42] and will be particularly useful in situations where the person seeking the information has no intention of bringing court proceedings but, for example, merely wishes to identify moles within its organization and dismiss them.[43] In some situations claimants are also able

---

[37] *Marie Claire Album v. Hartstone Hosiery* [1993] *FSR* 692.

[38] CDPA s. 100, s. 196. The copies must be exposed or otherwise immediately available for sale or hire; a local police station must be duly notified beforehand of the action to be taken; and the seizure must be in a public place or on public premises from a person who does not have a permanent or regular place of business there. Notice of what has been seized has to be given in prescribed form. No force may be used; though, if police officers are present, they may be able to use the discretionary power of arrest. See Police and Criminal Evidence Act 1984, ss. 24–5.

[39] CPR r. 31.

[40] It seems likely that the case law on *Norwich Pharmacal* orders will be applicable to CPR r. 31 Orders. It is therefore unlikely that an order will include the names of customers of a competing business: *Jade Engineering (Coventry) v. Antiference Window Systems* [1996] *FSR* 461, 465–7.

[41] An application for such an order can be resisted e.g. journalists may be protected from having to reveal their sources under the Contempt of Court Act 1981, s. 10, or reliance may be placed on ECHR Art 10: see *Goodwin v. UK* (1996) 22 *EHRR* 123. But there are limits: *Ashworth Security Hospital v. MGM Ltd* [2002] 1 *WLR* 2033 (paras. 61–66, 71–73).

[42] *Norwich Pharmacal v. CCE* [1974] *AC* 133; *Ashworth Hospital*, ibid. This order, made under the court's inherent jurisdiction, is available against a person who has committed no wrong, but they must have been 'involved' in the wrongdoing. For example, the Commissioners of Customs and Excise have been required to reveal the names of importers of a patented drug: *Norwich Pharmacal*, ibid; and British Telecom the names of mobile phone users alleged to be involved in passing-off: *The Coca-Cola Co. v. British Telecommunications* [1999] *FSR* 518, 523.

[43] *Ashworth Hospital*, ibid (para. 60) (where the claimant was entitled to an order against a newspaper requiring that it reveal the source of confidential patient records leaked from the claimant's high-security hospital). According to Lord Woolf, the claimant must clearly identify the wrongdoing on which he relies and specify the purposes for which disclosure will be used. The court order may impose restriction as to how the information may be used.

to petition for an order for the discovery of names.[44] This order may require parties to identify, for example, persons serving as the source of goods in their possession or providing access to works online.[45] The order may even address third parties, who are not themselves named as a wrongdoer, if they are shown to have become involved in the transaction in question.[46] In the normal course of things, such discovery is unlikely to include the names of customers of a competing business.[47]

The situations in which third parties may be forced to disclose information that might be pertinent to an intellectual property infringement action were recently discussed by the ECJ in *Promusicae*.[48] The case arose when Promusicae, which is a non-profit organization of producers and publishers of musical and audiovisual recordings, asked the Spanish internet service provider Telefónica to provide them with the names and addresses of people who were using the KaZaa peer-to-peer file-exchange program to share music which, according to Promusicae, was an infringement of intellectual property rights. After a preliminary ruling accepted Promusicae's requests, Telefónica appealed to a Spanish court which subsequently referred the matter to the ECJ, asking whether Community law requires member states to recognize an obligation to communicate personal data in the context of civil proceedings, so as to ensure effective protection of copyright. The ECJ held that the relevant Directives:[49]

did not require the Member States to lay down...an obligation to communicate personal data in order to ensure effective protection of copyright in the context of civil proceedings. [The Court went on to say, however, that] Community law requires that, when transposing those directives, the Member States take care to rely on an interpretation of them which allows a fair balance to be struck between the various fundamental rights protected by the Community legal order. Further, when implementing the measures transposing those directives, the authorities and courts of the Member States must not only interpret their national law in a manner consistent with those directives but also make sure that they do not rely on an interpretation of them which would be in conflict with those fundamental rights or with the other general principles of Community law, such as the principle of proportionality.[50]

By placing the onus of balancing the 'various fundamental rights protected by the Community legal order' on national courts, the ECJ has adopted the rhetoric of balance (frustratingly) familiar in British intellectual property law. As the *Norwich Pharmacal* order may satisfy this test, it seems that the ECJ may not have much of an impact on established British practice in this area.

---

[44] See S. Gee, *Commercial Injunctions* (2004), 688–93. For Scotland, see Intellectual Property (Enforcement, etc) Regulations 2006 (SI 2006/1028), r.4 (introducing order).

[45] See, e.g., *Jade Engineering* [1996] *FSR* 461 (order for discovery of name of foreign supplier); *Polydor v. Brown* [2005] *EWHC* 3191 (ascertaining defendant's name in a file-sharing case by getting a *Norwich Pharmacal* order against the internet service provider).

[46] *See, e.g., Norwich Pharmacal* [1974] *AC* 133 (requiring Commissioners of Customs and Excise to reveal the names of importers of a patented drug); *Coca Cola. v. BT* [1999] *FSR* 518 (requiring the supplier of telephone services to disclose the address of one of its customers who was implicated in passing-off); *Eli Lilly v. Neopharma* [2008] *EWHC* 415 (Ch). *See also Jade Engineering*, ibid (no need for wrongdoer to be in the U.K. to justify order).

[47] *Jade Engineering*, ibid, 465–7.

[48] *Productores de Música de España (Promusicae) v. Telefónica de España* C–275/06 (29 Jan. 2008).

[49] These were the Electronic Commerce Directive, the Information Society Directive, the Enforcement Directive, and the Directive on privacy and electronic communications.

[50] *Promusicae*, C–275/06 (29 Jan. 2008), para 71.

To enable intellectual-property-right owners to preserve evidence prior to trial, the British courts developed the so-called *Anton Piller* order,[51] now called a *search order*.[52] In essence a search order permits a claimant (and their solicitor) to inspect the defendant's premises and to seize or copy any information that is relevant to the alleged infringement. Applications for search orders are made either to a patents judge in the High Court or the Patents County Court, or to a Chancery judge.[53] As the order aims to ensure that evidence is not destroyed, the application is made without giving notice to the other party. Given their potentially draconian nature,[54] search orders will only be made if the matter is urgent or otherwise desirable in the interests of justice.[55] Before an order will be granted, the courts require claimants to show that they have an extremely strong *prima facie* case of infringement and that the potential damage to them is very serious. The claimant must also provide clear evidence that the defendant has incriminating material in their possession and that there is a real possibility that the evidence will be destroyed.[56] The search order is subject to procedural safeguards,[57] such as the need for a supervising solicitor (unconnected with the applicant) who is experienced in the operation of search orders.[58] The order may only be served on a weekday between 9.30 and 5.30 (unless the court orders otherwise), and supervising solicitors must explain the terms of the order to the respondents in everyday language and advise them of their rights.[59] Failure to comply with an order is a contempt of court, resulting in imprisonment or a fine.[60]

The application for a search order may be combined with an interim injunction against infringement and a *freezing order* (formerly known as a *Mareva* injunction) ordering the retention of property pending the outcome of the litigation.[61] In addition, the search order may require that the defendant provide information about the source of the infringing copies or their intended destination.[62]

---

[51] *Anton Piller v. Manufacturing Processes* [1976] *Ch* 55. See M. Dockray, *Anton Piller Orders* (1992); S. Gee, *Mareva Injunctions and Anton Piller Relief* (4th edn. 1998); M. Hoyle, *The Mareva Injunction and Related Orders* (1997), ch. 8. For a Marxist interpretation of the development of the order see F. Carrigan, 'The Political Economy of *Anton Piller* Orders' (1995) 11 *Australian Journal of Law & Society* 33.

[52] CPA 1997 s. 7; CPR r. 25; Rule 25 Practice Direction.

[53] CPR Rule 25A Practice Direction, para. 8.5.

[54] *Universal Thermosensors v. Hibben* [1992] *FSR* 361; *Taylor Made Golf Company v. Rata and Rata* [1996] *FSR* 528, 535. In *Bank Mellat v. Nikpour* [1985] *FSR* 87, 92 Donaldson LJ described the order as one of two 'nuclear weapons' of English law.

[55] CPR r. 25.2(2)(b).

[56] The applicant should disclose all material facts. Rule 25A Practice Direction, para. 3.3. See *Naf Naf SA v. Dickens* [1993] *FSR* 424.

[57] CPR Rule 25A Practice Direction. See Hoyle, *The Mareva Injunction*, 110 (use of such orders has declined since adoption of safeguards in *Universal Thermosensors* [1992] *FSR* 361 and the Practice Direction (*Mareva* Injunctions and *Anton Piller* Orders) 1994 [1994] *RPC* 617).

[58] CPR Rule 25A Practice Direction, paras. 7.2 and 8.1 (supervising solicitor must not be an employee or member of the applicant's firm of solicitors). Other safeguards were imposed as a result of *Universal Thermosensors*, ibid.

[59] CPR Rule 25A Practice Direction, para. 7.4. Where the supervising solicitor is a man and the respondent is likely to be an unaccompanied woman, at least one other person named in the order must be a woman and must accompany the supervising solicitor: para. 7.4(5).

[60] *Taylor Made* [1996] *FSR* 528 (fine of £75,000). See the Notice to the Respondent in the sample order annexed to CPR Rule 25A Practice Direction.

[61] CPR r. 25(f). (Sometimes called 'asset preservation orders').

[62] There is a statutory exception to the privilege against self-incrimination: Supreme Court Act 1981 s. 72.

5 PRESUMPTIONS

Normally in civil actions, the obligation falls upon the claimant to prove their case on the balance of probabilities. However, in a number of situations intellectual property legislation creates presumptions that alter the normal burden of proof. The most important is that it is presumed that registered rights have been granted validly. Thus, the obligation falls on the alleged infringer of a patent, a registered trade mark, or a registered design to prove that the right is invalid (or obtain revocation). Presumptions also operate in the field of unregistered design rights, copyright, publication right, performers rights, and the database right. These relate to the identity of the author,[63] publisher, performer, or (in the case of database right) the maker,[64] and the date on which a work (etc.) was published.[65] In copyright law, where an author is dead it is presumed that the work was original and that it was first published where and when the claimant alleges.[66]

6 UNJUSTIFIED THREATS TO SUE

The cost and burden of intellectual property litigation means that the mere threat of litigation has the scope to act as a potent commercial weapon.[67] To ensure that the threat to sue is not misused, special provisions offer remedies against unjustified threats to litigate.[68] These exist in the case of patents, trade marks, registered designs, and the unregistered design right. From 1 October 2005, equivalent provisions also exist for Community designs, whether registered or unregistered.[69] There are no statutory provisions that protect against unjustified threats to sue in relation to copyright, passing-off, or breach of confidence. In these cases, persons unjustifiably threatened with litigation have to resort to other means.[70]

---

[63] CDPA ss. 104(2)–(4); *Waterlow Publishers v. Rose* [1995] *FSR* 207, 218. These presumptions do not operate for the purposes of the publication right: Related Rights Reg. 17(2)(b). As regards films, additional presumptions operate concerning statements as to who was the director or producer of the film, as well as who was the principal director, author of the screenplay, author of dialogue, or composer of music.

[64] See Database Reg. r. 22(1).

[65] As regards copyright in sound recordings and computer programs, it is presumed that statements naming the copyright owner, or giving the date or place of first publication, are true: CDPA s. 105. See *Microsoft Corporation v. Electrowide* [1997] *FSR* 580, 594. Where copies of the database as published bear a label or a mark stating that the database was first published in a specified year, the label or mark shall be admissible as evidence of the facts stated and shall be presumed to be correct until the contrary is proved: Database Reg. 22(3).

[66] CDPA s. 104(5).

[67] Another technique that is used to avoid unnecessary litigation is the issuing of certificates of contested validity. As well as acting as a victory trophy, the certificate may deter subsequent litigation. RDA s. 25; PA s. 65; TMA s. 73.

[68] See I. Davies and T. Scourfield, 'Threats: is the current regime still justified?' [2007] *EIPR* 259; G. Schwartz and M. Gardner, 'Groundless threats of proceedings for IP infringement' [2006] *Communications Law* 85. The earliest statutory action was in the Patents, Designs and Trade Marks Act 1883 (46 & 47 Vict. ch. 57) s. 32.

[69] Community Designs Regulations 2005 (SI 2005/2339), para 2. The Regulations also introduced provisions making it an offence to falsely claim that a design is registered (para 3) similar to those in RDA s. 35.

[70] For a general discussion see *Reckitt Benkiser UK v. Home Pairfum* [2004] *FSR* (37) 774.

6.1 THREATS TO SUE: PATENTS, TRADE MARKS, DESIGNS

Special statutory provisions exist in the case of patents,[71] trade marks,[72] registered designs,[73] and the unregistered design right[74] to protect parties against unjustified threats to sue. These statutory provisions 'ensure that threats of infringement proceedings are not made casually or recklessly, because of the potential damage and concern they can cause'.[75] As a result, if owners threaten to sue, they must ensure that the threat can be justified.

In order to qualify for relief against a groundless threat, a claimant must establish that an actionable threat has been made and that as a result they have been aggrieved. If the defendant fails to justify the threat, the court will grant relief. We will deal with these factors in turn.

6.1.1 Actionable threats

In order for a claimant to be entitled to the relief provided, they must show that an actionable threat has been made. It should be noted that, in the case of patents,[76] registered designs,[77] and trade marks,[78] special provisions limit the circumstances in which groundless threats are actionable. In essence these exclude threats made in relation to primary acts of infringement: rival manufacturers may threaten each other.[79] While the legislative philosophy underlying these exclusions is 'difficult to detect',[80] it is clear that they greatly weaken the scope of the threats provisions.

Threats can take many different forms. Although actionable threats will usually be explicit, they may also be implicit,[81] and may arise from a single letter or a circular.[82] In an interesting development in the scope of the threats action, an injunction was granted to restrain the making of threats for infringement of a Community Design Right where a defendant had made use of the on-line auctions site eBay's complaint policy. The action arose when the claimant advertised children's motor bikes for sale on eBay. The defendant wrote to eBay claiming that he was the owner of Community Design Right in the children's motorbikes. In situations such as this, to avoid litigation eBay takes what the court described as 'the line of least resistance'. This means that, once the identity of the person making the complaints is verified, eBay will remove the listing. eBay not, and could not be expected to, check the accuracy of the infringement claims. On the basis that 'unsupported and unchallengeable allegations of infringement

---

[71] PA s. 70.   [72] TMA s. 21.   [73] RDA s. 26: e.g. *Jaybeam v. Abru Aluminium* [1975] *FSR* 334.

[74] CDPA s. 253.   [75] *Prince v. Prince Sports Group* [1998] *FSR* 21, 33.

[76] PA s. 70(4) provides that s. 70 does not apply where the threat is to bring infringement proceedings for 'making or importing a product for disposal of or using a process'.

[77] RDA s. 26(2A) and CDPA s. 253(3) state that proceedings may not be brought under the respective threat provisions 'in respect of a threat to bring proceedings for an infringement alleged to consist of the making or importing of anything'.

[78] TMA s. 21(1) excludes threats involving 'the application of the mark to goods or their packaging; the importation of goods to which, or to the packaging of which, the mark has been applied; or the supply of services under the mark'.

[79] *Cavity Trays v. RMC Panel Products* [1996] *RPC* 361.

[80] *Brain v. Ingledew Brown Bennison & Garrett (No. 3)* [1997] *FSR* 511, 525; *Unilever plc v. The Procter & Gamble Co.* [2000] *FSR* 344, where Simon Brown LJ calls the position today 'most curious and unsatisfactory'.

[81] *Bowden Controls v. Acco Cable Controls* [1990] *RPC* 427, 431; *Scandecor Development v. Scandecor Marketing* [1999] *FSR* 26, 47.

[82] When read in conjunction with other letters or circulars, the communication as a whole may be construed as giving rise to a threat of litigation: *Brain v. IBBG (No. 3)* [1997] *FSR* 511, 521–4. Later letters cannot nullify an earlier threat: *Prince v. Prince Sports* [1998] *FSR* 21, 33.

are potentially an exceedingly damaging abuse of registered rights', the court held that there was 'arguably a threat in the notification to eBay'.[83]

When considering whether a threat had been made, the document in question is looked at through the eyes of a reasonable and normal recipient.[84] In doing this, the court will take into account matters such as the circumstances of the business or the background information available to a reasonable recipient.[85] The courts will pay particular attention to the initial impression that the communication makes on a reasonable addressee. Mere notification of the existence of a patent, trade mark, or other right will not constitute a threat of proceedings. It has been suggested, however, that notification of a patent (and presumably other statutory intellectual property rights) may constitute an actionable threat if it is 'given in such a context that a threat is seen to be intended'.[86] It is necessary to show that a threat has been made against someone in particular: it is not enough for a claimant to show that a general threat has been made.[87]

6.1.2 Aggrieved

A person is able to bring an application for relief even though the threats have not been made against them. This means that right owners can bring an action where a shopkeeper who sells their products is threatened with litigation by a competitor. The availability of the action is limited by the requirement that claimants must show that they were 'aggrieved' by the threats. This excludes frivolous applications or applications by busybodies who have no real interest in the threats.[88] While a person can be aggrieved without having to prove actual damage at trial, they must show that something more than a merely fanciful or minimal commercial interest has been interfered with. The courts are more likely to infer an adverse effect where the threats are made directly against a party.[89] Where threats are made indirectly, claimants will need to demonstrate that they suffered actual or potential loss (that is not minimal).[90] This will be easier to prove where the threat was intended to scare off the claimant's customers.[91]

6.1.3 Groundless threats

Once a claimant has established that a threat has been made and that, as a result, they were aggrieved, the statutory provisions shift the onus onto the defendant to prove that the threats were justified.[92] To do this, the defendant will need to show that the right in question is

---

[83] *Quads 4 Kids v. Colin Campbell* [2006] *EWHC*, para 31.

[84] *Brain v. IBBG (No. 3)* [1997] *FSR* 511, 521; *Bowden Controls*, note 81 above, 431; *Lunar Advertising Company v. Burnham & Co.* (1928) 45 *RPC* 258, 260.

[85] *Brain v. Ingledew Brown Bennison & Garrett* [1996] *FSR* 341, 349. But 'without prejudice' discussions cannot be used as a basis for a threats claim: *Unilever v. Procter & Gamble*, 358 (CA); *Kooltrade v. XTS* [2001] *FSR* 158 (noting that 'without prejudice' is not a label that can be used to immunize an act from its normal consequences); *ALM Manufacturing v. Black & Decker* (21 May 2003) (refusing to strike out threats action and stating that the *Unilever* case left unclear the position in relation to threats made in the course of without prejudice negotiations where the person aggrieved was not party to the negotiations).

[86] *CIPA Guide*, 591. *Brain v. IBBG* [1997] *FSR* 511, 349. *Jaybeam* [1975] *FSR* 334, 340 (describing the letter as an over-ingenious attempt by solicitors to avoid producing an actionable threat); *L'Oreal v. Johnson & Johnson* [2000] *ETMR* 691, 703.

[87] *Speedycranes v. Thompson* [1978] *RPC* 221.

[88] *Brain v. IBBG (No. 3)* [1997] *FSR* 511, 519 (hurt feelings are not enough).

[89] *John Summers & Sons v. Cold Metal Press Co.* (1948) 65 *RPC* 75; *Prince v. Prince Sports* [1998] *FSR* 21, 33–4.

[90] *Brain v. IBBG (No. 3)* [1997] *FSR* 511, 520; *Summers*, ibid.

[91] *Dimplex v. De'Longhi* [1996] *FSR* 622.   [92] RDA s. 26(2); PA s. 70(2); CDPA s. 253(2); TMA s. 21(2).

valid[93] and that the acts in respect of which proceedings were threatened would constitute an infringement of the right. This means, for example, that where a threat was made after a patent application had been made but before the patent had been granted, it will not be possible to justify the threat if the patent is not granted before trial.[94]

6.1.4 Relief

If a claimant can show that they have been aggrieved as a result of an actionable threat and the defendant cannot establish that the threat was justified, the claimant is entitled to the relief provided in the relevant statutory provisions.[95] This includes a declaration that the threats are unjustifiable,[96] an injunction against the continuance of the threats,[97] and damages for any losses which were sustained as a result of the threats.[98]

6.2 THREATS TO SUE: COPYRIGHT, PASSING-OFF, AND BREACH OF CONFIDENCE

There are no statutory provisions that protect against unjustified threats to sue in relation to copyright, passing-off, or breach of confidence.[99] In these circumstances, a person who suffers damage as a result of an unjustified threat will have to seek relief through alternative avenues.[100] In some cases, an aggrieved party may be able to bring an action for the tort of abuse of process.[101] A more important option is provided by the action for injurious false-hood. To succeed in an action for injurious falsehood, a claimant must prove that the statements were untrue and malicious. They must also show that they suffered special damage as a result of the statements. The notion of malice has proved difficult to define. It seems to require that the threat must be issued with a view to injuring the claimant rather than defending the defendant's rights. Moreover, it has been said that an honest belief in an unfounded claim is not malicious.[102]

7 COURTS AND TRIBUNALS

One of the methods that have been adopted to deal with the technical nature of intellectual property litigation has been to develop special courts and tribunals. In this section we provide a brief overview of some of the courts and tribunals that operate in the UK.

---

[93] TMA s. 21(3).   [94] *Brain v. Ingledew Brown Bennison & Garrett (No. 2)* [1997] FSR 271, 275.

[95] RDA s. 26(2); PA s. 70(3); CDPA s. 253(1); TMA s. 21(2).

[96] For a discussion of the relationship between this and the inherent jurisdiction to grant declarations that a claimant does not infringe, see *L'Oreal v. Johnson & Johnson* [2000] ETMR 691.

[97] Injunctions should usually follow a successful threats action: *Prince v. Prince Sports* [1998] FSR 21, 36.

[98] Damage must be shown to have been caused by the threat: *Carflow Products v. Linwood Securities* [1998] FSR 691 (decision to withdraw product was a consequence of commencement of proceedings rather than a threat).

[99] During the passage of the 1988 CDPA, it was explained in Parliament that no such action was required in relation to copyright because the position as regards ownership of copyright is usually clear. See Lord Young, 501 *Hansard* (HL), 2 Nov. 1988, col. 338.

[100] See Laddie *et al.*, 952. A person may also seek a declaration of non-infringement. Once a letter or circular has been issued it seems that the legal contest is sufficiently joined to justify a court making such a declaration. See *Leco Instruments v. Land Pyrometers* [1982] RPC 133, 136.

[101] *Grainger v. Hill* (1838) 4 *Bing NC* 212. On the limits of the action see *Pitman Training v. Nominet* [1997] FSR 797; *Essex Electric v. IPC Computer* [1991] FSR 690. On the distinction between the tort of abuse of process and malicious prosecution see *Speed Seal Products v. Paddington* [1986] 1 *All ER* 91 (Fox LJ).

[102] *Greers v. Pearman and Corder* [1922] 39 RPC 406, 417; *Polydor v. Harlequin* [1980] FSR 26, 31.

7.1 THE VARIOUS TRIBUNALS

7.1.1 The High Court

Disputes to do with all forms of intellectual property can be brought before the Chancery Division of the High Court. Proceedings under the Patents Act are dealt with the by the Patents Court, which is a specialist court within the Chancery Division.[103] Proceedings before the Patents Court are heard before a specialist judge, sitting without a jury. The parties must be represented either by counsel instructed by a solicitor, or by a solicitor. The Patents Court has a reputation for the quality of its decisions.[104] Despite this, it has been said that litigation before the Patents Court is time-consuming, laborious, long-drawn-out, and as a consequence expensive.[105]

7.1.2 Patents County Court

The Patents County Court, which was established in 1990,[106] aims to provide a quicker, cheaper, and more accessible way of dealing with patent and design litigation.[107] The Patents County Court has jurisdiction to hear and determine any action or matter relating to patents or designs over which the High Court has jurisdiction. It is also able to hear claims or matters ancillary to or arising from such proceedings. This has been held to include ancillary copyright matters.[108]

While patent agents have the right of appearance before the Patents County Court,[109] discovery is not available 'as of right' and it is unusual for experiments to be conducted to prove a particular point. Procedures in the Patents County Court are otherwise similar to those in the Patents Court: there is cross-examination of witnesses,[110] and the court is equipped with a full range of remedies (such as interim and final injunctions and search orders).[111]

The question whether proceedings should be transferred from the Patents Court to the Patents County Court is left to the Patents County Court.[112] When deciding whether to transfer a matter, the County Court takes account of: the financial position of the parties;[113] whether it would be more convenient or fair for the hearing to be held in another court; the availability of a judge specializing in the type of claim in question; the relative complexity of the legal issues, the remedies, and the procedures involved;[114] the importance of the outcome to the public; and the facilities available at the court where the claim is being dealt with.[115]

---

[103] Practice Direction, pt. 49E Clause 1.3 defines patent to include Supplementary Protection Certificates and patent court business to include proceedings under the RDA.

[104] *Chaplin Patents Holding Co. v. Group Lotus* (CA) (*The Times*, 12 Jan. 1994).

[105] R. Nott, 'Patent Litigation in England' [1994] *EIPR* 3.

[106] CDPA pt. VI; Patents County Court (Designation and Jurisdiction) Order 1990 (SI 1990/1496). The court was established by CDPA s. 287. Patents County Court (Designation and Jurisdiction) Order 1994 (SI 1994/1609). So far only one court has been designated, namely the Central London County Court.

[107] *Chaplin v. Lotus* (CA) (*The Times*, 12 Jan. 1994) (Sir Thomas Bingham MR); *Memminger-Iro v. Trip-Lite* [1992] *RPC* 210, 216 (Aldous J). Cf. P. Ford, 'Patent Litigation: A Better Deal for Litigants?' [1990] *EIPR* 435, 436.

[108] *PSM v. Specialised Fastener Products* [1993] *FSR* 113, 116–17; *McDonald v. Graham* [1994] *RPC* 407, 434–5, 441.

[109] CDPA s. 292 (1). *Memminger-Iro* [1992] *RPC* 210, 221.   [110] Ibid, 220.

[111] CPA s. 7; CPR r. 25; CPR, *Practice Direction* para. 8.5. See *McDonald v. Graham* [1994] *RPC* 407, 435.

[112] CDPA s. 289. *Memminger-Iro* [1992] *RPC* 210, 224. *Wesley Jessen Corp v. Coopervision* (2 July 2001).

[113] CDPA s. 289(2).   [114] *Chaplin v. Lotus*, (CA) (*The Times*, 12 Jan. 1994).   [115] CPR r. 30.3.

Despite empirical evidence suggesting otherwise,[116] doubts have been raised over the success of the Patents County Court.[117] As Hoffmann J noted, it has led 'not so much to a saving in costs but to a shifting in the time at which those costs are incurred'.[118] More specifically, the requirement that the claimant set their case out at the preliminary stage leads to greater costs at an earlier stage, which may be unnecessary if the action is settled quickly.[119]

7.1.3 County Court

County courts have jurisdiction to hear cases on copyright,[120] unregistered designs, registered national and Community Trade Marks, passing-off, and performances,[121] but not patents, or registered designs.[122] The jurisdiction of the county court is local: a defendant should be sued in the county court in the district where they reside. Patent and trade mark agents have no right of audience. While certain forms of relief, such as search orders and delivery-up,[123] are not available,[124] the county court can award interim injunctions, damages, and accounts of profits.

7.1.4 Comptroller of Patents

The Comptroller of Patents and the Patent Office more generally have important powers to determine matters relating to the validity and revocation of patents.[125] On being authorized by the parties, the Comptroller has the ability to hear infringement actions and counter-claims for revocation.[126] The Comptroller also has jurisdiction over certain issues concerning unregistered design rights.[127] The Comptroller provides litigants with a cheaper, quicker, and more specialized and informal forum than is offered by the Patents Court.[128] One advantage of using the Comptroller is that the parties can be represented by patent agents rather than by counsel.[129] However, the jurisdiction has rarely been used. This may be because the Comptroller has no jurisdiction to grant injunctive relief and because failed proceedings do not give rise to any issue estoppel. Moreover, the courts have been extremely reluctant to stay court proceedings pending determination of the issues by the Comptroller.[130] Hoffmann J said that these factors mean that the Comptroller and the Patent Office can only be made to work as an alternative tribunal in infringement cases by the giving of undertakings by the parties which will

---

[116] J. Adams, 'Choice of Forum in Patent Disputes' [1995] *EIPR* 497, 501–2. In *McDonald v. Graham* [1994] *RPC* 407, 441 Evans LJ was more supportive.

[117] Nott, 'Patent Litigation in England' (also pointing to the unfortunate record of the court for being reversed on appeal); M. Lubbock, 'Access to Justice: The Woolf Report' [1997] *EIPR* 385, 389.

[118] *Composite Gutters v. Pre-Formed Components* [1993] *FSR* 305, 308; *Chaplin. v. Lotus* (CA) (*The Times*, 12 Jan. 1994).

[119] Nott, 'Patent Litigation in England', 4.

[120] *PSM v. Specialised Fastener* [1993] *FSR* 113, 116; *McDonald v. Graham* [1994] *RPC* 407.

[121] High Court and County Court Jurisdiction (Amendment) Order 2005, (SI 2005/587); CTMR, Art. 91; The Community Trade Mark Regulations 2006, (SI 2006/1027) r. 12; Arnold, 142.

[122] PA s. 130(1), RDA s. 27(1), TMA s. 75.

[123] County Courts Act 1994 s. 15 gives the court power to hear 'any action'.

[124] CPR Rule 25A Practice Direction, para. 8.5.

[125] The most important is the power to revoke the patent as invalid: PA s. 72, s. 73. The Comptroller may also grant compulsory licences, settle the terms of licence of right, and award compensation to employees. See Reid, chs. 7 and 8.

[126] PA s. 61(3).   [127] CDPA s. 246.   [128] Cf. *Ferro Corporation v. Escol Products* [1990] *RPC* 651.

[129] PA s. 102(1).

[130] Such a stay was ordered in *Hawker Siddley Dynamics Engineering v. Real Time Developments* [1983] *RPC* 395. *Hawker* was subsequently described as 'exceptional' (*Gen Set v. Mosarc* [1985] *FSR* 302) and as a 'very unusual case' (*Ferro* [1990] *RPC* 651).

enable it to decide finally on those issues which are before it and, even then, resort may still be had to the High Court in order to obtain injunctions.[131]

7.2 WHICH TRIBUNALS CAN BE USED FOR WHICH RIGHTS?

Not all actions can be brought before all of the courts. In the following section we attempt to explain in which tribunals proceedings can be brought for infringement of the different intellectual property rights.

7.2.1 Copyright

Copyright (including publication right and database right), moral rights, and performers' rights cases[132] can be brought before the county court,[133] or the High Court (Chancery Division). Where a copyright issue is ancillary to a designs question it may also be considered in the Patents County Court or High Court (Patents Court).[134]

7.2.2 Patents

UK patent infringement cases can be brought before the Comptroller (if the parties consent);[135] the Patents County Court (there is no value ceiling), or the High Court (Patents Court).[136] Such cases cannot be brought before the ordinary county courts. Since issues of validity may be heard before the Comptroller, or opposition proceedings may be taking place at the European Patent Office,[137] a possibility exists that proceedings will be duplicated. With domestic proceedings, some attempt is made to avoid such duplication by a provision that prohibits issues of validity from being raised before the Comptroller pending the outcome of a decision in the Patents Court. As between UK infringement (or invalidity) proceedings and oppositions at the EPO, the court has a discretion to order a stay which it will exercise according to the facts of the case: often the problem is how to balance the competing issues of costs of duplicating proceedings (perhaps unnecessarily) against the delays involved in staying local proceedings and awaiting the outcome of opposition at the EPO.[138]

7.2.3 Supplementary Protection Certificates

Supplementary Protection Certificate cases can be brought before the High Court (Patents Court).[139]

---

[131] *Ferro*, ibid, 652. For background to reform, see above p. 347.   [132] Arnold, 142.

[133] *PSM v. Specialised Fastener*, note 108 above, 116; *McDonald v. Graham* [1994] *RPC* 407; *Pasterfield v. Denham* [1999] *FSR* 168 (copyright, moral rights, and passing-off).

[134] *PSM*, ibid, 116.   [135] PA s. 61(3).

[136] PA s. 130(1). On proposals for Community patents, see above, pp. 348–9.

[137] EPC Art. 99; *Memminger-Iro* [1992] *RPC* 210.

[138] Delays at the EPO have promoted a number of applications for stay. See *Glaxo v. Genentech* [2008] *EWCA Civ* 23; *Unilin Beheer v. Berry Floor* [2007] *EWCA Civ* 364 (CA); *Hunt Technology v. Don and Low* [2005] *EWHC* 376 (Ch); *General Hospital Corporation's European Patent (UK)* [2000] *FSR* 633 (granting the stay and setting out relevant factors); *Kimberly-Clark Worldwide v. Procter & Gamble* [2000] *FSR* 235, 250–1; *Unilever v. Frisa* [2000] *FSR* 708 (stay granted); *Minnesota Mining and Minerals v. Rennicks* [2000] *FSR* 727 (refusing stay). The Irish practice is to order a stay unless there are convincing reasons why it should be refused: *GD Searle & Co & Monsanto's Patent* [2002] *FSR* (24) 381. See, W. Cook, 'Staying alive!' [2001] *EIPR* 304.

[139] CPR Practice Direction, pt. 49E, para. 1.3 defines patents to include Supplementary Protection Certificates.

7.2.4 Plant variety rights

Plant variety cases, including Community plant variety infringement cases, can be brought before the county court or the High Court (Chancery Division). There is also a special procedure whereby the Plant Varieties and Seeds Office can operate as an arbiter.[140] Since issues of validity of a Community plant variety may only be determined by the Community Office, the national court is directed to assume that the right is valid or, if proceedings are pending at the Community Office, to stay the national proceedings pending the determination of the validity of the right.[141]

7.2.5 Registered designs

UK registered design cases can be brought before the Patents County Court (there is no value ceiling) or the High Court (Patents Court).[142] Such cases cannot be brought before the ordinary county courts.[143] Since issues of validity may be heard by the Comptroller[144] and the Patents Court,[145] provision must be made for one set of proceedings to be stayed pending the determination in the other tribunal.

7.2.6 Community Design Right

The Community Designs Regulation requires member states to designate Community design courts which are given jurisdiction to decide issues relating to infringement of Registered and Unregistered Community Design Rights.[146] The High Court, and any county court designated as a patents county court under section 287(1) of the Copyright, Designs and Patents Act 1988 have been designated as Community designs courts for Community design matters.[147] Issues of validity can be determined by the Office of Harmonization in the Internal Market.[148]

7.2.7 Unregistered design right

UK unregistered design right cases can be brought before any of four tribunals. Questions of subsistence, term, and first ownership can be heard by the Comptroller.[149] The Comptroller cannot decide infringement questions, which are determined by the county court, the Patents County Court (there is no value ceiling), or the High Court.

7.2.8 Passing off

Passing-off cases can be brought before the county court or the High Court (Chancery Division).[150] Where a passing-off claim is ancillary to a designs question it may also be considered in the Patents County Court.[151]

---

[140] PVA s. 43.

[141] CPVR Art. 20 (nullity), Art. 21 (cancellation), Art. 105 (national court to treat as valid), Art. 106(2) (stay where proceedings have been initiated).

[142] CPR Practice Direction, pt. 49E para. 1.3 Patent Court business to include proceedings under the RDA.

[143] RDA s. 27.   [144] RDA s. 11 (cancellation).   [145] RDA s. 20 (rectification).

[146] CDR Art. 80.

[147] The Community Designs (Designation of Community Design Courts) Regulations 2005 (SI 2005/696). See also The Community Designs Regulations 2005 (SI 2005/2339).

[148] CDR Art. 52.

[149] CDPA s. 246. The Comptroller can refer the issue to the High Court: CDPA s. 251. For procedure, see the Design Right (Proceedings before the Comptroller) Rules 1989 (SI 1989/1130). Patent agents have rights of audience: r. 6(1).

[150] *McCain International v. Country Fair Foods* [1981] *RPC* 69; *CHC Software Care v. Hopkins & Wood* [1993] *FSR* 241, 248 (malicious falsehood based on infringement of copyright should be heard in Chancery Division).

[151] *PSM v. Specialised Fastener* [1993] *FSR* 113, 117.

7.2.9 Trade marks

Trade mark infringement cases can be brought before the High Court (Chancery Division), the Patents County Court, or certain specified county courts.[152] Issues of validity may be heard before the Comptroller, or in the case of Community Marks by the OHIM, as well as in counterclaims in infringement actions.[153]

7.2.10 Breach of confidence

Breach of confidence cases can be brought before the county court or the High Court (Chancery Division) and privacy actions are frequently heard in the Queen's Bench Division.

8 EXPERTS

Given the technical and novel nature of the subject matter of intellectual property law, it is not surprising that the courts frequently rely on experts for a range of different matters.[154] Courts can hear expert evidence in relation to matters of which the court is ignorant and needs to be informed. These include questions such as the meaning of a word in a patent claim, whether a substantial part of a copyright work has been reproduced,[155] or the likelihood of confusion in a passing-off or trade mark action.[156] It should be noted that, while courts can hear expert evidence on a range of matters, ultimately it is for the court to decide the factual issue in hand.

The permission of the court is required to call an expert or to put an expert's report in evidence.[157] As the use of expert evidence increases the cost of intellectual property litigation,[158] where possible matters requiring expert evidence should be dealt with by a single expert. In patent matters directions can be made for the production of joint reports.[159] An expert's report should be addressed to the court and not to the party from whom the expert has received instructions. The courts have emphasized that experts should be impartial, that is, they should not assume the role of an advocate.[160]

---

[152] CTMR Art. 91; The Community Trade Mark Regulations 2006 (SI 2006/1027) r. 12. The position in relation to domestic trade marks was clarified by the High Court and County Court Jurisdiction (Amendment) Order 2005 (SI 2005/587).

[153] CTMR Arts 50–1.

[154] On the practice of courts in relation to expert evidence and technical terms see *American Cyanamid v. Ethicon* [1979] *RPC* 215, 252–3.

[155] *Newspaper Licensing Agency v. Marks & Spencer plc* [2003] *AC* 551. But cf. *Procter Gamble Co v. Reckitt Benckiser (UK) Ltd* [2007] *EWCA Civ* 936 (no need for expert evidence in most design cases).

[156] Cf. *Guccio Gucci SpA v. Paolo Gucci* [1991] *FSR* 89, 91 where Browne-Wilkinson V-C admitted expert evidence in a passing-off case as to whether consumers were likely to be deceived, even though this was the very question that the court itself had to determine and therefore one on which evidence is not normally admitted.

[157] The rules on experts are codified in the CPR Rule 35 Practice Direction. These are intended to limit the use of oral expert evidence to that which is 'reasonably required'. These seem to codify the duties and responsibilities of experts identified in *The Ikarian Reefer* [1993] *FSR* 563.

[158] The need for experts is reduced by specialist courts such as the Patents Court and Patents County Court and by the use of scientific advisers. In order to avoid delays, patent judges require that the parties supply a scientific primer prior to trial. Moreover, CPR Part 49E Practice Direction specifies that where certain claims are to be made, that the parties set out the relevant matters in detail.

[159] CPR Part 49E Practice Direction.   [160] *Cantor Fitzgerald International v. Tradition* [2000] *RPC* 95.

9 JURISDICTIONAL ISSUES AND CONFLICTS OF LAW

Given the nature of intellectual property it should come as no surprise that many intellectual property actions have a transnational dimension.[161] For example, the claimant may be domiciled in country A and the defendant in country B. In these circumstances, it is necessary to decide whether the action should be brought in country A or B. More complex questions arise where the infringement occurs in a number of countries. This would be the case, for example, where the defendant manufactures infringing goods in country C and an importer sells them in country D. In these cases a claimant may wish to sue both infringers in a single action. Even more complicated scenarios arise, for example, where copyright infringement takes place on the internet.[162] Where disputes cross national boundaries, a number of questions arise. Here we focus on whether a court has jurisdiction to hear a matter, the type of law that should be applied, and the situations where foreign judgments will be recognized and enforced. A number of considerations arise in answering these questions: the convenience and efficiency of litigation; the impact on national sovereignty; the desirability of allowing litigants to choose the jurisdiction most favourable to their claim (forum shopping);[163] and national interests in attracting legal business.[164]

9.1 JURISDICTION

The question whether a court has jurisdiction to hear a matter where the infringement or breach of an intellectual property right crosses national boundaries depends on the situation in hand.[165]

9.1.1 Under the Brussels Regulation

The question whether a British court has jurisdiction over a matter is largely governed by the 'Brussels Regulation' (often also referred to as the 'Judgments Regulation').[166] The basic rule of the Regulation is that a person domiciled in a member state should be sued in the courts of that

---

[161] See Fawcett and Torremans; Wadlow (1998); I. Karet, 'Intellectual Property Litigation: Jurisdiction in Europe' (1998) 3 IPQ 317.

[162] Fawcett and Torremans, 236–7.   [163] Ibid, 198–201.

[164] The most controversial example of foreign courts offering extensive relief has been the Dutch kort geding procedure in which, following a speedy hearing of both parties, the judge determines appropriate relief on the basis of forecasting the outcome in full court procedure. See J. Brinkhof, 'Summary Proceedings and Other Provisional Measures in Connection with Patent Infringements' (1993) 24 IIC 762. For suggestions for reform see P. Torremans, 'Exclusive jurisdiction and cross-border IP (patent) infringement' [2007] EIPR 195.

[165] There has been discussion of a draft international convention on jurisdiction, the Hague Conference on Private International Law. Following that initiative, specific work has been undertaken towards resolving the specific intellectual property related issues. For an early analysis, see, Symposium, 'Constructing International Intellectual Property Law: The Role of National Courts' (2002) 77 Chicago–Kent Law Review 991, setting out the Hague draft at 1015; see especially J. Ginsburg and R. Dreyfuss, 'Draft Convention on Jurisdiction and Recognition of Judgments in Intellectual Property Matters', at 1065 ff. For further developments see the Project by the American Law Institute (and the Munich Max Planck Institute), Intellectual Property: Principles Governing Jurisdiction, Choice of Law, and Judgments in Transnational Disputes.

[166] EC Regulation 44/2001. This replaces the 1968 Brussels Convention, which in turn came into force in England on 1 Jan. 1987. Jurisdiction can be challenged according to CPR r. 11.

state (*actor sequitur forum rei*).[167] Consequently, a British copyright owner must normally bring an action against a French infringer in French courts: the domicile of the claimant and the familiarity of the court with the relevant law being largely irrelevant.[168] As Jacob J put it, in footballing terms the claimant must 'play away'.[169] There are five qualifications to this basic rule which need to be noted.[170]

(i)   Where the matter involves a tort, a claimant *may* bring an action in the place where the harmful event occurred:[171] Article 5(3).

(ii) Where there are a number of defendants, an action may be brought in the country where any one of the defendants is domiciled: Article 6(1).

(iii) An action can be brought in a country other than that of the defendant's domicile if both parties agree: Article 23.[172]

(iv) In proceedings concerned with the registration or validity of patents, trade mark, designs, or other similar rights required to be deposited or registered, the courts of that state have exclusive jurisdiction: Article 22(4).[173]

(v)   Different rules apply in relation to preliminary measures: Article 31.

We consider each of these exceptions in turn.

First, as regards 'tort', an action may be brought in the place where the harmful event occurred. This exception to the defendant's domicile rule could be of wide application in the field of intellectual property since most infringements of intellectual property are regarded as tortious. Doubts may exist, however, in relation to breach of confidence and the action relating to undisclosed private information.[174] Where the action does relate to a tort, the key question will be where the harmful event occurred.[175] One problem concerns whether, in the case of use on a web site, the event takes place in every country from which the site can be accessed. If so, the opportunities for forum shopping are dramatic. An alternative possibility is to limit

---

[167] Regulation 44/2001, Art. 2 (formerly Brussels Convention Art. 2). Domicile is determined under national law: Brussels Convention Art. 52. On the problems of knowing where a person is 'domiciled' see Wadlow (1998), 283.

[168] This has worried some of the UK judiciary. In *Coin Controls*, note 33 above Laddie J was concerned that as a result English courts might have to decide 'questions of foreign law as well as factual issues relating to the pronunciation and meaning of similar words spoken in other languages'. See also *Pearce v. Ove Arup* [1977] FSR 641.

[169] *Mecklermedia v. DC Congress* [1997] FSR 627, 633.

[170] Which are to be narrowly construed: see *Athanasios Kalfelis v. Bankhaus Schroeder*, Case 189/87 [1988] ECR 5565.

[171] Regulation, Art. 5(3) (formerly Brussels Convention Art. 5(3)).

[172] Formerly Brussels Convention, Art. 17. See, e.g. *Kitechnology v. Unicor Plastmaschinen* [1995] FSR 765, 774.

[173] Formerly Brussels Convention, Art. 16(4). See Wadlow (1998) 104ff.; 112ff.

[174] On what is a 'tort' see *Kalfelis*, note 170 above (all actions which seek to establish the liability of a defendant and which are not related to contract within the meaning of Art. 5(1)). The breadth of this statement is hard to reconcile with other parts of *Kalfelis* that seemed to exclude a claim for unjust enrichment from Art. 5(3). In matters of contract, jurisdiction is given to the courts of the place of performance of the obligation. It has been suggested that breach of confidence is not within Art. 5(3). But a more persuasive view is that where the action is based in equity, the decision as to whether to treat it as relating to a tort, unjust enrichment, or contract for the purposes of private international law should involve asking which category has the closest similarity to the circumstances of case case: on this see *Rickshaw Investments and Another v. Nicolai Baron von Uexkull* [2006] *Singapore Court Appeal* 39; see Wadlow (1998), 173–4; Wadlow [2008] *EIPR* 269.

[175] Regulation, Art. 5(3) (formerly Brussels Convention Art. 5(3)). On the place where the 'harmful event occurred', see *Bier v. Mines de Potasse d'Alsace*, Case 21/76 [1976] *ECR* 1735; *Shevill/Presse Alliance SA*, Case 68/93 [1995] *ECR* I–415. See Fawcett and Torremans, 154 ff.; Wadlow (1998), 90–6.

the place where the harmful event occurs to those jurisdictions which are targeted by the web site (as evidenced through e.g. references to particular currencies).[176] Such an approach has proved attractive to courts when determining substantive questions of liability in relation to 'e-commerce.'[177]

Second, the Regulation states that co-defendants may be sued in the country where one of them is domiciled.[178] In practice, this seemingly straightforward provision has been construed very narrowly indeed in the context of infringements of intellectual property rights. The ECJ has held that the provision is only applicable where a multiplicity of hearings based on the domicile of the defendant would present the possibility of contradictory judgments. In the context of a claim relating to infringement of a series of national patents brought against multiple defendants from the same corporate group (marketing the same product in Belgium, Germany, the UK, and elsewhere), the ECJ held that the Dutch court did not have jurisdiction to determine claims against non-Dutch co-defendants for infringements that took place outside the Netherlands.[179] The reason for this was said to be that the co-defendants were alleged to infringe different national laws, so there could be no possibility of contradictory judgments. The reasoning, it should be observed, applies beyond the field of patents to all national intellectual property rights.[180] The ECJ's judgment has reaped almost universal criticism, with the majority of commentators supporting the view that, at the very least, where an action is brought against the coordinator of the infringements, joinder of foreign participants is sensible in terms of 'procedural economy'.[181] Moreover, while it is strictly true that a patent application under the EPC results in a series of national patents, any rational commentator would rightly be puzzled by different conclusions from different national courts which were faced with the same patent and the same alleged infringement.

The third and fourth exceptions concern the situation where the parties have selected a forum (Article 23),[182] or the action concerns the registration or validity of patents, trade mark,

---

[176] See *Bonnier Media v. Smith* [2002] *ETMR* (86) 1050 (OH, CS) (where the defendant owned the domain name business.am.com and the claimant, owner of the UK trade mark for business.am, brought an action for infringement in Scotland (where the claimant sold a newspaper under the name 'business.A.M.') but, as there was doubt about the domicile of the defendant (the choices being Mauritius, England, or Greece), the Scottish Court found it had jurisdiction based on where the harmful event occurred. Lord Drummond Young held that a web site was to be regarded as having its delictual effect in all countries where its impact was 'significant' (para. 19). On the facts, a harmful event occurred in Scotland because the defendant's acts were aimed at the claimant's business centred in Scotland and were intended to have their main effect in Scotland.)

[177] See pp. 150–1 (discussing when a copy of a copyright work is 'issued' to the public) and pp. 918–19 (discussing where a trade mark is used).

[178] See *Kalfelis*, Case 189/87 [1988] *ECR* 5565.

[179] *Roche v. Primus*, Case C–539/03 [2006] *ECR* I–6535 (ECJ, 1st Ch). Effectively following *Fort Dodge Animal Health v. Akzo Nobel NV* [1998] *FSR* 222. *Pearce v. Ove Arup* [1997] *FSR* 641; *Coin Controls* [1997] *FSR* 660 (joinder of actions relating to UK, German, and Spanish patents) must now be regarded as suspect.

[180] Torremans, 'Exclusive Jurisdiction and Cross-Border IP (Patent) Infringement', 198.

[181] The so-called 'spider in the web' analysis adopted by the Dutch court in *Expandable Grafts Partnership v. Boston Scientific BV* [1999] *FSR* 352 (Court of Appeal of the Hague). A. Briggs, 'Jurisdiction over Defences and Connected Claims' (2006) *LMCLJ* 447, 450, 451 ('the merits in a patent dispute will often involve complex technical investigation; and the sense in requiring eight different patent courts to be seised with concurrent actions is elusive…infringement actions will now take an age to resolve; and the outcome is very unsatisfactory'); Torremans, ibid, 201 ('to exclude any possibility for consolidated jurisdiction in such cases appears undesirable and counterproductive'); A. Kur, 'A Farewell to Cross-Border Injunctions?' (2006) 37 *IIC* 844, 851 (predicting 'more litigation with a greater risk of diverging judgments, and…an increase in costs').

[182] The parties, however, cannot override the impact of Art 22(4) by agreement. But note the possible impact of the Hague Convention on Choice of Court Agreements (2005), available from <http://www.hcch.net>, discussed in Kur, 'A Farewell' at 852.

designs, or other similar rights required to be deposited or registered (Article 22(4)). In these cases the jurisdiction is *exclusive*: there is no question alternative jurisdictions. If a court of a contracting state is presented with a *claim* which is 'principally concerned' with a matter over which the courts of another contracting state have exclusive jurisdiction, it should decline jurisdiction.[183] While it should be relatively easy to determine whether the parties have a formal agreement governing the choice of jurisdiction (Article 23), it is more difficult to determine when Article 22(4) applies.[184]

Article 22 (4) applies to the registration or validity of patents, trade marks, designs, or other similar rights required to be deposited or registered. The phrase 'other similar rights' refers to other registrable rights such as plant varieties, Supplementary Protection Certificates, and utility models. As such, it does not apply where the intellectual property right is unregistered, as with copyright, unregistered design right, or passing-off.[185] Article 22(4) only applies to proceedings concerning the 'validity' of such rights.[186] Although in certain circumstances it is clear that an issue relating to a registered right does not concern validity (e.g. where the dispute is over ownership),[187] in many situations the matter is less clear. For example, in an action for infringement of a patent or design registration,[188] one of the most common 'defences' is that the registration is invalid. The problem here is that, while questions of validity and infringement are technically distinct, in British intellectual property law they are inextricably linked.[189]

The question whether an action is 'concerned with the registration or validity of patents, trade marks designs, or other similar rights' is a crucial one.[190] In *GAT v. Luk Lamellen*, the ECJ provided a very broad reading of the provision.[191] The case concerned whether a German court had jurisdiction to hear an action between two German companies in which one alleged that the other had infringed its French patents. In effect, the ECJ held that the German court lacked jurisdiction (since issues of validity had been raised before the Düsseldorf court). The ECJ stated that Article 16(4) was applicable 'whatever the form of proceedings in which the issue of a patent's validity is raised, be it by way of an action or a plea in objection, at the time the case is brought or at a later stage in the proceedings'.[192] The decision seems to suggest that a Court seised with jurisdiction must divest itself as soon as a defendant pleads a defence of invalidity.[193]

---

[183] For discussion of the meaning of 'claim' and an argument that it is distinguishable from the 'issues' in that it should concern the claimant's action, not the defendant's response, see Wadlow (1998), 183–4.

[184] See, e.g. *Coin Controls* [1997] *FSR* 660.　　　　[185] *Pearce v. Ove Arup* [1997] *FSR* 641.

[186] Torremans, 'Exclusive Jurisdiction and Cross-Border IP (Patent) Infringement', 199 (discussing different language versions and arguing that the term 'concerned with' should be read as 'having as their object').

[187] *Ferdinand Duijnstee v. Lodewijk Goderbauer*, Case 288/82 [1985] 1 *CMLR* 220.

[188] There will be less of a problem with trade marks, where invalidity is less frequently a defence, and issues of validity have less impact on the scope of rights: cf. *Prudential Assurance Co v. Prudential Insurance Co of America* [2003] *ETMR* (69) 858, 867 (para. 21).

[189] Nowhere is this more apparent than in the so-called *Gillette*' defence. See pp. 568–9.

[190] On the policy of Art. 16(4) see *Duijnstee*, Case 288/82 [1985] 1 *CMLR* 220, 227 (Rozes AG), 235 (ECJ).

[191] Case C–4/03 [2006] *ECR* I–6509 (ECJ, 1st Ch).

[192] Ibid, (para 25). See *Fort Dodge* [1998] *FSR* 222, 244 where Lord Woolf MR said that 'when there is a bona fide challenge to the validity of a United Kingdom patent, any proceedings for infringement must in English eyes be "concerned with" the validity of the patent'.

[193] Briggs, 'Jurisdiction over Defences and Connected Claims', 450, 451 (noting that the ECJ had said that such an event was unacceptable in *Preservatrice Foncière TIARD Compagnie d'Assurances v. Netherlands*, Case C–266/01 [2003] *ECR* I–4867).

There are a number of problems with the *GAT v LuK* ruling, the most obvious being that the same issues of patent validity might have to be simultaneously litigated in a number of countries with consequent costs and inconvenience.[194]

The fifth possible exception to the golden rule of the Brussels Regulation that a defendant should be sued in their state of domicile relates to 'provisional measures'. More specifically, Article 31 states that an application may be made to the courts of a contracting state for provisional measures (including protective measures that are available under the law of that state), even if under the Brussels Regulation the courts of another contracting state have jurisdiction over the substance of the matter. On one interpretation, this means that claimants can choose the forum in which they prefer to get an interim injunction, even if that court could not grant final relief. If this is correct, it means that forum shopping is possible at the interim stage.[195]

As the first two exceptions to the rule that an action be brought in the domicile of the defendant give rise to *alternative* jurisdictions, they enable claimants to choose the forum. The possibility of alternative jurisdictions creates the problem that simultaneous proceedings might produce inconsistent judgments. Consequently, the Brussels Regulation contains provisions which deal with pending actions (*lis pendens*). These provide that, where a court of a contracting state is presented with a claim (e.g. on the basis of domicile) which has already been commenced elsewhere (e.g. on the basis of harm), the later action should be stayed. More specifically, Article 27 states that where a later court is presented with *the same cause of action* between the *same parties* that court *must* decline jurisdiction.[196] In addition, a further provision gives the court a discretion to stay proceedings if it is presented with an action which is 'related' to one that is already being heard in the courts of another contracting state. This discretion only arises where the actions are 'related', that is, where they are so closely connected that it is expedient that the actions be tried together to avoid the risk of irreconcilable judgments.[197] In exercising the discretion, the court will take into account

---

[194] For earlier expression of the view that patent infringement actions should not be consolidated see *Plastus v. 3M*, [1995] *RPC* 438, 447 (patent infringement cases should be heard by a court situated in the country where the public will have to pay the higher prices if infringement is found to exist).

[195] The decision in *Fort Dodge* [1998] *FSR* 222, 246, that Art. 24 of the Convention (now Art. 31 of the Regulation) did not justify provisional proceedings being heard in the Netherlands for infringement of a UK patent because no final relief could be given in Dutch courts, is inconsistent with holdings of the ECJ in *Van Uden Maritime BV v. Kommanditgesellschaft in Firma Deco-Line*, Case C–391/95 [1998] *ECR* I–7091 (where preliminary measures were available in a Dutch court despite the existence of an arbitration clause depriving such a court of jurisdiction on the substantive issue).

[196] Brussels Regulation, Article 27 (formerly Brussels Convention, Art. 21). See, e.g. *Molins v. G. D. SpA* [2000] 1 *WLR* 1741 (deciding where proceedings were first started). An action for infringement of a trade mark is not the 'same action' as an action for passing off: *Mecklermedia* [1997] *FSR* 627, 637. While a wholly-owned subsidiary might be regarded as the 'same party', a mere licensee will not: ibid. If a French tribunal is considering opposition to registration of A's mark X on the basis of B's mark Y, and B commences an action in the UK against A for infringement of B's mark Y (registered in the UK) by use of X, and there is no issue as to the validity of B's mark Y, must the UK tribunal stay proceedings? See *Prudential v. Prudential of America* [2003] *ETMR* (69) 858, 867 (para. 47).

[197] On the approach to this, see *Sarrio v. Kuwait Investment Authority* [1999] *AC* 32; *Research in Motion (UK) Ltd v. Visto Corp* [2008] *EWCA Civ* 153 (rejecting mechanical approach). In *Mecklermedia*, ibid, an action brought by a defendant for infringement of a German registered trade mark ('Internet World') against the claimant's licensee was held not to be 'related' to an action for passing off by the claimant in relation to its goodwill in the same words in England. But an action brought in England by the claimant to English copyright in a film against a person also claiming to be the owner was related to an action by a third party in France relating to ownership of copyright in the same film everywhere except England: *ABCKO Music Records v. Jodorowski* [2003] *ECDR* (3) 13.

the domicile of the defendant, the applicable law, and whether any UK action will need to be decided in any case.[198]

9.1.2 Where the Brussels Regulation is not applicable

The Brussels Regulation applies where a person is domiciled in a contracting state. This is the case even if the claimant is domiciled outside the EC,[199] the right is granted by a state outside the EC, or the infringing acts took place outside of EC/EFTA territories. If the defendant is domiciled in the United Kingdom and a claim relates to infringement of American copyright by acts in the USA, the Regulation will apply and the UK court must accept jurisdiction. The Regulation will not necessarily apply where the defendant is not domiciled in a contracting state. Thus, if US citizen A was resident but not domiciled in the United Kingdom, and claimant B argued that the court should take jurisdiction over A for infringement of B's American copyright by acts in the USA, it seems that the traditional UK rules would apply.[200]

The traditional British rules on jurisdiction were long understood to preclude an action based on infringement of foreign intellectual property rights.[201] However, in light of the Court of Appeal decision in *Pearce v. Ove Arup Parnership* it seems that English courts might now accept jurisdiction in these situations. In this case, the Court of Appeal said that existing case law provided no assistance 'on the question whether an action for alleged infringement of a foreign copyright by acts done outside the United Kingdom, in a case where the existence and validity of the right is not in issue, is justiciable in an English court'.[202] However, the court might decline jurisdiction on the ground that a UK hearing is not 'convenient' under the principle of *forum non conveniens*.[203]

9.1.3 Community rights

Special rules exist on the allocation of jurisdiction in relation to ownership of European patents[204] and more generally for community rights (such as the Community Trade Mark, Design and Plant Variety Rights). For example, Article 90 of the Community Trade Mark Regulation incorporates the Brussels Regulation in modified form.[205] The basic rule of the Brussels Regulation is maintained, *viz.* that a person should sue in the jurisdiction where the defendant is domiciled. This is extended to those who are not domiciled but who have an 'establishment' in the jurisdiction. The Community Trade Mark Regulation also modifies the application of the Brussels Regulation by excluding Article 4, thereby conferring

---

[198] *ABCKO Music*, ibid.

[199] *Société Group Josi Reinsurance Company SA v. Compagnie d'Assurances Universal General Insurance Company*, Case C–412/98 (13 Jul. 2000) (an insurance case).

[200] Similarly, if a British claimant wanted to bring an action against a US company alleging infringement of copyright in the UK, the UK court might consider serving a claim form outside the jurisdiction. In contrast with the situation where jurisdiction exists under the Brussels Regulation, leave of the court is required to serve a claim from outside the jurisdiction. The claim must fall within one of the 'gateways' under the CPR r. 6.20. On the circumstances in which the service of proceedings out of the jurisdiction will be permitted see *Beecham Group v. Norton Healthcare* [1997] *FSR* 81; Fawcett and Torremans, 25–6.

[201] See Fawcett and Torremans, 279–90.   [202] [1999] *FSR* 524, 557.

[203] *Spiliada Maritime Corp. v. Cansulex* [1987] *AC* 460. See Fawcett and Torremans, 267.

[204] Protocol on Jurisdiction and the Recognition of Decisions in respect to the Right to the Grant of a European Patent, 1973. Art. 4 allocates jurisdiction to the courts of the contracting state whose law determines the right. In EPC Art. 60, this is the law of the state in which the employee is mainly employed.

[205] CTMR Art. 93; Council Regulation (EC) 6/2002 on Community Design Art. 82 applies very similar rules. Rather oddly, the CPVR bases its rules on the Lugano Convention. For problems, see Wadlow (1998), 276; Fawcett and Torremans, 357 ff.

jurisdiction on the Community Trade Mark Courts over defendants domiciled outside of contracting states (rather than applying national rules). If the defendant is not domiciled in the Community, the action should be brought where the claimant is domiciled. Where neither party is domiciled nor established in the Community, the action should be brought in the place where the Community Trade Mark Office is situated (i.e. Alicante). These rules are mandatory and applied in strict sequence. As a result, there is a reduced possibility of there being competing alternative jurisdictions and hence less scope for forum shopping. However, despite the strict scheme, Article 93(5) of the Community Trade Mark Regulation also allocates jurisdiction based on the place of infringement. If a claimant uses this forum, relief is territorially limited. Consequently, this route is less attractive than an action brought in the state of the defendant's domicile.[206] Moreover, Article 6 of the Brussels Convention is maintained, so that an action can also be brought against a co-defendant in a court other than the court where they are domiciled. Because the applicable right is a Community one, the limitation imposed to the applicability of the Article by the ECJ in *Roche* is inapplicable.

Because the Community systems for registered trade marks and designs co-exist beside harmonized national laws, provision is also made for dealing with simultaneous proceedings, and successive actions.[207] These require the latter court to stay proceedings pending the determination of the earlier one, or, if judgment has been given, to follow suit. Nevertheless, the detail of these rules is more complex. In *Prudential Assurance Co. v. Prudential Insurance Co. of America,* the Court of Appeal held that the claimant was not prevented from bringing an infringement action in England based on infringement of its Community Trade Marks PRU or PRUDENTIAL by the defendant's use of PRUMERICA, merely because the claimant had been unsuccessful when opposing a national registration of PRUMERICA in opposition proceedings before the French Trade Marks Registry, even though those proceedings had been unsuccessfully appealed.[208] While Article 105(2) of the CTMR requires the court to reject an action for infringement 'if a final judgment on the merits has been given on the same cause of action and between the same parties on the basis of an identical national trade mark valid for identical goods or services', the Court of Appeal found that the English action did not concern an 'identical trade mark': the French action related to the validity of PRUMERICA whereas the English one dealt with infringement of PRUDENTIAL.[209] This seems a rather formalistic way of applying Article 90.

9.2 APPLICABLE LAW

Once the court accepts it has jurisdiction, the next issue to determine is the law that applies. With the abolition of the so-called 'double actionability' rule in determining whether a tort is actionable,[210] the law to apply is usually that of the country for which protection is claimed (*lex protectionis*),[211] which will usually be where the infringement took place (*lex loci delicti*).[212]

---

[206] Wadlow (1998), 287–8.   [207] CTMR Art. 105, CDR Art. 95.   [208] [2003] *ETMR* (69) 858.

[209] Ibid, para. 39 (Chadwick LJ).

[210] Private International Law (Miscellaneous Provisions) Act 1995, s. 10.

[211] It has been argued that Berne Convention, Art. 5(2) contains international harmonization of the rule on the applicable law, namely that it should be the law of the country 'where protection is claimed'. However, there is dispute as to whether this wording implies the *lex fori* or *lex loci delicti*. For a discussion in the context of broadcasting, see Makeen, *Copyright in the Global Information Society* (2000), 185–92.

[212] Breach of confidence is probably not a 'tort' for these purposes, and defamation (and hence injurious falsehood) are not subject to the reform: Private International Law (Miscellaneous Provisions) Act 1995, s. 13. See Wadlow (1998), 342 ff.

For example, if a claimant brings an action in an English court against a defendant domiciled in the United Kingdom, alleging infringement of their Dutch copyright by acts in the Netherlands, the applicable law would be Dutch copyright law.[213] This is both the place where the act occurred and the law from which protection is claimed. Occasionally these places will differ, as where a person in the Netherlands authorizes an infringement in the United Kingdom: in such circumstances the governing law should be UK law. The 'universally acknowledged principle' that the *lex protectionis* is the applicable law in the case of non-contractual actions relating to intellectual property rights is to become a rule of European law, following the enactment of the so-called Rome II Regulation (which comes into force on 11 January 2009).[214] Parties are not allowed to agree that a different law should apply.[215]

While the law to apply is normally that of the country where the tort occurred, in certain cases, the law to be applied is determined by special rules. For example, disputes about the ownership of European patents for employee inventions are determined by the law of the state in which the employee is mainly employed.[216] Where the right infringed is a Community right, such as a Community Trade Mark, the relevant law is that of the Regulation concerned. However, where the Regulations do not apply, the relevant law is the law of the country in which the act of infringement took place.[217]

9.3 RECOGNITION OF JUDGMENTS

Where intellectual property matters cross jurisdictional boundaries, questions often arise about the recognition and enforcement of foreign judgments. This is largely governed by the Brussels Regulation. The general policy of the Regulation is that there should be free movement of judgments. This means that once a court has assumed jurisdiction over a matter, any determinations it makes should be recognized and, if necessary, enforced in other member states. So, for example, if a Dutch court held that a British-domiciled co-defendant infringed the Dutch claimant's copyright, then the order of that court should be enforced by English courts. The procedure for recognition is straightforward. The judgment must first be registered and then notice is served on the person subject to it.[218]

The requirement that a court of a contracting state automatically recognizes judgments from other contracting states is qualified in a number of ways.[219] The most important is that, where the originating court assumed jurisdiction in breach of Article 22, then recognition must be refused. Thus, if a Dutch court ordered the revocation of a British patent, UK courts would not have to recognize the judgment since it was made in respect of a claim principally concerned with validity. However, as the scope of Article 22(4) is unclear it will be difficult to predict whether a British court would be able to refuse to recognize the Dutch judgment that

---

[213] *Pearce v. Ove Arup* [1997] *FSR* 641, 542.

[214] Regulation (EC) No 864/2007 of the European Parliament and of the Council of 11 July 2007 on the law applicable to non-contractual obligations (Rome II) OJ L 199/40 (31 July 2007), Art 8. The concept of intellectual property is defined, by example, in recital 21. A different principle applies to cases of 'unfair competition': see Arts 6, 4. The Regulation does not regulate the rules on applicable law for violations of privacy and rights relating to personality, including defamation: Art 1(2)(g). For consideration of breach of confidence, see Wadlow [2008] *EIPR* 309.

[215] Rome II, Art 8(3) (excluding the operation of Art. 14). It is unclear whether, in the absence of expert testimony on the relevant applicable law, a court can choose to assume that the law of another country is the same as its own.

[216] EPC Art. 60.   [217] Rome II, Art 8(2); CTMR Art. 97; CDR Art. 88.   [218] CJJA s. 4.

[219] Brussels Convention Art. 27(1) and Art. 28. See also *Renault v. Maxicar*, Case C–38/98 [2000] *ECR* I–2973.

a UK patent had been infringed. This is especially the case if the Dutch court formed a conclusion as to the validity of the patent.[220] A court can also refuse to enforce a judgment which is irreconcilable with a judgment given in a dispute between the same parties in the state in which recognition is sought.[221] In *Italian Leather SpA v. WECO Polstermobel GmbH,* an Italian court ordered an interim injunction preventing the use of the claimant's mark LONGLIFE by a German defendant, whereas the German court had refused interim relief. When the German court was asked to enforce the Italian judgment in Germany, the court sought the advice of the ECJ as to whether the judgments were irreconcilable, and if so the consequences. The ECJ was clear that the judgments were irreconcilable, and that the German court was obliged to enforce its own rather than the Italian decision.[222]

9.4 PROPOSED EUROPEAN PATENT LITIGATION AGREEMENT OR EUROPEAN PATENT COURT

As we saw earlier, work has been going on for over a decade to establish a European Patent Court.[223] This has been undertaken under the auspices of the European Patent Litigation Agreement (EPLA), a voluntary agreement which needs to be ratified by member states of the European Patent Organisation for it to become operational. The main aim of the Agreement is to establish a central patent court to deal with matters of infringement. In part the desire to establish a central patent court grew out of the fact that, under existing law, patent infringement actions are heard in the national courts where the patent was allegedly infringed. This has created concerns about forum shopping, duplication of costs, and the resulting fragmentation of the internal market. To remedy these problems the European Patent Litigation Agreement proposes to establish a new international organization called the 'European Patent Judiciary' which will consist of the European Patent Court (comprising the Court of First Instance, the Court of Appeal, and a Registry) and an Administrative Committee. The draft Agreement contains rules on evidence and procedure, as well as how the decisions of the European Patent Judiciary are to take effect in member states of the European Union. Towards the end of 2007 these initiatives were being developed by the European Commission in a real political push to resolve the European patent litigation problem once and for all. One of the main stumbling blocks is the constitutional validity of the proposed Agreement, as well as the ongoing tension between the EPO and the Community.

10 ALTERNATIVE DISPUTE RESOLUTION

In many areas of law, the cost and hassle of litigation has encouraged the growth of mechanisms such as arbitration and mediation for resolving disputes outside the court framework. While alternative dispute resolution is used in many areas of law, it has not been widely used to

---

[220] Wadlow (1998), 539.   [221] Brussels, Art. 27(3).   [222] Case C–80/00 [2002] *ECR* I–4995.
[223] See above at p. 351.

resolve disputes concerning intellectual property.[224] It seems, however, that this may change.[225] One reason for this is that the Woolf Reforms offer increased incentives for parties to avoid using the court system.[226] The Civil Procedure Rules, for example, promote the use of alternative dispute resolution by providing that proceedings may be stayed pending alternative dispute resolution[227] and by allowing courts to make early neutral evaluations of the merits of the case (thus prompting settlement).[228] Another reason is that alternative dispute resolution is becoming more widely used by international bodies. A notable example is the recent extension of the WIPO Arbitration and Mediation Centre (established in 1994), to include compulsory arbitration under the Internet Corporation for Assigned Names and Numbers' (ICANN) Uniform Domain Name Dispute Resolution Policy.[229] ICANN's policy and procedures are incorporated into a subscriber's internet registration agreement, so that if a person makes a complaint to ICANN,[230] the registrant is required to submit to a mandatory administrative proceeding.[231] Proceedings only begin where a complainant asserts that (i) the domain name is identical or confusingly similar to a trade mark or service mark in which the complainant has rights (including 'common law' marks);[232] (ii) the registrant has no rights or legitimate interests in respect of the domain name;[233] and (iii) the domain name has been registered and

---

[224] See K. Mackie, 'ADR in Europe: Lessons from a Classic US Case: *IBM v. Fujitsu*' [1992] *EIPR* 183. M. Doherty and I. Griffiths, 'Costs in the Copyright Tribunal: Negotiate or Litigate?' [1999] *EIPR* 370. Research from the USA demonstrates that the likelihood of patent disputes being settled often depends on whether smaller or larger firms are involved: see Lanjouw and Schankerman, *Enforcing Intellectual Property Rights*, NBER Working Paper No. 1656 (Dec. 2001).

[225] See W. Kingston, 'The Case for Compulsory Arbitration: Empirical Evidence' [200] *EIPR* 154 and [1995] *European Journal of Law and Economics* 85.

[226] See J. Lambert, 'IP Litigation after Woolf' [1999] *EIPR* 427 and [2003] *EIPR* 406.

[227] CPR r. 26.4. Note also the cooling-off period for friendly settlement of opposition proceedings in the OHIM and the UK Registry.

[228] Prior to the *American Cyanamid* decision, note 154 above, litigants used to treat the grant of interlocutory relief as equivalent to such an early neutral evaluation. See pp. 1101–2.

[229] Approved by ICANN, 24 Oct. 1999. See <http://www.icann.org>. For introductory overviews to the rules and case law, see L. Helfer and G. Dinwoodie, 'Designing Non-National Systens: The Case of the Uniform Dispute Resolution Policy' [2001] 43 *William & Mary Law Review* 141; A. Engel, 'International Domain Disputes: Rules and Practice of the UDRP' [2003] *EIPR* 351; W. Bettink, 'Domain Name Dispute Resolution Under the UDRP: The First Two Years' [2002] *EIPR* 344; D. Hancock, 'An Assessment of ICANN's Mandatory Uniform Dispute Resolution Policy in Resolving Disputes Over Domain Names' (2001) *Journal of Information, Law and Technology*; A. Kur, *UDRP Study*, at <http://www.intellecprop.mpg.de ww/de/pub/bibliothek.cfm>

[230] Although WIPO provides 58 per cent of dispute resolution services, three other institutions, including NAF (National Arbitration Forum) (which has 34 per cent), also offer dispute resolution services.

[231] It applies to generic top-level domain names (e.g. .com, .net, .org). WIPO also provides dispute resolution services for 33 country-code domains. Nominet operates a similar policy for '.uk' domains, including '.co.uk' and '.plc.uk': see <http://www.nic.uk> and, for commentary, Osbourne and Willoughby (2001) 6(3) *Communications Law* 95–6. Nominet does not control some other second level domains, such as '.ac.uk' and '.gov.uk.'

[232] *Bennett Coleman & Co. v. Steven Lalwani* [2000] WIPO D2000–0014/15 (panelist, Prof. Cornish). It was on the basis of common law rights that author Jeanette Winterson was held entitled to jeanettewinterson.com: *Winterson v. Hogarth* [2000] *ETMR* 783. See also *Madonna Ciccone v. Dan Parisi* [2000] WIPO D2000–0847, and more recently *Pierce Brosnan v. Network Operations Center* [2003] WIPO D2003–0519; *Bridget Riley v. so so domains* [2003] D 2003–0600. Note the *Final Report of the WIPO Internet Domain Name Process* paras. 169–204 rejecting the extension of the UDRP to embrace personality rights (other than to the extent to which they are protected as trade marks, either through registration or at common law). For comment, see B. Isaac, 'Personal Names and the UDRP: A Warning to Authors and Celebrities' (2001) 12 *Ent LR* 43.

[233] While the respondent's ownership of the same mark will usually do, in at least one case the panel ignored this (a Tunisian registration for Madonna): *Madonna Ciccone*, ibid.

is being used in bad faith.[234] In the proceedings, the complainant must prove each of these three elements. The cost of the proceedings is borne by the complainant. The remedies available are the cancellation of the domain name or the transfer of the domain name registration to the complainant.

By early 2008, over 21,000 cases had been referred for resolution under the UDRP (the vast majority resulting in transfer of ownership of the domain name to the applicant) (12,234 to WIPO and 9,914 to the National Arbitration Forum).[235] Many tens of thousands of cases have also been heard under other specific policies. Perhaps surprisingly, the number of disputes has not diminished since the launch of the UDRP, suggesting this is not merely a transitional phenomenon. Many of the new complaints relate to registrations of variants of trade marks, which registrants hope to use to earn advertising revenue from 'click-through programs'. This practice, known as 'typo squatting', is regarded as falling within the scope of the policy.[236]

[234] Most obviously, by selling it at a price exceeding the registration cost.

[235] The success rate for applicants using WIPO panels is 82 per cent.

[236] See, e.g. the NAF decision of July 2007 in *Webkinz v. Texas International Property Associates* (relating to Webkinzz.com, Webkniz.com, and Weblinz.com).

48

CIVIL AND CRIMINAL REMEDIES

CHAPTER CONTENTS

In this chapter we look at the civil and criminal remedies that a claimant may obtain for violation of intellectual property rights. We begin by looking at the civil relief available before trial: interim injunctions and prevention of imports. We then go on to look at the civil remedies available at full trial: final injunction, delivery-up or destruction, damages, and account of profits. Next we look at the various criminal remedies that may be avail for a claimant. Finally, we look at some of the proposed reforms that may impact on intellectual property remedies.

1 INTERIM INJUNCTIONS

Although on most occasions a tribunal will make an order for a speedy trial, in many situations there may be a significant delay between the time when a rights holder discovers that their rights are being infringed and the time when the matter is heard at trial. In order to ensure that the rights holder's interests are not undermined during this period, provision exists for interim orders, sometimes referred to as 'interlocutory' relief. The most important of these is the interim injunction.[1] This is a court order to stay events pending a final determination. An interim injunction will only be granted if the matter is urgent or this is otherwise desirable

---

[1] CPR r. 25.1(a). *Ex parte* orders might be granted in appropriate cases, and these include injunctions against persons unknown: *Bloomsbury Publishing Ltd v. News Group Newspapers Ltd.* [2003] FSR 360. On the international and regional norms relating to *ex parte* orders, see TRIPS, Art 50(2) and Enforcement Directive, Art. 9. For the norms relating to interim injunctions, see TRIPS, Art 50(6) and Enforcement Directive, Art 8. On occasion, the ECJ has interpreted TRIPs, Art 50, in order to guide member states and avoid the emergence of divergent interpretations within the EC: see *Hermès v FHT* Case C–53/96 [1998] *ECR* I–3603 (interpreting the notion of 'provisional measure' for the purposes of TRIPS Art 50); *Dior and Others,* Joined Cases C–300/98 and

in the interests of justice.[2] Given the urgency, applications for interim injunctions are disposed of quickly. They are usually considered on the basis of sworn written evidence which has not been subjected to cross-examination. Consequently, there is a danger that the tribunal's interim decision will differ from the result after matters are fully aired at trial.[3] It is therefore important that, when a court grants interim relief, it does so in a way which minimizes the irreparable consequences to the parties that might arise from a hasty view of the merits of the case. In these circumstances, the courts must reconcile the conflicting demands of speed and correctness in decision making. On one hand, there is a desire to examine the issues as fully as possible to ensure that the interim decision is accurate. At the same time, since the evidence is necessarily inadequate, there is a desire to ignore the legal issues and focus instead on minimizing the injustices that will ensue from incorrect preliminary intervention.[4]

Applications for interim injunctions in the UK are usually assessed according to the approach set out by the House of Lords in *American Cyanamid v. Ethicon*.[5] It is important to note that some recent cases have been reluctant to follow these guidelines strictly. It should also be noted that the Human Rights Act 1998 has modified the approach that must be taken in cases which concern freedom of expression.

In *American Cyanamid* the claimant sought interim relief to restrain the defendant from infringing the claimant's patent for surgical sutures. The defendant company planned to argue at trial either that it had not infringed or that the claimant's patent was invalid. When considering whether to grant interim relief, the High Court and the Court of Appeal said that the key question was whether the claimant had established a strong prima facie case.[6] Overturning this approach, the House of Lords rejected previous suggestions to the effect that a prima facie case must be established before a court could grant interim relief. Instead, the Lords laid down a reduced threshold requirement: for a court to be vested with the discretion to grant an interim injunction, it was necessary for a claimant to establish that there was '*a serious question to be tried*'.[7] Once a claimant has established this, the House of Lords said that the court should then go on to consider a series of other matters. First, it should compare the possible effects of granting and not granting the injunction on the defendant and the claimant. Lord Diplock explained that this involved deciding whether the claimant's or defendant's interests were capable of being satisfied solely by financial means. If these considerations do not produce a clear indication of the best course of action, the court should consider the 'balance of convenience'. In turn, if there is no clear result from considering the balance of convenience, the court should look at the merits of the case.

The goal of *American Cyanamid* was to reduce the number of mini-trials that occurred at the interim stage and thereby speed up the process of granting interim relief. In turn, it was thought that this would avoid duplication and produce a more efficient judicial process. Nevertheless, the approach set out in *American Cyanamid* has been criticized on a number of

---

C–392/98 [2000] *ECR* I–11307; *Schieving-Nijstad vof and Others v. Robert Groeneveld*, Case C–89/99 (ECJ, Full chamber) [2001] *ECR* I–5851.

[2] CPR r. 25.2(2)(b). [3] *Films Rover International v. Cannon Film Cells* [1986] 3 *All ER* 772, 780.

[4] See J. Leubsdorf, 'The Standard for Preliminary Injunctions' (1978) 91 *Harvard Law Review* 525.

[5] *American Cyanamid v. Ethicon* [1975] *AC* 396.

[6] In the High Court, Graham J found that the claimant had established a strong *prima facie* case and that the balance of convenience favoured the grant of interim relief. In the Court of Appeal, where argument had lasted for two weeks, Russell LJ held that no prima facie case of infringement had been proved, and so did not go on to consider the balance of convenience: [1974] *FSR* 312.

[7] *American Cyanamid* [1975] *AC* 396, 407–9.

grounds.[8] First, it has been said that Lord Diplock failed to deal adequately with, or refer to, a number of existing House of Lords authorities which are difficult to reconcile with *American Cyanamid*.[9] Second, while the approach set out in *American Cyanamid* is supposed to be of general application, it is inflexible, especially where a claimant's case is strong.[10] Many commentators have noted that it gives rise to the perverse situation in which the availability of interim injunctive relief to a claimant with an open-and-shut case turns on questions of convenience. Third, it is also said that it is unrealistic to expect judges not to take into account obvious conclusions as to the merits of the case.[11] Fourth, ignoring the merits and basing the availability of relief on matters such as the adequacy of (including the ability to pay) damages sometimes favours established businesses unduly, at the expense of newer, financially weaker, competitors.[12] Fifth, the refusal to consider the merits overlooks the value to litigants of the kind of 'mini-trials' which took place prior to *American Cyanamid*. More specifically, it has been argued that, because interim relief required the merits of the parties' cases to be considered, the interim decision was often treated as indicating the final outcome of the case. In effect, interim relief was used as a cheap method of litigation and as a way of avoiding long-drawn-out final trials.[13]

For some time it was unclear whether the principles in *American Cyanamid* applied to all proceedings for interim injunctions against infringement of intellectual property rights.[14] In particular, it was suggested that *American Cyanamid* did not apply in passing-off cases.[15] This view was later rejected, and in *County Sound v. Ocean Sound* the Court of Appeal argued that the principles were well suited to a passing-off action.[16] In addition, after some doubts,[17] the *American Cyanamid* approach has also been applied to cases of breach of confidence and restraint of trade cases.[18]

While the general applicability of *American Cyanamid* to intellectual property cases has been accepted, a number of exceptions have been introduced to the *American Cyanamid* approach.[19] The most important of these was the recognition of the principle that, where the interim decision would be determinative of the action, the approach in *American Cyanamid* is not appropriate. This is because the problem which *American Cyanamid* seeks to redress, namely to minimize the harm when a preliminary decision turns out to have been incorrectly made, does not arise where the preliminary decision is going to be the only decision. In these cases the court should simply do its best to resolve the legal issues.[20]

[8] See P. Prescott, 'American Cyanamid v. Ethicon' (1975) 91 *LQR* 168.

[9] For example, *Stratford & Son v. Lindley* [1965] AC 269 (a requirement of a 'sufficient prima facie case') and *Hoffmann-La Roche v. Secretary of State for Trade and Industry* [1975] AC 295 (requiring a strong prima facie case).

[10] *Rubycliff v. Plastic Engineers* [1986] RPC 573, 583 (*American Cyanamid* recognized to be not 'a very popular decision, being rather formal and rigid'). A. Gore, 'Interlocutory Injunctions: A Final Judgment?' (1975) 38 *MLR* 672, 678. See also Leubsdorf, 'The Standard for Preliminary Injunctions', 540.

[11] *Alfred Dunhill v. Sunoptic* [1979] FSR 337, 372–3.   [12] Prescott, 'American Cyanamid'.

[13] Ibid at 169; Leubsdorf, 'The Standard for Preliminary Injunctions', 540.

[14] K. Gray, 'Interlocutory Injunctions Since *American Cyanamid*' (1981) 40 *CLJ* 307.

[15] *Newsweek v. BBC* [1978] RPC 441.   [16] *County Sound v. Ocean Sound* [1991] FSR 367, 372.

[17] *Fellowes v. Fisher* [1976] QB 122; *Office Overload v. Gunn* [1977] FSR 39, 43 (Lord Denning MR) (cf. Bridge LJ at 44).

[18] *Lawrence David v. Ashton* [1991] 1 All ER 385.

[19] A. Burrows, *Remedies for Torts and Breach of Contract* (1994) 432 ff.; *MacMillan Magazines v. RCN Publishing* [1998] FSR 9, 12.

[20] The general principle was established in *NWL v. Woods* [1979] 3 All ER 614. It has frequently been applied in intellectual property disputes: *Athletes Foot v. Cobra Sports* [1980] RPC 343 (where little dispute on facts and

In general, however, when considering the grant of interim relief the court should operate in two stages. First, the court should decide whether there is a serious question to be tried (or in freedom of expression cases, whether the claimant is likely to succeed). Second, if the court decides that this threshold has been passed, it should then go on to consider whether to exercise its discretion to grant an injunction. That is, it will consider whether it would be fair to grant interim relief.[21] We now examine these two stages in more detail.

1.1 SERIOUS QUESTION TO BE TRIED

The first task confronting a claimant seeking an interim injunction is that they must satisfy the threshold requirement that there is a serious question to be tried. In other words if the evidence reveals that the claimant does not have any real prospect of succeeding in their claim for a permanent injunction at trial, the court will not even consider the balance of convenience.[22] According to Lord Diplock, when determining whether there is a serious question to be tried the court should only investigate whether a known cause for action is revealed. In so doing it should take account of points of law that necessarily arise on the facts that are revealed at the interlocutory stage. However, the courts should not embark upon mini-trials of disputed questions of fact or difficult questions of law.

A claimant might fail to demonstrate that there is a serious question to be tried for a number of reasons. In some cases, a claimant might fail to show a realistic cause for action. For example, if a straightforward reading of existing case law suggests that no cause of action exists, the application will be refused.[23] Moreover, if the claimant's case is dependent on overseas authorities,[24] or the extension of an existing action to new circumstances, the court might take the view that this falls before the threshold.[25] In contrast, where the existing authorities are merely unclear, the court will usually decline to resolve the dispute and treat the situation as raising a serious question to be tried.

More commonly, a court will find that there is no arguable case because the affidavit evidence is so insubstantial that it is clear that the case will fail. In many cases, particularly in passing-off and trade mark cases, the court will be able to make a fairly confident judgment on factual matters such as whether a name or get-up is not distinctive,[26] and whether there is a misrepresentation[27] or a likelihood of confusion.[28] The fact that a reasonable person could

---

law not difficult); *Mirage Studios v. Counter-feat Clothing* [1991] *FSR* 145, 154; *Barnsley Brewery Company v. RBNB* [1997] *FSR* 462.

[21] *United Biscuits v. Burton Biscuits* [1992] *FSR* 14, 15.

[22] Although Lord Diplock equated this test with a claimant showing that the claim is not 'frivolous or vexatious', subsequent courts have preferred to ignore that rephrasing which carries with it the jurisprudential baggage of the striking-out action: see *Mothercare v. Robson Books* [1979] *FSR* 466, 472–4; *Consorzio del Proscuitto Di Parma v. Marks & Spencer* [1991] *RPC* 351, 372 per Nourse LJ; cf. Leggatt LJ, 383.

[23] *Mail Newspapers v. Insert Media* [1987] *RPC* 521, 529–30; *Schulke & Mayr v. Alkapharm* [1999] *FSR* 161, 166.

[24] *Lyngstrad v. Anabas Products* [1977] *FSR* 62, 68 (Oliver LJ).

[25] *Times Newspapers v. MGN* [1993] *EMLR* 443; *Marcus Publishing v. Hutton Wild Communications* [1990] *RPC* 576, 584.

[26] *Marcus Publishing,* ibid, 583; *County Sound* [1991] *FSR* 367, 372.

[27] *Consorzio Parma v. Marks & Spencer* [1991] *RPC* 351, 372 (describing this as a question of 'law depending on evidence already before the court which is of its nature complete and incontrovertible').

[28] *Morning Star Co-operative Society v. Express Newspapers* [1979] *FSR* 113 (no serious question that *Daily Star* would be confused with *Morning Star* to be tried).

bring the action in good faith will not matter if it is so hopeless a case that no interim relief should be available.[29] Having said that, a case may be 'thin' but arguable.[30] Another reason why the court might hold that there is no serious question to be tried is because the defendant has a very strong prospect of a successful defence.[31] It should be noted that the question is not whether there is an arguable defence: if the defence is only arguable, there is a serious question to be tried.[32]

An important qualification to the threshold for injunctive relief set out in *American Cyanamid* was introduced by section 12(3) of the Human Rights Act 1998. This provides that, where a court is considering whether to grant relief which might affect the exercise of the Convention right to freedom of expression, no relief should be granted that restrains publication prior to trial 'unless the court is satisfied that the applicant is likely to establish that publication should not be allowed'. The court is further instructed to take account of the extent to which the material has or is about to become available to the public. The courts also take account of whether it would be in the public interest for the material to be published.[33] The impact that section 12(3) has on the grant of injunctive relief was considered by the House of Lords in *Cream Holdings v Banerjee*.[34] This case arose when Banerjee, a disgruntled ex-employee of Cream Holdings (a company which ran nightclubs, dance parties, and similar events), sent confidential information about corruption within Cream to Echo (who publish the *Daily Post* and the *Liverpool Echo*). After some of the information was published, Cream sought injunctive relief to prevent further publication of the confidential information. The Court of Appeal, like the judge at first instance, granted an interlocutory injunction preventing the defendants from publishing the information until the matter could be heard at trial. The defendants appealed to the House of Lords, where the the key question before the Lords was the meaning of 'likely' in section 12(3).

Delivering the judgment of the House, Lord Nicholls began by explaining that when the Human Rights Bill was under consideration, concerns arose about the adverse impact that it might have on freedom of the press. In particular, the fear arose that 'applying the conventional *American Cyanamid* approach, orders imposing prior restraint on newspapers might readily be granted by the courts to preserve the status quo until trial whenever applicants claimed that a threatened publication would infringe their rights under Article 8 [ECHR]. Section 12(3) was enacted to allay these fears.'[35] Confirming that the test to be applied under section 12(3) was more stringent than that under *American Cyanamid*, the Lords said that the principal purpose of section 12(3) 'was to buttress the protection afforded to freedom of speech at the interlocutory stage. It sought to do so by setting a higher threshold for the grant of interlocutory injunctions against the media than the *American Cyanamid* guideline of a "serious question to be tried" or a "real prospect" of success at the trial'.[36]

---

[29] *Mothercare v. Robson Books* [1979] FSR 466, 472–3.

[30] *Metric Resources Corporation v. Leasemetrix* [1979] FSR 571, 580.

[31] *News Group Newspapers v. Rocket Records* [1981] FSR 89, 102.

[32] Cf. *Warner v. Channel Four* [1994] EMLR 1.

[33] Human Rights Act 1998, s. 12(4). The tribunal is also instructed to take into account 'any relevant privacy code'. See J. Griffiths and T. Lewis, 'The Human Rights Act 1998, s. 12: Press Freedom over Privacy?' [1999] *Ent LR* 361; Rogers and Tomlinson [2003] *European Human Rights Law Review* 36.

[34] *Cream Holdings v. Banerjee* [2005] AC 253.   [35] Ibid, para 15.

[36] Ibid. Affirming *Douglas v. Hello!* [2005] EMLR 199, 246–8, paras. 145–53 (Keene LJ); at 242–4, paras. 134–6 (Sedley LJ) (it requires the courts to look at the merits of the case and not merely apply the *American Cyanamid* test); *Theakston v. MGN* [2002] EMLR 398, 407 (discernibly more rigorous requirement); *Mills v. News Group Newspapers* [2001] EMLR 957, 966 (para. 18); Kerly, paras. 17.78 ff. Cf *Imutran v. Uncaged*

Lord Nicholls then went on to consider whether, as the *Echo* had argued, 'likely' in section 12(3) bears the meaning of 'more likely than not' or 'probably'. Rejecting this construction, Lord Nicholls said that such an interpretation would not be workable in practice, not least because it would 'produce results Parliament cannot have intended'. The reason for this is that if the *Echo*'s reading of section 12(3) was applied it would mean that the courts would not be able to make a restraining order to prevent disclosure in the period when the court was deciding whether the claim would succeed at trial: something which was very important in relation to confidential information which cannot be protected once it is published. Another situation in which Lord Nicholls felt that the court should be able to exercise their discretion was where the consequences of the disclosure would be extremely serious, 'such as a grave risk of personal injury to a particular person'.[37] Practical considerations such as these led Lord Nicholls to say 'that "likely" in section 12(3) cannot have been intended to mean "more likely than not" in all situations'.[38] He went on to say:

Section 12(3) makes the likelihood of success at the trial an essential element in the court's consideration of whether to make an interim order. But in order to achieve the necessary flexibility the degree of likelihood of success at the trial needed to satisfy section 12(3) must depend on the circumstances. There can be no single, rigid standard governing all applications for interim restraint orders. Rather, on its proper construction the effect of section 12(3) is that the court is not to make an interim restraint order unless satisfied the applicant's prospects of success at the trial are sufficiently favourable to justify such an order being made in the particular circumstances of the case.[39]

This in turn gave rise to a further question: what degree of likelihood makes the prospects of success 'sufficiently favourable'? In answering this, Lord Nicholls said that

the general approach should be that courts will be exceedingly slow to make interim restraint orders where the applicant has not satisfied the court he will probably ('more likely than not') succeed at the trial. In general, that should be the threshold an applicant must cross before the court embarks on exercising its discretion, duly taking into account the relevant jurisprudence on Article 10 and any countervailing Convention rights. But there will be cases where it is necessary for a court to depart from this general approach and a lesser degree of likelihood will suffice as a prerequisite.[40]

This would include, for example, situations where 'the potential adverse consequences of disclosure are particularly grave, or where a short-lived injunction is needed to enable the court to hear and give proper consideration to an application for interim relief pending the trial or any relevant appeal'. From this basis, the Lords allowed the appeal and discharged the injunction. The approach in *Cream* has been held by the Court of Appeal to be applicable in all cases of comparative advertising.[41]

1.2 IS IT FAIR THAT THE INJUNCTION BE GRANTED?

Where the claimant passes the threshold and establishes that there is a serious question to be tried, the court will then consider whether to exercise its discretion to grant an injunction. That is, it will consider whether it would be fair to grant interim relief. The aim is to reduce

Campaigns [2001] *EMLR* 21, para. 17 (Sir Andrew Morritt V-C denied that the two tests would produce different results).

[37] *Cream Holdings* [2005] *AC* 253, [2004] *UKHL* 44, para 18.   [38] Ibid, para 20.
[39] Ibid, para 22.
[40] Ibid.   [41] *Boehringer v. Vetplus* [2007] *FSR* (29) 737.

the chances of the provisional decision providing an unjust result.[42] In so doing, the court will focus on three factors: whether damages would be an adequate remedy, the balance of convenience, and the relative strength of the parties' cases.[43] In some situations, such as with copyright, the relevant statute may provide that, where a party has acted innocently, the remedies will be limited to damages.[44]

1.2.1 Adequacy of damages

The first matter to be considered is the adequacy of damages. Here, the court asks whether, if an injunction were refused, would damages awarded at full trial be a satisfactory remedy for the claimant? If damages are an adequate remedy for a claimant and the defendant is able to pay them, no relief should be granted.[45]

In considering whether damages would be an adequate remedy, the courts will consider whether the damage suffered by the claimant is reparable at all. That is, they ask whether the claimant's interest can be compensated by a financial remedy that may be granted at trial. If the damage is to a non-financial interest, such as privacy or personal reputation, it is highly unlikely that the claimant would be compensated for the loss in question. As a result, interim injunctions are less likely to be awarded in patent cases, compared with confidentiality or copyright cases where non-financial interests are often present.[46] In addition, if the claimant has been in the habit of licensing rights for royalties, it is likely that damages will be seen to be an adequate remedy.[47]

The courts also consider whether the defendant is likely to be able to pay such damages.[48] In general, the impact of this is that, the smaller a defendant's business, the more likely interim relief will be granted.[49] In some cases, in order to avoid unduly favouring rich claimants over poorer defendants, the courts have devised orders that allow a defendant to continue their allegedly infringing operations even where they cannot provide an undertaking. In these orders, the courts protect the claimant's rights by requiring the defendant to make payments into an account on a royalty-type basis.[50]

Where damages are not an adequate remedy, the courts will consider whether it is possible to formulate a cross-undertaking that compensates the defendant for any harm caused during the period when their activities were curtailed. If the cross-undertaking would be satisfactory, then an injunction should be granted. Usually the question is merely one of the adequacy

---

[42] *Barnsley Brewery Company* [1997] FSR 462, 472.

[43] In its initial formulation, Lord Diplock's speech appears to set out a series of matters to be considered sequentially, rather than a catalogue of factors—a matter criticized by Gore, 'Interlocutory Injunctions', 678. However, in a number of cases the latter approach has been preferred: see, e.g. *Fleming Fabrications v. Albion Cylinders* [1989] RPC 47, 56. Note that the 'adequacy of damages' issue is sometimes treated as part of the assessment of the balance of convenience. Indeed, Lord Diplock used the term 'balance of convenience' inconsistently in this respect. Nothing, however, appears to turn on the categorization.

[44] CDPA s. 233(2). Cf *Badge Sales v. PMS International Group* [2006] FSR 1 (despite limitation of final remedy available against innocent acquirers to damages, interim injunctive relief was granted).

[45] *Roussel-Uclaf v. Searle & Co.* [1977] FSR 125; *Baywatch Productions v. The Home Video Channel* [1997] FSR 22; *Weight Watchers (UK) v. Tesco Stores* (16 Apr. 2003).

[46] *Catnic v. Stressline* [1976] FSR 157.

[47] *Smith & Nephew v. 3M United Kingdom* [1983] RPC 92, 102. Cf. *Games Workshop v. Transworld Publishers* [1993] FSR 704, 714.

[48] *Dyrlund Smith v. Turbervill Smith* [1998] FSR 774.

[49] *Quantel v. Shima Seiki Europe* [1990] RPC 436 (no interim injunction in patent case where defendant gave bank guarantee of £2 million to cover damages).

[50] *Mirage v. Counter-feat* [1991] FSR 145, 154.

of damages, not of the claimant's ability to pay. The reason for this is that if there were any doubt as to the reliability of the cross-undertaking, the court might require the claimant to provide security. If the claimant acted promptly, the chances are that the cross-undertaking will be satisfactory and that the interim relief will be granted. (This is because money spent in preparations for trade is usually quantifiable.)[51] Moreover, pending trial the defendant can continue to trade in non-infringing ways (for example, by selling non-infringing items or selling goods under a different trade mark). This, however, will not be the case where timing is crucial to the defendant, for example, where the defendant is satisfying a short-term fashion or seasonal demand,[52] where a third-party competitor of the defendant is about to launch,[53] or where the defendant's whole business is in allegedly infringing goods.[54] If the defendant is already selling the allegedly infringing goods on the market, the cross-undertaking is liable to be inadequate. This is because it will be very difficult to quantify losses incurred from withdrawing from a (usually expanding) market.[55]

1.2.2 Balance of convenience

In deciding whether to grant an interim injunction, the court will consider the balance of convenience.[56] The facts that are taken into account will vary depending on the circumstances of the case. It has sometimes been suggested that the public interest should be taken into account in assessing the balance of convenience. For example, if granting injunctive relief might prevent the public having access to a life-saving drug, then such relief might be refused.[57] The court will also compare the likely impact that their decision will have on both parties. For example, in a case of alleged copying of a dress design, the Court of Appeal held that the risks to which the claimant was exposed were 'more dreadful' and their 'consequences more lasting and more irreparable'. As such, they granted an interim injunction.[58] In contrast, where there is only a remote risk of damage to the claimant, but the defendant would certainly suffer substantial unquantifiable damage, the balance of convenience will be against the grant of interim injunctive relief.[59] If the order would prevent the defendant from earning a living, it is more likely that the court will be reluctant to grant interim relief.[60]

Another factor often considered in the determination of the balance of convenience is whether the claimant brought the action promptly. If the claimant has delayed bringing the action, the court will usually refuse interim relief.[61] This is especially the case where, over the period where the claimant failed to act, the defendant spent a considerable amount of money, or put themselves at risk.[62] However, if the claimant can explain the delay or show that they acted diligently, the court is unlikely to treat this as a basis for refusing interim relief.[63] Another factor often considered in the determination of the balance of convenience is

---

[51] *Mothercare v. Robson Books* [1979] FSR 466, 475. Cf. *Polaroid v. Eastman Kodak* [1977] FSR 25, 35.

[52] *Aljose Fashions v. Alfred Young & Co.* [1978] FSR 364. Cf. *Monet of London v. Sybil Richards* [1978] FSR 368.

[53] *Silicon Graphics v. Indigo Graphic Systems* [1994] FSR 403, 418.

[54] *Mirage v. Counter-feat* [1991] FSR 145, 153.   [55] *Quantel* [1990] RPC 436.

[56] It has been said that the phrase is rather inept, and alternative phrases such as the 'balance of injustice' or 'prejudice' have sometimes been deployed.

[57] *Roussel-Uclaf* [1977] FSR 125, 131–2.   [58] *Monadress v. Bourne & Hollingsworth* [1981] FSR 118, 122.

[59] *John Walker v. Rothmans International* [1978] FSR 357, 363; *British Association of Aesthetic Plastic Surgeons v. Cambright* [1987] RPC 549; *John Wyeth v. Pharmachem* [1988] FSR 26, 33.

[60] *Raindrop Data Systems v. Systemics* [1988] FSR 354, 361.   [61] *Silicon Graphics* [1994] FSR 403.

[62] *Financial Times v. Evening Standard* [1991] FSR 7, 12–13 (delay of 11 days taken into account).

[63] *Mirage v. Counter-feat* [1991] FSR 145, 153 (three-month delay explained by claimant trying to enforce claim through trading standards authorities).

whether the defendant deliberately took a risk. If the defendant deliberately risked infringing, this might tip the balance of convenience in favour of an injunction.[64]

Where the factors are evenly balanced, Lord Diplock suggested that the best course is to preserve the status quo.[65] Subsequent cases have said that the status quo refers to the period preceding the issue of the 'statement of case' claiming a permanent injunction.[66] Thus, if a defendant is doing something they have not done before, all the injunction does is to postpone their activities;[67] if the injunction would stop them from continuing to do something they were already doing this would cause greater inconvenience. The courts have been careful to prevent the desire to preserve the status quo from being used tactically. In particular, they have been careful to ensure that a defendant cannot alter the status quo, for example by embarking on a high-risk strategy.[68]

1.2.3 The merits of the case

The third factor that the court will consider in deciding whether an interim injunction should be granted is the relative strength or merits of the parties' cases. According to the traditional reading of *American Cyanamid,* the court should only consider the merits of each party's case in the last resort. Applying the approach strictly, the courts have often refused to indicate which of the parties' cases they consider to be stronger, for fear that it might prejudice the ultimate outcome.[69]

While *American Cyanamid* suggests that the strength of the parties' cases should not be considered until this final stage, nonetheless in a number of cases the courts have been influenced by the merits of the claimant's case when considering factors such as the adequacy of damages and the balance of convenience.[70] This generated a growing feeling of unease that judges were not following *American Cyanamid.*[71] In *Series 5 Software* Laddie J criticized this trend, saying that he did 'not believe it is satisfactory to exercise the court's discretion to grant an interlocutory injunction by paying lip service to the guidance given in *American Cyanamid* while in practice applying different criteria'. Laddie J took the opportunity in *Series 5 Software* 'to look again at *American Cyanamid* to see what it decided'.[72] His primary concern was to consider the extent to which Lord Diplock's judgment prevents a court from considering the legal and factual merits of the case. Laddie J argued that Lord Diplock could not have been imposing the sea change attributed to him, given the fact that, in a subsequent decision, Lord Diplock himself said that to 'justify the grant of such a remedy the claimant must satisfy the court first that there is a strong prima-facie case'.[73] Laddie J argued that, when Lord Diplock said that the court should not consider the strength of the claimant's case, he

---

[64] *News Group v. Rocket* [1981] *FSR* 89, 107; *Elanco Products v. Mandops (Agrochemical Specialists)* [1979] *FSR* 46; *SmithKline Beecham plc v. Apotex Europe* (14 Feb. 2003) [2003] *EWCA Civ* 137 (para. 40).

[65] This has been referred to as a 'judicial last resort': *Barnsley Brewery Company* [1997] *FSR* 462.

[66] *Garden Cottage Foods v. Milk Marketing Board* [1983] 2 *All ER* 770, 774. But not always: *Dunhill v. Sunoptic* [1979] *FSR* 337, 376 (date may well vary in different cases).

[67] *Elanco Products* [1979] *FSR* 46.

[68] *Jian Tools for Sales Inc v. Roderick Manhattan Group Ltd* [1995] *FSR* 924, 943.

[69] *Sodastream v. Thorn Cascade* [1982] *RPC* 459, 467. For discussion of the prejudice argument, see Leubsdorf, 'The Standard for Preliminary Injunctions', 546–7.

[70] *Dunhill v. Sunoptic* [1979] *FSR* 337, 374; *County Sound* [1991] *FSR* 367, 372.

[71] Gray, 'Interlocutory Injunctions Since *American Cyanamid*', 338–9 refers to differences of appearance rather than substance.

[72] *Series 5 Software v. Clarke* [1996] 1 *All ER* 853; [1996] *FSR* 273 (the analysis appears to have been *obiter*).

[73] *Hoffmann-La Roche v. Sec State, Trade and Industry* [1975] *AC* 295, 360.

was merely referring to the 'mandatory initial hurdle'. Indeed, a close analysis of the factors which Lord Diplock thought were relevant suggested that even he would consider the strength of the case.[74] Laddie J therefore argued that the prospect of success was still a relevant factor when considering the balance of convenience. However, he did accept that Lord Diplock had intended that this should be conducted so as to avoid a mini-trial.

Laddie J's reformulation has met with a mixed reception. In *Barnsley Brewery Company v. RBNB*,[75] Robert Walker J signalled his approval, stating that while *Series 5* 'is sometimes regarded as surprising or even heretical', it provided a valuable reminder of the background to and basic message contained in *American Cyanamid*. However, other judges have ignored *Series 5*, preferring to stick to *American Cyanamid* and the acknowledged exceptions to it.[76] In *Guardian Media Groups v. Associated Newspapers*[77] the Court of Appeal said that the *American Cyanamid* principles had a degree of flexibility and:

do not prevent the court from giving proper weight to any clear view which the court can form at the time of the application for interim relief (and without the need for a mini-trial on copious affidavit evidence) as to the likely outcome at trial. That is particularly so when the grant or withholding of interim relief may influence the ultimate commercial outcome.

The better view appears to be that the strength of each case is a relevant factor for the court to take into account when it exercises its discretion. However, strength should only be considered where there is no credible dispute as to the evidence and it is clear that one party's case is likely to succeed.[78]

2 STOPPING IMPORTS

In many situations, the infringing products originate from other jurisdictions. In these circumstances, the claimant may try to prevent the infringement at its source. Alternatively, a claimant may try to intercept the infringing articles or materials at the point of import.[79] There are two legal mechanisms for stopping articles that infringe intellectual property rights at their point of import to the United Kingdom.[80] The most important of these are the European procedures specified in the Infringing Goods Regulation, as adopted by the Council in July 2003.[81] In 2006, using the European procedure then in place, over 130 million articles were confiscated, the bulk coming from China. The sorts of article seized included not just counterfeit clothes and perfume, and pirated CDs and DVDs, but potentially dangerous goods such as

---

[74] For example, Lord Diplock stated that if damages would satisfy a claimant no injunction should be granted 'however strong the plaintiff's claim'—implying that if damages were not adequate the strength of the claim was a relevant consideration.

[75] [1997] *FSR* 462, 472 (refusing injunction largely because claimant's case in passing-off, though not unarguable, was weak).

[76] *EMAP National Publications v. Security Publications* [1997] *FSR* 891; *Dyno-Rod v. Reeve* [1999] *FSR* 149, 151–2, 158–9.

[77] (20 Jan. 2000).   [78] *Intelsec Systems v. Grech-Cini* [1999] 4 *All ER* 11, 26.

[79] House of Commons Select Committee on Trade and Industry 8th Report (1998–9), *Trade Marks, Consumers and Fakes*, para. 102 (reporting 4,000 seizures between 1995 and 1997).

[80] TRIPS, Arts. 51 and 52 requires such measures.

[81] Council Regulation No. 1383/2003 which came into force in July 2004 (hereafter IGR) (replacing Council Regulation 3295/95 of 22 Dec. 1994 (as amended by Council Regulation 241/99 of 25 Jan. 1999).

medicines and electrical equipment.[82] The other set of procedures, which are now of limited scope, derives from domestic legislation.[83]

2.1 EUROPEAN PROCEDURE

The European Regulations[84] attempt to establish mechanisms which ensure that goods which infringe intellectual property rights, other than travellers' personal luggage,[85] can be retained by Customs authorities when they are introduced into or exported from the Community.[86] The Regulations define goods infringing intellectual property rights to cover 'counterfeit' goods infringing trade marks, 'pirated' goods infringing copyright and design rights, and goods which infringe patents, Supplementary Protection Certificates, plant varieties, PDOs, and PGIs.[87] The Regulations do not apply to parallel imports or over-runs.[88]

Provisions are made in the Infringing Goods Regulation for a pro-active intellectual-property-rights holder who gets wind of the fact that goods are going to be imported, to make an 'application for Customs action'. That is, the right holder can apply to the relevant Customs authorities designated by each member state (in the United Kingdom, HM Revenue and Customs—but the request can apply to authorities in other member states, too) to detain the goods, should they come into its hands.[89] As one would expect, right holders are required to describe the goods so that they can be 'readily recognised by the customs authorities' and to provide proof that they are the rights owner.[90] The applicants must accept liability towards the persons involved in the event that action is discontinued or goods are found to be non-infringing.[91] The Customs authorities must process the application by deciding whether the information is sufficient, determine the relevant 'action period', and forward details to the relevant offices. If the Customs office comes across goods which it suspects are infringing

---

[82] Commission Press Release IP/08/757 (19 May 2008).

[83] TMA s. 89; Trade Marks (Customs) Regulations 1994 (SI 1994/2625); CDPA s. 111.

[84] See generally O. Vrins and M. Schneider (eds), *Enforcement of Intellectual Property Rights through Border Measures: Law and Practice in the EU* (2006).

[85] IGR Art 3(3); Recital 11.

[86] In *The Polo/Lauren Co. LP v. PT Dwidua Langgeng Pratama International Freight Forwarders*, Case C–383/98 [2000] *ECR* I-2519 the ECJ interpreted Council Regulation 3295/94 as requiring EC customs authorities to seize counterfeit goods even though they were in transit between non-EEC countries (in this case T-shirts suspected of being counterfeits were being transported between Indonesia and Poland, via Austria), and the Court took the view that such legislation was justified under Art. 113 (now Art. 133 EC) because transit could affect the internal market 'as there is a risk that counterfeit goods placed under the external transit procedure may be fraudulently brought on to the Community market'.

[87] IGR., Art. 2. This further defines 'counterfeit goods', as goods which infringe registered trade marks where the trade mark used without consent is identical to or cannot be distinguished in its essential aspects from the registered mark; and which is used on the same type of goods; and 'pirated goods' as goods which are or embody copies made without the consent of the holder of the copyright or neighbouring rights or design right whether registered under national law or not.

[88] Ibid, Art. 4 (goods which have been manufactured with the right holder's consent but are placed in circulation without it, or which are manufactured or bear a trade mark 'under conditions other than those agreed with the holder of the right in question').

[89] Ibid, Art. 5. Apparently, in 2007 there were 10,000 such applications.

[90] Ibid, Art. 5(5). See *Commissioners of Customs and Excise v. Top High Development* [1998] *FSR* 464 (no reasonable grounds for seizure by customs authority where declarant had only applied for a trade mark and was not yet registered).

[91] Ibid, Art. 6. But fees and indemnities have been abandoned, to promote the use of these measures by SMEs. See, for early abolition of the fees in the UK, as of October 2003: Goods Infringing Intellectual Property Rights (Customs) Regulations 2003 (SI 2003/2316).

(within the decision) 'it shall suspend release of the goods or detain them'.[92] The office then informs the right holder and 'declarant or holder of the goods'. Right holders are given information necessary to assist them in establishing whether an intellectual property right has been infringed, including the opportunity to inspect the goods and to remove samples for analysis.[93]

Even if advance warning has not been given, but the relevant authority has sufficient grounds for suspecting that goods are infringing, the Regulation empowers the authority to prevent their transit temporarily.[94] The authority will attempt to contact the relevant intellectual-property-right holder, who must complete the standard 'application for Customs action' within three days.

The Customs office will not detain the goods indefinitely. Under the newly formulated Regulations, it seems that there are three possible scenarios which might ensue. First, the intellectual-property-right holder may take no further action. If so, the Customs office should release the goods after ten days. Second, the intellectual-property-right holder may commence an action for infringement in the relevant national tribunal. If this occurs, and the right holder informs the authority, detention of the goods can be continued pending the outcome of proceedings. However, since that may not be for some time, the owner of the goods has an option of seeking the release of the goods on condition that they provide an appropriate security. This option, it should be noted, is not available where the allegation is infringement of copyright, trade marks, PDO, or PGI. If the goods are found to be infringing at the substantive hearing, the competent authorities are empowered to destroy the goods and to take any measures which deprive the persons concerned of the economic benefits of the transaction.[95] Removing trade marks affixed to counterfeit goods is not normally regarded as sufficient.[96]

The third scenario is that the parties will agree to destruction of the goods without the need for proceedings. This new 'simplified procedure' for abandonment is optional for member states, and is only to be used by the Customs authorities if four conditions are met. First, the right holder must inform the authority within ten working days that the goods infringe intellectual property rights. Second, the authorities must have the written agreement of the 'declarant, the holder or the owner of the goods'. (If any object, the goods should not be destroyed.) Third, the right holder must agree. Fourth, before the goods are destroyed, samples must be kept as evidence, in case of further legal proceedings.

Concerns about the scope of the Infringing Goods Regulation, partly brought about by decisions of the European Court of Justice which limited its operation,[97] have led anti-counterfeiting bodies to call for reforms of the Regulation. While there is no formal process under way, it is an issue that may be on the reform agenda in the near future.

2.2 DOMESTIC PROCEDURE

A residual domestic procedure continues to coexist with the European Regulation, but does not apply to goods already in free circulation within the EEA. Under this procedure, copyright and trade mark owners may notify the Commissioners of HM Revenue and Customs that infringing goods, materials, or articles are about to be imported and request that this

---

[92] Ibid, Art. 9(1). If it fails to detect them, the authority is not liable to the right holder: Art. 19.
[93] Ibid, Art. 9(3).   [94] Ibid, Art. 4.   [95] Ibid, Art. 17.   [96] Ibid.
[97] *Class International BV v. Colgate-Palmolive Company* Case C–405/03 [2005] *ECR* I–8735 and *Montex Holdings Ltd v. Diesel SpA* Case C–281/05, (2006) *OJ C* 326/16.

be prohibited.[98] As regards copyright, the right only applies to printed copies of literary, dramatic, or musical works, or sound recordings, or film. As such, it does not cover things such as computer programs on disc or artistic works. Given that the copyright works covered by the domestic procedures fall within the scope of the EC Regulation (which pre-empts domestic procedures), its impact in this sphere is likely to be restricted to parallel imports and over-runs. As regards trade marks, the domestic procedure applies to all infringing goods, materials, or articles and so is broader in scope than the EC procedure. As with the EC procedure, the applicant must give certain information so that the Commissioners can establish that the applicant is the copyright or trade mark owner and that the goods (etc.) are infringing. The Commissioners may require an indemnity and security against any liability and expense which might accrue.[99] Once a notice is in force import of the goods is prohibited. If the Customs find such goods (other than for the private and domestic use of the person importing them), they will be seized and the owner informed.[100] The owner has one month to make a claim that the goods were not liable to seizure. If such notice is given the Commissioners are obliged to bring proceedings for 'condemnation' of the goods (either in the magistrates' court or the High Court).[101] If successful, the goods will usually be destroyed.[102]

3 FINAL INJUNCTION

A final or perpetual injunction is usually granted to intellectual-property-right owners who prove at trial that their rights have been infringed by the defendant.[103] A final injunction will order the defendant not to carry on with certain activities. As such, it is directed at future conduct, whereas financial remedies operate in relation to past acts. The injunction, being equitable in origin, is a discretionary remedy. This means that, while final injunctions are normally awarded, they are not granted automatically. Although the law of injunctions is a topic with implications that extend well beyond intellectual property rights, here we consider four specific issues.

3.1 GENERAL APPROACH

The question whether an injunction should be granted usually depends on the facts of the case.[104] Nevertheless, the courts have indicated a few of the circumstances where an injunction might be refused.[105] These include situations where the infringement is trivial, its value can be estimated

---

[98] CDPA s. 111; Copyright (Customs) Regulations 1989 (SI 1989/1178), amended by Copyright (EC Measures Relating to Pirated Goods and Abolition of Restrictions on the Import of Goods) Regulations 1995 (SI 1995/1445); TMA s. 89, s. 112; Trade Marks (Customs) Regulations 1994 (SI 1994/2625).

[99] CDPA s. 112.   [100] Customs and Excise Management Act 1979, Sched. 3, para. 1(2).

[101] Ibid, para. 8.   [102] CDPA s. 111(4); TMA s. 89(2).

[103] *Chiron v. Organon (No. 10)* [1995] *FSR* 325 (as a general rule a defendant who interferes with a proprietary right will be injuncted).

[104] *Proctor v. Bayley* (1889) 6 *RPC* 538, 541. In *LudlowMusic Inc. v. Williams (No. 2)* [2002] *FSR* 868, 896 an injunction was granted to prevent the making of future pressings of Williams' album, but not to sale of existing stocks.

[105] The leading authority is *Shelfer v. City of London* [1895] 1 *Ch* 287. Cf. CTMR Art. 98, which requires a Community trade mark court to grant an injunction 'unless there are special reasons for not doing so'. The notion of 'special reasons' was given a very narrow construction by the ECJ in *Nokia Corp. v. Joachim Wärdell*, Case C–316/05 (ECJ, 1st Ch.) [2007] 1 *CMLR* (37) 1167, the Court emphasizing the importance of uniformity

in financial terms and adequately compensated, and an injunction would be oppressive on the defendant;[106] where a claimant is only interested in money; where the claimant's action is vexatious; or where the infringing act is old and there is no future threat.[107] Moreover, in circumstances where licences of right are available to a defendant, injunctive relief will not normally be granted.[108] An injunction will not be refused simply because there is a public interest in widespread exploitation or dissemination of a particular product (such as a cure for HIV);[109] or the infringing material comprises only a small portion of the defendant's products.[110]

3.2 FORM OF INJUNCTION

It is normal practice to grant an injunction that corresponds to the rights that were infringed. For example, an injunction will usually be granted that restrains the defendant from infringing the patent in suit or restrains the defendant from passing off their goods as those of the claimant.[111] Such broadly worded relief is appropriate because 'claimants cannot be adequately protected by orders which are cabined or confined'.[112] Despite criticism that such vaguely worded relief is unfair to a defendant,[113] it has been stated by the Court of Appeal that the 'traditional form' of injunction sets out with as much clarity as the context admits what may not be done. This is because, while the wording of the order may look vague, the Patents Act and the claims form a context from which the specific meaning of the terms of the order can be understood.[114] Nevertheless, Aldous LJ has said that an order that simply restrained 'breach of confidence' would not be precise enough. Moreover, Aldous LJ reiterated that 'each case must be determined on its own facts and the discretion exercised accordingly'.

---

of remedial response in the context of a unitary Community-wide right. See also CDR Art. 89. Arts 11 and 12 of the Enforcement Directive 2004/48 might be interpreted as limiting the situations in which a national court may decline to grant injunctive relief to those where the 'person acted unintentionally and without negligence, if execution of the measures in question would cause him/her disproportionate harm and if pecuniary compensation to the injured party appears reasonably satisfactory.' For first impressions as to the impact (or absence thereof) of the Enforcement Directive see *Cantor Gaming v. Gameaccount Global Ltd* [2007] *EWHC* 1914 (Alexander QC) (sitting as Deputy Judge) (para 112).

[106] *Sterwin v. Brocades* [1979] *RPC* 481.

[107] *Raleigh v. Miller* (1949) 66 *RPC* 23; *Frayling Furniture v. Premier Upholstery* (5 Nov. 1999) (no injunction where infringement had taken place five years earlier apparently inadvertently and had not been repeated).

[108] RDA 1949, s. 11B(1)(a); PA s. 46(3)(c); CDPA s. 98(1)(a), s. 191K.

[109] *Chiron v. Organon (No. 10)* [1995] *FSR* 325. Cf. *Roussel Uclaf* [1977] *FSR* 125, 131.

[110] *Macmillan v. Reed* [1993] *FSR* 455; *Mawman v. Tegg* (1826) 2 *Russ* 385. Some flexibility here is regarded by many as desirable to prevent 'hold-outs', particularly by patent owners who do not manufacture products themselves and thus seek to maximise license fees: see M. Lemley & C. Shapiro, 'Patent Holdup and Royalty Stacking', 85 *Texas LR* 1991 (2007); S. Subramanian, 'Patent Trolls in Thickets' [2008] *EIPR* 182; *eBay Inc. v. MercExchange, LLC*, 126 *S. Ct.* 1837 (2006).

[111] Wadlow (2004), para. 10–37 ff.

[112] *Spectravest v. Aperknit* [1988] *FSR* 161, 174; *Aktiebolaget Volvo v. Heritage* [2000] *FSR* 253, 265–6.

[113] *Coflexip v. Stolt Comex Seaway* [1999] *FSR* 473, 476. Laddie J stated that, while the purpose of an injunction is to protect the claimant from further infringement, it is important that the order is also fair to the defendant. The standard approach did not always meet this objective. On the basis that most defendants are not untrustworthy but are respectable and honest traders, Laddie J said that a narrow injunction provided sufficient protection to the claimant. (He did acknowledge, however, that in the case of counterfeiting, usually involving infringement of copyright, trade marks, or passing-off, an injunction formulated in broader terms might be the only reasonable way of giving claimants the protection they need.) See also *Microsoft v. Plato Technology* [1999] *FSR* 834; [1999] *Masons Computer Law Reports* 370 (where the Court of Appeal declined to interfere with the narrow form of injunction granted); *Beautimatic v. Mitchell Pharmaceuticals* [2000] *FSR* 267, 284.

[114] *Coflexip* [1999] *FSR* 473.

Consequently, although the traditional form of injunction will often be appropriate, in some cases more narrowly couched orders will be required, depending on the right involved, the honesty of the defendant, and all other circumstances.[115]

3.3 SPRINGBOARD INJUNCTIONS

In the last few years, the courts have been asked to develop new forms of injunction on the grounds that it is 'just and convenient' to do so.[116] One such claim has been for injunctions which continue after the expiry of an intellectual property right (aka 'springboard relief'). Although the idea of a post-expiry injunction may seem strange, given the policy of fixing the duration of many intellectual property rights, such orders have been thought to be desirable in cases where infringing acts that have already taken place (during the term of the intellectual property right) have given a defendant a head start in the process of marketing legitimate goods in the post-expiry period. In *Dyson Appliances v. Hoover (No. 2)*, Judge Fysh QC in the Patents Court granted such an injunction against Hoover for a period of twelve months following expiry of Dyson's patent.[117] The case concerned the patent for Dyson's well-known 'bagless' vacuum cleaner. During the patent's life, Hoover had developed a cyclone-based vacuum cleaner and had been granted clearances by certifying authorities. In October 2000 the vacuum cleaner was held to infringe Dyson's patent. Dyson argued that it would be unfair if Hoover were able to relaunch the model when Dyson's patent expired in June 2001. The Court agreed. Having noted that the remedies prescribed in section 61 of the Patents Act were 'without prejudice to any other jurisdiction of the court', the judge held that such an order was 'just' and 'convenient' because it sought to place the claimant in the position it would have been in if its rights had been respected (and incidentally it saved the tribunal from having to calculate damages relating to such acts). The judge, however, did indicate that the scope of the injunction should be circumscribed to the model developed during the patent term, and to a period corresponding to the time which it had taken Hoover to develop the model and get the relevant clearances.

3.4 LONG-ARM INJUNCTIONS

The courts have proved less amenable to the idea of injunctions covering foreign territories (so-called 'long-arm relief'). In *Kirin-Amgen Inc v. Transkaryotic Therapies Inc (No. 2)*,[118] the claimant owned a patent relating to the production of erythropoietin (EPO) (using genetic engineering) which the defendant had been held to infringe. Although appeals were pending, the claimant sought to amend the relief it was seeking to include an order restraining the

---

[115] In *Department of Culture, Arts & Leisure v. Automobile Association* (29 Jan. 2001) Laddie J granted an injunction in the traditional form, but made comments to the effect that it would be an abuse of process if the claimant brought contempt proceedings based on alleged infringements which had not been established at trial.

[116] Supreme Court Act 1981, s. 37.

[117] [2001] *RPC* (27) 544. The case is remarkable, not least for its inclination to develop English law in line with Dutch practice, and the account taken of the ECJ's decision that the Dutch post-expiry remedy was legitimate in *Generics BV v. Smith Kline & French Laboratories* [1997] *ECR* I–3929. The ground for this jurisdiction had been laid by Jacob J in *Union Carbide v. BP Chemicals* [1998] *FSR* 1, 6. Such relief is also considered in *Kirin-Amgen Inc. v. Transkaryotic Therapies Inc. (No. 2)* [2002] *RPC* (3) 203, 222–3.

[118] Ibid, 216.

defendant from using outside the UK 'UK-derived cells' which could produce EPO. Refusing leave to amend in this way, Neuberger J held that the court could not 'at least in the absence of very exceptional circumstances, grant an injunction in a patent infringement case, restraining a person's activities abroad, even if those activities were only possible as a result of an infringement in this jurisdiction'. This view was informed by the terms of the statutory tort defined in section 60 of the Patents Act 1977, as well as a clear sense that acts occurring abroad were matters for foreign law. In another case, the Court of Session refused to grant an injunction relating to infringement of unregistered design right that extended beyond Scotland to cover England and Wales.[119]

One of the most important attributes of Community rights (Trade Marks, Designs, etc.) is that they result in a single action in a designated Community court which is given jurisdiction in respect of all the member states.[120]

3.5 INTERNET SERVICE PROVIDERS

Although the courts might well have been willing to extend their jurisdiction to cover internet service providers following implementation of the EC Information Society Directive, statutory provision is now made for the grant of injunctions against service providers, 'where that service provider has actual knowledge of another person using their service to infringe' copyright or a performer's property rights.[121]

4 DELIVERY-UP

As an adjunct to a final injunction,[122] a court may order the delivery up or destruction of infringing articles.[123] While the defendant usually chooses which option to take,[124] if they have shown themselves to be unreliable the court may demand delivery up.[125] The long-standing inherent equitable jurisdiction to make an order for delivery-up is not based on the idea that the claimant owns the infringing material.[126] Rather, it aims to ensure that a defendant is not tempted to put the infringing copies into circulation in breach of the injunction.[127] If the infringement relates to a separable part of an article, the order will be for delivery up of that

---

[119] *UVG Ambulances v. Auto Conversions* [2000] *ECDR* 479.   [120] CDR Art. 1(3),83; CTMR Art. 94.

[121] CDPA s. 97A, s. 191JA (as inserted by Copyright and Related Rights Regs 2003 (SI 2003/2498). Note also EC Enforcement Directive, 2004/48, Art. 11, third sentence.

[122] An order for delivery-up is a type of mandatory injunction and can be awarded in interim proceedings: see *Films Rover v. Cannon* [1986] 3 *All ER* 772.

[123] Burrows, *Remedies for Tort and Breach of Contract*, 458–61; P. Meagher, W. Gummow, and J. Lehane, *Equity: Doctrines and Remedies* (1992), ch. 27. Note CDR Art. 89(1)(b)–(c) (on finding of infringement of Community design right, court should order seizure of infringing products and materials used to manufacture infringing goods).

[124] *Lady Anne Tennant v. Associated Newspapers* [1979] *FSR* 298, 305.

[125] *Industrial Furnaces v. Reaves* [1970] *RPC* 605. The claimant is entitled to be present to ensure destruction is carried out: *Slazenger v. Feltham* (1889) 6 *RPC* 531.

[126] The position may also be different in relation to confidential information, where infringing material has been likened to 'trust property': *Industrial Furnaces,* ibid.

[127] *Mergethaler Linotype v. Intertype* (1926) 43 *RPC* 381. In *Chappell v. Columbia Gramophone Co.* [1914] 2 *Ch* 745 the Court of Appeal utilized the remedy to prevent the defendant benefiting from its infringement by making it deliver up sound recordings derived from infringing acts, even though these were not infringing articles. For discussion of the case, see *Union Carbide v. BP* [1998] *FSR* 1.

part.[128] In the case of trade marks and passing-off, if a sign can be removed the court will order that this be done rather than order delivery up of the goods.[129] No order can be made once the right has expired.[130] Moreover, the order does not extend to third parties who have come into possession of infringing articles.[131]

In the case of patents and trade marks, there is an express statutory power to order delivery-up and/or obliteration.[132] The statutory provisions, like the inherent jurisdiction, provide that in cases where it appears 'likely that such an order would not be complied with' the court can order delivery up to the claimant (or some other person) for erasure or destruction.

A more significant statutory extension has been made available in respect of the infringements of trade marks, performers' rights, unregistered design right, or copyright.[133] More specifically, a statutory procedure exists for the delivery up of infringing goods, illicit recordings, infringing articles, and infringing copies for the purposes of 'destruction' or 'forfeiture'. In most cases the power is only available where a person has infringing goods (etc.) in their possession, custody, or control 'in the course of business'. The power also applies where a person has in their possession anything specifically designed or adapted for making infringing goods (etc.), knowing or having reason to believe that it has been or is to be used to make infringing goods (etc.). The court may order delivery up to the right owner (or some other person), pending a further order either for destruction *or forfeiture* as the court thinks fit. The ability to order forfeiture goes well beyond the inherent power which is confined to delivery for destruction.[134]

In considering whether the discretionary order for destruction or forfeiture is appropriate, the court is directed to take into account 'whether other remedies available in an action for infringement would be adequate to compensate the right owner and protect their interests'. This has been described as 'a strange provision, the purpose of which is not entirely clear'.[135] As yet, there is little indication as to when a forfeiture order will be made.[136] However, one obvious case where the other remedies might be inadequate is where the defendant is bankrupt or unable to pay damages.[137] As the order might affect the rights of third parties having interests in the goods, third parties may appear in proceedings.[138]

---

[128] *Mergethaler,* ibid. Cf. *Industrial Furnaces* [1970] *RPC* 605.

[129] *Warwick Tyre v. New Motor and General Rubber* (1910) 27 *RPC* 161, 171.

[130] *Leggatt v. Hoods Darts Accessories* (1950) 67 *RPC* 134, 143.

[131] *Knowles v. John Bennett* (1895) 12 *RPC* 137, 148 (shipper).

[132] PA s. 61(1)(b); TMA s. 15; RDA ss. 24C and 24D; Community Design Regs 2005, Regs 1B and 1C (as amended by SI 2006/1208).

[133] TMA s. 16; CDPA ss. 195, 199 (criminal proceedings); CDPA ss. 204, 230, 231; CDPA ss. 99, 108 (criminal proceedings).

[134] Cf. TMA s. 97(6) (where forfeiture of 'infringing goods, materials or articles' acquired in the course of investigating or prosecuting 'an offence' requires destruction).

[135] Arnold, para. 6.52.

[136] In *Ocular Sciences v. Aspect Vision Care* [1997] *RPC* 289, 407 Laddie J refused delivery-up on the ground that it would cause much greater harm to the defendant than was necessary to safeguard the legitimate interests of the claimants.

[137] Laddie *et al.*, para. 24.35.

[138] TMA s. 19(3). For the sorts of interest that might be involved where destruction was sought of counterfeit beer held in a Belfast port, see *Miller Brewing Co. v. The Mersey Docks & Harbour Co* [2004] *FSR* (5) 81 (where various innocent third parties were held entitled to recovery of their reasonable costs).

5 DAMAGES

The most common remedy for infringement of intellectual property rights is an award of damages.[139] The damages recoverable are the same as with other torts: the aim is to restore the victim to the position they would have been in if no wrong had been committed: it does not aim to punish the defendant.[140]

In some cases, damages will not be available where the defendant's infringement was innocent. More specifically, damages will not be awarded in an action for infringement of a registered design or a patent where the defendant proves that at the date of infringement they were not aware and had no reasonable grounds for supposing that the design was registered or the patent existed.[141] In either case, a person will not be deemed to have been aware or have had reasonable grounds for supposing that the design was registered or patent existed merely because the article is marked 'registered' or 'patented'. This does not apply, however, where the marking is accompanied by the registration or patent number.[142] In the case of copyright, rights in performances, and unregistered design right, the legislation provides that damages will not be awarded in an action for infringement where it is shown that at the time of the infringement the defendant did not know, and had no reason to believe, that copyright (etc.) subsisted in the work to which the action relates.[143] In certain cases of infringement of performers' rights by a person who 'innocently acquired' an illicit recording, the only remedy available is damages 'not exceeding a reasonable royalty in respect of the act complained of'.[144] In contrast, in the case of trade mark infringement and passing-off,[145] it seems that damages will be awarded even against an innocent defendant. It is difficult to conceive of any rational basis for such inconsistent approaches.

The normal measure of damages is 'the depreciation caused by the infringement of the value of the intellectual property right as a chose in action'.[146] As we will see the courts have also allowed claims relating to indirect or consequential losses. It is for the claimant to prove the loss, though this is not a matter of scientific precision.[147] Given the varied circumstances in which infringement can occur, the courts have been reluctant to lay down more detailed rules

---

[139] PA 1977, s. 61(1)(c); CDPA 1988, ss. 96(2), 191(3), 229(2); RDA, s. 24(2); TMA 1994, s. 14(2): PVA 1997, s. 13(2); CPVR Art. 94.

[140] *General Tire & Rubber v. Firestone Tyre & Rubber* [1976] *RPC* 197, 214. On the extent to which damages are restitutionary, see J. Edelman, *Gain-Based Damages* (2002).

[141] RDA 1949, s. 24B; PA 1977, s. 62(1); CDPA ss. 191J, 233.

[142] See *Lancer Boss v. Henley Forklift Co.* [1974] *FSR* 14 (relevant factors in determining innocence include whether the goods were marked 'patented' with a number; how widely distributed the goods were; whether the defendant copied the goods; whether any investigations had been made); *Texas Iron Works Inc's Patent* [2000] *RPC* 207.

[143] CDPA ss. 97(1), 191J, 233(1). *Nottinghamshire Healthcare v. News Group* [2002] *RPC* (49) 962 (para. 52) (a very limited defence). Note also CDPA s. 233(2) as regards innocent acquirers, applied in *Badge Sales* [2006] *FSR* 1. See pp. 157–9 above.

[144] CDPA s. 184(2).

[145] *Gillette UK v. Edenwest* [1994] *RPC* 279, 291–4; cf. *Marengo v. Daily Sketch* (1948) *RPC* 242 (leaving undecided whether there could be damages for innocent passing-off); C. Best, 'Damages against the Innocent Infringer in Passing Off and Trade Mark Infringement' (1985) 1 *IPJ* 205.

[146] *Sutherland Publishing v. Caxton Publishing* [1936] *Ch* 323, 336. Cf. *Ludlow v. Williams* [2002] *FSR* 868, 882 (describing this as not a particularly helpful formulation).

[147] *Watson Laidlaw v. Potts, Cassels & Williamson* (1914) 31 *RPC* 104, 109; *Khawam v. Chellaram* [1964] *RPC* 337, 343.

as to how damages should be computed.[148] In the following sections, we look at some of the factors that are taken into account when assessing the damages that are payable.[149]

The financial remedies that are available in an intellectual property action (both damages and account of profits) need to be viewed in the light of the Intellectual Property (Enforcement, etc.) Regulations 2006.[150] Regulation 3, which applies to cases of knowing infringement, explains that damages should reflect the 'actual prejudice' suffered by the claimant. Regulation 3(3) elaborates that 'all appropriate aspects shall be taken into account', including 'the negative economic consequences, including any lost profits, which the claimant has suffered, and any unfair profits made by the defendant', as well as 'elements other than economic factors, including the moral prejudice caused to the claimant by the infringement'. Alternatively, 'where appropriate', damages may be awarded 'on the basis of royalties or fees which would have been due had the defendant obtained a licence'. The Enforcement Regulations appear to require courts to revisit the traditional rule that required a claimant to elect between 'damages', perhaps coupled with 'additional damages', and an 'account of profits'.[151] Under the Regulations, these remedies may be cumulative, as long as there is no 'double recovery' for the same loss.

5.1 LOST PROFITS

One way in which damages may be calculated is by reference to the profits which the claimant lost as a result of the competing sales of infringing goods (or services) made by the defendant. For example, if prior to an infringement the patentee of a widget was selling 200 widgets per year, but only sold 150 widgets after the infringement (the defendant selling 50 widgets), the damages are likely to be calculated as the profits the patentee would have made on the 50 widgets.[152] Clearly, this method of calculation will only be used where the intellectual-property-right owner exploits the right by manufacturing goods. Although the courts have indicated that proof of lost profits need not be minutely accurate, a claimant will often encounter difficulties.[153] In particular, problems may arise in relation to causation.[154] For example, where an infringer sells an infringing product at a cost which is less than that of the claimant's product, it will often be difficult to be certain that, absent infringement, sales which went to the defendant would have gone to the claimant.[155] Other difficulties may arise: discovering how many infringing items the defendant sold; establishing that the claimant's expected sales

---

[148] *Meters v. Metropolitan Gas Meters* (1910) 28 *RPC* 157, 163. For general comments, see *Kuwait Airways Corp. v. Iraqi Airways Co* [2002] 2 *AC* 833 *per* Lord Nicholls (paras. 69–73).

[149] Many of the intellectual property statutes provide that where licences of right are made available an award of damages is not to exceed double the amount which would have been payable as a licensee if such a licence on those terms had been granted before the earliest infringement: RDA 1949, s. 11B(1)(a); PA s. 46(3)(c); CDPA ss. 98(1)(a), 191K, 239(1)(c).

[150] SI 2006/1028 (effective for infringements occurring after 29 April 2006).

[151] See, *Redrow Homes Ltd. v. Betts Bros. Plc.* [1998] 1 *All ER* 385, 393 (HL) (explaining requirement on basis that the two remedies are 'inconsistent').

[152] The approach has been described as 'inescapably hypothetical, even speculative': *Douglas v. Hello! (No. 8)* [2004] *EMLR* (2) 13 (para. 17).

[153] *Watson Laidlaw* (1914) 31 *RPC* 104, 113.

[154] See *Coflexip SA v. Stolt Offshore MS* [2003] *FSR* (41) 728 (considering problems of causation in relation to defendant's acquisition of contracts, in execution of which it used claimant's patented process).

[155] *Columbia Pictures Industries v. Robinson* [1988] *FSR* 531, 535. See also *Prior v. Lansdowne Press* [1977] *RPC* 511.

figures were justified; proving that the claimant would have had sufficient stock to cover the defendant's sales; or that the defendant's sales would not have gone to a competitor of the claimant (rather than the claimant).[156] In certain circumstances, the courts have got over these difficulties by presuming that the claimant would have made the sales.[157]

5.2 ROYALTY

If a claimant is unable to claim damages on the basis of lost profits, the court may make an award on a royalty basis. That is, the court can award the claimant a notional fee for each infringing act.[158] Here the damages compensate for the misappropriation and represent the fee that the defendant would have paid for a licence for the use of the rights they infringed. Such a royalty will be easy to determine where a claimant has been in the practice of granting licences: it will be the 'going rate'. In these cases, the claimant will need to show that the circumstances in which the going rate was being paid by others are the same or comparable with those in which the intellectual-property-right holder and infringer are assumed to strike their bargain.[159] The defendant's own financial position is not regarded as a relevant circumstance and so it is not open to the defendant to argue that they could not have afforded to pay a reasonable rate.[160]

Where claimants have not been in the practice of granting licences, they will have to find some other basis from which the court can estimate an appropriate royalty. This 'may consist of the practice, as regards royalty, in the relevant trade or in analogous trades; perhaps of expert opinion expressed in publications... possibly of the profitability of the invention; and any other factor on which the judge can decide the measure of loss'.[161] The aim of the evidence is to establish what royalty a willing licensee would have been prepared to pay and a willing licensor to accept.[162] That is, the goal is to establish what terms would have been reached between the actual licensor and the actual licensee, bearing in mind their strengths and weaknesses and the market as it exists, on the assumption that each was willing to negotiate with the other.[163] The process of calculation is 'intended to represent a robust and inexpensive cutting of a Gordian knot'.[164]

Where neither avenue suggests itself as the most appropriate, the choice between the 'lost profits' and 'royalty' approaches to the calculation of damages is left to the claimant (even in 'licence of right cases').[165] In some circumstances it may be appropriate to choose both. For

---

[156] *Cow v. Cannon Rubber Manufacturers* [1961] *RPC* 236, 240.

[157] *Catnic Components v. Hill & Smith* [1983] *FSR* 512, 524. Cf. *Blayney (t/a Aardvark Jewellery) v. Clogau St. Davids Gold Mines* [2003] *FSR* (19) 360 (CA).

[158] Where the claimant has granted licences at a royalty rate, it is 'almost a rule of law' to assess damages as the amount the defendant infringer would have had to pay for the number of infringing articles at the royalty rate had they had a licence: *Meters,* note 148 above, 164; *Catnic Components,* ibid, 518. But the lost profits approach is preferred in cases of trade marks and passing-off: *Games Workshop* [1993] *FSR* 704, 713–14; *Dormeuil Frères v. Feraglow* [1990] *RPC* 449.

[159] *General Tire v. Firestone* [1976] *RPC* 197, 213.

[160] *Irvine v. TalkSport Ltd* [2003] *FSR* (35) 619 (para. 106) (CA) (Jonathan Parker LJ).

[161] *General Tire,* [1976] *RPC* 197, 214.

[162] Ibid, 225; *Ludlow v. Williams* [2002] *FSR* 868, 889–90 (court should err on side of generosity). Cf. *SPE International v. Professional Preparation Contractors* (10 May 2002) Rimer J (court should err on side of under-compensation).

[163] Ibid, 221.   [164] *Douglas v. Hello! (No. 8)* [2004] *EMLR* (2) 13 (para. 61).

[165] *Gerber Garment Technology v. Lectra Systems* [1997] *RPC* 443, 486. In *Douglas,* ibid (para. 13), a case on damages for breach of confidence, Lindsay J did not require the claimant to elect between damages based on

example, if a defendant sold 25 infringing works and the claimant would only have made 15 sales, then the claimant may claim for lost profits on those 15 sales plus a royalty in relation to the other 10 sales.[166]

5.3 SECONDARY LOSSES

Although the sum awarded is usually calculated on the basis of the loss to the value of the intellectual property right as a chose in action,[167] other secondary losses may also be recovered.[168] These are sometimes referred to as consequential or parasitic damages. The ability to claim such losses may be particularly important where goods incorporating intellectual property are marketed at low profit margins and the profits are largely made from the sale of associated goods or services. Such losses can be claimed if they are foreseeable, caused by the wrong,[169] and not excluded from recovery by public policy.[170] A conceivable but remote result could not be deemed to be reasonably foreseeable. Applying these principles the courts have held, for example, that a copyright infringer would not be liable for cash-flow consequences for the copyright owner;[171] nor would an infringer be liable for losses on sales of the claimant's goods as a result of the defendant's distribution of an infringing catalogue.[172]

5.4 EXEMPLARY DAMAGES

According to the House of Lords in *Rookes v. Barnard*,[173] a court may award exemplary damages where, in cynical disregard of a claimant's rights, a defendant infringed those rights calculating that they would make a profit which would exceed the compensation payable to the claimant. The award is proper 'whenever it is necessary to teach a wrongdoer that a tort does not pay'.[174] The House of Lords made it clear in *Kuddus v. Chief Constable of Leicestershire Constabulary* that the availability of exemplary damages is not confined (as had been

---

lost sales and damages calculated on a royalty basis, taking the view that the court should award the higher of the two—in this case, based on lost profits (though might penalize the claimant for running mutually exclusive claims through a costs award).

[166] *Watson Laidlaw* (1914) 31 *RPC* 104; *Catnic v. Hill & Smith* [1983] *FSR* 512, 522; *Gerber Garment Technology*, ibid, 486 (CA); *Blayney* [2003] *FSR* (19) 360 (CA).

[167] *Sutherland Publishing Company v. Caxton Publishing* [1936] 1 *All ER* 177, 180.

[168] Cf. *Catnic v. Hill & Smith* [1983] *FSR* 512, 534 (loss of profits due to sale of non-patented lintels not recoverable).

[169] *Work Model Enterprises v. Ecosystem & Clix Interiors* [1996] *FSR* 356, 362 (a matter of common sense).

[170] *Gerber Garment Technology* [1997] *RPC* 443, 452. In *Kuwait Airways* [2002] 2 *AC* 833 (paras. 69–73) Lord Nicholls treated causation as encompassing two stages: a 'but for' test, and an enquiry into whether the loss was one for which the defendant 'ought fairly or reasonably or justly to be held liable'. The latter includes aspects of foreseeability and public policy, though normally evokes 'an immediate intuitive response'.

[171] *Claydon Architectural Metalwork v. Higgins & Sons* [1997] *FSR* 475.

[172] *Work Model Enterprises* [1996] *FSR* 396; *Paterson Zochonis v. Merfarken Packaging* [1983] *FSR* 273, 295 (Robert Goff LJ) (where it was said to be undesirable as a matter of policy to extend the scope of recoverable damages in this way to cover a different proprietary interest). See also *Dyson v. Hoover* [2001] *RPC* (27) 544, 572, where Judge Fysh QC would not have granted a claimant damages for sales of non-infringing vaccum cleaners that used the mark VORTEX where the mark VORTEX had earlier been used to refer to vacuum cleaners that did infringe the patent.

[173] [1964] *AC* 1129, 1226–7.

[174] See Law Commission, Report No. 247: *Aggravated, Exemplary and Restitutionary Damages* (1997), para. 1.110, 62.

previously thought) to causes of action where the remedy had been recognized prior to *Rookes v. Barnard*.[175] Nevertheless, such damages will rarely be awarded.[176]

5.5 ADDITIONAL STATUTORY DAMAGES

In relation to copyright and rights in performances,[177] as well as unregistered design rights,[178] a court may consider all the circumstances, particularly the flagrancy of the infringement and any benefit accruing to the defendant,[179] and award such additional damages as the justice of the case requires.[180] The nature of additional damages is unclear. In particular, it is unclear whether they are compensatory, exemplary, or restitutionary.[181] However, it has been held that their award is the exception rather than the rule, and a claimant needs to show special circumstances which would justify the imposition of an additional financial penalty.[182] Ideally this should be done by full pleading, and the determination as to whether such damages should be awarded may be dealt with by the trial judge or the inquiry.[183] However, if there are issues on which evidence has not been given during the trial which might be relevant, the court will probably leave the assessment of additional damages to the inquiry stage.[184] Factors which may be relevant in deciding to award additional damages include: (i) whether the defendant acted deliberately or 'couldn't care less';[185] (ii) whether the defendant was acting on legal advice;[186] (iii) whether the defendant was merely out to make money or had other motives;[187] (iv) whether the claimant and defendant were involved in negotiating a licence;[188] (v) the impact of the defendant's action on the claimant (e.g. disruption or upset);[189] (vi) whether there are any other mitigating circumstances;[190] and (vii) possibly the means of the defendant.[191] Additional damages are not available in addition to an account of profits.[192]

---

[175] [2002] *AC* 122.

[176] *Morton-Norwich Products v. Intercen* [1981] *FSR* 337, 353 Graham J (it would require a very strong case with very peculiar circumstances before a court would exercise that power).

[177] CDPA ss. 97(2), 191J (that is, the performers' property rights but not for infringement of the non-property or recording rights).

[178] CDPA s. 229(3). *Fulton v. Totes Isotoner* [2003] *RPC* (27) 499.

[179] *Fulton*, ibid (para. 116) (flagrancy implies something approaching premeditated commercial amorality rather than just business risk or sharp practice); *Ravenscroft v. Herbert* [1980] *RPC* 193, 208 (benefit implies that the defendant has reaped a pecuniary advantage in excess of damages they would otherwise have to pay).

[180] CDPA s. 97. This amended and replaced CA 1956, s. 17(3) which had confined such damages to circumstances where 'effective relief would not otherwise be available'.

[181] *Redrow Homes* [1998] 1 *All ER* 385, 391 *per* Lord Jauncey (no need to decide whether punitive or compensatory); 393 *per* Lord Clyde (probably aggravated); *Ludlow v. Williams* [2002] *FSR* 868, 891–2 (restitutionary); *Nottinghamshire Healthcare* [2002] *RPC* (49) 962 (paras. 48–51) (can include a restitutionary element but not a punitive one). C. Michalos, 'Copyright and Punishment: The Nature of Additional Damages' [2000] *EIPR* 470.

[182] *Ravenscroft* [1980] *RPC* 193, 208 (flagrancy implies the existence of scandalous conduct, deceit, and such like; it includes deliberate and calculated infringement).

[183] *ZYX Music GmbH v. King* [1997] 2 *All ER* 129, 149 (CA) (whether the justice of the case requires an award of additional damages can only be determined on the inquiry).

[184] *O'Mara Books v. Express Newspapers* [1999] *FSR* 49, 57–8.

[185] *Nottinghamshire Healthcare* [2002] *RPC* (49) 962 (paras. 52–3).

[186] *Pro Sieben Media v. Carlton UK Television* [1998] *FSR* 43, 61–2.

[187] *ZYX Music GmbH v. King* [1995] *FSR* 566, 587; affirmed [1997] 2 *All ER* 129 (CA).

[188] *Ludlow v. Williams* [2002] *FSR* 868.

[189] *Nottinghamshire Healthcare* [2002] *RPC* (49) 962 (paras. 55, 60).

[190] Such as an apology: *Nottinghamshire Healthcare,* ibid (para. 60).

[191] *O'Mara Books* [1999] *FSR* 49, 57–8.   [192] *Redrow Homes* [1998] 1 *All ER* 385.

6 ACCOUNT OF PROFITS

In relation to most intellectual property rights,[193] a claimant may elect for an 'account of profits', instead of claiming damages.[194] An accounting of profits is an equitable remedy which deprives the defendant of any profits made as a result of their infringement. Because account of profits has its origins in the Court of Chancery, it has been treated as an alternative financial remedy to damages.[195] It cannot be claimed in addition to damages, even where the loss to the claimant and profit to the defendant are unrelated so that when combined the two remedies would not result in double liability.[196] Usually, election is solely a matter for the claimant, but as the remedy for account of profits is equitable (and therefore discretionary), the court may refuse it.[197] Where there is more than one claimant (for example a proprietor and exclusive licensee) or more than one defendant, it has been held that a single election must be made: as regards a single course of action, a claimant may not have an account against one defendant, and damages against another.[198] The rule requiring an election between either damages or an account of the profits is no longer strictly applied to infringements occurring after 29 April 2006. Instead, 'lost profit' is one of the factors that the courts take into account when determining damages. The profits to be sought would be those actually made by the defendant through his infringement of copyright.[199] If appropriate, the court will apportion a part of the total profit as that attributable to the infringement.[200]

Traditionally the remedy of account was said to have been conditional on the availability of injunctive relief. However, at least where the remedies for infringement of intellectual property rights are specified by statute, this precondition seems to have been abandoned.[201] In the case of patents, passing-off, registered designs and trade marks,[202] no order of an account will

---

[193] For registered design right see RDA s. 24A.

[194] PA s. 61(1)(d); CDPA s. 96(2); TMA s. 14(2); *My Kinda Town v. Soll* [1982] FSR 147 (passing off); *Peter Pan v. Corsets Silhouette* [1963] 3 *All ER* 402 (breach of confidence).

[195] For the history, see L. Bently and C. Mitchell, 'Combining Money Awards for Patent Infringement: *Spring Form Inc v. Toy Brokers Ltd*' [2003] *Restitution Law Review* 79.

[196] *Neilson v. Betts* (1871) LR 5; HL 1; *Redrow Homes* [1998] 1 *All ER* 385, 393 (HL) (explaining requirement on basis that the two remedies are inconsistent); PA s. 61(2). Cf. *Watson Laidlaw* (1914) 31 *RPC* 104, 119 (explaining the requirement of an election as a mechanism to prevent overlapping). See, more generally, S. Waterson, 'Alternative and Cumulative Remedies: What is the Difference?' [2003] 11 *Restitution Law Review* 7.

[197] *Sir Terence Conran v. Mean Fiddler Holdings* [1997] FSR 856, 861; *Van Zeller v. Mason* (1907) 25 *RPC* 37, 41; *Electrolux v. Electrix* (1953) 70 *RPC* 158.

[198] *Spring Form Inc. v. Toy Brokers* [2002] *FSR* (17) 276, 288, 290.

[199] CDPA, s. 96(2). There is no defense of innocence: *Wienerworld Ltd. v. Vision Video Ltd.* [1998] *FSR* 832. If there are multiple claimants (such as a copyright owner and his licensee) or multiple defendants, the one election applies to all: *Spring Form* [2002] *FSR* (17) 276 (a patent case).

[200] *Potton v. Yorkclose* [1990] FSR 11. See also *Cala Homes (South) v. Alfred McAlpine Homes East (No.2)* [1996] *FSR* 36, 44 (rejecting submission that profit made should be compared with profit the defendant might have made using non-infringing means); *Celanese International Corporation v. BP Chemicals Ltd.* [1999] *RPC* 203, 225 (a patent case).

[201] L. Bently, 'Accounting of Profits Gained from Infringement of Copyright: When Will It End?' [1990] *EIPR* 5, 7–8.

[202] PA 1977, s. 62(1); RDA, s. 24B see *Conran v. Mean Fiddler*, note 197 above, 861 (account refused where infringement of trade mark was innocent and causal connection between use of mark and profits of bar would be difficult to establish); Wadlow (2004), paras. 9–81 to 9–85; *Gillette v. Edenwest* [1994] *RPC* 279, 290 (accepting that different principles might operate so that, while damages were available for innocent infringement of trade marks or passing-off, an account was not); *Edelsten v. Edelsten* (1863) 1 *DeG J & S* 18, 46 ER 72; *Spalding v. Gamage* (1915) 32 *RPC* 273, 283. See also pp. 157–9 above.

be made where a defendant acted innocently. That is, no order will be made if at the date of infringement the defendant was not aware and had no reasonable grounds for supposing that the intangible property right existed. For some time it was thought that the decision to elect for an account of profits had to be made at the time of judgment. However, since a claimant would not necessarily have sufficient information on which to base the election, greater flexibility has been introduced so that the election should optimally take place only when the claimant can make an informed decision.[203]

The main difficulty raised by the remedy of an account concerns the way the profits are calculated. In part this is because it will be very rare for the infringement of the intellectual property right to be the single cause of any profit. It is more likely that only part of the product sold by the defendant will have been infringing. In such cases the court must try to determine what profits have been caused, in a legal sense, by those acts.[204] Under what is called the 'incremental approach', it has been suggested that, to determine the profits payable, the courts should compare the profit the defendant made with that which they would have made had they not used the infringing material or process: the 'increment' being the profits attributable to the infringement.[205] However, this approach has been rejected on a number of occasions in favour of a less refined approach, where the courts simply apportion the total net profits.[206]

With the 'apportionment approach', the court first ascertains the total net profits made by the defendant from the activity in question.[207] In calculating net profits the court will deduct relevant expenses such as costs, overheads, and taxes[208] from the revenue received in relation to the infringing project. The court then attempts to locate a principled means for dividing up the profits, so as to define the portion attributable to the infringement. This is not a mathematical exercise but one of reasonable approximation.[209] So if the infringing process is one of five steps in the production of a particular product, in the absence of evidence suggesting otherwise, one-fifth of the profits from the sale of the product would be attributed to the infringement. The courts have recently favoured the view that the proportion of profits attributable to the infringing activity might best be determined by looking at the corresponding costs of the process of production.[210] In some, though probably rare, circumstances the court will ask itself what is the importance of the infringing activity or part to the ultimate profits.[211]

As with damages, where licences of right are made available the amount to be rendered in an account of profits is not to exceed double the amount which would have been payable by the defendant as a licensee if such a licence on those terms had been granted before the earliest infringement.[212]

---

[203] *Island Records v. Tring International* [1995] FSR 560; *Brugger v. Medicaid* [1996] FSR 362, 364.

[204] *Celanese v. BP* [1999] RPC 203. See also *Union Carbide v. BP* [1998] FSR 1, 6 ('there must plainly be limits as to how far one can go on what is a derivation').

[205] An approach that seemed to have been taken in *Siddell v. Vickers* (1888) 5 RPC 416 and *My Kinda Town v. Soll* [1983] RPC 15.

[206] *Potton v. Yorkclose* [1990] FSR 11 (incremental approach is only suitable where the infringement was in the process of producing the work); *Cala Homes v. McAlpine* [1996] FSR 36, 44; *Celanese v. BP* [1999] RPC 203. See T. Moody-Stuart, 'Quantum in Accounts of Profits: The Acid Test' [1999] EIPR 147.

[207] *Potton,* ibid.　　[208] *Celanese v. BP* [1999] RPC 203, 249.　　[209] *My Kinda Town* [1993] RPC 15.

[210] *Potton v. Yorkclose* [1995] FSR 153, 18 (in the absence of some special reason to the contrary, the profits of a single part are attributed to different parts or aspects of the project in the same proportion as the costs and expenses are attributed to them).

[211] *Celanese v. BP* [1999] RPC 203, 225. Cf. *Potton,* ibid, 18.

[212] PA s. 46(3)(c); CDPA ss. 98(1)(a), 191K, 239(1)(c).

7 TIME LIMITS

Delay in bringing proceedings may lead to an action for infringement being barred, under either statutory provisions or equitable principles. An action for infringement of copyright, patent, or trade mark must be commenced within six years of the wrongful act.[213] If proceedings are commenced within the requisite period, it will only be struck out for want of prosecution if there is real prejudice to the defendant, as well as inordinate delay.[214]

Where a claimant expressly or impliedly represents that the defendant's conduct is non-infringing, they will thereafter be estopped from asserting their right. Where the claimant knows of their right against the defendant and that the defendant mistakenly believes that they are entitled to do what they are doing, yet the claimant stands by without asserting their right, they will be taken to have acquiesced in the wrong.[215]

8 CRIMINAL REMEDIES

For the most part, there has been little demand for criminal sanctions to protect intellectual property rights. In part this has been because the rights holders have preferred the lower standard of proof associated with the civil action.[216] Recently, there has been increased interest in the scope of criminal liabilities and sanctions, especially in the case of piracy and counterfeiting.[217] Criminal prosecution is attractive because of the publicity that a criminal trial can attract and the deterrent effect of the sanction.[218] There are four categories of crime that concern us here. These are: crimes relating to copyright and trade mark infringements under the relevant statutes; the common law crime of conspiracy to defraud; the crimes created by the Trade Descriptions Act 1968; and finally, special crimes created by the intellectual property statutes which are intended to protect the integrity of intellectual property registers.

If a right owner chooses to pursue a criminal prosecution, they can do so by three routes. First, the right owner or a representative[219] may commence criminal proceedings by 'laying an information' (or complaint) at a magistrates' court,[220] on the basis of which the court will issue a summons.[221] Alternatively, the claimant may seek the assistance of the police, which might

---

[213] Limitation Act 1980, s. 2.

[214] *Birkett v. James* [1978] AC 297; *Compagnie Française de Télévision v. Thorn* [1978] RPC 735.

[215] See *Film Investors Overseas Services SA v. Home Video Channel* [1997] EMLR 347, 365; *Farmers Build v. Carrier Bulk Materials Handling* [1999] RPC 461, 486–9 (mere delay in bringing proceedings is not acquiescence).

[216] See Worsdall and Clark, chs. 5 and 6.

[217] For example, Copyright, etc. and Trade Marks (Offences and Enforcement) Act 2002.

[218] In addition, criminal prosecutions are likely to be quicker than civil actions, and a losing prosecutor may avoid paying costs: Prosecution of Offences Act 1985, ss. 16–18. TRIPS, Art. 61 requires members to provide for criminal procedures and penalties at least in cases of wilful trade mark counterfeiting and copyright piracy 'on a commercial scale'.

[219] For example, a representative organization such as the Federation Against Copyright Theft (FACT), the Federation Against Software Theft, or a collecting society. See *Thames & Hudson v. Designs & Artists Copyright Society* [1995] FSR 153.

[220] There should be a separate 'information' for each individual copyright work: *R v. Ward* [1988] Crim LR 57.

[221] Any citizen may bring a private prosecution: Prosecution of Offences Act 1985, s. 6(1). See G. Harbottle, 'Criminal Remedies for Copyright and Performers' Rights Infringement under the Copyright, Designs and Patents Act 1988' [1994] Ent LR 12.

be advantageous because the police may obtain a search warrant and police action carries a significant social stigma. However, if a charge is made by the police, the prosecution must be conducted either by the Department of Public Prosecutions or the Crown Prosecution Service: it cannot then be handed back to the claimant.[222] This may be a dangerous tactic, because the Crown Prosecution Service might decide not to prosecute.[223] The right holder may also enlist the help of administrative authorities, in particular Trading Standards Departments or local Weights and Measures Authorities. These authorities are obliged to enforce the Trade Descriptions Act and the criminal provisions of the Trade Marks Act. Also, they may soon be placed under a duty to enforce criminal provisions relating to copyright and performances.[224] A provision to this effect has been enacted, but it has yet to be brought into force.

8.1 STATUTORY OFFENCES

In order to buttress the civil remedies and to help combat piracy, bootlegging, and counterfeiting, a number of statutory criminal offences have been introduced in relation to copyright, performers' rights, and trade mark law. There is no criminal sanction for the infringement of patents or designs (whether registered or unregistered).

In relation to copyright, criminal liability is not confined to those normally considered to be pirates.[225] Rather, criminal infringement covers most acts of primary and secondary infringement,[226] though in all cases criminal relief requires proof of knowledge or reason to know that copyright was being or would be infringed.[227] It should be clear, therefore, that a successful criminal prosecution can result either in a fine or imprisonment, and the maximum penalty is ten years' imprisonment.[228] In sentencing, the courts have indicated that they consider copyright infringement to be an offence of 'real dishonesty' equivalent to cheating or stealing.[229] Conscious of the prevalence of such offences and the difficulties of detection,[230] the courts have emphasized that criminal copyright infringement is to be regarded as a very serious matter. Even small-scale infringement, such as the copying of 48 videos, has led to

---

[222] See *R v. Ealing Justices, ex p. Dixon* [1989] 2 *All ER* 1050 (proceedings begun by police could not be prosecuted by FACT); cf. *R v. Croydon Justices, ex p. Holmberg* (1992) 157 *JP* 277.

[223] The Director of Public Prosecutions is under a duty to prosecute certain offences and may (in its discretion) prosecute others: Prosecution of Offences Act 1985, ss. 3, 6(2).

[224] CDPA s. 107A (introduced by the Criminal Justice and Public Order Act 1994, s. 165). In Northern Ireland, enforcement is the responsibility of the Dept. of Economic Development: CDPA s. 107A(3). A similar enforcement provision exists with respect to performances. No such duty or authority applies in relation to proceedings in Scotland.

[225] *Thames & Hudson v. DACS* [1995] *FSR* 153. On pirates see, D. Halbert, 'Intellectual Property Piracy: The narrative construction of deviance' (1997) 10 *International Journal for the Semiotics of Law* 55.

[226] CDPA ss. 107–10. Note also: CDPA s. 297 (fraudulently receiving programmes), s. 297A (making, etc. unauthorized decoders), s. 296ZB (circumventing technological measures), s. 198 (illicit recordings of performances); Related Rights Reg. 17(1), 17(3) (applying offences to publication right but with modified penalties). There are no criminal offences in relation to the database right.

[227] CDPA ss. 107–10. The presumptions of authorship, etc. do not apply, and problems of proving copyright ownership may arise: *Musa v. Le Maitre* [1987] *FSR* 272.

[228] CDPA s. 107(4), as amended by the Copyright and Trade Marks (Offences and Enforcement) Act 2002. Note that the maximum period for communicating the work to the public is two years: s. 107(2A), (4A) (following SI 2003/2498 r. 26). A maximum of six months applies to showing a film, or playing a sound recording in public: CDPA s. 107(3), (5).

[229] *R v. Carter* [1983] *FSR* 303; *R v. Ian Dukett* [1998] 2 *Cr App R* (S) 59; *R v. Roy John Gibbons* (1995) 16 *Cr App R* (S) 398.

[230] *R v. Paul Godfrey Kemp* (1995) 16 *Cr App R* (S) 941; *R v. Gibbons*, ibid.

custodial sentences.[231] The greater the numbers of copies made[232] and the greater the value of each copy,[233] the more severe the sentence.

Criminal offences also exist to protect performers.[234] These largely correspond to civil infringements and deal with the making, importing, and commercial dealing in illicit recordings, without sufficient consent. Sufficient consent is defined, in relation to performers' rights, as the consent of the performers or owner of the performers' property rights; and in relation to recording rights the consent of the performer or the owner of the recording rights. Criminal liability is also imposed for infringement by making available a work, for example on the internet, where the act took place in the course of business or 'to such an extent as to affect prejudicially the owner of the making available right'.[235] Liability depends on proof of knowledge or reason to believe that the recordings are 'illicit'.[236] The penalties are equivalent to those for infringement of copyright: so that a person convicted on indictment may receive a prison sentence of up to ten years.[237]

Special criminal provisions also exist to deal with trade mark infringement.[238] In particular, section 92 of the Trade Marks Act 1994 states that a person commits an offence if they apply to goods or their packaging a sign 'identical to, or likely to be mistaken for, a registered trade mark' without the consent of the proprietor and 'with a view to gain for himself or another, or with intent to cause loss to another'.[239] It is now clear that this requires a showing of trade mark use.[240] The section goes on to create further offences that capture parties who deal commercially in goods bearing such a sign or are otherwise involved in ancillary or preliminary acts that enable such exploitation.[241] The requirement that the sign be 'identical to, or likely to be mistaken for, a registered trade mark' uses language that differs from that

---

[231] *R v. Kemp*, ibid (six months). See also *R v. Lloyd* [1997] 2 *Cr App R (S)* 151 (six months); *R v. Gross* [1996] 2 *Cr App R* 189 (nine months); *R v. Gibbons*, ibid (seven months).

[232] *R v. Lewis* [1997] 1 *Cr App R (S)* 208 (sentence of 12 months for a person who ran a computer bulletin board for 'swapping' computer games. The system contained over 1,000 games, and thus was a significant enterprise); *R. v. Dowd* [2005] *EWCA Crim* 3582 Openshaw J (sentence depends 'on the nature and scale of the operation involved, as well as the motive (of the offender) and the consequences of his offending'. Even where there is no profit motive, but there is a risk of serious economic loss to others, sentence should reflect fact that infringement is 'a seriously antisocial act, which should be strongly discouraged'); *R v. Kirkwood* [2006] 2 *Cr App R (S)* 39 (small-scale operation copying and distributing music, films, and video games, that developed from defendant's hobby, justified sentence of 21 months because infringement extended for 3 years); *R v. Alphor Holborough* (7 Nov. 2002) (CA) (three years' imprisonment for conspiracy to defraud based on sale of about 20,000 devices for over £400,000); *R v. Harold Christopher Carey* [1999] 1 *Cr App R (S)* 322 (four years for sale of 650,000 smart cards); *R v. Maxwell King* [2001] *Cr App R (S)* 28 (150 hours of community service for inciting the supply of 20 devices to enable unauthorized access to cable TV contrary to the Computer Misuse Act 1990, s. 3).

[233] *R v. Dukett* [1998] 2 *Cr App R (S)* 59 (27 months' imprisonment for 4 copyright offences of distributing CD–ROMs was justified because, while the numbers sold were relatively small, each CD contained material worth several thousand pounds).

[234] CDPA s. 198. See Arnold, ch. 7.   [235] s.198(1A), (5A) (with a possible sentence of two years).

[236] On what is acceptable proof, see *Radford v. Kent County Council* (unreported, 18 Feb. 1998) (Queen's Bench Division).

[237] CDPA s. 198(5)—for making, importing, and distributing illicit recordings (as amended by the Copyright, etc, and Trade Marks (Enforcement and Offences) Act 2002); other offences carry a maximum of six months' imprisonment.

[238] *S v. London Borough of Havering* (20 Nov. 2002) (para. 10) (explaining rationale for criminal protection).

[239] On the meaning of 'with a view to' in TMA s 92(1)(c), see *R v. Zaman* [2003] *FSR* (13) 230.

[240] *R v. Johnstone* [2003] *FSR* (42) 748.

[241] But not importing: which may be a failure to implement Council Regulation 3295/94 Art. 11. See Worsdall and Clark, para. 7.41.

used in civil infringement.[242] Moreover, it is only an offence to apply the sign (etc.) to goods for which it is registered, or 'if the trade mark has a reputation in the UK, and the use of the sign takes...unfair advantage of; or is...detrimental to, the distinctive character or repute of the mark'. There is near-absolute liability which does not depend on proof of the trader's knowledge of the existence of a registered mark.[243]

It is a defence to a criminal prosecution to show that the accused 'believed on reasonable grounds that the use of the sign in the manner in which it was used...was not an infringement of the registered trade mark'.[244] As Lord Nicholls has explained, '[t]hose who act honestly and reasonably are not to be visited with criminal sanctions'. Thus the defence applies equally to situations where a defendant did not believe the mark was registered, and where a defendant believed a mark was registered but that the act was non-infringing.[245] It is for the defendant to establish on the balance of probabilities an affirmative case of reasonable belief.[246]

The criminal penalties for infringement of trade marks are similar to those for criminal copyright infringement. A summary conviction can result in a custodial sentence of six months or a fine of up to £5,000; a conviction on indictment can result in a fine or imprisonment for up to ten years. The courts have not been swayed by pleas that counterfeiting has not misled anyone,[247] and have repeatedly emphasized that trade mark infringement is 'properly a criminal offence' akin to stealing goodwill.[248] Consequently, it has been said that it is important that sentences be serious enough to operate as a deterrent.[249] The punishment will depend largely on the gravity and the scale of the infringement and the persistence of the defendant.[250] As to gravity, the courts have treated the counterfeiting of pharmaceuticals as particularly heinous, because of the potential effects on public safety.[251] As to scale, the Court of Appeal has held three years was an appropriate sentence for applying false trade marks to perfume such as Chanel No. 5, on a scale of 5,000–10,000 bottles per week.[252] With regard to persistence, an isolated lapse by a generally honest businessman will merely warrant a fine,[253] though small-scale dealing in counterfeit watches has been held to warrant a prison sentence of three months.[254]

On convicting a defendant either for criminal copyright infringement, trade mark infringement, or registered design infringement the courts also have the power to order delivery up of infringing copies or goods and to make certain compensation and confiscation orders.[255] Moreover, criminal proceedings concerning copyright are not subject to any statute of limitations.

---

[242] TMA s. 10(2). Note also IGR Art. 1(2) referring to an identical sign or one 'which cannot be distinguished in its essential aspects from such trade mark' in the definition of counterfeit goods.

[243] *Torbay Council v. Singh* [1999] 2 *Cr App R* 451, 455.   [244] TMA s. 92(5).

[245] *R v. Johnstone* [2003] *FSR* (42) 748, 763.

[246] Ibid, 764 (para. 46). This is a legal or persuasive burden, but was deemed by the House of Lords to be a justified derogation from the presumption of innocence contained in ECHR Art. 6(2). Lord Nicholls, at 766, (paras. 52–3) found there to be 'compelling reasons' why the defence should place the persuasive burden on the accused.

[247] *R v. Priestly* [1996] 2 *Cr App R (S)* 144.   [248] *R v. Bhad* [1999] 2 *Cr App R (S)* 139.

[249] *R v. Adam* [1998] 2 *Cr App R (S)* 403.

[250] *R v. Kelly* [1996] 1 *Cr App R (S)* 61 (defendant's persistence in dishonest conduct justified imprisonment).

[251] *R v. Yanko* [1996] 1 *Cr App R (S)* 217 (4–5 years for counterfeiting of medicinal products (steroids) under signs SYNTEX and ANAPOLON was not excessive).

[252] *R v. Priestly* [1996] 2 *Cr App R (S)* 144. See also *R v. Ansari, Horner, Ling & Ansari* [2000] *Cr App R (S)* 94 (three years).

[253] *R v. Bhad* [1999] 2 *Cr App R (S)* 139.

[254] *R v. Kelly* [1996] 1 *Cr App R (S)* 61 (possession of 30 watches).

[255] Powers of Criminal Courts Act 1973, ss. 35, 43 (property deprivation order); Magistrates' Courts Act 1980, s. 40 (power to award compensation up to £5,000); Criminal Justice Act 1988, as amended by the Proceeds of Crime Act 1995 and Criminal Justice Act 1988 (Confiscation Orders) Order 1995 (SI 1995/3145) (court may

8.2 CONSPIRACY TO DEFRAUD

In some cases, the general common law crime of conspiracy to defraud may be used to protect intellectual property rights. This crime will be committed where someone dishonestly tries to obtain an economic advantage without the need to show that anyone was deceived.[256] It will only be useful in cases of organized piracy where there is some agreement between the parties. One advantage of bringing a charge of common law conspiracy to defraud is that the courts' discretion to imprison or fine an adult offender is unlimited.[257] With the recent increase in penalties for criminal copyright infringement, the use of conspiracy charges is likely to diminish.

8.3 TRADE DESCRIPTIONS ACT 1968

Another source of criminal sanctions for intellectual property infringement is the Trade Descriptions Act 1968. Under this Act, a person commits an offence if, in the course of trade or business,[258] they apply a false trade description to goods, or supply or offer to supply any goods bearing such a false description.[259] Although typical trade descriptions cases cover misdescriptions as to quality, 'trade description' is defined broadly to include, inter alia, indications of 'approval by any person or conformity with a type approved by any person' and as to the 'person by whom manufactured, produced, processed or reconditioned'.[260] As a result, the application of a trade mark to goods may be a false trade description.[261] In some cases, it has been held that a disclaimer to the effect that the goods are 'replicas' or 'counterfeits' is sufficient to negate the initial misdescription.[262] There are also certain defences, which can protect innocent distributors of counterfeit goods.[263]

---

make confiscation order under Powers of Criminal Courts Act 1973, s. 43 in relation to offences under TMA s. 92 and CDPA s. 107). RDA s. 24C-D).

[256] *Scott v. Metropolitan Police Commissioner* [1975] *AC* 819; *R v. Bridgeman & Butt* [1996] *FSR* 538. In *Scott*, the defendant bribed cinema employees to hand over films so that they could be surreptitiously copied. The House of Lords held that this amounted to a conspiracy to defraud the owners of the copyright.

[257] See Criminal Law Act 1977, s. 5. *R. v. Dowd* [2005] *EWCA Crim* 3582 (defendant, member of an internet group which hacked into technologically protected copyright software, was not motivated by malice but seriously damaged commercial interests; sentenced to 12 months). But see *R v. Holborough* [2002] *EWCA Crim* 2631 (taking into account the statutory limitation on sentencing of the specific offence—that is, selling unauthorized decoders contrary to CDPA s. 297A, then subject to a maximum of two years' imprisonment—when reducing the defendant's sentence for conspiracy to defraud to three years).

[258] Although the courts will infer the existence of a business from numbers of articles in a person's possession (see, e.g. *Elder v. Crowe* [1996] *SCCR* 38) it is thought the requirement might make it difficult to convict counterfeiters who operate through 'car boot sales'.

[259] TDA s. 1.   [260] TDA s. 2.

[261] TDA s. 34; *Horner v. Kingsley Clothing* [1989] *Crim LR* 911 (sweatshirts bearing Marc O Polo mark did bear false trade description that goods were produced by Marc O Polo). Cf. *R v. Veys* [1993] *FSR* 366 (Manchester United FC merchandise did not signify approval or that manufactured by the club).

[262] *Kent County Council v. Price* (unreported, 1993) (89 T-shirts bearing marks were being sold on a market stall, and were accompanied by cards stating they were 'Brand Copies'. In addition the stallholder told customers orally that the goods were copies. It was held that the Crown Court was justified in reaching the conclusion that there was no false trade description). But cf. *Lewis v. Fuell* [1990] *Crim LR* 658 (oral disclaimer did not nullify trade description of use of ROLEX on watches). See Worsdall and Clark, para. 5–20.

[263] TDA s. 24; s. 28(3) (that defendant did not know and could not with reasonable diligence have ascertained that the goods did not conform to the description applied to the goods). See Worsdall and Clark, paras. 5.21–22.

The Trade Descriptions Act is enforced by trading standards officers employed by local authorities (which are under a statutory duty to enforce the Act). The officers are empowered to make test purchases, enter premises, and inspect and seize goods. They do not have power to arrest offenders.[264] The authorities also bring proceedings, but if prosecution is not thought to be appropriate they have power to issue 'formal cautions'. Offences under the 1968 Act carry a maximum of two years' imprisonment.[265] As mentioned below, much of the Trade Descriptions Act 1968 has been repealed and replaced by the Consumer Protection from Unfair Trading Regulations 2008.

8.4 PROTECTING REGISTRATION

A number of criminal sanctions exist which aim to maintain the veracity of the registration regimes. In particular, it is an offence to make false entries on the register[266] and to make unauthorized claims to rights.[267] An interesting variation is contained in section 201 of the Copyright, Designs and Patents Act 1988, which makes it an offence for a person 'falsely to represent that he is authorised by another to give consent . . . in relation to a performance unless he believes on reasonable grounds that he is so authorised'.

9 REFORM

There are a number of plans for reform that may impact on the way that intellectual property matters are litigated both in the UK and at the EU. Domestically, the UK has introduced a Bill that makes changes to the way that intellectual property enforcement is conducted at the local level.[268] It is unlikely that these reforms, if passed, will have much of an impact on intellectual property practice. In addition, Parliament has just passed the Consumer Protection from Unfair Trading Regulations 2008,[269] to implement the 2005 EU Unfair Commercial Practices Directive.[270] These Regulations, operative from 26 May 2008, repeal and replace much of the Trade Descriptions Act 1968 with provisions imposing criminal penalties where businesses mislead consumers (by act or omission), for example as to the main characteristics of a product (including the geographical or commercial origin of the product). These provisions will thus apply to many cases of wrongful use of registered trade marks and passing off. Brand owners had hoped that the proposed new Regulations would give private businesses the right to bring private civil actions (as Ireland has chosen to do), but the Government declined to do so, confining liability to criminal proceedings, and leaving enforcement, as under the Trade Descriptions Act, to the Office of Fair Trading and Trading Standards.

There are also reforms under way at the EU level. The harmonization of criminal remedies has long been a key part of Community plans to combat piracy. Although earlier drafts of the Enforcement Directive contained provisions dealing with criminal penalties, these were removed from the Directive that was passed in 2004. While the removal of

---

[264] TDA ss. 27–8.

[265] *R v. Ahmadi* (1993) 15 *Cr App R (S)* 254 (six months for supplying recycled toner cartridges); *R v. Shekhar Kumar* (1992) 13 *Cr App R (S)* 498 (hirer of 26 counterfeit videos fined £5,000).

[266] PA s. 109, TMA s. 59, RDA s. 34.

[267] For example, see PA s. 110, TMA s. 60; Trade Marks (International Registration) Order 1996 (SI 1996/714) r. 18; Community Trade Mark Regulations 1996 (SI 1996/1908) r. 8; RDA s. 35.

[268] *Regulatory Enforcement and Sanctions Bill* (6 Feb 2008).

[269] SI 2008/1277.   [270] 2005/29/EC (11 May 2005).

these controversial provision helped to ensure that the Enforcement Directive was passed, the Commission believed that the effectiveness of the Directive could not be been achieved without a 'sufficiently dissuasive set of penalties applicable throughout the Community'.[271] To remedy this problem, on 12 July 2005 the Commission released a proposed Directive on criminal measures aimed at ensuring the enforcement of intellectual property rights.[272] An amended version of the proposed Directive was adopted by the European Parliament on 25 April 2007.[273]

The proposed Directive, as amended by the European Parliament, applies to copyright (and related rights), database rights, trademarks, design rights, geographical indications, and trade names (as protected under national law). While earlier drafts included provisions relating to misuse of patents, these were removed in later amendments. As a result the proposed Directive does not apply to patents, utility models, or plant variety rights (including those rights obtained by Supplementary Protection Certificates). The proposed Directive specifies that criminal penalties shall be available for infringements on a 'commercial scale' (defined as any infringement that aims to obtain a commercial advantage, but does not include private acts for personal and not-for-profit uses).[274] Member states are also to provide a range of additional penalties including destruction of goods, winding up, and a ban on access to public assistance or subsidies.[275] As well as setting minimum penalty levels,[276] the proposed Directive provides for extended powers of confiscation.[277] It also requires member states to protect against misuse of threats of criminal sanctions, as well as ensuring that the rights of defendants are duly protected.[278] Despite the changes that have been made, the amended draft Directive has been subject to criticism. Because it is not limited to commercial piracy and counterfeiting, it has been said that the aiding and abetting provisions might place undue risks on businesses. As with the criminal provisions in the early drafts of the Enforcement Directive (which were later removed), questions have been raised about the Commission's competence to legislate in relation to criminal matters.[279]

---

[271] Recital 5.

[272] Commission proposal for a Directive on criminal measures aimed at ensuring the enforcement of intellectual property rights COM(2005) 276 final 12 July 2005).

[273] 374 votes to 278 (with 17 abstentions) COM (2006) 0168–C6–0233/2006–2005/0127 (COD); Amended proposal for a Directive of the European Parliament and of the Council on criminal measures aimed at ensuring the enforcement of intellectual property rights (COM/2006/0168 final—COD 2005/0127), OJ C 74 E/527 (20 Mar. 2008).

[274] Article 3 (defined in Art. 2).   [275] Art. 4(2).   [276] Art. 5.   [277] Art. 6.   [278] Art. 8.

[279] The Law Society of England and Wales, *Proposal for a Directive on criminal measures aimed at ensuring the enforcement of intellectual property rights* (Aug 2006), para 5–12 (highlighting problems from *Commission v. Council*, Case C–176/03. See also House of Lords European Union Committee, *The Criminal Law Competence of the EC: follow-up Report*, 11th Report of Session 2006–2007, (2007). See also *Commission v. Council*, Case C–440/05 (23 Oct 2007), a non-IP case, in which the ECJ recognized that, while criminal law and procedure is not generally a matter for Community competence, the Community could require member states to introduce criminal penalties to ensure fully effective operation of harmonized measures, but may not mandate the type or level of penalties).

INDEX